Chambers
Compact
Thesaurus

Chambers

CHAMBERS
An imprint of Chambers Harrap Publishers Ltd
7 Hopetoun Crescent
Edinburgh, EH7 4AY

Previous edition published 2001
This edition published by Chambers Harrap Publishers Ltd 2008

A CIP catalogue record for this book is available from the British Library.

ISBN: 978 0550 10331 4

Designed and typeset by The Charlesworth Group
Printed in Italy by Rotolito Lombarda Spa

Contents

Contributors

Managing Editor
Ian Brookes

Editors
Vicky Aldus
Pat Bulhosen
Sheila Ferguson
Lorna Gilmour
Andrew Holmes
Joyce Littlejohn

Editorial Assistance
Kay Cullen
Dorothea Gschwandtner

Data Management
Patrick Gaherty
Ruth O'Donovan

Production and Prepress Controller
Karen Stuart

Preface

A thesaurus is a book that contains lists of synonyms – that is, words that have a similar meaning to another word. A thesaurus allows you to look up a common word and find a range of other words that have the same or nearly the same meaning. *Chambers Compact Thesaurus* lists over 320,000 synonyms, allowing you to find a suitable word for every occasion. The synonyms are listed in alphabetical order, and information is provided on the context in which a particular synonym is appropriate – for example in formal, technical or colloquial language.

Looking up a word in this thesaurus may help you to find a more exact term for an essay or report, a livelier phrase for a speech, or a simpler expression for a letter. This will enable you to say what you have to say using the full range of words available to you. Moreover, browsing through a thesaurus also offers you a fascinating insight into the richness and variety of the English language.

But this book offers much more than lists of alternative words. It also contains lists of antonyms – words that have an opposite meaning. This allows you the further option of describing things in terms of their opposites. Thus you can describe something that is dull not only as 'boring', but also as 'not interesting'.

Another feature of this thesaurus is the inclusion of panels containing related words. For example, look up the word *language* and you will find not only a number of alternative words (*communication, conversation, discourse* …) but also a list of the major languages of the world from *Afrikaans* to *Zulu*. This feature complements the lists of synonyms and makes the thesaurus even more useful as resource for solving puzzles and word games.

A second type of panel offers warnings about words that are easily confused, for example *abuse* and *misuse*, or *incredible* and *incredulous*. This feature makes the thesaurus even more useful by making sure you are looking up the most suitable word for your needs.

A thesaurus is not the same thing as a dictionary. Synonyms listed in a thesaurus are not necessarily precise definitions of the word under which they are found, and there may be subtle distinctions between the words. For this reason it always advisable to use a thesaurus in conjunction with a dictionary. *Chambers Compact Thesaurus* has been designed as a companion volume for *Chambers Compact Dictionary*. Taken together, these books form a helpful and reliable guide to the English language.

How to use the thesaurus

Headwords are shown in bold letters at the beginning of each entry.

Different meanings are shown in numbered sections, introduced by a phrase in italics to indicate which sense of the word is being discussed.

Lists of related words are shown in panels after some entries.

Phrasal verbs are grouped alphabetically at the end of some entries. These are indicated by the symbol ►.

Synonyms or alternative words are listed in alphabetical order.

Antonyms, words that mean the opposite of the headword, are introduced by the symbol 🖬.

---

gelatinous *adj* congealed, gluey, glutinous, gooey *colloq*, gummy, jellied, jelly-like, mucilaginous *formal*, rubbery, sticky, viscid, viscous

geld *v* castrate, emasculate, neuter, unman, unsex

gem *n* **1** *precious gems:* gemstone, jewel, precious stone, stone **2** *his last joke was a real gem:* crème de la crème, masterpiece, pièce de résistance, pride and joy *colloq*, prize, treasure

Gems and gemstones include:
diamond, white sapphire, zircon, cubic zirconia, marcasite, rhinestone, pearl, moonstone, onyx, opal, mother-of-pearl, amber, citrine, fire opal, topaz, agate, tiger's eye, jasper, morganite, ruby, garnet, rose quartz, beryl, cornelian, coral, amethyst, sapphire, turquoise, lapis lazuli, emerald, aquamarine, bloodstone, jade, peridot, tourmaline, jet

gen *n* background, data, details, dope *colloq*, facts, info *colloq*, information, knowledge, low-down *colloq*
► **gen up on** be well-informed about, bone up on *colloq*, brush up on *colloq*, find out about, read up on, research, study, swot up on *colloq*

genealogy *n* ancestry, birth, breeding, derivation, descent, dynasty, extraction, family, family history, family tree, line, lineage, parentage, pedigree

general *adj* **1** *a general statement:* accepted, across-the-board, all-inclusive, blanket, broad, comprehensive, extensive, global, overall, panoramic, popular, prevailing, prevalent, sweeping, total, universal, wide-ranging, widespread **2** *a very general picture:* approximate, broad, ill-defined, imprecise, indefinite, inexact, loose, rough, unspecific, vague **3** *as a general rule:* common, conventional, customary, everyday, habitual, normal, ordinary, public, regular, standard, typical, usual **4** *a general store:* assorted, diverse, heterogeneous *formal*, miscellaneous, mixed, varied, variegated *formal*
🖬 **1** limited, particular **2** detailed, precise, specific **3** rare

generality *n* **1** *talked in generalities:* approximateness, general statement, generalization, impreciseness, indefiniteness, inexactness, looseness, sweeping statement, vagueness **2** *the generality of his appeal:* breadth, catholicity, commonness, comprehensiveness, ecumenicity, extensiveness, miscellaneity, popularity, prevalence, universality
🖬 **1** detail, exactness, particular
2 uncommonness

increasingly *adv* all the more, cumulatively, more and more, more so, progressively, to an increasing degree/extent

incredible *adj* **1** *give some incredible excuse:* absurd, beyond/past belief, far-fetched, implausible, impossible, improbable, inconceivable, preposterous, unbelievable, unimaginable, unthinkable **2** *walk an incredible distance:* amazing, astonishing, astounding, exceptional, extraordinary, fantastic, great, marvellous, remarkable, surprising, wonderful
☒ 1 believable, credible

incredible or *incredulous*? *Incredible* means 'unbelievable'; *incredulous* means 'showing disbelief'. If you are told an *incredible* story, you may be *incredulous*.

Warnings about confusable words are shown in panels after some entries.

incredulity *n* cynicism, disbelief, distrust, doubt, mistrust, scepticism, suspicion, unbelief
☒ credulity

incredulous *adj* cynical, disbelieving, distrustful, distrusting, doubtful, doubting, dubious, sceptical, suspicious, unbelieving, uncertain, unconvinced
☒ credulous

increment *n* accretion *formal*, accrual *formal*, accrument *formal*, addendum *formal*, addition, advancement, augmentation *formal*, enlargement, expansion, extension, gain, growth, increase, step-up, supplement
☒ decrease

incriminate *v* accuse, arraign, blame, charge, impeach, implicate, inculpate *formal*, indict *technical*, involve, point the finger at *colloq*, put the blame on
☒ exonerate

Labels in italics show when synonyms or antonyms are restricted to certain areas of language use.

inculcate *v* din into, drill into, drum into, engrain, fix, hammer into, implant, impress, imprint, indoctrinate, infuse, instil, teach

inculpate *v* accuse, arraign, blame, censure, charge, impeach, implicate, incriminate, indict *technical*, involve, put the blame on, recriminate
☒ exonerate

incumbent *adj* binding, compulsory, mandatory *formal*, necessary, obligatory, prescribed, up to
♦ *n* functionary, member, office-bearer, office-holder, officer, official

Parts of speech, eg adjective, noun, verb, are shown by abbreviations. A new part of speech within an entry is indicated by the symbol ♦.

incur *v* arouse, bring upon yourself, earn, experience, expose yourself to, gain, lay yourself open to, meet with, provoke, run up, suffer, sustain

incurable *adj* **1** *an incurable disease:* fatal, hopeless, inoperable, terminal, unhealable, untreatable **2** *an incurable romantic:* beyond hope, beyond redemption, dyed-in-the-wool, hardened, hopeless, incorrigible, inveterate
☒ 1 curable

Abbreviations used in the thesaurus

adj	adjective
adv	adverb
Austr	Australian
colloq	colloquial
conj	conjunction
interj	interjection
n	noun
prep	preposition
pron	pronoun
®	trademark
Scot	Scottish
US	United States
v	verb

A

abandon *v* **1** *abandon a baby:* break (it) off with *colloq*, chuck *colloq*, desert, ditch *colloq*, dump *colloq*, forsake *formal*, give the elbow to *colloq*, jilt *colloq*, leave (behind), leave high and dry *colloq*, leave in the lurch *colloq*, maroon, run out on *colloq*, strand, walk out on **2** *abandon the boat:* bail out, break away, break free from, break loose, depart from, escape, evacuate, get out, go away from, leave, quit *colloq*, vacate, withdraw from **3** *abandon your responsibilities:* abdicate *formal*, abort, cease *formal*, cede *formal*, desist *formal*, discontinue *formal*, drop *colloq*, forgo *formal*, forswear *formal*, give up, jack in *colloq*, kick the habit *colloq*, leave, leave it at that *colloq*, let go, pack in *colloq*, part with *formal*, quit *colloq*, relinquish *formal*, renounce *formal*, resign (from), sacrifice, scrap *colloq*, stop (doing), surrender, waive, yield *formal* **4** *abandon yourself to despair:* be overcome by, give way to, give yourself up to, yield to
🔁 **1** maintain, remain (with), stay (with), support **3** begin, continue, start
◆ *n* carelessness, impetuosity, recklessness, thoughtlessness, unrestraint, wildness
🔁 care, carefulness, caution, inhibition(s), moderation, restraint

abandoned *adj* **1** *abandoned buildings:* derelict, deserted, desolate, empty, forlorn, forsaken *formal*, neglected, unoccupied, unused, vacant **2** *abandoned young people:* corrupt, crazy, debauched, dissolute, immoral, mad, profligate *formal*, reprobate *formal*, uninhibited, wanton, wicked, wild
🔁 **1** occupied, (well-)kept **2** conscious, restrained, (self-)controlled

abandonment *n* **1** *her abandonment of the children:* decampment *formal*, dereliction *formal*, desertion, ditching *colloq*, forsaking *formal*, jilting *colloq*, leaving (behind), marooning, neglect, running out on *colloq*, stranding **2** *abandonment of an activity:* abdication *formal*, cessation *formal*, cession *formal*, discontinuance *formal*, discontinuation *formal*, dropping *colloq*, giving-up, relinquishment *formal*, renunciation *formal*, resignation (from), sacrifice, scrapping *colloq*, stopping, surrender, waiving

abase *v* belittle *formal*, debase *formal*, demean *formal*, disparage *formal*, humble, humiliate, malign *formal*, mortify *formal*
🔁 elevate, honour, raise

abashed *adj* affronted, ashamed, bewildered, confounded, confused, discomfited *formal*, discomposed *formal*, disconcerted *formal*, discountenanced *formal*, dumbfounded, embarrassed, floored *colloq*, humbled, humiliated, mortified, nonplussed, perturbed *formal*, shamefaced, taken aback
🔁 at ease, audacious *formal*, composed

abate *v* **1** *the storm abated:* attenuate *formal*, decline *formal*, decrease, die down, diminish *formal*, dwindle, ease, fall off, lessen, let up *colloq*, moderate, reduce, sink, subside, taper off, wane **2** *abate anger:* alleviate, decrease, ease, fade, lessen, let up *colloq*, mitigate, moderate, pacify,

quell, relieve, remit *formal*, slacken, slow, soothe, subside, wane, weaken
🔁 **1** increase, strengthen

abatement *n* **1** *the abatement of the storm:* attenuation *formal*, decline *formal*, diminution *formal*, dwindling, dying-down, easing, lessening, lowering, reduction, subsidence **2** *abatement of anger:* alleviation, assuagement *formal*, decrease, easing, lessening, mitigation, moderation, palliation *formal*, relief, remission *formal*, slackening, wane, weakening

abbey *n* cathedral, cloister, convent, friary, minster, monastery, nunnery, priory, seminary

abbreviate *v* abridge, abstract, clip, compress, condense, constrict *formal*, contract, curtail *formal*, cut (down), digest, lessen, précis, reduce, shorten, shrink, summarize, trim, truncate *formal*
🔁 amplify, expand, extend, lengthen

abbreviation *n* abridgement, abstract, acronym, clipping, compression, contraction, curtailment, digest, initialism, précis, reduction, résumé, short form, shortened form, shortening, summarization *formal*, summary, synopsis, truncated form *formal*, truncation *formal*
🔁 amplification, expansion, extension, long form

abdicate *v* **1** *the king abdicated:* give up, give up the throne, quit *colloq*, relinquish/renounce the throne *formal*, resign, resign from the throne, retire *formal*, stand down **2** *abdicate responsibility:* abandon, abjure *formal*, abnegate *formal*, cede *formal*, disown, forgo *formal*, give up, quit *colloq*, refuse to accept any longer, reject, relinquish *formal*, renounce *formal*, repudiate *formal*, shirk *colloq*, surrender, turn your back on *colloq*, wash your hands of *colloq*, yield *formal*

abdication *n* **1** *the abdication of the king:* giving up of the throne, renunciation/relinquishment of the throne *formal*, resignation, retirement, standing-down **2** *abdication of responsibilities:* abandonment, abjuration *formal*, abnegation *formal*, disowning, giving-up, refusal, rejection, relinquishment *formal*, renunciation *formal*, repudiation *formal*, surrender

abdomen *n* belly, guts *colloq*, midriff, stomach, tum *colloq*, tummy *colloq*

abdominal *adj* coeliac, colic, gastric, intestinal, ventral, ventricular, visceral

abduct *v* appropriate *formal*, carry off, hold to ransom, kidnap, lay hold of, make off with, rape, run away/off with *colloq*, seduce, seize, shanghai, snatch, spirit away, take (away) by force, take as hostage

aberrant *adj* anomalous, atypical *formal*, corrupt, defective, deviant, deviating, different, divergent, eccentric, freakish *colloq*, incongruous *formal*, irregular, odd, peculiar, quirky *colloq*, rogue
🔁 normal, regular, typical

aberration *n* **1** *an aberration in behaviour:* abnormality, anomaly, delusion, deviation, divergence, eccentricity, instability, irregularity,

lapse, nonconformity, oddity, oversight, peculiarity, straying, wandering **2** *scientific aberrations:* abnormality, anomaly, deviation, divergence, irregularity, mistake, oddity, peculiarity, variation
≠ 1 conformity, normality, regularity

abet *v* aid, assist, condone, egg on *colloq*, encourage, endorse, help, promote, sanction, spur, succour *formal*, support
≠ discourage, hinder, prevent

abhor *v* abominate *formal*, can't abide/bear, can't stand *colloq*, despise, detest, execrate *formal*, hate, hate someone's guts *colloq*, have an aversion to, loathe, recoil from, shrink from, shudder at, spurn
≠ adore, love

abhorrence *n* abomination *formal*, animosity *formal*, aversion, contempt, detestation *formal*, disgust, distaste, enmity *formal*, execration *formal*, hate, hatred, horror, loathing, malice *formal*, odium *formal*, repugnance *formal*, revulsion
≠ adoration, love

abhorrent *adj* abominable, detestable, disgusting, distasteful, execrable *formal*, hated, hateful, heinous *formal*, horrible, horrid, loathsome, nauseating, obnoxious, odious *formal*, offensive, repellent, repugnant, repulsive, revolting
≠ attractive, delightful

abide *v* **1** *I can't abide that smell:* accept, bear, brook, endure, put up with, stand *colloq*, stomach *colloq*, take, tolerate **2** *truths that abide:* continue, endure, last, persist, remain
▶ **abide by** accept, adhere to *formal*, agree to, carry out, comply with *formal*, conform to *formal*, discharge *formal*, follow, fulfil, go along with, go by the book *colloq*, hold to, keep to, obey, observe, respect, stand by, stick to the rules *colloq*, submit to *formal*, toe the line *colloq*, uphold
≠ flout *colloq*, ignore, reject

abiding *adj* chronic, constant, continual, continuous, durable, enduring, eternal, everlasting, firm, immortal, immutable *formal*, lasting, lifelong, long-lasting, long-running, long-term, permanent, persistent, stable, unchangeable, unchanging, unending
≠ ephemeral *formal*, short-lived, short-term, transient *formal*

ability *n* **1** *the ability to teach:* capability, capacity, facility, faculty, potential *formal*, potentiality *formal*, power(s), propensity *formal*, resources **2** *someone of great ability:* adeptness, adroitness, aptitude, calibre, competence, competency *formal*, deftness, dexterity, endowment, expertise, flair *colloq*, forte, genius *colloq*, gift, knack *colloq*, know-how *colloq*, motivation, proficiency, prowess, qualification, savoir-faire, savvy *colloq*, skill, strength, talent, the hang *colloq*, touch *colloq*, what it takes *colloq*
≠ 1 inability **2** incompetence, weakness

ability or *capability*? *Ability* is the more general term, referring to the possession of particular skills, knowledge, powers, etc, or the simple fact of something being possible: *his ability to write a catchy tune; our ability to work together. Capability* may refer to the possession of an aptitude, especially one

that derives from a person's character: *my mother's organizational capabilities.*

abject *adj* **1** *abject poverty:* degraded, execrable *formal*, forlorn, hopeless, humiliating, miserable, outcast, pathetic, pitiable, shameful, wretched **2** *an abject coward:* base, contemptible, debased, degenerate, deplorable, despicable, dishonourable, ignoble *formal*, ignominious *formal*, low, mean, servile, sordid, vile, worthless **3** *an abject apology:* base, debased, dishonourable, grovelling, ignoble *formal*, ignominious *formal*, servile, sordid, submissive
≠ 2 exalted **3** proud

abjure *v* abandon, abdicate *formal*, abnegate *formal*, deny, disavow *formal*, disclaim *formal*, disown, forswear *formal*, reject, relinquish *formal*, renege on *formal*, renounce, retract *formal*
≠ agree, assent, support

ablaze *adj* **1** *fuel tanks ablaze:* afire *formal*, aflame *formal*, alight, blazing, burning, flaming, ignited, in flames, incandescent, lighted, on fire **2** *a house ablaze with lights:* aglow, brilliant, flashing, gleaming, glowing, illuminated, incandescent *formal*, lit up, luminous, radiant, sparkling **3** *eyes ablaze with passion:* ardent, aroused, enthusiastic, excited, exhilarated, fervent, fiery, frenzied, impassioned, incensed, passionate, raging, stimulated

able *adj* accomplished, adept, adroit, all there *colloq*, capable, clever, competent, cut out for *colloq*, deft, dexterous, effective, efficient, experienced, expert, fit, fitted, gifted, ingenious, intelligent, masterly, on the ball *colloq*, powerful, practised, proficient, qualified, skilful, skilled, strong, talented, up to it *colloq*, wised up *colloq*
≠ incapable, incompetent, ineffective, unable

able-bodied *adj* burly, fine, fit, hale, hale and hearty, hardy, healthy, hearty, in good health, lusty, powerful, robust, rugged, sound, stalwart, staunch, stout, strapping, strong, sturdy, tough, vigorous
≠ delicate, disabled, handicapped, infirm

abnegation *n* abjuration *formal*, abstinence, eschewal *formal*, forbearance *formal*, giving-up, relinquishment *formal*, renunciation *formal*, repudiation *formal*, self-denial, self-sacrifice, surrender, temperance

abnormal *adj* aberrant *formal*, anomalous *formal*, atypical *formal*, curious, deviant, different, divergent, eccentric, erratic, exceptional, extraordinary, idiosyncratic, irregular, odd, oddball *colloq*, outré *formal*, paranormal, peculiar, preternatural *formal*, queer, singular *formal*, strange, uncanny, uncommon, unexpected, unnatural, unusual, wayward, weird
≠ normal, regular, typical

abnormality *n* aberration *formal*, anomaly, atypicality *formal*, bizarreness, deformity, deviation, difference, divergence, dysfunction, eccentricity, exception, flaw, irregularity, malformation, oddity, peculiarity, singularity *formal*, strangeness, unnaturalness, unusualness
≠ normality, regularity

abode *n* domicile *formal*, dwelling, dwelling-place, habitat, habitation, home, lodgings, pad *colloq*, residence *formal*

abolish *v* abrogate *formal*, annihilate, annul, axe *colloq*, blot out, cancel, destroy, discontinue *formal*, do away with, eliminate, end, eradicate, expunge *formal*, exterminate, get rid of, invalidate, nullify *formal*, obliterate, overthrow, overturn, put an end to, quash, repeal, rescind, revoke, stamp out, stop, subvert, suppress, terminate *formal*, vitiate *formal*, wipe out
🔁 authorize, continue, create, establish, institute, introduce, retain

abolition *n* abrogation *formal*, annihilation, annulment *formal*, axe *colloq*, blotting-out, cancellation, destruction, dissolution *formal*, doing away with, elimination, ending, eradication *formal*, extermination *formal*, extinction, extirpation *formal*, invalidation *formal*, nullification *formal*, obliteration *formal*, overthrow, quashing, repeal, rescindment *formal*, rescission *formal*, revocation *formal*, subversion *formal*, suppression, termination *formal*, voiding *formal*, withdrawal
🔁 authorization, continuation, creation, introduction, retention

abominable *adj* abhorrent, appalling, atrocious, base, contemptible, cursed, damnable, despicable, detestable, disgusting, execrable *formal*, foul, hateful, heinous *formal*, horrible, horrid, loathsome, nauseating, obnoxious, odious *formal*, offensive, repellent, reprehensible *formal*, repugnant *formal*, repulsive, revolting, terrible, vile, wretched
🔁 delightful, desirable, pleasant

abominate *v* abhor, condemn, despise, detest, execrate *formal*, hate, have an aversion to, loathe
🔁 adore, love

abomination *n* 1 *murder is an abomination:* anathema *formal*, atrocity, curse, disgrace, evil, horror, offence, outrage, plague, torment 2 *his abomination of all things rural:* abhorrence *formal*, aversion, detestation *formal*, disgust, distaste, execration *formal*, hate, hatred, hostility, loathing, odium *formal*, repugnance *formal*, revulsion
🔁 2 adoration, delight

aboriginal *adj* ancient, autochthonous *formal*, earliest, first, indigenous, local, native, original, primal, primeval, primitive

abort *v* 1 *abort a pregnancy:* have a miscarriage, miscarry, terminate 2 *abort a plan:* axe *colloq*, bring/come to an end, call off, check, cut short, end, fail, frustrate, halt, nullify *formal*, pull the plug on *colloq*, stop, suspend, thwart
🔁 2 begin, continue, start

abortion *n* miscarriage, termination

abortive *adj* barren, failed, fruitless, futile, idle, ineffective, ineffectual *formal*, sterile, unavailing *formal*, unproductive, unsuccessful, useless, vain
🔁 fruitful, successful

abound *v* 1 *rumours abound:* be plentiful, crowd, exuberate *formal*, flourish, increase, luxuriate *formal*, proliferate *formal*, superabound *formal*, swarm, swell, thrive *formal* 2 *a site abounding with wildlife:* be full, brim over, overflow, superabound *formal*, swarm, teem

about *prep* 1 *write about a subject:* apropos of *formal*, as regards, concerned with, concerning, connected with, dealing with, in the matter of, on, on the subject of, re, referring to, regarding, relating to, with reference to, with regard to, with

respect to 2 *somewhere about the house:* adjacent to, beside, close to, near, nearby 3 *walk about the town:* all over, around, encircling *formal*, encompassing *formal*, round, surrounding, throughout
♦ *adv* 1 *about twenty:* almost, approaching, approximately, around, circa *formal*, in the region of, more or less, nearing, nearly, roughly 2 *run about:* from place to place, here and there, hither and thither *old use*, to and fro

about-turn *n* about-face, (complete) reversal, enantiodromia *formal*, turnabout, U-turn *colloq*, volte-face

above *prep* 1 *above the clouds:* atop *formal*, higher than, on top of, over 2 *above the rank of sergeant:* higher than, over, senior to, superior to 3 *temperatures above the average:* beyond, exceeding, in excess of, surpassing *formal* 4 *above suspicion:* beyond, not liable to, not open to, superior to
🔁 1 below, under 2 below
♦ *adv* 1 *noise from above:* aloft *formal*, high up, higher, on high *formal*, overhead 2 *as mentioned above:* before, earlier, previously
🔁 1 below, underneath 2 below
♦ *adj* above-mentioned, above-stated *formal*, aforementioned *formal*, aforesaid *formal*, earlier, foregoing *formal*, preceding, previous, prior *formal*

above-board *adj* candid, fair and square *colloq*, forthright, frank, guileless *formal*, honest, honourable, legitimate, on the level *colloq*, open, reputable, square *colloq*, straight, straightforward, true, trustworthy, truthful, upright, veracious *formal*
🔁 dishonest, shady, underhand

abrade *v* chafe, erode, grate, graze, grind, rub, scour, scrape, scratch, wear away/down

abrasion *n* abrading, chafe, chafing, cut, erosion, excoriation *formal*, friction, grating, graze, grinding, rubbing, scouring, scrape, scraping, scratch, scratching, wearing away, wearing-down

abrasive *adj* 1 *abrasive material:* attritional *formal*, chafing, corrosive, erodent *formal*, erosive *formal*, frictional *formal*, grating, harsh, rough, scraping, scratching 2 *an abrasive person:* biting, brusque, caustic, harsh, hurtful, nasty, sharp, unpleasant
🔁 1 smooth 2 kind, pleasant

abreast *adv* 1 *walk abreast:* beside/alongside each other, level, next to each other, side by side 2 *keep abreast of the news:* acquainted, au courant, au fait, conversant *formal*, familiar, in the picture *colloq*, in touch, informed, knowledgeable, on the ball *colloq*, up-to-date, well up, with your finger on the pulse *colloq*
🔁 2 out of touch, unaware, unfamiliar

abridge *v* abbreviate, abstract, clip *colloq*, compress, concentrate, condense, contract, curtail, cut (down), decrease, digest, lessen, lop *colloq*, précis, prune, reduce, shorten, summarize, synopsize *formal*
🔁 amplify, expand, pad out *colloq*

abridgement *n* 1 *the abridgement of the story:* concentration, contraction, cutting, decrease, diminishing, diminution *formal*, reduction, restriction, shortening, truncation *formal* 2 *an abridgement of a report:* abrégé *formal*, abstract, conspectus *formal*, digest, epitome,

outline, précis, résumé, short version, shortened version, summary, synopsis
☒ 1 expansion, padding (out) *colloq*

abroad *adv* 1 *go abroad on business:* in/to a foreign country, in/to foreign parts, out of the country, overseas 2 *news spread abroad:* about, around, at large, circulating, current, extensively, far and wide, publicly, widely
☒ 1 at home

abrogate *v* abolish, annul, axe *colloq*, cancel, countermand *formal*, disenact *formal*, dissolve *formal*, do away with, end, invalidate, repeal, repudiate *formal*, rescind *formal*, retract *formal*, reverse, revoke, scrap *colloq*, stop
☒ establish, institute, introduce

abrupt *adj* 1 *come to an abrupt end:* dramatic, hasty, hurried, instant, instantaneous, precipitate *formal*, quick, rapid, snap *colloq*, sudden, surprising, swift, unannounced, unceremonious, unexpected, unforeseen 2 *an abrupt manner:* blunt, brisk, brusque, curt, direct, gruff, impolite, offhand, rough, rude, short *colloq*, snappish *colloq*, snappy *colloq*, terse, uncivil 3 *an abrupt slope:* declivitous *formal*, precipitous *formal*, sharp, sheer, steep
☒ 1 gradual, leisurely, slow 2 ceremonious, expansive, friendly, polite

abscond *v* beat it *colloq*, bolt, clear out *colloq*, decamp, disappear, do a bunk *colloq*, do a moonlight (flit) *colloq*, do a runner *colloq*, escape, flee, fly, make a quick getaway *colloq*, make off, quit *colloq*, run away, run for it *colloq*, run off, scram *colloq*, skedaddle *colloq*, take French leave *formal*, vamoose *colloq*, vanish

absence *n* 1 *absence from school:* absenteeism, non-appearance, non-attendance, non-existence, truancy 2 *absence of evidence:* dearth *formal*, deficiency, lack, need, omission, paucity *formal*, privation *formal*, scarcity, unavailability, vacancy, vacuity *formal*, want *formal*
☒ 1 appearance, attendance, presence
2 presence

absent *adj* 1 *absent from the meeting:* away, gone, in absentia *formal*, lacking, missing, not around, not here, not present, not there, off, out, truant, unavailable, when someone's back is turned *colloq* 2 *an absent wave of the hand:* absent-minded, blank, daydreaming, distracted *formal*, dreamy, elsewhere, faraway, inattentive, oblivious, preoccupied, unaware, unheeding, vacant *formal*
☒ 1 here, present, there 2 alert, attentive, aware

absent-minded *adj* absent, absorbed, abstracted, distracted, distrait(e) *formal*, dreaming, dreamy, engrossed, faraway, forgetful, having a bad memory, heedless, impractical, in a world of your own *colloq*, inattentive, miles away *colloq*, musing, not all there *colloq*, oblivious, pensive, preoccupied, scatterbrained, scatty *colloq*, somewhere else *colloq*, unaware, unconscious, unheeding, unthinking, with a memory like a sieve *colloq*, withdrawn, wool-gathering
☒ attentive

absolute *adj* 1 *an absolute disaster:* categorical, certain, complete, conclusive, consummate *formal*, decided, decisive, definite, definitive, downright, entire, exhaustive, final, full, genuine, indubitable *formal*, out-and-out, outright, perfect, positive, pure, rank, sheer,

supreme, sure, thorough, total, unadulterated, unambiguous, unconditional, undivided, unequivocal, unlimited, unmitigated, unmixed, unquestionable, unquestionable, unrestrained, unrestricted, utter 2 *absolute power:* almighty, autarchical *formal*, authoritarian, plenary, supreme, unlimited, unrestricted 3 *an absolute ruler:* almighty, autarchical *formal*, authoritarian, autocratic, despotic, dictatorial, omnipotent *formal*, sovereign, totalitarian, tyrannical

absolutely *adv* categorically, certainly, completely, conclusively, dead *colloq*, decidedly, decisively, definitely, entirely, exactly, exhaustively, finally, fully, genuinely, in every way/respect, infallibly, perfectly, positively, precisely, purely, supremely, surely, thoroughly, totally, truly, unambiguously, unconditionally, unequivocally, unquestionably, utterly, wholeheartedly, wholly

absolution *n* acquittal, amnesty, deliverance, discharge *formal*, emancipation, exculpation *formal*, exoneration *formal*, forgiveness, freedom, liberation, mercy, pardon, purgation *formal*, redemption, release, remission *formal*, shrift *formal*, vindication *formal*

absolve *v* acquit *formal*, clear, deliver, discharge *formal*, emancipate, exculpate *formal*, excuse, exonerate *formal*, forgive, free, have mercy on, justify *formal*, let off *colloq*, liberate, loose, pardon, release, remit *formal*, set free, show mercy towards, vindicate *formal*

absorb *v* 1 *absorb liquid:* consume *formal*, devour *colloq*, draw in, drink in, engulf, imbibe *formal*, ingest *formal*, soak up, suck up, take in 2 *absorb facts:* assimilate, digest, hold, receive, retain, take in, understand 3 *absorb your attention:* captivate, engage, engross, enthral, fascinate, fill (up), hold, involve, monopolize, not be able to put down *colloq*, occupy, preoccupy 4 *absorbed into a bigger company:* assimilate, incorporate, integrate, swallow up *colloq*
☒ 1 exude *formal*, give out

absorbed *adj* captivated, engrossed, enthralled, fascinated, interested, involved, occupied, preoccupied, riveted, taken up with

absorbent *adj* absorptive *formal*, assimilative *formal*, blotting, permeable, pervious, porous, receptive, resorbent *formal*, retentive, soaking, sorbefacient *formal*
☒ waterproof, water-repellent

absorbing *adj* amusing, captivating, compelling, compulsive, diverting, engrossing, enjoyable, entertaining, enthralling, fascinating, gripping, interesting, intriguing, preoccupying, riveting, spellbinding
☒ boring, off-putting

absorption *n* 1 *the absorption of liquid:* consumption *formal*, devouring *colloq*, drawing-in, ingestion *formal*, osmosis *technical*, soaking-up, taking-in 2 *absorption of your attention:* attentiveness, captivating, concentration, engagement, engrossing, holding, intentness, involvement, monopoly, occupation, preoccupation, riveting

abstain *v* 1 *abstain from food:* avoid, decline *formal*, deny yourself *formal*, desist *formal*, do/go without, eschew *formal*, forbear *formal*, forgo *formal*, give up, hold back, keep from, refrain *formal*, refuse, reject, renounce *formal*, resist, shun, stop, stop short of, think twice before doing something *colloq* **2** *abstain in an election:* not vote, refuse to vote

◨ **1** indulge

abstemious *adj* abstinent *formal*, ascetic, austere, disciplined, frugal, moderate, restrained, self-abnegating *formal*, self-denying, self-disciplined, sober, sparing, temperate

◨ gluttonous, intemperate, luxurious

abstention *n* declining to vote, not voting, refusal to vote

abstinence *n* **1** *abstinence from sensual desires:* abstaining, abstemiousness *formal*, avoidance, continence *formal*, declension *formal*, desistance *formal*, eschewal *formal*, forbearance *formal*, giving-up, going-without, non-indulgence, refraining *formal*, refusal, renunciation *formal*, restraint, self-control, self-denial, self-discipline, self-restraint **2** *abstinence from alcohol:* asceticism, frugality, moderation, nephalism *formal*, sobriety *formal*, teetotalism, temperance

◨ **1** indulgence, self-indulgence

abstract *adj* **1** *abstract nouns:* conceptual, non-concrete, notional **2** *abstract reasoning:* abstruse *formal*, academic, arcane *formal*, complex, conceptual, deep, general, generalized, hypothetical, indefinite, intellectual, metaphysical, notional, philosophical, profound, recondite *formal*, subtle, theoretical, unpractical, unrealistic **3** *abstract paintings:* contrived, non-realistic, non-representational

◨ **1** concrete **2** actual, concrete, practical, real **3** figurative, realistic, representational

♦ *n* abridgement, compression, conspectus *formal*, digest, epitome *formal*, outline, précis, recapitulation, résumé, summary, synopsis

♦ *v* **1** *abstract a report:* abbreviate, abridge, compress, condense, cut (down), digest, outline, précis, shorten, summarize **2** *abstract coal from the ground:* detach, dissociate *formal*, extract, isolate, remove, separate, take away/out, withdraw

◨ **1** expand, lengthen **2** insert, put in

abstracted *adj* absent, absent-minded, absorbed, bemused, distracted, dreaming, dreamy, engrossed, forgetful, heedless, impractical, inattentive, musing, oblivious, pensive, preoccupied, scatterbrained, scatty *colloq*, unaware, unconscious, unheeding, unthinking, withdrawn, wool-gathering

◨ alert, attentive, on the ball *colloq*

abstraction *n* **1** *academic abstractions:* concept, conception, formula, generality, generalization, hypothesis, idea, notion, theorem, theory, thought **2** *he roused himself from his abstraction:* absent-mindedness, absorption *formal*, bemusedness *formal*, distraction *formal*, dream, dreaminess, inattention, pensiveness *formal*, preoccupation, remoteness, withdrawal **3** *water abstraction:* extraction, isolation, separation, withdrawal

abstruse *adj* arcane *formal*, complex, cryptic, deep, difficult to understand, enigmatic *formal*, esoteric *formal*, incomprehensible, inscrutable *formal*, mysterious, obscure, perplexing, profound, puzzling, recondite *formal*, unfathomable

◨ obvious, simple

absurd *adj* asinine *formal*, comical, crazy, daft *colloq*, derisory, fantastic, farcical, foolish, funny, harebrained, humorous, idiotic, illogical, implausible *formal*, inane, incongruous *formal*, irrational, laughable, ludicrous, meaningless, nonsensical, paradoxical, preposterous, ridiculous, risible *formal*, senseless, silly, stupid, unreasonable, untenable *formal*

◨ logical, rational, reasonable, sensible

absurdity *n* balderdash *colloq*, charade, claptrap *colloq*, craziness, daftness *colloq*, drivel *colloq*, farce, fatuousness, folly, foolishness, gibberish *colloq*, humour, idiocy, illogicality, implausibility *formal*, inanity, incongruity *formal*, irrationality *formal*, joke, ludicrousness, meaninglessness, nonsense, paradox, ridiculousness, rubbish, senselessness, silliness, stupidity, travesty, twaddle *colloq*, unreasonableness

◨ (good) sense, logicality, rationality, reasonableness

abundance *n* affluence *formal*, amplitude *formal*, bags *colloq*, bonanza, bounty *formal*, copiousness *formal*, excess, extravagance, exuberance *formal*, fortune, fullness, generosity, glut, great supply, heaps *colloq*, land of milk and honey, lashings *colloq*, lavishness, loads *colloq*, lots *colloq*, luxuriance *formal*, masses *colloq*, munificence *formal*, oodles *colloq*, opulence *formal*, overflow, piles *colloq*, plenitude *formal*, plenty, plethora *formal*, prodigality *formal*, profusion *formal*, riches, richness, scads *US colloq*, stacks *colloq*, wealth

◨ dearth *formal*, paucity *formal*, scarcity, shortage

abundant *adj* affluent, ample, bounteous *formal*, bountiful, copious, exuberant, filled, full, galore, generous, in plenty, lavish, luxuriant *formal*, more than enough, opulent *formal*, overflowing, plentiful, profuse, rich, teeming, well-supplied

◨ insufficient, scant, scarce, sparse

abuse *n* **1** *the abuse of drugs:* exploitation, imposition, misapplication *formal*, misuse **2** *child abuse:* beating, cruelty, damage, harm, hurt, ill-treatment, injury, maltreatment, mistreatment, molestation, torture **3** *shout abuse:* affront *formal*, calumniation *formal*, calumny *formal*, castigation *formal*, censure, contumely *formal*, curse, cursing, defamation, denigration *formal*, derision *formal*, diatribe *formal*, disparagement *formal*, insult(s), invective *formal*, libel, malediction *formal*, offence, reproach, scolding, slander, swearing, swear-word, tirade *formal*, upbraiding *formal*, vilification *formal*, vitriol *formal*, vituperation *formal*

◨ **2** attention, care **3** compliment(s), praise

♦ *v* **1** *abuse authority:* exploit, misapply *formal*, misuse, take advantage of **2** *abuse children:* batter, beat, damage, exploit, harass sexually, harm, hit, hurt, ill-treat, injure, maltreat, molest, oppress, rape, torture, wrong **3** *abuse immigrants:* be rude to, bully, call names, calumniate *formal*, castigate *formal*, curse, defame, denigrate *formal*, disparage *formal*, hurl abuse at, insult, libel, malign *formal*, oppugn *formal*, pick on, rail, revile *formal*, scold, slander, slate *colloq*, smear, swear at, treat like dirt *colloq*, upbraid *formal*, victimize

◨ **2** care for, cherish, look after **3** compliment, praise

abuse or *misuse*? *Abuse* refers to the use of something for the wrong purposes: *substance abuse*, eg glue-sniffing. *Misuse* refers to the use of substances or objects in an incorrect way: *Bacteria may acquire resistance to a particular antibiotic by its overuse or misuse.*

abusive *adj* blasphemous, brutal, calumniating *formal*, castigating *formal*, censorious *formal*, contumelious *formal*, cruel, defamatory, denigrating *formal*, derogatory, destructive, disparaging, harmful, hurtful, injurious, insulting, libellous, maligning, offensive, opprobrious *formal*, pejorative, railing *formal*, reproachful, reviling, rude, scathing, scolding, slanderous, upbraiding *formal*, vilifying *formal*, vituperative *formal*
F͟∃ complimentary, polite

abut *v* adjoin *formal*, be next to, border, conjoin *formal*, impinge, join, touch, verge on

abysmal *adj* appalling, awful, complete, disgraceful, dismal, dreadful, shocking, utter

abyss *n* barathrum *formal*, bottomless pit, canyon, chasm, crater, crevasse, depth(s), fissure, gorge, gulf, pit, void

academic *adj* 1 *academic qualifications:* educational, instructional, pedagogical *formal*, scholastic 2 *she's a very academic child:* bookish, brainy *colloq*, donnish, educated, erudite *formal*, highbrow, intellectual, learned, literary, scholarly, serious, smart *colloq*, studious, well-educated, well-read 3 *an academic, not practical, approach:* abstract, conjectural *formal*, hypothetical, impractical, irrelevant, ivory-tower, notional *formal*, speculative, theoretical
F͟∃ 3 practical, relevant
♦ *n* bookworm, don, educator, fellow, instructor, lecturer, man/woman of letters, master, pedant, professor, scholar, student, teacher, trainer, tutor

accede *v* 1 *accede to a request:* accept, acquiesce *formal*, admit, agree to, assent to *formal*, back down, bow to, comply with *formal*, concur *formal*, consent to *formal*, give in 2 *accede to the throne:* assume *formal*, attain *formal*, come to, inherit, succeed (to) *formal*

accelerate *v* 1 *the car accelerated:* gain momentum, go faster, open up *colloq*, pick up/gather speed, put on a spurt *colloq*, quicken, speed, speed up 2 *accelerate a process:* advance, expedite *formal*, facilitate, festinate *technical*, forward, further, hasten *formal*, hurry, precipitate *formal*, promote, speed up, spur on, step up, stimulate
F͟∃ 1 decelerate, slow down 2 delay, slow down

acceleration *n* 1 *the acceleration of a car:* momentum, rate of increase, speeding-up 2 *acceleration of a process:* advancement *formal*, expedition *formal*, forwarding, furtherance *formal*, hastening *formal*, promotion, speeding-up, stepping-up, stimulation
F͟∃ 1 deceleration 2 delay, slowing-down

accent *n* 1 *speak with a strong Irish accent:* accentuation, articulation, beat, brogue, cadence *formal*, diction *formal*, emphasis, enunciation *formal*, force, inflection, intensity, intonation, modulation *formal*, pitch, pronunciation, pulsation *formal*, pulse, rhythm, stress, tone,

twang *colloq* 2 *the accent is on ease of use:* emphasis, highlighting, importance, priority, prominence, underlining

accentuate *v* deepen, drive the point home *colloq*, emphasize, give prominence to, heighten, highlight, intensify, make great play of *colloq*, point up *colloq*, put the emphasis on, show up *colloq*, strengthen, stress, underline, underscore
F͟∃ play down *colloq*, weaken

accept *v* 1 *accept an offer:* acquire, gain, get, jump at *colloq*, not say no to, obtain, receive, reply in the affirmative *formal*, say yes to, secure, take, take up 2 *accept advice:* embrace *formal*, take, take on board *colloq*, take someone's point *colloq*, welcome 3 *accept a decision:* abide by *formal*, accede to *formal*, acknowledge, acquiesce in *formal*, admit, adopt, agree to, allow, approve, back down, bow to, comply with *formal*, concur with *formal*, consent to *formal*, give in, go along with, recognize, take on 4 *accept responsibility:* bear, take on, undertake 5 *accept blame:* acknowledge, admit, be responsible for, bear 6 *accept your explanation:* be certain of, believe (in), buy *colloq*, fall for *colloq*, swallow *colloq*, trust 7 *accept into the family:* integrate, receive, receive warmly, welcome 8 *accept ill-treatment:* abide, be resigned to, bear, come to terms with, endure, face up to, let go of, make the best of *colloq*, put up with, resign yourself to, stand, stomach *colloq*, swallow *colloq*, take, tolerate, yield to
F͟∃ 1 refuse, turn down 7 reject

acceptable *adj* 1 *homework that is just acceptable:* adequate, all right, moderate, OK *colloq*, passable, reasonable, satisfactory, so-so *colloq*, tolerable, unexceptional 2 *acceptable not to smoke:* admissible, agreeable, allowable, appropriate, desirable, permissible, the done thing *colloq*, tolerable 3 *a most acceptable present:* delightful, desirable, gratifying, pleasant, welcome
F͟∃ 1 unacceptable, unsatisfactory
2 unacceptable

acceptance *n* 1 *acceptance of a job:* accepting, acquiring, gaining, getting, obtaining, receipt, securing, taking (up) 2 *acceptance of advice:* embracing *formal*, taking, taking on board *colloq*, taking someone's point *colloq*, welcoming 3 *acceptance of the decision:* accession *formal*, acknowledgement, acquiescence *formal*, admission, adoption, affirmation *formal*, agreement, approval, assent *formal*, backing-down, concurrence *formal*, consent *formal*, endorsement *formal*, giving-in, going along with, OK *colloq*, ratification *formal*, recognition, stamp of approval *colloq*, taking on 4 *acceptance of responsibility:* acknowledgement, admission, assumption, taking on, undertaking 5 *the idea gained acceptance:* belief, credence, faith, trust 6 *acceptance into the family:* integration, receiving, recognition, welcome 7 *acceptance of your situation:* bearing, endurance, facing up to, making the best of *colloq*, putting up with, resignation, tolerance
F͟∃ 1 refusal 6 rejection

accepted *adj* acceptable, acknowledged, admitted, agreed, appropriate, approved, authorized, common, confirmed, conventional, correct, customary, established, normal, orthodox, ratified, received, recognized, regular,

sanctioned, standard, time-honoured,
traditional, universal, usual
🔁 controversial, unconventional, unorthodox

access *n* **1** *gain access to the building*: approach,
course, door, drive, driveway, entering, entrance,
entry, gateway, key, means of approach/entry,
passage, path, road, way in **2** *deny access to the
prisoner*: accessibility, admission, admittance,
entrée *formal*, ingress *formal*, permission to
enter/see, right of entry
🔁 **1** egress *formal*, exit, outlet

accessible *adj* **1** *accessible from the motorway*:
achievable, attainable, get-at-able *colloq*,
reachable **2** *financial help that is accessible to
everyone*: available, convenient, handy, near,
nearby, obtainable, on hand, procurable *formal*,
ready **3** *an accessible book/painting*: easy to
understand, intelligible, understandable,
user-friendly
🔁 **1** inaccessible, off the beaten track *colloq*, out
of the way *colloq*, remote **3** incomprehensible,
unintelligible

accession *n* **1** *accession to the throne*: assumption
formal, attaining *formal*, inheritance, succession
formal **2** *accessions to the library*: acquisition,
addition, gift, increase, possession, purchase

accessory *n* **1** *computer accessories*: addition,
adjunct *formal*, appendage *formal*, attachment,
component, extension, extra, fitting, supplement
2 *accessories to match an outfit*: adornment,
complement, decoration, embellishment *formal*,
frill, ornament, supplement, trimming **3** *an
accessory to a crime*: abettor *formal*, accomplice,
aid, assistant, associate, colleague, confederate,
conniver *formal*, help, helper, particeps criminis
technical, partner
♦ *adj* additional, ancillary, auxiliary,
contributory, extra, incidental, secondary,
subordinate, subsidiary, supplemental *formal*,
supplementary

accident *n* **1** *an accident with boiling water*: blow
colloq, calamity, casualty, disaster, misadventure
formal, mischance *formal*, misfortune *formal*,
mishap, tragedy **2** *a car accident*: collision,
contretemps *formal*, crash, fatality, pile-up *colloq*,
prang *slang*, shunt *slang*, smash-up *colloq*,
wreck *colloq* **3** *happen by accident*: chance,
coincidence, contingency *formal*, fate, fluke *colloq*,
fortuity *formal*, fortune, good fortune,
good luck, happenstance *formal*, hazard,
luck, serendipity *formal*

accidental *adj* **1** *accidental overdose*: casual,
chance, haphazard, inadvertent, incidental,
unanticipated, uncalculated, uncertain,
unexpected, unforeseen, unintended,
unintentional, unlooked-for, unplanned,
unpremeditated, unwitting **2** *accidental
discoveries*: adventitious *formal*, aleatory *formal*,
casual, chance, fluky *colloq*, fortuitous *formal*,
haphazard, inadvertent, incidental, random,
serendipitous *formal*, unanticipated, uncertain,
unexpected, unforeseen, unlooked-for,
unplanned, unpremeditated, unwitting
🔁 **1** calculated, deliberate, intentional,
premeditated **2** deliberate, premeditated

accidentally *adv* adventitiously *formal*,
bechance *formal*, by accident, by chance, by
mistake, fortuitously *formal*, haphazardly,
inadvertently, incidentally, randomly,

serendipitously *formal*, unexpectedly,
unintentionally, unwittingly
🔁 deliberately, intentionally

acclaim *v* applaud, celebrate, cheer, clap,
commend, eulogize *formal*, exalt, extol, fanfare,
give a good press to *colloq*, give rave reviews to
colloq, hail, honour, laud *formal*, praise, rave
about *colloq*, salute, toast, welcome
🔁 condemn, criticize, give a bad press to *colloq*
♦ *n* acclamation *formal*, applause, approbation
formal, approval, bouquets, celebration,
cheering, cheers, clapping, commendation,
eulogy *formal*, exaltation, extolment *formal*,
homage, honour, laudation *formal*, ovation,
plaudits *formal*, praise, shouting, tribute,
welcome
🔁 bad press *colloq*, brickbats *colloq*,
condemnation, criticism, disapproval,
vituperation *formal*

acclamation *n* applause, approbation *formal*,
approval, bravos, celebration, cheering,
clapping, commendation, congratulations,
enthusiasm, eulogy *formal*, exaltation,
felicitations *formal*, homage, honour, ovation,
paean *formal*, panegyric *formal*, praise, shouting,
tribute, welcome
🔁 condemnation, criticism, disapproval

acclimatize *v* accommodate, acculturate *formal*,
accustom, adapt, adjust, attune, conform,
familiarize, find your feet *colloq*, find your
way around, find/get your bearings *colloq*,
get used to, habituate *formal*, inure *formal*,
naturalize *formal*

accolade *n* award, honour, praise, tribute

accommodate *v* **1** *accommodate someone in a
hotel*: billet, board, cater for, domicile *formal*,
house, lodge, provide shelter for, put a roof over
someone's head *colloq*, put up, shelter, take in
2 *the hall accommodates 400 guests*: have room/
space for, hold, take **3** *accommodate customers*:
aid, assist, be helpful to, give/lend a (helping)
hand to *colloq*, help, oblige, provide, serve,
supply **4** *accommodate yourself to new
developments*: acclimatize, accustom, adapt,
adjust, comply, compose, conform, fit,
harmonize, modify, reconcile, settle

accommodating *adj* agreeable, complaisant
formal, considerate, co-operative, friendly,
helpful, hospitable, indulgent, kind, obliging,
pliable *formal*, sympathetic, unselfish, willing
🔁 disobliging, selfish

accommodation *n* **1** *find accommodation*: a roof
over someone's head *colloq*, board, housing,
lodging, quarter(s), shelter **2** *reach an
accommodation*: agreement, compromise,
conformity, harmony, negotiation(s),
reconciliation, settlement

Types of accommodation include:
flat, apartment, bedsit, bedsitter, digs *colloq*,
lodgings, hostel, halls of residence, rooms,
residence, dwelling, shelter, pad *colloq*, squat
colloq; bed and breakfast, board, guest house,
hotel, youth hostel, villa, timeshare, motel,
inn, pension, boarding-house; barracks, billet,
married quarters. See also **house**

---

accompaniment *n* **1** *a musical accompaniment*:
background, backing, backup, obbligato
technical, support, vamp **2** *wine as an*

accompaniment to food: accessory, addition, adjunct *formal,* coexistence *formal,* complement, concomitant *formal,* supplement

accompany *v* **1** *accompany someone on holiday:* associate with, attend, chaperone, come (along) with, conduct, consort *formal,* convoy *formal,* escort, follow, go (along) with, hang around with *colloq,* partner, squire *formal,* usher **2** *a book accompanied by a study guide:* belong to, coexist *formal,* coincide *formal,* complement, go with, supplement **3** *accompany someone on the guitar:* play with, provide backing/support for

accomplice *n* abettor, accessory, aide, ally, assistant, associate, collaborator, colleague, confederate, conspirator, helper, henchman, mate, participator, partner, right-hand man, sidekick *colloq*

accomplish *v* achieve, attain, bring about, bring home the bacon *colloq,* bring off, carry out, complete, conclude, consummate *formal,* deliver the goods *colloq,* discharge, do, effect *formal,* effectuate *formal,* engineer, execute, finish, fulfil, hack it *colloq,* manage, obtain, perform, produce, pull it off *colloq,* realize

accomplished *adj* adept, adroit, consummate *formal,* cultivated, experienced, expert, gifted, masterly, polished, practised, professional, proficient, skilful, skilled, talented

🗲 incapable, inexpert, unskilled

accomplishment *n* **1** *the accomplishment of a task:* achievement, attainment, carrying-out, completion, conclusion, consummation *formal,* discharge *formal,* doing, effecting *formal,* execution, finishing, fruition, fulfilment, futurition *formal,* management, perfection, performance, production, realization **2** *her great accomplishments:* ability, aptitude *formal,* art, capability, faculty *formal,* forte, gift, proficiency, skill, talent **3** *no mean accomplishment:* achievement, deed, exploit, feat, stroke *colloq,* triumph

accord *v* **1** *not accord with the truth:* agree, be in agreement/harmony, concur *formal,* conform, correspond, harmonize, match, suit **2** *accord someone recognition:* allow, bestow *formal,* confer, endow, give, grant, tender, vouchsafe *formal*

🗲 **1** disagree **2** deny

♦ *n* accordance *formal,* agreement, assent, concert *formal,* concurrence *formal,* conformity, congruence *formal,* congruity *formal,* correspondence, harmony, sympathy, unanimity, unity

🗲 conflict, discord, disharmony

according *adj* **1** *play according to the rules:* after, after the manner of, as per, consistent with, in accordance with, in conformity with, in keeping with, in line with, in the light of, in the manner of, obedient to **2** *be paid according to experience:* as per, commensurate with *formal,* depending on, in proportion to, in relation to

accordingly *adv* **1** *he was dishonest and was distrusted accordingly:* as a result, consequently, correspondingly, ergo *formal,* for that reason, hence *formal,* in consequence, so, therefore, thus *formal* **2** *act accordingly:* appropriately, consistently, properly, suitably

accost *v* approach, attack, buttonhole *colloq,* confront, detain, halt, importune, molest, solicit, stop, waylay

account *n* **1** *an account of what happened:* chronicle, commentary, description, detail(s), explanation, history, memoir, narration, narrative, portrayal, presentation, record, report, sketch, statement, story, tale, version **2** *pay an account:* bill, charges, invoice, statement, tab **3** *the accounts of a business:* books, inventory, ledger, register **4** *a matter of no account:* consequence, distinction *formal,* esteem *formal,* importance, regard *formal,* significance

♦ *v* adjudge *formal,* appraise *formal,* assess, believe, consider, count, deem *formal,* esteem *formal,* hold, look upon, reckon, value, view as

▶ **account for 1** *account for the missing money:* answer for, clear up, come up with an explanation, elucidate *formal,* explain, give reasons for, illuminate, justify, rationalize, say why, vindicate *formal* **2** *exports account for half our income:* be responsible for, constitute *formal,* give, make up, provide, represent, supply **3** *account for an enemy:* defeat, destroy, kill

accountability *n* amenability, answerability, liability, obligation, reporting, responsibility

accountable *adj* amenable, answerable, bound, chargeable, charged with, liable, obligated *formal,* obliged, responsible

accoutrements *n* adornments, appointments, appurtenances *formal,* bits and pieces *colloq,* decorations, equipment, furnishings, gear, kit, odds and ends *colloq,* outfit, paraphernalia, trimmings

accredited *adj* appointed, approved, authorized, certificated *formal,* certified, commissioned, deputed *formal,* endorsed, licensed, official, qualified, recognized

accrue *v* accumulate, amass, build up, collect, compile

accumulate *v* accrue, acquire, aggregate *formal,* amass, assemble, augment *formal,* build up, collect, cumulate *formal,* gain, gather, grow, hoard, increase, multiply, pile up, snowball *colloq,* stash *colloq,* stockpile, store

🗲 diffuse *formal,* disseminate *formal*

accumulation *n* accrual, acquisition, aggregate *formal,* assembly, augmentation *formal,* building-up, build-up, collection, conglomeration, cumulation *formal,* gain, gathering, growth, hoard, increase, mass, multiplication, pile, reserve, stack, stock, stockpile, store

🗲 dissemination *formal*

accuracy *n* authenticity, carefulness, closeness, correctness, exactitude *formal,* exactness, faithfulness, fidelity *formal,* meticulousness, precision, truth, truthfulness, veracity *formal,* veridicality *formal,* verity *formal*

🗲 inaccuracy

accurate *adj* **1** *an accurate report:* authentic, close, correct, exact, fair, faithful, faultless, letter-perfect *formal,* literal, perfect, sound, strict, true, truthful, unerring, valid, veracious *formal,* veridical *formal,* word-for-word, word-perfect **2** *accurate calculations:* bang on *colloq,* correct, exact, meticulous, precise, right, rigorous, spot on *colloq,* valid **3** *an accurate throw:* precise, well-aimed, well-directed

🗲 **2** imprecise, inexact **3** inaccurate

accursed *adj* abominable, anathematized *formal*, bedevilled *formal*, condemned, damned, despicable, doomed, execrable *formal*, hateful, wretched
◼ blessed

accusation *n* allegation, arraignment *formal*, blame, charge, complaint, crimination *formal*, denunciation, gravamen *formal*, impeachment, imputation *formal*, incrimination, inculpation *formal*, indictment, recrimination

accuse *v* 1 *accused of murder*: allege, arraign *formal*, attribute, book *colloq*, bring/press charges, cite *formal*, confront, criminate *formal*, denounce, frame *colloq*, impeach, implicate, impugn *formal*, impute *formal*, incriminate, indict, inform against, make accusations, make allegations, prosecute, put on trial 2 *accuse someone of cheating*: blame, censure *formal*, hold responsible, point the finger at *colloq*, recriminate *formal*, throw the book at *colloq*

accustom *v* accommodate, adapt, adjust, attune *formal*, conform, familiarize, get acquainted with, get familiar with, get used to, habituate *formal*, inure *formal*

accustomed *adj* 1 *accustomed to the dark*: acclimatized, acquainted, at home *colloq*, given, habituated *formal*, in the habit of, inured *formal*, used, wont *formal* 2 *sitting in her accustomed chair*: consuetudinary *formal*, conventional, customary, established, everyday, familiar, fixed, general, habitual *formal*, normal, ordinary, prevailing, regular, routine, traditional, usual, wonted *formal*
◼ 1 unaccustomed, unused

ace *n* champion, dab hand *colloq*, expert, genius, hotshot *colloq*, maestro, master, virtuoso, whizz *colloq*, winner
♦ *adj* brilliant, excellent, first-class, great, outstanding, perfect, superb

acerbic *adj* abrasive, acrimonious, astringent *formal*, biting, caustic, harsh, mordant *formal*, rancorous *formal*, sharp, stinging, trenchant *formal*, vitriolic *formal*
◼ friendly, kind, mild

ache *v* 1 *my legs ache*: agonize, be in agony, be painful, be sore, hurt, kill *colloq*, pain, pound, smart, sting, suffer, throb, twinge 2 *aching to tell her*: crave, desire, hanker, hunger, itch, long, pine, thirst, yearn
♦ *n* 1 *an ache in my neck*: agony, anguish, hurt, pain, pang, pounding, smarting, soreness, stinging, suffering, throb, throbbing, twinge 2 *an ache for home*: craving, hankering, itch, longing, yearning

achieve *v* accomplish, acquire, attain, bring about, carry out, complete, consummate *formal*, do, earn, effect *formal*, effectuate *formal*, execute, finish, fulfil, gain, get, manage, obtain, perform, procure *formal*, produce, reach, realize, succeed, win
◼ fail, miss

achievement *n* 1 *the achievement of our aims*: accomplishment, acquirement *formal*, attainment, completion, consummation *formal*, execution, fruition, fulfilment, performance, procurement *formal*, realization, success 2 *great achievements*: accomplishment, act, action, activity, deed, effort, exploit, feat, performance

achiever *n* doer, go-getter *colloq*, high flyer *colloq*, performer, succeeder, success story *colloq*

acid *adj* 1 *an acid taste*: acerbic, acetic *formal*, acetous *formal*, acidic, acidulous *formal*, bitter, caustic, corrosive, pungent, sharp, sour, tart, vinegary 2 *an acid remark*: acerbic *formal*, astringent *formal*, biting, bitter, critical, cutting, harsh, hurtful, incisive, mordant *formal*, morose, sarcastic, stinging, trenchant *formal*, unkind, vitriolic *formal*
◼ 1 alkaline 2 complimentary, kind

> **Types of acid include:**
> acetic, acrylic, amino, aqua fortis, aqua regia, ascorbic, benzoic, boric, carbolic, chloric, citric, DNA (deoxyribonucleic acid), fatty, folic, formic, hydrochloric, hydrocyanic, lactic, malic, nitric, nitrohydrochloric, nitrous, palmitic, pectic, phenol, phosphoric, prussic, RNA (ribonucleic acid), salicylic, spirits of salt, stearic, sulphuric, tannic, tartaric, uric

acknowledge *v* 1 *acknowledge a fact*: accede *formal*, accept, acquiesce *formal*, admit, affirm *formal*, agree to, allow, avouch *formal*, concede, confess, declare, grant, own up to, recognize 2 *acknowledge him with a nod*: address, greet, hail *formal*, notice, recognize, salute *formal* 3 *acknowledge a letter*: answer, react to, reply to, respond to, write back 4 *acknowledge someone's help*: be grateful, express your thanks/gratitude, express/show your appreciation, recognize, say thank you, thank
◼ 1 deny, disagree with 2 ignore

acknowledged *adj* accepted, accredited, approved, attested *formal*, avowed *formal*, confirmed, declared, professed, recognized

acknowledgement *n* 1 *an acknowledgement of defeat*: acceptance, admission, confession, declaration, profession, recognition 2 *a gesture of acknowledgement*: greeting, nod, notice, recognition, salutation *formal*, smile, wave 3 *an acknowledgement of a letter*: affirmation *formal*, answer, reaction, reply, response 4 *an acknowledgement of assistance*: credit, expression of gratitude/appreciation/thanks, gratefulness, tribute

acme *n* apex *formal*, apogee *formal*, climax, crown, culmination, height, high point, optimum, peak, pinnacle, summit, zenith *formal*
◼ low point, nadir *formal*

acolyte *n* adherent, assistant, attendant, follower, helper

acoustic *adj* audile *formal*, auditory *formal*, aural *formal*, hearing, sound

acquaint *v* accustom, advise, apprise *formal*, brief, disclose, divulge, enlighten, familiarize, inform, let know, make aware of, make conversant *formal*, notify, reveal, tell

acquaintance *n* 1 *friends and acquaintances*: associate, colleague, companion, confrère *formal*, contact 2 *my acquaintance with them*: association, companionship, familiarity, fellowship, intimacy, relationship, social contact 3 *some acquaintance with art*: awareness, cognizance *formal*, experience, familiarity, knowledge, understanding

acquainted *adj* 1 *acquainted with him*: friendly, on friendly terms, on good terms 2 *acquainted*

with that book: abreast, apprised *formal*, au fait, aware, cognizant *formal*, conversant *formal*, familiar, in the know *colloq*, knowledgeable, well-versed
F 2 ignorant, unaware, unfamiliar

acquiesce *v* accede *formal*, accept, agree, allow, approve, concur *formal*, consent, defer, give in *colloq*, submit
F disagree, object, resist

acquiescence *n* acceptance, agreement, approval, assent *formal*, compliance *formal*, concurrence *formal*, consent, deference, submission, yielding
F disagreement, resistance

acquiescent *adj* acceding *formal*, accepting, agreeable, agreeing, amenable, approving, complaisant *formal*, compliant *formal*, concurrent *formal*, consenting, deferential, obedient, servile, submissive, yielding

acquire *v* 1 *acquiring a piece of land*: achieve, appropriate *formal*, attain, bag *slang*, buy, collar *slang*, come by, earn, gain, gather, get, net, obtain, pick up *colloq*, procure *formal*, purchase, realize, receive, secure, snap up *colloq*, splash out on *colloq*, win 2 *acquiring shares in the company*: accumulate, amass, appropriate *formal*, collect, gather, get, snap up *colloq*
F 1 forfeit, relinquish, sell

acquisition *n* 1 *his latest acquisition*: accession, buy, gain, possession, property, purchase, takeover 2 *the acquisition of a skill*: achievement, appropriation *formal*, attainment, gaining, obtaining, procurement *formal*, securing

acquisitive *adj* avaricious *formal*, avid *formal*, covetous, grasping, greedy, predatory *formal*, rapacious *formal*, voracious *formal*

acquisitiveness *n* avarice *formal*, avidity *formal*, covetousness, graspingness, greed, predatoriness *formal*, rapacity *formal*, voracity *formal*

acquit *v* 1 *acquitted of the crime*: absolve *formal*, clear, deliver, discharge, dismiss, exculpate *formal*, excuse, exonerate *formal*, free, let off *colloq*, let off the hook *colloq*, liberate, release, relieve, repay, reprieve, satisfy, settle, vindicate *formal* 2 *acquit yourself well*: act, bear *formal*, behave, comport *formal*, conduct, do, make a good/bad job *colloq*, perform
F 1 condemn, convict

acquittal *n* absolution *formal*, clearance, compurgation *formal*, deliverance, discharge, dismissal, exculpation *formal*, excusing, exoneration *formal*, freeing, liberation, release, relief, reprieve, vindication *formal*
F condemnation, conviction

acrid *adj* 1 *an acrid smell*: acerbic, acid, burning, caustic, harsh, pungent, sharp, sour, stinging, tart 2 *an acrid comment*: acerbic *formal*, acrimonious, astringent *formal*, biting, bitter, caustic, cutting, harsh, incisive, malicious, mordant *formal*, nasty, sarcastic, sardonic, trenchant *formal*, venomous, virulent *formal*, vitriolic *formal*

acrimonious *adj* abusive, acerbic *formal*, astringent *formal*, biting, bitter, caustic, censorious, crabbed *colloq*, cutting, ill-tempered, irascible *formal*, petulant *formal*, rancorous *formal*, severe, sharp, spiteful, splenetic *formal*, trenchant *formal*, venomous, virulent, vitriolic *formal*, waspish
F irenic *formal*, kindly, peaceable

acrimony *n* acerbity *formal*, acridity *formal*, asperity *formal*, astringency *formal*, bitterness, causticity *formal*, gall, harshness, ill temper, ill-will, irascibility *formal*, mordancy *formal*, petulance *formal*, rancour *formal*, resentment, sarcasm, spite, spleen *formal*, trenchancy *formal*, venom, virulence *formal*, vitriol *formal*

acrobat *n* aerialist *formal*, balancer, contortionist, equilibrist *formal*, gymnast, somersaulter, trapeze artist, tumbler

act *v* 1 *act in a certain way*: acquit yourself *formal*, be, be active, be busy, behave, comport yourself *formal*, conduct yourself *formal*, do, exert yourself *formal*, go about, move, react, take action, take measures, take steps 2 *the drug will act soon*: be efficacious *formal*, function, have an effect, operate, take effect, work 3 *the gear acts as a brake*: do, do the job of, function, operate, serve, work 4 *act upset*: affect *formal*, assume *formal*, dissemble *formal*, dissimulate *formal*, fake, feign *formal*, pretend, put on, sham *colloq*, simulate *formal* 5 *act in a play*: characterize, enact, go on the stage, imitate, impersonate, mime, mimic, perform, play, portray, represent
♦ *n* 1 *acts of bravery*: accomplishment, achievement, action, deed, doing, enterprise, execution, exploit, feat, manoeuvre, move, operation, step, stroke, undertaking 2 *put on an act*: affectation *formal*, counterfeit, dissemblance *formal*, dissimulation *formal*, fake, feigning *formal*, front *colloq*, make-believe, pretence, sham *colloq*, show *colloq* 3 *an act of parliament*: bill, decree, edict, law, measure, ordinance, resolution, ruling, statute 4 *a juggler's act*: gig *colloq*, item, performance, routine, sketch, skit *colloq*, turn
► **act on** 1 *act on orders*: carry out, comply with, conform to, follow, fulfil, heed, obey, take 2 *alcohol acting on his brain*: affect, alter, change, influence, modify, transform
► **act up** behave badly, cause trouble, give bother, mess about *colloq*, misbehave, muck around *colloq*, play up *colloq*

acting *adj* covering, deputy, in place of, interim, pro tem, provisional, relief, reserve, stand-by, stand-in, standing in for, stopgap, substitute, supply, surrogate, temporary
♦ *n* artistry, characterization, drama, dramatics, footlights, histrionics, imitating, impersonation, melodrama, performance, performing, performing arts, play-acting, portrayal, stagecraft, theatre, theatricals

action *n* 1 *his prompt action*: accomplishment, achievement, act, activity, course of action, deed, effort, endeavour, enterprise, exploit, feat, measure, move, performance, proceeding, process, step, undertaking 2 *put an idea into action*: doing, effect, exercise, exertion, force, functioning, mechanism, motion, movement, operation, performance, practice, work 3 *the action of a chemical on metal*: effect, influence, operation 4 *people of action*: activity, energy, force, get-up-and-go *colloq*, liveliness, power, spirit, vigour, vitality 5 *killed in action*: affray *formal*, battle, clash, combat, conflict, encounter, engagement, fight, fray, skirmish, warfare

6 *a legal action:* case, lawsuit, litigation, prosecution, suit

activate *v* actuate *formal*, animate *formal*, arouse, bestir *formal*, energize, excite, fire, galvanize, get going, impel *formal*, initiate, mobilize, move, prompt, propel, push/press the button *colloq*, rouse, set going, set in motion, set off, start, start working, stimulate, stir, switch/turn/put on, throw the switch *colloq*, trigger (off), trip
🔁 arrest, deactivate, stop

active *adj* **1** *an active person:* astir *formal*, busy, forceful, forward, frenetic, hard-working, hyperactive, indefatigable *formal*, industrious, manic, occupied, on the go *colloq*, spirited, vibrant, vital **2** *active for his age:* agile, alert, animated, energetic, lively, nimble, quick, sprightly, spry, vigorous **3** *active members:* committed, contributing, devoted, engaged, enterprising, enthusiastic, involved, militant **4** *the system is active:* functioning, in force, in operation, running, working
🔁 **1** passive **3** inactive

activity *n* **1** *the office is full of activity:* action, activeness, business, bustle, comings and goings *colloq*, commotion, exercise, exertion, hurly-burly *colloq*, industry, labour, life, liveliness, motion, movement, toing and froing *colloq* **2** *holiday activities:* act, deed, distraction, diversion, endeavour, enterprise, hobby, interest, job, occupation, pastime, project, pursuit, scheme, something to do, task, undertaking, venture, work
🔁 **1** inactivity, passivity

actor, actress *n* artist, dramatic artist, extra, impersonator, leading lady, leading man, mime artist, mummer, performer, play actor, player, Roscius *formal*, Thespian *formal*, understudy, walk-on

actual *adj* absolute, authentic, bona fide, certain, concrete, confirmed, de facto *formal*, definite, existent, factual, genuine, indisputable, legitimate, material, physical, positive, real, real live *colloq*, realistic, substantial, tangible, true, truthful, unquestionable, verified
🔁 apparent, imaginary, theoretical

actuality *n* corporeality *formal*, fact, factuality *formal*, historicity *formal*, materiality *formal*, reality, substance, substantiality *formal*, truth

actually *adv* **1** *she actually saw him fall:* absolutely, as a matter of fact, as it happens, de facto *formal*, in fact, in reality, in truth, indeed, really, truly **2** *gliding is actually a very safe sport:* as it happens, even, surprisingly, though it may seem strange

actuate *v* activate, arouse, instigate, kindle, motivate, move, prompt, rouse, set going, set in motion, set off, start, start working, stimulate, stir, switch/turn on, trigger (off)

acumen *n* astuteness, cleverness, discernment, discrimination, gumption *colloq*, ingenuity, insight, intelligence, intuition, judgement, judiciousness *formal*, keenness, penetration, perception, percipience *formal*, perspicacity *formal*, perspicuity *formal*, quickness, sagacity *formal*, sapience *formal*, sense, sharpness, shrewdness, smartness *colloq*, wisdom, wit

acute *adj* **1** *an acute shortage:* critical, crucial, cutting, dangerous, decisive, distressing, extreme, grave, intense, serious, severe, sharp, urgent, violent, vital **2** *an acute mind:* astute, canny, clever, discerning, incisive, insightful, judicious, keen, observant, penetrating, perceptive, percipient *formal*, perspicacious *formal*, sapient *formal*, sensitive, sharp, shrewd, smart *colloq* **3** *an acute illness:* critical, dangerous, grave, intense, serious, severe
🔁 **1** mild, slight **3** chronic, mild, persistent

acutely *adv* extremely, gravely, intensely, keenly, seriously, sharply, strongly, very

adage *n* aphorism *formal*, apophthegm *formal*, axiom, byword, maxim, paroemia *formal*, precept, proverb, saw, saying

adamant *adj* determined, firm, fixed, hard, immovable, inflexible, insistent, intransigent *formal*, obdurate *formal*, resolute, rigid, set, stiff, stubborn, tough, unbending, uncompromising, unrelenting, unshakable, unyielding
🔁 flexible, hesitant, yielding

adapt *v* **1** *adapt to a new environment:* acclimatize yourself, accommodate yourself, adjust, familiarize yourself, get used/accustomed, habituate yourself *formal*, orientate yourself **2** *adapt a building:* adjust, alter, change, comply, conform, convert, customize, fashion, fit, harmonize, match, modify, prepare, qualify, remodel, shape, suit, tailor

adaptable *adj* adjustable, alterable, amenable, changeable, compliant, conformable, convertible, easy-going, flexible, malleable, modifiable, plastic, variable, versatile
🔁 inflexible, refractory *formal*

adaptation *n* **1** *adaptation to a different situation:* acclimatization, accommodation, adjustment, familiarization, getting used/accustomed, habituation *formal* **2** *adaptation of a novel for TV:* adjustment, alteration, change, conformity, conversion, customization, fashioning, fitting, harmonization, matching, modification, preparation, refashioning, refitting, remodelling, reshaping, revision, reworking, shaping, shift, transformation, variation

add *v* **1** *add an introduction to the book:* adjoin *formal*, affix *formal*, annex *formal*, append *formal*, attach, augment *formal*, build on, combine, complete, improve, include, increase, put in, put on, supplement, throw in *colloq* **2** *add numbers:* count (up), tot up *colloq*, total, work out/calculate the total **3** *'Thanks,' I added:* carry on, continue, go on to say, tack on
🔁 **1** decrease, reduce, take away **2** deduct, remove, subtract, take (away)
▶ **add up 1** *add up numbers:* add, add together, calculate, compute, count (up), reckon, sum up, tally, tot up *colloq*, total **2** *the total adds up to 100:* amount, come to, constitute *formal*, include, spell, **3** *it doesn't add up:* be consistent, be plausible, be reasonable, fit, hang together, indicate, make sense, mean, ring true, signify, stand to reason

added *adj* additional, adjunct *formal*, another, extra, fresh, further, more, new, spare, supplementary

addendum *n* addition, adjunct *formal*, allonge *formal*, appendage *formal*, appendix, attachment *formal*, augmentation *formal*, codicil *formal*, endorsement *formal*, postscript, supplement

addict *n* **1** *a drug addict*: coke-head *slang*, dope-fiend *colloq*, drug taker, drug user, freak *slang*, head *slang*, junkie *colloq*, mainliner *slang*, tripper *slang*, user *colloq* **2** *a chess addict*: adherent, buff *colloq*, devotee, enthusiast, fan, fiend *colloq*, follower, freak *colloq*

addicted *adj* **1** *addicted to drugs*: dependent, hooked *colloq*, strung out *colloq* **2** *addicted to TV*: absorbed, dedicated, devoted, fond, hooked *colloq*, inclined, obsessed

addiction *n* **1** *alcohol addiction*: craving, dependence, habit, monkey *slang* **2** *addiction to chocolate*: compulsion, craving, habit, mania, obsession

addition *n* **1** *the index is a welcome addition*: accessory, addendum, additive, adjunct *formal*, afterthought, annexe, appendage *formal*, appendix, appurtenance *formal*, attachment, extra, increment, postscript, rider, supplement **2** *the addition of a separate phone line*: accession *formal*, accretion *formal*, adding, annexation *formal*, enlargement, extension, gain, increase, increasing **3** *addition of numbers*: computation, counting, inclusion, reckoning, summing-up, totalling, totting-up *colloq*
⊞ 2 removal, taking-away **3** deduction, subtraction

additional *adj* added, adscititious *formal*, adventitious *formal*, another, excrescent *formal*, extra, fresh, further, increased, more, new, other, spare, supervenient *formal*, supplementary

additionally *adv* also, as well, besides, for good measure *colloq*, further, furthermore, in addition, into the bargain *colloq*, moreover, over and above, too

additive *n* addition, extra, preservative, supplement

addled *adj* befuddled, bewildered, confused, flustered, mixed-up, muddled, perplexed
⊞ clear

address *n* **1** *write down an address and phone number*: abode *formal*, apartment, dwelling, flat, home, house, inscription, location, lodging, place, (place of) residence *formal*, poste restante, situation, whereabouts **2** *an address to the nation*: apostrophe *formal*, discourse, disquisition *formal*, dissertation, lecture, monologue, oration, sermon, soliloquy, speech, talk **3** *forms of address*: greeting, invocation *formal*, salutation *formal*, welcome
♦ *v* **1** *address an audience*: give a talk/speech to, lecture, make/deliver a speech, orate *formal*, sermonize *formal*, speak to, talk to **2** *address a remark to someone*: communicate, convey, direct, intend for, remit *formal*, send **3** *how should I address a duke?*: call, designate, speak/write to

adduce *v* allude to, cite, evidence *formal*, mention, point out, present, proffer *formal*, put forward, refer to

adept *adj* able, accomplished, ace *colloq*, adroit, capable, clever, competent, deft, experienced, expert, good, hot stuff *colloq*, masterly, nimble, no flies on someone *colloq*, polished, practised, proficient, sharp *colloq*, skilled, versed
⊞ bungling, incompetent, inept

adequacy *n* ability, acceptability, capability, commensurateness *formal*, competence, fairness, fitness, indifference, mediocrity, passability, reasonableness, requisiteness *formal*, satisfactoriness, serviceability, sufficiency, suitability, tolerability, tolerableness
⊞ inadequacy, insufficiency

adequate *adj* **1** *adequate amounts of food*: commensurate *formal*, enough, requisite *formal*, sufficient **2** *adequate hospital treatment*: able, acceptable, all right *colloq*, average, capable, competent, fair to middling *colloq*, fit, indifferent, nothing (much) to write home about *colloq*, OK *colloq*, passable, patchy *colloq*, reasonable, run of the mill *colloq*, satisfactory, serviceable, suitable, tolerable, undistinguished, unexceptional, will do *colloq*
⊞ 1 insufficient **2** inadequate

adhere *v* **1** *mud adhering to their boots*: accrete *formal*, attach, cement, cleave to *formal*, cling, coalesce, cohere, combine, fasten, fix, glue, grip, hold, join, link, paste, stick, stick together **2** *adhere to the agreement*: abide by, comply with, follow, fulfil, heed, keep, obey, observe, respect, stand by, stick *colloq* **3** *adhere to an opinion*: defend, espouse *formal*, go along with, hold, stand by, stick up for, support

adherent *n* admirer, advocate, aficionado *formal*, buff *colloq*, devotee, disciple, enthusiast, fan, follower, freak *colloq*, henchman, nut *colloq*, partisan, satellite, sectary *formal*, supporter, upholder, votary *formal*

adhesion *n* adherence, adhesiveness, attachment, bond, cohesion, grip, holding together, sticking together

adhesive *adj* adherent *formal*, adhering, attaching, clinging, cohesive, gluey *colloq*, glutinous *formal*, gummed, gummy *colloq*, holding, mucilaginous *formal*, self-adhesive, sticking, stick-on, sticky, tacky
♦ *n* cement, fixative, glue, gum, mucilage *formal*, paste, sticky tape, tape

adieu *n* au revoir, cheerio *colloq*, cheers *colloq*, farewell, goodbye, leave-taking, valediction *formal*, valedictory *formal*

adjacent *adj* abutting *formal*, adjoining, alongside, beside, bordering, close, closest, conterminant *formal*, conterminate *formal*, conterminous *formal*, contiguous *formal*, juxtaposed *formal*, near, nearest, neighbouring, next, next-door, proximate *formal*, touching, vicinal *formal*
⊞ distant, remote

adjoin *v* abut *formal*, add, annex, append *formal*, attach, border, combine, connect, couple, interconnect, join, juxtapose *formal*, link, meet, neighbour, touch, unite, verge

adjoining *adj* abutting *formal*, adjacent, bordering, combining, conjoining *formal*, connecting, contiguous *formal*, impinging *formal*, interconnecting, joining, juxtaposed *formal*, linking, near, neighbouring, next, next door, proximate *formal*, touching, uniting, verging, vicinal *formal*

adjourn *v* **1** *adjourn a meeting*: break off, defer, delay, discontinue *formal*, interrupt, pause, postpone, prorogue *formal*, put off, stay, stop temporarily, suspend **2** *adjourn to the lounge*: repair *formal*, retire *formal*, withdraw
⊞ 1 assemble, convene

adjournment *n* break, deferment *formal*, deferral *formal*, delay, discontinuation *formal*, dissolution *formal*, intermission, interruption, interval, pause, postponement, prorogation *formal*, putting-off, recess *US*, stay, suspension

adjudicate *v* adjudge *formal*, arbitrate, decide, determine, judge, pronounce, referee, settle, umpire

adjust *v* **1** *adjust to new circumstances*: acclimatize yourself, accommodate yourself, adapt, become acclimatized, become/grow accustomed, conform, get used to *colloq*, habituate yourself *formal*, harmonize, orientate yourself, reconcile yourself **2** *adjusting the water pressure*: accommodate, adapt, align, alter, amend, arrange, balance, change, coapt *formal*, compose, convert, dispose, fine-tune *colloq*, fit, fix, make adjustments, modify, rectify, refashion, regulate, remodel, repair, reshape, revise, set, settle, shape, square, suit, temper, tune, tweak *colloq*

adjustable *adj* adaptable, convertible, flexible, modifiable, movable
🖼 fixed, immovable

adjustment *n* **1** *minor adjustments to the engine*: accommodation, adaptation, alteration, amendment, arrangement, arranging, change, conversion, fitting, fixing, modification, ordering, rearrangement, rearranging, rectification, regulation, remodelling, revision, setting, settlement, shaping, tuning **2** *adjustment to a new job*: acclimatization, accommodation, adaptation, conforming, getting used to, habituation *formal*, harmonization, naturalization, orientation, reconciliation

ad-lib *v* extemporize *formal*, improvise, invent, make up, speak off the cuff/off the top of your head *colloq*
♦ *adj* extemporaneous *formal*, extempore *formal*, extemporized *formal*, impromptu, improvised, made-up, off the top of your head *colloq*, off-the-cuff *colloq*, spontaneous, unpremeditated, unprepared, unrehearsed, without preparation
🖼 prepared
♦ *adv* extemporaneously *formal*, extempore *formal*, impromptu, impulsively, off the cuff *colloq*, off the top of your head *colloq*, spontaneously

administer *v* **1** *administer a country*: conduct, control, direct, govern, head, lead, manage, officiate, organize, oversee, preside over, regulate, rule, run, superintend, supervise **2** *administer a drug*: adhibit *formal*, apply, disburse *formal*, dispense *formal*, distribute, dole out *colloq*, execute, give, give out, impose, measure out, mete out, provide, supply

administration *n* **1** *reduce the cost of administration*: administering, control, direction, execution, governing, leadership, management, organization, overseeing, paperwork, red tape *colloq*, ruling, running, superintendence, supervision **2** *a country's administration*: directorship, executive, governing body, government, leadership, management, ministry, regime, term of office

administrative *adj* authoritative, directorial *formal*, executive, governmental, gubernatorial *formal*, legislative, management, managerial, organizational, regulatory, supervisory

administrator *n* boss *colloq*, chairman/chairwoman, chief, chief executive, controller, custodian *formal*, director, executive, governor, guardian *formal*, head, leader, manager, managing director, organizer, overseer, president, ruler, superintendent, supervisor, trustee *formal*

admirable *adj* choice, commendable, creditable, deserving, estimable *formal*, excellent, exquisite, fine, laudable *formal*, masterly, meritorious *formal*, praiseworthy, rare, respected, superior, valuable, wonderful, worthy
🖼 contemptible, deplorable, despicable

admiration *n* adoration, adulation, affection, amazement, appreciation, approbation *formal*, approval, astonishment, delight, fureur *formal*, (high) esteem *formal*, (high) regard, idolism, kudos, pleasure, praise, respect, reverence, surprise, veneration *formal*, wonder, worship, yen *colloq*
🖼 contempt, disrespect, scorn

admire *v* **1** *admire his honesty*: adore, applaud, approve, esteem (highly) *formal*, have a high opinion of, hold in high regard/esteem *formal*, laud *formal*, like very much, look up to, praise, prize *formal*, respect, revere, take your hat off to *colloq*, think highly of, think the world of *colloq*, venerate *formal*, worship **2** *admire a car*: appreciate, approve of, like, value
🖼 **1** censure, despise

admirer *n* **1** *a great admirer of classical music*: adherent, aficionado *formal*, buff *colloq*, devotee, disciple, enthusiast, fan, fiend *colloq*, follower, freak *colloq*, idolater, idolizer, supporter, worshipper **2** *a woman's admirers*: beau *formal*, boyfriend, gallant *formal*, girlfriend, lover, suitor, sweetheart, wooer *formal*
🖼 **1** critic, opponent

admissible *adj* acceptable, allowable, allowed, justifiable, lawful, legitimate, licit *formal*, passable, permissible, permitted, tolerable, tolerated
🖼 illegitimate, inadmissible

admission *n* **1** *refuse admission*: access, entrance, ingress *formal*, permission, right of access **2** *admission is £5*: admission fee, entrance, entrance fee, entry charge **3** *an admission of guilt*: acceptance, acknowledgement, affirmation, allowance, avowal *formal*, concession, confession, declaration, disclosure, divulgence, exposé, granting, mea culpa *formal*, peccavi *formal*, profession, recognition, revelation
🖼 **1** exclusion, prohibition **3** contradiction, denial

admit *v* **1** *admit I was wrong*: accept, acknowledge, affirm *formal*, agree, allow, blurt out *colloq*, come clean *colloq*, concede, confess, declare, disclose, divulge, eat your words *colloq*, grant, own up, profess, recognize, reveal, unburden yourself **2** *be admitted to the palace*: accept, allow to enter, give access, give admission, initiate, introduce, intromit *formal*, let in, receive, take in
🖼 **1** deny, hide **2** exclude, let out, shut out

admittance *n* acceptance, admission, admitting, entrance, ingress *formal*, initiation, introduction, letting in, reception, (right of) access, (right of) entry
🖼 exclusion

admixture *n* alloy, amalgam, amalgamation, blend, combination, commixture *formal*, compound, fusion, intermixture *formal*, mix, mixture, tincture *formal*

admonish *v* berate *formal*, censure, chide, correct, counsel, discipline, exhort, rebuke, reprimand, reprove, scold, tell off *colloq*, upbraid, warn

admonition *n* berating *formal*, censure, correction, counsel, exhortation, rebuke, reprehension *formal*, reprimand, reproof, scolding, telling-off *colloq*, warning

adolescence *n* boyhood, development, girlhood, immaturity, juvenescence *formal*, juvenility *formal*, minority, puberty, pubescence *formal*, teenage years, teens, youth, youthfulness

adolescent *adj* 1 *an adolescent son*: developing, growing, juvenescent *formal*, juvenile, pubescent *formal*, teenage, young, youthful 2 *adolescent behaviour*: childish, immature, juvenile, puerile
♦ *n* juvenile, minor, teenager, young adult, young person, youth

adopt *v* 1 *adopt children*: foster, take as your own, take in 2 *adopt a policy*: accept, appropriate *formal*, approve, assume, back, choose, embrace *formal*, endorse, espouse *formal*, follow, maintain, nominate, ratify, select, support, take on, take up
🔁 1 disown 2 reject

adoption *n* 1 *the adoption of children*: (long-term) fostering, taking as your own, taking-in 2 *the adoption of a suggestion*: acceptance, approbation *formal*, appropriation *formal*, approval, backing, choice, embracement *formal*, embracing *formal*, endorsement, espousal *formal*, ratification, selection, support, taking-on, taking-up

adorable *adj* appealing, attractive, bewitching, captivating, charming, darling, dear, delightful, enchanting, fetching, lovable, pleasing, precious, sweet, winning, winsome, wonderful
🔁 abominable, hateful

adoration *n* 1 *adoration for someone*: admiration, cherishing, devotion, doting on, esteem *formal*, (high) regard, love 2 *adoration of God*: exaltation, glorification, homage, idolization, magnification, praise, reverence, veneration, worship
🔁 1 abhorrence, detestation

adore *v* 1 *adore your parents*: admire, be devoted to, be fond of, cherish, dote on, esteem (highly) *formal*, hold dear, honour, love, revere, think the world of *colloq*, venerate *formal*, worship 2 *adore apricots*: be fond of, be partial to, enjoy, enjoy greatly, have a weakness for *colloq*, like very much, love, not be able to resist *colloq*, relish
🔁 2 abhor *formal*, hate

adorn *v* adonize *formal*, apparel, array *formal*, beautify *formal*, bedeck *formal*, bedight *formal*, bedizen *formal*, begem *formal*, bejewel *formal*, bestick *formal*, crown, deck, decorate, doll up *colloq*, embellish, emblazon *formal*, enhance, enrich, festoon *formal*, furbish *formal*, garnish, gild, grace, impearl *formal*, miniate *formal*, ornament, tart up *colloq*, trim

adornment *n* 1 *bodily adornment*: beautification, bedizenment *formal*, decorating, embellishment, enrichment, garniture *formal*, ornamentation 2 *gold adornments*: accessory, decoration, falbala *formal*, fallal *formal*, fallalery *formal*, fandangle *formal*, figgery *formal*, flounce, frill, frippery,

furbelow *formal*, garnish, garnishry *formal*, gilding *formal*, jewellery, ornament, trappings, trimmings

adrift *adj* 1 *the boat had been cut adrift*: anchorless, at sea, drifting, off course 2 *feel adrift and lonely*: aimless, directionless, goalless, insecure, rootless, unsettled
🔁 1 anchored 2 stable

adroit *adj* able, adept, clever, deft, dexterous, expert, masterful, proficient, skilful
🔁 clumsy, inept, maladroit

adroitness *n* ability, adeptness, cleverness, competence, deftness, dexterity, expertise, facility, finesse, mastery, proficiency, skilfulness, skill
🔁 clumsiness, ineptitude

adulation *n* blandishment *formal*, bootlicking, fawning, flattery, hero worship, idolization, personality cult, praise, sycophancy

adulatory *adj* blandishing *formal*, bootlicking, fawning, flattering, fulsome *formal*, obsequious *formal*, praising, servile, sycophantic, unctuous *formal*
🔁 unflattering

adult *adj* 1 *adult responsibilities*: developed, full-grown, fully-grown, grown-up, mature, of age, ripe, ripened 2 *adult magazines*: obscene, pornographic, sexually explicit
🔁 1 immature

adulterate *v* attenuate *formal*, bastardize *formal*, contaminate, corrupt, debase, defile, degrade, deteriorate, devalue, dilute, make impure, pollute, taint, vitiate *formal*
🔁 purify, refine

adultery *n* a bit on the side *colloq*, affair, cheating *colloq*, entanglement, extramarital relations/relationship, extramarital sex, infidelity, playing around *slang*, playing the field *slang*, unchastity, unfaithfulness
🔁 faithfulness, fidelity

advance *v* 1 *medical procedures have advanced*: come forward, come on in leaps and bounds *colloq*, forge ahead, go ahead, go forward, make great strides *colloq*, make headway, make progress, move forward, move on, proceed, progress, surge forward 2 *advance the date of the wedding*: bring forward, make earlier 3 *the army is advancing*: accelerate, expedite *formal*, hasten *formal*, send forward, speed (up) 4 *her pleading advanced his cause*: assist, benefit, facilitate, foster, further, grow, help, increase, promote, support, upgrade 5 *advance an idea*: adduce *formal*, allege, bring forward, cite, furnish, offer, present, proffer *formal*, provide, put forward, submit, suggest, supply 6 *advance a sum of money*: give, lend, loan, pay, pay beforehand, pay in advance
🔁 1 retreat 2 put back 3 retard *formal* 4 hinder, impede
♦ *n* 1 *recent advances in medicine*: advancement *formal*, amelioration *formal*, betterment *formal*, breakthrough, development, forward movement, furtherance *formal*, going forward, growth, headway, improvement, increase, marching forward, moving forward, onward movement, progress, progression, step 2 *an advance of £500*: credit, deposit, down payment, loan, prepayment, retainer
🔁 1 recession, retreat

advanced *adj* **1** *an advanced design*: ahead, ahead of the times, at the cutting/leading edge, avant-garde, complex, foremost, forward, forward-looking, higher, hi-tech, leading, precocious, progressive, sophisticated, state-of-the-art, ultra-modern, up-to-date **2** *an advanced course of studies*: complex, high-level
▣ 1 backward, retarded **2** elementary

advancement *n* **1** *advancement in a career*: betterment, furtherance, preferment *formal*, promotion **2** *the advancement of science*: advance, development, gain, growth, headway, improvement, progress, rise
▣ 1 demotion **2** retardation

advances *n* addresses, approach(es), attentions, moves, overtures, proposition

advantage *n* **1** *the advantages of technology*: aid, asset, assistance, avail *formal*, beauty *colloq*, benefit, blessing, boon, convenience, fruit, gain, good, good point, help, interest, pay-off *colloq*, plus, plus point, pro, profit, service, use, usefulness, utility, virtue, welfare **2** *an advantage over other candidates*: dominance, edge, everything going for you *colloq*, head start *colloq*, lead, leverage, precedence, pre-eminence, superiority, sway, the odds in your favour *colloq*, upper hand
▣ 1 disadvantage, drawback, hindrance

advantageous *adj* beneficial, convenient, favourable, furthersome *formal*, gainful, helpful, of assistance, of service, opportune *formal*, profitable, propitious *formal*, remunerative, rewarding, useful, valuable, worthwhile
▣ adverse, damaging, disadvantageous

advent *n* accession *formal*, appearance, approach, arrival, beginning, birth, coming, dawn, entrance, inception *formal*, introduction, occurrence, onset

adventure *n* **1** *exciting adventures*: chance, enterprise, escapade, experience, exploit, hazard, incident, occurrence, risk, speculation, undertaking, venture **2** *a life of adventure*: danger, enterprise, excitement, peril, risk, romance

adventurer *n* hero, heroine, opportunist, traveller, venturer, voyager, wanderer

adventurous *adj* **1** *an adventurous person*: audacious, bold, daring, enterprising, gutsy *colloq*, headstrong, impetuous, intrepid, rash, reckless, risky, spunky *colloq*, venturesome **2** *an adventurous life*: dangerous, enterprising, exciting, hazardous, perilous, risky, romantic
▣ 1 cautious, chary, prudent **2** unadventurous

adversary *n* antagonist, competitor, contestant, enemy, foe, opponent, opposer, rival
▣ ally, friend, supporter

adverse *adj* antagonistic, conflicting, contrary, counter, counter-productive, detrimental, disadvantageous, harmful, hostile, hurtful, inauspicious *formal*, inexpedient *formal*, injurious, inopportune *formal*, negative, opposing, opposite, uncongenial, unfavourable, unfortunate, unfriendly, unlucky, unpropitious *formal*, untoward *formal*
▣ advantageous, favourable

adversity *n* affliction, bad luck, calamity, catastrophe, disaster, distress, hard times, hardship, hell *colloq*, ill fortune, ill luck, living hell *colloq*, misery, misfortune, reverse, sorrow, suffering, the pits *slang*, trial, tribulation *formal*, trouble, woe, wretchedness
▣ prosperity

advertise *v* **1** *advertise a product*: hype *colloq*, market, merchandise, plug *colloq*, praise, promote, publicize, push *colloq*, sell, tout **2** *advertise the time of a performance*: announce, broadcast, declare, display, inform, make known, make public, notify, proclaim, promulgate *formal*, publish

advertisement *n* ad *colloq*, advert *colloq*, announcement, bill, blurb, circular, commercial, display, handbill, handout, hype *colloq*, jingle, leaflet, marketing, notice, placard, plug *colloq*, poster, promotion, propaganda, publicity, trailer

advice *n* **1** *give someone advice*: caution, constructive criticism, counsel, counselling, direction, dos and don'ts, encouragement, guidance, help, injunction, instruction, opinion, recommendation, suggestion, tip, view, warning, wisdom, word **2** *a remittance advice*: communication, information, memorandum, notice, notification

advisability *n* appropriateness, aptness, desirability, expediency *formal*, judiciousness, prudence, soundness, suitability, wisdom
▣ folly, inadvisability

advisable *adj* appropriate, apt, beneficial, best, correct, desirable, fit, fitting, judicious, politic *formal*, profitable, proper, prudent, recommended, sensible, sound, suggested, suitable, wise, wisest
▣ foolish, inadvisable

advise *v* **1** *he advised them to see a lawyer*: caution, commend, counsel, enjoin *formal*, forewarn, give guidance, give/offer/make recommendations, give/offer/make suggestions, guide, instruct, recommend, suggest, teach, tutor, urge, warn **2** *a poster advising clients of their rights*: acquaint, apprise *formal*, give notice, inform, make known, notify, report, tell

adviser *n* aide, authority, coach, confidant(e), consultant, counsel, counsellor, guide, guru, helper, instructor, mentor, right-hand man/woman, teacher, therapist, tutor

advisory *adj* advising, consultative, consultatory *formal*, consulting, counselling, helping, recommending

advocacy *n* adoption, advancement *formal*, backing, campaigning, championing, defence, encouragement, espousal *formal*, justification, patronage, promotion, promulgation *formal*, propagation, proposal, recommendation, support, upholding

advocate *v* adopt, advise, argue for, back (up), be behind *colloq*, be pro *colloq*, believe in, campaign for, champion, countenance *formal*, defend, encourage, endorse, espouse *formal*, favour, justify, lobby, patronize, plead for, press for, promote, propose, recommend, subscribe to, support, sympathize with, throw your weight behind *colloq*, uphold, urge
▣ deprecate *formal*, disparage *formal*, impugn *formal*
♦ *n* **1** *an advocate of human rights*: campaigner, champion, defender, exponent, pleader, promoter, proponent, speaker, spokesperson,

supporter, upholder, vindicator **2** *the advocate in a court of law:* attorney, barrister, counsel, lawyer
F 1 critic, opponent

aegis *n* advocacy, auspices, backing, championship, favour, guardianship, patronage, protection, sponsorship, support, wing

aeroplane see aircraft

affability *n* amiability, amicability, approachability, benevolence, benignity *formal*, congeniality, conversableness *formal*, cordiality, courtesy, friendliness, geniality, good humour, good nature, graciousness, kindliness, mildness, obligingness, openness, pleasantness, sociability, warmth
F coolness, reserve, reticence, unfriendliness

affable *adj* agreeable, amiable, amicable, approachable, benevolent, congenial, cordial, courteous, expansive, friendly, genial, good-humoured, good-natured, gracious, kindly, mild, obliging, open, pleasant, sociable, warm
F cool, reserved, reticent, unfriendly

affair *n* **1** *spokesman for foreign affairs:* activity, business, circumstance, concern, episode, event, happening, incident, interest, issue, matter, occurrence, operation, proceeding, project, question, responsibility, subject, topic, transaction, undertaking **2** *have an affair:* amour, fling *colloq*, intrigue, liaison, love affair, relationship, romance

affect *v* **1** *changes that affect the schedule:* act on, alter, apply to, bear upon, change, concern, do to, have an effect/influence on, impact, impinge upon, influence, involve, modify, prevail over, regard, relate to, sway, transform **2** *deeply affected by the poverty:* disturb, impress, move, overcome, perturb *formal*, stir, touch, trouble, upset **3** *the disease affects the body:* attack, strike, take hold of **4** *affect an attitude:* adopt, assume *formal*, counterfeit, fake, feign *formal*, imitate, pretend, profess, put on, sham, simulate

---

affect or *effect*? *Affect* is always a verb. Its most common meaning is 'to have an influence on' or 'change the circumstances of': *The accident affected his eyesight. Effect* is used as a noun or a verb: as a noun it means 'result or consequence': *recover from the effects of his illness.* As a verb it is used in formal styles to mean 'to cause or bring about': *effect a reconciliation with his parents.*

---

affectation *n* act, airs, airs and graces, appearance, artificiality, façade, false display, imitation, insincerity, mannerism, pose, pretence, pretentiousness, sham, show, simulation, theatricism
F artlessness, ingenuousness

affected *adj* artificial, assumed *formal*, contrived, counterfeit, fake, feigned *formal*, insincere, la-di-da *colloq*, literose *formal*, mannered, minikin *formal*, phoney *colloq*, pompous, precious, pretentious, put-on, sham, simulated, stiff, studied, twee, unnatural
F genuine, natural

affecting *adj* impressive, moving, pathetic, piteous, pitiable, pitiful, poignant, sad, stirring, touching, troubling

affection *n* amity *formal*, attachment, care, caring, desire, devotion, favour, feeling, fondness, friendliness, goodwill, inclination, kindness, liking, love, partiality, passion, penchant *formal*, predilection *formal*, predisposition *formal*, proclivity *formal*, propensity *formal*, tenderness, warmth
F antipathy, dislike

affectionate *adj* amiable, attached, caring, cordial, devoted, doting, fond, friendly, kind, loving, tender, warm, warm-hearted
F cold, undemonstrative

affiliate *v* ally, amalgamate, annex, associate, band together, combine, confederate *formal*, conjoin *formal*, connect, incorporate, join, merge, syndicate, unite

affiliation *n* alliance, amalgamation, association, bond, coalition, combination, confederation, connection, federation, incorporation, joining, league, link, membership, merger, relationship, tie, union

affinity *n* **1** *a natural affinity with his audience:* attraction, bond, chemistry *colloq*, compatibility, fondness, good terms, liking, partiality, predisposition *formal*, propensity *formal*, rapport **2** *an affinity with Europeans:* analogy, comparability, correspondence, likeness, resemblance, similarity, similitude *formal*
F 1 hatred **2** dissimilarity

affirm *v* assert, asseverate *formal*, attest *formal*, aver *formal*, avouch *formal*, avow *formal*, certify, confirm, corroborate, declare, endorse, maintain, pronounce, ratify, state, swear, testify, witness
F deny, refute

affirmation *n* affirmance *formal*, assertion, asseveration *formal*, attestation *formal*, averment *formal*, avouchment *formal*, avowal *formal*, certification, confirmation, corroboration, declaration, deposition *formal*, endorsement, oath, pronouncement, ratification, statement, testimony, witness

affirmative *adj* agreeing, approving, assenting, concurring, confirming, consenting, corroborative, emphatic, positive
F dissenting, negative

affix *v* add, adjoin *formal*, annex, append, attach, bind, connect, fasten, glue, join, paste, pin on, stick, subjoin *formal*, tack, tag
F detach

afflict *v* beset *formal*, burden, distress, grieve, harass, harm, hurt, oppress, pain, plague, smite *old use*, strike, torment, torture, trouble, try, visit, wound
F comfort, solace *formal*

---

afflict or *inflict*? *Afflict* means 'to cause pain or distress to': *Pre-fight nerves afflict almost everyone. Inflict* means 'to impose something unpleasant or unwanted': *They inflicted heavy casualties on the enemy.*

---

affliction *n* adversity, calamity, cross, curse, depression, disaster, disease, distress, grief, hardship, illness, misery, misfortune, ordeal, pain, plague, sickness, sorrow, suffering, torment, trial, tribulation *formal*, trouble, woe, wretchedness blessing, comfort, consolation *formal*, solace *formal*

affluence *n* abundance, fortune, megabucks *slang*, opulence *formal*, plenty, profusion, property, prosperity, riches, substance, tidy sum *colloq*, wealth, wealthiness
F3 poverty

affluent *adj* comfortable, flush *colloq*, in the money *colloq*, loaded *slang*, moneyed, opulent *formal*, prosperous, rich, rolling in it *colloq*, wealthy, well-heeled *colloq*, well-off, well-to-do
F3 impoverished, poor

afford *v* **1** *afford school fees:* allow, be able to pay, bear, have enough for, manage, pay for, spare, sustain **2** *privileges afforded by the membership:* furnish, generate, give, grant, impart, offer, produce, provide, supply, yield

affray *n* brawl, brush, contest, disturbance, feud, fight, fisticuffs *colloq*, fracas, fray, free-for-all *colloq*, mêlée, quarrel, riot, row, scrap *colloq*, scuffle, set-to, skirmish, squabble, tussle, wrangle

affront *v* abuse, anger, annoy, displease, incense, insult, irritate, offend, outrage, pique, provoke, slight, vex
F3 appease, compliment
♦ *n* abuse, aspersion *formal*, discourtesy, disrespect, indignity, injury, insult, kick in the teeth *colloq*, offence, outrage, provocation, rudeness, slap in the face *colloq*, slight, slur, snub, vexation, wrong
F3 compliment

afoot *adj* about, abroad *formal*, around, brewing, circulating, current, going about, in the air, in the pipeline *colloq*, in the wind

afraid *adj* **1** *afraid of spiders:* aghast *formal*, alarmed, anxious, apprehensive, cowardly, craven, daunted, distrustful, faint-hearted, fearful, frightened, intimidated, nervous, panic-stricken, petrified, reluctant, scared, suspicious, terrified, timid, timorous, tremulous *formal* **2** *I'm afraid she's badly hurt:* concerned, regretful, sorry
F3 1 bold, brave, confident, unafraid

afresh *adv* again, anew, newly, once again, once more, over again

after *prep* **1** *life after death:* following, subsequent to **2** *after her mother:* given the same name as, in honour of **3** *after the way I've been treated:* as a result of, because of, in consequence of, owing to
F3 1 before

aftermath *n* after-effects, consequences, effects, end, outcome, repercussions, results, upshot, wake

afterwards *adv* after that, later (on), next, subsequently, then

again *adv* afresh, anew, another time, encore, once again, once more, one more time, over again, yet again

against *prep* **1** *against the wall:* abutting *formal*, adjacent to, close up to, in contact with, on, touching **2** *against corporal punishment:* antagonistic to, anti *colloq*, confronting, facing, fronting, hostile to, in contrast to, in defiance of, in opposition to, in the face of, opposed to, opposing, opposite to, resisting, versus
F3 2 for, in favour of, pro *colloq*

age *n* **1** *the Ice Age:* date, day, days, duration, eon, epoch, era, generation, period, span, time, years **2** *the experience of age:* advancing/declining years, decline, decrepitude *formal*, dotage, elderliness, maturity, old age, senescence *formal*, senility, seniority
F3 2 salad days *colloq*, youth
♦ *v* come of age, decline, degenerate, deteriorate, grow old/up, mature, mellow, obsolesce *formal*, ripen, season, wither

aged *adj* advanced (in years), ageing, ancient *colloq*, elderly, geriatric, getting on *colloq*, grey, have seen better days *colloq*, hoary, no spring chicken *colloq*, not as young as you were *colloq*, old, over the hill *colloq*, past it *colloq*, patriarchal, senescent *formal*, superannuated, with one foot in the grave *colloq*
F3 young, youthful

agency *n* **1** *a recruitment agency:* bureau, business, company, department, firm, office, organization, work **2** *pollution, through the agency of the motor car:* action, activity, effect, force, influence, instrumentality, intervention, means, mechanism, medium, operation, power, workings

agenda *n* calendar, diary, list, menu, plan, programme, schedule, scheme of work, timetable, to-do list

agent *n* **1** *a travel agent:* assignee, broker, delegate, deputy, doer, emissary, envoy, factor, functionary, go-between, intermediary, middleman, minister, mover, negotiator, operative, operator, performer, proxy, rep *colloq*, representative, substitute, trustee, worker **2** *a secret agent:* double agent, mole *colloq*, operative *US*, spy **3** *water-purifying agents:* agency, cause, channel, force, instrument, means, vehicle

agglomeration *n* accumulation, aggregate, aggregation *formal*, augmentation *formal*, build-up, collection, gathering, increase, store

aggrandize *v* advance, amplify, dignify, elevate, enhance, enlarge, ennoble, enrich, exaggerate, exalt, glamorize, glorify, inflate, magnify, make more powerful, make richer, promote, upgrade, widen
F3 belittle, debase

aggravate *v* **1** *aggravate the problem:* add fuel to the fire/flames *colloq*, add insult to injury *colloq*, compound, exacerbate *formal*, exaggerate, heighten, increase, inflame, intensify, magnify, make worse, rub salt in the wound *colloq*, worsen **2** *she was really aggravated by his lateness:* annoy, exasperate, get on someone's nerves *colloq*, get up someone's nose *colloq*, harass, incense, irk, irritate, needle *colloq*, pester, provoke, rub up the wrong way *colloq*, tease, vex
F3 1 alleviate, improve **2** appease, mollify, soothe

aggravation *n* annoyance, exasperation, hassle *colloq*, irksomeness, irritation, provocation, teasing, vexation

aggregate *n* accumulation, amount, collection, combination, entirety, generality, grand total, sum, sum total, total, total/whole amount, totality, whole

aggression *n* **1** *aggression against a neighbouring state:* antagonism, assault, attack, belligerence, encroachment, incursion, infringement, injury,

intrusion, invasion, offence, offensive, onslaught, provocation, raid, strike **2** *the youth's aggression:* aggressiveness, bellicosity *formal*, belligerence, combativeness, hostility, militancy, pugnacity *formal*
F₃ 1 peace, resistance **2** gentleness, passivity

aggressive *adj* **1** *an aggressive person:* argumentative, belligerent, brutal, contentious, cut-throat *colloq*, destructive, ferocious, hostile, intrusive, invasive, offensive, provocative, pugnacious *formal*, quarrelsome, ruthless, savage **2** *an aggressive sales rep:* assertive, bold, forceful, go-ahead, in-your-face *slang*, pushy *colloq*, vigorous, zealous
F₃ 1 friendly, peaceable, submissive, **2** timid, unassertive

aggressor *n* assailant, assaulter, attacker, intruder, invader, offender, provoker
F₃ victim

aggrieved *adj* annoyed, bitter, distressed, hurt, ill-used, injured, insulted, maltreated, offended, pained, resentful, saddened, unhappy, upset, wronged
F₃ happy, pleased

aghast *adj* amazed, appalled, astonished, astounded, confounded, dismayed, horrified, horror-struck, shocked, startled, stunned, stupefied, thunderstruck

agile *adj* **1** *an agile person:* active, athletic, brisk, fleet, flexible, limber, lithe, lively, mobile, nimble, quick, sprightly, spry, swift **2** *an agile mind:* acute, alert, astute, clever, quick-witted, sharp
F₃ 1 clumsy, stiff **2** slow

agility *n* **1** *agility of movement:* activeness, briskness, flexibility, liveliness, mobility, nimbleness, quickness, swiftness **2** *agility of thought:* alertness, astuteness, quick-wittedness, sharpness
F₃ 1 clumsiness, stiffness **2** slowness

agitate *v* **1** *the news agitated them:* alarm, confuse, discompose, disconcert, disquiet, distract, disturb, flurry, fluster, perturb *formal*, ruffle, trouble, unnerve, unsettle, upset, worry **2** *agitate for reform:* argue, arouse, campaign, estimulate, excite, ferment, fight, incite, inflame, rouse, stir up, work up **3** *agitate the mixture:* beat, churn, rattle, rock, shake, stir, toss, whisk
F₃ 1 calm, tranquillize

agitated *adj* anxious, disconcerted, distraught, disturbed, flustered, in a lather *colloq*, nervous, ruffled, troubled, unnerved, unsettled, upset, worried
F₃ calm, composed

agitator *n* activist, agent provocateur, firebrand, fomenter, inciter, instigator, rabble-rouser, revolutionary, stirrer *colloq*, subversive, troublemaker

agnostic *n* doubter, doubting Thomas *colloq*, sceptic, unbeliever

ago *adv* earlier, from that time, gone, past, previously, since

agog *adj* avid, curious, eager, enthralled, enthusiastic, excited, impatient, in suspense, keen, on tenterhooks *colloq*, on the edge of your seat *colloq*
F₃ incurious

agonize *v* labour, strain, strive, struggle, trouble, worry, wrestle

agonizing *adj* distressing, excruciating, harrowing, painful, racking, tormenting, torturous, worrying

agony *n* affliction, anguish, distress, hurt, misery, pain, spasm, suffering, throes, torment, torture, tribulation, woe, wretchedness

agree *v* **1** *agree with someone:* accord *formal*, be at one, be of one mind, be of the same opinion, come to/reach an agreement, compromise, concur, get on, go along with *colloq*, go with *colloq*, make concessions, meet halfway *colloq*, see eye to eye *colloq*, settle, share the view **2** *agree to your request:* accede *formal*, accept, acquiesce in *formal*, admit, allow, assent *formal*, comply, concede, consent, give the go-ahead *colloq*, give the thumbs-up *colloq*, grant, permit, rubber-stamp *colloq*, say yes to, yield **3** *the reports do not agree:* conform, correspond, fit, match, suit, tally
F₃ 1 disagree **2** refuse **3** conflict, differ, disagree

agreeable *adj* **1** *agreeable weather:* acceptable, delightful, enjoyable, fine, nice, pleasant **2** *an agreeable person:* amicable, attractive, charming, congenial, delightful, friendly, good-natured, likeable, nice, pleasant, sympathetic **3** *agreeable to a suggestion:* amenable, compliant, willing
F₃ 1 disagreeable, nasty **2** unpleasant **3** reluctant to accept, unwilling

agreement *n* **1** *a trade agreement:* arrangement, bargain, compact *formal*, concordat *formal*, contract, covenant, deal, deed, indenture *formal*, pact, settlement, treaty, understanding **2** *be in agreement:* affinity, assent *formal*, complaisance *formal*, consensus, harmony, sympathy, unanimity, union **3** *the agreement of the reports:* accord *formal*, compatibility, concord *formal*, concurrence, conformity, consistency, consonance *formal*, correspondence, fitting, matching, similarity, tally
F₃ 2 disagreement **3** inconsistency

agricultural *adj* agrarian, agronomic, bucolic *formal*, cultivated, farmed, farming, geoponic *formal*, georgic *formal*, pastoral, praedial *formal*, rural

agriculture *n* agribusiness *technical*, agronomics, agronomy, agroscience, cultivation, farming, geoponics, husbandry, tillage

aground *adv* ashore, high and dry, on the rocks
F₃ afloat

ahead *adv* **1** *glance ahead:* at the head, forward, in front, leading, onward **2** *ahead on points:* advanced, at an advantage, in the forefront, in the lead, superior, to the fore, winning **3** *plan ahead:* before, earlier on, in advance

aid *v* **1** *aid an invalid:* accommodate *formal*, assist, co-operate with, favour, help, oblige *formal*, rally round, relieve, second, serve, subsidize, succour *formal*, support, sustain **2** *aid a process:* boost, ease, encourage, expedite *formal*, facilitate, hasten *formal*, promote, speed up
F₃ 1 not lift a finger *colloq* **2** hinder, impede, obstruct
♦ *n* **1** *aid for refugees:* assistance, benefit, contribution, donation, encouragement, favour, funding, gift, grant, patronage, relief, service, sponsorship, subsidy, subvention *formal* **2** *turn to*

someone for aid: a (helping) hand *colloq*, a leg up *colloq*, a shot in the arm *colloq*, assistance, back-up, boost, help, prop, succour *formal*, support
🔁 2 hindrance, impediment, obstruction

aide *n* adjutant, adviser, advocate, aide-de-camp, assistant, attaché, confidant, disciple, follower, right-hand man, right-hand person, supporter

ail *v* afflict, bother, distress, fail, irritate, pain, sicken, trouble, upset, weaken, worry
🔁 comfort, flourish

ailing *adj* debilitated *formal*, diseased, failing, feeble, frail, ill, indisposed *formal*, infirm, invalid, languishing, off-colour *colloq*, out of sorts *colloq*, poorly, sick, sickly, suffering, under the weather *colloq*, unfit, unsound, unwell, weak
🔁 fit, flourishing, healthy, thriving

ailment *n* affliction, complaint, disability, disease, disorder, illness, indisposition *formal*, infection, infirmity, malady, sickness, weakness

aim *v* 1 *aim the gun at his head:* direct, level, point, shoot at, sight, take aim, target, train, zero in on *colloq* 2 *what I aim to achieve:* aspire, attempt, design, endeavour, intend, mean, plan, propose, purpose, resolve, seek, set your sights on, strive, try, want, wish
♦ *n* ambition, aspiration, course, design, desire, direction, dream, end, goal, hope, intention, mark, mission, mission statement, motive, object, objective, plan, purpose, scheme, target, wish

aimless *adj* 1 *aimless movement:* chance, directionless, drifting, erratic, haphazard, purposeless, rambling, random, stray, undirected, unguided, unmotivated, unpredictable, unsettled, wandering, wayward 2 *an aimless gesture:* futile, goalless, pointless, purposeless, undirected
🔁 1 determined, positive, purposeful
2 purposeful

air *n* 1 *birds flying in the air:* atmosphere, ether *formal*, heavens, oxygen, sky 2 *need some air:* blast, breath, breeze, draught, fresh air, puff, waft, wind, zephyr *formal* 3 *an air of distraction:* ambience *formal*, appearance, aspect, aura, bearing, carriage, character, demeanour *formal*, effect, feeling, impression, look, manner
♦ *v* 1 *air a room:* aerate, freshen, ventilate 2 *air an opinion:* broadcast, circulate, communicate, declare, disclose, disseminate, divulge, expose, express, give vent to, have your say *colloq*, make known, make public, publicize, publish, reveal, speak your mind *colloq*, state, tell, utter, voice

aircraft

> *Types of aircraft include:*
> aeroplane, plane, jet, jumbo, Concorde, airbus, helicopter, monoplane, two-seater, air-ambulance, freighter, seaplane, glider, hang-glider, microlight, hot-air balloon; fighter, spitfire, bomber, kite *colloq*, jump-jet, dive-bomber, chopper *colloq*, spy plane, delta-wing, swing-wing, troop-carrier, airship, turbojet, VTOL (vertical take-off and landing), warplane, zeppelin

airing *n* 1 *give clothes an airing:* aeration, freshening, ventilation 2 *the airing of opinions:* broadcast, circulation, communication, declaration, disclosure, dissemination *formal*, divulgence, exposure, expression, making

known, publication, revelation, statement, uttering, voicing

airless *adj* badly/poorly ventilated, close, heavy, muggy, musty, oppressive, stale, stifling, stuffy, suffocating, sultry, unventilated
🔁 airy, fresh

airs *n* affectation *formal*, affectedness *formal*, arrogance, artificiality, haughtiness, hauteur *formal*, pomposity *formal*, posing, pretensions, pretentiousness, superciliousness, swank *colloq*

airtight *adj* closed, impenetrable, impermeable, sealed, tight-fitting

airy *adj* 1 *an airy room:* blowy, breezy, draughty, gusty, open, roomy, spacious, well-ventilated, windy 2 *gave an airy wave:* casual, cheerful, happy, high-spirited, jaunty, light-hearted, lively, nonchalant, offhand
🔁 1 airless, close, heavy, oppressive, stuffy

aisle *n* alleyway, corridor, gangway, lane, passage, passageway, path, walkway

alarm *n* 1 *drew back in alarm:* anxiety, apprehension, consternation, dismay, distress, fear, fright, horror, nervousness, panic, perturbation *formal*, scare, shock, terror, trepidation, uneasiness 2 *a burglar alarm:* alarm-bell, alert, bell, danger signal, distress signal, siren, tocsin *formal*, warning
🔁 1 calmness, composure
♦ *v* affright *formal*, agitate, daunt, dismay, distress, frighten, make afraid, panic, perturb *formal*, put the wind up *colloq*, rattle *colloq*, scare, startle, terrify, unnerve
🔁 calm, reassure, soothe

alarming *adj* daunting, dismaying, distressing, disturbing, dreadful, frightening, ominous, perturbing *formal*, scary, shocking, startling, terrifying, threatening, unnerving, worrying
🔁 reassuring

alarmist *n* doomwatcher, pessimist, scaremonger
🔁 optimist

alcohol *n* booze *slang*, drink, Dutch courage *colloq*, fire-water *colloq*, hard stuff *colloq*, intoxicant, liquor, spirits, strong drink, the bottle *colloq*

alcoholic *adj* brewed, distilled, fermented, hard, inebriating, intoxicating, strong
♦ *n* alkie *slang*, boozer *slang*, dipso *slang*, dipsomaniac, drinker, drunk, drunkard, hard drinker, heavy drinker, inebriate, lush *slang*, piss artist *slang*, soak *slang*, tippler *colloq*, toper *slang*, tosspot *slang*, wino *slang*

alcove *n* bay, booth, carrel, compartment, corner, cubbyhole, cubicle, niche, nook, recess

alert *adj* active, agile, attentive, awake, brisk, careful, circumspect, heedful, lively, nimble, observant, on the ball *colloq*, on the lookout, on the qui vive *formal*, on your toes *colloq*, perceptive, prepared, quick, ready, sharp-eyed, sharp-witted, spirited, vigilant, wary, watchful, wide-awake, with your eyes open/peeled *colloq*
🔁 listless, slow, unprepared
♦ *v* alarm, forewarn, inform, notify, signal, tip off, warn

alias *n* allonym *formal*, anonym *formal*, assumed name, false name, nickname, nom de guerre, nom de plume, pen name, pseudonym, sobriquet *formal*, stage name

♦ *adv* aka *colloq*, also called, also known as, formerly, otherwise, otherwise known as, under the name of

alibi *n* cover-up, defence, excuse, explanation, justification, pretext, reason, story

alien *adj* **1** *an alien culture*: exotic, extraneous, extraterrestrial, foreign, remote **2** *alien surroundings*: incongruous, outlandish, strange, unfamiliar **3** *alien to her nature*: antagonistic, conflicting, contrary, incompatible, inimical *formal*, opposed, repugnant *formal*
♦ *n* foreigner, immigrant, newcomer, outsider, stranger
⊞ native, resident

alienate *v* antagonize, disaffect *formal*, divorce, estrange, make hostile, separate, set against, turn away, turn off
⊞ unite

alienation *n* antagonization, disaffection *formal*, disunion, diversion, divorce, estrangement, indifference, isolation, remoteness, rupture, separation, severance, turning away
⊞ endearment

alight¹ *adj* **1** *the rubbish was alight*: ablaze, blazing, burning, fiery, flaming, ignited, lighted, lit, on fire **2** *eyes alight with excitement*: alive, bright, brilliant, illuminated, lit up, lively, radiant, shining

alight² *v* **1** *passengers alighting from buses*: come down, debark *formal*, descend, disembark *formal*, dismount *formal*, get down, get off **2** *birds alighting on the branches*: come to rest, land, light, perch, settle, touch down
⊞ **1** ascend, board, get on, get onto, rise

align *v* **1** *align yourself with a political party*: affiliate, agree, ally, associate, combine, co-operate, join, join forces, side, sympathize, unite **2** *align two pieces of wood*: adjust, arrange, co-ordinate, even (up), line up, make parallel, order, range, regularize, regulate, straighten

alignment *n* **1** *alignment with a political party*: affiliation, agreement, alliance, association, co-operation, siding, sympathy **2** *alignment of the pieces*: arrangement, line, lining up, order, ranging, straightening

alike *adj* akin, analogous *formal*, cognate *formal*, comparable, corresponding, duplicate, equal, equivalent, even, identical, indistinguishable, much the same, parallel, resembling, similar, the same, uniform
⊞ different, dissimilar, unlike
♦ *adv* analogously, correspondingly, equally, in common, in the same way, similarly

alive *adj* **1** *are your parents alive?*: animate, breathing, existent, extant *formal*, having life, in existence, in the land of the living *colloq*, live, living, (still) going strong *colloq* **2** *I like her because she is so alive*: active, alert, animated, awake, brisk, energetic, full of life, lively, spirited, vibrant, vigorous, vital, vivacious, zestful **3** *alive with tourists*: abounding in, crawling with *colloq*, full of, overflowing with, swarming with *colloq*, teeming with **4** *alive to the danger*: alert to, aware of, cognizant of *formal*, heedful of, sensitive to
⊞ **1** dead, extinct **2** apathetic, lifeless **4** blind to, deaf to, unaware of

all *adj* **1** *all people are equal*: each, each and every, every, every one of, every single **2** *danced all*

night: complete, entire, every bit of, from start to finish, full, in its entirety, perfect, the whole of, total, utter
⊞ **1** no, none
♦ *n* aggregate, comprehensiveness, entirety, everybody, everyone, everything, sum, the lot *colloq*, total, total amount, universality, utmost, whole, whole amount
⊞ none, nothing
♦ *adv* altogether, completely, entirely, fully, totally, utterly, wholesale, wholly

allay *v* alleviate, blunt, calm, check, compose, diminish, ease, lessen, moderate, mollify, pacify, quell, quiet, reduce, relieve, smooth, soften, soothe, tranquillize
⊞ exacerbate, intensify

allegation *n* accusation, affirmation, assertion, asseveration *formal*, avowal *formal*, charge, claim, declaration, deposition *formal*, plea, profession, statement, testimony

allege *v* affirm, assert, attest *formal*, claim, contend, declare, hold, insist, maintain, plead, profess, put forward, state

alleged *adj* claimed, declared, described, designated, doubtful, dubious, inferred, ostensible *formal*, professed, putative *formal*, reputed, so-called, stated, supposed, suspect

allegiance *n* adherence, constancy, devotion, duty, faithfulness, fealty *formal*, fidelity, friendship, loyalty, obedience, obligation, solidarity, support
⊞ disloyalty, enmity

allegorical *adj* emblematic *formal*, figurative, metaphorical, parabolic *formal*, representative, significative *formal*, symbolic, symbolizing, typical

allegory *n* analogy, apologue *formal*, comparison, emblem *formal*, fable, legend, metaphor, myth, parable, story, symbol, symbolism, tale

allergic *adj* **1** *allergic to shellfish*: affected, hypersensitive, sensitive, susceptible **2** *allergic to Mondays*: antagonistic, averse, disinclined, dyspathetic *formal*, hostile, opposed

allergy *n* **1** *an allergy to dogs*: hypersensitivity, sensitivity, susceptibility **2** *an allergy to work*: antagonism, antipathy *formal*, aversion, disinclination *formal*, dyspathy *formal*, hostility, opposition

alleviate *v* abate, allay, assuage, check, cushion, deaden, diminish, dull, ease, lessen, mitigate, moderate, mollify, palliate *formal*, reduce, relieve, soften, soothe, subdue, temper
⊞ aggravate

alleviation *n* abatement, assuagement, deadening, diminution *formal*, dulling, easing, lessening, mitigation, moderation, mollification, palliation *formal*, reduction, relief, soothing
⊞ aggravation

alley *n* alleyway, back street, close, gate, lane, mall, passage, passageway, pathway, walk

alliance *n* affiliation, agreement, association, bloc, bond, cartel, coalition, combination, compact, confederation, conglomerate, connection, consortium, federation, guild, league, marriage, pact, partnership, syndicate, treaty, union

◨ divorce, enmity, estrangement, hostility, separation

allied *adj* affiliated, amalgamated, associated, bound, combined, connected, coupled, hand in glove *colloq*, in cahoots *colloq*, in league, joined, joint, kindred, linked, married, related, unified, united, wed
◨ estranged

allocate *v* admeasure *formal*, allot, allow, apportion, assign, budget, designate, dispense, distribute, divide, earmark, mete (out), parcel out, ration, set aside, share out

allocation *n* **1** *the allocation of funds:* allotment, apportionment, distribution, giving-out **2** *an allocation of tickets:* allowance, budget, cut *colloq*, grant, lot, measure, portion, quota, ration, share, slice of the cake *colloq*, stint

allot *v* admeasure *formal*, allocate, allow, apportion, assign, budget, designate, dispense, distribute, divide, dole out *colloq*, earmark, grant, mete, ration, set aside, share out

allotment *n* **1** *dig an allotment:* land, plot of land **2** *an allotment of funds:* allocation, allowance, apportionment, division, grant, lot, measure, partition, percentage, portion, quota, ration, share, stint

all-out *adj* complete, comprehensive, determined, exhaustive, full, full-scale, intensive, maximum, no-holds-barred *colloq*, powerful, resolute, thorough, thoroughgoing, total, undivided, unlimited, unremitting, unrestrained, unstinted, utmost, vigorous, wholesale
◨ half-hearted, perfunctory

allow *v* **1** *allow me to go out and play:* agree to, approve, authorize, consent (to) *formal*, enable, endure, give leave, give the go-ahead *colloq*, give the green light *colloq*, give your consent (to) *formal*, let, OK *colloq*, okay *colloq*, permit, put up with, sanction, say yes to, suffer, tolerate, warrant **2** *I have to allow that she is good-natured:* acknowledge, admit, agree, concede, confess, grant, own **3** *allow two hours for the journey:* afford, allocate, allot, apportion, assign, give, provide, spare
◨ **1** forbid, prevent **2** deny
▶ **allow for** arrange for, bear in mind, consider, foresee, include, keep in mind, make allowances for, make provision for, plan for, provide for, take into account
◨ discount

allowable *adj* acceptable, admissible, all right, appropriate, approved, justifiable, lawful, legal, legit *colloq*, legitimate, licit *formal*, permissible, sanctionable *formal*
◨ unacceptable

allowance *n* **1** *an annual allowance:* annuity, benefit, contribution, expense allowance, expenses, grant, income, maintenance, payment, pension, pocket money, remittance, stipend, subsistence allowance **2** *able to claim an allowance:* concession, deduction, discount, rebate, reduction, subsidy, weighting **3** *a prisoner's allowance of cigarettes:* allocation, amount, lot, portion, quota, ration, share **4** *make allowances for her inexperience:* excuse, mitigation

alloy *n* admixture *formal*, amalgam, blend, coalescence, combination, composite, compound, fusion, mixture

all right *adj* **1** *just about all right:* acceptable, adequate, allowable, average, fair, good enough, OK *colloq*, passable, reasonable, satisfactory, unobjectionable **2** *are you all right?:* fine, healthy, right as rain *colloq*, safe, secure, sound, unharmed, unhurt, unimpaired, uninjured, well, whole
◨ **1** inadequate, unacceptable
♦ *adv* acceptably, adequately, appropriately, OK *colloq*, passably, reasonably, satisfactorily, suitably, unobjectionably, well enough
◨ unacceptably, unsatisfactorily

allude *v* adumbrate *formal*, hint, imply, infer, insinuate, intimate, mention, refer, remark, speak of, suggest, touch on/upon

> *allude* or *elude*? If you *allude* to something, you refer to it; if something *eludes* you, you cannot remember it or understand it.

allure *v* attract, beguile, cajole, captivate, charm, coax, disarm, enchant, entice, entrance, fascinate, give the come-on *colloq*, interest, lead on, lure, persuade, seduce, tempt, win over, work on *colloq*
◨ repel
♦ *n* appeal, attraction, captivation, charm, enchantment, enticement, fascination, glamour, lure, magnetism, seduction, temptation

alluring *adj* arousing, attractive, beguiling, bewitching, captivating, come-hither *colloq*, desirable, enchanting, engaging, enticing, fascinating, fetching, interesting, intriguing, seductive, sensuous, sexy, tempting, winning
◨ repellent, unattractive

allusion *n* citation, hint, implication, insinuation, intimation, mention, observation, quotation, reference, remark, suggestion

> *allusion* or *illusion*? An *allusion* to something is an indirect reference to it; an *illusion* is a false belief or appearance.

ally *n* accessory, accomplice, associate, collaborator, colleague, confederate, consort, co-worker, friend, helper, partner, sidekick *colloq*, supporter
◨ antagonist, enemy
♦ *v* affiliate, amalgamate, associate, band together, collaborate, combine, confederate, connect, fraternize, go into partnership, join, join forces, league, link, marry, side, team up, unify, unite
◨ estrange, separate

almanac *n* annual, calendar, register, yearbook

almighty *adj* **1** *almighty God:* absolute, all-powerful, great, invincible, omnipotent *formal*, plenipotent *formal*, supreme **2** *an almighty crash:* awful, desperate, enormous, intense, overpowering, overwhelming, severe, terrible
◨ **1** impotent, weak

almost *adv* about, all but, approaching, approximately, as good as, close to/on, just about, more or less, nearing, nearly, not far from, not quite, practically, pretty much/well *colloq*, quasi- *formal*, to all intents and purposes, virtually, well-nigh

alone *adj* abandoned, apart, by itself, by yourself, cloistered, deserted, desolate, detached, forlorn, forsaken, isolated, lonely, lonesome, on your own, on your tod *colloq*, only, separate, sequestered *formal*, single, single-handed, sole, solitary, solo, unaccompanied, unaided, unattended, unconnected, unescorted, unique
☒ accompanied, escorted, together

aloof *adj* antisocial, chilly, cold, cool, detached, distant, forbidding, formal, haughty, inaccessible, indifferent, offish, remote, reserved, standoffish, supercilious, unapproachable, unforthcoming, unfriendly, uninterested, unresponsive, unsociable, unsympathetic
☒ concerned, friendly, sociable

aloud *adv* audibly, clearly, distinctly, intelligibly, loudly, noisily, out loud, plainly, resoundingly, sonorously, vociferously
☒ silently

alphabet

> *Alphabets and writing systems include:*
> Arabic, Byzantine, Chalcidian alphabet, cuneiform, Cyrillic, devanagari, estrangelo, finger-alphabet, futhark, Georgian, Glagol, Glossic, Greek, Gurmukhi, Hebrew, hieroglyphs, hiragana, ideograph, Initial Teaching Alphabet (ITA), International Phonetic Alphabet (IPA), kana, kanji, katakana, Kufic, linear A, linear B, logograph, nagari, naskhi, ogam, pictograph, romaji, Roman, runic, syllabary

already *adv* **1** *I've read the book already:* before now, beforehand, heretofore *formal*, hitherto *formal*, just now, previously **2** *he can already count:* by now, by that time, by then, by this time, even now, even then, so early, so soon (as this)

also *adv* additionally, along with, and, as well, as well as, besides, further, furthermore, in addition, including, moreover, plus, too

alter *v* adapt, adjust, amend, change, convert, diversify, emend, make different, metamorphose *formal*, modify, qualify, recast, reform, remodel, reshape, revise, shift, transform, transmute *formal*, transpose, turn, vary

alteration *n* adaptation, adjustment, amendment, change, conversion, difference, diversification, metamorphosis *formal*, modification, reformation, remodelling, reshaping, revision, shift, transfiguration, transformation, transmutation *formal*, transposition, variance, variation, vicissitude *formal*

altercation *n* argument, clash, disagreement, discord, dispute, dissension, fracas, logomachy *formal*, quarrel, row, squabble, wrangle

alternate *v* **1** *alternate between the two jobs:* alter, change, chop and change *colloq*, fluctuate, interchange, intersperse, oscillate, rotate, substitute, take turns, vary **2** *they alternated as club president:* follow one another, interchange, reciprocate, replace each other, rotate, take it in turns, take turns
♦ *adj* **1** *alternate weekends:* alternating, every other, every second **2** *alternate bouts of depression*

and happiness: consecutive, in turns, interchanging, one after the other, reciprocal, rotating

> **alternate** or **alternative**? *Alternate* refers to something happening or coming every second day, week, etc or in turns: *He visits them on alternate Tuesdays; alternate bursts of hot and cold water. Alternative* refers to the choice of two possibilities: *If that doesn't work, we'll have to think of an alternative plan.*

alternative *n* back-up, choice, option, other, preference, recourse, selection, substitute
♦ *adj* **1** *an alternative possibility:* another, different, other, second, substitute **2** *alternative medicine:* fringe, nontraditional, unconventional, unorthodox
☒ **2** conventional, orthodox, regular, standard, traditional

although *conj* albeit *formal*, despite the fact that, even if, even supposing, even though, granted that, howbeit *formal*, in spite of the fact that, notwithstanding *formal*, though, while, whilst *formal*

altitude *n* elevation, height, loftiness, stature, tallness

altogether *adv* **1** *altogether more efficient:* absolutely, completely, entirely, fully, perfectly, quite, thoroughly, totally, utterly, wholly **2** *the meal came to £40 altogether:* all in all, all told, in all, in total, in toto

altruistic *adj* benevolent, charitable, considerate, disinterested, generous, humane, humanitarian, philanthropic, public-spirited, selfless, self-sacrificing, unselfish
☒ selfish

always *adv* **1** *I want to stay here always:* all the time, eternally, evermore, for ever, in perpetuum, perpetually **2** *always criticizing others:* again and again, consistently, constantly, continually, endlessly, every time, forever, habitually, invariably, regularly, repeatedly, unceasingly, unfailingly, without exception
☒ **1** never

amalgam *n* admixture *formal*, aggregate *formal*, alloy, blend, coalescence, combination, commixture *formal*, compound, fusion, mixture, synthesis, union

amalgamate *v* alloy, ally, blend, coalesce, combine, commingle *formal*, compound, fuse, homogenize *formal*, incorporate, integrate, intermix, merge, mingle, synthesize, unify, unite
☒ separate

amalgamation *n* admixture *formal*, alliance, blend, coalescence, combination, commingling *formal*, compound, fusion, homogenization *formal*, incorporation, integration, joining, merger, synthesis, unification, union, unity
☒ separation

amass *v* accrue, accumulate, acquire, agglomerate *formal*, agglutinate *formal*, aggregate *formal*, assemble, collect, foregather *formal*, gain, garner *formal*, gather, heap (up), hoard, pile (up), store (up)

amateur *n* buff *colloq*, dabbler, dilettante, enthusiast, fancier, ham *colloq*, lay person, layman, non-professional
☒ professional

amateurish *adj* clumsy, crude, inept, inexpert, lay, non-professional, unpaid, unprofessional, unqualified, unskilful, untrained
🠒 expert, professional, skilled

amaze *v* astonish, astound, bewilder, blow your mind *colloq*, bowl over *colloq*, confound, daze, disconcert, dismay, dumbfound, flabbergast *colloq*, floor *colloq*, gobsmack *colloq*, knock for six *colloq*, knock you down with a feather *colloq*, shock, stagger, startle, strike dumb *colloq*, stun, stupefy, surprise, wow *colloq*

amazement *n* admiration, astonishment, bewilderment, confusion, dismay, marvel, perplexity, shock, stupefaction *formal*, surprise, wonder, wonderment *formal*

ambassador *n* **1** *a country's ambassador:* consul, diplomat, emissary *formal*, envoy, legate *formal*, plenipotentiary *formal*
2 *an ambassador of peace:* agent, delegate, deputy, minister, representative

ambience *n* air, atmosphere, aura, character, climate, environment, feel, feeling, flavour, impression, milieu, mood, spirit, surroundings, tenor, tone, vibes *colloq*, vibrations *colloq*

ambiguity *n* ambivalence, confusion, double entendre, double meaning, doubt, doubtfulness, dubiety *formal*, dubiousness, enigma, equivocality, equivocation, imprecision, indeterminateness, obscurity, paradox, polysemy, puzzle, uncertainty, unclearness, vagueness, woolliness
🠒 clarity

ambiguous *adj* back-handed, confused, confusing, cryptic, double-edged, double-meaning, doubtful, dubious, enigmatic, equivocal, imprecise, inconclusive, indefinite, indeterminate, multivocal, obscure, paradoxical, puzzling, two-edged, uncertain, unclear, vague, woolly
🠒 clear, definite

ambit *n* compass, confines, extent, range, scope

ambition *n* **1** *her ambition was to climb Everest:* aim, aspiration, craving, design, desire, dream, goal, hankering, hope, hunger, ideal, intent, longing, object, objective, purpose, target, wish, yearning **2** *a woman of great ambition:* commitment, drive, eagerness, enterprise, get-up-and-go *colloq*, initiative, push, striving, thrust, what it takes *colloq*, zeal
🠒 **2** apathy, diffidence

ambitious *adj* **1** *an ambitious person:* aspiring, assertive, bold, desirous, driving, eager, energetic, enterprising, enthusiastic, full of get-up and go *colloq*, go-ahead *colloq*, hopeful, industrious, intent, keen, not backward in coming forward *colloq*, power-hungry *colloq*, purposeful, pushy *colloq*, striving, zealous **2** *an ambitious undertaking:* arduous, bold, challenging, demanding, difficult, elaborate, exacting, formidable, grandiose, hard, impressive, strenuous
🠒 **1** lazy, unassuming **2** modest, uninspiring

ambivalence *n* clash, conflict, confusion, contradiction, doubt, fluctuation, hesitation, inconclusiveness, inconsistency, irresoluteness, opposition, uncertainty, vacillation *formal*, wavering
🠒 certainty

ambivalent *adj* clashing, conflicting, confused, contradictory, debatable, doubtful, fluctuating, hesitant, inconclusive, inconsistent, irresolute, mixed, opposed, uncertain, undecided, unresolved, unsettled, unsure, vacillating *formal*, warring, wavering
🠒 unequivocal

amble *v* dawdle, drift, meander, mosey along *colloq*, perambulate *formal*, promenade *formal*, ramble, saunter, stroll, toddle *colloq*, walk, wander
🠒 march, stride

ambush *n* ambuscade *formal*, snare, surprise attack, trap, waylaying
♦ *v* ambuscade *formal*, attack, bushwhack, ensnare, entrap, jump *colloq*, lay a trap for, lie in wait, pounce on *colloq*, surprise, trap, turn on *colloq*, waylay

ameliorate *v* alleviate, amend, benefit, better, ease, elevate, enhance, improve, mend, mitigate, promote, relieve
🠒 exacerbate, worsen

amenable *adj* accommodating, acquiescent *formal*, agreeable, complaisant *formal*, compliant, flexible, liable, open, persuadable, responsible, responsive, submissive, susceptible, tractable *formal*, willing
🠒 intractable, unwilling

amend *v* adjust, alter, ameliorate *formal*, better, change, correct, emend *formal*, emendate *formal*, enhance, fix, improve, mend, modify, qualify, rectify, redress, reform, remedy, repair, revise
🠒 impair, worsen

> *amend* or *emend*? If you *amend* a document, you alter or improve it; if you *emend* a text you correct errors in it.

amendment *n* addendum *formal*, addition, adjunct, adjustment, alteration, attachment, change, clarification, correction, corrigendum *formal*, emendation *formal*, enhancement, improvement, modification, qualification, rectification *formal*, reform, remedy, revision
🠒 deterioration, impairment

amends *n* atonement, compensation, expiation, indemnification, indemnity, recompense, redress, reparation, requital, restitution, restoration, satisfaction

amenity *n* advantage, convenience, facility, resource, service, utility

amiable *adj* affable, agreeable, approachable, charming, cheerful, companionable, congenial, easy to get along/on with, engaging, friendly, genial, good-natured, good-tempered, kind, likeable, obliging, pleasant, sociable, warm
🠒 curt, hostile, unfriendly

> *amiable* or *amicable*? *Amiable* is used to describe a person who is friendly, good-tempered and pleasant; *amicable* is used to describe relationships or agreements that are conducted in a friendly way without anger.

amicable *adj* civil, civilized, cordial, friendly, good-natured, harmonious, peaceful
🠒 hostile

amid *prep* amidst, among, amongst, in the middle of, in the midst of, in the thick of, midst, surrounded by

amiss *adj* awry, defective, false, faulty, imperfect, improper, inaccurate, inappropriate, incorrect, out of kilter, out of order, unsuitable, untoward, wonky *colloq*, wrong
🖻 right, well

amity *n* accord, brotherliness, comity *formal*, concord, cordiality, fellowship, fraternity, friendliness, friendship, goodwill, harmony, kindness, peace, peacefulness, sympathy, understanding
🖻 discord, hostility

ammunition *n* bombs, bullets, cartridges, grenades, gunpowder, mines, missiles, projectiles, rockets, shells, shot, slugs

amnesty *n* absolution, dispensation, forgiveness, immunity, indulgence, lenience, mercy, pardon, remission, reprieve

amok *adv* berserk, crazy, frenzied, in a frenzy, insanely, like a lunatic, madly, uncontrollably, violently, wildly

among *prep* amid, amidst, amongst, between, in the middle of, in the midst of, in the thick of, midst, surrounded by, together with, with

amorous *adj* affectionate, amatory *formal*, erotic, fond, impassioned, in love, lovesick, loving, lustful, passionate, randy *colloq*, tender
🖻 cold, indifferent

amorphous *adj* featureless, formless, inchoate *formal*, indeterminate, indistinct, irregular, nebulous, shapeless, undefined, unformed, unshapen, unstructured, vague
🖻 definite, distinctive, shapely

amount *n* aggregate, bulk, entirety, expanse, extent, lot, magnitude, mass, measure, number, quantity, quota, sum, sum total, supply, total, volume, whole
▶ **amount to 1** *amount to a total:* add up to, aggregate, come to, equal, make, run to, tot up to *colloq*, total **2** *giving presents to potential customers amounts to bribery:* be equivalent to, be tantamount to, boil down to, come down to, correspond to, mean

amphibian

Amphibians include:
frog, bullfrog, tree frog, toad, horned toad, midwife toad, natterjack, newt, eft, salamander, conger eel, axolotl

---

ample *adj* **1** *ample opportunity/space:* abundant, commodious *formal*, considerable, copious, great, (more than) enough, plentiful, plenty, profuse, spacious, substantial, sufficient, unrestricted **2** *of ample proportions:* big, broad, expansive, extensive, full, generous, large, substantial, voluminous *formal*, wide
🖻 **1** inadequate, insufficient, meagre

amplify *v* **1** *amplify sound:* boost, deepen, enhance, heighten, increase, intensify, make louder, raise, strengthen **2** *amplify a statement:* add to, augment, broaden, bulk out, develop, elaborate on, enlarge on, expand, expatiate on *formal*, extend, fill out, flesh out, go into more detail about, increase, lengthen, supplement, widen
🖻 **1** decrease, reduce, soften

amplitude *n* bulk, capaciousness *formal*, capacity, copiousness *formal*, expanse, extent, fullness, greatness, largeness, magnitude, mass, plenitude *formal*, profusion, spaciousness, vastness, volume, width

amputate *v* curtail, cut off, dissever, dock, lop, remove, separate, sever, truncate

amulet *n* charm, fetish, juju, lucky charm, pentacle *formal*, periapt *formal*, phylactery *formal*, talisman

amuse *v* **1** *the joke amused them:* charm, cheer (up), crack up *colloq*, crease up *colloq*, delight, enthral, gladden, make laugh, please, tickle *colloq*, tickle your funny bone *colloq* **2** *amuse yourselves while I'm away:* absorb, disport *formal*, divert, engross, entertain, interest, occupy, regale, relax
🖻 **1** displease

amusement *n* **1** *a look of amusement at the joke:* delight, enjoyment, fun, hilarity, laughter, merriment, mirth, pleasure **2** *to the amusement of the onlookers:* distraction, diversion, entertainment **3** *Victorian amusements:* game, hobby, interest, pastime, recreation, sport

amusing *adj* charming, comical, delightful, droll, enjoyable, entertaining, facetious, funny, hilarious, humorous, interesting, jocular, jolly, laughable, ludicrous, pleasant, waggish, witty
🖻 boring, dull

anaemic *adj* ashen, bloodless, chalky, colourless, enervated, feeble, frail, ineffectual, infirm, insipid, livid, pale, pallid, pasty, sallow, sickly, wan, weak, whey-faced
🖻 full-blooded, ruddy, sanguine

anaesthetic *n* analgesic, anodyne, epidural, general anaesthetic, local anaesthetic, narcotic, opiate, painkiller, palliative, premedication, sedative, soporific, stupefacient, stupefactive

anaesthetize *v* deaden, desensitize, dope, drug, dull, numb, stupefy

analogous *adj* agreeing, comparable, correlative, corresponding, equivalent, kindred, like, matching, parallel, relative, resembling, similar
🖻 disparate

analogy *n* agreement, comparison, correlation, correspondence, equivalence, likeness, metaphor, parallel, relation, resemblance, semblance *formal*, similarity, simile, similitude *formal*

analyse *v* anatomize *formal*, assay *formal*, break down, consider, dissect, divide, estimate, evaluate, examine, inquire, interpret, investigate, judge, reduce, resolve, review, scrutinize, separate, sift, study, take apart, test

analysis *n* anatomization *formal*, assay *formal*, breakdown, check, check-up, dissection, division, estimation, evaluation, examination, explanation, explication, exposition, inquiry, inspection, interpretation, investigation, judgement, opinion, reasoning, reduction, resolution, review, scrutiny, separation, sifting, study, test

analytical *adj* analytic, critical, detailed, diagnostic, dissecting, explanatory, expository, in-depth, inquiring, inquisitive, interpretative, investigative, logical, methodical, questioning, rational, searching, studious, systematic

anarchic *adj* anarchistic, chaotic, confused, disordered, disorganized, lawless, libertarian, mutinous, nihilist, rebellious, revolutionary, riotous, ungoverned
🖬 orderly, submissive

anarchist *n* insurgent, libertarian, nihilist, rebel, revolutionary, terrorist

anarchy *n* anarchism, chaos, confusion, disorder, insurrection, lawlessness, misrule, mutiny, pandemonium, rebellion, revolution, riot, unrule
🖬 control, order, rule

anathema *n* 1 *views that were anathema to him:* abhorrence, abomination, aversion, bane, bête noire, bugbear, object of loathing, taboo 2 *to declare an anathema:* curse, proscription, taboo

anatomy *n* 1 *part of the human anatomy:* build, composition, constitution, construction, frame, framework, make-up, structure 2 *to study anatomy:* dissection, vivisection, zootomy

ancestor *n* antecedent, forebear, forefather, forerunner, precursor, predecessor, primogenitor *formal*, progenitor
🖬 descendant

ancestral *adj* familial, genealogical, genetic, hereditary, lineal *formal*, parental

ancestry *n* ancestors, blood, derivation, descent, extraction, family, family tree, forebears, forefathers, genealogy, heredity, heritage, line, lineage, origin, parentage, pedigree, progenitors, race, roots, stock

anchor *v* affix, attach, berth, fasten, fix, make fast, moor, tie up

---

Types of anchor include:
car, double fluked, drogue, grapnel, kedge, killick, mushroom, navy, sea, stocked, stockless, yachtsman

---

ancient *adj* 1 *ancient monuments:* aged, age-old, antique, archaic, as old as the hills *colloq*, early, fossilized, immemorial, old, prehistoric, primeval, primordial, pristine *formal*, time-worn 2 *those ideas are positively ancient:* antediluvian, antiquated, atavistic *formal*, bygone, obsolete, old-fashioned, outmoded, out of date, passé, superannuated *formal*
🖬 1 contemporary, recent 2 modern, up-to-date

ancillary *adj* accessory, additional, adjuvant *formal*, adminicular *formal*, auxiliary, contributory, extra, helping, secondary, subordinate, subsidiary, supplementary, supporting

and *conj* also, as well (as), besides, by the way, furthermore, in addition (to), including, moreover, plus, then, together (with), too, what's more *colloq*

anecdote *n* reminiscence, sketch, story, tale, yarn

anew *adv* afresh, again, once again, once more

angel *n* 1 *an angel of God:* divine messenger, heavenly being, heavenly messenger 2 *she's an absolute angel:* darling, gem, ideal, paragon, saint, treasure
🖬 1 devil, fiend

The nine orders of angels are:
seraph, cherub, throne, domination/ dominion, virtue, power, principality, archangel, angel

---

angelic *adj* adorable, beatific *formal*, beautiful, celestial, cherubic, divine, empyrean *formal*, ethereal *formal*, heavenly, holy, innocent, lovely, pious, pure, saintly, seraphic, unworldly, virtuous
🖬 devilish, fiendish

anger *n* annoyance, antagonism, bitterness, chagrin, choler *formal*, displeasure, dudgeon *formal*, exasperation, fury, gall, indignation, ire, irritability, irritation, outrage, pique, rage, rancour, resentment, temper, vexation, wrath
🖬 forbearance, forgiveness
♦ *v* affront, aggravate *colloq*, annoy, antagonize, bother, enrage, exasperate, gall, incense, infuriate, irk, irritate, madden, make angry, make your blood boil *colloq*, miff *colloq*, nark *slang*, needle, nettle, offend, outrage, piss off *slang*, provoke, rile, ruffle, vex, wind up *colloq*
🖬 appease, calm, please

angle *n* 1 *met at an odd angle:* bend, corner, crook, crotch, edge, elbow, flexure, gradient, hook, inclination, intersection, knee, nook, point, projection 2 *look it from a different angle:* approach, aspect, direction, facet, outlook, perspective, point of view, position, side, slant, standpoint, viewpoint
♦ *v* direct, face, point, slant, turn

angry *adj* aggravated *colloq*, annoyed, bitter, cross, disgruntled *colloq*, displeased, enraged, exasperated, furious, heated, hopping mad *colloq*, hot, hot under the collar *colloq*, in a lather *colloq*, in a paddy *colloq*, in a temper, incensed, indignant, infuriated, irate, irritated, livid, mad *colloq*, on the warpath *colloq*, outraged, passionate, pissed off *slang*, raging, resentful, seeing red *colloq*, seething, up in arms *colloq*, uptight *colloq*
🖬 calm, content, happy

Colloquial ways of expressing becoming angry and losing your temper include:
blow up, blow a fuse, blow a gasket, blow your cool, blow your stack, blow your top, boil over, burst a blood vessel, do your nut, explode, flip your lid, fly into a rage, fly off the handle, go mad, go off the deep end, go up the wall, have a conniption, hit the ceiling, hit the roof, lose your cool, lose your patience, lose your rag, raise Cain, raise hell, see red, throw a tantrum, throw a wobbly, foam at the mouth, get all steamed up, go ape *US*, go ballistic, lose your marbles

---

anguish *n* agony, anxiety, desolation, distress, . dole *formal*, dolour *formal*, grief, heartache, heartbreak, misery, pain, sorrow, suffering, torment, torture, tribulation, woe, wretchedness
🖬 happiness, solace

anguished *adj* afflicted, distressed, dolorous *formal*, harrowed, miserable, stressed, stricken, suffering, tormented, tortured, wretched

angular *adj* bony, gaunt, gawky, lank, lanky, lean, rawboned, scrawny, skinny, spare, thin

animal *n* 1 *wild animals:* beast, creature, mammal 2 *that man is an animal:* barbarian, beast, brute,

monster, pig *colloq*, savage, swine *colloq*
♦ *adj* **1** *animal fats:* animalic *formal*, zoic *formal*
2 *animal instincts:* bestial, bodily, brutish, carnal, fleshly, inhuman, instinctive, physical, savage, sensual, wild

---

Animals include:
cat, dog, hamster, gerbil, mouse, rat, rabbit, hare, fox, badger, beaver, mole, otter, weasel, ferret, ermine, mink, hedgehog, squirrel, horse, pig, cow, bull, goat, sheep; monkey, lemur, gibbon, ape, chimpanzee, orang-utan, baboon, gorilla; seal, sealion, dolphin, walrus, whale; lion, tiger, cheetah, puma, panther, cougar, jaguar, ocelot, leopard; aardvark, armadillo, wolf, wolverine, hyena, mongoose, skunk, racoon, wombat, platypus, koala, polecat; deer, antelope, gazelle, eland, impala, reindeer, elk, caribou, moose; wallaby, kangaroo, bison, buffalo, gnu, camel, zebra, llama, panda, giant panda, grizzly bear, polar bear, giraffe, hippopotamus, rhinoceros, elephant. See also **amphibian, bird, butterfly, cat, cattle, dog, fish, horse, insect, invertebrate, mammal, marsupial, mollusc, monkey, moth, reptile, rodent**

---

animate *adj* alive, breathing, conscious, live, living
🔁 inanimate
♦ *v* activate, arouse, buck up *colloq*, embolden *formal*, encourage, energize, enliven, excite, fire, galvanize, goad, impel, incite, inspire, inspirit *formal*, instigate, invigorate, kindle, move, quicken, reactivate, revive, rouse, spark, spur, stimulate, stir, urge, vitalize, vivify *formal*
🔁 dull, inhibit

animated *adj* active, alive, ardent, bright and breezy *colloq*, brisk, buoyant, eager, ebullient, energetic, enthusiastic, excited, fervent, full of beans *colloq*, glowing, impassioned, lively, passionate, quick, radiant, spirited, vehement, vibrant, vigorous, vital, vivacious
🔁 inert, lethargic, sluggish

animation *n* action, activity, ebullience, elation, energy, enthusiasm, excitement, exhilaration, fervour, high spirits, life, liveliness, passion, pep *colloq*, radiance, sparkle, spirit, sprightliness, verve, vibrancy, vigour, vitality, zeal, zest, zing *colloq*
🔁 dullness, inertia

animosity *n* abhorrence, acrimony, animus *formal*, antagonism, bitterness, enmity, feud, hate, hatred, hostility, ill feeling, ill-will, loathing, malevolence, malice, malignity, odium *formal*, rancour, resentment, spite
🔁 goodwill

annals *n* archives, chronicles, history, journals, memoirs, records, registers, reports

annex *v* **1** *a letter was annexed to the agreement:* add, adjoin, affix, append, attach, connect, fasten, incorporate, join, unite **2** *to annex a country:* acquire, appropriate, arrogate *formal*, conquer, occupy, seize, take over, usurp

---

annex or *annexe*? *Annex*, stressed on the second syllable, is a verb meaning to add or acquire: *The USSR annexed Latvia in World War II.* The noun, stressed on the first syllable, may be spelt *annex* or *annexe*, but the form with *-e* is more common.

---

annexation *n* acquisition, appropriation, arrogation *formal*, conquest, occupation, seizure, takeover, usurping

annexe *n* addition, attachment, expansion, extension, supplement, wing

annihilate *v* abolish, assassinate, bring to their knees *colloq*, conquer, defeat, destroy, eliminate, eradicate, erase, exterminate, extinguish, extirpate *formal*, liquidate *colloq*, murder, obliterate, raze, rout, rub out *colloq*, thrash *colloq*, trounce *colloq*, wipe out

annihilation *n* abolition, assassination, defeat, destruction, elimination, eradication, erasure, extermination, extinction, extirpation *formal*, liquidation *colloq*, murder, obliteration

anniversary

Names of wedding anniversary include:
1st cotton, 2nd paper, 3rd leather, 4th flowers/fruit, 5th wood, 6th iron/sugar, 7th copper/wool, 8th bronze/pottery, 9th pottery/willow, 10th tin, 11th steel, 12th silk/linen, 13th lace, 14th ivory, 15th crystal, 20th china, 25th silver, 30th pearl, 35th coral, 40th ruby, 45th sapphire, 50th gold, 55th emerald, 60th diamond, 70th platinum

---

annotate *v* comment, elucidate, explain, explicate *formal*, gloss, interpret, marginalize *formal*, note

annotation *n* comment, commentary, elucidation, exegesis, explanation, explication *formal*, footnote, gloss, note

announce *v* advertise, blazon (abroad), broadcast, declare, disclose, divulge, give out, intimate, make known, make public, make/issue a statement, notify, preconize *formal*, proclaim, promulgate *formal*, propound *formal*, publicize, publish, report, reveal, state
🔁 suppress

announcement *n* **1** *an announcement about new jobs:* advertisement, broadcast, bulletin, communiqué, declaration, disclosure, dispatch, intimation, message, notification, proclamation, publication, publicity, report, revelation, statement **2** *I heard the the announcement of the news:* declaration, disclosure, divulgence, giving-out, intimation, making known/public, notification, proclamation, publication, publicizing, reporting, revelation

announcer *n* anchor, anchorman, anchorwoman, broadcaster, commentator, compère, herald, host, master of ceremonies, MC, messenger, newscaster, newsreader, presenter, town crier

annoy *v* aggravate *colloq*, anger, bother, brass off *colloq*, bug *colloq*, cheese off *colloq*, displease, disturb, drive bananas *colloq*, drive crazy/nuts *colloq*, drive round the bend/twist *colloq*, drive up the wall *colloq*, exasperate, gall, get on your nerves *colloq*, get on your wick *colloq*, get someone's blood up *colloq*, get someone's goat *colloq*, get under your skin *colloq*, get up your nose *colloq*, get your back up *colloq*, get your dander up *colloq*, give someone the hump *colloq*, harass, hassle *colloq*, irk, irritate, madden, make someone's hackles rise *colloq*, make your blood boil *colloq*, molest, nag, pester, plague, provoke, rile, rub up the wrong way *colloq*, ruffle,

tease, tick/hack off *US colloq*, trouble, vex, wind up *colloq*
🔁 comfort, gratify, please

annoyance *n* **1** *that's a real annoyance*: bind *colloq*, bore, bother, disturbance, drag *colloq*, headache *colloq*, irritant, nuisance, pain *colloq*, pain in the arse/backside *slang*, pain in the ass/ butt *US slang*, pain in the neck *colloq*, pest, provocation, tease, trouble **2** *express your annoyance*: aggravation *colloq*, anger, displeasure, exasperation, harassment, irritation, vexation
🔁 **2** pleasure

annoyed *adj* angry, bugged *colloq*, cheesed off *colloq*, cross, displeased, driven crazy *colloq*, driven nuts *colloq*, exasperated, got the hump *colloq*, harassed, hassled *colloq*, in a huff *colloq*, indignant, irritated, miffed *colloq*, narked *colloq*, peeved *colloq*, piqued, provoked, upset, vexed
🔁 pleased

annoying *adj* aggravating *colloq*, bothersome, disturbing, exasperating, galling, harassing, intrusive, irksome, irritating, maddening, offensive, pesky *US*, provoking, teasing, tiresome, troublesome, trying, unwelcome, vexatious
🔁 pleasing, welcome

annual *n* almanac, calendar, register, yearbook
♦ *adj* yearly

annul *v* abolish, abrogate, cancel, countermand, declare null and void, invalidate, negate, nullify, quash, recall, repeal, rescind, retract, reverse, revoke, suspend, void
🔁 enact, restore

annulment *n* abolition, abrogation, cancellation, countermand, invalidation, negation, nullification, quashing, recall, repeal, rescindment, rescission *formal*, reverse, revocation *formal*, suspension, voiding
🔁 enactment, restoration

anodyne *adj* bland, deadening, inoffensive, neutral

anoint *v* **1** *anointed him with oil*: apply oil/ lubrication, daub, embrocate *formal*, grease, lubricate, oil, rub, smear **2** *anointed her successor*: bless, consecrate, dedicate, ordain, sanctify

anomalous *adj* abnormal, atypical, deviant, eccentric, exceptional, freak *colloq*, freakish, incongruous, inconsistent, irregular, odd, peculiar, rare, singular, unusual
🔁 normal, ordinary, regular

anomaly *n* aberration, abnormality, departure, deviation, divergence, eccentricity, exception, freak, incongruity, inconsistency, irregularity, misfit, oddity, peculiarity, rarity

anonymous *adj* **1** *an anonymous letter*: incognito, innominate *formal*, nameless, unacknowledged, unattested *formal*, unidentified, unknown, unnamed, unsigned, unspecified **2** *an anonymous place*: faceless, impersonal, nondescript, unexceptional
🔁 **1** identifiable, named, signed **2** distinctive

another *adj* **1** *have you got another sandwich?*: added, additional, extra, further, more, second, spare **2** *that's another story*: alternative, different, not the same, other, some other, variant

answer *n* **1** *give a polite answer to an enquiry*: acknowledgement, comeback *colloq*, reaction,

rebuttal, rejoinder, replication *formal*, reply, response, retaliation, retort, riposte **2** *the answer to your problem*: explanation, key, quick fix *colloq*, resolution, result, solution, unravelling
♦ *v* **1** *answer an e-mail*: acknowledge, get/come back to *colloq*, react, refute, reply, respond, retaliate, write back **2** *answer a need*: fill, fulfil, match up to, meet, satisfy **3** *answer (to) a description*: agree, conform, correlate, correspond to, fit, pass, serve, suit
▶ **answer back** argue, be cheeky, contradict, disagree, dispute, rebut, retaliate, retort, riposte, sass *US colloq*, talk back
▶ **answer for 1** *I can't answer for her loyalty*: be liable for, be responsible for, speak for, vouch for **2** *answer for their crimes*: be punished for, pay for

answerable *adj* accountable, blameworthy, chargeable, liable, responsible, to blame

antagonism *n* animosity, antipathy, conflict, contention, discord, dissension, enmity, friction, hostility, ill feeling, ill-will, opposition, rivalry
🔁 agreement, rapport, sympathy

antagonist *n* adversary, competitor, contender, contestant, enemy, foe, opponent, rival
🔁 ally, supporter

antagonistic *adj* adverse, at variance, averse, belligerent, conflicting, contentious, hostile, ill-disposed, incompatible, opposed, unfriendly
🔁 friendly, sympathetic

antagonize *v* alienate, anger, annoy, disaffect, embitter, estrange, incense, insult, irritate, offend, provoke, repel
🔁 disarm

antecedent *n* **1** *antecedents of the aeroplane*: forerunner, precedent, precursor **2** *with Welsh antecedents*: ancestors, extraction, forebears, forefathers, genealogy

anthem *n* canticle, chant, chorale, hymn, paean *formal*, psalm, song, song of praise

anthology *n* collection, compendium, compilation, digest, miscellany, omnibus edition, selection, spicilege *formal*, treasury

anticipate *v* **1** *the statement anticipated all our objections*: beat to it *colloq*, forestall, intercept, obviate *formal*, preclude *formal*, pre-empt, prevent **2** *eagerly anticipated the reply*: await, expect, hope for, look forward to **3** *anticipate a United victory*: expect, figure on *US*, forecast, foresee, look for, predict, prepare for, reckon on, think likely

anticipation *n* **1** *in anticipation of the shortage*: expectation, prediction, preparation **2** *eager anticipation*: bated breath *colloq*, excitement, expectancy, hope

anticlimax *n* bathos *formal*, comedown, damp squib *colloq*, disappointment, fiasco, let-down, non-event *colloq*, not all that it was cracked up to be *colloq*

antics *n* buffoonery, capers, clowning, doings, foolery, frolics, horseplay, mischief, monkey-tricks, playfulness, pranks, silliness, skylarking, stunts, tomfoolery, tricks

antidote *n* **1** *an antidote to a sting*: antitoxin, antivenin *technical*, counter-agent, countermeasure, cure, mithridate *formal*, neutralizer, theriac **2** *the antidote to depression*: corrective, cure, remedy

antipathy *n* abhorrence, animosity, animus *formal*, antagonism, aversion, bad blood, disgust, dislike, distaste, enmity, hate, hatred, hostility, ill-will, incompatibility, loathing, odium *formal*, opposition, repulsion
🔁 affection, rapport, sympathy

antiquated *adj* anachronistic, ancient, antediluvian, archaic, bygone, dated, démodé, fossilized, obsolete, old hat *colloq*, old-fashioned, on the way out *colloq*, outdated, outmoded, out of date, outworn, passé
🔁 forward-looking, modern

antique *adj* ancient, antiquarian, antiquated, archaic, obsolete, old, old-fashioned, outdated, quaint, veteran, vintage
♦ *n* antiquity, bygone, curio, curiosity, heirloom, museum piece, object of virtu, period piece, rarity, relic

antiquity *n* **1** *a food much valued in antiquity:* ancient times, the distant past, the olden days, time immemorial **2** *an object of great antiquity:* age, agedness, old age, oldness
🔁 **1** modern times, the present day **2** modernity, novelty

antiseptic *adj* aseptic, clean, disinfectant, germ-free, hygienic, medicated, pure, sanitary, sanitized, sterile, sterilized, uncontaminated, unpolluted
♦ *n* bactericide, cleanser, disinfectant, germicide, purifier

antisocial *adj* **1** *an antisocial person:* alienated, reserved, retiring, unapproachable, uncommunicative, unfriendly, unsociable, withdrawn **2** *antisocial behaviour:* anarchic, antagonistic, asocial, belligerent, disorderly, disruptive, hostile, lawless, rebellious, unacceptable
🔁 **1** gregarious, sociable **2** acceptable

antithesis *n* **1** *this is the antithesis of an action film:* converse, opposite, opposite extreme, reverse **2** *the antithesis between old and new ways:* contradiction, contrast, opposition, reversal

anxiety *n* anguish, apprehension, care, concern, disquiet, disquietude *formal*, distress, dread, foreboding, fretfulness, impatience, misgiving, nervousness, restlessness, strain, stress, suspense, tension, uneasiness, worriment *formal*, worry
🔁 calm, composure, serenity

anxious *adj* **1** *anxious about the exam:* afraid, apprehensive, concerned, dismayed, distressed, disturbed, fearful, fretful, having butterflies in your stomach/tummy *colloq*, impatient, in a stew *colloq*, in suspense, nervous, on tenterhooks, overwrought, restless, solicitous *formal*, taut, tearing your hair out *colloq*, tense, tormented, tortured, troubled, uneasy, worried **2** *anxious to impress the new boss:* eager, enthusiastic, expectant, keen, longing, yearning
🔁 **1** calm, composed

apace *adv* at full speed, at top speed, double-quick, fast, hastily, quickly, rapidly, speedily, swiftly, without delay

apart *adv* **1** *stand some distance apart:* afar, aloof, aside, away, cut off, distant, distinct, excluded, isolated, piecemeal, separate, separated, to one side **2** *live apart:* alone, by yourself, divorced, independently, individually, not together, on your own, privately, separated, separately, singly **3** *tear apart:* in bits, in pieces, into parts, piecemeal, to bits, to pieces
🔁 **1** connected **2** together **3** together

apathetic *adj* blasé, cold, cool, emotionless, half-hearted, impassive, indifferent, lethargic, listless, lukewarm, numb, passive, unambitious, unconcerned, unemotional, unfeeling, uninterested, uninvolved, unmoved, unresponsive
🔁 concerned, enthusiastic, feeling, involved, responsive

apathy *n* accidie *formal*, acedia *formal*, coldness, coolness, impassivity, indifference, inertia, insensibility, lack of concern, lack of enthusiasm, lack of interest, languor *formal*, lethargy, listlessness, passivity, sluggishness, torpor, unconcern, uninterestedness
🔁 concern, enthusiasm, interest

ape *v* caricature, copy, counterfeit, echo, imitate, mimic, mirror, mock, parody, parrot, take off
♦ *n* baboon, chimpanzee, gibbon, gorilla, monkey, orang-utan

aperture *n* breach, chink, cleft, crack, eye, fissure, foramen *technical*, gap, hole, interstice *formal*, mouth, opening, orifice *technical*, passage, perforation, rent, slit, slot, space, vent

apex *n* acme *technical*, apogee, climax, consummation, crest, crown, crowning point, culmination, fastigium, height, high point, peak, pinnacle, point, summit, tip, top, vertex, zenith
🔁 nadir

aphorism *n* adage, apothegm *formal*, axiom, dictum, epigram *formal*, gnome *formal*, maxim, precept, proverb, saw, saying, witticism

aphrodisiac *n* love potion, stimulant
♦ *adj* amative *formal*, amatory *formal*, erogenous, erotic, erotogenous *formal*, stimulant, venerous *formal*

aplomb *n* assurance, audacity, balance, calmness, composure, confidence, coolness, equanimity, poise, sangfroid, savoir-faire, self-assurance, self-confidence, self-possession
🔁 discomposure

apocryphal *adj* concocted, doubtful, dubious, equivocal, fabricated, fictitious, imaginary, legendary, mythical, questionable, spurious, unauthenticated, unsubstantiated, unsupported, unverified
🔁 authentic, true

apologetic *adj* conscience-stricken, contrite, penitent, regretful, remorseful, repentant, rueful, sorry
🔁 defiant, impenitent, unrepentant

apologize *v* acknowledge, ask forgiveness, ask pardon, be apologetic, beg someone's pardon, confess, eat humble pie *colloq*, eat your words *colloq*, explain, justify, plead, regret, say sorry, say you are sorry, swallow your pride *colloq*

apology *n* acknowledgement, confession, defence, excuse, explanation, justification, palliation *formal*, plea, regrets, saying sorry, vindication
🔁 defiance

apostasy *n* defection, desertion, disloyalty, falseness, heresy, perfidy *formal*, recidivism *formal*, recreance *formal*, recreancy *formal*,

renegation *formal*, renunciation, treachery, unfaithfulness
▪ loyalty, orthodoxy

apostate *n* defector, deserter, heretic, recidivist *formal*, recreant *formal*, renegade, tergiversator *formal*, traitor, turncoat
▪ follower

apostle *n* **1** *Jesus Christ's apostles:* disciple, evangelist, messenger, missionary, preacher, proselytizer, reformer **2** *apostles of a united Europe:* advocate, champion, crusader, pioneer, proponent, supporter

appal *v* alarm, daunt, disconcert, disgust, dismay, frighten, horrify, intimidate, outrage, scare, shock, terrify, unnerve
▪ encourage, reassure

appalling *adj* alarming, atrocious, awful, daunting, dire, disgusting, dreadful, frightening, frightful, ghastly, grim, harrowing, hideous, horrible, horrid, horrific, horrifying, intimidating, loathsome, nightmarish, outrageous, shocking, terrible, terrifying, unnerving
▪ encouraging, reassuring

apparatus *n* **1** *a piece of gym apparatus:* appliances, contraptions, devices, equipment, gadgets, gear, implements, machinery, machines, materials, outfit, tackle, tools, utensils **2** *the apparatus of government:* framework, means, mechanism, network, set-up, structure, system

apparel *n* clothes, clothing, costume, dress, garb, garments, outfit, wardrobe

apparent *adj* **1** *his distrust was all too apparent:* clear, conspicuous, declared, distinct, evident, manifest, marked, noticeable, obvious, open, patent, perceptible, plain, standing out, unmistakable, visible **2** *their apparent calmness:* ostensible, outward, seeming, superficial, visible
▪ **1** hidden, obscure

apparently *adv* on the face of it, on the surface, ostensibly, outwardly, reputedly, seemingly, superficially, to all appearances

apparition *n* chimera *formal*, ghost, manifestation, materialization, phantom, presence, spectre, spirit, spook *colloq*, vision, visitant *formal*

appeal *n* **1** *an appeal for calm:* adjuration *formal*, application, approach, claim, entreaty, imploration *formal*, invocation, orison *formal*, petition, plea, prayer, request, solicitation, suit, supplication **2** *the appeal of the countryside:* allure, attraction, attractiveness, beauty, charisma, charm, enchantment, fascination, interest, magnetism, winsomeness **3** *an appeal in a lawcourt:* reconsideration, re-evaluation, re-examination, retrial, review
♦ *v* **1** *appeal for help:* address, apply, ask (for), beg, beseech, call, call upon, claim, entreat, implore, invoke, petition, plead, pray, request, solicit, sue *formal*, supplicate *formal* **2** *it really appeals to me:* allure, attract, charm, draw, engage, entice, fascinate, interest, invite, lure, please, tempt

appear *v* **1** *she appeared from nowhere:* arise, arrive, be present, come along, come into sight, come into view, crop up, emerge, enter, issue, loom, materialize, occur, pop up *colloq*, show (up), surface, turn up **2** *he appears to be well-educated:* come across as, give the impression of

being, look, seem, show signs of, take the guise of **3** *appear in a show:* act, be a guest in, be on stage, perform, play, take part, turn out **4** *his book appeared in the shops:* be published, become available, come out
▪ **1** disappear, vanish

appearance *n* **1** *the sudden appearance of a dolphin:* advent, appearing, arrival, attendance, coming, coming into view, début, emergence, introduction, presence, rise **2** *a man of cheerful appearance:* air, aspect, bearing, complexion, demeanour *formal*, expression, face, figure, image, look, looks, manner, mien *formal*, (outward) form, visage *formal* **3** *keep up an appearance:* façade, front, guise, illusion, image, impression, outward impression, pretence, semblance, show
▪ **1** disappearance

appease *v* conciliate, make peace with, mitigate, pacify, placate, propitiate, reconcile, satisfy
▪ aggravate

appellation *n* description, designation, epithet, name, sobriquet *formal*, title

append *v* add, adjoin *formal*, affix, annex *formal*, attach, conjoin *formal*, fasten, join, subjoin *formal*, tack on

appendage *n* addendum, addition, adjunct, appendix, supplement, tailpiece

appendix *n* addendum, addition, adjunct, appendage, codicil, epilogue, postscript, rider, supplement

appetite *n* **1** *a good appetite:* hunger, relish, stomach, taste, zest **2** *the public's appetite for sensationalism:* craving, desire, eagerness, hunger, inclination, liking, longing, lust, passion, propensity, taste, thirst, yearning, zeal

appetizing *adj* appealing, delicious, inviting, mouthwatering, palatable, piquant, savoury, scrumptious *colloq*, succulent, tasty, tempting
▪ disgusting, distasteful

applaud *v* **1** *the audience applauded:* cheer, clap, give a big hand to *colloq*, give a round of applause, give an ovation/a standing ovation to, put your hands together for, show your appreciation to **2** *applaud the government's efforts:* acclaim, approve, commend, compliment, congratulate, eulogize *formal*, extol *formal*, laud *formal*, praise

applause *n* a big hand *colloq*, acclaim, acclamation, accolade, approval, bravos, cheering, cheers, clapping, commendation, congratulation, encomium *formal*, ovation, praise, standing ovation
▪ censure, criticism

appliance *n* apparatus, contraption, contrivance, device, gadget, implement, instrument, machine, mechanism, tool

applicable *adj* apposite *formal*, appropriate, apt, fit, fitting, legitimate, pertinent *formal*, proper, relevant, suitable, suited, useful, valid
▪ inapplicable, inappropriate

applicant *n* aspirant, candidate, claimant, competitor, contestant, inquirer, interviewee, petitioner, postulant *technical*, suitor

application *n* **1** *an application for bail:* appeal, claim, demand, inquiry, petition, request, suit

2 *no application to the modern world:* aptness, bearing, function, germaneness, pertinence *formal*, praxis, purpose, relevance, significance, use, value **3** *work with great application:* assiduity *formal*, attentiveness, commitment, dedication, diligence, effort, hard work, industry, keenness, perseverance, sedulousness *formal*

apply *v* **1** *apply for a new contract:* appeal, ask for, claim, fill in a form for, inquire, order, petition, put in an application for, put in for, request, requisition, solicit, sue, write away/off for **2** *apply yourself to a task:* address, be industrious, buckle down, commit, commit/devote yourself, concentrate, dedicate, devote, direct, give, make an effort, persevere, settle down, study, work hard **3** *apply force:* administer, assign, bring into play, bring to bear, direct, draw on, employ, engage, execute, exercise, exert, harness, implement, ply, practise, put into practice/operation, resort to, use, utilize, wield **4** *that rule does not apply here:* appertain *formal*, be relevant, be significant, fit, pertain *formal*, relate, suit **5** *apply an ointment:* adhibit *formal*, anoint, cover with, lay on, paint, put on, rub, smear, spread on, treat with

appoint *v* **1** *appoint someone to be the spokesperson:* allot, assign, charge, choose, command, commission, co-opt, delegate, designate, detail, direct, elect, employ, engage, hire, install, name, nominate, pick, recruit, select, take on **2** *appointed Tuesday as the day of the meeting:* allot, arrange, decide, decree, designate, destine, determine, establish, fix, ordain, set, settle

F⃥ **1** discharge, dismiss, reject

appointed *adj* allotted, arranged, assigned, chosen, decided, decreed, designated, destined, determined, established, fixed, ordained, preordained, set, settled

appointment *n* **1** *a 3 o'clock appointment:* arrangement, arrangement to meet, consultation, date, engagement, interview, meeting, rendezvous **2** *took up her appointment as director:* job, office, place, position, post, situation **3** *the appointment of a new coach:* choice, choosing, commissioning, delegation, election, naming, nomination, selection

apportion *v* admeasure *formal*, allocate, allot, assign, deal (out), dispense, distribute, divide, dole out *colloq*, grant, hand out, measure out, mete (out), ration (out), share (out)

apportionment *n* allocation, allotment, assignment, dealing, dispensation, distribution, division, grant, handout *colloq*, ration(ing), share

apposite *adj* applicable, appropriate, apropos *formal*, apt, befitting *formal*, germane, pertinent *formal*, relevant, suitable, suited, to the point, to the purpose

F⃥ inapposite

appraisal *n* appreciation, assay *formal*, assessment, estimate, estimation, evaluation, examination, inspection, judgement, once-over *colloq*, opinion, rating, reckoning, review, survey, valuation

appraise *v* assay *formal*, assess, estimate, evaluate, examine, inspect, judge, rate, review, size up *colloq*, sum up, survey, value

appraise or *apprise*? If you *appraise* someone or something, you form an opinion about their quality, value, etc. If you are *apprised* of something, you are told about it.

appreciable *adj* considerable, definite, discernible, noticeable, perceptible, recognizable, significant, substantial

F⃥ imperceptible, insignificant, negligible

appreciate *v* **1** *to appreciate a painting:* admire, cherish, enjoy, esteem, like, prize, regard, relish, respect, savour, take kindly to, think highly of, treasure, value, welcome **2** *appreciate the finer points of croquet:* acknowledge, be aware of, be conscious of, be sensitive to, comprehend, grasp, know, perceive, realize, recognize, see, sympathize with, understand **3** *I appreciate your help:* be appreciative of, be grateful for, be indebted to someone for, express your gratitude/appreciation for, thank someone for **4** *appreciate in value:* enhance, gain, go up, grow, improve, increase, inflate, mount, rise, strengthen

F⃥ **1** despise, hate **2** ignore, overlook **4** depreciate, go down

appreciation *n* **1** *their appreciation of the meal:* admiration, enjoyment, esteem, liking, regard, relish, respect, valuing **2** *send a present to show your appreciation:* gratefulness, gratitude, indebtedness, obligation, thankfulness **3** *a sound appreciation of business:* acknowledgement, assessment, awareness, cognizance *formal*, comprehension, estimation, grasp, judgement, knowledge, perception, realization, recognition, responsiveness, sensitivity, sympathy, understanding, valuation **4** *wrote an appreciation of the Lake Poets:* analysis, assessment, commentary, critique, evaluation, notice, praise, review **5** *the appreciation of our assets:* enhancement, escalation, gain, growth, improvement, increase, inflation, rise

F⃥ **1** ingratitude **5** depreciation

appreciative *adj* **1** *appreciative of their efforts:* beholden *formal*, grateful, indebted, obliged, pleased, thankful **2** *an appreciative audience:* admiring, encouraging, enthusiastic, knowledgeable, respectful, responsive, sensitive **3** *we are appreciative that things can be improved:* conscious, mindful

F⃥ **1** ungrateful

apprehend *v* **1** *apprehend a thief:* arrest, bust *colloq*, capture, catch, collar *colloq*, detain, grab *colloq*, nab *colloq*, nick *colloq*, run in *colloq*, seize **2** *apprehend the situation:* believe, comprehend, conceive, grasp, perceive, realize, recognize, see, twig *colloq*, understand

apprehension *n* **1** *felt apprehension in my stomach:* alarm, anxiety, butterflies *colloq*, concern, disquiet, doubt, dread, fear, foreboding, misgiving, mistrust, nervousness, perturbation *formal*, qualm, suspicion, the willies *colloq*, trepidation, uneasiness, worry **2** *the apprehension of a suspect:* arrest, capture, detention, seizure, taking **3** *apprehension of the facts:* belief, comprehension, conception, discernment, grasp, perception, realization, recognition, understanding

apprehensive *adj* afraid, alarmed, anxious, bothered, concerned, distrustful, doubtful,

fearful, mistrustful, nervous, on tenterhooks *colloq*, suspicious, uneasy, worried
Fa assured, confident

apprentice *n* beginner, learner, newcomer, novice, probationer, pupil, recruit, rookie *US colloq*, starter, student, trainee, tyro
Fa expert

apprise *v* acquaint, advise, brief, communicate, enlighten, inform, intimate, notify, tell, tip off *colloq*, warn

apprise or *appraise*? See panel at **appraise**

approach *v* 1 *approaching the house*: advance towards, arrive, catch up, come nearer/closer, draw near, gain on, get closer to, meet, move towards, near, reach 2 *dared to approach the star*: accost, address, greet, make conversation with, speak to 3 *approach the task carefully*: begin, commence, deal with, embark on, introduce, mention, set about, tackle, treat, undertake 4 *approached him for help*: appeal to, apply to, broach, contact, get in touch with, get on to, invite, make advances, make overtures, sound out 5 *a speed approaching 200 km/h*: approximate, come close to, come near to, compare with, reach
♦ *n* 1 *the approach of winter*: advance, advent, arrival, coming 2 *the approach to the cottage*: access, avenue, doorway, drive, driveway, entrance, passage, road, threshold, way 3 *received an approach to appear in a soap opera*: advances, appeal, application, invitation, overture(s), plea, proposal, proposition, request 4 *impressed with his overall approach to the game*: course of action, manner, means, method, modus operandi, procedure, strategy, style, system, tactics, technique

approachable *adj* 1 *I find him a very approachable person*: affable, agreeable, congenial, easy to get on/along with, friendly, informal, open, sociable, warm 2 *the record remains approachable*: accessible, attainable, get-at-able *colloq*, reachable
Fa 1 aloof, unapproachable 2 inaccessible, remote

appropriate *adj* accepted, applicable, appurtenant *formal*, apropos *formal*, apt, becoming, befitting, correct, felicitous *formal*, fit, fitting, germane, meet *formal*, opportune, pertinent *formal*, proper, relevant, right, seasonable, seemly, spot-on *colloq*, suitable, timely, to the point, well-chosen, well-timed
Fa inappropriate, irrelevant, unsuitable
♦ *v* 1 *appropriate a position of power*: arrogate *formal*, assume, commandeer, confiscate, expropriate *formal*, impound, requisition, seize, take, take possession of, usurp 2 *appropriate the company's cash*: embezzle, filch, make off with, misappropriate, nick *colloq*, peculate *formal*, pilfer, pinch *colloq*, pocket, purloin *formal*, steal, swipe *colloq*, thieve

approval *n* 1 *gained his family's approval*: acceptance, acclaim, acclamation, admiration, applause, appreciation, approbation *formal*, commendation, esteem, favour, good opinion, honour, liking, praise, recommendation, regard, respect 2 *received formal approval for the deal*: acceptance, agreement, approbation *formal*, assent, authorization, blessing, certification, concurrence *formal*, confirmation, consent, endorsement, go-ahead *colloq*, green light *colloq*,

imprimatur *formal*, leave, licence, mandate, nod *colloq*, OK *colloq*, permission, ratification, rubber stamp *colloq*, sanction, support, thumbs-up *colloq*, validation, wink *colloq*
Fa 1 condemnation, disapproval

approve *v* 1 *I approve of her actions*: acclaim, admire, applaud, appreciate, be pleased with, commend, esteem, favour, hold in high regard, like, praise, recommend, regard, think well/highly of 2 *approve a proposal*: accede to, accept, adopt, agree to, allow, assent to, authorize, back, bless, buy *colloq*, carry, concur *formal*, confirm, consent to, countenance, endorse, give the go-ahead to *colloq*, give the green light to *colloq*, give the nod to *colloq*, give the thumbs-up to *colloq*, mandate, OK *colloq*, pass, permit, ratify, rubber-stamp *colloq*, sanction, second, support, uphold, validate
Fa 1 condemn, disapprove 2 reject

approved *adj* accepted, authorized, correct, favoured, official, orthodox, permissible, permitted, preferred, proper, recognized, recommended, sanctioned
Fa unauthorized, unorthodox

approximate *adj* ballpark *colloq*, close, estimated, guessed, inexact, like, loose, near, relative, rough, similar
Fa exact
♦ *v* approach, be similar to, be tantamount to, border on, come close to, resemble, verge on

approximately *adv* about, approaching, around, circa, close to, give or take *colloq*, in round numbers, in the region/neighbourhood/vicinity of, just about, loosely, more or less, nearly, not far off, odd, or thereabouts, roughly, round about, rounded up/down, some, something like, somewhere in the region of
Fa exactly

approximation *n* 1 *the number is only an approximation*: ballpark figure *colloq*, conjecture, estimate, guess, guesstimate *colloq*, rough calculation, rough idea 2 *an approximation to the truth*: correspondence, likeness, resemblance, semblance

apropos *adj* accepted, applicable, apt, becoming, befitting, correct, felicitous *formal*, fitting, opportune, pertinent *formal*, proper, relevant, right, seasonable, seemly, suitable, timely, to the point, well-chosen
Fa inappropriate
♦ *prep* in connection with, in relation to, in respect of, on the subject of, re, regarding, respecting, with reference to, with regard to, with respect to

apt *adj* 1 *an apt criticism*: acceptable, accurate, applicable, apposite, appropriate, correct, fit, fitting, germane, proper, relevant, seasonable, seemly, spot-on *colloq*, suitable, timely 2 *apt to do something*: disposed, given, inclined, liable, likely, prone, ready, subject, tending
Fa 1 inapt, unsuitable

aptitude *n* ability, bent, capability, capacity, cleverness, disposition, facility, faculty, flair, gift, inclination, intelligence, leaning, natural ability, proficiency, quickness, skill, talent, tendency
Fa inaptitude

aquatic *adj* fluid, fluvial *formal*, liquid, marine, maritime, nautical, river, sea, water, watery

arable *adj* cultivable, fecund *formal*, fertile, fruitful, ploughable, productive, tillable

arbiter *n* **1** *take the case to an independent arbiter:* adjudicator, judge, referee, umpire **2** *an arbiter of style:* authority, controller, expert, master, pundit

arbitrary *adj* **1** *an arbitrary choice:* capricious, chance, discretionary, illogical, inconsistent, instinctive, irrational, personal, random, subjective, unreasonable, unreasoned, whimsical **2** *arbitrary rule:* absolute, autocratic, despotic, dictatorial, dogmatic, domineering, high-handed, imperious, magisterial, overbearing, tyrannical

⊟ 1 circumspect, rational, reasoned

arbitrate *v* adjudicate, decide, determine, judge, mediate, pass judgement, referee, settle, sit in judgement, umpire

arbitration *n* adjudication, arbitrament *formal*, decision, determination, intervention, judgement, mediation, negotiation, settlement

arbitrator *n* adjudicator, arbiter, go-between, intermediary, judge, mediator, moderator, negotiator, referee, umpire

arc *n* arch, bend, bow, curvature, curve, curved line, semicircle

arcade *n* cloister, colonnade, covered way, gallery, loggia *technical*, mall, peristyle, piazza, portico, precinct, shopping mall, shopping precinct, stoa

arcane *adj* abstruse, concealed, cryptic, enigmatic, esoteric, hidden, mysterious, mystical, obscure, occult, profound, recondite, secret

arch *n* **1** *the arches of a bridge:* archway, bow, bridge, dome, semicircle, span, vault **2** *the arch of the foot:* arc, bend, concavity, curvature, curve
♦ *v* arc, bend, bow, camber, curve, vault
♦ *adj* cunning, mischievous, mysterious, playful, sly

archaeology

> *Archaeological terms include:*
> agger, amphitheatre, amphora, artefact, barrow, beaker, blade, bogman, bowl, bracteate, burin, cairn, cartouche, cave art/rock art, cist, cromlech, cup, dolmen, earthwork, eolith, flake, flask, flint, handaxe, henge, hieroglyph, hill fort, hoard, hypocaust, incised decoration, jar, jug, kitchen-midden, kurgan, ley lines, loom weight, lynchet, megalith, microlith, mosaic, mound, mummy, neolith, obelisk, palmette, palstave, papyrus, potassium-argon dating, radiocarbon dating, rock shelter, sondage, spindle, stele, stone circle, tell, tumulus, urn, vallum, whorl

archaic *adj* **1** *archaic gods:* ancient, antiquated, antique, bygone, old, primitive **2** *archaic notions of chivalry:* antediluvian, medieval, obsolete, old hat *colloq*, old-fashioned, out of the ark *colloq*, outdated, outmoded, out of date, passé, primitive, quaint

⊟ 1 modern **2** current, modern

archetypal *adj* characteristic, classic, exemplary *formal*, ideal, model, original, representative, standard, stock, typical

archetype *n* classic, epitome, exemplar *formal*, form, ideal, model, original, paradigm, pattern, precursor, prototype, standard, stereotype, type

architect *n* **1** *the architect of the building:* designer, draughtsman, master builder, planner **2** *the architect of modern economics:* author, constructor, creator, engineer, founder, instigator, inventor, maker, mastermind *colloq*, originator, prime mover, shaper

architecture *n* **1** *study architecture:* architectonics *technical*, building, construction, designing, planning **2** *the architecture of the cosmos:* arrangement, composition, design, framework, make-up, structure, style

> *Architectural and building terms include:*
> alcove, annexe, architrave, baluster, bargeboard, baroque, bas relief, capstone, classical, coping stone, Corinthian, corner-stone, cornice, coving, dado, dogtooth, dome, Doric, drawbridge, dry-stone, duplex, Early English, eaves, Edwardian, elevation, Elizabethan, façade, fascia, festoon, fillet, finial, flamboyant, Flemish bond, fletton, fluting, frieze, frontispiece, gargoyle, gatehouse, Georgian, Gothic, groin, groundplan, half-timbered, Ionic, jamb, lintel, mullion, Norman, pagoda, pantile, parapet, pinnacle, plinth, Queen-Anne, rafters, Regency, reveal, ridge, rococo, Romanesque, roof, rotunda, roughcast, sacristy, scroll, soffit, stucco, terrazzo, Tudor, Tuscan, wainscot, weathering. See also **wall**

archives *n* annals, chronicles, deeds, documents, ledgers, memorabilia, memorials, papers, records, registers, roll

arctic *adj* **1** *the Arctic Ocean:* boreal *formal*, far north, hyperborean *formal*, polar **2** *arctic weather:* bitterly cold, freezing, freezing cold, frozen, glacial, subzero

⊟ 1 Antarctic

ardent *adj* avid, dedicated, devoted, eager, enthusiastic, fervent, fervid, fierce, fiery, hot, impassioned, intense, keen, passionate, spirited, strong, vehement, warm, zealous

⊟ apathetic, unenthusiastic

ardour *n* animation, avidity, dedication, devotion, eagerness, empressement *formal*, enthusiasm, fervour, fire, heat, intensity, keenness, lust, passion, spirit, vehemence, warmth, zeal, zest

⊟ apathy, coolness, indifference

arduous *adj* backbreaking, burdensome, daunting, difficult, exhausting, fatiguing, formidable, gruelling, hard, harsh, heavy, laborious, onerous, punishing, rigorous, severe, strenuous, taxing, tiring, tough, uphill, wearying

⊟ easy

area *n* **1** *the Muslim areas of the city:* catchment area, department, district, enclave, environment, environs, locality, neighbourhood, parish, patch, precinct, province, quarter, region, reserve area, sector, terrain, zone **2** *a wide area of land:* breadth, expanse, part, portion, section, stretch, tract, width **3** *an area of knowledge:* branch, department, domain, extent, field, province, range, realm, sphere, territory

arena *n* **1** *a gladiatorial arena:* amphitheatre, area, bowl, coliseum, field, ground, hippodrome, ring, stadium **2** *the political arena:* area of conflict, battlefield, battleground, department, domain, province, realm, scene, sphere, world

arguable *adj* contentious, controvertible *formal*, debatable, disputable, moot, open to question, questionable, uncertain, undecided
🖃 certain, incontrovertible, indisputable

argue *v* **1** *argue about money:* altercate *formal*, be at each other's throats *colloq*, be at loggerheads *colloq*, bicker, cross swords *colloq*, disagree, dispute, fall out, feud, fight, haggle, have a bone to pick *colloq*, have a row, have it out (with) *colloq*, have words *colloq*, quarrel, remonstrate, row, squabble, take/join issue, wrangle **2** *I would argue that we should stop:* assert, claim, contend, declare, expostulate *formal*, hold, maintain, plead, reason **3** *argue the point:* debate, discuss, question **4** *argued them out of leaving:* convince, persuade, talk out of **5** *it argues for a more disciplined approach:* be evidence for, demonstrate, denote, display, exhibit, imply, indicate, manifest, prove, show, suggest

argument *n* **1** *arguments about money:* altercation *formal*, argy-bargy *colloq*, barney *colloq*, bust-up *colloq*, clash, conflict, controversy, debate, difference of opinion, ding-dong *colloq*, disagreement, discussion, dispute, dust-up *colloq*, feud, fight, heated exchange, quarrel, row, ruckus, rumpus, running battle *colloq*, set-to *colloq*, shouting-match *colloq*, slanging-match *colloq*, spat *US*, squabble, tiff *colloq*, wrangle **2** *impressed by her argument:* argumentation, assertion, case, claim, contention, debate, declaration, defence, demonstration, evidence, expostulation *formal*, logic, rationale, reason, reasoning **3** *the argument of the book:* outline, plot, summary, synopsis, theme, thesis

argumentative *adj* belligerent, cantankerous, captious *formal*, contentious, contrary, disputatious *formal*, dissentious *formal*, litigious *formal*, opinionated, perverse, polemical, quarrelsome, stroppy *colloq*
🖃 complaisant

arid *adj* **1** *an arid landscape:* baked, barren, dehydrated, desert, desiccated, dry, infertile, moistureless, parched, shrivelled up, torrefied *formal*, torrid, unproductive, waste, waterless **2** *an arid debate:* boring, colourless, drab, dreary, dry, dull, jejune, lifeless, monotonous, spiritless, sterile, tedious, uninspired, uninteresting, vapid
🖃 **1** fertile **2** exciting, lively

aright *adv* accurately, aptly, correctly, exactly, fitly, properly, rightly, suitably, truly

arise *v* **1** *whatever may arise:* appear, begin, come into being/existence, come to light, come up, commence, crop up *colloq*, emerge, happen, issue, occur, present itself, start **2** *points that arose from the report:* be a result of, be caused by, come, derive, ensue, flow, follow, proceed, result, spring, stem **3** *arise from the sofa:* ascend, climb, get to your feet, get up, go up, lift yourself, mount, rise, rise up, soar, stand up, tower

aristocracy *n* elite, gentility, gentry, haut monde *formal*, high society, nobility, noblemen,

noblewomen, optimates *formal*, patricians *formal*, patriciate *formal*, peerage, privileged class, ruling class, top drawer *colloq*, upper class, upper crust *colloq*
🖃 common people, hoi polloi *colloq*, lower classes, plebs *colloq*, proles *colloq*, proletariat, riff-raff *colloq*, working class

aristocrat *n* eupatrid *formal*, grandee *formal*, lady, lord, nob *colloq*, noble, nobleman, noblewoman, optimate *formal*, patrician, peer, peeress, toff *colloq*
🖃 commoner

aristocratic *adj* blue-blooded, courtly, dignified, elegant, elite, highborn, lordly, noble, patrician, refined, thoroughbred, titled, upper-class, upper-crust *colloq*, well-born
🖃 plebeian, vulgar

arm[1] *n* **1** *with folded arms:* appendage, brachium *technical*, limb, upper limb **2** *the air arm of the fighting forces:* branch, department, detachment, division, extension, offshoot, projection, section, wing **3** *an arm of the sea:* bay, channel, cove, creek, estuary, firth, inlet, passage

arm[2] *v* accoutre *formal*, array *formal*, brace, equip, forearm, fortify *formal*, furnish *formal*, gird, issue, outfit, prepare, prime, protect, provide, rearm, reinforce, rig, steel, strengthen, supply

armada *n* fleet, flotilla, naval force, navy, squadron

armaments *n* ammunition, arms, artillery, cannon, guns, munitions, ordnance, weaponry, weapons

armistice *n* agreement to end/cease/suspend hostilities, ceasefire, peace, peace treaty, truce

armour *n* chain mail, iron-cladding, mail, panoply, protective covering

armoured *adj* armour-plated, bomb-proof, bullet-proof, iron-clad, protected, reinforced, steel-plated

armoury *n* ammunition dump, (arms) depot, arsenal, garderobe, magazine, ordnance depot, repository, stock, stockpile

arms *n* **1** *to take up arms:* ammunition, armaments, artillery, firearms, guns, instruments of war, munitions, ordnance, weaponry, weapons **2** *my family's arms:* armorial bearings, blazonry, coat-of-arms, crest, escutcheon, heraldic device, heraldry, insignia, shield

army *n* **1** *a captain in the army:* armed force, infantry, land forces, military, militia, soldiers, troops **2** *an army of workers:* cohorts, crowd, horde, host, legions, mob, multitude, pack, swarm, throng

aroma *n* bouquet, fragrance, fumet(te) *formal*, odour, perfume, redolence *formal*, savour, scent, smell

aromatic *adj* balmy, fragrant, fresh, odoriferous *formal*, perfumed, pungent, redolent *formal*, savoury, scented, spicy, sweet-smelling
🖃 acrid, foul-smelling

around *prep* **1** *wrapped the paper around the present:* about, circumambient *formal*, circumjacent *formal*, encircling, enclosing, encompassing, framed by, on all sides of, on every side of, round, surrounding **2** *around a*

dozen: about, approximately, circa, close to, more or less, nearly, roughly
♦ *adv* **1** *heard gunfire all around*: about, all over, everywhere, here and there, in all directions, on all sides, throughout, to and fro **2** *a common sight in the countryside around*: at hand, close, close by, near, nearby

arouse *v* **1** *arouse suspicion*: animate, call forth, cause, excite, incur, induce, inflame, instigate, kindle, prompt, provoke, quicken, sharpen, spark, stimulate, summon up, trigger, whet **2** *arouse someone to anger*: agitate, evoke, excite, galvanize, get going, goad, incite, provoke, rouse, spur, startle, stir up, whip up **3** *arouse from sleep*: awaken, wake up, waken **4** *arouse sexually*: excite, get going, stimulate, turn on *colloq*
⊟ 2 calm, lull, quieten

arraign *v* accuse, call to account, charge, impeach, impugn, incriminate, indict, prosecute

arrange *v* **1** *arrange a meeting*: agree, decide, fix (up) *colloq*, make (an appointment), organize, pencil in *colloq*, plan, set up, settle on **2** *arrange for someone to cover you*: contrive, co-ordinate, design, determine, devise, fix, organize, plan, prepare, project, settle **3** *arrange the records into alphabetical order*: adjust, align, array, catalogue, categorize, class, classify, codify, dispose, distribute, file, grade, group, lay out, line up, list, marshal, order, position, range, regulate, set out, sift, sort (out), systematize, tidy **4** *arrange music*: adapt, harmonize, instrument, orchestrate, score, set
⊟ 3 disorganize, muddle, untidy

arrangement *n* **1** *make arrangements*: detail(s), groundwork, plan(s), planning, preparation(s), preparing **2** *come to a very satisfactory arrangement*: agreement, compromise, contract, modus vivendi, settlement, terms **3** *I like the arrangement of the paintings*: array, classification, design, display, disposition, format, grouping, layout, line-up, method, order, organization, plan, planning, positioning, preparation, schedule, scheme, set-up, structure, system **4** *a new arrangement of the song*: adaptation, harmonization, instrumentation, interpretation, orchestration, score, setting, version

arrant *adj* absolute, barefaced, blatant, brazen, complete, downright, egregious *formal*, extreme, flagrant, gross, incorrigible, infamous, notorious, out-and-out, outright, rank, thorough, thoroughgoing, unmitigated, utter, vile

array *n* arrangement, assemblage *formal*, assortment, collection, display, disposition, exhibition, exposition, formation, line-up, marshalling, muster, order, parade, show
♦ *v* **1** *the troops were arrayed in two lines*: align, arrange, assemble, display, dispose, draw up, exhibit, group, line up, marshal, muster, order, parade, position, range, show **2** *arrayed in a flowing robe*: accoutre *formal*, adorn, apparel *formal*, attire *formal*, bedizen *formal*, clothe, deck, decorate, dress, habilitate *formal*, robe

arrears *n* amount owed, balance, debt(s), deficit, liabilities, outstanding payment/amount, sum of money owed

arrest *v* **1** *arrest a criminal*: apprehend, book *colloq*, bust *colloq*, capture, catch, collar *colloq*, detain, do *colloq*, grab *colloq*, nab *colloq*, nail *colloq*,

nick *colloq*, pick up *colloq*, run in *colloq*, seize, take into custody **2** *arrest someone's progress*: block, check, delay, halt, hinder, impede, inhibit, interrupt, nip in the bud *colloq*, obstruct, restrain, retard, slow (down), stall, stem, stop **3** *arrest your attention*: absorb, attract, capture, catch, engage, engross, fascinate, grip, intrigue, rivet
♦ *n* apprehension, capture, detention, seizure, taking into custody

arresting *adj* amazing, conspicuous, engaging, extraordinary, impressive, notable, noteworthy, noticeable, outstanding, remarkable, striking, stunning, surprising
⊟ inconspicuous, unremarkable

arrival *n* **1** *the arrival of the president*: advent *formal*, appearance, approach, coming, emergence, entrance, entry, occurrence **2** *to welcome new arrivals*: débutant(e), entrant, fresher, freshman *US*, guest, incomer, newcomer, visitant *formal*, visitor
⊟ 1 departure

arrive *v* **1** *arrive at the airport*: appear, be present, blow in *colloq*, check in, clock in, come, come in, come on the scene, dock, drop in *colloq*, enter, get here, get there, get to, happen, land, make it *colloq*, materialize, occur, pull in, put in an appearance, reach, reach your destination, roll up *colloq*, show (up) *colloq*, surface *colloq*, touch down, turn up *colloq* **2** *the new series arrives in the UK on Friday*: appear, be produced, become available, come on the market **3** *arrive at a decision*: come to, reach **4** *he thinks he's really arrived*: get to the top *colloq*, make it *colloq*, succeed
⊟ 1 depart, leave

arrogance *n* boasting, conceit, condescension, contempt, contumely *formal*, disdain, egotism, haughtiness, hauteur *formal*, high-handedness, hubris *formal*, imperiousness, insolence, lordiness, nerve *colloq*, pomposity, presumption, pride, scorn, self-importance, snobbishness, superciliousness, superiority, vanity
⊟ bashfulness, humility, unassumingness

arrogant *adj* assuming, big-headed *colloq*, boastful, conceited, condescending, contemptuous, disdainful, egotistic, full of yourself, haughty, high and mighty *colloq*, high-handed, hoity-toity *colloq*, hubristic *formal*, imperious, insolent, lordly, overbearing, patronizing, presumptuous, proud, scornful, self-important, snobbish, stuck-up *colloq*, supercilious, superior, toffee-nosed *colloq*, uppity *colloq*
⊟ bashful, humble, unassuming

arrogate *v* appropriate, assume, commandeer, misappropriate, possess yourself of, presume, seize, usurp

arrogation *n* appropriation, assumption, commandeering

arrow *n* **1** *shoot with an arrow*: bolt, dart, flight, shaft **2** *follow the arrows*: indicator, marker, pointer

arsenal *n* ammunition dump, armoury, (arms) depot, garderobe, magazine, ordnance depot, repository, stock, stockpile

arson *n* fire-raising, incendiarism, pyromania

arsonist *n* fire-bug, fire-raiser, incendiary, pyromaniac

art *n* **1** *to be interested in art*: artistry, artwork, craft, craftsmanship, design, draughtsmanship, drawing, fine art, painting, sculpture, visual arts **2** *the art of public speaking*: adroitness, aptitude, craft, dexterity, expertise, facility, finesse, flair, gift, ingenuity, knack, mastery, method, profession, skill, talent, technique, trade, virtuosity **3** *performed the role with great art*: artfulness, astuteness, craftiness, cunning, deceit, guile, shrewdness, slyness, trickery, wiliness

---

Schools of art include:
abstract, action painting, Aestheticism, Art Deco, Art Nouveau, Barbizon, Baroque, Bohemian, Byzantine, classical revival, classicism, Conceptual Art, Constructivism, Cubism, Dadaism, Expressionism, Fauvism, Florentine, folk art, Futurism, Gothic, Hellenistic, Impressionism, junk art, Mannerism, medieval art, Minimal Art, Modernism, the Nabis, Naturalism, Neoclassicism, Neoexpressionism, Neoimpressionism, Neo-Plasticism, Op Art, plastic art, Pop Art, Postimpressionism, Post-Modernism, Purism, quattrocento, Realism, renaissance, Rococo, Romanesque, Romanticism, Suprematism, Surrealism, Symbolism, Venetian, Vorticism. See also **painting, picture, sculpture**

Arts and crafts include:
painting, oil painting, watercolour, fresco, portraiture; architecture, drawing, sketching, caricature, illustration; graphics, film, video; sculpture, modelling, woodcarving, woodcraft, marquetry, metalwork, enamelling, cloisonné, engraving, etching, pottery, ceramics, mosaic, jewellery, stained glass, photography, lithography, calligraphy, collage, origami, spinning, weaving, batik, silk-screen printing, needlework, tapestry, embroidery, patchwork, crochet, knitting. See also **embroidery**

---

artefact *n* item, object, piece of jewellery, something, thing, tool

artful *adj* clever, crafty, cunning, deceitful, designing, devious, dexterous, foxy, ingenious, masterly, resourceful, scheming, sharp, shrewd, skilful, sly, smart, subtle, tricky, vulpine *formal*, wily
Fa artless, ingenuous, naïve

article *n* **1** *articles in a magazine*: account, commentary, composition, essay, feature, item, monograph, offprint, paper, piece, report, review, story, write-up **2** *took several articles out of her bag*: artefact, commodity, constituent, item, object, part, piece, portion, something, thing, thingummy *colloq*, thingummybob *colloq*, thingummyjig *colloq*, unit **3** *article 25 of the contract*: clause, paragraph, point, section

articulate *adj* clear, coherent, comprehensible, distinct, eloquent, expressive, fluent, intelligible, lucid, meaningful, understandable, vocal, well-spoken
Fa inarticulate, incoherent
♦ *v* enunciate, express, pronounce, say, speak, state, talk, utter, verbalize, vocalize, voice

articulated *adj* attached, connected, coupled, fastened, fitted together, hinged, interlocked, joined, joint, linked

articulation *n* delivery, diction, enunciation, expression, pronunciation, saying, speaking, talking, utterance, verbalization, vocalization, voicing

artifice *n* **1** *an artifice to gain their confidence*: contrivance, device, dodge, ruse, scheme, stratagem, strategy, subterfuge, tactic, trick, wile **2** *spoke without artifice*: artfulness, chicanery, cleverness, craft, craftiness, cunning, deceit, deception, fraud, guile, slyness, subtlety, trickery

artificial *adj* **1** *artificial flowers*: imitation, man-made, manufactured, mock, non-natural, plastic, processed, simulated, synthetic **2** *an artificial smile*: affected, assumed, bogus, contrived, counterfeit, fake, false, feigned, forced, insincere, made-up, mannered, phoney *colloq*, pretended, pseud *colloq*, pseudo *colloq*, sham, simulated, specious, spurious, studied
Fa 1 natural, real **2** genuine

artisan *n* artificer, craftsman, craftswoman, expert, journeyman, mechanic, operative, skilled worker, technician

artist

Types of artist include:
architect, graphic designer, designer, draughtsman, draughtswoman, illustrator, cartoonist, photographer, printer, engraver, goldsmith, silversmith, blacksmith, carpenter, potter, weaver, sculptor, painter; craftsman, craftswoman, master

---

artist or *artiste*? An *artist* is someone who paints pictures or is skilled in one of the fine arts. An *artiste*, or *artist*, is a performer in a theatre or circus or on television; *artiste* is now regarded as old-fashioned or affected.

---

artiste *n* actor, actress, comedian, comedienne, comic, dancer, entertainer, performer, player, singer, trouper, variety artist, vaudevillian

artistic *adj* **1** *an artistic person*: creative, cultivated, cultured, gifted, imaginative, refined, sensitive, skilled, talented **2** *an artistic design*: aesthetic, attractive, beautiful, decorative, elegant, exquisite, graceful, harmonious, ornamental, stylish, tasteful
Fa 2 inelegant

artistry *n* ability, accomplishment, brilliance, craft, craftsmanship, creativity, deftness, expertise, finesse, flair, genius, mastery, proficiency, sensitivity, skill, style, talent, touch, workmanship
Fa ineptitude

artless *adj* candid, childlike, direct, frank, genuine, guileless, honest, ingenuous, innocent, naïve, natural, open, plain, pure, simple, sincere, straightforward, true, trusting, unpretentious, unsophisticated, unwary, unworldly
Fa artful, cunning

as *conj* **1** *continued talking as she ate*: all the time that, at the same time (that/as), when, while, whilst **2** *stood up tall as a tree*: for example, for instance, like, such as **3** *cooked it just as her mother had taught her*: in the same manner that, in the same way that, like **4** *I'll go to bed as I am so tired*: as a result of, because, considering that, on account of, owing to, seeing that, since, the reason is...

ascend *v* arise, climb, float up, fly up, gain height, go up, lift off, mount, move up, rise, scale, slope upwards, soar, take off, tower
F∃ descend, go down

ascendancy *n* authority, command, control, dominance, domination, dominion, edge, hegemony *formal*, influence, lordship, mastery, power, predominance, pre-eminence, prevalence, superiority, supremacy, sway, upper hand *colloq*
F∃ decline, subordination

ascent *n* **1** *the ascent of Everest:* ascending, ascension, climb, climbing, escalation, mounting, rise, rising, scaling **2** *a steep ascent: acclivity formal,* elevation, gradient, hill, incline, ramp, slope **3** *their rapid ascent to power:* advance, advancement *formal,* progress, rise
F∃ **1** descent

ascertain *v* confirm, detect, determine, discover, establish, find out, fix, get to know, identify, learn, locate, make certain, pin down *colloq,* settle, suss out *colloq,* verify

ascetic *adj* abstemious, abstinent, austere, harsh, plain, puritanical, rigorous, self-controlled, self-denying, self-disciplined, severe, Spartan, stern, strict
♦ *n* abstainer, anchorite, celibate, dervish, fakir, hermit, monk, nun, puritan, recluse, solitary, yogi

ascribe *v* accredit *formal,* assign, attribute, charge, credit, give credit to, impute *formal,* put down

ashamed *adj* **1** *ashamed of your behaviour:* abashed, apologetic, blushing, confused, conscience-stricken, contrite, crestfallen, discomfited, discomposed, distressed, embarrassed, guilty, having your tail between your legs *colloq,* humbled, humiliated, mortified, not able to look someone in the face *colloq,* red-faced, remorseful, sheepish, sorry **2** *ashamed to admit his mistakes:* bashful, hesitant, modest, reluctant, self-conscious, unwilling
F∃ **1** defiant, proud, shameless **2** proud

ashen *adj* anaemic, blanched, bleached, colourless, ghastly, grey, leaden, livid, pale, pallid, pasty, wan, white
F∃ ruddy

aside *adv* **1** *asked her to move aside:* apart, away, on one side, out of the way, separately, to one side **2** *his money aside, he doesn't have much going for him:* apart, notwithstanding
♦ *n* digression, monologue, parenthesis, soliloquy, stage whisper, whisper

asinine *adj* absurd, daft *colloq,* fatuous, foolish, gormless *colloq,* half-witted, idiotic, imbecilic, inane, moronic, nonsensical, potty *colloq,* senseless, silly, stupid
F∃ intelligent, sensible

ask *v* **1** *ask a question:* canvass, cross-examine, cross-question, give a grilling to *colloq,* grill *colloq,* inquire, interrogate, interview, poll, pose, posit *formal,* postulate *formal,* press, propose, propound *formal,* pump *colloq,* put a question to, put forward, put on the spot *colloq,* query, question, quiz *colloq,* suggest, want to know the answer to **2** *ask for advice:* appeal, approach, beg,

beseech, bid, clamour, crave, demand, entreat, implore, invite, order, petition, plead, pray, request, require, requisition, seek, solicit, sue, summon, supplicate **3** *ask them to dinner:* entertain, have over, have round, invite

askance *adv* contemptuously, disapprovingly, disdainfully, distrustfully, doubtfully, dubiously, indirectly, mistrustfully, obliquely, sceptically, scornfully, sideways, suspiciously

askew *adv* asymmetrically, at an oblique angle, crookedly, lopsidedly, obliquely, out of line, sideways, skew *colloq,* skew-whiff *colloq*
F∃ level, straight
♦ *adj* asymmetric, at an oblique angle, crooked, lopsided, oblique, off-centre, out of line, skew *colloq,* skew-whiff *colloq*
F∃ level, straight

asleep *adj* comatose *colloq,* dead to the world *colloq,* dormant *formal,* dozing, fast asleep, flaked out *colloq,* having forty winks *colloq,* inactive, inert, napping, numb, out like a light *colloq,* reposing *formal,* resting, sleeping, snoozing, sound asleep, unconscious

aspect *n* **1** *many aspects of life:* dimension, facet, factor, feature, position, side **2** *look at it from a different aspect:* angle, direction, light, outlook, point of view, position, standpoint, view **3** *take on a more promising aspect:* air, appearance, bearing, countenance, expression, face, look, manner

asperity *n* acerbity, acrimony, astringency, bitterness, causticity *formal,* churlishness, crabbedness, crossness, harshness, irascibility, irritability, peevishness, roughness, severity, sharpness, sourness
F∃ mildness

asphyxiate *v* choke, smother, stifle, strangle, strangulate, suffocate, throttle

aspiration *n* aim, ambition, craving, desire, dream, endeavour, goal, hankering, hope, ideal, intent, longing, object, objective, purpose, wish, yearning

aspire *v* aim, crave, desire, dream, hanker, have as an ambition/aim/goal, hope, intend, long, purpose, pursue, seek, wish, yearn

aspiring *adj* ambitious, aspirant, budding, eager, endeavouring, enterprising, hopeful, keen, longing, striving, wishful, would-be

ass *n* **1** *ride an ass:* burro, donkey, hinny, jackass, moke *colloq,* mule, pony **2** *call someone an ass:* blockhead *colloq,* dimwit *colloq,* dipstick *slang,* fool, idiot, imbecile, nerd *slang,* nincompoop *colloq,* ninny *colloq,* nitwit *colloq,* numskull *colloq,* twerp *colloq,* twit *colloq,* wally *slang*

assail *v* **1** *assailed by the newspapers:* attack, bombard, criticize, invade, lay into, malign, maltreat, set about, set upon, strike, tear into *colloq* **2** *assailed by doubts:* bedevil, beset, perplex, plague, torment, trouble, worry

assailant *n* abuser, adversary, aggressor, assailer, assaulter, attacker, enemy, invader, mugger, opponent, reviler

assassin *n* contract killer *colloq,* cut-throat, executioner, gunman, hatchet man *colloq,* hit-man *colloq,* killer, liquidator *colloq,* murderer, slayer

assassinate *v* bump off *colloq*, dispatch, do in *colloq*, eliminate *colloq*, hit *colloq*, kill, liquidate *colloq*, murder, slay, take someone's life, whack *colloq*

assault *n* **1** *an assault on the enemy lines*: act of aggression, attack, blitz, charge, incursion, invasion, offensive, onslaught, raid, storm, storming, strike **2** *charged with assault*: ABH *colloq*, abuse, actual bodily harm, battery, GBH *colloq*, grievous bodily harm, molestation, mugging *colloq*, rape, violence
♦ *v* abuse, attack, beat up *colloq*, do over *colloq*, fall on, go for *colloq*, hit, interfere with, lay into *colloq*, molest, mug *colloq*, set upon, strike

assemblage *n* accumulation, collection, crowd, flock, gathering, group, mass, multitude, rally, throng

assemble *v* **1** *assembled his troops*: accumulate, amass, bring together, collect, convene, gather, marshal, mass, mobilize, muster, rally, round up, summons **2** *they assembled in the courtyard*: come together, congregate, convene, gather, get together, group, join up, mass, meet, mobilize, muster, rally **3** *assemble a toy car*: build, collate, compose, connect, construct, fabricate, fit together, join, make, manufacture, piece together, put together, set up
🔁 **1** disperse, scatter **2** disperse, scatter **3** dismantle

assembly *n* **1** *an assembly of elders*: agora *technical*, assemblage, body, body of people, collection, company, conference, congregation, congress, convention, convocation *formal*, council, crowd, flock, gathering, gemot, gorsedd, group, indaba, kgotla, meeting, multitude, panegyry *formal*, rally, synod, throng **2** *the assembly of the shelves*: building, construction, fabrication, manufacture, putting together

assent *v* accede *formal*, accept, acquiesce *formal*, agree, allow, approve, comply *formal*, concede *formal*, concur *formal*, consent, grant, permit, sanction, submit, subscribe, yield
🔁 disagree
♦ *n* acceptance, accord *formal*, acquiescence *formal*, agreement, approbation *formal*, approval, compliance *formal*, concession, concurrence *formal*, consent, permission, sanction

assert *v* **1** *assert a fact*: affirm, argue, attest, confirm, declare, profess, pronounce, state, swear, testify to **2** *assert your rights*: claim, contend, defend, establish, insist on, maintain, protest, stand up for, stress, uphold, vindicate
🔁 **1** deny, refute

assertion *n* affirmation, allegation, attestation, avowal *formal*, claim, contention, declaration, insistence, predication *formal*, profession, pronouncement, statement, vindication, word
🔁 denial

assertive *adj* aggressive, assuming, bold, confident, decided, dogmatic, dominant, domineering, emphatic, firm, forceful, forward, insistent, not backward in coming forward *colloq*, opinionated, overbearing, positive, presumptuous, pushy *colloq*, self-assured, self-confident, strong-willed, sure of yourself
🔁 diffident, timid

assess *v* **1** *assess a situation*: appraise, check out *colloq*, consider, estimate, evaluate, gauge, judge,

review, size up, weigh **2** *assess the value of something*: calculate, compute, determine, estimate, fix, rate, value

assessment *n* **1** *the assessment of a situation*: appraisal, consideration, estimation, evaluation, judgement, opinion, recce *colloq*, review, testing **2** *a tax assessment*: computation, demand, imposition, levy, rate, tariff, toll, valuation

asset *n* **1** *an asset to the school*: advantage, aid, benefit, blessing, boon, help, liability, plus *colloq*, plus point *colloq*, resource, strength, strong point, virtue **2** *the assets of a company*: capital, estate, funds, goods, holdings, means, money, possessions, property, reserves, resources, savings, securities, valuables, wealth

assiduous *adj* attentive, conscientious, constant, dedicated, devoted, diligent, hard-working, indefatigable, industrious, persevering, persistent, sedulous *formal*, steady, studious, unflagging, untiring
🔁 negligent

assign *v* allocate, allot, appoint, apportion, choose, commission, consign, delegate, designate, detail, determine, dispense, distribute, fix, give, grant, install, name, nominate, select, set, specify, stipulate

assignation *n* appointment, arrangement, date, engagement, rendezvous, secret meeting

assignment *n* **1** *written assignments*: charge, commission, duty, errand, job, obligation, position, post, project, responsibility, task **2** *his assignment to the job*: allocation, appointment, consignment, delegation, designation, distribution, grant, nomination, selection

assimilate *v* **1** *to assimilate new ideas*: absorb, incorporate, learn, pick up, take in **2** *to be assimilated into a new culture*: absorb, acclimatize, accommodate, accustom, adapt, adjust, blend, integrate, mingle, mix, unite
🔁 **2** reject

assist *v* **1** *assist someone with their expenses*: abet, aid, back (up), collaborate, co-operate, do your bit *colloq*, give a leg up to *colloq*, give/lend a hand, help, rally round, reinforce, relieve, second, succour *formal*, support, sustain **2** *assist the performance of a task*: advance, benefit, enable, encourage, expedite, facilitate, further, make easier, serve
🔁 **1** hinder **2** thwart

assistance *n* a helping hand *colloq*, a leg up *colloq*, aid, backing, benefit, boost, collaboration, co-operation, furtherance, help, reinforcement, relief, service, succour *formal*, support
🔁 hindrance, resistance

assistant *n* **1** *the manager's assistant*: ancillary, auxiliary, backer, deputy, right-hand man, second, second-in-command, subordinate, supporter **2** *a personal assistant*: abettor, accessory, accomplice, aide, ally, associate, collaborator, colleague, confederate, helper, partner **3** *a shop assistant*: checkout person, sales clerk *US*, salesman, salesperson, saleswoman

associate *v* **1** *associate good looks with success*: connect, correlate, couple, identify, link, pair, speak of in the same breath *colloq*, think of together **2** *associate with bad company*: be involved, consort *formal*, fraternize, hang around/out *colloq*, hobnob *colloq*, keep company,

mingle, mix, rub shoulders *colloq*, socialize
3 *associate with other wine makers:* affiliate, ally, amalgamate, attach, band together, combine, confederate, connect, couple, join, league, link, relate, syndicate, unite, yoke
♦ *n* affiliate, ally, assistant, collaborator, colleague, companion, compeer, comrade, confederate, co-worker, fellow, follower, friend, helper, mate, partner, peer, sidekick *colloq*

association *n* **1** *an association of wine makers:* affiliation, alliance, band, cartel, clique, club, coalition, company, confederacy, confederation, consortium, corporation, federation, fellowship, fraternity, group, guild, league, organization, partnership, society, sodality *formal*, syndicate, union **2** *formed a strong association:* bond, companionship, connection, correlation, familiarity, friendship, intimacy, involvement, link, relation, relationship, tie

assorted *adj* different, differing, diverse, heterogeneous *formal*, manifold, miscellaneous, mixed, motley, multifarious *formal*, several, sundry, varied, variegated *formal*, various
🖃 homogeneous, uniform

assortment *n* arrangement, bunch, choice, collection, diversity, group(ing), jumble, lot, medley, miscellany, mix, mixture, olla-podrida, potpourri, salmagundi, selection, variety

assuage *v* **1** *assuage grief/pain:* allay, alleviate, calm, ease, lessen, lighten, lower, lull, mitigate, moderate, mollify, pacify, palliate, reduce, relieve, soften, soothe **2** *assuage your thirst:* alleviate, appease, quench, satisfy, slake *formal*
🖃 **1** exacerbate, worsen

assume *v* **1** *I assume you have read the introduction:* accept, believe, deduce, expect, fancy, guess, imagine, infer, postulate *formal*, presume, presuppose, suppose, surmise, take as read, take for granted, take it... *colloq*, take someone's word for it *colloq*, think, understand **2** *assume a false identity:* affect, counterfeit, feign, pretend, put on, simulate, take on **3** *assume great importance:* adopt, come to have, take on **4** *assume command:* adopt, appropriate, arrogate, commandeer, embrace, enter upon, pre-empt, seize, take over, take upon yourself, undertake, usurp

assumed *adj* affected, bogus, counterfeit, fake, false, feigned, fictitious, hypothetical, made-up, phoney *colloq*, pretended, pseudonymous *formal*, putative *formal*, sham, simulated, supposititious *formal*
🖃 actual, real, true

assumption *n* **1** *make an assumption:* belief, conjecture, expectation, fancy, guess, hypothesis, idea, inference, notion, postulate, postulation *formal*, premise, presumption, presupposition, supposition, surmise, theory **2** *her assumption of power:* adoption, appropriation *formal*, arrogation *formal*, commandeering, embarkation, embrace, pre-emption *formal*, seizure, takeover, taking upon yourself, undertaking, usurpation *formal*

assurance *n* **1** *gave a sworn assurance:* affirmation, assertion, declaration, guarantee, oath, pledge, promise, security, undertaking, vow, word **2** *act with great assurance:* aplomb, assuredness, audacity, belief in yourself, boldness, certainty, confidence, conviction, courage, nerve, self-assurance, self-confidence, self-reliance, sureness
🖃 **2** doubt, shyness, uncertainty

assure *v* **1** *assured me he would be safe:* comfort, convince, encourage, hearten, persuade, reassure, soothe **2** *success is assured:* affirm, attest, certify, confirm, ensure, guarantee, pledge, promise, seal, secure, swear, vow, warrant

assured *adj* **1** *an assured return on investment:* certain, confirmed, cut and dried *colloq*, definite, ensured, fixed, guaranteed, indisputable, irrefutable, positive, promised, secure, settled, sure **2** *gave an assured performance:* assertive, audacious, bold, confident, self-assured, self-confident, self-possessed, sure of yourself
🖃 **1** uncertain **2** bashful, shy

astonish *v* amaze, astound, bewilder, confound, daze, dumbfound, flabbergast *colloq*, floor *colloq*, shock, stagger, startle, stun, stupefy, surprise, take aback, take your breath away, wow *colloq*

astonished *adj* amazed, astounded, bewildered, bowled over *colloq*, confounded, dazed, dumbfounded, flabbergasted *colloq*, knocked for six *colloq*, shocked, staggered, startled, stunned, surprised, taken aback

astonishing *adj* amazing, astounding, bewildering, breathtaking, impressive, mind-boggling *colloq*, shocking, staggering, startling, striking, stunning, surprising

astonishment *n* amazement, bewilderment, confusion, consternation, disbelief, dismay, shock, stupefaction *formal*, surprise, wonder

astound *v* amaze, astonish, bewilder, bowl over *colloq*, knock for six *colloq*, overwhelm, shock, startle, stun, stupefy, surprise, take your breath away

astounding *adj* amazing, astonishing, bewildering, breathtaking, overwhelming, shocking, staggering, startling, stunning, stupefying, surprising

astray *adv* adrift, amiss, awry, lost, missing, off course, off the mark, off the rails *colloq*, wrong

astringent *adj* **1** *an astringent liquid:* acerbic, acid, caustic, styptic *technical* **2** *astringent criticism:* biting, caustic, hard, harsh, mordant *formal*, scathing, severe, stern, trenchant
🖃 **2** bland

astronaut *n* cosmonaut, space traveller, spaceman, spacewoman

astute *adj* canny, clever, crafty, cunning, discerning, intelligent, keen, knowing, penetrating, perceptive, perspicacious *formal*, prudent, sagacious *formal*, sharp, shrewd, sly, subtle, wily, wise
🖃 slow, stupid

asylum *n* **1** *seek political asylum:* haven, place of safety, port in a storm *colloq*, refuge, retreat, sanctuary, shelter **2** *an asylum for the mentally ill:* funny farm *colloq*, institution, loony bin *colloq*, madhouse *colloq*, mental hospital, nuthouse *colloq*, psychiatric hospital

asymmetrical *adj* awry, crooked, disproportionate, distorted, irregular, lopsided, malformed, unbalanced, unequal, uneven, unsymmetrical
🖃 symmetrical

asymmetry *n* crookedness, disproportionateness, distortion, imbalance, inequality, irregularity, lopsidedness, malformation, unevenness
🖃 symmetry

atheism *n* disbelief, freethinking, godlessness, heathenism, impiety, infidelity, irreligion, nihilism *technical*, non-belief, paganism, rationalism, scepticism, unbelief, ungodliness

atheist *n* disbeliever, freethinker, heathen, heretic, humanist, infidel, nihilist *technical*, non-believer, nullifidian *formal*, pagan, rationalist, sceptic, unbeliever

athlete *n* competitor, contender, contestant, gymnast, player, runner, sportsman, sportswoman

athletic *adj* 1 *an athletic person:* active, brawny, energetic, fit, muscular, powerful, robust, sinewy, sporty, strapping, strong, sturdy, vigorous, well-knit, well-proportioned, wiry 2 *athletic events:* gymnastic, sporting
🖃 1 puny

athletics *n* aerobics *technical*, callisthenics, exercises, field events, games, gymnastics, matches, races, sports, track events

atmosphere *n* 1 *the earth's atmosphere:* aerospace, air, ether, heavens, sky 2 *this café has a nice atmosphere:* air, ambience, aura, background, character, climate, environment, feel, feeling, flavour, milieu, mood, quality, setting, spirit, surroundings, tenor, tone

The different layers of the atmosphere are: troposphere, stratosphere, mesosphere, thermosphere, ionosphere, exosphere

atom *n* bit, crumb, fragment, grain, hint, iota, jot, mite, molecule, morsel, particle, scintilla, scrap, shred, speck, spot, trace, whit

atone *v* appease, compensate, expiate, indemnify, make amends, make good, make right, make up for, offset, pay for, propitiate, recompense, reconcile, redeem, redress, remedy, repent

atonement *n* amends, appeasement, compensation, expiation, eye for an eye *colloq*, indemnity, payment, penance, propitiation, recompense, redress, reimbursement, reparation, repayment, requital, restitution, restoration, satisfaction

atrocious *adj* abominable, appalling, brutal, cruel, dreadful, fiendish, flagitious *formal*, ghastly, grievous, heinous *formal*, hideous, horrendous, horrible, merciless, monstrous, nefarious *formal*, ruthless, savage, shocking, terrible, vicious, wicked
🖃 admirable, fine

atrocity *n* abomination, atrociousness, barbarity, brutality, cruelty, enormity, evil, flagitiousness *formal*, heinousness *formal*, hideousness, horror, monstrosity, outrage, savagery, viciousness, vileness, villainy, violation, wickedness

atrophy *n* decay, decline, degeneration, deterioration, diminution, emaciation, marasmus *technical*, shrivelling, tabefaction *technical*, wasting (away), withering
♦ *v* decay, decline, degenerate, deteriorate,

diminish, dwindle, emaciate, fade, shrink, shrivel, tabefy *technical*, waste (away), wither

attach *v* 1 *attach a label:* add, adhere, affix, annex, bind, connect, couple, fasten, fix, join, link, make secure, nail, pin, secure, stick, tie, unite, weld 2 *attach yourself to a group:* affiliate with, ally, associate with, combine with, join, latch on to *colloq*, unite 3 *a centre attached to the university:* affiliate, assign, associate, connect, link, second
🖃 1 detach, unfasten

attached *adj* 1 *very attached to her family:* affectionate, devoted, fond, friendly, liking, loving, tender 2 *is she attached?:* engaged, going steady *colloq*, in a relationship, involved with someone, married, spoken for
🖃 1 unloving 2 on your own, single, unattached

attachment *n* 1 *insert the attachment here:* accessory, accoutrement *formal*, addition, adjunct, appendage *formal*, appurtenance *formal*, extension, extra, fitting, fixture, supplement, supplementary part 2 *formed an attachment to her:* affection, affinity, attraction, bond, devotion, fondness, friendship, liking, link, love, loyalty, partiality, tenderness, tie

attack *v* 1 *physically attack a person:* ambush, assail, assault, beat up *colloq*, besiege, charge, do over *colloq*, fall on, go for, have someone's guts for garters *slang*, jump *colloq*, knock into the middle of next week *slang*, lay into, leave for dead *colloq*, make a dead set at *colloq*, mug *colloq*, pounce on, raid, rush, set about, set upon, storm, strike, take to the cleaners *slang* 2 *attacked in the press:* abuse, berate *formal*, bitch about *colloq*, blame, calumniate *formal*, censure, criticize, decry *formal*, denounce, find fault with, fulminate against *formal*, have a go at *colloq*, impugn *formal*, knock *colloq*, malign, pan *colloq*, pick holes in *colloq*, rebuke, reprove, revile, run down *colloq*, slag off *colloq*, slam *colloq*, slate *colloq*, tear to shreds *colloq*, tear/pull to pieces *colloq*, vilify *formal* 3 *the disease attacks the nerves:* affect, destroy, infect 4 *attack a task with relish:* begin, commence, deal with, embark on, get started on, set about, start, tackle, undertake
🖃 1 defend, protect
♦ *n* 1 *a military attack:* act of aggression, assault, battery, blitz, bombardment, charge, foray, incursion, invasion, irruption *formal*, offensive, onslaught, push, raid, rush, sally, sortie, storming, strike 2 *an attack on his reputation:* abuse, censure, criticism, flak *colloq*, impugnment *formal*, invective *formal*, knocking *colloq*, revilement *formal*, slamming *colloq*, slating *colloq*, vilification *formal* 3 *suffered a panic attack:* access *formal*, bout, convulsion, fit, paroxysm, seizure, spasm, stroke

attacker *n* abuser, aggressor, assailant, critic, detractor, invader, mugger *colloq*, persecutor, raider, reviler
🖃 defender, supporter

attain *v* accomplish, achieve, acquire, arrive at, complete, earn, effect, find, fulfil, gain, get, grasp, hit, net, obtain, procure, reach, realize, secure, touch, win

attainable *adj* accessible, achievable, at hand, conceivable, doable *colloq*, feasible, imaginable, manageable, obtainable, possible, potential,

practicable, probable, reachable, realistic, viable, within reach
🔁 unattainable

attainment *n* **1** *artistic attainments:* ability, accomplishment, achievement, aptitude, art, capability, competence, facility, feat, gift, proficiency, skill, success, talent **2** *the attainment of his ambitions:* accomplishment, acquirement *formal*, completion, consummation, fulfilment, mastery, procurement *formal*, realization

attempt *v* **1** aim, aspire, do your level best *colloq*, endeavour, experiment, give it a go/try/whirl *colloq*, have a go/shot/crack/stab *colloq*, have a try, see if you can do, seek, set out, strive, tackle, try, try your hand, try your hand at *colloq*, undertake, venture
♦ *n* bash *colloq*, bid, crack *colloq*, effort, endeavour, experiment, go, push, shot *colloq*, stab *colloq*, struggle, trial, try, undertaking, venture

attend *v* **1** *attend a meeting:* appear, be here, be present, be there, frequent, go to, go/come along, put in/make an appearance, show (up) *colloq*, turn up *colloq*, visit **2** *attend to what was said:* concentrate, follow, hear, heed, listen, mark, mind, note, notice, observe, pay attention, take note/notice, watch **3** *attend on royalty:* accompany, chaperone, escort, follow, guard, usher **4** *attend the sick:* care for, help, look after, minister to, nurse, serve, take care of, tend, wait upon
▶ **attend to** control, deal with, direct, follow up (on), handle, heed, look after, manage, oversee, process, see to, supervise, take care of

attendance *n* appearance, audience, crowd, gate, house, presence, showing (up) *colloq*, turnout *colloq*

attendant *n* aide, assistant, auxiliary, companion, custodian, escort, follower, guard, guide, helper, marshal, page, retainer, servant, steward, usher, waiter
♦ *adj* accompanying, associated, attached, concomitant *formal*, consequent, incidental, related, resultant, subsequent

attention *n* **1** *let your attention wander:* advertence *formal*, advertency *formal*, alertness, awareness, concentration, consideration, contemplation, focus of your thoughts, heed, mind, mindfulness, notice, observation, preoccupation, recognition, regard, thought, vigilance **2** *attract great public attention:* awareness, concern, consideration, contemplation, high profile *colloq*, limelight *colloq*, notice, observation, recognition, regard, thought **3** *receive medical attention:* care, help, service, therapy, treatment **4** *flattered by his attentions:* compliments, courtesy, gallantry, politeness, respect
🔁 **1** daydreaming, disregard, inattention **2** disregard, inattention **3** negligence

attentive *adj* **1** *try to remain attentive at all times:* advertent *formal*, alert, all ears *colloq*, awake, aware, careful, concentrating, conscientious, heedful, listening, mindful, noticing, observant, on the qui vive, vigilant, watchful, watching **2** *attentive to her wishes:* accommodating, chivalrous, civil, conscientious, considerate, courteous, devoted, gallant, gracious, kind, obliging, polite, thoughtful
🔁 **1** heedless, inattentive **2** inconsiderate

attest *v* adjure *formal*, affirm, assert, asseverate *formal*, aver *formal*, bear witness to, certify, confirm, corroborate, declare, demonstrate, display, endorse, evidence *formal*, evince *formal*, manifest, prove, show, verify, vouch for

attire *n* accoutrements *formal*, apparel *formal*, clothes, clothing, costume, dress, finery, garb, garments, gear *colloq*, habiliments *formal*, habit *formal*, outfit, rig-out *colloq*, togs *colloq*, wear

attired *adj* adorned, arrayed, clothed, decked out *colloq*, dressed, habilitated *formal*, rigged out *colloq*, turned out

attitude *n* **1** *an optimistic attitude:* approach, aspect, disposition, feeling, manner, mentality, mindset, mood, opinion, outlook, perspective, point of view, position, view, way of thinking, Weltanschauung, world-view **2** *strike an attitude:* bearing, carriage *formal*, deportment *formal*, pose, posture, stance, stand

attract *v* allure, appeal to, bewitch, bring in, captivate, charm, draw, enchant, engage, entice, excite, fascinate, incline, induce, interest, invite, lure, magnetize, pull, pull in, seduce, tempt
🔁 disgust, repel

attraction *n* **1** *the attraction of an exotic lifestyle:* affinity, allure, appeal, bait, captivation, charm, draw, enchantment, enticement, fascination, inducement, interest, invitation, lure, magnetism, pull, seduction, temptation **2** *tourist attractions:* activity, building, entertainment, feature, sight
🔁 **1** repulsion

attractive *adj* **1** *an attractive person:* beautiful, bonny *Scot*, charismatic, cute, desirable, elegant, engaging, fair, fetching, glamorous, good-looking, gorgeous, handsome, lovely, picturesque, pleasant, pleasing, prepossessing, pretty, sexy, striking, stunning, winsome **2** *an attractive suggestion:* agreeable, appealing, captivating, charming, engaging, enticing, fascinating, interesting, inviting, irresistible, magnetic, seductive, tempting, winning, winsome

attribute *v* accredit *formal*, apply, ascribe, assign, blame, charge, credit, impute *formal*, put down, refer
♦ *n* aspect, characteristic, facet, feature, idiosyncrasy, indicator, mark, note, peculiarity, point, property, quality, quirk, side, sign, streak, symbol, trait, virtue

attrition *n* **1** *rocks worn down by attrition:* abrasion, chafing, detrition *formal*, erosion, friction, rubbing, scraping **2** *a process of attrition:* attenuation *formal*, harassment, wearing away, wearing down

attuned *adj* acclimatized, accustomed, adapted, adjusted, assimilated, co-ordinated, familiarized, harmonized, regulated, set, tuned

atypical *adj* aberrant, abnormal, anomalous, deviant, divergent, eccentric, exceptional, extraordinary, freakish, uncharacteristic, untypical, unusual
🔁 typical

auburn *adj* chestnut, copper, henna, reddish-brown, russet, rust, tawny, Titian

audacious *adj* **1** *an audacious person:* brazen, cheeky, disrespectful, forward, impertinent,

impudent, insolent, pert, presumptuous, rude, shameless **2** *an audacious robbery:* adventurous, bold, brave, courageous, daring, enterprising, fearless, intrepid, rash, reckless, risky, venturesome *formal*
≠ 1 cautious, reserved, timid

audacity *n* adventurousness, boldness, bravery, brazenness, cheek, courage, daring, dauntlessness, defiance, disrespectfulness, effrontery, enterprise, fearlessness, forwardness, impertinence, impudence, insolence, intrepidity, pertness, pluck, presumption, rashness, recklessness, risk, rudeness, shamelessness, valour
≠ caution, reserve, timidity

audible *adj* appreciable, clear, detectable, discernible, distinct, hearable, heard, perceptible, recognizable
≠ inaudible, silent, unclear

audience *n* **1** *an appreciative audience:* assembly, auditorium, congregation, crowd, devotees, fans, following, gathering, house, listeners, onlookers, public, ratings, regulars, spectators, turnout, viewers **2** *an audience with the Pope:* conference, consultation, hearing, interview, meeting, reception

audit *n* analysis, balancing, check, examination, inspection, investigation, review, scrutiny, statement, verification
♦ *v* analyse, balance, check, examine, go over, go through, inspect, investigate, review, scrutinize, verify, work through

augment *v* add to, amplify, boost, build up, enhance, enlarge, expand, extend, grow, heighten, increase, inflate, intensify, magnify, make greater, multiply, put on, raise, reinforce, strengthen, swell
≠ decrease

augur *v* be a sign of, betoken *formal*, bode *formal*, forebode *formal*, foretell, harbinger *formal*, herald, portend *formal*, predict, presage *formal*, promise, prophesy, signify

augury *n* foreboding, forerunner, forewarning, harbinger, haruspication *formal*, herald, omen, portent, prediction, prodrome *formal*, prognostication, promise, prophecy, sign, token, warning

august *adj* awe-inspiring, dignified, exalted, glorious, grand, imposing, impressive, lofty, magnificent, majestic, noble, solemn, stately

aura *n* air, ambience, atmosphere, emanation, feel, feeling, hint, mood, nimbus *formal*, quality, suggestion, vibes *colloq*, vibrations

auspices *n* aegis, authority, care, charge, guidance, patronage, supervision

auspicious *adj* bright, cheerful, encouraging, favourable, felicitous *formal*, fortunate, happy, hopeful, lucky, opportune, optimistic, promising, propitious *formal*, prosperous, rosy, timely
≠ inauspicious, ominous, unfavourable

austere *adj* **1** *austere surroundings:* basic, bleak, forbidding, grim, plain, simple, sombre, spartan, stark, unadorned, unornamented **2** *an austere man:* abstemious, ascetic, chaste, cold, distant, exacting, formal, grave, hard, harsh, inflexible, puritanical, restrained, rigid, rigorous,

self-abnegating *formal*, self-denying, self-disciplined, serious, severe, sober, solemn, stern, strict, stringent, unbending, unfeeling
≠ 1 elaborate, ornate **2** genial

austerity *n* abstemiousness, abstinence, asceticism, economy, formality, hardness, harshness, inflexibility, plainness, puritanism, self-denial, self-discipline, simplicity
≠ elaborateness, extravagance, materialism

authentic *adj* **1** *an authentic signature:* actual, bona fide, certain, genuine, lawful, legal, legitimate, real, the genuine article *colloq*, the real McCoy *colloq*, the real thing *colloq*, valid **2** *an authentic description:* accurate, correct, credible, dependable, factual, faithful, honest, kosher *colloq*, reliable, true, true-to-life, trustworthy
≠ 1 counterfeit, fake, false, spurious **2** inaccurate, unfaithful

authenticate *v* accredit *formal*, attest, authorize, certify, confirm, corroborate, endorse, guarantee, prove, ratify, substantiate, validate, verify, vouch for, warrant

authenticity *n* accuracy, authoritativeness, certainty, correctness, credibility, dependability, faithfulness, fidelity, genuineness, honesty, legality, legitimacy, reliability, trustworthiness, truth, truthfulness, validity, veracity
≠ invalidity, spuriousness

author *n* **1** *made a living as an author:* biographer, composer, contributor, dramatist, essayist, journalist, librettist, lyricist, novelist, pen, penman, penwoman, playwright, poet, reporter, screenwriter, songwriter, writer **2** *the author of the universe:* architect, creator, designer, founder, initiator, inventor, maker, mover, originator, parent, planner, prime mover, producer

authoritarian *adj* absolute, autocratic, despotic, dictatorial, disciplinarian, doctrinaire, dogmatic, domineering, harsh, imperious, inflexible, oppressive, rigid, severe, strict, totalitarian, tough, tyrannical, unyielding
≠ liberal

authoritative *adj* **1** *an authoritative person:* assertive, audacious, bold, confident, imposing, masterful, self-assured, self-confident, self-possessed, sure of yourself **2** *an authoritative study:* accepted, accurate, approved, authentic, authorized, convincing, decisive, definitive, dependable, factual, faithful, learned, legitimate, magisterial, official, reliable, sanctioned, scholarly, sound, true, trustworthy, truthful, valid
≠ 2 unofficial, unreliable

authority *n* **1** *appeal to the authorities:* administration, bureaucracy, council, establishment, government, management, officialdom, state, the powers that be *colloq*, they *colloq* **2** *wield great authority:* clout *colloq*, command, control, dominion, force, influence, jurisdiction, muscle *colloq*, power, rule, sovereignty, supremacy, sway **3** *give official authority:* authorization, carte blanche, credentials, licence, permission, permit, power, prerogative, right, sanction, warrant **4** *an authority on antiques:* buff *colloq*, connoisseur, expert, master, professional, pundit, sage, scholar, specialist

authorization *n* accreditation *formal*, approval, authority, commission, confirmation, consent, credentials, empowering, entitlement, go-ahead *colloq*, green light *colloq*, leave, licence, mandate, OK *colloq*, okay *colloq*, permission, permit, ratification, sanction, validation, warranty

authorize *v* accredit *formal*, allow, approve, commission, confirm, consent to, empower, enable, entitle, give authority to, give permission, give the go-ahead *colloq*, give the green light *colloq*, legalize, let, license, make legal, OK *colloq*, okay *colloq*, permit, ratify, sanction, validate, warrant

autobiography *n* diary, journal, life story, memoirs, story of your life

autocracy *n* absolutism, authoritarianism, despotism, dictatorship, fascism, totalitarianism, tyranny
◼ democracy

autocrat *n* absolutist, authoritarian, despot, dictator, fascist, (little) Hitler *colloq*, totalitarian, tyrant

autocratic *adj* absolute, all-powerful, authoritarian, despotic, dictatorial, domineering, imperious, overbearing, totalitarian, tyrannical
◼ democratic, liberal

autograph *n* countersignature, endorsement, initials, inscription, mark, name, signature
◆ *v* countersign, endorse, initial, put your mark on, sign, write your name on

automatic *adj* **1** *an automatic washing machine*: automated, computerized, mechanical, mechanized, programmed, push-button, robotic, self-activating, self-propelling, self-regulating, unmanned **2** *an automatic response*: certain, inescapable, inevitable, instinctive, involuntary, knee-jerk *colloq*, mechanical, natural, necessary, reflex, routine, spontaneous, unavoidable, unconscious, uncontrollable, unthinking, unwilled

autonomy *n* autarky, free will, freedom, home rule, independence, self-determination, self-government, self-rule, self-sufficiency, sovereignty
◼ compulsion, subjection

auxiliary *n* ancillary, backer, helper, partner, right-hand man, second, second-in-command, subordinate, supporter
◆ *adj* accessory, aiding, ancillary, assistant, assisting, back-up, emergency, extra, helping, reserve, secondary, spare, subsidiary, substitute, supplementary, supporting, supportive

available *adj* accessible, at hand, at your disposal, convenient, disposable, forthcoming, free, handy, obtainable, on hand, on tap *colloq*, procurable *formal*, ready, to hand, unoccupied, untaken, up for grabs *colloq*, up your sleeve *colloq*, usable, vacant, within reach, yours for the asking/taking *colloq*
◼ taken, unavailable

avalanche *n* barrage, cascade, deluge, flood, inundation, landslide, landslip, torrent, wave

avant-garde *adj* advanced, contemporary, enterprising, experimental, far-out *slang*, forward-looking, futuristic, go-ahead *colloq*, innovative, innovatory, inventive, modern, original, pioneering, progressive, unconventional, way-out *slang*
◼ conservative

avarice *n* acquisitiveness, covetousness, greed, greediness, materialism, meanness, miserliness, selfishness
◼ generosity, liberality

avaricious *adj* acquisitive, covetous, grasping, greedy, mean, mercenary, miserly, pleonectic *formal*, rapacious *formal*
◼ generous, liberal

avenge *v* get back at *colloq*, get even with *colloq*, get your own back *colloq*, pay back, punish, repay, requite, retaliate, take revenge for, take vengeance for

average *n* centre, mean, median, medium, mid-point, mode, norm, par, rule, run, standard
◆ *adj* **1** *the average age*: intermediate, mean, medial, median, medium, middle **2** *the average reader*: common, everyday, normal, ordinary, regular, routine, standard, typical, unexceptional, usual **3** *a distinctly average performance*: fair, fair to middling, indifferent, mediocre, middling, moderate, no great shakes *colloq*, not much cop *colloq*, not up to much *colloq*, nothing much to write home about *colloq*, nothing special, passable, run-of-the-mill *colloq*, satisfactory, so-so *colloq*, tolerable, undistinguished, unexceptional
◼ **1** extreme **3** exceptional, remarkable

averse *adj* antagonistic, antipathetic *formal*, disinclined, hostile, ill-disposed, loath, opposed, reluctant, unfavourable, unwilling
◼ keen, sympathetic, willing

aversion *n* abhorrence *formal*, abomination, antagonism, detestation *formal*, disgust, disinclination *formal*, dislike, distaste, hate, hatred, horror, hostility, loathing, opposition, phobia, reluctance, repugnance *formal*, repulsion, revulsion, unwillingness
◼ desire, liking, sympathy

avert *v* avoid, deflect, evade, fend off, forestall, frustrate, head off, obviate *formal*, parry, preclude *formal*, prevent, stave off, stop, turn aside, turn away, ward off

aviation *n* aeronautics, aircraft industry, flight, flying

Aviation terms include:
aeronautics, aeroplane, aerospace, aileron, aircraft, airfield, air hostess, airline, air-miss, airplane *US*, airport, airship, airspace, air steward, airstrip, air-traffic control, airway, altitude, automatic pilot, biplane, black box, captain, chocks away *colloq*, cockpit, console, control tower, crash-dive, crash-landing, dive, drag, fixed-wing, flap, flight, flight crew, flight deck, flight recorder, fly-by, fly-by-wire, fly-past, fuselage, George *slang*, glider, ground-control, ground-speed, hangar, helicopter, hop, hot-air balloon, jet, jet engine, jet propulsion, jetstream, joystick, jumbo jet, landing, landing-gear, landing-strip, lift-off, loop-the-loop, Mach number, maiden flight, mid-air collision, monoplane, night-flying, nose dive, overshoot, parachute, pilot, plane, pressurized cabin, prang *slang*, propeller, rotor blade, rudder, runway, solo flight, sonic boom, sound barrier, spoiler, supersonic,

swing-wing, take-off, taxi, test flight, test pilot, thrust, touchdown, undercarriage, undershoot, vapour trail, vertical take-off and landing (VTOL), windsock, wingspan. See also **aircraft**

avid *adj* ardent, covetous, crazy *colloq*, dedicated, devoted, eager, earnest, enthusiastic, fanatical, fervent, grasping, great, greedy, hungry, insatiable, intense, keen, mad *colloq*, passionate, ravenous, thirsty, zealous
⊟ indifferent

avoid *v* abstain from, avert, balk at, bypass, circumvent *formal*, dodge *colloq*, duck *colloq*, elude, escape, eschew *formal*, evade, forbear *formal*, get out of, get round, give a miss *colloq*, give a wide berth to *colloq*, hedge against *colloq*, hold back from, keep away from, keep your distance from, make a detour, prevent, refrain from *formal*, run away from, shirk *colloq*, shun, shy away from, sidestep, stay away from, steer clear of, wriggle/worm your way out of *colloq*

avoidable *adj* avertible *formal*, eludible *formal*, escapable, preventable
⊟ inescapable, inevitable

avowed *adj* acknowledged, admitted, confessed, declared, open, overt, professed, self-confessed, self-proclaimed, sworn

await *v* **1** *I wonder what awaits us:* be in store for, lie in wait for, wait for **2** *eagerly awaiting his next book:* expect, hope for, look for, look forward to, wait for

awake *adj* alert, alive, aroused, attentive, aware, conscious, not sleeping a wink *colloq*, observant, sensitive, stirring, tossing and turning *colloq*, vigilant, wakeful, watchful, wide awake
⊟ asleep, sleeping
♦ *v* arouse, awaken, rouse, stir, wake, wake up, waken

awakening *n* activation, animating, arousal, awaking, birth, enlivening, revival, rousing, stimulation, vivification *formal*, wakening, waking

award *n* **1** *an award for bravery:* certificate, citation, commendation, decoration, gong *slang*, medal, presentation, prize, trophy **2** *an award for compensation:* adjudication, allotment, allowance, bestowal, conferral, decision, dispensation, endowment, gift, grant, judgement, order
♦ *v* accord, adjudge *formal*, allocate, allot, allow, apportion *formal*, assign, bestow, confer, determine, dispense, distribute, endow, gift, give, grant, present

aware *adj* **1** *aware of the problem:* alert, alive to, appreciative, attentive, conscious, heedful, mindful, observant, sensible *formal*, sensitive, sentient *formal*, sharp, vigilant **2** *environmentally aware:* acquainted, apprised *formal*, au courant, clued up *colloq*, cognizant *formal*, conversant, enlightened, familiar, in the know *colloq*, informed, knowing, knowledgeable, on the ball *colloq*, shrewd
⊟ **1** insensitive, oblivious, unaware

awe *n* admiration, amazement, apprehension, astonishment, dread, fear, honour, respect, reverence, stupefaction *formal*, terror, veneration *formal*, wonder
⊟ contempt

awe-inspiring *adj* amazing, astonishing, awesome, breathtaking, daunting, dazzling, exalted, fearsome, formidable, imposing, impressive, intimidating, magnificent, majestic, moving, numinous *formal*, overwhelming, solemn, spectacular, striking, stunning, stupefying, stupendous, sublime, wonderful
⊟ contemptible, tame

awful *adj* abysmal, alarming, appalling, atrocious, dire, disgusting, distressing, dreadful, fearful, frightful, ghastly, gruesome, heinous *formal*, hideous, horrible, horrid, horrific, horrifying, nasty, shocking, spine-chilling, terrible, ugly, unpleasant
⊟ excellent, wonderful

awkward *adj* **1** *a rather awkward young man:* all thumbs *colloq*, bungling, clumsy, cumbersome, gauche, graceless, ham-fisted, inelegant, inept, inexpert, lubberly, maladroit *formal*, unco-ordinated, ungainly, ungraceful, unskilful, unwieldy **2** *feeling awkward in their presence:* embarrassed, ill at ease, shy, uncomfortable **3** *put me in an awkward position:* annoying, delicate, difficult, embarrassing, fiddly, inconvenient, invidious, perplexing, problematic, tricky, troublesome, uncomfortable **4** *an awkward customer:* irritable, obstinate, oversensitive, prickly, rude, stubborn, touchy, unco-operative, unpleasant
⊟ **1** elegant, graceful **2** at ease, comfortable, relaxed **3** easy, straightforward **4** amenable, pleasant

awry *adj* **1** *her clothing was all awry:* askew, asymmetrical, cock-eyed, crooked, misaligned, off-centre, skew-whiff, twisted, uneven, wonky *colloq* **2** *something is awry:* amiss, wrong
⊟ **1** straight, symmetrical
♦ *adv* **1** *knocked it awry:* askew, out of true, skew-whiff **2** *our plans had gone awry:* amiss, wrong
⊟ **1** straight

axe *n* **1** *chop wood with an axe:* battle-axe, chopper, cleaver, hatchet, tomahawk **2** *got the axe after poor results:* boot *colloq*, chop *colloq*, dismissal, sack *colloq*, termination
♦ *v* **1** *axed 300 workers:* cut *colloq*, discharge, dismiss, eliminate, fire *colloq*, get rid of, remove, sack *colloq*, terminate, throw out **2** *axed the show because of poor ratings:* cancel, cut *colloq*, discontinue, get rid of, remove, terminate, withdraw

axiom *n* adage, aphorism, byword, dictum, fundamental, maxim, precept, principle, truism, truth

axiomatic *adj* accepted, aphoristic *formal*, apophthegmatic *formal*, assumed, certain, fundamental, given, gnomic *formal*, granted, indubitable *formal*, manifest, presupposed, proverbial, self-evident, understood, unquestioned

axis *n* centre-line, hinge, horizontal, pivot, vertical

axle *n* pin, pivot, rod, shaft, spindle

B

babble *v* **1** *everyone was babbling at once*: chatter, gabble, gibber, jabber, prate, rabbit on *colloq*, waffle *colloq* **2** *the stream babbled*: burble, gurgle
♦ *n* babel, burble, chatter, clamour, gabble, hubbub

babe *n* babe in arms, baby, child, infant

babel *n* **1** *a babel of voices*: babble, clamour, din, hubbub, hullabaloo, uproar **2** *the babel of everyday life*: bedlam, chaos, commotion, confusion, disorder, hullabaloo, pandemonium, tumult, turmoil, uproar

baby *n* babe, bairn *Scot*, child, infant, neonate *technical*, newborn baby, sprog *slang*, suckling, tiny tot, toddler
♦ *adj* diminutive, dwarf, little, midget, mini *colloq*, miniature, minute, small, small-scale, tiny, wee *Scot*

babyish *adj* baby, childish, immature, infantile, juvenile, puerile, sissy *colloq*, soft *colloq*, young
🔁 mature, precocious

back *n* **1** *lie on your back*: backbone, dorsum *technical*, spine, tergum **2** *the back of the house*: backside, end, hind part, hindquarters, posterior, rear, rear end, stern, tail, tail end **3** *write on the back of the envelope*: other side, reverse, reverse side
🔁 **1** face, front
♦ *v* **1** *he backed out of the room*: back away, backtrack, go backwards, recede, recoil, regress *formal*, retire, retreat, reverse, withdraw **2** *backed by loyal friends*: abet, advocate, aid, assist, bolster, boost, champion, countenance, encourage, endorse, favour, get/be behind *colloq*, help, promote, sanction, side with, support, sustain, throw your weight behind *colloq* **3** *investors backing the new company*: aid, assist, finance, sponsor, subsidize, support, underwrite
🔁 **1** advance, approach **2** discourage, weaken
♦ *adj* **1** *the back door*: end, hind, hindmost, posterior, rear, reverse, tail **2** *back copies*: bygone, earlier, elapsed, former, obsolete, out of date, outdated, past, previous
🔁 **1** front
♦ *adv* backwards, behind, to the rear
🔁 forwards
▶ **back away** draw back, fall back, give ground, move back, recede, recoil, retreat, step back, withdraw
▶ **back down** back-pedal, backtrack, climb down, concede, give in, retreat, submit, surrender, withdraw, yield
▶ **back out** abandon, cancel, chicken out *colloq*, get cold feet *colloq*, give up, go back on, pull out *colloq*, recant, resign, withdraw
▶ **back up 1** *my friends backed me up*: aid, assist, bolster, champion, second, support **2** *he backed up her story*: bear out, confirm, corroborate, endorse, reinforce, substantiate, support, validate

backbiting *n* abuse, aspersion *formal*, bitchiness *colloq*, calumny *formal*, cattiness *colloq*, criticism, defamation, denigration *formal*, detraction *formal*, disparagement, gossip, libel, malice, mud-slinging *colloq*, revilement *formal*, scandalmongering, slagging off *colloq*, slander, spite, spitefulness, vilification *formal*, vituperation *formal*
🔁 praise

backbone *n* **1** *the fall broke his backbone*: spinal column, spine, vertebrae, vertebral column **2** *the backbone of an organization*: basis, core, foundation, mainstay, nucleus, support **3** *he hadn't the backbone to stand up to her*: bottle *colloq*, courage, determination, firmness, grit, mettle, nerve, pluck, resolve, steadfastness, strength, (strength of) character, tenacity, toughness, willpower
🔁 **3** spinelessness, weakness

backbreaking *adj* arduous, crushing, exhausting, gruelling, hard, heavy, killing, laborious, punishing, strenuous
🔁 easy

backer *n* **1** *the company's new backers*: benefactor, patron, promoter, sponsor, subscriber, supporter, underwriter **2** *a defeat for the president and his backers*: advocate, champion, promoter, second, seconder, sponsor, supporter, well-wisher

backfire *v* **1** *the engine backfired*: blow up, detonate, discharge, explode **2** *the plans backfired*: be counterproductive, be self-defeating, blow up in your face *colloq*, boomerang, come home to roost *colloq*, defeat itself, fail, flop *colloq*, miscarry, rebound, recoil, ricochet, score an own goal *colloq*

background *n* **1** *a background of political unrest*: backdrop, circumstances, context, environment, factors, framework, influences, milieu, scene, setting, surroundings **2** *a privileged background*: breeding, culture, education, family, history, origins, social standing, status, tradition, upbringing **3** *a background in science*: credentials, education, experience, grounding, preparation, qualifications, record

backhanded *adj* ambiguous, double-edged, dubious, equivocal, ironic, sarcastic, sardonic, two-edged
🔁 sincere, wholehearted

backing *n* **1** *he has the backing of his colleagues*: advocacy, aid, approval, assistance, championing, commendation, encouragement, endorsement, favour, help, moral support, patronage, promotion, sanction, seconding, support **2** *financial backing for the deal*: assistance, finance, funds, grant, help, patronage, sponsorship, subsidy, support

backlash *n* kickback, reaction, repercussion, reprisal, response, retaliation

backlog *n* accumulation, build-up, excess, heap, mountain *colloq*

back-pedal *v* backtrack, change your mind, climb down, concede, do a U-turn *colloq*, give in, have second thoughts, retract, retreat, submit, surrender, tergiversate *formal*, withdraw, yield

backslide *v* apostatize *formal*, fall from grace, go astray, go back, lapse, leave the straight and narrow *colloq*, regress *formal*, relapse, renege, revert, sin, slip, stray
🔁 persevere

backslider *n* apostate, recidivist *formal*, recreant *formal*, renegade, reneger

backsliding *n* apostasy, lapse, regression *formal*, relapse

backup *n* additional equipment/resources, aid, assistance, help, reinforcement, support

backward *adj* **1** *a backward step:* rearward, retrograde, retrogressive, reverse, to the back **2** *a backward country/society:* underdeveloped, undeveloped, unsophisticated **3** *too backward to ask her out:* bashful, hesitant, hesitating, retiring, shrinking, shy, timid **4** *a backward child:* having learning difficulties, retarded, slow, subnormal ⊟ **1** forward **2** advanced, developed **3** precocious

backwards *adv* rearwards, regressively, retrogressively, to the back

backwash *n* **1** *the backwash of a ship:* flow, path, wake, wash, waves **2** *the resulting backwash of complaints:* after-effect(s), aftermath, consequence(s), repercussions, result(s), reverberations

backwoods *n* back of beyond, bush, middle of nowhere *colloq*, outback, sticks *colloq*

bacteria *n* bacilli, bugs *colloq*, germs, microbes, micro-organisms, viruses

bad *adj* **1** *the bad effects of smoking:* adverse, appalling, atrocious, damaging, dangerous, deleterious *formal*, destructive, detrimental, disagreeable, distressing, dreadful, harmful, hurtful, injurious, nasty, ruinous, undesirable, unfortunate, unhealthy, unpleasant, unwholesome **2** *a bad person:* corrupt, criminal, degenerate, dishonest, evil, immoral, reprehensible *formal*, reprobate *formal*, sinful, vile, wicked **3** *bad workmanship:* a load of crap/shit *slang*, a load of garbage *colloq*, a load of rubbish *colloq*, awful *colloq*, botched *colloq*, crappy *slang*, crummy *slang*, defective, deficient, faulty, imperfect, inadequate, incompetent, inferior, lousy *colloq*, mediocre, mismanaged, naff *slang*, pathetic *colloq*, poor, poxy *slang*, ropy *colloq*, second-rate, substandard, terrible *colloq*, third-rate, unacceptable, unsatisfactory **4** *bad at speaking French:* awful *colloq*, crappy *slang*, crummy *slang*, hopeless, inadequate, incompetent, ineffective, ineffectual *formal*, lousy *colloq*, pathetic *colloq*, poor, terrible *colloq*, useless **5** *I feel bad today:* ill, in pain, indisposed, poorly, sick, under the weather *colloq*, unwell **6** *feel bad about what happened:* despondent, gloomy, unhappy **7** *bad meat:* contaminated, decayed, high, mouldy, off, putrefactive *formal*, putrescent *formal*, putrid, rancid, rotten, sour, spoilt, tainted **8** *a bad child:* badly-behaved, bolshie *colloq*, disobedient, ill-behaved, mischievous, naughty, refractory *formal*, stroppy *colloq*, unruly, wayward **9** *have a bad cold:* acute, critical, grave, harsh, intense, serious, severe **10** *a bad time to call:* inappropriate, inauspicious *formal*, inconvenient, unfavourable, unfortunate, unsuitable ⊟ **1** good, mild, pleasant **2** virtuous **3** skilful, skilled **4** skilful, skilled **5** well **6** happy **7** fresh **8** obedient, well-behaved **10** auspicious *formal*, convenient, favourable, good

badge *n* **1** *a school badge:* brand, crest, device, emblem, ensign, escutcheon, identification, insignia, logo, mark, shield, sign, stamp, token, trademark **2** *a badge of power:* indication, indicator, mark, sign, symbol, token

badger *v* bully, chivvy, harass, harry, hassle *colloq*, hound, importune *formal*, nag, pester, plague, torment

badinage *n* banter, chaff, drollery, humour, jocularity, mockery, persiflage *formal*, raillery, repartee, ribbing *colloq*, teasing, waggery, word-play

badly *adv* **1** *a badly directed play:* awfully *colloq*, carelessly, defectively, faultily, imperfectly, improperly, inadequately, incompetently, incorrectly, ineffectually *formal*, negligently, pathetically *colloq*, poorly, terribly *colloq*, unacceptably, unsatisfactorily, uselessly, wrongly **2** *badly hurt:* acutely, critically, crucially, desperately, gravely, painfully, seriously, severely **3** *behave very badly:* criminally, dishonestly, evilly, immorally, offensively, shamefully, sinfully, unfairly, wickedly **4** *turn out badly:* adversely, unfavourably, unfortunately, unhappily, unsuccessfully **5** *want something badly:* deeply, desperately, enormously, exceedingly, extremely, greatly, intensely, tremendously, very much ⊟ **1** well **2** mildly, slightly **3** well **4** favourably, fortunately

bad-tempered *adj* cantankerous *formal*, choleric, crabbed *colloq*, crabby *colloq*, cross, cross as a bear with a sore head *colloq*, crotchety *colloq*, fractious, grouchy *colloq*, grumpy, having a short fuse *colloq*, having got out of bed on the wrong side *colloq*, impatient, in a (bad) mood, in a huff *colloq*, in a sulk *colloq*, irritable, narky, petulant *formal*, querulous *formal*, quick-tempered, ratty *colloq*, shirty *colloq*, snappy, stroppy *colloq* ⊟ equable, genial, good-tempered

baffle *v* **1** *baffled by the problem:* bamboozle *colloq*, bemuse, bewilder, confound, confuse, disconcert, dumbfound, flummox *colloq*, mystify, perplex, puzzle, stump *colloq*, throw *colloq* **2** *baffling his plans:* bar, block, check, confound, defeat, foil, frustrate, hinder, throw *colloq*, thwart, upset ⊟ **1** enlighten **2** help

baffling *adj* bemusing, bewildering, confusing, disconcerting, mysterious, perplexing, puzzling, unfathomable ⊟ enlightening, explanatory

bag *v* **1** *try to bag a hare:* capture, catch, kill, land, shoot, trap **2** *they've bagged all the best seats:* acquire, appropriate, come by, commandeer, gain, get, grab, obtain, reserve, take ♦ *n* container, receptacle

baggage *n* accoutrements *formal*, bags, belongings, effects, equipment, gear, impedimenta *formal*, luggage, paraphernalia, suitcases, things

baggy *adj* ballooning, billowing, droopy, floppy, loose, loose-fitting, oversize, roomy, sagging, shapeless, slack ⊟ firm, tight

bail *n* bond, collateral, guarantee, pledge, security, surety, warranty
► **bail out 1** *my parents bailed me out:* aid, assist, finance, help, relieve, rescue **2** *he bailed out just before the plane blew up:* escape, get clear, get out, retreat, withdraw

bait *n* allurement, attraction, bribe, enticement, incentive, incitement, inducement, lure, snare, temptation

🔄 disincentive

♦ *v* annoy, badger, give a hard time to *colloq*, harass, harry, hassle *colloq*, hound, irk, irritate, needle *colloq*, persecute, plague, provoke, tease, torment

balance *v* 1 *balance a book on your head:* level, poise, square, stabilize, steady 2 *balance work with leisure:* compensate for, counteract, counterbalance, counterweigh, equalize, equate, juggle, match, neutralize, offset, set 3 *balance the cost against the benefits:* appraise, compare, consider, estimate, evaluate, review, weigh

🔄 1 overbalance, unbalance

♦ *n* 1 *lose your balance:* equilibrium, equipoise, stability, steadiness 2 *a balance between family and career:* correspondence, equality, equilibrium, equity, equivalence, evenness, parity, stability, stasis *technical*, symmetry 3 *balance of mind:* aplomb *formal*, assurance, calmness, composure, cool-headedness, equanimity, level-headedness, poise, sangfroid *formal*, self-possession 4 *pay the balance on delivery:* difference, excess, remainder, residue, rest, surplus

🔄 1 imbalance, instability 2 imbalance, instability

balanced *adj* 1 *a balanced report:* equitable, even-handed, fair, impartial, objective, unbiased, unprejudiced 2 *a balanced diet:* complete, healthy, well-rounded 3 *a balanced person:* calm, cool-headed, equable, level-headed, self-possessed, sensible

🔄 1 biased, prejudiced

balcony *n* 1 *a balcony on the third floor:* loggia, portico, terrace, veranda 2 *we had seats in the balcony:* gallery, gods, upper circle

bald *adj* 1 *a bald head:* bald as a coot *colloq*, bald-headed, depilated *formal*, glabrate *technical*, glabrous *technical*, hairless, smooth 2 *a bald landscape:* bare, barren, bleak, exposed, naked, severe, stark, treeless, unsheltered 3 *a bald statement:* blunt, direct, downright, forthright, outright, outspoken, plain, simple, straight, straightforward, unadorned

🔄 1 hairy, hirsute

balderdash *n* balls *slang*, bilge *colloq*, bollocks *slang*, bullshit *slang*, bunk *colloq*, bunkum *colloq*, claptrap *colloq*, cobblers *colloq*, drivel, gibberish, hot air *colloq*, nonsense, piffle *colloq*, poppycock *colloq*, rot *colloq*, rubbish, shit *slang*, tommyrot *colloq*, trash, tripe, twaddle

balding *adj* becoming bald, losing your hair, receding, thin on top

baldness *n* alopecia *formal*, bald-headedness, bareness, calvities *technical*, calvousness *formal*, glabrousness *formal*, hair loss, hairlessness, psilosis *technical*

🔄 hirsuteness

bale *n* bundle, pack, package, parcel

▶ **bale out** same as **bail out** (sense 2)

baleful *adj* 1 *a baleful influence:* deadly, destructive, evil, harmful, hurtful, injurious, malevolent, malignant, noxious, pernicious, ruinous 2 *a baleful look:* malevolent, menacing, ominous, sinister, threatening, venomous

🔄 1 favourable 2 favourable

balk, baulk *v* 1 *he balked at telling her the truth:* dodge, eschew *formal*, evade, flinch, hesitate, jib, recoil, refuse, resist, shirk, shrink 2 *balking our plans:* baffle, bar, check, counteract, defeat, foil, forestall, frustrate, hinder, impede, obstruct, prevent, stall, thwart

ball¹ *n* 1 *a golf ball:* drop, globe, globule, orb, pellet, sphere 2 *a musket ball:* bullet, pellet, projectile, shot, slug *colloq*

ball² *n* carnival, dance, dinner-dance, masquerade, party, soirée

ballad *n* carol, ditty, folk-song, poem, shanty, song

ballet *n* ballet-dancing, dancing, leg-business

Terms used in ballet include:
à pointe, arabesque, attitude, ballerina, prima ballerina, ballon, barre, battement, batterie, battu, bourrée, capriole, chassé, choreography, ciseaux, company, corps de ballet, coryphée, divertissement, écarté, élévation, entrechat, fish dive, five positions, fouetté, fouetté en tournant, glissade, jeté, grand jeté, leotard, pas de deux, pas de seul, pirouette, plié, pointes, sur les pointes, ports de bras, principal male dancer, régisseur, répétiteur, ballet shoe, point shoe, splits, stulchak, tutu

---

balloon *v* 1 *sails ballooning in the wind:* bag, belly, billow, blow up, bulge, dilate, distend *formal*, enlarge, expand, inflate, puff out, swell 2 *the debt has ballooned:* enlarge, expand, increase, inflate, rocket, soar

ballot *n* election, plebiscite, poll, polling, referendum, vote, voting

ballyhoo *n* 1 *a lot of ballyhoo about nothing:* agitation, clamour, commotion, disturbance, excitement, fuss, hubbub, hue and cry, hullabaloo, noise, racket, to-do, tumult 2 *the ballyhoo about his new film:* advertising, build-up, hype, promotion, propaganda, publicity

balm *n* 1 *soothing balm for the skin:* anodyne, balsam, bromide, cream, curative, embrocation, emollient, lenitive, lotion, ointment, palliative, restorative, salve, unguent 2 *balm to a troubled spirit:* anodyne, calmative, comfort, consolation, curative, lenitive, palliative, restorative, sedative

🔄 1 irritant 2 irritant, vexation

balmy *adj* clement, mild, pleasant, summery, temperate, warm

🔄 inclement

bamboozle *v* 1 *bamboozled by technical jargon:* bemuse, bewilder, confound, confuse, daze, disconcert, dumbfound, mystify, perplex, puzzle 2 *bamboozled by a slick salesman:* cheat, con *colloq*, deceive, dupe, fool, gull *colloq*, hoodwink, swindle, trick

ban *v* 1 *smoking is banned in public buildings:* bar, disallow, forbid, outlaw, prohibit, proscribe *formal*, restrict, suppress, veto 2 *banned from driving:* banish, bar, disallow, disqualify, exclude, forbid, ostracize, outlaw, prohibit

🔄 1 allow, authorize, permit 2 allow, authorize, permit

♦ *n* bar, boycott, embargo, injunction, interdiction *formal*, outlawry, prohibition, proscription *formal*, restriction, sanctions, stoppage, suppression, taboo, veto

🔄 dispensation, permission

banal *adj* bland, boring, clichéed, commonplace, corny *colloq*, dull, everyday, hackneyed, humdrum, mundane, ordinary, overused, stale, stereotyped, stock, threadbare, tired, trite, unimaginative, unoriginal, vapid, wearing thin
🖅 fresh, imaginative, original

banality *n* **1** *the banality of his writing:* dullness, ordinariness, prosaicism, staleness, tiredness, triteness, triviality, unimaginativeness, unoriginality, vapidity **2** *conversation full of banalities:* bromide, cliché, commonplace, platitude, prosaicism, triviality, truism
🖅 **1** originality

band¹ *n* bandage, belt, binding, bond, chain, connection, cord, ligature, link, ribbon, strap, strip, tape, tie

band² *n* **1** *bands of looters:* association, body, clique, club, company, contingent, crew, crowd, flock, gang, gathering, group, herd, horde, party, society, throng, troop **2** *the band played on:* ensemble, group, music/musical group, orchestra, pop group
♦ *v* affiliate, ally, amalgamate, close ranks, collaborate, consolidate, federate, gather, group, join, join forces, merge, pull together, stand together, stick together *colloq*, unite
🖅 disband, disperse

bandage *n* compress, dressing, gauze, ligature, plaster, swaddle, swathe, tourniquet
♦ *v* bind (up), cover, dress, swaddle, swathe

bandit *n* brigand, buccaneer, crook, desperado, gangster, gunman, highwayman, marauder, outlaw, pirate, plunderer, robber, thief

bandy¹ *v* exchange, interchange, pass, reciprocate, swap, throw, toss, trade

bandy² *adj* bent, bowed, bow-legged, crooked, curved, misshapen

bane *n* **1** *migraines are the bane of my life:* affliction, annoyance, bête noire, blight, burden, curse, evil, irritation, nuisance, pest, pestilence, plague, scourge, torment, trial, trouble, vexation **2** *vowed to be the bane of his enemy:* adversity, affliction, calamity, destruction, disaster, distress, downfall, evil, misery, misfortune, ordeal, ruin, woe
🖅 **1** blessing **2** saviour

bang *n* **1** *a loud bang:* boom, clang, clap, clash, detonation, explosion, noise, peal, pop, report *formal*, shot, slam, thud, thump **2** *a nasty bang on the head:* bash, blow, bump, crack, hit, knock, punch, smack, sock *colloq*, stroke, thump, wallop *colloq*, whack *colloq*
♦ *v* **1** *started banging on the door:* bash, drum, hammer, hit, knock, pound, rap, strike, thump **2** *fireworks banged all round us:* boom, burst, clang, clatter, crash, detonate, explode, resound, thunder
♦ *adv* absolutely, directly, exactly, hard, headlong, precisely, right, slap, smack, straight

banish *v* **1** *banish someone from a country:* ban, bar, cast out, debar, deport, drive away, eject, evict, exclude, exile, expatriate, expel, extradite, outlaw, repatriate, rusticate *formal*, send away, shut out, throw out, transport **2** *banish thoughts from your mind:* discard, dismiss, dispel, drive away, eliminate, eradicate, get rid of, oust, remove, shut out
🖅 **1** recall, welcome

banishment *n* deportation, eviction, exclusion, exile, expatriation, expulsion, extradition, outlawry *formal*, transportation
🖅 recall, return, welcome

banisters *n* balustrade, handrail, rail, railing

bank¹ *n* **1** *an account with a bank:* building society, clearing bank, finance company/house, financial institution, high-street bank, merchant bank, savings bank **2** *a blood bank:* accumulation, cache, depository, fund, hoard, pool, repository, reserve, reservoir, stock, stockpile, store, treasury
♦ *v* accumulate, deposit, keep, lay by, put aside, save (up), save for a rainy day *colloq*, stockpile, store
🖅 spend
▶ **bank on** believe in, bet on, count on, depend on, pin your hopes on *colloq*, rely on, trust

bank² *n* **1** *the banks of a river:* edge, embankment, levee, margin, shore, side, slope **2** *a bank of ground:* earthwork, heap, hillock, incline, knoll, mass, mound, parados, pile, rampart, ridge, rise, slope
♦ *v* **1** *the plane banked to the right:* incline, pitch, slant, slope, tilt, tip **2** *snow was banked up beside the road:* accumulate, amass, heap, mass, mound, pile, stack

bank³ *n* array, group, line, panel, rank, row, sequence, series, succession, tier, train

banknote *n* bill, flimsy *slang*, greenback *US*, note, paper money, treasury note

bankrupt *adj* **1** *the company went bankrupt:* beggared, broke *colloq*, bust *colloq*, destitute, gone to the wall *colloq*, gone under *colloq*, impecunious *formal*, impoverished, in the red *colloq*, in(to) liquidation, insolvent, on the rocks *colloq*, on your uppers *colloq*, penurious *formal*, ruined **2** *spiritually and morally bankrupt:* deficient, depleted, deprived, exhausted, lacking, wanting
🖅 **1** flourishing, in the black *colloq*, prospering, rich, solvent, wealthy
♦ *v* cripple, ruin
♦ *n* beggar, debtor, insolvent, pauper

bankruptcy *n* beggary *formal*, disaster, failure, financial ruin, indebtedness, insolvency, liquidation, penury *formal*, ruin, ruination *formal*
🖅 solvency, wealth

banner *n* banderol *formal*, burgee *formal*, colours, ensign, fanion *formal*, flag, gonfalon *formal*, labarum *formal*, pennant, pennon, standard, streamer, vexillum *formal*

banquet *n* dinner, dinner party, feast, meal, repast *formal*, spread

banter *n* badinage, chaff, chaffing, jesting, joking, kidding *colloq*, mockery, persiflage, pleasantry, raillery, repartee, ribbing *colloq*, word play
♦ *v* chaff, jest, joke, kid *colloq*, make fun of, mock, pull someone's leg *colloq*, rag *colloq*, rib *colloq*

baptism *n* **1** *the child's baptism:* affusion *formal*, aspersion *formal*, christening, dedication, immersion, naming, purification, sprinkling **2** *a baptism of fire:* beginning, début, inauguration, initiation, introduction, launch, launching

baptize *v* **1** *baptize a child:* call, christen, cleanse, immerse, name, purify, sprinkle **2** *baptized into* *the Catholic Church:* enrol, initiate, introduce, recruit

bar *n* 1 *drinking in a bar:* boozer *slang*, counter, hostelry *colloq*, inn, lounge, lounge bar, pub *colloq*, public house, saloon, taproom, tavern, watering-hole *colloq* 2 *an iron bar:* batten, crosspiece, paling, pole, rail, railing, rod, shaft, stake, stanchion, stick 3 *a bar of soap:* block, cake, chunk, ingot, lump, nugget, slab, wedge 4 *a bar to his progress:* barrier, check, deterrent, drawback, hindrance, impediment, obstacle, obstruction, stop 5 *called to the Bar:* barristers, counsel, court, lawyers, tribunal
♦ *v* 1 *barred from trading:* ban, block, blockade, check, debar, disqualify, exclude, forbid, hinder, obstruct, preclude *formal*, prevent, prohibit, restrain, stop, suspend 2 *bar the door:* barricade, bolt, fasten, latch, lock, padlock, secure
♦ *prep* apart from, but for, except, excepting, excluding, omitting, save, with the exception of

barb *n* 1 *the barb on a fish hook:* arrow, bristle, fluke, needle, point, prickle, spike, thorn 2 *critical barbs at leaders:* affront, dig *colloq*, gibe, insult, sarcasm, scorn, sneer

barbarian *n* boor, brute, hooligan, ignoramus, lout, oaf, philistine, ruffian, savage, vandal, wild person
♦ *adj* brute, brutish, coarse, crude, hooligan, loutish, rough, savage, uncivilized, uncouth, uncultivated, uncultured, unsophisticated, vulgar, wild

barbaric *adj* 1 *barbaric cruelty:* barbarous, bestial, brutal, brutish, cruel, ferocious, fierce, inhuman, murderous, ruthless, savage, vicious 2 *a barbaric race:* barbarous, coarse, crude, primitive, rude, savage, uncivilized, uncouth, vulgar, wild
≠ 1 humane 2 civilized, gracious

barbarism *n* 1 *the barbarism of the crime:* bestiality, brutality, cruelty, ferocity, fierceness, inhumanness, murderousness, ruthlessness, savagery, viciousness 2 *reverting to barbarism:* brutishness, coarseness, crudeness, rudeness, savagery, uncivilizedness, uncouthness, vulgarity, wildness

barbarity *n* 1 *the barbarity of the attack:* atrocity, brutality, cruelty, ferocity, inhumanity, ruthlessness, savagery, viciousness 2 *a return to barbarity:* barbarousness, brutishness, savagery, wildness
≠ 1 humanity 2 civility, civilization

barbarous *adj* 1 *barbarous behaviour:* barbarian, barbaric, bestial, brutal, brutish, cruel, ferocious, fierce, heartless, inhuman, murderous, ruthless, savage, vicious, wild 2 *barbarous by modern standards:* crude, ignorant, primitive, rough, rude, uncivilized, uncultured, unlettered, unrefined, unsophisticated, vulgar
≠ 2 civilized, cultured, educated

barbed *adj* 1 *barbed wire:* hooked, jagged, pointed, prickly, pronged, spiked, spiny, thorny, toothed 2 *a barbed remark:* acid, caustic, critical, cutting, hostile, hurtful, nasty, snide, unkind

bare *adj* 1 *a bare body:* denuded, exposed, in the nude, in the raw *colloq*, naked, nude, stripped, unclothed, uncovered, undressed, with nothing on 2 *bare shelves/rooms:* empty, unfurnished, vacant 3 *a bare landscape:* barren, bleak, desolate, exposed, treeless, unforested, unsheltered, unwooded, woodless 4 *the bare facts/minimum:* absolute, bald, basic, cold, essential, hard, mere, plain, sheer, simple, stark, straightforward, unadorned
≠ 1 clothed 2 decorated, full 3 forested, sheltered, wooded 4 detailed

barefaced *adj* arrant, audacious, bald, blatant, bold, brazen, flagrant, glaring, manifest, naked, obvious, open, palpable, patent, shameless, transparent, unabashed, unconcealed, undisguised

barefooted *adj* barefoot, discalced *formal*, shoeless, unshod
≠ shod

barely *adv* almost not, by a whisker *colloq*, by the skin of your teeth *colloq*, hardly, just, only just, scarcely

bargain *n* 1 *a bargain between the two countries:* agreement, arrangement, concordat *formal*, contract, covenant, deal, negotiation, pact, pledge, promise, transaction, treaty, understanding 2 *looking for bargains in the sale:* discount, giveaway *colloq*, good buy, reduction, snip *colloq*, special offer, steal *colloq*, value for money
♦ *v* barter, beat down, buy, deal, haggle, negotiate, sell, trade, traffic, transact
▶ **bargain for** anticipate, be prepared for, consider, contemplate, expect, figure on, foresee, imagine, include, look for, plan for, reckon on, take into account

bargaining *n* barter(ing), buying, dealing(s), haggling, horsetrading, negotiation, selling, trade, trafficking, transaction, wheeler-dealing, wheeling and dealing

barge *n* canal-boat, flatboat, houseboat, lighter, narrow-boat
♦ *v* elbow, force your way, jostle, plough, press, push (in), push your way, rush, shove
▶ **barge in** break in, burst in, butt in, cut in, gatecrash, interfere, interrupt, intrude
▶ **barge into** bump into, collide with, hit, smash

bark[1] *v* 1 *the dog barked:* bay, growl, howl, snarl, woof, yap, yelp 2 *bark orders at someone:* bawl, cry, shout, snap, snarl, thunder, yell
♦ *n* bay, growl, howl, snarl, woof, yap, yelp

bark[2] *n* casing, cortex *technical*, covering, husk, integument, peel, rind, shell, skin

barmy *adj* 1 *a barmy old man:* batty *colloq*, crackers *colloq*, crazy, dippy *colloq*, dotty *colloq*, insane, loony *colloq*, loopy *colloq*, mad, need your head examining *colloq*, nuts *colloq*, nutty *colloq*, off your head/rocker/nutter *colloq*, off your trolley *colloq*, out to lunch *colloq*, round the bend/twist *colloq* 2 *a barmy idea:* crazy, daft *colloq*, foolish, idiotic, silly, stupid
≠ 1 of sound mind, rational, sane 2 sensible

baroque *adj* convoluted, decorated, elaborate, embellished, extravagant, fanciful, fantastic, flamboyant, florid, ornate, overdecorated, overwrought, rococo, showy, whimsical
≠ austere, plain, simple, unadorned

barrack *v* heckle, interrupt, jeer, shout down

barracks *n* accommodation, billet, camp, casern, encampment, fort, garrison, guardhouse, lodging, quarters

barrage n 1 *a barrage of fire:* assault, attack, battery, bombardment, broadside, burst, cannonade, gunfire, hail, onset, onslaught, rain, salvo, shelling, volley 2 *a barrage of criticism:* assault, attack, burst, deluge, flood, hail, mass, onslaught, profusion, rain, shower, storm, stream, torrent

barrel n butt, cask, keg, rundlet *formal*, tierce *formal*, tun, water-butt

barren adj 1 *barren land:* arid, desert, desolate, empty, uncultivable, unfruitful, unproductive, waste 2 *barren activity:* dry, dull, empty, flat, fruitless, pointless, profitless, purposeless, unfruitful, uninteresting, unproductive, unrewarding, useless, valueless, vapid 3 *a barren cow:* childless, infecund *formal*, infertile, sterile, unbearing, unprolific
🔁 1 fertile, fruitful, productive 2 fruitful, productive, useful 3 fertile

barricade n bar, barrier, blockade, bulwark, defence, fence, obstacle, obstruction, palisade, rampart, stockade
♦ v bar, block, close (up), defend, fortify, obstruct, shut (off), strengthen

barrier n 1 *security barriers:* bar, barricade, blockade, boundary, fence, fortification, frontier, gate, obstacle, railing, rampart, roadblock, stockade, wall 2 *a barrier to success:* check, difficulty, drawback, handicap, hindrance, hurdle, impediment, limitation, obstacle, obstruction, restraint, restriction, stumbling-block

barring prep except (for), except (in the event of), unless

bartender n barkeeper, barmaid, barman, publican

barter v bargain, deal, exchange, haggle, negotiate, sell, swap, trade, traffic
♦ n bargaining, dealing, exchange, haggling, negotiation, swapping, trade, trading, trafficking

base¹ n 1 *the base of the statue:* bed, bottom, foot, foundation, foundation stone, fundus *technical*, keystone, pedestal, plinth, prop, rest, stand, stay, substructure, support, underneath, understructure 2 *the base of the theory:* basis, component, core, essence, essential, foundation, fundamental, heart, key, origin, principal, root, source 3 *an army base:* camp, centre, depot, headquarters, home, post, settlement, starting-point, station
♦ v 1 *research based on fact:* build, construct, depend, derive, establish, found, ground, have as a basis, hinge, rest 2 *based in Edinburgh:* install, locate, position, site, situate, station

base² adj abject, contemptible, corrupt, depraved, despicable, disgraceful, disreputable, evil, ignominious, immoral, infamous, low, lowly, low-minded, mean, reprobate, scandalous, shameful, sordid, unprincipled, vile, vulgar, wicked, worthless

baseless adj gratuitous, groundless, unauthenticated, uncalled-for, unconfirmed, unfounded, unjustified, unsubstantiated, unsupported
🔁 justifiable, substantiated

basement n cellar, crypt, vault

bash v belt, hit, knock, punch, slug, smack, smash, sock *colloq*, strike, wallop *colloq*, whack *colloq*
♦ n 1 *have a bash at something:* attempt, crack *colloq*, go, shot *colloq*, stab *colloq*, try, whirl *colloq* 2 *throw a bash:* party, rave-up, thrash *colloq*

bashful adj abashed, backward, blushing, coy, diffident, embarrassed, modest, retiring, self-conscious, self-effacing, sheepish, shrinking, shy, timid, timorous, unforthcoming
🔁 aggressive, assertive, bold, confident

bashfulness n blushes, coyness, diffidence, embarrassment, modesty, self-consciousness, self-effacement, sheepishness, shyness, timidity
🔁 assertiveness, boldness, confidence

basic adj 1 *basic human rights:* central, elementary, essential, fundamental, important, indispensable, inherent, intrinsic, key, necessary, primary, radical, root, staple, underlying, vital 2 *basic rate of pay:* lowest level, minimum, standard, starting 3 *basic accommodation:* austere, crude, plain, primitive, simple, spartan, stark, unadorned, unsophisticated
🔁 1 inessential, minor, peripheral 2 premium, with commission

basically adv at bottom, at heart, essentially, fundamentally, in essence, in the main, inherently, intrinsically, mainly, primarily, principally, radically, substantially, when it comes down to it

basics n 1 *the basics of music theory:* essentials, (first) principles, fundamentals, introduction, rudiments 2 *let's get down to basics:* bedrock, brass tacks *colloq*, core, essentials, facts, fundamentals, necessaries, nitty-gritty *colloq*, nuts and bolts *colloq*, practicalities, realities, rock bottom

basin n 1 *a pudding basin:* bowl, dish, sink 2 *the basin of a river:* bed, cavity, channel, crater, depression, dip, hollow

basis n 1 *research that forms the basis of the book:* base, bedrock, bottom, core, cornerstone, essence, essential(s), first principles, foundation, fundamental point, fundamental(s), ground(s), groundwork, heart, hypostasis *formal*, key, keynote, main ingredient, premise, principle, quintessence *formal*, rationale, starting-point 2 *on a particular basis:* approach, arrangement, condition(s), footing, method, principle, procedure, system, terms, way

bask v 1 *bask in the sun:* laze, lie, loll, lounge, relax, sunbathe 2 *bask in someone's approval:* delight in, enjoy, lap up, luxuriate in *formal*, relish, revel in, savour, take pleasure in, wallow in

basket n bassinet, coop, creel, hamper, pannier, punnet, skep, trug

bass adj deep, deep-pitched, deep-toned, low, low-pitched, low-toned, resonant, rich, sonorous

bastard n illegitimate, illegitimate child, love child, natural child

bastardize v adulterate, cheapen, contaminate, corrupt, debase, defile, degrade, demean, depreciate, devalue, distort, pervert

bastion *n* bulwark, citadel, defence, fortress, mainstay, pillar, prop, redoubt *formal*, stronghold

batch *n* 1 *a batch of papers*: amount, assortment, bunch, cluster, collection, consignment, lot, mass, pack, parcel, quantity, set 2 *a new batch of pupils*: assemblage, assortment, bunch, contingent, crowd, group, lot, set

bath *n* 1 *be in the bath*: balneary *formal*, bathtub, hamman, Jacuzzi®, sauna, slipper bath, spa, steam bath, steam room, thermae, tub, Turkish bath, whirlpool 2 *have/take a bath*: dip, douche, scrub, shower, soak, tub, wash
♦ *v* bathe, clean, have/take a bath, shower, soak, wash

bathe *v* 1 *bathe in the sea*: bath, swim, take a dip 2 *bathe a wound*: cleanse, immerse, moisten, rinse, soak, steep, wash, wet
♦ *n* dip, paddle, soak, swim, wash

bathos *n* anticlimax, comedown, let-down

baton *n* rod, staff, stick, truncheon

battalion *n* 1 *an infantry battalion*: army, brigade, company, contingent, detachment, division, force, garrison, legion, platoon, regiment, section, squadron, troops, unit 2 *a battalion of people*: herd, horde, host, mass, multitude, throng

batten *n* bar, board, strip
♦ *v* board up, clamp down, fasten, fix, nail down, secure, tighten

batter *v* 1 *waves battering the pier*: beat, buffet, damage, dash, erode, lash, pelt, pound, pummel, smash, wear down, wear out 2 *battering his wife*: abuse, assault, bash, beat, bruise, disfigure, hit, hurt, ill-treat, injure, knock about, maltreat, strike, thrash *colloq*, wallop *colloq*, whack *colloq*
► **batter down** break down, demolish, destroy, ruin, smash, wreck

battered *adj* 1 *a battered child*: abused, beaten, bruised, ill-treated, injured 2 *a battered old shed*: crumbling, crushed, damaged, dilapidated, ramshackle, shabby, tumbledown, weather-beaten

battery *n* 1 *a battery of tests*: cycle, sequence, series, set, succession 2 *assault and battery*: attack, beating, grievous bodily harm, mugging *colloq*, striking, thrashing, violence 3 *the military battery*: artillery, cannon, cannonry, emplacements, guns

battle *n* 1 *a battle against the enemy*: action, Armageddon, armed conflict, attack, brawl, campaign, clash, combat, conflict, confrontation, crusade, encounter, engagement, fight, final battle, fray, free-for-all, hostilities, skirmish, strife, struggle, tournament, war, warfare 2 *a political battle*: altercation *formal*, campaign, clash, competition, conflict, confrontation, contest, controversy, debate, disagreement, dispute, race, row, struggle
♦ *v* 1 *to battle against the enemy*: campaign, combat, contend, contest, crusade, fight, strive, struggle, war 2 *to battle against the authorities*: agitate, argue, campaign, contend, contest, crusade, dispute, fight, quarrel, struggle

battle-axe *n* disciplinarian, dragon, harridan, martinet, Tartar, termagant, virago

battle-cry *n* 1 *the soldiers' fierce battle-cries*: rallying cry/call, war cry 2 *the battle-cry of the 1990s*: catchword, motto, slogan, watchword

battlefield *n* arena, battleground, field of battle, front, front line, theatre of operations, war/combat zone

batty *adj* barmy *colloq*, bats *colloq*, bonkers *colloq*, crackers *colloq*, crazy, daft *colloq*, demented, dippy *colloq*, dotty *colloq*, eccentric, insane, loony *colloq*, loopy *colloq*, mad, need your head examining *colloq*, nuts *colloq*, nutty *colloq*, odd, off your head/rocker/nutter *colloq*, out to lunch *colloq*, peculiar, round the bend/twist *colloq*
🆇 rational, sane, sensible

bauble *n* bagatelle, bibelot, flamfew *formal*, gewgaw, gimcrack, kickshaw, knick-knack, ornament, plaything, toy, trifle, trinket

baulk see **balk**

bawd *n* brothel-keeper, madam, panderess, pimp, procuress

bawdy *adj* blue, coarse, dirty, erotic, gross, improper, indecent, indecorous, indelicate, lascivious, lecherous, lewd, libidinous *formal*, licentious, lustful, obscene, pornographic, prurient *formal*, ribald, risqué, rude, salacious *formal*, smutty, suggestive, vulgar
🆇 chaste, clean

bawl *v* 1 *the baby bawled*: blubber, cry, squall, wail, weep 2 *bawl loudly at someone*: bellow, call (out), cry (out), holler *colloq*, howl, roar, scream, screech, shout, vociferate *formal*, yell
► **bawl out** rebuke, reprimand, scold, yell at

bay[1] *n* arm, bight, cove, estuary, firth, gulf, inlet, lagoon, loch, sound

bay[2] *n* alcove, booth, carrel, compartment, cubicle, niche, nook, opening, recess, stall

bay[3] *v* bark, bawl, bell, bellow, clamour, cry, howl, roar, yelp

bayonet *n* blade, dagger, knife, pike, poniard, spear
♦ *v* impale, knife, pierce, spear, stab, stick

bazaar *n* 1 *an Egyptian bazaar*: exchange, fair, market, marketplace, mart, sale, souk 2 *a church bazaar*: bring-and-buy, fair, fête, sale

be *v* 1 *cease to be*: be alive, breathe, exist, live 2 *to be somewhere in Canada*: be located, be situated, dwell, inhabit, lie, live, reside, stand 3 *the house will be here for centuries*: abide, continue, endure, last, obtain, persist, prevail, remain, stand, stay, survive 4 *whatever will be, will be*: arise, befall *formal*, come about, come to pass, develop, happen, occur, take place, transpire 5 *to be greater than ten*: add up to, amount to, make (up) 6 *you three will be the committee*: constitute, form, make (up), represent

beach *n* coast, coastline, littoral *formal*, sand, sands, seaboard, seashore, seaside, shingle, shore, strand, water's edge

beachcomber *n* forager, scavenger, scrounger

beacon *n* beam, bonfire, danger signal, fire, flare, light, lighthouse, pharos *formal*, rocket, sign, signal, warning light

bead *n* 1 *a string of beads*: ball, jewel, pearl, pellet, spheroid 2 *beads of sweat*: blob, bubble, dot, drip, drop, droplet, glob *colloq*, globule

beak n bill, mandibles, neb, nib, nose, proboscis, rostrum, snout

beaker n cup, glass, mug, tankard, tumbler

beam n 1 *a beam of light:* bar, flare, flash, gleam, glimmer, glint, glow, ray, shaft, stream 2 *a wooden beam:* bar, board, boom, cantilever, girder, joist, lath, lintel, plank, rafter, scantling, spar, stanchion, stringer, summer, support, timber, transom
♦ v 1 *beam a TV signal:* aim, broadcast, direct, emit, relay, send, transmit 2 *sunlight beaming through the window:* effulge *formal*, emit, flash, glare, gleam, glimmer, glitter, glow, radiate, shine, sparkle 3 *beaming in delight:* grin, smile

bean

> **Varieties of bean and pulse include:**
> adzuki bean, alfalfa, beansprout, black-eyed pea, broad bean, butter bean, carob bean, chick pea, chilli bean, dal, dwarf runner bean, fava bean, French bean, garbanzo pea, green bean, haricot bean, kidney bean, legume, lentil, lima bean *US*, locust bean, mange tout, marrowfat pea, mung bean, navy bean *US*, okra, pea, pinto bean *US*, red kidney bean, runner bean, scarlet runner *US*, snap bean, soya bean, split pea, string bean, sugar bean, tonka bean, wax bean *US*

bear v 1 *bear gifts:* bring, carry, convey, fetch, hump *colloq*, move, take, tote *colloq*, transport 2 *bear someone's weight:* hold (up), shoulder, support, sustain, uphold 3 *bear children:* beget, breed, bring forth, give birth to, produce 4 *trees bearing fruit:* bring forth, develop, generate, give up, produce, propagate, yield 5 *he can't bear noise:* abide, accept, admit, allow, endure, like, live with, permit, put up with, stand, stomach *colloq*, suffer, take, tolerate 6 *bear signs of a struggle:* carry, display, have, show 7 *bear the cost:* accept, pay, shoulder, support 8 *bear malice towards someone:* cherish, entertain, harbour, have, hold, maintain 9 *bear left at the junction:* bend, curve, go, move, turn, veer
▶ **bear out** back up, confirm, corroborate, demonstrate, endorse, justify, prove, ratify, substantiate, support, uphold, validate, verify, vindicate
▶ **bear up** carry on, cope, endure, grin and bear it *colloq*, keep your pecker up *colloq*, persevere, soldier on, survive, withstand
▶ **bear with** be patient with, endure, forbear, make allowances for, put up with, suffer, tolerate

bearable adj acceptable, admissible, endurable, manageable, sufferable, supportable, sustainable, tolerable
🔁 intolerable, unbearable

beard n beaver, bristle, facial hair, five o'clock shadow, goatee, imperial, stubble, tuft, vandyke, whiskers
♦ v brave, challenge, confront, dare, defy, face, oppose, stand up against

bearded adj bewhiskered, bristly, bushy, hairy, hirsute, pogoniate *technical*, shaggy, stubbly, unshaven, whiskered
🔁 beardless, clean-shaven, smooth

bearer n 1 *the bearer of bad news:* conveyor, courier, messenger, runner 2 *the bearers of a coffin:* carrier, conveyor, porter, transporter 3 *the bearer*

of a document: beneficiary, consignee, holder, payee, possessor

bearing n 1 *have no bearing on the matter:* concern, connection, influence, pertinence *formal*, reference, relation, relevance, significance 2 *a noble bearing:* air, aspect, attitude, behaviour, carriage, comportment *formal*, demeanour *formal*, deportment *formal*, gait, manner, mien *formal*, poise, posture 3 *find your bearings:* aim, course, direction, location, orientation, position, situation, track, way, whereabouts

beast n 1 *birds and beasts:* animal, brute, creature 2 *don't be such a selfish beast:* barbarian, brute, devil, fiend, monster, ogre, pig, savage, swine

beastly adj 1 *beastly weather:* awful, disagreeable, foul, horrible, horrid, nasty, rotten, terrible, unpleasant 2 *he's been beastly to me:* brutal, cruel, horrible, horrid, nasty, rotten, unpleasant

beat v 1 *beat someone to death:* bang, bash, batter, belt *colloq*, biff *colloq*, birch, box, buffet, cane, clout *colloq*, club, cudgel, drub, fill in *colloq*, flay, flog, hammer, hit, knock, knout *old use*, knubble *old use*, lambast, lash, lay into, pound, pummel, punch, slap, smack, strap, strike, swipe, tan *colloq*, thrash, thump, thwack, vapulate *old use*, wallop *colloq*, welt, whack *colloq*, wham, whip 2 *hear his heart beating:* flutter, palpitate, pound, pulsate, pulse, quiver, race, throb, thump, tremble, vibrate 3 *waves beating against the rocks:* batter, dash, pound, strike 4 *beat a drum:* bang, hit, strike 5 *a bird's wings beating:* flap, flutter, quiver, shake, vibrate 6 *beat the eggs:* blend, combine, mix, stir, whisk 7 *beat metal:* fashion, forge, form, hammer, knock, malleate *formal*, shape, stamp 8 *beat the opposition:* annihilate, be more than a match for, best, clobber *colloq*, conquer, defeat, drub, hammer *colloq*, have the edge on, lick *colloq*, outplay, overcome, overpower, overwhelm, rout, slaughter *colloq*, subdue, subjugate *formal*, thrash *colloq*, trounce, vanquish *formal*, wipe the floor with *colloq*, worst 9 *beat the record:* exceed, excel, outdo, outstrip, surpass, transcend
♦ n 1 *the beat of a drum:* bang, blow, hit, knocking, pounding, strike, striking, stroke 2 *the beat of a heart:* flutter, palpitation, pounding, pulsation, pulse, stroke, throb, thump, vibration 3 *the beat of the music:* accent, cadence *formal*, measure, metre, rhythm, stress, tempo, time 4 *a police officer's beat:* circuit, course, journey, path, round, rounds, route, walk, way
♦ adj exhausted, fatigued, jiggered *colloq*, tired, wearied, worn out, zonked (out) *slang*
▶ **beat up** assault, attack, batter *colloq*, beat the living daylights out of *colloq*, do over *colloq*, knock about, knock around, knock into the middle of next week *colloq*, knock someone's block off *colloq*, mug *colloq*, rough up *colloq*

beaten adj 1 *beaten metal:* fashioned, forged, formed, hammered, shaped, stamped, worked, wrought 2 *beaten paths:* trampled, trodden, well-trodden, well-used, well-worn 3 *beaten egg whites:* blended, mixed, whipped, whisked

beatific adj 1 *a beatific smile:* blissful, ecstatic, glorious, joyful, rapturous 2 *a beatific vision:* angelic, blessed, divine, ecstatic, exalted, glorious, heavenly, rapturous, seraphic, sublime

beatify v bless, exalt, glorify, macarize *formal*, sanctify

beating *n* **1** *a beating from his father:* battering, caning, chastisement, clubbing, corporal punishment, drubbing, flogging, hitting, lashing, punching, slapping, smacking, tanning *colloq,* the cane/birch/strap, thrashing, thumping, walloping *colloq,* whacking *colloq,* whipping **2** *their beating in the final:* annihilation, clobbering *colloq,* conquest, defeat, downfall, hammering *colloq,* overpowering, overthrow, overwhelming, rout, ruin, slaughter *colloq,* thrashing *colloq,* trouncing, vanquishing *formal*

beau *n* admirer, boyfriend, escort, fiancé, guy *colloq,* lover, suitor, sweetheart

beautician *n* beauty specialist, cosmetician, friseur, hairdresser, visagiste *formal*

beautiful *adj* alluring, appealing, attractive, bonny *Scot,* charming, comely *formal,* delightful, exquisite, fair, fine, good-looking, gorgeous, handsome, lovely, magnificent, out of this world *colloq,* pleasing, pretty, pulchritudinous *formal,* radiant, ravishing, smashing *colloq,* striking, stunning
🖛 hideous, plain, ugly

beautify *v* adorn, array, bedeck, deck, decorate, doll up *colloq,* embellish, enhance, garnish, glamorize, grace, improve, ornament, smarten (up), spruce up, tart up *colloq,* titivate *colloq*
🖛 disfigure, spoil

beauty *n* **1** *the beauty of a woman:* allure, appeal, attractiveness, charm, delight, exquisiteness, (good) looks, gorgeousness, handsomeness, loveliness, prettiness, pulchritude *formal,* radiance **2** *think her a real beauty:* belle, charmer, corker *colloq,* cracker *colloq,* femme fatale, good-looker *colloq,* knockout *colloq,* peach *colloq,* siren, smasher *colloq,* stunner *colloq,* Venus **3** *one of the beauties of the plan:* advantage, attraction, benefit, blessing, bonus, boon, dividend, glory, good point, good thing, merit, plus point, virtue
🖛 **1** repulsiveness, ugliness **2** frump
3 disadvantage

beaver
▶ **beaver away** persevere, persist, plug away *colloq,* put a lot of effort in, slave away *colloq,* slog *colloq,* work, work hard

becalmed *adj* at a halt, at a standstill, motionless, still, stranded, stuck

because *conj* as, as a result of, by reason of *formal,* by virtue of *formal,* due to, for, forasmuch as *formal,* in view of the fact that, on account of, owing to, seeing as *colloq,* since, thanks to, the reason is…

beckon *v* **1** *beckon to someone:* gesticulate, gesture, motion, nod, signal, wave **2** *fame beckoned him:* allure, attract, call, draw, entice, invite, lure, pull, tempt

become *v* **1** *become old-fashioned:* be changed into, change into, come to be, develop into, get, grow (into), mature into, pass into, turn, turn out to be, wax **2** *that outfit becomes you:* befit, enhance, flatter, grace, harmonize with, look good on, set off, suit

becoming *adj* **1** *a hat in a more becoming style:* attractive, charming, comely, elegant, fetching, flattering, graceful, pretty, tasteful **2** *becoming behaviour:* appropriate, befitting, compatible, congruous, consistent, fit, fitting, suitable
🖛 **2** unbecoming

bed *n* **1** *get out of bed:* bunk, couch, divan, kip *slang,* the hay *slang,* the sack *slang* **2** *a river bed:* base, bottom, channel, floor, watercourse **3** *a bed of rock:* base, basis, foundation, groundwork, layer, matrix, stratum, substratum **4** *bed of flowers:* area, border, garden, patch, plot, row, space, strip
♦ *v* base, bury, embed, fix, ground, implant, inlay, insert, plant, settle
▶ **bed down** doss down *slang,* go to bed, hit the hay *slang,* hit the sack *slang,* kip down *slang,* settle down, sleep, turn in

---

Kinds of bed include:
berth, box bed, bunk bed, camp-bed, cot, cradle, crib, day bed, divan bed, double bed, foldaway bed, folding bed, four-poster, hammock, mattress, pallet, palliasse, Put-u-up®, put-you-up, single bed, sofa bed, trucklebed, trundlebed, twin bed, water-bed, Z-bed

---

bedclothes *n* bedding, bed-linen, covers

bedeck *v* adorn, array, beautify, deck, decorate, embellish, festoon, garnish, ornament, trick out, trim

bedevil *v* afflict, annoy, confound, distress, frustrate, harass, irk, irritate, plague, torment, torture, trouble, vex, worry

bedlam *n* babel, chaos, clamour, commotion, confusion, furore, hubbub, hullabaloo, madhouse, noise, pandemonium, tumult, turmoil, uproar
🖛 calm

bedraggled *adj* dirty, dishevelled, drenched, dripping, messy, muddied, muddy, soaked, soaking (wet), sodden, soiled, unkempt, untidy, wet
🖛 clean, neat, tidy

bedridden *adj* confined to bed, flat on your back *colloq,* incapacitated, laid up *colloq*

bedrock *n* basics, basis, essence, essentials, first principles, foundation, fundamental point, fundamentals, heart, premise, rationale, starting-point

beef *v* complain, criticize, disagree, dispute, gripe *colloq,* grouse, grumble, moan, object
🖛 approve
▶ **beef up** build up, consolidate, give new energy to, invigorate, reinforce, strengthen, toughen
🖛 weaken

beefy *adj* brawny, bulky, burly, corpulent *formal,* fleshy, heavy, hefty, hulking, muscular, robust, stalwart, stocky, sturdy
🖛 slight

beer *n* ale, bitter, bottled beer, draught, lager, light ale, mild, Pils, Pilsener, real ale, stout

beetle *v* dash, hurry, nip, run, rush, scamper, scoot, scurry, tear, zip

beetling *adj* jutting, leaning over, overhanging, pendent *formal,* poking out, projecting, protruding, sticking out

befall *v* betide *formal,* chance, ensue, fall (upon), follow, happen (to), materialize, occur, result, supervene *formal,* take place

befitting *adj* appropriate, apt, becoming, correct, fit, fitting, meet *old use*, proper, right, seemly, suitable
🔁 unbecoming

before *prep* 1 *before breakfast:* earlier than, not later than, on the eve of, previous to, prior to, sooner than 2 *perform before the king:* in front of, in the presence of, in the sight of 3 *all of his life before him:* ahead of, in front of
♦ *adv* 1 *have been here before:* already, earlier, formerly, previously 2 *go on before:* ahead, in advance, in front

beforehand *adv* already, before, earlier, in advance, previously, sooner

befriend *v* aid, assist, back, benefit, fall in with, favour, get to know, help, make a friend of, make friends with, stand by, stick up for, succour *formal*, support, sustain, take under your wing
🔁 neglect, oppose

befuddle *v* 1 *befuddled by legal jargon:* baffle, bewilder, confuse, muddle, puzzle 2 *befuddled by drink:* daze, disorient, stupefy

beg *v* 1 *beg someone to do something:* appeal, ask, beseech, crave, entreat, implore, importune, petition, plead, pray, request, solicit, supplicate, turn to 2 *beg for money:* ask for money, bum *colloq*, cadge, mooch (off) *US colloq*, scrounge *colloq*, sponge *colloq*

beget *v* 1 *ignorance begets prejudice:* breed, bring about, cause, create, effect *formal*, engender, give rise to, occasion, result in 2 *beget a child:* breed, father, generate, procreate, produce, propagate, sire, spawn

beggar *n* bludger *slang*, bum *colloq*, cadger *colloq*, down-and-out, freeloader *colloq*, mendicant, moocher *US colloq*, panhandler, pauper, schnorrer *US slang*, scrounger *colloq*, sponger *colloq*, supplicant, tramp, vagrant
♦ *v* baffle, challenge, defy, exceed, surpass, transcend

beggarly *adj* 1 *a beggarly existence:* abject, contemptible, despicable, low, mean, needy, pathetic, pitiful, wretched 2 *a beggarly amount:* inadequate, low, meagre, mean, miserly, niggardly, paltry, stingy
🔁 1 affluent 2 generous

begin *v* 1 *begin a task:* activate, actuate, commence, do first, embark on, found, get cracking *colloq*, get going, initiate, instigate, institute, introduce, kick off *colloq*, launch into, open, set about, set in motion, set off, set the ball rolling *colloq*, start, take the plunge *colloq* 2 *begin to happen:* appear, arise, commence, crop up, emerge, get going, open, originate, spring, start
🔁 1 cease, conclude, end, finish, stop 2 cease, conclude, end, finish, stop

beginner *n* apprentice, cub, fledgling, fresher, freshman, greenhorn *colloq*, initiate, learner, neophyte, novice, probationer, raw recruit, recruit, rookie *colloq*, starter, student, tenderfoot, tiro, trainee
🔁 expert, old hand, veteran

beginning *n* 1 *the beginning of a new age:* birth, commencement, conception, dawn, day one *colloq*, emergence, establishment, first base *colloq*, fountainhead, fresh start, genesis, inauguration, inception, inchoation *formal*, incipience *formal*, initiation, institution, introduction, kick-off *colloq*, launch, new leaf *colloq*, onset, origin, outset, pastures new, rise, source, square one *colloq*, start, starting-point, the word go *colloq* 2 *the beginning of the book:* first part, intro *colloq*, introduction, opening, opening part, preface, prelude, start 3 *her humble beginnings:* birth, origin, root
🔁 1 conclusion, end, finish 2 conclusion, end

begrudge *v* be jealous of, covet, envy, grudge, mind, object to, resent
🔁 allow

beguile *v* 1 *beguiled by her beauty:* attract, bewitch, captivate, charm, delight, distract, divert, enchant, engross, entertain, occupy 2 *beguiled into giving him money:* cheat, cozen, deceive, delude, dupe, fool, hoodwink, mislead, trick

beguiling *adj* alluring, appealing, attractive, bewitching, captivating, charming, delightful, diverting, enchanting, entertaining, enticing, interesting, intriguing, seductive
🔁 offensive, repulsive

behave *v* 1 *behave aggressively:* acquit yourself, act, be, comport yourself *formal*, conduct yourself, perform, react, respond 2 *tell the children to behave themselves:* act properly/ politely, act your age *colloq*, be good, be on your best behaviour, be well behaved, keep your nose clean *colloq*, mind your manners, mind your p's and q's *colloq*, not mess about/muck about *colloq*, not put a foot wrong *colloq*, stay out of trouble, stop fooling around *colloq* 3 *electrons behave like this:* act, function, operate, perform, react, work
🔁 2 act up *colloq*, be up to no good *colloq*, get into trouble, misbehave

behaviour *n* 1 *the child's behaviour:* attitude, comportment *formal*, conduct, dealings, demeanour *formal*, deportment *formal*, habits, manner, manners, reaction, response, way of acting, ways 2 *the behaviour of chemical elements:* action, functioning, operation, performance, reaction

behead *v* decapitate, execute, guillotine

behest *n* bidding, command, instruction, order, request

behind *prep* 1 *a shed behind the garage:* at the back of, at the rear of, in back of *US*, on the other side of 2 *walk behind the others:* after, at the back of, at the rear of, close on, following 3 *behind schedule:* late, later than, overdue, running late, slow, slower than usual 4 *we are behind you in your decision:* backing, endorsing, for, on the side of, supporting 5 *the reasons behind the change in policy:* accounting for, at the bottom of, causing, explaining, giving rise to, initiating, instigating, responsible for
🔁 1 in front of 2 ahead of
♦ *adv* 1 *with a garden behind:* at the back/rear, in the rear 2 *with the stragglers following behind:* after, at the back, following, next, subsequently 3 *fall behind with work/payments:* behindhand, in arrears, in debt, late, overdue
♦ *n* arse *colloq*, ass *US colloq*, backside, bottom, bum *colloq*, butt *US colloq*, buttocks, posterior *colloq*

behold *v* consider, contemplate, descry, discern, espy, gaze at, look at, mark, note, observe, perceive, regard, scan, see, survey, view, watch, witness

♦ *interj* ecce, lo, look, mark, observe, see, voici, voila, watch

beholden *adj* bound, grateful, indebted, obligated, obliged, owing, thankful, under obligation

behove *v* be advantageous, be essential, be necessary, be proper, be seemly, be to your advantage, befit, benefit, profit

beige *adj* buff, camel, coffee, ecru, fawn, greige, khaki, mushroom, neutral, oatmeal, sandy, tan

being *n* **1** *brought into being:* actuality, animation, existence, haecceity *technical*, life, reality, substance **2** *thrilled to the core of his being:* essence, life, nature, soul, spirit, substance **3** *every living being on the planet:* animal, beast, creature, entity, human, human being, individual, man, mortal, person, thing, woman

belabour *v* attack, beat, belt, flay, flog, hit, thrash, whip

belated *adj* behindhand, delayed, late, overdue, tardy, unpunctual
☒ punctual, timely

belch *v* **1** *the baby belched:* bring up wind, burp, eructate *formal*, hiccup **2** *chimneys belching out smoke:* discharge, disgorge, eject, emit, give off, give out, spew, vent
♦ *n* burp, eructation *formal*, hiccup

beleaguered *adj* **1** *a beleaguered person:* badgered, beset, bothered, harassed, persecuted, pestered, plagued, vexed, worried **2** *a beleaguered city:* besieged, blockaded, surrounded, under siege

belie *v* **1** *the statistics belie the theory:* confute *formal*, contradict, deny, disprove, gainsay *formal*, negate, refute, run counter to **2** *her looks belie her age:* conceal, disguise, falsify, misrepresent

belief *n* **1** *my belief is that he is wrong:* conviction, feeling, impression, intuition, judgement, notion, opinion, point of view, theory, view, viewpoint **2** *belief in his innocence:* assurance, certainty, confidence, credit, expectation, faith, presumption, reliance, sureness, trust **3** *religious beliefs:* creed, doctrine, dogma, faith, ideology, ism, principle, teaching, tenet, theory
☒ **2** disbelief, doubt

believable *adj* acceptable, conceivable, credible, imaginable, likely, not beyond the realms of possibility, plausible, possible, probable, reliable, trustworthy, (well) within the bounds of possibility, with a ring of truth
☒ implausible, inconceivable, incredible, unbelievable, unconvincing

believe *v* **1** *I believe she's a professor:* assume, be of the opinion that, conjecture, consider, deem *formal*, gather, guess, hold, imagine, judge, maintain, opine *formal*, postulate *formal*, reckon, speculate, suppose, think, understand **2** *believe his story:* accept, be certain of, be convinced by, be persuaded by, buy *colloq*, fall for *colloq*, fall for/ swallow hook line and sinker *colloq*, swallow *colloq*, take on board *colloq*, take someone's word for it, trust, wear *colloq*
☒ **2** disbelieve, doubt, question
▸ **believe in 1** *I believe in God:* be convinced of, be sure of the existence/reality of **2** *believe in hard work:* accept the importance of, approve of, be in favour of, be persuaded by, depend on, encourage, favour, have confidence in, rate *colloq*, recommend, rely on, set great store by *formal*, swear by, trust, value highly

believer *n* adherent, convert, devotee, disciple, follower, proselyte, supporter, upholder, zealot
☒ sceptic, unbeliever

belittle *v* decry, demean, deprecate *formal*, deride, detract from, diminish, dismiss, disparage, lessen, minimize, play down, ridicule, run down, scorn, trivialize, underestimate, underrate, understate, undervalue
☒ exaggerate, praise

bellicose *adj* aggressive, antagonistic, argumentative, combative, contentious, militant, pugnacious *formal*, quarrelsome, violent, warlike, warring
☒ peaceable

belligerence *n* aggression, antagonism, argumentativeness, combativeness, contentiousness, militancy, pugnacity *formal*, quarrelsomeness, sabre-rattling, unfriendliness, violence, war, war-mongering
☒ complaisance

belligerent *adj* aggressive, antagonistic, argumentative, combative, contentious, disputatious *formal*, militant, pugnacious *formal*, quarrelsome, sabre-rattling, truculent *formal*, violent, warlike, war-mongering, warring
☒ peaceable

bellow *v* bawl, clamour, cry, holler *colloq*, howl, raise your voice, roar, scream, shout, shriek, yell

belly *n* abdomen, beer belly, bread basket *slang*, corporation *colloq*, gut, guts, insides, intestines, paunch, pot-belly, stomach, tummy *colloq*, venter *technical*

belong *v* **1** *this book belongs to me:* be owned by, be the possession of, be the property of, be under the ownership of, be yours **2** *belong to a rugby club:* be a member of, be affiliated to, be an adherent of, be associated with, be connected with, be in **3** *this lid belongs to that pan:* attach to, be connected with, be part of, fit, go with, link up with, relate to, tie up with **4** *Where do these toys belong?:* be categorized, be classified, be included, be sorted, fit in, go, have as its place/home

belonging *n* acceptance, affinity, association, attachment, closeness, compatibility, fellow-feeling, fellowship, kinship, link(s), loyalty, rapport, relationship
☒ antipathy

belongings *n* accoutrements *formal*, appurtenances *formal*, chattels, gear *colloq*, goods, paraphernalia, (personal) effects, possessions, property, stuff *colloq*, things *colloq*

beloved *adj* admired, adored, cherished, darling, dear, dearest, favourite, loved, much loved, pet, precious, prized, revered, treasured, worshipped
♦ *n* betrothed, boyfriend, darling, dear, dearest, fiancé, fiancée, girlfriend, husband, inamorata *formal*, inamorato *formal*, love, lover, partner, pet, precious, spouse, sweet, sweetheart, wife

below *adv* **1** *the flat below:* beneath, down, lower, lower down, under, underneath **2** *see below for details:* at a later place, further on, later
☒ **2** above
♦ *prep* **1** *below the water:* beneath, lower than,

under, underneath **2** *workers below management level*: inferior to, lesser than, lower (in rank) than, subject to, subordinate to
🔄 **2** above

belt *n* **1** *a leather belt*: baldric *formal*, ceinture *formal*, cestus *formal*, cincture *formal*, cingulum *formal*, cummerbund *formal*, girdle, girth, sash, strap, waistband **2** *a belt of land*: area, district, extent, layer, region, stretch, strip, swathe, tract, zone **3** *a belt on the jaw*: bang, bashing, box, clout *colloq*, hit, knock, pelt, punch, slap, smack, strike, swipe, thump, wallop *colloq*, whack *colloq*
♦ *v* **1** *his father belted him*: bang, bash, biff *colloq*, birch, box, cane, clout *colloq*, flay, flog, hit, knock, lash, pelt, punch, slap, smack, strap, strike, swipe, tan *colloq*, thump, thwack, wallop *colloq*, whack *colloq*, whip **2** *belt along the road*: career, charge, dash, fly, rush, speed, tear, zip
▶ **belt up** be quiet, keep your trap shut *slang*, pipe down *colloq*, put a sock in it *slang*, shut up, shut your mouth/face *slang*

bemoan *v* bewail, deplore, grieve for, lament, mourn, regret, rue, sigh for, sorrow over, weep for
🔄 gloat

bemuse *v* befuddle, bewilder, confuse, daze, muddle, perplex, puzzle
🔄 enlighten, illuminate

bemused *adj* befuddled, bewildered, confused, dazed, muddled, overwhelmed, perplexed, puzzled
🔄 clear, clear-headed, lucid

bench *n* **1** *sit on a bench*: form, pew, seat, settle **2** *work at a bench*: board, counter, stall, table, workbench, worktable **3** *appear before the bench*: court, courtroom, judge, judicature, judiciary, magistrate, tribunal

benchmark *n* criterion, example, guideline(s), level, model, norm, pattern, point of reference, reference, reference-point, scale, standard, touchstone, yardstick

bend *v* **1** *bend down to pick up a pin*: bow, crouch, incline, kneel, lean, stoop **2** *bend the wire*: arch, bow, buckle, contort, curve, deflect, flex, loop, make curved, turn, twist, warp **3** *the road bends*: curve, deflect, deviate, diverge, incurve *formal*, meander, swerve, turn, twist, veer, wind, zigzag **4** *bend to their will*: affect, compel, influence, mould, persuade, sway
🔄 **2** straighten
♦ *n* angle, arc, bow, corner, crook, curvature, curve, deflection, divergence, dog-leg, elbow, flexure *technical*, hairpin bend, hook, incurvation *formal*, kink, loop, turn, twist, zigzag

beneath *adv* below, lower, lower down, under, underneath
🔄 above
♦ *prep* **1** *lying beneath the tree*: below, lower than, under, underneath **2** *thinks the job is beneath her*: unbecoming to, unbefitting, unworthy of
🔄 **1** above

benediction *n* benison *formal*, blessing, consecration, favour, grace, invocation, prayer, thanksgiving
🔄 anathema, curse, execration *formal*

benefactor *n* angel *colloq*, backer, contributor, donor, friend, giver, helper, patron, philanthropist, promoter, provider, sponsor, subscriber, subsidizer, supporter, well-wisher
🔄 opponent, persecutor

beneficent *adj* benevolent, benign, bountiful, charitable, compassionate, generous, helpful, kind, liberal, munificent *formal*, unselfish
🔄 mean

beneficial *adj* advantageous, favourable, helpful, improving, profitable, promising, propitious *formal*, rewarding, salutary, serviceable, useful, valuable, wholesome
🔄 detrimental, harmful, useless

beneficiary *n* heir, heiress, inheritor, legatee, payee, receiver, recipient, successor

benefit *n* **1** *the benefits of exercise*: advantage, asset, blessing, bonus, boon, dividend, favour, fringe benefit, gain, good, good point, pay-off *colloq*, perk, profit **2** *of benefit to children*: aid, assistance, avail, good help, service, use, welfare **3** *living on state benefits*: allowance, credit, dole *colloq*, income, income support, payment, pension, sick pay, social security, support, welfare *US colloq*
🔄 **1** disadvantage **2** damage, harm
♦ *v* advance, aid, assist, avail, be of advantage to, be of service to, better, do good to, enhance, further, help, improve, profit, promote, serve
🔄 harm, hinder, undermine

benevolence *n* altruism, care, charitableness, compassion, considerateness, friendliness, generosity, goodwill, humaneness, humanitarianism, kind-heartedness, kindness, magnanimity, mercy, philanthropy, pity, tolerance
🔄 meanness

benevolent *adj* altruistic, benign, caring, charitable, compassionate, considerate, generous, gracious, humane, humanitarian, kind, kind-hearted, kindly, magnanimous, merciful, philanthropic, soft-hearted, tolerant, well-disposed
🔄 malevolent, mean, selfish

benighted *adj* backward, ignorant, illiterate, uncultured, uneducated, unenlightened, unknowing, unschooled

benign *adj* **1** *a benign view of his behaviour*: affable, amiable, benevolent, charitable, cordial, friendly, generous, genial, gentle, good, gracious, kind, liberal, obliging, sympathetic **2** *benign conditions*: agreeable, auspicious *formal*, beneficial, favourable, opportune, propitious *formal*, providential, salubrious *formal*, wholesome **3** *benign climate*: healthy, mild, salubrious *formal*, temperate, warm **4** *a benign tumour*: curable, harmless, non-malignant, treatable
🔄 **1** hostile **2** harmful, unpleasant **3** unpleasant **4** dangerous, malignant

bent *adj* **1** *a bent pin*: angled, arched, bowed, contorted, crooked, curved, doubled, folded, twisted, warped **2** *an old bent man*: bowed, crooked, hunched, stooped **3** *a bent policeman*: corrupt, criminal, crooked *colloq*, dishonest, fraudulent, illegal, untrustworthy
🔄 **1** straight **2** upright **3** honest, trustworthy
♦ *n* ability, aptitude, capacity, disposition, facility, faculty, flair, fondness, forte, gift, inclination, knack, leaning, penchant *formal*, predilection *formal*, predisposition *formal*,

preference, proclivity *formal*, propensity *formal*, talent, tendency

bequeath *v* 1 *bequeathed in her will*: assign, bestow, commit, consign, endow, entrust, give, grant, leave, make over, transfer, will 2 *social problems bequeathed by past generations*: hand down, impart, pass on, transmit

bequest *n* bequeathal *formal*, bestowal *formal*, devisal *formal*, donation, endowment, estate, gift, heritage, inheritance, legacy, settlement, trust

berate *v* blast *colloq*, castigate *formal*, censure, chastise, chew out *US colloq*, chide, criticize, dress down *colloq*, give a rocket to *colloq*, give hell *colloq*, jump down the throat of *colloq*, rail at, read the riot act to *colloq*, rebuke, reprimand, reproach, reprove, revile, scold, slate *colloq*, tear a strip off *colloq*, tell off, upbraid, vituperate *formal*
Ⓕ praise

bereaved *adj* 1 *the bereaved family*: deprived, orphaned, widowed 2 *bereaved of all their possessions*: deprived, dispossessed, divested, robbed

bereavement *n* death, deprivation, grief, loss, passing, passing-away, sadness, sorrow

bereft *adj* deprived, destitute, devoid, lacking, wanting

berserk *adj* crazed, crazy, demented, deranged, frantic, frenzied, furious, hysterical, insane, mad, maniacal, manic, off your head *colloq*, out of your mind *colloq*, rabid, raging, raving, uncontrollable, violent, wild
Ⓕ calm, sane

berth *n* 1 *a comfortable berth*: bed, billet, bunk, hammock 2 *the boat left its berth*: anchorage, dock, harbour, mooring, port, quay, wharf
♦ *v* anchor, dock, drop/cast anchor, land, moor, tie up
Ⓕ up anchor, weigh anchor

beseech *v* adjure *formal*, appeal to, ask, beg, call on, crave, entreat, exhort *formal*, implore, importune *formal*, obsecrate *formal*, petition, plead, pray, solicit, sue *formal*, supplicate

beset *v* assail, attack, bedevil, harass, hassle *colloq*, hem in, pester, plague, surround, torment, worry

besetting *adj* compulsive, constant, dominant, habitual, inveterate, irresistible, obsessive, persistent, prevalent, recurring, troublesome, uncontrollable

beside *prep* abreast of, abutting, adjacent to, alongside, bordering, by, close to, near, neighbouring, next door to, next to, overlooking

besides *adv* additionally, also, as well, further, furthermore, in addition, moreover, too, what's more *colloq*
♦ *prep* apart from, as well as, aside from, excluding, in addition to, other than, over and above

besiege *v* 1 *besiege a town*: beleaguer, blockade, confine, encircle, encompass, lay siege to, surround 2 *besieged by reporters*: confine, encircle, encompass, hem in, shut in, surround 3 *besiege someone with questions*: assail, badger, beleaguer, beset, bother, harass, hound, importune, nag, plague, trouble, worry

besmirch *v* blacken, damage, defame, defile, dirty, dishonour, slander, smear, soil, stain, sully, tarnish
Ⓕ enhance

besotted *adj* bewitched, doting, hypnotized, infatuated, obsessed, smitten, spellbound
Ⓕ disenchanted, indifferent

bespeak *v* attest, demonstrate, denote, display, evidence, evince, exhibit, imply, indicate, proclaim, reveal, show, signify, suggest

best *adj* a cut above the rest *colloq*, ace *colloq*, excellent, finest, first-class, first-rate, foremost, greatest, highest, incomparable, leading, matchless, nonpareil *formal*, number one *colloq*, of highest quality, one in a million *colloq*, optimal, optimum, outstanding, peerless, pre-eminent, prime, second to none *colloq*, star *colloq*, superlative, supreme, the pick of the bunch *colloq*, the tops *colloq*, top, unbeatable, unequalled, unrivalled, unsurpassed
Ⓕ worst
♦ *adv* excellently, exceptionally, extremely, greatly, incomparably, matchlessly, most, outstandingly, superlatively, supremely, to the greatest/highest degree, unsurpassedly
Ⓕ least, worst
♦ *n* 1 *students who are the best in their year*: choice, cream, elite, finest, first, pick, prime, star, the pick of the bunch *colloq*, top 2 *do your best*: damnedest *colloq*, greatest effort, hardest, utmost
Ⓕ 1 worst
♦ *v* annihilate, be more than a match for, clobber *colloq*, conquer, defeat, hammer *colloq*, have the edge on, lick *colloq*, outplay, outsmart, outwit, overcome, overpower, overwhelm, rout, slaughter *colloq*, subdue, thrash *colloq*, trounce, vanquish *formal*, worst

bestial *adj* animal, barbaric, barbarous, beastly, brutal, brutish, cruel, degraded, depraved, feral *formal*, gross, inhuman, savage, sordid, vile
Ⓕ civilized, humane

bestir *v* activate, actuate, animate, arouse, awaken, energize, exert, galvanize, incite, motivate, stimulate
Ⓕ calm, lull, quell

bestow *v* accord, allot, apportion, award, bequeath, commit, confer, donate, endow, entrust, give, grant, impart, lavish, present
Ⓕ deprive, withhold

bestride *v* overshadow, sit astride, stand astride, straddle

bet *v* 1 *bet money on a horse*: bid, chance, gamble, have a flutter *colloq*, hazard, lay, place, play for money *colloq*, pledge, punt, put, risk, speculate, stake, venture 2 *I bet she did it on purpose*: be certain, be convinced, be sure, expect, not be surprised
♦ *n* 1 *place a bet*: accumulator, ante, bid, flutter *colloq*, gamble, lottery, pledge, risk, speculation, stake, sweepstake, venture, wager 2 *my bet is that he'll stay*: conviction, feeling, impression, intuition, judgement, notion, opinion, point of view, theory, view, viewpoint 3 *your best bet*: alternative, choice, course of action, option

bête noire *n* abomination, anathema, aversion, bane, bugbear, curse, pet aversion, pet hate
Ⓕ favourite

betide *v* befall, chance, ensue, happen, occur, overtake, supervene *formal*

betoken v 1 *his expression betokened amusement:* bespeak, declare, denote, evidence, indicate, manifest, mark, represent, signal, signify, suggest 2 *the signs betoken disaster:* augur, bode, forebode, portend, presage, prognosticate, promise

betray v 1 *betray a friend:* abandon, be disloyal to, be unfaithful to, blow the whistle on *colloq*, break faith with, desert, double-cross, forsake, grass *slang*, inform on, sell (out) *colloq*, sell down the river *colloq*, shop *colloq*, squeal on *colloq*, stab in the back *colloq*, tell on *colloq*, turn traitor, walk out on *colloq* 2 *betray your true feelings:* bring to light, disclose, divulge, expose, give away, let slip, manifest, reveal, show, tell, unmask
⧉ 1 be loyal to, defend, protect 2 conceal, hide

betrayal n breaking faith, disloyalty, double-crossing, double-dealing, duplicity, falseness, perfidy *formal*, sell-out, treachery, treason, unfaithfulness
⧉ faithfulness, loyalty, protection

betrayer n apostate, conspirator, double-crosser, grass *slang*, informer, Judas, renegade, supergrass *slang*, traitor, whistle-blower *colloq*
⧉ protector, supporter

betrothal n engagement, espousal *formal*, fiançailles *formal*, plighting of your troth, promise, proposal of marriage, troth, vow(s)

betrothed adj affianced *formal*, contracted, engaged, engaged to be married, espoused *formal*, promised

better adj 1 *a better job:* a cut above *colloq*, finer, greater, more acceptable, more advantageous, more fitting, more valuable, of higher quality, preferable, superior, surpassing, worthier 2 *hope you're better soon:* cured, fitter, (fully) recovered, healed, healthier, improving, on the mend *colloq*, progressing, recovering, restored, stronger, well
⧉ 1 inferior 2 worse
♦ v 1 *to better someone's chances:* ameliorate *formal*, correct, enhance, enrich, forward, further, improve, make better, mend, promote, raise, rectify, reform 2 *to better a score:* beat, cap, exceed, go one better than, improve on, outdo, outstrip, overtake, surpass, top
⧉ 1 deteriorate, worsen

betterment n advancement, amelioration *formal*, edification, enhancement, enrichment, furtherance, improvement, melioration *formal*
⧉ deterioration, impairment

between prep amid, amidst, among, amongst, halfway, in the middle (of), mid

bevel n angle, basil, bezel, bias, cant, chamfer, diagonal, mitre, oblique, slant, slope, tilt
♦ v angle, bias, cant, chamfer, mitre, slant, slope, tilt

beverage n draught, drink, liquid, liquor, potable *formal*, potation *formal*, refreshment

bevy n assembly, band, bunch, collection, company, crowd, flock, gaggle, gathering, group, pack, throng, troupe

bewail v bemoan, cry over, deplore, grieve over, lament, moan, mourn, regret, repent, rue, sigh over, sorrow over
⧉ gloat, glory, vaunt

beware v 1 *beware if you go out after dark:* be careful, be cautious, be on the lookout, be on your guard, be wary, look out, mind (out), take heed, watch out 2 *beware of pickpockets:* avoid, be on the lookout for, be on your guard against, guard against, look out for, shun, steer clear of, watch out for

bewilder v baffle, bamboozle *colloq*, bemuse, confound, confuse, disconcert, disorient, mix up, muddle, mystify, perplex, puzzle, stump *colloq*

bewildered adj (all) at sea *colloq*, baffled, bamboozled *colloq*, bemused, confused, disoriented, muddled, mystified, nonplussed, perplexed, puzzled, stunned, taken aback
⧉ collected, unperturbed

bewilderment n confusion, disconcertion, disorientation, mystification, perplexity, puzzlement
⧉ composure, confidence

bewitch v allure, beguile, captivate, charm, delight, enchant, enrapture, enthral, entrance, fascinate, hypnotize, mesmerize, obsess, possess, seduce, spellbind, transfix
⧉ disenchant, repel

beyond prep 1 *the fields beyond the house:* apart from, away from, further than, on the far side of, on the other side of, remote from 2 *beyond the age of 16:* above, after, greater than, later than, over, past, upwards of 3 *beyond someone's control:* further than the limitations of, out of range of, out of reach of, outside

bias n 1 *racial bias:* bent, bigotry, favouritism, inclination, intolerance, leaning, one-sidedness, partiality, predilection *formal*, prejudice, proclivity *formal*, propensity *formal*, stereotyping, tendency, unfairness 2 *cut on the bias:* angle, cross, diagonal, oblique, slant
⧉ 1 fairness, impartiality
♦ v angle, distort, earwig *old use*, influence, load, load the dice *colloq*, predispose, prejudice, slant, sway, twist, warp, weight

biased adj angled, bigoted, blinkered, distorted, influenced, loaded, one-sided, partial, partisan, predisposed, prejudiced, slanted, subjective, swayed, tendentious, twisted, unfair, warped, weighted
⧉ fair, impartial, objective

Bible n 1 *study the Christian Bible:* Apocrypha, canon, epistles, good book *colloq*, Gospels, Holy Bible, holy Scriptures, holy writ, law, letters, New Testament, Old Testament, Pentateuch, prophets, revelation, Scriptures, writings 2 *the gardener's bible:* authority, companion, dictionary, directory, encyclopedia, guidebook, handbook, lexicon, manual, primer, reference book, textbook

---

The books of the Bible are:
the Old Testament: Genesis, Exodus, Leviticus, Numbers, Deuteronomy, Joshua, Judges, Ruth, 1 Samuel, 2 Samuel, 1 Kings, 2 Kings, 1 Chronicles, 2 Chronicles, Ezra, Nehemiah, Esther, Job, Psalms, Proverbs, Ecclesiastes, Song of Solomon (Song of Songs), Isaiah, Jeremiah, Lamentations, Ezekiel, Daniel, Hosea, Joel, Amos, Obadiah, Jonah, Micah, Nahum, Habakkuk, Zephaniah, Haggai, Zechariah, Malachi; *the New Testament:* Matthew, Mark, Luke, John, Acts of the Apostles, Romans, 1 Corinthians, 2 Corinthians, Galatians, Ephesians, Philippians, Colossians, 1 Thessalonians,

2 Thessalonians, 1 Timothy, 2 Timothy, Titus, Philemon, Hebrews, James, 1 Peter, 2 Peter, 1 John, 2 John, 3 John, Jude, Revelation; *the Apocrypha:* 1 Esdras, 2 Esdras, Tobit, Judith, Additions to Esther, Wisdom of Solomon, Ecclesiasticus, Baruch, Letter of Jeremiah, Prayer of Azariah, Song of the Three Young Men, History of Susanna, Bel and the Dragon, Prayer of Manasseh, 1 Maccabees, 2 Maccabees

bibliography *n* book list, catalogue, list of books, record

bicker *v* altercate *formal*, argue, clash, disagree, dispute, fall out, fight, quarrel, row, scrap *colloq*, spar, squabble, wrangle
▄ agree, make up

bicycle *n* all-terrain bike, bike *colloq*, cycle, mountain bike, push-bike *colloq*, racer, tandem, two-wheeler, unicycle

bid *v* **1** *bid for a painting:* advance, offer, proffer, propose, put forward, submit, tender **2** *bidden to attend the hearing:* ask, call (for), charge, command, demand, direct, enjoin *formal*, instruct, invite, order, request, summon, tell **3** *bid them farewell:* call, greet, say, tell, wave, wish
♦ *n* **1** *put in a bid for a house:* advance, amount, offer, price, proposal, submission, sum, tender **2** *a bid for freedom:* attempt, effort, endeavour, go *colloq*, try, venture

bidding *n* behest *formal*, call, charge, command, demand, direction, injunction, instruction, invitation, order, request, summons

big *adj* **1** *a big house:* bumper *colloq*, cavernous, colossal, considerable, enormous, extensive, extra large, giant, gigantic, ginormous *colloq*, great, huge, humungous *colloq*, immense, jumbo *colloq*, large, mammoth, massive, mega *slang*, sizeable, spacious, substantial, vast, voluminous *formal*, whopping *colloq* **2** *a big person:* beefy, brawny, bulky, burly, corpulent *formal*, enormous, fat, hefty *colloq*, huge, hulking, large, massive, muscular, obese, stout, tall **3** *love your big brother:* elder, older **4** *a big decision:* critical, fundamental, important, major, momentous, radical, salient, serious, significant, weighty **5** *a big name in the fashion world:* distinguished, eminent, famous, important, influential, leading, main, noteworthy, outstanding, principal, prominent, significant, valued, well-known **6** *that's big of you:* benevolent, generous, gracious, kind-hearted, magnanimous, unselfish
▄ **2** little, small **3** younger **4** insignificant **5** insignificant, unknown **6** mean, miserly, selfish

bigot *n* chauvinist, dogmatist, fanatic, male chauvinist pig (MCP), racist, sectarian, sexist, zealot
▄ humanitarian, liberal

bigoted *adj* biased, blinkered, closed, dogmatic, fanatical, illiberal, intolerant, narrow, narrow-minded, opinionated, partial, prejudiced, twisted, warped
▄ broad-minded, enlightened, liberal, tolerant

bigotry *n* bias, chauvinism, discrimination, dogmatism, fanaticism, intolerance, jingoism, narrow-mindedness, partiality, prejudice, racialism, racism, sectarianism, sexism, unfairness
▄ tolerance

bigwig *n* big cheese *colloq*, big gun *colloq*, big noise *colloq*, big shot *colloq*, dignitary, heavyweight *colloq*, mogul, nob *colloq*, notable, panjandrum, personage, somebody, VIP
▄ nobody, nonentity

bile *n* anger, bad temper, bitterness, choler, gall, ill-humour, irascibility, irritability, peevishness, rancour, short temper, spleen, testiness

bilge *n* claptrap *colloq*, cobblers *colloq*, codswallop *colloq*, drivel, gibberish, hot air *colloq*, nonsense, piffle *colloq*, poppycock *colloq*, rot *colloq*, rubbish, tommyrot *colloq*, trash, tripe, twaddle

bilious *adj* **1** *a bilious old man:* bad-tempered, choleric, crabby, cross, crotchety, grouchy, grumpy, ill-humoured, ill-tempered, irritable, peevish, short-tempered, testy **2** *feeling bilious:* nauseated, out of sorts *colloq*, queasy, sick, sickly **3** *bilious colours:* disgusting, garish, nauseating, sickly

bilk *v* bamboozle *colloq*, cheat, con *colloq*, deceive, defraud, diddle *colloq*, do *colloq*, do out of *colloq*, fleece *slang*, sting *slang*, swindle, trick

bill¹ *n* **1** *a gas bill:* account, charges, check *US*, invoice, reckoning, score, statement, tab *US colloq*, tally **2** *advertising bills:* ad *colloq*, advert *colloq*, advertisement, announcement, broadsheet, bulletin, circular, flyer, handbill, handout, leaflet, notice, placard, playbill, poster, programme **3** *a parliamentary bill:* act, measure, (piece of) legislation, proposal, statute
♦ *v* **1** *bill you at the end of the month:* charge, debit, invoice, list costs, send a statement, send an account/invoice **2** *be billed to appear in a show:* advertise, announce, give notice, post

bill² *n* beak, mandible, neb, nib, rostrum

billet *n* **1** *an army billet:* accommodation, barracks, berth, housing, living quarters, lodging, quarters **2** *a billet as a caretaker:* employment, job, occupation, office, position, post, situation
♦ *v* accommodate, lodge, quarter, station

billow *v* balloon, bulge, expand, fill out, heave, puff out, rise, roll, surge, swell, undulate
♦ *n* **1** *billows crashing on the rocks:* breaker, flood, surge, wave **2** *billows of smoke:* cloud, flood, rush, surge

billowy *adj* **1** *billowy clouds:* billowing, rolling, surging, swirling **2** *billowy waters:* billowing, heaving, rippling, rolling, surging, swelling, swirling, undulating, waving

bin *n* basket, box, chest, container, receptacle

bind *v* **1** *bind with string:* attach, chain, fasten, fetter, lash, rope, secure, shackle, stick, strap, tape, tether, tie, truss **2** *bind a wound:* bandage, cover, dress, wrap **3** *bound by the terms of the contract:* compel, confine, constrain, force, hamper, impel, necessitate, oblige, require, restrain, restrict **4** *bound together by a common grief:* bond, join, tie, unify, unite
♦ *n* **1** *it's a bind having to find babysitters:* bore, drag *colloq*, inconvenience, irritation,

nuisance **2** *we're in a bind*: difficulty, dilemma, hole, impasse, predicament, quandary, spot *colloq*, tight spot *colloq*

binding *adj* compulsory, conclusive, indissoluble, irrevocable, mandatory, necessary, obligatory, permanent, requisite, rigorous, strict, stringent, tight, unalterable, unbreakable, valid
♦ *n* border, cover, covering, edging, tape, trimming, wrapping

binge *n* beano *colloq*, bender *colloq*, blind *colloq*, bout, do *colloq*, fling, jag, orgy, spree
🖪 fast

biography *n* account, autobiography, curriculum vitae, cv, history, life, life story, profile, prosopography *formal*

biology

Biological terms include:
bacteriology, biochemistry, biology, bionics, botany, cybernetics, cytology, Darwinism, neo-Darwinism, ecology, embryology, endocrinology, evolution, Haeckel's law, genetics, Mendelism, Lamarckism, marine biology, natural history, palaeontology, pathology, physiology, systematics, taxonomy, zoology; amino acid, anatomy, animal behaviour, animal kingdom, bacillus, bacteria, biologist, botanist, cell, chromosome, class, coccus, conservation, corpuscle, cultivar, cytoplasm, deoxyribonucleic acid (DNA), diffusion, ecosystem, ectoplasm, embryo, endoplasmic reticulum (ER), enzyme, evolution, excretion, extinction, flora and fauna, food chain, fossil, gene, genetic engineering, genetic fingerprinting, population genetics, germ, Golgi apparatus, hereditary factor, homeostasis, living world, meiosis, membrane, metabolism, micro-organism, microbe, mitosis, molecule, mutation, natural selection, nuclear membrane, nucleus, nutrition, order, organism, osmosis, parasitism, photosynthesis, pollution, protein, protoplasm, reproduction, respiration, reticulum, ribonucleic acid (RNA), ribosome, secretion, survival of the fittest, symbiosis, virus

---

bird

Birds include:
sparrow, thrush, starling, blackbird, bluetit, chaffinch, greenfinch, bullfinch, dunnock, robin, wagtail, swallow, tit, wren, martin, swift, crow, magpie, dove, pigeon, skylark, nightingale, linnet, warbler, jay, jackdaw, rook, raven, cuckoo, woodpecker, yellowhammer; duck, mallard, eider, teal, swan, goose, heron, stork, flamingo, pelican, kingfisher, moorhen, coot, lapwing, peewit, plover, curlew, snipe, avocet, seagull, guillemot, tern, petrel, crane, bittern, albatross, gannet, cormorant, auk, puffin, dipper; eagle, owl, hawk, sparrowhawk, falcon, kestrel, osprey, buzzard, vulture, condor; emu, ostrich, kiwi, peacock, penguin; chicken, grouse, partridge, pheasant, quail, turkey; canary, budgerigar, budgie *colloq*, cockatiel, cockatoo, lovebird, parakeet, parrot, macaw, toucan, myna bird, mockingbird, kookaburra, bird of paradise

---

birth *n* **1** *the birth of a baby*: arrival, childbirth, confinement, delivery, labour, nativity, parturition *formal*, patter of tiny feet *colloq* **2** *of noble birth*: ancestry, background, blood, breeding, derivation, descent, extraction, family, genealogy, house, line, lineage, origin(s), parentage, pedigree, race, stock, strain **3** *the birth of modern science*: advent *formal*, appearance, arrival, beginning, commencement, dawn, derivation, emergence, fountainhead, genesis, origin(s), rise, root, seed, source, start, starting-point
🖪 **1** death **3** conclusion, end, finish

birthday *n* anniversary, day of birth

birthmark *n* blemish, discoloration, mole, naevus, patch

birthplace *n* **1** *Mozart's birthplace*: home, home town, mother country, native country, native town, place of birth **2** *the birthplace of modern art*: cradle, fount, home, place of origin, provenance, root(s), source

birthright *n* due, inheritance, legacy, prerogative, privilege, right

biscuit *n* cookie, cracker, hardtack, rusk, wafer

bisect *v* bifurcate *formal*, cross, cut in half, divide, divide in two, halve, intersect, separate, split

bisexual *adj* **1** *worms are bisexual*: androgynous, gynandromorphic *technical*, gynandromorphous *technical*, hermaphrodite, monoclinous **2** *a bisexual man*: AC/DC *colloq*, ambidextrous *colloq*, bi *colloq*, epicene
🖪 **2** heterosexual, homosexual

bishop *n* archbishop, diocesan, metropolitan, patriarch, prelate, primate, suffragan

bit *n* **1** *a tiny bit*: atom, chip, chunk, crumb, dash, drop, flake, fragment, grain, hint, iota, jot, lump, mite, morsel, mouthful, part, particle, piece, portion, scintilla, scrap, segment, shred, slice, sliver, small piece, soupçon, speck, tittle, touch, trace, vestige, whit **2** *wait a bit*: few minutes, few moments, jiffy *colloq*, minute, moment, short time, tick *colloq*, while

bitch *n* **1** *a bitch and her puppies*: female dog **2** *that woman's a bitch*: cat *colloq*, cow *slang*, harpy, shrew, virago, vixen
♦ *v* bad-mouth *colloq*, complain, criticize, find fault with, gripe *colloq*, grumble, moan, slag off *colloq*, talk about behind their back, whine *colloq*, whinge *colloq*

bitchy *adj* backbiting, catty, cruel, cutting, malicious, mean, nasty, rancorous *formal*, shrewish, snide, spiteful, venomous, vicious, vindictive, vixenish
🖪 kind, loving

bite *v* **1** *bite an apple*: champ, chew, crunch, eat, gnaw, masticate *formal*, munch, nibble, peck **2** *the dog bit her hand*: nip, rend, sink/get your teeth into, snap, tear, wound **3** *acid biting into the skin*: smart, sting, tingle **4** *the rise in costs was beginning to bite*: grip, hold, pinch, take effect, work
♦ *n* **1** *an insect bite*: nip, prick, puncture, snap, sting, wound **2** *have a bite to eat*: bit, light meal, morsel, mouthful, piece, refreshment, snack, taste **3** *a pasta dish with a little bite*: kick *colloq*, piquancy, punch *colloq*, pungency, spiciness

biting *adj* **1** *a biting wind*: bitter, cold, freezing, harsh, nipping, penetrating, piercing, severe, sharp, stinging **2** *a biting remark*: bitter, caustic, cutting, cynical, hurtful, incisive, mordant *formal*, raw, scathing, sharp, stinging, tart, trenchant *formal*
1 mild **2** bland

bitter *adj* **1** *a bitter taste*: acerbic *formal*, acid, acrid *formal*, astringent *formal*, pungent, sharp, sour, tangy, tart, unsweetened, vinegary **2** *bitter about the way he was treated*: acrimonious *formal*, aggrieved, angry, begrudging, embittered, hostile, indignant, rancorous *formal*, resentful, sour, sullen, with a chip on your shoulder *colloq* **3** *a bitter remark*: acerbic *formal*, acrimonious *formal*, caustic, cynical, rancorous *formal*, scathing, sour, spiteful, venomous, vindictive, virulent *formal*, vitriolic *formal*, vituperative *formal* **4** *a bitter experience*: cruel, disappointing, distressing, fierce, harrowing, harsh, heartbreaking, heart-rending, intense, merciless, painful, sad, savage, severe, tragic, unhappy **5** *bitter winds*: arctic, biting, freezing, freezing cold, harsh, penetrating, piercing, raw, sharp, stinging
1 sweet **2** contented **4** happy, mild **5** warm

bitterness *n* **1** *the bitterness of lemon juice*: acidity, pungency, sharpness, sourness, tanginess, tartness, vinegar **2** *his bitterness against his ex-wife*: acerbity *formal*, acrimony *formal*, anger, cynicism, embitterment, grudge, hostility, indignation, malevolence *formal*, rancour *formal*, resentment, sourness, spite, venom, vindictiveness, virulence *formal* **3** *the bitterness of her disappointment*: cruelty, distress, ferocity, harshness, intensity, pain, painfulness, sadness, severity, tragedy, unhappiness **4** *the bitterness of the wind*: bite, coldness, harshness, penetration, rawness, sharpness

bizarre *adj* abnormal, curious, deviant, eccentric, extraordinary, fantastic, freakish, grotesque, ludicrous, odd, oddball *colloq*, offbeat *colloq*, outlandish, peculiar, queer, strange, uncommon, unconventional, unusual, wacky *colloq*, way-out *slang*, weird
normal, ordinary, standard

blab *v* blurt out, disclose, divulge, gossip, leak *colloq*, let slip, reveal, squeal *colloq*, tattle, tell
hide, hush up

black *adj* **1** *a black cat*: black as coal *colloq*, coal-black, dusky, ebony, inky, jet, jet-black, nigrescent *formal*, pitch-black, raven, sable, sooty, swarthy **2** *black athletes*: coloured, dark-skinned, melanistic *technical*, Negro, Negroid, swarthy **3** *a black night*: Cimmerian *formal*, crepuscular *formal*, dark, dim, dusky, fuliginous *formal*, moonless, overcast, pitch-black, starless, Stygian *formal*, subfusc *formal*, tenebrous *formal*, unilluminated, unlit **4** *black with dirt*: dirty, filthy, grimy, grubby, muddy, soiled, sooty, stained, unclean **5** *the future looks black*: awful, bleak, depressing, dismal, distressing, gloomy, hopeless, sad **6** *a black despair*: depressed, gloomy, lugubrious *formal*, melancholy, miserable, mournful, sad, sombre **7** *in a black mood*: angry, bitter, resentful, sullen
1 white **2** white **3** bright **4** clean **5** bright
♦ *v* **1** *black someone's eye*: blacken, bruise, hit, injure, punch **2** *they blacked the imported goods*:

ban, bar, blacklist, boycott, embargo, taboo **3** *sections of the report have been blacked*: censor, gag, suppress, withhold
▶ **black out 1** *black out with the pain*: collapse, faint, flake out *colloq*, lose consciousness, pass out **2** *shutters which black out the light*: cover up, darken, eclipse

blackball *v* ban, bar, blacklist, drum out, exclude, expel, give the cold shoulder to *colloq*, ostracize, oust, reject, repudiate, shut out, snub, throw out, veto, vote against

blacken *v* **1** *face blackened by soot*: darken, dirty, make dirty, smudge, soil **2** *blacken someone's reputation*: besmirch, calumniate *formal*, decry *formal*, defame, defile, detract, discredit, dishonour, impugn *formal*, libel, malign, revile, run down *colloq*, slander, smear, stain, sully, taint, tarnish, vilify *formal*
2 enhance, praise

blackguard *n* bleeder *colloq*, blighter *colloq*, bounder *colloq*, devil, knave, miscreant, rascal, reprobate, rogue, rotter *colloq*, scoundrel, scumbag *colloq*, stinker *colloq*, swine *colloq*, villain, wretch

blacklist *v* ban, bar, boycott, debar, disallow, exclude, expel, ostracize, outlaw, preclude *formal*, proscribe *formal*, reject, repudiate, shut out, snub, taboo, veto
accept, allow

blackmail *n* chantage *formal*, exaction, extortion, intimidation
♦ *v* bleed *colloq*, coerce, compel, demand, exact, extort, force, hold to ransom, lean on *colloq*, milk *colloq*, squeeze *colloq*, threaten

blackmailer *n* bloodsucker, extortioner, extortionist, vampire

blackout *n* **1** *a city-wide blackout*: electricity failure, power cut, power failure **2** *suffer from blackouts*: coma, faint, flaking-out *colloq*, loss of consciousness, oblivion, swoon, syncope *technical*, unconsciousness **3** *a news blackout*: censorship, concealment, cover-up *colloq*, embargo, secrecy, suppression, withholding

blade *n* cutting edge, dagger, edge, knife, razor, scalpel, sword, vane

blame *v* **1** *blamed him for the accident*: accuse, attribute liability, charge, find guilty, hold responsible, point the finger at *colloq*, say something is someone's fault, scapegoat, tax **2** *I don't blame you for leaving*: berate *formal*, censure, chide, condemn, criticize, disapprove, find fault with, rebuke, reprehend, reprimand, reproach, reprove, tear into *colloq*, upbraid
1 exonerate, vindicate **2** vindicate
♦ *n* **1** *take the blame for something*: accountability, censure, charge, culpability *formal*, fault, guilt, incrimination, liability, rap *slang*, responsibility **2** *got a lot of blame for his actions*: accusation, berating *formal*, censure, condemnation, criticism, recrimination, reprimand, reproach, reproof, stick *slang*

blameless *adj* above reproach, faultless, guiltless, innocent, irreproachable, perfect, sinless, stainless, unblamable, unblemished, unimpeachable, upright, virtuous, without fault
blameworthy, guilty

blameworthy *adj* at fault, culpable *formal*, discreditable, disreputable, flagitious *formal*,

guilty, indefensible, inexcusable, reprehensible, reproachable, shameful, unworthy
☒ blameless

blanch v 1 *blanch at the sight:* go/become/turn white, grow/become pallid, grow/become/turn pale, whiten 2 *blanch vegetables:* boil, scald
☒ 1 blush, colour, redden

bland adv 1 *a bland person/statement:* boring, characterless, dull, flat, humdrum, inoffensive, monotonous, mundane, nondescript, ordinary, tedious, unexciting, uninspiring, uninteresting 2 *a bland dish:* flavourless, insipid, mild, tasteless, weak
☒ 1 exciting, lively, stimulating 2 piquant, rich, tasty

blandishments n blarney, cajolery, coaxing, compliments, fawning, flattery, ingratiation, inveiglement *formal,* persuasiveness, soft soap *colloq,* sweet talk *colloq,* sycophancy, wheedling

blank adj 1 *a blank page:* bare, clean, clear, empty, plain, unfilled, unmarked, unwritten-on, void, white 2 *a blank look:* apathetic, deadpan, emotionless, empty, expressionless, glazed, impassive, indifferent, inscrutable, lifeless, poker-faced, uninterested, vacant, vacuous, without feeling
♦ n 1 *my mind is a blank:* emptiness, empty space, nothingness, vacuity, vacuum, void 2 *fill in the blanks on the form:* empty space, gap, space

blanket n 1 *blankets on a bed:* bedcover, bedspread, cover, covering, coverlet 2 *a blanket of snow:* carpet, cloak, coat, coating, cover, covering, film, layer, mantle, overlay, sheet
♦ v cloak, cloud, coat, conceal, cover, eclipse, hide, mask, obscure, overlay
♦ adj across-the-board, all-embracing, all-inclusive, comprehensive, global, inclusive, overall, sweeping, total, wide-ranging

blare v blast (out), boom (out), clang, honk, hoot, peal, resound, ring, roar, sound loudly, thunder, trumpet

blarney n blandishments, cajolery, coaxing, flattery, persuasiveness, soft soap *colloq,* spiel *colloq,* sweet talk *colloq,* wheedling

blasé adj apathetic, bored, cool, indifferent, jaded, lukewarm, nonchalant, offhand, phlegmatic *formal,* unconcerned, unexcited, unimpressed, uninspired, uninterested, unmoved, weary
☒ enthusiastic, excited, responsive

blaspheme v 1 *blaspheme in public:* curse, cuss *colloq,* desecrate, execrate *formal,* imprecate *formal,* profane, swear, utter oaths, utter profanities 2 *blaspheme someone:* abuse, anathematize *formal,* curse, damn, revile

blasphemous adj godless, impious, imprecatory *formal,* irreligious, irreverent, profane, sacrilegious, ungodly

blasphemy n 1 *an act of blasphemy:* desecration, impiety, impiousness, irreverence, outrage, profaneness, profanity, sacrilege, ungodliness, unholiness, violation 2 *uttering blasphemies:* curse, cursing, execration *formal,* expletive, imprecation *formal,* oaths, profanity, swearing

blast n 1 *a bomb blast:* bang, burst, clap, crack, crash, detonation, discharge, explosion, outburst, volley 2 *a blast of cold air:* draught, gale, gust, rush, squall, storm, tempest 3 *a blast of noise:*

blare, blaring, boom, booming, clamour, clang, honk, hoot, peal, roar, roaring, scream, shriek, sound, thunder, wail
♦ v 1 *a bomb blasted the building:* blow to pieces, blow up, burst, demolish, destroy, explode, ruin, shatter 2 *music blasting out:* blare (out), boom (out), clang, honk, hoot, peal, roar, scream, shriek, sound, thunder, wail 3 *blasted for his failure:* berate *formal,* criticize, rebuke, reprimand, reprove, tell off, upbraid
▶ **blast off** be launched, lift off, take off

blatant adj arrant, barefaced, brazen, conspicuous, flagrant, glaring, manifest, obtrusive, obvious, open, ostentatious, out and out, outright, overt, patent, sheer, undisguised, unmitigated

---

blatant or *flagrant*? *Blatant* means 'glaringly or shamelessly obvious': *a blatant lie. Flagrant* implies a greater degree of condemnation and means 'scandalous, very obvious and wicked': *a flagrant misuse of his powers.*

---

blaze n 1 *firemen fighting the blaze:* bonfire, conflagration *formal,* fire, flames, flare-up, inferno 2 *a blaze of light:* beam, brilliance, burst, flash, glare, gleam, glitter, glow, light, outburst, radiance
♦ v 1 *the fire was blazing:* burn, burst into flames, catch fire, flame, flare (up), ignite 2 *blazing with light:* be brilliant, be radiant, beam, flare, flash, glare, gleam, glitter, glow, light, shine 3 *blazing with anger:* blow up, boil, burn, burst, erupt, explode, fire, flash, rage, see red *colloq,* seethe

blazon v announce, broadcast, celebrate, flaunt, flourish, make known, proclaim, publicize, trumpet, vaunt
☒ deprecate, hush up

bleach v blanch, decolorize, decolour, etiolate *technical,* fade, lighten, make pale, make white, pale, peroxide, whiten

bleak adj 1 *a bleak future:* cheerless, comfortless, dark, depressing, desperate, discouraging, disheartening, dismal, drab, dreary, gloomy, grim, hopeless, joyless, miserable, sombre, unpromising, wretched 2 *a bleak landscape:* bare, barren, desolate, empty, exposed, open, unsheltered, windswept, windy 3 *a bleak winter's day:* chilly, cold, dreary, dull, raw, weather-beaten
☒ 1 bright, cheerful 3 bright, fine, pleasant

bleary adj bleary-eyed, blurred, blurry, cloudy, dim, rheumy, tired, watery

bleat v 1 *sheep bleating:* baa, blat *US,* call, cry 2 *bleating about price increases:* complain, grumble, moan, whine *colloq,* whinge *colloq*

bleed v 1 *bleed from a wound:* exsanguinate *technical,* extravasate, exude, flow, gush, haemorrhage, lose blood, ooze, run, seep, shed blood, spurt, trickle, weep 2 *bleed of resources:* deplete *formal,* drain, exhaust, milk, sap, squeeze, suck dry 3 *bleed money from someone:* extort, extract, milk *colloq,* squeeze *colloq*

blemish n 1 *a blemish on her skin:* blot, blotch, deformity, discoloration, disfigurement, mark, smudge, speck, stain 2 *a blemish on his character:* defect, disgrace, dishonour, fault, flaw, imperfection, stain, taint
♦ v 1 *leaves blemished by black spots:* blot, deface,

disfigure, mar, mark, spot, stain, tarnish
2 *a reputation blemished by scandal:* compromise, damage, flaw, impair, mar, spoil, stain, sully, taint, tarnish

blench *v* cower, falter, flinch, quail, quake, quiver, recoil, shrink, shudder, shy, start, wince

blend *v* **1** *blend the ingredients:* admix *formal*, alloy, amalgamate, beat, coalesce, combine, commingle *formal*, commix *formal*, compound, fuse, homogenize, intermix *formal*, intertwine, interweave, merge, mingle, mix, stir, synthesize, unite, whisk **2** *colours that blend with this one:* complement, fit, go (well) with, go together, harmonize, match, set off, suit
◼ **1** divide, separate
♦ *n* admixture *formal*, alloy, amalgam, amalgamation, combination, commixture *formal*, composite, compound, concoction, cross between two things, fusion, merging, mix, mixture, synthesis, union, uniting

bless *v* **1** *the bishop blessed the new priests:* anoint, consecrate, dedicate, hallow, ordain, sanctify **2** *bless God's name:* exalt, extol, glorify, laud *formal*, magnify, praise **3** *the priest blessed the congregation:* ask God's favour for, ask God's protection for
◼ **1** curse **2** condemn

blessed *adj* **1** *the blessed saints:* adored, divine, hallowed, holy, revered, sacred, sanctified **2** *a blessed event:* fortunate, glad, happy, joyful, joyous, lucky, prosperous **3** *blessed with a good memory:* endowed, favoured, graced, provided
◼ **1** cursed **2** sad, unhappy

blessing *n* **1** *a blessing by the priest:* benediction, benison *formal*, consecration, darshan *technical*, dedication, grace, invocation *formal*, kiddush, thanksgiving **2** *count your blessings:* advantage, benefit, bounty, favour, gain, gift, godsend, good fortune, good thing, help, profit, windfall **3** *give a proposal your blessing:* agreement, approbation *formal*, approval, authority, backing, concurrence *formal*, consent, leave, permission, sanction, support
◼ **2** blight, curse **3** condemnation

blight *n* **1** *affected by planning blight:* affliction, bane, calamity, contamination, corruption, curse, decay, evil, misfortune, pollution, scourge, trouble, woe **2** *potato blight:* cancer, canker, disease, fungus, infestation, mildew, rot
◼ **1** benefaction, blessing, boon, bounty, favour, godsend, help
♦ *v* annihilate, blast, crush, damage, dash, destroy, frustrate, injure, mar, ruin, shatter, spoil, undermine, wreck
◼ bless

blind *adj* **1** *a blind man:* eyeless, sightless, unseeing, unsighted, visionless **2** *blind to their needs:* ignorant, imperceptive, inattentive, inconsiderate, indifferent, insensitive, neglectful, oblivious, thoughtless, unaware, unconscious, unobservant **3** *love is blind:* careless, hasty, heedless, impetuous, impulsive, indiscriminate, injudicious, irrational, mad, mindless, rash, reckless, uncritical, unreasoning, unthinking, wild **4** *a blind alley:* closed, obstructed **5** *a blind bend:* hidden, obscured, out of sight
◼ **1** sighted
♦ *v* **1** *blinded in the accident:* cause to lose your vision, deprive of sight, deprive of vision, gouge

the eyes out of, make blind, put the eyes out of **2** *blinded by the car's headlights:* block your vision, dazzle, obscure your vision **3** *blinded by prejudice:* cause to lose reason/sense, deceive, mislead
♦ *n* **1** *a window blind:* Austrian blind, cover, curtain, roller blind, screen, shutter, Venetian blind, (window) shade **2** *operate as a blind for illegal activities:* camouflage, cloak, cover, cover-up *colloq*, distraction, façade, front, mask, masquerade, smokescreen

blindly *adv* **1** *feel your way blindly:* sightlessly, unseeingly, without sight, without vision **2** *follow someone blindly:* carelessly, impetuously, impulsively, incautiously, indiscriminately, irrationally, madly, mindlessly, rashly, recklessly, senselessly, thoughtlessly, uncritically, unthinkingly, wildly
◼ **2** cautiously, critically

blink *v* **1** *his eye blinked:* nictate *formal*, nictitate *formal*, wink **2** *the light blinked:* flash, flicker, gleam, glimmer, glitter, scintillate, shine, sparkle, twinkle

bliss *n* blessedness, blissfulness, ecstasy, elation, euphoria, gladness, happiness, heaven, joy, nirvana, paradise, rapture, seventh heaven, utopia
◼ damnation, hell, misery

blissful *adj* delighted, ecstatic, elated, enchanted, enraptured, euphoric, happy, idyllic, joyful, joyous, rapturous
◼ miserable, wretched

blister *n* abscess, bleb *technical*, boil, bulla, canker, carbuncle, cyst, furuncle, papilla, papula, pimple, pompholyx, pustule, sore, swelling, ulcer, vesicle, vesicula, wen

blistering *adj* **1** *blistering heat:* extreme, hot, intense, scorching, withering **2** *blistering criticism:* caustic, cruel, fierce, sarcastic, savage, scathing, vicious

blithe *adj* carefree, careless, casual, cheerful, heedless, light-hearted, thoughtless, uncaring, unconcerned, unthinking, untroubled
◼ morose, serious, thoughtful

blitz *n* **1** *the blitz during the war:* attack, blitzkrieg, bombardment, campaign, offensive, onslaught, raid, strike **2** *have a blitz on the garden:* all-out effort, attack, attempt, campaign, effort, endeavour, exertion

blizzard *n* snowstorm, squall, storm, tempest

bloated *adj* **1** *a bloated face:* blown up, dilated, distended *formal*, enlarged, expanded, inflated, puffy, swollen **2** *feeling bloated:* blown up, full, stuffed
◼ **1** shrivelled, shrunken, thin

blob *n* ball, bead, bubble, dab, drop, droplet, glob *colloq*, globule, gob, lump, mass, pearl, pellet, pill, splash, spot

bloc *n* alliance, axis, cabal, cartel, clique, coalition, entente, faction, federation, group, league, ring, syndicate, union

block *n* **1** *a block of offices:* building, development, structure **2** *a block of stone:* bar, brick, cake, chunk, cube, hunk, lump, mass, piece, slab, square, wedge **3** *a block of seats/tickets:* batch, cluster, quantity, section, series **4** *a block in the tube:* blockage, impediment, jam, obstacle, obstruction, stoppage **5** *a block to success:* bar, barrier, delay, deterrent, drawback,

hindrance, impediment, let, obstacle, resistance, stumbling-block
♦ *v* **1** *block a pipe*: be in the way, bung up *colloq*, choke, clog, close, dam up, impede, obstruct, plug, seal, stop up **2** *block progress*: arrest, bar, check, deter, frustrate, halt, hinder, impede, obstruct, scotch, stonewall, stop, thwart

blockade *n* **1** *the blockade of the city*: closure, encirclement, investment *technical*, restriction, siege, stoppage **2** *set up blockades*: barricade, barrier, block, obstacle, obstruction
♦ *v* **1** *blockade the ports*: besiege, encircle, obstruct, surround **2** *blockaded from entering the town*: check, hinder, keep from, prevent, prevent entering/reaching, prevent using, stop

blockage *n* block, blocking, congestion, hindrance, impediment, jam, log-jam, obstruction, occlusion *formal*, stoppage

blockhead *n* dimwit *colloq*, dipstick *slang*, dork *slang*, dunce, fool, geek *slang*, idiot, imbecile, jerk *slang*, nerd *slang*, nincompoop *colloq*, ninny *colloq*, nitwit *colloq*, numskull *colloq*, twerp *colloq*, twit *colloq*, wally *slang*
🖻 brain, genius

bloke *n* boy, chap *colloq*, character, fellow, guy *colloq*, individual, male, man

blond, blonde *adj* **1** *blond hair*: bleached, fair, flaxen, golden, light-coloured, tow-coloured **2** *is she blonde or brunette?*: fair, fair-haired, golden-haired

blood *n* **1** *lose blood*: gore, lifeblood, vital fluid **2** *of aristocratic blood*: ancestry, birth, descendants, descent, extraction, family, kindred, kinship, lineage, relations

bloodcurdling *adj* appalling, chilling, dreadful, fearful, frightening, hair-raising, horrendous, horrible, horrid, horrifying, scary, spine-chilling, terrifying

bloodless *adj* **1** *a bloodless coup*: non-violent, peaceful, strife-free, unwarlike **2** *her bloodless face*: anaemic, ashen, chalky, colourless, drained, pale, pallid, pasty, sallow, sickly, wan **3** *a bloodless affair*: cold, feeble, insipid, languid, lifeless, listless, passionless, spiritless, torpid, unemotional, unfeeling
🖻 **1** bloody, violent **2** bloody, ruddy **3** vigorous

bloodshed *n* blood-bath, bloodletting, butchery, carnage, decimation, killing, massacre, murder, pogrom, slaughter, slaying

bloodsucker *n* blackmailer, extortioner, extortionist, leech *colloq*, parasite *colloq*, sponger *colloq*

bloodthirsty *adj* barbaric, barbarous, brutal, cruel, ferocious, homicidal, inhuman, murderous, ruthless, sanguinary *formal*, savage, vicious, warlike

bloody *adj* **1** *a bloody wound*: bleeding, bloodstained, gory, sanguinary *formal*, sanguine *formal*, sanguinolent *formal* **2** *a bloody crime*: bloodthirsty, brutal, cruel, ferocious, fierce, gory, murderous

bloom *n* **1** *colourful blooms*: blossom, bud, efflorescence *technical*, florescence, flower **2** *in the bloom of youth*: beauty, heyday, perfection, prime, strength, vigour **3** *skin with a healthy bloom*: beauty, blush, flush, freshness, glow, lustre, radiance, rosiness

♦ *v* **1** *the flowers were blooming*: blossom, bud, flower, open **2** *the children are blooming*: blossom, develop, flourish, grow, mature, thrive
🖻 **1** fade, wither

blooming *adj* **1** *blooming plants*: blossoming, florescent *technical*, flowering **2** *a blooming complexion*: bonny, healthy, rosy, ruddy
🖻 **2** ailing

blossom *n* bloom, bud, efflorescence *technical*, florescence, flower
♦ *v* **1** *the plants were blossoming*: bloom, burgeon *formal*, flower **2** *blossom into a beautiful young woman*: bloom, burgeon *formal*, develop, flourish, mature **3** *her career blossomed*: flourish, prosper, succeed, thrive
🖻 **1** fade, wither

blot *n* **1** *an ink blot*: blemish, blotch, mark, smear, smudge, speck, splodge, spot, stain **2** *a blot on his reputation*: black mark, blemish, defect, disgrace, fault, flaw, imperfection, stain, taint, tarnishing
♦ *v* **1** *blot a surface*: mark, smudge, spot, stain **2** *blot liquid*: absorb, dry (up), soak (up) **3** *blotted his character*: disgrace, mar, spoil, stain, sully, taint, tarnish
▶ **blot out 1** *clouds blotting out the sun*: conceal, darken, eclipse, efface *formal*, hide, obliterate, obscure, screen, shadow **2** *blot out a memory*: delete, erase, expunge *formal*

blotch *n* blemish, blot, mark, patch, smudge, splash, splodge, splotch, spot, stain

blotchy *adj* blemished, inflamed, patchy, reddened, spotted, spotty

blow[1] *v* **1** *the wind was blowing*: blast, flurry, gust **2** *the breeze blew leaves along the road*: blast, buffet, drive, fan, fling, move, sweep, waft, whirl, whisk **3** *hair blowing in the breeze*: float, flow, flutter, stream, waft, whirl, whisk **4** *blow into a paper bag*: breathe, breathe out, exhale *formal*, pant, puff (out) **5** *blow a horn*: blare, blast, pipe, play, sound, toot, trumpet **6** *blow a lot of money*: dissipate *formal*, fritter away, misspend, pour down the drain *colloq*, spend freely, spend like water *colloq* **7** *blow a chance*: make a mess of, miss out on, miss the boat *colloq*, ruin, screw up *slang*, spoil, waste, wreck
♦ *n* blast, draught, flurry, gale, gust, puff, squall, tempest, wind
▶ **blow out** extinguish *formal*, put out, smother, snuff out
▶ **blow over** cease, die down, disappear, dissipate *formal*, end, finish, fizzle out, pass, peter out, subside, vanish
▶ **blow up 1** *the bomb blew up*: blast, burst, detonate, explode, go off, go up **2** *blow up a balloon*: dilate, distend *formal*, expand, fill (out), inflate, puff up, pump up **3** *blew up the story out of all proportion*: exaggerate, overstate, puff up **4** *my boss suddenly blew up at me*: become angry, blow your top *colloq*, flip (your lid) *colloq*, fly off the handle *colloq*, get into a rage, go ape *US slang*, go ballistic *colloq*, go mad *colloq*, hit the roof *colloq*, lose your temper

blow[2] *n* **1** *a blow on the head*: bang, bash, belt *colloq*, biff *slang*, box, buffet, clap, clip, clout *colloq*, cuff, hit, hook, knock, punch, rap, slap, smack, sock *slang*, stroke, swipe, thump, wallop *colloq*, whack *colloq* **2** *a bitter blow*: affliction, bolt from the blue *colloq*, bombshell, calamity, catastrophe, comedown, disappointment, disaster, jolt, misfortune, reverse, rude awakening *colloq*, setback, shock, shocker *colloq*, upset

blow-out *n* **1** *a blow-out on the motorway*: burst tyre, flat *colloq*, flat tyre, puncture **2** *a blow-out for his birthday*: bash *colloq*, beanfeast *colloq*, binge *colloq*, celebration, feast, knees-up *colloq*, party, rave *colloq*, rave-up *colloq*

blowy *adj* blustery, breezy, fresh, gusty, squally, stormy, windy

blowzy *adj* bedraggled, dishevelled, messy, slipshod, sloppy, slovenly, tousled, ungroomed, unkempt, untidy
🗲 neat, smart

blubber *v* blub, cry, sniffle, snivel, sob, weep, whimper

bludgeon *v* **1** *bludgeon to death*: batter, beat, clobber *colloq*, club, cosh *colloq*, cudgel, hit, strike **2** *bludgeoned into agreeing*: badger, browbeat, bulldoze, bully, coerce, compel, dragoon, force, harass, hector, intimidate, pressurize, terrorize
♦ *n* baton, club, cosh, cudgel, truncheon

blue *adj* **1** *a blue dress*: aquamarine, azure, cerulean, cobalt, cyan, indigo, navy, navy blue, royal blue, sapphire, sky-blue, turquoise, ultramarine **2** *feeling blue*: dejected, depressed, despondent, dismal, dispirited, down in the dumps *colloq*, downcast, downhearted, fed up *colloq*, gloomy, glum, low, melancholy, miserable, morose, sad, unhappy **3** *a blue joke*: adult *colloq*, bawdy, coarse, dirty, erotic, improper, indecent, lewd, near the bone *colloq*, near the knuckle *colloq*, obscene, offensive, pornographic, raunchy *colloq*, risqué, smutty, steamy *colloq*, vulgar
🗲 **2** cheerful, happy **3** clean, decent

blueprint *n* **1** *a blueprint for the town's future*: draft, guide, outline, pilot, plan, programme, project, scheme, sketch, strategy **2** *a blueprint of the engine*: archetype, design, draft, model, outline, pattern, plan, prototype, representation, scheme, sketch

blues *n* dejection, depression, despondency, doldrums, dumps *colloq*, gloom, gloominess, glumness, melancholy, miseries, moodiness
🗲 euphoria

bluff¹ *v* bamboozle *colloq*, deceive, delude, fake, feign, fool, hoodwink, lie, mislead, pretend, sham
♦ *n* braggadocio *formal*, bravado, deceit, deception, fake, feint, fraud, humbug, idle boast, lie, pretence, sham, show, subterfuge, trick

bluff² *adj* affable, blunt, candid, direct, downright, frank, genial, good-natured, hearty, open, outspoken, plain-spoken, straightforward
🗲 diplomatic, refined
♦ *n* bank, brow, cliff, crag, escarp, escarpment, foreland, headland, height, peak, precipice, promontory, ridge, scarp

blunder *n* bloomer *colloq*, boob *colloq*, booboo *colloq*, clanger *colloq*, cock-up *slang*, error, fault, faux pas, gaffe, howler *colloq*, indiscretion, misjudgement, mistake, oversight, slip, slip-up *colloq*, solecism *formal*
♦ *v* **1** *afraid I've blundered again*: botch *colloq*, bungle, cock up *slang*, err, fluff *colloq*, get wrong, go wrong, goof *colloq*, make a mistake, miscalculate, misjudge, mismanage, screw up

slang, slip up *colloq* **2** *blunder into a table*: bumble, flounder, stumble

blunt *adj* **1** *a blunt knife*: dull, edgeless, not sharp, pointless, rounded, unsharpened, worn **2** *blunt to the point of rudeness*: abrupt, brusque, calling a spade a spade *colloq*, candid, curt, direct, downright, explicit, forthright, frank, honest, impolite, insensitive, not beating about the bush *colloq*, not mincing your words *colloq*, outspoken, plain-spoken, rude, speaking your mind *colloq*, stark, straightforward, tactless, unceremonious, uncivil
🗲 **1** pointed, sharp **2** subtle, tactful
♦ *v* abate, allay, alleviate, anaesthetize, dampen, deaden, dull, hebetate *formal*, numb, soften, take the edge off, weaken
🗲 intensify, sharpen

blur *v* **1** *rain blurred the windscreen*: blotch, smear, smudge, spot, stain **2** *blurred memories/views*: becloud, befog, cloud, darken, dim, dull, fog, make vague/indistinct, mist, obscure, veil
♦ *n* **1** *a blur on the picture*: blotch, smear, smudge, spot, stain **2** *my memories are a blur*: cloudiness, confusion, dimness, fog, fuzziness, haze, indistinctness, mist, muddle, obscurity

blurb *n* advertisement, commendation, copy, hype *colloq*, puff, spiel *colloq*

blurred *adj* clouded, cloudy, dim, faint, foggy, fuzzy, hazy, ill-defined, indistinct, lacking definition, misty, obscure, out of focus, unclear, vague
🗲 clear, distinct

blurt
▶ **blurt out** blab *colloq*, call out, come out with, cry (out), disclose, divulge, ejaculate *formal*, exclaim, give the game away *colloq*, gush, leak, let out, let slip, let the cat out of the bag *colloq*, reveal, spill the beans *colloq*, spout, tell, utter
🗲 bottle up, hush up

blush *v* colour, flush, glow, go red, redden, turn red
🗲 blanch
♦ *n* colour, flush, glow, reddening, rosiness, ruddiness

blushing *adj* erubescent *formal*, flushed, glowing, red, rosy
🗲 pale, white

bluster *v* **1** *blustering about how fit she was*: boast, brag, crow, show off, strut, swagger, talk big *colloq*, vaunt **2** *blustering to get his own way*: bully, harangue, hector, rant, roar, storm
♦ *n* bluff, boasting, braggadocio *formal*, bravado, crowing, swagger

blustery *adj* gusty, squally, stormy, tempestuous, violent, wild, windy
🗲 calm

board *n* **1** *a wooden board*: beam, panel, plank, sheet, slab, slat, timber **2** *a board of directors*: advisers, advisory group, commission, committee, council, directorate, directors, governors, head office, jury, management, panel, trustees **3** *bed and board*: food, grub *slang*, meals, nosh *slang*, provisions, rations, sustenance, victuals *formal*
♦ *v* catch, embark, embus *formal*, emplane *formal*, enter, entrain *formal*, get in/into, get on, mount
▶ **board up** close (up), cover (up), seal, shut (up)

boast *v* **1** *boasted about his qualifications:* blow your own horn *US colloq,* blow your own trumpet *colloq,* bluster, brag, crow, exaggerate, gasconade *formal,* loudmouth *colloq,* overstate, rodomontade *formal,* show off, sing your own praises, strut, swagger, swank *colloq,* talk big *colloq,* trumpet, vaunt **2** *boasts a new sauna:* enjoy, exhibit, possess, pride yourself on
▪ **1** belittle *formal,* deprecate *formal*
♦ *n* blustering, bragging, crowing, fanfaronade *formal,* gasconade *formal,* gasconism *formal,* hot air *colloq,* jactation *formal,* overstatement, rodomontade *formal,* self-praise, swank *colloq,* vaunt

boastful *adj* big-headed *colloq,* bragging, conceited, crowing, egotistical, proud, puffed up, self-flattering, swaggering, swanky *colloq,* swollen-headed *colloq,* vain, vainglorious *formal*
▪ humble, modest, self-effacing

boat

Types of boat or ship include:
canoe, dinghy, lifeboat, rowing-boat, kayak, coracle, skiff, punt, sampan, dhow, gondola, pedalo, catamaran, trimaran, yacht; cabin-cruiser, motor-boat, motor-launch, speedboat, trawler, barge, scow, narrow boat, houseboat, dredger, junk, smack, lugger; hovercraft, hydrofoil; clipper, cutter, ketch, packet, brig, schooner, square-rigger, galleon; ferry, paddle-steamer, tug, freighter, liner, container-ship, tanker; warship, battleship, destroyer, submarine, U-boat, frigate, aircraft-carrier, cruiser, dreadnought, corvette, minesweeper, man-of-war

---

boatman *n* bargee, ferryman, gondolier, oarsman, oarswoman, rower, sailor, voyageur, waterman, yachtsman, yachtswoman

bob *v* **1** *a balloon bobbing up and down:* bounce, float, move up and down, oscillate *formal,* quiver, shake, wobble **2** *bobbed back into the house:* hop, jerk, jolt, jump, leap, skip, spring **3** *the maid bobbed her head and left the room:* bow, curtsey, nod
▶ **bob up** appear, arise, emerge, materialize, pop up, rise, show up *colloq,* spring up, surface

bode *v* augur *formal,* betoken *formal,* forebode *formal,* foreshadow *formal,* foreshow *formal,* foretell, forewarn *formal,* herald, indicate, intimate, portend *formal,* predict, presage *formal,* prophesy, purport *formal,* signify, threaten, warn

bodily *adj* actual, carnal, concrete, corporeal *formal,* fleshly, material, physical, real, substantial, tangible
▪ spiritual
♦ *adv* altogether, as a whole, as one, collectively, completely, en masse, entirely, fully, in toto, totally, wholly
▪ piecemeal

body *n* **1** *his whole body was aching:* anatomy, build, figure, form, frame, physique **2** *arms folded across his body:* torso, trunk **3** *a body floating in the river:* cadaver, carcase, corpse, dead body, stiff *slang* **4** *sit in the body of the church:* central part, largest part, main part **5** *a charitable body:* association, authority, bloc, cartel, company, confederation, congress, corporation, council, group, organization, society, syndicate **6** *a huge body of people:* band, collection, crowd, group, mass, mob, multitude, phalanx, throng

7 *red wine with a good body:* consistency, density, essence, firmness, fullness, richness, solidity, substance

bodyguard *n* defender, guard, guardian, minder *slang,* protector

boffin *n* backroom-boy *colloq,* brain, designer, egghead *colloq,* engineer, genius, intellect, intellectual, inventor, mastermind, planner, scientist, thinker, wizard *colloq*

bog *n* fen, marsh, marshland, mire, morass, quag, quagmire, quicksands, slough, swamp, swampland, wetlands
▶ **bog down** delay, encumber, halt, hinder, hold up, impede *formal,* mire *formal,* overwhelm, retard *formal,* set back, slow down, slow up, stall, stick

boggle *v* amaze, astound, bowl over *colloq,* confuse, flabbergast *colloq,* overwhelm, stagger, surprise

boggy *adj* fenny, marshy, miry, morassy, muddy, oozy, paludal *formal,* quaggy, soft, spongy, swampy, waterlogged
▪ arid

bogus *adj* artificial, counterfeit, dummy, fake, false, forged, fraudulent, imitation, phoney *colloq,* pseud *colloq,* pseudo *colloq,* sham, spurious
▪ genuine, real, true, valid

bohemian *adj* alternative, artistic, arty *colloq,* avant-garde, bizarre, eccentric, exotic, nonconformist, oddball *colloq,* offbeat, off-the-wall *colloq,* original, unconventional, unorthodox, way-out *slang*
▪ bourgeois, conventional, orthodox
♦ *n* beatnik, drop-out, hippie, nonconformist
▪ conformist

boil¹ *v* **1** *boil the vegetables:* brew, bring to the boil, cook, heat, simmer, steam, stew **2** *wait till the water boils:* bubble, come to the boil, foam, froth, heat, seethe, simmer, steam **3** *boil with anger:* blow your top *colloq,* erupt, explode, fly into a rage *colloq,* fulminate *formal,* fume, go off the deep end *colloq,* hit the roof *colloq,* rage, rave, storm
▶ **boil down 1** *boil the sauce down:* concentrate, condense, distil, reduce **2** *boil the report down to the essential points:* abridge, abstract, digest, reduce, summarize

boil² *n* abscess, blister, carbuncle, gumboil, inflammation, pimple, pustule, tumour, ulcer

boiling *adj* **1** *boiling water:* bubbling, scalding, steaming, turbulent **2** *it's boiling in here:* baking, blistering, broiling *US,* hot, roasting, scorching, sweltering, torrid **3** *boiling with rage:* angry, enraged, flaming, fuming, furious, incensed, indignant, infuriated

boisterous *adj* active, clamorous, disorderly, energetic, exuberant, hyperactive, lively, loud, noisy, obstreperous, riotous, rollicking, romping, rough, rowdy, rumbustious *colloq,* spirited, turbulent, unrestrained, unruly, wild
▪ calm, docile, quiet, restrained

bold *adj* **1** *a bold adventurer:* adventurous, audacious, bold as a lion *colloq,* brave, confident, courageous, daring, dauntless, enterprising, fearless, gallant, heroic, intrepid, plucky, spirited, undaunted, valiant, valorous *formal,* venturesome **2** *a bold young hussy:* barefaced,

bold as brass *colloq*, brash, brassy *colloq*, brazen, cheeky *colloq*, forward, impudent, insolent, pert *colloq*, saucy *colloq*, shameless, unabashed **3** *bold colours*: bright, colourful, conspicuous, eye-catching, flamboyant, flashy, loud, prominent, pronounced, showy, striking, strong, vivid
Fᴀ 1 cautious, cowardly, nervous, shy, timid **2** diffident, modest, shy, timid **3** faint, restrained

bolshie *adj* awkward, bloody-minded *colloq*, difficult, obstinate, prickly, problem, rude, stroppy *colloq*, stubborn, unco-operative, unhelpful, unpleasant
Fᴀ amenable, co-operative, helpful, pleasant

bolster *v* aid, assist, augment *formal*, boost, brace, buoy up, buttress, firm up, help, invigorate, maintain, prop, reinforce, revitalize, shore up, stay, stiffen, strengthen, supplement, support
Fᴀ undermine
♦ *n* cushion, pillow, support

bolt *n* **1** *a bolt on a door*: bar, catch, fastener, latch, lock, rod, shaft **2** *nuts and bolts*: peg, pin, rivet, screw
♦ *v* **1** *bolt the door*: bar, fasten, latch, lock, secure **2** *bolt for the exit*: abscond *formal*, dash, escape, flee, fly, hurtle, run (away), run off, rush, sprint **3** *bolt your food down*: cram, devour, gobble, gorge, gulp, guzzle, stuff, wolf (down)

bomb *n* atom bomb, bombshell, car bomb, charge, depth charge, explosive, fire-bomb, grenade, hydrogen bomb, incendiary, letter bomb, mine, missile, Molotov cocktail, neutron bomb, nuclear bomb, petrol bomb, plastic bomb, projectile, rocket, shell, time bomb, torpedo
♦ *v* attack, blow up, bombard, destroy, shell, torpedo

bombard *v* **1** *bombard the airport*: assail, attack, besiege, blast, blitz, bomb, raid, shell, strafe, torpedo **2** *bombard with questions*: attack, bother, harass, hound, pester

bombardment *n* **1** *aerial bombardment*: air raid, assault, attack, barrage, blitz, bombing, cannonade, fire, flak, fusillade, salvo, shelling **2** *bombardment of questions*: attack, besieging, bothering, harassing, hounding, onslaught, pestering

bombastic *adj* affected, euphuistic *formal*, fustian *formal*, grandiloquent *formal*, grandiose, high-flown, inflated, magniloquent *formal*, ostentatious, pompous, portentous *formal*, pretentious, turgid, verbose, windy, wordy
Fᴀ reserved, restrained

bona fide *adj* actual, authentic, genuine, honest, kosher, lawful, legal, legitimate, real, the real McCoy *colloq*, true, valid
Fᴀ bogus

bonanza *n* blessing, boon, godsend, stroke of luck, sudden wealth, windfall

bond *n* **1** *bonds of friendship*: affiliation, affinity, attachment, binding, chemistry, connection, link, rapport, relation, relationship, tie(s), union, vinculum *formal* **2** *the legal bond of marriage*: agreement, contract, covenant, deal, obligation, pact, pledge, promise, transaction, treaty, word **3** *freed from his bonds*: binding, chain, cord, fetter, manacle, shackle

♦ *v* attach, bind, connect, fasten, fuse, glue, gum, join, paste, seal, stick, unite, weld

bondage *n* **1** *captives freed from bondage*: captivity, confinement, imprisonment, incarceration *formal*, restraint **2** *a life of bondage*: enslavement, serfdom, servitude, subjection, subjugation, subservience, thraldom *formal*, vassalage *formal*, yoke
Fᴀ 1 freedom **2** freedom, independence

bone

> **Human bones include:**
> clavicle, coccyx, collar-bone, femur, fibula, hip-bone, humerus, ilium, ischium, mandible, maxilla, metacarpal, metatarsal, patella, pelvic girdle, pelvis, pubis, radius, rib, scapula, shoulder-blade, skull, sternum, stirrup-bone, temporal, thigh-bone, tibia, ulna, vertebra

bonny *adj* **1** *a bonny lass*: attractive, beautiful, blooming, fair, fine, lovely, pretty **2** *bonny and blithe*: cheerful, cheery, joyful, merry
Fᴀ 1 ugly

bonus *n* **1** *pay a bonus*: commission, dividend, fringe benefits, gift, gratuity, handout, honorarium, lagniappe *formal*, premium, prize, reward, tip **2** *the good weather is a bonus*: advantage, benefit, extra, gain, perk *colloq*, perquisite *formal*, plus *colloq*
Fᴀ 1 disincentive **2** disadvantage

bony *adj* angular, drawn, emaciated, gangling, gaunt, lanky, lean, rawboned, scraggy, scrawny, skeletal, skinny, thin
Fᴀ fat, plump

book *n* booklet, publication, tome, tract, volume, work
♦ *v* **1** *book a ticket*: arrange (in advance), bag *colloq*, charter, engage, make a reservation for, order, organize, procure, reserve, schedule **2** *booked for assault*: accuse (of), blame, charge
Fᴀ 1 cancel
▶ **book in** check in, enrol, record your arrival, register

> **Types of book include:**
> hardback, paperback, bestseller; fiction, novel, story, thriller, detective, romantic novel, penny dreadful; children's book, primer, picture-book, annual; reference book, encyclopedia, dictionary, lexicon, thesaurus, concordance, anthology, compendium, omnibus, atlas, guidebook, gazetteer, directory, pocket companion, handbook, manual, cookbook, yearbook, almanac, catalogue; notebook, exercise book, textbook, scrapbook, album, sketchbook, diary, jotter, pad, ledger; libretto, manuscript, hymn-book, hymnal, prayer-book, psalter, missal, lectionary. See also **literature**

bookish *adj* academic, bluestocking, cultured, donnish, erudite, highbrow, intellectual, learned, lettered, literary, scholarly, scholastic, studious, well-read
Fᴀ lowbrow, unlettered

books *n* accounts, balance sheet, financial statement, ledgers, records

boom *v* **1** *cannons boomed in the distance*: bang, blare, blast, crash, explode, resound, reverberate, roar, roll, rumble, thunder **2** *business is booming*: develop, do well, escalate, expand, explode, flourish, gain, go from strength to strength, grow, increase, intensify, leap, mushroom, progress, prosper, strengthen, succeed, surge, swell, thrive

🔁 2 collapse, fail, slump

♦ *n* 1 *a boom of thunder:* bang, blare, blast, burst, clap, crash, explosion, loud noise, reverberation, roar, roll, rumble, thunder 2 *a boom in sales:* advance, boost, development, escalation, expansion, explosion, gain, growth, improvement, increase, jump, leap, progress, spurt, success, surge, upsurge, upswing, upturn

🔁 2 collapse, depression, failure, recession, slump

boomerang *v* 1 *the ball boomeranged:* backfire, bounce back, rebound, recoil, ricochet, spring back 2 *his actions boomeranged on him:* backfire, rebound

boon *n* 1 *grant a boon:* blessing, bonus, favour, gift, grant, gratuity, help, kindness, present, windfall 2 *this device is a boon for cooks:* advantage, benefit, blessing, bonus, godsend, help, plus *colloq*

🔁 1 blight 2 disadvantage

boor *n* barbarian, clod *colloq*, clodhopper *colloq*, country bumpkin *colloq*, lout, oaf, peasant *colloq*, philistine, rustic, vulgarian, yahoo, yokel

boorish *adj* coarse, crude, ignorant, ill-bred, ill-mannered, impolite, loutish, oafish, rough, rude, uncivilized, uncouth, uneducated, unrefined, vulgar

🔁 cultured, genteel, polite, refined

boost *v* 1 *boost confidence:* bolster, encourage, foster, inspire, lift, support, uplift 2 *boost sales:* advance, aid, amplify, assist, augment *formal*, develop, encourage, enhance, enlarge, expand, further, heighten, help, improve, increase, maximize, promote, put up, raise, supplement 3 *boost a product:* advertise, hype *colloq*, plug *colloq*, praise, promote, publicize

🔁 1 undermine 2 deteriorate, hinder, lower

♦ *n* 1 *a boost to morale:* encouragement, fillip, inspiration, lift, shot in the arm *colloq*, stimulus, support, uplift 2 *a boost in sales:* addition, advance, aid, amplification, assistance, augmentation *formal*, development, enhancement, enlargement, expansion, furtherance, help, improvement, increase, increment, rise, supplement 3 *a boost for a product:* advertisement, hype *colloq*, plug *colloq*, praise, promotion, publicity

🔁 1 blow, setback 2 deterioration, setback

boot *n* bootee, climbing-boot, Doc Martens®, football boot, galosh, gumboot, overshoe, riding-boot, wader, walking-boot, wellington

♦ *v* kick, shove

▶ **boot out** dismiss, eject, expel, fire *colloq*, give someone notice, give someone the heave *colloq*, give someone their cards *colloq*, kick out *colloq*, lay off, make redundant, sack *colloq*, shed, suspend

booth *n* box, carrel, compartment, cubicle, hut, kiosk, stall, stand

bootless *adj* barren, fruitless, futile, ineffective, pointless, profitless, sterile, unavailing, unproductive, unsuccessful, useless, vain, worthless

🔁 profitable, useful

booty *n* gains, haul, loot, pickings, pillage, plunder, prize, profits, spoil(s), swag *slang*, takings, winnings

border *n* 1 *south of the border:* boundary, frontier, line, marches, marchlands, state line 2 *herbaceous borders:* bed, edge, flower bed, verge 3 *the border of the lake:* borderline, bound, bounds, brim, brink, circumference, confine, confines, edge, fringe, limit, margin, perimeter, periphery, rim, surround, verge 4 *a hanky with a lace border:* frieze, frill, hem, skirt, trimming, valance

♦ *v* 1 *Sweden borders Norway:* abut *formal*, adjoin *formal*, be adjacent to, be next to, connect, impinge on *formal*, join, lie next to, touch 2 *streets bordered with trees:* bound, circumscribe *formal*, edge, flank, fringe, hem, rim, skirt, surround, trim

▶ **border on** approach, approximate to, be almost, be nearly, resemble, verge on

borderline *adj* ambivalent, doubtful, iffy *colloq*, indecisive, indefinite, indeterminate, marginal, problematic, uncertain

🔁 certain, clear-cut, definite

bore¹ *v* annoy, be tedious to, bore the pants off *colloq*, exhaust, fatigue, irk, irritate, jade, make tired, pall on, send to sleep *colloq*, tire, turn off *colloq*, wear out, weary

🔁 excite, interest

♦ *n* bind *colloq*, bother, drag *colloq*, headache *colloq*, nuisance, pain *colloq*, pain in the neck *colloq*, turn-off *colloq*

🔁 delight, pleasure

bore² *v* burrow, dig (out), drill, hollow (out), mine, penetrate, perforate, pierce, puncture, sap, sink, tap, tunnel, undermine

bored *adj* bored out of your mind *colloq*, bored stiff *colloq*, bored to tears *colloq*, brassed off *colloq*, browned off *colloq*, cheesed off *colloq*, ennuied *formal*, ennuyé *formal*, exhausted, fed up, in a rut *colloq*, sick and tired *colloq*, tired, turned off *colloq*, unexcited, uninterested, wearied

🔁 excited, interested

boredom *n* acedia *formal*, apathy, dullness, ennui *formal*, flatness, humdrum, malaise *formal*, monotony, sameness, tediousness, tedium, weariness, world-weariness

🔁 excitement, interest

boring *adj* commonplace, dreary, dry, dull, dull as ditchwater *colloq*, flat, humdrum, insipid, jejune *old use*, monotonous, prosaic, repetitious, routine, samey *colloq*, soul-destroying *colloq*, stale, stultifying *old use*, tedious, tiresome, tiring, uneventful, unexciting, unimaginative, uninspired, uninteresting, unvaried, with the novelty worn off *colloq*

🔁 exciting, interesting, original, stimulating

borrow *v* 1 *borrow a friend's car:* cadge, charter, have the use of, hire, lease, rent, scrounge, sponge *colloq*, take out a loan, take/have on loan, use temporarily 2 *borrow words/ideas:* acquire, adopt, appropriate *formal*, derive, draw, obtain, take (over), use

🔁 1 lend

borrowing *n* 1 *borrowing of money:* charter, hire, leasing, loan, rental, temporary use, use 2 *English borrowings in German:* acquisition, adoption, calque *technical*, derivation, loan, loan-translation, loan-word, takeover, use

🔁 1 lending

bosom n 1 *a lady with a large bosom:* boobs *slang*, breasts, bristols *slang*, bust, chest, knockers *slang*, tits *slang* 2 *in the bosom of the family:* centre, core, heart, midst, protection, sanctuary, shelter
♦ *adj* close, confidential, dear, devoted, faithful, intimate, loving

boss n administrator, captain, chief, director, employer, executive, foreman, gaffer *colloq*, governor, head, leader, manager, master, overseer, owner, superintendent, superior, supervisor, supremo
♦ *v* browbeat, bulldoze, bully, dominate, domineer, give orders to, lay down the law *colloq*, order about, order around, push around *colloq*, throw your weight about *colloq*, tyrannize

bossy adj assertive, authoritarian, autocratic, demanding, despotic, dictatorial, dominating, domineering, high-handed, imperious, lordly, oppressive, overbearing, tyrannical
◰ unassertive

botch v balls up *slang*, bungle, cock up *slang*, fluff *colloq*, foul up *colloq*, fuck up *taboo slang*, louse up *slang*, make a bad job of *colloq*, make a hash of *colloq*, make a mess of, mar, mess (up), mismanage, muff *colloq*, ruin, screw up *slang*, spoil
◰ accomplish, succeed
♦ *n* balls-up *slang*, bungle, cock-up *slang*, failure, farce *colloq*, hash *colloq*, mess, muddle, shambles *colloq*
◰ success

both adj each, the one and the other, the pair, the two

bother v 1 *not bother to reply:* concern yourself, make the/an effort, think necessary, trouble 2 *the heat bothered us:* alarm, annoy, concern, dismay, distress, trouble, upset, vex, worry 3 *don't bother her:* annoy, bug *colloq*, disturb, harass, hassle *colloq*, incommode *formal*, inconvenience, irritate, molest, nag, pester, plague, put out, trouble
♦ *n* 1 *not worth the bother:* bustle, difficulty, effort, exertion, flurry, fuss, hassle *colloq*, inconvenience, pains, problem, trouble 2 *office paperwork is a real bother:* aggravation *colloq*, annoyance, difficulty, irritation, nuisance, pain in the neck *colloq*, pest *colloq*, problem, strain, vexation, worry

bothersome adj 1 *bothersome neighbours:* aggravating *colloq*, annoying, exasperating, infuriating, irksome, irritating, tiresome, troublesome, vexatious, vexing 2 *a bothersome chore:* boring, inconvenient, irksome, laborious, tedious, tiresome, wearisome

bottle n container
▸ **bottle up** conceal, contain, curb, disguise, hide, hold back, inhibit, keep back, keep in check, restrain, shut in, suppress
◰ unbosom, unburden

bottleneck n block, blockage, congestion, hold-up, narrowing, obstacle, obstruction, snarl-up, traffic jam

bottom n 1 *the bottom of the statue:* base, foot, foundation, pedestal, plinth, substructure, support, underpinning 2 *the bottom of a shoe:* sole, underneath, underside 3 *at the bottom of the sea:* bed, depths, floor 4 *at the bottom of the garden:* end, far end, farthest end, furthest end 5 *children at the bottom of the class:* least important position,

lowest level 6 *sitting on his bottom:* arse *slang*, ass *colloq*, backside *colloq*, behind, bum *colloq*, butt *US colloq*, buttocks, posterior *colloq*, rear, rump, seat, tail *colloq*
◰ 1 top 2 top 3 surface 5 top
♦ *adj* lower, lowest, undermost

bottomless adj 1 *a bottomless pit:* boundless, deep, fathomless, immeasurable, profound, unfathomed, unplumbed 2 *a bottomless supply of funds:* boundless, immeasurable, inexhaustible, infinite, limitless, measureless, unlimited
◰ 1 shallow 2 limited

bough n branch, limb

boulder n rock, stone

boulevard n avenue, drive, mall, parade, promenade, thoroughfare

bounce v 1 *the ball bounced:* rebound, recoil, ricochet, spring back 2 *children bouncing about:* bound, jump, leap, spring
♦ *n* 1 *a ball with a lot of bounce:* bound, elasticity, give, rebound, recoil, resilience, spring, springiness 2 *he's full of bounce today:* animation, dynamism, ebullience, energy, exuberance, get-up-and-go *colloq*, go *colloq*, liveliness, spiritedness, vigour, vitality, vivacity, zip *colloq*
▸ **bounce back** get back to normal, get better, improve, recover

bouncing adj blooming, bonny, healthy, lively, robust, strong, thriving, vigorous

bound¹ adj 1 *bound to go wrong:* certain, definite, destined, doomed, fated, sure 2 *bound by law to attend:* beholden, committed, compelled, constrained, duty-bound, forced, liable, obliged, pledged, required 3 *he was bound to a chair:* attached, chained, clamped, fastened, fettered, fixed, held, lashed, roped, secured, shackled, strapped, tethered, tied (up), trussed

bound² adj coming, going, headed, heading, off (to), on your way to, proceeding, travelling

bound³ v bob, bounce, hurdle, jump, leap, spring, vault
♦ *n* bob, bounce, jump, leap, spring, vault

bound⁴ n 1 *within the bounds of his property:* border, borderline, brink, circumference, confine(s), demarcation, edge, extremity, limit, line, margin, perimeter, termination, verge 2 *within the bounds of good taste:* check, curb, limit, limitation, restraint, restriction
♦ *v* 1 *a lake bounded by trees:* border, edge, enclose, flank, fringe, outline, skirt, surround 2 *bounded by rules:* circumscribe *formal*, contain, control, moderate, regulate, restrain, restrict

boundary n 1 *the boundary of the forest:* bounds, confines, edge, extremity, fringe, limits, line, margin, perimeter, termination, verge 2 *the western boundary of the country:* border, borderline, demarcation, edge, frontier

bounded adj 1 *a garden bounded by a high wall:* bordered, circumscribed *formal*, delimited *formal*, demarcated, edged, encircled, enclosed, encompassed, surrounded, walled in 2 *bounded by laws and rules:* circumscribed *formal*, confined, controlled, encompassed, hemmed in, limited, restrained, restricted *formal*

bounder n blackguard, blighter *colloq*, cad, cur, dastard, dirty dog *colloq*, knave, miscreant, pig *colloq*, rat *colloq*, rogue, rotter *colloq*, swine *colloq*

boundless *adj* **1** *boundless love:* endless, everlasting, illimitable, immeasurable, immense, indefatigable, inexhaustible, infinite, interminable, limitless, measureless, never-ending, unbounded, unconfined, unending, unflagging, unlimited **2** *boundless wealth:* countless, immeasurable, immense, incalculable, innumerable, limitless, measureless, numberless, unlimited, untold, vast
🖅 **1** limited, restricted **2** limited, restricted

bounds *n* **1** *the bounds of the estate:* borders, boundaries, circumference, confines, demarcations, edges, extremities, fringes, limits, marches, margins, perimeter, periphery **2** *the bounds of decency:* confines, limits, parameters, restrictions, scope

bountiful *adj* **1** *a bountiful provider:* bounteous *formal*, generous, lavish, liberal, munificent *formal*, open-handed, ungrudging, unstinting **2** *a bountiful harvest:* abundant, ample, boundless, copious, exuberant, lavish, luxuriant *formal*, overflowing, plenteous *formal*, plentiful, princely, profuse, prolific
🖅 **1** mean **2** meagre, sparse

bounty *n* **1** *a bounty was offered for his capture:* allowance, bonus, donation, gift, grant, gratuity, premium, present, recompense, reward, tip **2** *indebted to her bounty:* almsgiving, beneficence *formal*, charity, generosity, kindness, largesse, liberality, munificence *formal*, philanthropy

bouquet *n* **1** *a bouquet of flowers:* boutonnière, bunch, buttonhole, corsage, garland, nosegay, posy, spray, wreath **2** *the wine's bouquet:* aroma, fragrance, odoriferousness *formal*, odour, perfume, redolence *formal*, scent, smell

bourgeois *adj* banal, commonplace, conformist, conservative, conventional, dull, hidebound, humdrum, middle-class, ordinary, pedestrian, traditional, trite, unadventurous, uncreative, unimaginative, uninspired, unoriginal
🖅 bohemian, original, unconventional

bout *n* **1** *a bout of bad weather:* course, go *colloq*, period, run, session, spell, spree, stint, stretch, term, time, turn **2** *a bout of illness:* attack, fit, touch **3** *a heavyweight bout:* battle, competition, contest, encounter, engagement, fight, heat, match, round, set-to, struggle

bovine *adj* **1** *bovine animals:* cattlelike, cowlike **2** *his bovine response:* dense *colloq*, dim-witted, doltish *colloq*, dull, dumb *colloq*, slow, slow-witted, stupid, thick *colloq*
🖅 **2** quick

bow¹ *v* **1** *bow your head:* arch, bend, bob, crook, crouch, curtsy, curve, genuflect *formal*, incline, kowtow, make obeisance *formal*, nod, salaam, stoop **2** *bow to someone's demands:* accede *formal*, accept, acquiesce *formal*, capitulate, comply, concede, consent, defer, give in, give way to, submit, succumb, surrender, yield **3** *the rebels refused to be bowed:* conquer, crush, humble, humiliate, overpower, subdue, subjugate *formal*, vanquish *formal*
♦ *n* bending, bob, curtsy, genuflexion *formal*, inclination, kowtow, nod, obeisance *formal*, prostration *formal*, salaam, salutation
► **bow out** abandon, back out, chicken out *colloq*, defect, desert, give up, leave, pull out, quit *colloq*, resign, retire, stand down, step down, withdraw

bow² *n* beak, front, head, prow, rostrum, stem
🖅 stern

bowdlerize *v* blue-pencil, censor, clean up, cut, edit, excise, expunge, expurgate, modify, purge, purify

bowels *n* **1** *pain in the bowels:* colon, entrails, guts, innards *colloq*, insides *colloq*, intestines, viscera *technical* **2** *in the bowels of the earth:* belly, cavity, centre, core, depths, heart, inside, interior, middle

bower *n* alcove, arbour, bay, grotto, recess, shelter

bowl¹ *n* basin, container, dish, receptacle, vessel

bowl² *v* **1** *bowl a ball:* fling, hurl, pitch, roll, throw **2** *the wheel bowled along the road:* revolve, roll, rotate, spin, whirl
► **bowl over 1** *bowled over by the news:* affect deeply, amaze, astonish, astound, dumbfound, flabbergast *colloq*, floor *colloq*, impress greatly, overwhelm, stagger, stun, surprise **2** *bowl over a person:* fell, knock down, push into, topple, unbalance

box¹ *n* bijou, carton, case, casket, chest, coffret, container, pyx, pyxis, receptacle
♦ *v* case, encase, pack, package, wrap
► **box in** block in, cage, circumscribe *formal*, confine, contain, coop up, corner, enclose, fence in, hem in, imprison, restrain, restrict, shut in, surround, trap

box² *v* **1** *learn to box:* engage in fisticuffs, fight, spar **2** *box someone's ears:* batter, buffet, clout *colloq*, cuff, hit, punch, slap, slug *colloq*, sock *slang*, strike, thump, wallop *colloq*, whack *colloq*

boxer *n* fighter, prizefighter, pugilist *formal*, sparring partner

---

Weight divisions in professional boxing:
heavyweight, cruiserweight/junior-heavyweight, light-heavyweight, super-middleweight, middleweight, light-middleweight/junior-middleweight, welterweight, light-welterweight/junior-welterweight, lightweight, junior-lightweight/superfeatherweight, featherweight, super-bantamweight/junior-featherweight, bantamweight, super-flyweight/junior-bantamweight, flyweight, light-flyweight/junior-flyweight, mini-flyweight/straw-weight/minimum weight

---

boxing *n* fisticuffs, prizefighting, pugilism *formal*, sparring

boy *n* adolescent, child, fellow, junior, kid *colloq*, lad, nipper *colloq*, schoolboy, stripling, teenager, whippersnapper *colloq*, young man, youngster, youth

boycott *v* **1** *boycotting the country's products:* ban, bar, black, blacklist, disallow, embargo, eschew *formal*, outlaw, prohibit, proscribe, refuse, reject **2** *they boycotted him after the scandal:* avoid, ban, bar, black, blacklist, cold-shoulder *colloq*, exclude, ignore, ostracize, reject, send to Coventry *colloq*, spurn
🖅 **1** advocate, patronize **2** champion, defend, encourage, support

boyfriend *n* admirer, beau, bloke *colloq*, cohabitee, common-law spouse, date *colloq*, fellow *colloq*, fiancé, live-in lover, lover, man, partner, significant other *colloq*, steady *colloq*, suitor, sweetheart, toyboy *colloq*, young man

boyish *adj* adolescent, childish, childlike, innocent, juvenile, young, youthful

brace[1] *n* beam, buttress, clamp, fastener, prop, reinforcement, shoring, stanchion *formal*, stay, strut, support, truss, vice
♦ *v* bolster, buttress, fortify *formal*, hold up, prop (up), reinforce, secure, shore (up), steady, strengthen, support

brace[2] *n* couple, duo, pair, twosome

bracelet *n* band, bangle, circlet

bracing *adj* brisk, crisp, energetic, energizing, enlivening, exhilarating, fortifying, fresh, invigorating, refreshing, reviving, rousing, stimulating, strengthening, tonic, vigorous
🔁 debilitating, draining, enervating *formal*, weakening

brackish *adj* bitter, briny, saline, salt, saltish, salty
🔁 clean, clear, fresh

brag *v* blow your own horn *US colloq*, blow your own trumpet *colloq*, bluster, boast, crow *colloq*, show off, swagger, talk big *colloq*, vaunt
🔁 be modest, deprecate *formal*, run down *colloq*

braggart *n* big mouth *colloq*, blusterer, boaster, braggadocio, fanfaron, gascon, loud-mouth *colloq*, rodomontader, show-off, swaggerer, swashbuckler, windbag *colloq*

bragging *n* bluster, boastfulness, boasting, hot air *colloq*, showing-off, vauntery *formal*
🔁 modesty, unobtrusiveness

braid *v* entwine, interlace, intertwine, interweave, lace, plait, ravel, twine, twist, weave, wind
🔁 undo, unravel

brain *n* 1 *an injury to the brain:* cerebrum *technical*, encephalon *technical*, grey matter *colloq*, sensorium *formal* 2 *have a good brain:* acumen *formal*, brains *colloq*, common sense, head, intellect, intelligence, mind, nous *colloq*, reason, sagacity *formal*, savvy *colloq*, sense, shrewdness, understanding, wit 3 *the real brain in the family:* boffin *colloq*, brainbox *colloq*, cleverclogs *colloq*, egghead *colloq*, expert, genius, highbrow, intellectual, mastermind, prodigy, pundit, scholar

---

Parts of the brain include:
brainstem, cerebellum, cerebral cortex (grey matter), cerebrum, corpus callosum, forebrain, frontal lobe, hindbrain, hypothalamus, medulla oblongata, mesencephalon, midbrain, occipital lobe, optic thalamus, parietal lobe, pineal body, pituitary gland, pons, spinal cord, temporal lobe, thalamus

---

brainless *adj* crazy, daft, foolish, half-witted, idiotic, mindless, senseless, silly, stupid, thoughtless
🔁 sensible, shrewd, wise

brainteaser *n* conundrum, mind-bender, poser, problem, puzzle, riddle

brainwashing *n* conditioning, indoctrination, mind-bending, persuasion, pressurizing, re-education

brainy *adj* bright, brilliant, clever, gifted, intellectual, intelligent, sapient *formal*, smart
🔁 dull, stupid

brake *n* check, constraint, control, curb, drag, rein, restraint, restriction, retardment *formal*
♦ *v* check, decelerate, drag, halt, pull up, reduce speed, slow, stop
🔁 accelerate

branch *n* 1 *the branches of a tree:* arm, bough, limb, offshoot, prong, ramus *technical*, shoot, sprig, stem 2 *a different branch of the company:* department, discipline, division, local/regional office, office, part, section, subdivision, subsection, subsidiary, wing
▶ **branch off** bifurcate *formal*, diverge, divide, fork, furcate *formal*, separate
▶ **branch out** broaden out, develop, diversify, enlarge, expand, extend, increase, multiply, proliferate, ramify *formal*, subdivide

brand *n* 1 *different brands of soap:* brand-name, emblem, hallmark, label, logo, make, sign, stamp, symbol, trademark, tradename 2 *the British brand of humour:* class, kind, line, quality, sort, species, type, variety 3 *identify cattle by their brand:* identification, identifying mark, mark, tag
♦ *v* 1 *brand as a troublemaker:* censure, denounce, discredit, disgrace, label, mark, stamp, stigmatize, typecast 2 *brand cattle:* burn (in), mark, scar, stamp

brandish *v* display, exhibit, flash, flaunt, flourish, parade, raise, shake, swing, wave, wield

brash *adj* 1 *a brash young man:* assertive, assured, audacious, bold, brazen, cocky, forward, impertinent, impudent, insolent, pushy *colloq*, rude, self-confident, temerarious *formal* 2 *a brash move:* foolhardy, hasty, impetuous, impulsive, incautious *formal*, indiscreet, precipitate *formal*, rash, reckless
🔁 1 modest, reserved, unassuming, unobtrusive 2 cautious, prudent, wary

brass *n* audacity, brass neck *colloq*, brass nerve *colloq*, brazenness, cheek *colloq*, chutzpah *colloq*, effrontery *formal*, gall, impertinence, impudence, insolence, nerve *colloq*, presumption, rudeness, temerity *formal*
🔁 circumspection *formal*, timidity

brassy *adj* 1 *brassy music:* blaring, dissonant, grating, hard, harsh, jangling, jarring, loud, noisy, piercing, raucous, strident 2 *a brassy blonde:* bold, brash, brazen, forward, insolent, loud, loud-mouthed *colloq*, pushy *colloq*, saucy *colloq*, shameless

brat *n* guttersnipe *colloq*, jackanapes *colloq*, kid, nipper *colloq*, puppy *colloq*, rascal, whippersnapper *colloq*, youngster

bravado *n* bluster, boast, boasting, bombast *formal*, braggadocio *formal*, bragging, fanfaronade *formal*, parade, pretence, rodomontade *formal*, show, showing-off, swagger, talk, vaunting *formal*
🔁 modesty, restraint

brave *adj* audacious *formal*, bold, courageous, daring, dauntless *formal*, doughty *formal*, fearless, gallant, gritty *colloq*, gutsy *colloq*, hardy, heroic, intrepid, lion-hearted, plucky, spunky *colloq*, stout-hearted, unafraid, undaunted, unflinching, valiant, valorous *formal*
🔁 afraid, chicken *colloq*, cowardly, craven, faint-hearted, spineless *colloq*, timid, wimpish *colloq*, yellow *colloq*
♦ *v* bear, challenge, confront, dare, defy,

endure, face, face up to, put up with *colloq*, stand up to, suffer, withstand

▣ capitulate, give in, yield

bravery *n* audacity, boldness, courage, daring, dauntlessness, fearlessness, fortitude, gallantry, grit *colloq*, guts *colloq*, hardiness, heroism, intrepidity *formal*, mettle, pluck, spirit, spunk *colloq*, stout-heartedness, valiance *formal*, valour

▣ cowardice, faint-heartedness, fearfulness, timidity

brawl *n* affray, altercation *formal*, argument, broil, bust-up *colloq*, clash, disorder, dispute, Donnybrook, dust-up *colloq*, fight, fisticuffs, fracas, fray, free-for-all, melee, punch-up *colloq*, quarrel, row, ruckus *US colloq*, rumpus, scrap, scuffle, skirmish, squabble

♦ *v* altercate *formal*, argue, dispute, fight, quarrel, row *colloq*, scrap *colloq*, scuffle, squabble, tussle, wrangle, wrestle

brawn *n* beef *colloq*, beefiness *colloq*, might, muscle, muscles, muscularity, power, robustness, sinews, strength

brawny *adj* athletic, beefy *colloq*, burly, hardy, hefty, hulking, husky *colloq*, muscular, powerful, robust, sinewy, solid, strapping, strong, sturdy, vigorous, well-built

▣ frail, skinny, slight, weak, weedy

bray *v* 1 *the donkey brayed*: heehaw, neigh, screech, trumpet, whinny 2 *she brayed with laughter*: bellow, blare, hoot, roar, screech

brazen *adj* 1 *a brazen young woman*: audacious *formal*, bold, brash, brassy, forward, immodest, impudent, insolent, pert, pushy *colloq*, saucy, shameless, unabashed, unashamed 2 *a brazen lie*: barefaced, blatant, flagrant, shameless, unashamed

▣ 1 modest, shamefaced, shy 2 cautious

breach *n* 1 *a breach of the rules*: breaking, contravention, disobedience, infraction, infringement, offence, transgression, trespass, violation 2 *a breach in international relations*: alienation, difference, disaffection *formal*, disagreement, dissension, dissociation, division, estrangement *formal*, parting, quarrel, rift, rupture, schism, separation, severance, split, variance 3 *a breach in the defences*: aperture, break, chasm, cleft, crack, crevice, fissure, gap, gulf, hole, opening, rift, rupture, space

♦ *v* 1 *breach an agreement*: break, contravene, infringe, violate 2 *breach the sea wall*: break (open), burst through, open up, rupture, split

bread *n* 1 *bread and jam*: bagel, baguette, bap, brioche, chapati, cob, croissant, crusts, French stick, loaf, matzo, nan, paratha, pitta, plait, pumpernickel, roll, sandwich 2 *our daily bread*: diet, fare, food, nourishment, nutriment *formal*, provisions, subsistence *formal*, sustenance *formal*, victuals *formal* 3 *earn your daily bread*: cash, funds, money

breadth *n* 1 *the breadth of the garden*: broadness, latitude, magnitude, measure, size, thickness, wideness, width 2 *a great breadth of interests*: amplitude *formal*, compass, comprehensiveness, expanse, extensiveness, extent, range, reach, scale, scope, span, spread, sweep, vastness

break *v* 1 *break a plate*: crack, demolish, destroy, disintegrate, divide, fracture, ruin, separate, shatter, shiver, smash, snap, splinter, split 2 *break*

the law: breach, contravene, dishonour, disobey, flout, infringe, violate 3 *the television has broken*: conk out *colloq*, crash *colloq*, cut out *colloq*, fail, go kaput *colloq*, go on the blink *colloq*, malfunction *formal*, pack up *colloq*, stop working 4 *break for lunch*: halt, pause, rest, stop 5 *break a silence*: bring to an end, cut off *colloq*, discontinue *formal*, interfere with, interrupt, suspend 6 *the news broke his spirit*: demoralize, enfeeble, impair, overcome, subdue, tame, undermine, weaken 7 *the injury broke her skin*: open (up), perforate, pierce, puncture 8 *break the news*: announce, disclose, divulge, impart, inform, reveal, tell 9 *break a record*: beat, better, exceed, excel, outdo, surpass 10 *the weather broke*: change (for the better/worse), improve, vary, worsen 11 *break a code*: crack, decipher, solve, work/figure out

▣ 1 mend, put together 2 abide by, keep, obey, observe 3 mend 4 start again 6 encourage, strengthen

♦ *n* 1 *a break in the surface of the earth*: breach, cleft, crack, crevice, fissure, fracture, gap, gash, hole, opening, rift, rupture, separation, split, tear 2 *a break in diplomatic relations*: breach, estrangement *formal*, schism, separation, split 3 *a break in the fighting*: breather *colloq*, halt, interruption, let-up *colloq*, lull, pause, respite, rest, stop, time-out *colloq* 4 *an ad break*: interlude, intermission, interval 5 *go away for a short break*: holiday, time off, vacation *US* 6 *a lucky break*: advantage, chance, fortune, opening, opportunity, (stroke of) luck

▸ **break away** 1 *he broke away from his captors*: escape, flee, fly, make a run for it *colloq*, run away 2 *break away from a union*: depart, detach, leave, part company, quit, secede, separate, split (off) 3 *the wing broke away from the plane*: detach, separate, split (off)

▸ **break down** 1 *the van broke down*: conk out *colloq*, fail, pack up *colloq*, seize up *colloq*, stop, stop working 2 *negotiations broke down*: collapse, fail, fall through *colloq*, founder 3 *break down in tears*: be overcome, collapse, crack up *colloq*, go to pieces *colloq*, lose control 4 *break down the figures*: analyse, detail, dissect, itemize, separate

▸ **break in** 1 *break in with unhelpful remarks*: butt in, cut in, interject, interpose *formal*, interrupt, intervene, intrude 2 *break in and steal the money*: burgle, enter illegally, raid, rob 3 *break in a horse*: accustom, condition, train 4 *break in a pair of walking boots*: condition, get used to, wear

▸ **break off** 1 *break off a piece of ice*: detach, disconnect, dissever *formal*, divide, part, separate, sever, snap off *colloq* 2 *break off a conversation*: bring to an end, cease, discontinue *formal*, end, finish, halt, interrupt, pause, stop, suspend, terminate *formal*

▸ **break out** 1 *war broke out in 1939*: arise, begin (suddenly), burst out *colloq*, commence *formal*, emerge, erupt, flare up *colloq*, happen, occur, start 2 *break out of prison*: abscond *formal*, bolt, escape, flee 3 *'Just a minute,' she broke out*: burst out *colloq*, exclaim, shout 4 *break out into a rash*: come out in, erupt

▸ **break through** 1 *break through the defences*: emerge, overcome, pass, penetrate 2 *break through in show business*: gain ground, leap forward, make headway, progress, succeed

▸ **break up** 1 *break up a machine*: demolish, destroy, disintegrate, dismantle, splinter, take apart 2 *break up a crowd*: divide, part, separate, split (up) 3 *the couple broke up*: divorce, separate, split up *colloq* 4 *the meeting*

broke up: adjourn, disband, discontinue *formal*, disperse, dissolve, finish, stop, suspend, terminate *formal*
▶ **break with** ditch *colloq*, drop *colloq*, finish with, jilt *colloq*, part with, reject, renounce *formal*, repudiate *formal*, separate from *colloq*

breakable *adj* brittle, delicate, flimsy, fragile, frail, frangible *formal*, friable *formal*
🞄 durable, long-lasting, shatterproof, sturdy, unbreakable

breakaway *adj* apostate *formal*, dissenting, heretical, rebel, renegade, schismatic *formal*, seceding *formal*, secessionist *formal*

breakdown *n* **1** *the breakdown of the car:* failure, malfunction *formal* **2** *the breakdown of the talks:* collapse, failure, interruption, stoppage **3** *a nervous breakdown:* collapse, cracking-up *colloq*, going to pieces *colloq* **4** *a breakdown of the figures:* analysis, categorization, classification, dissection, itemization

breaker *n* billow, roller, wave, white horses

break-in *n* burglary, house-breaking, larceny, raid, robbery, trespass

breakthrough *n* advance, development, discovery, find, finding, headway, improvement, innovation, invention, leap, milestone, progress, quantum leap (forward), step, step/leap forward

break-up *n* **1** *the break-up of a marriage:* disintegration, dissolution *formal*, divorce, finish, parting, rift, separation, split, splitting-up *colloq*, termination *formal* **2** *the break-up of the company:* dispersal, dissolution, termination *formal*

breakwater *n* groyne, jetty, mole, pier, sea wall, spur

breast *n* **1** *lay your head on my breast:* bosom, chest, front **2** *a woman's breasts:* boob *slang*, bristol *slang*, bust, cleavage, knocker *slang*, mamma *technical*, nipple, teat, tit *slang*

breath *n* **1** *take deep breaths to relax:* air, breathing, exhalation *formal*, flatus *formal*, gasp, gulp, inhalation *formal*, pant, respiration, sigh **2** *a breath of fresh air:* breeze, gust, pneuma *formal*, puff, waft **3** *a breath of autumn in the air:* aroma, odour, smell, whiff **4** *a breath of scandal:* hint, murmur, suggestion, suspicion, undertone, whisper

breathe *v* **1** *breathe deeply:* exhale *formal*, expire *formal*, gasp, inhale *formal*, pant, puff, respire *formal*, sigh **2** *not breathe a word to anyone:* articulate, express, impart, murmur, say, tell, utter, voice, whisper **3** *breathe new life into a project:* imbue, infuse, inject, inspire, instil, transfuse *formal*

breather *n* break, breathing-space *colloq*, halt, pause, recess, relaxation, respite *formal*, rest

breathless *adj* **1** *breathless from climbing:* choking, exhausted, gasping, out of breath, panting, puffed (out), puffing, short-winded, wheezing, winded **2** *breathless with anticipation:* agog, eager, excited, expectant, feverish, impatient, in suspense

breathtaking *adj* amazing, astonishing, awe-inspiring, exciting, impressive, magnificent, overwhelming, spectacular, stunning, thrilling

breed *v* **1** *animals that breed in the spring:* bear, bring forth, give birth to, hatch, multiply, procreate, propagate *formal*, pullulate *formal*, reproduce **2** *breed dogs:* bring up, propagate *formal*, raise, rear **3** *breed suspicion:* arouse, cause, create, cultivate, develop, engender *formal*, foster, generate, give rise to, make, nurture, occasion, originate, produce
♦ *n* **1** *breeds of cattle:* family, hybrid, line, lineage, pedigree, progeny *formal*, race, species, stamp, stock, strain, variety **2** *a new breed of leader:* class, kind, type

breeding *n* **1** *the breeding of cattle:* development, genetic engineering, nurture, raising, rearing, upbringing **2** *the birds' season for breeding:* procreation *formal*, reproduction **3** *a man of noble breeding:* ancestry, lineage, stock, upbringing **4** *have breeding:* civility *formal*, culture, education, gentility, (good) manners, polish, politeness, refinement, training, urbanity *formal*
🞄 **4** bad manners, vulgarity

breeding-ground *n* hotbed *colloq*, nest, nursery, school, training ground

breeze *n* air, breath, draught, flurry, gust, puff, waft, wind
♦ *v* flit *colloq*, glide, hurry, sail, sally *colloq*, sweep, trip

breezy *adj* **1** *a breezy day:* airy, blowing, blustery, fresh, gusty, squally, windy **2** *a breezy manner:* animated, blithe, bright, buoyant, carefree, casual, cheerful, confident, debonair, easy-going *colloq*, informal, jaunty, light, lively, vivacious
🞄 **1** calm, still, windless **2** quiet, sad, serious, staid

brevity *n* **1** *the brevity of the speech:* abruptness, briefness, conciseness, concision *formal*, crispness, curtness, economy, incisiveness, laconism *formal*, pithiness, shortness, succinctness, terseness *formal* **2** *the brevity of life:* briefness, ephemerality *formal*, impermanence *formal*, shortness, transience *formal*, transitoriness *formal*
🞄 **1** long-windedness, prolixity *formal*, verbosity *formal*, wordiness **2** longevity *formal*, permanence

brew *v* **1** *brew tea:* boil, cook, infuse, prepare, seethe *formal*, soak, steep, stew **2** *brew beer:* ferment **3** *a storm is brewing:* build up, develop, foment, gather **4** *brew a plot:* concoct, contrive, devise, foment, hatch, plan, plot, project, scheme
♦ *n* **1** *boil up a hot brew:* beverage, concoction *formal*, distillation, drink, fermentation, infusion, liquor, potion, preparation **2** *a powerful brew of sex and violence:* blend, mixture

bribe *n* allurement, back-hander *colloq*, boodle *colloq*, douceur, enticement, hush money *colloq*, incentive, inducement, kickback, pay-off *colloq*, payola *US colloq*, protection money *colloq*, refresher *colloq*, slush fund *colloq*, sweetener *colloq*
♦ *v* buy/pay off, corrupt, fix *colloq*, grease *colloq*, grease someone's palm *colloq*, reward, square, suborn, take care of *colloq*

bribery *n* corruption, graft *colloq*, inducement, palm-greasing *colloq*

bric-à-brac *n* baubles, curios, knick-knacks, ornaments, trinkets, trumpery

brick *n* **1** *bricks and mortar:* adobe, block, breeze block, briquette, firebrick, header, klinker, rock,

stone, stretcher **2** *you're a brick for helping*: buddy
US, chum, kind person, mate, pal, real friend

bridal *adj* conjugal, connubial *formal*, marital,
marriage, matrimonial, nuptial, wedding

bride *n* honeymooner, marriage partner, newly-
wed, spouse, wife

bridegroom *n* groom, honeymooner, husband,
marriage partner, newly-wed, spouse

bridge *n* **1** *a bridge over the river*: arch, causeway,
link, span **2** *act as a bridge between the different
factions*: bond, connection, link, tie
♦ *v* **1** *a huge tree which bridges the river*: cross,
go over, reach across, span, traverse *formal*
2 *bridge two cultures*: bind, connect, couple, join,
link, unite

Types of bridge include:
suspension bridge, arch bridge, cantilever
bridge, flying bridge, flyover, overpass,
footbridge, railway bridge, viaduct, aqueduct,
humpback bridge, toll bridge, pontoon bridge,
Bailey bridge, rope bridge, drawbridge,
swing bridge

---

bridle *v* **1** *bridle your temper*: check, contain,
control, curb, govern, master, moderate, repress,
restrain, subdue **2** *bridle at someone's attitude*: be
offended, become indignant, bristle, get angry
♦ *n* check, control, curb, halter, rein, restraint

brief *adj* **1** *a brief report/visit*: abridged, aphoristic
formal, compressed, concise, condensed, crisp,
pithy, short, succinct, terse, thumbnail **2** *his
manner is brief to the point of rudeness*: abrupt,
blunt, brusque, curt, laconic *formal*, sharp, short,
surly **3** *a brief visit*: cursory, fleeting, limited,
momentary, passing, quick, short, swift **4** *this
brief life*: ephemeral, fleeting, fugacious *formal*,
momentary, short-lived, temporary, transient,
transitory
F3 1 extensive, lengthy, long-winded, protracted
formal, verbose *formal*
♦ *n* **1** *with a brief to reduce crime*: directive,
instructions, mandate, orders, remit,
responsibility **2** *an editorial brief*: advice, briefing,
data, directions, information, instructions **3** *a
brief of the day's events*: abridgement, abstract,
digest, outline, précis, summary **4** *a legal brief*:
argument, case, data, defence, dossier, evidence
♦ *v* advise, direct, explain, fill in *colloq*, gen up
colloq, give someone the run-down/low-down
colloq, guide, inform, instruct, prepare, prime,
put someone in the picture *colloq*

briefing *n* **1** *a press briefing*: conference,
intimation *formal*, meeting **2** *a briefing on what
to do*: advice, directions, filling-in *colloq*,
gen *colloq*, guidance, information, instructions,
low-down *colloq*, orders, preparation, priming,
run-down *colloq*

briefly *adv* **1** *speak briefly*: concisely, cursorily,
precisely, quickly, succinctly, summarily, tersely,
to the point **2** *briefly, the answer is no*: in a few
words, in a nutshell *colloq*, in a word, in brief
F3 1 at length, fully

brigade *n* **1** *a military brigade*: company,
contingent, corps, crew, force, squad, team,
troop, unit **2** *the anti-hunting brigade*: band, body,
contingent, crew, group, party, squad

brigand *n* bandit, desperado, freebooter,
gangster, highwayman, marauder, outlaw,
plunderer, robber

bright *adj* **1** *bright lights*: beaming, blazing,
blinding, brilliant, dazzling, effulgent *formal*,
flashing, glaring, gleaming, glistening, glittering,
glowing, illuminated, incandescent *formal*,
intense, luminous, lustrous *formal*, radiant,
refulgent *formal*, resplendent *formal*, shimmering,
shining, sparkling, twinkling **2** *bright colours*:
blazing, brilliant, dazzling, glaring, glowing,
intense, luminous, radiant, vivid **3** *look bright*:
cheerful, glad, happy, jolly, joyful, lively, merry,
vivacious *formal* **4** *the future looks bright*:
auspicious *formal*, encouraging, favourable,
hopeful, optimistic, promising, propitious *formal*,
rosy **5** *bright students*: acute, astute, brainy *colloq*,
bright as a button *colloq*, clever, intelligent,
keen, perceptive, quick, quick-witted, sharp,
smart **6** *a bright day*: cloudless, fine, pleasant,
sunny, unclouded
F3 1 dim, dull, soft **2** colourless, drab, dull, pale,
soft **3** depressed, down *colloq*, gloomy, sad
4 depressing, gloomy, inauspicious *formal*
5 stupid, thick *colloq* **6** cloudy, dark, overcast

brighten *v* **1** *brighten up a room*: illuminate, light
up, lighten, make bright **2** *brighten up the silver*:
burnish, polish, rub (up), shine **3** *his eyes
brightened*: gleam, glow, shine **4** *she brightened at
the prospect*: buck up *colloq*, cheer up, enliven
formal, gladden, liven up, pep up *colloq*,
perk up *colloq*
F3 1 darken, shadow **2** dull, tarnish **3** dull

brilliance *n* **1** *brilliance at the piano*: aptitude,
cleverness, distinction, excellence, genius,
greatness, talent, virtuosity **2** *the brilliance of the
light*: brightness, coruscation *formal*, dazzle,
effulgence *formal*, fulgency *formal*, intensity,
radiance, refulgence *formal*, resplendence *formal*,
sparkle, vividness **3** *the brilliance of the spectacle*:
glamour, glory, magnificence, resplendence
formal, splendour

brilliant *adj* **1** *a brilliant flautist*: accomplished,
celebrated, exceptional, expert, famous, gifted,
illustrious, masterly, outstanding, remarkable,
skilful, superb, talented, wonderful **2** *a brilliant
light*: blazing, bright, dazzling, effulgent *formal*,
fulgent *formal*, glaring, glittering, intense,
refulgent *formal*, resplendent *formal*, scintillating,
shining, sparkling, vivid **3** *a brilliant spectacle*:
glorious, magnificent, resplendent *formal*, showy,
splendid **4** *a brilliant mind*: astute, brainy *colloq*,
bright, clever, erudite *formal*, intelligent, quick
5 *this is a brilliant game*: fantastic, great, superb,
wonderful
F3 1 ordinary, run-of-the-mill, undistinguished,
untalented **2** dull **4** stupid **5** awful, bad

brim *n* border, brink, circumference, edge, limit,
lip, margin, perimeter, rim, top, verge
♦ *v* be filled with, be full of, be overflowing
with, overflow with

bring *v* **1** *bring a drink*: bear *formal*, carry, convey,
deliver, fetch, take, transport **2** *I'll bring you home
later*: accompany, conduct, escort, guide, lead,
take, usher **3** *bring misery*: cause, create,
engender *formal*, force, produce, prompt,
provoke, result in
▶ **bring about** accomplish, achieve, cause,
create, effect *formal*, fulfil, generate, manage,
occasion, produce, realize
▶ **bring down 1** *bring down the government*:
defeat, destroy, oust, overthrow, topple *colloq*,

unseat, vanquish *formal* **2** *bring down blood pressure*: cause to fall/drop, lower, reduce
► **bring forward** advance, make earlier, put forward
Ⅎ postpone, put back
► **bring in 1** *bring in new laws*: inaugurate *formal*, initiate, introduce, originate, pioneer, set up, usher in **2** *bring in £400*: accrue *formal*, earn, fetch, gross, net, produce, realize *formal*, return, yield
► **bring off** accomplish, achieve, discharge *formal*, execute *formal*, fulfil, perform, pull off *colloq*, succeed in, win
► **bring on 1** *bring on a headache*: cause, generate, give rise to, induce *formal*, lead to, occasion *formal*, precipitate *formal*, prompt, provoke **2** *bring on the plant's growth*: accelerate, advance, expedite *formal*, foster, improve, nurture
► **bring out 1** *bring out a point in a story*: draw out, emphasize, enhance, highlight, make someone aware of, stress **2** *bring out a book*: introduce, issue, launch, print, produce, publish
► **bring round 1** *bring round someone who is unconscious*: awaken, bring to, resuscitate, revive, rouse **2** *bring someone round to your way of thinking*: cajole, coax, convert, convince, persuade, win over
► **bring up 1** *bring up children*: care for, educate, foster, nurture, raise, rear, teach, train **2** *bring up a matter for discussion*: broach, introduce, mention, propose, raise, submit **3** *bring up food*: puke *colloq*, regurgitate, throw up *colloq*, vomit

brink *n* **1** *on the brink of the river*: bank, border, boundary, brim, edge, extremity, fringe, limit, lip, margin, rim, threshold, verge **2** *on the brink of war*: edge, threshold, verge

brisk *adj* **1** *a brisk pace*: active, agile, bustling, busy, energetic, lively, nimble, quick, snappy, spirited, vigorous **2** *a brisk manner*: businesslike, lively, no-nonsense *colloq*, quick **3** *brisk trade*: busy, good, rapid **4** *brisk weather*: bracing, cold, crisp, exhilarating, fresh, invigorating, refreshing, stimulating
Ⅎ **1** slow, unenergetic **2** lethargic, slow **3** slow, sluggish

bristle *n* **1** *shave off bristles*: hair, stubble, whisker **2** *bristles on an animal's back*: awn, barb, prickle, quill, spine, thorn
♦ *v* **1** *bristling at his attitude*: be angry, be incensed at, bridle at, draw yourself up, seethe (with) **2** *bristling with police*: abound in *formal*, be thick with *colloq*, hum with *colloq*, swarm with, teem with

bristly *adj* **1** *a bristly chin*: bearded, hairy, hirsute *formal*, prickly, rough, stubbly, unshaven, whiskered **2** *a plant with bristly leaves*: barbellate, hirsute *formal*, hispid *technical*, prickly, spiky, spiny, thorny
Ⅎ **1** clean-shaven, smooth **2** smooth

brittle *adj* **1** *a brittle crust*: breakable, crisp, crumbling, crumbly, delicate, easily broken, fragile, frail, frangible *formal*, friable *formal*, shattery **2** *a brittle situation*: delicate, fragile, unstable **3** *a brittle manner*: curt, irritable, nervous, nervy *colloq*, tense **4** *a brittle laugh*: grating, harsh, sharp, short hard
Ⅎ **1** durable, resilient, sturdy **2** constant, secure, stable

broach *v* hint at, introduce, mention, propose, raise, suggest

broad *adj* **1** *broad avenues/valleys*: ample, capacious *formal*, extensive, large, latitudinous

formal, roomy, spacious, vast, wide, widespread **2** *a broad education*: all-embracing, catholic *formal*, compendious *formal*, comprehensive, eclectic *formal*, encyclopedic, extensive, far-reaching, general, inclusive, sweeping, universal, unlimited, wide-ranging **3** *the broad meaning of the term*: general, not detailed, vague **4** *broad support*: extensive, general, widespread **5** *a broad hint*: clear, obvious, plain, unconcealed, undisguised
Ⅎ **1** narrow **2** limited, restricted **3** detailed, narrow, precise, specific **4** limited **5** disguised, veiled

broad or ***wide***? *Broad* refers to the extent across something and often has the connotation of spaciousness or ampleness, whereas *wide* refers to the distance separating, or the gap between, sides or edges: *a person's broad back; broad shoulders; wide sleeves; a wide doorway*.

broadcast *v* **1** *broadcast TV programmes*: air, beam, cable, relay, show, televise, transmit **2** *broadcast the decision widely*: advertise, announce, circulate, disseminate *formal*, make known, promulgate *formal*, publicize, publish, report, scatter, spread
♦ *n* access television, community broadcasting, programme, satellite programme, show, simulcast, simultaneous transmission, teletext, television première, transmission

broaden *v* **1** *the road broadens out*: branch out, enlarge, expand, extend, open up, spread, stretch, widen **2** *broaden the scope of the inquiry*: augment *formal*, develop, diversify, enlarge, expand, extend, increase, open up, widen
Ⅎ **1** narrow **2** narrow, reduce, restrict

broad-minded *adj* dispassionate, enlightened, forbearing, free-thinking, impartial, indulgent, liberal, open-minded, permissive, progressive, receptive, tolerant, unbiased, unprejudiced
Ⅎ biased, intolerant, narrow-minded, prejudiced

broadside *n* **1** *fire a broadside at a ship*: assault, attack, blast, bombardment, cannonade, counterblast, volley **2** *verbal broadsides*: brickbat *colloq*, criticism, denunciation, diatribe *formal*, fulmination *formal*, harangue *formal*, invective *formal*, philippic *formal*, stick *colloq*

brochure *n* booklet, broadsheet, circular, flyer, folder, handbill, handout, leaflet, pamphlet, prospectus

broil *v* barbecue, cook, fry, grill, roast

broiling *adj* baking, blistering, boiling, roasting, scorching, sweltering

broke *adj* bankrupt, bust *colloq*, cleaned out *colloq*, destitute, impecunious *formal*, impoverished, indigent *formal*, insolvent *formal*, not having two pennies to rub together *colloq*, on your beam ends *colloq*, on your uppers *colloq*, penniless, penurious *formal*, poor, poverty-stricken, ruined, skint *colloq*, stony-broke *colloq*, strapped (for cash) *colloq*
Ⅎ affluent, rich, solvent

broken *adj* **1** *a broken pipe*: broken to smithereens *colloq*, burst, demolished, destroyed, fractured, ruptured, separated, severed, shattered, smashed **2** *broken machinery*: bust *colloq*, damaged, defective, duff *colloq*, faulty, gone wrong, inoperative *formal*, kaput *colloq*, malfunctioning *formal*, not working, on the blink *colloq*, out of order/action, wonky *colloq* **3** *broken sleep:* disconnected, discontinuous *formal*, disjointed, erratic, fragmentary, intermittent, interrupted, spasmodic **4** *speak broken German:* disjointed, halting, hesitating, imperfect, stammering **5** *a broken man:* beaten, crushed, defeated, demoralized, down *colloq*, oppressed, subdued, tamed, vanquished *formal* **6** *physically broken after his illness:* exhausted, feeble, knackered *colloq*, weak

☒ **1** intact, mended, whole **2** in order/action, mended, working **3** continuous, uninterrupted **4** fluent

broken-down *adj* **1** *a broken-down machine:* bust *colloq*, damaged, defective, duff *colloq*, faulty, inoperative *formal*, kaput *colloq*, on the blink *colloq*, out of order **2** *a broken-down old house:* collapsed, decayed, decrepit, dilapidated, in disrepair, ruined

broken-hearted *adj* dejected, desolate, despairing, despondent, devastated, disconsolate *formal*, dolorous *formal*, down *colloq*, down in the dumps *colloq*, forlorn *formal*, grief-stricken, heartbroken, inconsolable, miserable, mournful, prostrated *formal*, sad, sorrowful, unhappy, wretched

broker *n* agent, arbitrageur *technical*, dealer, factor, handler, intermediary, jobber, middleman, negotiator, stockbroker, stockjobber

bromide *n* anodyne *formal*, banality, cliché, commonplace, platitude, truism

bronze *adj* auburn, chestnut, copper, copper-coloured, reddish-brown, rust, tan, Titian

brooch *n* badge, breastpin, clasp, clip, pin

brood *v* **1** *brood over lost opportunities:* agonize, dwell on, fret *colloq*, go over, meditate, mope *colloq*, mull over, muse, ponder, rehearse *formal*, ruminate *formal*, worry about **2** *hens brooding:* hatch, incubate, sit
♦ *n* **1** *a brood of animals:* chicks, clutch, hatch, issue, litter, offspring, progeny, young **2** *we took our brood on holiday:* children, family

brook¹ *n* beck, burn, channel, gill, inlet, rivulet, runnel, stream, watercourse

brook² *v* accept, allow, bear, countenance *formal*, endure, permit, put up with, stand, stomach *colloq*, support, tolerate, withstand

brothel *n* bagnio, bawdy-house, bordello, cathouse *US slang*, house of ill fame, house of ill repute, knocking-shop *slang*, whorehouse

brother *n* **1** *brothers and sisters:* relation, relative, sibling **2** *brothers in the struggle against injustice:* associate, chum *colloq*, colleague, companion, comrade, fellow, friend, mate *colloq*, pal *colloq*, partner **3** *brothers in a monastery:* friar, monk

brotherhood *n* **1** *feelings of brotherhood:* camaraderie, comradeship, fellowship, friendliness, friendship **2** *a brotherhood of monks:* alliance, association, clique, community, confederacy, confederation, fellowship, fraternity, guild, league, society, union

brotherly *adj* affectionate, amicable, benevolent, caring, friendly, kind, loving, philanthropic, sympathetic
☒ callous, unbrotherly

brow *n* **1** *sweat on your brow:* forehead, temples **2** *the brow of the hill:* brink, cliff, peak, ridge, summit, tip, top, verge

browbeat *v* bulldoze *colloq*, bully, coerce, domineer, dragoon, force, intimidate, oppress, overbear, threaten, tyrannize
☒ coax, flatter, sweet-talk *colloq*

brown *adj* **1** *brown in colour:* auburn, bay, beige, brunette, chestnut, chocolate, coffee, dark, dusky, fawn, ginger, hazel, mahogany, russet, rust, rusty, sepia, tan, tawny, umber **2** *brown from lying in the sun:* bronze, bronzed, browned, sunburnt, tanned
♦ *v* cook, fry, grill, seal, toast

browned off *adj* bored, bored stiff *colloq*, brassed off *colloq*, cheesed off *colloq*, discontented, discouraged, disgruntled *colloq*, disheartened, fed up, pissed off *slang*, weary
☒ fascinated, interested, intrigued

browse *v* **1** *browse through a book:* dip into, flick through, leaf through, peruse *formal*, scan, skim, survey **2** *sheep browsing in the fields:* eat, feed, graze, nibble, pasture

bruise *v* **1** *bruise your leg:* blacken, blemish, discolour, injure, mark, wound **2** *bruise someone's feelings:* crush, grieve, hurt, injure, insult, offend, upset **3** *bruise fruit:* blemish, crush, damage, mark, spoil
♦ *n* blemish, contusion *formal*, discoloration, ecchymosis *technical*, injury, mark

brunt *n* (full) force, (full) weight, impact, impetus, pressure, shock, strain, thrust

brush¹ *n* besom, broom, sweeper, whisk
♦ *v* **1** *brush the room:* burnish, clean, flick, polish, shine, sweep **2** *her hand brushed mine:* contact, graze, kiss, rub, scrape, stroke, touch
▶ **brush aside** belittle *formal*, dismiss, disregard, flout, ignore, override, pooh-pooh *colloq*
▶ **brush off** cold-shoulder *colloq*, dismiss, disown, disregard, ignore, rebuff, reject, repudiate *formal*, repulse, slight, snub, spurn
▶ **brush up 1** *brush up your Spanish:* bone up on *colloq*, cram *colloq*, improve, polish up, read up, relearn, revise, study, swot *colloq* **2** *go and brush up:* clean (yourself up), freshen up, tidy (yourself up)

brush² *n* brushwood, bush, bushes, ground cover, scrub, shrubs, thicket, undergrowth

brush³ *n* argument, clash, conflict, confrontation, disagreement, dust-up *colloq*, encounter, fight, fracas, scrap *colloq*, set-to *colloq*, skirmish, tussle

brush-off *n* cold shoulder *colloq*, discouragement, dismissal, kiss-off *US slang*, rebuff, refusal, rejection, repudiation *formal*, repulse, slight, snub
☒ encouragement

brusque *adj* abrupt, blunt, curt, discourteous, gruff, impolite, sharp, short, tactless, terse, uncivil, undiplomatic
☒ courteous, polite, tactful

brutal *adj* **1** *a brutal murder:* bloodthirsty, callous, cruel, ferocious, inhuman, inhumane, merciless, pitiless, remorseless, ruthless, savage, vicious

2 *a brutal instinct:* animal, beastly, bestial *formal*, brutish **3** *brutal frankness:* harsh, heartless, insensitive, severe, unfeeling
🔁 **1** humane, kindly **2** civilized **3** gentle, kind, sensitive

brutality *n* atrocity, barbarism, barbarity, bloodthirstiness, brutishness, callosity *formal*, callousness, cruelty, ferocity, inhumanity, ruthlessness, savagery, viciousness, violence
🔁 gentleness, kindness

brute *n* animal, beast, bully, devil, fiend, lout, monster, ogre, sadist, savage, swine, yahoo
♦ *adj* **1** *brute force:* bodily, instinctive, mindless, physical, senseless, unthinking **2** *brute pleasures:* bodily, carnal, coarse, depraved, fleshly, gross, physical, sensual

brutish *adj* **1** *a brutish lout:* barbarian, brutal, coarse, crass, crude, gross, loutish, savage, stupid, uncivilized, uncouth, vulgar **2** *the brutish cruelty of the soldiers:* barbaric, barbarous, bestial *formal*, brutal, cruel, savage
🔁 **1** civilized, polite, refined

bubble *n* **1** *a bubble of blood from his nose:* ball (of air), bead, blister, drop, droplet, globule, vesicle *formal* **2** *a bath full of bubbles:* effervescence, fizz, foam, froth, head, lather, spume, suds **3** *the bubble of all their dreams burst:* delusion, fantasy, illusion
♦ *v* **1** *champagne bubbling in a glass:* effervesce, fizz *colloq*, foam, froth, sparkle **2** *water bubbling in a pot:* boil, burble, gurgle, seethe **3** *bubble with enthusiasm:* be elated, be excited, be filled, bounce *colloq*, sparkle

bubbly *adj* **1** *a bubbly drink:* carbonated, effervescent, fizzy *colloq*, foaming, frothy, sparkling, sudsy **2** *a bubbly personality:* alive and kicking, animated *formal*, bouncy *colloq*, ebullient *formal*, elated, excited, exuberant, full of beans *colloq*, happy, lively, merry, vivacious
🔁 **1** flat, still **2** lethargic

buccaneer *n* corsair, filibuster, freebooter, pirate, privateer, sea-robber, sea-rover, sea-wolf

buck
▶ **buck up 1** *tried to buck him up:* cheer (up), encourage, enliven, hearten, inspirit *formal*, perk up *colloq*, stimulate **2** *she bucked up when he arrived:* cheer (up), improve, perk up *colloq*, rally, take heart **3** *buck up or we'll be late!:* get a move on *colloq*, get your skates on *colloq*, hasten *formal*, hurry (up), step on it *colloq*

bucket *n* bail, can, pail, pitcher, scuttle, vessel

buckle *n* **1** *a buckle on a belt:* catch, clasp, clip, fastener, hasp **2** *a buckle in metal:* bulge, contortion *formal*, distortion, kink, twist, warp
♦ *v* **1** *buckle your belt:* catch, clasp, close, connect, fasten, hitch, hook, secure **2** *the metal buckled:* bend, bulge, cave in *colloq*, collapse, crumple, distort, fold, twist, warp, wrinkle

bucolic *adj* agrarian, agricultural, countrified *colloq*, country, pastoral, rural, rustic *formal*
🔁 industrial, urban

bud *n* embryo, germ, knosp *formal*, plumule *formal*, shoot, sprig, sprout
♦ *v* burgeon *formal*, develop, grow, pullulate *formal*, shoot, sprout
🔁 waste away, wither

budding *adj* burgeoning *formal*, developing, embryonic, fledgling, flowering, growing,

incipient *formal*, nascent *formal*, potential, promising
🔁 experienced, mature

budge *v* **1** *he wouldn't budge from the sofa:* move, roll, shift, slide, stir **2** *I couldn't budge the table:* dislodge, move, push, remove, shift, slide **3** *not budge from your position:* bend, change, change your mind, compromise, give (way), give in, yield **4** *once he's made up his mind, you can't budge him:* convince, influence, persuade, sway

budget *n* allocation, allotment, allowance, finances, (financial) estimate, funds, means, quota, resources, what you can afford
♦ *v* allocate, allot, allow, apportion *formal*, estimate, plan, ration, set aside

buff[1] *adj* fawn, khaki, sandy, straw, tan, yellowish, yellowish-brown
♦ *v* brush, burnish, polish, rub, shine, smooth

buff[2] *n* addict, admirer, aficionado, connoisseur, devotee, enthusiast, expert, fan, fiend *colloq*, freak *colloq*, maven *US*

buffer *n* **1** *railways buffers:* bulwark, bumper, cushion, fender, pad, pillow, shock-absorber **2** *a buffer between the two countries:* bulwark, intermediary, safeguard, screen, shield

buffet[1] *n* **1** *a railway buffet:* café, cafeteria, counter, snackbar **2** *a buffet was laid out:* cold meal, help yourself *colloq*, self-service, smorgasbord

buffet[2] *v* bang, batter, beat, box, bump, clout *colloq*, cuff, hit, knock, pound, pummel, push, shove, slap, strike, thump
♦ *n* bang, blow, box, bump, clout *colloq*, cuff, knock, push, shove, slap, smack, thump

buffoon *n* clown, comedian, comic, droll, fool, harlequin, jester, joker, wag

buffoonery *n* clowning, drollery, jesting, nonsense, pantomime, silliness, tomfoolery, waggishness

bug *n* **1** *crawling with bugs:* creepy-crawly *colloq*, flea, insect **2** *a stomach bug:* bacterium, disease, germ, infection, microbe, micro-organism, virus **3** *a bug in a computer program:* blemish, defect, error, failing, fault, flaw, gremlin *colloq*, imperfection **4** *bitten by the decorating bug:* craze, fad, obsession **5** *concealed a bug in the room:* hidden microphone, listening device, phone-tap *colloq*, wire-tap *colloq*
♦ *v* **1** *their attitude bugs me:* annoy, bother, disturb, harass, irk, irritate, needle *colloq*, vex, wind up *colloq* **2** *I think they have bugged my office:* eavesdrop (on) *formal*, listen in (on/to), phone-tap *colloq*, tap, wire-tap *colloq*

bugbear *n* anathema, bane, bête noire, dread, fiend, horror, nightmare, pet hate

build *v* **1** *build a new hotel:* assemble, construct, erect, fabricate, fashion, form, knock together, make, put together, put up, raise, shape **2** *build trust:* develop, enlarge, extend, improve, increase, intensify **3** *the pressure is building:* develop, escalate, extend, increase, intensify
🔁 **1** demolish, destroy, knock down *colloq* **2** lessen **3** lessen
♦ *n* body, figure, form, frame, physique, shape, size, structure
▶ **build up 1** *build up a navy:* assemble, enlarge, extend, piece together, put together **2** *build up your strength:* amplify, boost, develop, enhance,

expand, extend, fortify *formal*, heighten, improve, increase, intensify, reinforce **3** *tension is building up*: develop, escalate, extend, heighten, increase, intensify **4** *built him up as the next big thing*: advertise, hype *colloq*, plug *colloq*, promote

building *n* architecture, construction, development, dwelling *formal*, edifice *formal*, erection, fabrication, structure

---

Types of building include:
house, bungalow, cottage, block of flats, apartment, condominium *US*, cabin, farmhouse, villa, mansion, chateau, castle, palace; church, chapel, cathedral, abbey, monastery, temple, pagoda, mosque, synagogue; shop, store, garage, factory, warehouse, silo, office block, tower block, skyscraper, theatre, cinema, gymnasium, sports hall, restaurant, café, hotel, pub *colloq*, public house, inn, school, college, museum, library, hospital, prison, power station, observatory; barracks, fort, fortress, monument, mausoleum; shed, barn, outhouse, stable, mill, lighthouse, pier, pavilion, boat-house, beach-hut, summerhouse, gazebo, dovecote, windmill. See also **house, shop**

---

build-up *n* **1** *a build-up of fat*: accretion *formal*, accumulation, development, enlargement, escalation, expansion, gain, growth, increase **2** *build-up of nuclear weapons*: accumulation, heap, load, mass, stack, stockpile, store **3** *build-up to the competition*: hype *colloq*, plug *colloq*, promotion, publicity
⊟ 1 contraction, decrease, reduction

built-in *adj* **1** *built-in wardrobes*: fitted, in-built, included, integral **2** *built-in safeguards*: essential, fundamental, implicit, in-built, included, incorporated, inherent, integral, intrinsic, necessary

bulb

Plants grown from bulbs and corms include:
acidanthera, allium, amaryllis,, anemone, bluebell (endymion), chincherinchee, chionodoxa, crocosmia, crocus, autumn crocus (colchicum), cyclamen, daffodil, crown imperial (fritillaria), galtonia, garlic, gladioli, grape hyacinth (muscari), hyacinth, iris, ixia, jonquil, lily, montbretia, narcissus, nerine, ranunculus, scilla, snowdrop (galanthus), sparaxis, tulip, winter aconite

---

bulbous *adj* bloated, bulging, convex, distended *formal*, pulvinate(d) *technical*, rounded, swelling, swollen

bulge *n* **1** *a bulge on the wall*: bump, distension *formal*, hump, lump, projection *formal*, protuberance *formal*, swelling **2** *a bulge in the production figures*: increase, intensification, rise, surge, upsurge
♦ *v* bulb, distend *formal*, expand, hump, project, protrude, puff out *colloq*, sag *colloq*, swell

bulk *n* **1** *the vast bulk of the ship*: amplitude *formal*, bigness, body, dimensions, extent, immensity, largeness, magnitude, mass, size, substance, volume, weight **2** *the bulk of the recruits*: lion's share *colloq*, majority, most, nearly all, preponderance

bulky *adj* awkward, big, colossal, cumbersome, enormous, heavy, hefty, huge, immense, large,

mammoth, massive, substantial, unmanageable, unwieldy, voluminous *formal*, weighty
⊟ handy, insubstantial, small

bulldoze *v* **1** *bulldoze buildings*: clear, flatten, knock down, level, raze **2** *bulldoze someone into buying*: browbeat, bully *colloq*, coerce *formal*, force, intimidate, push, steamroller *colloq* **3** *bulldoze plans through a committee*: force, push (through), steamroller *colloq*

bullet *n* ball, cartouche, cartridge, missile, pellet, projectile, shot, slug *colloq*

bulletin *n* **1** *television news bulletins*: announcement, communication, communiqué, dispatch, message, newsflash, notification, report, statement **2** *an office bulletin*: leaflet, news sheet, newsletter, newspaper

bullish *adj* buoyant, cheerful, confident, hopeful, optimistic, positive, sanguine *formal*, upbeat *colloq*

bully *n* browbeater, bully-boy, heavy *colloq*, intimidator, persecutor, tormentor, tough *colloq*
♦ *v* **1** *don't let him bully you*: bullyrag, intimidate, oppress, overbear, persecute, pick on, push around *colloq*, terrorize, torment, tyrannize, victimize **2** *bullied me into going*: browbeat, bulldoze, bullyrag, coerce, cow, domineer, force, intimidate
⊟ 2 coax, encourage, persuade

bulwark *n* **1** *the bulwarks of the fort*: bastion, buttress, embankment, fortification, mainstay, outwork, partition, rampart, redoubt *technical* **2** *a bulwark against terrorism*: buffer, defence, guard, mainstay, safeguard, security, support

bumbling *adj* **1** *a bumbling figure*: awkward, blundering, clumsy, lumbering, stumbling **2** *a bumbling amateur*: blundering, botching, bungling, incompetent, inefficient, inept, maladroit *formal*
⊟ 2 competent, efficient

bump *v* **1** *bump into the wall*: bang, collide (with), crash, hit, knock, prang *colloq*, slam *colloq*, strike **2** *bump along a track*: bounce, jar, jerk, jolt, jostle, rattle, shake
♦ *n* **1** *hear a bump*: bang, crash, knock, smash, thud, thump **2** *we had a bump in the car*: blow, collision, crash, hit, impact, jar, jolt, knock, shock, smash **3** *a bump on your head*: bulge, hump, injury, knur, lump, nodule, papilla *technical*, protrusion *formal*, protuberance *formal*, swelling, tumescence *formal* **4** *a bump on a road*: bulge, hump, lump, protuberance, sleeping policeman
▶ bump into chance upon *formal*, come across, encounter, happen upon *formal*, light upon *formal*, meet (unexpectedly), meet by chance, run into *colloq*
▶ bump off assassinate, blow away *colloq*, do in *colloq*, eliminate *colloq*, kill, liquidate *colloq*, murder, remove, rub out *colloq*, top *colloq*

bumper *adj* abundant, enormous, excellent, exceptional, great, large, massive, plentiful
⊟ small, tiny

bumpkin *n* boor, clodhopper, country bumpkin, country yokel, hayseed *colloq*, hick *colloq*, hillbilly *colloq*, oaf, peasant, provincial, rustic

bumptious *adj* arrogant, assertive, boastful, cocky *colloq*, conceited, egotistic, forward, full of

yourself, overbearing, overconfident, presumptuous, pushy *colloq*, self-important, swaggering
🔁 humble, modest, unassertive

bumpy *adj* 1 *a bumpy road*: irregular, knobbly, knobby, lumpy, pot-holed, rough, uneven 2 *a bumpy ride*: bouncy, choppy, jerky, jolting, rough
🔁 1 level, smooth 2 even, smooth, uncomfortable

bunch *n* 1 *a bunch of grapes*: bundle, clump, cluster, sheaf, tuft 2 *a bunch of keys/papers*: agglomeration *formal*, assortment, batch, collection, fascicle *formal*, fascicule *formal*, heap, lot, mass, number, pile, quantity, stack, wad 3 *a bunch of flowers*: bouquet, corsage, nosegay, posy, spray 4 *a bunch of people*: band, crew, crowd, flock, gang, gathering, group, mob, multitude, party, swarm, team, troop
♦ *v* assemble *formal*, cluster, collect, congregate *formal*, crowd, flock, gather, group, herd, huddle, mass, pack
🔁 disperse, scatter, spread out

bundle *n* 1 *a bundle of sticks*: bale, bunch, faggot, fascicle *formal*, fascicule *formal*, roll, sheaf, truss 2 *carry bundles of clothes*: bag, box, carton, pack, package, packet, parcel 3 *a bundle of books/paper*: accumulation, assortment, collection, group, heap, mass, pile, quantity, set, stack
♦ *v* 1 *bundle papers together*: bale, bind, cluster, fasten, gather, pack, parcel, tie, truss, wrap 2 *bundle someone into a van*: hurry, push roughly, rush, shove

bungle *v* blunder, bodge *colloq*, botch *colloq*, cock up *slang*, fluff *colloq*, foul up *colloq*, fudge, louse up *colloq*, make a mess of, mess up *colloq*, mismanage, muff *colloq*, ruin, screw up *slang*, spoil

bungler *n* blunderer, botcher *colloq*, butterfingers *colloq*, duffer *colloq*, incompetent

bungling *adj* awkward, blundering *colloq*, botching *colloq*, cack-handed *colloq*, clumsy, ham-fisted *colloq*, ham-handed *colloq*, incompetent, inept, maladroit *formal*, unskilful

bunkum *n* balderdash *colloq*, balls *slang*, baloney *colloq*, bilge *colloq*, bosh *colloq*, bunk *colloq*, cobblers *colloq*, garbage *colloq*, hogwash US *colloq*, hooey *colloq*, horsefeathers *colloq*, nonsense, piffle *colloq*, poppycock *colloq*, rot *colloq*, rubbish, stuff and nonsense *colloq*, tommyrot *colloq*, trash *colloq*, tripe *colloq*, twaddle *colloq*

buoy *n* beacon, float, marker, mooring, signal
▶ **buoy up** boost, cheer (up), encourage, hearten, lift, raise, support, sustain
🔁 depress, discourage

buoyant *adj* 1 *a buoyant mood*: animated, blithe, bouncy *colloq*, bright, bullish, carefree, cheerful, debonair, happy, joyful, light-hearted, lively, optimistic, peppy *colloq*, vivacious 2 *a buoyant raft*: afloat, floatable, floating, light, weightless
🔁 1 depressed, despairing 2 heavy

burble *v* babble, gurgle, lap, murmur, purl

burden *n* 1 *put down a heavy burden*: cargo, deadweight, load, weight 2 *the burdens of office*: affliction, anxiety, care, duty, encumbrance *formal*, millstone, obligation, pressure, responsibility, sorrow, strain, stress, trial, trouble, weight, worry
♦ *v* bother, crush, encumber *formal*, handicap, lie heavy/hard on, oppress, overload, overwhelm, strain, weigh down
🔁 relieve, unburden

burdensome *adj* crushing, difficult, exacting, heavy, irksome, onerous, oppressive, taxing, troublesome, trying, wearisome, weighty
🔁 easy, light

bureau *n* 1 *the Federal Bureau of Investigation*: agency, branch, department, division, office, service 2 *sit at a bureau*: desk, writing-desk

bureaucracy *n* 1 *a bureaucracy of thousands of civil servants*: administration, civil service, government, ministry, the authorities, the system 2 *try to reduce bureaucracy*: administration, beadledom, officialdom, officiousness, red tape *colloq*, rules and regulations

bureaucrat *n* administrator, apparatchik, civil servant, committee member, functionary, (government) minister, mandarin, office-holder, officer, official

bureaucratic *adj* administrative, complicated, governmental, ministerial, official, procedural

burglar *n* cat-burglar, housebreaker, robber, thief

burglary *n* break-in, housebreaking, robbery, stealing, theft

burial *n* burying, entombment *formal*, exequies *formal*, funeral, inhumation *formal*, interment *formal*, obsequies *formal*

burial place *n* catacomb, cemetery, churchyard, crypt, God's acre, graveyard, mausoleum, necropolis, tumulus, vault

burlesque *n* caricature, mickey-taking *colloq*, mock, mockery, parody, ridicule, satire, send-up *colloq*, spoof *colloq*, take-off *colloq*, travesty
♦ *adj* caricatural *formal*, comic, derisive, farcical, hudibrastic *formal*, mocking, parodying, satirical
🔁 serious

burly *adj* beefy, big, brawny, heavy, hefty, hulking, muscular, powerful, stocky, strapping, strong, sturdy, thickset, well-built
🔁 puny, slim, small, thin

burn *v* 1 *the fire's burning*: be in flames, be on/catch fire, be/catch ablaze, blaze, burst into flames, flame, flare (up), flash, flicker, glow, go up in flames, go up in smoke, smoke, smoulder 2 *burn rubbish*: burn down, conflagrate *formal*, consume, cremate, deflagrate *formal*, destroy, gut, ignite, incinerate, kindle, light, put a match to, set fire to 3 *burn your hand on the oven*: brand, cauterize *formal*, scald, scorch 4 *burn toast*: char, scorch, sear, singe, toast 5 *make your throat burn*: bite, hurt, smart, sting, tingle 6 *burn with anger*: fume, seethe, simmer 7 *burn to be with someone*: be eager, desire, itch, long, yearn

burning *adj* 1 *a burning skyscraper*: ablaze, afire, aflame, alight, blazing, fiery, flaming, glowing, smouldering 2 *burning eyes*: blazing, fiery, flaming, flashing, gleaming, glowing 3 *a burning forehead/a burning hot day*: hot, scalding, scorching 4 *a burning sensation*: acute, biting, piercing, prickling, searing, smarting, stinging, tingling 5 *a burning smell*: acrid, caustic, pungent 6 *burning desire*: ardent, consuming, eager, earnest, fervent, fervid *formal*, frantic, frenzied, impassioned, intense, passionate, vehement

7 *a burning issue*: crucial, essential, important, pressing, significant, urgent, vital
☒ **3** cold **6** apathetic **7** unimportant

burnish *v* brighten, buff, glaze, polish (up), shine

burp *v* belch, bring up wind, eructate *formal*

burrow *n* den, earth, hole, lair, set, shelter, tunnel, warren
♦ *v* **1** *burrow into the sand*: delve, dig, excavate, mine, tunnel, undermine **2** *burrow for the keys*: delve, rummage, search

burst *v* **1** *the tyre burst*: break (open), crack, disintegrate, fragment, puncture, rupture, shatter, shiver, split, tear **2** *the water burst into the tunnel*: erupt, gush, rush, spout **3** *burst into a room*: barge, break in on, dart, hurry, push your way *colloq*, race, run, rush **4** *shells that burst on impact*: blow up, explode
♦ *n* **1** *have a burst on the motorway*: blow-out *colloq*, puncture **2** *a burst of gunfire*: discharge, fusillade *formal*, outburst, rush, volley **3** *a sudden burst of activity*: fit, outbreak, outburst, outpouring, rush, spate, spurt, surge, torrent
▶ **burst out 1** *burst out crying*: begin, commence *formal*, start **2** *'That's what I've been trying to tell you,' she burst out*: blurt out *colloq*, call out, cry (out), exclaim, utter

bury *v* **1** *bury the dead*: entomb *formal*, inearth *formal*, inhume *formal*, inter *formal*, lay to rest, put six feet under *colloq*, sepulchre *formal* **2** *bury your face in your hands*: conceal, cover, enclose, engulf, enshroud *formal*, hide, immerse **3** *posts buried deep into the ground*: embed, implant, plant, sink, submerge **4** *bury yourself in work*: absorb, engage, engross, immerse, occupy
☒ **1** disinter *formal*, exhume **2** expose, uncover

bush *n* **1** *a rose bush*: hedge, plant, shrub, thicket **2** *go camping in the bush*: backwoods, brush, scrub, scrubland, wilds

bushy *adj* **1** *bushy hair*: bristling, bristly, fluffy, fuzzy, luxuriant, rough, shaggy, spreading, stiff, thick, unruly, wiry **2** *a bushy plant*: bristling, bristly, dasyphyllous *formal*, dumose *formal*, dumous *formal*
☒ **1** neat, thin, tidy, trim, well-kept

busily *adv* actively, assiduously, briskly, diligently, earnestly, energetically, hard, industriously, purposefully, speedily, strenuously

business *n* **1** *a career in business*: bargaining, buying, commerce, industry, manufacturing dealings, merchandising, selling, trade, trading, transactions **2** *set up a new business*: company, concern, conglomerate, consortium, corporation, enterprise, establishment, firm, flagship, franchise, holding company, industry, multinational, operation, organization, parent/subsidiary company, private enterprise, syndicate, venture **3** *what business are you in?*: calling, career, employment, job, line, métier, occupation, profession, trade, vocation, work **4** *it's not my business to look after him*: duty, job, responsibility, task **5** *it's none of your business*: affair, concern, issue, matter, problem **6** *any other business to discuss*: issue, matter, point, question, subject, topic

businesslike *adj* correct, efficient, matter-of-fact, methodical, orderly, organized, painstaking, practical, pragmatic, precise, professional, systematic, thorough, well-ordered
☒ disorganized, inefficient, sloppy *colloq*, wasteful

businessman, businesswoman *n* capitalist, entrepreneur, executive, financier, industrialist, magnate, merchant, trader, tycoon

busker *n* street-entertainer, street-musician

bust *n* **1** *a bust of the President*: head, sculpture, statue, torso **2** *a woman's bust*: boobs *slang*, bosom, breast, breasts, bristols *slang*, chest, knockers *slang*, tits *slang*

bustle *v* bestir *formal*, dash, fuss, hasten *formal*, hurry, rush, rush to and fro, scamper, scramble, scurry, tear *colloq*, to and fro *colloq*
♦ *n* a hive of activity *colloq*, activity, ado *formal*, agitation, comings and goings *colloq*, commotion, excitement, flurry, fuss, haste *formal*, hurly-burly, hurry, hustle and bustle, pother *formal*, scramble, stir, the rush

bustling *adj* active, astir *formal*, busy, buzzing, crowded, energetic, full, hectic, humming, lively, rushing, swarming, teeming, thronged *formal*
☒ quiet, restful, sleepy

busy *adj* **1** *be busy at the moment*: busy as a bee *colloq*, employed, engaged, hard at it *colloq*, having a previous engagement/prior appointment, occupied, otherwise engaged, tied up *colloq*, unavailable, working **2** *a busy day*: active, energetic, eventful, frantic, full, hectic, strenuous, tiring **3** *a busy street*: active, bustling, crowded, full, hectic, lively, swarming, teeming, vibrant **4** *busy preparing for the meeting*: engrossed, involved, occupied, working **5** *a busy person*: active, assiduous, diligent, fully stretched *colloq*, having a lot on *colloq*, having a lot to do, having your hands full *colloq*, industrious, on the go *colloq*, rushed off your feet *colloq*, sedulous *formal*, snowed under *colloq*, under pressure *colloq*, up to your eyes in something *colloq*
☒ **1** available, free **2** empty, leisured, quiet **3** empty, quiet **4** unoccupied **5** at a loose end *colloq*, idle, lazy
♦ *v* absorb, concern, employ, engage, engross, immerse, interest, involve, occupy

busybody *n* eavesdropper, gossip, interferer, intruder, meddler, nosy parker *colloq*, pantopragmatic *formal*, pry, quidnunc *formal*, scandalmonger, snoop, snooper, troublemaker

butcher *n* **1** *buy meat from the butcher's*: meat counter, meat retailer, meat seller **2** *the butcher who killed ten people*: destroyer, killer, (mass) murderer, slaughterer, slayer
♦ *v* assassinate, destroy, exterminate, kill, liquidate, massacre, slaughter, slay

butchery *n* blood-letting, bloodshed, carnage, killing, mass destruction, (mass) murder, massacre, slaughter

butt¹ *n* **1** *the butt of a gun/tool*: base, butt end, end, foot, haft, handle, shaft, stock **2** *the butt of a cigarette*: dog-end *colloq*, fag-end *colloq*, stub, tail end, tip **3** *sit on your butt*: arse *slang*, bottom, bum *colloq*, buttocks, posterior *colloq*

butt² *n* dupe, laughing-stock, mark, object, scapegoat, subject, target, victim

butt[3] *v* buffet, bump, hit, jab, knock, poke, prod, push, ram, shove, thrust
▶ **butt in 1** *butt in while someone is talking:* cut in, interject *formal*, interpose *formal*, interrupt **2** *butt in on other people's business:* interfere, intrude, meddle, put your oar in *colloq*, stick your nose in *colloq*

butter
▶ **butter up** blarney, cajole, coax, flatter, kowtow, pander to, praise, soft-soap *colloq*, suck up to *colloq*, wheedle

butterfly

Types of butterfly include:
red admiral, white admiral, apollo, cabbage white, chalkhill blue, common blue, brimstone, meadow brown, Camberwell beauty, clouded yellow, comma, large copper, small copper, fritillary, Duke of Burgundy fritillary, heath fritillary, gatekeeper, grayling, hairstreak, purple hairstreak, white letter hairstreak, hermit, monarch, orange-tip, painted lady, peacock, purple emperor, ringlet, grizzled skipper, swallowtail, tortoiseshell

buttocks *n* arse *slang*, ass *US slang*, behind *colloq*, bottom, breech, bum *colloq*, butt *US colloq*, derrière, gluteus *technical*, haunches, hind-quarters, nates, posterior *colloq*, rear, rump, seat

button *n* **1** *buttons on a shirt:* catch, clasp, fastener, fastening **2** *press the button:* disc, knob, switch

buttonhole *v* accost, catch, corner *colloq*, detain, grab *colloq*, importune *formal*, nab *colloq*, take aside, waylay

buttress *n* abutment *formal*, brace, mainstay, pier, prop, reinforcement, shore, stanchion *formal*, stay, strut, support
♦ *v* **1** *walls buttressed by towers:* bolster up, brace, hold up, prop up, reinforce, shore up, strengthen, support, underpin **2** *the regime was buttressed by the CIA:* back up, bolster up, reinforce, strengthen, support, sustain, underpin
⊠ **1** undermine, weaken **2** undermine, weaken

buxom *adj* ample, bosomy, busty, chesty, comely *formal*, plump, voluptuous, well-endowed, well-rounded
⊠ petite, slim, small

buy *v* **1** *buy a car:* acquire, get, invest in, obtain, pay for, pick up *colloq*, procure *formal*, purchase, shop for, snap up *colloq*, speculate, splash out on *colloq*, stock up on **2** *he had bought the judge:* bribe,

buy off, fix *colloq*, grease someone's palm *colloq*, suborn
⊠ **1** sell
♦ *n* acquisition, bargain, deal, purchase

buyer *n* client, consumer, customer, emptor *formal*, patron *formal*, purchaser, shopper, vendee *formal*
⊠ seller, vendor *formal*

buzz *v* **1** *bees buzzing round:* bombilate *formal*, bombinate *formal*, drone, hum, murmur, susurrate *formal*, whirr **2** *buzz with excitement:* bustle, hum, pulse, race, throb
♦ *n* **1** *the buzz of bees:* bombilation *formal*, bombination *formal*, buzzing, drone, hum, murmur, purr, susurration *formal*, susurrus *formal*, tinnitus *technical*, whirr **2** *give me a buzz when you get the news:* (phone) call, ring **3** *the latest buzz:* gossip, hearsay, latest, rumour, scandal **4** *winning gives me a buzz:* excitement, high *colloq*, kick(s) *colloq*, stimulation, thrill

by *prep* **1** *a low table by the chair:* alongside, beside, close to, near, next to **2** *enter by the window:* along, over, through, via **3** *earn money by working hard:* by means of, through, through the agency of, under the aegis of *formal* **4** *get home by noon:* at, before, no later than **5** *by any standard:* according to, in relation to
♦ *adv* **1** *two policemen were standing by:* at hand, close (by), handy, near **2** *put some money by:* aside, away **3** *he walked by:* away, beyond, past

bygone *adj* ancient, antiquated, departed, erstwhile *formal*, forepast *formal*, forgotten, former, lost, olden, one-time, past, previous
⊠ forthcoming, future, modern, recent

bypass *v* avoid, circumvent *formal*, dodge *colloq*, find a way round, get round, ignore, neglect, omit, sidestep, skirt *colloq*
♦ *n* detour, diversion, ring road

by-product *n* **1** *cattle feed is a by-product of making whisky:* derivative, spin-off **2** *by-products of modern life:* after-effect, consequence, fallout *colloq*, repercussion, result, side effect

bystander *n* eyewitness, looker-on, observer, onlooker, passer-by, rubberneck *colloq*, spectator, watcher, witness
⊠ participant

byword *n* **1** *caution must be our byword:* catchword, dictum, maxim, motto, slogan **2** *the old byword 'silence is golden':* adage, aphorism, apophthegm *formal*, precept, proverb, saw, saying

C

cab *n* **1** *hire a cab:* hackney carriage, minicab, taxi, taxicab **2** *the cab in a lorry:* cabin, compartment, driver's compartment, quarters

cabal *n* clique, coalition, conclave, coterie, faction, junta, junto, league, party, plotters, set

cabaret *n* comedy, dancing, entertainment, show, singing

cabin *n* **1** *a log cabin:* bothy *Scot*, chalet, cottage, hut, lodge, shack, shanty, shed, shelter **2** *a ship's cabin:* berth, compartment, quarters, room, sleeping quarters

cabinet *n* **1** *a medicine cabinet:* case, chest, closet, cupboard, dresser, locker **2** *the Labour Cabinet:* administration, executive, government, ministers, senate

cable *n* **1** *tie with cable:* chain, cord, guy, hawser, line, rope, stay **2** *electric cable:* flex, lead, wire **3** *send a message by cable:* facsimile, fax, telegram, telegraph, Telemessage®, wire
♦ *v* fax, send a telegram/telemessage/wire, send by telegraph, telegraph, wire

cache *n* accumulation, collection, fund, hidden treasure, hoard, repository *formal*, reserve, stash *colloq*, stock, stockpile, store, storehouse, supply, treasure-store

cachet *n* approval, distinction, eminence, esteem *formal*, estimation, favour, prestige, reputation, street cred *colloq*

cackle *v* chortle, chuckle, giggle, laugh loudly, laugh unpleasantly

cacophonous *adj* discordant, dissonant, grating, harsh, horrisonant *formal*, inharmonious, jarring, raucous, strident
☲ harmonious, pleasant

cacophony *n* caterwauling, discord, disharmony, dissonance, harshness, horrisonance *formal*, jarring, raucousness, stridency
☲ harmony

cad *n* blackguard, bleeder *colloq*, blighter *colloq*, bounder *colloq*, devil, knave, miscreant, rascal, rat *colloq*, reprobate, rogue, rotter *colloq*, scoundrel, scumbag *colloq*, stinker *colloq*, swine *colloq*, villain

cadaver *n* body, carcase, corpse, dead body, remains, stiff *slang*

cadaverous *adj* ashen, corpse-like, death-like, emaciated, gaunt, haggard, like death warmed up *colloq*, pale, skeletal, thin, wan

cadence *n* **1** *the cadence of his voice:* accent, inflection, intonation, lilt, modulation **2** *the cadence of the verse:* accent, beat, lilt, measure, metre, pattern, pulse, rate, rhythm, stress, swing, tempo, throb

cadge *v* beg, bum *colloq*, scrounge, sponge *colloq*

café *n* bistro, brasserie, buffet, cafeteria, coffee bar, coffee shop, cybercafé, restaurant, snackbar, tea room, tea shop

cafeteria *n* buffet, café, canteen, restaurant, self-service café, self-service canteen, self-service restaurant

cage *n* aviary, coop, corral, enclosure, hutch, lock-up, pen, pound
♦ *v* confine, coop up, impound, imprison, incarcerate, lock up, shut up

caged *adj* confined, cooped up, encaged, fenced in, impounded, imprisoned, incarcerated *formal*, locked up, restrained, shut up
☲ free, let out, released

cagey *adj* careful, cautious, chary, circumspect *formal*, discreet, guarded, non-committal, playing your cards close to your chest *colloq*, secretive, wary
☲ frank, indiscreet, open

cajole *v* beguile, butter up *colloq*, coax, entice, flatter, get round, inveigle *formal*, lure, persuade, seduce, soft-soap *colloq*, sweet-talk *colloq*, tempt, wheedle
☲ bully, compel, force

cajolery *n* beguilement, blandishments *formal*, blarney, coaxing, enticement, flattery, inducement(s), inveigling *formal*, persuasion, soft soap *colloq*, sweet talk *colloq*, wheedling
☲ bullying, compulsion, force

cake *n* **1** *tea and cakes:* bun, fancy, flan, gateau, madeleine, pastry, pie, tart **2** *a cake of soap:* bar, block, chunk, cube, loaf, lump, mass, slab
♦ *v* **1** *his boots were caked with mud:* coat, cover, encrust, plaster **2** *blood had caked round his mouth:* coagulate, congeal, consolidate, dry, harden, solidify, thicken

calamitous *adj* cataclysmic, catastrophic, deadly, devastating, dire, disastrous, dreadful, fatal, ghastly, grievous, ruinous, tragic, woeful
☲ fortunate, good, happy

calamity *n* adversity, affliction, catastrophe, disaster, downfall, misadventure, mischance, misfortune, mishap, reverse, ruin, scourge, tragedy, tribulation, trouble
☲ blessing, godsend

calculate *v* **1** *the probabilities are calculated using this equation:* compute, count, derive, determine, enumerate, estimate, figure, gauge, measure, rate, reckon (up), value, weigh, work out **2** *a plan calculated to make him jealous:* aim, design, intend, plan

calculated *adj* considered, deliberate, intended, intentional, planned, premeditated, purposed *formal*, purposeful, wilful
☲ unintended, unplanned

calculating *adj* contriving, crafty, cunning, designing, devious, Machiavellian, manipulative, scheming, sharp, shrewd, sly
☲ artless, naïve

calculation *n* **1** *she did a mental calculation:* computation, estimate, estimation, figuring, forecast, judgement, reckoning, sum, working-out **2** *an act of deliberate calculation:* deliberation, planning, premeditation

calibre *n* **1** *a.38 calibre long-barrelled revolver:* bore, diameter, gauge, measure, size **2** *candidates of the right calibre:* ability, capacity, character, competence, distinction, endowments, excellence, faculty, gifts, merit, quality, strength, talent, worth

call *v* **1** *he is called John:* baptize, brand, christen, denominate *formal*, describe as, designate, dub, entitle, label, name, rename, style, term, title **2** *call more loudly:* bawl, bellow, cry (out), exclaim, roar, scream, shout, shriek, yell **3** *call me to arrange it:* buzz *colloq*, contact, give someone a buzz *colloq*, give someone a ring, give someone a tinkle *colloq*, phone (up), ring (up), telephone **4** *call a doctor:* ask for, ask to come in/round, contact, order, send for, summon *formal* **5** *call to collect the money:* call in/round, come by, drop in, pay a visit, pop in *colloq*, stop by **6** *call a meeting:* assemble, bid, convene *formal*, invite, summon *formal*
♦ *n* **1** *loud calls were heard outside:* cry, exclamation, scream, shout, shriek, yell **2** *the doctor paid a call:* visit **3** *a telephone call:* bell *colloq*, buzz *colloq*, ring, tinkle *colloq* **4** *calls for his resignation:* appeal, command, order, plea, request **5** *no call to talk to him like that:* cause, excuse, grounds, justification, need, occasion, reason, right **6** *there's no call for this product:* demand, need
▶ **call for 1** *she called for her bags:* collect, fetch, go for, pick up **2** *they called for his release:* press for, push for, require, suggest **3** *this calls for some thought:* entail *formal*, involve, justify, make necessary, necessitate *formal*, need, occasion, require, warrant *formal*
▶ **call off** abandon, break off, cancel, discontinue, drop, rescind *formal*, revoke *formal*, scrub *colloq*, shelve *colloq*, withdraw
▶ **call on 1** *call on a friend:* go and see, look in on, pay someone a (short) visit, visit **2** *call on the government to resign:* appeal to, ask, bid, demand, entreat *formal*, plead with, press for, request, supplicate *formal*, urge

calling *n* business, career, employment, field, job, line, line of business/work, métier, mission, occupation, profession, province, pursuit, trade, vocation, work

callous *adj* cold, cold-blooded, cold-hearted, hardened, hard-hearted, harsh, heartless, indifferent, indurate *formal*, insensate *formal*, insensitive, obdurate *formal*, stony, stony-hearted, uncaring, unfeeling, unsympathetic
◰ caring, kind, sensitive, sympathetic

callow *adj* fledgling, green *colloq*, immature, inexperienced, jejune *formal*, juvenile, naïve, raw, unfledged, unsophisticated, untried
◰ experienced

calm *adj* **1** *his calm leadership:* collected, composed, cool, cool-headed, dispassionate, impassive, imperturbable, laid back *colloq*, placid, poised, quiet, relaxed, sedate, self-controlled, self-possessed, serene, steady, unapprehensive, undisturbed, unemotional, unexcitable, unexcited, unflappable *colloq*, unflustered, unmoved, unperturbed, unruffled, untroubled **2** *calm waters:* peaceful, quiet, serene, smooth, still, tranquil, undisturbed, waveless **3** *calm weather:* mild, peaceful, quiet, serene, still, tranquil, unclouded, windless
◰ **1** anxious, excitable, upset, worried **2** rough, stormy, wild **3** rough, stormy, wild, windy
♦ *n* **1** *the calm before the storm:* calmness, hush, peace, peacefulness, quiet, quietude *formal*, repose *formal*, serenity, stillness, tranquillity **2** *a*

feeling of calm: ataraxia *formal*, calmness, composure, contentment, cool *colloq*, equanimity *formal*, impassiveness, impassivity, peace, peacefulness, placidity *formal*, quiet, quietude *formal*, repose *formal*, restfulness, sangfroid *formal*, serenity, stillness, tranquillity, unflappability *colloq*
◰ **1** storminess **2** excitement, restlessness, trouble
♦ *v* allay, appease *formal*, assuage *formal*, hush, lull, mollify *formal*, pacify, placate *formal*, quieten, relax, sedate, settle (down), soothe, still, tranquillize
◰ excite, upset, worry
▶ **calm down** compose yourself, cool down *colloq*, hush, keep your head *colloq*, lighten up *colloq*, quieten down, relax, settle down, simmer down *colloq*

calumny *n* abuse, aspersion, backbiting, defamation, denigration *formal*, derogation *formal*, detraction *formal*, disparagement *formal*, insult, libel, misrepresentation, obloquy *formal*, revilement *formal*, slagging-off *colloq*, slander, smear *colloq*, vilification *formal*, vituperation *formal*

camaraderie *n* affinity, brotherhood, brotherliness, closeness, companionship, comradeship, esprit de corps, fellowship, good fellowship, togetherness

camera

Types of camera include:
automatic, bellows, binocular, box Brownie®, camcorder, camera obscura, cine, cinematographic, compact, daguerreotype, digital, disc, disposable, film, Instamatic®, large-format, miniature, subminiature, panoramic, plate, dry-plate, half-plate, quarter-plate, wet-plate, point-and-press, Polaroid®, press, reflex, folding reflex, single-lens reflex (SLR), twin-lens reflex (TLR), security, sliding box, sound, still, stereo, Super 8®, TV, video. See also **photographic**

Parts of a camera include:
accessory shoe, AF lenses, aperture, aperture setting control, autofocus (AF), autofocus sensor, automatic focusing system, battery chamber, blind, cable release, card door, card on/off key, card window, compact lens, compound lens, data panel/display, diaphragm, exposure meter, exposure mode button, film advance/transport, film gate, film holder, fisheye lens, flash contact, flash setting, focal plane shutter, focus control/setting, focusing hood, focusing ring, frame counter, function adjustment button, function selector key, iris diaphragm, leaf shutter, lens, lens cap, lens release, light control, long-focus lens, magazine, medium focal-length lens, meter cell, mirror, mirror lens, mirror shutter, object lens, pentaprism, program card, program reset button, rangefinder window, reflex viewer, registration pin, release button, rewind handle/crank, shutter, shutter release, shutter speed control, shutter/film speed indicator, spool, spool knob, take-up reel/spool, telephoto lens, viewfinder eyepiece, viewfinder, viewing lens, wide-angle lens, zoom lens

---

camouflage *n* **1** *hide behind their camouflage:* blind, cloak, concealment, cover, cover-up,

deception, disguise, façade, front, guise, mask, masquerade, screen **2** *animals which use camouflage:* protective colouring
♦ *v* cloak, conceal, cover, cover up, disguise, hide, mask, obscure, screen, veil
🔁 reveal, uncover

camp[1] *n* **1** *a Scout camp:* bivouac, camping-ground, camping-site, campsite, encampment, tents **2** *the union camp:* caucus, clique, crowd, faction, group, party, section, set, side
♦ *v* pitch tents, rough it *colloq*, set up camp, sleep outdoors

camp[2] *adj* affected, artificial, campy, effeminate, exaggerated, homosexual, mannered, ostentatious, over the top *colloq*, poncy *colloq*, posturing, queer, theatrical

campaign *n* **1** *the election campaign:* course of action, crusade, drive, movement, operation, promotion, push, strategy **2** *a bombing campaign:* attack, battle, crusade, drive, expedition, offensive, operation, push, strategy, war
♦ *v* advocate, battle, crusade, drive, fight, promote, push, strive, struggle, work

camp-follower *n* hanger-on, henchman, lackey, toady

can *n* canister, container, jerrycan, pail, receptacle, tin

canal *n* **1** *the Grand Union canal:* channel, watercourse, waterway, zanja **2** *the alimentary canal:* channel, passage, tube

cancel *v* **1** *cancel a concert:* abandon, abort, axe *colloq*, call off, drop, postpone, scrap *colloq*, scrub *colloq*, shelve *colloq* **2** *cancel a reservation:* abolish, abrogate *formal*, annul *formal*, countermand *formal*, discontinue *formal*, dissolve, eliminate, invalidate *formal*, nullify *formal*, override, quash, repeal, rescind *formal*, retract *formal*, revoke *formal*, stop, vitiate *formal* **3** *cancel a name from a list:* delete, eliminate, erase, obliterate, stop
▶ **cancel out** balance, compensate, counteract, counterbalance, make up for, neutralize, nullify, offset, redeem

cancellation *n* **1** *a flight cancellation:* abandoning, abandonment, calling-off, revocation *formal*, shelving *colloq*, stopping **2** *the cancellation of a law:* abolition, annulment *formal*, elimination, invalidation *formal*, neutralization, nullifying *formal*, quashing, repeal, revocation *formal* **3** *the cancellation of a name from a list:* deletion, dropping, elimination, scrubbing *colloq*

cancer *n* **1** *she suffers from skin cancer:* carcinoma *technical*, growth, malignancy, malignant growth, tumour **2** *the cancer of racism:* blight, canker, corruption, disease, evil, pestilence, plague, rot, scourge, sickness

candelabrum *n* candlestick, menorah

candid *adj* blunt, clear, forthright, frank, guileless, honest, ingenuous, open, outspoken, plain, plain-spoken, sincere, straightforward, truthful, unequivocal
🔁 devious, evasive, guarded

candidate *n* **1** *candidates for a job:* applicant, aspirant, competitor, contender, contestant, nominee, possibility, runner **2** *candidates for an exam:* entrant

candle *n* cerge, tallow-candle, taper, wax-light

candour *n* artlessness, bluntness, directness, forthrightness, frankness, guilelessness, honesty, ingenuousness, openness, outspokenness, plain-dealing, plainness, sincerity, straightforwardness, truthfulness, unequivocalness
🔁 deviousness, evasiveness, guardedness

candy *n* chocolates, confectionery, sweets, toffees

cane *n* alpenstock, crook, ferule *formal*, rod, staff, stick, walking-stick

canker *n* **1** *a social canker:* bane, blight, cancer, corrosion, corruption, disease, evil, pestilence, plague, rot, scourge, sickness **2** *canker in an animal's ear:* boil, infection, lesion, sore, ulcer

cannabis *n* bhang, blow *slang*, dope *colloq*, ganja *colloq*, grass *colloq*, hash *colloq*, hashish, hemp, kef *colloq*, leaf *slang*, locoweed *US slang*, marijuana, pot *colloq*, puff *colloq*, punk *slang*, skunk *slang*, spliff *colloq*, tea *colloq*, weed *slang*

cannibal *n* anthropophagite *technical*, man-eater, people-eater

cannibalism *n* anthropophagy *technical*, endophagy, exophagy, man-eating, people-eating

cannon *n* artillery, battery, big gun *colloq*, field gun, howitzer, mortar, ordnance

---

cannon or *canon*? A *cannon* is a large gun. A *canon* is a Christian priest who helps to run the work of a cathedral and also a general rule or belief: *the canons of literary taste.*

---

cannonade *n* barrage, bombardment, broadside, salvo, shelling, volley

canny *adj* acute, artful, astute, careful, cautious, circumspect *formal*, clever, judicious *formal*, knowing, no flies on someone *colloq*, perspicacious *formal*, prudent, sagacious *formal*, sharp, shrewd, sly, subtle, wise, worldly-wise
🔁 foolish, imprudent

canon *n* **1** *a cathedral canon:* clergyman, minister, prebendary, priest, reverend, vicar **2** *the canons of literary taste:* criterion, dictate, precept, principle, regulation, rule, standard, statute, yardstick

canonical *adj* accepted, approved, authoritative, authorized, orthodox, recognized, regular, sanctioned

---

Names of canonical hours include:
matins, lauds, terce, sext, none, vespers, compline

---

canopy *n* awning, baldachin, cover, covering, shade, shelter, sunshade, tester, tilt, umbrella

cant *n* **1** *insincere cant:* hypocrisy, insincerity, sanctimoniousness **2** *underworld cant:* argot, jargon, lingo, slang, vernacular

cantankerous *adj* bad-tempered, contrary, crabbed *colloq*, crabby *colloq*, cross, crotchety *colloq*, crusty, difficult, grouchy, grumpy, ill-humoured, irascible, irritable, peevish, quarrelsome, quick-tempered, testy
🔁 easy-going *colloq*, good-natured, pleasant

canter *n* jog, jogtrot, lope, run, trot
♦ *v* amble, jog, lope, run, trot

canvass *v* **1** *the politician canvassed for votes:* agitate, ask for votes, campaign, drum up support, electioneer, seek votes, solicit votes **2** *canvass all options*: analyse, evaluate, examine, explore, find out, inquire into, inspect, investigate, poll, scan, scrutinize, sift, study, survey

canyon *n* abyss, chasm, gorge, gully, ravine, valley

cap *n* **1** *he put on his cap*: balmoral, baseball cap, beret, bonnet, flat cap, forage-cap, glengarry, hat, kalpak, kepi, muffin-cap, peaked cap, school cap, skullcap, tammy, tam-o'-shanter **2** *the cap of a jar*: bung, cover, lid, plug, stopper, top
♦ *v* **1** *cap someone's story*: beat, better, eclipse, exceed, excel, outdo, outshine, surpass, transcend **2** *mountains capped with snow*: coat, cover, crown, top **3** *cap tax levels*: control, curb, limit, restrain, restrict

capability *n* ability, accomplishment, aptitude, capacity, competence, efficiency, facility, faculty, means, potential, power, proficiency, qualification, skilfulness, skill, talent
🖿 inability, incompetence

---

capability or *ability*? See panel at **ability**

---

capable *adj* **1** *a capable person*: able, accomplished, adept, businesslike, clever, competent, efficient, experienced, gifted, masterly, proficient, qualified, skilful, smart, talented **2** *capable of murder*: apt to, disposed to, having the inclination/tendency to, inclined to, liable to, tending to **3** *a rifle capable of firing ten rounds a minute*: able, fitted, suited
🖿 **1** incompetent, useless **2** incapable **3** incapable

capacious *adj* ample, big, broad, commodious *formal*, comprehensive, expansive, extensive, generous, huge, large, roomy, sizeable, spacious, substantial, vast, voluminous *formal*, wide
🖿 cramped, small

capacity *n* **1** *the capacity to act*: ability, aptitude, capability, competence, efficiency, faculty, genius, gift, potential, power, proficiency, resources, skill, talent **2** *to maximum capacity*: compass, dimensions, extent, largeness, magnitude, proportions, range, room, scope, size, space, volume **3** *in her capacity as president*: function, job, office, position, post, role

cape¹ *n* cloak, mantle, pelerine, pelisse, poncho, robe, shawl, wrap

cape² *n* head, headland, neck, ness, peninsula, point, promontory, tongue

caper *v* bounce, bound, cavort, dance, frisk, frolic, gambol, hop, jump, leap, romp, skip, spring
♦ *n* **1** *he amused them with his capers and jokes*: antic, dido *US colloq*, escapade, high jinks, jape, jest, lark, mischief, prank, stunt **2** *are you involved in this caper too?*: affair, business

capital *n* **1** *need capital to expand the business*: assets, cash, finance, funds, investment(s), liquid assets, means, money, principal, property, reserves, resources, savings, stock, wealth, wherewithal **2** *the capital of France*: administrative centre, most important city, seat of government **3** *write in capitals*: block capital, block letter, capital letter, majuscule *formal*, uncial *formal*, upper-case letter
♦ *adj* **1** *the capital city*: cardinal, central, chief, first, foremost, important, leading, main, major, primary, prime, principal **2** *a capital offence*: punishable by death, serious
🖿 **1** minor, unimportant **2** minor

capitalism *n* free enterprise, laissez-faire, private enterprise, private ownership

capitalist *n* fat cat *slang*, financier, investor, magnate, mogul, moneybags *colloq*, moneyman, money-spinner *colloq*, person of means, plutocrat, tycoon

capitalize
▶ *capitalize on* cash in on *colloq*, exploit, make the most of, profit from, take advantage of

capitulate *v* back down, give in, give up, relent, submit, succumb, surrender, throw in the towel/sponge *colloq*, yield

capitulation *n* backing-down, giving-in, giving-up, relenting, submission, succumbing, surrender, yielding

caprice *n* fad, fancy, fickleness, fitfulness, impulse, inconstancy, notion, quirk, vagary, vapour, whim, whimsy

capricious *adj* **1** *her capricious moods*: changeable, erratic, fickle, fitful, impulsive, inconstant, mercurial, quirky, uncertain, unpredictable, variable, wayward, whimsical **2** *capricious weather conditions*: changeable, erratic, fitful, freakish, inconstant, mercurial, uncertain, unpredictable, variable
🖿 **1** sensible, steady **2** steady

capsize *v* invert, keel over, overturn, roll over, tip over, turn over, turn turtle, upset

capsule *n* **1** *a capsule of medicine*: container, lozenge, pill, receptacle, tablet **2** *a seed capsule*: pod, sheath, shell **3** *a space capsule*: craft, module, probe

captain *n* **1** *captain of a ship*: commander, master, officer, pilot, skipper **2** *captain of a team*: boss *colloq*, chief, head, leader, master, skipper

caption *n* heading, inscription, legend, note, title, wording

captivate *v* allure, attract, beguile, bewitch, charm, dazzle, delight, enamour, enchant, enrapture, enthral, fascinate, hypnotize, infatuate, mesmerize, seduce, win
🖿 appal, disgust, repel

captivating *adj* alluring, attractive, beautiful, beguiling, bewitching, charming, dazzling, delightful, enchanting, enthralling, fascinating, seductive, winsome
🖿 ugly, unattractive

captive *n* detainee, hostage, internee, prisoner, slave
♦ *adj* **1** *captive soldiers*: confined, detained, enchained, enslaved, held in custody, imprisoned, in bondage, incarcerated *formal*, interned, locked up/away, restricted, secure, shut up **2** *a captive animal*: caged, confined, ensnared, imprisoned, locked up/away, restrained, secure, shut up
🖿 **1** free, liberated **2** free, liberated

captivity *n* bondage, confinement, constraint, custody, detention, duress, imprisonment, incarceration *formal*, internment, restraint, servitude *formal*, slavery
🖿 freedom, liberation

capture *v* **1** *capture a prisoner:* apprehend, arrest, catch, collar *colloq*, ensnare, entrap, hunt down, nab *colloq*, nick *colloq*, pick up, recapture, secure, seize, snare, take, take possession of, trap **2** *capture a mood:* embrace, encapsulate, record, represent
♦ *n* arrest, catching, collaring *colloq*, nabbing *colloq*, nicking *colloq*, seizure, taking, taking captive, taking prisoner, trapping

car *n* automobile, jalopy *colloq*, motor, motor car, motor vehicle, (set of) wheels *colloq*, vehicle

---
Types of car include:
saloon, hatchback, fastback, estate, sports car, cabriolet, convertible, limousine, limo *colloq*, banger *colloq*, Mini®, bubble-car, coupé, station wagon, shooting brake, veteran car, vintage car, four-wheel drive, Jeep®, buggy, Land Rover®, Range Rover®, patrol car, taxi, cab. See also **motor vehicle**

---

carafe *n* bottle, decanter, flagon, flask, jug, pitcher

carbuncle *n* anthrax, boil, inflammation, pimple, sore

carcase *n* **1** *the carcase of an animal:* body, cadaver, corpse, dead body, remains **2** *the carcase of a building:* framework, hulk, shell, skeleton, structure

cardinal *adj* capital, central, chief, essential, first, foremost, fundamental, greatest, highest, important, key, leading, main, paramount, pre-eminent, primary, prime, principal

care *n* **1** *handle with care:* carefulness, caution, circumspection *formal*, forethought, meticulousness, pains, prudence *formal*, vigilance *formal*, watchfulness **2** *children need care:* attention, concern, consideration, heed, looking-after, minding, protection, regard, tending, watching-over **3** *in their care:* charge, control, custody, guardianship, keeping, protection, responsibility, safekeeping, supervision, tutelage, ward **4** *forget all your cares:* affliction, anxiety, burden, concern, pressure, responsibility, strain, stress, tribulation *formal*, trouble, vexation *formal*, worry
🔁 **1** carelessness **2** carelessness, inattention, neglect, thoughtlessness
♦ *v* be concerned, be interested, bother, give a damn *colloq*, mind, worry
🔁 be indifferent, ignore, neglect, not give a hoot/hang/hoot/damn/toss *colloq*, not give a monkey's *colloq*, not give a tinker's cuss/brass farthing *colloq*
▶ **care for 1** *care for the children:* attend, look after, maintain, mind, minister to, nurse, protect, provide for, take care of, tend, watch over **2** *care for someone:* be close to, be fond of, be in love with, be keen on, cherish, feel affection for, love **3** *would you care for a cup of tea?:* desire, like, want

career *n* calling, employment, job, life-work, livelihood, métier, occupation, profession, pursuit, trade, vocation
♦ *v* bolt, dash, gallop, hurtle, race, run, rush, shoot, speed, tear

carefree *adj* blithe, breezy, cheerful, cheery, easy-going *colloq*, happy, happy-go-lucky, insouciant *formal*, laid back *colloq*, light-hearted, nonchalant *formal*, unconcerned, untroubled, unworried

🔁 anxious, despondent, distressed, troubled, worried

careful *adj* **1** *be careful when you cross the road:* alert, attentive, aware, cautious, chary, circumspect *formal*, heedful, judicious *formal*, mindful, prudent *formal*, vigilant, wary, watchful **2** *be careful what you say to him:* cautious, chary, circumspect *formal*, discreet, guarded, judicious *formal*, prudent *formal*, tactful, wary **3** *a careful arrangement of flowers:* accurate, assiduous, conscientious, detailed, diligent, fastidious, methodical, meticulous, painstaking, particular, precise, punctilious *formal*, rigorous, scrupulous, showing great attention to detail, systematic, thorough, thoughtful
🔁 **1** careless, inattentive, reckless, thoughtless **2** careless, reckless, thoughtless **3** careless

careless *adj* **1** *a careless person:* absent-minded, forgetful, heedless, inattentive, inconsiderate, indiscreet, irresponsible, negligent, reckless, remiss, tactless, thoughtless, uncaring, unconcerned, unguarded, unmindful, unthinking **2** *careless work:* casual, cursory, disorderly, disorganized, hasty, inaccurate, lax, messy, neglectful, offhand, perfunctory, slack, slapdash, slipshod, sloppy *colloq*, superficial, untidy **3** *careless charm:* artless, breezy, carefree, casual, cheerful, easy-going *colloq*, happy-go-lucky, insouciant *formal*, laid back *colloq*, light-hearted, nonchalant *formal*, simple, untroubled, unworried
🔁 **1** careful, thoughtful **2** accurate, careful, meticulous

caress *v* canoodle *colloq*, cuddle, embrace, fondle, grope *colloq*, hug, kiss, nuzzle, pet, rub, stroke, touch
♦ *n* cuddle, embrace, fondle, hug, kiss, pat, petting, stroke, touch

caretaker *n* concierge, curator, custodian, doorkeeper, janitor, keeper, ostiary, porter, steward, superintendent, warden, watchman

careworn *adj* exhausted, fatigued, gaunt, haggard, tired, weary, worn, worn-out
🔁 lively, sprightly

cargo *n* baggage, consignment, contents, freight, goods, haul, lading, load, pay-load, shipment, tonnage

caricature *n* burlesque, cartoon, imitation, lampoon, mimicry, parody, satire, send-up *colloq*, take-off *colloq*, travesty
♦ *v* mimic, mock, parody, ridicule, satirize, send up *colloq*, take off *colloq*

carnage *n* bloodbath, bloodshed, butchery, ethnic cleansing, genocide, holocaust, killing, mass murder, massacre, murder, slaughter

carnal *adj* animal, bodily, corporeal *formal*, erotic, fleshly, human, impure, lascivious, lecherous, lewd, libidinous *formal*, licentious, lustful, natural, physical, sensual, sexual
🔁 chaste, pure, spiritual

carnival *n* celebration, fair, festival, fête, fiesta, gala, holiday, jamboree, jubilee, merrymaking, revelry

carnivorous *adj* creophagous *technical*, meat-eating, zoophagous

carol *n* Christmas song, hymn, noel, song, wassail

carouse v booze *slang*, drink, drink freely, imbibe *formal*, make merry, party, quaff, revel, roister, wassail

carousing n drinking, merrymaking, partying

carp v censure, complain, criticize, find faults, knock *colloq*, nag, nit-pick *colloq*, quibble, reproach, ultracrepidate *formal*
🗷 compliment, praise

carpenter n cabinet-maker, joiner, woodworker

carpet n 1 *fit a new carpet*: Aubusson, Axminster, covering, floor-covering, kali, Kidderminster, kilim, mat, matting, rug, Wilton 2 *a carpet of leaves*: bed, blanket, covering, layer

carriage n 1 *I arrived in a carriage*: cab, car, coach, gig, hackney, hansom, landau, trap, vehicle, wagon 2 *her noble carriage*: air, attitude, bearing, behaviour, conduct, demeanour *formal*, deportment *formal*, manner, mien *formal*, posture, presence, stance 3 *pay for carriage*: carrying, conveyance, delivery, freight, postage, transport, transportation

carrier n 1 *parcels sent by a carrier*: bearer, conveyor, delivery-person, messenger, porter, roundsperson, runner, transporter, vehicle 2 *the carrier of a disease*: bearer, transmitter, vector

carry v 1 *carry the boxes*: bring, cart *colloq*, conduct, convey, deliver, drive, fetch, haul, hump *colloq*, lug *colloq*, move, pipe, relay, shift, take, tote *colloq*, transfer, transport 2 *they carry all the weight*: bear, hold (up), maintain, shoulder, stand, suffer, support, sustain, take someone's weight, underpin, uphold 3 *carry a disease*: be infected with, pass on, transmit 4 *the proposal was carried*: accept, adopt, authorize, pass, ratify, sanction, vote for, vote in favour of 5 *drug-smuggling carries a risk*: bear, entail *formal*, have (as a consequence), involve, lead to, mean 6 *the newspaper carried the story*: broadcast, communicate, contain, cover, display, disseminate *formal*, present, print, release, show 7 *carry several brands*: have, have for sale, retail, sell, stock
► **carry on** 1 *carry on until the end*: continue, endure, go on, keep on, keep up, last, maintain, persevere, persist, proceed, progress, restart, resume, return to 2 *carry on a business*: administer, conduct, manage, operate, run 3 *children carrying on*: behave foolishly, mess around *colloq*, misbehave, play up *colloq* 4 *carrying on with a colleague at work*: be involved, have an affair
► **carry out** accomplish, achieve, bring off, conduct, deliver (the goods) *colloq*, discharge, do, effect *formal*, execute, fulfil, implement, perform, put into effect/operation/practice, realize, undertake

cart n barrow, dray, handcart, truck, wagon, wheelbarrow
♦ v bear, carry, convey, haul, hump *colloq*, lug *colloq*, move, shift, tote *colloq*, transfer, transport

carton n box, case, container, pack, package, packet, parcel

cartoon n 1 *newspaper cartoons*: caricature, drawing, lampoon, parody, picture, send-up *colloq*, sketch, take-off *colloq* 2 *watch cartoons on TV*: animated film, animation, comic strip

cartridge n canister, capsule, case, cassette, charge, container, cylinder, magazine, round, shell, tube

carve v 1 *carve meat*: chop, cut (up), hack, slice 2 *carve stone*: chip, chisel, cut, fashion, form, hew, sculpt, sculpture, shape, whittle 3 *carve a design*: engrave, etch, incise, indent
► **carve up** distribute, divide, parcel out, partition, separate, share (out), split (up)

carving n bust, dendroglyph *technical*, incision, lithoglyph, petroglyph, sculpture, statue, statuette

cascade n avalanche, cataract, chute, deluge, falls, flood, fountain, gush, outpouring, rush, shower, torrent, waterfall
♦ v descend, fall, flood, gush, overflow, pitch, plunge, pour, rush, shower, spill, surge, tumble

case¹ n 1 *if this is the case*: circumstances, condition, context, contingency *formal*, event, position, situation, state 2 *a bad case of pneumonia*: example, instance, occasion, occurrence, specimen 3 *a court case*: action, argument, cause, dispute, lawsuit, proceedings, process, suit, trial 4 *send in the next case*: client, invalid, patient, victim

case² n 1 *a case for jewels*: box, cabinet, capsule, carton, cartridge, casing, casket, chest, container, cover, crate, holder, jacket, receptacle, sheath, shell, showcase, trunk, wrapper 2 *a case of clothes*: attaché case, bag, briefcase, flight bag, hand-luggage, holdall, overnight-bag, portfolio, portmanteau, suitcase, travel bag, trunk, valise, vanity-case

cash n 1 *pay by cash*: banknotes, bullion, change, coins, currency, hard currency, hard money, legal tender, money, notes, ready money 2 *have no cash for a holiday*: bread *slang*, capital, dosh *slang*, dough *slang*, funds, lolly *slang*, readies *slang*, ready money *slang*, resources, wherewithal
♦ v encash, exchange, liquidate, realize, turn into cash

cashier¹ n accountant, bank clerk, banker, bursar, clerk, financial controller, purser, teller, treasurer

cashier² v discharge, dismiss, drum out, expel, get rid of, give someone the boot *colloq*, sack *colloq*, throw out, unfrock *colloq*

cask n barrel, butt, firkin, hogshead, keg, tub, tun, vat

casket n 1 *keep jewels in a casket*: box, case, chest, coffer, jewel-box, kist, pyxis 2 *lay the corpse in a casket*: box, coffin, pine overcoat *slang*, sarcophagus, wooden overcoat *slang*

cast v 1 *cast a stone*: drive, fling, heave, hurl, impel, launch, lob, pitch, shy, sling, throw, toss 2 *cast light*: diffuse, direct, emit, give off, give out, project, radiate, scatter, shed, spread 3 *cast your eyes/a glance*: catch sight, glance, glimpse, look (at), see, view 4 *cast doubt/suspicion*: place, put, put a question mark over *colloq*, put in jeopardy, throw 5 *cast your vote*: mark with a cross, record, register, vote 6 *cast a statue*: fashion, form, found, model, mould, shape
♦ n 1 *the cast of a film*: actors, characters, company, dramatis personae, entertainers, performers, players, troupe 2 *take off the cast*: casting, covering, form, model, mould, shape

▶ **cast down** crush, deject, depress, desolate, discourage, dishearten, sadden
▣ cheer up, encourage

caste *n* background, class, degree, estate, grade, group, lineage, order, position, race, rank, social class, social standing, station, status, stratum

castigate *v* berate, censure, chasten, chastise, chide, criticize, discipline, dress down *colloq*, haul over the coals *colloq*, punish, rap on the knuckles *colloq*, rebuke, reprimand, reprove, scold, tear a strip off *colloq*, upbraid

castle *n* château, citadel, fort, fortress, keep, stronghold, tower

---

Parts of a castle include:
approach, bailey, barbican, bartizan, bastion, battlements, brattice, buttress, chapel, corbel, courtyard, crenel, crenellation, curtain wall, ditch, donjon, drawbridge, dungeon, embrasure, enclosure wall, fosse, gatehouse, inner wall, keep, lookout tower, merlon, moat, motte, mound, outer bailey, parapet, portcullis, postern, rampart, scarp, stockade, tower, turret, ward, watchtower

---

castrate *v* emasculate, evirate *formal*, geld, neuter, unman, unsex

casual *adj* 1 *a casual glance:* apathetic, blasé, couldn't-care-less *colloq*, cursory, easy-going *colloq*, free-and-easy *colloq*, happy-go-lucky *colloq*, indifferent, informal, insouciant *formal*, lackadaisical, laid back *colloq*, lukewarm, negligent, nonchalant, offhand, relaxed, unconcerned 2 *casual clothes:* comfortable, informal, leisure, relaxed 3 *casual work:* intermittent, irregular, occasional, part-time, provisional, short-term, temporary 4 *a casual meeting:* accidental, chance, fortuitous, incidental, random, serendipitous *formal*, unexpected, unforeseen, unintentional, unpremeditated
▣ 1 concerned, worried 2 formal 3 full-time, permanent, regular 4 deliberate, planned

casualty *n* 1 *the enemy suffered huge casualties:* dead person, death, fatality, injured, injured person, injury, loss, missing, wounded 2 *a casualty of the job cuts:* sufferer, victim

casuistry *n* chicanery, equivocation, sophism, sophistry, speciousness

cat *n* grimalkin *old use*, kitten, mog *colloq*, moggy *colloq*, mouser, puss *colloq*, pussy *colloq*, pussy cat *colloq*, tabby, tomcat

---

Breeds of cat include:
Abyssinian, American shorthair, Balinese, Birman, Bombay, British longhair, British shorthair, Burmese, Carthusian, chinchilla, Cornish rex, Cymric, Devon rex, domestic tabby, Egyptian Mau, Exotic shorthair, Foreign Blue, Foreign spotted shorthair, Foreign White, Havana, Himalayan, Japanese Bobtail, Korat, Maine Coon, Manx, Norwegian Forest, Persian, rag-doll, rex, Russian Blue, Scottish Fold, Siamese, silver tabby, Singapura, Somali, Tiffany, Tonkinese, Tortoiseshell, Turkish Angora, Turkish Van

---

cataclysm *n* blow, calamity, catastrophe, collapse, debacle, devastation, disaster, upheaval

catacomb *n* 1 *buried in the catacombs:* burial-vault, crypt, ossuary *formal*, tomb, vault 2 *escaped*

via the catacombs: underground passages, underground rooms, underground tunnels

catalogue *n* 1 *a furniture catalogue:* brochure, checklist, classification, directory, gazetteer, guide, index, inventory, list, manifest, record, register, roll, roster, table 2 *a catalogue of events:* calendar, prospectus, schedule
♦ *v* alphabetize, classify, compile/make a list, file, index, list, record, register

catapult *v* fire, fling, hurl, hurtle, launch, pitch, propel, shoot, sling, throw, toss

cataract *n* cascade, deluge, downpour, falls, force, rapids, torrent, waterfall

catastrophe *n* adversity, affliction *formal*, blow, calamity, cataclysm *formal*, debacle, devastation, disaster, mischance, misfortune, reverse, ruin, tragedy, trouble, upheaval

catastrophic *adj* awful, calamitous, cataclysmic *formal*, devastating, disastrous, dreadful, fatal, terrible, tragic

catcall *n* barracking, boo, gibe, hiss, jeer, raspberry *colloq*, whistle

catch *v* 1 *catch a ball:* clutch, grab, grasp, grip, hold, seize, snatch, take 2 *catch an animal:* capture, corner, ensnare, entrap, hook, hunt down, net, round up, seize, snare, trap 3 *catch a prisoner:* apprehend, arrest, capture, collar *colloq*, corner, hunt down, lay hold of, nab *colloq*, nick *colloq*, seize 4 *catch what someone says:* comprehend, follow, get the hang of *colloq*, grasp, hear, make out, perceive, recognize, take in, twig *colloq*, understand 5 *catch someone doing something wrong:* catch red-handed/in the act, detect, discover, expose, find (out), surprise, unmask 6 *catch a cold:* become ill with, become infected with, contract *formal*, develop, get, go down with, pick up, succumb to *formal* 7 *catch someone's attention:* attract, draw, grasp, hold
▣ 1 drop 2 free, release 3 free, release 4 miss
♦ *n* 1 *a catch on the box:* bolt, clasp, clip, fastener, hasp, hook, latch, lock, sneck *Scot* 2 *what's the catch?:* difficulty, disadvantage, drawback, fly in the ointment *colloq*, hitch, obstacle, problem, snag
▶ **catch on** 1 *the new style is catching on quickly:* become all the rage *colloq*, become fashionable, become popular 2 *catch on to what she said:* comprehend, follow, grasp, take in, understand
▶ **catch up** draw level, gain on, overtake

catching *adj* communicable, contagious, infectious, transmissible, transmittable

catch phrase *n* byword, catchword, formula, motto, saying, slogan

catchy *adj* 1 *a catchy tune:* haunting, melodic, memorable, popular, tuneful, unforgettable 2 *a catchy title:* appealing, attractive, captivating, memorable, unforgettable
▣ 1 boring, dull, instantly forgettable 2 boring, dull, instantly forgettable

catechize *v* cross-examine, examine, give the third degree *colloq*, grill *colloq*, interrogate, question, test

categorical *adj* absolute, clear, conclusive, definite, direct, downright, emphatic, explicit, express, positive, total, unconditional, unequivocal, unqualified, unreserved, utter
▣ qualified, tentative, vague

categorize *v* arrange, class, classify, grade, group, list, order, rank, sort, tabulate

category *n* class, classification, department, division, genre, grade, group, grouping, head, heading, kind, list, listing, order, rank, section, sort, title, type, variety

cater *v* 1 *cater for a wedding:* provision *formal*, supply, victual *formal* 2 *cater for people's needs:* furnish, provide, serve, supply 3 *cater to someone's desires:* indulge, pander

caterwaul *v* bawl, cry, howl, scream, screech, shriek, squall, wail, yowl

catharsis *n* abreaction *technical*, cleansing, epuration, purging, purification, purifying, release

cathartic *adj* abreactive *technical*, cleansing, purging, purifying, releasing

cathedral *n* dome, duomo, minster

catholic *adj* all-embracing, all-encompassing, all-inclusive, broad, broad-based, broad-minded, comprehensive, diverse, eclectic *formal*, general, global, inclusive, liberal, open-minded, tolerant, universal, varied, wide, wide-ranging, widespread
🔀 bigoted, limited, narrow, narrow-minded

cattle *n* beasts, bulls, cows, livestock, oxen, stock

Breeds of cattle include:
Aberdeen Angus, Africander, Alderney, Ankole, Ayrshire, Blonde d'Aquitaine, Brahman, Brown Swiss, cattabu, cattalo, Charolais, Chillingham, Devon, dexter, Durham, Friesian, Galloway, Guernsey, Hereford, Highland, Holstein, Jersey, Latvian, Limousin, Longhorn, Luing, Red Poll, Romagnola, Santa Gertrudis, Shetland, Shorthorn, Simmenthaler, Teeswater, Ukrainian, Welsh Black

catty *adj* back-biting, bitchy, ill-natured, malevolent, malicious, mean, rancorous *formal*, spiteful, venomous, vicious
🔀 kind, pleasant

caucus *n* 1 *hold a caucus:* assembly, conclave, convention, gathering, get-together, meeting, parley, session 2 *a caucus of party members:* assembly, clique, conclave, gathering, set

causative *adj* causing, factitive *technical*, factive, root

cause *n* 1 *the cause of evil:* agency, agent, author, basis, beginning, creator, factor, mainspring, maker, mover, origin, originator, prime mover, producer, root, source, spring 2 *a cause for concern:* basis, grounds, impulse, incentive, inducement, justification, motivation, motive, reason, stimulus 3 *a worthy cause:* aim, belief, end, enterprise, ideal, movement, object, principle, purpose, undertaking
🔀 1 consequence, effect, result
♦ *v* be at the root of, be the cause of, begin, breed, bring about, compel, create, effect *formal*, force, generate, give rise to, incite, induce, lead to, make, make happen, motivate, occasion, originate, precipitate, produce, prompt, provoke, result in, stimulate, trigger (off)
🔀 prevent, stop

caustic *adj* 1 *caustic chemicals:* acid, burning, corrosive, stinging 2 *a caustic remark:* acrimonious *formal*, astringent *formal*, biting, cutting, mordant *formal*, pungent, sarcastic,

scathing, severe, snide, stinging, trenchant *formal*, virulent
🔀 1 soothing 2 kind, mild

cauterize *v* burn, disinfect, scorch, sear, singe, sterilize

caution *n* 1 *proceed with caution:* alertness, care, carefulness, circumspection *formal*, deliberation, discretion, forethought, heed, heedfulness, mindfulness, prudence *formal*, vigilance *formal*, wariness, watchfulness 2 *give a caution:* admonition *formal*, advice, caveat *formal*, counsel, injunction, tip-off *colloq*, warning
🔀 1 carelessness, recklessness
♦ *v* admonish *formal*, advise, alert, counsel, tip off *colloq*, urge, warn

cautious *adj* alert, cagey *colloq*, careful, chary, circumspect *formal*, discreet, gingerly *colloq*, guarded, heedful, judicious *formal*, prudent *formal*, shrewd, softly-softly *colloq*, tentative, unadventurous, vigilant *formal*, wary, watchful
🔀 foolhardy, rash, reckless

cavalcade *n* array, cortège, march-past, parade, procession, retinue, train, troop

cavalier *n* 1 *cavaliers of the King's army:* Bashi-Bazouk, cavalryman, chasseur, chevalier, equestrian, horse soldier, horseman, Ironside, knight, spahi 2 *a dashing cavalier:* escort, gallant, gentleman, partner
♦ *adj* arrogant, casual, condescending, curt, disdainful, free-and-easy, haughty, insolent, lofty, lordly, offhand, patronizing, scornful, supercilious, swaggering

cavalry *n* cavalrymen, dragoons, equestrians, horse soldiers, horsemen, hussars, lancers, troopers

cave *n* cavern, cavity, dugout, grotto, hole, hollow, pothole, tunnel, underground chamber
▶ **cave in** collapse, fall (in), give way, slip, subside, yield

caveat *n* admonition *formal*, caution, warning

cavern *n* cave, cavity, grotto, hollow, pothole, tunnel, underground chamber, vault

cavernous *adj* dark, deep, echoing, gaping, gloomy, huge, immense, spacious, vast, yawning

cavil *v* carp, complain, criticize, find faults, nag, nit-pick *colloq*, quibble
🔀 compliment, praise

cavity *n* aperture, crater, dent, gap, hole, hollow, lacuna, orifice *technical*, pit, sinus, ventricle, well

cavort *v* caper, dance, frisk, frolic, gambol, prance, romp, skip, sport

cease *v* 1 *the rain finally ceased:* abate, come to a halt, come to an end, die, discontinue *formal*, end, fail, finish, fizzle out *colloq*, halt, let up, peter out *colloq*, stop, terminate 2 *cease talking for a moment:* break off, bring to a halt, bring to an end, call a halt to, conclude, desist from *formal*, discontinue *formal*, end, finish, halt, leave (off), pack in *colloq*, quit *colloq*, refrain from, stop, suspend, terminate
🔀 1 begin, commence, start 2 begin, commence, start

ceaseless *adj* constant, continual, continuous, endless, eternal, everlasting, incessant, interminable, never-ending, non-stop,

perpetual, persistent, unceasing, unending, uninterrupted, unremitting, untiring
Fa irregular, occasional

cede *v* abandon, abdicate *formal*, concede, give up, grant, hand over, relinquish, renounce *formal*, resign, surrender, transfer, turn over, yield

ceiling *n* **1** *a decorated ceiling:* awning, beams, canopy, overhead, overhead covering, plafond, rafters, roof, vault **2** *a 15 per cent ceiling on foreign holdings:* cut-off point, limit, maximum, most, upper limit

celebrate *v* **1** *I feel like celebrating:* enjoy yourself, go on the razzle *colloq*, go out, go out on the town *colloq*, have a ball *colloq*, have fun, have/throw a party, kill the fatted calf *colloq*, live it up *colloq*, paint the town red *colloq*, put the flags out *colloq*, rave *colloq*, rejoice, revel, whoop it up *colloq* **2** *celebrate a birthday:* commemorate, do something in someone's honour, drink to, honour, keep, mark, observe, remember, toast **3** *the priest celebrated Communion:* bless, perform, solemnize

celebrated *adj* acclaimed, distinguished, eminent, exalted, famed, famous, great, illustrious, legendary, notable, noted, outstanding, popular, prominent, renowned, revered, well-known, with your name in lights *colloq*
Fa forgotten, obscure, unknown

celebration *n* festivity, jollification, merrymaking, rave *colloq*, rave-up *colloq*, revelry, spree *colloq*

celebrity *n* big name *colloq*, big shot *colloq*, bigwig *colloq*, dignitary, famous person, household name, legend, legend in their own lifetime, living legend, luminary *formal*, name, notable *formal*, personage *formal*, personality, star, superstar, VIP *colloq*, worthy *formal*
Fa nobody, nonentity, unknown

celerity *n* dispatch, expedition, fastness, fleetness, quickness, rapidity, speed, swiftness, velocity
Fa slowness

celestial *adj* **1** *celestial beings:* angelic, astral, divine, elysian, eternal, ethereal, godlike, heavenly, immortal, paradisaic, seraphic, spiritual, sublime, supernatural, transcendental **2** *the celestial spheres:* astral, empyrean, ethereal, heavenly, starry
Fa 1 earthly, mundane **2** earthly, mundane

celibacy *n* abnegation *formal*, abstinence, bachelorhood, chastity, continence, purity, self-denial, self-restraint, singleness, spinsterhood, virginity

celibate *adj* abstinent, bachelor, chaste, pure, single, spinster, virgin

cell *n* **1** *a prison cell:* chamber, compartment, cubicle, dungeon, enclosure, jail, lock-up, prison, room **2** *living cells:* cytoplasm, gamete, matrix, nucleus, organism, protoplasm *technical*, protoplast *technical*, spore, unit, zygote **3** *a political cell:* caucus, clique, faction, group, nucleus, party, section, set, unit

cellar *n* basement, crypt, storeroom, vault, wine cellar

cement *n* adhesive, bonding, concrete, glue, grouting, matrix, mortar, paste, plaster, pointing, screed
♦ *v* affix, attach, bind, bond, glue, gum, join, solder, stick, unite, weld

cemetery *n* burial ground, burial place, burial site, charnel house *formal*, churchyard, God's acre *formal*, graves, graveyard, necropolis *formal*, tombs

censor *v* ban, blue-pencil, bowdlerize, cut, delete, edit, expurgate, make cuts
♦ *n* bowdlerizer, editor, examiner, expurgator, inspector

---

censor or *censure*? To *censor* books, films, etc is to examine them, deleting parts of them or forbidding publication: *His letters home were censored.* To *censure* someone is to criticize them severely: *The President was severely censured for abusing his powers.*

---

censorious *adj* captious *formal*, carping, cavilling, condemnatory, critical, disapproving, disparaging, fault-finding, hypercritical, severe
Fa approving, complimentary

censure *v* admonish *formal*, blame, castigate *formal*, come down heavy on *colloq*, condemn, criticize, denounce, disapprove of, haul over the coals *colloq*, pull to pieces *colloq*, rebuke, remonstrate *formal*, reprehend, reprimand, reproach, reprove, scold, tell off *colloq*, upbraid *formal*
Fa approve, compliment, praise
♦ *n* admonishment *formal*, admonition *formal*, blame, castigation *formal*, condemnation, criticism, denunciation, disapproval, obloquy *formal*, rebuke, remonstrance *formal*, reprehension, reprimand, reproach, reproof, scolding, telling-off *colloq*, upbraiding *formal*, vituperation *formal*
Fa approval, compliments, praise

central *adj* **1** *a central area:* inner, interior, medial, median, mid, middle **2** *the central issue:* basic, chief, core, crucial, dominant, essential, focal, foremost, fundamental, key, main, major, most important, pivotal, primary, prime, principal, significant, vital
Fa 1 peripheral **2** minor, secondary

centralize *v* amalgamate, bring/gather together, compact, concentrate, condense, converge, focus, incorporate, rationalize, streamline, unify
Fa decentralize

centre *n* bull's-eye *colloq*, core, crux, focal point, focus, heart, hub, kernel, linchpin, middle, midpoint, nucleus, pivot
Fa edge, outskirts, periphery
♦ *v* concentrate, converge, focus, gravitate, hinge, pivot, revolve

ceramics *n* bisque, earthenware, faience, ironstone, porcelain, pottery, raku, ware

cereal *n* **1** *farmers growing cereals:* barley, corn, grain, maize, millet, oats, rye, sorghum, wheat **2** *breakfast cereal:* cornflakes, muesli, oatmeal, porridge

ceremonial *adj* formal, official, ritual, ritualistic, solemn, stately
Fa casual, informal
♦ *n* ceremony, custom, formality, protocol, rite, ritual, solemnity

ceremonial or *ceremonious*? *Ceremonial* means 'relating to or appropriate for a ceremony': *ceremonial dress; a ceremonial occasion*. *Ceremonious* means 'very formal or polite': *He ushered her through with a ceremonious bow*.

ceremonious *adj* courteous, courtly, deferential, exact, formal, grand, official, polite, precise, punctilious *formal*, ritual, scrupulous, solemn, starchy *colloq*, stately, stiff
🔼 informal, relaxed, unceremonious

ceremony *n* **1** *a traditional ceremony:* anniversary, bar mitzvah, celebration, commemoration, custom, dedication, formality, function, graduation, inauguration, induction, initiation, investiture, liturgy, observance, ordinance, rite, sacrament, service, tradition, unveiling **2** *we don't stand on ceremony:* ceremonial, decorum *formal*, etiquette, form, formality, niceties, pageantry, pomp, propriety *formal*, protocol, ritual, show

certain *adj* **1** *I'm certain he's telling the truth:* assured, confident, convinced, persuaded, positive, sure **2** *his guilt is certain:* absolute, clear, conclusive, evident, incontrovertible *formal*, indisputable, indubitable *formal*, irrefutable *formal*, no ifs and buts *colloq*, no two ways about it *colloq*, obvious, open-and-shut *colloq*, plain, sure as eggs is eggs *colloq*, true, undeniable, undoubted, unquestionable **3** *success is certain:* bound to happen, cut and dried *colloq*, destined, doomed, fated, home and dry *colloq*, in the bag *colloq*, ineluctable *formal*, inescapable, inevitable, inexorable *formal*, meant to happen, unavoidable **4** *below a certain income:* decided, definite, determined, established, fixed, particular, precise, settled **5** *a certain person:* individual, particular, special, specific **6** *to a certain extent:* partial, some
🔼 **1** doubtful, hesitant, uncertain, unsure **3** unlikely

certainly *adv* absolutely, assuredly, by all means, clearly, definitely, doubtlessly, for sure, naturally, no doubt, obviously, of course, plainly, positively, surely, undeniably, undoubtedly, unquestionably, without a doubt

certainty *n* **1** *he spoke with great certainty:* assurance, assuredness, confidence, conviction, faith, positiveness, sureness, trust **2** *it's a certainty that she'll get the job:* dead cert *colloq*, fact, foregone conclusion, inevitability, reality, safe bet *colloq*, sure thing *colloq*, truth
🔼 **1** doubt, hesitation, uncertainty

certificate *n* authorization, award, credentials, diploma, document, endorsement, guarantee, licence, pass, qualification, testimonial, voucher, warrant

certify *v* **1** *he is certified to practise medicine:* accredit *formal*, authorize, endorse, license, warrant **2** *the document has been certified as legal:* assure, attest *formal*, authenticate, aver *formal*, bear witness to, confirm, corroborate *formal*, declare, endorse, guarantee, pronounce, ratify, recognize, substantiate, testify, validate, verify, vouch, witness

certitude *n* assuredness, certainty, confidence, conviction, (full) assurance, plerophoria *formal*, plerophory *formal*, positiveness, sureness
🔼 doubt

cessation *n* abeyance *formal*, break, ceasing, conclusion, desistance *formal*, discontinuance *formal*, discontinuation, discontinuing, end, ending, halt, halting, hiatus *formal*, intermission, interruption, interval, let-up, pause, recess, remission, respite, rest, standstill, stay, stoppage, stopping, suspension, termination
🔼 beginning, commencement, start

chafe *v* **1** *chafe someone's skin:* abrade *formal*, excoriate *formal*, grate, irritate, rasp, rub, scrape, scratch, wear **2** *chafe at the rules:* be angry, be annoyed, be enraged, be exasperated, be incensed, be peeved *colloq*, be vexed

chaff *n* cases, husks, pods, shells

chagrin *n* annoyance, disappointment, discomfiture *formal*, discomposure *formal*, displeasure, disquiet, dissatisfaction, embarrassment, exasperation, fretfulness, humiliation, indignation, irritation, mortification, shame, vexation
🔼 delight, pleasure
♦ *v* annoy, disappoint, displease, disquiet, dissatisfy, embarrass, exasperate, humiliate, irk, irritate, mortify, peeve *colloq*, vex

chain *n* **1** *a metal chain:* bond, coupling, fetter, link, manacle, restraint, shackle, trammel **2** *a hotel chain:* company, firm, group **3** *a chain of islands:* concatenation *formal*, line, row, set, string, train **4** *a chain of events:* concatenation *formal*, progression, sequence, series, succession
♦ *v* bind, fasten, fetter, handcuff, hitch, manacle, restrain, secure, shackle, tether, tie
🔼 free, liberate, release

chair *n* **1** *sit on a chair:* armchair, bench, form, recliner, seat, stool, swivel-chair **2** *Sally is the new chair:* chairman, chairperson, chairwoman, convener, director, master of ceremonies, MC, organizer, president, speaker, toastmaster
♦ *v* act as chairperson/chairman/chairwoman, convene, direct, lead, preside over, supervise

chalk
▶ **chalk up 1** *chalk the points up on a board:* log, put down, record, register, score, tally **2** *chalk up another victory:* accumulate, achieve, attain, gain, score **3** *chalk his failure up to inexperience:* ascribe, attribute, charge, credit, put down

chalky *adj* **1** *chalky soil:* calcareous *formal*, cretaceous *formal* **2** *every one of them was chalky white:* ashen, colourless, pale, pallid, wan, white

challenge *v* **1** *he challenged him to a duel:* confront, dare, defy, invite, provoke, summon, throw down the gauntlet *colloq* **2** *challenged his authority:* call into question, demur *formal*, disagree with, dispute, object to, protest, query, question, take exception to **3** *challenged my ability:* stretch, tax, test, try
♦ *n* **1** *we will face many challenges:* hazard, hurdle, obstacle, problem, risk, test, trial **2** *take up the challenge to fight:* bidding, call, confrontation, dare, defiance, provocation, summons **3** *a challenge to their authority:* calling into question, confrontation, defiance, disagreement, dispute, objection, opposition, protest, questioning

challenging adj demanding, exacting, stretching, taxing, testing
🔁 undemanding

chamber n 1 *the City Chambers:* assembly room, auditorium, hall, meeting-place 2 *she stayed in her chamber:* apartment, bedroom, boudoir, room 3 *the chambers of the heart:* cavity, compartment, ventricle 4 *the upper chamber of parliament:* assembly, council, house, legislature, parliament

champion n 1 *the school chess champion:* ace, champ *colloq*, conqueror, hero, title-holder, victor, winner 2 *a champion of animal rights:* advocate, backer, defender, guardian, patron, protector, supporter, upholder, vindicator
♦ v advocate, back, defend, espouse *formal*, maintain, promote, protect, stand up for, support, uphold

chance n 1 *meet someone by chance:* accident, coincidence, destiny, fate, fluke *colloq*, fortuity *formal*, fortune, luck, providence, serendipity *formal* 2 *take a chance:* gamble, risk, speculation 3 *what are the chances of that happening?:* likelihood, odds, possibility, probability, prospect 4 *a second chance:* break *colloq*, chance of a lifetime *colloq*, golden opportunity *colloq*, occasion, opening, opportunity, your best shot *colloq*
🔁 1 certainty 2 certainty
♦ v 1 *he chanced everything and lost:* gamble, hazard, risk, speculate, stake, venture, wager 2 *I wouldn't chance it if I were you:* chance your luck *colloq*, push your luck *colloq*, risk, take a chance, try, venture 3 *it so chanced that they met in the same spot:* arise, come about, crop up, develop, follow, happen, occur, result, take place
♦ adj accidental, arbitrary, casual, flukey *colloq*, fortuitous, haphazard, inadvertent, incidental, random, serendipitous *formal*, unanticipated, unexpected, unforeseen, unintended, unintentional, unlooked-for
🔁 certain, deliberate, foreseen, intentional
▶ **chance on/upon** bump into *colloq*, come across, discover, find by chance, meet, meet unexpectedly, run into *colloq*, stumble on

chancy adj dangerous, dicey *colloq*, dodgy *colloq*, fraught, hazardous, problematical, risky, speculative, tricky, uncertain
🔁 safe, secure

change v 1 *water changes into ice:* adapt, adjust, alter, become, become different, convert, develop, evolve, go, metamorphose, mutate *technical*, reform, shift, transform, transmutate, turn 2 *prices keep changing:* adapt, adjust, alter, be in a state of flux, fluctuate, move, shift, vacillate, vary 3 *change the rules:* adapt, adjust, alter, amend, convert, customize, develop, make different, modify, reform, remodel, renew, reorganize, restructure, revise, transfigure, transform, transmutate, vary 4 *change one thing for another:* alternate, chop and change *colloq*, exchange, interchange, replace, rotate, substitute, swap, switch, trade, transfer, transpose 5 *change buses:* connect, make a connection, transfer
♦ n 1 *make some major changes:* about-face, about-turn, adaptation, adjustment, alteration, amendment, conversion, customization, development, difference, innovation, modification, move, movement, reconstruction, reform, remodelling, renewal, reorganization, restructuring, reversal, revision, revolution, shake-up, shift, trend, turnabout, upheaval, U-turn *colloq*, volte-face 2 *a change in the weather:* development, difference, ebb and flow, fluctuation, metamorphosis, movement, mutation *technical*, reversal, shift, state of flux, transfiguration, transformation, transition, transmutation, turnabout, vacillation, variation, variety, vicissitude *formal* 3 *let's eat out for a change:* difference, diversion, innovation, novelty, variety 4 *a change of clothes:* alternation, exchange, interchange, replacement, rotation, substitute, substitution, swap, switch, trade, transposition 5 *have you got any change?:* cash, coins, coppers, silver

changeable adj capricious, chameleonic, chameleon-like, erratic, fickle, fluctuating, fluid, inconstant, irregular, kaleidoscopic, labile *formal*, mercurial, mutable *formal*, Protean, shifting, uncertain, unpredictable, unreliable, unsettled, unstable, unsteady, vacillating, variable, varying, vicissitudinous *formal*, volatile, wavering
🔁 constant, reliable, settled

channel n 1 *a channel for rainwater:* conduit, duct, flume, furrow, groove, gutter, passage, trough 2 *a collision of ships in the channel:* canal, main, neck, passage, sound, strait, watercourse, waterway 3 *channels of communication:* agency, agent, approach, avenue, course, means, medium, passage, path, route, way
♦ v conduct, convey, direct, force, guide, send, transmit

chant n 1 *the football supporters' chants:* cry, shout, slogan, warcry 2 *a religious chant:* chorus, incantation, mantra, melody, plainsong, psalm, recitation, refrain, song
♦ v chorus, intone *formal*, recite, sing

chaos n anarchy, bedlam, confusion, disorder, disorganization, disruption, lawlessness, madhouse, mess, pandemonium, riot, shambles *colloq*, snafu *US slang*, tohu bohu *formal*, tumult, upheaval, uproar
🔁 order

chaotic adj all over the place/shop *colloq*, anarchic, at sixes and sevens *colloq*, confused, deranged, disordered, disorganized, disrupted, higgledy-piggledy *colloq*, lawless, orderless, riotous, shambolic *colloq*, snafu *US slang*, topsy-turvy, tumultuous, uncontrolled, unruly
🔁 ordered, organized

chap n bloke *colloq*, boy, character, fellow, guy *colloq*, individual, man, person, sort, type

chaperone, chaperon n companion, duenna, escort
♦ v accompany, attend, escort, guard, look after, mind, protect, safeguard, shepherd, take care of, watch over

chapped adj chafed, cracked, raw, sore

chapter n 1 *read chapter 3:* clause, division, part, portion, section, topic 2 *a new chapter in my life:* episode, period, phase, stage, time

char v brown, burn, carbonize, scorch, sear, singe

character n 1 *the cruel side of his character:* attributes, characteristics, constitution, disposition, identity, individuality, make-up, nature, peculiarity, persona *formal*, personality, psyche, stamp, temper, temperament, trait, what makes someone tick *colloq* **2** *the character of the countryside:* attributes, calibre, characteristics, essence, essential quality, ethos, feature, nature, property, quality, type **3** *a stain on his character:* good name, honour, image, reputation, status **4** *he has character:* courage, determination, honesty, integrity, moral fibre, strength, strength of purpose, uprightness **5** *this house has character:* appeal, arresting qualities, attractive features, attractiveness, charm, distinctive features, interesting features, specialness, style **6** *she's quite a character:* case *colloq*, eccentric, eccentric person, oddball *colloq*, oddity, original **7** *the characters who live in the village:* human being, individual, person, sort, type **8** *the characters in a play:* part, person, role **9** *using Latin characters:* cipher, device, emblem, figure, hieroglyph, ideograph, letter, logo, mark, rune, sign, symbol, type

characteristic *n* attribute, essential quality, factor, feature, hallmark, idiosyncrasy, mannerism, mark, peculiarity, property, quality, symptom, trait
♦ *adj* distinctive, distinguishing, idiosyncratic, individual, peculiar, representative, special, specific, symbolic, symptomatic, typical
▰ uncharacteristic, untypical

characterize *v* **1** *materialism that characterizes Western life:* brand, designate, distinguish, identify, mark, specify, stamp, typify **2** *characterize a person:* describe, portray, present, represent

charade *n* fake, farce, mockery, pantomime, parody, pretence, sham, travesty

charge *v* **1** *charge a high price:* ask, ask for, ask someone to pay, bill, debit, demand, demand in payment, exact, levy, set/fix a price **2** *charge with a crime:* accuse, arraign *formal*, blame, impeach, incriminate, indict **3** *charge towards the enemy:* assail, assault, attack, rush (forward), storm, tear
♦ *n* **1** *an extortionate charge:* amount, cost, dues, expenditure, expense, fee, levy, outlay, payment, price, rate, rent, rental, toll **2** *place charges against him:* accusation, allegation, arraignment *formal*, blame, impeachment, imputation *formal*, incrimination, indictment **3** *join in the charge:* assault, attack, incursion, onrush, onslaught, rush, sortie, storming **4** *left the children in her charge:* care, custody, guardianship, keeping, protection, safekeeping, trust, ward **5** *it comes under your charge:* duty, obligation, responsibility

charitable *adj* **1** *a charitable organization:* beneficent, benevolent, bounteous *formal*, eleemosynary *formal*, generous, humanitarian, open-handed, philanthropic **2** *a charitable nature:* benevolent, benign, broad-minded, compassionate, considerate, forgiving, generous, gracious, humanitarian, indulgent, kind, kindly, lenient, liberal, magnanimous *formal*, sympathetic, tolerant, understanding
▰ **2** inconsiderate, uncharitable, unforgiving

charity *n* **1** *a registered charity:* caritas, foundation, fund, trust, voluntary organization **2** *live on charity:* aid, alms, almsgiving, assistance, contribution, donation, funding, gift, handout, relief **3** *an act of charity:* affection, altruism, beneficence *formal*, benevolence, benignness, bountifulness, clemency, compassion, considerateness, generosity, goodness, goodwill,

humanity, indulgence, kindness, love, philanthropy, tender-heartedness, thoughtfulness, tolerance, unselfishness
▰ **3** malice, selfishness

charlatan *n* bogus caller/official, cheat, con man *colloq*, confidence trickster, fake, fraud, impostor, mountebank, phoney *colloq*, pretender, quack, sham, swindler

charm *n* **1** *his irresistible charm:* allure, allurement, appeal, attraction, attractiveness, captivation, delightfulness, desirability, fascination, magnetism, what it takes *colloq* **2** *lucky charm:* amulet, fetish, grisgris, idol, juju, mascot, obi, ornament, periapt, porte-bonheur, talisman, trinket **3** *the magician's charm:* abracadabra, enchantment, magic, sorcery, spell
♦ *v* allure, attract, beguile, bewitch, cajole, captivate, delight, draw, enamour, enchant, enrapture, fascinate, intrigue, mesmerize, please, seduce, win
▰ disgust, repel

charming *adj* alluring, appealing, attractive, captivating, cute, delightful, enchanting, engaging, fetching, irresistible, lovely, pleasant, pleasing, seductive, sweet, winning, winsome
▰ repulsive, ugly, unattractive

chart *n* **1** *a chart showing the patient's temperature:* bar chart, blueprint, diagram, flow chart, flow sheet, graph, map, nomogram *technical*, nomograph *technical*, pie chart, plan, table **2** *number one in the charts:* hit parade, league, list, top twenty
♦ *v* **1** *chart an area:* delineate, draft, draw, map, map out, mark, outline, place, plot, sketch **2** *chart one's progress:* document, follow, keep a record of, monitor, note, observe, put on record, record, register

charter *n* accreditation *formal*, authority, authorization, bond, concession, contract, covenant, deed, document, franchise, indenture, licence, permit, prerogative, privilege, right, sanction, warrant
♦ *v* **1** *charter an aircraft:* commission, employ, engage, hire, lease, rent **2** *chartered to practise medicine:* authorize, sanction

chary *adj* careful, cautious, circumspect *formal*, guarded, heedful, leery, prudent *formal*, reluctant, suspicious, uneasy, unwilling, wary
▰ heedless, unwary

chase *v* **1** *the police chased the thief:* be hot on someone's heels *colloq*, follow, give chase, hunt, pursue, run after, rush after, shadow, tail, track, trail **2** *he chased us away from the door:* drive, expel, hound, send away
♦ *n* coursing, hunt, hunting, pursuit, running after, trail

chasm *n* **1** *a chasm in the rocks:* abyss, breach, canyon, cavity, cleft, crack, crater, crevasse, fissure, gap, gorge, gulf, hollow, opening, ravine, rift, split, void **2** *a chasm between two people:* alienation, breach, disagreement, estrangement, gap, gulf, quarrel, rift, separation, split

chassis *n* bodywork, frame, framework, fuselage, skeleton, structure, substructure, undercarriage

chaste *adj* **1** *a chaste person:* abstinent, celibate, continent, decent, immaculate, innocent, moral, pure, single, undefiled, unmarried, unsullied, virginal, virtuous **2** *a chaste style:* austere, modest, plain, restrained, simple, unadorned, unembellished

F3 1 corrupt, immoral, promiscuous **2** decorated, unrestrained

chasten *v* castigate *formal*, chastise *formal*, correct, curb, discipline, punish, repress, reprove, subdue, tame

chastise *v* **1** *parents who physically chastise their children:* beat, cane, flog, lash, punish, scourge, smack, spank, strap, wallop *colloq*, whip **2** *chastised for his negligence:* admonish, berate *formal*, castigate *formal*, censure, correct, discipline, dress down *colloq*, haul over the coals *colloq*, reprimand, reprove, scold, take to task *colloq*, upbraid *formal*

F3 2 encourage, praise

chastity *n* abstinence, celibacy, continence, immaculateness, innocence, maidenhood, modesty, purity, singleness, temperateness, unmarried state, virginity, virtue

F3 immorality, promiscuity

chat *v* babble *colloq*, chatter, chew the rag/fat *colloq*, chinwag *colloq*, converse *formal*, gas *colloq*, gossip, jabber *colloq*, jaw *colloq*, natter *colloq*, prattle *colloq*, rabbit (on) *colloq*, talk, waffle *colloq*
♦ *n* chinwag *colloq*, confab *colloq*, conversation, cosy chat, gossip, heart-to-heart, natter *colloq*, small talk, talk, tête-à-tête

chatter *v* babble, chat, chinwag *colloq*, gab *colloq*, gas *colloq*, gossip, jabber *colloq*, jaw *colloq*, natter *colloq*, prattle, rabbit (on) *colloq*, talk the hind legs off a donkey *colloq*, waffle *colloq*, witter *colloq*
♦ *n* babble, chinwag *colloq*, chit-chat, confab *colloq*, conversation, gossip, jabber *colloq*, jaw *colloq*, natter *colloq*, prattle, talk, tête-à-tête, witter *colloq*

chatterbox *n* babbler, big mouth *colloq*, blabbermouth *colloq*, chatterer, conversationalist, gabber *colloq*, gasbag *colloq*, gossip, gossiper, jabberer, loudmouth *colloq*, natterer *colloq*, windbag *colloq*

chatty *adj* **1** *a chatty person:* conversational, effusive, gabby *colloq*, garrulous, gossipy, gushing, long-winded, loquacious *formal*, mouthy *colloq*, talkative, verbose **2** *a chatty letter:* colloquial, conversational, familiar, friendly, informal, newsy

F3 1 quiet, taciturn

chauvinism *n* bias, flag-waving, jingoism, male chauvinism, nationalism, partisanship, prejudice, sexism

chauvinist *adj* biased, flag-waving, jingoist, male chauvinist, nationalist, prejudiced, sexist

cheap *adj* **1** *a cheap car:* a good buy, a snip *colloq*, a steal *colloq*, affordable, bargain, budget, cheap-rate, concessional rate, cut-price, dirt-cheap *colloq*, discounted, economical, economy, giveaway, going for a song *colloq*, inexpensive, knock-down, low-cost, low-price, marked-down, no-frills, on a shoestring *colloq*, on special offer, reasonable, reduced, reduced rate, rock-bottom, sale, slashed, ten a penny *colloq*, value for money **2** *a cheap copy:* cheap and nasty, cheapjack, cheapo *colloq*, inferior, paltry, poor, second-rate, shoddy, tacky *colloq*, tasteless, tatty, tawdry, two-bit, worthless **3** *cheap comments:*

contemptible, despicable, low, mean, sordid, vulgar

F3 1 costly, dear, expensive **2** good quality, superior **3** admirable, noble

cheapen *v* belittle, degrade, demean, depreciate, derogate *formal*, devalue, discredit, downgrade, lower

cheat *v* **1** *cheat someone:* bamboozle *colloq*, bilk *colloq*, bluff, con *colloq*, cozen, deceive, defraud, diddle *colloq*, do *colloq*, double-cross, dupe, fleece *colloq*, fool, gull, hoodwink, mislead, pull the wool over someone's eyes *colloq*, put one over on *colloq*, rip off *colloq*, short-change, sting *colloq*, swindle, take for a ride *colloq*, take to the cleaners *colloq*, trick, two-time *colloq*, welsh **2** *cheat death:* check, deny, deprive, frustrate, prevent, thwart
♦ *n* charlatan, cheater, con man *colloq*, confidence trickster, cozener, crook, deceiver, dodger, double-crosser, extortioner, fraud, impostor, rogue, shark *colloq*, swindler, trickster

check *v* **1** *check a ticket:* analyse, compare, confirm, corroborate *formal*, cross-check, examine, give the once-over *colloq*, go through, inquire into, inspect, investigate, look at (closely), make sure, monitor, police, probe, research, scan, screen, scrutinize, study, substantiate *formal*, take stock, test, validate *formal*, verify **2** *check the spread of a disease:* arrest, bar, bridle, bring to a standstill, contain, control, curb, damp, delay, halt, hinder, impede, inhibit, limit, obstruct, rein in, repress, restrain, retard *formal*, slow (down), staunch, stem, stop, thwart
♦ *n* **1** *a health check:* analysis, audit, check-up, confirmation, examination, inquiry, inspection, investigation, monitoring, once-over *colloq*, probe, research, scrutiny, test, verification **2** *ask for the check:* account, bill, charges, invoice, reckoning, statement, tab *US*, tally
▶ **check in** book in, enrol, record your arrival, register
▶ **check out 1** *check out of a hotel:* leave, pay the bill, settle up **2** *check out the procedure:* examine, investigate, look into, recce *colloq*, study, test
▶ **check up** analyse, ascertain, assess, confirm, evaluate, inquire into, inspect, investigate, make sure, probe, verify

check-up *n* analysis, appraisal, audit, confirmation, evaluation, examination, inquiry, inspection, investigation, monitoring, probe, research, scrutiny, test, verification

cheek *n* audacity, brass neck *colloq*, brazenness, chutzpah *colloq*, disrespect, effrontery *formal*, gall *colloq*, impertinence, impudence, insolence, lip *colloq*, mouth *colloq*, nerve *colloq*, sauce *colloq*, temerity *formal*

cheeky *adj* audacious, brazen, disrespectful, forward, fresh *colloq*, impertinent, impudent, insolent, lippy *colloq*, overfamiliar, pert, sassy *US colloq*, saucy *colloq*

F3 polite, respectful

cheer *v* **1** *the audience cheered him:* acclaim, applaud, clap, hail, root for *colloq*, salute, support, welcome **2** *your confidence cheers me:* brighten, buck up *colloq*, buoy up, comfort, console, encourage, enliven, gladden, hearten, inspirit *formal*, perk up *colloq*, raise/lift the spirits of, solace *formal*, uplift, warm

F3 1 boo, jeer **2** discourage, dishearten
♦ *n* **1** *the cheers of the crowd:* acclamation,

applause, bravo, clapping, hurrah, ovation, plaudits *formal* **2** *be of good cheer:* cheerfulness, gladness, happiness, high spirits, hopefulness, joyfulness, light-heartedness, merriment
🖃 **1** criticism

▶ **cheer up 1** *tried to cheer her up:* brighten, buck up *colloq*, comfort, console, encourage, hearten, liven (up), perk up *colloq*, rally **2** *she cheered up when he arrived:* brighten, buck up *colloq*, liven (up), perk up *colloq*, rally, take heart

cheerful *adj* **1** *a cheerful person:* animated, blithe, breezy, bright, buoyant, carefree, cheery, chirpy, contented, enthusiastic, exuberant, gay, genial, glad, good-humoured, happy, hearty, in good spirits, jaunty, jolly, jovial, joyful, joyous, laughing, light-hearted, lively, merry, optimistic, smiling, sparkling, spirited, sunny **2** *painted in a cheerful yellow:* agreeable, attractive, bright, comforting, delightful, encouraging, heartening, inspiring, pleasant, pleasing, stirring, sunny, warm
🖃 **1** dejected, depressed, sad **2** depressing, disheartening

cheerio *interj* adieu, au revoir, bye *colloq*, bye-bye *colloq*, cheers *colloq*, farewell, goodbye, see you *colloq*, see you later *colloq*, so long *colloq*, ta-ta *colloq*

cheerless *adj* **1** *a cheerless room:* austere, barren, bleak, cold, comfortless, dank, dark, depressing, desolate, dingy, dismal, drab, dreary, dull, gloomy, grim, lonely, miserable, sombre, sunless, uninviting **2** *a cheerless group of people:* dejected, desolate, despondent, disconsolate, dismal, dolorous *formal*, forlorn, gloomy, grim, joyless, melancholy, miserable, mournful, sad, sombre, sorrowful, sullen, unhappy
🖃 **1** bright, cheerful **2** bright, cheerful

cheers *interj* **1** *cheers, everyone!:* all the best, bottoms up, down the hatch, happy landings, here's looking at you, here's mud in your eye, here's to..., here's to you, prosit, skol, slàinte, to absent friends, your good health **2** *cheers, you've been a great help:* bless you, many thanks *colloq*, much obliged, ta *colloq*, thank you, thank you very much, thanks a lot *colloq* **3** *cheers for now:* adieu, au revoir, bye *colloq*, bye-bye *colloq*, farewell, goodbye, see you *colloq*, see you later *colloq*, so long *colloq*, ta-ta *colloq*

cheery *adj* animated, breezy, bright, buoyant, carefree, cheerful, chirpy, contented, enthusiastic, exuberant, gay, genial, glad, happy, hearty, in good spirits, jaunty, jolly, jovial, joyful, laughing, light-hearted, lively, merry, optimistic, smiling, sparkling, spirited
🖃 downcast, sad

cheese

Varieties of cheese include:
Amsterdam, Bel Paese, Bleu d'Auvergne, Blue Cheshire, Blue Vinny, Boursin, Brie, Caboc, Caerphilly, Camembert, Carré, Cheddar, Cheshire, Churnton, cottage cheese, cream cheese, Crowdie, curd cheese, Danish blue, Derby, Dolcelatte, Dorset Blue, Double Gloucester, Dunlop, Edam, Emmental, Emmentaler, ewe-cheese, Feta, fromage frais, Gloucester, Gorgonzola, Gouda, Gruyère, Huntsman, Jarlsberg, Killarney, Lancashire, Leicester, Limburg(er), Lymeswold, mascarpone, mouse-trap, mozzarella, Neufchâtel, Orkney, Parmesan, pecorino, Petit Suisse, Pont-l'Évêque, Port Salut, processed cheese, quark, Red Leicester, Red Windsor, ricotta, Roquefort, sage Derby, Saint-Paulin, Stilton, stracchino, Vacherin, vegetarian cheese, Wensleydale

chemical elements

The chemical elements (with their symbols) are:
actinium (Ac), aluminium (Al), americium (Am), antimony (Sb), argon (Ar), arsenic (As), astatine (At), barium (Ba), berkelium (Bk), beryllium (Be), bismuth (Bi), boron (B), bohrium (Bh), bromine (Br), cadmium (Cd), caesium (Cs), calcium (Ca), californium (Cf), carbon (C), cerium (Ce), chlorine (Cl), chromium (Cr), cobalt (Co), copper (Cu), curium (Cm), darmstadtium (Ds), dubnium (Db), dysprosium (Dy), einsteinium (Es), erbium (Er), europium (Eu), fermium (Fm), fluorine (F), francium (Fr), gadolinium (Gd), gallium (Ga), germanium (Ge), gold (Au), hafnium (Hf), hahnium (Ha), hassium (Hs), helium (He), holmium (Ho), hydrogen (H), indium (In), iodine (I), iridium (Ir), iron (Fe), krypton (Kr), lanthanum (La), lawrencium (Lr), lead (Pb), lithium (Li), lutetium (Lu), magnesium (Mg), manganese (Mn), meitnerium (Mt), mendelevium (Md), mercury (Hg), molybdenum (Mo), neodymium (Nd), neon (Ne), neptunium (Np), nickel (Ni), niobium (Nb), nitrogen (N), nobelium (No), osmium (Os), oxygen (O), palladium (Pd), phosphorus (P), platinum (Pt), plutonium (Pu), polonium (Po), potassium (K), praseodymium (Pr), promethium (Pm), protactinium (Pa), radium (Ra), radon (Rn), rhenium (Re), rhodium (Rh), roentgenium (Rg), rubidium (Rb), ruthenium (Ru), rutherfordium (Rf), samarium (Sm), scandium (Sc), seaborgium (Sg), selenium (Se), silicon (Si), silver (Ag), sodium (Na), strontium (Sr), sulphur (S), tantalum (Ta), technetium (Tc), tellurium (Te), terbium (Tb), thallium (Tl), thorium (Th), thulium (Tm), tin (Sn), titanium (Ti), tungsten (W), uranium (U), vanadium (V), xenon (Xe), ytterbium (Yb), yttrium (Y), zinc (Zn), zirconium (Zr)

chemistry

Terms used in chemistry include:
analytical chemistry, biochemistry, inorganic chemistry, organic chemistry, physical chemistry; acid, alkali, analysis, atom, atomic number, atomic structure, subatomic particles, base, bond, buffer, catalysis, catalyst, chain reaction, chemical bond, chemical compound, chemical element, chemical equation, chemical reaction, chemist, chlorination, combustion, compound, corrosion, covalent bond, crystal, cycle, decomposition, diffusion, dissociation, distillation, electrochemical cell, electrode, electron, electrolysis, emulsion, fermentation, fixation, formula, free radical, gas, halogen, hydrolysis, immiscible, indicator, inert gas, ion, ionic bond, isomer, isotope, lipid, liquid, litmus paper, litmus test, mass, matter, metallic bond, mixture, mole, molecule, neutron, noble gas, nucleus, oxidation, periodic table, pH, polymer, proton,

radioactivity, reaction, reduction, respiration, salt, solids, solution, solvent, substance, suspension, symbol, synthesis, valency, zwitterion. See also **acid, chemical elements, gas, minerals**

chequered *adj* diverse, mixed, varied, with good and bad times/parts, with its fair share of rough and tumble, with sad and happy times/parts, with ups and downs

cherish *v* 1 *he cherished his children*: adore, care for, hold dear, look after, love, nurture, support, sustain, take (good) care of, treasure 2 *cherish a memory*: hold dear, prize, treasure, value 3 *cherish a hope*: entertain, foster, harbour, nurture, sustain

cherub *n* angel, seraph

cherubic *adj* adorable, angelic, appealing, cute, heavenly, innocent, lovable, lovely, seraphic, sweet

chest *n* 1 *a man with a hairy chest*: breast, sternum *technical*, thorax 2 *a treasure chest*: box, case, casket, coffer, crate, strongbox, trunk

chew *v* bite, champ, chomp, crunch, gnaw, grind, masticate *formal*, munch
▶ **chew over** consider, deliberate upon, meditate on, mull over, muse on, ponder, ruminate on *formal*, weigh up

chic *adj* à la mode, dapper, elegant, fashionable, modish, smart, snazzy *colloq*, sophisticated, stylish, trendy *colloq*
🔁 outmoded, unfashionable

chicanery *n* artifice, cheating, deceitfulness, deception, deviousness, dishonesty, dodge *colloq*, double-dealing, duplicity, fraud, guile, hoodwinking, intrigue, jiggery-pokery, *colloq*, sharp practice, sophistry, subterfuge, trickery, underhandedness, wiles

chide *v* admonish *formal*, berate *formal*, blame, censure, criticize, lecture, objurgate *formal*, rebuke, reprehend, reprimand, reproach, reprove, scold, tell off, upbraid *formal*
🔁 praise

chief *adj* arch, central, controlling, directing, dominant, essential, foremost, grand, head, highest, key, leading, main, major, most important, outstanding, predominant, pre-eminent, premier, prevailing, primary, prime, principal, supervising, supreme, uppermost, vital
🔁 minor, unimportant
♦ *n* big cheese *colloq*, big gun *colloq*, big noise *colloq*, boss, captain, chair, chairman, chairperson, chairwoman, chief executive, chieftain, commander, director, gaffer *colloq*, governor, head, leader, lord, manager, managing director, master, overlord, premier, president, prime minister, principal, ringleader, ruler, superintendent, superior, supremo, suzerain, top dog *colloq*

chiefly *adv* especially, essentially, for the most part, generally, in the main, mainly, mostly, on the whole, predominantly, primarily, principally, usually

child *n* 1 *a small child*: baby, boy, brat *colloq*, girl, infant, juvenile, kid *colloq*, little boy, little girl, little one, minor, nipper *colloq*, sprog *colloq*, tiny tot *colloq*, toddler, tot *colloq*, young one, youngster 2 *they have two children*: daughter,

descendant, issue *formal*, offspring *formal*, progeny *formal*, son

childbirth *n* accouchement *formal*, childbearing, confinement, delivery, labour, lying-in, maternity, parturition *technical*, puerperal *formal*, travail *formal*

childhood *n* adolescence, babyhood, boyhood, girlhood, infancy, minority, schooldays, youth

childish *adj* babyish, boyish, foolish, frivolous, girlish, immature, infantile, irresponsible, juvenile, puerile, silly
🔁 mature, sensible

childish or *childlike*? You describe someone as *childish* if you think they are behaving in a silly immature way: *Stop being so childish!* *Childlike* is a neutral term: *childlike innocence.*

childlike *adj* artless, credulous, guileless, ingenuous, innocent, naïve, natural, simple, trustful, trusting

chill *n* 1 *a wintry chill in the air*: bite, cold, coldness, coolness, crispness, iciness, nip, rawness 2 *catch a chill*: cold, fever, flu, influenza, virus 3 *a chill ran down my spine*: anxiety, apprehension, dread, fear, shiver
🔁 1 warmth
♦ *v* 1 *chill the wine*: cool, cool down, freeze, ice, make/become cold(er), refrigerate 2 *the look on his face chilled me*: depress, discourage, dishearten, dismay, frighten, scare, terrify
🔁 1 heat, warm
♦ *adj* biting, bleak, chilly, cold, cool, freezing, frigid, icy, nippy *colloq*, parky *colloq*, raw, sharp, wintry
🔁 hot, warm
▶ **chill out** calm down, have a rest, relax, take it easy *colloq*

chilly *adj* 1 *a chilly north wind*: biting, brisk, cold, cool, crisp, freezing, fresh, frigid, icy, nippy *colloq*, parky *colloq*, raw, sharp, wintry 2 *a chilly response*: aloof, cool, distant, frigid, hostile, stony, unenthusiastic, unfriendly, unresponsive, unsympathetic, unwelcoming
🔁 1 warm 2 friendly

chime *v* boom, clang, ding, dong, jingle, peal, resound, reverberate, ring, sound, strike, tinkle, tintinnabulate *formal*, toll
▶ **chime in** 1 *chime in when someone is talking*: butt in *colloq*, chip in *colloq*, cut in *colloq*, interrupt 2 *his analysis chimed in with mine*: agree, be consistent, be similar, blend, correspond, fit in, harmonize

chimera *n* delusion, dream, fancy, fantasy, figment of the imagination, hallucination, idle fancy, illusion, spectre, will-o'-the-wisp

chimney *n* femerall, flue, funnel, lum, shaft, vent

china *n* 1 *a vase made of china*: ceramic, earthenware, porcelain, pottery, terracotta 2 *use the best china*: crockery, cups and saucers, dinner service, dishes, plates, tableware

Chinese calendar

The animals representing the years in which people are born:
rat, buffalo, tiger, rabbit (or hare), dragon, snake, horse, goat (or sheep), monkey, rooster, dog, pig

chink *n* aperture, cleft, crack, crevice, cut, fissure, gap, opening, rift, slit, slot, space, split

chip *n* 1 *fish and chips:* (French) fry, fried potato 2 *a chip in the paintwork:* crack, dent, flaw, nick, notch, scratch 3 *a bone chip:* flake, fragment, paring, scrap, shard, shaving, shred, sliver, splinter, wafer 4 *gambling chips:* counter, disc, token
♦ *v* 1 *chip away at a stone:* chisel, whittle 2 *chip a front tooth:* break (off), crack, damage, nick, notch, snick 3 *the stone chips easily:* break, crack, crumble, fragment
► **chip in** 1 *chip in to buy a present:* club together, contribute, donate, have a collection, have a whip-round *colloq*, make a donation, pay, subscribe 2 *chip in when someone is talking:* butt in *colloq*, chime in *colloq*, cut in *colloq*, interpose *formal*, interrupt

chirp *v* cheep, chirrup, peep, pipe, sing, trill, tweet, twitter, warble, whistle
♦ *n* cheep, chirrup, peep, piping, song, trill, tweet, twitter, warbling, whistle

chirpy *adj* blithe, bright, cheerful, cheery, gay, happy, jaunty, merry, perky *colloq*
☒ downcast, sad

chit-chat *n* chat, chatter, chinwag *colloq*, confab *colloq*, conversation, cosy chat, gossip, heart-to-heart, idle gossip, natter *colloq*, small talk, talk, tête-à-tête, tittle-tattle

chivalrous *adj* 1 *chivalrous conduct toward ladies:* courteous, gallant, gentlemanly, gracious, honourable, noble, polite, well-mannered 2 *chivalrous knights:* bold, brave, courageous, gallant, heroic, noble, valiant
☒ 1 ungallant 2 cowardly, ungallant

chivalry *n* 1 *treats women with old-fashioned chivalry:* courtesy, courtliness, gallantry, gentlemanliness, good manners, graciousness, honour, politeness 2 *knightly chivalry:* boldness, bravery, courage, gallantry, honour, integrity

chivvy *v* annoy, badger, goad, harass, hassle *colloq*, hound, hurry (up), importune *formal*, nag, pester, plague, pressure, prod, torment, urge

choice *n* 1 *a choice of several dishes:* range, selection, variety 2 *make a choice between two things:* choosing, decision, election, opting, picking, preference, selection 3 *have no choice but to go:* alternative, answer, option, solution
♦ *adj* best, excellent, exclusive, exquisite, fine, first-class, first-rate, hand-picked, plum, precious, prime, prize, select, special, superior, valuable
☒ inferior, poor

choke *v* 1 *choked her with his bare hands:* asphyxiate, strangle, throttle 2 *choked by fumes:* asphyxiate, overpower, overwhelm, smother, stifle, suffocate 3 *choke the drains:* bar, block, clog, close, congest, constrict, dam (up), obstruct, occlude *formal*, plug, stop 4 *choke on food:* cough, gag, retch
► **choke back** check, contain, control, curb, fight back, inhibit, repress, restrain, suppress

choleric *adj* angry, bad-tempered, crabbed *colloq*, crabby *colloq*, crotchety *colloq*, fiery, hot-tempered, ill-tempered, irascible, irritable, petulant, quick-tempered, testy, touchy
☒ calm, placid

choose *v* 1 *choose a new leader:* adopt, appoint, decide on, designate, elect, espouse *formal*, fix on, go for, opt for, pick (out), plump for *colloq*, select, settle on, single out, take, take up, vote for 2 *choose to do something:* decide, desire, favour, make up your mind, prefer, see fit, want, wish

choosy *adj* discriminating, exacting, faddy, fastidious, finicky, fussy, particular, pernickety *colloq*, picky *colloq*, selective
☒ undemanding

chop *v* axe, carve, cleave, cut, dissect, divide, hack, hew, lop, saw, sever, slash, slice, split, truncate
► **chop up** cube, cut (up), cut into pieces, dice, divide, mince, shred, slice (up)

choppy *adj* blustery, broken, rough, ruffled, squally, stormy, tempestuous, turbulent, uneven, wavy
☒ calm, peaceful, still

chore *n* duty, errand, job, piece of work, routine, task

chortle *v* cackle, chuckle, guffaw, laugh, snigger, snort

chorus *n* 1 *join in the chorus:* burden, refrain, strain 2 *a chorus of complaints:* call, response, shout 3 *chorus and orchestra:* choir, choral group, choristers, ensemble, singers, vocalists

christen *v* 1 *christened by the priest:* baptize, give a name to, immerse, name, sprinkle 2 *christened it the 'emerald forest':* call, designate, dub, name, style, term, title 3 *christen the wine glasses:* begin using, inaugurate, use for the first time

Christmas *n* Noel, Xmas, Yule, Yuletide

chronic *adj* 1 *a chronic illness:* constant, continual, deep-rooted, deep-seated, incessant, ingrained, long-lasting, long-standing, long-term, persistent, recurring 2 *a chronic worrier:* confirmed, habitual, hardened, inveterate 3 *the film was chronic:* appalling, atrocious, awful, dreadful, terrible
☒ 1 temporary 3 excellent

chronicle *n* account, annals, archives, calendar, diary, epic, history, journal, narrative, record, register, saga, story
♦ *v* enter, list, narrate, put on record, record, recount, register, relate, report, set down, tell, write down

chronicler *n* annalist, archivist, chronographer, chronologer, diarist, historian, historiographer, narrator, recorder, reporter, scribe

chronological *adj* consecutive, historical, in order, in sequence, ordered, progressive, sequential, serial

chubby *adj* fat, flabby, fleshy, paunchy, plump, podgy, portly, rotund *formal*, round, stout, tubby
☒ skinny, slim

chuck *v* 1 *chuck a frisbee:* cast, fling, heave, hurl, jettison, pitch, shy, sling, throw, toss 2 *recycle rubbish instead of just chucking it:* discard, dump, get rid of 3 *chuck a habit:* abandon, give the elbow *colloq*, give up, pack in *colloq*, quit *colloq* 4 *chuck your boyfriend:* abandon, dump *colloq*, forsake *formal*, give the brush-off *colloq*, give the elbow *colloq*, give up, jilt, pack in *colloq*, reject

chuckle *v* chortle, giggle, laugh, laugh quietly, snigger, titter

chum *n* buddy *colloq*, companion, comrade, crony *colloq*, friend, mate *colloq*, pal *colloq*
⊠ enemy

chummy *adj* affectionate, close, friendly, intimate, matey *colloq*, pally *colloq*, sociable, thick *colloq*

chunk *n* block, dollop, hunk, lump, mass, piece, portion, slab, wedge, wodge *colloq*

church *n* **1** *a historic church:* abbey, bethel, cathedral, chantry, chapel, house of God, house of prayer, kirk, Lord's house, meeting-house, minster, place of worship, shrine, tabernacle **2** *the church of Scientology:* cult, denomination, grouping, sect, tradition **3** *the church is waiting for the Second Coming:* assembly, body of Christ, bride of Christ, community, congregation, fellowship, people of God

---

Parts of a church or cathedral include:
aisle, almonry, altar, ambulatory, apse, arcade, arch, belfry, bell screen, bell tower, chancel, chapel, choir, clerestory, cloister, confessional, credence, crossing, crypt, fenestella, font, frontal, gallery, keystone, lectern, narthex, nave, parvis, pew, pinnacle, piscina, porch, portal, predella, presbytery, pulpit, reredos, ringing chamber, rood, rood screen, sacristy, sanctuary, sedile, shrine, slype, spire, squint, stall, steeple, stoup, tomb, tower, transept, triforium, vault, vestry

---

Names of church services include:
baptism, christening, Christingle, communion, Holy Communion, confirmation, dedication, Eucharist, evening service, evensong, funeral, Lord's Supper, marriage, Mass, High Mass, Midnight Mass, nuptial Mass, Requiem Mass, Holy Matrimony, memorial service, morning prayers, morning service. See also **canonical, places of worship**

---

churlish *adj* bad-tempered, boorish, crabbed *colloq*, discourteous, harsh, ill-bred, ill-mannered, ill-tempered, impolite, loutish, morose, oafish, rude, sullen, surly, uncivil, unmannerly
⊠ polite, urbane

churn *v* **1** *my stomach is churning:* be sick, heave, puke *colloq*, retch, throw up *colloq*, turn, vomit **2** *churn up mud:* agitate, beat, move about violently, swirl **3** *the waters churned:* boil, convulse, foam, froth, move about violently, seethe, swirl, toss
▶ **churn out** knock up, produce in great quantities, pump out, throw together, turn out

chute *n* channel, funnel, gutter, incline, ramp, runway, shaft, slide, slope, trough

cigarette *n* cancer-stick *slang*, cig *colloq*, ciggy *colloq*, coffin-nail *slang*, dog end *colloq*, fag *colloq*, fag end *colloq*, filter-tip, gasper *colloq*, high-tar, joint *colloq*, king-size, low-tar, menthol, roll-up, roll-your-own, smoke, spliff *colloq*, whiff

cinch *n* child's play *colloq*, doddle *colloq*, like falling off a log *colloq*, piece of cake *colloq*, pushover *colloq*, snip *colloq*, stroll *colloq*, walkover *colloq*

cinders *n* ashes, charcoal, clinker, coke, embers, slag

cinema *n* **1** *the world of cinema:* big screen *colloq*, films, flicks *old use*, movies, pictures, silver screen *colloq* **2** *watching a film at the cinema:* entertainment centre, film theatre, fleapit *colloq*, movie theatre, movies, multiplex, picture-house, picture-palace

cipher *n* **1** *he has documents written in cipher:* code, coded message, cryptogram, cryptograph, secret system **2** *you're only a cipher:* nobody, nonentity, yes-man

circle *n* assembly, band, clique, club, company, coterie, crowd, fellowship, fraternity, gang, group, set, society
♦ *v* **1** *the enemy had circled us:* belt, circumnavigate *formal*, circumscribe *formal*, encircle, enclose, encompass, envelop, gird, hedge in, hem in, loop, ring, surround **2** *vultures were circling overhead:* circulate, gyrate, move round, pivot, revolve, rotate, swivel, turn, wheel, whirl

---

Types of circle include:
annulus, ball, band, belt, circuit, circumference, coil, compass, cordon, coronet, crown, curl, cycle, disc, discus, eddy, ellipse, epicycle, girdle, globe, gyration, halo, hoop, lap, loop, orb, orbit, oval, perimeter, plate, revolution, ring, rotation, round, saucer, sphere, spiral, turn, tyre, vortex, wheel, whirlpool, whirlwind, wreath

---

circuit *n* **1** *a racing circuit:* course, race track, running-track, tour, track **2** *three circuits of the track:* beat, course, lap, orbit, perambulation *formal*, revolution, round, route **3** *within the circuit of the gardens:* ambit, bounds, circumference, compass, limit, range **4** *a judge on the Northern circuit:* area, district, region

circuitous *adj* **1** *a circuitous route:* devious, indirect, labyrinthine *formal*, meandering, roundabout, tortuous, winding **2** *a circuitous argument:* devious, indirect, meandering, oblique, periphrastic *formal*, rambling, roundabout
⊠ 1 direct, straight **2** direct, straight

circular *adj* annular, disc-shaped, hoop-shaped, ring-shaped, round, spherical
♦ *n* advertisement, announcement, flyer, handbill, leaflet, letter, notice, pamphlet

circulate *v* **1** *circulate information:* broadcast, diffuse, disseminate *formal*, distribute, give out, issue, pass round, promulgate *formal*, propagate, publicize, publish, spread (around), transmit **2** *let the air circulate:* flow, go round, gyrate, revolve, rotate, swirl, whirl

circulation *n* **1** *problems with his circulation:* blood-flow **2** *the circulation of air:* circling, flow, motion, movement, rotation **3** *public circulation of images:* dissemination *formal*, distribution, propagation, publication, publicity, spread, transmission

circumference *n* border, boundary, bounds, circuit, confines, edge, extremity, fringe, limits, margin, outline, perimeter, periphery, rim, verge

circumlocution *n* convolution *formal*, diffuseness, discursiveness, euphemism, indirectness, periphrasis *formal*, pleonasm *formal*, prolixity *formal*, redundancy, roundaboutness, tautology, verbosity *formal*, wordiness

circumlocutory *adj* convoluted *formal*, diffuse, discursive, euphemistic, indirect, periphrastic *formal*, pleonastic *formal*, prolix *formal*, redundant, roundabout, tautological, verbose *formal*, wordy

circumscribe *v* **1** *a square circumscribed by a circle:* encircle, enclose, encompass, surround **2** *circumscribed by rules:* bound, confine, curtail, define, delimit, delineate, demarcate, hem in, limit, pen in, restrain, restrict

circumspect *adj* attentive, canny, careful, cautious, discreet, discriminating, guarded, judicious *formal*, observant, politic *formal*, prudent *formal*, sagacious *formal*, vigilant *formal*, wary, watchful, wise
🖅 reckless, unguarded, unwary

circumspection *n* canniness, care, caution, chariness, discretion, guardedness, prudence *formal*, vigilance *formal*, wariness
🖅 recklessness

circumstance *n* **1** *won't do it under any circumstances:* condition, how the land lies, lie of the land, occurrence, position, situation, state, state of affairs **2** *the circumstances of the case:* background, detail, element, environment, event, fact, factor, happening, item, particular, respect **3** *in impoverished circumstances:* case, environment, financial position, lifestyle, means, plight, resources, situation, status **4** *a victim of circumstance:* fate, fortune

circumstantial *adj* conjectural, contingent, deduced, evidential *formal*, hearsay, incidental, indirect, inferential, presumed, presumptive *formal*, provisional

circumvent *v* **1** *to circumvent the rules:* avoid, bypass, evade, get out of, get past, get round, sidestep, steer clear of **2** *an attempt to circumvent the police:* outwit, thwart

cistern *n* basin, reservoir, sink, tank, vat

citadel *n* acropolis, bastion, castle, fortification, fortress, keep, stronghold, tower

citation *n* **1** *he was given a special citation from the group:* award, commendation, honour **2** *according to the citation:* cutting, excerpt, illustration, mention, passage, quotation, quote, reference, source

cite *v* adduce *formal*, advance, allude to, bring up, evidence *formal*, exemplify, give an example, mention, name, quote, refer to, specify

citizen *n* burgher, city-dweller, denizen *formal*, freeman, householder, inhabitant, local, oppidan *formal*, resident, subject, taxpayer, townsman, townswoman, urbanite

city *n* big smoke *colloq*, city centre, concrete jungle, conurbation, downtown, ghetto, inner city, megalopolis, metropolis, metropolitan area, municipality, town, urban district, urban sprawl

civic *adj* borough, city, communal, community, local, metropolitan, municipal, public, urban

civil *adj* **1** *civil affairs:* civic, civilian, communal, community, domestic, home, interior, internal, local, municipal, national, public, secular, state **2** *a civil person:* accommodating, affable,

civilized, complaisant, courteous, courtly, mannerly, obliging, polite, respectful, urbane, well-bred, well-mannered
🖅 **1** international, military, religious **2** discourteous, rude, uncivil

civility *n* affability, amenity, comity *formal*, courteousness, courtesy, (good) manners, graciousness, pleasantness, politeness, respect, tact, urbanity
🖅 discourtesy, rudeness, uncouthness

civilization *n* **1** *ancient civilizations:* community, culture, human society, people, society **2** *the march of civilization:* advancement, cultivation, development, education, enlightenment, progress, refinement, sophistication, urbanity
🖅 **2** barbarity, primitiveness

civilize *v* advance, cultivate, educate, enlighten, humanize, improve, instruct, polish, refine, socialize, sophisticate

civilized *adj* **1** *a civilized society:* advanced, cultivated, cultured, developed, educated, enlightened, refined, sophisticated, urbane **2** *queue in a civilized manner:* polite, reasonable, sensible
🖅 **1** barbarous, coarse, primitive, uncivilized, unsophisticated **2** unreasonable

clad *adj* attired *formal*, clothed, covered, dressed, rigged out *colloq*, wearing

claim *v* **1** *he claims that he is right:* affirm, allege, assert, aver *formal*, avow *formal*, contend, hold, insist, maintain, postulate *formal*, profess, purport *formal*, state **2** *claim a refund:* ask, be entitled to, collect, demand, exact, lay claim to, put in for, request, require, requisition *formal*, take
♦ *n* **1** *make a false claim:* affirmation, allegation, assertion, averment *formal*, avowal *formal*, contention, declaration, insistence, profession **2** *a claim for a tax refund:* application, call, demand, petition, request, requirement **3** *a claim to the throne:* entitlement, privilege, right

claimant *n* applicant, candidate, litigant, petitioner, pretendant, pretender, suppliant, supplicant

clairvoyance *n* ESP, extrasensory perception, fortune-telling, psychic powers, telepathy

clairvoyant *adj* extra-sensory, prophetic, psychic, telepathic, visionary
♦ *n* augur, diviner, fortune-teller, oracle, prophet, prophetess, psychic, seer, soothsayer, telepath, visionary

clamber *v* ascend, climb, mount, scale, scrabble, scramble, shin, shinny *US*

clammy *adj* **1** *clammy fingers:* damp, moist, slimy, sticky, sweating, sweaty **2** *a clammy atmosphere:* close, damp, dank, heavy, moist, muggy, sticky

clamorous *adj* blaring, deafening, insistent, lusty, noisy, riotous, tumultuous, uproarious, vehement, vociferous
🖅 quiet, silent

clamour *v* ask for noisily, call for, claim, demand, insist, press for, urge
♦ *n* agitation, blare, commotion, din, hubbub, noise, outcry, racket, shouting, uproar, vociferation *formal*
🖅 quietness, silence

clamp *n* brace, bracket, clasp, fastener, grip, immobilizer, press, vice
♦ *v* brace, clench, clinch, fasten, fix, grip, hold, immobilize, press, secure, squeeze
► **clamp down on** come down hard on, confine, control, crack down on, limit, put a stop to, restrain, restrict, stop, suppress

clan *n* 1 *the Macleod clan:* family, house, line, race, sept, tribe 2 *a member of a secret clan:* band, brotherhood, circle, clique, confraternity, coterie, faction, fraternity, group, sect, set, society

clandestine *adj* backroom *colloq*, behind-door *colloq*, cloak-and-dagger *colloq*, closet, concealed, covert, furtive, hidden, private, secret, sly, sneaky, stealthy, surreptitious, undercover, underground, underhand, under-the-counter *colloq*
☒ open

clang *v* bong, chime, clank, clash, clatter, clink, clunk, jangle, peal, ring, toll
♦ *n* bong, clank, clash, clatter, clink, clunk, ring

clanger *n* bloomer *colloq*, blunder, boob *colloq*, booboo *colloq*, cock-up *slang*, error, fault, faux pas, gaffe, howler *colloq*, inaccuracy, indiscretion, misjudgement, mistake, oversight, slip, slip-up *colloq*, solecism *formal*

clank *n* clang, clash, clatter, clink, clunk, jangle, ring, toll
♦ *v* clang, clash, clatter, clink, clunk, jangle, ring, toll

clannish *adj* cliquey, cliquish, exclusive, insular, narrow, parochial, sectarian, select, unfriendly
☒ friendly, open

clap *v* 1 *they clapped loudly:* acclaim, applaud, cheer, put your hands together for 2 *he clapped him on the shoulder:* bang, pat, slap, smack, strike, wallop *colloq*, whack *colloq*

claptrap *n* bilge *colloq*, blarney, bunk *colloq*, bunkum *colloq*, cobblers *colloq*, codswallop *colloq*, drivel, gibberish, hot air *colloq*, nonsense, piffle *colloq*, poppycock *colloq*, rot *colloq*, rubbish, tommyrot *colloq*, trash, tripe, twaddle

clarification *n* elucidation *formal*, explanation, exposition, illumination, interpretation, simplification
☒ obfuscation *formal*

clarify *v* 1 *clarifying a point:* clear up, elucidate *formal*, explain, illuminate, make clear, make plain, resolve, simplify, spell out, throw light on 2 *clarifying water:* clear, filter, purify, refine
☒ 1 confuse, obscure 2 cloud

clarity *n* 1 *the clarity of the explanation:* comprehensibility, explicitness, intelligibility, lucidity, obviousness, plainness, simplicity, unambiguousness 2 *clarity of the water:* clearness, transparency 3 *clarity of the image:* clearness, definition, precision, sharpness
☒ 1 vagueness 3 imprecision, obscurity

clash *v* 1 *clashing their spears against their shields:* bang, clang, clank, clatter, crash, jangle, jar, rattle, strike 2 *the Japanese have clashed with Greenpeace ships:* conflict, contend, disagree, feud, fight, grapple, quarrel, war, wrangle 3 *two events clash:* coincide, co-occur *formal*, happen at the same time 4 *the styles clash:* be discordant, be incompatible, jar, look unpleasant, not go together, not go with, not match

☒ 4 be compatible, go well together, harmonize, match
♦ *n* 1 *a noisy clash:* bang, clang, clank, clatter, crash, jangle, noise, striking 2 *a clash with the police:* brush, conflict, confrontation, disagreement, feud, fight, fighting, quarrel, showdown, warring, wrangle

clasp *n* 1 *fastening a clasp:* buckle, catch, clip, fastener, fastening, hasp, hook, pin 2 *in a tight clasp:* cuddle, embrace, grasp, grip, hold, hug
♦ *v* 1 *the child clasped her doll:* cling to, clutch, embrace, enfold, grasp, grip, hold, hug, press, squeeze 2 *she clasped the brooch on to her cloak:* attach, clip, connect, fasten, hook, pin

class *n* 1 *a French class:* course, lecture, lesson, period, seminar, teach-in, tutorial, workshop 2 *he's in my class at school:* form, grade, set, study group, year 3 *social class:* caste, level, rank, social division, social order, social status, (social) background, (social) standing, sphere, standing in society, status 4 *a class of animal:* caste, category, classification, denomination *formal*, division, genre, genus, grade, group, grouping, kind, league, order, phylum *technical*, rank, section, set, sort, species, style, type 5 *he has class:* distinction, elegance, sophistication, style, stylishness, taste
♦ *v* arrange, brand, categorize, classify, designate, grade, group, order, pigeonhole, rank, rate, sort

---

Social classes/groups include:
aristocracy, nobility, gentry, landed gentry, gentlefolk, elite, nob *colloq*, high society, top drawer *colloq*, upper class, ruling class, jet set, middle class, lower class, working class, bourgeoisie, proletariat, hoi-polloi, commoner, serf, plebeian, pleb *colloq*. See also **nobility**

---

classic *adj* 1 *a classic film:* best, brilliant, consummate *formal*, excellent, finest, first-class, first-rate, masterly, outstanding 2 *a classic example:* characteristic, definitive, exemplary, ideal, model, paradigmatic *formal*, prime, quintessential *formal*, regular, representative, standard, true, typical, usual 3 *classic style:* abiding, ageless, archetypal, enduring, established, immortal, lasting, time-honoured, timeless, traditional, undying
☒ 1 second-rate 2 unrepresentative
♦ *n* established work, exemplar, great, masterpiece, masterwork, model, pièce de résistance, prototype, standard

classical *adj* 1 *classical style/form:* elegant, harmonious, plain, pure, refined, restrained, symmetrical, traditional, well-proportioned 2 *classical music:* concert, serious, symphonic, traditional 3 *classical drama:* ancient Greek, ancient Roman, Attic, Grecian, Hellenic, Latin
☒ 1 modern

classification *n* arrangement, cataloguing, categorization, classing, codification, grading, grouping, sorting, systematization, tabulation, taxonomy *technical*

classify *v* arrange, catalogue, categorize, class, codify, file, grade, group, order, pigeonhole, rank, sort, systematize, tabulate, type

classy *adj* elegant, exclusive, expensive, fine, grand, high-class, posh *colloq*, ritzy *colloq*, select,

sophisticated, stylish, superior, swanky *colloq*,
swish *colloq*, top-drawer, up-market
⊟ dowdy, plain, unstylish

clatter *n* bang, clang, clank, clunk, crash, jangle,
jar, rattle
♦ *v* bang, clang, clank, clunk, crash, jangle,
jar, rattle

clause *n* article, chapter, condition, heading,
item, loophole, paragraph, part, passage,
phrase, point, provision, proviso, rider, section,
specification, subsection

claw *n* chela *technical*, gripper, nail, nipper,
pincer, talon, unguis *technical*
♦ *v* graze, lacerate, mangle, maul, rip, scrape,
scratch, tear

clean *adj* **1** *clean laundry*: antiseptic, aseptic, clean
as a new pin *colloq*, cleansed, decontaminated,
flawless, fresh, hygienic, immaculate, laundered,
perfect, pure, purified, sanitary, speckless, spick
and span, spotless, sterile, sterilized,
unadulterated, unblemished, uncontaminated,
unpolluted, unsoiled, unspotted, unstained,
unsullied, washed **2** *a clean life*: chaste, decent,
good, guiltless, honest, honourable, innocent,
moral, pure, reputable, respectable, righteous,
squeaky-clean *colloq*, upright, upstanding,
virtuous **3** *a clean sheet of paper*: blank, fresh, new,
unmarked, unused **4** *a clean game*: above board
colloq, according to the rules, even-handed, fair,
just, proper **5** *clean lines*: clean-cut, neat, regular,
simple, smooth, straight, tidy, well-defined
⊟ **1** dirty, polluted **2** dishonourable, indecent
4 dirty, rough **5** ragged
♦ *adv* completely, directly, entirely, fully, quite,
straight, totally

Ways to clean include:
bath, bathe, bleach, brush, buff, cleanse, clear,
comb, decontaminate, deodorize, disinfect,
distil, dry-clean, dust, filter, floss, flush,
freshen, freshen up, fumigate, groom,
Hoover®, launder, mop, muck out, pasteurize,
pick, polish, purge, purify, refine, rinse, rub,
sandblast, sanitize, scour, scrape, scrub,
shampoo, shine, shower, soak, soap, sponge,
spring-clean, spruce, spruce up, steep,
sterilize, swab, sweep, swill, tidy, vacuum,
valet, wash, wipe

---

cleaner *n* char, charlady, charwoman, daily

cleanse *v* **1** *cleanse a wound*: bathe, clean, deterge
formal, disinfect, rinse, sterilize, wash **2** *cleansed
from sin/cleanse your soul*: absolve, clear, lustrate
formal, make free from, purge, purify
⊟ **1** dirty **2** defile

cleanser *n* cleaner, detergent, disinfectant,
purifier, scourer, scouring powder, soap, soap
powder, solvent

clear *adj* **1** *a clear explanation*: coherent,
comprehensible, crystal-clear, explicit,
intelligible, lucid, plain, precise, unambiguous,
unequivocal **2** *it is clear that he is lying*: apparent,
beyond doubt, beyond question, certain,
conspicuous, definite, distinct, evident,
incontrovertible, manifest, obvious, patent,
plain, positive, sure, unambiguous, unequivocal,
unmistakable, unquestionable **3** *a clear outline*:
conspicuous, definite, distinct, pronounced,
well-defined **4** *clear thinking*: keen, logical,
penetrating, perceptive, quick, reasonable,

sensible, sharp **5** *clear water*: clean, colourless,
crystalline, diaphanous *formal*, glassy, limpid,
pellucid *formal*, see-through, translucent,
transparent, unclouded **6** *a clear day*: bright,
cloudless, fair, fine, light, sunny, unclouded,
undimmed **7** *a clear driveway*: empty, free, open,
unblocked, unhindered, unimpeded,
unobstructed **8** *a clear conscience*: blameless,
guiltless, in the clear, innocent **9** *a clear call*:
audible, clear as a bell *colloq*, distinct, perceptible
⊟ **1** ambiguous, confusing, unclear, vague
2 ambiguous, unclear **3** unclear, vague
4 muddled **5** cloudy, opaque **6** cloudy, dull,
misty, rainy **7** blocked **8** guilty **9** faint,
inaudible, indistinct
♦ *v* **1** *clear something of dirt*: clean, cleanse, filter,
fine, free, refine, rid, tidy, wipe **2** *clear the rubble
from the site*: get rid of, move, remove, shift, take
away, tidy **3** *clear the room*: empty, evacuate,
vacate **4** *clear the drain*: decongest, disentangle,
extricate, free, loosen, rid, unblock, unclog,
unstop **5** *clear a fence*: go over, jump (over), leap
over, vault **6** *clear the accused*: absolve, acquit,
exculpate *formal*, excuse, exonerate, free, justify,
let go, liberate, pardon, release, vindicate
7 *cleared for publication*: allow, approve,
authorize, give permission, give the go-ahead
colloq, give the green light *colloq*, pass, permit,
sanction **8** *we cleared £1000 on the deal*: bring (in),
earn, gain, make, make a profit of, net, take home
⊟ **1** dirty **4** block **6** condemn **7** prohibit
▶ **clear out 1** *been told to clear out*: beat it *colloq*,
clear off *colloq*, depart, get lost *slang*, get out, go
away, hop it *colloq*, leave, piss off *slang*, push off
colloq, shove off *colloq*, withdraw **2** *clear out a
cupboard*: empty, sort (out), tidy (up) **3** *clear out
rubbish*: dispose of, get rid of, throw out
▶ **clear up 1** *clear up a problem*: answer, clarify,
crack *colloq*, elucidate, explain, iron out, resolve,
solve, sort out, straighten (out) **2** *clear
up a room*: order, put in order, rearrange, sort,
straighten (up), tidy **3** *the weather cleared up*:
become fine, become sunny, brighten(up), clear,
improve, stop raining

clearance *n* **1** *the clearance of the rubble*:
cleansing, clearing, emptying, moving, removal,
shifting, taking-away **2** *the clearance of the slums*:
clearing, demolition, emptying, evacuation,
removal, vacating **3** *official clearance*:
authorization, consent, endorsement, go-ahead
colloq, green light *colloq*, leave, OK *colloq*,
permission, sanction, say-so *colloq* **4** *enough
clearance for the van*: allowance, gap, headroom,
margin, room, space

clear-cut *adj* clear, cut and dried *colloq*, definite,
distinct, explicit, plain, precise, specific,
straightforward, trenchant, unambiguous,
unequivocal, well-defined
⊟ ambiguous, vague

clearing *n* dell, gap, glade, opening, space

clearly *adv* distinctly, evidently, incontestably,
incontrovertibly, indisputably, manifestly,
markedly, obviously, openly, patently, plainly,
undeniably, undoubtedly, unmistakably,
without doubt

cleave[1] *v* chop, crack, cut, dissever *formal*,
disunite, divide, halve, hew, open, part, rend,
separate, sever, slice, split, sunder *formal*
⊟ join, unite

cleave[2] *v* adhere, attach, cling, hold, stick

cleft *n* breach, break, chasm, chink, crack, cranny, crevice, fissure, fracture, gap, opening, rent, split

clemency *n* compassion, forbearance, forgiveness, generosity, humanity, indulgence, kindness, leniency, magnanimity *formal*, mercifulness, mercy, moderation, pity, sympathy
⋤ harshness, ruthlessness

clench *v* clasp, close (tightly), clutch, fasten, grasp, grip, grit, hold, seal, shut

clergy *n* churchmen, clergymen, clerics, holy orders, ministry, priesthood, the church, the cloth

clergyman *n* canon, chaplain, churchman, cleric, curate, deacon, deaconess, dean, divine, ecclesiastic, father, imam, man of God, man of the cloth, minister, muezzin, mullah, padre, parson, pastor, presbyter, priest, rabbi, rector, reverend, vicar

clerical *adj* 1 *clerical work:* administrative, filing, keyboarding, office, official, pen-pushing *colloq*, secretarial, typing, white-collar 2 *clerical vestments:* canonical, ecclesiastical, episcopal, ministerial, pastoral, priestly, sacerdotal

---

Types of clerical vestment include:
alb, amice, biretta, cassock, chasuble, chimer, clerical collar, dog-collar *colloq*, cope, cotta, cowl, dalmatic, ephod, frock, Geneva bands, Geneva gown, habit, hood, maniple, mantle, mitre, mozzetta, pallium, rochet, scapular, scarf, skullcap, soutane, stole, surplice, tallith, tippet, tunicle, wimple, yarmulka

---

clerk *n* account-keeper, administrative officer, administrator, assistant, copyist, notary, official, pen-pusher *colloq*, protocolist, record-keeper, secretary, stenographer, typist

clever *adj* 1 *a clever student:* able, adroit, apt, brainy *colloq*, bright, brilliant, capable, discerning, expert, gifted, intelligent, keen, knowing, knowledgeable, perceptive, quick, quick-witted, sagacious *formal*, sapient *formal*, sharp, sharp-witted, shrewd, smart, talented, witty 2 *a clever plan:* cunning, ingenious, inventive, resourceful, sensible, shrewd
⋤ 1 foolish, ignorant, senseless, stupid 2 foolish

cliché *n* banality, bromide, commonplace, hackneyed phrase/expression, (old) chestnut, platitude, stereotype, truism

click *v* 1 *the machine clicked:* beat, clack, clink, snap, snick, snip, tick 2 *what he had said suddenly clicked:* fall into place, make sense 3 *I finally clicked to the truth:* (begin to) understand, cotton on *colloq*, twig *colloq*
♦ *n* beat, clack, clink, snap, snick, snip, tick

client *n* buyer, consumer, customer, patient, patron, purchaser, regular, shopper, user

clientèle *n* business, buyers, clients, consumers, customers, following, market, patronage, patrons, purchasers, regulars, shoppers, trade, users

cliff *n* bluff, crag, escarpment, face, overhang, precipice, promontory, rock-face, scar, scarp, tor

climactic *adj* critical, crucial, decisive, exciting, paramount
⋤ trivial

climate *n* 1 *a cold climate:* temperature, weather, weather conditions 2 *a hostile political climate:* ambience, atmosphere, environment, feeling, milieu, mood, setting, temper, tendency, trend

climax *n* acme, apex, apogee *formal*, culmination, head, height, high point, highlight, peak, pinnacle, summit, top, zenith
⋤ low point, nadir *formal*

climb *v* 1 *climb the stairs:* ascend, clamber, go up, mount, scale, shin up, surmount 2 *climb into the car:* clamber, move, scramble, shift
3 *unemployment is climbing:* go up, increase, rise, shoot up, soar
▸ **climb down** admit that you are wrong, back down, concede, eat your words *colloq*, retract, retreat

clinch *v* close, conclude, confirm, decide, determine, land *colloq*, seal, secure, settle, verify

cling *v* 1 *cling to a branch:* clasp, clutch, embrace, grasp, grip, hold on to, hug 2 *the wet shirt clung to his back:* adhere, cleave, fasten, stick 3 *cling to old ideas:* adhere, be faithful to, defend, hold to, stand by, stay true to, stick to, support

clinic *n* doctor's, health centre, hospital, infirmary, medical centre, outpatients' department

clinical *adj* 1 *clinical trials of the drug:* hospital, medical, patient 2 *a clinical design:* austere, basic, plain, simple, stark, unadorned 3 *a clinical attitude:* analytic, business-like, cold, detached, disinterested, dispassionate, emotionless, impassive, impersonal, objective, scientific, unemotional, unfeeling, uninvolved
⋤ 2 decorated, ornamented 3 biased, subjective, warm

clip *n* 1 *a paper clip:* fastener, pin, staple 2 *a clip from a newspaper:* citation, cutting, excerpt, extract, passage, quotation, section, snippet 3 *a clip round the ear:* box, clout *colloq*, cuff, punch, slap, thump *colloq*, wallop *colloq*, whack *colloq*
♦ *v* 1 *clipped the pen to her pocket:* attach, fasten, fix, hold, pin, staple 2 *clip a bush:* crop, curtail, cut, cut short, dock, pare, poll, pollard, prune, shear, shorten, snip, trim, truncate

clipping *n* citation, clip, cutting, excerpt, extract, passage, quotation, section, snippet

clique *n* band, bunch, circle, clan, coterie, crowd, faction, fraternity, gang, group, in-crowd, pack, set, society

cloak *n* 1 *wear a cloak:* cape, cope, cover, mantle, robe, shawl, wrap 2 *a cloak of secrecy:* blind, cover, front, mantle, mask, pretext, screen, shield, shroud, veil
♦ *v* camouflage, conceal, cover, disguise, hide, mask, obscure, screen, shield, shroud, veil

clock
▸ **clock up** attain, chalk up, notch up, reach, record, register

---

Types of clock or watch include:
alarm-clock, digital clock, analogue clock, mantel clock, bracket clock, carriage clock, quartz clock, cuckoo clock, longcase clock, grandfather clock, grandmother clock, travelling clock, speaking clock, Tim *colloq*; wristwatch, fob-watch, repeating watch, chronograph, pendant watch, ring-watch, stopwatch; chronometer, sundial

---

clog

102

clog v block, bung up, burden, choke, congest, dam (up), encumber, hamper, hinder, impede, jam, obstruct, occlude *formal*, stop up
⊟ free, unblock

cloister n aisle, ambulatory, arcade, corridor, portico, walkway

cloistered adj cloistral *formal*, confined, enclosed, hermitic *formal*, insulated, isolated, protected, reclusive *formal*, restricted, secluded, sequestered *formal*, sheltered, shielded, withdrawn
⊟ open

close[1] v 1 *close a box*: bar, bolt, fasten, lock (up), padlock, secure, shut, shut up 2 *close a road*: block, clog, obstruct, occlude *formal*, shut 3 *close a bottle*: cork, plug, seal, shut, stop up 4 *close a meeting*: adjourn, bring to an end, cease *formal*, complete, conclude, discontinue *formal*, draw to an end, end, finish, round off, stop, terminate, wind up 5 *the shop closes at 6 o'clock*: close for the night, shut 6 *the factory closed in March*: cease operating, cease operations, close down, close permanently, fail, fold *colloq*, go bankrupt, go bust *colloq*, go to the wall *colloq*, shut down 7 *close a gap*: lessen, narrow, seal 8 *its jaws closed on his arm*: fuse, join, unite 9 *close a deal*: clinch, conclude, confirm, decide, determine, establish, seal, secure, settle, verify
⊟ 1 open, separate 4 begin, start 5 open, open for business 7 widen 8 widen
♦ n adjournment, cessation *formal*, completion, conclusion, culmination, dénouement, end, ending, finale, finish, stop, termination, winding-up
⊟ beginning, start
▶ **close in** approach, come nearer, draw near, encircle, surround

close[2] n court, courtyard, cul-de-sac, enclosure, lane, mews, quadrangle, square

close[3] adj 1 *the shop is close*: a stone's throw *colloq*, adjacent, adjoining, at hand, close by, in close proximity, in the vicinity, in your own backyard *colloq*, near, nearby, neighbouring, not far, on your doorstep *colloq* 2 *his birthday is close*: at hand, imminent, impending, near, not far 3 *a close friend*: attached, best, bosom, close-knit, dear, devoted, familiar, inseparable, intimate, loving 4 *this colour is close to the original one*: comparable, corresponding, like, near, similar 5 *a close game*: evenly matched, hard-fought, neck and neck *colloq*, well-matched 6 *a close atmosphere*: airless, fuggy, heavy, humid, muggy, oppressive, sticky, stifling, stuffy, suffocating, sultry, sweltering, unventilated 7 *close with money*: mean, miserly, niggardly, parsimonious *formal*, penny-pinching, stingy, tight *colloq* 8 *she's close about her plans*: confidential, private, quiet, reticent, secret, secretive, taciturn, uncommunicative, unforthcoming 9 *a close translation*: accurate, exact, faithful, literal, precise, strict, true 10 *pay close attention*: careful, concentrated, detailed, fixed, intense, keen, painstaking, rigorous, searching, thorough 11 *a close crowd*: compact, condensed, cramped, crowded, dense, packed, solid
⊟ 1 distant, far 2 distant, far 3 cool, distant, unfriendly 6 airy, fresh, well-ventilated 7 generous 8 open 9 loose, rough

closet n cupboard, storage room, wardrobe
♦ adj covert, furtive, hidden, private, secret, surreptitious, undercover, underground, unrevealed
⊟ having come out, open

closure n 1 *the closure of the factory*: cessation of operations *formal*, closing-down, failure, folding *colloq*, permanent closing, shutdown 2 *the closure of the road*: block, blocking, obstruction, shutting, stopping-up

clot n clotting, clump, coagulation, glob, lump, mass, thrombosis, thrombus
♦ v coagulate, coalesce, congeal, curdle, gel, set, solidify, thicken

cloth n 1 *an expensive cloth*: fabric, material, stuff, textile, upholstery 2 *dusting with a cloth*: dish-cloth, duster, face-cloth, flannel, floorcloth, rag, towel

clothe v accoutre *formal*, apparel *formal*, attire *formal*, bedizen *formal*, caparison *formal*, cover, deck, drape, dress, fit out, habit *formal*, invest *formal*, outfit, put on, rig, robe, vest
⊟ disrobe, strip, undress

clothes n apparel *formal*, attire *formal*, clobber *colloq*, clothing, costume, dress, garb, garments, gear *colloq*, get-up *colloq*, habiliments *formal*, outfit, raiment *formal*, togs *colloq*, vestments, vesture *formal*, wardrobe, wear

Clothes include:
suit, trouser suit, dress suit, catsuit, jumpsuit, tracksuit, shell suit, wet suit; dress, frock, evening-dress, shirtwaister, caftan, kimono, sari; skirt, A-line skirt, mini skirt, dirndl, pencil-skirt, pinafore-skirt, divided-skirt, grass skirt, wrapover skirt, culottes, kilt, sarong; cardigan, jumper, jersey, sweater, polo-neck, turtle-neck, guernsey, pullover, twin-set, shirt, dress-shirt, sweat-shirt, tee-shirt, T-shirt, waistcoat, blouse, smock, tabard, tunic; uniform; trousers, jeans, Levis®, 501s®, denims, slacks, cords, flannels, drainpipes, bell-bottoms, dungarees, leggings, pedal-pushers, ski pants, breeches, plus-fours, jodhpurs, Bermuda shorts, hot pants, shorts; lingerie, bra, brassière, body stocking, camisole, liberty bodice, corset, girdle, garter, suspender belt, suspenders, shift, slip, petticoat, teddy, basque, briefs, pants, panties, French knickers, camiknickers, hosiery, pantihose, tights, stockings; underpants, boxer-shorts, Y-fronts, vest, string vest, singlet; swimsuit, bathing-costume, bikini, swimming costume, swimming trunks, leotard, salopettes; nightdress, nightie *colloq*, pyjamas, bed-jacket, bedsocks, dressing-gown, housecoat, negligee; scarf, glove, mitten, muffler, earmuffs, leg-warmers, sock, tie, bow-tie, necktie, cravat, stole, shawl, belt, braces, cummerbund, veil, yashmak. See also **clerical, footwear, hat**

cloud v 1 *a dust storm clouded the sun*: cover, darken, dim, dull, eclipse, fog, mantle, mist, obfuscate *formal*, obscure, overshadow, shade, shadow, shroud, veil 2 *the sky clouded*: darken, dim, dull, mist 3 *it has clouded their judgment*: blur, confuse, fog, muddle, obfuscate *formal*, obscure
⊟ 2 clear 3 clear

Types of cloud include:
cirrus, cirrostratus, cirrocumulus,
altocumulus, altostratus, cumulus,
stratocumulus, nimbostratus, fractostratus,
fractocumulus, cumulonimbus, stratus,

cloudy *adj* 1 *a cloudy sky*: dark, dim, dull, foggy,
gloomy, grey, hazy, heavy, leaden, lowering,
misty, murky, overcast, sombre, sunless 2 *a
cloudy liquid*: milky, muddy, opaque 3 *cloudy
issues*: blurred, blurry, confused, foggy, hazy,
indistinct, misty, muddled, nebulous, obscure
Fa 1 bright, cloudless, sunny 2 clear 3 clear,
distinct, plain

clout *v* box, cuff, hit, punch, slap, slug *slang*,
smack, sock *slang*, strike, thump *colloq*, wallop
colloq, whack *colloq*
♦ *n* 1 *gave him a clout*: box, cuff, hit, punch, slap,
slug *slang*, smack, sock *slang*, strike, thump *colloq*,
wallop *colloq*, whack *colloq* 2 *political clout*:
authority, influence, muscle *colloq*, power,
prestige, pull *colloq*, standing, weight

cloven *adj* bisected, cleft, divided, split
Fa solid

clown *n* 1 *clowns at a circus*: buffoon, comedian,
comic, fool, harlequin, jester, joker, pierrot, zany
2 *some clown has parked in front of the gates*:
blockhead, dimwit *colloq*, dipstick *slang*, dork
slang, fool, geek *slang*, idiot, imbecile, jerk *slang*,
nerd *slang*, nincompoop *colloq*, ninny *colloq*,
nitwit *colloq*, numskull *colloq*, twerp *colloq*, twit
colloq, wally *slang*
♦ *v* act foolishly, act/play the fool, fool around,
jest, joke, mess around *colloq*, muck about *colloq*

cloying *adj* disgusting, excessive, nauseating,
oversweet, sickening, sickly
Fa pleasant, pleasing

club *n* 1 *a football club*: association, brotherhood,
circle, clique, company, federation, fraternity,
group, guild, league, order, organization, set,
social club, society, union 2 *hit with a club*: bat,
blackjack *US*, bludgeon, cosh *colloq*, cudgel,
mace, staff, stick, truncheon
♦ *v* bash, batter, beat, bludgeon, clobber *colloq*,
clout *colloq*, cosh *colloq*, hit, pummel, strike

clue *n* 1 *police are searching for clues*: evidence,
hint, indication, intimation, lead, pointer, sign,
suggestion, tip, tip-off, trace 2 *he doesn't have a
clue what's going on*: idea, inkling, notion,
suspicion

clump *n* accumulation, agglomeration *formal*,
agglutination *formal*, bunch, bundle, cluster,
collection, group, lot, mass, thicket, tuft
♦ *v* 1 *clump around*: clomp, lumber, plod, stamp,
stomp, thud, thump, tramp, trudge 2 *clump
together*: accumulate, amass, bunch, bundle,
cluster, group

clumsy *adj* 1 *a clumsy person*: accident-prone, all
thumbs *colloq*, awkward, blundering, bungling,
gauche, gawky *colloq*, ham-fisted, heavy-handed,
inept, lumbering, maladroit *formal*, unco-
ordinated, ungainly, ungraceful, unhandy,
unskilful, wooden 2 *clumsy objects*: awkward,
bulky, cumbersome, heavy, ill-made, ungainly,
unwieldy 3 *a clumsy attempt to comfort her*:
awkward, crude, insensitive, rough, tactless,
uncouth
Fa 1 careful, co-ordinated, graceful, natural,
skilful 2 elegant 3 sensitive, tactful

cluster *n* agglomeration *formal*, assemblage
formal, assembly, assortment, band, batch,
bunch, clump, collection, crowd, gathering,
group, huddle, inflorescence *technical*, knot,
mass, panicle *technical*, raceme *technical*, truss
♦ *v* assemble, bunch, collect, come together,
congregate, flock, gather, group (together)

clustered *adj* assembled, bunched, gathered,
glomerate *formal*, grouped, massed

clutch *v* catch, clasp, cling to, embrace, get/take
hold of, grab, grasp, grip, hang on to, hold,
seize, snatch
♦ *n* 1 *in someone's clutches*: claws, control,
custody, dominion, grasp, grip, hands, keeping,
mercy, possession, power, sway 2 *a clutch of eggs*:
group, hatching, incubation, set, setting

clutter *n* chaos, confusion, disarray, disorder,
jumble, litter, mess, muddle, untidiness
♦ *v* cover, fill (untidily), litter, make a mess,
make untidy, mess (up), scatter, strew

coach *n* 1 *travel by coach*: bus, charabanc *old use*,
express coach, Greyhound *US*, motor-bus *old use*,
motor-coach *old use* 2 *a train of twelve coaches*: car,
carriage, wagon 3 *a football coach*: educator,
instructor, mentor, teacher, trainer, tutor
4 *a coach and horses*: brougham, cab, carriage, gig,
hackney, hansom, landau, trap, wagon
♦ *v* cram, drill, instruct, prepare, prime, teach,
train, tutor

coagulate *v* clot, congeal, curdle, gel, solidify,
thicken

coalesce *v* affiliate, amalgamate, blend, cohere,
combine, commingle *formal*, commix *formal*,
consolidate, fuse, incorporate, integrate, join
(together), merge, mix, unite

coalition *n* affiliation, alliance, amalgamation,
association, bloc, combination, compact *formal*,
confederacy, confederation, conjunction *formal*,
federation, fusion, integration, joining, league,
merger, union

coarse *adj* 1 *a coarse texture*: bristly, hairy, lumpy,
prickly, rough, rugged, scaly, uneven 2 *coarse sea
salt*: unfinished, unpolished, unprocessed,
unpurified, unrefined 3 *coarse humour*: bawdy,
blue *colloq*, crude, earthy, foul-mouthed,
immodest, improper, indecent, indelicate,
obscene, offensive, raunchy *colloq*, ribald, rude,
smutty, vulgar 4 *coarse manners*: boorish, gross,
ill-mannered, impolite, loutish, offensive, rough,
rude, vulgar
Fa 1 fine, smooth 2 fine, smooth 3 clean
4 polite, refined, sophisticated

coarsen *v* blunt, deaden, desensitize, dull,
harden, indurate *formal*, roughen
Fa sensitize

coarseness *n* bawdiness, crassitude, crudity,
earthiness, immodesty, indecency, indelicacy,
obscenity, offensiveness, ribaldry, smut,
smuttiness, vulgarity
Fa delicacy, politeness, sophistication

coast *n* beach, coastline, foreshore, littoral
formal, seaboard, seashore, seaside, shore,
strand
♦ *v* cruise, drift, freewheel, glide, sail, slide, taxi

coat *n* 1 *an animal's coat*: fleece, fur, hair, hide,
pelt, skin, wool 2 *a coat of dust*: blanket, cladding,
coating, cover, covering, film, finish, glaze,
integument *technical*, laminate, lamination, layer,

mantle, overlay, pellicle, sheet, varnish, veneer
♦ *v* apply, cake, cover, daub, encrust, layer, paint, pave, plaster, put on/over, smear, spread

---

Types of coat include:
overcoat, greatcoat, redingote, car-coat, duffel coat, fleece, fur coat, Afghan, blanket, frock-coat, tail-coat, jacket, bomber jacket, dinner-jacket, donkey-jacket, hacking-jacket, reefer, pea-jacket, shooting-jacket, safari jacket, Eton jacket, matinee jacket, tuxedo, blazer, raincoat, trench-coat, mackintosh, mac *colloq*, Burberry, parka, anorak, cagoul, windcheater, jerkin, blouson, cape, cloak, poncho

---

coating *n* blanket, coat, covering, crust, dusting, film, finish, glaze, lamination, layer, membrane, overlay, patina *formal*, sheet, skin, varnish, veneer

coax *v* beguile, cajole, entice, flatter, get round, induce, inveigle *formal*, persuade, prevail upon, soft-soap *colloq*, sweet-talk *colloq*, talk into, tempt, wheedle, win over/round

cobble *v*
▶ **cobble together** improvise, knock up, make/produce quickly, make/produce roughly, put together

cock *n* chanticleer, cockerel, rooster
♦ *v* incline, lift, point, raise, slant, tip

cock-eyed *adj* **1** *leaning at a cockeyed angle:* askew, asymmetrical, awry, crooked, lopsided, skew-whiff **2** *a cock-eyed plan:* absurd, barmy *colloq*, crazy, daft *colloq*, ludicrous, nonsensical, preposterous
ⓕ 2 sensible, sober

cocky *adj* arrogant, brash, bumptious, cocksure, conceited, egotistical, hubristic *formal*, overconfident, self-assured, self-confident, self-important, swaggering, swollen-headed, vain
ⓕ humble, modest, shy

cocoon *v* **1** *he was cocooned in his duvet:* cover, envelop, wrap **2** *cocoon children from the outside world:* cloister, cushion, defend, insulate, isolate, overprotect, preserve, protect

coddle *v* baby, cosset, indulge, mollycoddle, overprotect, pamper, pet, spoil

code *n* **1** *a code of conduct:* conduct, convention, custom, ethics, etiquette, laws, manners, morality, morals, practice, principles, regulations, rules, system **2** *written in code:* cipher, cryptogram, cryptograph, Morse code, secret language, secret message, secret writing **3** *the product code on the base of the PC:* bar code, dialling code, international code, letters, local code, machine code, national code, numbers, postal code, postcode, signs, symbols, zip code

coerce *v* bludgeon, browbeat, bulldoze *colloq*, bully, compel, constrain, dragoon, drive, force, intimidate, lean on *colloq*, pressgang, pressure, pressurize, strongarm *colloq*, twist someone's arm *colloq*, use force

coercion *n* browbeating, bullying, compulsion, constraint, direct action, duress, force, intimidation, pressure, strongarm tactics, threats

coffer *n* box, case, casket, chest, moneybox, repository, safe, strongbox, treasury, trunk

cogent *adj* compelling, conclusive, convincing, effective, forceful, forcible, influential, irresistible, persuasive, potent, powerful, strong, unanswerable, urgent, weighty
ⓕ ineffective, unsound, weak

cogitate *v* cerebrate *formal*, consider, contemplate, deliberate, meditate, mull over, muse, ponder, reflect, ruminate *formal*, think deeply

cognate *adj* affiliated, agnate *technical*, akin, alike, allied, analogous, associated, congeneric, connected, consanguine, corresponding, kindred, related, similar
ⓕ unconnected, unrelated

cognition *n* apprehension, awareness, comprehension, consciousness, discernment, insight, intelligence, perception, rationality, reason, reasoning, thinking, understanding

cognizant *adj* acquainted, aware, conscious, conversant, familiar, informed, knowledgeable, versed, witting
ⓕ unaware

cohabit *v* live in sin *colloq*, live together, live together as man and wife, live with, shack up *slang*, sleep together

cohere *v* **1** *the groups cohered around a common aim:* adhere, bind, cling, coalesce, combine, consolidate, fuse, stick, unite **2** *the argument does not cohere:* add up, agree, correspond, hang together, harmonize, hold, make sense, square
ⓕ 1 separate

coherence *n* agreement, concordance *formal*, congruity *formal*, connection, consistency, consonance *formal*, correspondence, harmony, sense, union, unity
ⓕ incoherence

coherent *adj* **1** *a coherent plan:* consistent, logical, orderly, organized, rational, reasoned, sensible, systematic, well-planned, well-structured **2** *coherent speech:* articulate, clear, comprehensible, easy to understand, intelligible, meaningful
ⓕ 1 disjointed, incoherent **2** incoherent, incomprehensible, meaningless, unintelligible

cohesion *n* agreement, connection, consistency, correspondence, harmony, sense, union, unity, wholeness

cohort *n* **1** *Roman cohorts:* band, body, brigade, column, company, contingent, division, legion, regiment, squad, squadron, troop **2** *Robespierre and his cohorts:* accomplice, assistant, associate, buddy *colloq*, companion, follower, mate *colloq*, myrmidon, partner, sidekick *colloq*, supporter

coil *v* convolute *formal*, curl, entwine, loop, snake, spiral, twine, twist, wind, wreathe
♦ *n* convolution *formal*, corkscrew, curl, helix, loop, ring, roll, spiral, twist, volution *formal*, whorl

coin *n* cash, change, copper, loose change, money, piece, silver, small change, specie *formal*
♦ *v* **1** *coin a new word:* conceive, create, devise, dream up, fabricate, formulate, invent, make up, neologize, originate, produce, think up **2** *coin money:* forge, mint, produce

---

Types of coin include:
angel, bezant, bob *colloq*, copper, crown, dandiprat, denarius, dime, doubloon, ducat, farthing, florin, groat, guilder, guinea, half-crown, half guinea, halfpenny, half sovereign,

ha'penny, krugerrand, louis d'or, moidore, napoleon, nickel, noble, obol, penny, pound, quid *colloq*, rap, real, sesterce, shilling, sixpence, solidus, sou, sovereign, spade guinea, stater, tanner *colloq*, thaler, threepenny bit

coincide *v* 1 *the two events coincided*: clash, concur *formal*, happen at the same time, happen together, synchronize, take place simultaneously 2 *our opinions coincide*: accord, agree, be consistent, be the same, concur *formal*, correspond, harmonize, match, square, tally

coincidence *n* 1 *meet by coincidence*: accident, chance, fluke *colloq*, fortuity *formal*, luck, serendipity *formal* 2 *the coincidence of these two events*: clash, clashing, coexistence, concurrence *formal*, conjunction *formal*, correlation *formal*, correspondence, happening at the same time, happening together, synchronization, taking place simultaneously

coincidental *adj* accidental, casual, chance, flukey *colloq*, fortuitous *formal*, lucky, serendipitous *formal*, unintentional, unplanned
🖛 arranged, deliberate, planned

coitus *n* coition *formal*, copulation, coupling, going to bed with someone, love-making, mating, sex, sexual intercourse, sleeping with someone, union

cold *adj* 1 *a cold wind*: arctic, biting, bitter, brumal *formal*, brumous *formal*, chill, chilled, chilly, cool, freezing, fresh, frigid, frore *old use*, frosty, frozen, gelid *formal*, glacial, ice-cold, icy, keen, nippy *colloq*, numbed, parky *colloq*, polar, raw, rimy, shivery, Siberian, unheated, wintry 2 *I'm cold*: chilled, chilly, freezing, frozen, numbed, shivery 3 *a cold stare*: antagonistic, hostile, stony, unfriendly, unsympathetic 4 *a cold woman*: aloof, callous, clinical, distant, frigid, heartless, indifferent, insensitive, lukewarm, passionless, phlegmatic *formal*, remote, reserved, standoffish, uncaring, undemonstrative, unemotional, unexcitable, unfeeling, unmoved, unresponsive
🖛 1 hot, warm 2 hot, warm 3 friendly, responsive, warm 4 responsive, warm
♦ *n* chill, chilliness, coldness, coolness, frigidity, frost, ice, iciness, rawness, snow, winter
🖛 heat, warmth

cold-blooded *adj* barbaric, barbarous, brutal, callous, cruel, heartless, inhuman, merciless, pitiless, ruthless, savage, unfeeling
🖛 compassionate, merciful

cold-hearted *adj* callous, cold, detached, flinty, heartless, indifferent, inhuman, insensitive, stony-hearted, uncaring, uncompassionate, unfeeling, unkind, unsympathetic
🖛 warm-hearted

collaborate *v* 1 *collaborate with the police*: associate with, combine forces, co-operate, join, join forces, participate, team up, unite, work as partners, work jointly, work together 2 *collaborate with the enemy*: collude, conspire, fraternize, turn traitor

collaboration *n* 1 *in collaboration with local industry*: alliance, association, combined/joint/ collective effort, co-operation, participation, partnership, teamwork, union 2 *collaboration with the enemy*: collusion, conspiring, fraternizing

collaborator *n* 1 *collaborators in the research*: assistant, associate, colleague, co-worker, partner, team-mate 2 *traitors and collaborators*: accomplice, colluder, conspirator, fraternizer, quisling, traitor, turncoat

collapse *v* 1 *the bridge collapsed*: cave in, come apart, crumble, disintegrate, fall apart, fall down, fall in, fall to pieces, founder, give way, sink, subside 2 *the business collapsed*: break down, come to an end, come to nothing, disintegrate, fail, fall through, finish, flop *colloq*, fold *colloq*, founder, slump 3 *collapse with exhaustion*: black out, crumple, faint, keel over, lose consciousness, pass out, swoon
♦ *n* 1 *the collapse of the roof*: cave-in, coming apart, disintegration, falling to pieces, falling-down, falling-in, foundering, giving way, sinking, subsidence 2 *the collapse of the talks*: breakdown, disintegration, downfall, failure, falling-through, flop *colloq*, foundering, ruin 3 *his collapse in the street*: blackout, fainting, keeling-over, loss of consciousness, passing-out, swoon

collar *n* bertha, dog-collar, gorget, neckband, rebato, ring, ruche, ruff
♦ *v* apprehend, arrest, capture, catch, grab, nab *colloq*, nick *colloq*, seize

collate *v* arrange, collect, compose, gather, order, organize, put in order, sort

collateral *n* assurance, deposit, guarantee, pledge, security, surety

colleague *n* aide, ally, assistant, associate, auxiliary, collaborator, companion, comrade, confederate, confrère, co-worker, fellow worker, helper, partner, team-mate, workmate

collect *v* 1 *collect firewood*: accumulate, aggregate *formal*, amass, gather, heap, hoard, pile up, stockpile 2 *a crowd collected*: amass, assemble, come together, congregate, convene, converge, form, gather, mass, muster, rally 3 *collect them from the station*: call for, come for, fetch, get, go and bring, go and get, go and take, meet, pick up 4 *collect for a charity*: acquire, ask for money, ask people to give, raise money, solicit 5 *collect stamps*: acquire, amass, save 6 *collect your thoughts*: assemble, compose, gather (together), prepare
🖛 2 disperse, scatter 3 drop off

collected *adj* calm, composed, controlled, cool, imperturbable, placid, poised, self-controlled, self-possessed, serene, unperturbed, unruffled, unshaken
🖛 agitated, anxious, worried

collection *n* 1 *a collection of model cars*: accumulation, assortment, conglomeration, heap, hoard, mass, pile, stockpile, store 2 *a collection of people*: assemblage *formal*, assembly, cluster, gathering, group, mass 3 *the collection of information*: accumulation, acquisition, gathering 4 *a collection of poems*: anthology, collected works, compilation, set 5 *a collection for charity*: contribution(s), donation(s), gift(s), offering, offertory, subscription, whip-round *colloq*

collective *adj* 1 *collective agreement*: collaborative, combined, common, concerted, co-operative, corporate, democratic, joint, shared, unanimous, united 2 *their collective funds*: aggregate, combined, composite, cumulative, joint, shared
🖛 1 individual 2 individual
♦ *n* commune, community, co-operative, kibbutz, kolkhoz, moshav

collective nouns

Collective nouns (by animal) include:
shrewdness of *apes*, cete of *badgers*, sloth of *bears*, swarm of *bees*, obstinacy of *buffalos*, clowder of *cats*, drove of *cattle*, brood of *chickens*, bask of *crocodiles*, murder of *crows*, herd of *deer*, pack of *dogs*, school of *dolphins*, dole of *doves*, team of *ducks*, parade of *elephants*, busyness of *ferrets*, charm of *finches*, shoal of *fish*, skulk of *foxes*, army of *frogs*, gaggle/skein of *geese*, tribe of *goats*, husk of *hares*, cast of *hawks*, brood of *hens*, bloat of *hippopotami*, string of *horses*, pack of *hounds*, troop of *kangaroos*, kindle of *kittens*, exaltation of *larks*, leap of *leopards*, pride of *lions*, swarm of *locusts*, tittering of *magpies*, troop of *monkeys*, watch of *nightingales*, family of *otters*, parliament of *owls*, pandemonium of *parrots*, covey of *partridges*, muster of *peacocks*, muster of *penguins*, nye of *pheasants*, litter of *pigs*, school of *porpoises*, bury of *rabbits*, colony of *rats*, unkindness of *ravens*, crash of *rhinoceroses*, building of *rooks*, pod of *seals*, flock of *sheep*, murmuration of *starlings*, ambush of *tigers*, rafter of *turkeys*, turn of *turtles*, descent of *woodpeckers*, gam of *whales*, rout of *wolves*, zeal of *zebras*

collector

Names of collectors include:
antiquary (*antiques*), tegestollogist (*beer mats*), lepidopterist (*butterflies*), cartophilist (*cigarette cards*), numismatist (*coins/medals*), discophile (*gramophone records*), chirographist (*handwriting*), phillumenist (*matches/matchboxes*), deltiologist (*postcards*), philatelist (*stamps*), arctophile (*teddy bears*)

college *n* academy, adult education centre, college of further education, educational establishment, educational institution, institute, poly *formerly*, polytechnic *formerly*, school, seminary, technical college, university

collide *v* **1** *the cars collided*: bump (into), crash (into), go into, hit, meet head on, plough into, prang *colloq*, run into, smash (into) **2** *their opinions collided*: be at variance, be in conflict, be incompatible, clash, conflict, disagree

collision *n* **1** *a collision with a lorry*: accident, bump, crash, impact, pile-up, prang *colloq*, smash, wreck **2** *a collision between two stubborn men*: clash, conflict, confrontation, disagreement, feud, fight, fighting, opposition, quarrel, showdown, warring, wrangle

colloquial *adj* casual, chatty, conversational, demotic *formal*, everyday, familiar, idiomatic, informal, popular, vernacular
☒ formal

collude *v* collaborate, connive, conspire, intrigue, machinate *formal*, plot, scheme

collusion *n* cahoots *colloq*, collaboration, complicity, connivance, conspiracy, deceit, intrigue, league, machination *formal*, plot, scheme, scheming

colonist *n* colonial, immigrant, pioneer, settler

colonize *v* occupy, people, pioneer, populate, put down roots in, settle

colonnade *n* arcade, cloisters, columniation *formal*, covered walk, peristyle *formal*, portico, stoa

colony *n* **1** *Britain's former colonies*: dependency, dominion, outpost, possession, protectorate, province, satellite, satellite state, settlement, territory **2** *a colony of settlers*: association, community, group, settlement

colossal *adj* Brobdingnagian *formal*, enormous, gargantuan, gigantic, great, herculean, huge, immense, mammoth, massive, monstrous, monumental, vast, whopping *colloq*
☒ minute, tiny

colour *n* **1** *the car comes in six different colours*: coloration, hue, shade, tinge, tint, tone **2** *skin colour*: coloration, complexion, pigmentation, tone **3** *a range of hair colours*: colorant, coloration, dye, paint, pigment, tincture, tint, wash **4** *the colour of her cheeks*: glow, pinkness, rosiness, ruddiness **5** *give colour to a scene*: animation, brilliance, life, liveliness, richness, vividness **6** *a nation's colours*: badge, banner, emblem, ensign, flag, insignia, standard
♦ *v* **1** *colour a picture*: crayon, dye, highlight, paint, stain, tinge, tint, wash **2** *her cheeks coloured*: blush, flush, go/turn red, redden **3** *colour your judgement*: affect, bias, distort, influence, pervert, prejudice, slant, sway, taint **4** *colour an account*: distort, exaggerate, falsify, misrepresent, overstate

The range of colours includes:
red, crimson, scarlet, vermilion, cherry, cerise, magenta, maroon, burgundy, ruby, orange, tangerine, apricot, coral, salmon, peach, amber, brown, chestnut, mahogany, bronze, auburn, rust, umber, copper, cinnamon, chocolate, tan, sepia, taupe, beige, fawn, yellow, lemon, canary, ochre, saffron, topaz, gold, chartreuse, green, eau de nil, emerald, jade, bottle, avocado, sage, khaki, turquoise, aquamarine, cobalt, blue, sapphire, gentian, indigo, anil, navy, violet, purple, mauve, plum, lavender, lilac, pink, rose, magnolia, cream, ecru, milky, white, grey, silver, charcoal, ebony, jet, black

colourful *adj* **1** *a colourful coat*: bright, brilliant, garish, gaudy, kaleidoscopic, many-coloured, multicoloured, parti-coloured, rich, variegated, vibrant, vivid **2** *a colourful description*: animated, exciting, graphic, interesting, lively, picturesque, rich, stimulating, vibrant, vivid
☒ **1** colourless, drab

colourless *adj* **1** *a colourless substance*: bleached, faded, in black and white, monochrome, neutral, transparent, uncoloured **2** *his face was colourless*: anaemic, ashen, pale, sickly, wan, washed out **3** *a colourless person*: boring, characterless, drab, dreary, dull, insipid, lacklustre, plain, tame, uninteresting, unmemorable
☒ **1** colourful **3** bright, exciting

column *n* **1** *a Greek column*: asta *technical*, Atlas, caryatid, obelisk, pier, pilaster, pillar, post, shaft, support, telamon, upright **2** *a column of figures*: line, list, rank, row **3** *a column of people*: file, line, parade, procession, queue, rank, row, string **4** *a column in a newspaper*: article, feature, item, piece, story

columnist *n* correspondent, critic, editor, journalist, reporter, reviewer, writer

coma *n* catalepsy *technical*, insensibility, lethargy, oblivion, sopor, stupor, torpor, unconsciousness

comatose *adj* **1** *comatose in hospital:* cataleptic *technical*, in a coma, insensible, out, out cold, soporose, unconscious **2** *lying comatose on the sofa:* dazed, drowsy, insensible, lethargic, out, out cold, sleepy, sluggish, somnolent *formal*, stunned, stupefied, torpid, unconscious
F3 **1** conscious **2** conscious

comb *v* **1** *comb your hair:* arrange, dress, groom, neaten, tidy, untangle **2** *comb the countryside:* go over with a fine-tooth comb *colloq*, go through, hunt, rake, ransack, rummage, scour, screen, search, sift, sweep, turn upside down *colloq*

combat *n* action, battle, bout, clash, conflict, contest, duel, encounter, engagement, fight, fighting, hostilities, skirmish, struggle, war, warfare
♦ *v* battle, contend with, contest, defy, do battle with, fight, oppose, resist, strive against, struggle against, take up arms against, wage war on, war with, withstand

combatant *n* adversary, antagonist, belligerent, contender, enemy, fighter, opponent, serviceman, servicewoman, soldier, warrior

combative *adj* aggressive, antagonistic, argumentative, bellicose *formal*, belligerent, contentious, militant, pugnacious *formal*, quarrelsome, truculent *formal*, warlike
F3 pacific, peaceful

combination *n* **1** *a combination of several businesses:* alliance, amalgamation, association, coalition, combine, confederacy, confederation, conjunction, consortium, co-operation, co-ordination, federation, integration, merger, syndicate, synergy, unification, union **2** *a combination of dyes:* amalgam, amalgamation, blend, coalescence, composite, compound, cross, fusion, mix, mixture, solution, synthesis

combine *v* **1** *combine the two substances:* admix *formal*, alloy, amalgamate, bind, blend, bond, bring together, compound, fuse, homogenize *formal*, incorporate, integrate, marry, merge, mingle, mix, put together, stir, synthesize, weld **2** *businesses combining into one company:* ally, amalgamate, associate, club together, connect, co-operate, incorporate, integrate, join, join forces, link, merge, pool, team up, unify, unite
F3 **1** detach, divide, separate **2** detach, divide, separate

combustible *adj* **1** *combustible gas:* explosive, flammable, ignitable, incendiary, inflammable **2** *a combustible mood:* charged, excitable, explosive, sensitive, stormy, tense, volatile
F3 **1** flameproof, incombustible, non-flammable

combustion *n* burning, firing, igniting, ignition

come *v* **1** *they came to me:* advance, approach, draw near, move forward, move towards, near, travel towards **2** *come into the room:* appear, arrive, barge in *colloq*, burst in *colloq*, enter, materialize, reach, show up *colloq*, turn up *colloq* **3** *come to the party:* attend, put in an appearance, show up *colloq*, turn up *colloq* **4** *come to power:* achieve, attain, gain, pass into, reach, secure **5** *the time for action has come:* arrive, come about, come

to pass, happen, occur, present itself, take place, transpire **6** *she comes from Belgium:* be, be... by birth, be a native of, hail, have as its source/origin, have as your home, originate **7** *his arrogance comes from his insecurity:* arise, be caused by, develop, evolve, follow, have as its source/origin, issue, result from, stem **8** *it may come to war:* become, develop into, enter, evolve into, go as far as, pass into, turn **9** *the idea came to me:* come to the mind of, dawn on, occur to, strike
F3 **1** go **2** depart, leave **3** depart, leave **4** fall from

▶ **come about** arise, befall *formal*, come to pass, happen, occur, result, take place, transpire

▶ **come across 1** *I came across him on holiday:* bump into *colloq*, encounter, meet by chance, run into *colloq* **2** *come across an old photo:* chance upon *formal*, discover, find (by chance), happen upon *formal*, notice, stumble across

▶ **come along 1** *the project is coming along nicely:* advance, develop, make headway, make progress, progress **2** *how's she coming along after her operation?:* get better, improve, mend, rally, recover, recuperate, show an improvement

▶ **come apart** break (up), collapse, crumble, disintegrate, fall to bits/pieces, separate, split, tear

▶ **come between** alienate, cause a rift between, disunite, divide, estrange *formal*, part, separate, split up

▶ **come by** acquire, get, get hold of, obtain, procure *formal*, secure

▶ **come down 1** *numbers have come down:* decline, decrease, descend, drop, fall, reduce **2** *he's come down in the world:* decline, degenerate, deteriorate, worsen

▶ **come down on** admonish, berate *formal*, blame, chide, criticize, find fault with, rebuke, reprehend, reprimand, reprove, slate *colloq*, tear into *colloq*, upbraid

▶ **come down to** amount to, be equivalent to, be tantamount to, boil down to, correspond to, mean

▶ **come down with** become ill with, become infected with, catch, contract *formal*, develop, fall ill with, get, go down with, pick up, succumb to *formal*

▶ **come forward** offer (yourself), offer your services, step forward, volunteer

▶ **come in** appear, arrive, enter, show up *colloq*
F3 go out

▶ **come in for** be subjected to, endure, experience, get, receive, suffer, undergo

▶ **come into** acquire, be left, have bequeathed to you, inherit, receive

▶ **come off** be effective, be successful, end up, go well, happen, occur, succeed, take place, work (out)

▶ **come on 1** *he's really coming on at the piano:* advance, develop, get better, improve, make progress, proceed, progress, show an improvement, succeed **2** *she's coming on after her illness:* get better, improve, mend, rally, recover, recuperate, show an improvement, thrive **3** *autumn is coming on:* appear, begin, take place

▶ **come out 1** *the magazine comes out monthly:* appear, be produced, be published, become available **2** *the real story came out eventually:* be revealed, become known, come to light, emerge **3** *everything came out all right in the end:* conclude, end (up), finish, result **4** *come out as a homosexual:* admit, come out of the closet, declare openly, declare yourself to be

▶ **come out with** blurt out, declare, exclaim, say, state

▶ **come round 1** *come round from the anaesthetic:* awake, recover, recover/regain consciousness, wake **2** *they came round eventually:* accede, agree, be converted to, be persuaded, be won over, change your mind, concede, grant, relent, yield

▶ **come through 1** *we came through in the end:* prevail, succeed, triumph **2** *she's come through a lot:* endure, survive, withstand

▶ **come to 1** *come to after the operation:* awake, recover, recover/regain consciousness, wake **2** *come to a total:* add up to, aggregate, amount to, equal, make, run to, total

▶ **come up** arise, crop up, happen, occur, present itself, rise, turn up

▶ **come up to** approach, bear comparison with, compare with, live up to, make the grade, match up to, measure up to, meet, reach

▶ **come up with** advance, conceive, dream up, offer, present, produce, propose, put forward, submit, suggest, think of

comeback *n* rally, reappearance, recovery, resurgence, return, revival

comedian *n* clown, comic, funny man, funny woman, gagster *colloq*, humorist, joker, stand-up, wag *colloq*, wit

comedown *n* **1** *a comedown after his former job:* decline, deflation, degradation, demotion, descent, humiliation, reversal, reverse **2** *the film was a comedown after all the hype:* anticlimax, deflation, disappointment, let-down

comedy *n* **1** *a comedy on TV:* burlesque, farce, pantomime, satire, sitcom, situation comedy, slapstick, vaudeville **2** *his talent for comedy:* clowning, drollery, facetiousness, funniness, hilarity, humour, jesting, joking, wit
Ed 1 tragedy

comely *adj* attractive, beautiful, blooming, bonny, buxom, fair, good-looking, lovely, pretty, pulchritudinous *formal*

come-on *n* allurement, encouragement, enticement, inducement, lure, temptation

come-uppance *n* chastening, deserts, dues, just deserts, merit, punishment, recompense, requital, retribution, what you deserve

comfort *n* **1** *a life of comfort:* contentment, cosiness, ease, enjoyment, freedom from difficulties, freedom from pain, freedom from worry/unhappiness, luxury, opulence *formal*, plenty, snugness, well-being **2** *no comfort for her grief:* aid, alleviation, cheer, compensation, condolence, consolation, encouragement, help, reassurance, relief, solace *formal*, succour *formal*, support
Ed 1 discomfort **2** distress
♦ *v* alleviate, assuage, bring solace to *formal*, cheer, console, ease, encourage, gladden, hearten, help, reassure, relieve, soothe, strengthen, succour *formal*, support

comfortable *adj* **1** *a comfortable room:* agreeable, comfy *colloq*, cosy, delightful, easy, enjoyable, pleasant, relaxing, restful, snug **2** *comfortable clothes:* loose-fitting, roomy, well-fitting **3** *a comfortable lifestyle:* affluent, luxurious, opulent *formal*, prosperous, well-off, well-to-do, without financial problems **4** *not feel comfortable talking about it:* at ease, confident, contented, happy, relaxed, safe, unembarrassed

Ed 1 uncomfortable, unpleasant **2** tight, uncomfortable **3** poor **4** awkward, embarrassed, nervous, offended, threatened, uneasy

comforting *adj* cheering, consolatory, consoling, encouraging, heartening, heart-warming, helpful, inspiriting *formal*, reassuring, soothing
Ed worrying

comic *adj* absurd, amusing, comical, diverting, droll, facetious, farcical, funny, hilarious, humorous, jocular, joking, laughable, ludicrous, priceless *colloq*, rich *colloq*, ridiculous, side-splitting, witty, zany
Ed serious, tragic
♦ *n* buffoon, clown, comedian, funny man, funny woman, gagster *colloq*, humorist, joker, stand-up, wag *colloq*, wit

comical *adj* absurd, amusing, droll, farcical, funny, hilarious, humorous, laughable, ludicrous, ridiculous, witty
Ed sad, unamusing

coming *adj* **1** *in the coming months:* advancing, approaching, due, forthcoming, future, imminent, impending, near, nearing, next, upcoming **2** *the coming man:* aspiring, promising, rising, up-and-coming
♦ *n* advent, approach, arrival, birth, dawn

command *v* **1** *command a subordinate:* adjure *formal*, bid, charge, demand, direct, enjoin, give orders to, instruct, order **2** *command a battalion:* control, direct, dominate, govern, have charge/command/control of, head, lead, manage, preside over, reign, rule, superintend, supervise **3** *command respect:* be given, gain, get, obtain, receive, secure
♦ *n* **1** *give a command:* behest *formal*, bidding, charge, commandment, decree, dictate, direction, directive, edict, injunction, instruction, mandate, order, precept, requirement **2** *be in command:* ascendancy, authority, charge, control, domination, dominion, government, leadership, management, mastery, power, rule, superintendence, supervision, sway

commandeer *v* appropriate *formal*, arrogate *formal*, confiscate, expropriate *formal*, hijack, impound, requisition *formal*, seize, sequester *formal*, sequestrate *formal*, take possession of, usurp

commander *n* admiral, boss *colloq*, captain, chief, commander-in-chief, commanding officer, director, general, head, leader, officer

commanding *adj* **1** *in a commanding lead:* advantageous, controlling, directing, dominant, dominating, powerful, strong, superior **2** *a commanding personality:* assertive, authoritative, autocratic, confident, forceful, imposing, impressive, peremptory *formal*, powerful **3** *the castle's commanding position:* dominating, lofty

commemorate *v* **1** *commemorate a victory:* celebrate, honour, immortalize, mark, memorialize *formal*, pay tribute to, recognize, remember, salute **2** *a ritual to commemorate the summer solstice:* celebrate, keep, observe, solemnize

commemoration *n* **1** *we do it in commemoration of her:* celebration, dedication, honour, honouring, memory, recognition, remembrance, salute, tribute **2** *the commemoration of Remembrance Sunday:* ceremony, observance

commemorative *adj* as a tribute to, celebratory, dedicatory, honouring, in honour of, in memoriam, in memory of, in recognition of, in remembrance of, marking, memorial, remembering, saluting

commence *v* **1** *commence a lesson:* begin, embark on, inaugurate, initiate, launch, make a beginning, make a start, open, originate, start **2** *the term commences in August:* begin, go ahead, open, start
🔁 **1** cease *formal*, end, finish **2** cease *formal*, end, finish

commend *v* **1** *commend her for her achievement:* acclaim, applaud, compliment, eulogize *formal*, extol, laud *formal*, praise, speak highly of **2** *commend this book:* advocate, approve, propose, put in a good word for, recommend, suggest **3** *commend the child to your care:* commit, confide, consign, deliver, entrust, give, hand over, trust, yield
🔁 **1** censure, criticize

commendable *adj* admirable, creditable, estimable, excellent, exemplary, laudable *formal*, meritorious *formal*, noble, praiseworthy, worthy
🔁 blameworthy, poor

commendation *n* acclaim, acclamation, accolade, applause, approbation *formal*, approval, credit, encomium *formal*, good word, high/good opinion, panegyric *formal*, praise, recognition, recommendation, special mention
🔁 blame, criticism

commensurate *adj* **1** *salaries commensurate with those of doctors:* comparable, compatible with, corresponding, corresponding to, equivalent **2** *finding jobs commensurate with their education and experience:* according to, appropriate to, compatible with, consistent with, corresponding, corresponding to, due, equivalent, fitting, in proportion to, proportionate

comment *v* **1** *she commented that it wasn't her fault:* give an opinion, interject *formal*, interpose *formal*, mention, note, observe, opine *formal*, point out, remark, say **2** *comment on the news:* discuss, elucidate *formal*, explain, give an opinion, interpret, talk about
♦ *n* **1** *make a comment:* observation, opinion, remark, statement **2** *comments written in the margin:* annotation, commentary, criticism, elucidation *formal*, explanation, exposition, footnote, marginal note, note

commentary *n* **1** *a commentary on a football match:* account, analysis, description, narration, report, review, voice-over **2** *a commentary on 'The Waste Land':* analysis, annotation, critique, elucidation *formal*, exegesis *formal*, explanation, exposition *formal*, interpretation, notes, treatise

commentator *n* **1** *a sports commentator:* broadcaster, commenter, correspondent, narrator, newscaster, reporter, sportscaster **2** *a commentator on the text:* annotator, critic, exegete *formal*, expositor *formal*, interpreter

commerce *n* business, buying and selling, dealing, dealings, exchange, marketing, merchandising, private enterprise, trade, traffic, trafficking

commercial *adj* **1** *buildings for commercial use:* business, industrial, trade, trading **2** *a commercial transaction:* entrepreneurial, financial, monetary **3** *a commercial success:* popular, profitable, profit-making, saleable, sellable **4** *Christmas has become too commercial:* materialistic, mercenary, profit-orientated, venal
♦ *n* ad *colloq*, advert *colloq*, advertisement, announcement, bill, blurb, circular, display, handbill, handout, hype *colloq*, jingle, leaflet, marketing, notice, placard, plug *colloq*, poster, promotion, propaganda, publicity

commiserate *v* comfort, console, express/offer sympathy, send/offer condolences, sympathize

commiseration *n* comfort, compassion, condolence, consolation, pity, solace *formal*, sympathy

commission *n* **1** *he gave me a commission to write his biography:* appointment, assignment, authority, charge, duty, employment, errand, function, job, mandate, mission, piece of work, responsibility, task, warrant **2** *set up a commission to investigate the crash:* advisory group/body, board, committee, council, delegation, deputation, representatives **3** *earn a commission on a sale:* allowance, brokerage, cut *colloq*, fee, percentage, rake-off *colloq*, royalty, share
♦ *v* appoint, arrange, ask for, assign, authorize, contract, delegate, depute, employ, empower, engage, mandate, nominate, order, place/put in an order for, request, select, send

commit *v* **1** *commit a crime:* carry out, do, effect *formal*, enact, execute, get up to, indulge in, perform, perpetrate *formal* **2** *commit you with a task:* assign, commend, confide, consign, deliver, deposit, entrust, give, hand over, trust **3** *commit yourself to do something:* bind, covenant, decide, dedicate, engage, obligate *formal*, pledge, promise

commitment *n* **1** *show commitment:* adherence, allegiance, dedication, devotion, effort, hard work, involvement, loyalty **2** *too many commitments:* duty, engagement, liability, obligation, responsibility, tie, undertaking **3** *make a commitment:* assurance, covenant, guarantee, pledge, promise, undertaking, vow
🔁 **1** vacillation, wavering

committed *adj* active, card-carrying *colloq*, dedicated, devoted, diligent, engagé *formal*, enthusiastic, fervent, hardworking, industrious, involved, loyal, red-hot, studious, zealous
🔁 apathetic, uncommitted

commodious *adj* ample, capacious *formal*, comfortable, expansive, extensive, large, roomy, spacious
🔁 cramped

commodity *n* article, goods, item, merchandise, produce, product, stock, thing, wares

common *adj* **1** *a common name:* customary, daily, everyday, familiar, frequent, habitual, regular, routine, two a penny *colloq*, usual **2** *have a common belief:* collective, joint, mutual, shared **3** *common land:* communal, community, public **4** *common knowledge:* accepted, commonplace, conventional, general, popular, prevalent, universal, widespread **5** *the common cold:* average, ordinary, plain, run-of-the-mill, simple,

standard, undistinguished, unexceptional, workaday **6** *a common young man:* coarse, common as muck *colloq*, crude, ill-bred, loutish, low, plebeian, uncouth, unrefined, vulgar
🔄 **1** noteworthy, rare, uncommon, unusual **5** different, special **6** refined, tasteful

commonly *adv* as a rule, for the most part, generally, normally, routinely, typically, usually
🔄 rarely

commonplace *adj* banal, boring, common, everyday, frequent, hackneyed, humdrum, mundane, ordinary, pedestrian, routine, stale, stock, threadbare, trite, unexceptional, uninteresting, widespread
🔄 exceptional, memorable

common sense *n* astuteness, discernment, good sense, gumption *colloq*, hard-headedness, judgement, judiciousness *formal*, level-headedness, native intelligence, nous *colloq*, practicality, pragmatism, prudence *formal*, realism, reason, savvy *colloq*, sense, sensibleness, shrewdness, soundness, wisdom
🔄 folly, stupidity

common-sense *adj* astute, commonsensical, discerning, down-to-earth, hard-headed, judicious *formal*, level-headed, matter-of-fact, practical, pragmatic, prudent *formal*, realistic, reasonable, sensible, shrewd, sound, wise
🔄 foolish, unrealistic, unreasonable

commonwealth

Members of the Commonwealth are:
Antigua and Barbuda, Australia, the Bahamas, Bangladesh, Barbados, Belize, Botswana, Brunei, Cameroon, Canada, Cyprus, Dominica, Fiji, the Gambia, Ghana, Grenada, Guyana, India, Jamaica, Kenya, Kiribati, Lesotho, Malawi, Malaysia, the Maldives, Malta, Mauritius, Mozambique, Namibia, Nauru, New Zealand, Nigeria, Pakistan, Papua New Guinea, St Christopher and Nevis, St Lucia, St Vincent and the Grenadines, Samoa, Seychelles, Sierra Leone, Singapore, Solomon Islands, South Africa, Sri Lanka, Swaziland, Tanzania, Tonga, Trinidad and Tobago, Tuvalu, Uganda, United Kingdom, Vanuatu, Zambia

commotion *n* ado, agitation, ballyhoo *colloq*, brouhaha *colloq*, bustle, clamour, confusion, disorder, disturbance, excitement, ferment, fracas, furore, fuss, hubbub, hullabaloo *colloq*, hurly-burly, racket, riot, row, rumpus, stir, to-do *colloq*, tumult, turmoil, upheaval, uproar

communal *adj* collective, common, community, general, joint, public, shared
🔄 personal, private

commune *n* collective, colony, community, co-operative, kibbutz, settlement
♦ *v* communicate, converse, discourse, get in touch, make contact

communicable *adj* catching, contagious, conveyable, infectious, infective *formal*, spreadable, transferable, transmissible, transmittable

communicate *v* **1** *communicate information:* announce, broadcast, convey, declare, diffuse, disclose, disseminate *formal*, divulge, express, impart, inform, intimate, make known, pass on, proclaim, publish, relay, report, reveal, spread,

transmit, unfold **2** *communicate a disease:* pass on, spread, transfer, transmit **3** *communicate with a friend:* commune, contact, converse, correspond, get/be in touch, keep the lines open, phone, speak, talk, telephone, write

communication *n* **1** *be in communication with someone:* connection, contact **2** *a secret communication:* information, intelligence, intimation **3** *the communication of information:* disclosure, dissemination *formal*, transmission

communicative *adj* candid, chatty, expansive, forthcoming, frank, free, friendly, informative, open, talkative, unreserved
🔄 quiet, reserved, reticent, secretive

communion *n* **1** *communion with nature:* accord *formal*, affinity, closeness, communing, concord *formal*, empathy, fellowship, harmony, intercourse *formal*, rapport, sympathy, togetherness, unity **2** *Holy Communion:* Eucharist, Lord's Supper, Mass, Sacrament

communiqué *n* announcement, bulletin, dispatch, message, newsflash, (official) communication, report, statement

communism *n* Bolshevism, collectivism, Leninism, Maoism, Marxism, revisionism, socialism, sovietism, Stalinism, Titoism, totalitarianism, Trotskyism

community *n* **1** *the local community:* area, district, locality, neighbourhood, sector **2** *the Bangladeshi community:* colony, group, people, populace, population, public, residents, section **3** *promote a sense of community:* brotherhood, fellowship, fraternity **4** *a religious community:* association, brotherhood, commune, fellowship, fraternity, kibbutz, sisterhood, society

commute *v* **1** *commute by train:* journey, shuttle, travel to and from, travel to work **2** *commute the death sentence:* adjust, curtail, decrease, lighten, mitigate, modify, reduce, remit, shorten, soften

commuter *n* passenger, strap-hanger *colloq*, traveller

compact[1] *adj* **1** *a compact mass of leaves:* close, compressed, condensed, dense, firm, impenetrable, pressed together, solid **2** *a compact definition:* brief, concise, condensed, pithy, short, succinct, terse **3** *a compact gadget:* little, neat, pocket
🔄 **1** diffuse **2** diffuse, rambling **3** large
♦ *v* compress, condense, consolidate, cram, flatten, pack down, press down, press together, squeeze, tamp

compact[2] *n* agreement, alliance, arrangement, bargain, bond, concordat, contract, covenant, deal, entente, indenture, pact, settlement, treaty, understanding

companion *n* **1** *his faithful companion:* accomplice, ally, associate, buddy *colloq*, colleague, comrade, confederate, confidant(e), consort, crony *colloq*, fellow, follower, friend, intimate, mate *colloq*, pal *colloq*, partner, sidekick *colloq* **2** *paid companion to an old lady:* aide, assistant, attendant, chaperon(e), escort

companionable *adj* affable, amiable, congenial, convivial, familiar, friendly, genial, gregarious, neighbourly, outgoing, sociable
🔄 unfriendly

companionship n association, camaraderie, company, comradeship, conviviality, esprit de corps, fellowship, friendship, intimacy, rapport, social intercourse, togetherness

company n **1** *a manufacturing company:* association, business, business organization, cartel, concern, conglomerate, consortium, corporation, establishment, firm, holding company, house, limited company, limited liability company, multinational, partnership, private limited company, public limited company (PLC or plc), subsidiary, syndicate, trust **2** *a theatre company:* assembly, band, body, circle, community, crew, crowd, ensemble, gathering, group, party, set, society, team, throng, troop, troupe **3** *expecting company:* callers, guests, visitors **4** *be glad of company:* companionship, comradeship, contact, conviviality, fellowship, friendship, presence, togetherness

comparable adj akin, alike, analogous, cognate *formal*, commensurate, corresponding, equal, equivalent, like, parallel, proportional, proportionate, related, similar, tantamount
🖬 dissimilar, unequal, unlike

---

comparable or *comparative*? *Comparable* means 'of the same kind, to the same degree, etc': *cheaper than any comparable hotel.* *Comparative* means 'judged by comparing with something else': *After they had stopped playing so noisily there was a period of comparative silence.*

---

comparative adj by/in comparison, relative

compare v **1** *compare the new edition with the old one:* balance, contrast, correlate, juxtapose, measure, note the differences between, weigh **2** *compare her to an angel:* analogize *formal*, correlate, draw a parallel between, draw analogies with, equate, liken, regard as the same, show the similarities between **3** *not compare with his predecessor:* be as good as, be comparable to, bear comparison with, equal, hold a candle to *colloq*, match, parallel

comparison n **1** *make an unfair comparison:* contrast, differences, differentiation, distinction, juxtaposition **2** *there's no comparison between analogue and digital TV:* analogy, comparability, correlation, likeness, parallel, relationship, resemblance, similarity

compartment n **1** *a train compartment:* berth, carriage, section **2** *the freezer compartment in a fridge:* alcove, area, bay, booth, carrel, cell, chamber, cubbyhole, cubicle, locker, niche, part, partition, pigeonhole, section **3** *keep work and home life in separate compartments:* area, category, division, part, section, subdivision

compass n **1** *within the compass of the city walls:* area, boundary, bounds, circle, circuit, circumference, enclosure, extent, limit(s), round, space, zone **2** *a topic beyond the compass of this book:* field, limit(s), range, reach, realm(s), scale, scope, space, sphere, stretch

compassion n benevolence, care, concern, consideration, fellow-feeling, gentleness, humanity, kindness, leniency, mercy, pity, sorrow, sympathy, tender-heartedness, tenderness, understanding
🖬 cruelty, indifference

compassionate adj benevolent, caring, clement, humane, humanitarian, kind-hearted, kindly, lenient, merciful, pitying, sympathetic, tender, tender-hearted, understanding, warm-hearted
🖬 cruel, indifferent

compatible adj **1** *compatible views:* accordant *formal*, conformable, congruent *formal*, congruous *formal*, consistent, consonant *formal*, harmonious, in harmony, matching, reconcilable, similar, well-matched **2** *compatible companions:* having rapport, in harmony, like-minded, similar, suited, sympathetic, well-matched, well-suited
🖬 **1** contradictory, incompatible **2** antagonistic, incompatible

compatriot n countryman, countrywoman, fellow citizen, fellow countryman, fellow countrywoman, fellow national

compel v browbeat, bulldoze *colloq*, bully, coerce, constrain, dragoon, drive, force, hustle, impel, insist on, intimidate, lean on *colloq*, make, oblige, press-gang, pressure, pressurize, put the screws on *colloq*, strongarm *colloq*, twist someone's arm *colloq*

compelling adj **1** *a compelling novel:* absorbing, compulsive, enthralling, fascinating, gripping, irresistible, mesmeric, riveting, spellbinding, unputdownable *colloq* **2** *a compelling factor in his decision:* imperative, overriding, pressing, urgent, weighty **3** *a compelling argument:* cogent, conclusive, convincing, forceful, incontrovertible, irrefutable, persuasive, powerful
🖬 **1** boring **3** unconvincing, weak

compendium n **1** *an exhaustive compendium of news articles:* digest, summary, synopsis **2** *a gardeners' compendium:* companion, handbook, manual, vade-mecum

compensate v **1** *compensate you for any loss:* indemnify, recompense, refund, reimburse, remunerate, repay **2** *compensate for doing wrong:* atone, make amends, make good, make reparation, make up for, redress **3** *how the body compensates for the lack of oxygen:* balance, cancel, counteract, counterbalance, counterpoise *formal*, countervail *formal*, neutralize, nullify, offset

compensation n **1** *pay compensation:* damages, indemnification, indemnity, payment, recompense, refund, reimbursement, remuneration, reparation, repayment, requital **2** *make compensation for wrongdoing:* amends, atonement, redress, reparation, restitution

compere n anchorman, anchorwoman, announcer, emcee, host, link person, master of ceremonies, MC, presenter

compete v **1** *compete against/with other firms:* battle, challenge, contend, contest, fight, jostle, oppose, pit yourself, rival, strive, struggle, vie **2** *compete in a contest:* contend, enter, go in for, participate, race, run, take part

competence n ability, aptitude, capability, capacity, expertise, facility, proficiency, skill, technique
🖬 incompetence

competent adj **1** *a competent manager:* able, accomplished, adept, capable, efficient, expert, masterly, proficient, qualified, skilful, skilled, trained, well-qualified **2** *competent work:*

acceptable, adequate, appropriate, fit, passable, reasonable, respectable, satisfactory, sufficient, suitable

🔁 **1** incapable, incompetent, inefficient, unable **2** excellent, outstanding

competition n **1** *a swimming competition:* bout, championship, contest, cup, event, game, match, meet, quiz, race, tournament **2** *they are in competition with the organization:* challenge, combativeness, competitiveness, conflict, contention, contest, opposition, rivalry, strife, struggle, vying **3** *beat the competition:* challengers, competitors, field, opponents, opposition, rivals

competitive adj **1** *a competitive player:* aggressive, ambitious, antagonistic, combative, contentious, keen, pushy colloq **2** *a competitive business:* aggressive, antagonistic, contentious, cut-throat colloq, dog-eat-dog colloq

competitiveness n aggression, aggressiveness, ambition, ambitiousness, antagonism, combativeness, contentiousness, keenness, pugnacity formal, pushiness colloq, rivalry

🔁 backwardness, sluggishness

competitor n **1** *the competitors in the race:* candidate, challenger, contender, contestant, entrant, participant, player **2** *the company is outperforming its competitors:* adversary, antagonist, competition, opponent, opposition, rival

compilation n **1** *a compilation of songs:* album, anthology, arrangement, assemblage formal, chrestomathy formal, collectanea formal, collection, compendium, corpus, florilegium formal, miscellany, omnibus, potpourri, selection, thesaurus, treasury **2** *the compilation of data:* accumulation, amassment formal, arrangement, collation, collection, organization

compile v accumulate, amass, arrange, assemble, collate, collect, cull, garner, gather, marshal, organize, put together

complacency n contentment, gloating, gratification, pleasure, pride, satisfaction, self-satisfaction, smugness

🔁 diffidence, discontent

complacent adj contented, gloating, gratified, pleased, proud, satisfied, self-satisfied, smug

🔁 diffident, discontented

complacent or *complaisant*? *Complacent* means 'smugly pleased with yourself or your own abilities': *One of the dangers of success is that you can become complacent. Complaisant* means 'being cheerfully willing to do what others want': *Francesca's complaisant kindness was too much for him.*

complain v **1** *always complaining about something:* air your grievances, beef colloq, belly-ache colloq, bemoan, bewail, bleat colloq, carp, criticize, expostulate formal, find fault, fuss, gripe colloq, groan, grouse colloq, grumble, kick up a fuss, lament, moan, nag, object, protest, remonstrate formal, repine formal, whine, whinge colloq **2** *complain to the manager:* file/lodge a complaint, have a bone to pick colloq, take something up with someone **3** *complain of an illness:* ache, be in pain, feel pain, hurt, suffer from

complainer n belly-acher colloq, grouser colloq, grumbler, moaner, niggler, nit-picker colloq, whiner colloq, whinger colloq

complaint n **1** *make an official complaint:* accusation, charge, grievance, objection, protest, representation **2** *tired of listening to her complaints:* beefing colloq, belly-aching colloq, bleating colloq, carping, censure, criticism, fault-finding, grievance, gripe colloq, grouse colloq, grumble, moan, objection, whingeing colloq **3** *a chest complaint:* affliction formal, ailment, condition, disease, disorder, illness, indisposition formal, malady formal, malaise formal, sickness, trouble, upset

complaisant adj accommodating, agreeable, amenable, biddable, compliant, conciliatory, conformable, deferential, docile, obedient, obliging, tractable formal

🔁 obstinate, perverse

complaisant or *complacent*? See panel at **complacent**

complement n **1** *the wine was a fine complement to the dinner:* accessory, addition, companion **2** *a full complement of workers:* aggregate, capacity, entirety, quota, sum, total, totality
♦ v combine well with, complete, crown, go well together, go well with, match, round off, set off

complement, compliment or *supplement*? One thing is a *complement* to another when it makes a pleasant contrast or makes the combination of the two things pleasantly balanced: *Yoghurt can be used as a complement to spicy dishes.* You pay someone a *compliment* when you praise them. A *supplement* is something added to something else that is already complete or to make up for a deficiency: *a magazine supplement; take vitamin supplements.*

complementary adj companion, compatible, corresponding, interdependent, interrelated, matching, perfecting

🔁 contradictory, incompatible

complementary, complimentary or *supplementary*? Two things are *complementary* if they complement each other: *use complementary colours in all the furnishings.* You say something *complimentary* to someone as an expression of admiration or praise to them; a *complimentary* ticket is one given free of charge. You use *supplementary* to describe something that is added: *ask a supplementary question.*

complete adj **1** *the complete works of Shakespeare:* comprehensive, detailed, entire, exhaustive, full, total, unabbreviated, unabridged, unedited, unexpurgated, unshortened **2** *a complete dinosaur skeleton:* entire, full, intact, integral, total, unbroken, undivided, whole **3** *the work is now complete:* accomplished, achieved, completed, concluded, done, ended, finalized, finished, over, settled, terminated formal **4** *complete nonsense:* absolute, downright, out-and-out, outright, perfect, thorough, total, unconditional, unmitigated, unqualified, utter

🔁 **1** abridged **2** partial **3** incomplete **4** partial
♦ v **1** *complete a job:* accomplish, achieve, clinch colloq, close, conclude, consummate formal,

discharge, end, execute, finalize, finish, fulfil, perform, polish off *colloq*, realize, settle, terminate *formal*, wind up **2** *complete a collection*: cap, crown, finish off, make up, perfect, round off **3** *complete a form*: answer, fill in, fill out

completely *adv* absolutely, altogether, entirely, every inch *colloq*, from first to last *colloq*, fully, heart and soul *colloq*, hook line and sinker *colloq*, in every respect *colloq*, in full, lock stock and barrel *colloq*, perfectly, quite, root and branch *colloq*, solidly, thoroughly, through and through, totally, utterly, wholly

completion *n* accomplishment, achievement, attainment, close, conclusion, consummation *formal*, culmination, discharge, end, execution, finalization, finish, fruition, fulfilment, perfection, realization, termination *formal*

complex *adj* **1** *a complex problem*: Byzantine *formal*, complicated, convoluted *formal*, difficult, intricate, involved, ramified, tortuous **2** *a complex structure*: complicated, composite, compound, diverse, elaborate, intricate, involved, multiple, ramified, varied
🖃 **1** easy, simple **2** simple
♦ *n* **1** *a museum complex*: institute, organization, structure **2** *a complex of ideas about gender*: aggregation *formal*, composite, network, organization, scheme, structure, system **3** *an inferiority complex*: disorder, fixation, hang-up *colloq*, neurosis, obsession, phobia, preoccupation, thing *colloq*

complexion *n* **1** *a fair complexion*: colour, colouring, pigmentation, skin, tone **2** *the political complexion of the party*: cast, character, kind, nature, stamp, type **3** *this puts a different complexion on things*: appearance, aspect, look

complexity *n* **1** *the complexities of the problem*: complication, convolution *formal*, diverseness, elaboration, entanglement, intricacy, involvement, ramification, tortuousness **2** *the complexity of the structure*: complication, compositeness, diverseness, elaboration, intricacy, involvement, multifariousness, multiplicity, ramification, variety
🖃 **1** simplicity **2** simplicity

compliance *n* **1** *with the compliance of both parties*: agreement, assent, concurrence *formal*, conformity **2** *her slavish compliance to his wishes*: acquiescence *formal*, complaisance *formal*, conformability, deference, obedience, passivity, submission, submissiveness, yielding
🖃 **2** defiance, disobedience

compliant *adj* accommodating, acquiescent *formal*, biddable, complaisant *formal*, conformable, deferential, docile, obedient, passive, pliable, submissive, subservient, tractable *formal*, yielding
🖃 disobedient, intractable

complicate *v* compound, confuse, entangle, involve, jumble, make difficult, make involved, mix up, muddle, tangle
🖃 simplify

complicated *adj* **1** *a complicated problem*: complex, cryptic, difficult, perplexing, problematic, puzzling **2** *a complicated system*: complex, convoluted *formal*, elaborate, fiddly *colloq*, intricate, involved, tortuous
🖃 **1** easy, simple **2** simple

complication *n* **1** *legal complications*: difficulty, drawback, obstacle, problem, ramification, repercussion, snag **2** *a complication of emotions*: complexity, confusion, intricacy, mixture, tangle, web

complicity *n* abetment *formal*, collaboration, collusion, connivance, involvement
🖃 innocence

compliment *n* **1** *pay someone a compliment*: accolade, admiration, approval, bouquet, encomium *formal*, eulogy *formal*, flattering remark, flattery, homage *formal*, honour, laudation *formal*, praise, tribute **2** *my compliments to the chef*: commendation, congratulations, felicitation *formal*, praise **3** *sends his compliments*: best wishes, devoirs *formal*, greetings, regards, remembrances, respects, salutation *formal*
🖃 **1** criticism, insult **2** criticism
♦ *v* admire, applaud, commend, congratulate, eulogize *formal*, extol, felicitate *formal*, flatter, laud *formal*, praise, salute, speak highly/well of
🖃 condemn, insult

> *compliment*, *complement* or *supplement*? See panel at **complement**

complimentary *adj* **1** *a complimentary remark*: admiring, appreciative, approving, commendatory, congratulatory, eulogistic *formal*, favourable, flattering, panegyrical *formal* **2** *complimentary ticket*: courtesy, free, gratis, honorary, on the house *colloq*
🖃 **1** critical, insulting, unflattering

> *complimentary* or *complementary*? See panel at **complementary**

comply *v* abide by, accede *formal*, accommodate, accord *formal*, acquiesce *formal*, agree, assent, conform, consent, defer, discharge, follow, fulfil, meet, obey, oblige, observe, perform, respect, satisfy, submit, yield
🖃 defy, disobey

component *n* bit, constituent, constituent part, element, factor, ingredient, integral part, item, module, part, piece, section, unit
♦ *adj* basic, constituent, essential, inherent, integral, intrinsic

comport *v* acquit, act, bear, behave, carry, conduct, deport *formal*, perform

compose *v* **1** *the board is composed of four directors*: comprise, constitute, form, make up **2** *Beethoven composed nine symphonies*: arrange, assemble, build, concoct, construct, create, devise, fashion, form, frame, invent, make (up), produce, put together, think of/up, write **3** *compose yourself!*: calm, calm down, collect, control, pacify, quiet, settle, soothe, steady, still

composed *adj* at ease, calm, calmed down, collected, controlled, cool, cool and collected, cool as a cucumber *colloq*, imperturbable, level-headed, quiet, quietened down, relaxed, sedate, self-controlled, self-possessed, serene, tranquil, unflappable *colloq*, unruffled, unworried
🖃 agitated, troubled, worried

composer *n* arranger, author, bard, creator, maker, musician, originator, poet, producer, songsmith, songwriter, tunesmith, writer

composite *adj* agglutinate *formal*, blended, combined, complex, compound, conglomerate, fused, heterogeneous *formal*, mixed, patchwork, synthesized

🔁 homogeneous, uniform

♦ *n* agglutination *formal*, alloy, amalgam, blend, combination, compound, conglomerate, fusion, mixture, pastiche, patchwork, synthesis

composition *n* 1 *the chemical composition of the substance:* arrangement, character, combination, configuration, conformation *formal*, constitution, form, make-up, mixture, organization, structure 2 *the composition of a painting:* arrangement, balance, consonance, form, harmony, layout, organization, proportion, structure, symmetry 3 *a musical composition:* accompaniment, adaptation, arrangement, creation, drawing, exercise, novel, opera, opus, painting, picture, piece, poem, story, study, symphony, work, work of art 4 *the composition of a play:* arranging, compilation, concoction, creation, design, devising, formation, formulation, invention, making, production, putting together, writing

compost *n* dressing, fertilizer, humus, manure, mulch, peat

composure *n* aplomb *formal*, assurance, calm, confidence, coolness, dignity, ease, equanimity, imperturbability, level-headedness, poise, self-assurance, self-control, self-possession, serenity, tranquillity

🔁 agitation, discomposure, nervousness

compound¹ *n* admixture *technical*, alloy, amalgam, amalgamation, blend, combination, composite, composition, conglomerate, fusion, hybrid, medley, mixture, synthesis

♦ *adj* blended, combined, complex, composite, conglomerate, fused, intricate, mixed, multiple, synthesized

♦ *v* 1 *substances compounded into a resin:* alloy, amalgamate, blend, coalesce, combine, fuse, intermingle, mingle, mix, put together, synthesize, unite 2 *the difficulties were compounded by sanctions:* add insult to injury *colloq*, add to, aggravate, augment *formal*, complicate, exacerbate, heighten, increase, intensify, magnify, make worse, worsen

compound² *n* corral, court, enclosure, fold, paddock, pen, pound, stockade, yard

comprehend *v* 1 *comprehend a situation:* appreciate, apprehend, assimilate, conceive, discern, fathom, grasp, know, make sense of, penetrate, perceive, realize, see, take in, tumble to *colloq*, twig *colloq*, understand 2 *this course comprehends a group of subjects:* comprise, contain, cover, embrace, encompass, include, involve, take in

🔁 1 misunderstand

comprehensible *adj* accessible, clear, coherent, easy to understand, explicit, graspable, intelligible, lucid, plain, simple, straightforward, understandable

🔁 incomprehensible, obscure

comprehension *n* appreciation, apprehension, conception, discernment, grasp, insight, intelligence, judgement, ken *colloq*, knowledge, perception, realization, sense, understanding

🔁 incomprehension, unawareness

comprehensive *adj* across-the-board, all-embracing, all-inclusive, blanket, broad, compendious, complete, encyclopedic, exhaustive, extensive, full, general, inclusive, overall, sweeping, thorough, wide, widespread

🔁 incomplete, partial, selective

compress *v* 1 *compress petrol and air:* compact, concentrate, condense, consolidate, constrict, cram, crush, flatten, impact, jam, press, pressurize, squash, squeeze, stuff, tamp, wedge 2 *compress an article:* abbreviate, abridge, astrict *old use*, coarctate *formal*, condense, contract, reduce, shorten, summarize, synopsize, telescope

🔁 2 diffuse, expand

comprise *v* 1 *the course comprises a number of topics:* be composed of, comprehend *formal*, consist of, contain, cover, embody, embrace *formal*, encompass, include, incorporate, involve, take in 2 *the countries that comprise Great Britain:* compose, constitute, form, make up

compromise *v* 1 *the president has to compromise with the parliament:* adapt, adjust, agree, arbitrate, bargain, come to/reach an understanding, concede, give and take, make concessions, meet halfway, negotiate, settle 2 *compromise the success of the project:* endanger, expose, imperil, jeopardize, risk, undermine, weaken 3 *compromise your integrity:* bring into disrepute, bring shame to, damage, discredit, dishonour, shame

♦ *n* accommodation, adjustment, agreement, balance, bargain, concession, co-operation, deal, give-and-take, mediation, negotiation, settlement, trade-off, understanding

🔁 disagreement, intransigence

compulsion *n* 1 *use compulsion to obtain something:* coercion, constraint, demand, duress, force, insistence, obligation, pressure 2 *feel a compulsion to do something:* desire, drive, impulse, longing, necessity, need, obsession, preoccupation, temptation, urge

compulsive *adj* 1 *a compulsive desire to laugh:* besetting, compelling, driving, irresistible, overpowering, overwhelming, uncontrollable, urgent 2 *a compulsive gambler:* addicted, dependent, habitual, hardened, hooked *colloq*, hopeless, incorrigible, incurable, irredeemable, obsessive, pathological *colloq* 3 *compulsive viewing:* absorbing, compelling, enthralling, fascinating, gripping, irresistible, mesmeric, riveting, spellbinding

compulsory *adj* binding, contractual, de rigueur, essential, forced, imperative, mandatory, necessary, obligatory, required, requisite, set, stipulated

🔁 discretionary, optional, voluntary

compunction *n* contrition, guilt, hesitation, misgiving, penitence, qualm, regret, reluctance, remorse, repentance, shame, sorrow, unease, uneasiness

🔁 callousness, defiance

compute *v* add up, assess, calculate, count (up), enumerate, estimate, evaluate, figure, measure, rate, reckon, tally, total

comrade *n* ally, associate, buddy *colloq*, colleague, companion, confederate, confidant(e), crony *colloq*, fellow, friend, intimate, mate *colloq*, pal *colloq*, partner, sidekick *colloq*

con *v* bamboozle *colloq*, cheat, deceive, defraud, do *colloq*, double-cross, dupe, fleece *colloq*, hoax, hoodwink, inveigle *formal*, mislead, rip off *colloq*, rook, swindle, trick
♦ *n* cheat, confidence trick, deception, fiddle *colloq*, fraud, racket, scam *colloq*, swindle, trick

concatenation *n* chain, connection, course, interlinking, linking, nexus, procession, progress, progression, sequence, series, string, succession, thread, trail, train

concave *adj* bending inwards, cupped, curved in, depressed, excavated, hollow, hollowed, incurvate *formal*, incurved *formal*, indented, scooped, sunken
F⊒ convex

conceal *v* **1** *conceal a body:* bury, camouflage, cloak, cover, disguise, hide, keep hidden, keep out of sight, mask, obscure, screen, secrete *formal*, shroud, stash *colloq*, submerge, tuck away, veil **2** *conceal a secret:* cover up *colloq*, hide, hush up *colloq*, keep dark, keep quiet, keep secret, put the lid on *colloq*, suppress, sweep under the carpet *colloq*, whitewash *colloq*
F⊒ 1 uncover **2** disclose, reveal

concealed *adj* covered, disguised, hidden, inconspicuous, screened, tucked away, unseen
F⊒ clear, plain

concealment *n* **1** *the concealment of weapons:* hiding, secretion *formal* **2** *seeking concealment from our pursuers:* camouflage, cover, hideaway, hideout, hiding, protection, shelter **3** *concealment of information:* cover-up *colloq*, hiding, keeping dark, secrecy, smokescreen *colloq*, suppression, whitewash *colloq*
F⊒ 1 uncovering **2** uncovering **3** openness, revelation

concede *v* **1** *concede his errors:* accept, acknowledge, admit, allow, confess, grant, own (up), recognize **2** *they conceded two goals:* cede *formal*, forfeit, give up, hand over, relinquish, sacrifice, surrender, yield
F⊒ 1 deny

conceit *n* arrogance, boastfulness, cockiness, complacency, conceitedness, egotism, immodesty, narcissism, pride, self-admiration, self-importance, self-love, self-satisfaction, swagger, vainglory *formal*, vanity
F⊒ diffidence, modesty

conceited *adj* arrogant, big-headed *colloq*, boastful, cocky *colloq*, complacent, egotistical, full of yourself, immodest, narcissistic, proud, puffed up, self-important, self-satisfied, smug, stuck-up *colloq*, swollen-headed, too big for your boots *colloq*, vain, vainglorious *formal*
F⊒ diffident, humble, modest, self-effacing

conceivable *adj* believable, credible, imaginable, likely, possible, probable, tenable, thinkable
F⊒ inconceivable, unimaginable

conceive *v* **1** *it is hard to conceive of a world without computers:* appreciate, apprehend, believe, comprehend, envisage, fancy, grasp, imagine, perceive, picture, realize, see, suppose, think, understand, visualize **2** *conceive an idea:* come up with, contrive, create, design, develop, devise, form, formulate, invent, originate, produce, think of/up **3** *conceive a baby:* become fertilized, become impregnated, become inseminated, become pregnant, reproduce

concentrate *v* **1** *power remains concentrated in a tiny group of people:* accumulate, amass, centralize, centre, cluster, collect, congregate, consolidate, converge, crowd, focus, gather **2** *the students concentrated hard:* apply yourself, attend, consider, give your (undivided) attention, mind, pay/devote attention, put/keep your mind, think **3** *concentrate a liquid:* boil down, compress, condense, distil, evaporate, reduce, thicken
F⊒ 1 disperse **3** dilute
♦ *n* apozem *technical*, decoction, decocture, distillation, elixir *formal*, essence, extract, juice, quintessence *formal*

concentrated *adj* **1** *a concentrated sauce:* compressed, condensed, dense, evaporated, reduced, rich, strong, thickened, undiluted **2** *a concentrated effort:* all-out, concerted, deep, hard, intense, intensive, vigorous
F⊒ 1 diluted **2** half-hearted

concentration *n* **1** *total concentration:* absorption, application, attention, deep/close thought, devotion, engrossment, intensity, single-mindedness **2** *a concentration of people:* accumulation, agglomeration *formal*, centralization, cluster, collection, conglomeration, congregation, consolidation, convergence, crowd, focusing, grouping **3** *the concentration of the liquid:* boiling-down, compression, consolidation, denseness, distillation, evaporation, reduction, thickness
F⊒ 1 distraction **2** dispersal **3** dilution

concept *n* abstraction, conception, conceptualization, hypothesis, idea, image, impression, notion, picture, plan, theory, thought, view, visualization

conception *n* **1** *we have different conceptions of loyalty:* concept, idea, image, impression, notion, picture, thought, view **2** *he has no conception of the real world:* appreciation, clue, idea, image, impression, inkling, knowledge, perception, picture, understanding, visualization **3** *the conception of the project:* beginning, birth, design, formation, inauguration, initiation, invention, launching, origin, origination, outset **4** *from conception to birth:* fecundation *formal*, fertilization, impregnation, insemination, pregnancy, reproduction

concern *v* **1** *the situation concerns me:* alarm, bother, distress, disturb, make anxious, make worried, perturb *formal*, prey on your mind, trouble, upset, worry **2** *don't concern yourself with his problems:* busy, devote, give your attention to, interest, involve **3** *this matter doesn't concern you:* affect, involve, touch **4** *this letter concerns your application:* appertain to *formal*, apply to, be about, be connected with, bear on, deal with, have to do with, involve, pertain to *formal*, refer to, regard, relate to
♦ *n* **1** *a cause for concern:* anguish, anxiety, apprehension, care, disquiet, distress, disturbance, perturbation *formal*, pressure, sorrow, strain, unease, worry **2** *thank you for your concern:* attention, attentiveness, care, consideration, heed, regard, thought **3** *it's not my concern:* affair, business, charge, duty, field, interest, involvement, job, matter, problem, responsibility, task **4** *a business concern:*

association, business, company, corporation, enterprise, establishment, firm, organization, partnership, syndicate
F≡ 1 joy **2** indifference

concerned *adj* **1** *I'm concerned about my future:* anxious, apprehensive, bothered, distressed, disturbed, perturbed *formal*, troubled, uneasy, unhappy, upset, worried **2** *thank you for being so concerned:* attentive, caring, charitable, considerate, gracious, helpful, kind, sensitive, thoughtful, unselfish **3** *he's concerned with this issue:* affected, connected, implicated, interested, involved, related
F≡ 1 apathetic, indifferent, unconcerned **2** inconsiderate, selfish, thoughtless

concerning *prep* about, apropos *formal*, as regards, in the matter of, on the subject of, re, referring to, regarding, relating to, relevant to, respecting, with reference to, with regard to, with respect to

concert *n* **1** *a musical concert:* appearance, engagement, entertainment, gig, performance, presentation, production, prom, recital, show, soirée **2** *work in concert with others:* accord *formal*, agreement, concord *formal*, concordance *formal*, consonance *formal*, harmony, unanimity, union, unison
F≡ 2 disunity

concerted *adj* collaborative, collective, combined, co-operative, co-ordinated, joint, shared, united
F≡ disorganized, separate, unco-ordinated

concession *n* **1** *made some concessions for his age:* adjustment, allowance, compromise **2** *a concession of territory:* ceding *formal*, giving-up, grant, handover, relinquishment, sacrifice, surrender, yielding **3** *tax concessions:* allowance, bending of the rules *colloq*, cut, decrease, exception, favour, grant, reduction, (special) privilege, (special) right **4** *his concession that he might have been wrong:* acceptance, acknowledgement, admission, allowance, recognition

conciliate *v* appease, disarm, disembitter, mollify, pacify, placate, propitiate, reconcile, soften, soothe
F≡ antagonize

conciliation *n* appeasement, mollification, pacification, peacemaking, placation, propitiation, reconciliation
F≡ alienation, antagonization

conciliator *n* dove, intercessor, intermediary, mediator, negotiator, peacemaker, reconciler
F≡ troublemaker

conciliatory *adj* appeasing, assuaging, disarming, irenic *formal*, mollifying, pacific, pacificatory *formal*, peaceable, peacemaking, placatory *formal*, propitiative *formal*, propitiatory *formal*, reconciliatory
F≡ antagonistic

concise *adj* abbreviated, abridged, brief, compact, compendious, compressed, condensed, crisp, epigrammatic *formal*, pithy, short, succinct, summary, synoptic *formal*, terse, to the point
F≡ diffuse, wordy

conclave *n* assembly, cabal, cabinet, confabulation *formal*, conference, council, parley *colloq*, powwow *colloq*, (secret) meeting, session

conclude *v* **1** *concluded the party with a song:* bring to an end, close, complete, consummate *formal*, discontinue *formal*, end, finish, polish off *colloq*, terminate *formal*, wind up *colloq* **2** *the meeting concluded at noon:* cease *formal*, close, come/draw to an end, culminate, end, finish, terminate *formal*, wind up *colloq* **3** *he concluded that she was right:* assume, come to the conclusion, conjecture *formal*, decide, deduce, gather, infer, judge, reason, reckon, suppose, surmise **4** *they concluded a deal:* accomplish, agree, arrange, clinch *colloq*, close, decide, determine, effect *formal*, establish, negotiate, pull off *colloq*, resolve, settle, work out, wrap up *colloq*
F≡ 1 begin, commence, start **2** begin, commence, start

conclusion *n* **1** *my conclusion is that you are right:* assumption, conviction, decision, deduction, inference, judgement, opinion, resolution, settlement, verdict **2** *the logical conclusion of his actions:* consequence, issue, outcome, result, upshot **3** *the book's conclusion:* close, completion, consummation *formal*, culmination, end, finale, finish, termination *formal* **4** *the conclusion of a deal:* accomplishment, agreement, arrangement, clinching *colloq*, effecting *formal*, establishment, negotiation, pulling-off *colloq*, resolution, settling, working-out

conclusive *adj* clear, convincing, decisive, definite, definitive, final, incontrovertible, indisputable, irrefutable, unanswerable, unarguable, undeniable
F≡ inconclusive, questionable

concoct *v* **1** *concoct a potion:* blend, brew, cook (up), decoct *formal*, make, mix, prepare, put together, rustle up *colloq* **2** *concoct a story:* contrive, cook up *colloq*, devise, fabricate, formulate, hatch, invent, plan, plot

concoction *n* blend, brew, combination, compound, creation, mixture, potion, preparation

concomitant *adj* accompanying, associative, attendant, co-existent, coincidental, complementary, concurrent, contemporaneous *formal*, conterminous *formal*, incidental, simultaneous, synchronous, syndromic *formal*
F≡ accidental, unrelated
♦ *n* accompaniment, by-product, epiphenomenon *formal*, incidental, secondary, side effect, symptom

concord *n* **1** *a country heading towards concord:* accord, agreement, amicability, amity *formal*, consensus, consonance *formal*, entente, friendship, harmony, peace, rapport, unanimity, unison **2** *sign a concord:* agreement, compact, treaty
F≡ 1 discord

concourse *n* **1** *the station concourse:* entrance, foyer, hall, lobby, lounge, piazza, plaza **2** *a concourse of people:* assembly, collection, crowd, crush, gathering, meeting, multitude, press, swarm, throng

concrete *adj* **1** *concrete objects:* actual, material, physical, real, solid, substantial, tangible, touchable, visible **2** *concrete evidence:* definite, explicit, factual, firm, genuine, positive, solid, specific
F≡ 2 abstract, vague

concubine *n* courtesan, kept woman, lover, mistress, paramour

concupiscence *n* desire, horniness *colloq*, lasciviousness, lechery, lewdness, libidinousness *formal*, libido, lubricity *formal*, lust, lustfulness, randiness *colloq*

concupiscent *adj* horny *colloq*, lascivious, lecherous, lewd, libidinous *formal*, lubricious *formal*, lustful, randy *colloq*

concur *v* accede *formal*, accord *formal*, acquiesce *formal*, agree, approve, assent *formal*, be in harmony, comply, consent, harmonize
F3 disagree

concurrence *n* **1** *concurrence on the decision:* acceptance, acquiescence *formal*, agreement, approval, assent *formal*, common ground, convergence **2** *the concurrence of the two events:* coexistence, coincidence, contemporaneity *formal*, juxtaposition *formal*, simultaneity *formal*, synchrony
F3 1 difference, disagreement

concurrent *adj* coexistent, coexisting, coincident, coinciding, concomitant, contemporaneous, simultaneous, synchronous

condemn *v* **1** *condemn him for his actions:* berate *formal*, blame, castigate *formal*, censure *formal*, criticize, denounce, deplore, deprecate *formal*, disapprove, disparage *formal*, reprehend *formal*, reproach, reprove *formal*, revile, slam *colloq*, upbraid *formal* **2** *condemn a prisoner:* convict, damn, give/pass a sentence, punish, sentence **3** *condemned to a life of poverty:* consign, doom, ordain **4** *condemn a building:* declare unfit, declare unsafe, demolish, destroy
F3 1 approve, praise **2** acquit, pardon

condemnation *n* blame, castigation *formal*, censure *formal*, criticism, denunciation, deprecation *formal*, disapproval, disparagement *formal*, reproach, reproof, thumbs-down *colloq*
F3 approval, praise

condemnatory *adj* accusatory, accusing, censorious *formal*, critical, damnatory, denunciatory *formal*, deprecatory *formal*, disapproving, proscriptive *formal*, reprobative *formal*, reprobatory *formal*, unfavourable
F3 approving, complimentary, indulgent, laudatory *formal*

condensation *n* **1** *condensation of liquid:* boiling-down, concentration, consolidation, distillation, evaporation, reduction **2** *condensation of a text:* abridgement, compression, contraction, curtailment, digest, précis, synopsis

condense *v* **1** *condense a book:* abbreviate, abridge, compact, compress, contract, curtail, cut (down), encapsulate, précis, shorten, summarize **2** *condense liquid:* boil down, coagulate, compress, concentrate, distil, evaporate, reduce, solidify, thicken
F3 1 expand **2** dilute

condensed *adj* **1** *a condensed book:* abbreviated, abridged, abstracted, compact, concise, contracted, curtailed, cut (down), reduced, shortened, summarized **2** *condensed liquid:* clotted, coagulated, compressed, concentrated, dense, evaporated, reduced, rich, strong, thickened, undiluted
F3 1 expanded **2** diluted

condescend *v* **1** *condescend to do something:* bend, deign, demean yourself, descend, humble yourself, lower yourself, see fit, stoop **2** *condescend to people:* be snobbish to, patronize, talk down to, treat condescendingly

condescending *adj* disdainful, haughty, lofty, lordly, patronizing, snobbish, snooty, stuck-up *colloq*, supercilious, superior, toffee-nosed *colloq*
F3 gracious, humble

condescension *n* airs, disdain, haughtiness, loftiness, lordliness, snobbishness, superciliousness, superiority
F3 humility

condition *n* **1** *the condition of his health:* case, circumstances, plight, position, predicament, quandary, situation, state **2** *the conditions in which people work:* atmosphere, background, circumstances, climate, context, environment, factors, milieu, setting, set-up, situation, state, surroundings, way of life **3** *only under these conditions:* demand, essential, limit, limitation, necessity, obligation, precondition, prerequisite, provision, proviso, qualification, requirement, restriction, rule, stipulation, terms **4** *out of condition:* fettle, fitness, form, health, kilter, nick *colloq*, order, shape, state, state of health, working order **5** *a heart condition:* ailment, complaint, defect, disease, disorder, illness, infirmity, malady *formal*, problem, weakness
♦ *v* **1** *a shampoo that conditions:* improve, make healthy, restore, revive, tone, treat **2** *conditioned by experience:* accustom, adapt, adjust, brainwash, educate, equip, groom, indoctrinate, influence, mould, prepare, prime, season, temper, train, tune

conditional *adj* based, contingent, dependent, limited, provisional, qualified, restricted, subject, tied
F3 absolute, unconditional

condolence *n* commiseration, compassion, consolation, pity, support, sympathy
F3 congratulation

condom *n* female condom, Femidom®, French letter *slang*, johnnie *slang*, prophylactic, protective, rubber *slang*, scumbag *US slang*, sheath

condone *v* allow, brook, disregard, excuse, forgive, ignore, let pass, overlook, pardon, tolerate, turn a blind eye to *colloq*
F3 censure, condemn

conducive *adj* advantageous, beneficial, contributing, contributory, encouraging, favourable, helpful, instrumental, leading, productive, promoting, tending, useful
F3 adverse, detrimental, unfavourable

conduct *v* **1** *conduct a meeting:* administer, be in charge of, carry out, chair, control, direct, do, handle, manage, orchestrate, organize, perform, regulate, run **2** *conduct him out of the building:* accompany, bring, direct, escort, guide, lead, pilot, show, steer, take, usher **3** *conduct heat:* bear, carry, convey, transmit **4** *conduct yourself:* acquit, act, behave, comport *formal*
♦ *n* **1** *good conduct:* actions, attitude, bearing, behaviour, comportment *formal*, demeanour *formal*, deportment *formal*, manners, practice, ways **2** *responsible for the conduct of the meeting:* administration, control, direction, guidance,

leadership, management, operation, organization, running, supervision

conduit *n* canal, channel, chute, culvert, ditch, drain, duct, flume, gutter, main, passage, passageway, pipe, tube, tunnel, watercourse, waterway

confectionery *n* bonbon, candy, chocolates, fudge, rock, sweets, tablet *Scot*, toffees, truffle, Turkish delight

confederacy *n* alliance, coalition, compact *formal*, confederation, federation, league, partnership, union

confederate *n* abettor, accessory, accomplice, ally, assistant, associate, collaborator, colleague, conspirator, friend, partner, supporter
♦ *adj* allied, associated, combined, federal, federate, united

confederation *n* alliance, amalgamation, association, coalition, compact *formal*, confederacy, federation, league, partnership, union

confer *v* **1** *the judges conferred*: consult, converse, debate, deliberate, discuss, exchange views, talk **2** *the government confers citizenship*: accord, award, bestow, give (out), grant, impart, present

conference *n* colloquium, congress, consultation, convention, convocation *formal*, debate, dialogue, discussion, forum, meeting, seminar, summit, symposium

confess *v* **1** *confess your guilt*: accept blame, accept responsibility, acknowledge, admit, come clean *colloq*, come out with it *colloq*, disclose, divulge, get off your chest *colloq*, make a clean breast of *colloq*, make known, own up, spill the beans *colloq*, tell all *colloq*, unbosom, unburden **2** *I confess I don't like her much*: acknowledge, admit, affirm, assert, concede, confide, declare, grant, own, profess
🔄 **1** conceal, deny **2** conceal, deny

confession *n* **1** *the suspect made a confession*: acknowledgement, admission, disclosure, divulgence, making known, owning-up, revelation, unbosoming, unburdening **2** *a confession of faith*: acknowledgement, affirmation, assertion, declaration, profession
🔄 **1** concealment, denial **2** concealment, denial

confidant, confidante *n* bosom friend, close friend, companion, crony *colloq*, friend, intimate, mate *colloq*, pal *colloq*

confide *v* admit, breathe, confess, disclose, divulge, get off your chest *colloq*, impart, intimate, pour out your heart, reveal, tell, unbosom yourself, unburden yourself, whisper
🔄 conceal, hide, suppress

confidence *n* **1** *have confidence in someone*: belief, certainty, conviction, credence, dependence, faith, reliance, trust **2** *he has enough confidence*: aplomb *formal*, assurance, belief in yourself, boldness, courage, self-assurance, self-confidence, self-possession, self-reliance **3** *betray a confidence*: confidential matter, intimate matter, private matter, secret
🔄 **1** distrust **2** diffidence

confident *adj* **1** *confident that it will happen*: certain, convinced, definite, positive, sure **2** *a confident person*: assured, bold, cool, courageous, dauntless, fearless, positive,
self-assured, self-confident, self-possessed, self-reliant, sure of yourself, unselfconscious
🔄 **1** doubtful **2** diffident, insecure

confidential *adj* classified, intimate, off-the-record, personal, private, restricted, secret, sensitive, top secret

confidentially *adv* behind closed doors, between ourselves, between you and me *colloq*, between you me and the gatepost/bedpost *colloq*, entre nous, in camera *formal*, in confidence, in privacy, in private, in secret, on the quiet, personally, privately, within these four walls
🔄 openly

configuration *n* arrangement, cast, composition, conformation *formal*, contour, disposition *formal*, figure, form, outline, shape

confine *v* **1** *confine trade through the ports*: circumscribe *formal*, constrain, control, fix, keep within limits, limit, regulate, restrict **2** *confine in prison*: cage, coop up, enclose, hold captive, hold in custody, hold prisoner, immure *formal*, impound, imprison, incarcerate *formal*, intern, keep in, lock up/away, restrain, shackle, shut (up), trammel
🔄 **1** derestrict **2** free
♦ *n* border, bound, boundary, circumference, edge, frontier, limit, limitation, parameter, perimeter, restriction, scope

confined *adj* circumscribed *formal*, constrained, enclosed, limited, narrow, restricted
🔄 free, unrestricted

confinement *n* **1** *solitary confinement*: captivity, custody, detention, house arrest, imprisonment, incarceration *formal*, internment **2** *attended by the midwife during her confinement*: birth, childbirth, delivery, labour, parturition *technical*
🔄 **1** freedom, liberty

confirm *v* **1** *it has confirmed my greatest fears*: authenticate, back, corroborate, demonstrate, endorse, evidence, give credence to, prove, substantiate, support, validate, verify **2** *confirmed him as president*: approve, authorize, endorse, establish, ratify, sanction, warrant **3** *confirm that he will go*: affirm, assert, asseverate *formal*, assure, aver *formal*, guarantee, pledge, promise **4** *confirmed me in my decision*: clinch *colloq*, fix, fortify, harden, reinforce, settle, strengthen, support, uphold
🔄 **1** deny, refute

confirmation *n* **1** *confirmation of his guilt*: authentication, corroboration, evidence, proof, ratification, substantiation, testimony, validation, verification **2** *she nodded in confirmation*: acceptance, affirmation, agreement, approval, assent, backing, corroboration, endorsement, ratification, support, verification
🔄 **1** denial **2** denial

confirmed *adj* chronic, dyed-in-the-wool, entrenched, established, fixed, habitual, hardened, incorrigible, incurable, inured *formal*, inveterate, long-established, long-standing, rooted, seasoned, set, through and through

confiscate *v* appropriate *formal*, arrogate *formal*, commandeer, expropriate *formal*, impound, remove, seize, sequester *formal*, take away, take possession of
🔄 restore, return

confiscation *n* appropriation *formal*, commandeering, distrainment *formal*, distraint *formal*, escheat *formal*, expropriation *formal*, forfeiture *formal*, impounding, removal, seizure, sequestration *formal*, takeover
◢ restoration

conflagration *n* blaze, deflagration *formal*, fire, holocaust, inferno

conflict *n* **1** *a conflict of ideas:* antagonism, antipathy *formal*, bust-up *colloq*, clash, confrontation, contention, difference of opinion, disagreement, discord, dispute, dissension, feud, friction, hostility, ill-will, opposition, quarrel, row, strife, unrest, variance **2** *armed conflict:* battle, brawl, bust-up *colloq*, clash, combat, contest, encounter, engagement, fight, fracas, scrap *colloq*, set-to *colloq*, skirmish, war, warfare
◢ **1** agreement, concord, harmony
♦ *v* **1** *his ideas conflict with mine:* be at loggerheads, be at odds, be at variance, be in opposition, be inconsistent with, clash, contradict, differ, disagree, oppose **2** *two armies conflicting:* battle, clash, combat, contend, contest, fight, strive, struggle, war
◢ **1** agree, harmonize

confluence *n* concurrence, conflux *formal*, convergence, junction, meeting, meeting-point

conform *v* **1** *conform to a law:* accommodate, adapt, adjust, comply, fall in with, follow, obey, observe **2** *conform in your behaviour:* be conventional, be uniform, do the same thing, follow, follow the crowd *colloq*, go with the flow/ stream *colloq*, jump on the bandwagon *colloq*, toe the line *colloq* **3** *conform to a pattern:* accord, agree, correspond, harmonize, match, square, tally
◢ **1** disobey **2** rebel **3** conflict, differ

conformist *n* conventionalist, rubber-stamp *colloq*, stick-in-the-mud *colloq*, traditionalist, yes-man *colloq*
◢ bohemian, nonconformist

conformity *n* **1** *in conformity with the law:* accommodation, adaptation, adjustment, agreement, allegiance, compliance, conformance, obedience, observance **2** *conformity to a stereotype:* agreement, congruity *formal*, consonance *formal*, correspondence, harmony, likeness, resemblance, similarity **3** *conformity in behaviour:* conventionality, orthodoxy, traditionalism, uniformity
◢ **1** disobedience **3** nonconformity, rebellion

confound *v* **1** *confounded by his strange behaviour:* amaze, astonish, astound, baffle, bamboozle *colloq*, bewilder, confuse, dumbfound, flabbergast *colloq*, flummox *colloq*, mystify, nonplus, perplex, puzzle, stun, stupefy, surprise **2** *confound their plans:* beat, defeat, demolish, destroy, frustrate, overthrow, overwhelm, ruin, thwart, upset

confront *v* **1** *confront a problem:* address, brave, come to grips with *colloq*, come to terms with, contend with, cope with, deal with, face, face up to, meet head on *colloq*, tackle **2** *confront the enemy:* accost, brave, challenge, defy, encounter, face, face up to, meet, oppose, resist, stand up to, withstand **3** *confront him with the facts:* challenge, present, show

confrontation *n* battle, clash, collision, conflict, contest, disagreement, encounter, engagement, fight, quarrel, set-to *colloq*, showdown

confuse *v* **1** *confused his listeners:* baffle, bemuse, bewilder, confound, disconcert, disorient, floor *colloq*, fluster, mystify, perplex, puzzle, throw *colloq*, tie in knots *colloq* **2** *confuse their names:* mistake, mix up, muddle **3** *got the wires confused:* disarrange, disorder, entangle, jumble, mingle, mix up, muddle, tangle **4** *to confuse matters further:* complicate, compound, involve, make difficult, make involved, make more difficult
◢ **1** clarify, enlighten **4** simplify

confused *adj* **1** *a confused person:* all at sea *colloq*, at sixes and sevens *colloq*, baffled, bemused, bewildered, confounded, dazed, disconcerted, disorientated, floored *colloq*, flummoxed *colloq*, flustered, having your knickers in a twist *slang*, having your wires crossed *colloq*, in a flap *colloq*, in a flat spin *colloq*, like a headless chicken *colloq*, mystified, nonplussed, not knowing whether you are coming or going *colloq*, perplexed, puzzled **2** *a confused jumble of furniture:* chaotic, disarranged, disordered, disorderly, disorganized, higgledy-piggledy *colloq*, jumbled, mixed-up, muddled, out of order, untidy
◢ **2** orderly

confusing *adj* ambiguous, baffling, bewildering, complicated, contradictory, cryptic, difficult, inconsistent, involved, misleading, muddling, perplexing, puzzling, tortuous, unclear
◢ clear, definite

confusion *n* **1** *create confusion in the country:* chaos, commotion, disorder, turmoil, upheaval **2** *the confusion of his room:* clutter, disarrangement, disarray, disorder, disorganization, jumble, mess, muddle, shambles *colloq*, untidiness **3** *cause confusion among his listeners:* bafflement, bewilderment, mystification, perplexity, puzzlement **4** *clear up the confusion:* misunderstanding, mix-up, muddle
◢ **1** order **2** order **3** clarity

congeal *v* cake, clot, coagulate, coalesce, concentrate, curdle, gel, harden, set, solidify, stiffen, thicken
◢ dissolve, liquefy, melt

congenial *adj* **1** *she longs for congenial company:* agreeable, companionable, compatible, complaisant, favourable, friendly, genial, like-minded, pleasant, pleasing, suitable, sympathetic, well-suited **2** *a congenial atmosphere:* agreeable, cosy, delightful, homely, pleasant, pleasing, relaxing
◢ **1** disagreeable, unpleasant **2** disagreeable, unpleasant

congenital *adj* **1** *a congenital disease:* connate *technical*, constitutional, hereditary, inborn, inbred, inherent, inherited, innate, natural **2** *a congenital liar:* chronic, complete, entrenched, habitual, hardened, incorrigible, incurable, inured *formal*, inveterate, seasoned, thorough, utter

congested *adj* **1** *congested roads:* blocked, clogged, crammed, crowded, full, jammed, overcrowded, overflowing, packed, stuffed, teeming **2** *a congested nose:* blocked, choked, clogged
◢ **2** clear

congestion *n* **1** *congestion on the roads:* blockage, bottleneck, clogging, gridlock, jam, overcrowding, snarl-up, traffic jam **2** *nasal congestion:* blockage, blocking, clogging

conglomerate *n* association, business, business organization, cartel, company, concern, consortium, corporation, establishment, firm, multinational, partnership, trust

conglomeration *n* accumulation, agglomeration, aggregation, assemblage, collection, composite, hotchpotch, mass, medley

congratulate *v* compliment, felicitate *formal*, pat on the back *colloq*, praise, say well done to, send/offer best wishes to, send/offer good wishes to, take your hat off to *colloq*, wish happiness to, wish well
Fa commiserate

congratulations *n* best wishes, bouquet(s) *colloq*, compliments, felicitations *formal*, good wishes, greetings, pat on the back *colloq*
Fa commiserations, condolences

congregate *v* accumulate, assemble, clump, cluster, collect, convene, converge, crowd, flock, form, gather, mass, meet, muster, rally, rendezvous, throng
Fa disperse

congregation *n* assembly, crowd, fellowship, flock, group, host, laity, mass, meeting, multitude, parish, parishioners, throng

congress *n* **1** *hold a national congress:* assembly, conclave *formal*, conference, convention, convocation *formal*, council, diet, forum, gathering, meeting, synod **2** *approval by the congress:* assembly, conclave *formal*, council, legislature, parliament, synod

congruence *n* agreement, coincidence, compatibility, concinnity *formal*, concurrence *formal*, conformity, consistency, correspondence, harmony, identity, match, parallelism, resemblance, similarity
Fa incongruity

conical *adj* cone-shaped, funnel-shaped, infundibular *formal*, infundibulate *formal*, pointed, pyramidal, pyramid-shaped, tapered, tapering, turbinate *formal*

conjectural *adj* academic, assumed, hypothetical, posited *formal*, postulated *formal*, speculative, supposed, suppositional, surmised, tentative, theoretical
Fa factual, real

conjecture *v* assume, estimate, fancy, guess, hypothesize, imagine, infer, presume, presuppose, reckon, speculate, suppose, surmise, suspect, theorize
♦ *n* assumption, estimate, extrapolation, fancy, guess, guesstimate *colloq*, guesswork, hypothesis, inference, notion, presumption, presupposition, projection, speculation, supposition, surmise, suspicion, theory

conjugal *adj* bridal, connubial *formal*, epithalamic *formal*, hymeneal *formal*, marital, married, matrimonial, nuptial, spousal *formal*, wedded

conjunction *n* amalgamation, association, coexistence, coincidence, combination, concurrence *formal*, co-occurrence, juxtaposition *formal*, unification, union

conjure *v* **1** *he conjured at the children's party:* do magic, do tricks, perform magic, perform tricks

2 *conjure spirits to appear:* call up, compel, evoke, invoke, make appear, raise, rouse, summon
▶ **conjure up** awaken, call/bring to mind, create, evoke, excite, produce, recall, recollect

conjurer *n* illusionist, magician, prestidigitator *formal*, prestigiator *formal*

conk
▶ **conk out** break down, fail, go haywire *colloq*, go on the blink *colloq*, pack up *colloq*

connect *v* **1** *connect two objects:* affix, attach, bracket, bridge, clamp, concatenate *formal*, couple, fasten, fuse, join, link, secure, tie, unite **2** *what connects the two events?:* ally, associate, concatenate *formal*, correlate, couple, join, link, relate (to), tie
Fa 1 cut off, detach, disconnect

connected *adj* **1** *connected by a string:* coupled, fastened, joined, linked, secured, tied, united **2** *two connected murders:* affiliated, akin, allied, associated, coupled, joined, linked, related
Fa 1 disconnected, unconnected **2** unconnected

connection *n* **1** *a connection between pipes:* attachment, bond, clasp, coupling, fastening, joint, junction, link, tie **2** *a connection between smoking and cancer:* analogy, association, correlation, correspondence, interrelation, link, parallel, relation, relationship, relevance **3** *severed connections with his family:* alliance, association, attachment, bond, communication, contact, link, relation, relationship, tie **4** *use your connections to get a job:* acquaintance, contact, friend, person of importance, person of influence, relation, relative, sponsor
Fa 1 disconnection

connivance *n* abetment, abetting, collusion, complicity, condoning, consent

connive *v* **1** *connive with someone to commit an offence:* cabal *formal*, coact *formal*, collude, complot *formal*, conspire, intrigue, plot, scheme **2** *connive at wrongdoing:* allow, brook, condone, disregard, gloss over, ignore, let go, let pass, overlook, pass over, tolerate, turn a blind eye to *colloq*, wink at

conniving *adj* colluding, conspiring, plotting, scheming

connoisseur *n* aficionado, authority, buff *colloq*, cognoscente, devotee, expert, gastronome, gourmet, judge, pundit, specialist

connotation *n* association, colouring, implication, insinuation, intimation, nuance, overtone, suggestion, undertone

connote *v* betoken *formal*, hint at, imply, import *formal*, indicate, insinuate, intimate, purport *formal*, signify, suggest

conquer *v* **1** *conquer an enemy:* beat, best, crush, defeat, get the better of, master, overcome, overpower, overthrow, prevail over, quell, rout, subdue, subjugate *formal*, suppress, triumph over, trounce *colloq*, vanquish *formal*, worst **2** *conquer your fears:* beat, defeat, get the better of, master, overcome, quell, rise above, suppress, surmount, triumph over, vanquish *formal* **3** *conquer a country:* acquire, annex, appropriate *formal*, obtain, occupy, overrun, possess, seize, take, take possession of, win
Fa 1 give in, surrender, yield **2** give in, surrender, yield

conqueror *n* conquistador *formal*, lord, master, subjugator *formal*, vanquisher *formal*

conquest *n* **1** *the conquest of the country:* acquisition, annexation, appropriation *formal*, coup, invasion, occupation, overrunning, possession, seizing, subjection, subjugation *formal* **2** *the invaders' conquest of the natives:* beating, crushing, defeat, mastery, overpowering, overthrow, rout, subjection, subjugation *formal*, triumph, trouncing *colloq*, vanquishment *formal*, victory, win **3** *his latest conquest:* acquisition, catch, lover

conscience *n* ethics, moral code, moral sense, morals, principles, qualms, scruples, sense of right, sense of right and wrong, standards, still small voice, voice within

conscience-stricken *adj* ashamed, compunctious *formal*, contrite, guilt-ridden, guilty, penitent, regretful, remorseful, repentant, sorry
🔁 unashamed, unrepentant

conscientious *adj* assiduous, attentive, careful, dedicated, diligent, dutiful, faithful, hard-working, methodical, meticulous, painstaking, particular, punctilious, responsible, scrupulous, thorough
🔁 careless, irresponsible, unreliable

conscious *adj* **1** *he was fully conscious:* alert, alive, awake, responsive, sensible, sentient *formal* **2** *conscious of the honour being done to him:* alert, aware, cognizant *formal*, mindful, percipient *formal*, sensible *formal* **3** *a conscious effort to be polite:* calculated, deliberate, intentional, knowing, on purpose, premeditated, studied, volitional *formal*, voluntary, wilful
🔁 **1** unconscious **2** unaware **3** involuntary, unintentional

consciousness *n* **1** *enter his consciousness:* apprehension, awareness, cognizance *formal*, intuition, knowledge, mind, perception, realization, recognition, sensibility *formal*, sentience *formal* **2** *lose consciousness:* alertness, awareness, being awake, wakefulness
🔁 **2** unconsciousness

conscript *v* call up, draft, enlist, muster, recruit, round up, take on
🔁 volunteer
♦ *n* draftee, enlistee, recruit
🔁 volunteer

consecrate *v* **1** *the church is consecrated to the Virgin Mary:* dedicate, devote, hallow, make holy, revere, sanctify, venerate **2** *he was consecrated as bishop:* anoint, bless, dedicate, ordain

consecutive *adj* back to back *colloq*, continuous, following, in turn, on the trot *colloq*, one after the other, running, sequential, serial, seriate *formal*, straight, succeeding, successive, unbroken, uninterrupted
🔁 discontinuous

consensus *n* agreement, concord *formal*, concurrence *formal*, consent, consentience *formal*, harmony, majority view, unanimity, unity
🔁 disagreement

consent *v* accede *formal*, accept, acquiesce *formal*, agree, allow, approve, assent *formal*, authorize, comply, concur *formal*, give the go-ahead *colloq*, give the green light *colloq*, give the thumbs-up *colloq*, go along with, grant, permit, yield
🔁 decline, oppose, refuse
♦ *n* acceptance, acquiescence *formal*, agreement, approval, assent *formal*, authorization, clearance, compliance, concurrence *formal*, go-ahead *colloq*, green light *colloq*, permission, sanction
🔁 disagreement, opposition, refusal

consequence *n* **1** *the disaster had far-reaching consequences:* effect, end, implication, issue, outcome, repercussion, result, reverberation, side effect, upshot **2** *of no consequence:* concern, distinction, eminence, import *formal*, importance, moment *formal*, note, prominence, significance, substance, value, weight
🔁 **1** cause **2** insignificance, unimportance

consequent *adj* ensuing, following, resultant, resulting, subsequent

consequently *adv* accordingly, as a result, consequentially, ergo *formal*, hence *formal*, inferentially *formal*, necessarily, so that, subsequently, then, therefore, thus *formal*, with the result that

conservation *n* **1** *the conservation of the environment:* care, ecology, environmentalism, maintenance, preservation, protection, safeguarding, safe-keeping, upkeep **2** *the conservation of energy:* economy, husbandry, saving
🔁 **1** destruction

conservatism *n* conservativeness, conventionalism, orthodoxy, traditionalism
🔁 radicalism

conservative *adj* **1** *conservative politicians:* die-hard, establishmentarian, reactionary, right-wing, Tory **2** *conservative opinions:* careful, cautious, conventional, guarded, hidebound, inflexible, middle-of-the-road, moderate, orthodox, set in your ways, traditional, traditionalist, unprogressive
🔁 **1** left-wing, radical **2** innovative
♦ *n* die-hard, moderate, reactionary, right-winger, stick-in-the-mud, Tory, traditionalist
🔁 left-winger, radical

conservatory *n* **1** *grow plants in the conservatory:* glasshouse, greenhouse, hothouse **2** *study music at the conservatory:* academy, college, conservatoire, drama college, institute, music school, school

conserve *v* **1** *conserve energy:* hoard, keep back, keep in reserve, save, store up **2** *conserve the rainforests:* keep, maintain, preserve, protect, safeguard, save, take care of
🔁 **1** squander, use, waste

consider *v* **1** *consider a problem:* chew over *colloq*, cogitate *formal*, contemplate, deliberate, examine, give thought to, meditate, mull over, muse, ponder, reflect, ruminate *formal*, study, weigh (up) **2** *consider other people's wishes:* bear/keep in mind, give thought to, remember, respect, take into account/consideration **3** *consider it an honour:* believe, count, deem *formal*, feel, hold, judge, rate, regard as, think

considerable *adj* abundant, ample, appreciable, big, generous, great, large, lavish, marked, noticeable, perceptible, plentiful,

reasonable, remarkable, respectable, significant, sizeable, substantial, tidy *colloq*, tolerable
🔁 insignificant, slight, small, unremarkable

considerably *adv* abundantly, appreciably, greatly, markedly, much, noticeably, remarkably, significantly, substantially
🔁 slightly

considerate *adj* attentive, caring, charitable, compassionate, concerned, generous, gracious, helpful, kind, obliging, selfless, sensitive, solicitous, sympathetic, thoughtful, unselfish
🔁 inconsiderate, selfish, thoughtless

consideration *n* **1** *take into serious consideration:* analysis, attention, cogitation *formal*, contemplation, deliberation, examination, heed, inspection, meditation, reflection, regard, review, rumination *formal*, scrutiny, thought **2** *no consideration for other people:* attention, care, compassion, concern, generosity, graciousness, helpfulness, kindness, regard, respect, selflessness, sensitivity, sympathy, thoughtfulness, unselfishness **3** *the cost is a major consideration:* circumstance, fact, factor, issue, point
🔁 **1** disregard **2** thoughtlessness

considering *prep* bearing in mind, in the light of, in view of, making allowances for, taking into account/consideration
♦ *adv* all in all, all things considered

consign *v* **1** *his teachings are consigned to oblivion:* banish, commit, relegate **2** *the money was consigned to the treasury:* assign, commend, convey, deliver, entrust, give over, hand over, ship, transfer, transmit

consignment *n* batch, cargo, delivery, goods, load, shipment

consist *v* **1** *his diet consists of raw fruit and vegetables:* amount to, be composed of, be formed of, be made up of, comprise, contain, embody, embrace, include, incorporate, involve **2** *the poem's beauty consists in its simplicity:* be contained, have as its main feature, inhere, lie, reside

consistency *n* **1** *the consistency of the porridge:* cohesion, density, firmness, smoothness, thickness, viscosity *technical* **2** *show consistency in character:* constancy, dependability, evenness, identity, lack of change, persistence, regularity, reliability, sameness, stability, steadfastness, steadiness, unchangeableness, uniformity **3** *there is no consistency between the theories:* accordance, agreement, compatibility, congruity *formal*, consonance *formal*, correspondence, harmony
🔁 **3** inconsistency

consistent *adj* **1** *his playing is always consistent:* constant, dependable, regular, same, stable, steady, unchanging, undeviating, unfailing, uniform **2** *not consistent with his colleague's version:* accordant *formal*, agreeing, coinciding, compatible, conforming, congruous *formal*, consonant *formal*, corresponding, harmonious, matching
🔁 **1** erratic, irregular **2** inconsistent

consolation *n* aid, alleviation, assuagement *formal*, cheer, comfort, ease, encouragement, help, reassurance, relief, solace *formal*, soothing, succour *formal*, support, sympathy
🔁 discouragement

console¹ *v* calm, cheer, comfort, commiserate with, encourage, hearten, help, reassure, relieve, solace *formal*, soothe, succour *formal*, support, sympathize with
🔁 agitate, upset

console² *n* board, buttons, control panel, controls, dashboard, dials, instruments, keyboard, knobs, levers, panel, switches

consolidate *v* **1** *consolidate power/support:* fortify *formal*, make (more) secure, make (more) stable, make strong(er), reinforce, secure, stabilize, strengthen **2** *consolidate businesses:* amalgamate, combine, fuse, join, merge, unify, unite

consolidation *n* **1** *consolidation of power:* fortification *formal*, reinforcement, securing, stabilization, strengthening **2** *consolidation of businesses:* affiliation, alliance, amalgamation, association, combination, confederation, federation, fusion, joining, merger, unification, uniting

consonance *n* accordance *formal*, agreement, compatibility, concord *formal*, conformity, congruity *formal*, consistency, correspondence, harmony
🔁 dissonance

consonant *adj* accordant *formal*, according, agreeing, compatible, conforming, congruous *formal*, consistent, correspondent, harmonious, in accordance, in harmony
🔁 dissonant

consort *n* associate, companion, escort, husband, partner, spouse, wife
♦ *v* associate, fraternize, keep company, mingle, mix, spend time

consortium *n* affiliation, agreement, alliance, association, bloc, cartel, coalition, combination, compact, company, confederation, conglomerate, corporation, federation, guild, league, marriage, organization, pact, partnership, syndicate, treaty, union

conspicuous *adj* **1** *his red hair made him conspicuous:* apparent, discernible, easily seen/noticed, evident, glaring, manifest, marked, noticeable, observable, obvious, perceptible, prominent, recognizable, standing out a mile *colloq*, striking, visible **2** *conspicuous spending:* blatant, clear, flagrant, flashy, marked, obvious, ostentatious, patent, showy, standing out a mile *colloq*
🔁 **1** concealed, hidden, inconspicuous **2** concealed, hidden, inconspicuous

conspiracy *n* cabal, collaboration, collusion, connivance, fix *colloq*, frame-up *colloq*, intrigue, league, machination *formal*, plot, scheme, stratagem

conspirator *n* collaborator, colluder, conspirer, intriguer, plotter, schemer

conspire *v* **1** *conspire to oust the president:* collaborate, collude, connive, hatch a plot, intrigue, machinate *formal*, manoeuvre, plot, scheme **2** *events conspired to keep us apart:* ally, associate, combine, connect, co-operate, join, join forces, link, unite, work/act together

constancy *n* **1** *the constancy of the temperature:* firmness, permanence, regularity, stability, steadiness, unchangeability, uniformity **2** *a comrade's constancy:* dependability, devotion,

faithfulness, fidelity, loyalty, steadfastness, steadiness, trustworthiness
☒ 1 change, irregularity 2 fickleness

constant *adj* 1 *a constant barrage of questions:* ceaseless *formal*, chronic, continual, continuous, endless, eternal, everlasting, incessant, interminable, never-ending, non-stop, perpetual, persistent, relentless, unbroken, unflagging, uninterrupted, unremitting, unwavering, without respite 2 *his temperature is constant:* changeless, even, firm, immutable *formal*, invariable, permanent, regular, stable, steady, unalterable, unchanging, uniform, unvarying 3 *a constant friend:* dependable, devoted, faithful, firm, loyal, staunch, steadfast, steady, true, trustworthy
☒ 1 fitful, occasional 2 irregular, variable 3 disloyal, fickle

constantly *adv* ad nauseam, all the time, always, ceaselessly *formal*, continually, continuously, endlessly, everlastingly, incessantly, interminably, non-stop, permanently, perpetually, relentlessly
☒ occasionally

constellation

The constellations (with common English names) are:
Andromeda, Antlia (Air Pump), Apus (Bird of Paradise), Aquarius (Water Bearer), Aquila (Eagle), Ara (Altar), Aries (Ram), Auriga (Charioteer), Boötes (Herdsman), Caelum (Chisel), Camelopardalis (Giraffe), Cancer (Crab), Canes Venatici (Hunting Dogs), Canis Major (Great Dog), Canis Minor (Little Dog), Capricornus (Sea Goat), Carina (Keel), Cassiopeia, Centaurus (Centaur), Cepheus, Cetus (Whale), Chamaeleon (Chameleon), Circinus (Compasses), Columba (Dove), Coma Berenices (Berenice's Hair), Corona Australis (Southern Crown), Corona Borealis (Northern Crown), Corvus (Crow), Crater (Cup), Crux (Southern Cross), Cygnus (Swan), Delphinus (Dolphin), Dorado (Swordfish), Draco (Dragon), Equuleus (Little Horse), Eridanus (River Eridanus), Fornax (Furnace), Gemini (Twins), Grus (Crane), Hercules, Horologium (Clock), Hydra (Sea Serpent), Hydrus (Water Snake), Indus (Indian), Lacerta (Lizard), Leo (Lion), Leo Minor (Little Lion), Lepus (Hare), Libra (Scales), Lupus (Wolf), Lynx, Lyra (Harp), Mensa (Table), Microscopium (Microscope), Monoceros (Unicorn), Musca (Fly), Norma (Level), Octans (Octant), Ophiuchus (Serpent Bearer), Orion, Pavo (Peacock), Pegasus (Winged Horse), Perseus, Phoenix, Pictor (Easel), Pisces (Fishes), Piscis Austrinus (Southern Fish), Puppis (Ship's Stern), Pyxis (Mariner's Compass), Reticulum (Net), Sagitta (Arrow), Sagittarius (Archer), Scorpius (Scorpion), Sculptor, Scutum (Shield), Serpens (Serpent), Sextans (Sextant), Taurus (Bull), Telescopium (Telescope), Triangulum (Triangle), Triangulum Australe (Southern Triangle), Tucana (Toucan), Ursa Major (Great Bear), Ursa Minor (Little Bear), Vela (Sails), Virgo (Virgin), Volans (Flying Fish), Vulpecula (Fox). See also **star**

---

consternation *n* alarm, anxiety, bewilderment, dismay, disquietude *formal*, distress, dread, fear, fright, horror, panic, perturbation *formal*, shock, terror, trepidation *formal*
☒ composure

constituent *n* 1 *voting by constituents:* elector, voter 2 *the constituents of the mixture:* bit, component, component part, content, element, factor, ingredient, part, principle, section, unit
☒ 2 whole
♦ *adj* basic, component, essential, inherent, integral, intrinsic

constitute *v* 1 *six counties constitute the province:* compose, comprise, form, make up 2 *his remarks constitute a challenge to the leadership:* add up to, amount to, be, be equivalent to, be regarded as, be tantamount to, form, make, mean, represent 3 *constitute a committee:* appoint, authorize, charter, commission, create, empower, establish, form, found, institute, set up

constitution *n* 1 *a country's constitution:* basic principles, bill of rights, charter, code, codified law, laws, rules, statutes 2 *the constitution of the committee:* composition, configuration *formal*, formation, make-up, organization, structure 3 *he has a poor constitution:* condition, health, make-up, physical condition, physique 4 *of a nervous constitution:* character, disposition, nature, temperament

constitutional *adj* according to the law, authorized, by law, codified, governmental, lawful, legal, legislative, legitimate, ratified, statutory, vested
♦ *n* airing, amble, promenade, saunter, stroll, turn, walk

constrain *v* 1 *constrained to tell the truth:* coerce, compel, drive, force, impel, necessitate, oblige, pressure, pressurize, urge 2 *constrained by responsibilities:* bind, check, confine, constrict, curb, hinder, hold back, limit, restrain, restrict

constrained *adj* forced, guarded, inhibited, reserved, reticent, stiff, uneasy, unnatural
☒ free, relaxed

constraint *n* 1 *actions performed under constraint:* coercion, compulsion, duress, force, necessity, obligation, pressure 2 *a budget constraint:* check, curb, damper, hindrance, impediment, limitation, restraint, restriction

constrict *v* 1 *constrict an air passage:* choke, compress, contract, cramp, make narrow, narrow, pinch, shrink, squeeze, strangle, strangulate, tighten 2 *constricted by lower budgets:* bind, check, confine, constrain, curb, hamper, hinder, hold back, impede, inhibit, limit, obstruct, restrict
☒ 1 expand

constriction *n* 1 *feel a constriction in the chest:* blockage, compression, constringency *formal*, cramp, narrowing, pressure, squeezing, stenosis *technical*, stricture *technical*, tightening, tightness 2 *constrictions in the budget:* check, constraint, curb, hindrance, impediment, limitation, reduction, restriction
☒ 1 expansion

construct *v* 1 *construct a building:* assemble, build, elevate, erect, establish, fabricate, make, manufacture, put up, raise, set up 2 *construct a theory:* compose, create, design, devise, establish, fabricate, fashion, form, formulate, found, put together, shape
☒ 1 demolish, destroy

construction *n* 1 *the construction of houses:* assembly, building, elevation, erection,

establishment, fabrication, making, manufacture **2** *the cathedral is a magnificent construction:* building, edifice, figure, form, framework, shape, structure **3** *the construction put on his remarks:* deduction, inference, interpretation, meaning, reading
🔁 **1** demolition, destruction

constructive *adj* advantageous, beneficial, helpful, positive, practical, productive, useful, valuable
🔁 destructive, negative, unhelpful

construe *v* deduce, explain, expound *formal*, infer, interpret, read, regard as, see as, take to mean, understand

consult *v* **1** *consult an expert:* ask someone's opinion, ask/seek advice, ask/seek information, pick someone's brains *colloq*, question, turn to **2** *the judges consulted in whispers:* confer, debate, deliberate, discuss **3** *consult a map:* look up, refer to, turn to

consultant *n* adviser, authority, expert, specialist

consultation *n* **1** *US consultations with Turkey and Iraq:* conference, deliberation, dialogue, discussion, forum, meeting, talk **2** *a consultation with a specialist:* appointment, examination, hearing, interview, meeting, session

consultative *adj* advising, advisory, consultatory *formal*, consulting, counselling, helping

consume *v* **1** *consume food:* devour, drink (up), eat, eat up, gobble, guzzle *colloq*, ingest *formal*, polish off *colloq*, scoff *colloq*, swallow, take, tuck in *colloq* **2** *consume energy:* absorb, deplete *formal*, dissipate *formal*, drain, exhaust, expend *formal*, fritter away, get through, go through, spend, squander, use, use up, utilize *formal*, waste **3** *consumed by fire:* annihilate, demolish, destroy, devastate, gut, lay waste, ravage **4** *consumed with jealousy:* absorb, devour, dominate, eat up *colloq*, engross, grip, monopolize, obsess, overwhelm, preoccupy

consumer *n* buyer, client, customer, end-user, patron, purchaser, shopper, user

consuming *adj* absorbing, compelling, devouring, dominating, engrossing, gripping, immoderate, monopolizing, obsessive, overwhelming, preoccupying

consummate *adj* **1** *a consummate performer:* accomplished, distinguished, gifted, matchless, perfect, polished, practised, proficient, skilled, superb, superior, supreme, transcendent, ultimate **2** *a consummate liar:* absolute, complete, total, unqualified, utter
🔁 **1** imperfect
♦ *v* accomplish, achieve, complete, conclude, effectuate *formal*, execute *formal*, finish, fulfil, perfect, perform, realize

consummation *n* accomplishment, achievement, actualization *formal*, completion, conclusion, culmination, effectuation *formal*, execution *formal*, finish, fulfilment, perfection, performance, realization

consumption *n* **1** *consumption of food:* devouring, drinking, eating, guzzling *colloq*, ingestion *formal*, scoffing *colloq*, swallowing, tucking-in *colloq* **2** *consumption of energy:*

absorption, depletion *formal*, draining, exhaustion, expending *formal*, expenditure *formal*, getting-through, going-through, spending, squandering, using-up, utilization *formal*, waste

contact *n* **1** *in contact with an object:* contiguity *formal*, juxtaposition *formal*, meeting, proximity, touch, touching **2** *in contact with old friends:* association, communication, connection, touch **3** *use your contacts to get a job:* acquaintance, connection, friend, network of contacts, person of importance, person of influence, relation, relative
♦ *v* call, communicate with, e-mail, fax, get hold of, get in touch with, get onto, get through to, notify, phone, reach, ring, speak to, telephone, write to

contagious *adj* **1** *a contagious disease:* catching, communicable, epidemic, infectious, pandemic, spreading, transmissible, transmittable **2** *contagious laughter:* catching, compelling, infectious, irresistible

contain *v* **1** *the panel contains ten members:* comprise, embody, embrace, enclose, have inside, include, incorporate, involve **2** *the lift contains fifteen people:* accommodate, carry, hold, seat, take, take in **3** *attempts to contain the disease:* check, control, curb, hold in, keep back, keep in check, keep under control, limit, prevent from spreading, repress, restrain, stifle, stop, suppress
🔁 **1** exclude

container *n* holder, receptacle, repository *formal*, vessel

Types of container include:
bag, barrel, basin, basket, bath, beaker, bin, bottle, bowl, box, bucket, can, canister, carton, case, cask, casket, cauldron, chest, churn, cistern, crate, crock, cup, cylinder, dish, drum, dustbin, glass, hamper, jar, jug, keg, kettle, locker, mug, pack, packet, pail, pan, pannier, pitcher, pot, punnet, purse, sack, suitcase, tank, tea caddy, tea chest, teapot, tin, trough, trunk, tub, tube, tumbler, tureen, urn, vase, vat, waste bin, waste-paper basket, water-butt, well

contaminate *v* adulterate, corrupt, debase, defile, foul, harm, infect, make impure, pollute, soil, spoil, stain, sully, taint, tarnish, vitiate *formal*
🔁 purify

contamination *n* adulteration, corruption, debasement, defilement, filth, foulness, impurity, infection, pollution, soiling, spoiling, stain, sullying, taint, tarnish, vitiation *formal*
🔁 purification

contemplate *v* **1** *contemplate leaving:* consider, deliberate, envisage, examine, have in mind/view, intend, plan, propose, think about **2** *contemplate the meaning of life:* cogitate *formal*, consider, deliberate, dwell, examine, meditate, mull over, muse, ponder, reflect on, ruminate *formal*, study, think about, turn over in your mind, weigh (up) **3** *contemplate the view:* examine, inspect, look at, observe, regard, scrutinize, survey, view

contemplation *n* **1** *religious contemplation:* cerebration *formal*, cogitation *formal*, consideration, deliberation, meditation, mulling-over, musing, pondering, reflection, rumination

formal, study, thought, weighing (up)
2 *contemplation of the view:* examination, gazing, inspection, observation, regard, scrutiny, survey, view

contemplative *adj* cerebral *formal*, deep in thought, intent, introspective, meditative, musing, pensive, rapt, reflective, ruminative *formal*, thoughtful
🖅 impulsive, thoughtless

contemporary *adj* **1** *contemporary art:* avant-garde, current, fashionable, futuristic, latest, modern, new-fangled *colloq*, present, present-day, present-time, recent, today's, topical, trendy *colloq*, ultra-modern, up-to-date, up-to-the-minute, with it *colloq* **2** *contemporary with Shakespeare:* coetaneous *formal*, coeval *formal*, coexistent, concurrent *formal*, contemporaneous, simultaneous, synchronous
🖅 **1** old-fashioned, out of date

contempt *n* condescension, contumely *formal*, derision, detestation *formal*, disdain, dislike, disregard, disrespect, hatred, loathing, mockery, ridicule, scorn
🖅 admiration, regard, respect

contemptible *adj* abject, base, degenerate, despicable, detestable, ignominious *formal*, loathsome, low, mean, paltry, shameful, unworthy, vile, worthless
🖅 admirable, honourable

contemptuous *adj* arrogant, condescending, contumelious *formal*, derisive, derisory, disdainful, disrespectful, haughty, high and mighty, insolent, insulting, jeering, mocking, scornful, sneering, supercilious, withering
🖅 humble, polite, respectful

contend *v* **1** *contend with a problem:* address, brave, come to grips *colloq*, come to terms, cope, deal, face, face up to, grapple, meet head on *colloq*, tackle **2** *he contends that he is right:* affirm, allege, argue, assert, asseverate *formal*, aver *formal*, claim, declare, hold, maintain, profess, state **3** *contend with an opponent:* battle, challenge, clash, combat, compete, contest, dispute, fight, grapple, oppose, strive, struggle, tussle, vie, war, wrestle

content¹ *n* **1** *the contents of the package:* component parts, components, constituents, elements, ingredients, items, load, parts, things inside, what is contained **2** *the contents of the book:* chapter, division, section, subject, subject matter, theme, topic **3** *the content of the poem:* burden, contents, essence, gist, ideas, material, matter, meaning, significance, subject matter, substance, text, theme **4** *the fat content of the spread:* capacity, measure, size, volume

content² *adj* at ease, comfortable, contented, fulfilled, glad, happy, pleased, satisfied, willing
🖅 dissatisfied, troubled
♦ *n* comfort, contentment, delight, ease, fulfilment, gladness, gratification, happiness, peace, peacefulness, pleasure, satisfaction, serenity
🖅 discontent
♦ *v* delight, gratify, pacify, placate, please, satisfy
🖅 displease

contented *adj* comfortable, content, fulfilled, glad, happy, pleased, satisfied
🖅 annoyed, discontented, troubled, unhappy

contention *n* **1** *it is my contention that he is wrong:* argument, assertion, belief, claim, conviction, judgement, opinion, point of view, position, stand, theory, thesis, view, viewpoint **2** *a matter of contention:* argument, controversy, debate, disagreement, discord, dispute, dissension, enmity, feuding, hostility, strife, struggle, wrangling

contentious *adj* **1** *a contentious issue:* controversial, debatable, disputable, disputed, doubtful, polemical, questionable **2** *a contentious person:* antagonistic, argumentative, bickering, captious, perverse, pugnacious *formal*, quarrelsome, querulous
🖅 **1** straightforward; uncontroversial **2** co-operative, peaceable

contentment *n* comfort, complacency, content, contentedness, ease, fulfilment, gladness, gratification, happiness, peace, peacefulness, pleasure, satisfaction, serenity
🖅 discomfort, discontent, dissatisfaction, uneasiness, unhappiness

contest *n* **1** *the contest for the leadership:* battle, combat, conflict, controversy, debate, dispute, encounter, fight, set-to *colloq*, skirmish, struggle, vying **2** *a beauty contest:* championship, competition, event, game, match, race, tournament
♦ *v* **1** *contest a decision:* argue against, call into question, challenge, debate, deny, dispute, doubt, litigate *technical*, oppose, question, refute **2** *contesting for the title:* battle, compete, contend, fight, strive, struggle, tussle, vie
🖅 **1** accept

contestant *n* aspirant, candidate, competitor, contender, entrant, opponent, participant, player

context *n* background, circumstances, conditions, factors, frame of reference, framework, general situation, position, setting, situation, state of affairs, surroundings

contiguous *adj* abutting *formal*, adjacent, adjoining, beside, bordering, close, conjoining *formal*, conterminous *formal*, juxtaposed *formal*, juxtapositional *formal*, near, neighbouring, next, tangential, touching, vicinal *technical*

continent *n* mainland, terra firma

The continents of the world are:
Africa, Antarctica, Asia, Australia, Europe, North America, South America

contingency *n* **1** *prepared for every contingency:* accident, chance, chance event, emergency, event, eventuality, happening, incident, juncture *formal*, possibility **2** *the contingency of the future:* arbitrariness, fortuity *formal*, randomness, uncertainty

contingent *n* batch, body, company, complement, delegation, deputation, detachment, division, group, party, quota, representatives, section, set
♦ *adj* based, conditional, dependent, relative, subject

continual *adj* constant, eternal, everlasting, frequent, incessant, interminable, perpetual, persistent, recurrent, regular, repeated, repetitive
🖅 broken, erratic, fluctuating, intermittent, occasional, temporary

continual or *continuous*? *Continual* means 'very frequent, happening again and again': *I've had continual interruptions all morning.* *Continuous* means 'without a pause or break': *continuous rain.*

continually *adv* all the time, always, ceaselessly *formal*, constantly, endlessly, eternally, everlastingly, frequently, habitually, incessantly, interminably, non-stop, perpetually, persistently, recurrently, regularly, repeatedly
▪ intermittently, occasionally

continuance *n* **1** *the origin and continuance of life on this planet*: continuation, endurance, permanence, persistence, protraction *formal* **2** *for the continuance of his stay*: duration, period, term

continuation *n* **1** *a continuation of previous events*: development, furtherance, recommencement, renewal, resumption, sequel, starting again **2** *the continuation of the road*: addition, extension, lengthening, prolongation, protraction *formal*
▪ **1** cessation *formal*, termination *formal*

continue *v* **1** *continue doing something*: carry on, go on, keep on (with), not stop, persevere in, persist in, press on, proceed, soldier on *colloq*, stick at *colloq*, sustain **2** *we'll continue this discussion later*: begin again, carry on, go on with, pick up the threads *colloq*, pick up where you have left off *colloq*, proceed again, recommence, renew, resume, start again, take up again **3** *the course continues next term*: begin again, carry on, go on, proceed, recommence, resume, start again **4** *if the storm continues*: abide, endure, extend, hold out, keep on, last, lengthen, persist, remain, stay, survive **5** *'I'm not sure,' she continued*: go on, resume, start talking again **6** *continue on your way*: carry on, keep going, keep moving, keep on, keep travelling, keep walking
▪ **5** stop

continuity *n* cohesion, connection, continuousness, flow, interrelationship, linkage, progression, sequence, succession, unchangeableness, uninterruptedness
▪ discontinuity

continuous *adj* ceaseless, consecutive, constant, continued, endless, extended, interminable, lasting, never-ending, non-stop, not stopping, prolonged, solid, unbroken, unceasing, unending, uninterrupted, unremitting, with no let-up *colloq*, without a break
▪ broken, discontinuous, sporadic

contort *v* bend out of shape, convolute *formal*, deform, disfigure, distort, gnarl, knot, misshape, twist, warp, wrench

contortionist *n* acrobat, gymnast

contour *n* curve, figure, form, lines, outline, profile, relief, shape, silhouette

contraband *n* **1** *the authorities seized alleged contraband*: banned/black-market goods, hot goods *colloq*, prohibited/unlawful goods, proscribed goods *formal* **2** *charged with contraband*: bootlegging, forbidden/illegal traffic, smuggling

contract *v* **1** *the muscles contract*: become shorter, become smaller, compress, constrict, decrease, diminish, draw in, lessen, narrow, reduce, shorten, shrink, shrivel, tense, tighten **2** *net sales have contracted by 42 per cent*: decrease, diminish, lessen, reduce, shrink **3** *'does not' is contracted to 'doesn't'*: abbreviate, abridge, shorten **4** *contract pneumonia*: become ill with, become infected with, catch, develop, get, go/come down with, pick up, succumb to *formal* **5** *he has contracted to play for this team*: agree, agree terms, arrange, bargain, engage, negotiate, pledge, promise, settle, stipulate, undertake
▪ **1** enlarge, expand, lengthen **2** expand
♦ *n* agreement, arrangement, bargain, bond, commitment, compact *formal*, concordat *formal*, convention, covenant, deal, engagement, pact, settlement, transaction, treaty, understanding

contraction *n* **1** *the word 'don't' is a contraction of 'do not'*: abbreviation, abridgement, shortened form, shortening **2** *the contraction of muscles*: astringency *technical*, compression, constriction, drawing-in, lessening, narrowing, reduction, shrinkage, shrivelling, tensing, tightening
▪ **2** expansion, growth

contradict *v* **1** *contradict someone*: challenge, counter, gainsay *formal*, go against, impugn *formal*, oppose **2** *contradict a statement*: challenge, confute *formal*, counter, deny, disaffirm *formal*, dispute, impugn *formal*, rebut, refute *formal* **3** *one statement contradicts another*: be at odds, be at variance, be in conflict, be inconsistent with, clash, conflict, contrast, disagree, fly in the face of *colloq*, go against, negate *formal*
▪ **1** agree with **2** agree with **3** agree with, confirm, corroborate *formal*

contradiction *n* **1** *the contradiction between theory and practice*: antithesis *formal*, clash, conflict, disagreement, incongruity *formal*, inconsistency, odds, paradox, variance **2** *contradiction of an earlier report*: challenge, confutation *formal*, counter-argument, denial, disaffirmance *formal*, disaffirmation *formal*, dispute, negation *formal*, opposition, rebuttal, refutation *formal*
▪ **2** agreement

contradictory *adj* antithetical *formal*, clashing, conflicting, contrary, discrepant *formal*, dissentient *formal*, incompatible, incongruous *formal*, inconsistent, irreconcilable, opposed, opposing, opposite, paradoxical
▪ consistent

contraption *n* apparatus, contrivance, device, gadget, invention, machine, mechanism, rig, thingumajig *colloq*

contrary *adj* **1** *they hold contrary opinions*: adverse, antagonistic, clashing, conflicting, counter, incompatible, inconsistent, irreconcilable, opposed, opposing, opposite, reverse **2** *a contrary child*: awkward, cantankerous, difficult, disobliging, headstrong, intractable, obstinate, perverse, refractory *formal*, stroppy *colloq*, stubborn, wayward
▪ **1** like **2** obliging
♦ *n* antithesis *formal*, converse, opposite, reverse

contrast *n* antithesis *formal*, difference, differentiation, disparity *formal*, dissimilarity, dissimilitude *formal*, distinction, divergence, opposite, opposition
▪ resemblance, similarity
♦ *v* **1** *contrast two people*: compare, differentiate, discriminate, distinguish **2** *her expression*

contrasted sharply with her dress: be at odds, be at variance, be in conflict, be inconsistent with, clash, conflict, contradict, differ, disagree, go against, oppose

contravene v breach, break, defy, disobey, flout, infringe, transgress *formal*, violate
🖾 obey, observe, uphold

contretemps n **1** a contretemps outside the club: brush, clash, tiff **2** various contretemps which halted progress: accident, difficulty, hitch, misadventure, misfortune, mishap, predicament

contribute v **1** contribute money to charity: bestow *formal*, chip in *colloq*, donate, endow, furnish, give, give a donation, grant, present, provide, subscribe, supply **2** poor design contributed to the disaster: add to, be instrumental in, bring about, cause, conduce *formal*, create, generate, give rise to, help, lead to, make, make happen, occasion, originate, play a part in, produce, promote, result in **3** contribute an article for a magazine: compose, create, edit, prepare, provide, supply, write

contribution n **1** a contribution of £1000: bestowal *formal*, donation, endowment, gift, grant, gratuity, handout, input, offering, present, subscription **2** a contribution to a magazine: article, column, feature, item, piece, report, review, story

contributor n **1** the contributor to a good cause: backer, benefactor, donor, giver, patron, sponsor, subscriber, supporter **2** a newspaper contributor: author, columnist, correspondent, critic, freelance, journalist, reporter, reviewer, writer

contrite adj ashamed, chastened, conscience-stricken, guilt-ridden, humble, penitent, penitential, regretful, remorseful, repentant, sorry

contrition n compunction *formal*, penitence, regret, remorse, repentance, sackcloth and ashes, self-reproach, shame, sorrow

contrivance n **1** an ingenious mechanical contrivance: apparatus, appliance, contraption, device, equipment, gadget, gear, implement, invention, machine, mechanism, tool **2** a contrivance to deceive the public: artifice *formal*, design, dodge, expedient, intrigue, machination *formal*, plan, plot, ploy, ruse, scheme, stratagem, trick

contrive v **1** somehow contrived to blame me: arrange, find a way, manage, succeed **2** contrive a meeting between them: concoct, construct, create, devise, engineer, fabricate, invent, manoeuvre, orchestrate, plan, plot, scheme, set up *colloq*, stage-manage, wangle *colloq*

contrived adj artificial, elaborate, false, forced, laboured, mannered, overdone, set-up *colloq*, strained, unnatural
🖾 genuine, natural, spontaneous

control n **1** under military control: authority, charge, command, direction, discipline, dominance, government, guidance, influence, jurisdiction *formal*, management, mastery, oversight, power, reign, rule, superintendence, supervision, supremacy, sway **2** she had herself fully in control: check, constraint, curb, repression, restraint, self-control, self-discipline, self-restraint **3** price controls: brake, check, constraint, curb, hindrance, impediment, limit, limitation, regulation, restriction **4** his hands on the controls:

button, dial, instrument, knob, lever, switch
♦ v **1** control a group: be in charge of, be in the driving seat *colloq*, be in the saddle *colloq*, be the boss *colloq*, call the tune/shots *colloq*, command, direct, dominate, govern, have authority over, head, lead, manage, oversee, preside over, pull the strings *colloq*, rule, rule the roost *colloq*, run the show *colloq*, superintend, supervise, wear the trousers *colloq* **2** control a machine: make go, operate, run, work **3** control the temperature: adjust, monitor, regulate **4** control wages: check, constrain, curb, keep a tight rein on *colloq*, limit, put the brakes on *colloq*, regulate, restrict **5** control your temper: check, contain, curb, hold back, keep, repress, restrain, subdue

controversial adj at issue, contentious, debatable, disputable, disputed, doubtful, polemical, questionable

controversy n altercation *formal*, argument, contention, debate, difference of opinion, disagreement, discord, discussion, dispute, dissension, friction, polemic *formal*, quarrel, squabble, strife, war of words, wrangle
🖾 accord, agreement

contusion n bruise, bump, discoloration, ecchymosis *technical*, injury, knock, lump, swelling

conundrum n brainteaser, enigma, poser, problem, puzzle, riddle, word game

convalescence n getting better, improvement, recovery, recuperation, rehabilitation, restoration

convene v **1** convene a meeting: call (together), convoke *formal*, muster, rally, summon **2** the court convened: assemble, collect, congregate, gather, meet, muster, rally

convenience n **1** did it for your convenience: advantage, benefit, good, help, service, use **2** the convenience of this gadget: ease of use, handiness, serviceability, usefulness, utility **3** the convenience of the arrangement: advantage, advantageousness, appropriateness, expediency *formal*, fitness, handiness, opportuneness, propitiousness *formal*, suitability **4** the convenience of the railway station: accessibility, availability, handiness, propinquity *formal* **5** all modern conveniences: amenity, appliance, device, facility, gadget, labour-saving device, resource, service
🖾 **1** inconvenience **2** inconvenience **3** inconvenience **4** inconvenience

convenient adj **1** a convenient arrangement: beneficial, expedient *formal*, fit, fitting, suitable **2** a convenient gadget: handy, helpful, labour-saving, useful **3** the flat is convenient for the shops: accessible, at hand, at your fingertips *colloq*, handy, just/only round the corner *colloq*, near/close at hand, nearby, within reach, within walking/driving distance **4** is this a convenient time to call?: appropriate, fit, fitting, opportune, suitable, timely, well-timed
🖾 **1** awkward, inconvenient **2** awkward, inconvenient **3** inconvenient **4** awkward, inconvenient

convention n **1** break an unwritten convention: code, custom, etiquette, formality, matter of form, practice, propriety *formal*, protocol, punctilio *formal*, tradition, usage **2** a convention of scientists: assembly, conclave *formal*, conference, congress, convocation *formal*, council, gathering, meeting, synod **3** *the Geneva convention:* agreement, arrangement, bargain, bond, commitment, compact *formal*, concordat *formal*, covenant, deal, engagement, pact, settlement, transaction, treaty, understanding

conventional *adj* **1** *conventional opinions:* conformist, conservative, correct, formal, hidebound, mainstream, orthodox, proper, straight **2** *conventional methods:* common, customary, mainstream, normal, ordinary, orthodox, regular, routine, run-of-the-mill *colloq*, standard, traditional, usual **3** *conventional wisdom:* accepted, customary, expected, mainstream, orthodox, prevailing, prevalent, received, traditional, usual **4** *a rather conventional work:* common or garden *colloq*, commonplace, ordinary, routine, run-of-the-mill *colloq*, stereotyped, trite, unoriginal
F3 1 unconventional **2** alternative, exotic, unconventional, unusual **3** unconventional **4** alternative, exotic, unconventional, unusual

converge *v* **1** *crowds converged on the car:* approach, close in, concentrate, focus, form, gather, mass, move towards **2** *the roads converge at the bridge:* coincide, combine, come together, join, meet, merge, unite
F3 1 disperse **2** diverge

convergence *n* coincidence, combination, confluence *formal*, intersection, junction, meeting, merging, union
F3 divergence, separation

conversant *adj* acquainted, au fait, experienced, familiar, knowledgeable, proficient, skilled, versed
F3 ignorant

conversation *n* chat, chinwag *colloq*, colloquy *formal*, communication, confab *colloq*, cosy chat, dialogue, discourse, discussion, exchange, gossip, heart-to-heart, natter *colloq*, small talk, talk, tête-à-tête

conversational *adj* casual, chatty, colloquial, communicative, informal, relaxed

converse[1] *v* chat, chatter, commune *formal*, communicate, confer, discourse *formal*, discuss, gossip, talk

converse[2] *n* antithesis *formal*, contrary, obverse, opposite, other side of the coin *colloq*, other way round *colloq*, reverse
♦ *adj* antithetical *formal*, contrary, counter, obverse, opposing, opposite, reverse

conversion *n* **1** *the conversion of the building into flats:* adaptation, adjustment, alteration, change, customization, metamorphosis *technical*, modification, mutation, reconstruction, remodelling, reorganization, reshaping, transfiguration, transformation, transmutation, turning **2** *conversion of pounds into euros:* change, exchange, substitution, switch **3** *conversion to Judaism:* persuasion, proselytization, rebirth, reformation

convert *v* **1** *convert the building:* adapt, adjust, alter, change, customize, modify, rebuild, reconstruct, refashion, reform, remodel, reorganize, reshape, restructure, restyle, revise, transfigure, transform **2** *a sofa which converts into a bed:* change, metamorphose *technical*, switch, transfigure, transform, transmute, turn **3** *convert*

inches into centimetres: change, exchange, substitute, switch from, turn into **4** *convert someone to Christianity:* cause to change beliefs/religion, convince, persuade, proselytize, reform, win over
♦ *n* adherent, believer, disciple, neophyte, proselyte

convertible *adj* adaptable, adjustable, exchangeable, interchangeable, modifiable, permutable *formal*

convex *adj* bending outwards, bulging, curved out, gibbous, protuberant, rounded, swelling
F3 concave, hollow

convey *v* **1** *convey information:* announce, communicate, disclose, express, hand on, impart *formal*, make known, pass on, relate, reveal, tell, transmit **2** *convey passengers:* bear, bring, carry, channel, conduct, deliver, drive, fetch, forward, guide, move, pipe, send, shift, transfer, transport

conveyance *n* **1** *a four-wheeled conveyance:* bicycle, bus, car, carriage, coach, lorry, motorcycle, truck, van, vehicle, wagon **2** *the conveyance of prisoners:* movement, transfer, transference, transport, transportation **3** *the conveyance of property:* bequeathal, ceding, consignment, granting, transfer, transference, transmission

convict *v* find guilty, judge
♦ *n* criminal, felon, inmate, jailbird *colloq*, lag *slang*, prisoner

conviction *n* **1** *religious convictions:* belief, creed, faith, opinion, principle, tenet, view **2** *speak with conviction:* assurance, certainty, certitude *formal*, confidence, earnestness, fervour, firmness **3** *his conviction for manslaughter:* condemnation, judgement, pronouncement of guilt, sentence

convince *v* **1** *convince him of the truth:* assure, persuade, prove to **2** *convince him to keep quiet:* bring round, influence, persuade, prevail upon *formal*, sway, talk into, win over

convincing *adj* cogent *formal*, compelling, conclusive, credible, forceful, impressive, incontrovertible, likely, persuasive, plausible, powerful, probable, telling
F3 improbable, unconvincing

convivial *adj* cheerful, cordial, festive, friendly, fun-loving, genial, hearty, jolly, jovial, lively, merry, sociable
F3 taciturn

conviviality *n* bonhomie, cheer, cordiality, festivity, gaiety, geniality, jollity, joviality, liveliness, merrymaking, mirth, sociability

convocation *n* assemblage *formal*, assembly, conclave *formal*, congregation, congress, convention, council, diet, forgathering *formal*, meeting, synod

convoluted *adj* complex, complicated, involved, meandering, tortuous, twisting, winding
F3 straight, straightforward

convolution *n* **1** *convolutions in the design:* coil, coiling, curlicue *formal*, gyrus *technical*, helix, loop, spiral, turn, twist, whorl, winding **2** *convolutions in relationships:* complexity, complication, entanglement, intricacy, involvement, tortuousness

convoy *n* **1** *a convoy of trucks:* company, fleet, group, line, train **2** *the president's convoy:* attendance, escort, guard, protection

convulse *v* **1** *his body was convulsing with pain:* jerk, shake uncontrollably/violently, suffer a fit/seizure **2** *much of Asia was convulsed by civil war:* disturb, seize, unsettle

convulsion *n* **1** *he went into convulsions and died:* attack, contraction, cramp, fit, paroxysm, seizure, spasm, tic, tremor **2** *major political convulsions:* agitation, commotion, disorder, disturbance, eruption, furore, outburst, tumult, turbulence, turmoil, unrest, upheaval

convulsive *adj* fitful, jerky, spasmodic, sporadic, uncontrolled, violent

cook *v* heat, prepare, put on, put together, rustle up *colloq*, warm
▶ **cook up** brew, concoct, contrive, devise, fabricate, improvise, invent, make up, plan, plot, prepare, scheme

Ways of cooking include:
bake, barbecue, boil, braise, broil, brown, casserole, coddle, curry, deep-fry, fricassee, fry, grill, microwave, oven-roast, parboil, poach, pot-roast, roast, sauté, scramble, simmer, spit-roast, steam, stew, stir-fry, toast

Terms used in cookery include:
bake blind, bind, blend, bone, brown, caramelize, carve, chill, chop, cream, crumble, cure, defrost, deglaze, devil, drizzle, dust, fillet, flash fry, fold in, freeze, glaze, grate, grind, ice, joint, jug, knead, knock back, liquidize, marinate, mash, mince, mix, mull, peel, peppered, pickle, plate (up), potted, prep *colloq*, preserve, prove, purée, reduce, re-heat, rest, rise, sear, sieve, sift, skim, smoke, souse, stir, strain, stuff, sweat, thicken, truss, whisk; *Terms used in French cookery include:* à la crème, à la Grècque, au gratin, au poivre, Bolognese, brûlée, cacciatore, chasseur, cordon bleu, coulis, en cocotte, en croute, farci, frappé, galette, gougère, haute cuisine, Lyonnaise, mornay, Niçoise, nouvelle cuisine, Provençal, roux, sur le plat; *Terms used in Indian cookery include:* akhni, aloo, balti, bargar, bhajee or bhaji, bhindi or bindi, bhoona or bhuna, dhal, dhansak, dopiaza, dum, gosht, kalia, karahi, kofta, korma, madras, masala, Moglai, paneer, tandoori, tikka, vindaloo

cool *adj* **1** *a cool breeze:* bracing, breezy, chilly, cold, crisp, draughty, fresh, nippy **2** *a cool drink:* chilled, cold, ice-cold, iced, refreshing **3** *stay cool under pressure:* calm, collected, composed, cool as a cucumber *colloq*, dispassionate, impassive, imperturbable, laid back *colloq*, level-headed, poised, relaxed, sedate, self-possessed, unapprehensive, undisturbed, unemotional, unexcitable, unexcited, unflappable *colloq*, unflustered, unmoved, unperturbed, unruffled, untroubled **4** *a cool reception:* aloof, apathetic, cold, distant, frigid, frosty, half-hearted, lukewarm, reserved, standoffish, undemonstrative, unenthusiastic, unfriendly, uninterested, unresponsive, unwelcoming **5** *look cool in that outfit:* elegant, fashionable, smart, sophisticated, streetwise *colloq*, stylish, trendy *colloq* **6** *a really cool party:* excellent, fantastic, great, marvellous, wonderful

1 hot, warm **2** hot **3** angry, excited **4** friendly, welcoming
♦ *v* **1** *cool a drink:* air-condition, chill, fan, freeze, ice, make cold, make colder, refrigerate **2** *cool tempers:* abate *formal*, allay, assuage *formal*, calm, dampen, diminish, lessen, moderate, quiet, reduce, temper
1 heat, warm **2** excite
♦ *n* **1** *keep/lose your cool:* calmness, collectedness, composure, control, coolness, poise, self-control, self-possession, temper **2** *the cool of the early morning:* breeze, chill, cold, crispness, defervescence *technical*, defervescency *technical*, draught, freshness, nippiness

cooling *n* air-conditioning, chilling, defervescence *technical*, defervescency *technical*, refrigeration, ventilation
heating, warming
♦ *adj* freezing, refrigerant, refrigerative, refrigeratory
warming

coop *n* box, cage, enclosure, hutch, pen, pound
▶ **coop up** cage, enclose, immure *formal*, impound, imprison, incarcerate *formal*, keep in, lock up/away, pen, shut (up)

co-operate *v* **1** *co-operate on a project:* band together, collaborate, combine, conspire, join forces, participate, pool resources, pull together, team up, unite, work together **2** *co-operate with the police:* aid, assist, help, play ball *colloq*

co-operation *n* **1** *we can do it with a bit of co-operation:* collaboration, concerted action, co-ordination, give-and-take, joint action, participation, teamwork, unity, working together **2** *police are asking for the public's co-operation:* aid, assistance, help, helpfulness, helping hand, participation
1 competition, opposition, rivalry **2** opposition

co-operative *adj* **1** *co-operative efforts:* collaborative, collective, combined, concerted, co-ordinated, joint, shared, united, working together **2** *he is very co-operative:* accommodating, assisting, coactive *formal*, compliant *formal*, helpful, helping, obliging, responsive, supportive, willing
2 rebellious, unco-operative

co-ordinate *v* **1** *co-ordinate an event:* arrange, correlate, integrate, mesh, order, organize, regulate, synchronize, systematize **2** *need to co-ordinate to create a plan:* collaborate, co-operate, integrate, work together **3** *co-ordinate colours:* harmonize, match **4** *colours which co-ordinate:* go together, harmonize, match

cope *v* carry on, get by, get through, make do, manage, succeed, survive
▶ **cope with** contend with, deal with, endure, grapple with, handle, manage, struggle with, weather, wrestle with
not hack it *colloq*

copious *adj* abundant, ample, bags of *colloq*, bounteous *formal*, bountiful, extensive, full, generous, great, huge, inexhaustible, lavish, liberal, luxuriant *formal*, overflowing, plenteous *formal*, plentiful, profuse, rich
meagre, scarce

cop-out *n* alibi, dodge, evasion, fraud, pretence, pretext

copse n brush, bush, coppice, grove, thicket, wood

copulate v bang *taboo slang*, bed *slang*, bonk *taboo slang*, enjoy, fuck *taboo slang*, get your leg over *slang*, go all the way *slang*, go to bed with *colloq*, have *slang*, have it off with *slang*, have sex, have sexual intercourse, horse, hump *taboo slang*, lay *slang*, line, make it with *slang*, make love, mate, screw *taboo slang*, shag *taboo slang*, stuff *taboo slang*

copy n 1 *keep a copy of the letter for your files*: carbon copy, duplicate, facsimile, fax, image, photocopy, Photostat®, print, replica, reproduction, tracing, transcript, transcription, Xerox® 2 *beware of cheap copies*: counterfeit, duplicate, fake, forgery, imitation, likeness, replica, reproduction 3 *the copy which we are to follow*: archetype, model, pattern 4 *buy a copy of the magazine*: example, issue, sample, specimen
☲ 1 original 2 original
♦ v 1 *copy a document*: duplicate, fax, photocopy, Photostat®, print, replicate *formal*, reproduce, scan, trace, transcribe, Xerox® 2 *copy a CD illegally*: counterfeit, duplicate, forge, pirate, plagiarize, replicate *formal*, reproduce 3 *copy a gesture*: emulate, imitate, mirror, parrot, repeat, replicate *formal*, reproduce, simulate

coquettish adj amorous, come-hither *colloq*, dallying, flighty, flirtatious, flirty, inviting, teasing, vampish *colloq*

cord n 1 *bound with cords*: cable, flex, line, rope, string, tie, twine 2 *the umbilical cord*: bond, connection, link

cordial adj 1 *a cordial nature*: affable, affectionate, agreeable, amicable, cheerful, friendly, genial, hearty, pleasant, sociable, warm, warm-hearted, welcoming 2 *her cordial dislike of her mother-in-law*: earnest, heartfelt, sincere, wholehearted
☲ 1 aloof, cool, hostile

cordiality n affability, affection, agreeableness, cheerfulness, friendliness, geniality, heartiness, sociability, warmth, welcome
☲ coolness, hostility

cordon n barrier, chain, fence, line, ring
► **cordon off** close off, encircle, enclose, fence off, isolate, separate, surround

core n 1 *the earth's core*: centre, heart, kernel, middle, nucleus 2 *the core of the problem*: crux, essence, gist, heart, nitty-gritty *colloq*, nub, quintessence *formal*, substance
☲ 1 exterior, surface

corn n arable crop, barley, cereal, cereal crop, grain, maize, oats, rye, wheat

corner n 1 *round the corner*: angle, bend, crook, curve, fork, intersection, joint, junction, turning 2 *tucked away in a corner*: cavity, cranny, crevice, hideaway, hideout, hole, niche, nook, recess, retreat 3 *in a tight corner*: hardship, hole *colloq*, nowhere to turn *colloq*, pickle *colloq*, plight, predicament, straits, tight spot *colloq*, tricky situation
♦ v 1 *corner an animal*: block off, catch, cut off, force into a corner, hunt down, run to earth, trap 2 *corner the market*: control, dominate, have sole rights in, hog *colloq*, monopolize

corny adj 1 *a corny chat-up line*: banal, clichéd, commonplace, dull, feeble, hackneyed, old-fashioned, overused, platitudinous, stale, stereotyped, trite 2 *a corny love song*: maudlin, mawkish, sentimental
☲ 1 new, original

corollary n 1 *the obvious corollary is that he is lying*: conclusion, deduction, illation *formal*, induction, inference 2 *the corollary is that the project will finish late*: conclusion, consequence, result, upshot

coronation n accession to the throne, crowning, enthronement

coronet n circlet, crown, diadem, garland, tiara, wreath

corporal adj anatomical, bodily, carnal, corporeal, fleshly, material, physical, somatic *formal*
☲ spiritual

corporate adj allied, amalgamated, collaborative, collective, combined, communal, concerted, joint, merged, pooled, shared, united

corporation n 1 *a business corporation*: association, business, cartel, company, concern, conglomerate, consortium, establishment, firm, holding company, house, multinational, organization, partnership, syndicate, trust 2 *the Corporation of London*: authorities, authority, council, governing body

corporeal adj actual, bodily, fleshly, human, material, mortal, physical
☲ spiritual

corps n band, body, brigade, company, contingent, crew, detachment, division, regiment, squad, squadron, team, unit

corpse n body, cadaver, carcase, dead body, remains, stiff *slang*

corpulent adj adipose *formal*, beefy, bulky, burly, fat, fleshy, large, obese, overweight, plump, podgy, portly, pot-bellied, roly-poly, rotund *formal*, stout, tubby, well-padded
☲ thin

corpus n aggregation *formal*, body, collection, compilation, entirety, whole

corral n coop, enclosure, fold, kraal, pound

correct adj 1 *the correct answer*: accurate, actual, bang on *colloq*, exact, faultless, flawless, precise, real, right, spot on *colloq*, true, truthful, unerring, word-perfect 2 *correct behaviour*: acceptable, accepted, appropriate, fitting, OK *colloq*, proper, suitable 3 *the correct procedure*: conventional, proper, regular, standard
☲ 1 inaccurate, incorrect, wrong
♦ v 1 *correct an error*: adjust, ameliorate *formal*, amend, cure, disabuse *formal*, emend *formal*, improve, put right, put straight, put the record straight *colloq*, rectify, redress, regulate, remedy, revise, right, set right 2 *correct a child*: admonish *formal*, discipline, punish, rebuke, reprimand, reprove, scold

correction n 1 *corrections to the text*: adjustment, alteration, amelioration *formal*, amendment, emendation *formal*, improvement, modification, rectification, remedying 2 *the correction of wayward children*: admonition *formal*, chastisement, discipline, punishment, rebuke, reprimand, reproof

corrective adj 1 *corrective surgery*: curative, emendatory *formal*, medicinal, palliative, remedial, restorative, therapeutic **2** *a corrective school:* disciplinary, penal, punitive, reformatory, rehabilitative

correlate *v* **1** *workplace flexibility correlates with productivity growth:* agree, be connected, be related, correspond, equate, parallel, tie in **2** *trying to correlate data from different systems:* associate, compare, connect, co-ordinate, link, relate, show a connection/relationship, tie in

correlation *n* association, connection, correspondence, equivalence, interaction, interdependence, interrelationship, link, reciprocity, relationship

correspond *v* **1** *this corresponds to the first question:* accord *formal*, agree, be analogous *formal*, be consistent, be equivalent, be in agreement, be similar, coincide, complement, concur *formal*, conform, correlate *formal*, dovetail, fit (together), harmonize, match, match up, square, tally **2** *we still correspond regularly:* communicate, exchange letters, keep in touch, write

correspondence *n* **1** *frequent correspondence:* communication, letters, mail, post, writing **2** *correspondence between two issues:* agreement, analogy, coincidence, comparability, comparison, concurrence *formal*, conformity, congruity *formal*, consonance *formal*, correlation *formal*, equivalence, harmony, match, relation, resemblance, similarity
☒ **2** divergence, incongruity

correspondent *n* contributor, journalist, reporter, writer

corresponding *adj* analogous *formal*, comparable, complementary, equivalent, identical, interrelated, like, matching, parallel, reciprocal, similar

corridor *n* aisle, hall, hallway, lobby, passage, passageway

corroborate *v* authenticate, back up, bear out, certify, confirm, document, endorse, evidence *formal*, prove, ratify, substantiate, support, sustain, underpin, uphold, validate, verify
☒ contradict

corroborative *adj* confirmative *formal*, confirmatory *formal*, confirming, endorsing, evidential *formal*, evidentiary *formal*, substantiating, supporting, supportive, validating, verificatory *formal*, verifying

corrode *v* **1** *the metal was corroded by rust:* consume, destroy, eat away, erode, oxidize, rot, rust, tarnish, waste, wear away **2** *iron corrodes quickly:* be eaten away, be worn away, crumble, deteriorate, disintegrate, oxidize, rot, rust, tarnish

corrosive *adj* acid, caustic, consuming, corroding, destructive, erosive *technical*, wasting, wearing

corrugated *adj* channelled, creased, crinkled, fluted, folded, furrowed, grooved, ridged, rumpled, striate *technical*, wrinkled

corrupt *adj* **1** *a corrupt lawyer:* bent *colloq*, bribable, crooked *colloq*, dishonest, fraudulent, rotten, shady *colloq*, unethical, unprincipled, unscrupulous, untrustworthy, venal **2** *a corrupt lifestyle:* degenerate, depraved, dissolute, evil, immoral, tainted, wicked
☒ **1** ethical, fair, honest, trustworthy **2** upright, virtuous
♦ *v* **1** *the judges had been corrupted:* bribe, buy (off) *colloq*, grease someone's palm *colloq*, suborn **2** *corrupt innocent children:* be a bad influence on, contaminate, debase, debauch, defile, deprave, lead astray *colloq*, pervert, pollute, taint, vitiate *formal*
☒ **2** purify

corruption *n* **1** *engage in fraud and corruption:* bribery, criminality, crookedness *colloq*, dishonesty, extortion, fraud, graft *US*, shadiness *colloq*, sharp practice, subornation, unscrupulousness, villainy, wheeling and dealing *colloq* **2** *the corruption of Charles II's court:* debauchery, degeneration, degradation, depravity, evil, immorality, impurity, iniquity, perversion, rottenness, vice, wickedness
☒ **1** fairness, honesty, trustworthiness **2** virtue

corset *n* basque, bodice, corselet, foundation garment, girdle, panty girdle, roll-on, stays

cortège *n* cavalcade, entourage, parade, procession, retinue, suite, train

cosmetic *adj* **1** *a cosmetic substance:* beautifying, beauty **2** *cosmetic changes:* external, minor, peripheral, shallow, slight, superficial, surface, trivial
☒ **2** basic, essential

cosmetics *n* make-up

Types of cosmetics include:
blusher, cleanser, eyebrow pencil, eyelash dye, eyeliner, eye shadow, face cream, face mask, face pack, face powder, false eyelashes, foundation, greasepaint, kohl pencil, lip gloss, lip liner, lipstick, loose powder, maquillage, mascara, moisturizer, nail polish, nail varnish, pancake make-up, pressed powder, rouge, toner, war paint *colloq*

---

cosmic *adj* **1** *cosmic forces:* in/from space, universal **2** *changes of cosmic proportion:* grandiose, huge, immeasurable, immense, infinite, limitless, measureless, vast

cosmonaut *n* astronaut, space traveller, spaceman, spacewoman

cosmopolitan *adj* **1** *a very cosmopolitan city:* international, multicultural, multiracial, universal **2** *a cosmopolitan outlook:* broad-minded, cultured, sophisticated, urbane, well-travelled, worldly, worldly-wise
☒ **2** insular, parochial

cosmos *n* creation, galaxy, solar system, universe, worlds

cosset *v* baby, coddle, indulge, mollycoddle, pamper, pet, spoil

cost *n* **1** *the cost of a product:* amount, asking price, charge, damage *colloq*, disbursement *formal*, expenditure, expense, fee, figure, outlay, payment, price, rate, selling price, valuation, value, worth **2** *cover costs:* budget, expenditure, expenses, outgoings, outlay, overheads, spending **3** *the cost to her health:* detriment, harm, hurt, injury, loss, penalty, price, sacrifice, suffering
♦ *v* **1** *it costs £500:* amount to, be priced at, be valued at, be worth, come to, fetch, go for, knock

you back *colloq*, pay, retail at, sell for, set you back *colloq* **2** *to cost a job*: calculate, cost out, estimate, price, quote, value, work out **3** *cost him his life*: cause harm/injury to, cause the loss/sacrifice of, deprive of, harm, hurt, injure

costly *adj* **1** *a costly service*: dear, excessive, exorbitant, expensive, high-cost, high-priced, pricey *colloq*, steep *colloq* **2** *beautiful and costly fabrics*: lavish, precious, priceless, rich, splendid, valuable **3** *a costly mistake*: catastrophic, damaging, deleterious *formal*, destructive, detrimental, disastrous, harmful, loss-making, ruinous
Ⅎ **1** cheap, inexpensive **2** cheap, inexpensive

costume *n* apparel *formal*, attire *formal*, clothes, clothing, dress, ensemble, fancy dress, garments, get-up *colloq*, habit, livery, outfit, robes, style of dress, uniform, vestments

cosy *adj* **1** *a cosy room*: comfortable, comfy *colloq*, homely, snug, warm **2** *safe and cosy in bed*: comfortable, comfy *colloq*, safe, secure, sheltered, snug, warm **3** *a cosy chat*: congenial, intimate
Ⅎ **1** cold, uncomfortable **2** cold, uncomfortable

coterie *n* association, cabal, camp, circle, clique, club, community, faction, gang, group, set

cottage *n* cabin, chalet, hut, lodge, shack

couch *n* bed, chaise-longue, chesterfield, day bed, divan, ottoman, settee, sofa, sofa bed
♦ *v* express, frame, phrase, set, utter, word

cough *v* bark, clear your throat, hack, hawk, hem
♦ *n* bark, clearing your throat, frog in your throat *colloq*, hack, hawking, hem, tussis *technical*
► **cough up** fork out *colloq*, give, pay, pay out, pay up, shell out *colloq*, stump up *colloq*

council *n* **1** *the town council*: administration, cabinet, governing body, government, local authority, ministry, parliament, senate **2** *the Arts Council*: advisers, advisory body, advisory group, board, commission, committee, directorate, directors, governors, jury, panel, trustees, working party **3** *a ministerial council*: assembly, body, body of people, company, conference, congregation, congress, convention, convocation *formal*, group, meeting, rally

council or *counsel*? A *council* is 'a body of people who organize, control, advise or take decisions': *a county council*. *Counsel* is a rather formal word for 'advice': *give wise counsel*.

counsel *n* **1** *she came to me for counsel*: admonition *formal*, advice, consultation, direction, exhortation *formal*, guidance, information, opinion, recommendation, suggestion **2** *counsel for the defence*: advocate, attorney, barrister, lawyer, solicitor
♦ *v* admonish *formal*, advise, advocate, caution, direct, exhort *formal*, give guidance, give your opinion, guide, instruct, recommend, suggest, urge, warn

count *v* **1** *count sheep*: add (up), calculate, check, compute, enumerate, number, reckon, score, tally, tell, tot up *colloq*, total **2** *that doesn't count*: be important, carry weight, cut some ice *colloq*, make a difference, matter, mean something,

qualify, signify **3** *count yourself lucky*: consider, deem *formal*, esteem *formal*, hold, judge, look upon, reckon, regard, think **4** *there are ten of us if you count the children*: allow for, include, take account of, take into account
♦ *n* **1** *there were twenty at the last count*: calculation, computation, enumeration, numbering, poll, reckoning, tally, totting-up *colloq* **2** *the final count of survivors is five*: full amount, sum, total, whole
► **count on** bank on, depend on, expect, lean on, reckon on, rely on, trust
► **count out** eliminate, exclude, include out, leave out, omit, pass over
Ⅎ consider, include

countenance *n* appearance, expression, face, features, look, mien *formal*, physiognomy *formal*, visage *formal*
♦ *v* allow, approve, brook, condone, endorse, endure, put up with, sanction, stand for, tolerate

counter[1] *n* **1** *serve at the counter*: stand, surface, table, work surface, worktop **2** *a counter in a game*: chip, coin, disc, marker, piece, token

counter[2] *v* **1** *counter a blow*: combat, hit back at, meet, parry, resist, retaliate, return **2** *counter someone's argument*: answer, dispute, hit back at, offset, oppose, respond, retaliate, retort, return
♦ *adv* against, contrary to, conversely, in opposition
♦ *adj* adverse, against, conflicting, contradictory, contrary, contrasting, opposed, opposing, opposite

counteract *v* **1** *measures to counteract an invasion*: act against, check, defeat, foil, frustrate, hinder, oppose, resist, thwart **2** *trying to counteract the effects*: annul, check, counterbalance, countervail *formal*, invalidate, negate *formal*, neutralize, offset, undo
Ⅎ **1** assist, support **2** assist, support

counterbalance *v* balance, compensate for, counterpoise *formal*, countervail *formal*, equalize, make up for, neutralize, offset, undo

counterfeit *adj* artificial, bogus, copied, fake, faked, false, feigned *formal*, forged, fraudulent, imitation, phoney *colloq*, pirate, pretended, pseud *colloq*, pseudo *colloq*, sham, simulated, spurious
Ⅎ authentic, genuine, real
♦ *n* copy, fake, forgery, fraud, imitation, reproduction, sham
♦ *v* copy, fabricate, fake, falsify, feign *formal*, forge, imitate, impersonate, pirate, pretend, reproduce, sham, simulate

countermand *v* abrogate *formal*, annul, cancel, override, overturn, quash, repeal, rescind *formal*, reverse, revoke *formal*

counterpart *n* equal, equivalent, fellow, match, mate, opposite number, parallel, twin

countless *adj* endless, immeasurable, incalculable, infinite, innumerable, limitless, measureless, myriad, numberless, umpteen *colloq*, unnumbered, untold, without end
Ⅎ finite, limited

countrified *adj* agrarian, agricultural, bucolic *formal*, hick *colloq*, pastoral, provincial, rural, rustic
Ⅎ oppidan *formal*, urban

country n 1 *the country of Germany:* kingdom, nation, power, principality, realm, republic, state 2 *the country will not put up with a dictator:* citizens, community, electors, inhabitants, people, populace, population, residents, voters 3 *live in the country:* back of beyond *colloq*, backwater *colloq*, backwoods *colloq*, bush, countryside, farmland, green belt, middle of nowhere *colloq*, moorland, outback, provinces *colloq*, rural area, sticks *colloq*, wilds *colloq* 4 *this is good farming country:* area, district, land, locality, neighbourhood, region, terrain, territory
Fa 3 city, town
♦ *adj* agrarian, agricultural, bucolic *formal*, pastoral, provincial, rural, rustic
Fa urban

countryman, countrywoman n 1 *my fellow countrywomen:* compatriot, fellow citizen, fellow national 2 *crafts practised by local countrymen:* backwoodsman, bumpkin *colloq*, bushwhacker, clodhopper, farmer, hayseed *colloq*, hick *colloq*, hillbilly *colloq*, hind *Scot*, peasant, provincial, rustic, yokel

countryside n country, farmland, green belt, moorland, outdoors, rural area

county n area, district, province, region, shire, state, territory

coup n 1 *a military coup:* coup d'état, (military) takeover, overthrow, palace revolution, putsch, rebellion, revolt, revolution, uprising 2 *a big coup for the company:* accomplishment, deed, exploit, feat, manoeuvre, masterstroke, stroke, stunt, tour de force

coup d'état n coup, (military) takeover, overthrow, palace revolution, putsch, rebellion, revolt, revolution, uprising

coup de grâce n clincher *colloq*, death blow, kibosh *colloq*, kiss of death *colloq*, quietus *formal*

couple n 1 *a couple of policemen:* brace, duo, pair 2 *they're a happy couple:* husband and wife, item *colloq*, lovers, newlyweds, pair, partners, twosome
♦ *v* 1 *the engine is coupled to a drive shaft:* attach, bind, buckle, clasp, conjoin *formal*, connect, fasten, hitch, join, link, unite, yoke 2 *illness coupled with extreme exhaustion:* ally, combine, join, link, unite

coupon n certificate, check, slip, ticket, token, voucher

courage n audacity, backbone, boldness, bottle *colloq*, bravery, daring, dauntlessness, fearlessness, fortitude *formal*, gallantry, grit *colloq*, guts *colloq*, heroism, intrepidity, mettle, nerve *colloq*, pluck, spirit, spunk *colloq*, valour
Fa cowardice, fear

courageous adj adventurous, audacious, bold, brave, daring, dauntless, fearless, gallant, gutsy *colloq*, hardy, heroic, indomitable, intrepid, lion-hearted, plucky, spunky *colloq*, stout-hearted, valiant, valorous *formal*
Fa afraid, cowardly

courier n 1 *the courier delivered the parcels:* bearer, carrier, dispatch rider, emissary, envoy, estafette, herald, legate, messenger, nuncio, pursuivant, runner 2 *a guided tour by the courier:* company representative, escort, guide, tour guide, travel guide

course n 1 *a university course:* classes, curriculum, lectures, lessons, programme, schedule, studies, syllabus 2 *the course of events:* advance, development, flow, furtherance, march, movement, order, progress, progression, sequence, series, succession, unfolding 3 *during the course of the evening:* duration, lapse, passage, passing, period, span, spell, term, time 4 *follow a course:* ambit, channel, circuit, direction, flight path, lane, line, orbit, passage, path, road, route, run, tack, track, trail, trajectory, way 5 *course of action:* approach, manner, method, mode *formal*, plan, policy, procedure, process, programme, schedule, system, tack, way 6 *I always do well at this course:* circuit, golf course, ground, racecourse, racetrack, track 7 *ordered chicken for the second course:* afters *colloq*, appetizer, dessert, dish, entrée, entremets, hors d'oeuvres, main course, part, pudding, remove, stage, starters, sweet 8 *a course of medical treatment:* programme, regimen, schedule, sequence, series
♦ *v* 1 *water coursing down the cliff:* dash, flow, gush, move, pour, run, stream, surge 2 *coursing hares:* chase, follow, hunt, pursue, race, run after, track

court n 1 *a federal court:* assizes, bar, bench, judiciary, lawcourt, session, trial, tribunal 2 *tennis courts:* alley, arena, enclosure, game area, green, ground, playing area, ring, track 3 *a court within the castle grounds:* cloister, courtyard, enclosure, esplanade, forecourt, patio, plaza, quad *colloq*, quadrangle, square, yard 4 *banished from the royal court:* castle, palace, royal residence 5 *King James and his court:* attendants, cortège, entourage, household, retinue, suite, train
♦ *v* 1 *court a young lady:* date *colloq*, go out with, go steady with *colloq*, go with, woo 2 *courting publicity:* cultivate, seek, solicit, try to win 3 *court trouble:* attract, incite, invite, prompt, provoke

---

Types of court include:
Admiralty Division, assizes, Central Criminal Court, Chancery Division, children's court, circuit court, civil court, coroner's court, county court, court-martial, court of appeals, court of claims, Court of Common Pleas, Court of Exchequer, court of justice, Court of Protection, Court of Session, criminal court, crown court, district court, divorce court, European Court of Justice, family court, federal court, High Court, High Court of Justiciary, House of Lords, industrial tribunal, International Court of Justice, juvenile court, Lord Chancellor's Court, magistrates' court, municipal court, Old Bailey, police court, Privy Council, sheriff court, small claims court, Supreme Court

---

courteous adj chivalrous, civil, courtly, debonair, gallant, gentlemanly, gracious, ladylike, mannerly, polite, respectful, urbane, well-bred, well-mannered
Fa discourteous, impolite, rude

courtesy n chivalry, civility, gallantry, (good) breeding, (good) manners, graciousness, kindness, politeness, respect, urbanity
Fa discourtesy, rudeness

courtier n attendant, follower, lady, lady-in-waiting, liegeman, lord, noble, nobleman, page, steward, train-bearer

courtly *adj* aristocratic, ceremonious, chivalrous, civil, decorous, dignified, elegant, formal, gallant, gracious, high-bred, lordly, polished, polite, refined, stately
▨ inelegant, provincial, rough

courtship *n* affair, courting, dating, going steady, going-out, romance, wooing

courtyard *n* area, atrium, cloister, court, enclosure, esplanade, forecourt, patio, plaza, quad *colloq*, quadrangle, square, yard

cove *n* bay, bight, creek, estuary, fiord, firth, inlet

covenant *n* **1** *break a covenant*: arrangement, commitment, compact *formal*, concordat *formal*, convention, engagement, pact, pledge, promise, stipulation, treaty, trust, undertaking **2** *a tax covenant*: bond, contract, deed, indenture *formal*
♦ *v* agree, contract, engage, pledge, promise, stipulate, undertake

cover *v* **1** *cover with a blanket*: bury, camouflage, conceal, disguise, hide, mask, obscure, screen, shroud, veil, wreathe **2** *his boots were covered with mud*: cake, coat, daub, encase, envelop, plaster, spread **3** *clouds covered the moon*: be over, blanket, overlay **4** *she covered her head with a veil*: accoutre *formal*, attire *formal*, clothe, swaddle, wrap **5** *cover me while I run for the exit*: defend, guard, protect, safeguard, shelter, shield **6** *the new law covers three main areas*: comprise, contain, embody, embrace, encompass, include, incorporate, involve, take in **7** *her talk covered several topics*: consider, deal with, describe, examine, give details of, review, survey, treat **8** *he was sent to cover the story*: investigate, report on, review **9** *cover 25 miles*: cross, do, go, go across, journey, travel (over), traverse *formal* **10** *cover for a colleague*: be a replacement/substitute for, deputize, relieve, replace, stand in for, take over from **11** *the estate covers some 500 acres*: continue, extend over, measure, stretch **12** *£50 to cover expenses*: be enough for, make up for, pay for, recompense **13** *the insurance will cover it*: indemnify *formal*, insure, protect, provide for
▨ **1** uncover **4** strip **5** expose **6** exclude **7** exclude
♦ *n* **1** *find cover at their house*: concealment, defence, guard, hiding-place, protection, refuge, sanctuary, shelter, shield **2** *huddle under the covers*: bedclothes, bedspread, blankets, covering, duvet **3** *protect it with a cover*: binding, canopy, cap, case, coat, coating, covering, envelope, film, jacket, layer, lid, mantle, skin, top, wrapper **4** *as a cover for illegal activity*: camouflage, concealment, cover-up, disguise, façade, front, mask, pretence, screen, smokescreen, veil, whitewash *colloq* **5** *insurance cover*: assurance, compensation, indemnification *formal*, indemnity *formal*, insurance, protection
▶ **cover up** conceal, dissemble *formal*, gloss over, hide, hush up *colloq*, keep dark, keep secret, repress, suppress, whitewash *colloq*
▨ disclose, reveal

coverage *n* account, analysis, description, investigation, item, report(s), reportage, reporting, story

covering *n* blanket, case, casing, clothing, coat, coating, cover, crust, film, housing, layer, overlay, protection, roof, roofing, shell, shelter, skin, top, veneer, wrapping

♦ *adj* accompanying, descriptive, explanatory, introductory

covert *adj* clandestine, concealed, disguised, hidden, private, secret, sidelong, sneaky, stealthy, subreptitious *formal*, surreptitious, under the table *colloq*, underhand, veiled
▨ open

cover-up *n* concealment, façade, front, pretence, screen, smokescreen, whitewash *colloq*

covet *v* begrudge, crave, desire, envy, fancy *colloq*, hanker for, hunger/thirst for, long for, lust after, want, yearn for

covetous *adj* acquisitive, avaricious *formal*, craving, desirous *formal*, envious, grasping, greedy, hankering, hungering, jealous, longing, rapacious *formal*, thirsting, wanting, yearning

covey *n* bevy, cluster, flight, flock, group, nid, skein

cow *v* browbeat, bully, daunt, domineer, frighten, intimidate, scare, subdue, terrorize, unnerve
▨ encourage

coward *n* chicken *colloq*, craven, cry-baby *colloq*, faint-heart, poltroon, recreant *old use*, scaredy-cat *colloq*, sissy *colloq*, sook *Austral colloq*, wimp *colloq*, yellow-belly *colloq*
▨ hero

cowardice *n* cowardliness, faint-heartedness, pusillanimity *formal*, spinelessness, timorousness
▨ bravery, courage, valour

cowardly *adj* chicken *colloq*, chicken-hearted, chicken-livered, craven, faint-hearted, fearful, gutless *colloq*, lily-livered *colloq*, pusillanimous *formal*, scared, soft, spineless, timorous, unheroic, weak, weak-kneed, wimpish *colloq*, yellow *colloq*, yellow-bellied *colloq*
▨ audacious, bold, brave, courageous, daring, doughty, intrepid, valiant

cowboy *n* **1** *cowboys to look after cattle*: bronco-buster *US*, buckaroo, cattleherder, cattleman, cowhand, cowpoke, cowpuncher, drover, gaucho, herder, herdsman, rancher, ranchero, stockman, vaquero, waddy, wrangler **2** *that builder was a real cowboy*: bungler, incompetent, nonprofessional, rogue
▨ **2** professional

cower *v* cringe, crouch, draw back, flinch, recoil, shrink

coy *adj* **1** *a coy smile*: arch, bashful, coquettish, demure, diffident, flirtatious, kittenish, modest, prim, prudish, retiring, self-effacing, shrinking, shy, skittish **2** *coy about his future plans*: evasive, reserved, reticent, withdrawn
▨ **1** bold, forward

crabbed, crabby *adj* awkward, bad-tempered, cantankerous, captious, churlish, cross, crotchety *colloq*, difficult, fretful, grouchy *colloq*, ill-tempered, iracund *formal*, iracundulous *formal*, irascible *formal*, irritable, misanthropic *formal*, perverse, prickly *colloq*, snappish, snappy, sour, splenetic *formal*, surly, testy
▨ calm, placid

crack *v* **1** *crack your skull*: break, burst, fracture, fragment, shatter, snap, splinter, split **2** *fireworks cracked overhead*: bang, boom, burst, clap, crackle, crash, detonate, explode, go bang, pop, snap

3 *she cracked him on the head:* bang, bash, bump, clout *colloq*, hit, slap, wallop *colloq*, whack *colloq* **4** *crack under pressure:* break down, collapse, go to pieces, lose control **5** *crack a code:* decipher, figure out, find the answer to, solve, unravel, work out
♦ *n* **1** *a crack in the window pane:* breach, break, cavity, chink, cleft, cranny, crevice, fissure, flaw, fracture, gap, line, rift, rupture, split **2** *with a loud crack:* bang, boom, burst, clap, crash, detonation, explosion, pop, report *formal*, snap **3** *a crack on the jaw:* bang, blow, bump, clap, clout *colloq*, hit, slap, smack, whack *colloq* **4** *have a crack at something:* attempt, bash *colloq*, go, shot *colloq*, stab *colloq*, try, whirl *colloq* **5** *a nasty crack about her weight:* dig *colloq*, gag *colloq*, gibe, joke, one-liner, quip, repartee, wisecrack, witticism
♦ *adj* brilliant, choice, excellent, expert, first-class, first-rate, hand-picked, outstanding, superior, top-notch *colloq*
▶ **crack down on** act against, check, clamp down on, crush, end, put a stop to, repress, stop, suppress
▶ **crack up** break down, collapse, go mad, go to pieces, have a nervous breakdown

crackdown *n* clampdown, crushing, end, repression, stop, suppression

cracked *adj* **1** *a cracked glass:* broken, damaged, defective, faulty, fissured, flawed, imperfect, split **2** *you're cracked if you believe that:* barmy *colloq*, batty *colloq*, crackbrained *colloq*, crackpot *colloq*, crazed, crazy, daft *colloq*, deranged, insane, loony *colloq*, nuts *colloq*, nutty *colloq*, off your rocker *colloq*, round the bend *colloq*
✎ **1** flawless, perfect **2** sane

crackers *adj* batty *colloq*, crackbrained *colloq*, cracked, crackpot *colloq*, crazy, daft *colloq*, loony *colloq*, mad, nuts *colloq*, nutty *colloq*, round the bend *colloq*
✎ sane

crackle *v* crack, crepitate *formal*, decrepitate *formal*, rustle, sizzle, snap
♦ *n* crack, crepitation *formal*, crepitus *formal*, decrepitation *formal*, rustle, sizzle, snap

crackpot *n* freak *colloq*, loony *colloq*, nutter *colloq*, oddball *colloq*, weirdo *colloq*

cradle *n* **1** *a baby's cradle:* bassinet, bed, carry-cot, cot, crib, travel-cot **2** *the cradle of civilization:* beginning, birthplace, fount, fountain-head, origin, source, spring, starting-point, wellspring
♦ *v* hold, nestle, nurse, rock, support

craft *n* **1** *a book written with craft and wit:* ability, aptitude, art, artistry, cleverness, dexterity, expertise, expertness, flair, knack, mastery, skilfulness, skill, talent, technique, workmanship **2** *he knew his craft:* business, calling, employment, job, line, occupation, pursuit, trade, vocation, work **3** *the craft was low on fuel:* aircraft, boat, landing craft, ship, spacecraft, spaceship, vessel

craftsman, craftswoman *n* artisan, artist, expert, maker, master, skilled worker, smith, technician, wright

craftsmanship *n* artistry, dexterity, expertise, mastery, skill, technique, workmanship

crafty *adj* artful, astute, calculating, canny, conniving, cunning, designing, devious, foxy, scheming, sharp, shrewd, sly, subtle, wily
✎ artless, guileless, naïve

crag *n* bluff, cliff, escarpment, peak, pinnacle, ridge, rock, scarp, tor

craggy *adj* **1** *a craggy cliff:* cragged, jagged, rocky, rough, rugged, stony, uneven **2** *a craggy face:* jagged, rough, rugged, uneven
✎ **2** smooth

cram *v* **1** *cram sweets into your mouth:* compact *formal*, compress, force, jam, pack, press, ram, squeeze, stuff **2** *cram a bag full of clothes:* fill (up), overfill, pack, stuff **3** *they all crammed into the phone box:* crowd, crush, jam, overcrowd, pack, press, squeeze **4** *cram for an exam:* bone up *colloq*, grind *colloq*, mug up *colloq*, revise, study hard, swot *colloq*

cramp *n* ache, contraction, convulsion, crick, muscular contraction, pain, pang, spasm, stiffness, stitch, twinge
♦ *v* confine, constrain, hamper, hamstring, handicap, hinder, impede, inhibit, limit, obstruct, restrain, restrict, shackle

cramped *adj* closed in, confined, congested, crowded, full, hemmed in, jam-packed, narrow, overcrowded, overfull, packed, poky *colloq*, restricted, squashed, squeezed, tight, uncomfortable
✎ spacious

crane *n* block and tackle, davit, derrick, hoist, tackle, winch

crank *n* character, crackpot *colloq*, eccentric, freak *colloq*, loony *colloq*, madman, nutter *colloq*, oddball *colloq*, weirdo *colloq*

cranky *adj* **1** *a cranky new age cult:* bizarre, dotty *colloq*, eccentric, freakish, idiosyncratic, odd, peculiar, strange, unconventional, wacky *colloq* **2** *a cranky old woman:* awkward, bad-tempered, cantankerous, crabby *colloq*, cross, crotchety *colloq*, difficult, ill-tempered, irritable, prickly *colloq*, snappy, surly, tart, testy
✎ **1** normal, sensible **2** calm, placid

cranny *n* chink, cleavage, cleft, crack, crevice, fissure, gap, hole, interstice *formal*, nook, opening

crash *n* **1** *a car crash:* accident, bump, collision, pile-up, prang *colloq*, smash *colloq*, smash-up *colloq*, wreck **2** *a loud crash:* bang, boom, clang, clank, clash, clatter, din, explosion, racket, smash, thud, thump, thunder **3** *stock-market crash:* bankruptcy, collapse, depression, downfall, failure, fall, ruin
♦ *v* **1** *crash into a tree:* bang, bump, collide, drive into, go into, hit, knock, plough into, run into, smash into **2** *the glass crashed into pieces:* break, dash, disintegrate, fragment, shatter, shiver, smash, splinter **3** *the stock market crashed:* collapse, fail, fall, fold (up), founder, go bust *colloq*, go into liquidation, go to the wall *colloq*, go under, pitch, plunge, topple **4** *the computer crashed:* break down, cut out, fail, go on the blink *colloq*, malfunction *formal*, pack up *colloq*, stop working
♦ *adj* accelerated, concentrated, emergency, intensive, rapid, round-the-clock, urgent

crass *adj* blundering, coarse, crude, indelicate, insensitive, oafish, obtuse *formal*, rude, stupid, tactless, unrefined, unsophisticated, unsubtle, witless
✎ refined, sensitive

crate *n* box, case, container, packing-box, packing-case, tea chest

crater *n* cavity, depression, dip, hole, hollow, pit

crave *v* be dying for *colloq*, covet, desire, dream of, fancy *colloq*, hanker after, hunger for, long for, lust after, need, pant for, pine for, sigh for, thirst for, want, wish, yearn for
🖃 dislike

craven *adj* afraid, chicken *colloq*, chicken-hearted, chicken-livered, cowardly, faint-hearted, fearful, gutless *colloq*, lily-livered, mean-spirited, poltroon *old use*, pusillanimous *formal*, recreant *old use*, scared, soft, spineless, timorous, unheroic, weak-kneed, yellow *colloq*
🖃 bold, brave, courageous

craving *n* appetite, desire, hankering, hunger, longing, lust, panting, pining, sighing, thirst, urge, wish, yearning
🖃 dislike, distaste

crawl *v* 1 *the baby crawled along the floor:* creep, drag, go on all fours, move on your hands and knees, move/advance slowly, slither, squirm, wriggle 2 *I'll apologize but I won't crawl to him:* be all over *colloq*, bow and scrape, creep *colloq*, cringe, curry favour, fawn, flatter, grovel, suck up *colloq*, toady 3 *the city centre is crawling with police:* be full of, bristle, seethe, swarm, teem

craze *n* enthusiasm, fad, fashion, frenzy, infatuation, mania, mode, novelty, obsession, passion, preoccupation, rage *colloq*, the latest *colloq*, thing *colloq*, trend, vogue

crazed *adj* berserk, crazy, demented, deranged, insane, loony *colloq*, lunatic, mad, nuts *colloq*, off your rocker *colloq*, out of your mind, round the bend *colloq*, round the twist *colloq*, unbalanced, unhinged, wild

crazy *adj* 1 *go crazy with fear:* berserk, bonkers *colloq*, crazed, demented, deranged, disturbed, doolally *colloq*, having lost your marbles *colloq*, having several cards short of a full deck *colloq*, insane, loony *colloq*, loopy *colloq*, lunatic, mad, needing your head examining *colloq*, not all there *colloq*, nuts *colloq*, nutty *colloq*, nutty as a fruitcake *colloq*, off your rocker *colloq*, out of your mind, out to lunch *colloq*, round the bend *colloq*, round the twist *colloq*, unbalanced, unhinged, wild, with one sandwich short of a picnic *colloq* 2 *what a crazy idea!:* absurd, barmy *colloq*, batty *colloq*, crackbrained *colloq*, crackpot *colloq*, daft *colloq*, foolhardy, foolish, half-baked *colloq*, hare-brained *colloq*, idiotic, impracticable, ludicrous, nonsensical, outrageous, peculiar, potty *colloq*, preposterous, ridiculous, senseless, silly, stupid, unrealistic, unwise, wild 3 *crazy about golf:* ardent, avid, daft *colloq*, devoted, enamoured, enthusiastic, fanatical, fond, infatuated, keen, mad, nuts *colloq*, passionate, smitten, wild, zealous
🖃 1 sane 2 sensible 3 indifferent

creak *v* grate, grind, groan, rasp, scrape, scratch, screech, squeak, squeal

creaky *adj* grating, grinding, groaning, rasping, rusty, scraping, scratching, screeching, squeaking, squeaky, squealing, unoiled

cream *n* 1 *face cream:* cosmetic, emollient *technical*, emulsion, liniment, lotion, oil, ointment, paste, salve, unguent 2 *the cream of the crop:* best, choice/select part, crème de la crème, elite, flower, pick, pick of the bunch, prime
♦ *adj* off-white, pale, pasty, whitish-yellow, yellowish-white

creamy *adj* 1 *a creamy suit:* cream-coloured, off-white, pale, pasty, whitish-yellow, yellowish-white 2 *a creamy sauce:* buttery, milky, oily, rich, smooth, thick, velvety

crease *v* corrugate, crimp, crinkle, crumple, fold, furrow, groove, pleat, pucker, ridge, rumple, tuck, wrinkle
♦ *n* corrugation, crinkle, fold, furrow, groove, line, pleat, pucker, ridge, ruck, tuck, wrinkle
▶ **crease up** amuse, have rolling in the aisles *colloq*, make laugh, make someone fall about *colloq*, make someone split their sides *colloq*

create *v* 1 *create a new work:* bring into being, bring into existence, build, coin, compose, concoct, construct, design, develop, devise, engender, erect, fabricate, form, formulate, found, frame, generate, give rise to, hatch, initiate, invent, make, mould, originate, produce, shape 2 *create problems:* bring about, cause, cause to happen, engender, give rise to, lead to, occasion, produce, result in 3 *create a new position in the department:* appoint, establish, found, inaugurate, install, institute, invent, invest, ordain, set up
🖃 1 destroy

creation *n* 1 *the creation of a new work:* birth, conception, concoction, construction, development, fabrication, formation, generation, genesis *formal*, invention, making, origination, production 2 *the creation of the welfare state:* constitution, construction, development, establishment, formation, foundation, initiation, institution 3 *the whole of creation:* cosmos, everything, life, nature, universe, world 4 *it's his own creation:* achievement, brainchild, chef d'oeuvre, composition, concept, design, handiwork, innovation, invention, masterpiece, pièce de résistance, product, work, work of art
🖃 1 destruction

creative *adj* artistic, clever, fertile, full of ideas, gifted, imaginative, ingenious, inspired, intuitive, inventive, original, productive, resourceful, talented, visionary
🖃 unimaginative

creativity *n* artistry, cleverness, fertility, imagination, imaginativeness, ingenuity, inspiration, inventiveness, originality, productiveness, resourcefulness, vision
🖃 unimaginativeness

creator *n* 1 *the creator of the movement:* architect, author, builder, composer, designer, father, founder, initiator, inventor, mother, originator, producer 2 *the Creator of the universe:* first cause, God, Maker, prime mover

creature *n* 1 *a creature of the forest:* animal, beast, being, bird, fish, insect, living thing, organism 2 *he's a harmless enough creature:* being, body, human, human being, individual, man, mortal, person, soul, woman

credence *n* 1 *give credence to a theory:* believability, credibility, credit, plausibility, support 2 *I have little credence in this report:* belief, confidence, dependence, faith, reliance, trust
🖃 2 distrust

credentials n 1 *he certainly has the credentials for the job:* ability, capability, qualifications, skills, suitability 2 *asked to see his credentials:* accreditation *formal*, authorization, certificate, deed, diploma, documents, identity card, licence, papers, passport, permit, proof of identity, reference, testimonial, warrant

credibility n 1 *the credibility of the story:* likelihood, plausibility, probability, reasonableness, reliability, trustworthiness 2 *he has lost all his credibility:* integrity, plausibility, reliability, trustworthiness
🖅 1 implausibility

credible adj 1 *a credible explanation:* believable, conceivable, convincing, imaginable, likely, persuasive, plausible, possible, probable, reasonable, tenable, thinkable, with a ring of truth *colloq* 2 *a credible witness:* believable, convincing, dependable, honest, reliable, sincere, trustworthy
🖅 1 implausible, incredible, unbelievable
2 unreliable

> *credible, creditable* or *credulous*? *Credible* means 'believable, even if untrue': *a credible theory. Creditable* means 'worthy of praise or respect': *a very creditable performance. Credulous* means 'too easily fooled': *Only the most credulous of voters would believe all the party's election promises.*

credit n 1 *get the credit for his success:* acclaim, acknowledgement, approval, commendation, laudation *formal*, praise, recognition, thanks, tribute 2 *he is a credit to his parents:* asset, boast, feather in your cap *colloq*, glory, honour, pride, pride and joy *colloq* 3 *he lost credit because of his actions:* distinction, esteem, estimation, honour, prestige, reputation 4 *give a story no credit:* belief, confidence, credence, faith, trust 5 *be in credit:* the black *colloq* 6 *buy on credit:* deferred payment, hire purchase, the never-never *colloq*, the slate *colloq*, the tab *colloq*, tick *colloq*
🖅 1 blame, discredit, shame 5 insolvency, overdraft, the red *colloq*
♦ v 1 *credited with the invention:* accredit *formal*, ascribe, assign, attribute, charge, impute *formal*, put down 2 *the reports are difficult to credit:* accept, believe, buy *colloq*, fall for *colloq*, have faith in, rely on, subscribe to, swallow *colloq*, trust
🖅 2 disbelieve

creditable adj admirable, commendable, estimable, excellent, exemplary, good, honourable, laudable *formal*, meritorious *formal*, praiseworthy, respectable, worthy
🖅 blameworthy, shameful

creditor n debtee *formal*, lender, person/business you owe money to
🖅 debtor

credulity n credulousness, dupability, gullibility, naïvety, uncriticalness
🖅 scepticism

credulous adj dupable, gullible, naïve, overtrusting, trusting, uncritical, unsuspecting, wide-eyed
🖅 sceptical, suspicious

> *credulous, credible* or *creditable*? See panel at **credible**

creed n articles, belief, canon, catechism, credo, doctrine, dogma, faith, persuasion, principles, teaching, tenets

creek n bay, bight, cove, estuary, fiord, firth, inlet

creep v crawl, edge, inch, slink, slither, sneak, squirm, steal, tiptoe, worm, wriggle, writhe
♦ n 1 *you little creep!:* bootlicker *colloq*, fawner, sneak, sycophant, toady, yes-man *colloq* 2 *gave me the creeps:* disquiet, fear, horror, revulsion, terror, unease

creeper n climber, climbing plant, liana, rambler, runner, trailer, trailing plant, trailing vine

creepy adj disturbing, eerie, frightening, hair-raising, horrible, horrifying, macabre, menacing, nightmarish, ominous, scary *colloq*, sinister, spine-chilling, spooky *colloq*, terrifying, threatening, unpleasant, weird

crescent-shaped adj bow-shaped, falcate *formal*, falcated *formal*, falciform *formal*, lunate *formal*, lunated *formal*, lunular *formal*, sickle-shaped

crest n 1 *the crest of the hill:* apex *formal*, crown, head, peak, pinnacle, ridge, summit, top 2 *a bird's crest:* aigrette, caruncle, cockscomb, comb, mane, panache, plume, tassel, tuft 3 *the family crest:* badge, coat of arms, device, emblem, insignia, regalia, symbol

crestfallen adj cheesed off *colloq*, dejected, depressed, despondent, disappointed, disconsolate *formal*, discouraged, disheartened, dispirited, down in the dumps *colloq*, downcast, downhearted, sad
🖅 elated

crevasse n abyss, bergschrund, chasm, cleft, crack, fissure, gap

crevice n break, chink, cleft, crack, cranny, fissure, gap, hole, interstice *formal*, opening, rift, slit, split

crew n 1 *the ship's crew:* company, complement 2 *a building crew:* company, corps, force, squad, team, troop, unit 3 *hanging out with a rough crew:* band, bunch, gang, group, lot, mob, pack, set

crib n bassinet, bed, carry-cot, cot, travel-cot
♦ v cheat, copy, lift *colloq*, pinch *colloq*, pirate, plagiarize, purloin *formal*, steal

crick n convulsion, cramp, pain, spasm, stiffness, twinge

crier n announcer, bearer of tidings, herald, messenger, proclaimer, town crier

crime n 1 *commit a crime:* atrocity, felony, illegal act, malfeasance *formal*, misdeed, misdemeanour, offence, outrage, sin, transgression, unlawful act, violation 2 *moves to combat crime:* delinquency, iniquity, law-breaking, lawlessness, malfeasance *formal*, misconduct, sin, vice, villainy, wickedness, wrongdoing

> **Crimes include:**
> theft, robbery, burglary, larceny, pilfering, mugging, poaching; assault, rape, grievous bodily harm, GBH *colloq*, battery, manslaughter, homicide, murder, assassination; fraud, bribery, corruption, embezzlement, extortion, blackmail; arson,

treason, terrorism, hijack, piracy, computer hacking, kidnapping, stalking, sabotage, vandalism, hooliganism, criminal damage, drug-smuggling, forgery, counterfeiting, perjury, joy-riding, drink-driving, drunk and disorderly

criminal *n* convict, culprit, delinquent, felon, law-breaker, malefactor *formal*, miscreant, offender, villain, wrongdoer
♦ *adj* **1** *a criminal action:* bent *colloq*, corrupt, crooked *colloq*, culpable *formal*, dishonest, evil, felonious *formal*, illegal, illicit, indictable, iniquitous, law-breaking, lawless, nefarious *formal*, unlawful, villainous, wicked, wrong **2** *a criminal waste:* deplorable, disgraceful, disgusting, infamous, obscene *colloq*, outrageous, reprehensible, scandalous, shameful
Fa 1 honest, lawful, legal, upright

crimp *v* corrugate, crease, crinkle, crumple, flute, fold, furrow, gather, groove, pleat, pucker, ridge, rumple, tuck, wrinkle

cringe *v* **1** *the sight made me cringe:* blench, cower, draw back, flinch, quail, recoil, shrink, shy, start, tremble, wince **2** *I hate the way he cringes to his superiors:* bow and scrape, crawl *colloq*, creep *colloq*, curry favour, fawn, flatter, grovel, suck up *colloq*, toady

crinkle *n* corrugation, crease, fold, furrow, groove, line, pleat, pucker, ridge, ruck, ruffle, rumple, tuck, wave, wrinkle
♦ *v* corrugate, crease, crimp, crumple, fold, furrow, groove, pleat, pucker, ridge, rumple, tuck, wrinkle

crinkly *adj* corrugated, creased, crimped, crinkled, crumpled, fluted, folded, furrowed, gathered, grooved, kinky, pleated, puckered, ridged, rumpled, tucked, wrinkled, wrinkly
Fa smooth, straight

cripple *v* **1** *crippled by the accident:* debilitate *formal*, disable, hamstring, handicap, incapacitate *formal*, injure, lame, maim, mutilate, paralyse, weaken **2** *this will cripple the country's economy:* damage, destroy, hamper, impair, impede, ruin, sabotage, spoil, vitiate *formal*

crippled *adj* disabled, handicapped, incapacitated *formal*, lame, paralysed

crisis *n* calamity, catastrophe, critical situation, difficulty, dilemma, disaster, emergency, exigency *formal*, extremity, fix *colloq*, hole *colloq*, hot water *colloq*, jam *colloq*, mess *colloq*, predicament, quandary, trouble

crisp *adj* **1** *a crisp biscuit:* brittle, crispy, crumbly, crunchy, firm, friable *formal*, hard **2** *crisp air:* bracing, brisk, chilly, cool, fresh, invigorating, refreshing **3** *a crisp reply:* brief, clear, incisive, pithy, short, snappy *colloq*, succinct, terse
Fa 1 flabby, limp, soggy **2** muggy **3** vague, wordy

criterion *n* benchmark, canon, exemplar *formal*, gauge, measure, model, norm, principle, rule, scale, standard, test, touchstone, yardstick

critic *n* **1** *a music critic:* analyst, authority, commentator, expert, judge, pundit, reviewer **2** *a critic of the government:* attacker, backbiter *colloq*, carper *colloq*, censor, censurer, fault-finder, judge, knocker *colloq*, nit-picker *colloq*

critical *adj* **1** *at a critical stage:* all-important, climacteric *formal*, crucial, deciding, decisive, essential, exigent *formal*, fateful, historic, important, major, momentous, pivotal, serious, urgent, vital **2** *in a critical condition:* dangerous, grave, perilous *formal*, precarious, serious **3** *a critical remark:* captious, carping, cavilling *colloq*, censorious, derogatory, disapproving, disparaging, fault-finding, hypercritical, judgemental, niggling, nit-picking *colloq*, quibbling, scathing, uncomplimentary, vituperative *formal* **4** *a critical look:* analytical, diagnostic, discerning, evaluative, penetrating, perceptive, probing
Fa 1 unimportant **3** appreciative, complimentary

criticism *n* **1** *scathing criticism:* animadversion *formal*, brickbat *colloq*, censure, condemnation, disapproval, disparagement, fault-finding, flak *colloq*, knocking *colloq*, niggle *colloq*, nit-picking *colloq*, slamming *colloq*, slating *colloq*, stick *colloq* **2** *media criticism:* analysis, appraisal, appreciation, assessment, commentary, critique, evaluation, judgement, review, write-up
Fa 1 commendation, praise

criticize *v* **1** *many people criticized him for his actions:* animadvert *formal*, attack, badmouth *colloq*, censure, come down on *colloq*, condemn, decry *formal*, denigrate *formal*, denounce, disapprove of, disparage, do a hatchet job on *colloq*, excoriate *formal*, find fault with, give someone some stick *colloq*, go to town on *colloq*, haul over the coals *colloq*, knock *colloq*, nag *colloq*, nit-pick *colloq*, pan *colloq*, pick holes in *colloq*, pull to pieces *colloq*, put the boot in *colloq*, rubbish *colloq*, run down *colloq*, slag off *colloq*, slam *colloq*, slate *colloq*, snipe *colloq*, tear a strip off *colloq*, tear to shreds *colloq*, vituperate *formal* **2** *he criticizes films for the Chicago Tribune:* analyse, appraise, assess, evaluate, judge, review
Fa 1 commend, praise

critique *n* analysis, appraisal, appreciation, assessment, commentary, essay, evaluation, judgement, review, write-up

croak *v* **1** *the raven croaked:* caw, squawk **2** *'Help me!' he croaked:* gasp, grunt, rasp, speak harshly, wheeze

crock *n* jar, pot, vessel

crockery *n* china, dishes, earthenware, porcelain, pottery, stoneware, tableware

croft *n* farm, farmland, plot, smallholding

crony *n* accomplice, ally, associate, buddy *colloq*, chum *colloq*, colleague, companion, comrade, friend, mate *colloq*, pal *colloq*, sidekick *colloq*

crook *n* cheat, con man *colloq*, criminal, fraud, law-breaker, robber, rogue, shark *colloq*, swindler, thief, villain
♦ *v* angle, bend, bow, curve, flex, hook

crooked *adj* **1** *a crooked line:* bent, bowed, curved, uneven **2** *the picture is crooked:* angled, askew, asymmetric, awry, lopsided, off-centre, skew-whiff *colloq*, slanting, tilted, uneven **3** *crooked limbs:* bent, bowed, buckled, contorted, deformed, distorted, misshapen, twisted, warped **4** *crooked streets:* anfractuous *formal*, tortuous, winding, zigzag **5** *crooked business practices:* bent *colloq*, corrupt, criminal, deceitful, dishonest, fraudulent, illegal, illicit, nefarious *formal*, shady *colloq*, shifty, underhand, unethical, unlawful, unprincipled, unscrupulous

F₃ 1 straight **2** straight **3** straight **4** straight **5** honest

croon *v* hum, lilt, sing, vocalize, warble

crop *n* **1** *grow crops*: fruits, gathering, growth, harvest, produce, reaping, vintage, yield **2** *this year's crop of graduates*: batch, collection, group, lot, set
♦ *v* clip, cut, lop, mow, pare, prune, shear, shorten, snip, trim

▶ **crop up** appear, arise, come to pass, come up, emerge, happen, occur, present itself, take place

cross *n* **1** *we all have our crosses to bear*: adversity, affliction *formal*, burden, grief, load, misery, misfortune, pain, suffering, trial, tribulation *formal*, trouble, woe, worry **2** *a cross between a horse and a donkey*: amalgam, blend, combination, crossbreed, hybrid, mix, mixture, mongrel
♦ *v* **1** *cross the river*: bridge, ford, go across, pass over, span, travel across, traverse *formal* **2** *the point where the roads cross*: converge, criss-cross, intersect, intertwine, interweave, join, meet **3** *cross animals*: blend, crossbreed, cross-fertilize, cross-pollinate, hybridize, interbreed, mix, mongrelize **4** *I wouldn't want to cross her*: block, check, foil, frustrate, hamper, hinder, impede, obstruct, oppose, resist, thwart
♦ *adj* **1** *a cross old woman*: angry, annoyed, bad-tempered, cantankerous, crabby *colloq*, crotchety *colloq*, fractious, fretful, grouchy *colloq*, grumpy, ill-tempered, impatient, irascible, irritable, peeved *colloq*, prickly *colloq*, put out, shirty *colloq*, short, snappish, snappy, splenetic *formal*, sullen, surly, vexed **2** *a cross street*: crosswise, diagonal, intersecting, oblique, opposite, transverse

F₃ 1 placid, pleasant

Types of cross include:
ankh, Avelian, botoné, Calvary, capital, cardinal, Celtic, Constantinian, Cornish, crosslet, crucifix, encolpion, fleury, fylfot, Geneva, Greek, Jerusalem, Latin, Lorraine, Maltese, moline, papal, patriarchal, potent, quadrate, rood, Russian, saltire, St Andrew's, St Anthony's, St George's, St Peter's, swastika, tau, Y-cross

---

cross-examine *v* cross-question, examine, give someone the third degree *colloq*, grill *colloq*, interrogate, pump *colloq*, question, quiz

crossing *n* **1** *meet at the crossing*: crossroads, intersection, junction **2** *a pedestrian crossing*: crosswalk *US*, pedestrian crossing, pelican crossing, Toucan crossing, zebra crossing **3** *a sea crossing*: journey, passage, trip, voyage

crosswise *adv* across, aslant, athwart, catercorner *formal*, catercornered *formal*, crisscross, crossways, diagonally, obliquely, over, sideways, transversely

crotchety *adj* bad-tempered, cantankerous, crabbed *colloq*, crabby *colloq*, cross, crusty, fractious, grouchy *colloq*, grumpy, iracund *formal*, iracundulous *formal*, irascible, irritable, obstreperous, peevish, petulant, prickly, surly, testy

F₃ calm, placid, pleasant

crouch *v* bend, bow, duck, hunch, kneel, squat, stoop

crow *v* blow your own horn *US colloq*, blow your own trumpet *colloq*, bluster, boast, brag, exult, gloat, rejoice, show off, triumph, vaunt

crowd *n* **1** *a crowd of people*: army, assembly, collection, company, drove, flock, herd, horde, host, masses, mob, multitude, pack, people, populace, press, public, swarm, throng **2** *all the college crowd*: bunch, circle, clique, fraternity, group, lot, set **3** *performers who always get a good crowd*: attendance, audience, gate, house, listeners, spectators, turnout, viewers
♦ *v* **1** *they crowded around the pop star*: cluster, congregate, converge, flock, gather, huddle, mass, mob, muster, stream, surge, swarm, throng **2** *we were all crowded into a van*: bundle, compress, cram, jam, pack, pile, press, push, shove, squeeze, stuff, thrust **3** *a mob crowded the streets*: congest, jam, overflow, pack **4** *I hate people crowding me*: elbow, jostle, push, shove

crowded *adj* busy, chock-a-block *colloq*, congested, crammed, cramped, filled, full, full to bursting *colloq*, jammed, jam-packed *colloq*, overcrowded, overflowing, overfull, overpopulated, packed, swarming, teeming

F₃ deserted, empty

crown *n* **1** *a crown of gold*: circlet, coronet, diadem, garland, tiara, wreath **2** *won the heavyweight crown*: distinction, garland, glory, honour, kudos, laurels, prize, reward, trophy **3** *serve the crown*: emperor, empress, king, monarch, monarchy, queen, royalty, ruler, sovereign **4** *the crown of the hill*: acme *formal*, apex *formal*, crest, peak, pinnacle, summit, tip, top **5** *the crown of his career*: acme *formal*, apex *formal*, climax, crest, culmination, height, peak, pinnacle, summit
♦ *v* **1** *crown the king*: anoint, dignify, enthrone, honour, induct, install, invest **2** *crowned her with flowers*: adorn, festoon **3** *crowned his first season with another win*: be the culmination of, cap, complete, consummate *formal*, finalize, fulfil, perfect, round off

crowning *adj* climactic *formal*, consummate *formal*, culminating, paramount, perfect, sovereign, supreme, top, ultimate, unmatched, unsurpassed
♦ *n* coronation, enthronement, incoronation *formal*, installation, investiture

crucial *adj* **1** *a crucial issue*: central, essential, historic, important, major, momentous, pressing, urgent, vital **2** *at the crucial moment*: critical, deciding, decisive, key, pivotal, psychological

F₃ 1 trivial, unimportant **2** trivial, unimportant

crucify *v* **1** *Christ was crucified*: execute, kill on the cross, put to death on a cross **2** *crucified by the critics*: criticize, mock, persecute, ridicule, slam *colloq*, slate *colloq*, tear to pieces *colloq* **3** *crucified by remorse*: punish, rack, torment, torture

crude *adj* **1** *crude materials*: coarse, natural, raw, rough, unfinished, unpolished, unprocessed, unrefined **2** *a crude shelter*: basic, makeshift, rough, rude *formal*, unfinished **3** *a crude carving*: basic, primitive, rude *formal*, rudimentary, simple **4** *a crude remark*: bawdy, blue *colloq*, coarse, dirty, earthy, gross, hot *colloq*, indecent, juicy *colloq*, lewd, obscene, offensive, raunchy *colloq*, risqué, rude, smutty, uncouth, vulgar

F₃ 1 finished, refined **4** decent, polite, tasteful

cruel *adj* **1** *the cruel treatment of the prisoners:* atrocious, barbaric, barbarous, brutal, excruciating, ferocious, hellish, inhumane, sadistic, savage, severe, vicious **2** *a cruel tyrant:* bloodthirsty, callous, cold-blooded, evil, fiendish, fierce, flinty, grim, hard-hearted, heartless, implacable, indurate *formal*, inhuman, merciless, murderous, pitiless, remorseless, ruthless, sadistic, savage, severe, stony-hearted, unfeeling, unrelenting, vicious **3** *a cruel remark:* bitter, callous, cutting, malevolent *formal*, malicious, mean, nasty, spiteful, unfeeling, unkind, vicious
🔁 **1** compassionate, kind, merciful
2 compassionate, kind, merciful **3** kind

cruelty *n* abuse, barbarity, bestiality, bloodthirstiness, brutality, callousness, ferocity, hard-heartedness, harshness, heartlessness, inhumanity, mercilessness, murderousness, ruthlessness, sadism, savagery, severity, viciousness, violence
🔁 compassion, kindness, mercy

cruise *n* holiday, journey, sail, trip, voyage
♦ *v* **1** *cruising round the Mediterranean:* journey, sail, travel **2** *cruising along comfortably:* coast, drift, freewheel, glide, sail, slide, taxi

crumb *n* atom, bit, flake, grain, iota, jot, mite, morsel, particle, piece, scrap, shred, sliver, soupçon, speck

crumble *v* **1** *the plaster is crumbling:* break up, collapse, come away, decay, decompose, degenerate, deteriorate, disintegrate, fragment **2** *crumble the biscuits with a rolling-pin:* break up, crush, grind, pound, powder, pulverize **3** *the organization began to crumble:* break down, collapse, decay, degenerate, deteriorate, disintegrate, fail, fall apart, fall to pieces

crumbly *adj* **1** *crumbly biscuits:* brittle, short **2** *crumbly earth:* friable *formal*, powdery, pulverulent *formal*

crummy *adj* cheap, contemptible, crappy *slang*, grotty *colloq*, inferior, miserable, pathetic *colloq*, poor, rotten, rubbishy *colloq*, second-rate, shoddy, third-rate, trashy, useless, worthless
🔁 excellent

crumple *v* **1** *he crumpled to the floor:* collapse, fall **2** *don't crumple your dress:* crease, crinkle, crush, fold, rumple, wrinkle **3** *his face crumpled:* pucker, screw up

crunch *v* **1** *crunch a biscuit:* bite, champ, chew, chomp, crush, grind, masticate *formal*, munch **2** *crunching the glass underfoot:* crush, grind, smash
♦ *n* crisis, critical situation, crux, emergency, moment of truth, pinch *colloq*, test

crusade *n* **1** *a crusade against the invaders:* holy war, jihad **2** *the crusade against nuclear power:* campaign, cause, drive, movement, offensive, push, strategy, struggle, undertaking
♦ *v* battle, campaign, drive, fight, push, strive, struggle, work

crusader *n* campaigner, champion, enthusiast, fighter, missionary, reformer, zealot

crush *v* **1** *crush the almonds:* break (up), comminute *formal*, compress, crumble, crunch, grind, mash, mill, pound, press, pulp, pulverize, shatter, smash, squash, squeeze, triturate *formal* **2** *crushed the letter in his hand:* crinkle, crumple,

screw up, wrinkle **3** *the rebels were crushed:* conquer, overcome, overpower, overwhelm, put down, quash, quell, subdue, suppress, vanquish *formal* **4** *crushed by the criticism:* devastate, humiliate, put down *colloq*, shame, upset
♦ *n* **1** *injured in the crush:* crowd, jam, pack, press, squash **2** *a crush on the French teacher:* infatuation, liking, love, obsession, pash *colloq*, passion

crust *n* caking, casing, coat, coating, concretion, covering, film, incrustation *technical*, layer, mantle, scab, shell, skin, surface

crusty *adj* **1** *crusty bread:* baked, well-baked, well-done **2** *a crusty shell had formed:* breakable, brittle, crispy, crumbly, crunchy, firm, friable *formal*, hard **3** *a crusty old man:* bad-tempered, cantankerous, crabbed *colloq*, crabby *colloq*, cross, fractious, grouchy *colloq*, grumpy, irascible, irritable, obstreperous, peevish, petulant, prickly, short-tempered, splenetic *formal*, surly, testy, touchy
🔁 **1** soft, soggy **2** soft, soggy **3** calm, placid, pleasant

crux *n* centre, core, essence, heart, kernel, nub, nucleus, the bottom line *colloq*

cry *v* **1** *cry with pain:* bawl, be in/shed tears, blubber, burst into tears *colloq*, cry your eyes out *colloq*, howl, snivel, sob, wail, weep, whimper, whine **2** *cry out in surprise:* bawl, bellow, call (out), exclaim, howl, roar, scream, screech, shout, shriek, yell
♦ *n* **1** *the baby's cries:* bawl, blubbering, howl, snivel, sob, sobbing, tears, wail, weeping, whimper, whine **2** *we heard loud cries outside:* bawl, bellow, call, exclamation, howl, roar, scream, screech, shout, shriek, yell
▶ **cry off** back out, cancel, change your mind, decide against, excuse yourself, withdraw
▶ **cry out for** call for, demand, necessitate *formal*, need, require, want

crypt *n* burial chamber, catacomb, mausoleum, tomb, undercroft, vault

cryptic *adj* abstruse *formal*, ambiguous, dark, enigmatic, equivocal, esoteric *formal*, mysterious, obscure, perplexing, puzzling, veiled
🔁 clear, obvious, straightforward

crystallize *v* **1** *the substance crystallized:* harden, materialize, solidify **2** *the idea crystallized:* clarify, form, make/become clear, make/become definite, take shape

cub *n* **1** *fox cubs:* baby, offspring, pup, puppy, whelp **2** *an inexperienced cub:* apprentice, beginner, fledgling, fresher, freshman, greenhorn *colloq*, initiate, learner, neophyte, novice, probationer, raw recruit, recruit, rookie *colloq*, starter, student, tenderfoot, tiro, trainee

cubbyhole *n* **1** *she had to work from a tiny cubbyhole:* den, hideaway, tiny room **2** *stowed it away in a cubbyhole:* compartment, hole, niche, pigeonhole, recess, slot

cube *n* block, cuboid, dice, die, hexahedron

cuddle *v* **1** *cuddle the baby:* clasp, embrace, enfold, hold, hug, nestle, nurse, pet **2** *kissing and cuddling in the front room:* canoodle *colloq*, caress, embrace, fondle, hug, neck *colloq*, pet, smooch *colloq*, snog *colloq*, snuggle

cuddly *adj* cuddlesome, huggable, plump, soft

cudgel *n* alpeen, bastinado, bat, bludgeon, club, cosh *colloq*, mace, shillelagh, stick, truncheon
♦ *v* bash, batter, beat, bludgeon, clobber *colloq*, clout, club, cosh *colloq*, hit, pound, strike, thwack

cue *n* hint, nod, prompt, reminder, sign, signal

cuff *v* beat, belt *colloq*, biff *colloq*, box, buffet, clip, clobber *colloq*, clout, hit, knock, slap, smack, strike, thump, whack *colloq*

cuisine *n* cookery, cooking

cul-de-sac *n* blind alley, dead end, no through road

cull *v* **1** *information culled from newspapers:* amass, choose, collect, gather, glean, pick (out), pluck, select, sift **2** *cull wild animals:* destroy, kill, slaughter, thin (out)

culminate *v* climax, close, come to a climax, conclude, end (up), finish, peak, terminate, wind up *colloq*
🔁 begin, start

culmination *n* acme *formal*, apex *formal*, climax, completion, conclusion, consummation *formal*, crown, finale, height, high point, peak, pinnacle, summit, top, zenith *formal*
🔁 beginning, start

culpable *adj* answerable, at fault, blamable, blameworthy, censurable, guilty, in the wrong, liable, offending, peccant *formal*, responsible, sinful, to blame, wrong
🔁 blameless, innocent

culprit *n* criminal, delinquent, felon, guilty party, law-breaker, miscreant, offender, villain, wrongdoer

cult *n* **1** *a religious cult:* belief, denomination, faction, faith, movement, party, religion, school, sect **2** *the film became a cult among horror fans:* craze, fad, fashion, in-thing *colloq*, trend, vogue

cultivate *v* **1** *cultivating poppies:* bring on, farm, grow, harvest, plant, produce, raise, sow, tend **2** *cultivating the soil:* dig, farm, fertilize, plough, prepare, tend, till, work **3** *cultivate your children's talents:* aid, assist, back, develop, encourage, forward, foster, further, help, nurture, promote, support **4** *cultivate a friendship:* advance, encourage, forward, foster, further, nurture, pursue, work on **5** *cultivating influential people:* court, woo **6** *cultivate your mind:* develop, enhance, enlighten, enrich, improve, polish, refine, train
🔁 3 neglect 6 neglect

cultivated *adj* civilized, cultured, discerning, discriminating, educated, enlightened, genteel, highbrow, polished, refined, scholarly, sophisticated, urbane, well-informed, well-read

cultural *adj* **1** *cultural events:* aesthetic, artistic, broadening, civilizing, developmental, edifying, educational, educative, elevating, enlightening, enriching, improving **2** *cultural heritage:* anthropological *technical*, communal, ethnic, folk, national, societal *formal*, traditional, tribal

culture *n* **1** *popular culture:* history, humanities, learning, literature, music, painting, philosophy, the arts **2** *people from different cultures:* civilization, customs, heritage, society, traditions, way of life **3** *developing a culture of binge drinking:* behaviour, habits, lifestyle, mores

formal, way of life **4** *the organic culture of crops:* growth, nurturing, production

cultured *adj* artistic, arty *colloq*, cultivated, educated, enlightened, erudite, highbrow, intellectual, learned, polished, refined, scholarly, sophisticated, urbane, well-educated, well-informed, well-read
🔁 ignorant, uncultured, uneducated

culvert *n* channel, conduit, drain, duct, gutter, sewer, watercourse

cumbersome *adj* **1** *a cumbersome machine:* awkward, bulky, burdensome, cumbrous *formal*, heavy, incommodious *formal*, inconvenient, onerous, unmanageable, unwieldy, weighty **2** *a cumbersome process:* badly organized, complex, complicated, difficult, inefficient, involved, slow, wasteful
🔁 1 convenient, manageable 2 efficient, simple

cumulative *adj* collective, growing, increasing, mounting, multiplying, snowballing *colloq*

cunning *adj* **1** *a cunning person:* artful, astute, canny, crafty, cunning as a fox *colloq*, deep, devious, guileful, knowing, sharp, shrewd, sly, subtle, tricky, wily **2** *a cunning plan:* clever, fiendish, imaginative, ingenious, inventive, resourceful **3** *the artist's cunning brushwork:* clever, deft, dexterous, skilful
🔁 1 gullible, ingenuous, naïve
♦ *n* **1** *the legendary cunning of the fox:* artfulness, astuteness, cleverness, craftiness, deviousness, guile, resourcefulness, sharpness, shrewdness, slyness, subtlety, trickery, wiles **2** *the cunning of du Maurier's narrative structure:* adroitness, cleverness, deftness, finesse, imaginativeness, ingenuity, inventiveness, skill, subtlety

cup *n* **1** *drink from a cup:* beaker, chalice, goblet, mug, tankard **2** *win a cup:* award, prize, trophy **3** *claret cup:* punch

cupboard *n* cabinet, chest, chest of drawers, closet, dresser, locker, pantry, sideboard, tallboy, wardrobe, Welsh dresser

cupidity *n* acquisitiveness, avarice, avidity *formal*, covetousness, graspingness, greed, greediness, rapaciousness *formal*, rapacity *formal*, voracity *formal*

curative *adj* alleviative *formal*, corrective, febrifugal *technical*, healing, healthful, health-giving, medicinal, remedial, restorative, salutary, therapeutic, tonic, vulnerary *formal*

curator *n* attendant, caretaker, conservator, custodian, guardian, keeper, steward, warden, warder

curb *v* bridle, check, constrain, contain, control, hamper, hinder, hold back, impede, inhibit, keep in check, keep under control, moderate, muzzle, reduce, repress, restrain, restrict, retard *formal*, subdue, suppress
🔁 encourage, foster
♦ *n* brake, bridle, check, constraint, control, damper, deterrent, hamper, hindrance, holding-back, impediment, limitation, rein, repression, restraint, restriction, retardant *formal*, suppression

curdle *v* clot, coagulate, congeal, solidify, sour, thicken, turn, turn sour

cure *v* **1** *cure a disease:* alleviate, ease, heal, make better, make well, relieve, remedy, treat **2** *he was completely cured:* heal, make better, make well, restore **3** *cure a fault:* correct, fix, help, make

better, mend, rectify, remedy, repair **4** *cure meat:* dry, kipper, pickle, preserve, salt, smoke
♦ *n* **1** *find a cure for cancer:* alleviation, antidote, corrective, cure-all, elixir *formal*, healing, medicine, panacea, remedy, restorative, specific *technical*, therapy, treatment **2** *a cure for the problem:* alleviation, corrective, remedy, solution

curio *n* antique, bibelot, bygone, curiosity, knick-knack, object of virtu, objet d'art, objet de vertu, trinket

curiosity *n* **1** *he paid for his curiosity:* inquisitiveness, interest, nosiness *colloq*, prying, querying, questioning, snooping **2** *curiosities of a bygone age:* antique, bygone, curio, knick-knack, novelty, objet d'art, trinket **3** *a perennial curiosity for visitors:* exotica, freak, marvel, oddity, phenomenon, rarity, spectacle, wonder

curious *adj* **1** *a curious child:* inquiring, inquisitive, interested, keen to know, nosy *colloq*, prying, querying, questioning, snooping, wanting to know **2** *a curious sight:* bizarre, exotic, extraordinary, freakish, funny, mysterious, novel, odd, out of the ordinary, peculiar, puzzling, quaint, queer, rare, remarkable, strange, unconventional, unique, unorthodox, unusual, weird
F➚ **1** indifferent, uninterested **2** normal, ordinary, usual

curl *v* **1** *she curls her hair:* crimp, frizz, kink, wave **2** *the snake curled round my wrist:* bend, coil, corkscrew, curve, loop, snake, spiral, twine, twist, wave, wind **3** *smoke curling up from the fire:* corkscrew, meander, ripple, scroll, snake, spiral, twirl, twist, wreathe
F➚ **1** uncurl **2** uncurl
♦ *n* **1** *a head covered in curls:* kink, ringlet, wave **2** *curls of smoke:* coil, curlicue, helix, ring, spiral, swirl, twist, whorl

curly *adj* coiling, corkscrew, crimped, curled, curling, frizzy, fuzzy, kinky, permed, twisting, wavy
F➚ straight

currency *n* **1** *foreign currency:* bills, cash, coinage, coins, legal tender, money, notes **2** *an idea which gained currency:* acceptance, circulation, dissemination *formal*, exposure, popularity, prevalence, publicity, vogue

current *adj* **1** *the current fashion:* contemporary, existing, extant *formal*, fashionable, in *colloq*, in fashion, in vogue, modern, ongoing, popular, present, present-day, present-time, trendy *colloq*, up-to-date, up-to-the-minute **2** *still current in the 1800s:* common, general, (generally) accepted, going around *colloq*, in circulation, popular, prevailing, prevalent, reigning, widespread
F➚ **1** obsolete, old-fashioned
♦ *n* **1** *the river has a strong current:* course, drift, ebb, flow, movement, stream, swirl, tide, undercurrent **2** *a current of air:* draught, flow, jet, movement **3** *a current of feeling against him:* drift, feeling, mood, movement, tendency, tenor, trend

curriculum *n* core curriculum, course, course of studies, course of study, educational programme, module, national curriculum, subjects, syllabus, timetable

curse *v* **1** *he cursed under his breath:* blaspheme, cuss *colloq*, imprecate *formal*, swear, use bad language **2** *he cursed me for my stupidity:* blast, condemn, damn, denounce, fulminate *formal*,

imprecate *formal* **3** *she had been cursed:* accurse *formal*, anathematize *formal*, damn, put a jinx on *colloq* **4** *a family cursed with bad luck:* afflict, beset, blight, plague, scourge, torment, trouble
F➚ **3** bless **4** bless
♦ *n* **1** *uttered a curse under his breath:* bad language, blasphemy, execration *formal*, expletive, four-letter word *colloq*, imprecation *formal*, oath, obscenity, profanity, swear-word **2** *under an ancient curse:* anathema, execration *formal*, jinx, malediction *formal*, spell **3** *the curse of drug addiction:* affliction, bane, calamity, disaster, evil, misfortune, ordeal, plague, scourge, torment, tribulation *formal*, trouble
F➚ **2** blessing **3** advantage

cursed *adj* abominable, annoying, blasted *colloq*, blooming *colloq*, confounded, damned, dashed *colloq*, detestable, dratted *colloq*, execrable *formal*, flipping *colloq*, hateful, infernal, loathsome, odious, pernicious, vile

cursory *adj* brief, careless, casual, desultory, dismissive, fleeting, hasty, hurried, offhand, passing, perfunctory, quick, rapid, slapdash, slight, summary, superficial
F➚ painstaking, thorough

curt *adj* abrupt, blunt, brief, brusque, gruff, offhand, rude, sharp, short, short-spoken, snappish, summary, tart, terse, unceremonious, uncivil, ungracious
F➚ voluble

curtail *v* **1** *the company's efforts to curtail the costs:* cut, cut back (on), cut down, decrease, lessen, limit, pare, pare down/back, prune, reduce, restrict, shrink, slim, trim **2** *we had to curtail the meeting:* abbreviate, abridge, cut short, guillotine, shorten, truncate
F➚ **1** increase **2** extend, lengthen

curtailment *n* **1** *the curtailment of government spending:* cut, cutback, decrease, docking, lessening, limitation, paring, pruning, reduction, restriction, retrenchment *formal*, slimming, trimming **2** *the curtailment of time spent in meetings:* abbreviation, abridgement, contraction, cutting, decrease, guillotine, lessening, limitation, reduction, restriction, shortening, truncation
F➚ **1** increase **2** extension, increase, lengthening

curtain *n* backdrop, drape *US*, drapery, hanging, net curtain, portière, screen, tapestry, window hanging

curtsy *v* bob, bow, genuflect *formal*

curvaceous *adj* bosomy, buxom, curvy, shapely, voluptuous, well-proportioned, well-rounded, well-stacked
F➚ skinny

curve *v* **1** *the road curved through the forest:* arc, arch, bend, bow, coil, incurve *formal*, round, swerve, turn, twist, wind **2** *she curved a finger to beckon him on:* bend, crook, hook, incurve *formal* **3** *the surface curved outwards:* bow, bulge, swell
♦ *n* arc, arch, bend, bow, camber, crescent, curvature, flexure, loop, turn, winding

curved *adj* **1** *a curved line:* arched, arcuate *technical*, bending, bent, bowed, curviform, serpentine, sinuous, sweeping, tortuous, twisted **2** *a curved surface:* arched, arcuate *technical*, bowed, bulging, concave, convex, cupped, curviform, humped, rounded, scooped, swelling
F➚ **1** straight **2** straight

cushion *n* beanbag, bolster, buffer, hassock, headrest, mat, pad, padding, pillow, pulvinus *technical*, shock absorber, squab
♦ *v* **1** *tried to cushion the blow:* absorb, dampen, deaden, diminish, lessen, mitigate, muffle, reduce, soften, stifle, suppress **2** *the airbag cushions the driver in the event of a crash:* bolster, buttress, protect, support

cushy *adj* comfortable, easy, jammy *colloq*, plum *colloq*, soft *colloq*, undemanding
✦ demanding, tough

custodian *n* caretaker, castellan, conservator, curator, guard, guardian, keeper, overseer, protector, superintendent, warden, warder, watchdog, watchman

custody *n* **1** *gain custody of her children:* care, charge, custodianship, guardianship, keeping, possession, preservation, protection, responsibility, safekeeping, supervision, trusteeship, wardship **2** *in police custody:* arrest, captivity, confinement, detention, imprisonment, incarceration *formal*

custom *n* **1** *national customs:* convention, ethos, etiquette, fashion, form, formality, institution, observance, practice, rite, ritual, style, tradition, usage, use, way, way of behaving **2** *it was her custom to feed the birds every day:* habit, manner, policy, practice, procedure, routine, way **3** *take my custom elsewhere:* business, patronage *formal*, trade

customarily *adv* as a rule, commonly, conventionally, generally, habitually, normally, ordinarily, regularly, routinely, traditionally, usually
✦ occasionally, rarely, unusually

customary *adj* **1** *a customary practice:* accepted, common, conventional, established, everyday, familiar, general, normal, ordinary, prevailing, routine, set, traditional, usual **2** *his customary good humour:* accustomed, habitual, normal, regular, usual
✦ **1** rare, unusual

customer *n* buyer, client, clientèle, consumer, patron, punter *colloq*, purchaser, regular, shopper

customize *v* adapt, adjust, alter, convert, fine-tune *colloq*, fit, modify, suit, tailor

cut *v* **1** *cut a piece off something:* carve, chop, dock, hack, hew, lop, prune, sever, slice **2** *cut paper:* slice, slit, split **3** *cut meat:* carve, chop (up), cleave *formal*, dice, divide, mince, shred, slice **4** *cut hair:* clip, crop, pare, shave, shear, shorten, snip, trim **5** *cut grass:* clip, crop, dock, mow, prune, shorten, snip, trim **6** *cut glass:* chisel, engrave, incise, score **7** *cut your finger:* lacerate, nick, slash, stab, wound **8** *cut costs:* curb, curtail, decrease, diminish, lower, prune, reduce, slash *colloq* **9** *cut a story:* abbreviate, abridge, condense, curtail, edit, expurgate *formal*, make shorter, précis, shorten, summarize **10** *cut a scene from a film:* delete, edit, excise *formal*, omit **11** *when I said hello, she cut me:* avoid, cold-shoulder *colloq*, cut dead *colloq*, ignore, look right through *colloq*, not give someone the time of day *colloq*, pretend not to see/notice, send to Coventry *colloq*, slight, snub, spurn **12** *cut a supply:* block, break off, bring to an end, disconnect, discontinue *formal*, end, halt, stop, suspend **13** *cut that noise!:* cease,

formal, desist *formal*, discontinue *formal*, knock off *colloq*, lay off *colloq*, leave off *colloq*, pack in *colloq*, quit *colloq*, refrain, stop
♦ *n* **1** *a cut in his finger:* gash, incision, laceration, nick, notch, rip, score, slash, slit, wound **2** *go for a cut at the barber's:* clip, crop, shave, trim **3** *spending cuts:* cutback, decrease, economy, lessening, lowering, reduction, retrenchment *formal*, saving **4** *a cut of meat:* bit, part, piece, section, slice **5** *a power cut:* breakdown, breaking-down, cutting-out, failure, fault, malfunctioning *formal* **6** *a cut of the profits:* allocation, portion, proportion, quota, ration, share, slice *colloq*, slice of the cake *colloq*, whack *colloq* **7** *the cut of a garment:* fashion, form, shape, style

▶ **cut across** go beyond, leave behind, rise above, surmount, transcend
▶ **cut back 1** *cut back spending:* check, curb, curtail, decrease, downsize *colloq*, economize, lessen, lower, reduce, retrench *formal*, scale down, slash *colloq* **2** *cut back the hedges:* crop, lop, prune, trim
▶ **cut down 1** *cut down a tree:* chop down, fell, hew, level, lop, raze, saw **2** *cut down carbon emissions:* curb, curtail, decrease, diminish, lessen, lower, reduce
▶ **cut in** barge in *colloq*, break in, butt in, interject *formal*, interpose *formal*, interrupt, intervene, intrude
▶ **cut off 1** *cut off his head:* amputate, break off, chop off, detach, remove, sever, take off, tear off **2** *feel cut off from friends:* detach, insulate, isolate, keep apart, seclude, separate **3** *cut off supplies:* block, break off, bring to an end, disconnect, discontinue *formal*, end, halt, stop, suspend **4** *he cut her off in mid-sentence:* break off, interrupt
▶ **cut out 1** *cut out a coupon:* excise *formal*, extract, remove, separate, take out, tear out **2** *cut out a scene from a play:* cut, delete, drop, edit, excise *formal*, exclude, leave out, omit **3** *the engine cut out:* break down, conk out *slang*, fail, go wrong, malfunction *formal*, pack up *colloq*, stop working
▶ **cut up** carve, chop (up), dice, divide, mince, slash, slice (up)

cutback *n* curtailment, cut, decrease, economy, lessening, lowering, reduction, retrenchment *formal*, saving, slashing *colloq*

cutlery

Items of cutlery include:
knife, butter knife, carving knife, fish knife, steak knife, cheese knife, breadknife, vegetable knife, fork, fish fork, carving fork, spoon, dessertspoon, tablespoon, teaspoon, soupspoon, caddy spoon, salt spoon, apostle spoon, ladle, salad servers, fish slice, cake server, sugar tongs, chopsticks, canteen of cutlery

---

cut-price *adj* bargain, cheap, cut-rate, discount, low-priced, reduced, sale

cut-throat *adj* **1** *a cut-throat business:* dog-eat-dog *colloq*, fierce, highly/fiercely competitive, keen, keenly contested **2** *a cut-throat killer:* brutal, cruel, pitiless, relentless, ruthless

cutting *adj* **1** *a cutting comment:* acid, bitchy *colloq*, caustic, hurtful, incisive, malicious, mordant *formal*, pointed, sarcastic, scathing, sharp, snide, stinging, trenchant *formal*,

wounding **2** *a cutting wind:* biting, bitter, chill, keen, penetrating, piercing, raw, sharp
♦ *n* clipping, excerpt, extract, piece

cycle *n* **1** *the beginning of a new cycle:* age, eon, epoch, era, order, period, phase **2** *a five-year cycle:* circle, pattern, revolution, rota, rotation, round, sequence, series, succession

cyclone *n* hurricane, storm, tempest, tornado, tropical storm, typhoon, whirlwind

cylinder *n* barrel, bobbin, column, drum, reel, spindle, spool

cynic *n* doubter, killjoy, knocker *colloq*, misanthrope *formal*, pessimist, sceptic, scoffer, spoilsport *colloq*

cynical *adj* **1** *a cynical view of politicians:* contemptuous, critical, derisive, ironic, mocking, negative, sarcastic, sardonic, scornful, sneering **2** *cynical about love:* disenchanted, disillusioned, distrustful, doubtful, doubting, pessimistic, sceptical, suspicious

cynicism *n* **1** *the cynicism of his writing:* contempt, irony, misanthropy *formal*, mocking, sarcasm, scoffing, scorn, sneering **2** *her cynicism about organized religion:* disbelief, disenchantment, disillusionment, distrust, doubt, pessimism, scepticism, suspicion

cyst *n* atheroma *technical*, bladder, bleb, blister, growth, sac, utricle, vesicle, wen

D

dab *v* daub, pat, press, swab, tap, touch, wipe
♦ *n* **1** *a dab of paint*: bit, dash, drop, fleck, smear, smudge, speck, spot, tinge, trace **2** *a dab of his brush*: pat, press, stroke, tap, touch

dabble *v* **1** *dabbling with drugs*: dally, play, potter, tinker, toy, trifle **2** *ducks dabbled in the water*: dampen, dip, moisten, paddle, splash, splatter, sprinkle, wet

dabbler *n* amateur, dallier, dilettante, lay person, tinkerer, trifler
🖪 expert, professional

daft *adj* **1** *a daft suggestion*: absurd, barmy *colloq*, batty *colloq*, crackbrained *colloq*, crackpot *colloq*, crazy, dotty *colloq*, dumb *colloq*, fatuous, foolhardy, foolish, half-baked *colloq*, hare-brained *colloq*, idiotic, impracticable, imprudent, inane, irrational, irresponsible, ludicrous, nonsensical, odd, outrageous, peculiar, potty *colloq*, preposterous, ridiculous, senseless, silly, stupid, unrealistic, unwise, wacky *colloq*, wild **2** *I wasn't so daft as to believe him*: berserk, bonkers *colloq*, crazed, crazy, demented, deranged, disturbed, insane, loony *colloq*, loopy *colloq*, lunatic, mad, mental *colloq*, needing your head examining *colloq*, nuts *colloq*, nutty *colloq*, nutty as a fruitcake *colloq*, off your rocker *colloq*, out of your mind, round the bend *colloq*, round the twist *colloq*, simple, touched, unbalanced, unhinged, wild **3** *daft about football*: ardent, avid, devoted, enamoured, enthusiastic, fanatical, fond, infatuated, keen, mad, nuts *colloq*, passionate, potty *colloq*, smitten, sweet *colloq*, wild, zealous
🖪 **1** sensible **2** sane **3** indifferent

dagger *n* bayonet, blade, dirk, jambiya, knife, kris, kukri, misericord, poniard, skene, skene-dhu, stiletto, yatagan

daily *adj* **1** *our daily lives*: common, commonplace, customary, everyday, habitual, ordinary, regular, routine **2** *a daily occurrence*: circadian *formal*, diurnal *formal*, everyday, quotidian *formal*
♦ *adv* day after day, day by day, every day

dainty *adj* **1** *dainty and feminine*: charming, delicate, elegant, exquisite, fine, graceful, little, neat, petite, pretty, refined, small, trim **2** *a dainty morsel*: appetizing, delectable, delightful, enjoyable, juicy, luscious, mouth-watering, palatable, savoury, succulent, tasty **3** *a dainty appetite*: choosy *colloq*, discriminating, fastidious, finicky, fussy, particular, scrupulous
🖪 **1** clumsy, gross **2** unpalatable
♦ *n* bonbon, bonne-bouche, delicacy, fancy, sweetmeat, titbit

dais *n* platform, podium, rostrum, stage, stand

dale *n* coomb, dell, dingle, gill, glen, strath, vale, valley

dally *v* **1** *can't dally here talking*: dawdle, delay, linger, loiter, procrastinate *formal*, tarry *formal* **2** *dallied with the idea*: flirt, frivol, play, toy, trifle
🖪 **1** hasten, hurry

dam *n* barrage, barricade, barrier, blockage, embankment, obstruction, wall
♦ *v* barricade, block, check, confine, obstruct, restrict, staunch, stem

damage *v* abuse, deface, desecrate, destroy, harm, hurt, impair, incapacitate, injure, mar, mutilate, play/wreak havoc with, ruin, sabotage, spoil, tamper with, vandalize, vitiate *formal*, weaken, wreck
🖪 fix, mend, repair
♦ *n* **1** *extensive damage after the fire*: abuse, defacement, destruction, detriment, devastation, harm, havoc, hurt, impairment, injury, loss, mischief, mutilation, ruin, suffering, vandalism **2** *pay damages*: compensation, fine, indemnity, reimbursement, reparation, restitution, satisfaction
🖪 **1** repair

damaging *adj* bad, deleterious *formal*, detrimental, disadvantageous, harmful, hurtful, injurious, pernicious, prejudicial, ruinous, unfavourable
🖪 favourable, helpful

dame *n* **1** *Dame Edith Evans*: aristocrat, baroness, dowager, lady, noblewoman, peeress **2** *a couple of dames at the bar*: broad *slang*, female, woman

damn *v* **1** *damn you!*: accurse *formal*, anathematize *formal*, blaspheme, blast, curse, doom, execrate *formal*, fulminate *formal*, imprecate *formal*, maledict *formal*, swear, use bad language **2** *damned for her beliefs*: berate *formal*, castigate *formal*, censure, come down on *colloq*, condemn, criticize, decry *formal*, denigrate *formal*, denounce, denunciate, excoriate *formal*, inveigh *formal*, knock *colloq*, pan *colloq*, pick holes in *colloq*, pull to pieces *colloq*, revile, run down *colloq*, slam *colloq*, slate *colloq*, tear to shreds *colloq*
🖪 **1** bless **2** commend, praise
♦ *n* brass farthing *slang*, dash *slang*, hoot *slang*, iota, jot, monkey's *slang*, tinker's cuss *slang*, toss *slang*, two hoots *slang*

damnable *adj* abominable, atrocious, cursed, despicable, detestable, execrable *formal*, horrible, infernal, iniquitous, offensive, wicked
🖪 admirable, praiseworthy

damnation *n* anathema, condemnation, denunciation, doom, excommunication, hell, perdition, proscription *formal*

damned *adj* **1** *a damned soul*: accursed, anathematized, condemned, cursed, doomed, lost, reprobate **2** *a damned disgrace*: abominable, annoying, blasted *colloq*, blooming *colloq*, confounded, darned *colloq*, dashed *colloq*, despicable, detestable, dratted *colloq*, execrable *formal*, fiendish, flipping *colloq*, fucking *taboo slang*, loathsome, odious, pernicious, unpleasant, vile
🖪 **1** blessed

damning *adj* accusatorial *formal*, condemning, damnatory *formal*, implicating, implicative *formal*, incriminating, inculpatory *formal*

damp *adj* clammy, dank, dewy, drizzly, humid, misty, moist, muggy, rainy, soggy, vaporous, wet
🖪 arid, dry
♦ *n* clamminess, dampness, dankness, dew,

drizzle, fog, humidity, mist, moisture, wet, wetness
🖪 dryness
▶ **damp down** calm, check, deaden, decrease, diminish, dull, lessen, moderate, reduce, restrain

dampen *v* **1** *dampen a cloth:* damp, moisten, spray, wet **2** *that dampened my enthusiasm:* check, damp down, dash, deaden, decrease, depress, deter, diminish, discourage, dishearten, dismay, dull, inhibit, lessen, moderate, muffle, put a damper on, reduce, restrain, smother, stifle
🖪 **1** dry **2** encourage

damper *n* check, discouragement, inhibition, restraint

dampness *n* clamminess, damp, dankness, dew, drizzle, fog, humidity, mist, moisture, rain, vapour, wet, wetness

damsel *n* girl, lass, maiden, young lady, young woman

dance *v* **1** *learn to dance:* hoof it *colloq*, hop *colloq*, jig *colloq*, move to music, pirouette, rock, shake a leg *colloq*, spin, sway, trip the light fantastic, twirl, whirl **2** *dance for joy:* bounce, caper, frisk, frolic, gambol, juke, jump, kantikoy, leap, prance, skip, spin, stomp, sway, swing, tread a measure, whirl **3** *lights dancing on the water:* flash, flicker, leap, move lightly, play, shimmer, sparkle, sway, twinkle, waver
♦ *n* ball, hop *colloq*, knees-up *colloq*, shindig *colloq*, social

Dances include:
waltz, quickstep, foxtrot, tango, polka, one-step, military two-step, valeta, Lancers, rumba, samba, mambo, bossanova, beguine, fandango, flamenco, mazurka, bolero, paso doble, can-can; rock 'n' roll, jive, twist, stomp, bop, jitterbug, mashed potato; black bottom, Charleston, cha-cha, turkey-trot; Circassian circle, Paul Jones, jig, reel, quadrille, Highland fling, morris-dance, clog dance, hoe-down, hokey-cokey, Lambeth Walk, conga, belly-dance; galliard, gavotte, minuet

Types of dancing include:
ballet, tap, ballroom, old-time, disco, folk, country, Irish, Highland, Latin-American, flamenco, clog-dancing, line-dancing, morris dancing, limbo-dancing, break-dancing, robotics. See also **ballet**

Dance functions include:
disco, dance, social, tea dance, ceilidh, barn dance, ball, fancy dress ball, charity ball, hunt ball, hop *colloq*, knees-up *colloq*, shindig *colloq*, rave *colloq*, prom *US*

dancer *n* ballerina, ballet dancer, coryphee, danseur, danseuse

dandy *n* Adonis, beau, blade, coxcomb, dapperling, dude, exquisite, fop, man about town, peacock, popinjay, swell, toff
♦ *adj* capital, excellent, fine, first-rate, great, splendid

danger *n* **1** *in danger of falling:* endangerment *formal*, imperilment *formal*, insecurity, jeopardy, liability, precariousness, vulnerability **2** *the dangers of smoking:* hazard, menace, peril, pitfall, risk, threat

🖪 **1** safety, security **2** safety

dangerous *adj* alarming, breakneck, chancy, daring, dicey *colloq*, exposed, fraught with danger, grave, hairy *colloq*, hazardous, high-risk, insecure, menacing, minacious *formal*, ominous, perilous, precarious, reckless, risky, threatening, treacherous, unsafe, vulnerable
🖪 harmless, safe, secure

dangle *v* **1** *a bracelet dangled from his wrist:* droop, flap, hang, sway, swing, trail **2** *they dangled an incentive before me:* hold out, lure, wave

dank *adj* clammy, damp, dewy, moist, slimy, soggy, sticky, wet
🖪 dry

dapper *adj* active, brisk, chic, dainty, natty *colloq*, neat, nimble, smart, spruce, spry, stylish, trim, well-dressed, well-groomed, well-turned-out
🖪 dishevelled, dowdy, scruffy, shabby, sloppy

dappled *adj* bespeckled, chequered, dotted, flecked, freckled, mottled, piebald, pied, speckled, spotted, stippled, variegated

dare *v* **1** *I stepped forward as far as I dared:* adventure, be brave/bold enough, brave, endanger, gamble, have the courage, hazard, risk, stake, venture **2** *he dared me to ask for more:* challenge, goad, provoke, taunt, throw down the gauntlet *colloq*
♦ *n* challenge, gauntlet, goad, provocation, risk, taunt, ultimatum, venture

daredevil *n* adventurer, desperado, madcap, stuntman
🖪 coward
♦ *adj* adventurous, audacious, bold, brave, daring, dauntless, fearless, intrepid, plucky, valiant

daring *adj* adventurous, audacious, bold, brave, courageous, dauntless, fearless, intrepid, plucky, undaunted, valiant
🖪 afraid, cautious, timid
♦ *n* adventurousness, audacity, boldness, bravery, courage, defiance, fearlessness, foolhardiness, gall, grit *colloq*, guts *colloq*, intrepidity, nerve *colloq*, pluck, prowess, spirit, valour
🖪 caution, cowardice, timidity

dark *adj* **1** *a dark room:* badly lit, black, cloudy, dim, dimly lit, dingy, dusky, foggy, gloomy, misty, murky, overcast, poorly lit, shadowy, shady, sunless, tenebrous *formal*, unilluminated, unlit **2** *dark hair/skin:* black, brown, brunette, dark-haired, dark-skinned **3** *a dark manner:* bleak, cheerless, dejected, dismal, drab, forbidding, gloomy, grim, joyless, menacing, morose, mournful, ominous, sad, sombre **4** *the dark days of war:* awful, black, bleak, dismal, distressing, frightening, gloomy, hopeless, sad, unpleasant, worrying **5** *dark secrets:* abstruse *formal*, arcane *formal*, cryptic, enigmatic, esoteric *formal*, hidden, intricate, mysterious, obscure, puzzling, recondite *formal*, secret, unintelligible
🖪 **1** bright, clear, light **2** fair, light **3** bright, cheerful **4** happy, joyful **5** comprehensible
♦ *n* **1** *afraid of the dark:* blackness, cloudiness, darkness, dimness, dusk, evening, gloom, half-light, murkiness, night, nightfall, night-time, shade, shadiness, shadows, sunlessness, tenebrity *formal*, tenebrosity *formal*, twilight **2** *we*

were kept in the dark: concealment, ignorance, mystery, obscurity, secrecy
🔁 **1** brightness, daylight, light, lightness
2 enlightenment, openness

darken *v* **1** *a cloud darkened the sky:* blacken, cloud (over), dim, eclipse, fade, fog, obnubilate *old use,* obscure, overshadow, shade, shadow **2** *the news darkened his mood:* deject, depress, make gloomy, sadden
🔁 **1** lighten **2** brighten

darling *n* **1** *come here, darling:* angel, beloved, dear, dearest, favourite, honey, love, pet, sweetheart, treasure **2** *the darling of the fashion world:* apple of your eye, blue-eyed boy *colloq,* favourite, pet, teacher's pet *colloq*
♦ *adj* adored, beloved, cherished, dear, dearest, precious, treasured

darn *v* mend, repair, sew (up), stitch

dart *v* **1** *he darted away through the garden:* bolt, bound, dash, flash, flit, fly, leap, race, run, rush, scoot *colloq,* scurry, spring, sprint, tear **2** *dart a glance:* cast, send, shoot, throw
♦ *n* arrow, barb, bolt, shaft

dash *v* **1** *he dashed into the office:* bolt, bound, dart, dive, fly, hurry, hurtle, nip *colloq,* pop *colloq,* race, run, rush, speed, sprint, tear **2** *waves dashing against rocks:* beat, break, crash, fling, hurl, lash, pound, slam, smash, strike **3** *dash your hopes:* blight, confound, crush, dampen, depress, destroy, devastate, disappoint, discourage, dishearten, frustrate, let down, ruin, sadden, shatter, smash, spoil, thwart
♦ *n* **1** *a dash of olive oil:* bit, drop, flavour, grain, hint, little, pinch, smidgen *colloq,* soupçon, suggestion, tinge, touch, trace **2** *a dash to the car park:* bolt, dart, race, run, rush, sprint, spurt
▶ **dash off** jot down, scrawl, scribble

dashing *adj* **1** *a dashing young hero:* animated, bold, daring, energetic, exuberant, gallant, lively, plucky, spirited, vigorous **2** *a dashing outfit:* attractive, debonair, elegant, fashionable, flamboyant, showy, smart, stylish
🔁 **1** lethargic **2** dowdy

dastardly *adj* base, contemptible, cowardly, craven, despicable, faint-hearted, lily-livered, low, mean, pusillanimous *formal,* underhand, vile, wicked
🔁 heroic, noble

data *n* details, documents, facts, figures, information, input, material, particulars, research, statistics

date *n* **1** *at a later date:* age, century, day, decade, epoch, era, millennium, month, period, stage, time, week, year **2** *I have a date with him:* appointment, assignation *formal,* engagement, meeting, rendezvous **3** *she's my date for the dance:* boyfriend, escort, friend, girlfriend, partner, steady *colloq*
♦ *v* **1** *date back to the 18th century:* belong to, come/exist from, go back, originate **2** *buy styles that won't date:* become old-fashioned/obsolete, go out, go out of use, obsolesce *formal* **3** *date someone:* be together, court, go out with, go steady, take out

dated *adj* antiquated, archaic, obsolescent, obsolete, old hat *colloq,* old-fashioned, outdated,

outmoded, out of date, passé, superseded, unfashionable
🔁 fashionable, up-to-the-minute

daub *v* coat, cover, paint, plaster, smear, smirch, smudge, spatter, splatter, stain, sully
♦ *n* blot, blotch, smear, splash, splodge, splotch, spot, stain

daughter *n* child, descendant, disciple, female child, girl, inhabitant, lass, lassie, offspring

daunt *v* alarm, cow, demoralize, deter, disconcert, discourage, dishearten, disillusion, dismay, dispirit, frighten, intimidate, overawe, put off, scare, take aback, unnerve
🔁 encourage, hearten

dauntless *adj* bold, brave, courageous, daring, fearless, intrepid, plucky, resolute, undaunted, valiant
🔁 discouraged, disheartened

dawdle *v* dally, delay, dilly-dally *colloq,* go at a snail's pace, go slowly, hang about, lag, linger, loiter, potter, take too long, take your time, tarry *formal,* trail
🔁 hurry

dawn *n* **1** *I woke at dawn:* break of day, crack of dawn, daybreak, daylight, first light, morning, sunrise **2** *the dawn of the space age:* advent *formal,* arrival, beginning, birth, commencement *formal,* emergence, genesis *formal,* inception *formal,* onset, origin, rise, start
🔁 **1** dusk **2** end
♦ *v* **1** *the morning dawned:* become/grow light, break, brighten, gleam, glimmer, lighten **2** *a new era was about to dawn:* appear, be born, begin, come into being, commence *formal,* develop, emerge, open, originate, rise
▶ **dawn on** click *colloq,* come into your mind, hit *colloq,* occur to, realize, sink in, strike

day *n* **1** *during the day:* daylight, daytime **2** *in my day:* age, date, epoch, era, generation, period, time
🔁 **1** night

daybreak *n* break of day, cock-crow(ing), crack of dawn, dawn, daylight, first light, morning, sunrise, sun-up
🔁 sundown, sunset

daydream *n* castles in the air, dream, fantasy, figment, imagining, musing, pipe dream, reverie, vision, wish
♦ *v* be lost in space, dream, fancy, fantasize, imagine, let your thoughts wander, muse, not pay attention, stare into space, switch off *colloq*

daylight *n* **1** *get home in the daylight:* day, daytime, light, natural light, sunlight **2** *shortly after daylight:* break of day, crack of dawn, dawn, daybreak, first light, morning, sunrise
🔁 **1** dark, night

daze *v* **1** *the blow on the head dazed him:* numb, paralyse, shock, stun, stupefy **2** *dazed by the night's events:* amaze, astonish, astound, baffle, bewilder, blind, confuse, dazzle, dumbfound, flabbergast *colloq,* perplex, shock, stagger, startle, stun, surprise, take aback
♦ *n* bewilderment, confusion, distraction, numbness, shock, stupor, trance

dazed *adj* **1** *dazed and bleeding:* numbed, out *colloq,* paralysed, shocked, stunned, stupefied, unconscious **2** *she was left dazed by the performance:* amazed, astonished, astounded, baffled, bewildered, confused, dazzled, dumbfounded, flabbergasted *colloq*, perplexed, shocked, speechless, staggered, startled, stunned, surprised, taken aback

dazzle *v* 1 *dazzled by the headlights:* blind, blur, confuse, daze 2 *dazzled by her beauty:* amaze, astonish, awe, bedazzle, bewitch, bowl over *colloq*, dumbfound, fascinate, hypnotize, impress, knock out *colloq*, overawe, overpower, overwhelm, scintillate, strike, stupefy, wow *colloq*
♦ *n* brightness, brilliance, glare, gleam, glitter, magnificence, razzmatazz *colloq*, scintillation, sparkle, splendour

dazzling *adj* awe-inspiring, breathtaking, brilliant, glaring, glittering, glorious, grand, impressive, radiant, ravishing, scintillating, sensational, shining, sparkling, spectacular, splendid, stunning, superb

dead *adj* 1 *he's been dead for a month:* dead as a doornail *colloq*, deceased *formal*, defunct, departed, extinct, gone, inanimate, late, lifeless, no more, perished 2 *dead leaves:* exanimate *formal*, inanimate, inert, insensate *formal*, insentient *formal*, lifeless 3 *a dead language:* discontinued, extinct, no longer spoken, obsolete 4 *that issue is dead:* dated, dead as a dodo *colloq*, no longer of interest, old hat *colloq*, out of date, passé 5 *this town is dead:* boring, dull, humdrum, quiet, tedious, unexciting, uninteresting, with nothing happening 6 *my fingers have gone dead:* gone to sleep, not feeling anything, numb, paralysed, unfeeling 7 *a cold, dead voice:* apathetic, cold, dull, emotionless, frigid, indifferent, insensitive, lukewarm, numb, torpid, unresponsive, unsympathetic 8 *the dead centre:* absolute, complete, downright, entire, exact, outright, perfect, thorough, total, unqualified, utter
Ⓕ 1 alive 3 living 7 lively
♦ *adv* absolutely, completely, entirely, exactly, perfectly, precisely, quite, thoroughly, totally, utterly, very

deaden *v* 1 *deaden the pain:* abate, allay, alleviate, anaesthetize, assuage, blunt, check, desensitize, diminish, dull, lessen, mitigate, moderate, numb, paralyse, reduce, soothe, subdue, suppress, take the edge off, weaken 2 *deaden the sound:* dampen, diminish, dull, hush, lessen, muffle, mute, quieten, reduce, smother, stifle, subdue, suppress
Ⓕ 1 heighten 2 amplify

deadlock *n* dead end, halt, impasse, stalemate, standstill, stoppage

deadly *adj* 1 *deadly poison:* dangerous, destructive, fatal, lethal, malignant, mortal, murderous, noxious, pernicious, toxic, venomous 2 *deadly enemies:* fierce, grim, hated, implacable, mortal, murderous, savage 3 *in deadly earnest:* extreme, great, intense, marked, serious 4 *a deadly lecture:* boring, dull, monotonous, tedious, unexciting, uninteresting 5 *deadly aim:* accurate, effective, precise, sure, true, unerring, unfailing
Ⓕ 1 harmless 4 exciting
♦ *adv* absolutely, completely, dreadfully, entirely, perfectly, quite, thoroughly, totally, utterly

deadpan *adj* blank, dispassionate, empty, expressionless, impassive, inexpressive, inscrutable, poker-faced, straight-faced, unexpressive

deaf *adj* 1 *he is profoundly deaf:* deaf as a post *colloq*, hard of hearing, stone-deaf, with impaired hearing 2 *she was deaf to my pleas:* heedless, impervious, indifferent, oblivious, unconcerned, unmindful, unmoved
Ⓕ 2 aware, conscious

deafening *adj* booming, ear-splitting, overwhelming, piercing, resounding, reverberating, ringing, roaring, thunderous, very loud, very noisy
Ⓕ quiet

deal *v* 1 *he quickly dealt the cards:* allot, apportion *formal*, assign, bestow *formal*, dispense, distribute, divide, dole out, give out, mete out, share 2 *a merchant dealing in silk:* bargain, buy and sell, do business, export, handle, market, operate, stock, trade, traffic 3 *deal a blow:* administer, deliver, direct, inflict, mete
♦ *n* 1 *a great deal of money:* amount, degree, extent, load, lot, portion, quantity, share 2 *their trade deal with the EU:* agreement, arrangement, bargain, buy, contract, pact, transaction, understanding 3 *it's your deal:* distribution, hand, round
▶ **deal with** 1 *deal with a situation:* attend to, concern, cope with, get to grips with, handle, look after, manage, process, see to, sort out, tackle, take care of 2 *her novel deals with the future:* be about, concern, consider, cover, treat

dealer *n* marketer, merchandiser, merchant, pusher *colloq*, retailer, salesman, salesperson, saleswoman, tout *colloq*, trader, trafficker, vendor, wholesaler

dealings *n* business, commerce, intercourse *formal*, negotiations, operations, relations, trade, traffic, trafficking, transactions, truck *colloq*

dear *adj* 1 *a dear friend:* adored, beloved, cherished, close, darling, endearing, esteemed *formal*, familiar, favoured, favourite, intimate, loved, precious, respected, treasured, valued 2 *dear prices:* costly, exorbitant, expensive, high-cost, high-priced, not cheap, overpriced, pricey *colloq*, steep *colloq*
Ⓕ 1 disliked, hated 2 cheap
♦ *n* angel, beloved, darling, honey, loved one, pet, precious, sweetheart, treasure

dearly *adv* 1 *he loves her dearly:* adoringly, affectionately, devotedly, fondly, intimately, lovingly, tenderly, with affection, with favour/ respect 2 *I wish it dearly:* deeply, extremely, greatly, profoundly, very much 3 *pay dearly:* at a great cost, at a high price, with great loss

dearth *n* absence, deficiency, famine, inadequacy, insufficiency, lack, need, paucity *formal*, poverty, scantiness, scarcity, shortage, sparsity, want *formal*
Ⓕ abundance, excess

death *n* 1 *people in danger of death:* curtains *colloq*, decease *formal*, demise *formal*, departure, end, expiration *formal*, fatality, finish, last farewell *colloq*, loss, loss of life, passing, passing away, perishing, quietus *formal*, the grave 2 *the death of the welfare state:* annihilation, cessation *formal*, demise *formal*, destruction, dissolution, downfall, end, eradication *formal*, extermination,

extinction, extirpation *formal*, finish, obliteration *formal*, ruin, termination *formal*, undoing
Ⓕ 1 birth, life

deathless *adj* eternal, everlasting, immortal, imperishable, incorruptible, memorable, never-ending, timeless, undying, unforgettable

deathly *adj* **1** *her face had a deathly pallor*: ashen, cadaverous, colourless, ghastly, grim, haggard, pale, pallid, wan **2** *a deathly illness*: deadly, extreme, fatal, intense, mortal, utmost

debacle *n* cataclysm, catastrophe, collapse, defeat, devastation, disaster, disintegration, downfall, failure, farce, fiasco, havoc, overthrow, reversal, rout, ruin, ruination, stampede, turmoil

debar *v* ban, bar, blackball, deny, eject, exclude, expel, forbid, hamper, hinder, keep out, obstruct, preclude *formal*, prevent, prohibit, proscribe *formal*, restrain, segregate, shut out, stop
Ⓕ admit, allow

debase *v* **1** *jargon debases the English language*: adulterate, alloy, contaminate, corrupt, defile, devalue, dilute, pollute, taint, vitiate *formal* **2** *people often feel debased by the legal process*: abase, cheapen, degrade, demean, discredit, disgrace, dishonour, humble, humiliate, lower, reduce
Ⓕ 1 purify **2** exalt

debased *adj* **1** *a debased form of religion*: adulterated, cheapened, contaminated, corrupt, defiled, devalued, impure, polluted, tainted **2** *morally debased*: abased, base, corrupt, debauched, degenerate, degraded, discredited, disgraced, dishonoured, fallen, humbled, humiliated, low, perverted, shamed, sordid, vile
Ⓕ 1 pure **2** elevated

debasement *n* **1** *the debasement of liberal education*: adulteration, contamination, corruption, devaluation, pollution **2** *sexual debasement*: abasement, cheapening, corruption, defilement, degeneration, degradation, depravation, disgrace, dishonour, humiliation, perversion, shame
Ⓕ 1 purification **2** elevation

debatable *adj* arguable, contentious, contestable, controversial, disputable, doubtful, dubious, moot, open to question, problematical, questionable, uncertain, undecided, unsettled, unsure
Ⓕ certain, incontrovertible, unquestionable

debate *n* altercation *formal*, argument, consideration, contention, controversy, deliberation, discussion, disputation *formal*, dispute, forum, polemic, reflection
♦ *v* **1** *we have debated this endlessly*: altercate *formal*, argue, contend, contest, discuss, dispute, kick around *colloq*, reason, talk about/over, wrangle **2** *he debated whether to mention it*: cogitate *formal*, consider, deliberate, meditate on, mull over, ponder, reflect, think over, weigh

debauch *v* **1** *accused of debauching public morals*: corrupt, deprave, lead astray, pervert, pollute, ruin, subvert **2** *he debauched a number of teenage girls*: ravish, ruin, seduce, violate
Ⓕ 1 cleanse, purge, purify

debauched *adj* abandoned, carousing, corrupt, corrupted, debased, decadent, degenerate, degraded, depraved, dissipated, dissolute,

excessive, immoral, intemperate, lewd, licentious *formal*, overindulgent, perverted, promiscuous, riotous, wanton
Ⓕ decent, pure, virtuous

debauchery *n* carousal, corruption, decadence, degeneracy, degradation, depravity, dissipation *formal*, dissoluteness, excess, intemperance, lewdness, libertinism *formal*, licentiousness *formal*, lust, orgy, overindulgence, rakishness, revel, wantonness
Ⓕ restraint, temperance

debilitate *v* cripple, devitalize *formal*, enervate *formal*, enfeeble *formal*, exhaust, impair, incapacitate, sap, undermine, weaken, wear out
Ⓕ energize, invigorate, strengthen

debilitating *adj* crippling, enervating *formal*, enervative *formal*, enfeebling *formal*, exhausting, fatiguing, impairing, incapacitating, tiring, undermining, weakening, wearing out
Ⓕ invigorating, strengthening

debility *n* asthenia *technical*, atonicity, atony, decrepitude *formal*, enervation *formal*, enfeeblement *formal*, exhaustion, faintness, fatigue, feebleness, frailty, incapacity, infirmity, lack of energy/vitality, languor *formal*, malaise *formal*, tiredness, weakness
Ⓕ strength, vigour

debonair *adj* affable, charming, courteous, dashing, elegant, refined, smooth, suave, urbane, well-bred

debris *n* bits, detritus *formal*, drift, fragments, litter, pieces, remains, rubbish, rubble, ruins, sweepings, trash, waste, wreck, wreckage

debt *n* **1** *£500 in debt*: arrears, bill, claim, debit, due, duty, hock, liability, money owing/due, overdraft, Queer Street *colloq*, score, the red *colloq* **2** *in someone's debt for their kindness*: commitment, indebtedness, liability, obligation
Ⓕ 1 asset, credit

debtor *n* bankrupt, borrower, defaulter, insolvent, mortgagor
Ⓕ creditor

debunk *v* cut down to size *colloq*, deflate, disprove, explode, expose, lampoon, mock, puncture, ridicule, show up

début *n* beginning, coming-out, entrance, first appearance, first night, first performance, first recording, first time, inauguration, initiation, introduction, launching, première, presentation

decadence *n* corruption, debasement, debauchery, decay, decline, degeneracy, degenerateness, degeneration, depravity, deterioration, dissipation *formal*, dissolution, fall, immorality, licentiousness *formal*, perversion, retrogression *formal*, self-indulgence
Ⓕ flourishing, rise

decadent *adj* corrupt, debased, debauched, degenerate, degraded, depraved, dissipated, dissolute, immoral, licentious *formal*, self-indulgent
Ⓕ moral

decamp *v* abscond, absquatulate *colloq*, bolt, desert, do a bunk *colloq*, do a moonlight flit *colloq*, do a runner *colloq*, escape, flee, flit, fly, hightail it *colloq*, make off, run away, scarper *colloq*, skedaddle *colloq*, take off, vamoose *colloq*

decapitate *v* behead, execute, guillotine, unhead

decay *v* **1** *the corpse quickly decayed:* corrode, decompose, fester, go bad, perish, putrefy *formal*, rot, rust, spoil **2** *the authority of the Prime Minister was decaying:* atrophy, corrode, crumble, decline, degenerate, deteriorate, disintegrate, dwindle, fail, shrivel, sink, waste away, weaken, wear away, wither
🖅 **2** flourish, grow
♦ *n* **1** *tooth decay:* decomposition, going bad, perishing, putrefaction *formal*, putrescence *formal*, putridity *formal*, rot, rotting **2** *urban decay:* atrophy, collapse, crumbling, decadence, decline, degeneration, deterioration, disintegration, fading, failing, wasting, weakening, withering

decayed *adj* addled, bad, carious, carrion, corroded, decomposed, mildewed, mouldy, off, perished, putrefied *formal*, putrid *formal*, rank, rotten, sour, spoiled, stale, wasted, withered

decease *n* death, demise *formal*, departure, dissolution, dying, expiration *formal*, passing, passing away

deceased *adj* dead, defunct, departed, expired, extinct, finished, former, gone, late, lost
♦ *n* dead person, departed

deceit *n* abuse, artifice, cheating, chicanery, craftiness, cunning, deception, double-dealing, duplicity *formal*, fake, feint, fraud, fraudulence, guile, hypocrisy, imposition, misrepresentation, pretence, ruse, sham, slyness, stratagem, subterfuge, swindle, treachery, trickery, underhandedness, wile, wiliness
🖅 frankness, honesty, openness

deceitful *adj* counterfeit, crafty, cunning, deceiving, deceptive, designing, dishonest, dissembling *formal*, double-dealing, duplicitous *formal*, false, fraudulent, guileful, hypocritical, illusory, insincere, knavish, lying, mendacious *formal*, perfidious *formal*, sly, sneaky, treacherous, tricky *colloq*, two-faced *colloq*, underhand, untrustworthy, untruthful
🖅 honest, open

deceive *v* abuse, bamboozle *colloq*, beguile, betray, bluff, camouflage, cheat (on), con *colloq*, delude, dissemble *formal*, double-cross *colloq*, dupe, ensnare, entrap, fool, gull, have on *colloq*, hoax, hoodwink, impose upon, kid *colloq*, lead on, lead up the garden path *colloq*, misguide, mislead, outsmart, outwit, pull a fast one on *colloq*, pull someone's leg *colloq*, pull the wool over someone's eyes *colloq*, put one over on *colloq*, put up a smokescreen *colloq*, seduce, set a trap for, string along *colloq*, swindle, take for a ride *colloq*, trick, two-time *colloq*

deceiver *n* abuser, betrayer, charlatan, cheat, con man *colloq*, crook *colloq*, deluder, diddler *colloq*, dissembler *formal*, double-dealer *colloq*, fake, fraud, hoaxer, hypocrite, impostor, inveigler *formal*, mountebank, seducer, swindler, trickster

decelerate *v* brake, put the brakes on, reduce speed, slow down

decency *n* **1** *her sense of decency:* correctness, decorum *formal*, fitness, good taste, propriety *formal*, respectability, seemliness *old use*, uprightness **2** *the decency to tell me:* civility,

courteousness, courtesy, etiquette, good manners, graciousness, politeness
🖅 **1** impropriety **2** discourtesy

decent *adj* **1** *decent behaviour:* appropriate, becoming, befitting, chaste, decorous *formal*, ethical, fit, fitting, modest, nice, presentable, proper, pure, respectable, seemly *old use*, suitable, tasteful, upright, virtuous, worthy **2** *a decent person:* accommodating, courteous, generous, gracious, helpful, kind, obliging, polite, thoughtful **3** *decent pubs:* acceptable, adequate, competent, OK *colloq*, reasonable, satisfactory, sufficient, tolerable
🖅 **1** indecent **2** disobliging

decentralize *v* deconcentrate, delegate, devolve, localize, regionalize, spread downwards/outwards
🖅 centralize

deception *n* **1** *to obtain property by deception:* artifice, bluff, cheating, chicanery, craftiness, cunning, deceit, deceptiveness, dissembling *formal*, double-dealing, duplicity *formal*, flim-flam *colloq*, fraud, fraudulence, guile, hypocrisy, illusion, insincerity, misrepresentation, pretence, subterfuge, treachery, trickery, underhandedness **2** *the victim of a deception:* bluff, cheat, con *colloq*, deceit, fraud, hoax, illusion, imposture, leg-pull *colloq*, lie, pretence, put-up job *colloq*, ruse, sham, snare, stratagem, subterfuge, swindle, trick, wile
🖅 **1** honesty, openness

deceptive *adj* **1** *appearances can be deceptive:* ambiguous, fake, fallacious *formal*, false, illusive, illusory, misleading, mock, specious, spurious, unreliable **2** *deceptive advertising:* cheating, crafty, crooked, cunning, dishonest, dissembling *formal*, duplicitous *formal*, fraudulent, sly, underhand
🖅 **1** reliable, true, unambiguous **2** artless, genuine, open

decide *v* **1** *decide to do something:* come to/arrive at a decision, come to/reach a conclusion, determine, make up your mind, reach/make a decision, resolve **2** *decide an issue:* adjudicate, arbitrate, conclude, determine, establish, fix, give a judgement/ruling, judge, resolve, rule, settle **3** *decide on a new car:* choose, go for *colloq*, opt for, pick, plump for *colloq*, select, settle

decided *adj* **1** *they were at a decided advantage:* absolute, categorical, certain, clear, clear-cut, definite, distinct, emphatic, express, indisputable, marked, obvious, positive, pronounced, unambiguous, undeniable, undisputed, unequivocal, unmistakable, unquestionable **2** *a woman of very decided opinions:* decisive, deliberate, determined, firm, forthright, purposeful, resolute, unhesitating, unswerving, unwavering
🖅 **1** inconclusive **2** irresolute

decidedly *adv* absolutely, certainly, clearly, decisively, definitely, distinctly, downright, obviously, positively, quite, unequivocally, unmistakably, unquestionably, very

decider *n* clincher, coup de grâce, determiner, floorer

deciding *adj* chief, conclusive, critical, crucial, crunch *colloq*, decisive, determining, final, influential, prime, principal, significant, supreme
🖅 insignificant

decipher *v* 1 *decipher the code*: crack *colloq*, decode, understand, unravel, unscramble 2 *decipher her notes*: construe *formal*, figure out *colloq*, interpret, make out, translate, understand, unravel, work out
🖅 1 encode

decision *n* 1 *the jury came to a decision*: adjudication, arbitration, conclusion, decree, finding, judgement, opinion, outcome, pronouncement, resolution, result, ruling, settlement, verdict 2 *a man of decision and action*: decisiveness, determination, firmness, forcefulness, purpose, resolve, strong-mindedness

decisive *adj* 1 *a decisive victory*: absolute, conclusive, critical, crucial, deciding, definite, definitive, determining, fateful, final, influential, momentous, prime, principal, significant 2 *a decisive person*: decided, determined, firm, forceful, forthright, positive, purposeful, resolute, strong, strong-minded, unswerving, unwavering
🖅 1 inconclusive, insignificant 2 indecisive

deck *v* adorn, array *formal*, beautify, bedeck *formal*, decorate, embellish, enrich, festoon, garland, garnish, grace, ornament, prettify, rig *colloq*, tart up *colloq*, tog *colloq*, trick out, trim

declaim *v* harangue, hold forth, lecture, orate *formal*, perorate *formal*, proclaim, rant, sermonize, speak boldly/dramatically, spiel *colloq*, spout *colloq*

declamation *n* address, harangue, lecture, oration, rant, sermon, speech, speechifying, tirade

declamatory *adj* bold, bombastic, discursive, dramatic, fustian *formal*, grandiloquent, grandiose, high-flown, inflated, magniloquent *formal*, oratorical, orotund *formal*, overblown, pompous, rhetorical, stagy, stilted, theatrical

declaration *n* 1 *a declaration issued at the end of the talks*: announcement, broadcast, decree, edict, manifesto, notification, proclamation, promulgation *formal*, pronouncement, statement 2 *he signed a declaration*: acknowledgement, affidavit *formal*, affirmation, assertion, attestation *formal*, averment *formal*, avowal *formal*, confession, confirmation, disclosure, profession, revelation, statement, testimony

declare *v* 1 *he declared his intention*: announce, broadcast, decree, make known, proclaim, promulgate *formal*, pronounce, publish 2 *she declared that there was no lawful impediment*: affirm, assert, attest *formal*, aver *formal*, avow *formal*, certify, claim, confess, confirm, disclose, maintain, make known, profess, pronounce, reveal, show, state, swear, testify, validate, witness

decline *v* 1 *the birth rate declined*: abate *formal*, become/get less, decrease, diminish, drop, dwindle, ebb, fade, fall, flag, go/come down, lessen, plummet, plunge, sink, slide, subside, wane, weaken, wither 2 *she declined the invitation*: avoid, balk, deny, forgo, give the thumbs-down to *colloq*, refuse, reject, repudiate, say no to, turn down 3 *his health began to decline*: decay, degenerate, deteriorate, fall off, lapse, regress *formal*, sink, slip, worsen 4 *the sun declined*: descend, dip, sink, slant, slope

🖅 1 grow, increase 2 accept 3 improve 4 rise
♦ *n* 1 *a decline in bird numbers*: abatement *formal*, decay, decrease, degeneration, deterioration, diminution *formal*, downturn, dwindling, failing, failure, fall, falling-off, lessening, recession, reduction, slump, waning, weakening, worsening 2 *the sun's gradual decline*: declination, declivity *formal*, descent, deviation, dip, divergence, hill, incline, slope
🖅 1 improvement 2 rise

decode *v* construe *formal*, crack *colloq*, decipher, figure out *colloq*, interpret, make out, translate, transliterate, uncipher, understand, unravel, unscramble, work out
🖅 encode

decomposable *adj* biodegradable, decompoundable, degradable, destructible

decompose *v* break down, break up, crumble, decay, disintegrate, dissolve, fester, putrefy *formal*, rot, separate, spoil

decomposition *n* corruption, decay, disintegration, dissolution, going bad, perishing, putrefaction *formal*, putrescence *formal*, putridity *formal*, rot, rotting
🖅 combination, unification

décor *n* colour scheme, decoration, furnishings, ornamentation, scenery

decorate *v* 1 *they decorated the tree*: adorn, array *formal*, beautify, bedaub *formal*, bedizen *formal*, deck, embellish, enrich, festoon, garland, garnish, grace, ornament, prettify, tart up *colloq*, trick out, trim 2 *decorate the spare room*: colour, do up *colloq*, paint, paper, refurbish, renovate, smarten, wallpaper 3 *decorated for his bravery*: bemedal, cite, crown, garland, give a medal to, give an award to, give an honour to, honour

decoration *n* 1 *interior decoration*: adornment, beautification, elaboration, embellishment, enhancement, enrichment, ornamentation, trimming 2 *Christmas decorations*: adornment, bauble, bunting, embellishment, flourish, frill, furnishings, garnish, knick-knack, ornament, scroll, trimming, trinket 3 *military decorations*: award, badge, colours, cross, crown, emblem, garland, honour, insignia, laurel, medal, order, ribbon, star, title, wreath

decorative *adj* adorning, beautifying, elaborate, embellishing, enhancing, fancy, non-functional, ornamental, ornate, pretty, rococo
🖅 plain

decorous *adj* appropriate, becoming, befitting, comely, comme il faut, correct, courtly, decent, dignified, fit, mannerly, modest, polite, proper, refined, sedate, seemly *old use*, staid, suitable, well-behaved
🖅 indecorous

decorum *n* behaviour, breeding, conformity, decency, deportment *formal*, dignity, etiquette, good form, good manners, grace, modesty, politeness, propriety *formal*, protocol, respectability, restraint, seemliness *old use*
🖅 bad manners, impropriety *formal*

decoy *n* allurement, attraction, bait, diversion, dummy, ensnarement, enticement, inducement, lure, pitfall, pretence, snare, temptation, trap
♦ *v* allure, attract, bait, deceive, draw, ensnare, entice, entrap, inveigle *formal*, lead, lure, seduce, tempt

decrease *v* abate *formal*, contract, curtail, cut back/down, decline, diminish, drop, dwindle, ease, fall (off), go/come down, lessen, let up, lower, make/become less, peter out, plummet, plunge, reduce, scale down, shrink, slacken, slide, slim (down), subside, taper (off), trim, wane

Ｆａ increase

♦ *n* abatement *formal*, contraction, cutback, decline, diminution *formal*, downturn, drop, dwindling, ebb, fall, falling-off, lessening, loss, lowering, reduction, shrinkage, step-down, subsidence

Ｆａ increase

decree *n* act, command, directive, edict, enactment, fiat, firman *formal*, hatti-sherif *formal*, indiction *formal*, interlocution *formal*, irade *formal*, judgement, law, mandate, manifesto, order, ordinance, precept, proclamation, psephism *formal*, regulation, rescript *formal*, rule, ruling, statute

♦ *v* command, decide, determine, dictate, direct, enact, enjoin *formal*, lay down, ordain, order, prescribe, proclaim, pronounce, rule

decrepit *adj* **1** *a decrepit building:* battered, broken-down, clapped-out *colloq*, crumbling, dilapidated, falling apart/to bits, in bad condition/shape, old, ramshackle, rickety, run-down, tumbledown, worn-out **2** *a decrepit person:* aged, doddering, elderly, feeble, frail, infirm, senescent *formal*, tottering, weak, worn-out

decrepitude *n* **1** *fallen into decrepitude:* decay, degeneration, deterioration, dilapidation, ruin **2** *old age and decrepitude:* debility, disability, dotage, feebleness, incapacity, infirmity, old age, senescence *formal*, senility, weakness

Ｆａ **1** good repair **2** youth

decry *v* animadvert *formal*, attack, belittle, blame, carp, censure *formal*, come down on *colloq*, condemn, criticize, declaim against *formal*, denigrate *formal*, denounce, depreciate, derogate *formal*, devalue, disapprove of, disparage, do a hatchet job on *colloq*, excoriate *formal*, find fault with, inveigh against *formal*, knock *colloq*, nit-pick *colloq*, pan *colloq*, pull to pieces *colloq*, run down *colloq*, slate *colloq*, snipe *colloq*, tear a strip off *colloq*, tear to shreds *colloq*, traduce *formal*, underrate, undervalue

Ｆａ praise, value

dedicate *v* **1** *he dedicated himself to medicine:* assign, commit, devote, give, give over to, offer, pledge, present, sacrifice, surrender **2** *dedicate a book:* address, inscribe, name **3** *the church is dedicated to a saint:* bless, consecrate, hallow, make holy, sanctify, set apart

dedicated *adj* **1** *a dedicated teacher:* committed, devoted, diligent, enthusiastic, given over to, hard-working, industrious, purposeful, single-hearted, single-minded, wholehearted, zealous **2** *a dedicated rail link:* bespoke, custom-built, customized

Ｆａ **1** apathetic, uncommitted

dedication *n* **1** *success takes work and dedication:* adherence, allegiance, attachment, commitment, devotion, enthusiasm, faithfulness, loyalty, self-sacrifice, single-mindedness, wholeheartedness, zeal **2** *the book's dedication is to the author's wife:* address, inscription **3** *the church's dedication*

ceremony: blessing, consecration, hallowing, presentation, sanctification

Ｆａ **1** apathy

deduce *v* come to the conclusion, conclude, derive, draw, gather, glean, infer, reason, surmise, understand

deduct *v* decrease by, knock off *colloq*, reduce by, remove, subtract, take away/off, withdraw

Ｆａ add

deduction *n* **1** *an astute deduction:* assumption, conclusion, corollary, finding, inference, presumption, reasoning, result, surmising **2** *the deduction of tax at 22%:* abatement *formal*, allowance, decrease, diminution *formal*, discount, reduction, removal, subtraction, taking away/off, withdrawal

Ｆａ **2** addition, increase

deed *n* **1** *heroic deeds:* accomplishment, achievement, act, action, activity, exploit, fact, feat, performance, reality, truth, undertaking **2** *the deeds to my mother's house:* agreement, contract, document, indenture *formal*, record, title, transaction

deem *v* account, believe, conceive, consider, esteem *formal*, estimate, hold, imagine, judge, reckon, regard, suppose, think

deep *adj* **1** *a deep pit:* bottomless, cavernous, fathomless, immeasurable, immersed, profound, unfathomed, unplumbed, yawning **2** *a deep feeling of unease:* ardent, earnest, extreme, fervent, grave, heart-felt, intense, passionate, profound, serious, severe, strong, very great, vigorous **3** *he's a very deep person:* astute, clever, discerning, intellectual, learned, perceptive, perspicacious *formal*, profound, reserved, sagacious *formal*, serious, wise **4** *his voice was deep and powerful:* bass, booming, low, low-pitched, powerful, resonant, resounding, rich, sonorous, strong **5** *a deep colour:* brilliant, dark, glowing, intense, rich, strong, vivid, warm **6** *it's all a bit deep for me:* abstruse *formal*, difficult, esoteric *formal*, mysterious, obscure, recondite *formal*

Ｆａ **1** open, shallow **2** light **3** frivolous, shallow, superficial **4** high, high-pitched **5** light, pale **6** clear, open, plain

♦ *adv* a great distance, a long way, far

♦ *n* briny *colloq*, high seas, main, ocean, sea

deepen *v* **1** *further setbacks deepened the gloom:* build up, deteriorate, extend, get worse, grow, heighten, increase, intensify, magnify, reinforce, strengthen, worsen **2** *the tunnels were deepened:* dig out, excavate, hollow, scoop out

deeply *adv* acutely, ardently, completely, distressingly, earnestly, extremely, feelingly, fervently, from the bottom of your heart *colloq*, gravely, intensely, mournfully, movingly, passionately, profoundly, sadly, seriously, severely, strongly, thoroughly, to the quick, very much, vigorously

Ｆａ slightly

deep-seated *adj* confirmed, deep, deep-rooted, entrenched, fixed, ingrained, settled

Ｆａ eradicable, temporary

deer *n* buck, doe, hart, reindeer, roe, stag

deface *v* blemish, damage, deform, destroy, disfigure, impair, injure, mar, mutilate, obliterate, spoil, sully, tarnish, vandalize

Ｆａ repair

de facto *adj* actual, effective, existing, real
   ▫ de jure
   ♦ *adv* actually, in effect, in fact, in reality, really
   ▫ de jure

defamation *n* aspersion *formal*, backbiting, calumny *formal*, denigration *formal*, derogation *formal*, disparagement, innuendo, libel, malediction *formal*, obloquy *formal*, opprobrium *formal*, scandal, slander, slur, smear, smear campaign, traducement *formal*, vilification *formal*
   ▫ commendation, praise

defamatory *adj* calumnious *formal*, contumelious *formal*, denigrating *formal*, derogatory, disparaging, injurious, insulting, libellous, maledictory *formal*, pejorative, slanderous, vilifying *formal*
   ▫ appreciative, complimentary

defame *v* asperse *formal*, besmirch, blacken, calumniate *formal*, cast aspersions *formal*, denigrate *formal*, discredit, disgrace, dishonour, disparage, drag through the mud *colloq*, infame *old use*, libel, malign, run down *colloq*, slander, sling/throw mud at *colloq*, smear, speak evil of, stigmatize, traduce *formal*, vilify *formal*, vituperate *formal*
   ▫ compliment, praise

default *v* backslide, defraud, dodge, evade, fail to pay, neglect, swindle
   ♦ *n* absence, defect, deficiency, dereliction *formal*, failure, fault, lack, lapse, neglect, negligence, non-payment, omission, want *formal*

defaulter *n* absentee, non-appearer, non-payer, offender

defeat *v* **1** *defeat the occupying force:* annihilate *colloq*, beat, bring someone to their knees, conquer, crush, devastate *colloq*, eclipse, excel, get the better of, hammer *colloq*, lick *colloq*, make mincemeat (out) of *colloq*, overcome, overpower, overthrow, overwhelm, quell, reject, repel, rout, ruin, run rings round *colloq*, slaughter *colloq*, smash *colloq*, subdue, subjugate *formal*, surpass, thrash *colloq*, throw out, thump *colloq*, trounce *colloq*, vanquish *formal*, worst **2** *the crossword defeated me:* baffle, balk, block, checkmate, confound, disappoint, foil, frustrate, get the better of, obstruct, perplex, puzzle, thwart
   ♦ *n* **1** *a decisive defeat at Stalingrad:* beating, conquest, crushing, debacle, overcoming, overthrow, rejection, repulsion, rout, ruin, subjugation *formal*, thrashing *colloq*, trouncing *colloq*, vanquishment *formal* **2** *a temporary defeat for my hopes:* breakdown, checkmate, disappointment, downfall, failure, frustration, reverse, setback, thwarting

defeatist *n* doomwatcher, pessimist, prophet of doom, quitter, yielder
   ▫ optimist
   ♦ *adj* despairing, despondent, fatalistic, gloomy, helpless, hopeless, pessimistic, resigned
   ▫ optimistic

defecate *v* crap *slang*, do number two *colloq*, ease yourself, egest *formal*, empty/move your bowels, evacuate, excrete, pass a motion, poo *colloq*, relieve yourself, shit *slang*, void excrement

defect *n* absence, blemish, bug *colloq*, deficiency, deformity, error, failing, fault, flaw, frailty, imperfection, inadequacy, lack, mistake, omission, shortcoming, shortfall, snag, spot, taint, want *formal*, weak spot, weakness
   ♦ *v* abandon, apostatize *formal*, break faith, change sides, desert, rebel, renege *formal*, revolt, tergiversate *formal*, turn traitor

defection *n* abandonment, apostasy *formal*, backsliding, betrayal, defalcation *formal*, dereliction *formal*, desertion, disloyalty, mutiny, perfidy *formal*, rebellion, renegation *formal*, revolt, tergiversation *formal*, treason

defective *adj* abnormal, broken, bust *colloq*, deficient, duff *colloq*, faulty, flawed, imperfect, in disrepair, malfunctioning *formal*, on the blink *colloq*, out of order
   ▫ in order, operative *formal*, working

---

defective or *deficient*? *Defective* means 'having a fault or flaw': *The crash was caused by defective wiring in the signalling system*. *Deficient* means 'inadequate, lacking in what is needed': *a diet deficient in essential vitamins and minerals*.

---

defector *n* apostate *formal*, backslider, betrayer, deserter, Judas, mutineer, quisling, rat *colloq*, rebel, recreant, renegade *formal*, tergiversator *formal*, traitor, turncoat

defence *n* **1** *the best defence against vermin:* barricade, bastion, bulwark, buttress, cover, deterrence, deterrent, fortification, fortress, garrison, guard, immunity, keep, outpost, protection, rampart, resistance, safeguard, screen, security, shelter, shield, stronghold **2** *a country's defences:* air force, armaments, armed forces, army, military, military resources, navy, soldiers, troops, weapons **3** *his defence was that he was insane:* alibi, apologia *formal*, argument, case, excuse, exoneration *formal*, explanation, explication *formal*, extenuation *formal*, justification, plea, pleading, testimony, vindication
   ▫ **1** assault, attack **3** accusation, attack

defenceless *adj* exposed, helpless, impotent, open to attack, powerless, unarmed, undefended, unguarded, unprotected, vulnerable, weak
   ▫ guarded, protected

defend *v* **1** *we shall defend our city:* barricade, buttress, cover, fortify *formal*, garrison, guard, keep from harm, preserve, protect, safeguard, screen, secure, shelter, shield, watch over **2** *the PM stoutly defended the policy:* argue for, back, bolster, champion, endorse, exonerate *formal*, explain, justify, make a case for, plead, speak up for, stand by, stand up for, stick up for *colloq*, support, uphold, vindicate
   ▫ **1** attack **2** accuse, attack

defendant *n* accused, appellant, litigant *technical*, offender, prisoner, respondent

defender *n* **1** *the city's defenders finally surrendered:* bodyguard, guard, keeper, protector **2** *a staunch defender of French culture:* advocate, apologist, backer, champion, counsel, endorser, guardian, patron, preserver, sponsor, supporter, upholder, vindicator
   ▫ **1** attacker **2** accuser

defensible *adj* **1** *a scientifically defensible argument:* arguable, justifiable, maintainable, pardonable, permissible, plausible, tenable, valid, vindicable **2** *defensible borders:* impregnable, safe, secure, unassailable
Ⓕ **1** indefensible, insecure **2** insecure

defensive *adj* **1** *defensive barriers:* cautious, defending, opposing, protecting, protective, safeguarding, wary, watchful **2** *a defensive tone in his voice:* apologetic, self-defensive, self-justifying

defer¹ *v* adjourn, delay, hold over, postpone, procrastinate *formal*, prorogue *formal*, protract *formal*, put back, put off, put on ice *colloq*, put on the back burner *colloq*, shelve, suspend, take a raincheck on *colloq*, waive
Ⓕ bring forward

defer² *v* accede *formal*, acquiesce *formal*, bow, capitulate, comply, give in, give way, kowtow, respect, submit, surrender, yield

deference *n* **1** *treating his mother with polite deference:* attentiveness, civility, consideration, courtesy, esteem *formal*, honour, politeness, regard, respect, reverence, thoughtfulness **2** *I bowed with suitable deference:* acquiescence *formal*, compliance *formal*, obedience, submission, submissiveness, yielding
Ⓕ **1** contempt **2** resistance

deferential *adj* attentive, civil, complaisant *formal*, considerate, courteous, dutiful, ingratiating, morigerous *formal*, obeisant *formal*, obsequious *formal*, polite, regardful *formal*, respectful, reverent, reverential, thoughtful
Ⓕ arrogant, immodest

deferment *n* adjournment, delay, holding-over, moratorium, postponement, procrastination *formal*, prorogation *formal*, putting-off, shelving, stay, suspension, waiving

defiance *n* challenge, confrontation, contempt, contumacy *formal*, disobedience, disregard, insolence, insubordination, opposition, rebelliousness, recalcitrance *formal*, resistance, truculence *formal*
Ⓕ acquiescence, compliance, submissiveness

defiant *adj* aggressive, antagonistic, bold, challenging, contemptuous, contumacious *formal*, disobedient, insolent, insubordinate, intransigent, militant, obstinate, provocative, rebellious, recalcitrant *formal*, refractory *formal*, resistant, scornful, truculent *formal*, unco-operative
Ⓕ acquiescent, compliant, submissive

deficiency *n* **1** *vitamin deficiency:* absence, dearth, deficit, inadequacy, insufficiency, lack, scantiness, scarcity, shortage, want **2** *serious deficiencies in police training:* defect, failing, fault, flaw, frailty, imperfection, shortcoming, weakness
Ⓕ **1** excess, surfeit **2** perfection

deficient *adj* **1** *a diet deficient in protein:* exiguous *formal*, inadequate, insufficient, lacking, meagre, scanty, scarce, short, skimpy, wanting *formal* **2** *deficient data protection systems:* imperfect, inadequate, incomplete, inferior, poor, unsatisfactory, unworthy
Ⓕ **1** excessive **2** satisfactory

deficient or *defective*? See panel at **defective**

deficit *n* arrears, default, deficiency, lack, loss, shortage, shortfall
Ⓕ excess

defile *v* **1** *land defiled by a previous owner:* contaminate, dirty, infect, make impure/unclean, pollute, soil, spoil, stain, taint, tarnish **2** *the grave had been defiled:* blacken, corrupt, debase, defame, degrade, denigrate *formal*, desecrate, disgrace, dishonour, inquinate *formal*, profane, stain, sully, taint, tarnish, treat sacrilegiously, violate, vitiate *formal*
Ⓕ **1** clean, cleanse, purify **2** honour
♦ *n* gorge, gully, pass, passage, ravine, valley

definable *adj* ascertainable, definite, describable, determinable, exact, explicable *formal*, fixed, identifiable, perceptible, precise, specific
Ⓕ indefinable

define *v* **1** *define the boundaries:* bound, circumscribe *formal*, delimit, delineate *formal*, demarcate, establish, fix, limit, mark out **2** *define the meaning:* characterize, clarify, describe, designate, detail, determine, elucidate *formal*, explain, expound *formal*, interpret, specify, spell out

definite *adj* **1** *no definite proof:* clear, clear-cut, exact, explicit, firm, marked, noticeable, obvious, particular, precise, specific **2** *very definite about what she wants:* assured, certain, decided, determined, fixed, guaranteed, positive, settled, sure
Ⓕ **1** vague **2** indefinite, provisional

definite or *definitive*? *Definite* means 'clear' or 'certain': *I'll give you a definite answer later. Definitive* means 'settling things once and for all': *a definitive study of Ben Jonson.*

definitely *adv* absolutely, categorically, certainly, clearly, doubtless, easily, indeed, indubitably *formal*, no denying, obviously, plainly, positively, surely, undeniably, undoubtedly, unmistakably, unquestionably, without doubt, without question

definition *n* **1** *a postmodern definition of truth:* clarification, description, determination, elucidation *formal*, explanation, exposition *formal*, interpretation, meaning, sense, significance **2** *prints with good definition:* clarity, clearness, contrast, distinctness, focus, precision, sharpness, visibility

definitive *adj* **1** *a definitive answer:* absolute, categorical, conclusive, convincing, decisive, exact, final **2** *the definitive book on the subject:* authoritative, complete, exhaustive, final, perfect, reliable, standard, ultimate
Ⓕ **1** interim

deflate *v* **1** *the balloon deflated:* collapse, contract, empty, exhaust, flatten, let down, puncture, shrink, squash, squeeze, void **2** *deflate his opinion of himself:* chasten, dash, debunk, disappoint, disconcert, dispirit, humble, humiliate, mortify, put down *colloq* **3** *share prices started deflating:* decrease, depreciate, depress, devalue, diminish, lessen, lower, reduce
Ⓕ **1** inflate **2** boost **3** increase, inflate

deflect *v* avert, bend, change course, deviate, diverge, drift, glance off, ricochet, sidetrack, swerve, turn (aside), twist, veer, wind

deflection *n* aberration *formal*, bend, changing course, deviation, divergence, drift, glancing-off, refraction *formal*, ricochet, sidetracking, swerve, turning, turning aside, twisting, veer

deflower *v* assault, defile, desecrate, despoil *formal*, force, harm, mar, molest, rape, ravish *formal*, ruin, spoil, violate

deform *v* buckle, contort, damage, disfigure, distort, maim, malform, mar, misshape, mutilate, ruin, spoil, twist, warp

deformation *n* bend, buckle, contortion, curve, defacement, diastrophism *technical*, disfiguration, distortion, malformation, misshapenness, mutilation, twist, twisting, warp

deformed *adj* bent, buckled, contorted, corrupted, crippled, crooked, defaced, disfigured, distorted, gnarled, maimed, malformed, mangled, marred, misshapen, mutilated, ruined, twisted, warped

deformity *n* abnormality, defect, disfigurement, imperfection, irregularity

defraud *v* beguile, cheat, con *colloq*, cozen *formal*, deceive, delude, diddle *colloq*, do *colloq*, dupe, embezzle, fiddle *colloq*, fleece *colloq*, fool, hoodwink, mislead, outwit, rip off *colloq*, rob, rook, sting *colloq*, swindle, trick

defray *v* discharge, meet, pay, recompense, refund, reimburse, repay, settle
◼ incur

deft *adj* able, adept, adroit, agile, clever, dexterous, expert, handy, neat, nifty, nimble, proficient, skilful
◼ awkward, clumsy

defunct *adj* **1** *a now defunct branch of the royal family:* dead, deceased, departed, expired, extinct, gone **2** *the defunct British Leyland:* bygone, expired, inoperative *formal*, invalid, obsolete, outmoded, passé
◼ **1** alive, live **2** functioning, operative *formal*

defy *v* **1** *defy the authorities:* beard, brave, challenge, confront, dare, defeat, despise, disobey, disregard, disrespect, face, flout, frustrate, ignore, provoke, rebel against, repel, resist, scorn, slight, spurn, stand up to, thwart, withstand **2** *her writings defy categorization:* avoid, baffle, elude, foil, frustrate
◼ **1** obey **2** allow, permit

degeneracy *n* corruption, debasement, debauchery, decadence, degeneration, degradation, depravation, deterioration, dissoluteness, effeteness *formal*, fallenness, immorality, perversion, sinfulness, vileness, wickedness
◼ morality, uprightness

degenerate *adj* abandoned, base, corrupt, debased, debauched, decadent, degenerated, degraded, depraved, deteriorated, dissolute, effete *formal*, fallen, ignoble, immoral, low, mean, perverted, profligate *formal*, sinful, vile, wicked
◼ moral, upright
◆ *v* decay, decline, decrease, deteriorate, fail, fall off, go down the tube *colloq*, go downhill *colloq*, go to pot *colloq*, lapse, regress *formal*, rot, sink, slip, worsen
◼ improve

degeneration *n* atrophy, debasement, decay, decline, decrease, deterioration, drop, failure, falling-off, lapse, regression *formal*, sinking, slide, slip, worsening
◼ improvement

degradation *n* **1** *misery and degradation:* abasement, corruption, debasement, debauchery, decadence, degeneracy, degeneration, deprivation, disgrace, dishonour, dissoluteness, fallenness, humiliation, ignominy, immorality, mortification, perversion, shame, sinfulness, vileness, wickedness **2** *the degradation of the environment:* decline, degeneration, deterioration
◼ **1** virtue **2** enhancement

degrade *v* **1** *stripping degrades women:* abase, adulterate, belittle, cheapen, corrupt, debase, defile, demean, deteriorate, devalue, discredit, disgrace, dishonour, humble, humiliate, impair, lower, mortify, pervert, shame, sully, weaken **2** *degraded to a lower rank:* cashier, demote, depose, deprive, downgrade, drum out *colloq*, reduce/lower in rank, relegate, take down a peg or two *colloq*, unseat
◼ **1** exalt **2** promote

degrading *adj* base, belittling, cheapening, contemptible, debasing, demeaning, discrediting, disgraceful, dishonourable, humiliating, ignoble, mortifying, shameful, undignified, unworthy
◼ enhancing

degree *n* **1** *to a great degree:* amount, extent, intensity, level, measure, range, stage, standard, step, strength **2** *the highest degree of security:* class, grade, level, limit, mark, order, point, position, rank, rung, stage, standing, status, unit

dehydrate *v* desiccate *formal*, drain, dry, dry out, dry up, effloresce *formal*, evaporate, exsiccate *formal*, lose water, parch

deification *n* **1** *her deification as a fertility goddess:* apotheosis *formal*, divinification *formal*, divinization *formal*, elevation, exaltation, glorification, immortalization, worship **2** *the deification of pop stars:* adulation, elevation, extolling, glorification, idealization, idolization

deify *v* **1** *he was deified as a god of war:* adore, adulate, apotheosize, exalt, glorify, pray to, revere, venerate *formal*, worship **2** *North Korea deifies its leaders:* aggrandize *formal*, elevate, exalt, extol, glorify, idealize, idolize, immortalize, venerate *formal*

deign *v* condescend, consent, demean yourself, lower yourself, stoop

deity *n* demigod, divine being, divinity, eternal, god, goddess, godhead, idol, immortal, power, spirit, supreme being

dejected *adj* blue *colloq*, cast down, crestfallen, crushed, demoralized, depressed, despondent, disconsolate *formal*, discouraged, disheartened, dismal, dispirited, doleful, down, down in the dumps *colloq*, downcast, downhearted, gloomy, glum, low, melancholy, miserable, morose, sad, spiritless, wretched
◼ cheerful, happy, high-spirited

dejection *n* blues *colloq*, depression, despair, despondency, disconsolateness *formal*, disconsolation *formal*, discouragement, dispiritedness, dolefulness, downheartedness,

dumps *colloq*, gloom, gloominess, low spirits, melancholy, misery, moroseness, sadness, sorrow, unhappiness, wretchedness
🔁 happiness, high spirits

de jure *adv* legally, rightfully
🔁 de facto
♦ *adj* legal, rightful
🔁 de facto

delay *v* 1 *delayed by strike action:* check, detain, filibuster, halt, hamper, hinder, hold back, hold up, impede, keep, obstruct, restrain, set back, stonewall, stop 2 *she delayed leaving:* adjourn, defer, hold over, postpone, procrastinate *formal*, put off, put on ice *colloq*, put on the back burner *colloq*, shelve, stall, suspend 3 *let us delay no longer:* dawdle, dilly-dally *colloq*, dither, hang on, hold back, lag (behind), linger, loiter, tarry *formal*
🔁 1 accelerate 2 bring forward 3 hurry, keep up
♦ *n* 1 *delays for holidaymakers:* check, halt, hindrance, hold-up, impediment, interruption, interval, lull, obstruction, setback, stay, stoppage, wait 2 *a delay of the trial:* adjournment, cunctation *formal*, deferment, holding-over, mora *formal*, moratorium, postponement, procrastination *formal*, putting-off, reprieve, respite, shelving, stay, suspension, waiving 3 *without delay:* dawdling, dilly-dallying *colloq*, lingering, loitering, stalling, tarrying *formal*
🔁 1 continuation, hastening 3 hurry

delectable *adj* 1 *a delectable pudding:* appetizing, dainty, delicious, flavoursome, luscious, mouth-watering, palatable, savoury, scrumptious *colloq*, succulent, tasty, yummy *colloq* 2 *a delectable young woman:* adorable, agreeable, attractive, charming, delightful, enchanting, engaging, exciting, pleasant, pleasing
🔁 1 unpalatable 2 unpleasant

delectation *n* amusement, comfort, contentment, delight, diversion, enjoyment, entertainment, gratification, happiness, pleasure, refreshment, relish, satisfaction
🔁 distaste

delegate *n* agent, ambassador, commissioner, deputy, emissary, envoy, legate, messenger, proxy, representative, spokesman, spokesperson, spokeswoman
♦ *v* appoint, assign, authorize, charge, commission, commit, consign, depute, designate, devolve, empower, entrust, give, hand over, leave, name, nominate, ordain, pass on/over

delegation *n* 1 *a delegation was sent to the talks:* commission, contingent, deputation, embassy, legation, mission, representatives 2 *delegation of responsibility:* committal, consignment, devolution, empowerment, passing on/over, transference

delete *v* blot out, blue-pencil, cancel, cross out, cut (out), edit (out), efface *formal*, erase, excise *formal*, expunge *formal*, obliterate, remove, rub out, strike (out), take out
🔁 add, insert

deleterious *adj* bad, damaging, destructive, detrimental, harmful, hurtful, injurious, noxious *formal*, pernicious, prejudicial, ruinous
🔁 enhancing, helpful

deliberate *adj* 1 *a deliberate attempt to start a fight:* advised, calculated, conscious, considered,

designed, intentional, planned, prearranged, preconceived, premeditated, preplanned, willed 2 *a slow and deliberate backswing:* careful, cautious, circumspect *formal*, heedful, leisurely, measured, methodical, ponderous, prudent, resolute, slow, steady, studied, thoughtful, unhesitating, unhurried, unwavering
🔁 1 accidental, unintentional 2 hasty
♦ *v* cogitate *formal*, consider, consult, debate, discuss, evaluate, excogitate *formal*, meditate, mull over, muse, ponder, reflect, ruminate *formal*, think (over), weigh (up)

deliberately *adv* 1 *the fire was started deliberately:* by design, calculatingly, consciously, in cold blood, intentionally, knowingly, on purpose, pointedly, wilfully, with malice aforethought, wittingly 2 *he worked calmly and deliberately:* carefully, cautiously, circumspectly *formal*, methodically, ponderously, prudently, slowly, steadily, thoughtfully, unhurriedly
🔁 1 accidentally, by accident, by mistake, unintentionally 2 hastily

deliberation *n* 1 *arrived at after much deliberation:* brooding, calculation, cogitation *formal*, consideration, evaluation, excogitation *formal*, forethought, meditation, mulling, musing, pondering, reflection, rumination *formal*, study, thought, weighing-up 2 *secret deliberations:* conferring, consultation, debate, discussion 3 *he played with great deliberation:* care, carefulness, caution, circumspection *formal*, prudence, slowness, steadiness, thoughtfulness, unhurriedness

delicacy *n* 1 *jewels of exquisite delicacy:* daintiness, elegance, exquisiteness, fineness, fragility, lightness, precision 2 *she's shown great delicacy and tact:* care, consideration, diplomacy, discretion, discrimination, finesse, niceness, sensitivity, subtlety, tact 3 *mouthwatering delicacies:* dainty, luxury, relish, savoury, speciality, sweetmeat, taste, titbit, treat
🔁 1 coarseness, roughness 2 tactlessness

delicate *adj* 1 *a delicate design:* dainty, elegant, exquisite, fine, graceful, slight 2 *she's feeling rather delicate:* ailing, debilitated *formal*, faint, frail, in poor health, infirm, sickly, unwell, weak 3 *delicate china:* breakable, brittle, easily damaged/broken, flimsy, fragile, frail, insubstantial 4 *a delicate situation:* awkward, controversial, critical, difficult, problematic, sensitive, touchy, tricky 5 *delicate handling:* careful, considerate, diplomatic, discreet, kid-glove *colloq*, sensitive, softly-softly *colloq*, tactful 6 *delicate colours:* bland, faint, mild, muted, pale, pastel, soft, subdued, subtle 7 *a delicate instrument:* accurate, exact, precise, precision, sensitive
🔁 1 coarse 2 healthy, strong 3 strong 4 easy 6 bold, strong

delicious *adj* 1 *a delicious pastry:* ambrosial *formal*, appetizing, choice, delectable *formal*, good, juicy, morish *colloq*, mouth-watering, nectareous *formal*, palatable, savoury, scrumptious *colloq*, succulent, tasty, tempting, toothsome, yummy *colloq* 2 *a delicious irony:* agreeable, captivating, charming, delightful, enchanting, enjoyable, entertaining, fascinating, gratifying, pleasant, pleasing, pleasurable
🔁 1 unpalatable 2 unpleasant

delight n amusement, bliss, contentment, ecstasy, elation, enjoyment, entertainment, euphoria, gladness, glee, gratification, happiness, joy, jubilation, pleasure, rapture, transport
🔁 disgust, displeasure
♦ v 1 *the prospect of being parents delighted them:* amuse, bowl over *colloq*, captivate, charm, cheer, enchant, enrapture, entertain, excite, gladden, gratify, please, ravish, thrill, tickle, tickle pink *colloq* 2 *delight in something:* appreciate, boast of, enjoy, glory in, like, love, relish, revel in, savour, take pleasure in, take pride in, wallow in
🔁 1 disappoint, dismay, displease 2 dislike, hate

delighted adj captivated, charmed, ecstatic, elated, enchanted, enraptured, entranced, euphoric, excited, glad, gleeful, gratified, happy, happy as Larry/a sandboy *colloq*, joyful, joyous *formal*, jubilant, over the moon *colloq*, overjoyed, pleased, pleased as Punch *colloq*, thrilled, tickled pink *colloq*
🔁 disappointed, dismayed

delightful adj ace *colloq*, agreeable, amusing, appealing, attractive, captivating, charming, delectable *formal*, diverting, divine *colloq*, enchanting, engaging, enjoyable, entertaining, exciting, fascinating, gratifying, great *colloq*, magic *colloq*, out of this world *colloq*, pleasant, pleasing, pleasurable, the tops *colloq*, thrilling
🔁 disagreeable, displeasing, distasteful, horrid, nasty, unpleasant

delimit v bound, define, demarcate, determine, establish, fix, mark

delineate v bound, chart, define, depict, describe, design, determine, draw, establish, fix, mark, outline, portray, render, represent, set forth, sketch, trace

delinquency n crime, criminality, law-breaking, misbehaviour, misconduct, misdeed, misdemeanour, offence, transgression *formal*, wrongdoing

delinquent n criminal, culprit, hooligan, law-breaker, miscreant *formal*, offender, ruffian, vandal, wrongdoer, young offender
♦ adj criminal, culpable *formal*, guilty, law-breaking, lawless, negligent, offending, remiss *formal*
🔁 blameless, careful

delirious adj 1 *delirious because of fever:* babbling, beside yourself, crazy, demented, deranged, frantic, frenzied, incoherent, insane, irrational, light-headed, mad, out of your mind, raving, unhinged, wild 2 *delirious with excitement:* beside yourself, carried away, ecstatic, elated, euphoric, jubilant, over the moon *colloq*, overjoyed
🔁 1 sane

delirium n 1 *feverish delirium:* craziness, derangement, fever, frenzy, hallucination, hysteria, incoherence, insanity, irrationality, lunacy, madness, passion, raving, wildness 2 *the delirium of first love:* ecstasy, elation, euphoria, excitement, joy, jubilation, passion, wildness
🔁 1 sanity

deliver v 1 *deliver a parcel:* bring, carry, convey, dispatch *formal*, distribute, give, give out, send, supply, take 2 *he was delivered to the UN Special Court:* cede *formal*, commit, entrust, grant, hand over, relinquish, surrender, transfer, yield

3 *deliver a speech:* announce, declare, enunciate *formal*, express, give voice to, make, proclaim, pronounce, speak, utter, voice 4 *a punch delivered to the head:* administer, aim, deal, direct, give, inflict, launch, strike 5 *deliver the promised benefits:* carry out, do, fulfil, implement, provide, supply 6 *delivered from my enemies:* emancipate *formal*, liberate, ransom *formal*, redeem *formal*, release, rescue, save, set free

deliverance n emancipation *formal*, escape, extrication, freedom, liberation, ransom *formal*, redemption *formal*, release, rescue, salvation

delivery n 1 *a delivery of bricks:* carriage, consignment, conveyance, dispatch *formal*, distribution, shipment, supply, transfer, transmission, transport, transportation 2 *his delivery was stilted:* articulation, elocution, enunciation *formal*, intonation, speech, utterance 3 *she had a difficult delivery:* childbirth, confinement, labour, parturition *formal*, travail *formal*

dell n dean, dingle, hollow, vale, valley

delude v bamboozle *colloq*, beguile, cheat, deceive, double-cross *colloq*, dupe, fool, have on *colloq*, hoax, hoodwink, lead on, misguide, misinform, mislead, pull a fast one on *colloq*, pull someone's leg *colloq*, pull the wool over someone's eyes *colloq*, take for a ride *colloq*, take in, trick, two-time *colloq*

deluge n avalanche, downpour, flood, inundation, overflowing, rush, spate, torrent, wave
♦ v drown, engulf, flood, inundate, overwhelm, submerge, swamp

delusion n deception, fallacy, false belief/ impression, fancy, hallucination, illusion, misapprehension, misbelief, misconception, misinformation, tricking

> *delusion* or *illusion*? A *delusion* is a false belief arising in your own mind, whereas an *illusion* is a false impression coming into your mind from the world outside it.

de luxe adj choice, costly, elegant, exclusive, expensive, fine, grand, lavish, luxurious, luxury, opulent *formal*, palatial, plush *colloq*, quality, rich, select, special, splendid, sumptuous, superior

delve v 1 *delved into her family's past:* burrow, dig into, examine, explore, go/look into, hunt in/ through, investigate, probe, research, search 2 *he delved into his rucksack:* burrow, dig into, hunt in/ through, poke, root, rummage, search

demagogue n agitator, firebrand, haranguer, orator, rabble-rouser, tub-thumper

demand v 1 *he demanded an apology:* ask, call for, claim, dictate, exact, hold out for, inquire, insist on, interrogate, order, petition, press for, question, request, solicit, stipulate, tell, urge 2 *the task demands patience:* call for, cry out for, involve, necessitate *formal*, need, require, take
♦ n 1 *she made unreasonable demands:* claim, clamour, desire, inquiry, insistence, interrogation, order, petition, plea, pressure, question, request 2 *demand for natural gas:* call, exigency *formal*, necessity, need, requirement, want

demanding *adj* a tall order *colloq*, back-breaking, challenging, difficult, exacting, exhausting, exigent *formal*, harassing, hard, insistent, nagging, pressing, taxing, testing, tough, trying, urgent, wearing
F3 easy, easy-going, undemanding

demarcate *v* bound, define, delimit, determine, establish, fix, mark (out)

demarcation *n* **1** *the demarcation of the border*: bound, boundary, confine, division, enclosure, limit, line, margin **2** *the demarcation of duties*: delimitation, determination, differentiation, distinction, division, establishment, fixing, marking off/out, separation

demean *v* abase, belittle, condescend, debase, degrade, demote, deprecate, descend, humble, humiliate, lower, stoop
F3 enhance, exalt

demeanour *n* air, bearing *formal*, behaviour, comportment *formal*, conduct, deportment *formal*, manner, mien *formal*

demented *adj* berserk, bonkers *colloq*, crazed, deranged, disturbed, insane, loony *colloq*, loopy *colloq*, lunatic, mad, needing your head examining *colloq*, nuts *colloq*, nutty *colloq*, nutty as a fruitcake *colloq*, off your rocker *colloq*, out of your mind, round the bend *colloq*, round the twist *colloq*, unbalanced, unhinged, wild
F3 sane

demise *n* **1** *smoking caused his early demise*: cessation *formal*, death, decease, departure, end, expiration *formal*, passing, termination *formal* **2** *the demise of British manufacturing*: collapse, downfall, failure, fall, ruin

democracy *n* autonomy, commonwealth, government by the people, republic, self-government

democratic *adj* autonomous, egalitarian, popular, populist, representative, republican, self-governing

demolish *v* **1** *the church is being demolished*: break up, bulldoze, destroy, dismantle, flatten, knock down, level, pull down, pulverize, raze, tear down **2** *demolish the opponents*: annihilate *colloq*, beat, bring someone to their knees, conquer, crush, devastate *colloq*, excel, get the better of, hammer *colloq*, lick *colloq*, overcome, overpower, overthrow, overwhelm, quell, repel, rout, ruin, slaughter *colloq*, subdue, subjugate *formal*, surpass, thrash *colloq*, vanquish *formal* **3** *demolish an argument*: destroy, overturn, ruin, undo, wreck
F3 1 build up, construct, erect

demolition *n* **1** *the demolition of the old flats*: breaking-up, destruction, dismantling, flattening, knocking-down, levelling, pulling-down, razing, tearing-down **2** *demolition of the opposing team*: annihilation *colloq*, beating, hammering *colloq*, licking *colloq*, overpowering, overthrow, overwhelming, rout, slaughter *colloq*, surpassing, thrashing *colloq*

demon *n* **1** *possessed by demons*: afrit, cacodemon, daemon, devil, evil spirit, fallen angel, fiend, ghoul, imp, incubus, rakshas, succubus **2** *a tyrant and a demon*: beast, brute, devil, fiend, monster, rogue, savage, villain **3** *a demon at chess*: ace *colloq*, addict, buff, dab hand *colloq*, fanatic, fiend, freak *colloq*, wizard

demonic *adj* crazed, devilish, diabolical, fiendish, frantic, frenetic, frenzied, furious, hellish, infernal, mad, maniacal, manic, possessed, satanic

demonstrable *adj* arguable, attestable, certain, clear, evident, evincible *formal*, obvious, positive, provable, self-evident, verifiable
F3 unverifiable

demonstrate *v* **1** *demonstrate the harmful effects of smoking*: determine, establish, prove, show, substantiate *formal*, validate *formal*, verify **2** *demonstrated their commitment to reform*: bear witness to *formal*, bespeak *formal*, betoken *formal*, betray, display, evince *formal*, exhibit, express, indicate, manifest *formal*, register, show, testify to *formal* **3** *he demonstrated how to use the cooker*: describe, explain, expound *formal*, illustrate, make clear, show, teach **4** *crowds demonstrating against the council*: march, parade, picket, protest, rally, sit in

demonstration *n* **1** *a demonstration of their power*: affirmation *formal*, confirmation, display, evidence, evincement *formal*, exhibition, expression, indication, manifestation *formal*, proof, substantiation *formal*, testimony, validation *formal*, verification **2** *a demonstration of the new technology*: description, elucidation *formal*, explanation, exposition *formal*, illustration, presentation, test, trial **3** *police broke up the demonstration*: civil disobedience, demo *colloq*, march, mass rally, parade, picket, protest, rally, sit-in

demonstrative *adj* affectionate, effusive, emotional, expansive, expressive, extrovert, gushing, loving, open, unreserved, warm
F3 cold, introvert, reserved, restrained

demoralize *v* **1** *job losses demoralized the workforce*: cast down, crush, daunt, deject, depress, disconcert, discourage, dishearten, dispirit, lower, make despondent, undermine, weaken **2** *demoralized by his depraved father*: contaminate, corrupt, debase, defile, deprave, pervert
F3 1 encourage, inspire confidence **2** improve

demote *v* cashier, degrade, downgrade, humble, reduce in rank, relegate
F3 promote, upgrade

demotic *adj* colloquial, enchorial *formal*, enchoric *formal*, popular, vernacular, vulgar

demur *v* balk, be unwilling, cavil, disagree, dispute, dissent, doubt, express doubts, hesitate, object, protest, refuse, scruple, take exception
♦ *n* compunction *formal*, demurral *formal*, disagreement, dissent, doubt, hesitation, misgiving, objection, protest, qualm, reservation, scruple

demure *adj* coy, grave, modest, prim, prissy, prudish, quiet, reserved, reticent, retiring, serious, shy, sober, staid, strait-laced, timid, unassuming
F3 forward, wanton

den *n* **1** *a wolf's den*: hideout, hole, hollow, lair **2** *a den of forgers*: dive *colloq*, haunt, joint *colloq*, meeting-place, patch, pitch **3** *study in his den*: hideaway, retreat, sanctuary, shelter, study

denial *n* **1** *his denial that he was implicated*: abjuration *formal*, contradiction, disaffirmation *formal*, disagreement, disavowal *formal*, disclaimer, dismissal, dissent, negation *formal*, opposition, renunciation, repudiation **2** *the denial of a visa*: dismissal, prohibition, rebuff, refusal, rejection, veto **3** *his denial of his heritage*: disavowal, disowning, renunciation, repudiation

denigrate *v* abuse, assail, belittle, besmirch *formal*, calumniate *formal*, cast aspersions on *formal*, criticize, decry *formal*, defame *formal*, deprecate, disparage, fling/sling/throw mud *colloq*, impugn *formal*, malign *formal*, pick holes in *colloq*, revile *formal*, run down, slander, vilify *formal*, vilipend *formal*
☒ acclaim, praise

denizen *n* citizen, dweller, habitant, habitué, inhabitant, occupant, resident

denomination *n* **1** *the major Protestant denominations*: belief, Church, communion, constituency, creed, cult, faith, order, persuasion, religion, religious body/group, school, sect **2** *the highest denomination of bank note*: class, designation, face value, grade, kind, sort, unit, value, worth

denote *v* **1** *red denotes urgency*: be a sign of, betoken *formal*, designate, express, imply, indicate, mark, mean, show, signify, typify **2** *the name is believed to have denoted a village in a clearing*: imply, mean, refer to, signify, suggest **3** *the quantity is denoted by the letter C*: betoken *formal*, express, mean, represent, stand for, symbolize

dénouement *n* climax, close, conclusion, culmination, finale, finish, last act, outcome, pay-off *colloq*, resolution, solution, upshot

denounce *v* accuse, arraign *formal*, attack, betray, castigate *formal*, censure, condemn, criticize, declaim *formal*, decry *formal*, deplore *formal*, fulminate *formal*, impugn *formal*, inculpate *formal*, indict, inform against, revile *formal*, vilify *formal*
☒ acclaim, praise

dense *adj* **1** *a dense crowd/forest*: close, close-knit, close-packed, compact, compressed, condensed, crammed, crowded, heavy, jammed together, packed, solid, thick, tightly packed **2** *dense smoke*: concentrated, impenetrable, opaque, thick **3** *a bit dense when it comes to maths*: crass, dim *colloq*, dim-witted *colloq*, dull, obtuse *formal*, slow, slow-witted, stupid, thick *colloq*
☒ **1** sparse, thin **3** clever, quick-witted

density *n* closeness, compactness, consistency, denseness, impenetrability, thickness, tightness
☒ sparseness

dent *n* concavity, crater, depression, dimple, dint, dip, hollow, indentation, pit
♦ *v* depress, gouge, indent, push in

denude *v* bare, defoliate, deforest, divest, expose, strip, uncover
☒ cover

denunciation *n* accusation, attack, castigation *formal*, censure, condemnation, criticism, decrial *formal*, denouncement, fulmination *formal*, incrimination, invective *formal*, obloquy *formal*
☒ acclaim, praise

deny *v* **1** *deny the allegations*: abjure *formal*, contradict, disaffirm *formal*, disagree with, disprove, gainsay *formal*, negate *formal*, nullify *formal*, oppose, rebut, refute *formal*, repudiate **2** *deny him access to his children*: decline *formal*,

dismiss, forbid, prohibit, rebuff, refuse, reject, turn down, veto, withhold **3** *deny your heritage*: disavow *formal*, disclaim, disown, recant *formal*, renounce, repudiate, turn your back on
☒ **1** admit **2** allow

deodorant *n* air-freshener, anti-perspirant, deodorizer, disinfectant, fumigant, fumigator

deodorize *v* aerate, disinfect, freshen, fumigate, purify, refresh, sweeten, ventilate

depart *v* **1** *she departed for Paris*: absent yourself, bunk off *colloq*, clear off *colloq*, decamp, disappear, do a bunk *colloq*, do a moonlight flit *colloq*, do a runner *colloq*, escape, exit, get going, go, hightail it *colloq*, hit the road/trail *colloq*, leave, make a bolt/break for it *colloq*, make off, make tracks *colloq*, make yourself scarce *colloq*, migrate, pull out, push along/off *colloq*, quit *colloq*, remove, retire, retreat, scarper *colloq*, scat *colloq*, scoot *colloq*, scram *colloq*, set off, set out, shove off *colloq*, skedaddle *colloq*, sling your hook *colloq*, split *colloq*, start out, take off *colloq*, take to your heels *colloq*, take your leave, up sticks *colloq*, vamoose *colloq*, vanish, withdraw **2** *he departed from the script*: branch off, deviate, differ, digress, diverge, fork, swerve, turn aside, vary, veer
☒ **1** arrive, return **2** keep to

departed *adj* dead, deceased *formal*, expired *formal*, gone, late, passed away

department *n* **1** *the accounts department*: agency, branch, bureau, district, division, office, organization, region, section, sector, station, subdivision, unit, wing **2** *that's not really my department*: area, concern, domain, field, function, interest, line, province, realm, responsibility, speciality, sphere

departure *n* **1** *a hasty departure*: escape, exit, exodus, going, going away/off, leave-taking, leaving, removal, retirement, retreat, setting-off, setting-out, withdrawal **2** *a radical departure from his previous work*: branching (out), change, deviation, difference, digression, divergence, forking, innovation, shift, variation, veering
☒ **1** arrival, return

depend *v* **1** *the cost depends on the quantity*: be based on, be contingent on *formal*, be decided by, be dependent on, be determined by, be subject to, hang on, hinge on, rest on, revolve around, ride on, turn on *formal* **2** *depend on her for support*: bank on *colloq*, build upon, calculate on, count on, expect, have confidence in, lean on, need, not manage without, reckon on, rely on, trust in

dependable *adj* a safe pair of hands *colloq*, certain, conscientious, faithful, honest, reliable, responsible, stable, steadfast, steady, sure, tried and tested *colloq*, trustworthy, trusty, unfailing
☒ fickle, unreliable

dependant *n* charge, child, client, hanger-on, henchman, minion, minor, parasite, protégé, relative, subordinate, ward

dependence *n* **1** *our dependence on gas imports*: confidence, expectation, faith, need, reliance, trust **2** *alcohol dependence*: abuse, addiction, attachment, helplessness, subordination, subservience
☒ **1** independence

dependency *n* **1** *a tiny British dependency*: colony, protectorate, province **2** *her dependency on her parents*: helplessness, immaturity, reliance, subordination, support, weakness **3** *drug dependency:* abuse, addiction, attachment, habit, subservience

dependent *adj* **1** *I don't want to be dependent:* helpless, immature, leaning, reliant, subject, subordinate, supported, sustained, vulnerable, weak **2** *the profit is dependent on the quantity bought:* based, conditional, contingent *formal*, controlled, decided, determined, dictated, influenced, relative, subject, subordinate
Fa 2 independent

depict *v* **1** *depicted in a painting:* describe, draw, illustrate, outline, paint, picture, portray, represent, show, sketch, trace **2** *novels depicting Victorian life:* characterize, delineate *formal*, describe, detail, illustrate, outline, portray, record, recount, render, represent, reproduce, show, trace

depiction *n* **1** *a depiction of a sea battle:* drawing, illustration, image, likeness, outline, picture, portrayal, rendering, sketch **2** *depictions of rural life:* characterization, delineation *formal*, description, detailing, outline, portrayal, representation, sketch

deplete *v* attenuate *formal*, bankrupt, consume, decrease, diminish, drain, eat into, empty, erode, evacuate, exhaust, expend, impoverish, lessen, reduce, run down, spend, use up, weaken, whittle away
Fa augment *formal*, increase

depletion *n* attenuation *formal*, consumption, decrease, deficiency, diminution *formal*, dwindling, evacuation, exhaustion, expenditure, impoverishment, lessening, lowering, reduction, shrinkage, using up, weakening
Fa augmentation *formal*, increase, supply

deplorable *adj* abominable, appalling, blameworthy, despicable, dire, disastrous, disgraceful, dishonourable, disreputable, distressing, grievous, heartbreaking, lamentable, melancholy, miserable, outrageous, pitiable, regrettable, reprehensible, sad, scandalous, shameful, unfortunate, wretched
Fa commendable, excellent

deplore *v* **1** *she deplores violence:* berate *formal*, blame, castigate *formal*, censure *formal*, condemn, criticize, denounce, deprecate *formal*, disapprove of, disparage *formal*, reprehend *formal*, reproach, reprove *formal*, revile, slam *colloq*, slate *colloq*, upbraid *formal* **2** *they deplored the appalling loss of life:* bemoan, bewail, cry, grieve for, lament, mourn, pine, regret, rue, shed tears, weep
Fa 1 extol

deploy *v* arrange, dispose *formal*, distribute, position, scatter, spread out, station, use, utilize

depopulate *v* dispeople, empty, unpeople

deport¹ *v* banish, exile, expel, extradite, ostracize, oust, repatriate, transport

deport² *v* acquit *formal*, act, bear, behave, carry, comport *formal*, conduct, hold, manage

deportation *n* banishment, exile, expulsion, extradition, ostracism, ousting, repatriation, transportation

deportment *n* air, appearance, aspect, bearing, behaviour, carriage, comportment *formal*,

conduct, demeanour *formal*, etiquette, manner, mien *formal*, pose, posture, stance

depose *v* demote, dethrone, discharge, disestablish, dismiss, displace, downgrade, fire *colloq*, oust, overthrow, remove, sack *colloq*, topple, unseat

deposit *v* **1** *she deposited the box in front of him:* bung *colloq*, drop, dump *colloq*, lay, locate, park, place, plant, precipitate *technical*, put (down), set (down), settle, sit **2** *deposit money in the bank:* amass, bank, consign, entrust, file, hoard, lodge, put away, put by, save, store, stow
♦ *n* **1** *a deposit of £100:* down payment, earnest *formal*, instalment, money, part payment, pledge, retainer, security, stake **2** *deposits of salt:* accumulation, alluvium *technical*, deposition *formal*, dregs, lees, precipitate, precipitation, sediment, silt, sublimate, warp

deposition *n* **1** *the deposition of the ruler:* dethronement, dismissal, displacement, ousting, removal, toppling, unseating **2** *the witness's deposition:* affidavit, declaration, evidence, information, statement, testimony

depository *n* arsenal, bonded warehouse, depot, repository, store, storehouse, warehouse

depot *n* **1** *military depot:* arsenal, cache, depository, repository, store, storehouse, warehouse **2** *bus depot:* garage, station, terminal, terminus

deprave *v* contaminate, corrupt, debase, debauch, defile, degrade, demoralize, infect, lead astray, pervert, pollute, seduce, subvert
Fa improve, reform

depraved *adj* base, corrupt, criminal, debased, debauched, degenerate, dissolute, evil, immoral, iniquitous, licentious *formal*, obscene, perverted, reprobate, shameless, sinful, vile, wicked
Fa moral, upright

depravity *n* baseness, corruption, debasement, debauchery, degeneracy, dissoluteness, evil, immorality, iniquity, perversion, reprobacy, sinfulness, turpitude *formal*, vice, vileness, wickedness
Fa uprightness

deprecate *v* berate *formal*, blame, castigate *formal*, censure *formal*, condemn, criticize, denounce, deplore *formal*, disapprove of, disparage *formal*, knock *colloq*, object to, protest at, reject, reprehend *formal*, reproach, reprove *formal*, revile, slam *colloq*, slate *colloq*, upbraid *formal*
Fa approve, commend

> *deprecate* or *depreciate*? *Deprecate* is a formal word meaning 'to disapprove of': *The government deprecated the soldiers' actions.* *Depreciate* most commonly means 'to fall or cause to fall in value': *Property shares have depreciated rapidly.* A rarer meaning of *depreciate* is 'to speak of as having little value or importance': *to depreciate your achievements.*

deprecatory *adj* apologetic, censorious *formal*, condemnatory *formal*, disapproving, dismissive, protesting, regretful, reproachful
Fa commendatory *formal*, encouraging

depreciate *v* **1** *the dollar depreciated against the euro:* decline, decrease/fall/go down in value,

deflate, devalue, downgrade, drop, fall, lessen, lower, reduce, slump **2** *she liked to depreciate my taste in art*: belittle, defame *formal*, denigrate *formal*, disparage *formal*, make light of, malign *formal*, revile *formal*, run down, slight, underestimate, underrate, undervalue
F3 1 appreciate **2** overrate

depreciation *n* **1** *the depreciation of the pound*: cheapening, deflation, depression, devaluation, fall, mark-down, reduction in price/value, slump **2** *continual depreciation of my efforts*: belittlement, denigration *formal*, disparagement *formal*, underestimation

depredation *n* denudation *formal*, desolation, despoiling *formal*, destruction, devastation, harrying, laying waste, looting, marauding, pillage, plunder, raiding, ransacking, ravaging, robbery, theft

depress *v* **1** *the state of our marriage depresses me*: break someone's heart *colloq*, bring down, burden, cast down, daunt, deject, discourage, dishearten, get down *colloq*, make sad, oppress, overburden, sadden, upset, weigh down **2** *alcohol depresses the nervous system*: debilitate, drain, exhaust, impair, lessen, level, lower, press, reduce, sap, tire, undermine, weaken **3** *a lack of buyers has depressed prices*: bring down, cheapen, cut, depreciate, devalue, lower, reduce, slash *colloq*
F3 1 cheer **2** fortify *formal*, vitalize **3** increase, raise

depressant *n* calmant, calmative, downer, relaxant, sedative, tranquillizer
F3 stimulant

depressed *adj* **1** *depressed by recent bad fortune*: blue *colloq*, cast down, crestfallen, dejected, despondent, discouraged, disheartened, dispirited, distressed, down, down in the dumps *colloq*, downcast, downhearted, fed up *colloq*, gloomy, glum, low, low in spirits, low-spirited, melancholy, miserable, moody, morose, pessimistic, sad, unhappy **2** *unemployment in depressed areas*: deprived, destitute, disadvantaged, needy, poor, poverty-stricken, run-down **3** *a depressed point on the body*: concave, dented, hollow, indented, pushed in, recessed, sunken
F3 1 cheerful **2** affluent, thriving **3** convex, protuberant

depressing *adj* black, bleak, cheerless, daunting, dejecting, discouraging, disheartening, dismal, dispiriting, distressing, dreary, gloomy, grave, grey, heartbreaking, hopeless, melancholy, sad, saddening, sombre, unhappy
F3 cheerful, encouraging, happy

depression *n* **1** *nothing could cure her depression*: blues *colloq*, dejection, desolation, despair, despondency, discouragement, doldrums, downheartedness, dumps *colloq*, gloom, gloominess, glumness, hopelessness, low spirits, melancholia *technical*, melancholy, pessimism, sadness, unhappiness **2** *mass unemployment during the depression*: crash, decline, hard times, inactivity, recession, slowdown, slump, stagnation, standstill **3** *the ball rolled into a small depression*: basin, bowl, cavity, concavity, dent, dimple, dint, dip, dish, excavation, hole, hollow, impression, indentation, pit, sink, valley

F3 1 cheerfulness, euphoria, happiness **2** boom, prosperity **3** convexity, protuberance *formal*

deprivation *n* **1** *deprivation of sleep*: denial, dispossession, lack, removal, withdrawal, withholding **2** *deprivation in inner cities*: destitution *formal*, disadvantage, hardship, need, penury *formal*, poverty, privation *formal*, want

deprive *v* bereave, confiscate, denude *formal*, deny, dispossess, divest, expropriate *formal*, refuse, rob, strip, take away, withhold
F3 endow, provide

deprived *adj* bereft, destitute, disadvantaged, impoverished, in need, lacking, needy, poor, underprivileged
F3 prosperous

depth *n* **1** *20 metres in depth*: deepness, drop, extent, measure, profoundness, profundity *formal* **2** *depth of feeling*: earnestness, fervour, gravity, intensity, passion, seriousness, severity, strength, thoroughness, vigour **3** *a person of great depth*: acumen, astuteness, awareness, cleverness, discernment, insight, intuition, penetration, perception, profundity *formal*, shrewdness, wisdom **4** *the depths of their knowledge*: amount, extensiveness, extent, profundity *formal*, scope **5** *depth of colour*: brilliance, darkness, glow, intensity, richness, strength, vividness, warmth **6** *the depths of the sea*: abyss, bed, bottom, deep, floor, gulf, middle, midst, remotest area
F3 1 shallowness **6** surface

deputation *n* commission, committee, delegation, embassy, legation, mission, representatives

depute *v* accredit *formal*, appoint, authorize, charge, commission, consign, delegate, designate, empower, entrust, hand over, mandate, nominate, second

deputize *v* act for, cover, double, relieve, replace, represent, stand in for, sub for *colloq*, substitute, take over, take the place of, understudy

deputy *n* agent, ambassador, assistant, commissioner, delegate, envoy, legate, lieutenant, locum, proxy, representative, second-in-command, spokesperson, stand-in, subordinate, substitute, surrogate, vice-chairperson, vice-president, vice-regent
♦ *adj* assistant, coadjutor, depute, representative, stand-in, subordinate, substitute, suffragan, surrogate, vice-

deranged *adj* berserk, bonkers *colloq*, confused, crazy, delirious, demented, disordered, distraught, disturbed, frantic, insane, irrational, loony *colloq*, loopy *colloq*, lunatic, mad, needing your head examining *colloq*, non compos mentis, nuts *colloq*, nutty *colloq*, nutty as a fruitcake *colloq*, of unsound mind, off your rocker *colloq*, out of your mind, out to lunch *colloq*, round the bend *colloq*, round the twist *colloq*, unbalanced, unhinged, unsettled
F3 calm, sane

derangement *n* aberration, agitation, confusion, delirium, dementia, disorder, distraction, disturbance, hallucination, insanity, lunacy, madness, mania
F3 order, sanity

derelict *adj* abandoned, deserted, desolate, dilapidated, discarded, falling to pieces,

forsaken, in disrepair, neglected, ramshackle, ruined, run-down, tumbledown
♦ *n* beggar, dosser, down-and-out, drifter, good-for-nothing, hobo, ne'er-do-well, no-good, no-hoper, outcast, tramp, vagrant, wretch

dereliction *n* **1** *saved the church from dereliction:* abandonment, desertion, desolation, dilapidation, disrepair, forsaking, neglect, ruin(s) **2** *dereliction of duty:* abandonment, abdication, apostasy *formal*, betrayal, desertion, evasion, failure, faithlessness, forsaking, neglect, negligence, relinquishment, remissness, renegation *formal*, renunciation
▣ **2** devotion, faithfulness, fulfilment

deride *v* belittle, disdain, disparage *formal*, gibe, insult, jeer, knock *colloq*, make fun of, mock, pooh-pooh *colloq*, rag, ridicule, satirize, scoff, scorn, sneer, taunt, tease
▣ praise, respect

de rigueur *adj* conventional, correct, decent, decorous *formal*, done, fitting, necessary, proper, required, right, the done thing *colloq*

derision *n* contempt, disdain, disparagement *formal*, disrespect, hissing, insult, mockery, ragging, ridicule, satire, scoffing, scorn, sneering, taunting, teasing
▣ praise, respect

derisive *adj* contemptuous, disdainful, disrespectful, insulting, irreverent, jeering, mocking, scoffing, scornful, taunting
▣ flattering, respectful

---

derisive or *derisory*? *Derisive* means 'mocking': *derisive laughter. Derisory* means 'ridiculous; deserving mockery or derision': *The management offered a derisory pay increase.*

---

derisory *adj* absurd, contemptible, insulting, laughable, ludicrous, outrageous, paltry, preposterous, ridiculous, risible *formal*, tiny

derivation *n* ancestry, basis, beginning, deduction, descent, etymology, extraction, foundation, genealogy, inference, origin, root, source

derivative *adj* acquired, borrowed, copied, cribbed *colloq*, derived, hackneyed, imitative, obtained, plagiarized, rehashed *colloq*, secondary, second-hand, trite, unoriginal
▣ innovative, inventive, original
♦ *n* branch, by-product, derivation, descendant, development, offshoot, outgrowth, product, spin-off

derive *v* **1** *derive pleasure from something:* acquire, borrow, draw, extract, gain, get, obtain, procure *formal*, receive **2** *the word derives from Old Norse:* arise, descend, develop, emanate *formal*, evolve, flow, follow, have as the source, have its origin/roots in, issue, originate, proceed *formal*, spring, stem

derogatory *adj* belittling, critical, defamatory *formal*, denigratory *formal*, depreciative *formal*, disapproving, disparaging *formal*, injurious, insulting, offensive, pejorative, slighting, uncomplimentary, unfavourable, vilifying *formal*
▣ complimentary, favourable, flattering

descend *v* **1** *the plane descended gently:* alight, arrive, dip, dismount, drop, fall, go down, incline, move down, plummet, plunge, sink,

slope, subside, swoop, tumble **2** *I won't descend to associate with someone like that:* condescend, deign, lower yourself, sink, stoop **3** *the place descended into chaos:* decline, degenerate, deteriorate, go downhill *colloq*, go to the dogs *colloq* **4** *descended from Vikings:* emanate *formal*, issue, originate, proceed *formal*, spring, stem **5** *the family descended on us:* arrived suddenly, invade, swoop, take over
▣ **1** ascend, rise

descendants *n* children, issue, line, lineage, offspring, posterity, progeny, scions, seed *formal*, successors
▣ ancestors

descent *n* **1** *a steep descent:* decline, declivity *formal*, dip, drop, fall, going-down, gradient, incline, plunge, sinking, slant, slope, subsiding **2** *the West's moral descent:* comedown, debasement, decadence, decline, degeneracy, degradation, deterioration **3** *they are of foreign descent:* ancestry, extraction, family tree, genealogy, heredity, line, lineage, origin, parentage, stock
▣ **1** ascent, rise

describe *v* **1** *describe a situation:* characterize, define, delineate *formal*, depict, detail, draw, elucidate *formal*, explain, express, give details of, illustrate, narrate, outline, portray, present, recount, relate, report, represent, specify, talk, tell, write **2** *describe someone as clever:* brand, call, consider, designate, hail, label, portray, style, think **3** *skaters describing circles on the ice:* delineate *formal*, draw, mark out, outline, sketch, trace

description *n* **1** *a description of the proposed changes:* account, characterization, chronicle, commentary, delineation *formal*, depiction, elucidation *formal*, explanation, exposition *formal*, narration, outline, portrait, portrayal, presentation, profile, report, representation, sketch, statement **2** *cheeses of every description:* brand, breed, category, class, designation, kind, make, order, sort, specification, type, variety

descriptive *adj* colourful, detailed, elucidatory *formal*, explanatory, expressive, graphic, illustrative, pictorial, striking, vivid

descry *v* catch sight of, detect, discern, discover, distinguish, espy *old use*, glimpse, mark, notice, observe, perceive, recognize, see, spot

desecrate *v* abuse, blaspheme, contaminate, debase, defile, dishallow, dishonour, insult, pervert, pollute, profane, vandalize, violate

desecration *n* blasphemy, debasement, defilement, dishonouring, impiety, insult, pollution, profanation, sacrilege, violation

desert[1] *n* barrenness, void, wasteland, wilderness, wilds
♦ *adj* arid, bare, barren, desolate, dried up, dry, empty, infertile, lonely, moistureless, parched, solitary, sterile, uncultivated, uninhabited, unproductive, waste, wild

---

Deserts of the world, with locations, include: Sahara, N Africa; Arabian, SW Asia; Gobi, Mongolia and NE China; Patagonian, Argentina; Great Basin, SW USA; Chihuahuan, Mexico; Great Sandy, NW Australia; Nubian, Sudan; Great Victoria, SW Australia; Thar, India and Pakistan; Sonoran,

SW USA; Kara Kum, Turkmenistan; Kyzyl-Kum, Kazakhstan; Takla Makan, N China; Kalahari, SW Africa

desert² *v* **1** *desert his family*: abandon, abscond *formal*, cast off *formal*, forsake *formal*, give up, jilt *colloq*, leave, leave high and dry *colloq*, leave in the lurch *colloq*, maroon, quit *colloq*, rat on *colloq*, relinquish *formal*, renounce *formal*, run out on *colloq*, strand, walk out on **2** *the soldier deserted*: abscond *formal*, decamp, defect, flee, fly, go AWOL, run away **3** *desert a political party*: abandon, apostasize *formal*, betray, change sides, deny, forsake *formal*, give up, recant *formal*, relinquish *formal*, renounce *formal*, tergiversate *formal*, turn your back on
⊟ 1 stand by, support **3** support

desert³ *n* **1** *the villains got their just deserts*: comeuppance *colloq*, due, payment, recompense, remuneration, retribution, return, reward, right, what you deserve **2** *everyone shall receive their deserts*: merit, virtue, worth

deserted *adj* **1** *a deserted mining village*: abandoned, bereft, derelict, desolate, empty, forsaken *formal*, god-forsaken, isolated, left, neglected, underpopulated, uninhabited, unoccupied, vacant **2** *a deserted wife*: abandoned, bereft, betrayed, forsaken *formal*, isolated, lonely, neglected, solitary, stranded
⊟ 1 populous

deserter *n* absconder, apostate *formal*, backslider, betrayer, defector, delinquent, escapee, fugitive, rat *colloq*, renegade, runaway, traitor, truant, turncoat

desertion *n* **1** *desertion of his family*: abandonment, absconding *formal*, casting-off *formal*, forsaking *formal*, give up, jilting *colloq*, leaving, quitting *colloq*, relinquishment *formal*, renunciation *formal* **2** *desertion from the armed forces*: absconding *formal*, decamping, defection, dereliction *formal*, flight, going AWOL, running-away, truancy **3** *desertion of a political party*: abandonment, apostasy *formal*, betrayal, denial, forsaking *formal*, giving-up, relinquishment *formal*, renegation *formal*, renunciation *formal*, tergiversation *formal*
⊟ 3 support

deserve *v* be entitled to, be worthy of, earn, have a right to, incur, justify, merit, rate, warrant, win

deserved *adj* apposite *formal*, appropriate, apt, condign *formal*, due, earned, fair, fitting, just, justifiable, justified, legitimate, meet *formal*, merited, proper, right, rightful, suitable, warranted, well-earned
⊟ gratuitous, undeserved

deserving *adj* admirable, commendable, estimable, exemplary, laudable *formal*, meritorious *formal*, praiseworthy, righteous, upright, virtuous, worthy
⊟ undeserving, unworthy

desiccated *adj* **1** *desiccated leaves*: dehydrated, dried, dry, exsiccated *formal*, parched, powdered **2** *a desiccated book on philosophy*: arid, dead, dry, sterile

desiccation *n* aridity, dehydration, dryness, exsiccation *formal*, parching, sterility, xeransis *formal*

design *v* **1** *designing a new kitchen*: delineate *formal*, draft, draw, draw up, outline, plan, plot, sketch **2** *design a course to suit your needs*: conceive, construct, create, develop, fabricate, fashion, form, hatch, invent, make, model, originate, think up **3** *tax cuts designed to spur growth*: aim, contrive, devise, gear, intend, mean, plan, plot, project, propose, purpose, scheme, shape, tailor
♦ *n* **1** *the design for the Spitfire*: blueprint, delineation *formal*, diagram, draft, drawing, guide, map, model, outline, pattern, plan, prototype, scheme, sketch **2** *a simple geometric design*: arrangement, cipher, composition, construction, device, emblem, figure, form, format, logo, make-up, monogram, motif, organization, pattern, shape, structure, style **3** *more by accident than design*: aim, desire, dream, end, enterprise, goal, hope, intention, meaning, object, objective, plan, plot, point, project, purpose, scheme, target, undertaking, wish

designate *v* **1** *designated as a listed building*: call, christen, describe, dub, entitle, name, style, term, title **2** *designated to be chairman*: appoint, assign, choose, define, denote, earmark, elect, indicate, nominate, select, set aside, show, specify, stipulate

designation *n* **1** *quality designations such as 'Grand Cru'*: appellation *formal*, description, epithet, label, name, nickname, sobriquet, style, tag *colloq*, term, title **2** *its designation as European City of Culture*: category, classification, definition, denoting, description, indication, marking, specification, stipulation **3** *the PM's designation of his own successor*: appointment, election, nomination, selection

designer *n* architect, author, contriver, creator, deviser, fashioner, inventor, maker, originator, planner, producer, stylist

designing *adj* artful, calculating, conspiring, crafty, cunning, deceitful, devious, guileful, intriguing, plotting, scheming, sharp, shrewd, sly, tricky, underhand, wily
⊟ artless, naïve

desirability *n* **1** *the desirability of qualifications*: advantage, advisability, benefit, excellence, merit, popularity, preference, profit, usefulness, worth **2** *the desirability of the woman*: allure, attraction, attractiveness, seductiveness, sexiness *colloq*
⊟ 1 disadvantage, inadvisability, undesirability

desirable *adj* **1** *a desirable qualification*: advantageous, advisable, agreeable, appropriate, beneficial, eligible, expedient, good, in demand, pleasant, pleasing, popular, preferable, profitable, sensible, sought-after, worthwhile **2** *a desirable woman*: alluring, attractive, beddable *slang*, fetching, seductive, sexy *colloq*, tantalizing, tempting
⊟ 1 undesirable **2** unattractive

desire *v* **1** *he desired a change of scenery*: be dying for *colloq*, covet, crave, fancy, give the world for *colloq*, hanker after, have designs on *colloq*, have your eyes on *colloq*, hunger for, like, long for, need, set your heart on, want, wish for, yearn for **2** *desire a man*: be crazy about *colloq*, burn for, fancy *colloq*, have a crush on *colloq*, lust after, take a shine to *colloq*, take to
♦ *n* **1** *a strong desire to move abroad*: appetite,

aspiration, craving, fancy, hankering, itch *colloq*, longing, lust, need, predilection *formal*, predisposition *formal*, preference, proclivity *formal*, want, wish, yearning, yen *colloq* **2** *a relationship based more on friendship than desire:* ardour, concupiscence *formal*, lasciviousness, libido, lust, passion, sensuality, sex drive, sexual attraction, sexuality

desired *adj* accurate, appropriate, correct, exact, expected, fitting, necessary, particular, proper, required, right
◢ undesired, unintentional

desirous *adj* ambitious, anxious, aspiring, avid, burning, craving, eager, enthusiastic, hopeful, hoping, itching, keen, longing, ready, willing, wishing, yearning
◢ reluctant, unenthusiastic

desist *v* abstain, break off, cease *formal*, discontinue *formal*, end, forbear *formal*, give up, halt, leave off, pause, peter out, refrain, remit *formal*, stop, suspend
◢ continue, resume

desk *n* ambo, bureau, davenport, écritoire, lectern, reading-desk, secretaire, writing-table

desolate *adj* **1** *the desolate steppes of Kazakhstan:* abandoned, arid, bare, barren, bleak, depressing, deserted, dismal, dreary, forsaken, gloomy, God-forsaken, isolated, lonely, solitary, unfrequented, uninhabited, unoccupied, waste **2** *she was desolate without him:* bereft, broken-hearted, dejected, depressed, despondent, disheartened, dismal, distressed, downcast, forlorn, forsaken, gloomy, heartbroken, melancholy, miserable, sad, unhappy, wretched
◢ **1** populous **2** cheerful
♦ *v* confound, devastate, discomfit *formal*, disconcert, floor *colloq*, get down, nonplus, overwhelm, shatter *colloq*, take aback, upset

desolation *n* **1** *the troops left a trail of desolation:* destruction, devastation, laying waste, ravages, ruin **2** *the rocky desolation of the steep slopes:* barrenness, bleakness, emptiness, forlornness, isolation, loneliness, remoteness, solitude, wildness **3** *the desolation of her private life:* anguish, broken-heartedness, dejection, depression, despair, despondency, distress, gloom, grief, melancholy, misery, sadness, sorrow, unhappiness, wretchedness

despair *v* be despondent, be discouraged, collapse, give in, give up, hit rock bottom *colloq*, lose heart, lose hope, surrender, throw in the towel *colloq*
◢ hope
♦ *n* anguish, dejection, depression, desperation, despondency, distress, gloom, hopelessness, inconsolability, inconsolableness, melancholy, misery, pessimism, wretchedness
◢ cheerfulness, resilience

despairing *adj* anguished, dejected, depressed, desolate, desperate, despondent, disconsolate *formal*, discouraged, disheartened, dismayed, distraught, downcast, grief-stricken, heartbroken, hopeless, inconsolable, miserable, pessimistic, sorrowful, suicidal, wretched
◢ cheerful, hopeful

desperado *n* bandit, brigand, criminal, cut-throat, gangster, gunman, hoodlum *colloq*, law-breaker, mugger *colloq*, outlaw, ruffian, terrorist, thug

desperate *adj* **1** *groups of desperate people huddled inside:* abandoned, anguished, dejected, depressed, desolate, despondent, disconsolate *formal*, discouraged, disheartened, dismayed, distraught, downcast, grief-stricken, heartbroken, hopeless, inconsolable, miserable, pessimistic, sorrowful, suicidal, wretched **2** *a desperate rescue attempt:* audacious, bold, dangerous, daring, determined, do-or-die, foolhardy, frantic, frenzied, hasty, hazardous, impetuous, incautious, precipitate *formal*, rash, reckless, risky, violent, wild **3** *in desperate need of more doctors:* acute, compelling, critical, crucial, dangerous, dire, extreme, grave, great, pressing, serious, severe, urgent **4** *desperate to leave school:* crying out for, dying *colloq*, in great need, needing very much, wanting very much
◢ **1** hopeful **2** cautious

desperately *adv* acutely, badly, critically, dangerously, dreadfully, extremely, fearfully, frightfully, gravely, greatly, hopelessly, seriously, severely, urgently

desperation *n* agony, anguish, anxiety, depression, despair, despondency, distress, gloom, hopelessness, misery, pain, sorrow, trouble, worry, wretchedness

despicable *adj* abominable, contemptible, degrading, detestable, disgraceful, disgusting, disreputable, loathsome, mean, reprehensible *formal*, reprobate, shameful, vile, worthless, wretched
◢ admirable, noble

despise *v* abhor *formal*, condemn, deplore *formal*, deride *formal*, detest, disdain, dislike, hate, have a down on *colloq*, loathe, look down on, mock, revile *formal*, scorn, shun, slight, sneer, spurn, undervalue
◢ admire

despite *prep* against, defying, in spite of, in the face of, notwithstanding *formal*, regardless of, undeterred by

despoil *v* denude *formal*, depredate *formal*, deprive, destroy, devastate, dispossess, divest, loot, maraud, pillage, plunder, ransack, ravage, rifle, rob, spoliate *formal*, strip, vandalize, wreck
◢ adorn, enrich

despondency *n* blues *colloq*, broken-heartedness, dejection, depression, despair, desperation, disconsolateness *formal*, discouragement, dispiritedness, distress, downheartedness, gloom, glumness, grief, heartache *colloq*, hopelessness, inconsolability, inconsolableness, melancholia, melancholy, misery, sadness, sorrow, wretchedness
◢ cheerfulness, hopefulness

despondent *adj* blue *colloq*, dejected, depressed, despairing, discouraged, disheartened, distressed, doleful, down, down in the dumps *colloq*, downcast, gloomy, glum, heartbroken, inconsolable, low, melancholy, miserable, mournful, sad, sorrowful, wretched
◢ cheerful, heartened, hopeful

despot *n* absolute ruler, absolutist, autocrat, boss, dictator, oppressor, tyrant

despotic *adj* absolute, arbitrary, arrogant, authoritarian, autocratic, dictatorial, domineering, high-handed, imperious, oppressive, overbearing, tyrannical democratic, egalitarian, liberal, tolerant

despotism *n* absolutism, autocracy, dictatorship, oppression, repression, totalitarianism, tyranny

democracy, egalitarianism, liberalism, tolerance

dessert *n* afters *colloq*, pud *colloq*, pudding, sweet, sweet course, sweet dish

destination *n* **1** *early retirement is my destination:* aim, ambition, aspiration, design, end, goal, intention, object, objective, purpose, target **2** *arriving at our destination:* end of the line, final port of call, journey's end, station, stop, terminus

destined *adj* **1** *destined to become a soldier:* appointed, certain, designed, doomed, fated, foreordained *formal*, inescapable, inevitable, intended, meant, ordained *formal*, predetermined *formal*, set apart, unavoidable **2** *destined for London:* assigned, booked, bound, directed, en route, headed, heading, routed, scheduled

destiny *n* doom, fate, fortune, future, karma, kismet, lot *formal*, luck, portion *formal*, predestination *formal*, predestiny *formal*

destitute *adj* **1** *a charity for destitute children:* badly off, bankrupt, broke *colloq*, cleaned out *colloq*, distressed, down-and-out *colloq*, hard up, impecunious *formal*, impoverished, indigent *formal*, on the breadline *colloq*, on your beam-ends *colloq*, penniless, penurious *formal*, poor, poverty-stricken, skint *slang*, stony-broke *colloq*, strapped for cash *colloq* **2** *a region destitute of natural resources:* bereft *formal*, deficient, depleted, deprived, devoid of *formal*, innocent of, lacking, needy, wanting

1 prosperous, rich

destitution *n* bankruptcy, beggary, distress, impecuniousness *formal*, impoverishment, indigence *formal*, pauperdom *formal*, pennilessness, penury *formal*, poverty, starvation, straits

prosperity, wealth

destroy *v* **1** *the flats were completely destroyed:* break, crush, demolish, devastate, dismantle, extirpate *formal*, flatten, gut, knock down, lay waste, level, obliterate, overthrow, pull down, ransack, ravage, raze, ruin, sabotage, shatter, smash, spoil, stamp out, subdue, tear down, thwart, torpedo, undermine, undo, unshape, waste, wreck **2** *the dog had to be destroyed:* annihilate, dispatch, eliminate, eradicate, extinguish, kill, nullify *formal*, put down, put out of its misery, put to sleep, slaughter, slay *formal*, vitiate *formal*

1 build up **2** create

destroyer *n* annihilator, demolisher, desolater, despoiler, kiss of death, locust, ransacker, ravager, vandal, wrecker

creator

destruction *n* **1** *extensive destruction caused by forest fires:* crushing, defeat, demolition, depredation *formal*, desolation, devastation, dismantling, downfall, havoc, knocking-down, levelling, obliteration, overthrow, pulling-down, ravagement, razing, ruin, ruination, shattering, smashing, tearing-down, undoing, vandalism, wastage, wreckage **2** *the destruction of the enemy:* annihilation, elimination, end, eradication,

extermination, extinction, killing, liquidation, massacre, murder, nullification *formal*, slaughter

2 creation

destructive *adj* **1** *destructive storms:* baneful *formal*, catastrophic, damaging, deadly, deleterious *formal*, detrimental, devastating, disastrous, disruptive, fatal, harmful, hurtful, injurious, lethal, malignant, mischievous, noxious *formal*, nullifying *formal*, pernicious, ruinous, slaughterous *formal* **2** *destructive criticism:* adverse, contrary, denigrating *formal*, derogatory, discouraging, disparaging, hostile, negative, subversive, undermining, unfavourable, unfriendly, vicious

1 creative **2** constructive, favourable

desultory *adj* aimless, capricious *formal*, chaotic, disconnected, disorderly, erratic, fitful, half-hearted, haphazard, inconsistent, irregular, loose, rambling, random, spasmodic, unco-ordinated, undirected, unmethodical, unsystematic

methodical, systematic

detach *v* **1** *detach the reply slip:* cut off, disconnect, disengage, disentangle, disjoin, dissociate, divide, free, isolate, loosen, remove, segregate, separate, sever, take/tear off, uncouple, undo, unfasten, unfix, unhitch **2** *detach yourself from something:* cut off, dissociate, estrange *formal*, free, isolate, loosen, segregate, separate, sever, split

1 attach **2** involve

detached *adj* **1** *a detached house:* disconnected, discrete, dissociated, divided, free, loose, separate, severed **2** *a detached and impersonal writing style:* aloof, clinical, cold, disinterested, dispassionate, impartial, impersonal, independent, indifferent, neutral, objective, remote, unconcerned, unemotional

1 connected **2** involved

detachment *n* **1** *an air of aristocratic detachment:* aloofness, coolness, disinterestedness, dispassionateness, fairness, impartiality, impassivity, indifference, lack of bias, lack of emotion, neutrality, objectivity, remoteness, reserve, unconcern **2** *the detachment of the umbilical cord:* disconnection, disengagement, disentangling, disunion *formal*, isolation, loosening, removal, separation, severance, uncoupling, undoing, unfastening, withdrawal **3** *a detachment of troops:* brigade, corps, force, patrol, squad, task force, unit

1 bias, concern, prejudice

detail *n* **1** *look at every detail of the plan:* aspect, attribute, circumstance, component, element, fact, factor, feature, ingredient, item, particular, point, respect, specific, specification **2** *her great attention to detail:* complexity, complication, elaboration, intricacy **3** *bogged down in minor details:* fine point, minutiae, nicety, technicality, trifle, triviality

♦ *v* **1** *all the policy's failings were detailed:* catalogue, delineate *formal*, depict, describe, enumerate, itemize, list, point out, portray, recount, rehearse *formal*, relate, set out, specify, spell out, tabulate **2** *he detailed me to make the arrest:* allocate, appoint, assign, charge, choose, commission, delegate

detailed *adj* **1** *a detailed account of the battle:* comprehensive, blow-by-blow *colloq*,

descriptive, exact, exhaustive, full, in-depth, itemized, meticulous, minute, particular, precise, specific, thorough **2** *highly detailed carving:* complex, complicated, convoluted *formal*, elaborate, intricate
🖻 **1** cursory, general **2** simple, unfussy

detain *v* **1** *I won't detain you any further:* check, delay, hinder, hold (up), hold back, impede, inhibit *formal*, keep (back), make late, retard *formal*, slow, stay, stop **2** *detained for questioning:* arrest, confine, hold, imprison, incarcerate *formal*, intern, keep, keep/hold in custody, lock up, put in prison, restrain
🖻 **2** release

detect *v* **1** *he detected a sadness in her voice:* ascertain, catch, discern, distinguish, identify, make out, note, notice, observe, perceive, recognize, sight, spot, spy **2** *help the police detect crime:* bring to light, catch, disclose, discover, expose, find, reveal, track down, turn up, uncover, unearth, unmask

detection *n* **1** *the early detection of heart disease:* ascertaining, discernment, distinguishing, identification, note, noticing, observation, perception, recognition, sighting **2** *the criminals have avoided detection:* disclosure, discovery, exposé, exposure, revelation, smelling-out, sniffing-out, tracking-down, uncovering, unearthing, unmasking

detective *n* dick *colloq*, gumshoe *colloq*, operative *US*, plain-clothes officer, police officer, private eye *colloq*, (private) investigator, shamus *colloq*, sleuth *colloq*, sleuth-hound *colloq*, tail *colloq*

detention *n* captivity, confinement, constraint, custody, detainment, imprisonment, incarceration *formal*, internment, punishment, quarantine, restraint
🖻 release

deter *v* caution, check, daunt, discourage, disincline *formal*, dissuade *formal*, frighten, hinder, inhibit, intimidate, prevent, prohibit, put off, restrain, scare off, stop, talk out of, turn off *colloq*, warn
🖻 encourage

detergent *n* abstergent *technical*, cleaner, cleanser, soap, washing powder, washing-up liquid

deteriorate *v* **1** *the situation is deteriorating:* decline, degenerate, depreciate, drop, ebb, fail, fall off, get worse, go down the tube *colloq*, go downhill *colloq*, go to pot *colloq*, go/run to seed *colloq*, lapse, relapse, retrograde *formal*, retrogress *formal*, slide, slip, wane, worsen **2** *the varnish has deteriorated:* break up, decay, decompose, disintegrate, fade, fall apart, fall to pieces, go bad, weaken
🖻 **1** get better, improve

deterioration *n* atrophy, corrosion, debasement, decline, degeneration, degradation, disintegration, downturn, drop, ebb, exacerbation *formal*, failure, falling-off, lapse, pejoration *formal*, relapse, retrogression *formal*, slide, slipping, waning, worsening
🖻 improvement

determinate *adj* absolute, certain, clear-cut, conclusive, decided, decisive, defined, definite, definitive, distinct, established, explicit, express,

fixed, positive, precise, quantified, settled, specific, specified
🖻 indeterminate

determination *n* **1** *you need determination to succeed:* backbone, conviction, dedication, dig your heels in *colloq*, drive, firmness, firmness of purpose, fortitude *formal*, grit *colloq*, guts *colloq*, hang on like grim death *colloq*, hold your ground *colloq*, insistence, moral fibre, perseverance, persistence, purpose, push, resoluteness, resolve, single-mindedness, stamina, stay the course *colloq*, steadfastness, strength of character, tenacity, will, willpower **2** *a determination is needed on the future of the Bill:* conclusion, decision, decree, judgement, opinion, resolution *formal*, settlement, verdict
🖻 **1** irresolution

determine *v* **1** *it determines if you'll pass or fail:* affect, condition, control, dictate, direct, govern, guide, impel, influence, ordain, prompt, regulate **2** *to determine what really happened:* ascertain, check, detect, discover, establish, find out, identify, learn, verify **3** *a right to determine their own future:* agree on, choose, clinch *colloq*, conclude, decide, elect, establish, finish, fix on, make up your mind, purpose *formal*, resolve *formal*, settle

determined *adj* bent, convinced, dead set *colloq*, decided, dedicated, dogged, firm, fixed, hell-bent *colloq*, insistent, intent, out *colloq*, persevering, persistent, purposeful, resolute, resolved, set, single-minded, steadfast, strong, strong-minded, strong-willed, stubborn, tenacious, uncompromising, unflinching, unwavering
🖻 irresolute, wavering

deterrent *n* bar, barrier, block, check, curb, difficulty, discouragement, disincentive, hindrance, impediment, obstacle, obstruction, repellent, restraint
🖻 encouragement, incentive

detest *v* abhor *formal*, abominate *formal*, can't stand *colloq*, deplore, despise, dislike, execrate *formal*, hate, loathe, recoil from
🖻 adore, love

detestable *adj* abhorrent *formal*, abominable *formal*, accursed *formal*, contemptible, despicable, disgusting, distasteful, execrable *formal*, hateful, heinous, loathsome, obnoxious, odious, offensive, repellent, reprehensible *formal*, repugnant, repulsive, revolting, shocking, sordid, vile
🖻 admirable, adorable

detestation *n* abhorrence *formal*, abomination *formal*, anathema, animosity, antipathy, aversion, disgust, dislike, execration *formal*, hate, hatred, hostility, loathing, odium *formal*, repugnance, revulsion
🖻 adoration, approval, love

dethrone *v* depose, oust, topple, uncrown, unseat, unthrone
🖻 crown, enthrone

detonate *v* blast, blow up, discharge, explode, fulminate *formal*, ignite, kindle, let off, set off, spark off

detonation *n* bang, blast, blow-up, boom, burst, discharge, explosion, fulmination *formal*, igniting, ignition, report *formal*

detour *n* bypass, bypath, byroad, byway, circuitous route, deviation, digression, diversion, indirect route, roundabout route, scenic route

detract *v* devaluate, diminish, lessen, lower, mar, reduce, spoil, subtract from, take away from
🠺 add to, enhance, praise

detractor *n* backbiter, belittler, defamer, denigrator *formal*, disparager *formal*, enemy, muck-raker, reviler, scandalmonger, slanderer, traducer *formal*, vilifier *formal*
🠺 defender, flatterer, supporter

detriment *n* damage, disadvantage, disservice, evil, harm, hurt, ill, impairment, injury, loss, mischief, prejudice, wrong
🠺 advantage, benefit

detrimental *adj* adverse, damaging, destructive, disadvantageous, harmful, hurtful, inimical *formal*, injurious *formal*, mischievous, pernicious, prejudicial
🠺 advantageous, beneficial, favourable

detritus *n* debris, fragments, garbage, junk, litter, remains, rubbish, rubble, scum, waste, wreckage

devalue *v* decrease, deflate, devalorize *formal*, devaluate, lower, reduce

devastate *v* **1** *a fire devastated the hotel*: demolish, desolate, despoil, destroy, flatten, lay waste, level, pillage, plunder, ransack, ravage, raze, ruin, sack, spoil, waste, wreck **2** *she's devastated by the news*: confound, discomfit *formal*, discompose, disconcert, floor *colloq*, nonplus, overcome, overwhelm, perturb *formal*, shatter *colloq*, shock, take aback, traumatize

devastating *adj* **1** *devastating storms*: catastrophic, damaging, destructive, disastrous, harmful **2** *a devastating argument*: effective, incisive, overwhelming, shattering *colloq*, shocking, stunning

devastation *n* annihilation, damage, demolition, desolation, destruction, havoc, pillage, plunder, ravages, ruin(s), spoliation, waste, wreckage

develop *v* **1** *pupils develop at different rates*: advance, branch out, enlarge, evolve, expand, flourish, foster, grow, improve, mature, nurture, progress, prosper, spread **2** *she developed his original idea*: amplify, dilate on *formal*, elaborate, enhance, expand on, unfold, work out **3** *secretly developed an atomic weapons programme*: acquire, begin, commence *formal*, contract *formal*, create, establish, found, generate, institute, invent, originate, produce, set about/off, start **4** *a problem which developed last week*: arise, come about, ensue, follow, grow, happen, result **5** *develop an illness*: become ill with, become infected with, catch, contract *formal*, get, go down with, pick up, succumb to *formal*

development *n* **1** *the development of trade links*: advance, blossoming, elaboration, enlargement, evolution, expansion, extension, flourishing, furtherance, growth, improvement, increase, issue, maturity, progress, progression, promotion, prosperity, refinement, spread, unfolding **2** *an important development in the case*: change, circumstance, event, happening, incident, occurrence, outcome, phenomenon,

result, situation **3** *a property development*: area, block, centre, complex, estate, land

deviant *adj* aberrant, abnormal, anomalous, bent, bizarre, divergent, eccentric, freakish, irregular, kinky *colloq*, oddball *colloq*, perverse, perverted, quirky, twisted, variant, wayward, with a screw loose *colloq*, with bats in the belfry *colloq*
🠺 normal
♦ *n* crank *colloq*, dropout, freak, geek *slang*, goof *slang*, kook *colloq*, misfit, odd sort, oddball *colloq*, oddity, pervert, weirdo *colloq*
🠺 straight

deviate *v* change, deflect, depart, differ, digress, diverge, drift, err, go astray, go off the rails *colloq*, part, stray, swerve, turn (aside), vary, veer, wander, yaw

deviation *n* aberration, abnormality, alteration, anomaly, change, deflection, departure, detour, difference, digression, discrepancy, disparity *formal*, divergence, drift, eccentricity, fluctuation, freak, inconsistency, irregularity, quirk, shift, turning-aside, variance, variation
🠺 conformity, regularity

device *n* **1** *the device was easy to use*: apparatus, appliance, contraption, contrivance, gadget, gizmo *colloq*, implement, instrument, machine, mechanism, tool, utensil **2** *a device to give him a little more time*: artifice, dodge *colloq*, gambit, machination *formal*, manoeuvre, plan, plot, ploy, ruse, scheme, stratagem, strategy, stunt, trick, wile **3** *a decorative device*: badge, coat of arms, colophon, crest, design, emblem, insignia, logo, motif, seal, shield, symbol, token

devil *n* **1** *devils summoned from Hell*: Adversary, arch-fiend, Beelzebub, demon, Evil One, evil spirit, fiend, imp, Lucifer, Mephistopheles, Old Harry *colloq*, Old Nick *colloq*, Prince of Darkness, Satan **2** *the devils who killed my son*: beast, brute, demon, imp, monster, ogre, rascal, rogue, savage, terror, wretch

devilish *adj* accursed, atrocious, damnable, demonic, diabolic, diabolical, disastrous, dreadful, evil, excruciating, execrable *formal*, fiendish, hellish, infernal, nefarious *formal*, outrageous, satanic, shocking, vile, wicked

devil-may-care *adj* careless, casual, cavalier, easy-going, flippant, frivolous, happy-go-lucky, heedless, insouciant *formal*, nonchalant, reckless, swaggering, swashbuckling, unconcerned, unworried

devious *adj* **1** *a devious scheme to defraud him*: artful, calculating, crafty, crooked *colloq*, cunning, deceitful, designing, dishonest, disingenuous *formal*, double-dealing, evasive, insidious, insincere, misleading, scheming, slippery *colloq*, sly, surreptitious, treacherous, tricky *colloq*, underhand, unscrupulous, wily **2** *she followed a devious route*: circuitous, deviating, erratic, indirect, rambling, roundabout, tortuous, wandering, winding
🠺 **1** straightforward **2** direct

devise *v* arrange, come up with, compose, conceive, concoct, construct, contrive, cook up *colloq*, create, design, dream up, fabricate, forge, form, formulate, frame, hatch, imagine, invent, originate, plan, plot, project, put together, scheme, shape, think up, work out

devoid adj bare, barren, bereft, deficient *formal*, deprived, destitute, empty, free, lacking, vacant, void, wanting, without
⊞ endowed

devolution n decentralization, delegation of power, dispersal, distribution, transference of power
⊞ centralization

devolve v commission, consign, convey, delegate, deliver, depute, entrust, fall to, hand down, rest with, transfer

devote v allocate, allot, apply, appropriate, assign, commit, consecrate, consign, dedicate, enshrine, give, give yourself, offer, pledge, put in, reserve, sacrifice, set apart, set aside, surrender

devoted adj ardent, attentive, caring, committed, concerned, constant, dedicated, devout, faithful, fond, loving, loyal, staunch, steadfast, tireless, true, unswerving
⊞ disloyal, indifferent

devotee n addict, adherent, admirer, aficionado, buff *colloq*, disciple, enthusiast, fan, fanatic, fiend *colloq*, follower, freak *colloq*, hound, merchant *colloq*, supporter, zealot

devotion n 1 *touched by her continued devotion:* adherence, admiration, adoration, affection, allegiance, ardour, attachment, closeness, commitment, consecration, constancy, dedication, earnestness, faithfulness, fervour, fidelity *formal*, fondness, love, loyalty, passion, regard, reverence, solidarity, staunchness, steadfastness, support, trueness, warmness, zeal 2 *the monk's life of devotion:* devoutness, faith, godliness, holiness, piety, sanctity, spirituality 3 *they perform devotions four times a day:* observance, prayer, worship
⊞ 1 inconstancy 2 irreverence

devotional adj devout, dutiful, holy, pietistic, pious, religious, reverential, sacred, solemn, spiritual

devour v 1 *he devoured the pork pie:* bolt, consume, cram, eat, eat up, feast on, finish off, gobble, gorge, gormandize, gulp, guzzle, knock back *colloq*, polish off *colloq*, put away *colloq*, relish, revel in, scoff *colloq*, stuff *colloq*, swallow, tuck into *colloq*, wolf down *colloq* 2 *the advancing desert devoured the town:* absorb, consume, destroy, devastate, dispatch, engulf, envelop, lay waste, ravage 3 *devour a book:* appreciate, be engrossed in, drink in, enjoy, feast on, relish, take in

devout adj 1 *a devout Catholic:* church-going, committed, godly, holy, orthodox, pious, practising, prayerful, religious, reverent, saintly 2 *a devout socialist:* ardent, constant, deep, devoted, earnest, faithful, fervent, genuine, heartfelt, intense, passionate, profound, serious, sincere, staunch, steadfast, unswerving, vehement, wholehearted, zealous
⊞ 1 irreligious 2 insincere

devoutly adv 1 *devoutly religious:* piously, prayerfully, religiously, reverently 2 *she devoutly hoped he was right:* ardently, deeply, earnestly, faithfully, fervently, passionately, sincerely, staunchly, steadfastly, wholeheartedly, zealously

dewy adj blooming, innocent, roral *formal*, roric *formal*, rorid *formal*, roscid *formal*, starry-eyed, youthful

dexterity n ability, address, adeptness, adroitness, agility, aptitude, art, artistry, deftness, effortlessness, expertise, expertness, facility, finesse, handiness, ingenuity, knack, legerdemain, mastery, nimbleness, proficiency, readiness, skilfulness, skill, sleight
⊞ awkwardness, clumsiness, ineptitude

dexterous adj able, accomplished, adept, adroit, agile, clever, deft, expert, facile, handy, neat-handed, nifty *colloq*, nimble, nimble-fingered, nippy, proficient, skilful
⊞ awkward, clumsy, inept

diabolical adj 1 *a diabolical singing voice:* appalling, atrocious, damnable, disastrous, dreadful, excruciating, execrable *formal*, outrageous, shocking 2 *Satan's diabolical minions:* demonic, devilish, evil, fiendish, hellish, infernal, monstrous, satanic, sinful, wicked

diadem n circlet, coronet, crown, headband, mitre, round, tiara

diagnose v analyse, detect, determine, distinguish, explain, identify, interpret, investigate, isolate, pinpoint, recognize

diagnosis n 1 *diagnosis of this condition can be difficult:* detection, discovery, identification, pinpointing, recognition 2 *tests to confirm the diagnosis:* conclusion, interpretation, judgement, opinion, prognosis, pronouncement, result, verdict

diagnostic adj analytical, demonstrative, distinguishing, indicative, interpretative, interpretive, recognizable, symptomatic

diagonal adj angled, cornerways, crooked, cross, crossing, crosswise, oblique, slanting, sloping

diagonally adv aslant, at an angle, cornerwise, crossways, crosswise, obliquely, on the bias, on the cross, on the slant, slantwise

diagram n bar chart, chart, cutaway, delineation *formal*, draft, drawing, exploded view, figure, flow chart, graph, illustration, layout, outline, picture, pie chart, plan, representation, schema, sketch, table

diagrammatic adj diagrammatical, graphic, illustrative, representational, schematic, tabular
⊞ imaginative, impressionistic

dial n circle, clock, control, disc, face
♦ v call (up), give a buzz/a bell *colloq*, phone, ring, telephone

dialect n accent, argot, diction, idiom, jargon, language, lingo *colloq*, localism, patois, provincialism, regionalism, speech, variety, vernacular

dialectic adj analytical, argumentative, deductive, dialectical, disputatious *formal*, inductive, logical, logistic, polemical, rational, rationalistic
♦ n analysis, argumentation, contention, debate, deduction, dialectics, discussion, disputation *formal*, induction *formal*, logic, polemics, ratiocination *formal*, rationale, reasoning

dialogue n 1 *a dialogue with the protestors:* chat, colloquy *formal*, communication, conference, conversation, converse *formal*, debate *formal*, discourse, discussion, exchange, gossip, interchange *formal*, interlocution *formal*, talk, tête-à-tête **2** *not much dialogue in this scene*: lines, script

diametrically *adv* absolutely, antithetically *formal*, completely, directly, utterly

diaphanous *adj* chiffony, cobwebby, delicate, filmy, fine, gauzy, gossamer, gossamery, light, pellucid *formal*, see-through, sheer, thin, translucent, transparent, veily
🔁 heavy, opaque, thick

diarrhoea *n* Delhi belly *colloq*, dysentery, gippy tummy, holiday tummy, looseness of the bowels, Montezuma's revenge, Spanish tummy *colloq*, the runs *colloq*, the trots *colloq*
🔁 constipation

diary *n* appointment book, chronicle, day-book, engagement book, Filofax®, journal, logbook, year-book

diatribe *n* abuse, attack, criticism, denunciation, harangue, insult, invective *formal*, knocking *colloq*, onslaught, philippic *formal*, rebuke, reprimand, reproof, reviling, running-down *colloq*, slamming *colloq*, slating *colloq*, tirade, upbraiding, vituperation *formal*
🔁 eulogy, praise

dicey *adj* chancy, dangerous, difficult, dodgy *colloq*, dubious, hairy *colloq*, iffy *colloq*, problematic, risky, tricky, uncertain, unpredictable
🔁 certain

dicky *adj* ailing, frail, infirm, shaky, unsound, unsteady, weak
🔁 healthy, robust

dictate *v* **1** *he dictates letters to his PA*: announce, pronounce, read, read aloud, read out, say, speak, transmit, utter **2** *her attempts to dictate policy*: command, decree, demand, direct, impose, insist, instruct, lay down, order, prescribe *formal*, promulgate *formal*, rule, set down
♦ *n* behest *formal*, bidding, charge, command, decree, direction, edict, injunction, law, mandate, order, ordinance *formal*, precept, promulgation *formal*, requirement, rule, ruling, statute, ultimatum, word

dictator *n* absolute ruler, autarchist *formal*, autocrat, Big Brother *colloq*, despot, oppressor, supremo *colloq*, tyrant

dictatorial *adj* absolute, all powerful, arbitrary, autarchic *formal*, authoritarian, autocratic, bossy *colloq*, despotic, dogmatic, domineering, imperious, omnipotent *formal*, oppressive, overbearing, peremptory *formal*, repressive, totalitarian, tyrannical
🔁 democratic, egalitarian, liberal

dictatorship *n* absolute rule, authoritarianism, autocracy, despotism, fascism, Hitlerism, police state, reign of terror, totalitarianism, tyranny
🔁 democracy, egalitarianism

diction *n* articulation, delivery, elocution, enunciation *formal*, expression, fluency, inflection, intonation, phrasing, pronunciation, speech

dictionary *n* concordance, encyclopedia, glossary, lexicon, thesaurus, vocabulary, wordbook

dictum *n* **1** *a dictum from the Central Committee*: command, decree, dictate, edict, fiat *formal*, order, precept, pronouncement, ruling **2** *the old dictum 'mother knows best'*: aphorism, axiom, maxim, proverb, saying, utterance

didactic *adj* educational, educative *formal*, informative, instructive, moral, moralizing, pedagogic *formal*, prescriptive

die *v* **1** *he died in terrible pain*: bite the dust *colloq*, breathe your last, cash in your chips *slang*, depart, depart this life, draw your last breath, expire *formal*, give up the ghost *colloq*, go the way of all flesh *colloq*, have had it *colloq*, kick the bucket *slang*, lose your life, meet your maker *colloq*, pass away, pass on, peg out *colloq*, perish, pop off *colloq*, push up daisies *colloq*, shuffle off this mortal coil *colloq*, snuff it *slang* **2** *our hopes died*: come to an end, decay, decline, decrease, disappear, dissolve, dwindle, ebb, end, fade, finish, lapse, melt away, pass, peter out *colloq*, sink, subside, vanish, wane, wilt, wither **3** *the machine died*: break down, conk out *slang*, fail, lose power, stop **4** *I'm dying for a cigar*: be crazy *colloq*, be desperate, be mad *colloq*, be nuts *colloq*, be raring *colloq*, be wild *colloq*, desire, long for, pine for, yearn
🔁 **1** live

▶ **die away** become faint, become weak, disappear, fade, fade away
▶ **die down** decline, decrease, quieten, stop, subside
▶ **die out** become rarer/less common, disappear, peter out *colloq*, vanish

die-hard *n* blimp *colloq*, fanatic, hardliner, intransigent *formal*, old fogey *colloq*, reactionary, rightist, stick-in-the-mud *colloq*, ultra-conservative, zealot

diet *n* **1** *a diet rich in fish and seafood*: comestibles *formal*, fare, food, foodstuffs, nutrition, provisions *old use*, rations, subsistence, sustenance *formal*, viands *formal*, victuals *formal* **2** *I'll need to go on a diet*: abstinence, fast, regimen
♦ *v* abstain, fast, lose weight, reduce, slim, weight-watch *colloq*

differ *v* **1** *his story differed from mine*: be a departure from, be dissimilar, be unlike, contradict, contrast, depart from, deviate, diverge, vary **2** *the two Ministers differ on this issue*: altercate *formal*, argue, be at odds with, be at variance, clash, conflict, contend, debate, disagree, dispute, dissent *formal*, fall out, not see eye to eye, oppose, quarrel, take issue
🔁 **1** conform **2** agree

difference *n* **1** *a huge difference in size*: antithesis *formal*, contrast, deviation, differentiation, discrepancy, disparity *formal*, dissimilarity, dissimilitude *formal*, distinction, distinctness, divergence, diversity, exception, incongruity *formal*, singularity, unlikeness, variance, variation, variety **2** *you need to resolve your differences*: altercation *formal*, argument, clash, conflict, contention, controversy *formal*, disagreement, disputation *formal*, dispute, misunderstanding, quarrel, row, set-to **3** *we'll refund the difference*: balance, remainder, residue, rest
🔁 **1** conformity **2** agreement

different *adj* **1** *we have completely different views*: a far cry *colloq*, at odds, at variance, clashing,

contrasting, deviating, different as chalk and cheese *colloq*, dissimilar, divergent, inconsistent, opposed, poles/worlds apart *colloq*, unlike **2** *they sell lots of different cheeses:* assorted, discrete *formal*, disparate *formal*, diverse, many, miscellaneous, numerous, several, sundry, varied, various **3** *try a different tactic:* another, other, variant **4** *her approach to music-making is certainly different:* anomalous, bizarre, distinct, distinctive, extraordinary, individual, odd, original, out of the ordinary, peculiar, rare, remarkable, special, strange, unconventional, unique, unusual
F3 1 identical, similar **3** same **4** conventional, ordinary

differentiate *v* contrast, discriminate, distinguish, individualize, mark off, particularize, separate, tell apart

differentiation *n* contrast, demarcation, discrimination, distinction, distinguishing, individualization, modification, particularization, separation
F3 assimilation, association, confusion, connection

difficult *adj* **1** *proving difficult to find a job:* arduous, back-breaking, burdensome, demanding, exacting, exhausting, formidable, gruelling, hard, laborious, onerous, strenuous, tiring, tough, uphill, wearisome **2** *a difficult crossword:* abstract, abstruse *formal*, arcane *formal*, baffling, complex, complicated, dark, esoteric *formal*, hard, intractable *formal*, intricate, involved, knotty, obscure, perplexing, problematical, puzzling, recondite *formal*, thorny, tricky **3** *a very difficult young man:* awkward, demanding, intractable *formal*, obstinate, perverse, recalcitrant *formal*, refractory *formal*, stubborn, tiresome, troublesome, trying, unco-operative, unmanageable
F3 1 easy **2** intelligible, simple, straightforward **3** helpful, manageable

difficulty *n* **1** *climbed out the car with difficulty:* arduousness, awkwardness, exigency *formal*, hardship, labour, painfulness, strain, strenuousness, struggle, trial, tribulation *formal*, trouble **2** *one or two difficulties to resolve:* barrier, bitch *slang*, block, bugger *slang*, catch-22 *colloq*, cleft stick, complication, devil *colloq*, dilemma, dire straits *colloq*, distress, embarrassment, fix *colloq*, fly in the ointment *colloq*, hang-up *colloq*, hiccup *colloq*, hindrance, hole *colloq*, hot/deep water *colloq*, how-d'you-do *colloq*, hurdle, impediment, jam *colloq*, mess *colloq*, objection, obstacle, obstruction, opposition, pain in the arse *slang*, perplexity, pickle *colloq*, pitfall, plight, predicament, pretty pass *colloq*, problem, quandary, shit creek *slang*, snag, spot *colloq*, stumbling-block, tall order *colloq*, tight spot *colloq*
F3 1 ease

diffidence *n* backwardness, bashfulness, hesitancy, humility, inhibition, insecurity, meekness, modesty, reluctance, reserve, self-consciousness, self-distrust, self-doubt, self-effacement, shyness, timidity, unassertiveness
F3 confidence

diffident *adj* abashed, bashful, hesitant, inhibited, insecure, meek, modest, nervous, reluctant, reserved, self-conscious, self-effacing,

shamefaced, sheepish, shrinking, shy, tentative, timid, unassertive, unsure, withdrawn
F3 assertive, confident

diffuse *v* circulate, dispense, disperse, disseminate, dissipate *formal*, distribute, permeate, promulgate *formal*, propagate, scatter, spread
F3 concentrate
♦ *adj* **1** *diffuse outbreaks of rain:* diffused, disconnected, dispersed, scattered, unconcentrated **2** *an overly diffuse prose style:* circumlocutory *formal*, discursive, imprecise, long, long-winded, loquacious *formal*, periphrastic *formal*, profuse, prolix *formal*, rambling, vague, verbose, waffling *colloq*, wordy
F3 1 concentrated **2** succinct

dig *v* **1** *dig a small hole:* burrow, channel, cultivate, delve, excavate, gouge, harrow, hollow, make a hole, mine, penetrate, pierce, plough, quarry, scoop, till, tunnel, turn over, work **2** *he dug me in the ribs:* jab, poke, prod, punch **3** *she was digging for information:* delve, go into, investigate, probe, research, search
♦ *n* **1** *a dig in the ribs:* jab, poke, prod, punch **2** *he couldn't resist a dig at her:* compliment, crack, gibe, insinuation, insult, jeer, sneer, taunt, wisecrack
▶ **dig up** bring to light, discover, disinter, exhume *formal*, expose, extricate, find, retrieve, root out, track down, uncover, unearth
F3 bury, obscure

digest *v* **1** *had trouble digesting some foods:* absorb, assimilate, break down, dissolve, incorporate, macerate *formal*, process **2** *hadn't fully digested the day's news:* absorb, assimilate, consider, contemplate, grasp, meditate, mull over, ponder, study, take in, understand **3** *the information was digested into a summary:* abridge, comprehend *formal*, compress, condense, reduce, shorten, summarize
♦ *n* abbreviation, abridgement, abstract, compendium, compression, précis, reduction, résumé, summary, synopsis

digestion *n* absorption, assimilation, breaking-down, eupepsia *formal*, ingestion *formal*, transformation

digestive system

> *Parts of the human digestive system include:* alimentary canal, anus, bile, buccal cavity, colon, digestive enzymes, duodenum, gall bladder, gastric juices, ileum, intestine, large intestine, small intestine, jejenum, liver, mouth, oesophagus (gullet), pancreas, pancreatic juice, rectum, salivary glands, stomach

dignified *adj* august, ceremonious, courtly, decorous *formal*, distinguished, exalted, formal, grand, grave, honourable, imposing, impressive, lofty, lordly, majestic, noble, reserved, solemn, stately
F3 lowly, undignified

dignify *v* adorn, advance, aggrandize *formal*, apotheosize *formal*, distinguish, elevate, enhance, ennoble, exalt, glorify, grace, honour, promote, raise
F3 degrade, demean

dignitary *n* big gun *colloq*, big name *colloq*, big shot *colloq*, bigwig *colloq*, high-up, luminary formal, notable, personage, somebody, top brass *colloq*, VIP *colloq*, worthy

dignity *n* courtliness, decorum *formal*, elevation, eminence, excellence, grandeur, greatness, honour, honourability, importance, loftiness, majesty, nobility, nobleness, poise, pride, propriety *formal*, respectability, self-esteem, self-possession, self-respect, solemnity, standing, stateliness, status

digress *v* be sidetracked, depart, deviate, diverge, drift, go off at a tangent, go off the subject, ramble, stray, turn aside, wander

digression *n* apostrophe *formal*, aside, departure, deviation, divagation *formal*, divergence, diversion, excursus *formal*, footnote, obiter dictum *formal*, parenthesis, straying, wandering

dilapidated *adj* broken-down, crumbling, decayed, decaying, decrepit, falling apart, in ruins, neglected, ramshackle, rickety, ruined, run-down, shabby, shaky, tumbledown, uncared-for, worn-out

dilapidation *n* collapse, decay, demolition, destruction, deterioration, disintegration, disrepair, ruin, waste

dilate *v* bloat, broaden, distend *formal*, enlarge, expand, extend, increase, inflate, spread (out), stretch, swell, widen
🖃 constrict, contract, shorten

dilatory *adj* dawdling, delaying, lackadaisical, lazy, lingering, postponing, procrastinating *formal*, slack, slow, sluggish, snail-like, stalling, tardy *formal*, tarrying *formal*, time-wasting
🖃 prompt

dilemma *n* catch-22 *colloq*, conflict, difficulty, embarrassment, mess, no-win situation *colloq*, perplexity, plight, predicament, problem, puzzle, quandary, spot *colloq*, tight corner *colloq*, vicious circle

dilettante *n* aesthete *formal*, amateur, dabbler, potterer, sciolist *formal*, trifler
🖃 professional

diligence *n* application, assiduity, assiduousness, attention, attentiveness, care, conscientiousness, constancy, dedication, earnestness, industry, intentness, laboriousness, perseverance, pertinacity *formal*, sedulousness *formal*, thoroughness
🖃 laziness

diligent *adj* assiduous, attentive, busy, careful, conscientious, constant, dedicated, earnest, hard-working, industrious, meticulous, painstaking, persevering, persistent, sedulous *formal*, studious, thorough, tireless
🖃 lazy, negligent

dilly-dally *v* dally, dawdle, delay, dither, falter, hesitate, hover, linger, loiter, potter, procrastinate *formal*, shilly-shally *colloq*, take your time, tarry *formal*, vacillate, waver

dilute *v* adulterate, attenuate *formal*, decrease, diffuse, diminish, lessen, make thinner, make weaker, mitigate *formal*, moderate, reduce, temper, thin (out), tone down, water down, weaken
🖃 concentrate

dim *adj* 1 *it's rather dim outside:* cloudy, crepuscular *formal*, dark, dingy, dull, dusky,

feeble, gloomy, grey, lacklustre, leaden, overcast, shadowy, sombre, tenebrous *formal*, unlit 2 *her torch picked out the dim figures:* blurred, confused, faint, feeble, foggy, fuzzy, hazy, ill-defined, imperfect, indistinct, misty, obfuscated *formal*, obscure, pale, unclear, vague, weak 3 *he's not as dim as he looks:* dense, dim-witted *colloq*, doltish, dumb *colloq*, gormless *colloq*, obtuse, slow-witted, stupid, thick *colloq* 4 *dim prospects:* adverse, discouraging, gloomy, inauspicious *formal*, unfavourable, unpromising
🖃 1 bright 2 distinct 3 bright, intelligent
4 hopeful, promising
♦ *v* become blurred, become faint, blur, cloud, darken, dull, fade, obscure, pale, shade, tarnish
🖃 brighten, illuminate

dimension *n* 1 *the dimensions of the room:* area, breadth, capacity, depth, extent, height, largeness, length, magnitude, mass, measure, measurement, proportions, scope, size, volume, width 2 *the dimensions of a problem:* bulk, extent, greatness, importance, magnitude, range, scale, size 3 *add a new dimension to the matter:* aspect, element, facet, factor, feature, side

diminish *v* 1 *the threat of conflict had diminished:* abate *formal*, become/grow less, become/grow weaker, contract, cut, decline, decrease, deflate, die away, die out, dwindle, ebb, fade, lessen, lower, peter out *colloq*, recede, reduce, retrench *formal*, shrink, sink, slacken, subside, taper off, wane, weaken 2 *she diminished me in front of others:* belittle, defame, denigrate *formal*, deprecate *formal*, derogate *formal*, devalue, disparage *formal*, vilify *formal*
🖃 1 grow, increase 2 exaggerate

diminution *n* abatement *formal*, contraction, curtailment, cut, cutback, decay, decline, decrease, deduction, ebb, lessening, reduction, retrenchment *formal*, shortening, shrinkage, subsidence, weakening
🖃 enlargement, growth, increase

diminutive *adj* compact, dinky *colloq*, dwarfish, elfin, homuncular *formal*, Lilliputian, little, microscopic, midget, mini *colloq*, miniature, minute, petite, pint-size(d) *colloq*, pocket(-sized), pygmy, small, small-scale, teeny *colloq*, teeny-weeny *colloq*, tiny, undersized, wee *Scot*
🖃 big, large, oversized

dimple *n* concavity, depression, dint, fovea *technical*, hollow, indentation, umbilicus

dimwit *n* blockhead, bonehead *colloq*, dullard, dunce, dunderhead, fool, idiot, ignoramus, nitwit, numskull *colloq*, twit *colloq*

din *n* babble, brouhaha, clamour, clangour, clash, clatter, commotion, crash, hubbub, hullabaloo *colloq*, loud noise, noise, outcry, pandemonium, racket, row, shout, shouting, tumult, uproar, yelling
🖃 calm, quiet

dine *v* banquet, eat, feast, feed, have dinner, lunch, sup

dingy *adj* 1 *a dingy basement:* cheerless, colourless, dark, dim, dismal, drab, dreary, dull, dusky, gloomy, murky, obscure, run-down, sombre 2 *dingy patterned wallpaper:* dirty, discoloured, faded, grimy, seedy, shabby, soiled, worn
🖃 1 bright 2 clean

dinky *adj* dainty, fine, mini *colloq*, miniature, natty *colloq*, neat, petite, small, trim

dinner *n* banquet, blow-out *colloq*, evening meal, feast, main meal, meal, refection *formal*, repast *formal*, spread, supper, tea

dinosaur

> *Dinosaurs include:*
> Ornithischia, Saurischia; Allosaurus, Apatosaurus, Barosaurus, Brachiosaurus, Brontosaurus, Camptosaurus, Coelophysis, Compsognathus, Corythosaurus, Deinonychus, Diplodocus, Heterodontosaurus, Iguanodon, Ophiacodon, Ornithomimus, Pachycephalosaurus, Parasaurolophus, Plateosaurus, Stegosaurus, Styracosaurus, Triceratops, Tyrannosaurus

dint *n* blow, concavity, dent, depression, hollow, impression, indentation, stroke

dip *v* **1** *dip the prawn into the sauce:* bathe, douse, duck, dunk, immerse, lower, plunge, sink, soak, souse, submerge **2** *the sun dipped below the cloud:* decline, decrease, descend, drop, fall, go down, lower, sink, slump, subside **3** *the track dips:* decline, descend, drop, fall, go down, sink, slope ♦ *n* **1** *a dip in the road:* basin, concavity, decline, decrease, dent, depression, descent, drop, fall, hole, hollow, incline, indentation, lowering, slope, slump **2** *a dip in the sea:* bathe, dive, drenching, ducking, immersion, infusion *formal*, plunge, soaking, swim **3** *an avocado dip:* cream, dressing, sauce
► **dip into 1** *dip into a book:* browse, flick through, leaf through, look at, look through, run through, skim, thumb through **2** *dip into your savings:* draw on, spend, use

diplomacy *n* **1** *a little diplomacy is required:* cleverness, craft, delicacy, discretion, finesse, judiciousness *formal*, prudence *formal*, savoir-faire, sensitivity, skill, subtlety, tact, tactfulness **2** *let's use diplomacy rather than military force:* international relations, manoeuvring, negotiation, politics, statecraft, statesmanship

diplomat *n* ambassador, arbitrator, attaché, chargé d'affaires, conciliator, consul, emissary, envoy, go-between, legate, mediator, moderator, negotiator, peacemaker, plenipotentiary, politician, statesman

diplomatic *adj* **1** *diplomatic relations:* ambassadorial, consular **2** *a very diplomatic way of describing it:* clever, discreet, judicious *formal*, politic, prudent *formal*, sensitive, skilful, subtle, tactful

dire *adj* **1** *a dire predicament:* alarming, appalling, atrocious, awful, calamitous, catastrophic, disastrous, distressing, dreadful, frightful, horrible, shocking, terrible **2** *dire warnings about the economy:* crucial, desperate, drastic, extreme, grave, ominous, pressing, urgent, vital

direct *adj* **1** *a direct flight:* non-stop, straight, through, unbroken, undeviating, uninterrupted, unswerving **2** *direct answers:* bluff, blunt, candid, explicit, forthright, frank, honest, outspoken, plainspoken, sincere, straight, straightforward, unambiguous, unequivocal, up-front *colloq* **3** *I have direct experience of that:* face-to-face, first-hand, immediate, personal

⊟ 1 circuitous, indirect **2** equivocal **3** indirect
♦ *v* **1** *she's directing all operations:* administer, be in charge of, be in control of, be the boss of *colloq*, call the shots *colloq*, control, govern, handle, lead, manage, mastermind, organize, oversee, preside over, regulate, run, superintend, supervise **2** *directed to make this a priority:* adjure *formal*, charge, command, give orders, instruct, issue instructions, order **3** *we were directed to the entrance:* conduct, escort, guide, lead, point, show, show/point the way, steer, usher **4** *directed my camera towards the plane:* aim, focus, intend, level, mean, point, turn

direction *n* **1** *under my direction:* administration, control, government, guidance, handling, leadership, management, overseeing, regulation, running, superintendency, supervision **2** *heading in the wrong direction:* bearing, course, line, orientation, path, road, route, track, way **3** *change the direction of your career:* course, current aim, drift, inclination, orientation, tendency, tenor, trend **4** *give someone directions:* brief, briefing, guidance, guidelines, indication, instructions, orders, plan, recommendations, regulations, rules

directive *n* bidding, charge, command, decree, dictate, edict, fiat *formal*, imperative, injunction, instruction, mandate, notice, order, ordinance, regulation, ruling

directly *adv* **1** *directly after the talks ended:* as soon as possible, at once, exactly, forthwith, immediately, instantaneously, instantly, presently, promptly, pronto *colloq*, quickly, right, right away, soon, speedily, straight, straightaway, without delay **2** *he spoke simply and directly:* bluntly, candidly, clearly, explicitly, frankly, honestly, plainly, sincerely, straightforwardly, unambiguously, unequivocally

director *n* administrator, board of directors, boss, chair, chairman, chairperson, chairwoman, chief, chief executive, conductor, controller, executive, governor, head, leader, manager, managing director, organizer, overseer, president, principal, producer, régisseur, superintendent, supervisor, top dog *colloq*

dirge *n* coronach, dead-march, elegy, funeral song, lament, monody, requiem, threnody

dirt *n* **1** *carrots covered in dirt:* clay, dust, earth, loam, mud, soil **2** *dog dirt:* crap *slang*, crud *slang*, excrement, filth, grime, grot *colloq*, grunge *slang*, gunge *colloq*, gunk *slang*, mire, muck, pollution, slime, sludge, smudge, soot, stain, tarnish, yuck *colloq* **3** *the dirt TV beams into our homes:* impurity, indecency, lewdness, obscenity, pornography, salaciousness, sleaze *colloq*, smut *colloq*, sordidness

dirty *adj* **1** *a pool of dirty water:* clouded, cloudy, cruddy *colloq*, dark, defiled, dull, dusty, filthy, flea-bitten *colloq*, foul, greasy, grimy, grotty *colloq*, grubby, messy, miry, mucky, muddy, polluted, scruffy, shabby, slimy, soiled, sooty, squalid, stained, sullied, tarnished, unclean, unhygienic, unwashed, yucky *colloq* **2** *dirty magazines:* bawdy, blue *colloq*, coarse, contaminated, corrupt, filthy, improper, indecent, lewd, obscene, pornographic, raunchy

colloq, ribald, risqué, salacious, sleazy colloq, smutty, sordid, suggestive, vulgar
⊠ 1 clean 2 decent
♦ v adulterate, begrime formal, besmirch formal, blacken, contaminate, defile, foul, mess up, muddy, pollute, smear, smirch, smudge, soil, splash, spoil, stain, sully, tarnish
⊠ clean, cleanse

disability n affliction formal, ailment, complaint, defect, disablement, disorder, disqualification, handicap, illness, impairment formal, inability, incapability, incapacity, infirmity, malady formal, unfitness, weakness

disable v 1 disable a person: cripple, damage, debilitate formal, disqualify, enfeeble formal, hamstring, handicap, immobilize, impair formal, incapacitate formal, invalidate, lame, make unfit, paralyse, prostrate, weaken 2 disable a machine: deactivate, immobilize, paralyse, put out of action, render inoperative formal, stop

disabled adj bed-ridden, crippled, debilitated formal, enfeebled formal, handicapped, immobilized, impaired formal, incapacitated formal, indisposed formal, infirm, lame, maimed, out of action, paralysed, physically challenged colloq, unfit, weak, weakened, wrecked
⊠ able, able-bodied

disadvantage n 1 the plan has several disadvantages: Achilles heel colloq, chink in your armour colloq, defect, downside colloq, drawback, flaw, fly in the ointment colloq, handicap, hang-up colloq, hindrance, impediment, inconvenience, liability, limitation, minus colloq, nuisance, penalty, snag, spanner in the works colloq, trouble, weak link in the chain colloq, weak point, weakness 2 this would be to my disadvantage: damage, detriment, disservice, hardship, harm, hurt, injury, lack, loss, prejudice, privation formal
⊠ 1 advantage, asset, benefit

disadvantaged adj deprived, handicapped, impoverished, in distress, in need, in want, poor, poverty-stricken, struggling, underprivileged
⊠ privileged

disadvantageous adj adverse, damaging, deleterious formal, detrimental, hapless formal, harmful, hurtful, ill-timed, inconvenient, inexpedient, injurious, inopportune, prejudicial, unfavourable, unfortunate, unlucky
⊠ advantageous, auspicious formal, favourable

disaffected adj alienated, antagonistic, discontented, disgruntled, disloyal, dissatisfied, estranged formal, hostile, mutinous, rebellious, unfriendly
⊠ friendly, loyal, satisfied

disaffection n alienation, animosity, antagonism, aversion, coolness, disagreement, discontentment, discord, disharmony, dislike, disloyalty, dissatisfaction, estrangement formal, hostility, ill-will, resentment, unfriendliness
⊠ contentment, loyalty

disagree v 1 disagree with someone: agree to differ, argue, be at loggerheads with, be at odds with, beg to differ, bicker, clash, conflict, contend, contest, contradict, differ, dispute, dissent formal, diverge, fall out colloq, fight, not see eye to eye with, quarrel, squabble, take issue, wrangle 2 disagree with an idea: argue against, be against, contradict, disapprove of, dissent formal,
object, oppose, take issue with, think wrong 3 the food disagreed with me: cause illness, make unwell, upset
⊠ 1 agree 2 accept, approve 3 agree

disagreeable adj 1 disagreeable old man: awkward, bad-tempered, brusque, churlish, contrary, cross, difficult, disobliging, grouchy colloq, ill-humoured, ill-natured, impolite, irritable, nasty, peevish, rude, surly, unfriendly, unhelpful 2 a disagreeable taste: abominable, disgusting, dreadful, horrible, nasty, objectionable, obnoxious, offensive, repellent, repugnant formal, repulsive, unpleasant, unsavoury
⊠ 1 amiable, pleasant 2 agreeable, pleasant

disagreement n 1 disagreements between referees and managers: altercation formal, argument, clash, conflict, contention, difference of opinion, discord formal, disputation formal, dispute, dissension, dissent, falling-out colloq, friction, misunderstanding, quarrel, row, squabble, strife, tiff colloq, wrangle 2 the talks ended in disagreement: deviation, difference, discrepancy, disparity formal, dissimilarity, dissimilitude formal, divergence, diversity, incompatibility, incongruity formal, inconsistency, unlikeness, variance
⊠ 1 agreement

disallow v abjure formal, ban, cancel, debar, disaffirm formal, disavow formal, disclaim formal, dismiss, disown, embargo, exclude, forbid, interdict formal, prohibit, proscribe formal, rebuff, refuse, reject, repudiate, say no to, veto
⊠ allow, permit

disappear v 1 the plane disappeared from sight: dematerialize, dissolve, ebb, evanesce formal, evaporate, fade, get lost, go missing, go out of sight, make tracks colloq, melt away, pass from sight, recede, vanish, wane 2 the prisoner simply disappeared: depart, escape, exit, flee, fly, go, hide, retire, scarper colloq, vamoose colloq, withdraw 3 the threat of war disappeared: become extinct, cease formal, die away, die out, end, expire formal, pass, perish
⊠ 1 appear 3 begin, emerge, start

disappearance n 1 the gradual disappearance of the comet: departure, evaporation, exit, fading, going, loss, melting away, passing, passing from sight, vanishing, withdrawal 2 her disappearance while out on bail: departure, desertion, exit, flight, going 3 the disappearance of river dolphins: dying-out, end, evanescence formal, expiry, extinction, passing
⊠ 1 appearance, manifestation 3 beginning, start

disappoint v baffle, dash someone's hopes, defeat, depress, disconcert, discourage, disenchant, disgruntle, dishearten, disillusion, dismay, dispirit, dissatisfy, fail, foil, frustrate, hamper, hinder, let down, sadden, thwart, vex
⊠ delight, please, satisfy

disappointed adj cast down, deflated, depressed, despondent, discouraged, disenchanted, disgruntled, disheartened, disillusioned, dissatisfied, distressed, downhearted, frustrated, let down, miffed colloq, saddened, thwarted, upset, vexed
⊠ pleased, satisfied

disappointing *adj* anticlimactic, depressing, disagreeable, disconcerting, discouraging, inadequate, inferior, insufficient, not all it's cracked up to be *colloq*, sorry, underwhelming *colloq*, unhappy, unsatisfactory, unworthy
🔁 encouraging, pleasant, satisfactory

disappointment *n* **1** *the disappointment of our hopes*: bitter pill (to swallow) *colloq*, chagrin, cold comfort *colloq*, despondency, discontent, discouragement, disenchantment, disillusionment, dispiritedness, displeasure, dissatisfaction, distress, failure, frustration, regret, sadness **2** *the match was a disappointment*: anticlimax, blow, calamity, comedown, damp squib *colloq*, disaster, failure, fiasco, let-down, misfortune, non-event, setback, swiz *colloq*, swizzle *colloq*, washout *colloq*, wipeout *colloq*
🔁 **1** satisfaction **2** delight, pleasure

disapprobation *n* blame, censure, condemnation, criticism, denunciation, disapproval, disfavour, dislike, disparagement *formal*, displeasure, dissatisfaction, exception, objection, remonstration *formal*, reproach, reproof
🔁 approbation *formal*, approval

disapproval *n* blame, censure, condemnation, criticism, denunciation, disapprobation *colloq*, dislike, disparagement *formal*, displeasure, dissatisfaction, exception, objection, rebuke, rejection, remonstration *formal*, reproach, reproof, the thumbs-down *colloq*, veto
🔁 approbation *formal*, approval

disapprove *v* animadvert *formal*, be against, blame, censure, condemn, denounce, deplore, deprecate *formal*, disallow *formal*, discountenance *formal*, dislike, disparage, find unacceptable, frown on, give the thumbs-down *colloq*, have a low opinion of, hold in contempt, look down on, look down your nose at *colloq*, not hold with, object to, reject, spurn, take a dim view of, take exception to, think badly of, think little of, veto
🔁 agree, approve, have a high opinion of

disapproving *adj* censorious, condemnatory, critical, deprecatory *formal*, derogatory, disapprobative *formal*, disapprobatory *formal*, disparaging *formal*, improbative *formal*, improbatory *formal*, pejorative, reproachful

disarm *v* **1** *the rebel forces eventually disarmed*: demilitarize, demobilize, disband, lay down arms/weapons **2** *disarmed the bomb*: deactivate, immobilize, make powerless, put out of action, render inoperative *formal*, unarm **3** *he managed to disarm the critics*: appease, charm, conciliate, mollify, persuade, placate, win over
🔁 **1** arm

disarmament *n* arms control/limitation/reduction, deactivation, demilitarization, demobilization, laying down of arms/weapons

disarming *adj* charming, conciliatory, irresistible, likeable, mollifying, persuasive, winning

disarrange *v* confuse, derange, dislocate, disorder, disorganize, disturb, jumble, mess, shuffle, unsettle, untidy
🔁 arrange, tidy

disarray *n* chaos, clutter, confusion, disorder, disorganization, indiscipline, jumble, mess, muddle, shambles *colloq*, tangle
🔁 order

disaster *n* **1** *an air disaster*: accident, act of God, adversity, blow, calamity, cataclysm, catastrophe, misadventure, mischance, misfortune, mishap, reversal, reverse, ruin, ruination, setback, stroke, tragedy **2** *the entire play was a disaster*: debacle, failure, fiasco, flop *colloq*, non-starter, rout, wash out *colloq*
🔁 **2** success, triumph

disastrous *adj* adverse, appalling, calamitous, cataclysmic, catastrophic, destructive, devastating, dire, dreadful, fatal, harmful, injurious, miserable, ravaging, ruinous, shocking, terrible, tragic

disavowal *n* abjuration *formal*, contradiction, denial, disaffirmation *formal*, dissent, rejection, renunciation, repudiation

disband *v* break up, demob *colloq*, demobilize, dismiss, disperse, dissolve, go separate ways, part company, scatter, separate
🔁 assemble, gather, muster

disbelief *n* discredit, distrust, doubt, dubiety *formal*, incredulity, mistrust, questioning, rejection, scepticism, suspicion, unbelief
🔁 belief, conviction

disbelieve *v* be unconvinced, discount, discredit, distrust, doubt, mistrust, question, reject, repudiate, suspect, take something with a pinch of salt *colloq*
🔁 accept, believe, give credence to, trust

disbeliever *n* agnostic, atheist, doubter, doubting Thomas, nullifidian *formal*, questioner, sceptic, scoffer, unbeliever
🔁 believer

disburse *v* cough up *colloq*, expend *formal*, fork out *colloq*, lay out, pay out, shell out *colloq*, spend

disbursement *n* disbursal *formal*, disposal *formal*, expenditure, outlay, payment, spending

disc *n* **1** *a small disc of metal*: circle, counter, discus, face, plate, ring, saucer **2** *twelve songs on each disc*: album, CD, gramophone record, LP, record, vinyl **3** *photos stored on disc*: CD-ROM, compact disk, disk, diskette, floppy disk, hard disk, microfloppy

discard *v* abandon, cast aside, chuck away/out *colloq*, dispense with, dispose of, ditch *colloq*, drop, dump *colloq*, forsake *formal*, get rid of, jettison, reject, relinquish, remove, repudiate, scrap, shed, throw away, throw out, toss out
🔁 adopt, retain

discern *v* ascertain, descry *formal*, detect, determine, differentiate, discover, discriminate, distinguish, judge, make out, notice, observe, perceive, recognize, see

discernible *adj* apparent, appreciable, clear, conspicuous, detectable, discoverable, distinct, distinguishable, manifest *formal*, noticeable, observable, obvious, patent, perceptible, plain, recognizable, visible
🔁 imperceptible

discerning *adj* acute, astute, clear-sighted, clever, critical, discriminating, eagle-eyed, ingenious, intelligent, penetrating, perceptive, percipient *formal*, perspicacious *formal*, piercing, prudent *formal*, quick, sagacious *formal*, sapient *formal*, sensitive, sharp, shrewd, sound, subtle, wise

discernment *n* acumen, acuteness, ascertainment *formal*, awareness, clear-sightedness, cleverness, discrimination, (good) taste, ingenuity, insight, intelligence, judgement, keenness, penetration, perception, perceptiveness, percipience *formal*, perspicacity *formal*, sagacity *formal*, sharpness, shrewdness, understanding, wisdom

discharge *v* **1** *discharged from the army:* absolve, acquit, clear, dismiss, exculpate *formal*, exonerate *formal*, free, let go, liberate, pardon, release, relieve, set free **2** *discharge from employment:* axe *colloq*, boot out *colloq*, discard, dismiss, eject, expel, fire *colloq*, get rid of, give the boot to *colloq*, give the elbow *colloq*, oust, remove, sack *colloq*, turf out *colloq* **3** *discharge your duties:* carry out, dispense *formal*, do, fulfil, perform **4** *they discharged their guns:* detonate, explode, fire, let off, set off, shoot **5** *discharge fumes:* disembogue *formal*, disgorge, emit, excrete *formal*, exude, give off, gush, leak, let off/out, ooze, release **6** *discharge a debt:* clear, honour, meet, pay, satisfy, settle
◆ **1** detain **2** appoint, hire **3** neglect
♦ *n* **1** *her discharge from hospital:* absolution, acquittal, clearance, exculpation *formal*, exoneration *formal*, liberation, release **2** *discharge from employment:* cashiering, dismissal, expulsion, firing *colloq*, ousting, removal, sacking *colloq*, the boot *colloq*, the elbow *colloq*, the sack *colloq* **3** *a watery discharge:* ejection, emission, excretion *formal*, exuding, flow, pus, release, secretion, suppuration *formal* **4** *the discharge of his duties:* accomplishment, achievement, doing, execution, fulfilment, performance **5** *discharge of a debt:* clearance, honouring, payment, settling
◆ **1** confinement, detention **2** appointment, hiring **3** absorption **4** neglect

disciple *n* adherent, believer, convert, devotee, follower, learner, proselyte, pupil, student, supporter, upholder, votary

disciplinarian *n* authoritarian, autocrat, despot, (hard) taskmaster, martinet, stickler, tyrant

discipline *n* **1** *combat disciplines:* drill, exercise, practice, regimen, routine, training **2** *lack of discipline in the classroom:* castigation *formal*, chastisement *formal*, correction, punishment **3** *discipline is required in my work:* control, orderliness, regulation, restraint, self-control, self-restraint, strictness **4** *the discipline of political economy:* area of study, branch, course of study, field of study, speciality, subject
◆ **3** indiscipline
♦ *v* **1** *disciplined in the martial arts:* break in, drill, educate, exercise, ground, inculcate *formal*, instruct, inure *formal*, train **2** *discipline myself during study periods:* check, control, correct, govern, limit, regulate, restrain, restrict **3** *offenders need to be disciplined:* castigate *formal*, chasten, chastise *formal*, correct, make an example of, penalize, punish, rebuke, reprimand, reprove, teach someone a lesson

disclaim *v* abandon, abjure *formal*, decline, deny, disavow *formal*, disown, refuse, reject, renounce, repudiate, wash your hands of *colloq*
◆ accept, confess

disclaimer *n* abjuration *formal*, abnegation *formal*, contradiction, denial, disaffirmation *formal*, disavowal *formal*, disownment *formal*, rejection, renunciation, repudiation, retraction *formal*

disclose *v* blab *colloq*, blurt out, bring to light, broadcast, communicate, confess, discover, divulge *formal*, exhibit, expose, impart *formal*, lay bare, leak *colloq*, let slip, let the cat out of the bag *colloq*, make known, make public, publish, relate, reveal, show, spill the beans *colloq*, squeal *colloq*, tell, uncover, unveil
◆ conceal, cover, dissemble, hide, keep dark, keep secret, mask, obscure

disclosure *n* **1** *the judge ordered the disclosure of the figures:* acknowledgement, admission, announcement, broadcast, confession, declaration, divulgence *formal*, publication **2** *leaked newspaper disclosures:* bringing to light, discovery, exposé, exposure, laying bare, leak *colloq*, revelation, uncovering

discoloration *n* blemish, blot, blotch, dyschroa *technical*, ecchymosis, mark, patch, splotch, spot, stain, streak

discolour *v* disfigure, fade, mar, mark, rust, soil, stain, streak, tarnish, tinge, weather

discomfit *v* abash, baffle, confound, confuse, demoralize, discompose, disconcert, embarrass, faze *colloq*, fluster, frustrate, outwit, perplex, perturb *formal*, rattle *formal*, ruffle, thwart, unsettle

discomfiture *n* abashment, chagrin, confusion, demoralization, disappointment, discomposure, embarrassment, frustration, humiliation, unease

discomfort *n* **1** *a little pain and discomfort:* ache, hurt, malaise *formal*, pain, pang, soreness, twinge **2** *the discomfort in his voice:* annoyance, apprehension, disquiet, distress, embarrassment, hardship, irritation, restlessness, trouble, unease, vexation, worry **3** *the discomforts of travelling:* annoyance, bother, difficulty, disadvantage, drawback, inconvenience, irritation, nuisance, trouble, worry
◆ **2** comfort, ease

discomposure *n* agitation, annoyance, anxiety, disquietude *formal*, disturbance, fluster, inquietude *formal*, irritation, perturbation *formal*, restlessness, unease, upset
◆ composure *formal*

disconcert *v* alarm, baffle, bewilder, confuse, discombobulate *US slang*, dismay, disturb, embarrass, faze *colloq*, fluster, nonplus, perplex, perturb *formal*, put off/out, put someone's nose out of joint *colloq*, rattle *colloq*, ruffle, shake, startle, surprise, take aback, throw off balance, unnerve, unsettle, upset

disconcerting *adj* alarming, awkward, baffling, bewildering, bothersome, confusing, daunting, dismaying, distracting, disturbing, embarrassing, off-putting *colloq*, perplexing, perturbing *formal*, unnerving, upsetting

disconnect *v* cut off, detach, disengage, divide, part, separate, sever, split, uncouple, undo, unhitch, unhook, unplug
◼ attach, connect, join, unite

disconnected *adj* abrupt, confused, disjointed, garbled, illogical, incoherent, irrational, jumbled, loose, mixed-up, rambling, staccato, unco-ordinated, unintelligible, wandering
◼ coherent, connected

disconsolate *adj* crushed, dejected, depressed, desolate, despondent, dispirited, down, down in the dumps *colloq*, downcast, forlorn, gloomy, grief-stricken, heartbroken, heavy-hearted, hopeless, inconsolable, low, low-spirited, melancholy, miserable, sad, unhappy, wretched
◼ cheerful, joyful

discontent *n* disaffection, displeasure, disquiet, dissatisfaction, fretfulness, impatience, misery, regret, restlessness, uneasiness, unhappiness, unrest, vexation, wretchedness
◼ content, happiness, satisfaction

discontented *adj* browned off *colloq*, cheesed off *colloq*, complaining, disaffected, disgruntled, displeased, dissatisfied, exasperated, fed up *colloq*, impatient, miserable, pissed off *slang*, restless, unhappy, wretched
◼ contented, happy, satisfied

discontinue *v* abandon, abolish, break off, cancel, cease *formal*, come to a stop, come to an end, do away with, drop, end, finish, halt, interrupt, quit *colloq*, refrain, scrap *colloq*, stop, suspend, terminate *formal*
◼ begin, continue, produce

discontinuity *n* breach, disconnectedness, disconnection, disjointedness, disruption, disunion, incoherence, interruption, rupture
◼ coherence, continuity

discontinuous *adj* broken, disconnected, fitful, intermittent, interrupted, irregular, periodic, punctuated, spasmodic
◼ continuous

discord *n* **1** *signs of discord between the allies:* argument, clashing, conflict, contention, difference, difference of opinion, disagreement, discordance *formal*, dispute, dissension, dissent, disunity, division, friction, incompatibility, opposition, row, split, strife, wrangling **2** *the piece faded into discord:* cacophony *formal*, discord of sounds, disharmony, dissonance *formal*, harshness, jangle, jangling, jarring
◼ **1** agreement, concord **2** harmony

discordant *adj* **1** *their seemingly discordant views:* at odds, at variance, clashing, conflicting, contradictory, differing, disagreeing, dissenting, hostile, incompatible, incongruous *formal*, inconsistent, opposing **2** *discordant harmonies:* atonal *technical*, cacophonous *formal*, dissonant, flat, grating, harsh, jangling, jarring, sharp, strident
◼ **1** agreeing **2** harmonious

discount *n* allowance, concession, cut, cut price, deduction, mark-down, rebate, reduction
♦ *v* **1** *my plan was immediately discounted:* disbelieve, disregard, gloss over, ignore, overlook, pass over **2** *all holidays have been discounted:* deduct, knock off *colloq*, mark down, reduce, slash *colloq*, take off
◼ **1** pay attention to **2** increase

discourage *v* **1** *don't let this discourage you:* cast down, dampen, daunt, deject, demoralize, depress, disappoint, dishearten, dismay, dispirit, put a damper on, put off, unnerve **2** *smoking should be discouraged:* advise against, deter, dissuade, hinder, hold back, prevent, put off, restrain, talk out of
◼ **1** encourage, hearten **2** encourage, persuade

discouraged *adj* crestfallen, dashed, daunted, deflated, dejected, demoralized, depressed, disheartened, dismayed, dispirited, downcast, glum, let-down, pessimistic
◼ encouraged, heartened

discouragement *n* **1** *a feeling of discouragement in the dressing room:* dejection, depression, despair, despondency, disappointment, dismay, downheartedness, gloom, hopelessness, pessimism **2** *discouragements to saving for retirement:* barrier, curb, damper, deterrent, disincentive, hindrance, impediment, obstacle, opposition, restraint
◼ **1** encouragement **2** incentive

discouraging *adj* dampening, daunting, dehortatory *formal*, demoralizing, depressing, disappointing, disheartening, dispiriting, dissuasive *formal*, dissuasory *formal*, inauspicious *formal*, off-putting, unfavourable, unpropitious *formal*
◼ encouraging, heartening

discourse *n* **1** *let us continue our discourse:* chat, colloquy *formal*, communication, confabulation *formal*, conversation, converse *formal*, dialogue, discussion, talk **2** *a lengthy discourse on EU enlargement:* address, disquisition *formal*, dissertation, essay, homily, lecture, oration *formal*, sermon, speech, treatise
♦ *v* confer, converse, debate, discuss, lecture, preach, speak, talk

discourteous *adj* abrupt, bad-mannered, boorish, brusque, curt, disrespectful, gruff, ill-bred, ill-mannered, impertinent, impolite, impudent, insolent, offensive, offhand, rude, short, unceremonious, uncivil, uncouth, ungracious, unmannerly, unpleasant
◼ courteous, polite

discourtesy *n* **1** *noted for their discourtesy on holiday:* bad manners, brusqueness, curtness, disrespectfulness, ill-breeding, impertinence, impoliteness, incivility, indecorousness *formal*, indecorum *formal*, insolence, rudeness, ungraciousness, unmannerliness **2** *to leave now would be a discourtesy:* affront, insult, rebuff, slight, snub
◼ **1** courtesy, politeness

discover *v* **1** *I discovered that he had left yesterday:* ascertain *formal*, come to know, detect, determine, discern, establish, fathom (out), find out about, get onto *colloq*, get wind of *colloq*, get wise to *colloq*, learn, notice, perceive, realize, recognize, rumble *colloq*, see, spot, suss out *colloq*, twig *colloq* **2** *she discovered the body on the beach:* come across, come to light, dig up, disclose, ferret out, find, light on, locate, reveal, stumble across/on, turn up, uncover, unearth **3** *he discovered a new branch of number theory:* compose, create, devise, invent, originate, pioneer, work out
◼ **1** conceal, cover (up) **2** miss

discoverer *n* **1** *a discoverer of superconductivity:* creator, deviser, founder, initiator, inventor, originator, pioneer **2** *the discoverer of King Tut's tomb*: explorer, finder

discovery *n* **1** *an unpleasant discovery*: detection, determination, discernment, disclosure, finding, learning, location, realization, recognition, revelation **2** *an important discovery in quantum physics*: breakthrough, devising, exploration, find, finding(s), innovation, introduction, invention, origination, pioneering, research

discredit *v* **1** *discredit someone*: belittle, bring into disrepute, cast aspersions on *formal*, damage, defame, degrade, disgrace, dishonour, disparage *formal*, give someone a bad name, put in a bad light, reflect (badly) on, reproach, slander, slur, smear, tarnish, vilify *formal* **2** *discredit a theory*: challenge, debunk, deny, disbelieve, discard, distrust, doubt, explode, invalidate, mistrust, question, refute *formal*, reject, shake your faith in
F31 honour **2** believe, prove
♦ *n* aspersion *formal*, blame, censure, disgrace, dishonour, disrepute, humiliation, ignominy *formal*, infamy, opprobrium *formal*, reproach, scandal, shame, slur, smear, stigma

discreditable *adj* blameworthy, degrading, disgraceful, dishonourable, disreputable, improper, infamous, reprehensible *formal*, scandalous, shameful
F3 creditable

discreet *adj* careful, cautious, circumspect *formal*, considerate, delicate, diplomatic, guarded, judicious *formal*, politic *formal*, prudent *formal*, reserved, sensible, tactful, wary, wise
F3 indiscreet, tactless

---

discreet or *discrete*? *Discreet* means 'not saying or doing anything that might cause trouble': *My secretary won't ask awkward questions; she's very discreet*. *Discrete* means 'not attached to others': *a suspension of discrete particles in a liquid*.

---

discrepancy *n* conflict, contradiction, deviation, difference, disagreement, discordance *formal*, disparity *formal*, dissimilarity, divergence, incongruity *formal*, inconsistency, inequality, variance, variation

discrete *adj* detached, disconnected, discontinuous, disjoined, disjunct *formal*, distinct, individual, separate, unattached

discretion *n* **1** *he relied on her discretion*: care, carefulness, caution, circumspection *formal*, consideration, diplomacy, discernment, good sense, guardedness, judgement, judiciousness *formal*, predilection *formal*, prudence *formal*, reserve, tact, volition *formal*, wariness, wisdom **2** *£50 to use at your own discretion*: choice, desire, freedom, inclination, preference, will, wish
F31 indiscretion

discretionary *adj* elective, open, optional, voluntary
F3 automatic, compulsory, fixed, mandatory

discriminate *v* **1** *able to discriminate between right and wrong*: differentiate, discern, distinguish, draw/make a distinction, segregate, separate, tell apart, tell/recognize the differences **2** *he discriminated against me*: be biased, be intolerant, be prejudiced, treat differently, victimize
F31 confound, confuse **2** favour

discriminating *adj* astute, critical, cultivated, discerning, fastidious, keen, particular, perceptive, selective, sensitive, shrewd, tasteful

discrimination *n* **1** *I'm against all forms of discrimination*: bias, bigotry, favouritism, inequity, intolerance, narrow-mindedness, prejudice, segregation, unfairness **2** *she showed little taste or discrimination*: acumen, acuteness, astuteness, discernment, insight, judgement, keenness, penetration, perception, perspicacity *formal*, refinement, sensitivity, shrewdness, subtlety, taste

discriminatory *adj* biased, discriminative, favouring, inequitable, loaded, one-sided, partial, partisan, preferential, prejudiced, prejudicial, unfair, unjust, weighted
F3 fair, impartial, unbiased

discursive *adj* circuitous, diffuse, digressing, long-winded, meandering, prolix *formal*, rambling, verbose, wandering, wide-ranging, wordy
F3 terse

discuss *v* analyse, argue, confabulate *formal*, confer, consider, consult, converse, debate, deliberate, discourse *formal*, examine, exchange views on, go into, kick around *colloq*, parley *old use*, put your heads together *colloq*, review, study, talk about/over, weigh up

discussion *n* analysis, argument, colloquium *formal*, conference, consideration, consultation, conversation, debate, deliberation, dialogue, discourse *formal*, examination, exchange, forum, negotiations, parley *old use*, powwow *colloq*, review, scrutiny, seminar, study, symposium, talk, talks

disdain *n* arrogance, contempt, contumely *formal*, deprecation *formal*, derision, dislike, disparagement *formal*, haughtiness, scorn, sneering, snobbishness
F3 admiration, respect
♦ *v* belittle, cold shoulder *colloq*, contemn *formal*, deride *formal*, despise, disavow *formal*, disregard, ignore, look down on, pooh-pooh *colloq*, rebuff, reject, scorn, slight, sneer at, snub, spurn, turn down, undervalue
F3 admire, respect

disdainful *adj* aloof, arrogant, contemptuous, derisive, disparaging *formal*, haughty, insolent, pompous, proud, scornful, slighting, sneering, supercilious, superior
F3 respectful

disease *n* affliction *formal*, ailment, bug *colloq*, complaint, condition, contagion, disability, disorder, epidemic, ill-health, illness, indisposition, infection, infirmity, malady *formal*, sickness, virus *colloq*
F3 health

Diseases and disorders include:
Addison's disease, AIDS, alopecia, Alzheimer's disease, anaemia, angina, anorexia nervosa, anthrax, arthritis, asbestosis, asthma, athlete's foot, autism, Bell's palsy, beriberi, Black Death, botulism, Bright's disease, bronchitis, brucellosis, bubonic plague, bulimia, cancer, cerebral palsy, chickenpox, cholera, cirrhosis, coeliac disease, common cold, consumption, croup, cystic fibrosis, diabetes, diphtheria, dropsy, dysentery, eclampsia, emphysema,

encephalitis, endometriosis, enteritis, farmer's lung, flu *colloq*, foot-and-mouth disease, gangrene, German measles, gingivitis, glandular fever, glaucoma, gonorrhoea, haemophilia, hepatitis, herpes, Hodgkin's disease, Huntington's disease, hydrophobia, impetigo, influenza, Lassa fever, legionnaire's disease, leprosy, leukaemia, lockjaw, malaria, mastoiditis, measles, meningitis, motor neurone disease, multiple sclerosis (MS), mumps, muscular dystrophy, myalgic encephalomyelitis (ME), nephritis, osteomyelitis, osteoporosis, Paget's disease, Parkinson's disease, peritonitis, pneumonia, poliomyelitis, psittacosis, psoriasis, pyorrhoea, rabies, rheumatic fever, rheumatoid arthritis, rickets, ringworm, rubella, scabies, scarlet fever, schistosomiasis, schizophrenia, scurvy, septicaemia, shingles, silicosis, smallpox, syphilis, tapeworm, tetanus, thrombosis, thrush, tinnitus, tuberculosis (TB), typhoid, typhus, vertigo, whooping cough, yellow fever

diseased *adj* ailing, blighted, contaminated, ill, infected, infirm, sick, unhealthy, unsound, unwell
🞐 healthy, well

disembark *v* alight *formal*, arrive, debark *formal*, deplane *formal*, detrain *formal*, dismount, get off, land, leave, step off
🞐 embark

disembodied *adj* bodiless, discarnate *formal*, ghostly, immaterial, incorporeal *formal*, intangible, phantom, spectral *formal*, spiritual

disembowel *v* disbowel, draw, embowel, eviscerate *formal*, exenterate *formal*, gralloch, gut, paunch

disenchanted *adj* blasé, cynical, disappointed, discouraged, disillusioned, fed up *colloq*, indifferent, jaundiced, let down, soured

disenchantment *n* cynicism, disappointment, disillusion, disillusionment, revulsion

disengage *v* detach, disconnect, disentangle, disunite, extricate, free, liberate, loosen, release, separate, uncouple, undo, unfasten, unhitch, unhook, untie, withdraw
🞐 connect, engage, unite

disengaged *adj* apart, detached, separate, unattached, unconnected
🞐 connected, joined, united

disentangle *v* **1** *disentangled ropes from the propeller:* detach, disconnect, disengage, extricate, free, loose, release, separate, straighten, undo, unfasten, unfold, unknot, unravel, unsnarl, untangle, untwist, unwind **2** *to disentangle fact from fiction:* clarify, distance, distinguish, resolve, separate, simplify
🞐 **1** entangle

disfavour *n* **1** *fall into disfavour:* discredit, disrepute, ignominy *formal*, opprobrium *formal*, unpopularity **2** *look with disfavour at someone:* disapprobation *formal*, disapproval, disesteem *formal*, dislike, displeasure, disregard, dissatisfaction, distaste, low opinion
🞐 **2** favour

disfigure *v* blemish, damage, deface, deform, distort, injure, maim, make ugly, mar, mutilate, ruin, scar, spoil
🞐 adorn, embellish

disfigurement *n* defacement, deformity, distortion, impairment, injury, mutilation, scar, uglification
🞐 adornment

disgorge *v* belch, discharge, effuse *formal*, eject, empty, expel, spew, spout

disgrace *n* black mark, blot, debasement *formal*, defamation, degradation, disapprobation *formal*, discredit, disfavour, dishonour, disrepute, disrespect, humiliation, ignominy *formal*, infamy, loss of face, obloquy *formal*, opprobrium *formal*, reproach, scandal, shame, slur, smear, stain, stigma
🞐 esteem, honour
♦ *v* abase, belittle, blame, blot someone's copybook, bring shame on, cause to lose face, debase, defame, degrade, denigrate *formal*, discredit, disfavour, dishonour, disparage *formal*, drag through the mud *colloq*, humiliate, put someone's nose out of joint, put to shame, reproach, shame, slur, stain, stigmatize, sully, taint
🞐 honour, respect

disgraced *adj* branded, degraded, discredited, dishonoured, humiliated, in the doghouse *colloq*, shamed, stigmatized
🞐 honoured, respected

disgraceful *adj* appalling, awful, blameworthy, contemptible, culpable *formal*, despicable, dishonourable, disreputable, dreadful, ignominious *formal*, outrageous, reprehensible *formal*, scandalous, shameful, shocking, terrible, unworthy
🞐 honourable, respectable

disgruntled *adj* annoyed, brassed off *colloq*, browned off *colloq*, cheesed off *colloq*, discontented, displeased, dissatisfied, exasperated, fed up *colloq*, grumpy, hacked off *colloq*, irritated, malcontent *formal*, peeved, peevish, petulant, put out, resentful, sulky, sullen, testy, vexed
🞐 pleased, satisfied

disguise *n* camouflage, cloak, concealment, costume, cover, deception, façade, false picture, front, mask, masquerade, misrepresentation, pretence, screen, shroud, travesty, veil
♦ *v* **1** *disguised himself as an old man:* be under cover, camouflage, cloak, conceal, cover, cover up, dress up, hide, impersonate, mask, repress, screen, shroud, suppress, veil **2** *she disguised her religion well:* deceive, dissemble *formal*, fake, falsify, feign *formal*, fudge, gloss over, misrepresent, pretend, put up a smokescreen *colloq*, whitewash *colloq*
🞐 **1** expose, reveal

disguised *adj* camouflaged, cloaked, covert *formal*, fake, false, feigned *formal*, hidden, incognito, made up, masked, undercover, unrecognizable, veiled

disgust *v* displease, make your gorge rise, nauseate, offend, outrage, put off, repel, revolt, sicken, turn off *colloq*, turn your stomach *colloq*
🞐 delight, please
♦ *n* abhorrence *formal*, aversion, detestation *formal*, disapproval, displeasure, distaste, hatred, loathing, nausea, repugnance *formal*, repulsion, revulsion

disgusted *adj* appalled, offended, outraged, put off, repelled, repulsed, revolted, sickened, up in arms *colloq*
➡ attracted, delighted

disgusting *adj* abominable, appalling, bad, detestable, disgraceful, distasteful, foul, gross *colloq*, nasty, nauseating, nauseous, objectionable, obscene, odious, offensive, off-putting, outrageous, rebarbative *formal*, repellent, repugnant *formal*, repulsive, revolting, shocking, sickening, unappetizing, unpalatable, unpleasant, vile, yucky *colloq*
➡ acceptable, delightful, pleasant

dish *n* course, delicacy, fare, food, recipe, speciality
▶ **dish out** allocate, distribute, dole out, give out, hand out, hand round, inflict, mete out, pass round, share out
▶ **dish up** dispense, ladle, offer, present, scoop, serve, spoon

disharmony *n* clash, conflict, disaccord *formal*, discord, discordance *formal*, dissonance *formal*, friction, incompatibility
➡ harmony

dishearten *v* cast down, crush, dampen, dash, daunt, deject, depress, deter, disappoint, discourage, dismay, dispirit, make depressed, put a damper on, weigh down
➡ encourage, hearten

disheartened *adj* crestfallen, crushed, daunted, dejected, depressed, disappointed, discouraged, dismayed, dispirited, downcast, downhearted
➡ encouraged, heartened

dishevelled *adj* bedraggled, disarranged *formal*, disordered, in a mess, messy, ruffled, rumpled, slovenly, tousled, uncombed, unkempt, untidy
➡ neat, tidy

dishonest *adj* bent *colloq*, cheating, corrupt, crafty, crooked *colloq*, cunning, deceitful, deceptive, devious, dishonourable, disreputable, double-dealing, duplicitous *formal*, false, fishy *colloq*, fraudulent, iffy *colloq*, irregular, lying, mendacious *formal*, perfidious *formal*, shady *colloq*, shifty *colloq*, sly, swindling, treacherous, unprincipled, unscrupulous, untrustworthy, untruthful
➡ honest, scrupulous, trustworthy

dishonesty *n* cheating, chicanery, corruption, criminality, crookedness *colloq*, deceit, double-dealing, duplicity *formal*, falsehood, falsity, fraud, fraudulence, improbity *formal*, insincerity, irregularity, perfidy *formal*, shadiness *colloq*, sharp practice, treachery, trickery, unscrupulousness, untruthfulness
➡ honesty, truthfulness

dishonour *v* **1** *dishonour the family's name*: abuse, affront, debase, debauch, defame, defile, degrade, demean, discredit, disgrace, humiliate, insult, offend, shame, stain, sully **2** *dishonour an agreement/a cheque*: break, default on, refuse, reject, renege on, turn down
➡ **1** honour **2** accept, honour
♦ *n* abasement, abuse, aspersion *formal*, debasement *formal*, degradation, discourtesy, discredit *formal*, disfavour *formal*, disgrace, disrepute, humiliation, ignominy *formal*, indignity, infamy, insult, offence, opprobrium *formal*, outrage, reproach, scandal, shame, slight, slur, stigma

➡ honour

dishonourable *adj* contemptible, corrupt, despicable, discreditable, disgraceful, disreputable, ignoble, ignominious *formal*, infamous, perfidious *formal*, scandalous, shady *colloq*, shameful, shameless, treacherous, unethical, unprincipled, unscrupulous, untrustworthy, unworthy
➡ honourable

disillusion *v* disabuse *formal*, disappoint, disenchant

disillusioned *adj* disabused *formal*, disappointed, disenchanted, let down, undeceived

disincentive *n* barrier, constraint, damper, determent, deterrent, discouragement, dissuasion, hindrance, impediment, obstacle, repellent, restriction, turn-off
➡ encouragement, incentive

disinclination *n* antipathy *formal*, averseness, aversion, dislike, hesitation, loathness, objection, opposition, reluctance, repugnance *formal*, resistance, unwillingness
➡ enthusiasm, inclination

disinclined *adj* averse *formal*, hesitant, indisposed, loath, opposed, reluctant, resistant, unenthusiastic, unwilling
➡ enthusiastic, inclined, willing

disinfect *v* clean, cleanse, decontaminate, fumigate, purge, purify, sanitize, sterilize
➡ contaminate, infect

disinfectant *n* antiseptic, bactericide, decontaminant, fumigant, germicide, sanitizer, sterilizer

disingenuous *adj* artful, crafty, cunning, deceitful, designing, devious, dishonest, duplicitous *formal*, feigned *formal*, guileful, insidious, insincere, shifty, sly, two-faced, uncandid, wily
➡ artless, frank, ingenuous, naïve

disinherit *v* abandon, cut off, cut off without a penny *colloq*, cut someone out of your will, dispossess, impoverish, reject, renounce, repudiate, turn your back on *colloq*

disintegrate *v* break apart, break up, crumble, decay, decompose, fall apart, fall to pieces, moulder, rot, separate, shatter, smash, splinter

disinterest *n* detachment, disinterestedness, dispassionateness, fairness, impartiality, neutrality, unbiasedness

disinterested *adj* detached, dispassionate, equitable, even-handed, fair, impartial, just, neutral, objective, open-minded, unbiased, uninvolved, unprejudiced, unselfish
➡ biased, concerned, prejudiced

disinterested or *uninterested*? Disinterested means 'not influenced by private feelings or selfish motives': *I think we need the opinions of a few disinterested observers.* Uninterested means 'not showing any interest': *uninterested in politics.*

disjointed *adj* **1** *disjointed drug-fuelled ramblings*: aimless, bitty, confused, directionless, disordered, incoherent, loose, rambling, spasmodic, unconnected, wandering
2 *a disjointed and fragmented society*: broken,

dislike *n* animosity, animus *formal*, antagonism, antipathy *formal*, aversion, detestation, disapprobation *formal*, disapproval, disesteem *formal*, disgust, disinclination *formal*, displeasure, distaste, enmity, hatred, hostility, loathing, repugnance *formal*, resentment
■ liking, predilection *formal*
♦ *v* abhor *formal*, abominate, be no love lost between *colloq*, be sick to the back teeth of *colloq*, despise, detest, disapprove, disfavour *formal*, disrelish *formal*, execrate *formal*, hate, loathe, not be someone's cup of tea *colloq*, not stand the sight of *colloq*, object to, regard with distaste, scorn, shun
■ favour, like

dislocate *v* **1** *dislocate a bone:* disconnect, disengage, disjoint, disorder, displace, disunite, do in *colloq*, luxate *technical*, misplace, pull, put out, put out of joint/place, shift, sprain, strain, twist **2** *dislocate plans:* confuse, disorganize, disrupt, disturb, throw into confusion

dislocation *n* disarray, disorder, disorganization, disruption, disturbance
■ order

dislodge *v* displace, eject, extricate, force out, move, oust, remove, shift, uproot

disloyal *adj* apostate *formal*, deceitful, double-dealing, faithless, false, perfidious *formal*, traitorous, treacherous, two-faced, unfaithful, unpatriotic, untrue
■ constant, faithful, loyal, trustworthy

disloyalty *n* adultery, apostasy *formal*, betrayal, breach of trust, deceit, double-dealing, falseness, falsity, inconstancy *formal*, infidelity, perfidiousness *formal*, perfidy *formal*, sedition *formal*, treachery, treason, unfaithfulness
■ faithfulness, loyalty

dismal *adj* **1** *feeling rather dismal:* bleak, cheerless, depressing, despondent, discouraging, forlorn, gloomy, hopeless, long-faced *colloq*, low-spirited, lugubrious *formal*, melancholy, miserable, sad, sombre, sorrowful **2** *dismal weather:* bleak, cheerless, depressing, desolate, dingy, drab, dreary, dull, gloomy
■ **1** cheerful **2** bright

dismantle *v* demolish, disassemble, pull apart, separate, strip (down), take apart, take to pieces
■ assemble, put together

dismay *n* agitation, alarm, apprehension *formal*, consternation *formal*, disappointment, discouragement, distress, dread, fear, fright, horror, terror, trepidation *formal*
■ boldness, encouragement
♦ *v* alarm, bother, cast down, concern, daunt, depress, disappoint, disconcert, discourage, dishearten, disillusion, dispirit, distress, disturb, frighten, horrify, perturb *formal*, put off, scare, shock, take aback, unnerve, unsettle, upset, worry
■ encourage, hearten

dismember *v* amputate, break up, disjoint, dislocate, dissect, divide, mutilate, separate, sever
■ assemble, join, unify

dismiss *v* **1** *the class was dismissed:* banish, discharge, discord, dissolve, drop, free, let go, release, remove, send away **2** *dismiss employees:* boot out *colloq*, cashier, discharge, expel, fire *colloq*, give notice, give someone the sack/push/ boot/elbow *colloq*, give someone their cards *colloq*, give someone their papers, lay off, make redundant, relegate, remove, sack *colloq*, send packing *colloq*, show someone the door *colloq*, suspend **3** *dismiss it from your mind:* banish, discount, disregard, pour cold water on, put away, put out of your mind, reject, repudiate, set aside, shelve, spurn
■ **1** gather, retain **2** appoint, hire **3** accept, think about

dismissal *n* boot *colloq*, discharge, elbow *colloq*, expulsion, firing *colloq*, laying-off, marching-orders, notice, papers *colloq*, push *colloq*, redundancy, removal, sack *colloq*, sacking *colloq*
■ appointment, hiring

dismissive *adj* contemptuous, disdainful, dismissory *formal*, off-hand, scornful, sneering
■ concerned, interested

dismount *v* alight *formal*, descend, disembark *formal*, get down, light *formal*, unmount *formal*
■ mount

disobedience *n* contrariness, contumacity *formal*, contumacy *formal*, defiance, indiscipline, infraction *formal*, insubordination *formal*, mutiny, rebellion, recalcitrance *formal*, revolt, unruliness, waywardness, wilfulness
■ obedience

disobedient *adj* contrary, contumacious *formal*, defiant, disorderly, froward *formal*, insubordinate *formal*, intractable *formal*, mischievous, naughty, obstreperous, rebellious, recalcitrant *formal*, recusant *formal*, refractory *formal*, unruly, wayward, wilful
■ obedient

disobey *v* contravene *formal*, defy, disregard, flout, go against someone's wishes, ignore, infringe, overstep, rebel, resist, step out of line, transgress *formal*, violate *formal*
■ comply with, obey

disobliging *adj* awkward, bloody-minded, disagreeable, discourteous, rude, unaccommodating, uncivil, unco-operative, unhelpful, unwilling
■ helpful, obliging

disorder *n* **1** *the department was in a state of disorder:* chaos, clutter, confusion, disarray, disorderliness, disorganization, jumble, mess, muddle, shambles *colloq*, untidiness **2** *public disorder:* brawl, breach of the peace, brouhaha, clamour, commotion, confusion, disruption, disturbance, fight, fracas, mêlée, quarrel, riot, rout, rumpus, tumult, unrest, uproar **3** *a rare eye disorder:* affliction *formal*, ailment, complaint, condition, disability, disease, illness, malady *formal*, sickness
■ **1** neatness, order **2** law and order, peace

disordered *adj* **1** *a disordered pile of folders:* cluttered, confused, disorganized, jumbled, messy, muddled, untidy, upside-down **2** *a disordered mind:* confused, deranged, disturbed, maladjusted, troubled, unbalanced, upset
■ **1** organized, tidy

disorderly *adj* **1** *a disorderly jumble of letters:* at sixes and sevens *colloq*, chaotic, cluttered, confused, disorganized, in disarray, irregular, jumbled, messy, untidy **2** *drunk and disorderly:* boisterous, disobedient, lawless, obstreperous, rebellious, refractory *formal*, rough, rowdy, tumultuous, turbulent, uncontrollable, undisciplined, unmanageable, unruly, wild
🔁 **1** neat, tidy **2** well-behaved

disorganization *n* chaos, confusion, disarray, disorder, disruption, muddle, shambles *colloq*, untidiness
🔁 order, tidiness

disorganize *v* break up, confuse, destroy, disarrange, discompose, disorder, disrupt, disturb, jumble, mess up, mix up, muddle, play havoc with, unsettle, upset
🔁 organize

disorganized *adj* **1** *a disorganized office:* chaotic, confused, disordered, haphazard, jumbled, muddled, shambolic *colloq*, topsy-turvy, unsorted, unsystematized **2** *she is often disorganized at meetings:* careless, muddled, unmethodical, unorganized, unstructured, unsystematic, untogether *colloq*
🔁 **1** organized, tidy **2** methodical, organized

disorientate *v* confuse, disorient, faze *colloq*, mislead, muddle, perplex, puzzle, upset

disorientated *adj* adrift, astray, at sea, bewildered, confused, disoriented, lost, mixed up, muddled, perplexed, puzzled, unbalanced, unsettled, upset

disown *v* abandon, abnegate *formal*, cast off, deny, disallow, disavow *formal*, disclaim, forsake *formal*, reject, renounce, repudiate, turn your back on
🔁 accept, acknowledge

disparage *v* belittle, calumniate *formal*, cast aspersions on *formal*, criticize, decry, defame, degrade, denigrate *formal*, deprecate *formal*, deride *formal*, derogate *formal*, detract from, discredit, disdain, dishonour, dismiss, malign, minimize, ridicule, run down, scorn, slander, traduce *formal*, underestimate, underrate, undervalue, vilify *formal*, vilipend *formal*
🔁 praise

disparagement *n* aspersion *formal*, belittlement, condemnation, contempt, contumely *formal*, criticism, debasement, decrial *formal*, decrying *formal*, degradation, denunciation, deprecation *formal*, derision *formal*, derogation *formal*, detraction, discredit, disdain, ridicule, scorn, slander, underestimation, vilification *formal*
🔁 praise

disparaging *adj* critical, deprecatory *formal*, derisive, derogatory, dismissive, insulting, mocking, scornful, snide *colloq*
🔁 flattering, praising

disparate *adj* contrary, contrasting, different, discrepant *formal*, dissimilar, distinct, diverse, unequal, unlike
🔁 equal, similar

disparity *n* bias, contrast, difference, discrepancy, disproportion, dissimilarity, dissimilitude *formal*, distinction, gap, gulf, imbalance, incongruity *formal*, inequality,

inequity *formal*, unevenness, unfairness, unlikeness
🔁 equality, parity, similarity

dispassionate *adj* calm, calm and collected, composed, cool, detached, disinterested, equitable, fair, impartial, impersonal, neutral, objective, self-controlled, self-possessed, unbiased, unemotional, unexcited, unprejudiced
🔁 biased, emotional, involved

dispatch, despatch *v* **1** *she dispatched an e-mail:* accelerate, consign, convey, expedite, express, forward, mail, post, remit, send, transmit **2** *she dispatched her business:* conclude, discharge, dispose of, finish, perform, settle **3** *he quickly dispatched the injured deer:* assassinate, bump off *colloq*, do in *colloq*, execute, kill, knock off *colloq*, murder, put to death, slaughter
🔁 **1** receive
♦ *n* **1** *received a dispatch from the battlefield:* account, article, bulletin, communication, communiqué, item, letter, message, news, piece, report **2** *we have to act with dispatch:* alacrity *formal*, celerity *formal*, expedition, haste, promptitude *formal*, promptness, rapidity, speed, swiftness
🔁 **2** slowness

dispel *v* allay, banish, chase away, dismiss, disperse, disseminate *formal*, dissipate *formal*, drive away, eliminate, expel, get rid of, melt away, rid, rout, scatter

dispensable *adj* disposable, expendable, gratuitous, inessential, needless, non-essential, replaceable, superfluous, unnecessary, useless
🔁 essential, indispensable

dispensation *n* **1** *she needed special dispensation to compete:* exception, exemption, immunity, licence, permission, release, relief, remission, reprieve **2** *the dispensation of justice:* allocation, allotment, apportionment, bestowal *formal*, distribution, endowment *formal*, handing out, issue, sharing out **3** *I'd rather live under the previous dispensation:* administration, application, arrangement, authority, direction, discharge, economy *formal*, order, organization, plan, scheme, system

dispense *v* **1** *dispensed £10,000 in grants:* bestow, confer *formal*, deal out, distribute, divide out, dole out, give out, hand out, mete out **2** *courts dispensing justice:* administer, apply, carry out, discharge, effectuate *formal*, enforce, execute, implement, operate
► **dispense with** abolish, cancel, discard, dispose of, disregard, do away with, do without, forgo, get rid of, give up, ignore, not need, omit, relinquish, renounce, rescind *formal*, revoke *formal*, waive

disperse *v* break up, diffuse, disband, dismiss, dispel, disseminate *formal*, dissipate *formal*, dissolve, distribute, go their separate ways, melt away, scatter, separate, spread, thin out
🔁 gather

dispersion *n* broadcast, circulation, diaspora *technical*, diffusion, dispersal, dissemination *formal*, dissipation *formal*, distribution, scattering, spreading

dispirit *v* dampen, dash, deject, depress, deter, discourage, dishearten, put a damper on, sadden
🔁 encourage, hearten

dispirited *adj* brassed off *colloq*, browned off *colloq*, cast down, cheesed off *colloq*, crestfallen, dejected, depressed, despondent, discouraged, disheartened, down *colloq*, down in the dumps *colloq*, downcast, fed up *colloq*, gloomy, glum, low, morose, sad
🖅 encouraged

displace *v* 1 *stones displaced by the tide*: dislocate, dislodge, disturb, misplace, move, relocate, shift 2 *they displaced him in a coup*: boot out *colloq*, depose, discharge, dislodge, dismiss, eject, evict, expel, force out, oust, remove, replace, succeed, supersede, supplant, turf out *colloq*

displacement *n* disarrangement, dislocation, dislodging, disturbance, misplacement, moving, shifting
🖅 arrangement, order

display *v* 1 *we displayed our products*: advertise, demonstrate, exhibit, present, promote, publicize, put on show, show, unveil 2 *he displayed his sadness*: betray, disclose, evince *formal*, expose, manifest *formal*, reveal, show 3 *she displayed her charms for all to see*: blazon, boast, flaunt, flourish, parade, show off
🖅 1 conceal 2 disguise
♦ *n* array, demonstration, disclosure, evidence, evincement *formal*, exhibit, exhibition, manifestation *formal*, pageant, parade, presentation, revelation, show, spectacle

displease *v* aggravate *colloq*, anger, annoy, bug *colloq*, discompose *formal*, dissatisfy, disturb, exasperate, incense, infuriate, irk, irritate, offend, perturb *formal*, provoke, put out *colloq*, upset, vex
🖅 please, satisfy

displeased *adj* aggravated *colloq*, angry, annoyed, disgruntled, exasperated, furious, infuriated, irritated, offended, peeved, piqued, put out *colloq*, upset
🖅 pleased

displeasure *n* anger, annoyance, chagrin, disapprobation *formal*, disapproval, discontentment, disfavour, disgust, dissatisfaction, distaste, exasperation, indignation, ire, irritation, offence, perturbation *formal*, pique, resentment, wrath
🖅 pleasure

disport *v* amuse, cavort, cheer, delight, divert, entertain, frisk, frolic, gambol, play, revel, romp, sport

disposable *adj* biodegradable, expendable, non-returnable, throwaway

disposal *n* 1 *the disposal of the troops*: arrangement, grouping, order 2 *two regiments at our disposal*: command, control, direction 3 *the disposal of waste*: clearance, discarding, jettisoning, removal, riddance, scrapping, throwing-away

dispose *v* 1 *dispose of a problem*: attend to, deal with, decide, determine, finish, handle, look after, see to, settle, sort out, tackle, take care of 2 *dispose of old books*: chuck out *colloq*, clear out, destroy, discard, dump *colloq*, get rid of, get shot of *colloq*, jettison, scrap, shed, throw away/out 3 *dispose troops*: align, arrange, group, line up, order, organize, place, position, put, situate 4 *dispose of a person*: bump off *colloq*, destroy, do away with, do in *colloq*, kill, murder, put to death

🖅 2 keep

disposed *adj* apt, eager, inclined, liable, likely, minded, predisposed *formal*, prepared, prone, ready, subject, willing
🖅 disinclined *formal*

disposition *n* 1 *a friendly disposition*: bent, character, constitution, habit, humour, inclination, leaning, make-up, mood, nature, predilection *formal*, predisposition *formal*, proclivity *formal*, proneness, propensity *formal*, spirit, temper, temperament, tendency 2 *the disposition of troops*: alignment, arrangement, grouping, line-up, order, pattern, placing, positioning, sequence, system 3 *the disposition of property*: allocation, conveyance, disposal, distribution, giving-over, transfer

dispossess *v* deprive, dislodge, divest, eject, evict, expel, oust, rob, strip, take away
🖅 give, provide

disproportion *n* asymmetry *formal*, discrepancy, disparity *formal*, imbalance, incommensurateness *formal*, inequality, insufficiency, lopsidedness, unevenness
🖅 balance, equality

disproportionate *adj* excessive, incommensurate *formal*, out of proportion, unbalanced, unequal, uneven, unreasonable
🖅 balanced, commensurate *formal*

disprove *v* confute *formal*, contradict, controvert *formal*, debunk *colloq*, deny, discredit, expose, give the lie to, invalidate, negate *formal*, prove false, rebut, refute *formal*
🖅 confirm, prove

disputable *adj* arguable, controversial, debatable, doubtful, dubious, litigious *formal*, moot, questionable, uncertain
🖅 indisputable, unquestionable

disputation *n* argument, argumentation, controversy, debate, deliberation, dispute, dissension *formal*, polemics, quodlibet *technical*

disputatious *adj* argumentative, cantankerous, captious, contentious, litigious *formal*, polemical, pugnacious *formal*, quarrelsome

dispute *v* 1 *I disputed his assertion*: call into question, challenge, contend, contest, contradict, debate, deny, discuss, doubt, question 2 *neighbour disputed with neighbour*: argue, bicker, clash, quarrel, squabble, wrangle
🖅 1 agree
♦ *n* 1 *a legal dispute*: contention, controversy, debate, disagreement 2 *a noisy dispute*: altercation *formal*, argument, conflict, contention, feud, quarrel, row, squabble, strife, wrangle
🖅 1 agreement 2 settlement

disqualified *adj* debarred *formal*, disentitled *formal*, eliminated, ineligible, precluded *formal*, struck off
🖅 accepted, eligible, qualified

disqualify *v* 1 *disqualified from the competition*: debar *formal*, declare ineligible, disentitle *formal*, eliminate, preclude *formal*, prohibit, rule out, strike off, suspend 2 *poor eyesight disqualified him from service*: debilitate *formal*, disable, handicap, immobilize, impair *formal*, incapacitate, invalidate
🖅 1 accept, qualify

disquiet *n* agitation, alarm, anguish, anxiety, concern, disquietude *formal*, distress,

disturbance, dread, fear, foreboding, fretfulness, inquietude *formal*, nervousness, perturbation *formal*, restlessness, trouble, uneasiness, upset, worry
⊟ calm, reassurance
♦ *v* agitate, annoy, bother, concern, discompose *formal*, distress, disturb, fret, harass, hassle *colloq*, incommode *formal*, make anxious, make uneasy, perturb *formal*, pester, plague, ruffle, shake, trouble, unnerve, unsettle, upset, vex, worry
⊟ calm, reassure

disquisition *n* discourse *formal*, dissertation, essay, explanation, exposition *formal*, monograph, paper, sermon, thesis, treatise

disregard *v* 1 *I disregarded her protestations:* brush aside, discount, disobey, flout, gloss over, ignore, laugh off *colloq*, make light of, neglect, overlook, pass over, set aside, take no notice of, turn a blind eye to *colloq* 2 *she completely disregarded him:* cold shoulder *colloq*, denigrate *formal*, despise, disdain, disparage *formal*, insult, shun, slight, snub
⊟ 1 heed, listen to, pay attention to 2 respect
♦ *n* contempt, denigration *formal*, disdain, disrespect, inattention, indifference
⊟ attention, heed, notice

disrepair *n* collapse, decay, deterioration, dilapidation, rack and ruin, ruin, shabbiness
⊟ good repair

disreputable *adj* base, contemptible, corrupt, discreditable, disgraceful, dishonourable, dodgy *colloq*, dubious, ignominious *formal*, infamous, low, mean, notorious, opprobrious *formal*, outrageous, scandalous, shady *colloq*, shameful, shifty *colloq*, shocking, suspicious, unprincipled, unrespectable, unworthy
⊟ honourable, respectable

disrepute *n* discredit, disesteem *formal*, disfavour, disgrace, dishonour, disreputation, ignominy *formal*, infamy, obloquy *formal*, shame
⊟ esteem *formal*, honour

disrespect *n* cheek, contempt, discourtesy, dishonour, disregard, impertinence, impoliteness, impudence, incivility, insolence, irreverence, misesteem *formal*, rudeness, scorn
⊟ civility, consideration, politeness, respect

disrespectful *adj* cheeky, contemptuous, discourteous, impertinent, impolite, impudent, inconsiderate, insolent, insulting, irreverent, rude, sassy *US colloq*, uncivil, unmannerly
⊟ civil, considerate, polite, respectful

disrobe *v* bare, denude, disapparel *formal*, divest *formal*, remove, shed, strip, take off, unclothe, uncover, undress
⊟ cover, dress

disrupt *v* break up, butt in, cause confusion in, confuse, disarrange, disorganize, disturb, hamper, impede, interfere with, interrupt, intrude, put a spoke in someone's wheel *colloq*, sabotage, throw a spanner in the works *colloq*, throw into disorder/disarray, unsettle, upset

disruption *n* confusion, disarray, disorder, disorderliness, disorganization, disturbance, interference, interruption, stoppage, turmoil, upheaval, upset

disruptive *adj* boisterous, disorderly, distracting, disturbing, noisy, obstreperous, troublesome, turbulent, undisciplined, unruly, unsettling, upsetting
⊟ manageable, well-behaved

dissatisfaction *n* anger, annoyance, chagrin, disappointment, disapprobation *formal*, disapproval, discomfort, discontent, dislike, displeasure, exasperation, frustration, irritation, regret, resentment, restlessness, unhappiness, vexation
⊟ satisfaction

dissatisfied *adj* angry, annoyed, brassed off *colloq*, browned off *colloq*, cheesed off *colloq*, disappointed, discontented, disenchanted, disgruntled, disillusioned, displeased, exasperated, fed up *colloq*, frustrated, irritated, pissed off *slang*, unfulfilled, unhappy, unsatisfied
⊟ fulfilled, satisfied

dissatisfy *v* anger, annoy, disappoint, discontent, disgruntle, displease, exasperate, frustrate, give cause for complaint, irritate, put out, vex

dissect *v* 1 *he dissected two frogs:* anatomize *formal*, cut up, dismember, vivisect 2 *critics dissecting my work:* analyse, break down, examine, explore, inspect, investigate, pore over, probe, scrutinize, study

dissection *n* 1 *corpses required for dissection:* autopsy *technical*, cutting up, dismemberment, necropsy, vivisection 2 *the dissection of my plan:* analysis, breakdown, examination, exploration, inspection, investigation, probe, scrutiny, study

dissemble *v* affect *formal*, camouflage, cloak, conceal, counterfeit, cover up *colloq*, disguise, dissimulate *formal*, fake, falsify, feign, hide, mask, play possum, pretend, sham, simulate
⊟ admit

dissembler *n* charlatan, con man *colloq*, deceiver, dissimulator *formal*, fake, feigner, fraud, hypocrite, impostor, pretender, trickster, whited sepulchre

disseminate *v* broadcast, circulate, diffuse, disperse, distribute, proclaim, promulgate *formal*, propagate, publicize, publish, scatter, sow, spread

dissemination *n* broadcasting, circulation, diffusion, dispersion, distribution, promulgation *formal*, propagation, publication, publishing, spread

dissension *n* argument, conflict, contention, difference of opinion, disagreement, discord, dispute, dissent, friction, quarrel, strife, variance
⊟ agreement

dissent *v* differ, disagree, dispute, object, protest, quibble, refuse
⊟ assent
♦ *n* controversy, difference, difference of opinion, disagreement, discord, dispute, dissension, friction, objection, opposition, protest, resistance
⊟ agreement, conformity

dissenter *n* demonstrator, disputant, dissident, heretic, nonconformist, objector, protestant, protester, rebel, recusant, revolutionary, schismatic, sectary

dissentient *adj* conflicting, differing, disagreeing, dissenting, dissident, heretical,

opposing, protesting, rebellious, recusant, revolutionary
◨ arguing

dissertation *n* critique, discourse *formal*, disquisition *formal*, essay, exposition *formal*, monograph, paper, prolegomena *technical*, propaedeutic, thesis, treatise

disservice *n* bad turn, con trick *colloq*, dirty trick *colloq*, disfavour, harm, hurt, injury, injustice, kick in the teeth *colloq*, sharp practice, unkindness, wrong
◨ favour

dissidence *n* disagreement, discordance, dispute, dissent, feud, recusancy, rupture, schism, variance
◨ agreement, peace

dissident *adj* conflicting, differing, disagreeing, discordant, dissenting, heretical, heterodox *formal*, nonconformist, opposing, protesting, rebellious, revolutionary
◨ acquiescent, orthodox
♦ *n* agitator, dissenter, heretic, nonconformist, objector, protester, rebel, recusant, revolutionary, schismatic
◨ assenter

dissimilar *adj* contrasting, deviating, different, disparate *formal*, distinct, divergent, diverse, heterogeneous *formal*, incompatible, mismatched, unlike, unrelated, various, varying
◨ alike, like, similar

dissimilarity *n* contrast, difference, discrepancy, disparity *formal*, dissimilitude *formal*, distinction, divergence, diversity, heterogeneity *formal*, incomparability, incompatibility, unlikeness, unrelatedness, variety
◨ compatibility, similarity

dissimulate *v* affect *formal*, camouflage, cloak, conceal, cover up *colloq*, disguise, dissemble *formal*, fake, feign, hide, lie, mask, pretend

dissipate *v* 1 *he dissipated his inheritance:* burn up, consume, deplete, drain, exhaust, expend, fritter away, lavish, run/get through, spend, squander, use up, waste 2 *the clouds dissipated:* break up, diffuse, disappear, dispel, disperse, dissolve, drive away, evaporate, melt away, scatter, vanish
◨ 1 accumulate 2 appear, gather

dissipated *adj* abandoned, corrupt, debauched, degenerate, depraved, dissolute, intemperate *formal*, licentious *formal*, profligate *formal*, rakish, self-indulgent, wasted, wild
◨ conserved, upright, virtuous

dissipation *n* 1 *the dissipation of all fears:* consumption, depletion, diffusion, disappearance, dispersal, evaporation, expenditure, squandering 2 *a life of idle dissipation:* abandonment, corruption, debauchery, depravity, excess, extravagance, immorality, intemperance *formal*, licence, licentiousness *formal*, prodigality, self-indulgence
◨ 1 conservation 2 virtue

dissociate *v* 1 *dissociate one thing from another:* break off/up, cut off, detach, disassociate, disband, disconnect, disengage, disrupt, disunite, divorce, isolate, segregate, separate, set apart, sever 2 *dissociate yourself from something:*

cut off, disconnect, distance, quit *colloq*, secede *formal*, separate, withdraw
◨ 1 associate, join

dissociation *n* break, cutting-off, detachment, disconnection, disengagement, dissevering, distancing, disunion *formal*, division, divorce, isolation, segregation, separation, setting apart, severance, severing, split
◨ association, union

dissolute *adj* abandoned, corrupt, debauched, degenerate, depraved, dissipated, immoral, intemperate *formal*, lewd, licentious *formal*, profligate *formal*, rakish, self-indulgent, unrestrained, wanton, wild
◨ restrained, virtuous

dissolution *n* 1 *the dissolution of an organization/a marriage:* annulment, break-up, conclusion, discontinuation *formal*, divorce, ending, suspension, termination *formal* 2 *the dissolution of the monarchy:* break-up, destruction, overthrow 3 *dissolution of family life:* break-up, collapse, decomposition, disappearance, disintegration, disposal, division, evaporation, separation

dissolve *v* 1 *sugar dissolves in water:* deliquesce *technical*, go into solution, liquefy, melt, solvate 2 *the marriage/partnership dissolved:* break up, bring to an end, disband, discontinue *formal*, disintegrate, dismiss, disperse, end, finish, separate, terminate *formal*, wind up 3 *my fears gradually dissolved:* crumble, disappear, disperse, dissipate *formal*, dwindle, evanesce *formal*, evaporate, melt away, vanish 4 *dissolve into tears:* be overcome with, begin, break, burst, collapse, lose control, start

dissonance *n* 1 *diplomatic dissonance:* difference, disagreement, discord, discrepancy, disparity *formal*, dissension, incompatibility, incongruity *formal*, inconsistency, variance 2 *Mozart's use of dissonance:* cacophony, discord, discordance, disharmony, grating, harshness, jangle, jarring, stridency
◨ 1 agreement, harmony 2 agreement, harmony

dissonant *adj* 1 *several dissonant voices among his colleagues:* anomalous *formal*, differing, disagreeing, incompatible, incongruous *formal*, inconsistent, irreconcilable, irregular 2 *dissonant music:* cacophonous, clashing, discordant, grating, harsh, jangling, jarring, raucous, strident, tuneless, unmelodious, unmusical
◨ 1 compatible, harmonious 2 compatible, harmonious

dissuade *v* deter, discourage, disincline, persuade not to, put off, stop, talk out of
◨ persuade

dissuasion *n* caution, deterrence, deterring, discouragement, expostulation *formal*, remonstrance *formal*, remonstration *formal*
◨ persuasion

distance *n* 1 *the distance between the two posts:* breadth, depth, extent, gap, height, interval, length, range, reach, separation, space, span, stretch, width 2 *distance won't be a problem:* farness, inaccessibility, remoteness 3 *a blend of helpfulness and distance makes a good neighbour:* aloofness, coldness, coolness, formality, remoteness, reserve, stiffness, unfriendliness

▣ **1** closeness **2** accessibility **3** approachability, closeness, warmth

♦ *v* break, cut off, dissociate, remove, secede *formal*, separate, withdraw

distant *adj* **1** *a distant land:* abroad, back of beyond *colloq*, dispersed, far, faraway, far-flung, far-off, isolated, outlying, out-of-the-way, remote **2** *a distant relative:* not close, remote, slight **3** *she's polite but distant:* aloof, antisocial, cold, cool, detached, formal, reserved, restrained, stand-offish *colloq*, stiff, unapproachable, uncommunicative, unfriendly, unresponsive, withdrawn
▣ **1** close, nearby **2** close **3** approachable, warm

distaste *n* abhorrence *formal*, antipathy *formal*, aversion, disfavour, disgust, dislike, displeasure, horror, loathing, repugnance *formal*, revulsion
▣ liking

distasteful *adj* abhorrent, detestable, disagreeable, disgusting, displeasing, loathsome, objectionable, obnoxious, offensive, repellent, repugnant *formal*, repulsive, revolting, undesirable, uninviting, unpleasant, unsavoury
▣ pleasing

distend *v* balloon, bloat, bulge, dilate, enlarge, expand, fill out, inflate, intumesce *technical*, puff, stretch, swell, widen
▣ deflate

distended *adj* astrut, bloated, dilated, emphysematous *technical*, enlarged, expanded, inflated, puffed-out, puffy, stretched, swollen, tumescent, varicose
▣ deflated

distension *n* bloating, dilation, emphysema *technical*, enlargement, expansion, extension, intumescence, spread, swelling, tumescence

distil *v* condense, derive, draw out, drip, evaporate, express, extract, flow, leak, press out, purify, rectify *technical*, refine, sublimate, trickle, vaporize

distillation *n* condensation, essence, evaporation, extract, extraction, spirit

distinct *adj* **1** *a distinct change in his attitude:* apparent, clear, clear-cut, defined, definite, evident, manifest *formal*, marked, noticeable, obvious, plain, recognizable, sharp, unambiguous, unmistakable, well-defined **2** *two distinct parts:* detached, different, discrete *formal*, disparate *formal*, dissimilar, individual, separate, unassociated, unconnected
▣ **1** indistinct, vague

> *distinct* or *distinctive*? *Distinct* means 'clearly or easily seen, heard, smelt, etc': *a distinct smell of alcohol; a distinct Scottishness in her pronunciation.* *Distinctive* means 'distinguishing one person or thing from others': *She has a very distinctive walk; the distinctive call of a barn owl.*

distinction *n* **1** *obvious distinctions between the two:* contradistinction *formal*, contrast, difference, differentiation, discernment, discrimination, dissimilarity, dissimilitude *formal*, division, separation **2** *a writer of great distinction:* celebrity, consequence *formal*, credit, eminence, excellence, fame, greatness, honour, importance, merit,

prestige, prominence, quality, renown, reputation, repute, significance, superiority, worth **3** *the distinction of being a losing finalist five times:* characteristic, feature, individuality, mark, peculiarity, quality
▣ **2** obscurity, unimportance

distinctive *adj* characteristic, different, distinguishing, extraordinary, idiosyncratic, individual, noteworthy, original, particular, peculiar, singular *formal*, special, typical, unique
▣ common, ordinary

distinctly *adv* clearly, definitely, evidently, manifestly *formal*, markedly, noticeably, obviously, plainly, unambiguously, unmistakably

distinguish *v* **1** *distinguish right from wrong:* categorize, characterize, classify, determine, differentiate, discriminate, mark, mark off, particularize, set apart, single out, stamp, tell apart, tell the difference between, typify **2** *she could distinguish voices:* ascertain, descry *formal*, detect, discern, discriminate, identify, make out, notice, perceive, pick out, recognize, see **3** *distinguish yourself academically:* acquit yourself well, bring acclaim to, bring fame to, bring honour to, dignify, do well, excel, glorify

distinguishable *adj* **1** *it is distinguishable by its colour:* appreciable, conspicuous, discernible, evident, manifest *formal*, noticeable, observable, obvious, perceptible, plainly seen, recognizable **2** *no real distinguishable identity:* bold, clear, conspicuous, plain, strong, vivid
▣ **1** indistinguishable

distinguished *adj* acclaimed, aristocratic, celebrated, conspicuous, eminent, esteemed *formal*, extraordinary, famed, famous, honoured, illustrious, marked, noble, notable, noted, outstanding, prominent, refined, renowned, striking, well-known
▣ insignificant, obscure, unimpressive

distinguishing *adj* characteristic, diacritical *formal*, different, differentiating, discriminative, discriminatory, distinctive, individual, individualistic, marked, peculiar, singular *formal*, typical, unique

distort *v* **1** *distorting the shape of the tent:* bend, buckle, contort, deform, disfigure, misshape, twist, warp **2** *the newspaper distorted the facts:* bias, colour, cook the books *colloq*, falsify, garble, misrepresent, pervert, slant, tamper with, twist

distorted *adj* **1** *a distorted grimace:* awry, bent, deformed, disfigured, misshapen, out of shape, skew, skewed, twisted, warped, wry **2** *a distorted view of the story:* biased, false, misrepresented, perverted
▣ **1** straight **2** accurate

distortion *n* **1** *facial distortions:* bend, buckle, contortion, crookedness, deformity, skew, slant, twist, warp **2** *accused of wilful distortion:* bias, colouring, falsification, garbling, misrepresentation, perversion, twisting

distract *v* **1** *TV distracted him from homework:* deflect, divert, draw away, put off, sidetrack, turn aside/away **2** *read a book to distract myself:* amuse, divert, engross, entertain, occupy **3** *doubt distracted his thoughts:* bewilder, confound, confuse, discompose, disconcert, disturb, fluster, perplex, puzzle

distracted *adj* **1** *distracted by grief*: agitated, anxious, beside yourself, crazy, distraught, distressed, frantic, grief-stricken, hysterical, mad, overwrought, raving, upset, wild, worked up **2** *went about with a distracted look*: absent-minded, abstracted, dreaming, inattentive, miles away *colloq*, not with it *colloq*, preoccupied, wandering
🖃 **1** calm, untroubled **2** attentive

distracting *adj* annoying, bewildering, confusing, disconcerting, disturbing, irritating, off-putting *colloq*, perturbing *formal*

distraction *n* **1** *traffic noise is a distraction*: confusion, derangement *formal*, disturbance, diversion, interference, interruption **2** *a variety of distractions available*: amusement, diversion, divertissement, entertainment, game, hobby, pastime, recreation, sport

distraught *adj* agitated, anxious, beside yourself, crazy, distracted, distressed, frantic, het up *colloq*, hysterical, in a state *colloq*, mad, overwrought, raving, upset, wild, worked up
🖃 calm, untroubled

distress *n* **1** *emotional distress*: affliction *formal*, agony, anguish, anxiety, desolation, discomfort, grief, heartache, misery, pain, perturbation *formal*, sadness, sorrow, suffering, torment, torture, tribulation *formal*, unease, woe *formal*, worry, wretchedness **2** *poor families were helped in their distress*: adversity, calamity, destitution, difficulties, hardship, indigence *formal*, misfortune, need, penury *formal*, poverty, privation *formal*, trial, trouble
🖃 **1** content **2** comfort, ease
♦ *v* afflict *formal*, agonize, break someone's heart, cause suffering to, cut up *colloq*, disturb, grieve, harass, harrow, hurt, make anxious, make miserable, pain, perturb *formal*, sadden, torment, trouble, upset, vex, worry
🖃 comfort

distribute *v* **1** *we distributed food parcels*: allocate, allot, apportion *formal*, deal (out), dish out, dispense, divide, dole out, give out, hand out, issue, measure out, mete out, pass round, share **2** *distributing the post*: circulate, deliver, hand out, issue, spread, supply **3** *the birds are distributed in several valleys*: diffuse, disperse, scatter
🖃 **2** collect

distribution *n* **1** *distribution of the mail*: conveyance, dealing, delivery, handling, supply, transport, transportation **2** *the distribution of grants*: allocation, apportionment *formal*, division, giving-out, handing-out, sharing **3** *a wider distribution*: circulation, dispersal, dissemination *formal*, scattering, spreading **4** *a scattered distribution of field guns*: arrangement, classification, grouping, organization, placement, position
🖃 **1** collection

district *n* area, block, community, constituency, domain, locale, locality, neighbourhood, parish, place, precinct, quarter, region, sector, territory, vicinity, ward, zone

distrust *v* be sceptical about, be suspicious of, disbelieve, discredit, doubt, have doubts about, mistrust, question, suspect
🖃 trust
♦ *n* chariness, disbelief, discredit, doubt, doubtfulness, misgiving, mistrust, qualm, question, questioning, scepticism, suspicion, wariness
🖃 confidence, faith, trust

distrustful *adj* chary, cynical, disbelieving, distrusting, doubtful, doubting, dubious, mistrustful, sceptical, suspicious, uneasy, untrustful, untrusting, wary
🖃 trustful, unsuspecting

disturb *v* **1** *the car alarm disturbed me*: bother, break someone's train of thought, butt in on, disrupt, distract, interrupt, pester, put off **2** *he was disturbed by what he had seen*: agitate, annoy, bother, concern, discomfit *formal*, discompose, disconcert, dismay, distress, fluster, make anxious, perturb *formal*, stir, trouble, unsettle, upset, worry **3** *his files had been disturbed*: confuse, disarrange, disorder, disorganize, muddle, throw into confusion, unsettle, upset
🖃 **2** reassure **3** order

disturbance *n* **1** *the move caused a great deal of disturbance*: agitation, annoyance, bother, confusion, disorder, disruption, distraction, hindrance, interference, interruption, intrusion, muddle, trouble, upheaval, upset **2** *a late-night disturbance*: brawl, commotion, disorder, fracas, fray, hullabaloo, racket, riot, row, rumpus, tumult, turmoil, uproar **3** *emotional disturbance*: complaint, disorder, illness, neurosis, sickness
🖃 **1** peace **2** order

disturbed *adj* **1** *the news left me disturbed*: anxious, apprehensive, bothered, concerned, confused, discomposed, flustered, troubled, uneasy, upset, worried **2** *emotionally disturbed*: hung-up *colloq*, maladjusted, mentally ill, neurotic, paranoid, psychotic, screwed-up *colloq*, unbalanced, upset
🖃 **1** calm

disturbing *adj* agitating, alarming, bewildering, confusing, disconcerting, discouraging, dismaying, disquieting, distressing, disturbant *formal*, disturbative *formal*, frightening, perturbing *formal*, startling, threatening, troubling, unsettling, upsetting, worrying
🖃 comforting, reassuring

disunited *adj* alienated, disrupted, divided, estranged *formal*, separated, split
🖃 unify

disunity *n* alienation, breach, conflict, disagreement, discord, discordance *formal*, dissension, dissent, division, estrangement *formal*, rupture, schism, split, strife
🖃 unity

disuse *n* abandonment, decay, desuetude *formal*, discontinuance *formal*, neglect
🖃 use

disused *adj* abandoned, decayed, discontinued *formal*, neglected, unused
🖃 used

ditch *n* canal, channel, drain, dyke, furrow, gully, gutter, level, moat, trench, watercourse
♦ *v* abandon, chuck *colloq*, discard, dispose of, drop, dump *colloq*, get rid of, jettison, scrap, throw away/out

dither *v* be in two minds *colloq*, delay, dilly-dally *colloq*, hang back, hesitate, shilly-shally *colloq*, take your time, vacillate, waver

◆ *n* bother, flap *colloq*, fluster, flutter, indecision, panic, pother *colloq*, stew *colloq*, tizzy *colloq*
🔁 decision

divan *n* chaise-longue, chesterfield, couch, day bed, lounge, lounger, ottoman, settee, sofa

dive *v* 1 *dive into water*: descend, dip, drop, fall, go down/under, jump, leap, nose-dive, pitch, plummet, plunge, submerge, swoop 2 *dive for cover*: bolt, dash, fly, hurry, leap, move quickly, rush, tear
◆ *n* 1 *a dive into the pool*: dash, drop, fall, header, jump, leap, lunge, nose-dive, plummet, plunge, spring, swoop 2 *make a dive for the door*: dart, dash, leap, rush 3 *I've been thrown out of all these dives*: dump *colloq*, hole *colloq*, joint *colloq*

diverge *v* 1 *the path diverged into two*: bifurcate *formal*, branch (off), divide, fork, part, radiate, separate, split, spread (out), subdivide 2 *diverged in their opinions*: be at variance, clash, conflict, contradict, differ, disagree, dissent, vary 3 *to diverge from the truth*: depart, deviate, digress, divagate *formal*, drift, stray, wander
🔁 1 converge 2 agree

divergence *n* branching-out, clash, conflict, deflection, departure, deviation, difference, digression, disagreement, disparity *formal*, parting, separation, variation
🔁 agreement

divergent *adj* conflicting, deviating, different, differing, disagreeing, dissimilar, diverging, diverse, separate, tangential, variant, varying
🔁 similar

divers *adj* different, manifold *formal*, many, miscellaneous, multifarious *formal*, numerous, several, some, sundry, varied, various, varying

diverse *adj* 1 *diverse cheeses*: all means of, assorted, heterogeneous *formal*, miscellaneous, mixed, several, sundry, various
2 *diverse opinions*: contrasting, different, differing, discrete *formal*, dissimilar, distinct, separate, unlike, varied, varying
🔁 1 identical, similar 2 identical, similar

diversify *v* alter, assort, branch out, bring variety to, change, expand, extend, mix, modify, spread out, variegate *formal*, vary

diversion *n* 1 *traffic diversions*: alternative route, detour, deviation, redirection, rerouteing, switching 2 *chess is an excellent diversion*: amusement, distraction, divertissement, entertainment, fun, game, hobby, pastime, play, recreation, relaxation, sport 3 *a diversion from his usual themes*: alteration, change, deviation, redirection

diversionary *adj* deflecting, distracting, divertive

diversity *n* 1 *Britain's cultural diversity*: difference, dissimilarity, dissimilitude *formal*, diversification, heterogeneity *formal*, pluralism *formal*, range, variance, variegation *formal*, variety 2 *a diversity of views*: assortment, medley, miscellany, mixture, range, variety
🔁 1 likeness, similarity

divert *v* 1 *the plane was diverted*: avert, deflect, draw/turn away, redirect, reroute, sidetrack, switch 2 *diverted them with jokes*: absorb, amuse, delight, distract, engross, entertain, interest, intrigue, occupy

diverting *adj* amusing, enjoyable, entertaining, fun, funny, humorous, pleasant, pleasurable, witty
🔁 irritating

divest *v* 1 *divest of power*: deprive, despoil *formal*, dispossess, remove, strip 2 *divest of clothes*: denude *formal*, deprive, disrobe, doff *old use*, remove, strip, unclothe, undress
🔁 2 clothe

divide *v* 1 *the wall that divided the city*: bisect, branch, break up/down, cut (up), detach, disconnect, diverge, fork, part, segregate, separate, sever, split 2 *divide the pudding into four bowls*: allocate, allot, apportion *formal*, deal out, dispense, distribute, dole out, hand out, measure out, share 3 *her presence has divided the group*: alienate, break up, come between, disunite, estrange *formal*, separate, set someone against another, split (up) 4 *divide the population into three classes*: arrange, categorize, classify, grade, group, order, rank, segregate, sort
🔁 1 join 2 collect 3 unite
▶ **divide up** allocate, allot, apportion *formal*, dole out, measure out, parcel out, share (out)

dividend *n* 1 *shareholders' dividends*: bonus, cut *colloq*, divvy *colloq*, gain, portion, share, surplus, whack *colloq* 2 *our hard work will reap dividends*: benefit, bonus, extra, gain, plus

divination *n* augury, clairvoyance, divining, dukkeripen, foretelling, fortune-telling, hariolation *formal*, necromancy, prediction, presage, prognostication *formal*, prophecy, rhabdomancy *formal*, second sight, soothsaying, taghairm *Scot*

divine *adj* 1 *he had almost divine powers*: angelic, celestial, godlike, godly, heavenly, mystical, saintly, seraphic, spiritual, superhuman, supernatural 2 *God's divine law*: consecrated, exalted, glorious, holy, religious, sacred, sanctified, spiritual, supreme, transcendent 3 *a divine singing voice*: beautiful, charming, delightful, excellent, glorious, heavenly, lovely, wonderful
🔁 1 human 2 mundane
◆ *n* churchman, churchwoman, clergyman, clergywoman, cleric, ecclesiastic, minister, parson, pastor, prelate, priest, reverend
◆ *v* apprehend, conjecture *formal*, deduce, foretell, guess, infer, intuit *formal*, perceive, prognosticate *formal*, suppose, surmise, suspect, understand

diviner *n* astrologer, augur, dowser, haruspex, oracle, prophet, seer, sibyl, soothsayer, water-finder

divinity *n* 1 *worship a divinity*: deity, god, goddess, spirit 2 *claims to divinity*: divineness, godhead, godliness, holiness, sanctity 3 *he studied divinity*: religion, religious education, religious knowledge, religious studies, theology

division *n* 1 *a division into two separate states*: cutting (up), detaching, disunion, dividing, parting, separation, severance 2 *a division in the ranks of the ruling party*: alienation, breach, conflict, difference of opinion, disagreement, discord, disunion, estrangement *formal*, feud, rift, rupture, schism, split 3 *the division of labour*: allocation, allotment, apportionment *formal*, distribution, sharing (out) 4 *your divisions are to be merged*: arm, branch, category, class,

compartment, department, group, part, section, sector, segment **5** *the division between Kuwait and Iraq*: border, boundary, demarcation line, divide, dividing-line, frontier, partition
⊞ 1 union **2** unity **3** collection **4** whole

divisive *adj* alienating, damaging, discordant *formal*, disruptive, estranging *formal*, inharmonious, injurious, troublemaking, troublesome
⊞ harmonious, unifying

divorce *n* annulment, breach, break-up, dissolution, disunion, division, partition, rupture, separation, severance, split, split-up
◆ *v* annul, break up, bust up *colloq*, detach, disconnect, dissociate, dissolve, disunite, divide, isolate, part, separate, sever, split up
⊞ marry, unite

divulge *v* betray, blow the gaff *colloq*, break the news *colloq*, broadcast, communicate, confess, declare, disclose, expose, impart *formal*, leak *colloq*, let slip, let the cat out of the bag *colloq*, make known, proclaim, promulgate *formal*, publish, put your cards on the table *colloq*, reveal, spill the beans *colloq*, tell, uncover

dizzy *adj* **1** *he felt dizzy*: faint, giddy, light-headed, off-balance, reeling, shaky, vertiginous *formal*, weak at the knees, with your head swimming, wobbly, woozy *colloq* **2** *made dizzy by all the legal jargon*: bewildered, confused, dazed, muddled **3** *a dizzy blonde*: ditsy *US colloq*, feather-brained, foolish, irresponsible, scatterbrained, silly

do *v* **1** *I did it yesterday*: accomplish, achieve, carry out, complete, conclude *formal*, discharge, effectuate *formal*, end, execute, finish, fulfil, implement, perform, present, put into practice, put on, undertake, work **2** *do as I please*: act, behave, comport yourself *formal*, conduct yourself **3** *do the teas*: arrange, be in charge of, be responsible for, cause, create, deal with, fix, get ready, look after, make, manage, organize, prepare, produce, take care of **4** *will this do?*: be adequate, be enough, be satisfactory, be sufficient, fit the bill, satisfy, serve, suffice *formal* **5** *what do you do?*: be employed as, earn a living as, have a job, work as **6** *that should do it*: crack *colloq*, deal with, figure out, find the answer to, get to the bottom of *colloq*, resolve *formal*, sort out, tackle, try to solve, work out **7** *she is doing French*: learn, major in, master, read, study, take, work at/on **8** *do deliveries for you*: furnish, offer, provide, supply **9** *do 100 miles per hour*: achieve, go at, reach, travel at **10** *how are you doing?*: come along, come on, develop, fare, get along, get on, make a good/bad job of, manage, progress **11** *they did me good and proper*: cheat, con *colloq*, deceive, defraud, dupe, fleece *colloq*, have *colloq*, hoodwink, rip off *colloq*, swindle, take for a ride *colloq*, trick
◆ *n* affair, bash *colloq*, celebration, event, function, gathering, knees-up *colloq*, occasion, party, rave-up *colloq*, soirée

▶ **do away with 1** *do away with this unfair law*: abolish, annul *formal*, discard, discontinue *formal*, dispose of, eliminate, get rid of, nullify *formal*, remove **2** *he did away with his mother*: assassinate, bump off *colloq*, do in *colloq*, exterminate, kill, knock off *colloq*, murder, slaughter, slay
▶ **do down** blame, censure, condemn, criticize, find fault with

▶ **do in** assassinate, bump off *colloq*, exterminate, kill, knock off *colloq*, murder, slaughter, slay
▶ **do out of** cheat out of, con out of *colloq*, deprive of, diddle out of *colloq*, fleece *colloq*, prevent from having, swindle out of, trick out of
▶ **do up 1** *do up your zip*: button, fasten, lace, pack, tie, zip up **2** *we did up the cottage*: decorate, modernize, recondition, redecorate, renovate, repair, restore
▶ **do without** abstain from *formal*, deny yourself, dispense with, forgo *formal*, give up, go without, manage without, refrain, relinquish *formal*

docile *adj* amenable, compliant *formal*, controllable, controlled, co-operative, manageable, obedient, obliging, submissive, tractable, yielding
⊞ truculent, unco-operative

docility *n* amenability, biddableness, complaisance *formal*, compliance *formal*, ductility *formal*, manageability, meekness, obedience, pliability, pliancy, submissiveness, tractability
⊞ truculence, unco-operativeness

dock¹ *n* boat-yard, harbour, jetty, marina, pier, port, quay, waterfront, wharf
◆ *v* anchor, berth, drop anchor, land, moor, put in, tie up

dock² *v* **1** *dock an animal's tail*: clip, crop, curtail, cut, shorten, truncate **2** *dock someone's pay*: decrease, deduct, diminish, lessen, reduce, remove, subtract, withhold

docket *n* bill, certificate, chit, chitty, counterfoil, documentation, label, paperwork, receipt, tab, tag, tally, ticket
◆ *v* catalogue, file, index, label, mark, register, tab, tag, ticket

doctor *n* bones *colloq*, clinician, consultant, doc *colloq*, medic *colloq*, medical officer, physician, quack *colloq*
◆ *v* **1** *doctoring evidence*: adulterate, alter, change, dilute, disguise, falsify, interfere with, misrepresent, pervert, tamper with **2** *doctored her drink*: add drugs/poison to, adulterate, contaminate, drug, lace, spike *colloq*, weaken **3** *my cats have been doctored*: castrate, neuter, spay, sterilize

> **Types of medical doctor include:**
> general practitioner (GP), family doctor, family practitioner, locum, hospital doctor, houseman, intern, resident, registrar, consultant, medical officer (MO), dentist, veterinary surgeon, vet *colloq*.

doctrinaire *adj* biased, dogmatic, fanatical, inflexible, insistent, opinionated, pedantic, rigid
⊞ flexible

doctrine *n* belief, canon, conviction, credo, creed, dogma, opinion, precept, principle, teaching, tenet

document *n* affidavit *technical*, certificate, charter, deed, evidence, form, instrument *formal*, paper, proof, record, report
◆ *v* **1** *we need to document what we have done*: chart, chronicle, cite, detail, keep on record, list, put on record, record, register, report **2** *our position on this is well documented*: back up, corroborate

formal, give weight to, prove, substantiate *formal*, support, validate *formal*, verify

documentary *adj* charted, chronicled, detailed, recorded, written

doddering *adj* aged, decrepit, elderly, feeble, frail, infirm, tottering, weak

doddery *adj* aged, doddering, faltering, feeble, infirm, shaky, tottery, unsteady, weak
　🖅 hale, youthful

dodge *v* **1** *dodged the water bomb:* duck *colloq*, fend off, get out of, jump away, shift, sidestep, swerve, veer **2** *dodging fares on the Tube:* avoid, bypass, elude, evade, get out of, get round, shirk, shun, steer clear of
　♦ *n* contrivance, deception, device, machination *formal*, manoeuvre, ploy, ruse, scheme, sharp practice, stratagem, subterfuge, trick, wile

dodger *n* avoider, bilker, evader, shirker, sidestepper

dodgy *adj* chancy, dangerous, delicate, dicey *colloq*, dicky *colloq*, difficult, problematical, risky, shifty *colloq*, suspect, tricky, uncertain, unreliable, unsafe
　🖅 easy, safe

doer *n* accomplisher, achiever, activist, bustler, dynamo, executor, go-getter *colloq*, live wire *colloq*, organizer, power-house *colloq*, worker
　🖅 contemplatist, thinker

doff *v* discard, lift, raise, remove, shed, take off, throw off, tip, touch
　🖅 don

dog *n* **1** *cats and dogs:* bitch, canine, cur, hound, mongrel, mutt *colloq*, pooch *colloq*, pup, puppy **2** *you dog!:* rascal, rogue, scoundrel, villain, wretch
　♦ *v* follow, harry, haunt, hound, plague, pursue, shadow, tail, track, trail, trouble, worry

---

Breeds of dog include:
Afghan hound, Alsatian, basset-hound, beagle, Border collie, borzoi, bulldog, bull-mastiff, bull-terrier, cairn terrier, chihuahua, chow, cocker spaniel, collie, corgi, dachshund, Dalmatian, Doberman pinscher, foxhound, fox-terrier, German Shepherd, golden retriever, Great Dane, greyhound, husky, Irish wolfhound, Jack Russell, King Charles spaniel, Labrador, lhasa apso, lurcher, Maltese, Old English sheepdog, Pekingese, pit bull terrier, pointer, poodle, pug, Rottweiler, saluki, sausage-dog, schnauzer, Scottie, Scottish terrier, Sealyham, setter, sheltie, shih tzu, springer spaniel, St Bernard, terrier, West Highland terrier, Westie, whippet, wolf-hound, Yorkshire terrier

---

dogged *adj* determined, firm, indefatigable, indomitable *formal*, intent, obdurate *formal*, obstinate, persevering, persistent, pertinacious *formal*, relentless, resolute, single-minded, staunch, steadfast, steady, stubborn, tenacious, tireless, unfaltering, unflagging, unshakable, unyielding
　🖅 apathetic, irresolute

doggedness *n* determination, endurance, firmness, indomitability *formal*, obstinacy, perseverance, persistence, pertinacity *formal*, relentlessness, resolution, single-mindedness,

steadfastness, steadiness, stubbornness, tenaciousness, tenacity

dogma *n* article (of faith), belief, code (of belief), conviction, credo, creed, doctrine, maxim, opinion, precept, principle, teaching, tenet

dogmatic *adj* **1** *dogmatic Catholicism:* authoritative, canonical, categorical, doctrinal, ex cathedra, oracular **2** *her dogmatic management style:* arbitrary, arrogant, assertive, authoritarian, categorical, dictatorial, doctrinaire, domineering, emphatic, imperious, insistent, intolerant, opinionated, overbearing, pontifical, positive, unchallengeable, unquestionable

dogmatism *n* arbitrariness, assertiveness, bigotry, dictatorialness, imperiousness, opinionatedness, peremptoriness *formal*, presumption

dogsbody *n* doormat, drudge, factotum, galley-slave, gofer, lackey, maid-of-all-work, man-of-all-work, menial, skivvy *colloq*, slave

doings *n* achievements, actions, activities, acts, adventures, affairs, concerns, dealings, deeds, enterprises, events, exploits, feats, goings-on, handiwork, happenings, proceedings, transactions

doldrums *n* acedia *formal*, apathy, blues *colloq*, boredom, dejection, depression, downheartedness, dullness, dumps *colloq*, ennui *formal*, gloom, inertia, lassitude *formal*, listlessness, low-spiritedness, malaise *formal*, sluggishness, stagnation, tedium, torpor

dole *n* allowance, benefit, credit, income, Job Seekers Allowance (JSA), payment, social security, support, unemployment benefit
　▶ **dole out** administer, allocate, allot, apportion *formal*, assign, deal (out), dish out, dispense, distribute, divide (up), give out, hand out, issue, mete out, ration, share (out)

doleful *adj* blue *colloq*, cheerless, depressing, disconsolate *formal*, dismal, distressing, dolorous *formal*, down in the dumps *colloq*, dreary, forlorn, gloomy, lugubrious *formal*, melancholy, miserable, mournful, painful, pathetic, pitiful, rueful, sad, sombre, sorrowful, woebegone *formal*, woeful, wretched
　🖅 cheerful

doll *n* Barbie®, dolly, figure, figurine, marionette, moppet, plaything, puppet, Sindy®, toy
　▶ **doll up** deck out, dress up, preen, primp, tart up *colloq*, titivate, trick out

dollop *n* ball, blob, bunch, clump, glob, gob, gobbet, helping, lump, portion, serving

dolorous *adj* anguished, distressing, doleful, grievous, harrowing, heart-rending, lugubrious *formal*, melancholy, miserable, mournful, painful, rueful, sad, sombre, sorrowful, woebegone *formal*, woeful, wretched
　🖅 happy

dolour *n* anguish, distress, grief, heartache, heartbreak, lamentation, misery, mourning, sadness, sorrow, suffering

dolt *n* ass *colloq*, blockhead *colloq*, chump *colloq*, clot *colloq*, dimwit *colloq*, dipstick *slang*, dope *colloq*, fool, idiot, imbecile, nerd *slang*, nincompoop *colloq*, ninny *colloq*, nitwit *colloq*, numskull *colloq*, nutcase *colloq*, simpleton, twerp *colloq*, twit *colloq*, wally *slang*

domain n 1 *the emperor's domain:* dominion, empire, estate, kingdom, lands, province, realm, region, territory 2 *the domain of fine art:* area, concern, department, discipline, field, jurisdiction, province, realm, region, section, speciality, sphere, world

dome n arched roof, cupola, hemisphere, mound, rotunda, vault

domestic adj 1 *our happy domestic life:* domesticated, domiciliary *formal*, family, home, home-loving, homely, household, house-trained, personal, pet, private, stay-at-home, tame 2 *domestic flights into Gatwick:* home, indigenous, internal, native
F3 2 export, foreign, international
♦ n au pair, char, charwoman, daily, daily help, domestic help, hired help, housekeeper, maid, major-domo, servant

domestic appliance

> *Types of domestic appliance include:*
> washing machine, washer, washer/drier, tumble-drier, clothes airer, iron, steam iron, steam press, trouser press; dishwasher, vacuum cleaner, upright cleaner, cylinder cleaner, wet-and-dry cleaner, Hoover®, floor polisher, carpet sweeper, carpet shampooer; oven, Aga®, barbecue, cooker, Dutch oven, electric cooker, fan oven, gas stove, kitchen range, microwave oven, stove, hob, hotplate, grill, electric grill, griddle, rotisserie, spit, waffle iron, deep fryer, slow cooker, sandwich maker, toaster; food processor, mixer, blender, liquidizer, ice-cream maker, juicer, juice extractor, food slicer, electric knife, knife sharpener, kettle, tea/coffee maker, percolator, coffee mill, electric tin opener, timer, water filter; refrigerator, fridge *colloq*, icebox, fridge/freezer, freezer, deep-freeze; hostess-trolley, humidifier, ionizer, fire extinguisher

domesticate v acclimatize, accustom, assimilate, break, break in, familiarize, habituate *formal*, house-train, naturalize, tame, train

domesticated adj 1 *domesticated cats:* broken (in), house-trained, naturalized, pet, tame, tamed 2 *I'm very domesticated:* domestic, home-loving, homely, house-proud, housewifely
F3 1 feral, wild

domesticity n domestic science, domestication, home economics, homecraft, homemaking, housecraft, housekeeping

domicile n abode *formal*, dwelling *formal*, habitation *formal*, home, house, lodging(s), mansion, quarters, residence, residency, settlement
♦ v establish, make your home, put down roots, settle, take up residence

dominance n ascendancy *formal*, authority, command, control, domination, hegemony *formal*, leadership, mastery, paramountcy *formal*, power, pre-eminence, rule, supremacy, sway

dominant adj 1 *a dominant figure in the boardroom:* all-powerful, assertive, authoritative, controlling, governing, influential, powerful, ruling, strong 2 *the dominant company in the industry:* chief, commanding, important, key, leading, main, major, most important, outstanding, paramount, predominant, pre-eminent, prevailing, prevalent, primary, prime, principal, prominent, supreme
F3 1 submissive 2 subordinate

dominate v 1 *France and Germany used to dominate the EU:* command, control, direct, domineer, govern, have ascendancy over *formal*, have over a barrel *colloq*, have the upper/whip hand over *colloq*, have under your thumb *colloq*, intimidate, lead, master, monopolize, overbear, overrule, predominate, preside, prevail, rule, throw your weight around *colloq*, tyrannize 2 *the tower dominates the whole town:* dwarf, eclipse, overlook, overshadow, tower over

domination n ascendancy *formal*, authority, command, control, despotism, dictatorship, influence, leadership, mastery, oppression, power, predominance, pre-eminence, repression, rule, subjection, subordination, superiority, suppression, supremacy, sway, tyranny

domineering adj aggressive, arrogant, authoritarian, autocratic, bossy *colloq*, coercive, despotic, dictatorial, forceful, haughty, high-handed, imperious, iron-handed, masterful, oppressive, overbearing, peremptory *formal*, pushy *colloq*, tyrannical
F3 meek, servile

dominion n 1 *its dominion over Lebanon:* ascendancy *formal*, authority, command, control, direction, domination, government, jurisdiction, lordship, mastery, power, rule, sovereignty, supremacy, sway 2 *the empire's dominions:* colony, country, domain, empire, kingdom, province, realm, territory

don v clothe yourself in, dress in, get into, put on, slip into
F3 doff
♦ n academic, lecturer, professor, scholar, teacher, tutor

donate v bequeath, bestow *formal*, chip in *colloq*, club together *colloq*, confer *formal*, contribute, cough up *colloq*, fork out *colloq*, give, give away, make a donation, make a gift, pledge, present, shell out *colloq*, subscribe
F3 receive

donation n alms, benefaction *formal*, bequest, charity, contribution, gift, grant, gratuity, largess(e), offering, present, presentation, subscription

done adj 1 *the work is done:* accomplished, complete, completed, concluded *formal*, consummated *formal*, ended, executed, finished, fulfilled, over, realized, settled, terminated *formal* 2 *it simply isn't done:* acceptable, appropriate, conventional, correct, decorous *formal*, fitting, proper, right, seemly *old use*, suitable 3 *the stew isn't done yet:* baked, boiled, browned, cooked, finished, fried, prepared, ready, roasted, stewed, well-done
♦ interj absolutely, accepted, agreed, arranged, decided, OK *colloq*, right, settled

Don Juan n Casanova, gigolo, ladies' man, lady-killer, lover, philander(er), romeo, womanizer

donkey n ass, burro, hinny, jackass, jenny, moke *colloq*, mule

donnish *adj* academic, bookish, erudite, formalistic, intellectual, learned, pedagogic, pedantic, scholarly, scholastic, serious

donor *n* angel *colloq*, backer, benefactor, contributor, donator, fairy godmother *colloq*, giver, philanthropist, provider, supporter
🔁 beneficiary

doom *n* **1** *mariners lured to their doom:* destiny, fate, fortune, lot, portion **2** *warnings of impending doom:* catastrophe, death, death-knell, destruction, disaster, downfall, rack and ruin, ruin, ruination **3** *God's doom awaits you:* condemnation, judgement, pronouncement, sentence, verdict
♦ *v* condemn, consign, damn, decree, destine, fate, judge, predestine *formal*, pronounce, sentence

doomed *adj* bedevilled, condemned, cursed, damned, destined, fated, hopeless, ill-fated, ill-omened, ill-starred, luckless, ruined, star-crossed, unlucky

door *n* **1** *the door of the house:* doorway, entrance, entry, exit, hatch, opening, portal **2** *shutting the door to the poor:* access, entrance, gateway, open door, opening, opportunity, road, route, way, way in

doorkeeper *n* commissionaire, concierge, doorman, gatekeeper, janitor, ostiary *formal*, porter, usher

dope *n* **1** *he deals in dope:* acid, amphetamine, barbiturate, cannabis, coke *colloq*, crack, drugs, E *slang*, ecstasy *slang*, grass *colloq*, hallucinogen, hash *colloq*, LSD, marijuana, narcotic, opiate, pot *colloq*, speed *colloq*, weed *colloq* **2** *he's no dope:* blockhead *colloq*, clot *colloq*, dimwit *colloq*, dolt, dunce, fool, half-wit *colloq*, idiot, nincompoop *colloq*, ninny *colloq*, nitwit *colloq*, simpleton, twerp *colloq*, twit *colloq* **3** *they had plenty of dope on her:* details, facts, gen *colloq*, info *colloq*, information, inside information, low-down *colloq*, particulars, specifics
♦ *v* anaesthetize, doctor, drug, inject, knock out, medicate, narcotize, sedate, spike *colloq*, stupefy

dopey *adj* **1** *feeling a bit dopey this morning:* dozy, drowsy, groggy, lethargic, nodding, sleepy, somnolent *formal*, torpid *formal* **2** *she's so dopey:* daft, dozy, foolish, silly, simple, stupid
🔁 **1** alert, awake **2** bright, clever

dormant *adj* **1** *dormant during the winter months:* asleep, comatose *technical*, fallow, hibernating, inactive, inert, latent, quiescent *formal*, resting, sleeping, sluggish, slumbering, torpid *formal* **2** *all this talent had lain dormant:* latent, potential, undeveloped, undisclosed, unrealized
🔁 **1** active, awake **2** developed, realized

dose *n* amount, dosage, draught, measure, portion, potion, prescription, quantity, shot
♦ *v* administer, dispense, medicate, prescribe, treat

dot *n* atom, circle, dab, decimal point, fleck, full stop, iota, jot, mark, particle, pin-point, point, speck, spot
♦ *v* dab, mark, pepper, punctuate, scatter, speckle, spot, sprinkle, stipple, stud

dotage *n* decrepitude *formal*, feebleness, imbecility, infirmity, old age, second childhood, senility, weakness

dote *v*
▶ **dote on** admire, adore, hold dear, idolize, indulge, love, pamper, spoil, treasure, worship

doting *adj* adoring, affectionate, devoted, fond, indulgent, loving, soft, tender

dotty *adj* barmy *colloq*, batty *colloq*, crazy, daft *colloq*, eccentric, feeble-minded, loony *colloq*, peculiar, potty *colloq*, touched, weird
🔁 sensible

double *adj* **1** *double doors:* bifarious *formal*, binal *formal*, binate *formal*, coupled, doubled, dual, duplicate, paired, twice, twin, twofold, two-ply **2** *a double meaning:* ambiguous, ambivalent, double-edged, double-meaning, equivocal, paradoxical, two-edged
🔁 **1** half, single
♦ *v* **1** *double your income:* duplicate, enlarge, fold, increase twofold, magnify, multiply by two, repeat **2** *double as someone/something:* have a dual/second role, have a second job/purpose **3** *double for someone:* be an understudy, stand in, substitute, understudy
♦ *n* clone, copy, counterpart, doppelgänger, duplicate, facsimile, image, impersonator, lookalike, match, replica, ringer *colloq*, spitting image *colloq*, twin
▶ **double back** backtrack, circle, dodge, evade, go back the way you came, loop, retrace your steps, return, reverse

double-cross *v* betray, cheat, con *colloq*, defraud, hoodwink, mislead, pull a fast one on *colloq*, swindle, take for a ride *colloq*, trick, two-time *colloq*

double-dealing *n* betrayal, cheating, crookedness *colloq*, defrauding, dissembling *formal*, duplicity *formal*, hoodwinking, mendacity *formal*, misleading, perfidy *formal*, swindling, treachery, tricking, two-facedness, two-timing *colloq*

double entendre *n* ambiguity, double meaning, innuendo, play on words, pun, suggestiveness, wordplay

doubly *adv* again, bis *formal*, especially, extra, twice, twofold

doubt *n* **1** *I have doubts about this government:* apprehension, distrust, hesitation, incredulity, misgiving, mistrust, mixed feeling, qualm, reservation, scepticism, suspicion, uneasiness **2** *we were full of doubt:* ambiguity, confusion, difficulty, dilemma, hesitation, indecision, perplexity, problem, quandary, uncertainty
🔁 **1** confidence, faith, trust **2** belief, certainty
♦ *v* **1** *no reason to doubt her word:* be suspicious, disbelieve *formal*, distrust, fear, have misgivings/qualms about, mistrust, query, question, suspect, take with a pinch of salt *colloq* **2** *I doubt that will happen:* be dubious, be uncertain, be undecided, demur *formal*, hesitate, vacillate, waver
🔁 **1** believe, have confidence in, trust **2** be certain, decide

doubter *n* agnostic, cynic, disbeliever, doubting Thomas, questioner, sceptic, scoffer, unbeliever
🔁 believer

doubtful *adj* **1** *it is doubtful that he will win:* debatable, improbable, in doubt, open to question, touch and go *colloq*, uncertain, unlikely **2** *doubtful about his future:* apprehensive, distrustful, having reservations/misgivings, hesitant, in two minds *colloq*, irresolute, sceptical, suspicious, tentative, uncertain, undecided, uneasy, unsure, vacillating, wavering **3** *writing of doubtful origin:* ambiguous, debatable, dubious, fishy *colloq*, iffy *colloq*, inconclusive, obscure, questionable, shady *colloq*, suspect, unclear, vague

F3 1 certain **2** certain, confident, decided **3** definite, settled, trustworthy

doubtless *adv* certainly, clearly, indisputably, most likely, no doubt, of course, precisely, presumably, probably, seemingly, supposedly, surely, truly, undoubtedly, unquestionably, without doubt

dour *adj* austere, churlish, dismal, dreary, forbidding, gloomy, grim, gruff, morose, sour, sullen, unfriendly, unsmiling
F3 bright, cheerful

douse, dowse *v* **1** *douse the car with petrol:* deluge, dip, drench, duck, dunk, flood, immerge, immerse, plunge, saturate, soak, souse, splash, steep, submerge, wet **2** *douse the flames:* blow out, extinguish, put out, quench, smother, snuff

dovetail *v* accord *formal*, agree, coincide, conform, correspond, fit together, harmonize, interlock, join, link, match, tally

dowdy *adj* dingy, drab, frowsy, frumpish, ill-dressed, old-fashioned, shabby, slovenly, tatty *colloq*, unfashionable
F3 fashionable, smart

down[1] *adv* to a lower level/position, to the bottom, to the floor, to the ground
F3 up
♦ *adj* **1** *feeling down:* blue *colloq*, dejected, depressed, dispirited, down in the dumps *colloq*, downcast, downhearted, low, melancholy, miserable, sad, unhappy, wretched **2** *the computer is down:* bust *colloq*, conked out *slang*, crashed, inoperative *formal*, not working, out of action, out of order
F3 1 happy **2** operational
♦ *v* **1** *he was downed in the fifth round:* bring down, floor, knock down, prostrate, throw, topple **2** *she downed her drink and left:* consume, drink, gulp, knock back *colloq*, put away *colloq*, swallow, swig *colloq*, swill *colloq*, toss off *colloq*

down[2] *n* bloom, fine hair, floccus, floss, flue, fluff, fuzz, nap, pappus *technical*, pile, shag, soft feathers, wool

down-and-out *adj* derelict, destitute, impoverished, on your uppers, penniless, ruined
♦ *n* dosser *slang*, hobo *US*, loser *colloq*, tramp, vagabond, vagrant

down-at-heel *adj* dingy, dowdy, drab, frayed, frowsy, poor, ragged, run-down, seedy *colloq*, shabby, slovenly, tattered, tatty *colloq*

downbeat *adj* **1** *lines delivered in his downbeat style:* calm, casual, downcast, informal, insouciant *formal*, laid back *colloq*, nonchalant, relaxed, unhurried, unworried **2** *she's downbeat about her chances:* cheerless, cynical, depressed, despondent, downcast, fearing the worst, gloomy, low, negative, pessimistic
F3 1 upbeat **2** happy

downcast *adj* blue *colloq*, crestfallen, daunted, dejected, depressed, despondent, disappointed, disconsolate *formal*, discouraged, disheartened, dismayed, dispirited, down, downhearted, fed

up *colloq*, gloomy, glum, low, miserable, sad, unhappy, wretched
F3 cheerful, elated, happy

downfall *n* collapse, debacle, debasement, degradation, destruction, disgrace, failure, fall, overthrow, ruin, undoing
F3 rise

downgrade *v* deflate, degrade, demote, depose, lower, reduce/lower in rank, relegate
F3 improve, upgrade

downhearted *adj* daunted, dejected, depressed, despondent, disappointed, disconsolate *formal*, discouraged, disheartened, dismayed, dispirited, downcast, gloomy, glum, low-spirited, sad, unhappy
F3 cheerful, enthusiastic

downpour *n* cloudburst, deluge, flood, inundation, rainstorm, torrent

downright *adv* absolutely, categorically, clearly, completely, plainly, thoroughly, totally, utterly
♦ *adj* absolute, categorical, clear, complete, out-and-out, outright, plain, sheer, thorough, total, unequivocal, unqualified, utter, wholesale

down-to-earth *adj* commonsense, commonsensical, hard-headed, matter-of-fact, mundane, no-nonsense, plain-spoken, practical, realistic, sane, sensible, unsentimental
F3 fantastic, idealistic, impractical

down-trodden *adj* abused, bullied, burdened, exploited, helpless, oppressed, overwhelmed, powerless, subjugated *formal*, subservient, trampled on, tyrannized, victimized, weighed-down

downward *adj* declining, descending, downhill, going/moving down, sliding, slipping
F3 upward

dowry *n* dot, dower, endowment, faculty, gift, inheritance, legacy, marriage portion, marriage settlement, portion, provision, share, talent, wedding-dower

doze *v* catnap, drift off, drop off, go off, kip *colloq*, nap, nod off, sleep, snooze *colloq*, take a nap, zizz *slang*
♦ *n* catnap, forty winks *colloq*, kip *colloq*, nap, shut-eye *colloq*, siesta, snooze *colloq*, zizz *slang*

drab *adj* boring, cheerless, colourless, dingy, dismal, dreary, dull, featureless, flat, gloomy, grey, lacklustre, lifeless, shabby, sombre, tedious
F3 bright, cheerful

draft *n* **1** *an early draft:* abstract, blueprint, delineation *formal*, drawing, outline, plan, preliminary version, protocol *formal*, rough, rough sketch, sketch **2** *a bank draft:* bill of exchange, cheque, letter of credit, money order, postal order
♦ *v* compose, delineate *formal*, design, draw (up), formulate, outline, plan, sketch

drag *v* **1** *I dragged my chair over to the fire:* draw, haul, lug, pull, tow, trail, tug, yank **2** *the hours dragged by:* become boring/tedious, crawl, creep, go on and on, go on for ever, go slowly, lag, wear on
♦ *n* annoyance, bind *colloq*, bore, bother, headache *colloq*, nuisance, pain *colloq*, pain in the neck *colloq*, pest, trouble

▶ **drag out** draw out, extend, hang on, lengthen, persist, prolong, protract *formal*, spin out

▶ **drag up** bring up, introduce, mention, raise, rake up, remind, revive

dragoon *v* browbeat, bully, coerce, compel, constrain, drive, force, harass, impel, intimidate, strongarm *colloq*

drain *v* **1** *we'll need to drain the mine shaft*: bleed, draw off, dry, empty, evacuate, extract, milk, pump off, remove, strain, tap, void *formal*, withdraw **2** *waste draining into the stream*: discharge *formal*, effuse *formal*, exude *formal*, flow out, leak, ooze, seep out, trickle **3** *studying really drains you*: consume, deplete *formal*, drink up, exhaust, sap, strain, swallow, tax, use up
🔁 **1** fill
♦ *n* **1** *the council laid new drains*: channel, conduit, culvert, ditch, duct, gutter, outlet, pipe, sewer, trench **2** *a drain on resources*: consumption, depletion *formal*, exhaustion, sap, strain, tax

drama *n* **1** *radio dramas*: acting, comedy, dramatics, dramaturgy, melodrama, piece, play, scene, show, spectacle, stagecraft, theatre, tragedy **2** *the drama of the hostage rescue*: crisis, excitement, sensation, tension, thrill, turmoil

dramatic *adj* **1** *a dramatic change*: abrupt, distinct, marked, noticeable, significant, striking, sudden **2** *a dramatic penalty shoot-out*: effective, exciting, expressive, graphic, impressive, sensational, spectacular, stirring, striking, tense, thrilling, unexpected, vivid **3** *he has a rather dramatic manner*: artificial, exaggerated, flamboyant, histrionic, melodramatic, theatrical **4** *dramatic art*: stage, theatrical, Thespian

dramatist *n* dramaturge, dramaturgist, playwright, play-writer, screen writer, scriptwriter, tragedian

dramatize *v* **1** *a book that can't be dramatized*: adapt, arrange for, present as a play/film, put on, stage **2** *she likes to dramatize everything*: act, blow up out of all proportion *colloq*, exaggerate, ham (up) *colloq*, lay it on thick *colloq*, make a big thing of *colloq*, overdo, overstate, play-act

drape *v* adorn, arrange, cloak, cover, decorate, droop, drop, envelop, fold, hang, overlay, shroud, suspend, veil, wrap

drapery *n* arras, backdrop, blind(s), cloth, covering(s), curtain(s), hanging(s), tapestry, valance

drastic *adj* desperate, dire, Draconian, extreme, far-reaching, forceful, harsh, radical, rigorous, severe, strong
🔁 cautious, moderate

draught *n* **1** *a draught coming through the window*: current, flow, influx *formal*, movement, puff **2** *a draught of ale*: cup, drink, potion, quantity **3** *an arduous draught for the horses*: dragging, drawing, pulling, traction

draw *v* **1** *draw a picture*: chart, delineate *formal*, depict, design, doodle, map out, paint, pencil, portray, represent, scribble, sketch, trace **2** *the procession drew nearer*: advance, approach, come, go, move, proceed, progress, travel **3** *I drew my chair towards the table*: drag, haul, lug, pull, tow, trail, tug **4** *draw water from a well*: bring out, extract, produce, pull out, remove, take out, withdraw **5** *draw a breath*: breathe in, inhale

formal, inspire *formal*, respire *formal* **6** *draw money from a bank*: get, obtain, procure *formal*, receive, take **7** *draw attention to something*: allure, attract, bring in, elicit, entice, influence, lure, persuade, prompt **8** *draw a conclusion*: come to, conclude, deduce, gather, infer, reason **9** *draw lots*: choose, decide on, go for, pick, plump for *colloq*, select **10** *they drew 3-3*: be all square *colloq*, be equal, be even, tie **11** *draw someone out*: encourage to talk, induce to talk/speak, make feel less nervous, put at ease
🔁 **3** push **7** repel
♦ *n* **1** *London is a powerful draw for young people*: allure, appeal, attraction, bait, enticement, interest, lure, magnetism **2** *the game ended in a draw*: dead heat, stalemate, tie

▶ **draw back** flinch, recoil, retract, retreat, shrink, start back, wince, withdraw

▶ **draw on** apply, employ, exploit, have recourse to, make use of, put to use, quarry, rely on, use, utilize *formal*

▶ **draw out 1** *the train drew out of the station*: depart, leave, move out, pull out, set out, start **2** *the film was drawn out excessively*: elongate, extend, lengthen, prolong, protract *formal*, spin out, stretch

▶ **draw up 1** *I'll draw up a plan*: compose, draft, formulate, frame, prepare, put in writing, write out **2** *the car drew up*: halt, pull up, run in, stop

drawback *n* barrier, catch, damper, defect, deficiency, difficulty, disadvantage, discouragement, fault, flaw, fly in the ointment *colloq*, handicap, hindrance, hitch, hurdle, impediment, imperfection, liability, limitation, nuisance, obstacle, problem, snag, stumbling-block, trouble, weak spot
🔁 advantage, benefit

drawing *n* cartoon, composition, delineation *formal*, depiction, diagram, graphic, illustration, outline, picture, portrait, portrayal, representation, sketch, study

drawl *v* draw out your vowels, drone, haw-haw, protract, speak slowly, twang

drawn *adj* fatigued, fraught, gaunt, haggard, harassed, hassled *colloq*, pinched, sapped, strained, stressed, taut, tense, tired, washed out, worn

dread *v* be afraid of, be anxious/worried about, be frightened (to death) by, be scared of, be terrified by, cringe at, fear, flinch, get cold feet about *colloq*, quail, shrink from, shudder, shy, tremble
🔁 look forward to
♦ *n* alarm, apprehension, blind panic, (blue) funk *colloq*, cold sweat, dismay, disquiet, fear, fit of terror, fright, hair standing on end, horror, misgiving, perturbation *formal*, qualm, terror, trepidation *formal*, worry
🔁 confidence, security
♦ *adj* alarming, awe-inspiring, awful, dire, dreaded, dreadful, feared, frightening, frightful, ghastly, grisly, gruesome, horrible, terrible, terrifying

dreadful *adj* alarming, appalling, awful, dire, frightening, frightful, ghastly, grievous, grim, heinous *formal*, hideous, horrendous, horrible, horrific, nasty, outrageous, shocking, terrible, terrifying, tragic, unpleasant
🔁 comforting, wonderful

dream n 1 *I had a strange dream:* daydream, delusion, fantasy, hallucination, illusion, imagination, nightmare, phantasmagoria, reverie, trance, vision 2 *my dream of playing for Yorkshire:* aim, ambition, aspiration, castles in the air, design, desire, expectation, goal, hope, ideal, plan, speculation, wish, yearning 3 *went about in a dream all day:* daydream, fantasy, inattention, pipe dream, reverie 4 *their new house is a dream:* beauty, ideal, joy, marvel, perfection
◆ v 1 *dreamed I was abducted by aliens:* envisage, fancy, fantasize, hallucinate, have a dream, imagine 2 *dreaming about my holiday:* be lost in space, daydream, fancy, fantasize, imagine, let your thoughts wander, muse, not pay attention, stare into space, switch off *colloq* 3 *dreamed of becoming a doctor:* crave, desire, long, want very much, yearn
◆ adj excellent, ideal, model, perfect, superb, supreme, wonderful
▶ **dream up** conceive, concoct, conjure up, contrive, create, devise, fabricate, hatch, imagine, invent, spin, think up

dreamer n daydreamer, Don Quixote, fantasist, idealist, romancer, romantic, star-gazer, theorizer, utopian, visionary, Walter Mitty
▣ pragmatist, realist

dreamlike adj chimerical, ethereal *formal*, hallucinatory, illusory, insubstantial, phantasmagoric, phantasmagorical, phantom, surreal, trance-like, unreal, unsubstantial, visionary

dreamy adj 1 *walking around in a dreamy swoon:* dim, ethereal, faint, fantastic, hazy, imaginary, indistinct, misty, shadowy, unclear, unreal, vague 2 *a dreamy boy absorbed in books:* absent, absent-minded, abstracted, daydreaming, fanciful, fantasizing, faraway, idealistic, impractical, musing, pensive, preoccupied, romantic, thoughtful, visionary, with your head in the clouds *colloq* 3 *dreamy music:* calming, gentle, lulling, relaxing, romantic, soft, soothing
▣ 1 clear, real 2 down-to-earth, practical

dreary adj bleak, boring, cheerless, colourless, commonplace, dark, depressing, dismal, drab, dull, featureless, gloomy, humdrum, lifeless, monotonous, mournful, overcast, routine, run-of-the-mill, sombre, tedious, uneventful, uninteresting, unvaried, wearisome
▣ cheerful, interesting

dredge v
▶ **dredge up** dig up, discover, drag up, draw up, fish up, raise, rake up, scoop up, uncover, unearth

dregs n 1 *coffee dregs:* deposit, detritus *formal*, dross, grounds, lees, precipitate *technical*, residue, residuum *formal*, scourings, scum, sediment, sublimate, trash, waste 2 *society's dregs:* dossers *slang*, down-and-outs, outcasts, rabble, riff-raff, scum, tramps, vagrants

drench v douse, drown, duck, flood, imbue, immerse, inundate, permeate, saturate, soak, soak to the skin, souse, steep, swamp, wet

dress n 1 *a black dress:* frock, gown, robe 2 *employees had to wear smart dress:* apparel *formal*, attire *formal*, clothes, clothing, costume, ensemble, garb, garment(s), gear *colloq*, get-up *colloq*, habiliment *formal*, outfit, togs *colloq*
◆ v 1 *she dressed in a fetching outfit:* accoutre formal, adorn, array *formal*, attire *formal*, clothe, deck, decorate, don, drape, fit (out), garb, garnish, get into, put on, rig, robe, slip into, throw on *colloq*, trim, turn out, wear 2 *dress your hair:* adjust, arrange, comb, dispose, do, groom, preen, prepare, primp, straighten, tidy 3 *they dressed my wounds:* bandage, bind up, clean, cover, put a plaster on, swathe, tend, treat 4 *dress meat:* clean, get ready, prepare
▣ 1 strip, undress
▶ **dress down** berate *formal*, carpet *colloq*, castigate *formal*, chide, give someone an earful *colloq*, haul over the coals *colloq*, rebuke, reprimand, reprove, scold, tear off a strip *colloq*, tell off *colloq*, upbraid *formal*
▶ **dress up 1** *it had been dressed up but it was still the same car:* adorn, beautify, deck, decorate, disguise, embellish, gild, improve, ornament 2 *she dressed up for the occasion:* doll up *colloq*, dress for dinner, dress formally

dressing n 1 *a salad dressing:* condiment, relish, salad dressing, sauce 2 *put on fresh dressings daily:* bandage, compress, Elastoplast®, gauze, ligature, lint, pad, plaster, poultice, spica, tourniquet

dressmaker n couturier, midinette, modiste, needlewoman, seamstress, sewing woman, tailor, tailoress

dressy adj classy *colloq*, elaborate, elegant, formal, natty *colloq*, ornate, ritzy *colloq*, smart, stylish, swish *colloq*
▣ dowdy, scruffy

dribble v 1 *perspiration dribbled down his face:* drip, drop, exude *formal*, leak, ooze, run, seep, trickle 2 *he's dribbling on his T-shirt:* drivel, drool, slaver, slobber
◆ n drip, droplet, leak, seepage, sprinkling, trickle

dried adj arid, dehydrated, desiccated, drained, mummified, parched, shrivelled, wilted, withered, wizened

drift v 1 *we drifted out to sea:* be carried along, coast, float, freewheel, go with the stream, roam, rove, stray, waft, wander 2 *the snow drifted:* accumulate, amass, bank, drive, gather, pile up
◆ n 1 *a snow drift:* accumulation, bank, heap, mass, mound, pile 2 *the drift towards recession:* course, current, digression, direction, flow, movement, rush, sweep, tendency, trend, variation 3 *he didn't catch my drift:* aim, core, course, design, direction, essence, gist, implication, import *formal*, intention, meaning, point, purport *formal*, scope, significance, substance, tendency, tenor, thrust, trend, vein

drifter n beachcomber, hobo *US*, itinerant, nomad, rolling stone, rover, swagman, tramp, traveller, vagabond, vagrant, wanderer

drill n 1 *an electric drill:* awl, bit, borer, gimlet 2 *we were taught military drill:* coaching, discipline, exercise, grounding, inculcation *formal*, indoctrination, instruction, practice, preparation, procedure, repetition, routine, training, tuition
◆ v 1 *he drilled his men relentlessly:* coach, discipline, exercise, ground, inculcate *formal*, instruct, practise, put someone through their paces, rehearse, school, teach, train 2 *drilled three small holes:* bore, make a hole in, penetrate, perforate, pierce, prick, punch, puncture

drink *v* **1** *she drank her tea:* absorb, down, drain, gulp, guzzle, have, imbibe, knock back *colloq*, partake of *formal*, quaff, sip, sup, swallow, swig *colloq*, swill **2** *he's drinking too much:* be a hard drinker, be a heavy drinker, booze *slang*, carouse, drink like a fish *colloq*, get drunk, get pissed *slang*, have (a drop) too much, have a drink problem, have one over the eight *colloq*, have one too many, hit the bottle *colloq*, indulge, knock back a few *colloq*, lush *slang*, polish off *colloq*, revel, tank up *colloq*, tipple *colloq* **3** *drink someone's health:* drink to, propose a toast to, salute, toast, wish someone success

♦ *n* **1** *drinks such as tea:* beverage, brew, cold drink, draught, gulp, hot drink, infusion, liquid, refreshment, sip, soft drink, swallow, swig *colloq*, thirst-quencher **2** *staying off drink:* alcohol, booze *slang*, hard stuff *colloq*, liquor, spirits, stiffener *colloq*, strong drink, the bottle *colloq*, tipple *colloq*, tot

---

Alcoholic drinks include:
ale, beer, cider, lager, shandy, stout, Guinness®; alcopop; aquavit, Armagnac, bourbon, brandy, Calvados, Cognac, gin, pink gin, sloe gin, rum, grog, rye, vodka, whisky, Scotch, hot toddy; wine, red wine, vin rouge, vin rosé, white wine, vin blanc, champagne, bubbly *colloq*, hock, mead, perry, vino *colloq*, plonk *colloq*, absinthe, advocaat, Benedictine, Chartreuse, black velvet, bloody Mary, Buck's fizz, Campari, cocktail, Cointreau®, crème de menthe, daiquiri, eggnog, ginger wine, kirsch, Marsala, Martini®, ouzo, Pernod®, piña colada, port, punch, retsina, sake, sangria, schnapps, sherry, snowball, tequila, Tom Collins, vermouth. See also **wine**

Types of non-alcoholic drink include:
Assam tea, Indian tea, Earl Grey, China tea, lapsang souchong, green tea, herbal tea, fruit tea, camomile tea, peppermint tea, rosehip tea, lemon tea, tisane, julep, mint-julep; coffee, café au lait, café filtre, café noir, cappuccino, espresso, Irish coffee, Turkish coffee; cocoa, hot chocolate, Horlicks®, Ovaltine®, milk, milk shake, float; fizzy drink, pop *colloq*, cherryade, Coca Cola®, Coke® *colloq*, cream soda, ginger beer, lemonade, limeade, Pepsi®, root beer, sarsaparilla, cordial, squash, barley water, Ribena®, fruit juice, mixer, bitter lemon, Canada Dry®, ginger ale, soda water, tonic water, mineral water, Perrier®, seltzer, Vichy water, Lucozade®, Wincarnis®, beef tea

---

drinkable *adj* clean, fit to drink, potable, safe

drinker *n* alkie *slang*, boozer *slang*, dipso *slang*, dipsomaniac, drunk, drunkard, hard/serious drinker, heavy drinker, imbiber, inebriate, lush *slang*, piss artist *slang*, soak *slang*, tippler *colloq*, toper *slang*, tosspot *slang*, wino *slang*
🖾 abstainer, teetotaller

drip *v* dribble, drizzle, drop, filter, leak, ooze, percolate, plop, splash, sprinkle, trickle, weep
♦ *n* **1** *drips of sweat:* bead, dribble, drop, leak, plop, splash, tear, trickle **2** *he's a bit of a drip:* bore, dork *colloq*, nerd *colloq*, ninny *colloq*, softy *colloq*, weakling, wet *colloq*, wimp *colloq*

drive *v* **1** *she drove the car:* be at the controls, be behind/at the wheel, go/come (by car), motor, ride, steer, travel (by car) **2** *I drove her home:* carry, chauffeur, convey, give someone a lift, move, run, send, take, take someone somewhere, transport **3** *pistons drive the engine:* control, direct, handle, hurl, impel, manage, operate, press, propel, run, thrust **4** *we drove the cattle into the next field:* herd, round up, shepherd, urge **5** *poverty drove them to emigrate:* coerce, compel, constrain, force, goad, guide, impel, leave someone with no choice/option, move, oblige, press, prod, push, spur, urge **6** *our captain drove us on:* actuate, compel, force, impel, incite, lead, motivate, move, persuade, pressure, pressurize, prompt, provoke, spur **7** *I drove the nails in:* dash, dig, hammer, knock, plunge, ram, sink, strike, thrust, thump **8** *she drove herself mercilessly:* burden, kill yourself *colloq*, overburden, overdo it, overtax, overwork, tax, work too hard

♦ *n* **1** *a drive down to the seaside:* excursion, jaunt, journey, outing, ride, run, spin *colloq*, trip, turn *colloq* **2** *I walked up the drive:* avenue, driveway, road, roadway **3** *the whole team is full of drive:* action, ambition, determination, effort, energy, enterprise, get-up-and-go *colloq*, initiative, motivation, pizzazz *colloq*, resolve, spirit, tenacity *formal*, verve, vigour, vim *slang*, will, zip *colloq* **4** *our energy efficiency drive:* action, appeal, battle, campaign, crusade, effort, fight, push *colloq*, struggle **5** *can shift 50% of the car's drive to the rear wheels:* power, pressure, propulsion, surge, thrust, transmission **6** *sex drive:* desire, impulse, instinct, need, pressure, urge

▶ **drive at** aim at, allude to, get at *colloq*, have in mind, hint, imply, indicate, insinuate, intend, intimate, mean, refer to, signify, suggest

drivel *n* balderdash *old use*, bunkum *colloq*, claptrap *colloq*, crap *slang*, garbage, gibberish, gobbledegook, hogwash *colloq*, mumbo-jumbo *colloq*, nonsense, poppycock *colloq*, rot *colloq*, rubbish, tripe *colloq*, twaddle *colloq*, waffle *colloq*

driver *n* cabbie, chauffeur, motorist, trucker

driving *adj* compelling, dynamic, energetic, forceful, forthright, heavy, sweeping, vigorous, violent

drizzle *n* (light) rain, mist, mizzle, shower, spray
♦ *v* mizzle, rain, shower, spit, spot, spray, sprinkle

droll *adj* amusing, bizarre, clownish, comic, comical, diverting, eccentric, entertaining, farcical, funny, humorous, jocular, laughable, ludicrous, odd, peculiar, queer, ridiculous, risible *formal*, waggish, whimsical, witty, zany

drone *v* **1** *planes droned overhead:* bombilate, bombinate, buzz, chant, drawl, hum, purr, thrum, vibrate, whirr **2** *the lecturer droned on and on:* go on and on, intone, speak interminably, talk monotonously
♦ *n* **1** *the drone of bees:* buzz, chant, hum, murmuring, purr, thrum, vibration, whirr, whirring **2** *a no-good drone:* dreamer, hanger-on, idler, layabout, lazy person, lazybones *colloq*, leech, loafer, parasite, scrounger *colloq*, slacker, sponger *colloq*

drool *v* **1** *the dog drooled on my knee:* dribble, drivel, salivate, slaver, slobber, water at the mouth **2** *drool over the new baby:* dote, enthuse, gloat, gush, slobber over

droop *v* **1** *the cloak drooped over his shoulders:* bend, bow, dangle, drop, fall down, hang down, sag, sink, slump, stoop, wilt **2** *my spirits drooped:* decline, drop, fade, faint, fall down, falter, flag, languish, lose heart, slouch, slump, wilt, wither
Ⅎ 1 straighten **2** flourish, rise

drop *v* **1** *the grouse dropped out of the sky:* decline, descend, dive, droop, fall, plummet, plunge, sink, tumble **2** *I dropped the rope:* let fall, let go, lower **3** *water dropped gently onto the floor:* dribble, drip, leak, plop, trickle **4** *temperatures dropped suddenly:* decline, decrease, diminish, dwindle, lessen, lower, plummet, plunge, sink, slacken off, weaken **5** *he dropped his friends:* abandon, chuck *colloq*, desert, disown, ditch *colloq*, forsake *formal*, give up, jilt, reject, relinquish *formal*, renounce *formal*, repudiate *formal*, run out on *colloq*, throw over *colloq*, walk out on **6** *we were ordered to drop the plan:* cease *formal*, discontinue *formal*, dispense with *formal*, end, exclude, finish, forgo *formal*, leave out, miss out, omit, quit *colloq*, relinquish *formal*, renounce *formal*, repudiate *formal*, stop, terminate *formal* **7** *he was dropped from the team:* boot out *colloq*, discharge, dismiss, fire *colloq*, make redundant, sack *colloq*, turf out *colloq* **8** *he dropped me at the station:* deliver, deposit, hand in, set down, unload
Ⅎ 1 rise
♦ *n* **1** *drops of water:* bead, blob, bubble, drip, droplet, globule, globulet *formal*, goutte *formal*, gutta *formal*, spheroid *formal*, tear, trickle **2** *add a drop of sherry into the mixture:* bit, dab, dash *colloq*, little, modicum *formal*, mouthful, nip, pinch, sip, smidgen *colloq*, splash, spot *colloq*, sprinkle, tad *US*, tot, trace **3** *a sheer drop of 50 metres:* abyss, chasm, cliff, declivity *formal*, descent, fall, plunge, precipice, slope **4** *a drop in sales:* cutback, decline, decrease, depreciation, deterioration, devaluation, downturn, falling-off, fall-off, lowering, plunge, reduction, slump
► **drop back** fall back, fall behind, lag (behind), retreat *formal*
► **drop in** call (round), call by, come by, come over, come round, pop in *colloq*, visit
► **drop off 1** *she dropped off in front of the television:* catnap, doze *colloq*, drift off, fall asleep, go off, have forty winks *colloq*, nod off *colloq*, snooze *colloq* **2** *sales gradually dropped off:* decline, decrease, diminish, dwindle, fall off, lessen, plummet, plunge, sink, slacken off
► **drop out** back out *colloq*, cry off *colloq*, give up, leave, quit *colloq*, withdraw
► **drop out of** abandon, back out of, cry off from *colloq*, leave, opt out of, pull out of, quit *colloq*, renounce *formal*, withdraw from

dropout *n* Bohemian, deviant, dissenter, dissentient *formal*, hippie, malcontent *formal*, non-conformist, rebel, renegade *formal*

droppings *n* dung, egesta *formal*, excrement, excreta *technical*, faeces *formal*, manure, ordure, spraint, stools

dross *n* debris, dregs, lees, refuse, remains, rubbish, scum, slag, trash, waste

drought *n* aridity, dehydration, desiccation *formal*, dryness, parchedness, shortage, want, water shortage

drove *n* company, crowd, crush, flock, gathering, herd, horde, host, mob, multitude, pack, press, swarm, throng

drown *v* **1** *she drowned during the floods:* deluge, drench, engulf, flood, go under, immerse, inundate, sink, submerge **2** *their voices drowned by catcalls:* extinguish, overcome, overpower, overwhelm, swamp, wipe out

drowsiness *n* dopiness *colloq*, doziness *colloq*, grogginess *colloq*, lethargy, oscitancy *formal*, sleepiness, sluggishness, somnolence *formal*, tiredness, torpor *formal*, weariness

drowsy *adj* dopey *colloq*, dozy, dreamy, half-asleep, hardly able to keep your eyes open, lethargic, nodding, sleepy, somnolent *formal*, tired, torpid *formal*, weary, yawning
Ⅎ alert, awake

drubbing *n* beating, clobbering *colloq*, defeat, flogging, hammering, licking *colloq*, pounding, pummelling, thrashing *colloq*, trouncing, walloping, whipping

drudge *n* dogsbody *colloq*, factotum, galley-slave, hack, labourer, lackey, menial, servant, skivvy *colloq*, slave, toiler, worker
♦ *v* beaver *colloq*, grind *colloq*, keep your nose to the grindstone *colloq*, labour, plod, plug away *colloq*, slave, slog away *colloq*, toil, work, work your fingers to the bone *colloq*
Ⅎ idle, laze

drudgery *n* chore, donkeywork *colloq*, grind *colloq*, hack-work, labour, menial work, skivvying, slavery, slog *colloq*, sweat, sweated labour, toil

drug *n* cure, medication, medicine, potion, remedy
♦ *v* anaesthetize, deaden, dope *colloq*, dose, knock out *colloq*, make unconscious, medicate, numb, sedate, stupefy, tranquillize

Types of drug include:
anaesthetic, analgesic, antibiotic, antidepressant, antihistamine, barbiturate, hallucinogenic, narcotic, opiate, sedative, steroid, stimulant, tranquillizer; chloroform, aspirin, codeine, paracetamol, morphine, penicillin, diazepam, Valium®, Prozac®, cortisone, insulin, digitalis, laudanum, quinine, progesterone, oestrogen; cannabis, marijuana, smack, LSD, acid, ecstasy, E *slang*, heroin, opium, cocaine, crack, dope *colloq*, amphetamine, downer, speed *slang*. See also **medicine**

drug addict *n* coke-head *slang*, dope-fiend *colloq*, drug abuser, freak *slang*, head *slang*, junkie *colloq*, mainliner *slang*, tripper *slang*, user *colloq*

drugged *adj* comatose *technical*, doped *colloq*, high *colloq*, knocked out *colloq*, on a trip *colloq*, spaced out *colloq*, stoned *colloq*, stupefied, turned on *colloq*, zonked *colloq*

drum *v* beat, knock, pulsate, rap, reverberate, tap, tattoo, throb, thrum
► **drum into** din into, drive home, hammer, harp on, inculcate, instil, reiterate
► **drum out** discharge, dismiss, expel, throw out *colloq*
► **drum up** attract, canvass, collect, gather, get, obtain, petition, round up, solicit, summon

drunk *adj* bevvied *colloq*, bibulous *colloq*, blind drunk *colloq*, blotto *colloq*, bombed *slang*, canned *slang*, crapulent *formal*, drunk as a lord/newt *colloq*, drunken, happy *colloq*, having had a few *colloq*, inebriated *formal*, intoxicated *formal*, legless *colloq*, lit up *slang*, loaded *slang*, merry *colloq*, one over the eight *colloq*, paralytic *slang*, pickled *colloq*, pissed *slang*, plastered *colloq*, roaring drunk *colloq*, sloshed *slang*, smashed *slang*, soused *colloq*, sozzled *colloq*, squiffy *colloq*, stewed *slang*, stoned *slang*, tanked up *slang*, the worse for drink *colloq*, tiddly *colloq*, tight *colloq*, tipsy *colloq*, under the influence, under the table *colloq*, wasted *slang*, well-oiled *colloq*, woozy *colloq*, wrecked *slang*

Fa abstinent, sober, teetotal, temperate
♦ *n* alcoholic, alkie *slang*, boozer *slang*, dipso *slang*, dipsomaniac, drinker, drunkard, hard drinker, heavy drinker, inebriate, lush *slang*, piss artist *slang*, soak *slang*, sot *slang*, tippler *colloq*, toper *slang*, tosspot *slang*, wino *slang*

drunkard *n* alcoholic, alkie *slang*, boozer *slang*, dipso *slang*, dipsomaniac, drinker, drunk, hard drinker, heavy drinker, inebriated, lush *slang*, piss artist *slang*, soak *slang*, sot *slang*, tippler *colloq*, toper *slang*, tosspot *slang*, wino *slang*

drunken *adj* 1 *drunken fans celebrating a win:* bombed *slang*, boozy *slang*, crapulent *formal*, drunk, happy *colloq*, inebriate *formal*, intoxicated *formal*, lit up *slang*, loaded *slang*, merry *colloq*, pissed *slang*, sloshed *slang*, stoned *slang*, tiddly *colloq*, tight *colloq*, tipsy *colloq* 2 *a drunken party:* bacchanalian, crapulent *formal*, debauched, dissipated, intemperate, riotous
Fa 1 sober

drunkenness *n* alcoholism, bibulousness *colloq*, crapulence *formal*, debauchery, dipsomania, hard/serious drinking, inebriation *formal*, inebriety *formal*, insobriety *formal*, intemperance, intoxication, tipsiness *colloq*
Fa sobriety

dry *adj* 1 *the dry desert landscape:* arid, barren, dehydrated, desiccated *formal*, dry as a bone *colloq*, moistureless, parched, rainless, scorched, shrivelled, thirsty, torrid, unwatered, wilted, withered, xeric *technical* 2 *his essay was rather dry:* boring, dreary, dry as dust *colloq*, dull, flat, monotonous, tedious, uninteresting, wearisome 3 *dry humour:* cutting, cynical, deadpan, droll, ironic, laconic, low-key, sarcastic, subtle, witty
Fa 1 damp, wet 2 imaginative, interesting
♦ *v* dehydrate, desiccate *formal*, parch, scorch, shrivel, wilt, wither
Fa soak, wet
▶ **dry up** 1 *this market has started to dry up:* come to an end, die out, disappear, fade, fail, stop, stop being productive 2 *he dried up briefly then continued his act:* forget your lines, shut up, stop talking

dryness *n* 1 *the parched dryness of the soil:* aridity, aridness, barrenness, dehydration, drought 2 *dryness of the mouth:* dehydration, parchedness, thirst, thirstiness
Fa 1 wetness

dual *adj* binary, combined, coupled, double, duplex, duplicate, matched, paired, twin, twofold, two-piece

dub *v* bestow *formal*, call, christen, confer, designate, entitle, label, name, nickname, style, tag, term

dubiety *n* doubt, doubtfulness, hesitation, incertitude *formal*, indecision, misgiving,

mistrust, qualm, scepticism, suspicion, uncertainty
Fa certainty

dubious *adj* 1 *she was a bit dubious about it all:* doubtful, hesitant, irresolute, sceptical, suspicious, uncertain, undecided, unsettled, unsure, vacillating, wavering 2 *dubious business ethics:* ambiguous, debatable, fishy *colloq*, iffy *colloq*, obscure, questionable, shady *colloq*, shifty *colloq*, suspect, suspicious, unreliable, untrustworthy
Fa 1 certain 2 trustworthy

duck *v* 1 *she ducked just in time:* bend, bob, bow down, crouch, drop, squat, stoop 2 *he managed to duck the meeting:* avoid, dodge *colloq*, elude, evade, shirk, shun, sidestep, steer clear of, worm your way out of *colloq*, wriggle out of *colloq* 3 *duck him into the pool:* dip, dive, douse, dunk, immerse, lower, plunge, souse, submerge, wet

duct *n* canal, channel, conduit, funnel, passage, pipe, tube, vessel

ductile *adj* amenable, biddable, compliant *formal*, flexible, malleable, manageable, manipulable, plastic, pliable, pliant, tractable, yielding
Fa intractable, refractory *formal*

dud *n* failure, flop, washout *colloq*
♦ *adj* broken, bust *colloq*, duff *colloq*, failed, inoperative *formal*, kaput *colloq*, nugatory *formal*, valueless, worthless
Fa working

due *adj* 1 *I have a tax rebate due:* in arrears, outstanding, owed, owing, payable, unpaid 2 *treat it with due attention:* appropriate, correct, deserved, fitting, justified, merited, proper, right, rightful, suitable 3 *driving without due care:* adequate, ample, enough, plenty of, requisite *formal*, sufficient 4 *he's due now:* anticipated, expected, long-awaited, required, scheduled
Fa 1 paid 3 inadequate
♦ *adv* dead *colloq*, directly, exactly, precisely, straight
♦ *n* 1 *give him his due:* birthright, come-uppance *colloq*, (just) deserts, merits, prerogative, privilege, rights 2 *pay dues:* charge(s), contribution, fee, levy, membership fee, subscription

duel *n* 1 *shot in a duel:* affair of honour, battle, combat, engagement, fight, single combat 2 *the duel between the two golfers:* clash, competition, contest, encounter, engagement, rivalry, struggle

duffer *n* blunderer, bonehead *colloq*, bungler, clod *colloq*, clot *colloq*, dimwit *colloq*, dolt *colloq*, fool, idiot, ignoramus, oaf

dulcet *adj* agreeable, gentle, harmonious, mellifluous *formal*, mellow, melodious, pleasant, soft, soothing, sweet, sweet-sounding

dull *adj* 1 *a dull documentary:* bland, boring, dismal, dreary, dull as ditchwater *colloq*, flat, heavy, humdrum, insipid, lifeless, monotonous, pedestrian, plain, ponderous, stereotyped, stultifying, tedious, tiresome, uneventful, unexciting, unimaginative, uninteresting, wearisome 2 *a dull grey colour:* dark, dim, drab, dreary, gloomy, lacklustre, matt, murky, opaque, sombre 3 *a dull mind:* bird-brained *colloq*, dense, dim, dimwitted *colloq*, dumb *colloq*, slow, slow on

the uptake *colloq*, stupid, thick *colloq*,
unintelligent **4** *dull weather*: cloudy, dark, dim,
dreary, gloomy, grey, leaden, overcast, sombre
5 *feel dull*: heavy, idle, inactive, inert, lethargic,
slow, sluggish, torpid *formal* **6** *a dull pain*:
distressing, faint, mild, troublesome,
uncomfortable, weak **7** *a dull sound/thud*: feeble,
indistinct, muffled, muted, weak **8** *the dull edge of
the knife*: blunt, edgeless, unsharpened
☒ **1** exciting, interesting, lively **2** bright
3 clever, intelligent **4** fine, sunny **5** energetic,
lively **6** acute, intense, sharp **7** sharp **8** sharp
♦ *v* **1** *the barrage dulled their resistance*: allay,
alleviate, assuage, blunt, decrease, diminish,
lessen, mitigate *formal*, moderate, reduce, relieve,
soften, tone down **2** *morphine dulled his pain*:
deaden, drug, numb, paralyse, stupefy,
tranquillize **3** *the defeat failed to dull her optimism*:
dampen, deject, depress, discourage, dishearten,
sadden, subdue **4** *her red hair had dulled with age*:
darken, dim, fade, obscure, wash out

dullard *n* blockhead *colloq*, bonehead *colloq*,
chump *colloq*, clod *colloq*, clot *colloq*, dimwit
colloq, dolt *colloq*, dope *colloq*, dunce,
dunderhead *colloq*, idiot, ignoramus, imbecile,
moron, nitwit *colloq*, numskull *colloq*, oaf,
simpleton
☒ brain

dullness *n* **1** *the dullness of his suburban life*:
dreariness, dryness, flatness, monotony,
tediousness, tedium, torpor *formal*, vacuity
formal, vapidity *formal* **2** *restoration will remove the
painting's dullness*: dimness, dinginess, drabness,
gloominess, greyness
☒ **1** excitement, interest **2** brightness, clarity,
sharpness

duly *adv* accordingly, appropriately, befittingly
formal, correctly, decorously *formal*, deservedly,
fitly, fittingly, properly, rightfully, suitably, sure
enough

dumb *adj* **1** *struck dumb*: at a loss for words,
inarticulate, lost for words, mum *colloq*, mute,
shtoom *slang*, silent, speechless, tongue-tied,
without speech **2** *a dumb thing to do*: brainless
colloq, dense, dim-witted *colloq*, foolish, gormless
colloq, stupid, thick *colloq*, unintelligent

dumbfounded *adj* amazed, astonished,
astounded, baffled, bewildered, bowled over
colloq, confounded, confused, dumb,
flabbergasted *colloq*, floored *colloq*, gobsmacked
colloq, knocked for six *colloq*, lost for words,
nonplussed, overcome, overwhelmed,
paralysed, speechless, staggered, startled,
stunned, taken aback, thrown *colloq*

dummy *n* **1** *a dummy CCTV camera*: copy,
counterfeit, duplicate, imitation, representation,
reproduction, sample, substitute **2** *tailors'
dummies*: figure, form, lay-figure, mannequin,
model **3** *the baby's dummy*: pacifier, teat **4** *only a
dummy would say that*: blockhead *colloq*, chump
colloq, clot *colloq*, dimwit *colloq*, fool, idiot,
imbecile, nitwit *colloq*, numskull *colloq*, oaf
♦ *adj* **1** *dummy guns*: artificial, bogus, fake, false,
imitation, mock, phoney *colloq*, sham **2** *a dummy
run*: practice, simulated, trial

dump *v* **1** *dump your empties at the bottle bank*:
bung *colloq*, deposit, discharge, drop, empty out,
fling down, let fall, offload, park, place, plonk
colloq, pour out, put down, throw down, tip out,
unload **2** *they dumped the stolen car*: chuck away
colloq, discard, dispose of, ditch, get rid of,
jettison, scrap, throw away, throw out, tip **3** *he
dumped his girlfriend*: abandon, chuck *colloq*, ditch
colloq, forsake *formal*, leave, walk out on
♦ *n* **1** *took his refuse to the dump*: junkyard, rubbish
heap, rubbish tip, scrapyard, tip **2** *this hostel's a
bit of a dump*: hole *colloq*, hovel, joint *colloq*, mess,
pigsty *colloq*, shack, shanty, slum, tip *colloq*

dumpy *adj* chubby, chunky, plump, podgy,
pudgy, short, squab, squat, stout, stubby, tubby
☒ tall

dun *adj* dingy, dull, greyish-brown, mouse-
coloured, mud-coloured

dunce *n* blockhead *colloq*, bonehead *colloq*,
dimwit *colloq*, dipstick *slang*, fool, idiot,
imbecile, nerd *slang*, nincompoop *colloq*, ninny
colloq, nitwit *colloq*, numskull *colloq*, twerp *colloq*,
twit *colloq*, wally *slang*
☒ brain, intellectual

dung *n* animal waste, droppings, excrement,
faeces *formal*, manure, ordure, spraint

dungeon *n* cage, cell, gaol, jail, keep, lock-up,
oubliette, prison, vault

dupe *v* bamboozle *colloq*, cheat, con *colloq*,
deceive, defraud, delude, fool, hoax, hoodwink,
outwit, rip off *colloq*, swindle, take in, trick
♦ *n* fall guy *colloq*, fool, gull, instrument, mug
colloq, pawn, puppet, push-over *colloq*,
simpleton, stooge *colloq*, sucker *colloq*, victim

duplicate *v* clone, copy, do again, double, echo,
facsimile, fax, photocopy, repeat, replicate
formal, reproduce, Xerox®
♦ *adj* corresponding, identical, matched,
matching, paired, twin, twofold
♦ *n* carbon (copy), clone, copy, (dead) ringer
colloq, double, facsimile, fax, forgery, imitation,
lookalike *colloq*, match, mate, model, photocopy,
replica, reproduction, spitting image *colloq*,
twin, Xerox®

duplication *n* cloning, copying, dittography
formal, doubling, gemination *formal*,
photocopying, repetition, replication *formal*,
reproduction

duplicity *n* artifice, betrayal, chicanery, deceit,
deception, dishonesty, dissimulation *formal*,
double-dealing, falsehood, fraud, guile,
hypocrisy, mendacity *formal*, perfidy *formal*,
treachery

durability *n* constancy, durableness *formal*,
endurance, imperishability, lastingness,
longevity *formal*, permanence, persistence,
stability, strength
☒ fragility, impermanence, weakness

durable *adj* **1** *durable materials*: hard-wearing,
heavy-duty, long-lasting, reinforced, reliable,
resistant, robust, solid, sound, stable, strong,
sturdy, substantial, tough **2** *a durable peace was
reached*: abiding, constant, dependable, enduring,
fast, firm, fixed, lasting, long-lasting, permanent,
persistent, persisting, reliable, sound, stable,
substantial, unchanging
☒ **1** fragile, perishable, weak **2** changeable

duration *n* continuance, continuation, extent,
fullness, length, length of time, period, span,
spell, stretch, time, time scale, time span
☒ shortening

duress *n* arm-twisting *colloq*, coercion, compulsion, constraint, enforcement, exaction, force, pressure, restraint, threat

during *prep* at/in the time of, for the time of, in, in the course of, throughout

dusk *n* dark, darkness, evening, gloaming, gloom, nightfall, shade, shadows, sundown, sunset, twilight
Fa brightness, dawn

dusky *adj* 1 *the fading dusky light*: cloudy, crepuscular *formal*, dark, dim, foggy, fuliginous *formal*, gloomy, hazy, misty, murky, shadowy, subfusc *formal*, tenebrous *formal*, twilit 2 *dusky maidens*: black, brown, dark-coloured, dark-complexioned, dark-skinned, swarthy, tawny
Fa 1 bright 2 white

dust *n* clay, dirt, earth, grime, grit, ground, particles, powder, smut, soil, soot
♦ *v* 1 *dust the room*: brush, burnish, clean, mop, polish, spray, wipe 2 *dust the fillets with flour*: cover, powder, scatter, spread, sprinkle

dust-up *n* argument, argy-bargy *colloq*, brawl, brush, commotion, conflict, disagreement, disturbance, encounter, fight, fracas, punch-up *colloq*, quarrel, scrap *colloq*, scuffle, set-to *colloq*, skirmish, tussle

dusty *adj* 1 *the loft was dusty*: dirty, dust-covered, filthy, grimy, grubby, sooty 2 *the soil is rather dusty*: chalky, crumbly, friable *formal*, granular, powdery, sandy
Fa 1 clean 2 hard, solid

dutiful *adj* compliant *formal*, conscientious, considerate, deferential, devoted, filial, obedient, respectful, reverential, submissive, thoughtful

duty *n* 1 *the Queen's official duties*: assignment, burden, business, calling, charge, chore, commission, function, job, mission, obligation, office, onus, part, requirement, responsibility, role, service, task, work 2 *a strong sense of duty*: allegiance, faithfulness, fidelity *formal*, loyalty, obedience, respect 3 *duty on imported drinks*: customs, dues, excise, levy, tariff, tax, toll

dwarf *n* 1 *dwarves and clowns then took to the stage*: Lilliputian, midget, person of restricted growth, pygmy, Tom Thumb 2 *the wizard turned him into a dwarf*: gnome, goblin
♦ *adj* baby, diminutive, Lilliputian, mini *colloq*, miniature, petite, pocket, pygmy, small, stunted, tiny, undersized
Fa large
♦ *v* 1 *to dwarf a plant*: arrest, atrophy *formal*, check, retard, stunt 2 *this will dwarf all other issues*: dominate, overshadow, stand head and shoulders above *colloq*, tower over

dwell *v* abide *formal*, be domiciled *formal*, hang out *colloq*, inhabit, live, lodge, people, populate, reside *formal*, rest, settle, stay
► **dwell on** brood on, elaborate, emphasize, expatiate *formal*, harp on, linger over, meditate on, mull over, reflect on, ruminate on *formal*, think about, turn over in your mind
Fa pass over

dweller *n* denizen *formal*, inhabitant, occupant, occupier, resident

dwelling *n* abode *formal*, cottage, domicile *formal*, dwelling-house, establishment, habitation *formal*, home, house, hut, lodge, lodging, quarters, residence, shanty, tent

dwindle *v* become/grow less, decline, decrease, die out, diminish, disappear, ebb, fade, fall, lessen, peter out *colloq*, shrink, shrivel, subside, tail off, taper off, vanish, wane, waste away, weaken, wither
Fa grow, increase

dye *n* agent, colour, colouring, hue, pigment, shade, stain, tinge, tint, wash
♦ *v* colour, imbue, pigment, shade, stain, tinge, tint

dyed-in-the-wool *adj* card-carrying, complete, confirmed, deep-rooted, die-hard, entrenched, established, fixed, hard-core, hardened, inflexible, inveterate, long-standing, settled, thorough, through and through, unchangeable, uncompromising, unshakable
Fa superficial

dying *adj* at death's door, close/near to death, ebbing, fading, failing, final, going, moribund *formal*, mortal, not long for this world, on your deathbed, on your last legs *colloq*, passing, perishing, vanishing, with one foot in the grave *colloq*
Fa reviving

dynamic *adj* active, driving, effective, energetic, forceful, full of energy, go-ahead *colloq*, go-getting *colloq*, high-powered, lively, magnetic *colloq*, potent, powerful, self-starting, spirited, strong, vigorous, vital
Fa apathetic, inactive

dynamism *n* drive, energy, enterprise, forcefulness, get-up-and-go *colloq*, go *colloq*, initiative, liveliness, pep *colloq*, pizzazz *colloq*, push *colloq*, vigour, vim *colloq*, zap *colloq*, zip *colloq*
Fa apathy, inactivity, slowness

dynasty *n* authority, dominion, empire, house, jurisdiction, line, rule, sovereignty, succession

dyspeptic *adj* bad-tempered, crabbed, crabby, crotchety, gloomy, grouchy, peevish, short-tempered, snappish, testy, touchy

E

each *adj* every, every individual, every single
♦ *pron* each and every one, each in their own way, each one
♦ *adv* apiece, individually, per capita, per head, per person, respectively, separately, singly

eager *adj* **1** *an eager golfer*: ardent, avid, diligent, earnest, enthusiastic, fervent, keen, wholehearted, zealous **2** *eager to leave home*: anxious, impatient, intent, keen, longing, wishing, yearning **3** *eager for fame*: greedy, hungry, thirsty
F∃ 1 indifferent, reluctant, unenthusiastic

eagerly *adv* ardently, avidly, earnestly, enthusiastically, fervently, impatiently, intently, keenly, wholeheartedly, zealously
F∃ apathetically, listlessly

eagerness *n* **1** *his eagerness to please*: avidity, hunger, impatience, impetuosity, longing, yearning, zeal **2** *the eagerness of his supporters*: ardour, earnestness, enthusiasm, fervency, fervidity *formal*, fervour, keeness, thirst
F∃ 2 apathy, disinterest

ear *n* **1** *he had the ear of his new boss*: attention, attentiveness, heed, notice, regard **2** *an ear for language*: ability, appreciation, discrimination, hearing, perception, sensitivity, skill, taste

> *Parts of the ear include:*
> anvil (incus), auditory canal, auditory nerve, auricle, cochlea, concha, eardrum, Eustachian tube, hammer (malleus), helix, labyrinth, lobe, oval window, pinna, round window, semicircular canal, stirrup (stapes), tragus, tympanum, vestibular nerve, vestibule

early *adj* **1** *early stages*: first, initial, opening, undeveloped **2** *his early demise*: advanced, forward, precocious, premature, untimely **3** *early theatre*: ancient, autochthonous *technical*, primeval *formal*, primitive, primordial *formal*
♦ *adv* **1** *early in the day*: at dawn, at daybreak, in the (early) morning **2** *we booked early*: ahead of schedule, ahead of time, beforehand, in advance, in good time, with time to spare **3** *I arrived early*: before the usual/arranged/expected time, prematurely, too soon
F∃ 1 late

earmark *v* **1** *he was earmarked for early promotion*: designate, mark out **2** *the money earmarked for tuition fees*: allocate, keep back, label, put aside, reserve, set aside, tag

earn *v* **1** *earn a good salary*: be/get paid, bring in *colloq*, clear, collect, draw, gain, get, gross, make, net, obtain, pocket, pull in *colloq*, realize, reap, receive, take home **2** *earn a reputation for honesty*: achieve, attain, be owed, be someone's by right, deserve, merit, obtain, rate, secure, warrant, win
F∃ 1 lose, spend

earnest¹ *adj* **1** *an earnest apology*: assiduous *formal*, committed, dedicated, grave, heartfelt, intense, serious, sincere, solemn, thoughtful, zealous **2** *earnest prayers*: ardent, conscientious, devoted, eager, enthusiastic, fervent, firm, fixed, intent, keen, resolute, steady
F∃ 1 flippant, frivolous **2** apathetic

earnest² *n* assurance, deposit, down payment, guarantee, pledge, security, token

earnestly *adv* **1** *he earnestly believed she would return*: firmly, resolutely, seriously, sincerely **2** *they prayed earnestly for the child's recovery*: eagerly, fervently, intently, keenly, warmly, zealously
F∃ 2 flippantly, listlessly

earnestness *n* **1** *the earnestness of his apology*: gravity, seriousness, sincerity **2** *the earnestness with which she worked*: ardour, determination, eagerness, enthusiasm, fervency, fervour, intentness, keenness, passion, purposefulness, resolution, vehemence, zeal
F∃ 1 flippancy **2** apathy

earnings *n* emolument *formal*, fee, gain, gross pay, honorarium, income, net pay, pay, proceeds, receipts, remuneration, return, revenue, reward, salary, stipend, take home pay, wages
F∃ expenditure, outgoings

earth *n* **1** *they travelled the earth*: globe, orb, planet, sphere, world **2** *the earth was soaked with rain*: clay, dirt, ground, humus, land, loam, sod, soil, turf

earthenware *n* ceramics, crockery, pots, pottery, stoneware

earthly *adj* **1** *our earthly life*: fleshly, human, material, materialistic, mortal, mundane, physical, profane, secular, sensual, tellurian *formal*, telluric *formal*, temporal, terrestrial *formal*, worldy **2** *no earthly explanation*: conceivable, feasible, imaginable, likely, possible, slightest
F∃ 1 heavenly, spiritual

earthquake *n* aftershock, earth-tremor, quake, seism, shake, tremor

earthy *adj* **1** *his earthy language*: bawdy, blue *colloq*, coarse, crude, indecorous *formal*, raunchy *colloq*, ribald, rude, vulgar **2** *earthy common sense*: down-to-earth, natural, robust, rough, rude, uninhibited, unsophisticated
F∃ 1 modest **2** inhibited, modest, refined

ease *n* **1** *the ease with which she sang*: adroitness, deftness, dexterity, effortlessness, facility, naturalness, skilfulness **2** *a life of luxury and ease*: affluence, bed of roses *colloq*, comfort, easy street *colloq*, lap of luxury, leisure, life of Riley *colloq*, opulence *formal*, prosperity, wealth **3** *set her mind at ease*: contentment, enjoyment, happiness, peace, quiet, relaxation, repose *formal*, rest
F∃ 1 difficulty **3** discomfort
♦ *v* **1** *ease the pain*: abate *formal*, allay, alleviate, ameliorate *formal*, assuage, calm, comfort, diminish, grow/become less, lessen, lighten, mitigate *formal*, moderate, palliate *formal*, quieten, reduce, relax, relent, relieve, salve, soothe **2** *websites ease the way for entrepreneurs*: facilitate *formal*, smooth **3** *ease it into position*: edge, guide, inch, manoeuvre, slide, steer
F∃ 1 aggravate, intensify, worsen **2** aggravate, worsen

▶ **ease off** abate *formal*, become less, decrease, die away, die down, diminish, moderate, relent, slacken, subside, wane
F∃ increase

easily *adv* **1** *she chatted easily with the group:* comfortably, effortlessly, fluently, readily, simply, straightforwardly **2** *easily the best:* by far, certainly, clearly, definitely, doubtlessly, far and away, indisputably, simply, surely, undeniably, undoubtedly
Ⅎ 1 laboriously

easy *adj* **1** *the maths test was easy:* a cinch *colloq*, a doddle *colloq*, a piece of cake *colloq*, a pushover *colloq*, child's play *colloq*, easy as ABC *colloq*, like falling off a log *colloq*, manageable, natural, painless, simple, straightforward, uncomplicated, undemanding **2** *her easy manner:* calm, carefree, casual, comfortable, easy-going, effortless, informal, laid-back *colloq*, leisurely, natural, relaxed, unforced
Ⅎ 1 demanding, difficult, exacting, hard **2** tense, uneasy

easy-going *adj* **1** *an easy-going roommate:* amenable, calm, carefree, even-tempered, happy-go-lucky *colloq*, imperturbable *formal*, insouciant *formal*, laid-back *colloq*, nonchalant, placid, relaxed, serene **2** *he's not so easy-going with his own children:* lenient, relaxed, tolerant, undemanding
Ⅎ 2 critical, intolerant, strict

eat *v* **1** *eat healthy food:* bolt down, chew, consume, devour, gobble, gulp down, ingest *formal*, munch, partake of *formal*, polish off *colloq*, put away *colloq*, scoff *colloq*, swallow, tuck into *colloq*, wolf down *colloq* **2** *we often eat out:* breakfast, dine, feed, graze *colloq*, have a snack, lunch **3** *acid eats the enamel away:* corrode, crumble, decay, dissolve, erode, rot, wear away

eatable *adj* **1** *eatable plants:* comestible *formal*, digestible, edible **2** *her food is just not eatable:* good, palatable, wholesome
Ⅎ 1 inedible **2** unpalatable

---

eatable or *edible*? If something is *edible*, it is by nature safe or good to eat, whereas if it is *eatable*, it is in a condition that makes it possible to eat it (whether or not it is safe to do so). Poisonous mushrooms are *eatable* but they are not *edible*, while a bag of flour is perfectly *edible* but would scarcely be *eatable*.

---

eavesdrop *v* bug *colloq*, listen in, monitor, overhear, snoop *colloq*, spy, tap *colloq*

eavesdropper *n* listener, monitor, snoop *colloq*, snooper *colloq*, spy

ebb *v* **1** *the tide ebbed:* fall, fall back, flow back, go out, recede, retrocede *formal* **2** *his confidence ebbed away:* abate *formal*, decay, decline, decrease, degenerate, deteriorate, diminish, drop, dwindle, fade away, flag, lessen, peter out *colloq*, recede, shrink, sink, slacken, subside, wane, weaken
Ⅎ 1 rise **2** increase, rise
♦ *n* **1** *the ebb of the tide:* ebb tide, fall, flowing back, going out, low tide, low water, retreat **2** *her health is at a low ebb:* decay, decline, decrease, degeneration, deterioration, drop, dwindling, lagging, lessening, slackening, subsidence, wane, waning, weakening
Ⅎ 1 flow, rise **2** increase

ebony *adj* black, dark, jet, jet-black, jetty, sable, sooty

ebullience *n* breeziness, brightness, buoyancy, chirpiness *colloq*, effusiveness, elation, enthusiasm, excitement, exhilaration, exuberance, high spirits, vivacity, zest
Ⅎ apathy, dullness, lifelessness

ebullient *adj* breezy, bright, buoyant, chirpy *colloq*, effervescent, effusive, elated, enthusiastic, excited, exhilarated, exuberant, gushing, irrepressible, vivacious, zestful
Ⅎ apathetic, dull, lifeless

eccentric *adj* aberrant *formal*, abnormal, bizarre, dotty *colloq*, erratic, freakish, idiosyncratic, kooky *US colloq*, loony *colloq*, loopy *colloq*, nutty *colloq*, odd, off-beat *colloq*, outlandish, peculiar, queer, quirky, singular, strange, unconventional, wacky *colloq*, way-out *colloq*, weird
Ⅎ conventional, normal, orthodox
♦ *n* case *colloq*, character *colloq*, crackpot *colloq*, crank *colloq*, fish out of water *colloq*, freak *colloq*, geek *slang*, kook *US colloq*, nonconformist, nut *colloq*, nutter *colloq*, odd fish *colloq*, oddball *colloq*, oddity, square peg in a round hole *colloq*, weirdo *colloq*

eccentricity *n* **1** *the increasing eccentricity of its founder:* aberration *formal*, abnormality, anomaly, bizarreness, capriciousness *formal*, freakishness, idiosyncrasy, nonconformity, oddity, peculiarity, singularity, strangeness, unconventionality, weirdness **2** *individual eccentricities and habits:* aberration *formal*, anomaly, idiosyncrasy, quirk, weirdness
Ⅎ 1 conventionality, ordinariness

ecclesiastic *n* canon, chaplain, churchman, churchwoman, clergyman/clergywoman, cleric, curate, deacon, deaconess, dean, father, man/woman of God, man/woman of the cloth, minister, padre, parson, pastor, presbyter, priest, rector, reverend, vicar

ecclesiastical *adj* church, churchly, clerical, divine, holy, pastoral, priestly, religious, sacerdotal *formal*, spiritual
Ⅎ secular, temporal

echelon *n* degree, grade, level, place, position, rank, rung, status, tier

echo *n* **1** *the echo rang out:* reflection, reiteration, repetition, resounding, reverberation, ringing **2** *second-rate echoes of Picasso:* clone, copy, duplicate, image, imitation, mirror image, parallel, reflection, repeat, reproduction **3** *an echo of a bygone age:* allusion, evocation *formal*, hint, memory, remembrance, reminder, trace
♦ *v* **1** *the scream echoed in the empty hall:* reflect, reiterate, repeat, resound, reverberate, ring **2** *her statement echoed our thoughts on the matter:* copy, imitate, mimic, mirror, parallel, parrot, reflect, repeat, reproduce, resemble

eclectic *adj* all-embracing, broad, catholic, comprehensive, diverse, diversified, general, heterogeneous *formal*, liberal, many-sided, multifarious *formal*, selective, varied, wide-ranging
Ⅎ exclusive, narrow, one-sided

eclipse *v* **1** *the moon eclipsed the sun:* blot out, cast a shadow over, cloud, conceal, cover, darken, dim, obscure, shroud, veil **2** *his success eclipsed that of his father:* dwarf, exceed, excel, leave someone standing, outdo, outshine, overshadow, put into the shade, run rings around *colloq*, surpass, transcend
♦ *n* **1** *a lunar eclipse:* blotting-out, concealing,

covering, darkening, dimming, obscuration *formal*, shading, veiling **2** *the eclipse of Gaelic Ireland*: decline, ebb, failure, fall, loss, weakening

economic *adj* **1** *an economic boost*: business, commercial, industrial, trade **2** *she moved home for economic reasons*: budgetary, financial, fiscal, monetary **3** *outsourcing is the most economic solution*: cost-effective, money-making, productive, profitable, profit-making, remunerative, viable

---

economic or *economical*? *Economic* means 'relating to economics or the economy of a country': *economic history; the country's economic future*. It also means 'giving an adequate profit or fair return', as in *We must charge an economic rent. Economical* means 'not wasteful, expensive, or extravagant': *This car is very economical on petrol; the economical use of limited supplies.*

---

economical *adj* **1** *an economical way to heat the house*: careful, frugal, parsimonious *formal*, prudent *formal*, saving, scrimping, skimping, sparing, thrifty **2** *an economical little car*: budget, cheap, cost-effective, efficient, inexpensive, low-budget, low-cost, low-priced, modest, reasonable
🔄 **1** wasteful **2** expensive, uneconomical

economize *v* be economical, budget, buy cheaply, cut back, cut corners *colloq*, cut costs, cut expenditure, cut your coat according to your cloth *colloq*, keep down costs, live on the cheap, retrench *formal*, save, scrimp and save, tighten your belt *colloq*, use less
🔄 squander, waste

economy *n* **1** *the country's economy*: business resources, financial organization, financial resources, financial state, financial system, system of wealth **2** *redundancy forced her to make economies*: care, carefulness, frugality, husbandry, parsimony, providence, prudence *formal*, restraint, saving, scrimping, skimping, thrift
🔄 **2** extravagance

ecstasy *n* bliss, delight, elation, euphoria, exultation, fervour, frenzy, joy, jubilation, pleasure, rapture, transports of delight
🔄 misery, torment

ecstatic *adj* blissful, delirious, elated, enraptured, euphoric, fervent, frenzied, high as a kite *colloq*, in seventh heaven *colloq*, joyful, jubilant, jumping for joy *colloq*, on cloud nine *colloq*, over the moon *colloq*, overjoyed, rapturous, rhapsodic *formal*, tickled pink *colloq*
🔄 downcast

eddy *n* maelstrom, swirl, swirling, twist, vortex, whirlpool
♦ *v* swirl, whirl

edge *n* **1** *the edge of the forest*: border, boundary, brim, brink, extremity, fringe, frontier, limit, line, lip, margin, outer limit, outline, perimeter, periphery, rim, side, threshold, verge **2** *the edge of madness*: brink, threshold, verge **3** *his education gave him the edge*: advantage, ascendancy *formal*, dominance, superiority, upper hand *colloq*, whip hand *colloq* **4** *there was an edge to his comments*: acerbity *formal*, acuteness, bite, causticity *formal*, incisiveness, keenness, pungency, severity, sharpness, sting, trenchancy *formal*, zest

♦ *v* crawl, creep, ease, elbow, inch, pick your way, sidle, steal, worm

edgy *adj* anxious, ill at ease, irritable, keyed-up, nervous, nervy *colloq*, on edge, tense, touchy, uptight *colloq*
🔄 at ease, calm

edible *adj* comestible *formal*, digestible, eatable, fit to eat, good, harmless, palatable, wholesome
🔄 inedible

---

edible or *eatable*? See panel at **eatable**

---

edict *n* act, command, decree, fiat, injunction, law, mandate, manifesto, order, proclamation, pronouncement, pronunciamento, regulation, rule, ruling, statute, ukase

edification *n* coaching, education, elevation, enlightenment, guidance, improvement, instruction, teaching, upbuilding, uplifting

edifice *n* building, construction, erection, structure

edify *v* build up, coach, educate, elevate, enlighten, guide, improve, inform, instruct, nurture, school, teach, tutor, uplift

edit *v* **1** *click to edit your personal details*: adapt, annotate, blue pencil, check, correct, emend *formal*, modify, polish, rearrange, redact *formal*, reorder, rephrase, revise, rewrite **2** *edit a series of short stories*: compile, select **3** *edit a newspaper*: be in charge of, be responsible for, direct, head (up)

edition *n* copy, impression, issue, number, printing, publication, version, volume

educable *adj* instructible, teachable, trainable
🔄 ineducable

educate *v* coach, cultivate, develop, discipline, drill, edify, enlighten, improve, inculcate *formal*, indoctrinate, inform, instruct, prepare, prime, school, teach, train, tutor

educated *adj* **1** *an educated man*: brainy *colloq*, civilized, cultivated, cultured, enlightened, erudite *formal*, informed, knowledgeable, learned, lettered, literate, refined, sagacious *formal*, well-read, wise **2** *an educated guess*: enlightened, informed, knowledgeable, sagacious *formal*, trained, wise
🔄 **1** uncultured, uneducated

education *n* **1** *the education of children*: coaching, development, drilling, edification, enlightenment, fostering, guidance, improvement, inculcation *formal*, indoctrination, informing, instruction, nurture, preparation, scholarship, schooling, teaching, training, tuition, tutoring, upbringing **2** *a man of great education*: cultivation, culture, knowledge, letters, scholarship

educational *adj* **1** *educational qualifications*: academic, didactic *formal*, educative, pedagogic *formal*, pedagogical *formal*, scholastic *formal*, teaching **2** *educational and entertaining*: cultural, didactic *formal*, edifying, educative, enlightening, improving, informative, instructive
🔄 **2** uninformative

Educational establishments include:
kindergarten, nursery school, infant school, primary school, middle school, combined school, comprehensive school, secondary school, secondary modern, upper school, high

school, grammar school, grant-maintained school, voluntary school, foundation school, community school, preparatory school, public school, private school, boarding-school, college, sixth-form college, college of further education, city technical college (CTC), technical college, university, adult-education centre, academy, seminary, finishing school, business school, secretarial college, Sunday school, convent school, summer-school

---

Educational terms include:
adult education, A-level, assisted places scheme, (international) baccalaureate, board of governors, break time, bursar, campus, catchment area, certificate, classroom, coeducation, common entrance, course, course of studies, curriculum, degree, diploma, discipline, double-first, educational programme, eleven-plus, enrolment, examination, exercise book, final exam, finals, further education, GCSE (General Certificate of Secondary Education), governor, graduation, half-term, head boy, head girl, head teacher, higher education, Higher Grade, homework, intake, invigilator, lecture, literacy, matriculation, matron, mixed-ability teaching, modular course, module, national curriculum, newly qualified teacher, NVQ (national vocational qualification), numeracy, O-level, opting out, parent governor, PTA (parent teacher association), playground, playtime, prefect, primary education, proctor, professor, pupil, quadrangle, qualification, refresher course, register, report, scholarship, school term, secondary education, special education, Standard Grade, statemented, streaming, student, student grant, student loan, study, subject, syllabus, teacher, teacher training, test paper, textbook, thesis, timetable, truancy, university entrance, work experience

---

educative *adj* catechetic *formal*, catechismal *formal*, catechistic(al) *formal*, didactic *formal*, edifying, educational, enlightening, improving, informative, instructive
Ⅎ uninformative

educator *n* academic, coach, educationalist, instructor, lecturer, pedagogue *formal*, professor, schoolmaster, schoolmistress, schoolteacher, teacher, trainer, tutor

eerie *adj* bloodcurdling, creepy *colloq*, frightening, ghostly, mysterious, scaring, scary, spine-chilling *colloq*, spooky *colloq*, strange, uncanny, unearthly, unnatural, weird

efface *v* blank out, blot out, cancel, cross out, delete, destroy, eliminate, eradicate, erase, excise *formal*, expunge *formal*, extirpate *formal*, obliterate, remove, rub out, wipe out

effect *n* **1** *the effects of global warming*: aftermath, conclusion, consequence, fruit, impact, issue, outcome, result, upshot **2** *her tantrums had no effect*: efficacy *formal*, force, impact, impression, influence, power, strength **3** *something to the effect that she was bankrupt*: drift, import *formal*, meaning, purport *formal*, sense, significance, tenor **4** *personal effects*: accoutrements *formal*, baggage, belongings, chattels *formal*, gear *colloq*, goods, luggage, movables, paraphernalia, possessions, property, stuff *colloq*, things *colloq*, trappings
♦ *v* accomplish, achieve, bring about, carry out,

cause, complete, create, effectuate *formal*, execute, fulfil, generate *formal*, give rise to, initiate, make, perform, produce

---

effect or **affect**? See panel at **affect**

---

effective *adj* **1** *the treatment was effective*: adequate, capable, efficacious *formal*, efficient, productive, successful, useful **2** *effective exchange rates of the euro*: active, current, functioning, in force, operative, valid **3** *an effective design*: attractive, cogent *formal*, convincing, exciting, forceful, impressive, persuasive, potent, powerful, striking, telling **4** *decline in the effective demand for timber*: actual, essential, practical, virtual
Ⅎ **1** ineffective, powerless **4** theoretical

---

effective or **effectual**? *Effective* has a number of meanings: 'producing, or likely to produce, the intended result': *Aspirin is effective against many types of pain*; 'powerful': *He's a very effective speaker*; 'in operation': *The new regulations become effective at midnight*; 'in reality, even if not in theory': *Although not the king, he was the effective ruler of the country for twenty years*. *Effectual* puts more emphasis on the actual achievement of the desired result than *effective* does. If the police take *effective* measures to combat the rising crime rate, these measures have the desired effect, or are expected to, whereas if the police take *effectual measures*, there is no doubt that these measures are succeeding in reducing the crime rate.

---

effectiveness *n* ability, capability, clout *colloq*, cogency *formal*, efficacy *formal*, efficiency, force, influence, potency *formal*, power, strength, success, use, validity, vigour, weight
Ⅎ ineffectiveness, uselessness

effectual *adj* **1** *an effectual plan*: capable, effective, forcible, influential, operative, powerful, productive, serviceable, sound, successful, useful **2** *effectual contracts*: authoritative, binding, lawful, legal, valid
Ⅎ **1** ineffective, useless

effeminate *adj* delicate, feminine, sissy *colloq*, unmanly, wimpish *colloq*, womanly
Ⅎ manly

effervesce *v* **1** *the water was effervescing*: boil, bubble, ferment, fizz, foam, froth, sparkle **2** *to effervesce with sparkling conversation*: be animated, be ebullient *formal*, be exhilarated, be lively, be vivacious

effervescence *n* **1** *the nose-tickling effervescence of champagne*: bubbles, bubbling, ferment, fermentation, fizz, foam, foaming, froth, frothing, sparkle **2** *the effervescence of his performance*: animation, buoyancy, ebullience *formal*, enthusiasm, excitedness, excitement, exhilaration, exuberance, high spirits, liveliness, vim *colloq*, vitality, vivacity, zing *colloq*, zip *colloq*

effervescent *adj* **1** *effervescent water*: bubbling, bubbly, carbonated, fermenting, fizzing, fizzy, foaming, frothy, sparkling **2** *his effervescent personality*: animated, buoyant, ebullient *formal*, enthusiastic, excited, exhilarated, exuberant, lively, sparkling, vital, vivacious
Ⅎ **1** flat, still **2** dull

effete *adj* **1** *a rather effete man:* feeble, ineffectual *formal*, weak **2** *our effete society:* barren, corrupt, debased, decadent, decayed, degenerate, enfeebled, spoiled, sterile, tired out, weak, worn out
🖪 **1** vigorous **2** vigorous

efficacious *adj* active, adequate, capable, competent, effective, effectual, operative, potent, powerful, productive, strong, successful, sufficient, useful
🖪 ineffective, useless

efficacy *n* ability, capability, competence, effect, effectiveness, energy, force, influence, potency, power, strength, success, use, usefulness, virtue
🖪 ineffectiveness, uselessness

efficiency *n* ability, capability, competence, effectiveness, expertise, organization, productivity, proficiency, skilfulness, skill
🖪 incompetence, inefficiency

efficient *adj* **1** *an efficient worker:* able, capable, competent, effective, expert, organized, productive, proficient, skilful, well-organized, workmanlike **2** *an efficient business:* businesslike, effective, organized, productive, rationalized, streamlined, well-conducted, well-ordered, well-organized, well-run
🖪 **1** incompetent, inefficient **2** inefficient

effigy *n* carving, dummy, figure, guy, icon, idol, image, likeness, picture, portrait, representation, statue

effluent *n* discharge, effluence *formal*, effluvium *formal*, efflux *formal*, emanation *formal*, emission, exhalation *formal*, outflow, pollutant, pollution, sewage, waste

effort *n* **1** *pushing the car took real effort:* application, beef *colloq*, elbow grease *colloq*, energy, exertion, force, hard work, labour, muscle power, muscles *colloq*, pains, power, strain, stress, striving, struggle, sweat, sweat of your brow *colloq*, toil, travail *formal*, trouble **2** *she made a half-hearted effort:* attempt, bash *colloq*, crack *colloq*, endeavour, go *colloq*, shot *colloq*, stab *colloq*, try, whirl *colloq* **3** *paid handsomely for his efforts:* accomplishment, achievement, attainment, creation, deed, exploit, feat, opus, product, production, result, work

effortless *adj* easy, facile, painless, simple, smooth, straightforward, uncomplicated, undemanding, unexacting
🖪 complicated, demanding, difficult, exacting

effrontery *n* arrogance, audacity, boldness, brashness, brass *colloq*, brazenness, cheek *colloq*, cheekiness, chutzpah *colloq*, disrespect, face *colloq*, gall, impertinence, impudence, insolence, lip *colloq*, nerve *colloq*, presumption, temerity
🖪 respect, timidity

effulgent *adj* brilliant, glorious, glowing, incandescent *formal*, radiant, refulgent *formal*, resplendent *formal*, shining, splendid

effusion *n* discharge, effluence *formal*, efflux *formal*, emission, gush, outburst, outflow, outpouring, shedding, stream, voidance *formal*

effusive *adj* all mouth *colloq*, big-mouthed *colloq*, demonstrative, ebullient *formal*, enthusiastic, expansive, extravagant, exuberant, fulsome, gabby *colloq*, gassy *colloq*, gushing, lavish, lyrical, OTT *colloq*, over the top *colloq*,

overflowing, profuse, rhapsodic *formal*, talkative, unreserved, unrestrained, voluble
🖪 reserved, restrained

egg
▶ **egg on** coax, drive, encourage, excite, exhort *formal*, goad, incite, prick, prod, prompt, push, spur, stimulate, talk into, urge
🖪 discourage

egghead *n* academic, boffin, bookworm, brain, Einstein, genius, intellect, intellectual, know-all *colloq*, know-it-all *colloq*, scholar, thinker

ego *n* self, self-confidence, self-esteem, self-image, self-importance, self-worth, (sense of) identity

egoism *n* amour-propre, egocentricity, egomania, egotism, narcissism, self-absorption, self-centredness, self-importance, self-interest, selfishness, self-love, self-regard, self-seeking
🖪 altruism

egoist *n* egomaniac, egotist, narcissist, self-seeker

egoistic *adj* egocentric, egoistical, egomaniacal, egotistic, egotistical, narcissistic, self-absorbed, self-centred, self-important, self-involved, self-pleasing, self-seeking
🖪 altruistic

egotism *n* bigheadedness *colloq*, blowing your own horn *US colloq*, blowing your own trumpet *colloq*, boastfulness, braggadocio *formal*, conceitedness, egocentricity, egoism, egomania, narcissism, no thought for others, pride, self-admiration, self-centredness, self-conceit, self-importance, selfishness, self-love, self-regard, snobbery, superiority, swank *colloq*, vanity
🖪 humility

egotist *n* big mouth *colloq*, bighead *colloq*, bluffer, boaster, braggadocio, braggart, clever clogs *colloq*, clever dick *colloq*, egoist, egomaniac, self-admirer, show-off, smart alec *colloq*, swaggerer

egotistic *adj* bigheaded *colloq*, boasting, bragging, conceited, egocentric, egoistic, narcissistic, proud, self-admiring, self-centred, self-important, selfish, superior, swollen-headed *colloq*, vain
🖪 humble

egregious *adj* arrant, flagrant, glaring, grievous, gross, heinous, infamous, insufferable, intolerable, monstrous, notorious, outrageous, rank, scandalous, shocking
🖪 slight

egress *n* departure, emergence, escape, exit, exodus, issue, leaving, outlet, vent, way out

ejaculate *v* **1** *to ejaculate a fluid:* come *colloq*, discharge, eject, emit, expel, release, spurt **2** *'Oh no!' he ejaculated:* blurt (out), call (out), cry (out), exclaim, scream, shout (out), utter, yell

ejaculation *n* **1** *ejaculation of semen:* climax, coming *colloq*, discharge, ejection, emission, expulsion, orgasm, release, spurt **2** *'Amen!' and other such religious ejaculations:* call, cry, exclamation, scream, shout, utterance, yell

eject *v* **1** *how do you eject the CD on this thing?:* discharge, disgorge, emit, evacuate, excrete *formal*, expel, exude *formal*, release, spew, spout, vomit **2** *ejected the contents of her stomach:* discharge, disgorge, emit, evacuate, excrete

formal, release, spew, spout, vomit
3 *unceremoniously ejected from the theatre:* banish, boot out *colloq*, chuck out *colloq*, deport, drive out, evict, exile, expel, get rid of, kick out, oust, remove, show someone the door *colloq*, throw out, turf out *colloq*, turn out **4** *well-off until he was ejected from his job:* boot out *colloq*, dismiss, fire *colloq*, get rid of, give someone their cards *colloq*, kick out, sack *colloq* **5** *he ejected from the jet just before impact:* bail out, get out, propel, throw out, thrust out

ejection *n* banishment, deportation, discharge, dismissal, eviction, exile, expulsion, firing *colloq*, ousting, removal, sacking *colloq*, the boot *colloq*, the sack *colloq*

eke
▶ **eke out 1** *eke out supplies:* be economical with, economize on, fill out, go easy with *colloq*, husband, make something stretch, spin out, stretch **2** *eke out a living:* scrape, scratch, scrimp and save

elaborate *adj* **1** *elaborate plans:* careful, complex, complicated, detailed, exact, extensive, laboured, minute, painstaking, perfected, precise, studied, thorough **2** *elaborate designs:* complex, complicated, decorated, extravagant, fancy, fussy, intricate, involved, ornamental, ornate, ostentatious, rococo, showy
🔁 **2** plain, simple
♦ *v* amplify, develop, enhance, enlarge on, expand on, expatiate *formal*, explain, flesh out, improve, polish, refine
🔁 précis, simplify

elapse *v* go by, go on, lapse, pass, slip away, slip by

elastic *adj* **1** *a lightweight, elastic fabric:* bouncy, buoyant, flexible, plastic, pliable, pliant, resilient, rubbery, springy, stretchable, stretchy, supple, yielding **2** *this was the most elastic way of working:* accommodating, adaptable, adjustable, compliant *formal*, easy *colloq*, flexible, fluid, tolerant
🔁 **1** rigid **2** inflexible

elasticity *n* **1** *the skin's natural elasticity:* bounce, buoyancy, flexibility, give *colloq*, plasticity, pliability, resilience, springiness, stretch, stretchiness, suppleness **2** *elasticity of labour supply:* adaptability, adjustability, flexibility, tolerance
🔁 **1** rigidity **2** inflexibility

elated *adj* blissful, delighted, ecstatic, euphoric, excited, exhilarated, exultant, joyful, joyous *formal*, jubilant, on cloud nine *colloq*, over the moon *colloq*, overjoyed, rapturous, rhapsodic *formal*
🔁 despondent, downcast

elation *n* bliss, delight, ecstasy, euphoria, exhilaration, exultation, glee, high spirits, joy, joyfulness, joyousness *formal*, jubilation, rapture, transports of delight
🔁 depression, despondency

elbow *v* barge *colloq*, bump, crowd, jostle, knock, nudge, push, shoulder, shove *colloq*

elbow-room *n* breathing-space, freedom, latitude, Lebensraum, leeway, play, room, scope, space

elder *adj* ancient, first-born, older, senior
🔁 younger

elderly *adj* aged, aging, grey-haired, hoary, long in the tooth *colloq*, not as young as you were *colloq*, not getting any younger *colloq*, not long for this world *colloq*, old, over the hill *colloq*, past it *colloq*, senescent *formal*, senile
🔁 young, youthful
♦ *n* fossils *slang*, has-beens *colloq*, OAPs, old people, old-age pensioners, older adults, older generation, oldies *colloq*, pensioners, retired people, senior citizens, wrinklies *colloq*

eldest *adj* first, first-born, oldest
🔁 youngest

elect *v* adopt, appoint, choose, decide on, designate, determine, opt for, pick, plump for *colloq*, prefer, select, vote for
♦ *adj* **1** *an elect group:* choice, elite, hand-picked, picked, select **2** *the president elect:* chosen, designate, designated, prospective, to be

election *n* appointment, ballot, choice, choosing, decision, determination, hustings, picking, poll, preference, referendum, selection, vote, voting

elector *n* constituent, electorate, selector, voter

electric *adj* **1** *an electric light:* battery-operated, cordless, electric-powered, live, mains-operated, powered, rechargeable **2** *the atmosphere was electric:* charged, dynamic, electrifying, exciting, rousing, startling, stimulating, stirring, tense, thrilling
🔁 **2** flat, unexciting

electricity

Electricity and electronic terms include:
alternating current (AC), alternator, amp, ampere, amplifier, analogue signal, anode, band-pass filter, battery, bioelectricity, capacitance, capacitor, cathode, cathode-ray tube, cell, commutator, condenser, conductivity, coulomb, digital signal, diode, direct current (DC), Dolby (system), dynamo, eddy current, electrode, electrolyte, electromagnet, electron tube, farad, Faraday cage, Foucault current, frequency modulation, galvanic, galvanometer, generator, grid system, henry, impedance, induced current, inductance, integrated circuit, isoelectric, isoelectronic, logic gate, loudspeaker, microchip, mutual induction, ohm, optoelectronics, oscillator, oscilloscope, piezoelectricity, polarity, power station, reactance, resistance, resistor, rheostat, semiconductor, siemens, silicon chip, solenoid, solid state circuit, static electricity, step-down transformer, step-up transformer, superconductivity, switch, thermionics, thermistor, thyristor, transformer, transistor, triode, truth table, turboalternator, tweeter, valve, volt, voltage amplifier, voltaic, watt, Wheatstone bridge, woofer

---

Types of electrical components and devices include:
adaptor, ammeter, armature, battery, bayonet fitting, cable, ceiling rose, circuit breaker, conduit, continuity tester, copper conductor, dimmer switch, dry-cell battery, earthed plug, electrical screwdriver, electricity meter, extension lead, fluorescent tube, fuse, fusebox, fuse carrier, high voltage tester, insulating tape, lampholder, light bulb, multimeter,

neon lamp, socket, test lamp, three-core cable, three-pin plug, transducer, transformer, two-pin plug, universal test meter, voltage doubler, wire strippers

electrify *v* amaze, animate, astonish, astound, charge, excite, fire, galvanize, invigorate, jolt, rouse, shock, stagger, stimulate, stir, thrill
fa bore

elegance *n* beauty, chic, dignity, discernment, distinction, exquisiteness, fashionableness, gentility, grace, gracefulness, grandeur, luxury, poise, polish, politeness, propriety *formal*, refinement, smartness, sophistication, style, sumptuousness, taste, tastefulness
fa inelegance

elegant *adj* artistic, beautiful, charming, chic, cultivated, cultured, delicate, exquisite, fashionable, fine, genteel, graceful, handsome, lovely, modish, neat, polished, refined, smart, smooth, sophisticated, stylish, tasteful
fa inelegant, unfashionable, unrefined

elegiac *adj* doleful, funereal, keening, lamenting, melancholic, mournful, plaintive, sad, threnetic *formal*, threnetical *formal*, threnodial *formal*, threnodic *formal*, valedictory
fa happy

elegy *n* dirge, funeral poem, funeral song, lament, plaint, requiem, threnode *formal*, threnody *formal*

element *n* 1 *the elements of our discussion*: component, constituent, factor, feature, fragment, ingredient, member, part, piece, strand 2 *the elements of a subject*: basics, essentials, foundations, fundamentals, principles, rudiments 3 *an element of truth*: grain, hint, small amount, soupçon, suspicion, touch, trace 4 *the criminal element in society*: clique, faction, group, individual(s), party, set 5 *exposed to the elements*: atmospheric conditions, atmospheric forces, climate, storms, weather, wind and rain
fa 1 whole

elemental *adj* basic, forceful, fundamental, immense, natural, powerful, primitive, radical, rudimentary, uncontrolled

elementary *adj* basic, clear, easy, fundamental, introductory, primary, principal, rudimentary, simple, straightforward, uncomplicated
fa advanced, complicated

elephantine *adj* awkward, bulky, clumsy, enormous, heavy, huge, hulking, immense, large, lumbering, massive, vast, weighty

elevate *v* 1 *elevate the leg*: heighten, hike up *colloq*, hoist, lift, raise 2 *elevate His name in praise*: exalt, lift up, magnify, raise 3 *elevated to the captaincy*: advance, aggrandize, ennoble, exalt, kick upstairs *colloq*, move up the ladder *colloq*, promote, put on a pedestal *colloq*, upgrade 4 *the compliment elevated my spirits*: boost, brighten, buoy up, cheer, give a lift to, gladden, rouse, uplift
fa 1 lower 3 downgrade 4 depress

elevated *adj* 1 *with her elevated circumstances*: dignified, exalted, grand, great, important, lofty, noble 2 *elevated thoughts*: advanced, dignified, exalted, grand, lofty, moral, noble, sublime *formal* 3 *elevated ground*: high, hoisted, lifted (up), raised, rising, uplifted

elevation *n* 1 *her instant elevation to celebrity*: advancement, aggrandizement, go-getting *colloq*, leg-up *colloq*, preferment, promotion, rise, step up the ladder *colloq*, upgrading 2 *the prestige of his presence and the elevation of his sentiments*: dignity, eminence, exaltation, grandeur, loftiness, nobility, sublimity *formal* 3 *an elevation of seventy feet*: altitude, height, rise 4 *on a slight elevation*: hill, mound, mount, rise
fa 1 demotion

elf *n* banshee, brownie, fairy, gnome, goblin, hobgoblin, imp, leprechaun, puck, sprite, troll

elfin *adj* charming, delicate, elfish, elflike, frolicsome, impish, mischievous, petite, playful, puckish, small, sprightly

elicit *v* bring out, call forth *formal*, cause, derive, draw out, educe *formal*, evoke, exact, extort, extract, obtain, worm out *colloq*, wrest

eligible *adj* acceptable, appropriate, desirable, fit, fitting, proper, qualified, suitable, worthy
fa ineligible

eliminate *v* 1 *eliminate all nuclear weapons*: cut out, delete, dispense with, dispose of, disregard, do away with, drop, eradicate, extinguish, get rid of, put an end/a stop to, remove, rub out, stamp out, take out 2 *eliminated in the third round*: annihilate *colloq*, beat, conquer, defeat, disregard, exclude, expel, hammer *colloq*, knock out *colloq*, lick *colloq*, omit, overwhelm, reject, thrash *colloq* 3 *eliminate that line of enquiry*: disregard, exclude, omit 4 *eliminate TB-infected badgers*: bump off *colloq*, do away with, do in *colloq*, exterminate, kill, liquidate *colloq*, murder, rub out *colloq*, wipe out *colloq*
fa 1 accept, include

elite *n* aristocracy, best, cream, crème de la crème, elect, establishment, gentry, high society, jet set *colloq*, nobility, pick, pick of the bunch *colloq*, upper classes
♦ *adj* aristocratic, best, choice, exclusive, first-class, noble, select, upper-class

elixir *n* concentrate, cure-all, essence, extract, mixture, nostrum, panacea, pith, potion, principle, quintessence, remedy, solution, syrup, tincture

elliptical *adj* 1 *an elliptical orbit*: egg-shaped, oval, oviform, ovoid(al) 2 *his language is often elliptical*: abstruse *formal*, ambiguous, concentrated, concise, condensed, cryptic, incomprehensible, laconic, oblique, obscure, recondite *formal*, terse, unfathomable
fa 2 clear, direct

elocution *n* articulation, delivery, diction, enunciation *formal*, oratory *formal*, phrasing, pronunciation, rhetoric, speech, utterance, voice production

elongate *v* draw out, extend, lengthen, make longer, prolong, protract *formal*, stretch

elongated *adj* extended, lengthened, long, prolonged, protracted, stretched

elope *v* abscond, bolt, decamp, disappear, do a bunk *colloq*, escape, flee, leave, make off, run away, run off, slip away, steal away

eloquence *n* articulateness, blarney *colloq*, diction, expression, expressiveness, facility, facundity *formal*, flow of words, fluency,

forcefulness, gassiness *colloq*, gift of the gab *colloq*, oratory, persuasiveness, rhetoric
🔁 inarticulateness

eloquent *adj* articulate, effective, expressive, fluent, forceful, glib, graceful, moving, persuasive, plausible, stirring, vivid, vocal, voluble, well-expressed, well-spoken
🔁 inarticulate, tongue-tied

elsewhere *adv* abroad, in/to another place, not here, somewhere else
🔁 here

elucidate *v* clarify, clear up, exemplify, explain, explicate *formal*, expound *formal*, fill in, give an example, illuminate, illustrate, interpret, make clear, simplify, spell out, state simply, throw/shed light on, unfold
🔁 confuse

elucidation *n* annotation, clarification, comment, commentary, explanation, explication *formal*, exposition *formal*, footnote, gloss, illumination, illustration, interpretation, marginalia

elude *v* circumvent *formal*, dodge *colloq*, duck *colloq*, escape, evade, flee, get away from, give someone the slip, shake off, shirk, slip through someone's fingers *colloq*, throw someone off the scent

---
elude or *allude*? See panel at **allude**
---

elusive *adj* **1** *that elusive divine presence:* baffling, difficult to describe, indefinable, intangible, puzzling, subtle, transient, transitory, unanalysable **2** *her answer was elusive:* baffling, misleading, puzzling **3** *the elusive Mr Shepherd:* difficult to find, dodgy *colloq*, evasive, hard to catch, shifty *colloq*, slippery, tricky

emaciated *adj* all skin and bone *colloq*, anorexic, attenuated *formal*, cadaverous *formal*, drawn, gaunt, haggard, lean, meagre, pinched, scrawny, skeletal, skinny, thin, thin as a rake *colloq*, wasted
🔁 plump, well-fed

emaciation *n* atrophy *formal*, gauntness, haggardness, leanness, scrawniness, thinness
🔁 plumpness

emanate *v* **1** *this man emanated light:* discharge, emit, exhale *formal*, give off, give out, radiate, send out **2** *application programs have emanated from the US:* arise, come, derive, emerge, flow, issue, originate, proceed, spring, stem

emanation *n* discharge, effluence, effluent, effluvium *formal*, efflux *formal*, effluxion *formal*, effusion *formal*, emission, flow, radiation

emancipate *v* deliver, discharge, enfranchise, free, liberate, loose, manumit *formal*, release, set free, set loose, unchain, unfetter, unshackle, untie, unyoke
🔁 enslave

emancipation *n* deliverance, discharge, enfranchisement, freedom, liberation, liberty, manumission *formal*, release, setting free, unbinding, unchaining, unfettering
🔁 enslavement

emasculate *v* **1** *the rescue dogs were emasculated as a matter of course:* castrate, geld, neuter, spay

2 *emasculate his opponents:* cripple, debilitate, enervate *formal*, impoverish, soften, weaken
🔁 **2** boost, vitalize

embalm *v* conserve, mummify, preserve

embankment *n* causeway, dam, earthwork, levee, rampart

embargo *n* ban, bar, barrier, blockage, check, hindrance, impediment, interdiction *formal*, obstruction, prohibition, proscription *formal*, restraint, restriction, seizure, stoppage
♦ *v* ban, bar, block, check, impede, interdict *formal*, obstruct, prohibit, proscribe *formal*, restrain, restrict, seize, stop
🔁 allow

embark *v* board (ship), go aboard, take ship
🔁 disembark
▶ **embark on** begin, commence, engage, enter (on), initiate, launch into, set about, start, undertake, venture into
🔁 complete, finish

embarrass *v* confuse, discomfit *formal*, discompose, disconcert, discountenance *formal*, distress, fluster, humiliate, make awkward/ashamed, mortify, shame, show up, upset

embarrassed *adj* abashed, ashamed, awkward, confused, discomfited *formal*, disconcerted, distressed, guilty, humiliated, mortified, self-conscious, shamed, sheepish *colloq*, shown up, uncomfortable, upset
🔁 unembarrassed

embarrassing *adj* awkward, compromising, discomfiting *formal*, disconcerting, discountenancing *formal*, distressing, humiliating, indelicate *formal*, mortifying, painful, sensitive, shameful, shaming, touchy *colloq*, tricky, uncomfortable, upsetting

embarrassment *n* **1** *the embarrassment of not remembering:* awkwardness, bashfulness, chagrin *formal*, confusion, discomfiture *formal*, discomposure, distress, guilt, humiliation, mortification, self-consciousness, shame **2** *a greater embarrassment arose:* constraint, difficulty, dilemma, fix *colloq*, mess, pickle *colloq*, plight, predicament, scrape *colloq* **3** *an embarrassment of riches:* abundance, excess, profusion *formal*, superabundance, surplus

embassy *n* consulate, delegation, deputation, legation, ministry, mission

embed *v* drive, fix, hammer, implant, insert, plant, root, set, sink

embellish *v* adorn, beautify, bedeck *formal*, bespangle *formal*, deck, decorate, dress up, elaborate, embroider, enhance, enrich, exaggerate, festoon, garnish, gild, grace, ornament, trim, varnish
🔁 denude *formal*, simplify

embellishment *n* adornment, decoration, elaboration, embroidery, enhancement, enrichment, exaggeration, garnish, gilding, ornament, ornamentation, trimming

embers *n* ashes, charcoal, cinders, residue

embezzle *v* appropriate, defalcate *formal*, filch *colloq*, have your fingers/hand in the till *colloq*, misappropriate *formal*, nab *colloq*, nick *colloq*, peculate *formal*, pilfer, pinch *colloq*, purloin *formal*, rip off *colloq*, rob, steal, swindle

embezzlement *n* appropriation *formal*, defalcation *formal*, filching *colloq*, fraud, misappropriation *formal*, nabbing *colloq*, nicking *colloq*, pilfering, stealing, theft

embezzler *n* cheat, con man *colloq*, crook *colloq*, defalcator *formal*, diddler *colloq*, fraud, peculator *formal*, robber, thief

embittered *adj* angry, bitter, disaffected, disenchanted, disillusioned, exasperated, piqued, rankled, resentful, sour

emblazon *v* **1** *emblazoned with the company logo*: adorn, blazon, colour, decorate, depict, embellish, illuminate, ornament, paint **2** *the minstrels emblazoned King Arthur's deeds*: extol, glorify, laud *formal*, praise, proclaim, publicize, publish, trumpet

emblem *n* badge, crest, device, figure, image, insignia, logo, mark, representation, sign, symbol, token

emblematic *adj* emblematical, figurative, representative, representing, symbolic, symbolical

embodiment *n* epitome, example, exemplification, expression, incarnation, manifestation *formal*, model, personification, realization, representation, type

embody *v* **1** *the sense of the literature it embodies*: exemplify, express, incorporate, manifest *formal*, personify, represent, stand for, symbolize, typify **2** *the idea of justice embodied in the law*: assimilate, bring together, collect, combine, contain, include, incorporate, integrate, take in

embolden *v* animate, cheer, encourage, fire, give courage to, hearten, inflame, inspire, invigorate, make brave/bold, nerve, reassure, rouse, stimulate, stir, strengthen, vitalize
▭ dishearten

embrace *v* **1** *she embraced her son*: canoodle *colloq*, clasp, cuddle, grasp, hold, hug, neck *colloq*, put/throw your arms around, smooch *colloq*, squeeze, take into your arms **2** *architecture which embraced bits of everything*: comprise *formal*, contain, cover, encompass, include, incorporate, involve, span, take in **3** *embraced this custom with gusto*: accept, espouse *formal*, receive eagerly, receive wholeheartedly, take on board *colloq*, take up, welcome
♦ *n* clasp, clinch *colloq*, cuddle, hold, hug, necking *colloq*, slap and tickle *colloq*, smooch *colloq*, squeeze

embrocation *n* cream, epithem *formal*, lotion, ointment, salve

embroider *v* **1** *she embroidered her initials on the linen*: decorate, sew, stitch **2** *he embroidered his stories with colourful detail*: colour, dress up, elaborate, embellish, enhance, enrich, exaggerate, garnish

embroidery *n* fancywork, needlepoint, needlework, sewing, tapestry, tatting

Types of embroidery stitch include:
backstitch, blanket, bullion, chain, chevron, cross, feather, fishbone, French knot, half-cross, herringbone, lazy-daisy, longstitch, long-and-short, moss, Oriental couching, Romanian couching, running, satin, stem, straight, Swiss darning, tent

embroil *v* catch up in, draw into, enmesh, entangle, implicate, incriminate, involve, mix up

embryo *n* **1** *embryo research*: foetus, unborn child **2** *the embryo of the plan*: basics, beginning, germ, nucleus, root, rudiments

embryonic *adj* beginning, early, elementary, germinal, immature, inchoate *formal*, incipient *formal*, primary, rudimentary, undeveloped, unformed
▭ developed

emend *v* alter, amend, correct, edit, improve, polish, rectify, redact *formal*, refine, revise, rewrite

emend or *amend*? See panel at **amend**

emendation *n* alteration, amendment, correction, corrigendum *formal*, editing, improvement, rectification *formal*, redaction *formal*, refinement, revision, rewriting

emerge *v* **1** *emerge from the office*: appear, arise, come forth, come into view, come out, develop, emanate, issue, materialize, proceed, rise, surface, turn up **2** *the facts emerged*: appear, become known, come out, come to light, crop up *colloq*, transpire, turn out
▭ **1** disappear

emergence *n* advent *formal*, appearance, arrival, coming, dawn, development, disclosure, issue, rise, springing-up, unfolding
▭ disappearance

emergency *n* accident, calamity, catastrophe, crisis, danger, difficulty, dilemma, disaster, exigency *formal*, fix *colloq*, hot water *colloq*, mess *colloq*, pickle *colloq*, pinch, plight, predicament, quandary, scrape *colloq*, strait
♦ *adj* alternative, back-up, extra, fall-back, reserve, spare, substitute

emergent *adj* budding, coming (out), developing, embryonic, emerging, independent, rising
▭ declining, disappearing

emetic *adj* emetical, vomitive, vomitory
♦ *n* vomit, vomitive, vomitory

emigrate *v* depart, leave your home/native country, migrate, move, move abroad, relocate, resettle

emigration *n* departure, exodus, expatriation, journey, migration, moving abroad, relocation, removal

eminence *n* celebrity, dignity, distinction, esteem, fame, greatness, illustriousness, importance, notability, note, pre-eminence, prestige, prominence, rank, renown, reputation

eminent *adj* celebrated, conspicuous, distinguished, elevated, esteemed, famous, grand, great, high-ranking, illustrious, important, notable, noteworthy, outstanding, pre-eminent, prestigious, prominent, renowned, respected, superior, well-known
▭ obscure, unimportant, unknown

eminently *adv* conspicuously, exceedingly, exceptionally, extremely, greatly, highly, notably, outstandingly, par excellence, prominently, remarkably, signally, strikingly, surpassingly, very, well

emissary *n* agent, ambassador, courier, delegate, deputy, envoy, go-between, herald, intermediary, messenger, representative, scout, spy

emission *n* diffusion, discharge, ejection, emanation, exhalation, exudation, giving-off, giving-out, issue, production, radiation, release, transmission

emit *v* diffuse, discharge, eject, emanate, excrete *formal*, express, exude, give off, give out, issue, leak, let out, ooze, pour out, produce, radiate, release, send forth, send out, shed, throw out, vent
F absorb

emollient *adj* **1** *rich, emollient shampoo*: assuaging, assuasive *formal*, balsamic *formal*, demulcent *formal*, lenitive *formal*, mitigative *formal*, mollifying, softening **2** *an emollient reply was drafted*: appeasing, calming, conciliatory, placatory, propitiatory *formal*
♦ *n* balm, cream, lenitive *formal*, liniment *formal*, lotion, moisturizer, oil, ointment, poultice, salve, unguent *formal*

emolument *n* allowance, benefit, compensation, earnings, fee, gain, hire, honorarium, pay, payment, profit(s), recompense, remuneration, return, reward, salary, stipend, wages

emotion *n* anger, ardour, despair, dread, ecstasy, excitement, fear, feeling, fervour, grief, happiness, hate, joy, passion, reaction, sadness, sensation, sense, sentiment, sorrow, vehemence, warmth

emotional *adj* **1** *she was rarely emotional*: ardent, demonstrative, enthusiastic, excitable, feeling, fervent, fiery, heated, hot-blooded, impassioned, loving, moved, overcharged, passionate, responsive, roused, sensitive, sentimental, temperamental, tempestuous, tender, warm, zealous **2** *the emotional force of his songs*: emotive, exciting, heart-warming, moving, pathetic, poignant, schmaltzy *colloq*, sentimental, soppy *colloq*, soul-stirring, stirring, tear-jerking *colloq*, thrilling, touching **3** *on this highly emotional issue*: contentious, delicate, emotive, sensitive, tricky
F **1** calm, cold, detached, unemotional

emotionless *adj* blank, clinical, cold, cold-blooded, cool, detached, distant, frigid, glacial, impassive, imperturbable *formal*, indifferent, phlegmatic *formal*, remote, toneless, undemonstrative, unemotional, unfeeling
F emotional

emotive *adj* awkward, controversial, delicate, inflammatory, sensitive, touchy

empathize *v* be sensitive towards, comfort, feel for, identify with, put yourself in someone's shoes *colloq*, share, support, understand

emperor *n* imperator, kaiser, mikado, ruler, shogun, sovereign, tsar

emphasis *n* **1** *emphasis on practical work*: accent, attention, importance, insistence, intensity, mark, moment, positiveness, power, pre-eminence, priority, prominence, significance, strength, stress, underscoring, urgency, weight **2** *the emphasis is on the second syllable*: accent, accentuation, force, stress, weight

emphasize *v* **1** *emphasize the differences*: accent, accentuate, bring to the fore, call attention to, drive the point home *colloq*, dwell on, feature, heighten, highlight, insist on, intensify, play up, point up, press home, punctuate, spotlight, strengthen, stress, underline, weight **2** *emphasize a syllable*: accent, accentuate, put stress on, stress
F **1** play down, understate

emphatic *adj* absolute, categorical, certain, decided, definite, direct, distinct, distinctive, earnest, energetic, forceful, forcible, important, impressive, insistent, marked, momentous, positive, powerful, pronounced, significant, striking, strong, telling, unequivocal, unmistakable, vigorous, vivid
F hesitant, tentative, understated

empire *n* **1** *the empire of the Incas*: commonwealth, domain, dominion, kingdom, province, realm, territory **2** *the empire of reason*: authority, command, control, dominion, government, jurisdiction, power, rule, sovereignty, supremacy, sway

empirical *adj* experiential *formal*, experimental, observed, practical, pragmatic
F conjectural, speculative, theoretical

employ *v* **1** *the firm employs 200 people*: appoint, apprentice, commission, engage, enlist, fill, hire, occupy, put on the payroll, recruit, retain, sign up, take on, take up **2** *employing mechanical means*: apply, bring into play, bring to bear, draw on, exercise, exert, exploit, make use of, ply, put to use, use, utilize

employed *adj* active, busy, earning, engaged, hired, in employment, in work, occupied, preoccupied, with a job, working
F jobless, unemployed

employee *n* artisan, assistant, blue-collar worker, craftsman, hand, job-holder, labourer, member of staff, office worker, operative, tradesman, wage-earner, white-collar worker, worker, working man, working person, working woman.

employer *n* boss *colloq*, business, company, director, establishment, executive, firm, gaffer *colloq*, head, management, manager, organization, owner, proprietor, skipper *colloq*

employment *n* **1** *his current employment*: business, calling, craft, job, line *colloq*, métier, occupation, profession, pursuit, service, situation, trade, vocation, work **2** *the employment of illegal immigrants*: apprenticeship, employ, engagement, enlistment, hire, hiring, recruitment, signing-up, taking-on **3** *the employment of the reservists*: adoption, exercising, exploitation, use, utilization
F **1** unemployment

emporium *n* bazaar, establishment, fair, market, market-place, mart, shop, store

empower *v* **1** *empowered them to impose sanctions*: accredit *formal*, authorize, certify, commission, entitle, license, permit, qualify, sanction, warrant **2** *information and education empower people*: enable, equip, give power/means to

emptiness *n* **1** *the emptiness of the Pacific*: bareness, barrenness, desolation, hiatus *formal*, hollowness, hunger, vacantness, void, voidness **2** *a feeling of emptiness swept over her*: aimlessness, futility, ineffectiveness, insubstantiality,

meaninglessness, purposelessness, senselessness, unreality, uselessness, worthlessness
🔁 1 fullness

empty *adj* **1** *the house was empty:* available, bare, barren, clear, containing nothing, deserted, desolate, free, hollow, unfilled, uninhabited, unoccupied, vacant, void, with nothing in it **2** *an empty gesture:* aimless, fruitless, futile, idle, ineffective, ineffectual *formal,* insincere, insubstantial, meaningless, senseless, trivial, unreal, useless, vain, worthless **3** *an empty period of life:* aimless, futile, hollow, meaningless, purposeless, senseless, useless, vain, worthless **4** *his empty gaze scared her:* blank, deadpan, expressionless, inane, vacant, vacuous
🔁 1 full 2 meaningful 3 eventful, interesting
♦ *v* clear, discharge, drain, evacuate, exhaust, flow out, go out, gut, issue, leave, pour out, turn out, unload, use up, vacate, void
🔁 fill

empty-headed *adj* batty *colloq,* daft *colloq,* dopey *colloq,* dotty *colloq,* feather-brained *colloq,* foolish, frivolous, inane, scatter-brained *colloq,* scatty *colloq,* silly, stupid
🔁 intelligent

emulate *v* compete with, contend with, copy, echo, follow, imitate, match, mimic, model yourself on, rival, take a leaf out of someone's book *colloq,* vie with

emulation *n* challenge, competition, contention, contest, copying, echoing, following, imitation, matching, mimicry, rivalry, strife

enable *v* **1** *enabled by a special act of Parliament:* accredit *formal,* allow, authorize, commission, empower, endue, entitle, license, permit, qualify, sanction, validate *formal,* warrant **2** *enabled her to continue her studies:* allow, clear/pave the way for, equip, facilitate, further, help, make easier, make possible, permit, prepare
🔁 1 forbid, inhibit, prevent

enact *v* **1** *emergency legislation could be enacted:* authorize, command, decree, establish, legislate, make law, ordain, order, pass, ratify, rule, sanction **2** *a scene enacted up and down the country:* act out, appear as, depict, perform, play, portray, represent
🔁 1 repeal, rescind

enactment *n* **1** *others have called for the enactment of a bill of rights:* approval, authorization, ordinance, passing, ratification, regulation, sanction **2** *the number of enactments:* act, bill, command, commandment, decree, edict, law, legislation, order, ordinance, rule, sanction, statute **3** *an enactment of his fantasies:* acting, performance, performing, play, playing, portrayal, representation, staging
🔁 1 repeal 2 repeal

enamoured *adj* bewitched, captivated, charmed, enchanted, enthralled, entranced, fascinated, fond, in love with, infatuated, keen, mad, smitten, taken, wild

encampment *n* base, bivouac, camp, camping-ground, campsite, quarters, tents

encapsulate *v* abridge, capture, compress, condense, contain, digest, epitomize, exemplify, include, précis, represent, sum up, summarize, take in, typify

enchant *v* **1** *enchanted by his playing:* allure, attract, captivate, charm, delight, enamour, enrapture, fascinate, thrill **2** *a wizard enchants two sisters:* beguile, bewitch, enthral, entrance, hypnotize, mesmerize, spellbind
🔁 1 repel

enchanter *n* conjurer, magician, magus, mesmerist, necromancer, reim-kennar, sorcerer, spellbinder, warlock, witch, wizard

enchanting *adj* alluring, appealing, attractive, bewitching, captivating, charming, delightful, endearing, entrancing, fascinating, irresistible, lovely, mesmerizing, pleasant, ravishing, winsome, wonderful
🔁 boring, repellent

enchantment *n* **1** *the many enchantments of this isle:* allure, allurement, appeal, attractiveness, bliss, charm, delight, ecstasy, fascination, glamour, rapture **2** *as if I were under an enchantment:* charm, conjuration *formal,* hypnotism, incantation, magic, mesmerism, necromancy *formal,* sorcery, spell, witchcraft, wizardry
🔁 1 disenchantment

enchantress *n* **1** *a spell cast by an enchantress:* Circe, conjurer, lamia, magician, necromancer *formal,* sorceress, spellbinder, witch **2** *fancied herself as a sexual enchantress:* charmer, femme fatale, seductress, siren, vamp

encircle *v* circle, circumscribe *formal,* close in, compass, crowd, enclose, encompass, enfold, envelop, gird *formal,* girdle, hem in, orbit, ring, surround

enclose *v* **1** *a wall encloses the garden:* bound, cage, circle, circumscribe *formal,* close in, cocoon, confine, corral, cover, encase, encircle, encompass, pen, envelop, fence, frame, hedge, hem in, hold, pen, ring, shut in, surround **2** *please enclose a self-addressed envelope:* comprehend *formal,* contain, include, insert, put in, send with

enclosure *n* **1** *herded into the enclosure:* area, arena, cloister, close, compound, corral, court, fold, kraal, paddock, pen, pound, ring, run, stockade, sty, yard **2** *the enclosure of a large self-addressed envelope:* addition, inclusion, insertion

encompass *v* **1** *a small wall encompassed the cottage:* circle, circumscribe *formal,* close in, confine, encircle, enclose, envelop, gird *formal,* hem in, hold, ring, shut in, surround **2** *it encompasses a number of themes:* admit, comprehend *formal,* comprise *formal,* contain, cover, embody, embrace, include, incorporate, involve, span, take in

encore *n* additional/extra performance, repeat, repetition

encounter *v* **1** *encounter difficulties:* be faced with, be/come up against, confront, cope with, deal with, experience, face **2** *the moment she encounters Romeo:* bump into *colloq,* chance upon *formal,* come across, happen on *formal,* meet, run across, run into *colloq,* stumble across **3** *sent to encounter guerilla troops:* clash with, combat, come into conflict with, contend, cross swords with *colloq,* do battle with, engage, fight, grapple with, strive, struggle, tussle
♦ *n* **1** *their first encounter since the semi-finals:*

brush, confrontation, contact, meeting, rendezvous **2** *a bad-tempered encounter at a checkpoint*: action, battle, clash, collision, combat, conflict, contest, dispute, engagement, fight, run-in, set-to *colloq*, skirmish, struggle

encourage *v* **1** *encouraged by the positive response*: animate, be supportive to, buoy up, cheer, comfort, console, embolden, exhort *formal*, give moral support to, hearten, incite, inspire, motivate, rally, reassure, rouse, spur, stimulate, stir, urge **2** *encourage someone to do something*: convince, egg on *colloq*, exhort *formal*, influence, persuade, prompt, sway, talk into, win over **3** *encouraged expansion*: advance, advocate, aid, assist, back, boost, favour, forward, foster, further, help, promote, strengthen, support
F3 1 depress, discourage **2** discourage, dissuade **3** discourage

encouragement *n* **1** *a great encouragement*: cheer, consolation, exhortation *formal*, incentive, incitement, inspiration, motivation, pep talk *colloq*, persuasion, reassurance, stimulation, succour *formal*, urging **2** *the council's encouragement of music*: aid, assistance, backing, boost, furtherance, help, promotion, shot in the arm *colloq*, stimulus, support
F3 1 disapproval, discouragement

encouraging *adj* auspicious *formal*, bright, cheerful, cheering, comforting, heartening, hopeful, inspiring, promising, reassuring, rosy, satisfactory, stimulating, uplifting
F3 discouraging

encroach *v* impinge, infiltrate, infringe, intrude, invade, make inroads, muscle in on *colloq*, overrun, overstep, tread on someone's toes *colloq*, trespass, usurp

encroachment *n* incursion *formal*, infiltration, infringement, intrusion, invasion, overstepping, trespassing

encumber *v* **1** *encumbered with heavy loads*: burden, check, constrain, cramp, hamper, handicap, hinder, impede, inconvenience, obstruct, oppress, overload, prevent, restrain, retard *formal*, saddle, slow down, strain, stress, weigh down **2** *encumbering every available space*: block, congest, cram, jam, pack, stuff

encumbrance *n* albatross, burden, constraint, cross, cumbrance *formal*, difficulty, handicap, hindrance, impediment, inconvenience, liability, load, millstone, obligation, obstacle, obstruction, responsibility, restraint, strain, stress, weight

encyclopedic *adj* all-embracing, all-encompassing, all-inclusive, broad, compendious, complete, comprehensive, exhaustive, thorough, universal, vast, wide-ranging
F3 incomplete, narrow

end *n* **1** *end of the twentieth century*: cessation *formal*, close, completion, conclusion, culmination, dénouement, ending, epilogue, finale, finish, termination *formal* **2** *end of the earth*: border, boundary, edge, extremity, limit, margin, tip **3** *cigarette ends litter the garden*: butt, fragment, left-over, leftovers, remainder, remnant, scrap, stub, tip, vestige **4** *for political ends*: aim, design, goal, intent *formal*, intention, motive, object, objective, point, purpose, reason, target **5** *go to*

any lengths to achieve that end: consequence, issue, outcome, result, upshot **6** *the end came quickly*: death, demise *formal*, destruction, dissolution, doom, downfall, extermination, extinction, ruin **7** *look after the financial end of things*: area, aspect, branch, department, field, part, section, side
F3 1 beginning, start **6** birth
◆ *v* **1** *their marriage ended soon after that*: be over, break off, cease *formal*, come/bring to an end, culminate, die out, expire, fade away, finish, round off, run out, stop **2** *the track ends with a long guitar solo*: break off, close, complete, conclude *formal*, discontinue *formal*, finish, terminate *formal*, wind up *colloq* **3** *injury ended his hope of a medal*: abolish, annihilate, destroy, dissolve, exterminate, extinguish, ruin
F3 1 begin, commence *formal*, start **2** begin, commence *formal*, start

endanger *v* compromise, expose, hazard, imperil *formal*, jeopardize, put at risk, put in danger, put in jeopardy, risk, threaten
F3 protect

endearing *adj* adorable, appealing, attractive, captivating, charming, delightful, enchanting, engaging, lovable, sweet, winsome

endearment *n* affection, attachment, diminutive, fondness, hypocorism *formal*, love, pet-name, sweet nothing

endeavour *v* aim, aspire, attempt, do your best, labour, seek *formal*, strive, struggle, take pains, try, try your hand at, undertake, venture
◆ *n* aim, attempt, bash *colloq*, crack *colloq*, effort, enterprise, go *colloq*, shot *colloq*, stab *colloq*, striving, try, undertaking, venture

ending *n* cessation *formal*, climax, close, completion, conclusion, consummation *formal*, culmination, dénouement, end, epilogue, finale, finish, resolution, termination *formal*
F3 beginning, start

endless *adj* **1** *endless possibilities*: boundless, infinite, limitless, measureless, unending, unlimited, without end **2** *bored me with her endless questions*: boring, ceaseless *formal*, constant, continual, continuous, eternal, interminable, monotonous, perpetual, undying **3** *an endless expanse of clear blue*: constant, continuous, entire, unbroken, uninterrupted, whole
F3 1 finite, limited **2** temporary

endorse *v* **1** *appearing to endorse the policy change*: adopt, advocate, affirm *formal*, approve, authorize, back, be/get behind, confirm, favour, ratify, recommend, sanction, subscribe to, support, sustain, throw your weight behind *colloq*, uphold, vouch for, warrant **2** *you need to endorse the cheque*: countersign, sign

endorsement *n* **1** *the bill gained parliamentary endorsement*: advocacy, affirmation *formal*, approval, authorization, backing, commendation, confirmation, OK *colloq*, ratification, recommendation, sanction, seal of approval, support, testimonial, warrant **2** *write an endorsement on a copy of the letter*: countersignature, signature

endow *v* **1** *endowed many charities*: bequeath money for *formal*, finance, fund, provide for, set up **2** *endow with higher mental functions*: bless with, endue with, give, present, provide

endowment *n* **1** *founded by an endowment*: award, benefaction *formal*, bequest *formal*, bestowal *formal*, donation, dowry, finance, fund, gift, grant, income, legacy, present, provision, revenue, settlement **2** *physical endowments*: ability, aptitude, attribute, capability, capacity, faculty, flair, genius, gift, power, qualification, quality, talent

endurable *adj* bearable, manageable, sufferable, supportable, sustainable, tolerable, withstandable
◳ intolerable, unbearable

endurance *n* backbone, bottle *colloq*, durability, fortitude *formal*, guts *colloq*, patience, perseverance, persistence, resignation, resolution, spunk *colloq*, stability, stamina, staying power, stickability *colloq*, stoicism, strength, sufferance, tenacity, toleration

endure *v* **1** *endure hardship*: abide, allow, bear, brave, cope with, encounter, experience, face, go through, meet, permit, put up with, stand, stick, stomach *colloq*, submit to, suffer, support, sustain, swallow, take, tolerate, undergo, weather, withstand **2** *a peace that will endure for ever*: abide *formal*, continue, hold, last, live, persist, prevail, remain, stay, survive

enduring *adj* abiding, chronic, continuing, durable, eternal, firm, immortal, imperishable, lasting, long-lasting, long-standing, permanent, perpetual, persistent, persisting, prevailing, remaining, stable, steadfast, steady, surviving, unfaltering, unwavering
◳ brief, changeable, ephemeral, fleeting, momentary, passing

enemy *n* adversary, antagonist, competitor, foe *formal*, opponent, opposer, other side, rival, the competition, the opposition
◳ ally, friend

energetic *adj* active, animated, boisterous, brisk, bursting with energy *colloq*, dynamic, forceful, full of beans *colloq*, go-getting *colloq*, high-powered, indefatigable, lively, potent, powerful, punchy *colloq*, spirited, strenuous, strong, tireless, vigorous, zestful, zippy *colloq*
◳ idle, inactive, lethargic, sluggish

energize *v* activate, animate, arouse, electrify, enliven, galvanize, invigorate, liven, motivate, pep up *colloq*, quicken, stimulate, stir, vitalize, vivify
◳ daunt

energy *n* activity, animation, ardour, brio *colloq*, drive, dynamism, effectiveness, effervescence, efficiency, enthusiasm, exertion, fire, force, forcefulness, get-up-and-go *colloq*, intensity, life, liveliness, might *formal*, pizzazz *colloq*, potency, power, push *colloq*, sparkle, spirit, stamina, strength, verve, vigour, vitality, vivacity, zeal, zest, zip *colloq*
◳ inertia, lethargy, weakness

enervated *adj* debilitated *formal*, devitalized, done in *colloq*, effete *formal*, enfeebled *formal*, exhausted, fatigued, feeble, incapacitated, limp, paralysed, run-down *colloq*, sapped, spent, tired, undermined, unmanned, unnerved, washed-out *colloq*, weak, weakened, worn out
◳ active, energetic

enfeeble *v* debilitate *formal*, deplete, devitalize, diminish, enervate *formal*, exhaust, fatigue, geld,

reduce, sap, undermine, unhinge, unnerve, weaken, wear out
◳ strengthen

enfold *v* **1** *darkness enfolded them*: encircle, enclose, encompass, envelop, enwrap, fold, shroud, swathe, wrap (up) **2** *plump arms enfolded her*: clasp, embrace, hold, hug

enforce *v* administer, apply, carry out, discharge, execute, fulfil, implement, impose

enforced *adj* binding, compelled, compulsory, constrained, dictated, forced, imposed, involuntary, necessary, obliged, ordained, prescribed, required, unavoidable

enforcement *n* administration, application, discharge, execution, fulfilment, implementation, imposition, prosecution

enfranchise *v* emancipate *formal*, free, give suffrage to *formal*, give the right to vote to, give the vote to, liberate, manumit *formal*, release
◳ disenfranchise

enfranchisement *n* emancipation *formal*, freedom, freeing, giving the right to vote, liberating, liberation, manumission *formal*, release, suffrage *formal*, voting rights
◳ disenfranchisement

engage *v* **1** *engage in conversation*: become involved in/with, do, embark on, enter into, involve, join in, participate, practise, take part, take up, undertake **2** *engage the eye*: allure, attract, captivate, catch, charm, draw, gain, win **3** *engage her interest*: absorb, busy, employ, engross, fill, grip, hold, occupy, preoccupy, tie up **4** *engage a caretaker*: appoint, commission, contract, employ, enlist, enrol, hire, put on the payroll, recruit, sign up/on, take on **5** *engage first gear*: attach, enmesh, fit together, interact, interconnect, interlock, join, mesh **6** *engage the enemy*: assail, attack, battle with, clash with, combat, encounter, fight, join in battle with, take on, wage war with
◳ **2** repel **4** discharge, dismiss **5** disengage

engaged *adj* **1** *engaged in his work*: absorbed, active, busy, employed, engrossed, immersed, involved, occupied, preoccupied, tied up *colloq* **2** *engaged to be married*: affianced *formal*, betrothed *formal*, committed, espoused *formal*, pledged, plighted *formal*, promised, spoken for *colloq* **3** *the phone is engaged*: busy, in use, taken, tied up *colloq*, unavailable

engagement *n* **1** *engagement with their overseas counterparts*: appointment, arrangement, assignation, commitment, date, fixture, interview, meeting, rendezvous **2** *she called off her engagement*: agreement, assurance, betrothal *formal*, bond, commitment, contract, obligation, pledge, promise, troth *formal*, vow **3** *defeated Red Army troops in several engagements*: action, assault, attack, battle, clash, combat, conflict, confrontation, contest, encounter, fight, offensive, strife, struggle, war

engaging *adj* adorable, agreeable, appealing, attractive, captivating, charming, delightful, enchanting, fascinating, fetching, likeable, lovable, pleasant, pleasing, sweet, winning, winsome
◳ repellent, repulsive

engender *v* arouse, beget *old use*, breed, bring about, cause, create, effect *formal*, encourage, excite, generate, give rise to, incite, induce, inspire, instigate, kindle, lead to, nurture, occasion, produce, propagate, provoke

engine *n* apparatus, appliance, contraption, device, dynamo, generator, implement, instrument, locomotive, machine, machinery, mechanism, motor, tool

Types of engine include:
diesel, donkey, fuel-injection, internal-combustion, jet, petrol, steam, turbine, turbojet, turboprop, V-engine

Parts of an automotive engine and its ancillaries include:
air filter, alternator, camshaft, camshaft cover, carburettor, choke, connecting rod, con-rod *colloq*, cooling fan, crankshaft, crankshaft pulley, cylinder block, cylinder head, drive belt, exhaust manifold, exhaust valve, fan belt, flywheel, fuel and ignition ECU (electronic control unit), fuel injector, gasket, ignition coil, ignition distributor, inlet manifold, inlet valve, oil filter, oil pump, oil seal, petrol pump, piston, piston ring, power-steering pump, push-rod, radiator, rocker arm, rocker cover, rotor arm, spark plug, starter motor, sump, tappet, thermostat, timing belt, timing pulley, turbocharger

engineer *n* **1** *the helpdesk engineer restored the hard drive:* mechanic, operator, technician **2** *the engineer of the plan:* architect, builder, designer, deviser, inventor, mastermind, originator, planner
♦ *v* arrange, bring about, cause, contrive, control, create, devise, direct, effect *formal*, manage, manipulate, manoeuvre, mastermind, orchestrate, originate, plan, plot, rig, scheme, set up, stage-manage

Types of engineer include:
chemical engineer, civil engineer, electrical engineer, mechanical engineer, software engineer, sound engineer

engrave *v* **1** *her name engraved on the bracelet:* carve, chase, chisel, cut, etch, impress, imprint, incise, inscribe, mark, print **2** *engraved on her mind:* brand, embed, engrain, fix, impress, imprint, lodge, set, stamp

engraving *n* block, carving, chiselling, cut, cutting, dry-point *technical*, etching, impression, imprint, inscription, intaglio, mark, plate, print, woodcut

engross *v* absorb, arrest, captivate, engage, enthral, fascinate, grip, hold, interest, intrigue, involve, occupy, preoccupy, rivet

engrossed *adj* absorbed, captivated, caught up, engaged, enthralled, fascinated, fixated, gripped, immersed, intent, intrigued, lost, mesmerized, occupied, preoccupied, rapt, riveted, taken up, wrapped
☒ bored, disinterested

engrossing *adj* absorbing, captivating, compelling, enthralling, fascinating, gripping, interesting, intriguing, riveting, suspenseful, unputdownable *colloq*
☒ boring

engulf *v* absorb, bury, consume, deluge, devour, drown, engross, envelop, flood,

immerse, inundate, overrun, overtake, overwhelm, plunge, submerge, swallow up, swamp

enhance *v* add to, augment *formal*, boost, elevate, embellish, emphasize, enrich, exalt, heighten, improve, increase, intensify, lift, magnify, raise, reinforce, strengthen, stress, swell, upgrade
☒ minimize, reduce

enhancement *n* augmentation *formal*, boost, elevation, enrichment, heightening, improvement, increase, intensification, magnification, reinforcement

enigma *n* brain-teaser, conundrum, dilemma, mystery, paradox, poser *colloq*, problem, puzzle, quandary, riddle

enigmatic *adj* arcane *formal*, baffling, cryptic, esoteric *formal*, incomprehensible, inexplicable, mysterious, mystifying, obscure, paradoxical, perplexing, puzzling, recondite *formal*, strange, unfathomable
☒ simple, straightforward

enjoin *v* **1** *enjoined to remain silent:* advise, charge, command, decree, demand, direct, instruct, ordain, order, require, urge **2** *enjoined from using the patent:* ban, bar, disallow *formal*, forbid, interdict *formal*, prohibit, proscribe *formal*

enjoy *v* **1** *enjoy dancing:* appreciate, be fond of, delight in, fancy *colloq*, like, love, rejoice in, relish, revel in, savour, take pleasure in **2** *enjoy a benefit:* be blessed with, be endowed with, be favoured with, have, possess
☒ **1** dislike, hate

enjoyable *adj* agreeable, amusing, delectable *formal*, delicious, delightful, entertaining, fine, fun, good, gratifying *formal*, lovely, nice, pleasant, pleasing, pleasurable, satisfying
☒ disagreeable

enjoyment *n* **1** *enjoyment of music:* amusement, delectation *formal*, delight, diversion, entertainment, fun, gladness, gratification *formal*, happiness, indulgence, joy, pleasure, recreation, relish, satisfaction, zest **2** *enjoyment of rights:* advantage, benefit, blessing, favour, possession, privilege, use
☒ **1** displeasure

enlarge *v* **1** *enlarge the garden:* add to, amplify, augment *formal*, broaden, develop, elongate *formal*, expand, extend, heighten, increase, lengthen, make bigger, make larger, stretch, supplement, widen **2** *glands enlarging:* become bigger, become larger, dilate, distend *technical*, expand, inflate, intumesce, swell, widen **3** *enlarge a photograph:* blow up, magnify, make bigger **4** *enlarge on something:* elaborate on, expand on, expatiate on *formal*, go into details
☒ **1** shrink **2** shrink

enlargement *n* **1** *enlargement of the workforce:* amplification, augmentation *formal*, development, expansion, extension, increase, inflation, magnification, multiplication, stretching **2** *enlargement of a gland:* dilation, distension *technical*, expansion, intumescence, oedema *technical*, swelling **3** *a photographic enlargement:* blow up, magnification
☒ **3** contraction, decrease, reduction

enlighten v advise, apprise, counsel, cultivate, edify, educate, illuminate, inform, instruct, make aware, teach, tutor
🔄 confuse

enlightened adj aware, broad-minded, civilized, conversant, cultivated, cultured, educated, erudite *formal*, informed, intellectual, knowledgeable, learned, liberal, literate, open-minded, reasonable, refined, sophisticated, wise
🔄 confused, ignorant

enlightenment n awareness, broad-mindedness, civilization, comprehension, cultivation, edification, education, erudition *formal*, information, insight, instruction, knowledge, learning, literacy, open-mindedness, refinement, sapience *formal*, sophistication, teaching, understanding, wisdom
🔄 confusion, ignorance

enlist v 1 *enlist in the army:* enrol, enter, join up, muster, register, sign up, volunteer 2 *enlist someone's help:* conscript, employ, engage, gather, hire, obtain, procure *formal*, recruit, secure, sign up, take on

enliven v animate, brighten, buoy up, cheer (up), excite, exhilarate, fire, give a lift to *colloq*, gladden, hearten, inspire, invigorate, kindle, liven (up), pep up *colloq*, perk up *colloq*, quicken, revitalize, rouse, spark, stimulate, vivify *formal*, wake up
🔄 subdue

en masse adv all at once, all together, as a group, as a whole, as one, en bloc, ensemble, in a body, together, wholesale

enmity n acrimony *formal*, animosity, antagonism, antipathy, aversion, bad blood, bitterness, discord, feud, hate, hatred, hostility, ill-will, malevolence *formal*, malice, rancour, strife, venom
🔄 friendship, reconciliation

ennoble v aggrandize *formal*, dignify, elevate, enhance, exalt, glorify, honour, magnify, nobilitate *formal*, raise, uplift

ennui n accidie *formal*, acedia *formal*, boredom, dissatisfaction, languor, lassitude, listlessness, tedium, the doldrums *colloq*, tiredness

enormity n abomination, atrociousness, atrocity, crime, depravity, evil, evilness, horror, iniquity, monstrosity, outrage, outrageousness, viciousness, vileness, violation, wickedness

---

enormity or *enormousness*? Of these two nouns, only *enormousness* should be used when referring to size: *the enormousness of his ambitions*. *Enormity* means 'great wickedness, seriousness (of a crime, etc)': *the enormity of his assault on the little girl*.

---

enormous adj astronomic, colossal, considerable, gargantuan, gigantic, great big *colloq*, gross, huge, immense, jumbo *colloq*, large-scale, mammoth, massive, monstrous, prodigious, stupendous, tremendous, vast, whopping *colloq*
🔄 small, tiny

enormously adv exceedingly, exceptionally, extraordinarily, extremely, hugely, immensely, massively, to a vast/huge/immense extent, tremendously

enormousness n expanse, extensiveness, greatness, hugeness, immenseness, largeness, magnitude, massiveness, vastness

enough n abundance, adequacy, ample supply, amplitude *formal*, plenty, sufficiency
♦ adv adequately, amply, fairly, moderately, passably, reasonably, satisfactorily, sufficiently, tolerably

en passant adv by the way, cursorily, in passing, incidentally, while on the subject

enquire, enquirer, enquiring, enquiry see inquire, inquirer, inquiring, inquiry

enrage v agitate, anger, annoy, bug *colloq*, drive someone round the bend *colloq*, drive someone up the wall *colloq*, exasperate, incense, incite, inflame, infuriate, irk, irritate, madden, make angry, make someone's blood boil *colloq*, make someone's hackles rise *colloq*, needle *colloq*, provoke, push too far *colloq*, put/get someone's back up *colloq*, rile, vex, wind up *colloq*
🔄 calm, placate

enraged adj aggravated *colloq*, angered, angry, annoyed, exasperated, fuming, furious, incensed, inflamed, infuriated, irate, irritated, livid, mad *colloq*, raging, storming, wild *colloq*
🔄 calm

enrapture v beguile, bewitch, captivate, charm, delight, enchant, enthral, entrance, fascinate, ravish, spellbind, thrill, transport

enrich v 1 *enrich the soil:* add to, aggrandize *formal*, ameliorate *formal*, augment *formal*, cultivate, develop, endow, enhance, improve, refine, supplement 2 *enriched by enamel plaques:* adorn, beautify, decorate, embellish, garnish, gild, grace, ornament
🔄 1 impoverish

enrol v 1 *enrol for dance classes:* enter, go in for, join up, put your name down, register, sign on, sign up 2 *enrol more foster carers:* admit, engage, enlist, recruit, sign up 3 *enrol the minutes of the meeting:* enter, inscribe *formal*, list, note, put down, record

enrolment n acceptance, admission, enlisting, enlistment, joining up, recruitment, registration, signing on/up

en route adv in transit, on the move, on the road, on the way

ensconce v entrench, establish, install, locate, lodge, nestle, place, protect, put, screen, settle, shelter, shield

ensemble n 1 *form a unique ensemble:* accumulation, aggregate *formal*, collection, entirety, group, set, sum, total, whole, whole (bang) shoot *colloq*, whole caboodle *colloq* 2 *a jacket and jeans ensemble:* co-ordinates, costume, get-up *colloq*, outfit, rig-out *colloq*, suit 3 *a string ensemble:* band, cast, chorus, circle, company, group, troupe

enshrine v apotheosize *formal*, consecrate, exalt, hallow, idolize, immortalize, revere, sanctify

enshroud v cloak, cloud, conceal, cover, enclose, enfold, envelop, enwrap, hide, obscure, pall, shroud, veil, wrap

ensign n badge, banner, coat of arms, colours, crest, flag, jack, pennant, shield, standard

enslave *v* bind, dominate, enchain, subject, subjugate *formal*, trap, yoke
🔄 emancipate, free

enslavement *n* bondage, captivity, dulosis *formal*, enthralment *formal*, oppression, repression, serfdom, servitude, slavery, subjection, subjugation *formal*, thraldom *formal*, vassalage
🔄 emancipation

ensnare *v* capture, catch, embroil, enmesh, entangle, entrap, net, snare, trap

ensue *v* arise, befall *formal*, come next, derive, flow, follow, happen, issue, occur, proceed, result, stem, succeed, transpire, turn out
🔄 precede

ensure *v* 1 *ensure co-operation*: certify, effect *formal*, guarantee, make certain, make sure, secure, warrant 2 *ensure the future of family units*: guard, make safe, protect, safeguard, secure

entail *v* bring about, call for, cause, demand, give rise to, involve, lead to, necessitate, need, occasion, produce, require, result in

entangle *v* 1 *entangled in the net*: enmesh, ensnare, intertwine, knot, mix up, ravel, snare, tangle, twist 2 *entangled in the court system*: complicate, confuse, embroil, implicate, involve, jumble, muddle
🔄 1 disentangle

entanglement *n* 1 *entanglement in fishing nets*: ensnarement, entrapment, jumble, knot, mesh, snare, tangle, tie, trap 2 *political entanglements*: complication, confusion, difficulty, embarrassment, involvement, mess, mix-up, muddle, predicament, snarl-up 3 *entanglements with the opposite sex*: affair, involvement, liaison
🔄 1 disentanglement 2 disentanglement

entente *n* agreement, arrangement, compact *formal*, deal, entente cordiale, friendship, pact, treaty, understanding

enter *v* 1 *enter by the back door*: arrive, board, break in, burst in, come in to, cross the threshold, get in (to), go in (to), pop in *colloq*, sneak in 2 *alcohol enters the bloodstream*: get in (to), insert, introduce, penetrate 3 *he entered the army from school*: become a member of, engage in, enlist, enrol, go in for, infiltrate, join, participate, put your name down for, sign up, worm your way in 4 *entering a new era*: begin, commence *formal*, embark upon, set about, start, take up 5 *entered politics*: engage in, take part, undertake 6 *enter the notes carefully*: input, inscribe, list, lodge, log, note, put down, put on record, record, register, set down, submit, take down
🔄 1 depart 2 exit 6 delete

enterprise *n* 1 *engaged in some momentous enterprise*: campaign, effort, endeavour, operation, plan, programme, project, scheme, task, undertaking, venture 2 *enterprise and competitiveness are important*: adventurousness, ambition, boldness, courage, drive, energy, enthusiasm, get-up-and-go *colloq*, initiative, oomph *colloq*, push *colloq*, resourcefulness, spirit, vitality 3 *a family-run enterprise*: business, company, concern, establishment, firm, industry, operation
🔄 2 apathy

enterprising *adj* active, adventurous, ambitious, aspiring, bold, daring, eager, energetic, enthusiastic, entrepreneurial, go-ahead *colloq*, imaginative, keen, pushy *colloq*, resourceful, self-reliant, spirited, venturesome, vigorous, zealous
🔄 lethargic, unenterprising

entertain *v* 1 *entertain the children*: amuse, captivate, charm, cheer, delight, divert, engage, engross, interest, occupy, please 2 *entertain visiting dignitaries*: accommodate, ask over/round, have guests, have round, host, invite over/round, play host to, provide hospitality, put up, receive, regale, treat 3 *refused to entertain the notion*: cherish, conceive, consider, contemplate, countenance *formal*, foster, harbour, imagine, nurture, think about
🔄 1 bore 3 reject

entertainer

Entertainers include:
acrobat, actor, actress, artiste, busker, chat-show host, clown, comedian, comic, conjurer, contortionist, dancer, disc jockey, DJ *colloq*, escapologist, fire-eater, game-show host, hypnotist, ice-skater, impressionist, jester, juggler, magician, mime artist, mimic, mind-reader, minstrel, musician, performer, player, presenter, prima ballerina, singer, song-and-dance act, stand-up comic, striptease-artist, stripper *colloq*, trapeze-artist, tight-rope walker, unicyclist, ventriloquist. See also **musician, singer**

---

entertaining *adj* amusing, comical, delightful, diverting, enjoyable, fun, funny, humorous, interesting, pleasant, pleasing, pleasurable, recreational, witty
🔄 boring

entertainment *n* 1 *computer games as entertainment*: activity, amusement, distraction, diversion, enjoyment, fun, hobby, leisure, pastime, play, pleasure, recreation, sport 2 *a pre-match entertainment*: extravaganza, performance, play, presentation, show, spectacle

---

Forms of entertainment include:
cinema, cartoon show, DVD, radio, television, theatre, pantomime; club, dance, disco, concert, recital, musical, opera, variety show, music hall, revue, karaoke, cabaret, night-club, casino; magic show, puppet show, Punch-and-Judy show, circus, gymkhana, waxworks, zoo, rodeo, carnival, pageant, fête, festival, firework party, barbecue. See also **theatrical**

---

enthral *v* absorb, beguile, bewitch, captivate, charm, delight, enchant, engross, enrapture, entrance, fascinate, grip, hypnotize, intrigue, mesmerize, rivet, spellbind, thrill
🔄 bore

enthralling *adj* beguiling, captivating, charming, compelling, compulsive, enchanting, entrancing, fascinating, gripping, hypnotizing, intriguing, mesmeric, mesmerizing, riveting, spellbinding, thrilling
🔄 boring

enthuse *v* bubble over, drool, effervesce, excite, fire, gush, inspire, motivate, praise, rave, wax lyrical

enthusiasm *n* 1 *she dances with great enthusiasm*: ardour, commitment, devotion, eagerness, earnestness, excitement, fervour, fire, frenzy,

keenness, passion, relish, spirit, vehemence, warmth, wholeheartedness, zeal, zest **2** *revival of enthusiasm for Gaelic*: craze, hobby, interest, mania, passion, pastime, rage, thing *colloq*
  F3 1 apathy

enthusiast *n* admirer, aficionado, buff *colloq*, devotee, fan, fanatic, fiend *colloq*, follower, freak *colloq*, lover, supporter, zealot

enthusiastic *adj* ardent, avid, committed, crazy *colloq*, daft *colloq*, devoted, eager, earnest, ebullient *formal*, excited, exuberant, fanatical, fervent, keen, mad *colloq*, nuts *colloq*, passionate, potty *colloq*, spirited, vehement, vigorous, warm, wholehearted, wild *colloq*, zealous
  F3 apathetic, unenthusiastic

entice *v* attract, beguile, cajole, coax, draw, induce, inveigle *formal*, lead on, lure, persuade, seduce, sweet-talk *colloq*, tempt

enticement *n* **1** *an enticement to tourists*: allurement, attraction, bait, inducement, inveiglement *formal*, lure, persuasion, temptation **2** *murmur sweet enticements*: beguilement, blandishment *formal*, cajolery, coaxing, come-on *colloq*, seduction, sweet-talk *colloq*

entire *adj* absolute, complete, full, intact, perfect, sound, total, whole
  F3 incomplete, partial

entirely *adv* absolutely, altogether, completely, every inch, exclusively, fully, in every respect, in every way, in toto, only, perfectly, solely, thoroughly, totally, unreservedly, utterly, wholly
  F3 partially

entirety *n* completeness, fullness, totality, whole, wholeness

entitle *v* **1** *entitled to the money*: accredit *formal*, allow, authorize, empower, enable, give someone the right, license, make eligible, permit, qualify, sanction, warrant **2** *an article entitled 'Men's Liberation'*: call, christen, designate, dub, give the title, know as, label, name, style, term, title

entity *n* being, body, creature, existence, individual, object, organism, substance, thing

entombment *n* burial, inhumation *formal*, interment, sepulture *formal*

entourage *n* associates, attendants, companions, company, cortège, coterie, court, escort, followers, following, retainers, retinue, staff, suite, train

entrails *n* bowels, giblets, guts *colloq*, innards *colloq*, insides *colloq*, internal organs, intestines, offal, umbles, viscera, vital organs

entrance[1] *n* **1** *the entrance to the garden*: access, anteroom, approach, door, doorway, drive, driveway, entry, foyer, gate, gateway, hall, lobby, opening, passageway, porch, threshold, vestibule, way in **2** *she made a grand entrance*: appearance, arrival, debut, initiation, introduction, start **3** *entrance costs a pound*: access, admission, admittance, entrée, entry, ingress *formal*, right of entry
  F3 1 exit **2** departure

entrance[2] *v* beguile, bewitch, captivate, charm, delight, enchant, enrapture, enthral, fascinate, hypnotize, mesmerize, ravish, spellbind, transport
  F3 repel

entrant *n* **1** *new entrants to the profession*: apprentice, beginner, convert, fresher, freshman, initiate, learner, new arrival, newcomer, novice, probationer, pupil, starter, student, trainee **2** *two entrants were disqualified*: applicant, candidate, competitor, contender, contestant, entry, opponent, participant, player, rival

entrap *v* **1** *used to entrap sunlight*: ambush, capture, catch, embroil, enmesh, ensnare, entangle, net, snare, trap **2** *entrapped by the power of his presence*: allure, beguile, deceive, delude, entice, implicate, inveigle *formal*, lure, seduce, trick

entreat *v* appeal to, ask, beg, beseech *formal*, crave, implore, importune *formal*, invoke *formal*, petition, plead with, pray, request, solicit, supplicate *formal*

entreaty *n* appeal, cry, invocation *formal*, petition, plea, prayer, request, solicitation, suit, supplication *formal*

entrench *v* anchor, dig in, embed, ensconce, establish, fix, ingrain, install, lodge, plant, root, seat, set, settle, take up position
  F3 dislodge

entrenched *adj* deep-rooted, deep-seated, diehard, dyed-in-the-wool, firm, fixed, implanted, inbred, indelible, ineradicable, inflexible, ingrained, intransigent *formal*, rooted, set, stick-in-the-mud *colloq*, unshakable, well-established

entrepreneur *n* agent, broker, business executive, businessman, businesswoman, contractor, dealer, financier, impresario, industrialist, magnate, manager, middleman, money-maker, promoter, speculator, tycoon

entrepreneurial *adj* budgetary, business, commercial, contractual, economic, financial, industrial, managerial, monetary, professional, trade

entrust *v* assign, authorize, charge, commend, commit, confide, consign, delegate, deliver, depute, hand over, invest, make someone responsible for, put in charge, trust, turn over

entry *n* **1** *her entry into fashionable society*: appearance, entering, introduction **2** *unlawful entry*: access, admission, admittance, entrance, entrée, introduction **3** *an entry in a catalogue*: account, description, item, listing, memorandum, minute, note, record, statement **4** *a late entry to the race*: applicant, candidate, competitor, contestant, entrant, opponent, participant, player, rival **5** *the rear entry*: access, anteroom, approach, door, doorway, entrance, foyer, gate, gateway, hall, lobby, opening, passage, porch, threshold, vestibule, way in
  F3 5 exit

entwine *v* braid, embroil, entangle, interlace, interlink, intertwine, interweave, intwine, knit, knot, plait, ravel, twine, twist, weave, wind, wreathe
  F3 unravel

enumerate *v* calculate, cite, count, detail, itemize, list, mention, name, number, quote, recite, reckon, recount, relate, specify, spell out, tell

enunciate *v* **1** *enunciate each word clearly*: articulate, express, pronounce, say, sound, speak, utter, vocalize, voice **2** *principles he enunciated:* affirm *formal*, announce, declare, express, proclaim, promulgate *formal*, propound *formal*, put forward, state, utter

envelop *v* blanket, cloak, conceal, cover, encase, encircle, enclose, encompass, enfold, engulf, enwrap, hide, obscure, shroud, surround, swathe, veil, wrap

envelope *n* case, casing, coating, cover, covering, holder, jacket, sheath, shell, skin, wrapper, wrapping

enviable *adj* advantageous, blessed, desirable, excellent, favoured, fine, fortunate, lucky, privileged, sought-after
🖅 unenviable

envious *adj* begrudging, covetous, dissatisfied, green (with envy), green-eyed *colloq*, grudging, jaundiced, jealous, resentful

environment *n* ambience, atmosphere, background, circumstances, climate, conditions, context, domain, element, habitat, influences, locale, medium, milieu, mood, scene, setting, situation, surroundings, territory, the lie of the land *colloq*

environmentalist *n* conservationist, ecofreak *colloq*, ecologist, econut *colloq*, Friend of the Earth, green *colloq*, preservationist

environs *n* circumjacencies *formal*, district, locality, neighbourhood, outskirts, precincts, purlieus, suburbs, surrounding area, surroundings, vicinage *formal*, vicinity

envisage *v* anticipate, conceive of, contemplate, envision, foresee, image, imagine, picture, preconceive, predict, see, see coming, think of, visualize

envoy *n* agent, ambassador, attaché, consul, courier, delegate, deputy, diplomat, emissary, go-between, intermediary, legate, mediator, messenger, minister, representative

envy *n* covetousness, dissatisfaction, grudge, ill-will, jealousy, malice, resentfulness, resentment, spite
♦ *v* begrudge, covet, crave, grudge, resent

ephemeral *adj* brief, evanescent *formal*, fleeting, flitting, fugacious *formal*, fungous *formal*, impermanent, momentary, passing, short, short-lived, temporary, transient, transitory
🖅 enduring, lasting, perpetual

epic *adj* ambitious, colossal, elevated, exalted, grand, grandiloquent *formal*, great, heroic, huge, imposing, impressive, large, large-scale, lofty, long, majestic, sublime *formal*, vast
🖅 ordinary
♦ *n* history, legend, long story/poem, myth, narrative, saga

epicure *n* bon vivant, bon viveur, connoisseur, epicurean, gastronome, glutton, gourmand, gourmet, hedonist, sensualist, Sybarite, voluptuary

epicurean *adj* gastronomic, gluttonous, gormandizing, gourmet, hedonistic, libertine, luscious, lush, luxurious, self-indulgent, sensual, Sybaritic, unrestrained, voluptuous

epidemic *adj* endemic, extensive, pandemic *formal*, pervasive, prevailing, prevalent, rampant, rife, sweeping, wide-ranging, widespread
♦ *n* growth, increase, outbreak, plague, rash, rise, scourge, spate, spread, upsurge, wave

epigram *n* aphorism, apophthegm *technical*, bon mot, gnome, maxim, proverb, quip, saying, witticism

epigrammatic *adj* aphoristic, brief, concise, incisive, ironic, laconic, piquant, pithy, pointed, pungent, sharp, short, succinct, terse, witty

epilogue *n* afterword, appendix, coda, conclusion, postscript, PS, swan song
🖅 foreword, preface, prologue

episode *n* **1** *an embarrassing episode:* adventure, affair, business, circumstance, event, experience, happening, incident, matter, occasion, occurrence **2** *filming an episode of a sitcom:* chapter, instalment, part, passage, scene, section

episodic *adj* anecdotal, digressive, disconnected, disjointed, intermittent, irregular, occasional, periodic, picaresque *formal*, spasmodic, sporadic

epistle *n* bulletin, communication, correspondence, encyclical, letter, line, message, missive, note

epitaph *n* commemoration, funeral oration, inscription, lapidary expression *technical*, obituary, rest in peace, RIP

epithet *n* appellation *formal*, denomination *formal*, description, descriptive adjective, descriptive phrase/expression, designation, name, nickname, sobriquet, tag, title

epitome *n* **1** *epitome of evil:* archetype, embodiment, essence, example, exemplar *formal*, model, personification, prototype, quintessence *formal*, representation, type **2** *the epitome begins with two letters:* abridgement, abstract, digest, outline, précis, résumé, summary, synopsis

epitomize *v* **1** *epitomizing the soldier-poet:* embody, encapsulate, exemplify, illustrate, incarnate *formal*, personify, represent, sum up, symbolize, typify **2** *passages epitomized from her novel:* abbreviate, abridge, abstract, compress, condense, contract, curtail, cut, précis, reduce, shorten, summarize
🖅 **2** elaborate, expand

epoch *n* age, date, era, period, time

equable *adj* **1** *an equable person:* calm, composed, cool and collected, easy-going, even-tempered, imperturbable *formal*, laid-back *colloq*, level-headed, placid, serene, tranquil, unexcitable, unfazed *colloq*, unflappable *colloq* **2** *an equable climate:* consistent, constant, even, moderate, regular, smooth, stable, steady, temperate, unchanging, uniform, unvarying
🖅 **1** excitable **2** extreme, variable

---

equable or *equitable*? Equable means 'even-tempered': *That child would infuriate the most equable parent* ; 'not extreme and without great variation': *an equable climate*. Equitable means 'fair, just': *a more equitable distribution of profits.*

---

equal *adj* **1** *of equal height:* alike, commensurate, comparable, corresponding, equivalent, identical, like, matched, the same **2** *equal partners:* balanced, constant, even, evenly matched, fifty-fifty *colloq*, level, neck and neck *colloq*, on an equal footing, regular, symmetrical, unchanging, uniform, unvarying, well balanced

3 *equal pay:* fair, impartial, just, neutral, non-partisan, unbiased **4** *equal to a task:* able, adequate, capable, competent, fit, strong, sufficient, suitable, suited
₣ **1** different **2** unequal **3** biased **4** unsuitable
♦ *n* **1** coequal, compeer, counterpart, equivalent, fellow, match, mate, parallel, peer, twin
♦ *v* **1** *equal a number:* add up to, amount to, balance, be the same as, coincide with, correspond to, equalize, equate with, make, match, parallel, square with, tally with, total **2** *equal someone's score:* be level with, be on a par with, come up to, emulate, match, measure up to, rival

equality *n* **1** *equality of size and shape:* balance, comparability, correspondence, equivalence, evenness, identity, likeness, par, parallelism, parity, proportion, sameness, similarity, symmetry, uniformity **2** *equality for all people:* egalitarianism, equal opportunities, equal rights, fairness, impartiality, justice, neutrality, non-partisanship
₣ **2** inequality, partisanship

equalize *v* balance, compensate, draw level, equal, equate, even out, keep pace, level, make even, match, redress the balance, regularize, smooth, square, standardize

equanimity *n* aplomb *formal*, assurance, calm, composure, confidence, coolness, dignity, ease, impassivity, imperturbability *formal*, level-headedness, placidity, poise, sangfroid *formal*, self-assurance, self-control, self-possession, serenity, tranquillity, unflappability *colloq*
₣ alarm, anxiety, discomposure

equate *v* **1** *equate wealth with happiness:* bracket together, compare with, connect with, identify with, juxtapose with, liken to, link with, match with, pair with, regard as the same **2** *costs equate to a quarter of the income:* agree with, balance, be equal, correspond to, correspond with, equalize, offset, parallel, square with, tally with

equation *n* agreement, balancing, comparison, correspondence, equality, equivalence, identity, juxtaposition *formal*, likeness, match, matching, pairing, parallel, similarity

equestrian *n* cavalier, cavalryman, courier, cowboy, cowgirl, herder, horseman, horsewoman, hussar, jockey, knight, rancher, rider, trooper
♦ *adj* equine *formal*, horse-riding, mounted, riding

equilibrium *n* **1** *in equilibrium:* balance, counterpoise *formal*, equipoise *formal*, evenness, poise, stability, stasis *technical*, steadiness, symmetry **2** *regained her equilibrium:* aplomb *formal*, assurance, calmness, composure, confidence, coolness, dignity, equanimity, imperturbability *formal*, level-headedness, poise, sangfroid *formal*, self-assurance, self-control, self-possession, serenity, tranquillity, unflappability *colloq*
₣ **1** imbalance, instability **2** anxiety

equip *v* accoutre *formal*, arm, array *formal*, deck out, dress, endow, fit out, fit up, furnish, issue, kit out, prepare, provide, rig, stock, supply

equipment *n* accessories, accoutrements *formal*, apparatus, baggage, furnishings, furniture, gear, kit, luggage, material, outfit, paraphernalia, rig-out *colloq*, stuff, supplies, tackle, things, tools

equipoise *n* balance, ballast, counterbalance, counterpoise *formal*, counter-weight, equibalance *formal*, equilibrium, equiponderance *formal*, evenness, poise, stability, steadiness, symmetry
₣ imbalance

equitable *adj* disinterested, dispassionate, due, ethical, even-handed, fair, fair-and-square, honest, impartial, just, legitimate, objective, proper, reasonable, right, rightful, square, unbiased, unprejudiced
₣ inequitable, unfair

equitable or *equable*? See panel at **equable**

equity *n* disinterestedness, equitableness, even-handedness, fair play, fair-mindedness, fairness, honesty, impartiality, integrity, justice, justness, objectivity, reasonableness, rectitude *formal*, righteousness, uprightness
₣ inequity

equivalence *n* agreement, comparability, conformity, correlation, correspondence, equality, identity, interchangeability, likeness, parallel, parity *formal*, sameness, similarity, substitutability
₣ dissimilarity, unlikeness

equivalent *adj* alike, commensurate *formal*, comparable, corresponding, equal, even, homologous *technical*, identical, interchangeable, like, same, similar, substitutable, tantamount *formal*, twin
₣ different, unlike
♦ *n* alternative, correlative *formal*, correspondent, counterpart, double, equal, fellow, homologue *technical*, match, opposite number, parallel, peer, twin

equivocal *adj* ambiguous, ambivalent, confusing, dubious, evasive, indefinite, misleading, oblique, obscure, questionable, suspicious, uncertain, vague
₣ clear, definite, unequivocal

equivocate *v* beat about the bush *colloq*, change your mind, change your tune *colloq*, chop and change *colloq*, dodge, evade, fence, hedge, hedge your bets *colloq*, mislead, prevaricate, pussyfoot *colloq*, run with the hare and hunt with the hounds *colloq*, shilly-shally *colloq*, tergiversate *formal*, vacillate *formal*, waffle *colloq*

equivocation *n* dodging the issue, double talk, evasion, hedging, prevarication, pussyfooting *colloq*, quibbling, shifting, shuffling, tergiversation *formal*, waffle *colloq*, weasel words *colloq*
₣ directness

era *n* eon, age, century, cycle, date, day, days, epoch, generation, period, season, stage, time, times

eradicate *v* abolish, annihilate, crack down on, destroy, efface *formal*, eliminate, erase, expunge *formal*, exterminate, extinguish, extirpate *formal*, get rid of, obliterate, remove, root out, stamp out, suppress, uproot, weed out, wipe out

eradication *n* abolition, annihilation, deracination *formal*, destruction, effacement *formal*, elimination, expunction *formal*, extermination, extinction, extirpation *formal*, obliteration, removal, riddance, suppression

erasable *adj* effaceable *formal*, eradicable, removable, washable
☒ ineradicable, permanent

erase *v* blot out, cancel, delete, efface *formal*, eradicate, excise *formal*, expunge *formal*, get rid of, obliterate, put out of your mind, remove, rub out, wipe out

erasure *n* cancellation, cleansing, deletion, effacement *formal*, elimination, eradication, erasement *formal*, expunction *formal*, obliteration, removal

erect *v* assemble, build, construct, create, elevate, establish, lift, mount, pitch, put together, put up, raise, rear, set up
♦ *adj* **1** *the dog's ears were erect*: raised, standing, straight, upright, upstanding, vertical **2** *erect nipples*: firm, hard, rigid, stiff

erection *n* **1** *the erection of thirty houses*: assembly, building, construction, creation, elevation, establishment, fabrication, manufacture, pile *colloq*, raising **2** *a red brick erection*: building, construction, edifice, pile *colloq*, structure **3** *sustain his erection*: rigidity, stiffness, tumescence *technical*

ergo *adv* accordingly, consequently, for this reason, hence *formal*, in consequence, so, then, therefore, this being the case, thus *formal*

erode *v* abrade *formal*, consume, corrode, deplete, destroy, deteriorate, disintegrate, eat away, eat into, excoriate *formal*, fragment, grind down, spoil, undermine, wear away, wear down

erosion *n* abrasion *formal*, attrition *formal*, corrosion, denudation *formal*, destruction, deterioration, disintegration, excoriation *formal*, undermining, wear, wearing away

erotic *adj* adult *colloq*, amatory *formal*, amorous, aphrodisiac, blue *colloq*, carnal, dirty *colloq*, erogenous, lascivious, lustful, pornographic, raunchy *colloq*, seductive, sensual, sexually arousing, sexy *colloq*, steamy *colloq*, stimulating, suggestive, titillating, venereal, voluptuous

err *v* **1** *you erred by ordering white wine*: balls up *slang*, bark up the wrong tree *colloq*, be incorrect, be wrong, blunder, boob *colloq*, cock up *slang*, get hold of the wrong end of the stick *colloq*, louse up *slang*, make a booboo *colloq*, make a mistake, make a slip, miscalculate, misconstrue, misjudge, mistake, misunderstand, put your foot in it *colloq*, slip up *colloq* **2** *to err is human*: deviate, do wrong, fall from grace, go astray, misbehave, offend, sin, transgress *formal*

errand *n* assignment, charge, chore, commission, duty, job, message, mission, task, undertaking

errant *adj* **1** *an errant husband*: aberrant *formal*, criminal, deviant, disobedient, erring, lawless, loose, offending, peccant *formal*, sinful, sinning, stray, straying, wayward, wrong **2** *a knight errant*: itinerant, journeying, nomadic, peripatetic *formal*, rambling, roaming, roving, wandering

erratic *adj* aberrant *formal*, abnormal, capricious *formal*, changeable, desultory *formal*, eccentric, fitful, fluctuating, inconsistent, inconstant, intermittent, irregular, meandering, shifting,

sporadic, unpredictable, unreliable, unsettled, unstable, unsteady, variable, varying, volatile, wandering
☒ consistent, stable, steady

erring *adj* criminal, deviant, disobedient, errant, guilty, lawless, loose, offending, peccant *formal*, sinful, sinning, stray, straying, wayward, wrong

erroneous *adj* fallacious *formal*, false, faulty, flawed, illogical, inaccurate, incorrect, inexact, invalid, misguided, misplaced, mistaken, specious, spurious, unfounded, untrue, wrong
☒ correct, right

error *n* aberration *formal*, blunder, boob *colloq*, fallacy, fault, faux pas, flaw, gaffe, howler *colloq*, inaccuracy, lapse, literal, misapprehension, miscalculation, misconception, misinterpretation, misjudgement, misprint, mistake, misunderstanding, mix-up, omission, oversight, slip, slip of the tongue, slip-up *colloq*, solecism *formal*, wrong

ersatz *adj* artificial, bogus, counterfeit, fake, imitation, man-made, phoney *colloq*, sham, simulated, substitute, synthetic

erstwhile *adj* bygone, ex, former, late, old, once, one-time, past, previous, sometime

erudite *adj* academic, brainy *colloq*, cultured, educated, highbrow, intellectual, knowledgeable, learned, lettered, literate, profound, scholarly, well-educated, well-read, wise
☒ ignorant, illiterate

erudition *n* culture, education, facts, knowledge, knowledgeableness, learnedness, learning, letters, profundity *formal*, reconditeness *formal*, scholarliness, scholarship, wisdom

erupt *v* belch, break, break out, burst, discharge, eject, emit, eruct, eructate *formal*, expel, explode, flare up, gush, pour forth, spew, spout, vent, vomit

eruption *n* **1** *a volcanic eruption*: discharge, ejection, emission, explosion **2** *a violent eruption of booing and shouting*: flare-up, outbreak, venting **3** *an eruption of spots*: inflammation, outbreak, rash

escalate *v* accelerate, amplify, ascend, climb, develop, enlarge, expand, extend, go through the roof *colloq*, grow, heighten, hit the roof *colloq*, increase, intensify, magnify, mount, mushroom, raise, rise, rocket *colloq*, soar, spiral, step up
☒ decrease, diminish

escalator *n* elevator, lift, moving staircase, moving walkway, travolator

escapable *adj* avertible, avoidable, eludible, evadable
☒ inevitable

escapade *n* adventure, antic, caper, exploit, fling, frolic, lark *colloq*, prank, romp, skylarking *colloq*, spree, stunt, trick

escape *v* **1** *escape from prison*: abscond, bolt, break free, break loose, break out, decamp, do a moonlight flit *colloq*, do a runner/bunk *colloq*, flee, flit, fly, get away, make a bolt/break for it *colloq*, make your escape, make your getaway, run away, run for your life *colloq*, scarper *colloq*, scat *colloq*, scoot *colloq*, scram *colloq*, shake off, slip, slip away, slip through someone's fingers

colloq, take to your heels *colloq* **2** *escaping injury:* avoid, circumvent *formal*, dodge *colloq*, duck *colloq*, elude, evade, shun, sidestep, skip, steer clear of **3** *pull out the plug and let the water escape:* discharge, drain, flow, gush, issue, leak, ooze, pass, pour out/forth, seep, spurt, trickle **4** *his name escapes me:* be on the tip of your tongue *colloq*, forget, not be able to put your finger on *colloq*, not be remembered/recalled, not know, not place
♦ *n* **1** *made his escape:* absconding, bolt, breakout, bunk *colloq*, decampment, flight, flit, getaway, jailbreak **2** *a narrow escape:* avoidance, circumvention *formal*, dodging *colloq*, ducking *colloq*, evasion **3** *gas escape:* discharge, drain, efflux *formal*, emanation, emission, gush, issue, leak, leakage, outflow, outpour, seepage, spurt **4** *alcohol was her escape:* distraction, diversion, dreaming, escapism, fantasizing, fantasy, pastime, recreation, relaxation, safety-valve, wishful thinking

escapee *n* absconder, defector, deserter, fugitive, jailbreaker, refugee, runaway, truant

escapism *n* distraction, diversion, dreaming, fantasizing, fantasy, pastime, recreation, relaxation, safety-valve, wishful thinking
☲ realism

escapist *n* daydreamer, dreamer, fantasizer, non-realist, ostrich *colloq*, wishful thinker
☲ realist

eschew *v* abandon, abjure *formal*, abstain from *formal*, avoid, disdain, forgo *formal*, forswear *formal*, give up, keep clear of, refrain from, renounce *formal*, repudiate, shun, spurn
☲ embrace

escort *n* **1** *his charming escort:* aide, attendant, beau, bodyguard, chaperon(e), companion, date *colloq*, defender, guide, partner, protector, squire **2** *a police escort:* attendants, company, convoy, cortège, entourage, guard, retinue, suite, train
♦ *v* accompany, attend on, bring, chaperon(e), come (along) with, conduct, defend, guard, guide, lead, partner, protect, shepherd, take, take out, usher, walk

esoteric *adj* abstruse *formal*, arcane *formal*, confidential, cryptic, hidden, inscrutable, inside, mysterious, mystic, mystical, obscure, occult, private, recondite *formal*, secret
☲ familiar, well-known

especial *adj* exceptional, exclusive, express, extraordinary, marked, notable, noteworthy, outstanding, particular, peculiar, pre-eminent, remarkable, signal, singular, special, specific, striking, uncommon, unique, unusual

especially *adv* **1** *she was especially beautiful:* exceptionally, extraordinarily, markedly, notably, outstandingly, remarkably, strikingly, supremely, uncommonly, unusually, very **2** *he had the ring made especially for her:* exclusively, expressly, particularly, specially, uniquely **3** *especially her:* above all, chiefly, mainly, most of all, pre-eminently, primarily, principally

espionage *n* bugging *colloq*, counter-intelligence, fifth column, industrial espionage, infiltration, intelligence, intercepting, investigation, probing, reconnaissance, snooping *colloq*, spying, surveillance,

undercover operations/work, wiretapping *colloq*

espousal *n* adoption, advocacy, backing, championing, championship, choice, defence, embracing, maintenance, promotion, support

espouse *v* adopt, advocate, back, champion, choose, defend, embrace, maintain, opt for, patronize, stand up for, support, take up

espy *v* behold, catch sight of, detect, discern, discover, distinguish, glimpse, make out, notice, observe, perceive, see, sight, spot, spy

essay *n* article, assignment, commentary, composition, critique, discourse *formal*, disquisition *formal*, dissertation, leader, paper, piece, review, thesis, tract, treatise
♦ *v* attempt, endeavour, go for, have a bash *colloq*, have a crack *colloq*, have a go *colloq*, have a stab *colloq*, strain, strive, struggle, tackle, take on, test, try, undertake

essence *n* **1** *the essence of the matter:* actuality, attributes, centre, character, characteristics, core, crux, essential character, heart, kernel, marrow, meaning, nature, pith, point, principle, quality, quintessence *formal*, reality, significance, substance **2** *captures the essence of Italy:* being, entity, life, soul, spirit **3** *vanilla essence:* concentrate, concentration, distillate *formal*, distillation, extract, spirits

essential *adj* **1** *cover the essential points:* basic, central, characteristic, constituent, definitive, fundamental, inherent, innate, intrinsic, key, main, principal, typical, underlying **2** *experience is essential:* crucial, important, indispensable, necessary, needed, required, requisite, vital
☲ **1** incidental **2** dispensable, inessential
♦ *n* basic, fundamental, gist, key point(s), main point(s), must *colloq*, necessary, necessity, prerequisite, principle, requirement, requisite, sine qua non *formal*

establish *v* **1** *establish ourselves in Montreal:* base, form, lodge, plant, secure, settle **2** *establish a community:* base, begin, bring into being, create, form, found, inaugurate, install, institute, introduce, open, organize, secure, set up, start **3** *having established his whereabouts:* affirm *formal*, attest, authenticate, certify, confirm, corroborate *formal*, demonstrate, prove, ratify, show, substantiate *formal*, validate *formal*, verify
☲ **1** uproot **2** uproot **3** refute

established *adj* conventional, ensconced, entrenched, experienced, fixed, proved, proven, respected, secure, settled, steadfast, traditional, tried and tested
☲ impermanent, unreliable

establishment *n* **1** *the establishment of multi-denominational schools:* creation, formation, forming, foundation, founding, inauguration, inception *formal*, installation, institution, organization, setting up **2** *a family-run establishment:* business, company, concern, corporation, enterprise, firm, institute, institution, organization, shop, store **3** *a pillar of the English establishment:* ruling class, the authorities, the powers that be, the system

estate *n* **1** *her estate passed to her son:* assets, belongings, effects, goods, holdings, possessions, property **2** *he has deer on his estate:* holdings, land, landholding, lands, manor, property, real estate

3 *a housing estate:* area, centre, development, land, region, tract **4** *fallen from his former lofty estate:* class, condition, place, position, rank, situation, standing, state, status

estate agent *n* property agent, real-estate agent, realtor *US*

esteem *n* account, admiration, appreciation, approbation *formal*, consideration, count, credit, estimation, good opinion, honour, judgement, love, reckoning, regard, respect, reverence, veneration *formal*
♦ *v* account, adjudge *formal*, admire, believe, cherish, consider, count, deem *formal*, hold, honour, judge, rate, reckon, regard, regard highly, respect, revere, reverence, think, treasure, value, venerate *formal*, view

esteemed *adj* admirable, admired, distinguished, excellent, highly-regarded, honourable, honoured, prized, reputable, respectable, respected, revered, treasured, valued, venerated *formal*, well-respected, well-thought-of, worthy

estimable *adj* admirable, commendable, creditable, distinguished, esteemed, excellent, good, honourable, laudable *formal*, meritorious *formal*, notable, noteworthy, praiseworthy, reputable, respectable, respected, valuable, valued, worthy
☒ despicable, insignificant

estimate *v* assess, calculate roughly, conjecture *formal*, evaluate, gauge, guess, reckon, value, work out approximately
♦ *n* **1** *get several estimates before you choose:* approximate cost/price/value/quantity, approximation, assessment, ballpark figure *colloq*, computation, estimation, evaluation, guesstimate *colloq*, judgement, quotation, reckoning, rough calculation, (rough) guess, valuation **2** *I revised my estimate of her mother:* assessment, belief, conclusion, consideration, evaluation, judgement, opinion, reckoning, thinking, view

estimation *n* **1** *correct in his estimation:* assessment, belief, calculation, computation, conception, conclusion, consideration, estimate, evaluation, feeling, judgement, opinion, reckoning, view, (way of) thinking **2** *Trollope rose in my estimation:* appreciation, credit, esteem, regard **3** *a written estimation:* approximate cost/price/value/quantity, assessment, estimate, evaluation, rough calculation, (rough) guess, valuation

estrange *v* alienate, antagonize, break up, disaffect, disunite, divide, divorce, drive a wedge between *colloq*, drive apart, part, put a barrier between *colloq*, separate, set against, set at variance, sever, split up, withdraw, withhold
☒ attract, bind, unite

estranged *adj* alienated, antagonized, disaffected, divided, divorced, separate, separated
☒ reconciled, united

estrangement *n* alienation, antagonization, antipathy, breach, break-up, disaffection, dissociation, disunity, division, hostility, parting, separation, severance, split, unfriendliness, withdrawal, withholding

estuary *n* arm, bay, cove, creek, firth, fjord, inlet, mouth, sea-loch

et cetera *adv* and so forth, and so on, and suchlike, and the like, and the rest, and what have you *colloq*, and/or whatever *colloq*, et al

etch *v* bite, burn, carve, corrode, cut, dig, engrave, furrow, groove, impress, imprint, incise, ingrain, inscribe, stamp

etching *n* carving, cut, engraving, impression, imprint, inscription, print, sketch

eternal *adj* **1** *eternal bliss:* ceaseless, deathless, endless, everlasting, immortal, imperishable, indestructible, infinite, limitless, never-ending, undying, unending **2** *eternal truths:* abiding, enduring, lasting, perennial, timeless, unchanging **3** *eternal quarrelling:* constant, continuous, endless, incessant, interminable, never-ending, non-stop, perpetual, persistent, relentless, remorseless, unremitting *formal*
☒ **1** ephemeral, temporary **2** changeable

eternally *adv* **1** *eternally yours:* ceaselessly, endlessly, everlastingly, for ever, indestructibly **2** *I am eternally paying him compliments:* always, constantly, for ever, incessantly, interminably, lastingly, perpetually
☒ **1** briefly, temporarily

eternity *n* **1** *for all eternity:* deathlessness, endlessness, everlasting, everlasting life, everlastingness, immortality, immutability, imperishability, infinity, perpetuity **2** *be together in eternity:* after-life, heaven, hereafter, next world, paradise, world to come, world without end **3** *she took an eternity to get dressed:* age, ages, ages and ages, donkey's years *colloq*, long time

ethereal *adj* **1** *ethereal breeze:* airy-fairy, dainty, delicate, diaphanous *formal*, exquisite, fine, gossamer, immaterial, impalpable, insubstantial, intangible, light, subtle, tenuous **2** *ethereal creatures:* celestial, elemental, empyreal *formal*, empyrean *formal*, heavenly, rarefied, refined, spiritual, unearthly, unworldly
☒ **2** earthly, solid

ethical *adj* above reproach, commendable, correct, decent, decorous *formal*, fair, fitting, good, high-minded, honest, honourable, just, moral, noble, principled, proper, right, righteous, upright, virtuous
☒ unethical

ethics *n* beliefs, code, conscience, equity, moral code, moral philosophy, moral principles, moral standards, moral values, morality, morals, principles, principles of behaviour, principles of right and wrong, propriety *formal*, rules, standards, values

ethnic *adj* aboriginal, autochthonous *formal*, cultural, folk, indigenous, national, native, racial, traditional, tribal

ethos *n* attitude, beliefs, character, code, disposition, ethics, flavour, manners, morality, principles, rationale, spirit, standards, tenor

etiquette *n* ceremony, civility *formal*, code, code of behaviour, code of conduct, code of practice, conventions, correctness, courtesy, customs, decency, decorum *formal*, form, formalities, good form, good manners, manners, politeness, propriety *formal*, protocol *formal*, rules, standards, unwritten law

etymology *n* derivation, lexicology, linguistics, origin, philology, semantics, source, word history, word origins, word-lore

eulogize *v* acclaim, applaud, approve, celebrate, commend, compliment, congratulate, exalt, extol, glorify, honour, hype *colloq*, laud *formal*, magnify, panegyrize *formal*, plug *colloq*, praise, rave about *colloq*, sing/sound the praises of, wax lyrical
🔄 condemn

eulogy *n* acclaim, acclamation, accolade, applause, commendation, compliment, encomium *formal*, exaltation, glorification, laud *formal*, laudation *formal*, laudatory *formal*, paean *formal*, panegyric *formal*, plaudit, praise, tribute
🔄 condemnation

euphemism *n* evasion, genteelism, indirect expression, polite term, politeness, softening, substitution, understatement
🔄 dysphemism

euphemistic *adj* evasive, genteel, indirect, neutral, polite, soft-toned, understated, vague

euphonious *adj* canorous *formal*, clear, consonant *formal*, dulcet, dulcifluous *formal*, dulciloquent *formal*, euphonic *formal*, harmonious, mellifluous *formal*, mellow, melodic, melodious, musical, silvery, soft, sweet, sweet-sounding, sweet-toned, symphonious *formal*, tuneful
🔄 cacophonous

euphoria *n* bliss, buoyancy, cheerfulness, ecstasy, elation, enthusiasm, exaltation, exhilaration, exultation, glee, high *colloq*, high spirits, intoxication, joy, jubilation, rapture, transport, well-being
🔄 depression, despondency

euphoric *adj* blissful, buoyant, cheerful, ecstatic, elated, enraptured, enthusiastic, exhilarated, exultant, exulted, gleeful, happy, high *colloq*, intoxicated, joyful, joyous *formal*, jubilant, rapturous
🔄 depressed, despondent

euthanasia *n* happy/merciful release, mercy killing, quietus, release

evacuate *v* 1 *evacuate the area*: abandon, clear (out) *colloq*, decamp, depart, desert, forsake *formal*, go away from, leave, move out of, pull out of *colloq*, quit *colloq*, relinquish, remove, retire from, retreat, vacate, withdraw 2 *evacuate the bowels*: clear, defecate *formal*, discharge, eject, eliminate, empty, excrete *formal*, expel, make empty, purge, void

evacuation *n* 1 *the evacuation of the building*: abandonment, clearance, departure, desertion, exodus, flight, forsaking *formal*, leaving, quitting *colloq*, relinquishment, retreat, vacating 2 *an evacuation of civilians*: leaving, removal, retirement, withdrawal 3 *evacuation of the bowels*: defecation *formal*, discharge, ejection, elimination, emptying, expulsion, purging, urination

evade *v* 1 *evade your duties*: avoid, balk, chicken out *colloq*, circumvent *formal*, cop out *colloq*, dodge *colloq*, duck *colloq*, elude, escape, fend off, get round, shirk, shun, sidestep, skive *colloq*, steer clear of 2 *evade a question*: avoid, beat about the bush *colloq*, dodge *colloq*, duck *colloq*, equivocate,

fence, fudge, hedge *colloq*, parry, prevaricate, quibble
🔄 1 confront, face

evaluate *v* appraise *formal*, assess, calculate, compute, determine, estimate, gauge, judge, measure, rank, rate, reckon, size up, value, weigh

evaluation *n* appraisal *formal*, assessment, calculation, computation, determination, estimate, estimation, judgement, opinion, reckoning, valuation

evanescent *adj* brief, disappearing, ephemeral, evaporating, fading, fleeting, impermanent, insubstantial, momentary, passing, perishable, short-lived, temporary, transient, transitory, unstable, vanishing
🔄 permanent

evangelical *adj* 1 *evangelical Christianity*: Bible-bashing *colloq*, Bible-believing, Bible-punching *colloq*, Bible-thumping *colloq*, biblical, crusading, fundamentalist, missionary, orthodox, scriptural 2 *a typically evangelical ex-smoker*: campaigning, crusading, enthusiastic, evangelistic, missionary, propagandist, propagandizing, proselytizing, zealous

evangelist *n* campaigner, crusader, missionary, missioner, preacher, revivalist

evangelize *v* baptize, campaign, convert, crusade, gospelize, missionarize, missionize, preach, propagandize, proselytize, spread the word

evaporate *v* 1 *alcohol evaporates*: dematerialize, disappear, dispel, disperse, dissolve, evanesce *formal*, fade, melt (away), vanish 2 *his anger evaporated*: disappear, disperse, dissolve, fade, melt (away), vanish 3 *evaporated milk*: dehydrate, desiccate *formal*, dry, exhale, vaporize

evaporation *n* condensation, dehydration, dematerialization, desiccation *formal*, dissolution, distillation, drying, fading, melting, vanishing, vaporization

evasion *n* 1 *tax evasion*: avoidance, circumvention *formal*, ducking *colloq*, escape, fencing, hedging *colloq*, prevarication, shirking, shunning, steering clear of, subterfuge, tergiversation *formal*, trickery 2 *evasions rather than straight answers*: deceit, deception, dodge *colloq*, dodging *colloq*, ducking *colloq*, equivocation, excuse, fudging, hedging *colloq*, prevarication, quibble, trickery
🔄 2 directness, frankness

evasive *adj* cagey *colloq*, cunning, deceitful, deceptive, devious, equivocating, fudging, indirect, misleading, oblique, prevaricating, quibbling, secretive, shifty *colloq*, slippery *colloq*, tricky, unforthcoming, vague, waffling *colloq*
🔄 direct, frank

eve *n* brink, day before, edge, period before, threshold, time before, verge

even *adj* 1 *on an even surface*: flat, flush, horizontal, level, parallel, plane, smooth, true, uniform 2 *at an even rate*: consistent, constant, regular, stable, steady, unchanging, uniform, unvarying, unwavering 3 *ranked even*: alike, balanced, equal, evenly matched, fifty-fifty *colloq*, level, like, matching, neck and neck *colloq*, on an equal footing, same, side by side, similar,

symmetrical **4** *an even temper:* calm, composed, cool, equable, even-tempered, placid, serene, tranquil, unexcitable, unflappable *colloq*, unperturbable *formal*, unruffled **5** *even chance:* balanced, equitable, even-handed, fair, impartial, just, neutral, non-partisan
F3 1 uneven **3** unequal
♦ *adv* **1** *things got even worse:* all the more, more, still, to a greater extent/degree, yet **2** *you can walk or even run:* also, as well, likewise, oddly, still more, surprisingly, too, unexpectedly, unusually **3** *sad, even depressed:* indeed, more exactly, more precisely **4** *could not even write his own name:* at all, hardly, scarcely, so much as
♦ *v* **1** *even the surface:* align, balance, flatten, level, make uniform, plane, regularize, smooth, stabilize, steady, straighten, strike a balance *colloq* **2** *even the score:* balance, equalize, make equal, match, square

even-handed *adj* balanced, disinterested, dispassionate, equitable, fair, fair and square, impartial, just, neutral, non-discriminatory, reasonable, square, unbiased, unprejudiced, without fear or favour
F3 discriminatory, inequitable

evening *n* close of day, dusk, eve, eventide, nightfall, sundown, sunset, twilight

event *n* **1** *an event that changed her life:* adventure, affair, business, case, circumstance, episode, eventuality *formal*, experience, fact, happening, incident, matter, milestone, occasion, occurrence, possibility **2** *team events:* competition, contest, engagement, fixture, game, item, match, meeting, race, round, tournament **3** *the venture had no successful event:* aftermath, conclusion, consequence, effect, end, issue, outcome, result, termination *formal*, upshot

even-tempered *adj* calm, composed, cool, cool and collected, equable, imperturbable *formal*, laid-back *colloq*, level-headed, peaceable, peaceful, placid, serene, stable, steady, tranquil, unfazed *colloq*, unflappable *colloq*
F3 erratic, excitable

eventful *adj* action-packed *colloq*, active, busy, critical, crucial, exciting, full, historic, important, interesting, lively, memorable, momentous, notable, noteworthy, remarkable, significant, unforgettable
F3 dull, ordinary

eventual *adj* closing, concluding, ensuing, final, future, impending, last, later, planned, projected, prospective, resulting, subsequent, ultimate

eventuality *n* case, chance, circumstance, contingency, crisis, emergency, event, happening, happenstance *formal*, likelihood, mishap, outcome, possibility, probability

eventually *adv* after all, at last, at length, at the end of the day *colloq*, finally, in the end, in the final analysis *colloq*, in the fullness of time, in the long run, sooner or later, subsequently, ultimately, when all is said and done *colloq*

ever *adv* **1** *ever the optimist:* always, at all times, constantly, continually, endlessly, eternally, evermore, for ever, incessantly, permanently, perpetually, till doomsday, till hell freezes over *colloq*, till the cows come home *colloq*, till your dying day, until the end of time **2** *if you ever need*

me: at all, at any time, in any case, in any circumstances, on any account, on any occasion
F3 1 never

everlasting *adj* **1** *everlasting life:* endless, eternal, immortal, imperishable, indestructible, infinite, never-ending, permanent, perpetual, timeless, undying **2** *everlasting noise:* constant, continuous, endless, incessant, interminable, never-ending, non-stop, perpetual, persistent, relentless, remorseless, unremitting *formal*
F3 1 temporary, transient

evermore *adv* always, eternally, ever, ever after, for ever, for ever and a day, for ever and ever, henceforth *formal*, hereafter *formal*, in perpetuum *formal*, till doomsday, to the end of time, unceasingly

every *adj* **1** *every child:* each, every individual, every single **2** *make every effort:* all possible, as much as possible **3** *have every confidence:* all, complete, entire, full, total

everybody *n* all and sundry, each one, each person, every person, everyone, one and all, the whole world

everyday *adj* accustomed, average, basic, common, common-or-garden *colloq*, commonplace, conventional, customary, daily, day-to-day, familiar, frequent, habitual, informal, monotonous, normal, ordinary, plain, regular, routine, run-of-the-mill, simple, standard, stock, unimaginative, usual, workaday
F3 exceptional, special, unusual

everyone *n* all and sundry, all the world and his wife *colloq*, each one, each person, every man Jack *colloq*, every person, every Tom, Dick and Harry *colloq*, everybody, one and all, the whole world, Uncle Tom Cobleigh and all *colloq*

everything *n* all, all things, each thing, everything but the kitchen sink *colloq*, lock, stock and barrel, the aggregate *formal*, the entirety, the lot, the sum, the total, the whole bag of tricks *colloq*, the whole caboodle *colloq*, the whole kit and caboodle *colloq*, the whole lot, the whole shebang *colloq*, the whole shooting-match *colloq*, the works *colloq*

everywhere *adv* all around, all over, every place *US colloq*, far and near, far and wide, here there and everywhere *colloq*, high and low, in/ to all places, in/to each place, left *colloq*, near and far, right and centre *colloq*, the world over, throughout, ubiquitous

evict *v* cast out, chuck out *colloq*, dislodge, dispossess, eject, expel, expropriate *formal*, force out, force to leave, kick out *colloq*, oust, put out, remove, show someone the door *colloq*, throw out, throw out on the streets *colloq*, turf out *colloq*, turn out, turn out of house and home *colloq*

eviction *n* clearance, defenestration *formal*, dislodgement, dispossession, ejection, expropriation *formal*, expulsion, removal, the boot *colloq*, the bum's rush *colloq*, the elbow *colloq*, the push *colloq*

evidence *n* **1** *the evidence suggests that:* affirmation *formal*, confirmation, corroboration *formal*, data, documentation, grounds, proof, substantiation *formal*, support, verification

2 *without her evidence there's no case:* affidavit *technical*, attestation *formal*, declaration, testimony **3** *there was no evidence of a break-in:* demonstration, hint, indication, manifestation *formal*, mark, sign, suggestion, symptom, token, trace
♦ *v* affirm *formal*, attest *formal*, betray, confirm, demonstrate, denote *formal*, display, establish, evince *formal*, exhibit, indicated, manifest *formal*, prove, reveal, show, signify, witness

evident *adj* apparent, clear, clear-cut, conspicuous, discernible, distinct, incontestable, incontrovertible, indisputable, manifest *formal*, noticeable, obvious, patent, perceptible, plain, tangible, undoubted, unmistakable, visible

evidently *adv* **1** *evidently hurt by her remark:* apparently, clearly, doubtless(ly), indisputably, manifestly *formal*, obviously, patently, plainly, undoubtedly **2** *she's evidently decided not to come:* apparently, as it would seem/appear, ostensibly *formal*, outwardly, seemingly, so it seems/ appears, to all appearances

evil *adj* **1** *evil and vicious thugs:* bad, base, black, corrupt, cruel, depraved, heinous *formal*, immoral, iniquitous *formal*, malevolent *formal*, malicious, malignant, mischievous, nefarious *formal*, reprehensible *formal*, sinful, sinister, vicious, vile, wicked, wrong **2** *evil spirits:* bad, demonic, devilish, diabolic, malevolent *formal* **3** *the evil effects of drugs:* bad, deadly, deleterious *formal*, destructive, detrimental, harmful, hurtful, injurious, pernicious, poisonous **4** *he had fallen on evil days:* adverse, calamitous, catastrophic, dire, disastrous, inauspicious *formal*, ruinous, unfortunate, unlucky, unpropitious *formal* **5** *a uniquely evil smell:* foul, noisome *formal*, noxious, offensive, stinking
🔁 **1** good **4** fortunate
♦ *n* **1** *struggle between good and evil:* badness, baseness, corruption, depravity, devilishness, heinousness *formal*, immorality, iniquity *formal*, malignity *formal*, mischief, misconduct, sin, sinfulness, vice, viciousness, vileness, wickedness, wrong, wrongdoing **2** *safe against future evils:* adversity, affliction *formal*, blow, calamity, catastrophe, curse, disaster, distress, harm, hurt, ill, injury, misery, misfortune, pain, ruin, sorrow, suffering, woe

evildoer *n* bad person, criminal, delinquent, miscreant, offender, reprobate, rogue, scoundrel, sinner, villain, wrongdoer

evince *v* attest *formal*, bespeak *formal*, betoken *formal*, betray, confess, declare, demonstrate, display, establish, evidence *formal*, exhibit, express, indicate, manifest *formal*, reveal, show, signify
🔁 conceal, suppress

eviscerate *v* disembowel, draw, exenterate *formal*, gralloch, gut

evocation *n* activation, arousal, calling, echo, elicitation, excitation, inducing, invocation, kindling, recall, stimulation, stirring, suggestion, summoning-up

evocative *adj* expressive, graphic, indicative, memorable, redolent *formal*, reminiscent, suggestive, vivid

evoke *v* arouse, awaken, bring about, bring back memories of, call, call forth, call up, cause, conjure up, elicit, excite, induce, invoke, kindle,

make someone think of, provoke, raise, recall, stimulate, stir, summon (up)
🔁 suppress

evolution *n* derivation, descent, development, expansion, growth, increase, opening-out, progress, progression, ripening, unfolding, unravelling, unrolling, working-out

evolve *v* derive, descend, develop, elaborate, emerge, enlarge, expand, grow, increase, mature, open out, progress, result, unfold, unravel, unroll, work out

exacerbate *v* add fuel to the fire/flames *colloq*, add insult to injury *colloq*, aggravate, compound the problem, deepen, embitter, enrage, exaggerate, exasperate, fan the flames *colloq*, heighten, increase, inflame, infuriate, intensify, irritate, make things/matters worse, make worse, provoke, rub salt in the wound *colloq*, sharpen, vex, worsen
🔁 soothe

exact *adj* **1** *the exact location:* accurate, bang on *colloq*, blow-by-blow *colloq*, correct, definite, detailed, explicit, express, factual, faithful, faultless, flawless, identical, just, literal, on the button *colloq*, on the nail *colloq*, precise, right, specific, spot on *colloq*, strict, true, unerring, veracious *formal*, word-perfect **2** *exact in measuring the food:* careful, exacting, methodical, meticulous, orderly, painstaking, particular, precise, punctilious *formal*, rigorous, scrupulous, thorough
🔁 **1** imprecise, inexact **2** careless
♦ *v* bleed *colloq*, call for, claim, command, compel, demand, extort, extract, force, impose, insist on, milk *colloq*, require, squeeze, wrest, wring

exacting *adj* arduous, challenging, demanding, difficult, firm, hard, harsh, laborious, onerous, painstaking, rigorous, severe, stern, strict, stringent, taxing, tiring, tough, unsparing, unyielding
🔁 easy

exactitude *n* accuracy, care, carefulness, conscientiousness, correctness, detail, exactness, faultlessness, meticulousness, orderliness, painstakingness, perfectionism, precision, rigorousness, rigour, scrupulousness, strictness, thoroughness
🔁 carelessness, imprecision, inaccuracy

exactly *adv* **1** *he described the scene exactly:* accurately, carefully, correctly, explicitly, expressly, faithfully, faultlessly, literally, methodically, particularly, precisely, religiously, rigorously, scrupulously, specifically, strictly, to the letter, unerringly, veraciously *formal*, verbatim, without error **2** *at exactly eight o'clock:* absolutely, bang on *colloq*, definitely, indeed, just, on the button *colloq*, on the dot *colloq*, on the nail *colloq*, plumb *colloq*, precisely, quite, smash *colloq*, spot on *colloq*, to a T *colloq*, truly, unequivocally
🔁 **1** inaccurately, roughly, vaguely
♦ *interj* absolutely, agreed, certainly, indeed, just so, of course, precisely, quite, right, true

exactness *n* accuracy, care, carefulness, correctness, exactitude, faultlessness, meticulousness, orderliness, precision, rigorousness, rigour, scrupulousness, strictness, thoroughness
🔁 carelessness, imprecision, inaccuracy

exaggerate *v* aggrandize *formal*, amplify, blow something up out of all proportion *colloq*, colour, dramatize, embellish, embroider, emphasize, enhance, enlarge, lay/pile it on *colloq*, lay/pile it on thick *colloq*, lay/pile it on with a trowel *colloq*, magnify, make a drama out of a crisis *colloq*, make a mountain out of a molehill *colloq*, make too much of, overdo, overdramatize, overemphasize, overplay, oversell, overstate, shoot a line *colloq*, stress, stretch the truth
F⃥ play down, understate

exaggerated *adj* amplified, bombastic, burlesqued, caricatured, embellished, euphuistic *technical*, exalted, excessive, extravagant, hyperbolic *formal*, inflated, overblown, overcharged, overdone, overestimated, overstated, pretentious, tall *colloq*
F⃥ played down, understated

exaggeration *n* amplification, burlesque, caricature, embellishment, emphasis, enlargement, excess, extravagance, hyperbole *formal*, magnification, overemphasis, overestimation, overstatement, parody, pretentiousness
F⃥ meiosis, understatement

exalt *v* 1 *exalts her as a genius*: acclaim, adore, applaud, bless, eulogize, extol, glorify, honour, laud *formal*, magnify, praise, revere, reverence, venerate *formal*, worship 2 *physically tired, but spiritually exalted*: aggrandize *formal*, delight, elate, elevate, enliven, excite, exhilarate, overjoy, prefer, promote, raise, transport, upgrade

exaltation *n* 1 *click up my heels in pure joy and exaltation*: bliss, ecstasy, elation, excitement, exhilaration, high spirits, joy, jubilation, rapture 2 *songs of exaltation*: acclaim, adoration, eulogy, glorification, glory, honour, praise, reverence, veneration *formal*, worship

exalted *adj* 1 *exalted rank*: elevated, eminent, grand, high, idealistic, lofty, lordly, moral, noble, regal, stately, virtuous 2 *with an exalted smile*: blissful, ecstatic, elated, happy, in high spirits, in seventh heaven *colloq*, joyful, jubilant, rapturous

exam *n* examination, exercises, final, oral, paper, practical, questions, quiz, test, viva, viva voce

examination *n* 1 *examination of the object*: analysis, appraisal *formal*, assessment, audit, check, critique, inquiry, inspection, investigation, observation, once-over *colloq*, perusal, post-mortem, probe, research, review, scan, scrutiny, search, study, survey 2 *given a medical examination*: analysis, assessment, check-up, exploration, investigation, post-mortem 3 *take an English examination*: exam, oral, quiz, test, viva 4 *the examination by the prosecution*: cross-examination, cross-questioning, inquisition, interrogation, questioning

examine *v* 1 *he examined the charts carefully*: analyse, appraise *formal*, assay *technical*, assess, audit, case *slang*, check (out), check over, consider, explore, inspect, investigate, look at, look into, observe, peruse, ponder, pore over, research, review, scan, scrutinize, sift, study, survey, vet, weigh up 2 *examined her cuts*: assess, check over, inspect, look at, scrutinize, study, vet

3 *we were examined on French vocabulary*: question, quiz, test

examinee *n* applicant, candidate, competitor, contestant, entrant, interviewee

examiner *n* adjudicator, analyst, arbiter, assayer *technical*, assessor, auditor, censor, critic, examinant *formal*, inspector, interlocutor *formal*, interviewer, judge, marker, questioner, reader, reviewer, scrutator *formal*, scrutineer, scrutinizer, tester

example *n* 1 *throughout the examples given*: archetype *formal*, exemplar *formal*, pattern, prototype, sample, specimen, type 2 *an example of the Art Deco style*: case, case in point, criterion, epitome, exemplification, illustration, instance, representation, standard, typical case 3 *an excellent example to her peers*: guide, ideal, model, paradigm *formal*, role model 4 *let that be an example to you*: admonition *formal*, caution, lesson, precedent, punishment, warning

exasperate *v* anger, annoy, bug *colloq*, drive up the wall *colloq*, enrage, gall, get on someone's nerves *colloq*, get to *colloq*, goad, incense, infuriate, irk, irritate, madden, make someone's blood boil *colloq*, needle *colloq*, provoke, put someone's back up *colloq*, rankle, rile, rouse, vex, wind up *colloq*
F⃥ appease, pacify

exasperated *adj* aggravated *colloq*, angered, angry, annoyed, at the end of your tether *colloq*, bugged *colloq*, fed up *colloq*, galled, goaded, incensed, indignant, infuriated, irked, irritated, maddened, needled *colloq*, nettled *colloq*, peeved *colloq*, piqued, provoked, riled, vexed
F⃥ calm, satisfied

exasperating *adj* aggravating *colloq*, annoying, bothersome, disagreeable, galling, infuriating, irksome, irritating, maddening, pernicious, provoking, troublesome, vexatious, vexing

excavate *v* burrow, cut, delve, dig (out), dig up, disinter, exhume *formal*, gouge, hollow, mine, quarry, reveal, scoop, tunnel, uncover, unearth

excavation *n* burrow, cavity, colliery, crater, cutting, dig, diggings, ditch, dugout, hole, hollow, mine, pit, quarry, shaft, trench, trough

exceed *v* be greater/larger than, be more than, be superior to, beat, better, cap, eclipse, go beyond, go over, outdo, outnumber, outreach, outrun, outshine, outstrip, outweigh, overdo, overstep, overtake, pass, surpass, top, transcend

exceedingly *adv* amazingly, astonishingly, enormously, especially, exceptionally, excessively, extraordinarily, extremely, greatly, highly, hugely, immensely, inordinately, superlatively, surpassingly, unprecedentedly, unusually, vastly, very, very much

excel *v* 1 *he excels at sport*: be excellent, be outstanding, be pre-eminent, be skilful, predominate, shine, stand out, succeed 2 *she excelled all singers of her day*: be better than, be superior to, beat, better, eclipse, outclass, outdo, outperform, outrank, outrival, surpass

excellence *n* distinction, eminence, fineness, goodness, greatness, merit, perfection, pre-eminence, purity, quality, skill, superiority, supremacy, transcendence, value, virtue, worth

excellent *adj* ace *colloq,* admirable, brill *colloq,* brilliant, commendable, cool *slang,* crucial *slang,* distinguished, eminent, exceptional, exemplary, fantastic, faultless, fine, first-class, first-rate, flawless, good, great, groovy *slang,* high-quality, inspired, marvellous, matchless, mega *slang,* neat *colloq,* notable, noted, noteworthy, out of this world *colloq,* outstanding, perfect, praiseworthy, pre-eminent, prime, radical *slang,* remarkable, second to none *colloq,* select, shit-hot *slang,* smashing *colloq,* splendid, sterling *formal,* stonking *slang,* superb, superior, superlative, surpassing, terrific *colloq,* top-notch *colloq,* unequalled, unparalleled, very good, way-out *slang,* wicked *slang,* wonderful, worthy
▭ inferior, second-rate

except *prep* apart from, aside from, bar, barring, besides, but, but for, except for, excepting, excluding, leaving out, less, minus, not counting, omitting, other than, save, with the exception of
♦ *v* bar, exclude, leave out, omit, pass over, reject, rule out

exception *n* abnormality, anomaly *formal,* departure, deviation, freak, inconsistency, irregularity, oddity, peculiarity, quirk, rarity, special case

exceptionable *adj* abhorrent, deplorable, disagreeable, disgusting, objectionable, offensive, repugnant *formal,* unacceptable, unpleasant
▭ acceptable, agreeable

exceptional *adj* **1** *an exceptional pianist:* brilliant, excellent, extraordinary, marvellous, notable, noteworthy, outstanding, phenomenal, prodigious *formal,* remarkable, superior, unequalled **2** *these are exceptional circumstances:* aberrant *formal,* abnormal, anomalous *formal,* atypical, extraordinary, irregular, odd, out of the ordinary, peculiar, rare, singular *formal,* special, strange, uncommon, unusual
▭ **1** mediocre **2** normal

exceptionally *adv* **1** *he was exceptionally shy:* amazingly, especially, extraordinarily, extremely, notably, outstandingly, remarkably, wonderfully **2** *an exceptionally heavy baby:* abnormally, irregularly, rarely, uncommonly, unusually

excerpt *n* citation, clip, clipping, cutting, extract, fragment, part, passage, pericope *technical,* piece, portion, quotation, quote, scrap, section, selection .

excess *n* **1** *an excess of fat:* glut, more than enough, overabundance, oversupply, superabundance, surplus, too much **2** *trim off the excess:* glut, leftovers, more than enough, overabundance, overflow, oversupply, remainder, residue, superfluity *formal,* surplus **3** *the excesses of youth:* debauchery, dissipation *formal,* dissoluteness, extravagance, immoderateness, immoderation, intemperance *formal,* overindulgence, prodigality *formal,* unrestraint
▭ **2** deficiency **3** restraint
♦ *adj* additional, extra, left-over, redundant, remaining, residual, spare, superfluous, supernumerary *formal,* surplus, too much
▭ inadequate

excessive *adj* disproportionate, exorbitant, extravagant, extreme, immoderate, inordinate, lavish, needless, OTT *colloq,* over the top *colloq,* overdone, steep *colloq,* superabundant, superfluous, too much, uncalled-for, undue, unnecessary, unneeded, unreasonable, unwarranted
▭ insufficient

excessively *adv* disproportionately, exaggeratedly, exorbitantly, extravagantly, extremely, immoderately, inordinately, intemperately, needlessly, overly, overmuch, superfluously, to a fault, too much, unduly, unnecessarily, unreasonably
▭ inadequately, insufficiently

exchange *v* bandy, bargain, barter, change, commute, convert, interchange, reciprocate, replace, stand in for, substitute, swap, switch, trade, transpose
♦ *n* **1** *an exchange of gunfire:* give and take *colloq,* interchange, reciprocity *formal,* replacement, substitution, swap, switch **2** *the exchange of goods:* commerce, dealing, market, trade, trade-off, traffic **3** *a heated exchange:* argument, chat, conversation, discussion

excise[1] *n* customs, duty, impost *formal,* levy, surcharge, tariff, tax, toll, VAT

excise[2] *v* cut, cut out, delete, destroy, eradicate, erase, expunge *formal,* expurgate *formal,* exterminate, extirpate *formal,* extract, remove, rescind *formal*

excision *n* deletion, destruction, eradication, expunction, expurgation *formal,* extermination *formal,* extirpation *formal,* removal

excitable *adj* choleric *formal,* edgy *colloq,* emotional, fiery, hasty, highly-strung, hot-headed, hot-tempered, irascible, mercurial *formal,* nervous, passionate, quick-tempered, sensitive, susceptible, temperamental, volatile
▭ calm, stable

excite *v* **1** *excite a feeling:* agitate, animate, arouse, awaken, disturb, engender, evoke, fire, ignite, impress, inflame, inspire, kindle, move, rouse, stir up, thrill, touch, turn on *colloq,* upset **2** *excite an action:* bring about, galvanize, generate, incite, induce, instigate, motivate, provoke, stimulate, sway **3** *excite sexually:* arouse, awaken, stimulate, titillate, turn on *colloq*
▭ **1** calm

excited *adj* agitated, animated, aroused, beside yourself, eager, elated, enthusiastic, exhilarated, fired up *colloq,* frantic, frenzied, high *colloq,* hyper *colloq,* in high spirits, moved, on tenterhooks *colloq,* on the edge of your seat *colloq,* overwrought, restless, roused, stimulated, stirred, thrilled, thrilled to bits *colloq,* turned on *colloq,* uptight *colloq,* wild, worked up, wrought-up
▭ apathetic, calm

excitement *n* **1** *the excitement of winning:* adventure, agitation, animation, discomposure, eagerness, elation, emotion, enthusiasm, exhilaration, ferment, fever, kick(s) *colloq,* passion, perturbation *formal,* pleasure, restlessness, stimulation, thrill **2** *urban excitements:* action, activity, ado, commotion, flurry, furore, fuss, stir, tumult, unrest
▭ **1** apathy **2** calm

exciting adj action-packed colloq, breathtaking, cliff-hanging colloq, dramatic, electrifying, enthralling, exhilarating, inspiring, interesting, intoxicating, moving, nail-biting colloq, provocative, rousing, sensational, sexy colloq, stimulating, stirring, striking, thrilling
🔁 dull, unexciting

exclaim v bellow, blurt (out), call, come out with, cry (out), declare, ejaculate formal, proclaim, roar, shout, shriek, utter, vociferate formal, yell

exclamation n bellow, call, cry, ejaculation formal, expletive, interjection, outcry, roar, shout, shriek, utterance, yell

exclude v 1 exclude women from the priesthood: ban, bar, blacklist, disallow, forbid, interdict formal, keep out, ostracize, prohibit, refuse, shut out, veto 2 excluding tax: delete, drop colloq, eliminate, ignore, leave out, miss out, omit, preclude formal, reject, rule out, skip colloq 3 excluded from school: boot out colloq, eject, evict, excommunicate, expel, kick out colloq, remove, throw out, turf out colloq
🔁 1 admit 2 consider, include

exclusion n 1 exclusion of rational thought: elimination, omission, preclusion formal, refusal, rejection, repudiation, ruling out 2 exclusion from away games: ban, bar, boycott, embargo, interdict formal, prohibition, proscription formal, veto 3 exclusion from school: boycott, ejection, eviction, exception, expulsion, removal
🔁 1 inclusion 2 allowance 3 admittance

exclusive adj exclusive live coverage: individual, only, peculiar, single, sole, unique, unshared 2 for the exclusive use of her parents: only, single, sole, unshared 3 her exclusive London address: chic, choice, classy colloq, cliquey, closed, discriminative, elegant, fashionable, limited, narrow, plush colloq, posh colloq, private, restricted, restrictive, ritzy colloq, select, snazzy colloq, snobbish, swish colloq, up-market, upper-crust

excommunicate v anathematize formal, ban, banish, bar, blacklist, debar, denounce, disfellowship, eject, exclude, execrate formal, expel, outlaw, proscribe formal, remove, repudiate, unchurch

excoriate v animadvert formal, attack, blame, carp, censure, come down on colloq, condemn, decry formal, denigrate formal, denounce, disapprove of, disparage formal, find fault with, give someone some stick colloq, knock colloq, nag colloq, nit-pick colloq, run down colloq, slam colloq, slate colloq, snipe colloq, vituperate formal

excrement n crap slang, droppings, dung, egesta technical, excretion, faeces formal, frass, guano, ordure, poop slang, scats, shit slang, stool formal, turd, waste matter

excrescence n appendage, boil, bump, cancer, growth, intumescence formal, knob, lump, outgrowth, projection, prominence, protuberance formal, swelling, tumour, wart

excrete v crap slang, defecate formal, discharge, eject, evacuate, expel, exude, pass, secrete, shit slang, urinate formal, void

excretion n crap slang, defecation formal, discharge, droppings, dung, evacuation,

excrement, excreta formal, faeces formal, ordure, perspiration, shit slang, stool formal, urination formal

excruciating adj acute, agonizing, atrocious, bitter, burning, extreme, harrowing, insufferable, intense, intolerable, painful, piercing, racking, savage, severe, sharp, tormenting, unbearable

exculpate v absolve, acquit, clear, deliver, discharge, excuse, exonerate formal, forgive, free, justify, let off, pardon, release, vindicate
🔁 blame, condemn

excursion n 1 their annual excursion: airing, breather, day trip, drive, expedition, jaunt, journey, junket colloq, outing, ramble, ride, tour, trip, walk 2 excursion into TV drama: departure, detour, digression, diversion, straying, wandering

excusable adj allowable, defensible, explainable, forgivable, justifiable, minor, pardonable, permissible, slight, understandable
🔁 blameworthy

excuse v 1 he can excuse her anything: absolve, acquit, exculpate formal, exonerate formal, forgive, ignore, indulge, make allowances for, overlook, pardon, tolerate 2 we were excused from the table: discharge, exempt, free, let off, liberate, release, relieve, spare 3 I won't excuse or explain my conduct: apologize for, condone, defend, explain, justify, mitigate formal, vindicate
🔁 1 criticize 2 punish
◆ n 1 there's no excuse for torture: alibi, apology, defence, exoneration formal, explanation, grounds, justification, mitigating circumstances formal, mitigation formal, plea, vindication 2 a feeble excuse: alibi, cop-out colloq, cover-up colloq, defence, evasion, explanation, front colloq, grounds, pretence, pretext, reason

execrable adj abhorrent, abominable, accursed, appalling, atrocious, damnable, deplorable, despicable, detestable, disgusting, foul, hateful, heinous formal, horrible, loathsome, nauseous, obnoxious, odious, offensive, repulsive, revolting, shocking, vile
🔁 admirable, estimable

execrate v abhor, abominate, anathematize formal, blast colloq, condemn, curse, damn, denounce, denunciate, deplore, despise, detest, excoriate formal, fulminate formal, hate, imprecate, inveigh against formal, loathe, revile, vilify formal
🔁 commend, praise

execute v 1 executed by militia: behead, crucify, decapitate formal, electrocute, guillotine, hang, kill, liquidate colloq, put to death, shoot 2 execute a business plan: accomplish, achieve, administer, bring off, carry out, complete, consummate formal, deliver, discharge, dispatch, do, effect formal, enact, enforce, engineer, expedite formal, finish, fulfil, implement, perform, put into effect, put into practice, realize, render, serve, stage, validate 3 she executed the vault perfectly: accomplish, achieve, bring off, carry out, complete, do, perform

execution n 1 execution for treason: capital punishment, death penalty, death sentence, killing, putting to death 2 execution of policy: accomplishment, achievement, administration, completion, consummation formal, discharge, dispatch, effect, effecting *formal*, enactment, enforcement, fulfilment, implementation, operation, performance, realization **3** *flawless execution:* delivery, manner, mode, performance, presentation, rendering, rendition, staging, style, technique

---
Means of execution include:
beheading, burning, crucifixion, decapitation, electrocution, firing squad, garrotting, gassing, guillotining, hanging, lethal injection, lynching, shooting, stoning, stringing up *colloq*

---

executioner *n* assassin, axeman, exterminator, firing squad, hangman, headsman, hit man *colloq*, killer, liquidator *colloq*, murderer, slayer

executive *n* **1** *a TV executive:* administrator, controller, director, governor, leader, manager, official, organizer **2** *the executive of the housing association:* administration, big guns *colloq*, big shots *colloq*, government, hierarchy, leadership, management, top brass *colloq*
♦ *adj* administrative, controlling, decision-making, directing, directorial, governing, guiding, law-making, leading, managerial, organizational, organizing, regulating, supervisory

exegesis *n* clarification, explanation, explication *formal*, exposition *formal*, expounding *formal*, interpretation, opening-up

exemplar *n* archetype *formal*, copy, criterion, embodiment *formal*, epitome, example, exemplification *formal*, ideal, illustration, instance, model, paradigm *formal*, paragon, pattern, prototype, specimen, standard, type, yardstick

exemplary *adj* **1** *exemplary conduct:* admirable, commendable, correct, estimable *formal*, excellent, faultless, flawless, good, honourable, ideal, laudable *formal*, meritorious *formal*, model, perfect, praiseworthy, worthy **2** *award exemplary damages:* admonitory *formal*, cautionary, warning ◪ **1** imperfect, unworthy

exemplify *v* be an example of, characterize, cite, demonstrate, depict, display, embody, epitomize, exhibit, illustrate, instance, manifest *formal*, personify, represent, show, typify

exempt *v* absolve, discharge, dismiss, exclude, excuse, exonerate *formal*, free, grant immunity to, let off, liberate, make an exception, release, relieve, spare, waive
♦ *adj* absolved, clear, discharged, dismissed, excluded, excused, free, immune, liberated, not liable, not subject, released, spared ◪ liable

exemption *n* absolution *formal*, discharge, dispensation *formal*, exception, exclusion, exoneration *formal*, freedom, immunity, indemnity, indulgence, privilege, release ◪ liability

exercise *v* **1** *exercise great caution:* apply, bring into play, bring to bear, discharge, employ, exert, exploit, implement, make use of, practise, try, use, utilize, wield **2** *she exercises daily:* do exercises, drill, exert yourself, keep fit, practise, train, work out *colloq* **3** *her illness is greatly exercising our minds:* afflict, agitate, annoy, burden, distress, disturb, perturb *formal*, preoccupy, trouble, upset, vex, worry

♦ *n* **1** *aerobic exercise:* activity, aerobics, callisthenics, drill, effort, eurhythmics, exertion, gymnastics, isometrics, jogging, keep-fit, labour, movement, PE, physical education, physical jerks *colloq*, physical training, practice, PT, running, sports, training, warm-up, workout *colloq* **2** *by the exercise of the will alone:* accomplishment, application, discharge, employment, exertion, fulfilment, implementation, use, utilization **3** *a cost-cutting exercise:* application, assignment, operation, practice **4** *comprehension exercises:* discipline, lesson, piece of work, problem, task, work

exert *v* apply, bring into play, bring to bear, employ, exercise, expend, spend, use, utilize, wield

exertion *n* **1** *physical exertion:* effort, assiduousness, attempt, diligence, endeavour, exercise, industry, labour, pains, perseverance, strain, stress, struggle, toil, travail *formal*, trial, work **2** *exertion of control:* action, application, employment, exercise, operation, use, utilization ◪ **1** idleness, rest

exhale *v* blow, breathe (out), discharge, emanate *formal*, emit, evaporate, expel, expire *formal*, give off, issue, respire, steam ◪ inhale

exhaust *v* **1** *her complaining exhausts me:* do in *colloq*, drain, enervate *formal*, fag out *colloq*, fatigue, knock out *colloq*, nearly/almost kill *colloq*, overtax, overwork, sap, strain, take it out of *colloq*, tax, tire (out), weaken, wear out, weary, whack *colloq* **2** *exhausted our supplies:* bankrupt, consume, deplete *formal*, dissipate *formal*, drain, dry, empty, expend, finish, impoverish, sap, spend, squander, use up, waste ◪ **1** refresh **2** renew
♦ *n* discharge, emanation *formal*, emission, exhalation, fumes, smoke, steam, vapour

exhausted *adj* **1** *exhausted from the flight:* all in *colloq*, burnt out *colloq*, bushed *colloq*, dead beat *colloq*, dead tired, dog-tired *colloq*, done (in) *colloq*, drained, enervated *formal*, enfeebled *formal*, fagged out *colloq*, fatigued, jaded, knackered *colloq*, ready to drop *colloq*, tired out, washed-out, weak, whacked *colloq*, worn out, zonked *colloq* **2** *exhausted gas supply:* consumed, depleted *formal*, drained, dry, empty, finished, spent, used up, void, worn out ◪ **1** vigorous **2** replenished

exhausting *adj* arduous, backbreaking, debilitating *formal*, draining, enervating *formal*, formidable, gruelling, hard, laborious, punishing, severe, strenuous, taxing, testing, tiring, wearing ◪ invigorating, refreshing

exhaustion *n* debility *formal*, enervation *formal*, fatigue, feebleness, jet-lag, lethargy, tiredness, weakness, weariness ◪ freshness, liveliness

exhaustive *adj* all-embracing, all-inclusive, all-out, complete, comprehensive, definitive, detailed, encyclopedic, extensive, far-reaching, full, full-scale, in-depth, intensive, sweeping, thorough, total ◪ incomplete, restricted

exhibit *v* air, array *formal*, demonstrate, disclose, display, expose, express, flaunt, indicate, make

clear, make plain, manifest *formal*, offer, parade, present, put on display, reveal, set forth, set out, show, unveil
🔁 conceal, hide
♦ *n* demonstration, display, exhibition, illustration, model, presentation, show, showing

exhibition *n* **1** *an exhibition of skill:* airing, demonstration, disclosure, display, expression, manifestation *formal*, performance, presentation, revelation, show **2** *a painting exhibition:* display, exhibit, expo *colloq*, exposition *formal*, fair, show, showcase, showing, spectacle

exhibitionist *n* extrovert, poser, poseur, self-advertiser, show-off

exhilarate *v* animate, brighten, cheer up, delight, elate, enliven, excite, gladden, invigorate, lift, make excited, make happy, perk up *colloq*, raise/lift the spirits of, revitalize, stimulate, thrill, vitalize
🔁 bore, discourage

exhilarating *adj* breathtaking, cheerful, cheering, delightful, enlivening, exciting, gladdening, heady, invigorating, mind-blowing *colloq*, revitalizing, stimulating, thrilling
🔁 boring, discouraging

exhilaration *n* animation, ardour, cheerfulness, dash, delight, élan *formal*, elation, enthusiasm, exaltation, excitement, gaiety, gladness, glee, gusto, happiness, high spirits, hilarity, invigoration, joy, joyfulness, liveliness, mirth, revitalization, stimulation, thrill, vivacity, zeal
🔁 boredom, discouragement

exhort *v* admonish *formal*, advise, beseech *formal*, bid, call upon, caution, counsel, encourage, enjoin *formal*, entreat *formal*, goad, implore, incite, inflame, inspire, instigate, persuade, press, prompt, spur, urge, warn

exhortation *n* admonition *formal*, advice, beseeching *formal*, bidding, caution, counsel, encouragement, enjoinder *formal*, entreaty *formal*, goading, incitement, lecture, paraenesis *formal*, persuasion, protreptic *formal*, sermon, urging, warning

exhume *v* dig up, disentomb, disinhume *formal*, disinter, excavate, resurrect, unbury, unearth
🔁 bury

exigency *n* **1** *exigencies of rural life:* demand, necessity, need, requirement **2** *exigencies of war:* crisis, criticalness, difficulty, distress, emergency, imperativeness, plight, predicament, pressure, quandary, stress, urgency

exigent *adj* critical, crucial, demanding, exacting, insistent, necessary, pressing, stringent, urgent

exiguous *adj* bare, insufficient, meagre, negligible, scant, scanty, slight, slim, sparse

exile *n* **1** *her exile to France:* banishment, deportation, expatriation, expulsion, ostracism, separating, separation, transportation, uprooting **2** *life of an exile:* deportee, displaced person, émigré, ex-pat, expatriate, outcast, outlaw, pariah, refugee
♦ *v* ban, banish, bar, cast out, deport, drive out, eject, excommunicate, expatriate, expel, extradite, ostracize, oust, outlaw, repatriate, separate, uproot

exist *v* **1** *you can't exist without water:* abide, be, breathe, continue, endure, have being, have breath, have existence, have life, live **2** *exist on shoestring budgets:* eke out a living, eke out an existence, live, subsist, survive **3** *opportunities exist for new graduates:* be available, be present, continue, happen, last, occur, prevail, remain

existence *n* **1** *the existence of God:* actuality, being, breath, continuance, continuation, endurance, fact, life, living, reality, subsistence, survival **2** *an easier existence:* life, lifestyle, mode of living *formal*, way of life, way of living **3** *all the riddles of existence:* creation, the world
🔁 **1** death, non-existence

existent *adj* abiding, actual, alive, around *colloq*, current, enduring, existing, extant *formal*, living, obtaining *formal*, present, prevailing, real, remaining, standing, surviving
🔁 non-existent

exit *n* **1** *his sudden exit:* departure, exodus, farewell, flight, going, leave-taking, leaving, retirement, retreat, withdrawal **2** *the side exit:* door, doorway, egress *formal*, gate, outlet, vent, way out
🔁 **1** arrival, entrance **2** entrance
♦ *v* depart, go, issue, leave, retire, retreat, take your leave, withdraw
🔁 arrive, enter

exodus *n* departure, escape, evacuation, exit, fleeing, flight, hegira, leaving, long march, mass departure, mass evacuation, migration, retirement, retreat, withdrawal

exonerate *v* **1** *exonerated the defendant:* absolve, acquit, clear, declare innocent, discharge, exculpate *formal*, excuse, justify, pardon, vindicate **2** *exonerated from confronting them:* discharge, excuse, exempt, free, let off, liberate, release, relieve, spare
🔁 **1** incriminate

exoneration *n* **1** *exoneration from the accusation:* absolution, acquittal, amnesty, clearing, discharge, dismissal, exculpation *formal*, excusing, justification, pardon, vindication **2** *exoneration from income tax:* discharge, excusing, exemption, freeing, immunity, indemnity, liberation, release, relief
🔁 **1** incrimination

exorbitant *adj* a rip-off *colloq*, daylight robbery *colloq*, enormous, excessive, extortionate, extravagant, immoderate, inordinate, monstrous, preposterous, undue, unreasonable, unwarranted
🔁 fair, moderate, reasonable

exorcism *n* adjuration *formal*, casting out, deliverance, expulsion, exsufflation *old use*, freeing, purification

exorcize *v* adjure *formal*, cast out, drive out, expel, exsufflate *old use*, free, purify

exotic *adj* **1** *exotic plants:* alien, external, foreign, imported, introduced, non-native, tropical **2** *exotic names:* bizarre, colourful, curious, different, extraordinary, extravagant, fascinating, glamorous, impressive, outlandish, outrageous, peculiar, remarkable, sensational, strange, striking, unfamiliar, unusual
🔁 **1** native **2** common, ordinary

expand *v* amplify, become/make larger/bigger, blow up, branch out, broaden, develop, dilate *formal*, distend *formal*, diversify, enlarge, escalate, extend, fatten, fill out, grow, increase, inflate, intensify, intumesce *formal*, lengthen, magnify, multiply, open out, pad, puff out, spread, stretch, swell, thicken, unfold, unfurl, widen

🔁 contract

▶ **expand on** dilate on *formal*, elaborate on, embroider, enlarge on, expatiate on *formal*, go into details

expanse *n* area, breadth, extensiveness, extent, field, plain, range, region, space, stretch, sweep, tract, vastness

expansion *n* amplification, augmentation *formal*, broadening, development, diffusion *formal*, dilatation *formal*, dilation *formal*, distension *formal*, diversification, enlargement, expanse, extension, growth, increase, inflation, lengthening, magnification, multiplication, spread, swelling, thickening, unfolding, unfurling

🔁 contraction

expansive *adj* **1** *expansive gardens*: broad, extensive, wide **2** *expansive reforms*: all-embracing, broad, comprehensive, extensive, thorough, wide-ranging, widespread **3** *he was in an expansive mood and enjoyed chatting*: affable, communicative, effusive, friendly, genial, loquacious *formal*, open, outgoing, sociable, talkative, uninhibited, warm

🔁 **2** narrow, restricted **3** cold, reserved

expatiate *v* amplify, develop, dilate *formal*, dwell on, elaborate, embellish, enlarge, expand, expound

expatriate *n* displaced person, emigrant, émigré, exile, ex-pat, outcast, refugee
♦ *v* banish, deport, drive out, exile, expel, extradite, ostracize, oust, proscribe *formal*, repatriate, uproot
♦ *adj* banished, deported, emigrant, émigré, exiled, expelled, uprooted

expect *v* **1** *I expect you're right*: assume, believe, conjecture *formal*, guess *colloq*, imagine, presume, reckon, suppose, surmise *formal*, think, trust **2** *expect the money soon*: anticipate, await, bank on, bargain for, contemplate, envisage, forecast, foresee, hope for, look for, look forward to, predict, project, watch for **3** *we expect you to comply*: call for, count on, demand, hope for, insist on, look for, rely on, require, want, wish

expectancy *n* anticipation, conjecture *formal*, curiosity, eagerness, expectation, hope, suspense, waiting

expectant *adj* **1** *an expectant crowd*: anticipating, anxious, apprehensive, awaiting, curious, eager, hopeful, in suspense, looking forward, on tenterhooks, ready, watchful, with bated breath **2** *an expectant mother*: enceinte *formal*, expecting *colloq*, going to have a baby, gravid *technical*, in the club *colloq*, in the family way *colloq*, preggers *slang*, pregnant, with a bun in the oven *slang*, with child *formal*

expectantly *adv* apprehensively, eagerly, expectingly, hopefully, in anticipation, in suspense, optimistically

expectation *n* anticipation, assumption, assurance, belief, calculation, confidence, conjecture *formal*, demand, eagerness, forecast,

hope, insistence, optimism, outlook, possibility, prediction, presumption, probability, projection, promise, prospect, reliance, requirement, supposition, surmise, suspense, trust, want, wish

expecting *adj* enceinte *formal*, expectant, going to have a baby, gravid *technical*, in the club *colloq*, in the family way *colloq*, pregnant, with child *formal*

expedience *n* advantage, advantageousness, advisability, appropriateness, aptness, benefit, convenience, desirability, effectiveness, expediency, fitness, helpfulness, judiciousness *formal*, practicality, pragmatism, profitability, profitableness, properness, propriety *formal*, prudence *formal*, suitability, usefulness, utilitarianism, utility

expedient *adj* advantageous, advisable, appropriate, beneficial, convenient, fitting, in your own interest, opportune, politic, practical, pragmatic, profitable, prudent *formal*, sensible, suitable, tactical, useful

🔁 inexpedient

♦ *n* contrivance, device, dodge *colloq*, manoeuvre, means, method, plan, ploy, scheme, shift, stopgap, stratagem, tactic, trick

expedite *v* accelerate, assist, discharge, dispatch, facilitate, further, hasten, hurry, hurry through, precipitate *formal*, press, promote, quicken, speed up, step up

🔁 delay

expedition *n* **1** *expeditions all over Europe*: journey, adventure, campaign, crusade, enterprise, excursion, exploration, hike, mission, outing, pilgrimage, project, quest, raid, ramble, safari, sail, tour, trek, trip, undertaking, voyage **2** *his expedition of forty men*: company, crew, group, party, team **3** *with great expedition*: alacrity *formal*, celerity *formal*, haste, promptness, speed, swiftness

expeditious *adj* active, alert, brisk, diligent, efficient, fast, hasty, immediate, instant, meteoric *colloq*, prompt, quick, rapid, ready, speedy, swift

🔁 slow

expel *v* **1** *expelled from the country*: ban, banish, bar, boot out *colloq*, cast out, chuck out *colloq*, dismiss, drive out, eject, evict, exile, expatriate, kick out *colloq*, oust, outlaw, proscribe *formal*, reject, throw out **2** *expel trapped air*: belch, cast out, discharge, eject, evacuate, spew out, void

🔁 **1** welcome

expend *v* **1** *expend considerable resources*: afford, blow *colloq*, buy, disburse *formal*, fork out *colloq*, fritter, lay out *colloq*, overspend, pay, procure *formal*, purchase *formal*, shell out *colloq*, spend, splash out *colloq*, squander, waste **2** *expend energy*: consume, deplete *formal*, dissipate *formal*, drain, employ, empty, exhaust, get through, go through, sap, use (up), utilize

🔁 **1** save **2** conserve

expendable *adj* dispensable, disposable, inessential, non-essential, replaceable, unimportant, unnecessary

🔁 indispensable, necessary

expenditure *n* **1** *huge amounts of public expenditure*: costs, disbursement *formal*, expense, expenses, outgoings, outlay, output, payment,

spending, squandering, waste **2** *the expenditure of effort*: application, consumption, dissipation *formal*, draining, employment, sapping, use, utilization
⊟ 1 income

expense *n* **1** *underestimate the expense of moving house*: charge, cost, disbursement *formal*, expenditure, fee, loss, outlay, paying-out, payment, price, rate, spending **2** *expenses will be reimbursed*: costs, incidental expenses, incidentals, miscellaneous expenses, outgoings, outlay, out-of-pocket expenses, overheads, spending **3** *at the expense of his life*: detriment, disadvantage, harm, loss, sacrifice

expensive *adj* costing a bomb *colloq*, costing a lot, costing an arm and a leg *colloq*, costing the earth *colloq*, costly, daylight robbery *colloq*, dear, exorbitant, extortionate, extravagant, high-priced, lavish, overpriced, pricey *colloq*, sky-high *colloq*, steep *colloq*
⊟ cheap, inexpensive

experience *n* **1** *management experience*: contact, exposure, familiarity, involvement, know-how *colloq*, knowledge, learning, observation, participation, practice, skill, training, understanding **2** *life-changing experience*: adventure, affair, case, circumstance, encounter, episode, event, happening, incident, occurrence, ordeal
⊟ 1 inexperience
♦ *v* become familiar with, encounter, endure, face, feel, go through, know, live through, meet, participate in, perceive, suffer, sustain, try, undergo

experienced *adj* **1** *an experienced driver*: accomplished, adept, au courant, au fait, capable, competent, expert, familiar, knowledgeable, practised, professional, proficient, qualified, skilful, skilled, trained, tried, well-versed **2** *picked an experienced squad for the tournament*: having been around *colloq*, mature, seasoned, sophisticated, streetwise *colloq*, veteran, wise, worldly wise
⊟ 1 inexperienced, unskilled **2** inexperienced, unsophisticated

experiment *n* analysis, attempt, demonstration, dry run, dummy run, examination, experimentation, inquiry, investigation, observation, pilot study, piloting, procedure, proof, research, test, testing, trial, trial and error, trial run, try-out, venture
♦ *v* carry out tests, conduct an experiment, examine, explore, investigate, observe, research, sample, test, try (out), verify

experimental *adj* at the trial/exploratory stage, empirical *formal*, exploratory, investigative, observational, peirastic *formal*, pilot, preliminary, provisional, speculative, tentative, test, trial, trial-and-error

expert *n* ace *colloq*, authority, buff *colloq*, connoisseur, dab hand *colloq*, egghead *colloq*, maestro, master, maven *US colloq*, mavin *US colloq*, old hand *colloq*, old master, past master, pro *colloq*, professional, pundit, specialist, virtuoso, wise guy *colloq*
♦ *adj* able, accomplished, ace *colloq*, adept, brilliant, crack *colloq*, dexterous, excellent, experienced, knowledgeable, masterly, practised, professional, proficient, qualified,

skilful, skilled, specialist, top-notch *colloq*, up on *colloq*, virtuoso, well up on *colloq*
⊟ amateurish, novice

expertise *n* ability, cleverness, command, deftness, dexterity, expertness, facility, knack *colloq*, know-how *colloq*, knowledge, mastery, professionalism, proficiency, savoir-faire, skilfulness, skill, virtuosity
⊟ inexperience, inexpertness

expiate *v* atone for, do penance for, make amends for, make up for, pay for, purge, redress

expiation *n* amends, atonement, penance, ransom, recompense, redemption, redress, reparation, shrift

expire *v* **1** *my visa has expired*: be no longer valid, cease, close, come to an end, conclude *formal*, discontinue *formal*, end, finish, lapse, run out, stop, terminate *formal* **2** *she expired soon after*: bite the dust *colloq*, breathe your last, cash in your chips *slang*, decease *formal*, depart, depart this life, die, give up the ghost *colloq*, have had it *colloq*, kick the bucket *slang*, lose your life, meet your maker *colloq*, pass away, pass on, peg out *colloq*, perish, pop off *colloq*, snuff it *slang*
⊟ 1 be valid, begin **2** be born, live

expiry *n* cessation *formal*, close, conclusion *formal*, discontinuation *formal*, end, expiration, finish, lapse, termination *formal*
⊟ beginning, continuation

explain *v* **1** *explain the offside rule*: clarify, decipher, decode, define, delineate *formal*, demonstrate, describe, disclose, elaborate, elucidate *formal*, explicate *formal*, expound *formal*, illustrate, interpret, make clear, resolve, set out, simplify, solve, spell out, teach, throw/shed light on, translate, unfold, unravel, untangle **2** *explain your behaviour*: account for, defend, excuse, explain away, give a reason for, justify, lie behind, rationalize, vindicate
⊟ 1 confound, obscure

explanation *n* **1** *explanation of the IVF process*: account, annotation, clarification, comment, commentary, deciphering, decoding, definition, delineation *formal*, demonstration, description, elucidation *formal*, exegesis *formal*, explication *formal*, expounding *formal*, illustration, interpretation, unfolding **2** *no explanation for your rudeness*: account, alibi, answer, apologia *formal*, defence, excuse, justification, meaning, motive, rationalization, reason, vindication, warrant

explanatory *adj* demonstrative, descriptive, elucidatory *formal*, exegetical *formal*, explicative *formal*, expository *formal*, illustrative, interpretative *formal*, interpretive *formal*, justifying

expletive *n* anathema *formal*, bad language, blasphemy, curse, execration *formal*, four-letter word *colloq*, imprecation *formal*, oath, obscenity, profanity, swear-word

explicable *adj* accountable, definable, determinable, explainable, exponible *formal*, intelligible, interpretable *formal*, justifiable, resolvable, solvable, understandable

explicate *v* clarify, define, demonstrate, describe, elucidate *formal*, explain, expound *formal*, illustrate, interpret, make clear, set forth, spell out, unfold, unravel, untangle
⊟ confuse, obscure

explicit *adj* **1** *given explicit instructions:* absolute, categorical, certain, clear, clearly expressed, declared, definite, detailed, direct, distinct, exact, express, positive, precise, specific, stated, straightforward, unambiguous, unequivocal **2** *threat of explicit violence:* candid, direct, forthright, frank, open, outspoken, plain, plain-spoken, straightforward, uninhibited, unreserved, unrestrained
🖛 **1** implicit, unspoken, vague **2** reserved, restrained

explode *v* **1** *the bomb exploded:* blast, blow up, burst, detonate, discharge, erupt *formal,* go bang *colloq,* go off, go up, set off **2** *explode with rage:* blow a fuse *colloq,* blow up, blow your cool *colloq,* blow your top *colloq,* boil over *colloq,* burst a blood vessel *colloq,* burst out, do your nut *colloq,* erupt, flare up, fly into a rage *colloq,* fly off the handle *colloq,* go off the deep end *colloq,* go up the wall *colloq,* hit the ceiling *colloq,* hit the roof *colloq,* lose your cool *colloq,* lose your rag *colloq,* lose your temper, see red *colloq* **3** *explode the myth:* debunk, discredit, disprove, give the lie to, invalidate, rebut, refute *formal,* repudiate **4** *the population exploded:* accelerate, boom, escalate, grow rapidly, increase suddenly, leap, mushroom, rocket, surge
🖛 **3** confirm, prove

exploit *n* accomplishment, achievement, act, action, activity, adventure, attainment, deed, feat, stunt
♦ *v* **1** *exploits the beauty of the countryside:* apply, capitalize on, cash in on *colloq,* draw on, employ, make capital out of, milk *colloq,* profit by, put to good use, take advantage of, tap, turn to account, use, use to good advantage, utilize **2** *exploit the young and vulnerable:* abuse, bleed *colloq,* fleece *colloq,* ill-treat, impose on, manipulate, milk *colloq,* misuse, oppress, play off against *colloq,* profiteer, pull a fast one on *colloq,* put something across someone *colloq,* rip off *colloq,* take advantage of, take for a ride *colloq,* take liberties, walk all over *colloq*

exploration *n* **1** *exploration of police practice:* analysis, examination, inquiry, inspection, investigation, observation, probe, research, scrutiny, study **2** *exploration of the region:* expedition, reconnaissance, safari, search, survey, tour, travel, trip, voyage

exploratory *adj* analytic, experimental, fact-finding, investigative, pilot, probing, searching, tentative, trial

explore *v* **1** *explore the possibilities:* analyse, consider, examine, inquire into, inspect, investigate, look into, probe, research, review, scrutinize, study, survey **2** *dream of exploring Africa:* do *colloq,* prospect, reconnoitre, scout, search, see the world *colloq,* survey, tour, travel, traverse *formal*

explorer *n* discoverer, navigator, prospector, reconnoitrer, scout, surveyor, tourer, traveller

explosion *n* **1** *the explosion destroyed a bus:* bang, blast, boom, burst, clap, crack, detonation, discharge, eruption, fit, outbreak, outburst, report *formal,* roll, rumble, thunder **2** *population explosion:* boom, dramatic growth, leap, sudden increase, surge **3** *explosion of anger:* eruption, fit, flare-up, outburst, paroxysm, rage, tantrum

explosive *n* bomb, cordite, dynamite, gelignite, gunpowder, jelly, nitroglycerine, Semtex®, TNT
♦ *adj* **1** *an explosive device:* charged, dangerous, hazardous, perilous *formal,* unstable, volatile **2** *an explosive situation:* charged, critical, fraught, nerve-racking, sensitive, tense, unstable, volatile **3** *explosive atmosphere:* angry, fiery, overwrought, raging, sensitive, stormy, touchy, unrestrained, unstable, violent, volatile, wild, worked-up **4** *explosive growth:* abrupt, burgeoning, dramatic, meteoric *colloq,* mushrooming, rapid, rocketing, sudden, unexpected
🖛 **2** calm, stable **3** composed

exponent *n* **1** *exponent of Judaism:* adherent, advocate, backer, champion, defender, promoter, proponent *formal,* spokesman, spokesperson, spokeswoman, supporter, upholder **2** *exponent of the six-string bass:* adept, expert, master, performer, player, practitioner, specialist

export *v* deal with, sell abroad/overseas, trade, traffic in, transport
♦ *n* exported product/commodity/goods, foreign trade, international trade, trade, transfer

expose *v* **1** *he was exposed as a fraud:* betray, blow the whistle *colloq,* bring out into the open, bring to light, denounce, detect, disclose, display, divulge, exhibit, lay bare, make known, manifest *formal,* present, reveal, show, take the lid off *colloq,* uncover, unearth, unmask, unveil **2** *exposed to radiation:* endanger, hazard, imperil, jeopardize, make vulnerable, put at risk, put in jeopardy, risk **3** *expose the public to art:* acquaint with, bring into contact with, familiarize with, introduce to, lay open to, subject to
🖛 **1** conceal, cover up **2** protect

exposé *n* account, article, disclosure, divulgence, exposure, revelation, uncovering

exposed *adj* bare, exhibited, in the open, laid bare, on display, on show, on view, open, open to the elements, revealed, shown, susceptible, unprotected, vulnerable, without protection
🖛 covered, sheltered

exposition *n* **1** *exposition of capitalism:* account, analysis, clarification, commentary, critique, description, discourse *formal,* elucidation *formal,* exegesis *formal,* explanation, explication *formal,* illumination, illustration, interpretation, monograph, paper, presentation, study, thesis, unfolding **2** *a technology exposition:* demonstration, display, exhibition, expo *colloq,* fair, show

expository *adj* declaratory *formal,* descriptive, elucidative *formal,* exegetic *technical,* explanatory, explicatory *formal,* hermeneutic, illustrative, interpretative, interpretive *formal*

expostulate *v* argue, dissuade, plead, protest, reason, remonstrate *formal*

exposure *n* **1** *the exposure of his past crimes:* airing, denunciation, detection, disclosure, discovery, divulgence, exposé, manifestation *formal,* publicity, revelation, uncovering, unmasking, unveiling **2** *exposure of her underwear:* display, exhibition, manifestation *formal,* presentation, showing, uncovering **3** *repeated exposure to violence can desensitize you:* acquaintance, awareness, contact, experience, familiarity, knowledge **4** *exposure to price* *fluctuation:* danger, hazard, risk, susceptibility, vulnerability **5** *worldwide exposure:* advertising, hype *colloq*, plug *colloq*, promotion, public attention, publicity

expound *v* analyse, clarify, comment on, describe, dissect, elucidate *formal*, explain, explicate *formal*, illuminate, illustrate, interpret, preach, sermonize, set forth, set out, spell out, unfold, unravel, untangle

express *v* **1** *he expresses himself very well:* air, announce, articulate, assert, communicate, convey, declare, enunciate *formal*, formulate, give voice to, intimate, point out, pronounce, put across, put into words, put/get over, report, say, speak, state, tell, testify, utter, vent, ventilate, verbalize, voice, word **2** *I can't express my gratitude:* couch, demonstrate, denote, depict, disclose, divulge, embody, exhibit, indicate, manifest *formal*, reveal, show **3** *what is this image meant to express?:* designate, represent, signify, stand for, symbolize
♦ *adj* **1** *I gave express instructions on the matter:* categorical, certain, clear, clear-cut, distinct, exact, explicit, manifest *formal*, plain, precise, stated, unambiguous, unequivocal, well-defined **2** *with the express purpose of incriminating her:* particular, sole, special, specific, unambiguous **3** *an express delivery service:* brisk, expeditious *formal*, fast, high-speed, non-stop, quick, rapid, speedy, swift
▨ 1 vague

expression *n* **1** *dazed expression:* air, appearance, aspect, countenance *formal*, gesture, grimace, look, mien *formal*, scowl **2** *romantic expression of their love:* communication, demonstration, embodiment, exhibition, illustration, indication, manifestation *formal*, representation, show, sign, style, symbol **3** *sincere expression of sympathy:* announcement, articulation, assertion, communication, declaration, intimation, proclamation, pronouncement, speech, statement, utterance, verbalization, voicing, wording **4** *such a quaint expression:* idiom, language, phrase, phrasing, saying, set phrase, term, turn of phrase, word, wording **5** *range of expression:* delivery, diction, enunciation, idiom, intonation, locution *formal*, modulation, phrasing, style, tone **6** *she sings with great expression:* artistry, creativity, depth, emotion, feeling, force, imagination, intensity, passion, power, vigour, vividness

expressionless *adj* blank, deadpan, dull, emotionless, empty, glassy, impassive, inscrutable, poker-faced *colloq*, straight-faced, vacuous
▨ expressive

expressive *adj* **1** *large, expressive eyes:* animated, articulate, communicative, demonstrative, eloquent, emphatic, evocative, forceful, informative, lively, meaningful, moving, poignant, revealing, significant, striking, suggestive, sympathetic, telling, thoughtful, vivid **2** *expressive of his growing anger:* demonstrating, indicative, revealing, showing, suggesting

expressly *adv* absolutely, categorically, clearly, decidedly, definitely, distinctly, especially, exactly, explicitly, intentionally, manifestly *formal*, on purpose, particularly, plainly, pointedly, precisely, purposely, solely, specially, specifically, unambiguously, unequivocally

expropriate *v* annex, appropriate *formal*, arrogate *formal*, assume, commandeer, confiscate, dispossess, disseise *technical*, impound, requisition *formal*, seize, sequester *formal*, take, take away, unhouse, usurp

expulsion *n* **1** *expulsion from the union:* banishment, discharge, dismissal, ejection, eviction, exclusion, exile, rejection, removal, sacking *colloq*, the boot *colloq*, the sack *colloq*, throwing out **2** *expulsion of gas:* belching, discharge, ejection, evacuation, excretion, voiding

expunge *v* abolish, annihilate, annul, blot out, cancel, cross out, delete, destroy, efface *formal*, eradicate, erase, exterminate, extinguish, extirpate *formal*, get rid of, obliterate, raze, remove, rub out, wipe out

expurgate *v* blue-pencil, bowdlerize, censor, clean up, cut, emend, purge, purify, sanitize

exquisite *adj* **1** *an exquisite necklace:* attractive, beautiful, charming, dainty, delicate, delightful, elegant, fine, fragile, lovely, pleasing, pretty **2** *an exquisite tapestry:* choice, excellent, fine, flawless, outstanding, perfect, precious, rare **3** *she had quite exquisite taste:* cultivated, cultured, discerning, discriminating, impeccable, meticulous, refined, sensitive **4** *the exquisite anguish of his loss:* acute, intense, keen, piercing, poignant, sharp
▨ 1 ugly **2** flawed **3** unrefined

extant *adj* alive, existent, existing, in existence, living, remaining, subsistent, subsisting, surviving
▨ dead, extinct, non-existent

extempore *adv* ad lib, impromptu, off the cuff *colloq*, off the top of your head *colloq*, on the spur of the moment, spontaneously
♦ *adj* ad-lib, extemporaneous, impromptu, improvised, off-the-cuff *colloq*, spontaneous, unplanned, unprepared, unrehearsed, unscripted
▨ planned

extemporize *v* ad-lib, improvise, make up, play it by ear, think on your feet

extend *v* **1** *extends for four miles along the coast:* carry on, come (up/down) to, continue, go as far as, go down/up to, last, reach, run, spread, stretch **2** *extended to include reform:* amplify, augment *formal*, broaden, develop, drag out, draw out, elongate *formal*, enlarge, expand, increase, intensify, lengthen, prolong, protract *formal*, spin out, step up, stretch, unwind, widen **3** *I extend my congratulations:* bestow *formal*, confer *formal*, give, grant, hold out, impart, offer, present, proffer *formal*, reach out
▨ 2 contract, shorten **3** withhold

extended *adj* amplified, developed, enlarged, expanded, increased, lengthened, lengthy, long

extension *n* **1** *extension of the rail network:* broadening, continuation, development, elongation *formal*, enhancement, enlargement, expansion, increase, lengthening, prolongation, protraction *formal*, stretching, widening **2** *planning permission for the extension:* addendum *formal*, addition, add-on, adjunct, annexe, appendix, supplement, wing **3** *seeking an extension to the deadline:* delay, more/additional time, postponement

extensive *adj* **1** *extensive knowledge:* all-inclusive, boundless, broad, complete, comprehensive, thorough, unlimited, wide, wide-ranging **2** *extensive use of the death penalty:* extended, far-reaching, general, large-scale, pervasive, prevalent, widespread **3** *an extensive property:* capacious *formal*, commodious *formal*, fair-sized, huge, large, lengthy, long, roomy, sizeable, spacious, substantial, vast, voluminous *formal*, wide
   1 narrow **2** restricted **3** small

extent *n* **1** *the extent of the intimidatory violence:* amount, area, breadth, bulk, coverage, degree, duration, expanse, length, level, magnitude, measure, quantity, size, spread, stretch, term, time, volume, width **2** *in both size and geographical extent:* bounds, compass, dimension(s), lengths, limit, play, range, reach, scope, sphere, stretch, sweep

extenuate *v* diminish, excuse, lessen, minimize, mitigate *formal*, modify, qualify, soften

extenuating *adj* diminishing, exculpatory *formal*, excusing, extenuative *formal*, extenuatory *formal*, justifying, lessening, minimizing, mitigating *formal*, moderating, modifying, palliative, qualifying, softening

exterior *n* appearance, coating, covering, external surface, externals, façade, face, finish, outer surface, outside, shell, skin, surface
   inside, interior
♦ *adj* external, extrinsic, outer, outermost, outside, outward, peripheral, superficial, surface, surrounding
   inside, interior

exterminate *v* abolish, annihilate, destroy, eliminate, eradicate, extirpate *formal*, kill, massacre, slaughter, wipe out

extermination *n* annihilation, destruction, elimination, eradication, extirpation *formal*, genocide, killing, massacre

external *adj* **1** *external surface:* apparent, exterior, extraneous, extrinsic, outer, outermost, outside, outward, peripheral, superficial, surface, visible **2** *external students:* extramural, independent, non-resident, outside, visiting
   1 internal **2** resident

extinct *adj* **1** *the polar bear may soon be extinct:* abolished, dead, defunct, died out, ended, exterminated, gone, lost, non-existent, obsolete, terminated, vanished, wiped out **2** *extinct volcano:* burnt out, extinguished, inactive, out, quenched **3** *extinct customs like doffing your hat:* antiquated, bygone, expired, invalid, obsolete, outmoded, passé, terminated *formal*
   1 existent, existing, living **2** active, erupting

extinction *n* abolition, annihilation, death, destruction, dying-out, eradication, excision, extermination, obliteration, termination *formal*, vanishing

extinguish *v* **1** *extinguish the light:* blow out, choke, dampen down, douse, put out, quench, smother, snuff out, stifle, stub out **2** *extinguish popular superstitions:* abolish, annihilate, destroy, eliminate, end, eradicate, erase, expunge *formal*,

exterminate, extirpate *formal*, kill, remove, suppress

extirpate *v* abolish, annihilate, cut out, deracinate *formal*, destroy, eliminate, eradicate, erase, expunge *formal*, exterminate, extinguish, remove, root out, uproot, wipe out

extol *v* acclaim, applaud, celebrate, commend, eulogize *formal*, exalt, glorify, laud *formal*, magnify, praise, rhapsodize *formal*, sing the praises of
   blame, denigrate *formal*

extort *v* blackmail, bleed *colloq*, bully, coerce, exact, extract, force, get out of, milk *colloq*, squeeze, wrest, wring

extortion *n* blackmail, coercion, demand, exaction, force, milking *colloq*, oppression, racketeering

extortionate *adj* exacting, excessive, exorbitant, grasping, hard, harsh, immoderate, inordinate, oppressive, outrageous, preposterous, rapacious *formal*, severe, unreasonable

extra *adj* **1** *set an extra place at table:* added, additional, ancillary, another, auxiliary, fresh, further, more, new, other, subsidiary, supplementary **2** *there were extra seats available:* excess, excessive, left-over, redundant, reserve, spare, superfluous, supernumerary *formal*, surplus, unnecessary, unneeded, unused
   1 integral **2** essential
♦ *n* **1** *optional extras:* accessory, addendum *formal*, addition, additive, adjunct, appendage, attachment, bonus, complement, extension, supplement **2** *employ extras in the film:* bit player, minor role, spear-carrier, supernumerary, walk-on
♦ *adv* **1** *she took extra care:* especially, exceptionally, extraordinarily, extremely, particularly, remarkably, uncommonly, unusually **2** *you pay extra to fly from Glasgow:* above and beyond, additionally, along with, also, and so on, as well, besides, in addition, into the bargain *colloq*, let alone, not forgetting, not to mention, together with, too

extract *v* **1** *extract a tooth:* cut out, deracinate *formal*, draw out, prise, pull out, remove, take out, uproot **2** *extract a confession under torture:* draw, elicit, exact, gather, get, glean, obtain, prise, worm, wrest, wring **3** *extracted a bottle of brandy from her handbag:* draw out, get out, pluck, pull out, take out, withdraw **4** *extract essential oils:* distil, draw, gather, wring **5** *information extracted from trade journals:* abstract, choose, cite, copy, cull, quote, reproduce, select
   1 insert **3** insert
♦ *n* **1** *malt extract:* concentrate, decoction, distillate *formal*, distillation, essence, juice, spirits **2** *extracts from her diary:* abstract, citation, clip, clipping, cutting, excerpt, passage, quotation, selection

extraction *n* **1** *the extraction of teeth:* drawing, pulling, removal, taking out, uprooting, withdrawal **2** *a method of extraction of individual oils:* derivation, distillation, obtaining, separation **3** *of noble extraction:* ancestry, birth, blood, derivation, descent, family, lineage, origin, parentage, pedigree, race, stock
   1 insertion

extradite *v* banish, deport, exile, expel, repatriate, send back, send home

extradition *n* banishment, deportation, exile, expulsion, sending back

extraneous *adj* additional, alien, exterior, external, extra, extrinsic, foreign, immaterial, inapplicable, inapposite *formal*, inappropriate, inapt, incidental, inessential, irrelevant, needless, non-essential, peripheral, redundant, strange, superfluous, supplementary, tangential, unconnected, unessential, unnecessary, unneeded, unrelated
🔁 essential, integral

extraordinary *adj* amazing, astounding, bizarre, curious, exceptional, fantastic, marvellous, notable, noteworthy, odd, out of this world *colloq*, outstanding, particular, peculiar, rare, remarkable, significant, singular *formal*, special, strange, surprising, uncommon, unconventional, unexpected, unique, unprecedented, unusual, wonderful
🔁 commonplace, ordinary

extravagance *n* 1 *typical Hollywood extravagance*: improvidence *formal*, imprudence *formal*, overspending, prodigality *formal*, profligacy *formal*, recklessness, squandering, thriftlessness, waste, wastefulness 2 *extravagances of her imagination*: exaggeration, excess, folly, immoderation, lavishness, outrageousness, pretentiousness, profusion, recklessness, wildness
🔁 1 thrift 2 moderation, restraint

extravagant *adj* 1 *she's extravagant with her inheritance*: improvident *formal*, imprudent *formal*, prodigal *formal*, profligate *formal*, reckless, spendthrift, squandering, thriftless, wasteful 2 *an extravagant Oriental palace*: excessive, flamboyant, flashy *colloq*, lavish, ornate, ostentatious, OTT *colloq*, over the top *colloq*, unrestrained, wild 3 *extravagant claims for its effectiveness*: exaggerated, excessive, fanciful, fantastic, immoderate, outrageous, preposterous, pretentious, unrestrained, wild 4 *extravagant room prices*: costly, dear, excessive, exorbitant, expensive, extortionate, overpriced, steep *colloq*
🔁 1 thrifty 2 moderate, restrained 3 moderate, realistic 4 reasonable

extravaganza *n* display, pageant, show, spectacle, spectacular

extreme *adj* 1 *extreme curiosity*: acute, downright, exceptional, extraordinary, great, greatest, highest, immoderate, inordinate, intense, maximum, out-and-out, remarkable, supreme, ultimate, unreasonable, utmost, uttermost 2 *the extreme end of the garden*: distant, endmost, faraway, far-off, farthest, final, last, most remote, outermost, outlying, remotest, terminal, ultimate, uttermost 3 *extreme nationalists*: excessive, extremist, fanatical, hardline, immoderate, radical, unreasonable, zealous 4 *extreme measures to lose weight*: dire, Draconian, drastic, harsh, rigid, severe, stern, strict, stringent, uncompromising, unrelenting, unyielding
🔁 1 mild 3 moderate
♦ *n* acme *formal*, apex *formal*, climax, depth, edge, end, excess, extremity, height, limit, line, mark, maximum, peak, pinnacle, pole,

termination *formal*, top, ultimate, utmost, zenith *formal*

extremely *adv* acutely, awfully *colloq*, decidedly, dreadfully *colloq*, exceedingly, exceptionally, excessively, extraordinarily, frightfully *colloq*, greatly, highly, immoderately, inordinately, intensely, really, remarkably, severely, terribly *colloq*, terrifically *colloq*, thoroughly, uncommonly, unreasonably, unusually, utterly, very

extremism *n* excessiveness, fanaticism, radicalism, terrorism, unreasonableness, zeal, zealotry *formal*
🔁 moderation

extremist *n* diehard, fanatic, fundamentalist, hardliner, militant, radical, terrorist, ultra, zealot
🔁 moderate

extremity *n* 1 *the western extremity of the island*: acme *formal*, apex *formal*, apogee *formal*, border, bound, boundary, brink, edge, end, frontier, height, limit, margin, peak, periphery, pole, terminal, termination, terminus, tip, top, verge 2 *the extremity of her grief*: depth, excess, extreme, height, maximum, minimum, peak, pinnacle, top 3 *pain in the extremities of the body*: arm, fingers and toes, foot, hand, leg, limb 4 *extremities of human life*: adversity, crisis, danger, emergency, exigency *formal*, hardship, indigence *formal*, misfortune, plight, trouble

extricate *v* clear, deliver, detach, disengage, disentangle, extract, free, get out, let loose, liberate, release, relieve, remove, rescue, withdraw
🔁 involve

extrinsic *adj* alien, exotic, exterior, external, extraneous, foreign, imported, outside
🔁 intrinsic

extrovert *n* conversationalist, joiner, life and soul of the party, mingler, mixer, outgoing person, sociable person, socializer

extroverted *adj* amiable, amicable, demonstrative, exuberant, friendly, hearty, outgoing, sociable
🔁 introverted

extrude *v* force out, mould, press out, squeeze out

exuberance *n* 1 *childlike exuberance*: animation, buoyancy, cheerfulness, eagerness, ebullience *formal*, effervescence, effusiveness, elation, energy, enthusiasm, excitement, exhilaration, fulsomeness, high spirits, life, liveliness, pizzazz *colloq*, vigour, vitality, vivacity *formal*, zest 2 *exuberance of the Gothic style*: abundance, copiousness, exaggeration, excessiveness, lavishness, lushness, luxuriance, plenitude *formal*, prodigality *formal*, profusion *formal*, rankness, richness, superabundance
🔁 1 apathy, lifelessness 2 scantiness

exuberant *adj* 1 *an exuberant child*: animated, buoyant, cheerful, ebullient *formal*, effervescent, effusive, elated, energetic, enthusiastic, exaggerated, excited, exhilarated, full of life, fulsome, high-spirited, irrepressible, lively, sparkling, spirited, unrestrained, vigorous, vivacious, zestful 2 *exuberant compliments*: exaggerated, fulsome, lavish 3 *exuberant foliage*: abundant, lavish, lush, luxurious, overflowing, plenteous *formal*, plentiful, profuse, rank, rich, thriving

Ⅎ 1 apathetic **3** scarce

exude *v* **1** *exude confidence:* display, emanate, emit, exhibit, manifest *formal*, ooze, radiate, show **2** *exude a thick yellow pus:* bleed, discharge, excrete, flow out, issue, leak, perspire, secrete, seep, sweat, trickle, weep, well

exult *v* be delighted, be joyful, be over the moon *colloq*, celebrate, crow, delight, gloat, glory, rejoice, relish, revel, triumph

exultant *adj* cock-a-hoop *colloq*, delighted, elated, enraptured, exulting, gleeful, joyful, joyous *formal*, jubilant, over the moon *colloq*, overjoyed, rejoicing, revelling, transporting, triumphant

Ⅎ depressed

exultation *n* celebration, crowing, delight, elation, eulogy *formal*, glee, gloating, glory, glorying, joy, joyfulness, joyousness *formal*, jubilation, merriness, paean *formal*, rejoicing, revelling, transport, triumph

Ⅎ depression

eye *n* **1** *an eye for spotting possibilities:* appreciation, awareness, discernment, discrimination, judgement, perception, recognition, sensitivity, taste **2** *keen eyes and quick hands:* eyesight, faculty of sight, observation, power of seeing, sight, vision **3** *to my eye, as lovely as her mother:* belief, estimation, judgement, mind, opinion, point of view, view, viewpoint

4 *under the policeman's eye:* lookout, notice, observation, surveillance, view, vigilance, watch, watchfulness

♦ *v* assess, contemplate, examine, gaze at, glance at, inspect, look at, look up and down, observe, peruse, regard, scan, scrutinize, stare at, study, survey, view, watch

> *Parts of the eye include:*
> anterior chamber, aqueous humour, blind spot, choroid, ciliary body, cone, conjunctiva, cornea, eyelash, fovea, iris, lacrimal duct, lens, lower eyelid, ocular muscle, optic nerve, papilla, posterior chamber, pupil, retina, rod, sclera, suspension ligament, upper eyelid, vitreous humour

eye-catching *adj* arresting, attractive, beautiful, captivating, conspicuous, gorgeous, imposing, impressive, noticeable, prominent, showy, spectacular, striking, stunning

Ⅎ plain, unattractive

eyesight *n* faculty of sight, observation, perception, power of seeing, sight, view, vision

eyesore *n* atrocity, blemish, blight, blot, blot on the landscape, carbuncle, defacement, disfigurement, disgrace, horror, mess, monstrosity, scar, ugliness

eyewitness *n* bystander, looker-on, observer, onlooker, passer-by, spectator, viewer, watcher, witness

F

fable *n* allegory, apologue *formal*, epic, fabrication, fiction, invention, legend, moral tale, myth, old wives' tale *colloq*, parable, saga, story, tale, tall story *colloq*, yarn

fabled *adj* famed, famous, legendary, remarkable, renowned
F3 unknown

fabric *n* **1** *synthetic fabrics:* cloth, material, stuff, textile **2** *the fabric of society:* constitution, construction, foundations, framework, infrastructure, make-up, organization, structure

> *Fabrics include:*
> alpaca, angora, astrakhan, barathea, bouclé, cashmere, chenille, duffel, felt, flannel, fleece, Harris tweed®, mohair, paisley, pashm, serge, sheepskin, Shetland wool, tweed, vicuña, wool, worsted; brocade, buckram, calico, cambric, candlewick, canvas, chambray, cheesecloth, chino, chintz, cord, corduroy, cotton, crepe, denim, drill, jean, flannelette, gaberdine, gingham, jersey, lawn, linen, lisle, madras, moleskin, muslin, needlecord, piqué, poplin, sateen, seersucker, terry towelling, ticking, Viyella®, webbing, winceyette; grosgrain, damask, Brussels lace, chiffon, georgette, gossamer, voile, organza, organdie, tulle, net, crêpe de chine, silk, taffeta, shantung, velvet, velour; polycotton, polyester, rayon, nylon, Crimplene®, Terylene®, Lurex®, Lycra®, lamé; hessian, horsehair, chamois, kid, leather, leather-cloth, nubuck, sharkskin, suede

fabricate *v* **1** *had fabricated the evidence:* concoct, cook up *colloq*, counterfeit, fake, falsify, forge, invent, make up, trump up **2** *the basic structure is fabricated at the dockyard:* assemble, build, construct, create, devise, erect, fashion, form, frame, make, manufacture, produce, put together, shape
F3 2 demolish, destroy

fabrication *n* **1** *her story was a complete fabrication:* cock-and-bull story *colloq*, concoction, fable, fairy story *colloq*, fake, falsehood, fiction, figment, forgery, invention, myth, story, untruth **2** *the fabrication of nuclear cores:* assemblage *formal*, assembly, building, construction, erection, manufacture, production
F3 1 truth

fabulous *adj* **1** *had a fabulous time:* amazing, astonishing, astounding, breathtaking, cool *colloq*, fantastic, great, inconceivable, incredible, magic *colloq*, marvellous, out of this world *colloq*, phenomenal, radical *colloq*, remarkable, spectacular, super *colloq*, superb, top-notch *colloq*, unbelievable, unimaginable, way-out *slang*, wonderful **2** *a fabulous beast:* fabled, fantastic, fictional, fictitious, imaginary, invented, legendary, made-up, mythical, unreal
F3 2 real

façade *n* **1** *the glass façade of the building:* exterior, face, front, frontage **2** *behind her façade of cool sophistication:* appearance, cloak, cover, disguise, guise, mask, pretence, semblance, show, veil, veneer

face *n* **1** *she has a lovely face:* clock *colloq*, countenance, dial *colloq*, features, kisser *colloq*, mug *colloq*, pan *colloq*, phiz *colloq*, physiognomy *formal*, puss *slang*, visage *formal* **2** *put on a brave face:* air, appearance, aspect, demeanour *formal*, expression, look, mien *formal* **3** *pull a face:* frown, grimace, pout, scowl **4** *the south face of the building:* aspect, cover, exterior, façade, front, frontage, outside, side, surface **5** *changing the face of the city:* appearance, aspect, form, look(s), nature **6** *save/lose face:* admiration, honour, name, prestige, reputation, respect, standing
♦ *v* **1** *a house facing the river:* be opposite, front, give on to, look onto, overlook **2** *face the consequences of his actions:* brave, come up against, confront, cope with, deal with, defy, encounter, experience, face up to, have to reckon with, meet, oppose, resist, tackle, withstand **3** *a wall faced with stone:* clad, coat, cover, dress, line, overlay, polish, smooth, veneer

> **face up to** accept, acknowledge, come to terms with, confront, cope with, deal with, meet head-on, recognize, resign yourself to, stand up to

facelift *n* **1** *she's had a facelift:* cosmetic surgery, plastic surgery, rhytidectomy *technical* **2** *give the library a facelift:* redecoration, renovation, restoration

facet *n* **1** *different facets of her personality:* angle, aspect, characteristic, element, factor, feature, side **2** *the facets of a diamond:* edge, face, plane, side, surface

facetious *adj* amusing, comic, comical, droll, flippant, frivolous, funny, humorous, jesting, jocose, jocular, joking, light-hearted, playful, tongue-in-cheek, witty
F3 serious

facile *adj* easy, fluent, glib, plausible, quick, ready, shallow, simple, simplistic, slick, smooth, superficial, uncomplicated
F3 complicated, profound

facilitate *v* accelerate, advance, assist, ease, encourage, expedite *formal*, forward, further, help, promote, smooth, smooth the way, speed up

facility *n* **1** *a facility for learning languages:* ability, ease, effortlessness, fluency, gift, knack, proficiency, quickness, readiness, skilfulness, skill, smoothness, talent **2** *sports facilities:* advantage, aid, amenity, appliance, convenience, equipment, means, mod con *colloq*, opportunity, resource, service, utility

facing *n* **1** *the wooden facing was torn from the building in the storm:* cladding, coating, covering, dressing, façade, overlay, revetment *technical*, surface, veneer **2** *attach the facing inside the neckline:* false front, lining, reinforcement, trimming

facsimile *n* carbon, carbon copy, copy, duplicate, fax, image, imitation, photocopy,

Photostat®, print, replica, repro, reproduction, transcript, Xerox®

fact *n* **1** *facts and figures*: act, circumstance, component, datum, deed, detail, element, event, factor, fait accompli, feature, gen *colloq*, happening, incident, info *colloq*, information, ins and outs *colloq*, item, low-down *colloq*, occurrence, particular, point, score *colloq*, specific **2** *the fact of the matter is she lied*: actuality, certainty, factuality, reality, truth
Ⅻ **2** fiction

faction *n* **1** *rival factions of the party*: band, cabal, camp, caucus, clique, contingent, coterie, division, ginger group, group, junta, lobby, minority, party, pressure group, ring, section, sector, set, side, splinter group **2** *a country split by faction and civil war*: argument, conflict, contention, disagreement, discord, disharmony, division, friction, infighting, quarrels, strife, trouble

factious *adj* at loggerheads, at odds, clashing, conflicting, contentious, discordant, disputatious *formal*, dissident, divisive, insurrectionary, mutinous, partisan, quarrelling, quarrelsome, rebellious, refractory *formal*, rival, sectarian, seditious, troublemaking, tumultuous, turbulent, warring
Ⅻ calm, co-operative

factor *n* aspect, cause, characteristic, circumstance, component, consideration, constituent, contingency, detail, determinant *formal*, element, facet, fact, feature, influence, ingredient, item, part, point

factory *n* assembly line, foundry, manufactory, mill, plant, works, workshop

factual *adj* accurate, actual, authentic, correct, detailed, exact, faithful, genuine, historical, literal, objective, precise, real, realistic, strict, true, true-to-life, truthful, unbiased, unprejudiced
Ⅻ false, fictional, fictitious, imaginary

faculties *n* capabilities, intelligence, powers, reason, senses, wits

faculty *n* **1** *she has lost her critical faculty*: ability, aptitude, bent, capability, capacity, facility, flair, gift, knack, power, proficiency, skill, talent **2** *the Faculty of Medicine*: department, division, organization, section

fad *n* affectation *formal*, craze, enthusiasm, fancy, mania, mode, (passing) fashion, rage *colloq*, trend, vogue, whim

faddy *adj* choosy *colloq*, fastidious, finicky, fussy, hard-to-please, nit-picking *colloq*, particular, pernickety *colloq*, picky *colloq*

fade *v* **1** *the curtains had faded in the strong sun*: become paler, bleach, dim, discolour, dull, etiolate *technical*, lose colour, pale, tone down, wash out, whiten **2** *hope faded of finding any survivors*: become weaker, decline, die (away), diminish, disappear, dissolve, droop, dwindle, ebb (away), evanesce *formal*, fail, fall, fizzle out *colloq*, flag, melt (away), pale, perish, peter out *colloq*, recede, shrivel, vanish, wane, waste away, weaken, wilt, wither
Ⅻ **1** darken **2** brighten

faeces *n* body waste, crap *slang*, droppings, dung, excrement, excreta *technical*, ordure, shit *slang*, stools, turd, waste matter

fag *n* **1** *nipped out for a fag*: cancer-stick *slang*, cig *colloq*, cigarette, ciggy *colloq*, coffin-nail *slang*, filter-tip, gasper *colloq*, roll-up, smoke, whiff **2** *it's such a fag having to clear up every night*: bind, bore, bother, chore, drag *colloq*, inconvenience, irritation, nuisance, pest

fagged *adj* all in *colloq*, beat *colloq*, exhausted, fatigued, jaded, knackered *colloq*, on your last legs *colloq*, wasted, weary, worn out, zonked *slang*
Ⅻ refreshed

fail *v* **1** *his attempt at humour failed*: abort, be unsuccessful, break down, collapse, come undone *colloq*, fall flat *colloq*, fall through, fizzle out *colloq*, flop *colloq*, flunk *colloq*, fold *colloq*, founder, get nowhere, go wrong, miscarry, not come off *colloq*, not come up to scratch *colloq*, not come up with the goods *colloq*, not make it *colloq*, score an own goal *colloq* **2** *fail to pay the bill*: forget, neglect, not do something, omit **3** *failed her friends*: abandon, desert, disappoint, forsake *formal*, leave, let down, neglect **4** *the engine failed*: break down, conk out *slang*, crash *colloq*, cut out, go kaput *colloq*, go wrong, malfunction *formal*, not start, not work, pack up *colloq*, stop **5** *the business failed*: become insolvent, collapse, crash *colloq*, flop *colloq*, fold *colloq*, founder, go bankrupt, go broke *colloq*, go bust *colloq*, go into the red *colloq*, go to the wall *colloq*, go under, sink **6** *his health failed*: collapse, decay, decline, deteriorate, diminish, droop, dwindle, ebb, fade, flag, sink, wane, weaken
Ⅻ **1** succeed **4** work **5** prosper

failing *n* blemish, defect, deficiency, drawback, error, failure, fault, flaw, foible, imperfection, lapse, shortcoming, weak spot, weakness
Ⅻ advantage, strength
♦ *prep* in default of, in the absence of, lacking, wanting, without

failure *n* **1** *our efforts ended in failure*: abortion, breakdown, collapse, coming to nothing, defeat, downfall, flop *colloq*, frustration, lack of success, let-down *colloq*, miscarriage **2** *the trip was a failure*: calamity, disappointment, disaster, fiasco, flop *colloq*, misfortune, miss, no go *colloq*, shambles *colloq*, slip-up *colloq*, washout *colloq*, wipeout *colloq* **3** *his failure to fill in the form*: default, dereliction *formal*, disregard, forgetfulness, neglect, negligence, omission, oversight **4** *feel that you are a failure*: also-ran *colloq*, born loser, dead loss *colloq*, dropout *colloq*, flop *colloq*, has-been *colloq*, loser, misfit, no-hoper *colloq*, non-starter *colloq*, reject, victim, washout *colloq*, waste of space *colloq*, write-off *colloq* **5** *the failure of the machine*: breakdown, conking-out *slang*, crash *colloq*, cutting-out, malfunctioning *formal*, packing-up *colloq*, shutdown, stalling, stopping **6** *the failure of the business*: bankruptcy, collapse, crash *colloq*, flop *colloq*, folding *colloq*, foundering, going to the wall *colloq*, going under *colloq*, insolvency, ruin **7** *the failure of his health*: breakdown, collapse, decline, deterioration, ebbing, fading, flagging, sinking, waning, weakening
Ⅻ **2** success **3** observance **4** success **6** prosperity

faint *adj* **1** *a faint mark*: bleached, blurred, dim, dull, faded, feeble, hazy, indistinct, light, mild, obscure, pale, slight, soft, unclear, vague, weak **2** *a faint noise*: hushed, indistinct, low, muffled, muted, weak **3** *I feel faint*: dizzy, exhausted, feeble, giddy, light-headed, unsteady, weak, woozy *colloq* **4** *a faint smile*: feeble, half-hearted, slight, unenthusiastic, weak
🔁 **1** clear, strong **2** strong
♦ *v* black out, collapse, drop, flake out *colloq*, keel over *colloq*, lose consciousness, pass out
♦ *n* blackout, collapse, loss of consciousness, syncope *technical*, unconsciousness

faint-hearted *adj* diffident, half-hearted, irresolute, lily-livered, spiritless, timid, timorous, weak, yellow *colloq*
🔁 confident, courageous

faintly *adv* **1** *felt faintly ridiculous*: a bit, a little, slightly **2** *his heart was beating faintly*: feebly, softly, vaguely, weakly

fair[1] *adj* **1** *a fair referee*: above board, detached, disinterested, dispassionate, equitable, even-handed, going/done/played by the book *colloq*, honest, honourable, impartial, just, kosher *colloq*, lawful, legit *colloq*, legitimate, objective, on the level *colloq*, proper, right, square, straight up *colloq*, trustworthy, unbiased, unprejudiced, upright **2** *a fair chance of success*: decent, moderate, modest, reasonable, respectable, satisfactory **3** *fair hair*: blond(e), light, yellow **4** *a tall, fair boy*: blond(e), fair-haired, fair-headed, light-haired **5** *fair skin*: cream, light, pale **6** *a fair mark*: acceptable, adequate, all right, mediocre, middling, not bad, OK *colloq*, passable, reasonable, satisfactory, so-so *colloq*, sufficient, tolerable **7** *fair weather*: bright, clear, cloudless, dry, fine, sunny, unclouded
🔁 **1** unfair **3** dark **4** dark **6** excellent, poor **7** cloudy, inclement

fair[2] *n* bazaar, carnival, craft fair, exchange, exhibition, expo *colloq*, exposition, festival, fête, gala, market, show, trade fair

fairly *adv* **1** *fairly long hair*: adequately, moderately, pretty, quite, rather, reasonably, somewhat, tolerably **2** *fairly shaking with anticipation*: absolutely, fully, positively, really, veritably **3** *treat their workers fairly*: equitably, honestly, impartially, justly, lawfully, legally, objectively, properly, unbiasedly
🔁 **3** unfairly

fairness *n* decency, disinterestedness, equitableness, equity, even-handedness, impartiality, justice, legitimacy, legitimateness, rightfulness, rightness, unbiasedness, uprightness
🔁 unfairness

fairy *n* brownie, elf, fay, fée, hob, hobgoblin, imp, leprechaun, nymph, peri, pixie, Puck, Robin Goodfellow, rusalka, sprite

fairy tale *n* **1** *a book of traditional fairy tales*: fairy story, fantasy, fiction, folk-tale, myth, romance **2** *some fairy tale about meeting an old friend*: cock-and-bull story *colloq*, fabrication, invention, lie, tall story *colloq*, untruth

faith *n* **1** *had a lot of faith in his ability*: assurance, belief, confidence, conviction, credence *formal*, credit *formal*, dependence, reliance, trust **2** *a mixed faith service*: belief, church, creed,

denomination, doctrine, dogma, persuasion, religion, sect, teaching **3** *kept faith with the team*: commitment, dedication, devotion, faithfulness, fidelity, honour, loyalty, obedience
🔁 **1** mistrust **3** treachery, unfaithfulness

faithful *adj* **1** *a faithful friend*: committed, constant, dedicated, dependable, devoted, loyal, obedient, reliable, staunch, steadfast, true, trustworthy, trusty, unflagging, unswerving, unwavering **2** *a faithful description*: accurate, close, exact, precise, strict, true, truthful
🔁 **1** disloyal, treacherous **2** inaccurate, vague
♦ *n* adherents, believers, brethren, communicants, congregation, followers, supporters

faithfulness *n* **1** *the faithfulness of his friend*: allegiance, commitment, constancy, dedication, dependability, devotion, fidelity, loyalty, reliability, staunchness, steadfastness, trustworthiness **2** *the faithfulness of a description*: accuracy, closeness, exactness, scrupulousness, strictness
🔁 **1** disloyalty, treachery **2** inaccuracy

faithless *adj* **1** *a faithless friend*: adulterous, disloyal, false, false-hearted, fickle, inconstant, perfidious *formal*, traitorous, treacherous, unfaithful, unreliable, untrue, untrustworthy, untruthful **2** *a faithless sinner*: disbelieving, doubting, nullifidian *formal*, unbelieving
🔁 **1** faithful **2** believing

faithlessness *n* adultery, apostasy, betrayal, deceit, disloyalty, fickleness, inconstancy, infidelity, perfidy *formal*, treachery, unfaithfulness
🔁 faithfulness

fake *adj* affected *formal*, artificial, assumed, bogus, counterfeit, false, forged, fraudulent, imitation, mock, phoney *colloq*, pretend *colloq*, pseud *colloq*, pseudo, reproduction, sham, simulated, spurious
🔁 genuine
♦ *v* affect *formal*, assume, copy, counterfeit, fabricate, feign, forge, imitate, pirate, pretend, put on, sham, simulate
♦ *n* **1** *the painting was a fake*: copy, counterfeit, forgery, fraud, hoax, imitation, replica, reproduction, sham, simulation **2** *he's a complete fake*: charlatan, impostor, mountebank, phoney *colloq*, quack *colloq*

fall *v* **1** *he fell over at school*: collapse, crash, fall down, keel over, pitch (forward), slide, slip, slump, stumble, topple, trip, tumble **2** *fell into a chair*: come down, descend, dive, drop, go down, incline, nose-dive, pitch, plummet, plunge, sink, slant, slide, slope **3** *prices fell sharply*: decline, decrease, diminish, dive, dwindle, fall off, go down, lessen, nose-dive, plummet, plunge, recede, slump, subside **4** *fall asleep*: become, come to be, grow (into), pass (into), turn **5** *fall in battle*: be killed, be slain *formal*, die, lose your life, perish **6** *the town fell in the battle*: be conquered, be defeated, be taken, be vanquished *formal*, capitulate, give in, lose control, pass into enemy hands, surrender, yield **7** *my birthday falls on a Tuesday this year*: come about, happen, occur, take place
🔁 **2** rise **3** increase
♦ *n* **1** *had a nasty fall*: collapse, crash, keeling-over, slide, slip, stumble, topple, trip, tumble **2** *a fall in oil prices*: crash, cut, decline, decrease,

drop, dwindling, fall-off, lessening, nose-dive, plummeting, plunge, reduction, slump **3** *the fall of the city:* capitulation, capture, collapse, conquest, defeat, demise *formal*, destruction, downfall, failure, giving-in, loss of control, overthrow, resignation, ruin, surrender, yielding
► **fall apart** break, break into pieces, break up, collapse, come away, come/go to pieces, crack up, crumble, decay, decompose, disintegrate, dissolve, fall to bits/pieces, go to bits, rot, shatter
► **fall back** depart, disengage, draw back, pull back, recoil, retreat, withdraw
► **fall back on** call into play, call on, employ, have recourse to, look to, make use of, resort to, turn to, use
► **fall behind** drop back, lag (behind), not keep up, trail
🔁 keep pace, keep up, make progress
► **fall for 1** *she really fell for him:* be attached to, be crazy about *colloq*, become infatuated with, desire, fall head over heels in love with *colloq*, fall in love with, fancy *colloq*, have a crush on *colloq*, take to **2** *fell for his lies:* accept, be deceived by, be fooled by, be taken in by, buy *colloq*, swallow *colloq*
► **fall in** cave in, collapse, come down, crash, give way, sink, subside
► **fall in with** accept, agree with, assent to *formal*, comply with, co-operate with, go along with, support
► **fall off** decline, decrease, deteriorate, drop (off), lessen, slacken, slow, slump, worsen
► **fall on** assail, assault, attack, descend on, lay into, pounce on, set upon, snatch
► **fall out** argue, bicker, clash, differ, disagree, fight, quarrel, squabble
🔁 agree
► **fall through** abort, collapse, come to grief, come to nothing, fail, founder, go wrong, miscarry
🔁 come off, succeed
► **fall to** apply yourself, begin, commence *formal*, get stuck in, set about, set to, start

fallacious *adj* casuistical *formal*, deceptive, delusive, delusory, erroneous, false, fictitious, illogical, illusory, inaccurate, incorrect, inexact, misleading, mistaken, sophistic *formal*, sophistical *formal*, spurious, untrue, wrong
🔁 correct, true

fallacy *n* casuistry *formal*, delusion, error, false idea, falsehood, flaw, illusion, inconsistency, misapprehension, miscalculation, misconception, mistake, mistaken belief, myth, sophism *formal*, sophistry *formal*
🔁 truth

fallen *adj* **1** *fallen in battle:* dead, died, killed, lost, perished, slain *formal*, slaughtered **2** *fallen women:* degenerate, disgraced, immoral, loose, promiscuous, shamed
🔁 **2** chaste

fallible *adj* errant, erring, flawed, frail, human, ignorant, imperfect, mortal, uncertain, weak
🔁 infallible

fallow *adj* barren, dormant, idle, inactive, resting, uncultivated, undeveloped, unplanted, unploughed, unproductive, unsown, unused

false *adj* **1** *false information:* erroneous, fallacious *formal*, faulty, illusory, inaccurate, incorrect, inexact, invalid, misleading, mistaken, untrue, wrong **2** *false ID:* artificial, assumed, bogus, counterfeit, fabricated, fake, feigned, fictitious, forged, fraudulent, imitation, invented, mock, phoney *colloq*, pretend *colloq*, pretended, sham, simulated, synthetic, trumped-up *colloq* **3** *false friends:* deceitful, dishonest, disloyal, double-dealing, duplicitous *formal*, faithless, hypocritical, insincere, lying, perfidious *formal*, traitorous, treacherous, two-faced, unfaithful, unreliable, untrustworthy
🔁 **1** right, true **2** genuine, real **3** faithful, genuine, reliable

falsehood *n* **1** *told a falsehood:* fabrication, fairy story, fib, fiction, invention, lie, story, tall story *colloq*, untruth **2** *an act of falsehood:* bullshit *slang*, deceit, deception, dishonesty, double dealing, duplicity *formal*, fabrication, hypocrisy, insincerity, invention, perfidy *formal*, perjury *technical*, treachery, two-facedness, untruthfulness
🔁 **1** truth **2** truthfulness

falsification *n* adulteration, alteration, change, deceit, dissimulation *formal*, distortion, forgery, misrepresentation, perversion, tampering

falsify *v* adulterate, alter, cook *colloq*, counterfeit, distort, doctor, fake, fiddle, forge, manipulate, massage, misrepresent, misstate, pervert, rig, tamper with, twist

falter *v* **1** *faltered on the rough ground:* be shaky, be unsteady, stumble, totter **2** *falter while talking:* fluff your lines *colloq*, stammer, stumble, stutter **3** *faltered before accepting his offer:* be in two minds *colloq*, delay, dilly-dally *colloq*, drag your feet *colloq*, flag, flinch, hesitate, quail, shake, shilly-shally *colloq*, sit on the fence *colloq*, take your time *colloq*, vacillate, waver

faltering *adj* **1** *the faltering peace process:* failing, flagging, hesitant, irresolute, tentative, uncertain, unsteady, weak **2** *a faltering voice:* hesitant, stammering, stumbling, tentative, timid, uncertain
🔁 **1** firm, strong **2** confident

fame *n* celebrity, distinction, eminence, esteem *formal*, glory, greatness, illustriousness, importance, name, notability, note, prominence, renown, reputation, stardom

famed *adj* acclaimed, celebrated, esteemed *formal*, famous, noted, recognized, renowned, well-known, widely-known
🔁 unknown

familiar *adj* **1** *the place looks familiar:* accustomed, common, commonplace, conventional, customary, everyday, frequent, habitual, household, known, ordinary, recognizable, repeated, routine, run-of-the-mill, unmistakable, usual, well-known **2** *they're getting very familiar with each other:* casual, chummy *colloq*, close, comfortable, confidential, easy, free, free-and-easy, friendly, informal, intimate, near, open, pally *colloq*, relaxed, sociable, unceremonious, unreserved **3** *familiar with the procedure:* abreast, acquainted, au courant, au fait, aware, conversant, knowledgeable, versed, well up **4** *don't be so familiar!:* bold, disrespectful, forward, impertinent, over-familiar, over-friendly, presumptuous, pushy *colloq*, smarmy *colloq*
🔁 **1** strange, unfamiliar **2** formal, reserved **3** ignorant, unfamiliar **4** respectful

familiarity *n* **1** *an easy familiarity with her students:* casualness, chumminess *colloq*, closeness, ease, friendliness, informality, intimacy, liberty, naturalness, nearness, openness, palliness *colloq*, sociability, unceremoniousness **2** *his familiarity with the subject:* acquaintance, awareness, comprehension, experience, grasp, knowledge, mastery, skill, understanding **3** *reprimanded for her familiarity with the chairman:* boldness, disrespect, forwardness, impertinence, impudence, intrusiveness, liberties, liberty, over-familiarity, over-friendliness, presumption, pushiness *colloq*

familiarize *v* acclimatize, accustom, brief, coach, habituate *formal*, indoctrinate, instruct, make acquainted, make aware, make familiar, prime, school, teach, train

family *n* **1** *pictures of all of his family:* ancestors, children, descendants, extended family, folk *colloq*, forebears, household, issue, kids *colloq*, kin, kindred, kinsmen, little ones *colloq*, next of kin, offspring, parents, people, progeny, relations, relatives, scions **2** *the McDonald family:* ancestry, birth, blood, clan, descent, dynasty, extraction, house, line, lineage, parentage, pedigree, race, stock, strain, tribe **3** *a family of plants:* class, classification, genus, group, kind, species, stirps *technical*, type

> *Members of a family include:*
> ancestor, forebear, forefather, descendant, offspring, heir; husband, wife, spouse, parent, father, dad, daddy *colloq*, old man *colloq*, mother, mum *colloq*, mummy *colloq*, mom *US colloq*; grandparent, grandfather, grandmother, granny, nanny *colloq*, grandchild, son, daughter, brother, half-brother, sister, half-sister, sibling, uncle, aunt, nephew, niece, cousin, godfather, godmother, godchild, stepfather, stepdad, stepmother, stepmum, foster-parent, foster-child

famine *n* dearth, deprivation, destitution *formal*, hunger, lack, malnutrition, scarcity, shortage of food, starvation, want *formal*
🔁 plenty

famous *adj* acclaimed, celebrated, distinguished, eminent, esteemed *formal*, famed, glorious, great, having (made) a name for yourself, honoured, illustrious, infamous, legendary, notable, noted, notorious, popular, prominent, remarkable, renowned, respected, venerable, well-known, world-famous
🔁 obscure, unheard-of, unknown

fan¹ *n* addict, adherent, admirer, aficionado, backer, buff *colloq*, devotee, enthusiast, fiend *colloq*, follower, freak *colloq*, lover, nut *colloq*, supporter

fan² *v* **1** *fanned herself with her hat:* air, air-condition, air-cool, blow, cool, freshen, refresh, ventilate **2** *fanned the flames of discontent:* agitate, arouse, excite, ignite, incite, increase, instigate, intensify, kindle, provoke, rouse, stimulate, stir up, whip up, work up
♦ *n* air cooler, air-conditioner, blower, cooler, extractor fan, propeller, vane, ventilator
▶ **fan out** move out, open out, spread out

fanatic *n* **1** *religious fanatics:* bigot, devotee, extremist, fundamentalist, maniac, militant, radical, visionary, zealot **2** *rock music fanatics:* addict, devotee, enthusiast, fan, fiend *colloq*, freak *colloq*

fanatical *adj* bigoted, burning, dogmatic, extreme, extremist, fervent, frenzied, fundamentalist, immoderate, mad, militant, narrow-minded, obsessive, overenthusiastic, passionate, rabid, radical, single-minded, wild, zealous
🔁 moderate, unenthusiastic

fanaticism *n* activism, bigotry, dedication, dogmatism, enthusiasm, extremism, fervour, frenzy, fundamentalism, infatuation, madness, militancy, monomania, narrow-mindedness, obsessiveness, single-mindedness, wildness, zeal
🔁 moderation

fanciful *adj* **1** *a fanciful tale:* airy-fairy, fabulous, fairy-tale, fantastic, illusory, imaginary, legendary, make-believe, mythical, romantic, unreal, unrealistic, visionary, whimsical **2** *a rather fanciful hat:* creative, curious, decorated, elaborate, extravagant, fantastic, imaginative, ornate
🔁 **1** ordinary, real, realistic **2** plain, simple

fancy *v* **1** *do you fancy a coffee?:* desire, favour, feel like, go for, have in mind, like, long for, not mind, not say no to, prefer, take a liking to, take to, want, wish, yearn for **2** *I think he fancies your sister:* be attracted to, be interested in, be mad about *colloq*, desire, find attractive, go for, have a crush on *colloq*, have a soft spot for, have eyes for *colloq*, have the hots for *slang*, lust after, take to, think the world of, want *colloq* **3** *they'll marry soon, I fancy:* believe, conceive, conjecture *formal*, guess, imagine, picture, reckon, suppose, surmise *formal*, think
🔁 **1** dislike
♦ *n* **1** *a fancy for strawberry ice cream:* caprice, craving, desire, fondness, impulse, inclination, itch *colloq*, liking, longing, penchant *formal*, predilection *formal*, preference, urge, want, whim, wish, yearning, yen *colloq* **2** *a strange fancy that he could fly:* dream, fantasy, idea, illusion, impression, notion, opinion, thought, vision
🔁 **1** aversion, dislike **2** fact, reality
♦ *adj* baroque, decorated, elaborate, elegant, embellished, extravagant, fanciful, fantastic, far-fetched, lavish, ornamented, ornate, ostentatious, rococo, showy
🔁 ordinary, plain, simple

fanfare *n* fanfarade, flourish, trump, trumpet call

fang *n* prong, tooth, tusk, venom-tooth

fantasize *v* build castles in the air *colloq*, daydream, dream, hallucinate, imagine, invent, live in a dream *colloq*, romance

fantastic *adj* **1** *a fantastic opportunity:* ace *colloq*, amazing, brill *colloq*, brilliant, cool *colloq*, enormous, excellent, extreme, first-rate, great, impressive, incredible, magic *colloq*, marvellous, neat *US colloq*, out of this world *colloq*, overwhelming, radical *colloq*, sensational, super *colloq*, superb, terrific, top notch *colloq*, tremendous, unbelievable, wonderful **2** *fantastic creatures:* absurd, bizarre, eccentric, exotic, extravagant, fabulous, fanciful, illusory, imaginary, imaginative, odd, outlandish, romantic, strange, unreal, visionary, weird
🔁 **1** ordinary **2** real

fantasy *n* **1** *a fantasy about travelling the world:* apparition, daydream, delusion, dream, fancy, figment of the imagination, flight of fancy, hallucination, mirage, nightmare, pipe-dream, reverie, vision **2** *the realm of fantasy:* cloud-cuckoo-land *colloq,* creativity, delusion, fancy, illusion, imagination, invention, moonshine, myth, nightmare, speculation, unreality
F₂ **2** reality

far *adv* **1** *travelled far and wide:* a good way, a great distance, a long way, nowhere near, some distance **2** *far bigger:* considerably, decidedly, extremely, greatly, immeasurably, incomparably, markedly, miles *colloq,* much, very much
F₂ **1** close, near **2** barely
♦ *adj* distant, faraway, far-flung, far-off, far-removed, further, inaccessible, outlying, out-of-the-way, remote, removed, secluded
F₂ accessible, close, nearby

faraway *adj* **1** *faraway lands:* distant, far, far-flung, far-off, outlying, remote **2** *a faraway look in her eyes:* absent, absent-minded, abstracted, dreamy, lost, preoccupied
F₂ **1** nearby **2** alert

farce *n* **1** *a bedroom farce:* buffoonery, burlesque, comedy, parody, satire, slapstick **2** *the interview process was a complete farce:* absurdity, joke, mockery, nonsense, parody, sham, shambles *colloq,* travesty

farcical *adj* absurd, comic, derisory, diverting, laughable, ludicrous, nonsensical, preposterous, ridiculous, silly, stupid
F₂ sensible

fare *n* **1** *pay your fare:* charge, cost, fee, passage, price, ticket **2** *simple country fare:* board, diet, eatables, eats *colloq,* food, meals, menu, nosh *colloq,* nourishment, nutriment, rations, sustenance *formal,* table, viands *formal,* victuals *formal*
♦ *v* be, do, get along, get on, go, go on, happen, make out, manage, proceed, progress, prosper, succeed, turn out

far-fetched *adj* crazy, dubious, fanciful, fantastic, implausible, improbable, incredible, preposterous, unbelievable, unconvincing, unlikely, unrealistic
F₂ plausible

farm *n* acreage, acres, co-operative, croft, farmland, farmstead, grange, holding, homestead, land, ranch, station
♦ *v* cultivate, operate, plant, plough, till, work the land
▶ **farm out** contract out, delegate, pass/give to others, subcontract

farmer *n* agriculturalist, agriculturist, agronomist *technical,* crofter, grazier, husbandman, rancher, smallholder, yeoman

farming *n* agribusiness *technical,* agriculture, agronomy, agroscience, crofting, cultivation, geoponics, husbandry, tilling

far-reaching *adj* broad, comprehensive, extensive, global, important, momentous, significant, sweeping, thorough, wide, wide-ranging, widespread
F₂ insignificant, limited, restricted

far-sighted *adj* acute, canny, cautious, circumspect *formal,* discerning, far-seeing,

forward-looking, judicious *formal,* politic *formal,* prescient *formal,* provident, prudent *formal,* shrewd, wise
F₂ imprudent, unwise

farther *adj* further, more distant, more extreme, remoter
♦ *adv* to a great distance, to a more distant/remote/onward/advanced point

farthest *adj* furthest, most distant, most extreme, remotest

fascinate *v* absorb, allure, attract, beguile, captivate, charm, delight, draw, enchant, engross, enrapture, enthral, entice, hypnotize, intrigue, lure, mesmerize, rivet, spellbind, transfix
F₂ bore, repel

fascinated *adj* absorbed, beguiled, bewitched, captivated, charmed, curious, delighted, engrossed, enthralled, enticed, entranced, hooked *colloq,* hypnotized, infatuated, intrigued, mesmerized, smitten, spellbound
F₂ bored, uninterested

fascinating *adj* absorbing, alluring, bewitching, captivating, charming, compelling, delightful, enchanting, engaging, engrossing, enticing, exciting, gripping, interesting, intriguing, irresistible, mesmerizing, riveting, seductive, stimulating, tempting
F₂ boring, uninteresting

fascination *n* allure, appeal, attraction, captivation, charm, compulsion, delight, draw, enchantment, interest, lure, magic, magnetism, pull, sorcery, spell
F₂ boredom, repulsion

fascism *n* absolutism, authoritarianism, autocracy, dictatorship, Hitlerism, totalitarianism

fascist *adj* absolutist, authoritarian, autocratic, Hitlerist, Hitlerite, totalitarian
♦ *n* absolutist, authoritarian, autocrat, Blackshirt, Hitlerist, Hitlerite, totalitarian

fashion *n* **1** *different fashions of colouring the glass:* approach, cut, design, form, kind, line, look, make, manner, method, mode, pattern, shape, sort, style, system, type, way **2** *the fashion for body piercings:* craze, custom, fad, latest *colloq,* mode, practice, rage *colloq,* style, tendency, trend, vogue **3** *the world of fashion:* clothes, couture, designer label, fashion business, haute couture, high fashion
♦ *v* adapt, adjust, alter, create, design, fit, form, model, mould, shape, tailor

fashionable *adj* à la mode, all the rage *colloq,* chic, contemporary, cool *colloq,* current, designer, elegant, funky *colloq,* glitzy *colloq,* hip *colloq,* in, in thing *colloq,* in vogue, latest, modern, modish, natty *colloq,* popular, ritzy *colloq,* smart, snazzy *colloq,* stylish, swanky *colloq,* swinging *colloq,* trendy *colloq,* up-to-date, up-to-the-minute, with it *colloq*
F₂ unfashionable

fast¹ *adj* **1** *fast cars:* accelerated, brisk, express, flying, hasty, high-speed, hurried, nippy *colloq,* quick, rapid, speedy, swift **2** *her hand was stuck fast:* fastened, firm, fixed, immobile, immovable, secure, tight
F₂ **1** slow, unhurried **2** loose
♦ *adv* **1** *the bullet train goes very fast:* apace, at a

rate of knots *colloq*, hastily, hell for leather *colloq*, hurriedly, in a hurry, lickety-spit *colloq*, like a bat out of hell *colloq*, like a flash *colloq*, like a shot *colloq*, like greased lightning *colloq*, like lightning *colloq*, like mad/crazy *colloq*, like the clappers *colloq*, like the wind *colloq*, quickly, rapidly, speedily, swiftly **2** *clung fast to his principles*: doggedly, firmly, fixedly, immovably, resolutely, securely, stubbornly, tightly **3** *fast asleep*: deeply, fully, sound
Ea 1 gradually, slowly

fast² *v* abstain *formal*, deny yourself, diet, go hungry, refrain, slim, starve
♦ *n* abstinence, diet, fasting, starvation
Ea gluttony, self-indulgence

fasten *v* **1** *fastened the picture to the wall*: affix, anchor, attach, bind, bolt, chain, clamp, connect, fix, nail, pin, rivet, tack, tether, unite **2** *fastened their seat belts*: buckle, button, clip, close, do up, join, lace, latch, link, lock, seal, secure, shut, tie, zip up **3** *fastened his attention on the dial*: aim, concentrate, direct, fix, focus, point, rivet
Ea 1 unfasten **2** undo, untie

fastidious *adj* choosy *colloq*, dainty, difficult, discriminating, faddy, finicky, fussy, hard-to-please, hypercritical, meticulous, overnice, particular, pernickety *colloq*, picky *colloq*, precise, punctilious, squeamish
Ea undemanding

fat *adj* **1** *a short fat man*: beefy *colloq*, buxom, chubby, corpulent *formal*, dumpy, fat as a pig *colloq*, flabby *colloq*, fleshy, gross *colloq*, heavy, large, obese, overweight, paunchy, plump, podgy, portly, pot-bellied, rotund *formal*, round, solid, sonsy *Scot*, steatopygous *formal*, stout, tubby **2** *a fat solution*: adipose *formal*, fatty, greasy, oily, oleaginous *formal*, pinguid *formal*, sebaceous *formal* **3** *a fat book*: big, broad, heavy, solid, substantial, thick, wide **4** *fat profits*: considerable, generous, handsome, large, sizeable
Ea 1 slim, thin **2** low-fat **3** narrow, slim, thin **4** meagre, miserable, poor, slim
♦ *n* **1** *rolls of fat around her waist*: blubber, bulk, chubbiness, corpulence *formal*, fatness, flab *colloq*, paunch, plumpness, pot (belly), solidness, stoutness **2** *fats such as cream*: animal fat, blubber, lard, oil, polyunsaturated fat, suet, tallow, vegetable fat

fatal *adj* calamitous, catastrophic, deadly, destructive, disastrous, final, incurable, lethal, malignant, mortal, terminal
Ea harmless

fatal or *fateful*? *Fatal* means 'causing death or disaster': *a fatal accident; She made the fatal mistake of telling him what she really thought.* *Fateful* means 'of great importance, having important consequences, etc': *At last the fateful day arrived, the day she was to be married.*

fatalism *n* acceptance, endurance, foreordination *formal*, passivity, predestination *formal*, preordination *formal*, resignation, stoicism

fatality *n* casualty, catastrophe, dead, death, disaster, loss, mortality

fate *n* catastrophe, chance, death, defeat, destiny, destruction, disaster, doom, fortune,

God's will, karma, kismet, lot, luck, providence, ruin

fated *adj* certain, destined, doomed, foreordained, ineluctable *formal*, inescapable, inevitable, predestined, preordained, sure, unavoidable
Ea avoidable

fateful *adj* critical, crucial, decisive, important, momentous, pivotal, significant
Ea unimportant

fateful or *fatal*? See panel at **fatal**

father *n* **1** *looks like his father*: ancestor, begetter *formal*, dad *colloq*, daddy *colloq*, old man *colloq*, pa *colloq*, papa *colloq*, parent, pater *formal*, paterfamilias *formal*, patriarch, pop *colloq*, procreator *formal*, progenitor *formal*, sire *formal* **2** *the fathers of the tribe*: ancestor, elder, forebear, forefather, patriarch, predecessor, progenitor **3** *the father of modern medicine*: architect, author, creator, founder, initiator, inventor, leader, maker, originator, patron, prime mover **4** *forgive me, father*: abbé, clergyman, curé, padre, parson, pastor, priest
♦ *v* engender, give life to, procreate *formal*, produce

fatherland *n* home, homeland, land of your birth, mother-country, motherland, native land, old country

fatherly *adj* affectionate, avuncular *formal*, benevolent, benign, forbearing, indulgent, kind, kindly, paternal, patriarchal, protective, supportive, tender
Ea cold, harsh, unkind

fathom *v* **1** *to fathom the depth of the bay*: estimate, gauge, measure, plumb, probe, sound **2** *it's hard to fathom what happened*: comprehend, get to the bottom of, grasp, interpret, penetrate, perceive, search out, see, understand, work out

fatigue *n* debility *formal*, enervation *formal*, exhaustion, lassitude, lethargy, listlessness, tiredness, weakness, weariness
Ea energy
♦ *v* debilitate *formal*, drain, enervate *formal*, exhaust, sap, take it out of *colloq*, tax, tire, weaken, wear out, weary
Ea invigorate, refresh

fatigued *adj* all in *colloq*, beat *colloq*, bushed *colloq*, dead-beat *colloq*, done in *colloq*, exhausted, fagged (out) *colloq*, jaded, jiggered, knackered *colloq*, overtired, tired, tired out, wasted, weary, whacked *colloq*, zonked *colloq*
Ea refreshed

fatness *n* bulk, bulkiness, corpulence *formal*, flab *colloq*, grossness, heaviness, largeness, obesity, plumpness, podginess, portliness, rotundity *formal*, stoutness, tubbiness

fatten *v* bloat, broaden, build up, feed, feed up, fill out, nourish, nurture, overfeed, pinguefy, stuff, swell, thicken, widen

fatty *adj* buttery, creamy, fat, greasy, lipoid *formal*, oily, oleaginous *formal*, oleic *formal*, pinguid, sebaceous *formal*, unctuous *formal*, waxy

fatuous *adj* absurd, asinine, brainless, daft, dense, foolish, idiotic, inane, ludicrous, lunatic,

mindless, moronic, puerile, ridiculous, silly, stupid, vacuous, weak-minded, witless
Fa sensible

fault *n* **1** *a fault in the program*: blemish, bug *colloq*, defect, deficiency, failing, flaw, foible, glitch *colloq*, hitch *colloq*, imperfection, omission, oversight, shortcoming, weak point, weakness **2** *it was a fault on the part of the manager*: blunder, boob *colloq*, booboo *colloq*, error, foible, indiscretion, lapse, misdeed, misdemeanour *formal*, mistake, offence, peccadillo, sin, slip, slip-up *colloq*, wrong, wrongdoing **3** *it's your fault*: accountability, answerability, blameworthiness, culpability *formal*, liability, responsibility
♦ *v* blame, call to account, censure, criticize, find fault with, impugn *formal*, knock *colloq*, pick holes in *colloq*, pull to pieces *colloq*, slam *colloq*, slate *colloq*
Fa approve, praise

fault-finding *n* carping, cavilling, complaining, criticism, finger-pointing *colloq*, grumbling, hair-splitting *colloq*, hypercriticism, nagging, niggling, nit-picking *colloq*, quibbling, ultracrepidation *formal*
Fa praise
♦ *adj* captious, carping, cavilling, censorious, critical, grumbling, hypercritical, nagging, nit-picking *colloq*, querulous *formal*, ultracrepidarian *formal*
Fa complimentary

faultless *adj* accurate, blameless, correct, exemplary, flawless, immaculate, impeccable, model, perfect, pure, spotless, unblemished, unsullied
Fa faulty, flawed, imperfect

faulty *adj* **1** *faulty equipment*: broken, bust *colloq*, damaged, defective, duff *colloq*, imperfect, inoperative *formal*, kaput *colloq*, malfunctioning *formal*, not working, on the blink *colloq*, out of action, out of order **2** *a faulty argument*: casuistic *formal*, defective, erroneous, fallacious *formal*, flawed, illogical, inaccurate, incorrect, invalid, weak, wrong
Fa **1** working **2** sound

faux pas *n* blunder, boob *colloq*, booboo *colloq*, clanger *colloq*, gaffe, goof *colloq*, howler *colloq*, impropriety *formal*, indiscretion, mistake, slip-up *colloq*, solecism *formal*

favour *n* **1** *won the teacher's favour*: aid, approbation *formal*, approval, assistance, backing, esteem *formal*, favouritism, friendliness, goodwill, kindness, partiality, patronage, preference, support, sympathy **2** *he did me a favour*: benefit, courtesy, good deed, good turn, kindness, service
Fa **1** disapproval
♦ *v* **1** *the crowd favoured the underdog*: advocate, approve, back, champion, choose, endorse, go for *colloq*, like, opt for, pick, plump for *colloq*, prefer, recommend, sanction, select, support, take kindly to **2** *the boggy pitch favoured the home side*: aid, assist, benefit, encourage, help, promote
Fa **1** dislike **2** hinder

favourable *adj* **1** *a favourable reaction*: agreeable, amicable, approving, complimentary, encouraging, enthusiastic, friendly, heartening, kind, positive, reassuring, sympathetic, understanding, well-disposed **2** *a favourable impression*: agreeable, effective, good, pleasing,

positive, promising **3** *favourable conditions*: advantageous, appropriate, auspicious *formal*, beneficial, convenient, encouraging, fair, good, opportune, promising, propitious *formal*, suitable
Fa **1** negative **2** negative **3** unhelpful

favourably *adv* **1** *favourably placed to win*: advantageously, auspiciously *formal*, conveniently, fortunately, helpfully, opportunely, profitably, propitiously *formal*, well **2** *received favourably by the crowds*: agreeably, approvingly, enthusiastically, positively, sympathetically, well
Fa **1** unfavourably **2** unfavourably

favoured *adj* advantaged, blessed, chosen, elite, favourite, predilected *formal*, preferred, privileged, recommended, selected

favourite *adj* beloved, best-loved, chosen, dearest, esteemed *formal*, favoured, most-liked, pet, preferred, special, treasured
Fa hated
♦ *n* beloved, blue-eyed boy *colloq*, choice, darling, first choice, idol, number one, pet, pick, preference, teacher's pet *colloq*, the apple of your eye *colloq*
Fa bête noire, pet hate

favouritism *n* bias, inequality, inequity, injustice, nepotism, one-sidedness, partiality, partisanship, preference, preferential treatment, prejudice, unfairness
Fa equality, impartiality

fawn[1] *adj* beige, buff, khaki, sand-coloured, sandy, yellowish-brown

fawn[2] *v* bootlick *colloq*, bow and scrape, butter up *colloq*, court, crawl *colloq*, creep *colloq*, cringe *colloq*, curry favour, dance attendance, flatter, grovel, ingratiate yourself, kowtow, lick someone's boots *colloq*, pay court, smarm *colloq*, soft-soap *colloq*, suck up to *colloq*, toady

fawning *adj* abject, bootlicking *colloq*, bowing and scraping, crawling *colloq*, cringing *colloq*, deferential, flattering, grovelling, ingratiating, obsequious, servile, sycophantic, toadying, toadyish, unctuous *formal*
Fa cold, proud

fear *n* **1** *couldn't hide her fear*: agitation, alarm, apprehension, aversion, consternation *formal*, dismay, distress, dread, fearfulness, foreboding, fright, horror, panic, terror, trepidation *formal* **2** *a fear of flying*: aversion, bête noire, dread, horror, phobia, worry **3** *fear about the test results*: anxiety, concern, disquiet, doubt, misgivings, qualms, suspicion, unease, uneasiness, worry **4** *no fear of being misunderstood*: chance, expectation, likelihood, possibility, probability, prospect, risk, scope
Fa **1** bravery, confidence, courage
♦ *v* **1** *feared for his life*: be afraid of, be in a cold sweat *colloq*, be scared of, dread, freak out *colloq*, get the wind up *colloq*, have a horror of, have a phobia about, panic, shrink from, shudder at, take fright at, tremble, your stomach turns *colloq* **2** *feared for the future*: be anxious about, be concerned about, be uneasy about, have misgivings/qualms about, tremble for, worry **3** *fear God*: hold in reverence, revere, reverence, stand in awe of, venerate *formal*, wonder at **4** *I fear I can't help you*: anticipate, be afraid, expect, foresee, suspect

fearful adj **1** *fearful of what would happen:* afraid, agitated, alarmed, anxious, apprehensive, faint-hearted, frightened, hesitant, in dread, nervous, nervy, panicky, petrified, quivering, scared, shaking, spineless *colloq*, tense, timid, trembling, uneasy, yellow *colloq* **2** *a fearful noise:* appalling, atrocious, awful, dire, distressing, dreadful, fearsome *formal*, frightful, ghastly, grim, gruesome, harrowing, hideous, horrible, horrific, monstrous, shocking, terrible
  F3 **1** brave, courageous, fearless **2** delightful, wonderful

fearfully adv **1** *glanced fearfully at his face:* anxiously, apprehensively, hesitantly, in fear and trembling, nervously, timidly **2** *fearfully insecure:* awfully *colloq*, dreadfully *colloq*, exceedingly, extremely, frightfully *colloq*, highly, intensely, terribly *colloq*, unusually

fearless adj bold, brave, confident, courageous, daring, dauntless, doughty *formal*, gallant, game *colloq*, gritty *colloq*, gutsy *colloq*, heroic, indomitable *formal*, intrepid, lion-hearted, plucky, spunky *colloq*, unafraid, unapprehensive, unblenching, unblinking, undaunted, unflinching, valiant, valorous *formal*
  F3 afraid, timid

fearsome adj alarming, appalling, awe-inspiring, awesome, awful, daunting, dismaying, formidable, frightening, frightful, hair-raising, horrendous, horrible, horrific, horrifying, menacing, terrible, unnerving
  F3 delightful

feasibility n achievability, expedience, possibility, practicability, reasonableness, viability, workability

feasible adj accomplishable, achievable, attainable, doable, likely, possible, practicable, practical, realistic, realizable, reasonable, viable, workable
  F3 impossible

feast n **1** *a Christmas feast:* banquet, beano *colloq*, binge *colloq*, blow-out *colloq*, dinner, junket, repast *formal*, slap-up meal *colloq*, spread **2** *a feast for the eyes:* abundance, cornucopia, delight, profusion *formal*, wealth **3** *the feast of St Anthony:* celebration, feast day, festival, festivities, fête, gala, holiday, holy day, religious festival, revels, saint's day
  ♦ v eat, eat your fill, entertain, gorge, indulge in, partake of *formal*, regale, treat, wine and dine

feat n accomplishment, achievement, act, action, attainment, deed, exploit, performance

feather n aigrette, crest, down, egret, penna *technical*, pinion, plume, plumula, plumule, quill, tuft

feathery adj **1** *feathery creatures:* feathered, plumate, plumed, plumose, plumous **2** *a plant with feathery leaves:* downy, featherlike, fleecy, fluffy, pennaceous *technical*, penniform, plumy, wispy **3** *feathery clouds:* delicate, fluffy, light, soft, wispy

feature n **1** *a new feature on the car:* aspect, attraction, attribute, characteristic, facet, factor, focal point, hallmark, highlight, mark, peculiarity, point, property, quality, side, speciality, trait **2** *a person's facial features:* clock *colloq*, countenance *formal*, dial *colloq*, face, kisser *colloq*, lineaments *formal*, looks, mug *colloq*,

pan *colloq*, phiz *colloq*, physiognomy *formal*, visage *formal* **3** *a magazine feature:* article, column, comment, item, piece, report, story
  ♦ v **1** *hope to feature her new album:* accentuate, emphasize, highlight, play up, present, promote, show, spotlight **2** *many big stars will feature in the show:* act, appear, figure, participate, perform, star

febrile adj burning, delirious, fevered, feverish, fiery, flushed, hot, pyretic *formal*

feckless adj aimless, feeble, futile, hopeless, incompetent, ineffectual *formal*, irresponsible, useless, weak, worthless
  F3 efficient, sensible

fecund adj feracious *formal*, fertile, fructiferous *formal*, fructuous *formal*, fruitful, productive, prolific, teeming
  F3 infertile

fecundity n feracity *formal*, fertility, fructi-ferousness *formal*, fruitfulness, productiveness
  F3 infertility

federal adj allied, amalgamated, associated, combined, confederated, in league, integrated, unified

federate v amalgamate, associate, combine, confederate, integrate, join together, league, syndicate, unify, unite
  F3 disunite, separate

federation n alliance, amalgamation, association, coalition, combination, confederacy, confederation, copartnership, federacy, league, syndicate, union

fed up adj annoyed, at the end of your tether *colloq*, blue *colloq*, bored, brassed off *colloq*, browned off *colloq*, cheesed off *colloq*, depressed, discontented, dissatisfied, down *colloq*, gloomy, glum, hacked off *colloq*, have had enough, have had it up to here *colloq*, pissed off *slang*, sick and tired *colloq*, tired, weary
  F3 contented

fee n account, bill, charge, cost, emolument *formal*, honorarium, pay, payment, price, recompense, remuneration, retainer, subscription, terms, toll

feeble adj **1** *felt feeble after her fall:* ailing, debilitated *formal*, decrepit, delicate, enervated *formal*, exhausted, failing, faint, frail, helpless, infirm, powerless, puny, sickly, weak **2** *a feeble excuse:* flimsy, futile, inadequate, ineffective, ineffectual *formal*, lame, poor, tame, thin, unconvincing, unsuccessful, weak **3** *a feeble person:* incompetent, indecisive, ineffective, ineffectual *formal*, weak, wet *colloq*, wimpish *colloq*
  F3 **1** powerful, strong

feeble-minded adj deficient, dim-witted *colloq*, dumb *colloq*, half-witted, idiotic, imbecilic, moronic, retarded, simple, slow on the uptake *colloq*, slow-witted, soft in the head *colloq*, stupid, two bricks short of a load *colloq*, weak-minded
  F3 bright, intelligent

feed v **1** *feed the baby:* cater for, give food to, nourish, nurture, provide for, suckle **2** *what do frogs feed on?:* consume, dine (on), eat, partake of *formal*, take in **3** *animals feeding:* browse, crop, graze, pasture, ruminate *formal* **4** *feed your sense of self-worth:* encourage, foster, fuel, gratify, nurture, strengthen **5** *feed data into a computer:*

give, insert, introduce, provide, put, supply
♦ *n* fodder, food, forage, pasture, provender, silage

feel *v* **1** *she had never felt such pain:* be overcome by, bear, endure, enjoy, experience, give way to, go through, harbour, know, live through, nurse, suffer, undergo **2** *just feel this silk:* caress, clutch, finger, fondle, fumble, grasp, handle, hold, manipulate, massage, maul, paw, rub, stroke, touch **3** *it feels soft:* appear, look, seem **4** *I feel that it was my fault:* believe, consider, deem *formal*, hold, judge, reckon, think **5** *felt that he wasn't telling the truth:* be aware of, feel in your bones, know, notice, observe, perceive, realize, sense, understand
♦ *n* **1** *the feel of the material:* consistency, finish, surface, texture, touch **2** *have a feel for computer-programming:* ability, aptitude, bent, faculty, flair, gift, knack, skill, talent, touch **3** *the feel of a place:* air, ambience, atmosphere, aura, feeling, impression, mood, quality, vibes *colloq*
▶ **feel for** be moved by, be sorry for, commiserate (with), empathize with, grieve for, pity, sympathize (with), weep for

feeler *n* **1** *the butterfly's feelers:* antenna, horn, palp *technical*, palpus, sense-organ, tentacle **2** *put out feelers:* advance, approach, ballon d'essai, overture(s), probe, trial balloon

feeling *n* **1** *her feelings for him:* affection, appreciation, ardour, compassion, concern, emotion, fervour, fondness, love, passion, pity, sensibility, sensitivity, sentience *formal*, sentiment, sentimentality, susceptibility, sympathy, understanding, warmth **2** *he plays the violin with real feeling:* emotion, intensity, passion **3** *a feeling that all was not well:* hunch, idea, impression, inkling, instinct, intuition, notion, opinion, perception, point of view, sensation, sense, suspicion, theory, thought **4** *hurt someone's feelings:* affections *formal*, ego, emotions, passions, self-esteem, sensitivities, susceptibilities **5** *create a feeling of comfort:* air, atmosphere, aura, feel, impression, mood, quality, vibes *colloq*

feign *v* act, affect *formal*, assume, counterfeit, dissemble *formal*, dissimulate *formal*, fake, forge, imitate, invent, make a show of, pretend, put it on, put on, sham, simulate

feint *n* artifice, blind, bluff, deception, distraction, dodge *colloq*, expedient, gambit, manoeuvre, mock-assault, play, pretence, ruse, stratagem, subterfuge, wile

felicitous *adj* **1** *a felicitous choice of words:* apposite, appropriate, apropos *formal*, apt, fitting, fortunate, opportune, suitable, timely, well-chosen, well-timed, well-turned **2** *a felicitous play of light:* delightful, fortunate, happy, inspired, propitious *formal*
🖎 **1** inappropriate

felicity *n* **1** *a state of near perfect felicity:* bliss, delectation *formal*, delight, ecstasy, happiness, joy **2** *the felicity of the choice of venue:* applicability, appropriateness, aptness, propriety *formal*, suitability, suitableness
🖎 **1** sadness **2** inappropriateness

feline *adj* catlike, graceful, leonine, seductive, sensual, sinuous, sleek, slinky, smooth, stealthy

fell *v* cut down, demolish, flatten, floor, hew, knock down, level, overthrow, raze, raze to the ground, strike down

fellow *n* **1** *a jolly good fellow:* bloke *colloq*, boy, chap *colloq*, character, guy *colloq*, individual, lad *colloq*, male, man, person **2** *the minister and his fellows:* associate, buddy *colloq*, chum *colloq*, colleague, companion, compeer, comrade, confrère, contemporary, counterpart, co-worker, crony *colloq*, equal, friend, match, mate, pal *colloq*, partner, peer, twin
♦ *adj* associate, associated, co-, related, similar

fellow feeling *n* compassion, empathy, sympathy, understanding

fellowship *n* **1** *the fellowship of the other staff:* affability, amiability, camaraderie, chumminess *colloq*, communion, companionship, comradeship, familiarity, friendship, intimacy, matiness *colloq*, palliness *colloq* **2** *a fellowship for those who love horticulture:* affiliation, association, brotherhood, club, fraternity, guild, league, order, sisterhood, society, union

female *adj* feminine, girlish, ladylike, she-, womanly
🖎 male

feminine *adj* **1** *a very feminine girl:* delicate, female, gentle, graceful, ladylike, pretty, tender, womanly **2** *a rather feminine way of throwing the ball:* effeminate, girlish, sissy *colloq*, unmanly, weak, womanish
🖎 **1** masculine **2** manly

femininity *n* delicacy, feminineness, gentleness, girlishness, gracefulness, prettiness, tenderness, womanhood, womanishness, womanliness
🖎 masculinity

feminism *n* female emancipation, women's lib(eration), women's movement, women's rights

femme fatale *n* charmer, enchantress, seductress, siren, temptress, vamp

fen *n* bog, marsh, morass, quag, quagmire, slough, swamp

fence *n* barricade, barrier, defence, enclosure, paling, palisade, rail, railing, rampart, stockade, windbreak
♦ *v* **1** *the area had been fenced:* bound, circumscribe *formal*, confine, coop, encircle, enclose, fortify *formal*, pen, protect, restrict, secure, separate, shut in, surround, wall **2** *fencing with his opponent:* beat about the bush *colloq*, dodge *colloq*, equivocate, evade, hedge, parry, prevaricate, pussyfoot *colloq*, quibble, shilly-shally *colloq*, stonewall, tergiversate *formal*, vacillate *formal*

fend *v* **1** *fend for yourself:* look after, maintain, provide, support, sustain, take care of **2** *fend off an attack:* avert, beat off, deflect, divert, hold at bay, keep off, parry, repel, repulse, resist, shut out, stave off, turn aside, ward off

feral *adj* bestial, brutal, brutish, ferocious, fierce, savage, unbroken, undomesticated, untamed, vicious, wild
🖎 domesticated, tame

ferment *v* **1** *leave the beer to ferment:* boil, brew, bubble, effervesce, fester, foam, froth, rise, seethe, smoulder, work **2** *fermenting trouble:* agitate, arouse, cause, excite, foment, heat, incite, inflame, provoke, rouse, stir up, work up

♦ *n* agitation, brouhaha, commotion, confusion, disruption, excitement, fever, frenzy, furore, fuss, hubbub, stew, stir, tumult, turbulence, turmoil, unrest, uproar
▨ calm

ferocious *adj* **1** *a ferocious beast*: barbaric, barbarous, bloodthirsty, brutal, cruel, feral *formal*, fierce, inhuman, merciless, murderous, pitiless, ruthless, sadistic, savage, untamed, vicious, violent, wild **2** *ferocious hunger*: deep, extreme, intense, severe, strong, vigorous, wild
▨ **1** tame **2** gentle, mild

ferocity *n* barbarity, bloodthirstiness, brutality, cruelty, extremity, fierceness, inhumanity, intensity, ruthlessness, sadism, savagery, severity, viciousness, violence, wildness
▨ gentleness, mildness

ferret *v* forage, go through, hunt, rifle, rummage, scour, search
► **ferret out** dig up, discover, elicit, extract, find, hunt down, nose out, root out, run to earth, search out, suss out *colloq*, trace, track down, unearth, worm out

ferry *n* boat, car ferry, ferry-boat, packet, packet boat, ship, shuttle, vessel
♦ *v* carry, convey, drive, move, ply, run, ship, shuttle, take, taxi, transport

fertile *adj* **1** *fertile soil*: abundant, fecund *formal*, fruitful, luxuriant *formal*, productive, rich **2** *a fertile imagination*: creative, imaginative, inspired, inventive, productive, prolific, resourceful, visionary **3** *fertile animals*: able to have children, fecund *formal*, generative, potent, prolific, reproductive, virile
▨ **1** unfruitful, unproductive **2** barren **3** barren, infertile, sterile

fertility *n* **1** *the fertility of the land*: abundance, fecundity *formal*, fruitfulness, luxuriance *formal*, productiveness, richness **2** *fertility tests*: generativeness, potency, prolificness, reproductiveness, virility
▨ **1** aridity **2** barrenness, sterility

fertilization *n* fecundation *formal*, implantation, impregnation, insemination, procreation *formal*

fertilize *v* **1** *fertilize an egg*: fecundate *formal*, fructify *formal*, impregnate, inseminate, make fruitful, make pregnant, procreate *formal* **2** *fertilize land*: compost, dress, dung, enrich, feed, manure, mulch, top-dress

fertilizer *n* bone meal, compost, dressing, dung, humus, manure, mulch, plant food, top-dressing

fervent *adj* ardent, devout, eager, earnest, emotional, energetic, enthusiastic, excited, fiery, full-blooded, heartfelt, impassioned, intense, passionate, sincere, spirited, vehement, vigorous, warm, wholehearted, zealous
▨ apathetic, cool, indifferent

fervour *n* animation, ardour, eagerness, earnestness, emotion, energy, enthusiasm, excitement, fire, intensity, passion, sincerity, spirit, vehemence, verve, vigour, warmth, wholeheartedness, zeal
▨ apathy, indifference

fester *v* **1** *the wound was festering*: discharge, gather, infect, maturate *technical*, suppurate, ulcerate **2** *the food was festering*: decay, decompose, go bad, perish, putrefy *formal*, rot

3 *hatred was festering*: anger, annoy, chafe, gall, irk, rankle, smoulder

festival *n* anniversary, carnival, celebration, commemoration, entertainment, fair, feast, festivities, fête, fiesta, gala, gala day, holiday, jubilee, party

festive *adj* carnival, celebratory, cheerful, cheery, convivial, cordial, festal, gala, happy, hearty, holiday, jolly, jovial, joyful, joyous *formal*, jubilant, light-hearted, merry
▨ gloomy, sober, sombre

festivity *n* **1** *all joined in the festivities*: banqueting, celebration, entertainment, feasting, festival, fun, fun and games, junketing, merrymaking, party, revel, revelry **2** *an atmosphere of festivity*: amusement, carousal, celebration, cheerfulness, cheeriness, conviviality, enjoyment, fun, jollity, joviality, jubilation, merriment, merrymaking, pleasure, revelry

festoon *v* adorn, array *formal*, bedeck *formal*, deck, decorate, drape, garland, garnish, hang, ornament, swathe, wreathe
♦ *n* chaplet, garland, swag, swathe, wreath

fetch *v* **1** *fetch a bucket*: bring, carry, collect, conduct, convey, deliver, escort, get, go and get, transport **2** *should fetch a good price*: bring in, earn, go for, make, realize, sell for, yield

fetching *adj* alluring, attractive, captivating, charming, cute, enchanting, fascinating, pretty, sweet, winsome
▨ repellent

fête *n* bazaar, carnival, fair, festival, gala, garden party, sale of work
♦ *v* entertain, honour, lionize, regale, treat, welcome

fetid *adj* disgusting, filthy, foul, malodorous *formal*, mephitic *formal*, nauseating, noisome *formal*, noxious *formal*, odorous, offensive, rancid, rank, reeking, sickly, smelly, stinking
▨ fragrant

fetish *n* **1** *a foot fetish*: fixation, idée fixe, mania, obsession, thing *colloq* **2** *a wooden fetish*: amulet, charm, cult object, idol, image, ju-ju, talisman, totem

fetter *v* bind, chain, confine, constrain, curb, encumber, entrammel, hamper, hamstring, hinder, impede, manacle, obstruct, restrain, restrict, shackle, tie (up), truss
▨ free

fetters *n* **1** *the fetters of marriage*: bondage, checks, constraints, curbs, hindrances, inhibitions, obstructions, restraints, restrictions **2** *led in fetters to the dock*: bonds, bracelets, chains, handcuffs, irons, manacles, shackles

feud *n* animosity, antagonism, argument, bad blood, bickering, bitterness, conflict, disagreement, discord, dispute, enmity, hostility, ill will, quarrel, rivalry, row, strife, vendetta
▨ agreement, peace
♦ *v* altercate *formal*, argue, be at odds, bicker, brawl, clash, contend, dispute, duel, fight, quarrel, row, squabble, war, wrangle
▨ agree

fever *n* **1** *the baby had a fever*: ague, delirium, feverishness, (high) temperature, pyrexia technical **2** *World Cup fever gripped the country:* agitation, ecstasy, excitement, ferment, frenzy, heat, passion, restlessness, turmoil, unrest

feverish *adj* **1** *feeling weak and feverish:* burning, delirious, flushed, hot, red, with a temperature **2** *feverish fans hoping for a glimpse:* agitated, bothered, excited, flustered, frantic, frenzied, hot and bothered *colloq*, impatient, in a dither *colloq*, in a kerfuffle *colloq*, in a tizz *colloq*, in a tizzy *colloq*, nervous, overwrought, passionate, restless, worked up
☒ **1** cool **2** calm

few *adj* inadequate, inconsiderable, insufficient, sporadic
☒ many
♦ *pron* a couple, a handful, a small number, hardly any, not many, one or two, scarcely any, some
☒ many

fiancé, fiancée *n* betrothed, bridegroom-to-be, bride-to-be, future/prospective husband, future/prospective wife, husband-to-be, intended, wife-to-be

fiasco *n* calamity, catastrophe, collapse, damp squib *colloq*, debacle, disaster, failure, flop *colloq*, mess, rout, ruin, washout *colloq*
☒ success

fiat *n* authorization, command, decree, dictum, diktat, directive, edict, injunction, mandate, OK *colloq*, order, ordinance, permission, precept, proclamation, sanction, warrant

fib *n* concoction, evasion, falsehood, fantasy, fiction, invention, lie, misrepresentation, story, tale, untruth, white lie, whopper *colloq*, yarn
♦ *v* dissemble *formal*, evade, fabricate, falsify, fantasize, invent, lie, prevaricate

fibre *n* **1** *natural fibres:* cloth, fibril, filament, material, pile, strand, stuff, substance, tendril, texture, thread **2** *moral fibre:* backbone, calibre, character, courage, determination, disposition, firmness (of purpose), make-up, nature, resoluteness, resolution, stamina, strength, strength of character, temperament, toughness, willpower

fickle *adj* capricious *formal*, changeable, disloyal, faithless, flighty, inconstant, irresolute, labile *formal*, mercurial *formal*, treacherous, unfaithful, unpredictable, unreliable, unstable, unsteady, vacillating, variable, volatile
☒ constant, stable, steady

fickleness *n* capriciousness *formal*, changeability, changeableness, disloyalty, faithlessness, flightiness, inconstancy, instability, treachery, unfaithfulness, unpredictability, unreliability, unsteadiness, volatility
☒ constancy

fiction *n* **1** *a master of crime fiction:* fable, fantasy, legend, myth, novels, parable, romance, story, storytelling, tale, yarn **2** *her tale was a complete fiction:* cock-and-bull story *colloq*, concoction, fabrication, falsehood, fib *colloq*, invention, lie, pretence, tall story *colloq*, untruth
☒ **1** non-fiction **2** fact, truth

fictional *adj* fabulous, imaginary, invented, legendary, literary, made-up, make-believe, mythical, mythological, non-existent, unreal
☒ factual, real

fictitious *adj* apocryphal, assumed, bogus, concocted, counterfeit, fabricated, fake, false, imaginary, improvised, invented, made-up, non-existent, sham, spurious, supposed, untrue
☒ genuine, true

fiddle *v* **1** *fiddling with her necklace:* fidget, fuss, play, toy **2** *fiddling in his affairs:* fool around, interfere, meddle, mess around, tamper, tinker, trifle **3** *fiddled the accounts:* cheat, cook the books *colloq*, diddle *colloq*, falsify, graft *colloq*, juggle, swindle
♦ *n* con *colloq*, fix *colloq*, fraud, graft *colloq*, racket, rip-off *colloq*, sharp practice, swindle

fiddling *adj* insignificant, negligible, paltry, petty, trifling, trivial
☒ important, significant

fidelity *n* **1** *his fidelity was never in doubt:* allegiance, constancy, dependability, devotedness, devotion, faithfulness, loyalty, reliability, trustworthiness **2** *the fidelity of her account:* accuracy, authenticity, closeness, exactness, faithfulness, precision, strictness
☒ **1** disloyalty, inconstancy, infidelity, treachery, unfaithfulness **2** inaccuracy

fidget *v* **1** *fidgeting in his seat:* fret, jerk, jiggle, jump, shuffle, squirm, toss and turn, twitch, wriggle, writhe **2** *fidgeting with her watch:* fiddle, fuss, mess about, play around, tamper, tinker, toy, twiddle

fidgety *adj* agitated, excited, impatient, jittery *colloq*, jumpy, like a cat on hot bricks *colloq*, nervous, on edge, restive *formal*, restless, twitchy, uneasy, uptight *colloq*
☒ still

field *n* **1** *a farmer's field:* grassland, green, ground, lawn, meadow, paddock, pasture, pitch, playing-field **2** *not in my field:* area, department, discipline, domain, environment, line, province, range, regime, scope, speciality, sphere, territory **3** *narrowed the field to six:* applicants, candidates, competition, competitors, contenders, contestants, entrants, opponents, opposition, participants, possibles, runners
♦ *v* **1** *my team was fielding:* catch, pick up, retrieve, return, stop **2** *he was fielding questions from the press:* answer, cope with, deal with, deflect, handle, parry

fiend *n* **1** *battling a fiend from hell:* beast, brute, demon, devil, evil spirit, monster, ogre, savage **2** *a health fiend:* addict, aficionado, buff *colloq*, devotee, enthusiast, fan, fanatic, freak *colloq*, nut *colloq*

fiendish *adj* **1** *a fiendish person/plot:* aggressive, barbaric, bloodthirsty, brutal, cruel, cunning, devilish, diabolical, ferocious, infernal, inhuman, malevolent, monstrous, ruthless, savage, unspeakable, vicious, wicked **2** *a fiendish problem:* challenging, clever, complex, complicated, difficult, horrendous, imaginative, ingenious, intricate, involved, obscure

fierce *adj* **1** *a fierce warrior:* aggressive, bloodthirsty, brutal, cruel, dangerous, ferocious, frightening, grim, menacing, merciless, murderous, relentless, ruthless, savage, stern, terrible, threatening, vicious, wild **2** *fierce competition:* cut-throat, furious, grave, hot, intense, keen, passionate, powerful, raging, relentless, severe, strong

⊟ 1 gentle, kind **2** calm

fiercely *adv* aggressively, bitterly, brutally, cruelly, dangerously, fanatically, ferociously, furiously, implacably, intensely, keenly, menacingly, mercilessly, murderously, passionately, powerfully, relentlessly, ruthlessly, savagely, severely, strongly, tempestuously, terribly, threateningly, tooth and nail *colloq*, viciously, violently, wildly
⊟ gently, kindly

fiery *adj* **1** *the fiery glow of the embers:* ablaze, afire, aflame, aglow, blazing, burning, flaming, flushed, glowing, hot, red-hot, sultry, torrid **2** *a fiery temperament:* ardent, excitable, fervent, fierce, hot-headed, impatient, impetuous, impulsive, passionate, violent **3** *a fiery curry:* hot, piquant, pungent, seasoned, sharp, spiced, spicy
⊟ 1 cold **2** impassive

fight *v* **1** *the two boys were fighting in the garden:* box, brawl, clash, come to blows, cross swords, fence, grapple, lay into *colloq*, scrap *colloq*, scuffle, skirmish, struggle, take on, tussle, weigh into *colloq*, wrestle **2** *armies fighting in the desert:* attack, battle, be at war, clash, combat, do battle, engage, make war, skirmish, wage war, war **3** *always fighting about money:* altercate *formal*, argue, be at each other's throats *colloq*, be at odds, bicker, fall out *colloq*, feud, have a row, quarrel, squabble, wrangle **4** *fighting against oppression:* campaign against, contest, dispute, hold out against, object to, oppose, resist, stand up to, take issue with, withstand **5** *fighting for justice:* champion, strive for, work for
♦ *n* **1** *get involved in a fight:* action, aggro *colloq*, attack, bashing *colloq*, battle, bloodshed, bout, bovver *colloq*, brawl, brush, clash, combat, conflict, confrontation, contest, disturbance, Donnybrook, duel, encounter, engagement, exchange, fracas, fray, free-for-all, hostilities, mêlée, pasting *colloq*, punch-up *colloq*, riot, rout, row, ruckus, ruction, ruffle, scrap *colloq*, scuffle, set-to *colloq*, shindy, skirmish, struggle, tussle, war, warfare **2** *a fight about working hours:* altercation *formal*, argument, difference of opinion, disagreement, discord *formal*, dispute, dissension *formal*, dust-up *colloq*, quarrel, row **3** *the fight for freedom:* battle, campaign, crusade, drive, movement, struggle **4** *lose all his fight:* aggression, determination, drive, firmness, resoluteness, spirit, tenacity, will to live, willpower
▶ **fight back 1** *United fought back to win:* counter-attack, defend yourself, hold out against, put up a fight, reply, resist, retaliate, retort **2** *fight back tears:* bottle up *colloq*, check, contain, control, curb, force back, hold back, repress, restrain, suppress
▶ **fight off** beat off, hold off, keep/hold at bay, put to flight, rebuff, repel, resist, rout, stave off, ward off

fighter *n* adversary, antagonist, attacker, boxer, combatant, contender, contestant, disputant, gladiator, man-at-arms, mercenary, opponent, prizefighter, pugilist *formal*, rival, soldier, sparring partner, swordsman, trouper, warrior, wrestler

figment *n* concoction, fabrication, fiction, invention

figurative *adj* allegorical, descriptive, emblematic, metaphorical, naturalistic, parabolic, pictorial, representative, symbolic
⊟ literal

figure *n* **1** *a six-figure salary:* amount, digit, integer, number, numeral, sum, total **2** *good at figures:* arithmetic, calculations, mathematics, maths, mental arithmetic, statistics **3** *the figure of a man:* form, outline, shape, silhouette **4** *she has a nice figure:* body, build, frame, physique, torso **5** *a public figure:* celebrity, character, dignitary, leader, notable, person, personage, personality, worthy **6** *see figure 1:* design, diagram, drawing, emblem, illustration, image, pattern, picture, representation, sign, sketch, symbol
♦ *v* **1** *I figured he'd understand:* believe, conclude, consider, estimate, guess, judge, reckon, think **2** *she didn't figure in the final film:* appear, be included in, be mentioned in, crop up, feature
▶ **figure out** calculate, compute, count, decipher, estimate, fathom, get the picture *colloq*, latch onto *colloq*, make out, puzzle out, reason, reckon, see, tumble to *colloq*, twig *colloq*, understand, work out

figurehead *n* **1** *the president is merely a figurehead:* dummy, front man, image, man of straw, mouthpiece, name, nominal head, puppet, titular head, token **2** *a figurehead on a ship's prow:* bust, carving, figure

filament *n* cable, cord, fibre, hair, pile, strand, string, tendril, thread, whisker, wire

filch *v* knock off *colloq*, lift *colloq*, misappropriate *formal*, nick *colloq*, palm, peculate *formal*, pilfer, pinch *colloq*, purloin *formal*, rip off *colloq*, rob, snaffle *colloq*, snitch *colloq*, steal, swipe *colloq*, take, thieve

file¹ *n* **1** *put the papers in the file:* binder, box, case, dossier, folder **2** *his police file:* data, details, document, dossier, information, papers, particulars, portfolio, record **3** *a long file of troops:* column, cortège, line, procession, queue, row, stream, string, trail, train
♦ *v* **1** *file papers:* catalogue, categorize, classify, enter, note, organize, pigeonhole, process, put in place, store **2** *file a complaint:* make, put in, record, register, submit **3** *file for divorce:* apply, ask, request **4** *file out of the building:* march, parade, process, stream, troop, walk in line

file² *v* abrade, grate, hone, plane, polish, rasp, rub (down), sand, scour, scrape, shape, smooth, whet

filial *adj* affectionate, daughterly, devoted, dutiful, familial, fond, loving, loyal, respectful
⊟ disloyal, unfilial

filibuster *n* delay, hindrance, impediment, obstruction, peroration *formal*, postponement, procrastination *formal*, speechifying *formal*
♦ *v* delay, hinder, impede, obstruct, perorate *formal*, prevent, procrastinate *formal*, put off, speechify *formal*
⊟ expedite

filigree *n* fretwork, interlace, lace, lacework, lattice, latticework, scrollwork, tracery, wirework

fill *v* **1** *fill a box with books:* cram, crowd, furnish, make full, occupy, pack, provide, replenish *formal*, satisfy, stock, stuff, supply **2** *fill a hole in the pipe:* block, bung, clog, close, cork, plug, seal,

stop (up) **3** *scent filled the air*: charge, imbue, impregnate, permeate, pervade, riddle, saturate, soak, spread throughout, suffuse *formal* **4** *fill a post*: fulfil, hold, occupy, perform, take up
🗲 **1** empty **2** drain
♦ *n* abundance, all you can take, all you want, ample, enough, more than enough, plenty, sufficiency, sufficient
▶ **fill in 1** *fill in a form*: answer, complete, fill out **2** *filling in for the boss*: act for, deputize, replace, represent, stand in, substitute, understudy **3** *filled me in on the details*: acquaint, advise, brief, bring up to date, inform
▶ **fill out 1** *fill out a form*: answer, complete, fill in **2** *the child filled out*: become plumper/chubbier, become/grow fatter, put on/gain weight

filling *n* contents, filler, inside, padding, stuffing, substance, wadding
♦ *adj* ample, big, generous, heavy, large, nutritious, rich, satisfying, solid, square, stodgy, substantial
🗲 insubstantial

film *n* **1** *a family film*: documentary, DVD, feature film, flick *colloq*, footage, motion picture, movie *colloq*, picture, screenplay, short, video **2** *a film for a camera*: cartridge, cassette, reel, spool, video, videocassette **3** *a film of dust covered the furniture*: blanket, coat, coating, cover, covering, dusting, glaze, layer, membrane, screen, sheet, skin, tissue, veil
♦ *v* photograph, record on film, shoot, televise, video, videotape
▶ **film over** become blurred, blur, cloud over, dull, glaze, mist over

Kinds of film include:
action, adult, adventure, animated, avant-garde, biopic, B-movie, black comedy, blockbuster, Bollywood, buddy, burlesque, Carry-on, cartoon, chapter-play, cinéma-vérité, classic, cliff-hanger, comedy, comedy thriller, comic-book hero, cowboy and Indian, crime, cult, detective, disaster, Disney, documentary, Ealing comedy, epic, erotic, escapist, ethnographic, expressionist, family, fantasy, farce, film à clef, film noir, flashback, gangster, historical romance, Hollywood, horror, James Bond, kitchen sink, love story, low-budget, medieval, melodrama, multiple-story, murder mystery, musical remake, newsreel, new wave, nouvelle vague, period epic, police thriller, political, pornographic, psychological thriller, realist, re-make, rites of passage, robbery, romantic, romantic comedy, satirical, science-fiction, screenplay, serial, sexual fantasy, short, silent, social comedy, social problem, space-age, space exploration, spy, surrealist, tear-jerker *colloq*, thriller, tragedy, tragicomedy, travelogue, underground, war, western, whodunnit

filmy *adj* chiffony, cobwebby, delicate, diaphanous *formal*, fine, flimsy, floaty, fragile, gauzy, gossamer, gossamery, insubstantial, light, see-through, sheer, shimmering, thin, translucent, transparent
🗲 opaque

filter *v* clarify, drain, dribble, filtrate *formal*, leach, leak, ooze, percolate, purify, refine, riddle, screen, seep, sieve, sift, strain, trickle
♦ *n* colander, gauze, membrane, mesh, netting, riddle, sieve, sifter, strainer

filth *n* **1** *surfaces covered in filth*: contamination, corruption, crap *slang*, crud *slang*, defilement, dirt, dung, effluent, excrement, faeces *formal*, foulness, garbage, grime, grot *colloq*, grunge *slang*, gunge *colloq*, gunk *slang*, impurity, manure, muck, pollution, putrefaction *formal*, putrescence *formal*, refuse, rubbish, sewage, slime, sludge, sordidness, squalor, trash, yuck *colloq* **2** *how can you watch such filth?*: blue films *colloq*, coarseness, dirty books, hard porn *colloq*, obscenity, porn *colloq*, pornography, raunchiness *colloq*, sexploitation *colloq*, sleaze *colloq*, smut *colloq*, vulgarity
🗲 **1** cleanliness, cleanness, purity

filthy *adj* **1** *filthy hands*: base, black, contaminated, contemptible, crappy *slang*, decaying, despicable, dirty, faecal *formal*, foul, grimy, gross, grubby, impure, low, mean, mucky, muddy, nasty, polluted, putrefying *formal*, putrid *formal*, rotten, slimy, soiled, sooty, sordid, squalid, unclean, unwashed, vile, yucky *colloq* **2** *filthy jokes*: adult *colloq*, bawdy, blue *colloq*, coarse, corrupt, depraved, dirty, explicit, foul, foul-mouthed, indecent, lewd, obscene, offensive, pornographic, smutty, suggestive, vulgar **3** *a filthy trick*: contemptible, despicable, low, nasty, vile, worthless, wretched
🗲 **1** clean, pure **2** decent

final *adj* **1** *the final episode*: closing, concluding, end, eventual, finishing, last, last-minute, latest, terminal, terminating *formal*, ultimate **2** *my decision is final*: conclusive, decisive, definite, definitive, determinate *formal*, incontrovertible, indisputable, irrefutable, irrevocable, settled
🗲 **1** first, initial

finale *n* climax, close, conclusion, crowning glory, culmination, curtain, dénouement, end, ending, epilogue, final act

finality *n* certitude, conclusiveness, conviction, decidedness, decisiveness, definiteness, firmness, incontrovertibility, inevitability, inevitableness, irreversibility, irrevocability, resolution, ultimacy *formal*, unavoidability

finalize *v* agree, clinch *colloq*, close, complete, conclude, decide, finish, put the finishing touches to *colloq*, put the icing on the cake *colloq*, resolve, round off, settle, sew up *colloq*, work out, wrap up *colloq*

finally *adv* **1** *we'd finally arrived*: at last, at length, eventually, in the end, ultimately **2** *it was finally decided*: conclusively, decisively, definitely, for ever, for good, irreversibly, irrevocably, once and for all, permanently **3** *finally, let's speak to the newsroom*: in conclusion, lastly, to close, to conclude

finance *n* **1** *corporate finance*: accounting, banking, business, commerce, economics, funding, investment, money, money management, sponsorship, stock market, subsidy, trade **2** *the company's finances*: accounts, affairs, assets, bank account, budget, capital, cash, funding, funds, income, liquidity, means, money, resources, revenue, savings, wealth, wherewithal
♦ *v* back, capitalize, float, fund, guarantee, pay for, set up, sponsor, subsidize, support, underwrite

Terms used in accounting and finance include: above the line, accounting period, accounts rendered, accounts payable, accounts receivable, accrual basis, allowable expense, annual accounts, annual report, appreciation, APR [= Annual Percentage Rate], asset-stripping, audit, authorized capital, bad debt, balance sheet, below the line, benefit in kind, bookkeeping, break-even point, budgetary control, capital expenditure, capital gain, capitalization, cash flow, circulating capital, collateral, compound interest, consolidated accounts, cost accounting, cost-benefit analysis, creative accounting, credit control, creditor, current assets, current liabilities, debit, debt/equity ratio, debtor, deferred credit, deferred expenditure, deferred liability, deficit, depreciating asset, depreciation, direct costs, disinvestment, dividend, double-entry bookkeeping, earnings per share, equity, fiduciary loan, fictitious assets, financial year, first cost, fiscal year, fixed assets, fixed capital, fixed costs, fixtures and fittings, floating capital, frozen assets, funds flow statement, gearing, going concern, gross margin, gross profit, gross receipts, grossing up, historic cost, income, intangible assets, interim accounts, ledger, liability, liquid assets, liquidation, liquidity, loan capital, loss, net assets, net profit, nominal capital, overheads, outgoings, payroll, petty cash, poison pill, profit and loss account, rate of return, realization of assets, refinance, replacement cost, reserves, return on capital, revenue expenditure, ring fencing (funds), running costs, secured loan, simple interest, statutory income, statutory returns, takeover, hostile takeover, tangible assets, tax loss, taxable profits, total costs, trading account, trial balance, turnover, unit costs, variable costs, wasting asset, watering, white knight, windfall profit, write off

financial *adj* budgetary, commercial, economic, entrepreneurial, fiscal, monetary, money, pecuniary *formal*

financier *n* banker, financialist, investor, money-maker, speculator, stockbroker

find *v* **1** *found the source of the Nile:* bring to light, chance upon *formal*, come across, come by, detect, dig out, discover, expose, happen upon *formal*, learn, locate, reveal, stumble across/on, trace, track down, uncover, unearth **2** *found my watch:* locate, recover, regain, retrieve, track down, turn up **3** *find fame:* achieve, acquire, attain, earn, gain, get, obtain, procure *formal*, reach, win **4** *find it difficult to believe:* consider, declare, deem *formal*, gauge, judge, rate, think

🔁 **1** lose **2** lose

♦ *n* acquisition, asset, bargain, boon, catch, coup, discovery, godsend, good buy

▶ **find out 1** *trying to find out the truth:* ascertain, cotton on to *colloq*, detect, discover, establish, gather, get wind of *colloq*, identify, learn, note, observe, perceive, pinpoint, realize, see, suss out *colloq* **2** *the police eventually found him out:* bring to light, catch, detect, disclose, expose, get at, lay bare, reveal, rumble *slang*, suss out *colloq*, tumble to *colloq*, uncover, unmask

finding *n* **1** *the report's findings:* breakthrough, discovery, find, innovation **2** *the finding of the legal inquiry:* award, conclusion, decision, decree, judgement, order, pronouncement, recommendation, verdict

fine[1] *adj* **1** *a fine example of classical architecture:* admirable, attractive, beautiful, brilliant, choice, excellent, exceptional, exquisite, first-class, good, great, handsome, lovely, magnificent, nice, outstanding, select, splendid, superior **2** *I feel fine:* fit, flourishing, healthy, in good health, strong, vigorous, well **3** *that's fine, but don't do it again:* acceptable, agreeable, all right, good, OK *colloq*, satisfactory **4** *fine weather:* bright, clear, clement, cloudless, dry, fair, sunny, temperate **5** *a fine thread:* dainty, delicate, flimsy, fragile, gauzy, light, narrow, sheer, slender, slight, slim, thin **6** *a fine powder:* crushed, fine-grained, gossamer, ground, powdery **7** *fine hotels:* elegant, expensive, fashionable, smart, stylish **8** *a fine distinction:* accurate, critical, exact, hair-splitting *colloq*, nice, precise

🔁 **1** mediocre **4** cloudy, dull, inclement, stormy **5** coarse, thick

fine[2] *n* amercement *formal*, damages, forfeit, forfeiture, mulct *formal*, penalty, punishment
♦ *v* amerce *formal*, mulct *formal*, penalize, punish, sting *colloq*

finery *n* bedizenment *formal*, best bib and tucker *colloq*, best clothes, decorations, frippery, gaudery, glad rags *colloq*, jewellery, ornaments, showiness, splendour, Sunday best, trappings

finesse *n* adeptness, adroitness, cleverness, deftness, delicacy, diplomacy, discretion, elegance, expertise, flair, gracefulness, know-how *colloq*, neatness, polish, quickness, refinement, savoir-faire, skill, sophistication, subtlety, tact
♦ *v* bluff, manipulate, manoeuvre, trick

finger *v* caress, feel, fiddle with, fondle, handle, manipulate, meddle with, paw, play about with, stroke, touch, toy with

finicky *adj* **1** *a finicky eater:* choosy *colloq*, critical, discriminating, faddy, fastidious, finickety, fussy, hypercritical, meticulous, nit-picking *colloq*, particular, pernickety *colloq*, picky *colloq*, scrupulous, selective **2** *a finicky clasp on the necklace:* delicate, difficult, fiddly, intricate, tricky

🔁 **1** easy-going **2** easy

finish *v* **1** *the work is finished at last:* accomplish, achieve, attain, be done with *colloq*, be over, be through *colloq*, bring/come to an end, call it a day *colloq*, carry out, cease *formal*, close, complete, conclude *formal*, culminate, deal with, discharge, discontinue *formal*, do, end, fulfil, get shot of *colloq*, pack in *colloq*, perfect, polish off *colloq*, round off, settle, sew up *colloq*, stop, terminate *formal*, wind up *colloq*, wrap up *colloq* **2** *finished all the milk:* consume, deplete *formal*, devour, drain, drink, eat, empty, exhaust, expend *formal*, run out of, use, use up **3** *the battle completely finished them:* annihilate, bring down, conquer, crush, defeat, destroy, exterminate, get rid of, get the better of, overcome, overpower, overthrow, overwhelm, rout, ruin, wipe out *colloq*

🔁 **1** begin, commence *formal*, start
♦ *n* **1** *there were only two riders at the finish:* accomplishment, achievement, cessation *formal*, close, completion, conclusion, culmination,

curtains *colloq*, end, ending, finale, fulfilment, perfection, termination *formal*, winding-up *colloq*, wind-up *colloq* **2** *a glossy finish:* appearance, coating, glaze, gloss, grain, lacquer, lustre, polish, shine, smoothness, surface, texture, veneer

F3 1 beginning, commencement *formal*, start

finished *adj* **1** *the finished article:* at an end, complete, completed, concluded, dealt with, over, over and done with *colloq*, sewn up *colloq*, through *colloq*, wrapped up *colloq* **2** *this company is finished:* defeated, done for *colloq*, doomed, ruined **3** *a finished performance:* accomplished, consummate, expert, faultless, flawless, impeccable, masterly, perfect, polished, professional, proficient, refined, sophisticated, urbane, virtuoso

F3 1 incomplete, unfinished **3** incompetent

finite *adj* bounded, calculable, countable, definable, demarcated, fixed, limited, measurable, numbered, restricted, terminable

F3 infinite

fire *n* **1** *a fire in a warehouse:* blaze, bonfire, burning, combustion, conflagration *formal*, flames, holocaust, inferno **2** *under fire from local militia:* attack, barrage, bombardment, bombing, cannonade, flak, fusillade, gunfire, salvo, shelling, sniping **3** *an electric fire:* convector, fan, heater, radiator **4** *fire in his belly:* animation, ardour, creativity, eagerness, energy, enthusiasm, excitement, feeling, fervour, heat, intensity, inventiveness, life, liveliness, passion, radiance, sparkle, spirit, verve, vigour, vivacity ♦ *v* **1** *fired the boiler:* ignite, kindle, light, put a match to, set ablaze, set alight, set fire to, set on fire **2** *fire a missile:* detonate, discharge, explode, hurl, launch, let off, set off, shoot, trigger **3** *fired from her job:* axe *colloq*, boot out *colloq*, discharge, dismiss, eject, get rid of, give someone the sack/push/boot/elbow *colloq*, give someone their cards *colloq*, sack *colloq*, show someone the door *colloq* **4** *fired her with enthusiasm:* animate, arouse, electrify, enliven, excite, galvanize, incite, inflame, inspire, motivate, rouse, spark off, stimulate, stir (up), trigger off, whet

firearm *n* automatic, gun, handgun, musket, pistol, revolver, rifle, shotgun, weapon

fireworks *n* **1** *a fireworks display:* explosions, feux d'artifice, illuminations, pyrotechnics **2** *there'll be fireworks when he finds out:* fit, frenzy, hysterics, outburst, rage, rows, sparks, storm, temper, trouble, uproar

firm¹ *adj* **1** *firm ground:* close-grained, compact, compressed, concentrated, dense, hard, hardened, inelastic, inflexible, rigid, set, solid, solidified, stiff, substantive, unyielding **2** *a firm grip:* anchored, embedded, established, fast, fastened, fixed, immovable, motionless, riveted, secure, set, stable, stationary, steady, strong, sturdy, tight, unshakable **3** *a firm decision:* decided, definite, established, fixed, settled, unalterable, unchangeable **4** *a firm supporter of reform:* adamant, constant, decided, determined, dogged, hard, inflexible, obdurate *formal*, obstinate, resolute, resolved, staunch, steadfast, strict, stubborn, tenacious, unfaltering, unflinching, unshakable, unswerving, unwavering **5** *firm friends:* close, committed, constant, dependable, long-lasting,

long-standing, stable, staunch, steadfast, steady, sure, true, unchanging

F3 1 flabby, soft **2** unsteady **3** changeable **4** hesitant

firm² *n* association, business, company, concern, conglomerate, corporation, enterprise, establishment, house, institution, organization, partnership, syndicate

firmly *adv* **1** *closed the door firmly:* immovably, securely, stably, steadily, strongly, tightly **2** *firmly believe:* decisively, definitely, determinedly, doggedly, enduringly, immovably, inflexibly, resolutely, robustly, staunchly, steadfastly, strictly, strongly, sturdily, unalterably, unchangeably, unflinchingly, unshakably, unwaveringly

F3 1 loosely **2** hesitantly, uncertainly, unsoundly

firmness *n* **1** *firmness of the ground:* compactness, density, fixity, hardness, immovability, inelasticity, inflexibility, rigidity, solidity, stiffness, tautness, tension, tightness **2** *firmness of character:* changelessness, constancy, conviction, dependability, determination, doggedness, indomitability *formal*, obduracy *formal*, reliability, resistance, resolution, resolve, stability, staunchness, steadfastness, steadiness, strength, strength of will, strictness, sureness, willpower

F3 1 softness **2** uncertainty

first *adj* **1** *first day at school:* beginning, inaugural, initial, introductory, opening, preliminary, primary **2** *from first principles:* basic, elementary, fundamental, primary **3** *the first men:* earlier, earliest, eldest, oldest, original, primeval *formal*, primitive, primordial *formal*, prior, senior **4** *first violin:* best, cardinal, chief, foremost, greatest, head, highest, key, leading, main, paramount, predominant, pre-eminent, prime, principal, ruling, sovereign, supreme, uppermost

F3 1 final, last ♦ *adv* at first, at the outset, before anything else, beforehand, first and foremost, first of all, in preference, in the first place, initially, originally, rather, sooner, to begin with, to start with ♦ *n* beginning, commencement *formal*, inception *formal*, introduction, opening, origin(s), original, outset, première, prototype, square one *colloq*, start, the word go *colloq*, unveiling

first-born *adj* aîné(e) *formal*, elder, eldest, older, oldest, primogenital *formal*, primogenitary *formal*, primogenitive *formal*, senior

firsthand *adj* actual, direct, hands-on *colloq*, immediate, in service, on the job, personal

F3 indirect ♦ *adv* directly, immediately, personally, straight from the horse's mouth *colloq*

F3 indirectly

first name *n* baptismal name, Christian name, forename, given name

first-rate *adj* A1 *colloq*, ace *colloq*, admirable, cool *slang*, crack *colloq*, excellent, exceptional, fine, first-class, leading, matchless, mega *slang*, out of this world *colloq*, outstanding, peerless, premier, prime, radical *slang*, second-to-none, splendid, super *colloq*, superb, superior, superlative, supreme, top, top-flight, top-notch *colloq*

F3 inferior

fiscal *adj* budgetary, capital, economic, financial, monetary, money, pecuniary *formal*, treasury

fish *v* **1** *fishing for trout:* angle, go fishing, trawl **2** *fished in her bag for a pen:* delve, grope, hunt, search
▶ **fish out** come up with, dredge up, extract, find, haul out, produce, pull out, retrieve, take out

---

Types of fish include:
bloater, brisling, cod, coley, Dover sole, haddock, hake, halibut, herring, jellied eel, kipper, mackerel, pilchard, plaice, rainbow trout, salmon, sardine, sole, sprat, trout, tuna, turbot, whitebait; bass, Bombay duck, bream, brill, carp, catfish, chub, conger eel, cuttlefish, dab, dace, dogfish, dory, eel, goldfish, guppy, marlin, minnow, monkfish, mullet, octopus, perch, pike, piranha, roach, shark, skate, snapper, squid, stickleback, stingray, sturgeon, swordfish, tench, whiting; clam, cockle, crab, crayfish, crawfish *US*, kingprawn, lobster, mussel, oyster, prawn, scallop, shrimp, whelk. See also **shark**

---

fishing *n* angling, fly-fishing, trawling

fishy *adj* **1** *a fishy taste:* fish-like, piscatorial *formal*, piscatory *formal*, piscine *formal* **2** *something fishy about the whole business:* doubtful, dubious, funny, implausible, improbable, irregular, odd, queer, questionable, shady, suspect, suspicious
  F≥ **2** honest, legitimate

fission *n* breaking, cleavage, division, parting, rending, rupture, schism, scission, severance, splitting

fissure *n* breach, break, chasm, chink, cleavage *formal*, cleft, crack, cranny, crevasse, crevice, fault, foramen, fracture, gap, gash, grike *technical*, hole, interstice *formal*, opening, rent, rift, rupture, scissure *formal*, slit, split, sulcus

fist *n* hand, mitt *slang*, palm, paw *colloq*

fit[1] *adj* **1** *fit as a fiddle:* able-bodied, flourishing, hale and hearty, hardy, healthy, in good condition, in good form, in good health, in good shape, in shape, in trim, robust, sound, strong, sturdy, vigorous, well **2** *fit for the task:* able, appropriate, apt, capable, competent, convenient, correct, decorous *formal*, due, eligible, equipped, fitting, pertinent *formal*, prepared, proper, qualified, ready, right, suitable, trained, worthy
  F≥ **1** unfit **2** unsuitable, unworthy
♦ *v* **1** *do the shoes fit you?:* be a good fit, be the right shape for, be the right size for, fit like a glove *colloq* **2** *the two pieces fit together snugly:* connect, dovetail, go, interlock, join, meet, put together **3** *this version should fit your requirements:* accommodate, agree, be consistent, be consonant *formal*, be right, be suitable, belong, concur *formal*, conform, correspond, follow, go, harmonize, match, meet, suit, tally **4** *fit a washing-machine:* arrange, attach, fix, insert, install, place, position, put in, put in position/ place **5** *fit the room with all the necessary equipment:* arm, equip, make ready, make suitable, prepare, prime, tailor
▶ **fit in** accord *formal*, agree, belong, concur *formal*, conform, correspond, match, slot, square, squeeze
▶ **fit out** accoutre *formal*, arm, equip, furnish, kit out, prepare, provide, rig out, supply

fit[2] *n* **1** *had a fit:* attack, convulsion, ictus *technical*, paroxysm, seizure, spasm **2** *a fit of hysterics:* bout, burst, eruption, explosion, outbreak, outburst, spell, surge, tantrum

fitful *adj* broken, disconnected, disturbed, erratic, haphazard, intermittent, irregular, occasional, spasmodic, sporadic, uneven
  F≥ regular, steady

fitness *n* **1** *fitness for the job:* adequacy, applicability, appropriateness, aptness, competence, condition, eligibility, pertinence *formal*, preparedness, qualifications, readiness, suitability **2** *health and fitness:* condition, good health, haleness, health, healthiness, robustness, shape, strength, trim, vigour
  F≥ **1** unsuitability **2** unfitness

fitted *adj* **1** *fitted wardrobe:* built-in, fixed, permanent **2** *fitted with shelves:* appointed, armed, equipped, furnished, prepared, provided, rigged out **3** *a fitted suit:* close-fitting, figure-hugging, tailored, trim

fitting *adj* appropriate, apt, correct, decorous *formal*, deserved, desirable, fit, proper, right, suitable
  F≥ improper, unsuitable
♦ *n* **1** *light fittings:* accessory, attachment, component, connection, fitment, fixture, part, piece, unit **2** *the price includes fittings:* accessories, accoutrements *formal*, appointments *formal*, equipment, extras, fitments, fixtures, furnishings, furniture, installations

fix *v* **1** *fix the hook to the wall:* anchor, attach, bind, cement, clamp, connect, couple, embed, fasten, glue, harden, implant, install, join, link, locate, nail, pin, plant, position, rivet, root, screw, secure, set, situate, solidify, stabilize, station, stick, stiffen, tie **2** *fix a date:* agree on, arrange, arrive at, decide, define, determine, establish, finalize, name, resolve, set, settle, sort, specify **3** *fix the washing machine:* adjust, correct, mend, patch up, put right, rectify, remedy, repair, restore, see to **4** *fix your eyes/attention:* aim, concentrate, direct, focus, level, turn **5** *fix your hair:* adjust, arrange, comb, do, dress, groom, order, prepare, put in order, straighten, tidy **6** *fix a race:* fake, falsify, manipulate, rig, tamper with **7** *fix some food for you:* cook, get ready, make, prepare, put together
  F≥ **1** move, shift **3** damage **5** untidy
♦ *n* **1** *in a bit of a fix:* bind *colloq*, corner, difficulty, dilemma, hole *colloq*, jam *colloq*, mess, muddle, pickle *colloq*, plight, predicament, quandary, scrape *colloq*, the soup *colloq*, (tight) spot *colloq* **2** *an addict needing a fix:* dose, hit, injection, score *colloq*, shot, slug *colloq*
▶ **fix up 1** *fixed up a meeting:* agree on, arrange, bring about, lay on, organize, plan, settle **2** *fixed up the flat:* decorate, do up, equip, furnish, refurbish, repair, sort out

fixation *n* complex, compulsion, fetish, hang-up *colloq*, idée fixe, infatuation, mania, obsession, phobia, preoccupation, thing *colloq*

fixed *adj* arranged, cast/set in stone *colloq*, constant, decided, definite, entrenched, established, fast, firm, immobile, inflexible, permanent, planned, rigid, rooted, secure, set, settled, steady
  F≥ flexible, mobile, variable, varying

fixity *n* constancy, fixedness, immutability *formal,* permanence, persistence, stability, steadiness

fixture *n* **1** *fixtures and fittings:* equipment, furnishings, furniture, installations **2** *a sports fixture:* competition, contest, event, game, match, meeting, race, round

fizz *v* bubble, effervesce, fizzle, foam, froth, hiss, sparkle

fizzle
▶ **fizzle out** collapse, come to grief, come to nothing, die away, die down, disappear, dissipate *formal,* evaporate, fail, fall through, flop *colloq,* fold *colloq,* peter out *colloq,* stop, subside, taper off

fizzy *adj* aerated, bubbling, bubbly, carbonated, effervescent, foaming, frothy, gassy, sparkling

flabbergasted *adj* amazed, astonished, astounded, bowled over *colloq,* confounded, dazed, dumbfounded, nonplussed, overcome, overwhelmed, speechless, staggered, stunned

flabby *adj* drooping, fat, feeble, flaccid, fleshy, floppy, hanging, lax, limp, loose, overweight, plump, sagging, slack, soft, weak, yielding
🗗 firm, lean, strong, toned

flaccid *adj* clammy, drooping, flabby, floppy, lax, limp, loose, nerveless, relaxed, sagging, slack, soft, toneless, weak
🗗 firm, hard

flag¹ *v* **1** *flagged down a passing car:* hail, motion, salute, signal, signal to stop, wave, wave down **2** *flagged for special attention:* indicate, label, mark, note, tag

flag² *v* abate *formal,* decline, die, diminish, droop, dwindle, ebb, fade, fail, faint, fall (off), falter, flop, grow tired, hang down, lessen, peter out, sag, sink, slow, slump, subside, taper off, tire, wane, weaken, weary, wilt
🗗 revive

flagellation *n* beating, castigation *formal,* chastisement *formal,* flaying, flogging, lashing, scourging, thrashing, vapulation *formal,* whaling, whipping

flagging *adj* abating *formal,* declining, decreasing, diminishing, drooping, dwindling, ebbing, fading, failing, faltering, lessening, sagging, sinking, slowing, subsiding, tiring, waning, weakening, wilting
🗗 returning, reviving

flagon *n* bottle, carafe, decanter, ewer, flask, jug, pitcher, vessel

flagrant *adj* arrant, atrocious, audacious, barefaced, blatant, bold, brazen, conspicuous, disgraceful, dreadful, egregious *formal,* enormous, glaring, gross, heinous, infamous, notorious, open, ostentatious, outrageous, overt, rank, scandalous, shameless, unashamed, undisguised
🗗 covert, secret

---
flagrant or *blatant*? See panel at **blatant**
---

flail *v* batter, beat, strike, swing wildly, thrash, thresh, wave uncontrolledly, whip

flair *n* **1** *a flair for languages:* ability, acumen, aptitude, bent, facility, faculty, feel, genius, gift,

knack, mastery, natural ability, skill, talent **2** *she dresses with real flair:* discernment, elegance, panache, style, stylishness, taste
🗗 **1** inability, ineptitude

flak *n* abuse, animadversions *formal,* aspersions *formal,* bad press *colloq,* blame, brickbats *colloq,* censure, complaints, condemnation, criticism, disapprobation *formal,* disapproval, disparagement *formal,* fault-finding, hostility, invective *formal,* opposition, stick *colloq*

flake *n* bit, chip, desquamation *technical,* exfoliation, fragment, furfur, paring, particle, peeling, scale, scurf, shaving, sliver, splinter, wafer
♦ *v* blister, chip, desquamate *technical,* exfoliate, peel, scale, splinter
▶ **flake out** collapse, drop, faint, fall asleep, keel over, pass out, relax completely

flaky *adj* desquamative *technical,* desquamatory, dry, exfoliative, furfuraceous, laminar, layered, scabrous, scaly, scurfy

flamboyance *n* brilliance, colour, dash, élan, extravagance, glamour, ostentation, panache, pizzazz *colloq,* showiness, style, theatricality
🗗 diffidence, restraint

flamboyant *adj* bright, brilliant, colourful, dashing, dazzling, elaborate, exciting, extravagant, flashy, florid, gaudy, glamorous, ornate, ostentatious, rich, showy, striking, theatrical
🗗 modest, restrained

flame *v* beam, blaze, burn, burst into flames, catch fire, flare, flash, glare, gleam, glow, radiate, shine, sparkle
♦ *n* **1** *the flames licked around the window:* blaze, brightness, conflagration *formal,* fire, gleam, glow, heat, light, warmth **2** *the flames of love:* ardour, eagerness, enthusiasm, excitement, fervency, fervour, fire, intensity, keenness, passion, radiance, warmth, zeal **3** *an old flame:* boyfriend, girlfriend, lover, partner, sweetheart

flaming *adj* **1** *a flaming torch:* aflame, alight, blazing, brilliant, burning, fiery, glowing, in flames, on fire, raging, red-hot, scintillating, smouldering **2** *a flaming red:* blazing, bright, brilliant, intense, vivid **3** *a flaming temper:* angry, enraged, furious, incensed, infuriated, mad, raging, violent

flammable *adj* combustible, ignitable, inflammable
🗗 fire-resistant, flameproof, flame-resistant, incombustible, non-flammable

flank *n* **1** *the enemy's flank:* border, edge, side, wing **2** *the animal's flank:* haunch, hip, loin, quarter, thigh
♦ *v* border, bound, confine, edge, fringe, line, screen, skirt, wall

flannel *n* blarney, flattery, nonsense, rot *colloq,* rubbish, soft soap *colloq,* sweet talk *colloq,* waffle *colloq*

flap *v* agitate, beat, flutter, move from side to side, move up and down, shake, sway, swing, swish, thrash, thresh, vibrate, wag, waggle, wave
♦ *n* **1** *a flap of material:* aileron, apron, covering, fly, fold, lapel, lappet, lug, overhang, overlap, skirt, tab, tag, tail **2** *the flap of its wings:* flutter, fluttering, shake, sway, swing, swish, wag,

waggle, wave **3** *got into a flap:* agitation, commotion, dither, fluster, flutter, fuss, panic, state *colloq*, stew *colloq*, tizzy *colloq*

flare *v* **1** *the fire flared when he threw on the petrol:* blaze, burn, burst, erupt, explode, flame, flash, flicker, glare, gleam, glitter, glow, sparkle **2** *the horse's nostrils flared:* broaden, flare out, splay, spread out, widen
♦ *n* **1** *a sudden flare as the curtains caught fire:* blaze, burst, dazzle, flame, flash, flicker, glare, gleam, glimmer **2** *sent up a flare to show their position:* beacon, beam, distress signal, light, rocket, signal, warning signal **3** *the flare of her skirt:* broadening, splay, spread, widening
► **flare up** blaze, blow up *colloq*, boil over *colloq*, break out, burst out, erupt, explode *colloq*

flash *v* **1** *lights flashed:* beam, blaze, coruscate *formal*, dance, flare, flicker, fulgurate *formal*, glare, gleam, glimmer, glint, glisten, glitter, light up, scintillate, shimmer, shine, sparkle, twinkle **2** *the train flashed past:* bolt, bound, career, dart, dash, fly, race, rush, shoot, speed, streak, tear, zoom **3** *flashed her engagement ring:* brandish, display, flaunt, flourish, show off
♦ *n* **1** *a flash of lightning:* beam, blaze, bolt, burst, flare, flicker, fork, glare, gleam, glimmer, glint, glitter, ray, shaft, shimmer, spark, sparkle, streak, twinkle **2** *a flash of inspiration:* burst, display, exhibition, outbreak, outburst, show, sudden appearance
♦ *adj* expensive, fashionable, gaudy, glamorous, kitsch, ostentatious, pretentious, showy, smart, vulgar

flashy *adj* bold, cheap, flamboyant, flash, garish, gaudy, glamorous, glitzy *colloq*, jazzy, kitsch, loud, ostentatious, pretentious, showing poor taste, showy, tacky *colloq*, tasteless, tawdry, vulgar
F3 plain, tasteful

flask *n* bottle, carafe, decanter, flacket, flagon, lekythos, matrass

flat *n* apartment, bed-sit(ter), flatlet, maisonette, pad *colloq*, penthouse, rooms, suite, tenement
♦ *adj* **1** *a flat surface:* even, flat as a pancake *colloq*, homaloidal *technical*, horizontal, level, levelled, low, plane, smooth, unbroken, uniform **2** *lying flat on the floor:* outstretched, prone, prostrate, reclining, recumbent, spread-eagled, supine *formal* **3** *a flat dish:* not deep, not tall, not thick, shallow **4** *a flat tyre:* blown-out *colloq*, burst, collapsed, deflated, punctured, ruptured **5** *her life seemed flat after he left:* bland, boring, dead, dull, empty, insipid, lacklustre, lifeless, monotonous, pointless, spiritless, stale, tedious, unexciting, uninteresting, vapid, watery, weak **6** *a flat refusal:* absolute, categorical, complete, definite, direct, downright, explicit, final, out and out, outright, plain, point-blank, positive, straight, total, unconditional, unequivocal, unqualified, utter **7** *feel flat:* dejected, depressed, discouraged, down *colloq*, downcast, inactive, low, miserable, slack, slow, sluggish **8** *charge a flat rate:* arranged, definite, firm, fixed, planned, rigid, set, standard, stock
F3 **1** bumpy, vertical **2** upright **3** deep, tall, thick **5** exciting, full **6** equivocal **7** cheerful, happy, lively **8** negotiable, variable
♦ *adv* absolutely, categorically, completely, directly, entirely, exactly, outright, plainly, point-blank, precisely, straight, totally, utterly

flatly *adv* absolutely, categorically, completely, peremptorily *formal*, point-blank, positively, uncompromisingly, unconditionally, unhesitatingly

flatness *n* **1** *the flatness of the land:* evenness, horizontality, levelness, smoothness, uniformity **2** *the flatness of her life:* boredom, dullness, emptiness, insipidity, languor *formal*, monotony, staleness, tastelessness, tedium, vapidity

flatten *v* **1** *flatten the creases:* compress, crush, even out, iron, level, make even, make flat, plane, press, roll, smooth, squash **2** *the whole building was flattened:* demolish, fell, floor, knock down, knock to the ground, raze, tear down

flatter *v* **1** *he's always flattering you:* adulate, butter up *colloq*, compliment, court, creep *colloq*, curry favour with, eulogize *formal*, fawn, humour, inveigle *formal*, kowtow, make up to *colloq*, play up to *colloq*, praise, soft-soap *colloq*, suck up to *colloq*, sweet-talk *colloq*, sycophantize *formal*, toady **2** *that dress flatters you:* become, befit, embellish, enhance, grace, look good on, make someone look attractive, show off, show to advantage, suit
F3 **1** criticize

flatterer *n* adulator, back-scratcher *colloq*, bootlicker, crawler *colloq*, creeper *colloq*, encomiast *formal*, eulogizer *formal*, fawner, groveller, lackey, lickspittle, sycophant *formal*, toady
F3 critic, opponent

flattering *adj* **1** *flattering remarks:* adulatory, complimentary, effusive, fawning, fulsome, gratifying, honeyed, honey-tongued, ingratiating, kind, laudatory *formal*, obsequious *formal*, servile, smooth-spoken, smooth-tongued, sugared, sugary, sycophantic *formal*, unctuous *formal* **2** *a flattering photograph:* becoming, enhancing, favourable
F3 **1** candid, uncompromising, unflattering **2** unflattering

flattery *n* adulation, blandishments *formal*, blarney, cajolery, compliments, eulogy *formal*, fawning, flannel *colloq*, fulsomeness, ingratiation, laudation *formal*, praise, servility, soft soap *colloq*, sweet talk *colloq*, sycophancy *formal*, toadyism
F3 criticism

flatulence *n* borborygmus *formal*, eructation *formal*, farting *colloq*, flatus *formal*, gas, gassiness, ventosity *formal*, wind, windiness

flatulent *adj* gassy, ventose *formal*, windy

flaunt *v* air, boast, brandish, dangle, display, exhibit, flash, flourish, parade, show off, sport, vaunt

flaunt or *flout*? To *flaunt* something is 'to show it off or display it ostentatiously': *She was flaunting her new coat in front of her colleagues.* *Flout* means 'to treat with contempt, to refuse to obey or comply with': *He constantly flouts the law.*

flavour *n* **1** *a nutty flavour:* aroma, odour, piquancy, relish, savour, smack, tang, taste, zest, zing *colloq* **2** *a cosmopolitan flavour:* aspect, atmosphere, character, essence, feel, feeling, nature, property, quality, soul, spirit, style, tone

3 *adds a flavour of the East:* hint, suggestion, tinge, tone, touch
♦ *v* ginger up, imbue, infuse, lace, season, spice

flavouring *n* additive, essence, extract, flavour, piquancy, relish, seasoning, tang, zest, zing *colloq*

flaw *n* **1** *a flaw in the wood:* blemish, break, chip, cleft, crack, crevice, defect, fissure, fracture, imperfection, mark, rent, rift, speck, split, spot, tear **2** *a flaw in his character:* defect, error, failing, fault, foible, shortcoming, weak spot, weakness

flawed *adj* **1** *a flawed diamond:* blemished, broken, chipped, cracked, damaged, defective, faulty, imperfect, marked, marred, spoilt **2** *a flawed argument:* defective, erroneous, fallacious, faulty, unsound
1 flawless, perfect

flawless *adj* faultless, immaculate, impeccable, intact, perfect, sound, spotless, stainless, unblemished, unbroken, undamaged, unimpaired, whole
blemished, flawed, imperfect

flay *v* **1** *they had been flayed and left for dead:* flog, scourge, skin, skin alive, whip **2** *the critics flayed his latest film:* castigate *formal*, excoriate *formal*, execrate *formal*, lambast *formal*, pull to pieces *colloq*, revile, tear a strip off *colloq*, upbraid

fleck *v* dapple, dot, dust, freckle, mark, mottle, spatter, speckle, spot, sprinkle, stipple, streak
♦ *n* dot, freckle, mark, point, speck, speckle, spot, streak

fledgling *n* apprentice, beginner, greenhorn *colloq*, learner, neophyte, newcomer, novice, novitiate, recruit, rookie *colloq*, tenderfoot, tiro, trainee

flee *v* abscond, bolt, clear off *colloq*, cut and run, decamp, depart, disappear, escape, fly, get away, leave, make off, make yourself scarce, retreat, run away, rush, scarper *colloq*, scoot *colloq*, scram *colloq*, take flight, take off, take to your heels *colloq*, vamoose *colloq*, vanish, withdraw
stay

fleece *n* coat, down, wool
♦ *v* bilk, bleed *colloq*, cheat, con *colloq*, defraud, diddle *colloq*, fiddle *colloq*, gull *colloq*, have someone on *colloq*, mulct, overcharge, plunder, pull a fast one *colloq*, rip off *colloq*, rob, squeeze *colloq*, sting *colloq*, string along *colloq*, swindle, take for a ride *colloq*, take to the cleaners *colloq*

fleecy *adj* downy, eriophorous *formal*, floccose *formal*, flocculate *formal*, fluffy, hairy, lanuginose *formal*, nappy, pilose *formal*, shaggy, soft, velvety, woolly
bald, smooth

fleet *n* armada, flotilla, naval force, navy, squadron, task force
♦ *adj* fast, flying, light-footed, mercurial, meteoric, nimble, quick, rapid, speedy, swift, winged
slow

fleeting *adj* brief, ephemeral, evanescent *formal*, flying, fugacious *formal*, here today and gone tomorrow *colloq*, momentary, passing, quick, rushed, short, short-lived, sudden, temporary, transient, transitory
lasting, permanent

flesh *n* **1** *an animal's flesh:* body, brawn, fat, meat, muscle, pulp, skin, tissue **2** *he was there in the flesh:* matter, physicality, solidity, stuff, substance, weight **3** *pleasures of the flesh:* carnal nature, carnality, corporeality, human nature, physical nature, physicality, sensuality, sinful nature
► **flesh out** add/give details, elaborate, make complete, make more substantial

fleshly *adj* animal, bestial, bodily, brutish, carnal, corporal, corporeal, earthly, earthy, erotic, human, lustful, material, physical, sensual, sexual, wordly
spiritual

fleshy *adj* ample, beefy, brawny, chubby, chunky, corpulent *formal*, fat, flabby *colloq*, hefty, meaty, obese, overweight, paunchy, plump, podgy, portly, rotund *formal*, stout, tubby, well-padded
slim, thin

flex *n* cable, cord, lead, wire
♦ *v* angle, bend, bow, contract, crook, curve, double up, ply, stretch, tighten
extend, straighten

flexibility *n* **1** *the flexibility of the plastic:* bendability, elasticity, flexion, give, pliability, pliancy, resilience, spring, springiness, suppleness, tensility *formal* **2** *she has shown great flexibility in doing whatever is asked of her:* adaptability, adjustability, agreeability, amenability, complaisance *formal*
2 inflexibility

flexible *adj* **1** *young children are very flexible:* agile, bendable, bendy *colloq*, double-jointed, elastic, limber, lithe, malleable, mobile, mouldable, plastic, pliable, pliant, springy, stretchy, supple, yielding **2** *a flexible approach to the problem:* accommodating, adaptable, adjustable, amenable, changeable, manageable, open, open-ended, variable, yielding
1 inflexible, rigid **2** fixed, inflexible, rigid

flick *v* click, dab, flip, hit, jerk, lash, rap, snap, strike, swish, tap, touch, whip
♦ *n* click, dab, flip, jerk, rap, snap, swish, tap, touch
► **flick through** browse through, flip through, glance at, glance over, leaf through, scan, skim, skip, thumb through

flicker *v* bat, blink, flare, flash, flutter, glimmer, glint, glitter, gutter, quiver, shimmer, sparkle, twinkle, vibrate, waver, wink
♦ *n* **1** *the flicker of a light:* flash, gleam, glimmer, glint, glitter, spark, sparkle, twinkle **2** *a flicker of hope:* atom, drop, indication, iota, trace

flight[1] *n* **1** *the power of flight:* aeronautics, air transport, air travel, aviation, flying **2** *a long-haul flight:* journey, shuttle, trip, voyage **3** *a flight of steps:* set, staircase, stairs, stairway, steps

flight[2] *n* absconding, breakaway, departure, escape, exit, exodus, fleeing, getaway, retreat, running away/off, rush, withdrawal

flighty *adj* bird-brained *colloq*, capricious *formal*, changeable, fickle, frivolous, hare-brained *colloq*, impetuous, impulsive, inconstant, irresponsible, light-headed, mercurial, rattle-brained, rattle-headed, scatterbrained, silly, skittish, thoughtless, unbalanced, unstable, unsteady, volatile, wild
responsible, sensible, steady

flimsy adj 1 flimsy structures: fragile, insubstantial, jerry-built, makeshift, ramshackle, rickety, shaky, slight 2 flimsy clothing: delicate, ethereal, filmy, fine, light, lightweight, sheer, thin 3 a flimsy excuse: feeble, implausible, inadequate, meagre, poor, shallow, superficial, thin, trifling, trivial, unconvincing, weak
F∃ 1 strong, sturdy 2 strong, thick 3 convincing, plausible

flinch v avoid, balk, blench, cower, cringe, crouch, dodge colloq, draw back, duck colloq, flee, pull back, quail, quake, recoil, retreat, shake, shirk, shiver, shrink, shudder, shy away, start, tremble, wince, withdraw

fling v cast, catapult, chuck colloq, heave, hurl, jerk, launch, let fly, lob, pitch, propel, send, send flying, sling, throw, toss
♦ n 1 a fling of the dice: cast, heave, hurl, lob, pitch, shot, throw, toss 2 a final fling before he starts work: attempt, binge, crack colloq, gamble, go, indulgence, spree, trial, try, turn, venture, whirl

flip v cast, click, flap, flick, jerk, pitch, snap, spin, throw, toss, turn, twirl, twist
♦ n click, flap, flick, jerk, snap, spin, toss, turn, twirl, twist
▶ **flip through** browse through, flick through, glance at, glance over, leaf through, scan, skim, skip, thumb through

flippancy n cheek colloq, cheekiness colloq, disrespect, disrespectfulness, facetiousness, frivolity, glibness, impertinence, irreverence, levity, light-heartedness, persiflage formal, pertness, sauciness colloq, shallowness, superficiality, thoughtlessness
F∃ earnestness, seriousness

flippant adj cheeky colloq, disrespectful, facetious, frivolous, glib, impertinent, impudent, insouciant formal, irresponsible, irreverent, light-hearted, offhand, pert, rude, saucy colloq, shallow, superficial, thoughtless
F∃ respectful, serious

flirt v chat up, dally, eye up, lead on, make a pass at, make eyes at, make up to, ogle, philander
♦ n chippy slang, coquet(te), floozie slang, gillet, heart-breaker, hussy, philanderer, tease, trifler, vamp, wanton
▶ **flirt with** consider, dabble in, entertain, play with, toy with, trifle with, try

flirtation n affair, amour formal, chatting up, coquetry, dalliance, dallying, intrigue, philandering, romance, sport, teasing, toying, trifling

flirtatious adj amorous, come-hither colloq, come-on colloq, coquettish, flirty, loose, promiscuous, provocative, sportive, teasing, wanton

flit v bob, dance, dart, dash, flash, flitter, flutter, fly, pass, rush, skim, slip, speed, whisk, wing

float v 1 floating down the river: be buoyant, bob, drift, glide, sail, slide, stay afloat, swim 2 floating in the air: glide, hang, hover, suspend, waft, wander 3 float a business: be in at the beginning of, establish, get going, get off the ground, get the show on the road, initiate, launch, promote, set up 4 float an idea with you: present, propose, put forward, recommend, submit, suggest
F∃ 1 sink

floating adj 1 a floating restaurant: afloat, bobbing, buoyant, drifting, hovering, sailing, swimming, unsinkable, wafting 2 floating voters: fluctuating, free, migratory, movable, transitory, unattached, uncommitted, unsettled, variable, wandering
F∃ 1 sinking, submerged 2 fixed, settled

flock v assemble, bunch, cluster, collect, come together, congregate, converge, crowd, gather, group, herd, huddle, mass, mill, swarm, throng, troop
♦ n 1 a flock of sheep: bunch, cluster, collection, crowd, drove, group, herd, mass, pack 2 the priest's flock: assembly, congregation, crowd, gathering, group, multitude, throng

flog v 1 flogged for telling lies: beat, belt, birch, cane, chastise, drub, flagellate formal, flay, horsewhip, lash, punish, scourge, strap, thrash, wallop colloq, whack colloq, whip 2 flogging stolen phones: deal in, handle, hawk, offer for sale, peddle, put up for sale, sell, trade

flogging n beating, belting, birching, caning, flagellation formal, flaying, hiding, horsewhipping, lashing, scourging, strapping, thrashing, walloping colloq, whacking colloq, whipping

flood v 1 the whole town was flooded: brim over, deluge, drench, drown, engulf, fill, immerse, inundate, overflow, overwhelm, saturate, smother, soak, submerge, surge, swamp, swell 2 water flooded out of the pipe: flow, gush, pour, rush, stream, surge
♦ n 1 the flood caused devastation: deluge, downpour, flash flood, flow, inundation, outpouring, overflow, rush, spate, stream, torrent 2 a flood of phone calls: abundance, excess, glut, plethora formal, profusion formal, superfluity formal, torrent
F∃ 1 drought, trickle 2 dearth, lack, trickle

floor n 1 a laminate floor: base, basis, flooring, ground 2 on the third floor: deck, landing, level, stage, storey, tier
♦ v 1 completely floored by his remark: baffle, beat, bewilder, confound, defeat, discomfit formal, disconcert, dumbfound, frustrate, nonplus, overwhelm, perplex, puzzle, stump colloq, throw 2 floored in the second round: fell, knock down, level, prostrate, strike down

flop v 1 flopped down in a chair: collapse, dangle, droop, drop, fall, hang, sag, slump, topple, tumble 2 their first business venture flopped: be unsuccessful, bomb US colloq, collapse, crash colloq, fail, fall flat, fold colloq, founder, go broke colloq, go bust colloq, go into the red colloq, go to the wall colloq, misfire, pack up colloq, sink
♦ n also-ran colloq, debacle, disaster, failure, fiasco, has-been colloq, no-hoper colloq, non-starter colloq, shambles colloq, wash-out colloq

floppy adj baggy, dangling, droopy, flabby, hanging, limp, loose, sagging, soft
F∃ firm

flora n botany, herbage, plant life, plantage, plants, vegetable kingdom, vegetation

florid adj 1 a florid style of writing: baroque, bombastic, elaborate, embellished, extravagant, flamboyant, flowery, fussy, grandiloquent formal, melismatic technical, ornate, overelaborate, pompous, rococo, verbose

2 *a florid complexion:* blushing, flushed, purple, red, reddish, red-faced, rubicund *formal*, ruddy
☒ **1** plain, simple **2** pale

flotsam *n* debris, detritus *formal*, floating wreckage, jetsam, junk, oddments, odds and ends, rubbish, wreckage

flounce[1] *v* bob, bounce, fling, jerk, spring, stamp, storm, throw

flounce[2] *n* falbala, frill, fringe, ruffle, trimming, valance

flounder *v* **1** *her resignation left the company floundering:* be confused, be in difficulties, be out of your depth, blunder, dither, falter, fumble, go under, not know which way to turn, reel, struggle **2** *floundering in the water:* be in difficulties, be out of your depth, flail about, go under, grope, thrash about, wallow

flourish *v* **1** *the business is flourishing:* be strong, bear fruit, bloom, blossom, boom, burgeon *formal*, develop, do well, flower, get on, grow, increase, progress, prosper, succeed, thrive, wax **2** *flourishing a sword:* brandish, display, exhibit, flaunt, parade, shake, show off, swing, swish, twirl, vaunt, wag, wave, wield
☒ **1** decline, fail, languish
♦ *n* **1** *he opened the box with a flourish:* display, élan, fanfare, gesture, panache, parade, pizzazz *colloq*, show, sweep, wave **2** *decorative flourishes:* curlicue, decoration, ornament, serif, swirl, twist

flourishing *adj* blooming, blossoming, booming, prosperous, successful, thriving

flout *v* break, defy, disdain, disobey, disregard, jeer at, laugh at, mock, reject, ridicule, scoff at, scorn, show contempt for, sneer at, spurn, treat with contempt, violate *formal*
☒ obey, regard, respect

flow *v* **1** *the water flows into the tank:* babble, bubble, cascade, circulate, drift, drip, flood, glide, gurgle, gush, jet, leak, move, ooze, overflow, pour, proceed, ripple, roll, run, rush, seep, slide, slip, spew, spill, spout, spurt, squirt, stream, surge, sweep, swirl, teem, trickle, well, whirl **2** *it all flows from poor planning in the initial stages:* arise, derive, emanate *formal*, emerge, issue, originate, proceed, result, spring, stem
♦ *n* abundance, cascade, course, current, deluge, drift, effusion *formal*, flood, flux, gush, outpouring, plenty, plethora *formal*, spate, spurt, stream, tide

flower *n* **1** *a bunch of flowers:* bloom, blossom, bud, efflorescence *technical*, florescence, floret, floweret, inflorescence **2** *the flower of the city:* best, choice, cream, crème de la crème, elite, finest, pick, select
♦ *v* bloom, blossom, bud, burgeon *formal*, come out, develop, flourish, grow, mature, open, prosper, sprout, succeed, thrive

---

Parts of a flower include:
anther, calyx, capitulum, carpel, corolla, corymb, dichasium, filament, gynoecium, monochasium, nectary, ovary, ovule, panicle, pedicel, petal, pistil, raceme, receptacle, sepal, spadix, spike, stalk, stamen, stigma, style, thalamus, torus, umbel

---

Flowers include:
African violet, alyssum, anemone, aster, aubrietia, azalea, begonia, bluebell, busy lizzie

---

(impatiens), calendula, candytuft, carnation, chrysanthemum, cornflower, cowslip, crocus, cyclamen, daffodil, dahlia, daisy, delphinium, forget-me-not, foxglove (digitalis), freesia, fuchsia, gardenia, geranium, gladioli, hollyhock, hyacinth, iris (flag), lily, lily-of-the-valley, lobelia, lupin, marigold, narcissus, nasturtium, nemesia, nicotiana, night-scented stock, orchid, pansy, petunia, pink (dianthus), phlox, poinsettia, polyanthus, poppy, primrose, primula, rose, salvia, snapdragon (antirrhinum), snowdrop, stock, sunflower, sweet pea, sweet william, tulip, verbena, viola, violet, wallflower, zinnia. See also **bulb, plant, shrub, wild flower**

---

flowery *adj* baroque, bombastic, elaborate, euphuistic *technical*, fancy, florid, grandiloquent *formal*, high-flown, ornate, pompous, rhetorical, verbose
☒ plain, simple

flowing *adj* **1** *flowing rivers:* bubbling, cascading, gushing, oozing, overflowing, pouring, rushing, seeping, streaming, surging, sweeping, welling **2** *flowing traffic:* moving, rushing, streaming, surging **3** *a single flowing movement:* continuous, easy, effortless, fluent, smooth, unbroken, uninterrupted **4** *flowing hair:* falling, hanging, hanging freely, hanging loose, rolling

fluctuate *v* alter, alternate, change, chop and change *colloq*, ebb and flow, go up and down, hesitate, oscillate *formal*, rise and fall, seesaw, shift, sway, swing, undulate, vacillate, vary, waver
☒ be steady

fluctuation *n* alternation, ambivalence, capriciousness *formal*, change, fickleness, inconstancy, instability, irresolution, oscillation *formal*, shift, swing, unsteadiness, vacillation *formal*, variability, variation, wavering

fluency *n* articulateness, assurance, command, control, ease, eloquence, facility, facundity *formal*, glibness, readiness, slickness, smoothness, volubility *formal*
☒ incoherence

fluent *adj* articulate, easy, effortless, elegant, eloquent, flowing, fluid, glib, graceful, mellifluous *formal*, natural, ready, silver-tongued, slick, smooth, voluble *formal*
☒ broken, inarticulate, tongue-tied

fluff *n* down, dust, floss, fuzz, lint, nap, pile
♦ *v* balls up *slang*, blot your copybook *colloq*, blow *colloq*, boob *colloq*, botch, bungle, cock up *slang*, do badly, foul up *colloq*, fumble, make a bad job of, make a mess of, mess up *colloq*, mismanage, muck up, muddle, muff, put your foot in it *colloq*, screw up *slang*, spoil
☒ bring off

fluffy *adj* downy, feathery, fleecy, furry, fuzzy, hairy, shaggy, silky, soft, velvety, woolly

fluid *n* gas, juice, liquid, liquor, solution, vapour
♦ *adj* **1** *fluid substances:* aqueous, flowing, liquefied, liquid, melted, molten, running, runny, watery **2** *a fluid situation:* adaptable, adjustable, changeable, flexible, fluctuating, inconstant, mobile, open, protean *formal*, shifting, unsettled, unstable, unsteady, variable **3** *fluid movements:* easy, effortless, elegant, flowing, graceful, natural, smooth
☒ **1** solid **2** fixed, inflexible

fluke *n* accident, blessing, break, chance, coincidence, fortuity *formal*, freak *colloq*, lucky break, quirk, serendipity *formal*, stroke of luck, windfall

fluky *adj* accidental, chance, coincidental, fortuitous *formal*, fortunate, freakish *colloq*, lucky, serendipitous *formal*, uncertain

flummoxed *adj* at a loss, at sea, baffled, bewildered, confounded, confused, foxed, mystified, nonplussed, perplexed, puzzled, stumped, stymied

flunkey *n* assistant, bootlicker, cringer, drudge, footman, hanger-on, lackey, manservant, menial, minion, slave, toady, underling, valet, yes-man

flurry *n* **1** *snow flurries*: blast, bout, burst, gust, outbreak, shower, spell, spurt, squall **2** *a flurry of activity*: agitation, bustle, commotion, disturbance, excitement, flap *colloq*, fluster, fuss, hubbub, hurry, perturbation *formal*, stir, to-do *colloq*, tumult, whirl
♦ *v* agitate, bewilder, bother, confuse, disconcert, discountenance *formal*, disturb, fluster, flutter, fuss, hassle *colloq*, hustle, perturb *formal*, rattle *colloq*, ruffle, unsettle, upset

flush¹ *v* **1** *she flushed with shame*: blush, burn, colour, crimson, flame, glow, go/turn red, redden, suffuse *formal* **2** *flush the dirt out of the pipe*: cleanse, clear, eject, empty, evacuate, expel, hose, rinse, swab, wash
♦ *n* bloom, blush, colour, freshness, glow, redness, rosiness, ruddiness, vigour
♦ *adj* **1** *for once I was feeling flush*: generous, lavish, moneyed, overflowing, prosperous, rich, wealthy, well-heeled, well-off, well-to-do **2** *the shelf was flush with the wall*: even, flat, level, plane, smooth, square, true

flush² *v* discover, disturb, drive out, eject, expel, force out, rouse, run to earth, uncover

flushed *adj* **1** *the sky was flushed with the sunset*: ablaze, aflame, aglow, crimson, glowing, red, rosy, rubicund *formal*, ruddy, scarlet **2** *he looked flushed with shame*: blushing, burning, crimson, embarrassed, hot, red, scarlet **3** *flushed with success*: animated, aroused, elated, enthused, excited, exhilarated, exultant, inspired, intoxicated, sanguine, thrilled
◩ **1** pale **2** pale

fluster *v* agitate, bother, confound, confuse, discompose, disconcert, distract, disturb, embarrass, faze *colloq*, make nervous, perturb *formal*, put off, rattle *colloq*, ruffle, unnerve, unsettle, upset
◩ calm
♦ *n* agitation, confusion, disturbance, dither *colloq*, embarrassment, flap *colloq*, flurry, panic, perturbation *formal*, state *colloq*, tizz *colloq*, tizzy *colloq*, turmoil, upset
◩ calm

fluted *adj* channelled, corrugated, furrowed, grooved, ribbed, ridged

flutter *v* agitate, bat, beat, dance, flap, flicker, flitter, fluctuate, hover, palpitate, pulsate, quiver, ripple, ruffle, shake, shiver, toss, tremble, twitch, vibrate, wave, waver
♦ *n* **1** *the flutter of wings*: beat, flapping, flicker, palpitation, quiver, ripple, ruffle, shiver, shudder, tremble, tremor, twitch, vibration,

wave **2** *had a flutter on the horses*: bet, gamble, risk, speculation, wager

flux *n* alteration, change, development, flow, fluctuation, fluidity, instability, modification, motion, movement, mutation, transition, unrest
◩ rest, stability

fly¹ *v* **1** *the ball flew into the air*: ascend, flit, float, flutter, glide, hover, mount, rise, soar, take off, wing **2** *fly an aeroplane*: control, guide, manoeuvre, operate, pilot, steer **3** *fly a flag*: display, exhibit, present, reveal, show, wave **4** *she flew into the room and hugged him*: bolt, career, dart, dash, go/pass quickly, hasten *formal*, hurry, jet, race, rush, shoot, speed, sprint, tear, zoom
► **fly at** attack, bite someone's head off *colloq*, charge, fall upon, go for, hit, jump down someone's throat *colloq*, lash out at, lay into, let fly, let someone have it, strike

fly² *adj* alert, artful, astute, canny, careful, cunning, nobody's fool *colloq*, on the ball *colloq*, prudent *formal*, sagacious *formal*, sharp, shrewd, smart *colloq*

fly-by-night *adj* cowboy, discreditable, disreputable, dubious, ephemeral, here today gone tomorrow *colloq*, irresponsible, questionable, shady, short-lived, undependable, unreliable, untrustworthy
◩ reliable

flying *adj* **1** *flying insects*: airborne, flapping, floating, fluttering, gliding, hovering, mobile, soaring, wind-borne, winged **2** *a flying visit*: brief, fast, fleeting, hasty, hurried, rapid, rushed, speedy

foam *n* bubbles, effervescence, fizz, froth, head, lather, spume, suds
♦ *v* boil, bubble, effervesce, fizz, froth, lather, seethe, spume

foamy *adj* bubbly, foaming, frothy, lathery, spumescent *formal*, spumy, sudsy

fob
► **fob off** deceive, dump, foist, get rid of, impose, inflict, palm off *colloq*, pass off, put off, unload

focus *n* axis, centre, core, crux, focal point, heart, hinge, hub, kernel, linchpin, nucleus, pivot, target
♦ *v* aim, bring into focus, centre, concentrate, converge, direct, fix, home in, pinpoint, spotlight, turn, zero in *colloq*, zoom in

fodder *n* feed, food, foodstuff, forage, lucerne, nourishment, pabulum, provender, proviant, rations, silage

foe *n* adversary, antagonist, combatant, enemy, ill-wisher, opponent, rival
◩ friend

foetus *n* embryo, unborn child

fog *n* **1** *patches of fog over high ground*: cloud, gloom, haze, haziness, mist, mistiness, murkiness, pea-souper, smog **2** *a fog of misunderstanding*: bafflement, bewilderment, blur, confusion, daze, disorientation, haze, obscurity, perplexity, puzzlement, stupor, trance, vagueness
♦ *v* **1** *the windows were fogged with condensation*: blur, cloud, darken, dim, mist, obscure, steam up **2** *his mind was fogged by uncertainty*: baffle,

bewilder, blur, cloud, confuse, dull, muddle, obfuscate *formal*, perplex

foggy *adj* 1 *a foggy morning*: clouded, cloudy, dark, dim, gloomy, grey, hazy, misty, murky, overcast, smoggy 2 *a foggy recollection of his dream*: dim, hazy, indistinct, obscure, shadowy, unclear, vague
Fa 1 clear 2 distinct

foible *n* defect, eccentricity, failing, fault, habit, idiosyncrasy, imperfection, oddity, oddness, peculiarity, quirk, shortcoming, strangeness, weak point, weakness

foil[1] *v* baulk, block, check, circumvent *formal*, counter, defeat, frustrate, hamper, hinder, nullify, obstruct, outwit, prevent, scupper *colloq*, scuttle *colloq*, stop, thwart
Fa abet

foil[2] *n* antithesis *formal*, background, balance, complement, contrast, relief, setting

foist *v* fob off, force, get rid of, impose, introduce, palm off *colloq*, pass off, thrust, unload, wish on

fold[1] *v* 1 *fold the paper in half*: bend, crease, crimp, crinkle, crumple, double, gather, overlap, pleat, ply, tuck, turn down, turn under 2 *folded his son in his arms*: clasp, embrace, enclose, enfold, entwine, envelop, hug, intertwine, squeeze, wrap (up) 3 *the business folded*: close, collapse, crash, fail, flop *colloq*, go bust *colloq*, go out of business, go to the wall *colloq*, pack up *colloq*, shut down
♦ *n* bend, corrugation, crease, crinkle, furrow, gather, knife-edge, layer, line, overlap, pleat, ply, pucker, tuck, turn, wrinkle

fold[2] *n* 1 *the sheep in the fold*: compound, court, enclosure, kraal, paddock, pen, pound, ring, stockade, yard 2 *newcomers are welcomed to the fold*: assembly, church, congregation, fellowship, flock, gathering, parishioners

folder *n* binder, envelope, file, folio, holder, pocket, portfolio, wallet

foliage *n* foliation, foliature, frondescence *technical*, greenery, leafage, leaves, vegetation, verdure *formal*, vernation

folk *n* 1 *country folk*: clan, ethnic group, nation, people, population, public, race, society, tribe 2 *home to see my folks*: family, kin, kindred, parents, relations, relatives
♦ *adj* ancestral, ethnic, indigenous, national, native, popular, traditional, tribal

folklore *n* beliefs, customs, fables, folktales, legends, lore, mythology, myths, stories, superstitions, tales, tradition

follow *v* 1 *night follows day*: come after, come next, replace, step into the shoes of, succeed, supersede, supplant, take the place of 2 *a dog following a scent*: be at someone's heels, catch, chase, dog, give chase, go after, hound, hunt, pursue, run after, shadow, stalk, tail, track, trail 3 *you lead and I'll follow*: accompany, attend, escort, go (along) with, go behind, tag along, trail, tread behind, walk behind 4 *it follows logically from the proposal*: arise, develop, emanate, ensue, flow, issue, proceed, result, spring 5 *you've got to follow the rules*: accept, adhere to, carry out, comply with *formal*, conform to, heed, mind, note, obey, observe, practise, yield to

6 *just couldn't follow his argument*: appreciate, comprehend, fathom, grasp, latch onto *colloq*, take in, twig *colloq*, understand 7 *do you follow football?*: be a fan of, be a supporter of, be devoted to, be interested in, keep up to date with, keep up with, support
Fa 1 precede 3 abandon, desert 5 disobey
▶ **follow through** bring to completion, complete, conclude, continue, finish, fulfil, implement, pursue, see through
▶ **follow up** check out, consolidate, continue, investigate, look into, pursue, reinforce, research

follower *n* adherent, admirer, apostle, attendant, backer, believer, buff *colloq*, companion, convert, devotee, disciple, emulator, enthusiast, fan, freak *colloq*, hanger-on, helper, imitator, pupil, retainer, sidekick *colloq*, supporter

following *adj* consequent, ensuing, later, next, resulting, subsequent, succeeding, successive
Fa previous
♦ *n* adherents, admirers, audience, backers, backing, body of support, circle, clientèle, coterie, entourage, fan base, fans, followers, patronage, patrons, public, retinue, suite, support, supporters

folly *n* 1 *an act of utter folly*: absurdity, craziness, fatuousness *formal*, foolishness, idiocy, illogicality, imbecility, imprudence *formal*, inanity, indiscretion, insanity, irresponsibility, ludicrousness, lunacy, madness, nonsense, rashness, recklessness, ridiculousness, senselessness, silliness, stupidity 2 *a Gothic folly*: belvedere, gazebo, monument, tower
Fa 1 prudence, sanity, wisdom

fond *adj* 1 *fond of someone/something*: addicted to, attached to, enamoured of *formal*, having a soft spot for, hooked on *colloq*, keen on, liking, partial to 2 *a fond embrace*: adoring, affectionate, amorous, caring, devoted, doting, indulgent, loving, tender, warm 3 *fond expectations*: absurd, credulous, deluded, foolish, impractical, naïve, over-optimistic, vain

fondle *v* caress, cuddle, hug, pat, pet, stroke

fondness *n* affection, attachment, devotion, enthusiasm, fancy, inclination, kindness, leaning, liking, love, partiality, penchant *formal*, predilection *formal*, preference, soft spot, susceptibility, taste, tenderness, weakness
Fa aversion, hate

food *n* 1 *Italian food*: board, chow *slang*, comestibles, cooking, cuisine, delicacy, diet, dish, eatables *colloq*, eats *colloq*, fare, feed, fodder, foodstuffs, grub *slang*, meals, menu, nosh *slang*, nourishment, nutriment, nutrition, provisions, rations, refreshments, scoff *slang*, speciality, stores, subsistence, sustenance, table, tuck *colloq*, viands *formal*, victuals *formal* 2 *food for thought*: mental stimulation, something to be seriously considered, something to think about

---

Kinds of food include:
soup, broth, minestrone, bouillabaisse, borsch, cockaleekie, consommé, gazpacho, goulash, vichyssoise; chips, French fries, ratatouille, sauerkraut, bubble-and-squeak, nut cutlet, cauliflower cheese, chilladas, hummus, macaroni cheese; pasta, cannelloni, fettuccine, ravioli, spaghetti bolognese, tortellini, lasagne;

fish and chips, fishcake, fish-finger, fisherman's pie, kedgeree, gefilte fish, kipper, pickled herring, scampi, calamari, prawn cocktail, caviar; meat, casserole, cassoulet, hotpot, shepherd's pie, cottage pie, chilli con carne, biriyani, chop suey, moussaka, paella, samosa, pizza, ragout, risotto, tandoori, vindaloo, Wiener schnitzel, smorgasbord, stroganoff, Scotch woodcock, welsh rarebit, faggot, haggis, sausage, frankfurter, hot dog, fritter, hamburger, bacon, egg, omelette, quiche, tofu, Quorn®, Yorkshire pudding, toad-in-the-hole; ice cream, charlotte russe, egg custard, fruit salad, fruit cocktail, gateau, millefeuilles, pavlova, profiterole, Sachertorte, soufflé, summer pudding, Bakewell tart, trifle, yogurt, sundae, syllabub, queen of puddings, Christmas pudding, tapioca, rice pudding, roly-poly pudding, spotted dick, zabaglione; doughnut, Chelsea bun, Eccles cake, éclair, flapjack, fruitcake, Danish pastry, Genoa cake, Battenburg cake, Madeira cake, lardy cake, hot-cross-bun, ginger nut, gingerbread, ginger snap, macaroon, digestive, digestive biscuit, oatcake, Garibaldi biscuit; bread, French bread, French toast, pumpernickel, cottage loaf, croissant; baguette, brioche, bagel, gravy, fondue, salad cream, mayonnaise, French dressing; sauces: tartare, Worcestershire, bechamel, white, barbecue, tomato ketchup, hollandaise, Tabasco®, apple, mint, cranberry, horseradish, pesto. See also **cheese, fish, fruit, meat, nut, pasta, pastry, sugar, sweet, vegetable**

fool *n* ass *colloq*, birdbrain *colloq*, blockhead, buffoon, butt, chump *colloq*, clot *colloq*, clown, comic, cretin, dimwit, dope *colloq*, dork *slang*, dumbo *slang*, dunce, dupe, fat-head, geek *slang*, git *slang*, halfwit, idiot, ignoramus, imbecile, jerk *slang*, jester, laughing-stock, moron, mug *colloq*, nincompoop *colloq*, ninny *colloq*, nit *colloq*, nitwit *colloq*, pillock *slang*, plonker *slang*, prat *slang*, prick *slang*, simpleton, stooge, sucker *colloq*, twerp *colloq*, twit *colloq*, wally *slang*
♦ *v* **1** *conmen fooled her into handing over her money*: bamboozle *colloq*, beguile, bluff, cheat, con *colloq*, deceive, delude, diddle *colloq*, dupe, gull, have on *colloq*, hoax, hoodwink, make a fool of, mislead, play tricks, put one over on, string along *colloq*, swindle, take in, trick **2** *I was only fooling*: feign, jest, joke, kid *colloq*, make believe *colloq*, pretend, sham, tease **3** *fooling about*: horse around *colloq*, lark about, mess about *colloq*, mess around *colloq*, monkey about, monkey around, play about

foolery *n* antics, buffoonery, capers, carry-on, childishness, clowning, drollery, farce, folly, fooling, high jinks, horseplay, larks, mischief, monkey tricks, nonsense, practical jokes, pranks, shenanigans, silliness, tomfoolery, waggery, zanyism

foolhardy *adj* bold, daredevil, daring, ill-advised, imprudent *formal*, impulsive, incautious, irresponsible, rash, reckless, temerarious *formal*
🖃 cautious, prudent *formal*

foolish *adj* absurd, barmy *colloq*, batty *colloq*, crack-brained *colloq*, crazy, daft *colloq*, dotty *colloq*, dumb *colloq*, fatuous *formal*, gormless *colloq*, half-baked, half-witted, hare-brained, idiotic, ignorant, ill-advised, ill-considered,

inane, inept, injudicious *formal*, insane, ludicrous, mad, moronic, needing to have your head examined *colloq*, nonsensical, not in your right mind *colloq*, nutty *colloq*, out of your mind *colloq*, pointless, potty *colloq*, ridiculous, risible *formal*, senseless, short-sighted, silly, simple, simple-minded, stupid, unintelligent, unreasonable, unwise, with a screw missing *colloq*
🖃 judicious *formal*, prudent *formal*, wise

foolishly *adv* absurdly, fatuously *formal*, idiotically, ill-advisedly, imprudently *formal*, incautiously, indiscreetly, ineptly, injudiciously *formal*, mistakenly, ridiculously, senselessly, short-sightedly, stupidly, unwisely
🖃 wisely

foolishness *n* absurdity, balls *slang*, baloney *colloq*, bilge *colloq*, bullshit *slang*, bunk *colloq*, bunkum *colloq*, claptrap *colloq*, cobblers *colloq*, crap *slang*, craziness, daftness *colloq*, folly, foolery, hogwash *colloq*, imprudence *formal*, inanity, incaution *formal*, indiscretion, ineptitude, irresponsibility, lunacy, madness, nonsense, piffle *colloq*, poppycock *colloq*, rot *colloq*, rubbish, senselessness, silliness, stupidity, unreason *formal*, unwisdom *formal*, weakness
🖃 prudence *formal*, wisdom

foolproof *adj* certain, dependable, fail-safe, guaranteed, idiot-proof, infallible, safe, sure, sure-fire *colloq*, trustworthy, unfailing
🖃 unreliable

foot *n* **1** *an animal's feet*: heel, hoof, leg, pad, paw, pes *technical*, sole, toe, trotter **2** *at the foot of the hill*: border, bottom, end, extremity, far end, foundation, limit
🖃 **2** head, summit, top

footing *n* **1** *male and female staff should be on an equal footing*: base, basis, conditions, foundation, grade, ground, position, rank, relations, relationship, standing, state, status, terms **2** *lost his footing on the rocks*: balance, foothold, grip, position, support

footnotes *n* annotation, commentary, gloss, marginal note, marginalia, note, scholia *formal*

footprint *n* footmark, step, trace, track, trail, tread, vestige *formal*

footstep *n* footfall, plod, step, tramp, tread, trudge

footwear

Types of footwear include:
shoe, court-shoe, brogue, casual, lace-up *colloq*, slip-on *colloq*, slingback, sandal, espadrille, stiletto heel, platform heel, moccasin, Doc Martens®, slipper, mule, pantofle, flip-flop *colloq*, boot, walking-boot, climbing-boot, riding-boot, overshoe, wader, bootee, wellington boot, welly *colloq*, galosh, gumboot, football boot, rugby boot, tennis shoe, plimsoll, pump, sneaker, trainer, ballet shoe, clog, sabot, snow-shoe, beetle-crushers *slang*, brothel-creepers *slang*

forage *n* feed, fodder, food, foodstuffs, pasturage, provender
♦ *v* assault, cast about, hunt, invade, loot, plunder, raid, ransack, ravage, rummage, scavenge, scour, scratch, search, seek

foray *n* assault, attack, incursion, inroad, invasion, offensive, raid, ravage, reconnaissance, sally, sortie, swoop

forbear *v* abstain *formal*, avoid, cease *formal*, decline, desist *formal*, eschew *formal*, hesitate, hold, hold back, keep from, omit, pause, refrain, restrain yourself, stay, stop, withhold

forbearance *n* abstinence *formal*, avoidance, clemency, endurance, leniency, long-suffering, mildness, moderation, patience, refraining, resignation, restraint, self-control, sufferance, temperance, tolerance, toleration
 ⊞ intolerance

forbearing *adj* clement, easy, forgiving, indulgent, lenient, long-suffering, merciful, mild, moderate, patient, restrained, self-controlled, tolerant
 ⊞ intolerant, merciless

forbid *v* ban, blacklist, block, debar, deny, disallow, exclude, hinder, inhibit, interdict *formal*, not allow, not let, outlaw, preclude *formal*, prevent, prohibit, proscribe *formal*, refuse, rule out, veto
 ⊞ allow, approve, let, permit

forbidden *adj* banned, debarred, excluded, illicit, out of bounds, outlawed, prohibited, proscribed *formal*, taboo, vetoed

forbidding *adj* awesome, daunting, foreboding, formidable, frightening, grim, harsh, menacing, off-putting, ominous, severe, sinister, stern, threatening, unfriendly, uninviting
 ⊞ approachable, congenial, friendly

force *v* **1** *forced her to give up her job*: bulldoze, bully, coerce, compel, constrain, drive, impel, impose, inflict, lean on *colloq*, make, necessitate *formal*, oblige, press, pressgang, pressure, pressurize, propel, push, put pressure on, put the screws on *colloq*, railroad, twist someone's arm *colloq*, urge **2** *forced open the door*: blast, crack, force open, prise, wrench, wrest, wring
 ♦ *n* **1** *an act of force*: aggression, arm-twisting *colloq*, coercion, compulsion, constraint, duress, enforcement, impulse, influence, necessity, pressure, strongarm tactics *colloq*, the screws *colloq*, the third degree *colloq*, violence **2** *the force of his passion*: determination, drive, dynamism, dynamo, effectiveness, effort, emphasis, energy, exertion, impetus, influence, intensity, might, momentum, muscle, passion, persuasiveness, power, significance, stamina, strength, stress, vehemence, vigour, vitality **3** *the main force of the argument*: essence, gist, meaning, sense, significance, substance, thrust **4** *forces are massing on the border*: army, battalion, body, corps, detachment, division, patrol, platoon, regiment, squad, squadron, troop, unit
 ⊞ **2** weakness

forced *adj* **1** *a forced laugh*: affected *formal*, artificial, contrived, false, feigned, insincere, laboured, overdone, stiff, stilted, strained, unnatural, wooden **2** *forced repatriation*: compelled, compulsory, enforced, involuntary, mandatory *formal*, obligatory
 ⊞ **1** natural, sincere, spontaneous **2** voluntary

forceful *adj* **1** *a forceful attack*: assertive, dynamic, energetic, forcible, mighty, potent, powerful, strong, urgent, vigorous **2** *a forceful argument*: cogent *formal*, compelling, convincing, effective,

emphatic, impressive, persuasive, potent, powerful, strong, telling, valid, vehement, weighty
 ⊞ **1** feeble, weak **2** feeble, weak

forcible *adj* **1** *forcible entry into the flat*: aggressive, by/using force, coercive, forced, violent **2** *a forcible policy on immigration*: cogent, compelling, compulsory, effective, energetic, forceful, impressive, mighty, potent, powerful, strong, telling, vehement, weighty
 ⊞ **2** feeble, weak

forcibly *adv* **1** *forcibly removed from the demonstration*: against your will, by force, compulsorily, obligatorily, under compulsion, under duress, using force, vigorously, violently **2** *forcibly denied the charges*: emphatically, vehemently, vigorously, violently

ford *n* causeway, crossing, drift

forebear *n* ancestor, antecedent, father, forefather, forerunner, predecessor, primogenitor *formal*, progenitor *formal*
 ⊞ descendant

foreboding *n* **1** *filled with foreboding*: anxiety, apprehension, apprehensiveness, dread, fear, intuition, misgiving, presentiment *formal*, prognostication *formal*, sixth sense, suspicion, worry **2** *forebodings of disaster*: omen, prediction, premonition, sign, token, warning

forecast *v* anticipate, augur *formal*, calculate, conjecture *formal*, divine *formal*, estimate, expect, foresee, foretell, forewarn, portend *formal*, predict, prognosticate *formal*, prophesy, tip off
 ♦ *n* augury *formal*, conjecture *formal*, expectation, forewarning, guess, guesstimate *colloq*, outlook, prediction, prognosis *formal*, prognostication *formal*, projection, prophecy, speculation, tip

forefather *n* ancestor, antecedent, father, forebear, forerunner, predecessor, primogenitor *formal*, progenitor *formal*
 ⊞ descendant

forefront *n* avant-garde, firing line, fore, front, front line, lead, leading/foremost position, spearhead, van, vanguard
 ⊞ rear

foregoing *adj* above, aforementioned *formal*, antecedent *formal*, earlier, former, precedent *formal*, preceding, previous, prior
 ⊞ following

foregone *adj* anticipated, cut-and-dried, fixed, foreseen, inevitable, open-and-shut, predetermined *formal*, predictable, preordained *formal*
 ⊞ unpredictable

foreground *n* centre, fore, forefront, front, leading/foremost position, limelight, prominence
 ⊞ background

forehead *n* brow, front, metope *technical*, temples

foreign *adj* **1** *foreign affairs*: alien, borrowed, distant, ethnic, exotic, external, faraway, immigrant, imported, international, migrant, outside, overseas, remote **2** *the idea was completely foreign to her*: extraneous, inapposite *formal*, incongruous *formal*, odd, outlandish,

outside, peculiar, strange, uncharacteristic, unconnected, unfamiliar, unknown
Fa 1 indigenous, native

foreigner *n* alien, immigrant, incomer, newcomer, outsider, stranger, visitor
Fa native

foreknowledge *n* clairvoyance, foresight, forewarning, precognition *technical*, premonition, prescience, prevision *formal*, prognostication *formal*, second sight

foreman *n* boss *colloq*, charge hand, gaffer *colloq*, ganger, honcho *US colloq*, leader, manager, overman, overseer, steward, superintendent, supervisor

foremost *adj* advanced, cardinal, central, chief, first, highest, leading, main, most important, paramount, pre-eminent, premier, primary, prime, principal, supreme, top, uppermost

foreordained *adj* appointed, destined, fated, foredoomed, prearranged, predestined *formal*, predetermined *formal*, preordained

forerunner *n* 1 *a forerunner of the camera:* harbinger, herald, precursor, sign, token 2 *his Irish forerunners:* ancestor, antecedent, forefather, predecessor
Fa 2 successor

foresee *v* anticipate, divine *formal*, envisage, expect, forebode, forecast, foreknow, foretell, predict, prognosticate *formal*, prophesy

foreshadow *v* augur *formal*, bode *formal*, indicate, portend *formal*, predict, prefigure *formal*, presage *formal*, promise, prophesy, signal, signify, suggest

foresight *n* anticipation, care, caution, circumspection *formal*, discernment, discrimination, far-sightedness, forethought, forward planning, judiciousness *formal*, perspicacity *formal*, planning, precaution, preparedness, provision, prudence *formal*, vision
Fa improvidence

forest *n* greenwood, monte, plantation, trees, urman, wood, woodland, woods

forestall *v* anticipate, avert, balk, frustrate, get ahead of, head off, hinder, impede, intercept, obstruct, obviate *formal*, parry, preclude *formal*, pre-empt, prevent, stave off, stop, thwart, ward off

forestry *n* afforestation *technical*, arboriculture, dendrology, forest management, forestation, silviculture, woodcraft, woodmanship

foretaste *n* appetizer, example, foretoken, forewarning, indication, premonition, preview, sample, specimen, trailer, warning, whiff

foretell *v* augur *formal*, divine *formal*, forecast, foresee, foreshadow, forewarn, indicate, predict, presage *formal*, prognosticate *formal*, prophesy, signify

forethought *n* anticipation, caution, circumspection *formal*, discernment, far-sightedness, foresight, forward planning, judiciousness *formal*, perspicacity *formal*, planning, precaution, preparation, provision, prudence *formal*
Fa carelessness, improvidence

forever *adv* 1 *I'll love you forever:* always, eternally, ever, evermore, for all time, for good *colloq*, permanently, till kingdom come *colloq*, till the cows come home *colloq*, till the end of time, until hell freezes over *colloq* 2 *forever asking stupid questions:* all the time *colloq*, always, constantly, continually, endlessly, incessantly, interminably *formal*, perpetually, persistently

forewarn *v* advise, alert, apprise *formal*, caution, dissuade *formal*, give advance warning to, previse *formal*, tip off, warn

foreword *n* frontmatter, introduction, preface, preliminary matter, prelims, prolegomenon *formal*, prologue
Fa appendix, epilogue, postscript

forfeit *v* abandon, forgo, give up, hand over, lose, relinquish *formal*, renounce *formal*, sacrifice, surrender
♦ *n* amercement, confiscation, damages, fine, loss, penalty, relinquishment, sequestration *technical*, surrender

forfeiture *n* attainder, confiscation, déchéance *formal*, escheat *technical*, foregoing, giving up, loss, relinquishment, sacrifice, sequestration, surrender

forge[1] *v* 1 *forge an alliance:* beat into shape, beat out, cast, construct, create, devise, fashion, form, found, frame, hammer out, invent, make, mould, put together, shape, work 2 *forge a document:* copy, counterfeit, fake, falsify, feign, imitate, simulate

forge[2]
▶ **forge ahead** advance, go/move forward, make headway, make progress, move steadily, progress, push forward

forger *n* coiner, contriver, counterfeiter, fabricator, faker, falsifier, framer

forgery *n* 1 *the document was a forgery:* copy, counterfeit, dud *colloq*, fake, fraud, imitation, phoney *colloq*, replica, reproduction, sham 2 *the business of forgery:* counterfeiting, faking, falsification, fraud, imitation, reproduction
Fa 1 original

forget *v* 1 *I completely forgot:* fail to remember, go in one ear and out the other *colloq*, have a memory like a sieve *colloq*, have no recollection of, lose sight of, not place, omit, overlook, slip your mind 2 *let's just forget all about it:* dismiss, disregard, ignore, lose sight of, neglect, put aside, put behind you, put out of your mind, think no more of, unlearn
Fa 1 recall, recollect, remember 2 attend to

forgetful *adj* absent-minded, abstracted, careless, distracted, dreamy, heedless, inattentive, lax, neglectful, negligent, not all there *colloq*, oblivious, pensive *formal*, preoccupied, remiss, scatterbrained, unheeding, with a memory like a sieve *colloq*
Fa attentive, heedful, mindful

forgetfulness *n* absent-mindedness, abstraction, amnesia, carelessness, dreaminess, heedlessness, inattention, lapse, laxness, oblivion, obliviousness, obliviscence *formal*, wool-gathering
Fa attentiveness, heedfulness

forgivable *adj* excusable, innocent, minor, pardonable, petty, slight, trifling, venial
Fa unforgivable

forgive *v* absolve, acquit, bury the hatchet *colloq*, clear, condone, exculpate *formal*, excuse, exonerate *formal*, forgive and forget, let bygones be bygones, let it go, let off, overlook, pardon, remit, shake hands *colloq*, shake on it *colloq*, spare, think no more of *colloq*
🔁 censure, punish

forgiveness *n* absolution, acquittal, amnesty, clemency, exoneration *formal*, leniency, mercy, pardon, remission
🔁 blame, censure, punishment

forgiving *adj* clement, compassionate, forbearing, humane, indulgent, kind, lenient, magnanimous *formal*, merciful, mild, soft-hearted, tolerant
🔁 censorious, harsh, merciless

forgo *v* abandon, abjure *formal*, abstain from *formal*, do without, eschew *formal*, forfeit, give up, go without, pass up, refrain from, relinquish *formal*, renounce *formal*, resign, sacrifice, surrender, waive, yield

forgotten *adj* blotted out, buried, bygone, disregarded, gone, ignored, irrecoverable, irretrievable, left behind, lost, neglected, obliterated, omitted, out of mind, overlooked, past, past recall, past recollection, unrecalled, unremembered, unretrieved
🔁 remembered

fork *v* bifurcate *formal*, branch (off), divaricate *formal*, diverge, divide, go separate ways, part, separate, split
♦ *n* bifurcation *formal*, branching, divarication *formal*, divergence, division, furcation *formal*, intersection, junction, separation, split
▶ **fork out** cough up *colloq*, give, pay (up), shell out *colloq*, stump up *colloq*

forked *adj* bifurcate *formal*, branched, branching, divaricated *formal*, divided, forficate *formal*, furcal *formal*, furcate *formal*, furcular *formal*, pronged, separated, split, tined *formal*, Y-shaped

forlorn *adj* **1** *she looked utterly forlorn:* bereft, despairing, desperate, disconsolate *formal*, friendless, helpless, homeless, hopeless, lonely, lost, miserable, pathetic, pitiable, sad, unhappy, wretched **2** *a forlorn landscape:* abandoned, cheerless, deserted, desolate, destitute, forgotten, forsaken, lonely, lost, neglected, uncared-for
🔁 **1** cheerful **2** cared-for

form *n* **1** *in the form of a circle:* appearance, configuration *formal*, design, disposition *formal*, formation, guise, manifestation *formal*, pattern, shape **2** *a rigid form of government:* construction, cut, formation, frame, framework, model, mould, order, structure, system **3** *I could just pick out the form of a man:* figure, frame, outline, shape, silhouette **4** *a form of punishment:* character, description, genre, genus, kind, manner, nature, order, sort, species, style, type, variety **5** *she is in form 3W:* class, grade, stream, year **6** *on top form:* condition, fettle, fitness, health, shape, spirits, trim **7** *it was considered bad form to be late:* behaviour, convention, custom, etiquette, manners, polite behaviour, protocol, ritual, the done thing *colloq* **8** *fill in a form:* application (form), document, paper, questionnaire, sheet
♦ *v* **1** *was asked to form a government:* acquire, arrange, assemble, build, construct, create, develop, devise, establish, fashion, forge, found,

line up, make, manufacture, model, mould, order, organize, produce, put together, set up, shape **2** *a team formed of six members:* be a part of, compose, comprise, constitute, make (up), serve as **3** *a band of colour formed in the sky:* appear, become visible, come into existence, crystallize, develop, grow, materialize, show up, take shape

formal *adj* **1** *formal approval of the plan:* approved, ceremonial, conventional, correct, customary, established, fixed, methodical, official, ordered, organized, orthodox, prescribed, proper, regular, ritual, set, solemn, standard, stately, traditional **2** *rather a formal manner:* aloof, ceremonious, exact, inflexible, precise, prim, punctilious, remote, reserved, rigid, starchy, stiff, stilted, strait-laced, strict, unbending **3** *a formal garden:* controlled, conventional, ordered, regular, symmetrical
🔁 **2** casual, informal

formality *n* **1** *it's just a formality but you have to sign in:* ceremony, convention, custom, form, matter of form, procedure, protocol, ritual, rule **2** *the formality of the occasion:* bureaucracy, ceremoniousness, ceremony, correctness, decorum *formal*, etiquette, politeness, propriety *formal*, punctilio *formal*, red tape, ritual
🔁 **2** informality

format *n* appearance, arrangement, configuration *formal*, construction, design, dimensions, form, layout, look, make-up, order, pattern, plan, presentation, shape, structure, style, type

formation *n* **1** *in a V-shaped formation:* arrangement, composition, configuration *formal*, constitution, construction, design, disposition *formal*, figure, format, grouping, layout, make-up, order, organization, pattern, phalanx *formal*, structure **2** *the formation of a company:* appearance, building, construction, creation, development, establishment, founding, generation, inauguration, institution, making, manufacture, production, shaping, starting

formative *adj* controlling, determinative *formal*, determining, developmental, dominant, growing, guiding, impressionable, influential, malleable, mouldable, moulding, pliant, sensitive, shaping, susceptible, teachable
🔁 destructive

former *adj* above, antecedent, bygone, departed, earlier, erstwhile *formal*, ex-, first, first-mentioned, foregoing, historical, late, long ago, long-gone, of yore *formal*, old, old-time, one-time, past, preceding, previous, prior, quondam *formal*, sometime
🔁 current, following, future, present

formerly *adv* at an earlier time, at one time, before, earlier, erst *formal*, erstwhile *formal*, heretofore *formal*, historically, hitherto *formal*, in the past, once, previously
🔁 currently, later, now

formidable *adj* alarming, awesome, challenging, colossal, daunting, dreadful, fearful, frightening, frightful, great, horrific, horrifying, huge, impressive, intimidating, mammoth, menacing, mind-blowing *colloq*, overwhelming, powerful, prodigious *formal*, redoubtable, scary *colloq*, spooky *colloq*, staggering, terrific, terrifying, threatening, tremendous

formless *adj* amorphous, chaotic, confused, disorganized, inchoate *formal*, incoherent, indefinite, indeterminate, indigest *formal*, nebulous, shapeless, unformed, unshaped, vague
Fa definite, orderly

formula *n* blueprint, code, convention, form, method, precept, prescription, principle, procedure, proposal, recipe, rubric, rule, technique, way

formulate *v* **1** *formulated a plan:* conceive, create, define, design, detail, develop, devise, draw up, evolve, form, found, give form to, invent, itemize, map out, originate, plan, prepare, put down, set down, specify, think up, work out **2** *struggled to formulate a response:* articulate, compose, express, frame, give form to, state

fornication *n* coitus *formal*, copulation *formal*, going to bed/sleeping with someone, love-making, making love, sex, sexual intercourse, sexual relations

forsake *v* abandon, cast off, desert, discard, disown, ditch *colloq*, forgo *formal*, give up, have done with *colloq*, jettison, jilt *colloq*, leave, leave in the lurch *colloq*, quit *colloq*, reject, relinquish *formal*, renounce *formal*, repudiate, set aside, surrender, throw over, turn your back on *colloq*

forsaken *adj* abandoned, cast off, derelict, deserted, desolate, destitute, discarded, disowned, dreary, forlorn, friendless, God-forsaken, ignored, isolated, jilted *colloq*, left in the lurch *colloq*, lonely, marooned, neglected, outcast, rejected, remote, shunned, solitary

forswear *v* abandon, abjure *formal*, cut out *colloq*, deny, disavow *formal*, disclaim, disown, do without, drop, forgo *formal*, forsake *formal*, give up, jack in *colloq*, lie, pack in *colloq*, perjure yourself, recant *formal*, reject, renege, renounce *formal*, repudiate, retract *formal*
Fa revert to

fort *n* battlements, castle, citadel, donjon, fortification, fortress, garrison, keep, redoubt, station, stronghold, tower, turret, watchtower

forte *n* aptitude, bent, gift, métier, skill, speciality, strength, strong point, talent
Fa inadequacy, weak point

forth *adv* away, forwards, into existence, into view, off, onwards, out, outside

forthcoming *adj* **1** *their forthcoming wedding:* approaching, coming, expected, future, imminent, impending, projected, prospective **2** *no explanation was forthcoming about his absence:* accessible, at your disposal, available, obtainable, on tap *colloq*, ready, up for grabs *colloq*, yours for the asking/taking *colloq* **3** *she wasn't very forthcoming about her new job:* chatty, communicative, conversational, direct, expansive, frank, informative, loquacious *formal*, open, sociable, talkative, voluble *formal*
Fa **3** reserved, reticent

forthright *adj* blunt, bold, candid, direct, frank, honest, open, outspoken, plain, plain-spoken, straightforward
Fa devious, secretive

forthwith *adv* at once, directly, immediately, instantly, pronto *colloq*, quickly, right away, straightaway, without delay

fortification *n* **1** *the town's fortifications:* barricade, bastion, battlements, bulwark, castle, citadel, defence, earthwork, embattlement, entrenchment, fort, fortress, keep, munition, outwork, palisade, parapet, rampart, redoubt, stockade, stronghold **2** *the fortification of the defences:* buttressing, protection, reinforcement, strengthening

fortify *v* **1** *efforts to fortify the town:* brace, buttress, cover, defend, embattle, garrison, guard, protect, reinforce, secure, shore up, strengthen **2** *fortified herself with a glass of brandy:* boost, brace, buoy up, cheer, encourage, energize, hearten, invigorate, reassure, revive, strengthen, support, sustain
Fa **1** weaken

fortitude *n* backbone, bravery, courage, determination, endurance, firmness, forbearance *formal*, grit *colloq*, hardihood, mettle, nerve, patience, perseverance, pluck, resolution, spine *colloq*, stoicism, strength of mind, tenacity, valour, willpower
Fa cowardice, fear

fortress *n* battlements, castle, citadel, fastness, fortification, garrison, keep, stronghold, tower

fortuitous *adj* accidental, arbitrary, casual, chance, fluky *colloq*, fortunate, haphazard, incidental, lucky, providential, random, unexpected, unforeseen, unintentional, unplanned
Fa anticipated, intentional, planned

fortunate *adj* **1** *it was fortunate we'd packed our rain things:* advantageous, auspicious *formal*, convenient, encouraging, favourable, felicitous *formal*, happy, lucky, opportune, promising, propitious *formal*, providential, timely, well-timed **2** *people less fortunate than ourselves:* blessed, favoured, privileged, prosperous, successful, well-off
Fa **1** unfortunate, unhappy, unlucky **2** unfortunate

fortunately *adv* conveniently, encouragingly, happily, luckily, providentially *formal*
Fa unfortunately

fortune *n* **1** *he squandered the family fortune:* affluence, assets, estate, income, means, opulence, possessions, property, prosperity, riches, substance, success, treasure, wealth **2** *his watch cost a fortune:* big bucks *slang*, bomb *colloq*, bundle *colloq*, lot of money, megabucks *slang*, mint *colloq*, packet *colloq*, pile *colloq* **3** *his fortune in life:* accident, chance, coincidence, cup, destiny, doom, fate, future, history, life, lot, luck, portion, providence, serendipity *formal* **4** *the fortunes of the company:* circumstances, condition, experience, position, situation, state of affairs

fortune-teller *n* augur, clairvoyant, diviner, oracle, prophet, prophetess, psychic, seer, sibyl, soothsayer, telepath, visionary

forum *n* **1** *a forum for debate:* arena, environment, meeting-place, rostrum, setting, stage **2** *hold a forum on globalization:* assembly, conference, debate, discussion, meeting, symposium

forward *adj* **1** *a forward movement:* advance, advancing, enterprising, fore, foremost,

forward-looking, front, frontal *formal*, future, go-ahead *colloq*, head, leading, onward, progressing, progressive, prospective **2** *rather forward of you to ask for his phone number:* aggressive, assertive, audacious, barefaced, bold, brash, brazen, cheeky *colloq*, cocky *colloq*, confident, familiar, fresh *colloq*, impertinent, impudent, over-assertive, over-confident, overfamiliar, presuming, presumptuous, pushy *colloq*, thrusting **3** *forward planning:* advance, advanced, early, precocious, premature, well-advanced, well-developed
Fa 1 backward, retrograde **2** modest, shy **3** late, retarded
♦ *adv* ahead, forth, forwards, into the open, into view, on, onward, onwards, out
♦ *v* **1** *steps to forward research:* accelerate, advance, aid, assist, back, encourage, expedite *formal*, facilitate, favour, foster, further, hasten, help, hurry, promote, speed (up), step up, support **2** *any post will be forwarded:* deliver, dispatch, mail, pass on, post, send (on), ship, transport

forward-looking *adj* avant-garde, dynamic, enlightened, enterprising, far-sighted, go-ahead *colloq*, goey *colloq*, go-getting *colloq*, innovative, liberal, modern, progressive, reforming
Fa conservative, retrograde

forwardness *n* aggressiveness, audacity, boldness, brashness, brazenness, cheek *colloq*, cheekiness *colloq*, confidence, impertinence, impudence, over-confidence, pertness, presumption, presumptuousness, pushiness *colloq*
Fa reserve

forwards *adv* ahead, forth, forward, on, onwards, out

fossil *n* ammonite, coprolite, graptolite *technical*, petrified remains/impression, relic, reliquiae, remains, remnant, trilobite

fossilized *adj* **1** *a fossilized tree:* hardened, ossified, petrified, stony **2** *fossilized filing systems:* anachronistic, antediluvian, antiquated, archaic, dead, extinct, obsolete, old-fashioned, out of date, outmoded, passé, prehistoric
Fa 2 up-to-date

foster *v* **1** *attempts to foster peace:* advance, aid, assist, back, boost, cultivate, encourage, further, help, nurse, promote, support, sustain, uphold **2** *fostered a child:* bring up, care for, feed, look after, nourish, nurture, raise, rear, take care of
Fa 1 discourage, neglect

foul *adj* **1** *a foul smell:* abominable, contaminated, decayed, defiled, dirty, disgusting, fetid, filthy, foul-smelling, impure, infected, loathsome, nauseating, odious, offensive, polluted, putrefactive *formal*, putrescent *formal*, putrid, rank, repulsive, revolting, rotten, rotting, sickening, smelly, soiled, squalid, stinking, tainted, unclean **2** *foul language:* abusive, blasphemous, blue *colloq*, coarse, dirty, filthy, gross, indecent, indelicate, lewd, low, obscene, off-colour, offensive, profane, ribald, smutty, vulgar **3** *foul deeds:* abhorrent, base, contemptible, despicable, detestable, disagreeable, disgraceful, disgusting, execrable *formal*, heinous *formal*, horrible, iniquitous *formal*, loathsome, low, mean, nasty, nefarious *formal*, offensive, repulsive, revolting, shameful, vicious,

vile, wicked **4** *foul weather:* bad, blustery, dirty, disagreeable, nasty, rainy, rough, squally, stormy, unpleasant, wet, wild
Fa 1 clean **2** clean **4** fine
♦ *v* **1** *dogs had fouled the pavement:* blacken, contaminate, defile, dirty, muddy, pollute, soil, stain, sully, taint **2** *fouled the fishing net on a rock:* catch, ensnare, entangle, snarl, tangle, twist **3** *the drain was fouled with leaves:* block, choke, clog, foul up, jam, obstruct
Fa 1 clean **2** disentangle **3** clear

foul-mouthed *adj* abusive, blasphemous, coarse, foul-spoken *formal*, obscene, offensive, profane

found *v* **1** *founded the company in 1963:* bring into being, constitute, create, develop, endow, establish, inaugurate, initiate, institute, organize, originate, set up, start **2** *a case founded on unproven evidence:* base, build, construct, erect, fix, ground, locate, plant, position, raise, rest, root, set, settle

foundation *n* **1** *the building's foundations:* base, basis, bedrock, bottom, foot, footing, ground, substance, substratum, substructure, underpinning, understructure **2** *the argument's foundation:* alpha and omega, base, basis, bedrock, core, essence, essential(s), first principles, fundamental point, fundamental(s), groundwork, heart, hypostasis *formal*, key, keynote, main ingredient, premise, principle, quintessence *formal*, rationale, reason(s), starting-point, support, thrust **3** *the foundation of a new university:* constitution, creation, endowment, establishment, founding, groundwork, inauguration, initiation, institution, organization, setting-up

founder[1] *n* architect, author, benefactor, builder, constructor, creator, designer, developer, discoverer, establisher, father, initiator, institutor, inventor, maker, mother, organizer, originator, prime mover

founder[2] *v* **1** *the ship foundered:* capsize, go down, go to the bottom, sink, submerge **2** *the plan foundered:* abort, break down, collapse, come to grief, come to nothing, fail, fall through, go wrong, miscarry, misfire
Fa 1 float **2** succeed

foundling *n* enfant trouvé, orphan, outcast, stray, urchin, waif

fountain *n* **1** *a water fountain:* fount, jet, reservoir, source, spout, spray, spring, spurt, waterworks, well, wellspring **2** *the fountain of all knowledge:* beginning, birth, cause, commencement *formal*, fount, fountainhead, inception *formal*, mainspring, origin, rise, source, well, wellhead

fowl *n* bantam, bird, chicken, cock, duck, goose, hen, pheasant, poultry, turkey, wildfowl

foxy *adj* artful, astute, canny, crafty, cunning, devious, fly, guileful, knowing, sharp, shrewd, sly, tricky, wily
Fa naïve, open

foyer *n* antechamber, anteroom, entrance hall, hall, lobby, reception, vestibule

fracas *n* affray, aggro *colloq*, barney, brawl, disturbance, Donnybrook *formal*, fight, free-for-all, melee, quarrel, riot, rout, row, ruckus, ruction, ruffle, rumpus, scuffle, shindy, trouble, uproar

fraction *n* amount, bit, part, proportion, ratio, subdivision

fractious *adj* awkward, bad-tempered, captious, choleric *formal*, crabby *colloq*, cross, crotchety *colloq*, fretful, grouchy *colloq*, grumpy *colloq*, irritable, peevish, petulant, quarrelsome, querulous *formal*, recalcitrant *formal*, refractory *formal*, testy, touchy, unruly
🔁 complaisant, placid

fracture *n* aperture, breach, break, breakage, cleft, crack, fissure, gap, opening, rent, rift, rupture, schism, slit, split, splitting
♦ *v* break, chip, crack, rupture, splinter, split
🔁 join

fragile *adj* **1** *a fragile package:* breakable, brittle, dainty, delicate, fine, flimsy, frail, frangible *formal*, insubstantial, slight, unstable **2** *feel fragile after an illness:* delicate, feeble, infirm, weak
🔁 **1** durable, robust, sturdy, tough **2** strong

fragility *n* breakableness, brittleness, delicacy, feebleness, frailty, frangibility *formal*, infirmity, weakness
🔁 durability, robustness, strength

fragment *n* bit, chink, chip, crumb, fraction, morsel, part, particle, piece, portion, remainder, remains, remnant, scrap, shard, shiver, shred, sliver, snip, snippet, splinter
♦ *v* break, break up, come apart, come to pieces, crumble, disintegrate, disunite, divide, shatter, shiver, smash to pieces/smithereens, splinter, split (up)
🔁 hold together, join

fragmentary *adj* bitty, broken, disconnected, discontinuous, disjointed, incoherent, incomplete, partial, piecemeal, scattered, scrappy, separate, sketchy, uneven
🔁 complete, whole

fragrance *n* aroma, attar, balm, bouquet, odour, otto, perfume, redolence *formal*, scent, smell, sweet smell

fragrant *adj* aromatic, balmy, odoriferous *formal*, odorous, perfumed, redolent *formal*, scented, sweet, sweet-smelling
🔁 unscented

frail *adj* breakable, brittle, delicate, easily broken, feeble, flimsy, fragile, frangible *formal*, infirm, insubstantial, puny, slight, susceptible, unsound, unwell, vulnerable, weak
🔁 robust, strong, tough

frailty *n* **1** *the frailty of the old man:* brittleness, delicacy, fallibility, fragility, infirmity, susceptibility, vulnerability, weakness **2** *a frailty of the plan:* blemish, defect, deficiency, failing, fault, flaw, foible, imperfection, shortcoming, weak point
🔁 **1** robustness, strength, toughness **2** strength

frame *n* **1** *a building with a metal frame:* body, bodywork, build, carcase, casing, chassis, construction, fabric, figure, form, foundation, framework, physique, shape, shell, size, skeleton, structure, substructure, support **2** *a picture frame:* border, edge, mount, mounting, setting, surround
♦ *v* **1** *framed the wording of the document carefully:* assemble, build, compose, conceive, concoct, construct, contrive, cook up *colloq*, create, devise,

draft, draw up, erect, establish, fabricate, fashion, forge, form, formulate, make, manufacture, map out, model, mould, plan, plot, put together, set up, shape, sketch **2** *a window framed in honeysuckle:* box in, case, encase, enclose, mount, surround **3** *I've been framed:* cook up a charge *colloq*, fit up *colloq*, incriminate, pin on *colloq*, plant, set up *colloq*, trap

frame-up *n* fabrication, fit-up *colloq*, fix *colloq*, put-up job *colloq*, trap, trumped-up charge *colloq*

framework *n* **1** *the framework of the building:* bare bones, casing, fabric, foundation, frame, groundwork, lattice, rack, shell, skeleton, structure, substructure, trestle, trestlework **2** *within the framework of the document:* constraints, frame, outline, parameters, plan, scheme

franchise *n* authorization, charter, concession, consent *formal*, enfranchisement *formal*, exemption, freedom, immunity, liberty, licence, permission, prerogative, privilege, right, suffrage *formal*, warrant

frank *adj* bluff, blunt, candid, direct, downright, explicit, forthright, free, genuine, honest, open, outspoken, plain, plain-spoken, sincere, straight, straight from the shoulder *colloq*, straightforward, truthful, up-front *colloq*
🔁 evasive, insincere
♦ *v* cancel, mark, postmark, stamp

frankly *adv* **1** *answered frankly:* bluntly, candidly, directly, explicitly, freely, honestly, openly, plainly, straight, truthfully **2** *frankly, I don't care:* honestly, in truth, to be blunt, to be frank, to be honest, truthfully
🔁 **1** evasively, insincerely

frankness *n* bluntness, candour, directness, forthrightness, honesty, ingenuousness *formal*, openness, outspokenness, plain speaking, sincerity, truthfulness
🔁 reserve

frantic *adj* agitated, at your wits' end *colloq*, berserk, beside yourself, desperate, distracted, distraught, distressed, fraught, frenetic, frenzied, furious, hectic, mad, out of control, overwrought, panic-stricken, raging, raving, wild
🔁 calm, composed

fraternity *n* **1** *a spirit of fraternity:* brotherhood, camaraderie, companionship, comradeship, fellowship, kinship **2** *the legal fraternity:* association, circle, clan, club, community, company, guild, league, order, set, society, union

fraternize *v* affiliate, associate, consort *formal*, gang up with *colloq*, go around, hang about *colloq*, hobnob *colloq*, keep company, mingle, mix, pal up with *colloq*, rub shoulders *colloq*, socialize, sympathize, unite
🔁 ignore, shun

fraud *n* **1** *credit-card fraud:* cheating, chicanery *formal*, con *colloq*, counterfeit, deceit, deception, diddle *colloq*, double-dealing, duplicity *formal*, embezzlement, fake, fix *colloq*, forgery, fraudulence, guile, hoax, racket, riddle *colloq*, rip-off *colloq*, scam *colloq*, sham, sharp practice, swindling, swiz *colloq*, trick, trickery **2** *the man's a complete fraud:* bluffer, charlatan, cheat, con man *colloq*, double-dealer, embezzler, fake, hoaxer, impostor, mountebank, phoney *colloq*, pretender, quack, sham, swindler, trickster

fraudulent *adj* bogus, cheating, counterfeit, criminal, crooked *colloq*, deceitful, deceptive, dishonest, double-dealing, duplicitous *formal*, exploitative, false, phoney *colloq*, shady *colloq*, sham, shameless, swindling, unscrupulous
🖃 genuine, honest

fraught *adj* 1 *a journey fraught with dangers*: abounding, accompanied, attended, bristling, charged, filled, full, laden *formal*, replete *formal* 2 *feeling a bit fraught on the flight*: agitated, anxious, distraught, distressed, overwrought, stressed out *colloq*, tense, under stress, uptight *colloq*, worried
🖃 1 calm, untroublesome

fray *v* 1 *the rope is fraying*: become ragged, become threadbare, unravel, wear, wear thin 2 *tempers were fraying*: irritate, make nervous, make tense, overtax, push too far, put on edge, strain, stress, tax, vex
♦ *n* battle, brawl, challenge, clash, combat, conflict, disturbance, dust-up *colloq*, fight, free-for-all, quarrel, riot, row, rumpus, scuffle, set-to

frayed *adj* ragged, tattered, thin, threadbare, unravelled, worn, worn thin

freak *n* 1 *a circus freak*: deformity, freak of nature, irregularity, malformation *formal*, monster, monstrosity, mutant, mutation 2 *by some freak of fate, I married his father*: aberration, abnormality, anomaly, caprice *formal*, curiosity, oddity, quirk, turn, twist, vagary, whim 3 *she was regarded as a bit of a freak*: oddball *colloq*, oddity, strange person, weirdo *colloq* 4 *a computer freak*: addict, aficionado, buff *colloq*, devotee, enthusiast, fan, fanatic, fiend *colloq*, nut *colloq*
♦ *adj* aberrant *formal*, abnormal, atypical, bizarre, capricious *formal*, chance, erratic, exceptional, fluky *colloq*, fortuitous *formal*, odd, queer, surprise, unexpected, unpredictable, unusual
🖃 common, normal

freakish *adj* aberrant *formal*, abnormal, arbitrary, capricious *formal*, changeable, erratic, fanciful, fantastic, fitful, freaky, grotesque, malformed, monstrous, odd, outlandish, strange, unconventional, unpredictable, unusual, weird, whimsical
🖃 normal, ordinary

free *adj* 1 *free tickets*: at no cost, at no extra cost, buckshee *slang*, complimentary, for nothing, free of charge, gratis, on the house *colloq*, without charge 2 *free to move*: at large, at liberty, free as a bird *colloq*, loose, on the loose, out, unattached, unconfined, unrestrained 3 *a free country*: autonomous, democratic, emancipated, independent, liberated, self-governing, self-ruling, sovereign 4 *free of dirt*: clear of, devoid of *formal*, exempt from, immune to, lacking, safe from, unaffected by, without 5 *free time*: available, empty, idle, spare, unemployed, unoccupied, untaken, vacant, with time on your hands 6 *a free passageway*: clear, open, unblocked, unhampered, unimpeded, unobstructed 7 *free with his money*: charitable, generous, giving, hospitable, lavish, liberal, munificent *formal*, open-handed, unstinting 8 *with his free hand*: loose, unattached, unfastened, unsecured 9 *a free translation*: broad, general, imprecise, inexact, loose, rough, vague 10 *his free manner*: casual,

doing as you please *colloq*, doing your own thing *colloq*, easy, easy-going, fluid, natural, relaxed, smooth, spontaneous, uninhibited
🖃 2 bound, confined, fettered, imprisoned, restricted, tied 4 affected by, liable to 5 at work, busy, engaged, occupied, reserved, tied up *colloq* 6 blocked, obstructed 7 mean, stingy 8 attached 9 exact, literal, precise, rigorous 10 formal, inhibited, tense
♦ *v* 1 *free a prisoner*: disengage, disentangle, emancipate, extricate, let go, let out, liberate, loose, release, rescue, set free, set loose, turn loose, unbind, unchain, unleash, untie 2 *free someone from debt*: absolve, acquit, except, excuse, exempt, relieve, rid, save, unburden
🖃 1 confine, imprison 2 burden
♦ *adv* 1 *given away free*: for free, for love, for nothing, freely, gratis, without charge 2 *advice was given free*: abundantly, copiously, extravagantly, generously, lavishly, liberally
🖃 2 meanly

freedom *n* 1 *prisoners granted their freedom*: deliverance, emancipation, exemption, immunity, impunity, liberty, release 2 *a country's freedom*: autonomy, democracy, emancipation, home rule, independence, self-government, sovereignty 3 *given the freedom to make his own decisions*: flexibility, free hand, free rein, informality, latitude, leeway, licence, margin, opportunity, play, power, prerogative, privilege, range, right, scope
🖃 1 captivity, confinement 3 restriction

freely *adv* 1 *I freely admit I can be annoying*: easily, of your own free will, of your own volition, readily, spontaneously, voluntarily, willingly 2 *give freely*: abundantly, amply, extravagantly, generously, lavishly, liberally 3 *speak freely*: bluntly, candidly, frankly, openly, plainly, unreservedly
🖃 2 grudgingly 3 cautiously, evasively

freethinker *n* agnostic, deist, doubter, infidel, nonconformist, rationalist, sceptic, unbeliever

free will *n* autarky *technical*, autonomy *formal*, freedom, independence, liberty, self-determination, self-sufficiency, spontaneity, volition *formal*

freeze *v* 1 *the pond has frozen*: congeal, glaciate *technical*, harden, ice over, ice up, set, solidify, stiffen 2 *I'm going to freeze some raspberries*: chill, cool, deep-freeze, ice, refrigerate 3 *we froze at the bus stop*: catch a chill, get cold, quiver, shiver, turn blue with cold, your teeth be chattering 4 *she heard something and froze*: fix, halt, immobilize, stand still, stop, stop dead in your tracks, suspend 5 *petrol prices have been frozen for six months*: fix, hold, peg, suspend
♦ *n* 1 *the big freeze of 1963*: freeze-up, frost 2 *a freeze on pay rises*: embargo, halt, interruption, moratorium, postponement, shutdown, standstill, stay, stoppage, suspension

freezing *adj* arctic, biting, bitter, bitterly cold, chilly, cold, cutting, frosty, glacial, icy, numb, numbing, penetrating, piercing, polar, raw, Siberian, stinging, wintry
🖃 hot, warm

freight *n* 1 *a freight train*: cargo, contents, goods, load, merchandise, payload 2 *freight charges*: carriage, consignment, conveyance, freightage, haulage, lading, portage, shipment, transportation

frenetic *adj* berserk, demented, distraught, excited, frantic, frenzied, hectic, hyperactive, hysterical, insane, mad, maniacal, obsessive, overwrought, unbalanced, wild
Fᴇ calm, placid

frenzied *adj* amok, at your wits' end, berserk, beside yourself, crazed, demented, desperate, distracted, distraught, feverish, frantic, frenetic, furious, hectic, hysterical, mad, obsessive, out of control, overwrought, panic-stricken, raving, uncontrolled, wild
Fᴇ calm, composed

frenzy *n* **1** *the fans had worked themselves up into a frenzy:* agitation, delirium, distraction, fever, hysteria, insanity, lunacy, madness, mania, turmoil, wildness **2** *a frenzy of rage:* bout, burst, convulsion, fit, fury, outburst, paroxysm, passion, rage, seizure, spasm, transport
Fᴇ **1** calm, composure

frequency *n* commonness, constancy, frequentness, incidence, oftenness, periodicity *formal*, prevalence, recurrence, repetition
Fᴇ infrequency

frequent *adj* common, commonplace, constant, continual, customary, everyday, familiar, habitual, happening often, incessant, normal, persistent, predominant, prevailing, prevalent, recurring, regular, repeated, usual
Fᴇ infrequent
♦ *v* associate with, attend, go to frequently, go to regularly, hang about with *colloq*, hang out at *colloq*, hang out with *colloq*, haunt, patronize, visit

frequenter *n* client, customer, habitué, haunter, patron, regular, regular visitor, visitor

frequently *adv* commonly, continually, customarily, habitually, many a time, many times, more times than you've had hot dinners *colloq*, much, nine times out of ten *colloq*, often, oftentimes, over and over, persistently, repeatedly
Fᴇ infrequently, seldom

fresh *adj* **1** *a fresh sheet of paper:* additional, extra, further, more, other, supplementary **2** *fresh ideas:* brand-new, different, exciting, innovative, latest, modern, new, new-fangled *colloq*, novel, original, recent, revolutionary, unconventional, unusual, up-to-date **3** *a fresh breeze:* bracing, bright, brisk, chilly, clean, clear, cool, crisp, fair, invigorating, keen, pure, refreshing, unfaded, unpolluted **4** *fresh fruit:* crude, natural, raw, uncured, undried, unpreserved, unprocessed **5** *he felt fresh after his holiday:* a new person *colloq*, alert, bouncing, energetic, fresh as a daisy *colloq*, invigorated, lively, raring to go *colloq*, ready for more *colloq*, refreshed, renewed, rested, restored, revived, stimulated, vibrant, vigorous, vital, yourself again *colloq* **6** *a fresh complexion:* blooming, bright, clear, fair, glowing, healthy, pink, rosy **7** *don't get fresh with me, miss!:* bold, brazen, cheeky *colloq*, cocky *colloq*, disrespectful, familiar, forward, impudent, insolent, overfamiliar, pert, presumptuous, saucy *colloq*
Fᴇ **2** hackneyed, old **3** stale **4** preserved, processed, tinned **5** tired

freshen *v* **1** *the cool breeze freshened the room:* air, clean, clear, deodorize, purify, ventilate **2** *decided to freshen the paintwork in the bedroom:* enliven, liven (up), refresh, reinvigorate, restore, revitalize, revive, rouse, stimulate, tart up *colloq*
Fᴇ **2** tire
▶ **freshen up** get spruced up, get washed, spruce yourself up, tidy yourself up, wash yourself

freshman *n* first-year, fresher, underclassman

freshness *n* bloom, brightness, cleanness, clearness, glow, newness, novelty, originality, shine, sparkle, vigour, wholesomeness
Fᴇ staleness, tiredness

fret *v* **1** *don't fret, he'll be fine:* agonize, anguish, be anxious, be distressed, be upset, brood, make a fuss, mope, pine, worry **2** *nothing seems to fret her:* anger, annoy, bother, exasperate, infuriate, irritate, nettle, rile, torment, trouble, vex

fretful *adj* anxious, distressed, disturbed, edgy *colloq*, fearful, restless, tense, troubled, uneasy, unhappy, upset, uptight *colloq*, worried
Fᴇ calm

friable *adj* brittle, crisp, crumbly, powdery, pulverizable *formal*
Fᴇ solid

friar *n* abbot, brother, mendicant, monk, prior, religioner, religious

friction *n* **1** *some friction between the two colleagues:* animosity, antagonism, arguing, bad blood, bad/ill feeling, clashing, conflict, disagreement, discord *formal*, disharmony, disputation *formal*, dispute, dissension *formal*, hostility, opposition, quarrelling, resentment, rivalry, strife **2** *worn away by friction:* abrading *formal*, abrasion *formal*, attrition *formal*, chafing, erosion, excoriation *formal*, gnawing, grating, irritation, rasping, resistance, rubbing, scraping, traction, wearing away

friend *n* **1** *an old school friend:* acquaintance, ally, associate, best friend, bosom friend, buddy *colloq*, chum *colloq*, close friend, companion, comrade, confidant(e), crony *colloq*, good friend, intimate, mate *colloq*, pal *colloq*, partner, playmate, soul mate, well-wisher **2** *a friend of the National Theatre:* backer, benefactor, patron, sponsor, subscriber, supporter, well-wisher
Fᴇ **1** enemy **2** opponent

friendless *adj* abandoned, alone, by yourself, cold shouldered *colloq*, companionless, deserted, forlorn, forsaken, isolated, lonely, lonely-heart, lonesome, ostracized, shunned, solitary, unattached, unbefriended, unbeloved, unloved, unpopular, with no one to turn to

friendliness *n* affability, amiability, approachability, companionability, congeniality, conviviality, Gemütlichkeit, geniality, kindliness, kindness, matiness *colloq*, neighbourliness, sociability, warmth
Fᴇ coldness, unsociableness

friendly *adj* **1** *the boys are all very friendly:* affable, affectionate, agreeable, amiable, amicable, approachable, companionable, comradely, convivial, cordial, genial, good-natured, helpful, hospitable, kind, kindly, maty *colloq*, neighbourly, outgoing, pally *colloq*, receptive, sociable, sympathetic, warm, well-disposed **2** *she's very friendly with my sister:* chummy *colloq*, close, familiar, fond, inseparable, intimate, maty *colloq*, pally *colloq*, thick *colloq*, tight *colloq* **3** *a friendly atmosphere:* amicable, close, congenial, convivial, cordial, familiar, warm, welcoming

🔃 **1** hostile, unfriendly, unsociable **2** distant **3** cold

friendship *n* affection, affinity, alliance, amiability, amity *formal*, attachment, closeness, companionship, comradeship, concord, familiarity, fellowship, fondness, friendliness, friendly relationship, goodwill, harmony, intimacy, kindliness, love, rapport, understanding, warmth
🔃 animosity, enmity

fright *n* **1** *trembling with fright:* alarm, apprehension, blind panic *colloq*, blood running cold *colloq*, blue funk *colloq*, cold sweat *colloq*, consternation *formal*, creeps *colloq*, dismay, disquiet, dread, fear, fearfulness, funk *colloq*, hair standing on end *colloq*, heebie-jeebies *colloq*, horror, jitters *colloq*, knocking knees *colloq*, panic, perturbation *formal*, shivers *colloq*, shock, terror, trepidation *formal*, willies *colloq* **2** *it was such a fright:* bolt from the blue *colloq*, bombshell *colloq*, panic, scare, shock

frighten *v* alarm, appal, daunt, dismay, give someone a fright, horrify, intimidate, make someone jump out of their skin *colloq*, make your blood run cold *colloq*, make your hair stand on end *colloq*, panic, petrify, put the frighteners on *colloq*, put the wind up *colloq*, rattle *colloq*, scare, scare out of your wits *colloq*, scare stiff, scare the living daylights out of *colloq*, scare the shit out of *slang*, shock, startle, terrify, terrorize, unman, unnerve
🔃 calm, reassure

frightened *adj* afraid, alarmed, cowed, dismayed, frozen, having kittens *colloq*, in a blue funk *colloq*, panicky, panic-stricken, petrified, quivery, scared, scared out of your wits *colloq*, scared stiff, scared to death *colloq*, shaking like a leaf *colloq*, startled, terrified, terrorized, terror-stricken, trembly, unnerved, with your heart in your mouth *colloq*
🔃 calm, courageous

frightening *adj* alarming, bloodcurdling, creepy, daunting, fearsome, forbidding, formidable, grim, hair-raising, hairy *colloq*, petrifying, scary *colloq*, spine-chilling, spooky *colloq*, terrifying, traumatic

frightful *adj* **1** *a frightful mess:* abhorrent, appalling, awful, dire, disagreeable, dreadful, fearful, ghastly, grim, horrible, horrid, shocking, terrible, unbearable, unpleasant, unspeakable **2** *a frightful scream:* alarming, fearful, ghastly, grim, grisly, gruesome, harrowing, hideous, horrible, loathsome, macabre, nasty, odious, repulsive, revolting, terrifying
🔃 **1** agreeable, pleasant

frigid *adj* **1** *the frigid wastes of the tundra:* arctic, bitter, chill, chilly, cold, freezing, frosty, frozen, glacial, icy, polar, Siberian, wintry **2** *a frigid atmosphere:* aloof, chilly, cool, distant, formal, icy, lifeless, passionless, passive, unfeeling, unloving, unresponsive
🔃 **1** hot **2** approachable, enthusiastic, responsible

frigidity *n* aloofness, chill, chilliness, cold-heartedness, coldness, frostiness, iciness, impassivity, lifelessness, passivity, stiffness, unapproachability, unresponsiveness
🔃 responsiveness, warmth

frill *n* **1** *a blouse with frills:* flounce, fold, fringe, furbelow, gathering, orphrey, purfle, ruche, ruching, ruff, ruffle, trimming, tuck, valance **2** *the basic model without the frills:* accessory, addition, decoration, embellishment, extra, fanciness, fandangle, finery, frilliness, frippery, ornamentation, ostentation, superfluity, trimmings

frilly *adj* crimped, fancy, frilled, gathered, lacy, ornate, ruffled, trimmed
🔃 plain

fringe *n* **1** *on the fringes of society:* border, borderline, edge, limit, margin, outskirts, perimeter, periphery, rim, verge **2** *a shawl with long fringe:* border, edging, frill, tassel, trimming, valance
♦ *adj* alternative, avant-garde, experimental, unconventional, unofficial, unorthodox
🔃 conventional, mainstream
♦ *v* border, edge, enclose, skirt, surround, trim

fringed *adj* bordered, edged, fimbriated *technical*, fringy, tasselled, tasselly, trimmed

frippery *n* adornments, baubles, decorations, fanciness, fandangles, finery, flashiness, foppery, frilliness, frills, froth, fussiness, gaudiness, gewgaws, glad rags, knickknacks, meretriciousness *formal*, nonsense, ornaments, ostentation, pretentiousness, showiness, tawdriness, trifles, trinkets, trivia, triviality
🔃 plainness, simplicity

frisk *v* **1** *lambs frisking in the fields:* bounce, caper, cavort, dance, frolic, gambol, hop, jump, leap, play, prance, romp, skip, sport, trip **2** *frisked at the entrance:* body-search, check, inspect, search, shake down *US*

frisky *adj* active, alive and kicking *colloq*, bouncy, dashing, exuberant, frolicsome, full of beans *colloq*, high *colloq*, high-spirited, hyper *colloq*, in high spirits, lively, playful, rollicking, romping, spirited
🔃 quiet, subdued

fritter *v* blow *slang*, dissipate *formal*, get through, go through, idle, misspend, misuse, overspend, spend like water *colloq*, squander, waste

frivolity *n* facetiousness, flippancy, folly, foolishness, fun, gaiety, inanity, jest, levity, light-heartedness, nonsense, pettiness, senselessness, silliness, superficiality, triviality
🔃 seriousness

frivolous *adj* facetious, flighty, flippant, foolish, futile, idle, inane, jocular, juvenile, light, light-hearted, merry, petty, pointless, puerile, senseless, shallow, silly, superficial, trifling, trivial, unimportant, vain, zany
🔃 sensible, serious

frizzy *adj* corrugated, crimped, crisp, curled, curly, frizzed, wiry
🔃 straight

frolic *v* bounce, caper, cavort, dance, frisk, gambol, hop, lark around, leap, make merry, play, prance, rollick, romp, skip, sport
♦ *n* amusement, antics, caper, escapade, fun, fun and games, gaiety, game, high jinks, jollity, lark, merriment, mirth, prank, razzle *colloq*, razzle-dazzle *colloq*, revel, romp, sport, spree

frolicsome *adj* coltish, frisky, gay, lively, merry, playful, rollicking, skittish, sportive, sprightly
🔃 quiet, serious, solemn

front *n* **1** *the front of the building:* aspect, bow, cover, exterior, façade, face, facing, frontage, obverse, outside **2** *in the front of the painting:* forefront, foreground, forepart **3** *soldiers at the front:* firing line, front line, vanguard **4** *put on a front of being happy:* air, appearance, blind, countenance *formal*, cover, cover-up, disguise, expression, exterior, façade, look, manner, mask, pretence, pretext, show
🔁 **1** back, rear **2** back, rear
♦ *adj* first, fore, foremost, head, leading
🔁 back, last, rear
♦ *v* confront, face, look out on, look over, meet, oppose, overlook

frontier *n* border, borderline, boundary, bounds, confines, edge, limit, marches, perimeter, verge

frost *n* **1** *frost on the windows:* hoar-frost, ice, Jack Frost, rime **2** *there was a frost overnight:* coldness, freeze, freeze-up

frosty *adj* **1** *a frosty morning:* arctic, bitterly cold, chilly, cold, freezing, frigid, frozen, glacial, icy, nippy *colloq*, parky *colloq*, polar, rimy, Siberian, wintry **2** *a rather frosty reception:* aloof, cold, cool, discouraging, hostile, icy, standoffish, stiff, unfriendly, unwelcoming
🔁 **1** hot, warm **2** enthusiastic, friendly, responsive, warm, welcoming

froth *n* bubbles, effervescence, fizz, foam, head, lather, scum, spume, suds
♦ *v* bubble, effervesce, ferment, fizz, foam, lather, spume

frothy *adj* **1** *a frothy milk shake:* bubbling, bubbly, fizzy *colloq*, foaming, foamy, spumescent *formal*, spumous *formal*, spumy *formal*, sudsy, yeasty **2** *a frothy novel:* empty, frivolous, insubstantial, slight, trifling, trivial, vain
🔁 **1** flat **2** significant, substantial

frown *v* give someone a dirty look *colloq*, glare, glower, grimace, look daggers at *colloq*, lour, pout, scowl
♦ *n* dirty look *colloq*, glare, glower, grimace, raised eyebrow, scowl
▶ **frown on** disapprove of, discourage, dislike, have a low opinion of, not take kindly to, object to, raise your eyebrows, take a dim view of, think badly of
🔁 approve of, go along with

frozen *adj* **1** *the frozen wastes:* arctic, bitterly cold, chilled, freezing, frigid, frosted, frosty, frozen-stiff, hard, icebound, ice-cold, ice-covered, iced, icy, polar, raw, Siberian, solidified **2** *frozen in his tracks:* fixed, immobile, motionless, numb, rigid, stiff
🔁 **1** warm

frugal *adj* careful, economical, inadequate, meagre, miserly, niggardly, paltry, parsimonious *formal*, penny-pinching, penny-wise, provident, prudent *formal*, scanty, scrimping and saving *colloq*, sparing, stingy, thrifty
🔁 generous, wasteful

fruit *n* **1** *the fruit of the earth:* crop, fruitage, harvest, produce **2** *her hard work has borne fruit:* advantage, benefit, consequence, effect, outcome, product, profit, result, return, reward, yield

---

Varieties of fruit include:
apple, Bramley, Cox's Orange Pippin, Golden Delicious, Granny Smith, crab apple; pear, William, Conference; orange, Jaffa, mandarin, mineola, clementine, satsuma, tangerine, Seville; apricot, peach, plum, nectarine, cherry, sloe, damson, greengage, grape, gooseberry, goosegog *colloq*, rhubarb; banana, pineapple, lemon, lime, ugli fruit, star fruit, lychee, passion fruit, date, fig, grapefruit, kiwi fruit, mango, avocado; melon, honeydew, cantaloupe, watermelon; strawberry, raspberry, blackberry, bilberry, loganberry, elderberry, blueberry, boysenberry, cranberry; redcurrant, blackcurrant

---

fruitful *adj* **1** *fruitful land:* abundant, fecund *formal*, feracious *formal*, fertile, fruit-bearing, plentiful, productive, prolific, rich, teeming **2** *a fruitful partnership:* advantageous, beneficial, effective, effectual *formal*, efficacious *formal*, productive, profitable, rewarding, successful, useful, well-spent, worthwhile
🔁 **1** barren **2** fruitless

fruitfulness *n* fecundity *formal*, feracity *formal*, fertility, productiveness, profitability, usefulness
🔁 fruitlessness

fruition *n* achievement, attainment, completion, consummation *formal*, enjoyment, fulfilment, maturity, perfection, realization, success

fruitless *adj* abortive, barren, futile, hopeless, idle, ineffectual *formal*, pointless, sterile, unproductive, unsuccessful, useless, vain, worthless
🔁 fruitful, productive, profitable, successful

fruity *adj* **1** *a fruity voice:* full, mellow, resonant, rich **2** *fruity jokes:* bawdy, blue *colloq*, indecent, indelicate, juicy, racy, risqué, salacious, saucy, sexy, smutty, spicy, suggestive, titillating, vulgar
🔁 **2** decent

frumpy *adj* badly-dressed, dated, dingy, dowdy, drab, dreary, ill-dressed, out of date
🔁 chic, well-groomed

frustrate *v* **1** *it frustrates me that I can't get a job:* anger, annoy, circumvent *formal*, depress, disappoint, discourage, dishearten, dissatisfy, embitter, irritate, stymie *colloq* **2** *frustrated her plans:* baffle, balk, block, check, counter, defeat, foil, forestall, hamper, hinder, impede, inhibit, neutralize, nobble *colloq*, nullify, obstruct, spike *colloq*, stop, thwart
🔁 **1** encourage **2** further, promote

frustrated *adj* angry, annoyed, blighted, disappointed, discontented, discouraged, disheartened, dissatisfied, embittered, repressed, resentful, thwarted
🔁 fulfilled, satisfied

frustration *n* **1** *almost screaming with frustration:* anger, annoyance, disappointment, discouragement, dissatisfaction, irritation, resentment, vexation **2** *the frustration of his plans:* balking, blocking, circumvention *formal*, contravention, curbing, defeat, failure, foiling, non-fulfilment, obstruction, thwarting
🔁 **1** fulfilment **2** furthering, promoting

fuddled *adj* bemused, confused, drunk, groggy, hazy, inebriated, intoxicated, muddled, muzzy, sozzled, stupefied, tipsy, woozy
🔁 clear, sober

fuddy-duddy *n* back number *colloq*, conservative, fogey, fossil, museum piece, old

fogey *colloq*, square *colloq*, stick-in-the-mud *colloq*, stuffed shirt *colloq*
♦ *adj* carping, censorious, old-fashioned, old-fogeyish, prim, stick-in-the-mud, stuffy
◪ up-to-date

fudge *v* avoid, dodge, equivocate, evade, fake, falsify, fiddle *colloq*, fix *colloq*, hedge, misrepresent, shuffle, stall

fuel *n* **1** *solid fuel*: combustible, motive power, propellant **2** *provided fuel for their argument*: ammunition, encouragement, goading, incentive, incitement, material, provocation, stimulus
♦ *v* encourage, fan, feed, fire, incite, inflame, nourish, stoke up, sustain
◪ damp down, discourage

fug *n* fetidness *formal*, frowstiness, fustiness, reek, staleness, stink, stuffiness
◪ airiness

fuggy *adj* airless, close, fetid, foul, frowsty, fusty, noisome *formal*, noxious *formal*, stale, stuffy, suffocating, unventilated
◪ airy

fugitive *n* deserter, escapee, refugee, runaway
♦ *adj* **1** *a fugitive convict*: refugee, runaway **2** *a fugitive impression*: brief, elusive, ephemeral, evanescent *formal*, fleeting, flying, fugacious *formal*, momentary, passing, short, short-lived, temporary, transient, transitory
◪ **2** permanent

fulfil *v* **1** *fulfil a duty*: accomplish, carry out, complete, conclude *formal*, consummate *formal*, discharge, effect *formal*, execute, finish, implement, perfect, perform **2** *fulfil your potential*: achieve, fill, live up to, realize, satisfy **3** *fulfil an obligation*: comply with, conform to, meet, obey, observe, satisfy
◪ **1** neglect **2** fail **3** fall short

fulfilled *adj* content, gratified, happy, pleased, satisfied
◪ discontented, dissatisfied, unhappy

fulfilment *n* accomplishment, achievement, completion, consummation *formal*, discharge, execution, implementation, observance, perfection, performance, realization, satisfaction, success
◪ failure

full *adj* **1** *a room full of people*: bulging, bursting at the seams *colloq*, chock-a-block *colloq*, crammed, crowded, filled, filled to capacity, flush, full to the brim, jammed, laden, loaded, overflowing, packed, packed like sardines *colloq*, packed out *colloq*, stuffed, well-stocked **2** *a full set of stickers*: complete, entire, intact, total, unabridged, unexpurgated, whole **3** *a full inspection*: abundant, all-inclusive, ample, broad, comprehensive, copious, detailed, exhaustive, extensive, filled, generous, plentiful, profuse, sufficient, thorough, vast **4** *feel full*: bursting *colloq*, gorged, replete *formal*, sated, satiated *formal*, satisfied, stuffed **5** *a full sound*: clear, deep, distinct, fruity, loud, resonant, rich, strong **6** *at full speed*: greatest, highest, maximum, top, utmost **7** *lead a full life*: active, busy, eventful, frantic, hectic, lively, tiring **8** *a full figure*: buxom, chubby, corpulent *formal*, fat, large, obese, overweight, plump, rotund *formal*, round,

shapely, stout **9** *a full skirt*: baggy, loose-fitting, voluminous *formal*, wide
◪ **1** empty **2** incomplete, partial **3** superficial **4** hungry **6** minimum **7** empty, unoccupied
♦ *adv* bang *colloq*, directly, exactly, right, smack *colloq*, squarely, straight

full-blooded *adj* committed, dedicated, devoted, enthusiastic, hearty, thorough, vigorous, wholehearted
◪ half-hearted

full-grown *adj* adult, developed, full-scale, fully-developed, fully-fledged, fully-grown, grown-up, mature, of age, ripe
◪ undeveloped, young

fullness *n* **1** *praised the fullness of the report*: abundance, ampleness, completeness, comprehensiveness, extensiveness, plenty, profusion, richness, strength, thoroughness, totality, variety, vastness, wholeness **2** *the fullness of a sound*: loudness, resonance, richness **3** *a sense of fullness after eating*: fill, glut, repletion *formal*, satedness, satiation *formal*, satiety *formal*, satisfaction **4** *fullness of figure*: breadth, curvaceousness, largeness, plumpness, shapeliness, width **5** *the fullness in her breasts before she fed her baby*: dilation *formal*, enlargement, growth, inflammation, swelling, tumescence *technical*
◪ **1** incompleteness **3** emptiness

full-scale *adj* all-encompassing, all-out, complete, comprehensive, exhaustive, extensive, in-depth, intensive, major, sweeping, thorough, thoroughgoing, wide-ranging
◪ partial

fully *adv* altogether, completely, entirely, in all respects, perfectly, positively, quite, satisfactorily, sufficiently, thoroughly, totally, unreservedly, utterly, wholly, without reserve
◪ partly

fully-fledged *adj* experienced, full-blown, fully-developed, graduate, mature, professional, proficient, qualified, senior, trained
◪ inexperienced

fulminate *v* animadvert *formal*, condemn, criticize, curse, declaim *formal*, decry *formal*, denounce, fume, inveigh *formal*, protest, rage, rail, thunder, vituperate *formal*
◪ praise

fulmination *n* condemnation, criticism, decrial *formal*, denunciation, detonation, diatribe *formal*, invective *formal*, obloquy *formal*, philippic *formal*, thundering, tirade
◪ praise

fulsome *adj* adulatory, buttery *colloq*, cloying, effusive, excessive, extravagant, fawning, gross, immoderate, ingratiating, inordinate, insincere, nauseating, nauseous, over the top *colloq*, overdone, saccharine, sickening, slimy *colloq*, smarmy *colloq*, sycophantic, unctuous
◪ sincere

fumble *v* blunder, botch, bungle, feel, flounder, grope, mishandle, mismanage, scrabble, spoil

fume *v* **1** *a fuming chimney*: boil, smoke, smoulder, steam **2** *silently fumed at his insensitivity*: be furious, be livid, blow your cool *colloq*, boil, burst a blood vessel *colloq*, hit the roof *colloq*, rage, rant, rant and rave *colloq*, rave, seethe, storm

fumes *n* exhalation *formal*, exhaust, fog, gas, haze, pollution, reek, smell, smog, smoke, stench, stink, vapour

fumigate *v* cleanse, deodorize, disinfect, purify, sanitize, sterilize

fuming *adj* angry, boiling, enraged, furious, incensed, livid, raging, seething, steamed up *colloq*
◻ calm

fun *n* amusement, buffoonery, celebration, cheerfulness, distraction, diversion, enjoyment, entertainment, foolery, games, gladness, hilarity, horseplay, jesting, jocularity, joking, jollity, joy, laughs, laughter, merrymaking, mirth, play, pleasure, recreation, relaxation, romp, skylarking, sport, tomfoolery
♦ *adj* amusing, delightful, diverting, enjoyable, entertaining, lively, pleasurable, recreational, witty

function *n* **1** *in her function as social secretary:* activity, business, capacity, charge, chore, concern, duty, employment, job, mission, occupation, office, part, post, purpose, responsibility, role, situation, task, use **2** *a social function:* affair, dinner, do *colloq*, gathering, luncheon, party, reception
♦ *v* act, be in working order, behave, go, have the job of, operate, perform, play the part of, run, serve, work
◻ break down, conk out *slang*, malfunction *formal*

functional *adj* **1** *functional clothing:* hard-wearing, plain, practical, serviceable, useful, utilitarian, utility **2** *a functional model:* operational, operative, running, working
◻ **1** decorative **2** useless

functionary *n* bureaucrat, dignitary, employee, office-bearer, office-holder, officer, official

fund *n* **1** *contribute to the restoration fund:* endowment, foundation, grant, investment, kitty, pool, reserve, treasury **2** *raise funds for the repairs:* assets, backing, capital, cash, finance, means, money, resources, savings, wealth **3** *a fund of funny stories:* accumulation, cache, collection, hoard, mine, repository, reserve, reservoir, source, stack, stock, store, storehouse, supply, well
♦ *v* back, capitalize, endow, finance, float, pay for, promote, provide finance for, sponsor, subsidize, support, underwrite

fundamental *adj* basal *formal*, basic, cardinal, central, chief, crucial, elemental *formal*, elementary, essential, first, important, indispensable, initial, integral, key, main, necessary, original, primary, prime, principal, profound, rudimentary *formal*, underlying, vital

fundamentally *adv* at bottom, at heart, basically, deep down, essentially, in essence, inherently, intrinsically, primarily

fundamentals *n* basics, brass tacks *colloq*, essentials, facts, first principles, laws, necessaries, nitty-gritty *colloq*, nuts and bolts *colloq*, practicalities, rudiments

funeral *n* burial, cremation, entombment *formal*, exequies *formal*, inhumation *formal*, interment *formal*, obsequies *formal*, wake

funereal *adj* dark, deathlike, depressing, dismal, dreary, exequial *formal*, funebral *formal*, funebrial *formal*, gloomy, grave, lamenting, lugubrious *formal*, mournful, sad, sepulchral, serious, solemn, sombre, woeful
◻ happy, lively

funk *v* balk at, blench, chicken out of *colloq*, cop out *colloq*, dodge *colloq*, duck out of, flinch from, recoil from, shirk from

funnel *v* channel, convey, direct, filter, go, move, pass, pour, siphon, transfer

funny *adj* **1** *his act was so funny:* a hoot *colloq*, a scream *colloq*, absurd, amusing, comic, comical, corny *colloq*, diverting, droll, entertaining, facetious, farcical, hilarious, humorous, hysterical, killing *colloq*, laughable, rich, ridiculous, riotous, risible *formal*, rum *colloq*, side-splitting, silly, uproarious, witty **2** *a funny smell:* bizarre, curious, dubious, mysterious, odd, oddball *colloq*, off-beat *colloq*, peculiar, perplexing, puzzling, queer, remarkable, shady *colloq*, strange, suspicious, unusual, wacky *colloq*, way-out *colloq*, weird
◻ **1** sad, serious, solemn **2** normal, ordinary, usual

fur *n* coat, down, fell, fleece, hair, hide, pelage, pelt, skin, wool

furious *adj* **1** *her father was furious:* angry, boiling, enraged, foaming at the mouth *colloq*, frenzied, fuming, gone off the deep end *colloq*, hopping mad *colloq*, hot under the collar *colloq*, in a huff *colloq*, in a lather *colloq*, in a paddy *colloq*, in a stew *colloq*, incensed, indignant, inflamed, infuriated, irate, livid, mad *colloq*, purple with rage, raging, seething, sizzling *colloq*, up in arms *colloq* **2** *a furious argument:* boisterous, fierce, frantic, intense, stormy, tempestuous, vehement, vigorous, violent, wild
◻ **1** calm, pleased **2** restrained

furnish *v* appoint, bestow *formal*, decorate, endue, equip, fit out, give, grant, offer, present, provide, rig, stock, supply
◻ divest

furniture *n* appliances, appointments, effects, equipment, fittings, furnishings, household goods, movables, possessions, things

> *Types of furniture include:*
> table, dining-table, gateleg table, refectory table, lowboy, side-table, coffee-table, card table; chair, easy chair, armchair, rocking-chair, recliner, dining-chair, carver, kitchen chair, stool, swivel-chair, high-chair, suite, settee, sofa, couch, studio couch, chesterfield, pouffe, footstool, bean-bag; bed, four-poster, chaise-longue, daybed, bed-settee, divan, camp-bed, bunk, water-bed, cot, cradle; desk, bureau, secretaire, bookcase, cupboard, cabinet, china cabinet, Welsh dresser, sideboard, buffet, dumb-waiter, fireplace, overmantel, fender, firescreen, hallstand, umbrella-stand, mirror, magazine rack; wardrobe, armoire, dressing-table, vanity unit, washstand, chest-of-drawers, tallboy, chiffonier, commode, ottoman, chest, coffer, blanket box

furore *n* commotion, disturbance, excitement, flap *colloq*, frenzy, fury, fuss, hullabaloo,

outburst, outcry, rage, stir, storm, to-do, tumult, uproar
🖅 calm

furrow *n* **1** *ploughing furrows in the earth:* channel, groove, hollow, rut, sulcus *technical*, track, trench, trough **2** *a furrow in his brow:* crease, crinkle, crow's foot, line, wrinkle
♦ *v* channel, corrugate, crease, draw together, flute, gouge, groove, knit, seam, wrinkle

further *adj* **1** *any further questions:* additional, extra, fresh, more, new, other, supplementary **2** *it was further than I remembered:* farther, more distant, more extreme, remoter
🖅 **2** nearer
♦ *v* accelerate, advance, aid, assist, champion, contribute to, ease, encourage, expedite *formal*, facilitate, forward, foster, hasten, help, promote, push *colloq*, speed (up)
🖅 frustrate, stop
♦ *adv* additionally, also, as well, besides, furthermore, in addition, moreover, too, what's more *colloq*

furtherance *n* advancement, advancing, advocacy, backing, boosting, carrying-out, championship, encouragement, facilitation, help, preferment *formal*, promoting, promotion, pursuit

furthermore *adv* additionally, also, as well, besides, further, in addition, moreover, too, what's more *colloq*

furthest *adj* extreme, farthest, furthermost, outermost, outmost, remotest, ultimate, utmost, uttermost
🖅 nearest

furtive *adj* clandestine *formal*, cloaked, covert, hidden, secret, secretive, sly, sneaky, stealthy, surreptitious, underhand, veiled
🖅 open

fury *n* anger, ferocity, fierceness, force, frenzy, intensity, ire, madness, passion, power, rage, severity, turbulence, vehemence, violence, wildness, wrath
🖅 calm, peacefulness

fuse *v* agglutinate *formal*, amalgamate, blend, coalesce, combine, commingle *formal*, integrate, intermingle *formal*, intermix, join, meld, melt, merge, smelt, solder, synthesize, unite, weld

fusion *n* amalgamation, blending, coalescence, federation, integration, melting, merger, smelting, synthesis, union, welding

fuss *n* a song and dance *colloq*, agitation, ballyhoo *colloq*, bother, bustle, carry-on *colloq*, commotion, confusion, excitement, flap *colloq*, flurry, fluster, furore, hassle *colloq*, hoo-ha *colloq*, hurry, kerfuffle *colloq*, palaver, row, squabble, stir, storm in a teacup *colloq*, tizzy *colloq*, to-do *colloq*, trouble, upset, worry
🖅 calm
♦ *v* be in a tizzy *colloq*, bother, bustle, complain,

fidget, flap *colloq*, fret, grumble, make a song and dance *colloq*, panic, stir *colloq*, take pains, worry

fussiness *n* busyness, choosiness, fastidiousness, finicalness, meticulousness, niceness, niggling, particularity, perfectionism, pernicketiness
🖅 unfussiness

fusspot *n* fidget, hyper-critic, nit-picker *colloq*, old woman *colloq*, perfectionist, stickler, worrier

fussy *adj* **1** *fussy about his food:* choosy *colloq*, demanding, difficult, discriminating, faddy, fastidious, finical, finicky, hard to please, nit-picking *colloq*, particular, pedantic, pernickety *colloq*, pettifogging, picky *colloq*, quibbling, scrupulous, selective **2** *fussy decorations:* baroque, busy, cluttered, elaborate, fancy, ornate, overdecorated, rococo
🖅 **1** casual, uncritical **2** plain, simple

fusty *adj* **1** *a fusty gentlemen's club:* antiquated, archaic, old-fashioned, old-fogeyish *colloq*, outdated, out of date, passé **2** *the old house smelled fusty:* airless, damp, dank, frowsty, fuggy, ill-smelling, malodorous *formal*, mouldering, mouldy, musty, rank, stale, stuffy, unventilated
🖅 **1** up-to-date **2** airy

futile *adj* abortive, barren, empty, forlorn, fruitless, hollow, idle, in vain, ineffective, ineffectual *formal*, pointless, profitless, to no avail, unavailing, unproductive, unprofitable, unsuccessful, useless, vain, wasted, worthless
🖅 fruitful, profitable

futility *n* aimlessness, barrenness, emptiness, fruitlessness, hollowness, ineffectiveness, pointlessness, unproductiveness, uselessness, vanity, waste, worthlessness
🖅 purpose, success, use

future *n* coming times, expectations, hereafter, outlook, prospects, time to come, tomorrow
🖅 past
♦ *adj* approaching, coming, designate, destined, eventual, expected, fated, forthcoming, imminent, impending, in the offing, later, next, planned, prospective, subsequent, to be, to come, unborn
🖅 past

fuzz *n* down, fibre, flock, floss, fluff, fug, hair, lint, nap, pile

fuzzy *adj* **1** *fabric with a fuzzy surface:* downy, fleecy, fluffy, frizzy, furry, hairy, linty, napped, velvety, woolly **2** *a fuzzy image:* blurred, confused, distorted, faint, foggy, fuddled, hazy, ill-defined, indefinite, indistinct, muffled, muzzy *colloq*, shadowy, unclear, unfocused, vague, woolly
🖅 **2** clear, distinct, focused

G

gab *v* babble, blabber, blather, blether, buzz, chatter, drivel, gossip, jabber, jaw, prattle, talk, tattle, yak *colloq*
♦ *n* blab, blarney, blethering, chat, chatter, chitchat, conversation, gossip, loquacity *formal*, prattle, prattling, small talk, tittle-tattle, tongue-wagging, yackety-yak *colloq*, yak *colloq*

gabble *v* babble, blab, blabber, blether, cackle, chatter, gaggle, gibber, jabber, prattle, rattle, splutter, spout, sputter
♦ *n* babble, blabber, blethering, cackling, chatter, drivel, gibberish, nonsense, prattle, twaddle, waffle

gad
▶ **gad about** dot about, flit about, gallivant, ramble, range, roam, rove, run around, stray, traipse, travel, wander

gadabout *n* gallivanter, pleasure-seeker, rover, runabout, stravaiger *Scot*, wanderer

gadget *n* apparatus, appliance, contraption, contrivance, device, gimmick, gismo *colloq*, implement, instrument, invention, mechanism, novelty, thing, thingummy *colloq*, tool, whatnot *colloq*, whatsit *colloq*, widget *colloq*

gaffe *n* bloomer *colloq*, blunder, boob *colloq*, boo-boo *colloq*, brick *colloq*, clanger *colloq*, faux pas, gaucherie, goof *colloq*, howler *colloq*, indiscretion, mistake, slip, solecism *formal*

gaffer *n* boss *colloq*, foreman, ganger, manager, overman, overseer, superintendent, supervisor

gag[1] *v* **1** *they were bound and gagged:* muzzle, put a gag on, restrain, smother, stifle, throttle **2** *the press had been gagged:* block, check, curb, muffle, quiet, silence, still, suppress **3** *gagged at the thought of food:* choke, heave, nearly vomit, retch

gag[2] *n* crack *colloq*, funny *colloq*, jest, joke, one-liner, pun, quip, wisecrack, witticism

gaiety *n* **1** *a time of great gaiety:* blitheness, brightness, buoyancy, celebration, cheerfulness, delight, exuberance, festivity, frolics, fun, gladness, glee, good humour, happiness, high spirits, hilarity, joie de vivre, jollity, joviality, joy, joyfulness, light-heartedness, liveliness, merriment, merrymaking, mirth, pleasure, revelry, vivacity *formal* **2** *the gaiety of the decorations:* brightness, brilliance, cheerfulness, colour, colourfulness, glitter, show, showiness, sparkle
🔁 **1** sadness **2** drabness

gaily *adv* **1** *children laughing gaily:* blithely, brightly, cheerfully, happily, joyfully, light-heartedly, merrily **2** *gaily coloured banners:* brightly, brilliantly, cheerfully, colourfully, flamboyantly
🔁 **1** sadly **2** dully

gain *v* **1** *gain an advantage:* achieve, acquire, bring in, capture, clear, earn, gather, get, gross, harvest, make, net, obtain, procure *formal*, produce, profit, realize, reap, secure, win, yield **2** *gained the far shore:* achieve, arrive at, attain, come to, get to, reach, realize **3** *gain speed:* add, advance, collect, gather, improve, increase, pick up, progress

🔁 **1** lose **3** lose
♦ *n* **1** *the gains from introducing the policy:* advantage, benefit, dividend, earnings, emolument *formal*, headway, improvement, income, interest, pickings, proceeds, profit, progress, return, revenue, reward, takings, winnings, yield **2** *a side-effect of the drug is weight gain:* accretion *formal*, acquisition, addition, attainment, augmentation *formal*, growth, increase, increment, rise
🔁 **1** loss **2** loss
▶ **gain on** approach, catch up, close in on, close with, get nearer/closer to, level with, narrow the gap, outdistance, overtake
🔁 leave behind

gainful *adj* advantageous, beneficial, financially rewarding, fructuous *formal*, fruitful, lucrative, moneymaking, paying, productive, profitable, remunerative, rewarding, useful, worthwhile
🔁 useless

gainsay *v* challenge, contradict, contravene *formal*, controvert *formal*, deny, disaffirm *formal*, disagree with, dispute, oppose
🔁 agree

gait *n* bearing, carriage, manner, pace, step, stride, tread, walk

gala *n* carnival, celebration, fair, festival, festivity, fête, jamboree, jubilee, pageant, party, procession

galaxy *n* **1** *the largest star in our galaxy:* cluster, constellation, nebula, solar system, star system, stars, the Milky Way **2** *a galaxy of Hollywood stars:* array, assembly, collection, gathering, group, host, mass

gale *n* **1** *warnings of gales in the west:* cyclone, hurricane, squall, storm, tornado, typhoon, wind **2** *gales of laughter:* blast, burst, eruption, explosion, fit, outbreak, outburst

gall[1] *n* **1** *had the gall to ask for more money:* brass *colloq*, brass neck *colloq*, brazenness, cheek *colloq*, chutzpah *colloq*, effrontery *formal*, impertinence, impudence, insolence, neck *colloq*, nerve *colloq*, presumption, presumptuousness, sauciness *colloq* **2** *came out of prison full of gall against the system:* acrimony *formal*, animosity, animus *formal*, antipathy, bitterness, enmity, hostility, malevolence *formal*, malice, rancour, sourness, spite, venom, virulence
🔁 **1** modesty, reserve **2** friendliness

gall[2] *v* aggravate *colloq*, annoy, bother, exasperate, get to, harass, irk, irritate, nag, nettle, peeve, pester, plague, provoke, rankle, rile, ruffle, vex
🔁 please

gallant *adj* **1** *a gallant effort to win:* audacious, bold, brave, courageous, daring, dashing, dauntless, fearless, heroic, intrepid, plucky, valiant **2** *gallant young men:* attentive, considerate, courteous, courtly, gentlemanly, gracious, honourable, noble, polite, thoughtful
🔁 **1** cowardly **2** ungentlemanly

gallantry *n* **1** *a medal for gallantry:* audacity, boldness, bravery, courage, courageousness, daring, dauntlessness, fearlessness, heroism,

honour, intrepidity, manliness, pluck, spirit, valiance *formal*, valour **2** *the gallantry of his attention:* attentiveness, chivalry, consideration, courteousness, courtesy, courtliness, gentlemanliness, graciousness, honour, nobility, politeness, thoughtfulness
🔁 **1** cowardice **2** ungentlemanliness

gallery *n* **1** *the national portrait gallery:* art gallery, exhibition area, museum **2** *our seats were in the gallery:* balcony, circle, gods *colloq* **3** *a covered gallery around the piazza:* arcade, colonnade, passage, portico, walk, walkway

galling *adj* aggravating *colloq*, annoying, bothersome, embittering, exasperating, harassing, humiliating, infuriating, irksome, irritating, nettling, plaguing, provoking, rankling, vexatious, vexing
🔁 pleasing

gallivant *v* dot about, flit about, gad about, ramble, range, roam, rove, run around, stravaig *Scot*, stray, traipse, travel, wander

gallop *v* bolt, canter, career, dart, dash, fly, hasten *formal*, hurry, race, run, rush, scurry, shoot, speed, sprint, tear, zoom
🔁 amble

gallows *n* gibbet, scaffold, the rope

galore *adj* everywhere, heaps of *colloq*, in abundance, in numbers, in profusion *formal*, lots of, millions of *colloq*, plenty, stacks of *colloq*, to spare, tons of *colloq*
🔁 scarce

galvanize *v* animate, arouse, awaken, electrify, energize, enliven, excite, fire, inspire, invigorate, jolt, move, prod, provoke, rouse, shock, spur, startle, stimulate, stir, urge, vitalize

gambit *n* artifice, device, machination *formal*, manoeuvre, move, play, ploy, ruse, stratagem, tactic(s), trick, wile

gamble *v* back, bet, chance, chance it, game, have a flutter *colloq*, hazard, play, play for money, play the horses, punt, put money on, risk, speculate, stake, take a chance, take a risk, try your luck, venture, wager
♦ *n* bet, chance, flutter *colloq*, hazard, leap in the dark *colloq*, lottery, pot luck, punt, risk, speculation, toss-up *colloq*, venture, wager

gambler *n* better, daredevil, desperado, punter, risk-taker, speculator

gambol *v* bounce, bound, caper, cavort, dance, frisk, frolic, hop, jump, leap, prance, romp, skip, spring

game¹ *n* **1** *fun and games:* amusement, distraction, diversion, entertainment, frolic, fun, jest, joke, merriment, pastime, play, prank, recreation, romp, sport, trick **2** *a game of football:* bout, competition, contest, event, match, meet, meeting, round, tournament **3** *shooting game:* animals, bag, flesh, game birds, meat, prey, quarry, spoils, wild animals, wild fowl **4** *he's in the building game:* activity, business, enterprise, line, occupation, profession, trade **5** *what was his game, do you think?:* device, intention, plot, ploy, ruse, scheme, stratagem, strategy, tactic(s), trick

Types of indoor game include:
board game, backgammon, checkers *US*, chess, Cluedo®, draughts, halma, ludo, mah-jongg, Monopoly®, nine men's morris,

Scrabble®, snakes and ladders, Trivial Pursuit®; card game, baccarat, beggar-my-neighbour, bezique, blackjack, brag, bridge, canasta, chemin de fer, crib *colloq*, cribbage, faro, gin rummy, rummy, happy families, nap *colloq*, napoleon, newmarket, old maid, patience, Pelmanism, picquet, poker, draw poker, stud poker, pontoon, vingt-et-un, snap, solitaire, twenty-one, whist, partner whist, solo whist; bagatelle, pinball, billiards, snooker, pool, bowling, ten-pin bowling, bowls, darts, dice, craps, dominoes, roulette, shove ha'penny, table tennis, ping pong

Types of children's games include:
battleships, blind man's buff, charades, Chinese whispers, consequences, fivestones, forfeits, hangman, hide-and-seek, I-spy, jacks, jackstraws, musical chairs, noughts and crosses, pass the parcel, piggy-in-the-middle, pin the tail on the donkey, postman's knock, sardines, Simon says, spillikins, spin the bottle, tiddlywinks

game² *adj* **1** *game for anything:* desirous *formal*, eager, enthusiastic, inclined, interested, prepared, ready, willing **2** *a game fighter:* bold, brave, courageous, daring, fearless, gallant, intrepid, lion-hearted, plucky, resolute, spirited, unflinching, valiant
🔁 **1** unwilling **2** afraid, cowardly, fearful

gamekeeper *n* keeper, venerer *old use*, warden

gamut *n* area, compass, field, range, scale, scope, sequence, series, spectrum, sweep, variety

gang *n* **1** *a gang of teenagers:* band, circle, clique, club, company, coterie, crowd, gathering, group, herd, horde, lot, mob, pack, party, ring, set, shift, troupe **2** *a gang of builders:* band, crew, group, squad, team

gangling *adj* angular, awkward, bony, gangly, gauche, gawky, lanky, loose-jointed, rangy, raw-boned, skinny, spindly, tall, ungainly

gangster *n* bandit, brigand, criminal, crook *colloq*, desperado, heavy *slang*, hoodlum, mobster, racketeer, robber, rough, ruffian, terrorist, thug, tough

gaol see **jail**

gaoler see **jailer**

gap *n* **1** *a gap in the hedge:* aperture, blank, breach, cavity, chink, cleft, crack, cranny, crevice, difference, discontinuity *formal*, disparity *formal*, divergence, divide, fracture, gulf, hole, lacuna *formal*, opening, orifice *formal*, rent, rift, space, vacuity *formal*, void **2** *a two-week gap:* break, hiatus, interlude, intermission, interruption, interval, lull, pause, recess

gape *v* **1** *gaping at the man in their bathroom:* gawk *colloq*, gawp *colloq*, gaze, goggle, rubberneck *US slang*, stare, wonder **2** *a door gaped open:* crack, open, part, split, yawn

gaping *adj* broad, cavernous, open, vast, wide, yawning
🔁 tiny

garage *n* **1** *backed the car into the garage:* car port, lock-up, outbuilding, shed **2** *called at the garage for petrol:* petrol station, service station

garb n **1** *in military garb:* apparel *formal*, array *formal*, attire *formal*, clothes, clothing, costume, dress, garment, gear *colloq*, get-up *colloq*, habiliment, outfit, raiment *formal*, rig-out *colloq*, robes, togs *colloq*, uniform, vestments, wear **2** *dressed aromatherapy up in the garb of a science:* appearance, aspect, fashion, form, guise, look, style
♦ v apparel *formal*, array *formal*, attire *formal*, clothe, cover, dress, habilitate *formal*, rig out *colloq*, robe

garbage n **1** *a garbage dump:* bits and pieces, debris, detritus *formal*, dross, filth, junk, leftovers, litter, muck, odds and ends, refuse, remains, rubbish, scourings, scraps, slops, sweepings, swill, trash *US*, waste **2** *talks such garbage:* balls *slang*, bilge *colloq*, bollocks *slang*, bullshit *slang*, bunk *colloq*, bunkum *colloq*, claptrap *colloq*, cobblers *colloq*, gibberish, hot air *colloq*, nonsense, piffle *colloq*, poppycock *colloq*, rot *colloq*, rubbish, shit *slang*, tommyrot *colloq*, trash, tripe, twaddle

garble v confuse, corrupt, distort, doctor, falsify, jumble, misinterpret, misrepresent, mix up, muddle, mutilate, pervert, scramble, slant, tamper with, twist, warp
🔁 decipher

garden n **1** *sitting in her garden:* allotment, backyard, plot, yard **2** *the public gardens:* common, green, park, parkland

gargantuan adj big, Brobdingnagian *formal*, colossal, elephantine, enormous, giant, gigantic, huge, immense, large, leviathan *formal*, mammoth, massive, monstrous, monumental, prodigious *formal*, titanic, towering, tremendous, vast
🔁 minute, small, tiny

garish adj cheap, flash *colloq*, flashy, flaunting, gaudy, glaring, glittering, glitzy *colloq*, loud, lurid, meretricious *formal*, raffish, showy, tasteless, tawdry, tinselly, vulgar
🔁 quiet, tasteful

garland n bays, chaplet, coronal, coronet, crown, decoration, festoon, flowers, headband, laurels, lei, stemma, wreath
♦ v adorn, crown, deck, decorate, festoon, wreathe

garments n apparel *formal*, attire *formal*, clothes, clothing, costume, dress, garb *colloq*, gear *colloq*, get-up *colloq*, outfit, togs *colloq*, uniform, wear

garner v **1** *garnering vegetables:* amass, assemble, collect, cull, deposit, gather, heap, hoard, husband, lay up, pile up, put by, reserve, save, stack up, stockpile, store, stow away **2** *garnering accolades:* accumulate, acquire, amass, collect, gain, gather, get
🔁 **1** dissipate **2** scatter

garnish v adorn, beautify, deck (out), decorate, embellish, enhance, festoon, grace, ornament, set off, trim
🔁 divest
♦ n adornment, decoration, embellishment, enhancement, ornament, ornamentation, relish, trimming

garrison n **1** *a garrison of 100 men:* armed force, command, detachment, troops, unit **2** *the troops returned to their garrison:* barracks, base, camp, casern, encampment, fort, fortification, fortress, post, station, stronghold, zareba

♦ v **1** *the army has garrisoned the port:* defend, guard, man, occupy, protect **2** *soldiers garrisoned in the town:* assign, place, position, post, station

garrulous adj babbling, chattering, chatty, effusive, gabby, gassy, glib, gossiping, gushing, long-winded, loquacious *formal*, mouthy, prating, prattling, prolix *formal*, talkative, verbose, voluble *formal*, windy, wordy, yabbering
🔁 taciturn, terse

gas

Types of gas include:
acetylene, ammonia, black damp, butane, carbon dioxide, carbon monoxide, chloroform, choke damp, CS gas, cyanogen, ether, ethylene, fire damp, helium, hydrogen sulphide, krypton, laughing gas, marsh gas, methane, mustard gas, natural gas, neon, nerve gas, niton, nitrous oxide, ozone, propane, radon, tear gas, town gas, xenon

gash v cut, gouge, incise, lacerate, nick, rend, score, slash, slit, split, tear, wound
♦ n cut, gouge, incision, laceration, nick, rent, score, slash, slit, split, tear, wound

gasp v blow, breathe, catch your breath, choke, gulp, heave, pant, puff, wheeze
♦ n blow, breath, choke, exclamation, gulp, pant, puff

gastric adj abdominal, coeliac, enteric, intestinal, stomach, stomachic

gate n access, barrier, door, doorway, entrance, exit, gateway, opening, passage, portal *formal*

gather v **1** *a crowd gathered at the town hall:* assemble, attract, build, cluster, collect, come/ bring together, congregate, convene, converge, crowd, draw, group, marshal, mass, meet, muster, rally, round up, summon **2** *gather all the toys together:* accumulate, amass, build, cluster, collect, garner, group, heap, hoard, hoard up, mass, pile up, pull in, rake in, round up, stash away *colloq*, stockpile **3** *I gather she's leaving:* assume, believe, conclude, deduce, hear, infer, learn, surmise, understand **4** *gather flowers:* collect, crop, cull, garner, glean, harvest, pick, pluck, reap, select **5** *gather speed:* add, advance, build up, develop, gain, grow, improve, increase, pick up, progress **6** *gather the material together:* fold, pleat, pucker, ruffle, shirr, tuck
🔁 **1** disperse, scatter **2** distribute, scatter

gathering n assemblage *formal*, assembly, band, company, conclave *formal*, congregation, convention, convocation *formal*, crowd, flock, get-together, group, horde, jamboree, mass, meeting, mob, party, rally, round-up, throng, turnout

gauche adj awkward, clumsy, farouche, gawky, graceless, ignorant, ill-bred, ill-mannered, inelegant, inept, insensitive, maladroit *formal*, shy, tactless, uncultured, ungainly, ungraceful, unpolished, unsophisticated
🔁 elegant, graceful, urbane

gaudy adj bright, brilliant, colourful, flash *colloq*, flashy, flaunting, garish, glaring, glitzy *colloq*, harsh, kitsch, loud, meretricious *formal*, multicoloured, ostentatious, raffish, showy, shrieking, snazzy *colloq*, stark, tasteless, tawdry, tinselly, too bright, vulgar
🔁 drab, plain, simple

gauge *v* apprise *formal*, ascertain *formal*, assess, calculate, check, compute, count, determine, estimate, evaluate, figure, guess, guesstimate *colloq*, judge, measure, rate, reckon, value, weigh
♦ *n* **1** *a temperature gauge*: basic, benchmark, criterion, example, exemplar *formal*, guide, guideline, indicator, measure, meter, model, norm, pattern, rule, sample, standard, test, touchstone, yardstick **2** *the gauge of a bullet*: area, bore, calibre, capacity, degree, depth, extent, height, magnitude, measure, scope, size, span, thickness, width

gaunt *adj* **1** *she came out of hospital looking thin and gaunt*: angular, bony, cadaverous *formal*, emaciated, haggard, hollow-eyed, lank, lean, scraggy, scrawny, skeletal, skin and bones, skinny, spindly, thin, wasted **2** *a gaunt landscape*: bare, barren, bleak, desolate, dismal, dreary, forbidding, forlorn, grim, harsh, stark
🖃 **1** plump

gauzy *adj* delicate, diaphanous *formal*, filmy, flimsy, gossamer, insubstantial, light, see-through, sheer, thin, transparent, unsubstantial
🖃 heavy, thick

gawk *v* gape, gaze, goggle, look, ogle, stare

gawky *adj* awkward, clumsy, gangling, gauche, graceless, inept, lanky, loutish, lumbering, maladroit *formal*, oafish, unco-ordinated, ungainly
🖃 graceful

gay *adj* **1** *a club for gay men*: bent *derog*, bisexual, butch *colloq*, camp *colloq*, dykey *derog*, homosexual, lesbian, queer *derog* **2** *feeling light-hearted and gay*: animated, blithe, bright, carefree, cheerful, debonair, exuberant, fun-loving, happy, in good/high spirits, jolly, joyful, light-hearted, lively, merry, playful, pleasure-seeking, sprightly, sunny, vivacious **3** *gay colours*: bright, brilliant, colourful, festive, flamboyant, flashy, garish, gaudy, rich, showy, sparkling, vivid
🖃 **1** heterosexual, straight *slang* **3** gloomy, sad
♦ *n* dyke *derog*, fag *derog*, faggot *derog*, fairy *derog*, homo *derog*, homosexual, lesbian, nancy *derog*, pansy *derog*, poof *derog*, queen *slang*, queer *derog*, woofter *derog*
🖃 heterosexual, straight *colloq*

gaze *v* contemplate, eye, gape, gawk *colloq*, goggle, look, regard, stare, stare fixedly/intently, view, watch, wonder
♦ *n* fixed look, gape, look, stare

gazebo *n* belvedere, hut, pavilion, shelter, summerhouse

gazette *n* dispatch, journal, magazine, newspaper, news-sheet, notice, organ, paper, periodical

gear *n* **1** *put all the fishing gear in the van*: accessories, accoutrements *formal*, apparatus, appliances, contrivances, equipment, implements, instruments, kit, outfit, stuff *colloq*, supplies, tackle, things *colloq*, tools, utensils **2** *a system of gears*: cog, cogwheel, engrenage *formal*, gearing, gearwheel, machinery, mechanism, ratchet, toothed wheel, tooth-wheel, works **3** *can I leave all my gear at your flat?*: baggage, belongings, effects *formal*, kit, luggage, paraphernalia, personal possessions, possessions, stuff *colloq*, things **4** *wears all the*

latest gear: apparel *formal*, attire *formal*, clothes, clothing, dress, garb *colloq*, garments, get-up *colloq*, togs *colloq*
♦ *v* adapt, design, devise, fit, organize, prepare, tailor

gel, jell *v* **1** *the jam will eventually gel*: coagulate, congeal, crystallize, harden, set, solidify, thicken **2** *the idea gelled*: come together, develop, finalize, form, materialize, take shape **3** *we gelled straightaway*: click *colloq*, get along, get on, hit it off *colloq*, see eye to eye
🖃 **1** liquefy

gelatinous *adj* congealed, gluey, glutinous, gooey *colloq*, gummy, jellied, jelly-like, mucilaginous *formal*, rubbery, sticky, viscid, viscous

geld *v* castrate, emasculate, neuter, unman, unsex

gem *n* **1** *precious gems*: gemstone, jewel, precious stone **2** *his last joke was a real gem*: crème de la crème, masterpiece, pièce de résistance, pride and joy *colloq*, prize, treasure

---

Gems and gemstones include:
diamond, white sapphire, zircon, cubic zirconia, marcasite, rhinestone, pearl, moonstone, onyx, opal, mother-of-pearl, amber, citrine, fire opal, topaz, agate, tiger's eye, jasper, morganite, ruby, garnet, rose quartz, beryl, cornelian, coral, amethyst, sapphire, turquoise, lapis lazuli, emerald, aquamarine, bloodstone, jade, peridot, tourmaline, jet

---

gen *n* background, data, details, dope *colloq*, facts, info *colloq*, information, knowledge, low-down *colloq*
▶ **gen up on** be well-informed about, bone up on *colloq*, brush up on *colloq*, find out about, read up on, research, study, swot up on *colloq*

genealogy *n* ancestry, birth, breeding, derivation, descent, dynasty, extraction, family, family history, family tree, line, lineage, parentage, pedigree

general *adj* **1** *a general statement*: accepted, across-the-board, all-inclusive, blanket, broad, comprehensive, extensive, global, overall, panoramic, popular, prevailing, prevalent, sweeping, total, universal, wide-ranging, widespread **2** *a very general picture*: approximate, broad, ill-defined, imprecise, indefinite, inexact, loose, rough, unspecific, vague **3** *as a general rule*: common, conventional, customary, everyday, habitual, normal, ordinary, public, regular, standard, typical, usual **4** *a general store*: assorted, diverse, heterogeneous *formal*, miscellaneous, mixed, varied, variegated *formal*
🖃 **1** limited, particular **2** detailed, precise, specific **3** rare

generality *n* **1** *talked in generalities*: approximateness, general statement, generalization, impreciseness, indefiniteness, inexactness, looseness, sweeping statement, vagueness **2** *the generality of his appeal*: breadth, catholicity, commonness, comprehensiveness, ecumenicity, extensiveness, miscellaneity, popularity, prevalence, universality
🖃 **1** detail, exactness, particular
2 uncommonness

generally *adv* as a rule, at large, broadly, by and large, chiefly, commonly, customarily, for the most part, habitually, in general, in most cases, largely, mainly, mostly, normally, on the whole, ordinarily, predominantly, universally, usually

generate *v* arouse, breed, bring about, bring into being, cause, create, engender, form, give rise to, initiate, make, occasion, originate, produce, propagate, whip up
 prevent

generation *n* 1 *the younger generation*: age, age group, days, epoch, era, period, time 2 *the generation of energy*: breeding, creation, engendering, formation, genesis *formal*, origination, procreation *formal*, production, propagation, reproduction

generic *adj* 1 *a generic term*: all-encompassing, all-inclusive, blanket, collective, common, comprehensive, general, inclusive, sweeping, universal, wide 2 *generic drugs*: non-proprietary, non-registered, non-trademarked, unbranded
 1 particular 2 branded, proprietary, registered, trademarked

generosity *n* benevolence, big-heartedness, bounty, charity, goodness, kindness, lavishness, liberality, magnanimity, munificence *formal*, open-handedness, philanthropy, selflessness, unselfishness
 meanness, selfishness

generous *adj* 1 *generous with his time*: bountiful, free, free-handed, lavish, liberal, open-handed, unsparing, unstinting 2 *a generous person*: altruistic, beneficent *formal*, benevolent, big *colloq*, big-hearted, charitable, good, high-minded, kind, lofty, magnanimous, munificent *formal*, noble, philanthropic, public-spirited, selfless, unselfish 3 *generous portions of food*: abundant, ample, copious, full, lavish, overflowing, plentiful, rich
 1 mean, miserly 2 selfish 3 meagre

genesis *n* beginning, birth, commencement *formal*, creation, dawn, engendering, formation, foundation, founding, generation, inception *formal*, initiation, origin, outset, propagation, root, source, start
 end, finish

genial *adj* affable, agreeable, amiable, amicable, cheerful, convivial, cordial, easy-going *colloq*, friendly, good-humoured, good-natured, happy, hearty, jolly, jovial, kind, kindly, pleasant, sociable, warm, warm-hearted
 cold, unfriendly

geniality *n* affability, agreeableness, amiability, cheerfulness, cheeriness, congenialness, conviviality, cordiality, friendliness, gladness, good nature, happiness, jollity, joviality, kindliness, kindness, pleasantness, warm-heartedness, warmth
 coldness, unfriendliness

genie *n* demon, fairy, jann, jinnee, jinni, spirit

genitals *n* balls *slang*, clitoris, cock *slang*, cunt *slang*, dick *slang*, fanny *slang*, genitalia *formal*, labia majora/minora, penis, prick *slang*, private parts, privates *colloq*, pudenda *technical*, pudendum, pussy *slang*, reproductive organs, scrotum, sexual organs, testicles, uterus, vagina, vulva, willy *colloq*, womb

genius *n* 1 *a genius on the violin*: adept, boffin *colloq*, brain, brains *colloq*, egghead *colloq*, expert, intellect, intellectual, maestro, master, mastermind, past master, prodigy, sage, virtuoso 2 *his genius at cards*: ability, aptitude, bent, brains *colloq*, brightness, brilliance, capacity, cleverness, faculty, fine mind, flair, gift, grey matter *colloq*, inclination, intellect, intelligence, knack, little grey cells *colloq*, nous *colloq*, propensity *formal*, talent, wisdom

genocide *n* ethnic cleansing, ethnocide, extermination, massacre, slaughter

genre *n* brand, category, character, class, fashion, form, genus *technical*, group, kind, school, sort, strain, style, type, variety

genteel *adj* aristocratic, civil, courteous, courtly, cultivated, cultured, elegant, fashionable, formal, gentlemanly, graceful, ladylike, mannerly, polished, polite, refined, respectable, stylish, urbane, well-bred, well-mannered
 crude, rough, unpolished, vulgar

gentility *n* 1 *a member of the gentility*: aristocracy, blue blood, breeding, elite, gentle birth, gentry, good family, high birth, nobility, nobles, rank, upper class 2 *treated with great gentility*: civility, courtesy, courtliness, culture, decorum *formal*, elegance, etiquette, formality, mannerliness, manners, politeness, propriety *formal*, refinement, respectability, urbanity
 1 crudeness, discourteousness, roughness

gentle *adj* 1 *a gentle soul*: amiable, benign, calm, charitable, compassionate, humane, kind, kindly, lenient, merciful, mild, placid, serene, soft, soft-hearted, sympathetic, tender, tender-hearted, tranquil 2 *a gentle slope*: easy, gradual, imperceptible, light, moderate, slight, slow, smooth 3 *a gentle voice*: peaceful, quiet, serene, smooth, soft, soothing 4 *a gentle breeze*: balmy, calm, light, mild, moderate, pleasant
 1 harsh, rough, unkind, wild 2 severe, steep 4 strong, violent

gentlemanly *adj* civil, civilized, courteous, cultivated, gallant, genteel, gentlemanlike, honourable, mannerly, noble, obliging, polished, polite, refined, reputable, suave, urbane, well-bred, well-mannered
 impolite, rough

gentry *n* aristocracy, elite, gentility, nobility, nobles, upper class

genuine *adj* 1 *genuine leather*: actual, authentic, bona fide, factual, lawful, legal, legitimate, natural, original, pukka, real, real McCoy *colloq*, sound, true, unadulterated, veritable 2 *a very genuine man*: candid, earnest, frank, honest, natural, open, sincere, truthful, with integrity
 1 artificial, counterfeit, fake, false 2 deceitful, insincere

genus *n* breed, category, class, division, genre, group, kind, order, race, set, sort, species, subdivision, taxon *technical*, type

germ *n* 1 *pick up germs from dirty handkerchiefs*: bacillus, bacterium, bug *colloq*, microbe, micro-organism, virus 2 *the germ of an idea*: beginning, bud, cause, commencement *formal*, embryo, inception *formal*, nucleus, origin, root, rudiment, seed, source, spark, sprout, start

germane *adj* akin, allied, applicable, apposite *formal*, appropriate, apropos *formal*, apt, connected, fitting, material, pertinent *formal*, proper, related, relevant, suitable

Ea irrelevant

germinal *adj* developing, embryonic, generative, preliminary, rudimentary, seminal, undeveloped

germinate *v* bud, burgeon *formal*, develop, grow, originate, shoot, spring up, sprout, swell, take root

gestation *n* conception, development, drafting, evolution, incubation, maturation *formal*, planning, pregnancy, ripening

gesticulate *v* gesture, indicate, make a sign, motion, sign, signal, wave

gesticulation *n* chironomy *formal*, gesture, indication, motion, movement, sign, signal, wave

gesture *n* act, action, gesticulation, indication, motion, movement, sign, signal, wave
♦ *v* beckon, gesticulate, indicate, motion, point, sign, signal, wave

get *v* 1 *get lots of presents*: achieve, acquire, be given, bring in, buy, clear, come by, earn, gain, make, obtain, procure *formal*, purchase *formal*, realize, receive, secure, win 2 *it's getting dark*: become, come to be, go, grow, turn 3 *get him to help*: coax, convince, induce, influence, persuade, prevail upon *formal*, sway, talk into, urge, win over 4 *we got there at about 6*: arrive, come, go, move, reach 5 *could you get me a chair?*: bring, capture, catch, collect, fetch, grab, pick up, seize, take 6 *get a disease*: be afflicted by, become infected with, catch, come down with, contract *formal*, develop, pick up 7 *get to see the exhibition*: arrange, have the opportunity, manage, organize, succeed 8 *I'll get breakfast for you*: cook, fix *US*, get ready, prepare, put together, rustle up *colloq* 9 *get the joke*: comprehend *formal*, fathom, follow, get the hang of *colloq*, get the point *colloq*, grasp, see, twig *colloq*, understand 10 *get a thief/an animal*: arrest, capture, catch, collar *colloq*, hit, hunt down, kill, lay hold of, nab *colloq*, nick *colloq*, snare, trap 11 *his snoring really gets me*: annoy, bother, bug *colloq*, drive crazy *colloq*, exasperate, get on someone's nerves *colloq*, infuriate, irritate, provoke, rub someone up the wrong way *colloq*, vex

Ea 1 lose 4 leave

▶ **get about** go/travel (widely), move about, move around

▶ **get across** bring home to, communicate, convey, get over, impart, put across, put over, transmit

▶ **get ahead** advance, do well, flourish, get on, get somewhere *colloq*, get there *colloq*, go great guns *colloq*, go places *colloq*, go up in the world *colloq*, make good, make it, make the big time *colloq*, make your mark *colloq*, progress, prosper, succeed, thrive

Ea fail, fall behind

▶ **get along** 1 *I wondered how you were getting along*: cope, develop, fare, get by, manage, progress, survive 2 *they've never really got along*: agree, be on friendly terms, be on the same wavelength, get on, harmonize, hit it off *colloq*

▶ **get at** 1 *hoping to get at the truth*: attain, discover, find, obtain, reach 2 *the jury had been got at*: bribe, corrupt, influence, suborn 3 *I don't know what you're getting at*: hint, imply, insinuate, intend, mean, suggest 4 *stop getting at Paul*:

attack, criticize, find fault with, knock *colloq*, make fun of, pick holes in *colloq*, pick on, slam *colloq*, slate *colloq*

▶ **get away** break away, break free, break out, depart, escape, flee, get out, leave, run away

▶ **get back** 1 *what time will you get back?*: go/come back, go/come home, return 2 *trying to get back his losses*: recoup, recover, regain, repossess, retrieve 3 *swore to get back at him for what he had done*: avenge yourself on, get even with, pay back, retaliate, take vengeance on

▶ **get by** cope, exist, fare, get along, hang on *colloq*, keep the wolf from the door *colloq*, keep your head above water *colloq*, make ends meet *colloq*, manage, scrape through *colloq*, see it through *colloq*, subsist *formal*, survive, weather the storm *colloq*

▶ **get down** 1 *these reality TV shows really get me down*: depress, dishearten, dispirit, sadden 2 *she got down from the ladder*: alight, descend, dismount, get off

▶ **get in** 1 *the plane gets in at 9.35*: arrive, come, come in, land 2 *rain had got in through the broken window*: come in, enter, infiltrate, penetrate

▶ **get off** 1 *get off a train*: alight, climb off, descend, disembark *formal*, dismount, get out (of), leave 2 *can't get the lid off*: detach, remove, separate, shed

▶ **get on** 1 *got on the bus*: ascend, board, climb on, embark, get in, get into, mount 2 *we've never really got on*: be on friendly terms with, get along, hit it off with *colloq* 3 *you're getting on very well with that task*: cope, fare, make out, manage, prosper, succeed 4 *the students just got on with their work*: advance, continue, press on, proceed, progress

▶ **get out** 1 *got out of prison*: break out, clear off *colloq*, clear out, depart, escape, evacuate, extricate yourself, flee, free yourself, leave, quit *colloq*, vacate, withdraw 2 *she got out a pen*: produce, take out 3 *the news got out*: be leaked, become known, become public, circulate, come out, leak out, spread

▶ **get out of** avoid, dodge *colloq*, escape, evade, shirk, skive *colloq*

▶ **get over** 1 *getting over a bout of flu*: be restored, get well/better, pull through, recover from, recuperate from, respond to treatment, shake off, survive 2 *getting over a few problems*: deal with, defeat, get round, master, overcome, surmount 3 *getting it over to an audience*: communicate, convey, explain, get across, impart, put over

▶ **get round** 1 *getting round an obstacle*: avoid, bypass, circumvent *formal*, evade 2 *he got round her to help out*: coax, induce, persuade, prevail upon *formal*, sway, talk round, win over

▶ **get together** assemble, collaborate, collect, congregate, gather, join, meet, organize, rally, unite

▶ **get up** arise, rise, stand (up)

getaway *n* absconding, break, breakout, decampment, escape, flight, start

get-together *n* assembly, do *colloq*, function, gathering, meeting, party, rally, reception, reunion, social, soirée

get-up *n* clothes, clothing, garments, gear *colloq*, outfit, rig-out *colloq*, set, togs *colloq*

ghastly *adj* 1 *a ghastly accident*: appalling, awful, dreadful, frightening, frightful, grim, gruesome, hideous, horrendous, horrible, horrid, horrifying, loathsome, nasty, repellent, shocking, terrible, terrifying 2 *look/feel ghastly*: awful,

dreadful, ill, lousy *colloq*, off colour *colloq*, poorly, ropy *colloq*, rotten, sick, terrible, under the weather *colloq*, unwell **3** *a ghastly mistake:* appalling, awful, bad, critical, dangerous, dreadful, frightful, grave, serious, shocking, terrible, unrepeatable
F3 1 attractive, delightful **2** healthy, well

ghost *n* **1** *Banquo's ghost:* apparition, phantom, presence, shade, shadow, soul, spectre, spirit, spook *colloq*, visitant, wraith **2** *the ghost of a smile:* hint, impression, semblance, shadow, suggestion, trace

ghostly *adj* creepy, eerie, ghostlike, illusory, phantom, shadowy, spectral, spooky *colloq*, supernatural, unearthly, weird, wraith-like

ghoulish *adj* grisly, gruesome, macabre, morbid, revolting, sick, unhealthy, unwholesome

giant *n* behemoth, colossus, Cyclops, Goliath, Hercules, monster, ogre, titan
♦ *adj* Brobdingnagian, colossal, cyclopean, enormous, gargantuan, gigantic, great big *colloq*, huge, immense, jumbo *colloq*, king-size, large, mammoth, massive, monumental, prodigious, titanic, vast, whopping *colloq*

gibber *v* babble, blab, blabber, blather, cackle, cant, chatter, gabble, jabber, prattle

gibberish *n* balderdash, bunkum *colloq*, cobblers *colloq*, drivel, gobbledygook *colloq*, jargon, mumbo-jumbo *colloq*, nonsense, poppycock *colloq*, rubbish, tommyrot *colloq*, twaddle
F3 sense

gibe, jibe *n* crack *colloq*, derision, dig *colloq*, jeer, mockery, quip, ridicule, scoff, sneer, taunt, teasing
♦ *v* deride *formal*, jeer, make fun of, mock, ridicule, scoff, sneer, taunt, tease

giddiness *n* **1** *a fit of giddiness:* dizziness, faintness, light-headedness, nausea, vertigo, wobbliness, wooziness **2** *her giddiness at seeing him:* animation, dizziness, excitement, exhilaration, frenzy, thrill

giddy *adj* **1** *feeling giddy after the ride:* dizzy, faint, light-headed, reeling, unsteady, vertiginous *formal*, woozy *colloq* **2** *giddy with excitement:* dizzy, elated, excited, exhilarated, frenzied, high *colloq*, stimulated, stirred, thrilled, wild

gift *n* **1** *a wedding gift:* bequest, bonus, bounty, contribution, donation, endowment, freebie *colloq*, gratuity, inheritance, largesse, legacy, offering, present, tip **2** *a gift for languages:* ability, aptitude, attribute, bent, capability, capacity, facility, faculty, flair, genius, knack, power, proficiency, skill, talent
♦ *v* bestow *formal*, confer *formal*, contribute, donate, give, offer, present

gifted *adj* able, accomplished, adept, bright, brilliant, capable, clever, endowed, expert, intelligent, masterly, proficient, sharp, skilful, skilled, smart *colloq*, talented

gigantic *adj* Brobdingnagian, colossal, enormous, gargantuan, giant, great big *colloq*, huge, immense, jumbo *colloq*, king-size, mammoth, massive, monumental, titanic, vast, whopping *colloq*
F3 Lilliputian, tiny

giggle *v* chortle, chuckle, laugh, snicker, snigger, titter
♦ *n* chortle, chuckle, laugh, snicker, snigger, titter

gild *v* adorn, array *formal*, beautify, bedeck *formal*, brighten, coat, deck, dress up, embellish, embroider, enhance, enrich, festoon, garnish, grace, ornament, paint, trim

gilded *adj* gilt, gold, golden, gold-layered, gold-plated

gimcrack *adj* cheap, rubbishy, shoddy, tacky *colloq*, tawdry, trashy, trumpery
F3 solid, well-made

gimmick *n* attraction, contrivance, device, dodge, gadget, novelty, ploy, publicity, ruse, scheme, stratagem, stunt, trick

gingerly *adv* attentively, carefully, cautiously, charily, delicately, hesitantly, judiciously *formal*, prudently *formal*, tentatively, warily, watchfully, with caution
F3 boldly, carelessly

gird *v* **1** *girded themselves for the fray:* brace, fortify *formal*, get ready, prepare, ready, steel **2** *girded with a sash:* belt, bind, encircle, enclose, encompass, enfold, fasten, girdle, hem in, pen, ring, surround

girdle *n* band, belt, ceinture *formal*, cestus *formal*, cincture *formal*, cingulum *formal*, corset, cummerbund *formal*, sash, waistband
♦ *v* bind, bound, circle, encircle, enclose, encompass, gird, go round, hem, ring, surround

girl *n* adolescent, child, daughter, girlfriend, kid *colloq*, lass, maiden, nipper *colloq*, schoolgirl, sweetheart, teenager, young lady, young woman

girlfriend *n* bird *slang*, chick *slang*, cohabitee, common-law spouse, date, fiancée, girl, lass, live-in lover, lover, mistress, old flame, partner, significant other *colloq*, steady *colloq*, sweetheart, young lady

girlish *adj* adolescent, childish, childlike, immature, innocent, unmasculine, youthful

girth *n* **1** *the girth of the tree:* breadth, bulk, circumference, measure, perimeter, size, span, thickness **2** *the horse's girth:* band, strap

gist *n* core, crux, direction, drift, essence, idea, import *formal*, keynote, marrow, matter, meaning, nub, nucleus, pith, point, quintessence *formal*, sense, significance, substance

give *v* **1** *gave her the prize:* accord *formal*, administer, award, bequeath, bestow *formal*, commit, confer *formal*, contribute, deliver, devote, distribute, donate, endow, entrust, furnish, gift, grant, hand over, leave, lend, let someone have, make over, offer, present, proffer *formal*, provide, slip, supply, turn over, will **2** *give me the news:* announce, communicate, convey, declare, impart *formal*, pronounce, publish, set forth, tell, transfer, transmit, utter **3** *give someone credit:* admit, allow, cede *formal*, concede, give up, give way, surrender, yield **4** *give trouble:* cause, create, do, make, occasion, perform, produce **5** *give an impression:* display, exhibit, indicate, manifest *formal*, present, reveal, set forth, show **6** *give attention to something:* aim, concentrate, direct, focus, turn **7** *give someone a fright:* cause to experience/undergo, create, do,

give rise to, make, occasion, perform **8** *give something a value*: allow, estimate, grant, offer **9** *the branch gave under his weight*: bend, break (down), buckle, collapse, fall, fall apart, give way, sink, yield **10** *give a party*: arrange, be responsible for, hold, lay on, organize, put on, take charge of, throw *colloq* **11** *be given to understand something*: cause, dispose, incline, induce, lead, make, move, prompt
F3 1 take, withhold
▶ **give away** betray, concede, disclose, divulge, expose, inform on, leak, let out, let slip, reveal, uncover
F3 keep
▶ **give in** admit/concede defeat, call it a day *colloq*, capitulate, chuck it in *colloq*, give up, give way, jack in *colloq*, pack it in *colloq*, quit *colloq*, show the white flag *colloq*, submit, succumb, surrender, throw in the towel/sponge *colloq*, yield
F3 hold out
▶ **give off** discharge, emit, exhale, exude, give out, pour out, produce, release, send out, throw out, vent
▶ **give on to** lead to, open on to, overlook
▶ **give out 1** *give the exam papers out*: allot, deal, dish out *colloq*, disperse, distribute, dole out, hand out, mete out, pass around, share out **2** *it was given out that he had died*: advertise, announce, broadcast, circulate, communicate, declare, disseminate, impart, make known, notify, publish, transmit **3** *his heart just gave out*: break down, conk out *slang*, pack up *colloq*, stop working **4** *supplies had given out*: be depleted *formal*, be exhausted, come to an end, run out
▶ **give up 1** *trying to give up smoking*: abandon, cease *formal*, cut out *colloq*, discontinue *formal*, forswear *formal*, leave off, quit *colloq*, relinquish *formal*, renounce, sacrifice, stop, waive **2** *gave up in despair*: capitulate, concede, concede defeat, give in, quit *colloq*, surrender, throw in the towel *colloq*, turn in *colloq*

give-and-take *n* adaptability, compliance, compromise, flexibility, goodwill, negotiation, willingness

given *adj* **1** *a given number*: definite, distinct, individual, particular, specific, specified **2** *not given to losing her temper*: disposed, inclined, liable, likely, prone
♦ *prep* assuming, bearing in mind, considering, in the light of, in view of, making allowances for, taking into account/consideration

giver *n* angel *colloq*, backer, benefactor, contributor, donor, fairy godmother *colloq*, friend, helper, patron, philanthropist, promoter, provider, sponsor, subscriber, subsidizer, supporter, well-wisher
F3 opponent, persecutor

glacial *adj* **1** *a glacial wind*: arctic, biting, bitter, brumous *formal*, chill, chilly, cold, freezing, frigid, frosty, frozen, gelid *formal*, icy, piercing, polar, raw, Siberian, stiff, wintry **2** *a glacial atmosphere*: antagonistic, cold, hostile, icy, inimical *formal*, unfriendly
F3 2 warm

glad *adj* **1** *glad to see us*: bright, cheerful, cheery, chuffed *colloq*, contented, delighted, elated, gleeful, gratified, happy, joyful, merry, over the moon *colloq*, overjoyed, pleased, satisfied, thrilled, tickled pink *colloq*, welcome **2** *glad to*

help: disposed *formal*, eager, happy, inclined, keen, pleased, prepared, ready, willing
F3 1 sad, unhappy **2** reluctant, unwilling

gladden *v* brighten, buck up *colloq*, cheer, delight, elate, encourage, enliven, exhilarate, gratify, hearten, please, raise the spirits of, rejoice
F3 sadden

gladly *adv* cheerfully, fain *old use*, freely, happily, readily, willingly, with good grace, with pleasure
F3 reluctantly, sadly, unwillingly

gladness *n* brightness, cheerfulness, delight, felicity *formal*, gaiety, glee, happiness, high spirits, hilarity, jollity, joy, joyousness *formal*, mirth, pleasure
F3 sadness

glamorous *adj* alluring, appealing, attractive, beautiful, captivating, charming, colourful, dazzling, elegant, enchanting, exciting, fascinating, flashy *colloq*, glittering, glitzy *colloq*, glossy, gorgeous, lovely, ritzy *colloq*, smart, stylish, thrilling, well-dressed
F3 boring, drab, plain

glamour *n* allure, appeal, attraction, attractiveness, beauty, captivation, charm, elegance, enchantment, excitement, fascination, glitter, magic, prestige, thrill

glance *v* browse, catch a glimpse of, dip, flick, flip, glimpse, leaf, look, look quickly/briefly at, peek, peep, scan, skim, thumb, view
♦ *n* butcher's *colloq*, dekko *colloq*, gander *colloq*, glimpse, look, peek, peep, quick/brief look
▶ **glance off** bounce off, rebound, ricochet, spring back

glare *v* **1** *she glared at him*: frown, give someone a dirty look *colloq*, glower, look, look daggers *colloq*, scowl, stare **2** *the lights glared*: beam, blaze, dazzle, flame, flare, reflect, shine
♦ *n* **1** *his fiery glare*: black look *colloq*, dirty look *colloq*, frown, look, scowl, stare **2** *the glare of the spotlights*: blaze, brightness, brilliance, dazzle, flame, flare, glow, spotlight

glaring *adj* blatant, conspicuous, flagrant, gross, lurid, manifest *formal*, obvious, open, outrageous, overt, patent
F3 concealed, hidden, minor

glass *n* **1** *a glass of water*: beaker, goblet, tumbler **2** *a collection of china and glass*: crystal, glassware, vitrics **3** *a pair of glasses*: eyeglasses, lorgnette, monocle, opera-glasses, pince-nez, specs *colloq*, spectacles

glassy *adj* **1** *a glassy surface*: clear, crystal clear, glasslike, glossy, icy, mirrorlike, polished, shiny, slippery, smooth, transparent **2** *a glassy stare*: blank, cold, dazed, deadpan, dull, empty, expressionless, fixed, glazed, lifeless, unmoving, vacant, vacuous

glaze *v* burnish, coat, cover, enamel, gloss, lacquer, polish, varnish
♦ *n* coat, coating, enamel, finish, gloss, lacquer, lustre, polish, shine, varnish

gleam *n* beam, brightness, flare, flash, flicker, glimmer, glint, glitter, gloss, glow, lustre, ray, shaft, shimmer, sparkle
♦ *v* beam, flare, flash, glance, glimmer, glint, glisten, glitter, glow, radiate, scintillate, shimmer, shine, sparkle

glean *v* accumulate, amass, collect, cull, find out, garner, gather, harvest, learn, pick (up), reap, select

glee *n* cheerfulness, delight, elation, exhilaration, exuberance, exultation, fun, gaiety, gladness, gratification, hilarity, jocularity, jollity, joviality, joy, joyfulness, joyousness *formal*, liveliness, merriment, mirth, pleasure, triumph, verve

gleeful *adj* beside yourself, cheerful, cock-a-hoop *colloq*, delighted, elated, exuberant, exultant, gratified, happy, jovial, joyful, joyous *formal*, jubilant, merry, mirthful, over the moon *colloq*, overjoyed, pleased, triumphant
▪ sad

glib *adj* easy, facile, fluent, gabby *colloq*, gassy *colloq*, insincere, loquacious *formal*, plausible, quick, ready, silver-tongued, slick, smooth, smooth-talking, smooth-tongued, suave, talkative, voluble *formal*, with the gift of the gab *colloq*
▪ implausible, tongue-tied

glide *v* coast, drift, float, flow, fly, move smoothly/effortlessly, pass, roll, run, sail, skate, skim, slide, slip

glimmer *v* blink, flash, flicker, gleam, glisten, glitter, glow, shimmer, shine, sparkle, twinkle, wink
♦ *n* **1** *the glimmer of lights*: flash, flicker, gleam, glint, glow, ray, shimmer, shine, sparkle, twinkle **2** *a glimmer of hope*: flicker, grain, hint, inkling, ray, suggestion, trace

glimpse *n* glance, look, peek, peep, quick/brief look, sight, sighting, squint, view
♦ *v* catch sight of, espy, see, sight, spot, spy, view

glint *v* flash, gleam, glimmer, glisten, glitter, reflect, scintillate, shimmer, shine, sparkle, twinkle
♦ *n* flash, gleam, glimmer, glistening, glitter, reflection, shimmer, shine, sparkle, twinkle

glisten *v* coruscate *formal*, flash, flicker, gleam, glimmer, glint, glitter, shimmer, shine, sparkle, twinkle

glitter *v* coruscate *formal*, dazzle, flash, flicker, gleam, glimmer, glint, glisten, scintillate, shimmer, shine, spangle, sparkle, twinkle
♦ *n* **1** *the glitter of their jewels*: brightness, brilliance, coruscation *formal*, flash, flicker, gleam, glimmer, glint, lustre, radiance, scintillation, sheen, shimmer, shine, sparkle, splendour, twinkle **2** *an evening of glamour and glitter*: flashiness, glamour, glitz *colloq*, razzle-dazzle *colloq*, razzmatazz *colloq*, showiness, tinsel

gloat *v* boast, crow, delight in, exult, glory, rejoice, relish, revel in, rub it in *colloq*, triumph, vaunt

global *adj* **1** *a global business*: international, universal, worldwide **2** *a global report*: all-encompassing, all-inclusive, comprehensive, encyclopedic, exhaustive, general, thorough, total, wide-ranging
▪ **1** parochial **2** limited

globe *n* **1** *a wooden globe*: ball, orb, round, sphere **2** *all over the globe*: earth, planet, world

globular *adj* ball-shaped, globate, orbicular *formal*, round, spherical, spheroid *formal*

globule *n* ball, bead, bubble, drop, droplet, globulet, particle, pearl, pellet, vesicle *technical*, vesicula

gloom *n* **1** *sitting in the gloom of the evening*: blackness, cloud, cloudiness, dark, darkness, dimness, dullness, dusk, murkiness, obscurity, shade, shadow, twilight **2** *he was sunk in gloom*: dejection, depression, desolation, despair, despondency, glumness, grief, hopelessness, low spirits, melancholy, misery, pessimism, sadness, sorrow, the blues *colloq*, unhappiness, woe
▪ **1** brightness **2** cheerfulness, happiness

gloomy *adj* **1** *a gloomy corner of the garden*: crepuscular *formal*, dark, dim, dingy, dismal, dreary, dull, obscure, overcast, shadowy, sombre, tenebrous *formal*, unlit **2** *feeling sad and gloomy*: cheerless, dejected, depressed, desolate, despondent, disconsolate *formal*, dismal, dispirited, down, down in the dumps *colloq*, downcast, downhearted, glum, in low spirits, low, melancholy, miserable, morose, pessimistic, sad, sorrowful **3** *painted a gloomy picture of his life*: cheerless, depressing, desolate, dismal, drear, dreary, melancholy, miserable, pessimistic, sad
▪ **1** bright **2** cheerful, happy **3** cheerful, happy

glorify *v* **1** *glorify God*: adore, bless, exalt, extol, honour, laud *formal*, magnify, praise, revere, sanctify, thank, venerate *formal*, worship **2** *glorify violence/war*: celebrate, elevate, enshrine, eulogize *formal*, hail, idolize, immortalize, lionize, magnify, panegyrize, romanticize
▪ **1** denounce, vilify *formal*

glorious *adj* **1** *our glorious history*: celebrated, distinguished, eminent, excellent, famed, famous, grand, great, honoured, illustrious, magnificent, majestic, noble, noted, renowned, splendid, supreme, triumphant, victorious **2** *a glorious shade of pink*: beautiful, dazzling, delightful, excellent, gorgeous, great *colloq*, heavenly, marvellous, perfect, splendid, super *colloq*, superb, terrific *colloq*, wonderful **3** *glorious weather*: bright, brilliant, fine, radiant, shining
▪ **1** unknown

glory *n* **1** *brought glory on the team*: acclaim, accolade, celebrity, distinction, eminence, fame, greatness, honour, illustriousness, kudos, prestige, recognition, renown, triumph **2** *to the glory of God*: adoration, blessing, exaltation, gratitude, homage, praise, thanksgiving, tribute, veneration, worship **3** *restoring the house to its former glory*: beauty, brightness, brilliance, dignity, grandeur, impressiveness, magnificence, majesty, pomp, radiance, resplendence, splendour
♦ *v* boast, crow, delight, exult, gloat, pride yourself, rejoice, relish, revel, triumph

gloss¹ *n* **1** *polished to a high gloss*: brightness, brilliance, gleam, lustre, polish, sheen, shimmer, shine, sparkle, varnish **2** *a gloss of good manners*: appearance, camouflage, disguise, façade, front, mask, semblance, show, surface, veil, veneer, window-dressing
▶ **gloss over** avoid, camouflage, conceal, cover up, deal with quickly, disguise, draw a veil over, evade, explain away, hide, ignore, mask, smooth over, veil, whitewash

gloss² *n* annotation, comment, commentary, definition, elucidation *formal*, explanation, explication *formal*, footnote, interpretation, note,

scholion *formal*, translation
♦ *v* add glosses to, annotate, comment, construe, define, elucidate *formal*, explain, interpret, translate

glossy *adj* bright, brilliant, burnished, enamelled, glassy, glazed, gleaming, lustrous, polished, sheeny, shimmering, shining, shiny, silky, sleek, smooth, sparkling
🔁 matt

glove *n* gage, gauntlet, mitt, mitten, mousquetaire glove, oven glove

glow *n* 1 *the glow of the fire*: brightness, brilliance, gleam, glimmer, incandescence *formal*, light, luminosity *formal*, phosphorescence *technical*, radiance, richness, splendour, vividness 2 *he felt a warm glow in his stomach*: ardour, enthusiasm, excitement, fervour, happiness, intensity, passion, satisfaction, warmth 3 *a glow in her cheeks*: blush, burning, flush, pinkness, reddening, redness, rosiness
♦ *v* 1 *her eyes glowed*: burn, gleam, glimmer, radiate, shine, smoulder 2 *their faces glowed*: blush, colour, flush, grow/look pink, redden

glower *v* frown, give someone a dirty look *colloq*, glare, look daggers *colloq*, scowl, stare
♦ *n* black look *colloq*, dirty look *colloq*, frown, glare, look, scowl, stare

glowing *adj* 1 *glowing embers*: bright, flaming, flushed, incandescent *formal*, luminous, phosphorescent *technical*, red, rich, ruddy, smouldering, vibrant, vivid, warm 2 *a glowing review*: complimentary, ecstatic, enthusiastic, eulogistic *formal*, favourable, laudatory *formal*, panegyrical *formal*, rave *colloq*, rhapsodic
🔁 1 colourless, dull 2 restrained

glue *n* adhesive, cement, fixative, gum, mortar, paste, size
♦ *v* affix, agglutinate *formal*, bond, cement, fix, gum, paste, seal, stick

gluey *adj* adhesive, glutinous *formal*, gummy, sticky, viscid, viscous

glum *adj* churlish, crabbed, crestfallen, dejected, depressed, despondent, doleful, down *colloq*, down in the dumps *colloq*, forlorn, gloomy, gruff, grumpy, ill-humoured, low *colloq*, miserable, moody, morose, pessimistic, sad, sour, sulky, sullen, surly, unhappy
🔁 ecstatic, happy

glut *n* excess, overabundance, overflow, saturation, superabundance, superfluity, surfeit, surplus
🔁 lack, scarcity
♦ *v* choke, clog, cram, deluge, fill, flood, gorge, inundate, overfeed, overload, oversupply, sate, satiate, saturate, stuff

glutinous *adj* adhesive, cohesive, gluey, gummy, mucilaginous *formal*, mucous, sticky, viscid *formal*, viscous

glutton *n* gobbler, gorger *colloq*, gormandizer, gourmand, greedy guts *colloq*, guzzler *colloq*, overeater, pig *colloq*
🔁 ascetic

gluttonous *adj* edacious *formal*, esurient *formal*, gluttonish, gourmandizing, greedy, gutsy *colloq*, hoggish *colloq*, insatiable, omnivorous *formal*, piggish *colloq*, rapacious *formal*, ravenous, voracious
🔁 abstemious, ascetic

gluttony *n* edacity *formal*, esurience *formal*, gourmandise, gourmandism, greed, greediness, insatiability, piggishness *colloq*, voracity
🔁 abstinence, asceticism

gnarled *adj* bumpy, contorted, distorted, gnarly, knotted, knotty, leathery, lumpy, rough, rugged, twisted, weather-beaten, wrinkled

gnash *v* grate, grind, grit, scrape

gnaw *v* 1 *gnawing on a bone*: bite, chew, consume, crunch, devour, eat, erode, masticate *formal*, munch, nibble, wear 2 *worry about losing her job had been gnawing at her for weeks*: fret, harass, harry, haunt, nag, niggle, plague, prey, torment, trouble, worry

go *v* 1 *it's time to go*: begin, depart, disappear, go away, leave, make tracks *colloq*, melt away, quit *colloq*, repair *formal*, retreat, scat *colloq*, scoot *colloq*, scram *colloq*, set off, set out, start, take your leave, vanish, withdraw 2 *this car goes really fast*: advance, drive, journey, leave, move, proceed, progress, travel, walk 3 *set the machine going*: act, be in working order, function, operate, perform, run, work 4 *the road goes as far as Leeds*: continue, extend, lead, reach, span, spread, stretch, unfold 5 *time goes quickly*: elapse, go by, lapse, pass, proceed, roll on, slip away, tick away 6 *go mad*: be changed into, become, come to be, get, grow, turn 7 *the machine goes 'beep'*: emit, give off, make a sound, release, send out, sound 8 *the books go here*: be found, be located, be situated, belong, fit in, have as its usual place 9 *the interview went well*: end up, eventuate *formal*, fare, manage, occur, pan out *colloq*, proceed, progress, result, turn out, work out 10 *where does all the money go?*: be consumed, be exhausted, be finished, be spent, be used up 11 *100 jobs will go*: be axed *colloq*, be discarded, be dismissed, be fired *colloq*, be given their cards *colloq*, be got rid of, be made redundant, be sacked *colloq*, be shown the door *colloq*, be thrown away 12 *most of the income goes on rent*: be allotted to, be assigned to, be awarded to, be given to, be spent on
🔁 1 stay 2 stop 3 break down, fail
♦ *n* 1 *have a go*: attempt, bash *colloq*, bid, effort, endeavour, shot *colloq*, stab *colloq*, try, turn, whirl *colloq* 2 *she's always full of go*: animation, dynamism, energy, force, get-up-and-go *colloq*, life, pizzazz *colloq*, push *colloq*, spirit, vigour, vitality

▶ **go about** address, approach, attend to, begin, do, engage in, perform, set about, tackle, undertake

▶ **go ahead** advance, begin, carry on, continue, make progress, move, proceed, progress

▶ **go along with** abide by, accept, agree with, comply with *formal*, concur with *formal*, follow, obey, support

▶ **go around** be passed round, be spread around, be talked about, circulate, go about

▶ **go away** abscond, depart, disappear, get knotted *colloq*, leave, retreat, sling your hook *colloq*, vanish, withdraw

▶ **go back** backslide, retreat, return, revert

▶ **go back on** break your promise, change your mind, default on, deny, renege on

▶ **go by** 1 *as time went by*: elapse, flow, lapse, pass 2 *go by the rules*: comply with *formal*, follow, heed, obey, observe

▶ **go down** 1 *prices have gone down*: be reduced, collapse, decline, decrease, descend, drop, fall 2 *as the sun went down*: drop, fall, set, sink 3 *the* area has really gone down: decline, degenerate, deteriorate, fail, founder, go under **4** *the team went down 2-0*: be beaten, be defeated, come a cropper *colloq*, fail, lose, suffer defeat **5** *the play went down badly*: be met, be reacted to, be received

▶ **go for 1** *I'd go for the blue one*: admire, aim for, choose, enjoy, favour, like, prefer, select **2** *the dog just went for her*: assail, assault, attack, lunge at, rush at, set about

▶ **go in for 1** *go in for a new hobby*: adopt, embrace, engage in, espouse *formal*, follow, practise, pursue, take up, undertake **2** *go in for a competition*: enter, go into, participate in, take part in

▶ **go into** analyse, check out, consider, delve into, discuss, dissect, examine, inquire into, investigate, look into, probe, research, review, scrutinize, study

▶ **go off 1** *she went off this morning*: abscond, depart, disappear, leave, quit *colloq*, set out, vanish **2** *a bomb went off*: be discharged, be fired, blast, blow up, burst, detonate, explode, go bang *colloq* **3** *the milk has gone off*: deteriorate, go bad, go stale, rot, sour, turn

▶ **go on 1** *the work went on*: carry on, continue, endure, last, persist, proceed, remain, stay **2** *always going on about some band or other*: chatter, gab *colloq*, gas *colloq*, natter *colloq*, rabbit *colloq*, ramble on, talk the hind legs off a donkey *colloq*, witter *colloq*

▶ **go out 1** *went out by the back door*: depart, exit, leave, withdraw **2** *go out with a boy*: court, date, go steady *colloq*, go with, see each other

▶ **go over** check, discuss, examine, inspect, list, look over, peruse, read, rehearse, repeat, review, revise, scan, study, think about

▶ **go through 1** *I shudder to think what he's been through*: be subjected to, bear, endure, experience, stand, suffer, tolerate, undergo, withstand **2** *went through the evidence*: check, examine, explore, hunt, investigate, look through, search **3** *went through all their money*: consume, exhaust, get through, spend, squander, use up

▶ **go together** accord *formal*, blend, complement, co-ordinate, fit, harmonize, match, suit

▶ **go under 1** *the business went under*: close down, collapse, default, die, fail, flop *colloq*, fold *colloq*, founder, go bankrupt, go bust *colloq*, go out of business, go to the wall *colloq* **2** *the stricken ship slowly went under*: drown, founder, go down, sink, submerge, succumb

▶ **go with 1** *that bag goes with your suit*: blend, complement, co-ordinate, correspond, fit, harmonize, match, suit **2** *I went with her to the hospital*: accompany, escort, take, usher **3** *the health problems that go with obesity*: happen with, occur with, take place with

▶ **go without** abstain, deny yourself, do without, forgo, lack, manage without, want

goad *v* annoy, arouse, drive, harass, hound, impel, incite, induce, inspire, instigate, irritate, jolt, motivate, nag, pressurize, prick, prod, prompt, provoke, push, spur, stimulate, taunt, urge, vex

go-ahead *n* agreement, approval, assent, authorization, clearance, confirmation, consent, green light *colloq*, OK *colloq*, permission, sanction, thumbs-up *colloq*, warranty

🔁 ban, embargo, veto

♦ *adj* aggressive, ambitious, dynamic, energetic, enterprising, forward, forward-looking, go-getting *colloq*, opportunist, pioneering, progressive, pushy *colloq*, up-and-coming, vigorous

🔁 sluggish, unenterprising

goal *n* aim, ambition, aspiration, design, end, ideal, intention, mark, object, objective, purpose, target

gobble *v* bolt, consume, cram, devour, gorge, gulp, guzzle, put away *colloq*, scoff *colloq*, stuff, swallow, wolf *colloq*

gobbledygook *n* balderdash, buzz words, computerese, drivel, jargon, journalese, nonsense, prattle, psychobabble, rubbish, twaddle

go-between *n* agent, broker, contact, dealer, factor, intermediary, liaison, mediator, medium, messenger, middleman

goblin *n* bogey, brownie, demon, elf, fiend, gnome, gremlin, hobgoblin, imp, kelpie, kobold, nixie, red-cap, spirit, sprite

God *n* Allah, Almighty, Brahma, Creator, Deity, Divine Being, Eternal, Everlasting, Father, Godhead, Holy One, Jehovah, Judge, King, Lord, Maker, prime mover, Providence, Saviour, Supreme Being, Yahweh, Zeus

god, goddess *n* deity, divine being, divinity, graven image, icon, idol, power, spirit

God-forsaken *adj* abandoned, bleak, depressing, deserted, desolate, dismal, dreary, forlorn, gloomy, isolated, lonely, miserable, remote, wretched

godless *adj* agnostic, atheistic, bad, evil, faithless, heathen, impious, irreligious, irreverent, nullifidian *formal*, pagan, profane, sacrilegious, sinful, ungodly, unholy, unrighteous, wicked

🔁 godly, pious

godlike *adj* celestial, deiform *formal*, divine, exalted, heavenly, holy, perfect, sacred, saintly, sublime, superhuman, theomorphic *formal*, transcendent

godly *adj* believing, devout, God-fearing, good, holy, innocent, moral, pious, pure, religious, righteous, saintly, virtuous

🔁 godless, impious

godsend *n* benediction, blessing, bonanza, boon, miracle, stroke of luck, windfall

🔁 blow, setback

goggle *v* gawk *colloq*, gawp *colloq*, gaze, stare, wonder

going-over *n* **1** *the doctor gave him a thorough going-over*: analysis, check, check-up, examination, inspection, investigation, review, scrutiny, study, survey **2** *the headmaster gave him a real going-over*: beating, castigation *formal*, chastisement *formal*, chiding, criticism, dressing-down *colloq*, pasting, rebuke, reprimand, row, scolding, thrashing, trouncing *colloq*, whipping

goings-on *n* activities, affair, business, events, funny business *colloq*, happenings, misbehaviour, mischief, occurrences, scenes

gold *n* bar, bullion, ingot, nugget, precious metal

golden *adj* **1** *golden hair*: blond(e), bright, brilliant, dazzling, fair, flaxen, gilded, gilt,

gleaming, gold, gold-coloured, lustrous,
resplendent *formal*, shining, yellow **2** *a golden
period*: auspicious *formal*, bright, delightful,
excellent, favourable, flourishing, glorious,
happy, joyful, precious, promising, propitious
formal, prosperous, rewarding, rosy, successful,
treasured

golf club

Types of golf club include:
driver, brassie, spoon, wood, iron, driving
iron, midiron, midmashie, mashie iron,
mashie, spade mashie, mashie niblick,
pitching niblick, niblick, putter, pitching
wedge, sand wedge

gone *adj* **1** *found his wife was gone*: absent, astray,
away, departed, disappeared, lost, missing,
vanished **2** *all the money was gone*: done, elapsed,
finished, lost, missing, over, over and done with
colloq, spent, used **3** *now that her mother was gone*:
dead, defunct, departed, extinct

goo *n* crud *slang*, grease, grime, grot *colloq*,
grunge *slang*, gunge *colloq*, gunk *slang*, matter,
mire, muck, mud, ooze, scum, slime, sludge,
slush, stickiness, yuck *colloq*

good *adj* **1** *do good work*: acceptable, adequate,
commendable, excellent, exceptional, fine, first-
class, first-rate, great *colloq*, passable, reasonable,
satisfactory, satisfying, superb, superior,
tolerable **2** *have a good day*: agreeable, cheerful,
desirable, enjoyable, exceptional, fantastic, fine,
great *colloq*, marvellous, nice, pleasant, pleasing,
pleasurable, super *colloq*, superb, terrific,
wonderful **3** *good at her job*: able, accomplished,
adept, brilliant, capable, clever, competent,
dependable, dexterous, efficient, expert, fit,
gifted, professional, proficient, reliable, skilful,
skilled, talented **4** *a good neighbour*: altruistic,
benevolent, charitable, considerate, friendly,
gracious, kind, kind-hearted, philanthropic,
sympathetic, well-disposed **5** *a good Christian*:
admirable, ethical, exemplary, honest,
honourable, moral, noble, righteous, salt of the
earth *colloq*, trustworthy, upright, virtuous,
worthy **6** *good luck*: advantageous, appropriate,
auspicious *formal*, beneficial, convenient,
favourable, fitting, fortunate, helpful, lucky,
profitable, propitious *formal*, suitable, useful,
worthwhile **7** *a good little girl*: compliant *formal*,
good as gold *colloq*, obedient, polite, respectful,
under control, well-behaved, well-mannered
8 *in good health*: fine, fit as a fiddle *colloq*, hale and
hearty, healthy, in the pink *colloq*, sound, strong,
the picture of health *colloq*, vigorous **9** *a good
reason*: genuine, right, sensible, sound, valid
10 *be good friends*: best, bosom, close, dear,
intimate, loving **11** *give it a good clean*: complete,
considerable, large, sizeable, substantial,
thorough, whole
€ **1** poor **2** bad **3** incompetent **4** inconsiderate,
unkind **5** immoral, wicked **6** inconvenient,
useless **7** disobedient, naughty **8** poor **9** bad
♦ *n* **1** *struggle between good and evil*: ethics,
goodness, honesty, honour, integrity, morality,
morals, rectitude *formal*, right, righteousness,
uprightness, virtue **2** *it's no good complaining*:
advantage, avail, gain, merit, profit, purpose,
service, use, usefulness, worth **3** *for your own
good*: behalf, benefit, convenience, interest, sake,

welfare, well-being
♦ *interj* agreed, all right, fine, indeed, just so, OK
colloq, perfect, right, very well

goodbye *interj* adieu, all the best *colloq*, au
revoir, auf Wiedersehen, be seeing you *colloq*,
bye *colloq*, bye-bye *colloq*, cheerio *colloq*, cheers
colloq, ciao, farewell, have a nice day *colloq*,
mind how you go *colloq*, see you (later) *colloq*,
see you around *colloq*, so long *colloq*, take care
colloq, ta-ta *colloq*
♦ *n* adieu, au revoir, farewell, leave-taking,
parting, swan song, valediction *formal*

good-for-nothing *adj* feckless *formal*, idle,
indolent *formal*, irresponsible, lazy, no-good,
profligate *formal*, reprobate, useless, worthless
€ conscientious, successful
♦ *n* black sheep *colloq*, bum *slang*, idler,
layabout, lazy-bones *colloq*, loafer *colloq*,
ne'er-do-well, profligate *formal*, reprobate,
waster, wastrel
€ achiever, success, winner

good-humoured *adj* affable, amiable,
approachable, cheerful, congenial, friendly,
genial, good-tempered, happy, jovial, pleasant
€ ill-humoured

good-looking *adj* attractive, beautiful, comely
old use, fair, handsome, lovely, personable,
presentable, pretty
€ plain, ugly

goodly *adj* ample, considerable, good, large,
significant, sizeable, substantial, sufficient, tidy
colloq
€ inadequate

good-natured *adj* approachable, benevolent,
friendly, generous, gentle, good-tempered,
helpful, kind, kind-hearted, kindly,
neighbourly, patient, sympathetic, tolerant,
warm-hearted
€ ill-natured

goodness *n* altruism, beneficence *formal*,
benefit, benevolence, compassion, excellence,
friendliness, generosity, goodwill, graciousness,
helpfulness, honesty, integrity, kindness, mercy,
probity *formal*, rectitude *formal*, righteousness,
unselfishness, uprightness, virtue,
wholesomeness
€ badness, selfishness, wickedness

goods *n* **1** *all his worldly goods*: accoutrements
formal, appurtenances *formal*, belongings,
chattels, effects, gear *colloq*, paraphernalia,
possessions, property, stuff *colloq*, things **2** *the
goods have already been shipped*: commodities,
freight, lines, merchandise, products, stock,
things, wares

goodwill *n* amity *formal*, benevolence,
compassion, favour, friendliness, friendship,
generosity, kindness, zeal
€ ill-will

goody-goody *adj* pious, priggish,
sanctimonious, self-righteous, ultra-virtuous
formal, unctuous *formal*

gooey *adj* **1** *a gooey mess*: gluey, glutinous, gungy
colloq, mucilaginous *formal*, soft, sticky, syrupy,
tacky, thick, viscid *formal*, viscous **2** *gooey love
stories*: maudlin, mawkish, nauseating,
sentimental, sloppy, slushy, syrupy

gore *v* impale, penetrate, pierce, spear, stab,
stick, wound

♦ *n* blood, bloodiness, bloodshed, butchery, carnage, cruor *technical*, grume, slaughter

gorge *n* abyss, canyon, chasm, cleft, crevice, defile, fissure, gap, gully, pass, ravine, rift
♦ *v* bolt, cram, devour, feed, fill, glut, gobble, gulp, guzzle, overeat, sate, stuff, surfeit, swallow, wolf *colloq*
Fa fast

gorgeous *adj* 1 *gorgeous tapestries*: brilliant, dazzling, delightful, enjoyable, fine, glamorous, glorious, good, grand, impressive, lovely, luxurious, magnificent, marvellous, opulent *formal*, pleasing, resplendent, rich, showy, splendid, sumptuous, superb, wonderful 2 *a gorgeous blonde*: attractive, beautiful, fine, glamorous, good-looking, handsome, lovely, pretty, pulchritudinous *formal*, ravishing *colloq*, sexy *colloq*, stunning *colloq*, sweet
Fa 1 dull, plain

gory *adj* blood-soaked, bloodstained, bloody, brutal, grisly, murderous, sanguinary *formal*, savage, violent

gospel *n* 1 *the gospel according to Mark*: good news, life of Christ, message of Christ, New Testament, teaching of Christ 2 *spread the gospel of Christianity*: credo, creed, doctrine, evangel *formal*, kerygma *technical*, teaching 3 *take something as gospel*: certainty, fact, truth, verity *formal*

gossamer *adj* airy, cobwebby, delicate, diaphanous *formal*, fine, flimsy, gauzy, insubstantial, light, see-through, sheer, shimmering, silky, thin, translucent, transparent
Fa heavy, opaque, thick

gossip *n* 1 *a magazine full of celebrity gossip*: chitchat, hearsay, idle talk, mud-slinging *colloq*, prattle, report, rumour, scandal, smear campaign *colloq*, tittle-tattle, whisper 2 *he's such a gossip*: babbler, blether, busybody, chatterbox, gossip-monger, nosey parker *colloq*, prattler, scandalmonger, talebearer, tattler, tell-tale, whisperer
♦ *v* babble, blather, blether, chat, chatter, chew the rag/fat *colloq*, chinwag *colloq*, gabble, gas *colloq*, jabber *colloq*, jaw *colloq*, natter, prattle, rabbit (on) *colloq*, rumour, spread gossip, spread/circulate a rumour, talk, tattle, tell tales, waffle *colloq*, whisper

gouge *v* chisel, claw, cut, dig, extract, gash, groove, hack, hollow, incise, scoop, score, scratch, slash

gourmand *n* glutton, gorger *colloq*, gormandizer, guzzler *colloq*, hog *colloq*, omnivore *formal*, pig *colloq*
Fa ascetic

gourmet *n* bon vivant, connoisseur, epicure, epicurean, foodie *colloq*, gastronome

govern *v* 1 *govern a country*: administer, be in charge of, be in power, be responsible for, command, conduct, control, direct, guide, head, hold office, influence, lead, manage, order, oversee, pilot, preside, reign, rule, steer, superintend, supervise 2 *govern your temper*: bridle, check, constrain, contain, control, curb, discipline, dominate, hold/keep back, keep in check, master, quell, regulate, rein in, restrain, subdue, tame

governess *n* companion, duenna, gouvernante *old use*, guide, instructress, mentor, teacher, tutoress, tutress

governing *adj* commanding, controlling, dominant, dominative *formal*, guiding, leading, overriding, predominant, prevailing, regulatory, reigning, ruling, supreme, transcendent, uppermost

government *n* 1 *blame the government*: administration, authorities, cabinet, congress, council, Establishment, executive, leadership, ministry, parliament, powers that be *colloq*, régime, state 2 *the party in government*: authority, charge, command, control, direction, domination, dominion, guidance, management, power, regulation, restraint, rule, sovereignty, superintendence, supervision, surveillance, sway

> **Government systems include:**
> absolutism, autocracy, commonwealth, communism, democracy, despotism, dictatorship, empire, federation, hierocracy, junta, kingdom, monarchy, plutocracy, puppet government, republic, theocracy, triumvirate. See also **parliaments and political assemblies**

governor *n* administrator, boss *colloq*, chief, commander, commissioner, controller, director, executive, guide, head, leader, manager, master, overseer, president, regulator, ruler, superintendent, supervisor, viceroy, warden

gown *n* costume, dress, dressing-gown, frock, garb *colloq*, garment, habit, robe

grab *v* 1 *grabbed him by the shoulder*: catch, catch/take/lay hold of, clutch, collar *colloq*, grasp, grip, seize, snatch 2 *grabbed the best seats*: annex, appropriate *formal*, bag *colloq*, capture, commandeer, nab *colloq*, nail *colloq*, seize, snap up, snatch, swipe *colloq*, take, usurp
♦ *n* capture, catch, clutch, grasp, grip, snatch

grace *n* 1 *her natural grace*: attractiveness, beauty, breeding, charm, consideration, courtesy, cultivation, decency, decorum, ease, elegance, etiquette, finesse, fluency, good taste, gracefulness, loveliness, manners, poise, polish, propriety *formal*, refinement, shapeliness, smoothness, tastefulness 2 *divine grace*: beneficence *formal*, benevolence, charity, clemency *formal*, compassion, consideration, favour, forgiveness, generosity, goodness, goodwill, indulgence, kindliness, kindness, leniency, mercifulness, mercy, pardon, quarter, reprieve, virtue 3 *say grace*: benediction, blessing, prayer, thanksgiving
Fa 2 cruelty, harshness
♦ *v* adorn, decorate, dignify, distinguish, embellish, enhance, enrich, favour, garnish, honour, ornament, set off, trim
Fa detract from, spoil

graceful *adj* 1 *a graceful movement*: agile, appealing, attractive, beautiful, deft, easy, elegant, flowing, fluid, natural, nimble, slender, smooth, supple 2 *a graceful apology*: charming, cultivated, cultured, dignified, fine, polished, refined, suave, tasteful
Fa 1 awkward, clumsy, graceless, ungainly
2 awkward, graceless

graceless *adj* 1 *graceless dancing*: awkward, barbarous, clumsy, forced, gawky, inelegant,

shameless, unattractive, ungainly, ungraceful **2** *a graceless manner:* coarse, crude, gauche, ill-mannered, impolite, improper, indecorous *formal*, inelegant, rough, rude, uncouth, unmannerly, unsophisticated, vulgar
1 graceful **2** refined

gracious *adj* **1** *a gracious smile:* accommodating, beneficent *formal*, benevolent, charitable, clement, compassionate, considerate, courteous, forgiving, friendly, generous, hospitable, indulgent, kind, kind-hearted, kindly, lenient, magnanimous, merciful, mild, obliging, pleasant, polite, refined, sweet, well-mannered **2** *set in gracious surroundings:* comfortable, elegant, luxurious, sumptuous, tasteful
1 ungracious

gradation *n* arrangement, array *formal*, change, degree, grading, level, mark, ordering, progress, progression, rank, sequence, series, shading, sorting, stage, step, succession

grade *n* category, class, classification, condition, degree, echelon *formal*, group, level, mark, notch, order, place, position, quality, rank, rating, rung, size, stage, standard, standing, station, status, step, type
♦ *v* arrange, assess, brand, categorize, class, classify, evaluate, group, label, mark, order, pigeonhole, range, rank, rate, size, sort, type, value

gradient *n* acclivity *formal*, bank, declivity *formal*, grade, hill, incline, rise, slope

gradual *adj* continuous, easy, even, gentle, leisurely, measured, moderate, progressive, regular, slow, steady, step-by-step, unhurried
precipitate, steep, sudden

gradually *adv* bit by bit, by degrees, cautiously, continuously, evenly, gently, gingerly, imperceptibly, inch by inch, little by little, moderately, piecemeal, progressively, regularly, slowly, steadily, step by step, successively

graduate *v* **1** *graduate from medical school:* complete studies, pass, qualify **2** *a graduated reading scheme:* arrange, calibrate, categorize, classify, grade, group, mark off, measure out, order, proportion, range, rank, sort **3** *graduated from being a clerk to running the department:* advance, be promoted, go/forge ahead, make headway, move forward, move up, progress
♦ *n* alumna, alumnus, bachelor, consultant, doctor, expert, fellow, graduand, master, member, professional, qualified/skilled person, specialist, valedictorian, whizz kid *colloq*

graft[1] *v* affix *formal*, engraft, implant, insert, join, splice, transplant
♦ *n* bud, growth, implant, implantation, scion, shoot, splice, sprout, transplant

graft[2] *n* **1** *several years of hard graft:* effort, hard work, labour, slog *colloq*, sweat of your brow *colloq*, toil **2** *an administration charged with graft:* bribery, con tricks *colloq*, corruption, dirty tricks/dealings *colloq*, dishonesty, extortion, rip-off *colloq*, scam *slang*, shady business *colloq*, sharp practices *colloq*, sting *colloq*, wheeling and dealing *colloq*

grain *n* **1** *a grain of sand:* atom, bit, crumb, fragment, granule, mite, molecule, morsel, particle, piece, scintilla, scrap, speck **2** *a grain of truth:* hint, iota, jot, modicum, scrap, soupçon,

speck, suggestion, trace **3** *grains of corn:* barley, cereals, corn, kernel, maize, oats, rye, seed, wheat **4** *the grain of the wood:* fabric, fibre, marking, nap, pattern, surface, texture, weave

grand *adj* **1** *the grand hall:* ambitious, exalting, excellent, fine, first-rate, glorious, grandiose, imposing, impressive, large, lavish, lofty, lordly, luxurious, magnificent, majestic, monumental, noble, opulent *formal*, ostentatious, outstanding, palatial, pompous, pretentious, regal, showy, splendid, stately, striking, sublime, sumptuous, superb **2** *the grand master:* arch, chief, great, head, highest, illustrious, leading, main, pre-eminent, principal, senior, supreme **3** *have a grand day out:* cool *slang*, delightful, enjoyable, excellent, fantastic, first-rate, great *colloq*, marvellous, mega *slang*, outstanding, smashing *colloq*, splendid, super *colloq*, superb, terrific *colloq*, wicked *slang*, wonderful **4** *a grand total:* all-inclusive, complete, comprehensive, final, in full, inclusive
1 common, humble, plain, poor, simple

grandeur *n* dignity, eminence, fame, greatness, illustriousness, importance, impressiveness, lavishness, luxuriousness, magnificence, majesty, nobility, opulence *formal*, pomp, prominence, renown, splendour, state, stateliness
humbleness, lowliness, simplicity

grandfather *n* grand(d)ad, grand(d)addy, grandpa

grandiloquent *adj* bombastic, euphuistic, exaggerated, flowery, fustian, grandiloquous *formal*, high-flown, high-sounding, inflated, magniloquent *formal*, orotund *formal*, pompous, pretentious, rhetorical, swollen, turgid
plain, restrained, simple

grandiose *adj* ambitious, extravagant, flamboyant, grand, high-flown, high-sounding, imposing, impressive, lofty, magnificent, majestic, monumental, ostentatious, over-the-top *colloq*, pompous, pretentious, showy, splendid, stately, striking
unpretentious

grandmother *n* gran, grandma, granny, nan

grant *v* **1** *granted three wishes:* allocate, allot, apportion *formal*, assign, award, bestow *formal*, confer *formal*, dispense, donate, furnish *formal*, give, impart, present, provide, supply, transmit **2** *he is funny, I grant you:* accede to *formal*, accept, acknowledge, admit, agree to, allow, concede, consent to *formal*, permit, vouchsafe *formal*
1 withhold **2** deny
♦ *n* allowance, annuity, award, bequest, bursary, concession, contribution, donation, endowment, gift, honorarium, pension, scholarship, subsidy

granular *adj* crumbly, friable, grainy, granulated, gritty, lumpy, rough, sandy

granule *n* atom, bead, crumb, fragment, grain, molecule, particle, pellet, piece, scrap, seed, speck

graph *n* bar chart, bar graph, chart, curve, diagram, grid, nomogram *technical*, nomograph, pie chart, plot, scatter diagram, table

graphic *adj* **1** *a graphic account of the attack:* blow-by-blow, clear, cogent *formal*, descriptive, detailed, effective, explicit, expressive, lively, lucid, realistic, specific, striking, telling, vivid,

well-defined **2** *graphic novels*: delineative *formal*, diagrammatic, drawn, illustrative, pictorial, representational, visual
🖅 **1** impressionistic, vague

grapple *v* **1** *grappled with the man*: battle, clash, clasp, close, clutch, combat, contend, engage, fight, grab, grip, hold, lay hold of, seize, snatch, struggle, tussle, wrestle **2** *grapple with a problem*: address, confront, cope with, deal with, encounter, face, get to grips with, tackle
🖅 **1** release **2** avoid, evade

grasp *v* **1** *grasping a set of keys*: catch, clasp, clench, clutch, grab, grapple, grip, hold, lay hold of, seize, snatch **2** *grasp a concept*: apprehend *formal*, catch on, comprehend, follow, get *colloq*, latch onto, master, perceive, realize, see, take in, understand
♦ *n* **1** *a strong grasp*: clasp, clutches, command, control, dominion, embrace, grip, hold, mastery, possession, power, rule **2** *his grasp of arithmetic is poor*: apprehension, awareness, comprehension, familiarity, knowledge, mastery, perception, understanding

grasping *adj* acquisitive, avaricious *formal*, close-fisted, covetous, greedy, mean, mercenary, miserly, niggardly, parsimonious *formal*, rapacious *formal*, selfish, stingy, tight-fisted
🖅 generous

grass *n* common, downs, field, grassland, green, lawn, lea *old use*, mead *old use*, meadow, pampas, pasture, prairie, savanna, steppe, sward *old use*, turf, veld, veldt

grate *v* **1** *grated the cheese*: grind, mince, pulverize, rasp, rub, scrape, scratch, shred, triturate *formal* **2** *her voice really grates on me*: aggravate *colloq*, annoy, exasperate, gall, get on someone's nerves *colloq*, get someone's goat *colloq*, get under your skin *colloq*, irk, irritate, jar, peeve *colloq*, rankle, set your teeth on edge, vex

grateful *adj* appreciative, beholden *formal*, indebted, obligated, obliged, thankful
🖅 ungrateful

gratification *n* contentment, delight, elation, enjoyment, glee, indulgence, joy, kicks *colloq*, pleasure, relish, satisfaction, thrill
🖅 disappointment, frustration

gratify *v* **1** *gratified by the welcome*: charm, cheer, delight, gladden, make happy, please, thrill **2** *gratify a desire*: fulfil, humour, indulge, pander to, placate, satisfy
🖅 **1** frustrate **2** thwart

grating[1] *adj* **1** *a grating noise*: disagreeable, discordant, grinding, harsh, rasping, raucous, scraping, scratching, screeching, squeaky, strident **2** *a grating laugh*: annoying, disagreeable, exasperating, galling, irksome, irritating, jarring, offensive, unpleasant
🖅 **1** harmonious **2** pleasing

grating[2] *n* frame, grate, graticule *technical*, grid, grille, lattice, trellis

gratis *adv* at no cost, buckshee *slang*, complimentary, for nothing, free, free of charge, on the house *colloq*, without charge

gratitude *n* acknowledgement, appreciation, gratefulness, indebtedness, obligation, recognition, thankfulness, thanks
🖅 ingratitude, ungratefulness

gratuitous *adj* **1** *gratuitous violence*: groundless, needless, superfluous, unasked-for, uncalled-for, undeserved, unfounded, unjustified, unmerited, unnecessary, unprovoked, unsolicited, unwarranted, wanton, without reason **2** *gratuitous advice*: complimentary, for nothing, free, free of charge, gratis, unpaid, unrewarded, voluntary
🖅 **1** justified, provoked

gratuity *n* baksheesh, bonus, boon, bounty, donation, gift, largesse, perk *colloq*, perquisite *formal*, pourboire, present, recompense, reward, tip

grave[1] *n* **1** *buried in a grave*: barrow, burial mound, burial place, burial site, cairn, crypt, last resting-place, mausoleum, pit, sepulchre, tomb, tumulus, vault **2** *an early grave*: curtains *colloq*, death, decease *formal*, demise *formal*, departure, expiration *formal*, fatality, last farewell *colloq*, loss, loss of life, passing, passing away

grave[2] *adj* **1** *a grave expression*: dignified, earnest, gloomy, grim, long-faced, pensive, quiet, reserved, restrained, sedate, serious, severe, sober, solemn, sombre, staid, subdued, thoughtful **2** *a grave mistake*: acute, critical, crucial, dangerous, exigent *formal*, hazardous, important, menacing, momentous, perilous *formal*, pressing, serious, severe, significant, threatening, urgent, vital, weighty
🖅 **1** cheerful, smiling **2** light, slight, trivial

gravel *n* chesil, grail *old use*, grit, hogging, pebbles, shingle, stones

gravelly *adj* **1** *gravelly ground*: glareous *old use*, grainy, granular, gritty, pebbly, sabulose *formal*, sabulous *formal*, shingly **2** *a gravelly voice*: croaky, grating, gruff, guttural, harsh, hoarse, rough, thick, throaty
🖅 **1** fine **2** clear, velvety

gravestone *n* headstone, memorial, stone, tombstone

graveyard *n* burial ground, burial place, burial site, cemetery, charnel house *formal*, churchyard, God's acre *formal*, necropolis *formal*

gravitate *v* **1** *all the women gravitated towards him*: be attached to, be drawn to, drift, head for, incline, lean, move, tend **2** *the sediment gravitates to the bottom*: descend, drift, drop, fall, precipitate, settle, sink

gravity *n* **1** *the gravity of the charges*: acuteness, consequence, danger, exigency *formal*, hazard, importance, momentousness, peril *formal*, seriousness, severity, significance, urgency, weightiness **2** *the gravity of her expression*: dignity, earnestness, gloominess, grimness, reserve, restraint, seriousness, severity, sobriety *formal*, solemnity, sombreness, thoughtfulness **3** *force of gravity*: attraction, gravitation, heaviness, pull, weight
🖅 **1** triviality **2** levity

graze[1] *v* browse, crop, feed, fodder, pasture, ruminate *formal*

graze[2] *v* **1** *grazed his knee*: abrade *formal*, bruise, chafe, rub, scrape, scratch, skin **2** *the glider grazed the treetops*: brush, glance off, kiss, shave, skim, touch
♦ *n* abrasion, scrape, scratch

grease *n* dripping, fat, lard, lubrication, oil, tallow

greasy *adj* **1** *a greasy substance:* adipose *formal*, buttery, fatty, lardy, oily, oleaginous *formal*, oleic *formal*, sebaceous *formal*, slimy, smeary, waxy **2** *a greasy manner:* oily, oleaginous *formal*, slimy, smooth, unctuous *formal*

great *adj* **1** *a great hall:* big, boundless, colossal, enormous, extensive, gigantic, ginormous *colloq*, great big *colloq*, huge, immense, impressive, jumbo *colloq*, large, mammoth, massive, mega *slang*, spacious, vast, whopping *colloq* **2** *with great care:* considerable, excessive, extreme, inordinate, pronounced, sizeable, substantial **3** *a great novelist:* august *formal*, celebrated, distinguished, eminent, famed, famous, illustrious, notable, noted, noteworthy, outstanding, prominent, remarkable, renowned **4** *great works of art:* fine, glorious, grand, imposing, impressive, magnificent, splendid **5** *a great moment in our history:* chief, critical, crucial, essential, important, leading, main, major, momentous, paramount, primary, principal, salient, serious, significant, vital **6** *had a great time:* ace *colloq*, admirable, cool *slang*, excellent, fabulous, fantastic, first-rate, marvellous, mega *slang*, smashing *colloq*, splendid, super *colloq*, superb, terrific *colloq*, top-notch *colloq*, tremendous, wicked *slang*, wonderful **7** *a great driver:* able, accomplished, ace *colloq*, adept, brilliant, crack *colloq*, dexterous, excellent, experienced, expert, knowledgeable, masterly, practised, professional, proficient, qualified, skilful, skilled, specialist, top-notch *colloq*, up on *colloq*, virtuoso, well up on *colloq*
 1 limited, small **2** slight **3** unknown **5** insignificant, unimportant **7** amateurish, novice

greatly *adv* abundantly, considerably, enormously, exceedingly, extremely, highly, hugely, immensely, impressively, markedly, mightily, much, notably, noticeably, remarkably, significantly, substantially, tremendously, vastly

greatness *n* **1** *the leader's greatness:* distinction, eminence, excellence, fame, genius, glory, grandeur, heroism, illustriousness, importance, note, renown, significance **2** *the greatness of the task:* intensity, magnitude, momentousness, power, seriousness, significance, weight
 1 insignificance, pettiness **2** smallness

greed *n* **1** *it was pure greed eating all the cakes:* bingeing *colloq*, edacity *formal*, esurience *formal*, gluttony, gourmandism, hoggishness *colloq*, insatiability, piggishness *colloq*, ravenousness, stuffing yourself *colloq*, voracity *formal* **2** *greed for material things:* acquisitiveness, avarice *formal*, covetousness, craving, cupidity *formal*, desire, eagerness, impatience, longing, rapacity *formal*, selfishness
 1 abstemiousness, self-restraint

greedy *adj* **1** *greedy young piglets:* bingeing *colloq*, edacious *formal*, esurient *formal*, gluttonous, gormandizing, hoggish *colloq*, hungry, insatiable, omnivorous *formal*, piggish *colloq*, ravenous, starving, voracious *formal* **2** *greedy for success:* acquisitive, avaricious *formal*, covetous, craving, cupidinous *formal*, desirous, eager, grabbing,

grabby *colloq*, grasping, impatient, on the make *colloq*, rapacious *formal*, selfish
 1 abstemious

green *adj* **1** *green fields:* blooming, budding, flourishing, fresh, glaucous *formal*, grassy, healthy, leafy, lush, raw, tender, unripe, unseasoned, verdant *formal*, verdurous *formal*, vigorous, virescent *formal*, viridescent *formal* **2** *green policies:* conservationist, eco-friendly, ecological, environmental, environmentally aware, environmentally friendly **3** *too green to know what to do:* ignorant, immature, inexperienced, inexpert, naïve, new, raw, recent, simple, unqualified, unsophisticated, untrained, unversed, wet behind the ears *colloq*, young **4** *green with envy:* covetous, envious, grudging, jealous, resentful
 3 experienced, expert, mature, qualified
 ♦ *n* common, grass, grassland, lawn, meadow, pasture, turf

greenery *n* foliage, greenness, vegetation, verdancy *formal*, verdure *formal*, virescence *formal*, viridescence *formal*, viridity *formal*

greenhorn *n* apprentice, beginner, fledgling, initiate, learner, neophyte, newcomer, novice, recruit, rookie *colloq*, tenderfoot, tiro
 old hand *colloq*, veteran

greenhouse *n* conservatory, glasshouse, hothouse, orangery, pavilion, vinery

greet *v* accost, acknowledge, address, hail, kiss, meet, nod to, receive, salute, say hello to, shake hands with, wave to, welcome
 ignore

greeting *n* acknowledgement, address, hallo, handshake, nod, reception, salutation, seasonal greeting, the time of day, wave, welcome

greetings *n* best wishes, compliments, congratulations, good wishes, kind/warm regards, love, regards, respects, salutations, wishes

gregarious *adj* affable, companionable, convivial, cordial, extrovert, friendly, hospitable, outgoing, sociable, social, warm
 unsociable

grey *adj* **1** *a grey face:* ashen, colourless, leaden, neutral, pale, pallid, wan **2** *a grey morning:* bleak, cheerless, cloudy, dark, dim, dismal, dreary, dull, foggy, misty, murky, overcast **3** *a grey mood:* bleak, cheerless, colourless, depressing, dismal, dreary, dull, gloomy, uninteresting **4** *a grey area:* ambiguous, debatable, doubtful, open to question, uncertain, unclear

grid *n* frame, graticule *technical*, grating, gridiron, grill, grille, lattice, network, trellis

grief *n* affliction *formal*, agony, anguish, bereavement, dejection, depression, desolation, despair, despondency, distress, heartache, heartbreak, lamentation *formal*, misery, mourning, pain, regret, remorse, sadness, sorrow, suffering, tribulation *formal*, trouble, unhappiness, woe
 delight, happiness

grief-stricken *adj* afflicted *formal*, anguished, broken, broken-hearted, crushed, dejected, depressed, desolate, despairing, despondent, devastated, disconsolate *formal*, distressed,

grieving, heartbroken, inconsolable, mourning, overcome, overwhelmed, sad, sorrowful, sorrowing, troubled, unhappy, woebegone *formal*, wretched
F3 delighted, overjoyed

grievance *n* **1** *take your grievances to your line manager*: bone to pick *colloq*, charge, complaint, gripe *colloq*, grouse *colloq*, grumble *colloq*, moan *colloq*, objection, protest, trial, tribulation *formal*, trouble **2** *a source of grievance*: affliction *formal*, damage, hardship, injury, injustice, offence, resentment, trouble, unfairness, wrong

grieve *v* **1** *grieving for his wife*: ache, brood, cry, lament, mope, mourn, pine away, sob, sorrow, suffer, wail, weep **2** *it grieved her to do it*: afflict, break someone's heart, crush, dismay, distress, horrify, hurt, offend, pain, sadden, shock, upset, wound
F3 **1** rejoice **2** gladden, please

grievous *adj* **1** *grievous errors*: appalling, atrocious, burdensome, calamitous, damaging, deplorable, devastating, distressing, dreadful, flagrant, glaring, grave, harmful, intolerable, monstrous, outrageous, overwhelming, severe, shameful, shocking, sorrowful *formal*, tragic, unbearable **2** *grievous injuries*: afflicting *formal*, damaging, hurtful, injurious, painful, sore, wounding

grim *adj* **1** *a grim face*: depressing, dour, fierce, forbidding, formidable, gloomy, harsh, menacing, morose, severe, stern, sullen, surly, threatening, unattractive **2** *grim news from the front*: appalling, awful, dire, dreadful, fearsome, frightening, ghastly, grisly, gruesome, harrowing, horrendous, horrible, horrid, shocking, sinister, terrible, unpleasant, unspeakable **3** *grim determination*: determined, dogged, inexorable, obdurate *formal*, persistent, resolute, stubborn, tenacious, unshakable, unyielding
F3 **1** attractive **2** pleasant

grimace *n* face, frown, pout, scowl, smirk, sneer
♦ *v* frown, make a face, mouth, pout, pull a face, scowl, smirk, sneer

grime *n* crud *slang*, dirt, dust, filth, grot *colloq*, grunge *slang*, gunge *colloq*, muck, mud, soot, yuck *colloq*

grimy *adj* besmirched *formal*, dirty, dusty, filthy, grubby, mucky, muddy, smudgy, smutty, soiled, sooty, stained
F3 clean

grind *v* **1** *grind the peppercorns*: comminute *formal*, crumble, crush, granulate, grate, kibble *formal*, levigate *formal*, mill, pound, powder, pulverize, scrape, triturate *formal* **2** *grinding the knives*: abrade, file, polish, rub, sand, sharpen, smooth, whet **3** *the two pieces of metal ground together*: grate, rasp, rub, scrape
♦ *n* chore, drudgery, exertion, labour, round, routine, slavery, sweat, task, toil
▶ **grind down** afflict *formal*, crush, harass, harry, hound, oppress, persecute, plague, torment, trouble, tyrannize, wear down

grip *n* **1** *a firm grip on the rope*: clasp, clench, clutch, embrace, grasp, hold, hug **2** *the army lost its grip on the city*: clutches, command, control, domination, influence, mastery, power **3** *his*

clothes were in a small grip: bag, case, hold-all, kitbag, overnight bag, shoulder-bag, suitcase, travelling bag, valise
♦ *v* **1** *gripped her arm*: catch, clasp, clench, cling, clutch, get/catch/grab hold of, grab, grasp, hold, latch onto, seize **2** *gripped by the drama*: absorb, compel, engage, engross, enthral, entrance, fascinate, hypnotize, involve, mesmerize, rivet, spellbind, thrill

gripe *v* beef *colloq*, bellyache *colloq*, bitch *colloq*, carp *colloq*, complain, groan, grouch *colloq*, grouse *colloq*, grumble, have a bone to pick *colloq*, moan, nag, protest, whine *colloq*, whinge *colloq*
♦ *n* beef *colloq*, bitch *colloq*, complaint, grievance, griping *colloq*, groan, grouch *colloq*, grouse *colloq*, grumble, moan, objection, protest

gripping *adj* absorbing, compelling, compulsive, engrossing, enthralling, entrancing, exciting, fascinating, riveting, spellbinding, suspenseful, thrilling, unputdownable *colloq*

grisly *adj* abhorrent, abominable, appalling, awful, disgusting, dreadful, frightful, ghastly, gory, grim, gruesome, hideous, horrible, horrid, horrifying, loathsome, macabre, repulsive, revolting, shocking, terrible
F3 delightful

grit *n* **1** *a piece of grit in her eye*: dust, gravel, pebbles, sand, shingle **2** *the grit to get on with the job*: backbone *colloq*, bravery, courage, determination, doggedness, endurance, guts *colloq*, hardness, mettle, perseverance, resolution, resolve, steadfastness, strength, tenacity, toughness
♦ *v* clench, gnash, grate, grind, rasp, scrape

gritty *adj* **1** *a gritty texture*: abrasive, dusty, grainy, granular, gravelly, pebbly, powdery, rough, sabulose *formal*, sabulous *formal*, sandy, shingly **2** *gritty determination*: brave, courageous, determined, dogged, hardy, mettlesome, plucky, resolute, spirited, spunky *colloq*, steadfast, tenacious, tough
F3 **1** fine, smooth **2** cowardly, spineless *colloq*

grizzle *v* **1** *grizzling about the cold*: complain, grumble, moan, snivel, whine, whinge **2** *the baby was grizzling in her cot*: cry, fret, sniffle, snivel, snuffle, whimper, whinge

grizzled *adj* canescent *formal*, grey, grey-haired, grey-headed, greying, griseous *technical*, hoar, hoary, pepper-and-salt

groan *n* **1** *a groan of pain*: cry, lament, moan, sigh, wail, whimper, whine **2** *moans and groans about the weather*: beef *colloq*, complaint, grievance, griping *colloq*, grouch *colloq*, grouse *colloq*, grumble, moan, objection, outcry, protest
♦ *v* **1** *groaning in pain*: cry, lament, moan, sigh, wail, whimper, whine **2** *groaning about the train strike*: beef *colloq*, bellyache *colloq*, complain, grouse *colloq*, grumble, object, protest, whine *colloq*, whinge *colloq*

grocer *n* dealer, greengrocer, purveyor *formal*, storekeeper, supermarket, supplier, victualler *formal*

groggy *adj* befuddled, bewildered, confused, dazed, dizzy, dopey, faint, muzzy *colloq*, punch drunk, reeling, shaky, staggering, stunned, stupefied, unsteady, weak, wobbly, woozy *colloq*
F3 healthy, lucid, strong

groom *v* **1** *groomed himself in front of the mirror:* adjust, arrange, do, fix, neaten, prepare, put in order, smarten, smooth, spruce up, tidy (up) **2** *groomed the horses:* brush, clean, curry, dress, preen **3** *groomed for her new post:* coach, drill, educate, instruct, make ready, prepare, prime, school, teach, train, tutor
♦ *n* **1** *the bride and groom:* bridegroom, honeymooner, husband, marriage partner, newly-wed, spouse **2** *a groom at the stables:* stable hand, stable lad/lass, stableboy, stableman

groove *n* canal, chamfer, channel, cut, ditch, furrow, gouge, gutter, hollow, indentation, rabbet *technical*, rebate, ridge, rut, score, slot, sulcus, track, trench, trough

grooved *adj* chamfered, channelled, exarate *formal*, fluted, furrowed, rabbeted *technical*, rutted, scored, scrobiculate, sulcal *formal*, sulcate *formal*
F3 ridged

grope *v* **1** *groped for the light switch:* feel, flounder, fumble, pick, scrabble **2** *groping for an answer:* cast about, fish, hunt, probe, scrabble, search

gross *adj* **1** *gross misconduct:* blatant, egregious *formal*, flagrant, glaring, grievous, manifest *formal*, obvious, outrageous, outright, plain, serious, shameful, sheer, shocking, utter **2** *gross language:* bawdy, blue *colloq*, coarse, crude, dirty, earthy, filthy, improper, indecent, lewd, obscene, offensive, pornographic, ribald, risqué, rude, smutty, tasteless, vulgar **3** *I had put on weight and felt absolutely gross:* big, bulky, colossal, corpulent *formal*, fat, heavy, huge, hulking, immense, large, massive, obese, overweight **4** *the gross behaviour of the mob:* boorish, coarse, insensitive, tasteless, uncultured, unpleasant, unrefined, unsophisticated, vulgar **5** *gross earnings:* aggregate *formal*, all-inclusive, before deductions, before tax, complete, comprehensive, entire, inclusive, total, whole
F3 **2** polite **3** slight **4** tasteful **5** net
♦ *v* accumulate, aggregate *formal*, bring in, earn, make, rake in *colloq*, take, total

grotesque *adj* absurd, bizarre, deformed, distorted, extravagant, fanciful, fantastic, freakish, hideous, ludicrous, macabre, malformed, misshapen, monstrous, odd, outlandish, peculiar, ridiculous, strange, surreal, twisted, ugly, unnatural, unsightly, weird, whimsical
F3 graceful, normal

grotto *n* catacomb, cave, cavern, chamber, subterranean (chamber), underground chamber

grouch *n* **1** *he is such a grouch:* belly-acher *colloq*, complainer, crosspatch *colloq*, fault-finder, grouser, grumbler, malcontent *formal*, moaner, murmurer, mutterer, whiner *colloq*, whinger *colloq* **2** *a list of grouches against the landlord:* complaint, grievance, gripe *colloq*, grouse *colloq*, grumble, moan, objection, whinge *colloq*

grouchy *adj* bad-tempered, cantankerous *formal*, captious, churlish, complaining, cross, crotchety *colloq*, discontented, dissatisfied, grumbling, grumpy, ill-tempered, irascible, irritable, peevish, petulant, querulous *formal*, sulky, surly, testy, truculent *formal*
F3 contented

ground *n* **1** *stony ground:* bottom, clay, dirt, dry land, dust, earth, foundation, land, loam, soil, surface, terra firma, terrain **2** *a football ground:* arena, field, park, pitch, stadium **3** *the palace grounds:* acres, campus, domain, estate, fields, gardens, holding, land, park, plot, property, surroundings, terrain, territory **4** *no grounds for such harsh treatment:* account, argument, base, basis, call, cause, excuse, foundation, inducement, justification, motive, occasion, principle, reason, score, vindication **5** *coffee grounds:* deposit, dregs, lees, precipitate *technical*, residue, scourings, sediment
♦ *v* **1** *her fiction is grounded in real life:* base, establish, fix, found, set, settle **2** *grounded his students in science:* acquaint with, coach, drill, educate, familiarize with, inform, initiate, instruct, introduce, prepare, teach, train, tutor

groundless *adj* baseless, empty, false, illusory, imaginary, uncalled-for, unfounded, unjustified, unprovoked, unsubstantiated, unsupported, unwarranted, without reason
F3 justified, reasonable, well-founded

groundwork *n* base, basis, cornerstone, essentials, footing, foundation, fundamentals, homework, preliminaries, preparation, research, spadework, underpinnings

group *n* **1** *a group of people:* assembly, association, band, body, bracket, bunch, circle, class, clique, club, cluster, company, congregation, contingent, coterie, crew, crowd, detachment, faction, family, flock, gang, gathering, guild, knot, league, organization, pack, party, school, set, society, squad, team, troop, unit **2** *a group of things:* batch, body, bunch, category, class, classification, clump, cluster, collection, combination, conglomeration *formal*, element, genus, grouping, lot, pack, set, species, unit **3** *a rock group:* band, circle, company
♦ *v* **1** *we all grouped together for a family photo:* assemble, bunch, clump, cluster, collect, congregate, gather, huddle, mass **2** *group them according to size:* arrange, associate, band, bracket, categorize, class, classify, grade, line up, link, marshal, order, organize, range, rank, sort

grouse *v* beef *colloq*, bellyache *colloq*, bitch *colloq*, carp *colloq*, complain, find fault, gripe *colloq*, grouch *colloq*, grumble, moan, whine *colloq*, whinge *colloq*
F3 acquiesce
♦ *n* bellyache *colloq*, complaint, grievance, gripe *colloq*, groan, grouch *colloq*, grumble, moan, objection, protest, whine *colloq*, whinge *colloq*

grove *n* arbour, avenue, coppice, copse, covert, plantation, spinney, thicket, wood, woodland

grovel *v* **1** *had to grovel to get out of the work:* bow and scrape *colloq*, butter someone up *colloq*, cower, crawl, creep, cringe, defer, demean yourself, fawn, flatter, ingratiate yourself, kiss up to *colloq*, kowtow, lick someone's boots *colloq*, suck up *colloq*, toady **2** *grovelling in the dirt:* bow down, cower, crawl, creep, crouch, fall on your knees, kneel, lie down, lie low, prostrate yourself, stoop

grow *v* **1** *he's really grown:* become larger, become taller/bigger, broaden, deepen, develop, elongate, enlarge, expand, extend, fill out, increase in size/height, lengthen, swell, thicken, widen **2** *the shrub grew quickly:* bud, burgeon *formal,* develop, flower, germinate, mature, shoot, spring, sprout **3** *the population is growing:* develop, enlarge, escalate, expand, extend, increase, multiply, mushroom, proliferate *formal,* rise, spread, stretch, swell, wax **4** *grow cold:* become, change, come to be, develop, get, go, turn **5** *she is growing as a person:* advance, flourish, improve, make headway, progress, prosper, succeed, thrive **6** *the novel grew from a particular incident she imagined:* arise, issue, originate, spring, stem **7** *growing vegetables:* breed, cultivate, farm, harvest, plant, produce, propagate, raise, sow
F3 **1** shrink **3** decrease **5** fail

growl *v* bark, howl, roar, rumble, snap, snarl, yap, yelp

grown-up *adj* adult, full-grown, fully-developed, fully-fledged, fully-grown, mature, of age
F3 immature, young
♦ *n* adult, man, woman
F3 child

growth *n* **1** *the growth in the use of mobile phones:* advance, aggrandizement *formal,* amplification, augmentation *formal,* development, enlargement, evolution, expansion, extension, headway, improvement, increase, magnification, multiplication, progress, proliferation *formal,* prosperity, rise, spread, success **2** *the growth of the plant:* budding, burgeoning *formal,* development, flowering, germination, maturation *formal,* shooting, springing, sprouting **3** *a benign growth:* excrescence, intumescence *technical,* lump, outgrowth, protuberance, swelling, tumour
F3 **1** decline, decrease, failure

grub *v* burrow, delve, dig, excavate, explore, ferret, forage, hunt, probe, root, rummage, scour, search, uncover, unearth
♦ *n* **1** *grubs on the leaves:* caterpillar, chrysalis, larva, maggot, pupa, worm **2** *come and get some grub:* eats *colloq,* food, meals, nosh *slang,* nutrition, provision, refreshment(s), sustenance, tuck *colloq*

grubby *adj* dirty, filthy, grimy, messy, mucky, scruffy, seedy, shabby, soiled, squalid, unwashed
F3 clean

grudge *n* animosity, animus *formal,* antagonism, antipathy, aversion, bitterness, dislike, enmity, envy, grievance, hard feelings, hate, hatred, ill-will, jealousy, malevolence *formal,* malice, pique, rancour *formal,* resentment, spite, venom
F3 favour
♦ *v* be jealous of, begrudge, covet, dislike, envy, mind, object to, resent, take exception to

grudging *adj* envious, half-hearted, hesitant, jealous, reluctant, resentful, unenthusiastic, unwilling

gruelling *adj* arduous, backbreaking, crushing, demanding, difficult, draining, exhausting, grinding, hard, harsh, laborious, punishing, severe, strenuous, taxing, tiring, tough, trying
F3 easy

gruesome *adj* abhorrent, abominable, appalling, awful, disgusting, dreadful, frightful, ghastly, grim, grisly, hideous, horrible, horrid, horrific, loathsome, macabre, monstrous, repellent, repugnant, repulsive, revolting, shocking, sickening, terrible
F3 pleasant

gruff *adj* **1** *a gruff manner:* abrupt, bad-tempered, blunt, brusque, churlish, crabbed *colloq,* crotchety *colloq,* curt, discourteous, grumpy, impolite, rude, sour, sullen, surly, testy, tetchy, unfriendly **2** *a gruff voice:* croaking, guttural, harsh, hoarse, husky, rasping, rough, thick, throaty
F3 **1** courteous, friendly, polite

grumble *v* **1** *grumbling about having to go to work:* beef *colloq,* bellyache *colloq,* bleat, carp *colloq,* complain, find fault, gripe *colloq,* grouch *colloq,* moan, object, protest, whine *colloq,* whinge *colloq* **2** *his tummy was grumbling:* growl, gurgle, murmur, rumble
♦ *n* **1** *had no grumbles about the hotel:* beef *colloq,* bitch *colloq,* bleat *colloq,* complaint, grievance, gripe *colloq,* grouch *colloq,* grouse *colloq,* moan, objection, protest, whinge *colloq* **2** *a grumble of discontent:* growl, gurgle, murmur, muttering, roar, rumble

grumpy *adj* bad-tempered, cantankerous *formal,* churlish, crabbed *colloq,* cross, crotchety *colloq,* discontented, grouchy *colloq,* having got out of bed on the wrong side *colloq,* ill-tempered, in a huff *colloq,* in a sulk *colloq,* irritable, petulant, ratty *colloq,* snappy, sulky, sullen, surly, tetchy
F3 contented

guarantee *n* assurance, bond, collateral, contract, covenant, earnest *formal,* endorsement, insurance, oath, pledge, promise, security, surety, testimonial, warranty, word of honour
♦ *v* answer for, assure, back, certify, endorse, ensure, give an assurance, insure, make certain, make sure, pledge, promise, protect, provide security/collateral/surety for, secure, sponsor, support, swear, underwrite, vouch for, warrant

guarantor *n* angel *colloq,* backer, bailsman, bondsman, covenantor, guarantee, referee, sponsor, supporter, surety, underwriter, voucher, warrantor

guard *v* be alert, beware, cover, defend, escort, keep watch, look out, mind, oversee, patrol, police, preserve, protect, safeguard, save, screen, secure, shelter, shield, supervise, take care, watch
♦ *n* **1** *a guard stood at the gates:* bodyguard, conductor, custodian, defender, escort, guardian, keeper, lookout, minder *slang,* patrol, picket, protector, scout, security, sentinel, sentry, warder, watch, watchman **2** *a fire guard:* barrier, buffer, bumper, cushion, defence, fence, fender, pad, protection, safeguard, screen, shield, wall

guarded *adj* cagey *colloq,* careful, cautious, chary, circumspect *formal,* discreet, non-committal, reluctant, reserved, restrained, reticent, secretive, wary, watchful
F3 communicative, frank

guardian *n* attendant, caretaker, champion, curator, custodian, defender, escort, guard, keeper, preserver, protector, steward, trustee, warden, warder

guardianship *n* aegis *formal*, attendance, care, curatorship, custodianship, custody, defence, guard, guidance, hands, keeping, patronage, preservation, protection, safekeeping, stewardship, trust, trusteeship, tutelage, wardenship, wardship

guerrilla *n* bushwhacker, franc-tireur, freedom fighter, guerrillero, haiduck, irregular, maquisard, partisan, resistance fighter, sniper, terrorist

guess *v* assume, believe, conjecture *formal*, consider, estimate, fancy, feel, guesstimate *colloq*, hypothesize, imagine, judge, make a guess, postulate *formal*, predict, put something at, reckon, speculate, suppose, surmise *formal*, suspect, think, work out
♦ *n* **1** *made a wild guess:* ballpark figure *colloq*, conjecture *formal*, estimate, guesstimate *colloq*, prediction, shot in the dark *colloq*, speculation, supposition *formal*, surmise *formal* **2** *my guess is she'll accept the job:* assumption, belief, conjecture *formal*, fancy, feeling, hunch, hypothesis, idea, intuition, judgement, notion, opinion, prediction, reckoning, supposition *formal*, surmise *formal*, suspicion, theory

guesswork *n* assumption, conjecture, estimation, guesstimate *colloq*, hypothesis, intuition, prediction, reckoning, speculation, supposition *formal*, surmise *formal*, theory

guest *n* boarder, caller, lodger, patron, regular, resident, visitant *formal*, visitor

guesthouse *n* B & B, boarding-house, hostel, hostelry, hotel, inn, pension, rooming-house, xenodochium *formal*

guidance *n* advice, assistance, charge, control, counsel, counselling, direction, directions, guidelines, help, hint(s), indication(s), information, instruction, instructions, leadership, management, pointer(s), recommendation(s), rule, suggestion(s), teaching, tip(s)

guide *v* **1** *guided them along the path:* accompany, attend, conduct, direct, escort, hold someone's hand *colloq*, lead, manoeuvre, navigate, pilot, point, show, show the way, steer, usher **2** *guided the company:* be in charge of, command, control, direct, govern, manage, oversee, preside over, rule, superintend, supervise **3** *guided the students through the application process:* advise, counsel, educate, give directions/recommendations to, influence, instruct, teach, train
♦ *n* **1** *a guide to London:* ABC, catalogue, directory, guidebook, handbook, key, manual **2** *a tour guide:* attendant, chaperon(e), companion, conductor, courier, director, escort, helmsman, leader, navigator, pilot, ranger, steersman, usher **3** *our solicitor acted as our guide throughout:* adviser, counsellor, guru, instructor, mentor, teacher, tutor **4** *use this essay as a guide:* archetype *formal*, beacon, benchmark, criterion, example, exemplar *formal*, gauge, guideline, indication, key, mark, marker, measure, model, norm, pattern, pointer, sign, signal, signpost, standard, tombstone, yardstick

guideline *n* advice, benchmark, constraint, criterion, direction, framework, indication, information, instruction, measure, parameter, principle, procedure, recommendation,

regulation, rule, standard, suggestion, terms, touchstone, yardstick

guild *n* alliance, association, brotherhood, chapel, club, company, corporation, federation, fellowship, fraternity, incorporation, league, lodge, order, organization, society, sorority, union

guile *n* artfulness, artifice, cleverness, craft, craftiness, cunning, deceit, deception, deviousness, double-dealing, duplicity *formal*, fraud, gamesmanship, knavery, slyness, treachery, trickery, trickiness, wiliness
🗷 artlessness, guilelessness

guileless *adj* artless, candid, direct, frank, genuine, honest, ingenuous *formal*, innocent, naïve, natural, open, simple, sincere, straight, straightforward, transparent, trusting, truthful, unreserved, unsophisticated, unworldly
🗷 artful, cunning

guilt *n* **1** *he confessed his guilt:* blame, blameworthiness, criminality, culpability *formal*, disgrace, dishonour, misconduct, responsibility, unlawfulness, wrong, wrongdoing **2** *a feeling of guilt:* compunction *formal*, conscience, contrition, disgrace, dishonour, guilty conscience, penitence, regret, remorse, repentance, self-accusation, self-condemnation, self-reproach, shame
🗷 **1** innocence, righteousness **2** shamelessness

guiltless *adj* above reproach, blameless, clean, clear, faultless, immaculate, impeccable, inculpable *formal*, innocent, irreproachable, pure, sinless, spotless, stainless, unblamable, undefiled, unimpeachable, unspotted, unsullied, untainted, untarnished
🗷 guilty, tainted

guilty *adj* **1** *guilty of a crime:* at fault, blamable, blameworthy, convicted, criminal, culpable *formal*, delinquent, evil, illegal, illicit, offending, responsible, sinful, to blame, unlawful, wicked, wrong **2** *felt guilty for causing so much trouble:* ashamed, bad, compunctious *formal*, conscience-stricken, contrite, guilt-ridden, penitent, regretful, remorseful, repentant, shamefaced, sheepish, sorry, with a bad conscience
🗷 **1** blameless, guiltless, innocent **2** shameless

guise *n* air, appearance, aspect, behaviour, custom, demeanour *formal*, disguise, façade, face, features, form, front, likeness, manner, mask, pretence, semblance, shape, show

gulf *n* **1** *sailing in the gulf:* basin, bay, bight, cove, inlet **2** *the gulf between rich and poor:* abyss, breach, canyon, chasm, cleft, crevice, division, fissure, gap, gorge, hole, hollow, opening, ravine, rift, separation, split, void

gullet *n* craw, crop, maw, oesophagus *technical*, throat

gullibility *n* credulity, foolishness, innocence, naïvety, simplicity, trustfulness
🗷 astuteness

gullible *adj* credulous, easily deceived, foolish, green, impressionable, inexperienced, ingenuous, innocent, naïve, suggestible, trustful, trusting, unsophisticated, unsuspecting, wet behind the ears *colloq*
🗷 astute

gully *n* canyon, channel, ditch, gorge, gutter, ravine, valley, watercourse

gulp *v* bolt, devour, gobble, guzzle, knock back *colloq*, quaff, stuff, swallow, swig, swill, tuck into *colloq*, wolf *colloq*
F3 nibble, sip
♦ *n* draught, mouthful, swallow, swig

gum *n* adhesive, cement, fixative, glue, paste, resin
♦ *v* affix *formal*, cement, clog, fix, glue, paste, seal, stick
► **gum up** choke, clog, hinder, impede, obstruct

gummy *adj* adhesive, gluey, gooey, sticky, tacky, viscid *formal*, viscous

gumption *n* ability, acumen, acuteness, astuteness, cleverness, common sense, discernment, enterprise, initiative, nous, resourcefulness, sagacity *formal*, savvy *colloq*, shrewdness, wit
F3 foolishness

gun *n* airgun, automatic repeater, bazooka, blunderbuss, cannon, carbine, Colt®, firearm, flintlock, fusil, handgun, howitzer, machine-gun, mortar, musket, pistol, revolver, rifle, shooter *colloq*, shooting iron *colloq*, shotgun, Winchester®

gunman *n* assassin, bandit, bravo, desperado, gangster, gunslinger, hatchet man *colloq*, hit man *colloq*, killer, mobster *US colloq*, murderer, shootist, sniper, terrorist, thug

gurgle *v* **1** *the stream gurgled down the hillside*: babble, bubble, burble, crow, lap, murmur, plash, ripple, splash **2** *a baby gurgling*: babble, burble, crow
♦ *n* **1** *the gurgle of the water in the pipes*: babble, bubbling, murmur, ripple **2** *a gurgle from the baby*: babble, burble, crow

guru *n* authority, expert, guiding light, instructor, leader, luminary, maharishi, master, mentor, pundit, sage, Svengali, swami, teacher, tutor

gush *v* **1** *blood gushed from the wound*: burst, cascade, flood, flow, issue, jet, pour, run, rush, spout, spurt, stream, surge, well **2** *gushing about her new record*: babble, blather, bubble over, chatter, drivel, effervesce, effuse, enthuse, fuss, go on *colloq*, jabber
♦ *n* burst, cascade, flood, flow, jet, outburst, outflow, outpouring, rush, spate, spout, spurt, stream, surge, tide, torrent

gushing *adj* cloying, effusive, emotional, excessive, fulsome, gushy, mawkish, over-enthusiastic, saccharine, sentimental, sickly
F3 restrained, sincere

gust *n* blast, blow, breeze, burst, eruption, fit, flurry, gale, outbreak, outburst, puff, rush, squall, storm, surge, wind
♦ *v* blast, blow, bluster, breeze, burst out, erupt, puff, rush, squall, surge

gusto *n* appreciation, delight, élan, energy, enjoyment, enthusiasm, exhilaration, exuberance, fervour, pleasure, relish, verve, zeal, zest
F3 apathy, distaste

gusty *adj* blowy, blustering, blustery, breezy, squally, stormy, tempestuous, windy
F3 calm

gut *n* **1** *remove the guts from the animal*: belly, bowels, entrails, innards *colloq*, insides, intestines, stomach, viscera, vital organs **2** *have the guts to own up*: audacity, backbone *colloq*, boldness, bottle *colloq*, bravery, courage, fortitude *formal*, grit *colloq*, mettle, nerve, pluck, spunk *colloq*, tenacity
♦ *v* **1** *gut fish*: clean (out), disembowel, draw, eviscerate *formal*, exenterate *formal* **2** *fire gutted the hotel*: destroy, devastate, ravage **3** *their house had been gutted by intruders*: clear, clear out, empty, loot, plunder, ransack, rifle, rob, sack, strip
♦ *adj* basic, deep-seated, emotional, heartfelt, innate, instinctive, intuitive, involuntary, natural, spontaneous, strong, unthinking

gutless *adj* abject, chicken *colloq*, chicken-hearted *colloq*, chicken-livered *colloq*, cowardly, craven, faint-hearted, feeble, irresolute, lily-livered *colloq*, spineless *colloq*, timid, weak
F3 courageous

gutsy *adj* bold, brave, courageous, determined, gallant, game, indomitable, mettlesome, passionate, plucky, resolute, spirited, staunch
F3 quiet, timid

gutter *n* channel, conduit, culvert, ditch, drain, duct, passage, pipe, sewer, sluice, trench, trough, tube

guttural *adj* croaking, deep, grating, gravelly, gruff, harsh, hoarse, husky, low, rasping, rough, thick, throaty
F3 dulcet

guy *n* bloke *colloq*, boy, chap *colloq*, character, fellow, individual, lad, man, person, youth

guzzle *v* bolt, devour, gobble, gormandize, gulp, knock back *colloq*, polish off *colloq*, put away *colloq*, quaff, scoff *colloq*, stuff, swallow, swig, swill, tuck into *colloq*, wolf *colloq*

gyrate *v* circle, pirouette, revolve, rotate, spin, spiral, swirl, swivel, turn, twirl, wheel, whirl

gyration *n* circle, convolution *formal*, pirouette, revolution, rotation, spin, spinning, spiral, swirl, swivel, turn, twirl, wheeling, whirl, whirling

H

habit *n* **1** *has some odd habits:* bent, custom, inclination, leaning, manner, mannerism, matter of course, mode, policy, practice, procedure, proclivity *formal*, propensity *formal*, quirk, routine, rule, second nature, tendency, usage, way(s), wont **2** *a cocaine habit:* addiction, dependence, fixation, obsession, weakness **3** *a monk's habit:* clothing, costume, dress, garment, gear *colloq*, get-up *colloq*, outfit, robe, togs *colloq*, uniform, vestment

habitable *adj* fit to live in, good enough to live in, inhabitable, suitable to live in

habitat *n* abode *formal*, domain, dwelling, element, environment, home, locality, surroundings, terrain, territory

habitation *n* **1** *unfit for human habitation:* housing, inhabitance, inhabitancy, inhabitation, lodging, occupancy, occupation, quarters, residence, tenancy **2** *few human habitations in the area:* abode *formal*, accommodation, apartment, cottage, digs *colloq*, domicile *formal*, dwelling *formal*, dwelling-place *formal*, flat, home, house, hut, joint *colloq*, living quarters, lodging, mansion, pad *colloq*, quarters, residence *formal*, residency *formal*, roof over your head *colloq*

habitual *adj* **1** *his habitual morning walk:* accustomed, common, customary, established, familiar, fixed, natural, normal, ordinary, recurrent, regular, routine, set, standard, traditional, usual, wonted *formal* **2** *a habitual drinker:* addicted, chronic, confirmed, constant, dependent, hardened, inveterate, obsessive, persistent
🖙 **1** infrequent, occasional

habituate *v* acclimatize, accustom, adapt, break in, condition, discipline, familiarize, harden, inure, make familiar with, make used to, school, season, tame, train

habitué *n* denizen, frequenter, patron, regular, regular customer

hack¹ *v* chop, clear, cut, fell, gash, hew, lacerate, mangle, mutilate, notch, saw, slash

hack² *n* drudge, journalist, scribbler, writer

hackneyed *adj* banal, clichéed, cliché-ridden, common, commonplace, corny *colloq*, overused, overworked, pedestrian, platitudinous *formal*, run-of-the-mill *colloq*, stale, stereotyped, stock, threadbare, time-worn, tired, trite, unimaginative, uninspired, unoriginal, wearing thin, worn-out, yawn-making *colloq*
🖙 fresh, new, original

hag *n* battle-axe *colloq*, crone, fury, gorgon, harpy, harridan, shrew, termagant, virago, vixen, witch

haggard *adj* careworn, drained, drawn, gaunt, ghastly, hollow-cheeked, pale, pallid, pinched, shrunken, thin, wan, wasted
🖙 hale

haggle *v* bargain, barter, beat down, bicker, chaffer, dicker *US*, dispute, higgle, negotiate, quarrel, squabble, wrangle

hail¹ *v* **1** *hailed his friend in the street:* acknowledge, address, greet, nod to, salute, say hello to, wave to **2** *hail a cab:* call out to, flag down, signal to, wave to **3** *hailed as a masterpiece:* acclaim, applaud, cheer, exalt, honour, laud *formal*, praise, welcome **4** *hail from Malawi:* be born in, come, have your home/roots in, originate

hail² *n* barrage, bombardment, rain, shower, storm, torrent, volley
♦ *v* assail, attack, batter, bombard, pelt, rain, shower

hair *n* **1** *long blonde hair:* locks, mane, mop, shock, tresses **2** *the dog's hair:* coat, fleece, fur, hide, pelt, wool

hair's-breadth *n* fraction, hair, inch, jot, whisker *colloq*
🖙 mile

hairdo *n* coiffure, cut, haircut, hairstyle, set, style

hairdresser *n* barber, coiffeur, coiffeuse, hairstylist, stylist

hairless *adj* bald, bald-headed, beardless, clean-shaven, shaven, shorn, tonsured
🖙 hairy, hirsute

hair-raising *adj* alarming, bloodcurdling, creepy *colloq*, eerie, exciting, frightening, horrifying, petrifying, scary, shocking, spine-chilling, startling, terrifying, thrilling

hairstyle *n* coiffure, cut, haircut, hairdo *colloq*, set, style

hairy *adj* bearded, bushy, crinigerous *formal*, crinite *formal*, crinose *formal*, fleecy, furry, fuzzy, hirsute, pilose *formal*, shaggy, unshaven, woolly
🖙 bald, clean-shaven

halcyon *adj* balmy, calm, carefree, flourishing, gentle, golden, happy, mild, pacific, peaceful, placid, prosperous, quiet, serene, still, tranquil, undisturbed
🖙 stormy

hale *adj* able-bodied, athletic, blooming, fit, flourishing, healthy, hearty, in fine fettle *colloq*, in the pink *colloq*, robust, sound, strong, vigorous, well, youthful
🖙 ill

half *n* bisection, equal part/share, fifty per cent, fraction, hemisphere, portion, section, segment, semicircle, share
♦ *adj* bisected, divided, divided in two, fractional, halved, hemispherical, incomplete, limited, moderate, part, partial, semi-, slight
🖙 whole
♦ *adv* barely, inadequately, incompletely, insufficiently, moderately, partially, partly, slightly
🖙 completely

half-baked *adj* crackpot *colloq*, crazy, foolish, harebrained *colloq*, ill-conceived, ill-judged, impractical, senseless, short-sighted, silly, stupid, undeveloped, unplanned
🖙 sensible, thought out

half-caste *n* Creole, griff(e), mestee, mestiza, mestizo, metif, Métis, Métisse, miscegen, miscegene, miscegine, mongrel, mulatta, mulatto, mulattress, person of mixed race, quadroon, quarter-blood, quarteroon, quintroon, sambo

half-hearted *adj* apathetic, cool, feeble, indifferent, lacklustre, listless, lukewarm, neutral, passive, unconcerned, unenthusiastic, uninterested, weak
🖃 enthusiastic, whole-hearted

halfway *adv* centrally, in/to the middle, midway
♦ *adj* central, equidistant, intermediate, mean, median, mid, middle, midway

halfwit *n* ass *colloq*, birdbrain *colloq*, blockhead, buffoon, butt, chump *colloq*, clot *colloq*, clown, comic, cretin, dimwit, dope *colloq*, dork *slang*, dumbo *slang*, dunce, dupe, fat-head, fool, geek *slang*, idiot, ignoramus, imbecile, jester, laughing-stock, moron, mug *colloq*, nincompoop *colloq*, ninny *colloq*, nit *colloq*, nitwit *colloq*, pillock *slang*, plonker *slang*, prat *slang*, prick *slang*, simpleton, stooge, sucker *colloq*, twerp *colloq*, twit *colloq*, wally *slang*
🖃 brain

half-witted *adj* barmy *colloq*, batty *colloq*, crack-brained *colloq*, crackpot *colloq*, crazy, dim-witted *colloq*, dotty *colloq*, dull, dumb *colloq*, feeble-minded, foolish, idiotic, moronic, nutty *colloq*, potty *colloq*, silly, simple, simple-minded, stupid, two bricks short of a load *colloq*
🖃 clever

hall *n* 1 *decorate the hall:* corridor, entrance-hall, foyer, hallway, lobby, passage, passageway, vestibule 2 *the school hall:* assembly room, auditorium, chamber, concert-hall, conference hall

hallmark *n* 1 *a hallmark on gold:* mark/stamp of authenticity, official mark/stamp 2 *the hallmark of her music:* badge, brand-name, device, distinctive feature, emblem, indication, indicator, mark, sign, stamp, symbol, trademark, typical quality

hallowed *adj* age-old, blessed, consecrated, dedicated, established, holy, honoured, inviolable, revered, sacred, sacrosanct, sanctified

hallucinate *v* daydream, dream, fantasize, freak out *slang*, imagine, imagine things, see things, see visions, trip *slang*

hallucination *n* apparition, daydream, delirium, delusion, dream, fantasy, figment, figment of the imagination, illusion, mirage, phantasmagoria, trip *colloq*, vision

halo *n* aura, aureola, aureole, circle of light, corona, crown, gloria, gloriole, glory, halation, nimbus, radiance, ring

halt *v* arrest, block, break off, bring/draw to a close, call it a day *colloq*, cease *formal*, check, come/bring to a stop, crush, curb, desist *formal*, discontinue *formal*, draw up, end, finish, hold back, impede, obstruct, pause, pull up, put an end to, quit *colloq*, rest, stem, stop, terminate *formal*, wait
🖃 continue, start
♦ *n* arrest, break, breathing-space, cessation *formal*, close, deadlock, desistance *formal*,

discontinuance *formal*, discontinuation *formal*, end, interruption, interval, pause, respite, rest, stalemate, standstill, stop, stoppage, termination *formal*
🖃 continuation, start

halting *adj* awkward, broken, faltering, fumbling for words, hesitant, imperfect, laboured, stammering, stumbling, stuttering, uncertain, unsteady
🖃 certain, fluent

halve *v* bisect, cut down, cut in half, dichotomize *formal*, divide, divide equally, lessen, reduce, sever, share, split, split in two

halved *adj* bisected, cut, dimidiate *formal*, divided, shared, split

hammer *v* 1 *hammer on the door:* bang, bash, batter, beat, drive, drum, fashion, form, hit, knock, make, mould, pound, shape, slap, strike 2 *hammered by the critics:* attack, blame, censure, condemn, criticize, decry *formal*, denigrate *formal*, knock *colloq*, run down *colloq*, slam *colloq*, slate *colloq*, tear a strip off *colloq* 3 *hammer the opposition:* annihilate, beat, clobber *colloq*, defeat, lick *colloq*, outplay, overcome, overwhelm, rout, slaughter *colloq*, thrash *colloq*, trounce 4 *hammer an idea into someone:* din, drive home, drum, force, instil, reiterate 5 *hammer away at his essay:* drudge, grind, keep on, labour, persevere, persist, plug, pound, slog
♦ *n* beetle, gavel, mallet
▶ **hammer out** accomplish, achieve eventually, bring about, carry through, complete, finish, negotiate, produce, resolve, settle, sort out, thrash out, work out

hamper *v* baulk, block, bridle, check, cramp, curb, encumber, fetter, foil, frustrate, hamstring, handicap, hinder, hold up, impede, inhibit, obstruct, prevent, restrain, restrict, retard *formal*, shackle, slow down, stop, stymie *colloq*, thwart
🖃 aid, facilitate
♦ *n* basket, box, container, creel, pannier

hamstring *v* baulk, block, check, cramp, cripple, disable, encumber, foil, frustrate, handicap, hinder, hold up, impede, incapacitate, paralyse, restrain, restrict, stop, stymie *colloq*, thwart

hand *n* 1 *a piece of paper in her hand:* fin *slang*, manus *technical*, mitt *slang*, palm, paw *colloq* 2 *give me a hand:* aid, assistance, help, helping hand, influence, part, participation, succour *formal*, support 3 *in someone's hands:* authority, care, charge, clutches, command, control, custody, management, possession, power, responsibility, supervision 4 *a big hand for the loser:* acclaim, applause, cheering, clapping, handclap, ovation 5 *the hands of a clock:* arrow, indicator, marker, needle, pointer 6 *a beautiful flowing hand:* calligraphy, fist *colloq*, handwriting, penmanship, script, writing 7 *a hired hand:* employee, farm-hand, hireling, labourer, operative, worker, workman
♦ *v* conduct, convey, deliver, give, hand over, offer, pass, present, submit, transmit, yield
▶ **hand down** bequeath, give, grant, leave, pass down, pass on, transfer, will
▶ **hand out** deal out, dish out *colloq*, dispense *formal*, disseminate *formal*, distribute, give out, mete out, pass out, share out

▶ **hand over** consign, deliver, donate, give, pass, present, release, relinquish, surrender, transfer, turn over, yield
🖭 keep, retain

handbill *n* advertisement, announcement, circular, flyer, leaflet, letter, notice, pamphlet

handbook *n* ABC, book of directions, companion, guide, guidebook, instruction book, manual, prospectus

handcuff *v* fasten, fetter, manacle, secure, shackle, tie

handcuffs *n* cuffs, darbies *colloq*, fetters, manacles, shackles, wristlets

handful *n* 1 *only a handful of times:* few, little, scattering, small amount, small number, smattering, sprinkling 2 *he's a bit of a handful:* bother, nuisance, pain *colloq*, pain in the neck *colloq*, pest, thorn in the flesh *colloq*
🖭 1 a lot, many

handicap *n* 1 *a physical handicap:* abnormality, defect, disability, disadvantage, drawback, impairment, impediment, limitation, shortcoming 2 *not having my own car is quite a handicap:* barrier, block, check, constraint, encumbrance, hindrance, obstacle, obstruction, penalty, restriction, stumbling-block
🖭 1 advantage 2 assistance
♦ *v* block, bridle, burden, check, curb, disable, disadvantage, encumber, hamper, hinder, hold back, impair, impede, limit, obstruct, put at a disadvantage, restrict, retard *formal*
🖭 assist, help

handicraft *n* art, craft, craftsmanship, craftwork, handiwork, handwork, skill, workmanship

handiwork *n* 1 *all my own handiwork:* achievement, action, doing, invention, product, production, responsibility, result, work, workmanship 2 *skilled at handiwork:* art, artisanship, craft, craftsmanship, craftwork, creation, design, handicraft, skill

handle *n* grip, haft, handgrip, hilt, knob, shaft, stock
♦ *v* 1 *handling the velvet:* feel, finger, fondle, grasp, grip, hold, paw *colloq*, pick up, touch 2 *handle a situation:* be in charge of, control, cope with, deal with, manage, supervise, tackle, take care of, treat 3 *handle a car:* control, drive, operate, steer, work 4 *handling stolen goods:* deal in, do business in, market, operate, stock, trade in, traffic

handling *n* administration, approach, conduct, direction, discussion, management, manipulation, operation, running, transaction, treatment

handout *n* 1 *living on government handouts:* alms, charity, dole, free sample, freebie *colloq*, gifts, issue, largesse, share 2 *a handout about the concert:* brochure, bulletin, circular, leaflet, literature, pamphlet, press release, statement

hand-picked *adj* choice, chosen, elect, elite, picked, recherché, screened, select, selected

handsome *adj* 1 *a handsome man:* attractive, dignified, dishy *colloq*, elegant, fair, fine, good-looking, gorgeous *colloq*, hunky *colloq*, personable, stately 2 *a handsome offer:* abundant, ample, bountiful, considerable, generous, large, lavish, liberal, magnanimous, plentiful, sizeable, unsparing, unstinting
🖭 1 ugly, unattractive 2 mean

handsomely *adv* abundantly, amply, bountifully, generously, lavishly, liberally, magnanimously, munificently *formal*, plentifully, richly, unsparingly, unstintingly
🖭 stingily

handwriting *n* autograph, calligraphy, fist *colloq*, hand, penmanship, scrawl *colloq*, scribble *colloq*, script, writing

handy *adj* 1 *a handy tray for your keyboard:* convenient, functional, helpful, practicable, practical, useful 2 *keep the scissors handy:* accessible, at hand, at your fingertips *colloq*, available, near, nearby, ready, to hand, within reach 3 *handy with a needle:* adept, adroit, clever, dexterous, expert, nimble, practical, proficient, skilful, skilled
🖭 2 inconvenient 3 clumsy

handyman *n* DIYer, factotum, Jack-of-all-trades, odd-jobber, odd-jobman

hang *v* 1 *balloons hanging from the ceiling:* be suspended, bend, dangle, drape, droop, drop, flop, hang down, lean, put up, sag, suspend, swing, trail 2 *hang a picture on the wall:* affix *formal*, append *formal*, attach, cement, fasten, fix, glue, paste, stick 3 *hang in the air:* cling, drift, flit, float, flutter, hover, linger, remain 4 *the prisoners were hanged:* execute, kill, lynch, put to death, send to the gallows/scaffold/gibbet, string up *colloq*
▶ **hang about** dawdle, frequent, hang around, haunt, linger, loiter, wait, waste time
▶ **hang about with** associate with, consort with, hang around with, keep company with, mix with
▶ **hang back** be reluctant, demur *formal*, hesitate, hold back, recoil, shrink back, shy away, stay behind
▶ **hang on** 1 *hang on a minute:* carry on, continue, endure, hold on, hold out, persevere, persist, remain, wait 2 *hung on to the rope:* cling, clutch, grasp, grip, hold fast 3 *it all hangs on his exam results:* be conditional on, be contingent on *formal*, be determined by, depend on, hinge on, rest on, turn on

hangdog *adj* abject, browbeaten, cowed, cringing, defeated, downcast, furtive, guilty, miserable, shamefaced, sneaking, wretched
🖭 bold

hanger-on *n* dependant, follower, freeloader, henchman, lackey, minion, parasite, sponger *colloq*, sycophant, toady

hanging *adj* dangling, draping, drooping, flapping, flopping, floppy, loose, pendent *formal*, pendulous *formal*, pensile *formal*, suspended, swinging, unattached, unsupported
♦ *n* dossal, dossel, drape, drapery, drop, drop-scene, frontal

hang-out *n* den, dive *colloq*, haunt, home, joint *colloq*, local, meeting-place, patch, watering-hole *colloq*

hangover *n* after-effects, crapulence *formal*, katzenjammer, morning after, the morning after the night before

hang-up *n* block, difficulty, fixation, idée fixe, inhibition, mental block, obsession, phobia, preoccupation, problem, thing *colloq*

hank *n* coil, fank *Scot*, length, loop, piece, roll, skein, twist

hanker *v*
▶ **hanker after/for** be dying for *colloq*, covet, crave, desire, hunger for, itch for, long for, pine for, set your heart on, thirst for, want, wish for, yearn for

hankering *n* craving, desire, hunger, itch, longing, pining, thirst, urge, wish, yearning

hanky-panky *n* cheating, chicanery, deception, devilry, dishonesty, funny business *colloq*, jiggery-pokery, machinations *formal*, mischief, monkey business *colloq*, nonsense, shenanigans *colloq*, subterfuge, trickery, tricks
🔁 openness

haphazard *adj* aimless, arbitrary, careless, casual, chance, disorderly, disorganized, hit-or-miss, indiscriminate, irregular, orderless, random, slapdash, slipshod, unmethodical, unplanned, unsystematic
🔁 methodical, orderly

hapless *adj* cursed, ill-fated, ill-starred, jinxed, luckless, miserable, star-crossed, unfortunate, unhappy, unlucky, wretched
🔁 lucky

happen *v* **1** *what happened at the party?*: arise, come about, come into being, crop up, develop, ensue, eventuate *formal*, follow, go on, materialize *colloq*, occur, present itself, result, supervene *formal*, take place, transpire *formal*, turn out, turn up **2** *happen to do something*: have the good/bad fortune to, have the good/bad luck to **3** *happen on something*: chance on, come across, discover, find, hit on, light on, stumble on

happening *n* accident, action, adventure, affair, business, case, chance, circumstance, episode, event, eventuality *formal*, experience, incident, occasion, occurrence, phenomenon, proceedings

happily *adv* **1** *playing happily on the beach*: agreeably, cheerfully, contentedly, delightedly, enthusiastically, gladly, gleefully, heartily, joyfully, joyously *formal*, merrily, willingly **2** *happily, no one was hurt*: auspiciously *formal*, by chance, fittingly, fortunately, luckily, opportunely *formal*, propitiously *formal*, providentially
🔁 **2** unhappily

happiness *n* bliss, blitheness *formal*, cheerfulness, cheeriness, contentment, delight, ecstasy, elation, enjoyment, euphoria, exuberance, felicity *formal*, gaiety, gladness, glee, good spirits, high spirits, joy, joyfulness, light-heartedness, merriment, merriness, pleasure
🔁 sadness, unhappiness

happy *adj* **1** *happy to be home*: blithe *formal*, carefree, cheerful, cock-a-hoop *colloq*, content, contented, delighted, ecstatic, elated, euphoric, exuberant, gay, glad, gleeful, gratified, happy as Larry/a sandboy *colloq*, in a good mood, in good/high spirits, in seventh heaven *colloq*, jolly, jovial, joyful, joyous *formal*, light-hearted, merry, on cloud nine *colloq*, on top of the world *colloq*, over the moon *colloq*, overjoyed, pleased, radiant, rapturous, satisfied, smiling, thrilled, tickled pink *colloq*, unconcerned, untroubled, unworried, walking/floating on air *colloq* **2** *a happy coincidence*: advantageous, apposite *formal*,

appropriate, apt, auspicious *formal*, beneficial, convenient, favourable, felicitous *formal*, fitting, fortunate, helpful, lucky, opportune, proper, propitious *formal*
🔁 **1** discontented, sad, unhappy
2 inappropriate, unfortunate

happy-go-lucky *adj* blithe *formal*, carefree, casual, cheerful, devil-may-care, easy-going, heedless, improvident, insouciant *formal*, irresponsible, light-hearted, nonchalant, reckless, unconcerned, untroubled, unworried
🔁 anxious, wary

harangue *n* address, diatribe, exhortation *formal*, lecture, peroration *formal*, speech, tirade
♦ *v* address, declaim *formal*, hold forth, lecture, preach, spout

harass *v* annoy, antagonize, badger, bother, disturb, dragoon, drive round the bend/twist *colloq*, exasperate, exhaust, fatigue, fret, harry, hassle *colloq*, have it in for *colloq*, hound, irritate, nag, persecute, pester, plague, provoke, put the frighteners on *colloq*, put the wind up *colloq*, stress, tire, torment, trouble, vex, wear out, worry

harassed *adj* careworn, distraught, distressed, harried, hassled *colloq*, hounded, pestered, plagued, pressured, pressurized, strained, stressed, stressed out *colloq*, tormented, troubled, under pressure, under stress, uptight *colloq*, vexed, worried
🔁 carefree

harassment *n* aggravation, annoyance, badgering, bedevilment, bother, distress, hassle *colloq*, irritation, molest, molestation, nuisance, persecution, pestering, pressuring, torment, trouble, vexation
🔁 assistance

harbinger *n* avant-courier, forerunner, foretoken *formal*, herald, indication, messenger, omen, portent, precursor, sign, warning

harbour *n* anchorage, dock, haven, marina, mooring, port, quay, refuge, shelter, wharf
♦ *v* **1** *harbour a criminal*: conceal, hide, house, protect, shelter, shield, take in **2** *harbour a feeling*: believe, cherish, cling to, entertain, foster, hold, imagine, maintain, nurse, nurture, retain

hard *adj* **1** *a hard surface*: compact, compacted, compressed, condensed, dense, firm, hard as stone/iron/rock *colloq*, impenetrable, inflexible, resistant, rigid, solid, stiff, strong, tough, unpliable, unyielding **2** *a hard question/problem*: baffling, bewildering, complex, complicated, difficult, intricate, involved, knotty, perplexing, puzzling **3** *building a wall is hard work*: arduous, backbreaking, difficult, exacting, exhausting, heavy, laborious, onerous, rigorous, strenuous, tiring, toilsome, tough **4** *a hard taskmaster*: callous, cold-hearted, cruel, distressing, hard as flint *colloq*, hard-hearted, harsh, implacable, merciless, obdurate *formal*, oppressive, painful, pitiless, ruling with a rod of iron *colloq*, ruthless, severe, standing no nonsense *colloq*, stern, strict, tyrannical, unfeeling, unpleasant, unrelenting, unsparing, unsympathetic, unyielding **5** *hard times*: austere, difficult, disagreeable, distressing, grim, harsh, painful, severe, tough, uncomfortable, unpleasant **6** *a hard worker*: assiduous, busy, conscientious, diligent,

energetic, enthusiastic, hard-working, industrious, keen, sedulous *formal*, zealous **7** *a hard push*: forceful, heavy, intense, powerful, sharp, strong, violent **8** *a hard winter*: bitter, cold, freezing, harsh, raw, severe **9** *hard evidence*: actual, certain, definite, indisputable, real, true, undeniable, unquestionable, verified **10** *hard drugs*: addictive, habit-forming, harmful, heavy, narcotic, potent, strong
Ⓕ **1** soft, yielding **2** easy, simple **4** compassionate, gentle, kind, pleasant **5** comfortable, easy **6** idle, lazy **8** mild **9** uncertain
♦ *adv* **1** *pushed hard against the door*: energetically, forcefully, heavily, intensely, powerfully, sharply, strongly, vigorously, violently, with all your might *formal* **2** *work hard*: assiduously, busily, conscientiously, diligently, eagerly, energetically, enthusiastically, industriously, intensely, keenly **3** *look/think hard*: attentively, carefully, closely, intently, keenly, sharply **4** *a hard-won victory*: after a struggle, arduously, laboriously, strenuously, vigorously, with difficulty **5** *snowing hard*: heavily, intensely, severely, steadily, strongly
Ⓕ **3** carelessly **4** effortlessly **5** lightly

hard-bitten *adj* callous, case-hardened, cynical, down-to-earth, hard-boiled, hard-headed, hard-nosed, inured, matter-of-fact, practical, realistic, ruthless, shrewd, tough, toughened, unsentimental
Ⓕ callow

hard-boiled *adj* cynical, down-to-earth, hard-headed, tough, unsentimental

hard-core *adj* blatant, dedicated, diehard, dyed-in-the-wool, extreme, intransigent, obstinate, rigid, staunch, steadfast
Ⓕ moderate

harden *v* **1** *the wax hardened*: anneal *technical*, bake, cake, congeal, freeze, indurate *formal*, petrify, reinforce, season, set, solidify, stiffen, temper, toughen, vulcanize **2** *hardened to the awful poverty*: accustom, brace, deaden, fortify *formal*, gird, habituate *formal*, indurate *formal*, inure, nerve, steel, stiffen, strengthen, toughen, train
Ⓕ **1** soften **2** weaken

hardened *adj* accustomed, callous, chronic, habitual, habituated, incorrigible, inured, inveterate, irredeemable, obdurate *formal*, reprobate, seasoned, shameless, toughened, unfeeling
Ⓕ callow, soft

hard-headed *adj* astute, businesslike, clear-thinking, cool-headed, down-to-earth, hard-bitten, hard-boiled, hard-nosed *colloq*, level-headed, practical, pragmatic, rational, realistic, sensible, sharp, shrewd, tough, unsentimental
Ⓕ idealistic, impractical, sentimental, unrealistic

hard-hearted *adj* callous, cold, cruel, hard, heartless, inhuman, merciless, pitiless, stony, stony-hearted, uncaring, unconcerned, unfeeling, unkind, unsympathetic
Ⓕ compassionate, concerned, kind, merciful

hard-hitting *adj* bold, condemnatory, critical, direct, forceful, frank, no-holds-barred *colloq*, pulling no punches *colloq*, straight, tough, uncompromising, unsparing, vigorous
Ⓕ mild

hardiness *n* boldness, courage, fortitude *formal*, intrepidity, resilience, resolution, robustness, ruggedness, sturdiness, toughness, valour
Ⓕ timidity

hardline *adj* extreme, immoderate, inflexible, intransigent *formal*, militant, strict, tough, uncompromising, undeviating, unyielding
Ⓕ flexible, moderate

hardly *adv* **1** *hardly alive*: almost not, barely, just, only just, scarcely **2** *that's hardly fair*: by no means, not at all, not quite

hardness *n* **1** *the hardness of the wood*: firmness, inflexibility, rigidity, solidity, toughness **2** *hardness of heart*: coldness, firmness, harshness, inhumanity, insensitivity, pitilessness, severity, sternness **3** *the hardness of the test*: difficulty, harshness, laboriousness, severity, toughness
Ⓕ **1** softness **2** mildness, softness **3** ease

hard-pressed *adj* harassed, hard put, hard-pushed, harried, in a corner *colloq*, overburdened, overtaxed, pushed, under pressure, up against it *colloq*, with your back to the wall *colloq*
Ⓕ untroubled

hardship *n* adversity, affliction, austerity, burdens, deprivation, destitution, difficulty, distress, misery, misfortune, need, pain, poverty, privation *formal*, suffering, trial, tribulation *formal*, trouble, want
Ⓕ comfort, ease, prosperity

hard-wearing *adj* durable, lasting, made/built to last, resilient, rugged, stout, strong, sturdy, tough, well-made
Ⓕ delicate

hard-working *adj* assiduous, busy, conscientious, diligent, energetic, enthusiastic, industrious, keen, sedulous *formal*, with your nose to the grindstone *colloq*, zealous
Ⓕ idle, lazy

hardy *adj* **1** *hardy plants*: durable, fit, healthy, heavy-duty, robust, sound, strong, sturdy, tough, vigorous **2** *a hardy fighter*: bold, brave, courageous, daring, fearless, heroic, indomitable, intrepid, plucky, stalwart, stoical, stout, stout-hearted, undaunted
Ⓕ **1** unhealthy, weak

hare-brained *adj* careless, crackpot *colloq*, daft, foolish, giddy, half-baked *colloq*, ill-conceived, inane, rash, reckless, scatterbrained *colloq*, scatty *colloq*, silly, stupid, wild
Ⓕ sensible

hark *v* give ear, hear, hearken *old use*, listen, mark, note, notice, pay attention, pay heed
▶ **hark back** go back, recall, recollect, regress *formal*, remember, revert, turn back

harlequin *n* buffoon, clown, comic, fool, jester, joker, zany

harm *n* abuse, adversity, damage, destruction, detriment, disservice, hurt, ill, impairment, injury, loss, misfortune, pain, ruin, suffering, wrong
Ⓕ benefit, service
♦ *v* abuse, be detrimental to, blemish, damage, destroy, hurt, ill-treat, impair, injure, maltreat, mar, misuse, molest, ruin, spoil, work against, wound
Ⓕ benefit, improve

harmful *adj* bad, damaging, dangerous, deleterious *formal*, destructive, detrimental, hazardous, injurious, noxious *formal*, pernicious, poisonous, toxic, unhealthy, unwholesome, wounding
🔁 harmless

harmless *adj* blameless, -friendly, gentle, innocent, innocuous, inoffensive, mild, non-toxic, safe
🔁 dangerous, destructive, harmful

harmonious *adj* 1 *harmonious voices*: euphonious, harmonizing, mellifluous *formal*, mellow, melodious, musical, pleasant, rhythmic, sweet-sounding, symphonious, tuneful 2 *harmonious colours*: balanced, compatible, concordant *formal*, congruous *formal*, co-ordinated, matching 3 *a harmonious relationship*: agreeable, amiable, amicable, compatible, cordial, friendly, like-minded, peaceable, peaceful, sympathetic
🔁 1 discordant

harmonize *v* 1 *the colours harmonize beautifully*: balance, blend, co-ordinate, go together, match, mix, suit, tone 2 *tried to harmonize their views*: accommodate, accord *formal*, adapt, agree, arrange, be congruent *formal*, be congruous *formal*, coincide, co-ordinate, fit in, get on with, reconcile
🔁 1 clash 2 conflict

harmony *n* 1 *singing in harmony*: euphony, mellifluousness *formal*, melodiousness, melody, tune, tunefulness 2 *live in harmony*: accord *formal*, agreement, amicability, amity *formal*, assent *formal*, compatibility, concord *formal*, concurrence *formal*, co-operation, friendliness, goodwill, like-mindedness, oneness, peace, rapport, sympathy, unanimity, understanding, unison, unity 3 *a harmony of styles*: balance, blending, concord *formal*, conformity, consonance *formal*, co-ordination, correspondence, symmetry
🔁 1 discord 2 conflict

harness *n* accoutrements *formal*, equipment, gear, reins, straps, tack, tackle
♦ *v* apply, channel, control, employ, exploit, make use of, mobilize, use, utilize

---

Parts of a horse's harness include:
backband, bellyband, bit, blinders *US*, blinkers, breeching, bridle, collar, crupper, girth, hackamore, halter, hames, headstall *US*, martingale, noseband, reins, saddle, saddlepad, stirrup, throatlatch/throatlash *US*, traces

---

harp
▶ **harp on** dwell on, go on and on about *colloq*, keep talking about, labour, nag, press, reiterate, renew, repeat

harpoon *n* arrow, barb, dart, grains, spear, trident

harridan *n* battle-axe *colloq*, dragon, fury, gorgon, harpy, hell-cat, nag, scold, shrew, tartar, termagant, virago, vixen, witch, Xanthippe

harried *adj* agitated, anxious, beset, bothered, distressed, harassed, hard-pressed, hassled *colloq*, plagued, pressured, pressurized, ravaged, tormented, troubled, worried
🔁 untroubled

harrowing *adj* agonizing, alarming, daunting, distressing, disturbing, excruciating, frightening, heart-rending, nerve-racking, perturbing *formal*, terrifying, tormenting, traumatic, upsetting
🔁 encouraging, heartening

harry *v* annoy, badger, bother, chivvy, disturb, harass, hassle *colloq*, molest, nag, oppress, persecute, pester, plague, torment, trouble, vex, worry

harsh *adj* 1 *harsh living conditions*: austere, barren, bitter, bleak, comfortless, desolate, grim, inhospitable, severe, Spartan, stark, wild 2 *a harsh punishment*: abrasive, acerbic *formal*, brutal, cruel, Draconian, grim, hard, inhuman, merciless, pitiless, ruthless, savage, severe, stern, strict, unfeeling, unsympathetic 3 *a harsh sound*: coarse, croaking, discordant, dissonant, ear-piercing, grating, grinding, gruff, guttural, hoarse, jangling, jarring, metallic, rasping, raucous, rough, sharp, shrill, strident, unpleasant 4 *harsh lights*: bold, bright, dazzling, flashy, garish, gaudy, glaring, lurid, showy
🔁 1 comfortable, lenient, mild 2 compassionate, feeling 3 gentle, harmonious, soft 4 gentle

harshness *n* 1 *the harshness of the winter*: bitterness, hardness, rigour, severity, starkness 2 *the harshness of the ruler*: abrasiveness, acerbity *formal*, acrimony *formal*, asperity *formal*, bitterness, brutality, coarseness, hardness, ill-temper, sourness, sternness, strictness
🔁 1 mildness 2 gentleness, softness

harum-scarum *adj* careless, erratic, haphazard, hare-brained *colloq*, hasty, ill-considered, impetuous, imprudent *formal*, irresponsible, precipitate *formal*, rash, reckless, scatterbrained *colloq*, scatty *colloq*, wild
🔁 sensible

harvest *n* 1 *work long hours at harvest*: accumulation, collection, harvesting, harvest-time, hoard, ingathering, reaping, stock, store, supply 2 *a good harvest of grain*: crop, fruits, produce, yield 3 *reap the harvest of all her hard work*: consequence, effect, fruits, product, result, return, returns, yield
♦ *v* accumulate, acquire, amass, collect, gain, garner, gather, gather in, glean, hoard, mow, obtain, pick, pluck, reap, secure

hash *n* 1 *made a hash of the exam*: botch, bungle, confusion, hotchpotch, jumble, mess, mishmash, mismanagement, mix-up, muddle 2 *corned beef hash*: goulash, hotpot, lob's course, lobscouse, stew

hashish *n* bhang, cannabis, dope *colloq*, ganja *colloq*, grass *colloq*, hash, hemp, marijuana, pot *colloq*

hassle *n* aggro *colloq*, altercation *formal*, argument, bickering, bother, difficulty, disagreement, dispute, fight, inconvenience, nuisance, problem, quarrel, squabble, struggle, trial, trouble, upset, wrangle
🔁 agreement, peace
♦ *v* annoy, badger, bother, bug *colloq*, chivvy, harass, harry, hound, pester, trouble
🔁 assist, calm

haste *n* 1 *set off with all haste to the station*: alacrity *formal*, briskness, bustle, celerity *formal*, expeditiousness *formal*, fastness, hurry, hustle, quickness, rapidity, rush, speed, swiftness, urgency, velocity **2** *apologized for her haste in naming her successor:* carelessness, foolhardiness, impetuosity, impulsiveness, rashness, recklessness

F✑ **1** slowness **2** carefulness

hasten *v* accelerate, advance, be quick, bolt, dash, dispatch, expedite *formal*, fly, forward, get a move on *colloq*, go fast/quickly, hotfoot it *colloq*, hurry (up), make haste *old use*, precipitate *formal*, press, push forward, put your foot down *colloq*, quicken, race, run, rush, speed (up), sprint, step on it/the gas *colloq*, step up, tear, urge

F✑ dawdle, delay

hastily *adv* **1** *a hastily worded note:* heedlessly, hurriedly, impetuously, impulsively, precipitately *formal*, rashly, recklessly **2** *hastily ate their lunch:* apace, chop-chop *colloq*, double-quick *colloq*, fast, promptly, quickly, rapidly, speedily, straightaway

F✑ **1** carefully, deliberately **2** slowly

hasty *adj* **1** *a hasty decision:* careless, headlong, heedless, hotheaded, hurried, impatient, impetuous, impulsive, precipitate *formal*, rash, reckless, rushed, thoughtless **2** *ate a hasty breakfast:* brief, brisk, cursory, expeditious *formal*, fast, fleeting, hurried, perfunctory, prompt, quick, rapid, rushed, short, speedy, swift, transitory

F✑ **1** careful, deliberate **2** slow

hat

Hats include:

trilby, bowler, fedora, top-hat, Homburg, derby *US*, pork-pie hat, flat cap, beret, bonnet, tam-o'-shanter, tammy, deerstalker, hunting-cap, stovepipe hat, stetson, ten-gallon hat, boater, sunhat, panama, straw hat, picture-hat, pill-box, cloche, beanie, poke-bonnet, mob-cap, turban, fez, sombrero, sou'wester, glengarry, bearskin, busby, peaked cap, sailor-hat, baseball cap, balaclava, hood, snood, toque, helmet, mortar-board, skullcap, yarmulka, mitre, biretta

---

hatch *v* **1** *hatched an egg:* breed, brood, incubate, sit on **2** *hatched a plot:* conceive, concoct, contrive, design, devise, dream up, formulate, invent, originate, plan, plot, project, scheme, think up

hatchet *n* axe, battle-axe, chopper, cleaver, machete, mattock, pickaxe, tomahawk

hate *v* **1** *hated her boss:* abhor *formal*, abominate *formal*, despise, detest, dislike, execrate *formal*, feel revulsion at, hate someone's guts *colloq*, have an aversion to, loathe, not stand, recoil from **2** *I hate to disturb you:* apologize, be loath, be reluctant, be sorry, be unwilling, regret

F✑ **1** like, love

♦ *n* abhorrence *formal*, abomination *formal*, animosity, antagonism, aversion, bitterness, dislike, enmity, grudge, hatred, hostility, ill-will, loathing, rancour *formal*, resentment

F✑ liking, love

hateful *adj* abhorrent *formal*, abominable, contemptible, despicable, detestable, disagreeable, disgusting, evil, execrable *formal*, foul, heinous, horrible, horrid, loathsome, nasty, obnoxious, odious, offensive, repellent *formal*,

repugnant *formal*, repulsive, revolting, unpleasant, vile

F✑ pleasing

hatred *n* abhorrence *formal*, abomination *formal*, animosity, animus *formal*, antagonism, antipathy *formal*, aversion, bitterness, detestation *formal*, disgust, dislike, enmity, execration *formal*, grudge, hate, hostility, ill-will, loathing, rancour *formal*, repugnance *formal*, resentment, revulsion

F✑ liking, love

haughtiness *n* airs, aloofness, arrogance, conceit, contempt, contemptuousness, disdain, hauteur, insolence, loftiness, pomposity, pride, snobbishness, snootiness *colloq*, superciliousness

F✑ friendliness, humility

haughty *adj* arrogant, cavalier, conceited, condescending, contemptuous, disdainful, egotistical, high and mighty, imperious, lofty, on your high horse *colloq*, overbearing, patronizing, proud, scornful, self-important, snobbish, snooty *colloq*, stuck-up *colloq*, supercilious, superior, swollen-headed, vain

F✑ humble, modest

haul *v* carry, cart, convey, convoy, drag, draw, heave, hump *colloq*, lug, move, pull, push, ship, tow, trail, transport, tug

♦ *n* booty, find, gain, loot, plunder, spoils, swag *slang*, takings, yield

haunches *n* buttocks, hips, huckles, hucks, hunkers, nates, thighs

haunt *v* **1** *a ghost haunts the house:* appear often in, curse, materialize, possess, show up *colloq*, spook, visit, walk **2** *he haunted the local bars:* frequent, hang about/around in *colloq*, patronize, visit (regularly) **3** *memories haunted her:* beset, burden, disturb, harry, obsess, oppress, plague, possess, prey on, recur, torment, trouble, worry

♦ *n* den, favourite spot, hang-out *colloq*, local, meeting-place, rendezvous, resort, stamping-ground

haunted *adj* **1** *a haunted castle:* cursed, eerie, ghostly, hag-ridden, jinxed, possessed, spooky *colloq* **2** *a haunted look:* obsessed, plagued, preoccupied, tormented, troubled, worried

haunting *adj* atmospheric, evocative, memorable, nostalgic, persistent, poignant, recurrent, unforgettable

F✑ unmemorable

have *v* **1** *has two cars:* accept, acquire, be given, gain, get, hold, keep, obtain, own, possess, procure *formal*, receive, secure, take, use **2** *not have much luck:* be subjected to, encounter, endure, enjoy, experience, feel, find, go through, meet, put up with, submit to, suffer, tolerate, undergo **3** *the flat has four rooms:* comprehend *formal*, comprise *formal*, consist of, contain, embody, embrace *formal*, include, incorporate, take in **4** *have a party:* arrange, hold, organize, participate in, take part in **5** *have to go now:* be compelled, be forced, be obliged, be required, must, ought, should **6** *have someone do something:* arrange, ask, bid, cause, coerce, command, compel, enjoin *formal*, force, get, make, oblige, order, persuade, prevail upon *formal*, request, require, talk into, tell **7** *have pity on someone:* demonstrate, display, exhibit, express, feel, manifest *formal*, show **8** *have food/drink:* consume, devour, down, drink, eat, gulp, guzzle, knock back *colloq*, partake of *formal*, put away *colloq*, swallow, take, tuck into *colloq* **9** *have a baby*: be delivered of, bear, bring into the world, give birth to **10** *I won't have such behaviour*: abide, accept, allow, brook, permit, put up with, stand, take, tolerate **11** *you've been had*: cheat, con *colloq*, deceive, diddle *colloq*, dupe, fool, swindle, take in, trick

⊠ 1 lack

▶ **have on 1** *had a blue jacket on*: be clothed in, be dressed in, wear **2** *I don't have much on this week*: have an appointment, have an engagement, have arranged, have planned **3** *he's just having you on*: kid *colloq*, play a joke on, pull someone's leg *colloq*, rag *colloq*, tease, trick

haven *n* **1** *a safe haven*: asylum, oasis, refuge, retreat, sanctuary, shelter **2** *a haven for boats*: anchorage, bay, dock, harbour, port

haversack *n* backpack, kitbag, knapsack, rucksack

havoc *n* chaos, confusion, damage, desolation, despoliation *formal*, destruction, devastation, disorder, disruption, mayhem, rack and ruin, ravaging, ruin, ruination, shambles *colloq*, waste, wreck, wreckage

hawk¹ *n* buzzard, falcon, goshawk, haggard, harrier, kite, sparrowhawk, tercel

hawk² *v* bark, cry, market, offer, offer for sale, peddle, sell, tout, vend

hawker *n* barrow-boy, chapman, colporteur, coster, costermonger, crier, door-to-door salesman, huckster, pedlar, vendor

haywire *adj* chaotic, confused, crazy, disordered, disorganized, mad, out of control, tangled, topsy-turvy, wild, wrong

hazard *n* accident, chance, danger, deathtrap, jeopardy, menace, peril *formal*, pitfall, risk, threat

⊠ safety

◆ *v* **1** *hazarding injury if he fell*: endanger, expose to danger, jeopardize, put at risk, put in jeopardy, risk **2** *I wouldn't hazard a guess*: chance, gamble, offer, put forward, speculate, stake, submit, suggest, venture

hazardous *adj* chancy, dangerous, difficult, hairy *colloq*, insecure, menacing, perilous *formal*, precarious, risky, threatening, tricky, uncertain, unpredictable, unsafe

⊠ safe, secure

haze *n* **1** *haze over the river*: cloud, cloudiness, dimness, film, fog, fogginess, mist, mistiness, obscurity, smog, smokiness, steam, vapour **2** *in a haze after the crash*: bewilderment, blur, confusion, indistinctness, muddle, uncertainty, vagueness

hazy *adj* **1** *a hazy morning*: clouded, cloudy, foggy, milky, misty, obscure, overcast, smoky, veiled **2** *a hazy memory*: blurred, dim, faint, fuzzy, ill-defined, indefinite, indistinct, muzzy, uncertain, unclear, vague

⊠ 1 bright, clear **2** clear, definite

head *n* **1** *hit him on the head*: bonce *colloq*, caput *technical*, conk *colloq*, cranium, noddle *colloq*, nut *colloq*, skull **2** *get it into your head*: brain, brains *colloq*, common sense, grey matter *colloq*, intellect, intelligence, little grey cells *colloq*, loaf *colloq*, mental abilities, mentality, mind, noddle *colloq*,

reasoning, sense, thought, understanding, upper storey *colloq*, wisdom, wit(s) **3** *the head of the stairs*: apex, climax, crest, crown, height, peak, summit, tip, top, vertex **4** *at the head of the march*: fore, forefront, front, lead, van, vanguard **5** *the head of the company*: administrator, boss *colloq*, captain, chair, chairman, chairperson, chairwoman, chief, commander, controller, director, governor, head teacher, headmaster, headmistress, leader, manager, managing director, president, principal, ruler, superintendent, supervisor **6** *a team with the minister at its head*: charge, command, control(s), directorship, leadership, management, supervision **7** *come to a head*: calamity, catastrophe, climax, crisis, critical point, crunch *colloq*, dilemma, emergency **8** *the head of a river*: fount, origin, rise, source, spring, wellhead, wellspring **9** *no head on the beer*: bubbles, fizz, foam, froth, lather, suds

⊠ 3 base, foot **4** back **5** subordinate

◆ *adj* chief, dominant, first, foremost, front, highest, leading, main, pre-eminent, premier, prime, principal, supreme, top, topmost

◆ *v* **1** *head the queue*: be at the front of, be first in, go first, lead **2** *head the government*: administer, be in charge of, be in control of, command, control, direct, govern, guide, lead, manage, oversee, rule, run, steer, superintend, supervise

▶ **head for** aim for, direct towards, go in the direction of, go/move/travel towards, make for, point to, steer for, turn for

▶ **head off** avert, cut off, deflect, divert, fend off, forestall, intercept, interpose *formal*, intervene, prevent, stop, turn aside, ward off

▶ **head up** be in charge of, be responsible for, direct, lead, manage, take charge of

headache *n* **1** *suffer from headaches*: cephalalgia *technical*, hemicrania, migraine, neuralgia **2** *a bit of a headache getting everybody in the car*: bane, bother, hassle *colloq*, inconvenience, nuisance, pest, problem, trouble, vexation, worry

heading *n* caption, category, class, classification, division, head, headline, name, rubric, section, subject, title

headland *n* cape, foreland, head, ness, point, promontory

headlong *adj* breakneck, careless, dangerous, hasty, head-first, impetuous, impulsive, precipitate *formal*, rash, reckless

◆ *adv* **1** *fell headlong into the river*: head first, head over heels **2** *rushed headlong into marriage*: carelessly, hastily, heedlessly, hurriedly, impetuously, impulsively, precipitately *formal*, prematurely, rashly, recklessly, thoughtlessly, wildly, without thinking

headman *n* captain, chief, leader, muqaddam, ruler, sachem

head-on *adj* **1** *a head-on crash*: direct, full-frontal, straight, straight-on **2** *a head-on confrontation*: confrontational, direct, eyeball-to-eyeball, full-frontal, straight, straight-on

headquarters *n* base (camp), centre of operations, head office, HQ, main office, nerve centre

headstrong *adj* contrary, intractable, intransigent *formal*, not listening to reason, obdurate *formal*, obstinate, perverse, pigheaded, recalcitrant *formal*, refractory *formal*, self-willed,

stubborn, ungovernable, unruly, wayward, wilful
≠ docile, tractable

headway n advance, development, ground, improvement, progress, way

heady adj **1** *heady news of victory:* ecstatic, euphoric, exciting, exhilarating, invigorating, rousing, stimulating, thrilling **2** *a heady perfume:* aromatic, intoxicatng, overpowering, spicy, strong

heal v **1** *heal the sick:* assuage *formal*, comfort, cure, make better, make well, palliate *formal*, remedy, restore, salve, soothe, treat **2** *heal a rift between them:* improve, make good, mend, patch up, put/set right, reconcile, settle

health n condition, constitution, fettle, fitness, form, good condition, good shape, healthiness, robustness, shape, soundness, state, strength, tone, trim, vigour, welfare, well-being
≠ illness, infirmity

healthy adj **1** *healthy children:* a picture of health *colloq*, able-bodied, blooming, fine, fit, fit as a fiddle *colloq*, flourishing, good, hale and hearty, hardy *colloq*, in condition, in fine fettle, in good shape, in the pink *colloq*, right as rain *colloq*, robust, sound, strong, sturdy, thriving, vigorous, well **2** *healthy food:* beneficial, good, healthful, nourishing, nutritious, wholesome **3** *healthy fresh air:* bracing, invigorating, refreshing, salubrious *formal*, stimulating **4** *a healthy economy:* robust, sound, strong, successful, vigorous **5** *a healthy respect for authority:* judicious *formal*, prudent *formal*, sensible, sound, wise
≠ **1** ill, infirm, sick **2** junk *colloq* **4** ailing

heap n **1** *a heap of clothes:* accumulation, agglomeration *formal*, assemblage *formal*, bundle, collection, hoard, lot, mass, mound, mountain, pile, stack, stockpile, store, supply **2** *heaps of time:* a lot, abundance, great deal, lashings, load(s) *colloq*, lots, mass, millions *colloq*, oodles *colloq*, plenty, pot(s) *colloq*, quantities, scores *colloq*, stack(s) *colloq*, tons *colloq*
♦ v **1** *heap the flour on the board:* accumulate, amass, assemble, bank, build, burden, collect, gather, hoard, load, mound, pile, stack, stockpile, store (up) **2** *heap criticism/praise on someone:* bestow *formal*, confer *formal*, lavish, shower

hear v **1** *hear a sound:* catch, eavesdrop, heed, latch onto *colloq*, listen, make out, overhear, pay attention, perceive, pick up, take in **2** *I hear she's pregnant:* ascertain *formal*, be informed, be told, discover, find out, gather, learn, pick up, understand **3** *hear a case:* adjudicate, consider, examine, inquire, investigate, judge, pass judgement, try

hearing n **1** *within hearing of the waiter:* ear, earshot, hearing distance, perception, range, reach, sound **2** *granted a hearing:* adjudication, audience, audition, examination, inquest, inquiry, inquisition, interview, investigation, judgement, review, trial

hearsay n buzz *colloq*, common knowledge, common talk, gossip, report, rumour, talk, tittle-tattle, word of mouth

heart n **1** *a kind heart:* character, disposition, mind, nature, soul, temperament **2** *a woman with a lot of heart:* affection, compassion, concern, emotion, feeling, kindness, love, passion, pity,

responsiveness, sentiment, sympathy, tenderness, warmth **3** *lose heart:* boldness, bravery, courage, determination, eagerness, enthusiasm, fearlessness, fortitude *formal*, guts *colloq*, heroism, intrepidity, keenness, pluck, resolution, spirit, stout-heartedness **4** *the heart of the matter:* centre, core, crux, essence, essential part, kernel, marrow, middle, nub, nucleus, pith, quintessence *formal*, substance
≠ **3** cowardice **4** periphery

Parts of the heart include:
aortic valve, ascending aorta, bicuspid valve, carotid artery, descending thoracic aorta, inferior vena cava, left atrium, left pulmonary artery, left pulmonary veins, left ventricle, mitral valve, myocardium, papillary muscle, pulmonary valve, right atrium, right pulmonary artery, right pulmonary veins, right ventricle, superior vena cava, tricuspid valve, ventricular septum

heartache n affliction *formal*, agony, anguish, anxiety, bitterness, dejection, despair, despondency, distress, grief, heartbreak, pain, remorse, sorrow, suffering, torment, torture, worry

heartbreak n agony, anguish, dejection, desolation, despair, distress, grief, misery, pain, sadness, sorrow, suffering
≠ elation, joy, relief

heartbreaking adj agonizing, bitter, cruel, disappointing, distressing, excruciating, grievous, harrowing, harsh, heart-rending, painful, pitiful, poignant, sad, tragic
≠ heartening, heartwarming

heartbroken adj anguished, broken-hearted, crestfallen, crushed, dejected, desolate, despondent, disappointed, disheartened, dispirited, downcast, grieved, in low spirits, inconsolable, miserable, sad, sorrowful, suffering
≠ delighted, elated

hearten v animate, boost, buck up *colloq*, cheer (up), comfort, console, encourage, energize, inspire, invigorate, pep up *colloq*, raise the spirits of, reassure, revitalize, rouse, stimulate
≠ depress, dishearten, dismay

heartfelt adj ardent, compassionate, deep, devout, earnest, fervent, genuine, honest, profound, sincere, unfeigned, warm, wholehearted
≠ false, insincere

heartily adv **1** *applauded heartily:* cordially, deeply, eagerly, earnestly, enthusiastically, feelingly, genuinely, gladly, profoundly, resolutely, sincerely, unfeignedly, vigorously, warmly, zealously **2** *heartily sick of her:* absolutely, completely, thoroughly, totally, very

heartless adj brutal, callous, cold, cold-blooded, cold-hearted, cruel, hard, hard-hearted, harsh, inconsiderate, inhuman, merciless, pitiless, ruthless, uncaring, unfeeling, unkind, unmoved, unsympathetic
≠ considerate, kind, merciful, sympathetic

heart-rending adj affecting, agonizing, distressing, harrowing, heartbreaking, moving, pathetic, piteous, pitiful, poignant, sad, tragic

heartsick *adj* dejected, depressed, despondent, disappointed, downcast, glum, heavy-hearted, melancholy, sad

heart-throb *n* dreamboat *colloq*, idol, pin-up, star

heart-to-heart *n* cosy chat, friendly talk, honest talk, personal conversation, private conversation, tête-à-tête

heartwarming *adj* affecting, cheering, encouraging, gladdening, gratifying, heartening, moving, pleasing, rewarding, satisfying, touching, uplifting
🖃 heartbreaking

hearty *adj* 1 *a hearty welcome:* affable, cheerful, cordial, eager, ebullient, effusive, enthusiastic, exuberant, friendly, genuine, heartfelt, jovial, sincere, unfeigned, unreserved, warm, wholehearted 2 *a hearty breakfast:* abundant, ample, filling, generous, large, nourishing, nutritious, sizeable, solid, substantial 3 *a hearty handshake:* boisterous, energetic, hardy, healthy, robust, sound, stalwart, strong, vigorous
🖃 1 cold, half-hearted, inhibited, reserved 3 feeble, weak

heat *n* 1 *the heat of the day:* calefaction *technical*, closeness, fever, feverishness, heaviness, high temperature, hotness, sultriness, swelter, torridness, warmth 2 *in the heat of his anger:* anger, ardour, eagerness, earnestness, enthusiasm, excitement, fervency, fervour, fieriness, fury, impetuosity, intensity, passion, vehemence, warmth, zeal
🖃 1 cold(ness) 2 coolness
♦ *v* bake, boil, calefy *technical*, cook, microwave, reheat, roast, toast, warm, warm up
🖃 chill, cool (down)

heated *adj* angry, animated, bitter, enraged, excited, fierce, fiery, fired, frenzied, furious, impassioned, inflamed, intense, passionate, raging, roused, stimulated, stirred, stormy, tempestuous, vehement, violent, worked-up *colloq*
🖃 calm

heathen *n* barbarian, idolater, idolatress, infidel, nations, nullifidian *formal*, pagan, philistine, savage, unbeliever
🖃 believer
♦ *adj* barbaric, godless, idolatrous, infidel, irreligious, nullifidian *formal*, pagan, philistine, savage, unbelieving, uncivilized, unenlightened
🖃 believing, godly

heave *v* 1 *oxen heaved the cart:* drag, haul, hitch, hoist, lever, lift, pull, raise, rise, surge, tug 2 *heaved the anchor over the side:* cast, chuck *colloq*, fling, hurl, let fly, pitch, send, sling *colloq*, throw, toss 3 *her stomach was heaving:* be sick, gag, retch, spew, throw up *colloq*, vomit 4 *heave a sigh:* breathe, express, give, let out, utter

heaven *n* 1 *the angels in heaven:* abode of God *formal*, afterlife, bliss, elysian fields, Elysium, happy hunting-ground, hereafter, home of God, life to come, next world, nirvana, paradise, Swarga, up there *colloq*, utopia, Valhalla, Zion 2 *the comet shot across the heavens:* ether, firmament, skies, sky, the blue 3 *a week in the sun would be sheer heaven:* bliss, complete happiness, delight, ecstasy, happiness, joy, rapture, seventh heaven *colloq*, transports of delight
🖃 1 hell

heavenly *adj* 1 *the heavenly host:* angelic, beatific, blessed, celestial, cherubic, cosmic, divine, empyreal *formal*, empyrean *formal*, extraterrestrial, godlike, holy, immortal, otherworldly, seraphic, spiritual, sublime, supernatural, unearthly 2 *the chocolate mousse is heavenly:* beautiful, blissful, delightful, divine *colloq*, enchanting, enjoyable, exquisite, glorious, lovely, marvellous, out of this world *colloq*, perfect, rapturous, wonderful
🖃 1 infernal, mundane 2 hellish

heavily *adv* 1 *fell heavily:* awkwardly, clumsily, hard, laboriously, painfully, ponderously, slowly, sluggishly, weightily, woodenly 2 *a heavily built man:* closely, compactly, densely, solidly, thick, thickly 3 *heavily beaten:* completely, decisively, roundly, soundly, thoroughly, utterly 4 *heavily armed guards:* abundantly, copiously, excessively, to excess, too much
🖃 1 lightly 2 loosely

heaviness *n* 1 *the heaviness of the parcel:* bulk, density, heftiness, ponderousness, solidity, thickness, weight, weightiness 2 *a heaviness in the air:* burdensomeness, deadness, dejection, depression, despondency, drowsiness, gloom, gloominess, languor *formal*, lassitude *formal*, melancholy, onerousness, oppression, oppressiveness, sadness, seriousness, sleepiness, sluggishness, somnolence *formal*
🖃 2 lightness, liveliness

heavy *adj* 1 *heavy loads:* awkward, bulky, burdensome, cumbersome, dense, heavy as lead *colloq*, hefty, hulking, large, massive, ponderous, solid, substantial, thick, weighing a ton *colloq*, weighty 2 *heavy work:* arduous, demanding, difficult, exacting, hard, harsh, laborious, severe, strenuous, taxing, tough, troublesome 3 *a heavy discussion about politics:* deep, dry, dull, grave, intense, profound, serious, sombre, tedious, uninteresting 4 *heavy fighting:* considerable, excessive, extreme, great, immoderate, inordinate, intense, severe, strong 5 *a heavy blow on the head:* forceful, hard, intense, powerful, sharp, strong, violent 6 *heavy responsibilities:* burdensome, crushing, demanding, difficult, exacting, intolerable, irksome, onerous, oppressive, taxing, troublesome, trying, unbearable, wearisome, weighty 7 *with a heavy heart:* crushed, depressed, despondent, discouraged, downcast, gloomy, miserable, sad 8 *a heavy meal:* big, filling, indigestible, large, solid, starchy, stodgy, substantial 9 *tables heavy with food:* burdened, encumbered, full, groaning, laden, loaded, weighed down 10 *the weather is heavy:* close, humid, muggy, oppressive, steamy, sticky, sultry 11 *a heavy sky:* cloudy, dark, dull, gloomy, grey, leaden, overcast
🖃 1 light 2 easy 3 light 4 light 5 gentle 6 light 8 light 10 cool, fresh 11 bright

heavy-handed *adj* autocratic, despotic, domineering, forceful, harsh, inept, insensitive, oppressive, overbearing, severe, stern, tactless, thoughtless, unsubtle
🖃 skilful

heavy-hearted *adj* crushed, depressed, despondent, disappointed, discouraged, disheartened, downcast, downhearted, forlorn,

gloomy, glum, heartsick, melancholy, miserable, morose, mournful, sad, sorrowful
🔁 light-hearted

heckle *v* bait, barrack, catcall, disrupt, gibe, interrupt, jeer, pester, shout down, taunt

hectic *adj* bustling, busy, chaotic, excited, fast, feverish, frantic, frenetic, frenzied, furious, heated, tumultuous, turbulent, wild
🔁 leisurely

hector *v* badger, bluster, browbeat, bulldoze *colloq*, bully, bullyrag, chivvy, harass, huff, intimidate, menace, nag, provoke, threaten, worry

hedge *n* **1** *a hedge around a field:* barrier, boundary, dyke, fence, hedgerow, protection, screen, windbreak **2** *a hedge against inflation:* cover, guard, protection, safeguard, shield
♦ *v* **1** *hedge a permit with conditions:* confine, cover, edge, encircle, enclose, fortify *formal*, guard, hem in, insure, limit, protect, restrict, safeguard, shield, surround **2** *stop hedging and answer the question:* dodge *colloq*, duck *colloq*, equivocate, evade, prevaricate, quibble, sidestep, stall, temporize *formal*

hedonism *n* dolce vita, Epicureanism, epicurism, gratification, luxuriousness, pleasure-seeking, self-indulgence, sensualism, sensuality, sybaritism, voluptuousness
🔁 asceticism

hedonist *n* bon vivant, bon viveur, epicure, epicurean, pleasure-seeker, sensualist, sybarite, voluptuary
🔁 ascetic

hedonistic *adj* epicurean, luxurious, pleasure-seeking, self-indulgent, sybaritic, voluptuous
🔁 ascetic, austere

heed *v* attend to, bear in mind, consider, follow, listen, mark, mind, note, obey, observe, pay attention to, regard, take into account, take into consideration, take note/notice
🔁 disregard, ignore
♦ *n* animadversion *formal*, attention, care, caution, consideration, ear, heedfulness, mind, note, notice, regard, respect, thought, watchfulness
🔁 inattention, indifference, unconcern

heedful *adj* attentive, careful, cautious, chary, circumspect *formal*, mindful, observant, prudent *formal*, regardful *formal*, vigilant, wary, watchful
🔁 heedless, unthinking

heedless *adj* careless, foolhardy, inattentive, negligent, oblivious, precipitate *formal*, rash, reckless, regardless, thoughtless, unconcerned, unmindful, unobservant, unthinking, unwary
🔁 attentive, heedful, mindful, vigilant, watchful

hefty *adj* **1** *a hefty shot-putter:* beefy, big, brawny, burly, huge, hulking, large, massive, muscular, powerful, robust, stout, strapping, strong, vigorous **2** *a hefty blow:* awkward, bulky, colossal, forceful, hard, heavy, immense, massive, powerful, solid, substantial, unwieldy, vigorous, weighty **3** *a hefty sum of money:* ample, considerable, generous, sizeable, substantial
🔁 **1** slight, small **2** weak **3** small

height *n* **1** *the height of the tower is 100 feet:* altitude, elevation, highness, loftiness, stature, tallness **2** *from the height of the mountain:* apex, crest, crown, hill top, mountain top, peak, pinnacle, summit, top **3** *at the height of his fame:* apex, apogee, ceiling, climax, culmination, extremity, limit, maximum, peak, pinnacle, summit, ultimate, uttermost, vertex *technical*, zenith
🔁 **1** depth

heighten *v* add to, amplify, augment *formal*, boost, build up, elevate, enhance, exalt, improve, increase, intensify, lift, magnify, raise, sharpen, strengthen
🔁 decrease, diminish, lower

heinous *adj* abhorrent *formal*, abominable, atrocious, awful, contemptible, despicable, detestable, evil, execrable *formal*, facinorous *formal*, flagrant, grave, hateful, hideous, infamous, iniquitous, loathsome, monstrous, nefarious *formal*, odious, outrageous, revolting, shocking, unspeakable, vicious, villainous, wicked

heir, heiress *n* beneficiary, co-heir, inheritor, inheritress, inheritrix, legatee, parcener *technical*, scion, successor

helix *n* coil, corkscrew, curl, curlicue *technical*, loop, screw, spiral, twist, volute, whorl, wreathe

hell *n* **1** *heaven and hell:* Abaddon, abode of the devil *formal*, abyss, Acheron, blazes *colloq*, bottomless pit, down there *colloq*, fire, Gehenna, Hades, infernal regions, inferno, lower regions, Malebolge, nether world, perdition *formal*, Tartarus, Tophet, underworld **2** *it was hell at the sales:* agony, anguish, misery, nightmare, ordeal, suffering, torment, torture, tribulation *formal*, wretchedness
🔁 **1** heaven

hell-bent *adj* bent, determined, dogged, fixed, inflexible, intent, intransigent *formal*, obdurate *formal*, resolved, set, settled, tenacious, unhesitating, unwavering

hellish *adj* abominable, accursed, atrocious, barbaric, cruel, damnable, demonic, devilish, diabolical, disagreeable, dreadful, execrable *formal*, fiendish, infernal, monstrous, nasty, nefarious *formal*, satanic, savage, unpleasant, wicked
🔁 heavenly
♦ *adv* awfully, dreadfully, extremely, unpleasantly

helm *n* rudder, tiller, wheel

help *v* **1** *helped me with the work:* aid, assist, back, be of assistance, be of use, collaborate, contribute to, co-operate, do someone a good turn, do something for, do your bit *colloq*, encourage, give a boost to, guide, lend a hand, oblige, promote, rally round, serve, stand by, support **2** *the drugs should help the condition:* alleviate *formal*, ameliorate *formal*, assuage, cure, ease, facilitate, further, heal, improve, mitigate *formal*, relieve, remedy, soothe **3** *can't help laughing:* avoid, control, prevent yourself, refrain/abstain *formal*, stop
🔁 **1** hinder **2** worsen
♦ *n* **1** *with the help of her teachers:* advantage, advice, aid, assistance, backing, backup, benefit, boost, charity, collaboration, co-operation, encouragement, guidance, helping hand, relief, service, shot in the arm *colloq*, succour *formal*, support, use, utility **2** *you've been a great help:* advisor, aide, assistant, backer, collaborator, guide, helper, helping hand, supporter, tower of

strength *colloq* **3** *the drugs were no help:* alleviation *formal*, amelioration *formal*, balm, cure, mitigation *formal*, relief, remedy, restorative, salve
F3 **1** hindrance

helper *n* accomplice, adjutant, aide, ally, assistant, associate, attendant, auxiliary, collaborator, colleague, co-worker, deputy, employee, helpmate, maid, man/girl Friday, mate, PA, partner, right-hand man/woman, second, second-in-command, servant, subordinate, subsidiary, supporter, worker

helpful *adj* **1** *a helpful suggestion:* advantageous, beneficial, constructive, of service, of use, practical, profitable, useful, valuable, worthwhile **2** *a helpful person:* accommodating, benevolent, caring, charitable, considerate, co-operative, friendly, kind, neighbourly, obliging, supportive, sympathetic
F3 **1** futile, useless **2** cruel, unfriendly

helping *n* amount, bowlful, dollop *colloq*, piece, plateful, portion, ration, serving, share, spoonful

helpless *adj* abandoned, debilitated *formal*, defenceless, dependent, desolate, destitute, disabled, exposed, feeble, forlorn, friendless, helpless as a newborn babe *colloq*, impotent, incapable, incompetent, infirm, paralysed, powerless, unprotected, vulnerable, weak
F3 competent, independent, strong

helpmate *n* assistant, associate, better half, companion, consort, helper, helpmeet, husband, other half, partner, spouse, support, wife

helter-skelter *adv* carelessly, confusedly, hastily, hurriedly, impulsively, pell-mell, rashly, recklessly, wildly
♦ *adj* confused, disordered, disorganized, haphazard, higgledy-piggledy, hit-or-miss, jumbled, muddled, random, topsy-turvy, unsystematic

hem *n* border, edge, edging, fimbria *technical*, flounce, frill, fringe, margin, trim, trimming, valance
♦ *v* bind, border, edge, fimbriate *technical*, fold, fringe, skirt, trim
▶ **hem in** box in, close in, confine, constrain, enclose, hedge in, limit, pen in, restrict, shut in, surround, trap

hence *adv* accordingly, consequently, ergo *formal*, for this reason, therefore, thus

henceforth *adv* from now on, from this time on, hence, henceforward, hereafter, hereinafter, in the future

henchman *n* aide, associate, attendant, bodyguard, crony *colloq*, follower, hatchet man *colloq*, heavy *colloq*, hit man *colloq*, lackey, minder *colloq*, minion, right-hand man/woman, sidekick *colloq*, subordinate, supporter, underling

henpecked *adj* badgered, browbeaten, bullied, criticized, dominated, harassed, intimidated, meek, pestered, subjugated, tied to someone's apron strings *colloq*, timid, tormented, under someone's thumb *colloq*
F3 dominant

herald *n* **1** *a herald of what is to come:* augury *formal*, forerunner, harbinger *formal*, indication, omen, portent *formal*, precursor, sign, signal,

token **2** *the king's herald:* announcer, courier, crier, messenger, usher
♦ *v* **1** *fireworks herald the arrival of the pop star on stage:* advertise, announce, broadcast, make known, make public, proclaim, promulgate *formal*, publicize, trumpet **2** *the drug heralds a breakthrough in AIDS treatment:* augur *formal*, foreshadow, harbinger *formal*, indicate, pave the way *colloq*, portend *formal*, presage *formal*, promise, show, signal, usher in

heraldry

Heraldic terms include:
shield, crest, coat of arms, arms, badge, hatchment, emblazonry, emblem, ensign, insignia, regalia, mantling, helmet, supporters, field, charge, compartment, motto, dexter, centre, sinister, annulet, fleur-de-lis, martlet, mullet, rampant, passant, sejant, caboched, statant, displayed, couchant, dormant, urinant, volant, chevron, pile, pall, saltire, quarter, orle, bordure, gyronny, lozenge, impale, escutcheon, antelope, camelopard, cockatrice, eagle, griffin, lion, phoenix, unicorn, wivern, addorsed, bezant, blazon, canton, cinquefoil, quatrefoil, roundel, semé, tierced, undee, urdé

---

herb

Herbs and spices include:
angelica, anise, basil, bay, bergamot, borage, camomile, catmint, chervil, chives, comfrey, cumin, dill, fennel, garlic, hyssop, lavender, lemon balm, lovage, marjoram, mint, oregano, parsley, rosemary, sage, savory, sorrel, tarragon, thyme; allspice, caper, caraway seeds, cardamon, cayenne pepper, chilli, cinnamon, cloves, coriander, curry, ginger, mace, mustard, nutmeg, paprika, pepper, saffron, sesame, turmeric, vanilla

---

herculean *adj* arduous, colossal, daunting, demanding, difficult, enormous, exacting, exhausting, formidable, gigantic, great, gruelling, hard, heavy, huge, laborious, large, mammoth, massive, onerous, powerful, strenuous, strong, toilsome, tough, tremendous

herd *n* **1** *a herd of cattle:* collection, crowd, crush, drove, flock, horde, host, mass, mob, multitude, pack, press, swarm, throng **2** *the common herd:* mob, plebs *colloq*, proles *colloq*, rabble, riff-raff *colloq*, the masses
♦ *v* **1** *people herded together in the square:* assemble, collect, congregate, flock, gather, get together, huddle, muster, rally **2** *herded the fans into the stadium:* drive, force, goad, guide, lead, round up, shepherd, urge

herdsman *n* cowherd, cowman, drover, grazier, shepherd, stockman, vaquero *US*, wrangler

here *adv* **1** *come here:* around, in, in/to/at this place, present **2** *I must finish here:* at this point, at this stage, at this time, now
F3 **1** absent, away, missing, there **2** then

hereafter *adv* eventually, from now on, from this time forward/onwards, hence, henceforth, henceforward, in the future, later
♦ *n* afterlife, elysian fields, happy hunting-ground, heaven, life after death, life to come, next world, paradise

here and there *adv* from pillar to post *colloq*, hither and thither, in different places, sporadically, to and fro

hereditary *adj* **1** *a hereditary title:* ancestral, bequeathed, family, handed down, inherited, left, transferred, willed **2** *hereditary diseases:* congenital, genetic, inborn, inbred, inherent, inherited, innate, natural, transmissible

heresy *n* agnosticism, apostasy, atheism, blasphemy, dissent, dissidence, error, free-thinking, heterodoxy, nonconformity, revisionism, scepticism, schism, sectarianism, separatism, unbelief, unorthodoxy
🔁 orthodoxy

heretic *n* agnostic, apostate, atheist, dissenter, dissident, free-thinker, nonconformist, renegade, revisionist, sceptic, schismatic, sectarian, separatist, unbeliever
🔁 conformist

heretical *adj* agnostic, atheistic, blasphemous, dissenting, dissident, free-thinking, heterodox, iconoclastic, impious, irreverent, rationalistic, renegade, revisionist, sceptical, schismatic, sectarian, separatist, unbelieving, unorthodox
🔁 conformist, conventional, orthodox

heritage *n* **1** *part of his family's heritage:* bequest, birthright, due, endowment, estate, inheritance, legacy, lot, portion, share **2** *the cultural heritage of Britain:* ancestry, background, cultural traditions, culture, descent, dynasty, extraction, family, history, lineage, past, tradition

hermetic *adj* airtight, hermetical, sealed, shut, watertight

hermit *n* anchoress, anchorite, ancress, ascetic, eremite, loner, monk, pillarist, pillar-saint, recluse, solitary, stylite

hermitage *n* asylum, cloister, haven, hideaway, hideout, hiding place, refuge, retreat, sanctuary, shelter

hero *n* **1** *the hero of a play:* lead, leading actor, leading male role/part, male lead, protagonist **2** *heroes in battle:* cavalier, champion, conqueror, goody *colloq*, lion, man/person of courage, victor **3** *film heroes like Brando:* celebrity, god, heart-throb *colloq*, ideal, idol, paragon, pin-up, star, superstar
🔁 **1** villain

heroic *adj* adventurous, bold, brave, chivalrous, courageous, daring, dauntless, determined, doughty *formal*, fearless, gallant, intrepid, lion-hearted, noble, selfless, stout-hearted, undaunted, valiant, valorous *formal*
🔁 cowardly, timid

heroine *n* **1** *the heroine of a play:* diva, female lead, lead, leading actress/lady, leading female role/part, prima ballerina, prima donna, protagonist **2** *heroines in battle:* cavalier, celebrity, champion, conqueror, goody *colloq*, lion, victor, woman/person of courage **3** *a heroine of the silver screen:* celebrity, goddess, ideal, idol, paragon, pin-up, star, superstar
🔁 **1** villain

heroism *n* boldness, bravery, chivalry, courage, daring, dauntlessness, determination, doughtiness *formal*, fearlessness, fortitude

formal, gallantry, intrepidity, lion-heartedness, prowess, selflessness, stout-heartedness, valour
🔁 cowardice, pusillanimity *formal*, timidity

hero-worship *n* admiration, adoration, adulation, deification, exaltation, glorification, idealization, idolization, putting on a pedestal *colloq*, veneration *formal*, worship

hesitancy *n* demur *formal*, disinclination *formal*, doubt, doubtfulness, indecision, irresolution *formal*, misgiving, qualm, reluctance, reservation, scruples, uncertainty, unwillingness, wavering
🔁 certainty, willingness

hesitant *adj* delaying, demurring *formal*, disinclined *formal*, doubtful, dubious, half-hearted, halting, hesitating, indecisive, irresolute, reluctant, sceptical, shy, stalling, stammering, stuttering, tentative, timid, uncertain, unsure, unwilling, vacillating, wary, wavering
🔁 confident, decisive, fluent, resolute

hesitate *v* **1** *hesitated before answering:* delay, falter, halt, hang back, hold back, pause, stammer, stumble, stutter, think twice, wait **2** *don't hesitate to ask for help:* be disinclined *formal*, be reluctant, be uncertain, be unwilling, boggle, demur *formal*, dilly-dally *colloq*, dither, scruple, shilly-shally *colloq*, shrink from, stall, vacillate, waver
🔁 **2** decide

hesitation *n* cunctation *formal*, delay, demur *formal*, dilly-dallying *colloq*, disinclination *formal*, doubt, doubtfulness, faltering, hanging-back, hesitance, holding-back, indecision, irresolution *formal*, misgivings, pause, qualm(s), reluctance, scepticism, scruple(s), second thoughts, shilly-shallying *colloq*, stalling, stammering, stumbling, stuttering, uncertainty, unsureness, unwillingness, vacillation, waiting, wavering
🔁 assurance, eagerness

heterodox *adj* dissenting, dissident, free-thinking, heretical, iconoclastic, revisionist, schismatic, unorthodox, unsound
🔁 orthodox

heterogeneous *adj* assorted, catholic, contrary, contrasted, different, discrepant, disparate *formal*, dissimilar, divergent, diverse, diversified, incongruous *formal*, miscellaneous, mixed, motley, multiform *formal*, opposed, polymorphic *technical*, unlike, unrelated, varied
🔁 homogeneous

heterosexual *n* breeder *slang*, hetero *slang*, straight person
🔁 gay, homosexual
♦ *adj* hetero *slang*, straight
🔁 gay, homosexual

hew *v* **1** *hewing logs:* axe, chop, cut, fell, hack, lop, prune, saw, sever, split, trim **2** *a monument hewn out of the cliff face:* carve, chip, chisel, fashion, form, hammer, make, model, sculpt, sculpture, shape, whittle

heyday *n* bloom, boom time, culmination, flowering, flush, golden age, peak, pinnacle, prime

hiatus *n* aperture *formal*, blank, breach, break, chasm, discontinuance *formal*, discontinuity, gap, interruption, interval, lacuna *formal*, lapse, lull, opening, pause, rest, rift, space, suspension, void

hidden *adj* **1** *a hidden door:* camouflaged, concealed, covered, disguised, masked, out of sight, secret, shrouded, unseen, veiled **2** *a hidden meaning in the text:* abstruse, arcane *formal*, close, covert, cryptic, dark, indistinct, latent, mysterious, mystical, obscure, occult, recondite *formal*, secret, ulterior, under wraps *colloq*
☒ **1** apparent, on view, revealed, showing, visible **2** clear, distinct, obvious

hide¹ *v* **1** *hid the book under a cushion:* bury, conceal, cover, put out of sight, screen, stash away *colloq*, store, stow **2** *hid his true feelings:* bottle up *colloq*, camouflage, cloak, cover, disguise, dissemble *formal*, draw a veil over, keep dark, keep under wraps *colloq*, keep under your hat *colloq*, mask, obscure, put out of sight, secrete, suppress, sweep under the carpet *colloq*, veil, withhold **3** *hid from her pursuers:* conceal yourself, cover your tracks, disappear into thin air *colloq*, go into hiding, go to ground, hole up *colloq*, keep a low profile *colloq*, keep out of sight, lay a false scent *colloq*, lie doggo *colloq*, lie low, lurk, shelter, take cover
☒ **1** reveal, show **2** display, reveal, show

hide² *n* coat, fell, fleece, fur, leather, pelt, skin

hideaway *n* cloister, den, haven, hermitage, hideout, hiding place, hole, lair, nest, refuge, retreat, sanctuary, shelter

hidebound *adj* bigoted, conventional, entrenched, fixed, intolerant, intractable *formal*, narrow, narrow-minded, reactionary, rigid, set, strait-laced, ultra-conservative, uncompromising
☒ liberal, progressive

hideous *adj* abominable, appalling, awful, disgusting, dreadful, frightful, ghastly, grim, grotesque, gruesome, horrendous, horrible, horrid, horrifying, macabre, monstrous, outrageous, repellent, repulsive, revolting, shocking, terrible, terrifying, ugly, unsightly
☒ attractive, beautiful

hideout *n* cloister, den, haven, hermitage, hideaway, hiding place, hole, lair, refuge, retreat, sanctuary, shelter

hiding¹ *n* camouflage, concealment, cover, disguise, mask, screening, veiling

hiding² *n* battering, beating, belting *colloq*, caning, drubbing, flogging, licking *colloq*, spanking, tanning *colloq*, thrashing, walloping *colloq*, whacking *colloq*, whipping

hiding place *n* cache, cloister, cover, den, haven, hide, hideaway, hideout, hole, lair, refuge, retreat, sanctuary, shelter

hierarchy *n* echelons, grading, ladder, pecking order, ranking, scale, series, strata, structure, system

higgledy-piggledy *adv* any old how, anyhow, confusedly, haphazardly, indiscriminately, pell-mell, topsy-turvy, untidily
♦ *adj* confused, disorderly, disorganized, haphazard, indiscriminate, jumbled, muddled, topsy-turvy, untidy

high *adj* **1** *high buildings:* elevated, lofty, soaring, tall, towering **2** *a state of high tension:* extreme, forceful, great, intense, powerful, strong,

vigorous, violent **3** *in a high position in the government:* chief, distinguished, elevated, eminent, exalted, high-ranking, important, influential, leading, notable, powerful, principal, prominent, senior, top **4** *a higher form of life:* advanced, complex, elaborate, hi-tech, progressive, ultra-modern **5** *a high standard:* blue-chip, choice, classy *colloq*, commendable, de luxe, excellent, exemplary, fine, first-class, first-rate, gilt-edged, good, great, noteworthy, outstanding, perfect, quality, select, superior, superlative, surpassing, tiptop, top-class, unequalled, unparalleled **6** *have a high opinion of someone:* admiring, agreeable, appreciative, approving, complimentary, favourable, good, positive, well-disposed **7** *high moral principles:* admirable, ethical, honourable, lofty, moral, noble, upright, virtuous, worthy **8** *a high price:* costly, dear, excessive, exorbitant, expensive, extortionate, inflated, steep *colloq* **9** *a high voice:* acute, falsetto, high-pitched, penetrating, piercing, piping, sharp, shrill, soprano, tinny, treble **10** *high on drugs:* blasted *slang*, blitzed *slang*, bombed *slang*, doped *colloq*, freaked out *colloq*, hallucinating, having your mind blown *colloq*, inebriated, intoxicated, loaded *slang*, on a trip *colloq*, out of it *slang*, spaced out *colloq*, stoned *colloq*, turned on *colloq*, wasted *colloq*, wired *US colloq*, zonked *colloq* **11** *meat that smelt a bit high:* bad, decayed, off, putrid, rancid, rotting, smelling
☒ **1** low, short **2** low, slight **3** lowly, unimportant **4** low **5** inferior, low, poor **6** bad, low, poor **7** low **8** cheap **9** deep, low
♦ *n* **1** *feeling on a high:* boost, buzz *colloq*, kick, lift, thrill **2** *temperatures reached an all-time high:* height, peak, record, summit, top, zenith *formal*
☒ **2** low

high-born *adj* aristocratic, blue-blooded, noble, patrician, thoroughbred, well-born
☒ low-born

highbrow *n* academic, boffin *colloq*, brainbox *colloq*, brains *colloq*, clever clogs *colloq*, egghead *colloq*, genius, intellectual, know-all *colloq*, mastermind, scholar
♦ *adj* academic, bookish, brainy *colloq*, classical, cultivated, cultured, deep, intellectual, profound, scholarly, serious, sophisticated
☒ lowbrow

high-class *adj* choice, classy *colloq*, de luxe, elegant, élite, excellent, exclusive, first-rate, high-quality, luxurious, posh *colloq*, quality, select, super *colloq*, superior, top-class, top-flight, upper-class
☒ mediocre, ordinary

highfalutin, highfaluting *adj* affected, bombastic, grandiose, high-flown, high-sounding, la-di-da *colloq*, lofty, magniloquent *formal*, pompous, pretentious, supercilious, swanky *colloq*

high-flown *adj* affected, artificial, bombastic, elaborate, exaggerated, extravagant, flamboyant, florid, grandiloquent *formal*, grandiose, highfalutin, high-sounding, la-di-da *colloq*, lofty, ornate, ostentatious, pompous, pretentious, stilted, supercilious, turgid

high-handed *adj* arbitrary, arrogant, autocratic, bossy *colloq*, despotic, dictatorial, domineering, haughty, imperious, oppressive, overbearing, peremptory *formal*, tyrannical

highland *n* elevation, height, hill, mound, mount, mountain, plateau, ridge, rise, upland

highlight *n* best, climax, cream, focus, high point, high spot, most interesting/exciting part, most significant feature, peak
♦ *v* accent, accentuate, call attention to, emphasize, feature, focus on, illuminate, play up, point up, put emphasis on, set off, show up, spotlight, stress, underline

highly *adv* **1** *highly unlikely*: certainly, considerably, decidedly, exceptionally, extraordinarily, extremely, greatly, hugely, immensely, tremendously, vastly, very, very much **2** *think highly of someone*: appreciatively, approvingly, enthusiastically, favourably, warmly, well

highly-strung *adj* easily upset, edgy, excitable, jumpy, nervous, nervy, neurotic, on edge, overwrought, restless, sensitive, stressed, temperamental, tense, uptight *colloq*, wound up *colloq*
Ⓕ calm

high-minded *adj* elevated, ethical, fair, good, honourable, idealistic, lofty, moral, noble, principled, pure, righteous, upright, virtuous, worthy
Ⓕ immoral, unscrupulous

high-pitched *adj* acute, falsetto, penetrating, piercing, piping, sharp, shrill, soprano, tinny, treble
Ⓕ deep, low

high-powered *adj* aggressive, ambitious, assertive, driving, dynamic, energetic, enterprising, forceful, go-ahead *colloq*, insistent, powerful, pushy *colloq*, vigorous

high-priced *adj* costly, dear, excessive, exorbitant, expensive, extortionate, high, pricey, steep *colloq*, stiff *colloq*, unreasonable
Ⓕ cheap

high-sounding *adj* affected *formal*, artificial, bombastic, extravagant, flamboyant, florid, grandiloquent *formal*, grandiose, high-flown, magniloquent *formal*, orotund *formal*, ostentatious, overblown, pompous, ponderous, pretentious, stilted, strained

high-spirited *adj* active, animated, boisterous, bold, bouncy, daring, dashing, dynamic, ebullient, effervescent, energetic, exuberant, frolicsome, full of beans *colloq*, lively, sparkling, spirited, vibrant, vigorous, vivacious
Ⓕ placid, quiet, sedate

high spirits *n* animation, boisterousness, boldness, bounce *colloq*, buoyancy, capers, ebullience, energy, exhilaration, exuberance, good cheer, hilarity, joie de vivre, liveliness, sparkle, spirit, vivacity

highwayman *n* bandit, footpad, knight of the road, land-pirate, rank-rider, robber

hijack *v* commandeer, expropriate *formal*, seize, skyjack, take over

hike *v* **1** *hiked across the moors*: march, plod, ramble, tramp, trek, trudge, walk, wander **2** *will hike interest rates*: increase, jack up *colloq*, lift, pull up, push up *colloq*, put up, raise **3** *hike up your*

clothing: hitch, hoist, jack, jerk, lift, pull, raise, tug, yank *colloq*
♦ *n* march, ramble, tramp, trek, trudge, walk, wander

hilarious *adj* a scream *colloq*, amusing, comical, entertaining, farcical, funny, humorous, hysterical *colloq*, jolly, jovial, killing *colloq*, laughable, merry, noisy, riotous, rollicking, side-splitting, uproarious
Ⓕ grave, serious

hilarity *n* amusement, comedy, conviviality, exhilaration, exuberance, frivolity, fun, high spirits, jollity, laughter, levity, merriment, mirth
Ⓕ gravity, seriousness

hill *n* **1** *hills and valleys*: down, elevation, eminence, fell, foothill, height, hillock, hilltop, hummock, knoll, mesa *US*, mound, mount, mountain, prominence, rise, rising ground, tor **2** *a steep hill*: acclivity *formal*, ascent, declivity, descent, drop, gradient, incline, ramp, rise, slope

hillock *n* barrow, dune, hummock, knap, knob, knoll, knowe *Scot*, monticle, monticulus, mound, tump

hilt *n* grip, haft, handgrip, handle, heft, helve, shaft

hind *adj* after, back, caudal, hinder, posterior, rear, tail
Ⓕ fore

hinder *v* arrest, balk, block, check, curb, delay, encumber, foil, forestall, frustrate, halt, hamper, hamstring, handicap, hold back, hold up, impede, inhibit, interfere with, interrupt, obstruct, oppose, prevent, put a spoke in someone's wheel *colloq*, retard *formal*, slow down, stop, stymie *colloq*, thwart
Ⓕ aid, assist, help

hindmost *adj* concluding, endmost, farthest behind, final, furthest, furthest back, last, rearmost, remotest, tail, terminal, trailing, ultimate
Ⓕ foremost

hindrance *n* bar, barrier, block, check, curb, delay, deterrent, difficulty, disadvantage, drag, drawback, encumbrance, foil, handicap, hitch, hold-up, impediment, inconvenience, interference, interruption, limitation, obstacle, obstruction, restraint, restriction, snag, stoppage, stumbling-block, thwarting
Ⓕ aid, assistance, help

hinge *v* be contingent *formal*, centre, depend, hang, pivot, rest, revolve, turn

hint *n* **1** *household hints*: advice, help, pointer, suggestion, tip, wrinkle *colloq* **2** *hints that something was wrong*: allusion, clue, cue, implication, indication, inkling, innuendo, insinuation, intimation, mention, sign, suggestion, suspicion, tip-off, whisper **3** *a hint of garlic*: dash, nuance, soupçon, speck, sprinkling, suggestion, suspicion, taste, tinge, touch, trace, whiff
♦ *v* allude, imply, indicate, insinuate, intimate, mention, prompt, signal, suggest, tip off *colloq*, tip someone the wink *colloq*

hinterland *n* back-blocks, back-country, backveld, hinderland, interior

hip *n* buttocks, croup, haunch, hindquarters, huck, huckle, loin, pelvis, posterior, rump

hippie *n* beatnik, bohemian, deviant, dropout *colloq*, flower child, loner, rebel

hire *v* **1** *hire a car:* book, charter, commission, lease, let, rent, reserve **2** *hire a secretary:* appoint, employ, engage, enlist, retain, sign on, sign up, take on
F3 **2** dismiss, fire *colloq*
♦ *n* charge, cost, fee, lease, price, rent, rental

hire-purchase *n* credit, easy terms, instalment plan, never-never *colloq*

hirsute *adj* bearded, bewhiskered, bristly, crinal *formal*, crinate *formal*, crinigerous *formal*, crinite *formal*, crinose *formal*, hairy, hispid *technical*, shaggy, unshaven
F3 bald, hairless

hiss *v* **1** *the kettle hissed on the stove:* shrill, sibilate *formal*, sizzle, whistle, whizz **2** *the audience hissed and booed:* blow raspberries *colloq*, boo, catcall, deride *formal*, hoot, jeer, mock, ridicule, scoff at, scorn, shout down, taunt
♦ *n* **1** *the hiss of the hot iron:* buzz, hissing, sibilance *formal*, sibilation *formal*, whistle **2** *hisses from the crowd:* boo, catcall, contempt, derision *formal*, hoot, jeer, mockery, raspberry *colloq*, scoffing, scorn, taunting

historian *n* annalist, archivist, chronicler, chronologer, diarist, historiographer, narrator, recorder

historic *adj* celebrated, consequential *formal*, epoch-making, extraordinary, famed, famous, important, memorable, momentous, notable, outstanding, red-letter *colloq*, remarkable, renowned, significant
F3 insignificant, unimportant, unknown

---

historic or *historical*? *Historic* means 'famous or important in history': *a historic battle*. *Historical* means 'of or about history': *books on military and historical topics* ; or 'having actually happened or lived, in contrast to existing only in legend or fiction': *Is Macbeth a historical person?*

---

historical *adj* **1** *of historical interest:* ancient, bygone, former, of yore *formal*, old, past, prior **2** *a historical document:* actual, attested *formal*, authentic, chronicled, confirmed, documented, factual, real, recorded, verifiable, verified
F3 fictional, legendary

history *n* **1** *ancient history:* antiquity, bygone/olden days, days of old, days of yore *formal*, former times, past, the (good) old days, yesterday, yesteryear *formal* **2** *a history of the civil war:* account, annals, archives, autobiography, biography, chronicle, chronology, life, memoirs, narrative, record(s), report(s), saga, story, study, tale **3** *a long history of petty crime:* background, circumstances, credentials, education, experience, record

histrionic *adj* affected, artificial, bogus, dramatic, exaggerated, forced, ham, insincere, melodramatic, sensational, theatrical, unnatural

histrionics *n* affectation *formal*, artificiality, dramatics, insincerity, overacting, performance, ranting and raving *colloq*, scene, sensationalism, staginess, tantrums, theatricality, unnaturalness

hit *v* **1** *hit the ball hard:* bash, bat, batter, beat, belt *colloq*, biff *colloq*, box, buffet, clobber *colloq*, clout *colloq*, cuff, knock, pound, punch, slap, smack, sock *colloq*, strike, tap, thrash, thump, wallop *colloq*, whack *colloq*, zap *colloq* **2** *hit another car:* bang, bump, collide with, crash into, damage, meet head-on, plough into, run into, smash into **3** *her mother's death hit her hard:* affect, disturb, have an effect on, knock for six *colloq*, move, overwhelm, perturb *formal*, touch, trouble, upset **4** *the thought hit me:* be remembered, be thought of, come to, come to mind, dawn on, occur to, strike
♦ *n* **1** *a hit on the head:* bash, beating, belt *colloq*, biff *colloq*, blow, box, buffet, bump, clobbering *colloq*, clout *colloq*, collision, crash, cuff, impact, knock, punch, shot, slap, smack, smash, sock *colloq*, stroke, tap, thrashing, wallop *colloq*, whack *colloq* **2** *the show's been a huge hit:* success, triumph, winner *colloq*
F3 **2** failure
▶ **hit back** counter-attack, criticize in return, reciprocate, retaliate, strike back
▶ **hit on** arrive at, chance on, discover, guess, invent, light on, realize, stumble on, think of, uncover
▶ **hit out 1** *hit out wildly at his attacker:* assail, attack, lash out, strike out **2** *hit out at the newspaper coverage of the affair:* attack, condemn, criticize, denounce, inveigh *formal*, lash out, rail, vilify *formal*

hitch *v* **1** *hitched the horse to the wagon:* attach, bind, connect, couple, fasten, harness, join, tether, tie, unite, yoke **2** *hitched up her skirts:* heave, hike (up) *colloq*, hoist, jerk, pull, tug, yank *colloq*
F3 **1** unfasten, unhitch
♦ *n* barrier, block, catch, check, delay, difficulty, drawback, hiccup, hindrance, hold-up, impediment, mishap, obstacle, obstruction, problem, setback, snag, trouble

hitherto *adv* beforehand, heretofore *formal*, previously, so far, thus far, till now, until now, up to now

hit-or-miss *adj* aimless, apathetic, careless, casual, cursory, disorganized, haphazard, indiscriminate, lackadaisical, offhand, perfunctory, random, trial-and-error, undirected, uneven, unplanned
F3 directed, organized, planned

hoard *n* accumulation, aggregation *formal*, cache, collection, conglomeration *formal*, fund, heap, mass, pile, reserve, reservoir, stash *colloq*, stockpile, store, supply, treasure-trove
♦ *v* accumulate, amass, buy up, collect, gather, heap (up), keep, lay in, lay up, pile up, put away, put by, save, set aside, stack up, stash away *colloq*, stock up, stockpile, store, treasure
F3 spend, squander, use

---

hoard or *horde*? A *hoard* is a store or hidden stock of something: *He had a hoard of chocolate bars under the bed.* A *horde* is a crowd or large number of people: *Hordes of tourists come here every year.*

---

hoarder *n* collector, gatherer, magpie, miser, niggard, saver, squirrel

hoarse *adj* croaking, croaky, discordant, grating, gravelly, growling, gruff, guttural, harsh, husky, rasping, raspy, raucous, rough, throaty
F3 clear, smooth

hoary *adj* **1** *a hoary old trapper:* aged, ancient, antiquated, antique, canescent *formal*, grey, grey-haired, grizzled, old, senescent *formal*, silvery, venerable, white, white-haired **2** *that hoary old joke:* ancient, archaic, familiar, old, old-hat *colloq*, overused

hoax *n* bluff, cheat, con *colloq*, deception, fake, fast one *colloq*, frame-up *colloq*, fraud, humbug, jest, joke, leg-pull *colloq*, practical joke, prank, put-on, put-up job *colloq*, ruse, scam *colloq*, spoof *colloq*, swindle, trick
♦ *v* bamboozle *colloq*, bluff, cheat, con *colloq*, deceive, delude, double-cross *colloq*, dupe, fool, gull, have on *colloq*, hoodwink, lead up the garden path *colloq*, play a practical joke on, pull a fast one on *colloq*, pull someone's leg *colloq*, pull the wool over someone's eyes *colloq*, swindle, take for a ride *colloq*, take in, trick, two-time *colloq*

hoaxer *n* bamboozler *colloq*, hoodwinker, joker, mystifier, practical joker, prankster, spoofer *colloq*, trickster

hobble *v* dodder, falter, limp, shuffle, stagger, stumble, totter, walk awkwardly, walk lamely, walk with a limp

hobby *n* amusement, diversion, divertissement, entertainment, interest, leisure activity/pursuit, pastime, pursuit, recreation, relaxation, sideline

hobgoblin *n* apparition, bogey, bugaboo, bugbear, dwarf, elf, evil spirit, gnome, goblin, imp, spectre, spirit, sprite

hobnob *v* associate, consort *formal*, fraternize, go around, hang about *colloq*, keep company, mingle, mix, pal around *colloq*, socialize

hocus-pocus *n* abracadabra, artifice, cant, cheat, chicanery, conjuring, deceit, deception, delusion, gibberish, gobbledygook, hoax, humbug, imposture, jargon, legerdemain, mumbo-jumbo, nonsense, prestidigitation *formal*, rigmarole, sleight of hand, swindle, trickery, trompe-l'oeil

hog *n* boar, grunter, pig, porker, swine, wild boar
♦ *v* control, corner, dominate, keep to yourself, monopolize, take over

hogwash *n* balderdash *colloq*, balls *slang*, bilge *colloq*, bollocks *slang*, bullshit *slang*, bunk *colloq*, bunkum *colloq*, claptrap *colloq*, cobblers *colloq*, drivel, eyewash *colloq*, gibberish, hooey *colloq*, hot air *colloq*, nonsense, piffle *colloq*, poppycock *colloq*, rot *colloq*, rubbish, shit *slang*, tommyrot *colloq*, tosh *colloq*, trash, tripe, twaddle

hoi polloi *n* riff-raff *colloq*, the common people, the great unwashed *colloq*, the herd *colloq*, the masses, the ordinary people, the peasants *colloq*, the plebs *colloq*, the populace *formal*, the proles *colloq*, the proletariat, the rabble *colloq*, the third estate
▣ aristocracy, élite, nobility

hoist *v* elevate, erect, heave, jack up, lift, raise, rear, uplift, winch up
♦ *n* capstan, crane, elevator, jack, lift, pulley, tackle, winch

hoity-toity *adj* arrogant, conceited, disdainful, haughty, high and mighty *colloq*, lofty, overweening, pompous, proud, scornful, snobbish, snooty *colloq*, stuck-up *colloq*, supercilious, toffee-nosed *colloq*, uppity *colloq*

hold *v* **1** *hold a camera:* clasp, cling to, clutch, grasp, grip, have in your hand(s), seize **2** *hold someone in your arms:* clasp, cling to, clutch, embrace, enfold, hug, keep **3** *hold a licence:* have, own, possess, retain **4** *hold a meeting:* assemble, call, carry on, conduct, continue, convene, organize, preside over, run, summon **5** *hold someone's attention:* absorb, arrest, captivate, catch, engage, engross, enthral, fascinate, fill, keep, maintain, monopolize, occupy, rivet **6** *I hold you responsible:* assume, believe, consider, deem *formal*, esteem *formal*, judge, maintain, presume, reckon, regard, suppose, think, treat, view **7** *the deck wouldn't hold our weight:* bear, brace, buttress, carry, hold up, keep up, prop up, support, sustain, take **8** *held without charges:* arrest, check, confine, curb, detain, hold in custody, impound, imprison, incarcerate *formal*, lock up, restrain, stop **9** *the glue wouldn't hold:* adhere, cling, remain, stay, stick **10** *the memories that they held dear:* cherish, hold dear, keep, prize, treasure, value **11** *the bus holds 53 passengers:* accommodate, compromise *formal*, contain, have a capacity of, take **12** *hold office as prime minister:* continue, fill, fulfil, have, hold down, occupy, take up **13** *the fine weather will hold:* carry on, continue, keep up, last, remain, stay **14** *the theory still holds:* apply, be in force/operation, hold up, remain, remain valid/true, stay
▣ **1** drop **7** break, collapse, fall **8** free, liberate, release
♦ *n* **1** *a tight hold on the rail:* clasp, embrace, grasp, grip, hug **2** *the governor's hold over the country:* authority, clout *colloq*, control, dominance, dominion, grip, influence, leverage, mastery, power, sway
▶ **hold back 1** *police held back the crowds:* bar, check, contain, control, impede, keep back, obstruct, prevent, repress, restrain, retain **2** *struggling to hold back the tears:* check, curb, delay, inhibit, keep back, repress, retain, retard *formal*, stifle, stop, suppress **3** *held back from making an announcement:* delay, desist *formal*, forbear *formal*, hesitate, refrain *formal*, refuse, shrink
▶ **hold down 1** *hold down a job:* continue in, have, keep, occupy **2** *hold someone down:* dominate, keep down, oppress, suppress, tyrannize
▶ **hold forth** declaim *formal*, discourse, harangue, lecture, orate *formal*, preach, speak, spout *colloq*, talk
▶ **hold off 1** *held off his attackers:* fend off, fight off, keep at bay, keep off, rebuff, repel, stave off, ward off **2** *held off making a decision:* avoid, defer, delay, postpone, put off, wait
▶ **hold on 1** *held on tightly:* clasp, cling to, clutch, grasp, grip, seize **2** *just hold on while I check my e-mail:* be patient, hang on *colloq*, wait, wait a minute **3** *have to hold on until more work comes through:* carry on, continue, endure, hang on *colloq*, keep going, persevere, remain, survive
▶ **hold out 1** *held out his hand:* extend, give, offer, present, proffer *formal* **2** *trying to hold out for a better settlement:* carry on, continue, endure, hang on *colloq*, last, last out, persevere, persist, resist, stand fast, stand firm, withstand
▶ **hold over** adjourn, defer, delay, postpone, put off, shelve, suspend
▶ **hold up 1** *a row of pillars held up the roof:* bear, brace, carry, lift, prop up, raise, shore up,

support, sustain **2** *the discovery held up the building work:* delay, detain, hinder, impede, obstruct, retard *formal*, set/put back, slow **3** *held up by an armed robber:* break into, burglarize *US*, burgle, knock off *colloq*, knock over, mug *colloq*, nobble *colloq*, rob, steal from, stick up *colloq*
▶ **hold with** accept, agree with, approve of, countenance *formal*, go along with, subscribe to, support

holder *n* **1** *holder of two world records:* bearer, custodian, incumbent, keeper, owner, possessor, proprietor **2** *a toothbrush holder:* case, casing, container, cover, housing, receptacle, rest, sheath, stand

holdings *n* assets, bonds, estate, investments, land, possessions, property, real estate, resources, securities, shares, stocks, tenure

hold-up *n* **1** *a hold-up with deliveries:* bottleneck, delay, difficulty, hitch, obstruction, problem, setback, snag, stoppage, trouble **2** *a hold-up at a jeweller's:* break-in, burglary, heist *slang*, mugging *colloq*, raid, robbery, stick-up *slang*, stick-up job *slang*, theft

hole *n* **1** *dig a hole:* cave, cavern, cavity, chamber, chasm, crater, dent, depression, dimple, excavation, hollow, mine, pit, pocket, pothole, recess, scoop, shaft **2** *a hole in the roof:* aperture, breach, break, crack, eyelet, fissure, gap, gash, notch, opening, orifice *formal*, outlet, perforation, pore, puncture, rent, rift, shaft, slit, slot, space, split, tear, vent **3** *an animal's hole:* burrow, covert, den, lair, nest, set **4** *a hole in a theory:* defect, discrepancy, error, fault, flaw, inconsistency, loophole, mistake, weakness **5** *lives in a bit of a hole:* dump *colloq*, hovel, pigsty *colloq*, shack, slum, tip *colloq* **6** *we got ourselves in a bit of a hole:* difficulty, fix *colloq*, hot/deep water *colloq*, jam *colloq*, mess *colloq*, pickle *colloq*, plight, predicament, pretty pass *colloq*, quandary, snag, spot *colloq*
♦ *v* breach, break, crack, gash, perforate, pierce, puncture, rent, slit, spike, stab
▶ **hole up** conceal yourself, go into hiding, go to ground, hide, lie low, take cover

hole-and-corner *adj* back-door *colloq*, backstairs *colloq*, clandestine, covert, furtive, hush-hush *colloq*, secret, secretive, sneaky *colloq*, stealthy, surreptitious, underhand, under-the-counter *colloq*
🎝 open, public

holiday *n* **1** *go on holiday:* break, day off, furlough, half-term, leave, leave of absence, recess, rest, time off, trip, vacation **2** *a national holiday:* anniversary, bank holiday, celebration, feast day, festival, holy day, legal holiday, public holiday, saint's day

holier-than-thou *adj* complacent, goody-goody *colloq*, pietistic, pious, priggish, religiose, sanctimonious, self-approving, self-righteous, self-satisfied, smug, unctuous *formal*
🎝 humble, meek, modest

holiness *n* blessedness, consecration, dedication, devoutness, divinity, godliness, goodness, perfection, piety, purity, religiousness, righteousness, sacredness, saintliness, sanctity, sinlessness, spirituality, virtuousness
🎝 impiety

holler *n* bawl, bellow, cheer, cry, howl, roar, shout, shriek, whoop, yell, yelp, yowl
♦ *v* bawl, bellow, call, cry, howl, roar, shout, shriek, yell

hollow *adj* **1** *hollow cheeks:* caved-in, cavernous, concave, deep, deep-set, depressed, incurvate *formal*, indented, sunken **2** *a hollow Easter egg:* empty, unfilled, vacant, void **3** *a hollow pretence:* artificial, deceitful, deceptive, empty, false, fruitless, futile, hypocritical, insincere, meaningless, of no avail, pointless, pretended, profitless, Pyrrhic, sham, unavailing, useless, vain, valueless, worthless **4** *a hollow sound:* deep, dull, echoing, flat, low, muffled, reverberant, rumbling
🎝 **2** solid **3** real
♦ *n* **1** *a hollow in the surface:* basin, bowl, cave, cavern, cavity, channel, concavity *formal*, cranny, crater, cup, dent, depression, dimple, dip, excavation, groove, hole, indentation, niche, nook, pit, recess, trough, well **2** *a hollow between the hills:* cirque, dale, dell, glen, gorge, ravine, valley
♦ *v* burrow, channel, dent, dig, excavate, furrow, gouge, groove, indent, pit, scoop, tunnel

holocaust *n* annihilation, carnage, conflagration, destruction, devastation, ethnic cleansing, extermination, extinction, flames, genocide, hecatomb, immolation *formal*, inferno, mass murder, massacre, pogrom, sacrifice, slaughter

holy *adj* **1** *holy ground:* blessed, consecrated, dedicated, divine, hallowed, religious, revered, sacred, sacrosanct, sanctified, spiritual, venerated **2** *a holy man:* devout, faithful, God-fearing, godly, good, moral, perfect, pietistic, pious, pure, religious, righteous, saintly, sinless, virtuous
🎝 **1** unsanctified **2** impious, irreligious

homage *n* acknowledgement, admiration, adoration, adulation, awe, deference, devotion, esteem *formal*, honour, praise, recognition, regard, respect, reverence, tribute, veneration *formal*, worship

home *n* **1** *invite someone to your home:* abode *formal*, address, apartment, bungalow, cottage, digs *colloq*, domicile *formal*, dwelling *formal*, dwelling-place *formal*, flat, habitation *formal*, house, pad *colloq*, residence *formal*, roof over your head *colloq*, semi *colloq*, somewhere to live *colloq* **2** *living a long way from my home:* birthplace, country of origin, fatherland, home town, homeland, mother country, motherland, native country, native town, roots **3** *sent him to a home:* asylum, centre, children's home, hostel, institution, nursing home, old people's home, refuge, residential home, retirement home, retreat, safe place, sheltered housing **4** *the home of jazz:* birthplace, cradle, element, fount, natural environment, place of origin, source
♦ *adj* **1** *home cooking:* domestic, family, household, local **2** *home affairs:* domestic, inland, interior, internal, national, native
🎝 **2** foreign, international, overseas
♦ *v*
▶ **home in on** aim, concentrate, direct, focus, pinpoint, zero in on, zoom in on

homeland *n* country of origin, fatherland, mother country, motherland, native country, native land

homeless *adj* abandoned, destitute, displaced, dispossessed, dossing *slang*, down-and-out *colloq*, evicted, exiled, forsaken, itinerant, nomadic, of no fixed abode *formal*, of no fixed address, outcast, rootless, travelling, unsettled, vagrant, wandering
♦ *n* derelicts *formal*, dossers *slang*, down-and-outs *colloq*, squatters, tramps, travellers, unhoused, vagabonds, vagrants

homely *adj* **1** *a homely room:* cheerful, comfortable, cosy, familiar, friendly, homelike, homey, hospitable, informal, intimate, relaxed, snug, welcoming **2** *homely pleasures:* domestic, everyday, folksy, homespun, modest, natural, ordinary, plain, simple, unassuming, unpretentious, unsophisticated **3** *a homely person:* not much to look at *colloq*, plain, ugly, unattractive, unlovely, unprepossessing
🖪 **1** formal, grand **3** attractive, good-looking, lovely

homespun *adj* amateurish, artless, coarse, crude, folksy, homely, home-made, inelegant, plain, rough, rude, rustic, simple, uncomplicated, unpolished, unrefined, unsophisticated
🖪 sophisticated

homicidal *adj* bloodthirsty, deadly, death-dealing, lethal, maniacal, mortal, murderous, sanguinary *formal*, violent

homicide *n* assassination, bloodshed, killing, manslaughter, murder, slaughter, slaying

homily *n* address, discourse *formal*, harangue, lecture, oration *formal*, postil *formal*, preaching, sermon, speech, spiel *colloq*, talk

homogeneity *n* agreement, analogousness, comparability, consistency, consonancy *formal*, correspondence, identicalness, likeness, oneness, resemblance, sameness, similarity, similitude *formal*, uniformity
🖪 difference, disagreement

homogeneous *adj* akin, alike, all of a piece, (all) the same, analogous, cognate *formal*, comparable, compatible, consistent, correlative *formal*, corresponding, harmonious, identical, kindred, of the same kind, similar, uniform, unvaried, unvarying
🖪 different, heterogeneous

homogenize *v* amalgamate, blend, coalesce, combine, fuse, merge, unite

homologous *adj* analogous, comparable, correspondent, corresponding, equivalent, like, matching, parallel, related, similar
🖪 different, dissimilar

homosexual *n* dyke *derog*, fag *derog*, faggot *derog*, fairy *derog*, gay, homo *derog*, invert, lesbian, nancy *derog*, pansy *derog*, poof *derog*, queen *slang*, queer *derog*, woofter *derog*
🖪 heterosexual, straight *colloq*
♦ *adj* bent *derog*, butch *colloq*, camp *colloq*, dykey *derog*, gay, lesbian, queer *derog*

hone *v* **1** *honed the blade:* edge, file, grind, point, polish, sharpen, whet **2** *honed her skills:* develop, enhance, perfect, polish, refine, sharpen, work on
🖪 **1** blunt

honest *adj* **1** *an honest citizen:* dependable, ethical, genuine, high-minded, honourable, incorruptible, law-abiding, moral, principled, real, reliable, reputable, respectable, right-minded, scrupulous, true, trustworthy, upright, upstanding, virtuous **2** *give me your honest opinion:* blunt, candid, direct, forthright, frank, open, outright, outspoken, plain, plain-speaking, simple, sincere, straight, straightforward, truthful, up front *colloq* **3** *honest treatment:* above-board, equitable, fair, fair and square *colloq*, honest as the day is long *colloq*, impartial, just, lawful, legal, legitimate, objective, on the level *colloq*, straight as a die *colloq*
🖪 **1** dishonourable **2** dishonest **3** unjust

honestly *adv* **1** *honestly, he's impossible:* frankly, not to put too fine a point on it *colloq*, really, straight up *colloq*, to be honest, truly, truthfully **2** *spoke honestly about her problems:* directly, frankly, openly, plainly, sincerely, truthfully **3** *deal honestly with the public:* ethically, fairly, honourably, in good faith, justly, lawfully, legally, legitimately, morally, objectively, on the level *colloq*
🖪 **3** dishonestly, dishonourably

honesty *n* **1** *a man of complete honesty:* ethics, genuineness, honour, incorruptibility, integrity, morality, morals, principles, probity *formal*, rectitude *formal*, righteousness, scrupulousness, trustworthiness, uprightness, veracity, virtue **2** *the honesty of the account:* bluntness, candour, explicitness, forthrightness, frankness, openness, outspokenness, plain-speaking, sincerity, straightforwardness, truthfulness **3** *questioned the honesty of the proceedings:* balance, equity, even-handedness, fairness, impartiality, justness, legality, legitimacy, objectivity
🖪 **2** dishonesty **3** bias, partiality, prejudice

honorarium *n* emolument *formal*, fee, pay, recompense, remuneration, reward, salary

honorary *adj* ex officio, formal, honorific, in name only, nominal, titular, unofficial, unpaid
🖪 paid

honour *n* **1** *a man of honour:* decency, dignity, distinction, ethics, goodness, honesty, integrity, morality, morals, principles, probity *formal*, rectitude *formal*, righteousness, self-respect, trustworthiness, truthfulness, uprightness, virtue **2** *for the honour of the country:* credit, esteem *formal*, fame, glory, good name, regard, renown, reputation, repute **3** *an honour for bravery:* accolade, acknowledgement, award, commendation, compliment, crown, decoration, distinction, favour, laurel, privilege, prize, recognition, reward, title, tribute, trophy **4** *a man held in honour by the public:* acclaim, acclamation, admiration, adoration, applause, homage, praise, reverence, worship
🖪 **1** dishonour **2** disgrace
♦ *v* **1** *honoured for her work:* acclaim, acknowledge, admire, applaud, celebrate, commemorate, commend, compliment, crown, decorate, esteem *formal*, exalt, glorify, have a high regard for, pay homage to, pay tribute to, praise, prize, recognize, remember, respect, revere, value, venerate *formal*, worship **2** *honour a promise:* be true to, carry out, discharge, execute, fulfil, keep, observe, perform, respect **3** *honour a cheque/bill:* accept, clear, pay
🖪 **1** disgrace, dishonour

honourable *adj* admirable, decent, dependable, distinguished, ethical, fair, good, great, high-minded, high-principled, honest, just, moral, noble, notable, principled, reliable, reputable,

respectable, respected, right, righteous, sincere, straight, true, trustworthy, trusty, truthful, upright, upstanding, virtuous, worthy
ⓕ dishonest, dishonourable, unworthy

hood *n* cape line, capuche, cowl, domino, scarf

hoodlum *n* **1** *young hoodlums had smashed the windows:* bovver boy *slang*, brute, hooligan, lout, mobster, mugger *colloq*, rowdy, ruffian, thug, tough, vandal, yob *slang* **2** *a gang of hoodlums robbed the bank:* armed robber, criminal, felon, gangster, gunman, hood *colloq*, law-breaker, mobster *US colloq*, offender

hoodwink *v* bamboozle *colloq*, cheat, con *colloq*, deceive, defraud, delude, dupe, fool, get the better of, gull, have on *colloq*, hoax, mislead, outwit, pull a fast one on *colloq*, pull the wool over someone's eyes *colloq*, rook, swindle, take for a ride *colloq*, take in, trick

hoof *n* cloot, cloven hoof, foot, trotter, ungula *technical*

hoofed *adj* cloven-footed, cloven-hoofed, ungulate *technical*, unguligrade

hook *n* **1** *a hook on a skirt:* barb, catch, clasp, clip, fastener, hasp, peg **2** *the stick has a big hook on the end:* scythe, sickle **3** *a hook in the road:* angle, arc, bend, bow, crook, curve, elbow, loop **4** *floored him with a left hook:* blow, box, clip, clout *colloq*, cuff, hit, knock, punch, rap, stroke, thump, wallop *colloq*
♦ *v* **1** *the river hooks to the left:* bend, crook, curl, curve **2** *hooked three trout:* bag, capture, catch, enmesh, ensnare, entangle, entrap, grab, snare, trap **3** *the dress hooks down the back:* clasp, fasten, fix, hitch, secure

hooked *adj* **1** *a hooked shape:* barbed, bent, curled, curved, falcate *formal*, hamate *formal*, hamose *formal*, hamous *formal*, hamular *formal*, hamulate *formal*, sickle-shaped, uncate *formal*, unciform *formal*, uncinate *formal* **2** *a hooked nose:* aquiline, beaked, beaky **3** *hooked on reality TV shows:* addicted, dependent, devoted, enamoured, obsessed

hooligan *n* bovver boy *slang*, delinquent, hoodlum, lout, mobster, mugger *colloq*, rough, rowdy, ruffian, thug, tough, vandal, yob *slang*

hoop *n* band, circle, circlet, girdle, loop, ring, round, wheel

hoot *v* **1** *an owl hooting:* call, cry, screech, tu-whit tu-whoo, ululate *formal*, whoop **2** *the car hooted:* beep, toot, whistle **3** *the audience hooted:* boo, hiss, howl, howl down, jeer, mock, ridicule, shout, shriek, sneer, taunt, whoop
♦ *n* **1** *the hoot of an owl:* call, cry, screech, tu-whit tu-whoo, whoop **2** *the hoot of a car:* beep, toot, whistle **3** *the hoots of the audience:* boo, hiss, howl, jeer, mock, ridicule, shout, shriek, sneer, taunt, whoop

hop *v* **1** *hop up and down:* bound, dance, frisk, hobble, jump, leap, limp, prance, skip, spring, vault **2** *hop over to Paris:* fly quickly, nip, pop
♦ *n* **1** *with a hop and a skip:* bounce, bound, dance, jump, leap, skip, spring, step, vault **2** *a quick hop by plane:* excursion, jaunt, journey, (quick) flight, trip **3** *met at the local hop:* dance, disco, knees-up *colloq*, party, rave *colloq*, shindig *colloq*, social

hope *n* **1** *the team's hopes for success:* ambition, aspiration, craving, desire, dream, expectation,

prospect, wish, yearning **2** *eyes full of hope:* anticipation, assurance, belief, confidence, conviction, expectation, faith, hopefulness, longing, optimism, promise, yearning
ⓕ **1** despair **2** pessimism
♦ *v* **1** *we hope to deliver the goods this week:* anticipate, assume, be hopeful, believe, expect, foresee, have confidence, reckon on, trust **2** *desperately hoping for a win:* aspire, be hopeful, crave, desire, dream, hope against hope *colloq*, keep your fingers crossed *colloq*, long, look forward to, pin your hopes on *colloq*, wish, yearn
ⓕ **2** despair

hopeful *adj* **1** *feeling hopeful about the results:* aspirant, aspiring, assured, bullish *colloq*, buoyant, cheerful, confident, expectant, optimistic, positive, sanguine **2** *a hopeful sign:* auspicious *formal*, bright, cheerful, encouraging, favourable, gladdening, heartening, optimistic, pleasant, positive, promising, propitious *formal*, reassuring, rosy
ⓕ **1** despairing, pessimistic **2** discouraging

hopefully *adv* **1** *hopefully the weather will improve:* all being well, conceivably, I hope, if all goes well, it is to be hoped that, probably, with luck **2** *listened hopefully to the announcement:* bullishly *colloq*, confidently, eagerly, expectantly, optimistically, sanguinely *formal*, with anticipation, with hope

hopeless *adj* **1** *felt completely hopeless about her future:* defeatist, dejected, demoralized, despairing, desperate, despondent, downcast, downhearted, forlorn, gloomy, negative, pessimistic, wretched **2** *a hopeless quest:* beyond remedy, beyond repair, foolish, futile, grave, helpless, impossible, impracticable, incurable, irremediable, irreparable, irreversible, lost, pointless, poor, unachievable, unattainable, useless, vain, worthless **3** *hopeless at speaking French:* awful *colloq*, bad, incompetent, lousy *colloq*, pathetic *colloq*, useless, weak
ⓕ **1** hopeful, optimistic **2** curable **3** expert, skilled

horde *n* army, band, crew, crowd, drove, flock, gang, herd, host, mass, mob, multitude, pack, swarm, throng, troop

---

horde or *hoard*? See panel at **hoard**

---

horizon *n* **1** *a single building on the horizon:* prospect, range, range of vision, skyline, vista **2** *widen your horizons:* compass, outlook, perception, perspective, scope

horizontal *adj* flat, level, levelled, on its side, plane, smooth, supine

horny *adj* **1** *a horny shell:* callous, ceratoid *technical*, corneous *formal*, corny, hard **2** *feeling horny after the film:* ardent, concupiscent *formal*, lascivious, lecherous, libidinous *formal*, lustful, randy *colloq*, ruttish, sexy
ⓕ **2** cold, frigid

horrendous *adj* appalling, dreadful, frightening, frightful, horrific, horrifying, shocking, terrible, terrifying

horrible *adj* **1** *horrible scenes of murder:* abominable, appalling, awful, bloodcurdling, dreadful, frightening, frightful, ghastly, grim, gruesome, hair-raising, harrowing, hideous, horrific, horrifying, repulsive, revolting, scary

colloq, shocking, terrible, terrifying **2** *that fish smells horrible:* abominable, awful, detestable, disagreeable, disgusting, dreadful, frightful, ghastly, horrid, loathsome, nasty, obnoxious, offensive, repulsive, revolting, terrible, unkind, unpleasant
✷ 1 attractive **2** agreeable, lovely, pleasant

horrid *adj* **1** *a horrid sight:* abominable, appalling, awful, bloodcurdling, dreadful, frightening, frightful, ghastly, grim, gruesome, hair-raising, harrowing, hideous, horrific, horrifying, repulsive, revolting, shocking, terrible, terrifying **2** *you've been horrid to me:* awful, beastly *colloq,* cruel, dreadful, hateful, mean, nasty, obnoxious, unkind
✷ 2 lovely, pleasant

horrific *adj* appalling, awful, bloodcurdling, dreadful, frightening, frightful, ghastly, gruesome, harrowing, horrifying, scary *colloq,* shocking, terrible, terrifying

horrify *v* alarm, appal, disgust, dismay, frighten, intimidate, make your blood run cold *colloq,* make your hair stand on end *colloq,* nauseate, offend, outrage, panic, put the frighteners on *colloq,* put the wind up *colloq,* repel, revolt, scandalize, scare, scare out of your wits *colloq,* scare the living daylights out of *colloq,* scare to death *colloq,* shock, sicken, startle, terrify, terrorize
✷ delight, please

horror *n* **1** *recoil in horror:* abhorrence, abomination, alarm, apprehension, consternation *formal,* detestation *formal,* disgust, dismay, distaste, dread, fear, fright, hate, loathing, outrage, panic, repugnance, revulsion, shock, terror, trepidation *formal* **2** *the horror of the attack:* awfulness, frightfulness, ghastliness, hideousness, unpleasantness
✷ 1 approval, delight

horror-struck *adj* aghast, appalled, frightened, horrified, horror-stricken, petrified, shocked, stunned, terrified
✷ delighted, pleased

horse *n* bay, bronco, charger, cob, colt, dobbin, filly, hack, hackney, mare, mount, mustang, nag, roan, sorrel, stallion, steed

The points of a horse are:
back, breast, cannon, chestnut, crest of the neck, croup/crupper/rump, ear, elbow, eye, face, fetlock, forearm, forefoot, forehead, forelock, gaskin, haunch, head, hind leg, hip, hock, hoof, knee, loins, lower jaw, lower/under lip, mane, mouth, neck, nose, nostril, pastern, root/dock of the tail, shoulder, spur vein, stifle (joint), tail, throat, upper lip, withers

Breeds of horse include:
Akhal-Teké, Alter-Réal, American Quarter Horse, American Saddle Horse, American Trotter, Andalusian, Anglo-Arab, Anglo-Norman, Appaloosa, Arab, Ardennias, Auxois, Barb, Bavarian Warmblood, Boulonnais, Brabannçon, Breton, British Warmblood, Brumby, Budyonny, Calabrese, Charollais Halfbred, Cleveland Bay, Clydesdale, Comtois, Criollo, Danubian, Døle Gudbrandsdal, Døle Trotter, Don, Dutch Draught, East Bulgarian, East Friesian,

Einsiedler, Finnish, Frederiksborg, Freiberger, French Saddle Horse, French Trotter, Friesian, Furioso, Gelderland, German Trotter, Groningen, Hanoverian, Hispano, Holstein, Iomud, Irish Draught, Irish Hunter, Italian Heavy Draught, Jutland, Kabardin, Karabair, Karabakh, Kladruber, Knabstrup, Kustanair, Latvian Harness Horse, Limousin Halfbred, Lipizzaner, Lithuanian Heavy Draught, Lokai, Lusitano, Mangalarga, Maremmana, Masuren, Mecklenburg, Metis Trotter, Morgan, Muraköz, Murgese, Mustang, New Kirgiz, Nonius, North Swedish, Oldenburg, Orlov Trotter, Palomino, Paso Fino, Percheron, Peruvian Stepping Horse, Pinto, Pinzgauer Noriker, Plateau Persian, Poitevin, Rhineland Heavy Draught, Russian Heavy Draught, Salerno, Sardinian, Shagya Arab, Shire, Suffolk Punch, Swedish Halfbred, Tchenaran, Tennessee Walking Horse, Tersky, Thoroughbred, Toric, Trait du Nord, Trakehner, Vladimir Heavy Draught, Waler, Welsh Cob, Württemberg

Breeds of pony include:
Connemara, Dales, Dartmoor, Exmoor, Falabella, Fell, Hackney, Highland, New Forest, Przewalski's Horse, Shetland, Welsh Mountain Pony, Welsh Pony

horseman, horsewoman *n* cavalryman, dragoon, equestrian, horse soldier, hussar, jockey, knight, rider

horseplay *n* antics, buffoonery, capers, clowning, foolery, fooling, fooling around, fun and games, high jinks, monkey business *colloq,* practical jokes, pranks, rough-and-tumble, skylarking, tomfoolery

hortatory *adj* didactic *formal,* edifying, encouraging, exhortative *formal,* exhortatory *formal,* heartening, homiletic, hortative *formal,* inspiriting, instructive, pep *colloq,* practical, preceptive *formal,* stimulating

horticulture *n* arboriculture *formal,* cultivation, floriculture *formal,* gardening

hosanna *n* alleluia, laudation *formal,* praise, save us, worship

hose *n* channel, conduit, duct, pipe, tube, tubing

hosiery *n* hose, leg-coverings, leggings, socks, stockings, tights

hospitable *adj* amicable, bountiful, congenial, convivial, cordial, friendly, generous, genial, gracious, helpful, kind, kind-hearted, liberal, neighbourly, open-handed, receptive, sociable, warm, welcoming
✷ hostile, inhospitable, unfriendly

hospital *n* clinic, health centre, hospice, infirmary, institute, medical centre, sanatorium

hospitality *n* accommodation, cheer, congeniality, conviviality, entertainment, friendliness, generosity, helpfulness, kindness, liberality, neighbourliness, open-handedness, sociability, warmth, welcome
✷ hostility, unfriendliness

host[1] *n* **1** *the host of the show:* anchorman, anchorwoman, announcer, compère, emcee *colloq,* linkman, master of ceremonies, MC, media personality, presenter **2** *mine host proposed a toast:* innkeeper, landlady, landlord, proprietor,

proprietress, publican
♦ *v* compère, give, introduce, present

host² *n* army, array, band, crowd, crush, herd, horde, mass, mob, myriad, pack, swarm, throng, troop

hostage *n* captive, pawn, pledge, prisoner, security, surety

hostel *n* bed and breakfast, boarding-house, dosshouse *slang*, guesthouse, hotel, inn, motel, pension, residence *formal*, youth hostel

hostile *adj* 1 *given a hostile reception by the crowd*: antagonistic, bellicose *formal*, belligerent, ill-disposed, inhospitable, inimical, malevolent *formal*, opposed, unfriendly, unsympathetic, warlike 2 *a hostile climate*: adverse, contrary, inauspicious *formal*, opposite, unfavourable
 1 friendly, receptive, welcoming
2 favourable

hostilities *n* action, battle, bloodshed, conflict, fighting, strife, war, warfare

hostility *n* abhorrence *formal*, aggression, animosity, antagonism, aversion, bellicosity *formal*, belligerence, cruelty, dislike, enmity, estrangement *formal*, hate, hatred, ill-will, malevolence *formal*, malice, militancy, opposition, resentment, unfriendliness
 friendliness, friendship

hot *adj* 1 *a hot day*: baking, blistering, boiling, burning, fiery, heated, parching, piping, red hot, roasting, scalding, scorching, searing, sizzling, steaming, sultry, sweltering, torrid, tropical, warm 2 *a hot curry*: fiery, peppery, piquant, pungent, sharp, spicy, strong 3 *feeling hot and headachy*: burning, delirious, feverish, flushed, red, with a temperature 4 *his hot temper*: angry, boiling, enraged, fiery, fuming, furious, heated, incensed, indignant, inflamed, livid, raging, seething, violent 5 *hot competition*: cut-throat, fierce, furious, intense, keen, strong 6 *not very hot on the idea*: devoted, diligent, eager, earnest, enthusiastic, keen, warm, zealous 7 *hot news*: exciting, fresh, latest, new, recent, up-to-date 8 *hot goods*: contraband, illegally obtained/imported, ill-gotten, pilfered, stolen
 1 chilly, cold, cool 2 bland, mild 4 calm
7 old, stale

hotbed *n* breeding-ground, cradle, den, forcing-house, hive, nest, nursery, school, seedbed

hot-blooded *adj* ardent, bold, eager, excitable, fervent, fiery, heated, high-spirited, impetuous, impulsive, lustful, lusty, passionate, perfervid *formal*, precipitate *formal*, rash, sensual, spirited, temperamental, wild
 cool, dispassionate

hotchpotch *n* collection, confusion, hodgepodge *US*, jumble, medley, melange, mess, miscellany, mishmash, mix, mixture

hotel *n* boarding-house, guesthouse, hostel, hostelry, inn, motel, pension, pub *colloq*, public house, tavern

hotfoot *adv* at top speed, hastily, helter-skelter, hurriedly, in haste, pell-mell, posthaste, quickly, rapidly, speedily, swiftly, without delay
 dilatorily *formal*, slowly

hothead *n* daredevil, desperado, hotspur, madcap, madman, tearaway, terror

hotheaded *adj* excitable, explosive, fiery, foolhardy, hasty, headstrong, hot-tempered, impetuous, impulsive, irascible, quick-tempered, rash, reckless, short-tempered, volatile, volcanic, wild
 calm, cool

hothouse *n* conservatory, glasshouse, greenhouse, orangery, vinery

hot-tempered *adj* choleric, explosive, fiery, hasty, irascible, irritable, petulant, quick-tempered, short-tempered, testy, violent, volcanic
 calm, cool, imperturbable *formal*

hound *v* badger, bully, chase, chivvy, disturb, drive, follow, force, goad, harass, harry, hunt (down), nag, persecute, pester, prod, provoke, pursue, stalk, track, trail, urge

house *n* 1 *a three-bedroomed house*: building, domicile *formal*, dwelling *formal*, habitation *formal*, home, residence *formal* 2 *you woke the whole house when you came in*: family, family circle, home, household, ménage 3 *a publishing house*: business, company, corporation, enterprise, establishment, firm, organization 4 *the lower house of the parliament*: assembly, body, chamber, congress, legislature, parliament 5 *a full house at the theatre*: assembly, audience, auditorium, gathering, listeners, onlookers, spectators, turnout, viewers 6 *the house of York*: ancestry, blood, clan, dynasty, family, kindred, line, lineage, race, strain, tribe
♦ *v* 1 *housed in old army barracks*: accommodate, billet, board, harbour, have room/space for, lodge, put up, quarter, shelter, take in 2 *houses the princess's jewellery collection*: contain, cover, guard, hold, keep, place, protect, sheathe, shelter, store

> **Types of house include:**
> semi-detached, semi *colloq*, detached, terraced, town house, council house, cottage, thatched cottage, prefab *colloq*, pied-à-terre, bungalow, chalet bungalow; flat, bedsit, apartment, studio, maisonnette, penthouse, granny flat, duplex *US*, condominium *US*, manor, hall, lodge, grange, villa, mansion, rectory, vicarage, parsonage, manse, croft, farmhouse, homestead, ranchhouse, chalet, log cabin, shack, shanty, hut, igloo, hacienda

household *n* establishment, family, family circle, home, house, ménage, set-up
♦ *adj* 1 *household chores*: common, domestic, everyday, family, home, ordinary, plain 2 *a household name*: established, familiar, well-known

householder *n* freeholder, head of the household, home-owner, landlady, landlord, leaseholder, occupant, occupier, owner, proprietor, resident, tenant

housekeeping *n* domestic science, domestic work/matters, home economics, homemaking, household management, housewifery, running a home

house-trained *adj* domesticated, house-broken, tame, tamed, well-mannered
 unsocial

housing *n* 1 *affordable housing*: accommodation, dwellings *formal*, habitation *formal*, homes, houses, shelter 2 *the housing for the wheel*: case,

hovel n cabin, dump *colloq*, hole *colloq*, hut, shack, shanty, shed

hover v 1 *the butterfly hovered in the air:* drift, flap, float, flutter, fly, hang, poise 2 *he hovered by the door:* alternate, fluctuate, hang about, hesitate, linger, oscillate *formal*, pause, seesaw, vacillate *formal*, waver

however adv anyhow, even so, just the same, nevertheless, nonetheless, notwithstanding *formal*, regardless, still, though, yet

howl n bawl, bellow, cry, groan, hoot, moan, roar, scream, shout, shriek, wail, yell, yelp, yowl
♦ v bawl, bay, bellow, cry, groan, hoot, moan, roar, scream, shriek, wail, yelp, yowl

howler n bloomer *colloq*, blunder, boob *colloq*, clanger *colloq*, error, gaffe, malapropism, mistake, solecism *formal*

hub n axis, centre, core, focal point, focus, heart, linchpin, middle, nerve centre, pivot

hubbub n chaos, clamour, commotion, confusion, din, disorder, disturbance, hullabaloo, hurly-burly, noise, pandemonium, racket, riot, rumpus, tumult, uproar
☒ peace, quiet

huckster n barker, dealer, haggler, hawker, packman, pedlar, pitcher, salesperson, tinker, vendor

huddle v 1 *huddled together for warmth:* cram, crouch, cuddle, curl up, hunch, nestle, pack, press, snuggle, squeeze 2 *people huddled around the water cooler:* cluster, congregate, converge, crowd, flock, gather, gravitate, herd, meet, press, throng
☒ 2 disperse
♦ n 1 *a huddle of people at the bus stop:* clump, cluster, crowd, heap, jumble, knot, mass, muddle 2 *went into a huddle to make their decision:* conclave, conference, consultation, discussion, meeting, powwow *colloq*

hue n aspect, colour, complexion, dye, light, nuance, shade, tinge, tint, tone

hue and cry n ado, brouhaha, chase, clamour, furore, fuss, hullabaloo, outcry, ruction *colloq*, rumpus, to-do *colloq*, uproar

huff n anger, bad mood, mood, passion, pique, rage, sulks

huffy adj angry, crabbed *colloq*, cross, crotchety *colloq*, crusty, disgruntled, grumpy, irritable, miffed *colloq*, moody, moping, morose, offended, peevish, petulant, querulous *formal*, resentful, shirty *colloq*, short, snappy, sulky, surly, testy, touchy, waspish
☒ cheery, happy

hug v clasp, cling to, clutch, cuddle, embrace, enclose, enfold, follow closely, grip, hold, hold close, press, squeeze, stay close to
♦ n clasp, clinch, cuddle, embrace, hold, squeeze

huge adj bulky, colossal, enormous, extensive, gargantuan, giant, gigantic, great big, heavy, Herculean, immense, jumbo *colloq*, large, mammoth, massive, monstrous, monumental, prodigious *formal*, stupendous, titanic, tremendous, unwieldy, vast
☒ minute, tiny

hulk n 1 *the hulk of the tanker:* derelict, frame, hull, remains, shell, shipwreck, wreck 2 *be careful, you clumsy great hulk:* clod *colloq*, lout, lubber, lump, oaf

hulking adj awkward, bulky, clumsy, cumbersome, heavy, lumbering, massive, ungainly, unwieldy, weighty
☒ delicate, small

hull[1] n body, casing, covering, frame, framework, skeleton, structure

hull[2] n capsule, epicarp *technical*, husk, legume, peel, pod, rind, shell, shuck *US*, skin
♦ v husk, pare, peel, shell, shuck *US*, skin, strip, trim

hullabaloo n brouhaha, commotion, din, disturbance, furore, fuss, hubbub, hue and cry, noise, outcry, palaver, pandemonium, racket, ruction *colloq*, rumpus, to-do *colloq*, tumult, turmoil, uproar
☒ calm, peace

hum v 1 *heard an engine humming outside:* buzz, croon, drone, purr, sing, thrum, whirr 2 *hum a tune:* mumble, murmur 3 *humming with activity:* buzz, pulse, throb, vibrate
♦ n 1 *the hum of machinery:* buzz, buzzing, drone, pulsation, purring, throb, throbbing, thrum, vibration, whirr, whirring 2 *a hum of voices:* drone, mumble, murmur

human adj 1 *human life:* anthropoid *formal*, fallible, flesh and blood, fleshly, mortal, physical, rational, reasonable, susceptible, vulnerable, weak 2 *a very human gesture:* compassionate, considerate, humane, kind, sympathetic, understanding
☒ 2 inhuman
♦ n body, child, homo sapiens *technical*, human being, individual, man, mortal, person, soul, woman

humane adj benevolent, benign, charitable, compassionate, considerate, forbearing, forgiving, generous, gentle, good, good-natured, humanitarian, kind, kind-hearted, kindly, lenient, loving, merciful, mild, sympathetic, tender, understanding
☒ cruel, inhumane

humanitarian adj altruistic, benevolent, caring, charitable, compassionate, considerate, generous, humane, kind, philanthropic, public-spirited, sympathetic, understanding, unselfish, welfare
☒ selfish, self-seeking
♦ n altruist, benefactor, do-gooder, good Samaritan, philanthropist
☒ egoist, self-seeker

humanitarianism n beneficence *formal*, benevolence, charitableness, charity, compassionateness, generosity, goodwill, humanism, loving-kindness, philanthropy
☒ egoism, self-seeking

humanity n 1 *the struggle to save humanity:* Homo sapiens *technical*, human race, humankind, man, mankind, mortality, mortals, people, womankind 2 *showed great humanity to the poor:* benevolence, brotherly love, compassion, fellow-feeling, generosity, gentleness, goodness, goodwill, humaneness, kind-heartedness, kindness, mercy, pity,

sympathy, tenderness, thoughtfulness, tolerance, understanding
F2 2 cruelty, inhumanity

humanize *v* better, civilize, cultivate, domesticate, edify, educate, enlighten, improve, polish, refine, tame

humble *adj* **1** *a very humble man:* deferential, meek, modest, obsequious, polite, prideless, respectful, self-effacing, servile, submissive, subservient, sycophantic, unassertive, unassuming **2** *in a humble position in the company:* common, commonplace, inferior, insignificant, low, lowly, low-ranking, mean, modest, ordinary, plain, poor, simple, unassuming, undistinguished, unimportant, unostentatious, unpretentious, unrefined
F2 1 assertive, proud **2** important, pretentious
♦ *v* abase, belittle, bring down, bring low, bring/take someone down a peg or two *colloq*, chasten, crush, deflate, demean, discredit, disgrace, disparage *formal*, humiliate, lower, mortify, put someone in their place *colloq*, put to shame, shame, sink, subdue
F2 exalt

humbly *adv* cap in hand *colloq*, deferentially, diffidently, docilely, meekly, modestly, obsequiously, respectfully, servilely, sheepishly *colloq*, simply, submissively, subserviently, unassumingly, unpretentiously
F2 confidently, defiantly

humbug *n* **1** *political humbug:* cheating, con *colloq*, deceit, deception, fraud, hoax, pretence, sham, swindle, trick, trickery **2** *that's humbug and you know it:* balderdash *colloq*, balls *slang*, baloney *slang*, bluff, bunkum *colloq*, cant, claptrap *colloq*, cobblers *colloq*, eyewash *colloq*, hypocrisy, nonsense, poppycock *colloq*, rot *colloq*, rubbish, shit *slang* **3** *the guy's a complete humbug:* actor, bluffer, charlatan, cheat, con man *colloq*, fake, fraud, impostor, poser *colloq*, rogue, sham, swank *colloq*, swindler, trickster

humdrum *adj* banal, boring, commonplace, dreary, dull, everyday, monotonous, mundane, ordinary, repetitious, routine, run-of-the-mill, tedious, tiresome, uneventful, uninteresting, unvaried
F2 exceptional, lively, unusual, varied

humid *adj* clammy, close, damp, dank, heavy, moist, muggy, oppressive, steamy, sticky, sultry, wet
F2 dry

humidity *n* clamminess, closeness, damp, dampness, dankness, dew, heaviness, humidness, mist, moistness, moisture, mugginess, sogginess, steaminess, stickiness, sultriness, vaporosity *formal*, vaporousness, wetness
F2 dryness

humiliate *v* abase, abash, break, bring low, bring shame on, bring/take someone down a peg or two *colloq*, chasten, confound, crush, cut someone down to size *colloq*, deflate, degrade, demean, discomfit *formal*, discredit, disgrace, embarrass, humble, make someone lose face *colloq*, mortify, put down *colloq*, put someone in their place *colloq*, put to shame, shame, take the wind out of someone's sails *colloq*
F2 dignify, exalt

humiliating *adj* chastening, crushing, deflating, degrading, discomfiting *formal*, disgraceful, disgracing, embarrassing, humbling, humiliant *formal*, humiliative *formal*, humiliatory *formal*, ignominious, inglorious, mortifying, shaming, snubbing
F2 gratifying, triumphant

humiliation *n* abasement, affront, chastening, confounding, crushing, deflation, degradation, discomfiture *formal*, discredit, disgrace, dishonour, embarrassment, humbling, ignominy, indignity, loss of face *colloq*, mortification, put-down *colloq*, rebuff, shame, snub
F2 gratification, triumph

humility *n* deference, diffidence, humbleness, lowliness, meekness, modesty, self-abasement, self-effacement, servility, submissiveness, unassertiveness, unassumingness, unpretentiousness
F2 arrogance, assertiveness, pride

hummock *n* barrow, elevation, hillock, hump, knoll, mound, prominence

humorist *n* caricaturist, cartoonist, clown, comedian, comic, jester, joker, satirist, wag, wit

humorous *adj* absurd, amusing, comic, comical, droll, entertaining, facetious, farcical, funny, hilarious, jocular *formal*, laughable, ludicrous, playful, ridiculous, risible *formal*, satirical, side-splitting, waggish, whimsical, witty, zany *colloq*
F2 humourless, serious

humour *n* **1** *a great sense of humour:* absurdity, amusement, badinage, comedy, drollery, facetiousness, farce, fun, gags, hilarity, jesting, jocularity *formal*, jokes, repartee, ridiculousness, satire, wisecracks *colloq*, wit, wittiness **2** *in a bad humour:* disposition, frame/state of mind, mood, spirits, temper, temperament
♦ *v* accommodate, acquiesce in *formal*, comply with, cosset, favour, flatter, go along with, gratify, indulge, mollify, pamper, pander to, permit, please, satisfy, spoil, tolerate

humourless *adj* boring, dry, dull, glum, grave, grim, long-faced, morose, serious, solemn, sombre, tedious, unlaughing, unsmiling
F2 humorous, witty

hump *n* **1** *a camel with one hump:* bulge, bump, excrescence *formal*, hunch, intumescence *formal*, knob, lump, mass, mound, outgrowth, projection, prominence, protrusion, protuberance, swelling **2** *get the hump:* aggravation *formal*, annoyance, depression, exasperation, gloom, irritation, sadness, unhappiness, vexation
♦ *v* **1** *humped up her pillows:* arch, crook, curve **2** *hump heavy boxes up the stairs:* carry, heave, hoist, lift, lug, shoulder

hump-backed *adj* crookbacked, crooked, deformed, gibbous, humped, hunchbacked, hunched, kyphotic *technical*, misshapen, stooped
F2 straight, upright

humped *adj* arched, bent, crooked, curved, gibbous, hunched
F2 flat, straight

hunch *n* feeling, guess, idea, impression, inkling, intuition, premonition, presentiment *formal*, sixth sense, suspicion

♦ *v* arch, bend, crouch, curl up, curve, draw in, huddle, hump, squat, stoop

hunger *n* **1** *dying of hunger:* famine, famishment, malnutrition, starvation **2** *hunger pangs:* appetite, emptiness, esurience *formal*, esuriency *formal*, greed, greediness, hungriness, ravenousness, voracity *formal* **3** *hunger for power:* appetite, craving, desire, hankering, itch, longing, need, pining, thirst, want, yearning, yen
♦ *v* ache, crave, desire, hanker, have a craving for, have a longing for, itch, long, need, pine, starve, thirst, want, wish, yearn

hungry *adj* **1** *we got home tired and hungry:* could eat a horse *colloq*, empty, famished, greedy, hollow, insatiable, malnourished, peckish *colloq*, ravenous, starving, underfed, undernourished, voracious *formal* **2** *hungry for knowledge:* aching, avid, covetous, craving, desirous, eager, hankering, itching, longing, needing, pining, thirsty, yearning
 1 full, satisfied

hunk *n* block, chunk, clod, dollop, gobbet, lump, mass, piece, slab, wedge

hunt *v* **1** *hunting deer:* chase, dog, follow, hound, pursue, shadow, stalk, track, trail **2** *hunting for an envelope:* ferret, fish, forage, investigate, look for, rummage, scour, search, seek, try to find
♦ *n* chase, investigation, pursuit, quest, rummaging, scouring, search, stalking, tracking

hunter *n* chaser, chasseur, huntsman, jäger, montero, venator, venerer, woodman, woodsman

hurdle *n* **1** *a race over hurdles:* barrier, fence, hedge, jump, obstacle, railing, wall **2** *a hurdle in the way of success:* barrier, complication, difficulty, handicap, hindrance, impediment, obstacle, obstruction, problem, snag, stumbling-block

hurl *v* cast, catapult, chuck *colloq*, fire, fling, heave, launch, let fly, pitch, project, propel, send, sling, throw, toss

hurly-burly *n* agitation, bedlam, brouhaha, bustle, chaos, commotion, confusion, disorder, disruption, distraction, frenzy, furore, hassle *colloq*, hubbub, hustle, pandemonium, trouble, tumult, turbulence, turmoil, unrest, upheaval, uproar

hurricane *n* cyclone, gale, squall, storm, tempest, tornado, typhoon, whirlwind

hurried *adj* **1** *snatch a hurried lunch:* breakneck, brief, fast, precipitate *formal*, quick, rapid, rushed, speedy, swift **2** *a hurried glance at the figures:* careless, cursory, fast, fleeting, hasty, offhand, passing, perfunctory, rushed, shallow, short, slapdash, superficial
 1 leisurely, unhurried **2** careful, close

hurry *v* accelerate, cut and run *colloq*, dash, fly, get a move on *colloq*, get a wiggle on *colloq*, get cracking *colloq*, go all out *colloq*, hasten, hustle, make haste, press on, pull your finger out *colloq*, put your foot down *colloq*, quicken, run, run like hell *colloq*, rush, shake a leg *colloq*, show your heels *colloq*, speed (up), step on it *colloq*
 delay, slow down
♦ *n* bustle, celerity *formal*, commotion, confusion, expedition *formal*, fastness, flurry,

haste, hustle, quickness, rapidity, rush, speed, swiftness, urgency
 calm, leisureliness

hurt *v* **1** *my leg hurts:* ache, be painful, be sore, burn, pain, smart, sting, throb, tingle **2** *hurt her back:* bruise, burn, cut, damage, debilitate *formal*, disable, ill-treat, impair, injure, lacerate, maim, maltreat, scratch, torture, wound **3** *the scandal could hurt his image:* blemish, blight, damage, harm, impair, mar, spoil **4** *his words had hurt her deeply:* afflict *formal*, annoy, cause sadness, distress, grieve, offend, sadden, upset, wound
♦ *n* aching, affliction *formal*, bruise, burning, cut, damage, discomfort, distress, grief, harm, injury, misery, pain, sadness, scratch, smarting, soreness, sorrow, suffering, throbbing, tingling, upset, wound
♦ *adj* **1** *badly hurt in the bombing:* aching, bruised, burning, cut, grazed, injured, lacerated, maimed, painful, scarred, smarting, sore, throbbing, tingling, wounded **2** *deeply hurt by her father's rejection:* affronted, aggrieved, annoyed, distressed, grief-stricken, in anguish, miserable, offended, sad, saddened, sorrowful, upset

hurtful *adj* **1** *hurtful remarks:* catty, cruel, cutting, derogatory, distressing, injurious *formal*, malefactory *formal*, malicious, mean, nasty, offensive, scathing, spiteful, unkind, upsetting, vicious, wounding **2** *the hurtful effects of the sun:* damaging, deleterious *formal*, destructive, harmful, injurious *formal*, pernicious, ruinous
 1 helpful, innocuous, kind **2** advantageous

hurtle *v* career, charge, crash, dash, dive, fly, plunge, race, rattle, rush, shoot, speed, tear

husband *n* better half *colloq*, groom, hubby *colloq*, married man, mate, other half *colloq*, partner, spouse
♦ *v* budget, conserve, economize, eke out, hoard, preserve, put aside, put by, ration, reserve, save, save up, store, use carefully, use sparingly
 squander, waste

husbandry *n* **1** *animal husbandry:* agribusiness *technical*, agriculture, agronomics, agronomy, conservation, cultivation, farm management, farming, land management, tillage **2** *the husbandry of their meagre resources:* economy, frugality, good housekeeping, management, saving, thrift, thriftiness
 2 squandering, wastefulness

hush *v* calm, compose, dry up *colloq*, mollify, pipe down *colloq*, quieten, settle, shush, shut up *colloq*, silence, soothe, still, subdue
 disturb, rouse
♦ *n* calm, calmness, peace, peacefulness, quiet, quietness, repose *formal*, serenity, silence, stillness, tranquillity
 clamour, noise
♦ *interj* be quiet, hold your tongue, not another word, quiet, shut up
▶ **hush up** conceal, cover up, gag, keep dark, keep secret, smother, stifle, suppress
 publicize

hush-hush *adj* classified, confidential, restricted, secret, top-secret, under wraps *colloq*
 open, public

husk *n* bran, capsule, case, chaff, covering, epicarp *technical*, hull, legume, peel, pod, rind, shell, shuck *US*, skin

husky *adj* **1** *a husky voice*: coarse, croaking, croaky, deep, gravelly, gruff, guttural, harsh, hoarse, low, rasping, rough, thick, throaty **2** *husky rugby players*: beefy *colloq*, brawny, burly, hefty, muscular, strapping, strong, well-built

hussy *n* floosie *colloq*, loose woman, minx, scrubber *slang*, slag *slang*, slut *slang*, tart *slang*, temptress, tramp *slang*, vamp *colloq*

hustle *v* **1** *hustled her into a cab*: bundle, bustle, crowd, elbow, hasten, hurry, jostle, nudge, push, shove, thrust **2** *spent the morning hustling about*: bustle, dash, fly, hasten, hurry, rush **3** *hustled him into accepting*: force, nudge, pressurize, push ◆ *n* activity, agitation, bustle, commotion, fuss, hurly-burly, hurry, rush, stir, tumult

hut *n* booth, bothy *Scot*, cabin, den, lean-to, shack, shanty, shed, shelter

hybrid *n* amalgam, combination, composite, compound, conglomeration *formal*, cross, crossbreed, half-blood, half-breed, mixture, mongrel ◆ *adj* combined, composite, compound, crossbred, heterogeneous, mixed, mongrel ◪ pure-bred

hybridize *v* bastardize, cross, crossbreed, interbreed, reproduce together

hygiene *n* cleanliness, disinfection, purity, sanitariness, sanitation, sterility, wholesomeness ◪ insanitariness

hygienic *adj* aseptic, clean, disinfected, germ-free, healthy, pure, salubrious *formal*, sanitary, sterile, sterilized, wholesome ◪ contaminated, insanitary, polluted, unhygienic

hymn *n* anthem, cantata, canticle, carol, chant, choral(e), chorus, doxology, introit, motet, offertory, paean, paraphrase, psalm, song, song of praise, spiritual

hype *n* advertisement, advertising, ballyhoo, build-up, fuss, plugging *colloq*, promotion, publicity, puffing, razzmatazz *colloq* ◆ *v* advertise, build up, plug *colloq*, promote, publicize

hyperbole *n* exaggeration, excess, extravagance, magnification, overkill, overstatement ◪ litotes *technical*, meiosis *technical*, understatement

hypercritical *adj* captious, carping, cavilling, censorious, choosy *colloq*, fault-finding, finicky, fussy, hair-splitting, niggling, nit-picking *colloq*, over-particular, pedantic, pernickety *colloq*, picky *colloq*, quibbling, strict, ultracrepidarian *formal* ◪ tolerant, uncritical

hypnotic *adj* compelling, fascinating, irresistible, magnetic, mesmerizing, numbing,

sedative, sleep-inducing, somniferous *formal*, soporific, spellbinding, stupefactive *formal*

hypnotism *n* auto-suggestion, hypnosis, mesmerism, suggestion

hypnotize *v* beguile, bewitch, captivate, enchant, entrance, fascinate, magnetize, mesmerize, put into a state of unconsciousness, put to sleep, spellbind

hypochondria *n* hypochondrianism *technical*, hypochondriasis *technical*, neurosis, valetudinarianism *formal*

hypochondriac *n* hypochondriast *technical*, valetudinarian *formal* ◆ *adj* hypochondriacal *technical*, neurotic, valetudinarian *formal*

hypocrisy *n* cant, deceit, deceitfulness, deception, dishonesty, dissembling *formal*, double-dealing, double-talk, duplicity *formal*, falsity, insincerity, lip service, pharisaism, phoneyness *colloq*, pretence, pretended goodness, two-facedness ◪ sincerity

hypocrite *n* canter, charlatan, deceiver, dissembler *formal*, fraud, Holy Willie, impostor, mountebank, Pharisee, phoney *colloq*, pretender, pseud *colloq*, pseudo *colloq*, whited sepulchre

hypocritical *adj* deceitful, deceptive, dishonest, dissembling *formal*, double-dealing, duplicitous *formal*, false, fraudulent, hollow, insincere, lying, Pecksniffian, perfidious *formal*, pharisaical, phoney *colloq*, sanctimonious, self-righteous, specious, spurious, two-faced ◪ genuine, sincere, truthful

hypothesis *n* assumption, axiom, conjecture *formal*, postulate *formal*, premise *formal*, presumption, proposition, speculation, supposition, theorem, theory, thesis

hypothetical *adj* assumed, conjectural *formal*, imaginary, imagined, presumed, proposed, speculative, supposed, theoretical ◪ actual, real

hysteria *n* agitation, delirium, frenzy, hysterics, madness, mania, neurosis, panic, (screaming) habdabs *colloq* ◪ calm, composure, control

hysterical *adj* **1** *the crowd became hysterical*: berserk, beside yourself, crazed, delirious, demented, frantic, frenzied, in a panic, mad, neurotic, out of control, overwrought, raving, uncontrollable **2** *a hysterical joke*: extremely funny, hilarious, priceless *colloq*, rich *colloq*, side-splitting, uproarious ◪ **1** calm, composed, self-possessed

hysterics *n* agitation, delirium, frenzy, hysteria, madness, mania, neurosis, panic, (screaming) habdabs *colloq*

ice n **1** *rivers of ice*: frost, frozen water, glacier, icicle, rime **2** *there was ice in his voice*: chill, coldness, coolness, distance, frostiness, iciness, unresponsiveness
♦ v chill, cool, freeze (over), frost, glaze, harden, refrigerate

ice-cold adj algid *technical*, arctic, bitterly cold, chilled, chilled to the bone, freezing, frigid, frosted, frosty, frozen, frozen-stiff, gelid *formal*, glacial, icebound, iced, icy, polar, Siberian
🔁 hot, warm

icon n figure, idol, image, likeness, portrait, portrayal, representation, symbol

iconoclast n critic, denouncer, denunciator, dissenter, dissident, heretic, image-breaker, opponent, questioner, radical, rebel, sceptic, unbeliever
🔁 believer, devotee

iconoclastic adj critical, denunciatory *formal*, dissentient *formal*, dissident, heretical, impious, innovative, irreverent, questioning, radical, rebellious, sceptical, subversive
🔁 trustful, uncritical, unquestioning

icy adj **1** *icy winds*: arctic, biting, bitter, chill, chilly, cold, freezing, frigid, frosty, frozen, gelid *formal*, glacial, ice-cold, polar, raw, Siberian **2** *icy roads*: frostbound, frosty, frozen, glassy, icebound, rimy, slippery, slippy **3** *met with an icy response*: aloof, cold, cool, distant, formal, frigid, frosty, hostile, indifferent, reserved, restrained, stiff, stony, unfriendly
🔁 **1** hot **3** friendly, responsive, warm, welcoming

idea n **1** *got the idea she disliked me*: abstraction *formal*, belief, clue, concept, conception, conceptualization, conjecture *formal*, fancy, feeling, guess, hypothesis, image, impression, inkling, interpretation, judgement, notion, opinion, perception, suspicion, theory, thought, understanding, view, viewpoint, vision **2** *good idea*: brainwave, design, plan, proposal, proposition, recommendation, scheme, suggestion **3** *the idea is to help farmers*: aim, end, goal, intention, object, objective, point, purpose, reason, target

ideal n **1** *my ideal of beauty*: acme *formal*, archetype *formal*, benchmark, criterion, epitome, example, exemplar *formal*, image, model, nonpareil *formal*, paragon, pattern, perfection, prototype, standard, type, yardstick **2** *his liberal ideals*: ethical standards/values, ethics, moral standards/values, morals, principle
♦ adj **1** *the ideal person to ask*: absolute, archetypal *formal*, best, complete, consummate *formal*, dream, highest, model, optimal, optimum, perfect, quintessential *formal*, supreme, utopian **2** *in an ideal world*: abstract, conceptual, fanciful, hypothetical, idealistic, imaginary, impractical, philosophical, romantic, theoretical, unattainable, unreal, utopian, visionary

idealism n impracticality, perfectionism, romanticism, utopianism
🔁 pragmatism, realism

idealist n dreamer, optimist, perfectionist, romantic, romanticist, visionary
🔁 pragmatist, realist

idealistic adj impracticable, impractical, optimistic, perfectionist, quixotic, romantic, starry-eyed, unrealistic, utopian, visionary
🔁 practical, pragmatic, realistic

idealization n apotheosis *formal*, ennoblement, exaltation, glamorization, glorification, idolization, romanticization, romanticizing, worship

idealize v exalt, glamorize, glorify, idolize, romanticize, utopianize, worship
🔁 caricature

ideally adv at best, hypothetically, in a perfect world, in an ideal world, in theory, perfectly, theoretically

idée fixe n complex, fixation, fixed idea, hang-up, leitmotiv, monomania *formal*, obsession

identical adj alike, as like as two peas in a pod *colloq*, corresponding, duplicate, equal, equivalent, indistinguishable, interchangeable, like, matching, one and the same, same, self-same, similar, twin
🔁 different

identifiable adj ascertainable *formal*, detectable, discernible, distinguishable, known, noticeable, perceptible, recognizable, unmistakable
🔁 indefinable, unfamiliar, unidentifiable, unknown

identification n **1** *a positive identification*: classification, detection, diagnosis, labelling, naming, pointing-out, recognition, spotting **2** *a strong identification with her students*: association, connection, empathy, fellow feeling, involvement, rapport, relationship, sympathy **3** *see some identification*: badge, credentials, documents, ID, identity card, papers

identify v **1** *couldn't identify the plane*: ascertain *formal*, catalogue, classify, detect, diagnose, discern, discover, distinguish, establish, find out, know, label, make out, name, notice, perceive, pick out, pinpoint, place, point out, recognize, single out, specify, spot, tag **2** *he's identified with the far left*: associate, connect, couple, involve, place, relate, think of together **3** *identify with other sufferers*: associate with, empathize with, feel for, relate to, respond to, sympathize with

identity n **1** *her Cornish identity*: character, distinctiveness, ego, existence, individuality, name, particularity, personality, personhood, self, selfhood, singularity *formal*, uniqueness **2** *identity of purpose*: closeness, correspondence, equality, equivalence, indistinguishability, interchangeability, likeness, resemblance, sameness, selfsameness, similarity

ideologist n doctrinaire, ideologue, philosopher, teacher, theorist, thinker, visionary

ideology n belief(s), convictions, credo *formal*, creed *formal*, doctrine(s), dogma, faith, ideas, opinion(s), philosophy, principles, teaching, tenets, theory, thesis, world-view

idiocy *n* absurdity, craziness, daftness *colloq*, fatuousness *formal*, folly, foolhardiness, inanity, insanity, lunacy, senselessness, silliness, stupidity
◰ sanity, wisdom

idiom *n* **1** *familiar Scottish idioms:* colloquialism, expression, locution *formal*, phrase, turn of phrase, usage **2** *a knowledge of cockney idiom:* jargon, language, phraseology, speech, style, talk, usage, vernacular

idiomatic *adj* colloquial, correct, dialectal, dialectical, everyday, grammatical, idiolectal, native, vernacular
◰ unidiomatic

idiosyncrasy *n* characteristic, eccentricity, feature, freak, habit, individuality, mannerism, oddity, peculiarity, quality, quirk, singularity *formal*, speciality, trait

idiosyncratic *adj* characteristic, distinctive, eccentric, individual, odd, peculiar, personal, quirky, singular *formal*
◰ common, general

idiot *n* ass *colloq*, birdbrain *colloq*, chump *colloq*, clot *colloq*, clown, cretin, dimwit, dope *colloq*, dork *slang*, dumbo *slang*, dunce, fat-head, fool, geek *slang*, halfwit, ignoramus, imbecile, jerk *slang*, mug *colloq*, nerd *slang*, nincompoop *colloq*, ninny *colloq*, nit *colloq*, nitwit *colloq*, numskull *colloq*, pillock *slang*, plonker *slang*, prat *slang*, prick *slang*, simpleton, sucker *colloq*, thickhead *colloq*, twerp *colloq*, twit *colloq*, wally *slang*

idiotic *adj* absurd, barmy *colloq*, batty *colloq*, crack-brained *colloq*, crazy, daft *colloq*, dotty *colloq*, dumb *colloq*, fatuous *formal*, foolish, half-baked, half-witted, hare-brained, ignorant, ill-advised, ill-considered, inane, inept, injudicious *formal*, insane, ludicrous, mad, moronic, nonsensical, nutty *colloq*, pointless, potty *colloq*, ridiculous, risible *formal*, senseless, short-sighted, silly, simple, simple-minded, stupid, thick-headed *colloq*, unintelligent, unreasonable, unwise
◰ sane, sensible

idle *adj* **1** *machines lay idle:* dead, dormant, inactive, inoperative, jobless, mothballed, not working, on the dole *colloq*, redundant, unemployed, unoccupied, unused **2** *they're an idle bunch:* do-nothing, indolent *formal*, lackadaisical, lazy, lethargic, loafish, slothful *formal*, sluggish, work-shy **3** *idle threats:* empty, fruitless, futile, ineffective, ineffectual *formal*, pointless, unproductive, unsuccessful, useless, vain, worthless **4** *idle gossip:* casual, foolish, insignificant, petty, shallow, trivial, unimportant
◰ **1** active, hardworking **2** busy **4** deep, important
◆ *v* **1** *idling in bars:* bum around *slang*, dally, dawdle, do nothing, fart about *slang*, fritter, horse around *colloq*, kill time, laze, loaf, loiter, lounge, potter, relax, shirk, sit back, skive *colloq*, slack, sod about *slang*, take it easy, waste, while, while away **2** *the engine is idling:* be operational, be ready to work/run, move, tick over
◰ **1** be busy, work

idleness *n* ease, inaction, inactivity, indolence *formal*, inertia, laziness, lazing, leisure, loafing, pottering, shiftlessness, skiving *colloq*, sloth

formal, slothfulness *formal*, sluggishness, torpor, vegetating
◰ activity, employment, occupation

idler *n* clock-watcher, dawdler, dodger *colloq*, do-nothing, drone, good-for-nothing, laggard, layabout, lazybones *colloq*, loafer, lounger, malingerer, shirker, skiver *colloq*, slacker, sloth *formal*, sluggard, waster, wastrel

idol *n* **1** *a cinema idol:* beloved, blue-eyed boy *colloq*, darling, favourite, hero, heroine, pet, pin-up *colloq*, star, superstar **2** *worship idols:* deity, effigy, fetish, god, graven image, icon, image, likeness, mammet

idolater *n* admirer, adorer, devotee, iconolater, idolatress, idolist, idol-worshipper, votary, worshipper

idolatrous *adj* adoring, adulatory, glorifying, heretical, idolizing, idol-worshipping, lionizing, pagan, reverential, uncritical, worshipping

idolatry *n* admiration, adoration, adulation, deification, exaltation, fetishism, glorification, heathenism, hero-worship, icon worship, iconolatry, idolism, idolizing, paganism, reverence, worshipping
◰ vilification

idolize *v* admire, adore, adulate, deify, dote on, exalt, glorify, hero-worship, lionize, love, put on a pedestal *colloq*, revere, reverence, venerate *formal*, worship
◰ despise

idyllic *adj* blissful, charming, delightful, happy, heavenly, idealized, pastoral, peaceful, perfect, picturesque, romantic, rustic, unspoiled, wonderful
◰ noisy, spoiled, unpleasant

if *conj* as/so long as, assuming (that), in case of, in the event of, on condition that, provided, providing, supposing (that)

iffy *adj* dodgy *colloq*, doubtful, dubious, uncertain, undecided, unsettled

ignite *v* **1** *the gas ignited:* burn, burst into flames, catch fire, fire, flare up, inflame **2** *the incendiary bombs ignited a fire:* burn, kindle, light, put a match to, set alight, set fire to, spark off, touch off
◰ **1** quench **2** quench

ignoble *adj* **1** *an ignoble chapter in our history:* base, contemptible, despicable, disgraceful, dishonourable, heinous *formal*, infamous, shameful, vile **2** *a man of ignoble birth:* base, common, low, lowborn, lowly, mean, vulgar
◰ **1** honourable, noble, worthy **2** noble

ignominious *adj* abject, base, contemptible, degrading, despicable, discreditable, disgraceful, dishonourable, disreputable, embarrassing, humiliating, infamous, mortifying, scandalous, shameful, sorry, undignified
◰ glorious, honourable, triumphant

ignominy *n* contempt, degradation, discredit, disgrace, dishonour, disrepute, humiliation, indignity, infamy, mortification, obloquy *formal*, odium *formal*, opprobrium *formal*, reproach, scandal, shame, stigma
◰ credit, dignity, honour

ignoramus *n* ass *colloq*, blockhead, bonehead *colloq*, dimwit, dolt *colloq*, duffer *colloq*, dullard,

dunce, fool, halfwit, illiterate, imbecile, know-nothing, numskull *colloq*, simpleton
☒ highbrow, intellectual, scholar

ignorance *n* greenness *colloq*, illiteracy, inexperience, innocence, naïvety, oblivion, stupidity, thickness *colloq*, unawareness, unconsciousness, unfamiliarity, unintelligence
☒ education, intelligence, knowledge, wisdom

ignorant *adj* a brick short of a load *colloq*, backward, blind, clueless *colloq*, dense *colloq*, dumb *colloq*, ill-informed, illiterate, in the dark *colloq*, inexperienced, innocent, innumerate, naïve, nescient *formal*, not all there *colloq*, oblivious, stupid, thick *colloq*, thick as two short planks *colloq*, unacquainted, unaware, unconscious, uneducated, unenlightened, unfamiliar, uninformed, uninitiated, unlearned, unread, unschooled, untaught, untrained, unwitting
☒ clever, conversant *formal*, educated, knowledgeable, learned, wise

ignore *v* 1 *ignoring his family:* be oblivious to, disregard, neglect, not listen to *colloq*, pay no attention to, take no notice of 2 *ignoring the important issues:* brush aside, close/shut your eyes to *colloq*, disregard, look the other way *colloq*, neglect, omit, overlook, pass over, reject, run away from *colloq*, shrug off, turn a blind eye to *colloq*, turn a deaf ear to *colloq* 3 *I smiled but she ignored me:* blank, cold-shoulder *colloq*, cut (dead), rebuff, slight, snub, spurn, turn your back on *colloq*
☒ 1 heed 2 notice 3 welcome

ilk *n* brand, breed, character, class, description, kind, make, sort, stamp, style, type, variety

ill *adj* 1 *ill with a stomach bug:* afflicted *formal*, ailing, bedridden, dicky *colloq*, diseased, feeble, frail, groggy *colloq*, in a bad way *colloq*, indisposed *formal*, infirm, laid up, like death warmed up *colloq*, off-colour, out of sorts *colloq*, poorly, queasy, rough *colloq*, run down *colloq*, seedy, sick, under the weather *colloq*, unhealthy, unwell, valetudinarian *formal*, weak 2 *an ill omen:* adverse, bad, damaging, deleterious *formal*, destructive, detrimental, difficult, evil, harmful, harsh, inauspicious *formal*, infelicitous *formal*, injurious, ominous, ruinous, severe, sinister, threatening, unfavourable, unfortunate, unlucky, unpleasant, unpromising, unpropitious *formal* 3 *ill feelings:* antagonistic, belligerent, hostile, resentful, unfriendly, unkind
☒ 1 healthy, well 2 favourable, fortunate, good 3 friendly, kind
♦ *n* affliction *formal*, cruelty, destruction, disaster, evil, harm, hurt, injury, misfortune, pain, problem, sorrow, suffering, trial(s), tribulation *formal*, trouble, unpleasantness
☒ benefit, good
♦ *adv* 1 *this bodes ill for him:* adversely, badly, disapprovingly, inauspiciously *formal*, unfavourably, unfortunately, unkindly, unluckily, unsuccessfully, wrongfully 2 *we can ill afford more delays:* amiss, barely, by no means, hardly, inadequately, insufficiently, poorly, scantily, scarcely
☒ 1 well

ill-advised *adj* careless, foolish, hasty, ill-considered, imprudent *formal*, inappropriate, injudicious *formal*, misguided, rash, reckless, short-sighted, thoughtless, unwise

cautious, circumspect *formal*, politic *formal*, sensible, well-advised, wise

ill-assorted *adj* discordant, incompatible, incongruous *formal*, inharmonious, misallied, mismatched, uncongenial, unsuited
☒ harmonious, well-matched

ill-bred *adj* bad-mannered, boorish, coarse, crass, crude, discourteous, ill-mannered, impolite, indelicate, loutish, rude, uncivil, uncivilized, uncouth, unseemly *formal*, vulgar
☒ gentlemanly, ladylike, polite, well-bred

ill-considered *adj* careless, foolish, hasty, heedless, ill-advised, ill-judged, improvident *formal*, imprudent *formal*, injudicious *formal*, overhasty, precipitate *formal*, rash, unwise
☒ sensible, wise

ill-defined *adj* blurred, blurry, dim, fuzzy, hazy, imprecise, indefinite, indistinct, nebulous, shadowy, unclear, vague, woolly
☒ clear

ill-disposed *adj* against, antagonistic, anti *colloq*, averse *formal*, hostile, inimical *formal*, opposed, unco-operative, unfriendly, unsympathetic, unwelcoming
☒ well-disposed

illegal *adj* banned, barred, black-market, criminal, felonious *formal*, forbidden, fraudulent, illegitimate, illicit, interdicted *formal*, outlawed, prohibited, proscribed *formal*, unauthorized, unconstitutional, under-the-counter, unlawful, wrong, wrongful
☒ allowed, lawful, legal, permitted

illegality *n* crime, criminality, felony *technical*, illegitimacy, illicitness, lawlessness, unconstitutionality, unlawfulness, wrong, wrongfulness, wrongness
☒ legality

illegible *adj* faint, hard to read, hieroglyphic, indecipherable, indistinct, obscure, scrawled, unintelligible, unreadable
☒ clear, legible

illegitimate *adj* 1 *an illegitimate child:* adulterine, bastard, born out of wedlock, fatherless, love, misbegotten, natural, unfathered 2 *an illegitimate regime:* illegal, illicit, improper, lawless, unauthorized, unlawful, unlicensed, unwarranted 3 *an illegitimate argument:* illogical, inadmissible, incorrect, invalid, spurious, unsound
☒ 1 legitimate 2 legal 3 well-reasoned

ill-fated *adj* blighted, doomed, hapless *formal*, ill-omened, ill-starred, luckless, unfortunate, unhappy, unlucky
☒ lucky

ill-favoured *adj* hideous, homely *US*, plain, repulsive, ugly, unattractive, unlovely, unprepossessing, unsightly
☒ attractive, beautiful

ill-feeling *n* anger, animosity, animus *formal*, antagonism, bad blood, bitterness, disgruntlement, dissatisfaction, dudgeon, enmity, frustration, grudge, hard feelings, hostility, ill-will, indignation, malice, odium *formal*, offence, rancour *formal*, resentment, sourness, spite, wrath
☒ friendship, goodwill

ill-founded *adj* baseless, groundless, unconfirmed, unjustified, unsupported, without foundation
🖅 substantiated, verified

ill-humoured *adj* acrimonious *formal*, bad-tempered, cantankerous *formal*, crabbed *colloq*, crabby *colloq*, cross, crotchety *colloq*, disagreeable, grouchy *colloq*, grumpy, huffy, impatient, irascible, irritable, moody, morose, peevish, petulant *formal*, quick-tempered, sharp, snappish, snappy, sulky, sullen, tart, testy, waspish
🖅 amiable

illiberal *adj* **1** *illiberal social views*: bigoted, hidebound, intolerant, narrow-minded, petty, prejudiced, reactionary, small-minded **2** *an illiberal host*: close-fisted, mean, miserly, niggardly, parsimonious *formal*, stingy, tight, tight-fisted *colloq*, uncharitable, ungenerous
🖅 **1** broad-minded, liberal **2** generous

illicit *adj* banned, barred, black-market, clandestine, contraband, criminal, forbidden, furtive, illegal, illegitimate, ill-gotten, improper, prohibited, secretive, stealthy, surreptitious, unauthorized, under-the-counter, unlawful, unlicensed, wrong
🖅 legal, permissible

illiterate *adj* analphabetic *technical*, benighted *formal*, ignorant, uncultured, uneducated, unlearned, unlettered, unschooled, untaught, untutored
🖅 literate

ill-judged *adj* daft *colloq*, foolhardy, foolish, hasty, ill-advised, ill-considered, impolitic *formal*, imprudent *formal*, incautious, indiscreet, injudicious *formal*, misguided, overhasty, rash, reckless, short-sighted, unwise, wrong-headed
🖅 sensible

ill-mannered *adj* badly-behaved, boorish, churlish, coarse, crude, discourteous, ill-behaved, ill-bred, impolite, insensitive, insolent, loutish, rude, uncivil, uncouth, unmannerly
🖅 polite, well-mannered

ill-natured *adj* bad-tempered, churlish, crabbed *colloq*, cross, disagreeable, malevolent *formal*, malicious, malignant, mean, nasty, perverse, petulant *formal*, spiteful, sulky, sullen, surly, unfriendly, unkind, unpleasant, vicious, vindictive
🖅 good-natured

illness *n* affliction *formal*, ailment, attack, bout, complaint, condition, disability, disease, disorder, ill health, indisposition, infirmity, malady *formal*, poor health, sickness, touch

illogical *adj* absurd, casuistic *formal*, fallacious *formal*, fallible, faulty, inconsistent, incorrect, invalid, irrational, meaningless, senseless, sophistical *formal*, specious, spurious, unreasonable, unscientific, unsound, untenable, wrong
🖅 logical, rational, reasonable

illogicality *n* absurdity, fallaciousness *formal*, fallacy, inconsistency, invalidity, irrationality, senselessness, speciousness, unreason, unreasonableness, unsoundness
🖅 logicality

ill-starred *adj* blighted, doomed, hapless *formal*, ill-fated, inauspicious *formal*, star-crossed, unfortunate, unhappy, unlucky
🖅 fortunate

ill-tempered *adj* bad-tempered, choleric, cross, curt, grumpy, ill-humoured, ill-natured, impatient, irascible, irritable, sharp, spiteful, testy, tetchy, touchy, vicious
🖅 good-tempered

ill-timed *adj* awkward, crass, inappropriate, inconvenient, inept, inopportune, tactless, unfortunate, unseasonable, untimely, unwelcome, wrong-timed
🖅 well-timed

ill-treat *v* abuse, damage, harm, injure, maltreat, mishandle, mistreat, misuse, neglect, oppress, wrong

ill-treatment *n* abuse, damage, harm, ill-use, injury, maltreatment, manhandling, mishandling, mistreatment, misuse, neglect
🖅 care

illuminate *v* **1** *candles illuminated the room*: brighten, floodlight, illumine *formal*, light, light up, shine on, throw light on **2** *use examples to illuminate your point*: clarify, clear up, edify, elucidate, enlighten, explain, illustrate, instruct **3** *an illuminated manuscript*: adorn, decorate, embellish, illustrate, ornament
🖅 **1** darken **2** mystify

illuminating *adj* edifying, enlightening, explanatory *formal*, helpful, informative, instructive, revealing, revelatory *formal*
🖅 unhelpful

illumination *n* **1** *illumination from a small gas lamp*: beam, brightness, irradiation, light, lighting, lights, radiance, ray **2** *the handbook provided no illumination*: awareness, education, enlightenment, insight, instruction, learning, perception, revelation, understanding **3** *the illumination of manuscripts*: adornment, decoration, embellishment, illustration, ornamentation
🖅 **1** darkness

illusion *n* **1** *no illusions about the size of the task*: deception, delusion, error, fallacy *formal*, false impression, misapprehension, misconception, misjudgement **2** *illusions rather than supernatural beings*: apparition, chimera *formal*, fancy, fantasy, figment of the imagination, hallucination, mirage, phantom, spectre, will-o'-the-wisp
🖅 **1** truth **2** reality

> *illusion*, *allusion* or *delusion*? See **allusion**, **delusion**

illusory *adj* apparent, chimerical *formal*, deceptive, deluding, delusive, delusory, erroneous, fallacious *formal*, false, fancied, illusionary, illusive, imagined, misleading, mistaken, seeming, sham, specious, unreal, unsubstantial, untrue
🖅 actual, real

illustrate *v* **1** *the point was illustrated well*: clarify, demonstrate, depict, draw, elucidate *formal*, exemplify, exhibit, explain, instance, interpret, picture, show, sketch **2** *illustrate a book*: adorn, decorate, embellish, illuminate, miniate *formal*, ornament

illustrated *adj* decorated, embellished, illuminated, miniated *formal*, pictorial

illustration *n* **1** *attractive illustrations throughout:* adornment, artwork, chart, decoration, design, diagram, drawing, embellishment, figure, halftone, ornamentation, photograph, picture, plate, representation, sketch **2** *a helpful illustration of his point:* analogy, case, clarification, demonstration, elucidation *formal*, example, exemplar *formal*, exemplification, explanation, instance, interpretation, sample, specimen

illustrative *adj* **1** *an example for illustrative purposes:* descriptive, exemplifying, explanatory, explicatory *formal*, expository *formal*, illustrational *formal*, interpretative, representative, sample, specimen, typical **2** *an illustrative guide:* delineative *formal*, diagrammatic, graphic, illustratory *formal*, pictorial

illustrious *adj* acclaimed, brilliant, celebrated, distinguished, eminent, esteemed *formal*, exalted, excellent, famed, famous, glorious, great, honoured, magnificent, noble, notable, noted, outstanding, pre-eminent, prominent, remarkable, renowned, splendid, well-known ✦ ignoble, inglorious

ill-will *n* anger, animosity, animus *formal*, antagonism, antipathy, aversion, bad blood, dislike, enmity, grudge, hard feelings, hatred, hostility, ill-feeling, indignation, malevolence, malice, odium *formal*, rancour *formal*, resentment, spite, unfriendliness, wrath ✦ friendship, goodwill

image *n* **1** *conjure up an image:* concept, conception, fancy, idea, impression, notion, perception, thought, vision **2** *worship of images:* bust, doll, effigy, figure, figurine, graven image, icon, idol, likeness, picture, portrait, replica, representation, resemblance, statue, statuette **3** *print the image:* copy, facsimile, photograph, picture, reflection, reproduction **4** *he is the image of his father:* clone, copy, (dead) ringer *colloq*, doppelgänger, double, duplicate, likeness, lookalike, match, replica, representation, spitting image *colloq*, twin **5** *a poem full of strange images:* figurative expression, figure of speech, imagery, metaphor, rhetorical device, simile, turn of phrase

imaginable *adj* believable, conceivable, credible, feasible, likely, plausible, possible, probable, supposable, thinkable ✦ inconceivable, unimaginable

imaginary *adj* assumed, chimerical *formal*, dreamy, fabulous, fancied, fanciful, fantastic, fictional, fictitious, ghostly, hallucinatory, hypothetical, illusory, imagined, insubstantial, invented, legendary, made-up, make-believe, mythical, mythological, non-existent, notional, pretend, shadowy, spectral, supposed, unreal ✦ real

imagination *n* **1** *he has little imagination:* creativity, enterprise, fancifulness, imaginativeness, ingenuity, insight, inspiration, inventiveness, originality, resourcefulness, vision, wit **2** *see them in my imagination:* conceptualization, dream, fancy, illusion, mind's eye, vision ✦ **1** unimaginativeness **2** reality

imaginative *adj* clever, creative, enterprising, fanciful, fantastic, full of ideas, ingenious, innovative, inspired, inventive, original, resourceful, visionary, vivid, whimsical ✦ unimaginative

imagine *v* **1** *I can't imagine a happier scene:* conceive, conjure up, create, daydream, devise, dream, dream up, envisage, fancy, fantasize, form a picture of, invent, make believe, picture, plan, pretend, project, scheme, see, see in your mind's eye, think up, visualize **2** *I imagine so:* assume, believe, conjecture *formal*, deem *formal*, fancy, gather, guess, judge, presume, reckon, suppose, surmise *formal*, take it *colloq*, think

imbalance *n* bias, disparity *formal*, disproportion, inequality, inequity *formal*, partiality, unevenness, unfairness ✦ balance, parity

imbecile *n* ass *colloq*, blockhead, bungler, clot *colloq*, cretin, dimwit, dunce, fool, halfwit, idiot, moron, nitwit *colloq*, simpleton, twit *colloq* ✦ *adj* absurd, asinine, barmy *colloq*, crazy, daft *colloq*, doltish *colloq*, dopey *colloq*, dotty *colloq*, fatuous *formal*, foolish, idiotic, inane, ludicrous, moronic, silly, stupid, thick *colloq*, witless ✦ intelligent, sensible

imbecility *n* amentia *technical*, asininity, childishness, cretinism, fatuity *formal*, foolishness, idiocy, inanity, incompetence, stupidity ✦ intelligence, sense

imbibe *v* **1** *he had imbibed too much at Christmas:* consume, drink, gulp, ingest *formal*, knock back *colloq*, quaff *colloq*, sip, swallow, swig *colloq* **2** *imbibed a set of beliefs from his parents:* absorb, acquire, assimilate, drink in, gain, gather, lap up *colloq*, receive, soak up, take in

imbue *v* charge, fill, impregnate, inculcate, ingrain, inject, inspire, instil, permeate, pervade, saturate, steep, suffuse, tinge, tint

imitate *v* **1** *he can imitate all sorts of famous people:* ape, caricature, copy, do an impression of, do likewise, echo, emulate *formal*, follow, follow suit, impersonate, mimic, mirror, mock, parody, parrot, repeat, send up *colloq*, spoof *colloq*, take a leaf out of someone's book *colloq*, take as a model, take off *colloq* **2** *natural fabrics can now be imitated synthetically:* copy, counterfeit, duplicate, fake, forge, replicate *formal*, reproduce, simulate

imitation *n* **1** *accurate imitations of his teachers:* apery, aping, caricature, impersonation, impression, mimicry, mockery, mocking, parody, send-up *colloq*, spoof *colloq*, take-off *colloq*, travesty **2** *beware of cheap imitations:* copy, counterfeit, dummy, duplicate, emulation *formal*, fake, forgery, likeness, reflection, replica, reproduction, resemblance, sham, simulation ✦ *adj* artificial, dummy, ersatz, fake, man-made, mock, phoney *colloq*, pseudo *colloq*, reproduction, sham, simulated, synthetic ✦ genuine

imitative *adj* copying, derivative, emulating *formal*, me-too *colloq*, mimetic *formal*, mimicking, mock, parrot-like, plagiarized, second-hand, simulated, unoriginal ✦ original

imitator *n* ape, copier, copycat *colloq*, copyist, echo, emulator *formal*, epigone, follower, impersonator, impressionist, mimic, parodist, parrot, plagiarist

immaculate adj 1 the tablecloth is immaculate: clean, spick and span, spotless, stainless, unblemished, unsoiled 2 an immaculate reputation: blameless, faultless, flawless, guiltless, impeccable, incorrupt, innocent, perfect, pure, sinless, spotless, squeaky clean colloq, stainless, unblemished, undefiled, unsullied, untainted 1 dirty, filthy 2 corrupt, stained

immaterial adj inconsequential, insignificant, irrelevant, minor, of no account, petty, trifling, trivial, unimportant important, relevant

immature adj 1 immature birds: adolescent, incomplete, juvenile, under-age, undeveloped, unmellowed, unprepared, unready, unripe, young 2 he's very immature for someone his age: babyish, callow, childish, green colloq, inexperienced, infantile, ingenuous formal, juvenile, naïve, puerile, raw, wet behind the ears colloq 1 fully-developed 2 grown-up, mature

immaturity n 1 immaturity evident in his early poems: adolescence, greenness, immatureness, imperfection, rawness, unpreparedness, unripeness, youth 2 his immaturity and lack of manners: babyishness, callowness, childishness, greenness, immatureness, juvenility, puerility 1 experience 2 maturity

immeasurable adj bottomless, boundless, endless, fathomless, illimitable, immense, incalculable, inestimable, inexhaustible, infinite, interminable, limitless, never-ending, unbounded, unfathomable, unlimited, vast limited

immediacy n directness, imminence, instancy, instantaneity, promptness, simultaneity, spontaneity, swiftness, urgency indirectness

immediate adj 1 his immediate reaction was one of relief: direct, instant, instantaneous, prompt, speedy, sudden, swift, without delay 2 the immediate problem is lack of drinking water: critical, crucial, current, existing, high-priority colloq, important, present, pressing, top-priority colloq, urgent, vital 3 seated on her immediate right: abutting formal, adjacent, adjoining formal, close, closest, near, nearest, next, next-door, recent 4 the immediate cause of death: basic, chief, direct, fundamental, main, primary, principal 1 delayed 3 distant 4 indirect

immediately adv as soon as, at once, before you can say Jack Robinson colloq, before you know it colloq, directly, forthwith, in two shakes of a lamb's tail colloq, instantaneously, instantly, like a shot colloq, no sooner... than, now, promptly, pronto colloq, quickly, right away, right now, speedily, straight away, this minute/instant, unhesitatingly, without delay, without hesitation, without question, yesterday colloq eventually, never

immemorial adj age-old, ancestral, ancient, archaic, fixed, hoary, long-standing, of yore formal, time-honoured, timeless, traditional recent

immense adj Brobdingnagian, bumper colloq, colossal, elephantine, enormous, extensive, extremely large, giant, gigantic, ginormous colloq, great, huge, humungous colloq, jumbo colloq, mammoth, massive, mega colloq, monumental, titanic, tremendous, vast, whopping colloq minute, tiny

immensely adv acutely, enormously, extraordinarily, extremely, greatly, massively, unusually

immensity n bulk, enormousness, expanse, extensiveness, giganticness, greatness, hugeness, magnitude, massiveness, vastness minuteness

immerse v 1 immerse in water: baptize, bathe, dip, douse, drench, duck, dunk, plunge, saturate, sink, soak, souse, submerge, submerse 2 immersed himself in the task: absorb, bury, engage, engross, engulf, involve, occupy, preoccupy, wrap up in

immersed adj absorbed, buried, busy, consumed, deep, engrossed, involved, occupied, preoccupied, rapt, sunk, taken up, wrapped up

immersion n 1 immersion in the sea: baptism, bathe, dip, dipping, dousing, drenching, ducking, dunking, plunging, saturation, sinking, soaking, submersion 2 immersion in the music: absorption, concentration, engagement, engrossing, involvement, preoccupation

immigrant n alien, incomer, migrant, new arrival, newcomer, settler native

immigrate v come in, migrate, move in, remove, resettle, settle emigrate

imminence n approach, closeness, immediacy, instancy, menace, nearness, propinquity formal, threat remoteness

imminent adj about to happen, almost upon you, approaching, at hand, brewing, close, coming, fast approaching, forthcoming, impending, in the air, in the offing, looming, menacing, near, on the horizon, on the way, round the corner colloq, threatening far-off, remote

immobile adj at rest, fixed, frozen, immobilized, immovable, motionless, rigid, riveted, rooted, static, stationary, stiff, still, stock-still, unmoving mobile, moving

immobility n firmness, fixedness, fixity, immovability, inertness, motionlessness, stability, steadiness, stillness mobility

immobilize v disable, freeze, halt, inactivate, paralyse, put out of action/operation, stop, transfix mobilize

immoderate adj distemperate formal, exaggerated, excessive, extravagant, extreme, inordinate, intemperate, lavish, OTT colloq, outrageous, over the top colloq, self-indulgent, unbridled, uncontrolled, uncurbed, unlimited, unreasonable, unrestrained, wanton moderate

immoderately *adv* exaggeratedly, excessively, exorbitantly, extravagantly, extremely, inordinately, unduly, unjustifiably, unreasonably, unrestrainedly, wantonly, without measure
🎝 moderately

immoderation *n* dissipation *formal*, excess, excessively, exorbitance, extravagance, immoderateness, intemperance, lavishness, overindulgence, prodigality *formal*, unreason, unrestraint
🎝 moderation

immodest *adj* **1** *immodest about their success:* boastful, bold, brazen, cheeky *colloq*, cocky *colloq*, forward, impudent, shameless **2** *shockingly immodest behaviour:* coarse, immoral, improper, indecent, indecorous *formal*, lewd, obscene, revealing, risqué, saucy *colloq*
🎝 **1** modest **2** proper

immodesty *n* **1** *the immodesty of her boast:* audacity, boldness, brass *colloq*, forwardness, gall, impudence, shamelessness, temerity **2** *attacking immodesty and loose morals:* bawdiness, coarseness, impurity, indecorousness *formal*, indecorum *formal*, indelicacy, lewdness, obscenity
🎝 **1** modesty **2** propriety

immoral *adj* bad, base, corrupt, debauched, degenerate, depraved, dishonest, dissolute, evil, impure, indecent, iniquitous *formal*, licentious, loose, nefarious *formal*, reprobate, sinful, unethical, unprincipled, unscrupulous, vile, wicked, wrong
🎝 good, moral, right

immorality *n* badness, corruption, debauchery, depravity, dishonesty, dissoluteness, evil, impurity, indecency, iniquity *formal*, licentiousness, obscenity, sin, sinfulness, turpitude *formal*, vice, vileness, wickedness, wrong, wrongdoing
🎝 morality

immortal *adj* **1** *immortal gods:* abiding, ageless, ceaseless, constant, deathless, endless, enduring, eternal, everlasting, imperishable, indestructible, lasting, perennial, perpetual, sempiternal *formal*, timeless, undying, unfading **2** *his immortal words:* celebrated, distinguished, famous, honoured, memorable, unforgettable, well-known
🎝 **1** mortal
♦ *n* deity, divinity, genius, god, goddess, Olympian

immortality *n* **1** *the immortality of the soul:* deathlessness, endlessness, eternal life, eternity, everlasting life, imperishability, incorruptibility, indestructibility, perpetuity, timelessness **2** *with that opera he achieved musical immortality:* celebrity, distinction, fame, glorification, gloriousness, glory, greatness, honour, renown
🎝 **1** mortality

immortalize *v* celebrate, commemorate, enshrine, eternalize, glorify, laud *formal*, memorialize, perpetuate

immovable *adj* **1** *immovable objects:* anchored, constant, fast, firm, fixed, immobile, jammed, moored, riveted, rooted, secure, set, stable, stuck **2** *on this issue I am immovable:* adamant, constant, determined, dogged, firm, inflexible, intransigent *formal*, obstinate, resolute, set,

steadfast, stubborn, uncompromising, unshakable, unswerving, unwavering, unyielding
🎝 **1** movable **2** flexible

immune *adj* free, invulnerable, protected, resistant, safe, secure, spared, unsusceptible
🎝 affected, liable, subject, susceptible

immunity *n* **1** *promise immunity to witnesses:* exception, exemption, exoneration *formal*, freedom, impunity, indemnity, liberty, licence, permission, privilege, protection, release, right **2** *immunity to bacteria:* immunization, inoculation, protection, resistance, safety, vaccination
🎝 **2** susceptibility

immunization *n* injection, inoculation, jab, protection, vaccination

immunize *v* inject, inoculate, protect, safeguard, shield, vaccinate

immure *v* cage, cloister, confine, enclose, imprison, incarcerate, jail, shut up, wall in
🎝 free

immutability *n* changelessness, constancy, durability, fixedness, immutableness, invariability, permanence, stability, unalterableness, unchangeableness
🎝 mutability

immutable *adj* abiding, changeless, constant, enduring, fixed, inflexible, invariable, lasting, permanent, perpetual, sacrosanct, stable, steadfast, unalterable, unchangeable
🎝 changeable, mutable

imp *n* **1** *malevolent imps:* demon, devil, gnome, goblin, hobgoblin, puck, sprite **2** *you naughty little imp!:* brat, flibbertigibbet, gamin, minx, mischief-maker, mischievous child, prankster, rascal, rogue, scamp, trickster, troublemaker, urchin

impact *n* **1** *the impact of the reforms:* consequences, effect, impression, influence, meaning, power, repercussions, results, significance **2** *the driver died on impact:* bang, blow, brunt, bump, clash, collision, contact, crash, force, jolt, knock, shock, smash, whack
♦ *v* **1** *metal impacting on brick:* clash, collide, crash, crush, fix, hit, press together, strike **2** *the scheme impacted on hundreds of people:* affect, apply to, have an effect on, impinge, influence

impair *v* blunt, cripple, damage, debilitate *formal*, decrease, deteriorate, diminish, disable, enervate *formal*, enfeeble *formal*, harm, hinder, injure, lessen, mar, reduce, spoil, undermine, vitiate *formal*, weaken, worsen
🎝 enhance, improve

impaired *adj* damaged, defective, disabled, faulty, flawed, imperfect, poor, spoilt, unsound, vitiated *formal*, weak
🎝 enhanced

impairment *n* damage, deterioration, disability, disablement, dysfunction *formal*, fault, harm, hurt, injury, reduction, ruin, vitiation *formal*, weakness
🎝 enhancement

impale *v* disembowel, lance, perforate, pierce, prick, puncture, run through, skewer, spear, spike, spit, stab, stick, transfix

impalpable *adj* airy, delicate, elusive, fine, imperceptible, inapprehensible, incorporeal *formal*, indistinct, insubstantial, intangible, shadowy, tenuous, unsubstantial
🖛 palpable

impart *v* 1 *impart knowledge:* communicate, convey, disclose, divulge, make known, pass on, relate, report, reveal, tell, transmit 2 *imparts a delicate flavour:* accord *formal*, assign, bestow *formal*, confer *formal*, contribute, give, grant, lend, offer
🖛 2 withhold

impartial *adj* detached, disinterested, dispassionate, equal, equitable, even-handed, fair, fair-minded, just, neutral, non-partisan, objective, open-minded, unbiased, unprejudiced
🖛 biased, prejudiced

impartiality *n* detachment, disinterest, disinterestedness, dispassion, equality, equity, even-handedness, fairness, justice, neutrality, non-partisanship, objectivity, open-mindedness, unbiasedness
🖛 bias, discrimination, favouritism, prejudice

impassable *adj* blocked, closed, impenetrable, insuperable, insurmountable, obstructed, unassailable, unnavigable, unpassable
🖛 passable

impasse *n* blind alley, checkmate, cul-de-sac, dead end, deadlock, gridlock, halt, stalemate, standstill

impassioned *adj* animated, ardent, blazing, eager, emotional, enthusiastic, excited, fervent, fervid, fiery, forceful, furious, glowing, heated, inflamed, inspired, intense, passionate, rousing, spirited, stirring, vehement, vigorous, violent
🖛 apathetic, mild

impassive *adj* calm, composed, cool, dispassionate, emotionless, expressionless, imperturbable *formal*, indifferent, laid back *colloq*, phlegmatic *formal*, stoical, unconcerned, unemotional, unexcitable, unfeeling, unflappable *colloq*, unmoved, unruffled
🖛 moved, responsive

impatience *n* 1 *impatience with the pace of reform:* anxiety, edginess, frustration, intolerance, restlessness 2 *impatience in his tone:* abruptness, brusqueness, curtness, irritability, shortness 3 *impatience to continue:* eagerness, enthusiasm, keenness, zeal 4 *in their impatience to buy a house:* haste, hastiness, impetuosity, rashness
🖛 1 patience 2 calm 3 indifference 4 slowness

impatient *adj* 1 *he's impatient to get stuck in:* avid, champing at the bit *colloq*, eager, fervent, keen, raring, restless, straining/panting at the leash *colloq*, zealous 2 *impatient with his critics:* bad-tempered, edgy, ill-tempered, irritated, petulant, tense
🖛 1 apathetic 2 patient

impeach *v* accuse, arraign, attack, blame, censure, charge, criticize, denounce, disparage *formal*, impugn *formal*, indict *technical*, revile

impeachment *n* accusation, arraignment *technical*, charge, disparagement *formal*, indictment

impeccable *adj* blameless, correct, exact, exemplary, faultless, flawless, immaculate, irreproachable, perfect
🖛 corrupt, faulty, flawed

impede *v* bar, block, check, clog, curb, delay, disrupt, hamper, handicap, hinder, hold back, hold up, obstruct, restrain, retard *formal*, slow (down), stop, thwart
🖛 aid, further, promote

impediment *n* 1 *no impediment to the marriage:* bar, barrier, block, burden, check, curb, difficulty, encumbrance, handicap, hindrance, obstacle, obstruction, restraint, restriction, setback, snag, stumbling-block 2 *a speech impediment:* defect, handicap, stammer, stutter
🖛 1 aid

impedimenta *n* accoutrements *formal*, baggage, belongings, effects *formal*, equipment, gear, luggage, stuff *colloq*, things *colloq*

impel *v* compel, constrain, drive, force, goad, incite, inspire, instigate, motivate, move, oblige, press, pressure, pressurize, prod, prompt, propel, push, spur, stimulate, urge
🖛 deter, dissuade

impending *adj* about to happen, approaching, at hand, brewing, close, coming, forthcoming, imminent, in the air, in the offing, looming, menacing, near, on the horizon, on the way, threatening
🖛 far-off, remote

impenetrable *adj* 1 *impenetrable jungle:* dense, impassable, overgrown, solid, thick 2 *his impenetrable prose:* abstruse *formal*, baffling, cryptic, dark, enigmatic, incomprehensible, indiscernible, inscrutable, mysterious, obscure, puzzling, recondite *formal*, unfathomable, unintelligible
🖛 2 accessible, understandable

impenitence *n* defiance, hard-heartedness, impenitency, incorrigibility, obduracy *formal*, stubbornness
🖛 penitence

impenitent *adj* defiant, hardened, incorrigible, obdurate *formal*, remorseless, unabashed, unashamed, uncontrite, unreformed, unregenerate, unremorseful, unrepentant
🖛 contrite, penitent

imperative *adj* compulsory, critical, crucial, essential, indispensable, necessary, obligatory, pressing, urgent, vital
🖛 optional, unimportant

imperceptible *adj* faint, fine, gradual, impalpable, inappreciable, inaudible, indefinite, indiscernible, indistinct, indistinguishable, infinitesimal, microscopic, minuscule, minute, muffled, negligible, obscure, slight, small, subtle, tiny, unapparent, unclear, undetectable, vague
🖛 clear, noticeable, perceptible

imperceptibly *adv* bit by bit, gradually, inappreciably, indiscernibly, insensibly *formal*, little by little, slowly, subtly, unnoticeably, unobtrusively, unseen
🖛 perceptibly

imperfect *adj* blemished, broken, chipped, damaged, defective, deficient, faulty, flawed, impaired, inadequate, incomplete
🖛 perfect, whole

imperfection *n* 1 *imperfections in the cloth:* blemish, blot, blotch, break, crack, cut, deformity, dent, failing, fault, scratch, spot, stain, taint, tear 2 *imperfections in the tax system:* defect, deficiency, failing, fault, flaw, foible, shortcoming, weakness **3** *his hatred of imperfection:* deficiency, frailty, inadequacy, incompleteness, insufficiency

☒ **3** perfection

imperial *adj* glorious, grand, great, kingly, lofty, magnificent, majestic, monarchical, noble, queenly, regal, royal, sovereign, splendid, stately

---

imperial or *imperious? Imperial* means 'of an empire or emperor': *the imperial crown. Imperious* means 'expecting to be, or in the habit of being, obeyed': *She disliked his imperious manner.*

---

imperialism *n* acquisitiveness, adventurism, colonialism, empire-building, expansionism

imperil *v* compromise, endanger, expose, expose to risk, hazard, jeopardize, put in danger, put in jeopardy, risk, take a chance, threaten

imperious *adj* arrogant, assertive, autocratic, commanding, despotic, dictatorial, domineering, haughty, high-handed, lordly, masterful, overbearing, overweening *formal*, peremptory *formal*, tyrannical

☒ humble

imperishable *adj* abiding, deathless, enduring, eternal, everlasting, immortal, incorruptible, indestructible, inextinguishable, perennial, permanent, perpetual, undying, unfading, unforgettable

☒ perishable

impermanent *adj* brief, elusive, ephemeral *formal*, evanescent *formal*, fleeting, fly-by-night *colloq*, flying, fugacious *formal*, fugitive, inconstant, momentary, mortal, passing, perishable, short-lived, temporary, transient, transitory, unfixed, unsettled, unstable

☒ permanent

impermeable *adj* damp-proof, hermetic, impassable, impenetrable, impervious, non-porous, proof, resistant, sealed, waterproof, water-repellent, water-resistant

☒ permeable, porous

impersonal *adj* **1** *her voice was brisk and impersonal:* aloof, businesslike, clinical, cold, cool, detached, distant, formal, frigid, official, remote, stiff, stuffy, unemotional, unfeeling **2** *the law is supposed to be impersonal:* detached, dispassionate, neutral, objective, unbiased, unprejudiced

☒ **1** friendly, informal **2** biased

impersonate *v* act, ape, caricature, imitate, masquerade as, mimic, mock, parody, pass off as, portray, pose as, take off *colloq*

impersonation *n* apery, aping, caricature, imitation, impression, mimicry, parody, take-off *colloq*

impertinence *n* audacity, boldness, brass *colloq*, brass neck *colloq*, brazenness, cheek *colloq*, discourtesy, disrespect, effrontery, face *colloq*, forwardness, gall *colloq*, impoliteness, impudence, insolence, lip *colloq*, mouth *colloq*, nerve *colloq*, presumption, rudeness, sauce *colloq*, shamelessness

☒ civility, politeness, respect

impertinent *adj* audacious, bold, brash, brazen, cheeky *colloq*, discourteous, disrespectful, forward, fresh *colloq*, ill-mannered, impolite, impudent, insolent, pert, presumptuous, rude, sassy *US colloq*, saucy *colloq*, shameless, smart-arsed *slang*, unmannerly

☒ polite, respectful

imperturbability *n* calmness, complacency, composure, coolness, equanimity *formal*, self-possession, tranquillity

☒ jitteriness, touchiness

imperturbable *adj* calm, calm and collected *colloq*, collected, complacent, composed, cool, even-tempered, impassive, self-possessed, tranquil, unexcitable, unflappable *colloq*, unmoved, unruffled, untroubled

☒ excitable, ruffled

impervious *adj* **1** *impervious to water:* closed, damp-proof, hermetic, impenetrable, impermeable, non-porous, proof, resistant, sealed, waterproof, watertight **2** *impervious to criticism:* closed, immune, invulnerable, resistant, unaffected, unmoved, untouched

☒ **1** pervious, porous **2** responsive, vulnerable

impetuosity *n* dash, élan, foolhardiness, haste, hastiness, impatience, impetuousness, impulsiveness, precipitateness *formal*, rashness, recklessness, spontaneity, thoughtlessness, vehemence

☒ caution, circumspection *formal*, wariness

impetuous *adj* brash, foolhardy, hasty, headlong, ill-conceived, impatient, impulsive, precipitate *formal*, rash, reckless, spontaneous, spur-of-the-moment, thoughtless, uncontrolled, unplanned, unpremeditated, unreasoned, unthinking

☒ cautious, circumspect *formal*, wary

impetuously *adv* impulsively, passionately, precipitately *formal*, rashly, recklessly, spontaneously, unthinkingly, vehemently

☒ cautiously

impetus *n* **1** *the projectile lost its impetus:* energy, force, momentum, power **2** *provided a big impetus to business activity:* boost, drive, encouragement, goad, impulse, incentive, influence, inspiration, motivation, push, spur, stimulus, urging

impiety *n* blasphemy, godlessness, hubris *formal*, iniquity *formal*, irreligion, irreverence, profaneness, profanity, sacrilege, sacrilegiousness, sinfulness, ungodliness, unholiness, unrighteousness, wickedness

☒ piety, reverence

impinge *v* **1** *impinging on others' land:* encroach, infringe, intrude, invade, trespass **2** *impinging on their ability to do their jobs:* affect, have a bearing on, impact on, influence, touch (on)

impious *adj* blasphemous, godless, hubristic *formal*, iniquitous *formal*, irreligious, irreverent, profane, sacrilegious, sacriligious, sinful, ungodly, unholy, unrighteous, wicked

☒ pious, reverent

impish *adj* devilish, elfin, frolicsome, gamin, mischievous, naughty, pranksome, rascally, roguish, sportive, tricksome, tricksy, waggish

implacability *n* implacableness, inexorability, inflexibility, intractability *formal*, intransigence *formal*, irreconcilability, mercilessness,

pitilessness, rancorousness *formal*, relentlessness, remorselessness, ruthlessness, unforgivingness, vengefulness
▪ placability

implacable *adj* adamant, cruel, heartless, inexorable, inflexible, intractable *formal*, intransigent *formal*, irreconcilable, merciless, pitiless, rancorous *formal*, relentless, remorseless, ruthless, unappeasable, uncompromising, unforgiving, unrelenting, unyielding, vengeful
▪ compassionate, forgiving

implant *v* 1 *implant ideas*: fix, inculcate, instil, introduce, plant, root, sow 2 *implant a pacemaker*: engraft, graft, insert, place, put, transplant

implausible *adj* doubtful, dubious, far-fetched, flimsy, hard to believe, improbable, inconceivable, incredible, questionable, suspect, thin, transparent, unbelievable, unconvincing, unlikely, weak
▪ likely, plausible, reasonable

implement *n* apparatus, appliance, contrivance, device, gadget, instrument, tool, utensil
♦ *v* accomplish, bring about, carry out, complete, discharge *formal*, do, effect *formal*, enforce, execute *formal*, fulfil, perform, put into action/operation, put into effect, realize

implementation *n* accomplishment, action, carrying out, completion, discharge *formal*, effecting *formal*, enforcement, execution *formal*, fulfilling, fulfilment, operation, performance, performing, realization

implicate *v* 1 *implicated in the murder*: compromise, embroil, entangle, incriminate, inculpate *formal*, involve 2 *implicated in global warming*: associate, be (a) party to, be a part of, concern, connect, include, involve
▪ 1 absolve, exonerate *formal*

implicated *adj* associated, compromised, concerned, connected, embroiled, entangled, included, incriminated, inculpated *formal*, involved, party to, responsible, suspected
▪ exonerated

implication *n* 1 *the implication is that he was responsible*: conclusion, consequence, deduction, effect, inference, insinuation, meaning, overtone, ramification, repercussion, significance, suggestion, undertone 2 *their implication in a murder*: association, connection, embroilment, entanglement, incrimination, inculpation *formal*, involvement

implicit *adj* 1 *an implicit criticism of her policies*: deducible, hidden, hinted, implied, indirect, inferred, inherent, insinuated, latent, suggested, tacit, understood, unexpressed, unsaid, unspoken, unstated 2 *you have my implicit trust*: absolute, complete, entire, full, perfect, positive, sheer, steadfast, total, unconditional, unhesitating, unqualified, unquestioning, unreserved, utter, wholehearted
▪ 1 explicit 2 half-hearted

implicitly *adv* absolutely, completely, firmly, steadfastly, totally, unconditionally, unhesitatingly, unquestioningly, unreservedly, utterly, wholeheartedly
▪ explicitly

implied *adj* assumed, hinted, implicit, indirect, inherent, insinuated, suggested, tacit, undeclared, understood, unexpressed, unspoken, unstated
▪ stated

implore *v* appeal, ask, beg, beseech *formal*, crave, entreat, importune *formal*, plead, pray, press, request, solicit *formal*, supplicate *formal*

imply *v* 1 *he implied that I was dishonest*: give someone to understand/believe, hint, indicate, infer, insinuate, intimate, say indirectly, signal, signify, state, suggest 2 *the rate implies a return of 5%*: denote *formal*, entail, indicate, involve, mean, point to, require, signify

> *imply* or *infer*? *Imply* means 'to suggest or hint at something without actually stating it': *Are you implying that I'm a liar? Infer* means 'to form an opinion by reasoning from what you know': *I infer from your silence that you are angry.*

impolite *adj* bad-mannered, boorish, cheeky *colloq*, coarse, discourteous, disrespectful, ill-bred, ill-mannered, impertinent, inconsiderate, indecorous, insolent, loutish, rude, uncivil, ungentlemanly, ungracious, unladylike, unmannerly, unrefined, vulgar
▪ courteous, polite

impoliteness *n* abruptness, bad manners, boorishness, churlishness, coarseness, crassness, discourtesy, disrespect, gaucherie, impertinence, incivility, inconsiderateness, indelicacy, insolence, roughness, rudeness, unmannerliness
▪ courtesy, politeness

impolitic *adj* daft *colloq*, foolish, ill-advised, ill-considered, ill-judged, imprudent *formal*, indiscreet, inexpedient, injudicious *formal*, maladroit *formal*, misguided, rash, short-sighted, undiplomatic, unwise
▪ politic *formal*, prudent *formal*, wise

import *n* 1 *exports and imports*: foreign product/commodity/goods, foreign trade, imported product/commodity/goods 2 *a matter of great import*: consequence, importance, significance, substance, weight 3 *the import of his speech*: content, drift, essence, gist, implication, intention, meaning, message, nub, purport *formal*, sense, substance, thrust
♦ *v* bring in, buy in, introduce, land

importance *n* 1 *safety is of great importance to us*: concern, consequence *formal*, criticalness, graveness, interest, matter, momentousness, significance, substance, urgency, usefulness, value, weight, worth 2 *people of importance in society*: distinction, eminence, esteem *formal*, influence, mark, noteworthiness, power, prestige, prominence, standing, status
▪ 2 insignificance, unimportance

important *adj* 1 *an important chapter in our history*: central, chief, critical, crucial, essential, far-reaching, fateful, grave, historic, key, main, major, material, meaningful, momentous, noteworthy, paramount, pivotal, primary, principal, priority, relevant, salient, seminal *formal*, serious, significant, substantial, urgent, valuable, valued, vital, weighty 2 *the most important person in the school*: chief, distinguished,

eminent, esteemed *formal*, foremost, high-level, high-ranking, influential, leading, main, notable, noted, outstanding, powerful, pre-eminent, prestigious, prominent, valued
₣ 1 insignificant, trivial, unimportant 2 powerless

importunate *adj* dogged, impatient, insistent, persistent, pertinacious *formal*, pressing, tenacious, troublesome, urgent

importune *v* appeal, badger, beset, cajole, harass, hound, pester, plague, plead with, press, request, solicit, supplicate *formal*, urge

importunity *n* cajolery, entreaties, harassing, harassment, hounding, insistence, persistence, pestering, pressing, solicitation, urgency, urging

impose *v* 1 *impose a fine*: apply, burden, charge, decree, encumber, enforce, establish, exact, fix, foist, force, inflict, institute, introduce, lay (on), levy, place (on), put (on), saddle, set, thrust 2 *I hope we're not imposing*: abuse, break in, butt in, encroach, foist yourself, force yourself, intrude, obtrude, presume, put upon, take advantage of, take liberties, thrust yourself, trespass

imposing *adj* august, dignified, grand, impressive, lofty, majestic, splendid, stately, striking
₣ modest, unimposing

imposition *n* 1 *imposition of the tax*: application, decree, enforcement, establishment, exaction, fixing, infliction, institution, introduction, levying, setting 2 *VAT and other impositions*: burden, charge, constraint, duty, encumbrance, load, punishment, tariff, task, tax, toll 3 *felt it to be an imposition*: intrusion, liberty, presumption

impossibility *n* absurdity, hopelessness, impracticability, inability, inconceivability, ludicrousness, preposterousness, ridiculousness, unacceptability, unattainableness, unobtainableness, untenability, unviability
₣ possibility

impossible *adj* absurd, and pigs might fly *colloq*, beyond you, hopeless, impracticable, inconceivable, incredible, insoluble, intolerable, ludicrous, not by any stretch of the imagination *colloq*, out *colloq*, out of the question, outlandish, preposterous, ridiculous, unacceptable, unachievable, unattainable, unbearable, unbelievable, unimaginable, unobtainable, unreasonable, unthinkable, unworkable
₣ possible

impostor *n* charlatan, cheat, con man *colloq*, deceiver, defrauder, deluder, fake, fraud, hoodwinker, impersonator, mountebank, phoney *colloq*, pretender, quack, rogue, sham, swindler, trickster

imposture *n* artifice, cheat, con *colloq*, con trick *colloq*, counterfeit, deception, fraud, hoax, impersonation, quackery, swindle, trick

impotence *n* disability, enervation *formal*, feebleness, frailty, helplessness, impuissance *formal*, inability, inadequacy, incapacity, incompetence, ineffectiveness, inefficacy *formal*, infirmity, paralysis, powerlessness, uselessness, weakness
₣ strength

impotent *adj* crippled, debilitated *formal*, disabled, enervated *formal*, exhausted, feeble, frail, futile, helpless, impuissant *formal*, inadequate, incapable, incapacitated, incompetent, ineffective, infirm, paralysed, powerless, unable, useless, weak, worn out, worthless
₣ potent, strong

impound *v* 1 *impound the car*: appropriate *formal*, commandeer, confiscate, expropriate *formal*, remove, seize, take away, take possession of 2 *the two pit bulls were impounded*: cage, confine, coop up, hem in, immure *formal*, incarcerate *formal*, keep in, lock up, shut up

impoverish *v* 1 *impoverished by inflation*: bankrupt, beggar, break, pauperize *formal*, ruin 2 *impoverish the soil*: denude, deplete, diminish, drain, exhaust, reduce, weaken
₣ 1 enrich

impoverished *adj* 1 *impoverished farmers*: bankrupt, bust *colloq*, cleaned out *colloq*, destitute, down-and-out, impecunious *formal*, indigent *formal*, needy, not having two pennies to rub together *colloq*, on your beam ends *colloq*, on your uppers *colloq*, penniless, penurious *formal*, poor, poverty-stricken, ruined, skint *colloq*, stony-broke *colloq* 2 *impoverished soils*: bare, barren, dead, desolate, drained, empty, exhausted, waste, weakened
₣ 1 rich

impracticability *n* futility, hopelessness, impossibility, infeasibility, unsuitableness, unviability, unworkability, uselessness
₣ practicability

impracticable *adj* impossible, inoperable, out of the question, unachievable, unattainable, unfeasible, unserviceable, unviable, unworkable, useless
₣ feasible, practicable

---

impracticable or *impractical*? *Impracticable* means 'that cannot be carried out or put into practice': *The whole project has become completely impracticable*. When referring to suggestions, plans, etc, *impractical* means 'possible to carry out, but not sensible or convenient': *In a modern economy barter is totally impractical* ; 'not able to do or make things in a sensible and efficient way': *He was impractical and dreamy, with a head full of foolish notions*.

---

impractical *adj* 1 *providing the service has become impractical*: impossible, impracticable, inconvenient, unrealistic, unserviceable, unworkable 2 *his ideas are exciting but impractical*: abstract, academic, idealistic, ivory-tower, romantic, starry-eyed, theoretical, visionary
₣ 1 practical, workable 2 realistic, sensible

impracticality *n* hopelessness, idealism, impossibility, infeasibility, romanticism, unworkability, unworkableness
₣ practicality

imprecation *n* abuse, anathema, blasphemy, curse, denunciation, execration *formal*, malediction *formal*, profanity *formal*, vilification *formal*, vituperation *formal*

imprecise *adj* ambiguous, approximate, blurred, equivocal, estimated, hazy, ill-defined,

inaccurate, indefinite, inexact, inexplicit, loose, rough, sloppy, vague, woolly
⊠ exact, precise

impregnable *adj* fortified, impenetrable, indestructible, invincible, inviolable, invulnerable, irrefutable, safe, secure, solid, strong, unassailable, unbeatable, unconquerable, unquestionable
⊠ vulnerable

impregnate *v* **1** *impregnated with wax:* drench, fill, imbue, infuse, penetrate, permeate, pervade, saturate, soak, steep, suffuse **2** *impregnated by her lover:* fecundate *formal*, fertilize, inseminate, make pregnant

impregnation *n* **1** *the mare's impregnation:* fecundation *formal*, fertilization, fertilizing, fructification *formal*, fructifying *formal*, insemination **2** *impregnation with wax:* imbuing, saturation

impresario *n* director, exhibitor, manager, organizer, producer, promoter

impress *v* **1** *impress the manager:* affect, excite, grab *colloq*, influence, inspire, move, rouse, stir, strike, sway, touch **2** *impress on him the need for tact:* bring home, emphasize, fix deeply, highlight, imprint, inculcate, instil, mark, stamp, stress, underline

impressed *adj* affected, excited, grabbed *colloq*, influenced, knocked out *colloq*, marked, moved, overawed, stamped, stirred, struck, taken, touched, turned on *colloq*
⊠ unimpressed

impression *n* **1** *my impression is that they are not happy:* awareness, belief, consciousness, conviction, fancy, feeling, funny feeling *colloq*, gut feeling *colloq*, hunch, idea, illusion, memory, notion, opinion, recollection, sensation, sense, suspicion, thought, vibes *colloq* **2** *make a good impression:* control, effect, impact, influence, power, sway **3** *they left hardly any impression on the snow:* dent, imprint, indentation, mark, outline, pressure, print, stamp **4** *his famous impression of Frank Spencer:* burlesque, caricature, imitation, impersonation, mimicry, parody, send-up *colloq*, take-off *colloq*

impressionability *n* greenness, gullibility, ingenuousness *formal*, naïvety, receptiveness, receptivity, sensitivity, suggestibility, susceptibility, vulnerability

impressionable *adj* gullible, ingenuous *formal*, mouldable, naïve, open, persuadable, pliable, receptive, responsive, sensitive, suggestible, susceptible, vulnerable

impressive *adj* affecting, awe-inspiring, awesome, breathtaking, dazzling, effective, exciting, grand, imposing, inspiring, powerful, rousing, spectacular, stirring, striking
⊠ unimpressive, uninspiring

imprint *n* badge, colophon, emblem, impression, indentation, logo, mark, print, sign, stamp
♦ *v* brand, emboss, engrave, establish, etch, fix, impress, mark, print, stamp

imprison *v* bang up *colloq*, cage, confine, detain, immure *formal*, incarcerate *formal*, intern, jail, lock up, pen, put away *colloq*, put in prison, send down *colloq*, send to prison, shut in
⊠ free, release

imprisoned *adj* behind bars, caged, captive, confined, doing bird *colloq*, doing porridge *colloq*, doing time *colloq*, immured *formal*, incarcerated *formal*, inside *colloq*, jailed, locked up, put away *colloq*, sent down *colloq*
⊠ free

imprisonment *n* captivity, confinement, custody, detention, incarceration *formal*, internment
⊠ freedom, liberty

improbability *n* doubt, doubtfulness, dubiety *formal*, dubiousness, far-fetchedness, implausibility, preposterousness, ridiculousness, uncertainty, unlikelihood, unlikeliness
⊠ probability

improbable *adj* **1** *their profit projections look highly improbable:* doubtful, dubious, far-fetched, implausible, incredible, questionable, unbelievable, uncertain, unlikely **2** *one of the more improbable unions in musical history:* preposterous, ridiculous, unbelievable, unconvincing
⊠ **1** likely, probable **2** convincing

impromptu *adj* ad-lib, extempore, improvised, off the cuff, spontaneous, unprepared, unrehearsed, unscripted
⊠ rehearsed
♦ *adv* ad lib, extempore, off the cuff *colloq*, off the top of your head *colloq*, on the spur of the moment *colloq*, spontaneously, without preparation

improper *adj* **1** *improper behaviour:* indecent, indecorous *formal*, indelicate, risqué, rude, shocking, unbecoming *formal*, unseemly *formal*, vulgar **2** *improper accounting:* erroneous, false, incorrect, irregular, unlawful, wrong **3** *improper responses:* inadequate, inappropriate, incongruous *formal*, inopportune, out of place, unfitting, unsuitable
⊠ **1** decent **2** correct, lawful **3** appropriate, suitable

impropriety *n* **1** *deny any impropriety:* bad taste, gaucherie, immodesty, incongruity *formal*, indecency, indecorousness *formal*, indecorum *formal*, unseemliness *formal*, unsuitability, vulgarity **2** *forgive their naïve improprieties:* blunder, faux pas, gaffe, lapse, mistake, slip, solecism *formal*
⊠ **1** propriety *formal*

improve *v* **1** *improve the infrastructure:* ameliorate, amend, better, develop, do up *colloq*, enhance, fix up *colloq*, give a facelift to *colloq*, mend, modernize, put right, rectify, reform, rehabilitate, revamp, revise, set right, streamline, touch up, upgrade **2** *improve her violin playing:* cultivate, elevate, hone, perfect, polish, refine, strenghen, temper **3** *the weather is starting to improve:* advance, be on the up and up *colloq*, get better, look up *colloq*, make headway, pick up, take a turn for the better *informal* **4** *his health has improved:* be on the mend *colloq*, convalesce, gain strength, get better, make progress, perk up *colloq*, pick up, rally, recover, recuperate, rehabilitate
⊠ **1** ruin **2** weaken **3** worsen **4** deteriorate

improvement *n* **1** *great improvements in conditions:* advancement, amendment, betterment, correction, development, enhancement, gain, increase, reform **2** *the new*

system is a great improvement: advance, development, furtherance, progress, recovery, reformation, rehabilitation
Fa 1 setback **2** deterioration, worsening

improvident *adj* careless, extravagant, heedless, imprudent, inattentive, Micawberish, negligent, prodigal *formal*, profligate *formal*, reckless, shiftless, spendthrift, thoughtless, thriftless, underprepared, uneconomical, unprepared, unthrifty, wasteful
Fa economical, thrifty

improvisation *n* **1** *a talent for improvisation:* ad-libbing, extemporizing, invention, spontaneity **2** *came up with a hasty improvisation:* ad-lib, autoschediasm *formal*, expedient, impromptu, makeshift, vamp

improvise *v* **1** *to improvise a feast from scraps:* cobble together *colloq*, concoct, contrive, invent, knock up *colloq*, make do, put together quickly, rig up *colloq*, run up *colloq*, throw together *colloq* **2** *had to improvise:* ad-lib, compose/perform without preparation, extemporize, have a brainwave *colloq*, play by ear *colloq*, say whatever comes into your head/mind *colloq*, speak off the cuff *colloq*, speak off the top of your head *colloq*, vamp

improvised *adj* ad-lib, extemporaneous, extempore, extemporized, makeshift, off-the-cuff, spontaneous, unprepared, unrehearsed, unscripted
Fa rehearsed

imprudent *adj* careless, foolhardy, foolish, hasty, heedless, ill-advised, ill-considered, ill-judged, impolitic *formal*, improvident *formal*, indiscreet, injudicious *formal*, irresponsible, rash, reckless, short-sighted, thoughtless, unthinking, unwise
Fa cautious, prudent *formal*, wary, wise

impudence *n* boldness, brass neck *colloq*, brazenness, cheek *colloq*, effrontery *formal*, face *colloq*, impertinence, insolence, lip *colloq*, mouth *colloq*, nerve *colloq*, pertness, presumption, rudeness, sauciness *colloq*
Fa politeness

impudent *adj* audacious, bold, brazen, cheeky *colloq*, cocky, disrespectful, forward, fresh *colloq*, immodest, impertinent, impolite, insolent, pert, presumptuous, rude, saucy *colloq*, shameless, smart-arsed *slang*
Fa polite

impugn *v* assail, attack, berate *formal*, call in question, censure *formal*, challenge, criticize, dispute, oppose, question, resist, revile *formal*, traduce *formal*, vilify *formal*, vilipend *formal*, vituperate *formal*
Fa compliment, praise

impulse *n* caprice, desire, drive, feeling, inclination, instinct, notion, passion, urge, whim, wish

impulsive *adj* automatic, emotional, foolhardy, hasty, headstrong, ill-considered, ill-judged, impatient, impetuous, instinctive, intuitive, madcap, passionate, precipitate *formal*, quick, rash, reckless, spontaneous, sudden, thoughtless, unthinking
Fa cautious, premeditated

impulsiveness *n* emotion, foolhardiness, haste, hastiness, impatience, impetuosity,

impetuousness, instinct, intuitiveness, passion, precipitateness *formal*, precipitation *formal*, quickness, rashness, recklessness, spontaneity, suddenness, thoughtlessness
Fa caution

impunity *n* amnesty, dispensation, excusal, exemption, freedom, immunity, liberty, licence, permission, security
Fa liability

impure *adj* **1** *impure drugs:* adulterated, alloyed, blended, combined, contaminated, corrupt, debased, defiled, diluted, dirty, foul, infected, mixed, polluted, sullied, tainted, unclean, unrefined **2** *impure thoughts:* bawdy, coarse, crude, depraved, dirty, erotic, immodest, immoral, improper, indecent, lecherous, lewd, licentious, lustful, obscene, offensive, pornographic, promiscuous, ribald, risqué, sexy, shameless, smutty, suggestive, unchaste, vulgar
Fa 1 pure **2** chaste, decent

impurity *n* **1** *impurities in the petrol:* adulteration, blend, contamination, corruption, debasement, dilution, dirt, dirtiness, dross, filth, foreign body, foulness, grime, infection, mark, mixture, pollutant, pollution, spot, taint **2** *impurity and lustful desires:* coarseness, crudity, eroticism, immodesty, immorality, impropriety, indecency, lewdness, licentiousness, looseness, lustfulness, obscenity, offensiveness, pornography, promiscuity, shamelessness, smut, unchastity, vulgarity
Fa 2 purity

impute *v* accredit *formal*, ascribe, assign, attribute, charge, credit, put down to, refer

in *adj* all the rage *colloq*, cool *colloq*, current, fashionable, in vogue, modish, popular, smart, stylish, trendy *colloq*

inability *n* disability, handicap, impotence, inadequacy, incapability, incapacity, incompetence, ineffectiveness, ineptitude, powerlessness, uselessness, weakness
Fa ability

inaccessible *adj* beyond reach, god-forsaken, impenetrable, isolated, out of reach, out of the way, remote, unapproachable, unattainable, unavailable, unfrequented, unget-at-able *colloq*, unreachable
Fa accessible

inaccuracy *n* **1** *the inaccuracy of her claim:* erroneousness, error, fallaciousness *formal*, imprecision, inexactness, mistakenness, unreliability **2** *the report contains several inaccuracies:* blunder, boo-boo *colloq*, corrigendum *formal*, defect, erratum *formal*, error, fault, gaffe, howler *colloq*, miscalculation, mistake, slip, slip-up *colloq*
Fa 1 accuracy, precision **2** accuracy, precision

inaccurate *adj* defective, erroneous, fallacious *formal*, false, faulty, flawed, imperfect, imprecise, incorrect, inexact, loose, mistaken, out, unfaithful, unreliable, unsound, untrue, wrong
Fa accurate, correct, right, sound, true

inaccurately *adv* carelessly, clumsily, defectively, erroneously, falsely, imperfectly, imprecisely, incorrectly, inexactly,

loosely, unfaithfully, unreliably, wildly, wrongly
≠ accurately, correctly

inaction *n* idleness, immobility, inactivity, inertia, lethargy, lifelessness, motionlessness, passivity, rest, slowness, sluggishness, stagnation, torpor *formal*
≠ action

inactivate *v* cripple, disable, immobilize, knock the bottom out of *colloq*, mothball, paralyse, scupper *colloq*, stabilize, stop
≠ activate

inactive *adj* **1** *the production line is inactive:* dormant, idle, immobile, inert, inoperative *formal*, motionless, quiescent *formal*, stagnant, stationary, unused **2** *obese, inactive teenagers:* idle, indolent *formal*, lazy, lethargic, passive, sedentary, sleepy, slow, sluggish, torpid *formal*, vegetating **3** *she's been inactive since redundancy:* economically inactive, idle, jobless, out of work, unemployed, unoccupied
≠ **1** active, busy, functioning, in use, working **2** active **3** working

inactivity *n* **1** *the animal's inactivity during the winter:* abeyance *formal*, dormancy, hibernation, immobility, inaction, inertia, inertness, lifelessness, stagnation, stasis *technical*, torpor *formal*, vegetation **2** *inactivity and obesity:* dilatoriness *formal*, dullness, heaviness, idleness, indolence *formal*, languor, lassitude *formal*, laziness, lethargy, passivity, quiescence *formal*, sloth, sluggishness, torpor *formal*
≠ **1** activity **2** activeness

inadequacy *n* **1** *the inadequacy of milk supplies:* dearth, deficiency, deficit, insufficiency, lack, meagreness, paucity *formal*, scantiness, scarcity, shortage, want *formal* **2** *his inadequacy as a minister:* defectiveness, inability, incapability, incompetence, ineffectiveness, inefficacy *formal* **3** *inadequacies of the system:* defect, failing, fault, flaw, foible, imperfection, shortcoming, weakness
≠ **1** adequacy **3** strong point

inadequate *adj* **1** *inadequate rations:* deficient, insufficient, meagre, niggardly, scant, scanty, scarce, short, skimpy, sparse, too little/few, wanting **2** *an inadequate husband:* bad, careless, defective, disappointing, faulty, imperfect, incapable, incompetent, ineffective, ineffectual *formal*, inefficacious *formal*, inexpert, not good enough, not up to scratch *colloq*, substandard, unequal, unfit, unproficient, unqualified, unsatisfactory
≠ **1** adequate, enough **2** satisfactory

inadequately *adv* badly, carelessly, imperfectly, insufficiently, meagrely, poorly, scantily, sketchily, skimpily, sparsely, thinly
≠ adequately

inadmissible *adj* disallowed, immaterial, improper, inapposite *formal*, inappropriate, irrelevant, precluded *formal*, prohibited, unacceptable
≠ admissible

inadvertent *adj* accidental, careless, chance, involuntary, negligent, thoughtless, uncalculated, unconscious, unintended, unintentional, unplanned, unpremeditated, unwitting
≠ careful, conscious, deliberate

inadvertently *adv* accidentally, by accident, by chance, by mistake, carelessly, heedlessly, involuntarily, mistakenly, negligently, remissly, thoughtlessly, unconsciously, unintentionally, unthinkingly, unwittingly
≠ deliberately

inadvisable *adj* foolish, ill-advised, ill-considered, ill-judged, imprudent *formal*, indiscreet, inexpedient, injudicious *formal*, misguided, silly, unwise
≠ advisable, wise

inalienable *adj* absolute, inherent, inviolable, non-negotiable, non-transferable, permanent, sacrosanct, unassailable, unremovable, untransferable
≠ impermanent

inane *adj* absurd, empty, fatuous *formal*, foolish, frivolous, futile, idiotic, ludicrous, mindless, nonsensical, puerile, ridiculous, senseless, silly, stupid, trifling, unintelligent, vacuous, vain, vapid, worthless
≠ sensible

inanimate *adj* dead, defunct, dormant, dull, extinct, immobile, inactive, inert, insensate, insentient *technical*, lifeless, spiritless, stagnant, torpid *formal*, unconscious, wooden
≠ alive, animate, living

inanity *n* absurdity, asininity, daftness *colloq*, emptiness, fatuity *formal*, folly, foolishness, frivolity, imbecility, ludicrousness, puerility, ridiculousness, senselessness, silliness, stupidity, vacuity, vapidity, waffle *colloq*
≠ sense

inapplicable *adj* immaterial, inapposite *formal*, inappropriate, inapt, inconsequent *formal*, irrelevant, unconnected, unrelated, unsuitable, unsuited
≠ applicable, germane *formal*, pertinent *formal*

inapposite *adj* immaterial, inappropriate, irrelevant, out of place, unsuitable

inappropriate *adj* **1** *she was sold an inappropriate policy:* ill-fitted, ill-suited, incompatible, unfitting, unsuitable, unsuited **2** *an inappropriate remark:* ill-timed, improper, incongruous *formal*, indecorous *formal*, out of place, tactless, tasteless, unbecoming, unbefitting, unseemly *formal*, unsuitable
≠ **1** suitable **2** appropriate

inapt *adj* ill-fitted, ill-suited, ill-timed, inapposite *formal*, inappropriate, infelicitous *formal*, inopportune, irrelevant, out of place, unfortunate, unsuitable, unsuited
≠ apt

inarticulacy *n* hesitancy, inarticulateness, incoherence, incomprehensibility, indistinctness, mumbling, speechlessness, stammering, stumbling, stuttering, tongue-tiedness, unintelligibility
≠ articulacy

inarticulate *adj* **1** *an inarticulate cry:* blurred, incoherent, incomprehensible, indistinct, muffled, mumbled, unclear, unintelligible **2** *she was inarticulate and shy:* faltering, halting, hesitant, hesitating, quavery, stammering, stumbling, stuttering, tongue-tied **3** *inarticulate rage:* dumb, mute, silent, speechless, voiceless, wordless
≠ **1** clear **2** articulate **3** vocal

inattention *n* absent-mindedness, carelessness, daydreaming, disregard, distraction, dreaminess, forgetfulness, heedlessness, inattentiveness, negligence, preoccupation, thoughtlessness, unmindfulness

inattentive *adj* absent-minded, careless, daydreaming, disregarding, distracted, distrait *formal*, dreamy, forgetful, heedless, in a world of your own *colloq*, miles away *colloq*, negligent, preoccupied, regardless, remiss, somewhere else *colloq*, thoughtless, unmindful, wool-gathering ◻ attentive

inaudible *adj* dull, faint, imperceptible, indistinct, low, muffled, mumbled, murmured, muted, muttered, noiseless, silent, soft, stifled, whispered ◻ audible, loud

inaugural *adj* exordial *formal*, first, initial, introductory, launching, maiden, opening, original

inaugurate *v* **1** *inaugurate a scheme:* begin, commence *formal*, get going, initiate, institute, introduce, launch, open, originate, put into operation, set in motion, set up, set/start the ball rolling *colloq*, start, usher in **2** *inaugurate the president:* enthrone, induct, install, instate, invest, ordain **3** *inaugurate a new building:* commission, consecrate, dedicate, open officially

inauguration *n* **1** *the inauguration of a folk festival:* commencement *formal*, initiation, institution, launch, launching, opening, setting up, starting **2** *the inauguration of the Senator:* consecration, enthronement, induction, installation, installing, investiture, ordination

inauspicious *adj* bad, black, discouraging, ill-fated, ill-starred, infelicitous *formal*, ominous, threatening, unfavourable, unfortunate, unlucky, unpromising, unpropitious *formal*, untimely ◻ auspicious *formal*, promising

inborn *adj* congenital, connate *formal*, hereditary, in the family, inbred, ingrained, inherent, inherited, innate, instinctive, intuitive, native, natural ◻ learned

inbred *adj* connate *formal*, constitutional, ingenerate *formal*, ingrained, inherent, innate, native, natural ◻ learned

incalculable *adj* boundless, countless, endless, enormous, immeasurable, immense, inestimable, infinite, innumerable, limitless, measureless, numberless, unlimited, untold, vast, without number ◻ limited, restricted

incandescent *adj* aglow, bright, brilliant, dazzling, gleaming, glowing, shining, white-hot

incantation *n* abracadabra, chant, charm, conjuration *formal*, formula, hex, invocation, magic formula, mantra, mantram, rune, spell

incapable *adj* **1** *incapable of doing the job:* feeble, inadequate, incompetent, ineffective, ineffectual *formal*, inept, not hacking it *colloq*, not up to scratch *colloq*, out of your league *colloq*, unfit, unfitted, unqualified, unsuited, useless, weak **2** *drunk and incapable:* helpless, impotent, powerless, unfit ◻ **1** capable, experienced

incapacitate *v* cripple, debilitate *formal*, disable, immobilize, lay up, paralyse, put out of action, scupper *colloq*

incapacitated *adj* crippled, disabled, disqualified, drunk, hamstrung, immobilized, indisposed *formal*, laid up *colloq*, out of action, paralysed, prostrate, scuppered *colloq*, tipsy *colloq*, unfit, unwell ◻ operative

incapacity *n* disability, disqualification, feebleness, impotence, inability, inadequacy, incapability, incompetence, incompetency, ineffectiveness, ineffectuality *formal*, ineptitude, powerlessness, unfitness, uselessness, weakness ◻ capability

incarcerate *v* cage, commit, confine, coop up, detain, encage, gaol, immure *formal*, impound, imprison, intern, jail, lock up, put away, put in jail, put in prison, restrain, restrict, send down *colloq*, wall in ◻ free, release

incarceration *n* bondage, captivity, confinement, custody, detention, imprisonment, internment, jail, restraint, restriction ◻ freedom, liberation

incarnate *adj* corporeal *formal*, embodied, fleshly, human, in human form, in the flesh, made flesh, personified, typified

incarnation *n* appearance in the flesh, embodiment, human form, impersonation, manifestation, personification

incautious *adj* careless, foolhardy, foolish, hasty, ill-advised, ill-considered, ill-judged, imprudent *formal*, impulsive, inattentive, inconsiderate, injudicious *formal*, precipitate *formal*, rash, reckless, thoughtless, uncircumspect *formal*, unobservant, unthinking, unwary, unwatchful ◻ careful, cautious, vigilant

incendiary *adj* **1** *an incendiary bomb:* combustible, fire-raising, flammable, pyromaniac **2** *incendiary remarks:* dissentious, inciting, inflammatory, proceleusmatic *formal*, provocative, rabble-rousing, seditious, stirring, subversive ◻ **2** calming
♦ *n* **1** *incendiaries inflamed the mob:* agitator, demagogue, firebrand, insurgent, rabble-rouser, revolutionary **2** *incendiaries set fire to the embassy:* arsonist, firebug, fire-raiser, pétroleur, pétroleuse, pyromaniac **3** *planes bombed the ship with incendiaries:* bomb, charge, explosive, fire-bomb, grenade, mine, petrol bomb

incense[1] *n* aroma, balm, bouquet, fragrance, joss-stick, perfume, scent

incense[2] *v* aggravate *colloq*, agitate, anger, drive up the wall *colloq*, enrage, exasperate, excite, get someone's blood up *colloq*, get someone's dander up *colloq*, get under someone's skin *colloq*, hassle *colloq*, inflame, infuriate, irk, irritate, madden, make someone's blood boil *colloq*, nettle, provoke, rile, vex ◻ calm

incensed *adj* angry, enraged, exasperated, fuming, furibund *formal*, furious, in a paddy *colloq*, indignant, infuriated, irate, ireful, mad, maddened, on the warpath *colloq*, steamed up, up in arms *colloq*, wrathful ◻ calm

incentive *n* bait, carrot *colloq*, encouragement, enticement, goad, impetus, incitement, inducement, lure, motivation, motive, reason, reward, spur, stimulant, stimulus, sweetener *colloq*
🔁 deterrent, discouragement, disincentive

inception *n* beginning, birth, commencement *formal*, dawn, inauguration, initiation, installation, kick-off *colloq*, opening, origin, outset, rise, start
🔁 end

incessant *adj* ceaseless, constant, continual, continuous, endless, eternal, everlasting, interminable *formal*, never-ending, non-stop, perpetual, persistent, recurrent, unbroken, unceasing, unending, uninterrupted, unremitting
🔁 intermittent, periodic, sporadic, temporary

incidence *n* amount, commonness, degree, extent, frequency, occurrence, prevalence, range, rate

incident *n* **1** *an incident from my naval career:* adventure, affair, circumstance, episode, event, experience, happening, instance, matter, occasion, occurrence, proceeding **2** *an incident at the prison:* brush, clash, commotion, conflict, confrontation, disturbance, fight, fracas, mishap, row, scene, skirmish, upset

incidental *adj* **1** *incidental to our main purpose:* accompanying, ancillary, attendant, background, concomitant *formal*, contributory, minor, non-essential, peripheral, petty, related, secondary, small, subordinate, subsidiary, supplementary, trivial **2** *incidental effects:* accidental, by chance, chance, fortuitous *formal*, random
🔁 **1** essential, important **2** planned

incidentally *adv* **1** *the castle, incidentally, dates from the Norman era:* apropos, by the by *colloq*, by the way, en passant, in passing, parenthetically, secondarily **2** *the discovery was made only incidentally:* accidentally, by accident, by chance, casually, coincidentally, digressively, fortuitously *formal*, unexpectedly

incinerate *v* burn, carbonize, consume by fire, reduce to ashes

incipient *adj* beginning, commencing *formal*, developing, embryonic, impending, inaugural, inceptive *formal*, inchoate *formal*, nascent *formal*, newborn, originating, rudimentary, starting
🔁 developed

incise *v* carve, chisel, cut, cut into, engrave, etch, gash, nick, notch, sculpt, sculpture, slash, slit

incision *n* cut, gash, nick, notch, opening, slash, slit

incisive *adj* acid, acute, astute, biting, caustic, cutting, keen, mordant *formal*, penetrating, perceptive, perspicacious *formal*, piercing, pungent, sarcastic, sharp, shrewd, stinging, trenchant *formal*

incisiveness *n* acidity, acuteness, astucity *formal*, astuteness, keenness, penetration, perspicacity *formal*, pungency, sarcasm, sharpness, tartness, trenchancy *formal*

incite *v* agitate, animate, arouse, drive, egg on *colloq*, encourage, excite, foment, goad, impel, induce, inflame, instigate, prod, prompt, provoke, rouse, spur, stimulate, stir up, urge, whip up, work up
🔁 restrain

incitement *n* agitation, animation, drive, encouragement, goad, impetus, incentive, inducement, instigation, motivation, prod, prompting, provocation, rousing, spur, stimulation, stimulus, urging
🔁 discouragement

inciting *adj* incendiary, inflammatory, proceleusmatic *formal*, provocative, rabble-rousing, seditious, stirring, subversive
🔁 calming

incivility *n* bad manners, boorishness, coarseness, discourteousness, discourtesy, disrespect, ill-breeding, impoliteness, inurbanity, roughness, rudeness, unmannerliness, vulgarity
🔁 civility

inclemency *n* bitterness, foulness, harshness, rawness, roughness, severity, storminess, tempestuousness
🔁 clemency

inclement *adj* bitter, blustery, foul, harsh, intemperate, nasty, raw, rough, severe, squally, stormy, tempestuous
🔁 clement, fine

inclination *n* **1** *her artistic inclinations:* affection, affinity, attraction, bias, disposition, fondness, leaning, liking, partiality, penchant *formal*, predilection *formal*, predisposition *formal*, preference, proclivity *formal*, propensity *formal*, taste, tendency, trend **2** *an inclination of 45 degrees:* acclivity *formal*, angle, ascent, bank, bend, bow, declivity *formal*, gradient, incline, lift, nod, pitch, ramp, slant, slope, steepness, tilt
🔁 **1** disinclination, dislike

incline *v* **1** *a belief that inclines us to act in a certain way:* affect, bend, bias, dispose, influence, persuade, prejudice, sway, tend **2** *she inclined her head:* bank, bend, bow, curve, deviate, lean, list, nod, slant, slope, stoop, swing, tilt, tip, veer
♦ *n* acclivity *formal*, ascent, declivity *formal*, descent, dip, gradient, hill, ramp, rise, slope

inclined *adj* apt, disposed, given, liable, likely, of a mind, predisposed *formal*, tending, willing, wont *formal*

include *v* **1** *the list includes children's books:* admit, allow for, comprehend *formal*, comprise, contain, cover, embody, embrace *formal*, enclose, encompass, hold, incorporate, introduce, involve, let in on, rope in *colloq*, span, subsume *formal*, take in, take into account, throw in *colloq* **2** *include your personal details:* add, enter, insert, put in
🔁 **1** eliminate, exclude, omit **2** exclude

including *prep* containing, counting, included, inclusive of, together with, with
🔁 excluding

inclusion *n* addition, embodiment, encompassing, incorporation, insertion, involvement
🔁 exclusion

inclusive *adj* across-the-board, all-embracing, all-in, all-inclusive, blanket *colloq*, catch-all, comprehensive, full, general, overall, sweeping
🔁 exclusive, narrow

incognito *adj* camouflaged, disguised, in disguise, keeping your identity secret, masked,

nameless, under an assumed/a false name, unidentifiable, unidentified, unknown, unmarked, unrecognizable, veiled
₣ undisguised

incognizant *adj* ignorant, inattentive, unacquainted, unaware, unconscious, unenlightened, uninformed, unknowing, unobservant
₣ apprised *formal*, aware

incoherence *n* brokenness, confusion, disconnectedness, disjointedness, garbledness, illogicality, inarticulateness, incomprehensibility, inconsistency, jumble, mix-up, muddle, mumble, mutter, stammer, stutter, unintelligibility
₣ coherence

incoherent *adj* broken, confused, disconnected, disjointed, disordered, garbled, illogical, inarticulate, incomprehensible, inconsistent, jumbled, mixed-up, muddled, mumbled, muttered, rambling, scrambled, stammering, stuttering, unclear, unconnected, unintelligible, wandering
₣ coherent, intelligible

incombustible *adj* fireproof, fire-resistant, flameproof, flame-resistant, flame-retardant, non-flammable, non-inflammable, unburnable
₣ combustible

income *n* earnings, gains, interest, means, pay, proceeds, profits, receipts, remuneration, returns, revenue, salary, takings, wages
₣ expenditure, expenses

incoming *adj* **1** *incoming flights:* approaching, arriving, coming, ensuing, entering, homeward, returning **2** *the incoming Prime Minister:* new, next, succeeding
₣ **1** departing **2** outgoing

incommensurate *adj* disproportionate, excessive, extravagant, inadequate, inequitable *formal*, inordinate *formal*, insufficient, unequal
₣ appropriate

incommunicable *adj* indescribable, ineffable *formal*, inexpressible, unimpartable, unspeakable, unutterable
₣ communicable, expressible

incomparable *adj* beyond compare, brilliant, inimitable, matchless, nonpareil, paramount, peerless, superb, superlative, supreme, unequalled, unmatched, unparalleled, unrivalled, unsurpassed, without equal, without parallel
₣ ordinary, poor, run-of-the-mill

incomparably *adv* beyond compare, brilliantly, by far, easily, eminently, far and away, immeasurably, infinitely, superbly, superlatively, supremely
₣ poorly, slightly

incompatibility *n* antagonism, clash, conflict, contradiction, difference, disagreement, discrepancy, disparateness *formal*, disparity *formal*, incongruity *formal*, inconsistency, irreconcilability, mismatch, uncongeniality, variance
₣ compatibility

incompatible *adj* antagonistic, at odds, at variance, clashing, conflicting, contradictory, disagreeing, discordant, disparate *formal*, ill-matched, incongruous *formal*, inconsistent, irreconcilable, like a fish out of water *colloq*, like

a square peg in a round hole *colloq*, mismatched, uncongenial, unsuited, wrong
₣ compatible, complementary, going well together

incompetence *n* bungling, inability, inadequacy, incapability, ineffectiveness, ineffectuality *formal*, ineffectualness *formal*, inefficiency, ineptitude, ineptness, insufficiency, stupidity, unfitness, unsuitability, uselessness
₣ competence

incompetent *adj* amateurish, awkward, botched, bungling, clumsy, deficient, fumbling, inadequate, incapable, ineffective, inefficient, inept, inexpert, insufficient, not able to organize a piss-up in a brewery *slang*, stupid, unable, unfit, unqualified, unskilful, unsuitable, useless
₣ able, competent

incomplete *adj* abridged, broken, defective, deficient, fragmentary, imperfect, lacking, part, partial, piecemeal, scrappy, short, shortened, unaccomplished, undeveloped, unfinished, wanting *formal*
₣ accomplished, complete, exhaustive, total

incomprehensible *adj* above your head, abstruse *formal*, baffling, complex, complicated, deep, enigmatic, impenetrable, inscrutable, involved, mysterious, obscure, opaque, perplexing, profound, puzzling, recondite *formal*, unfathomable, unintelligible, unreadable
₣ comprehensible, intelligible

inconceivable *adj* absurd, implausible, impossible, incredible, ludicrous, mind-boggling *colloq*, outrageous, ridiculous, shocking, staggering, unbelievable, unheard-of, unimaginable, unthinkable
₣ conceivable, imaginable, not on

inconclusive *adj* ambiguous, indecisive, indefinite, indeterminate *formal*, left hanging *colloq*, open, open to question, uncertain, unconvincing, undecided, unsatisfying, unsettled, up in the air *colloq*, vague
₣ conclusive, open-and-shut *colloq*

incongruity *n* clash, conflict, contradiction, discrepancy, disparity *formal*, dissociability *formal*, dissociableness *formal*, inappropriateness, inaptness, incompatibility, inconsistency, inharmoniousness, irreconcilability, unsuitability
₣ consistency, harmoniousness

incongruous *adj* absurd, at odds, clashing, conflicting, contradictory, contrary, inappropriate, incompatible, inconsistent, irreconcilable, jarring, odd, out of keeping, out of place, strange, unsuitable
₣ compatible, consistent

inconsequential *adj* immaterial, inappreciable, insignificant, minor, negligible, petty, trifling, trivial, unimportant
₣ important, significant

inconsiderable *adj* insignificant, minor, negligible, petty, slight, small, trifling, trivial, unimportant
₣ considerable, large

inconsiderate *adj* careless, egotistic, heedless, insensitive, intolerant, rude, self-centred, selfish, tactless, thoughtless, uncaring, uncharitable, unconcerned, undiscerning, unkind, unthinking
₣ considerate, gracious, kind, thoughtful

inconsiderateness *n* carelessness, insensitivity, intolerance, rudeness, self-centredness, selfishness, tactlessness, thoughtlessness, unconcern, unkindness
☒ considerateness, kindness, thoughtfulness

inconsistency *n* **1** *inconsistencies in her evidence:* conflict, contradiction, contrariety *formal,* disagreement, discrepancy, disparity *formal,* divergence, incompatibility, incongruity *formal,* irreconcilability, odds, paradox, variance **2** *his inconsistency is frustrating:* changeableness, fickleness, inconstancy, instability, unpredictability, unreliability, unsteadiness
☒ **1** consistency **2** consistency, constancy

inconsistent *adj* **1** *activities inconsistent with stock exchange rules:* at odds, at variance, conflicting, contradictory, contrary, differing, discordant, in opposition, incompatible, incongruous *formal,* irreconcilable, out of place/keeping **2** *he's a rather inconsistent player:* capricious, changeable, erratic, fickle, inconstant, irregular, mercurial, unpredictable, unstable, unsteady, variable, varying
☒ **1** consistent **2** consistent, constant

inconsolable *adj* brokenhearted, desolate, despairing, devastated, disconsolate *formal,* grief-stricken, heartbroken, miserable, wretched

inconspicuous *adj* camouflaged, concealed, discreet, hidden, in the background, indistinct, insignificant, low-key, modest, ordinary, plain, quiet, retiring, unassuming, undistinguished, unobtrusive, unremarkable
☒ conspicuous, noticeable, obtrusive

inconstant *adj* capricious, changeable, changeful, erratic, fickle, fluctuating, inconsistent, irresolute, mercurial, mutable, uncertain, undependable, unfaithful, unreliable, unsettled, unstable, unsteady, vacillating *formal,* variable, varying, volatile, wavering, wayward
☒ constant

incontestable *adj* certain, clear, evident, incontrovertible, indisputable, indubitable *formal,* irrefutable *formal,* obvious, self-evident, sure, undeniable, unquestionable
☒ uncertain

incontinent *adj* debauched, dissipated, dissolute, lascivious, lecherous, lewd, licentious, loose, lustful, promiscuous, unbridled, unchaste, unchecked, uncontrollable, uncontrolled, ungovernable, ungoverned, unrestrained, wanton
☒ continent

incontrovertible *adj* beyond doubt, beyond question, certain, clear, indisputable, indubitable *formal,* irrefutable *formal,* self-evident, undeniable, unquestionable
☒ questionable, uncertain

inconvenience *n* annoyance, awkwardness, bind *colloq,* bore *colloq,* bother, burden, difficulty, disadvantage, disruption, disturbance, drag *colloq,* drawback, fuss, headache *colloq,* hindrance, inappropriateness, nuisance, pain *colloq,* problem, trouble, turn-off *colloq,* unsuitability, upset, vexation, worry
☒ convenience
♦ *v* annoy, bother, burden, discommode *formal,* disrupt, disturb, fuss, impose upon, irk, put out, trouble, upset, worry
☒ convenience

inconvenient *adj* annoying, awkward, bothersome, difficult, ill-timed, inappropriate, inexpedient, inopportune, troublesome, unmanageable, unseasonable, unsuitable, untimely
☒ convenient, handy, suitable

incorporate *v* **1** *incorporate some new features:* assimilate, contain, embody, embrace *formal,* include, integrate, take in **2** *it was incorporated into Indonesia:* absorb, amalgamate, assimilate, coalesce, fuse, include, integrate, merge, subsume *formal,* unite **3** *incorporate the oil into the mixture:* amalgamate, blend, combine, consolidate, fuse, meld, mingle, mix
☒ **1** exclude **2** separate **3** separate

incorporation *n* absorption, amalgamation, assimilation, association, blend, coalescence, combination, company, embodiment, federation, fusion, inclusion, integration, merger, society, subsuming *formal,* unification, unifying
☒ separation, splitting off

incorporeal *adj* bodiless, ethereal, ghostly, illusory, intangible, phantasmal, phantasmic, spectral, spiritual, unfleshy, unreal
☒ fleshy, real

incorrect *adj* **1** *an incorrect answer:* erroneous, fallacious *formal,* false, faulty, illegitimate, imprecise, inaccurate, inexact, mistaken, not right, ungrammatical, untrue, (way) off beam *colloq,* wrong **2** *incorrect behaviour:* improper, inappropriate, unseemly, unsuitable, untrue, wrong
☒ **1** accurate, correct **2** appropriate, suitable

incorrectness *n* erroneousness, error, fallacy *formal,* falseness, faultiness, impreciseness, imprecision, inaccuracy, inexactitude, inexactness, mistakenness, speciousness, unsoundness, unsuitability, wrongness
☒ accuracy, correctness

incorrigible *adj* beyond, beyond redemption, dyed-in-the-wool, hardened, hope, hopeless, incurable, inveterate, irredeemable
☒ redeemable

incorruptibility *n* honesty, honour, integrity, justness, morality, nobility, probity *formal,* trustworthiness, uprightness, virtue
☒ corruptibility

incorruptible *adj* ethical, high-principled, honest, honourable, just, moral, straight, trustworthy, unbribable, upright, virtuous
☒ corruptible, dishonest

increase *v* **1** *the number of tourists has increased:* advance, be on the increase, become greater, build up, climb, develop, escalate, expand, extend, go through the roof *colloq,* go up, grow, heighten, improve, intensify, mount, multiply, mushroom, progress, proliferate, rise, rocket, skyrocket, snowball, soar, spiral, spread, strengthen, swell **2** *increase the public's awareness:* add to, advance, augment *formal,* boost, breed, bring to a head *colloq,* bring to the boil *colloq,* broaden, build up, bump up *colloq,* deepen, develop, enhance, enlarge, expand, extend, further, heighten, hike up *colloq,* improve, intensify, magnify, prolong, propagate, raise, scale up, spread, step up, strengthen, widen

≠ **1** decline, fall **2** decrease, reduce
♦ *n* addition, advance, augmentation *formal*, boost, build-up, development, enlargement, escalation, expansion, extension, gain, growth, heightening, hike *colloq*, increment, intensification, mushrooming, proliferation, rise, rocketing, snowballing, spread, step-up, surge, upsurge, upturn
≠ decline, decrease, reduction

increasingly *adv* all the more, cumulatively, more and more, more so, progressively, to an increasing degree/extent

incredible *adj* **1** *give some incredible excuse*: absurd, beyond/past belief, far-fetched, implausible, impossible, improbable, inconceivable, preposterous, unbelievable, unimaginable, unthinkable **2** *walk an incredible distance*: amazing, astonishing, astounding, exceptional, extraordinary, fantastic, great, marvellous, remarkable, surprising, wonderful
≠ **1** believable, credible

---

incredible or *incredulous*? *Incredible* means 'unbelievable'; *incredulous* means 'showing disbelief'. If you are told an *incredible* story, you may be *incredulous*.

---

incredulity *n* cynicism, disbelief, distrust, doubt, mistrust, scepticism, suspicion, unbelief
≠ credulity

incredulous *adj* cynical, disbelieving, distrustful, distrusting, doubtful, doubting, dubious, sceptical, suspicious, unbelieving, uncertain, unconvinced
≠ credulous

increment *n* accretion *formal*, accrual *formal*, accrument *formal*, addendum *formal*, addition, advancement, augmentation *formal*, enlargement, expansion, extension, gain, growth, increase, step-up, supplement
≠ decrease

incriminate *v* accuse, arraign, blame, charge, impeach, implicate, inculpate *formal*, indict *technical*, involve, point the finger at *colloq*, put the blame on
≠ exonerate

inculcate *v* din into, drill into, drum into, engrain, fix, hammer into, implant, impress, imprint, indoctrinate, infuse, instil, teach

inculpate *v* accuse, arraign, blame, censure, charge, impeach, implicate, incriminate, indict *technical*, involve, put the blame on, recriminate
≠ exonerate

incumbent *adj* binding, compulsory, mandatory *formal*, necessary, obligatory, prescribed, up to
♦ *n* functionary, member, office-bearer, office-holder, officer, official

incur *v* arouse, bring upon yourself, earn, experience, expose yourself to, gain, lay yourself open to, meet with, provoke, run up, suffer, sustain

incurable *adj* *an incurable disease*: fatal, hopeless, inoperable, terminal, unhealable, untreatable **2** *an incurable romantic*: beyond hope, beyond redemption, dyed-in-the-wool, hardened, hopeless, incorrigible, inveterate
≠ **1** curable

incursion *n* assault, attack, foray, infiltration, inroads, invasion, irruption *formal*, onslaught, penetration, raid, sally, sortie

indebted *adj* appreciative, beholden *formal*, grateful, obliged, thankful

indecency *n* coarseness, crudity, foulness, grossness, immodesty, impurity, indecorum *formal*, lewdness, licentiousness, obscenity, offensiveness, vulgarity
≠ decency, modesty

indecent *adj* **1** *indecent suggestions*: bawdy, coarse, corrupt, crude, degenerate, depraved, dirty, filthy, foul, gross, immodest, immoral, improper, impure, indelicate, lewd, licentious, obscene, offensive, outrageous, perverted, pornographic, ribald, risqué, shocking, smutty, suggestive, vulgar **2** *indecent haste*: improper, inappropriate, indecorous *formal*, unbecoming, unseemly *formal*, unsuitable
≠ **1** decent, modest

indecipherable *adj* crabbed, cramped, illegible, indistinct, indistinguishable, tiny, unclear, unintelligible, unreadable
≠ readable

indecision *n* ambivalence, doubt, fluctuation, hesitancy, hesitation, indecisiveness, irresolution, shilly-shallying *colloq*, tentativeness, uncertainty, vacillation *formal*, wavering
≠ decisiveness, resolution

indecisive *adj* **1** *an indecisive leader*: ambivalent, blowing hot and cold *colloq*, chopping and changing *colloq*, doubtful, faltering, fluctuating, hesitant, hesitating, in two minds *colloq*, indefinite, irresolute, pussyfooting *colloq*, shilly-shallying *colloq*, sitting on the fence *colloq*, tentative, uncertain, undecided, undetermined, unsure, vacillating *formal*, wavering, weak-willed *colloq*, wishy-washy *colloq* **2** *an indecisive battle*: hanging in the balance *colloq*, inconclusive, indefinite, indeterminate *formal*, open, unclear, undecided, unsettled, up in the air *colloq*
≠ **1** decisive **2** decisive, open-and-shut *colloq*

indecorous *adj* boorish, churlish, coarse, crude, ill-bred, ill-mannered, immodest, impolite, improper, in bad taste, inappropriate, indecent, rough, rude, tasteless, uncivil, uncouth, undignified, ungentlemanly, unladylike, unmannerly, unseemly *formal*, unsuitable, untoward *formal*, vulgar
≠ decorous

indeed *adv* **1** *I do indeed know him*: absolutely, certainly, doubtlessly, for sure, positively, truly, undeniably, undoubtedly, without doubt **2** *found that the money had indeed been taken*: actually, doubtlessly, for sure, in fact, in truth, really, to be sure, undoubtedly

indefatigable *adj* diligent, dogged, indomitable, inexhaustible, patient, persevering, relentless, tireless, undying, unfailing, unflagging, unremitting, unresting, untireable, untiring, unweariable, unwearied, unwearying
≠ flagging, slothful

indefensible *adj* **1** *morally indefensible*: faulty, flawed, inexcusable, insupportable, specious, unforgivable, unjustifiable, unpardonable, untenable, wrong **2** *an indefensible place*: defenceless, disarmed, exposed, ill-equipped,

unarmed, unfortified *formal*, unguarded, unprotected, unshielded, vulnerable
F 1 defensible, excusable **2** defensible, guarded, protected

indefinable *adj* dim, hazy, impalpable, indescribable, indistinct, inexpressible, nameless, obscure, subtle, unclear, unrealized, vague
F definable

indefinite *adj* **1** *an indefinite period*: equivocal, ill-defined, indeterminate *formal*, inexact, loose, uncertain, unclear, undefined, undetermined, unfixed, unlimited, unresolved, unsettled, unspecified, vague **2** *indefinite instructions*: ambiguous, doubtful, ill-defined, imprecise, indeterminate *formal*, indistinct, inexact, obscure, uncertain, unclear, undefined, undetermined, unknown
F 1 definite, settled **2** clear, definite

indefinitely *adv* ad infinitum, continually, endlessly, eternally, for ever, without limit

indelible *adj* enduring, fast, imperishable, indestructible, ineffaceable, ineradicable, ingrained, lasting, permanent, unfading
F erasable

indelicacy *n* bad taste, coarseness, crudity, grossness, immodesty, impropriety *formal*, indecency, obscenity, offensiveness, rudeness, smuttiness, suggestiveness, tastelessness, vulgarity
F delicacy

indelicate *adj* blue *colloq*, coarse, crude, embarrassing, gross, immodest, improper, in bad taste, indecent, indecorous *formal*, low, obscene, off-colour *colloq*, offensive, risqué, rude, suggestive, tasteless, unbecoming, unseemly *formal*, untoward *formal*, vulgar
F delicate

indemnify *v* **1** *we'll indemnify them against any losses*: endorse, guarantee, insure, protect, secure, underwrite **2** *indemnified for the loss of his vessel*: compensate, pay, reimburse, remunerate, repair, repay, requite, satisfy

indemnity *n* **1** *full indemnity cover*: assurance, guarantee, insurance, protection, safeguard, security **2** *they paid indemnity for all cases*: compensation, immunity, redress, reimbursement, remuneration, reparation, repayment, requital, restitution **3** *indemnity from prosecution*: amnesty, exemption, immunity, impunity, privilege

indent *v* **1** *a slogan indented into the metal*: cut, dent, dint, mark, nick, notch, pink, scallop, serrate **2** *I had to indent for a new tunic*: ask for, demand, order, request, requisition *formal*

indentation *n* cut, dent, depression, dimple, dip, furrow, groove, hollow, nick, notch, pit, serration

indenture *n* agreement, bond, certificate, commitment, contract, covenant, deal, deed, settlement

independence *n* autarky *technical*, autonomy, freedom, home rule, individualism, liberty, self-determination, self-government, self-rule, separation, sovereignty
F dependence

independent *adj* **1** *an independent country*: absolute, autarchic *formal*, autarkic *technical*, autonomous, impartial, neutral, non-aligned, self-determining, self-governing, self-legislating, self-ruling, sovereign **2** *an independent young woman*: doing something off your own bat *colloq*, doing your own thing *colloq*, free, freelance, free-thinking, going your own way *colloq*, individualist, individualistic, liberated, paddling your own canoe *colloq*, self-reliant, self-sufficient, self-supporting, standing on your own two feet *colloq*, unaided, unconstrained, unconventional, unrestrained, with a mind of your own *colloq* **3** *two independent studies*: distinct, free-standing, individual, self-contained, separate, unattached, unconnected, unrelated
F 1 dependent

independently *adv* alone, autonomously, by yourself, individually, on your own, on your tod *colloq*, separately, solo, unaided, under your own steam *colloq*
F together

indescribable *adj* amazing, exceptional, extraordinary, incredible, indefinable, ineffable *formal*, inexpressible, unspeakable, unutterable
F describable

indestructible *adj* abiding, durable, endless, enduring, eternal, everlasting, immortal, imperishable, inextinguishable, infrangible *formal*, lasting, permanent, strong, tough, unbreakable, undecaying
F breakable, mortal

indeterminate *adj* ambiguous, ambivalent, equivocal, hazy, ill-defined, imprecise, indefinite, inexact, open-ended, uncertain, unclear, undecided, undefined, undetermined, unfixed, unknown, unpredictable, unspecified, unstated, vague
F fixed, known, specified

index *n* **1** *an index of names*: catalogue, directory, guide, key, list, table **2** *exam results as an index of effectiveness*: clue, hand, hint, indication, indicator, mark, needle, pointer, sign, symptom, token

indicate *v* **1** *shrugging indicates a lack of care*: be symptomatic of, denote *formal*, display, evince *formal*, express, imply, make known, manifest *formal*, mark, mean, represent, reveal, show, signify, suggest, tell **2** *indicate the way*: designate, point out, point to, show, specify **3** *the gauge indicates temperature*: read, record, register, show

indicated *adj* advisable, called-for, desirable, necessary, needed, recommended, required, suggested

indication *n* augury *formal*, clue, evidence, explanation, hint, intimation, manifestation *formal*, mark, note, omen, portent *formal*, record, register, sign, signal, suggestion, symptom, warning

indicative *adj* characteristic, demonstrative, denotative *formal*, exhibitive *formal*, indicant *formal*, indicatory *formal*, significant, suggestive, symbolic, symptomatic, typical

indicator *n* **1** *he read the figures on the indicator*: dial, display, gauge, marker, meter, pointer, signal, signpost **2** *a useful indicator of wealth*: gauge, guide, index, marker, sign

indict *v* accuse, arraign *technical*, charge, impeach, incriminate, inculpate *formal*, prosecute, put on trial, summon, summons
ⓕ absolve, exonerate *formal*

indictment *n* accusation, allegation, arraignment *technical*, charge, impeachment, incrimination, inculpation *formal*, prosecution, recrimination, summons
ⓕ exoneration

indifference *n* apathy, coldness, coolness, disinterestedness, disregard, heedlessness, impassivity, inattention, lack of concern, lack of feeling, lack of interest, negligence, neutrality, nonchalance, unconcern
ⓕ concern, interest

indifferent *adj* 1 *indifferent to her plight:* all the same to you *colloq*, aloof, apathetic, blasé, callous, careless, cold, cool, detached, disinterested, dispassionate, distant, easy *colloq*, heedless, impassive, neutral, nonchalant, uncaring, unconcerned, unemotional, unenthusiastic, unexcited, unfeeling, uninterested, uninvolved, unmoved, unresponsive, unsympathetic 2 *an indifferent display by United:* adequate, average, bad, could be better/worse *colloq*, fair, mediocre, medium, middling, moderate, not good, OK *colloq*, ordinary, passable, run of the mill *colloq*, so-so *colloq*, undistinguished
ⓕ 1 caring, interested 2 excellent

indigence *n* deprivation, destitution, distress, necessity, need, penury *formal*, poverty, privation *formal*, want
ⓕ affluence

indigenous *adj* aboriginal, autochthonous *formal*, home-grown, local, native, original
ⓕ foreign

indigent *adj* broke *colloq*, bust *colloq*, cleaned out *colloq*, destitute, down and out *colloq*, impecunious *formal*, impoverished, in dire straits, in need, in want, necessitous *formal*, needy, not having two pennies to rub together *colloq*, on your beam ends *colloq*, on your uppers *colloq*, penniless, penurious *formal*, poor, poverty-stricken, skint *colloq*, stony-broke *colloq*
ⓕ affluent

indigestion *n* acidity, cardialgia, dyspepsia, dyspepsy, heartburn, pyrosis, water-brash

indignant *adj* angry, annoyed, disgruntled, enraged, exasperated, fuming, furious, got the hump *colloq*, heated, in a huff *colloq*, incensed, infuriated, irate, livid, mad *colloq*, miffed *colloq*, narked *colloq*, outraged, peeved *colloq*, riled, up in arms *colloq*, wrathful
ⓕ delighted, pleased

indignation *n* anger, annoyance, contempt, exasperation, fury, ire, outrage, pique, rage, scorn, wrath
ⓕ delight, pleasure

indignity *n* abuse, affront, cold shoulder *colloq*, contempt, contumely *formal*, disgrace, dishonour, disrespect, humiliation, incivility, injury, insult, kick in the teeth *colloq*, mistreatment, obloquy *formal*, offence, opprobrium *formal*, outrage, putdown *colloq*, reproach, slap in the face *colloq*, slight, snub
ⓕ honour

indirect *adj* 1 *an indirect route:* circuitous, circumlocutory *formal*, curving, devious, discursive, divergent, meandering, oblique, periphrastic *formal*, rambling, roundabout, tortuous, wandering, winding, zigzag 2 *an indirect effect:* ancillary, incidental, secondary, subordinate, subsidiary, unintended
ⓕ 1 direct 2 primary

indirectly *adv* 1 *we are indirectly responsible for this mess:* by implication, circumlocutorily *formal*, in a roundabout way 2 *she referred indirectly to the problem:* circuitously *formal*, evasively, hintingly, in a roundabout way, obliquely, periphrastically *formal* 3 *I'd heard about it only indirectly:* on the grapevine *informal*, second-hand
ⓕ 1 directly 2 directly

indiscernible *adj* hidden, impalpable, imperceptible, indistinct, indistinguishable, invisible, microscopic, minuscule, minute, obscure, tiny, unapparent, unclear, undetectable, undiscernible
ⓕ apparent, clear

indiscreet *adj* careless, foolhardy, foolish, hasty, heedless, ill-advised, ill-considered, ill-judged, immodest, impolitic *formal*, imprudent *formal*, indelicate, injudicious *formal*, insensitive, rash, reckless, shameless, tactless, undiplomatic, unthinking, unwary, unwise
ⓕ cautious, discreet

indiscretion *n* 1 *she paid for her indiscretion with her life:* carelessness, folly, foolishness, immodesty, imprudence *formal*, indelicacy, rashness, recklessness, shamelessness, tactlessness 2 *my youthful indiscretions:* blunder, boob *colloq*, error, faux pas, gaffe, lapse, mistake, slip, slip-up *colloq*
ⓕ 1 caution, diplomacy, etiquette

indiscriminate *adj* aimless, careless, chaotic, confused, diverse, general, haphazard, hit and miss, hit or miss, miscellaneous, mixed, motley, random, sweeping, undifferentiating, undiscriminating, unmethodical, unselective, unsystematic, varied, wholesale
ⓕ precise, selective, specific

indiscriminately *adv* aimlessly, carelessly, generally, haphazardly, in the mass, randomly, unmethodically, unselectively, unsystematically, wholesale, without fear or favour
ⓕ deliberately, selectively

indispensable *adj* absolutely, basic, crucial, essential, fundamental, imperative, important, key, necessary, needed, needful, required, requisite, vital
ⓕ dispensable, unnecessary

indisposed *adj* 1 *the lady is indisposed:* ailing, confined to bed, groggy *colloq*, ill, incapacitated *formal*, laid up, like death warmed up *colloq*, out of sorts *colloq*, poorly, sick, under the weather *colloq*, unwell 2 *indisposed to discuss the matter:* averse, disinclined, loath, not of a mind (to), not willing, reluctant, unwilling
ⓕ 1 well 2 inclined

indisposition *n* 1 *her indisposition was inconvenient:* ailment, bad health, complaint, disease, disorder, ill health, illness, malady *formal*, sickness 2 *an indisposition to talk:* aversion, disinclination, dislike, distaste, hesitancy, reluctance, unwillingness
ⓕ 1 health 2 inclination

indisputable *adj* absolute, beyond question, certain, definite, incontestable, incontrovertible, indubitable *formal*, irrefutable *formal*, positive, sure, undeniable, undisputed, unquestionable
ᛟ doubtful, uncertain

indissoluble *adj* abiding, binding, enduring, eternal, fixed, imperishable, incorruptible, indestructible, inseparable, inviolable, lasting, permanent, sempiternal *formal*, solid, unbreakable
ᛟ impermanent, short-lived

indistinct *adj* 1 *indistinct shapes:* ambiguous, blurred, confused, dim, faded, faint, fuzzy, hazy, ill-defined, indefinite, indistinguishable, low, misty, obscure, out of focus, pale, shadowy, unclear, undefined, vague, woolly 2 *an indistinct murmur:* confused, dim, faint, indecipherable, indistinguishable, muffled, muted, muttered, unintelligible
ᛟ 1 clear, distinct, in focus 2 clear

indistinguishable *adj* alike, cloned, hard to make out the difference, identical, interchangeable, like as two peas in a pod *colloq*, same, tantamount, twin
ᛟ different, dissimilar, distinguishable, unalike

individual *n* being, body, character, creature, fellow, human being, mortal, party, person, sort, soul, type
♦ *adj* 1 *individual portions:* isolated, lone, separate, single, sole, solitary 2 *an individual singing style:* characteristic, distinct, distinctive, distinguishing, idiosyncratic, particular, peculiar, personal, personalized, respective, signature, special, specific 3 *a very individual personality:* distinct, idiosyncratic, original, singular *formal*, special, unique
ᛟ 1 collective 2 common 3 conventional, ordinary

individualism *n* anarchism, eccentricity, egocentricity, egoism, freethinking, free-thought, independence, libertarianism, originality, self-direction, self-interest, self-reliance
ᛟ conventionality

individualist *n* anarchist, bohemian, eccentric, egocentric, egoist, free spirit, freethinker, independent, libertarian, lone wolf, loner, maverick, nonconformist, original
ᛟ conventionalist

individualistic *adj* anarchistic, bohemian, eccentric, egocentric, egoistic, idiosyncratic, independent, individual, libertarian, non-conformist, original, particular, self-reliant, special, typical, unconventional, unique, unorthodox
ᛟ conventional

individuality *n* character, distinction, distinctiveness, originality, peculiarity, personality, separateness, singularity *formal*, uniqueness
ᛟ sameness

individually *adv* independently, one by one, separately, severally *formal*, singly
ᛟ together

indivisible *adj* impartible, indiscerptible *formal*, indissoluble, inseparable, undividable
ᛟ divisible

indoctrinate *v* brainwash, drill, ground, impress, inculcate, instil, instruct, propagandize, school, teach, train

indoctrination *n* brainwashing, catechesis *formal*, catechetics *formal*, drilling, grounding, inculcation, instilling, instruction, schooling, teaching, training

indolence *n* apathy, do-nothingism, heaviness, idleness, inactivity, inertia, inertness, languidness *formal*, languor *formal*, laziness, lethargy, listlessness, shirking *colloq*, slacking, sloth, sluggishness, torpidity *formal*, torpidness *formal*, torpitude *formal*, torpor *formal*
ᛟ activeness, enthusiasm, industriousness

indolent *adj* apathetic, do-nothing, fainéant *formal*, idle, inactive, inert, lackadaisical, languid *formal*, lazy, lethargic, listless, lumpish, shiftless, slack, slothful, slow, sluggard, sluggish, torpid *formal*
ᛟ active, enthusiastic, industrious

indomitable *adj* bold, brave, courageous, determined, fearless, firm, impregnable, intransigent, intrepid, invincible, lion-hearted, resolute, stalwart, staunch, steadfast, unassailable, unbeatable, unconquerable, undaunted, undefeatable, unflinching, unyielding, valiant
ᛟ compliant, submissive, timid

indubitable *adj* absolute, beyond dispute, beyond doubt, certain, evident, incontestable, incontrovertible, indisputable, irrebuttable *formal*, irrefragable *formal*, irrefutable *formal*, obvious, sure, unanswerable, unarguable, undeniable, undoubtable, undoubted, unquestionable
ᛟ arguable

induce *v* 1 *a crisis induced by high wheat prices:* bring about, cause, effect *formal*, generate, give rise to, incite, instigate, lead to, occasion, originate, produce, prompt, provoke, set in motion 2 *she induced him to stay:* actuate, coax, draw, encourage, impel, influence, inspire, motivate, move, persuade, press, prevail upon, talk into, tempt, urge
ᛟ 2 deter, discourage

inducement *n* attraction, bait, carrot *colloq*, encouragement, enticement, goad, impetus, incentive, incitement, influence, lure, motive, reason, reward, spur, stimulus, sweetener *colloq*
ᛟ disincentive

induct *v* consecrate, enthrone, inaugurate, initiate, install, invest, ordain, swear in

induction *n* 1 *his induction into the Hall of Fame:* consecration, enthronement, inauguration, initiation, installation, institution, introduction, investiture, ordination 2 *a logical induction:* conclusion, deduction, generalization, inference

indulge *v* 1 *he indulges his grandchildren:* cater to, cosset, favour, give in to, give way to, go along with, gratify, humour, mollycoddle, pamper, pander to, pet, regale, satisfy, spoil, treat, yield to 2 *indulge in something:* give free rein to, give way to, give yourself up to, luxuriate in, revel in, wallow in

indulgence *n* 1 *a life of indulgence:* dissipation, dissoluteness, excess, extravagance, fulfilment, gratification, immoderation, intemperance, luxury, satisfaction 2 *crave your indulgence:*

favour, generosity, lenience, pardon, remission, tolerance
1 restraint

indulgent *adj* compassionate, cosseting, easy-going *colloq*, fond, forbearing *formal*, forgiving, generous, humane, humouring, kind, lenient, liberal, merciful, mollycoddling, pampering, patient, permissive, spoiling, sympathetic, tender, tolerant, understanding
harsh, strict

industrial *adj* business, commercial, manufacturing, trade

industrialist *n* baron, capitalist, captain of industry, financier, magnate, manufacturer, producer, tycoon

industrious *adj* active, assiduous, busy, busy as a bee *colloq*, conscientious, dedicated, determined, diligent, dogged, energetic, hard, hard-working, indefatigable, laborious, on the go *colloq*, persevering, persistent, productive, sedulous *formal*, slogging your guts out *colloq*, steady, studious, tireless, vigorous, zealous
idle, lazy

industriously *adv* assiduously, conscientiously, diligently, doggedly, hard, perseveringly, sedulously, steadily, with your nose to the grindstone *colloq*
lazily

industry *n* **1** *the steel industry:* business, commerce, enterprise, field, line, manufacturing, production, service, trade **2** *his industry paid off:* activity, application, assiduity, assiduousness, concentration, conscientiousness, determination, diligence, effort, energy, hard work, industriousness, intentness, laboriousness, labour, perseverance, persistence, productiveness, sedulity *formal*, sedulousness *formal*, steadiness, stickability *colloq*, tirelessness, toil, vigour, zeal

inebriated *adj* bevvied *colloq*, bibulous *colloq*, blind drunk *colloq*, blotto *colloq*, bombed *slang*, canned *slang*, crapulant *formal*, drunk, drunk as a lord/newt *colloq*, drunken, happy *colloq*, have had a few *colloq*, intoxicated *formal*, legless *colloq*, lit up *slang*, loaded *slang*, merry *colloq*, one over the eight *colloq*, paralytic *slang*, pickled *colloq*, pissed *slang*, plastered *colloq*, roaring drunk *colloq*, sloshed *slang*, smashed *slang*, soused *slang*, sozzled *colloq*, squiffy *colloq*, stewed *slang*, stoned *slang*, tanked up *slang*, the worse for drink *colloq*, tiddly *colloq*, tight *colloq*, tipsy *colloq*, under the influence, under the table *colloq*, wasted *slang*, well-oiled *colloq*, woozy *colloq*, wrecked *slang*
abstinent, sober, teetotal, temperate

inedible *adj* bad, indigestible, not fit to eat, off, rancid, rotten, stale, unconsumable, uneatable, unpalatable
edible, wholesome

ineducable *adj* incorrigible, indocile, unteachable
educable

ineffable *adj* beyond words, incommunicable, indescribable, inexpressible, unimpartible, unspeakable, unutterable
describable

ineffective *adj* **1** *an ineffective drug:* abortive, fruitless, futile, idle, ineffectual *formal*, profitless,

to no avail, unavailing, unproductive, unsuccessful, useless, vain, worthless **2** *an ineffective ruler:* feeble, idle, impotent, inadequate, incompetent, inept, lame, powerless, weak
2 effective

ineffectual *adj* **1** *ineffectual methods:* abortive, fruitless, futile, inefficacious *formal*, unavailing, unproductive, useless, vain, worthless **2** *an ineffectual person:* feeble, impotent, inadequate, incompetent, inept, lame, powerless, weak
2 effectual

inefficacy *n* futility, inadequacy, ineffectiveness, ineffectuality *formal*, ineffectualness *formal*, unproductiveness, uselessness
efficacy

inefficiency *n* carelessness, disorganization, incompetence, ineptitude, laxity, muddle, negligence, slackness, sloppiness, waste, wastefulness
efficiency

inefficient *adj* careless, disorganized, incompetent, ineffective, inept, inexpert, lax, money-wasting, negligent, slack, slipshod, sloppy, time-wasting, uneconomic, unorganized, unworkmanlike, wasteful
efficient

inelegant *adj* awkward, clumsy, crude, gauche, graceless, ill-bred, laboured, rough, ugly, uncouth, uncultivated, uncultured, unfinished, ungainly, ungraceful, unpolished, unrefined, unsophisticated, vulgar
elegant

ineligible *adj* disqualified, incompetent *technical*, ruled out, unacceptable, undesirable, unequipped, unfit, unfitted, unqualified, unsuitable, unworthy
eligible

inept *adj* awkward, bungling, cack-handed *colloq*, clumsy, foolish, ham-fisted *colloq*, heavy-handed, inadequate, incapable, incompetent, inexpert, lousy *colloq*, maladroit *formal*, pathetic *colloq*, unskilful, unsuccessful, useless
competent, skilful

ineptitude *n* awkwardness, bungling, clumsiness, crassness, fatuity *formal*, gaucheness, gaucherie, incapability, incapacity *formal*, incompetence, ineptness, inexpertness, stupidity, unfitness, unhandiness, unskilfulness, uselessness
aptitude, skill

inequality *n* bias, contrast, difference, discrepancy, discrimination, disparity, disproportion, dissimilarity, diversity, imbalance, irregularity, nonconformity, prejudice, roughness, unequalness, unevenness, variation
balance, equality

inequitable *adj* biased, bigoted, discriminatory, intolerant, one-sided, partial, partisan, preferential, prejudiced, unequal, unfair, wrongful
equitable

inequity *n* abuse, bias, discrimination, inequality, injustice, maltreatment, mistreatment, one-sidedness, partiality, prejudice, unfairness, unjustness, wrongfulness
equity

inert *adj* **1** *his lifeless, inert body:* cold, comatose *formal*, dead, immobile, inactive, inanimate, lifeless, motionless, passive, static, stationary, still, stock-still, unmoving, unresponsive **2** *sitting inert on the couch:* apathetic, dormant, dull, idle, inactive, indolent *formal*, lazy, lethargic, listless, slack, sleepy, sluggish, stagnant, torpid
₣ **1** moving **2** animated, lively

inertia *n* apathy, idleness, immobility, inaction, inactivity, indolence *formal*, languor *formal*, laziness, lethargy, listlessness, motionlessness, passivity, sloth, slothfulness, stagnation, stillness, torpor *formal*, unresponsiveness
₣ activity, liveliness

inescapable *adj* assured, certain, destined, fated, ineluctable *formal*, inevitable, inexorable, irrevocable, sure, unalterable, unavoidable
₣ escapable, preventable

inessential *adj* accidental, dispensable, expendable, extraneous, extrinsic, irrelevant, needless, non-essential, optional, redundant, secondary, spare, superfluous, surplus, unasked-for, uncalled-for, unessential, unimportant, unnecessary
₣ essential, necessary
♦ *n* accessory, appendage, extra, extravagance, luxury, non-essential, superfluity, trimming
₣ essential

inestimable *adj* immeasurable, immense, incalculable, incomputable, infinite, invaluable, measureless, mind-boggling *colloq*, precious, priceless, prodigious *formal*, uncountable, unfathomable, unlimited, untold, vast, worth a fortune *colloq*
₣ insignificant

inevitable *adj* assured, automatic, certain, decreed, definite, destined, fated, fixed, ineluctable *formal*, inescapable, inexorable, irrevocable, necessary, ordained, predestined *formal*, settled, sure, unalterable, unavoidable, unpreventable
₣ alterable, avoidable, uncertain

inevitably *adv* assuredly, automatically, certainly, definitely, inescapably, inexorably, irrevocably, necessarily, surely, unavoidably
₣ avoidably

inexact *adj* approximate, erroneous, fallacious *formal*, fuzzy, imprecise, inaccurate, incorrect, indefinite, indeterminate *formal*, indistinct, lax, loose, muddled, woolly
₣ accurate, exact

inexactitude *n* approximation, impreciseness, imprecision, inaccuracy, incorrectness, indefiniteness, inexactness, looseness, miscalculation, woolliness
₣ accuracy, exactitude

inexcusable *adj* blameworthy, indefensible, intolerable, outrageous, reprehensible *formal*, shameful, unacceptable, unforgivable, unjustifiable, unpardonable
₣ excusable, justifiable

inexhaustible *adj* **1** *an inexhaustible supply:* abundant, boundless, endless, illimitable *formal*, infinite, limitless, measureless, never-ending, unbounded, unlimited, unrestricted **2** *an inexhaustible worker:* indefatigable, tireless,

unfailing, unflagging, untiring, unwearied, unwearying, weariless
₣ **1** limited

inexorable *adj* certain, definite, destined, fated, immovable, incessant, ineluctable *formal*, inescapable, inevitable, irresistible, irrevocable, ordained, relentless, remorseless, sure, unalterable, unavertable, unceasing, unfaltering, unpreventable, unrelenting, unstoppable, unyielding
₣ avoidable, preventable

inexorably *adv* certainly, definitely, implacably, ineluctably *formal*, inescapably, inevitably, irresistibly, irrevocably, mercilessly, pitilessly, relentlessly, remorselessly, resistlessly, surely

inexpedient *adj* detrimental, disadvantageous, foolish, ill-advised, ill-chosen, ill-judged, impolitic *formal*, impractical, imprudent *formal*, inadvisable, inappropriate, inconvenient, indiscreet, injudicious *formal*, misguided, senseless, unadvisable, undesirable, undiplomatic, unfavourable, unsuitable, unwise, wrong
₣ expedient

inexpensive *adj* bargain, budget, cheap, cut-rate, discounted, economical, low-cost, low-price, low-priced, modest, reasonable, reduced
₣ dear, expensive

inexperience *n* freshness, ignorance, immaturity, inexpertness, innocence, naïveness, newness, rawness, strangeness, unfamiliarity
₣ experience

inexperienced *adj* amateur, apprentice, callow, fresh, green *colloq*, ignorant, immature, inexpert, innocent, naïve, new, new to the job, out of your depth *colloq*, probationary, raw, unaccustomed, unacquainted, unfamiliar, uninformed, unqualified, unseasoned, unskilled, unsophisticated, untrained, untutored, wet behind the ears *colloq*, wide-eyed *colloq*, young
₣ experienced, mature

inexpert *adj* amateur, amateurish, awkward, blundering, bungling, cack-handed *colloq*, clumsy, ham *colloq*, ham-fisted *colloq*, incompetent, inept, maladroit *formal*, unhandy, unpractised, unprofessional, unqualified, unskilful, unskilled, untaught, untrained, untutored, unworkmanlike
₣ expert

inexplicable *adj* abstruse *formal*, baffling, bewildering, enigmatic, incomprehensible, incredible, insoluble, miraculous, mysterious, mystifying, perplexing, puzzling, strange, unaccountable, unbelievable, unexplainable, unfathomable, unintelligible, weird
₣ explicable

inexplicably *adv* bafflingly, incomprehensibly, incredibly, miraculously, mysteriously, mystifyingly, puzzlingly, strangely, unaccountably, unexplainably
₣ explicably

inexpressible *adj* incommunicable, indefinable, indescribable, ineffable *formal*, nameless, undescribable, unsayable, unspeakable, untellable, unutterable

inexpressive *adj* blank, cold, dead, deadpan, emotionless, empty, expressionless, impassive,

inscrutable, lifeless, poker-faced, unexpressive, vacant
🔄 expressive

inextinguishable *adj* deathless, enduring, eternal, everlasting, immortal, imperishable, indestructible, irrepressible, lasting, unconquerable, undying, unquellable, unquenchable, unsuppressible
🔄 impermanent, perishable

inextricable *adj* indissoluble, indistinguishable, indivisible, inseparable, intricate, irretrievable, irreversible

inextricably *adv* indissolubly, indistinguishably, indivisibly, inseparably, intricately, irresolubly, irretrievably, irreversibly

infallibility *n* **1** *belief in the Pope's infallibility:* faultlessness, impeccability, inerrancy, irrefutability *formal*, irreproachability, omniscience *formal*, perfection, supremacy, unerringness **2** *the clock's infallibility:* accuracy, dependability, reliability, safety, sureness, trustworthiness
🔄 **1** fallibility **2** fallibility

infallible *adj* accurate, certain, dependable, fail-safe, faultless, flawless, foolproof, impeccable, perfect, reliable, sound, sure, sure-fire *colloq*, trustworthy, unerring, unfailing
🔄 fallible

infamous *adj* abominable, bad, base, detestable, discreditable, disgraceful, dishonourable, disreputable, egregious *formal*, evil, hateful, ignominious *formal*, ill-famed, iniquitous *formal*, nefarious *formal*, notorious, outrageous, scandalous, shameful, shocking, vile, wicked
🔄 glorious, illustrious

infamy *n* baseness, depravity, discredit, disgrace, dishonour, disrepute, evil, ignominy *formal*, notoriety, shame, turpitude *formal*, vileness, villainy, wickedness
🔄 glory

infancy *n* **1** *a happy infancy:* babyhood, childhood, youth **2** *a science in its infancy:* beginning, birth, commencement *formal*, cradle, dawn, early stages, emergence, genesis, inception *formal*, origin(s), outset, rise, start
🔄 **1** adulthood

infant *n* babe *formal*, babe in arms *formal*, baby, bairn *Scot*, child, little one, toddler, tot *colloq*
🔄 adult
♦ *adj* dawning, developing, early, emergent, growing, immature, initial, juvenile, nascent *formal*, new, newborn, young, youthful
🔄 adult, mature

infantile *adj* adolescent, babyish, childish, immature, juvenile, puerile, young, youthful
🔄 adult, mature

infatuated *adj* besotted, bewitched, captivated, carried away, crazy *colloq*, daft *colloq*, enamoured, enraptured, entêté(e) *formal*, far gone *colloq*, fascinated, having a thing *colloq*, head over heels in love *colloq*, in love, mad *colloq*, mesmerized, nuts *colloq*, obsessed, ravished, smitten *colloq*, sold *colloq*, spellbound, sweet *colloq*, wild *colloq*
🔄 disenchanted, indifferent

infatuation *n* craze, crush *colloq*, fascination, fixation, fondness, love, mania, obsession, pash *colloq*, passion, shine *colloq*, thing *colloq*

🔄 disenchantment, indifference

infect *v* **1** *the diseased animal infected many others:* contaminate, pass on, spread to, transmit to **2** *a chemical infected the water:* blight, contaminate, corrupt, defile, mar, pervert, poison, pollute, spoil, taint **3** *we were infected by her fear:* affect, animate, excite, influence, inspire, move, touch

infection *n* bacteria, blight, bug *colloq*, complaint, condition, contagion, contamination, corruption, defilement, disease, epidemic, fouling, germ, illness, influence, pestilence, poison, pollution, sepsis *technical*, spoiling, taint, tainting, virus

infectious *adj* **1** *an infectious disease:* catching, communicable, contagious, contaminating, corrupting, deadly, defiling, epidemic, infective, noxious *formal*, polluting, septic *technical*, spreading, toxic, transmissible, transmittable, virulent **2** *infectious laughter:* catching, compelling, contagious, irresistible, spreading

infelicitous *adj* **1** *an infelicitous choice of words:* disadvantageous, inappropriate, incongruous *formal*, inopportune, unfitting, unfortunate, unsuitable, untimely **2** *an infelicitous event:* despairing, miserable, sad, sorrowful, unfortunate, unhappy, unlucky, wretched
🔄 **1** appropriate, apt **2** happy

infer *v* allude, assume, come to a conclusion, conclude, conjecture *formal*, deduce, derive, extrapolate, figure out *colloq*, gather, presume, reason, surmise, understand

infer or *imply*? See panel at **imply**

inference *n* assumption, conclusion, conjecture *formal*, consequence, construction, corollary *formal*, deduction, extrapolation *formal*, interpretation, presumption, reading, reasoning, surmise *formal*

inferior *adj* **1** *inferior status:* ancillary, humble, junior, lesser, low, lower, lowly, menial, minor, not in the same league *colloq*, secondary, second-class, subordinate, subservient, subsidiary **2** *inferior work:* awful, bad, cheap, crummy *colloq*, defective, imperfect, incompetent, low-quality, mediocre, naff *slang*, poor, ropy *colloq*, second-rate, shoddy, slipshod, substandard, unsatisfactory
🔄 **1** superior **2** excellent
♦ *n* junior, menial, minion, subordinate, underling, vassal
🔄 superior

inferiority *n* **1** *in a position of inferiority:* humbleness, insignificance, lowliness, meanness, subordination, subservience **2** *the inferiority of their products:* defectiveness, faultiness, imperfection, inadequacy, incompetence, low/poor/bad quality, mediocrity, shoddiness, unsatisfactoriness
🔄 **1** superiority **2** excellence, perfection

infernal *adj* **1** *Satan's infernal abode:* accursed, damned, demonic, devilish, diabolical, fiendish, Hadean, hellish, satanic **2** *infernal vandals:* atrocious, evil, execrable *formal*, malevolent *formal*, vile, wicked **3** *what an infernal mess!:* blasted *colloq*, blooming *colloq*, confounded, cursed, damned, darned *colloq*, dashed *colloq*, fiendish, flipping *colloq*, wretched
🔄 **1** heavenly

infertile *adj* **1** *infertile land*: arid, barren, dried-up, infecund *formal*, non-productive, parched, sterile, unfructuous *formal*, unfruitful, unproductive **2** *my wife is infertile*: arid, barren, childless, sterile
▣ **1** fertile, fruitful, productive **2** fertile

infertility *n* aridity, aridness, barrenness, effeteness *formal*, infecundity *formal*, sterility, unfruitfulness, unproductiveness
▣ fertility

infest *v* beset, bristle, crawl, flood, infiltrate, invade, overrun, overspread, penetrate, permeate, pervade, plague, ravage, spread through, swarm, take over, teem, throng

infested *adj* alive, beset, bristling, crawling, infiltrated, overrun, overspread, permeated, pervaded, plagued, ravaged, ridden, swarming, teeming, vermined

infidel *n* atheist, disbeliever, freethinker, heathen, heretic, irreligionist, nullifidian *formal*, pagan, sceptic, unbeliever
▣ believer

infidelity *n* **1** *marital infidelity*: adultery, affair, cheating, intrigue, unfaithfulness **2** *infidelity to Islam*: betrayal, disloyalty, duplicity *formal*, faithlessness, perfidy *formal*, treachery
▣ **1** fidelity **2** faithfulness

infiltrate *v* creep into, enter, filter, insinuate, intrude, invade, penetrate, percolate, permeate, pervade, seep, slip, soak

infiltration *n* entr(y)ism, insinuation, interpenetration *formal*, intrusion, invasion, penetration, percolation, permeation, pervasion

infiltrator *n* entr(y)ist, insinuator, intruder, penetrator, seditionary, spy, subversive, subverter

infinite *adj* **1** *an infinite number of stars*: bottomless, boundless, countless, endless, extensive, fathomless, huge, immeasurable, immense, incalculable, indeterminable *formal*, inestimable, inexhaustible, innumerable, interminable, limitless, never-ending, numberless, unbounded, uncountable, unfathomable, unlimited, untold, vast, without number **2** *he measured it with infinite care*: absolute, enormous, supreme, total
▣ **1** finite, limited

infinitesimal *adj* imperceptible, inappreciable, inconsiderable, insignificant, microscopic, minuscule, minute, negligible, teeny *colloq*, tiny, trifling, wee *Scot*
▣ enormous, great, large

infinity *n* boundlessness, countlessness, endlessness, enormousness, eternity, extensiveness, immeasurableness, immensity, inexhaustibility, limitlessness, perpetuity, vastness
▣ finiteness, limitation

infirm *adj* ailing, debilitated *formal*, decrepit, disabled, doddery, failing, faltering, feeble, frail, ill, lame, old, poorly, shaky, sickly, unsteady, unwell, weak, wobbly
▣ healthy, strong

infirmity *n* **1** *age and infirmity*: decrepitude, dodderiness, feebleness, frailty, ill health, illness, instability, malady *formal*, sickliness, sickness, vulnerability, weakness **2** *the infirmities of old age*: ailment, complaint, debility *formal*, disease, disorder, failing, malady *formal*, sickness, weakness
▣ **1** health, strength

inflame *v* **1** *her presence inflamed the crowd*: agitate, anger, arouse, enrage, exasperate, fire, foment, fuel, heat, ignite, impassion, incense, infuriate, kindle, madden, provoke, rile, rouse, stimulate, stir, stir (up), whip up, work up **2** *he has only further inflamed the situation*: aggravate, exacerbate *formal*, excite, fan, increase, intensify, make worse, worsen
▣ **1** cool, quench

inflamed *adj* angry, festered, fevered, feverish, flushed, glowing, heated, hot, infected, poisoned, red, reddened, septic, sore, swollen

inflammable *adj* burnable, combustible, flammable, ignitable
▣ fire-resistant, flameproof, flame-resistant, incombustible, non-flammable

inflammation *n* abscess, empyema *technical*, eruption, erythema, festering, heat, hotness, infection, irritation, painfulness, rash, redness, sepsis, septicity, sore, soreness, swelling, tenderness

inflammatory *adj* **1** *inflammatory remarks*: anarchic, demagogic, explosive, fiery, incendiary, incitative, inciting, inflaming, instigative, insurgent, intemperate, provocative, rabble-rousing, rabid, riotous, seditious **2** *inflammatory disorders*: allergic, festering, septic
▣ **1** calming, pacific

inflate *v* **1** *inflate a life-jacket*: aerate, bloat, blow up, dilate, distend *formal*, enlarge, expand, puff out, pump up, swell **2** *prices were inflated*: amplify, augment *formal*, boost, escalate, extend, hike up *colloq*, increase, intensify, push up *colloq*, raise, step up **3** *inflate the importance of something*: aggrandize *formal*, boost, exaggerate, magnify, overestimate, overrate, overstate
▣ **1** deflate **2** decrease, lower **3** play down, understate

inflated *adj* **1** *inflated tyres*: ballooned, bloated, blown up, dilated, distended *formal*, puffed out, swollen, tumefied *formal*, tumid *formal* **2** *inflated prices*: escalated, extended, increased, intensified, raised **3** *an inflated opinion of themselves*: bombastic, euphuistic *formal*, exaggerated, grandiloquent *formal*, magniloquent *formal*, ostentatious, overblown, pompous
▣ **1** deflated

inflation *n* escalation, expansion, hyperinflation, increase, rise
▣ deflation

inflection *n* change of tone/intonation, emphasis, modulation, pitch, rhythm, stress

inflexibility *n* **1** *annoyed by her boss's inflexibility*: intractability *formal*, intransigence *formal*, obduracy *formal*, obstinacy, stubbornness **2** *the material's inflexibility*: fixity, hardness, immovability, immutability, immutableness, inelasticity, rigidity, stiffness, stringency, unsuppleness
▣ **1** flexibility **2** flexibility

inflexible *adj* **1** *an inflexible mass*: fast, firm, fixed, hard, immovable, immutable, rigid, set, solid, steely, stiff, taut, unbendable, unchangeable, unelastic, uniform, unsupple, unvarying

2 *inflexible rules/people:* adamant, dyed-in-the-wool, entrenched, implacable, intolerant, intractable *formal*, intransigent *formal*, merciless, obdurate, obstinate, pitiless, relentless, resolute, rigorous, strict, stringent, stubborn, unaccommodating, unbending, uncompromising, unyielding
Fʒ 1 flexible, yielding **2** adaptable, flexible

inflict *v* administer, apply, burden, deal (out), deliver, enforce, exact, impose, lay, levy, mete out, perpetrate, wreak

---

inflict or *afflict*? See panel at **afflict**

---

infliction *n* administration, affliction, application, burden, castigation *formal*, chastisement *formal*, delivery, enforcement, exaction, imposition, penalty, perpetration, punishment, retribution *formal*, trouble, worry, wreaking

influence *n* authority, bias, clout *colloq*, control, direction, dominance, domination, effect, guidance, hold, impact, importance, mastery, power, prejudice, pressure, prestige, pull *colloq*, rule, standing, supremacy, sway, toll, weight
♦ *v* **1** *deprivation can influence life chances:* affect, change, colour, condition, control, determine, direct, guide, have an effect on, impact on, modify, mould, shape, transform **2** *she influenced him to change his mind:* arouse, dispose, impel, impress, incite, incline, induce, instigate, motivate, move, persuade, prejudice, prompt, rouse, stir, sway

influential *adj* authoritative, charismatic, compelling, controlling, convincing, dominant, effective, far-reaching, guiding, important, inspiring, instrumental, leading, meaningful, momentous, moving, persuasive, potent, powerful, prestigious, significant, strong, telling, weighty
Fʒ ineffective, unimportant

influx *n* arrival, flood, flow, incursion *formal*, inflow, ingress *formal*, inrush, intrusion, inundation, invasion, rush, stream

inform *v* **1** *inform me of any developments:* acquaint, advise, announce, apprise *formal*, brief, clue up *colloq*, communicate, enlighten, fill in *colloq*, illuminate, impart, instruct, keep posted *colloq*, leak, notify, put in the picture *colloq*, put wise *colloq*, relate, tell, tip off, wise up *colloq* **2** *inform on your friends:* betray, blab, blow the whistle on *colloq*, denounce, grass *slang*, incriminate, rat *colloq*, sell down the river *colloq*, shop *colloq*, snitch *colloq*, split *colloq*, squeal *colloq*, tell on *colloq* **3** *the ideals which inform his writing:* brand, characterize, distinguish, identify, mark, permeate, stamp, typify

informal *adj* casual, easy, easygoing, everyday, familiar, free, natural, relaxed, simple, unceremonious, unofficial, unpretentious
Fʒ formal, official, serious, solemn

informality *n* approachability, casualness, congeniality, cosiness, ease, familiarity, freedom, homeliness, naturalness, relaxation, simplicity, unceremoniousness, unpretentiousness
Fʒ ceremony, formality

informally *adj* **1** *we discussed the matter informally:* casually, easily, familiarly, freely, simply **2** *advised the PM informally:* on the quiet, privately, unofficially
Fʒ 1 formally **2** officially

information *n* advice, briefing, bulletin, bumf *slang*, clues, communiqué, counsel, data, databank, database, details, dope *colloq*, dossier, enlightenment, evidence, facts, file, gen *colloq*, info *colloq*, input, instruction, intelligence, knowledge, low-down *colloq*, message, news, notice, particulars, propaganda, record, report, tidings *formal*, word

informative *adj* chatty, communicative, constructive, edifying, educational, enlightening, forthcoming, gossipy, helpful, illuminating, instructive, newsy, revealing, useful
Fʒ uninformative

informed *adj* **1** *we'll keep you informed:* abreast, acquainted, au fait, briefed, conversant, enlightened, familiar, in the know *colloq*, posted, primed, up-to-date **2** *an informed opinion:* authoritative, erudite, expert, knowledgeable, learned, versed, well-briefed, well-informed, well-read, well-researched, well-versed
Fʒ 1 ignorant, unaware

informer *n* betrayer, finger *colloq*, grass *slang*, informant, Judas, mole *colloq*, nark *slang*, rat *colloq*, sneak, snitch *colloq*, spy, squealer *colloq*, stool pigeon *slang*, supergrass *slang*, tell-tale, traitor, whistle-blower *colloq*

infraction *n* breach, breaking, contravention, encroachment, infringement, transgression *formal*, violation
Fʒ compliance, observance

infrequent *adj* exceptional, few and far between *colloq*, intermittent, like gold dust *colloq*, occasional, rare, scanty, sparse, spasmodic, sporadic, uncommon, unusual
Fʒ frequent

infringe *v* **1** *it infringed copyright:* break, contravene, defy, disobey, flout, ignore, overstep, transgress *formal*, violate **2** *this infringes on our freedoms:* encroach, impinge, intrude, invade, trespass

infringement *n* **1** *infringement of the rules:* breach, breaking, contravention, defiance, disobedience, evasion, infraction *formal*, non-compliance, non-observance, transgression *formal*, violation **2** *an infringement of sovereignty:* encroachment, intrusion, invasion, trespass

infuriate *v* anger, annoy, antagonize, bug *colloq*, enrage, exasperate, get *colloq*, get on someone's nerves *colloq*, get under someone's skin *colloq*, incense, inflame, irritate, madden, make someone's blood boil *colloq*, provoke, rile, rouse, rub up the wrong way *colloq*, vex
Fʒ calm, pacify

infuriated *adj* agitated, angry, beside yourself, enraged, exasperated, flaming *colloq*, furious, heated, incensed, irate, irritated, maddened *colloq*, miffed *colloq*, narked *colloq*, peeved *colloq*, provoked, roused, vexed, violent, wild
Fʒ calm, gratified, pleased

infuriating *adj* aggravating *colloq*, annoying, exasperating, frustrating, galling, intolerable, irritating, maddening, pesky *colloq*, provoking, thwarting, unbearable, vexatious *formal*
Fʒ agreeable, pleasing

infuse *v* **1** *the party was infused with good humour:* charge, fill, imbue, inspire, inundate, suffuse **2** *to infuse new blood into the team:* breathe into, impart to, implant, inculcate, inject, instil, introduce **3** *teas made by infusing herbs:* brew, immerse, saturate, soak, steep

infusion *n* infusing, instillation, soaking, steeping

ingenious *adj* adept, adroit, astute, bright, brilliant, clever, crafty, creative, cunning, gifted, imaginative, innovative, inventive, masterly, original, resourceful, sharp, shrewd, skilful, sly, smart, talented, wily
☒ unimaginative

> *ingenious* or *ingenuous*? *Ingenious* means 'clever' or 'cleverly made or thought out': *an ingenious plan.* *Ingenuous* means 'naïvely trusting': *It was rather ingenuous of you to believe a compulsive liar like him.*

ingenuity *n* adroitness, astuteness, cleverness, creativeness, cunning, deftness, faculty, flair, genius, gift, ingeniousness, innovativeness, invention, inventiveness, knack, originality, resourcefulness, sharpness, shrewdness, skilfulness, skill, slyness
☒ clumsiness, dullness

ingenuous *adj* artless, candid, direct, forthright, frank, genuine, guileless, honest, innocent, naïve, open, plain, simple, sincere, trustful, trusting, undissembling *formal*, unsophisticated
☒ artful, cunning, deceitful, sly

ingenuousness *n* artlessness, candour, directness, forthrightness, frankness, genuineness, guilelessness, honesty, innocence, naïvety, openness, trustfulness, unreserve, unsophisticatedness
☒ artfulness, cunning, deceit, slyness, subterfuge

inglorious *adj* blameworthy, discreditable, disgraceful, dishonourable, disreputable, humiliating, ignoble, ignominious *formal*, infamous, mortifying, obscure, shameful, unheroic, unhonoured, unknown, unsuccessful, unsung
☒ glorious

ingrain *v* build in, dye, embed, engrain, entrench, fix, imbue, implant, impress, imprint, infix, instil, root

ingrained *adj* built-in, deep-rooted, deep-seated, embedded, entrenched, fixed, immovable, implanted, inborn, inbred, inbuilt, ineradicable, inherent, permanent, rooted

ingratiate *v* bow and scrape *colloq*, crawl, creep, curry favour, fawn, flatter, get in with, get into someone's good books *colloq*, get on the right side of *colloq*, grovel, lick someone's boots *colloq*, play up to, suck up to *colloq*, toady

ingratiating *adj* bootlicking *colloq*, crawling, fawning, flattering, obsequious, servile, smooth-tongued, suave, sycophantic *formal*, time-serving, toadying, unctuous

ingratitude *n* thanklessness, unappreciativeness, ungraciousness, ungratefulness, unthankfulness
☒ appreciation, gratitude, thankfulness

ingredient *n* component, constituent, element, factor, feature, item, part, unit

inhabit *v* colonize, dwell in *formal*, live in, make your home in, occupy, people, populate, possess, reside in *formal*, settle, stay in

inhabitant *n* citizen, dweller *formal*, habitant *formal*, inmate, lodger, native, occupant, occupier, resident, settler, tenant

inhabited *adj* colonized, developed, held, lived-in, occupied, peopled, populated, possessed, settled, tenanted
☒ uninhabited

inhalation *n* breath, breathing, inhaling, inspiration, respiration *technical*, spiration, suction

inhale *v* breathe in, draw, draw in, inbreathe *formal*, inspire, respire *technical*, suck in, whiff

inharmonious *adj* **1** *an inharmonious racket:* atonal, cacophonous, clashing, discordant, grating, harsh, jangling, jarring, raucous, strident, tuneless, unharmonious, unmelodious, unmusical, untuneful **2** *inharmonious personal relationships:* antipathetic *formal*, clashing, conflicting, contradictory, incompatible, inconsonant *formal*, irreconcilable, perverse, quarrelsome, stroppy *colloq*, unfriendly, unsympathetic
☒ **2** harmonious

inherent *adj* basic, built-in, essential, fundamental, hereditary, in the blood, inborn, inbred, inbuilt, ingrained, inherited, innate, intrinsic, native, natural

inherit *v* accede to *formal*, assume, be bequeathed, be left, come into, receive, succeed to, take over

inheritance *n* accession *formal*, bequest, birthright, descent, endowment, heredity, heritage, legacy, succession

inheritor *n* beneficiary, devisee *technical*, heir, heiress, heritor *formal*, heritress *formal*, heritrix *formal*, inheritress, inheritrix, legatary, legatee, recipient, reversionary, successor

inhibit *v* balk, bridle, check, constrain, curb, discourage, frustrate, hamper, hinder, hold back, impede, interfere with, obstruct, prevent, rein in, repress, restrain, restrict, slow down, stanch, stem, stop, suppress, thwart
☒ assist, encourage

inhibited *adj* constrained, embarrassed, frustrated, guarded, introverted, repressed, reserved, restrained, reticent, self-conscious, self-restrained, shy, subdued, uptight *colloq*, withdrawn
☒ open, relaxed, uninhibited

inhibition *n* **1** *lose all our inhibitions:* hang-up *colloq*, repression, reserve, reticence, self-consciousness, shyness **2** *an inhibition to investing in Albania:* bar, check, curb, frustration, hampering, hindrance, impediment, interference, obstruction, restraint, restriction, thwarting
☒ **1** openness **2** freedom

inhospitable *adj* **1** *an inhospitable place:* bare, barren, bleak, desolate, empty, forbidding, hostile, inimical *formal*, lonely, uncongenial, unfavourable, uninhabitable **2** *an inhospitable person:* aloof, antisocial, cold, cool, uncivil,

unfriendly, ungenerous, unkind, unneighbourly, unreceptive, unsociable, unwelcoming, xenophobic
F3 1 favourable, hospitable

inhuman *adj* **1** *an inhuman act of cruelty*: animal, barbaric, barbarous, bestial, brutal, cold-blooded, cruel, diabolical, fiendish, merciless, ruthless, sadistic, savage, vicious **2** *inhuman life forms*: animal, non-human, odd, strange
F3 2 human

> *inhuman* or *inhumane*? When referring to cruel conditions, treatment, behaviour, etc, *inhuman* is stronger than *inhumane*. *Inhumane* means 'cruel, showing lack of compassion', whereas *inhuman* means 'showing such cruelty and lack of compassion to a degree almost unbelievable in a human being'.

inhumane *adj* callous, cold-hearted, cruel, hard-hearted, harsh, heartless, inconsiderate, insensitive, pitiless, uncaring, unfeeling, unkind, unsympathetic
F3 compassionate, humane, kind

inhumanity *n* atrocity, barbarism, barbarity, brutality, brutishness, callousness, cold-bloodedness, cold-heartedness, cruelty, hard-heartedness, heartlessness, pitilessness, ruthlessness, sadism, savageness, unkindness, viciousness
F3 humanity

inimical *adj* adverse, antagonistic, antipathetic, contrary, destructive, disaffected, harmful, hostile, hurtful, ill-disposed, inhospitable, injurious, intolerant, noxious *formal*, opposed, pernicious, repugnant *formal*, unfavourable, unfriendly, unwelcoming
F3 favourable, friendly, sympathetic

inimitable *adj* consummate, distinctive, exceptional, incomparable, matchless, nonpareil, peerless, sublime, superlative, supreme, unequalled, unexampled, unique, unmatched, unparalleled, unrivalled, unsurpassable, unsurpassed

iniquitous *adj* abominable, accursed, atrocious, awful, base, criminal, dreadful, evil, flagitious *formal*, heinous *formal*, immoral, infamous, nefarious *formal*, reprehensible *formal*, reprobate, sinful, unjust, unrighteous, vicious, wicked
F3 virtuous

iniquity *n* abomination, baseness, crime, enormity, evil, evil-doing, heinousness *formal*, infamy, injustice, lawlessness, misdeed, offence, sin, sinfulness, transgression *formal*, ungodliness, unrighteousness, vice, viciousness, wickedness, wrong, wrongdoing
F3 virtue

initial *adj* basic, beginning, commencing *formal*, early, elementary, first, formative, foundational, inaugural, inceptive *formal*, inchoate *formal*, incipient *formal*, introductory, opening, original, primary, prime, starting
F3 final, last
♦ *v* countersign, endorse, sign, write your initials on

initially *adv* at first, at the beginning, at the start, first, first of all, firstly, originally, to begin with, to start with
F3 finally, in the end

initiate *v* **1** *they initiated the talks*: activate, begin, cause, commence *formal*, get off the ground *colloq*, get things moving *colloq*, get under way *colloq*, inaugurate, instigate, institute, introduce, kick off *colloq*, launch, open, originate, pioneer, prompt, set in motion *colloq*, set the ball rolling *colloq*, set the wheels in motion *colloq*, set up, start, stimulate, trigger **2** *initiated into the mysteries of quantum physics*: crash, drill, inculcate, instil, instruct, teach, train, tutor **3** *initiated into the organization*: accept, admit, enrol, induct, install, introduce, invest, let in, ordain, receive, sign up, welcome
♦ *n* authority, beginner, catechumen, connoisseur, convert, entrant, expert, greenhorn *colloq*, learner, member, neophyte, newcomer, novice, novitiate, probationer, proselyte, recruit, rookie *colloq*, sage, tenderfoot, tiro

initiation *n* **1** *the initiation of proceedings*: beginning, inauguration, inception *formal*, launching, opening, origination, setting-up, start **2** *my initiation into the movement*: admission, admittance, baptism, debut, enlistment, enrolment, entrance, entry, inauguration, induction, installation, introduction, investiture, ordination, reception, rite of passage

initiative *n* **1** *many new employees lack initiative*: ambition, creativity, drive, dynamism, energy, enterprise, get-up-and-go *colloq*, go *colloq*, innovativeness, inventiveness, originality, push *colloq*, resourcefulness **2** *the Russian initiative*: action, first move, first step, lead, opening move, recommendation, suggestion

inject *v* **1** *inject drugs*: immunize, inoculate, jab *colloq*, mainline *slang*, shoot (up) *slang*, syringe, vaccinate **2** *inject a little fun into the meeting*: add, bring (in), infuse, insert, instil, introduce

injection *n* **1** *an injection to help her sleep*: dose, fix *slang*, immunization, inoculation, jab *colloq*, shot *colloq*, vaccination **2** *an injection of money*: addition, infusion, insertion, instilling, introduction

injudicious *adj* foolish, hasty, ill-advised, ill-judged, ill-timed, impolitic *formal*, imprudent *formal*, inadvisable, incautious, inconsiderate, indiscreet, inexpedient, misguided, rash, stupid, unthinking, unwise, wrong-headed
F3 cautious, judicious *formal*, prudent *formal*, wise

injunction *n* admonition *formal*, command, dictate, dictum, direction, directive, instruction, mandate, order, precept, ruling

injure *v* **1** *injured by falling masonry*: blemish, blight, break, cripple, cut, damage, deface, deform, disable, disfigure, fracture, harm, hurt, impair, lame, maim, mangle, mar, mutilate, ruin, spoil, undermine, weaken, wound **2** *injured by her remarks*: abuse, ill-treat, maltreat, offend, put out, upset, wrong

injured *adj* **1** *an injured soldier*: crippled, damaged, disabled, harmed, hurt, lame, weakened, wounded **2** *the injured party agreed to settle out of court*: abused, aggrieved, cut to the quick, defamed, disgruntled, displeased, grieved, ill-treated, insulted, maligned, maltreated, misused, offended, pained, put out, unhappy, upset, wronged

injurious *adj* adverse, bad, baneful, calumnious *formal*, corrupting, damaging, deleterious *formal*, destructive, detrimental, disadvantageous, harmful, hurtful, iniquitous *formal*, insulting, libellous, noxious *formal*, pernicious, prejudicial, ruinous, slanderous, unconducive, unhealthy, unjust, wrongful
🖃 beneficial, favourable

injury *n* **1** *a leg injury:* abrasion, affliction *formal*, bruise, contusion *technical*, cut, damage, disfigurement, fracture, gash, harm, hurt, ill, impairment, laceration, lesion, mischief, mutilation, ruin, sore, trauma, wound **2** *injury to her feelings:* abuse, grievance, ill-treatment, injustice, insult, offence, wrong

injustice *n* abuse, bias, discrimination, disparity *formal*, favouritism, ill-treatment, inequality, inequity *formal*, iniquity *formal*, injury, offence, one-sidedness, oppression, partiality, partisanship, prejudice, unfairness, unjustness, wrong
🖃 fairness, justice

inkling *n* allusion, clue, faintest *colloq*, foggiest *colloq*, glimmering, hint, idea, indication, innuendo, insinuation, intimation, notion, pointer, sign, suggestion, suspicion, whisper *colloq*

inky *adj* black, coal-black, dark-blue, jet, jet-black, pitch-black, sooty

inlaid *adj* damascened, empaestic *formal*, enamelled, enchased, inset, lined, mosaic, set, studded, tessellated *formal*, tiled

inland *adj* central, inner, interior, internal, up-country

inlay *n* damascene, emblema *formal*, enamel, inset, lining, mosaic, setting, studding, tessellation *formal*, tiling

inlet *n* bay, bight, cove, creek, entrance, fiord, firth, opening, passage, sound

inmate *n* **1** *an inmate of the hospital:* case, client, patient **2** *prison inmates:* convict, detainee, prisoner

inn *n* bar, hostelry, hotel, local *colloq*, pub *colloq*, public house, tavern

innards *n* **1** *the innards of an animal:* entera, entrails, guts, insides, interior, internal organs, intestines, organs, umbles, viscera, vitals **2** *the innards of a machine:* inner workings, mechanism, works

innate *adj* congenital, connate *formal*, hereditary, inborn, inbred, indigenous, inherent, inherited, instinctive, intrinsic, intuitive, native, natural
🖃 acquired, learnt

inner *adj* **1** *an inner chamber:* inside, interior, internal, inward **2** *inner London:* central, interior, internal, middle **3** *the Prime Minister's inner circle:* close, confidential, intimate, personal, private **4** *nature's inner secrets:* deep, esoteric *formal*, hidden, obscure, secret **5** *the composer's inner life:* emotional, intellectual, mental, psychological, spiritual
🖃 **1** outer, outward **4** exposed, revealed

innermost *adj* basic, buried, closest, confidential, dearest, deep, deepest, esoteric *formal*, essential, hidden, inmost, intimate, personal, private, secret

innkeeper *n* bar-keeper, host, hostess, hotelier, hotel-keeper, innholder, landlady, landlord, mine host, padrone, publican, restaurateur

innocence *n* **1** *she had to prove her innocence:* blamelessness, chastity, faultlessness, guiltlessness, honesty, immaculateness, impeccability, incorruptibility, inculpability *formal*, integrity, irreproachability, purity, righteousness, sinlessness, spotlessness, stainlessness, unimpeachability, virginity, virtue **2** *the innocence of youth:* artlessness, childlikeness, credulity, frankness, guilelessness, gullibility, ignorance, inexperience, ingenuousness, naïveness, naïvety, naturalness, openness, simplicity, trustfulness, unsophistication, unworldliness **3** *in all innocence:* harmlessness, innocuousness, inoffensiveness, playfulness, safety
🖃 **1** guilt **2** experience **3** harmfulness

innocent *adj* **1** *innocent of the crime:* above suspicion, blameless, chaste, clear, faultless, guiltless, honest, immaculate, impeccable, incorrupt, inculpable *formal*, irreproachable, not guilty, pure, righteous, sinless, spotless, stainless, unblameworthy, unblemished, uncontaminated, uncorrupted, unimpeachable, unsullied, untainted, upright, virginal, virtuous **2** *young and innocent:* angelic, artless, childlike, credulous, frank, fresh, green *colloq*, guileless, gullible, inexperienced, ingenuous, innocent as a newborn babe *colloq*, naïve, natural, open, simple, trustful, trusting, unsophisticated, unworldly, wet behind the ears *colloq* **3** *an innocent mistake:* harmless, innocuous, inoffensive, playful, safe, unsuspicious
🖃 **1** guilty, to blame **2** experienced, sophisticated **3** harmful, offensive
♦ *n* babe, babe in arms, beginner, child, greenhorn, infant, ingénue, neophyte, novice, tenderfoot
🖃 connoisseur, expert

innocently *adv* artlessly, blamelessly, credulously, harmlessly, ingenuously, innocuously, inoffensively, like a lamb to the slaughter *colloq*, naïvely, simply, trustfully, trustingly, unoffendingly, unsuspiciously

innocuous *adj* bland, harmless, innocent, inoffensive, mild, playful, safe, unobjectionable, unobtrusive
🖃 harmful

innovation *n* **1** *a constant process of innovation:* alteration, change, departure, introduction, modernization, newness, novelty, progress, reform, variation **2** *many new technical innovations:* new idea, new method, new product

innovative *adj* adventurous, bold, creative, daring, enterprising, fresh, go-ahead, imaginative, inventive, new, original, progressive, reforming, resourceful
🖃 conservative, unimaginative

innuendo *n* allusion, aspersion *formal*, hint, implication, insinuation, intimation, overtone, slur, suggestion, whisper

innumerable *adj* countless, incalculable, infinite, many, numberless, numerous, umpteen *colloq*, uncountable, unnumbered, untold

inoculate *v* give a jab/shot to *colloq*, immunize, inject, protect, safeguard, vaccinate

inoculation *n* immunization, injection, jab *colloq*, protection, shot *colloq*, vaccination

inoffensive *adj* bland, harmless, innocent, innocuous, mild, peaceable, quiet, retiring, safe, unassertive, unobjectionable, unobtrusive
🗷 harmful, offensive, provocative

inoperable *adj* deadly, fatal, hopeless, incurable, intractable *formal*, irremovable, terminal, unhealable, unremovable, untreatable
🗷 operable

inoperative *adj* broken, broken-down, defective, futile, idle, inadequate, ineffective, ineffectual *formal*, inefficacious *formal*, inefficient, invalid, kaput *colloq*, non-functioning, not operative, not working, nugatory *formal*, out of action, out of commission, out of order, out of service, unserviceable, unused, unworkable, useless, worthless
🗷 operative, working

inopportune *adj* clumsy, ill-chosen, ill-timed, inappropriate, inauspicious *formal*, inconvenient, infelicitous *formal*, mistimed, tactless, unfortunate, unpropitious *formal*, unseasonable, unsuitable, untimely, wrong-timed
🗷 opportune

inordinate *adj* disproportionate, excessive, exorbitant, extreme, great, immoderate, outrageous, preposterous, undue, unreasonable, unrestrained, unrestricted, unwarranted
🗷 moderate, reasonable

input *v* capture, code, feed in, insert, key in, process, store
♦ *n* data, details, facts, figures, information, material, particulars, resources, statistics
🗷 output

inquest *n* examination, hearing, inquiry, inspection, investigation, post-mortem

inquietude *n* agitation, anxiety, apprehension, discomposure, disquiet, disquietude *formal*, jumpiness, nervousness, perturbation *formal*, restlessness, solicitude *formal*, unease, uneasiness, worry
🗷 composure

inquire, enquire *v* **1** *I inquired if any tables were free:* ask, query, question, quiz **2** *he inquired into their tax affairs:* examine, explore, inspect, interrogate, investigate, look into, probe, research, scan, scrutinize, search, snoop *colloq*, study

inquirer, enquirer *n* explorer, interrogator, investigator, questioner, researcher, searcher, seeker, student

inquiring, enquiring *adj* analytical, curious, doubtful, eager, inquisitive, interested, interrogatory, investigative, investigatory, nosy *colloq*, outward looking, probing, prying, questioning, sceptical, searching, wondering, zetetic *formal*
🗷 incurious, unquestioning

inquiry, enquiry *n* **1** *a murder inquiry:* hearing, inquest, inquisition, investigation, probe, scrutiny, search **2** *a public inquiry:* examination, exploration, investigation, reconnaissance, research, scrutiny, search, sounding, study, survey **3** *a polite inquiry:* query, question

inquisition *n* cross-examination, cross-questioning, examination, grilling *colloq*, inquest, inquiry, interrogation, investigation, questioning, quizzing, third degree *colloq*, witch hunt *colloq*

inquisitive *adj* curious, inquiring, interfering, intrusive, meddlesome, nosy, peeping, peering, probing, prying, questioning, scrutinizing, searching, snooping, snoopy *colloq*, spying

inroad *n* advance, assault, attack, charge, encroachment, foray, impingement, incursion, intrusion, invasion, irruption, offensive, onslaught, progress, raid, sally, sortie, trespass, trespassing

insane *adj* **1** *criminally insane:* barmy *colloq*, bonkers *colloq*, crackers *colloq*, crazy, demented, deranged, disturbed, loony *colloq*, loopy *colloq*, lunatic, mad, mental *colloq*, mentally ill, needing your head examining *colloq*, non compos mentis, not all there *colloq*, nuts *colloq*, nutty *colloq*, nutty as a fruitcake *colloq*, off your rocker *colloq*, off your trolley *colloq*, out of your mind, round the bend *colloq*, round the twist *colloq*, soft in the head *colloq*, unhinged **2** *an insane shot to play:* absurd, barmy *colloq*, crazy, daft *colloq*, foolish, idiotic, impractical, mad, nonsensical, potty *colloq*, ridiculous, senseless, stupid
🗷 **1** sane **2** sensible

insanitary *adj* contaminated, dirtied, dirty, disease-ridden, feculent *formal*, filthy, foul, impure, infected, infested, insalubrious *formal*, noisome *formal*, noxious *formal*, polluted, unclean, unhealthful *formal*, unhealthy, unhygienic, unsanitary, unsanitized
🗷 clean, sanitary

insanity *n* **1** *suffer from insanity:* craziness, delirium, dementia, derangement, frenzy, lunacy, madness, mania, mental illness, neurosis, psychosis *technical* **2** *the insanity of his decision:* absurdity, craziness, daftness *colloq*, folly, foolishness, irresponsibility, lunacy, madness, ridiculousness, senselessness, stupidity
🗷 **1** sanity **2** sensibleness

insatiable *adj* avid, craving, gluttonous, greedy, hungry, immoderate, inordinate, rapacious *formal*, ravenous, unappeasable, unquenchable, unsatisfiable, voracious

inscribe *v* **1** *her name was inscribed on the trophy:* brand, carve, cut, engrave, etch, impress, imprint, incise, mark, print, stamp **2** *the book is inscribed to you:* address, autograph, dedicate **3** *inscribe the names of the new intake:* enlist, enrol, record, register, sign, write

inscription *n* caption, dedication, engraving, epitaph, etching, legend, lettering, message, signature, words, writing

inscrutable *adj* arcane *formal*, baffling, cryptic, deep, enigmatic, hidden, impenetrable, incomprehensible, inexplicable, mysterious, puzzling, unexplainable, unfathomable, unintelligible, unreadable
🗷 comprehensible

insect

Insects include:
fly, gnat, midge, mosquito, tsetse-fly, locust,
dragonfly, cranefly, daddy longlegs *colloq*,
horsefly, mayfly, butterfly, moth, bee,

bumblebee, wasp, hornet, aphid, blackfly, greenfly, whitefly, froghopper, ladybird, water boatman, lacewing; beetle, cockroach, roach *US*, earwig, stick insect, grasshopper, cricket, cicada, flea, louse, nit, leatherjacket, termite, glowworm, woodworm, weevil, woodlouse

Parts of an insect include:
abdomen, antenna, cercus, compound eye, forewing, head, hindwing, legs, mandible, mouthpart, ocellus, ovipositor, segment, spiracle, thorax

insecure *adj* 1 *he's insecure about his acting:* afraid, anxious, apprehensive, doubtful, fearful, hesitant, lacking confidence, nervous, uncertain, unsure, worried 2 *their online system is insecure:* dangerous, defenceless, exposed, flimsy, frail, hazardous, loose, open to attack, perilous, precarious, shaky, unguarded, unprotected, unsafe, unstable, unsteady, vulnerable, weak ⊞ 1 confident, self-assured 2 protected, safe, secure

insecurity *n* 1 *emotional insecurity:* anxiety, apprehension, fear, lack of confidence, nervousness, uncertainty, uneasiness, unsureness, worry 2 *the insecurity of our defences:* danger, defencelessness, flimsiness, frailness, hazard, instability, peril, precariousness, shakiness, unsafeness, unsafety, unsteadiness, vulnerability, weakness ⊞ 1 confidence 2 safety, security

insensible *adj* 1 *knocked insensible:* anaesthetized, comatose *formal*, dead to the world *colloq*, insentient *formal*, knocked out *colloq*, numb, out *colloq*, out for the count *colloq*, senseless, unconscious, unresponsive, zonked *colloq* 2 *insensible of the danger:* blind, deaf, ignorant, oblivious, unaware, unconscious, unmindful 3 *insensible to my misfortunes:* aloof, callous, cold, detached, distant, emotionless, hard, insensitive, unaffected, unfeeling, unmoved, untouched 4 *varying by insensible gradations:* faint, imperceptible, indiscernible, indistinguishable, slight, unapparent, undetectable ⊞ 1 conscious 2 aware, knowing 3 sensitive

insensitive *adj* callous, crass, hardened, heartless, hypalgesic *technical*, immune, impassive, impenetrable, impervious, indifferent, oblivious, resistant, tactless, thick-skinned, thoughtless, tough, unaffected, uncaring, unconcerned, unfeeling, unmoved, unresponsive, unsusceptible, unsympathetic, untouched ⊞ affected, responsive, sensitive

insensitivity *n* bluntness, callousness, crassness, hard-headedness, hardness, imperviousness, indifference, obtuseness, resistance, tactlessness, toughness, unconcern, unresponsiveness ⊞ responsiveness, sensitivity

inseparable *adj* 1 *the sisters were inseparable:* bosom, close, constant, devoted, intimate 2 *liberty is inseparable from peace:* indissoluble, indivisible, inextricable, undividable ⊞ 2 separable

insert *v* embed, enclose, engraft, enter, implant, infix, inlay, inset, intercalate *formal*, interject,

interleave, interpolate *formal*, interpose *formal*, introduce, let in, place, press, push in, put, put in, set, slide in, slip in, stick in, thrust in
♦ *n* addition, advertisement, circular, enclosure, inlay, insertion, inset, notice, supplement

insertion *n* 1 *the insertion of new text:* addition, inclusion, intercalation *formal*, interpolation *formal*, introduction 2 *several insertions and one deletion:* addition, entry, implant, insert, inset, supplement

inside *n* belly *colloq*, centre, content, contents, core, guts *colloq*, heart, interior, middle ⊞ outside
♦ *adv* indoors, internally, inwardly, privately, secretly, within ⊞ outside
♦ *adj* 1 *an inside toilet:* implicit, inherent, inner, innermost, interior, internal, intrinsic, inward 2 *inside information:* classified, confidential, internal, private, reserved, restricted, secret

insider *n* co-worker, member, one of the in-crowd *colloq*, one of us *colloq*, participant, staff member

insides *n* abdomen, belly, bowels, entrails, guts, innards *colloq*, internal organs, intestines, organs, stomach, viscera

insidious *adj* artful, crafty, cunning, deceitful, deceptive, devious, dishonest, duplicitous *formal*, furtive, insincere, Machiavellian, perfidious *formal*, sly, sneaking, sneaky, stealthy, subtle, surreptitious, treacherous, tricky, wily ⊞ direct, straightforward

insight *n* acumen, apprehension, awareness, comprehension, discernment, grasp, intelligence, intuition, judgement, knowledge, observation, penetration, perception, perspicacity *formal*, realization, sensitivity, sharpness, shrewdness, understanding, vision, wisdom

insightful *adj* acute, astute, discerning, intelligent, knowledgeable, observant, penetrating, perceptive, percipient *formal*, perspicacious *formal*, prudent *formal*, sagacious *formal*, sharp, shrewd, understanding, wise ⊞ superficial

insignia *n* badge, brand, crest, decoration, emblem, ensign, hallmark(s), mark, medallion, regalia, ribbon, sign(s), symbol, trademark

insignificance *n* immateriality, inconsequence, inconsequentiality, insubstantiality, irrelevance, meaninglessness, meanness, negligibility, nugatoriness *formal*, paltriness, pettiness, smallness, tininess, triviality, unimportance, worthlessness ⊞ significance

insignificant *adj* cutting no ice *colloq*, immaterial, inconsequential, inconsiderable, insubstantial, irrelevant, meagre, meaningless, minor, negligible, no great shakes *colloq*, non-essential, not worth mentioning, nugatory *formal*, paltry, peripheral, petty, piddling *colloq*, scanty, slight, small, small-time *colloq*, tiny, trifling, trivial, unimportant ⊞ important, significant

insincere *adj* deceitful, devious, dishonest, disingenuous *formal*, disloyal, dissembling *formal*, double-dealing, duplicitous *formal*,

faithless, false, feigned, hollow, hypocritical, lying, mendacious *formal*, perfidious *formal*, phoney *colloq*, pretended, treacherous, two-faced, underhand, unfaithful, untrue, untruthful
F3 genuine, sincere

insincerity *n* artificiality, cant, deceitfulness, deviousness, dishonesty, disingenuousness *formal*, dissembling *formal*, dissimulation *formal*, duplicity *formal*, evasiveness, faithlessness, falseness, falsity, hollowness, humbug *colloq*, hypocrisy, lip service *colloq*, mendacity *formal*, perfidy *formal*, phoniness *colloq*, pretence, untruthfulness
F3 sincerity

insinuate *v* allude, get at *colloq*, hint, imply, indicate, intimate, mention, suggest, whisper *colloq*

insinuation *n* allusion, aspersion *formal*, hint, implication, innuendo, intimation, introduction, slant, slur, suggestion

insipid *adj* **1** *this soup is rather insipid:* bland, characterless, flavourless, tasteless, thin, unappetizing, watery, weak, wishy-washy *colloq* **2** *insipid chit-chat:* anaemic, banal, bland, boring, characterless, colourless, drab, dry, dull, flat, inanimate, lifeless, monotonous, spiritless, tame, tedious, trite, unimaginative, uninteresting, vapid, weak, wearisome, wishy-washy *colloq*
F3 1 appetizing, piquant, spicy, tasty **2** exciting, interesting, lively, stimulating

insist *v* **1** *I didn't want to go, but she insisted:* not take no for an answer *colloq*, persist, put your foot down *colloq*, refuse to accept an alternative, stand firm, stand your ground **2** *I insisted that the part be replaced:* ask for firmly, command, demand, dictate, entreat, order, require, urge **3** *she insisted that she was OK:* assert, aver *formal*, claim, contend, declare, emphasize, hold, maintain, reiterate, repeat, state, stress, swear, vow

insistence *n* **1** *it was at my insistence:* command, demand, dictate, entreaty, exhortation *formal*, insistency, pressing, urging **2** *her insistence that she wanted to leave:* assertion, attestation, avowal, claim, contention, declaration, maintenance, persistence, reiteration

insistent *adj* **1** *he's insistent that I stay in contact:* adamant, demanding, determined, dogged, emphatic, exigent *formal*, forceful, importunate, inexorable, persevering, pressing, resolute, tenacious, unrelenting, unyielding, urgent **2** *the phone's insistent ringing:* constant, incessant, persistent, relentless, repeated, unremitting

insobriety *n* crapulence *formal*, drunkenness, hard drinking, inebriation, inebriety, intemperance, intoxication, tipsiness *colloq*
F3 sobriety

insolence *n* abuse, arrogance, audacity, boldness, cheek *colloq*, cheekiness *colloq*, chutzpah *colloq*, contemptuousness, contumely *formal*, defiance, disrespect, effrontery *formal*, forwardness, gall *colloq*, hubris *formal*, impertinence, impudence, incivility, insubordination, insults, lip *colloq*, mouth *colloq*, nerve *colloq*, offensiveness, pertness, presumption, presumptuousness, rudeness, sauce *colloq*, sauciness *colloq*
F3 politeness, respect

insolent *adj* abusive, arrogant, audacious, bold, brash, brazen, cheeky *colloq*, contemptuous, defiant, disrespectful, forward, fresh *colloq*, ill-mannered, impertinent, impudent, insubordinate, insulting, presumptuous, rude, saucy *colloq*
F3 polite, respectful

insoluble *adj* baffling, complex, enigmatic, impenetrable, incomprehensible, indecipherable, inexplicable, inscrutable, intricate, involved, mysterious, mystifying, obscure, perplexing, puzzling, unexplainable, unfathomable, unsolvable
F3 explicable

insolvency *n* bankruptcy, default, destitution, failure, impecuniosity *formal*, impoverishment, indebtedness, liquidation, pennilessness, ruin
F3 solvency

insolvent *adj* bankrupt, broke *colloq*, bust *colloq*, destitute, failed, gone to the wall *colloq*, gone under *colloq*, impecunious *formal*, impoverished, in debt, in queer street *colloq*, in the red *colloq*, liquidated, on the rocks *colloq*, on your beam ends *colloq*, penniless, ruined, skint *colloq*, strapped (for cash) *colloq*
F3 solvent

insomnia *n* insomnolence *formal*, restlessness, sleeplessness, wakefulness
F3 sleep

insouciance *n* airiness, breeziness, carefreeness, ease, flippancy, heedlessness, indifference, jauntiness, light-heartedness, nonchalance, unconcern
F3 anxiety, care

insouciant *adj* airy, breezy, buoyant, carefree, casual, easy-going, flippant, free and easy, happy-go-lucky, heedless, indifferent, jaunty, light-hearted, nonchalant, unconcerned, untroubled, unworried
F3 anxious, careworn

inspect *v* appraise, assess, audit, check, examine, go over, investigate, look over, oversee, pore over, reconnoitre, scan, scrutinize, search, see over, study, superintend, supervise, survey, tour, vet, view, visit

inspection *n* analysis, appraisal, assessment, audit, check, check-up, dekko *colloq*, examination, investigation, look-over *colloq*, once-over *colloq*, recce *colloq*, review, scan, scrutiny, search, study, supervision, survey, tour, vetting, visit

inspector *n* appraiser, assessor, auditor, checker, controller, critic, examiner, investigator, overseer, reviewer, scanner, scrutineer, superintendent, supervisor, surveyor, tester, visitor

inspiration *n* **1** *his work lacks inspiration:* creativity, genius, imagination, inventiveness, originality **2** *her music is an inspiration to others:* arousing, encouragement, fillip, goad, incitement, influence, motivation, muse, spur, stimulation, stimulus, stirring **3** *one of my colleagues had an inspiration:* awakening, brainwave, bright idea, enlightenment, idea, illumination, insight, revelation, stroke of genius

inspire *v* **1** *he inspired me to take up the guitar:* animate, encourage, energize, enliven, enthral, enthuse, exhilarate, fire, galvanize, goad, hearten, imbue, impress, inflame, influence, infuse, instigate, kindle, motivate, provoke, quicken, rouse, spark off, spur, stimulate, stir, thrill, touch off, trigger **2** *the boat's handling inspires confidence:* arouse, awake, cause, engender, excite, ignite, induce, produce, prompt

inspired *adj* brilliant, dazzling, enthralling, exceptional, exciting, impressive, marvellous, memorable, outstanding, remarkable, splendid, superlative, thrilling, wonderful
◱ dull, uninspired

inspiring *adj* affecting, encouraging, enthralling, enthusiastic, exciting, exhilarating, heartening, impressive, interesting, invigorating, memorable, moving, rousing, stimulating, stirring, thrilling, uplifting
◱ dull, uninspiring

inspirit *v* animate, cheer, embolden, encourage, enliven, exhilarate, fire, galvanize, gladden, hearten, incite, inspire, invigorate, move, nerve, quicken, refresh, reinvigorate, rouse, stimulate

instability *n* capriciousness, changeableness, fickleness, fitfulness, flightiness, flimsiness, fluctuation, frailty, impermanence, inconstancy, insecurity, irresolution, oscillation, precariousness, shakiness, transience, uncertainty, unpredictability, unreliability, unsafeness, unsoundness, unsteadiness, vacillation, variability, volatility, wavering
◱ stability

install *v* **1** *install a new phone system:* establish, fit, fix, insert, introduce, lay, locate, lodge, place, plant, position, put (in), set up, settle, site, situate, station **2** *install her as president:* consecrate, inaugurate, induct, instate, institute, invest, ordain

installation *n* **1** *the installation of security measures:* fitting, insertion, location, placing, positioning, siting **2** *computer installations:* equipment, machinery, plant, system **3** *her installation as president:* consecration, inauguration, induction, instatement, investiture, ordination **4** *a military installation:* base, centre, establishment, headquarters, post, settlement, site, station

instalment *n* **1** *pay in instalments:* hire purchase, part payment, payment, portion, repayment **2** *the next instalment of the series:* chapter, division, episode, part, portion, section, segment

instance *n* **1** *several instances of bullying:* case, case in point, citation, example, exemplification, illustration, occasion, occurrence, sample **2** *at his instance:* behest *formal*, demand, entreaty, exhortation *formal*, importunity *formal*, incitement, initiative, insistence, instigation, pressure, prompting, request, solicitation, urging
♦ *v* adduce *formal*, cite, exemplify, give, mention, name, point to, quote, refer to, specify

instant *n* flash, jiffy *colloq*, juncture, minute, moment, occasion, second, split second, tick *colloq*, time, trice, twinkling, twinkling of an eye *colloq*, two shakes of a lamb's tail *colloq*
♦ *adj* **1** *an instant decision:* direct, fast, immediate, instantaneous, on-the-spot, prompt, quick, rapid, swift, unhesitating, urgent **2** *instant food:* convenience, easily prepared, quickly prepared, ready mixed
◱ **1** slow

instantaneous *adj* direct, immediate, instant, on-the-spot, prompt, rapid, sudden, unhesitating
◱ eventual

instantaneously *adv* at once, before you can say Jack Robinson *colloq*, directly, forthwith, immediately, in two shakes of a lamb's tail *colloq*, instantly, on the spot, promptly, pronto *colloq*, quickly, rapidly, right away, speedily, straight away, there and then, unhesitatingly, without delay, without hesitation
◱ eventually

instantly *adv* at once, directly, forthwith, immediately, instantaneously, now, on the spot, pronto *colloq*, right away, straight away, there and then, without delay
◱ eventually

instead *adv* alternatively, as an alternative, by/ in contrast, else, preferably, rather, replacement, substitute

instigate *v* begin, bring about, cause, egg on *colloq*, encourage, excite, foment, generate, goad, incite, induce, influence, initiate, inspire, kindle, move, persuade, press, prod, prompt, provoke, rouse, set on, spur, start, stimulate, stir up, urge, whip up

instigation *n* behest *formal*, bidding, encouragement, incentive, incitement, inducement, initiation, initiative, insistence, prompting, urging

instigator *n* agent provocateur, agitator, firebrand, fomenter, goad, incendiary, inciter, leader, mischief-maker, motivator, prime mover, provoker, ringleader, spur, troublemaker

instil *v* din into *colloq*, drill, imbue, implant, impress, inculcate, infuse, inject, insinuate, introduce, teach

instinct *n* **1** *strong paternal instincts:* drive, feeling, gut feeling/reaction *colloq*, hunch, impulse, inbred response, intuition, natural response, predisposition *formal*, sixth sense, tendency, urge **2** *an instinct for the job:* ability, aptitude, bent, faculty, feel, flair, gift, knack, talent

instinctive *adj* automatic, gut *colloq*, immediate, impulsive, inborn, inherent, innate, intuitive, involuntary, mechanical, native, natural, reflex, spontaneous, unintentional, unlearned, unpremeditated, untaught, unthinking, visceral
◱ conscious, deliberate, voluntary

instinctively *adv* automatically, intuitively, involuntarily, mechanically, naturally, spontaneously, unthinkingly, without thinking
◱ consciously, deliberately, voluntarily

institute *v* **1** *we instituted the award last year:* begin, commence *formal*, create, develop, enact, establish, found, inaugurate, initiate, introduce, launch, open, organize, originate, set up, start **2** *he was instituted into the priesthood:* appoint, induct, initiate, install, invest, ordain
◱ **1** abolish, cancel, discontinue *formal*
♦ *n* **1** *an institute for advanced research:* academy, college, conservatory, foundation, institution, organization, school, seminary **2** *the institutes of the sacred law:* custom, decree, law, principle, regulation, rule

institution *n* **1** *research institutions:* association, centre, club, concern, corporation, establishment, foundation, guild, home, hospital, institute, league, organization, society **2** *the institution of marriage:* convention, custom, law, practice, ritual, rule, system, tradition, usage **3** *the institution of the five-day week:* commencement *formal,* creation, enactment, establishment, formation, foundation, founding, inception *formal,* initiation, installation, introduction, setting-up, starting

institutional *adj* accepted, bureaucratic, clinical, conventional, customary, established, establishment, formal, impersonal, methodical, orderly, organized, orthodox, regimented, ritualistic, routine, set, systematic, uniform, unwelcoming
F individualistic, unconventional

instruct *v* **1** *he instructed me in geometry:* coach, discipline, drill, educate, ground, prepare, prime, school, teach, train, tutor **2** *I was instructed to leave the building:* advise, bid *formal,* charge, command, counsel, demand, direct, enjoin *formal,* enlighten, guide, inform, make known, mandate, notify, order, require, tell

instruction *n* **1** *give someone instructions:* advice, briefing, charge, command, direction, directive, guidance, information, injunction, mandate, order, recommendation, requirement, ruling **2** *instruction in anatomy:* classes, coaching, drilling, education, enlightenment, grounding, guidance, lesson(s), preparation, priming, schooling, teaching, training, tuition, tutelage, tutoring **3** *read the instructions carefully:* advice, book of words, brief, directions, guidance, guidelines, handbook, information, key, legend, manual, orders, recommendations, rules

instructive *adj* doctrinal, edifying, educational, educative, enlightening, helpful, illuminating, informative, uplifting, useful
F unenlightening

instructor *n* adviser, coach, counsellor, demonstrator, educator, exponent, guide, guru, lecturer, master, mentor, mistress, pedagogue, teacher, trainer, tutor

instrument *n* **1** *surgical instruments:* apparatus, appliance, contraption, contrivance, device, gadget, gismo *colloq,* implement, mechanism, tool, utensil **2** *navigational instruments:* gauge, guideline, indicator, measure, meter, rule, yardstick **3** *an instrument of diplomacy:* agency, agent, channel, factor, means., medium, organ, vehicle, way

instrumental *adj* active, auxiliary, conducive, contributory, helpful, important, influential, involved, significant, subsidiary, useful
F obstructive, unhelpful

insubordinate *adj* contumacious *formal,* defiant, disobedient, disorderly, impertinent, impudent, insurgent, mutinous, rebellious, recalcitrant *formal,* refractory *formal,* riotous, rude, seditious, turbulent, undisciplined, ungovernable, unruly
F compliant, docile, obedient

insubordination *n* defiance, disobedience, impertinence, impudence, indiscipline, insurrection, mutinousness, mutiny, rebellion, recalcitrance *formal,* revolt, riotousness, rudeness, sedition, ungovernability
F compliance, docility, obedience

insubstantial *adj* **1** *an insubstantial hut:* feeble, flimsy, frail, poor, slight, tenuous, thin, weak **2** *fears as insubstantial as ghosts:* chimerical *formal,* ephemeral *formal,* false, fanciful, idle, illusory, imaginary, immaterial, incorporeal, moonshine, unreal, vaporous
F **1** solid, strong **2** real

insufferable *adj* detestable, dreadful, impossible, intolerable, loathsome, more than you can bear, outrageous, revolting, shocking, too much to bear, unbearable, unendurable
F pleasant, tolerable

insufficiency *n* dearth, deficiency, inadequacy, lack, need, poverty, scarcity, short supply, shortage, want *formal*
F excess, sufficiency

insufficient *adj* deficient, in short supply, inadequate, lacking, meagre, not enough, scant, scanty, scarce, short, sparse, wanting
F enough, excessive, sufficient

insular *adj* biased, bigoted, blinkered, closed, cut off, detached, insulated, inward-looking, isolated, limited, narrow, narrow-minded, parish-pump *colloq,* parochial, petty, prejudiced, provincial, remote, restricted, separate, solitary, withdrawn, xenophobic
F open-minded

insularity *n* bias, bigotry, detachment, isolation, narrow-mindedness, parochiality, parochialness, pettiness, prejudice, solitariness, xenophobia
F open-mindedness, openness

insulate *v* cocoon, cover, cushion, cut off, detach, encase, envelop, exclude, isolate, lag, pad, protect, segregate, separate, sequester *formal,* shelter, shield, wrap

insulation *n* **1** *insulation for water pipes:* cladding, covering, cushioning, lagging, padding, protection, stuffing, wrapping **2** *insulation from potential difficulties:* cocooning, cover, cushioning, detachment, exclusion, isolation, protection, segregation, separation, shelter

insult *v* abuse, affront *formal,* bait, call names, calumniate *formal,* disparage *formal,* give the cold shoulder *colloq,* hurt, impugn *formal,* injure, kick in the teeth *colloq,* libel, malign, mortify, offend, outrage, rebuff, revile *formal,* ridicule, slander, slap in the face *colloq,* slight, slur, snub, taunt, traduce *formal,* wound
F compliment, praise
♦ *n* **1** *they shouted insults as he arrived:* barb, gibe, put-down *colloq,* slight, slur, snub, taunt **2** *an insult to the church:* affront *formal,* cold shoulder *colloq,* defamation, disparagement *formal,* indignity, insolence, libel, offence, revilement *formal,* rudeness
F **1** compliment **2** praise

insulting *adj* abusive, affronting *formal,* contemptuous, degrading, disparaging *formal,* hurtful, injurious, insolent, libellous, offensive, outrageous, reviling *formal,* rude, scurrilous, slanderous, slighting
F complimentary, respectful

insuperable *adj* formidable, impassable, insurmountable, invincible, overwhelming, unassailable, unconquerable
⊟ surmountable

insupportable *adj* 1 *the heat was insupportable:* detestable, dreadful, hateful, insufferable, loathsome, unacceptable, unbearable, unendurable 2 *an increasingly insupportable position:* indefensible, unjustifiable, untenable
⊟ 1 bearable 2 justifiable

insuppressible *adj* energetic, go-getting *colloq*, incorrigible, irrepressible, lively, obstreperous, uncontrollable, ungovernable, unruly, unstoppable, unsubduable
⊟ suppressible

insurance *n* assurance, cover, guarantee, indemnification, indemnity, policy, premium, protection, provision, safeguard, security, surety, warranty

insure *v* assure, cover, guarantee, indemnify, protect, underwrite, warrant

insurer *n* assurer, guarantor, indemnifier, protector, underwriter, warrantor

insurgent *n* insurrectionist, mutineer, partisan, rebel, resister, revolter, revolutionary, revolutionist, rioter, seditionist
♦ *adj* disobedient, insubordinate, insurrectionary, mutinous, partisan, rebellious, revolting, revolutionary, riotous, seditious

insurmountable *adj* hopeless, impossible, insuperable, invincible, overwhelming, unassailable, unconquerable
⊟ surmountable

insurrection *n* coup, coup d'état, insurgence, mutiny, putsch, rebellion, revolt, revolution, riot, rising, sedition, uprising

intact *adj* (all) in one piece, complete, entire, faultless, flawless, integral, perfect, sound, unbroken, undamaged, unharmed, unhurt, uninjured, unscathed, whole
⊟ broken, damaged, incomplete

intangible *adj* abstract, airy, elusive, fleeting, immeasurable, imponderable, indefinite, indescribable, insubstantial, invisible, obscure, shadowy, subtle, unclear, undefinable, unreal, vague
⊟ real, tangible

integral *adj* 1 *an integral part:* basic, component, constituent, elemental, essential, fundamental, indispensable, inherent, intrinsic, necessary, requisite *formal* 2 *an integral service:* complete, entire, full, intact, total, undivided, whole
⊟ 1 additional, extra, unnecessary

integrate *v* amalgamate, assimilate, blend, coalesce, combine, consolidate, desegregate, fuse, harmonize, homogenize, incorporate, intermix, join, knit, merge, mesh, mingle, mix, unite
⊟ divide, segregate, separate

integrated *adj* amalgamated, assimilated, blended, coalesced, cohesive, combined, connected, consolidated, desegregated, fused, harmonious, harmonized, incorporated, interrelated, joined, merged, meshed, mingled, mixed, part and parcel *colloq*, unified, united, unseparated
⊟ segregated, unintegrated

integration *n* amalgamation, assimilation, blend, combination, consolidation, desegregation, fusion, harmony, incorporation, merger, mix, unification, unity
⊟ segregation, separation

integrity *n* 1 *a woman of integrity:* decency, fairness, goodness, honesty, honour, incorruptibility, morality, principle, probity *formal*, purity, rectitude *formal*, righteousness, sincerity, truthfulness, uprightness, virtue 2 *the structural integrity of the building:* coherence, cohesion, completeness, entirety, totality, unification, unity, wholeness
⊟ 1 dishonesty 2 incompleteness

intellect *n* 1 *a person of considerable intellect:* brain(s), brainpower, brilliance, comprehension, genius, intelligence, judgement, mind, reason, sense, thought, understanding, wisdom 2 *one of our greatest intellects:* academic, egghead *colloq*, genius, highbrow, intellectual, mastermind, thinker
⊟ 1 stupidity

intellectual *adj* academic, bookish, cerebral *formal*, cultural, erudite *formal*, highbrow, intelligent, learned, logical, mental, scholarly, studious, thoughtful, well-educated, well-read
⊟ low-brow
♦ *n* academic, egghead *colloq*, genius, highbrow, intellect, mastermind, thinker
⊟ low-brow

intelligence *n* 1 *a man of great intelligence:* acumen, alertness, aptitude, brain(s) *colloq*, brainpower, brightness, brilliance, cleverness, comprehension, discernment, grey matter *colloq*, intellect, little grey cells *colloq*, nous *colloq*, perception, quickness, reason, sharpness, thought, understanding, wit(s) 2 *the gathering of intelligence:* account, advice, data, dope *colloq*, facts, findings, gen *colloq*, information, knowledge, low-down *colloq*, news, notice, notification, report, rumour, tip-off *colloq*, warning 3 *military intelligence:* espionage, observation, spying, surveillance
⊟ 1 foolishness, stupidity

intelligent *adj* acute, alert, all there *colloq*, brainy *colloq*, bright, brilliant, clever, discerning, educated, knowing, knowing a thing or two *colloq*, knowing how many beans make five *colloq*, knowledgeable, no flies on someone *colloq*, perceptive, perspicacious *formal*, quick, quick on the uptake *colloq*, quick-witted, rational, sagacious *formal*, sensible, sharp, smart, thinking, using your loaf *colloq*, well-informed
⊟ foolish, stupid, unintelligent

intelligentsia *n* academics, brains *colloq*, cognoscenti, eggheads *colloq*, highbrows, illuminati, intellectuals, literati

intelligibility *n* clarity, clearness, comprehensibility, comprehensibleness, distinctness, explicitness, legibility, lucidity, lucidness, plainness, precision, simplicity
⊟ unintelligibility

intelligible *adj* clear, comprehensible, decipherable, distinct, explicit, fathomable, legible, lucid, open, penetrable, plain, understandable
⊟ unintelligible

intemperance *n* crapulence *formal*, drunkenness, excess, extravagance, immoderation, inebriation *formal*, insobriety, intoxication, licence, overindulgence, self-indulgence, unrestraint
🖝 temperance

intemperate *adj* 1 *the intemperate fellows at his favourite drinking den:* dissolute, drunken, incontinent, inebriated *formal*, intoxicated 2 *intemperate language:* excessive, extravagant, extreme, immoderate, inordinate, irrestrainable, licentious, over the top *colloq*, passionate, prodigal, profligate, self-indulgent, severe, tempestuous, unbridled, uncontrollable, uncontrolled, ungovernable, unreasonable, unrestrained, violent, wild
🖝 1 sober 2 temperate

intend *v* 1 *I intend to move to France:* aim, be determined, be going, be looking, choose, contemplate, determine, expect, have a mind, mean, plan, plot, propose, purpose, resolve *formal*, scheme 2 *funds intended for regional development:* aim, consign, design, destine, determine, earmark, mark out, mean, set apart

intended *adj* deliberate, designate, designated, destined, future, intentional, planned, proposed, prospective
🖝 accidental
♦ *n* betrothed, fiancé, fiancée, husband-to-be, wife-to-be

intense *adj* 1 *intense desire:* acute, ardent, burning, concentrated, consuming, deep, eager, earnest, energetic, enthusiastic, excited, extreme, fervent, fervid *formal*, fierce, forceful, great, harsh, heightened, impassioned, intensive, keen, passionate, potent, powerful, profound, severe, sharp, strong, vehement, vigorous, violent, zealous 2 *an intense person:* emotional, heavy, impassioned, nervous, serious, tense, thoughtful
🖝 1 mild, moderate, weak 2 easy-going

---

intense or *intensive*? *Intense* means 'very great': *the intense heat from the furnace; intense bitterness. Intensive* means 'concentrated, thorough, taking great care': *an intensive search; the intensive care ward of a hospital.*

---

intensely *adv* ardently, deeply, extremely, fervently, fiercely, greatly, passionately, profoundly, strongly, very, with a vengeance *colloq*
🖝 mildly

intensification *n* acceleration, aggravation, augmentation *formal*, boost, building-up, build-up, concentration, deepening, emphasis, enhancement, escalation, exacerbescence *formal*, heightening, increase, magnification, reinforcement, stepping-up, strengthening, worsening
🖝 lessening

intensify *v* add fuel to the flames *colloq*, add to, aggravate, augment *formal*, boost, bring to a head *colloq*, broaden, build up, bump up *colloq*, concentrate, deepen, emphasize, enhance, escalate, exacerbate *formal*, fan, fire, fuel, heighten, hike up *colloq*, hot up *colloq*, increase, magnify, maximize, quicken, reinforce, sharpen, step up, strengthen, whet, widen, worsen
🖝 reduce, weaken

intensity *n* acuteness, ardour, concentration, depth, eagerness, earnestness, emotion, energy, enthusiasm, extremity, fanaticism, fervency, fervour, fierceness, fire, force, greatness, intenseness, keenness, passion, potency, power, profundity, severity, strain, strength, tension, vehemence, vigour, zeal

intensive *adj* all-out, comprehensive, concentrated, detailed, exhaustive, in-depth, intense, thorough, thoroughgoing
🖝 superficial

---

intensive or *intense*? See panel at **intense**

---

intent *adj* 1 *intent on doing something:* bent, committed, determined, eager, firm, keen, resolved, set 2 *an intent look:* absorbed, alert, attentive, close, concentrating, engrossed, enrapt, fixed, focused, hard, keen, occupied, preoccupied, rapt, searching, steady, watchful, wrapped up
🖝 2 absent-minded, distracted
♦ *n* aim, design, end, goal, idea, intention, meaning, object, objective, plan, point, purpose, target, view

intention *n* aim, ambition, aspiration, design, end, goal, idea, intent, meaning, object, objective, plan, point, purpose, target, view, wish

intentional *adj* calculated, conscious, considered, deliberate, designed, intended, meant, on purpose, planned, prearranged, preconceived, premeditated, purposeful, studied, weighed-up, wilful
🖝 accidental, unintentional

intentionally *adv* by design, deliberately, designedly, meaningly, on purpose, wilfully, with malice aforethought
🖝 accidentally

intently *adv* attentively, carefully, closely, fixedly, hard, keenly, searchingly, staringly, steadily, watchfully
🖝 absent-mindedly

inter *v* bury, entomb, inearth, inhume, inurn *formal*, lay to rest, sepulchre
🖝 exhume

interbreed *v* cross, crossbreed, cross-fertilize, hybridize, miscegenate *formal*, mongrelize, reproduce together

interbreeding *n* cross-breeding, crossing, hybridization, miscegenation *formal*

intercede *v* arbitrate, beseech *formal*, entreat *formal*, interpose *formal*, intervene, mediate, negotiate, petition, plead, speak

intercept *v* ambush, arrest, block, catch, check, commandeer, cut off, deflect, delay, frustrate, head off, impede, interrupt, obstruct, seize, stop, take, thwart

intercession *n* advocacy, agency, arbitration, beseeching *formal*, entreaty *formal*, good offices, interposition *formal*, intervention, mediation, negotiation, plea, pleading, prayer, solicitation, supplication *formal*

interchange *n* 1 *an interchange of ideas:* alternation, barter, crossfire, exchange, give-and-take *colloq*, interplay, reciprocation, swap, trading 2 *we stopped near the interchange:* crossing, crossroad(s), intersection, junction

♦ *v* alternate, exchange, reciprocate, replace, reverse, substitute, swap, switch, trade, transpose

interchangeable *adj* comparable, corresponding, equivalent, exchangeable, identical, reciprocal, similar, standard, synonymous, the same, transposable
🔁 different

intercourse *n* 1 *sexual intercourse:* bang *taboo slang,* bonk *taboo slang,* carnal knowledge, coition *formal,* coitus *formal,* copulation, fuck *taboo slang,* going to bed with someone *colloq,* intimacy, intimate relations, it *colloq,* love-making, nookie *colloq,* screw *taboo slang,* sex, sexual relations, shag *taboo slang,* sleeping with someone *colloq,* the sex act 2 *social intercourse:* association, commerce, communication, communion, congress, connection, conversation, converse, correspondence, dealings, intercommunication, trade, traffic

interdict *v* ban, bar, debar, disallow *formal,* embargo, forbid, outlaw, preclude *formal,* prevent, prohibit, proscribe *formal,* rule out, veto
🔁 allow
♦ *n* ban, bar, disallowance *formal,* embargo, injunction, interdiction *formal,* preclusion *formal,* prohibition, proscription *formal,* taboo, veto
🔁 permission

interest *n* 1 *an interest in dance:* allure, appeal, attention, attentiveness, attraction, care, charm, concern, curiosity, engagement, fascination, heed, inquisitiveness, involvement, notice, regard 2 *of no interest to her:* consequence, consideration, gravity, importance, magnitude, moment, note, priority, prominence, relevance, seriousness, significance, urgency, value, weight 3 *leisure interests:* activity, amusement, diversion, hobby, pastime, pursuit, recreation 4 *in your best interests:* advantage, benefit, gain, good, profit 5 *business interests:* business, claim, concern, equity, investment, involvement, participation, portion, share, stake, stock 6 *earn interest:* bonus, credits, dividend, gain, percentage, premium, proceeds, profit, receipts, return, revenue
🔁 1 boredom 2 meaninglessness 4 loss
♦ *v* absorb, amuse, appeal to, attract, captivate, concern, divert, engage, engross, fascinate, grip, intrigue, involve, move, occupy, rivet, touch
🔁 bore

interested *adj* 1 *she looked very interested:* absorbed, attentive, attracted, captivated, curious, engrossed, enthralled, enthusiastic, fascinated, gripped, having the... bug *colloq,* intent, intrigued, keen, riveted 2 *the interested parties:* affected, concerned, implicated, involved
🔁 1 apathetic, indifferent, uninterested 2 disinterested, unaffected

interesting *adj* absorbing, amusing, appealing, attractive, captivating, compelling, compulsive, curious, engaging, engrossing, entertaining, exciting, fascinating, gripping, intriguing, riveting, stimulating, thought-provoking, unputdownable *colloq,* unusual
🔁 boring, monotonous, tedious, uninteresting

interfere *v* 1 *he's been interfering again:* butt in *colloq,* interrupt, intervene, intrude, meddle, muscle in on *colloq,* poke/stick your nose in *colloq,* pry, put in your two cents' worth *US colloq,* put in your two pennyworth *colloq,* stick/put your oar in *colloq,* tamper 2 *illness interfered with*

my studies: balk, block, check, clash, conflict, cramp, get in the way of *colloq,* hamper, handicap, hinder, impede, inhibit, obstruct, thwart, trammel 3 *interfered with children:* abuse, assault, attack, molest, rape, sexually assault
🔁 1 mind your own business *colloq* 2 assist

interference *n* 1 *freedom from state interference:* interruption, intervention, intrusion, meddlesomeness, meddling, prying 2 *the defender's interference stopped him from scoring:* blocking, checking, clashing, conflict, hampering, handicap, hindrance, impediment, inhibiting, obstruction, opposition, thwarting, trammel(s)
🔁 2 assistance

interim *adj* acting, caretaker, improvised, makeshift, pro tem *colloq,* provisional, stand-in, stopgap, temporary
♦ *n* interregnum, interval, meantime, meanwhile

interior *adj* 1 *the interior light:* central, inner, innermost, inside, internal, inward 2 *interior thoughts:* emotional, hidden, impulsive, innate, inner, instinctive, intimate, intuitive, involuntary, mental, personal, private, psychological, secret, spiritual, spontaneous 3 *the interior forested areas:* central, domestic, home, inland, local, remote, up-country
🔁 1 exterior, external 3 coastal, external
♦ *n* centre, core, depths, heart, inside, inside part, middle, nucleus
🔁 exterior, outside

interject *v* call, cry, ejaculate *formal,* exclaim, interpolate *formal,* interpose *formal,* interrupt, introduce, shout, utter

interjection *n* call, cry, ejaculation *formal,* exclamation, interpolation *formal,* interruption, shout, utterance

interlace *v* braid, cross, enlace, entwine, interlock, intermix, intersperse, intertwine, interweave, interwreathe, knit, plait, reticulate *formal,* twine

interlink *v* clasp together, interconnect, intergrow, interlock, intertwine, interweave, knit, link, link together, lock together, mesh
🔁 divide, separate

interlock *v* clasp together, interconnect, interdigitate *formal,* intertwine, link, link together, lock together, mesh

interloper *n* encroacher, gate-crasher *colloq,* intruder, invader, trespasser, uninvited guest

interlude *n* break, breather *colloq,* breathing-space, delay, halt, hiatus *formal,* intermission, interval, let-up *colloq,* pause, recess, respite, rest, spell, stop, stoppage, wait

intermediary *n* agent, arbitrator, broker, go-between, mediator, middleman, negotiator

intermediate *adj* halfway, in-between, intermediary, intervening, mean, medial, median, mid, middle, midway, transitional
🔁 extreme

interment *n* burial, burying, exequies *formal,* funeral, inhumation *formal,* obsequies *formal,* obsequy *formal,* sepulture *formal*
🔁 exhumation

interminable *adj* boring, boundless, ceaseless *formal,* dragging, dull, endless, eternal,

everlasting, limitless, long, long-drawn-out, long-winded, loquacious *formal*, monotonous, never-ending, perpetual, prolix *formal*, tedious, unlimited, wearisome, without end
E brief, limited

intermingle *v* amalgamate, blend, combine, commingle *formal*, commix *formal*, fuse, interlace, intermix *formal*, interweave, merge, mix, mix together, mix up
E separate

intermission *n* break, breather *colloq*, breathing-space, cessation *formal*, halt, interlude, interruption, interval, let-up *colloq*, lull, pause, recess, remission, respite, rest, stop, stoppage, suspension

intermittent *adj* broken, cyclic, discontinuous *formal*, erratic, fitful, irregular, occasional, off and on, periodic, spasmodic, sporadic
E constant, continuous

intern *v* confine, detain, hold, hold in custody, imprison, jail
E free, release

internal *adj* **1** *the internal walls*: inner, inside, interior, inward **2** *France's internal affairs*: domestic, home, in-house, local **3** *internal processes of the mind*: emotional, intimate, mental, personal, private, psychological, spiritual, subjective
E **1** external

international *adj* cosmopolitan, general, global, intercontinental, universal, worldwide
E local, national, parochial

internecine *adj* bloody, civil, deadly, destructive, exterminating, family, fatal, fierce, internal, mortal, murderous, ruinous, violent

interplay *n* alternation, exchange, give-and-take *colloq*, interaction, interchange, reciprocation, transposition

interpolate *v* add, insert, intercalate *formal*, interject *formal*, interpose *formal*, introduce, put in

interpolation *n* addition, aside, insert, insertion, intercalation *formal*, interjection *formal*, introduction

interpose *v* **1** *interposed themselves between the Bosnians and the Serbs*: arbitrate, come between, intercede, interfere, intervene, intrude, mediate, put/place between, step in **2** *'I'm not going,' he interposed*: insert, interject, interrupt, introduce, intrude, put in

interpret *v* **1** *the speech was interpreted in a number of ways*: construe *formal*, explain, read, regard, take, understand **2** *this code will take a long time to interpret*: covert, decipher, decode, paraphrase, render, solve, translate **3** *to interpret the law*: clarify, construe *formal*, define, elucidate *formal*, explain, explicate *formal*, expound *formal*, make clear, make sense of, read between the lines *colloq*, throw/shed light on, understand **4** *his music is often difficult to interpret*: comprehend, explain, read, understand

interpretation *n* **1** *my interpretation of the data*: analysis, elucidation *formal*, explanation, explication *formal*, exposition *formal*, expounding *formal*, reading, sense, understanding **2** *interpretation of the scriptures*: anagogy *technical*, analysis, construe *formal*, elucidation *formal*,

exegesis *formal*, explanation, explication *formal*, exposition *formal*, expounding *formal*, reading, version **3** *his memorable interpretation of Hamlet*: depiction, execution, performance, reading, rendering, version **4** *one interpretation of Akhmatova's poem*: deciphering, decoding, paraphrase, rendering, translation, understanding, version

interpretative *adj* clarificatory, exegetic *formal*, explanatory, explicatory *formal*, expository *formal*, hermeneutic *technical*, interpretive

interpreter *n* annotator, commentator, elucidator *formal*, exegete *formal*, expositor *formal*, hermeneutist *technical*, linguist, translator

interrogate *v* cross-examine, cross-question, debrief, examine, give a going-over *colloq*, give a roasting *colloq*, give the third degree *colloq*, grill *colloq*, pump *colloq*, question, quiz

interrogation *n* cross-examination, cross-questioning, examination, going-over *colloq*, grilling *colloq*, inquest, inquiry, inquisition, pumping *colloq*, questioning, quizzing, third degree *colloq*

interrogative *adj* catechetical *formal*, curious, erotetic *formal*, inquiring, inquisitional *formal*, inquisitive, inquisitorial *formal*, interrogatory, probing, questioning, quizzical

interrupt *v* **1** *interrupt a conversation*: barge in *colloq*, barrack, break in, butt in *colloq*, chip in *colloq*, cut in, cut off, cut short, disturb, heckle, intrude, punctuate, put your oar in *colloq* **2** *interrupt an event*: break, cancel, cut off, delay, disconnect, disrupt, disturb, end, halt, hold up, postpone, punctuate, stop, suspend **3** *interrupt a view*: block, cut off, disturb, interfere with, obstruct

interruption *n* **1** *work without interruption*: barging-in *colloq*, breaking-off, butting-in *colloq*, cessation *formal*, cutting-in, delay, disconnection, discontinuance *formal*, disruption, disturbance, interference, intrusion, suspension **2** *no interruptions are allowed*: hitch, impediment, interjection, interpolation *formal*, obstacle, obstruction, question, remark **3** *a brief interruption between acts*: break, breather *colloq*, halt, intermission, interval, let-up *colloq*, pause, recess, stop

intersect *v* bisect, converge, criss-cross, cross, cut across, divide, meet, overlap

intersection *n* crossing, crossroads, interchange, junction, meeting

intersperse *v* dispense, distribute, diversify, dot, interlard *formal*, intermix, interpose *formal*, pepper, scatter, spread, sprinkle

intertwine *v* blend, coil, connect, cross, entwine, interlace, interlink, interweave, interwind, link together, mix, twine, twirl, twist, weave

interval *n* **1** *a short interval before we got underway again*: break, breather *colloq*, breathing-space *colloq*, delay, gap, interim, interlude, intermission, lull, meantime, meanwhile, pause, period, recess, rest, space, time, wait **2** *intervals of six feet or so*: distance, gap, opening, space **3** *intervals of five thousand years*: period, season, spell, time

intervene *v* **1** *the government intervened in the dispute:* arbitrate, intercede, interfere, interrupt, intrude, involve yourself in, mediate, negotiate, step in **2** *bad weather intervened:* arise, befall *formal*, come to pass, elapse *formal*, happen, occur, pass

intervening *adj* between, interjacent *formal*, interposing *formal*, intervenient *formal*, mediate *formal*

intervention *n* agency, arbitration, intercession, interference, interruption, intrusion, involvement, mediation, negotiation, stepping-in

interview *n* **1** *a job interview:* appraisal, assessment, evaluation, meeting, oral examination, viva **2** *an interview with the President:* audience, conference, consultation, dialogue, discussion, press conference, talk
♦ *v* **1** *interviewed by the police:* cross-examine, cross-question, interrogate, question, quiz **2** *two candidates were interviewed for the job:* assess, evaluate, examine, vet

interviewer *n* appraiser, assessor, correspondent, evaluator, examiner, inquisitor, interlocutor *formal*, interrogant *formal*, interrogator, investigator, questioner, reporter

interweave *v* blend, braid, coil, connect, criss-cross, cross, entwine, interconnect, interlace, interlink, interlock, intermingle, intertangle, intertwine, intertwist, interwind, interwork, interwreathe, knit, link together, mix, reticulate *formal*, splice, twine, twist, weave

intestinal *adj* abdominal, coeliac *technical*, duodenal, enteric, gastric, ileac, internal, stomachic *formal*, visceral

intestines *n* bowels, colon, entrails, guts, innards *colloq*, insides, offal, viscera, vitals

intimacy *n* **1** *the intimacy of their friendship:* affection, close relationship, closeness, confidence, confidentiality, familiarity, friendship, love, privacy, understanding, warmth **2** *intimacy between man and wife:* carnal knowledge, coition *formal*, coitus *formal*, copulation, going to bed with someone, intimate relations, love-making, sexual intercourse, sexual relations, sleeping with someone
☲ **1** distance

intimate¹ *adj* **1** *an intimate atmosphere:* affectionate, bosom, cherished, chummy *colloq*, close, cosy, dear, familiar, friendly, informal, matey *colloq*, near, pally *colloq*, thick *colloq*, tight *colloq*, warm **2** *an intimate conversation:* confidential, innermost, internal, personal, private, secret **3** *intimate knowledge of art:* deep, detailed, exhaustive, in-depth, penetrating, profound, thorough
☲ **1** cold, distant, unfriendly **3** superficial
♦ *n* associate, best friend, bosom friend, buddy *colloq*, chum *colloq*, close friend, confidant(e), crony *colloq*, friend, mate *colloq*, pal *colloq*
☲ stranger

intimate² *v* **1** *he intimated their decision to go:* announce, communicate, declare, hint, impart, imply, insinuate, let it be known, make known, signal, state, tell **2** *intimated that he was thinking of leaving:* allude, hint, imply, indicate, insinuate, suggest

intimately *adv* **1** *they got to know each other intimately:* affectionately, closely, familiarly, personally, tenderly, warmly **2** *we were now intimately connected:* confidentially, confidingly, privately **3** *she knew his music intimately:* deeply, exhaustively, fully, in detail, inside out, thoroughly
☲ **1** coldly, distantly **3** superficially

intimation *n* **1** *a public intimation of what will be in the manifesto:* announcement, communication, declaration, notice, reference, reminder, signal, statement, warning **2** *not even an intimation that she might leave:* allusion, hint, implication, indication, inkling, insinuation, suggestion

intimidate *v* alarm, appal, blackmail, browbeat, bulldoze, bully, coerce, compel, cow, daunt, dismay, domineer, extort, frighten, get at *colloq*, lean on *colloq*, menace, overawe, pressure, pressurize, put the frighteners on *colloq*, put the screws on *colloq*, scare, subdue, terrify, terrorize, threaten, turn the heat on *colloq*, twist someone's arm *colloq*, tyrannize, warn off

intimidation *n* arm-twisting *colloq*, big stick *colloq*, browbeating, bullying, coercion, compulsion, domineering, fear, frighteners *colloq*, frightening, menaces, pressure, screws *colloq*, terrifying, terror, terrorization, terrorizing, threatening, threatening behaviour, threats, tyrannization
☲ persuasion

intolerable *adj* awful *colloq*, detestable, dreadful *colloq*, impossible, insufferable, insupportable, loathsome, more than you can bear, the end *colloq*, the last straw *colloq*, the limit *colloq*, the straw that broke the camel's back *colloq*, too bad *colloq*, unacceptable, unbearable, unendurable
☲ tolerable

intolerance *n* ageism, anti-Semitism, bigotry, chauvinism, discrimination, dogmatism, extremism, fanaticism, illiberality, impatience, insularity, jingoism, narrow-mindedness, narrowness, opinionativeness, prejudice, racialism, racism, sexism, small-mindedness, uncharitableness, xenophobia
☲ tolerance

intolerant *adj* ageist, anti-Semitic, biased, bigoted, chauvinistic, discriminating, dogmatic, extremist, fanatical, illiberal, impatient, insular, jingoistic, narrow, narrow-minded, one-sided, opinionated, parochial, partisan, prejudiced, provincial, racialist, racist, sexist, small-minded, uncharitable, xenophobic
☲ tolerant

intonation *n* accentuation, cadence, emphasis, inflection, lilt, modulation, pitch, stress, timbre, tone

intone *v* chant, croon, declaim *formal*, enunciate, intonate, monotone, pronounce, recite, say, sing, speak, utter, voice

intoxicate *v* **1** *enough cider to intoxicate a rugby team:* befuddle, fuddle, inebriate *formal*, make drunk, stupefy **2** *his power intoxicated her:* animate, elate, enthuse, excite, exhilarate, inflame, inspire, stimulate, thrill

intoxicated *adj* **1** *intoxicated in public:* bevvied *colloq*, bibulous *colloq*, blind drunk *colloq*, blotto *colloq*, bombed *slang*, canned *slang*, crapulent *formal*, drunk, drunk as a lord/newt *colloq*,

drunken, happy *colloq*, have had a few *colloq*, inebriated *formal*, legless *colloq*, lit up *slang*, loaded *slang*, merry *colloq*, one over the eight *colloq*, paralytic *slang*, pickled *colloq*, pissed *slang*, plastered *colloq*, roaring drunk *colloq*, sloshed *slang*, smashed *slang*, soused *colloq*, sozzled *colloq*, squiffy *colloq*, stewed *slang*, stoned *slang*, tanked up *slang*, the worse for drink *colloq*, tiddly *colloq*, tight *colloq*, tipsy *colloq*, under the influence, under the table *colloq*, well-oiled *colloq*, woozy *colloq* **2** *intoxicated by success:* carried away *colloq*, elated, enthusiastic, excited, exhilarated, in high spirits, moved, stimulated, stirred, thrilled, worked up
◪ 1 sober

intoxicating *adj* **1** *intoxicating liquor:* alcoholic, going to your head *colloq*, inebriant *formal*, stimulant, strong **2** *the atmosphere is intoxicating:* dramatic, enthralling, exciting, exhilarating, heady, inspiring, moving, rousing, stimulating, stirring, thrilling
◪ 1 sobering

intoxication *n* **1** *in a state of intoxication:* alcoholism, bibulousness *colloq*, crapulence *formal*, debauchery, dipsomania, drunkenness, hard/serious drinking, inebriation *formal*, inebriety *formal*, insobriety *formal*, intemperance, methysis *technical*, tipsiness *colloq* **2** *the intoxication of success:* animation, elation, enthusiasm, euphoria, excitement, exhilaration, pleasure, rapture, stimulation, thrill
◪ 1 sobriety

intractability *n* awkwardness, cantankerousness, contrariness, incorrigibility, indiscipline, obduracy *formal*, obstinacy, perverseness, perversity, pig-headedness, stubbornness, unamenability, uncontrollableness, unco-operativeness, ungovernableness, unmanageableness, waywardness
◪ amenability

intractable *adj* **1** *intractable disputes:* awkward, difficult, insoluble, unmanageable **2** *an intractable customer:* awkward, cantankerous, contrary, difficult, disobedient, fractious, headstrong, intransigent *formal*, obdurate *formal*, obstinate, perverse, pig-headed, refractory *formal*, self-willed, stubborn, unamenable, unbending, uncontrollable, unco-operative, undisciplined, ungovernable, unruly, unyielding, wayward, wild, wilful
◪ 2 amenable

intransigent *adj* determined, hardline, immovable, implacable, inexorable, intractable *formal*, irreconcilable, obdurate *formal*, obstinate, relentless, rigid, stubborn, tenacious, tough, unamenable, unbending, unbudgeable, uncompromising, unpersuadable, unrelenting, unyielding, uppity *colloq*
◪ amenable, flexible

intrepid *adj* audacious, bold, brave, courageous, daring, dauntless, doughty *formal*, fearless, gallant, gritty *colloq*, gutsy *colloq*, heroic, lion-hearted, plucky, spirited, spunky *colloq*, stalwart, stout-hearted, undaunted, undismayed, unflinching, valiant, valorous *formal*
◪ afraid, cowardly, timid

intrepidness *n* audacity, boldness, bravery, courage, daring, dauntlessness, doughtiness

formal, fearlessness, fortitude *formal*, gallantry, guts *colloq*, heroism, intrepidity, lion-heartedness, nerve, pluck, prowess, spirit, stout-heartedness, undauntedness, valour
◪ cowardice, timidity

intricacy *n* complexedness, complexity, complexness, complication, convolution(s) *formal*, elaborateness, entanglement, intricateness, involution, involvement, sophistication
◪ simplicity, straightforwardness

intricate *adj* baffling, complex, complicated, convoluted *formal*, difficult, elaborate, enigmatic, entangled, fancy, involved, knotty, ornate, perplexing, puzzling, ravelled, rococo, sophisticated, tangled, tortuous, twisty
◪ plain, simple, straightforward

intrigue *n* **1** *political intrigues:* artifice, cabal, collusion *formal*, conniving, conspiracy, dodge *colloq*, double-dealing, machination *formal*, manoeuvre, plot, ruse, scheme, sharp practice *colloq*, stratagem, trickery, wile **2** *unaware of her husband's intrigues:* affair, amour, intimacy, liaison, love affair, romance
♦ *v* **1** *the chess match intrigued him:* absorb, arouse your curiosity, attract, captivate, charm, draw, fascinate, interest, pull, puzzle, rivet, tantalize **2** *the Cabinet was intriguing behind her back:* connive, conspire, machinate *formal*, manoeuvre, plot, scheme
◪ 1 bore

intriguer *n* collaborator, conniver, conspirator, intrigant(e), Machiavellian, machinator *formal*, plotter, schemer, wangler *colloq*, wheeler-dealer *colloq*, wire-puller *colloq*

intriguing *adj* absorbing, appealing, attractive, beguiling, captivating, charming, compelling, diverting, exciting, fascinating, interesting, puzzling, riveting, tantalizing, titillating
◪ boring, dull, uninteresting

intrinsic *adj* basic, built-in, central, congenital, constitutional, elemental, essential, fundamental, genuine, inborn, inbred, in-built, indigenous, inherent, interior, inward, native, natural, underlying
◪ extrinsic

introduce *v* **1** *she introduced many reforms:* begin, bring in, commence *formal*, develop, establish, found, inaugurate, initiate, institute, launch, open, organize, originate, put/set in motion, start, usher in **2** *he'll introduce the idea at the meeting:* advance, offer, propose, put forward, submit, suggest **3** *she introduced me to her yesterday:* acquaint, announce, familiarize, present **4** *a fanfare introduces the work:* begin, commence *formal*, lead in, lead into, precede, preface, start
◪ 1 conclude, end **2** remove, take away **4** conclude, end, finish

introduction *n* **1** *the introduction of the legislation:* beginning, commencement *formal*, debut, development, establishment, inauguration, initiation, institution, launch, organization, origination, presentation, start **2** *wrote an introduction to his volume of poems:* exordium *formal*, foreword, front matter, intro *colloq*, lead-in, opening, overture, preamble, preface, preliminaries, prelude, proem *formal*, prolegomenon *formal*, prologue **3** *brief*

introductions before the meeting started: acquainting, announcement, familiarization, presentation **4** *an introduction to Latin grammar:* basics, essentials, first principles, fundamentals, rudiments
F₃ 1 removal, withdrawal **2** appendix, conclusion

introductory *adj* **1** *an introductory course on geometry:* basic, elementary, essential, exordial *formal*, first, fundamental, inaugural, initial, initiatory *formal*, isagogic *formal*, opening, precursory *formal*, prefatory *formal*, preliminary, preparatory, rudimentary **2** *an introductory price of £4.99:* early, initial, opening, starting

introspection *n* brooding, contemplation, heart-searching, introversion, navel-contemplation *colloq*, navel-gazing *colloq*, pensiveness, self-analysis, self-centredness, self-examination, self-observation, soul-searching, thoughtfulness

introspective *adj* brooding, contemplative, introverted, inward-looking, meditative, musing, pensive, reserved, self-absorbed, self-analysing, self-centred, self-examining, self-observing, subjective, thoughtful, withdrawn
F₃ outward-looking

introverted *adj* introspective, inward-looking, quiet, reserved, self-absorbed, self-centred, self-examining, shy, withdrawn
F₃ extroverted

intrude *v* **1** *she kept intruding with silly questions:* barge in *colloq*, butt in *colloq*, chip in *colloq*, interfere, interject *formal*, interrupt, meddle, obtrude *formal* **2** *fans intruding onto the pitch:* encroach, gatecrash *colloq*, infringe, invade, trespass, violate
F₃ 1 stand back

intruder *n* burglar, gatecrasher *colloq*, housebreaker, infiltrator, interloper *formal*, invader, pilferer, prowler, raider, robber, thief, trespasser, unwelcome guest

intrusion *n* encroachment, gatecrashing *colloq*, incursion *formal*, infringement, interference, interruption, invasion, meddling, obtrusion *formal*, trespass, violation
F₃ withdrawal

intrusive *adj* **1** *security cameras were an intrusive presence:* disturbing, interfering, invasive, obtrusive, unwanted, unwelcome **2** *intrusive reporters asking questions:* annoying, forward, go-getting *colloq*, impertinent, importunate *formal*, interfering, interrupting, irritating, meddlesome, nosy *colloq*, officious, presumptuous, pushy *colloq*, snooping *colloq*, trespassing, troublesome, uninvited, unwanted, unwelcome
F₃ 1 unintrusive **2** welcome

intuition *n* **1** *my intuition told me something was wrong:* discernment, extrasensory perception, insight, instinct, perception, presentiment *formal*, sixth sense **2** *let your intuitions guide you:* feeling, feeling in your bones *colloq*, gut feeling *colloq*, hunch, insight, instinct
F₃ 1 reasoning

intuitive *adj* automatic, inborn, innate, instinctive, intuitional, involuntary, spontaneous, unlearned, untaught
F₃ reasoned

inundate *v* **1** *inundated by the rising tide:* deluge, drown, engulf, flood, immerse, overflow, saturate, soak, submerge, swamp **2** *inundated with inquiries:* bury, engulf, flood, overburden, overrun, overwhelm, submerge, swamp

inundation *n* **1** *a farmhouse threatened by inundation:* deluge, flood, spate, tidal wave, torrent **2** *an inundation of bills:* deluge, excess, flood, glut, surplus, tidal wave, torrent
F₃ 2 trickle

inure *v* acclimatize, accustom, desensitize, familiarize, habituate *formal*, harden, strengthen, temper, toughen, train

invade *v* **1** *invade a country:* assault, attack, burst in, descend on, enter (by force), infest, infiltrate, maraud, march into, occupy, overrun, penetrate, pervade, pillage, plunder, raid, seize, storm, swarm over, take over **2** *invade someone's privacy:* encroach, infringe, interrupt, intrude, obtrude *formal*, trespass, violate
F₃ 1 evacuate, withdraw

invader *n* aggressor, assailant, attacker, infringer, intruder, marauder, pillager, plunderer, raider, trespasser

invalid¹ *n* convalescent, patient, sufferer, valetudinarian *formal*
♦ *adj* ailing, bedridden, debilitated *formal*, disabled, feeble, frail, ill, infirm, poorly, sick, sickly, unwell, valetudinarian *formal*, weak
F₃ healthy

invalid² *adj* **1** *an invalid argument:* baseless, erroneous, fallacious *formal*, false, groundless, ill-founded, illogical, incorrect, irrational, mistaken, unacceptable, unfounded, unjustified, unscientific, unsound, unsubstantiated, untenable, unwarranted, weak, wrong **2** *the result was declared invalid:* abolished, cancelled, illegal, inoperative *formal*, null, null and void, nullified *formal*, overturned, quashed, rescinded *formal*, revoked *formal*, void, worthless
F₃ 1 sound, valid **2** binding, legal

invalidate *v* abrogate *formal*, annul, cancel, discredit, negate, nullify *formal*, overrule, overthrow, quash, rescind *formal*, revoke *formal*, terminate *formal*, undermine, undo, veto, vitiate *formal*, void, weaken
F₃ validate

invalidity *n* fallaciousness *formal*, fallacy *formal*, falsity, illogicality, inconsistency, incorrectness, irrationality, sophism, speciousness, unsoundness, voidness

invaluable *adj* costly, incalculable, indispensable, inestimable, precious, priceless, useful, valuable
F₃ cheap, worthless

invariable *adj* changeless, consistent, constant, fixed, habitual, immutable *formal*, inflexible, invariant *formal*, permanent, regular, rigid, set, stable, steady, unalterable, unchangeable, unchanging, uniform, unvarying, unwavering
F₃ changeable, variable

invariably *adv* always, consistently, constantly, habitually, inevitably, regularly, repeatedly, unfailingly, without exception, without fail
F₃ never

invasion *n* **1** *an invasion of a country:* attack, breach, foray, incursion *formal*, infiltration, occupation, offensive, onslaught, penetration,

raid, storming **2** *invasion of privacy:*
encroachment, infringement, interference,
interruption, intrusion, violation
🔁 **1** evacuation, withdrawal

invective *n* abuse, berating *formal*, castigation
formal, censure *formal*, contumely *formal*,
denunciation, diatribe, fulmination *formal*,
obloquy *formal*, philippic *formal*, rebuke,
recrimination, reprimand, reproach, revilement
formal, sarcasm, scolding, tirade, tongue-
lashing, vilification *formal*, vituperation *formal*
🔁 praise

inveigh *v* berate *formal*, blame, castigate *formal*,
censure *formal*, condemn, criticize, denounce,
expostulate *formal*, fulminate *formal*, lambast
formal, rail, recriminate, reproach, scold, sound
off, tongue-lash, upbraid, vituperate *formal*
🔁 praise

inveigle *v* allure, bamboozle *colloq*, beguile,
cajole, coax, con *colloq*, decoy, ensnare, entice,
entrap, lead on, lure, manipulate, manoeuvre,
persuade, seduce, sweet-talk *colloq*, wheedle,
wile

invent *v* **1** *it was invented in the 17th century:* be
the brainchild of, coin, come up with, conceive,
contrive, create, design, devise, discover, dream
up, fabricate, formulate, frame, hit upon,
improvise, innovate, originate, pioneer, think up
2 *invent an excuse:* concoct, cook up, dream up,
imagine, make up, trump up

invention *n* **1** *her latest invention:* brainchild,
construction, contrivance, creation, design,
development, device, discovery, gadget,
innovation, machine, system **2** *the invention of the
steam engine:* contriving, creation, design,
development, discovery, innovation **3** *his excuse
was pure invention:* concoction, deceit, fabrication,
fake, falsehood, falsification, fantasy, fib *colloq*,
fiction, figment, forgery, lie, myth, tall story
colloq, untruth **4** *she had huge powers of invention:*
artistry, creativity, genius, gift, imagination,
ingenuity, innovation, inspiration, inventiveness,
originality, resourcefulness, skill, talent
🔁 **3** truth

inventive *adj* artistic, clever, creative, fertile,
gifted, imaginative, ingenious, innovative,
inspired, original, resourceful, skilful, talented

inventor *n* architect, author, creator, designer,
developer, deviser, discoverer, engineer, father,
framer, innovator, maker, mother, originator,
producer, scientist

inventory *n* account, catalogue, checklist,
description, equipment, file, list, listing, record,
register, roll, roster, schedule, stock, supply,
tally

inverse *adj* contrary, converse, counter,
inverted, obverse, opposite, other, reverse,
reversed, transposed, upside down
♦ *n* contrary, converse, obverse, opposite,
reverse, the other side of the coin *colloq*

inversion *n* antithesis *formal*, contraposition
formal, contrariety *formal*, contrary, converse,
opposite, reversal, reverse, transposal,
transposition

invert *v* capsize, overturn, reverse, transpose,
turn around, turn back to front, turn inside out,
turn turtle, turn upside down, upset, upturn
🔁 right

invertebrate

Invertebrates include:
sponges: calcareous, glass, horny; *jellyfish, corals
and sea anemones:* Portuguese man-of-war, box
jellyfish, sea wasp, dead-men's fingers, sea
pansy, sea gooseberry, Venus's girdle;
echinoderms: sea lily, feather star, starfish,
crown-of-thorns, brittle star, sea urchin, sand
dollar, sea cucumber; *worms:* annelid worm,
arrow worm, blood fluke, bristle worm,
earthworm, eelworm, flatworm, fluke,
hookworm, leech, liver fluke, lugworm,
peanut worm, pinworm, ragworm,
ribbonworm, roundworm, sea mouse,
tapeworm, threadworm; *crustaceans:* acorn
barnacle, barnacle, brine shrimp, crayfish,
daphnia, fairy shrimp, fiddler crab, fish louse,
goose barnacle, hermit crab, krill, lobster,
mantis shrimp, mussel shrimp, pill bug,
prawn, sand hopper, seed shrimp, spider crab,
spiny lobster, tadpole shrimp, water flea,
whale louse, woodlouse; centipede, millipede.
See also **butterfly, insect, mollusc, moth**

---

invest *v* **1** *investing money in property:* fund, lay
out, put in, sink, spend, subsidize **2** *invest time/
energy in something:* contribute, dedicate, devote,
give, put in, spend **3** *he was invested with only
limited powers:* authorize, bestow *formal*, confer
formal, empower, endow, entrust, give, grant,
provide, sanction, supply, vest **4** *invest a person
in authority:* inaugurate, induct, install, ordain

investigate *v* analyse, check out *colloq*,
consider, delve into, examine, explore, give the
once-over *colloq*, go into, inquire into, inspect,
look into, probe, research, scrutinize, search, see
how the land lies *colloq*, see which way the wind
is blowing *colloq*, sift, study, suss out *colloq*

investigation *n* analysis, consideration,
examination, exploration, fact-finding mission/
visit, hearing, inquest, inquiry, inspection,
probe, research, review, scrutiny, search, sifting,
study, survey

investigative *adj* analytical, exploratory, fact-
finding, heuristic *formal*, inspecting,
investigating, research, researching, zetetic
formal

investigator *n* analyser, analyst, detective,
examiner, explorer, inquirer, inspector, private
detective, private eye *colloq*, prober, questioner,
researcher, reviewer, scrutineer, scrutinizer,
searcher, sleuth *colloq*

investiture *n* admission, coronation,
enthronement, inauguration, induction,
installation, instatement, investing, investment,
ordination

investment *n* **1** *my investments are doing nicely:*
asset, capital, cash, finance, funds, money,
property, reserve, resources, savings, wealth
2 *investment in this sector is now more profitable:*
backing, contribution, expenditure, financing,
funding, investing, outlay, speculation **3** *an
investment of £40,000:* capital, concern, interest,
outlay, share, stake, stock, transaction, venture
4 *a wise investment:* acquisition, asset, buy, risk

inveterate *adj* **1** *an inveterate drinker:* addicted,
chronic, confirmed, established, habitual, hard-
core, hardened, incorrigible, incurable, inured,
irreformable **2** *an inveterate socialist:* diehard,

dyed-in-the-wool, entrenched, established, long-standing, obstinate

𝄐 1 impermanent

invidious *adj* **1** *in an invidious position:* awkward, difficult, hateful, objectionable, offensive, slighting, undesirable, unpleasant **2** *an invidious comparison to make:* discriminating, discriminatory, unfair, unjust

𝄐 1 pleasant **2** fair

invigorate *v* animate, brace, buck up *colloq*, energize, enliven, excite, exhilarate, fortify *formal*, freshen, give a new lease of life to *colloq*, inspire, liven up, motivate, pep up *colloq*, perk up *colloq*, quicken, refresh, rejuvenate, revitalize, rouse, soup up *colloq*, stimulate, strengthen, vitalize

𝄐 dishearten, tire, weary

invigorating *adj* animating, bracing, energizing, exhilarating, fresh, generous, healthful, inspiriting *formal*, refreshing, rejuvenating, restorative, salubrious *formal*, stimulating, tonic, uplifting, vivifying

𝄐 disheartening, tiring, wearying

invincible *adj* impenetrable, impregnable, indestructible, indomitable *formal*, insuperable, invulnerable, unassailable, unbeatable, unconquerable, undefeatable, unshakable, unsurmountable, unyielding

𝄐 beatable, surmountable

inviolability *n* holiness, inalienability, inviolableness, inviolacy, invulnerability, sacredness, sacrosanctness, sanctity

𝄐 violability

inviolable *adj* hallowed, holy, inalienable, intemerate *formal*, sacred, sacrosanct, unalterable, untouchable

𝄐 alienable, violable

inviolate *adj* complete, entire, intact, intemerate *formal*, pure, sacred, stainless, unbroken, undamaged, undefiled, undisturbed, unharmed, unhurt, uninjured, unpolluted, unprofaned, unspoiled, unstained, unsullied, untouched, virgin, whole

𝄐 sullied

invisible *adj* **1** *so small that it is almost invisible:* imperceivable, imperceptible, indiscernible, indistinguishable, infinitesimal, microscopic, undetectable, unseen **2** *the problems exist but are largely invisible:* concealed, disguised, hidden, inconspicuous, out of sight, unnoticed, unobserved, unseen

𝄐 1 visible

invitation *n* **1** *an invitation to dinner:* bidding, call, overture, petition, request, solicitation *formal*, summons, welcome **2** *almost an invitation to break the law:* allurement, appeal, attraction, bait, challenge, come-on *colloq*, draw, encouragement, enticement, incitement, inducement, lure, provocation, temptation

invite *v* **1** *he invited her to the wedding:* ask, bid, have round/over, request the pleasure of someone's company *formal*, summon **2** *the council is inviting applications from contractors:* appeal, ask, ask for, bid, call, encourage, look for, petition, request *formal*, seek, solicit *formal*, welcome **3** *this will only invite more criticism:* allure, attract, bring

on, cause, draw, entice, generate, induce, lead, tempt

inviting *adj* agreeable, alluring, appealing, attractive, beguiling, bewitching, captivating, delightful, enchanting, engaging, enticing, entrancing, fascinating, intriguing, irresistible, pleasant, pleasing, seductive, tantalizing, tempting, welcoming, winning

𝄐 disagreeable, off-putting *colloq*, unappealing, unattractive, uninviting, unpleasant

invocation *n* **1** *an invocation for peace:* appeal, beseeching *formal*, conjuration *formal*, entreaty *formal*, imploration *formal*, petition, request *formal*, solicitation *formal* **2** *an invocation to God:* epiclesis *formal*, prayer, supplication *formal*

invoice *n* account bill, charges, reckoning, statement of account

invoke *v* **1** *invoke God for help:* appeal to, beg, beseech *formal*, call upon, conjure *formal*, entreat *formal*, implore, imprecate *formal*, petition, pray, request *formal*, solicit *formal*, supplicate *formal* **2** *invoke a law:* have recourse to, make use of, resort to, turn to

involuntary *adj* **1** *an involuntary movement:* automatic, blind, conditioned, forced, impulsive, instinctive, mechanical, reflex, spontaneous, unconscious, uncontrolled, unintentional, unthinking **2** *involuntary redundancies:* against your wishes, coerced, compelled, forced, reluctant, unwilling

𝄐 1 deliberate, intentional

involve *v* **1** *involving loss of earnings:* affect, assume, comprehend *formal*, concern, cover, denote *formal*, embrace *formal*, encompass, entail, imply, include, incorporate, mean, necessitate *formal*, presuppose, require, take in **2** *got involved by accident:* associate, cause to take part, connect, draw in, embroil, implicate, incriminate, inculpate *formal*, let yourself in for, mix up **3** *completely involved in her career:* absorb, engage, engross, grip, hold, interest, occupy, preoccupy, rivet

𝄐 1 exclude

involved *adj* **1** *those involved in the project:* associated, concerned, participating, taking part **2** *she's not involved in the fraud at all:* caught up, implicated, in on *colloq*, incriminated, inculpated *formal*, mixed up **3** *an involved explanation:* complex, complicated, confused, confusing, convoluted *formal*, difficult, elaborate, intricate, jumbled, knotty, tangled, tortuous

𝄐 1 uninvolved **2** uninvolved **3** simple

involvement *n* association, attachment, concern, connection, contribution, entanglement, implication, interest, part, participation, responsibility, share

invulnerability *n* impenetrability, impregnability, insusceptibility, invincibility, inviolability, safety, security, strength, unassailability

𝄐 vulnerability

invulnerable *adj* impenetrable, indestructible, invincible, safe, secure, unassailable

𝄐 vulnerable

inward *adj* **1** *an inward sense of relief:* confidential, hidden, inmost, inner, innermost, inside, interior,

internal, intimate, personal, private, secret
2 *inward trajectory:* entering, inbound, incoming
🖪 **1** external, outward **2** outward

inwardly *adv* at heart, deep down, deep inside you, in your heart of hearts, inside, privately, secretly, to yourself, within
🖪 externally, outwardly

iota *n* atom, bit, fraction, grain, hint, jot, mite, morsel, particle, scrap, speck, tad *colloq*, trace, whit

irascibility *n* bad temper, cantankerousness, crabbiness *colloq*, crossness, edginess *colloq*, fieriness, ill-temper, impatience, irritability, irritation, petulance, shortness, snappishness, testiness, touchiness
🖪 placidness

irascible *adj* bad-tempered, cantankerous, choleric, crabbed *colloq*, crabby *colloq*, cross, hasty, hot-tempered, ill-natured, ill-tempered, iracund *formal*, iracundulous *formal*, irritable, narky *colloq*, petulant, prickly *colloq*, querulous *formal*, quick-tempered, short-tempered, testy, touchy
🖪 placid

irate *adj* angry, annoyed, enraged, exasperated, fuming, furious, incensed, indignant, infuriated, irritated, livid, mad *colloq*, raging, ranting, up in arms, vexed, worked up
🖪 calm, composed

ire *n* anger, annoyance, choler, displeasure, exasperation, fury, indignation, passion, rage, wrath
🖪 calmness

iridescent *adj* dazzling, glittering, multicoloured, opalescent *formal*, pearly, polychromatic, prismatic, rainbow, rainbow-coloured, rainbow-like, shimmering, shot, sparkling, variegated *formal*

irk *v* aggravate *colloq*, anger, annoy, bug *colloq*, disgust, distress, exasperate, gall, get, get to, hassle *colloq*, incense, infuriate, irritate, make someone's blood boil *colloq*, miff *colloq*, nettle, peeve *colloq*, provoke, put out, rile, rub up the wrong way *colloq*, ruffle, vex, weary
🖪 please

irksome *adj* aggravating *colloq*, annoying, boring, bothersome, burdensome, disagreeable, exasperating, infuriating, irritating, tedious, tiresome, troublesome, trying, vexatious, vexing, wearisome
🖪 pleasing

iron *adj* adamant, determined, firm, hard, inflexible, rigid, steely, strong, tough
🖪 pliable, weak
♦ *v* flatten, press, smooth
▶ **iron out** clear up, deal with, eliminate, eradicate, get rid of, harmonize, put right, reconcile, resolve, settle, sort out, straighten out

ironic *adj* **1** *tiring of his ironic remarks:* contemptuous, derisive, ironical, mocking, rich *colloq*, ridiculing, sarcastic, sardonic, satirical, scoffing, scornful, sneering, wry **2** *it's ironic that the people who make this programme would never watch it:* absurd, ambiguous, incongruous, paradoxical

irons *n* bonds, chains, fetters, manacles, shackles, trammels

irony *n* **1** *his use of heavy irony:* mockery, ridicule, sarcasm, satire, scorn **2** *the irony is I thought she'd*

help me: ambiguity, contrariness, incongruity *formal*, paradox

irradiate *v* brighten, enlighten, expose, illume, illuminate, illumine, light up, lighten, radiate, shine on

irrational *adj* **1** *irrational opposition to the reform:* absurd, arbitrary, groundless, illogical, implausible, inconsistent, invalid, nonsensical, ridiculous, unreasonable, unsound **2** *her behaviour became irrational:* crazy, foolish, insane, ridiculous, senseless, silly, wild
🖪 **1** rational **2** reasonable

irrationality *n* absurdity, groundlessness, illogicality, insanity, lunacy, madness, preposterousness, ridiculousness, senselessness, unreason, unreasonableness, unsoundness
🖪 rationality

irreconcilable *adj* **1** *an irreconcilable clash of personalities:* hardline, implacable, inexorable, inflexible, intransigent *formal*, unappeasable **2** *irreconcilable views:* at odds, clashing, conflicting, contradictory, contrary, incompatible, incongruous *formal*, inconsistent, opposed, opposite
🖪 **1** reconcilable

irrecoverable *adj* irreclaimable, irredeemable, irremediable, irreparable, irretrievable, lost, unrecoverable, unsalvageable, unsavable
🖪 recoverable

irrefutable *adj* beyond doubt/question, certain, decisive, definite, incontestable, incontrovertible, indisputable, indubitable, positive, sure, unanswerable, undeniable, unquestionable

irregular *adj* **1** *an irregular surface:* asymmetric, bumpy, crooked, jagged, lopsided, lumpy, pitted, ragged, rough, uneven **2** *a very irregular bus service:* disorderly, disorganized, erratic, fitful, fluctuating, fragmentary, haphazard, inconsistent, intermittent, occasional, random, shaky, spasmodic, sporadic, uneven, unmethodical, unsteady, unsystematic, variable, wavering **3** *an irregular heartbeat:* aberrant, abnormal, anomalous, exceptional, extraordinary, freak, improper, odd, out of order, peculiar, strange, unconventional, unofficial, unorthodox, unusual **4** *irregular financial dealings:* cheating, deceitful, dishonest, false, fraudulent, immoderate, improper, indecent, lawless, unprincipled
🖪 **1** level, smooth, uniform **2** regular **3** conventional **4** honest

irregularity *n* **1** *the irregularities of the playing surface:* asymmetry, bumpiness, crookedness, jaggedness, lopsidedness, lumpiness, raggedness, roughness, unevenness **2** *temperature irregularities:* disorderliness, disorganization, fitfulness, fluctuation, haphazardness, inconsistency, inconstancy, intermittence, occasionalness, patchiness, randomness, spasm, uncertainty, unpunctuality, unsteadiness, variability, wavering **3** *heartbeat irregularity:* aberration, abnormality, anomaly, breach, deviation, eccentricity, freak, oddity, peculiarity, singularity *formal*, unconventionality, unorthodoxy **4** *tax irregularities:* cheating, deceit, dishonesty, fraud, fraudulence, lawlessness, malpractice

≠ 1 levelness, smoothness **2** regularity **3** conventionality

irregularly *adv* anyhow, by/in fits and starts *colloq*, disconnectedly, eccentrically, erratically, fitfully, haphazardly, intermittently, jerkily, now and again, occasionally, off and on, spasmodically, unevenly, unmethodically **≠** regularly

irrelevance *n* inappositeness *formal*, inaptness, inconsequence, innappropriateness, irrelevancy, red herring *colloq*, unimportance, unrelatedness **≠** bearing, relevance

irrelevant *adj* beside/off the point, having no bearing, immaterial, inapplicable, inapposite *formal*, inappropriate, inapt, inconsequent, making no difference *colloq*, neither here nor there *colloq*, not coming into it *colloq*, not matter *colloq*, out of place, peripheral, tangential, unconnected, unimportant, unrelated **≠** relevant

irreligious *adj* agnostic, atheistic, blasphemous, free-thinking, godless, heathen, heathenish, heretical, iconoclastic, impious, irreverent, nullifidian *formal*, pagan, profane, rationalistic, sacrilegious, sceptical, sinful, unbelieving, undevout, ungodly, unholy, unreligious, unrighteous **≠** pious, religious

irremediable *adj* deadly, fatal, final, hopeless, incorrigible, incurable, inoperable, irrecoverable, irredeemable, irreparable, irretrievable, irreversible, mortal, remediless, terminal, unmedicinable **≠** remediable

irremovable *adj* durable, fast, fixed, immovable, indestructible, ineradicable, ingrained, inoperable, obdurate *formal*, obstinate, permanent, persistent, rooted, set, stuck **≠** removable

irreparable *adj* incurable, irreclaimable, irrecoverable, irremediable, irretrievable, irreversible, unrepairable **≠** recoverable, remediable

irreplaceable *adj* essential, indispensable, matchless, peerless, precious, priceless, special, unique, unmatched, vital **≠** replaceable

irrepressible *adj* animated, boisterous, bubbly, buoyant, ebullient, effervescent, insuppressible, resilient, uncontainable, uncontrollable, ungovernable, uninhibited, unrestrainable, unstoppable, vivacious

irreproachable *adj* beyond reproach, blameless, faultless, flawless, guiltless, immaculate, impeccable, innocent, irreprehensible, perfect, pure, sinless, spotless, stainless, unblamable, unblemished, unimpeachable **≠** blameworthy, culpable *formal*

irresistible *adj* **1** *irresistible desire:* compelling, forceful, imperative, inescapable, inevitable, inexorable, irrepressible, overpowering, overwhelming, potent, pressing, unavoidable, uncontrollable, unpreventable, urgent **2** *irresistible beauty:* alluring, captivating,

charming, enchanting, enticing, fascinating, ravishing, seductive, tantalizing, tempting **≠ 1** avoidable, resistible **2** repulsive, unattractive

irresolute *adj* ambivalent, dithering, doubtful, dubious, faint-hearted, fickle, fluctuating, half-hearted, hesitant, hesitating, in two minds *colloq*, indecisive, pussyfooting *colloq*, shifting, shilly-shallying *colloq*, (sitting) on the fence *colloq*, tentative, uncertain, undecided, undetermined, unsettled, unstable, unsteady, unsure, vacillating *formal*, variable, wavering, weak **≠** decisive, resolute

irresponsible *adj* carefree, careless, erratic, flighty, heedless, ill-considered, immature, injudicious *formal*, light-hearted, negligent, rash, reckless, scatterbrained, thoughtless, unreliable, untrustworthy, unwise, wild **≠** cautious, dependable, responsible

irretrievable *adj* damned, hopeless, irrecoverable, irredeemable, irremediable, irreparable, irreversible, irrevocable *formal*, lost, unrecallable, unrecoverable, unsalvageable **≠** recoverable, reversible

irreverence *n* **1** *God will punish your irreverence:* blasphemy, godlessness, heresy, impiety, irreligion, profanity, sacrilege, ungodliness **2** *enjoyed his cheeky irreverence:* cheek *colloq*, cheekiness, discourtesy, disrespect, disrespectfulness, flippancy, impertinence, impoliteness, impudence, insolence, levity, mockery, rudeness, sauce *colloq* **≠ 2** reverence

irreverent *adj* **1** *irreverent unbelievers:* blasphemous, godless, heretical, impious, irreligious, profane, sacrilegious, ungodly **2** *an irreverent look at politics:* cheeky *colloq*, discourteous, disrespectful, flippant, impertinent, impolite, impudent, insolent, mocking, rude, saucy *colloq* **≠ 1** reverent **2** deferential, respectful

irreversible *adj* final, incurable, irremediable, irreparable, irretrievable, irrevocable, lasting, permanent, unalterable, unrectifiable **≠** curable, remediable, reversible

irrevocable *adj* changeless, final, fixed, immutable *formal*, invariable, irretrievable, irreversible, predetermined *formal*, settled, unalterable, unchangeable **≠** alterable, flexible, reversible

irrigate *v* dampen, flood, inundate, moisten, soak, spray, sprinkle, water, wet

irritability *n* bad temper, crossness, edge, edginess, fractiousness, fretfulness, grumpiness, hypersensitivity, ill-temper, impatience, irascibility, peevishness, petulance, prickliness, testiness, tetchiness, touchiness **≠** bonhomie, cheerfulness, complacence, good humour

irritable *adj* bad-tempered, cantankerous, crabby *colloq*, cross, crotchety *colloq*, crusty, edgy, fractious, fretful, grumpy, hypersensitive, ill-tempered, impatient, irascible, peevish, prickly, quick-tempered, ratty *colloq*, shirty *colloq*, short, short-tempered, snappish, snappy, stroppy *colloq*, testy, thin-skinned, touchy

☒ cheerful, good-tempered

irritant *n* annoyance, bother, goad, menace, nuisance, pain *colloq*, provocation, thorn in the flesh *colloq*, trouble, vexation
☒ pleasure, sweetness

irritate *v* **1** *his voice irritates me:* aggravate *colloq*, anger, annoy, bother, bug *colloq*, drive crazy/ nuts *colloq*, drive round the bend/up the wall *colloq*, enrage, exasperate, get *colloq*, get on your nerves *colloq*, get under your skin *colloq*, get your back up *colloq*, get your blood up *colloq*, goad, grate, harass, incense, infuriate, irk, jar, nettle, peeve *colloq*, provoke, put out, rile, rouse, rub up the wrong way *colloq*, vex **2** *irritate the skin:* chafe, fret, hurt, inflame, itch, rub, tickle
☒ **1** gratify, please

irritated *adj* angry, annoyed, bothered, cross, discomposed, displeased, edgy, exacerbated *formal*, exasperated, flustered, harassed, impatient, in a huff *colloq*, irked, irritable, miffed *colloq*, narked *colloq*, nettled, peeved *colloq*, piqued, put out *colloq*, ratty *colloq*, riled, roused, ruffled, uptight, vexed
☒ composed, gratified, pleased

irritating *adj* **1** *irritating habits:* aggravating *colloq*, annoying, bothersome, displeasing, disturbing, galling, grating, infuriating, irksome, maddening, nagging, pesky *colloq*, provoking, thorny, tiresome, troublesome, trying, upsetting, vexatious, vexing, worrisome **2** *an irritating cough:* abrasive, chafing, itchy, rubbing, sore, ticklish
☒ **1** pleasant, pleasing

irritation *n* **1** *express your irritation:* aggravation, anger, annoyance, crossness, displeasure, dissatisfaction, exasperation, fury, impatience, indignation, irritability, pique, snappiness, testiness, vexation **2** *it's only a minor irritation:* annoyance, bind *colloq*, bother, disturbance, drag *colloq*, nuisance, pain *colloq*, pain in the neck *colloq*, pest, thorn in the flesh *colloq*, trouble
☒ **1** delight, pleasure, satisfaction

island *n* archipelago, atoll, cay, eyot, holm, isle, islet, key, skerry

---

The world's largest islands include:
Australia, Greenland, New Guinea, Borneo, Madagascar, Sumatra, Baffin (Canada), Honshu (Japan), Great Britain, Victoria (Canada)

---

isolate *v* abstract, alienate, cut off, detach, disconnect, divorce, exclude, insulate, keep apart, maroon, quarantine, remove, seclude, segregate, separate, sequester *formal*, set apart, shut out/away, strand
☒ assimilate, incorporate, integrate

isolated *adj* **1** *an isolated community:* alone, apart, cut off, deserted, detached, God-forsaken, lonely, off the beaten track *colloq*, outlying, out-of-the-way, remote, secluded, segregated, separated, single, solitary, unfrequented **2** *an isolated occurrence:* abnormal, anomalous, atypical, exceptional, freak, single, solitary, special, uncommon, unique, unrelated, untypical, unusual

☒ **1** populous **2** common, typical

isolation *n* aloneness, detachment, exile, loneliness, remoteness, retirement, seclusion, segregation, separateness, separation, solitariness, solitude, withdrawal
☒ contact

issue *n* **1** *several issues to be debated:* affair, argument, concern, controversy, debate, dispute, matter, point, problem, question, subject, topic **2** *an issue of shares:* announcement, broadcast, circulation, delivery, dissemination *formal*, distribution, promulgation *formal*, publication, release, supply, supplying **3** *last week's issue of the magazine:* copy, edition, impression, instalment, number, printing, version **4** *the scheme was carried to a successful issue:* conclusion, consequence, effect, finale, outcome, pay-off *colloq*, result, upshot **5** *he died without issue:* children, descendants, family, heirs, offspring, progeny, scions *formal*, seed, successors, young **6** *an issue of blood:* discharge, effluence *formal*, effusion *formal*, gush, jet, outflow, rush, spurt
♦ *v* **1** *the stamps will be issued in December:* announce, broadcast, circulate, deal out, deliver, disseminate *formal*, distribute, give out, proclaim, promulgate *formal*, publish, put out, release, supply **2** *music issued from the speakers:* arise, burst forth, emanate, emerge, flow, gush, originate, proceed, result, rise, spring, stem **3** *blood issues from his wound:* burst forth, come out, discharge, emanate, emerge, emit, exude, flow, gush, ooze, produce, seep

itch *v* **1** *my nose itches:* crawl, irritate, prickle, tickle, tingle **2** *be itching to do something:* ache, burn, crave, die, hanker, long, pine, yearn
♦ *n* **1** *I've got an itch:* irritation, itchiness, prickling, tickle, tingling **2** *an insatiable itch to play again:* ache, burning, craving, desire, eagerness, hankering, hunger, keenness, longing, thirst, yearning

itching *adj* aching, avid, burning, dying, eager, greedy, hankering, impatient, inquisitive, longing, raring

item *n* **1** *a valuable item in my collection:* article, component, object, piece, thing **2** *an item on the agenda:* aspect, circumstance, consideration, detail, element, factor, feature, ingredient, matter, particular, point **3** *an item in the local paper:* account, article, bulletin, entry, feature, notice, paragraph, piece, report, story

itemize *v* count, detail, document, enumerate, instance, list, make an inventory, mention, number, overname, particularize, record, specify, tabulate

itinerant *adj* drifting, journeying, migratory, nomadic, peripatetic, rambling, roaming, rootless, roving, travelling, unsettled, vagabond, vagrant, wandering, wayfaring
☒ settled, stationary

itinerary *n* arrangements, circuit, course, journey, plan, programme, route, schedule, timetable, tour

J

jab *v* box, dig, elbow, lunge, nudge, poke, prod, punch, push, stab, tap, thrust
♦ *n* **1** *a jab in the ribs:* box, dig, nudge, poke, prod, punch, push, stab, tap **2** *a flu jab:* immunization, injection, shot

jabber *v* babble, blather, blether, chatter, gab, gabble, jaw, mumble, prate, prattle, rabbit, ramble, rattle, tattle, witter, yap

jack *v*
▶ **jack up 1** *jack up a car:* elevate, hoist, lift, raise **2** *jack up prices:* hike (up), increase, inflate, push up, put up

jacket *n* case, casing, cover, covering, envelope, folder, sheath, shell, skin, wrap, wrapper, wrapping

jackpot *n* award, bonanza, first prize, kitty, pool, pot, prize

jaded *adj* bored, cheesed off *colloq*, done in *colloq*, dulled, exhausted, fagged *colloq*, fatigued, fed up *colloq*, played-out, spent, tired, tired out, unenthusiastic, wearied, weary, worn out
🗲 fresh, refreshed

jag *n* barb, denticle *technical*, dentil, notch, point, projection, protrusion, snag, spur, tooth

jagged *adj* barbed, broken, craggy, denticulate *technical*, indented, irregular, nicked, notched, pointed, ragged, ridged, rough, saw-edged, serrated, snagged, snaggy, spiked, toothed, uneven
🗲 even, smooth

jail, gaol *n* choky *slang*, clink *slang*, custody, detention centre, guardhouse, inside *colloq*, jailhouse, lock-up, nick *colloq*, penitentiary, prison, quod *slang*, the can *slang*, the cooler *slang*, the jug *slang*, the slammer *slang*
♦ *v* confine, detain, immure, impound, imprison, incarcerate *formal*, intern, lock up, put away, send down, send to prison

jailer, gaoler *n* captor, guard, keeper, prison officer, screw *slang*, warden, warder

jam¹ *n* confiture, conserve, jelly, marmalade, preserve, spread

jam² *v* **1** *jammed into the back of the van:* confine, congest, cram, crowd, crush, force, insert, pack, press, push, ram, squash, squeeze, stuff, thrust, wedge **2** *the machine was jammed:* block, clog, close (off), obstruct, stall, stick
♦ *n* **1** *a jam of passengers:* congestion, crowd, crush, herd, horde, mob, multitude, pack, press, swarm, throng **2** *a traffic jam:* bottleneck, congestion, gridlock, hold-up, obstruction **3** *put her in quite a jam:* bind *colloq*, fix *colloq*, hole *colloq*, pickle *colloq*, plight, predicament, quandary, scrape *colloq*, straits, the soup *colloq*, (tight) spot *colloq*, trouble

jamboree *n* carnival, carousal, celebration, convention, festival, festivity, fête, field day, gathering, get-together, jubilee, junket, merriment, party, rally, revelry, shindig *colloq*, spree

jangle *v* **1** *jangling her keys:* chime, clang, clank, clash, clatter, clink, jar, jingle, rattle, vibrate

2 *jangle someone's nerves:* bother, disturb, irritate, make anxious, trouble, upset
♦ *n* cacophony, clang, clangour, clash, clatter, clink, din, discord, dissonance *formal*, jar, jarring, racket, rattle, reverberation, stridor
🗲 euphony

janitor *n* caretaker, concierge, custodian, doorkeeper, doorman, ostiary *technical*, porter

jar¹ *n* carafe, container, crock, flagon, flask, jug, mug, pitcher, pot, receptacle, urn, vase, vessel

jar² *v* **1** *jarred her wrist:* agitate, jerk, jolt, rattle, shake, vibrate **2** *a voice that jars on me:* annoy, disturb, grate, irk, irritate, jangle, nettle *colloq*, offend, trouble, upset **3** *a message that jars with our overall goals:* be at odds, be at variance, be in conflict, bicker, clash, disagree, quarrel

jargon *n* **1** *sporting jargon:* argot, buzz words, cant, idiom, journalese, legalese, parlance, psychobabble, slang, specialist language, usage, vernacular **2** *spouting all sorts of jargon:* gibberish, gobbledegook *colloq*, mumbo-jumbo *colloq*, nonsense

jarring *adj* cacophonous, discordant, disturbing, grating, harsh, irritating, jangling, jolting, rasping, strident, troubling, upsetting

jaundiced *adj* **1** *she's rather jaundiced about marriage:* biased, bigoted, bitter, cynical, disbelieving, distrustful, envious, hostile, jaded, jealous, misanthropic, pessimistic, prejudiced, resentful, sceptical, suspicious, unenthusiastic **2** *a jaundiced view of events:* biased, bigoted, distorted, preconceived, prejudiced

jaunt *n* drive, excursion, holiday, outing, ramble, ride, spin, stroll, tour, trip

jaunty *adj* **1** *a jaunty manner:* airy, bouncy, breezy, buoyant, carefree, cheeky, energetic, high-spirited, lively, perky, self-confident, sprightly **2** *a jaunty hat:* dapper, debonair, flashy, showy, smart, spruce, stylish, trim
🗲 **1** depressed **2** dowdy

jaw *n* **1** *the lower jaw:* chops *colloq*, mandible, maxilla *technical*, mouth, muzzle, trap *colloq* **2** *stopped by for a good jaw:* chat, chinwag *colloq*, confab *colloq*, conversation, discussion, gossip, natter *colloq*, talk **3** *the jaws of death:* claws, clutches, control, grasp, power, threshold
♦ *v* babble *colloq*, chat, chatter, gabble, gossip, jabber *colloq*, natter *colloq*, rabbit (on) *colloq*, talk

jazz
▶ **jazz up** brighten up, enliven, liven up, smarten up

Kinds of jazz include:
acid jazz, Afro-Cuban, avant-garde, bebop, boogie-woogie, bop, cool, Dixieland, free-form, fusion, hot jazz, jive, mainstream, modern, New Orleans, post-bop, ragtime, soul jazz, spiel, swing, third stream, West Coast

---

jazzy *adj* bold, fancy, flashy *colloq*, gaudy, lively, smart, snazzy *colloq*, spirited, stylish, swinging *colloq*, vivacious, wild, zestful
🗲 conservative, square

jealous *adj* 1 *jealous of her good looks:* begrudging, covetous, desirous, envious, green *colloq*, grudging, resentful 2 *a jealous husband:* anxious, distrustful, doubting, green-eyed *colloq*, insecure, possessive, suspicious, wary 3 *he's very jealous of his reputation:* careful, mindful, protective, vigilant, wary, watchful
🖬 2 contented, secure

jealousy *n* 1 *professional jealousy:* bitterness, covetousness, envy, grudge, grudgingness, ill-will, resentment, spite 2 *jealousy towards his wife:* distrust, doubt, insecurity, mistrust, possessiveness, suspicion, the green-eyed monster *colloq* 3 *values we guard with jealousy:* carefulness, mindfulness, protectiveness, vigilance, wariness, watchfulness

jeer *v* banter, barrack, boo, chaff, deride *formal*, gibe, heckle, hiss, knock *colloq*, make fun of, mock, razz *US colloq*, ridicule, scoff, scorn, shout down, sneer, taunt, tease, twit
♦ *n* abuse, banter, boo, catcall, derision *formal*, dig *colloq*, gibe, hiss, hoot, mockery, ridicule, scoff, sneer, taunt, teasing

jejune *adj* 1 *a jejune attempt at satire:* callow, childish, immature, juvenile, naïve, puerile, silly, simple, unsophisticated 2 *jejune and trashy entertainments:* arid, banal, barren, colourless, dry, dull, empty, insipid, prosaic, senseless, spiritless, trite, uninteresting, unoriginal, vapid, wishy-washy
🖬 1 mature 2 meaningful

jell see **gel**

jeopardize *v* endanger, expose, expose to danger, imperil *formal*, put at risk, put in jeopardy, risk, threaten
🖬 protect, safeguard

jeopardy *n* danger, endangerment, exposure, hazard, insecurity, peril *formal*, precariousness, risk, threat
🖬 safety, security

jerk *v* 1 *jerked on the cord:* jiggle, pluck, pull, tug, twitch, yank 2 *jerked his head back:* jolt, pull, throw, thrust, twitch, wrench, yank 3 *jerked to a sudden stop:* jolt, lurch
♦ *n* 1 *a sudden jerk of the head:* jar, jog, jolt, lurch, pluck, pull, shrug, throw, thrust, tug, twitch, wrench, yank 2 *the guy is such a jerk!:* clot *colloq*, dope *colloq*, fool, geek *slang*, idiot, nerd *slang*, pillock *slang*, prat *slang*, twerp *colloq*, twit *colloq*, wally *slang*

jerky *adj* bouncy, bumpy, convulsive, disconnected, fitful, incoherent, jolting, jumpy, lurching, rough, shaking, shaky, spasmodic, twitchy, uncontrolled, unco-ordinated
🖬 smooth

jerry-built *adj* built on the cheap, cheap, cheapjack, defective, faulty, flimsy, insubstantial, quickly built, ramshackle, rickety, shoddy, slipshod, thrown together, unstable, unsubstantial
🖬 stable, substantial, well-built

jersey *n* jumper, pullover, sweater, sweatshirt, top, woolly

jest *n* banter, crack *colloq*, fooling, gag *colloq*, hoax, joke, kidding *colloq*, leg-pull *colloq*, practical joke, prank, quip, trick, wisecrack *colloq*, witticism
♦ *v* fool, jeer, joke, kid *colloq*, mock, quip, tease, tell jokes

jester *n* buffoon, clown, comedian, comic, droll, fool, harlequin, humorist, joculator, joker, juggler, merry-andrew, merryman, motley, mummer, pantaloon, patch, prankster, quipster, wag, wit, zany

jet[1] *n* flow, fountain, gush, rush, spout, spray, sprayer, spring, sprinkler, spurt, squirt, stream
♦ *v* career, fly, rush, shoot, zoom

jet[2] *adj* black, ebony, inky, pitch-black, raven, sable, sooty

jetsam see **flotsam**

jettison *v* abandon, chuck *colloq*, discard, ditch *colloq*, dump *colloq*, eject, expel, get rid of, heave, offload, scrap, throw away, unload
🖬 load, take on

jetty *n* breakwater, dock, groyne, harbour, mole, pier, quay, wharf

jewel *n* 1 *a priceless collection of jewels:* gem, gemstone, jewellery, ornament, precious stone, rock *colloq*, sparkler *colloq* 2 *Durham is the jewel of the North:* crème de la crème, find, gem, masterpiece, paragon, pearl, pièce de résistance, pride and joy, prize, rarity, showpiece, treasure

jewellery *n* bijouterie, bijoux, finery, gauds, gemmery, gems, jewels, ornaments, regalia, treasure, trinkets

---

Types of jewellery include:
bangle, bracelet, charm bracelet, anklet, cufflink, tiepin, hatpin, brooch, cameo, earring, stud, nose-ring, ring, signet-ring, solitaire ring, necklace, rivière, necklet, choker, pendant, locket, chain, beads, amulet, torque, tiara, coronet, diadem

---

Jewish calendar

The Jewish calendar and its Gregorian equivalents:
Tishri (September-October), Hesshvan (October-November), Kislev (November-December), Tevet (December-January), Shevat (January-February), Adar (February-March), Adar Sheni (leap years only), Nisan (March-April), Iyar (April-May), Sivan (May-June), Tammuz (June-July), Av (July-August), Elul (August-September)

Jezebel *n* Delilah, femme fatale, harlot, hussy, jade, loose woman *colloq*, man-eater, scarlet woman, scrubber *slang*, seductress, tart *slang*, temptress, vamp *colloq*, wanton, whore, witch

jib *v* back off, balk, recoil, refuse, retreat, shrink, stall, stop short

jibe see **gibe**

jiffy *n* flash, instant, minute, moment, no time, sec, second, split second, tick, trice, twinkling, twinkling of an eye, two shakes of a lamb's tail *colloq*, two ticks
🖬 age

jig *v* bob, bounce, caper, dance, hop, jerk, jump, leap, prance, shake, skip, wiggle

jigger *v* balls up *slang*, botch up *colloq*, break, bugger up *slang*, destroy, kibosh *colloq*, louse up *colloq*, make a pig's ear of *colloq*, ruin, scupper *colloq*, spoil, undermine, wreck

jiggery-pokery *n* chicanery, deceit, deception, dishonesty, fraud, funny business, hanky-panky, mischief, monkey business *colloq*, subterfuge, trickery

jiggle *v* *jiggled the doorknob*: agitate, fidget with, jerk, jig, jog, joggle, shift **2** *jiggled his hips*: bounce, jerk, shake, twitch, waggle, wiggle, wobble

jilt *v* abandon, betray, brush off, cast aside, chuck *colloq*, desert, discard, ditch *colloq*, drop, leave, pack in *colloq*, reject, spurn

jingle *v* chime, chink, clatter, clink, ding, jangle, rattle, ring, tinkle, tintinnabulate *formal*
♦ *n* **1** *the jingle of bells*: chime, clang, clangour, clink, ding, jangle, rattle, ringing, tinkle, tintinnabulation *formal* **2** *an advertising jingle*: chant, chorus, ditty, doggerel, melody, poem, refrain, rhyme, song, tune, verse

jingoism *n* chauvinism, flag-waving, imperialism, insularity, nationalism, patriotism, warmongering

jinx *n* affliction *formal*, bad luck, black magic, charm, curse, evil eye, gremlin *colloq*, hex, hoodoo, malediction *formal*, plague, spell, voodoo
♦ *v* bedevil, bewitch, cast a spell on, curse, doom, plague

jitters *n* agitation, anxiety, fidgets, habdabs *colloq*, heebie-jeebies *colloq*, jimjams *colloq*, nerves, nervousness, tenseness, the creeps *colloq*, the shakes *colloq*, the shivers *colloq*, the willies *colloq*, trembling, uneasiness

jittery *adj* agitated, anxious, edgy *colloq*, fidgety, flustered, jumpy, nervous, nervy *colloq*, panicky, perturbed *formal*, quaking, quivering, shaky, shivery, trembling, uneasy
Fa calm, composed, confident

job *n* **1** *she has a good job*: business, calling, capacity, career, employment, line of work/business, livelihood, métier, occupation, position, post, profession, pursuit, situation, trade, vocation, work **2** *a simple job*: activity, assignment, chore, commission, enterprise, errand, function, mission, piece of work, proceeding, project, task, undertaking, venture **3** *that's not my job*: affair, assignment, concern, duty, function, part, place, province, responsibility, role, share, task

jobless *adj* idle, inactive, laid off, on the dole, out of work, redundant, unemployed, without work, workless
Fa employed

jockey *n* equestrian, horseman, horsewoman, rider
♦ *v* **1** *jockeying for top jobs*: cajole, coax, engineer, induce, inveigle *formal*, manage, manipulate, manoeuvre, negotiate, wheedle **2** *jockeying into the space*: ease, edge, manoeuvre

jocose *adj* comical, droll, facetious, funny, humorous, jesting, jovial, joyous, lepid *formal*, merry, mirthful, mischievous, playful, pleasant, sportive, teasing, waggish, witty
Fa morose

jocular *adj* amusing, comic, comical, droll, entertaining, facetious, funny, hilarious, humorous, jesting, jocose *formal*, joking, jovial, playful, roguish, teasing, waggish, whimsical, witty
Fa serious

jocularity *n* amusement, comedy, desipience *formal*, drollery, entertainment, facetiousness, fooling, fun, gaiety, hilarity, humour, jesting, jocoseness *formal*, jocosity *formal*, jolliness, joviality, laughter, merriment, playfulness, pleasantry, roguishness, sport, sportiveness, teasing, waggishness, whimsicality, wit

jog *v* **1** *jogged the baby up and down*: bounce, joggle, rock, shake **2** *jogged her arm*: bump, elbow, jar, jolt, nudge, poke, prod, push **3** *jogged my memory*: activate, arouse, prompt, remind, stimulate, stir **4** *jogged five miles*: canter, run, trot
♦ *n* **1** *a jog on the elbow*: bump, jerk, jolt, nudge, poke, prod, push, shake, shove **2** *a jog around the lake*: canter, run, trot

joie de vivre *n* blitheness *formal*, bounce *colloq*, buoyancy, cheerfulness, ebullience *formal*, enjoyment, enthusiasm, gaiety, get-up-and-go *colloq*, gusto, joy, joyfulness, merriment, mirth, pleasure, relish, zest
Fa depression

join *v* **1** *joined the two together*: add, ally, amalgamate, attach, bind, cement, combine, conjoin *formal*, connect, converge, couple, fasten, fuse, glue, knit, link, marry, merge, splice, tie, unify, unite, weld, yoke **2** *it joins the Thames at Oxford*: abut *formal*, adjoin *formal*, border (on), coincide, conjoin *formal*, meet, touch, verge on **3** *joined the Scouts*: accompany, affiliate, ally, associate with, become a member of, enlist, enrol, enter, sign up, team up with
Fa **1** divide, separate **3** leave
▶ **join in** chip in, contribute, co-operate, help, lend a hand, muck in *colloq*, partake, participate, pitch in, take part in
▶ **join up** enlist, enrol, enter, sign up

joint *n* **1** *the joints of the body*: articulation, connection, coupling, hinge, intersection, join, junction, juncture, knot, nexus *formal*, seam, union **2** *a sleazy joint*: bar, club, dive, haunt, nightclub, place, pub **3** *smoking a joint*: cigarette, reefer *colloq*, roach *colloq*, spliff *colloq*, stick *colloq*
♦ *adj* amalgamated, collective, combined, common, communal, consolidated, co-operative, joined, mutual, shared, united
♦ *v* carve, cut up, dismember, dissect, divide, sever

joke *n* **1** *telling jokes*: banter, crack *colloq*, funny story, gag *colloq*, hoot, jest, one-liner *colloq*, pun, quip, repartee, whimsy, wisecrack *colloq*, witticism, yarn **2** *played a joke on her*: hoax, jape, lark, practical joke, prank, spoof, sport, trick
♦ *v* **1** *he is always joking*: banter, clown, fool (around), jest, kid *colloq*, laugh, mock, pun, quip, tease, tell jokes, wisecrack *colloq* **2** *I was only joking*: have someone on *colloq*, kid *colloq*, pull someone's leg *colloq*, tease

joker *n* buffoon, card *colloq*, character, clown, comedian, comic, droll, hoaxer, humorist, jester, kidder, practical joker, prankster, quipster, sport, trickster, wag, wisecracker *colloq*

jolly *adj* **1** *a jolly person*: cheerful, cheery, exuberant, gleeful, happy, hearty, jovial, joyful, lively, merry, mirthful, playful **2** *we had a jolly time*: convivial, delightful, enjoyable, festive, happy, pleasurable

☲ **1** sad, unhappy

♦ *adv* certainly, exceptionally, extremely, greatly, highly, intensely, very

jolt *v* **1** *the boat jolted against the bank:* bang, bounce, bump, jar, jerk, jog, jostle, jounce, knock, lurch, nudge, push, shake, shove **2** *it jolted my confidence:* amaze, astonish, astound, discompose, disconcert, disturb, perturb *formal*, shake (up), shock, startle, stun, surprise, upset

♦ *n* **1** *stopped with a sudden jolt:* bang, blow, bump, hit, impact, jar, jerk, jog, knock, lurch, push, shake, shove, start **2** *quite a jolt for the firm's investors:* blow, bolt from the blue *colloq*, bombshell *colloq*, fright of your life, reversal, setback, shock, start, surprise, thunderbolt *colloq*, turn-up for the book *colloq*, upset

jostle *v* **1** *jostled through the crowds:* bang, bump, collide, crowd, elbow, hustle, jog, joggle, jolt, push, shake, shoulder, shove, squeeze **2** *jostling for victory:* battle, compete, contend, fight, struggle, vie

jot *n* ace, atom, bit, detail, fraction, gleam, glimmer, grain, hint, iota, mite, morsel, particle, scintilla, scrap, smidgen *colloq*, speck, tittle, trace, trifle, whit

▶ **jot down** enter, list, note (down), put down, record, register, scribble, take down, write down

journal *n* **1** *trade journals:* magazine, monthly, newspaper, paper, periodical, publication, review, weekly **2** *kept a regular journal:* account, chronicle, daybook, diary, gazette, log, record, register

journalism *n* broadcasting, feature-writing, Fleet Street, media, news, news coverage, press, radio, reportage, reporting, television, the fourth estate, writing

journalist *n* broadcaster, columnist, commentator, contributor, correspondent, editor, feature-writer, freelance, hack *colloq*, journo *colloq*, newshound, news-writer, paparazzo, reporter, reviewer, scribe *colloq*, stringer, sub *colloq*, subeditor

journey *n* crossing, cruise, drive, excursion, expedition, flight, jaunt, odyssey *formal*, outing, passage, peregrination *formal*, progress, ramble, ride, safari, tour, travels, trek, trip, voyage, wanderings

♦ *v* cruise, fly, gallivant, go, hike, peregrinate *formal*, proceed, ramble, range, roam, rove, sail, tour, tramp, travel, trek, voyage, wander

joust *v* compete, contest, fight, quarrel, skirmish, spar, vie, wrangle

♦ *n* **1** *knights at a joust:* fight, tilt, tournament, tourney **2** *a legal joust:* contest, encounter, fight, skirmish, trial

jovial *adj* affable, animated, cheerful, cheery, cordial, genial, gleeful, happy, in good spirits, jolly, lively, merry, mirthful, sociable

☲ depressed, gloomy, sad

joviality *n* affability, buoyancy, cheerfulness, cheeriness, ebullience, fun, gaiety, gladness, glee, happiness, hilarity, jollity, merriment, mirth

☲ moroseness, sadness

joy *n* **1** *my heart was filled with joy:* bliss, delight, ecstasy, elation, enjoyment, exultation, felicity *formal*, gladness, glee, gratification, happiness,

joyfulness, pleasure, rapture, rejoicing **2** *the joys of childhood:* delight, gem, pleasure, prize, thrill, treasure, treat **3** *get no joy from the inquiry desk:* accomplishment, achievement, positive result, satisfaction, success, victory

☲ **1** despair, grief

joyful *adj* cheerful, delighted, ecstatic, elated, euphoric, glad, gleeful, gratified, happy, in seventh heaven *colloq*, jubilant, merry, on cloud nine *colloq*, on top of the world *colloq*, over the moon *colloq*, overjoyed, pleased, thrilled, tickled pink *colloq*, triumphant

☲ mournful, sorrowful

joyless *adj* bleak, cheerless, dejected, depressing, despondent, discouraging, dismal, dispirited, doleful, dour, downcast, dreary, forlorn, gloomy, glum, grim, miserable, sad, sombre, unhappy

☲ joyful

joyous *adj* cheerful, ecstatic, festal, festive, glad, gladsome, gleeful, happy, joyful, jubilant, merry, rapturous

☲ sad

jubilant *adj* delighted, ecstatic, elated, euphoric, excited, exuberant, exultant, in seventh heaven *colloq*, joyful, on cloud nine *colloq*, on top of the world *colloq*, over the moon *colloq*, overjoyed, rejoicing, rhapsodic, thrilled, tickled pink *colloq*, triumphant

jubilation *n* celebration, ecstasy, elation, euphoria, excitement, exultation, festivity, jollification, joy, triumph

☲ depression, lamentation

jubilee *n* anniversary, commemoration, festival, holiday

Judas *n* betrayer, deceiver, quisling, renegade, tergiversator *formal*, traitor, turncoat

judge *n* **1** *appeared before the judge:* adjudicator, arbiter, arbitrator, assessor, beak *slang*, coroner, district attorney, his/her nibs *slang*, judiciary, justice, Law Lord, magistrate, mediator, moderator, procurator fiscal, recorder, referee, seneschal, sheriff, umpire **2** *a fine judge of cattle:* assessor, authority, connoisseur, critic, evaluator, expert, reviewer

♦ *v* **1** *to judge a case:* adjudge *formal*, adjudicate, arbitrate, decree, deliver/pronounce a verdict, examine, find, give sentence, mediate, pass sentence, referee, review, rule, sentence, sit in judgement, try, umpire **2** *she judged him to be in his forties:* appraise, ascertain, assess, believe, conclude, consider, decide, determine, discern, distinguish, estimate, evaluate, examine, form an opinion, gauge, rate, reckon, review, think, value, weigh (up) **3** *don't judge me!:* condemn, convict, criticize, damn, doom

judgement *n* **1** *read out her judgement to the court:* adjudication, arbitration, conclusion, decision, decree, finding, mediation, opinion, order, result, ruling, sentence, verdict **2** *a person of sound judgement:* acumen, common sense, discernment, discrimination, enlightenment, good sense, intelligence, judiciousness *formal*, penetration, perception, perspicacity *formal*, prudence *formal*, sagacity *formal*, sense, shrewdness, taste, understanding, wisdom **3** *in my judgement they ought to leave:* appraisal, assessment, belief, conviction, diagnosis, estimate, evaluation, opinion, view

judicial *adj* critical, discriminating, forensic, impartial, judiciary, legal, official

judicial or *judicious*? *Judicial* is a formal word meaning 'relating to judges and lawcourts'. *Judicious* means 'showing wisdom and good sense': *a judicious choice of words.*

judicious *adj* astute, careful, cautious, circumspect *formal*, clever, common-sense, considered, discerning, discriminating, informed, intelligent, prudent, reasonable, sagacious *formal*, sensible, shrewd, smart, sound, thoughtful, well-advised, well-judged, wise **ᴇᴈ** injudicious

jug *n* carafe, container, crock, decanter, ewer, flagon, jar, pitcher, receptacle, Toby jug, urn, vessel

juggle *v* adjust, alter, balance, change, cook *colloq*, disguise, doctor *colloq*, equalize, fake, falsify, manipulate, massage, rearrange, rig, tamper with

juice *n* essence, extract, fluid, liquid, liquor, nectar, sap, secretion, serum

juicy *adj* **1** *juicy tomatoes:* flowing, lush, moist, succulent, watery, wet **2** *some juicy gossip:* colourful, exciting, interesting, lurid, racy, risqué, scandalous, sensational, spicy, suggestive, thrilling, vivid **ᴇᴈ 1** dry

jumble *v* confuse, disarrange, disorganize, mix, mix up, muddle, shuffle, tangle **ᴇᴈ** order
♦ *n* chaos, clutter, confusion, disarray, disorder, hotch-potch, medley, mess, miscellany, mishmash *colloq*, mixture, mix-up, muddle, potpourri, shambles *colloq*

jumbled *adj* chaotic, confused, disarrayed, disordered, disorganized, miscellaneous, mixed-up, muddled, shuffled, tangled, tumbled, unsorted, untidy **ᴇᴈ** orderly, tidy

jumbo *adj* colossal, enormous, extra-large, giant, gigantic, huge, immense, mammoth, vast, whopping *colloq*

jump *v* **1** *jump over a fence:* bound, clear, go over/across, hop, hurdle, leap, skip, spring, vault **2** *jump about on the dance floor:* bounce, caper, cavort, dance, frisk, frolic, gambol, hop, leap, prance, romp, skip, sport **3** *jumped at the sight of a snake:* flinch, jerk, jump out of your skin, quail, quiver, recoil, shake, start, twitch, wince **4** *you can jump the next page:* avoid, bypass, cut out, disregard, ignore, leave out, miss, omit, overlook, pass over, skip **5** *share prices jumped:* advance, appreciate, ascend, escalate, gain, go up, increase, mount, rise, spiral, surge **6** *he was jumped by a gang of youths:* assault, attack, beat up *colloq*, set about *colloq*, mug *colloq*, pounce on, set upon, spring on, swoop on
♦ *n* **1** *cleared the fence with a great jump:* bound, hop, leap, pounce, skip, spring, vault **2** *woke up with a jump:* flinch, jar, jerk, jolt, lurch, quiver, shake, shiver, shock, spasm, start, twitch **3** *the sudden jump in gas prices:* advance, boost, elevation, escalation, hike *colloq*, increase, increment, mounting, rise, upsurge, upturn **4** *the*

horse cleared the first jump easily: barricade, barrier, fence, gate, hedge, hurdle, obstacle, rail
▶ **jump at** accept, agree to, grab, leap at, pounce on, seize, snatch
▶ **jump on** berate *formal*, blame, castigate *formal*, censure *formal*, chide, criticize, fly at, rebuke, reprimand, reproach, reprove, revile *formal*, scold, tick off, upbraid

jumper *n* jersey, pullover, sweater, sweatshirt, woolly

jumpy *adj* **1** *crowds make me jumpy:* agitated, anxious, apprehensive, edgy *colloq*, fidgety, jittery, nervous, on edge, panicky, restive *formal*, shaky, tense, twitchy *colloq*, uneasy **2** *jumpy videos shot on mobile phones:* bumpy, convulsive, fitful, incoherent, jerky, jolting, shaky, spasmodic **ᴇᴈ 1** calm, composed

junction *n* **1** *a road junction:* confluence, crossing, crossroads, interchange, intersection, meeting-point **2** *the junction between the nerve and the muscle:* bond, connection, coupling, intersection, join, joining, joint, juncture, link, linking, seam, union, welding

junction or *juncture*? A *junction* is a point or place where things meet: *a road junction; a junction box for wires.* A *juncture* is a point in time: *at this juncture.*

juncture *n* minute, moment, occasion, period, point, stage, time

jungle *n* **1** *tigers inhabit the dense jungle:* bush, equatorial rainforest, growth, rainforest, tropical forest **2** *a jungle of buildings:* chaos, clutter, confusion, disarray, disorder, heap, hotch-potch, labyrinth, mass, maze, medley, miscellany, mishmash, snarl, tangle, web

junior *adj* inferior, lesser, lower, minor, secondary, subordinate, subsidiary, younger **ᴇᴈ** senior
♦ *n* inferior, minion, minor, servant, subordinate, subsidiary

junk *n* bric-à-brac, clutter, debris, dregs, garbage, leavings, leftovers, litter, oddments, refuse, rubbish, rummage, scrap, trash, waste, wreckage
♦ *v* chuck *colloq*, discard, dispose of, ditch, dump *colloq*, get rid of, jettison, throw out

junta *n* cabal, camarilla, cartel, clique, conclave, confederacy, coterie, council, faction, gang, group, league, party, ring, set

jurisdiction *n* **1** *under the council's jurisdiction:* administration, authority, command, control, domination, dominion, influence, leadership, mastery, power, prerogative *formal*, province, right, rule, sovereignty, sway **2** *crimes in a neighbouring jurisdiction:* area, zone

jury *n* jurors, jurymen, jurywomen, panel

just *adj* **1** *a just ruler:* disinterested, equitable, ethical, even-handed, fair, fair-minded, good, honest, honourable, impartial, irreproachable, moral, neutral, objective, principled, righteous, sincere, truthful, unbiased, unprejudiced, upright, upstanding, virtuous **2** *a just punishment:* appropriate, apt, deserved, due, earned, fitting, justified, lawful, legal, legitimate, merited, proper, reasonable, rightful, sound, suitable, valid, well-deserved, well-founded, well-grounded

☞ **1** unjust **2** undeserved
♦ *adv* **1** *he's just left:* a moment ago, a short time ago, lately, recently **2** *that's just like him:* absolutely, completely, exactly, perfectly, precisely, quite, to a T *colloq* **3** *she's just a child:* barely, hardly, merely, nothing but, only, purely, scarcely, simply

justice *n* **1** *there is no justice in the world:* equitableness, equity, ethics, even-handedness, fair play, fair-mindedness, fairness, honesty, honour, impartiality, integrity, justifiableness, justness, lawfulness, legitimacy, morality, neutrality, objectivity, propriety *formal*, reasonableness, rectitude *formal*, right, righteousness, rightfulness, rightness, soundness, uprightness, validity **2** *sought justice in the courts:* amends, compensation, law, legality, penalty, punishment, recompense, redress, reparation, satisfaction **3** *a justice of the supreme court:* JP, judge, Justice of the Peace, magistrate, sheriff
☞ **1** bias, injustice, unfairness

justifiable *adj* acceptable, defensible, excusable, explainable, explicable *formal*, fit, forgivable, justified, lawful, legal, legitimate, pardonable, plausible, proper, reasonable, right, sensible, sound, supportable, sustainable, tenable, understandable, valid, warranted, well-founded, within reason
☞ unjustifiable

justification *n* apology, basis, defence, excuse, explanation, grounds, mitigation, plea, rationalization, reason, vindication, warrant

justify *v* **1** *justify the decision to go to war:* bear out, defend, excuse, explain, maintain, rationalize, show to be reasonable, substantiate *formal*, support, sustain, uphold, validate, vindicate, warrant **2** *tried to justify herself:* absolve, acquit, clear, defend, exculpate *formal*, excuse, exonerate *formal*, explain, forgive, pardon

justly *adv* **1** *always try to act justly:* conscientiously, equitably, even-handedly, fairly, honestly, impartially, lawfully **2** *justly criticized:* correctly, duly, justifiably, legitimately, properly, rightfully, rightly, with reason
☞ **1** unjustly **2** unjustly

jut *v* beetle, extend, extrude, overhang, project, protrude, stick out
☞ recede

juvenile *n* adolescent, boy, child, girl, infant, kid *colloq*, minor, teenager, young person, youngster, youth
♦ *adj* **1** *a juvenile offender:* adolescent, immature, junior, minor, wet behind the ears *colloq*, young, youthful **2** *juvenile behaviour:* babyish, callow, childish, green *colloq*, immature, inexperienced, infantile, puerile, unsophisticated
☞ **2** mature

juxtapose *v* place side by side, put next to each other, put/place together

juxtaposition *n* closeness, connection, contact, contiguity *formal*, immediacy, nearness, proximity, vicinity

K

kaleidoscopic *adj* **1** *a kaleidoscopic image:* many-coloured, many-splendoured, motley, multicoloured, poikilitic *technical*, polychromatic *formal*, polychrome *formal*, variegated **2** *a kaleidoscopic account of the fall of the Soviet Union:* changeable, ever-changing, fluctuating, fluid, manifold, multifarious *formal*
Fa 1 dull, monochrome, monotonous

kaput *adj* broken, conked out *colloq*, defunct, destroyed, extinct, finished, ruined, smashed, undone, wrecked

karate

> *Karate belts include:*
> *junior grades (Kyu):* red belt (beginner), white belt (8th Kyu), yellow belt (7th Kyu), orange belt (6th Kyu), green belt (5th Kyu), brown belt (4th-1st Kyu), black belt (1st Dan); *senior grades (Dans):* black belts (1st-8th Dan)

keel
▶ **keel over 1** *the boat keeled over:* capsize, collapse, founder, overturn, turn turtle, turn upside down **2** *she keeled over in the supermarket:* black out, drop, faint, fall down, lose consciousness, pass out, topple over

keen *adj* **1** *a keen gardener:* assiduous, avid, conscientious, devoted, diligent, eager, earnest, enthusiastic, fervent, impatient, industrious, intent **2** *a keen intelligence:* astute, clever, deep, discerning, discriminating, penetrating, perceptive, perspicacious *formal*, quick, quick-witted, sensitive, sharp, sharp-witted, shrewd, wise **3** *a keen sense of humour:* acid, acute, biting, incisive, intense, mordant *formal*, penetrating, piercing, pointed, pungent, sharp, trenchant *formal* **4** *keen competition:* cut-throat, dog-eat-dog *colloq*, fierce, intense, ruthless, strong **5** *keen on someone:* attached, caring, devoted, fond, having a soft spot *colloq*, liking, loving
Fa 1 apathetic **2** superficial **3** dull
♦ *v* cry, grieve, howl, lament, mourn, sob, sorrow, wail

keenness *n* **1** *keenness to start work:* diligence, eagerness, earnestness, enthusiasm, industriousness, industry, sedulity, sedulousness **2** *the keenness of his mind:* astuteness, cleverness, discernment, incisiveness, penetration, sagacity *formal*, sapience *formal*, sensitivity, sharpness, shrewdness, trenchancy *formal*, wisdom
Fa 1 apathy, reluctance **2** dullness

keep *v* **1** *keep it for later:* accumulate, amass, carry, collect, conserve, deal in, deposit, furnish, hang on to, heap, hoard, hold, hold on to, keep possession of, maintain, not part with, pile (up), place, possess, preserve, retain, save, stack, stock, store (up), sustain **2** *keep doing the same thing:* carry on, continue, keep on, maintain, persevere, persist, remain, stay **3** *keep rabbits:* be responsible for, care for, defend, feed, foster, guard, have charge of, have custody of, keep in good order, look after, maintain, manage, mind, nurture, protect, provide for, safeguard, shelter, shield, subsidize, superintend, support, sustain, tend,

watch (over) **4** *keep in custody:* arrest, block, check, confine, constrain, control, curb, delay, detain, deter, hamper, hinder, hold (up), hold back, impede, inhibit, interfere with, keep back, limit, obstruct, prevent, restrain, retard *formal*, withhold **5** *keep the Sabbath:* abide by, adhere to, carry out, celebrate, commemorate, comply with, effectuate *formal*, fulfil, hold, honour, keep faith with, keep up, maintain, mark, obey, observe, perform, perpetuate, recognize, respect, solemnize
♦ *n* **1** *pay for one's keep:* board, board and lodgings, food, livelihood, living, maintenance, means, nourishment, nurture, subsistence, support, sustenance, upkeep **2** *laid siege to the keep:* castle, citadel, donjon, dungeon, fort, fortress, stronghold, tower
▶ **keep back 1** *injuries have kept him back:* check, constrain, curb, delay, impede, limit, prohibit, restrain, retard *formal*, stop **2** *trying to keep back my emotions:* censor, conceal, hide, hold back, hush up, keep secret, reserve, restrict, retain, stifle, suppress, withhold
▶ **keep from 1** *kindly keep from smoking:* desist *formal*, forbear *formal*, halt, refrain from, resist, stop **2** *nothing will keep me from going:* get in the way of, prevent, stop
▶ **keep in 1** *keep your feelings in:* bottle up, conceal, control, hide, inhibit, keep back, quell, repress, restrain, stifle, stop up, suppress **2** *kept in after school:* confine, coop up, detain, shut in
▶ **keep off** avoid, avoid going near, give a wide berth to *colloq*, keep at a distance from, keep at arm's length, keep away from, not go near, stay away from, stay off, steer clear of
▶ **keep on 1** *keep on playing until late:* carry on, continue, endure, keep at it, last, maintain, persevere, persist, remain, soldier on *colloq*, stay, stay the course, stick at it *colloq* **2** *hoped the firm would keep her on:* hold onto, retain, stick with *colloq*
▶ **keep on at** badger, chivvy, go on at, harass, harry, importune *formal*, nag, pester, plague, pursue
▶ **keep to** adhere to, comply with, fulfil, obey, observe, respect, stick to
▶ **keep up** continue, maintain, preserve, sustain
▶ **keep up with** compete with, contend with, emulate, equal, keep pace with, match, rival, vie
Fa fall behind

keeper *n* **1** *the keeper of the castle:* administrator, caretaker, conservator *formal*, curator, governor, guardian, inspector, overseer, steward, superintendent, supervisor, warden **2** *gave his keepers the slip:* attendant, bodyguard, escort, gaoler, guard, jailer, minder *colloq*, warder

keeping *n* **1** *in his father's keeping:* aegis *formal*, auspices *formal*, care, charge, cure *technical*, custody, guardianship, maintenance, patronage, protection, retention, safe-keeping, supervision, surveillance, trust, tutelage **2** *in keeping with the architecture:* accord *formal*, agreement, balance, conformity, congruity *formal*, consistency, correspondence, harmony, proportion

keepsake *n* emblem, memento, pledge, relic, remembrance, reminder, souvenir, token

keg n barrel, butt, cask, drum, firkin, hogshead, tun, vat

ken n appreciation, awareness, cognizance formal, compass, comprehension, field, grasp, knowledge, perception, range, reach, scope, understanding

kernel n 1 apricot kernels: nut, seed, stone 2 the kernel of the plan: centre, core, crux, essence, germ, gist, grain, heart, nitty-gritty colloq, nub, nucleus, nuts and bolts colloq, quintessence formal, substance

key n 1 a key to her personality: answer, clue, explanation, explication formal, guide, indicator, interpretation, pointer, secret, solution 2 provide a key to the symbols: code, glossary, guide, index, legend, table, translation 3 in a low key: mood, pitch, style, tone
♦ adj basic, central, chief, crucial, decisive, essential, fundamental, important, leading, main, major, necessary, principal, vital

keynote n accent, centre, core, emphasis, essence, gist, heart, marrow, pith, stress, substance, theme

keystone n base, basis, core, cornerstone, foundation, ground, linchpin, mainspring, motive force, principle, root, source, spring

kick v 1 kicked the ball: boot, hit, strike 2 tried to kick the habit: abandon, break, desist from, give up, leave off, quit, stop
♦ n 1 a kick in the shins: blow, jolt, recoil, striking 2 got a kick out of skiing: buzz colloq, excitement, fun, high colloq, lark colloq, lift colloq, pleasure, stimulation, thrill 3 a drink with a bit of kick: bite colloq, effect, pep colloq, potency, power, punch colloq, strength, zing colloq, zip colloq
▶ **kick against** defy, hold out against, oppose, protest against, rebel against, resist, spurn, withstand
▶ **kick around** discuss, play with, talk about, toy with
▶ **kick off** begin, commence formal, get under way, inaugurate, initiate, introduce, open, open the proceedings, set the ball rolling colloq, start, start the ball rolling colloq
▶ **kick out** boot out colloq, chuck out colloq, discharge, dismiss, eject, evict, expel, get rid of, give the sack/push/boot/elbow to colloq, oust, reject, remove, sack colloq, show someone the door colloq, throw out

kick-off n beginning, commencement formal, inception formal, introduction, opening, outset, start, word go colloq

kid[1] n adolescent, boy, child, girl, infant, juvenile, lad, little one, nipper colloq, teenager, toddler, tot colloq, young one, young person, youngster, youth

kid[2] v 1 managed to kid the authorities: bamboozle colloq, con colloq, deceive, delude, dupe, fool, gull, hoodwink, trick 2 I was only kidding: fool, have on colloq, hoax, jest, joke, pretend, pull someone's leg colloq, tease

kidnap v abduct, capture, hijack, hold to ransom, seize, snatch, steal, take hostage

kill v 1 killed the enemy fighters: annihilate, assassinate, behead, blow away colloq, bump off colloq, butcher, decapitate formal, decimate colloq, destroy, dispatch colloq, do away with, do in colloq, do to death, electrocute, eliminate colloq, execute, exterminate, finish off, guillotine, hang, knock off colloq, liquidate colloq, massacre, murder, polish off colloq, put down, put to death, put to sleep, rub out colloq, send to the electric chair, shoot, slaughter, slay, smite formal, stab to death, take out colloq, take someone's life, waste colloq, wipe out colloq, zap colloq 2 kill a project: abolish, destroy, end, eradicate, put an end to, ruin 3 my feet are killing: ache, be painful, be sore, cause pain, hurt, pound, smart, sting, suffer, throb, twinge 4 don't kill yourself with all this work: drain, exhaust, fatigue, sap, strain, tire out, weary 5 kill time: fill, occupy, pass, spend, use (up), while away 6 kill the sound: deaden, dull, muffle, quash, quell, smother, stifle, suppress
♦ n climax, conclusion, coup de grâce, death, death-blow, dénouement, dispatch, end, finish

killer n assassin, butcher colloq, cut-throat, destroyer, executioner, exterminator, gunman, hatchet man colloq, hit-man colloq, homicide, liquidator colloq, murderer, slaughterer, slayer

killing n 1 brutal killing: assassination, bloodshed, butchery, carnage, destruction, elimination, execution, extermination, fatality, fratricide formal, genocide, homicide, infanticide formal, liquidation colloq, manslaughter, massacre, matricide formal, murder, patricide formal, slaughter, slaying, sororicide formal, uxoricide formal 2 make a killing from property developing: big hit, bonanza colloq, booty, clean-up colloq, coup, fortune, gain, hit, lucky break, profit, stroke of luck, success, windfall
♦ adj 1 a killing joke: absurd, amusing, comical, funny, hilarious, ludicrous, rib-tickling, side-splitting colloq, uproarious 2 the heat was killing: arduous, debilitating formal, draining, enervating formal, exhausting, fatiguing, hard, taxing, tiring, wearing

killjoy n complainer, cynic, dampener, damper, grouch, misery, moaner, pessimist, prophet of doom, sceptic, spoilsport, Weary Willie, wet blanket colloq, whiner
🔁 enthusiast, optimist, sport

kin n blood, clan, consanguinity formal, cousins, extraction, family, flesh and blood, lineage, people, relations, relatives, stock, tribe

kind n brand, breed, category, character, class, description, family, genre, genus, manner, nature, persuasion, race, set, sort, species, stamp, strain, style, temperament, type, variety
♦ adj affectionate, altruistic, amiable, amicable, benevolent, benign, big-hearted, bounteous formal, charitable, compassionate, congenial, considerate, cordial, courteous, forbearing, friendly, generous, genial, gentle, giving, good, good-hearted, good-natured, gracious, helpful, humane, humanitarian, indulgent, kind-hearted, kindly, lenient, loving, magnanimous, merciful, mild, neighbourly, nice, obliging, patient, philanthropic, pitying, selfless, soft-hearted, sympathetic, tactful, tender-hearted, thoughtful, tolerant, understanding, unselfish, warm, warm-hearted
🔁 cruel, inconsiderate, unhelpful

kind-hearted adj altruistic, amicable, benign, big-hearted, compassionate, considerate, generous, good-hearted, good-natured, gracious, helpful, humane, humanitarian, kind,

kindly, obliging, philanthropic, sympathetic, tender-hearted, warm, warm-hearted
🔳 cold-hearted, ill-natured

kindle v 1 *kindled a fire:* ignite, light, set alight, set fire to, set on fire 2 *kindle the emotions:* arouse, awaken, excite, fan, fire, incite, induce, inflame, inspire, provoke, rouse, stimulate, stir, thrill

kindliness n amiability, beneficence *formal*, benevolence, benignity *formal*, charity, compassion, friendliness, generosity, kindness, loving-kindness *formal*, sympathy, warmth
🔳 cruelty, meanness, unkindness

kindly adj agreeable, amicable, benevolent, big-hearted, charitable, compassionate, considerate, cordial, favourable, friendly, generous, gentle, good, good-natured, helpful, humane, indulgent, kind, kind-hearted, magnanimous, mild, nice, patient, pleasant, sympathetic, tender, thoughtful, understanding, warm
🔳 cruel, uncharitable

kindness n 1 *treated her with kindness:* affection, altruism, benevolence, charity, compassion, considerateness, consideration, courtesy, fellow feeling, friendliness, generosity, gentleness, good will, goodness, grace, helpfulness, hospitality, humaneness, humanitarianism, humanity, indulgence, kindliness, leniency, love, loving-kindness *formal*, magnanimity, mildness, niceness, patience, philanthropy, pleasantness, sympathy, thoughtfulness, tolerance, understanding, warm-heartedness, warmth 2 *do me the kindness of listening:* favour, good turn, help, service
🔳 1 cruelty, inhumanity 2 disservice

kindred n clan, connections, family, flesh and blood, folk, kinsfolk, lineage, people, relations, relationship, relatives
♦ adj affiliated, akin, allied, cognate *formal*, common, connected, corresponding, like, matching, related, similar

king n 1 *crowned him king:* chief, chieftain, emperor, lord, majesty, monarch, prince, ruler, sovereign, supremo 2 *the king of snooker:* big cheese *colloq*, big noise *colloq*, big shot *colloq*, chief, kingpin, leader, leading light *colloq*, master, star, supremo, the greatest *colloq*, top dog *colloq*

kingdom n commonwealth, country, division, domain, dominion, dynasty, empire, grouping, land, monarchy, nation, principality, province, realm, reign, sovereign state, state, territory

kingly adj august *formal*, dignified, glorious, grand, grandiose, imperial, imperious, imposing, lordly, majestic, monarchical *formal*, noble, regal, royal, sovereign, splendid, stately, sublime *formal*, supreme

kink n 1 *noticed a kink in the chain:* bend, coil, crimp, crinkle, curl, dent, entanglement, indentation, knot, loop, tangle, twirl, twist, wrinkle 2 *a kink of her personality:* caprice *formal*, deviation, eccentricity, fetish, foible, idiosyncrasy, perversion, quirk, whim
♦ v bend, coil, crimp, curl, curve, tangle, twist, wrinkle

kinky adj 1 *kinky behaviour:* bizarre, capricious *formal*, degenerate, depraved, deviant, eccentric, freakish, idiosyncratic, licentious, odd, outlandish, peculiar, perverted, queer, quirky, strange, unconventional, unnatural, warped,

weird, whimsical 2 *the kinky long tresses of his wig:* coiled, crimped, crumpled, curled, curly, frizzy, tangled, twisted, wavy, wrinkled

kinsfolk n clan, connections, cousins, family, relations, relatives

kinship n 1 *ties of kinship:* ancestry, blood, consanguinity *formal*, family, kin, lineage, relationship 2 *felt a certain kinship between them:* affinity, alliance, association, community, conformity, connection, correspondence, equivalence, kindred, likeness, relationship, similarity, tie

kiosk n booth, box, cabin, counter, news-stand, stall, stand

kismet n destiny, doom, fate, fortune, karma, lot, portion, predestiny *formal*, providence

kiss v 1 *kissed passionately:* bill and coo *colloq*, canoodle *colloq*, caress, neck *colloq*, osculate *formal*, peck *colloq*, smooch *colloq*, snog *slang* 2 *just kissed the surface of the pond:* brush, glance off, graze, lick, scrape, touch, touch gently / lightly
♦ n osculation *formal*, peck *colloq*, smack *colloq*, smacker *colloq*, snog *slang*

kit n 1 *scuba-diving kit:* accoutrements *formal*, apparatus, appurtenances *formal*, baggage, effects, equipment, gear, implements, instruments, luggage, outfit, paraphernalia, provisions, rig, set, stuff *colloq*, supplies, tackle, things *colloq*, tools, trappings, utensils 2 *football kit:* clobber *colloq*, clothing, colours, gear *colloq*, get-up *colloq*, outfit, rig-out *colloq*, strip *colloq*, togs *colloq*, uniform

▶ **kit out** arm, deck out, dress, equip, fit out, fix up, furnish, outfit, prepare, provide, rig out, supply

kitchen utensils

Kitchen utensils include:
baster, blender, bottle opener, breadbin, breadboard, butter curler, butter dish, can-opener, cheese board, cheese slicer, chopping-board, colander, corer, corkscrew, cruet set, dough hook, egg separator, egg slicer, egg-timer, fish slice, flour dredger, food processor, fork, garlic press, grater, herb mill, ice-cream scoop, icing syringe, jelly mould, kitchen scales, knife block, lemon squeezer, liquidizer, mandolin, measuring jug, meat thermometer, mezzaluna, mincer, mixing bowl, nutcracker, nutmeg grater, pasta maker, pastry board, pastry brush, pastry cutter, peeler, pepper mill, pie funnel, potato masher, pudding basin, punch bowl, rolling-pin, salad spinner, scissors, sharpening steel, shears, sieve, sifter, skewer, spatula, spice rack, stoner, storage jar, tea caddy, tea infuser, tea strainer, toast rack, tongs, tureen, vegetable brush, whisk, wine cooler, wine rack, yoghurt maker, zester; *types of knife:* boning knife, bread knife, butter knife, carving knife, cheese knife, cleaver, cocktail knife, cook's knife, fish knife, grapefruit knife, Kitchen Devils®, palette knife, paring knife, steak knife, table knife, vegetable knife; *types of spoon:* dessertspoon, draining spoon, ladle, measuring spoon, serving spoon, skimmer, straining spoon, tablespoon, teaspoon, wooden spoon

Types of cooking utensil include:
baking sheet, bun tin, cake tin, flan tin, loaf tin, muffin tin, pie plate, quiche dish, bain-marie, brochette, casserole, cocotte, deep-fat fryer, egg coddler, egg poacher, fish kettle, fondue set, frying-pan, grill pan, milk pan, preserving pan, pressure cooker, ramekin, roasting pan, saucepan, skillet, slow cooker, soufflé dish, steamer, stockpot, terrine, vegetable steamer, wok

kittenish *adj* coquettish, cute, flirtatious, frisky, frolicsome, playful, sportive
F3 staid

knack *n* ability, adroitness, aptitude, bent, capability, capacity, competence, dexterity, expertise, facility, faculty, flair, forte, genius, gift, handiness, hang *colloq*, proficiency, propensity *formal*, quickness, skilfulness, skill, talent, trick

knapsack *n* backpack, bag, duffel bag, flight bag, haversack, hold-all, kitbag, pack, rucksack, shoulder-bag

knave *n* cheat, rascal, reprobate, rogue, scallywag, scamp, scoundrel, swindler, swine, villain

knavery *n* chicanery, corruption, deceit, deception, devilry, dishonesty, double-dealing, duplicity *formal*, fraud, hanky-panky *colloq*, imposture, knavishness, mischief, monkey business *colloq*, roguery, trickery, villainy

knavish *adj* contemptible, corrupt, deceitful, deceptive, devilish, dishonest, dishonourable, fiendish, fraudulent, mischievous, rascally, reprobate, roguish, scoundrelly, unprincipled, unscrupulous, villainous, wicked
F3 honest, honourable, scrupulous

knead *v* form, knuckle, malax *formal*, malaxate *formal*, manipulate, massage, mould, ply, press, rub, shape, squeeze, work

kneel *v* bend, defer to, fall to your knees, genuflect *formal*, get down on your knees, kowtow, make obeisance *formal*

knell *n* chime, end, peal, ring, ringing, sound, toll

knickers *n* bikini briefs, bloomers, briefs, camiknickers, Directoire knickers, drawers *colloq*, knickerbockers, lingerie, panties, pants, smalls *colloq*, underwear

knick-knack *n* bagatelle, bauble, bric-à-brac, gewgaw, gimcrack, ornament, plaything, trifle, trinket

knife *n* blade, carver, craft knife, cutter, dagger, dirk, flick knife, jackknife, machete, penknife, pocket knife, scalpel, skene-dhu, Stanley knife®, Swiss army knife, switchblade
♦ *v* bayonet, cut, lacerate, pierce, rip, slash, stab, wound

knight *n* banneret, cavalier, cavalryman, champion, chevalier, equestrian, freelance, gallant, horseman, kemper, kempery-man, knight-errant, man-at-arms, soldier, warrior

knightly *adj* bold, chivalrous, courageous, courtly, dauntless, gallant, gracious, heroic, honourable, intrepid, noble, soldierly, valiant, valorous *formal*
F3 cowardly, ignoble

knit *v* **1** *knit the pieces together:* ally, bind, connect, draw together, fasten, interlace, intertwine, join, link, mend, secure, tie, unite **2** *knit a pullover:* crochet, knot, loop, purl, weave **3** *knit your brows:* crease, furrow, gather, wrinkle

knob *n* **1** *turned the knob and entered:* door-handle, handle, switch **2** *a raised knob on a shield:* ball, boss, bump, capitulum, lump, nub, projection, protrusion, protuberance, umbo *technical*

knock *v* **1** *knock on the door:* hit, pound, rap, slap, smack, strike, tap, thump **2** *knock someone on the head:* bang, batter, belt *colloq*, box, clip, clout *colloq*, cuff, hit, pound, punch, slap, smack, strike, swipe, thump, wallop *colloq*, whack *colloq* **3** *knocked her head against the wall:* bang, bash, bump, dash, hit, jolt, strike, whack *colloq* **4** *the press are always knocking her:* attack, censure *formal*, condemn, criticize, deprecate *formal*, disparage *formal*, find fault with, pan *colloq*, pick on *colloq*, run down *colloq*, slam *colloq*, slate *colloq*, tear to pieces *colloq*
F3 4 boost, praise
♦ *n* **1** *a knock at the door:* banging, hammering, hit, pounding, rap, tap **2** *took a knock on the head:* bang, belt *colloq*, blow, box, bump, clip *colloq*, clout *colloq*, cuff, pounding, rap, slap, smack, thump, wallop *colloq*, whack *colloq* **3** *took a while to recover from that knock:* bad experience, blow, defeat, failure, misfortune, rebuff, rejection, reversal, setback, stroke of bad luck
▶ **knock about 1** *her father knocked her about:* abuse, bash, batter, beat up, bruise, buffet, damage, hit, hurt, injure, maltreat, manhandle, mistreat, punch, strike, wound **2** *spent July knocking about in Europe:* gad, gallivant, ramble, range, roam, rove, saunter, traipse, travel, wander **3** *I used to knock about with her:* associate, consort *formal*, go around, hang around *colloq*
▶ **knock down 1** *knocked down his opponent:* batter, clout, fell, floor, level, pound, smash **2** *knock down a block of flats:* demolish, destroy, level, pull down, raze, wreck **3** *knocked down by a truck:* hit, knock over, run down, run over **4** *knocked down the price:* decrease, lower, reduce
▶ **knock off 1** *knocked off by a fellow gangster:* assassinate, bump off *colloq*, do away with, do in *colloq*, get rid of, kill, murder, slay, waste *slang*, whack *slang* **2** *knock off five pounds for a quick sale:* deduct, take away **3** *we usually knock off at five:* cease *formal*, clock off, clock out, finish, finish work, pack (it) in *colloq*, stop, terminate *formal* **4** *knock off a DVD player:* filch, lift *colloq*, nick *colloq*, pilfer, pinch *colloq*, rip off *colloq*, rob, snaffle *colloq*, snitch *colloq*, steal, swipe *colloq*
▶ **knock out 1** *knock someone out:* fell, floor, KO *colloq*, level, prostrate, render unconscious, strike down **2** *knocked out of a competition:* beat, defeat, eliminate, get the better of, overcome **3** *knocked out by that performance:* amaze, astonish, astound, bowl over *colloq*, impress, knock for six *colloq*, overwhelm, shock, startle, stun, surprise, take your breath away
▶ **knock up** build quickly, improvise, jerry-build, make quickly, put together hurriedly, throw together
F3 demolish

knockout *n* attraction, coup, hit, sensation, smash *colloq*, smash-hit *colloq*, stunner *colloq*, success, triumph, winner
F3 flop, loser

knoll *n* barrow, elevation, hill, hillock, hummock, knowe *Scot*, koppie, mound

knot v bind, entwine, knit, lash, leash, loop, secure, tether, tie, weave
♦ n **1** *tied in a secure knot*: bond, fastening, joint, ligature, loop, splice, tie, twist **2** *a knot of idlers*: band, bunch, circle, clump, cluster, crowd, gathering, group, ring **3** *a knot on a tree*: gnarl, knob, knub, knurl, lump, swelling

---

Types of knot include:
bend, Blackwall hitch, blood knot, bow, bowline, running bowline, carrick bend, clove hitch, common whipping, double-overhang, Englishman's tie (or knot), figure of eight, fisherman's bend, fisherman's knot, flat knot, granny knot, half hitch, highwayman's hitch, hitch, Hunter's bend, loop knot, overhand knot or thumb knot, reef knot or square knot, rolling hitch, round turn and two half hitches, seizing, sheepshank, sheet bend or common bend or swab hitch, slipknot, spade-end knot, surgeon's knot, tie, timber hitch, Turk's head, turle knot, wall knot, weaver's knot, Windsor knot

---

knotty *adj* **1** *a knotty problem*: anfractuous *formal*, baffling, Byzantine, complex, complicated, difficult, hard, intricate, mystifying, perplexing, problematical, puzzling, thorny, tricky, troublesome **2** *a knotty stump*: bumpy, gnarled, knobby, knotted, nodose, nodous, nodular, rough, rugged

know v **1** *to know French*: be clued up about *colloq*, be conversant with, be well-versed in, comprehend, have at your fingertips *colloq*, have fathomed, have something taped *colloq*, understand **2** *you know the rules*: apprehend, be aware of, be cognizant of *formal*, be conscious of, have experience of, know like the back of your hand *colloq*, understand **3** *I used to know George*: associate with, be acquainted with, be familiar with, be friends with, be on good terms with **4** *know what makes a good wine*: differentiate, discern, discriminate, distinguish, identify, make out, tell (apart)

know-all *n* clever clogs *colloq*, clever dick *colloq*, know-it-all, smart alec *colloq*, smart arse *slang*, smartypants *colloq*, wise guy *colloq*, wiseacre

know-how *n* ability, adeptness, adroitness, aptitude, bent, capability, competence, dexterity, experience, expertise, faculty, flair, gumption, ingenuity, knack, knowledge, proficiency, savoir-faire, savvy *colloq*, skill, talent

knowing *adj* astute, aware, conscious, cunning, discerning, expressive, meaningful, perceptive, shrewd, significant

knowingly *adv* by design, calculatedly, consciously, deliberately, designedly, intentionally, on purpose, purposely, studiedly, wilfully, willingly, wittingly

knowledge *n* **1** *general knowledge*: data, education, enlightenment, erudition *formal*, facts, information, instruction, know-how *colloq*, learning, letters, scholarship, schooling, tuition, wisdom **2** *I had no knowledge of him*: acquaintance, awareness, cognizance *formal*, consciousness, familiarity, intimacy **3** *my limited knowledge of baseball*: apprehension, cognition *formal*, comprehension, discernment, expertise, grasp, understanding
🔁 **1** ignorance **2** unawareness

knowledgeable *adj* **1** *very knowledgeable about chess*: a mine of information *colloq*, educated, enlightened, erudite *formal*, informed, intelligent, learned, lettered, scholarly, well-informed, well-read **2** *knowledgeable of my whereabouts*: acquainted, au fait, aware, conscious, conversant, experienced, familiar, in the know *colloq*
🔁 **1** ignorant

known *adj* acknowledged, admitted, avowed, celebrated, commonplace, confessed, familiar, famous, noted, obvious, patent, plain, proclaimed, published, recognized, revealed, well-known

knuckle
▶ **knuckle down** begin to study, buckle down, start to work hard
▶ **knuckle under** accede *formal*, acquiesce *formal*, buckle under, capitulate, defer, give in, give way, submit, succumb, surrender, yield

kowtow v bow and scrape *colloq*, cringe, curry favour, defer, fawn, flatter, grovel, kneel, pander, pay court, suck up *colloq*, toady *colloq*

kudos *n* acclaim, applause, distinction, esteem *formal*, fame, glory, honour, laudation *formal*, laurels, plaudits, praise, prestige, regard *formal*, renown, reputation, repute

L

label n 1 *stick a label on the package:* docket, mark, marker, sticker, tab, tag, ticket 2 *came under the label of feminism:* badge, brand, categorization, characterization, classification, description, designation, epithet, identification, name, nickname, tag, title 3 *the supermarket's own label:* brand, brand name, proprietary name, trademark
♦ v 1 *labelled all the pictures:* attach a label to, mark, stamp, tag, ticket 2 *labelled her a feminist:* brand, call, categorize, characterize, class, classify, define, describe, designate, dub, identify, name, term

laborious adj arduous, backbreaking, difficult, fatiguing, hard, heavy, onerous, strenuous, tedious, tiresome, tiring, toilsome, tough, uphill, wearisome, wearying
☲ easy, effortless

labour n 1 *manual labour:* chore, diligence, drudgery, effort, employment, exertion, grind *colloq*, hard work, industriousness, job, slog *colloq*, sweat *colloq*, task, toil, work 2 *cheap labour:* employees, hands, labourers, workers, workforce, workmen 3 *go into labour:* birth, childbirth, contractions, delivery, labour pains, pangs, parturition *technical*, throes
☲ 1 ease, leisure
♦ v 1 *labouring on a building site:* drudge, endeavour, exert yourself, grind *colloq*, kill yourself *colloq*, plod, slave, strive, struggle, sweat *colloq*, toil, travail *formal*, work, work hard 2 *to labour a point:* dwell on, elaborate, overdo, overemphasize, overstress, put too much emphasis on, strain 3 *labour hard to get results:* do your best *colloq*, endeavour, give your all *colloq*, go all out *colloq*, strive, struggle, work hard
☲ 1 idle, laze, lounge

laboured adj affected *formal*, awkward, complicated, contrived, difficult, forced, heavy, overdone, overwrought, ponderous, stiff, stilted, strained, studied, unnatural
☲ easy, natural

labourer n blue-collar worker, drudge, hand, hireling, manual worker, menial, navvy, unskilled worker, worker, workman

labyrinth n complexity, complication, confusion, enigma, entanglement, intricacy, jungle, maze, network, puzzle, riddle, tangle, warren, winding

labyrinthine adj Byzantine, complex, complicated, confused, convoluted *formal*, intricate, involved, knotty, mazelike, mazy, perplexing, puzzling, tangled, tortuous, winding
☲ simple, straightforward

lace n 1 *working in lace:* crochet, filigree, meshwork, netting, open work, tatting 2 *the lace of a shoe:* bootlace, cord, lacing, shoelace, string, thong, tie, twine
♦ v 1 *lace the panels together:* attach, bind, close, do up, fasten, intertwine, interweave, secure, string, thread, tie, twine 2 *lace a drink with whisky:* add to, blend, flavour, fortify *formal*, mix in, spike *colloq*, strengthen

lacerate v 1 *lacerate the skin:* claw, cut (open), gash, injure, maim, mangle, mutilate, rend, rip, slash, tear, wound 2 *lacerated by his satire:* afflict *formal*, distress, harrow, hurt, torment, wound

laceration n cut, gash, injury, maim, mutilation, rent, rip, slash, tear, wound

lachrymose adj crying, dolorous *formal*, lugubrious *formal*, melancholy, mournful, sad, sobbing, tearful, teary, weeping, weepy, woeful
☲ happy, laughing

lack n absence, dearth, deficiency, deprivation, destitution, emptiness, insufficiency, need, paucity *formal*, privation *formal*, scantiness, scarcity, shortage, vacancy, void, want *formal*
☲ abundance, profusion
♦ v be clean/fresh out of *colloq*, be deficient in, have a shortage of, have need of, miss, need, not have, not have enough of, require, want *formal*

lackadaisical adj abstracted, apathetic, dreamy, enervated *formal*, half-hearted, idle, indifferent, indolent *formal*, inert, languid *formal*, languorous *formal*, lazy, lethargic, limp, listless, lukewarm, spiritless
☲ active, dynamic, energetic, vigorous

lackey n 1 *the president's lackeys:* doormat *colloq*, fawner, flatterer, hanger-on, instrument, minion, parasite, pawn, sycophant, toady, tool, yes-man *colloq* 2 *uniformed lackeys:* attendant, footman, manservant, menial, servant, steward, valet

lacking adj defective, deficient, flawed, inadequate, minus, missing, needing, short of, wanting *formal*, without

lacklustre adj boring, commonplace, dim, drab, dry, dull, flat, insipid, leaden, lifeless, run-of-the-mill *colloq*, spiritless, tedious, unimaginative, uninspired, uninteresting, vapid
☲ bright, brilliant, inspired, lively

laconic adj abrupt, blunt, brief, concise, crisp, curt, economical, incisive, pithy, short, succinct, taciturn, terse, to the point
☲ verbose, wordy

lacuna n blank, break, cavity, gap, hiatus *formal*, omission, space, void

lad n 1 *he was just a lad:* boy, juvenile, kid *colloq*, schoolboy, son, youngster, youth 2 *out clubbing with the lads:* bloke *colloq*, chap, fellow, guy *colloq*

laden adj 1 *a laden shopping trolley:* chock-full, full, loaded, packed, stuffed 2 *words laden with regret:* burdened, charged, fraught, loaded, oppressed, weighed down, weighted
☲ 1 empty

la-di-da adj affected *formal*, conceited, foppish, highfalutin *colloq*, mannered, over-refined, posh, pretentious, put-on *colloq*, snobbish, snooty, stuck-up *colloq*, toffee-nosed *colloq*

ladle v bail, dip, dish, lade, scoop, shovel, spoon
► **ladle out** disburse, dish out, distribute, dole out, hand out

lady n dame, damsel, female, gentlewoman, matron, noblewoman, woman, young woman

ladylike adj courteous, courtly, cultured, decorous *formal*, elegant, genteel, matronly, modest, polished, polite, proper, queenly, refined, respectable, well-bred, well-mannered

lag *v* bring up the rear, dally, dawdle, delay, drag your feet *colloq*, fall behind, hang back, idle, kick your heels *colloq*, linger, loiter, lounge *colloq*, saunter, shilly-shally *colloq*, shuffle, straggle, tarry *formal*, trail
🔁 hurry, keep up, lead

laggard *n* dawdler, idler, lingerer, loafer, loiterer, lounger *colloq*, saunterer, slowcoach *colloq*, sluggard, snail, straggler
🔁 dynamo, go-getter *colloq*, live wire

lagoon *n* bayou *US*, bog, fen, lake, marsh, pond, pool, shallows, swamp

laid-back *adj* at ease, calm, casual, cool, easy-going, free and easy, imperturbable *formal*, leisurely, passionless, relaxed, unflappable *colloq*, unhurried, untroubled, unworried
🔁 tense, uptight *colloq*

laid up *adj* bedridden, disabled, hors de combat, housebound, ill, immobilized, incapacitated, injured, on the sick list, out of action, sick

lair

Lairs and homes of creatures include:
sett (*badger*); den (*bear*); lodge (*beaver*); hive (*bee*); nest (*bird*); byre (*cow*); eyrie (*eagle*); coop (*fowl*); earth (*fox*); form (*hare*); den (*lion*); fortress (*mole*); hole, nest (*mouse*); holt (*otter*); sty (*pig*); dovecote (*pigeon*); burrow, warren (*rabbit*); pen, fold (*sheep*); shell (*snail*); drey (*squirrel*); nest, vespiary (*wasp*)

---

laissez-faire *adj* free-enterprise, free-market, free-trade, live and let live *colloq*, non-interfering, non-interventionist, permissive

lake *n* basin, bayou *US*, billabong *Austr*, dam, lagoon, loch *Scot*, mere, pond, pool, reservoir, tarn

lam *v* batter, beat, biff *colloq*, clout *colloq*, hit, knock, leather, pelt, pound, pummel, strike, thrash, thump, wallop *colloq*, whack *colloq*

lambaste *v* **1** *lambasted her for her poor attitude:* berate *formal*, castigate *formal*, censure *formal*, criticize, rebuke, reprimand, reprove *formal*, roast *colloq*, scold, upbraid **2** *lambasted him with her handbag:* batter, beat, clout *colloq*, drub, flay, flog, leather, strike, tan *colloq*, thrash, thump, wallop *colloq*, whack *colloq*, whip

lame *adj* **1** *an accident had left him lame:* crippled, disabled, gammy *colloq*, halting, handicapped, hobbling, hurt, incapacitated *formal*, injured, limping, maimed, poorly *colloq* **2** *a lame excuse:* defective, feeble, flimsy, inadequate, poor, thin, unconvincing, unsatisfactory, weak
🔁 **1** able-bodied **2** convincing

lament *v* bemoan *formal*, bewail, complain, cry, deplore, grieve, groan, keen, moan, mourn, regret, sob, sorrow, ululate *formal*, wail, weep
🔁 celebrate, rejoice
♦ *n* complaint, dirge, elegy, groan, howl, keen, lamentation, moan, requiem, threnody *formal*, wail

lamentable *adj* deplorable, distressing, grievous, miserable, mournful, pitiful, regrettable, sorrowful, terrible, tragic, unfortunate, unsatisfactory, woeful, wretched

lamentation *n* deploration *formal*, dirge, elegy, grief, grieving, jeremiad, keen, keening, lament, moan, mourning, plaint *formal*, sobbing, sorrow, threnody *formal*, ululation *formal*, wailing, weeping
🔁 celebration, rejoicing

laminate *v* coat, cover, face, plate, veneer

lamp *n* bulb, lantern, light, light bulb

lampoon *n* burlesque, caricature, parody, pasquinade, satire, send-up *colloq*, skit, spoof, take-off *colloq*, travesty
♦ *v* burlesque, caricature, make fun of, mock, parody, pasquinade, ridicule, satirize, send up *colloq*, spoof, take off *colloq*

lampooner *n* caricaturist, parodist, pasquilant, pasquiler, pasquinader, satirist

lance *v* cut (open), incise, pierce, prick, puncture, slit
♦ *n* bayonet, harpoon, javelin, lancet, pike, spear

land *n* **1** *the ship reached land:* dry land, earth, ground, loam, soil, terra firma, terrain **2** *invested her wealth in land:* acreage, acres, agricultural land, country, countryside, estate, farmland, fields, grounds, manor, open space, property, real estate, rural area, tract **3** *my native land:* area, country, district, domain, fatherland, motherland, nation, native country, province, realm, region, state, territory
♦ *v* **1** *landed at Naples:* alight, berth, come to land, come to rest, disembark, dismount, dock, go ashore, unload **2** *to land an aeroplane:* bring down, bring to rest, come in to land, take down, touch down **3** *landed in a mess:* arrive, end up *colloq*, find yourself, get, reach, turn up, wind up *colloq* **4** *to land a good job:* achieve, acquire, capture, gain, get, net, obtain, procure *formal*, secure, win **5** *land you with another bill:* burden, encumber, oppress, saddle, tax, trouble, weigh down **6** *land a blow on the ear:* administer, deal, deliver, deposit, direct, fetch *colloq*, give, hit, inflict

landlady, landlord *n* freeholder, host, hotelier, hotel-keeper, innkeeper, mine host, owner, proprietor, publican, restaurateur, tenant

landmark *n* **1** *the country's most famous landmark:* beacon, boundary, cairn, feature, milepost, milestone, monument, signpost **2** *the ruling was a landmark in the civil-rights movement:* crisis, turning-point, watershed

landscape *n* aspect, countryside, outlook, panorama, perspective, prospect, scene, scenery, view, vista

landslide *n* avalanche, earthfall, landslip, mudslip, rockfall
♦ *adj* decisive, emphatic, overwhelming, runaway

lane *n* alley(way), avenue, byroad, byway, driveway, footpath, footway, passage(way), path(way), towpath, track, way

language *n* **1** *human language:* communication, conversation, discourse *formal*, parlance *formal*, speaking, speech, talk, terminology, uttering, verbalizing, vocabulary, vocalizing **2** *picturesque language:* diction, expression, phraseology, phrasing, rhetoric, style, utterance, wording

---

Languages of the world include:
Afrikaans, Albanian, Amharic, Arabic,

Armenian, Bantu, Basque, Bengali, Burmese, Belorussian, Bulgarian, Catalan, Chinese, Creole, Croatian, Czech, Danish, Dhivehi, Dutch, Dzongkha, English, Esperanto, Estonian, Farsi, Finnish, Flemish, French, Frisian, Gaelic, Georgian, German, Greek, Hawaiian, Hebrew, Hindi, Hindustani, Icelandic, Indonesian, Irish, Italian, Japanese, Kazakh, Khmer, Kurdish, Kyrgyz, Lao, Lapp, Latin, Latvian, Lithuanian, Magyar, Malagasy, Malay, Maltese, Mandarin, Manx, Maori, Nepali, Norwegian, Pashto, Pidgin, Polish, Portuguese, Punjabi, Quechua, Romansch, Romany, Romanian, Russian, Sanskrit, Serbian, Sesotho, Setswana, Sinhalese, Slovak, Slovenian, Somali, Spanish, Swahili, Swedish, Tagalog, Tajik, Tamil, Thai, Tibetan, Turkish, Turkmen, Ukrainian, Urdu, Uzbek, Vietnamese, Welsh, Xhosa, Yiddish, Zulu

languid *adj* debilitated *formal*, drooping, dull, enervated *formal*, faint, feeble, heavy, inactive, indifferent, inert, lackadaisical, languorous *formal*, lazy, lethargic, limp, listless, pining, sickly, slow, sluggish, spiritless, torpid *formal*, unenthusiastic, uninterested, weak, weary
🗷 alert, lively, vivacious

languish *v* decline, deteriorate, droop, fade, fail, faint, flag, rot, sicken, sink, waste, waste away, weaken, wilt, wither
🗷 flourish

languor *n* calm, debility *formal*, dreaminess, drowsiness, enervation *formal*, ennui, faintness, fatigue, feebleness, frailty, heaviness, indolence *formal*, inertia, lassitude *formal*, laziness, lethargy, listlessness, lull, oppressiveness, relaxation, silence, sleepiness, sloth, stillness, torpor *formal*, weakness, weariness
🗷 alacrity, gusto

lank *adj* 1 *lank hair*: drooping, lifeless, limp, lustreless, scraggy, straggling 2 *lank young people*: emaciated, gaunt, lanky, lean, long, rawboned, scrawny, skinny, slender, slim, tall, thin
🗷 1 burly

lanky *adj* gangling, gaunt, lean, scraggy, scrawny, slender, slim, tall, thin, weedy
🗷 short, squat

lap[1] *n* 1 *a lap of the track*: ambit, circle, circuit, compass, course, distance, loop, orbit, round, tour 2 *the last lap of the journey*: leg, section, stage
♦ *v* cover, encase, enfold, envelop, fold, overlap, surround, swaddle, swathe, wind, wrap

lap[2] *v* drink, lick, sip, sup
▶ **lap up** absorb, accept eagerly, listen in to, take in enthusiastically

lapse *n* 1 *a fatal lapse of judgement*: aberration *formal*, backsliding, dereliction *formal*, error, failing, fault, indiscretion, mistake, negligence, omission, oversight, relapse, slip 2 *a lapse in quality*: backsliding, decline, degeneration, descent, deterioration, downturn, drop, fall, slipping, worsening 3 *a lapse of several years*: break, gap, hiatus *formal*, intermission, interruption, interval, lull, pause
♦ *v* 1 *lapse into bad habits*: backslide, decline, degenerate, deteriorate, drift, drop, fall, go down the tube(s) *colloq*, go downhill *colloq*, go to pot *colloq*, go to rack and ruin *colloq*, go to the dogs *colloq*, sink, slide, slip, worsen 2 *I let my*

membership lapse: become void/invalid, cease, end, expire, run out, stop, terminate *formal*
🗷 2 continue

lapsed *adj* discontinued *formal*, ended, expired, finished, invalid, obsolete, out of date, outdated, run out, unrenewed
🗷 continued, renewed

larceny *n* burglary, expropriation *formal*, heist *slang*, misappropriation *formal*, pilfering, piracy, purloining *formal*, robbery, stealing, theft

larder *n* pantry, scullery, storage room, storeroom

large *adj* 1 *a large mansion*: ample, big, broad, bulky, bumper *colloq*, colossal, commodious *formal*, dirty great *colloq*, enormous, giant, gigantic, ginormous *colloq*, grand, grandiose, great, high, huge, humungous *colloq*, immense, jumbo *colloq*, king-sized, mammoth, massive, monumental, prodigious, sizeable, stupendous, substantial, tall, vast, voluminous *formal*, whopping *colloq* 2 *play a large role in my plans*: big, comprehensive, considerable, exhaustive, extensive, far-reaching, full
🗷 1 small, tiny

largely *adv* by and large, chiefly, considerably, extensively, for the most part, generally, greatly, in the main, mainly, mostly, predominantly, primarily, principally, to a large extent, widely

large-scale *adj* broad, country-wide, epic, expansive, extensive, far-reaching, global, nationwide, sweeping, vast, wholesale, wide, wide-ranging
🗷 minor

largesse *n* aid, allowance, alms, benefaction, bequest, bounty, charity, donation, endowment, generosity, gift, grant, handout, kindness, liberality, munificence *formal*, open-handedness, philanthropy, present
🗷 meanness

lark *n* 1 *got up to some dangerous larks*: antic, caper, cavorting, escapade, fling, fooling, frolic, game, horseplay, mischief, play, prank, revel, romp, skylark *colloq* 2 *this writing lark*: activity, business, chore, game *colloq*, job, task
♦ *v* caper, cavort, fool around/about, frolic, gambol, have fun, mess about, play, play tricks, rollick, romp, skylark *colloq*, sport

lascivious *adj* bawdy, blue *colloq*, coarse, crude, dirty, horny *colloq*, indecent, lecherous, lewd, libidinous *formal*, licentious, lustful, obscene, offensive, pornographic, prurient *formal*, randy *colloq*, ribald, salacious, scurrilous, sensual, smutty *colloq*, suggestive, unchaste, vulgar, wanton

lash *n* blow, hit, stroke, swipe, whip
♦ *v* 1 *lash an insolent slave*: batter, beat, flail, flog, hit, scourge, strike, thrash, wallop *colloq*, whack *colloq*, whip 2 *lash it to the deck*: affix, bind, fasten, join, make fast, rope, secure, strap, tether, tie 3 *waves lashing the shore*: beat, break on, buffet, dash, pound, smash, strike 4 *an animal lashing its tail*: flick, swish, switch, wag, whip
▶ **lash out 1** *lash out at someone*: attack, criticize, have a go at, hit out at, speak out against 2 *lash out on new clothes*: spend a fortune *colloq*, spend a lot of money, spend extravagantly, spend money like water *colloq*, splash out *colloq*

lass n bird slang, chick slang, girl, lassie, miss, schoolgirl, young woman

lassitude n apathy, drowsiness, dullness, enervation formal, exhaustion, fatigue, heaviness, languor formal, lethargy, listlessness, sluggishness, tiredness, torpor formal, weariness
🔁 energy, vigour

last¹ adj 1 we won our last match: latest, most recent, previous 2 a last cigarette: closing, concluding, ending, extreme, final, finishing, furthest, hindmost, latest, rearmost, remotest, terminal, ultimate, utmost 3 the last person I expected help from: least likely, least suitable, most unlikely, most unsuitable
🔁 1 next 2 first, initial 3 first, most likely
♦ adv after, at the back/rear, at the end, behind, finally, ultimately
🔁 first, firstly

last² v abide formal, carry on, continue, endure, exist, go on, hold on, hold out, keep (on), persist, remain, stand up, stay, subsist formal, survive, wear
🔁 cease, fade, stop

last-ditch adj all-out colloq, desperate, eleventh-hour colloq, final, frantic, frenzied, heroic, last-chance, last-gasp colloq, straining, struggling, wild

lasting adj abiding, ceaseless formal, continuing, durable, enduring, everlasting, external, interminable formal, lifelong, long-lived, long-standing, long-term, never-ending, permanent, perpetual, persisting, surviving, unceasing, unchanging, undying, unending
🔁 brief, fleeting, short-lived

lastly adv finally, in conclusion, in the end, to sum up, ultimately
🔁 firstly

latch n bar, bolt, catch, fastening, hasp, hook, lock
♦ v bar, bolt, catch, fasten, hook, lock, make secure
▶ **latch on to 1** latch on to someone: attach yourself to, follow, not want to leave 2 latch on to what is going on: apprehend formal, comprehend, grasp, learn, realize, twig colloq, understand

late adj 1 a late arrival: behind, behind schedule, behind time, behindhand, delayed, last-minute, overdue, slow, tardy formal, unpunctual 2 my late partner: dead, deceased, defunct, departed, former, old, past, preceding, previous
🔁 1 early, punctual
♦ adv behind schedule, behind time, behindhand, belatedly, dilatorily formal, in arrears, tardily formal, unpunctually
🔁 early, punctually

lately adv latterly, newly, not long ago, of late, recently

lateness n belatedness, delay, dilatoriness formal, retardation formal, tardiness formal, unpunctuality
🔁 earliness

latent adj concealed, dormant, hidden, inactive, invisible, lurking, passive, possible, potential, quiescent formal, secret, underlying, undeveloped, unexpressed, unrealized, unrevealed, unseen, veiled
🔁 active, apparent, conspicuous

later adv after, afterwards, at a future time/date, at a later time, in a while, in due course, in the (near) future, later on, next, some other time, subsequently
🔁 earlier
♦ adj following, next, subsequent, succeeding

lateral adj edgeways, flanking, indirect, marginal, oblique, side, sideward, sideways, slanting

latest adj current, fashionable, in colloq, modern, most recent, newest, now, ultimate, up-to-date, up-to-the-minute colloq, with it colloq
🔁 earliest

lather n 1 work the soap into a lather: bubbles, foam, froth, soapsuds, suds 2 worked herself up into a lather: agitation, anxiety, dither, fever, flap colloq, fluster, flutter, fuss, state colloq, stew colloq, sweat colloq, tizzy colloq
♦ v foam, froth, rub, whip up

latitude n breadth, carte blanche, clearance, extent, field, freedom, indulgence, laxity, leeway, liberty, licence, play, range, reach, room, scope, space, span, spread, sweep, unrestrictedness, width

latter adj closing, concluding, end, ensuing, final, last, last-mentioned, later, second, succeeding, successive
🔁 former

latter-day adj contemporary, current, modern, present-day

latterly adv lately, most recently, of late, recently
🔁 formerly

lattice n espalier, fretwork, grate, grating, grid, grille, lattice-work, mesh, network, openwork, reticulation formal, tracery, trellis, web

laud v acclaim, admire, applaud, approve, celebrate, extol, glorify, hail, honour, magnify, praise
🔁 blame, condemn, curse, damn

laudable adj admirable, commendable, creditable, estimable, excellent, exemplary, meritorious formal, of note, praiseworthy, sterling, worthy
🔁 damnable, execrable

laudation n acclaim, acclamation, accolade, adulation, blessing, celebrity, commendation, devotion, encomion formal, encomium formal, eulogy formal, extolment, glorification, glory, homage, kudos, paean formal, panegyric formal, praise, reverence, tribute, veneration formal
🔁 condemnation, criticism

laudatory adj acclamatory, adulatory, approbatory formal, approving, celebratory, commendatory, complimentary, encomiastic(al) formal, eulogistic formal, glorifying, panegyrical formal
🔁 damning

laugh v be in stitches colloq, be rolling in the aisles colloq, break up colloq, burst out laughing, cackle, chortle, chuckle, crease up colloq, dissolve into laughter, fall about colloq, giggle, guffaw, hoot, laugh like a drain colloq, peal, roar, roar with laughter, snigger, split your sides colloq, titter
♦ n 1 have a good laugh: chortle, chuckle, giggle, guffaw, hoot colloq, peel, roar, scream colloq,

snigger, titter **2** *do it for a laugh:* fun, hoax, jest, joke, lark, play, prank, sport, trick
▶ **laugh at** deride *formal,* jeer, make a fool of, make jokes about, make/poke fun of, mock, ridicule, scoff at, scorn, taunt
▶ **laugh off** belittle, brush aside, dismiss, disregard, ignore, make little of, minimize, shrug off

laughable *adj* absurd, comical, derisive, derisory, farcical, ludicrous, nonsensical, preposterous, ridiculous

laughing-stock *n* Aunt Sally, butt, dupe, fair game, figure of fun, stooge, target, victim

laughter *n* amusement, cheerfulness, chortling, chuckling, convulsions, giggling, glee, guffawing, happiness, hilarity, laughing, merriment, mirth, sniggering, tittering

launch *v* **1** *launch a missile:* discharge, dispatch, fire, float, project, propel, send off, set afloat, set in motion, throw **2** *launch a new career:* begin, commence *formal,* embark on, establish, found, inaugurate, initiate, instigate, institute, introduce, open, organize, set in motion *colloq,* set the ball rolling *colloq,* set up, start

laundry *n* **1** *do the laundry:* (dirty) clothes, wash, washing **2** *go to the laundry:* dry cleaner's, launderette, Laundromat® US

lavatory *n* bathroom, bog *colloq,* cloakroom, comfort station, john *US slang,* kazi *slang,* ladies' room, latrine, loo *colloq,* powder room, privy, public convenience, rest room *US,* the gents *colloq,* the ladies *colloq,* toilet, urinal, washroom, water closet, WC

lavish *adj* **1** *lavish floral arrangements:* abundant, copious, gorgeous, grand, lush, luxuriant, plentiful, profuse, prolific, rich, splendid, unlimited **2** *lavish hospitality:* bountiful, excessive, extravagant, free, generous, immoderate, intemperate, liberal, open-handed, prodigal, profligate, thriftless, unsparing, unstinting, wasteful, wild
▣ **1** scant **2** frugal, mean, thrifty
♦ *v* bestow *formal,* deluge, dissipate, expend, heap, pour, shower, spend, squander, waste

law *n* **1** *to pass a law:* act, charter, code, command, commandment, constitution, decree, directive, edict, enactment, legislation, order, ordinance, pronouncement, regulation, rule, statute **2** *the laws of physics:* axiom, canon, code, criterion, direction, formula, guideline, instruction, maxim, precept, principle, rule, standard, tenet **3** *to study law:* jurisprudence, legislation **4** *to go to law over something:* lawsuit, litigation

law-abiding *adj* complying, decent, dutiful, good, honest, honourable, lawful, obedient, orderly, righteous, upright, upstanding, virtuous
▣ lawless

law-breaker *n* convict, criminal, crook *colloq,* culprit, delinquent, felon, infractor *formal,* miscreant, offender, outlaw, sinner, transgressor, trespasser, villain *colloq,* wrongdoer

lawful *adj* allowable, authorized, constitutional, just, legal, legalized, legitimate, licit *formal,* permissible, proper, recognized, rightful, sanctioned, valid, warranted
▣ illegal, illicit, unlawful

lawless *adj* **1** *lawless behaviour:* anarchic(al), criminal, disorderly, illegal, insurgent, insurrectionary, law-breaking, mutinous, rebellious, reckless, revolutionary, riotous, seditious, unrestrained, unruly, wrongdoing **2** *a lawless place:* anarchic(al), chaotic, disorderly, ungoverned, unruly, wild
▣ **1** law-abiding **2** law-abiding

lawlessness *n* anarchy, chaos, disorder, insurgency, insurrection, mobocracy *colloq,* mob-rule, ochlocracy *formal,* piracy, racketeering, rebellion, revolution, sedition
▣ order

lawsuit *n* action, argument, case, cause, contest, dispute, indictment *technical,* legal action, legal proceedings, litigation, proceedings, process, prosecution, suit, trial

lawyer *n* advocate, attorney, barrister, brief *colloq,* counsel, legal adviser, legal representative, QC, solicitor

lax *adj* **1** *security was lax:* careless, casual, easy-going, heedless, inattentive, indulgent, lenient, neglectful, negligent, permissive, remiss, slack, slipshod, sloppy, tolerant **2** *lax interpretation of the law:* broad, general, imprecise, inaccurate, indefinite, inexact, loose, vague
▣ **1** careful, strict **2** exact, rigorous, specific

laxative *n* aperient *technical,* cathartic, eccoprotic, evacuant, loosener, purgative, purge, salts

laxity *n* **1** *laxity in enforcing regulations:* carelessness, freedom, heedlessness, indifference, indulgence, laissez-faire, latitude, latitudinarianism, leniency, neglect, negligence, nonchalance, permissiveness, slackness, sloppiness, slovenliness, softness, tolerance **2** *allow a certain laxity in spelling:* imprecision, indefiniteness, inexactness, looseness
▣ **1** severity, strictness **2** exactness

lay¹ *v* **1** *lay a parcel on the table:* deposit, establish, leave, lodge, place, plant, posit *formal,* put, set, set down, settle **2** *laid their plans:* arrange, design, devise, dispose *formal,* make, plan, prepare, set out, work out **3** *lay the blame:* allot, ascribe, assign, attribute, charge, impute **4** *lay a burden on someone:* apply, burden, encumber, impose, inflict, oppress, put, saddle, thrust, weigh down **5** *lay a bet:* bet, chance, gamble, hazard, place, risk, wager **6** *lay eggs:* bear, breed, deposit, engender, give birth to, oviposit *technical,* produce **7** *lay a woman:* bang *taboo slang,* bonk *taboo slang,* fuck *taboo slang,* go to bed with *colloq,* have *slang,* have it off with *slang,* have sex with, make it with *slang,* make love with, screw *taboo slang,* shag *taboo slang*
▶ **lay aside 1** *laid aside for the winter:* keep, put aside, save, store **2** *laid aside his ambition:* abandon, cast aside, discard, dismiss, postpone, put off, put out of your mind, reject, set aside, shelve
▶ **lay down 1** *lay down your weapons:* discard, drop, give, give up, relinquish *formal,* surrender, yield **2** *lay down strict guidelines:* affirm, assert, establish, formulate, ordain, postulate, prescribe, state, stipulate
▶ **lay in** accumulate, amass, build up, collect, gather, glean, hoard, stock up, stockpile, store (up)

▶ **lay into** assail, attack, have a go at, hit out at, lash out at, let fly at, pitch into, set about, tear into
▶ **lay off 1** *lay off workers*: discharge, dismiss, let go, make redundant, pay off, sack *colloq* **2** *lay off drinking*: cease *formal*, desist *formal*, discontinue *formal*, drop, give up, leave alone, leave off, let up, quit *colloq*, refrain, stop
▶ **lay on** cater, furnish, give, organize, provide, set up, supply
▶ **lay out 1** *laid out their plans*: detail, explain, present, put forward, reveal, set out **2** *laid out the gifts on the table*: arrange, display, exhibit, set out, spread out **3** *laid him out with a left hook*: demolish, fell, flatten, floor, knock out **4** *lay out fifty pounds*: contribute, disburse *formal*, fork out *colloq*, give, invest, pay, shell out *colloq*, spend
▶ **lay up** accumulate, amass, hoard, keep, put away, save, store up

---

lay or *lie*? *Lay* means 'to place in a flat, prone or horizontal position'. It is a transitive verb, ie it requires an object: *If you lay the pen down there, it will roll off the table.* *Lie* means 'to be or move into a flat, prone or horizontal position'. It is an intransitive verb, ie, it does not have an object. The past tense is *lay: She went into the bedroom and lay on the bed.*

---

lay² *adj* **1** *a lay preacher*: laic, secular **2** *a lay member of the board*: amateur, non-professional, non-specialist
🗷 **1** clerical, ordained **2** expert, professional

lay³ *n* ballad, lyric, madrigal, ode, poem, song

layabout *n* good-for-nothing, idler, laggard, lazy-bones *colloq*, loafer *colloq*, lounge-lizard *colloq*, lounger, ne'er-do-well, shirker *colloq*, skiver *colloq*, waster

layer *n* **1** *an extra layer against the cold*: blanket, coat, coating, cover, covering, film, lamina, mantle, sheet **2** *a layer in the rock*: band, bed, deposit, plate, ply, row, seam, stratum, thickness, tier, vein

lay-off *n* boot *colloq*, discharge, dismissal, elbow *colloq*, firing *colloq*, papers *colloq*, push *colloq*, redundancy, sack *colloq*, sacking *colloq*, unemployment

layout *n* **1** *got to know the layout of the building*: arrangement, design, format, geography, plan **2** *showed them the layouts for the catalogue*: design, draft, plan, sketch

layperson *n* **1** *used for washing by both priests and laypersons*: layman, laywoman, parishioner **2** *terms that confuse a layperson*: amateur, layman, laywoman, non-professional, outsider
🗷 **1** clergyman **2** expert, professional

laze *v* bum around *colloq*, idle, lie around, loaf *colloq*, loll, lounge, not pull your weight *colloq*, relax, sit around
🗷 work

laziness *n* dilatoriness *formal*, fainéance *formal*, idleness, inactivity, indolence *formal*, langour *formal*, lethargy, slackness, sloth, slothfulness, slowness, sluggishness, tardiness *formal*
🗷 industriousness

lazy *adj* bone idle *colloq*, fainéant *formal*, good-for-nothing, idle, inactive, indolent *formal*, inert, languid *formal*, languorous *formal*, lethargic, slack, slothful, slow, slow-moving, sluggish, tardy *formal*, torpid *formal*, work-shy
🗷 hard-working, industrious

lazy-bones *n* good-for-nothing, idler, laggard, layabout, loafer *colloq*, lounger *colloq*, ne'er-do-well, shirker *colloq*, skiver *colloq*, slouch, sluggard

leach *v* drain, extract, filter, filtrate, lixiviate *formal*, osmose *technical*, percolate, seep, strain

lead¹ *v* **1** *lead people through a maze*: conduct, escort, guide, pilot, steer, usher **2** *lead one's country*: be at the head of, be in charge of, call the shots *colloq*, command, direct, govern, head, manage, preside over, regulate, rule, supervise **3** *lead to misery*: bring about, bring on, call forth, cause, contribute to, produce, provoke, result in, tend towards **4** *lead someone to change their mind*: dispose, incline, induce, influence, move, persuade, prompt, sway **5** *leading the other competitors*: be in front of, be in the lead, come first, eclipse, exceed, excel, outdistance, outdo, outrun, outstrip, surpass, transcend **6** *lead your life*: experience, have, live, pass, spend, undergo
🗷 **1** follow
♦ *n* **1** *a huge lead over their rivals*: advantage, edge, gap, interval, margin, precedence, pre-eminence, supremacy **2** *you go in the lead*: advance position, first place, forefront, van, vanguard **3** *follow someone's lead*: direction, example, guidance, leadership, model, pattern **4** *the police had no leads in the case*: clue, guide, hint, indication, indicator, pointer, suggestion, tip, tip-off *colloq* **5** *played the lead in 'West Side Story'*: leading role, principal, principal part, starring part, title role
♦ *adj* chief, first, foremost, head, leading, main, premier, primary, prime, principal, star, top
▶ **lead off** begin, commence, get going, inaugurate, initiate, kick off *colloq*, open, start (off), start the ball rolling *colloq*
▶ **lead on** beguile, deceive, draw on, dupe, entice, lure, mislead, persuade, seduce, string along, tempt, trick
▶ **lead up to** introduce, pave/open the way for, prepare (the way) for

lead² *n* **1** *shot him full of lead*: ammunition, balls, bullets, pellets, shot, slugs **2** *weighed down with lead*: heavy weight, plumb, sinker, weight

leaden *adj* **1** *leaden skies*: ashen, cloudy, dingy, dismal, dreary, gloomy, grey, greyish, oppressive, overcast, sombre **2** *leaden prose*: dull, heavy, humdrum, laboured, lacklustre, languid *formal*, lifeless, listless, sluggish, spiritless, stilted *formal* **3** *leaden movements*: cumbersome, heavy, laboured, lead, plodding, stiff, wooden

leader *n* **1** *the leader of the group*: boss *colloq*, captain, chief, chieftain, commander, conductor, director, figurehead, governor, head, manager, mover and shaker, overseer, principal, ringleader, ruler, skipper, superintendent, superior, supervisor **2** *followed the leader*: courier, escort, guide, usher **3** *a leader in spinal-cord injury research*: architect, authority, developer, discoverer, expert, founder, front-runner, groundbreaker, guiding light, innovator, inventor, leading light, pathfinder, pioneer, trailblazer
🗷 **2** follower

leadership *n* administration, authority, captaincy, command, control, direction, directorship, domination, governorship, guidance, headship, management, pre-eminence, premiership, rule, superintendency, supervision, sway

leading *adj* chief, directing, dominant, first, foremost, front, governing, greatest, guiding, highest, main, number one, outstanding, paramount, pre-eminent, primary, principal, ruling, superior, supreme, top-rank
◫ subordinate

leaf *n* **1** *the leaves of a tree:* blade, bract, calyx, cotyledon *technical*, foliole, frond, leaflet, needle, pad, sepal **2** *the leaves of a book:* folio, page, sheet
♦ *v* browse, flip, glance, skim, thumb (through)

> **Leaf parts include:**
> auxiliary bud, blade, chloroplasts, epidermis, leaf axil, leaf cells, margin, midrib, petiole, sheath, stipule, stomata, tip, vein

> **Leaf shapes include:**
> abruptly pinnate, acerose, ciliate, cordate, crenate, dentate, digitate, doubly dentate, elliptic, entire, falcate, hastate, lanceolate, linear, lobed, lyrate, obovate, orbicular, ovate, palmate, peltate, pinnate, pinnatifid, reniform, runcinate, sagittate, spathulate, subulate, ternate, trifoliate

leaflet *n* bill, booklet, brochure, circular, flyer, handbill, handout, pamphlet, tract

leafy *adj* bosky, dasyphyllous *technical*, foliose, frondescent, frondose, green, leafed, leaved, shaded, shady, verdant *formal*, wooded, woody

league *n* **1** *a league of Saxon princes:* affiliation, alliance, association, band, cartel, coalition, combination, combine, compact, confederacy, confederation, conglomerate, consortium, co-operative, corporation, federation, fellowship, group, guild, partnership, syndicate, union **2** *not in the same league:* category, class, group, level

leak *n* **1** *a leak in the roof:* break, chink, crack, crevice, cut, fissure, hole, opening, puncture **2** *a leak of water:* discharge, drip, escape, leakage, leaking, oozing, percolation, seepage, seeping **3** *a leak from a government source:* bringing to light, disclosure, divulgence, exposé, exposure, revelation, uncovering
♦ *v* **1** *oiled leaked from the engine:* discharge, drip, escape, exude, ooze, percolate, seep, spill, trickle **2** *leaked the story to the press:* blab *colloq*, disclose, divulge *formal*, give away, impart *formal*, let on *colloq*, let slip, let the cat out of the bag *colloq*, make known, make public, pass on, relate, reveal, spill the beans *colloq*, squeal *colloq*, tell

leaky *adj* cracked, holey, leaking, perforated, permeable, porous, punctured, split

lean[1] *v* **1** *lean to the right:* bank, be at an angle, bend, incline, list, slant, slope, tilt **2** *lean your head on a pillow:* prop, recline, repose *formal*, rest
▶ **lean on 1** *able to lean on them for support:* bank on *colloq*, depend on, have confidence in, not manage without, rely on, trust in **2** *had to lean on them to make them pay:* force, persuade, pressurize, put pressure on
▶ **lean towards** be inclined to, favour, have a propensity for *formal*, have an inclination/preference for, prefer, tend towards

lean[2] *adj* **1** *a lean physique:* all skin and bones *colloq*, angular, bony, emaciated, gaunt, lank, scraggy, scrawny, skinny, slender, slim, thin **2** *lean rewards for your efforts:* arid, bare, barren,

inadequate, insufficient, poor, scanty, sparse, unfruitful, unproductive
◫ **1** fat, flabby

leaning *n* aptitude, attraction, bent, bias, disposition, fondness, inclination, liking, partiality, penchant *formal*, predilection *formal*, preference, proclivity *formal*, propensity *formal*, tendency

leap *v* **1** *leapt over the fence:* bound, clear, hop, jump, skip, spring, vault **2** *leap for joy:* bounce, caper, cavort, dance, frisk, frolic, gambol, hop, jump, romp, skip **3** *prices have leapt:* escalate, increase, mount, rise, rocket, skyrocket, soar, surge
◫ **3** drop, fall
♦ *n* **1** *an enormous leap over the stream:* bound, caper, entrechat *technical*, hop, jump, skip, spring, vault **2** *a leap in prices:* escalation, increase, rise, soaring, surge, upsurge, upswing
▶ **leap at** accept eagerly, agree to, fall for, grab, jump at, pounce on, seize, snatch, swallow

learn *v* **1** *she is quick to learn new ideas:* absorb, acquire, acquire skill in, assimilate, comprehend, digest, discern, familiarize yourself in, gain knowledge of, gather, get the hang of *colloq*, grasp, master, pick up, study, take in, train, understand **2** *learn the words to a song:* commit to memory, have off pat, learn by heart, memorize, remember **3** *learned that she had won a scholarship:* ascertain, become aware, become informed about, detect, determine, discover, find out, gather, get wind of *colloq*, hear, realize, see, understand

learned *adj* academic, cultured, erudite, intellectual, knowledgeable, lettered, literary, literate, scholarly, studious, versed, well-educated, well-informed, well-read, widely read
◫ illiterate, uneducated

learner *n* apprentice, beginner, greenhorn *colloq*, neophyte, novice, pupil, rookie *colloq*, scholar, student, tiro, trainee

learning *n* culture, edification, education, erudition, information, knowledge, letters, research, scholarship, schooling, study, tuition, wisdom

lease *v* charter, hire, let, loan, rent, sublet
♦ *n* agreement, chapter, contract

leash *n* check, control, cord, curb, discipline, hold, lead, rein, restraint, tether

least *adj* fewest, lowest, minimum, poorest, slightest, smallest
◫ most

leathery *adj* coriaceous *technical*, corious, durable, hard, hardened, rough, rugged, tough, wizened, wrinkled

leave[1] *v* **1** *leave at midday for the airport:* decamp, depart, disappear, do a bunk *colloq*, emigrate, exit, go, go away, hook it *colloq*, make tracks *colloq*, move, pull out, push along *colloq*, push off *colloq*, quit *colloq*, retire, retreat, scoot *colloq*, set out, take off *colloq*, take your leave, up sticks *colloq*, withdraw **2** *leave a job:* abandon, cease *formal*, chuck *colloq*, desert, desist *formal*, ditch *colloq*, drop, forsake, give up, jilt *colloq*, leave high and dry *colloq*, pull out, relinquish *formal*, renounce *formal*, run out on *colloq*, surrender, turn your back on *colloq* **3** *I'll leave that to my*

colleagues: allot, assign, commit, consign, deliver, entrust, hand over, make over, transmit **4** *leave property in your will*: bequeath *formal*, devise *technical*, endow, give over, hand down, leave behind, will
F3 1 arrive **4** inherit
▶ **leave off** abstain *formal*, break off, cease *formal*, desist *formal*, discontinue *formal*, end, give over *colloq*, halt, knock off *colloq*, lay off, quit *colloq*, refrain, stop, terminate *formal*
▶ **leave out** bar, cast aside, count out, cut (out), disregard, eliminate, except, exclude, ignore, neglect, omit, overlook, pass over, reject
F3 include

leave² *n* **1** *leave to go on holiday*: allowance, authorization, concession, consent, dispensation *formal*, freedom, green light *colloq*, indulgence, liberty, OK *colloq*, permission, sanction, say-so *colloq*, warrant **2** *annual leave*: break, compassionate leave, day off, furlough, holiday, leave of absence, sabbatical, sick leave, time off, vacation
F3 1 refusal, rejection

leaven *v* **1** *to leaven bread*: cause to rise, expand, ferment, puff up, raise, swell **2** *her writing is leavened with humour*: imbue, lighten, moderate, permeate, pervade, suffuse

leavings *n* bits, debris, detritus, dregs, dross, fragments, leftovers, oddments, pieces, refuse, remainder, remains, remnants, residue, rubbish, scraps, spoil, sweepings, waste

lecher *n* adulterer, Casanova, debauchee, dirty old man *colloq*, Don Juan, flasher *colloq*, fornicator, goat *colloq*, libertine, libidinist, profligate, rake, roué, seducer, sensualist, wanton, wolf *colloq*, womanizer

lecherous *adj* carnal, concupiscent *formal*, debauched, degenerate, dissipated, dissolute, horny *colloq*, lascivious, lewd, libidinous, licentious *formal*, lustful, promiscuous, prurient *formal*, randy *colloq*, raunchy *colloq*, salacious, unchaste, wanton, womanizing

lechery *n* carnality, concupiscence *formal*, debauchery, lasciviousness, lewdness, libertinism, libidinousness, licentiousness, lust, lustfulness, prurience *formal*, rakishness, randiness *colloq*, raunchiness *colloq*, salaciousness, sensuality, wantonness, womanizing

lecture *n* **1** *a lecture on Greek tragedy*: address, discourse *formal*, disquisition *formal*, homily *formal*, instruction, lesson, sermon, speech, talk **2** *administer a stern lecture*: berating *formal*, censure, chiding, dressing-down *colloq*, harangue, rebuke, reprimand, reproach, reproof, rocket *colloq*, scolding, talking-to *colloq*, telling-off *colloq*, upbraiding
♦ *v* **1** *to lecture about architecture*: address, expound, give a talk, give lessons in, hold forth, instruct, make a speech, speak, talk, teach **2** *lectured them for arriving late*: admonish, berate *formal*, censure, chide, harangue, haul over the coals *colloq*, pick holes in *colloq*, rebuke, reprimand, reprove, scold, tear/pull to pieces *colloq*, tell off *colloq*

lecturer *n* academic, declaimer *formal*, expounder, haranguer, instructor, orator, pedagogue, preacher, reader, sermonizer,

speaker, speechifier, speech-maker, talker, teacher, tutor

ledge *n* mantel, mantelpiece, mantelshelf, overhang, projection, ridge, shelf, sill, step

lee *n* cover, protection, refuge, sanctuary, shelter

leech *n* bloodsucker, extortioner, freeloader, hanger-on, parasite, scrounger *colloq*, sponger *colloq*, sycophant, toady, usurer

leer *v* eye, goggle, grin, look lecherously at, ogle, smirk, sneer, squint, stare, wink
♦ *n* grin, lecherous look, ogle, smirk, sneer, squint, stare, wink

leery *adj* careful, cautious, chary, distrustful, doubting, dubious, guarded, on your guard, sceptical, suspicious, uncertain, unsure, wary

lees *n* deposit, draff, dregs, grounds, precipitate *formal*, refuse, residue, sediment, settlings

leeway *n* elbow-room, flexibility, latitude, margin, play, room, scope, slack, space

left *adj* **1** *my left eye*: left-hand, port, sinistral *formal* **2** *the left wing of the party*: communist, liberal, progressive, radical, red *colloq*, revolutionary, socialist
F3 1 right **2** right

left-handed *adj* **1** *a left-handed person*: cack-handed *colloq*, corrie-fisted *Scot colloq*, sinistral **2** *a left-handed compliment*: ambiguous, dubious, equivocal, hypocritical, insincere

left-over *adj* excess, remaining, settled, surplus, uneaten, unused

leftovers *n* dregs, excess, leavings, refuse, remainder, remains, remnants, residue, scraps, surplus, sweepings

leg *n* **1** *to break your leg*: crus *technical*, limb, member, peg *colloq*, pin *colloq*, shank, stump *colloq* **2** *a chair leg*: brace, prop, support, underpinning, upright **3** *the last leg of the journey*: bit, lap, part, portion, section, segment, stage, stretch

legacy *n* bequeathal *formal*, bequest, birthright, endowment, estate, gift, heirloom, heritage, heritance *formal*, inheritance, patrimony *formal*

legal *adj* **1** *within the legal limit*: above-board, acceptable, admissible, allowable, allowed, authorized, constitutional, lawful, legalized, legitimate, licensed, licit *formal*, permissible, permitted, proper, right, rightful, sanctioned, sound, valid, warranted, within the law **2** *a legal drama series*: forensic, judicial **3** *legal requirements*: constitutional, judiciary, statutory
F3 1 illegal

Legal terms include:
criminal law: acquittal, age of consent, alibi, arrest, bail, caution, charge, confession, contempt of court, dock, fine, guilty, indictment, innocent, malice aforethought, pardon, parole, plead guilty, plead not guilty, prisoner, probation, remand, reprieve, sentence; *marriage and divorce*: adultery, alimony, annulment, bigamy, decree absolute, decree nisi, divorce, maintenance, settlement; *people*: accessory, accomplice, accused, advocate, Attorney General, barrister, brief *colloq*, clerk of the court, client, commissioner for oaths, convict, coroner, criminal, defendant, Director of Public Prosecutions (DPP), executor, felon, judge, jury, justice of

the peace (JP), juvenile, Law Lord, lawyer, Lord Advocate, Lord Chancellor, Lord Chief Justice, liquidator, magistrate, notary public, offender, plaintiff, procurator fiscal, receiver, Queen's Counsel (QC), sheriff, solicitor, witness, young offender; *property or ownership:* asset, conveyance, copyright, deed, easement, endowment, estate, exchange of contracts, fee simple, fee tail, foreclosure, freehold, inheritance, intestacy, lease, leasehold, legacy, local search, mortgage, patent, tenancy, title, trademark, will; *miscellaneous:* act of God, Act of Parliament, adjournment, affidavit, agreement, allegation, amnesty, appeal, arbitration, bar, bench, Bill of Rights, brief, by-law, charter, civil law, claim, codicil, common law, constitution, contract, covenant, courtcase, court martial, cross-examine, custody, damages, defence, demand, equity, eviction, evidence, extradition, grant, hearing, hung jury, indemnity, injunction, inquest, inquiry, judgment, judiciary, lawsuit, legal aid, liability, mandate, misadventure, miscarriage of justice, oath, party, penalty, power of attorney, precedent, probate, proceedings, proof, proxy, public inquiry, repeal, sanction, settlement, statute, subpoena, sue, summons, testimony, trial, tribunal, verdict, waiver, ward of court, warrant, will, writ

legality *n* admissibleness, constitutionality, lawfulness, legitimacy, permissibility, rightfulness, rightness, soundness, validity
🖬 illegality

legalize *v* accept, admit, allow, approve, authorize, decriminalize, legitimize, license, permit, ratify, sanction, validate, warrant

legate *n* agent, ambassador, commissioner, delegate, deputy, emissary, envoy, messenger, nuncio, representative

legatee *n* beneficiary, co-heir(ess), devisee, heir, inheritor, inheritrix, recipient

legation *n* commission, consulate, delegation, deputation, embassy, ministry, mission, representation

legend *n* **1** *an ancient legend:* fable, fiction, folk-tale, myth, narrative, romance, saga, story, tale, traditional story **2** *the legend below the statue:* caption, cipher, explanation, inscription, key, motto

legendary *adj* **1** *a legendary account of the city's origin:* fabled, fabulous, fanciful, fictional, fictitious, mythical, story-book, traditional **2** *a legendary performance:* acclaimed, celebrated, famous, glorious, honoured, illustrious, immortal, popular, remembered, renowned, well-known

legerdemain *n* artfulness, artifice, chicanery, contrivance, craftiness, cunning, deception, feint, hocus-pocus *colloq*, manipulation, manoeuvring, prestidigitation *formal*, sleight of hand, sophistry *formal*, subterfuge, thaumaturgics *formal*, trickery

legible *adj* clear, decipherable, distinct, easy to read, intelligible, neat, plain, readable
🖬 illegible

legion *n* **1** *Roman legions:* army, battalion, brigade, cohort, company, division, force, regiment, troop, unit **2** *legions of foreign tourists:*

drove, horde, host, mass, multitude, myriad, number, swarm, throng
♦ *adj* countless, illimitable, innumerable, multitudinous, myriad, numberless, numerous

legislate *v* authorize, codify, constitutionalize *formal*, decree, enact, establish, formulate, ordain, order, prescribe *formal*

legislation *n* **1** *housing legislation:* act, authorization, bill, charter, code, enactment, law, measure, ordinance, regulation, rules, ruling, statute **2** *the process of legislation:* codification, enactment, formulation, law-making, prescription *formal*

legislative *adj* congressional, judicial, jurisdictive *technical*, law-giving, law-making, parliamentary, senatorial

legislator *n* congressman, congresswoman, law-giver, law-maker, member of parliament, parliamentarian, senator

legislature *n* assembly, chamber, congress, house, parliament, senate

legitimate *adj* **1** *a legitimate act:* acknowledged, authorized, correct, genuine, lawful, legal, licit *formal*, proper, real, rightful, sanctioned, statutory, warranted **2** *a legitimate excuse:* acceptable, admissible, credible, fair, justifiable, justified, logical, plausible, rational, reasonable, sensible, sound, true, valid, warranted, well-founded
🖬 **1** illegal **2** invalid

legitimize *v* allow, authorize, charter, decriminalize, entitle, legalize, legitimate *formal*, license, permit, sanction, validate, warrant

leisure *n* break, ease, free time, freedom, holiday, liberty, recreation, relaxation, rest, retirement, spare time, time off, time out, vacation
🖬 work

leisurely *adj* carefree, comfortable, easy, easy-going, gentle, laid-back *colloq*, lazy, loose, relaxed, restful, slow, tranquil, unhasty, unhurried
🖬 hectic, rushed

lend *v* **1** *lend someone five pounds:* advance, allow to have, allow to use, let someone use, loan **2** *lend your support to something:* add, bestow *formal*, confer *formal*, contribute, donate, furnish *formal*, give, grant, impart *formal*, provide, supply
🖬 **1** borrow

length *n* **1** *the length of a bridge:* distance, extent, measure, reach, span **2** *the length of a loan:* duration, period, space, span, stretch, term **3** *a length of string:* piece, portion, section, segment

lengthen *v* continue, draw out, eke (out), elongate *formal*, expand, extend, grow longer, increase, pad out, prolong, protract, spin out, stretch
🖬 reduce, shorten

lengthwise *adv* endlong, endways, endwise, horizontally, lengthways, vertically

lengthy *adj* diffuse, drawn-out, extended, interminable, lengthened, long, long-drawn-out, long-winded, overlong, prolix *formal*, prolonged, protracted *formal*, rambling, tedious, verbose, wordy
🖬 brief, concise

leniency *n* clemency *formal*, compassion, forbearance, forgiveness, generosity, gentleness, humaneness, indulgence, kindness, lenience, magnanimity, mercy, mildness, moderation, permissiveness, soft-heartedness, softness, tenderness, tolerance
☒ severity

lenient *adj* compassionate, forbearing, forgiving, generous, gentle, humane, indulgent, kind, liberal, magnanimous, merciful, mild, moderate, soft-hearted, sparing, tender, tolerant
☒ severe, strict

lenitive *adj* alleviating, assuaging, calming, easing, mitigating *formal*, mollifying, palliative, relieving, soothing
☒ irritant

lens See panel at **spectacles**

leper *n* lazar, outcast, pariah, social outcast, undesirable, untouchable

lesbian *n* butch *colloq*, dyke *derog*, gay, homosexual, les *derog*, lez *derog*, lezzy *derog*, queer *derog*, sapphist, tribade
♦ *adj* butch *colloq*, dykey *derog*, gay, homosexual, Sapphic, tribadic

lesion *n* abrasion, bruise, contusion *technical*, cut, gash, hurt, impairment, injury, laceration, scrape, scratch, sore, trauma, wound

less *n* fewer, not as/so many, not as/so much, smaller amount
☒ more
♦ *adv* not as/so much, to a lesser degree/extent, to a smaller extent
☒ more

lessen *v* **1** *in time her anger lessened*: abate *formal*, contract, decline, decrease, de-escalate, die down, diminish, dwindle, ease (off), ebb, erode, fail, flag, go down, let up, moderate, peter out *colloq*, reduce, shrink, slow down, subside, wane, weaken **2** *lessen the impact of the blow*: abridge, contract, curtail, decrease, diminish, lighten, lower, minimize, narrow, reduce, shrink
☒ **1** grow, increase **2** increase

lessening *n* abatement *formal*, contraction, curtailment, deadening, decline, decrease, de-escalation, diminution *formal*, dwindling, easing, ebbing, erosion, failure, flagging, let-up, minimization, moderation, petering out *colloq*, reduction, shrinkage, slackening, waning, weakening
☒ increase

lesser *adj* inferior, lower, minor, secondary, slighter, smaller, subordinate
☒ greater

lesson *n* **1** *a cookery lesson*: class, coaching, course, instruction, lecture, period, seminar, sermon, teaching, tutorial **2** *she works hard at her lessons*: assignment, drill, exercise, homework, practice, schoolwork, task **3** *let that be a lesson to you*: deterrent, example, model, moral, warning

let[1] *v* **1** *let him watch television*: agree to, allow, assent to *formal*, authorize, consent to *formal*, enable, give leave *formal*, give permission, give the go-ahead *colloq*, give the green light to *colloq*, give the nod *colloq*, give the OK *colloq*, grant, OK *colloq*, permit, sanction, say the magic word *colloq*, tolerate **2** *let something happen*: allow,

cause, enable, make **3** *to let a flat*: hire, lease, let out, rent
☒ **1** forbid, prohibit
▶ **let down** abandon, betray, desert, disappoint, disenchant, disillusion, dissatisfy, fail, fall short, leave in the lurch *colloq*
☒ satisfy
▶ **let in** accept, admit, allow to enter, greet, include, incorporate, receive, take in, welcome
☒ bar, forbid, prohibit
▶ **let off 1** *let her off with a warning*: absolve, acquit, discharge, excuse, exempt, exonerate *formal*, forgive, liberate, pardon, release, reprieve, spare **2** *let off a fire extinguisher*: detonate, discharge, emit, explode, fire, give off, release
▶ **let on** blab *colloq*, disclose, divulge *formal*, give away, impart *formal*, let slip, let the cat out of the bag *colloq*, make known, make public, pass on, relate, reveal, spill the beans *colloq*, squeal *colloq*, tell
▶ **let out 1** *let the cat out*: discharge, free, let go, release **2** *let out a strange odour*: discharge, emit, expel, exude **3** *let out a secret*: betray, blab *colloq*, disclose, leak *colloq*, let slip, let the cat out of the bag *colloq*, make known, reveal, spill the beans *colloq*, squeal *colloq*, utter
▶ **let up** abate *formal*, cease *formal*, decrease, die down, diminish, ease (off), end, halt, lessen, moderate, slacken, stop, subside
☒ continue

let[2] *n* check, constraint, hindrance, impediment, interference, obstacle, obstruction, prohibition, restraint, restriction
☒ assistance

let-down *n* anticlimax, betrayal, desertion, disappointment, disillusionment, setback, washout *colloq*

lethal *adj* dangerous, deadly, deathly, destructive, devastating, disastrous, fatal, mortal, murderous, noxious *formal*, poisonous, ruinous, toxic
☒ harmless, safe

lethargic *adj* apathetic, debilitated *formal*, drowsy, dull, enervated *formal*, heavy, hebetant *formal*, idle, inactive, inert, languid *formal*, lazy, lifeless, listless, sleepy, slothful, slow, sluggish, somnolent *formal*, torpid *formal*, weary
☒ lively

lethargy *n* apathy, drowsiness, dullness, idleness, inaction, inactivity, indifference, inertia, langour *formal*, lassitude *formal*, laziness, lifelessness, listlessness, sleepiness, sloth, slowness, sluggishness, somnolence *formal*, stupor, torpor *formal*, weariness
☒ liveliness

letter *n* **1** *sent a letter home*: acknowledgement, chit, circular, communication, correspondence, dispatch, epistle *formal*, line, message, missive *formal*, note, reply **2** *a word of five letters*: character, grapheme *technical*, sign, symbol **3** *a man of letters*: academia, belles-lettres, books, culture, education, erudition *formal*, humanities, learning, literature, scholarship, writing

lettered *adj* academic, accomplished, cultivated, cultured, educated, erudite *formal*, highbrow *colloq*, informed, knowledgeable, learned, literary, literate, scholarly, studied, versed, well-educated, well-read, widely read
☒ ignorant

let-up *n* abatement *formal*, break, breather *colloq*, cessation *formal*, interval, lessening, lull, pause, recess, remission, respite, slackening
▣ continuation

level *adj* **1** *a level surface:* aligned, even, flat, flush, horizontal, plane, smooth, uniform **2** *a level contest:* aligned, balanced, equal, even, level pegging, matching, neck and neck, on a par **3** *uptake of services remains level:* constant, regular, stable, steady, unchanging, uniform **4** *keep a level head:* calm, composed, self-possessed, steady, unemotional, unflappable *colloq*
▣ **1** uneven **2** unequal **3** unsteady **4** emotional
♦ *n* **1** *the plane reached its cruising level:* altitude, elevation, height, highness **2** *move up to the next level:* class, degree, echelon *formal*, grade, layer, mark, plane, point, position, rank, stage, standard, standing, station, status, storey, stratum, zone **3** *a high level of pollution:* amount, degree, extent, magnitude, measure, quantity, size, volume
♦ *v* **1** *to level a building:* bulldoze, demolish, destroy, devastate, flatten, knock down, lay waste, pull down, raze, raze to the ground, tear down **2** *to level the score:* equalize, even up, make equal, make level, tie **3** *to level a road surface:* even out, even up, make flat, make level, plane, smooth, stabilize **4** *to level accusations at someone:* aim, concentrate, direct, focus, point, train, zero in on **5** *to level with someone:* admit, be frank, be upfront *colloq*, bring out in the open *colloq*, come clean *colloq*, confess, give it straight *colloq*, keep nothing back, open up, put your cards on the table *colloq*, speak plainly, tell all, tell it like it is *colloq*

level-headed *adj* balanced, calm, circumspect *formal*, composed, cool, cool-headed, dependable, even-tempered, imperturbable *formal*, prudent *formal*, rational, reasonable, sane, self-possessed, sensible, steady, unflappable *colloq*

lever *n* **1** *pull on a lever:* bar, handle, joystick, pull, switch **2** *open with a lever:* bar, crowbar, handspike, jemmy
♦ *v* dislodge, force, heave, hoist, jemmy, lift, move, prise, pry, raise, shift

leverage *n* advantage, ascendancy *formal*, authority, clout *colloq*, force, influence, power, pull *colloq*, purchase *formal*, rank, strength, weight

leviathan *n* behemoth, colossus, giant, hulk, mammoth, monster, sea monster, Titan, whale

levitate *v* drift, float, fly, glide, hang, hover, waft

levity *n* carefreeness, facetiousness, flippancy, frivolity, fun, hilarity, irreverence, light-heartedness, light-mindedness, silliness, triviality
▣ seriousness

levy *v* charge, collect, demand, exact, gather, impose, raise, tax
♦ *n* assessment, collection, contribution, due, duty, excise, fee, impost *technical*, subscription, tariff, tax, tithe, toll

lewd *adj* bawdy, blue *colloq*, carnal, concupiscent *formal*, debauched, degenerate, dissolute, impure, indecent, lascivious, lecherous, licentious, lustful, obscene, pornographic, promiscuous, randy *colloq*, raunchy *colloq*, salacious, smutty, suggestive, unchaste, vulgar
▣ chaste, decent

lewdness *n* bawdiness, carnality, concupiscence *formal*, crudity, debauchery, depravity, impurity, indecency, lasciviousness, lechery, licentiousness, lustfulness, obscenity, pornography, randiness *colloq*, salaciousness, smut, smuttiness, unchastity, vulgarity, wantonness
▣ chasteness, politeness

lexicon *n* dictionary, encyclopedia, glossary, phrase book, vocabulary, wordbook, word-list

liability *n* **1** *accept liability for the losses:* accountability, answerability, blameworthiness, culpability *formal*, obligation, responsibility **2** *the company's pension liabilities:* arrears, debit, dues, indebtedness, obligation **3** *an electoral liability:* burden, disadvantage, drag *colloq*, drawback, encumbrance, hindrance, impediment, inconvenience, millstone around your neck *colloq*, nuisance
▣ **1** indemnity, unaccountability **2** asset **3** advantage, asset

liable *adj* **1** *liable to burst out laughing:* amenable, apt, disposed, inclined, likely, open, predisposed *formal*, prone, subject, susceptible, tending **2** *liable for damages:* accountable, answerable, at fault, chargeable, exposed, responsible, to blame
▣ **1** unlikely **2** unaccountable

liaise *v* collaborate, communicate, contact, co-operate, exchange information, intercommunicate, interface, network, relate to, work together

liaison *n* **1** *liaison with other organizations:* collaboration, communication, connection, contact, co-operation, exchange of information, interchange, link, working together **2** *a liaison with a married woman:* love affair, affair, amour, entanglement, flirtation, intrigue, relationship, romance

liar *n* deceiver, false witness, falsifier, fibber *colloq*, perjurer, prevaricator

libation *n* drink offering, oblation *formal*, sacrifice

libel *n* aspersion *formal*, calumny *formal*, defamation, denigration, disparagement *formal*, false report, muck-raking *colloq*, mudslinging *colloq*, slander, slur, smear, untrue statement, vilification *formal*
♦ *v* abuse, badmouth US *colloq*, calumniate *formal*, cast aspersions on *formal*, defame, denigrate, disparage *formal*, drag someone's name through the mud *colloq*, malign, revile *formal*, slander, slur *colloq*, smear *colloq*, throw mud at *colloq*, traduce *formal*, vilify *formal*

libel or *slander*? In English law, *libel* is an untrue defamatory statement made in a permanent form such as print, writing or pictures or broadcast on radio or television, whereas *slander* is one made by means of the spoken word (not broadcast) or gesture. In Scots law, both are *slander*.

libellous *adj* abusive, calumniatory *formal*, defamatory, denigratory, derogatory, disparaging *formal*, false, injurious, maligning, scurrilous, slanderous, traducing *formal*, untrue, vilifying *formal*

liberal *adj* **1** *liberal views on censorship*: broad-based, broad-minded, catholic, enlightened, impartial, lenient, libertarian, open-minded, tolerant, unbiased, unprejudiced, wide-ranging **2** *the liberal wing of the party*: advanced, forward-looking, moderate, progressive, radical, reformist **3** *liberal with his advice*: altruistic, big-hearted, bountiful, generous, lavish, magnanimous, munificent, open-handed, philanthropic, unsparing **4** *a liberal serving of ice cream*: abundant, ample, bountiful, copious, generous, handsome, lavish, plentiful, profuse
🖪 **1** narrow-minded **2** conservative **3** mean, miserly

liberalism *n* free-thinking, humanitarianism, latitudinarianism, libertarianism, progressivism, radicalism
🖪 conservatism, narrow-mindedness

liberality *n* **1** *liberality towards strangers*: altruism, beneficence *formal*, benevolence, bounty, charity, free-handedness, generosity, kindness, large-heartedness, largesse, magnanimity, munificence *formal*, open-handedness, philanthropy **2** *govern with justice and liberality*: broad-mindedness, catholicity, impartiality, liberalism, libertarianism, open-mindedness, permissiveness, progressivism, tolerance, toleration
🖪 **1** meanness **2** illiberality

liberate *v* deliver, discharge, emancipate, free, let go, let loose, let out, manumit *formal*, ransom, redeem *formal*, release, rescue, set free, set loose, uncage, unchain, unfetter, unshackle
🖪 enslave, imprison, restrict

liberation *n* deliverance, emancipation, enfranchisement, freedom, freeing, liberating, liberty, loosing, manumission *formal*, ransoming, redemption *formal*, release, uncaging, unchaining, unfettering, unpenning, unshackling
🖪 enslavement, imprisonment, restriction

liberator *n* deliverer, emancipator, freer, manumitter *formal*, ransomer, redeemer, rescuer, saviour
🖪 enslaver, jailer

libertine *n* Casanova, debauchee, Don Juan, lecher, loose-liver, profligate, rake, reprobate, roué, seducer, sensualist, voluptary, womanizer
♦ *adj* debauched, degenerate, dissolute, lecherous, licentious *formal*, lustful, promiscuous, reprobate, salacious, womanizing

liberty *n* **1** *fought for their country's liberty*: autonomy, deliverance, emancipation, freedom, independence, liberation, manumission *formal*, release, self-determination, self-government, self-rule, sovereignty **2** *given liberty to do as he pleased*: authorization, dispensation, entitlement, franchise, licence, permission, prerogative, privilege, right, sanction **3** *treat with undue liberty*: disrespect, familiarity, impertinence, impropriety *formal*, impudence, insolence, overfamiliarity, presumption
🖪 **1** imprisonment **3** politeness, respect

libidinous *adj* carnal, concupiscent *formal*, cupidinous *formal*, debauched, horny *colloq*, impure, lascivious, lecherous, lewd, loose,

lustful, promiscuous, prurient *formal*, randy *colloq*, ruttish *formal*, salacious, sensual, unchaste, wanton, wicked
🖪 modest, temperate

libido *n* ardour, erotic desire, eroticism, lust, passion, randiness *colloq*, sex drive, sexual appetite, sexual desire, sexual urge, the hots *colloq*

libretto *n* book, lines, lyrics, script, text, words

licence *n* **1** *a driving licence*: authority, certificate, charter, document, grant, imprimatur, pass, permit, warrant **2** *given licence to roam freely*: accreditation *formal*, approval, authority, authorization, carte blanche, certification, consent, dispensation, entitlement, exemption, freedom, independence, leave, liberty, permission, prerogative, privilege, right, sanction, warranty **3** *sexual licence*: abandon, anarchy, debauchery, decadence, disorder, dissipation, dissoluteness, excess, immoderation, immorality, impropriety, indulgence, intemperance, irresponsibility, lawlessness, licentiousness, self-indulgence, unruliness
🖪 **2** prohibition, restriction **3** control, decorum, moderation, restraint

license *v* accredit *formal*, allow, authorize, certify, commission, consent *formal*, empower, entitle, franchise, give permission, permit, sanction, warrant
🖪 ban, prohibit

licentious *adj* abandoned, debauched, decadent, depraved, disorderly, dissipated, dissolute, immoral, impure, lascivious, lax, lecherous, lewd, libertine, lustful, profligate, promiscuous, unchaste, wanton
🖪 chaste, modest

licentiousness *n* abandon, cupidinousness *formal*, debauchery, dissipation, dissoluteness, immorality, impurity, lechery, lewdness, libertinism, lust, lustfulness, promiscuity, prurience *formal*, salaciousness, salacity, wantonness
🖪 modesty, temperance

lick *v* **1** *lick the chocolate*: clean, lap, moisten, taste, tongue, wash, wet **2** *waves licking the shore*: dart, flick, flicker, play over, ripple, touch **3** *licked the other team 6–0*: beat, conquer, defeat, hammer *colloq*, thrash *colloq*, trounce *colloq*, vanquish *formal*
♦ *n* bit, brush, dab, hint, little, sample, smidgeon, speck, spot, stroke, taste, touch

licking *n* beating, defeat, drubbing, flogging, hiding, smacking, spanking, tanning, thrashing, whipping

lid *n* cap, cover, covering, stopper, top

lie¹ *n* cock-and-bull story *colloq*, deceit, fabrication, falsehood, falsification, falsity, fib *colloq*, fiction, half-truth, invention, made-up story *colloq*, perjury, porky *colloq*, prevarication, tall story *colloq*, untruth, white lie, whopper *colloq*
🖪 truth
♦ *v* dissemble *formal*, dissimulate *formal*, equivocate, fabricate, falsify, fib *colloq*, forswear yourself *formal*, invent, lie through your teeth *colloq*, make up a story, misrepresent, perjure yourself, prevaricate, tell a lie

lie² *v* **1** *the town lies over the border:* be, be found, be located, stand, stay, stretch **2** *the truth lies elsewhere:* be found, be located, belong, dwell *formal*, exist, remain **3** *lie on the couch:* laze, lounge, recline, repose *formal*, rest, sprawl out, stretch out

lie or *lay*? See panel at **lay**¹

lieutenant *n* assistant, deputy, right-hand man/woman, second-in-command, subordinate

life *n* **1** *bring something to life:* aliveness, animation, being, breath, entity, existence, viability **2** *extra-terrestrial life:* animal life, fauna, fauna and flora, flora, human life, living things, plants **3** *the loss of many lives:* child, human being, individual, man, person, woman **4** *the life of this parliament:* career, course, duration, existence, life expectancy, lifespan, lifetime, span **5** *the machine has a limited life:* continuance, course, duration, lifespan, lifetime, period of usefulness, span, time, time of being active **6** *a life of Napoleon:* autobiography, biography, diaries, diary, journal, life story, memoirs **7** *put some life into proceedings:* activity, animation, cheerfulness, effervescence, élan, energy, enthusiasm, excitement, exuberance, high spirits, liveliness, oomph *colloq*, pizzazz *colloq*, sparkle, spirit, verve, vigour, vitality, vivacity, zest
⊠ 1 death

life-and-death *adj* all-important, critical, crucial, important, serious, vital

lifeblood *n* centre, core, essential part/factor, heart, inspiration, life-force, soul, spirit

lifeless *adj* **1** *a lifeless corpse:* cold, dead, deceased, defunct, gone, inanimate, insensible, stiff, unconscious **2** *a lifeless performance:* apathetic, colourless, dull, flat, insipid, lacklustre, lethargic, listless, passive, slow, sluggish, stiff, uninspired, uninspiring, wooden **3** *a lifeless desert:* arid, bare, barren, desolate, empty, stark, sterile, uninhabited, unproductive
⊠ 1 alive **2** exciting, lively

lifelike *adj* authentic, exact, faithful, graphic, natural, real, realistic, true, true-to-life, vivid
⊠ unnatural, unrealistic

lifelong *adj* abiding, constant, enduring, for all your life, lasting, lifetime, long-lasting, long-standing, permanent, persistent
⊠ impermanent, temporary

lifestyle *n* life, living conditions, manner of living, position, situation, way of life, way of living

lifetime *n* career, course, day(s), duration, existence, life, lifespan, period, span, time

lift *v* **1** *she lifted the chair:* elevate, hoist, hold high, hold up, pick up, raise, uplift, upraise **2** *he lifted their spirits:* boost, buoy up, elevate, exalt, raise, uplift **3** *the ban has been lifted:* annul, cancel, end, relax, remove, rescind *formal*, revoke *formal*, stop, terminate *formal*, withdraw **4** *lift people out of the war zone:* airlift, convey, fly, move, shift, transfer, transport **5** *the fog lifted:* clear, disappear, disperse, dissolve, scatter, thin out, vanish **6** *to lift potatoes:* dig out of the ground, dig up, pick, pull up, root out, unearth **7** *lift someone else's material:* borrow, copy, crib *colloq*, plagiarize, steal
⊠ 1 drop, lower **2** lower **3** start **5** come down **6** plant, sow
♦ *n* **1** *go up in a lift:* elevator, escalator, hoist, paternoster **2** *give you a lift home:* drive, hitch, ride, run, transport **3** *gave our spirits a lift:* boost, encouragement, fillip, pick-me-up, reassurance, shot in the arm *colloq*, spur, uplift
⊠ 3 discouragement

ligature *n* band, bandage, binding, bond, connection, cord, ligament, link, rope, strap, string, thong, tie, tourniquet

light¹ *n* **1** *light from the sun:* beam, blaze, brightness, brilliance, effulgence *formal*, flash, glare, gleam, glint, glow, illumination, incandescence, lambency *formal*, luminescence *formal*, luminosity *technical*, lustre, radiance, ray, shaft, shine **2** *put out that light!:* beacon, bulb, candle, flashlight *US*, lamp, lantern, lighter, match, taper, torch **3** *stay here until light:* cockcrow, crack of dawn, dawn, day, daybreak, daylight, daytime, first light, sunrise **4** *shed some light on the matter:* comprehension, elucidation *formal*, enlightenment, explanation, illumination, insight, knowledge, understanding **5** *presented in a different light:* angle, approach, aspect, dimension, manner, point of view, style, way
⊠ 1 darkness **3** night
♦ *v* **1** *to light a bonfire:* fire, ignite, kindle, set alight, set burning, set fire to **2** *to light a building:* brighten, floodlight, illuminate, light up
⊠ 1 extinguish **2** darken
♦ *adj* **1** *a light room:* bright, brilliant, glowing, illuminated, luminous, shining, sunny, well-lit **2** *light colours:* bleached, blond, blonde, faded, faint, fair, pale, pastel, whitish
⊠ 1 dark **2** dark

light² *adj* **1** *light fabrics:* airy, buoyant, delicate, feathery, fine, flimsy, floaty, insubstantial, lightweight, slight, thin, weightless **2** *a light breeze:* faint, gentle, mild, slight, weak **3** *light machinery:* easily moved, easy to carry around, portable, small **4** *light work:* easy, effortless, moderate, undemanding, unexacting, untaxing **5** *a light punishment:* lenient, mild, slight **6** *light movements:* agile, gentle, graceful, nimble, quick **7** *light comedy:* inconsequential, inconsiderable, petty, superficial, trifling, trivial, unimportant, worthless **8** *wanted to watch something light:* amusing, diverting, entertaining, frivolous, funny, humorous, light-hearted, pleasing, witty **9** *light food:* delicately flavoured, digestible, easy to digest, loose, modest **10** *light soil:* crumbly, easily dug, loose, porous
⊠ 1 heavy, thick, weighty **3** heavy **4** heavy **5** harsh, severe **7** important, serious **8** serious **9** heavy, rich **10** dense, solid

light³ *v*
▶ light on/upon chance on *formal*, come across, discover, encounter *formal*, find, happen upon *formal*, hit on, notice, spot, stumble on

lighten¹ *v* **1** *the sky lightened:* brighten, glow, light up, shine **2** *the sun had lightened her hair:* bleach, brighten, make brighter, make lighter
⊠ 1 darken **2** darken

lighten² *v* **1** *lighten the burden:* allay *formal*, alleviate *formal*, assuage *formal*, calm, ease, lessen, lift, make lighter, mitigate *formal*, reduce, relieve, unload **2** *lighten their spirits:* brighten, buoy up, cheer (up), elate, encourage, gladden,

hearten, inspire, inspirit *formal*, lift, perk up *colloq*, restore, revive, uplift
F3 1 burden **2** depress

light-fingered *adj* crafty, crooked *colloq*, dishonest, filching *colloq*, furtive, pilfering, shifty, shoplifting, sly, stealing, thieving, thievish
F3 honest

light-footed *adj* active, agile, graceful, lithe, nimble, sprightly, spry, swift
F3 clumsy, slow

light-headed *adj* airy, delirious, dizzy, faint, giddy, unsteady, vertiginous *formal*, woozy *colloq*

light-hearted *adj* amusing, blithe *formal*, bouncy *colloq*, bright, carefree, cheerful, chirpy *colloq*, elated, entertaining, frolicsome, gay, glad, happy, happy-go-lucky, high *colloq*, in good spirits, in high spirits, jolly, jovial, joyful, merry, playful, sunny, untroubled
F3 sad, serious, unhappy

lighthouse *n* beacon, danger/warning signal, fanal, pharos, tower

lightly *adv* **1** *lightly chilled wine*: delicately, faintly, gently, slightly, sparingly **2** *tread lightly*: airily, breezily, easily, effortlessly, gently, gingerly, softly **3** *not to be taken lightly*: carelessly, flippantly, frivolously, heedlessly, thoughtlessly **4** *let them off lightly*: easily, leniently, mildly
F3 2 heavily **3** soberly

lightness *n* **1** *the lightness of the fabric*: airiness, buoyancy, delicacy, delicateness, flimsiness, slightness, thinness, weightlessness **2** *lightness of movement*: agility, gentleness, grace, gracefulness, litheness, nimbleness **3** *lightness of spirit*: animation, blitheness *formal*, cheerfulness, cheeriness, gaiety, light-heartedness, liveliness
F3 1 heaviness, solidity **2** clumsiness **3** heaviness

lightning *n* ball lightning, clap of thunder, electric storm, forked lightning, lightning strike, sheet lightning, summer lightning, thunderbolt, thunderclap, thunderdart, thunderstorm

lightweight *adj* **1** *a lightweight material*: delicate, feathery, flimsy, insubstantial, light, thin, weightless **2** *a lightweight argument*: inconsequential, insignificant, negligible, nugatory *formal*, paltry, petty, slight, trifling, trivial, unimportant, worthless
F3 1 heavy **2** heavyweight, important, serious

like¹ *adj* akin, alike, allied, analogous *formal*, approximating, comparable, corresponding, equivalent, having an affinity, identical, much the same, of a kind, parallel, related, relating, resembling, same, similar
F3 dissimilar, unlike
♦ *n* counterpart, equal, equivalent, fellow, match, parallel, peer
♦ *prep* along the lines of, in the same way/manner as, on the lines of, similar to

like² *v* **1** *to like opera*: admire, adore, appreciate, approve of, be fond of, be keen on, care for, cherish, delight in, dig *colloq*, enjoy, esteem *formal*, find attractive, find enjoyable/interesting, find pleasant, go a bundle on *colloq*, have a soft spot for *colloq*, hold dear, love, prize, relish, revel in, take (kindly) to, take a shine to *colloq*, take pleasure in, take to, welcome **2** *would you like*

coffee or tea?: choose, decide on, desire, fancy *colloq*, feel inclined towards, go for *colloq*, prefer, select, want, wish
F3 1 dislike **2** reject

likeable *adj* agreeable, amiable, appealing, attractive, charming, congenial, engaging, genial, lovable, nice, pleasant, pleasing, sympathetic, winning, winsome
F3 disagreeable, unpleasant

likelihood *n* chance, liability, likeliness, possibility, probability, prospect
F3 improbability, unlikeliness

likely *adj* **1** *likely to become the manager*: anticipated, expected, inclined, liable, odds on *colloq*, prone, tending **2** *the likely outcome*: anticipated, expected, foreseeable, possible, predictable, probable, to be expected **3** *a likely explanation*: acceptable, believable, credible, feasible, plausible, reasonable **4** *a likely candidate*: acceptable, appropriate, fit, fitting, hopeful, pleasing, promising, proper, right
F3 1 unlikely **2** unlikely **4** unsuitable
♦ *adv* (as) like as not *colloq*, doubtlessly, in all probability, no doubt, presumably, probably

like-minded *adj* agreeing, compatible, harmonious, in accord *formal*, in agreement, in harmony, in rapport, of one mind, of the same mind, unanimous
F3 disagreeing

liken *v* analogize *formal*, associate, compare, correlate *formal*, equate, juxtapose, link, match, parallel, relate, set beside

likeness *n* **1** *noticed a likeness between them*: affinity, analogy *formal*, comparison, correspondence, parallelism, resemblance, similarity, similitude *formal* **2** *T-shirts bearing the likeness of Nelson Mandela*: bust, copy, drawing, effigy, facsimile, icon, image, painting, photograph, picture, portrait, replica, representation, reproduction, sculpture, sketch, statue, study **3** *Jesus appeared in the likeness of a man*: appearance, form, guise, semblance, shape
F3 1 dissimilarity, unlikeness

likewise *adv* by the same token, in like manner, in the same way, similarly

liking *n* affection, affinity, appreciation, attraction, bent, bias, desire, fancy, fondness, inclination, leaning, love, partiality, penchant *formal*, predilection *formal*, preference, proclivity *formal*, proneness, propensity *formal*, soft spot *colloq*, taste, tendency, thing *colloq*, weakness
F3 aversion, dislike, hatred

lilt *n* air, beat, cadence, measure, rhythm, rise and fall, song, sway, swing

lily-white *adj* blameless, chaste, faultless, incorrupt, innocent, irreproachable, milk-white, pure, spotless, uncorrupt, uncorrupted, unsullied, untainted, untarnished, virgin, virtuous
F3 corrupt

limb *n* **1** *stretch your limbs*: appendage, arm, extremity, leg, member **2** *the limbs of a tree*: bough, branch, fork, part, projection, spur **3** *the contemporary music limb of the National Youth Orchestra*: extension, offshoot, part, section, wing

limber *adj* agile, elastic, flexible, graceful, lissom, lithe, loose-jointed, loose-limbed, plastic, pliable, pliant, supple

▣ stiff
► **limber up** exercise, loosen up, prepare, warm up, work out

limbo *n* abeyance *formal*, the back burner *colloq*, uncertainty

limelight *n* attention, celebrity, eminence, fame, notability, notice, prominence, public eye, publicity, recognition, renown, spotlight, stardom

limit *n* **1** *push it to the limit:* ceiling, cut-off point, deadline, extreme, extremity, greatest amount, greatest extent, maximum, saturation point, terminus, ultimate, utmost **2** *the city limits:* border, bound(s), boundary, brink, confines, edge, end, frontier, parameters, perimeter, threshold, verge **3** *place a limit on:* check, constraint, curb, limitation, restraint, restriction
♦ *v* check, circumscribe *formal*, confine, constrain, control, curb, delimit, demarcate, hem in, hinder, hold in check, ration, reduce, restrain, restrict, specify

limitation *n* **1** *a limitation on parking:* block, check, constraint, control, curb, delimitation, demarcation, hindrance, impediment, restraint, restriction **2** *know your limitations:* defect, disadvantage, drawback, inability, inadequacy, incapability, shortcoming, weak point, weakness
▣ **1** extension **2** advantage, strong point

limited *adj* basic, checked, circumscribed *formal*, confined, constrained, controlled, defined, finite, fixed, imperfect, inadequate, incomplete, insufficient, minimal, narrow, qualified, restricted, scanty, small
▣ boundless, limitless

limitless *adj* boundless, countless, endless, illimited, immeasurable, incalculable, inexhaustible, infinite, interminable, measureless, never-ending, unbounded, undefined, unending, unlimited, unspecified, untold, vast
▣ limited

limp[1] *v* falter, hobble, hop, shamble, shuffle, stagger, stumble, totter, walk unevenly, walk with a limp
♦ *n* claudication *technical*, hitch, hobble, lameness, shuffle, uneven walk

limp[2] *adj* **1** *the lettuce was limp to the touch:* drooping, flabby, flaccid, flexible, floppy, lax, limber, loose, pliable, relaxed, slack, soft **2** *limp with exhaustion:* debilitated *formal*, enervated *formal*, exhausted, fatigued, feeble, frail, lethargic, spent, tired, weak, weary, worn out
▣ **1** firm, stiff **2** energetic, vigorous

limpid *adj* **1** *limpid waters:* bright, clear, crystal-clear, glassy, pellucid *formal*, pure, still, translucent, transparent, unruffled, untroubled **2** *a limpid explanation:* clear, coherent, comprehensible, flowing, intelligible, lucid
▣ **1** muddy, turbid *formal* **2** unintelligible

line[1] *n* **1** *mark a line under it:* band, bar, belt, dash, mark, rule, score, scratch, seam, slash, strand, streak, strip, stripe, stroke, underline, underscore **2** *a line of trees:* bank, chain, column, file, parade, procession, queue, rank, row, sequence, series, string, tier, trail **3** *the county line:* border, borderline, boundary, demarcation, edge, frontier, limit, margin, perimeter, periphery **4** *a fishing line:* cable, cord, filament, rope, strand,

string, thread, twine, wire **5** *the precise line of her jaw:* appearance, configuration *formal*, contour, delineation *formal*, figure, formation, outline, pattern, profile, shape, silhouette, style **6** *the lines on his face:* corrugation, crease, crow's feet, furrow, groove, wrinkle **7** *steer a straight line:* axis, channel, course, direction, path, route, track, trajectory, way **8** *follow a different line of enquiry:* approach, attitude, avenue, course (of action), ideology, method, modus operandi, policy, position, practice, procedure, scheme, system, way **9** *what line are you in?:* activity, area, business, calling, career, department, employment, field, interest, job, line of business / work, occupation, profession, province, pursuit, specialism, speciality, specialization, specialty, trade, vocation, work **10** *chat-up line:* patter, pitch, sales talk, spiel, talk **11** *drop you a line:* card, information, letter, memo, memorandum, message, note, postcard, report, word **12** *learn my lines:* book, libretto, part, script, text, words **13** *a shipping line:* business, company, firm, transport business **14** *behind enemy lines:* battleground, defences, firing-line, front, front line, position **15** *a new line of products:* brand, kind, make, sort, type, variety **16** *comes from an ancient line of kings:* ancestry, breed, descent, extraction, family, heritage, lineage, parentage, pedigree, race, stock, strain
♦ *v* border, bound, edge, fringe, rim, skirt, verge
► **line up 1** *line them up in a row:* align, array *formal*, assemble, group, marshal, order, range, regiment, straighten **2** *line up outside the shop:* assemble, fall in, form ranks, queue up, stand in line, wait in line **3** *line up a trip to Wales:* arrange, lay on *colloq*, obtain, organize, prepare, procure *formal*, secure

line[2] *v* back, cover, encase, face, fill, inlay, pad, panel, reinforce, stuff

lineage *n* ancestors, ancestry, birth, breed, descendants, descent, extraction, family, forebears, genealogy, heredity, house, line, offspring, pedigree, race, stock, succession

lineaments *n* appearance, aspect, configuration *formal*, countenance *formal*, face, features, lines, outline(s), physiognomy *formal*, profile, traits, visage *formal*

lined *adj* **1** *lined paper:* feint, ruled **2** *a lined face:* creased, furrowed, wizened, worn, wrinkled
▣ **1** blank, unlined **2** smooth

linen *n* bed linen, napery *formal*, napkins, pillowcases, sheets, table linen, tablecloths, tea towels, white goods

line-up *n* **1** *a superb line-up of guest stars:* arrangement, array, bill, cast, list, selection, team **2** *picked the mugger out of a line-up:* line, queue, row

linger *v* **1** *linger outside the door:* dally, dawdle, delay, dilly-dally *colloq*, hang around, idle, lag, loiter, remain, stay, tarry *formal*, wait **2** *linger a while before agreeing:* delay, hang on, procrastinate *formal*, stop, take your time, tarry *formal*, wait **3** *the pain still lingers:* continue, endure, last, persist, remain, survive
▣ **1** leave

lingerie *n* body stocking, bra, brassiere, camiknickers, camisole, frillies *colloq*, half-slip, inexpressibles, knickers, panties, panty girdle, slip, smalls *colloq*, suspender belt, teddy, underclothes, underclothing, undergarments, underwear, undies *colloq*, unmentionables

lingering *adj* dragging, long-drawn-out, persistent, prolonged, protracted *formal*, remaining, slow
🖃 quick

lingo *n* argot, cant, dialect, idiom, jargon, language, parlance, patois, patter, speech, talk, terminology, tongue, vernacular, vocabulary

liniment *n* balm, balsam, cream, embrocation, emollient, lotion, ointment, salve, unguent *formal*, wash

lining *n* backing, encasement, facing, inlay, interfacing, padding, panelling, reinforcement, stiffening

link *n* **1** *forged strong links with investors:* association, attachment, bond, communication, connection, liaison, partnership, relationship, tie, tie-up, union **2** *a link in a chain:* bond, joint, knot, loop, ring, tie **3** *the missing link:* component, constituent, division, element, member, part, piece
♦ *v* ally, amalgamate, associate, attach, bind, bracket, connect, couple, fasten, hook, join, merge, relate, team, tie, unite, yoke
🖃 separate, unfasten
▶ **link up** ally, amalgamate, connect, dock, hook up, join (up), join forces, meet up, merge, team up, unify
🖃 separate

link-up *n* alliance, amalgamation, association, connection, merger, partnership, relationship, tie-in, union
🖃 separation

lion-hearted *adj* bold, brave, courageous, daring, dauntless, dreadless, fearless, gallant, heroic, intrepid, resolute, stalwart, stout-hearted, valiant, valorous *formal*
🖃 cowardly

lionize *v* acclaim, adulate, aggrandize *formal*, celebrate, eulogize *formal*, exalt, fête, glorify, hero-worship, honour, idolize, magnify, praise, put on a pedestal *colloq*, sing the praises of, treat as a hero
🖃 vilify

lip *n* **1** *the lip of the cup:* border, brim, brink, edge, margin, rim, verge **2** *less of your lip!:* backchat, cheek *colloq*, effrontery, impertinence, impudence, insolence, rudeness, sauce *colloq*
🖃 **2** politeness

liquefaction *n* deliquescence *formal*, dissolution, dissolving, fusion, liquefying, melting, thawing
🖃 solidification

liquefy *v* deliquesce *formal*, dissolve, fluidize, flux, fuse, liquesce *formal*, liquidize, melt, run, smelt, thaw
🖃 solidify

liquid *n* drink, fluid, juice, liquor, lotion, sap, solution
♦ *adj* **1** *liquid medicines:* aqueous *formal*, clear, flowing, fluid, hydrous *formal*, liquefied, melted, molten, running, runny, sloppy, thawed, thin, watery, wet **2** *liquid notes:* flowing, mellow, melodious, smooth
🖃 **1** gas, solid

liquidate *v* **1** *liquidate a company:* break up, cash in, close down, convert to cash, disband,

dissolve, sell (off), wind up **2** *liquidate a loan:* clear, discharge, pay (off) **3** *liquidate your enemies:* abolish, annihilate, assassinate, destroy, dispatch, dissolve, do away with, eliminate, exterminate, finish off, kill, massacre, murder, put an end to, remove, rub out *colloq*, terminate, wipe out *colloq*

liquidize *v* blend, crush, mix, process, purée, synthesize

liquor *n* alcohol, booze *slang*, drink, Dutch courage *colloq*, firewater *colloq*, grog *colloq*, hard stuff *colloq*, hooch *colloq*, intoxicant, juice *colloq*, plonk *colloq*, sauce *colloq*, spirits, strong drink, vino *colloq*

lissom *adj* agile, flexible, graceful, light, limber, lithe, lithesome, loose-jointed, loose-limbed, nimble, pliable, pliant, supple, willowy
🖃 awkward, stiff

list[1] *n* agenda, calendar, catalogue, checklist, directory, enumeration, file, index, inventory, invoice, (list of) contents, listing, programme, recipe, record, register, roll, roster, rota, schedule, series, syllabus, table, tabulation, tally
♦ *v* alphabetize, bill, book, catalogue, classify, compile, enrol, enter, enumerate, file, index, itemize, note, programme, record, register, schedule, set down, tabulate, write down

list[2] *v* cant, heel (over), incline, lean (over), slant, slope, tilt, tip

listen *v* attend, give ear, hang on (someone's) words, hear, heed, lend an ear, mind, pay attention, prick up your ears, take notice
▶ **listen in** bug *colloq*, eavesdrop, monitor, overhear, tap, wiretap

listless *adj* apathetic, bored, depressed, dull, enervated *formal*, heavy, impassive, inactive, indifferent, indolent *formal*, inert, lackadaisical, languid *formal*, languishing, lethargic, lifeless, limp, passive, sluggish, spiritless, torpid *formal*, uninterested, vacant
🖃 energetic, enthusiastic

listlessness *n* apathy, enervation *formal*, ennui, inattention, indifference, indolence *formal*, languidness *formal*, languor *formal*, lethargy, lifelessness, sloth, sluggishness, spiritlessness, torpidity *formal*, torpor *formal*
🖃 liveliness

litany *n* **1** *recite a litany:* devotion, invocation *formal*, petition, prayer, supplication **2** *a litany of offences:* account, catalogue, enumeration, list, recital, recitation, repetition

literacy *n* ability to read, ability to write, articulacy, articulateness, cultivation, culture, education, erudition *formal*, intelligence, knowledge, learnedness, learning, proficiency, scholarship
🖃 illiteracy

literal *adj* **1** *a literal account of the conversation:* accurate, actual, close, exact, factual, faithful, genuine, precise, strict, true, undistorted, unembellished, unexaggerated, unvarnished, verbatim, word-for-word **2** *a literal cast of mind:* boring, colourless, down-to-earth, dull, humdrum, matter-of-fact, prosaic, tedious, unimaginative, uninspired
🖃 **1** deviating, imprecise, loose **2** imaginative

literally *adv* **1** *many people in Africa are literally starving:* actually, certainly, really, truly

2 *translate literally:* closely, exactly, faithfully, plainly, precisely, strictly, to the letter, verbatim, word for word
F₂ 2 imprecisely, loosely

literary *adj* **1** *literary society:* bookish, cultivated, cultured, educated, erudite *formal*, learned, lettered, literate, refined, scholarly, well-read, widely-read **2** *literary phrases:* formal, old-fashioned, poetic
F₂ 1 ignorant, illiterate **2** colloquial, everyday, informal

literate *adj* able to read, able to write, cultured, educated, intellectual, intelligent, knowledgeable, learned, proficient, well-educated

literature *n* **1** *a student of Russian literature:* letters, paper(s), printed works, published works, writings **2** *literature about insurance:* advertising material, brochure(s), bumf *colloq*, circular(s), data, facts, hand-out(s), information, leaflet(s), pamphlet(s), printed matter

Types of literature include:
allegory, anti-novel, autobiography, belles-lettres *formal*, biography, classic novel, criticism, drama, epic, epistle, essay, fiction, Gothic novel, lampoon, libretto, magnum opus, non-fiction, novel, novella, parody, pastiche, penny dreadful *colloq*, picaresque novel, poetry, polemic, postil, prose, roman novel, saga, satire, thesis, tragedy, treatise, triad, trilogy, verse. See also **poem, story**

lithe *adj* agile, double-jointed, flexible, limber, lissom, lithesome, loose-jointed, loose-limbed, pliable, pliant, supple
F₂ stiff

litigant *n* claimant, complainant, contender, contestant, disputant, litigator, party, plaintiff

litigation *n* action, case, contention, dispute, lawsuit, legal case, process, prosecution, suit

litigious *adj* argumentative, belligerent, contentious, disputatious, quarrelsome
F₂ easy-going

litter *n* **1** *pick up litter from the streets:* clutter, debris, detritus *formal*, fragments, garbage, grot *colloq*, jumble, junk *colloq*, mess, muck, odds and ends, refuse, rubbish, shreds, trash *US*, waste **2** *a litter of puppies:* brood, family, issue *formal*, offspring, progeny *formal*, young
♦ *v* clutter, disorder, make a mess, make untidy, scatter, strew
F₂ tidy

little *adj* **1** *a little boat:* baby, diminutive, dwarf, Lilliputian, microscopic, midget, mini, miniature, minute, petite, pint-size(d) *colloq*, short, slender, slight, small, teeny *colloq*, tiny, wee *colloq* **2** *a little while:* brief, ephemeral *formal*, fleeting, momentary, passing, short, short-lived, transient, transitory **3** *it's only a little thing:* inconsiderable, insignificant, minor, negligible, nominal, nugatory *formal*, paltry, petty, trifling, trivial, unimportant **4** *a nice little house:* attractive, cute, nice, pleasant, sweet
F₂ 1 big **2** lengthy, long **3** considerable, serious
♦ *adv* barely, hardly, not much, scarcely, seldom, slightly
♦ *n* bit, dab, dash, drop, fragment, hint, modicum, particle, pinch, small amount,

smattering, soupçon, speck, spot, taste, touch, trace, trickle, trifle
F₂ lot

liturgical *adj* ceremonial, eucharistic, formal, hieratic *formal*, ritual, sacerdotal *formal*, sacramental, solemn
F₂ secular

liturgy *n* celebration, ceremony, form, formula, observance, office, ordinance, rite, ritual, sacrament, service, usage, worship

live¹ *v* **1** *he is still living:* be, be alive, breathe, draw breath, exist, have life **2** *make enough money to live:* earn your living, endure, support yourself, survive **3** *her reputation still lives:* abide *formal*, continue, endure, last, persist, remain, stay, survive **4** *live in Leeds:* abide *formal*, be settled, dwell *formal*, hang out *colloq*, have your home, inhabit, lodge, reside *formal*, squat, stay **5** *live your life:* conduct *formal*, lead, pass, spend **6** *live well:* behave, comport yourself *formal*, conduct yourself *formal* **7** *live while you're young:* enjoy life, enjoy life to the full, make the most of your life, see life
F₂ 1 die
▶ **live on** depend for nourishment on, exist on, feed on, live off, rely on, subsist on *formal*

live² *adj* **1** *give birth to live young:* alive, animate, breathing, existent, having life, living **2** *a live flame:* alight, blazing, burning, flaming, glowing, hot, ignited **3** *live cables:* active, charged, connected, electrically charged **4** *a live bomb:* explosive, unexploded, unstable, volatile **5** *a live issue:* active, controversial, current, important, lively, pertinent *formal*, pressing, relevant, topical, urgent, vital
F₂ 1 dead **3** disconnected **4** defused **5** irrelevant

liveable *adj* **1** *at least the flat is liveable:* habitable, inhabitable **2** *make life liveable:* acceptable, adequate, bearable, comfortable, endurable, satisfactory, supportable, tolerable, worthwhile
F₂ 1 uninhabitable **2** unbearable

livelihood *n* income, job, living, maintenance, means, means of support, occupation, profession, source of income, subsistence, support, sustenance, trade, work

liveliness *n* activity, animation, boisterousness, brio *colloq*, briskness, dynamism, energy, oomph *colloq*, quickness, smartness, spirit, sprightliness, vitality, vivacity
F₂ apathy, inactivity

livelong *adj* complete, enduring, entire, full, long, protracted, whole
F₂ partial

lively *adj* **1** *a lively person:* active, alert, alive, animated, blithe, bouncy *colloq*, cheerful, dynamic, energetic, enthusiastic, high-spirited, jaunty, keen, perky, playful, quick, spirited, sprightly, spry, vigorous, vivacious **2** *a lively discussion:* animated, enthusiastic, exciting, heated, interesting, stimulating **3** *the city was lively:* brisk, bustling, busy, buzzing, crowded, exciting, hectic, swarming, teeming
F₂ 1 apathetic, moribund **2** dull **3** dull

liven *v* animate, brighten, buck up *colloq*, energize, enliven, hot up *colloq*, invigorate, pep up *colloq*, perk up *colloq*, put life into, rouse, spice (up), stir (up), vitalize
F₂ dishearten

liverish adj crabbed *colloq*, crabby *colloq*, crotchety *colloq*, crusty, disagreeable, grumpy, ill-humoured, irascible, irritable, peevish, quick-tempered, snappy, splenetic, testy, tetchy
🖃 calm, easy-going

livery n apparel *formal*, attire *formal*, clobber *colloq*, clothes, clothing, costume, dress, garb, garments, gear *colloq*, get-up *colloq*, habiliments *formal*, habit, regalia, suit, togs *colloq*, uniform, vestments

livid adj 1 *livid with rage*: angry, enraged, exasperated, fuming, furious, incensed, indignant, infuriated, irate, mad *colloq*, outraged, raging, seething 2 *a livid mark on her arm*: black-and-blue, bruised, discoloured, greyish, leaden, purple, purplish
🖃 1 calm

living adj 1 *her parents are still living*: alive, animate, breathing, existing, live 2 *a living tradition*: active, animated, continuing, current, extant *formal*, going strong *colloq*, lively, operative, strong, surviving, vigorous, vital 3 *the living image of him*: close, exact, genuine, identical, precise, true
🖃 1 dead 3 inexact
♦ n 1 *healthy living*: animation, being, existence, life 2 *make a living*: income, lifestyle, livelihood, maintenance, means of support, source of income, subsistence, support, sustenance

living-room n drawing-room, lounge, sitting-room

load n 1 *a lorry shed its load*: burden, cargo, charge, consignment, contents, freight, goods, lading, shipment 2 *a load on my mind*: albatross, burden, charge, duty, encumbrance, millstone, obligation, oppression, pressure, responsibility, strain, tribulation *formal*, trouble, weight, worry 3 *a load of money*: heap, horde, lot, score, ton
♦ v 1 *load a van*: charge, fill (up), freight, heap, lade, pack, pile, stack 2 *load with guilt*: burden, encumber, oppress, overburden, overwhelm, saddle, strain, tax, trouble, weigh down, weight, worry

loaded adj 1 *a loaded van*: burdened, charged, filled, full, heaped, laden, packed, piled, snowed under *colloq*, stacked, weighted 2 *loaded dice*: biased, to your disadvantage, weighted 3 *her family is loaded*: affluent, flush *colloq*, in the money *colloq*, rich, rolling in it *colloq*, wealthy, well-heeled *colloq*, well-off 4 *went into a bar and got loaded*: bevvied *colloq*, blind drunk *colloq*, blotto *colloq*, bombed *slang*, canned *slang*, drunk, drunk as a lord/newt *colloq*, inebriated *formal*, intoxicated *formal*, legless *colloq*, lit up *slang*, merry *colloq*, paralytic *slang*, pickled *colloq*, pissed *slang*, plastered *colloq*, roaring drunk *colloq*, sloshed *slang*, smashed *slang*, soused *colloq*, sozzled *colloq*, squiffy *colloq*, stewed *slang*, stoned *slang*, tanked up *slang*, the worse for drink *colloq*, tiddly *colloq*, tight *colloq*, tipsy *colloq*, under the influence, well-oiled *colloq*

loaf[1] n 1 *a loaf of bread*: block, brick, cake, cube, lump, mass, slab 2 *use your loaf*: brains *colloq*, common sense, gumption *colloq*, head, noddle, nous *colloq*, sense

loaf[2] v hang around *colloq*, idle, laze, loiter, lounge around *colloq*, mooch *colloq*, stand about, take it easy *colloq*
🖃 toil

loafer n idler, layabout *colloq*, lazybones *colloq*, lounger, ne'er-do-well, shirker, skiver *colloq*, sluggard, wastrel

loan n advance, allowance, credit, lending, mortgage
♦ v advance, allow, lend

loath adj against, averse *formal*, disinclined, grudging, hesitant, indisposed, opposed, reluctant, resisting, unwilling
🖃 willing

loathe v abhor *formal*, abominate *formal*, cannot stand, despise, detest, dislike, execrate *formal*, feel revulsion at, hate, have an aversion to, recoil from
🖃 adore, love

loathing n abhorrence *formal*, abomination *formal*, antipathy *formal*, aversion, detestation, disgust, dislike, execration *formal*, hate, hatred, horror, ill-will, odium, repugnance, repulsion, revulsion
🖃 affection, love

loathsome adj abhorrent *formal*, abominable *formal*, contemptible, despicable, detestable, disagreeable, disgusting, execrable *formal*, hateful, horrible, nasty, nauseating, obnoxious, odious, offensive, repellent, repugnant, repulsive, revolting, vile

lob v chuck *colloq*, fling, heave, hurl, launch, lift, loft, pitch, shy, throw, toss

lobby v call, campaign, demand, influence, persuade, press, pressure, promote, push *colloq*, solicit, urge
♦ n 1 *meet in the hotel lobby*: anteroom, corridor, entrance, entrance hall, foyer, hall, hallway, passage, passageway, porch, vestibule, waiting-room 2 *the anti-smoking lobby*: campaign, ginger group, lobbyists, pressure group

local adj city, community, district, limited, municipal, narrow, neighbourhood, parish, parish-pump, parochial, provincial, regional, restricted, small-town, town, urban, vernacular, village
🖃 national
♦ n 1 *enjoyed meeting the locals*: citizen, inhabitant, native, resident 2 *have a drink in my local*: bar, boozer *slang*, hostelry *colloq*, inn, pub, public house, tavern, watering-hole *colloq*

locale n area, environment, locality, location, locus *formal*, neighbourhood, place, position, scene, setting, site, spot, venue, zone

locality n area, district, environment, locale, neighbourhood, place, position, region, scene, setting, site, spot, surrounding area, vicinity

localize v 1 *the ability to localize sounds*: ascribe, assign, identify, narrow down, pinpoint, specify, zero in on 2 *localize the bleeding*: circumscribe *formal*, concentrate, confine, contain, delimit, delimitate, limit, restrain, restrict

locate v 1 *locate the source of the problem*: come across, detect, discover, find, hit upon *colloq*, identify, lay your hands on *colloq*, pinpoint, run to earth *colloq*, track down, uncover, unearth 2 *located on a hilltop*: build, establish, fix, place, position, put, seat, set, settle, site, situate, station

location n bearings, locale, locus *formal*, place, point, position, scene, setting, site, situation, spot, venue, whereabouts

lock¹ n bolt, catch, Chubb® lock, clasp, combination lock, fastening, mortise lock, padlock, spring lock, Yale® lock
♦ v 1 *lock the door:* bar, bolt, fasten, latch, padlock, seal, secure, shut 2 *locked in a power struggle:* clench, engage, entangle, entwine, interlock, join 3 *locked in an embrace:* clasp, clutch, embrace, encircle, enclose, grapple, grasp, hug
🔁 1 unlock
▶ **lock out** bar, debar, exclude, keep out, refuse admittance/entrance to, shut out
▶ **lock up** cage, close up, confine, detain, imprison, incarcerate *formal*, jail, pen, put behind bars, put under lock and key, secure, shut in, shut up, wall in
🔁 free

> **Parts of a lock include:**
> barrel, bolt, cylinder, cylinder hole, dead bolt, escutcheon, face plate, hasp, key, key card, keyhole, keyway, knob, latch, latch bolt, latch follower, latch lever, mortise bolt, pin, push button, rose, sash, sash bolt, spindle, spindle hole, spring, strike plate, staple

lock² n curl, plait, ringlet, strand, tress, tuft

locker n cabinet, compartment, container, cupboard

lock-up n 1 *spent four hours in a police lock-up:* can *slang*, cell, clink *slang*, cooler *slang*, gaol, jail, jug *slang*, penitentiary, prison, quod *slang* 2 *kept the goods in a lock-up:* depository, garage, storeroom, warehouse

locomotion n action, ambulation *formal*, headway, motion, movement, moving, perambulation *formal*, progress, progression, travel, travelling, walking

locution n 1 *his odd locution:* accent, articulation, diction, inflection, intonation, verbal style 2 *a quaint locution:* cliché, collocation, expression, idiom, phrase, phrasing, term, turn of phrase, wording

lodge n 1 *a hunting lodge:* cabin, chalet, cottage, gatehouse, house, hunting-lodge, hut 2 *a Masonic lodge:* association, branch, chapter, club, group, meeting-place, section, society 3 *a beaver's lodge:* den, haunt, lair, nest, retreat, shelter
♦ v 1 *lodged them in the basement:* accommodate, billet, board, harbour, put up *colloq*, quarter, shelter 2 *the villa where we lodged:* be settled, dwell *formal*, have your home, live, reside *formal*, room, sojourn *formal*, stay 3 *it lodged in my mind:* fix, get caught, get stuck, imbed, implant 4 *lodge a tax return:* bank, deposit, place, put in, register, submit 5 *lodge a complaint:* file, make, record, register, submit

lodger n boarder, guest, paying guest, resident, tenant

lodgings n a roof over your head *colloq*, abode *formal*, accommodation, billet, board, boarding-house, digs *colloq*, dwelling *formal*, pad *colloq*, place, quarters, residence *formal*, rooms

lofty adj 1 *lofty ideals:* dignified, distinguished, esteemed *formal*, exalted, grand, illustrious, imperial, imposing, majestic, noble, renowned, stately, sublime 2 *a lofty peak:* elevated, high, raised, sky-high, soaring, tall, towering 3 *a lofty attitude:* arrogant, condescending, disdainful, haughty, high and mighty *colloq*, lordly,

patronizing, proud, snooty, supercilious, superior, toffee-nosed *colloq*
🔁 2 low 3 humble, lowly, modest

log n 1 *pine logs:* block, chunk, piece, timber, trunk 2 *the ship's log:* account, chart, daybook, diary, journal, logbook, record, register, tally
♦ v book, chart, file, note, record, register, set down, tally, write up

logic n argument, argumentation, coherence, deduction, dialectics *technical*, judgement, ratiocination *formal*, rationale, reason, reasoning, sense

logical adj clear, cogent *formal*, coherent, consistent, deducible, intelligent, judicious *formal*, methodical, rational, reasonable, reasoned, relevant, sensible, sound, valid, well-founded, well-organized, well-reasoned, well-thought-out, wise
🔁 illogical, irrational

logistics n co-ordination, direction, engineering, management, masterminding, orchestration, organization, planning, plans, strategy, tactics

logo n badge, device, emblem, figure, image, insignia, mark, representation, sign, symbol, trademark

loiter v dally, dawdle, delay, dilly-dally *colloq*, hang about/around, idle, lag, linger, loaf *colloq*, lounge, mooch, saunter, take your time, tarry *formal*, waste time

loll v 1 *lolling about in gangs:* loaf *colloq*, lounge *colloq*, recline *formal*, relax, slouch, slump, sprawl 2 *his head lolled backwards:* dangle, droop, drop, flap, flop, hang, sag

lone adj 1 *a lone voice:* alone, isolated, only, separate, single, sole, solitary 2 *a lone parent:* divorced, separated, single, unattached, unmarried, without a partner 3 *a lone cottage:* abandoned, barren, deserted, desolate, forsaken, isolated, out-of-the-way, remote, secluded, unfrequented, uninhabited
🔁 1 accompanied

loneliness n aloneness, desolation, isolation, lonesomeness, seclusion, solitariness, solitude

lonely adj 1 *a lonely person:* abandoned, alone, companionless, destitute, forsaken, friendless, lone, lonesome, miserable, outcast, reclusive, rejected, sad, solitary, unaccompanied, unhappy, wretched 2 *this lonely place:* abandoned, barren, deserted, desolate, forsaken, God-forsaken, isolated, off the beaten track *colloq*, out-of-the-way, remote, secluded, unfrequented, uninhabited
🔁 2 crowded, populous

loner n hermit, individualist, lone wolf *colloq*, recluse, solitary, solitudinarian *formal*

lonesome adj 1 *I feel so lonesome:* abandoned, alone, companionless, destitute, forsaken, friendless, lonely, miserable, outcast, rejected, sad, solitary, unhappy, wretched 2 *a lonesome canyon:* abandoned, barren, deserted, desolate, forsaken, isolated, lonely, out-of-the-way, remote, secluded, unfrequented, uninhabited

long adj 1 *a long time:* extended, extensive, interminable, lengthy, marathon, slow, spread out, stretched (out), sustained 2 *a long explanation:* elongated, expansive, extensive,

interminable, lengthy, long-drawn-out, overlong, prolonged, protracted *formal*, spun out
F3 1 brief, fleeting, short **2** abbreviated, brief, short
♦ *v* covet, crave, desire, dream, hanker, hope, hunger, itch, lust, pine, thirst, want, wish, yearn, yen for *colloq*

long-drawn-out *adj* dragging on *colloq*, interminable, lengthy, long-drawn, long-winded, marathon, overextended, overlong, prolix *formal*, prolonged, protracted *formal*, spun out, tedious
F3 brief, curtailed

longing *n* ambition, aspiration, coveting, craving, desire, dream, hankering, hope, hunger, hungering, itch, pining, thirst, urge, wanting, wish, yearning, yen *colloq*
♦ *adj* anxious, ardent, avid, desirous *formal*, eager, hungry, wishful, wistful

long-lasting *adj* abiding, chronic, continuing, enduring, imperishable, lingering, long-standing, permanent, prolonged, protracted *formal*, unchanging, unfading
F3 ephemeral, short-lived, transient

long-lived *adj* durable, enduring, lasting, longevous *formal*, long-lasting, long-standing, macrobian *technical*, macrobiotic
F3 brief, ephemeral *formal*, short-lived

long-standing *adj* abiding, enduring, established, long-established, long-lasting, long-lived, time-honoured, traditional, well-established

long-suffering *adj* easy-going, forbearing, forgiving, indulgent, patient, resigned, stoical, tolerant, uncomplaining
F3 complaining

long-winded *adj* diffuse, discursive, garrulous, lengthy, long-drawn-out, overlong, prolix *formal*, prolonged, protracted *formal*, rambling, repetitious, tedious, verbose, voluble *formal*, wordy
F3 brief, terse

long-windedness *n* diffuseness, discursiveness, garrulity, lengthiness, longueur *formal*, macrology *formal*, prolixity *formal*, repetitiousness, tediousness, verbosity, volubility *formal*, wordiness
F3 brevity, curtness

look *v* **1** *look at the scenery*: check, consider, contemplate, examine, eye, eyeball *US colloq*, focus, gape, gawp *colloq*, gaze, get a load of *colloq*, get an eyeful of *colloq*, give a going-over *colloq*, give the once-over *colloq*, glance, inspect, observe, peep, regard, run your eyes over *colloq*, scan, scrutinize, see, stare, study, survey, take a butcher's *colloq*, take a dekko *colloq*, take a gander *colloq*, take a look, take a shufti *colloq*, take a squint *colloq*, take in, view, watch **2** *it looks good*: appear, exhibit the signs of being, give the appearance of being, seem, show up as **3** *the house looks onto the fields*: be opposite, face, front, front on, give onto, look onto, overlook
♦ *n* **1** *take a quick look*: butcher's *colloq*, contemplation, dekko *colloq*, examination, eyeful *colloq*, gander *colloq*, gape, gaze, glance, glimpse, inspection, observation, once-over *colloq*, peek, peep, review, shufti *colloq*, sight, squint *colloq*, stare, study, survey, view **2** *a faraway look*: air, appearance, aspect, bearing *formal*, complexion,

countenance *formal*, effect, expression, façade, face, features, guise, impression, manner, mien *formal*, semblance
▶ **look after** attend to, babysit, care for, childmind, guard, keep an eye on, maintain, mind, nurse, protect, sit, supervise, take care of, take charge of, tend, watch over
F3 disregard, ignore, neglect
▶ **look back** recall, reflect on, remember, reminisce, think back
▶ **look down on** act condescendingly towards, despise, disdain, disparage *formal*, hold in contempt, look down your nose at *colloq*, patronize, scorn, sneer at, spurn, talk down to, think of as inferior/unimportant, turn your nose up at *colloq*
F3 approve, esteem
▶ **look for** forage for, hunt for, hunt out, quest, search for, seek, try to find
▶ **look forward to** anticipate, await, envisage, envision, expect, hope for, long for, look for, wait for
▶ **look into** ask about, check out *colloq*, delve into, dig into, examine, explore, fathom, go into, inquire about, inspect, investigate, look over, plumb, probe, research, scrutinize, search into, study
▶ **look on** consider, count, deem *formal*, hold, judge, regard, think
▶ **look out** be alert, be careful, be on the qui vive *formal*, be on your guard, beware, guard yourself, keep an eye out, keep your eyes open/peeled/skinned, look/mind where you're going *colloq*, pay attention, watch out
▶ **look over** cast an/your eye over, check, check out *colloq*, examine, give a once-over to *colloq*, go through, inspect, look through, monitor, read through, scan, view
▶ **look to 1** *we are looking to move next year*: anticipate, await, expect, hope to, reckon on, think about **2** *to look to someone for help*: count on, rely on, turn to
▶ **look up 1** *look up facts*: consult, find, hunt for, research, search for, seek, track down **2** *look up my relatives*: call on, drop by, drop in on, look in on, pay a visit to, stop by, visit **3** *things are looking up*: advance, ameliorate *formal*, come on/along, develop, get better, improve, make headway, make progress, perk up *colloq*, pick up, progress
▶ **look up to** admire, esteem *formal*, have a high opinion of, honour, regard highly, respect, revere, think highly of

look-alike *n* clone, (dead) ringer *colloq*, doppelgänger, double, exact likeness, image, living image, replica, spit *colloq*, spitting image *colloq*, twin

lookout *n* **1** *act as lookout*: guard, sentinel, sentry, watchman **2** *man the lookout*: observation post, post, tower, watch, watch-tower **3** *that's your lookout, pal!*: affair, business, concern, pigeon *colloq*, problem, responsibility, worry

loom *v* **1** *the ship loomed out of the mist*: appear, become visible, emerge, rise, soar, take shape, tower **2** *her exams are looming*: be imminent, hang over, impend, menace, threaten

loop *n* bend, circle, coil, convolution *formal*, curl, curve, eyelet, hoop, kink, loophole, noose, oval, ring, spiral, turn, twirl, twist, whorl
♦ *v* bend, braid, circle, coil, connect, curl, curve round, encircle, fasten, fold, join, knot, roll, spiral, surround, tie, turn, twist, wind

loophole *n* escape, evasion, excuse, let-out, omission

loose *adj* **1** *a loose tooth*: insecure, movable, wobbly **2** *the horses are loose*: at large, escaped, free, let go, off, released, unattached, unconfined, uncoupled, undone, unfastened, unlocked, untethered, untied **3** *loose clothes*: baggy, flowing, hanging, loose-fitting, sagging, shapeless, slack, unbound, untied **4** *loose wording*: broad, general, ill-defined, imprecise, inaccurate, indefinite, indistinct, inexact, rambling, vague **5** *loose morals*: abandoned, corrupt, debauched, degenerate, disreputable, dissolute, fast, immoral, lax, promiscuous, unchaste, wanton
⊞ 1 firm, fixed, secure **2** fastened, tied up **3** tight **4** literal, precise, specific **5** chaste
♦ *v* **1** *loosed the horses*: detach, disconnect, disengage, free, let go, liberate, loosen, release, set free, unbind, unclasp, uncouple, undo, unfasten, unhook, unleash, unlock, unmoor, unpen, untie **2** *loosed the restrictions*: diminish, ease, lessen, loosen, moderate, reduce, relax, slacken, weaken
⊞ 1 bind, fasten, fix, secure **2** tighten

loosen *v* diminish, ease, loose, moderate, relax, slacken, unbind, undo, unfasten, untie, weaken
⊞ tighten
▶ **loosen up 1** *he needs to loosen up a bit*: chill out *colloq*, cool it *colloq*, ease up, go easy, hang loose *colloq*, lessen, let up, relax, unwind **2** *loosen up before playing squash*: exercise, limber up, prepare, warm up, work out

loot *n* booty, haul, pickings, plunder, prize, riches, spoils, stolen goods, stolen money, swag *colloq*
♦ *v* burgle, despoil *formal*, maraud, pillage, plunder, raid, ransack, ravage, rifle, rob, sack, steal, steal from

lop *v* chop, clip, crop, curtail, cut (off), detach, dock, hack, prune, reduce, remove, sever, shorten, take off, trim, truncate

lope *v* bound, canter, gallop, lollop, run, spring, stride

lop-sided *adj* askew, asymmetrical, crooked, off balance, one-sided, squint, tilting, unbalanced, unequal, uneven
⊞ balanced, symmetrical

loquacious *adj* babbling, blathering, chattering, chatty, gabby *colloq*, garrulous, gassy *colloq*, gossipy, multiloquent *formal*, multiloquous *formal*, talkative, voluble *formal*, wordy
⊞ reserved, succinct, taciturn, terse

loquacity *n* chattiness, effusiveness, garrulity, gassiness *colloq*, multiloquence *formal*, multiloquy *formal*, talkativeness, volubility *formal*
⊞ succinctness, taciturnity, terseness

lord *n* **1** *a noble lord*: aristocrat, baron, count, duke, earl, noble, nobleman, peer, viscount **2** *my lord and master*: captain, chief, commander, emperor, governor, king, leader, master, monarch, overlord, prince, ruler, sovereign, superior **3** *praise the Lord*: Almighty, Christ, Creator, Eternal One, Father, God, Holy One, Jehovah, Jesus Christ, King, Maker, Redeemer, Saviour, Son of God, Son of Man, the Word, Yahweh

lordly *adj* **1** *his lordly estate*: aristocratic, dignified, grand, grandiose, imperial, impressive, lofty, magnificent, majestic, noble, splendid, stately **2** *a lordly manner*: arrogant, big-headed *colloq*, condescending, dictatorial, disdainful, domineering, haughty, high and mighty *colloq*, high-handed, hoity-toity *colloq*, hubristic *formal*, imperious, overbearing, over-confident, patronizing, peremptory *formal*, proud, stuck-up *colloq*, supercilious, toffee-nosed *colloq*, too big for your boots *colloq*, uppity *colloq*
⊞ 1 lowly **2** humble

lore *n* beliefs, erudition *formal*, folklore, knowledge, learning, legends, sayings, scholarship, stories, superstitions, teaching, traditions, wisdom

lorry *n* articulated lorry, float, juggernaut, pantechnicon, pick-up, removal van, trailer, truck, vehicle, wagon

lose *v* **1** *lose your keys*: drop, forfeit, forget, mislay, misplace, miss, not find **2** *lose at tennis*: be beaten, be conquered, be defeated, be unsuccessful, come to grief *colloq*, fail, fall short, go down, suffer defeat, throw in the towel *colloq* **3** *lost their pursuers*: elude, evade, leave behind, outrun, shake off, throw off **4** *lost his father in the war*: be bereaved of, be deprived of, be dispossessed of, be divested of *formal*, have taken away, no longer have, stop having **5** *lose an opportunity*: disregard, fail to grasp, fritter, ignore, miss, neglect, not take advantage of, squander, waste **6** *lose your way*: depart from, stray from, wander from **7** *lose valuable time*: consume, deplete *formal*, dissipate *formal*, drain, exhaust, expend, spend, squander, use up, waste
⊞ 1 find, gain, keep **2** win **5** grasp, take advantage of **6** find **7** make
▶ **lose out** be at a disadvantage, be disadvantaged, be unsuccessful, miss out, suffer

loser *n* also-ran *colloq*, dead loss *colloq*, failure, flop *colloq*, has-been *colloq*, no-hoper *colloq*, non-starter *colloq*, runner-up, the defeated, washout *colloq*, write-off *colloq*
⊞ winner

loss *n* **1** *the loss of her keys*: disappearance, dropping, forfeiture, forgetting, mislaying, misplacement, missing **2** *to suffer loss*: bereavement, deprivation, disadvantage, dispossession, harm, hurt, impairment, privation *formal* **3** *losses in war*: casualty, death, fatality, missing, wounded **4** *the business made a loss*: debt, deficiency, deficit
⊞ 1 finding **2** gain **4** profit

lost *adj* **1** *to get lost*: astray, disappeared, disorientated, disoriented, mislaid, misplaced, missing, off course, strayed, vanished **2** *lost for an explanation*: at a loss, baffled, bewildered, confused, disoriented, nonplussed, perplexed, puzzled **3** *the ship was lost*: demolished, destroyed, ruined, wrecked **4** *my lost youth*: frittered away, missed, neglected, squandered, unrecoverable, wasted **5** *a lost civilization*: bygone, dead, defunct, extinct, long-forgotten, past, untraceable, vanished **6** *lost souls*: condemned, cursed, damned, doomed, fallen, irredeemable **7** *lost in thought*: absent-minded, absorbed, captivated, dreamy, engrossed, enthralled, fascinated, occupied, preoccupied, riveted, spellbound, taken up with
⊞ 1 found

lot *n* **1** *a lot of people:* a good/great deal, a quantity, dozens *colloq*, great number, heaps *colloq*, hundreds *colloq*, large amount, loads *colloq*, many, masses *colloq*, miles *colloq*, millions *colloq*, oodles *colloq*, piles *colloq*, stacks *colloq*, thousands *colloq*, tons *colloq* **2** *they are a strange lot:* assortment, batch, bunch *colloq*, bundle, collection, consignment, crowd, gathering, group, quantity, set **3** *accept your lot:* allowance, cut *colloq*, parcel, part, percentage, piece, portion, quota, ration, share **4** *your lot in life:* circumstances, destiny, fate, fortune, situation **5** *a vacant lot:* allotment, parcel, piece of ground, piece of land, plot

lotion *n* balm, balsam, cream, embrocation, emollient, liniment, ointment, salve

lottery *n* **1** *win the lottery:* bingo, draw, gambling game, raffle, sweepstake, tombola **2** *it's all a huge lottery:* chance, gamble, hazard, luck, risk, speculation, venture

loud *adj* **1** *a loud sound:* aggressive, blaring, booming, brazen, clamorous, deafening, ear-piercing, ear-splitting, emphatic, full-mouthed, insistent, loud-mouthed, noisy, penetrating, piercing, raucous, resonant, resounding, reverberating, roaring, rowdy, shrill, stentorian *formal*, strident, thundering, vehement, vociferous **2** *loud colours:* bold, brash, flamboyant, flash *colloq*, flashy, garish, gaudy, glaring, obtrusive, ostentatious, showy, tasteless, vulgar
F3 **1** quiet, soft **2** subdued

loudly *adv* clamorously, deafeningly, fortissimo *technical*, lustily, noisily, resoundingly, shrilly, streperously *formal*, strepitantly *formal*, stridently, strongly, uproariously, vehemently, vigorously, vociferously
F3 quietly, softly

loudmouth *n* big mouth *colloq*, blusterer, boaster, braggadocio, braggart, gasbag *colloq*, swaggerer, windbag *colloq*

loud-mouthed *adj* aggressive, blustering, boasting, bold, bragging, brazen, coarse, noisy, vulgar

lounge *v* idle, kill time, laze, lie about/around, lie back, loll (about), recline, relax, repose *formal*, slump, sprawl, take it easy *colloq*, waste time
♦ *n* day-room, drawing-room, living-room, parlour, sitting-room

louring, lowering *adj* black, cloudy, dark, darkening, forbidding, foreboding, gloomy, grey, grim, heavy, impending, menacing, ominous, overcast, threatening

lousy *adj* **1** *the weather was lousy:* awful *colloq*, bad, contemptible, crap *slang*, inferior, low, mingy *colloq*, miserable, no good, poor, rotten, second-rate, terrible *colloq* **2** *I feel lousy:* awful *colloq*, ill, off-colour, out of sorts *colloq*, poorly, queasy, seedy, sick, under the weather *colloq*, unwell
F3 **1** excellent, superb **2** well

lout *n* barbarian, boor, bumpkin *colloq*, clod *colloq*, clodhopper *colloq*, dolt, gawk, hick *colloq*, hobbledehoy *colloq*, lubber, oaf, slob *colloq*, yahoo, yob *colloq*, yobbo *colloq*

loutish *adj* boorish, bungling, churlish, clodhopping *colloq*, coarse, crude, doltish, gawky, gruff, ignorant, ill-bred, ill-mannered, impolite, oafish, rough, rude, rustic, uncivilized, uncouth, uneducated, unmannerly, unrefined, vulgar
F3 cultured, genteel, polite, refined

lovable *adj* adorable, appealing, attractive, bewitching, captivating, charming, cute, dear, delightful, enchanting, endearing, engaging, fetching, likeable, lovely, pleasing, sweet, winsome
F3 detestable, hateful

love *v* **1** *he loves his wife:* adore, be attracted to, be daft/nuts on *colloq*, be devoted to, be fond of, be infatuated with, be mad on *colloq*, be sold on *colloq*, be sweet on *colloq*, care for, cherish, desire, dote on, feel affection for, hold dear, idolize, like very much, long for, prize, think the world of, treasure, worship **2** *I love macaroons:* appreciate, be partial to, delight in, desire, enjoy, fancy, have a liking for, like very much, relish, savour, take pleasure in
F3 **1** detest, hate
♦ *n* **1** *the love of children:* adoration, adulation, affection, amorousness, ardour, attachment, brotherhood, care, concern, delight, desire, devotion, enjoyment, fondness, friendship, inclination, infatuation, intimacy, kindness, liking, lust, passion, rapture, regard, soft spot *colloq*, sympathy, taste, tenderness, warmth, weakness **2** *a love of power:* appreciation, delight, enjoyment, liking, partiality, pleasure, relish, soft spot *colloq*, weakness **3** *come here, my love:* angel, beloved, darling, dear, dear one, dearest, favourite, honey, pet, sweetheart, treasure
F3 **1** dislike, hate, hatred **2** detestation, loathing

loveless *adj* cold, cold-hearted, disliked, forsaken, friendless, frigid, hard, heartless, icy, insensitive, passionless, unappreciated, uncherished, unfeeling, unfriendly, unloved, unloving, unresponsive, unvalued
F3 passionate

lovelorn *adj* desiring, infatuated, languishing, longing, lovesick, pining, unrequited in love, yearning

lovely *adj* **1** *a lovely face:* adorable, attractive, beautiful, charming, delightful, enchanting, exquisite, fair, good-looking, handsome, pleasant, pleasing, pretty, sweet, winning **2** *have a lovely time:* agreeable, delightful, enjoyable, marvellous, pleasing, wonderful
F3 **1** hideous, ugly

love-making *n* carnal knowledge *formal*, coition *formal*, coitus *formal*, congress *formal*, copulation, foreplay, going to bed with someone *colloq*, intercourse, intimacy, mating, sex, sexual intercourse, sexual relations, sexual union, sleeping with someone *colloq*

lover *n* **1** *a gift from her lover:* admirer, beloved, bird *colloq*, bit on the side *colloq*, boyfriend, date *colloq*, fella *colloq*, fiancé(e), flame *colloq*, girlfriend, heart-throb *colloq*, lady love, live-in partner, loved one, man friend, mistress, other man, other woman, partner, significant other, suitor, sweetheart, toy boy *colloq*, vamp *colloq*, wolf *colloq*, woman friend **2** *a lover of opera:* admirer, buff *colloq*, devotee, enthusiast, fan, fanatic, fiend *colloq*, follower, freak *colloq*, supporter

lovesick *adj* desiring, infatuated, languishing, longing, lovelorn, pining, unrequited in love, yearning

loving *adj* adoring, affectionate, amorous, ardent, caring, devoted, doting, fond, friendly, kind, passionate, sympathetic, tender, warm, warm-hearted

low¹ *adj* 1 *low hills:* little, shallow, short, small, squat, stunted 2 *low land:* close to the ground, deep, depressed, flat, ground-level, sea-level, sunken 3 *of low birth:* common, humble, inferior, junior, low-born, lowly, low-ranking, mean, meek, mild, modest, obscure, ordinary, peasant, plain, plebeian, poor, simple, unimportant 4 *have a low opinion of someone:* adverse, antagonistic, bad, hostile, negative, opposing, poor, unfavourable 5 *low intelligence:* below standard, deficient, dull, foolish, inadequate, mediocre, slow, unintelligent 6 *feeling a bit low:* blue *colloq,* cheesed off *colloq,* depressed, despondent, disconsolate *formal,* disheartened, down *colloq,* down in the dumps *colloq,* downcast, downhearted, fed up *colloq,* gloomy, glum, low-spirited, miserable, sad, unhappy 7 *a low trick:* bad, base, coarse, contemptible, depraved, despicable, dishonourable, evil, heinous *formal,* immoral, indecent, mean, nasty, obscene, smutty, vulgar, wicked 8 *low prices:* cheap, inexpensive, moderate, modest, reasonable, reduced, rock-bottom, sale, slashed 9 *sales were low:* deficient, inadequate, insignificant, insufficient, little, meagre, paltry, poor, reduced, scant, scanty, sparse, trifling 10 *low notes:* bass, deep, low-pitched, resonant, rich, sonorous 11 *a low whisper:* gentle, hushed, muffled, muted, quiet, quietened, soft, subdued, whispered
🔁 1 high 2 high 3 high, important 4 good, high 6 cheerful 7 honourable 8 exorbitant, high 9 high 10 high 11 loud, noisy
♦ *n* all-time low, bottom, low point, lowest point, low-watermark, nadir *formal*
🔁 high

low² *v* bellow, moo

low-born *adj* humble, lowly, low-ranking, mean-born, obscure, peasant, plebeian, poor, unexalted
🔁 high-born, noble

lowbrow *adj* crude, ignorant, rude, uncultivated, uncultured, uneducated, unlearned, unlettered, unrefined, unscholarly
🔁 highbrow, intellectual

low-down *n* data, dope *colloq,* facts, gen *colloq,* info *colloq,* information, inside story, intelligence, news

lower *adj* 1 *the lower jaw:* bottom, nether, under, undermost 2 *lower levels of management:* inferior, junior, lesser, low-level, lowly, minor, secondary, second-class, subordinate
🔁 1 upper 2 higher
♦ *v* 1 *to lower a bucket:* descend, drop, let down, let fall, sink, take down 2 *to lower prices:* abate *formal,* bring down, cheapen, curtail, cut, decrease, diminish, lessen, reduce, slash 3 *lower your eyes:* bring low, look down, move downwards, set down 4 *lower your voice:* hush, quieten, speak (more) quietly 5 *not lower yourself by doing something:* abase, belittle, debase, degrade, demean, disgrace, dishonour, disparage *formal*

🔁 1 raise 2 increase 3 raise

lowering see **louring**

low-grade *adj* bad, below standard, inferior, not up to scratch *colloq,* poor, poor-quality, second-class, second-rate, substandard, third-rate
🔁 good, quality

low-key *adj* easy-going, muted, quiet, relaxed, restrained, slight, soft, subdued, subtle, understated
🔁 impressive, showy

lowly *adj* common, humble, inferior, junior, low-born, low-ranking, mean, meek, mild, modest, obscure, ordinary, peasant, plain, plebeian, poor, simple, submissive, subordinate, unimportant
🔁 lofty, noble, pretentious

low-pitched *adj* bass, deep, low, resonant, rich, sonorous
🔁 high, high-pitched

low-spirited *adj* cheesed off *colloq,* dejected, depressed, despondent, discouraged, down *colloq,* down in the dumps *colloq,* downhearted, fed up *colloq,* gloomy, glum, heavy-hearted, low, miserable, moody, sad, unhappy
🔁 cheerful, high-spirited

loyal *adj* committed, constant, dedicated, dependable, devoted, faithful, firm, patriotic, reliable, sincere, staunch, steadfast, true, truehearted, trustworthy, trusty, unchanging
🔁 disloyal, treacherous

loyalty *n* allegiance, commitment, constancy, dedication, dependability, devotion, faithfulness, fidelity, patriotism, reliability, sincerity, staunchness, steadfastness, trustworthiness
🔁 disloyalty, treachery

lozenge *n* cough-drop, gumdrop, jujube, pastille, tablet, troche *technical,* trochiscus *technical,* trochisk *technical*

lubber *n* barbarian, boor, bumpkin *colloq,* clod *colloq,* clodhopper *colloq,* dolt, gawk, hick *colloq,* hobbledehoy *colloq,* lout, oaf, slob *colloq,* yahoo, yob *colloq,* yobbo *colloq*

lubberly *adj* awkward, blundering, bungling, churlish, clodhopping *colloq,* clownish, clumsy, coarse, crude, dense, doltish, gawky, heavy-handed, loutish, lumbering, lumpish, oafish, uncouth, ungainly

lubricant *n* fat, grease, lard, lubrication, oil

lubricate *v* grease, lard, make smooth, oil, polish, smear, wax

lucid *adj* 1 *lucid writing:* clear, comprehensible, distinct, evident, explicit, intelligible, obvious, plain 2 *lucid thoughts:* clear-headed, intelligent, of sound mind, rational, reasonable, sane, sensible, sober, sound 3 *the lucid waters of the lake:* beaming, bright, brilliant, crystalline, diaphanous *formal,* effulgent *formal,* glassy, gleaming, limpid *formal,* luminous, pellucid *formal,* pure, radiant, resplendent, shining, translucent, transparent
🔁 1 unclear, unintelligible 3 dark, murky

luck *n* 1 *we met by pure luck:* accident, chance, destiny, fate, fluke *colloq,* fortuity *formal,* fortune, hazard 2 *wish me luck!:* good fortune, good luck, prosperity, success
🔁 2 misfortune

luckily *adv* as luck would have it, by accident, by chance, by good luck, fortuitously *formal*, fortunately, happily, providentially
☒ unfortunately

luckless *adj* calamitous, catastrophic, cursed, disastrous, doomed, hapless, hopeless, ill-fated, ill-starred, jinxed, miserable, star-crossed, unfortunate, unhappy, unlucky, unpropitious *formal*, unsuccessful
☒ fortunate, lucky

lucky *adj* auspicious *formal*, charmed, expedient, favoured, fortuitous *formal*, fortunate, in luck, jammy *colloq*, opportune, promising, propitious *formal*, prosperous, providential, successful, timely
☒ unlucky

lucrative *adj* advantageous, financially rewarding, gainful, high-paying, money-making, productive, profitable, profit-making, remunerative, well-paid, worthwhile
☒ unprofitable

lucre *n* bread *slang*, cash, dosh *slang*, dough *slang*, gain(s), income, mammon, money, pay, proceeds, profit(s), remuneration, riches, spoils, wealth, winnings

ludicrous *adj* absurd, amusing, comic, comical, crazy *colloq*, droll, eccentric, farcical, funny, hilarious, humorous, laughable, nonsensical, odd, outlandish, preposterous, ridiculous, risible *formal*, silly, zany
☒ serious

lug *v* bear, carry, drag, haul, heave, hump, pull, tote, tow, tug

luggage *n* baggage, belongings, gear *colloq*, impedimenta *formal*, paraphernalia, stuff *colloq*, things *colloq*

Types of luggage include:
case, suitcase, vanity-case, bag, holdall, portmanteau, valise, overnight-bag, kit-bag, flight bag, hand-luggage, travel bag, Gladstone bag, grip, rucksack, knapsack, haversack, backpack, briefcase, attaché case, portfolio, satchel, basket, hamper, trunk, chest, box

lugubrious *adj* dismal, doleful, dreary, funereal, gloomy, glum, melancholy, morose, mournful, sad, sepulchral, serious, sombre, sorrowful, woebegone, woeful
☒ cheerful, jovial, merry

lukewarm *adj* 1 *lukewarm water*: cool, slightly warm, tepid, warmish 2 *a lukewarm response to his advances*: apathetic, cool, half-hearted, impassive, indifferent, Laodicean, tepid, unconcerned, unenthusiastic, uninterested, unresponsive

lull *n* calm, calmness, hush, let-up, pause, peace, quiet, silence, stillness, tranquillity
☒ agitation
♦ *v* allay, assuage *formal*, calm, compose, ease, hush, pacify, quell, quiet, quieten down, silence, soothe, still, subdue
☒ agitate

lullaby *n* berceuse, cradle song

lumber¹ *n* 1 *store away lumber*: bits and pieces, clutter, jumble, junk, odds and ends, refuse, rubbish, trash 2 *cutting lumber*: timber, wood
♦ *v* burden, charge, encumber, hamper, impose, land, load, saddle

lumber² *v* clump, plod, shamble, shuffle, stamp, stumble, stump, trudge, trundle

lumbering *adj* awkward, blundering, bovine, bumbling, clumsy, elephantine, heavy, heavy-footed, hulking, like a bull in a china shop *colloq*, lumpish, massive, ponderous, ungainly, unwieldy
☒ agile, nimble

luminary *n* authority, big name *colloq*, bigwig *colloq*, celebrity, dignitary, expert, leader, leading light, notable, personage, star, superstar, VIP, worthy

luminescent *adj* bright, effulgent *formal*, fluorescent, glowing, luciferous *formal*, luminous, phosphorescent *formal*, radiant, shining

luminous *adj* bright, brilliant, dazzling, effulgent *formal*, fluorescent, glowing, illuminated, lighted, lit, luminescent *formal*, lustrous, radiant, shining

lump¹ *n* 1 *a lump of clay*: ball, bunch, cake, chunk, clod, clump, cluster, dab, hunk, mass, nugget, piece, wad, wedge 2 *a lump on the head*: bruise, bulge, bump, carbuncle, growth, protrusion, protuberance, swelling, tumescence *formal*, tumour
♦ *v* blend, cluster, coalesce, collect, combine, conglomerate, consolidate, fuse, gather, group, mass, mix together, pool, put together, unite

lump² *v* bear (with), brook, endure, put up with, stand, stomach *colloq*, suffer, swallow, take, thole *Scot*, tolerate

lumpish *adj* awkward, boorish, bungling, clumsy, doltish, dull-witted, elephantine, gawky, heavy, hulking, lethargic, lumbering, oafish, obtuse, stolid, stupid, ungainly

lumpy *adj* bumpy, bunched, cloggy, clotted, curdled, grainy, granular, knobbly, nodose *formal*, nodous *formal*
☒ even, smooth

lunacy *n* aberration, absurdity, craziness *colloq*, dementedness, dementia, derangement, folly, foolishness, idiocy, illogicality, imbecility, imprudence *formal*, inanity, insanity, irrationality, irresponsibility, madness, mania, nonsense, outrageousness, preposterousness, ridiculousness, senselessness, silliness, stupidity
☒ sanity

lunatic *n* dipstick *slang*, fruitcake *colloq*, headcase *colloq*, imbecile, insane person, loony *colloq*, madman, madwoman, maniac, manic-depressive, neurotic, nutcase *colloq*, nutter *colloq*, oddball *colloq*, psycho *colloq*, psychopath, psychotic
♦ *adj* absurd, barmy *colloq*, bonkers *colloq*, crackpot *colloq*, crazy *colloq*, daft *colloq*, demented, deranged, disturbed, foolish, hare-brained *colloq*, idiotic, illogical, inane, insane, irrational, loony *colloq*, loopy *colloq*, mad, nonsensical, nuts *colloq*, nutty *colloq*, potty *colloq*, psychotic, round the bend/twist *colloq*, senseless, silly, stupid, unbalanced
☒ sane

lunch *n* brunch, dinner, light lunch, luncheon, midday meal, packed lunch, ploughman's lunch, Sunday lunch

lunge *v* bound, charge, dart, dash, dive, fall upon, grab (at), hit (at), jab, leap, pitch into, plunge, poke, pounce, spring, stab, strike (at), thrust
♦ *n* bound, charge, cut, jab, leap, pass, plunge, poke, pounce, spring, stab, thrust

lurch *v* list, pitch, reel, rock, roll, stagger, stumble, sway, swerve, totter, veer

lure *v* allure, attract, beguile, decoy, draw, ensnare, entice, induce, inveigle *formal*, lead on, seduce, tempt
♦ *n* allurement, attraction, bait, carrot *colloq*, decoy, draw, enticement, inducement, seduction, temptation

lurid *adj* 1 *lurid headlines:* exaggerated, explicit, graphic, melodramatic, sensational, shocking, startling 2 *the story reached a lurid conclusion:* ghastly, gory, grisly, gruesome, horrific, macabre, revolting 3 *lurid clothes:* brightly coloured, brilliant, dazzling, garish, glaring, intense, loud, showy, vivid
🔁 1 restrained 3 pale

lurk *v* conceal yourself, crouch, hide, lie in wait, lie low, prowl, skulk, slink, sneak, snoop

luscious *adj* 1 *luscious food:* appetizing, delectable *formal*, delicious, juicy, morish *colloq*, mouth-watering, savoury, scrumptious *colloq*, succulent, sweet, tasty, yummy *colloq* 2 *a luscious blonde:* attractive, beautiful, desirable, gorgeous, ravishing, sensuous, sexy, smashing *colloq*, stunning, voluptuous

lush *adj* 1 *lush vegetation:* abundant, dense, flourishing, green, luxuriant, overgrown, profuse, prolific, teeming, verdant *formal* 2 *lush costumes:* extravagant, grand, lavish, luxurious, opulent, ornate, palatial, plush, rich, sumptuous
♦ *n* alcoholic, alkie *slang*, boozer *slang*, dipso *slang*, dipsomaniac, drinker, drunk, drunkard, hard drinker, heavy drinker, inebriated, piss artist *slang*, soak *slang*, sot *slang*, tippler *colloq*, toper *slang*, tosspot *slang*, wino *slang*

lust *n* 1 *motivated solely by lust:* concupiscence *formal*, horniness *colloq*, lasciviousness, lechery, lewdness, libido, licentiousness, prurience *formal*, randiness *colloq*, raunchiness *colloq*, sensuality, sexual desire, sexual drive, the hots *colloq* 2 *a lust for freedom:* appetite, avidity, covetousness, craving, cupidity *formal*, desire, greed, greediness, hunger, longing, passion, yearning
▶ **lust after** covet, crave, desire, hunger for, long for, need, thirst for, want, yearn for

lustful *adj* carnal, concupiscent *formal*, craving, cupidinous *formal*, hankering, horny *colloq*, lascivious, lecherous, lewd, libidinous *formal*, licentious, passionate, prurient *formal*, randy *colloq*, raunchy *colloq*, salacious, sensual, unchaste, wanton

lustily *adv* forcefully, hard, loudly, powerfully, robustly, stoutly, strongly, vigorously, with all your might, with might and main *formal*
🔁 feebly, weakly

lustiness *n* energy, haleness, hardiness, health, healthiness, power, robustness, stoutness, strength, sturdiness, toughness, vigour, virility

lustre *n* 1 *the lustre of fine steel:* brightness, brilliance, burnish, gleam, glint, glitter, gloss, glow, lambency *formal*, radiance, refulgence *formal*, resplendence, sheen, shimmer, shine, sparkle 2 *give the tournament some much-needed lustre:* credit, distinction, fame, glory, honour, illustriousness, merit, prestige, renown

lustrous *adj* bright, burnished, dazzling, gleaming, glistening, glittering, glossy, glowing, lambent *formal*, luminous, radiant, shimmering, shining, shiny, sparkling, twinkling
🔁 dull, lacklustre, matt

lusty *adj* blooming, energetic, forceful, gutsy *colloq*, hale, hale and hearty, healthy, hearty, lively, powerful, robust, rugged, strapping, strong, sturdy, tough, vigorous, virile
🔁 feeble, weak

luxuriance *n* abundance, copiousness, denseness, excess, exuberance, fecundity *formal*, fertility, lavishness, lushness, profusion, rankness, richness, sumptuousness

luxuriant *adj* 1 *luxuriant tropical forests:* abundant, ample, copious, dense, fecund *formal*, fertile, lavish, lush, overflowing, plenteous, plentiful, productive, profuse, prolific, rank, rich, riotous, sumptuous, superabundant, teeming, thriving 2 *luxuriant compositions:* baroque, elaborate, excessive, extravagant, fancy, flamboyant, florid *formal*, flowery, opulent, ornate, rococo
🔁 1 barren, infertile

luxuriate *v* bask, delight, enjoy yourself, flourish, have a ball *colloq*, relax in, relish, revel, savour, thrive, wallow

luxurious *adj* affluent, comfortable, costly, cushy *colloq*, de luxe, expensive, glitzy *colloq*, grand, lavish, magnificent, opulent, pampered, plush *colloq*, posh *colloq*, rich, self-indulgent, splendid, sumptuous, swanky *colloq*, well-appointed
🔁 austere, spartan

luxury *n* 1 *a life of luxury:* affluence, comfort, costliness, expensiveness, grandeur, grandness, gratification, hedonism, indulgence, magnificence, opulence, pleasure, richness, self-indulgence, splendour, sumptuousness 2 *life's little luxuries:* extra, extravagance, satisfaction, treat
🔁 1 austerity 2 essential

lying *adj* crooked *colloq*, deceitful, dishonest, dissembling *formal*, dissimulating *formal*, double-dealing, false, mendacious *formal*, two-faced *colloq*, untruthful
🔁 honest, truthful
♦ *n* crookedness *colloq*, deceit, dishonesty, double-dealing, duplicity *formal*, fabrication, falsification, falsity, fibbing *colloq*, invention, perjury, untruthfulness, white lies *colloq*
🔁 honesty, truthfulness

lynch *v* execute, hang, hang by the neck, kill, put to death, string up *colloq*

lyric *adj* direct, emotional, musical, passionate, personal, poetic, strong, subjective

lyrical *adj* 1 *lyrical ballads:* musical, poetic, romantic 2 *a lyrical account of her home town:* carried away, ecstatic, effusive, emotional, enthusiastic, expressive, impassioned, inspired, passionate, rapturous, rhapsodic

lyrics *n* book, libretto, text, words

M

macabre *adj* chilling, dreadful, eerie, frightening, frightful, ghastly, ghostly, gory, grim, grisly, gruesome, hideous, horrible, horrific, morbid, shocking, terrifying

mace *n* club, cudgel, rod, staff, stick

macerate *v* blend, liquefy, mash, pulp, soak, soften, steep

Machiavellian *adj* artful, astute, calculating, crafty, cunning, deceitful, designing, devious, double-dealing, foxy, guileful, intriguing, opportunist, perfidious *formal*, scheming, shrewd, sly, underhand, unscrupulous, wily

machination *n* artifice *formal*, cabal, conspiracy, design, device, dodge, intrigue, manoeuvre, plot, ploy, ruse, scheme, shenanigans *colloq*, stratagem, tactic, trick, wile

machine *n* **1** *a machine to slice bread:* apparatus, appliance, contraption, contrivance, device, engine, gadget, hardware, instrument, mechanism, motor, tool **2** *a machine of change:* agency, catalyst, influence, instrument, organ, organization, structure, system, tool, vehicle, workings **3** *he works and works, like a machine:* android, automaton, mechanical person, mechanism, robot, tool, zombie

machinery *n* **1** *regulates the temperature of the machinery:* apparatus, equipment, gadgetry, gear, instruments, mechanism, tackle, tools **2** *the machinery of government:* agency, channel(s), organization, procedure, structure, system, workings

---

Types of heavy machinery include:
all-terrain fork lift, bulldozer, caterpillar tractor, combine harvester, concrete mixer, concrete pump, crane, crawler crane, crawler tractor, digger, dragline excavator, dredger, dumper, dump truck, dustcart, excavator, fertilizer spreader, fire appliance, fork-lift truck, gantry crane, grader, grapple, gritter, hydraulic bale loader, hydraulic shovel, JCB®, muck spreader, pick-up loader, pile-driver, platform hoist, riding mower, road roller, road-sweeping lorry, Rotovator®, silage harvester, snowplough, straw baler, threshing machine, tower crane, tracklayer, tractor, tractor-scraper, truck crane, wheel loader

---

machinist *n* factory hand, mechanic, operative, operator, worker

machismo *n* maleness, manliness, masculinity, strength, toughness, virility

macrocosm *n* civilization, community, cosmos, creation, culture, humanity, planet, (single) entity, society, solar system, system, totality, universe, world
🖪 microcosm

mad *adj* **1** *are you mad?:* crazed, demented, deranged, frenzied, insane, lunatic, maniacal, manic, non compos mentis, of unsound mind, out of your mind, out of your senses, psychotic, unbalanced, unhinged, unstable **2** *dad was mad when he found out:* angry, blazing, enraged, fuming, furious, hopping mad, hot under the collar, incensed, infuriated, irate, livid, raging, seeing red **3** *some mad scheme to make money:* absurd, barmy *colloq*, crackbrained *colloq*, crackpot *colloq*, crazy *colloq*, daft *colloq*, foolhardy, foolish, hare-brained *colloq*, idiotic, illogical, insane, irrational, ludicrous, nonsensical, potty *colloq*, preposterous, silly, stupid, unreasonable, wild **4** *mad about football:* ardent, avid, crazy *colloq*, daft *colloq*, devoted, enthusiastic, fanatical, fond, infatuated, keen, nuts *colloq*, passionate, wild, zealous **5** *a mad dash for the door:* abandoned, energetic, excited, frantic, frenzied, furious, hasty, hurried, intense, rapid, reckless, uncontrolled, unrestrained, violent, wild
🖪 **1** sane **2** calm **3** sensible **4** apathetic **5** controlled

madcap *adj* bird-brained *colloq*, crazy, flighty, foolhardy, hare-brained *colloq*, heedless, hotheaded, ill-advised, imprudent *formal*, impulsive, lively, rash, reckless, silly, thoughtless, wild
♦ *n* adventurer, crackpot *colloq*, daredevil, desperado, firebrand, fury, hothead, tearaways

madden *v* aggravate *colloq*, agitate, anger, annoy, bug *colloq*, drive crazy/nuts *colloq*, drive round the bend/twist *colloq*, drive up the wall *colloq*, enrage, exasperate, get on your nerves *colloq*, get on your wick *colloq*, get someone's blood up *colloq*, get someone's goat *colloq*, get under your skin *colloq*, get up your nose *colloq*, get your back up *colloq*, get your dander up *colloq*, hassle *colloq*, incense, inflame, infuriate, irk, irritate, make your blood boil *colloq*, provoke, rub up the wrong way *colloq*, upset, vex
🖪 calm, pacify

maddening *adj* annoying, disturbing, exasperating, galling, infuriating, irritating, troublesome, upsetting, vexatious

made-up *adj* **1** *an obviously made-up excuse:* fabricated, fairy-tale, false, fictional, imaginary, invented, make-believe, mythical, specious, trumped-up *colloq*, unreal, untrue **2** *a beautifully made-up girl:* done up, painted, powdered, wearing make-up
🖪 **1** factual, real, true

madhouse *n* **1** *the shop was a madhouse today:* Babel, bedlam, chaos, disarray, disorder, pandemonium, turmoil, uproar **2** *put her in the madhouse when she got pregnant:* asylum, funny farm *colloq*, loony bin *colloq*, lunatic asylum, mental hospital, mental institution, nut-house *colloq*, psychiatric hospital

madly *adv* **1** *he rolled his eyes madly:* crazily *colloq*, deliriously, dementedly, distractedly, frenziedly, hysterically, insanely, wildly **2** *madly cleaning up:* energetically, excitedly, fast, frantically, furiously, hastily, hurriedly, intensely, rapidly, recklessly, violently, wildly **3** *madly in love:* devotedly, fervently, intensely, wildly **4** *not a madly popular choice:* exceedingly, exceptionally, extremely, unreasonably, utterly, wildly

madman, madwoman *n* basket case *colloq*, crackpot *colloq*, crank *colloq*, fruitcake *colloq*, headcase *colloq*, imbecile, loony *colloq*, lunatic, maniac, nut *colloq*, nutcase *colloq*, nutter *colloq*, oddball *colloq*, psycho *slang*, psychopath, psychotic, screwball *colloq*

madness *n* **1** *the king's madness was kept secret:* craziness *colloq*, delusion, dementia, derangement, distraction, insanity, lunacy, mania, mental instability, psychosis **2** *her madness at hearing what he had done:* agitation, anger, exasperation, frenzy, fury, hysteria, ire, rage, raving, wrath **3** *it was sheer madness to start this war:* absurdity, craziness, daftness *colloq*, folly, foolhardiness, foolishness, inanity, insanity, irrationality, nonsense, preposterousness, silliness, stupidity, unreasonableness, wildness
⊟ 1 sanity

maelstrom *n* bedlam, chaos, Charybdis, confusion, disorder, mess, pandemonium, tumult, turmoil, uproar, vortex, whirlpool

maestro *n* ace *colloq*, expert, genius, master, prodigy, virtuoso, wizard *colloq*

magazine *n* **1** *a weekly magazine:* colour supplement, journal, monthly, paper, periodical, publication, quarterly, supplement, weekly **2** *a magazine of weapons:* ammunition dump, arsenal, depot, ordnance, storehouse

magic *n* **1** *believe in magic:* black art, black magic, curse, enchantment, hoodoo, magical powers, necromancy *formal*, occult, occultism, sorcery, spell, supernatural, thaumaturgy *formal*, voodoo, witchcraft, wizardry, wonder-working **2** *perform magic for children's parties:* conjuring, deception, illusion, legerdemain, prestidigitation *formal*, sleight of hand, trickery **3** *the magic of film:* allure, allurement, charm, enchantment, enticement, fascination, glamour, magnetism, pull
♦ *adj* **1** *magic powers:* demonic, mysterious, occult, supernatural **2** *the whole trip was magic:* ace *colloq*, brill *colloq*, cool *slang*, excellent, great, marvellous, mega *slang*, smashing *colloq*, terrific *colloq*, tremendous, wicked *slang*, wonderful

magician *n* **1** *magicians like Merlin:* enchanter, miracle-worker, necromancer *formal*, sorcerer, spellbinder, spellworker, thaumaturge *formal*, warlock, witch, wizard, wonder-worker **2** *the magician did a few card tricks:* conjurer, illusionist, juggler **3** *a magician in the kitchen:* ace *colloq*, expert, genius, maestro, master, virtuoso, wizard *colloq*

magisterial *adj* arrogant, assertive, authoritarian, authoritative, bossy *colloq*, commanding, despotic, dictatorial, domineering, high-handed, imperious, lordly, masterful, overbearing, peremptory *formal*

magistrate *n* aedile, bailiff, beak *colloq*, JP, judge, justice, justice of the peace, stipendiary, tribune

magnanimity *n* altruism, beneficence *formal*, benevolence, big-heartedness, bountifulness, charitableness, charity, forgiveness, generosity, high-mindedness, kindness, largesse, liberality, mercy, munificence *formal*, nobility, open-handedness, philanthropy, selflessness, unselfishness
⊟ meanness, vindictiveness

magnanimous *adj* altruistic, beneficent *formal*, benevolent, big-hearted, bountiful, charitable, forgiving, generous, kind, kindly, liberal, merciful, munificent *formal*, noble, open-handed, philanthropic, selfless, ungrudging, unselfish
⊟ mean

magnate *n* baron, big noise *colloq*, big shot *colloq*, big timer *colloq*, bigwig *colloq*, captain of industry, entrepreneur, executive, fat cat *colloq*, financier, industrialist, leader, mogul, moneybags *colloq*, notable, personage, plutocrat, tycoon

magnet *n* **1** *it works by means of a magnet:* lodestone, magnetic body, solenoid **2** *a magnet for trade:* allurement, appeal, attraction, bait, centre of attraction, charm, draw, enticement, focal point, focus, lure
⊟ 2 repellent

magnetic *adj* absorbing, alluring, appealing, attractive, bewitching, captivating, charismatic, charming, enchanting, engaging, enthralling, entrancing, fascinating, gripping, hypnotic, irresistible, mesmerizing, seductive, tantalizing, tempting
⊟ repellent, repulsive

magnetism *n* allure, appeal, attraction, captivation, charisma, charm, draw, drawing power, enchantment, fascination, grip, hypnotism, lure, magic, mesmerism, power, pull, seductiveness, spell, temptation

magnification *n* **1** *the magnification of an image:* aggrandizement *formal*, amplification, augmentation *formal*, boost, deepening, dilation, enhancement, enlargement, expansion, heightening, increase, inflation, intensification, lionization **2** *magnification of his importance as a political figure:* dramatization, embellishment, embroidery, exaggeration, overdoing, overemphasis, overstatement
⊟ 1 diminution, reduction

magnificence *n* brilliance, excellence, glory, gorgeousness, grandeur, impressiveness, lavishness, luxuriousness, luxury, majesty, nobility, opulence *formal*, pomp, resplendence *formal*, splendour, stateliness, sublimity *formal*, sumptuousness
⊟ modesty, plainness, simplicity

magnificent *adj* august *formal*, brilliant, dazzling, elegant, exalted, excellent, fine, glorious, gorgeous, grand, grandiose, imposing, impressive, lavish, luxurious, majestic, marvellous, noble, opulent *formal*, resplendent *formal*, rich, royal, splendid, stately, striking, sublime *formal*, sumptuous, superb, wonderful
⊟ humble, modest, poor

magnify *v* **1** *magnify the size of the font:* amplify, boost, broaden, build up, deepen, dilate, enhance, enlarge, expand, extend, greaten, heighten, increase, intensify **2** *magnified his part in the rescue:* blow up *colloq*, blow up out of all proportion *colloq*, dramatize, embellish, embroider, exaggerate, make a mountain out of a molehill *colloq*, overdo, overemphasize, overplay, overstate
⊟ 1 diminish, reduce **2** belittle, play down

magniloquence *n* bombast, euphuism, fustian, grandiloquence *formal*, loftiness, orotundity *formal*, pomposity, pretentiousness, rhetoric, turgidity
⊟ simplicity, straightforwardness

magniloquent *adj* bombastic, declamatory, elevated, euphuistic, exalted, fustian, grandiloquent *formal*, high-flown, high-sounding, lofty, orotund *formal*, overblown, pompous, pretentious, rhetorical, sonorous, stilted, turgid
🗷 simple, straightforward

magnitude *n* **1** *the magnitude of the image:* amount, amplitude, bulk, capacity, dimensions, expanse, extent, greatness, largeness, mass, measure, proportions, quantity, size, space, strength, volume, weight **2** *the magnitude of his position:* consequence, distinction, eminence, fame, greatness, importance, intensity, moment, note, significance, weight

magnum opus *n* chef d'oeuvre, masterpiece, masterwork, pièce de résistance

maid *n* abigail, au pair, chambermaid, domestic, girl, handmaiden, housemaid, kitchenmaid, lady's maid, maid-of-all-work, maidservant, servant, serving-maid, skivvy *colloq*, soubrette, waitress

maiden *n* damsel *formal*, girl, lass, lassie, miss, nymph, virgin, young girl, young lady, young woman
♦ *adj* first, inaugural, initial, initiatory, introductory, new

maidenly *adj* becoming, chaste, decent, decorous *formal*, demure, female, gentle, girlish, modest, proper, pure, reserved, unbroached, undefiled, unmarried, unsullied, unwed, vestal, virgin, virginal, virtuous
🗷 immodest

mail¹ *n* **1** *deliver the mail:* airmail, communications, correspondence, delivery, direct mail, electronic mail, e-mail, international mail, junk mail *colloq*, letters, packages, packets, parcels, post, recorded mail, registered mail, snail mail *colloq*, special delivery, surface mail **2** *put it in the mail:* post, Post Office, postal service, postal system
♦ *v* dispatch, forward, post, send

mail² *n* armour, chain mail, iron-cladding, panoply, protective covering

maim *v* cripple, disable, disfigure, hurt, impair, incapacitate, injure, lame, mar, mutilate, put out of action, wound

main *adj* cardinal, central, chief, critical, crucial, dominant, essential, first, foremost, fundamental, head, key, leading, major, most important, necessary, outstanding, paramount, pivotal, predominant, pre-eminent, premier, primary, prime, principal, supreme, vital
🗷 insignificant, minor, unimportant
♦ *n* cable, channel, conduit, duct, line, pipe

mainly *adv* above all, as a rule, by and large, chiefly, commonly, especially, first and foremost, for the most part, generally, in general, in the main, largely, mostly, on the whole, overall, primarily, principally, usually

mainspring *n* cause, driving force, fountainhead, generator, impulse, incentive, inspiration, motivation, motive, origin, prime mover, reason, source, wellspring

mainstay *n* anchor, backbone, base, basis, bulwark, buttress, foundation, linchpin, pillar, prop, support

mainstream *adj* accepted, average, central, conventional, established, general, mainline, normal, orthodox, received, regular, standard, typical
🗷 heterodox, marginal, peripheral

maintain *v* **1** *to maintain fitness:* carry on, conserve, continue, keep (up), keep going, perpetuate, preserve, retain, sustain **2** *maintained the house:* care for, conserve, keep (up), keep in good condition/repair, look after, preserve, take care of **3** *maintained a family:* feed, finance, keep, nourish, nurture, provide for, supply, support, sustain **4** *she maintained that she had never met him:* affirm *formal*, announce, assert, asseverate *formal*, aver *formal*, avow *formal*, believe, claim, contend, declare, fight for, hold, insist, profess, stand by, state, support
🗷 **2** neglect **4** deny

maintenance *n* **1** *the maintenance of high standards:* carrying-on, conservation, continuance, continuation, perpetuation, preservation **2** *the maintenance of the vehicles:* care, conservation, preservation, protection, repairs, running, support, upkeep **3** *the maintenance of his family:* aliment, alimony, allowance, feeding, financing, keep, livelihood, living, nourishment, nurture, subsistence, support, sustenance, upkeep
🗷 **2** neglect

majestic *adj* **1** *a majestic display:* august *formal*, awesome, dignified, distinguished, elevated, exalted, glorious, grand, imposing, impressive, lofty, magnificent, marvellous, monumental, pompous, resplendent *formal*, splendid, sublime *formal*, superb **2** *majestic robes:* imperial, kingly, lordly, noble, princely, queenly, regal, royal, stately
🗷 **1** unimposing, unimpressive **2** lowly

majesty *n* **1** *the majesty of the Alps:* awesomeness, beauty, dignity, exaltedness, glory, grandeur, grandness, impressiveness, loftiness, magnificence, nobility, nobleness, pomp, resplendence *formal*, splendour, sublimity *formal* **2** *respect the majesty of the king:* nobility, nobleness, regality, royalty, stateliness

major *adj* bigger, chief, crucial, great, greater, higher, important, key, keynote, larger, leading, main, notable, older, outstanding, paramount, pre-eminent, prime, senior, serious, significant, superior, supreme, uppermost, vital, weighty
🗷 minor, trivial, unimportant

majority *n* **1** *the majority of the shareholders:* bulk, greater/larger part, lion's share *colloq*, mass, more than half, most, nearly all, preponderance, (the) many **2** *inherited when he attained his majority:* adulthood, age of consent, legal age, manhood, maturity, womanhood, years of discretion
🗷 **1** minority

make *v* **1** *made a tent out of an old sheet:* assemble, build, compose, construct, create, erect, fabricate, fashion, form, manufacture, mass-produce, model, mould, originate, produce, put together, put up, shape, turn out **2** *make a mess:* accomplish, bring about, cause, create, effect *formal*, engender, generate, give rise to, occasion, perform, produce, render **3** *made a phone call:* accomplish, achieve, carry out, deliver (the goods) *colloq*, discharge, do, effect *formal*, execute *formal*, get down to *colloq*, perform, undertake, wrap up *colloq* **4** *made him do it*: bulldoze *colloq*, coerce, compel, constrain, dragoon, drive, force, impel, oblige, press, pressure, pressurize, prevail upon, put the screws on *colloq*, require, strongarm *colloq*, urge **5** *made him team leader*: appoint, create, designate, elect, install, name, nominate, ordain, select, vote, vote in **6** *make a circle with your chairs*: arrange, compose, construct, create, devise, draw up, form, formulate, frame, prepare, produce **7** *he makes £50,000 a year*: acquire, bring in, clear, earn, gain, get, gross, net, obtain, realize *formal*, secure, take home, win **8** *six and two makes eight*: add up to, amount to, come to, compose, comprise, constitute, total **9** *make a big impression*: chalk up, gain, notch up *colloq*, score **10** *I'll make the dinner*: cook, fix *US colloq*, get ready, prepare, put together **11** *what do you make the total?*: calculate, compute, estimate, reckon (up), work out **12** *she'll make a great teacher*: achieve, act as, become, have the qualifications for, play the role/part of, serve as **13** *make a will*: complete, draw up, fill in, write out **14** *I'm sure we'll make it*: cope, fare *formal*, get along, get by, get on, manage, progress, succeed **15** *make an application*: complete, fill in/out, write out

🄴 **1** dismantle **7** lose, spend

♦ *n* brand, form, kind, manufacture, mark, model, sort, structure, style, type, variety

▶ **make for 1** *ships making for port*: aim for, go towards, head for, move towards **2** *all this argument doesn't make for a good atmosphere*: be conducive to, contribute to, facilitate, favour, forward, further, lead to, produce, promote

▶ **make off** beat a hasty retreat *colloq*, beat it *colloq*, bolt, clear off *colloq*, cut and run *colloq*, depart, fly, leave, make a getaway *colloq*, run away, run off, scarper *colloq*, skedaddle *colloq*, take to your heels *colloq*

▶ **make off with** appropriate *formal*, carry off, filch *colloq*, knock off *colloq*, nab *colloq*, nick *colloq*, pilfer, pinch *colloq*, purloin *formal*, run off with, steal, swipe, walk off with

▶ **make out 1** *could just make out the writing on the box*: decipher, detect, discern, discover, distinguish, manage to see/hear, perceive, recognize, see **2** *couldn't make out what he was on about*: comprehend, fathom, follow, grasp, understand, work out **3** *he was making out that you were incapable*: affirm *formal*, assert, aver *formal*, claim, declare, demonstrate, describe, establish, imply, maintain, prove

▶ **make over** assign, bequeath, convey, leave, sign over, transfer

▶ **make up 1** *make up a story*: compose, concoct, construct, create, devise, dream up, fabricate, formulate, frame, hatch, invent, originate, think up **2** *a cottage made up of four rooms*: compose, comprise, constitute, form **3** *they kissed and made up*: be reconciled, become friends again, bury the hatchet *colloq*, call it quits *colloq*, forgive and forget *colloq*, make peace, repent, settle differences, shake hands **4** *never been good at making herself up*: doll up *colloq*, paint, perfume, powder, put make-up on, put on your face *colloq*, rouge, tart up *colloq* **5** *make up the difference*: complete, fill, meet, provide, round off, supplement, supply

▶ **make up for** atone for *formal*, compensate for, make amends for, make recompense for, offset, redress

▶ **make up to** butter up, chat up *colloq*, court, curry favour with, fawn on, make overtures to, toady to

make-believe *n* charade, daydreaming, dream, dreaming, fabrication, fantasy, imagination, masquerade, play-acting, pretence, role-play, unreality
🄴 reality
♦ *adj* dream, fantasized, fantasy, feigned *formal*, imaginary, imagined, imitated, made-up, mock, pretend *colloq*, pretended, sham, simulated, unreal
🄴 real

maker *n* architect, author, builder, constructor, creator, director, fabricator, manufacturer, producer

makeshift *adj* cobbled together, expedient, improvised, make-do, provisional, rough and ready, stand-by, stopgap, substitute, temporary, thrown together
🄴 permanent

make-up *n* **1** *a counter selling make-up*: cosmetics, greasepaint, maquillage, paint, powder, war paint *colloq* **2** *the make-up of the board of directors*: arrangement, assembly, character, composition, configuration *formal*, constitution, construction, form, format, formation, nature, organization, structure, style **3** *it isn't in her make-up to be unkind*: character, disposition, nature, personality, style, temper, temperament

making *n* **1** *the making of the film*: assembly, building, composition, construction, creating, creation, fabrication, forging, manufacture, modelling, moulding, producing, production **2** *has the making of a professional photographer*: beginnings, capability, capacity, ingredients, materials, possibilities, potential, potentiality, promise, qualities **3** *the makings from the deal*: earnings, income, proceeds, profits, returns, revenue, takings
🄴 **1** dismantling

maladjusted *adj* alienated, confused, disordered, disturbed, dotty *colloq*, estranged *formal*, gaga *slang*, neurotic, psycho *slang*, round the bend *colloq*, schizo *slang*, screwed-up *colloq*, unstable
🄴 together *colloq*, well-adjusted

maladministration *n* blundering, bungling, corruption, dishonesty, incompetence, inefficiency, malfeasance *technical*, malpractice, malversation *formal*, misconduct, misfeasance, misgovernment, mishandling, mismanagement, misrule, stupidity

maladroit *adj* awkward, bungling, cack-handed *colloq*, clumsy, gauche, graceless, ham-fisted *colloq*, ill-timed, inconsiderate, inelegant, inept, inexpert, insensitive, tactless, thoughtless, undiplomatic, unhandy, unskilful

malady *n* affliction *formal*, ailment, breakdown, complaint, disease, disorder, illness, indisposition *formal*, infirmity, malaise *formal*, sickness

malaise *n* **1** *a feeling of slight malaise*: discomfort, disease, enervation *formal*, illness, indisposition *formal*, lassitude *formal*, melancholy *formal*, sickness, weakness **2** *a sense of growing malaise*: angst, anguish, anxiety, depression, discomfort, discontent, disquiet, dissatisfaction, doldrums,

enervation *formal*, lassitude *formal*, melancholy *formal*, unease, uneasiness, weariness
𝔼 1 well-being 2 happiness

malapropism *n* misapplication, misuse, wrong word

malapropos *adj* ill-timed, inapposite *formal*, inappropriate, inapt, inopportune, misapplied, tactless, uncalled-for, unseemly *formal*, unsuitable, untimely
𝔼 appropriate, tactful

malcontent *n* agitator, belly-acher *colloq*, complainer, grouch *colloq*, grouser *colloq*, grumbler, mischief-maker, moaner, nit-picker *colloq*, rebel, troublemaker, whinger *colloq*
♦ *adj* belly-aching *colloq*, disaffected, discontented, disgruntled, dissatisfied, dissentious *formal*, fault-finding, ill-disposed, morose, rebellious, resentful, restive *formal*, unhappy, unsatisfied
𝔼 contented

male *adj* boyish, he-, manlike, manly, masculine, virile
𝔼 female

malediction *n* anathema, anathematization, curse, cursing, damnation, damning, denunciation, execration *formal*, imprecation *formal*, malison *formal*
𝔼 blessing, praise

malefactor *n* convict, criminal, crook *colloq*, culprit, delinquent, evildoer, felon, law-breaker, miscreant *formal*, misfeasor *technical*, offender, outlaw, transgressor *formal*, villain, wrongdoer

malevolence *n* bitterness, cruelty, fierceness, hate, hatred, hostility, ill-will, malice, maliciousness, malignancy, malignity, rancour *formal*, spite, spitefulness, unfriendliness, vengefulness, venom, viciousness, vindictiveness
𝔼 benevolence

malevolent *adj* baleful *formal*, bitter, cruel, evil-minded, fierce, hostile, ill-natured, maleficent *formal*, malicious, malign, pernicious, rancorous *formal*, resentful, spiteful, unfriendly, vengeful, venomous, vicious, vindictive
𝔼 benevolent, kind

malformation *n* deformity, disfigurement, distortion, irregularity, misshapenness, warp

malformed *adj* bent, crooked, deformed, disfigured, distorted, irregular, misshapen, twisted, warped
𝔼 perfect

malfunction *v* break down, conk out *slang*, fail, go kaput *colloq*, go wrong, pack up *colloq*, stop working
♦ *n* breakdown, defect, failure, fault, flaw, glitch, impairment

malice *n* animosity, animus *formal*, bad blood, bitchiness *colloq*, bitterness, bloody-mindedness *colloq*, enmity, hate, hatred, hostility, ill-will, malevolence *formal*, maliciousness, rancour *formal*, resentment, spite, spleen, venom, vindictiveness
𝔼 love

malicious *adj* baleful *formal*, bitter, evil, evil-minded, hostile, ill-natured, malevolent *formal*, malign, pernicious, rancorous *formal*, resentful, spiteful, vengeful, venomous, vicious
𝔼 friendly, kind

malign *v* abuse, badmouth *colloq*, calumniate *formal*, defame, disparage *formal*, drag through the mud *colloq*, harm, injure, insult, kick in the teeth *colloq*, libel, run down *colloq*, slander, slur *colloq*, smear *colloq*, stab in the back *colloq*, traduce *formal*, vilify *formal*
𝔼 praise
♦ *adj* bad, destructive, evil, harmful, hostile, hurtful, injurious, malevolent *formal*, malignant
𝔼 benign, kind

malignant *adj* 1 *malignant powers*: destructive, evil, harmful, hostile, hurtful, malevolent *formal*, malicious, pernicious, rancorous *formal*, spiteful, venomous, vicious 2 *a malignant tumour*: cancerous, dangerous, deadly, fatal, incurable, lethal, life-threatening, uncontrollable, virulent
𝔼 1 kind 2 benign

malignity *n* animosity, animus *formal*, bad blood, balefulness *formal*, bitterness, deadliness, destructiveness, gall, harmfulness, hate, hatred, hostility, hurtfulness, ill-will, malevolence *formal*, malice, maliciousness, perniciousness, rancour *formal*, spite, vengefulness, venom, viciousness, vindictiveness, wickedness
𝔼 harmlessness, kindness

malinger *v* dodge *colloq*, loaf *colloq*, pretend, pretend to be ill, put it on *colloq*, shirk *colloq*, skive *colloq*, slack, swing the lead *colloq*
𝔼 work

malingerer *n* dodger *colloq*, lead-swinger *colloq*, loafer *colloq*, shirker *colloq*, skiver *colloq*, slacker
𝔼 worker

mall *n* galleria, plaza, shopping centre, shopping precinct

malleable *adj* 1 *a malleable material*: ductile *formal*, flexible, plastic, pliable, pliant, soft, supple, workable 2 *a malleable young girl*: adaptable, biddable, compliant *formal*, flexible, governable, impressionable, manageable, persuadable, pliable, pliant, receptive, susceptible, tractable *formal*, tractile *formal*
𝔼 1 rigid 2 intractable *formal*

malnutrition *n* anorexia (nervosa), hunger, inanition *formal*, starvation, underfeeding, undernourishment, unhealthy diet
𝔼 nourishment

malodorous *adj* evil-smelling, fetid, foul-smelling, miasmal *formal*, miasmatic *formal*, miasmatous *formal*, miasmic *formal*, miasmous *formal*, nauseating, niffy, noisomemephitic *formal*, offensive, putrid, rank, reeking, smelly, stinking
𝔼 sweet-smelling

malpractice *n* abuse, carelessness, dereliction of duty *formal*, impropriety, misconduct, misdeed, mismanagement, negligence, offence, unethical behaviour, unprofessional conduct, wrongdoing

maltreat *v* abuse, bully, damage, harm, hound, hurt, ill-treat, injure, mistreat, misuse, torture, treat badly, victimize
𝔼 care for

maltreatment *n* abuse, bullying, damage, harm, hurt, ill-treatment, ill-usage, ill-use, injury, mistreatment, misuse, torture, victimization
𝔼 care

mammal

> *Mammals include:*
> aardvark, African black rhinoceros, African
> elephant, anteater, antelope, armadillo,
> baboon, Bactrian camel, badger, bat, bear,
> beaver, bushbaby, cat, chimpanzee,
> chipmunk, cow, deer, dog, dolphin, duck-
> billed platypus, dugong, echidna, flying
> lemur, fox, gerbil, gibbon, giraffe, goat, gorilla,
> guinea pig, hamster, hare, hedgehog,
> hippopotamus, horse, human being, hyena,
> Indian elephant, kangaroo, koala, lemming,
> leopard, lion, manatee, marmoset, marmot,
> marsupial mouse, mole, mouse, opossum,
> orang utan, otter, pig, porcupine, porpoise,
> rabbit, raccoon, rat, sea cow, sea lion, seal,
> sheep, shrew, sloth, squirrel, tamarin, tapir,
> tiger, vole, wallaby, walrus, weasel, whale,
> wolf, zebra. See also **cat, cattle, dog, horse,
> marsupial, monkey, rodent**

mammoth *adj* Brobdingnagian, bumper *colloq*,
colossal, enormous, gargantuan, giant, gigantic,
ginormous *colloq*, herculean, huge, immense,
jumbo *colloq*, leviathan, massive, mighty,
monumental, prodigious, stupendous, vast,
whopping *colloq*
Fa minute, tiny

man *n* **1** *a kind man:* bloke *colloq*, boy, chap *colloq*,
fellow *colloq*, gentleman, guy *colloq*, lad *colloq*,
male **2** *all men are equal before the law:* adult,
human, human being, individual, mortal, person
3 *man is destroying the environment:* Homo
sapiens *technical*, human beings, human race,
humanity, humankind, mankind, mortals,
people **4** *employing 15 men:* attendant, employee,
factotum, hand, helper, houseboy, houseman,
jack-of-all-trades, labourer, man-of-all-work,
manservant, odd-jobman, page, servant, soldier,
valet, worker, workman **5** *Jill and her man are
coming round:* bloke *colloq*, boyfriend, fellow
colloq, guy *colloq*, husband, lover, partner,
spouse, toy boy *colloq*
♦ *v* be in charge of, crew, occupy, operate, staff,
take charge of, work

manacle *v* bind, chain, check, curb, fetter,
hamper, handcuff, put in chains, restrain,
shackle
Fa free, unshackle

manacles *n* bonds, bracelets *colloq*, chains,
cuffs, darbies *colloq*, fetters, handcuffs, irons,
shackles, wristlets

manage *v* **1** *managed the department:* administer,
be head of, be in charge of, be responsible for,
command, conduct, control, direct, govern,
guide, head (up), lead, organize, oversee, preside
over, rule, run, superintend, supervise **2** *managed
a spectacular coup:* accomplish, achieve, bring
about, bring off, effect *formal*, engineer, succeed
3 *tips on how to manage your time:* control, deal
with, guide, handle, influence, manipulate,
master, operate, use, wield, work **4** *it's hard to
manage on what we earn:* cope, fare *formal*, get
along, get by, get on, make do, make out *colloq*,
survive
Fa **1** mismanage **2** fail

manageable *adj* **1** *a manageable amount of work:*
acceptable, attainable, doable, feasible,
practicable, reasonable, tolerable, viable **2** *a
manageable child:* accommodating, amenable,

controllable, docile, flexible, governable, pliable,
pliant, submissive, tractable *formal*, yielding
Fa **2** unmanageable

management *n* **1** *in charge of management of the
company:* administration, care, charge, command,
conduct, control, direction, government,
handling, leadership, organization, overseeing,
ruling, running, superintendence, supervision
2 *talks between workers and management:* board,
bosses *colloq*, directorate, directors, employers,
executive, executives, governors, managers,
owners, proprietors, supervisors
Fa **1** mismanagement **2** workers

manager *n* administrator, boss *colloq*, chairman,
chief, chief executive, commissioner,
comptroller, controller, director, employer,
executive, gaffer *colloq*, governor, guv *colloq*,
head, head of department, honcho *US colloq*,
managing director, organizer, overseer,
president, superintendent, supervisor

mandate *n* authority, authorization, bidding,
charge, command, commission, decree, dictate,
direction, directive, edict, injunction,
instruction, law, order, ordinance, ruling,
sanction, statute, warrant

mandatory *adj* binding, compulsory, essential,
imperative, necessary, obligatory, required,
requisite *formal*
Fa optional

manful *adj* bold, brave, courageous, daring,
determined, gallant, hardy, heroic, indomitable,
intrepid, lion-hearted, manly, noble, noble-
minded, powerful, resolute, stalwart, stout,
stout-hearted, strong, unflinching, valiant,
vigorous
Fa half-hearted, timid

manfully *adv* boldly, bravely, courageously,
desperately, determinedly, gallantly, hard,
heroically, intrepidly, nobly, pluckily,
powerfully, resolutely, stalwartly, steadfastly,
stoutly, strongly, unflinchingly, valiantly,
vigorously
Fa half-heartedly, timidly

manger *n* crib, feeder, feeding trough, trough

mangle *v* **1** *the body had been mangled:* butcher,
crush, cut, deform, destroy, disfigure, distort,
hack, lacerate, maim, maul, mutilate, rend, tear,
twist, wreck **2** *mangled his speech because of nerves:*
botch *colloq*, bungle, butcher, make a mess of
colloq, mess up *colloq*, ruin, screw up *slang*, spoil

mangy *adj* dirty, filthy, mean, moth-eaten,
scabby, scruffy, seedy, shabby, shoddy, tatty
colloq, worn

manhandle *v* **1** *the porters manhandled the
baggage:* haul, heave, hump *colloq*, pull, push,
shove, tug **2** *the police manhandled the
demonstrators:* abuse, handle roughly, knock
about *colloq*, maltreat, maul, mistreat, misuse,
push, rough up *colloq*, shove

manhood *n* **1** *would never grow to manhood:*
adulthood, maturity **2** *a slur on his manhood:*
machismo *colloq*, maleness, manfulness,
manliness, masculinity, virility

mania *n* **1** *showing signs of mania:* aberration,
craziness *colloq*, dementia, derangement,
disorder, frenzy, hysteria, insanity, lunacy,
madness, psychosis, raving, wildness **2** *a mania*

for exercise: compulsion, craving, craze, desire, enthusiasm, fad *colloq*, fascination, fetish, fixation, infatuation, obsession, passion, preoccupation, rage, urge

maniac *n* **1** *a maniac on the loose:* crackpot *colloq*, crank *colloq*, deranged person, fruitcake *colloq*, headcase *colloq*, loony *colloq*, lunatic, madman, madwoman, nut *colloq*, nutcase *colloq*, nutter *colloq*, oddball *slang*, psycho *slang*, psychopath, psychotic, screwball *slang* **2** *a maniac for crime novels:* enthusiast, fan, fanatic, fiend *colloq*, freak *colloq*

manifest *adj* apparent, blatant, clear, conspicuous, distinct, evident, glaring, noticeable, obvious, open, patent, perceptible, plain, transparent, unconcealed, unmistakable, visible
◘ unclear
♦ *v* declare, demonstrate, display, establish, evince *formal*, exhibit, expose, express, illustrate, indicate, make clear/plain, present, prove, reveal, set forth, show
◘ conceal, hide

manifestation *n* appearance, declaration, demonstration, disclosure, display, evidence, exemplification, exhibition, exposition *formal*, exposure, expression, illustration, indication, mark, presentation, revelation, show, sign, token

manifesto *n* announcement, declaration, platform, policies, proclamation, publication, statement

manifold *adj* abundant, copious, diverse, kaleidoscopic, many, multifarious *formal*, multiple, multitudinous *formal*, numerous, several, varied, various

manipulate *v* **1** *managed to manipulate the press coverage:* capitalize on, cash in on *colloq*, control, direct, engineer, exploit, fit up *colloq*, frame *colloq*, guide, have in the palm of your hand *colloq*, have over a barrel *colloq*, influence, manoeuvre, negotiate, pull strings *colloq*, steer, twist round your little finger *colloq*, use/turn to your advantage, wangle *colloq*, wheel and deal *colloq*, work **2** *manipulated the figures:* cook *colloq*, doctor *colloq*, falsify, fiddle *colloq*, juggle with, massage, rig, tamper with **3** *controls that are easy to manipulate:* control, employ, handle, knead, operate, ply, process, use, utilize, wield, work

manipulator *n* **1** *a manipulator of the press:* controller, director, engineer, exploiter, influencer, manoeuvrer, negotiator, schemer, smart guy *colloq*, smoothy *colloq*, wheeler-dealer *colloq* **2** *the manipulator of the winch:* controller, handler, operator, user, wielder, worker

mankind *n* Homo sapiens *technical*, human beings, human race, humanity, humankind, man, mortals, people

manliness *n* boldness, bravery, courage, fearlessness, firmness, fortitude *formal*, hardihood, heroism, independence, intrepidity, machismo *colloq*, maleness, manfulness, manhood, masculinity, mettle, resolution, stalwartness, stout-heartedness, strength, valour, vigour, virility
◘ timidity, unmanliness

manly *adj* bold, brave, courageous, determined, fearless, firm, heroic, intrepid, macho *colloq*,

male, manful, masculine, powerful, robust, rugged, strong, sturdy, tough, vigorous, virile

man-made *adj* artificial, ersatz *colloq*, imitation, manufactured, simulated, synthetic
◘ natural

manner *n* **1** *in an unexpected manner:* approach, fashion, form, means, method, mode *formal*, practice, procedure, process, routine, style, technique, variety, way **2** *she has a friendly manner:* air *formal*, appearance, aspect *formal*, attitude, bearing *formal*, behaviour, character, conduct, demeanour *formal*, deportment *formal*, look, mien *formal*, posture, stance **3** *good manners:* bearing *formal*, behaviour, conduct, courtesy, decorum *formal*, demeanour *formal*, etiquette, formalities, good form, politeness, propriety *formal*, protocol, p's and q's *colloq*, social graces, the done thing *colloq*, way of behaving

mannered *adj* affected, artificial, euphuistic *formal*, posed, precious, pretentious, pseudo *colloq*, put-on *colloq*, stilted
◘ natural

mannerism *n* characteristic, feature, foible, habit, idiosyncrasy, peculiarity, quirk, trait

mannerly *adj* civil, civilized, courteous, decorous *formal*, deferential, formal, genteel, gentlemanly, gracious, ladylike, polished, polite, refined, respectful, well-behaved, well-bred, well-mannered
◘ unmannerly

mannish *adj* Amazonian, butch *colloq*, laddish *colloq*, masculine, tomboyish, unfeminine, unladylike, unwomanly, viraginian, viraginous, viragoish, virilescent *formal*
◘ womanish

mannishness *n* butchness *colloq*, masculinity, unfemininity, unladylikeness, unwomanliness, virilescence *formal*, virilism
◘ womanishness

manoeuvre *v* **1** *manoeuvred the boat into the dock:* direct, drive, exercise, guide, handle, jockey, manipulate, move, navigate, negotiate, pilot, steer **2** *manoeuvred a position of power for herself:* contrive, devise, engineer, intrigue, jockey for position *colloq*, manage, manipulate, negotiate, plan, plot, pull strings *colloq*, scheme, wangle *colloq*
♦ *n* **1** *military manoeuvres:* action, deployment, exercise, move, movement, operation **2** *a clever business manoeuvre won the contract:* artifice *formal*, device, dodge *colloq*, gambit, machination *formal*, manipulation, plot, ploy, ruse, scheme, skilful plan, stratagem, subterfuge, tactic, trick, wangle *colloq*

manor *n* barony, château, country house, hall, Hof, house, Schloss, seat, villa

manse *n* deanery, glebe-house, parsonage, rectory, vicarage

manservant *n* butler, gentleman's gentleman, retainer, valet

mansion *n* abode *formal*, castle, château, dwelling *formal*, habitation *formal*, hall, home, house, manor, manor-house, residence *formal*, Schloss, seat, villa

manslaughter *n* assassination, bloodshed, butchery, carnage, destruction, elimination, execution, extermination, fatality, fratricide *formal*, genocide, homicide, infanticide *formal*, killing, liquidation *colloq*, massacre, matricide *formal*, murder, patricide *formal*, slaughter, slaying, sororicide *formal*, uxoricide *formal*

mantle *n* **1** *wore a hooded mantle:* cape, cloak, hood, screen, shawl, shroud, veil, wrap **2** *a mantle of snow:* blanket, cloak, cloud, cover, covering, envelope, layer, mask, shroud, veil
♦ *v* blanket, cloak, cloud, conceal, cover, disguise, envelop, hide, mask, shroud, veil, wrap

manual *n* ABC, bible, book of words *colloq*, companion, directions, guide, guidebook, handbook, instruction book, instructions, prospectus, vade-mecum
♦ *adj* by hand, (done) with your hands, hand-operated, human, physical
▣ automatic, mental

manufacture *v* **1** *a plant manufacturing plastic goods:* assemble, build, construct, create, fabricate, fashion, forge, form, make, mass-produce, model, process, produce, put together, turn out **2** *manufactured an alibi:* concoct, construct, devise, dream up, fabricate, frame, invent, make up, think up
♦ *n* assembly, building, construction, creation, fabrication, fashioning, formation, forming, making, mass-production, modelling, processing, production

manufacturer *n* builder, constructor, creator, factory-owner, industrialist, maker, producer

manure *n* animal excrement, animal faeces *formal*, compost, droppings, dung, fertilizer, guana, muck, ordure

manuscript *n* document, paper, parchment, scroll, text, vellum

many *adj* a large number of, a lot of, billions of *colloq*, copious, countless, diverse, heaps of *colloq*, hundreds of *colloq*, innumerable, lots of *colloq*, manifold *formal*, masses of *colloq*, millions of *colloq*, multiple, multitudinous *formal*, numerous, oodles of *colloq*, piles of *colloq*, scads of *colloq*, scores of *colloq*, several, stacks of *colloq*, sundry, thousands of *colloq*, tons of *colloq*, umpteen *colloq*, varied, various
▣ few
♦ *n* a large number of people/things, a lot, a mass, a multitude, billions *colloq*, hundreds *colloq*, masses *colloq*, millions *colloq*, plenty, scores *colloq*, thousands *colloq*, zillions *colloq*

map *n* atlas, chart, gazetteer, graph, plan, plot, road-map, street guide, street plan, town plan
♦ *v* chart, delineate *formal*, mark, plan, plot, sketch
▶ **map out** draft, draw (up), outline, sketch, work out

mar *v* blemish, contaminate, damage, deface, deform, detract from, disfigure, harm, hurt, impair, injure, maim, mangle, mutilate, ruin, scar, spoil, stain, taint, tarnish, wreck
▣ enhance

maraud *v* depredate *formal*, despoil *formal*, forage, foray, harry, loot, pillage, plunder, raid, ransack, ravage, sack, spoliate *formal*

marauder *n* bandit, brigand, buccaneer, freebooter, highwayman, looter, outlaw, pillager, pirate, plunderer, predator, raider, ravager, robber, rover, rustler

march *v* **1** *soldiers marching down the road:* advance, file, hike, make headway, parade, progress, strut, tramp, tread, walk **2** *marched into the room:* flounce, pace, stalk, stride, strut, swagger, sweep, walk
♦ *n* **1** *proceeded at a march:* gait, pace, step, stride, walk **2** *a forced march:* footslog *colloq*, hike, route-march, tramp, trek, walk **3** *the march will head along the high street:* demo *colloq*, demonstration, parade, procession **4** *the march of time:* advance, development, evolution, headway, passage, progress

margin *n* **1** *police combed the margins of the field:* border, bound, boundary, brim, brink, confine(s), demarcation line, edge, frontier, limit(s), perimeter, periphery, rim, side, skirt, verge **2** *no margin for error:* allowance, difference, differential, extra, latitude, leeway, play, room, room for manoeuvre, scope, space, surplus

marginal *adj* **1** *marginal differences in price:* borderline, doubtful, insignificant, low, minimal, minor, minute, negligible, slight, small, tiny **2** *a marginal position:* on the edge, on the fringe, peripheral, side
▣ **1** major **2** central, core, mainstream

marijuana *n* bhang, blow *slang*, cannabis, dope *colloq*, ganja *colloq*, grass *colloq*, hash *colloq*, hashish, hemp, kef *colloq*, leaf *slang*, locoweed *US slang*, pot *colloq*, puff *colloq*, punk *slang*, skunk *slang*, spliff *colloq*, tea *colloq*, weed *slang*

marina *n* dock, harbour, mooring, port, yacht station

marinade *v* imbue, immerse, infuse, marinate, permeate, saturate, soak, souse, steep

marine *adj* **1** *marine life:* aquatic, oceanic, pelagic *formal*, saltwater, sea, seawater, thalassian *formal*, thalassic *formal* **2** *marine traffic:* maritime, nautical, naval, ocean-going, oceanic, sea, seafaring, seagoing

mariner *n* deckhand, Jack Tar *colloq*, limey *colloq*, matelot *colloq*, matlo *colloq*, matlow *colloq*, navigator, sailor, salt *colloq*, sea dog *colloq*, seafarer, seaman, tar *colloq*

marital *adj* conjugal, connubial *formal*, marriage, married, matrimonial, nuptial *formal*, wedded, wedding

maritime *adj* **1** *a major maritime power:* marine, nautical, naval, oceanic, sea, seafaring, seagoing **2** *maritime areas:* coastal, littoral *formal*, seaside

mark *n* **1** *left a mark on the coffee table:* blemish, blot, blotch, chip, cut, dent, fingerprint(s), impression, imprint, line, nick, notch, patch, score, scratch, smear, smudge, spot, stain, stigma *formal*, trace, track(s) **2** *a mark on his cheek:* blemish, blotch, bruise, patch, pimple, scar, scratch, smear, smudge, spot, zit *US colloq* **3** *as a mark of respect:* attribute, character, characteristic, clue, evidence, feature, hint, impression, indication, print, proof, quality, sign, stamp, symbol, symptom, token **4** *a mark of 9 out of 10:* assessment, evaluation, grade, letter, number, percentage, score **5** *the company's mark:* badge, brand, device, emblem, logo, monogram, motto, seal, stamp, symbol, trademark **6** *inflation reaching the 5% mark:* criterion, gauge, level, measure, norm, point, scale, stage, standard, yardstick **7** *his jibes always hit the mark:* aim, bull's-eye, end, goal, intention, object, objective,

purpose, target
◆ *v* **1** *marked the wood:* blemish, blot, bruise, chip, cut, dent, discolour, nick, scar, score, scratch, smudge, stain **2** *X marks the spot:* brand, characterize, distinguish, flag, identify, label, stamp, tag **3** *marked his essay:* appraise *formal*, assess, correct, evaluate, grade **4** *mark any CDs you'd like to buy:* designate, indicate, jot down, label, name, note (down), specify, write down **5** *the talks mark a major step forward between the two countries:* brand, characterize, distinguish, identify, stamp, typify **6** *mark an event:* celebrate, commemorate, honour, keep, observe, recognize, remember **7** *mark my words:* bear in mind, discern, heed *formal*, listen, mind, note, notice, observe, pay attention to, regard, see, spot, take heed of *formal*, take note of, take to heart
▶ **mark down** cut, decrease, lower, reduce, slash *colloq*
◪ mark up
▶ **mark out 1** *mark out a football pitch:* delimit, demarcate, draw lines, fix, show the boundaries of **2** *his hard work marked him out from the other boys:* differentiate, discriminate, distinguish, set apart, single out, tell apart, tell the difference between
▶ **mark up** hike up *colloq*, increase, jack up *colloq*, put up, raise

marked *adj* **1** *a surface marked with stains:* blemished, blotched, blotchy, bruised, freckled, pimply, scarred, scratched, spotted, spotty, stained **2** *a marked difference in size:* apparent, blatant, clear, considerable, conspicuous, decided, distinct, emphatic, evident, glaring, noted, noticeable, obvious, prominent, pronounced, remarkable, signal, striking, unmistakable **3** *a marked man:* condemned, doomed, suspected, watched
◪ **2** slight, unnoticeable

markedly *adv* blatantly, clearly, considerably, conspicuously, decidedly, distinctly, emphatically, evidently, glaringly, noticeably, obviously, prominently, remarkably, signally, strikingly, unmistakably

market *n* **1** *buy goods at the market:* agora *formal*, bazaar, exchange, fair, mall, market-place, mart, outlet, shopping centre **2** *no market for these goods:* call, demand, desire, need, occasion, requirement, want **3** *the housing market:* business, buying, dealings, industry, selling, trade, trading
◆ *v* hawk, offer for sale, peddle, retail, sell
◪ buy

marketable *adj* in demand, merchantable, saleable, sellable, sought after, vendible *formal*, wanted
◪ unsaleable

marksman, markswoman *n* bersagliere, crack shot, dead shot, sharpshooter, sniper

maroon *v* abandon, cast away, desert, forsake, isolate, leave (behind), leave high and dry *colloq*, leave in the lurch *colloq*, put ashore, strand, turn your back on

marriage *n* **1** *the marriage ceremony:* married relationship, married state, matrimony *formal*, nuptials *formal*, spousage *formal*, union, wedding **2** *the cake is a happy marriage of plum and almond:* affiliation, alliance, amalgamation, association, combination, confederation, connection,

coupling, fusion, link, merger, partnership, unification, union
◪ **1** divorce **2** separation

married *adj* conjugal *formal*, connubial *formal*, hitched *colloq*, husbandly, joined, marital, matrimonial *formal*, nuptial *formal*, spliced *colloq*, spousal *formal*, united, wed, wedded, wifely, wived, yoked
◪ divorced, single

marrow *n* centre, core, essence, gist, heart, kernel, nitty-gritty *colloq*, nub, nucleus, nuts and bolts *colloq*, pith, quick, quintessence *formal*, soul, spirit, stuff, substance

marry *v* **1** *the couple married in 1979:* become espoused *formal*, become husband and wife, elope, get hitched *colloq*, get married, get spliced *colloq*, intermarry, join in matrimony *formal*, lead to the altar *colloq*, make an honest woman of *colloq*, take the plunge *colloq*, tie the knot *colloq*, wed **2** *the process marries efficiency and innovation:* affiliate, ally, amalgamate, associate, combine, connect, couple, fuse, join (together), knit, link, match, merge, unite, weld
◪ **1** divorce **2** separate

marsh *n* bayou *US*, bog, fen, marshland, mire, morass, quagmire, slough, swamp

marshal *v* **1** *tried to marshal his thoughts:* align, arrange, array, assemble, collect, deploy, dispose, draw up, gather (together), group, line up, muster, order, organize, put in order, rank **2** *marshalled the children into the museum:* conduct, escort, guide, lead, shepherd, take, usher

marshy *adj* boggy, fennish, fenny, miry, muddy, paludal *formal*, paludinal *formal*, paludine *formal*, paludinous *formal*, quaggy, slumpy, spongy, squelchy, swampy, waterlogged, wet
◪ dry, firm, solid

marsupial

Marsupials include:
bandicoot, cuscus, kangaroo, rat kangaroo, tree kangaroo, wallaroo, koala, marsupial anteater, marsupial mouse, marsupial mole, marsupial rat, opossum, pademelon, phalanger, Tasmanian Devil, Tasmanian wolf, wallaby, rock wallaby, wombat

---

martial *adj* aggressive, army, bellicose *formal*, belligerent, brave, combative, heroic, militant, military, pugnacious *formal*, soldierly, warlike

martinet *n* disciplinarian, formalist, slave-driver *colloq*, stickler, taskmaster, taskmistress, tyrant

martyr *v* burn at the stake, crucify, give the third degree *colloq*, give the works *colloq*, make a martyr of, persecute, put on the rack, put to death, stone, throw to the lions, torment, torture

martyrdom *n* agony, anguish, death, excruciation, ordeal, persecution, suffering, torment, torture, witness

marvel *v* be amazed at, be flabbergasted *colloq*, gape, gawp *colloq*, gaze, goggle, not believe your eyes *colloq*, not expect, not know what to say *colloq*, stand in amazement, stare, wonder
◆ *n* **1** *he's a marvel in the kitchen:* eye-opener *colloq*, genius, phenomenon, prodigy, quite something *colloq*, sensation **2** *the marvels of modern science:* miracle, phenomenon, sensation,

something amazing/incredible, spectacle, surprise, wonder

marvellous *adj* **1** *a marvellous day out:* ace *colloq*, awesome *slang*, bad *slang*, brill *colloq*, cool *slang*, excellent, fantastic, great, magic *colloq*, magnificent, mega *slang*, splendid, super, superb, terrific, wicked *slang*, wonderful **2** *marvellous creatures:* amazing, astonishing, astounding, awesome, extraordinary, glorious, incredible, miraculous, remarkable, sensational, spectacular, stupendous, surprising, unbelievable
🔁 **1** awful, terrible **2** ordinary, run-of-the-mill

masculine *adj* **1** *a masculine voice:* butch *colloq*, macho *colloq*, male, manlike, manly, mannish, virile **2** *masculine pursuits like hunting:* bold, brave, confident, determined, fearless, gallant, heroic, powerful, red-blooded, resolute, robust, rugged, stout-hearted, strong, vigorous
🔁 **1** feminine

masculinity *n* boldness, bravery, courage, fearlessness, firmness, fortitude *formal*, hardihood, heroism, independence, intrepidity, machismo *colloq*, maleness, manfulness, manhood, manliness, mettle, resolution, stalwartness, stout-heartedness, strength, valour, vigour, virility
🔁 femininity

mash *v* beat, crush, grind, pound, pulp, pulverize, pummel, purée, smash, squash
♦ *n* crush, mush, pap, paste, pulp, purée, squash

mask *n* **1** *a mask of good humour:* blind, camouflage, cloak, concealment, cover, cover-up, disguise, façade, front, guise, pretence, screen, semblance, show, veil, veneer **2** *a swimming mask:* goggles, visor
♦ *v* camouflage, cloak, conceal, cover (up), disguise, hide, obscure, screen, shield, veil
🔁 expose, uncover

masquerade *n* **1** *a masquerade at the Lido:* costume ball, fancy-dress party, masked ball, masque **2** *a masquerade of sensitivity:* cloak, counterfeit, cover, cover-up, deception, disguise, front, guise, pose, pretence
♦ *v* disguise, dissimulate *formal*, impersonate, mask, pass yourself off, play, pose, pretend to be, profess to be

mass¹ *n* **1** *the trees were a mass of colour:* accumulation, aggregate *formal*, assemblage *formal*, batch, bunch, collection, combination, conglomeration *formal*, entirety, group, heap, load, lot, pile, sum, total, totality, whole **2** *masses of things to do:* abundance, bags *colloq*, band, crowd, heaps *colloq*, horde, loads *colloq*, lots *colloq*, mob, multitude, oodles *colloq*, piles *colloq*, quantity, scores *colloq*, throng, tons *colloq*, troop **3** *the mass of the work is completed:* body, bulk, greater part, majority, most, preponderance **4** *calculate the mass of the cube:* bulk, capacity, dimension, immensity, magnitude, size **5** *a mass of tissue:* block, chunk, hunk, lump, piece, wedge *colloq* **6** *the masses:* common people, crowd, herd, hoi polloi, lower classes, mob, plebs *colloq*, proletariat, rabble, riff-raff *colloq*, the rank and file, working class(es)
♦ *adj* across-the-board, blanket, comprehensive, extensive, general, indiscriminate, large-scale,

pandemic *formal*, popular, sweeping, universal, wholesale, widespread
🔁 limited, small-scale
♦ *v* accumulate, amass, assemble, cluster, collect, come/bring together, congregate, crowd, draw together, gather, muster, rally, swarm, throng
🔁 separate

mass² *n* Communion, Eucharist, Holy Communion, Lord's Supper, Lord's Table

massacre *n* annihilation, bloodbath, butchery, carnage, decimation, ethnic cleansing, extermination, genocide, holocaust, homicide, indiscriminate killing, killing, liquidation, murder, pogrom, slaughter, wholesale slaughter
♦ *v* annihilate, butcher, decimate, exterminate, kill (off), liquidate, mow down, murder, slaughter, slay, wipe out *colloq*

massage *n* acupressure, aromatherapy, kneading, manipulation, osteopathy, physiotherapy, pummelling, reflexology, Reichian therapy, rub, rubbing, rub-down, shiatsu
♦ *v* knead, manipulate, pummel, rub, rub down

massive *adj* big, bulky, colossal, enormous, extensive, gigantic, ginormous *colloq*, great, heavy, hefty, huge, hulking, immense, jumbo *colloq*, large, large-scale, mammoth, mighty, monumental, solid, substantial, vast, weighty, whopping *colloq*
🔁 small, tiny

mast *n* bar, boom, heel, pole, post, rod, shaft, spar, staff, stick, support, upright, yard

master *n* **1** *master of all he surveys:* boss *colloq*, captain, chief, commander, controller, director, employer, gaffer *colloq*, governor, guv *colloq*, head, honcho *US colloq*, lord, manager, overlord, overseer, owner, principal, ruler, skipper *colloq*, superintendent **2** *a master of disguise:* ace *colloq*, adept, buff *colloq*, dab hand *colloq*, egghead *colloq*, expert, genius, grand master, maestro, maven *colloq*, mavin *US colloq*, past master, pro *colloq*, professional, pundit, virtuoso, wise guy *colloq* **3** *the French master:* guide, guru, instructor, mentor, pedagogue *formal*, preceptor *formal*, schoolmaster, schoolmistress, schoolteacher, teacher, tutor
🔁 **1** servant, underling **2** amateur **3** learner, pupil
♦ *adj* **1** *a master key:* chief, controlling, foremost, grand, great, leading, main, most important, predominant, prime, principal **2** *a master stroke:* adept, dexterous, experienced, expert, masterly, practised, proficient, skilful, skilled
🔁 **1** subordinate **2** inept
♦ *v* **1** *mastered his fear and did the jump:* bridle, check, conquer, control, curb, defeat, govern, overcome, overpower, quell, rule, subdue, subjugate *formal*, suppress, tame, triumph over, vanquish *formal* **2** *mastered how to ride a bike:* acquire, get the hang of *colloq*, grasp, learn, manage

masterful *adj* arrogant, authoritative, autocratic, bossy *colloq*, controlling, despotic, dictatorial, dominating, domineering, high-handed, imperious, overbearing, peremptory *formal*, powerful, tyrannical
🔁 downtrodden, hen-pecked *colloq*, humble

masterful or *masterly*? *Masterful* means 'showing power, authority or determination': *The directors adopt a masterful approach to their employees*. *Masterly* means 'showing the skill of a master': *a masterly display of swordsmanship*.

masterly *adj* accomplished, ace *colloq*, adept, adroit, consummate *formal*, crack *colloq*, dexterous, excellent, expert, first-rate, polished, professional, skilful, skilled, superb, superior, supreme, top-notch *colloq*
🖬 clumsy, inept

mastermind *v* be behind, conceive, contrive, design, devise, direct, dream up, engineer, forge, frame, hatch, inspire, manage, organize, originate, plan, think up
♦ *n* architect, authority, brains *colloq*, creator, director, engineer, genius, initiator, intellect, manager, organizer, originator, planner, prime mover, virtuoso

masterpiece *n* chef d'oeuvre, creation, jewel, magnum opus, masterwork, pièce de résistance, work of art

mastery *n* 1 *his mastery of the flute*: ability, capability, command, comprehension, dexterity, expertise, familiarity, grasp, know-how, knowledge, proficiency, prowess *formal*, skill, understanding, virtuosity 2 *her complete mastery of the situation*: ascendancy *formal*, authority, command, control, direction, domination, dominion, rule, sovereignty, superiority, supremacy, triumph, upper hand *colloq*, victory
🖬 1 incompetence 2 subjugation

mat *n* 1 *a mat on the floor*: carpet, doormat, drugget, felt, rug, underfelt, underlay 2 *a mat on the table*: coaster, place mat, table mat 3 *a mat of hair*: cluster, knot, mass, tangle, twist

match[1] *n* 1 *a football match*: bout, competition, contest, event, game, meet, test, tournament, trial 2 *met her match in him*: counterpart, equal, peer, rival 3 *tested the print to see if it was a match*: companion, copy, counterpart, dead ringer *colloq*, double, duplicate, equal, equivalent, fellow, lookalike, replica, twin 4 *a match made in heaven*: affiliation, alliance, combination, coupling, marriage, merger, pairing, partnership, union
♦ *v* 1 *their standard of service is hard to match*: compare with, compete with, contend with, equal, keep up with, measure up to, oppose, parallel, pit against, rival, vie with 2 *their two accounts don't match*: accompany, accord *formal*, adapt, agree, blend, complement, connect, co-ordinate, correspond, fit, go together, go with, harmonize, relate, suit, tally, tone with
🖬 2 clash, conflict

match[2] *n* fuse, light, safety match, spill, taper, vesta

matching *adj* blending, complementary, co-ordinating, corresponding, coupled, equivalent, harmonizing, identical, like, paired, same, similar, twin
🖬 clashing, conflicting

matchless *adj* beyond compare, incomparable, inimitable, peerless, perfect, unequalled, unexcelled, unique, unmatched, unparalleled, unrivalled, unsurpassed, without equal
🖬 ordinary

mate *n* 1 *he's gone out with his mates*: associate, buddy *colloq*, chum *colloq*, colleague, companion, compeer *formal*, comrade, coworker, crony *colloq*, fellow worker, friend, pal *colloq*, partner, workmate 2 *a mate for life*: better half *colloq*, boyfriend, companion, girlfriend, hubbie *colloq*, husband, missis *colloq*, missus *colloq*, other half *colloq*, partner, spouse, wife 3 *a plumber's mate*: accomplice, apprentice, assistant, helper, partner, subordinate 4 *these socks have all lost their mates*: counterpart, equivalent, fellow, match, twin
♦ *v* 1 *attempts to get the pandas to mate*: breed, copulate, couple, pair 2 *mating thought and deed*: join, marry, match, wed

material *n* 1 *raw materials*: body, matter, medium, stuff, substance 2 *she used a soft flowing material for the curtains*: cloth, fabric, stuff, textile 3 *collecting material about the war*: constituents, data, details, evidence, facts, facts and figures, gen *colloq*, ideas, info *colloq*, information, lowdown *colloq*, notes, numbers, particulars, work
♦ *adj* 1 *the material world*: bodily, concrete, corporeal *formal*, earthly, palpable, physical, substantial, tangible, worldly 2 *information not material to the trial*: apposite *formal*, consequential, essential, germane *formal*, important, indispensable, key, meaningful, momentous, pertinent *formal*, relevant, serious, significant, vital, weighty
🖬 1 abstract, spiritual 2 irrelevant

materialistic *adj* mammonist, mammonistic, mercenary, money-grabbing
🖬 spiritual

materialize *v* appear, arise, become visible, come into being, happen, occur, show/reveal yourself, take place, take shape, turn up
🖬 disappear

materially *adv* basically, considerably, essentially, fundamentally, gravely, greatly, much, seriously, significantly, substantially
🖬 insignificantly

maternal *adj* caring, doting, kind, loving, motherlike, motherly, nourishing, nurturing, protective, vigilant
🖬 paternal

mathematics

Mathematical terms include:
acute angle, addition, algebra, algorithm, analysis, angle, apex, approximate, arc, area, argument, arithmetic, arithmetic progression, asymmetrical, average, axis, axis of symmetry, bar chart, bar graph, base, bearing, binary, binomial, breadth, calculus, capacity, cardinal number, Cartesian co-ordinates, chance, chord, circumference, coefficient, combination, commutative operation, complement, complementary angle, complex number, concave, concentric circles, congruent, conjugate angles, constant, continuous distribution, converse, convex, co-ordinate, correlation, cosine, covariance, cross section, cube, cube root, curve, decimal, degree, denominator, depth, derivative, determinant, diagonal, diameter, differentiation, directed number, distribution, dividend, division, divisor, edge, equal, equation, equidistant, even number, exponent, exponential, face, factor, factorial, Fibonacci sequence, formula, fraction, function, geometric

progression, geometry, gradient, graph, greater than, group, harmonic progression, height, helix, histogram, horizontal, hyperbola, hypotenuse, identity, infinity, integer, integration, irrational number, latitude, length, less than, linear, line, locus, logarithm, longitude, magic square, matrix, maximum, mean, measure, median, minimum, minus, mirror image, mirror symmetry, Möbius strip, mode, modulus, multiple, multiplication, natural logarithm, natural number, negative number, number, numerator, oblique, obtuse angle, odd number, operation, ordinal number, origin, parabola, parallel lines, parallel planes, parameter, percentage, percentile, perimeter, permutation, perpendicular, pi, pie chart, place value, plane figure, plus, point, positive number, prime number, probability, product, proportion, protractor, Pythagoras's theorem, quadrant, quadratic equation, quadrilateral, quartile, quotient, radian, radius, random sample, ratio, rational number, real numbers, reciprocal, recurring decimal, reflection, reflex angle, regression, remainder, right-angle, right-angled triangle, root, rotation, rotational symmetry, sample, scalar segment, secant, sector, set, side, simultaneous equation, sine, speed, spiral, square, square root, standard deviation, statistics, straight line, subset, subtractor, supplementary angles, symmetry, tangent, three-dimensional, total, transcendental number, triangulation, trigonometry, unit, universal set, variable, variance, vector, velocity, Venn diagram, vertex, vertical, volume, whole number, width, zero. See also **shape**

mating *n* breeding, coition *formal*, copulating, copulation, coupling, fusing, jointing, matching, pairing, sexual intercourse, twinning, uniting

matrimonial *adj* conjugal *formal*, marital, marriage, married, nuptial *formal*, spousal, wedded, wedding

matrimony *n* espousals *formal*, marriage, married relationship/state, nuptials *formal*, spousage *formal*, union

matted *adj* dishevelled, entangled, knotted, tangled, tangly, tousled, uncombed
🢒 tidy, untangled

matter *n* **1** *the matter to be considered*: affair, business, case, circumstance, concern, episode, event, happening, incident, issue, occurrence, point, proceeding, question, situation, subject, thing, topic **2** *it's of no matter*: consequence, import *formal*, importance, interest, momentousness, note, significance, value, weight **3** *what's the matter?*: bother, difficulty, distress, inconvenience, nuisance, problem, shortcoming, trouble, upset, weakness, worry **4** *dark matter in the universe*: body, content, material, medium, physical elements, stuff, substance **5** *matter seeped from the infected wound*: discharge, purulence *formal*, pus, secretion, suppuration *formal*
♦ *v* be important, be of importance, be relevant, carry weight, count, cut a lot of ice *colloq*, have influence, make a difference, make a stir *colloq*, make waves *colloq*, mean something

matter-of-fact *adj* deadpan *colloq*, down-to-earth, dry, dull, emotionless, flat, lifeless, pedestrian, prosaic, sober, straightforward, unemotional, unimaginative, unsentimental
🢒 emotional

mature *adj* **1** *a mature bird*: adult, full-grown, fully fledged, grown, grown-up, of age, well-developed **2** *a mature outlook*: balanced, complete, experienced, grown-up, perfect, perfected, responsible, sensible, well-thought-out, wise **3** *mature fruit*: mellow, ready, ripe, ripened, seasoned
🢒 **2** childish **3** immature
♦ *v* **1** *she has matured recently*: age, be fully developed, become adult, become sensible, come of age, develop, evolve, grow up **2** *the fruit matures on the tree*: age, become mellow, become ripe, develop, mellow, ripen

maturity *n* **1** *looked after until they reach maturity*: adulthood, coming of age, experience, full growth, majority, manhood, responsibility, sensibleness, wisdom, womanhood **2** *the maturity of the grapes*: mellowness, perfection, readiness, ripeness
🢒 **1** childishness **2** immaturity

maudlin *adj* emotional, gushy *colloq*, half-drunk, lachrymose *formal*, mawkish, mushy *colloq*, schmaltzy *colloq*, sentimental, sickly *colloq*, slushy *colloq*, soppy *colloq*, tearful, weepy *colloq*
🢒 pleasant

maul *v* abuse, assault, attack, batter *colloq*, beat (up), belt *colloq*, claw, do over *colloq*, ill-treat, knock about *colloq*, knock someone's block off *colloq*, lacerate, maltreat, mangle, manhandle, molest, mug *colloq*, mutilate, paw, rough up *colloq*, thrash, wallop *colloq*

maunder *v* babble, blather, chatter, gabble, jabber *colloq*, mutter, natter *colloq*, prattle *colloq*, rabbit (on) *colloq*, ramble, waffle *colloq*, witter *colloq*

mausoleum *n* burial chamber, catacomb, crypt, sepulchre, tomb, undercroft, vault

maverick *n* agitator, fish out of water *colloq*, individualist, nonconformist, outsider, rebel

maw *n* abyss, chasm, gulf, gullet, jaws, mouth, stomach, throat

mawkish *adj* emotional, feeble, flat, gushy *colloq*, maudlin, mushy *colloq*, nauseating, nauseous, offensive, schmaltzy *colloq*, sentimental, sickly *colloq*, slushy *colloq*, soppy *colloq*
🢒 matter-of-fact, pleasant

maxim *n* adage, aphorism, axiom, byword, epigram, gnome *formal*, motto, precept, proverb, rule, saw, saying

maximum *adj* biggest, greatest, highest, largest, most, supreme, top, topmost, utmost
🢒 minimum
♦ *n* acme *formal*, apogee *formal*, ceiling, extremity, height, limit, most, peak, pinnacle, summit, top (point), upper limit, utmost, uttermost, zenith *formal*
🢒 minimum

maybe *adv* conceivably, for all you know, peradventure *formal*, perchance *formal*, perhaps, possibly
🢒 definitely

mayhem *n* anarchy, bedlam, chaos, confusion, disorder, disorganization, disruption, lawlessness, madhouse, mess, riot, tumult, uproar

maze *n* **1** *a path through the maze:* labyrinth, network, puzzle, warren, web **2** *a maze of regulations:* complex, confusion, intricacy, jumble, jungle, network, tangle

meadow *n* field, grass, grassland, green, paddock, pasture, pastureland

meagre *adj* **1** *meagre rations:* deficient, exiguous *formal*, inadequate, insufficient, measly *colloq*, negligible, niggardly, paltry, poor, scanty, skimpy, slight, small, sparse, stingy **2** *the prisoners' meagre bodies:* bony, emaciated, gaunt, insubstantial, puny, scraggy, scrawny, slight, thin
🅴 **1** ample **2** fat

meagreness *n* deficiency, inadequacy, insufficiency, measliness *colloq*, puniness, scantiness, slightness, smallness, sparseness, stinginess

mealy-mouthed *adj* equivocal, euphemistic, flattering, glib, hesitant, indirect, mincing, overdelicate, over-squeamish, prim, reticent, smooth-tongued

mean[1] *v* **1** *what does 'plausible' mean?:* betoken *formal*, connote *formal*, convey, denote *formal*, designate, express, imply, indicate, intimate, purport *formal*, represent, show, signify, stand for, suggest, symbolize **2** *I meant to call him:* aim, aspire, design, have in mind, intend, plan, propose, purpose, think of, wish, wont **3** *the defeat means relegation for the team:* bring about, cause, effect *formal*, entail, give rise to, involve, lead to, produce, result in **4** *it was meant to happen:* appoint, design, destine, fate, intend, ordain *formal*

mean[2] *adj* **1** *mean with his money:* close-fisted, grasping, mingy *colloq*, miserly, niggardly, parsimonious *formal*, penny-pinching *colloq*, selfish, stingy *colloq*, tight *colloq*, tight-fisted **2** *don't be so mean to your sister:* bad-tempered, crabby *colloq*, cross, crotchety *colloq*, cruel, disagreeable, grouchy *colloq*, nasty, spiteful, unfriendly, unkind, unpleasant **3** *a mean little shack:* base, common, dirty, dismal, humble, lowly, miserable, obscure, ordinary, poor, shabby, squalid, wretched
🅴 **1** generous **2** kind **3** noble, splendid

mean[3] *adj* average, halfway, intermediate, median, medium, middle, middling, normal
🅴 extreme
♦ *n* average, compromise, golden mean, happy medium, median, medium, middle, middle course, middle way, mid-point, mode, norm
🅴 extreme

meander *v* **1** *the river meanders around the castle:* bend, curve, snake, turn, twist, wind, zigzag **2** *spent the afternoon meandering around the town:* amble, laze *colloq*, mooch *colloq*, mosey *colloq*, ramble, roam, rove, stroll, wander

meandering *adj* circuitous, convoluted *formal*, indirect, meandrous, rambling, roundabout, serpentine, sinuous, snaking, tortuous, turning, twisting, wandering, winding
🅴 direct, straight

meaning *n* **1** *the meaning of a word:* connotation *formal*, definition, drift, elucidation *formal*, essence, explanation, explication *formal*, expression, gist, implication, import *formal*, interpretation, message, sense, significance, signification *formal*, substance, thrust, trend **2** *the whole meaning of his ministry:* aim, aspiration, goal, idea, intention, object, objective, plan, purpose, wish **3** *being a mother gave her life a meaning:* point, purpose, significance, value, worth

meaningful *adj* **1** *an attempt to make education more meaningful:* important, material, purposeful, relevant, serious, significant, useful, valid, worthwhile **2** *with a meaningful glance at the clock:* eloquent, expressive, pointed, pregnant, speaking, suggestive, warning
🅴 **1** unimportant, worthless

meaningless *adj* **1** *meaningless jargon:* aimless, futile, incomprehensible, insignificant, insubstantial, irrational, motiveless, pointless, purposeless, senseless, trifling, trivial, unintelligible, useless **2** *made his whole life seem meaningless:* absurd, empty, hollow, nonsensical, vacuous, vain, worthless
🅴 **1** important, meaningful **2** worthwhile

meanness *n* **1** *meanness with money:* close-fistedness, close-handedness, illiberality, miserliness, niggardliness, parsimony *formal*, penuriousness *formal*, stinginess *colloq*, tight-fistedness **2** *crimes of unimaginable meanness:* mean-spiritedness, narrow-mindedness
🅴 **1** generosity **2** kindness

means *n* **1** *a means to an end:* agency, avenue, channel, course, instrument, manner, medium, method, mode *formal*, process, vehicle, way **2** *don't have the means to support that lifestyle:* affluence, assets, capital, fortune, funds, income, money, property, resources, riches, substance, wealth, wherewithal

meantime, meanwhile *adv* at the same time, concurrently, for now, for the moment, for the time being, in the interim, in the interval, in the meantime, in the meanwhile, simultaneously

measly *adj* beggarly, contemptible, meagre, mean, mingy *colloq*, miserable, miserly, niggardly, paltry, pathetic *colloq*, petty, piddling *colloq*, pitiful, poor, puny, scanty, skimpy, stingy *colloq*, trivial, ungenerous
🅴 generous

measurable *adj* appreciable, assessable, computable, determinable, fathomable, gaugeable, material, mensurable *formal*, noticeable, perceptible, quantifiable, quantitative, significant
🅴 measureless

measure *n* **1** *weights and measures:* amount, area, bulk, capacity, degree, depth, dimension(s), expanse, extent, height, length, magnitude, mass, proportion(s), quantity, range, scope, size, volume, weight, width **2** *a measure of the policy's success:* benchmark, criterion, gauge, level, meter, norm, rule, ruler, scale, standard, system, test, touchstone, unit(s), yardstick **3** *measures to eradicate poverty:* act, action, bill, course, deed, expedient, means, method, procedure, proceeding, resolution, statute, step **4** *a measure of whisky:* allocation, allotment, cut *colloq*,

division, lot, part, piece, portion, quota, rake-off *colloq*, ration, share
♦ *v* appraise *formal*, assess, calculate, compute, determine, estimate, evaluate, fathom, gauge, judge, measure off, measure out, meter, plumb, quantify, rate, read, record, size (up), sound, survey, time, value, weigh
► **measure off** circumscribe *formal*, delimit, demarcate, determine, fix, lay down, limit, mark out, measure (out), pace out
► **measure out** allot, apportion, assign, deal out, dispense, distribute, divide, dole out, hand out, issue, mete out, parcel out, pour out, proportion, share out
► **measure up** come up to scratch *colloq*, come up to standard, do, fit/fill the bill, make the grade, pass muster, shape up *colloq*, suffice *formal*
► **measure up to** come up to, compare with, equal, live up to, make the grade, match, match up to, meet, rival, touch

measured *adj* calculated, careful, considered, deliberate, planned, precise, premeditated, reasoned, regular, slow, steady, studied, unhurried, well-thought-out

measureless *adj* bottomless, boundless, endless, immeasurable, immense, incalculable, inestimable, infinite, innumerable, limitless, unbounded, vast
ｦ measurable

measurement *n* **1** *take a measurement of the floor*: amount, amplitude, area, bulk, capacity, depth, dimension, expanse, extent, height, length, magnitude, mass, proportion(s), quantity, range, size, unit, volume, weight, width **2** *the measurement of his success*: appraisal, appreciation, assessment, calculation, calibration, computation, estimation, evaluation, gauging, judgement, quantification, reading, sizing, survey, weighing

---

Units of measurement include:
SI base units: ampere, candela, kelvin, kilogram, metre, mole, second; *SI derivatives and other measurements:* acre, angstrom, atmosphere, bar, barrel, becquerel, bushel, cable, calorie, centimetre, century, chain, coulomb, cubic centimetre, cubic foot, cubic inch, cubic metre, cubic yard, day, decade, decibel, degree, dyne, erg, farad, fathom, fluid ounce, fresnel, foot, foot-pound, furlong, gallon, gill, gram, hand, hectare, hertz, horsepower, hour, hundredweight, inch, joule, kilometre, knot, league, litre, lumen, micrometre, mile, millennium, millibar, millilitre, minute, month, nautical mile, newton, ohm, ounce, pascal, peak, pint, pound, pound per square inch, radian, rod, siemens, span, square centimetre, square foot, square inch, square kilometre, square metre, square mile, square yard, steradian, stone, therm, ton, tonne, volt, watt, week, yard, year

---

meat *n* **1** *doesn't eat meat*: flesh **2** *get to the meat of the argument*: core, crux, essence, fundamentals, gist, heart, kernel, marrow, nub, nucleus, pith, point, substance

---

Kinds of meat include:
beef, pork, lamb, mutton, ham, bacon, gammon, chicken, turkey, goose, duck, rabbit, hare, venison, pheasant, grouse, partridge,

---

pigeon, quail; offal, liver, heart, tongue, kidney, brains, brawn, pig's knuckle, trotters, oxtail, sweetbread, tripe; steak, minced beef, sausage, rissole, faggot, beefburger, hamburger, black pudding, paté

Cuts of meat include:
shoulder, collar, hand, loin, hock, leg, chop, shin, knuckle, rib, spare-rib, breast, brisket, chine, cutlet, fillet, rump, scrag, silverside, topside, sirloin, flank, escalope, neck, saddle

---

meaty *adj* **1** *a big meaty bloke*: beefy, brawny, burly, fleshy, hearty, heavy, hunky *colloq*, muscular, solid, strapping, sturdy **2** *a meaty problem*: interesting, meaningful, pithy, profound, rich, significant, substantial

mechanic *n* artificer, engineer, machinist, mechanician, operative, operator, repairman, technician

mechanical *adj* **1** *a mechanical device*: automated, automatic, electric, machine-powered, power-driven **2** *a mechanical performance*: automatic, cold, dead, dull, emotionless, habitual, impersonal, instinctive, involuntary, lifeless, machine-like, matter-of-fact, perfunctory, routine, unconscious, unemotional, unfeeling
ｦ **2** conscious

mechanism *n* **1** *the mechanism to open the door*: action, apparatus, appliance, components, contraption, contrivance, device, engine, gadget, gears, guts *colloq*, instrument, machine, machinery, motor, movement, system, tool, workings, works **2** *a mechanism for learning*: agency, channel, functioning, means, medium, method, operation, performance, procedure, process, structure, system, technique, workings

medal *n* award, decoration, gong *slang*, honour, medallion, prize, reward, trophy

meddle *v* butt in, interfere, intervene, intrude, poke/stick your nose in *colloq*, pry, snoop *colloq*, stick/put your oar in *colloq*, tamper

meddlesome *adj* interfering, intruding, intrusive, meddling, mischievous, nosy *colloq*, prying

mediate *v* act as mediator/intermediary/peacemaker, arbitrate, conciliate, intercede, interpose *formal*, intervene, moderate, negotiate, reconcile, referee, resolve, settle, step in, umpire

mediation *n* arbitration, conciliation, good offices, intercession, interposition *formal*, intervention, negotiation, peacemaking, reconciliation

mediator *n* arbiter, arbitrator, conciliator, go-between, interceder, intercessor, intermediary, intervener, middleman, moderator, negotiator, Ombudsman, peacemaker, reconciler, referee, umpire

medical

Medical terms include:
abortion, allergy, amputation, analgesic, antibiotics, antiseptic, bandage, barium meal, biopsy, blood bank, blood count, blood donor, blood group, blood pressure, blood test, caesarean, cardiopulmonary resuscitation (CPR), case history, casualty, cauterization, cervical smear, check-up, childbirth, circulation, circumcision, clinic, complication,

compress, consultant, consultation, contraception, convulsion, cure, diagnosis, dialysis, dislocate, dissection, doctor, donor, dressings, enema, examination, gene, health screening, home visit, hormone replacement therapy (HRT), hospice, hospital, immunization, implantation, incubation, infection, inflammation, injection, injury, inoculation, intensive care, labour, miscarriage, mouth-to-mouth, nurse, ointment, operation, paraplegia, post-mortem, pregnancy, prescription, prognosis, prosthesis, psychosomatic, quarantine, radiotherapy, recovery, rehabilitation, relapse, remission, respiration, resuscitation, scan, side effect, sling, smear test, specimen, splint, sterilization, steroid, surgery, suture, symptom, syndrome, therapy, tourniquet, tranquillizer, transfusion, transplant, trauma, treatment, tumour, ultrasound scanning, vaccination, vaccine, virus, X-ray. See also **therapy**

medicinal *adj* curative, healing, health-giving, medical, remedial, restorative, therapeutic

medicine *n* analeptic *technical*, cure, drug, medicament, medication, panacea, pharmaceutical, prescription, remedy

Types of medicine include:
tablet, capsule, pill, painkiller, lozenge, pastille, gargle, linctus, tonic, laxative, suppository, antacid, ointment, eye drops, ear drops, nasal spray, inhaler, antibiotic, emetic, paregoric. See also **drug**

medieval *adj* **1** *medieval history:* archaic, dark-age, historic, of the Middle Ages **2** *his views about women are positively medieval:* antediluvian, antiquated, antique, archaic, obsolete, old-fashioned, old-world, outmoded, primitive, unenlightened

mediocre *adj* adequate, average, commonplace, fair to middling *colloq*, indifferent, inferior, insignificant, medium, middling, no great shakes *colloq*, not all that it is cracked up to be *colloq*, not much cop *colloq*, not up to much *colloq*, nothing much to write home about *colloq*, ordinary, passable, pedestrian, run-of-the-mill *colloq*, second-rate, so-so *colloq*, tolerable, undistinguished, unexceptional, uninspired
☒ distinctive, exceptional, extraordinary

mediocrity *n* **1** *the mediocrity of his work:* adequacy, averageness, indifference, inferiority, insignificance, ordinariness, passableness, poorness, unexceptionableness, unimportance **2** *these students are all complete mediocrities:* dead loss *colloq*, nobody, no-hoper *colloq*, nonentity, non-starter *colloq*, nothing
☒ **1** distinction, exceptionableness

meditate *v* brood, cogitate *formal*, concentrate, consider, contemplate, deliberate, design, devise, have in mind, intend, mull over, muse, plan, ponder, put on your thinking cap *colloq*, reflect, ruminate, scheme, speculate, study, think (over)

meditation *n* brooding, brown study, cerebration *formal*, cogitation *formal*, concentration, contemplation, deliberation, excogitation *formal*, mulling over, musing,

pondering, reflection, reverie, ruminating, rumination, speculation, study, thought

meditative *adj* cogitative *formal*, contemplative, deliberative, museful, pensive, reflective, ruminant, ruminative, studious, thoughtful

medium *adj* average, fair, intermediate, mean, medial, median, middle, middling, midpoint, midway, standard
♦ *n* **1** *find the medium between two viewpoints:* average, centre, compromise, golden mean, happy medium, intermediate point, mean, median, middle, middle ground, midpoint, mode, norm **2** *a communication medium:* agency, avenue, channel, form, instrument, means, means of expression, mode *formal*, organ, vehicle, way, way of expressing **3** *a suitable medium for life:* ambience, atmosphere, circumstances, conditions, element, environment, habitat, influences, milieu, setting, surroundings **4** *the medium said she was in contact with his mother:* clairvoyant, necromancer, psychic, spiritist, spiritualist

medley *n* assortment, collection, confusion, conglomeration *formal*, farrago, gallimaufry, hodge-podge, hotchpotch, jumble, melange, miscellany, mishmash, mix, mixed bag *colloq*, mixture, omnium-gatherum *colloq*, pastiche, patchwork, potpourri, salmagundi, smorgasbord, variety

meek *adj* compliant *formal*, deferential, docile, forbearing, gentle, humble, long-suffering, lowly, mild, modest, patient, peaceful, quiet, resigned, spineless *colloq*, spiritless, submissive, tame, timid, unassuming, unpretentious, weak, yielding
☒ arrogant, assertive, rebellious

meekness *n* acquiescence *formal*, compliance *formal*, deference, docility, forbearance, gentleness, humbleness, humility, long-suffering, lowliness, mildness, modesty, patience, peacefulness, resignation, self-abasement, self-disparagement, self-effacement, softness, spinelessness *colloq*, spiritlessness, submission, submissiveness, tameness, timidity, unpretentiousness, weakness
☒ arrogance, assertiveness

meet *v* **1** *guess who I met at the supermarket?:* bump into *colloq*, chance on, come across, encounter, happen upon *formal*, join up with, make contact with, run across, run into **2** *we are meeting at 6 o'clock:* assemble, collect, come together, congregate, convene *formal*, convoke *formal*, forgather *formal*, gather, get together, muster, rally, rendezvous **3** *meet the requirements:* answer, come up to, comply with, discharge, equal, execute, fulfil, match, measure up to, perform, satisfy **4** *met a lot of difficulties:* bear, come across, encounter, endure, experience, face, go through, suffer, undergo **5** *meet a challenge:* cope with, deal with, get to grips with, handle, look after, manage, tackle **6** *meet the cost:* discharge, honour, pay (for), settle **7** *where the two lines meet:* abut *formal*, adjoin *formal*, come together, connect, converge, cross, intersect, join, link (up), touch, unite
☒ **2** disperse, scatter **7** diverge, separate

meeting *n* **1** *a meeting with the bank manager:* appointment, assignation, confrontation, contact, date, encounter, engagement, introduction, rendezvous, tryst *formal* **2** *a board meeting:* assembly, gathering, session **3** *the meeting of two rivers:* abutment *formal*, concourse *formal*, confluence, conjunction *formal*, convergence, interface, intersection, junction, (point of) contact, union, venue, watersmeet

megalomania *n* conceitedness, delusions of grandeur, exaggerated sense of power, folie de grandeur, overestimation, self-importance

melancholy *adj* blue *colloq*, dejected, depressed, despondent, disconsolate *formal*, dismal, dispirited, down *colloq*, down in the dumps *colloq*, downcast, downhearted, gloomy, glum, heavy-hearted, in the doldrums *colloq*, low, low-spirited, lugubrious *formal*, miserable, moody, mournful, sad, sorrowful, unhappy, woebegone *formal*, woeful *formal*
🔁 cheerful, elated, joyful
♦ *n* blues *colloq*, dejection, depression, despondency, doldrums *colloq*, dumps *colloq*, gloom, low spirits, misery, pessimism, sadness, sorrow, unhappiness
🔁 cheerfulness, elation, joy

melange *n* assortment, collection, confusion, conglomeration *formal*, farrago, gallimaufry, hodge-podge, hotchpotch, jumble, medley, miscellany, mishmash *colloq*, mix, mixed bag *colloq*, mixture, omnium-gatherum *colloq*, pastiche, patchwork, potpourri, salmagundi, smorgasbord, variety

melee *n* **1** *a melee in the street:* affray, brawl, broil, fight, fracas, fray, free-for-all, ruckus, ruction, rumpus, scrum, scuffle, set-to, stramash *Scot*, tussle **2** *a melee of different things:* chaos, clutter, confusion, disorder, disorganization, jumble, mess, mix-up, muddle, tangle

mellow *adj* **1** *a mellow port:* full-flavoured, juicy, luscious, mature, mild, ripe, soft, sweet, tender **2** *feeling mellow after a few drinks:* affable, amiable, amicable, cheerful, cordial, easy-going, genial, gentle, good-natured, happy, jolly, jovial, kind, kind-hearted, placid, pleasant, relaxed, serene, tranquil **3** *mellow tones of the clarinet:* dulcet, euphonious *formal*, full, harmonious, melodious, rich, rounded, smooth, soft, sweet, tuneful
🔁 **1** unripe **2** cold **3** harsh
♦ *v* improve, mature, perfect, ripen, season, soften, sweeten, temper

melodious *adj* dulcet, euphonious *formal*, harmonious, melodic, musical, silvery, sweet, sweet-sounding, tuneful
🔁 discordant, grating, harsh

melodramatic *adj* exaggerated, extravagant, hammy *colloq*, histrionic, overdone, overdramatic, overemotional, sensational, stagy, theatrical

melody *n* **1** *hum the melody:* air, harmony, music, refrain, rhythm, song, strain, theme, tune **2** *a song with little melody:* euphony *formal*, harmoniousness, harmony, musicality, musicalness, sweetness, tunefulness

melt *v* **1** *the snow had melted overnight:* defrost, deliquesce *formal*, dissolve, fuse, liquefy, thaw, unfreeze **2** *melt someone's heart:* affect, calm, make/become tender, moderate, move, soften, touch
🔁 **1** freeze, solidify **2** harden

▶ **melt away** disappear, disappear into thin air *colloq*, disperse, dissolve, evanesce *formal*, evaporate, fade (away), vanish

member *n* **1** *members of a club:* adherent, associate, comrade, fellow, representative, subscriber **2** *his lower members:* appendage, arm, element, extremity, leg, limb, organ, part

membership *n* **1** *membership of a club:* adherence, affiliation, allegiance, enrolment, fellowship, participation **2** *the membership agreed the change to the rules:* adherents, associates, body, comrades, fellows, fellowship, members, representatives, subscribers

membrane *n* diaphragm, film, hymen, integument *technical*, layer, partition, septum, sheet, skin, tissue, veil, velum

memento *n* keepsake, memorial, record, relic, remembrance, reminder, souvenir, token, trophy, vestige

memoir *n* account, biography, chronicle, essay, journal, life, monograph, narrative, record, register, report

memoirs *n* annals, autobiography, chronicles, confessions, diaries, diary, experiences, journals, life story, memories, recollections, records, reminiscences

memorable *adj* consequential, distinctive, distinguished, extraordinary, historic, important, impressive, momentous, notable, noteworthy, outstanding, remarkable, significant, special, striking, unforgettable, unique
🔁 forgettable, trivial, unimportant

memorandum *n* memo *colloq*, memory-jogger *colloq*, message, note, reminder

memorial *n* cenotaph, mausoleum, memento, monument, plaque, record, remembrance, shrine, souvenir, statue, stone
♦ *adj* celebratory, commemorative, monumental

memorize *v* commit to memory, learn, learn by heart, learn by rote, remember
🔁 forget

memory *n* **1** *a good memory:* powers of recall, recall, recollection, remembrance, reminiscence, retention **2** *in memory of the dead:* commemoration, honour, observance, recognition, remembrance, tribute
🔁 **1** forgetfulness

menace *n* **1** *a voice full of menace:* browbeating, bullying, coercion, intimidation, ominousness, pressure, terrorism, terrorizing, threat, threatening behaviour, tyrannization, warning **2** *a menace to society:* danger, hazard, jeopardy, peril, risk, threat **3** *that kid's a menace:* annoyance, bother, nuisance, pain *colloq*, pest, thorn in your side/flesh *colloq*, troublemaker
♦ *v* alarm, appal, browbeat, bully, coerce, daunt, dismay, frighten, intimidate, loom, lour, press, pressure, pressurize, scare, terrify, terrorize, threaten

menacing *adj* alarming, Damoclean, dangerous, frightening, grim, impending *formal*, intimidating, intimidatory, looming, louring, minacious *formal*, minatory *formal*, ominous, portentous *formal*, sinister, threatening, warning

mend *v* **1** *mend a pair of shoes:* cobble, cure, darn, fix, heal, make whole, patch (up), put back

together, refit, renew, renovate, repair, restore, sew, stick **2** *she's slowly mending after the accident:* get better, improve, recover, recuperate **3** *try to mend relations with the president:* ameliorate *formal*, amend, correct, emend *formal*, improve, put in order, put right, rectify, reform, remedy, revise
E **1** break **2** deteriorate **3** destroy

mendacious *adj* deceitful, deceptive, dishonest, duplicitous *formal*, fallacious *formal*, false, fictitious, fraudulent, insincere, lying, perfidious *formal*, perjured, untrue, untruthful
E honest, truthful, veracious *formal*

mendacity *n* deceit, deceitfulness, dishonesty, distortion, duplicity *formal*, falsehood, falsification, fraudulence, insincerity, inveracity *formal*, lie, lying, misrepresentation, perfidy *formal*, perjury, untruth, untruthfulness
E honesty, truthfulness, veracity *formal*

mendicant *adj* begging, cadging *colloq*, petitionary *formal*, scrounging, supplicant *formal*
♦ *n* beachcomber, beggar, bum *colloq*, cadger *colloq*, down-and-out, hobo *US*, moocher *US colloq*, pauper, scrounger *colloq*, supplicant, tramp, vagabond, vagrant

menial *adj* base, boring, degrading, demeaning, dull, humble, humdrum, ignominious, low, lowly, routine, servile, slavish, subservient, unskilled
♦ *n* attendant, dogsbody *colloq*, domestic, drudge, labourer, minion, servant, skivvy *colloq*, slave, underling

menstruation *n* catamenia *technical*, courses, flow, menorrhoea, menses, menstrual cycle, monthlies *colloq*, monthly flow, period, the curse *colloq*, the usual *colloq*

mensuration *n* assessment, calculation, calibration, computation, estimation, evaluation, measurement, measuring, metage *technical*, survey, surveying, valuation

mental *adj* **1** *mental stimulation:* abstract, cerebral *formal*, cognitive *formal*, conceptual, intellectual, rational, theoretical, unconscious **2** *he must be mental:* barmy *colloq*, bonkers *colloq*, crazy, deranged, disturbed, having a screw loose *colloq*, insane, loony *colloq*, lunatic, mad, (mentally) unbalanced *colloq*, nuts *colloq*, off your head *colloq*, off your trolley *colloq*, psychotic
E **1** physical **2** sane

mentality *n* **1** *our mentality towards the old:* character, disposition, frame of mind, make-up, (mental) attitude, mind, mindset, outlook, personality, psychology, way of thinking **2** *a person of superior mentality:* brains *colloq*, comprehension, faculty, grey matter *colloq*, intellect, intelligence, little grey cells *colloq*, mind, rationality, understanding

mentally *adv* emotionally, in the mind, intellectually, inwardly, psychologically, subjectively, temperamentally

mention *v* **1** *he never mentioned their earlier meeting:* acknowledge, broach, cite, communicate, declare, disclose, divulge, impart, introduce, make known, name, quote, refer to, report, reveal, say, speak of, state **2** *I promised never to mention the subject again:* allude to, bring up, cite, hint at, intimate, point out, refer to, speak about briefly, touch on
♦ *n* acknowledgement, allusion, announcement,

citation, indication, notification, observation, recognition, reference, remark, statement, tribute

mentor *n* adviser, coach, counsellor, guide, guru, instructor, pedagogue, swami, teacher, therapist, tutor

menu *n* bill of fare, card, carte du jour, list, tariff

mercantile *adj* commercial, marketable, merchantable, saleable, trade, trading

mercenary *adj* **1** *a mercenary attitude to marriage:* acquisitive, avaricious *formal*, covetous, grasping, greedy, mammonistic, materialistic, money-grubbing *colloq*, money-orientated, on the make *colloq*, sordid **2** *a mercenary soldier:* hired, paid, venal
♦ *n* condottiere, free companion, freelance, galloglass, hired soldier, hireling, landsknecht, lansquenet, merc *colloq*, soldier of fortune

merchandise *n* cargo, commodities, freight, goods, produce, products, shipment, stock, vendibles *formal*, wares
♦ *v* **1** *we merchandise all types of timber:* buy and sell, carry, deal in, distribute, market, peddle, retail, sell, supply, trade, traffic in, vend *formal* **2** *a campaign to merchandise the new product range:* advertise, market, plug *colloq*, promote, publicize, push *colloq*, sell

merchant *n* broker, dealer, distributor, retailer, sales executive, salesman, salesperson, saleswoman, seller, shopkeeper, trader, trafficker, vendor, wholesaler

merciful *adj* compassionate, forbearing, forgiving, generous, gracious, humane, humanitarian, kind, lenient, liberal, mild, pitying, soft-hearted, sparing, sympathetic, tender-hearted, tolerant
E hard-hearted, merciless

merciless *adj* barbarous, callous, cruel, hard, hard-hearted, harsh, heartless, implacable, inexorable, inhuman, inhumane, intolerant, pitiless, relentless, remorseless, rigid, ruthless, severe, stern, unfeeling, unforgiving, unmerciful, unpitying, unsparing, unsympathetic
E compassionate, merciful

mercurial *adj* active, capricious *formal*, changeable, erratic, fickle, flighty, impetuous, impulsive, inconstant, irrepressible, light-hearted, lively, mobile, spirited, sprightly, temperamental, unpredictable, unstable, variable, volatile
E saturnine

mercy *n* **1** *showed no mercy to the prisoners:* clemency *formal*, compassion, forbearance, forgiveness, generosity, grace, humaneness, humanitarianism, kindness, leniency, mildness, pity, sympathy, tender-heartedness, tenderness **2** *it's a mercy they came to no harm:* blessing, boon, favour, godsend, good luck, relief, stroke of good luck
E **1** cruelty, harshness

mere *adj* absolute, bare, common, complete, no more than, paltry, petty, plain, pure, pure and simple, sheer, simple, stark, unadulterated, utter

merely *adv* barely, hardly, just, nothing but, only, purely, scarcely, simply

merge *v* amalgamate, be assimilated in, be engulfed, be swallowed up in, become lost in, blend, coalesce, combine, come/bring together, consolidate, converge, fuse, incorporate, intermix, join, join forces, meet, meld, melt into, mingle, mix, run into, team up, unite

merger *n* alliance, amalgamation, assimilation, blend, coalition, combination, confederation, consolidation, convergence, fusion, incorporation, union

merit *n* **1** *a film with little artistic merit:* claim, credit, excellence, good, goodness, high quality, justification, quality, talent, value, virtue, worth, worthiness **2** *the merits of studying abroad:* advantage, asset, plus *colloq*, recompense, reward, strong point, virtue
🔁 **1** worthlessness **2** drawback, fault, minus *colloq*
♦ *v* be entitled to, be worth, be worthy of, deserve, earn, have a right to, justify, warrant

merited *adj* appropriate, condign *formal*, deserved, due, earned, entitled, fitting, just, justified, rightful, warranted, worthy
🔁 inappropriate, unjustified

meritorious *adj* admirable, commendable, creditable, deserving, estimable, excellent, exemplary, good, honourable, laudable *formal*, praiseworthy, right, righteous, virtuous, worthy
🔁 unworthy

merriment *n* amusement, blitheness *formal*, buoyancy, carefreeness, cheerfulness, conviviality, festivity, frolic, fun, gaiety, high spirits, hilarity, jocundity *formal*, jollity, joviality, joyfulness, laughter, liveliness, mirth *formal*, mirthfulness *formal*, revelry
🔁 gloom, seriousness

merry *adj* **1** *a merry atmosphere:* amusing, blithe *formal*, carefree, cheerful, cheery, convivial, festive, glad, happy, high-spirited, in good spirits, jolly, jovial, joyful, light-hearted, mirthful *formal* **2** *got a bit merry at the pub:* happy, slightly drunk, squiffy *colloq*, tiddly, tipsy
🔁 **1** gloomy, melancholy **2** sober

merry-go-round *n* carousel, joy-wheel, roundabout, whirligig

merrymaking *n* carousal, carousing, celebration, conviviality, festivity, fun, gaiety, jollification, merriment, party, rejoicings, revel, revelry

mesh *n* entanglement, lattice, latticework, net, netting, network, snare, tangle, tracery, trap, trellis, web
♦ *v* combine, connect, co-ordinate, dovetail, engage, fit together, go/come together, harmonize, interlock, match

mesmerize *v* benumb, captivate, enthral, entrance, fascinate, grip, hold spellbound, hypnotize, magnetize, spellbind, stupefy, transfix

mess *n* **1** *your room's in a complete mess:* chaos, clutter, confusion, disarray, disorder, disorganization, dog's breakfast *colloq*, dog's dinner *colloq*, dump *colloq*, hole *colloq*, jumble, mix-up, muddle, pig's breakfast *colloq*, shambles *colloq*, squalor, tip *colloq*, turmoil, untidiness **2** *got in a mess with paying her tax:* difficulty, dilemma, fix *colloq*, hiccup *colloq*, hole *colloq*, hot/deep water *colloq*, jam *colloq*, pickle *colloq*, plight,

predicament, pretty pass *colloq*, quandary, stew *colloq*, (tight) spot *colloq*, trouble **3** *made a complete mess of the job:* balls-up *slang*, botch, bungle, cock-up *slang*, failure, farce *colloq*, hash *colloq*, muddle, shambles *colloq*
🔁 **1** order, tidiness
▶ **mess about/around** faff about/around *colloq*, fiddle around, fool around, frig about/around *slang*, fuck about/around *taboo slang*, muck about *colloq*, piss about/around *taboo slang*, play, play about, play around, potter about, waste time
▶ **mess about/around with 1** *someone's been messing about with my papers:* fool about/around with, interfere with, meddle with, play (about/around) with, tamper with **2** *don't let anyone mess about with you:* annoy, bother, fool with, muck about with *colloq*
▶ **mess up 1** *who's messed up my things?:* clutter up, confuse, dirty, disarrange, dishevel, disrupt, foul, jumble, muddle, tangle, throw into disorder, untidy **2** *he messed up on his first attempt:* bodge *colloq*, botch, bungle, cock up *slang*, fluff *colloq*, foul up *colloq*, louse up *slang*, make a hash of *colloq*, make a mess of, muck up *colloq*, muff *colloq*, ruin, screw up *slang*, spoil

message *n* **1** *sent a message that she'd be late:* bulletin, cable, communication, communiqué, dispatch, epistle *formal*, fax, letter, memo *colloq*, memorandum, missive *formal*, news, note, notice, piece of information, report, tidings *formal*, word **2** *the novel's message is clear:* drift, essence, gist, idea, implication, meaning, moral, point, purport *formal*, sense, significance, theme, thrust

messenger *n* agent, ambassador, bearer, carrier, courier, emissary *formal*, envoy, errand-boy, errand-girl, go-between, harbinger, herald, Hermes, runner

messy *adj* chaotic, cluttered, confused, dirty, dishevelled, disordered, disorganized, grubby, in disarray, littered, muddled, shambolic *colloq*, slobbish *colloq*, sloppy, slovenly, unkempt, untidy
🔁 neat, ordered, tidy

metallic *adj* **1** *a metallic surface:* copper, gleaming, gold, iron, lead, metal, nickel, polished, shiny, silver, steel, tin **2** *a metallic finish:* gleaming, glossy, polished, reflective, shiny, sparkling **3** *metallic sounds:* dissonant, grating, harsh, jangling, jarring, rough, tinny, unpleasant

metamorphose *v* alter, change, convert, modify, mutate *technical*, remake, remodel, reshape, transfigure *formal*, transform, translate, transmogrify *colloq*, transmute *formal*, transubstantiate

metamorphosis *n* alteration, change, change-over, conversion, modification, mutation *technical*, rebirth, regeneration, transfiguration, transformation, transmogrification *colloq*, transmutation *formal*

metaphor *n* allegory, analogy, figure of speech, image, picture, representation, symbol, trope *formal*

metaphorical *adj* allegorical, analogical, emblematic, figurative, representational, symbolic, visual
🔁 literal

metaphysical *adj* abstract, abstruse *formal*, basic, deep, esoteric *formal*, essential, eternal, fundamental, high-flown, ideal, immaterial, impalpable *formal*, incorporeal *formal*, insubstantial, intangible, intellectual, philosophical, profound, recondite *formal*, speculative, spiritual, subjective, supernatural, theoretical, transcendental, universal, unreal, unsubstantial

mete
▶ **mete out** administer, allot, apportion, assign, deal out, dispense, distribute, divide out, dole out, hand out, measure out, portion, ration out, share out

meteor *n* aerolite, aerolith, bolide, comet, fireball, meteorite, meteoroid, shooting star

meteoric *adj* brief, brilliant, dazzling, fast, flashing, instantaneous, lightning, momentary, overnight, quick, rapid, spectacular, speedy, sudden, swift, transient

meteorologist *n* climatologist, met man, weather forecaster, weather prophet, weathergirl, weatherlady, weatherman

method *n* **1** *teaching methods*: approach, arrangement, course, fashion, form, manner, means, mode *formal*, modus operandi, plan, practice, procedure, process, programme, route, rule, scheme, style, system, technique, way **2** *his approach lacks method*: arrangement, design, form, order, orderliness, organization, pattern, plan, planning, regularity, routine, structure, system

methodical *adj* businesslike, deliberate, disciplined, efficient, logical, meticulous, neat, ordered, orderly, organized, painstaking, planned, precise, regular, scrupulous, structured, systematic, tidy, well-ordered
⊠ chaotic, confused, irregular

meticulous *adj* accurate, careful, conscientious, detailed, exact, fastidious, fussy, painstaking, particular, precise, punctilious, rigorous, scrupulous, strict, thorough
⊠ careless, slapdash

metropolis *n* capital, city, industrial/cultural centre, large city, main city, megalopolis, municipality

mettle *n* **1** *a man of fine mettle*: calibre, character, disposition, make-up, nature, personal qualities, personality, temperament **2** *showed their mettle on the battlefield*: backbone *colloq*, boldness, bravery, courage, daring, determination, endurance, fearlessness, fortitude, gallantry, guts *colloq*, indomitability, intrepidity, nerve, pluck, resolve, spirit, spunk *colloq*, valour, vigour

mew *v* caterwaul, meow, mewl, miaow, whine

mewl *v* blubber, cry, grizzle, snivel, whimper, whine, whinge

miasma *n* effluvium *formal*, fetor *formal*, mephitis *formal*, odour, pollution, reek, smell, stench, stink

microbe *n* bacillus, bacterium, bug *colloq*, germ, micro-organism, pathogen, virus

microscopic *adj* extremely small, imperceptible, indiscernible, infinitesimal, minuscule, minute, negligible, tiny
⊠ enormous, huge

midday *n* lunchtime, noon, noonday *formal*, noontide *formal*, twelve, twelve noon, twelve o'clock

middle *adj* central, equidistant, halfway, intermediate, intervening, mean, medial, median, medium, mid, midway
♦ *n* **1** *in the middle of the room*: bull's eye *colloq*, centre, core, heart, inside, mean, median, midpoint, midst **2** *reached the middle of their journey*: halfway point, midpoint
⊠ **1** border, edge, extreme **2** beginning, end, extreme

middle-class *adj* bourgeois, conventional, gentrified, professional, suburban, white-colour

middleman *n* broker, distributor, entrepreneur, fixer, go-between, intermediary, negotiator, retailer

middling *adj* adequate, average, fair, indifferent, mediocre, medium, moderate, modest, OK *colloq*, ordinary, passable, run-of-the-mill, so-so *colloq*, tolerable, unexceptional, unremarkable

midget *n* dwarf, gnome, homunculus, Lilliputian, manikin, person of restricted growth, pygmy, Tom Thumb
⊠ giant
♦ *adj* baby, diminutive, dwarf, itsy-bitsy *colloq*, Lilliputian, little, miniature, minute, pocket, pocket-sized, pygmy, small, teeny *colloq*, teeny-weeny *colloq*, tiny, toy
⊠ giant

midst *n* bosom, centre, core, depths, heart, hub, interior, middle, midpoint, nucleus, thick

midway *adv* at the midpoint, betwixt and between, equidistant between, halfway, in the centre, in the middle

miffed *adj* aggrieved, annoyed, chagrined, disgruntled, displeased, hurt, in a huff *colloq*, irked, irritated, narked *colloq*, nettled, offended, peeved *colloq*, piqued, put out, resentful, upset, vexed
⊠ chuffed *colloq*, delighted, pleased

might *n* ability, capability, capacity, clout *colloq*, efficacy *formal*, energy, force, forcefulness, heftiness, muscle *colloq*, muscularity, potency, power, powerfulness, prowess, puissance *formal*, stamina, strength, sway, valour, vigour

mightily *adv* decidedly, energetically, exceedingly, extremely, forcefully, greatly, highly, hugely, intensely, lustily, manfully, much, powerfully, strenuously, strongly, very, very much, vigorously

mighty *adj* **1** *a mighty warrior*: dominant, doughty, forceful, grand, hardy, hefty, indomitable, influential, lusty, manful, muscular, potent, powerful, robust, stalwart, stout, strapping, strong, tough, vigorous **2** *a mighty oak tree*: bulky, colossal, enormous, gigantic, great, huge, immense, large, massive, monumental, prodigious, stupendous, titanic, towering, tremendous, vast
⊠ **1** frail, weak **2** small

migrant *n* drifter, emigrant, globetrotter, Gypsy, immigrant, itinerant, nomad, rover, tinker, transient, traveller, vagrant, wanderer
♦ *adj* drifting, globetrotting, Gypsy, immigrant, itinerant, migratory, nomadic, peripatetic,

roving, shifting, transient, travelling, vagrant, wandering

migrate *v* drift, emigrate, hike, journey, move, relocate, resettle, roam, rove, travel, trek, voyage, wander

migration *n* diaspora *technical*, emigration, journey, movement, relocation, roving, shift, transhumance *formal*, travel, trek, voyage, wandering

migratory *adj* drifting, globetrotting, Gypsy, immigrant, itinerant, migrant, nomadic, peripatetic, roving, shifting, transient, travelling, vagrant, wandering

mild *adj* 1 *mild manners:* amiable, calm, compassionate, easy-going, forbearing, gentle, good-natured, humane, kind, lenient, meek, merciful, peaceable, placid, sensitive, soft, soft-hearted, sympathetic, tender, tender-hearted, warm, warm-hearted 2 *mild weather:* balmy, calm, clement, fair, moderate, pleasant, temperate, warm 3 *mild food:* bland, insipid, mellow, smooth, soothing, subtle, tasteless
Ⓕ 1 aggressive, fierce, harsh 2 cold, stormy 3 sharp, spicy, strong

mildewy *adj* fetid *formal*, fusty, mucedinous *formal*, mucid *formal*, musty, rotten

mildness *n* 1 *the mildness of his tone:* calmness, compassion, docility, forbearance, gentleness, indulgence, kindness, leniency, lenity, meekness, mercy, passivity, placidity, softness, sympathy, tenderness, tranquillity, warmth 2 *the mildness of the climate:* calmness, clemency, moderation, temperateness, warmth 3 *the mildness of the flavourings:* blandness, insipidness, mellowness, smoothness, tastelessness
Ⓕ 1 aggressiveness, harshness, violence 2 storminess 3 sharpness

milieu *n* arena, background, element, environment, locale, location, medium, scene, setting, sphere, surroundings

militant *adj* activist, aggressive, assertive, belligerent, combative, embattled, fighting, pugnacious *formal*, vigorous, warring
Ⓕ pacifist, peaceful
♦ *n* activist, aggressor, belligerent, combatant, fighter, partisan, struggler

military *adj* armed, army, disciplined, martial, service, soldierly, warlike
♦ *n* air force, armed forces, army, forces, militia, navy, services, soldiers

Military terms include:
about turn, absent without leave (AWOL), action stations, action, adjutant, aide-de-camp (ADC), air cover, air-drop, Airborne Warning and Control System (AWACS), allies, ambush, arm, armed forces, armistice, army, arsenal, artillery, assault course, atomic warfare, attack, attention, barracks, base, battle fatigue, battle, beachhead, billet, bivouac, blockade, bomb, bombardment, brevet, bridgehead, briefing, brigade, bugle call, call up, camouflage, camp, campaign, canteen, carpet-bombing, cease-fire, charge, citation, colours, combat, command, commission, company, conquest, conscript, conscription, corps, counter-attack, court-martial, crossfire, debriefing, decamp, decoration, defeat,

defence, demilitarize, demob *colloq*, demotion, depot, desertion, detachment, detail, disarmament, discharge, dispatches, division, draft, drill, duty, encampment, enemy, enlist, ensign, epaulette, evacuation, excursion, expedition, fall out, fatigues, firing line, first post, flank, fleet, flight, flotilla, foe, foray, forced march, friendly fire, front line, fusillade, garrison, guard, incursion, infantry, insignia, inspection, installation, insubordination, intelligence, invasion, kitbag, landing, last post, latrine, leave, left wheel, liaison, lines, logistics, manoeuvres, march, marching orders, march past, married quarters, martinet, minefield, mission, mobilize, munitions, muster, mutiny, national service, navy, Navy, Army and Air Force Institutes (NAAFI), nuclear warfare, observation post, offensive, operational command, operational fleet, operations, orders, ordnance, outpost, padre, parade, parade ground, parley, parole, patrol, pincer movement, platoon, posting, prisoner of war (POW), quartermaster, quarters, quick march, radar, range, rank, ration, rearguard, recce *colloq*, recruit, regiment, reinforcements, requisition, retreat, reveille, rifle range, roll-call, rout, route march, salute, sentry, shell, shell-shock, signal, skirmish, slow march, sniper, sortie, squad, squadron, square-bashing *slang*, standard, stores, strategy, supplies, surrender, tactics, tank, target, task-force, tattoo, the front, training, trench, trench warfare, troop, truce, unit, vanguard, victory, wing. See also **rank, sailor, soldier**

militate
▶ **militate against** act/tell against, be a decisive factor against, be detrimental to, be disadvantageous to, be harmful to, contend, counter, counteract, damage, discourage, go/count against, hurt, oppose, prejudice, resist, weigh against
▶ **militate for** advance, aid, back, further, help, promote, speak for

militia *n* minutemen, National Guard, reserve, reservists, Territorial Army, yeomanry

milk *v* 1 *milk a cow:* bleed, drain, draw (off), express, extract, press, pump, siphon, squeeze, tap, wring 2 *milk the benefit system:* bleed *colloq*, exploit, impose on, manipulate, oppress, pump, rip off *colloq*, squeeze, take advantage of, use, wring

milky *adj* chalky, clouded, cloudy, milk-white, opaque, white

mill *n* 1 *steel mill:* factory, foundry, plant, processing plant, shop, works, workshop 2 *pepper mill:* crusher, grinder, quern, roller
♦ *v* comminute *formal*, crunch, crush, grate, grind, pound, powder, press, pulverize, roll
▶ **mill around** crowd around, move about, press around, stream, swarm, throng

millstone *n* 1 *the grain is crushed between two millstones:* grindstone, quernstone 2 *a millstone around her neck:* affliction, burden, cross to bear *colloq*, duty, encumbrance, load, obligation, onus, trouble, weight

mime *n* charade, dumb show, gesture, mimicry, mummery, pantomime

mimic ♦ *v* act out, gesture, imitate, impersonate, mimic, represent, simulate

mimic *v* ape, caricature, copy, echo, emulate *formal*, imitate, impersonate, look like, mirror, parody, parrot, resemble, send up *colloq*, simulate, take off *colloq*
♦ *n* caricaturist, copy, copycat *colloq*, copyist, imitator, impersonator, impressionist, mimicker, parrot

mimicry *n* aping, burlesque, caricature, copying, imitating, imitation, impersonation, impression, parody, take-off *colloq*

mince *v* 1 *mince the onion finely:* chop, crumble, cut, cut into very small pieces, dice, grind, hash 2 *not mince your words:* diminish, hold back, moderate, play down, soften, spare, speak indirectly, suppress, tone down, weaken 3 *minced into the room:* attitudinize, ponce, pose, posture, simper, strike a pose, walk affectedly, walk in an effeminate/a dainty way

mincing *adj* affected, coxcombic(al), dainty, effeminate, foppish, la-di-da *colloq*, minikin, nice, niminy-piminy, poncy *colloq*, precious, pretentious, sissy *colloq*

mind *n* 1 *turned her mind to the job in hand:* application, attention, comprehension, concentration, grey matter *colloq*, intellect, intelligence, judgement, little grey cells *colloq*, mentality, powers of reasoning, psyche *technical*, ratiocination *formal*, reason, sense, subconscious, thinking, thoughts, understanding, wits 2 *can't call him to mind:* memory, recall, recollection, remembrance, retention 3 *changed his mind:* attitude, belief, feeling, judgement, opinion, outlook, point of view, sentiment, view, viewpoint, way of thinking 4 *had a mind to refuse:* desire, disposition, fancy, inclination, intention, notion, tendency, urge, will, wish 5 *one of the greatest minds of the 20th century:* brain *colloq*, brainbox *colloq*, egghead *colloq*, expert, genius, intellect, intellectual, mastermind, scholar, thinker
♦ *v* 1 *do you mind if I open the window?:* be annoyed by, be bothered by, be offended by, care about, disapprove, dislike, object (to), resent, take offence (at) 2 *mind the step:* be careful, comply with, concentrate on, follow, heed, listen to, mark, note, obey, observe, pay attention, pay heed to, regard, respect, watch 3 *mind that you've got all your notes with you:* ensure, make certain, make sure, not forget, note, remember, take care 4 *could you mind the shop for an hour?:* attend to, guard, have charge of, keep an eye on *colloq*, look after, take care of, watch over
▶ **mind out** be careful, be on your guard, beware, keep your eyes open, look out, pay attention, take care, watch, watch out

mindful *adj* alert, alive (to), attentive, aware, careful, chary, cognizant *formal*, conscious, heedful, paying attention to, sensible *formal*, wary, watchful
🠪 heedless, inattentive

mindless *adj* 1 *mindless chatter:* bird-brained *colloq*, dopey *colloq*, dull, dumb *colloq*, foolish, gratuitous, illogical, irrational, negligent, senseless, stupid, thick *colloq*, thoughtless, unintelligent, witless 2 *mindless repetition:* automatic, instinctive, involuntary, mechanical, routine, tedious
🠪 1 intelligent, thoughtful

mine *n* 1 *a coal mine:* coalfield, colliery, deposit, excavation, lode, pit, quarry, seam, vein 2 *a mine of information:* fund, hoard, repository, reserve, reservoir, source, stock, store, storehouse, supply, treasury, wealth 3 *checked the road for mines:* bomb, depth charge, explosive, land mine
♦ *v* dig for, dig up, excavate, extract, quarry, tunnel, undermine, unearth

miner *n* coalminer, collier, pitman

mineral

Minerals include:
alabaster, albite, anhydrite, asbestos, aventurine, azurite, bentonite, blacklead, bloodstone, blue john, borax, cairngorm, calamine, calcite, calcspar, cassiterite, chalcedony, chlorite, chrysoberyl, cinnabar, corundum, dolomite, emery, feldspar, fluorite, fluorspar, fool's gold, French chalk, galena, graphite, gypsum, haematite, halite, haüyne, hornblende, hyacinth, idocrase, jacinth, jargoon, jet, kandite, kaolinite, lapis lazuli, lazurite, magnetite, malachite, meerschaum, mica, microcline, montmorillonite, olivine, orthoclase, peridot, plumbago, pyrites, quartz, rock salt, rutile, saltpetre, sanidine, silica, smithsonite, sodalite, spar, sphalerite, spinel, talc, uralite, uranite, vesuvianite, wurtzite, zircon

mingle *v* 1 *the noises of the market mingled with the singing from the church:* amalgamate, blend, coalesce, combine, compound, fuse, intermingle, intermix, join, merge, mix, unite 2 *mingled with her guests:* associate, circulate, commingle *formal*, hobnob *colloq*, rub shoulders *colloq*, socialize

miniature *adj* baby, diminutive, dwarf, little, midget, mini *colloq*, minute, pint-size(d) *colloq*, pocket-sized, reduced, scaled-down, small, small-scale, tiny, toy, wee *Scot*
🠪 giant

minimal *adj* least, littlest, minimum, minute, negligible, nominal, slightest, smallest, token

minimize *v* 1 *attempts to minimize costs:* curtail, cut, decrease, diminish, reduce, shrink, slash *colloq* 2 *accused the government of minimizing the risks to consumers:* belittle, decry *formal*, deprecate, discount, disparage *formal*, laugh off, make light of, make little of, play down, soft-pedal *colloq*, trivialize, underestimate, underrate
🠪 1 maximize 2 emphasize, play up

minimum *n* bottom, least, lowest, lowest number, lowest point, nadir *formal*, slightest, smallest quantity
🠪 maximum
♦ *adj* least, littlest, lowest, minimal, slightest, smallest, tiniest
🠪 maximum

minion *n* 1 *the president blamed one of his minions for the mistake:* attendant, drudge, flunkey, follower, hireling, lackey, menial, servant, underling 2 *the star arrived surrounded by her minions:* bootlicker *colloq*, darling, dependant, favourite, fawner, hanger-on, leech, parasite, sycophant, yes-man *colloq*

minister *n* 1 *a government minister:* administrator, agent, aide, ambassador, cabinet minister, consul, delegate, department secretary, dignitary, diplomat, emissary, envoy, executive, legate, office-holder, official, politician,

representative **2** *a Methodist minister:* chaplain, churchman, clergyman, cleric, curate, deacon, dean, ecclesiastic *formal,* elder, padre, parson, pastor, preacher, priest, rector, verger, vicar
♦ *v* accommodate, administer, attend, cater to, look after, nurse, serve, take care of, tend, wait on

ministration *n* aid, assistance, backing, care, favour, help, patronage, relief, service, succour *formal,* supervision, support

ministry *n* **1** *the Ministry of Defence:* administration, bureau, cabinet, department, government, office **2** *go into the ministry:* holy orders, the church, the priesthood

minor *adj* inconsiderable, inferior, insignificant, junior, lesser, light, little known, negligible, petty, secondary, second-class, slight, small, smaller, subordinate, subsidiary, trifling, trivial, unclassified, unimportant, unknown, younger
◻ important, major, significant

minstrel *n* bard, joculator, jongleur, musician, rhymer, singer, troubadour

mint *v* **1** *mint coins:* cast, coin, construct, devise, fashion, forge, make, manufacture, produce, punch, stamp, strike **2** *mint a new word:* coin, concoct, fabricate, fake, falsify, forge, hatch, invent, make up, trump up
♦ *adj* as new, brand-new, excellent, first-class, fresh, immaculate, new, perfect, unblemished, undamaged, unused
♦ *n* bomb *colloq,* bundle *colloq,* fortune, heap *colloq,* million *colloq,* packet *colloq,* pile *colloq,* riches, stack *colloq,* wealth

minuscule *adj* diminutive, fine, infinitesimal, itsy-bitsy *colloq,* Lilliputian, little, microscopic, miniature, minute, teeny *colloq,* teeny-weeny *colloq,* tiny, very small
◻ gigantic, huge

minute[1] *n* **1** *ten minutes:* flash, instant, jiffy *colloq,* moment, second, short (length of) time, tick *colloq* **2** *the minute something happens:* as soon as, directly, immediately, no sooner, the instant, the moment, the point

minute[2] *adj* **1** *minute particles of gold:* diminutive, inconsiderable, infinitesimal, insignificant, Lilliputian, microscopic, miniature, minuscule, negligible, slight, tiny, trifling, trivial, very small **2** *described in minute detail:* accurate, close, critical, detailed, exact, exhaustive, meticulous, painstaking, precise, punctilious, strict
◻ **1** gigantic, huge **2** cursory, superficial

minutely *adv* closely, critically, exactly, exhaustively, in detail, meticulously, painstakingly, precisely, scrupulously, systematically, with a fine-tooth comb *colloq*

minutes *n* details, memorandum, notes, proceedings, record(s), tapes, transactions, transcript

minutiae *n* complexities, details, fine details, finer points, intricacies, niceties, particulars, small print *colloq,* subtleties, trifles, trivialities

miracle *n* marvel, phenomenon, prodigy, womder

miraculous *adj* **1** *a miraculous recovery:* amazing, astonishing, astounding, extraordinary, incredible, marvellous, phenomenal, remarkable, unbelievable, wonderful **2** *miraculous events:* extraordinary, inexplicable, phenomenal,

remarkable, superhuman, supernatural, unaccountable, unbelievable
◻ **1** natural, normal

mirage *n* fantasy, hallucination, illusion, optical illusion, phantasm, phantasmagoria

mire *n* **1** *sucked into the mire:* bog, fen, glaur *Scot,* marsh, marshland, morass, quag, quagmire, slough, swamp **2** *the mire in the farmyard:* dirt, muck, mud, ooze, slime **3** *stuck in the mire of unemployment:* difficulties, fix *colloq,* hole *colloq,* jam *colloq,* mess, pickle *colloq,* spot *colloq,* stew *colloq,* trouble
♦ *v* bog down, deluge, overwhelm, sink

mirror *n* **1** *the bathroom mirror:* glass, looking-glass, reflector **2** *her twin is a mirror of herself:* clone, copy, dead ringer *colloq,* double, exact likeness, image, likeness, reflection, spitting image *colloq,* twin
♦ *v* ape, copy, depict, echo, emulate *formal,* follow, imitate, mimic, parrot, reflect, represent, show

mirth *n* amusement, blitheness *formal,* buoyancy, cheerfulness, enjoyment, frolics, fun, gaiety, glee, high spirits, hilarity, jocularity, jollity, laughter, light-heartedness, merriment, pleasure, revelry
◻ gloom, melancholy

mirthful *adj* amused, amusing, blithe *formal,* buoyant, cheerful, cheery, festive, frolicsome, funny, gay, glad, gladsome, happy, hilarious, jocund *formal,* jolly, jovial, laughable, laughing, light-hearted, light-spirited, merry, playful, pleasurable, sportive, uproarious, vivacious
◻ gloomy, glum, melancholy, mirthless

misadventure *n* accident, bad luck, calamity, cataclysm, catastrophe, debacle, disaster, failure, hard luck, ill fortune, ill luck, mischance, misfortune, mishap, reverse, setback, tragedy

misanthropic *adj* antisocial, egoistic, inhumane, malevolent, surly, unfriendly, unsociable, unsympathetic
◻ philanthropic

misanthropy *n* antisociality, egoism, inhumanity, malevolence, unsociableness
◻ philanthropy

misapply *v* abuse, exploit, misappropriate, misemploy, misuse, pervert, use unwisely/unsuitably

misapprehend *v* get a false impression, get hold of the wrong end of the stick *colloq,* get the wrong idea, miscomprehend, misconceive, misconstrue, misinterpret, misread, mistake, misunderstand
◻ apprehend

misapprehension *n* delusion, error, fallacy, false impression, misconception, misinterpretation, misreading, mistake, misunderstanding, wrong idea

misappropriate *v* abuse, defalcate *formal,* embezzle, filch *colloq,* have your fingers/hand in the till *colloq,* misapply, misspend, misuse, nab *colloq,* nick *colloq,* peculate *formal,* pervert, pilfer, pinch *colloq,* pocket, rob, steal, swindle, thieve

misappropriation *n* defalcation *formal,* embezzlement, misapplication, misuse, peculation *formal*, pilfering, pocketing, robbing, stealing, theft

misbegotten *adj* **1** *their misbegotten gains:* dishonest, disreputable, ill-gotten, illicit, purloined *formal*, shady, stolen, unlawful **2** *a misbegotten scheme:* abortive, hare-brained *colloq*, ill-advised, ill-conceived, poorly thought-out **3** *his misbegotten son:* bastard, born out of wedlock, illegitimate, natural

misbehave *v* act up *colloq*, be beyond the pale, be naughty, be rude, behave unacceptably/ badly, carry on *colloq*, disobey, fool about/ around, get up to mischief, mess about, muck about *colloq*, offend, play up *colloq*, transgress *formal*, trespass

misbehaviour *n* bad manners, carryings-on *colloq*, disobedience, impropriety *formal*, insubordination, mischief, misconduct, misdemeanour *formal*, mucking about *colloq*, naughtiness, unacceptable/bad behaviour

misbelief *n* delusion, error, fallacy, heresy, heterodoxy, illusion, misapprehension, misconception, mistake, misunderstanding, unorthodoxy, wrong belief

miscalculate *v* blunder, boob *colloq*, err, get wrong, go wrong, make a mistake, miscount, misjudge, overestimate, slip up, underestimate

miscarriage *n* **1** *have a miscarriage:* spontaneous abortion **2** *a miscarriage of justice:* aborting, abortion, breakdown, disappointment, error, failure, mishap, mismanagement, perversion, ruination
🔁 **2** fulfilment, success

miscarry *v* **1** *she miscarried:* abort, have a spontaneous abortion, lose the baby **2** *the plan miscarried:* bite the dust *colloq*, come a cropper *colloq*, come to grief, come to nothing, fail, fall through, flop *colloq*, fold *colloq*, founder, go amiss, go wrong, misfire, not come off *colloq*
🔁 **2** succeed

miscellaneous *adj* assorted, diverse, diversified, heterogeneous *formal*, indiscriminate, jumbled, mixed, motley, multifarious *formal*, sundry, varied, variegated *formal*, various

miscellany *n* anthology, assortment, collection, conglomeration *formal*, diversity, farrago, gallimaufry, hotch-potch, jumble, medley, mishmash *colloq*, mix, mixed bag *colloq*, mixture, omnium-gatherum *colloq*, pastiche, patchwork, potpourri, salmagundi, smorgasbord, variety

mischance *n* accident, bad break, blow, calamity, contretemps, disaster, ill-chance, ill-fortune, ill-luck, infelicity *formal*, misadventure, misfortune, mishap, tragedy

mischief *n* **1** *criminal mischief:* damage, disruption, evil, harm, hurt, injury, trouble **2** *got up to some mischief at school:* bad behaviour, carry-on *colloq*, devilment, escapade, funny business *colloq*, hanky-panky *colloq*, impishness, jiggery-pokery *colloq*, misbehaviour, monkey business *colloq*, naughtiness, pranks, roguishness, shenanigans *colloq*, tricks, wrongdoing **3** *her younger son's a little mischief:* devil, imp, monkey, nuisance, pest, rascal, rogue, scallywag, scamp, stirrer, tyke, villain

mischievous *adj* **1** *mischievous gossip:* destructive, detrimental, evil, harmful, hurtful, injurious, malicious, malignant, pernicious, spiteful, vicious, wicked **2** *a mischievous little girl:* bad, badly-behaved, disobedient, frolicsome, impish, misbehaving, naughty, playful, rascally, roguish, teasing, troublesome
🔁 **1** kind **2** good, well-behaved

misconceive *v* get hold of the wrong end of the stick *colloq*, misapprehend, misconstrue, misinterpret, misjudge, misread, mistake, misunderstand

misconception *n* delusion, error, fallacy, false impression, misapprehension, misinterpretation, misreading, mistake, misunderstanding, the wrong end of the stick *colloq*, wrong idea

misconduct *n* bad/unacceptable behaviour, impropriety *formal*, malpractice, misbehaviour, misdemeanour *formal*, mismanagement, unethical/unprofessional behaviour, wrongdoing

misconstrue *v* get hold of the wrong end of the stick *colloq*, misapprehend, misconceive, misinterpret, misjudge, misread, misreckon, mistake, mistranslate, misunderstand, take the wrong way

miscreant *n* criminal, dastard, evildoer, knave, malefactor *formal*, mischief-maker, profligate, rascal, reprobate, rogue, scallywag, scamp, scoundrel, sinner, troublemaker, villain, wretch, wrongdoer
🔁 worthy

misdeed *n* crime, delinquency, error, fault, felony, misconduct, misdemeanour *formal*, offence, peccadillo, sin, transgression *formal*, trespass, villainy, wrong, wrongdoing

misdemeanour *n* error, fault, indiscretion, infringement, lapse, malfeasance *formal*, misbehaviour, misconduct, misdeed, offence, peccadillo, transgression *formal*, trespass, wrong, wrongdoing

miser *n* cheapskate *colloq*, cheeseparer, meanie *colloq*, money-grubber *colloq*, niggard, penny-pincher *colloq*, Scrooge, skinflint, tight arse *slang*, tightwad *colloq*
🔁 spendthrift

miserable *adj* **1** *felt miserable after her husband left:* blue *colloq*, crushed, dejected, depressed, desolate, despondent, disconsolate *formal*, distressed, down *colloq*, down in the dumps *colloq*, downcast, downhearted, forlorn, gloomy, glum, heartbroken, low-spirited, melancholic *formal*, sad, sorrowful, unhappy, wretched **2** *miserable weather:* cheerless, depressing, disagreeable, dismal, dreary, forlorn, gloomy, joyless, unpleasant **3** *miserable living conditions:* impoverished, poor, shabby, squalid, wretched **4** *miserable treatment by the press:* base, contemptible, deplorable, despicable, detestable, disgraceful, ignominious, low, mean, shameful, vile **5** *earned a miserable £3 an hour:* meagre, measly *colloq*, niggardly, paltry, pathetic, pitiful, poor, scanty, worthless **6** *he's always a bit miserable in the mornings:* bad-tempered, crotchety *colloq*, grouchy *colloq*, grumpy, ill-tempered, irritable, sullen, surly

☲ **1** cheerful, happy **2** pleasant **3** happy **5** generous

miserliness *n* avarice, cheeseparing, close-fistedness, frugality, meanness, minginess *colloq*, niggardliness, parsimony, penny-pinching, penuriousness *formal*, stinginess *colloq*, tight-fistedness, tightness
☲ generosity, lavishness, prodigality *formal*

miserly *adj* beggarly, cheeseparing, close-fisted, mean, mingy *colloq*, money-grubbing *colloq*, niggardly, parsimonious, penny-pinching *colloq*, penurious *formal*, sparing, stingy *colloq*, tight, tight-fisted
☲ generous, spendthrift

misery *n* **1** *scenes of human misery:* adversity, affliction *formal*, agony, anguish, depression, despair, discomfort, distress, gloom, grief, melancholy *formal*, misfortune, sadness, sorrow, suffering, unhappiness, woe *formal*, wretchedness **2** *families living in absolute misery:* deprivation, destitution, hardship, indigence *formal*, oppression, penury *formal*, poverty, privation *formal*, want **3** *don't be such a misery:* complainer, grouch *colloq*, Jeremiah, killjoy, moaner, pessimist, prophet of doom, sourpuss *colloq*, spoilsport, wet blanket *colloq*, whiner *colloq*, whinger *colloq*
☲ **1** contentment **2** comfort

misfire *v* bite the dust *colloq*, come a cropper *colloq*, come to grief, fail, fall through, fizzle out, flop *colloq*, founder, go amiss, go awry, go wrong, miscarry, not come off *colloq*
☲ succeed

misfit *n* dropout, eccentric, fish out of water *colloq*, freak *colloq*, individualist, lone wolf, loner, maverick, nonconformist, odd one out *colloq*, oddball *colloq*, square peg in a round hole *colloq*, weirdo *colloq*
☲ conformist

misfortune *n* accident, adversity, affliction *formal*, bad luck, blow, calamity, catastrophe, disaster, evil, failure, hard luck, hardship, ill-luck, misadventure, mischance, mishap, reverse, setback, sorrow, tragedy, trial, tribulation *formal*, trouble, woe *formal*
☲ luck, success

misgiving *n* anxiety, apprehension, distrust, doubt, fear, hesitation, niggle, qualm, reservation, scruple, second thoughts, suspicion, uncertainty, unease, worry
☲ confidence

misguided *adj* deluded, erroneous, fallacious *formal*, foolish, ill-advised, ill-considered, ill-judged, imprudent, injudicious *formal*, misconceived, misdirected, misinformed, misled, misplaced, mistaken, rash, wrong
☲ sensible, wise

mishandle *v* balls up *slang*, botch *colloq*, bungle, make a hash of *colloq*, make a mess of, make a pig's ear of *colloq*, mess up, misjudge, mismanage, muff *colloq*, screw up *slang*
☲ cope, manage

mishap *n* accident, blow, calamity, catastrophe, disaster, ill-fortune, incident, misadventure, misfortune, reverse, setback, stroke of bad luck, trial, tribulation *formal*, trouble

mishmash *n* conglomeration *formal*, farrago, gallimaufry, hash, hodge-podge, hotchpotch, jumble, medley, mess, muddle, olio, olla-podrida, pastiche, potpourri, salad, salmagundi

misinform *v* bluff, deceive, hoodwink, lead up the garden path *colloq*, misdirect, misguide, mislead, take for a ride *colloq*

misinformation *n* baloney, bluff, bum steer *colloq*, disinformation, dope *colloq*, eyewash *colloq*, guff *colloq*, hype *colloq*, lies, misdirection, misleading, nonsense

misinterpret *v* distort, garble, get hold of the wrong end of the stick *colloq*, misapprehend, misconceive, misconstrue, misjudge, misread, mistake, misunderstand, take the wrong way

misjudge *v* have a wrong opinion about, miscalculate, misconstrue, misinterpret, mistake, misunderstand, overestimate, underestimate

mislay *v* be unable to find, forget where you have put, lose, lose sight of, lose track of, misfile, misplace, miss

mislead *v* deceive, delude, fool, fool into, hoodwink, lead astray, lead up the garden path *colloq*, misdirect, misguide, misinform, misrepresent, pull a fast one on *colloq*, pull the wool over someone's eyes *colloq*, send on a wild goose chase *colloq*, take for a ride *colloq*

misleading *adj* ambiguous, biased, confusing, deceiving, deceptive, delusive, equivocal, evasive, fallacious *formal*, illusory, loaded, tricky *colloq*, unreliable
☲ authoritative, informative, unequivocal

mismanage *v* balls up *slang*, botch *colloq*, bungle, foul up, make a balls of *slang*, make a hash of *colloq*, make a mess of, make a pig's ear of *colloq*, mess up, mishandle, misjudge, misrule, misspend, muff *colloq*, screw up *slang*

mismatched *adj* antipathetic *formal*, clashing, discordant, disparate *formal*, ill-assorted, incompatible, incongruous *formal*, irregular, misallied, mismated, unmatching, unreconcilable, unsuited
☲ compatible, matching

misogynist *n* anti-feminist, male chauvinist, male chauvinist pig *colloq*, male supremacist, misogamist, sexist, woman-hater
☲ feminist

misplace *v* be unable to find, forget where you have put, lose, lose sight of, lose track of, misapply, misassign, misfile, mislay, miss

misprint *n* corrigendum *formal*, erratum *formal*, error, literal, mistake, printing error, typo *colloq*, typographical error

misquote *v* distort, falsify, garble, misremember, misreport, misrepresent, misstate, muddle, pervert, twist

misrepresent *v* distort, exaggerate, falsify, garble, give a false/wrong account of, minimize, misconstrue, misinterpret, misquote, misreport, misstate, pervert, slant, twist

misrule *n* anarchy, chaos, confusion, disorder, disorganization, indiscipline, lawlessness, maladmininstration, misgovernment, mismanagement, riot, tumult, turbulence, turmoil, unreason

miss[1] *v* **1** *miss a target:* blow *colloq*, err, fail, fail to hit/get/catch, leave out, let go, let slip, lose, miscarry, mistake, misunderstand, muff *colloq*, omit, overlook, pass over, slip, trip **2** *miss a meeting:* be absent from, be away from, be too late for, fail to attend, not be part of, not go to, not go to see, not take part in **3** *miss an opportunity:* disregard, fail to seize, let go, let slip, neglect, not take advantage of, overlook **4** *he'd left a note but I missed it:* disregard, fail to notice, fail to notice the absence of, not notice, not spot, overlook **5** *swerved to miss the fallen tree:* avoid, bypass, circumvent *formal*, dodge, escape, evade, sidestep, skip **6** *was missing her family so much:* ache for, feel the loss of, grieve for, lament, long for, mourn, need, pine for, regret, sorrow for, want, wish, yearn for

Fa 1 catch, get, hit **2** take part in **3** seize **4** notice, spot

♦ *n* blunder, error, failure, fault, flop *colloq*, mistake, omission, oversight, slip

▶ **miss out** bypass, dispense with, disregard, ignore, jump, leave out, omit, pass over, skip

miss² *n* damsel, girl, lass, mademoiselle, maid, maiden, schoolgirl, teenager, young lady, young woman

missal *n* breviary, euchologion, formulary, mass-book, office-book, prayerbook, servicebook, Triodion

misshapen *adj* bent, contorted, crippled, crooked, deformed, distorted, grotesque, malformed, misproportioned, monstrous, twisted, ugly, warped

Fa regular, shapely

missile *n* arrow, ballistic missile, bomb, dart, flying bomb, grenade, guided missile, projectile, rocket, shaft, shell, shot, torpedo, weapon

missing *adj* absent, astray, disappeared, gone, gone astray, lacking, lost, mislaid, misplaced, nowhere to be found, strayed, unaccounted-for, wanting

Fa found, present

mission *n* **1** *a fact-finding mission:* assignment, business, campaign, chore, crusade, duty, errand, operation, task, undertaking, work **2** *his mission in life is to care for the sick:* aim, calling, charge, duty, goal, job, office, purpose, pursuit, quest, raison d'être, vocation, work **3** *a mission from the EU:* commission, delegation, deputation, embassy, legation, ministry, task-force

missionary *n* **1** *a missionary for peace:* ambassador, apostle, campaigner, champion, crusader, emissary, envoy, promoter, propagandist, proselytizer **2** *a Catholic missionary:* apostle, converter, evangelist, minister, preacher

missive *n* bulletin, communication, communiqué, dispatch, epistle *formal*, letter, line, memo *colloq*, memorandum, message, note, report

misspent *adj* dissipated, frittered away, idle, idled away, misapplied, misused, prodigal *formal*, profitless, squandered, thrown away, unprofitable, wasted

Fa profitable

misstate *v* distort, falsify, garble, misquote, misrelate, misremember, misreport, misrepresent, pervert, twist

mist *n* cloud, condensation, dew, dimness, drizzle, film, fog, haze, mizzle, smog, spray, steam, vapour, veil

▶ **mist over/up** become blurred, become cloudy, become hazy, blur, cloud over, dim, fog (up), glaze, obscure, steam up, veil

Fa clear

mistake *n* aberration, bad move *colloq*, bloomer *colloq*, blooper *colloq*, blunder, boob *colloq*, booboo *colloq*, botch-up *colloq*, clanger *colloq*, corrigendum *formal*, erratum *formal*, error, fault, faux pas, fluff *colloq*, gaffe, goof *colloq*, howler *colloq*, inaccuracy, indiscretion, lapse, misapprehension, miscalculation, misjudgement, misprint, mispronunciation, misreading, misspelling, misunderstanding, muff *colloq*, oversight, slip, slip of the tongue, slip-up *colloq*, solecism *formal*

♦ *v* **1** *I mistook what she said:* get wrong, get your wires crossed *colloq*, misapprehend, miscalculate, misconstrue, misjudge, misreadea, misunderstand **2** *often mistake him for his brother:* confound, confuse, mix up, muddle (up)

mistaken *adj* at fault, deceived, deluded, erroneous, fallacious *formal*, false, faulty, get the wrong idea *colloq*, having got hold of the wrong end of the stick *colloq*, ill-judged, in error, inaccurate, inappropriate, inauthentic, incorrect, inexact, misguided, misinformed, misled, unfounded, untrue, wide of the mark *colloq*, wrong

Fa correct, right

mistakenly *adv* by mistake, erroneously, fallaciously *formal*, falsely, inaccurately, inappropriately, incorrectly, misguidedly, unfairly, unjustly, wrongly

Fa appropriately, correctly, fairly, justly

mistimed *adj* ill-timed, inconvenient, infelicitous *formal*, inopportune, malapropos *formal*, unfortunate, unseasonable, unsynchronized, untimely

Fa opportune

mistreat *v* abuse, batter, beat up *colloq*, bully, harm, hurt, ill-treat, ill-use, injure, knock about *colloq*, maltreat, maul, mishandle, misuse, molest, treat badly, walk (all) over *colloq*

Fa cosset, pamper

mistreatment *n* abuse, battering, brutalization, bullying, cruelty, harm, hurt, ill-treatment, ill-usage, ill-use, injury, maltreatment, manhandling, mauling, mishandling, misuse, molestation, unkindness

Fa cosseting, pampering

mistress *n* **1** *kept a mistress for 20 years:* bit on the side *colloq*, concubine, courtesan, girlfriend, hetaera, inamorata, kept woman, lady-love, live-in lover, lover, paramour, partner, woman **2** *the French mistress:* governess, schoolteacher, teacher, tutor

mistrust *n* apprehension, caution, chariness, distrust, doubt, hesitancy, misgiving, qualm, reservations, scepticism, suspicion, uncertainty, wariness

Fa trust

♦ *v* be suspicious of, be wary of, beware, distrust, doubt, fear, have doubts about, have misgivings, have no faith in, have reservations, suspect

Fa trust

mistrustful *adj* apprehensive, cautious, chary, cynical, distrustful, doubtful, dubious, fearful, hesitant, leery *colloq*, sceptical, shy, suspicious, uncertain, wary
◨ trustful

misty *adj* blurred, cloudy, dim, foggy, fuzzy, hazy, indistinct, murky, nebulous, obscure, opaque, smoky, unclear, vague, veiled
◨ clear, distinct

misunderstand *v* get a false impression, get hold of the wrong end of the stick *colloq*, get the wrong idea, get wrong, get your wires crossed *colloq*, misapprehend, misconstrue, mishear, misinterpret, misjudge, misread, miss the point, mistake, not make head or tail of *colloq*
◨ understand

misunderstanding *n* **1** *there's was a misunderstanding about our order:* crossed wires *colloq*, error, false impression, misapprehension, misconception, misinterpretation, misjudgement, misreading, mistake, mix-up, the wrong end of the stick *colloq*, wrong idea **2** *they've had a bit of a misunderstanding:* argument, breach, clash, conflict, difference, difference of opinion, disagreement, discord *formal*, dispute, falling-out *colloq*, quarrel, rift, row, squabble, tiff *colloq*
◨ **1** understanding **2** agreement

misunderstood *adj* ill-judged, misappreciated, misconstrued, misheard, misinterpreted, misjudged, misread, misrepresented, mistaken, unappreciated, unrecognized

misuse *n* **1** *misuse of power:* abuse, corruption, exploitation, misapplication, misappropriation, misemployment, mishandling, perversion, squandering, waste, wrong use **2** *his misuse of his wife:* abuse, harm, ill-treatment, injury, maltreatment, mistreatment
♦ *v* **1** *misused a position of trust:* abuse, corrupt, distort, exploit, misapply, misemploy, pervert **2** *accused of misusing the animals in his care:* harm, hurt, ill-treat, ill-use, injure, mistreat, treat badly, wrong **3** *misused government funds:* dissipate, misappropriate, misemploy, squander, waste

> *misuse* or *abuse*? See panel at **abuse**

mite *n* atom, bit, grain, iota, jot, modicum, morsel, ounce, scrap, smidgen *colloq*, spark, tad *colloq*, touch, trace, whit

mitigate *v* abate *formal*, allay *formal*, alleviate, appease *formal*, assuage *formal*, blunt, calm, check, decrease, diminish, dull, ease, extenuate *formal*, lenify *formal*, lessen, lighten, moderate, modify, mollify, pacify, palliate *formal*, placate, quiet, reduce, remit *formal*, soften, soothe, still, subdue, temper, tone down, weaken
◨ aggravate, exacerbate, increase

mitigating *adj* extenuating, justifying, modifying, palliative *formal*, qualifying, tempering, vindicating, vindicatory

mitigation *n* abatement *formal*, allaying *formal*, alleviation, appeasement *formal*, assuagement *formal*, decrease, diminution, easement *formal*, extenuation *formal*, lessening, moderation, mollification, palliation *formal*, qualification, reduction, relief, remission *formal*, tempering
◨ aggravation, exacerbation, increase

mix *v* **1** *mix the sugar and butter:* alloy, amalgamate, blend, coalesce, combine, compound, emulsify, fold in, fuse, homogenize, incorporate, intermingle, intermix, interpolate *formal*, introduce, join, mash, merge, mingle, put together, stir, synthesize, unite, whisk **2** *doesn't mix with the other children:* associate, consort, fraternize, hobnob *colloq*, join, meet others, mingle, socialize **3** *the music and decor just don't mix:* agree, be compatible, be on the same wavelength *colloq*, complement, get along/on, go well with, harmonize, suit
◨ **1** divide, separate
♦ *n* **1** *an odd mix of comedy and horror:* alloy, amalgam, amalgamation, blend, coalition, combination, composite, compound, conglomerate *formal*, fusion, merger, mixture, synthesis, union **2** *an interesting mix of people:* assortment, medley, mishmash *colloq*, mixture
▶ **mix in** add in, blend, incorporate, introduce, merge
◨ extract, isolate
▶ **mix up 1** *mixed her up with someone else:* bewilder, confound, confuse, disturb, garble, get jumbled up, jumble, mistake, muddle (up), perplex, puzzle **2** *was mixed up in the robbery:* implicate, involve

mixed *adj* **1** *mixed race:* alloyed, amalgamated, blended, combined, composite, compound, crossbred, fused, hybrid, incorporated, interbred, mingled, mongrel, united **2** *mixed biscuits:* assorted, diverse, diversified, miscellaneous, motley, varied **3** *mixed feelings:* ambivalent, conflicting, contradicting, equivocal, uncertain, unsure

mixer *n* **1** *a food mixer:* beater, blender, food processor, liquidizer, whisk **2** *she's always been a good mixer:* everybody's friend, extrovert, joiner, life and soul of the party *colloq*, socializer
◨ **2** introvert, loner, recluse

mixing *n* **1** *the mixing of the cement:* amalgamation, blending, coalescence, combination, fusion, hybridization, interbreeding, interflow, intermingling, minglement *formal*, synthesis, union **2** *not much mixing between the boys and girls:* association, fraternization, mingling, socializing
◨ **1** separation

mixture *n* alloy, amalgam, amalgamation, assortment, blend, brew, coalescence, combination, composite, compound, concoction, conglomeration *formal*, cross, farrago, fusion, hotchpotch, hybrid, jumble, medley, melange, miscellany, mishmash *colloq*, mix, mixed bag *colloq*, pastiche, patchwork, potpourri, smorgasbord, synthesis, union, variety

mix-up *n* balls-up *slang*, complication, confusion, foul-up *colloq*, jumble, mess, mistake, misunderstanding, muddle, nonsense, snafu *US slang*, snarl-up, tangle

moan *n* **1** *uttered a loud moan:* groan, howl, lament, lamentation, sob, wail, whimper, whine **2** *enjoyed a good moan about their neighbours:* accusation, beef *colloq*, beefing *colloq*, bellyaching *colloq*, bleating *colloq*, carping, censure, charge, complaint, criticism, fault-finding, grievance, gripe *colloq*, groan, grouse *colloq*, grumble, whinge *colloq*, whingeing *colloq*
♦ *v* **1** *crowds of people shrieked and moaned:* grieve,

groan, howl, lament, mourn, sigh, sob, wail, weep, whimper **2** *some people moaned about the selection process:* beef *colloq*, belly-ache *colloq*, bleat *colloq*, carp, complain, gripe *colloq*, grouse *colloq*, grumble, kick up a fuss *colloq*, whine, whinge *colloq*
Fa 2 rejoice

mob *n* **1** *an unruly mob:* assemblage *formal*, body, brood, company, crew, crowd, drove, flock, gang, gathering, group, herd, horde, host, mass, multitude, pack, press, rabble, set, swarm, throng, tribe, troop **2** *his brand of politics appeals to the mob:* canaille, great unwashed, hoi polloi, masses, plebs *colloq*, populace, rabble, riff-raff *colloq*
♦ *v* **1** *mobbing the returning hero:* crowd round, gather round, jostle, pester, surround, swarm round **2** *the people mobbed the palace:* attack, beseige, charge, descend on, fall upon, overrun, set upon **3** *protestors mobbed the streets:* crowd, descend on, fill, overrun, pack, throng

mobile *adj* **1** *a mobile library:* able to move, ambulatory *formal*, itinerant, locomotive *formal*, migrant, motile *formal*, movable, moving, peripatetic *formal*, portable, roaming, roving, transportable, travelling, wandering **2** *mobile joints:* active, adaptable, adjustable, agile, energetic, flexible, nimble, supple **3** *her mobile features:* changeable, changing, ever-changing, expressive, lively
Fa 1 immobile

mobility *n* **1** *elderly people of limited mobility:* agility, flexibility, locomobility *formal*, locomotion *formal*, locomotivity *formal*, motility *formal*, motion, motivity *formal*, movability, movableness, portability, suppleness **2** *the mobility of her face:* animation, expressiveness, vivacity
Fa 1 immobility, inflexibility, rigidity

mobilize *v* activate, animate, assemble, call into action, call up, cause to take action, conscript, enlist, galvanize, get ready, make ready, marshal, muster, organize, prepare, rally, ready, summon

mob rule *n* lynch law, mobocracy *colloq*, ochlocracy, Reign of Terror

mock *v* **1** *they were mocking his accent:* chaff, deride *formal*, disparage *formal*, gibe, insult, jeer, kid *colloq*, knock *colloq*, laugh at, make fun of, poke fun at, rag *colloq*, rib *colloq*, ridicule, scoff, scorn, sneer, take the mickey out of *colloq*, take the piss out of *slang*, taunt, tease **2** *artificial drugs which mock natural hormones:* ape, emulate *formal*, imitate, mimic, simulate
♦ *adj* **1** *mock leather:* artificial, bogus, counterfeit, ersatz, fake, false, imitation, phoney *colloq*, pseudo, simulated, substitute, synthetic **2** *in mock horror:* faked, feigned, phoney *colloq*, pretend *colloq*, pretended, pseudo, sham, simulated

mocker *n* critic, derider *formal*, detractor, flouter, iconoclast *formal*, jeerer, lampooner, lampoonist, pasquinader, reviler *formal*, ridiculer, satirist, scoffer, scorner, sneerer, tease, tormentor, vilifier *formal*
Fa flatterer, supporter

mockery *n* **1** *subject a person to mockery:* contempt, contumely *formal*, derision *formal*,

disdain, disparagement *formal*, disrespect, jeering, kidding *colloq*, mickey-taking *colloq*, piss-taking *slang*, ragging *colloq*, ribbing *colloq*, ridicule, sarcasm, scoffing, scorn, sneer, sneering, taunting, teasing **2** *make a mockery of the legal system:* burlesque, caricature, farce, lampoon, parody, satire, send-up *colloq*, sham, spoof *colloq*, take-off *colloq*, travesty

mocking *adj* contemptuous, cynical, derisive, derisory, disdainful, disrespectful, impudent, insulting, irreverent, sarcastic, sardonic, satirical, scoffing, scornful, sneering, snide *colloq*, taunting

mode *n* **1** *a mode of thinking:* approach, condition, convention, form, manner, method, plan, practice, procedure, process, style, system, technique, way **2** *the current mode for ballgowns and trainers:* craze *colloq*, custom, dernier cri *colloq*, fad, fashion, latest thing *colloq*, look, rage *colloq*, style, trend, vogue

model *n* **1** *a model of a tank:* copy, dummy, facsimile, image, imitation, mock-up, replica, representation **2** *a good model to follow:* design, example, exemplar *formal*, ideal, original, paradigm *formal*, pattern, prototype, sample, standard, template **3** *a model of consistency:* archetype *formal*, embodiment, epitome, exemplar *formal*, paradigm *formal*, paragon, perfect example, prime example, prototype, standard **4** *a new model of car:* design, form, kind, mark, mode *formal*, sort, style, type, variety, version **5** *hopes to find work as a model:* artist's model, fashion model, mannequin, photographer's model, poser, sitter
♦ *adj* archetypal *formal*, exemplary, ideal, perfect, prototypical *formal*, typical
♦ *v* **1** *model a head:* base, carve, cast, create, design, fashion, form, make, mould, plan, sculpt, shape, work **2** *to model clothes:* display, show off, sport, wear

moderate *adj* **1** *met with moderate success:* adequate, average, fair, fair to middling *colloq*, fairish, indifferent, mediocre, medium, middle-of-the-road, middling, modest, no great shakes *colloq*, not much cop *colloq*, not up to much *colloq*, nothing much to write home about *colloq*, ordinary, passable, so-so *colloq*, tolerable **2** *moderate behaviour:* calm, controlled, cool, fair, just, mild, modest, reasonable, restrained, sensible, sober, steady, temperate, well-regulated
Fa 1 exceptional, extreme **2** excessive, immoderate
♦ *v* abate *formal*, allay *formal*, alleviate *formal*, appease *formal*, assuage *formal*, attenuate *formal*, calm, check, control, curb, decrease, diminish, dwindle, ease, keep in check, keep under control, lessen, mitigate *formal*, modulate, pacify, palliate *formal*, play down, regulate, repress, restrain, slacken, soften, soft-pedal, subdue, subside, tame, tone down
♦ *n* centrist, liberal, neutral person, nonextremist
Fa extremist, hardliner

moderately *adv* fairly, passably, quite, rather, reasonably, slightly, somewhat, to a certain degree, to some extent, within reason
Fa extremely

moderation *n* **1** *act with moderation:* abstemiousness, caution, composure, control, reasonableness, restraint, self-control, self-restraint, sobriety, temperance, temperateness **2** *the moderation of the union's demands:* abatement *formal*, alleviation *formal*, attenuation *formal*, curbing, decrease, lessening, mitigation *formal*, reduction, regulation, subsidence

₣ 1 indulgence, self-indulgence

modern *adj* **1** *a modern design:* all the rage *colloq*, avant-garde, contemporary, cool *colloq*, current, fashionable, futuristic, hip *colloq*, hot off the press *colloq*, in *colloq*, in fashion, in style, in vogue, latest, modernistic, modish, new, present, present-day, recent, spanking new *colloq*, stylish, trendy *colloq*, up-to-date, up-to-the-minute, voguish, with it *colloq* **2** *modern technology:* advanced, avant-garde, innovative, inventive, latest, modernistic, new, newfangled *colloq*, novel, spanking new *colloq*, state-of-the-art **3** *modern ideas:* avant-garde, forward-looking, fresh, go-ahead, hip *colloq*, innovative, latest, new, novel, progressive

₣ 1 old, old-fashioned, traditional **2** out of date, traditional **3** old-fashioned, out of date

modernity *n* contemporaneity, fashionableness, freshness, innovation, innovativeness, newness, novelty, originality, recentness

₣ antiquatedness, antiquity

modernize *v* bring up-to-date, do over *colloq*, do up *colloq*, fix up *colloq*, get with it *colloq*, improve, make modern, modify, move with the times *colloq*, progress, redesign, reform, refresh, refurbish, regenerate, rejuvenate, remake, remodel, renew, renovate, revamp, streamline, transform, update

₣ regress

modest *adj* **1** *a modest young man:* bashful, coy, discreet, humble, quiet, reserved, retiring, self-conscious, self-deprecating, self-effacing, shy, timid, unassuming, unpretentious **2** *earn a modest salary:* adequate, fair, limited, moderate, ordinary, passable, reasonable, satisfactory, small, tolerable, unexceptional **3** *a modest house:* inexpensive, plain, simple, unassuming, unpretentious **4** *modest behaviour:* chaste, decent, decorous *formal*, demure, discreet, proper, virtuous

₣ 1 arrogant, conceited, immodest **2** exceptional, excessive **3** expensive, extravagant, pretentious

modesty *n* **1** *impressed by his modesty:* bashfulness, coyness, humbleness, humility, quietness, reserve, reticence, self-consciousness, self-deprecation, self-effacement, shyness, timidity **2** *modesty of behaviour:* chasteness, decency, decorum *formal*, demureness, propriety **3** *a hotel of great modesty:* inexpensiveness, plainness, simplicity, unpretentiousness

₣ 1 conceit, immodesty, vanity **3** extravagance

modicum *n* atom, bit, crumb, dash, degree, drop, fragment, grain, hint, inch, iota, little, little bit, mite, molecule, ounce, particle, pinch, scrap, shred, small amount, speck, suggestion, tad *colloq*, tinge, touch, trace

modification *n* adaptation, adjustment, alteration, change, improvement, limitation, moderation, modulation *formal*, mutation, qualification, recasting, refinement, reformation, remoulding, reorganization, restriction, revision, reworking, tempering, transformation, variation

modify *v* **1** *modify your plans:* adapt, adjust, alter, change, convert, improve, recast, redesign, reform, remould, reorganize, reshape, revise, rework, transform, vary **2** *modify your ambitions:* abate *formal*, decrease, diminish, dull, lessen, limit, mitigate *formal*, moderate, qualify, reduce, soften, temper, tone down

modish *adj* à la mode, all the rage *colloq*, avant-garde, chic, contemporary, current, fashionable, hip *colloq*, in *colloq*, latest *colloq*, mod *colloq*, modern, modernistic, now, smart, stylish, trendy *colloq*, up-to-the-minute *colloq*, vogue, voguish, with it *colloq*

₣ dowdy, old-fashioned

modulate *v* adjust, alter, balance, change, harmonize, inflect, lower, moderate, modify, regulate, soften, temper, tune, vary

modulation *n* accent, adjustment, alteration, balance, change, harmonization, inflection, inflexion, intonation, lowering, moderation, modification, regulation, shade, shift, softening, tone, tuning, variation

modus operandi *n* manner, method, operation, plan, practice, praxis *formal*, procedure, process, rule, rule of thumb, system, technique, way

mogul *n* baron, big cheese *colloq*, big gun *colloq*, big noise *colloq*, big pot *colloq*, big shot *colloq*, big wheel *colloq*, bigwig *colloq*, magnate, Mr Big *colloq*, notable, potentate, supremo, top dog *colloq*, tycoon, VIP *colloq*

₣ nobody

moist *adj* clammy, damp, dank, dewy, dripping, drizzling, drizzly, humid, muggy, rainy, soggy, watery, wet, wettish

₣ arid, dry

moisten *v* damp, dampen, humidify, humify, irrigate, lick, make wet, moisturize, soak, water, wet

₣ dry

moisture *n* condensation, damp, dampness, dankness, dew, drizzle, humidity, liquid, mugginess, rain, spray, steam, vapour, water, wateriness, wet, wetness

₣ dryness

mole[1] *n* blemish, blotch, freckle, speckle, spot

mole[2] *n* agent, double agent, infiltrator, secret agent, spy

molest *v* **1** *molest a person with constant questions:* aggravate *colloq*, agitate, annoy, badger, bother, bug *colloq*, chivvy, disturb, exasperate, fluster, harass, harry, hassle *colloq*, hound, irritate, nag, needle *colloq*, persecute, pester, plague, provoke, tease, torment, trouble, upset, vex, worry **2** *accused of molesting a co-worker:* abuse, accost, assail, attack, harm, hurt, ill-treat, injure, interfere with, maltreat, mistreat, rape, ravish *formal*, (sexually) assault

mollify *v* abate *formal*, allay *formal*, appease, assuage *formal*, blunt, calm, compose, conciliate, cushion, ease, lessen, lull, mellow, mitigate *formal*, moderate, modify, pacify, placate, propitiate *formal*, quell, quiet, relax, relieve, soften, soothe, sweeten, temper

₣ aggravate, anger

mollusc

> *Molluscs include:*
> abalone, conch, cowrie, cuttlefish, clam,
> cockle, limpet, mussel, nautilus, nudibranch,
> octopus, oyster, periwinkle, scallop, sea slug,
> slug, freshwater snail, land snail, marine snail,
> squid, tusk shell, whelk

mollycoddle *v* baby, coddle, cosset, indulge,
mother, overprotect, pamper, pander to, pet,
ruin, spoil, spoon-feed
🔁 ill-treat, neglect

moment *n* **1** *stop for a moment:* flash, instant, jiffy
colloq, less than no time, minute, mo *colloq,* point
in time, sec, second, split second, tick *colloq,* trice,
twinkling of an eye, two shakes of a lamb's tail
colloq, two ticks *colloq,* (very) short time **2** *an event
of great moment:* concern, consequence, gravity,
import *formal,* importance, interest, note,
seriousness, significance, substance, value,
weight, weightiness, worth
🔁 **2** insignificance

momentarily *adv* briefly, fleetingly, for a
moment, for a second, for a short time, for an
instant, temporarily

momentary *adj* brief, ephemeral *formal,*
evanescent *formal,* fleeting, hasty, passing,
quick, short, short-lived, temporary, transient,
transitory
🔁 lasting, permanent

momentous *adj* consequential, critical, crucial,
decisive, earth-shaking, earth-shattering, epoch-
making, eventful, fateful, grave, historic,
important, major, of consequence, of
importance, of significance, pivotal, serious,
significant, vital, weighty, world-shattering
🔁 insignificant, trivial, unimportant

momentum *n* drive, driving-power, energy,
force, impact, impetus, impulse, incentive,
power, propulsion, push, speed, stimulus,
strength, thrust, urge, velocity

monarch *n* crowned head, emperor, empress,
king, potentate, prince, princess, queen, ruler,
sovereign, tsar

monarchy *n* **1** *we live in a monarchy:* domain,
dominion, empire, kingdom, realm, sovereign
state **2** *opposed to the Stuart monarchy:* absolutism,
autocracy, despotism, kingship, monocracy
formal, royalism, sovereignty, tyranny

monastery *n* abbey, charterhouse, cloister,
coenobium *formal,* convent, friary, nunnery,
priory, religious community

monastic *adj* anchoritic *formal,* ascetic, austere,
canonical, celibate, cloistered, coenobitic *formal,*
contemplative, eremitic *formal,* meditative,
reclusive, secluded, sequestered *formal,*
withdrawn
🔁 secular, worldly

monasticism *n* asceticism, austerity,
coenobitism *formal,* eremitism *formal,*
monachism *formal,* monkhood, recluseness,
reclusion, seclusion

monetary *adj* budgetary, capital, cash,
economic, financial, fiscal, money, pecuniary
formal

money *n* **1** *have you any money on you?:*
banknotes, brass *slang,* bread *slang,* cash, coins,
currency, dosh *slang,* dough *slang,* gelt *slang,*
gravy *slang,* greens *US slang,* legal tender, lolly
slang, loot *slang,* megabucks *slang,* moolah *slang,*
readies *colloq,* rhino *slang,* shekels *slang,*
spondulicks *slang,* the necessary *colloq* **2** *made her
money in property:* affluence, assets, brass *slang,*
capital, cash, finances, funds, means, megabucks
slang, prosperity, resources, riches, savings,
shekels *slang,* wealth

money-box *n* cash box, chest, coffer, piggy-
bank, safe

moneyed *adj* affluent, comfortable, flush *colloq,*
loaded *slang,* opulent *formal,* prosperous, rich,
rolling in it *colloq,* wealthy, well-heeled *colloq,*
well-off, well-to-do
🔁 impoverished, poor

money-grubbing *adj* acquisitive, grasping,
mammonish, mammonistic, mean, mercenary,
miserly, quaestuary *formal*

money-making *adj* commercial, lucrative,
paying, profitable, profit-making, remunerative,
successful

mongrel *n* cross, crossbreed, cur, half-breed,
hybrid, mixed breed
♦ *adj* bastard, crossbred, half-bred, hybrid, ill-
defined, mixed, of mixed breed
🔁 pedigree, pure-bred

monitor *v* check, detect, follow, keep an eye on,
keep track of, keep under surveillance, note,
observe, oversee, plot, record, scan, supervise,
survey, trace, track, watch
♦ *n* **1** *saw his face on the monitor:* CCTV, display,
recorder, scanner, screen, security camera, VDU
2 *the homework monitor:* adviser, head boy, head
girl, invigilator, observer, overseer, prefect,
supervisor, watchdog

monk *n* abbot, anchorite, beguin, brother,
cloisterer, coenobite, contemplative, conventual,
frater, friar, gyrovague, hermit, mendicant,
monastic, prior, religieux, religionary,
religioner, religious

monkey *n* **1** *watching the monkeys at the zoo:*
primate, simian **2** *he's a cheeky little monkey!:*
brat, imp, mischief-maker, rascal, rogue,
scallywag *colloq,* scamp, urchin
♦ *v* fiddle, fidget, fool, interfere, meddle, mess,
play, potter, tamper, tinker, trifle

> *Monkeys include:*
> ape, baboon, capuchin, colobus monkey, drill,
> guenon, guereza, howler monkey, langur, leaf
> monkey, macaque, mandrill, mangabey,
> marmoset, night monkey (or douroucouli),
> proboscis monkey, rhesus monkey, saki,
> spider monkey, squirrel monkey, tamarin, titi,
> toque, uakari (or cacajou), woolly monkey

monochrome *adj* black-and-white, monochroic
formal, monochromatic, monotone,
monotonous, sepia, unicolor *formal,* unicolorate
formal, unicolorous *formal,* unicolour *formal,*
unicoloured *formal*
🔁 kaleidoscopic, multicoloured

monocle *n* eyeglass, glass, lens

monogamous *adj* having only one marriage
partner, monandrous *formal,* monogamic *formal,*
monogynous *formal*
🔁 bigamous, polygamous

monogamy *n* monandry *formal*, monogyny *formal*, practice/custom of having only one marriage partner, state of having only one marriage partner
🔁 bigamy, polygamy

monolingual *adj* expressed in one language only, monoglot *formal*, speaking one language only, unilingual *formal*, using/involving one language only
🔁 polyglot

monolith *n* megalith, menhir, sarsen, shaft, standing stone

monolithic *adj* colossal, faceless, fossilized, giant, gigantic, hidebound, huge, immobile, immovable, inflexible, intractable, massive, monumental, rigid, solid, unchanging, undifferentiated, unmoving, unvaried, vast

monologue *n* address, homily, lecture, oration, sermon, soliloquy, speech, spiel *colloq*
🔁 conversation, dialogue, discussion

monomania *n* bee in one's bonnet *colloq*, fanaticism, fetish, fixation, hobby-horse *colloq*, idée fixe, mania, neurosis, obsession, ruling passion, thing *colloq*

monopolize *v* appropriate *formal*, control, corner, dominate, engross, have (all) to yourself, have exclusive/sole rights, hog *colloq*, keep to yourself, not share with others, occupy, preoccupy, take over, take up, tie up
🔁 share

monopoly *n* ascendancy *formal*, control, domination, exclusive right(s), monopsony *technical*, sole right(s)

monotonous *adj* all the same, boring, colourless, deadly *colloq*, dull, flat, ho-hum *colloq*, humdrum, mechanical, plodding, repetitious, repetitive, routine, run-of-the-mill *colloq*, samey *colloq*, soul-destroying, tedious, tiresome, toneless, unchanging, uneventful, unexciting, uniform, uninteresting, unvaried, unvarying, wearisome
🔁 colourful, lively, varied

monotony *n* boredom, dullness, flatness, repetition, repetitiveness, routine, routineness, sameness, tedium, tiresomeness, uneventfulness, uniformity, wearisomeness
🔁 colour, excitement, interest, liveliness, variety

monster *n* **1** *sea monsters*: dragon, frightening creature, imaginary creature, mythical creature **2** *that child is an absolute monster!*: barbarian, beast, brute, devil, fiend, savage **3** *a monster with two heads*: freak, freak of nature, malformation, miscreation, monstrosity, mutant, teratism *formal* **4** *a monster of a car*: behemoth, Brobdingnagian, colossus, giant, jumbo, leviathan, mammoth
♦ *adj* colossal, enormous, giant, gigantic, ginormous *colloq*, huge, immense, jumbo, mammoth, massive, mega *colloq*, monstrous, tremendous, vast, whopping *colloq*
🔁 minute, tiny

Monsters include:
bandersnatch, basilisk, bunyip, Charybdis, chimera, cockatrice, cyclops, dragon, Frankenstein's monster, giant, Gorgon, harpy, hippocampus, hydra, jabberwock, kraken, manticore, Medusa, Minotaur, orc, ogre, salamander, Scylla, Sphinx, troll, windigo, wivern, yowie

---

monstrosity *n* **1** *that building is real monstrosity*: atrocity, blot on the landscape, carbuncle, enormity, eyesore, obscenity **2** *it was hard to believe the monstrosity of his actions*: dreadfulness, evil, frightfulness, heinousness *formal*, hellishness, hideousness, horror, loathsomeness

monstrous *adj* **1** *monstrous behaviour*: abhorrent, abominable, atrocious, criminal, cruel, disgraceful, dreadful, evil, foul, frightful, grisly, heinous *formal*, horrible, horrifying, inhuman, nasty, outrageous, savage, scandalous, shocking, terrible, vicious, vile, wicked **2** *a monstrous creature*: abnormal, deformed, freakish, grotesque, gruesome, hideous, inhuman, malformed, misshapen, teratoid *technical*, unnatural **3** *a monstrous salary hike*: colossal, enormous, gigantic, huge, immense, mammoth, massive, tremendous, vast

monument *n* **1** *a monument in the churchyard*: barrow, cairn, cenotaph, column, cross, gravestone, headstone, marker, mausoleum, memorial, obelisk, pillar, relic, shrine, statue, tombstone **2** *a monument to his success*: commemoration, evidence, marker, memento, record, remembrance, reminder, testament, testimonial, token, witness

monumental *adj* **1** *a monumental achievement*: abiding, awe-inspiring, awesome, classic, enduring, epoch-making, historic, immortal, important, imposing, impressive, lasting, magnificent, majestic, memorable, notable, outstanding, overwhelming, permanent, remarkable, significant, striking, unforgettable **2** *a monumental tower block*: colossal, enormous, exceptional, extraordinary, great, huge, immense, massive, tremendous, vast **3** *a monumental inscription*: celebratory, commemorative, memorial
🔁 **1** insignificant, unimportant

mood *n* **1** *in a good mood today*: disposition, frame of mind, humour, spirit, state of mind, temper, tenor, vein, whim **2** *he's in one of his moods*: bad mood, bad temper, blues *colloq*, depression, doldrums, dumps *colloq*, low spirits, melancholy, pique, sulk, the sulks **3** *tried to lighten the mood*: ambience, atmosphere, climate, feel, feeling, spirit, tenor, tone

moody *adj* angry, bad-tempered, broody, cantankerous, capricious *formal*, changeable, crabby *colloq*, crotchety, crusty *colloq*, doleful, downcast, fickle, flighty, gloomy, glum, impulsive, in a (bad) mood, in a huff, irascible, irritable, melancholy, miserable, mopy, morose, petulant, short-tempered, sulky, sullen, temperamental, testy, touchy, unpredictable, unstable, volatile
🔁 cheerful, equable

moon *n* satellite
♦ *v* **1** *always mooning over some woman or other*: brood, daydream, dream, fantasize, mope, pine **2** *spent the summer mooning about the house*: drift, idle, languish, loaf, mooch *colloq*

moonlike *adj* crescent, crescentic, lunar, lunate *technical*, lunular *formal*, meniscoid *formal*, moon-shaped, moony, selenic *formal*

moonshine *n* **1** *the story was a load of moonshine*: baloney *colloq*, blather *colloq*, blether *colloq*, bosh *colloq*, bullshit *slang*, bunk *colloq*, bunkum *colloq*,

claptrap *colloq*, crap *slang*, eyewash *colloq*, fantasy, guff *colloq*, hogwash *colloq*, hot air *colloq*, nonsense, piffle *colloq*, rot *colloq*, rubbish, stuff, tommyrot *colloq*, tosh *colloq*, tripe *colloq*, twaddle *colloq* **2** *they brewed their own moonshine*: bootleg, hoo(t)ch, liquor, pot(h)een, spirits
🖪 **1** sense

moor¹ *v* berth, dock, drop anchor, fasten, fix, hitch, lash, make fast, secure, tie up
🖪 loose

moor² *n* fell, heath, moorland, upland

moot *v* advance, argue, bring up, broach, debate, discuss, introduce, pose, propose, propound *formal*, put forward, submit, suggest
♦ *adj* academic, arguable, contestable, controversial, crucial, debatable, difficult, disputable, disputed, doubtful, insoluble, knotty, open, open to debate, problematic, questionable, undecided, undetermined, unresolvable, unresolved, unsettled, vexed

mop *n* **1** *a floor mop*: sponge, squeegee, swab, wiper **2** *a mop of hair*: head of hair, mane, mass, mat, shock, tangle, thatch
♦ *v* clean, soak, sponge, swab, wash, wipe
▶ **mop up 1** *mop up the spilt drink*: absorb, clean up, soak up, sponge, swab, tidy up, wash, wipe up **2** *mop up the remaining items quickly*: account for, deal with, dispose of, eliminate, finish off, neutralize, round up, secure, take care of, wipe up

mope *v* brood, despair, droop, fret, grieve, languish, pine, sulk
♦ *n* depressive, grouch *colloq*, grump *colloq*, introvert, killjoy, melancholiac, melancholic, misery, moaner, moper *colloq*, pessimist
▶ **mope about** idle, languish, loll *colloq*, lounge *colloq*, mooch *colloq*, moon, wander

moral *adj* **1** *his behaviour was very moral*: blameless, chaste, clean-living, decent, ethical, good, high-minded, honest, honourable, incorruptible, just, noble, principled, proper, pure, right, righteous, straight, upright, upstanding, virtuous **2** *give moral support*: emotional, encouraging, psychological
🖪 **1** immoral
♦ *n* adage, aphorism, dictum, epigram, lesson, maxim, meaning, message, point, precept, proverb, saying, significance, teaching

morale *n* confidence, esprit de corps, heart, hopefulness, mood, optimism, self-confidence, self-esteem, spirit(s), state of mind

morality *n* chastity, conduct, decency, ethics, goodness, honesty, ideals, integrity, justice, manners, moral values, morals, principles, principles of behaviour, principles of right and wrong, propriety *formal*, purity, rectitude *formal*, righteousness, standards, uprightness, virtue
🖪 immorality

moralize *v* discourse *formal*, edify, ethicize *formal*, lecture, pontificate, preach, sermonize

morals *n* behaviour, conduct, ethics, habits, ideals, integrity, manners, moral code, moral values, morality, principles, principles of behaviour, principles of right and wrong, scruples, standards

morass *n* **1** *a muddy morass*: bog, fen, marsh, marshland, mire, quag, quagmire, quicksand, slough, swamp **2** *a legal morass*: can of worms

colloq, chaos, confusion, jam, jumble, mess, mix-up, muddle, tangle

moratorium *n* ban, delay, embargo, freeze, halt, postponement, respite, standstill, stay, stoppage, suspension
🖪 go-ahead *colloq*, green light *colloq*

morbid *adj* **1** *morbid tales*: dreadful, ghastly, ghoulish, grim, grisly, gruesome, hideous, horrible, horrid, macabre, obsessed with death **2** *a morbid outlook on life*: dejected, gloomy, lugubrious *formal*, melancholy, morose, pessimistic, sombre **3** *morbid tissue*: ailing, diseased, insalubrious *formal*, unhealthy, unwholesome

mordant *adj* acerbic *formal*, acid, acrimonious *formal*, astringent, biting, bitter, caustic, critical, cutting, edged, harsh, incisive, pungent, sarcastic, scathing, sharp, stinging, trenchant *formal*, venomous, vicious, waspish, wounding
🖪 gentle, mild, sparing

more *adv* **1** *I should try to sleep more*: better, further, longer, to a greater extent **2** *say something more*: additionally, besides, further
🖪 **1** less
♦ *n* a greater number/quantity, additional people/things, extra
🖪 less

moreover *adv* additionally, also, as well, besides, further, furthermore, in addition, what is more

morgue *n* charnel house, deadhouse, funeral parlour, mortuary

moribund *adj* **1** *a moribund patient*: comatose, declining, dying, expiring, fading, failing, in extremis, not long for this world *colloq*, on the way out *colloq*, on your last legs *colloq*, senile, wasting away, with one foot in the grave *colloq* **2** *a moribund business*: ailing, collapsing, crumbling, declining, doomed, dwindling, ebbing, feeble, lifeless, obsolescent, stagnant, stagnating, waning, wasting away, weak
🖪 **1** alive, lively, nascent *formal* **2** flourishing

morning *n* a.m., before noon, break of day, dawn, daybreak, daylight, sunrise

moron *n* ass *colloq*, birdbrain *colloq*, blockhead, buffoon, butt, chump *colloq*, clot *colloq*, clown, comic, cretin, dimwit, dolt, dope *colloq*, dork *slang*, dumbo *slang*, dunce, dupe, fat-head, fool, geek *slang*, halfwit, idiot, ignoramus, imbecile, jerk *slang*, jester, laughing-stock, mug *colloq*, nincompoop *colloq*, ninny *colloq*, nit *colloq*, nitwit *colloq*, pillock *slang*, plonker *slang*, prat *slang*, prick *slang*, schmuck *US slang*, simpleton, stooge, sucker *colloq*, twerp *colloq*, twit *colloq*, wally *slang*

moronic *adj* absurd, barmy *colloq*, batty *colloq*, crack-brained *colloq*, crazy, daft *colloq*, dotty *colloq*, dumb *colloq*, foolish, gormless *colloq*, half-baked, half-witted, hare-brained, idiotic, ignorant, ill-advised, ill-considered, inane, inept, insane, ludicrous, mad, needing to have your head examined *colloq*, nonsensical, not in your right mind *colloq*, nutty *colloq*, out of your mind *colloq*, pointless, potty *colloq*, ridiculous, senseless, shortsighted, silly, simple, simple-minded, stupid, unintelligent, unreasonable, unwise, with a screw missing *colloq*

morose *adj* bad-tempered, crabby *colloq*, depressed, gloomy, glum, grim, grouchy *colloq*, gruff, ill-tempered, lugubrious *formal*, melancholic, moody, mournful, pessimistic, saturnine, sombre, sour, sulky, sullen, surly, taciturn
🔁 cheerful, communicative

morsel *n* atom, bit, bite, crumb, fraction, fragment, grain, modicum, mouthful, nibble, part, particle, piece, scrap, slice, soupçon, taste, titbit

mortal *adj* **1** *these mortal remains:* bodily, corporeal *formal*, earthly, ephemeral *formal*, fleshly, human, perishable, temporal, transient, worldly **2** *dealt a mortal blow:* deadly, fatal, killing, lethal, murderous **3** *in mortal danger:* awful, dire, extreme, grave, great, intense, severe, terrible, unbearable **4** *mortal enemies:* bitter, cruel, deadly, implacable, relentless, unrelenting, vengeful
🔁 **1** immortal
♦ *n* being, body, creature, earthling, human, human being, individual, man, person, woman
🔁 god, immortal

mortality *n* **1** *aware of his own mortality:* death, earthliness, ephemerality *formal*, humanity, impermanence, perishability, transience, worldliness **2** *the rate of mortality:* carnage, casualty, death, death rate, fatality, killing, loss of life, slaughter
🔁 **1** immortality

mortgage *n* bond, debenture, lien *formal*, loan, pledge, security, wadset *Scot*

mortification *n* **1** *to his mortification, no one turned up:* abasement, annoyance, chagrin *formal*, chastening, confounding, discomfiture *formal*, disgrace, dishonour, embarrassment, humiliation, ignominy *formal*, loss of face, shame, vexation **2** *mortification of the flesh:* asceticism, conquering, control, denial, discipline, punishment, self-control, self-denial, subjugation *formal*

mortified *adj* ashamed, confounded, crushed, defeated, disgraced, dishonoured, embarrassed, horrified, humbled, humiliated, shamed

mortify *v* **1** *the public sacking mortified her:* abash, affront, annoy, bring low, chagrin *formal*, chasten, chastise, confound, crush, deflate, disappoint, discomfit *formal*, disgrace, dishonour, embarrass, horrify, humble, humiliate, offend, put to shame, shame, take down a peg or two *colloq* **2** *mortify the flesh:* conquer, control, deny, discipline, restrain, subdue, suppress

mortifying *adj* chastening, crushing, discomfiting *formal*, embarrassing, humbling, humiliating, ignominious, overwhelming, punishing, salutary, shaming, thwarting

mortuary *n* charnel house, deadhouse, funeral parlour, morgue

most *n* almost all, bulk, greatest/largest part, lion's share *colloq*, majority, mass, nearly all, overwhelming majority, preponderance

mostly *adv* above all, as a rule, chiefly, especially, for the most part, generally, in general, in the main, largely, mainly, on the whole, overall, predominantly, principally, usually

moth *n*

Types of moth include:
brown-tail, buff-tip, burnet, carpet, cinnabar, clothes, emperor, garden tiger, gypsy, death's head hawkmoth, privet hawkmoth, Kentish glory, lackey, lappet, leopard, lobster, magpie, oak hook-tip, pale tussock, peach blossom, peppered, puss, red underwing, silkworm, silver-Y, six-spot, swallowtail, turnip, wax, winter

moth-eaten *adj* ancient, antiquated, archaic, dated, decayed, decrepit, dilapidated, mangy, moribund, mouldy, musty, obsolete, old, old-fashioned, outdated, outworn, ragged, seedy, shabby, stale, tattered, threadbare, worn, worn-out
🔁 fresh, new

mother *n* **1** *looks very much like her mother:* ancestor, dam, ma *colloq*, mam *colloq*, mamma *colloq*, mater *formal*, materfamilias *formal*, matriarch, matron, mom *US colloq*, mommy *US colloq*, mum *colloq*, mummy *colloq*, mumsy *colloq*, old woman *colloq*, parent, procreator *formal*, progenitress *formal* **2** *philosophy is the mother of the sciences:* base, cause, derivation, foundation, fount, origin, roots, source, spring, wellspring
♦ *v* **1** *mothered four children:* bear, bring forth, care for, cherish, look after, nurse, nurture, produce, raise, rear, take care of, tend **2** *still mothers her grown-up sons:* baby, fuss over, indulge, overprotect, pamper, spoil

motherly *adj* affectionate, caring, comforting, fond, gentle, kind, loving, maternal, protective, tender, warm
🔁 neglectful, uncaring

motif *n* **1** *the motif of death in his work:* concept, device, idea, theme, topic **2** *a motif of flowers:* decoration, design, emblem, figure, form, logo, ornament, pattern, shape

motion *n* **1** *the motion of the train:* action, activity, change, flow, going, inclination, locomotion, mobility, motility *formal*, movement, moving, passage, passing, progress, transit, travel, travelling **2** *made a motion with his hand:* act, action, gesticulation, gesture, indication, movement, nod, sign, signal, wave **3** *proposed a motion to adjourn the meeting:* bid, manifesto, offer, plan, project, proposal, proposition, recommendation, scheme, suggestion
♦ *v* beckon, direct, gesticulate, gesture, nod, sign, signal, usher, wave

motionless *adj* at a standstill, at rest, fixed, frozen, halted, immobile, inanimate, inert, lifeless, paralysed, resting, rigid, stagnant, standing, static, stationary, still, stock-still, transfixed, unmovable, unmoving
🔁 active, moving

motivate *v* activate, actuate, arouse, cause, drive, encourage, excite, goad, impel, incite, induce, initiate, inspire, kindle, lead, move, persuade, prompt, propel, provoke, push, spur, stimulate, stir, trigger, urge
🔁 deter, discourage, inhibit, prevent

motivation *n* ambition, desire, drive, hunger, impulse, incentive, incitement, inducement, inspiration, instigation, interest, momentum, motive, persuasion, prompting, provocation, push, reason, spur, stimulus, urge, wish
🔁 discouragement, prevention

motive *n* basis, cause, consideration, design, desire, goad, ground(s), impulse, incentive, incitement, inducement, influence, inspiration, intention, lure, motivation, object, occasion, persuasion, purpose, rationale, reason, spur, stimulus, thinking, urge
🔳 deterrent, disincentive

motley *adj* 1 *a motley collection of chairs:* assorted, diverse, diversified, heterogeneous *formal*, miscellaneous, mixed, multifarious, varied 2 *a motley cat:* brindled, colourful, dappled, many-hued, mottled, multicoloured, particoloured, piebald, pied, spotted, streaked, striped, tabby, variegated
🔳 1 homogeneous, uniform 2 monochrome

motor vehicle

Parts of a motor vehicle include:
ABS (anti-lock braking system), accelerator, airbag, air brake, air-conditioner, air inlet, antidazzle mirror, antiglare switch, anti-roll bar, antitheft device, ashtray, axle, backup light *US*, battery, bench seat, bezel, bodywork, bonnet, boot, brake drum, brake light, brake pad, brake shoe, bumper, car radio, car phone, catalytic converter, central locking, centre console, chassis, child-safety seat, cigarette-lighter, clock, clutch, courtesy light, crankcase, cruise control, dashboard, differential gear, dimmer, disc brake, door, door-lock, drive shaft, drum brake, electric window, emergency light, engine, exhaust pipe, fender *US*, filler cap, flasher switch, fog lamp, folding seat, four-wheel drive, fuel gauge, gas tank *US*, gear, gearbox, gear-lever (or gear-stick), glove compartment, grill, handbrake, hazard warning light, headlight, headrest, heated rear window, heater, hood *US*, horn, hub-cap, hydraulic brake, hydraulic suspension, ignition, ignition key, indicator, instrument panel, jack, jump lead, kingpin, license plate *US*, lift gate *US*, monocoque, number plate, oil gauge, overrider, parcel shelf, parking-light, petrol tank, pneumatic tyre, power brake, prop shaft, quarterlight, rack and pinion, radial-ply tyre, rear light, rear-view mirror, reclining seat, reflector, rev counter *colloq*, reversing light, roof rack, screen-washer bottle, seat belt, shaft, shock absorber, sidelight, side-impact bar, side mirror, silencer, sill, solenoid, spare tyre, speedometer, spoiler, steering-column, steering-wheel, stick shift *US*, stoplight, sunroof, sun visor, suspension, temperature gauge, towbar, track rod, transmission, trunk *US*, tyre, vent, wheel, wheel arch, windscreen, windscreen-washer, windscreen-wiper, windshield *US*, wing, wing mirror. See also **engine**

mottled *adj* blotched, blotchy, brinded, brindle, brindled, dappled, flecked, freckled, marbled, piebald, poikilitic *technical*, speckled, splotchy, spotted, stippled, streaked, tabby, variegated
🔳 monochrome, uniform

motto *n* adage, aphorism, axiom, byword, catchword, cry, dictum, epigram *formal*, formula, gnome *formal*, golden rule, maxim, precept, proverb, rule, saw, saying, slogan, truism, watchword

mould¹ *n* 1 *pour the metal into the mould:* cast, die, form, frame, framework, matrix, pattern, shape,
template 2 *a player of a different mould:* arrangement, brand, build, calibre, cast, character, configuration *formal*, construction, cut, design, figure, form, format, formation, kind, line, make, model, nature, outline, pattern, quality, shape, sort, stamp, structure, style, type
◆ *v* 1 *moulded the clay into a head:* carve, cast, construct, create, design, fashion, forge, form, frame, make, model, sculpt, shape, stamp, work 2 *attempts to mould public opinion:* affect, control, direct, form, influence, shape

mould² *n* blight, fungus, mildew, mouldiness, must, mustiness, rot

moulder *v* corrupt, crumble, decay, decompose, disintegrate, humify, perish, rot, turn to dust, waste

mouldy *adj* bad, blighted, corrupt, decaying, fusty, mildewed, musty, putrid, rotten, spoiled, stale
🔳 fresh, wholesome

mound *n* 1 *a mound of earth:* bank, barrow, dune, earthwork, elevation, embankment, hill, hillock, hummock, knoll, ridge, rise, tump, tumulus 2 *mounds of papers covered the desk:* abundance, accumulation, bundle, collection, heap, hoard, lot, mountain, pile, stack, stockpile, store, supply

mount *v* 1 *mounted a display of the students' work:* arrange, display, exhibit, install, launch, organize, prepare, produce, put on, set up, stage 2 *food prices mounted:* accrue, accumulate, build (up), escalate, grow, increase, intensify, multiply, pile up, rise, soar, swell 3 *mounted the steps to the stage:* ascend, clamber up, climb (up), climb on (to), get astride, get on, get up, go up, jump on (to), scale
🔳 2 decrease, descend 3 descend, dismount, go down
◆ *n* 1 *his trusty mount:* horse, steed 2 *lay the mount around the picture:* backing, base, fixture, frame, mounting, stand, support

mountain *n* 1 *the Welsh mountains:* alp, elevation, fell, height, hill, massif, mound, mount, peak, pinnacle, tor 2 *mountains of washing to do:* abundance, accumulation, backlog, heap, lot, mass, mound, pile, stack

The highest mountains of the world include:
Everest, K2 (Qogir), Kangchenjunga, Lhotse, Makalu, Dhaulagiri, Cho Oyo, Manaslu, Nanga Parbat, Annapurna

Mountaineering and climbing terms include:
abseiling, abseil station, adze, adz *US*, Alpinism, arête, ascender, ascent, avalanche; axe, ax *US*, ice axe, hammer axe; base camp; belay, belayer, non-belayer, self-belaying; bivouac; bolting, debolting; bouldering, cam, carabiner or karabiner, chalk bag, chalk cliff climbing, chimney, chock, chockstone, cleft, climbing wall, col, cornice, corrie, crag, crampon, crevasse, descender, descent, Dülfer seat, étrier, fissure, glacier, gully; harness, climbing harness, sit harness; hand hold, helmet, helmet lamp, hut, ice climbing, ice ridge, ice screw, ice slope, ice step, Munro; nut, wallnut; overhang, pick, piolet, pitch; piton, abseil piton, corkscrew piton, drive-in ice piton, ice piton, ringed piton; prusik knot, prusik loop, rappelling, ridge, rock, rock face, rock spike, rock wall; rope, dynamic rope,

kernmantel rope, standing rope, on the rope, unrope; saddle, scree, sérac, Sherpa, shunt; sling, abseil sling, rope sling, sling seat, wrist sling; solo ascent, snow bridge, snow cornice, snow gaiters, snow goggles, spike, sport climbing, spur; stack, sea stack; summit, top out, trad route, traverse, tying in

mountainous *adj* 1 *mountainous terrain:* alpine, craggy, high, highland, hilly, lofty, rocky, soaring, steep, towering, upland 2 *a mountainous dish of ice cream:* colossal, enormous, gigantic, huge, immense, massive, towering, vast
Fa 1 flat 2 tiny

mourn *v* bemoan, bewail, deplore, grieve, keen, lament, miss, regret, sorrow, wail, weep
Fa rejoice

mourner *n* bereaved person, griever, keener, mute, sorrower

mournful *adj* broken-hearted, cast-down, dejected, depressed, desolate, disconsolate *formal*, dismal, doleful, downcast, elegiac *formal*, funereal, gloomy, grief-stricken, heartbroken, heavy-hearted, lugubrious *formal*, melancholy, miserable, sad, sombre, sorrowful, tragic, unhappy, woeful *formal*
Fa cheerful, happy, joyful

mourning *n* bereavement, desolation, grief, grieving, keening, lamentation, sadness, sorrow, sorrowing, wailing, weeping
Fa rejoicing

moustache *n* face fungus *colloq*, handlebar moustache, mustachio, toothbrush moustache, walrus, whiskers

mousy *adj* 1 *mousy hair:* brownish, colourless, diffident, drab, dull, greyish, plain, uninteresting 2 *a mousy little girl:* quiet, self-effacing, shy, timid, timorous *formal*, unassertive, unforthcoming, withdrawn
Fa 2 assertive, bright, extrovert, irrepressible

mouth *n* 1 *kissed her on the mouth:* cakehole *slang*, chops *colloq*, embouchure, gob *slang*, jaws, kisser *colloq*, lips, trap *slang*, traphole *slang* 2 *the mouth of the cave:* aperture, cavity, door, doorway, entrance, gateway, hatch, opening, orifice *formal*, portal, stoma *technical*, vent 3 *the mouth of the river:* bay, delta, estuary, inlet, outlet 4 *she's all mouth and no action:* babble, blustering, boasting, bragging, empty/idle talk, gas *colloq*, hot air *colloq* 5 *don't give me any of your mouth!:* backchat, brass neck *colloq*, cheek, disrespect, effrontery *formal*, gall *colloq*, impertinence, impudence, insolence, lip *colloq*, nerve *colloq*, rudeness, sauce *colloq*
♦ *v* articulate, enunciate, form, pronounce, say, utter, whisper

---

Parts of the mouth include:
cleft palate, gum, hard palate, hare lip, inferior dental arch, isthmus of fauces, labial commissure, lower lip, palatoglossal arch, palato-pharyngeal arch, soft palate, superior dental arch, tongue, tonsil, upper lip, uvula.
See also **tooth**

---

mouthful *n* bit, bite, bonne-bouche, drop, forkful, gulp, morsel, nibble, sample, sip, slug, spoonful, sup, swallow, taste, titbit

mouthpiece *n* 1 *he's the mouthpiece of the PM:* agent, delegate, propagandist, representative, spokesman, spokesperson, spokeswoman 2 *the newspaper's the unoffical government mouthpiece:* journal, organ, periodical, publication

movable *adj* 1 *a movable date:* adjustable, alterable, changeable, flexible, transferable 2 *a movable seat:* mobile, portable, portative *formal*, transportable
Fa 1 fixed, immovable 2 fixed, immovable

movables *n* belongings, chattels *formal*, effects *formal*, furniture, gear *colloq*, goods, impedimenta *formal*, plenishings *formal*, possessions, property, stuff *colloq*, things *colloq*

move *v* 1 *the handle just wouldn't move:* act, advance, budge *colloq*, change, go, make strides, pass, proceed, progress, shift, stir, take action, travel, walk 2 *could you move the table onto the lawn?:* bring, carry, fetch, relocate, shift, shunt, swing, switch, take, transfer, transport, transpose *formal* 3 *they're moving in June:* decamp, depart, go away, leave, migrate, move away, move house, relocate, remove, transfer 4 *his words moved her to retaliate:* actuate, arouse, cause, drive, excite, impel, incite, incline, induce, influence, inspire, lead, motivate, persuade, prompt, propel, provoke, push, rouse, stimulate, urge 5 *the film moved him greatly:* affect, agitate, disturb, excite, impress, stir, touch, upset 6 *I move that we adjourn for an hour:* advocate, propose, put forward, recommend, request, suggest
♦ *n* 1 *made no move to leave:* activity, gesticulation, gesture, manoeuvre, motion, movement 2 *nothing was broken in the move:* change of address, migration, relocation, removal, repositioning, transfer 3 *moves to prevent the passing of the bill:* act, action, activity, device, manoeuvre, measure, step, stratagem, tack

movement *n* 1 *the movement of his limbs:* act, action, activity, agitation, gesticulation, gesture, move, moving, passage, relocation, repositioning, shifting, stirring, transfer, transportation 2 *no movement in prices:* advance, breakthrough, change, current, development, drift, evolution, fall, flow, improvement, passage, progress, progression, rise, shift, swing, tendency, trend, variation 3 *the movement to abolish smoking in public:* campaign, coalition, crusade, drive, faction, group, organization, party, wing 4 *a watch's internal movement:* action, guts *colloq*, mechanism, system, workings, works 5 *the slow movement of a symphony:* bit, division, part, passage, piece, portion, section

movie *n* feature film, film, flick, motion picture, picture, silent, talkie, video

moving *adj* 1 *a moving walkway:* active, astir, dynamic, in motion, kinetic *technical*, manoeuvrable, mobile, motile *formal* 2 *a moving speech:* affecting, arousing, disturbing, emotional, emotive, exciting, impressive, inspirational, inspiring, pathetic, persuasive, poignant, stimulating, stirring, thrilling, touching, upsetting, worrying 3 *the moving force:* driving, dynamic, influential, inspiring, leading, motivating, stimulating, urging
Fa 1 fixed, immobile 2 unemotional

mow *v* clip, crop, cut, scythe, shear, trim
► **mow down** butcher, cut down, cut to pieces, decimate, massacre, shoot down, slaughter

much *adv* a great deal, a lot, considerably, frequently, greatly, often, significantly, to a great extent
♦ *adj* a great number of, a lot, abundant, ample, considerable, copious, extensive, great, lots *colloq*, plentiful, substantial, widespread
♦ *n* a great deal, a lot, heaps *colloq*, lashings *colloq*, loads *colloq*, lots *colloq*, plenty
🔁 little

muck *n* **1** *I got covered in muck:* crud *slang*, dirt, filth, grime, grunge *slang*, gunge *colloq*, mire, mud, scum, slime, sludge, yuck *colloq* **2** *horse muck:* dung, excrement, faeces *formal*, guano *technical*, manure, ordure, sewage
▶ **muck about/around 1** *muck about in the playground:* fool around, lark about/around *colloq*, mess about/around *colloq*, play about, play around **2** *his girlfriend was mucking him about again:* bother, inconvenience, lead a merry dance *colloq*, lead up the garden path *colloq*, make life hell for *colloq*, send on a wild goose chase *colloq*, trouble, upset **3** *don't muck about with my CDs!:* disarrange, dishevel, disorder, interfere, meddle, mess up, tamper, untidy
▶ **muck up** botch, bungle, cock up *slang*, louse up *slang*, make a mess of, mess up, ruin, screw up *slang*, spoil, wreck

mucky *adj* begrimed, bespattered, dirty, filthy, grimy, messy, miry, mud-caked, muddy, oozy, slimy, soiled, sticky
🔁 clean

mucous *adj* gelatinous, glutinous, gummy, mucilaginous *formal*, slimy, snotty, viscid, viscous

mud *n* clay, dirt, mire, ooze, silt, sludge, soil

muddle *n* chaos, clutter, confusion, disarray, disorder, disorganization, jumble, mess, mix-up, tangle
♦ *v* **1** *muddled up the cards and asked me to pick one:* disorder, disorganize, jumble (up), mess up, mix up, scramble, tangle, throw into disorder **2** *muddle the brain:* befuddle, bemuse, bewilder, confound, confuse, daze, perplex, puzzle
▶ **muddle through** cope, get along, get by, make

muddled *adj* **1** *a muddled heap of clothes:* chaotic, disarrayed, disordered, disorganized, higgledy-piggledy, jumbled, messy, mixed-up, scrambled, tangled **2** *gran's become rather muddled lately:* at sea *colloq*, befuddled, bewildered, confused, dazed, disorient(at)ed, incoherent, perplexed, unclear, vague, woolly
🔁 **1** ordered **2** clear

muddy *adj* **1** *a muddy field:* boggy, dirty, filthy, foul, grimy, grubby, marshy, miry, mucky, oozy, quaggy, slimy, slushy, swampy **2** *muddy water:* blurred, cloudy, dingy, dull, fuzzy, hazy, murky, opaque, smoky, turbid
🔁 **1** clean **2** clear
♦ *v* **1** *muddied his trousers:* bedash, bedaub, begrime, bespatter, cloud, dirty, smear, smirch, soil **2** *muddy the issue:* cloud, confuse, disorganize, jumble (up), make unclear, mix up, scramble, tangle
🔁 **1** clean **2** clarify

muff *v* botch, bungle, fluff *colloq*, mess up, mishit, mismanage, miss, spoil

muffle *v* **1** *a scarf was muffled around his neck:* cloak, cover (up), envelop, swaddle, swathe, wrap, wrap up **2** *muffle the sound:* dampen, deaden, dull, gag, hush, mute, muzzle, quieten, silence, smother, soften, stifle, suppress
🔁 **2** amplify

mug[1] *n* beaker, cup, pot, tankard

mug[2] *v* assault, attack, bash, batter *colloq*, beat up, do over *colloq*, jump (on), knock about, rob, rough up *colloq*, set upon, steal from, waylay

mug[3] *n* chump *colloq*, fool, gull, muggins *colloq*, simpleton, soft touch *colloq*, sucker *colloq*

mug[4] *n* clock *colloq*, countenance *formal*, face, features, kisser *colloq*, mush *colloq*, phiz *colloq*, visage *formal*
▶ **mug up** bone up, con, cram, get up, study, swot

muggy *adj* airless, clammy, close, damp, humid, moist, oppressive, sticky, stuffy, sultry, sweltering
🔁 dry

mulish *adj* defiant, difficult, headstrong, inflexible, intractable *formal*, intransigent *formal*, obstinate, perverse, pig-headed *colloq*, recalcitrant *formal*, refractory *formal*, rigid, self-willed, stiff-necked, stubborn, unreasonable, wilful, wrong-headed

mull
▶ **mull over** chew over, consider, contemplate, deliberate, examine, meditate, muse on, ponder, reflect on, ruminate *formal*, study, think about, think over, weigh up

multicoloured *adj* brindled, colourful, dappled, motley, particoloured, piebald, pied, spotted, striped, variegated

multifarious *adj* different, diverse, diversified, legion, manifold *formal*, many, miscellaneous, multiform *formal*, multiple, multitudinous, numerous, sundry, varied, variegated

multiple *adj* collective, manifold *formal*, many, numerous, several, sundry, various

multiplicity *n* abundance, array, diversity, heaps *colloq*, host, loads *colloq*, lot, lots *colloq*, manifoldness *formal*, mass, myriad, number, numerousness, oodles *colloq*, piles *colloq*, profusion, scores *colloq*, stacks *colloq*, tons *colloq*, variety

multiply *v* accumulate, augment *formal*, boost, breed, build up, expand, extend, grow, increase, intensify, proliferate, propagate, reproduce, spread
🔁 decrease, lessen

multitude *n* **1** *a multitude of people:* assembly, congregation, crowd, herd, horde, host, legion, lot, lots *colloq*, mass, mob, swarm, throng **2** *music that appeals to the multitude:* common herd, common people, crowd, herd, hoi polloi, mob, people, plebs *colloq*, populace, public, rabble, riff-raff *colloq*
🔁 **1** few, scattering

multitudinous *adj* abounding, abundant, considerable, copious, countless, great, infinite, innumerable, legion, manifold *formal*, many, myriad, numerous, profuse, swarming, teeming, umpteen *colloq*

mum *adj* close-lipped, close-mouthed, dumb, mute, quiet, reticent, secretive, silent, tight-lipped, uncommunicative, unforthcoming

mumble *v* murmur, mutter, rumble, slur, speak in a low voice, speak softly, speak unclearly, stutter, talk to yourself, talk under your breath

mumbo-jumbo *n* abracadabra, cant, chant, charm, claptrap, conjuration *formal*, double talk *colloq*, gibberish, gobbledygook *colloq*, hocus-pocus *colloq*, humbug *colloq*, incantation, jargon, magic, mummery, nonsense, rigmarole, rite, ritual, spell, superstition

munch *v* champ, chew, chomp, crunch, eat, masticate *formal*

mundane *adj* **1** *mundane tasks:* banal, boring, common, commonplace, customary, everyday, hackneyed, humdrum, normal, ordinary, prosaic, regular, routine, stale, trite, typical, usual, workaday **2** *soiling the silver moondust with the mundane feet of men:* earthly, fleshly, secular, temporal, terrestrial, worldly
    1 extraordinary **2** spiritual

municipal *adj* borough, city, civic, civil, community, metropolitan, public, town, urban

municipality *n* borough, burgh, city, council, département, department, district, local government, precinct, town, township

munificence *n* altruism, beneficence *formal*, benevolence, bounteousness *formal*, bounty, charitableness, generosity, generousness, hospitality, largesse *formal*, liberality, magnanimousness, open-handedness, philanthropy
    meanness

munificent *adj* altruistic, beneficent *formal*, benevolent, big-hearted, bounteous *formal*, bountiful, charitable, free-handed, generous, hospitable, lavish, liberal, magnanimous, open-handed, philanthropical, unstinting
    mean

murder *n* **1** *convicted of murder:* assassination, bloodshed, butchery, execution, foul play, fratricide *formal*, homicide, infanticide *formal*, killing, liquidation *colloq*, manslaughter, massacre, matricide *formal*, patricide *formal*, slaughter, slaying, sororicide *formal*, uxoricide *formal* **2** *driving in town is murder:* agony, anguish, hell, misery, nightmare, ordeal, suffering, torment, torture, wretchedness
    v **1** *murdered a business rival:* assassinate, blow away *colloq*, bump off *colloq*, butcher, do in *colloq*, eliminate *colloq*, kill, knock off *colloq*, liquidate *colloq*, massacre, put to death, rub out *colloq*, slaughter, slay, take out *colloq*, waste *colloq*, wipe out *colloq* **2** *murder a Beatles tune:* botch, destroy, make a mess of, mess up, ruin, spoil, wreck **3** *got absolutely murdered in the final match:* annihilate, beat, clobber *colloq*, defeat easily, hammer *colloq*, lick *colloq*, outplay, outsmart, outwit, overwhelm, rout, slaughter *colloq*, thrash *colloq*, trounce, wipe the floor with *colloq*

murderer *n* assassin, butcher, cut-throat, homicide, killer, slaughterer, slayer

murderous *adj* **1** *Macbeth's murderous rise to power:* barbarous, bloodthirsty, bloody, brutal, cruel, cut-throat, deadly, fatal, ferocious, homicidal, killing, lethal, mortal, savage **2** *a murderous schedule of matches:* arduous, dangerous, difficult, exhausting, killing *colloq*, punishing, strenuous, unpleasant

murky *adj* **1** *murky skies:* cheerless, cloudy, dark, dim, dismal, dreary, dull, foggy, gloomy, grey, misty, obscure, overcast, veiled **2** *murky water:* cloudy, dark, dingy, dirty, turbid **3** *a murky past:* dark, mysterious, questionable, secret, shady, suspicious
    1 bright, clear, fine **2** clear

murmur *n* **1** *the murmur of bees:* drone, grumble, humming, mumble, muttering, rumble, undertone, whisper **2** *accepted it without a murmur:* beefing *colloq*, belly-aching *colloq*, carping, complaint, grouse *colloq*, grumble, moan, objection, protest, whingeing *colloq*
    v **1** *she murmured a request:* intone, mumble, mutter, whisper **2** *the generator murmured:* burble, buzz, drone, hum, purl, purr, rumble, rustle, whisper

murmuring *adj* buzzing, droning, mumbling, murmurous, muttering, purring, rumbling, whispering
    n buzz(ing), drone, mumble, mumbling, murmuration *formal*, muttering, purr(ing), rumble, rumbling, susurrus *formal*, whisper(ing)

muscle *n* **1** *strong muscles:* ligament, sinew, tendon **2** *use a bit of muscle:* beef, brawn, clout *colloq*, force, forcefulness, might *formal*, potency, power, stamina, strength, sturdiness, weight
    ▶ **muscle in** butt in, elbow your way in, force your way in, impose yourself, interfere, intrude, jostle, push in, shove, strongarm

muscular *adj* **1** *a muscular build:* athletic, beefy *colloq*, brawny, burly, hefty, husky, potent, powerful, powerfully built, robust, rugged, stalwart, strapping, strong, sturdy, vigorous **2** *muscular tissue:* fibrous, sinewy
    1 flabby, puny, weak

muse *v* brood, chew, cogitate *formal*, consider, contemplate, deliberate, dream, meditate, mull over, ponder, reflect, review, ruminate *formal*, speculate, think, think over, weigh up

mush *n* **1** *a tasteless mush:* corn, cream, dough, mash, pap, paste, pulp, purée, slush, swill **2** *sentimental mush:* mawkishness, schmaltz *colloq*, sentimentality

mushroom *v* boom, burgeon *formal*, expand, flourish, grow, increase, luxuriate, proliferate, shoot up, spread, spring up, sprout

mushy *adj* **1** *mushy peas:* doughy, pappy, pulpous, pulpy, soft, squashy, squelchy, squidgy, wet **2** *a mushy ballad:* maudlin, mawkish, saccharine, schmaltzy *colloq*, sentimental, sloppy, slushy, sugary, syrupy, weepy

music

> *Types of music include:*
> acid house, ballet, ballroom, bluegrass, blues, boogie-woogie, chamber, choral, classical, country-and-western, dance, disco, Dixieland, doo-wop, electronic, folk, folk rock, funk *colloq*, garage, gospel, grunge, hard rock, heavy metal, hip-hop, honky-tonk, house, incidental, instrumental, jazz, jazz-funk, jazz-pop, jazz-rock, jive, karaoke, operatic, orchestral, pop, punk rock, ragtime, rap, reggae, rhythm and blues (R & B), rock and roll, rock, sacred, ska, skiffle, soft rock, soul, swing, thrash metal *slang*. See also **jazz**

musical *adj* dulcet, euphonious *formal*, harmonious, lyrical, mellifluous, mellow, melodic, melodious, sweet-sounding, tuneful
🔢 discordant, unmusical

Musical terms include:
accelerando, acciaccatura, accidental, accompaniment, acoustic, adagio, ad lib, a due, affettuoso, agitato, al fine, al segno, alla breve, alla cappella, allargando, allegretto, allegro, al segno, alto, amoroso, andante, animato, appoggiatura, arco, arpeggio, arrangement, a tempo, attacca, bar, bar line, double bar line, baritone, bass, beat, bis, breve, buffo, cadence, cantabile, cantilena, chord, chromatic, clef, alto clef, bass clef, tenor clef, treble clef, coda, col canto, con brio, concert, con fuoco, con moto, consonance, contralto, counterpoint, crescendo, crotchet, cross-fingering, cue, da capo, decrescendo, demisemiquaver, descant, diatonic, diminuendo, dissonance, dolce, doloroso, dominant, dotted note, dotted rest, downbeat, drone, duplet, triplet, quadruplet, quintuplet, sextuplet, encore, ensemble, expression, finale, fine, fingerboard, flat, double flat, forte, fortissimo, fret, glissando, grave, harmonics, harmony, hemidemisemiquaver, hold, imitation, improvisation, interval, augmented interval, diminished interval, second interval, third interval, fourth interval, fifth interval, sixth interval, seventh interval, major interval, minor interval, perfect interval, intonation, key, key signature, langsam, larghetto, largo, leading note, ledger line, legato, lento, lyric, maestoso, major, manual, marcato, mediant, medley, melody, metre, mezza voce, mezzo forte, microtone, middle C, minim, minor, moderato, mode, modulation, molto, mordent, movement, mute, natural, non troppo, note, obbligato, octave, orchestra, orchestration, ostinato, part, pause, pedal point, pentatonic, perdendo, phrase, pianissimo, piano, piece, pitch, pizzicato, presto, quarter tone, quaver, rallentando, recital, refrain, resolution, rest, rhythm, rinforzando, ritenuto, root, scale, score, semibreve, semiquaver, semitone, semplice, sempre, senza, sequence, shake, sharp, double sharp, slur, smorzando, solo, soprano, sostenuto, sotto voce, spiritoso, staccato, staff, stave, subdominant, subito, submediant, sul ponticello, supertonic, swell, syncopation, tablature, tacet, tanto, tempo, tenor, tenuto, theme, tie, timbre, time signature, compound time, simple time, two-two time, three-four time, four-four time, six-eight time, tone, tonic sol-fa, transposition, treble, tremolo, triad, trill, double trill, tune, tuning, turn, tutti, upbeat, unison, vibrato, vigoroso, virtuoso, vivace

Musical instruments include:
balalaika, banjo, cello, double-bass, guitar, harp, hurdy-gurdy, lute, lyre, mandolin, sitar, spinet, ukulele, viola, violin, fiddle *colloq*, zither; accordion, concertina, squeeze-box *colloq*, clavichord, harmonium, harpsichord, keyboard, melodeon, organ, Wurlitzer®, piano, grand piano, Pianola®, player-piano, synthesizer, virginals; bagpipes, bassoon, bugle, clarinet, cor anglais, cornet, didgeridoo, euphonium, fife, flugelhorn, flute, French horn, harmonica, horn, kazoo, mouth-organ, oboe, Pan-pipes, piccolo, recorder, saxophone,

sousaphone, trombone, trumpet, tuba; castanets, cymbal, glockenspiel, maracas, marimba, tambourine, triangle, tubular bells, xylophone; bass-drum, bongo, kettle-drum, snare-drum, tenor-drum, timpani, tom-tom

musician

Musicians include:
instrumentalist, accompanist, performer, player, composer, bard, virtuoso; bugler, busker, cellist, clarinettist, drummer, flautist, fiddler, guitarist, harpist, oboist, organist, pianist, piper, soloist, trombonist, trumpeter, violinist; singer, vocalist, balladeer, diva, prima donna; conductor, maestro; band, orchestra, group, backing group, ensemble, chamber orchestra, choir, duo, duet, trio, quartet, quintet, sextet, octet, nonet

musing *n* absent-mindedness, abstraction, brown study, cerebration *formal*, cogitation *formal*, contemplation, daydreaming, dreaming, introspection, meditation, ponderment *formal*, reflection, reverie, rumination *formal*, thinking, wool-gathering

muss *v* disarrange, dishevel, make a mess of, make untidy, ruffle, tousle

must *n* basic, duty, essential, fundamental, imperative, necessity, obligation, prerequisite, provision, requirement, requisite *formal*, sine qua non, stipulation

muster *v* **1** *mustered an army of 2000 men*: assemble, bring together, call together, call up, convene, convoke *formal*, enrol, gather (together), marshal, mobilize, rally, round up, summon (up) **2** *a crowd mustered on the village green*: assemble, collect, come together, congregate, convene, gather (together), group, mass, meet, rally, throng ♦ *n* assemblage *formal*, assembly, collection, concourse, congregation, convention, convocation *formal*, gathering, march past, mass, meeting, mobilization, parade, rally, review, round-up, throng

musty *adj* airless, damp, dank, decayed, decaying, fusty, mildewed, mildewy, mouldy, smelly, stale, stuffy

mutability *n* alterability, changeableness, interchangeability, permutability, variability, variation

mutable *adj* adaptable, alterable, changeable, changing, fickle, flexible, inconsistent, inconstant, interchangeable, irresolute, permutable, uncertain, undependable, unreliable, unsettled, unstable, unsteady, vacillating, variable, volatile, wavering
🔢 constant, invariable, permanent

mutation *n* adaptation, alteration, anomaly, change, deviation, evolution, metamorphosis *formal*, modification, transformation, transmogrification *colloq*, variation

mute *adj* aphasic *technical*, dumb, mum *colloq*, noiseless, silent, speechless, taciturn, uncommunicative, unexpressed, unpronounced, unspoken, voiceless, wordless
🔢 talkative, vocal
♦ *v* dampen, deaden, dull, lower, moderate, muffle, quieten, silence, smother, soften, soft-pedal *colloq*, stifle, subdue, suppress, tone down
🔢 intensify

muted adj dampened, discreet, dull, faint, low-key, muffled, quiet, restrained, soft, softened, stifled, subdued, subtle, suppressed

mutilate v 1 *mutilate a corpse:* butcher, cripple, cut to pieces, cut up, disable, disfigure, dismember, hack (up), injure, lacerate, lame, maim, mangle 2 *the text was mutilated by censors:* bowdlerize *formal,* butcher *colloq,* censor, cut, damage, distort, hack *colloq,* impair, mangle, mar, ruin, spoil

mutilation n amputation, damage, detruncation *formal,* disfigurement, dismembering, maiming

mutinous adj anarchistic, bolshie *colloq,* contumacious *formal,* disobedient, disorderly, insubordinate, insurgent, rebellious, refractory *formal,* revolutionary, riotous, seditious, subversive, uncontrollable, ungovernable, unruly
◨ compliant, obedient

mutiny n defiance, disobedience, insubordination, insurgence, insurrection, protest, rebellion, resistance, revolt, revolution, riot, rising, strike, uprising
♦ v defy, disobey, protest, rebel, resist, revolt, rise up, strike

mutt n 1 *a scraggy little mutt with white paws:* bitch, cur, dog, hound, mongrel, pooch *colloq* 2 *you stupid mutt!:* dolt, dunderhead *colloq,* fool, idiot, ignoramus, imbecile, moron, thickhead *colloq*

mutter v 1 *muttering something about buying a new coat:* mumble, murmur, rumble, stutter, talk to yourself, talk under your breath 2 *muttered about job cuts:* beef *colloq,* belly-ache *colloq,* carp, complain, criticize, find fault, fuss, gripe *colloq,* grouse *colloq,* grumble, object, protest, whine, whinge *colloq*

mutual adj collective, common, complementary, exchanged, interchangeable, interchanged, joint, reciprocal, shared

muzzle v censor, check, choke, fetter, gag, inhibit, mute, restrain, silence, stifle, suppress

muzzy adj 1 *have a muzzy head:* addled, befuddled, bewildered, confused, dazed, groggy, muddled, tipsy 2 *a muzzy image:* blurred, faint, fuzzy, hazy, indistinct, unclear, unfocused
◨ 2 clear

myopic adj 1 *myopic vision:* half-blind, near-sighted, purblind, short-sighted 2 *myopic attitudes:* ill-considered, imprudent *formal,* localized, narrow, narrow-minded, parochial, short-sighted, short-term, thoughtless, uncircumspect *formal,* unwise
◨ 1 long-sighted 2 far-sighted

myriad adj boundless, countless, immeasurable, incalculable, innumerable, limitless, multitudinous *formal,* untold
♦ n army, flood, horde, host, millions *colloq,* mountain *colloq,* multitude, scores *colloq,* sea, swarm, thousands *colloq,* throng, zillions *colloq*

mysterious adj 1 *died in mysterious circumstances:* abstruse *formal,* arcane *formal,* baffling, cryptic, curious, enigmatic, hidden, incomprehensible, inexplicable, inscrutable, insoluble, mystical, mystifying, obscure, perplexing, puzzling, recondite *formal,* strange, unfathomable, unsearchable 2 *the mysterious world of magic:* as if by magic, baffling, curious, dark, furtive, hidden, mystical, obscure, reticent, secret, secretive, strange, surreptitious, veiled, weird
◨ 1 comprehensible, straightforward

mystery n 1 *a murder mystery:* conundrum, enigma, problem, puzzle, question, question mark, riddle, secret 2 *a sect cloaked in mystery:* ambiguity, curiosity, furtiveness, incomprehensibility, inexplicability, inscrutability, mystique, obscurity, reticence, secrecy, strangeness, surreptitiousness, unfathomability, weirdness

mystical adj 1 *a mystical religion:* esoteric, hidden, metaphysical, mystic, occult, other-worldly, paranormal, preternatural *formal,* spiritual, strange, supernatural, transcendental 2 *the mystical world of the cryptic crossword:* abstruse *formal,* arcane *formal,* baffling, incomprehensible, inexplicable, mysterious, obscure, recondite *formal,* strange, unfathomable, weird
◨ 1 logical, rational

mystify v baffle, bamboozle *colloq,* bewilder, confound, confuse, perplex, puzzle

mystique n appeal, awe, charisma, charm, fascination, glamour, magic, mystery, secrecy, spell

myth n 1 *Greek myths:* allegory, bestiary, fable, fairy story, fairy tale, folk tale, legend, parable, saga, story, tale 2 *his country manor house was a complete myth:* delusion, fabrication, fallacy, fancy, fantasy, fib *colloq,* fiction, invention, lie, pretence, tall story *colloq,* untruth

mythical adj 1 *mythical creatures:* chimerical *formal,* fabled, fabulous *formal,* fairytale, fantastic *formal,* fictitious, legendary, mythological 2 *a mythical wealthy father:* fabricated, fanciful, fantasy, fictitious, imaginary, invented, made-up, make-believe *colloq,* non-existent, phoney *colloq,* pretend *colloq,* pretended, put-on *colloq,* unreal, untrue
◨ 1 historical 2 actual, real, true

mythological adj fabled, fabulous *formal,* fairytale, fictitious, folkloric *formal,* legendary, mythic, mythical

---

Mythological creatures and spirits include: abominable snowman (or yeti), afrit, basilisk, bunyip, Cecrops, centaur, Cerberus, Chimera, cockatrice, Cyclops, dragon, dryad, Echidna, elf, Erinyes (or Furies), Fafnir, fairy, faun, Frankenstein's monster, genie, Geryon, Gigantes, gnome, goblin, golem, Gorgon, griffin, Harpies, hippocampus, hippogriff, hobgoblin, imp, kelpie, kraken, lamia, leprechaun, Lilith, lindworm, Loch Ness monster, Medusa, mermaid, merman, Minotaur, naiad, nereid, nymph, ogre, ogress, orc, oread, Pegasus, phoenix, pixie, roc, salamander, sasquatch, satyr, sea serpent, Siren, Sphinx, sylph, troll, Typhoeus, unicorn, werewolf, windigo, wivern

---

mythology n folk tales, folklore, legend, lore, myths, stories, tales, tradition(s)

N

nab *v* apprehend *formal*, arrest, capture, catch, collar *colloq*, grab, nail *colloq*, nick *colloq*, nobble *colloq*, seize, snatch

nabob *n* bigwig *colloq*, billionaire, celebrity, financier, luminary *formal*, magnate, millionaire, multimillionaire, personage, tycoon, VIP

nadir *n* all-time low, bottom, depths, low point, lowest point, low-watermark, minimum, rock bottom *colloq*, zero
Ⅎ acme *formal*, apex *formal*, peak, zenith

nag¹ *v* **1** *nagged her to tidy her room:* badger, berate *formal*, complain, grouse *colloq*, harass, harry, hassle *colloq*, henpeck *colloq*, keep on at, moan, pester, pick on, plague, scold, torment, upbraid, vex **2** *the thought had been nagging him all night:* aggravate *colloq*, annoy, bother, bug *colloq*, get your back up *colloq*, irritate, niggle, tease, trouble, worry

nag² *n* hack, horse, jade, keffel, plug *colloq*, rip, Rosinante

nagging *adj* **1** *a nagging pain:* aching, continuous, critical, distressing, irritating, niggling, painful, persistent, upsetting, worrying **2** *nagging remarks:* critical, moaning, nit-picking *colloq*, scolding, shrewish, tormenting

nail *v* **1** *nailed the noticeboard to the wall:* attach, fasten, fix, hammer, join, pin, secure, tack **2** *finally nailed her attacker:* apprehend *formal*, arrest, capture, catch, collar *colloq*, corner, grab, nab *colloq*, nick *colloq*, nobble *colloq*, pin down, seize, snatch, trap **3** *nailed his lie:* detect, expose, identify, reveal, uncover, unearth, unmask
♦ *n* **1** *a plank full of rusty nails:* brad, clout, fastener, pin, rivet, screw, skewer, sparable, spike, sprig, tack **2** *cut his nails:* claw, fingernail, nipper, pincer, talon, toenail

naïve *adj* artless, born yesterday, candid, childlike, credulous, frank, green *colloq*, guileless, gullible, immature, inexperienced, ingenuous, innocent, jejune *formal*, natural, open, simple, trusting, unaffected, unpretentious, unrealistic, unsophisticated, unsuspecting, unsuspicious, unworldly, wet behind the ears *colloq*, wide-eyed
Ⅎ experienced, sophisticated

naïvety *n* artlessness, candidness, childlikeness, credulity, frankness, guilelessness, gullibility, immaturity, inexperience, ingenuousness, innocence, naturalness, openness, simplicity
Ⅎ experience, sophistication

naked *adj* **1** *a naked body:* bare, denuded, disrobed, exposed, in the altogether *colloq*, in the buff *colloq*, in the raw *colloq*, in your birthday suit *colloq*, naked as the day you were born *colloq*, not a stitch on *colloq*, nude, starkers *colloq*, stark-naked, stripped, unclothed, uncovered, undressed, with nothing on **2** *the naked truth:* bald, blatant, evident, exposed, flagrant, glaring, open, overt, patent, plain, simple, stark, unadorned, undisguised, unqualified, unvarnished **3** *the actor admitted he felt naked without a script to hide behind:* defenceless, exposed, helpless, powerless, uncovered,

unguarded, unprotected, vulnerable, weak **4** *a naked landscape:* bare, barren, denuded, exposed, grassless, stark, stripped, treeless
Ⅎ **1** clothed, covered **2** concealed, veiled

nakedness *n* **1** *covered her nakedness with a throw:* bareness, nudity, starkness, the altogether *colloq*, the buff *colloq*, undress **2** *the nakedness of the greed in his eyes:* baldness, bareness, barrenness, openness, plainness, simplicity, starkness

namby-pamby *adj* anaemic, colourless, feeble, insipid, maudlin, mawkish, pretty-pretty, prim, prissy, sentimental, spineless, vapid, weak, weedy, wet, wishy-washy

name *n* **1** *what's your husband's name?:* appellation *formal*, cognomen *formal*, denomination *formal*, designation, epithet, handle *colloq*, label, monicker *colloq*, nickname, style, tag, term, title **2** *have a good name for treating their staff well:* character, distinction, eminence, esteem *formal*, fame, honour, popularity, prestige, prominence, renown, reputation, repute, standing **3** *there were several famous names at the dinner:* a somebody *colloq*, authority, big name *colloq*, big noise *colloq*, bigwig *colloq*, celebrity, dignitary, expert, hero, leading light, luminary, star, VIP
♦ *v* **1** *named their son Peter:* baptize, call, christen, denominate *formal*, dub, entitle, give name to, identify, label, style, tag, term, title **2** *named as the PM's successor:* appoint, choose, cite, classify, commission, designate, mention, nominate, pick, select, specify

---

Kinds of name include:
full name, first name, given name, Christian name, baptismal name, second name, middle name; surname, family name, last name; maiden name; nickname, sobriquet, agnomen, pet name, term of endearment, diminutive; false name, pseudonym, alias, stage-name, nom-de-plume, assumed name, pen-name; proper name; place name; brand name, trademark; code name

---

named *adj* **1** *a named brand:* baptized, by the name of, christened, denominated *formal*, designated, dit, dubbed, entitled, labelled, termed, titled **2** *at the named price:* appointed, chosen, cited, classified, commissioned, designated, identified, mentioned, nominated, picked, selected, singled out, specified, styled
Ⅎ **1** nameless

nameless *adj* **1** *nameless people:* anonymous, innominate *formal*, obscure, undesignated, unidentified, unknown, unlabelled, unnamed, unspecified, untitled **2** *a feeling of nameless wonder:* indescribable, inexpressible, unheard-of, unmentionable, unspeakable, unutterable
Ⅎ **1** named

namely *adv* ie, in other words, specifically, that is, that is to say, to wit *formal*, viz

nap¹ *n* catnap, doze, forty winks *colloq*, kip *colloq*, lie-down, light sleep, rest, siesta, sleep, snooze *colloq*
♦ *v* catnap, doze, drop off, get some shut-eye

colloq, have forty winks *colloq*, kip *colloq*, lie down, nod (off), rest, sleep, sleep lightly, snooze *colloq*

nap² *n* down, downiness, fibre, fuzz, grain, pile, shag, surface, texture, weave

nappy *n* diaper, disposable (nappy), napkin, serviette, towel

narcissism *n* conceit, egocentricity, egomania, egotism, self-centredness, self-conceit, self-love, self-regard, vanity

narcissistic *adj* conceited, egocentric, egomaniacal, egotistic, self-centred, self-loving, vain

narcotic *n* anaesthetic, analgesic, anodyne, downer *slang*, drug, opiate, painkiller, palliative, sedative, sleeping pill, soporific, tranquillizer, upper *slang*
♦ *adj* anaesthetic, analgesic, calming, dulling, hypnotic, numbing, opiate, pain-dulling, painkilling, sedative, sleep-inducing, somnolent *formal*, soporific, stupefacient *formal*, stupefying, tranquillizing

narked *adj* annoyed, bothered, bugged *colloq*, exasperated, galled, irked, irritated, miffed *colloq*, nettled *colloq*, peeved *colloq*, piqued, provoked, riled, vexed

narrate *v* chronicle, describe, detail, explain, portray, read, recite, recount *formal*, rehearse *formal*, relate *formal*, report, set forth *formal*, set out, state, tell, unfold

narration *n* account, chronicle, description, detail, explanation, history, portrayal, reading, recital, recountal *formal*, rehearsal *formal*, report, sketch, statement, story, storytelling, tale, telling, voice-over

narrative *n* account, chronicle, description, detail, history, portrayal, reading, report, sketch, statement, story, tale

narrator *n* anecdotist, annalist, author, chronicler, commentator, describer, raconteur, recounter *formal*, relater, reporter, storyteller, writer

narrow *adj* 1 *jeans with narrow legs*: attenuated *formal*, close, confined, constricted, cramped, fine, slender, slim, small, spare, tapering, thin, tight 2 *a narrow area*: circumscribed *formal*, close, cramped, exiguous *formal*, incommodious *formal*, limited, meagre, restricted, scant, squeezed, tight 3 *a narrow outlook on the world*: biased, bigoted, close-minded, conservative, dogmatic, dyed-in-the-wool, hidebound, illiberal, insular, intolerant, narrow-minded, petty, prejudiced, reactionary, rigid, set, small-minded, strait-laced 4 *in the narrow sense of the word*: exact, literal, original, precise, strict, true
🡻 1 wide 2 broad 3 broad-minded, tolerant 4 broad
♦ *v* attenuate *formal*, circumscribe *formal*, confine, constrict, cramp, diminish, limit, reduce, restrict, taper
🡻 broaden, increase, widen

narrowing *n* attenuation *formal*, compression, constipation, constriction, contraction, curtailment, emaciation, reduction, stenosis *technical*, tapering, thinning
🡻 broadening, widening

narrowly *adv* 1 *swerved and narrowly avoided the child*: barely, by a hair's breadth *colloq*, by a whisker *colloq*, just, only just, scarcely 2 *the doorman studied him narrowly as he came in*: carefully, closely, exactly, painstakingly, precisely, scrutinizingly, strictly

narrow-minded *adj* biased, bigoted, blimpish, close-minded, conservative, diehard, dyed in the wool, entrenched, exclusive, hidebound, illiberal, inflexible, insular, intolerant, jaundiced, opinionated, parochial, petty, petty-minded, prejudiced, provincial, reactionary, rigid, set, small-minded, strait-laced, twisted, ultra-conservative, unreasonable, warped
🡻 broad-minded, liberal, tolerant

narrowness *n* 1 *the narrowness of the alleys*: attenuation *formal*, closeness, constriction, limitation, meagreness, nearness, restrictedness, slenderness, thinness, tightness 2 *narrowness of mind*: bias, bigotry, conservatism, exclusiveness, insularity, intolerance, narrow-mindedness, parochialism, pettiness, prejudice, rigidity, small-mindedness
🡻 1 breadth, width 2 broad-mindedness, tolerance

narrows *n* channel, passage, sound, straits, waterway

nascent *adj* advancing, beginning, budding, burgeoning *formal*, developing, embryonic, evolving, growing, incipient *formal*, naissant *formal*, rising, young
🡻 dying

nastiness *n* 1 *the nastiness of the hotel room*: defilement, dirtiness, disagreeableness, filth, filthiness, foulness, horribleness, impurity, offensiveness, pollution, repulsiveness, squalor, uncleanliness, unpleasantness, unsavouriness 2 *shocked by the nastiness of the comedian's material*: filth, indecency, obscenity, porn *colloq*, pornography, smuttiness *colloq* 3 *the sheer nastiness of the critic's review raised eyebrows*: malevolence *formal*, malice, meanness, spite, spitefulness, viciousness

nasty *adj* 1 *a nasty smell*: awful, dirty, disagreeable, disgusting, distasteful, filthy, foul, grotty *colloq*, hateful, horrible, loathsome, malodorous *formal*, noisome *formal*, objectionable, obnoxious, odious, offensive, polluted, rank, repellent *formal*, repugnant *formal*, repulsive, revolting, sickening, squalid, unpleasant, vile, yucky *colloq* 2 *nasty sick jokes*: blue *colloq*, dirty, filthy, indecent, obscene, offensive, pornographic, ribald, smutty *colloq* 3 *don't be so nasty to your sister*: bad-tempered, cruel, disagreeable, malevolent *formal*, malicious, mean, spiteful, unkind, unpleasant, vicious 4 *a nasty cut on his forehead*: alarming, critical, dangerous, difficult, disquieting, grave, serious, tricky, unpleasant, worrying 5 *nasty weather*: awful, disagreeable, filthy, foggy, foul, rainy, stormy, unpleasant, vile, wet
🡻 1 agreeable, decent, nice, palatable, pleasant 3 benevolent, kind 5 fine

nation *n* 1 *the African nations*: country, kingdom, land, realm, republic, state 2 *the queen spoke to the nation*: community, people, population, society 3 *Native American nations*: race, tribe

national adj **1** a national strike: comprehensive, countrywide, general, nationwide, widespread **2** national policy: civic, civil, domestic, federal, governmental, internal, public, social, state
♦ n citizen, inhabitant, native, resident, subject

nationalism n allegiance, chauvinism, jingoism, loyalty, patriotism, xenophobia

nationalistic adj chauvinistic, ethnocentrist formal, jingoistic, loyal, patriotic, xenophobic

nationality n birth, clan, ethnic group, nation, race, tribe

nationwide adj coast-to-coast, comprehensive, countrywide, extensive, general, national, overall, state, widespread

native adj **1** the native people of Australia: aboriginal, autochthonous formal, domestic, home, home-grown, indigenous, local, mother, original, vernacular **2** her native good humour: built-in, congenital, connate formal, hereditary, inborn, inbred, ingrained, inherent, inherited, innate, instinctive, intrinsic, intuitive, natal formal, natural
♦ n aborigine, autochthon formal, citizen, dweller, inhabitant, national, resident
⊟ alien, foreigner, outsider, stranger

nativity n birth, childbirth, delivery, parturition formal

natter v blather colloq, blether colloq, chat, chatter, chinwag colloq, confab colloq, confabulate, gab colloq, gabble colloq, gossip, jabber colloq, jaw colloq, prattle colloq, rabbit (on) colloq, talk, witter colloq
♦ n blather colloq, blether colloq, chat, chinwag colloq, chit-chat, confab colloq, conversation, gab colloq, gabble colloq, gossip, jaw colloq, prattle, talk

natty adj chic, dapper, elegant, fashionable, neat, ritzy colloq, smart, snazzy colloq, spruce, stylish, trim, well-dressed

natural adj **1** it's natural to be nervous before an exam: common, everyday, normal, ordinary, regular, routine, run-of-the-mill, standard, typical, usual **2** her natural talent for horse riding: built-in, congenital, connate formal, inborn, inbred, indigenous, ingrained, inherent, inherited, innate, instinctive, intuitive, native, normal **3** natural fibres: additive-free, authentic, chemical-free, genuine, organic, plain, pure, raw, real, unmixed, unprocessed, unrefined, untreated, virgin, whole **4** a natural manner on TV: artless, candid, frank, genuine, guileless, ingenuous, open, simple, sincere, spontaneous, unaffected, unpretentious, unsophisticated
⊟ **1** unnatural **2** acquired **3** artificial, man-made, synthetic **4** affected, contrived, disingenuous

naturalist n biologist, botanist, creationist, Darwinist, ecologist, evolutionist, life scientist, plant scientist, zoologist

naturalistic adj factual, graphic, lifelike, natural, photographic, realistic, real-life, representational, true-to-life
⊟ idealistic, unrealistic

naturalize v **1** became naturalized to their new life in Canada: acclimate formal, acclimatize, acculturate formal, accustom, adapt, assimilate, domesticate, endenizen formal, enfranchise, familiarize, habituate formal **2** English phrases

naturalized into the French language: accept, adopt, assimilate, incorporate, introduce

naturally adv **1** naturally, we were suprised to win: absolutely, as a matter of course, as you would expect, certainly, logically, natch colloq, obviously, of course, simply, typically **2** a naturally charming man: artlessly, candidly, frankly, genuinely, ingenuously, instinctively, normally, sincerely, spontaneously

naturalness n artlessness, candidness, frankness, genuineness, informality, ingenuousness, openness, plainness, pureness, purity, realism, simpleness, simplicity, sincerity, spontaneity, spontaneousness, unaffectedness, unpretentiousness, wholeness

nature n **1** a girl with a lovely nature: attributes, character, characteristic(s), chemistry colloq, complexion, constitution, disposition, essence, essential quality/character, features, humour, identity, make-up, mood, outlook, personality, quality, stamp, temper, temperament **2** explain the nature of your call: category, class, description, kind, sort, species, style, type, variety **3** the laws of nature: cosmos, creation, earth, environment, mother earth/nature, universe, world **4** enjoyed the beauties of nature: country, countryside, landscape, natural history, scenery

naught n nil, nothing, nothingness, nought, zero, zilch colloq

naughty adj **1** he's such a naughty child: bad, badly behaved, defiant, disobedient, exasperating, incorrigible, misbehaving, mischievous, perverse, playful, refractory formal, roguish, undisciplined, unruly, wayward **2** naughty photos of the star have appeared on the Internet: bawdy, blue colloq, coarse, indecent, lewd, obscene, off-colour, ribald, risqué, smutty, vulgar
⊟ **1** good, well-behaved **2** decent

nausea n **1** suffered from nausea and dizziness: biliousness, gagging, puking colloq, queasiness, retching, sickness, throwing up colloq, vomiting **2** a feeling of utter nausea at the photographs: abhorrence formal, aversion, detestation formal, disgust, distaste, hatred, loathing, repugnance formal, revulsion

nauseate v disgust, gross out US colloq, make sick, make your gorge rise, offend, repel, revolt, sicken, turn off colloq, turn your stomach colloq

nauseating adj abhorrent formal, detestable formal, disgusting, distasteful, loathsome, nauseous, odious, offensive, repellent, repugnant formal, repulsive, revolting, sickening

nauseous adj about to throw up colloq, ill, nauseated, queasy, sick, under the weather colloq

nautical adj boating, maritime, naval, oceanic, sailing, seagoing, yachting

> **Nautical terms include:**
> afloat, aft, air-sea rescue, amidships, ballast, beam, bear away, beat, bow-wave, breeches buoy, broach, capsize, cargo, cast off, chandler, circumnavigate, coastguard, compass bearing, convoy, course, cruise, current, Davy Jones's locker, dead reckoning, deadweight, disembark, dock, dockyard, dry dock, ebb tide, embark, ferry, fleet, float,

flotilla, flotsam, foghorn, fore, foreshore, go about, gybe, harbour, harbour-bar, harbour dues, harbour-master, haven, head to wind, heave to, heavy swell, heel, helm, high tide, inflatable life-raft, jetsam, jetty, knot, launch, lay a course, lay up, lee, lee shore, leeward, life buoy, life-jacket, life-rocket, list, low tide, make fast, marina, marine, maroon, mayday, moor, mooring, mutiny, navigation, neap tide, on board, pitch and toss, plane, put in, put to sea, quay, reach, reef, refit, ride out, riptide, roll, row, run, run aground, run before the wind, salvage, seafaring, sea lane, sea legs, seamanship, seasick, seaworthy, set sail, sheet in, shipping, shipping lane, ship's company, ship water, shipwreck, shipyard, shore leave, sink, slip anchor, slipway, stevedore, stowaway, tack, tide, trim, voyage, wake, wash, watch, wave, weather, weigh anchor, wharf, wreck. See also **sail**

naval *adj* marine, maritime, nautical, sea, seafaring, seagoing

navel *n* belly-button *colloq*, centre, hub, middle, omphalos *formal*, tummy-button *colloq*, umbilicus

navigable *adj* clear, crossable, negotiable, open, passable, surmountable, traversable *formal*, unblocked, unobstructed

navigate *v* cross, cruise, direct, drive, guide, handle, helm, journey, manoeuvre, negotiate, pilot, plan, plot, sail, skipper *colloq*, steer, voyage

navigation *n* cruising, directing, direction, guidance, guiding, helmsmanship, manoeuvring, pilotage, piloting, sailing, seamanship, steering, voyaging

> *Navigational aids include:*
> astro-navigation, bell buoy, channel-marker buoy, chart, chronometer, conical buoy, Decca® navigator system, depth gauge, dividers, echo-sounder, flux-gate compass, Global Positioning System (GPS), gyrocompass, lighthouse, lightship, log, loran (long-range radio navigation), magnetic compass, marker buoy, nautical table, parallel ruler, pilot, radar, sectored leading-light, sextant, VHF radio

navigator *n* guide, helmsman, mariner, pilot, seaman

navvy *n* common labourer, digger, ganger, labourer, manual worker, worker, workman

navy *n* armada, fleet, flotilla, ships, warships

nay *adv* absolutely, actually, certainly, in fact, in truth, indeed, really, to be sure

ne'er-do-well *n* black sheep *colloq*, good-for-nothing, idler, layabout, loafer *colloq*, shirker *colloq*, skiver *colloq*, waster, wastrel

near *adj* **1** *where's the nearest hospital?: a stone's* throw from *colloq*, accessible, adjacent, adjoining *formal*, alongside, at hand, bordering, close, close by, contiguous *formal*, convenient, local, nearby, neighbouring, within range, within reach **2** *in the near future*: approaching, close, coming, forthcoming, immediate, imminent, impending, in the offing, looming, proximate *formal* **3** *her nearest relative is an elderly aunt*: akin, close, closely related, dear, familiar, intimate, related

4 *a near match for the paint*: alike, close, comparable, corresponding, like, similar
☒ **1** far, far off, far-away **2** distant **3** remote
♦ *adv* a stone's throw away *colloq*, alongside, at close quarters, at hand, close, close by, nearby, not far away, within close range, within reach
♦ *prep* adjacent to, adjoining *formal*, alongside, bordering on, close to, contiguous to *formal*, in the neighbourhood of, nearby, next to, within reach of
♦ *v* advance towards, approach, close in on, come nearer/closer, come/move towards, draw near to, get closer to
☒ keep your distance, withdraw

nearby *adj* accessible, adjacent, adjoining, close, convenient, handy, near, neighbouring, within reach
☒ faraway
♦ *adv* a short distance away, at close quarters, close at hand, in the vicinity, in your own backyard *colloq*, near, not far away, on your doorstep *colloq*, within reach

nearly *adv* all but, almost, approximately, as good as, close to, closely, just about, more or less, practically, roughly, virtually, well-nigh
☒ completely, totally

nearness *n* **1** *the nearness of the flat to my office*: accessibility, closeness, contiguity *formal*, handiness, propinquity *formal*, proximity *formal*, vicinity **2** *hadn't realized the nearness of the date of the wedding*: closeness, immediacy, imminence **3** *her nearness to her family*: chumminess, closeness, dearness, familiarity, intimacy

near-sighted *adj* half-blind, myopic, purblind, short-sighted

neat *adj* **1** *kept his desk very neat*: clean, in apple-pie order *colloq*, ordered, orderly, organized, shipshape, shipshape and Bristol fashion *colloq*, spick-and-span *colloq*, straight, tidy, well-ordered, well-organized **2** *a neat little man*: clean, dapper, natty *colloq*, smart, spruce, trim **3** *threw it with a neat flick of the wrist*: adroit, clever, deft, dexterous, expert, nifty *colloq*, nimble, practised, skilful **4** *a neat gadget to clean your keyboard*: compact, convenient, dainty, efficient, handy, user-friendly, well-designed, well-made **5** *a neat solution*: apt, clever, convenient, elegant, ingenious, nice, sensible, simple **6** *those trainers are really neat*: admirable, cool *slang*, excellent, fabulous, fantastic, great, marvellous, mega *slang*, smashing *colloq*, super *colloq*, superb, terrific *colloq*, tremendous, wicked *slang*, wonderful **7** *neat whiskey*: pure, straight, unadulterated, undiluted, unmixed
☒ **1** untidy **2** scruffy, shabby, slovenly **3** clumsy **7** diluted

neaten *v* arrange, clean (up), groom, put to rights, round off, smarten (up), spruce up, straighten, tidy (up), trim
☒ mess up

neatly *adv* **1** *papers stacked neatly in piles*: efficiently, methodically, smartly, sprucely, stylishly, systematically, tidily **2** *a neatly designed storage system*: aptly, cleverly, conveniently, daintily, elegantly, handily, nicely **3** *caught the keys neatly*: accurately, adeptly, adroitly, agilely, deftly, dexterously, effortlessly, expertly, gracefully, nimbly, precisely, skilfully
☒ **1** untidily **2** inelegantly **3** inexpertly, unskilfully

neatness n 1 *surprised at the neatness of the room:* methodicalness, orderliness, smartness, spruceness, straightness, style, stylishness, tidiness, trimness 2 *the neatness of the solution he suggested:* aptness, cleverness, daintiness, efficiency, elegance, handiness, niceness, nicety 3 *the neatness of her movements:* accuracy, adeptness, adroitness, agility, deftness, dexterity, expertness, grace, gracefulness, nimbleness, preciseness, precision, skilfulness, skill ⊟ 1 disorderliness, untidiness 2 inelegance

nebulous adj abstract, ambiguous, amorphous *formal,* cloudy, confused, dim, fuzzy, hazy, imprecise, indefinite, indeterminate *formal,* indistinct, misty, obscure, shadowy, shapeless, uncertain, unclear, unformed, vague ⊟ clear

necessarily adv accordingly, automatically, axiomatically, by definition, certainly, compulsory, consequently, incontrovertibly, ineluctably *formal,* inescapably, inevitably, inexorably, naturally, nolens volens, of course, of necessity, perforce *formal,* therefore, thus, willy-nilly

necessary adj certain, compulsory, crucial, de rigueur, essential, imperative *formal,* indispensable, ineluctable *formal,* inescapable, inevitable, inexorable, mandatory *formal,* needed, needful *old use,* obligatory, required, requisite *formal,* sure, unavoidable, vital ⊟ inessential, unimportant, unnecessary

necessitate v call for, compel, constrain, demand, entail, exact, force, involve, make necessary, need, oblige, require, take

necessity n 1 *a knowledge of Italian is an absolute necessity for the job:* compulsion, demand, desideratum *formal,* essential, exigency *formal,* fundamental, indispensable, must *colloq,* need, obligation, prerequisite, requirement, requisite *formal,* sine qua non *formal,* want 2 *the necessity of breathing:* indispensability, needfulness, obligation 3 *the necessity of death:* certainty, inescapability, inevitability, inexorability 4 *living in a state of absolute necessity:* deprivation, destitution, hardship, indigence *formal,* need, penury *formal,* poverty, privation *formal,* want ⊟ 4 luxury

neck n cervix *technical,* halse, nape, scrag, scruff ◆ v canoodle *colloq,* caress, kiss, smooch *colloq,* snog *slang*

necklace n band, beads, carcanet, chain, choker, gorget, jewels, lavallière, locket, negligee, pearls, pendant, rivière, string, torc, torque

necromancer n conjurer, diviner, magician, sorcerer, sorceress, spiritist, spiritualist, thaumaturge *formal,* thaumaturgist *formal,* warlock, witch, wizard

necromancy n black art, black magic, conjuration *formal,* demonology, divination, enchantment, hoodoo, magic, magical powers, sorcery, spiritism, spiritualism, thaumaturgy *formal,* voodoo, witchcraft, witchery, wizardry, wonder-working

necropolis n burial ground, burial place, burial site, cemetery, charnel house *formal,* churchyard, God's acre *formal,* graveyard

need v 1 *I really need your help:* be dependent on, be desperate for, be necessary to have, be reliant

on, call for, crave, cry out for, demand, depend on, desire, have need of, have occasion for, lack, miss, necessitate *formal,* pine for, rely on, require, want, yearn for 2 *he needs to work hard:* be compelled/obliged to, have to, must, ought, should ◆ n 1 *the need for caution:* call, demand, necessity, obligation, want, wish 2 *our basic needs:* desideratum *formal,* essential, necessity, prerequisite, requirement, requisite *formal* 3 *people in great need:* destitution, exigency *formal,* insufficiency, lack, neediness, penury, poverty, privation, want

needed adj called for, compulsory, desired, essential, lacking, necessary, obligatory, required, requisite *formal,* wanted ⊟ unnecessary, unneeded

needful adj essential, indispensable, necessary, needed, required, requisite *formal,* stipulated, vital ⊟ excess, needless, superfluous

needle n 1 *needle and thread:* bodkin, hypodermic needle, knitting needle, nib, pin, stylus 2 *the needle on the dial:* arrow, hand, indicator, marker, pointer 3 *pine needles:* barb, bramble, briar, bristle, prickle, quill, spicule *formal,* spike, spine, splinter, thorn ◆ v aggravate *colloq,* annoy, bait, cheese off *colloq,* goad, harass, irk, irritate, nag, nettle *colloq,* niggle *colloq,* pester, piss off *slang,* prick, prod, provoke, rile, ruffle, spur, sting, taunt, torment, wind up *colloq*

needless adj dispensable, expendable, gratuitous, pointless, purposeless, redundant, superfluous, uncalled-for, undesired, unnecessary, unwanted, useless ⊟ essential, indispensable, necessary

needlework n crocheting, embroidery, fancywork, needlepoint, sewing, stitching, tapestry, tatting

needy adj deprived, destitute *formal,* disadvantaged, hard up *colloq,* impecunious *formal,* impoverished, in need, indigent *formal,* on the breadline *colloq,* penniless, penurious *formal,* poor, poverty-stricken, unable to keep the wolf from the door *colloq,* underprivileged ⊟ affluent, wealthy, well-off

nefarious adj abominable, atrocious, base, criminal, depraved, detestable, dreadful, evil, execrable *formal,* foul, heinous *formal,* horrendous, horrible, infamous, infernal, iniquitous *formal,* loathsome, monstrous, odious, opprobrious *formal,* outrageous, satanic, shameful, sinful, terrible, unholy, vicious, vile, villainous, wicked ⊟ exemplary

negate v 1 *the slight rise in takings was negated by the rent increase:* abrogate *formal,* annul, cancel, countermand *formal,* invalidate, neutralize, nullify *formal,* quash, repeal, rescind *formal,* retract *formal,* reverse, revoke *formal,* undo, void, wipe out 2 *her statement is negated by the evidence:* contradict, deny, discredit, disprove, explode *colloq,* gainsay *formal,* oppose, refute *formal,* reject, renounce, repudiate, squash *colloq* ⊟ 2 affirm

negation n 1 *the negation of the contract:* abrogation *formal,* cancellation, countermanding

formal, disavowal *formal*, neutralization, nullification *formal*, repeal, veto **2** *a negation of his beliefs*: contradiction, denial, disclaimer, rejection, renunciation **3** *darkness is the negation of light*: antithesis *formal*, contrary, converse *formal*, inverse *formal*, opposite, reverse
⊟ 2 affirmation

negative *adj* **1** *a negative answer*: annulling, contradictory, contrary, denying, dissenting *formal*, gainsaying *formal*, invalidating, neutralizing, nullifying *formal*, opposed, opposing, refusing **2** *feeling very negative about the whole project*: critical, cynical, defeatist, gloomy, pessimistic, spineless, unco-operative, unenthusiastic, unhelpful, uninterested, unwilling, weak
⊟ 1 affirmative, positive **2** constructive, positive
♦ *n* contradiction, denial, dissension *formal*, opposite, refusal, rejection

neglect *v* **1** *neglected his children after his wife died*: abandon, disdain, disregard, forsake *formal*, ignore, leave alone, leave out, overlook, pass by, rebuff, scorn, slight, spurn **2** *neglected to answer the letter*: be lax about, fail (in), forget, let slide, omit, overlook, shirk, skimp
⊟ 1 appreciate, cherish **2** attend to, pay attention to, remember
♦ *n* carelessness, default *formal*, dereliction of duty *formal*, disdain, disregard, disrepair, disrespect, failure, forgetfulness, heedlessness *formal*, ignoring, inattention, indifference, laxity, negligence, oversight, rebuff, remissness *formal*, scorn, slackness, slight, spurning
⊟ attention, care, concern

neglected *adj* abandoned, derelict, disregarded, overgrown, unappreciated, uncared-for, uncultivated, underestimated, undervalued, unhusbanded, unmaintained, untended, untilled, unweeded
⊟ cherished, treasured

neglectful *adj* careless, disregardful, forgetful, heedless *formal*, inattentive, indifferent, lax, negligent, oblivious, remiss *formal*, sloppy *colloq*, thoughtless, uncaring, unmindful
⊟ attentive, careful

negligence *n* carelessness, default *formal*, dereliction of duty *formal*, disregard, failure, forgetfulness, heedlessness *formal*, inattention, inattentiveness, indifference, laxity, neglect, omission, oversight, remissness *formal*, shortcoming, slackness, sloppiness *colloq*, thoughtlessness
⊟ attentiveness, care, regard

negligent *adj* careless, casual, cursory, dilatory *formal*, forgetful, heedless *formal*, inattentive, indifferent, lax, neglectful, nonchalant, offhand, remiss *formal*, slack, sloppy *colloq*, thoughtless, uncaring, unmindful
⊟ attentive, careful, scrupulous

negligible *adj* imperceptible, inappreciable, insignificant, minor, minute, not worth bothering about, paltry, petty, small, tiny, trifling, trivial, unimportant
⊟ significant

negotiable *adj* **1** *the final details of the plan are still negotiable*: arguable, contestable, debatable, open to discussion/question, questionable, undecided, unsettled **2** *the path across the moors is*

not negotiable in winter: clear, crossable, navigable, open, passable, surmountable, traversable *formal*, unblocked, unobstructed
⊟ 1 definite, fixed, non-negotiable

negotiate *v* **1** *negotiate an agreement*: agree, arbitrate, arrange, bargain, come to an agreement, complete, conclude *formal*, confer *formal*, consult, contract, deal, debate, discuss, execute *formal*, fulfil, haggle, hammer out, intercede, intervene, manage, mediate, parley *colloq*, pull off, reach a compromise, resolve *formal*, settle, talk, thrash out, transact, wheel and deal *colloq*, work out **2** *crashed when trying to negotiate a bend*: clear, cross, get round, pass (over/through), surmount, traverse *formal*

negotiation *n* **1** *the negotiation of a settlement*: arbitration, bargaining, hammering-out, mediation, pulling-off, reaching an agreement, thrashing-out, transaction **2** *negotiations are still under way*: conference, debate, diplomacy, discussion, haggling, parley *colloq*, parleying, talks, wheeling and dealing *colloq*

negotiator *n* adjudicator, ambassador, arbitrator, bargainer, broker, diplomat, go-between, haggler, intercessor, intermediary, mediator, moderator, parleyer *colloq*, wheeler-dealer *colloq*

neigh *v* bray, hinny, nicker, whinny

neighbourhood *n* **1** *a residential neighbourhood*: area, community, district, locale, locality, part, precinct, purlieus *formal*, quarter, region **2** *in the neighbourhood of the factory*: confines, environs, proximity *formal*, surroundings, vicinity

neighbouring *adj* abutting *formal*, adjacent, adjoining *formal*, bordering, close at hand, connecting, contiguous *formal*, local, near, near at hand, nearby, nearest, next, surrounding
⊟ distant, far away, remote

neighbourly *adj* affable, amiable, companionable, considerate, cordial, easy to get on/along with, friendly, generous, genial, helpful, hospitable, kind, obliging, sociable, warm

nemesis *n* destiny, destruction, downfall, fate, just punishment, punishment, retribution, ruin, vengeance

neologism *n* coinage, innovation, new expression, new phrase, new word, novelty, vogue word

neophyte *n* apprentice, beginner, greenhorn *colloq*, learner, new member, newcomer, novice, noviciate *formal*, novitiate *formal*, probationer, raw recruit, recruit, rookie, tiro, trainee

nepotism *n* bias, favouritism, jobs for the boys *colloq*, keeping it in the family, looking after your own, old-boy network *colloq*, old-school tie *colloq*, partiality, preferential treatment

nerve *n* **1** *kept his nerve as he crossed the ravine*: bottle *colloq*, bravery, cool-headedness, courage, daring, determination, endurance, fearlessness, firmness, force, fortitude *formal*, grit *colloq*, guts *colloq*, hardihood, intrepidity, mettle, pluck, resolution, spirit, spunk *colloq*, steadfastness, valour, vigour, will **2** *had the nerve to say I was boring*: audacity, boldness, brass neck *colloq*, brazenness, cheek *colloq*, chutzpah *colloq*, effrontery, face *colloq*, gall, impertinence,

impudence, insolence, lip *colloq*, mouth *colloq*, neck *colloq*, presumption, sauce *colloq*, temerity ▣ **1** weakness **2** timidity
♦ *v* bolster, brace, embolden, encourage, fortify *formal*, hearten, invigorate, steel, strengthen
▣ unnerve

nerveless *adj* afraid, cowardly, debilitated *formal*, enervated *formal*, feeble, inert, nervous, spineless, timid, unnerved, weak
▣ bold, brave, strong

nerve-racking *adj* anxious, difficult, disquieting, distressing, frightening, harrowing, maddening, nail-biting *colloq*, stressful, tense, trying, worrying

nerves *n* anxiety, apprehensiveness, butterflies *colloq*, butterflies in your stomach *colloq*, collywobbles *colloq*, fretfulness, heebie-jeebies *colloq*, jitters *colloq*, nervous tension, nervousness, strain, stress, tension, willies *colloq*, worry

nervous *adj* agitated, anxious, apprehensive, disquieted, edgy, excitable, fearful, fidgety, flustered, fretful, het up *colloq*, highly-strung, in a stew *colloq*, in a sweat *colloq*, in a tizzy *colloq*, jittery *colloq*, jumpy *colloq*, keyed up *colloq*, nervy *colloq*, neurotic, on edge, on pins and needles *colloq*, on tenterhooks, perturbed *formal*, quaking, screwed-up *slang*, shaking like a leaf/jelly *colloq*, shaky, strained, tense, timid, timorous, twitchy *colloq*, uneasy, uptight *colloq*, with butterflies in your stomach *colloq*, with your heart in your mouth *colloq*, worried, wound up *colloq*
▣ calm, relaxed

nervous breakdown *n* clinical depression, cracking-up *colloq*, crisis, depression, melancholia, mental breakdown, nervous disorder, neurosis

nervousness *n* agitation, anxiety, apprehensiveness, disquiet, edginess, excitability, fluster, habdabs *colloq*, heebie-jeebies *colloq*, perturbation *formal*, restlessness, strain, stress, tension, timidity, timorousness, touchiness *colloq*, tremulousness, uneasiness, willies *colloq*, worry
▣ calmness, coolness

nervy *adj* agitated, anxious, apprehensive, edgy, excitable, fearful, fidgety, flustered, het up *colloq*, highly-strung, jittery *colloq*, jumpy *colloq*, keyed up *colloq*, neurotic, on edge, on pins and needles *colloq*, shaking like a leaf/jelly *colloq*, shaky, strained, tense, twitchy *colloq*, uneasy, uptight *colloq*, with butterflies in your stomach *colloq*, with your heart in your mouth *colloq*, worried, wound up *colloq*
▣ calm, relaxed

nescient *adj* backward, clueless *colloq*, dense *colloq*, ignorant, ill-informed, illiterate, inexperienced, innumerate, stupid, thick *colloq*, thick as two short planks *colloq*, unacquainted, unaware, uneducated, unenlightened, unfamiliar, uninformed, uninitiated, unlearned, unread, unschooled, untaught, untrained, unwitting
▣ clever, conversant *formal*, educated, knowledgeable, learned

nest *n* **1** *a bird's nest*: bird-house *US*, breeding-ground, cote, den, dovecote, eyrie, lair,

nesting-box, nidification *formal*, perch, roost, vespiary **2** *made a nest for herself among the cushions*: den, haunt, hideaway, hideout, hiding place, mew, refuge, retreat, shelter

nest egg *n* bottom drawer, cache, deposit, fund(s), money saved for a rainy day *colloq*, reserve(s), savings, store

nestle *v* cuddle (up), curl up, huddle (together), nuzzle, snuggle (up)

nestling *n* baby, chick, fledgling, suckling, weanling

net[1] *n* drag, dragnet, drift, drift-net, drop-net, filigree, fishnet, lace, lattice, latticework, mesh, meshwork, netting, network, open work, reticulum *formal*, seine, seine net, snare, tracery, trap, web, webbing
♦ *v* **1** *netted six mackerel*: bag, capture, catch, enmesh, ensnare, entangle, snare, trap **2** *net a dangerous criminal*: capture, catch, collar *colloq*, nab *colloq*, nick *colloq*, take captive

net[2] *adj* **1** *a net salary*: after deductions, after tax, clear, final, lowest, nett, take-home **2** *the net result was we lost the match*: broad, final, general, inclusive, overall, total, ultimate
▣ **1** gross
♦ *v* accumulate, bring in, clear, earn, gain, get, make, obtain, pocket, pull in *colloq*, raise, rake in *colloq*, realize *formal*, receive, take, take home

nether *adj* **1** *down in the building's nether regions*: basal *formal*, below, beneath, bottom, inferior *formal*, lower, lower-level, under, underground **2** *the nether world*: hellish, infernal, Plutonian, Stygian, underworld

nettle *v* aggravate *colloq*, annoy, bug *colloq*, chafe, discountenance, drive round the bend/twist *colloq*, exasperate, fret, get on your nerves *colloq*, get your blood/back up *colloq*, goad, harass, hassle *colloq*, incense, irritate, needle, pique, provoke, rub up the wrong way *colloq*, ruffle, sting, tease, torment, vex

nettled *adj* aggrieved, angry, annoyed, cross, exasperated, galled, goaded, harassed, huffy, incensed, irritable, irritated, miffed *colloq*, narked *colloq*, needled *colloq*, offended, peeved *colloq*, piqued, provoked, riled, ruffled, stung, vexed

network *n* **1** *a network of passages*: circuitry, convolution *formal*, filigree, grill, labyrinth, lace, lattice, latticework, maze, mesh, meshwork, net, netting, open work, tracery, web, webbing **2** *a communication network*: arrangement, channels, complex, grid, interconnections, matrix, nexus *formal*, organization, structure, system, tracks

neurosis *n* abnormality, affliction, derangement, deviation, disturbance, fixation, hang-up, instability, maladjustment, (mental) disorder, obsession, phobia, psychological disorder

neurotic *adj* anxious, compulsive, deranged, deviant, disturbed, hysterical, irrational, maladjusted, nervous, obsessive, overwrought, paranoid, phobic, unhealthy, unstable

neuter *v* caponize, castrate, doctor, dress, emasculate, fix *colloq*, geld, spay, sterilize

neutral *adj* **1** *a neutral witness*: detached, disinterested, dispassionate, even-handed, impartial, indifferent, non-aligned,

non-committal, non-partisan, objective, open-minded, unbiased, uncommitted, undecided, uninvolved, unprejudiced **2** *a rather neutral personality*: anodyne, bland, colourless, drab, dull, expressionless, indistinct, inoffensive, insipid, nondescript, ordinary, unassertive, unexceptionable, uninteresting, unremarkable **3** *a neutral colour*: beige, fawn, grey, indefinite, indistinct, pale, pastel
⊟ 1 biased, partisan, prejudiced **2** exciting, remarkable **3** colourful

neutrality *n* detachment, disinterest, disinterestedness, impartiality, impartialness, non-alignment, non-intervention, non-involvement, unbiasedness

neutralize *v* annul, balance, cancel (out), compensate for, counteract, counterbalance, frustrate, incapacitate, invalidate, make up for, negate, nullify *formal*, offset, undo

never *adv* at no time, no way *colloq*, not at all, not ever, not for a moment, not in a million years *colloq*, not in a month of Sundays *colloq*, not on your life *colloq*, not on your nellie *colloq*, on no account, under no circumstances, when pigs fly *colloq*
⊟ always

never-ending *adj* boundless, constant, continuous, endless, eternal, everlasting, incessant, infinite, interminable, limitless, non-stop, permanent, perpetual, persistent, relentless, unbroken, unceasing, unchanging, unending, uninterrupted, unremitting, without end
⊟ fleeting, transitory

nevertheless *adv* all/just the same, anyhow, anyway, at the same time, but, by any means, by some means, even so, for all that, however, in any case/event, nonetheless, notwithstanding *formal*, regardless, still, yet

new *adj* **1** *new technology*: advanced, avant-garde, contemporary, current, futuristic, latest, modern, modish, newfangled *colloq*, present-day, recent, state-of-the-art, topical, trendy *colloq*, ultra-modern, up-to-date, up-to-the-minute, way out *colloq* **2** *full of new ideas*: brand-new, creative, different, experimental, fresh, ground-breaking, imaginative, ingenious, innovative, mint, newborn, newly discovered, novel, original, pioneering, resourceful, revolutionary, strange, unconventional, unfamiliar, unknown, unused, unusual, virgin **3** *felt a new man after the operation*: altered, born-again *colloq*, changed, improved, modernized, redesigned, refreshed, reinvigorated, remodelled, renewed, restored **4** *with new ingredients*: added, additional, another, extra, further, more, supplementary **5** *new to the work*: a stranger, alien, ignorant, inexperienced, unaccustomed, unacquainted, unfamiliar, unknown, unversed
⊟ 1 old-fashioned, outdated, out of date **2** just another, ordinary, usual **3** old **5** familiar

newcomer *n* **1** *the town welcomes newcomers*: alien, colonist, foreigner, immigrant, incomer, intruder, (new) arrival, outsider, settler, stranger **2** *a newcomer to the world of journalism*: apprentice, beginner, greenhorn *colloq*, learner, neophyte *formal*, novice, probationer, pupil, recruit, rookie *colloq*, trainee

newfangled *adj* contemporary, fashionable, futuristic, gimmicky, modern, modernistic, new, novel, recent, state-of-the-art, trendy *colloq*, ultra-modern
⊟ old-fashioned

newly *adv* **1** *newly arrived from the US*: freshly, just, lately, latterly, of late, recently **2** *an old story newly told*: afresh, anew, freshly

newness *n* freshness, innovation, novelty, oddity, originality, recency *formal*, strangeness, unfamiliarity, uniqueness, unusualness
⊟ oldness, ordinariness

news *n* **1** *tell us all your news*: advice, data, developments, dope *colloq*, facts, gen *colloq*, gossip, hearsay, info *colloq*, information, intelligence, latest, lowdown *colloq*, revelation, rumour, scandal, story, tidings *formal* **2** *watch the news on TV*: account, announcement, bulletin, communication, communiqué, dispatch, exposé, news item, newscast, newsflash, press release, report, statement

newspaper *n* broadsheet, daily, gazette, journal, magazine, organ, paper, periodical, press, publication, rag *colloq*, sheet, tabloid, weekly

newsworthy *adj* arresting, hitting/making the headlines, important, interesting, notable, noteworthy, remarkable, reportable, significant, stimulating, unusual

next *adj* **1** *in the next room*: adjacent, adjoining *formal*, along, alongside, beside, bordering, closest, contiguous *formal*, nearest, neighbouring, tangential *formal* **2** *catch the next train*: ensuing, following, later, subsequent *formal*, succeeding, successive
⊟ 2 preceding, previous
♦ *adv* afterwards, later, subsequently *formal*, then, thereafter *formal*

nibble *n* **1** *just have a nibble of this chocolate*: bit, bite, crumb, gnaw, morsel, munch, peck, piece, taste **2** *prepared a few nibbles*: appetizer, bite, canapé, snack, titbit
♦ *v* bite, chew, eat, gnaw, munch, nosh *slang*, peck, pick at, snack *colloq*

nice *adj* **1** *have a nice time*: acceptable, agreeable, amusing, appealing, delectable *formal*, delightful, enjoyable, entertaining, fine, good, lovely, pleasant, pleasurable, satisfying, welcome **2** *he seems a nice man*: agreeable, amiable, attractive, charming, civil, courteous, delightful, endearing, friendly, genial, good, good-humoured, good-natured, kind, kindly, likeable, pleasant, polite, respectable, sweet, sympathetic, understanding, well-mannered **3** *a nice distinction between drama and docudrama*: accurate, careful, close, delicate, discriminating, exact, fastidious, fine, meticulous, minute, particular, precise, refined, scrupulous, strict, subtle
⊟ 1 horrible, unpleasant **2** disagreeable, nasty, unpleasant **3** careless

nicely *adv* agreeably, delightfully, pleasantly, pleasingly, pleasurably, properly, respectably, satisfactorily, well
⊟ disagreeably, nastily, unpleasantly

niceness *n* agreeableness, amiability, attractiveness, charm, delightfulness, friendliness, kindness, likeableness, pleasantness, politeness, respectability disagreeableness, nastiness, unpleasantness

nicety *n* **1** *the niceties of the agreement*: delicacy, distinction, fine point, nuance, refinement, subtlety **2** *the nicety of the craftmanship*: accuracy, exactness, finesse, meticulousness, minuteness, precision, scrupulousness

niche *n* **1** *found her niche in the world of publishing*: calling, métier, place, position, slot, specialized/ specialist area, vocation **2** *a candle burned in a niche in the wall*: alcove, corner, cranny, cubbyhole, hollow, nook, opening, recess

nick *n* **1** *made a nick in the surface of the table*: chip, cut, dent, groove, indentation, mark, notch, scar, scratch **2** *been in the nick for armed robbery*: clink *slang*, cooler *slang*, inside *colloq*, jail, jailhouse, jug *slang*, police station, prison, slammer *slang* **3** *in good nick*: condition, fettle, form, health, shape, state
♦ *v* **1** *nicked the paintwork around the door*: chip, cut, damage, dent, indent, mark, notch, scar, score, scratch, snick **2** *my bike's been nicked again*: knock off *colloq*, lag *colloq*, pilfer, pinch *colloq*, pocket, snitch *colloq*, steal, swipe *colloq*, take **3** *was nicked for speeding*: apprehend *formal*, arrest, bust *slang*, capture, catch, collar *colloq*, nab *colloq*, pick up, run in *colloq*

nickname *n* diminutive, epithet, familiar name, pet name, sobriquet

nifty *adj* **1** *a nifty bit of parking*: adroit, agile, clever, deft, excellent, neat, skilful, slick **2** *a nifty gadget*: apt, clever, handy, neat, pleasing **3** *his new car's quite nifty*: fast, nippy, quick **4** *a nifty dresser*: chic, neat, sharp, smart, spruce, stylish

niggardliness *n* **1** *ashamed of her father's niggardliness*: cheese-paring *colloq*, closeness, grudgingness, meanness, miserliness, parsimony *formal*, stinginess *colloq*, tight-fistedness *colloq*, ungenerousness **2** *the niggardliness of her gift*: inadequacy, insufficiency, meagreness, paltriness, scantiness, skimpiness, smallness
1 generosity **2** bountifulness

niggardly *adj* **1** *a niggardly old man*: cheese-paring *colloq*, close, grudging, hard-fisted, mean, miserly, parsimonious *formal*, sparing, stingy *colloq*, tight-fisted *colloq*, ungenerous, ungiving **2** *a niggardly allowance*: inadequate, insufficient, meagre, measly *colloq*, miserable, paltry, scanty, skimpy, small
1 generous **2** bountiful

niggle *v* **1** *doubts had started to niggle her*: annoy, bother, bug *colloq*, irritate, trouble, upset, worry **2** *please stop niggling me about the cost*: carp, complain, criticize, hassle *colloq*, henpeck *colloq*, keep on at, moan, nag, nit-pick *colloq*, pick on, quibble

night *n* dark, darkness, dead of night, hours of darkness, night-time
day, daytime

nightclub *n* cabaret, club, disco, discotheque, nightspot, niterie *colloq*, nitery *colloq*

nightfall *n* crepuscule *formal*, dark, dusk, evening, gloaming *formal*, sundown, sunset, twilight
dawn, sunrise

nightmare *n* **1** *I had a terrible nightmare last night*: bad dream, hallucination, incubus *formal* **2** *the flight was an absolute nightmare*: agony, anguish,

awful experience, calamity, horror, ordeal, torment, torture, trial

nightmarish *adj* agonizing, alarming, creepy *colloq*, disturbing, dreadful, frightening, harrowing, horrible, horrific, scaring, terrifying, unreal

nihilism *n* abnegation *formal*, agnosticism, anarchy, atheism, cynicism, denial, disbelief, disorder, emptiness, lawlessness, negation, negativism, non-existence, nothingness, nullity *formal*, oblivion, pessimism, rejection, renunciation *formal*, repudiation, scepticism

nihilist *n* agitator, agnostic, anarchist, antinomian, atheist, cynic, disbeliever, extremist, negationist, negativist, pessimist, revolutionary, sceptic

nil *n* duck *colloq*, love, naught, none, nothing, nought, zero, zilch *colloq*

nimble *adj* **1** *he's very nimble for his age*: active, agile, brisk, deft, graceful, light-footed, lithe, lively, nippy *colloq*, prompt, quick, quick-moving, ready, smart, sprightly, spry, swift **2** *a nimble brain*: alert, clever, quick, quick-thinking, quick-witted, sharp-eyed, sharp-witted, smart
1 clumsy, slow **2** slow

nimbleness *n* adroitness, agility, alacrity *formal*, alertness, deftness, dexterity, finesse, grace, lightness, niftiness *colloq*, nippiness *colloq*, skill, smartness, sprightliness, spryness

nimbly *adv* actively, agilely, alertly, briskly, deftly, dexterously, easily, fast, proficiently, promptly, quickly, quick-wittedly, readily, sharply, smartly, snappily, speedily, spryly, swiftly
awkwardly, clumsily

nincompoop *n* blockhead *colloq*, chump *colloq*, clot *colloq*, dimwit, dolt, dunce, fool, idiot, ignoramus, nerd *slang*, nitwit *colloq*, numskull *colloq*, plonker *slang*, simpleton, twerp *colloq*, twit *colloq*, wally *slang*

nip¹ *v* **1** *the dog nipped her on the leg*: bite, catch, clip, grip, nibble, pinch, snip, squeeze, tweak **2** *nipped out to the newsagent's*: dash, fly, go, hurry, pop *colloq*, run, rush, tear

nip² *n* dram, draught, drop, mouthful, portion, shot, sip, swallow, taste, tot

nipple *n* breast, dug, mamilla *technical*, pap, papilla, teat, tit *slang*, udder

nippy *adj* **1** *it was a bit nippy in the old cabin*: biting, chilly, cold, nipping, piercing, raw, sharp, stinging **2** *at 43, he's still quite nippy on the tennis court*: active, agile, brisk, fast, nimble, quick, speedy, sprightly, spry
1 warm **2** slow

nirvana *n* bliss, ecstasy, enlightenment, exaltation, joy, paradise, peace, serenity, tranquillity

nit-picking *adj* captious, carping, cavilling, critical, finicky, fussy, hair-splitting, hypercritical, pedantic, quibbling

nitty-gritty *n* basics, bottom line *colloq*, brass tacks *colloq*, essentials, fundamentals, key points, main points, nuts and bolts *colloq*

nitwit *n* dimwit, dummy *colloq*, fool, idiot, nincompoop *colloq*, ninny *colloq*, nit *colloq*, numskull *colloq*, simpleton, twit *colloq*

no *adv* absolutely not, most certainly not, no thanks, no way *colloq*, nope *colloq*, not at all, not on your life *colloq*, not really, of course not, over my dead body *colloq*, under no circumstances

nob *n* aristocrat, big shot *colloq*, bigwig *colloq*, fat cat *colloq*, personage, toff *colloq*, VIP

nobble *v* 1 *accused of nobbling the jury:* bribe, buy (off), influence, intimidate, threaten, warn off 2 *the favourite had been nobbled:* disable, dope, drug, get at *colloq*, hamstring, incapacitate, interfere with 3 *the suspect was nobbled as he left his hotel:* arrest, catch, collar *colloq*, grab, nab *colloq*, nick *colloq*, seize 4 *somebody nobbled my watch:* grab, knock off *colloq*, nick *colloq*, pilfer, pinch, snitch *colloq*, steal, swipe *colloq*, take 5 *nobbled her attempt for promotion:* check, defeat, foil, frustrate, hinder, thwart

nobility *n* 1 *nobility of spirit:* dignity, eminence, excellence, generosity, honour, integrity, magnanimity, nobleness, superiority, uprightness, virtue, worthiness 2 *the nobility of their country estate:* grandeur, grandness, illustriousness, impressiveness, magnificence, majesty, splendour, stateliness 3 *a member of the nobility:* aristocracy, élite, gentry, high society, lords, nobles, nobs *colloq*, peerage, peers, toffs *colloq*
🗷 1 baseness 3 proletariat

> **Titles of the nobility include:**
> aristocrat, baron, baroness, baronet, count, countess, dame, dowager, duchess, duke, earl, governor, grand duke, knight, lady, laird, liege, liege lord, life peer, lord, marchioness, marquess, marquis, noble, nobleman, noblewoman, peer, peeress, ruler, seigneur, squire, thane, viscount, viscountess

noble *n* aristocrat, lady, lord, nobleman, noblewoman, peer
🗷 commoner
♦ *adj* 1 *from a noble family:* aristocratic, blue-blooded *colloq*, born with a silver spoon in your mouth *colloq*, high-born, high-ranking, landed, patrician, titled 2 *a noble pile in Gloucestershire:* dignified, distinguished, eminent, exalted, fine, grand, great, imposing, impressive, lofty, magnificent, majestic, splendid, stately, venerated 3 *fighting for a noble cause:* elevated, excellent, fine, generous, gentle, honourable, magnanimous, self-sacrificing, unselfish, virtuous, worthy
🗷 1 low-born 3 base, contemptible, ignoble

nobody *pron* no one, not a soul, not one person, nothing
🗷 somebody
♦ *n* cipher, lightweight *colloq*, mediocrity, menial, nonentity
🗷 somebody

nod *v* 1 *the receptionist nodded for me to go in:* acknowledge, bow, dip, gesture, incline, indicate, salute, sign, signal 2 *I asked if I could go and he nodded:* accept, agree, approve, assent *formal*, say yes to, support 3 *she soon nodded off in the hot sun:* doze (off), drop off *colloq*, drowse, fall asleep, nap, sleep, slumber *formal*
♦ *n* acknowledgement, beck, gesture, greeting, indication, salute, sign, signal

node *n* bud, bump, carbuncle, growth, knob, knot, lump, nodule, protuberance, swelling

noise *n* babble, blare, clamour, clash, clatter, commotion, cry, din, hubbub, outcry, pandemonium, racket, row, sound, talk, tumult, uproar
🗷 quiet, silence
♦ *v* announce, circulate, publicize, report, rumour

noiseless *adj* hushed, inaudible, mute, quiet, silent, soundless, still
🗷 loud, noisy

noisome *adj* bad, deleterious *formal*, disagreeable, disgusting, fetid *formal*, foul, harmful, hurtful, injurious, malodorous *formal*, mephitic *formal*, nauseating, noxious *formal*, obnoxious, offensive, pernicious, pestiferous *formal*, pestilential *formal*, poisonous, putrid, reeking, repulsive, smelly, stinking, unhealthy, unwholesome
🗷 balmy, pleasant, wholesome

noisy *adj* 1 *a noisy bar:* blaring, blasting, booming, clamorous, deafening, ear-splitting, loud, piercing, so loud you can't hear yourself think *colloq*, thundering, tumultuous, turbulent 2 *noisy children:* boisterous, obstreperous, roaring, rowdy, rumbustious, vocal, vociferous *formal*
🗷 1 peaceful, quiet, silent 2 quiet, silent

nomad *n* itinerant, migrant, rambler, roamer, rover, transient, traveller, vagabond, vagrant, wanderer

nomadic *adj* drifting, Gypsy, itinerant, migrant, migratory, peregrinating *formal*, peripatetic *formal*, roaming, roving, travelling, unsettled, vagrant, wandering

nom-de-plume *n* alias, assumed name, pen-name, pseudonym

nomenclature *n* classification, codification *formal*, locution *formal*, naming, phraseology, taxonomy *technical*, terminology, vocabulary

nominal *adj* 1 *nominal head of the organization:* formal, in name only, ostensible, professed, puppet, purported *formal*, self-styled, so-called, supposed, symbolic, theoretical, titular 2 *pay a nominal amount:* insignificant, minimal, small, symbolic, token, trifling, trivial
🗷 1 actual, genuine, real

nominate *v* 1 *nominated him for the award:* designate, present, propose, put up *colloq*, recommend, submit, suggest 2 *nominated as the president's successor:* appoint, assign, choose, commission, elect, elevate, name, select, term

nomination *n* 1 *here are the nominations for best actor:* proposal, recommendation, submission, suggestion 2 *his nomination as vice-president:* appointment, choice, designation, election, selection

nominee *n* appointee, assignee, candidate, contestant, entrant, runner

non-aligned *adj* impartial, independent, neutral, non-partisan, uncommitted, undecided, uninvolved

nonchalance *n* aplomb *formal*, calm, composure, cool, detachment, equanimity *formal*, imperturbability *formal*, indifference, insouciance *formal*, pococurant(e)ism *formal*, sangfroid *formal*, self-possession, unconcern
🗷 anxiousness, worriedness

nonchalant *adj* apathetic, blasé, calm, careless, casual, collected, cool, cool and collected *colloq*, cool as a cucumber *colloq*, detached, dispassionate, imperturbable *formal*, indifferent, insouciant *formal*, laid-back *colloq*, offhand, unconcerned
🔄 careful, concerned

non-committal *adj* ambiguous, careful, cautious, circumspect *formal*, diplomatic, discreet, equivocal, evasive, guarded, indefinite, neutral, playing your cards close to your chest *colloq*, politic *formal*, prudent *formal*, reserved, sitting on the fence *colloq*, tactful, tentative, unrevealing, vague, wary

non compos mentis *adj* crazy, deranged, insane, mentally ill, of unsound mind, unbalanced, unhinged
🔄 sane, stable

nonconformist *n* dissenter, dissentient *formal*, dissident, eccentric, fish out of water *colloq*, heretic, iconoclast, individualist, maverick, protester, radical, rebel, seceder, secessionist, square peg in a round hole *colloq*
🔄 conformist
♦ *adj* dissentient *formal*, dissident, eccentric, heretical, individualist, radical, rebel, uncooperative

nonconformity *n* deviation, dissent, eccentricity, heresy, heterodoxy, originality, secession, unconventionality
🔄 conformity, conventionality

nondescript *adj* anaemic, bland, common or garden *colloq*, commonplace, dull, featureless, indeterminate, indistinguishable, insipid, ordinary, plain, run of the mill *colloq*, unattractive, unclassified, undistinctive, undistinguished, unexceptional, uninspiring, uninteresting, unremarkable, vague
🔄 distinctive, remarkable

none *pron* nil, no one, nobody, not a single one, not a soul, not any, not even one, not one, nothing, zero

nonentity *n* cipher, lightweight *colloq*, mediocrity, menial, nobody, nothing
🔄 somebody

non-essential *adj* dispensable, excessive, expendable, extraneous, inessential, peripheral, redundant, superfluous, supplementary, unimportant, unnecessary, unneeded
🔄 essential, necessary

nonetheless *adv* anyhow, anyway, but, even so, however, nevertheless, notwithstanding *formal*, regardless, still, yet

non-existence *n* chimera *formal*, fancy, illusion, illusiveness, insubstantiality, unbeing, unreality
🔄 existence, reality

non-existent *adj* chimerical *formal*, fancied, fanciful, fantasy, fictional, fictitious, hallucinatory, hypothetical, illusory, imaginary, imagined, immaterial, incorporeal *formal*, insubstantial, legendary, missing, mythical, null, suppositional *formal*, unreal
🔄 actual, existing, real

non-flammable *adj* fire-proof, fire-resistant, flame-resistant, incombustible, not flammable, uninflammable
🔄 flammable, inflammable

non-intervention *n* apathy, hands-off policy *colloq*, inaction, inertia, laissez-faire, non-alignment, non-interference, non-involvement, non-participation, passivity

nonpareil *adj* beyond compare, incomparable, inimitable, matchless, unequalled, unique, unparalleled, unrivalled, without equal

non-partisan *adj* detached, dispassionate, even-handed, impartial, independent, neutral, objective, unbiased, unprejudiced
🔄 biased, partisan, prejudiced

nonplus *v* astonish, astound, baffle, bewilder, confound, confuse, discomfit *formal*, disconcert, discountenance *formal*, dismay, dumbfound, embarrass, faze *colloq*, flabbergast *colloq*, flummox *colloq*, mystify, perplex, puzzle, stump, stun, take aback

nonplussed *adj* astonished, astounded, at a loss, baffled, bewildered, confounded, disconcerted, dismayed, dumbfounded, embarrassed, fazed *colloq*, flabbergasted *colloq*, floored *colloq*, flummoxed *colloq*, out of your depth *colloq*, perplexed, puzzled, stumped *colloq*, stunned, taken aback

nonsense *n* balderdash, balls *slang*, baloney *colloq*, bilge *colloq*, blather, bosh *colloq*, bull *colloq*, bullshit *slang*, bunk *colloq*, bunkum *colloq*, claptrap *colloq*, cobblers *colloq*, codswallop *colloq*, crap *slang*, double Dutch *colloq*, drivel, flannel *colloq*, folly, foolishness, gibberish, gobbledygook, hooey *colloq*, humbug *colloq*, mumbo-jumbo *colloq*, piffle *colloq*, poppycock *colloq*, ridiculousness, rot *colloq*, rubbish, senselessness, shit *slang*, silliness, stuff and nonsense *colloq*, stupidity, tommy-rot *colloq*, tosh *colloq*, trash, tripe *colloq*, twaddle, waffle *colloq*
🔄 sense, wisdom

nonsensical *adj* absurd, barmy *colloq*, crackpot *colloq*, crazy *colloq*, dotty *colloq*, fatuous, foolish, hare-brained *colloq*, inane, incomprehensible, irrational, ludicrous, meaningless, nutty *colloq*, potty *colloq*, preposterous, ridiculous, senseless, silly, stupid, unintelligible, wacky *colloq*
🔄 logical, reasonable, sensible

non-stop *adj* ceaseless, constant, continuous, endless, incessant, interminable, never-ending, ongoing, persistent, relentless, round-the-clock, unbroken, unceasing, unending, unfaltering, uninterrupted, without interruption
🔄 intermittent, occasional
♦ *adv* ceaselessly, constantly, continuously, endlessly, incessantly, interminably, relentlessly, round-the-clock, steadily, unbrokenly, unceasingly, unendingly, unfalteringly, uninterruptedly, unrelentingly, unremittingly
🔄 intermittently, occasionally

non-violent *adj* dovish, irenic, pacifist, passive, peaceable, peaceful
🔄 violent

nook *n* 1 *a nook in the wall:* alcove, corner, cranny, cubbyhole, niche, recess 2 *a sheltered nook by the river:* cavity, den, hideaway, hideout, opening, refuge, retreat, shelter

noon *n* lunchtime, midday, twelve noon, twelve o'clock

norm *n* average, benchmark, criterion, gauge, mean, measure, model, pattern, reference, rule, standard, touchstone, usual rule, yardstick

normal *adj* accepted, accustomed, average, common, commonplace, conventional, everyday, general, habitual, mainstream, natural, ordinary, popular, rational, reasonable, regular, routine, run-of-the-mill *colloq*, standard, straight, typical, usual
▣ abnormal, irregular, peculiar

normality *n* averageness, balance, commonness, conventionality, naturalness, ordinariness, rationality, reason, reasonableness, regularity, routine, typicality, usualness
▣ abnormality, irregularity, peculiarity

normally *adv* as a rule, as usual, characteristically, commonly, conventionally, generally, naturally, ordinarily, regularly, routinely, typically, usually
▣ abnormally, exceptionally

northern *adj* Arctic, boreal *formal*, hyperborean *formal*, north, northerly, polar, septentrional *old use*
▣ southern

nose *n* **1** *the animal's nose:* beak *colloq*, bill, boko *colloq*, conk *slang*, hooter *colloq*, neb, proboscis *formal*, schnozzle *colloq*, snitch *colloq*, snoot *colloq*, snout **2** *a nose for a good story:* feel, flair, instinct, perception, sense
♦ *v* ease, edge, inch, nudge, push
▶ **nose around** poke around, poke your nose in *colloq*, pry, rubberneck *colloq*, search, snoop *colloq*
▶ **nose out** detect, discover, find out, inquire, reveal, sniff out *colloq*, uncover

nosedive *v* **1** *the plane suddenly nosedived:* dive, drop, plummet, plunge, submerge, swoop **2** *house prices are set to nosedive:* crash, decline, decrease, dive, drop, fall, get worse, go down, plummet, plunge
♦ *n* dive, drop, header, plummet, plunge, purler, swoop

nosegay *n* bouquet, bunch, posy, spray

nosh *n* board, comestibles, cooking, cuisine, delicacy, diet, dish, eatables *colloq*, eats *colloq*, fare, feed, fodder, food, foodstuffs, grub *slang*, meals, menu, nourishment, nutriment, nutrition, provisions, rations, refreshments, speciality, stores, subsistence, sustenance, table, tuck *colloq*, viands *formal*, victuals *formal*

nostalgia *n* homesickness, longing, pining, recollection(s), regret(s), regretfulness, remembrance, reminiscence(s), wistfulness, yearning

nostalgic *adj* emotional, homesick, longing, pining, regretful, reminiscent, sentimental, wistful, yearning

nostrum *n* cure, cure for all ills, cure-all, drug, elixir, medicine, panacea, pill, potion, remedy, universal cure/remedy

nosy *adj* curious, eavesdropping, inquisitive, interfering, meddlesome, probing, prying, snooping *colloq*

notability *n* **1** *the notability of his art collection:* distinction, eminence, esteem *formal*, fame, importance, impressiveness, noteworthiness, renown, significance **2** *film stars and other notabilities attended the gala:* big noise *colloq*, big shot *colloq*, bigwig *colloq*, celebrity, dignitary, heavyweight *colloq*, luminary, magnate, notable *formal*, personage *formal*, somebody *colloq*, someone *colloq*, top brass *colloq*, VIP *colloq*, worthy
▣ **2** nonentity

notable *adj* **1** *a notable achievement:* extraordinary, great, important, impressive, marked, memorable, momentous, noteworthy, noticeable, notorious, outstanding, particular, pre-eminent, rare, remarkable, significant, special, striking, uncommon, unforgettable, unusual **2** *our notable guests:* celebrated, distinguished, eminent, famous, illustrious, renowned, well-known
▣ **1** commonplace, ordinary, usual **2** ordinary
♦ *n* celebrity, dignitary, luminary, notability, personage, somebody, star, VIP, worthy
▣ nobody, nonentity

notably *adv* conspicuously, distinctly, eminently, especially, extraordinarily, impressively, markedly, noticeably, outstandingly, particularly, remarkably, signally, significantly, strikingly, uncommonly

notation *n* alphabet, characters, cipher, code, hieroglyphics, noting, record, script, shorthand, signs, symbols, system

notch *n* **1** *fits into a notch in the bottom of the shelf:* cleft, cut, dent, gash, gouge, groove, incision, indentation, mark, nick, score, scratch, snip **2** *she's gone up a few notches in my estimation:* degree, grade, level, stage, step
♦ *v* cut, dent, gash, gouge, groove, indent, mark, nick, score, scratch
▶ **notch up** achieve, attain, chalk up *colloq*, gain, make, record, register, score

notched *adj* crenellate(d) *formal*, emarginate *formal*, eroded, erose *formal*, jagged, jaggy, pinked, serrate(d), serrulate(d)

note *n* **1** *left a note for his wife:* account, comment, communication, epistle *formal*, jotting, letter, line, memo *colloq*, memorandum, message, missive *formal*, record, reminder **2** *made a note in the margin of the book:* annotation, comment, commentary, explanation, explication *formal*, footnote, gloss, marginalia *formal*, remark **3** *interest in the story provides a note of the band's growing popularity:* element, indication, inflection, mark, signal, symbol, token, tone **4** *politicians of note:* consequence, distinction, eminence, fame, greatness, illustriousness, pre-eminence, prestige, renown, reputation **5** *take careful note of the instructions:* attention, attentiveness, care, consideration, heed, mindfulness, notice, observation, regard
♦ *v* **1** *noted that the door was open:* detect, heed, mark, notice, observe, perceive, see, witness **2** *the detective noted the time before the interview began:* allude to, mention, observe, refer to, remark, say, state, touch on **3** *noted down a few points:* enter, jot down, log, put down, put in writing, record, register, write down

noted *adj* acclaimed, celebrated, distinguished, eminent, famous, great, illustrious, notable, of note, pre-eminent, prominent, recognized, renowned, respected, well-known
▣ obscure, unknown

notes *n* commentary, draft, impressions, jottings, minutes, outline, record, report, sketch, synopsis, transcript

noteworthy *adj* exceptional, extraordinary, important, impressive, marked, memorable, notable, outstanding, remarkable, significant, striking, unusual
🄴 commonplace, ordinary, unexceptional

nothing *n* 1 *got nothing for his pains:* bugger all *slang,* fuck all *taboo slang,* naught, not a thing, nought, sod all *slang,* sweet Fanny Adams *colloq,* zero, zilch *colloq* 2 *disappeared into nothing:* emptiness, lightweight *colloq,* non-existence, nothingness, nullity *formal,* oblivion, void 3 *he is a total nothing:* cipher, mediocrity, menial, nobody, nonentity
🄴 1 something

nothingness *n* emptiness, nihilism *formal,* nihility *formal,* non-existence, nullity *formal,* oblivion, vacuum, void
🄴 existence, life

notice *v* become aware of, behold *formal,* detect, discern, distinguish, espy *formal,* heed *formal,* make out, mark, mind, note, observe, pay attention to, perceive, remark, see, spot, take heed of *formal,* take note of
🄴 ignore, miss, overlook
♦ *n* 1 *published a death notice:* advice, announcement, appraisal *formal,* communication, declaration, information, instruction, intelligence, intimation, news, notification, order, warning 2 *stuck a notice on the church wall:* advertisement, bill, bulletin, circular, handbill, information sheet, leaflet, pamphlet, poster, sign 3 *the play got good notices in the press:* comment, crit *colloq,* criticism, critique, review, write-up 4 *took no notice of her:* attention, awareness, cognizance *formal,* consideration, heed *formal,* interest, note, observation, regard, thought, watchfulness

noticeable *adj* appreciable, clear, conspicuous, detectable, discernible, distinct, distinguishable, evident, manifest *formal,* measurable, observable, obvious, patent, perceptible, plain, significant, striking, unmistakable, visible
🄴 inconspicuous, unnoticeable

notification *n* advice, announcement, communication, declaration, disclosure, divulgence, information, informing, intelligence, message, notice, publication, statement, telling, warning

notify *v* acquaint, advise, alert, announce, apprise *formal,* broadcast, caution, communicate, declare, disclose, divulge, inform, make known, publish, reveal, tell, warn

notion *n* 1 *had no notion what he was talking about:* apprehension, assumption, belief, concept, conception, conceptualization *formal,* conviction, hypothesis, idea, impression, opinion, theory, thought, understanding, view 2 *took a notion to go to Paris for dinner:* caprice, desire, fancy, inclination, whim, wish

notional *adj* abstract, classificatory, conceptual, fancied, fanciful, hypothetical, ideational *formal,* illusory, imaginary, speculative, thematic, theoretical, unfounded, unreal, visionary
🄴 real

notoriety *n* disgrace, dishonour, disrepute, ignominy *formal,* infamy, obloquy *formal,* opprobrium *formal,* scandal

notorious *adj* 1 *a notorious art fraud:* blatant, disgraceful, dishonourable, disreputable, egregious *formal,* flagrant, glaring, ignominious *formal,* ill-famed, infamous, of ill repute, opprobrious *formal,* scandalous 2 *a tabloid notorious for its sensationalism:* familiar, famous, renowned, well-known

notoriously *adv* 1 *a notoriously difficult case:* blatantly, glaringly, notably, obviously, openly, overtly, particularly, patently 2 *behaved notoriously wherever he went:* arrantly, disgracefully, dishonourably, disreputably, egregiously *formal,* flagrantly, ignominiously *formal,* infamously, opprobriously *formal,* scandalously, spectacularly

notwithstanding *prep* despite, in spite of, regardless of

nought *n* naught, nil, nothing, nothingness, zero, zilch *colloq*

nourish *v* 1 *the kind of diet that nourishes young children:* feed, maintain, nurse, nurture, provide for, rear, support, sustain, take care of, tend 2 *nourished a hope to travel widely:* cherish, foster, have, maintain, sustain 3 *hoped to nourish the arts in her home town:* advance, aid, assist, boost, cultivate, encourage, forward, foster, further, help, promote, stimulate, strengthen

nourishing *adj* alimentative *technical,* beneficial, good, healthful, health-giving, invigorating, nutritious, nutritive *formal,* strengthening, substantial, wholesome

nourishment *n* diet, eats *colloq,* food, grub *slang,* nosh *slang,* nutriment, nutrition, subsistence, sustenance, tuck *colloq*

novel *adj* creative, different, fresh, ground-breaking, imaginative, ingenious, innovative, inventive, modern, new, original, pioneering, rare, resourceful, strange, uncommon, unconventional, unfamiliar, unique, unorthodox, unprecedented, unusual
🄴 familiar, hackneyed, ordinary
♦ *n* book, fiction, narrative, romance, story, tale

novelty *n* 1 *the novelty of mobile phones has begun to wear off:* creativity, difference, freshness, imaginativeness, innovation, newness, originality, rareness, strangeness, unconventionality, unfamiliarity, uniqueness, unusualness 2 *each Christmas cracker contains a hat, a joke and a novelty:* bauble, curiosity, gadget, gimcrack, gimmick, knick-knack, memento, souvenir, trifle, trinket

novice *n* amateur, apprentice, beginner, greenhorn *colloq,* learner, neophyte *formal,* newcomer, noviciate *formal,* probationer, pupil, raw recruit, recruit, rookie *colloq,* student, tiro, trainee
🄴 expert

noviciate *n* apprenticeship, initiation, trainee period, training, trial period

now *adv* 1 *we're living in Kent now:* at present, at the moment, at the present time, at this moment in time, at this time, currently, for the time being, just now, nowadays, presently *US,* right now, these days, today 2 *the doctor will see you now:* at once, directly, immediately, instantly, next, promptly, right away, straight away, without delay

nowadays *adv* at present, at the moment, at the present time, at this moment in time, at this time, currently, in this day and age, presently *US*, these days, today

noxious *adj* damaging, deadly, deleterious *formal*, destructive, detrimental, disgusting, foul, harmful, injurious, malignant, menacing, noisome *formal*, pernicious, poisonous, ruinous, threatening, toxic, unhealthy
🖬 innocuous, wholesome

nuance *n* degree, (fine) distinction, gradation, hint, nicety, overtone, refinement, shade, shading, subtlety, suggestion, suspicion, tinge, touch, trace

nub *n* centre, core, crux, essence, focus, gist, heart, kernel, marrow, meat, nucleus, pith, pivot, point

nubile *adj* adult, attractive, desirable, marriageable, mature, sexy *colloq*, voluptuous

nucleus *n* basis, centre, core, crux, focus, heart, kernel, marrow, meat, nub, pivot

nude *adj* bare, exposed, in the altogether *colloq*, in the buff *colloq*, in the raw *colloq*, in your birthday suit *colloq*, naked, naked as the day you were born *colloq*, not a stitch on *colloq*, starkers *colloq*, stark-naked, stripped, unclothed, uncovered, undressed, with nothing on
🖬 clothed, dressed

nudge *v* bump, elbow, jab, jog, poke, prod, push, shove
♦ *n* bump, dig, elbow, jab, poke, prod, prompt, push, shove

nudity *n* bareness, déshabillé, dishabille, nakedness, nudism, state of undress, the altogether *colloq*, undress

nugatory *adj* futile, inadequate, inconsequential, ineffectual *formal*, inoperative, insignificant, invalid, null and void, trifling, trivial, unavailing, useless, vain, valueless, worthless
🖬 important, significant

nugget *n* chunk, clump, hunk, lump, mass, piece, wad, wodge

nuisance *n* affliction *formal*, annoyance, bore, bother, burden, difficulty, drag *colloq*, drawback, inconvenience, irritant, irritation, pain *colloq*, pest, plague, problem, thorn in your side/flesh *colloq*, trial, tribulation *formal*, trouble, vexation

null *adj* abrogated *formal*, annulled, cancelled, ineffectual *formal*, inoperative, invalid, invalidated, nullified *formal*, powerless, revoked, useless, vain, void, worthless
🖬 valid

nullify *v* abolish, abrogate *formal*, annul, bring to an end, cancel, counteract, countermand *formal*, declare null and void, discontinue *formal*, invalidate, negate *formal*, offset, quash, renounce *formal*, repeal, rescind, reverse, revoke, set aside, void
🖬 validate

nullity *n* characterlessness, immateriality, incorporeality *formal*, ineffectualness *formal*,

invalidity, non-existence, powerlessness, uselessness, voidness, worthlessness
🖬 validity

numb *adj* *felt numb with cold*: anaesthetized, benumbed, dead, deadened, drugged, frozen, insensate *formal*, insensible *formal*, insensitive, paralysed, unfeeling, without feeling 2 *felt numb with shock*: dazed, immobilized, in shock, insensate *formal*, insensible *formal*, stunned
🖬 1 sensitive 2 animated
♦ *v* anaesthetize, benumb, daze, deaden, drug, dull, freeze, immobilize, paralyse, stun, stupefy
🖬 sensitize

number *n* 1 *enter your number into the machine*: character, cipher, data, decimal, digit, figure, fraction, integer, numeral, statistics, unit 2 *huge numbers of people fled the country*: aggregate, amount, collection, company, count, crowd, group, horde, multitude, quantity, score, sum, tally, throng, total 3 *a back number of the magazine*: copy, edition, impression, imprint, issue, printing, volume
♦ *v* 1 *the government numbered the deaths at 79*: add (up to), calculate, compute, count, enumerate, estimate, include, reckon, total 2 *your days are numbered*: delimit, limit, restrain, restrict, specify

numberless *adj* countless, endless, immeasurable, infinite, innumerable, many, multitudinous *formal*, myriad, uncounted, unnumbered, unsummed, untold

numbness *n* anaesthetization, deadness, dullness, insensateness *formal*, insensibility *formal*, insensitivity, paralysis, stupefaction, stupor, torpor, unfeelingness
🖬 sensitivity

numeral *n* character, cipher, digit, figure, integer, number, unit

numerous *adj* a good few *colloq*, abundant, copious, countless, endless, innumerable, legion, manifold *formal*, many, multitudinous *formal*, plentiful, profuse, quite a few, several, sundry, various
🖬 few, rare, scarce

numerousness *n* abundance, copiousness, countlessness, manifoldness *formal*, multeity *formal*, multiplicity *formal*, multitudinousness *formal*, plentifulness, plurality, profusion
🖬 scantiness, scarcity

numskull *n* birdbrain *colloq*, clot *colloq*, dimwit, dummy *colloq*, dunce, fat head *colloq*, fool, nit *colloq*, nitwit *colloq*, simpleton, thickhead *colloq*, twerp *colloq*, twit *colloq*

nun *n* abbess, anchoress, ancress, canoness, mother superior, prioress, sister, vestal, vowess

nuncio *n* ambassador, envoy, legate, representative

nunnery *n* abbey, cloister, convent, priory

nuptial *adj* bridal, conjugal *formal*, connubial *formal*, epithalamial *formal*, epithalamic *formal*, hymeneal *formal*, marital, matrimonial, wedded, wedding

nuptials *n* espousal *formal*, marriage, matrimony *formal*, spousals *formal*, wedding, wedding celebrations

nurse *v* 1 *nurse the sick*: attend to, care for, look after, take care of, tend, treat 2 *nursed her baby*:

breast-feed, feed, nourish, nurture, suckle, wet-nurse **3** *nurse a secret ambition to go into politics*: advance, aid, assist, boost, cherish, encourage, entertain, foster, further, harbour, help, keep, nourish, nurture, preserve, promote, support, sustain

> **Nurses include:**
> charge nurse, children's nurse, dental nurse, district nurse, healthcare assistant, health visitor, home nurse, Iain Rennie nurse, locality manager, Macmillan nurse, matron, midwife, nanny, night nurse, night sister, nursemaid, nursery nurse, nurse tutor, occupational health nurse, psychiatric nurse, Registered General Nurse (RGN), school nurse, sister, staff nurse, State Enrolled Nurse (SEN), State Registered Nurse (SRN), theatre sister, ward sister, wet nurse

nurture *n* **1** *provide nurture for his family*: diet, eats *colloq*, food, grub *slang*, nosh *slang*, nourishment, nutrition, subsistence, sustenance, tuck *colloq* **2** *the nurture of young talent*: advance, aid, assistance, boosting, care, cultivation, development, discipline, education, encouragement, feeding, fostering, furtherance, help, promotion, rearing, schooling, stimulation, tending, training, upbringing
♦ *v* **1** *nurtured her children*: care for, feed, foster, nourish, nurse, support, sustain, tend **2** *an organization that nurtures young musicians*: advance, aid, assist, boost, bring up, coach, cultivate, develop, discipline, educate, foster, further, help, instruct, promote, rear, school, stimulate, train, tutor

nut *n* **1** *a bag of mixed nuts*: kernel, pip, seed, stone **2** *she's a complete nut*: basket-case *colloq*, fruitcake *colloq*, headcase *slang*, insane person, loony *colloq*, lunatic, madman, madwoman, maniac, nutcase *colloq*, nutter *colloq*, oddball *slang*, psycho *slang*, psychopath **3** *a sci-fi nut*: admirer, aficionado,

buff *colloq*, devotee, enthusiast, fan, fanatic, fiend *colloq*, follower, freak *colloq*, supporter, zealot

> **Varieties of nut include:**
> almond, beech nut, brazil nut, cashew, chestnut, cobnut, coconut, filbert, hazelnut, macadamia, monkey nut, peanut, pecan, pistachio, walnut

nutriment *n* diet, eats *colloq*, food, grub *slang*, nosh *slang*, nourishment, nutrition, subsistence, sustenance, tuck *colloq*

nutrition *n* diet, eats *colloq*, food, grub *slang*, nosh *slang*, nourishment, nutriment, subsistence, sustenance, tuck *colloq*

nutritious *adj* beneficial, good, healthful, health-giving, nourishing, nutritive, strengthening, substantial, wholesome
⊠ bad, unwholesome

nuts *adj* **1** *he'll go nuts when he sees his car*: berserk, bonkers *colloq*, crazed, crazy, demented, deranged, disturbed, doolally *colloq*, insane, loony *colloq*, loopy *colloq*, lunatic, mad, nutty *colloq*, nutty as a fruitcake *colloq*, off your rocker *colloq*, out of your mind, out to lunch *colloq*, round the bend *colloq*, round the twist *colloq*, unbalanced, unhinged, wild **2** *nuts about computers*: ardent, avid, crazy, daft *colloq*, devoted, enamoured, enthusiastic, fanatical, fond, infatuated, keen, mad, passionate, smitten, wild, zealous
⊠ **1** sane **2** indifferent

nuts and bolts *n* basics, components, details, essentials, fundamentals, nitty-gritty *colloq*, practicalities

nuzzle *v* burrow, cuddle, fondle, nestle, nudge, pet, snuggle

nymph *n* damsel, dryad, girl, hamadryad, lass, maid, maiden, naiad, oread, sprite, sylph, undine

O

oaf *n* barbarian, boor, bumpkin *colloq*, clod *colloq*, dolt, gawk, hick *colloq*, hobbledehoy *colloq*, lout, lubber, slob *colloq*, yahoo, yobbo *colloq*

oafish *adj* boorish, bungling, churlish, clodhopping *colloq*, coarse, doltish, gawky, gross, ill-bred, ill-mannered, loutish, lubberly, lumpen, lumpish, rough, stolid, swinish, uncouth, unmannerly

oasis *n* 1 *oases of the central Sahara:* spring, watering-hole 2 *an oasis of calm:* haven, hideaway, hideout, island, refuge, retreat, sanctuary, sanctum *formal*

oath *n* 1 *an oath of loyalty:* affirmation *formal*, assurance, attestation *formal*, avowal *formal*, bond, pledge, promise, vow, word, word of honour 2 *he muttered a few foul oaths:* bad language, blasphemy, curse, expletive *formal*, four-letter word, imprecation *formal*, malediction *formal*, obscenity, profanity *formal*, swear-word

obdurate *adj* adamant, bloody-minded *colloq*, determined, dogged, firm, hard-hearted, headstrong, immovable, implacable, inflexible, intractable *formal*, intransigent *formal*, iron, obstinate, persistent, pig-headed *colloq*, self-willed, steadfast, stiff-necked, stony, strong-minded, stubborn, unbending, unfeeling, unrelenting, unyielding, wilful
🗷 submissive, tender

obedience *n* accordance, acquiescence *formal*, agreement, allegiance, amenability, compliance *formal*, conformability, deference, docility, dutifulness, duty, malleability, observance, passivity, respect, reverence, submission, submissiveness, subservience, tractability *formal*
🗷 disobedience, rebellion

obedient *adj* acquiescent *formal*, amenable, biddable, compliant *formal*, conforming, deferential, disciplined, docile, dutiful, law-abiding, malleable, obsequious *formal*, observant, pliable, respectful, submissive, subservient, tractable *formal*, well-trained, yielding
🗷 disobedient, rebellious, wilful

obeisance *n* 1 *a low obeisance to the queen:* bow, curtsy, genuflection *formal*, salaam, salutation *formal*, salute 2 *sentimental obeisance to the past:* deference, homage, kowtowing, respect, reverence, submission, veneration *formal*

obelisk *n* column, memorial, monument, needle, pillar

obese *adj* big, bulky, chubby, corpulent *formal*, Falstaffian, fat, flabby *colloq*, fleshy, gross *colloq*, heavy, large, outsize, overweight, paunchy, plump, podgy, ponderous, portly, roly-poly, rotund *formal*, round, stout, tubby, well-endowed
🗷 skinny, slender, thin

obesity *n* bulk, chubbiness, corpulence *formal*, fatness, flabbiness *colloq*, grossness *colloq*, overweight, plumpness, podginess, portliness, rotundness *formal*, stoutness, tubbiness
🗷 skinniness, slenderness, thinness

obey *v* 1 *obey your teachers:* be ruled by, defer (to), follow, give way to, heed, submit to, surrender to, take orders from, yield to 2 *obey the rules:* abide by, adhere to, comply with *formal*, conform to, follow, heed, keep (to), mind, observe, respect, respond to 3 *she reluctantly promised to obey:* acquiesce *formal*, comply *formal*, conform, do as you are told, give way, stick to the rules *colloq*, submit, surrender, take orders, toe the line *colloq* 4 *I was just obeying orders:* act upon, carry out, discharge, execute, fulfil, perform
🗷 1 disobey 2 disobey 3 disobey

obfuscate *v* blur, cloak, cloud, complicate, conceal, confuse, cover, disguise, hide, mask, muddle, obscure, overshadow, shade, shadow, shroud, veil

object[1] *n* 1 *an object of great beauty:* article, body, device, entity, gadget, item, something, thing 2 *the object of the tutorial:* aim, ambition, design, end, goal, idea, intent *formal*, intention, motive, objective, point, purpose, reason, target 3 *the object of intense hostility:* butt, focus, recipient, target, victim

object[2] *v* argue, beg to differ, challenge, complain, demur *formal*, disapprove, expostulate *formal*, oppose, protest, rebut, refuse, remonstrate *formal*, repudiate, resist, take a stand against, take exception, take issue, withstand
🗷 accede *formal*, acquiesce *formal*, agree, approve, assent *formal*

objection *n* argument, challenge, complaint, demur *formal*, disapproval, dissatisfaction, dissent, expostulation *formal*, grievance, opposition, protest, remonstration *formal*, scruple
🗷 agreement, approval, assent

objectionable *adj* abhorrent *formal*, contemptible, deplorable, despicable, detestable, disagreeable, hateful, intolerable, loathsome, nauseating, obnoxious, offensive, repellent *formal*, reprehensible *formal*, repugnant *formal*, repulsive, revolting, sickening, unacceptable, unpleasant
🗷 acceptable, delightful, pleasant

objective *adj* 1 *be as objective as possible:* detached, disinterested, dispassionate, equitable, even-handed, fair, impartial, just, neutral, open-minded, unbiased, uninvolved, unprejudiced 2 *objective information:* actual, authentic, factual, genuine, real, true
🗷 1 subjective
♦ *n* aim, ambition, design, end, goal, idea, intent *formal*, intention, mark, object, point, purpose, target

objectively *adv* disinterestedly, dispassionately, equitably, even-handedly, fairly, impartially, justly, neutrally, with an open mind

objectivity *n* detachment, disinterest, disinterestedness, equitableness, even-handedness, fairness, impartiality, justness, open mind, open-mindedness
🗷 bias, prejudice, subjectivity

obligate *v* bind, coerce, compel, constrain, force, impel, make, necessitate, press, pressure, pressurize, require

obligation *n* accountability, agreement, assignment, bond, burden, charge, command, commitment, compulsion, contract, covenant, debt, deed, demand, duress, duty, function, indebtedness, job, liability, onus, pressure, requirement, responsibility, task, trust

obligatory *adj* binding, compulsory, enforced, essential, imperative *formal*, mandatory *formal*, necessary, required, requisite *formal*, statutory, unavoidable
🗷 optional

oblige *v* 1 *obliged him to pay court costs:* bind, coerce, compel, constrain, force, give no option, impel, make, necessitate, obligate, press, pressure, pressurize, require 2 *happy to oblige:* accommodate, assist, do someone a favour, do someone a service, gratify, help, please, put yourself out for, serve

obliged *adj* 1 *obliged to pay court costs:* bound, compelled, constrained, duty-bound, forced, honour-bound, obligated, required, under an obligation, under compulsion 2 *I'd be obliged if you could wait:* appreciative, beholden *formal*, grateful, gratified, in debt (to), indebted, thankful

obliging *adj* accommodating, agreeable, civil, complaisant *formal*, considerate, co-operative, courteous, friendly, generous, good-natured, helpful, indulgent, kind, pleasant, polite, willing
🗷 unhelpful

oblique *adj* 1 *currents oblique to the shore:* angled, inclined, slanting, sloping, tilted 2 *an oblique glance:* furtive, sidelong, sideways 3 *oblique references:* circuitous, circumlocutory *formal*, devious, discursive, divergent, indirect, meandering, periphrastic *formal*, rambling, roundabout, tortuous, winding, zigzag
♦ *n* diagonal, slant, slash, stroke, virgule *formal*

obliquely *adv* 1 *always cut stems obliquely:* askance, askant, aslant, aslope, at an angle, diagonally, slantwise 2 *referred obliquely to:* circuitously, evasively, in a roundabout way, indirectly, not in so many words

obliterate *v* 1 *gender taboos were obliterated:* annihilate, destroy, eliminate, eradicate, expunge *formal*, extirpate *formal*, wipe out 2 *obliterated from his memory:* blot out, delete, efface *formal*, erase, rub out, strike out

obliteration *n* annihilation, blotting out, deletion, destruction, effacement *formal*, elimination, eradication, erasure, expunction *formal*, extirpation *formal*

oblivion *n* 1 *oblivion of sleep:* blankness, darkness, limbo, stupor, unconsciousness, void 2 *consigned to baseball oblivion:* nothingness, obscurity 3 *bulldozed into oblivion:* disuse, non-existence 4 *drug-induced oblivion:* absent-mindedness, blindness, carelessness, deafness, ignorance, inattentiveness, unawareness, unconsciousness, unmindfulness
🗷 4 awareness

oblivious *adj* absent-minded, blind, careless, deaf, forgetful, heedless, ignorant, inattentive, insensible *formal*, negligent, preoccupied, unaware, unconcerned, unconscious, unheeding, unmindful
🗷 aware, conscious

obloquy *n* 1 *years of contempt and obloquy:* abuse, animadversion *formal*, aspersion *formal*, attack, contumely *formal*, criticism, defamation, invective *formal*, slander, vilification *formal* 2 *marked with that obloquy for life:* bad press, blame, calumny *formal*, censure, detraction, discredit, disfavour, disgrace, dishonour, humiliation, ignominy *formal*, odium *formal*, opprobrium *formal*, reproach, shame, stigma *formal*

obnoxious *adj* abhorrent *formal*, contemptible, deplorable, detestable, disagreeable, disgusting, hateful, horrible, horrid, intolerable, loathsome, nasty, nauseating, objectionable, odious, offensive, repellent *formal*, repugnant *formal*, repulsive, revolting, sickening, unacceptable, unpleasant, vile
🗷 pleasant

obscene *adj* 1 *obscene literature:* bawdy, blue *colloq*, carnal *formal*, coarse, dirty, disgusting, filthy, foul, fruity *colloq*, gross, immodest, immoral, improper, impure, indecent, lewd, licentious, lubricious *formal*, near the knuckle/bone *colloq*, off-colour, pornographic, prurient *formal*, raunchy *colloq*, risqué, rude, scurrilous, sexy, shameless, sleazy *colloq*, smutty, suggestive, unchaste, vile, vulgar 2 *obscene luxury:* disgraceful, immoral, offensive, outrageous, scandalous, shameless, shocking
🗷 1 decent, wholesome

obscenity *n* 1 *obscenity legislation:* bawdiness, carnality *formal*, coarseness, dirtiness, eroticism, filthiness, foulness, grossness, immodesty, immorality, impropriety, impurity, indecency, indelicacy, lasciviousness, lewdness, licentiousness, lubricity *formal*, pornography, prurience *formal*, raunchiness *colloq*, salaciousness, shamelessness, sleaze *colloq*, suggestiveness, unchasteness, vulgarity 2 *the obscenity of apartheid:* atrocity, evil, heinousness *formal*, offence, outrage, vileness, wickedness 3 *ignore his obscenities:* bad language, curse, expletive *formal*, four-letter word, imprecation *formal*, malediction *formal*, profanity *formal*, swear-word

obscure *adj* 1 *some obscure eighties band:* God-forsaken, humble, inconspicuous, insignificant, little-known, minor, nameless, off the beaten track *colloq*, out-of-the-way, remote, undistinguished, unheard-of, unimportant, unknown, unrecognized, unsung 2 *impenetrably obscure poetry:* abstruse *formal*, arcane *formal*, complex, concealed, confusing, cryptic, deep, enigmatic, esoteric *formal*, hidden, impenetrable, incomprehensible, inexplicable, involved, mysterious, opaque, perplexing, puzzling, recondite *formal*, unclear, unexplained, unfathomable 3 *an obscure passageway:* cloudy, dark, dim, dusky, gloomy, hazy, misty, murky, shadowy, shady 4 *obscure markings:* blurred, doubtful, faint, fuzzy, indefinite, indistinct, uncertain, unclear, vague
🗷 1 famous, renowned 2 intelligible, straightforward 3 clear, plain 4 clear, definite
♦ *v* 1 *a pillar obscured the view:* block out, cloak, conceal, cover, disguise, eclipse, hide, mask,

screen, shade, shroud, veil **2** *obscure the important issues*: blur, cloud, complicate, confuse, darken, dim, muddle, obfuscate *formal*, overshadow
⊠ 1 clarify, reveal **2** clarify, illuminate

obscurity *n* **1** *on the way from obscurity to celebrity*: inconspicuousness, insignificance, lack of fame/recognition, lowliness, namelessness, unimportance **2** *avoid obscurity of expression*: abstruseness *formal*, ambiguity, complexity, impenetrability, incomprehensibility, intricacy, mystery, mysticism, reconditeness *formal*, unclearness **3** *his movements are veiled in obscurity*: confusion, mystery, mysticism
⊠ 1 fame **2** clarity, intelligibility, lucidity **3** clarity, intelligibility, lucidity

obsequious *adj* abject, arse-licking *slang*, bootlicking *colloq*, creepy *colloq*, cringing, deferential, fawning, flattering, grovelling, ingratiating, menial, oily, servile, slavish, smarmy *colloq*, submissive, subservient, sycophantic, toadying, unctuous

observable *adj* apparent, appreciable, clear, detectable, discernible, evident, measurable, noticeable, obvious, open, patent, perceivable, perceptible, recognizable, significant, visible

observance *n* **1** *observance of safety regulations*: adherence, attention, compliance *formal*, discharge *formal*, execution, following, fulfilment, heeding *formal*, honouring, keeping, notice, obedience, performance **2** *Easter observances of Iona*: celebration, ceremony, custom, festival, formality, practice, rite, ritual, service, tradition

observant *adj* **1** *an observant parent*: alert, attentive, eagle-eyed, hawk-eyed, heedful *formal*, mindful, on guard, on the lookout, perceptive, sharp, sharp-eyed, vigilant, watchful, wide-awake, with eyes like a hawk *colloq*, with your eyes skinned/peeled *colloq* **2** *an observant Jew*: committed, devoted, dutiful, obedient, orthodox, practising
⊠ 1 unobservant

observation *n* **1** *observation of wildlife*: consideration, examination, inspection, monitoring, noticing, review, scrutiny, study, viewing, watching **2** *his powers of observation*: discernment, notice, noticing, perception, seeing **3** *kept a record of her thoughts and observations*: annotation *formal*, comment, data, description, finding, information, note, reflection, result, statement, thought **4** *may I make an observation?*: comment, declaration, opinion, pronouncement, reflection, remark, statement, utterance

observe *v* **1** *observing animals*: contemplate, examine, inspect, keep an eye on *colloq*, keep tabs on *colloq*, keep under surveillance, keep watch on, keep your eyes skinned/peeled *colloq*, miss nothing, monitor, note, study, watch like a hawk *colloq* **2** *observe his change in demeanour*: behold *formal*, catch sight of, detect, discern, espy *formal*, note, notice, perceive, see, spot **3** *'It's cold,' she observed*: comment, declare, mention, remark, say, state, utter **4** *observe the law*: abide by, adhere to, comply with *formal*, conform to, discharge *formal*, execute, follow, fulfil, honour, obey, respect **5** *observe religious festivals*: celebrate, commemorate, honour, keep, mark, perform, recognize, remember, respect
⊠ 2 miss **4** break, violate

observer *n* **1** *a chance observer saw the gun being used*: beholder *formal*, bystander, eyewitness, looker-on, onlooker, sightseer, spectator, viewer, watcher, witness **2** *industry observers expected a deal*: commentator, reporter, witness

obsess *v* be uppermost in your mind, bedevil, consume, control, dominate, engross, grip, haunt, have a grip/hold on, hound, monopolize, plague, possess, preoccupy, prey on, rule, torment

obsessed *adj* bedevilled, beset, dominated, gripped, haunted, hounded, hung up on *colloq*, immersed in, in the grip of, infatuated, plagued, preoccupied
⊠ detached, indifferent, unconcerned

obsession *n* complex, compulsion, enthusiasm, fascination, fetish, fixation, hang-up *colloq*, idée fixe, infatuation, mania, one-track mind *colloq*, preoccupation, ruling passion, thing *colloq*

obsessive *adj* compulsive, consuming, fixed, gripping, haunting, maddening, tormenting

obsolescent *adj* ageing, dated, declining, disappearing, dying out, fading, moribund *formal*, old-fashioned, on the decline, on the wane, on the way out, out of date, outdated, past its prime, redundant, waning

obsolete *adj* ancient, antediluvian *colloq*, antiquated, antique, behind the times, bygone, dated, dead, discarded, discontinued *formal*, disused, extinct, in disuse, old, old hat *colloq*, old-fashioned, on the shelf *colloq*, on the way out, out of date, out of fashion, out of the ark *colloq*, outmoded, outworn, passé, past its prime, past its sell-by date *colloq*, superannuated
⊠ current, in use, modern, up-to-date

obstacle *n* bar, barricade, barrier, blockade, blockage, catch, check, curb, deterrent, difficulty, drawback, fly in the ointment *colloq*, handicap, hiccup *colloq*, hindrance, hitch, hurdle, impediment, interference, interruption, no-no *colloq*, obstruction, snag, spanner in the works *colloq*, stop, stoppage, stumbling-block
⊠ advantage, help

obstinacy *n* doggedness, firmness, frowardness *formal*, hard-heartedness, inflexibility, intransigence *formal*, mulishness, obduracy *formal*, perseverance, persistence, pertinacity *formal*, perversity, pig-headedness *colloq*, relentlessness, resoluteness, stubbornness, tenacity, wilfulness, wrong-headedness
⊠ co-operativeness, flexibility, submissiveness

obstinate *adj* adamant, bloody-minded *colloq*, determined, dogged, firm, hard-hearted, headstrong, immovable, inflexible, intractable *formal*, intransigent *formal*, persevering, persistent, pig-headed *colloq*, recalcitrant *formal*, refractory *formal*, self-willed, steadfast, strong-minded, stubborn, stubborn as a mule *colloq*, unbending, unrelenting, unyielding, wilful
⊠ flexible, tractable

obstreperous *adj* **1** *their obstreperous neighbour*: bloody-minded *colloq*, bolshie *colloq*, intractable *formal*, refractory *formal*, stroppy *colloq*, unruly **2** *an obstreperous racket*: boisterous, clamorous, disorderly, loud, noisy, raucous, riotous, rip-roaring, rowdy, tumultuous, turbulent, uproarious, vociferous, wild
⊠ 2 quiet

obstruct *v* **1** *obstructing the police:* arrest *formal,* brake, bridle, check, delay, encumber, frustrate, halt, hamper, hamstring, hinder, hold up, impede, inhibit, interfere with, interrupt, limit, prevent, retard *formal,* slow down, stall, stop, thwart **2** *smokers now obstruct the pavements:* bar, barricade, block, choke, clog, cut off, encumber, inhibit, restrict, shut off **3** *obstruct my vision:* block, cut off, hamper, limit, obscure, restrict
F₃ **1** assist, further

obstruction *n* **1** *a vehicle causing an obstruction:* bar, barricade, barrier, block, embargo, hindrance, impediment, obstacle **2** *dislodge the obstruction from his windpipe:* block, blockage, stoppage **3** *poor handwriting is an obstruction to understanding:* check, deterrent, difficulty, hindrance, impediment, restriction, sanction, stop, stumbling-block
F₃ **3** help

obstructive *adj* awkward, blocking, delaying, difficult, hindering, inhibiting, interrupting, restrictive, stalling, unco-operative, unhelpful
F₃ co-operative, helpful

obtain *v* **1** *obtain a visa:* acquire, come by, gain, gain possession of, get, get your hands on *colloq,* procure *formal,* secure, seize **2** *obtain the best results:* achieve, attain, earn, gain, secure **3** *the situation which now obtains in our schools:* be effective, be in force, be in use, be prevalent, be the case, exist, hold, hold sway, prevail, reign, rule, stand

obtainable *adj* **1** *the qualifications obtainable:* achievable, attainable, realizable, to be had **2** *readily obtainable:* accessible, at hand, on call, procurable *formal,* ready
F₃ **1** unobtainable **2** unavailable

obtrusive *adj* **1** *obtrusive yellow lines:* blatant, bold, conspicuous, flagrant, forward, noticeable, obvious, projecting, prominent **2** *an obtrusive photographer:* forward, interfering, intrusive, meddling, nosy *colloq,* prying, pushy *colloq*
F₃ **1** unobtrusive

obtuse *adj* crass, dense, dim *colloq,* dim-witted *colloq,* dull, dull-witted, dumb *colloq,* slow, slow-witted, stolid, stupid, thick *colloq,* thick-skinned, unintelligent
F₃ bright, sharp

obviate *v* anticipate, avert, counter, counteract, divert, forestall, preclude *formal,* prevent, remove

obvious *adj* apparent, as clear as daylight *colloq,* as plain as a pikestaff *colloq,* clear, clear-cut, conspicuous, crystal-clear, detectable, distinct, evident, glaring, manifest, noticeable, open, patent, perceptible, plain, prominent, pronounced, recognizable, right under your nose *colloq,* self-evident, self-explanatory, shouting from the rooftops *colloq,* staring you in the face *colloq,* sticking out a mile *colloq,* straightforward, transparent, unconcealed, undeniable, unmistakable, visible
F₃ indistinct, obscure, unclear

obviously *adv* **1** *running is obviously an aerobic activity:* certainly, clearly, of course, without doubt **2** *obviously relieved by the arrival of the police:* distinctly, evidently, manifestly *formal,* noticeably, patently, plainly, undeniably, undoubtedly, unmistakably, without doubt

occasion *n* **1** *waiting for the right occasion:* chance, circumstance, opportunity, time **2** *on one occasion:* affair, case, episode, event, experience, happening, incident, instance, juncture, occurrence, point, situation, time **3** *he had no occasion to say that:* call, cause, excuse, ground(s), justification, reason **4** *the occasion of their marriage:* affair, celebration, do *colloq,* function, get-together *colloq,* party
♦ *v* bring about, bring on, cause, create, effect *formal,* elicit, engender, evoke, generate, give rise to, induce, influence, inspire, lead to, make, originate, persuade, produce, prompt, provoke

occasional *adj* casual, incidental, infrequent, intermittent, irregular, odd, periodic, rare, sporadic, uncommon
F₃ constant, frequent, regular

occasionally *adv* at intervals, at times, every so often, from time to time, infrequently, intermittently, irregularly, now and again, now and then, off and on, on and off, on occasion, once in a while, periodically, sometimes, sporadically
F₃ always, frequently, often

occult *adj* abstruse *formal,* arcane *formal,* concealed, esoteric *formal,* hidden, magic, magical, mysterious, mystical, obscure, preternatural *formal,* recondite *formal,* secret, supernatural, transcendental *formal,* veiled
♦ *n* black arts, mysticism, supernaturalism, the supernatural

---

Terms associated with the occult include:
amulet, astral projection, astrologer, astrology, bewitch, black cat, black magic, black mass, cabbala, charm, chiromancer, chiromancy, clairvoyance, clairvoyant, conjure, coven, crystal ball, curse, divination, diviner, divining-rod, dream, ectoplasm, evil eye, evil spirit, exorcism, exorcist, extrasensory perception (ESP), familiar, fetish, fortune-teller, garlic, Hallowe'en, hallucination, hoodoo, horoscope, hydromancer, hydromancy, illusion, incantation, jinx, juju, magic, magician, medium, necromancer, necromancy, obi, omen, oneiromancer, oneiromancy, Ouija board®, palmist, palmistry, paranormal, pentagram, planchette, poltergeist, possession, psychic, relic, rune, satanic, Satanism, Satanist, séance, second sight, shaman, sixth sense, sorcerer, sorcery, spell, spirit, spiritualism, spiritualist, supernatural, superstition, talisman, tarot card, tarot reading, telepathist, telepathy, totem, trance, vision, voodoo, Walpurgis Night, warlock, white magic, witch, witchcraft, witch doctor, witch's broomstick, witch's sabbath

---

occupancy *n* domiciliation *formal,* habitation *formal,* holding, inhabitancy *formal,* occupation, owner-occupancy, ownership, possession, residence, tenancy, tenure, term, use

occupant *n* holder, householder, incumbent, inhabitant, inmate, leaseholder, lessee, occupier, owner-occupier, renter, resident, squatter, tenant, user

occupation *n* **1** *fill in your occupation:* activity, business, calling, career, craft, employ, employment, field, job, line, métier, post, profession, province, trade, vocation, walk of life, work **2** *shopping is her favourite occupation:* activity, craft, hobby, pastime, pursuit **3** *the occupation of France:* capture, conquest, control, foreign domination, foreign rule, invasion, overthrow, possession, seizure, subjugation *formal*, takeover **4** *the house is ready for occupation:* habitation *formal*, holding, occupancy, possession, residence, tenancy, tenure, use

occupational *adj* business, career, employment, job-related, professional, trade, vocational, work

occupied *adj* **1** *this seat is occupied:* busy, full, in use, taken, tenanted, unavailable **2** *a book will keep him occupied:* absorbed, busy, employed, engaged, engrossed, hard at it *colloq*, immersed, preoccupied, taken up, tied up, working
🖃 **1** unoccupied, vacant

occupy *v* **1** *her parents occupy the upper floor:* dwell in *formal*, inhabit, live in, make your home in, own, people, possess, reside in, settle, stay in, take possession of, tenant **2** *occupying herself with a newspaper:* absorb, amuse, busy, divert, employ, engage, engross, entertain, hold, immerse, interest, involve, preoccupy, take up **3** *troops occupied Panama:* capture, invade, overrun, seize, take over, take possession of **4** *occupy prominent positions:* fill, have, hold, take up, use (up)

occur *v* **1** *a chemical reaction occurs:* befall *formal*, chance, come about, come to pass, crop up, develop, eventuate *formal*, happen, materialize, result, take place, transpire *formal*, turn out, turn up **2** *the same concept occurs later:* appear, arise, be found, be present, exist, have its being, manifest itself *formal*, obtain *formal* **3** *it occurred to me:* come to mind, come to you, cross your mind, dawn on, enter your head, hit, present itself, sink in, spring to mind, strike, suggest itself

occurrence *n* **1** *a daily occurrence:* action, affair, case, circumstance, development, episode, event, happening, incident, instance, proceedings **2** *the occurrence of natural gas deposits:* appearance, arising, development, existence, incidence, manifestation *formal*, springing-up

ocean *n* briny *colloq*, main, profound, sea, the deep, the drink *colloq*

The world's oceans and largest seas include:
Pacific Ocean, Atlantic Ocean, Indian Ocean, Arctic Ocean, Antarctic (Southern) Ocean, South China Sea, Caribbean Sea, Mediterranean Sea, Bering Sea, Gulf of Mexico, Sea of Okhotsk

---

odd *adj* **1** *an odd sense of humour:* abnormal, atypical, barmy *colloq*, bizarre, crackers *colloq*, deviant, different, eccentric, exceptional, extraordinary, far-out *slang*, freaky *colloq*, funny, idiosyncratic, irregular, kinky *colloq*, oddball *colloq*, off the wall *colloq*, out of the ordinary *colloq*, outlandish, peculiar, queer, rare, remarkable, rum *colloq*, singular, strange, unconventional, unusual, wacky *colloq*, way-out *slang*, weird, wild, zany *colloq* **2** *I found it odd that she didn't come:* abnormal, atypical, barmy *colloq*, bizarre, curious, different, exceptional, extraordinary, freaky *colloq*, irregular, out of the ordinary *colloq*, outlandish, peculiar, queer, rare, remarkable, singular, strange, uncanny, uncommon, weird **3** *I have the odd drink:* casual,

fortuitous *formal*, haphazard, incidental, irregular, occasional, part-time, periodic, random, seasonal, temporary **4** *he's wearing odd socks:* left-over, miscellaneous, remaining, single, spare, sundry, superfluous, surplus, unmatched, unpaired, various
🖃 **1** normal **2** usual **3** regular

oddity *n* **1** *the oddities of ant life:* abnormality, anomaly, eccentricity, idiosyncrasy, peculiarity, phenomenon, queerness, quirk, rarity, strangeness, twist **2** *they regarded him as an oddity:* character, freak *colloq*, misfit

oddment *n* bit, end, fragment, leftover, offcut, patch, piece, remnant, scrap, shred, snippet

odds *n* chances, likelihood, probability

odious *adj* abhorrent *formal*, abominable *formal*, contemptible, despicable, detestable, disagreeable, disgusting, execrable *formal*, foul, hateful, heinous *formal*, horrible, horrid, loathsome, objectionable, obnoxious, offensive, repugnant *formal*, repulsive, revolting, unpleasant, vile
🖃 pleasant

odium *n* abhorrence *formal*, animosity *formal*, antipathy *formal*, censure, condemnation, contempt, detestation *formal*, disapprobation *formal*, disapproval, discredit, disfavour, disgrace, dishonour, dislike, disrepute, execration *formal*, hatred, infamy *formal*, obloquy *formal*, opprobrium *formal*, reprobation *formal*, shame

odorous *adj* aromatic, balmy, fragrant, odoriferous *formal*, perfumed, pungent, redolent *formal*, scented, sweet-smelling
🖃 odourless

odour *n* aroma, bouquet, fragrance, niff *colloq*, perfume, pong *colloq*, redolence *formal*, scent, smell, stench, stink *colloq*, whiff *colloq*

odyssey *n* adventure, journey, peregrination *formal*, travels, trek, voyage, wandering

off *adj* **1** *the meat is off:* bad, decomposed, high, mouldy, rancid, rotten, sour, spoilt, turned **2** *the concert is off:* abandoned, called off, cancelled, dropped, postponed, scrapped *colloq*, shelved *colloq* **3** *she's off work:* absent, away, gone, unavailable, unobtainable **4** *your calculation is way off:* below par, disappointing, incorrect, slack, substandard, unsatisfactory, wrong **5** *feel a bit off:* ill, indisposed *formal*, off form, out of sorts, poorly, sick, under the weather *colloq*, unwell
♦ *adv* apart, aside, at a distance, away, elsewhere, out

offbeat *adj* abnormal, bizarre, far-out *slang*, freaky *colloq*, kooky *colloq*, oddball *colloq*, out of the ordinary, strange, unconventional, unorthodox, untraditional, unusual, wacky *colloq*, way-out *slang*, weird

off-colour *adj* **1** *she looks a bit off-colour:* ill, indisposed *formal*, off form, out of sorts, poorly, run down *colloq*, sick, under the weather *colloq*, unwell **2** *off-colour remarks:* coarse, dirty, filthy, immoral, improper, impure, indecent, pornographic, risqué, rude, sexy, smutty, suggestive, vulgar

off-duty *adj* at leisure, free, not at work, off, off work, on holiday
🖃 on duty

offence *n* **1** *a criminal offence:* breach of the law, crime, illegal act, infraction *formal*, infringement, misdeed *formal*, misdemeanour *formal*, sin, transgression *formal*, trespass, violation *formal*, wrong, wrongdoing **2** *an offence to nature:* affront, atrocity, hurt, indignity, injury, insult, outrage, slight, snub **3** *to give offence:* anger, annoyance, antipathy *formal*, disapproval, exasperation, hard feelings, hurt, indignation, ire, outrage, pique, resentment, umbrage

offend *v* **1** *I didn't mean to offend you:* affront, anger, annoy, displease, exasperate, hurt, incense, injure, insult, miff *colloq*, needle *colloq*, outrage, provoke, put someone's back up *colloq*, put someone's nose out of joint *colloq*, raise someone's hackles *colloq*, rub someone up the wrong way *colloq*, snub, upset, wound, wrong **2** *animal cruelty offends me:* disgust, nauseate, put off, repel, revolt, sicken **3** *offend while on bail:* break the law, do wrong, err, go astray, sin, transgress *formal*, violate *formal*
🖃 **1** please

offended *adj* affronted, angered, annoyed, disgruntled, disgusted, displeased, exasperated, huffy *colloq*, hurt, in a huff *colloq*, incensed, miffed *colloq*, outraged, pained, piqued, put out *colloq*, resentful, smarting, stung, touchy *colloq*, upset, wounded
🖃 happy, pleased

offender *n* criminal, culprit, delinquent, guilty party, law-breaker, malefactor *formal*, miscreant, transgressor *formal*, wrongdoer

offensive *adj* **1** *an offensive smell:* abhorrent *formal*, abominable, detestable, disagreeable, disgusting, displeasing, foul, loathsome, nasty, nauseating, objectionable, obnoxious, odious, repellent *formal*, repugnant *formal*, revolting, sickening, unpleasant, vile **2** *his remarks were offensive:* abusive, affronting, annoying, discourteous, disrespectful, exasperating, hurtful, impertinent, impolite, insolent, insulting, rude, upsetting, wounding
🖃 **1** pleasant **2** polite
♦ *n* assault, attack, charge, drive, incursion *formal*, invasion, onslaught, push, raid, sortie, thrust

offer *v* **1** *offer my congratulations:* advance, extend, hold out, make available, present, proffer *formal*, propose, propound *formal*, put forward, recommend, submit, suggest **2** *local agencies offering aid:* afford *formal*, give, provide, supply **3** *a house offered for sale:* provide, put on the market, sell **4** *offer £100:* bid, propose, put in a bid, tender **5** *he offered to fetch her:* be at someone's service, come forward, make yourself available, show willing *colloq*, volunteer **6** *offer prayers/a sacrifice:* consecrate, dedicate, give, offer up, present, sacrifice **7** *offer resistance:* attempt, express, give, present, show, try
♦ *n* **1** *it's a very generous offer:* bid, proposal, tender **2** *she refused an offer of wine:* approach, attempt, overture, presentation, proposal, proposition, submission, suggestion

offering *n* **1** *offerings to help flood victims:* contribution, donation, gift, handout, present, subscription, tithe **2** *sacrifices and offerings are still made at sites:* celebration, consecration, dedication, oblation *formal*, sacrifice

offhand *adj* abrupt, blasé, brusque, careless, casual, cavalier, couldn't-care-less *colloq*, cursory, curt, discourteous, free-and-easy *colloq*, happy-go-lucky *colloq*, indifferent, informal, laid-back *colloq*, perfunctory, rude, take-it-or-leave-it *colloq*, terse, unceremonious, unconcerned, uninterested
♦ *adv* ad lib, extempore *formal*, immediately, impromptu, off the cuff *colloq*, off the top of one's head *colloq*, without checking, without thinking about it
🖃 calculated, planned

office *n* **1** *taking up office:* appointment, business, charge, commission, duty, employment, function, obligation, occupation, place, position, post, responsibility, role, service, situation, tenure, work **2** *work in an office:* base, bureau, place of business, workplace, workroom **3** *through the good offices of someone:* advocacy, aegis *formal*, aid, auspices *formal*, backing, back-up, favour, help, intercession *formal*, intervention, mediation, patronage, recommendation, referral, support, word

officer *n* administrator, agent, appointee, board member, bureaucrat, committee member, deputy, dignitary, envoy, executive, functionary, messenger, office-bearer, office-holder, official, public servant, representative

official *adj* **1** *an official website:* accepted, accredited *formal*, approved, authentic, authenticated, authoritative, authorized, bona fide, certified, endorsed, formal, kosher *colloq*, lawful, legal, legitimate, licensed, proper, recognized, sanctioned, validated **2** *official activities:* ceremonial, dignified, formal, ritual, solemn, stately
🖃 **1** unofficial
♦ *n* functionary, office-bearer, office-holder, officer

> *official* or *officious*? *Official* means 'done by someone in authority; relating to authority': *We think she has won, but we're still waiting for the official result of the race.* *Officious* means 'too eager to meddle, offering unwanted advice or assistance' or, more often, 'holding too rigidly to rules and regulations': *An officious little man told us that we would have to move our bicycles.*

officiate *v* be in charge, chair, conduct, manage, oversee, preside, run, superintend, take charge, take the chair

officious *adj* bossy *colloq*, bustling, dictatorial, domineering, forward, importunate *formal*, inquisitive, interfering, intrusive, meddlesome, meddling, obtrusive, opinionated, over-zealous, prying, pushy *colloq*, self-important

> *officious* or *official*? See panel at **official**

offish *adj* aloof, cool, haughty, standoffish, stuck-up *colloq*, unsociable
🖃 friendly, sociable

off-key *adj* **1** *singing off-key in the kitchen:* discordant, dissonant *formal*, inharmonious, jarring, out of tune **2** *an off-key tone:* inappropriate, out of keeping, unsuitable
🖃 **1** in tune

offload *v* **1** *pork was being offloaded from vehicles:* discharge, dump *colloq*, jettison, unload

2 *desperate to offload her children on anyone:* chuck *colloq*, disburden *formal*, drop, dump *colloq*, get rid of, shift, unburden, unload

off-putting *adj* daunting, demoralizing, discomfiting *formal*, disconcerting, discouraging, disheartening, dispiriting, disturbing, formidable, frightening, intimidating, unnerving, unsettling, upsetting

offset *v* balance (out), cancel out, compensate for, counteract, counterbalance, counterpoise *formal*, countervail *formal*, make up for, neutralize

offshoot *n* **1** *remove the offshoots to encourage more flowers:* appendage, arm, branch, limb, outgrowth **2** *an offshoot of the anti-nuclear movement:* appendage, branch, by-product, consequence, development, outcome, product, result, spin-off

offspring *n* brood, child, children, descendants, family, fruit of your loins *formal*, heirs, issue *formal*, kid(s) *colloq*, nipper(s) *colloq*, progeny *formal*, successors, young, young one(s)
F∃ parent(s)

often *adv* again and again, day in day out, frequently, generally, many a time, many times, month in month out, much, over and over again, regularly, repeatedly, time after time, time and (time) again, week in week out
F∃ never, rarely, seldom

ogle *v* eye, eye up, leer, look, make eyes at, stare

ogre *n* **1** *the adventures of the ogre and his donkey:* bogey, bogeyman, demon, devil, fiend, monster, troll **2** *his father is a bit of an ogre:* barbarian, beast, brute, fiend, monster, savage, villain

oil *v* anoint, grease, lubricate, make smooth
♦ *n* balm, cream, grease, liniment, lotion, lubricant, ointment, salve, unguent *formal*

oily *adj* **1** *oily fish:* buttery, fatty, greasy, oleaginous *formal* **2** *smiling in an oily manner:* flattering, glib, ingratiating, obsequious, servile, smarmy, smooth *colloq*, smooth-talking, suave, subservient, unctuous, urbane

ointment *n* balm, cream, embrocation *formal*, emollient *technical*, gel, liniment, lotion, salve

OK *adj* acceptable, accurate, adequate, all right, convenient, correct, fair, fine, good, in order, not bad *colloq*, passable, permitted, reasonable, satisfactory, so-so *colloq*, tolerable, up to par *colloq*, up to scratch *colloq*
♦ *n* agreement, approbation *formal*, approval, authorization, consent *formal*, endorsement, go-ahead *colloq*, green light *colloq*, permission, sanction, thumbs-up *colloq*
♦ *v* agree to, approve, authorize, consent to *formal*, give the go-ahead to *colloq*, give the green light to *colloq*, give the thumbs-up to *colloq*, pass, rubber-stamp, say yes to
♦ *interj* agreed, all right, fine, right, very good, very well, yes

old *adj* **1** *70 isn't old nowadays:* (a bit) long in the tooth *colloq*, advanced in years, aged, ageing, elderly, getting on *colloq*, grey, mature, no spring chicken *colloq*, not as young as you were *colloq*, not getting any younger *colloq*, not long for this world *colloq*, over the hill *colloq*, past it *colloq*, past your prime, senescent *formal*, senile, sensible, wise **2** *in the old days:* age-old, ancient,

antiquated, bygone, classic, earlier, earliest, early, original, prehistoric, primal, primeval, primitive, primordial, pristine *formal*, veteran, vintage **3** *the old methods are dying out:* age-old, enduring, lasting, long-established, long-lived, long-standing, old as the hills *colloq*, time-honoured, traditional **4** *I still listen to my old 78s:* antediluvian *colloq*, antique, archaic, behind the times, Dickensian *colloq*, obsolete, old-fashioned, on the way out *colloq*, out of date, out of the ark *colloq*, outdated, passé, past it *colloq*, past its sell-by date *colloq*, unfashionable **5** *the house was old and in need of repair:* broken down, cast-off, crumbling, decayed, decaying, decrepit, having seen better days *colloq*, ramshackle, shabby, torn, tumbledown, worn out **6** *I liked his old car much better:* earlier, erstwhile *formal*, ex-, former, one-time, previous, quondam *formal*, sometime
F∃ 1 young **2** new **4** contemporary, fashionable, modern, new, state-of-the-art, up-to-date **5** new **6** current

old-fashioned *adj* **1** *an old-fashioned gesture:* ancient, antediluvian *colloq*, antiquated, archaic, bygone, dead, fuddy-duddy *colloq*, obsolescent, obsolete, old, old hat *colloq*, old-time, on the way out *colloq*, out of date, out of the ark *colloq*, outdated, passé, past, past it *colloq*, past its sell-by date *colloq*, square *colloq*, written off **2** *an old-fashioned waistcoat and jacket:* ancient, dated, fuddy-duddy *colloq*, old, on the way out *colloq*, out of date, out of fashion, out of the ark *colloq*, outdated, outmoded, passé, past it *colloq*, past its sell-by date *colloq*, square *colloq*, unfashionable
F∃ 1 modern, up-to-date **2** modern, up-to-date

old-time *adj* antiquated, archaic, behind the times, bygone, dated, obsolete, old, old fashioned, out of date, out of fashion, outdated, outmoded, passé, past, unfashionable

old-world *adj* antiquated, archaic, bygone, old-fashioned, past, picturesque, quaint, traditional

omen *n* augury *formal*, auspice *formal*, foreboding, forecast, harbinger, indication, portent *formal*, prediction, premonition, presentiment *formal*, prodrome *formal*, prodromus *formal*, sign, token, warning

ominous *adj* fateful, foreboding, inauspicious *formal*, menacing, minatory *formal*, portentous *formal*, sinister, threatening, unfavourable, unlucky, unpromising, unpropitious *formal*
F∃ auspicious *formal*, favourable

omission *n* **1** *a serious omission:* dereliction *formal*, failure, gap, lack, lacuna *formal*, oversight **2** *the omission of punctuation:* avoidance, disregard, exclusion, lack, leaving-out, neglect
F∃ 2 inclusion

omit *v* cross out, delete, disregard, drop, edit out, eliminate, erase, except, exclude, expunge *formal*, fail, fail to mention, forget, leave out, leave undone, miss (out), neglect, overlook, pass over, rub out, skip
F∃ include, mention

omnibus *adj* all-embracing, compendious, comprehensive, encyclopedic, inclusive, wide-ranging
F∃ selective
♦ *n* anthology, collection, compendium, compilation, encyclopedia

omnipotence *n* absolute/total power, all-powerfulness, almightiness, complete authority, divine right, invincibility, mastery, plenipotence *formal*, sovereignty, supremacy
🔁 impotence

omnipotent *adj* all-powerful, almighty, invincible, plenipotent *formal*, supreme
🔁 impotent

omnipresent *adj* all-pervasive, all-present, infinite, limitless, pervasive, present everywhere, ubiquitary *formal*, ubiquitous, universal

omniscient *adj* all-knowing, all-seeing, all-wise, pansophic *formal*

omnivorous *adj* all-devouring, eating anything, gluttonous, indiscriminate, undiscriminating

once *adv* at one point, at one time, formerly, in the old days, in the past, in times gone by, in times past, long ago, on one occasion, once upon a time, one time, previously
♦ *conj* after, as soon as, immediately after, when

oncoming *adj* advancing, approaching, gathering, looming, nearing, onrushing, upcoming

one *adj* 1 *the one cake on the plate*: individual, lone, only, single, sole, solitary 2 *become one flesh*: alike, bound, complete, entire, equal, fused, harmonious, identical, joined, like-minded, married, united, wedded, whole

oneness *n* completeness, consistency, identicalness, identity, individuality, sameness, singleness, unity, wholeness

onerous *adj* arduous, back-breaking, burdensome, crushing, demanding, difficult, exacting, exhausting, exigent *formal*, fatiguing, hard, heavy, laborious, oppressive, strenuous, taxing, tiring, troublesome, wearying, weighty

one-sided *adj* 1 *a one-sided contest*: lopsided, unbalanced, unequal, uneven 2 *a one-sided debate*: biased, bigoted, discriminatory, inequitable, narrow-minded, partial, partisan, prejudiced, unfair, unjust 3 *a one-sided decision*: independent, one-way, separate, separated, unilateral
🔁 1 balanced 2 impartial 3 bilateral, multilateral

one-time *adj* erstwhile *formal*, ex-, former, late, previous, quondam *formal*, sometime

ongoing *adj* 1 *an ongoing crisis*: constant, continuing, continuous, incessant, non-stop, unbroken, unending, uninterrupted 2 *ongoing discussions*: advancing, current, developing, evolving, growing, in progress, progressing, unfinished, unfolding

onlooker *n* bystander, eyewitness, gawper *colloq*, looker-on, observer, rubberneck *colloq*, sightseer, spectator, viewer, watcher, witness

only *adv* at most, barely, exclusively, just, merely, no more than, not more than, nothing but, purely, simply, solely
♦ *adj* exclusive, individual, lone, one and only, single, sole, solitary, unique

onrush *n* career, cascade, charge, flood, flow, onset, onslaught, push, rush, stampede, stream, surge

onset *n* 1 *the onset of senile depression*: beginning, commencement *formal*, inception *formal*, kick-off

colloq, outbreak, outset, start 2 *the onset of the Prussian army*: assault, attack, charge, onrush, onslaught
🔁 1 end, finish

onslaught *n* assault, attack, blitz, bombardment, charge, drive, foray, offensive, onrush, push, raid, storming, thrust

onus *n* albatross *colloq*, burden, charge, duty, encumbrance, liability, load, millstone *colloq*, obligation, responsibility, task, weight

onwards *adv* ahead, beyond, forth *formal*, forward(s), in front, on
🔁 backward(s)

oodles *n* abundance, bags *colloq*, heaps *colloq*, lashings *colloq*, loads *colloq*, lots, masses, tons *colloq*
🔁 scarcity

oomph *n* animation, bounce *colloq*, energy, enthusiasm, exuberance, get-up-and-go *colloq*, pep *colloq*, pizzazz *colloq*, sexiness *colloq*, sparkle, vigour, vitality, vivacity, zing *colloq*

ooze *v* bleed, discharge, drain, dribble, drip, drop, emit, escape, excrete *formal*, exude, filter, filtrate *formal*, flow, leak, overflow with, percolate, pour forth, secrete, seep, trickle
♦ *n* alluvium *formal*, deposit, mire, muck, mud, sediment, silt, slime, sludge

oozy *adj* dewy, dripping, miry, moist, mucky, muddy, slimy, sloppy, sludgy, sweaty, uliginous *formal*, weeping

opacity *n* 1 *maximum opacity of a smoke plume*: cloudiness, density, dullness, filminess, impermeability, milkiness, murkiness, opaqueness, unclearness 2 *prose of baroque opacity*: impenetrability, incomprehensibility, obfuscation *formal*, obscurity, unintelligibility
🔁 1 transparency 2 clarity

opalescent *adj* dazzling, glittering, iridescent *formal*, multicoloured, pearly, polychromatic, prismatic, rainbow, rainbow-coloured, rainbow-like, shimmering, shot, sparkling, variegated *formal*

opaque *adj* 1 *opaque glass*: blurred, clouded, cloudy, dense, dim, dingy, dull, hazy, misty, muddied, muddy, murky, thick, turbid, unclear 2 *opaque and elliptical language*: abstruse *formal*, as clear as mud *colloq*, baffling, confusing, cryptic, difficult, enigmatic, esoteric *formal*, impenetrable, incomprehensible, obscure, puzzling, recondite *formal*, unclear, unfathomable, unintelligible
🔁 1 transparent 2 clear, obvious

open *adj* 1 *leave the window open*: ajar, coverless, gaping, lidless, topless, unbarred, unbolted, unclosed, uncovered, unfastened, unlatched, unlocked, unsealed, wide open, yawning 2 *open countryside*: accessible, available, clear, exposed, free, navigable, obtainable, passable, unblocked, unenclosed, unfenced, unobstructed, unoccupied, unprotected, unrestricted, unsheltered, vacant, wide 3 *the road is open again*: accessible, clear, free, navigable, passable, unblocked, unobstructed 4 *his open contempt*: apparent, blatant, clear, conspicuous, evident, flagrant, manifest *formal*, noticeable, obvious, overt, patent, plain, unconcealed, undisguised, unhidden, visible 5 *the date is still open to discussion*: arguable, debatable, moot, problematic, undecided, unresolved, unsettled

6 *she was quite open about her affair:* blunt, candid, direct, forthright, frank, guileless, honest, ingenuous, natural, simple, unreserved **7** *a lightweight, open fabric:* airy, cellular, holey, honeycombed, loosely woven, openwork, porous, spongelike **8** *an open secret:* accessible, general, public, unrestricted, well known, widely known **9** *open to misinterpretation:* accessible, disposed, exposed, liable, receptive, susceptible, vulnerable
E **1** closed, shut **2** restricted **4** concealed, hidden **5** decided, resolved **6** reserved **7** close **8** closed, private
♦ *v* **1** *open the bottle:* break open, broach, burst open, clear, crack, expose, force open, prise open, push open, slide open, unblock, unbolt, uncork, uncover, undo, unfasten, unlatch, unlock, unseal, untie **2** *open my heart:* bare, disclose, divulge, explain, expose, lay bare, pour out **3** *the buds will open:* come apart, extend, flower, separate, split, spread (out), unfold, unfurl, unroll **4** *she opened the fete:* begin, commence, get cracking *colloq,* inaugurate, initiate, kick off *colloq,* launch, set in motion, set the ball rolling *colloq,* start, take the plunge *colloq*
E **1** close, shut **2** hide **4** end, finish
▶ **open onto** command a view of, face, give onto, lead to, overlook

open-air *adj* afield, alfresco, outdoor, out-of-doors, outside
E indoor

open-and-shut *adj* clear, easily decided, easily solved, obvious, simple, straightforward

open-handed *adj* bounteous *formal,* bountiful, eleemosynary *formal,* free, generous, large-hearted, lavish, liberal, munificent *formal,* unstinting
E tight-fisted

opening *n* **1** *a small opening in the fence:* aperture, breach, break, chasm, chink, cleft, crack, crevice, fissure, gap, hole, inlet, interstice *formal,* orifice *formal,* outlet, rupture, slot, space, split, vent **2** *the opening of the race:* beginning, birth, dawn, first base *colloq,* inauguration, inception *formal,* kick-off *colloq,* launch, onset, outset, square one *colloq,* start, the word go *colloq* **3** *the opening he'd been looking for:* break *colloq,* chance, occasion, opportunity **4** *the factory didn't have any openings:* job, place, position, vacancy
E **2** close, end
♦ *adj* beginning, commencing *formal,* early, first, inaugural *formal,* initial, introductory, primary, starting
E closing

openly *adv* blatantly, bluntly, brazenly, candidly, directly, flagrantly, forthrightly, frankly, glaringly, honestly, immodestly, in full view, in public, overtly, plainly, shamelessly, unashamedly, unreservedly, with no holds barred *colloq*
E secretly, slyly

open-minded *adj* broad, broad-minded, catholic, dispassionate, enlightened, free, impartial, latitudinarian *formal,* liberal, objective, reasonable, receptive, tolerant, unbiased, unprejudiced
E bigoted, intolerant, narrow-minded, prejudiced

open-mouthed *adj* amazed, astounded, clamorous, dumbfounded, expectant,

flabbergasted *colloq,* shocked, spellbound, thunderstruck

operate *v* **1** *it operates on batteries:* act, function, go, perform, run, work **2** *she can operate that machine:* be in charge of, control, employ, handle, manage, manoeuvre, run, use, utilize, work

operation *n* **1** *the operation of the handbrake:* action, functioning, motion, movement, performance, running, working **2** *the operation of power:* control, handling, influence, management, manipulation, running, use, using, utilization, working **3** *it's a two-person operation:* activity, affair, business, deal, effort, enterprise, exercise, job, procedure, proceeding, process, task, transaction, undertaking **4** *operations outside the area:* action, assault, attack, campaign, charge, exercise, manoeuvre, raid, task **5** *a gall bladder operation:* excision, intervention, procedure, surgery

operational *adj* functional, functioning, going, in action, in service, in use, in working order, prepared, ready, usable, viable, workable, working
E out of order

operative *adj* **1** *procedures operative before 1982:* active, effective, efficient, functional, functioning, in action, in force, in operation, operational, serviceable, valid, viable, workable, working **2** *the transmitter is operative:* effective, functioning, in operation, serviceable, working **3** *'maybe' being the operative word:* crucial, important, key, relevant, significant, vital
E **1** out of service
♦ *n* **1** *the recruitment of skilled operatives:* artisan, employee, hand, labourer, machinist, mechanic, operator, worker, workman **2** *Shaft, the famous black operative:* detective, dick *colloq,* gumshoe *colloq,* private detective, private eye *colloq,* (private) investigator, shamus *colloq,* sleuth *colloq* **3** *CIA operatives:* agent, double agent, mole *colloq,* secret agent, spy

operator *n* **1** *a lathe operator:* driver, machinist, mechanic, mover, operative, practitioner, technician, worker **2** *operators of mobile radio networks:* administrator, contractor, dealer, director, handler, manager, trader **3** *a sharp operator:* machinator, manipulator, manoeuvrer, punter, shyster, speculator, wheeler-dealer *colloq*

opiate *n* anodyne, bromide, depressant, downer *colloq,* drug, narcotic, nepenthe *formal,* pacifier, sedative, soporific, stupefacient, tranquillizer

opine *v* believe, conceive, conclude, conjecture *formal,* declare, guess, judge, presume, say, suggest, suppose, surmise *formal,* suspect, think, venture, volunteer

opinion *n* assessment, assumption, attitude, belief, conception, conviction, estimation *formal,* feeling(s), idea, impression, judgement, mind, notion, perception, persuasion, point of view, school of thought, sentiment, stance, standpoint, theory, thought(s), view, viewpoint, way of thinking

opinionated *adj* adamant, arrogant, biased, bigoted, cocksure, dictatorial, doctrinaire, dogmatic, inflexible, obstinate, pigheaded, pompous, pontifical, prejudiced, self-important,

single-minded, stubborn, uncompromising, with preconceived ideas
🔁 open-minded

opponent *n* adversary, antagonist, challenger, competitor, contender, contestant, dissentient *formal*, dissident, enemy, foe, objector, opposer, opposition, rival
🔁 ally, friend, supporter

opportune *adj* advantageous, appropriate, apt, auspicious *formal*, convenient, favourable, felicitous *formal*, fit, fitting, fortunate, good, happy, lucky, pertinent *formal*, proper, propitious *formal*, providential, seasonable, suitable, timely, well-timed
🔁 inopportune *formal*, unsuitable

opportunism *n* expediency, exploitation, Machiavellianism, making hay while the sun shines *colloq*, pragmatism, realism, taking advantage, unscrupulousness

opportunity *n* break *colloq*, chance, hour, look-in *colloq*, moment, occasion, opening, possibility

oppose *v* **1** *those who oppose cruelty to animals:* argue against, attack, bar, be against, challenge, check, combat, confront, contest, contradict, counter, defy, disagree with, disapprove of, face, fight, fly in the face of *colloq*, hinder, obstruct, prevent, resist, stand up to, take a stand against, take issue with, thwart, withstand **2** *a wheeze (as opposed to a sneeze):* balance, compare, contrast, counterbalance, juxtapose *formal*, match, offset, play off, set against
🔁 **1** defend, support

opposed *adj* against, antagonistic, anti *colloq*, averse *formal*, clashing, conflicting, contrary, disagreeing, hostile, in opposition, incompatible, inimical *formal*, opposing, opposite
🔁 in favour

opposing *adj* antagonistic, antipathetic *formal*, at odds, at variance, clashing, combatant, conflicting, contending, contentious, contrary, differing, disputatious *formal*, enemy, fighting, hostile, incompatible, irreconcilable, opposed, opposite, oppugnant *formal*, rival, warring

opposite *adj* **1** *the chair opposite:* corresponding, face to face, facing, fronting **2** *take the opposite point of view:* adverse *formal*, antagonistic, antithetical *formal*, at odds, at variance, clashing, conflicting, contradictory, contrary, contrasted, different, differing, dissident *formal*, hostile, irreconcilable, opposed, poles apart *colloq*, reverse, unlike
🔁 **2** same
♦ *n* antithesis *formal*, contradiction, contrary, converse, flip side *colloq*, inverse, reverse, the other side of the coin *colloq*, the other side of the fence *colloq*
🔁 same

opposition *n* **1** *opposition to the plans:* antagonism, confrontation, disapproval, dislike, hostility, obstructiveness, resistance, unfriendliness **2** *playing for the opposition:* adversary, antagonist, competition, enemy, foe, opponent, opposing side, other side, rival
🔁 **1** co-operation, support **2** ally, supporter

oppress *v* **1** *oppress the people:* abuse, bring someone to their knees *colloq*, crush, enslave, maltreat, overpower, overwhelm, persecute, quash, quell, repress, subdue, subjugate, suppress, trample, treat like dirt *colloq*, treat like shit *slang*, tyrannize, use as a doormat *colloq* **2** *oppressed by the strict formality:* afflict, burden, crush, deject, depress, desolate *formal*, discourage, dishearten, dispirit, harass, lie heavy on, sadden, torment, vex, weigh down

oppressed *adj* abused, burdened, crushed, disadvantaged, downtrodden, enslaved, harassed, maltreated, misused, persecuted, repressed, subject, subjugated *formal*, troubled, tyrannized, underprivileged
🔁 free

oppression *n* abuse, brutality, cruelty, despotism, hardship, harshness, injustice, maltreatment, overpowering, overwhelming, persecution, repression, ruthlessness, subjection, subjugation *formal*, suppression, tyranny

oppressive *adj* **1** *oppressive legislation:* brutal, burdensome, cruel, crushing, despotic, domineering, Draconian, harsh, inhuman, intolerable, iron-fisted, merciless, onerous, overbearing, overwhelming, pitiless, repressive, ruthless, tyrannical, unjust **2** *oppressive humidity:* airless, close, heavy, muggy, stifling, stuffy, suffocating, sultry
🔁 **1** gentle, just **2** airy

oppressor *n* autocrat, bully, despot, dictator, (hard) taskmaster, intimidator, persecutor, slave-driver, subjugator *formal*, tormentor, torturer, tyrant

opprobrious *adj* abusive, calumniatory *formal*, calumnious *formal*, contemptuous, contumelious *formal*, damaging, defamatory, derogatory, insolent, insulting, invective *formal*, offensive, scandalous, scurrilous, venomous, vitriolic, vituperative *formal*

opprobrium *n* calumny *formal*, censure, contumely *formal*, debasement, degradation, discredit, disfavour, disgrace, dishonour, disrepute, ignominy *formal*, infamy, obloquy *formal*, odium *formal*, reproach, scurrility, shame, slur *colloq*, stigma

opt *v* choose, decide (on), elect, go for *colloq*, pick, plump for *colloq*, prefer, select, settle on, single out

optimistic *adj* assured, bright, bullish, buoyant, cheerful, confident, expectant, happy-go-lucky *colloq*, hopeful, idealistic, looking on the bright side/through rose-coloured spectacles *colloq*, Panglossian, Panglossic, pollyann(a)ish, positive, sanguine, upbeat *colloq*
🔁 pessimistic

optimum *adj* best, choice, flawless, highest, ideal, model, most favourable, optimal, perfect, superlative, supreme, top, utopian
🔁 worst

option *n* alternative, choice, possibility, preference, selection

optional *adj* discretionary, elective, free, unforced, voluntary
🔁 compulsory, mandatory *formal*, required

opulence *n* **1** *the only signs of opulence were the gold boxes:* affluence, easy street *colloq*, fortune, prosperity, riches, wealth **2** *the opulence of the*

palace: lavishness, luxury, plenty, richness, sumptuousness
▨ 1 penury *formal,* poverty

opulent *adj* **1** *the opulent elite:* affluent, moneyed, prosperous, rich, rolling in it *colloq,* wealthy, well-heeled *colloq,* well-off, well-to-do **2** *opulent decors:* lavish, luxurious, plush *colloq,* posh *colloq,* sumptuous **3** *the opulent curves of her body:* abundant, copious, luxuriant, plentiful, profuse, prolific, superabundant
▨ 1 penurious *formal,* poor

opus *n* brainchild, composition, creation, oeuvre, piece, production, work

oracle *n* **1** *consult an oracle:* augur, high priest, prophet, sage, seer, sibyl, soothsayer, wizard **2** *the Colonial Office's oracle on Africa:* adviser, authority, expert, guru *colloq,* mastermind *colloq,* mentor, pundit *colloq,* specialist **3** *began to utter oracles in Greek:* answer, augury, divination, prediction, prognostication *formal,* prophecy, revelation, vision

oracular *adj* abstruse *formal,* ambiguous, arcane *formal,* auspicious *formal,* authoritative, cryptic, Delphic, dictatorial, dogmatic, equivocal, grave, haruspical *formal,* mysterious, obscure, ominous, portentous, positive, predictive, prescient *formal,* prophetic, sage *formal,* significant, two-edged, venerable, wise

oral *adj* said, spoken, unwritten, uttered, verbal, vocal
▨ written

orate *v* declaim *formal,* discourse, harangue, hold forth, pontificate, sermonize, speak, speechify, talk

oration *n* address, declamation *formal,* discourse, harangue, homily, lecture, sermon, speech, spiel *colloq*

orator *n* declaimer, demagogue, lecturer, phrasemonger, public speaker, rhetorician, speaker, spellbinder, spieler *colloq*

oratorical *adj* bombastic *formal,* Ciceronian, declamatory *formal,* Demosthenic, elocutionary, eloquent, grandiloquent *formal,* high-flown, magniloquent *formal,* rhetorical, silver-tongued, smooth-tongued, sonorous

oratory *n* declamation, diction, elocution, eloquence, grandiloquence *formal,* public speaking, rhetoric, speech, speechifying, speech-making

orb *n* ball, circle, globe, globule, mound, ring, round, sphere, spherule

orbit *n* **1** *Mercury's orbit:* circle, circuit, circumgyration *formal,* course, cycle, path, revolution, rotation, track, trajectory **2** *within the European orbit:* ambit, compass, domain, influence, range, reach, scope, sphere of influence, sweep
♦ *v* circle, circumnavigate, encircle, revolve

orchestrate *v* arrange, compose, co-ordinate, fix, integrate, mastermind, organize, prepare, present, put together, score, stage-manage

ordain *v* **1** *ordain to the priesthood:* anoint, appoint, call, consecrate, elect, frock, invest **2** *James ordained these measures:* decree, dictate, fix, instruct, lay down, order, predetermine *formal,* prescribe *formal,* pronounce, require, rule,

set, will **3** *ordained to save the world:* destine, fate, foreordain *formal,* predestine *formal*

ordeal *n* affliction *formal,* agony, anguish, distress, nightmare, pain, persecution, suffering, test, torment, torture, trial, tribulation(s) *formal,* trouble(s)

order *n* **1** *he barked orders:* command, decree, dictate, direction, directive, edict, injunction, instruction, law, mandate, ordinance, precept, regulation, rule, stipulation, summons, warrant, writ **2** *she has a settee on order:* application, booking, call, commission, demand, notification, request, requirement, requisition, reservation **3** *in order of height:* arrangement, array, categorization, classification, codification, cycle, disposition *formal,* form, grouping, layout, line-up, method, organization, pattern, plan, regularity, rota, sequence, set-up, structure, symmetry, system, uniformity **4** *the order with which everything was done:* method, neatness, orderliness, system, tidiness **5** *restoring order to the city:* calm, discipline, harmony, law and order, lawfulness, peace, quiet, tranquillity **6** *a member of an ancient order:* association, brotherhood, club, community, company, denomination, fellowship, fraternity, guild, league, lodge, organization, secret society, sect, sisterhood, society, sorority, union **7** *higher orders of animals:* caste, class, degree, family, genus, grade, group, hierarchy, kind, level, pecking order *colloq,* position, rank, sort, species, station, type, variety
▨ 3 disorder **4** chaos, confusion **5** anarchy
♦ *v* **1** *he ordered me to shoot:* authorize, bid, command, decree, direct, enjoin *formal,* instruct, legislate, prescribe *formal,* require, rule **2** *I ordered her gift:* apply for, book, call for, request, requisition *formal,* reserve, send away for, write off for **3** *she ordered the tins in the cupboard:* arrange, catalogue, classify, codify, control, dispose, group, lay out, manage, marshal, organize, regulate, sort out, systematize, tidy up
▶ **order around** boss around, browbeat, bulldoze, bully, dominate, domineer, lay down the law *colloq,* order about, push around *colloq,* throw your weight about *colloq,* tyrannize

orderly *adj* **1** *arranged in an orderly fashion:* businesslike, efficient, in apple-pie order *colloq,* in order, methodical, neat, orderly, regular, systematic, tidy, trim, well-organized, well-regulated **2** *form an orderly queue please:* controlled, disciplined, law-abiding, restrained, ruly, well-behaved
▨ 1 chaotic **2** disorderly

ordinance *n* **1** *Germany's packaging ordinance:* canon, command, decree, dictum, directive, edict, enactment, fiat, injunction, law, regulation, rule, ruling, statute **2** *God's ordinance in the holy estate of matrimony:* ceremony, institution, observance, order, practice, rite, ritual, sacrament

ordinarily *adv* as a rule, commonly, conventionally, customarily, familiarly, generally, habitually, in general, normally, usually

ordinary *adj* average, banal, bland, common, common-or-garden *colloq,* commonplace, conventional, customary, dull, everyday, fair, familiar, habitual, indifferent, mainstream, mediocre, modest, mundane, nondescript,

normal, pedestrian, plain, prosaic, quotidian, regular, routine, run-of-the-mill *colloq*, simple, standard, typical, undistinguished, unexceptional, uninteresting, unmemorable, unpretentious, unremarkable, usual, workaday
☒ extraordinary, unusual

ordnance *n* arms, artillery, big guns *colloq*, cannon, guns, military supplies, munitions, weapons

organ *n* 1 *donating organs for transplantation*: component, constituent, device, element, implement, instrument, member, part, process, structure, tool, unit 2 *the official weekly organ of the DTI*: agency, forum, journal, magazine, medium, mouthpiece, newspaper, paper, periodical, publication, vehicle, voice

organic *adj* 1 *organic matter*: animate, biological, biotic *technical*, living, natural 2 *organic vegetables*: additive-free, natural, non-chemical, not artificial, pesticide-free 3 *an organic whole*: harmonious, ordered, organized, structured

organism *n* 1 *like every organism in a thriving garden*: animal, bacterium, being, body, cell, creature, entity, living thing, plant, structure 2 *the Church is an organism and an organization*: entity, set-up, structure, system, unity, whole

organization *n* 1 *a political organization*: association, authority, body, club, company, concern, confederation, conglomeration, consortium, corporation, council, federation, firm, group, institute, institution, league, operation, outfit, society, syndicate, union 2 *the organization of disco-dancing competitions*: administration, arrangement, co-ordination, development, establishment, management, running 3 *review the organization of the Diplomatic Service*: classification, composition, configuration *formal*, design, formation, grouping, method, methodology, order, pattern, plan, set-up, structure, system, unity, whole

organize *v* 1 *she organized her day*: administer, arrange, be in charge of, be responsible for, catalogue, classify, co-ordinate, dispose, group, manage, marshal, order, put in order, run, see to, sort out, standardize, structure, systematize, tabulate 2 *they organized the prom*: assemble, begin, construct, create, develop, establish, form, found, frame, institute, mould, originate, prepare, put together, set up, shape, start
☒ 1 disorganize

organized *adj* arranged, businesslike, efficient, in order, methodical, neat, ordered, orderly, planned, regular, structured, systematic, tidy, well-ordered, well-organized, well-regulated
☒ disorganized

orgy *n* 1 *a wild orgy*: bacchanalia, binge *colloq*, bout, carousal, debauch, party, revel(s), revelry, splurge *colloq*, wild party 2 *an orgy of thieving*: binge *colloq*, excess, frenzy, indulgence, splurge *colloq*, spree

orient *v* acclimatize, accommodate, accustom, adapt, adjust, align, familiarize, get your bearings, habituate *formal*, orientate

orientation *n* 1 *an orientation towards counselling skills*: alignment, attitude, bearings, direction, inclination, location, placement, position 2 *spent the first day undergoing orientation*: acclimatization, adaptation, adjustment, familiarization, getting your bearings, guiding, induction, initiation, leading, settling-in, training

orifice *n* aperture *formal*, breach, break, cleft, crack, crevice, fissure, gap, hole, inlet, mouth, opening, perforation, pore, rent, rift, slit, slot, space, vent

origin *n* 1 *the origins of the Hungarian nation*: base, basis, cause, derivation, etymology, foundation, fount, fountain, fountainhead, provenance *formal*, root(s), source, spring, well-spring 2 *some mosaics of Roman origin*: beginning, birth, commencement *formal*, conception, creation, dawn, dawning, emergence, foundation, genesis *formal*, inauguration, inception *formal*, launch, start 3 *a theatre-goer of French origin*: ancestry, birth, descent, extraction, family, heritage, lineage, parentage, paternity, pedigree, stock
☒ 2 end, termination

original *adj* 1 *the original manuscript*: archetypal, autochthonous *formal*, commencing, earliest, early, embryonic, first, first-hand, initial, opening, primal, primary, primeval, primitive, primordial, rudimentary, starting 2 *original screenplays*: creative, fresh, ground-breaking, imaginative, ingenious, innovative, inventive, new, novel, pioneering, resourceful, unconventional, unique, unorthodox, unusual 3 *the original sleeping beauty*: authentic, genuine, real, true
☒ 1 latest 2 hackneyed, unoriginal 3 copied
♦ *n* archetype, master, model, paradigm, pattern, prototype, standard, type
☒ copy

originality *n* boldness, cleverness, creative spirit, creativeness, creativity, daring, eccentricity, freshness, imagination, imaginativeness, individuality, ingenuity, innovation, innovativeness, inventiveness, newness, novelty, resourcefulness, singularity, unconventionality, unorthodoxy

originally *adv* at first, at the outset, at the start, by birth, by derivation, first, in origin, in the beginning, initially, to begin with

originate *v* 1 *youth hostels originated in Germany*: arise, be born, come, derive, emanate, emerge, evolve, flow, issue, proceed, result, rise, spring, stem 2 *the person who originates the message*: be the father/mother of, begin, commence *formal*, conceive, create, develop, discover, establish, form, generate, give birth to, inaugurate, introduce, invent, launch, pioneer, produce, set in motion, set up, start
☒ 1 end, terminate

originator *n* architect, author, creator, designer, developer, discoverer, establisher, father, founder, generator, initiator, innovator, inventor, mother, pioneer, prime mover, the brains *colloq*

ornament *n* 1 *enjoy them as garden ornaments*: accessory, adornment, decoration, embellishment, frill, garnish, pattern, trimming 2 *ornaments made of gold*: accessory, bauble, decoration, fallal, furbelow, gewgaw, jewel, trinket
♦ *v* adorn, beautify, brighten, deck, decorate, dress up, embellish, garnish, gild, trim

ornamental *adj* adorning, attractive, decorative, embellishing, embroidering, fancy, showy

ornamentation *n* adornment, decoration, elaboration, embellishment, embroidery, fallalery, frills, garniture, ornateness

ornate *adj* baroque, busy, decorated, elaborate, embellished, fancy, flamboyant, flash *colloq*, florid, flowery, fussy, grandiose, ornamented, ostentatious, rococo, showy, sumptuous
🖾 plain

orotund *adj* 1 *orotund voices:* booming, deep, full, loud, powerful, resonating, rich, round, sonorous, strong 2 *orotund speaking:* dignified, imposing, magniloquent *formal*, ornate, pompous, pretentious, strained

orthodox *adj* 1 *orthodox Jews:* accepted, authoritative, conformist, conservative, conventional, correct, customary, established, official, received, recognized, regular, traditional, usual, well-established 2 *orthodox religious views:* devout, established, faithful, sound, strict, traditional, true
🖾 1 nonconformist, unorthodox

orthodoxy *n* 1 *go against the conventional orthodoxy:* authoritativeness, conformism, conformity, conventionality, correctness, properness, received wisdom, traditionalism 2 *imposition of Christian orthodoxy:* conservatism, devotion, devoutness, faithfulness, inflexibility, soundness, strictness, trueness

oscillate *v* fluctuate, go from one extreme to the other, move backwards and forwards, move to and fro, seesaw *colloq*, sway, swing, vacillate, vary, vibrate, waver, yo-yo *colloq*, zigzag

oscillation *n* fluctuation, instability, seesawing *colloq*, shilly-shallying *colloq*, swing, swinging, vacillation, variation, wavering

ossify *v* fossilize, harden, indurate *formal*, make/become fixed, make/become hard, petrify *formal*, rigidify *formal*, solidify

ostensible *adj* alleged, apparent, claimed, feigned *formal*, outward, presumed, pretended, professed, purported *formal*, seeming, so-called, specious, superficial, supposed
🖾 genuine, real

ostensibly *adv* allegedly, apparently, outwardly, professedly, purportedly *formal*, reputedly, seemingly, superficially, supposedly

ostentation *n* affectation *formal*, boasting, display, exhibitionism, flamboyance, flashiness *colloq*, flaunting, flourish, pageantry, parade, pomp, pretension, pretentiousness, show, showiness, showing off, swank *colloq*, tinsel *colloq*, trappings, vaunting, window-dressing
🖾 unpretentiousness

ostentatious *adj* affected *formal*, conspicuous, demonstrative, extravagant, flamboyant, flash *colloq*, flashy *colloq*, flaunting, garish, gaudy, glitzy *colloq*, kitsch *colloq*, loud, obtrusive, OTT *colloq*, over the top *colloq*, pretentious, showy, vulgar
🖾 modest, restrained

ostracism *n* avoidance, banishment, barring, boycott, cold shoulder *colloq*, disfellowship *formal*, exclusion, excommunication, exile,

expulsion, isolation, proscription *formal*, rejection
🖾 acceptance, reinstatement, welcome

ostracize *v* avoid, banish, bar, boycott, cold-shoulder *colloq*, cut *colloq*, exclude, excommunicate, exile, expel, isolate, outlaw, reject, segregate, send to Coventry, shun, snub
🖾 accept, welcome

other *adj* 1 *other types of skin complaint:* contrasting, different, disparate *formal*, dissimilar, distinct, separate, unlike, variant 2 *other news just in:* additional, alternative, extra, further, more, spare, supplementary

otherwise *conj* failing that, if not, or, or else, unless
♦ *adv* 1 *his father thought otherwise:* along different lines, differently, in a different way, in other respects 2 *an otherwise flat landscape:* except for that, in other respects

otherworldly *adj* absent-minded, bemused, dreamy, ethereal, fey, preoccupied, rapt
🖾 mundane, solid, substantial, worldly

ounce *n* atom, crumb, drop, grain, iota, jot, modicum, morsel, particle, scrap, shred, speck, spot, trace, whit

oust *v* boot out *colloq*, depose, disinherit, dislodge, dismiss, displace, dispossess, drive out, eject, evict, expel, fire *colloq*, force out, get rid of, give someone the boot/elbow *colloq*, overthrow, put out, replace, sack *colloq*, show the door to *colloq*, throw out, thrust out, topple, turn out, unseat
🖾 install, settle

out *adj* 1 *she's out:* abroad, absent, away, elsewhere, gone, not at home, not in, outside 2 *I'm out the minute my head hits the pillow:* comatose *technical*, insensible *formal*, knocked out, KO'd *colloq*, out cold, unconscious 3 *the new Johnny Depp film is out:* available, in print, obtainable, published, ready 4 *the truth is out:* disclosed, divulged, evident, exposed, in the open, known, manifest *formal*, public, revealed 5 *alcohol is out when you're pregnant:* disallowed *formal*, excluded, forbidden, impossible, inadmissible, inappropriate, unacceptable, undesirable, unsuitable, unwelcome 6 *seaside breaks are out:* antiquated, dated, démodé, old hat *colloq*, old-fashioned, out of date, passé, unfashionable 7 *the fire is out:* dead, doused, expired, extinguished, finished, not burning, not shining, used up 8 *the flowers are out:* blooming, blossoming, in bloom, in flower, in full bloom 9 *out to make money:* bent, determined, insistent, intent, set
🖾 1 at home, here, in 2 conscious 3 out of printround, 4 concealed, hidden 5 allowed 6 in *colloq*, up-to-date

out-and-out *adj* absolute, arrant *formal*, complete, consummate *formal*, downright, dyed-in-the-wool *colloq*, inveterate, outright, perfect, thorough, thoroughgoing, total, uncompromising, unmitigated, unqualified, utter

outbreak *n* burst, epidemic, eruption, explosion, flare-up, flash, outburst, rash, recrudescence *formal*, sudden start, upsurge

outburst *n* attack, burst, eruption, explosion, fit, fit of temper, flare-up, gale, gush, outbreak, outpouring, paroxysm, seizure, spasm, storm, surge

outcast *n* castaway, evacuee, exile, leper, outsider, pariah, persona non grata, refugee, reject, untouchable

outclass *v* be much better than, beat, eclipse, excel over, leave standing, outdistance, outdo, outrank, outrival, outshine, outstrip, overshadow, put in the shade, surpass, top, transcend

outcome *n* after-effect, conclusion, consequence, effect, end result, issue, product, result, sequel, upshot

outcry *n* clamour, commotion, complaint, cry, dissent, exclamation, fuss, hue and cry, hullabaloo *colloq*, indignation, noise, objection, outburst, protest, protestation, racket *colloq*, row, tumult, uproar

outdated *adj* antediluvian, antiquated, antique, archaic, behind the times, dated, démodé, obsolescent, obsolete, old hat *colloq*, old-fashioned, old-fogeyish *colloq*, out of date, out of fashion, outmoded, passé, square *colloq*, superseded, unfashionable
🖃 fashionable, modern

outdistance *v* leave behind, leave standing, outpace, outrun, outstrip, overhaul, overtake, pass, pull ahead of, shake off, surpass

outdo *v* beat, cap *colloq*, come first, defeat, eclipse, exceed, excel, gain the upper/whip hand over *colloq*, get the better of, have the advantage over, outclass, outdistance, outshine, outstrip, overcome, run rings/circles round *colloq*, stand/be head and shoulders above *colloq*, surpass, transcend

outdoors *adv* alfresco, en plein air, in the open air, out, out-of-doors, outside
🖃 indoors

outer *adj* 1 *the outer layer*: exterior, external, outermost, outside, outward, peripheral, superficial, surface 2 *the outer islands*: distant, far-away, fringe, further, outlying, peripheral, remote
🖃 1 internal 2 inner

outface *v* beard, brave, brazen out, confront, defy, outstare, stare down
🖃 capitulate, succumb *formal*

outfit *n* 1 *a new outfit for the wedding*: clothes, costume, dress, ensemble, garb *colloq*, gear *colloq*, get-up *colloq*, suit, togs *colloq* 2 *the gastric lavage outfit*: apparatus, equipment, gear *colloq*, kit, paraphernalia, rig, tools, trappings 3 *the local car hire outfit*: business, clique, company, corporation, coterie, crew, firm, gang, group, organization, set, set-up, squad, team, unit
♦ *v* accoutre *formal*, apparel *formal*, appoint, attire *formal*, equip, fit out, fit up, furnish, kit out, provide, provision, stock, supply, turn out

outfitter *n* clothier, costumer, costumier, couturier, couturière, dressmaker, haberdasher, modiste, sartor, tailor

outflow *n* debouchment *formal*, discharge, disemboguement *formal*, drainage, ebb, effluence *formal*, effluent *formal*, effluvium *formal*, efflux *formal*, effluxion *formal*, effusion,

emanation, emergence, gush, jet, outfall, outpouring, outrush, rush, spout
🖃 inflow

outflowing *adj* debouching *formal*, discharging, effluent, emanant, gushing, leaking, rushing, spurting

outgoing *adj* 1 *she's really outgoing*: affable, affectionate, amiable, approachable, communicative, cordial, demonstrative, easy-going, expansive, extrovert, friendly, genial, gregarious, open, sociable, sympathetic, talkative, unreserved, warm 2 *the outgoing bishop*: departing, ex-, former, last, leaving, past, retiring
🖃 1 reserved 2 incoming

outgoings *n* costs, disbursal *formal*, disbursement *formal*, expenditure, expenses, outlay, overheads, spending
🖃 income

outgrowth *n* 1 *a natural outgrowth of civil-rights law*: by-product, consequence, effect, emanation, offshoot, product, spin-off 2 *a pair of outgrowths or appendages*: excrescence *formal*, protuberance *formal*, shoot, sprout, swelling

outing *n* excursion, expedition, jaunt, mystery tour, picnic, pleasure trip, spin, tour, trip *colloq*

outlandish *adj* alien, barbarous, bizarre, curious, eccentric, exotic, extraordinary, far-out *slang*, foreign, freaky *colloq*, grotesque, odd, oddball *colloq*, peculiar, preposterous, quaint, strange, unconventional, unfamiliar, unheard-of, unknown, unreasonable, unusual, wacky *colloq*, way-out *slang*, weird
🖃 familiar, ordinary

outlandishness *n* bizarreness, eccentricity, exoticness, grotesqueness, oddness, quaintness, queerness, strangeness, unusualness, weirdness
🖃 commonplaceness, familiarity

outlast *v* come through, outlive, outstay, ride, survive, weather

outlaw *n* bandit, brigand, criminal, desperado, exile, fugitive, highwayman, marauder, outcast, pirate, robber
♦ *v* ban, banish, bar, condemn, debar, disallow, embargo, exclude, excommunicate, forbid, interdict *formal*, prohibit, proscribe *formal*
🖃 allow, legalize

outlay *n* charge, cost, disbursement *formal*, expenditure, expenses, outgoings, payment, price, spending
🖃 income

outlet *n* 1 *a fast food outlet*: market, retail outlet, retailer, shop, store, supplier 2 *illegal socket outlets*: channel, conduit, culvert, duct, egress *formal*, escape, exit, opening, outfall, release, safety valve, valve, vent, way out 3 *an outlet for your feelings*: channel, means of expression, means of release, safety valve
🖃 2 entry, inlet

outline *n* 1 *here is a brief outline of the topic*: abstract, bare bones, bare facts, main points, précis, résumé, rough idea, sketch, summary, synopsis, thumbnail sketch 2 *the vague outline of his face*: configuration *formal*, contour, delineation *formal*, design, form, layout, lineament *formal*, plan, profile, shape, silhouette, sketch, tracing
♦ *v* 1 *the themes outlined in his introduction*: draft, give a rough idea of, rough out, summarize

2 *irregular shapes outlined the village:* delineate *formal*, rough out, sketch (out), trace

outlive *v* come through, live through, outlast, survive, weather
▪ predecease

outlook *n* **1** *an optimistic outlook:* angle, attitude, frame of mind, interpretation, opinion, perspective, point of view, slant, standpoint, view, viewpoint **2** *the outlook is grim for tenants:* expectations, forecast, future, prognosis, prospect **3** *a house with a pleasant outlook:* aspect, panorama, prospect, view

outlying *adj* distant, far-away, far-flung, far-off, inaccessible, isolated, off the beaten track *colloq*, outer, out-of-the-way, provincial, remote
▪ inner

outmanoeuvre *v* beat, circumvent *formal*, get the better of, outdo, outflank, outfox, outgeneral, outsmart, outthink, outwit

outmoded *adj* antediluvian, antiquated, archaic, behind the times, dated, démodé, obsolescent, obsolete, old hat *colloq*, old-fashioned, old-fogeyish *colloq*, out of date, out of fashion, passé, square *colloq*, superseded, unfashionable
▪ fashionable, fresh, modern, new

out of date *adj* antediluvian, antiquated, archaic, behind the times, dated, démodé, obsolescent, obsolete, old hat *colloq*, old-fashioned, old-fogeyish *colloq*, out of fashion, outdated, outmoded, passé, square *colloq*, superseded, unfashionable
▪ fashionable, fresh, modern, new

out-of-the-way *adj* distant, far-away, far-flung, far-off, inaccessible, isolated, little-known, lonely, obscure, off the beaten track *colloq*, outer, outlying, peripheral, remote, unfrequented

out of work *adj* idle, jobless, laid off, on the dole *colloq*, out of a job, redundant, unemployed, workless
▪ busy, employed, occupied

outpace *v* beat, outdistance, outdo, outrun, outstrip, overhaul, overtake, pass, surpass

outpouring *n* cascade, debouchment *formal*, deluge, disemboguement *formal*, effluence *formal*, efflux *formal*, effusion, emanation, flood, flow, flux, outflow, spate, spurt, stream, torrent

output *n* accomplishment, achievement, fruits, gain, harvest, manufacture, performance, product, production, productivity, return, yield

outrage *n* **1** *public outrage grew:* affront, anger, fury, horror, indignation, rage, shock, wrath **2** *an outrage against public decency:* affront, atrocity, barbarism, brutality, crime, enormity, evil, horror, injury, offence, scandal, violation
♦ *v* **1** *outraged at blanket smoking bans:* affront, anger, appal, disgust, enrage, horrify, incense, infuriate, injure, madden, offend, scandalize, shock **2** *exiled from the humanity he has outraged:* abuse, assault, defile, desecrate, ravage, ravish, violate

outrageous *adj* **1** *an outrageous miscarriage of justice:* abominable, atrocious, disgraceful, dreadful, foul, ghastly, gruesome, heinous *formal*, horrible, insufferable, intolerable, monstrous, offensive, scandalous, shocking,

terrible, unacceptable, unbearable, unspeakable, vile **2** *outrageous phone bills:* excessive, exorbitant, extortionate, immoderate, inordinate, obscene, preposterous, scandalous, unreasonable
▪ **2** acceptable, reasonable

outré *adj* bizarre, eccentric, extraordinary, far-out *slang*, freaky *colloq*, odd, oddball *colloq*, outrageous, shocking, strange, unconventional, unusual, way-out *slang*, weird

outrider *n* advance guard, attendant, bodyguard, escort, guard, herald, precursor, vanguard

outright *adj* **1** *an outright ban:* absolute, complete, direct, downright, out-and-out, perfect, pure, thorough, total, unconditional, unmitigated, unqualified, utter **2** *no outright winner is expected to emerge:* categorical, clear, definite, straightforward, undeniable, unequivocal, unmistakable
▪ **2** indefinite
♦ *adv* **1** *rejected outright:* absolutely, categorically, completely, entirely, positively, thoroughly, totally, utterly, wholly **2** *asked him outright if it was true:* categorically, directly, explicitly, openly, straightforwardly, without restraint **3** *killed outright:* at once, immediately, instantaneously, instantly, straight away, there and then

outrun *v* beat, exceed, excel, leave behind, lose, outdistance, outdo, outpace, outstrip, overhaul, overtake, pass, shake off, surpass

outset *n* beginning, commencement *formal*, inauguration, inception *formal*, kick-off *colloq*, opening, start
▪ conclusion, end

outshine *v* beat, best, dwarf, eclipse, excel, outclass, outdo, outrank, outstrip, overshadow, put in the shade, put to shame, surpass, top, transcend, upstage

outside *adj* **1** *an outside toilet:* exterior, external, extraneous, extreme, outdoor, outer, outermost, outward, superficial, surface **2** *an outside chance:* distant, faint, improbable, marginal, negligible, remote, slender, slight, slim, small, unlikely, vague
▪ **1** inside **2** likely, real, substantial
♦ *n* appearance, cover, exterior, façade, face, front, outer surface, surface
▪ inside

outsider *n* alien, emigrant, émigré, foreigner, gatecrasher, immigrant, interloper, intruder, misfit, newcomer, non-member, non-resident, odd one out *colloq*, outlander, stranger, visitor

outskirts *n* borders, boundary, edge, environs, fringes, frontier, limit, margin, perimeter, periphery, suburbia, suburbs
▪ centre

outsmart *v* beat, best, con *colloq*, deceive, dupe, get the better of, have on *colloq*, kid *colloq*, outfox, outmanoeuvre, outperform, outthink, outwit, pull a fast one on *colloq*, take for a ride *colloq*, trick

outspoken *adj* blunt, brusque, candid, direct, explicit, forthright, frank, free, plain, plain-spoken, rude, straightforward, unceremonious, unequivocal, unreserved
▪ diplomatic, reserved

outspread *adj* expanded, extended, fanned out, flared, open, opened, outstretched, spread out, stretched, unfolded, unfurled, wide, wide open

outstanding *adj* **1** *an outstanding performance:* celebrated, distinguished, eminent, excellent, exceptional, extraordinary, famed, famous, great, important, impressive, memorable, notable, noteworthy, pre-eminent, prominent, remarkable, renowned, special, superb, superior, superlative, well-known **2** *outstanding beauty:* arresting, conspicuous, exceptional, extraordinary, great, impressive, notable, noteworthy, prominent, remarkable, striking **3** *outstanding bills:* due, owing, payable, pending, remaining, uncollected, unpaid, unsettled **4** *outstanding jobs:* incomplete, left-over, remaining, unfinished, unresolved, unsettled
 ✦ **1** ordinary, unexceptional **3** paid, settled **4** finished

outstandingly *adv* amazingly, especially, exceptionally, extraordinarily, extremely, greatly, impressively, notably, remarkably, strikingly

outstrip *v* beat, better, eclipse, exceed, gain on, leave behind, leave standing, outdistance, outdo, outrun, outshine, overtake, pass, surpass, top, transcend

outward *adj* apparent, discernible, evident, exterior, external, noticeable, observable, obvious, ostensible, outer, outermost, outside, perceptible, professed, public, superficial, supposed, surface, visible
 ✦ inner, private

outwardly *adv* apparently, as far as you can see, at first sight, externally, on the face of it, on the outside, on the surface, seemingly, superficially, supposedly, to all appearances, visibly

outweigh *v* be greater than, be more than, be superior to, cancel out, compensate for, exceed, make up for, overcome, override, predominate, preponderate *formal*, prevail over, surpass, take precedence over

outwit *v* be cleverer than, beat, better, cheat, con *colloq*, deceive, defraud, dupe, get the better of, have on *colloq*, kid *colloq*, outmanoeuvre, outsmart, outthink, pull a fast one on *colloq*, swindle, take for a ride *colloq*, trick

outworn *adj* abandoned, ancient, antiquated, archaic, behind the times, defunct, discredited, disused, exhausted, hackneyed, moth-eaten *colloq*, obsolescent, obsolete, old hat *colloq*, old-fashioned, out of date, outdated, outmoded, past its sell-by date *colloq*, rejected, stale
 ✦ fresh, new

oval *adj* egg-shaped, ellipsoidal, elliptical, obovate *technical*, ovate, oviform, ovoid, vulviform *formal*

ovation *n* acclaim, acclamation, accolade, applause, bouquet *colloq*, bravos, cheering, cheers, clapping, handclapping, laudation *formal*, plaudits *formal*, praise(s), tribute
 ✦ abuse, catcalls

over *adj* accomplished, ancient history *colloq*, at an end, closed, completed, concluded *formal*, done with, ended, finished, forgotten, gone, in the past, no more, over and done with *colloq*, past, settled, terminated *formal*, up
 ✦ *adv* **1** *a seagull flew over:* above, aloft *formal*, beyond, on high, overhead **2** *she had to pay the asking price and something over:* additionally, extra, in addition, in excess, more
 ✦ *prep* **1** *flying over the lake:* above, beyond, on top of **2** *his ex-wife is over him in the company now:* above, higher than, in charge of, in command of, on top of, superior to **3** *over the speed limit:* exceeding, in excess of, more than

overabundance *n* embarras de choix, embarras de richesse, excess, glut, oversupply, plethora *formal*, profusion *formal*, superabundance *formal*, superfluity *formal*, surfeit, surplus, too much of a good thing *colloq*
 ✦ dearth, lack

overact *v* exaggerate, ham *colloq*, lay/pile it on *colloq*, lay/pile it on thick *colloq*, lay/pile it on with a trowel *colloq*, overdo, overplay
 ✦ underact, underplay

overall *adj* all-embracing, all-inclusive, all-over, blanket *colloq*, broad, complete, comprehensive, general, global, inclusive, sweeping, total, umbrella *colloq*, universal
 ✦ narrow, specific
 ✦ *adv* broadly, by and large, generally speaking, in general, on the whole

overawe *v* abash, alarm, awe, browbeat, cow, daunt, disconcert, dismay, frighten, intimidate, petrify, scare, terrify, unnerve
 ✦ comfort, reassure

overbalance *v* capsize, fall over, keel over, lose your balance, lose your footing, overturn, slip, somersault, tip over, topple over, trip, tumble, turn turtle, upset

overbearing *adj* arrogant, autocratic, bossy *colloq*, cavalier, contemptuous, despotic, dictatorial, disdainful, dogmatic, domineering, haughty, high-handed, imperious, la-di-da *colloq*, lordly, officious, oppressive, presumptuous, proud, smart-ass *colloq*, snobby *colloq*, snooty *colloq*, snotty *colloq*, stuck-up *colloq*, toffee-nosed *colloq*, too big for your boots *colloq*, tyrannical
 ✦ meek, unassertive

overblown *adj* amplified, bombastic, burlesqued, caricatured, embellished, exalted, excessive, extravagant, inflated, OTT *colloq*, over the top *colloq*, overcharged, overdone, overestimated, overstated, pretentious, self-important

overcast *adj* clouded (over), cloudy, dark, darkened, dismal, dreary, dull, foggy, gloomy, grey, hazy, leaden, louring, misty, sombre, sunless
 ✦ bright, clear

overcharge *v* cheat, diddle *colloq*, do *colloq*, extort, fleece *colloq*, rip off *colloq*, rook *colloq*, short-change, sting *colloq*, surcharge, swindle
 ✦ undercharge

overcome *v* be more than a match for, be victorious over, beat, best, clobber *colloq*, conquer, defeat, get the better of, hammer *colloq*, have the edge on, lick *colloq*, master, outplay, outsmart, outwit, overpower, overthrow, overwhelm, prevail, rise above, rout, slaughter *colloq*, subdue, subjugate *formal*, surmount, thrash *colloq*, triumph over, trounce, vanquish *formal*, wipe the floor with *colloq*, worst
 ✦ *adj* affected *formal*, bowled over *colloq*, broken,

lost for words *colloq*, moved, overpowered, overwhelmed, speechless, swept off your feet *colloq*

over-confident *adj* arrogant, blustering, brash, cocksure, cocky *colloq*, foolhardy, hubristic *formal*, incautious, over-optimistic, overweening, presumptuous, rash, sanguine, self-assured, swaggering, temerarious *formal*, uppish *colloq*, uppity *colloq*
⊞ cautious, diffident

overcritical *adj* captious, carping, cavilling, fault-finding, hair-splitting *colloq*, hard to please, hypercritical, nit-picking *colloq*, over-nice, overparticular, pedantic, pernickety *colloq*, purist, ultracrepidarian *formal*, Zoilean
⊞ easy-going, tolerant, uncritical

overcrowded *adj* chock-full, congested, crammed full, full to overflowing, jam-packed *colloq*, overloaded, overpopulated, overrun, packed (out), packed like sardines *colloq*, swarming, teeming
⊞ deserted, empty

overdo *v* camp it up *colloq*, carry to excess, exaggerate, go overboard *colloq*, go too far, ham it *colloq*, lay/pile it on *colloq*, lay/pile it on thick *colloq*, lay/pile it on with a trowel *colloq*, overact, overindulge, overplay, overstate, stretch a point *colloq*

overdone *adj* **1** *I can't eat steak if it's overdone:* burnt, burnt to a cinder *colloq*, burnt to a frazzle *colloq*, charred, dried up, overbaked, overcooked, spoiled **2** *I thought his triumphalism overdone:* effusive, exaggerated, excessive, fulsome, gushing, histrionic, immoderate, inordinate, over the top *colloq*, overelaborate, overplayed, overstated, undue, unnecessary
⊞ **1** raw, underdone **2** underplayed, understated

overdraft *n* arrears, borrowings, debt, deficit, insufficient funds, liabilities, overdrawn account, unpaid amounts

overdue *adj* behind schedule, behindhand, belated *formal*, delayed, due, late, owing, payable, pending, slow, tardy *formal*, unpaid, unpunctual, unsettled
⊞ early

overeat *v* binge *colloq*, eat too much, go on a binge, gorge, gormandize, guzzle, have eyes bigger than your stomach *colloq*, make a pig of yourself *colloq*, overindulge, pig out *colloq*, stuff yourself
⊞ abstain, starve

overeating *n* bingeing *colloq*, bulimia, gluttony, gormandism, gourmandise, gourmandism, guzzling, hyperphagia, overindulgence
⊞ abstemiousness, abstention

overemphasize *v* attach too much importance to, belabour, blow up out of all proportion *colloq*, exaggerate, labour, lay/put too much emphasis on, make a mountain out of a molehill *colloq*, make too much of, overdramatize, overstress
⊞ belittle, minimize, play down, underplay, understate

overflow *v* brim over, bubble over, deluge, discharge, flood, flow over, inundate, overrun, pour over, run over, shower, soak, spill (over), submerge, surge, swamp, teem, well over

♦ *n* flood, inundation, overabundance, overspill, spill, spillage, surplus

overflowing *adj* abounding, bountiful, brimful, copious, crowded, filled, full, inundant *formal*, plenteous *formal*, plentiful, profuse, rife, superabundant, swarming, teeming, thronged
⊞ lacking, scarce

overgrowth *n* escalation, hypertrophy *technical*, overabundance, overdevelopment, superabundance
⊞ decline, failure, shrinkage, wasting

overhang *v* beetle, bulge (out), extend, jut (out), project, protrude, stand out, stick out

overhanging *adj* beetling, bulging (out), jutting (out), pensile *formal*, projecting, protruding, standing out, sticking out

overhaul *v* **1** *completely overhauled the electoral system:* check, check over/up, examine, fix, go over, inspect, investigate, mend, recondition, re-examine, renovate, repair, revamp, service, survey **2** *Piquet finished third to overhaul him:* gain on, get ahead of, outdistance, outpace, outstrip, overtake, pass, pull ahead of
♦ *n* check, check-up, examination, going-over *colloq*, inspection, reconditioning, renovation, repair, service

overhead *adv* above, on high, up above, upwards
⊞ below, underfoot
♦ *adj* aerial, elevated, overhanging, raised

overheads *n* burden, disbursement *formal*, expenditure, expenses, oncost, operating costs, outgoings, regular costs, running costs
⊞ income, profit

overheated *adj* agitated, angry, excited, fiery, flaming, impassioned, inflamed, overexcited, overwrought, passionate, roused
⊞ calm, cool, dispassionate, impassive

overindulge *v* **1** *he overindulges when he's on holiday:* binge *colloq*, booze *slang*, debauch, eat/drink too much, gluttonize, gorge, gormandize, guzzle, make a pig of yourself *colloq*, pig out *colloq*, sate, satiate **2** *she overindulges her nephews:* cosset, mollycoddle, pamper, pander, pet, spoil, spoon-feed *colloq*
⊞ **1** abstain

overindulgence *n* binge *colloq*, debauch, excess, immoderation, intemperance, overeating, surfeit
⊞ abstemiousness, abstention

overjoyed *adj* delighted, ecstatic, elated, enraptured, euphoric, high as a kite *colloq*, in raptures, in seventh heaven *colloq*, in transports of delight, joyful, jubilant, like a child with a new toy *colloq*, on cloud nine *colloq*, on top of the world *colloq*, over the moon *colloq*, pleased as Punch *colloq*, rapturous, thrilled, tickled pink *colloq*
⊞ disappointed, sad

overlap *v* coincide, cover, flap over, imbricate *technical*, overlay, overlie, shingle

overlay *v* adorn, blanket, cover, decorate, envelop, inlay, laminate, ornament, varnish, veneer, wrap

overload *v* burden, encumber, lumber, oppress, overburden, overcharge, overtax, saddle, strain, tax, weigh down

overlook *v* **1** *her garden is overlooked by a block of flats*: command/have a view of, face, front onto, look onto, look over, open onto **2** *endometriosis is often overlooked*: disregard, forget, ignore, leave, let pass, let ride, miss, neglect, omit, pass over, slight, take no notice of **3** *I can't overlook your negligence*: condone, excuse, forgive, pardon, turn a blind eye to, wink at
F3 **2** notice, observe **3** condemn, penalize

overlooked *adj* unconsidered, unheeded, unhonoured, unnoted, unprized, unregarded, unremarked, unvalued
F3 appreciated, prized, sought-after, valued

overly *adv* exceedingly, excessively, immoderately, inordinately, over, too, unduly, unreasonably
F3 inadequately, insufficiently

overnice *adj* finical, nit-picking *colloq*, overfastidious, over-meticulous, overparticular, overprecise, overscrupulous, oversensitive, oversubtle, pernickety *colloq*
F3 casual, uncritical

overplay *v* aggrandize *formal*, amplify, blow something up out of all proportion *colloq*, colour, dramatize, embellish, embroider, emphasize, enhance, enlarge, exaggerate, lay/pile it on *colloq*, lay/pile it on thick *colloq*, lay/pile it on with a trowel *colloq*, magnify, make a mountain out of a molehill *colloq*, make too much of, overdo, overdramatize, overemphasize, oversell, overstate, shoot a line *colloq*, stress, stretch the truth
F3 play down, understate

overpopulated *adj* chock-full, congested, crammed full, full to overflowing, jam-packed *colloq*, overcrowded, overloaded, overrun, packed (out), packed like sardines *colloq*, swarming, teeming
F3 deserted, empty

overpower *v* **1** *he quickly overpowered his victim*: gain mastery over, gain the upper hand over, immobilize, master, overcome, overthrow, overwhelm, quash, quell, rout, subdue, subjugate *formal*, vanquish *formal* **2** *they overpowered the Italian pair to win*: beat, conquer, crush, defeat, gain mastery over, gain the upper hand over, immobilize, master, overcome, overthrow, quash, quell, rout, subdue, subjugate *formal*, trounce, vanquish *formal* **3** *overpowered by a feeling*: affect deeply/strongly, bowl over *colloq*, confuse, daze, dumbfound, flabbergast *colloq*, floor *colloq*, knock for six *colloq*, leave speechless, move, perplex, stagger, take aback, touch

overpowering *adj* compelling, extreme, forceful, irrefutable, irresistible, nauseating, oppressive, overwhelming, powerful, sickening, stifling, strong, suffocating, unbearable, uncontrollable, undeniable

overrate *v* attach too much importance to, blow up *colloq*, magnify, make too much of, overestimate, overpraise, overprize, overvalue
F3 underrate

override *v* **1** *ambition has overridden party loyalty*: be greater than, be more important than, be superior to, exceed, outweigh, overcome, prevail over, surpass **2** *to override a decision*: abrogate *formal*, annul, cancel, countermand *formal*, nullify *formal*, overrule, quash, rescind *formal*, reverse,

supersede, vanquish *formal* **3** *overriding their protests*: disregard, ignore, ride roughshod over *colloq*, set aside, trample over

overriding *adj* cardinal, compelling, determining, dominant, essential, final, first, major, most important, most significant, number one, overruling, paramount, pivotal, predominant, prevailing, primary, prime, principal, prior, ruling, supreme, ultimate
F3 insignificant, unimportant

overrule *v* abrogate *formal*, annul, cancel, countermand, disallow, invalidate, nullify *formal*, override, overturn, reject, rescind *formal*, reverse, revoke, set aside, vote down

overrun *v* **1** *overrun by ants*: infest, inundate, overgrow, overwhelm, penetrate, permeate, run riot *colloq*, spread like wildfire *colloq*, spread over, surge over, swamp, swarm over **2** *overrun the enemy positions*: attack, besiege, invade, occupy, overwhelm, penetrate, ravage, storm, surge over, swamp, swarm over **3** *the meeting overran by twenty minutes*: exceed, go over, overreach, overshoot, overstep

overseas *adj* distant, exotic, external, faraway, foreign, international, remote
F3 domestic, home
♦ *adv* abroad, in/to a foreign country, in/to foreign climes, in/to foreign parts, out of the country

overseer *n* boss *colloq*, chief, foreman, forewoman, gaffer *colloq*, manager, manageress, superintendent, supervisor

overshadow *v* **1** *overshadowed by the castle*: cloud, darken, dim, obscure, veil **2** *illness overshadowed her success*: blight, cloud, mar, put a damper on, spoil, take the edge off **3** *overshadowed by his brother*: be superior to, dominate, dwarf, eclipse, excel, outshine, put in the shade, rise above, surpass, tower above

oversight *n* **1** *human error and oversight*: blunder, boob *colloq*, carelessness, dereliction *formal*, error, fault, howler *colloq*, lapse, mistake, neglect, omission, slip-up *colloq* **2** *under the constant oversight of his parents*: administration, care, charge, control, custody, direction, handling, keeping, management, responsibility, superintendence, supervision, surveillance

overstate *v* aggrandize *formal*, amplify, blow something up out of all proportion *colloq*, colour, dramatize, embellish, embroider, emphasize, enhance, enlarge, exaggerate, lay/pile it on *colloq*, lay/pile it on thick *colloq*, lay/pile it on with a trowel *colloq*, magnify, make a mountain out of a molehill *colloq*, make too much of, overdo, overdramatize, overemphasize, oversell, shoot a line *colloq*, stress, stretch the truth
F3 play down, understate

overstatement *n* amplification, burlesque, caricature, embellishment, emphasis, enlargement, exaggeration, excess, extravagance, hyperbole *formal*, magnification, overemphasis, overestimation, parody, pretentiousness
F3 meiosis, understatement

overt *adj* apparent, conspicuous, evident, manifest *formal*, noticeable, observable, obvious,

open, patent, plain, professed, public, unconcealed, undisguised, visible
F2 covert, secret

overtake *v* **1** *overtake on the bend:* catch up with, draw level with, drive/run past, go past, leave behind, outdistance, outstrip, overhaul, pass, pull ahead of **2** *calamity overtook us:* befall *formal*, catch unawares, come upon, engulf, happen suddenly/unexpectedly to, happen to, overwhelm, strike, take by surprise

overthrow *v* **1** *overthrow the government:* abolish, beat, best, bring down, conquer, crush, defeat, depose, dethrone, displace, master, oust, overcome, overpower, overwhelm, quash, quell, subdue, topple, trounce, unseat, upset, vanquish *formal*, worst **2** *overthrows the paradigms of theory and practice:* invert, keel over, knock over, overbalance, overturn, spill, tip over, topple, turn over, upset, upturn
F2 **1** install, protect, reinstate, restore
♦ *n* defeat, deposition, destruction, dethronement, downfall, end, fall, humiliation, ousting, rout, ruin, suppression, undoing, unseating, vanquishing *formal*

overtone *n* association, connotation, feeling, flavour, hidden meaning, hint, implication, indirect reference, innuendo, insinuation, intimation, nuance, sense, suggestion, undercurrent

overture *n* **1** *his overtures were not immediately successful:* advance(s), approach, invitation, motion, move(s), offer, proposal, proposition, signal, suggestion **2** *no more than the overture to a long debate:* introduction, opening, opening move, (opening) gambit, prelude

overturn *v* **1** *a double-decker bus overturned:* capsize, invert, keel over, knock over, overbalance, skittle, spill, tip over, topple, turn over, upset, upturn **2** *overturned the verdict:* abolish, abrogate *formal*, annul, cancel, destroy, nullify *formal*, override, overrule, quash, repeal, rescind *formal*, reverse, revoke *formal*, set aside, veto **3** *overturning autocracy:* beat, bring down, conquer, crush, defeat, depose, dethrone, displace, oust, overcome, overpower, overthrow, overwhelm, topple, unseat, vanquish *formal*

overused *adj* bromidic, clichéed, commonplace, hackneyed, overworked, platitudinous *formal*, played out, stale, stereotyped, threadbare, tired, trite, unoriginal, worn
F2 fresh, new, original

overweening *adj* arrogant, cavalier, cocksure, cocky *colloq*, conceited, egotistical, excessive, extravagant, haughty, high-handed, hubristic *formal*, immoderate, inflated, insolent, lordly, opinionated, overblown, pompous, presumptuous, proud, self-confident, supercilious, swollen, vain, vainglorious *formal*
F2 diffident, modest, unassuming

overweight *adj* ample, bulky, buxom, chubby, chunky, corpulent *formal*, fat, flabby *colloq*, fleshy, gross *colloq*, heavy, hefty, huge, massive, obese, outsize, plump, podgy, portly, pot-bellied, stout, tubby, well-padded *colloq*, well-upholstered *colloq*
F2 emaciated, skinny, thin, underweight

overwhelm *v* **1** *overwhelmed in round three:* be more than a match for, be victorious over, beat,

best, clobber *colloq*, crush, defeat, destroy, devastate, get the better of, hammer *colloq*, have the edge on, lick *colloq*, outplay, outsmart, outwit, overcome, overpower, overthrow, prevail, quash, quell, rout, slaughter *colloq*, subdue, subjugate *formal*, thrash *colloq*, trounce, vanquish *formal*, wipe the floor with *colloq*, worst **2** *overwhelmed by the demand:* bury, deluge, engulf, inundate, overburden, overrun, snow under *colloq*, submerge, swamp **3** *overwhelmed by their concern:* affect deeply/strongly, bowl over *colloq*, confuse, daze, floor *colloq*, knock for six *colloq*, move, stagger, touch

overwhelming *adj* **1** *the overwhelming smell of turpentine:* compelling, extreme, forceful, irrefutable, irresistible, nauseating, oppressive, overpowering, powerful, sickening, stifling, strong, suffocating, unbearable, uncontrollable, undeniable **2** *an overwhelming majority:* great, huge, immense, large, vast
F2 **1** resistible **2** insignificant, negligible

overwork *v* **1** *I've been overworking:* bite off more than you can chew *colloq*, burn the candle at both ends *colloq*, burn yourself out *colloq*, do too much, overdo it, overexert yourself, overreach yourself, overstrain, overstretch yourself, run yourself into the ground *colloq*, strain yourself, sweat blood *colloq*, wear yourself out, work too hard, work your fingers to the bone *colloq* **2** *their boss overworked them:* burden, exhaust, exploit, oppress, overload, overtax, overuse, wear out, weary

overworked *adj* **1** *overworked employees:* exhausted, overstrained, overtaxed, stressed out *colloq*, worn out **2** *an overworked expression:* bromidic, clichéed, commonplace, hackneyed, platitudinous *formal*, played out, stale, stereotyped, threadbare, tired, trite, unoriginal, worn
F2 **1** fresh, new, original

overwrought *adj* agitated, beside yourself, distraught, edgy, excited, frantic, highly-strung, keyed up, nervous, nervy *colloq*, on edge, overcharged, overexcited, tense, uptight *colloq*, worked up, wound up
F2 calm

owe *v* **1** *owe a lot of money:* be in arrears, be in debt, be in the red *colloq*, be overdrawn, be up to your ears in debt *colloq*, get into debt, run up debts **2** *I owe everything to my father:* be in someone's debt, be under an obligation

owing *adj* due, in arrears, outstanding, overdue, owed, payable, unpaid, unsettled

own *adj* idiosyncratic, individual, particular, personal, private
♦ *v* enjoy, have, have (all) to yourself, have as your belongings/property, have got, have in your possession, hold, keep, monopolize, occupy, possess, retain, use
► **own up** acknowledge, admit, come clean *colloq*, confess, make a clean breast of it *colloq*, tell the truth

owner *n* freeholder, holder, home-owner, householder, keeper, landlady, landlord, master, mistress, possessor, proprietor, proprietress

ownership *n* dominion, freehold, possession, proprietary rights, proprietorship, right of possession, rights, title *technical*

ox *n* bison, buffalo, bull, bullock, steer, yak

P

pace *n* **1** *her pace suddenly quickened*: gait, step, stride, tread, walk **2** *running at a steady pace*: celerity *formal*, measure, motion, movement, progress, quickness, rapidity, rate, rate of progress, speed, swiftness, tempo, velocity
♦ *v* march, mark out, measure, patrol, pound, step, stride, tramp, walk, walk up and down

pacific *adj* **1** *a pacific foreign policy*: appeasing, complaisant *formal*, conciliatory, diplomatic, dovelike, dovish, equable, friendly, gentle, halcyon *formal*, irenic, nonbelligerent, non-violent, pacificatory *formal*, pacifist, peaceable, peaceful, peace-loving, peacemaking, placatory *formal*, propitiatory *formal* **2** *a pacific scene*: calm, halcyon *formal*, peaceful, placid, quiet, serene, smooth, still, tranquil, unruffled
🖃 **1** aggressive, belligerent, contentious, pugnacious *formal*

pacifism *n* non-violence, pacificism, passive resistance, satyagraha

pacifist *n* conchy *colloq*, conscientious objector, dove, pacificist, peace-lover, peacemaker, peace-monger
🖃 hawk, warmonger

pacify *v* **1** *he managed to pacify his critics*: allay, appease, assuage, calm, calm down, compose, conciliate, defuse, lull, moderate, mollify, placate, propitiate *formal*, put down, quell, quiet, quieten, soften, soothe, still **2** *Stalin's attempts to pacify the peasantry*: crush, put down, quell, silence, subdue, tame
🖃 **1** anger

pack *n* **1** *a pack containing 24 tins*: bale, box, bundle, burden, carton, container, load, package, packet, parcel, truss **2** *I stuffed the money in my pack*: backpack, bag, haversack, kitbag, knapsack, rucksack **3** *a pack of reporters*: band, bunch, company, crew, crowd, drove, flock, gang, group, herd, mob, set, troop
♦ *v* **1** *I packed goods in the warehouse*: bundle, cover, crate, package, parcel, put in, store, stow, tie up, wrap, wrap up **2** *hundreds packed the church*: charge, compact, compress, cram, crowd, fill, jam, load, mob, press, ram, squeeze, stuff, throng, wedge
▶ **pack in 1** *they pack in as many visitors as possible*: charge, cram in, crowd, fill, jam, load, mob, press, ram, squeeze, stuff, throng, wedge **2** *I'd love to pack in my job*: chuck *colloq*, end, give up, jack in *colloq*, leave, resign, stop, throw in *colloq*
▶ **pack off** bundle off, dismiss, dispatch, send away
▶ **pack up 1** *pack up your stuff*: clear up, put things away, tidy away, tidy up **2** *she packed up teaching*: call it a day *colloq*, end, finish, give up, jack in *colloq*, stop, throw in *colloq*, wrap up *colloq* **3** *the engine packed up last week*: break down, conk out *slang*, fail, malfunction *formal*, seize up *colloq*, stop working

package *n* **1** *a package containing books*: bale, box, carton, consignment, container, pack, packet, parcel **2** *a package of measures*: entity, group, package deal, set, unit, whole
♦ *v* batch, box, gift-wrap, pack (up), parcel (up), wrap (up)

packaging *n* box, container, packet, packing, presentation, wrapper(s), wrapping(s)

packed *adj* brimful, chock-a-block *colloq*, congested, crammed, crowded, filled, full, jammed, jam-packed *colloq*, overflowing, overloaded, packed like sardines *colloq*
🖃 deserted, empty

packet *n* **1** *put it in a packet*: bag, box, carton, case, container, Jiffy bag®, pack, package, packing, padded bag, padded envelope, parcel, wrapper, wrapping **2** *cost a packet*: a bob or two *colloq*, a lot, bomb *colloq*, bundle *colloq*, fortune, king's ransom, lots, mint *colloq*, pile *colloq*, pots *colloq*, pretty penny *colloq*, small fortune, tidy sum *colloq*

pact *n* agreement, alliance, arrangement, bargain, bond, cartel, compact *formal*, concordat *formal*, contract, convention, covenant, deal, entente, settlement, treaty, understanding
🖃 disagreement, quarrel

pad¹ *n* **1** *a thick pad of material*: bolster, buffer, cushion, padding, pillow, protection, stuffing, wad, wadding **2** *jot it down in your pad*: block, jotter, memo pad *colloq*, notebook, notepad, writing-pad **3** *an animal's pad*: foot, footprint, paw, print, sole **4** *a bachelor pad*: apartment, flat, hang-out *colloq*, home, penthouse, place, quarters, room, rooms
♦ *v* cushion, fill, line, pack, protect, stuff, wad, wrap
▶ **pad out** amplify, augment *formal*, elaborate, expand, fill out, flesh out, increase, inflate, lengthen, protract *formal*, spin out, stretch

pad² *v* lope, move, run, step, tiptoe, tramp, tread, trudge, walk

padding *n* **1** *foam rubber padding*: cushioning, filling, lining, packing, protection, stuffing, wadding **2** *a speech with a lot of padding*: bombast, hot air, prolixity *formal*, verbiage *formal*, verboseness, verbosity, waffle *colloq*, wordiness

paddle¹ *n* oar, scull, sweep
♦ *v* oar, propel, pull, punt, row, scull, steer

paddle² *v* dabble, plunge, slop, splash, wade

paddock *n* compound, corral, enclosure, field, fold, pen, pound, stockade, yard

paddy *n* bate, fit of temper, fury, passion, pet *colloq*, rage, taking, tantrum, temper, tiff

padlock *n* bolt, catch, clasp, fastening, lock, mortise lock, spring lock

padre *n* chaplain, churchman, clergyman, cleric, curate, deacon, deaconess, father, minister, parson, pastor, priest, rector, reverend, vicar

pagan *n* atheist, heathen, idolater, infidel, nonbeliever, nullifidian *formal*, unbeliever
🖃 believer
♦ *adj* atheistic, godless, heathen, idolatrous, infidel, irreligious, nullifidian *formal*, pantheistic

page¹ *n* **1** *write on a new page*: folio, leaf, recto, sheet, side, verso **2** *start a new page of your life*:

chapter, episode, epoch, era, event, incident, period, phase, stage

page² *n* attendant, bell-boy, bell-hop *US*, footman, messenger, pageboy, servant
♦ *v* announce, ask for, bid, call, send for

pageant *n* cavalcade, display, extravaganza, parade, play, procession, representation, scene, show, spectacle, tableau

pageantry *n* ceremony, display, drama, extravagance, flourish, glamour, glitter, grandeur, magnificence, melodrama, parade, pomp, show, showiness, spectacle, splendour, theatricality

pail *n* bail, bucket, can, churn, piggin, pitcher, scuttle, tub, vessel

pain *n* **1** *pain in his knee:* ache, aching, affliction *formal*, agony, anguish, cramp, discomfort, distress, hurt, irritation, pang, smart, smarting, soreness, spasm, stab, sting, stitch, suffering, tenderness, throb, throbbing, torment, torture, trouble, twinge **2** *the pain of losing someone close:* agony, anguish, anxiety, brokenheartedness, desolation, distress, grief, heartache, heartbreak, misery, pang, rack, sorrow, suffering, torment, torture, tribulation *formal*, woe, wretchedness **3** *that car alarm is a real pain:* annoyance, bore *colloq*, bother, burden, drag *colloq*, headache *colloq*, nuisance, pain in the arse *slang*, pain in the neck/backside *colloq*, pest, vexation
♦ *v* **1** *his wrist still pained him:* ache, be sore, be tender, hurt, irritate, smart, sting **2** *it pains me to think of their plight:* afflict, agonize, distress, grieve, make anxious, make miserable, sadden, torment, torture, trouble, upset, worry
2 delight, gratify, please

pained *adj* aggrieved, distressed, grieved, hurt, injured, offended, piqued, reproachful, sad, saddened, stung, unhappy, upset, vexed, worried, wounded
gratified, pleased

painful *adj* **1** *her leg was painful:* aching, agonizing, excruciating, hurting, inflamed, irritating, smarting, sore, stabbing, tender, throbbing **2** *a painful experience:* agonizing, disagreeable, disquieting *formal*, distressing, disturbing, harrowing, miserable, saddening, traumatic, unpleasant, upsetting, wretched **3** *redundancy was painful:* awkward, discomfiting *formal*, disconcerting, distressing, embarrassing, humiliating, mortifying, sensitive, shameful, shaming, touchy *colloq*, uncomfortable, upsetting **4** *negotiating was a painful process:* arduous, difficult, exacting, hard, laborious, rigorous, strenuous, tedious, tough, trying
1 painless, soothing **2** agreeable, pleasant **4** easy, simple

painfully *adv* agonizingly, alarmingly, clearly, deplorably, distressingly, dreadfully, excessively, excruciatingly, markedly, pitiably, pitifully, sadly, terribly, unfortunately, woefully, wretchedly

painkiller *n* anaesthetic, analgesic, anodyne, drug, lenitive, palliative, remedy, sedative

painless *adj* a piece of cake *colloq*, child's play *colloq*, cushy *colloq*, easy, effortless, like falling off a log *colloq*, pain-free, plain sailing *colloq*, simple, trouble-free, undemanding
difficult, painful

pains *n* assiduousness, bother, care, diligence, effort, labour, trouble

painstaking *adj* assiduous, attentive, careful, conscientious, dedicated, devoted, diligent, hardworking, industrious, meticulous, persevering, punctilious *formal*, scrupulous, searching, sedulous *formal*, thorough
careless, negligent

paint *n* colorant, colour, colouring, dye, pigment, stain, tint, vinyl, wash
♦ *v* **1** *he painted the wall blue:* apply, coat, colour, cover, daub, decorate, dye, glaze, lacquer, plaster, redecorate, respray, smear, spray, stain, tint, varnish, wash, whitewash **2** *he was expert at painting horses:* delineate *formal*, depict, describe, draw, evoke, narrate, picture, portray, recount *formal*, represent, sketch, tell

painter *n* artist, colourist, dauber, delineator *formal*, depicter, limner, miniaturist, oil painter, watercolourist

painting *n* delineation *formal*, fresco, illustration, landscape, likeness, miniature, mural, oil, oil painting, picture, portrait, portrayal, representation, still life, watercolour

Painting terms include:
abstract, alla prima, aquarelle, aquatint, art gallery, bleeding, bloom; brush, filbert brush, flat brush, round brush, sable brush; brush strokes, canvas, canvas board, capriccio, cartoon, charcoal, chiaroscuro, collage, composition, craquelure, diptych, drawing, easel, encaustic, facture, *fête champêtre*, *fête galante*, figurative, foreshortening, fresco, frieze, frottage, gallery, genre painting, gesso, gouache, grisaille, grotesque, hard edge, icon, illustration, impasto, landscape, mahlstick, miniature, monochrome, montage, mural, oil painting, paint, palette, palette knife, pastels, pastoral, paysage, pencil sketch, pentimento, perspective, picture, pieta, pigment, pochade box, pointillism, portrait, primer, scumble, seascape, secco, sfumato, sgraffito, silhouette, sketch, skyscape, still life, stipple, tempera, thinners, tint, tondo, tone, triptych, trompe l'oeil, turpentine, underpainting, vignette, wash, watercolour. See also **art, picture**.

pair *n* brace, couple, duo, set, twins, two, two of a kind, twosome
♦ *v* arrange in pairs, bracket, couple, join (up), link (up), marry, match (up), mate, put together, splice, team (up), twin, unite, wed
part, separate

paired *adj* associated, bracketed, coupled, double, in twos, joined, linked, matched, mated, twinned, yoked
single

pal *n* buddy *colloq*, chum *colloq*, companion, comrade, confidant(e), crony *colloq*, friend, intimate, mate *colloq*, partner, sidekick *colloq*, soul mate
enemy, opponent

palace *n* basilica, castle, château, dome, mansion, stately home

palatable *adj* **1** *spices make it more palatable:* appetizing, delectable *formal*, done to a turn

colloq, eatable, edible, flavorous, flavoursome, morish *colloq*, mouth-watering, savoury, scrummy *colloq*, scrumptious *colloq*, succulent, tasty, yummy *colloq* **2** *tax rises will not be palatable to the electorate:* acceptable, agreeable, attractive, enjoyable, nice, pleasant, pleasing, satisfactory
F₃ 1 unpalatable **2** disagreeable, unacceptable, unpleasant

palate *n* appetite, appreciation, enjoyment, enthusiasm, gout, heart, liking, relish, sense of taste, stomach, taste

palatial *adj* de luxe, grand, grandiose, imposing, luxurious, magnificent, majestic, opulent, plush *colloq*, posh *colloq*, regal, ritzy *colloq*, spacious, splendid, stately, sumptuous

palaver *n* activity, bother, business, bustle, carry-on, commotion, flap *colloq*, fluster, fuss, fuss about nothing, procedure, rigmarole, song and dance *colloq*, to-do *colloq*

pale *adj* **1** *he looked tired and pale:* anaemic, ashen, ashy, chalky, colourless, drained, livid, pallid, pasty, pasty-faced, peaky, sallow, wan, washed-out *colloq*, waxen, waxy, white, whitish **2** *pale blue:* bleached, colourless, dim, etoliated *formal*, faded, faint, feeble, insipid, light, low-key, muted, pastel, restrained, thin, vapid, washed-out *colloq*, weak
F₃ 1 ruddy **2** dark, intense, strong
♦ *v* **1** *the colours pale over time:* blanch, bleach, dim, fade, grow pale, grow white, whiten **2** *pale into insignificance:* dim, diminish, dwindle, fade, lessen, melt
F₃ 1 blush, colour

palisade *n* barricade, bulwark, defence, enclosure, fence, fortification, paling, stockade

pall¹ *n* **1** *a pall over a coffin:* cloak, mantle, shroud, veil **2** *cast a pall over proceedings:* cloud, damper, gloom, shadow

pall² *v* become bored, become tired, cloy, jade, lose its attraction, sate, satiate, sicken, tire, wear off, weary

palliate *v* abate *formal*, allay, alleviate, assuage *formal*, cloak, conceal, cover, diminish, ease, excuse, extenuate *formal*, lenify *formal*, lessen, lighten, minimize, mitigate, moderate, mollify, relieve, soften, soothe, temper

palliative *adj* alleviative, anodyne, assuasive *formal*, calmative, calming, demulcent *technical*, lenitive, mitigative *formal*, mitigatory *formal*, mollifying, paregoric, sedative, soothing
F₃ irritant
♦ *n* analgesic, anodyne, calmative, demulcent *technical*, lenitive, painkiller, paregoric, sedative, tranquillizer

pallid *adj* **1** *a pallid complexion:* anaemic, ashen, ashy, bloodless, colourless, etiolated *formal*, pale, pasty, pasty-faced, peelie-wally *Scot*, sallow, wan, waxen, waxy, whey-faced, whitish **2** *a pallid cover version:* bland, boring, dull, insipid, lifeless, spiritless, sterile, tame, tired, unexciting, uninspired, uninteresting, vapid, weak
F₃ 1 high-complexioned, ruddy, vigorous **2** exciting, lively

pallor *n* bloodlessness, chalkiness, etiolation *formal*, paleness, pallidness, sallowness, wanness, whiteness
F₃ ruddiness

pally *adj* affectionate, chummy *colloq*, close, familiar, friendly, intimate, thick *colloq*
F₃ unfriendly

palm *n* hand, mitt *slang*, paw *colloq*
♦ *v* appropriate, grab, snatch, take
▶ **palm off** fob off, foist, get rid of, impose, offload, pass off, thrust, unload

palmist *n* clairvoyant, fortune-teller, palm reader

palmistry *n* chirognomy, chiromancy, clairvoyancy, fortune-telling, palm reading

palpable *adj* **1** *a barely palpable outgrowth:* concrete, material, real, solid, substantial, tangible, touchable **2** *their delight was palpable:* apparent, blatant, clear, conspicuous, evident, glaring, manifest *formal*, obvious, patent, plain, unmistakable, visible
F₃ 1 intangible **2** elusive, impalpable, imperceptible

palpitate *v* beat, flutter, pound, pulsate, pulse, quake, quiver, shake, shiver, throb, thud, thump, tremble, vibrate

paltry *adj* **1** *fined the paltry sum of £5:* derisory, inconsiderable, low, meagre, measly *colloq*, negligible, petty, piddling *colloq*, small, trifling **2** *paltry matters:* contemptible, derisory, insignificant, mean, minor, miserable, petty, piddling *colloq*, poor, puny, slight, small, sorry, trivial, unimportant, worthless, wretched
F₃ 1 considerable, valuable **2** significant, substantial

pamper *v* coddle, cosset, fondle, gratify, humour, indulge, mollycoddle, overindulge, pander, pet, spoil, spoon-feed *colloq*, wait on someone hand and foot *colloq*
F₃ ill-treat, neglect

pampered *adj* coddled, cosseted, high-fed, indulged, mollycoddled, overfed, petted, spoilt
F₃ abused, neglected

pamphlet *n* booklet, brochure, circular, folder, handout, leaflet, notice

pan¹ *n* casserole, container, fryer, frying-pan, pancheon, pot, saucepan, skillet, vessel, wok
♦ *v* censure, criticize, find fault with, flay, hammer, knock *colloq*, pull to pieces *colloq*, roast *colloq*, rubbish *colloq*, slam *colloq*, slate *colloq*
F₃ praise
▶ **pan out** come to an end, culminate, eventuate *formal*, happen, result, turn out, work out, yield

pan² *v* circle, follow, move, scan, sweep, swing, track, traverse *formal*, turn

panacea *n* catholicon *formal*, cure-all, diacatholicon *formal*, elixir, nostrum, panpharmacon *formal*, universal remedy

panache *n* brio, dash, élan, energy, enthusiasm, flair, flamboyance, flourish, ostentation, spirit, style, verve, vigour, zest

pancake *n* bannock *Scot*, battercake *US*, blini, crêpe, griddle-cake, tortilla, waffle

pandemic *adj* common, extensive, far-reaching, general, global, pervasive, prevalent, rife, universal, widespread

pandemonium *n* bedlam, chaos, commotion, confusion, din, disorder, hubbub, hue and cry, hullabaloo, rumpus, to-do *colloq*, tumult, turbulence, turmoil, uproar
F₃ calm, order, peace

pander
▶ **pander to** cater to, fulfil, gratify, humour, indulge, pamper, please, provide, satisfy

panegyric *n* accolade, citation, commendation, encomium *formal*, eulogium *formal*, eulogy, homage, paean *formal*, praise, tribute
F3 censure, criticism
♦ *adj* commendatory, complimentary, encomiastic *formal*, eulogistic, favourable, flattering, glowing, laudatory *formal*, panegyrical *formal*, praiseful, praising
F3 censorious, critical, damning

panel *n* **1** *a wooden panel:* beam, board, cartouche, plank, sheet, slab, timber **2** *a panel of judges:* advisory group, board, commission, committee, council, directorate, jury, team, trustees **3** *a control panel:* board, buttons, console, controls, dashboard, dials, instrument panel, instruments, knobs, levers, switches

panelling *n* dado, panel-work, wainscot, wainscot(t)ing

pang *n* **1** *hunger pangs:* ache, gripe, pain, stab, stitch **2** *guilt pangs:* ache, prick, qualm, spasm, stab, twinge

panic *n* agitation, alarm, consternation *formal*, dismay, disquiet *formal*, fear, flap *colloq*, frenzy, fright, horror, hysteria, perturbation *formal*, terror, trepidation *formal*
F3 calmness, confidence
♦ *v* feel your hair stand on end *colloq*, flap *colloq*, get the jitters *colloq*, get the shakes *colloq*, get the willies *colloq*, go to pieces *colloq*, have kittens *colloq*, lose your cool *colloq*, lose your head, lose your nerve, overreact, run round like a headless chicken *colloq*, unnerve
F3 relax

panic-stricken *adj* aghast, alarmed, frantic, frenzied, frightened, horrified, hysterical, in a cold sweat, in a tizzy *colloq*, panicky, perturbed *formal*, petrified, scared, scared stiff, terrified, terror-stricken
F3 confident, relaxed

panorama *n* **1** *he took in the whole panorama:* bird's eye view, landscape, prospect, scene, scenery, view, vista, wide/broad view **2** *a great panorama of India's past:* overall picture, overview, perspective, survey

panoramic *adj* **1** *a panoramic view of the city:* broad, extensive, scenic, wide **2** *a panoramic historical perspective:* comprehensive, extensive, far-reaching, general, overall, sweeping, universal, wide-ranging, widespread
F3 **1** limited **2** limited, narrow, restricted

pant *v* **1** *she was panting with effort:* blow, breathe, gasp, heave, huff and puff *colloq*, palpitate, puff, sigh, throb, wheeze **2** *the crowd was panting for more:* ache, covet, crave, desire, hanker, long, pine, sigh, thirst, want, yearn, yen *colloq*
♦ *n* gasp, huff, puff, throb, wheeze

panting *adj* **1** *she broke off in a panting gasp:* breathless, gasping, out of breath, puffed, puffed out, puffing, short-winded, winded **2** *they're still panting for more:* anxious, craving, eager, hankering, impatient, longing

pantomime *n* charade, commedia dell'arte, farce, harlequinade, masque, panto *colloq*, show

pants *n* **1** *he stripped down to his pants and socks:* boxer shorts, briefs, camiknickers, drawers, frillies *colloq*, knickers, panties, panty girdle, shorts, smalls *colloq*, teddy, trunks, underpants, undies *colloq*, Y-fronts **2** *he wore a sports jacket with a pair of grey pants:* jeans, slacks, trousers

pap *n* **1** *tasteless pap:* goo *colloq*, mush, pulp, purée, semi-liquid food, soft food **2** *a television channel showing pap:* claptrap *colloq*, crap *slang*, drivel, gibberish, nonsense, rot *colloq*, rubbish, trash

paper *n* **1** *he read the paper:* broadsheet, daily, journal, magazine, newspaper, organ, periodical, rag *colloq*, tabloid, weekly **2** *forged papers:* authorization, certificate, credential, deed, document, ID, identification, identity card, paperwork, record, red tape *colloq* **3** *a paper on alternative medicine:* analysis, article, composition, dissertation, essay, examination, monograph *formal*, report, study, thesis, treatise, work
▶ **paper over** camouflage, conceal, cover up, disguise, hide, obscure, put out of sight

> *Types of paper include:*
> art paper, bank, blotting paper, bond, carbon paper, cartridge paper, crêpe paper, graph paper, greaseproof paper, manila, notepaper, parchment, rice paper, silver paper, sugar paper, tissue paper, toilet paper, tracing paper, vellum, wallpaper, wrapping paper, writing-paper; card, cardboard, pasteboard; A4, foolscap, quarto, atlas, crown

papery *adj* delicate, flimsy, fragile, frail, insubstantial, light, lightweight, paper-thin, thin, translucent

par *n* accordance, balance, correspondence, equal footing, equality, equilibrium, equivalence, level, mean, median *technical*, norm, parity *formal*, similarity, standard

parable *n* allegory, fable, lesson, moral tale, story, story with a moral

parade *n* **1** *the Mardi Gras parade:* cavalcade, ceremony, column, file, march, motorcade, procession, progression, review, train **2** *a parade of military might:* array *formal*, demonstration, display, exhibition, pageant, show, spectacle
♦ *v* **1** *two regiments paraded past:* file past, march, process **2** *he liked to parade his wealth:* brandish, display, exhibit, flaunt, show, show off, vaunt

paradigm *n* archetype *formal*, example, exemplar *formal*, framework, ideal, model, original, pattern, prototype

paradise *n* **1** *he believes he'll go to paradise when he dies:* afterlife, bliss, Eden, elysian fields, Elysium, Garden of Eden, happy hunting ground, heaven, hereafter, home of God, life to come, next world, Shangri-la, utopia **2** *I was in paradise when we scored:* bliss, complete happiness, delight, ecstasy, felicity *formal*, happiness, joy, rapture, seventh heaven *colloq*, transports of delight
F3 **1** Hades, hell

paradox *n* absurdity, anomaly *formal*, contradiction, enigma, incongruity *formal*, inconsistency, mystery, oddity, puzzle, riddle

paradoxical *adj* absurd, anomalous *formal*, baffling, conflicting, contradictory, enigmatic, illogical, impossible, improbable, incongruous *formal*, inconsistent, mysterious, puzzling, self-contradictory

paragon *n* archetype *formal*, crème de la crème, criterion, epitome, exemplar *formal*, ideal, masterpiece, model, nonpareil *formal*, pattern, prototype, quintessence *formal*, standard, the bee's knees *colloq*

paragraph *n* article, clause, item, part, passage, piece, portion, section, segment, subdivision, subsection

parallel *adj* 1 *two parallel lines of ships:* aligned, alongside, coextensive, collateral, equidistant 2 *parallel careers:* analogous *formal*, comparable, corresponding, equivalent, homologous *formal*, like, matching, resembling, similar, uniform
Fa 2 different, divergent
♦ *n* 1 *a war with no parallel in history:* analogue *formal*, counterpart, duplicate, equal, equivalent, match, twin 2 *parallels between the two crimes:* analogy, comparison, correlation *formal*, correspondence, equivalence, likeness, resemblance, similarity
♦ *v* 1 *his remarks paralleled those of the PM:* agree, be analogous *formal*, be equivalent, be like, be similar to, compare, conform, correlate *formal*, correspond, echo, liken, resemble 2 *her achievements might never be paralleled:* duplicate, equal, match
Fa 1 differ, diverge

paralyse *v* 1 *the crash paralysed his legs:* cripple, debilitate *formal*, disable, incapacitate, lame 2 *to paralyse someone with fear:* anaesthetize, deaden, dull, freeze, immobilize, numb, shock, terrify, transfix 3 *paralyse the transport system:* bring to a standstill, cripple, disable, halt, immobilize, stop

paralysed *adj* crippled, disabled, immobilized, incapacitated, lame, numb, paralytic, paraplegic, quadriplegic
Fa able-bodied

paralysis *n* 1 *paralysis in the legs:* deadness, debilitation *formal*, immobility, numbness, palsy, paraplegia, paresis *technical*, powerlessness, quadriplegia 2 *paralysis of the transport system:* breakdown, halt, immobility, shutdown, standstill, stoppage

paralytic *adj* 1 *a rare paralytic disease:* crippling, disabling, incapacitating, paralysing 2 *the rowing team got paralytic later that night:* drunk, inebriated, intoxicated, legless *colloq*, pie-eyed *colloq*, pissed *slang*, plastered *colloq*, sloshed *slang*, smashed *slang*, stewed *slang*, stoned *slang*
Fa 2 (stone-cold) sober

parameter *n* boundary, criterion, factor, framework, guideline, indication, limit, limitation, limiting factor, restriction, specification, variable

paramount *adj* cardinal, chief, first, first and foremost, foremost, highest, main, most important, of greatest importance, outstanding, predominant, pre-eminent, primary, prime, principal, supreme, topmost
Fa last, lowest

paramour *n* beau, beloved, bit on the side *colloq*, concubine, courtesan, fancy man *colloq*, fancy woman *colloq*, hetaera, inamorata, inamorato, kept woman, lover, mistress

paranoia *n* delusions, megalomania, monomania, obsession, persecution complex, psychosis

paranoid *adj* afraid, bewildered, confused, distrustful, fazed, fearful, suspicious

parapet *n* 1 *the parapet of the bridge:* barrier, fence, paling, rail, railing, wall 2 *troops crouched behind the parapet:* barbican, bastion, battlement, bulwark, defence, embankment, fortification, guard, rampart

paraphernalia *n* accessories, accoutrements *formal*, apparatus, baggage, belongings, bits and pieces *colloq*, effects *formal*, equipment, gear, implements, materials, odds and ends *colloq*, possessions, stuff, tackle, things, tools, trappings

paraphrase *v* express differently, gloss, interpret, put in other words, rehash *colloq*, render, rephrase, restate, reword, translate
♦ *n* different expression, gloss, interpretation, other form of words, rendering, rephrasing, restatement, rewording, translation, version

parasite *n* 1 *immune to the parasite:* bloodsucker, endophyte *technical*, endozoon, entozoon, epiphyte, epizoan, epizoon, leech 2 *parasites in society:* bloodsucker, bum *colloq*, cadger *colloq*, drone, freeloader *colloq*, hanger-on, leech, moocher *colloq*, passenger, scrounger *colloq*, sponger *colloq*

parasitic *adj* 1 *parasitic animals:* biogenous, epizoan *technical*, epizoic, leechlike, parasitical 2 *a parasitic person:* bloodsucking, cadging *colloq*, freeloading, scrounging *colloq*, sponging *colloq*

parcel *n* 1 *a parcel containing presents:* box, bundle, carton, pack, package, packet 2 *a parcel of land:* allotment, area, lot, patch, piece, plot, portion, tract 3 *a parcel of rogues:* band, company, crowd, flock, gang, group, herd, mob, troop 4 *a parcel of shares:* collection, deal, lot, pack, package, transaction
♦ *v* bundle (up), gift-wrap, pack (up), package, tie up, wrap (up)
▶ **parcel out** allocate, allot, apportion, carve up, deal out, dispense, distribute, divide (out), dole out, hand out, mete out, share out

parch *v* bake, blister, burn, dehydrate, desiccate *formal*, dry (up), scorch, sear, shrivel, wither

parched *adj* 1 *parched earth:* arid, baked, blistered, burnt, dehydrated, desiccated *formal*, dried up, dry, dry as a bone *colloq*, scorched, sear *formal*, seared, sere *formal*, shrivelled, waterless, withered 2 *I was parched after a long walk:* dehydrated, dry, gasping *colloq*, thirsty

parchment *n* certificate, charter, diploma, document, palimpsest, scroll, vellum

pardon *v* absolve, acquit *formal*, condone, exculpate *formal*, excuse, exonerate *formal*, forgive, free, let off, let off the hook *colloq*, liberate, overlook, release, remit *formal*, reprieve, vindicate *formal*
Fa discipline, punish
♦ *n* absolution, acquittal *formal*, amnesty, clemency, condonation *formal*, discharge, exculpation *formal*, excuse, exoneration *formal*, forbearance, forgiveness, indulgence, lenience, mercy, release, reprieve
Fa condemnation, punishment

pardonable *adj* allowable, condonable, excusable, forgivable, justifiable, minor, permissible, slight, understandable, venial, warrantable
Fa inexcusable

pare *v* **1** *pare the rind:* clip, crop, cut, dock, lop, peel, prune, shear, skin, trim, whittle **2** *pare down spending:* cut, cut back, decrease, reduce, trim

parent *n* **1** *a single parent:* begetter *old use*, biological/birth parent, custodial parent, father, foster parent, guardian, mother, procreator *formal*, progenitor *formal*, single parent, sire **2** *one of the parents of atomic energy:* architect, author, cause, creator, forerunner, origin, originator, prototype, root, source
♦ *v* be the father/mother of, beget *old use*, bring into the world, bring up, create, educate, foster, look after, nurture, procreate *formal*, raise, rear *formal*, take care of, teach, train

parentage *n* affiliation, ancestry, birth, derivation, descent, extraction, family, filiation, line, lineage, origin, paternity, pedigree, race, source, stirps *formal*, stock

parenthetical *adj* bracketed, elucidative *formal*, explanatory, extraneous, in parenthesis, incidental, inserted, interposed *formal*, intervening *formal*, qualifying
⊞ basic, original

pariah *n* black sheep *colloq*, castaway, exile, Ishmael, leper, outcast, outlaw, undesirable, unperson, untouchable

paring *n* clipping, cutting, flake, flaught, fragment, peel, peeling, rind, shaving, shred, skin, slice, sliver, snippet, trimming

parish *n* **1** *one of Bermuda's nine parishes:* community, district, town, village **2** *her parish can't do without her:* church, churchgoers, congregation, flock, fold, parishioners

parity *n* affinity, agreement, conformity, congruence *formal*, congruity *formal*, consistency, consonance *formal*, correspondence, equality, equivalence, likeness, par, parallelism, resemblance, sameness, semblance, similarity, similitude *formal*, uniformity, unity

park *n* grassland, grounds, woodland
♦ *v* **1** *he parked in the drive:* leave, position, station, stop **2** *park your bags:* deposit, leave, place, plonk *colloq*, put, set

Types of park include:
amusement park, arboretum, botanical garden, car park, estate, game reserve, industrial park, municipal park, national park, park-and-ride, parking lot, parkland, play area, playground, pleasance, pleasure garden, pleasure ground, recreation ground, reserve, sanctuary, theme park, wildlife park

parlance *n* argot, cant, diction, idiom, jargon, language, lingo *colloq*, phraseology, speech, talk, tongue

parliament *n* assembly, congress, convocation, council, diet, house, legislature, lower house, senate, upper house

Names of parliaments and political assemblies include:
House of Representatives, Senate (*Australia*); Nationalrat, Bundesrat (*Austria*); Narodno Sobraniye (*Bulgaria*); House of Commons, Senate (*Canada*); National People's Congress (*China*); Folketing (*Denmark*); People's Assembly (*Egypt*); Eduskunta (*Finland*); National Assembly, Senate (*France*);

Bundesrat, Bundestag, Landtag (*Germany*); Althing (*Iceland*); Lok Sabha, Rajya Sabha (*India*); Majlis (*Iran*); Dáil, Seanad (*Ireland*); Knesset (*Israel*); Camera del Deputati, Senato (*Italy*); Diet (*Japan*); Staten-Generaal (*Netherlands*); House of Representatives (*New Zealand*); Storting (*Norway*); Sejm (*Poland*); Cortes (*Portugal*); Congress of People's Deputies, Supreme Soviet (*Russia*); House of Assembly (*South Africa*); Cortes (*Spain*); Riksdag (*Sweden*); Nationalrat, Ständerat, Bundesrat (*Switzerland*); Porte (*Turkey*); House of Commons, House of Lords (*UK*); House of Representatives, Senate (*US*); National Assembly (*Vietnam*)

parliamentary *adj* congressional, democratic, elected, governmental, law-giving, law-making, legislative, legislatorial *formal*, official, popular, representative, republican, senatorial

parochial *adj* blinkered, confined, hick *colloq*, insular, inward-looking, limited, narrow, narrow-minded, parish-pump, petty, provincial, restricted, small-minded, small-town
⊞ international, national

parochialism *n* insularity, narrow-mindedness, narrowness, pettiness, provincialism, small-mindedness

parody *n* burlesque, caricature, imitation, lampoon, mimicry, pasquinade, satire, send-up *colloq*, skit, spoof *colloq*, take-off *colloq*, travesty
♦ *v* ape, burlesque, caricature, imitate, lampoon, mimic, satirize, send up *colloq*, spoof *colloq*, take off *colloq*

paroxysm *n* attack, convulsion, eruption, explosion, fit, flare-up, outbreak, outburst, seizure, spasm

parrot *v* ape, copy, echo, imitate, mimic, rehearse, reiterate, repeat

parrot-fashion *adv* automatically, by rote, mechanically, mindlessly, unthinkingly

parry *v* **1** *she parried questions about the incident:* avert, avoid, circumvent *formal*, dodge *colloq*, duck *colloq*, evade, shun, sidestep, steer clear of **2** *he parried every blow:* block, deflect, fend off, field, keep/hold at bay, rebuff, repel, repulse, stave off, turn aside, ward off

parsimonious *adj* cheese-paring, close, close-fisted, close-handed, frugal, grasping, mean, mingy *colloq*, miserly, niggardly, penny-pinching *colloq*, penurious *formal*, saving, scrimpy, sparing, stingy *colloq*, stinting, tight *colloq*, tight-fisted
⊞ generous, liberal, open-handed

parsimony *n* frugality, meanness, mingiedness *colloq*, miserliness, niggardliness, penny-pinching *colloq*, stinginess *colloq*, tight-fistedness, tightness *colloq*
⊞ generosity, liberality

parson *n* churchman, clergyman, cleric, minister, pastor, preacher, priest, rector, reverend, vicar

part *n* **1** *part of the kit:* aspect, bit, branch, component, constituent, department, dimension, division, element, excerpt, extract, facet, factor, fraction, fragment, ingredient, module, particle, percentage, piece, portion, proportion, scrap, section, sector, segment, share, side, slice, wing

2 *he has a big part to play:* capacity, character, charge, chore, duty, function, involvement, job, office, participation, responsibility, role, task, work **3** *this part of the book:* book, chapter, episode, instalment, passage, scene, section, volume **4** *it's quiet in these parts:* area, district, neighbourhood, quarter, region, sector, territory **5** *a person of many parts:* ability, accomplishment, attribute, calibre, capability, endowment, expertise, faculty, genius, gift, intellect, intelligence, skill, talent
🔄 **1** totality, whole
♦ *v* **1** *he parted the curtains:* cleave *formal*, detach, disconnect, disjoin *formal*, divide, separate, sever, split **2** *they parted on bad terms:* clear off *colloq*, depart from, divorce from, get divorced from, get going, go away from, go your separate ways, hit the road/trail *colloq*, leave, make tracks *colloq*, part company with, push along/off *colloq*, say goodbye, scarper *colloq*, separate from, split *colloq*, split up from, take off *colloq*, take your leave, withdraw from **3** *the company parted:* break up, disband, disperse, diverge, scatter, separate, split up
🔄 **2** join
▶ **part with** abandon, discard, forgo, give up, jettison, let go of, relinquish, renounce, surrender, yield
🔄 hold onto

partake *v* be involved, engage, enter, participate, share, take part
▶ **partake of 1** *partake of food:* consume, drink, eat **2** *partake of the divine nature:* demonstrate, evince *formal*, evoke, have, manifest *formal*, receive, share, show, suggest, take

partial *adj* **1** *a partial victory:* fragmentary, imperfect, in part, incomplete, limited, part, restricted, unfinished **2** *a very partial view:* affected, biased, coloured, discriminatory, inequitable, one-sided, partisan, predisposed *formal*, preferential, prejudiced, unfair, unjust
🔄 **1** complete, total **2** disinterested, fair, impartial, unbiased

partiality *n* **1** *accused of partiality:* bias, discrimination, inequitableness, inequity, injustice, partisanship, prejudice, unfairness **2** *a partiality for dark chocolate:* fondness, inclination, liking, love, predilection *formal*, predisposition *formal*, preference, proclivity *formal*

partially *adv* fractionally, in part, incompletely, not fully, partly, somewhat

participant *n* associate, competitor, contestant, contributor, co-operator, entrant, helper, member, participator, partner, party, shareholder, sharer, worker

participate *v* assist, be associated, be involved, contribute, co-operate, engage, enter, help, join in, partake *formal*, play a part, play a role, share, take part

participation *n* assistance, association, contribution, co-operation, involvement, partaking *formal*, partnership, sharing

particle *n* **1** *food particles:* bit, crumb, drop, fragment, grain, iota, jot, mite, morsel, piece, scrap, shred, sliver, smidgen *colloq*, speck, tad *colloq*, tittle, touch, trace, whit **2** *radioactive particles:* atom, isotope, molecule

particular *adj* **1** *on that particular day:* certain, distinct, exact, individual, peculiar, precise, special, specific **2** *of particular importance:* especial *formal*, exceptional, marked, notable, noteworthy, outstanding, peculiar, remarkable, thorough, uncommon, unusual **3** *she's rather particular:* choosy *colloq*, discriminating, exacting, fastidious, finicky, fussy, meticulous, painstaking, pernickety *colloq*, picky *colloq*, selective **4** *a very particular account:* accurate, detailed, exact, faithful, precise, thorough
🔄 **1** general
♦ *n* circumstance, detail, fact, feature, item, point, specific

particularity *n* **1** *ethnic particularities:* characteristic, distinctiveness, idiosyncrasy, individuality, peculiarity, property, quirk, singularity, trait, uniqueness **2** *the particularities of each situation:* circumstance, detail, fact, feature, instance, item, point

particularize *v* detail, enumerate, individualize, individuate *formal*, itemize, specify, stipulate

particularly *adv* **1** *she particularly asked for an aisle seat:* distinctly, especially, explicitly, expressly, specifically **2** *particularly high:* especially, exceptionally, extraordinarily, markedly, notably, remarkably, surprisingly, uncommonly, unusually

parting *n* **1** *an emotional parting:* adieu, departure, farewell, going, goodbye, leave-taking, leaving, valediction *formal* **2** *the parting of the Red Sea:* breaking, breaking-up, divergence, division, partition, rift, rupture, separation, split
🔄 **1** meeting **2** convergence
♦ *adj* closing, concluding, departing, dying, farewell, final, goodbye, last, leaving, valedictory *formal*
🔄 arriving, first, opening

partisan *n* **1** *the partisans of liberty:* adherent, backer, champion, devotee, disciple, fan, follower, party man, stalwart, supporter, upholder, votary **2** *Yugoslav partisans fighting in World War II:* freedom fighter, guerrilla, irregular, resistance fighter
♦ *adj* biased, discriminatory, factional, inequitable, one-sided, partial, predisposed, prejudiced, sectarian, unfair, unjust
🔄 impartial

partisanship *n* bias, factionalism, partiality, partyism, prejudice, sectarianism
🔄 impartiality

partition *n* **1** *desks divided by a partition:* barrier, diaphragm, divider, dividing screen, dividing wall, membrane *technical*, panel, room-divider, screen, separator, wall **2** *the partition of Ireland:* break-up, division, parting, segregation, separation, severance, splitting, subdivision
♦ *v* **1** *partion the office:* bar, divide, fence off, screen (off), separate, separate off, subdivide, wall off **2** *Korea was partioned:* break up, divide (up), parcel out, segregate, sever, share, split up

partly *adv* a little, fractionally, half, in part, in some measure, incompletely, moderately, partially, relatively, slightly, somewhat, to a certain degree, to a certain extent, to some degree, to some extent, up to a point
🔄 completely, fully, totally, wholly

partner *n* **1** *partners in crime:* accomplice, ally, collaborator, colleague, companion, comrade, confederate, co-operator, co-worker, helper, mate, oppo *colloq,* sidekick *colloq,* team-mate **2** *partners in a law firm:* associate, colleague, copartner **3** *bring your partner to the party:* boyfriend, companion, consort, friend, girlfriend, husband, other half *colloq,* spouse, wife

partnership *n* **1** *the partnership between teachers and parents:* affiliation, alliance, association, brotherhood, collaboration, combination, confederation, co-operation, fellowship, fraternity, participation, sharing, union **2** *a business partnership:* association, company, conglomerate, co-operative, corporation, firm, society, syndicate

party *n* **1** *a birthday party:* at-home, celebration, festivity, function, gathering, get-together, reception, reunion, social **2** *a search party:* band, body, company, contingent, crew, detachment, gang, group, squad, team, unit **3** *a political party:* affiliation, alliance, association, cabal, camp, combination, faction, grouping, league, side **4** *she is the guilty party:* defendant, individual, litigant, person, plaintiff

pass¹ *v* **1** *it passed low overhead:* drive, flow, go, make your way, move, proceed, progress, run, travel **2** *a bus passed me:* beat, draw level with, drive/run past, go past, lap, leave behind, lose, outdistance, outstrip, overhaul, overtake, pull ahead of **3** *we passed through several villages:* get across, get over, go across, go over, go through, move, run, traverse **4** *pass the salt:* give, hand, let someone have, reach, transfer, transmit **5** *time passes quickly:* advance, drag, elapse, go by, go past, proceed, slip away, slip by **6** *pass time wisely:* devote, employ, fill, occupy, spend, take up, use up, while away **7** *it passed all our expectations:* exceed, go beyond, go over, outdo, outstrip, surpass **8** *pass an exam:* be successful in, get through, graduate, pass with flying colours, qualify, sail/breeze through, scrape through, succeed **9** *the examiner passed him:* accept, approve, declare satisfactory, declare successful **10** *pass a new law:* accept, adopt, agree to, approve, authorize, enact, ratify, sanction, validate, vote for **11** *pass from one state to another:* become, change, develop, evolve, go, move, transfer, turn **12** *my prediction came to pass:* befall *formal,* come about, happen, occur, take place, transpire *formal* **13** *the estate passed to her daughter:* be bequeathed, be consigned, be endowed, be given, be granted, be handed down, be inherited, be left, be made over, be willed, transfer **14** *pass the ball:* kick, lunge, move, swing, throw **15** *pass urine:* discharge, emit, excrete *formal,* expel, let out, release

🔁 **2** fall behind **7** fail to reach **8** fail **9** fail

♦ *n* **1** *a pass to the goalkeeper:* kick, lunge, move, swing, throw **2** *you'll need to show him your pass:* authorization, identification, licence, passport, permission, permit, ticket, visa, warrant **3** *make a pass at someone:* advances, approach, overture, play, proposition, suggestion

▶ **pass away** decease *formal,* die, expire *formal,* give up the ghost *colloq,* kick the bucket *colloq,* pass on, peg out *colloq,* pop off *colloq*

▶ **pass for** appear to be, be mistaken for, be regarded as, be taken for

▶ **pass off 1** *it passed off without incident:* go off, happen, occur, take place **2** *the effects passed off quickly:* die down, disappear, fade away, vanish, wear off **3** *passed them off as free-range eggs:* counterfeit, fake, feign, palm off

▶ **pass out 1** *he felt faint then passed out:* black out, collapse, drop, faint, flake out *colloq,* keel over *colloq,* lose consciousness **2** *pass out the sweets:* allocate, allot, deal out, distribute, dole out, give out, hand out, share out

▶ **pass over** disregard, forget, ignore, leave, miss, neglect, not take into consideration, omit, overlook, take no notice of, turn a blind eye to, turn a deaf ear to

▶ **pass up** ignore, let slip, miss, neglect, not take advantage of, refuse, reject

pass² *n* canyon, col, defile, gap, gorge, passage, ravine

passable *adj* **1** *the meal was only passable:* acceptable, adequate, all right, allowable, average, fair, mediocre, moderate, no great shakes *colloq,* not much cop *colloq,* nothing to write home about *colloq,* OK *colloq,* ordinary, run-of-the-mill *colloq,* satisfactory, so-so *colloq,* tolerable, unexceptional **2** *the road is passable:* clear, navigable, open, traversable, unblocked, unobstructed

🔁 **1** excellent, unacceptable **2** blocked, impassable, obstructed

passably *adv* after a fashion, fairly, moderately, rather, reasonably, relatively, somewhat, tolerably

passage *n* **1** *the toilet is down the passage on your left:* aisle, corridor, doorway, entrance, exit, hall, hallway, lobby, opening, passageway, vestibule **2** *the passage between the two blocks of flats:* alley, avenue, lane, path, road, route, thoroughfare, track, way **3** *a narrow passage between the two lakes:* canal, channel, conduit, duct, flume, furrow, groove, gully, gutter, main, neck, sound, strait, trough, watercourse, waterway **4** *the passage of troops through the country:* course, flow, movement, running **5** *the passage from school to work:* advance, change, development, metamorphosis, mutation *technical,* progress, transfer, transition, turning **6** *the passage of a bill:* acceptance, adoption, approval, authorization, enactment, ratification, sanction, validation **7** *grant passage through a country:* access, admission, permission to travel through, safe conduct **8** *a passage from her latest book:* citation *formal,* clause, excerpt, extract, paragraph, piece, quotation, section, text, verse **9** *I wish you a safe passage:* crossing, journey, tour, trek, trip, voyage

passageway *n* aisle, alley, corridor, entrance, exit, hall, hallway, lane, lobby, passage, path, track, way

passé *adj* antiquated, dated, démodé, obsolete, old hat *colloq,* old-fashioned, out *colloq,* out of date, outdated, outmoded, outworn, past its best, unfashionable

🔁 fashionable, in

passenger *n* **1** *passengers stranded by strike action:* commuter, fare, fare-payer, hitchhiker, rider, traveller, voyager **2** *this company can't afford to carry passengers:* bum *colloq,* drone, freeloader *colloq,* hanger-on, parasite, sponger *colloq*

passer-by *n* bystander, eyewitness, gawper *colloq*, looker-on, observer, onlooker, rubberneck *colloq*, spectator, witness

passing *adj* 1 *a passing fad:* brief, ephemeral *formal*, fleeting, momentary, short, short-lived, temporary, transient *formal*, transitional 2 *a passing glance:* casual, cursory, hasty, incidental, quick, shallow, slight, superficial
🖃 1 lasting, permanent
♦ *n* death, decease *formal*, demise *formal*, departure, end, expiration *formal*, finish, loss, passing away, perishing, quietus *formal*, termination *formal*

passion *n* 1 *her performances lack passion:* ardour, emotion, feeling, fervour, fire, heat, intensity, spirit, vehemence, warmth, zeal 2 *he worked himself into a passion:* anger, explosion, fit, fury, indignation, outburst, rage, tantrum, temper, wrath 3 *his passion for his wife:* adoration, affection, ardour, craving, desire, fondness, infatuation, love, lust, sexual desire 4 *his passion for cricket:* avidity, craze, eagerness, enthusiasm, fanaticism, fascination, keenness, mania, obsession, zeal, zest
🖃 1 coolness, indifference

passionate *adj* 1 *a passionate libertarian:* ardent, aroused, avid, eager, enthusiastic, excited, fanatical, fervent, fierce, fiery, hot, impassioned, inflamed, intense, keen, stormy, strong, tempestuous, vehement, zealous 2 *he gets a bit too passionate at times on the touchline:* emotional, excitable, frenzied, hot-headed, impetuous, impulsive, intense, irritable, quick-tempered 3 *passionate lovers:* affectionate, ardent, aroused, erotic, loving, lustful, randy *colloq*, sensual, sexy, sultry, turned on *colloq*
🖃 1 laid back *colloq*, phlegmatic 3 frigid

passionless *adj* 1 *a passionless consultant:* calm, detached, dispassionate, impartial, neutral, restrained, unemotional, uninvolved 2 *a selfish and passionless woman:* cold, cold-blooded, cold-hearted, emotionless, frigid, frosty, icy, impassive, indifferent, insensible, uncaring, unfeeling, unloving, unresponsive, withdrawn
🖃 1 passionate 2 caring, sensitive, sympathetic

passive *adj* 1 *passive acceptance of the occupation:* compliant, docile, long-suffering, non-violent, patient, resigned, submissive, unassertive, unresisting, yielding 2 *passive bystanders:* aloof, apathetic, detached, dispassionate, distant, emotionless, inactive, indifferent, non-participating, remote, unemotional, unenterprising, uninvolved, unmoved
🖃 1 active, involved, lively 2 responsive

passport *n* 1 *show your passport:* authorization, ID, identity card, laissez-passer, papers, pass, permit, travel documents, visa 2 *the passport to success:* admission, avenue, door, doorway, entry, key, means of access, path, route, way

password *n* countersign, key, open sesame, parole, shibboleth, signal, watchword, word

past *adj* 1 *the age of the battleship is past:* completed, done, ended, finished, over, over and done with 2 *a past lover:* erstwhile *formal*, foregoing, foregone, former, last, late, latter, preceding, previous, recent, sometime 3 *past times:* ancient, bygone, defunct, early, elapsed, extinct, forgotten, gone, gone by, long ago, no more, olden
🖃 2 future, next
♦ *n* 1 *in the past:* antiquity, bygone times/days, days gone by, days of yore *formal*, former times, good old days, olden days, olden times 2 *the truth about his past:* background, experience, life, record, track record
🖃 1 future

pasta

Forms and shapes of pasta include:
agnolotti, anelli, angel's hair, bombolotti, bucatini, cannelloni, capelletti, casarecci, conchiglie, crescioni, ditali, farfalline, fedelini, fettuccine, fiochetti, fusilli, gnocchi, lasagne, linguini, lumache, macaroni, mafalde, manicotti, maruzze, mezzani, noodle, noodle farfel, penne, ravioli, rigatoni, ruote, spaghetti, stelline, tagliatelle, tortellini, trofie, vermicelli, ziti

---

paste *n* 1 *wallpaper paste:* adhesive, cement, glue, gum, mastic, putty 2 *fish paste:* blend, mixture, mush, pap, pulp, purée, spread
♦ *v* cement, fasten, fix, glue, gum, stick

pastel *adj* delicate, discreet, faint, light, light-coloured, low-key, muted, pale, soft, soft-hued, subdued, subtle
♦ *n* 1 *he drew it with a pastel:* chalk, crayon, pastille 2 *a pastel of a bowl of fruit:* drawing, sketch, vignette

pastiche *n* assortment, collection, confusion, conglomeration *formal*, farrago, gallimaufry, hodgepodge, hotchpotch, jumble, medley, melange, miscellany, mish, mishmash *colloq*, mix, mixed bag *colloq*, mixture, omnium-gatherum *colloq*, patchwork, potpourri, salmagundi, smorgasbord, variety

pastille *n* confection, cough drop, cough sweet, jujube, lozenge, pastel, tablet, troche

pastime *n* activity, amusement, distraction, diversion, entertainment, fun, game, hobby, leisure activity, play, recreation, relaxation, sport
🖃 employment, work

past master *n* ace *colloq*, adept, artist, dab hand *colloq*, expert, old hand *colloq*, proficient, virtuoso, wizard *colloq*
🖃 incompetent

pastor *n* canon, churchman, clergyman, cleric, divine, ecclesiastic, minister, parson, prebendary, priest, rector, vicar

pastoral *adj* 1 *a tranquil pastoral scene:* agrarian, agricultural, bucolic *formal*, country, idyllic, rural, rustic, simple 2 *his pastoral duties:* clerical, ecclesiastical, ministerial, priestly
🖃 1 urban

pastry

Types of pastry include:
American crust, biscuit-crumb, cheese pastry, choux, Danish, filo, flaky, hot-water crust, one-stage pastry, pâte à savarin, pâte brisée, pâte frolle, pâte sablée, pâte sucrée, plain pastry, pork-pie pastry, puff, rough-puff, shortcrust, suetcrust, sweet pastry

---

pasture *n* field, grass, grassland, grazing, grazing land, meadow, paddock, pasturage

pasty *adj* anaemic, pale, pallid, pasty-faced, sallow, sickly, unhealthy, wan
 ☒ healthy, ruddy

pat *v* caress, clap, dab, fondle, pet, stroke, tap, touch
 ♦ *n* caress, dab, stroke, tap, touch
 ♦ *adj* easy, facile, fluent, glib, ready, simplistic, slick, smooth
 ♦ *adv* exactly, faultlessly, flawlessly, fluently, perfectly, precisely
 ☒ imprecisely, inaccurately, wrongly

patch *n* **1** *a patch of land:* area, bed, lot, parcel, piece, plot, spot, tract **2** *elbow patches:* cloth, cover, covering, material, protection, shield **3** *a bad patch:* period, phase, spell, stretch, term, time
 ♦ *v* cover, fix, mend, reinforce, repair, sew, stitch

patchwork *n* farrago, gallimaufry, hash, hotchpotch, jumble, medley, mishmash *colloq*, mixture, pastiche

patchy *adj* **1** *her skin is patchy:* bitty, blotchy, dappled, mottled, spotty, uneven, variegated **2** *the service has been patchy:* bitty, erratic, fitful, inconsistent, irregular, random, sketchy, uneven, variable, varying
 ☒ **1** even, regular, unbroken **2** consistent, even, regular, uniform

patent *adj* apparent, blatant, clear, conspicuous, evident, flagrant, glaring, manifest *formal*, obvious, open, overt, palpable, plain, transparent, unequivocal, unmistakable, visible
 ☒ hidden, opaque
 ♦ *n* certificate, copyright, invention, licence, privilege, registered trademark, right

paternal *adj* benevolent, concerned, fatherlike, fatherly, protective, vigilant

path *n* **1** *I followed the path down the hill:* bridleway, footpath, pathway, towpath, track, trail, walk **2** *protestors blocked her path:* approach, course, direction, lane, passage, road, route, way

pathetic *adj* **1** *a pathetic sight:* affecting, dismal, distressing, heartbreaking, heart-rending, lamentable, miserable, moving, pitiable, pitiful, plaintive, poignant, poor, sad, sorry, touching, woeful, wretched **2** *his attempts were pathetic:* contemptible, deplorable, derisory, feeble, inadequate, meagre, miserable, poor, sorry, unsatisfactory, useless, woeful, worthless
 ☒ **1** cheerful **2** admirable, excellent, valuable

pathological *adj* addicted, chronic, compulsive, confirmed, dependent, habitual, hardened, inveterate, obsessive, persistent

pathos *n* inadequacy, misery, pitiableness, pitifulness, plaintiveness, poignancy, sadness

patience *n* **1** *he lost his patience:* calmness, composure, cool *colloq*, equanimity, even-temperedness, imperturbability *formal*, inexcitability, restraint, self-control, serenity, tolerance, tranquillity, unflappability *colloq* **2** *he bore it with patience:* diligence, doggedness, endurance, forbearance, fortitude, perseverance, persistence, stickability *colloq*, stoicism, tenacity
 ☒ **1** exasperation, impatience, intolerance **2** irresolution

patient *adj* **1** *he's very patient:* accommodating, calm, composed, cool *colloq*, even-tempered, forbearing, forgiving, indulgent, lenient, mild, restrained, serene, tolerant, understanding **2** *patient devotion to his wife:* long-suffering,

persevering, persistent, philosophical, resigned, self-possessed, stoical, uncomplaining
 ☒ **1** impatient, intolerant **2** exasperated, restless
 ♦ *n* case, client, invalid, sufferer

patois *n* argot, cant, dialect, jargon, lingo, lingua franca, local parlance, local speech, patter, slang, vernacular

patriarch *n* elder, father, founder, grand old man *colloq*, grandfather, greybeard, paterfamilias, sire

patrician *n* aristocrat, gentleman, grandee, noble, nobleman, peer
 ☒ commoner, plebeian
 ♦ *adj* aristocratic, blue-blooded *colloq*, gentle, high-born, high-class, lordly, noble, thoroughbred, well-born
 ☒ common, humble

patrimony *n* bequest, birthright, estate, heritage, inheritance, legacy, portion, possessions, property, revenue, share

patriot *n* chauvinist, flag-waver, jingo, jingoist, loyalist, nationalist

patriotic *adj* chauvinistic, flag-waving, jingoistic, loyal, loyalist, nationalist, nationalistic

patriotism *n* chauvinism, flag-waving, jingoism, loyalty, nationalism

patrol *v* be on the beat, defend, go the rounds, guard, inspect, keep guard on, keep watch on/over, make/do the/your rounds, monitor, police, protect, tour
 ♦ *n* **1** *the intruders were challenged by a patrol:* guard, night-watchman, patrolman, patrolwoman, police officer, security guard, sentinel, sentry, watchman **2** *on patrol:* beat, defence, guard, patrolling, policing, protection, round, surveillance, vigil, watch

patron *n* **1** *a patron of the arts:* advocate, angel *colloq*, backer, benefactor, champion, defender, fairy godmother *colloq*, friend, guardian, guardian angel, helper, philanthropist, promoter, protector, sponsor, supporter, sympathizer, upholder **2** *the shop's regular patrons:* buyer, client, customer, frequenter, purchaser, regular *colloq*, shopper, subscriber

---

Occupations with a patron saint include:
Accountants (Matthew), Actors (Genesius; Vitus), Advertisers (Bernardino of Siena), Architects (Thomas), Artists (Luke; Angelico), Astronauts (Joseph of Cupertino), Astronomers (Dominic), Athletes (Sebastian), Authors (Francis de Sales), Aviators (Our Lady of Loreto), Bakers (Honoratus), Bankers (Bernardino Feltre), Barbers (Cosmas and Damian), Blacksmiths (Eligius), Bookkeepers (Matthew), Book trade (John of God), Brewers (Amand; Wenceslaus), Builders (Barbara; Thomas), Butchers (Luke), Carpenters (Joseph), Chemists (Cosmas and Damian), Comedians (Vitus), Cooks (Lawrence; Martha), Dancers (Vitus), Dentists (Apollonia), Doctors (Cosmas and Damian; Luke), Editors (Francis de Sales), Farmers (Isidore), Firemen (Florian), Fishermen (Andrew; Peter), Florists (Dorothy; Thérèse of Lisieux), Gardeners (Adam; Fiacre), Glassworkers (Luke; Lucy), Gravediggers (Joseph of Arimathea), Grocers (Michael), Hotelkeepers (Amand; Julian the

Hospitaler), Housewives (Martha), Jewellers (Eligius), Journalists (Francis de Sales), Labourers (James; John Bosco), Lawyers (Ivo; Thomas More), Librarians (Jerome; Catherine of Alexandria), Merchants (Francis of Assisi), Messengers (Gabriel), Metalworkers (Eligius), Midwives (Raymond Nonnatus), Miners (Anne; Barbara), Motorists (Christopher), Musicians (Cecilia; Gregory the Great), Nurses (Camillus de Lellis; John of God), Philosophers (Thomas Aquinas; Catherine of Alexandria), Poets (Cecilia; David), Police (Michael), Postal workers (Gabriel), Priests (Jean-Baptiste Vianney), Printers (John of God), Prisoners (Leonard), Radio workers (Gabriel), Sailors (Christopher; Erasmus; Francis of Paola), Scholars (Thomas Aquinas), Scientists (Albert the Great), Sculptors (Luke; Louis), Secretaries (Genesius), Servants (Martha; Zita), Shoemakers (Crispin; Crispinian), Singers (Cecilia; Gregory), Soldiers (George; Joan of Arc; Martin of Tours; Sebastian), Students (Thomas Aquinas), Surgeons (Luke; Cosmas and Damian), Tailors (Homobonus), Tax collectors (Matthew), Taxi drivers (Fiacre), Teachers (Gregory the Great; John Baptist de la Salle), Theologians (Augustine; Alphonsus Liguori; Thomas Aquinas), Television workers (Gabriel), Undertakers (Dismas; Joseph of Arimathea), Waiters (Martha), Writers (Lucy)

patronage *n* **1** *lavish patronage of the arts*: backing, encouragement, financial help/aid/assistance, funding, promotion, sponsorship, support **2** *his regular patronage of the shop*: business, buying, commerce, custom, purchasing, shopping, subscription, trade

patronize *v* **1** *he never patronizes his patients*: act/speak condescendingly to, despise, disparage *formal*, look down on, look down your nose at *colloq*, scorn, talk down to, turn your nose up at *colloq* **2** *he patronizes the city's orchestra*: aid, assist, back, champion, encourage, finance, foster, fund, help, maintain, promote, protect, sponsor, support **3** *I patronize my local deli*: be a regular at *colloq*, buy from, deal with, frequent, shop at

patronizing *adj* condescending, contemptuous, disdainful, haughty, high-and-mighty *colloq*, high-handed, lofty, on your high horse *colloq*, overbearing, scornful, snobbish, snooty *colloq*, stooping, stuck-up *colloq*, supercilious, superior, toffee-nosed *colloq*
◼ humble, lowly

patter¹ *v* beat, drum, pat, pelt, pitter-patter, pound, scurry, scuttle, tap, trip
♦ *n* beating, pattering, pitter-patter, tapping

patter² *n* chatter, gabble, jabber, jargon, line, lingo *colloq*, monologue, pitch, spiel *colloq*, yak *colloq*

pattern *n* **1** *all the crimes followed the same pattern*: arrangement, method, order, plan, system **2** *a delicate floral pattern*: decoration, design, device, figure, markings, motif, ornament, ornamentation, style **3** *a knitting pattern*: blueprint, design, example, guide, ideal, instruction, model, norm, original, plan, prototype, standard, stencil, template **4** *a book of fabric patterns*: sample, swatch
♦ *v* copy, decorate, design, emulate, follow,

form, imitate, match, model, mould, order, shape, stencil, style, trim

patterned *adj* decorated, figured, moiré, ornamented, printed, watered
◼ plain

paucity *n* dearth, deficiency, exiguousness *formal*, fewness, insufficiency, lack, meagreness, paltriness, poverty, rarity, scantiness, scarcity, shortage, slenderness, slightness, smallness, sparseness, sparsity, want
◼ abundance

paunch *n* abdomen, beer belly, belly, corporation *colloq*, fat stomach, pot-belly

paunchy *adj* adipose *technical*, corpulent *formal*, fat, podgy, portly, pot-bellied, pudgy, rotund *formal*, tubby

pauper *n* bankrupt, beggar, church-mouse, down-and-out, have-not, indigent *formal*, insolvent, mendicant

pause *v* adjourn, break off, cease *formal*, delay, desist *formal*, discontinue *formal*, halt, hesitate, hold back, interrupt, let up *colloq*, rest, stop, take a break, take a breather *colloq*, take a rest *colloq*, take five *colloq*, wait
♦ *n* break, breather *colloq*, breathing space *colloq*, cessation *formal*, delay, gap, halt, hesitation, interlude, intermission, interruption, interval, let-up *colloq*, lull, respite, rest, stay, stoppage, time out *colloq*, wait

pave *v* asphalt, concrete, cover, flag, floor, macadamize, surface, tar, tarmac, tile

pavement *n* bed, causeway, floor, footpath, footway, path, sidewalk *US*, way

paw *n* foot, forefoot, pad
♦ *v* manhandle, maul, mishandle, molest, stroke, touch, touch up *colloq*

pawn¹ *n* cat's-paw *colloq*, dupe, instrument, plaything, puppet, stooge *colloq*, tool, toy

pawn² *v* deposit, hock, impignorate *formal*, lay in lavender *colloq*, mortgage, pledge, pop *colloq*, stake

pawnbroker *n* gombeen-man, lender, money-lender, mont-de-piété, monte di pietà, pawnshop, pop-shop *colloq*, uncle *slang*, usurer

pay *v* **1** *pay money to someone*: cough up *colloq*, dip (your hand) into your pocket *colloq*, disburse *formal*, discharge, expend *formal*, foot the bill *colloq*, fork out *colloq*, hand over, indemnify *formal*, invest, lay out, meet the cost of, outlay, pay out, pick up the tab *colloq*, recompense, refund, reimburse, remit *formal*, remunerate *formal*, repay, reward, settle, settle up, shell out *colloq*, spend, stump up *colloq* **2** *this job doesn't pay much*: bring in, return, yield **3** *crime doesn't pay*: be advantageous, be beneficial, be worthwhile, benefit, pay off, profit
♦ *n* commission, compensation, earnings, emoluments *formal*, fee, honorarium, income, payment, recompense, reimbursement, remuneration *formal*, reward, salary, stipend, wages
▸ **pay back 1** *pay back a loan with interest*: give back, pay off, recompense, refund, reimburse, repay, return, settle, square **2** *pay someone back for insulting you*: avenge yourself on, counter-attack, get even with, get your own back, punish, reciprocate, repay, retaliate, take revenge

▶ **pay for** answer for, atone, be punished for, compensate, count the cost (of), face the music *colloq*, get your deserts *colloq*, make amends, pay a penalty for, pay the price for, suffer

▶ **pay off 1** *pay off your debts:* clear, discharge, honour, meet, pay in full, repay, settle, square **2** *pay off a worker:* discharge, dismiss, fire *colloq*, lay off, make redundant, sack *colloq* **3** *pay off the judge:* bribe, buy off, fix *colloq*, grease someone's palm *colloq*, take care of **4** *the preparations paid off:* be successful, get results, succeed, work

▶ **pay out** disburse *formal*, fork out *colloq*, hand over, lay out, part with, remit *formal*, shell out *colloq*, spend

payable *adj* due, in arrears, mature, outstanding, owed, owing, to be paid, unpaid

payment *n* advance, allowance, amount, clearance, contribution, deposit, discharge, donation, fare, fee, hire, instalment, outlay, pay, premium, remittance *formal*, remuneration *formal*, reward, settlement, toll

pay-off *n* **1** *the joke's pay-off:* advantage, benefit, consequence, crunch *colloq*, moment of truth *colloq*, outcome, punchline *colloq*, result, reward, settlement, upshot **2** *several detectives were given pay-offs:* allurement, back-hander *colloq*, bribe, enticement, hush money *colloq*, inducement, protection money *colloq*, slush fund *colloq*, sweetener *colloq*

peace *n* **1** *some peace and quiet:* calm, calmness, composure, contentment, hush, peacefulness, placidity, quiet, quietness, relaxation, repose *formal*, rest, restfulness, serenity, silence, still, stillness, tranquillity **2** *the treaty brought peace to Europe:* accord *formal*, agreement, amicableness, amity *formal*, armistice, cease-fire, conciliation, concord *formal*, friendship, goodwill, harmony, non-aggression, non-violence, peace treaty, treaty, truce

☒ **1** disturbance, noise **2** disagreement, discord, war

peaceable *adj* amicable, conciliatory, cordial, easy-going *colloq*, even-tempered, friendly, gentle, good-natured, harmonious, inoffensive, irenic, mild, non-aggressive, non-violent, pacific, peace-loving, placid, unwarlike

☒ aggressive, belligerent, quarrelsome

peaceful *adj* **1** *a peaceful nation:* amicable, friendly, harmonious, pacific, peaceable, peace-loving **2** *a peaceful scene:* calm, gentle, placid, quiet, relaxing, reposeful *formal*, restful, serene, sleepy, still, tranquil, undisturbed, unruffled, untroubled

☒ **1** warlike **2** disturbed, noisy

peacemaker *n* appeaser, arbitrator, conciliator, intercessor, mediator, pacifier, pacifist, peace-monger

peacemaking *adj* appeasing, conciliatory, irenic(al), mediating, mediative, mediatorial, mediatory, pacific

peak *n* **1** *the highest peak in Wales:* alp, height, hill, massif, mount, mountain **2** *the mountaineers finally reached the peak:* apex, crest, crown, high point, pinnacle, point, summit, tip, top **3** *the peak of his career:* apex, apogee *formal*, climax, culmination, high point, maximum, pinnacle, summit, zenith *formal*

☒ **1** valley **3** nadir *formal*, trough

♦ *v* climax, come to a head, culminate

peaky *adj* ill, off-colour, pale, pallid, poorly, sick, sickly, under the weather *colloq*, unwell, wan, washed-out *colloq*

☒ healthy, in the pink *colloq*

peal *n* **1** *the peals of the church's bells:* carillon, chime, clang, knell, ring, ringing, tintinnabulation *formal*, toll **2** *peals of thunder:* boom, clap, crash, resounding, reverberation, roar, rumble

♦ *v* **1** *the bells tolled after the service:* chime, clang, resonate, resound, reverberate, ring (out), toll **2** *thunder pealed and rattled the windows:* boom, crash, reverberate, roar, roll, rumble

peasant *n* boor, bumpkin, churl, country bumpkin *colloq*, country person, lout, oaf, provincial, rustic, yokel

pebble *n* agate, chip, gallet, stone

peccadillo *n* boob *colloq*, delinquency, error, fault, indiscretion, infraction *formal*, lapse, minor offence, misdeed, misdemeanour, slip, slip-up *colloq*

peck *v* bite, hit, jab, nip, pick, prick, rap, strike, tap

peculiar *adj* **1** *a peculiar sound:* abnormal, bizarre, curious, droll, eccentric, exceptional, exotic, extraordinary, freakish, funny, grotesque, odd, offbeat, outlandish, quaint, queer, strange, unconventional, unusual, way-out *slang*, weird **2** *her peculiar ways:* characteristic, distinct, distinctive, distinguishing, idiosyncratic, individual, individualistic, particular, personal, remarkable, singular, special, specific, unique **3** *feel peculiar:* dizzy, ill, out of sorts, poorly, sick, under the weather *colloq*, unwell

☒ **1** normal, ordinary **2** general

peculiarity *n* **1** *the peculiarity of his behaviour:* abnormality, bizarreness, eccentricity, idiosyncrasy, oddity, weirdness **2** *one of their peculiarities:* attribute, characteristic, distinctiveness, exception, feature, hallmark, mark, particularity, property, quality, trait

pecuniary *adj* commercial, financial, fiscal, monetary, nummary *formal*, nummulary *formal*

pedagogic *adj* academic, didactic, educational, instructional, scholastic, teaching, tuitional

pedagogue *n* dogmatist, dominie, don, educationalist, educationist, educator, instructor, master, mistress, pedant, preceptor, schoolmaster, schoolmistress, teacher

pedagogy *n* didactics, instruction, pedagogics, teaching, training, tuition, tutelage

pedant *n* **1** *a pedant about grammar:* casuist, doctrinaire, dogmatist, Dryasdust, hair-splitter *colloq*, nit-picker *colloq*, perfectionist, pettifogger, precisian, precisionist, purist, quibbler **2** *a pedant in his ivory tower:* academic, egghead *colloq*, highbrow *colloq*, intellectual, scholar, scholastic

pedantic *adj* **1** *a pedantic point:* exact, finical, fussy, hair-splitting *colloq*, meticulous, nit-picking *colloq*, particular, perfectionist, precise, punctilious, purist, quibbling, scrupulous **2** *a long-winded, pedantic lecture:* academic, bookish, donnish, erudite, intellectual, schoolmasterly

☒ **1** casual, imprecise, informal

pedantry *n* **1** *noted for its pedantry:* academicness, bookishness, intellectualism, pedagogism, pedantism, pomposity, pretentiousness, stuffiness **2** *bogged down by pedantry:* cavilling, exactness, finicality, hair-splitting *colloq*, meticulousness, nit-picking *colloq*, punctiliousness, quibbling

peddle *v* flog *colloq*, hawk, market, offer/present for sale, push, sell, tout, trade, traffic, vend

pedestal *n* base, column, foot, foundation, mounting, pillar, platform, plinth, podium, stand, support

pedestrian *n* foot-traveller, hiker, walker
♦ *adj* banal, boring, commonplace, dull, flat, humdrum, indifferent, mediocre, mundane, no great shakes *colloq*, not up to much *colloq*, nothing much to write home about *colloq*, ordinary, plodding, prosaic, run-of-the-mill *colloq*, stodgy, turgid, unexciting, unimaginative, uninspired
🖪 exciting, imaginative

pedigree *n* ancestry, blood, breed, derivation, descent, extraction, family, family tree, genealogy, line, line of descent, lineage, parentage, race, stirps *formal*, stock, strain
♦ *adj* full-blooded, pure-bred, thoroughbred

pedlar *n* boxwallah, chapman, cheap-jack, colporteur, gutter-man, gutter-merchant, hawker, huckster, seller, street-trader, vendor, walker, yagger *Scot*

peek *v* glance, have a gander *colloq*, have a look-see *colloq*, look, peep, peer, spy
♦ *n* blink, dekko *colloq*, gander *slang*, glance, glimpse, look, look-see *colloq*, peep, shufti *colloq*

peel *v* decorticate *formal*, desquamate *formal*, flake (off), pare, remove, scale, skin, strip, take off
♦ *n* epicarp *technical*, exocarp, integument, peeling, rind, skin, zest

peep[1] *v* **1** *he peeped through the keyhole:* glimpse, look, peek, peer, spy, squint **2** *her toes peeped out through the sandals:* appear, emerge, issue
♦ *n* dekko *colloq*, gander *slang*, glance, glimpse, look, look-see *colloq*, peek, shufti *colloq*, squint

peep[2] *v* chatter, cheep, chirp, chirrup, pipe, squeak, tweet, twitter, warble
♦ *n* **1** *a gentle peep from the bird:* cheep, chirp, chirrup, squeak, tweet, twitter, warble **2** *I don't want to hear another peep out of you:* noise, sound, utterance, word

peephole *n* aperture, chink, cleft, crack, crevice, fissure, hole, interstice *formal*, Judas-hole, Judas-window, keyhole, opening, pinhole, slink, slit, spyhole

peer[1] *v* examine, gaze, inspect, look, peep, scan, scrutinize, snoop, spy, squint

peer[2] *n* **1** *a life peer:* aristocrat, baron, count, duke, earl, lord, marquess, marquis, noble, nobleman, patrician, viscount **2** *envied by his peers:* compeer, confrère, counterpart, equal, equivalent, fellow

peerage *n* aristocracy, lords and ladies, nobility, top drawer *colloq*, upper crust *colloq*

peeress *n* aristocrat, baroness, countess, dame, duchess, lady, marchioness, noble, noblewoman, viscountess

peerless *adj* beyond compare, excellent, incomparable, matchless, nonpareil *formal*, outstanding, paramount, second to none *colloq*, superlative, supreme, unbeatable, unequalled, unexcelled, unique, unmatched, unparalleled, unrivalled, unsurpassed, without equal

peeve *v* annoy, drive up the wall *colloq*, exasperate, gall, get on someone's nerves *colloq*, get someone's blood up *colloq*, get under someone's skin *colloq*, irk, irritate, rub someone up the wrong way *colloq*, vex

peeved *adj* annoyed, exasperated, galled, having the hump *colloq*, in a huff *colloq*, irked, irritated, miffed *colloq*, narked *colloq*, nettled, piqued, put out, riled, sore, upset, vexed

peevish *adj* cantankerous, churlish, complaining, crabbed *colloq*, cross, crotchety *colloq*, crusty, fractious, fretful, grumpy, ill-tempered, in a bad mood, irritable, moody, petulant, querulous, ratty *colloq*, short-tempered, snappy, sulky, sullen, surly, testy, tetchy, touchy
🖪 good-tempered

peevishness *n* acrimony, captiousness, ill-temper, irritability, perversity, pet, petulance, pique, protervity *formal*, querulousness, testiness

peg *n* brad, dowel, hook, knob, marker, nail, pin, post, screw, spike, stake
♦ *v* **1** *she pegged the sheet onto the line:* attach, fasten, fix, join, mark, secure **2** *peg prices:* control, fix, freeze, limit, set, stabilize
▶ **peg away** apply yourself, beaver away, hang in *colloq*, keep at it *colloq*, persevere, persist, plod along, plug away, stick at it *colloq*, work away

pejorative *adj* bad, belittling, deprecatory *formal*, derogatory, disparaging, negative, slighting, uncomplimentary, unflattering, unpleasant
🖪 complimentary

pellet *n* **1** *he was treated for pellet wounds:* ball, bullet, shot, slug *colloq* **2** *pellets of fish food:* capsule, drop, lozenge, pill

pell-mell *adv* at full tilt, feverishly, hastily, heedlessly, helter-skelter *colloq*, hurriedly, hurry-scurry *colloq*, impetuously, posthaste, precipitously, rashly, recklessly

pellucid *adj* bright, clear, glassy, limpid, pure, translucent, transparent

pelt[1] *v* **1** *pelted with eggs:* assail, attack, batter, beat, bombard, hit, hurl, shower, strike, throw **2** *rain pelted down:* bucket (down) *colloq*, pour, rain cats and dogs *colloq*, teem **3** *he pelted along:* belt *colloq*, career, charge, dash, hurry, race, run, rush, speed, sprint, tear, zip *colloq*

pelt[2] *n* coat, fell, fleece, fur, hide, skin

pen[1] *n* ballpoint, ballpoint pen, Biro®, felt-tip, felt-tip pen, fountain pen
♦ *v* compose, draft, jot down, scribble, write (down)

pen[2] *n* cage, compound, coop, corral, enclosure, fold, hutch, mew, pound, stall, sty
♦ *v* cage, confine, coop, enclose, fence, hedge, hem in, shut (up)

penal *adj* corrective, disciplinary, punitive, retaliatory, retributive

penalize *v* 1 *infringements will be penalized:* castigate *formal*, chastise *formal*, correct, discipline, fine, punish 2 *older workers are being unfairly penalized:* disadvantage, handicap
🔁 1 reward

penal servitude *n* bird *colloq*, hard labour, lag *colloq*, porridge *colloq*, stretch, time

penalty *n* 1 *the penalty is a fine of £100:* castigation *formal*, chastisement, fine, forfeit, mulct *formal*, punishment, retribution, sentence 2 *one of the penalties of old age:* disadvantage, downside *colloq*, drawback, handicap, minus *colloq*, snag, weak point
🔁 1 reward 2 advantage, benefit

penance *n* atonement, mortification, penalty, punishment, reparation, self-abasement, self-punishment

penchant *n* affinity, bent, bias, disposition *formal*, fondness, inclination, leaning, liking, partiality, predilection *formal*, predisposition *formal*, preference, proclivity *formal*, proneness, propensity *formal*, soft spot, taste, tendency, weakness
🔁 dislike

pendant *n* locket, medallion, necklace

pendent *adj* dangling, drooping, hanging, nutant *formal*, pendulous *formal*, pensile *formal*, suspended, swinging

pending *adj* approaching, awaiting settlement, coming, forthcoming, imminent, impending, in the balance *colloq*, in the offing, near, nearing, uncertain, undecided, unsettled, up in the air *colloq*
🔁 finished, settled
♦ *prep* awaiting, before, till, to, until, while, whilst

pendulous *adj* dangling, drooping, droopy, hanging, pendent *formal*, sagging, suspended, swaying, swinging

penetrable *adj* 1 *barely penetrable jungle:* accessible, open, passable, permeable, pervious, porous 2 *a thick but penetrable Scots burr:* clear, comprehensible, explicable, fathomable, intelligible, understandable
🔁 1 impenetrable 2 incomprehensible

penetrate *v* 1 *the needle penetrated her skin:* bore, perforate, pierce, prick, probe, puncture, sink, spike, stab 2 *pine scents penetrated the cabin:* enter, fill, get into, imbue, infiltrate, make your way, permeate, pervade, saturate, seep, suffuse 3 *Hegel's philosophy is difficult to penetrate:* comprehend, cotton on *colloq*, crack *colloq*, fathom, get to the bottom of *colloq*, grasp, make out, register, see, sink in, twig *colloq*, understand, work out

penetrating *adj* 1 *a cold, penetrating wind:* biting, incisive, piercing, sharp, stinging 2 *a penetrating sound:* carrying, clear, loud, piercing, shrill, strident 3 *a penetrating mind:* acute, deep, discerning, discriminating, keen, observant, perceptive, probing, profound, searching, shrewd, wise
🔁 1 blunt

penetration *n* 1 *penetration by the scalpel:* incision, perforation, piercing, pricking, puncturing, stabbing 2 *penetration by enemy spies:* entry, infiltration, inroad, interpenetration

formal, invasion, permeation, pervasion 3 *his thoughts are full of subtlety and penetration:* acumen, acuteness, astuteness, discernment, insight, keenness, perception, perspicacity *formal*, sharpness, shrewdness, wit

penis *n* cock *taboo slang*, dick *taboo slang*, knob *taboo slang*, membrum virile *formal*, pecker *slang*, phallus *formal*, prick *taboo slang*, rod *taboo slang*, tool *taboo slang*, willy *colloq*, winkle *taboo slang*

penitence *n* compunction *formal*, contrition, regret, remorse, repentance, ruefulness *formal*, self-reproach, shame, sorrow

penitent *adj* apologetic, ashamed, conscience-stricken, contrite, humble, regretful, remorseful, repentant, rueful *formal*, shamefaced, sorrowful, sorry
🔁 callous, hard-hearted, unrepentant

pen-name *n* allonym *formal*, assumed name, false name, nom-de-plume, pseudonym, stage-name

pennant *n* banderol, banner, colours, ensign, flag, gonfalon, jack, standard, streamer

penniless *adj* bankrupt, broke *colloq*, bust, cleaned out *colloq*, destitute, down and out *colloq*, impoverished, indigent *formal*, on the breadline *colloq*, on your beam-ends *colloq*, poor, poverty-stricken, ruined, skint *slang*, stony-broke *colloq*, strapped for cash *colloq*
🔁 affluent, rich, wealthy

penny-pincher *n* cheapskate *colloq*, cheeseparer, meanie *colloq*, miser, money-grubber *colloq*, niggard, Scrooge, skinflint

penny-pinching *adj* cheese-paring, close, frugal, mean, mingy *colloq*, miserly, niggardly, parsimonious *formal*, scrimping, stingy *colloq*, tight-fisted, ungenerous
🔁 generous, open-handed

pension *n* allowance, annuity, benefit, company pension, income, index-linked pension, old-age pension, personal pension, retirement pension, social assistance, state pension, superannuation, support, welfare

pensioner *n* old-age pensioner, retired person, senior citizen

pensive *adj* absent-minded, absorbed, cogitative *formal*, contemplative, dreamy, meditative, musing, pondering, preoccupied, reflective, ruminative, serious, sober, solemn, thinking, thoughtful, wistful
🔁 carefree

pent-up *adj* bottled-up *colloq*, bridled, curbed, held in, inhibited, repressed, restrained, stifled, suppressed

penurious *adj* 1 *a penurious young artist:* beggarly, bust *colloq*, cheese-paring *colloq*, destitute, flat broke *colloq*, hard up, impecunious *formal*, impoverished, in straitened circumstances, inadequate, indigent *formal*, parsimonious *formal*, penniless, poor, poverty-stricken, stingy *colloq*, tight *colloq* 2 *a penurious landlord:* close, close-fisted, grudging, mean, miserly, niggardly, tight-fisted *colloq*, ungenerous
🔁 1 generous, wealthy

penury *n* beggary, dearth, deficiency, destitution, impoverishment, indigence *formal*,

insolvency, mendicity *formal*, need, pauperism, poverty, straitened circumstances, straits, want
⇄ prosperity

people *n* **1** *people should use less energy:* folk(s), human beings, humanity, humankind, humans, individuals, mankind, mortals, persons, the human race **2** *the will of the people:* citizens, community, electorate, general public, inhabitants, masses, men women and children, mob, ordinary citizens, populace, population, public, rabble, rank and file, riff-raff *colloq*, society, the plebs *colloq* **3** *the British people:* clan, nation, race, tribe **4** *his people are from Wales:* family, folks, kith and kin, parents, relations, relatives
♦ *v* colonize, inhabit, occupy, populate, settle

pep *n* ebullience *formal*, effervescence, energy, exuberance, get-up-and-go *colloq*, high spirits, life, liveliness, pizzazz *colloq*, sparkle, spirit, verve, vigour, vitality
► **pep up** animate, energize, excite, exhilarate, inspire, invigorate, liven up, quicken, stimulate, vitalize
⇄ tone down

pepper *v* **1** *they peppered the ship with bullets:* assail, attack, blitz, bombard, pelt **2** *insects peppered the windscreen:* bespatter, dot, scatter, shower, spatter, sprinkle, strew

peppery *adj* **1** *a hot, peppery stew:* hot, piquant, pungent, seasoned, spicy **2** *a peppery retired colonel:* choleric, fiery, grumpy, hot-tempered, irascible, irritable, quick-tempered, snappish, testy, touchy *colloq* **3** *his peppery writing:* astringent, biting, caustic, incisive, sarcastic, sharp, stinging, trenchant *formal*, waspish

perceive *v* **1** *I perceive a number of ships on the horizon:* behold *formal*, catch sight of, detect, discern, discover, distinguish, espy *formal*, glimpse, make out, note, notice, observe, recognize, remark, see, spot, view **2** *quickly perceived that her future did not lie here:* appreciate, apprehend, be aware of, be cognizant of *formal*, comprehend, conclude, deduce, discern, feel, gather, get wind of *colloq*, grasp, know, learn, realize, recognize, see, sense, understand

perceptible *adj* apparent, appreciable, clear, conspicuous, detectable, discernible, distinct, distinguishable, evident, manifest *formal*, noticeable, observable, obvious, patent, perceivable, plain, tangible, visible
⇄ imperceptible, inconspicuous

perception *n* **1** *our perception of the European Union:* apprehension, conception, feeling, idea, impression, interpretation, knowledge, sense, understanding, view **2** *he lacks perception in these matters:* awareness, cognizance *formal*, consciousness, discernment, discrimination, grasp, insight, observation, recognition, responsiveness, sensitivity, understanding

perceptive *adj* alert, astute, aware, discerning, discriminating, keen, observant, penetrating, perspicacious *formal*, quick, quick-witted, responsive, sensitive, sharp, sharp-eyed, shrewd, understanding
⇄ unobservant

perch *v* **1** *she perched on the corner of the desk:* balance, rest, settle, sit **2** *the blackbird perched on the fence:* alight, land, roost

perchance *adv* conceivably, feasibly, maybe, perhaps, possibly

percipience *n* acuteness, alertness, astuteness, awareness, discernment, insight, intuition, judgement, penetration, perception, perspicacity *formal*, sagacity *formal*, sensitivity, understanding

percipient *adj* alert, alive, astute, aware, discerning, discriminating, intelligent, judicious *formal*, knowing, observant, penetrating, perceptive, perspicacious *formal*, quick-witted, sharp, wide-awake
⇄ obtuse, unaware

percolate *v* drain, drip, filter, leach, leak, ooze, pass through, penetrate, permeate, pervade, seep, sieve, sift, spread (slowly) through, strain, trickle through

perdition *n* annihilation, condemnation, damnation, destruction, doom, downfall, everlasting punishment, hell, hellfire, ruin, ruination

peregrination *n* excursion, expedition, exploration, globe-trotting, journey, odyssey, roaming, roving, tour, travel, travelling, trek, trekking, trip, voyage, wandering, wayfaring

peremptory *adj* abrupt, absolute, arbitrary, assertive, authoritative, autocratic, bossy *colloq*, commanding, curt, dictatorial, dogmatic, domineering, high-handed, imperious, irrefutable, lordly, overbearing, summary, tyrannical

perennial *adj* abiding, ceaseless *formal*, constant, continual, endless, enduring, eternal, everlasting, immortal, imperishable, incessant, lasting, never-ending, permanent, perpetual, persistent, unceasing, unchanging, undying, unending, unfailing, uninterrupted

perfect *adj* **1** *her perfect French:* blameless, excellent, faultless, flawless, immaculate, impeccable, incomparable, matchless, peerless, pure, sinless, spotless, superb, superlative, unblemished, unmarred, wonderful **2** *the perfect host:* accomplished, completed, consummate *formal*, exemplary, experienced, expert, finished, ideal, just the job *colloq*, model, skilful, textbook, ultimate **3** *a perfect copy:* accurate, correct, exact, faithful, precise, right, true **4** *perfect strangers:* absolute, complete, downright, entire, out-and-out, sheer, thorough, total, utter
⇄ **1** blemished, flawed, imperfect **2** inexperienced, unskilled **3** inaccurate, wrong
♦ *v* better, complete, consummate *formal*, elaborate, finish, fulfil, improve, polish, refine
⇄ mar, spoil

perfection *n* **1** *physical perfection:* excellence, faultlessness, flawlessness, immaculateness, impeccability, superiority **2** *the perfection of new techniques:* betterment, completion, consummation *formal*, improvement, polishing, realization, refinement **3** *this meal is perfection itself:* acme, crown, ideal, model, ne plus ultra, one in a million *colloq*, paragon, peak of perfection, pinnacle, ultimate
⇄ **3** flaw, imperfection

perfectionist *n* formalist, idealist, pedant, precisionist, purist, stickler

perfectly *adv* **1** *it's perfectly safe to cross the road:* absolutely, altogether, completely, entirely, fully,

quite, thoroughly, totally, utterly, wholly **2** *the new system worked perfectly:* correctly, exactly, faultlessly, flawlessly, ideally, immaculately, impeccably, superbly, to perfection, without blemish, wonderfully
Fa **1** partially **2** badly, imperfectly

perfidious *adj* corrupt, deceitful, dishonest, disloyal, double-dealing, double-faced, duplicitous *formal*, faithless, false, Machiavellian, Punic, traitorous, treacherous, treasonous, two-faced, unfaithful, untrustworthy
Fa faithful, honest, loyal

perfidy *n* betrayal, deceit, disloyalty, double-dealing, duplicity *formal*, faithlessness, falsity, infidelity, perfidiousness *formal*, traitorousness, treachery, treason
Fa faithfulness, honesty, loyalty

perforate *v* bore, burst, drill, gore, hole, make holes in, penetrate, pierce, prick, punch, puncture, rupture, spike, split, stab, tear

perforated *adj* bored, drilled, ethmoid *technical*, fenestrate(d), fenestrial, foraminous, holed, pierced, porous, punched, punctured

perforation *n* bore, dotted line, fenestration *technical*, foramen, hole, prick, puncture

perforce *adv* inevitably, necessarily, of necessity, unavoidably, willy-nilly

perform *v* **1** *she performed the test adequately:* accomplish, achieve, bring about, bring off, carry out, complete, conduct, discharge, do, effect *formal*, execute *formal*, fulfil, pull off, satisfy **2** *perform a play:* act, appear as, do, enact, play, present, put on, represent, stage **3** *the helicopter performs well:* behave, function, go, operate, produce, run, work

performance *n* **1** *an afternoon performance:* acting, appearance, interpretation, portrayal, presentation, production, representation, show **2** *the performance of his duties:* accomplishment, achievement, action, carrying out, completion, conducting, deed, discharge, doing, effecting *formal*, execution *formal*, fulfilment, implementation **3** *impressed with the car's performance:* behaviour, conduct, functioning, going, operation, running

performer *n* **1** *circus performer:* actor, actress, artiste, clown, comedian, comic, dancer, entertainer, musician, player, singer, Thespian, trouper. **2** *one of the firm's top performers:* achiever, author, doer, executor *formal*, operator

perfume *n* **1** *he bought her perfume for Christmas:* cologne, eau-de-toilette, fragrance, incense, scent, toilet water **2** *the flower's perfume:* aroma, balm, bouquet, essence, fragrance, odour, redolence *formal*, scent, smell, sweetness

perfunctory *adj* automatic, brief, careless, cursory, heedless, hurried, inattentive, indifferent, mechanical, negligent, offhand, quick, routine, slipshod, slovenly, stereotyped, superficial, wooden
Fa careful, enthusiastic

perhaps *adv* conceivably, feasibly, maybe, perchance *formal*, possibly

peril *n* danger, hazard, insecurity, jeopardy, menace, risk, threat, uncertainty
Fa safety, security

perilous *adj* chancy, dangerous, dire, exposed, fraught with danger, hazardous, insecure, menacing, precarious, risky, threatening, unsafe, unsure, vulnerable
Fa safe, secure

perimeter *n* border, boundary, bounds, circumference, confines, edge, fringe, frontier, limit(s), margin, outer limits, periphery
Fa centre, heart, middle

period *n* **1** *a period of a few weeks:* cycle, duration, interval, season, session, shift, space, span, spell, stint, stretch, term, time, turn, while **2** *the Edwardian period:* age, date, eon, epoch, era, generation, phase, stage, years **3** *a double period of Chemistry:* class, instruction, lecture, lesson, seminar, tutorial **4** *her monthly period:* menses *formal*, menstrual flow, menstruation, monthlies, the curse *colloq* **5** *a period ends the sentence:* full point, full stop, point **6** *you may not go, period:* conclusion, end, finish, full stop, stop

periodic *adj* cyclic, cyclical, infrequent, intermittent, occasional, once in a while, periodical, recurrent, recurring, regular, repeated, seasonal, sporadic

periodical *n* journal, magazine, monthly, organ, publication, quarterly, review, weekly

peripatetic *adj* ambulant *formal*, ambulatory *formal*, itinerant, journeying, migrant, migratory, mobile, nomadic, roaming, roving, travelling, vagabond, vagrant, wandering
Fa fixed

peripheral *adj* **1** *a peripheral character:* ancillary, beside the point *colloq*, borderline, incidental, irrelevant, lesser, marginal, minor, neither here nor there *colloq*, secondary, subsidiary, superficial, surface, unimportant, unnecessary **2** *peripheral neighbourhoods:* outer, outermost, outlying, surrounding
Fa **1** crucial, major **2** central

periphery *n* ambit, border, boundary, brim, brink, circuit, circumference, edge, fringe, hem, margin, outer regions, outskirts, perimeter, rim, skirt, verge
Fa centre, middle, nub

periphrastic *adj* circuitous, circumlocutory *formal*, discursive, indirect, long-drawn-out, oblique, rambling, roundabout, tortuous, wandering

perish *v* **1** *he perished in the war's first battle:* bite the dust *colloq*, breathe your last, depart, die, expire *formal*, have had it *colloq*, kick the bucket *colloq*, lose your life, pass away, peg out *colloq*, pop off *colloq* **2** *their civilization eventually perished:* collapse, come to an end, crumble, die away, disappear, fail, fall, vanish **3** *the lining perished:* crumble, decay, decompose, disintegrate, go off, rot

perishable *adj* biodegradable, decomposable, destructible, short-lived
Fa durable, imperishable

perjury *n* false evidence, false oath, false statement, false swearing, false testimony, false witness, falsification, forswearing *formal*, mendacity *formal*

perk *n* advantage, baksheesh, benefit, bonus, dividend, extra, freebie *colloq*, fringe benefit, golden handshake *colloq*, gratuity, perquisite *formal*, plus *colloq*, tip

▶ **perk up** brighten (up), buck up *colloq*, cheer up, improve, liven up, pep up *colloq*, rally, recover, revive, take heart

perky *adj* animated, bouncy, bright, bubbly, buoyant, cheerful, cheery, ebullient *formal*, effervescent, gay, jaunty, lively, peppy, spirited, sprightly, sunny, vivacious
▣ cheerless, dull, gloomy

permanence *n* constancy, durability, endurance, fixedness, imperishability, indestructibility, perpetuity, persistence, stability, steadfastness
▣ impermanence, transience

permanent *adj* **1** *a permanent reminder of the war:* constant, durable, enduring, eternal, everlasting, immutable, imperishable, indelible, indestructible, invariable, lasting, lifelong, long-lasting, perennial, perpetual, steadfast, unchangeable, unfading **2** *a permanent fixture:* constant, established, fixed, stable, unchanging
▣ **1** ephemeral *formal*, fleeting, temporary

permanently *adv* always, ceaselessly, constantly, continually, endlessly, eternally, ever more, everlastingly, for all time, for ever, for ever and ever, for keeps *colloq*, in perpetuity, incessantly, indelibly, once and for all, perpetually, till doomsday *colloq*, till hell freezes over *colloq*, till kingdom come *colloq*, till the cows come home *colloq*, unceasingly, unendingly, unremittingly
▣ temporarily

permeable *adj* absorbent, absorptive, passable, penetrable, porous, spongy
▣ impermeable, watertight

permeate *v* **1** *pessimism permeates the company:* diffuse, fill, imbue, impregnate, infiltrate, penetrate, pervade, spread through **2** *water permeating through the rock:* filter through, impregnate, pass through, penetrate, percolate, saturate, seep through, soak through, spread through

permissible *adj* acceptable, admissible, all right, allowable, allowed, authorized, kosher *colloq*, lawful, legal, legitimate, OK *colloq*, permitted, proper, sanctioned, tolerable
▣ banned, forbidden, prohibited

permission *n* agreement, allowance, approbation *formal*, approval, assent, authorization, clearance, consent, dispensation, freedom, go-ahead, green light *colloq*, leave, liberty, licence, permit, sanction, thumbs up *colloq*, warrant
▣ prohibition

permissive *adj* broad-minded, easy-going *colloq*, forbearing, free, indulgent, latitudinarian *formal*, lax, lenient, liberal, overindulgent, tolerant
▣ narrow-minded, rigid, strict

permit *v* admit, agree, allow, authorize, consent, empower, enable, give the go-ahead to *colloq*, give the green light to *colloq*, give the nod to *colloq*, give the thumbs up to *colloq*, grant, let, license, sanction, warrant

▣ forbid, prohibit
◆ *n* authorization, licence, pass, passport, permission, sanction, visa, warrant
▣ prohibition

permutation *n* alteration, change, commutation *formal*, configuration *formal*, shift, transformation, transmutation *formal*, transposition *formal*, variation

pernicious *adj* bad, damaging, dangerous, deadly, deleterious *formal*, destructive, detrimental, evil, fatal, harmful, hurtful, injurious, maleficent *formal*, malevolent *formal*, malicious, malignant, noisome *formal*, noxious *formal*, offensive, pestilent, poisonous, ruinous, toxic, unhealthy, unwholesome, venomous, wicked
▣ innocuous

pernickety *adj* careful, carping, choosy *colloq*, detailed, exacting, fastidious, fiddly, fine, finical, finicky, fussy, hair-splitting *colloq*, nice, nit-picking *colloq*, over-particular, over-precise, painstaking, particular, picky *colloq*, punctilious, tricky

peroration *n* **1** *the lawyer began his peroration:* closing remarks, conclusion, recapitulation, recapping *colloq*, reiteration, summary, summing-up **2** *his lengthy and tiresome perorations:* address, declamation *formal*, diatribe *formal*, lecture, oration *formal*, speech, talk

perpendicular *adj* **1** *perpendicular to the wall:* at right angles, plumb, straight, upright, vertical **2** *perpendicular cliffs:* precipitous, sheer, steep
▣ **1** horizontal

perpetrate *v* be responsible for, be to blame for, carry out, commit, do, effect *formal*, effectuate *formal*, execute, inflict, perform, wreak

perpetual *adj* **1** *a cave in perpetual darkness:* abiding, endless, enduring, eternal, everlasting, infinite, lasting, never-ending, perennial, permanent, unchanging, undying, unending, unfailing **2** *his perpetual complaints:* ceaseless, constant, continual, continuous, endless, incessant, interminable, never-ending, perennial, persistent, recurrent, repeated, unceasing, unremitting
▣ **1** ephemeral *formal*, temporary, transient *formal* **2** momentary, short-lived

perpetually *adv* ceaselessly, constantly, continually, endlessly, eternally, incessantly, interminably, permanently, persistently, unceasingly, unremittingly

perpetuate *v* commemorate, continue, eternalize, immortalize, keep alive, keep going, keep up, maintain, memorialize, preserve, sustain

perpetuity *n* all time, always, eternity, evermore, forever

perplex *v* baffle, bamboozle *colloq*, bewilder, confound, confuse, dumbfound, muddle, mystify, nonplus *colloq*, puzzle, stump

perplexed *adj* at a loss, baffled, bamboozled *colloq*, bewildered, confounded, confused, disconcerted, fuddled, muddled, mystified, nonplussed *colloq*, puzzled, stumped, worried

perplexing *adj* amazing, baffling, bewildering, complex, complicated, confusing, difficult, enigmatic, hard, inexplicable, intricate, involved, knotty, labyrinthine *formal*, mysterious, mystifying, paradoxical, puzzling, strange, taxing, thorny, weird

 easy, simple

perplexity *n* 1 *in perplexity:* bafflement, bewilderment, confusion, incomprehension, mystification, nonplus, puzzlement 2 *the perplexities of physics:* complexity, complication, difficulty, dilemma, enigma, intricacy, involvement, labyrinth, mystery, obfuscation *formal*, obscurity, paradox, puzzle

perquisite *n* advantage, baksheesh, benefit, bonus, dividend, extra, freebie *colloq*, fringe benefit, gratuity, perk, plus, tip

persecute *v* 1 *persecuted for their religious beliefs:* abuse, afflict, crucify, distress, ill-treat, maltreat, martyr, mistreat, oppress, torment, torture, tyrannize, victimize 2 *persecuted by cold-calling salesmen:* annoy, badger, bother, harass, hassle *colloq*, hound, hunt, molest, pester, pursue, worry

 1 pamper, spoil

persecution *n* abuse, crucifixion, discrimination, harassment, ill-treatment, maltreatment, martyrdom, mistreatment, molestation, oppression, punishment, subjugation *formal*, suppression, torture, tyranny, victimization

perseverance *n* application, assiduity, commitment, constancy, dedication, determination, diligence, doggedness, endurance, indefatigability, intransigence *formal*, persistence, pertinacity *formal*, purpose, purposefulness, resolution, resolve, stamina, steadfastness, stickability *colloq*, tenacity

persevere *v* be determined, be persistent, be resolute, carry on, continue, go on, go the whole distance *colloq*, hang in there *colloq*, hang on, hold on, keep going, leave no stone unturned *colloq*, mean business *colloq*, persist, plug away *colloq*, remain, soldier on, stand fast, stand firm, stick at it *colloq*, stick to your guns *colloq*, struggle on

 discontinue *formal*, give up, stop

persist *v* 1 *we shall persist:* be determined, be persistent, be resolute, carry on, continue, go on, hang on, hold on, insist, keep at it, keep going, keep on, persevere, plug away *colloq*, soldier on, stand fast, stand firm, stick at it *colloq* 2 *his symptoms persisted:* abide *formal*, continue, endure, hold, keep on, last, linger, remain

 1 desist *formal*, give up, stop

persistence *n* assiduity, assiduousness, constancy, determination, diligence, doggedness, endurance, grit *colloq*, indefatigability, perseverance, pertinacity *formal*, resolution, sedulity *formal*, stamina, steadfastness, stickability *colloq*, tenacity, tirelessness

persistent *adj* 1 *persistent rain:* ceaseless, constant, continual, continuous, endless, enduring, incessant, interminable, lasting, never-ending, perpetual, relentless, repeated, steady, unceasing, unrelenting, unremitting 2 *persistent effort:* assiduous, determined, diligent, dogged, indefatigable, intractable *formal*, obdurate *formal*, obstinate, persevering, pertinacious *formal*, purposeful, resolute, steadfast, stubborn, tenacious, tireless, unflagging, zealous

person *n* being, body, character, human, human being, individual, man, mortal, somebody, someone, soul, type, woman

persona *n* character, façade, face, front, image, mask, part, personality, public face, role

personable *adj* affable, agreeable, amiable, attractive, charming, good-looking, handsome, likeable, nice, outgoing, pleasant, pleasing, presentable, warm, winning

 disagreeable, unattractive, unpleasant

personage *n* big noise *colloq*, big shot *colloq*, bigwig *colloq*, celebrity, dignitary, headliner, luminary, name, notable, personality, public figure, somebody *colloq*, VIP *colloq*, worthy

personal *adj* 1 *give you my personal attention:* exclusive, in person, individual, particular, special 2 *your personal style:* characteristic, distinctive, idiosyncratic, individual, own, peculiar, subjective, unique 3 *her personal life:* confidential, intimate, private, secret 4 *personal remarks:* abusive, critical, disrespectful, hurtful, insulting, offensive, rude, upsetting, wounding

 2 general, universal 3 official, public

personality *n* 1 *his friendly personality:* character, disposition, individuality, make-up, nature, psyche, temper, temperament, traits 2 *a woman of great personality:* character, charisma, charm, magnetism 3 *we spotted several television personalities:* celebrity, dignitary, notable, personage, public figure, star, VIP *colloq*, worthy

personally *adv* 1 *this interests me personally:* individually, specially, subjectively 2 *she will respond personally:* alone, by yourself, in person, independently, solely 3 *take something personally:* as hurtful comments, as personal criticism, directed against you, insultingly, offensively

personification *n* delineation *formal*, embodiment, essence, image, incarnation, likeness, manifestation *formal*, portrayal, quintessence *formal*, recreation, representation, semblance

personify *v* be the incarnation of, embody, epitomize, exemplify, mirror, represent, symbolize, typify

personnel *n* crew, employees, human resources, labour force, liveware *colloq*, manpower, members, people, staff, workers, workforce

perspective *n* 1 *a panoramic perspective:* angle, aspect, prospect, scene, vantage point, view, viewpoint, vista 2 *a new perspective on life:* attitude, frame of mind, outlook, point of view, slant, standpoint 3 *get things into perspective:* equilibrium, proportion, relation

perspicacious *adj* alert, astute, aware, discerning, discriminating, judicious *formal*, keen, observant, penetrating, perceptive, percipient *formal*, quick, quick-witted, responsive, sagacious *formal*, sensitive, sharp, sharp-eyed, shrewd, understanding

 obtuse, unobservant

perspicacity *n* acumen, acuteness, astuteness, brains *colloq*, cleverness, discernment, discrimination, insight, keenness, penetration, perceptiveness, percipience *formal*, perspicaciousness *formal*, perspicuity *formal*, sagaciousness *formal*, sagacity *formal*, sharpness, shrewdness, wit

perspicuity *n* clarity, clearness, comprehensibility, comprehensibleness, distinctness, explicitness, intelligibility, limpidity *formal*, limpidness *formal*, lucidity, penetrability, plainness, precision, straightforwardness, transparency

perspicuous *adj* apparent, clear, comprehensible, crystal-clear, distinct, explicit, intelligible, limpid *formal*, lucid, manifest *formal*, obvious, plain, self-evident, straightforward, transparent, unambiguous, understandable

perspiration *n* diaphoresis, exudation *formal*, hidrosis, moisture, secretion, sudor *technical*, sweat, wetness

perspire *v* drip, exude *formal*, secrete, sudate *technical*, sweat, swelter

persuadable *adj* acquiescent *formal*, agreeable, amenable, compliant *formal*, flexible, impressionable, malleable, persuasible, pliable, receptive, susceptive
🖅 firm, inflexible, stubborn

persuade *v* bring round, cajole, coax, coerce, convert, convince, incite, induce, influence, inveigle *formal*, lead on, lean on *colloq*, lobby, lure, prevail upon, prompt, pull strings *colloq*, put the screws on *colloq*, satisfy, soft-soap *colloq*, sway, sweet-talk *colloq*, swing it *colloq*, talk into, tempt, twist someone's arm *colloq*, urge, wheedle, win over
🖅 deter, discourage, dissuade, put off, talk out of

persuasion *n* 1 *my powers of persuasion:* arm-twisting *colloq*, cajolery, clout *colloq*, coaxing, coercion, conversion, conviction, enticement, incitement, inducement, influence, power, prevailing, prompting, pull, sway, sweet-talking *colloq*, talking into, urging, wheedling, winning over 2 *a different political persuasion:* affiliation, belief, camp, conviction, denomination, faction, faith, opinion, party, philosophy, point of view, school (of thought), sect, side, view, viewpoint

persuasive *adj* cogent *formal*, compelling, convincing, effective, effectual *formal*, forceful, influential, moving, plausible, potent, pushy *colloq*, slick, smooth-talking *colloq*, sound, telling, touching, valid, weighty
🖅 unconvincing

pert *adj* bold, brash, brisk, cheeky, cocky *colloq*, daring, flippant, forward, fresh, gay, impertinent, impudent, insolent, jaunty, lively, perky *colloq*, presumptuous, saucy *colloq*, spirited, sprightly
🖅 coy, shy

pertain *v* appertain *formal*, apply, be appropriate, be part of, be relevant, bear on, befit, belong, come under, concern, have a bearing on, refer, regard, relate

pertinent *adj* ad rem *formal*, applicable, apposite, appropriate, apropos *formal*, apt, fitting, germane *formal*, material, relevant, suitable, to the point
🖅 inappropriate, irrelevant, unsuitable

pertness *n* audacity, boldness, brashness, brass *colloq*, brazenness, cheek, cheekiness, chutzpah

colloq, cockiness *colloq*, effrontery, face *colloq*, forwardness, freshness, impertinence, impudence, insolence, presumption, rudeness, sauciness *colloq*

perturb *v* agitate, alarm, bother, confuse, discompose, disconcert, disquiet, disturb, fluster, make anxious, ruffle, trouble, unsettle, upset, vex, worry
🖅 compose, reassure

perturbed *adj* agitated, alarmed, anxious, discomposed, disconcerted, disturbed, fearful, flurried, flustered, harassed, nervous, restless, shaken, troubled, uncomfortable, uneasy, unsettled, upset, worried
🖅 calm, composed

perusal *n* browse, check, examination, glance, inspection, look, read, run-through, scrutiny, skim, study

peruse *v* browse, check, examine, glance through, inspect, leaf through, look through, pore over, read, run through, scan, scrutinize, skim, study

pervade *v* affect, be disseminated through, charge, diffuse, fill, imbue, impregnate, infiltrate, infuse, pass through, penetrate, percolate, permeate, saturate, spread through, suffuse

pervasive *adj* common, diffuse, extensive, general, immanent *formal*, inescapable, omnipresent *formal*, prevalent, rife, ubiquitous, universal, widespread

perverse *adj* awkward, bloody-minded *colloq*, bolshie *colloq*, cantankerous, contrary, deviant, difficult, disobedient, headstrong, ill-tempered, improper, incorrect, intractable *formal*, intransigent *formal*, nit-picking *colloq*, obdurate *formal*, obstinate, pig-headed *colloq*, rebellious, refractory *formal*, senseless, stroppy *colloq*, stubborn, troublesome, uncontrollable, unmanageable, unreasonable, unruly, unyielding, wayward, wilful, wrong-headed
🖅 co-operative, obliging, reasonable

perversion *n* 1 *sexual perversion:* abnormality, corruption, debauchery, depravity, deviance, immorality, irregularity, kinkiness *colloq*, vice, wickedness 2 *a perversion of our ideology:* aberration *formal*, deviation, distortion, falsification, misapplication, misinterpretation, misrepresentation, misuse, travesty, twisting

perversity *n* awkwardness, contradictoriness, contrariness, contumacy *formal*, disobedience, frowardness, gee, intransigence *formal*, obduracy *formal*, obstinacy, rebelliousness, refractoriness *formal*, senselessness, stubbornness, troublesomeness, uncontrollability, unreasonableness, unruliness, waywardness, wilfulness, wrong-headedness

pervert *v* 1 *pervert the truth:* avert, deflect, distort, falsify, garble, misdirect, misinterpret, misrepresent, turn aside, twist, warp 2 *perverting the nation's youth:* abuse, corrupt, debase, debauch, degrade, deprave, lead astray, misapply, misuse, vitiate *formal*, warp
♦ *n* debauchee, degenerate, deviant, deviate, oddball *colloq*, perv *colloq*, weirdo *colloq*

perverted *adj* abnormal, corrupt, corrupted, debased, debauched, depraved, deviant, distorted, evil, immoral, kinky *colloq*, twisted,

unhealthy, unnatural, vitiated *formal*, warped, wicked
☒ natural, normal

pessimism *n* cynicism, defeatism, dejection, depression, despair, despondency, distrust, doomwatch, fatalism, gloom, gloominess, glumness, hopelessness, looking on the black side *colloq*, melancholy, negative thinking, Weltschmerz
☒ hopefulness, optimism

pessimist *n* alarmist, cynic, defeatist, dismal Jimmy *colloq*, doomster, doomwatcher, doubter, doubting Thomas, fatalist, gloom and doom merchant *colloq*, gloom-monger, killjoy *colloq*, melancholic, no-hoper *colloq*, prophet of doom, wet blanket *colloq*, worrier
☒ hopeful, optimist

pessimistic *adj* alarmist, bleak, cynical, defeatist, dejected, depressed, depressing, despairing, despondent, discouraging, dismal, distrustful, doubting, downhearted, fatalistic, gloomy, glum, hopeless, looking on the black side *colloq*, melancholy, morose, negative, off-putting, resigned, suspicious
☒ optimistic

pest *n* annoyance, bane, blight, bother, bug, curse, irritant, irritation, nuisance, pain *colloq*, pain in the neck *colloq*, scourge, thorn in the flesh *colloq*, trial, vexation

pester *v* annoy, badger, bother, disturb, drive round the bend *colloq*, drive up the wall *colloq*, fret, get at *colloq*, get on someone's nerves *colloq*, harass, hassle *colloq*, hound, irk, irritate, nag, pick on, plague, provoke, torment, worry

pestilence *n* cholera, contagion, disease, epidemic, infection, infestation, pandemic *formal*, plague, sickness

pestilent *adj* **1** *pestilent diseases*: catching, communicable, contagious, contaminated, corrupting, deleterious *formal*, destructive, detrimental, diseased, disease-ridden, harmful, infected, infectious, pernicious, plague-ridden, poisonous, ruinous **2** *pestilent spam e-mails*: annoying, bothersome, infuriating, irksome, irritating, tiresome, troublesome, vexing

pestilential *adj* annoying, bothersome, infuriating, irksome, irritating, pernicious, tiresome, troublesome, vexing

pet¹ *n* apple of your eye *colloq*, blue-eyed boy/girl *colloq*, darling, favourite, idol, jewel, teacher's pet *colloq*, treasure
♦ *adj* cherished, chosen, dear, dearest, favoured, favourite, particular, personal, preferred, prized, special
♦ *v* canoodle *colloq*, caress, cuddle, embrace, fondle, kiss, neck *colloq*, smooch *colloq*, snog *slang*, stroke

pet² *n* bad mood, bad temper, grumps *colloq*, huff *colloq*, hump *colloq*, paddy *colloq*, stew *colloq*, sulk(s), tantrum, temper, the pits *colloq*

peter
▶ **peter out** cease, come to an end, come to nothing, die away, diminish, dwindle, ebb, evaporate, fade, fail, fizzle out *colloq*, stop, taper off, wane

petite *adj* bijou, dainty, delicate, dinky, little, slight, small
☒ big, large

petition *n* **1** *a petition of over 5000 signatures*: appeal, list of signatures, protest, round robin **2** *a petition to the Almighty*: appeal, application, entreaty, invocation *formal*, plea, prayer, request, solicitation, supplication
♦ *v* adjure *formal*, appeal, ask, beg, beseech, bid, call upon, crave, entreat, implore, plead, pray, press, request, solicit, sue *formal*, supplicate *formal*, urge

pet name *n* diminutive, endearment, hypocorisma *formal*, nickname, term of endearment

petrified *adj* aghast, appalled, benumbed, dazed, dumbfounded, frozen, horrified, horror-stricken, numb, scared stiff, shocked, speechless, stunned, stupefied, terrified, terror-stricken, transfixed

petrify *v* **1** *his outburst petrified her*: alarm, appal, dumbfound, frighten, horrify, numb, panic, paralyse, stun, stupefy, terrify **2** *petrified into a mineral*: fossilize, ossify, turn to stone

pettish *adj* bad-tempered, cross, fractious, fretful, grumpy, huffy *colloq*, ill-humoured, irritable, peevish, petulant, querulous, snappish, splenetic *formal*, sulky, tetchy, thin-skinned, touchy *colloq*, waspish

petty *adj* **1** *arguments over petty matters*: inconsequential, inconsiderable, inessential, insignificant, lesser, little, measly *colloq*, minor, negligible, no great shakes *colloq*, paltry, piddling *colloq*, piffling *colloq*, secondary, slight, small, trifling, trivial, unimportant **2** *her attitude is rather petty*: grudging, mean, narrow-minded, small-minded, spiteful, ungenerous
☒ **1** important, significant **2** generous

petulance *n* bad temper, crabbedness *colloq*, crabbiness *colloq*, ill-humour, ill-temper, irritability, peevishness, pique, procacity *formal*, querulousness *formal*, spleen *formal*, sulkiness, sullenness, waspishness

petulant *adj* bad-tempered, browned off *colloq*, complaining, crabbed *colloq*, crabby *colloq*, cross, crotchety *colloq*, fretful, ill-humoured, impatient, in a paddy *colloq*, in a stew *colloq*, irritable, moody, peevish, querulous *formal*, ratty *colloq*, snappish, sour, sulky, sullen, touchy *colloq*, ungracious

phantom *n* apparition, figment, ghost, hallucination, illusion, revenant *formal*, spectre, spirit, spook *colloq*, vision, wraith

pharisaical *adj* goody-goody *colloq*, holier-than-thou, hypocritical, insincere, moralizing, pietistic, preachy, sanctimonious, self-righteous

Pharisee *n* dissembler *formal*, dissimulator *formal*, fraud, humbug *colloq*, hypocrite, phoney *colloq*, pietist, whited sepulchre

phase *n* aspect, chapter, condition, form, juncture, part, period, point, position, season, shape, spell, stage, state, step, time
▶ **phase in** bring in, ease in, initiate, introduce, start, start using
▶ **phase out** close, dispose of, ease off, eliminate, get rid of, remove, run down, stop, stop using, taper off, terminate *formal*, wind down, wind up, withdraw

phenomenal *adj* amazing, astonishing, astounding, breath-taking, exceptional, extraordinary, fantastic, incredible, marvellous, mind-blowing *colloq*, mind-boggling *colloq*, remarkable, sensational, singular, stupendous, too good to be true *colloq*, unbelievable, unheard of, unique, unparalleled, unprecedented, unusual, wonderful

phenomenon *n* **1** *scientific explanations of these phenomena*: appearance, circumstance, episode, event, experience, fact, happening, incident, occurrence, sight **2** *she was briefly a worldwide phenomenon*: curiosity, marvel, miracle, prodigy, rarity, sensation, spectacle, wonder

philander *v* dally, flirt, have an affair, play/fool around, sleep around *colloq*, womanize

philanderer *n* Casanova, dallier, Don Juan, flirt, ladies' man, lady-killer *colloq*, libertine, playboy, stud *colloq*, wolf *colloq*, womanizer

philanthropic *adj* alms-giving, altruistic, benevolent, bounteous *formal*, bountiful *formal*, charitable, generous, humane, humanitarian, kind, kind-hearted, liberal, munificent *formal*, open-handed, public-spirited, selfless, unselfish
🗲 misanthropic

philanthropist *n* alms-giver, altruist, backer, benefactor, contributor, donor, giver, helper, humanitarian, patron, sponsor
🗲 misanthrope

philanthropy *n* alms-giving, altruism, backing, beneficence *formal*, benevolence, bounteousness *formal*, bountifulness *formal*, charity, generosity, giving, help, humanitarianism, kind-heartedness, liberality, munificence *formal*, open-handedness, patronage, public-spiritedness, selflessness, social concern/awareness, social conscience, sponsorship, unselfishness
🗲 misanthropy

philippic *n* abuse, attack, criticism, denunciation, diatribe, harangue, insult, invective *formal*, onslaught, rebuke, reprimand, reproof, reviling, tirade, upbraiding, vituperation *formal*

philistine *n* barbarian, boor *colloq*, bourgeois, ignoramus, lout *colloq*, lowbrow, vulgarian, yahoo
♦ *adj* boorish, bourgeois, crass, ignorant, lowbrow, tasteless, uncultivated, uncultured, uneducated, unlettered, unread, unrefined

philosopher *n* analyser, deipnosophist *formal*, dialectician, epistemologist *technical*, expert, guru, logician, metaphysicist, philosophizer, sage, scholar, theorist, theorizer, thinker

philosophical *adj* **1** *a philosophical discussion*: abstract, analytical, contemplative, erudite, learned, logical, meditative, metaphysical, pensive, rational, reflective, theoretical, thoughtful, wise **2** *he was philosophical about the defeat*: calm, collected, composed, cool, dispassionate, imperturbable *formal*, logical, patient, phlegmatic *formal*, rational, realistic, resigned, self-possessed, stoic, stoical, unruffled

philosophy *n* **1** *study philosophy*: knowledge, reason, thinking, thought, wisdom **2** *her philosophy of non-violence*: attitude, beliefs, convictions, doctrine, ideology, point of view, principles, tenets, values, view, viewpoint, world-view

Philosophical terms include:
absolutism, aesthetics, agnosticism, altruism, antinomianism, a posteriori, a priori, ascetism, atheism, atomism, behaviourism, deduction, deism, deontology, determinism, dialectical materialism, dogmatism, dualism, egoism, empiricism, entailment, Epicureanism, epistemology, ethics, existentialism, fatalism, hedonism, historicism, humanism, idealism, identity, induction, instrumentalism, interactionism, intuition, jurisprudence, libertarianism, logic, logical positivism, materialism, metaphysics, monism, naturalism, nihilism, nominalism, objectivism, ontology, pantheism, phenomenalism, phenomenology, positivism, pragmatism, prescriptivism, rationalism, realism, reductionism, relativism, scepticism, scholasticism, sensationalism, sense data, solipsism, stoicism, structuralism, subjectivism, substance, syllogism, teleology, theism, transcendentalism, utilitarianism

phlegmatic *adj* calm, cool, cool and collected *colloq*, dispassionate, impassive, imperturbable *formal*, indifferent, matter-of-fact, placid, stoical, stolid, tranquil, unconcerned, unemotional
🗲 emotional, nervous, passionate

phobia *n* antipathy *formal*, anxiety, aversion, detestation *formal*, dislike, dread, fear, hang-up *colloq*, hatred, horror, irrational fear, loathing, neurosis, obsession, repulsion, revulsion, terror, thing *colloq*
🗲 liking, love

phone *n* **1** *I'm on the phone*: blower *colloq*, car phone, handset, mobile (phone), receiver, telephone **2** *give me a quick phone*: bell *colloq*, buzz *colloq*, call, phone call, ring, tinkle *colloq*
♦ *v* call (up), contact, dial, get in touch, give a bell *colloq*, give a buzz *colloq*, give a tinkle *colloq*, give someone a call, make a call, ring (up), telephone

phoney *adj* affected, assumed, bogus, contrived, counterfeit, ersatz, fake, false, feigned, forged, fraudulent, imitation, mock, pseudo *colloq*, put-on, sham, simulated, spurious, trick
🗲 genuine, real
♦ *n* fake, faker, fraud, humbug *colloq*, impostor, mountebank, pretender, pseud *colloq*, quack *colloq*

phosphorescent *adj* bright, glowing, luminescent, luminous, noctilucent *technical*, noctilucous, radiant, refulgent *formal*

photograph *n* image, likeness, mug shot *colloq*, photo, picture, print, shot, slide, snap, snapshot, still, transparency
♦ *v* capture on film, record, shoot, snap, take, take a photograph of, take a picture of, take a snapshot of

photographic *adj* **1** *photographic equipment*: cinematic, filmic, graphic, pictorial **2** *photographic memory*: accurate, detailed, exact, faithful, lifelike, minute, natural, naturalistic, precise, realistic, representational, retentive, visual, vivid

Photographic equipment includes:
camera, boom arm, flash umbrella, stand, tripod; developer bath, developing tank, dry mounting press, easel, enlarger, enlarger

timer, film-drying cabinet, fixing bath, focus magnifier, light-box, negative carrier, print washer, contact printer, print-drying rack, paper drier, safelight, stop bath, Vertoscope®, viewer; slide viewer, slide projector, film projector, screen

Photographic accessories include:
air-shutter release, battery, cable release, camera bag, eye-cup, eyepiece magnifier, film, cartridge film, cassette film, disc film, film pack, filter, colour filter, heat filter, polarizing filter, skylight filter, flashbulb, flashcube, flashgun, flash unit, hot shoe, lens, afocal lens, auxiliary lens, close-up lens, fish-eye lens, macro lens, supplementary lens, telephoto lens, teleconverter, wide-angle lens, zoom lens, lens cap, lens hood, lens shield, light meter, exposure meter, spot meter, diffuser, barn doors, honeycomb diffuser, parabolic reflector, snoot, slide mount, viewfinder, right-angle finder; camcorder battery discharger/charger/tester, cassette adaptor, remote control, tele-cine converter, video editor, video light, video mixer. See also **camera**

phrase *n* clause, comment, construction, expression, group of words, idiom, language, phraseology, remark, saying, usage, utterance, way/style of speaking
♦ *v* couch, express, formulate, frame, present, pronounce, put, say, utter, word

phraseology *n* argot, cant, diction, expression, idiom, language, parlance, patois, phrase, phrasing, speech, style, syntax, terminology, wording, writing

physical *adj* **1** *the physical world:* bodily, carnal, corporeal, earthly, fleshly, fleshy, incarnate, mortal, somatic *formal*, unspiritual **2** *a lack of physical evidence:* actual, concrete, material, palpable, real, solid, substantial, tangible, visible ▰ **1** mental, spiritual **2** abstract, theoretical

physician *n* consultant, doc *colloq*, doctor, general practitioner, GP, healer, houseman, intern, medic *colloq*, medical practitioner, medico *colloq*, quack *colloq*, registrar, specialist

physics

Terms used in physics include:
absolute zero, acceleration, acoustics, alpha particles, analogue signal, applied physics, Archimedes principle, area, atom, beta particles, Big Bang theory, boiling point, bubble-chamber, capillary action, centre of gravity, centre of mass, centrifugal force, chain reaction, charge, charged particle, circuit, circuit-breaker, couple, critical mass, cryogenics, density, diffraction, digital, dynamics, efficiency, elasticity, electric current, electric discharge, electricity, electrodynamics, electromagnetic spectrum, electromagnetic waves, electron, energy, engine, entropy, equation, equilibrium, evaporation, field, flash point, force, formula, freezing point, frequency, friction, fundamental constant, gamma ray, gas, gate, grand united theory (GUT), gravity, half-life, heat, heavy water, hydraulics, hydrodynamics, hydrostatics, incandescence,

indeterminacy principle, inertia, infrared, interference, ion, Kelvin effect, kinetic energy, kinetic theory, laser (light amplification by stimulated emission of radiation), latent heat, law, laws of motion, laws of reflection, laws of refraction, laws of thermodynamics, lens, lever, light, light emission, light intensity, light source, liquid, longitudinal wave, luminescence, Mach number, magnetic field, magnetism, mass, mechanics, microwaves, mirror, Mohs scale, molecule, moment, momentum, motion, neutron, nuclear, nuclear fission, nuclear fusion, nuclear physics, nucleus, optical centre, optics, oscillation, parallel motion, particle, periodic law, perpetual motion, phonon, photon, photosensitivity, polarity, potential energy, power, pressure, principle, process, proton, quantum chromodynamics (QCD), quantum electrodynamics (QED), quantum mechanics, quantum theory, quark, radiation, radioactive element, radioactivity, radioisotope, radio wave, ratio, reflection, refraction, relativity, resistance, resonance, rule, semiconductor, sensitivity, separation, SI unit, sound, sound wave, specific gravity, specific heat capacity, spectroscopy, spectrum, speed, states of matter, statics, substance, superstring theory, supersymmetry, surface tension, temperature, tension, theory, theory of relativity, thermodynamics, Thomson effect, transverse wave, ultrasound, ultraviolet, uncertainty principle, velocity, visible spectrum, viscosity, volume, wave, wave property, weight, white heat, work, X-ray. See also **electricity**

physiognomy *n* clock *colloq*, countenance *formal*, dial *colloq*, face, features, kisser *colloq*, look, mug *colloq*, phiz *colloq*, phizog *colloq*, visage *formal*, visnomy *old use*

physique *n* body, build, constitution, figure, form, frame, make-up, shape, structure

pick *v* **1** *he picked two people to help him:* choose, decide on, favour, fix on, go for, make up your mind, opt for, plump for *colloq*, prefer, select, settle on, single out **2** *to pick fruit:* collect, cull, gather, harvest, pluck, pull, take in **3** *pick a lock/safe:* break open, crack, force open, open, prise open **4** *pick a quarrel:* begin, cause, give rise to, lead to, produce, prompt, provoke, start
♦ *n* **1** *we had the pick of the clothes on sale:* choice, decision, favour, option, preference, selection **2** *the pick of the nation's young athletes:* best, choicest, cream, crème de la crème, elect, elite, flower, prize
▶ **pick at** eat small amounts of, nibble, peck, play with, toy with
▶ **pick off** fire at, hit, kill, remove, shoot, strike, take out
▶ **pick on** bait, blame, bully, criticize, find fault with, get at *colloq*, nag, needle *colloq*, persecute, torment
▶ **pick out** choose, discern, discriminate, distinguish, hand-pick, make out, notice, perceive, recognize, select, separate, single out, spot, tell apart
▶ **pick up 1** *she picked up the box:* hoist, lift, raise, take up **2** *I'll pick you up at eight:* call for, collect, fetch, give a lift/ride **3** *I picked up some Spanish:* acquire, gather, get to know, grasp, learn, master

4 *the economy should pick up:* get better, improve, make headway, make progress, perk up *colloq*, rally, recover **5** *police picked him up:* apprehend, arrest, collar *colloq*, nab *colloq*, nick *colloq*, run in *colloq*, take in *colloq*, take into custody **6** *pick up where we left off:* begin again, carry on, continue, go on, resume, start again **7** *pick up a bargain:* acquire, buy, chance upon *formal*, come across, discover, find, gain, hear, learn, obtain, purchase **8** *pick up an infection:* become ill with, become infected with, catch, contract, get, go down with **9** *pick up a radio signal:* detect, get, hear, receive

picket *n* **1** *police clashed with pickets:* demonstrator, dissident, objector, picketer, protester, rebel, striker **2** *the advance was spotted by pickets:* guard, lookout, outpost, patrol, sentry, watch **3** *an enclosure surrounded by pickets:* pale, paling, pike, post, spike, stake, stanchion, upright
♦ *v* blockade, boycott, demonstrate, enclose, go on a picket line, protest, surround

pickings *n* booty, earnings, gravy *slang*, loot, plunder, proceeds, profits, returns, rewards, spoils, take, yield

pickle *n* **1** *cheese and pickle:* chutney, condiment, flavouring, relish, sauce, seasoning, vinegar **2** *we're in a bit of a pickle:* bind *colloq*, crisis, difficulty, dilemma, exigency *formal*, fix *colloq*, hot water *colloq*, jam *colloq*, mess, pinch *colloq*, predicament, quandary, scrape *colloq*, spot *colloq*, straits, tight spot *colloq*
♦ *v* conserve, cure, marinade, preserve, salt, souse, steep

pick-me-up *n* boost, cordial, fillip, refreshment, restorative, roborant *technical*, shot in the arm *colloq*, stimulant, stimulus, tonic

pick-pocket *n* dip *colloq*, diver *colloq*, file *old use*, pick-purse, snatcher, thief, wire *colloq*

picnic *n* **1** *a picnic lunch:* excursion, fête champêtre, outdoor meal, outing, wayzgoose **2** *it's no picnic:* child's play *colloq*, cinch *colloq*, doddle *colloq*, piece of cake *colloq*, pushover *colloq*, simple task, walkover *colloq*

pictorial *adj* diagrammatic, expressive, graphic, illustrated, in photographs, in pictures, picturesque, representational, scenic, schematic, striking, vivid

picture *n* **1** *a clear picture of what we want to achieve:* account, delineation *formal*, depiction, description, impression, narrative, portrayal, report, semblance, similitude *formal*, story, tale **2** *the picture of health:* archetype *formal*, embodiment, epitome, essence, exemplar *formal*, personification, quintessence *formal* **3** *he's been in a number of pictures:* film, flick *colloq*, motion picture **4** *go to the pictures:* cinema, entertainment centre, film theatre, flicks *colloq*, movies, multiplex, picture-house, picture-palace
♦ *v* **1** *I can't picture that at all:* call to mind, conceive, envisage, envision, imagine, see, see in your mind's eye, visualize **2** *she is pictured holding a milk jug:* appear, delineate *formal*, depict, describe, draw, illustrate, paint, photograph, portray, represent, reproduce, show, sketch

---

Kinds of picture include:
abstract, cameo, canvas, caricature, cartoon, collage, design, doodle, drawing, effigy,

---

engraving, etching, fresco, graffiti, graphics, icon, identikit, illustration, image, kakemono, landscape, likeness, miniature, montage, mosaic, mug shot *colloq*, mural, negative, oil-painting, old master, painting, passport photo, Photofit®, photograph, photogravure, pin-up, plate, portrait, print, representation, reproduction, self-portrait, silhouette, sketch, slide, snap *colloq*, snapshot, still, still life, study, tableau, tapestry, tracing, transfer, transparency, triptych, trompe l'oeil, vignette, watercolour

picturesque *adj* **1** *a picturesque little village:* attractive, beautiful, charming, delightful, idyllic, lovely, pleasant, pleasing, pretty, quaint, scenic **2** *a picturesque name:* colourful, descriptive, graphic, impressive, striking, vivid
☒ **1** unattractive **2** boring, dull

piddling *adj* contemptible, derisory, inconsiderate, insignificant, low, meagre, mean, measly *colloq*, minor, miserable, negligible, paltry, petty, piffling *colloq*, poor, puny, slight, small, sorry, trifling, trivial, unimportant, worthless, wretched
☒ significant, substantial, valuable

pie *n* pastry, quiche, tart

piebald *adj* black and white, brindle(d), dappled, flecked, mottled, pied, skewbald, speckled, spotted, variegated

piece *n* **1** *a piece of land:* allocation, allotment, bar, bit, bite, block, chip, chunk, component, constituent, crumb, cut *colloq*, division, dollop, element, flake, fleck, fraction, fragment, hunk, length, lump, morsel, mouthful, offcut, part, percentage, portion, quantity, quota, sample, scrap, section, segment, share, shred, slab, slice, sliver, smithereen *colloq*, snippet, speck, splinter, tidbit *US*, titbit, unit, wedge **2** *he wrote a short piece on the subject:* article, composition, creation, example, illustration, instance, item, opus, report, review, specimen, story, study, work
▶ **piece together** assemble, attach, compose, fit, fix, join, mend, patch, put together, repair, restore, unite

pièce de résistance *n* chef-d'oeuvre, jewel, magnum opus, masterwork, masterpiece, prize, showpiece

piecemeal *adv* at intervals, bit by bit, by degrees, fitfully, in dribs and drabs *colloq*, intermittently, little by little, parcel-wise, partially, slowly
☒ completely, entirely, wholly
♦ *adj* discrete *formal*, fragmentary, intermittent, interrupted, partial, patchy, scattered, sporadic, unsystematic
☒ complete, entire, whole, wholesale

pied *adj* brindle(d), dappled, flecked, irregular, motley, mottled, multicoloured, parti-coloured, piebald, skewbald, spotted, streaked, varicoloured, variegated

pier *n* **1** *boats moored at the pier:* breakwater, dock, jetty, landing-stage, quay, wharf **2** *the piers of the jetty:* column, pile, pillar, post, support, upright

pierce *v* **1** *pierce the tomato's skin:* bayonet, bore, drill, enter, impale, lance, pass through, penetrate, perforate, prick, probe, punch, puncture, run through, skewer, spear, spike, stab, stick into, transfix **2** *pierce someone's spirit:* cut to the quick, hurt, move, pain, prick, stab, sting **3** *pierce the darkness:* burst through, enter, fill, light up, penetrate

pierced *adj* impaled, perforated, pertusate *formal*, pertuse(d) *formal*, punctured, stung

piercing *adj* **1** *a piercing cry:* ear-piercing, ear-splitting, high-pitched, keen, loud, penetrating, sharp, shrill **2** *a piercing intellect:* alert, astute, discerning, penetrating, perceptive, probing, searching, sharp, sharp-witted, shrewd **3** *a piercing wind:* Arctic, biting, bitter, cold, fierce, freezing, frosty, keen, numbing, raw, severe, wintry **4** *a piercing pain:* agonizing, excruciating, extreme, intense, lacerating, painful, severe, shooting, stabbing

piety *n* deference, devotion, devoutness, faith, godliness, holiness, piousness, religion, religiousness, respect, reverence, saintliness, sanctity, spirituality
⊟ impiety, irreligion

piffle *n* balderdash, balls *slang*, bullshit *slang*, bunk *colloq*, bunkum *colloq*, codswallop *colloq*, drivel, guff *colloq*, hooey *colloq*, nonsense, poppycock *colloq*, rot, rubbish, tarradiddle, tommy-rot *colloq*, tosh *colloq*, trash, tripe, twaddle *colloq*

pig *n* **1** *two pigs feeding on swill:* boar, grunter, hog, piggy *colloq*, piglet, sow, swine **2** *her ex-husband was a real pig:* beast, boor, brute, monster **3** *he made a real pig of himself at dinner:* glutton, gormandizer, gourmand, greedy guts *colloq*, guzzler *colloq*
♦ *v* gorge, guzzle, stuff, wolf *colloq*

pigeonhole *n* **1** *several letters in his pigeonhole:* box, compartment, cubbyhole, cubicle, locker, niche, place, section, slot **2** *she doesn't fit neatly into any pigeonhole:* category, class, classification, compartment
♦ *v* **1** *his music has already been pigeonholed by the media:* alphabetize, catalogue, categorize, classify, compartmentalize, file, label, slot, sort, tag **2** *let's pigeonhole the decision for a day or two:* defer, postpone, put off, put on the back burner *colloq*, shelve

pig-headed *adj* bull-headed, contrary, froward *old use*, headstrong, inflexible, intractable *formal*, intransigent *formal*, mulish, obstinate, perverse, self-willed, stiff-necked, stubborn, stupid, unyielding, wilful, wrong-headed
⊟ flexible, tractable

pigment *n* colour, colouring, dye, hue, paint, stain, tincture, tint

pile[1] *n* **1** *a pile of books:* accumulation, assemblage *formal*, assortment, bundle, collection, heap, hoard, mass, mound, mountain, stack, stockpile, store **2** *piles of work:* a great deal, a lot, heaps *colloq*, hundreds *colloq*, large quantity, lashings *colloq*, loads *colloq*, lots *colloq*, millions *colloq*, oodles *colloq*, quantities, stacks *colloq*, thousands *colloq*, tons *colloq* **3** *make a pile:* big bucks *slang*, bomb *colloq*, bundle *colloq*, fortune, megabucks *slang*, mint *colloq*, packet *colloq*, riches, wealth **4** *their country pile:* edifice, imposing/impressive building, large building
♦ *v* **1** *piling clothes into her suitcase:* accumulate, amass, assemble, build up, collect, gather, heap, hoard, load, mass, stack, stockpile, store **2** *they all*

piled into the lift: charge, crowd, crush, flock, flood, jam, pack, rush, squeeze, stream
▶ **pile up** accumulate, escalate, grow, increase, mount up, multiply, soar

pile[2] *n* bar, beam, column, foundation, piling, post, support, upright

pile[3] *n* down, fluff, fur, fuzz, hair, nap, plush, shag, (soft) surface, texture, wool

pile-up *n* accident, bump, collision, crash, prang *colloq*, smash *colloq*, smash-up *colloq*, wreck

pilfer *v* filch, have sticky fingers *colloq*, knock off *colloq*, lift *colloq*, nick *colloq*, nobble *colloq*, peculate *formal*, pinch *colloq*, purloin *formal*, rob, shoplift, snaffle *colloq*, snitch *colloq*, steal, swipe *colloq*, thieve

pilgrim *n* crusader, devotee, hadji, palmer, traveller, wanderer, wayfarer, worshipper

pilgrimage *n* crusade, expedition, hadj, journey, mission, tour, trip

pill *n* bolus, capsule, lozenge, pellet, tablet

pillage *v* depredate *formal*, despoil *formal*, freeboot, loot, maraud, plunder, raid, ransack, ravage, raze, rifle, rob, sack, spoil, spoliate *formal*, strip, vandalize
♦ *n* depredation *formal*, devastation, harrying, marauding, plunder, rapine *formal*, robbery, seizure, spoliation *formal*

pillar *n* **1** *six pillars supporting the roof:* cippus *technical*, column, mast, pier, pile, pole, post, prop, shaft, stanchion, support, upright **2** *a pillar of society:* bastion, mainstay, rock, support, tower of strength

pillory *v* brand, cast a slur on, denounce, hold up to shame, lash, laugh at, mock, pour scorn on, ridicule, show up, stigmatize

pillow *n* bed, bolster, cushion, headrest, rest

pilot *n* **1** *an RAF fighter pilot:* aircrew, airman, airwoman, aviator, captain, commander, crew, first officer, flight engineer, flyer **2** *a ship's pilot:* captain, coxswain, director, guide, helmsman, leader, navigator, steersman
♦ *v* conduct, control, direct, drive, fly, guide, handle, lead, manage, manoeuvre, navigate, operate, run, steer
♦ *adj* experimental, model, test, trial

pimp *n* fancy man, fleshmonger, go-between, hustler *slang*, mack *slang*, pander, panderer, procurer, solicitor, whoremonger

pimple *n* blackhead, boil, papula, papule, pustule, spot, swelling, zit *colloq*

pin *v* **1** *he pinned a notice to the wall:* affix, attach, clip, fasten, fix, join, nail, secure, staple, stick, tack **2** *the man was pinned to the ground by two officers:* constrain, hold down, hold fast, immobilize, press, restrain **3** *pin the blame on someone:* ascribe, attach, attribute, impute *formal*, lay, place, put
♦ *n* bolt, brooch, clip, dowel, fastener, nail, peg, rivet, screw, spike, staple, tack
▶ **pin down 1** *we need to pin down its location:* define, determine, identify, nail down *colloq*, pinpoint, put your finger on *colloq*, specify **2** *he's pinned down and unable to release the ball:* constrain, hold down, hold fast, nail down *colloq*, press, pressurize, restrain

pincers *n* forceps, forfex, tweezers

pinch *v* **1** *she pinched his leg*: compress, confine, cramp, crush, grasp, grip, hurt, nip, press, squeeze, tweak **2** *he pinched a bag of sweets*: appropriate *formal*, filch, knock off *colloq*, lift *colloq*, nick *colloq*, peculate *formal*, pilfer, purloin *formal*, snatch, steal, walk off with *colloq* **3** *we'll have to scrape and pinch if we want that TV*: budget, cut back, cut your coat according to your cloth *colloq*, economize, keep costs down, live on the cheap, save, scrape a living *colloq*, scrimp and save, tighten your belt *colloq* **4** *he was pinched coming out the station*: arrest, book *colloq*, bust *colloq*, capture, catch, collar *colloq*, detain, nab *colloq*, nail *colloq*, nick *colloq*, pick up *colloq*, run in *colloq*, seize
♦ *n* **1** *he gave her a playful pinch*: nip, squeeze, tweak **2** *a pinch of salt*: bit, dash, jot, mite, smidgen *colloq*, soupçon, speck, tad *colloq*, taste, touch, trace **3** *we're in something of a pinch*: crisis, difficulty, emergency, hardship, predicament, pressure, stress

pinched *adj* careworn, drawn, gaunt, haggard, narrowed, pale, peaky, starved, straightened, thin, worn

pine *v* **1** *pining for the fjords*: ache, crave, desire, hanker, hunger, long, sigh, thirst, wish, yearn **2** *pine away from grief*: fade, fret, grieve, languish, mourn, waste away, weaken

pinion *v* bind, chain, confine, fasten, fetter, hobble, immobilize, manacle, pin down, shackle, tie, truss

pink¹ *adj* flushed, reddish, rose, roseate, rosy, salmon
♦ *n* acme *formal*, best, extreme, flower, height, peak, perfection, summit, tiptop, top

pink² *v* crenellate, cut, incise, notch, perforate, prick, punch, scallop, score, serrate

pinnacle *n* **1** *the pinnacle of her career*: acme *formal*, apex, apogee *formal*, cap, crest, crown, culmination, eminence, height, peak, summit, top, vertex, zenith *formal* **2** *an ornamental pinnacle*: cone, needle, obelisk, pyramid, spire, steeple, turret

pinpoint *v* define, determine, discover, distinguish, home in on, identify, locate, nail down *colloq*, pin down, place, put your finger on *colloq*, specify, spot, zero in on *colloq*

pint-size *adj* diminutive, dwarf, little, midget, miniature, pint-sized, pocket, pocket-sized, small, tiny, wee *Scot*
◪ enormous, giant, huge

pioneer *n* **1** *pioneers of the American midwest*: colonist, explorer, frontiersman, frontierswoman, settler **2** *a pioneer in science*: developer, discoverer, founder, founding father, ground-breaker, innovator, inventor, leader, pathfinder, trail-blazer
♦ *v* begin, blaze a trail, break new ground, create, develop, discover, establish, found, initiate, instigate, institute, introduce, invent, launch, lead the way, make the first move, open up, originate, pave the way *colloq*, prepare the way for, set up, set/start the ball rolling *colloq*, spearhead, start

pious *adj* **1** *brought up in a pious household*: dedicated, devoted, devout, faithful, godly, good, holy, moral, religious, reverent, righteous, saintly, sanctified, spiritual, virtuous **2** *pious moralizing*: goody-goody *colloq*, holier-than-thou *colloq*, hypocritical, insincere, pi *colloq*, sanctimonious, self-righteous, unctuous
◪ **1** impious, irreligious, irreverent

pipe *n* **1** *a gas pipe*: channel, conduit, conveyor, cylinder, drainpipe, duct, flue, hose, line, main, overflow, passage, pipeline, piping, tube, tubing **2** *pipe and tobacco*: brier, calumet, clay, claypipe, dudeen, hookah, hubble-bubble, kalian, meerschaum, narghile, peace-pipe, water pipe
♦ *v* **1** *piping oil from the north sea*: bring, carry, channel, conduct, convey, deliver, duct, funnel, siphon, supply, take, transmit **2** *the blackbird piped its song*: cheep, chirp, chirrup, peep, play, shrill, sing, sound, trill, tweet, twitter, warble, whistle
▶ **pipe down** be quiet, shut up *colloq*, stop talking

pipe dream *n* castle in Spain *colloq*, castle in the air *colloq*, chimera *formal*, daydream, delusion, dream, fantasy, mirage, notion, pie in the sky *colloq*, reverie, romance, vagary *formal*

pipeline *n* channel, conduit, conveyor, duct, line, passage, pipe, tube

pipsqueak *n* creep *colloq*, hobbledehoy *colloq*, nobody, nonentity, nothing, squirt *colloq*, twerp *colloq*, upstart *colloq*, whippersnapper *colloq*
◪ somebody

piquancy *n* **1** *add some piquancy to this dish*: bite, flavour, ginger, pepperiness, pungency, relish, sharpness, spice, spiciness, tang **2** *the managers' feud added a piquancy to the match*: colour, edge *colloq*, excitement, interest, kick *colloq*, liveliness, pep *colloq*, pizzazz *colloq*, punch, raciness, spirit, vigour, vitality, zest, zip *colloq*

piquant *adj* **1** *piquant sauce*: biting, highly seasoned, peppery, pungent, salty, savoury, seasoned, sharp, spicy, stinging, tangy, tart, zesty **2** *a piquant irony*: colourful, fascinating, interesting, intriguing, juicy *colloq*, lively, provocative, racy, sharp, sparkling, spirited, stimulating
◪ **1** bland, insipid **2** banal, dull

pique *n* anger, annoyance, displeasure, gall, grudge, huff *colloq*, irritation, offence, resentment, umbrage, vexation
♦ *v* **1** *this piqued my interest*: arouse, excite, galvanize, goad, kindle, provoke, rouse, spur, stimulate, stir, whet **2** *I was piqued by her lack of interest*: affront, anger, annoy, displease, gall, get, incense, irk, irritate, miff *formal*, mortify, nettle *formal*, offend, peeve *formal*, put out, rile, sting, vex, wound

piqued *adj* angry, annoyed, displeased, irritated, miffed *colloq*, offended, peeved *colloq*, put out, resentful, riled, vexed

piracy *n* bootlegging, buccaneering, freebooting, hijacking, infringement, plagiarism, rapine *formal*, robbery, stealing, theft

pirate *n* **1** *pirates boarded our clipper*: brigand, buccaneer, corsair, filibuster, freebooter, marauder, marque, picaroon, raider, rover, sea rat, sea robber, sea rover, sea wolf, water rat **2** *pirates will be the death of the music industry*: infringer, plagiarist, plagiarizer
♦ *v* appropriate *formal*, borrow *colloq*, copy, crib *colloq*, lift *colloq*, nick *colloq*, pinch, plagiarize, poach, reproduce illegally, steal

pirouette n gyration, pivot, spin, turn, twirl, whirl
♦ v gyrate, pivot, spin, turn, twirl, whirl

pistol n dag, derringer US, gat colloq, gun, handgun, iron colloq, Luger®, piece colloq, revolver, rod colloq, sidearm, six-shooter

pit n 1 *dig a pit*: abyss, cavity, chasm, coalmine, crater, diggings, ditch, excavations, gulf, hole, mine, pothole, quarry, trench, workings 2 *shallow pits on his skin*: dent, depression, hollow, indentation, pockmark
♦ v blemish, dent, depress, dimple, indent, mark, notch, pockmark, pothole, scar
▶ **pit against** compete, match, oppose, set against

pitch¹ v 1 *he pitched the ball against the wall*: aim, bowl, cast, chuck colloq, direct, fire, fling, heave, hurl, launch, lob, sling, throw, toss 2 *she pitched into the sea*: dive, drop, fall, fall headlong, plummet, plunge, topple, tumble 3 *pitch camp*: erect, fix, place, plant, put up, set up, settle, station 4 *their vessel pitched alarmingly*: flounder, keel, list, lurch, move up and down, reel, roll, sway, wallow
♦ n 1 *cricket pitch*: arena, field, ground, park, playing-field, sports field, stadium 2 *her voice was at a high pitch*: frequency, level, modulation, sound, timbre, tonality, tone 3 *the steep pitch of the roof*: angle, cant, degree, gradient, inclination, incline, slant, slope, steepness, tilt 4 *reach a high pitch*: degree, extent, grade, height, intensity, level, mark, point, position 5 *his pitch went over my head*: chuck colloq, fling, hurl, lob, throw, toss 6 *my sales pitch*: chatter, gabble, jargon, line, patter, spiel colloq, talk, yak colloq
▶ **pitch in** be involved, co-operate, do your bit colloq, help, join in, lend a hand, muck in colloq, participate

pitch² n asphalt, bitumen, tar

pitch-black adj black, coal-black, dark, inky, jet-black, pitch-dark, unilluminated, unlit

pitcher n bottle, can, container, crock, ewer, jar, jug, urn, vessel

piteous adj distressing, heartbreaking, heart-rending, mournful, moving, pathetic, pitiable, pitiful, plaintive, poignant, sad, sorrowful, touching, woeful, wretched

┌─────────────────────────────────────┐
piteous, pitiable or *pitiful*? *Pitiful* means 'arousing or deserving pity': *She was a pitiful sight* ; and also 'so poor as to arouse contempt': *a pitiful attempt at catching the ball*. *Pitiable* means the same as *pitiful* but is less common: *He was in a pitiable condition*; *That was a pitiable attempt you made*. *Piteous* is a rather formal word meaning 'arousing or deserving pity': *She gave a piteous cry*.
└─────────────────────────────────────┘

pitfall n catch, danger, difficulty, drawback, hazard, peril, snag, snare, stumbling-block, trap

pith n consequence, core, crux, essence, essential part, forcefulness, gist, heart, import formal, importance, kernel, marrow, matter, meat, moment, nub, point, quintessence formal, salient point, significance, substance, value, vigour, weight

pithy adj brief, cogent formal, compact, concise, condensed, expressive, forceful, incisive,

meaningful, pointed, short, succinct, summary, telling, terse, trenchant formal
☒ verbose, wordy

pitiable adj contemptible, distressed, distressful, distressing, doleful, grievous, lamentable, miserable, mournful, pathetic colloq, poor, sad, sorry, woeful, woesome, wretched

┌─────────────────────────────────────┐
pitiable, piteous or *pitiful*? See panel at **piteous**
└─────────────────────────────────────┘

pitiful adj 1 *it was a really pitiful sight*: affecting, distressing, doleful, heart-breaking, heart-rending, miserable, mournful, moving, pathetic, piteous, pitiable, poor, sad, sorry, wretched 2 *a pitiful display by Wales*: base, contemptible, deplorable, despicable, hopeless, inadequate, insignificant, lamentable, low, meagre, mean, miserable, paltry, pathetic colloq, poor, shabby, vile, woeful, worthless

┌─────────────────────────────────────┐
pitiful, piteous or *pitiable*? See panel at **piteous**
└─────────────────────────────────────┘

pitiless adj brutal, callous, cold-blooded, cold-hearted, cruel, hard-hearted, harsh, heartless, inexorable, inhuman, inhumane, merciless, relentless, ruthless, severe, uncaring, unfeeling, unremitting, unsympathetic
☒ compassionate, gentle, kind, merciful

pittance n chickenfeed colloq, crumb, drop (in the ocean), modicum, peanuts slang, slave wages, trifle

pitted adj blemished, dented, depressed, holey, indented, marked, notched, pockmarked, potholed, rough, scarred

pity n 1 *he showed no pity to them*: commiseration, compassion, condolence, distress, emotion, feeling, fellow-feeling, forbearance formal, forgiveness, grace, kindness, mercy, regret, sadness, sorrow, sympathy, tenderness, understanding 2 *what a pity!*: bad luck, crying shame colloq, disappointment, misfortune, shame, unfortunate thing
☒ 1 anger, cruelty, scorn
♦ v be sympathetic towards, commiserate with, empathize with, feel for, feel sorry for, feel/have compassion for, grieve for, show understanding towards, sympathize with, weep for

pivot n 1 *the wheel turns on a pivot*: axis, axle, centre, fulcrum, hinge, hub, kingpin, linchpin, spindle, swivel 2 *the pivot of her life*: central point, centre, focal point, focus, fulcrum, heart, hub, linchpin
♦ v 1 *pivoted around to look at him*: revolve, rotate, spin, swing, swivel, turn 2 *the plot pivots on an unlikely coincidence*: be contingent formal, depend, hang, hinge, lie, rely, revolve, turn formal

pivotal adj axial, central, climactic, critical, crucial, decisive, determining, focal, important, vital

pixie n brownie, elf, fairy, goblin, leprechaun, sprite

placard n ad colloq, advert colloq, advertisement, bill, notice, poster, sign, sticker

placate v appease, assuage, calm (down), conciliate, lull, mollify, pacify, propitiate formal, quiet, soothe, win over
☒ anger, enrage, incense, infuriate

placatory *adj* appeasing, calming, conciliatory, mollifying, pacificatory *formal*, peacemaking, propitiative *formal*, propitiatory *formal*, soothing

place *n* **1** *the shop used to be in this very place:* locale, location, part, point, position, room, scene, seat, setting, site, situation, space, spot, venue, whereabouts **2** *the place where I grew up:* area, city, country, district, hamlet, locality, neighbourhood, region, state, town, village, whereabouts **3** *he has a place in London:* abode *formal*, accommodation, apartment, building, digs *colloq*, domicile *formal*, dwelling *formal*, establishment, flat, home, hotel, house, institution, pad *colloq*, property, residence *formal*, restaurant **4** *her place on the council:* appointment, footing, grade, job, niche, part, position, rank, role, situation, standing, status **5** *not your place to comment:* business, concern, duty, function, responsibility, right, role, task
♦ *v* **1** *place it over there:* deposit, establish, fix, install, lay, lay down, leave, locate, lodge, plant, position, put, put down, rest, set, set down, settle, situate, stand, station **2** *the survey placed us fifth:* arrange, categorize, class, classify, grade, group, put, rank, sort **3** *I can't quite place her:* categorize, establish, identify, know, pinpoint, recognize, remember **4** *place graduates in companies:* allocate, assign, find a job for, find accommodation for, find employment for

placement *n* **1** *the correct placement of sound equipment:* arrangement, deployment, disposition, distribution, emplacement *formal*, installation, locating, location, ordering, positioning, ranking, stationing **2** *a 12-week placement with Rolls-Royce:* appointment, employment, engagement, job

placid *adj* **1** *a placid person:* calm, composed, cool, easy-going *colloq*, equable, even-tempered, gentle, imperturbable, level-headed, mild, peaceable, self-possessed, serene, tranquil, undisturbed, unemotional, unexcitable, unflappable *colloq*, unmoved, unruffled, untroubled **2** *placid surroundings:* calm, pacific *formal*, peaceful, quiet, restful, still, tranquil
⊞ 1 agitated, disturbed, excitable

plagiarism *n* appropriation *formal*, borrowing *colloq*, copying, counterfeiting, cribbing *colloq*, infringement, lifting *colloq*, piracy, reproduction, theft

plagiarist *n* copier, imitator, pirate, robber, thief

plagiarize *v* appropriate *formal*, borrow, copy, counterfeit, crib *colloq*, imitate, infringe copyright, lift *colloq*, nick *colloq*, pirate, poach, reproduce, steal

plague *n* **1** *a cholera plague swept the camp:* Black Death, bubonic plague, cholera, contagion, disease, epidemic, infection, infestation, pandemic *formal*, pestilence, pneumonic plague, sickness **2** *a plague of rats:* epidemic, huge number, infestation, influx, invasion, swarm **3** *speed bumps can be a real plague:* affliction, annoyance, calamity, curse, nuisance, pain in the neck *colloq*, scourge, thorn in the flesh *colloq*, torment, trial
♦ *v* afflict, aggravate *colloq*, annoy, bedevil, bother, bug *colloq*, cause headaches to *colloq*, cause problems for, distress, disturb, dog, hamper, harass, hassle *colloq*, haunt, hinder, hound, irritate, persecute, pester, torment, torture, trouble, upset, vex, worry

plain *adj* **1** *plain cookery:* austere, basic, modest, ordinary, restrained, simple, Spartan, stark, unadorned, unelaborate, unpretentious, unsophisticated **2** *plain fabric:* muted, restrained, self-coloured, unadorned, uncoloured, undecorated, unembellished, unpatterned, unvariegated **3** *the evidence is plain:* apparent, clear, discernible, evident, manifest *formal*, noticeable, obvious, overt, patent, perceptible, plain as a pikestaff *colloq*, transparent, understandable, unmistakable, visible **4** *she's a bit plain:* homely *US*, ordinary, ugly, unattractive, unlovely, unprepossessing **5** *the instructions are plain:* accessible, clear, direct, intelligible, lucid, simple, straightforward, unambiguous, uncomplicated, understandable **6** *plain talking:* blunt, candid, direct, forthright, frank, honest, open, outspoken, plain-spoken, simple, sincere, straightforward, truthful, unambiguous, unassuming
⊞ 1 elaborate, fancy **2** patterned **3** obscure, unclear **4** attractive, beautiful, good-looking **5** complicated, obscure **6** deceitful, devious
♦ *adv* completely, quite, simply, thoroughly, totally, undeniably, utterly
♦ *n* flat, flatland, grassland, lowland, pampas, plateau, prairie, savannah, steppe, tableland, tundra

plain-spoken *adj* blunt, candid, direct, downright, explicit, forthright, frank, honest, open, outright, outspoken, straightforward, truthful, unequivocal

plaintive *adj* disconsolate *formal*, doleful, grief-stricken, heart-broken, heart-rending, high-pitched, melancholy, mournful, piteous, pitiful, sad, sorrowful, unhappy, wistful, woeful, wretched

plan *n* **1** *our plan is to join:* aim, arrangement, formula, idea, intention, means, method, plot, policy, procedure, programme, project, proposal, proposition, scenario, schedule, scheme, strategy, suggestion, system, way **2** *the plans for the new bridge:* blueprint, chart, delineation *formal*, design, diagram, drawing, illustration, layout, map, representation, scale drawing, sketch
♦ *v* **1** *planning his comeback:* arrange, contrive, design, develop, devise, draft, formulate, frame, invent, map out, mastermind, organize, outline, plot, prepare, programme, schedule, scheme, shape, sketch, think of, work out **2** *I plan to go next year:* aim, contemplate, envisage, foresee, intend, mean, propose, purpose, resolve *formal*, seek, want, wish

plane¹ *n* **1** *a horizontal plane:* flat, flat surface, level, level surface **2** *he thinks on a higher plane:* class, condition, degree, echelon, footing, level, position, rank, rung, stage, stratum
♦ *adj* even, flat, flush, homaloidal *technical*, horizontal, level, plain, planar *formal*, regular, smooth, uniform

plane² *n* aeroplane, aircraft, airliner, airplane *US*, bomber, fighter, glider, jet, jumbo, jumbo jet, seaplane, swing-wing, VTOL
♦ *v* fly, glide, sail, skate, skim, volplane, wing

planet

---

*Major planets within the Earth's solar system
(nearest the sun shown first) are:*
Mercury, Venus, Earth, Mars, Jupiter, Saturn,
Uranus, Neptune

---

plant *n* 1 *garden plants:* bush, flower, herb, shrub,
vegetable 2 *a new plant was opened recently:*
apparatus, equipment, factory, foundry, gear,
machinery, mill, shop, works, workshop, yard
♦ *v* 1 *she planted some seeds:* bury, implant, put
into the ground, scatter, seed, sow, transplant
2 *he planted himself on the sofa:* establish, fix,
found, imbed, lodge, place, position, put, root,
set, settle, situate 3 *he planted the bomb under the
table:* bury, conceal, disguise, hide, put out of
sight, put secretly, secrete *formal*

Plants include:
annual, biennial, perennial, herbaceous plant,
evergreen, succulent, cultivar, hybrid, house
plant, pot plant; flower, herb, shrub, bush,
tree, vegetable, grass, vine, weed, cereal, wild
flower, air-plant, water-plant, cactus, fern,
moss, algae, lichen, fungus; bulb, corm,
seedling, sapling, bush, climber. See also **bulb,
flower, grass, leaf, poisonous, shrub, wild
flower**

Parts of a plant include:
bark, cambium, cork cambium, cellulose,
conducting tissue, cotyledon, monocotyledon,
dicotyledon, flower, fruit, leaf, meristem,
phellogen, phloem, root, lateral root, root cap,
root hair, rootlet, seed, seed leaf, stem, tap
root, vascular bundle, vascular tissue, xylem

---

plaque *n* badge, brass, brooch, cartouche
technical, medal, medallion, panel, plaquette,
plate, shield, sign, slab, tablet

plaster *n* 1 *apply plaster to walls:* gypsum, mortar,
plaster of Paris, plasterboard, plasterwork,
stucco 2 *put a plaster on a wound:* adhesive
dressing, bandage, Band-aid®, dressing,
Elastoplast®, patch, sticking-plaster
♦ *v* bedaub, coat, cover, cover thickly, daub,
overlay, smear, spread

plastic *adj* 1 *plastic toys:* ductile, flexible,
malleable, mouldable, pliable, shapeable, soft,
supple 2 *plastic young minds:* compliant *formal*,
easily influenced, impressionable, malleable,
manageable, mouldable, pliable, pliant,
receptive, tractable *formal* 3 *his plastic smile:*
artificial, false, phoney *colloq*, synthetic,
unnatural
₣ 1 inflexible, rigid 2 inflexible, intractable
formal 3 natural

Types of plastic include:
Bakelite®, Biopol®, celluloid®, epoxy resin,
Perspex®, phenolic resin, plexiglass, polyester,
polyethylene, polymethyl methacrylate,
polynorbornene, polypropylene, polystyrene,
polythene, polyurethane, PTFE
(polytetrafluoroethylene), PVC (polyvinyl
chloride), uPVC, silicone, Teflon®,
transpolyisoprene, urea formaldehyde, vinyl

---

plasticity *n* flexibility, malleability, pliability,
pliableness, pliancy, softness, suppleness,
tractability *formal*
₣ inflexibility, rigidity

plate *n* 1 *a plate of stew:* asset, dish, helping,
platter, portion, salver, serving 2 *a thin steel plate:*
lamina *formal*, pane, panel, plaque, sheet, sign,
slab, tablet 3 *the book has many colour plates:*
illustration, lithograph, photograph, picture,
print
♦ *v* anodize, coat, cover, electroplate, galvanize,
gild, laminate, overlay, platinize, silver, tin, veneer

plateau *n* 1 *a grassy plateau:* highland, mesa,
plane, table, tableland, upland 2 *progress reached
a plateau:* grade, level, stability, stage

platform *n* 1 *she took to the platform to deliver her
speech:* dais, podium, rostrum, soapbox *colloq*,
stage, stand 2 *a liberal platform:* aims, ideas,
intentions, manifesto, objectives, party line,
policy, principles, programme, strategy, tenets

platitude *n* banality, bromide, chestnut *colloq*,
cliché, commonplace, hackneyed statement,
inanity, overworked phrase, stereotype, trite
expression, truism

platitudinous *adj* banal, clichéd, commonplace,
corny *colloq*, dull, flat, hackneyed, inane,
overworked, set, stale, stereotyped, stock, tired,
trite, truistic, vapid, well-worn

platonic *adj* 1 *the platonic ideal of a sports car:*
ideal, idealistic, incorporeal *formal*, intellectual,
spiritual, theoretical, transcendent 2 *our
relationship is purely platonic:* non-physical, non-
romantic, non-sexual
₣ 1 real 2 sexual

platoon *n* battery, company, group, outfit,
patrol, squad, squadron, team

platter *n* charger, dish, plate, salver, tray,
trencher

plaudits *n* acclaim, acclamation, accolade,
applause, approbation *formal*, approval,
bouquet *colloq*, clapping, commendation,
congratulations, good press *colloq*, hand *colloq*,
hurrahs, ovation, pat on the back *colloq*, praise,
rave review *colloq*, standing ovation
₣ criticism

plausible *adj* 1 *plausible evidence:* believable,
cogent *formal*, conceivable, convincing, credible,
imaginable, likely, logical, persuasive, possible,
probable, reasonable 2 *she's so plausible:* glib,
persuasive, smooth-talking
₣ 1 implausible, improbable, unlikely
2 unconvincing

play *v* 1 *play in the garden:* amuse yourself, caper,
cavort, divert yourself, enjoy yourself, frisk,
frolic, gambol, have fun, occupy yourself, play
games, revel, romp, sport 2 *play golf:* be involved
in, compete, do, join in, participate, take part
3 *France played Scotland:* challenge, compete
against, oppose, rival, take on, vie with
4 *he played Hamlet:* act, impersonate, perform,
play the part of, portray, represent 5 *light playing
on the water:* dance, flash, flicker, move lightly,
twinkle
₣ 1 work
♦ *n* 1 *all work and no play:* amusement, diversion,
enjoyment, entertainment, fun, game, hobby,
leisure, merrymaking, pastime, recreation, sport
2 *a play about the war:* comedy, drama, farce,

melodrama, performance, plot, show, tragedy
3 *enough play on the line:* action, flexibility, free
rein, freedom, freedom of movement, give *colloq,*
latitude, leeway, liberty, licence, looseness,
margin, movement, range, room, scope, slack,
space **4** *luck comes into play:* action, exercise,
interaction, interplay, operation, transaction
🖃 **1** work
▸ **play around with 1** *play around with his future:*
fiddle with, fidget with, interfere with, meddle
with, tamper with, toy with **2** *he played around:*
dally with, flirt with, fool with, mess around
with, philander with, trifle with, womanize with
▸ **play at** affect *formal,* go through the motions
colloq, make out, pretend (to be), put on an act
▸ **play down** downplay, gloss over, make light
of, minimize, underestimate, underplay,
understate, undervalue
🖃 emphasize, exaggerate, play up
▸ **play on** capitalize on, exploit, profit by,
take advantage of, trade on, turn to account
▸ **play out** act, be revealed, carry on, continue,
enact, go on, unfold
▸ **play up 1** *played up by the media:* accentuate,
call attention to, emphasize, exaggerate,
highlight, point up, spotlight, stress, underline
2 *she's always playing up:* annoy, be difficult to
control, be mischievous, be naughty, bother, give
trouble, hurt, misbehave, trouble **3** *the clutch is
playing up:* go wrong, go/be on the blink *colloq,*
malfunction, not work
▸ **play up to** blandish, bootlick *colloq,* butter up
colloq, curry favour with, fawn, flatter, ingratiate
yourself, soft-soap *colloq,* suck up to, toady

playboy *n* debauchee, ladies' man, lady-killer,
libertine, man about town *colloq,* philanderer,
rake, roué, socialite *colloq,* womanizer

player *n* **1** *chess players:* competitor, contestant,
participant, sportsman, sportswoman **2** *a banjo
player:* accompanist, artist, instrumentalist,
musician, performer, virtuoso **3** *the leading
players in the production:* actor, actress, artist,
artiste, comedian, entertainer, performer, trouper

playful *adj* **1** *as playful as a kitten:* frisky,
frolicsome, fun-loving, impish, kittenish, lively,
mischievous, puckish, roguish, spirited, sportive
2 *a playful remark:* facetious, humorous, jesting,
joking, teasing, tongue-in-cheek, waggish
🖃 **2** serious

playground *n* adventure playground,
amusement park, park, play area, playing-field,
pleasure ground, recreation ground

playmate *n* buddy *colloq,* chum *colloq,*
companion, comrade, friend, neighbour, pal
colloq, playfellow

plaything *n* amusement, bauble, game,
gewgaw, gimcrack, pastime, puppet, toy, trifle,
trinket

playwright *n* dramatist, dramaturge,
dramaturgist, screen writer, scriptwriter,
tragedian, writer

plea *n* **1** *a passionate plea for peace:* appeal,
entreaty, imploration *formal,* invocation *formal,*
petition, prayer, request, supplication **2** *a plea of
insanity:* claim, defence, excuse, explanation,
justification, pretext, vindication *formal*

plead *v* **1** *they were pleading for mercy:* appeal, ask,
beg, beseech *formal,* entreat, implore, make

supplication *formal,* petition, request, solicit
formal **2** *plead ignorance:* adduce *formal,* allege,
argue, assert, claim, maintain, put forward, state

pleasant *adj* **1** *a pleasant chat:* acceptable,
agreeable, amusing, charming, delightful,
enjoyable, entertaining, fine, gratifying, lovely,
nice, pleasing, refreshing, satisfying, welcome
2 *a pleasant person:* affable, amiable, charming,
cheerful, congenial, friendly, good-humoured,
likeable, lovely, nice, winsome
🖃 **1** nasty, unpleasant **2** nasty, unfriendly,
unpleasant

pleasantry *n* **1** *exchange pleasantries about the
weather:* casual remark, friendly remark, polite
comment **2** *she laughed at her own pleasantry:*
badinage, banter, bon mot, jest, joke, quip, sally,
witticism

please *v* **1** *the performance greatly pleased her:*
amuse, appeal to, attract, captivate, charm, cheer
(up), content, delight, divert, entertain, fulfil,
give pleasure to, gladden, gratify, humour,
indulge, make happy, satisfy, suit **2** *I want to
dress as I please:* choose, desire, like, prefer, see fit,
think fit, want, will, wish
🖃 **1** anger, annoy, displease, sadden

pleased *adj* cheerful, chuffed *colloq,* contented,
delighted, elated, euphoric, glad, gratified,
happy, over the moon *colloq,* satisfied, thrilled,
tickled pink *colloq*
🖃 annoyed, displeased

pleasing *adj* agreeable, amusing, attractive,
charming, delightful, engaging, enjoyable,
entertaining, fine, good, gratifying, nice,
pleasant, pleasurable, satisfying, winning
🖃 disagreeable, unpleasant

pleasurable *adj* agreeable, amusing, congenial,
delightful, diverting, enjoyable, entertaining,
fun, good, gratifying, groovy *colloq,* lovely, nice,
pleasant, welcome
🖃 bad, disagreeable

pleasure *n* **1** *great pleasure:* contentment, delight,
enjoyment, gladness, gratification, happiness,
joy, satisfaction, solace *formal* **2** *the pleasure of
playing:* delight, enjoyment, gem, glory, joy,
prize, thrill, treasure **3** *combine business with
pleasure:* amusement, entertainment, fun, leisure,
recreation **4** *what's your pleasure?:* choice, desire,
inclination, preference, will, wish
🖃 **1** displeasure, pain, sorrow, trouble
2 disappointment, sadness

pleat *v* crease, crimp, flute, fold, gather, pucker,
tuck

plebeian *adj* **1** *of plebeian stock:* low-born, lower-
class, mean, peasant, proletarian, working-class
2 *plebeian tastes:* base, coarse, common, ignoble,
low, non-U *colloq,* uncultivated, uncultured,
unrefined
🖃 **1** aristocratic, noble, patrician **2** refined,
sophisticated
♦ *n* common person, commoner, peasant,
person in the street, pleb *colloq,* prole *colloq,*
proletarian, worker
🖃 aristocrat, noble, patrician

plebiscite *n* ballot, poll, referendum, straw poll,
vote

pledge *n* **1** *gave a pledge that he would return:*
assurance, bond, commitment, covenant,
guarantee, oath, promise, undertaking, vow,

warrant, word, word of honour **2** *give money in pledge:* bail, collateral *formal,* deposit, guarantee, pawn, security, surety
♦ *v* **1** *pledged to return:* commit, contract, engage, give an undertaking, give your word, guarantee, promise, secure, swear, take an oath, undertake, vouch, vow **2** *pledged his watch:* guarantee, mortgage, put up as collateral *formal*

plenary *adj* absolute, complete, entire, full, general, integral, open, sweeping, thorough, unconditional, unlimited, unqualified, unrestricted, whole

plenipotentiary *n* ambassador, dignitary, emissary, envoy, legate, minister, nuncio

plenitude *n* abundance, amplitude *formal,* bounty, completeness, copiousness, cornucopia, entireness, excess, fullness, plenteousness *formal,* plentifulness, plenty, plethora *formal,* profusion, repletion *formal,* wealth
🅴 scarcity

plenteous *adj* abounding, abundant, ample, bounteous *formal,* bountiful, bumper *colloq,* copious, fertile, fruitful, generous, inexhaustible, infinite, lavish, liberal, luxuriant *formal,* overflowing, plentiful, productive, profuse, prolific
🅴 paltry, scarce

plentiful *adj* abundant, ample, bounteous *formal,* bountiful, bumper *colloq,* copious, fruitful, generous, inexhaustible, infinite, lavish, liberal, overflowing, productive, profuse
🅴 rare, scanty, scarce

plenty *n* **1** *we have plenty of money:* abundance, copiousness, enough, fullness, fund, mass, mine, plenteousness *formal,* plethora *formal,* profusion, quantity, store, sufficiency, volume **2** *times of plenty:* affluence, fortune, prosperity, riches, substance, wealth, wealthiness
🅴 **1** lack, scarcity, want **2** need

plethora *n* excess, glut, overabundance, overfullness, profusion, superabundance, superfluity *formal,* surfeit, surplus

pliability *n* **1** *the pliability of the material:* bendability, ductility, elasticity, flexibility, plasticity **2** *the pliability of her nature:* adaptability, amenability, compliance *formal,* docility, impressionableness, malleability, suggestibility, susceptibility, tractableness *formal*
🅴 inflexibility, rigidity

pliable *adj* **1** *pliable pieces of wood:* bendable, bendy *colloq,* elastic, flexible, lithe, malleable, plastic, pliant, supple **2** *a pliable person:* accommodating, adaptable, biddable, compliant *formal,* docile, flexible, impressionable, manageable, persuadable, receptive, responsive, susceptible, tractable *formal,* yielding
🅴 **1** inflexible, rigid **2** headstrong

pliant *adj* **1** *pliant pieces of wood:* bendable, bendy *colloq,* elastic, flexible, malleable, plastic, pliable, supple **2** *a pliant person:* accommodating, adaptable, biddable, compliant *formal,* docile, flexible, impressionable, manageable, persuadable, receptive, responsive, susceptible, tractable *formal,* yielding
🅴 **1** inflexible, rigid **2** headstrong

plight¹ *n* case, circumstances, condition, difficult/distressing situation, difficulty, dilemma, dire straits, extremity, hole *colloq,* jam

colloq, pickle *colloq,* predicament, quandary, scrape *colloq,* situation, state, straits, tight spot *colloq,* trouble

plight² *v* contract, covenant, engage, guarantee, pledge, promise, propose, swear, vouch, vow

plod *v* **1** *plod along the path:* clump, lumber, plough through, stomp, stump, tramp, trudge, walk heavily **2** *plod through the work:* drudge, grind, labour, peg away, persevere, plug away, slog, soldier on, toil

plodder *n* drudge, dullard, mug, sap, slogger, toiler
🅴 high-flier

plot *n* **1** *a plot to kill the president:* cabal, conspiracy, intrigue, machination *formal,* plan, ruse, scheme, stratagem **2** *the film had an improbable plot:* action, narrative, outline, scenario, story, storyline, subject, theme, thread **3** *a plot of land:* allotment, area, lot, parcel, patch, tract
♦ *v* **1** *plotted to forge banknotes:* collude, connive, conspire, contrive, intrigue, machinate *formal,* plan, scheme **2** *plotted a clever scheme:* concoct, contrive, cook up *colloq,* design, devise, draft, frame, hatch, plan **3** *plot a map of the area:* calculate, chart, draw, map (out), mark, sketch

plotter *n* conspirator, intriguer, machinator *formal,* planner, schemer

plough *v* break, cultivate, dig, furrow, ridge, spade, till, turn up, work
▶ **plough into** bump into, collide, crash into, drive into, hit, run/go into, smash into
▶ **plough through** move through laboriously, plod through, trudge through, wade through

ploy *n* artifice, contrivance, device, dodge, game, manoeuvre, move, ruse, scheme, stratagem, subterfuge, tactic, trick, wile

pluck *v* **1** *pluck feathers:* collect, draw, extract, gather, harvest, pick, pull, pull (off), remove, snatch, take in, tug, yank *colloq* **2** *pluck a guitar:* finger, pick, strum, twang
♦ *n* audacity, backbone, boldness, bravery, courage, daring, determination, fearlessness, fortitude *formal,* grit *colloq,* guts *colloq,* intrepidity, mettle, nerve *colloq,* resolution, spirit, valour *formal*
🅴 cowardice

plucky *adj* audacious, bold, brave, courageous, daring, determined, fearless, gritty *colloq,* gutsy *colloq,* heroic, intrepid, spirited, spunky *colloq,* valiant
🅴 cowardly, feeble, weak

plug *n* **1** *put a plug in the sink:* bung, cork, seal, spigot, stopper **2** *a plug for his new album:* ad *colloq,* advertisement, blurb, commercial, good word, hype *colloq,* mention, promotion, publicity, puff, push *colloq* **3** *a plug of tobacco:* cake, chew, twist, wad
♦ *v* **1** *plug a gap:* block, bung, choke, close, cork, fill, pack, seal, stop (up), stuff **2** *plugging her new chat show:* advertise, hype *colloq,* market, mention, promote, publicize, push *colloq,* tout
▶ **plug away** keep trying, peg away, persevere, plod on, slog away, soldier on

plum *adj* best, choice, cushy *colloq,* especially valued, excellent, first-class, prize

plumb *adv* **1** *plumb straight:* perpendicularly, sheer, straight down, straight up, up and down, vertically **2** *plumb in the middle:* bang *colloq*, dead, exactly, precisely, right, slap *colloq*, spot on *colloq* ♦ *v* delve into, examine, explore, fathom, gauge, investigate, measure, penetrate, probe, search (out), sound (out)

plume *n* aigrette, crest, feather, pappus *technical*, pinion, quill, tuft

plummet *v* decrease quickly, descend, dive, drop, drop/fall rapidly, fall, hurtle, nosedive, plunge, tumble
☒ soar

plump¹ *adj* ample, beefy *colloq*, buxom, chubby, corpulent *formal*, dumpy, fat, flabby *colloq*, fleshy, full, gross *colloq*, obese, podgy, portly, rotund *formal*, round, stout, tubby, well-rounded, well-upholstered *colloq*
☒ skinny, thin

plump² *v* collapse, deposit, descend, drop, dump *colloq*, fall, flop, put down, set down, sink, slump
► **plump for** back, choose, favour, opt for, prefer, select, side with, support

plumpness *n* chubbiness, corpulence *formal*, fatness, fleshiness, obesity *formal*, podginess, portliness, pudginess, rotundity *formal*, stoutness, tubbiness
☒ skinniness, thinness

plunder *v* depredate *formal*, despoil *formal*, devastate, fleece, lay waste, loot, maraud, pillage, raid, ransack, ravage, rifle, rob, sack, steal, strip
♦ *n* booty, ill-gotten gains, loot, pickings, pillage, prize, spoils, swag *slang*

plunge *v* **1** *plunged into the crowd:* career, charge, dash, dive, hurtle, jump, pitch, rush, swoop, tear, throw yourself, tumble **2** *share prices plunged:* decrease quickly, dive-bomb, drop, drop/fall rapidly, fall, go down, nosedive, plummet, sink, tumble **3** *plunged a knife into him:* drive, jab, push, ram, shove, stab, stick, thrust **4** *plunged into the water:* dip, immerse, sink, submerge
♦ *n* **1** *a headfirst plunge:* charge, descent, dive, drop, fall, immersion, jump, rush, submersion, swoop, tumble **2** *a sudden plunge in prices:* descent, drop, fall, nosedive, tumble

plurality *n* bulk, diversity, galaxy *colloq*, majority, mass, most, multiplicity *formal*, multitudinousness *formal*, number, numerousness, preponderance *formal*, profusion, variety

plus *n* advantage, asset, benefit, bonus, credit, extra, gain, good point, perk *colloq*, surplus
☒ disadvantage, drawback, minus *colloq*
♦ *prep* and, as well as, in addition to, not to mention *colloq*, over and above, together with, with
☒ minus

plush *adj* affluent, costly, de luxe, glitzy *colloq*, lavish, luxurious, luxury, opulent *formal*, palatial, posh *colloq*, rich, ritzy *colloq*, stylish, sumptuous, swanky *colloq*

plutocrat *n* billionaire, capitalist, Croesus, Dives, fat cat *colloq*, magnate, millionaire, moneybags *colloq*, multimillionaire, rich man, tycoon

ply¹ *v* **1** *ply her with sherry:* assail, beset, bombard, feed, furnish, harass, importune, keep supplying, lavish, provide, supply **2** *ply the same route:* ferry,

go, make regular journeys between/along, travel **3** *ply a trade:* carry on, exercise, follow, practise, pursue, work at **4** *ply a tool:* employ, handle, manipulate, use, utilize, wield

ply² *n* fold, layer, leaf, sheet, strand, thickness

poach *v* **1** *poached his ideas:* appropriate *formal*, borrow *colloq*, copy, lift *colloq*, nick *colloq*, pilfer, steal, take **2** *accused of poaching:* catch/hunt illegally, encroach, infringe, intrude, trespass

pocket *n* **1** *a trouser pocket:* bag, cavity, compartment, envelope, hollow, pouch, receptacle **2** *a drain on my pocket:* assets, budget, capital, finances, funds, means, money, resources, wherewithal **3** *pocket of resistance:* isolated area, patch, small area, small group
♦ *adj* abridged, compact, concise, little, mini *colloq*, miniature, pint-size *colloq*, portable, potted, small
♦ *v* appropriate *formal*, filch, gain, help yourself to, lift *colloq*, nick *colloq*, pilfer, pinch *colloq*, purloin *formal*, steal, take, win unfairly

pockmark *n* blemish, pit, pock, pockpit, scar

podgy *adj* chubby, chunky, corpulent *formal*, dumpy, fat, fleshy, paunchy, plump, roly-poly, rotund *formal*, squat, stout, stubby, stumpy, tubby
☒ skinny, thin

podium *n* dais, platform, rostrum, stage, stand

poem

> **Types of poem include:**
> ballad, bucolic, clerihew, couplet, ditty, eclogue, elegy, epic, epigram, epithalamium, epode, epopee, georgic, haiku, idyll, lay, limerick, lipogram, lyric, madrigal, monody, nursery rhyme, ode, palinode, pastoral, prothalamion, rhyme, rondeau, roundelay, song, sonnet, tanka, triolet, verse, verselet, versicle. See also **song**

poet *n* balladeer, bard, elegist, idyllist, lyricist, minstrel, poetaster, poeticule, rhymer, rhymester, rhymist, sonneteer, verse-maker, versifier

poetic *adj* **1** *poetic composition:* metrical, poetical, rhyming, rhythmical **2** *a poetic description:* artistic, beautiful, creative, expressive, flowing, graceful, imaginative, lyrical, moving, poetical, sensitive
☒ **1** prosaic **2** prosaic

poetry *n* **1** *a book of poetry:* lyrics, poems, rhyme, verse **2** *dedicated his life to poetry:* Parnassus, poesy, the Muses, versification, versing

pogrom *n* annihilation, bloodbath, butchery, carnage, decimation, ethnic cleansing, extermination, genocide, holocaust, homicide, indiscriminate killing, killing, liquidation, murder, slaughter, wholesale slaughter

poignancy *n* bitterness, distress, emotion, evocativeness, feeling, intensity, keenness, misery, pain, painfulness, pathos, piquancy, piteousness, pungency, sadness, sentiment, sharpness, tenderness, tragedy, wretchedness

poignant *adj* affecting, agonizing, distressing, emotional, heartbreaking, heartfelt, heart-rending, miserable, moving, painful, pathetic, piteous, sad, sorrowful, tearful, tender, touching, tragic, upsetting, wretched

point *n* **1** *the main points of the argument*: issue, item, matter, question, subject, topic **2** *the finer points of chess*: aspect, attribute, characteristic, detail, facet, feature, item, particular, property, quality, subject, topic **3** *what's your point?*: aim, end, goal, intention, motive, object, objective, purpose, reason, sense, use **4** *get straight to the point*: burden, central point, core, crux, drift, essence, gist, heart, heart of the matter, keynote, main point, marrow, meaning, meat, nub, pith, theme, thrust **5** *the point where the sea meets the sand*: area, locality, location, place, position, site, situation, spot **6** *a good point at which to stop*: instant, juncture, moment, period, position, stage, time **7** *noticed a tiny point on the page*: decimal point, dot, full point, full stop, mark, period, speck, spot, stop **8** *the point of a needle*: end, extremity, nib, sharp end, spike, taper, tine, tip, top **9** *sailed out past the point*: cape, foreland, head, headland, ness, promontory **10** *a record number of points*: goal, hit, mark, run, score, total
♦ *v* **1** *point a gun*: aim, direct, level, train **2** *this points to a bright future*: denote *formal*, designate, evidence *formal*, gesture at/towards, indicate, show, signal, signify, suggest
▶ **point out** allude to, bring up, draw/call attention to, identify, indicate, mention, point to, remind, reveal, show, specify
▶ **point up** call attention to, emphasize, highlight, stress, underline

point-blank *adv* abruptly, bluntly, candidly, directly, explicitly, forthrightly, frankly, openly, outright, plainly, rudely, straight, straightforwardly, unequivocally
♦ *adj* **1** *a point-blank response*: blunt, candid, direct, explicit, forthright, frank, open, outright, plain, straightforward, unreserved **2** *shot at point-blank distance*: close, near, touching

pointed *adj* **1** *a pointed implement*: acicular *technical*, aculeate(d) *formal*, barbed, cuspidate(d), edged, fastigiate *formal*, keen, lanceolate(d) *formal*, mucronate(d) *formal*, sharp, tapering **2** *a pointed comment*: biting, clear, cutting, forceful, incisive, obvious, penetrating, striking, telling, trenchant *formal*

pointer *n* **1** *the pointer on the dial*: arrow, hand, indicator, needle **2** *offered me some pointers*: advice, caution, clue, guide, guideline, hint, indication, indicator, piece of advice, recommendation, sign, suggestion, tip, warning **3** *waved a long pointer at the screen*: cane, pole, rod, stick

pointless *adj* *a mug's game colloq*, a waste of time/effort, absurd, aimless, foolish, fruitless, futile, inane, insignificant, meaningless, nonsensical, ridiculous, senseless, to no avail, unavailing, unproductive, unprofitable, useless, vain, valueless, worthless
◨ meaningful, profitable, useful

poise *n* aplomb *formal*, assurance, balance, calmness, composure, cool *colloq*, coolness *colloq*, dignity, elegance, equanimity *formal*, equilibrium, grace, presence of mind, self-assurance, self-control, self-possession, serenity
♦ *v* balance, hang, hover, position, steady, support, suspend

poised *adj* **1** *remain calm and poised at all times*: assured, calm, collected, composed, cool *colloq*, cool calm and collected *colloq*, dignified, graceful,

self-confident, self-controlled, self-possessed, serene, suave, unflappable *colloq*, unruffled *colloq*, urbane **2** *poised for action*: all set, expectant, prepared, ready, set, waiting

poison *n* **1** *poisons such as arsenic*: toxin, venom **2** *a poison spreading through society*: bane, blight, cancer, canker, contagion, contamination, corruption, malignancy, pollution
♦ *v* **1** *accused of poisoning their parents*: kill by poison **2** *the water was poisoned*: adulterate, blight, contaminate, defile, infect, pollute, spoil, taint **3** *poisoned his mind towards her*: corrupt, deprave, pervert, warp

poisonous *adj* **1** *poisonous mushrooms*: deadly, fatal, lethal, mortal, toxic, venomous **2** *a poisonous influence within the club*: cancerous, cankerous, contaminating, corrupting, harmful, malicious, malignant, noxious, pernicious, spiteful, vicious, virulent

---

Poisonous plants include:
aconite, amanita, anemone, banewort, belladonna, black nightshade, castor oil plant, common nightshade, cowbane, cuckoo pint, deadly nightshade, digitalis, dwale, foxglove, giant hogweed, helmet flower, hemlock, hemlock water dropwort, jimson-weed, laburnum, lantana, lords-and-ladies, meadow saffron, monkshood, naked boys, naked lady, oleander, poison ivy, stinkweed, stramonium, thorn apple, wake-robin, wild arum, windflower, wolfsbane

---

poke *v* butt, dig, elbow, hit, jab, nudge, prod, punch, push, shove, stab, stick, thrust
♦ *n* butt, dig, jab, nudge, prod, punch, shove, thrust
▶ **poke around** grope around, look (all over) for, rake through, rummage around, search for
▶ **poke out** beetle, extend, extrude, jut out, overhang, project, protrude, stick out

poky *adj* confined, cramped, crowded, incommodious *formal*, narrow, small, tight, tiny
◨ roomy, spacious

polar *adj* **1** *polar ice*: arctic, cold, freezing, frozen, glacial, icy, Siberian **2** *the polar opposite*: ambivalent, antithetical *formal*, completely/ utterly different, conflicting, contradictory, diametrically opposed, dichotomous *formal*, opposite

polarity *n* ambivalence, antithesis *formal*, contradiction, contrariety, dichotomy *formal*, duality, oppositeness, opposition, paradox

pole¹ *n* bar, mast, pillar, post, rod, shaft, spar, staff, stake, stick, support, upright

pole² *n* extreme, extremity, limit

polemic *n* argument, controversy, debate, dispute
♦ *adj* argumentative, contentious, controversial, disputatious *formal*, eristic(al) *formal*, polemical

polemicist *n* arguer, contender, controversialist, debater, disputant, disputer, logomachist *formal*, polemist

polemics *n* argument, argumentation, contention, controversy, debate, disputation *formal*, dispute, logomachy *formal*

police *n* constabulary, cops *colloq*, pigs *slang*, police force, rozzers *slang*, the (old) Bill *slang*, the Force *colloq*, the fuzz *slang*, the Law *colloq*

♦ *v* **1** *policing the area:* defend, guard, keep the peace, keep watch, patrol, protect **2** *police your emotions:* check, control, keep under control, monitor, observe, oversee, regulate, supervise, watch

police officer *n* bluebottle *slang,* bobby *colloq,* boy in blue *colloq,* bull *slang,* constable, cop *colloq,* copper *colloq,* flatfoot *slang,* nark *slang,* officer, PC, pig *slang,* policeman, policewoman, rozzer *colloq,* the (old) Bill *colloq,* the fuzz *slang,* the Law *colloq*

policy *n* **1** *a strict policy on Internet use:* code of practice, custom, guidelines, method, practice, procedure, protocol, rules, system **2** *recommend a change of policy on drugs:* approach, course, course of action, line, plan, position, programme, schedule, scheme, stance

polish *v* **1** *polish shoes:* brighten, buff, burnish, clean, furbish, rub (up), shine, smooth, wax **2** *polish up my Swedish:* brush up, cultivate, enhance, finish, improve, perfect, refine, touch up
  1 dull, tarnish
♦ *n* **1** *a tin of polish:* varnish, wax **2** *a high polish:* brightness, brilliance, burnish, finish, glaze, gloss, lustre, sheen, shine, smoothness, sparkle, veneer **3** *a performance of great polish:* breeding, class, cultivation, elegance, finesse, grace, poise, refinement, sophistication, style
  2 dullness **3** clumsiness
▶ **polish off 1** *polish off your food:* bolt, complete, consume, devour, dispose of, down, eat up, finish, gobble, put away, stuff, wolf *colloq* **2** *after the battle they polished off the stragglers:* bump off *colloq,* eliminate, kill, liquidate *colloq,* murder, rub out *colloq*

polished *adj* **1** *a highly polished surface:* burnished, glassy, gleaming, glossy, lustrous, shining, shiny, slippery, smooth, waxed **2** *gave a polished performance:* accomplished, adept, consummate *formal,* excellent, expert, faultless, flawless, impeccable, masterly, outstanding, perfect, perfected, professional, proficient, remarkable, skilful, superlative **3** *polished and debonair:* civilized, cultivated, elegant, genteel, graceful, polite, refined, sophisticated, suave, urbane, well-bred, well-mannered
  1 tarnished **2** inexpert **3** gauche

polite *adj* **1** *such a polite boy:* chivalrous, civil, considerate, courteous, cultured, deferential, diplomatic, gallant, gentlemanly, gracious, ladylike, obliging, refined, respectful, tactful, thoughtful, well-behaved, well-bred, well-mannered **2** *in polite society:* civilized, cultured, elegant, genteel, refined, sophisticated, suave, urbane, well-bred, well-mannered
  1 discourteous, impolite, rude

politeness *n* attention, civility, complaisance *formal,* considerateness, cordiality, courtesy, courtliness, cultivation, culture, deference, diplomacy, discretion, elegance, gentility, gentlemanliness, good manners, grace, graciousness, mannerliness, manners, polish, refinement, respect, respectfulness, tact, thoughtfulness
  discourtesy, impoliteness, rudeness

politic *adj* advantageous, advisable, diplomatic, expedient, judicious *formal,* opportune, prudent,

sagacious *formal,* sage *formal,* sensible, shrewd, tactful, wise
  impolitic

---

politic or *political*? Politic is a rather formal word meaning 'sensible': *He considered it politic to leave before there was any further trouble.* Political means 'relating to politics': *the political system of the USA; party political broadcasts.*

---

political *adj* administrative, bureaucratic, civil, constitutional, executive, governmental, judicial, ministerial, parliamentary, party political, public

---

Political ideologies include:
absolutism, anarchism, authoritarianism, Bolshevism, Christian democracy, collectivism, communism, conservatism, democracy, egalitarianism, fascism, federalism, holism, imperialism, individualism, liberalism, Maoism, Marxism, nationalism, Nazism, neocolonialism, neofascism, neo-Nazism, pluralism, republicanism, social democracy, socialism, syndicalism, Thatcherism, theocracy, totalitarianism, Trotskyism, unilateralism, Whiggism

---

politics *n* **1** *go into politics:* affairs of state, civics, diplomacy, government, local government, national government, party politics, political science, political views/beliefs, public affairs, regional government, statecraft, statesmanship **2** *office politics:* machination(s) *formal,* manipulation, manoeuvring, power game, power politics, power struggle, wheeler-dealing *colloq*

Terms used in politics include:
alliance, apartheid, ballot, bill, blockade, cabinet, campaign, civil service, coalition, constitution, council, *coup d'état,* détente, election, electoral register, ethnic cleansing, general election, go to the country, government, green paper, Hansard, judiciary, left wing, lobby, local government, majority, mandate, manifesto, nationalization, parliament, party, party line, prime minister's question time, privatization, propaganda, proportional representation, rainbow coalition, referendum, right wing, sanction, shadow cabinet, sovereignty, state, summit, summit conference, term of office, trade union, veto, vote, welfare state, three-line whip, whip, white paper

---

Political parties include:
Alliance, British National Party, Christian Democrats, Communist, Conservative and Unionist, Co-operative, Democratic, Democratic Unionist, Fianna Fáil, Fine Gael, Free Democrats, Green, Labour, Liberal, Liberal Democrats, National Front, Official Unionist, Plaid Cymru, Popular Front, Progressive, Republican, Respect, Scottish National Party, Sinn Féin, Scottish Socialist Party, Social Democrats, Social Democratic and Labour Party, United Kingdom Independence Party, Ulster Unionist, Veritas. See also **government systems, parliament**

poll n ballot, canvass, census, count, Gallup poll, head count, opinion poll, plebiscite, referendum, sampling, show of hands, straw poll, straw vote, survey, tally, vote, voting
♦ v 1 *poll a large number of votes*: gain, get, net, obtain, receive, return, win 2 *polled them to find out what they wanted*: ballot, canvass, interview, question, sample, solicit, survey 3 *to poll cattle*: clip, cut, dishorn, dod, pollard, shear, trim

pollute v adulterate, befoul, blacken, contaminate, corrupt, debase, defile, deprave, dirty, foul, infect, make dirty, mar, poison, soil, spoil, stain, sully, taint, tarnish, vitiate *formal*, warp

pollution n adulteration, blackening, contamination, corruption, debasement, defilement, depravity, dirtiness, filthiness, fouling, foulness, impurity, infection, muckiness *colloq*, staining, sullying, taint, tarnishing
₣ cleanness, purification, purity

polychromatic adj kaleidoscopic, many-coloured, many-hued, motley, mottled, multicoloured, parti-coloured, poikilitic *technical*, polychrome, rainbow, varicoloured, variegated
₣ black and white, monochromatic, monochrome

polyglot adj cosmopolitan, international, multilingual, multiracial, polyglottal *formal*, polyglottic *formal*
₣ monoglot
♦ n linguist, multilinguist

polymath n all-rounder, know-all *colloq*, mine of information, oracle, pansophist *formal*, polyhistor *formal*, walking encyclopedia *colloq*
₣ ignoramus

pomp n brilliance, ceremonial, ceremoniousness, ceremony, display, flourish, formality, glitter *colloq*, glory, grandeur, magnificence, majesty, ostentation, pageantry, parade, ritual, show, solemnity, spectacle, splendour, state
₣ austerity, simplicity

pomposity n 1 *behave with pomposity*: affectation *formal*, airs, arrogance, condescension, haughtiness, imperiousness, presumption, pretension, pretentiousness, pride, self-importance, superciliousness, vanity 2 *pomposity of language*: bombast, euphuism *formal*, fustian *formal*, grandiloquence *formal*, magniloquence *formal*, preachiness, rhetoric, stuffiness, turgidity
₣ 1 modesty 2 economy, simplicity

pompous adj 1 *a pompous individual*: affected *formal*, arrogant, conceited, condescending, grandiose, haughty, imperious, magisterial, ostentatious, overbearing, patronizing, presumptuous, pretentious, proud, self-important, snooty *colloq*, supercilious, vain 2 *pompous language*: bombastic, elaborate, euphuistic *formal*, flowery, grand, high-flown, la-di-da *colloq*, magniloquent *formal*, ostentatious, overblown, preachy *colloq*, stuffy, turgid, windy
₣ 1 modest, unaffected, unassuming 2 simple

pond n lake, mere, pool, puddle, tarn, waterhole, watering-hole

ponder v analyse, brood, cerebrate *formal*, cogitate *formal*, consider, contemplate, deliberate, examine, excogitate *formal*, give thought to, meditate, mull over, muse, puzzle over, ratiocinate *formal*, reason, reflect, ruminate over, study, think, weigh

ponderous adj 1 *ponderous writing*: dreary, dull, humourless, laborious, laboured, lifeless, long-winded, pedantic, pedestrian, plodding, prolix *formal*, serious, stilted, stodgy, stolid, tedious, verbose 2 *a plump and ponderous man*: awkward, bulky, clumsy, cumbersome, elephantine, graceless, heavy, heavy-footed, heavy-handed, hefty, huge, lumbering, massive, slow-moving, unwieldy, weighty
₣ 1 light, simple 2 delicate

ponderousness n gravitas, heaviness, humourlessness, laboriousness, seriousness, stodginess, stolidity, tedium, weightiness
₣ delicacy, lightness, subtlety

pontifical adj 1 *a pontifical mass*: apostolic, ecclesiastical, papal, prelatic 2 *a most arrogant and pontifical manner*: condescending, didactic, dogmatic, imperious, magisterial, overbearing, pompous, portentous, preachy *colloq*, pretentious, self-important, sermonizing
₣ 2 reticent, unassuming

pontificate v declaim *formal*, dogmatize, expound, harangue, hold forth, lay down the law *colloq*, lecture, moralize, perorate *formal*, preach, pronounce, sermonize, sound off

pony see **horse**

pooh-pooh v belittle, brush aside, deride *formal*, disdain, dismiss, disparage *formal*, disregard, make little of, minimize, play down, reject, ridicule, scoff, scorn, slight, sneer, sniff at, spurn, turn up your nose at *colloq*
₣ exaggerate, magnify

pool[1] n lake, mere, paddling-pool, pond, puddle, swimming-bath(s), swimming-pool, tarn, waterhole, watering-hole

pool[2] n 1 *put all the money into a pool*: accumulation, ante, bank, fund, jackpot, kitty, pot, purse, reserve, supply 2 *a pool of suppliers*: cartel, collective, combine, consortium, group, ring, syndicate, team
♦ v amalgamate, chip in *colloq*, combine, contribute, merge, muck in *colloq*, share

poor adj 1 *a poor man*: badly off, bankrupt, broke *colloq*, deprived, destitute, disadvantaged, distressed, exiguous *formal*, hard up, humble, impecunious *formal*, impoverished, in need, indigent *formal*, lowly, mean, miserable, needy, not having a penny to your name *colloq*, not having two pennies to rub together *colloq*, on the breadline *colloq*, on your beam-ends *colloq*, on your uppers *colloq*, penniless, penurious *formal*, poor as a church mouse *colloq*, poverty-stricken, reduced, skint *colloq*, stony-broke *colloq*, straitened, underprivileged, without means, without the wherewithal, wretched 2 *a poor performance*: bad, barren, below par, below standard, crummy *colloq*, defective, faulty, feeble, fruitless, imperfect, inferior, jerry, low, low-grade, low-quality, measly *colloq*, mediocre, naff *slang*, pathetic *colloq*, ropy *colloq*, rotten *colloq*, rubbish *colloq*, second-rate, shoddy, sorry, substandard, third-rate, unproductive, unsatisfactory, weak, worthless 3 *the soil was poor*: deficient, depleted, exhausted, inadequate, insufficient, lacking, meagre, paltry, scanty, skimpy, sparse 4 *poor you!*: hapless *formal*, ill-

fated, ill-starred, luckless, miserable, pathetic, pitiable, pitiful, sad, sorry, spiritless, unfortunate, unhappy, unlucky, wretched
F 1 affluent, rich, wealthy 2 good, impressive, superior 3 ample, sufficient 4 fortunate, lucky

poorly *adj* ailing, below par, groggy, ill, indisposed, off colour, out of sorts *colloq*, rotten *colloq*, seedy, sick, sickly, under the weather *colloq*, unwell
F healthy, well
♦ *adv* badly, faultily, feebly, inadequately, incompetently, inexpertly, inferiorly, insufficiently, meanly, rottenly, shabbily, shoddily, unsatisfactorily, unsuccessfully
F well

pop *v* 1 *flashbulbs popped:* bang, burst, crack, explode, go off, snap 2 *to pop out to the shops:* dash, go for a short time, go quickly, hurry, leave quickly, nip *colloq*, rush 3 *popped a sweet into her mouth:* drop, insert, push, put, shove, slide, slip, thrust
♦ *n* 1 *a sudden pop:* bang, boom, burst, crack, explosion, report *formal*, snap 2 *drinking pop:* cola, fizzy drink, fizzy lemonade, soda
▶ **pop off** die, have had it *colloq*, kick the bucket *slang*, pass away, pass on, peg out *colloq*, snuff it *slang*
▶ **pop up** appear, come along, crop up, materialize, occur, show up, turn up

pope *n* Bishop of Rome, His Holiness, Holy Father, pontiff, sovereign pontiff, Vicar of Christ

poppycock *n* balderdash, balls *slang*, baloney *colloq*, bilge *colloq*, blather, bosh *colloq*, bull *colloq*, bullshit *slang*, bunk *colloq*, claptrap *colloq*, cobblers *colloq*, codswallop *colloq*, crap *slang*, drivel, flannel *colloq*, folly, foolishness, gibberish, gobbledygook, hooey *colloq*, humbug *colloq*, nonsense, piffle *colloq*, rot *colloq*, rubbish, shit *slang*, silliness, stuff and nonsense *colloq*, stupidity, tommy-rot *colloq*, tosh *colloq*, trash, tripe *colloq*, twaddle, waffle *colloq*
F sense

populace *n* canaille, citizens, common herd, community, crowd, folk, general public, hoi polloi, inhabitants, masses, mob, multitude(s), natives, occupants, people, plebs *colloq*, proletariat, public, punters *colloq*, rabble *colloq*, rank and file *colloq*, residents, society
F aristocracy, élite, nobility

popular *adj* 1 *these shirts are very popular:* admired, all the rage *colloq*, approved, big *colloq*, cool *colloq*, desired, fashionable, favoured, favourite, hip *colloq*, in *colloq*, in demand, in favour, liked, modish, sought-after, trendy *colloq*, wanted, well-liked 2 *a popular actor:* acclaimed, celebrated, famous, idolized, noted, renowned, well-known 3 *according to popular belief:* accepted, common, conventional, current, customary, general, generally recognized, household, prevailing, prevalent, standard, stock, universal, usual, widespread 4 *a popular history of science:* accessible, general, mass-market, non-specialist, non-technical, ordinary, simple, simplified, understandable
F 1 disliked, out of favour, unpopular 2 obscure, unheard-of, unknown 3 rare, unusual 4 expert, professional, specialist, technical

popularity *n* acceptance, acclaim, adoration, adulation, approbation *formal*, approval,

currency, esteem *formal*, fame, favour, glory, idolization, kudos, lionization, mass appeal, recognition, regard, renown, reputation, repute, vogue, worship
F unpopularity

popularize *v* democratize, familiarize, generalize, give currency to, make accessible, make understandable, propagate, simplify, spread, universalize

popularly *adv* commonly, conventionally, customarily, generally, ordinarily, regularly, traditionally, universally, usually, widely

populate *v* colonize, dwell *formal*, inhabit, live in, occupy, overrun, people, settle

population *n* citizens, community, folk, inhabitants, natives, occupants, people, populace *formal*, residents, society

populous *adj* crawling, crowded, densely populated, overpeopled, overpopulated, packed, swarming, teeming
F deserted, empty

porcelain

Types of porcelain include:
biscuit, bisque, blue and white, bone china, Canton, Capodimonte, chinoiserie, Compagnie des Indes, copper red, eggshell, faience, famille-rose, famille-verte, First Period Worcester, hard paste, Imari, Kakiemon, Kraak, nankeen, Parian, salt-glazed, soapstone paste, soft paste, Yingqing

Famous makes of porcelain include:
Arita, Belleek, Bow, Bristol, Caughley, Chantilly, Chelsea, Coalport, Copeland, Derby, Dresden, Limoges, Meissen, Ming, Minton, Nanking, Rockingham, Royal Doulton, Royal Worcester, Satsuma, Sèvres, Vienna, Wedgwood, Worcester

porch *n* entrance-hall, foyer, hall, hallway, lobby, vestibule

pore[1]
▶ **pore over** brood, contemplate, dwell on, examine, examine closely, go over, peruse *formal*, ponder, read, scan, scrutinize, study, study intensely

pore[2] *n* aperture, foramen *technical*, hole, opening, orifice *formal*, outlet, perforation, vent

pornographic *adj* bawdy, blue, coarse, dirty, erotic, filthy, gross, indecent, lewd, obscene, off-colour, porn *colloq*, prurient *formal*, risqué, salacious, titillating

pornography *n* bawdiness, dirt, erotica, facetiae, filth, girlie magazines *colloq*, grossness, indecency, obscenity, porn *colloq*, porno *colloq*, sexploitation *colloq*, smut

porous *adj* absorbent, airy, cellular, foraminous *technical*, foveate, holey, honeycombed, open, penetrable, permeable, pervious, spongy
F impermeable, impervious

port *n* anchorage, dock, harbour, harbourage, haven, hithe, jetty, roads, roadstead, seaport

portable *adj* compact, convenient, conveyable, handy, lightweight, manageable, movable, transportable
F fixed, immovable

portend *v* adumbrate *formal*, announce, augur *formal*, be a sign of, be an indication of, bespeak *formal*, betoken *formal*, bode *formal*, forebode *formal*, forecast, foreshadow *formal*, foreshow *formal*, foretell, foretoken *formal*, forewarn *formal*, harbinger *formal*, herald, indicate, point to, predict, presage *formal*, prognosticate *formal*, promise, signify, threaten, warn of

portent *n* augury *formal*, foreboding, forecast, forerunner, foreshadowing *formal*, forewarning *formal*, harbinger *formal*, indication, omen, precursor, prefiguration, premonition, presage *formal*, presentiment *formal*, prodrome *formal*, prognostic *formal*, prognostication *formal*, sign, signification *formal*, threat, warning

portentous *adj* **1** *a portentous gloom:* fateful, foreboding, menacing, momentous, ominous, sinister, threatening **2** *a portentous few months:* amazing, astounding, awe-inspiring, crucial, earth-shaking, epoch-making, extraordinary, important, miraculous, remarkable, significant **3** *portentous moralizing:* pompous, ponderous, pontifical, self-important, solemn, weighty
E∃ 2 insignificant, unimportant, unimpressive

porter¹ *n* baggage-attendant, baggage-carrier, baggage-handler, bearer, carrier

porter² *n* caretaker, commissionaire, concierge, door attendant, door-keeper, doorman, gatekeeper, janitor

portion *n* **1** *a portion of the whole:* allocation, allotment, allowance, bit, cut *colloq*, division, fraction, fragment, helping, measure, morsel, parcel, part, percentage, piece, quantity, quota, rake-off *colloq*, ration, section, segment, serving, share, slice, tranche, wedge, whack *colloq* **2** *my portion in life:* chance, destiny, fate, fortune, kismet, lot, luck
♦ *v* allocate, allot, apportion, assign, carve up *colloq*, deal, distribute, divide, dole out *colloq*, parcel, partition, share out, slice up

portliness *n* ampleness, beefiness *colloq*, chubbiness, corpulence *formal*, dumpiness, fatness, fleshiness, fullness, heaviness, obesity, paunchiness, plumpness, rotundity *formal*, roundness, stoutness, tubbiness

portly *adj* ample, corpulent *formal*, fat, heavy, large, obese, overweight, plump, rotund *formal*, round, stocky, stout
E∃ slight, slim, thin

portrait *n* **1** *his portrait hung in the hall:* caricature, drawing, icon, image, likeness, miniature, painting, photograph, picture, portrayal, profile, representation, sketch **2** *an unflattering portrait of family life:* account, characterization, depiction, description, picture, portrayal, representation, story, study, thumbnail sketch, vignette

portray *v* **1** *portrayed her in oils:* draw, illustrate, paint, picture, represent, sketch **2** *portrayed as a scheming temptress:* characterize, depict, describe, evoke, illustrate, picture, represent **3** *she portrayed the Queen of Sheba:* act, characterize, impersonate, perform, personify, play, play/act the part of

portrayal *n* acting, characterization, delineation *formal*, depiction, description, drawing,

evocation, interpretation, painting, performance, picture, presentation, rendering, representation, sketch, study

pose *v* **1** *to pose for an artist:* arrange, model, position, sit **2** *posed as a gas inspector:* act, affect *formal*, attitudinize, feign, impersonate, masquerade, pass yourself off, pretend, put on airs, put on an act **3** *pose a question:* advance, ask, posit *formal*, postulate *formal*, propose, propound *formal*, put, put forward, set, submit, suggest **4** *pose a problem/threat:* cause, create, give rise to, lead to, present, produce, result in
♦ *n* **1** *adopt a defiant pose:* air, attitude, bearing *formal*, carriage *formal*, deportment *formal*, position, posture, stance **2** *his confident air was just a pose:* act, affectation *formal*, airs, façade, front, masquerade, pretence, role, sham

poser¹ *n* attitudinizer, charlatan, exhibitionist, impostor, phoney *colloq*, play-actor, poseur, poseuse, posturer, pseud *colloq*, sham, show-off

poser² *n* brain-teaser, conundrum, dilemma, enigma, mystery, problem, puzzle, riddle, vexed question

poseur *n* attitudinizer, charlatan, exhibitionist, impostor, phoney *colloq*, play-actor, poser, poseuse, posturer, pseud *colloq*, sham, show-off

posh *adj* **1** *his girlfriend is rather posh:* classy *colloq*, high-class, la-di-da *colloq*, rich, smart, stylish, upper-class **2** *a posh restaurant:* classy *colloq*, de luxe, elegant, exclusive, expensive, fancy, fashionable, grand, high-class, lavish, luxurious, opulent *formal*, plush *colloq*, select, smart, stylish, sumptuous, superior, swanky *colloq*, swish *colloq*, up-market
E∃ 2 cheap, inferior

posit *v* advance, assert, assume, pose, postulate *formal*, predicate *formal*, presume, propound *formal*, put forward, state, submit

position *n* **1** *a position on top of the hill:* area, locality, location, place, point, scene, setting, site, situation, spot, whereabouts **2** *an uncomfortable position:* arrangement, attitude, bearing *formal*, disposition, pose, posture, stance **3** *a position in the research department:* appointment, capacity, duty, employment, function, job, occupation, office, post, role, situation **4** *used her position:* grade, influence, level, place, prestige, rank, ranking, standing, status **5** *the position looks hopeless:* background, case, circumstances, condition, factor(s), plight, predicament, situation, state, state of affairs **6** *a radical position:* attitude, belief, opinion, outlook, point of view, stance, stand, standpoint, view, viewpoint
♦ *v* arrange, array *formal*, deploy, dispose, establish, fix, install, lay out, locate, place, put, set, settle, site, situate, stand, station

positive *adj* **1** *positive that I am right:* assured, certain, confident, convinced, sure **2** *feel positive about the future:* cheerful, confident, encouraged, encouraging, hopeful, optimistic, promising, upbeat *colloq* **3** *positive criticism:* constructive, helpful, practical, productive, useful **4** *made a positive identification:* actual, categorical, clear, clear-cut, conclusive, concrete, decisive, definite, direct, emphatic, explicit, express, firm, incontestable, incontrovertible, indisputable, irrefutable *formal*, precise, real, undeniable, unequivocal, unmistakable **5** *a positive nightmare:*

absolute, complete, consummate *formal*, out-and-out, outright, perfect, rank, sheer, thorough, unmitigated, utter, veritable

☒ **1** uncertain **3** negative **4** indefinite, vague

positively *adv* absolutely, assuredly, categorically, certainly, conclusively, decisively, definitely, emphatically, expressly, finally, firmly, incontestably, incontrovertibly, indisputably, surely, uncompromisingly, undeniably, unequivocally, unmistakably, unquestionably

possess *v* **1** *to possess nuclear weapons:* acquire, be endowed with, be gifted with, be in possession of, enjoy, gain, get, have, hold, own **2** *his soul was possessed:* acquire, get, obtain, occupy, seize, take, take over, take possession of **3** *what possessed you to say that?:* bewitch, control, dominate, enchant, haunt, infatuate, influence, obsess

possessed *adj* bedevilled, berserk, besotted, bewitched, consumed, controlled, crazed, cursed, demented, dominated, enchanted, frenzied, hag-ridden, haunted, infatuated, maddened, mesmerized, obsessed, raving

possession *n* control, custody, grip, hold, holding, occupation, ownership, proprietorship, tenancy, tenure, title

possessions *n* accoutrements *formal*, (all your) worldly goods *colloq*, assets, baggage, belongings, chattels, effects, estate, gear *colloq*, goods, goods and chattels, luggage, movables, paraphernalia, property, riches, stuff *colloq*, things *colloq*, wealth

possessive *adj* acquisitive, clinging, controlling, covetous, dominating, domineering, grasping, greedy, jealous, overprotective, selfish

☒ sharing, unselfish

possibility *n* **1** *there is a possibility it could happen:* attainability, chance, conceivability, danger, feasibility, hazard, hope, likelihood, odds, potentiality, practicability, probability, prospect, risk **2** *a place with possibilities:* advantages, capabilities, expectations, potential, potentiality *formal*, promise, prospects, talent **3** *that is one possibility:* alternative, choice, option, preference, recourse

☒ **1** impossibility, impracticability **2** disadvantages, liabilities

possible *adj* accomplishable, achievable, attainable, conceivable, credible, doable, feasible, imaginable, likely, odds-on *colloq*, on the cards *colloq*, potential, practicable, probable, promising, realizable, tenable, that can be done, viable, workable

☒ impossible, impracticable, unattainable, unthinkable

possibly *adv* **1** *possibly it will arrive tomorrow:* conceivably, hopefully *colloq*, maybe, peradventure *formal*, perhaps **2** *you can't possibly mean that:* at all, by any chance, by any means, conceivably

post[1] *n* baluster, banister, column, leg, newel, pale, palisade, picket, pillar, pole, prop, shaft, stake, stanchion, standard, strut, support, upright

♦ *v* **1** *posted the cutting on the notice board:* affix, attach, display, pin (up), put up, stick up **2** *posted the news on her website:* advertise, announce,

broadcast, circulate, make known, publicize, publish, report

post[2] *n* appointment, assignment, beat, employment, job, office, place, position, situation, station, vacancy

♦ *v* appoint, assign, locate, move, place, position, put, second, send, situate, station, transfer

post[3] *n* **1** *deliver the post:* airmail, communications, correspondence, delivery, direct mail, electronic mail, e-mail, international mail, junk mail *colloq*, letters, mail, packages, packets, parcels, recorded mail, registered mail, snail mail *colloq*, special delivery, surface mail **2** *the letter is in the post:* mail, Post Office, postal service, postal system

♦ *v* dispatch, forward, mail, send, transmit

poster *n* ad *colloq*, advert *colloq*, advertisement, announcement, bill, bulletin, notice, placard, sign, sticker

posterior *adj* after, back, behind, dorsal *technical*, ensuing, following, hind, hinder, later, latter, posticous, rear, rearward, subsequent, succeeding

☒ anterior, front, previous

♦ *n* arse *slang*, ass *colloq*, backside *colloq*, behind, bottom, bum *colloq*, butt *US colloq*, buttocks, haunches, hinder end, hindquarters, rear, rump, seat, tail *colloq*

posterity *n* children, descendants, future generations, heirs, issue *formal*, offspring, progeny *formal*, seed, succeeding generations, successors

posthaste *adv* at once, directly, double-quick *colloq*, full tilt *colloq*, hastily, immediately, promptly, pronto *colloq*, quickly, speedily, straight away, swiftly, with all speed

☒ eventually, gradually, slowly

post-mortem *n* analysis, autopsy, dissection, examination, necropsy, review

postpone *v* adjourn, defer, delay, do later, freeze, hold over, pigeonhole, procrastinate *formal*, prorogue *formal*, put back, put off, put on ice *colloq*, put on the back burner *colloq*, reschedule, shelve, suspend, take a raincheck on *colloq*

☒ advance, bring forward, forward

postponed *adj* adjourned, deferred, frozen, in abeyance *formal*, on ice *colloq*, on the back burner *colloq*, pigeonholed, put off, shelved, suspended

☒ advanced

postponement *n* adjournment, deferment, deferral, delay, freeze, moratorium, prorogation *formal*, put-off, respite, stay, suspension

postscript *n* addendum, addition, afterthought, afterword, appendix, codicil *technical*, epilogue, PS *colloq*, supplement

☒ introduction, prologue

postulate *v* advance, assume, hypothesize *formal*, lay down, posit *formal*, presume, presuppose, propose, stipulate, suppose, theorize

posture *n* **1** *her perfect posture:* attitude, bearing *formal*, carriage *formal*, deportment *formal*, disposition, pose, position, stance **2** *an aggressive posture:* attitude, belief, opinion, outlook, point of view, stance, stand, standpoint, view, viewpoint

♦ *v* affect *formal*, attitudinize, pose, put on airs, show off, strike attitudes, strut

posy *n* bouquet, buttonhole, corsage, nosegay, spray

pot *n* **1** *a cooking pot:* basin, bowl, cauldron, coffee pot, crucible, jar, pan, receptacle, teapot, urn, vase, vessel **2** *kept all the money in a central pot:* fund, kitty, purse, reserve

pot-bellied *adj* bloated, corpulent, distended, fat, gor-bellied, obese, overweight, paunchy, portly, tubby

pot-belly *n* beer belly, belly, corporation *colloq*, gut, paunch, pot, spare tyre *colloq*

potency *n* authority, capacity, cogency *formal*, control, effectiveness, efficaciousness *formal*, efficacy *formal*, energy, force, headiness *colloq*, influence, kick *colloq*, might *formal*, muscle *colloq*, persuasiveness, potential, power, puissance *formal*, punch *colloq*, strength, sway, vigour
▨ impotence, weakness

potent *adj* authoritative, cogent *formal*, commanding, compelling, convincing, dominant, dynamic, effective, efficacious *formal*, eloquent, energetic, forceful, impressive, influential, intoxicating, mighty, overpowering, persuasive, powerful, puissant *formal*, pungent, strong, vigorous
▨ impotent, weak

potentate *n* autocrat, chief, chieftain, despot, dictator, dynast, emperor, empress, head of state, king, leader, mogul, monarch, overlord, prince, queen, ruler, sovereign, tyrant

potential *adj* aspiring, budding, concealed, developing, dormant, embryonic, future, hidden, inherent, latent, likely, possible, probable, promising, prospective, undeveloped, unrealized, would-be
♦ *n* ability, aptitude, capability, capacity, flair, gift, possibility, powers, promise, resources, talent

potentiality *n* ability, aptitude, capability, capacity, likelihood, possibilities, potential, promise, prospect, virtuality

potion *n* beverage, brew, concoction, dose, draught, drink, elixir, medicine, mixture, philtre, potation, tonic

potpourri *n* assortment, collection, confusion, gallimaufry, hotchpotch, jumble, medley, melange, miscellany, mishmash *colloq*, mixture, pastiche, patchwork, smorgasbord

potter *v* amble, dawdle, dilly-dally *colloq*, loiter, mess about *colloq*, toddle *colloq*
▶ **potter about** fiddle about/around, fool about/around, mess about/around *colloq*, muck about/around *colloq*, play about/around, tinker about/around

pottery *n* ceramics, china, crockery

Terms used in pottery include:
armorial, art pottery, basalt, blanc-de-chine, bronzing, celadon, ceramic, china clay, cloisonné, crackleware, crazing, creamware, delft, earthenware, enamel, faience, fairing, figure, firing, flambé, flatback, glaze, grotesque, ground, ironstone, jasper, kiln, lustre, maiolica, majolica, maker's mark, mandarin palette, model, monogram,

---

overglaze, porcelain, sagger, scratch blue, sgraffito, slip, slip-cast, spongeware, Staffordshire, stoneware, terracotta, tin-glazed earthenware, transfer printing, underglaze, Willow pattern. See also **porcelain**

---

potty *adj* bananas *colloq*, barmy *colloq*, bonkers *colloq*, crackers *colloq*, crazy, daft *colloq*, demented, dippy *colloq*, dotty *colloq*, eccentric, foolish, nuts *colloq*, nutty *colloq*, silly, soft, touched

pouch *n* bag, container, marsupium *technical*, pocket, poke, purse, receptacle, reticule *formal*, sac, sack, sporran, wallet

pounce *v* ambush, attack, bound, catch off guard, catch/take unawares, descend, dive on, drop, fall on, grab, jump, leap, lunge, snatch, spring, strike, swoop, take by surprise
♦ *n* assault, attack, bound, dive, grab, jump, leap, lunge, spring, swoop

pound[1] *n* nicker *slang*, oncer *slang*, pound coin, pound sterling, quid *colloq*, smacker *slang*, smackeroo *slang*, sov *slang*

pound[2] *n* compound, corral, enclosure, fold, pen, yard

pound[3] *v* **1** *pounded on the door:* bang, bash, batter, beat, drum, hammer, pelt, pummel, smash, strike, thump **2** *pound the fruit into a pulp:* beat, bray, comminute *formal*, crush, granulate, grind, levigate *formal*, mash, pestle, powder, pulverize, smash, triturate *formal* **3** *his heart was pounding:* palpitate, pulsate, throb, thud, thump **4** *pound the streets:* pace, plod, stomp, tramp, tread, trudge, walk

pour *v* **1** *pour a drink:* decant, make flow, pour out, serve, spill, sprinkle, tip **2** *water was pouring from the hole:* cascade, come out, course, crowd, discharge, disembogue *formal*, disgorge *formal*, emit, flood, flow, gush, issue, jet, leak, ooze, run, rush, spew, spill, spout, spurt, stream, swarm, throng **3** *it's pouring outside:* bucket down *colloq*, come down in buckets/stair rods/torrents *colloq*, pelt down, piss down *slang*, rain, rain cats and dogs *colloq*, teem down

pout *v* glower, grimace, lour, mope, pull a face, scowl, sulk
▨ grin, smile
♦ *n* glower, grimace, long face, moue, scowl
▨ grin, smile

poverty *n* bankruptcy, dearth, deficiency, depletion, deprivation, destitution, distress, hardship, impecuniosity *formal*, impoverishment, inadequacy, indigence *formal*, insolvency, insufficiency, lack, meagreness, necessity, need, paucity, pennilessness, penury *formal*, poorness, privation *formal*, scarcity, shortage, want
▨ affluence, plenty, richness, wealth

poverty-stricken *adj* bankrupt, beggared, broke *colloq*, destitute, distressed, impecunious *formal*, impoverished, indigent *formal*, needy, obolary *formal*, on your beam-ends *colloq*, on your uppers *colloq*, penniless, penurious *formal*, poor, skint *colloq*, stony *colloq*, stony-broke *colloq*, strapped *colloq*
▨ affluent, rich

powder *n* bran, dust, grains, pounce, pulvil *formal*, pulvil(l)io *formal*, pulville *formal*, talc, triturate *formal*

◆ *v* **1** *powdered bones:* beat, bray, comminute *formal*, crush, granulate, grind, levigate *formal*, mash, pestle, pulverize, smash, triturate *formal* **2** *powder your nose:* cover, dust, sprinkle

powdery *adj* chalky, crumbly, dry, dusty, fine, floury, friable *formal*, grainy, granular, granulated, ground, levigate *formal*, loose, powdered, pulverized, pulverulent *formal*, sandy

power *n* **1** *in a position of power:* ascendancy *formal*, authority, clout *colloq*, clutches *colloq*, command, control, domination, dominion, influence, mastery, muscle *colloq*, pull *colloq*, rule, say, sovereignty, supremacy, sway, teeth *colloq* **2** *have the power of arrest:* authority, authorization, licence, prerogative, privilege, right, warrant **3** *a performance of great power:* effectiveness, energy, force, forcefulness, intensity, juice *colloq*, might *formal*, potency, powerfulness, strength, vigour **4** *he has the power to succeed:* ability, capability, capacity, competence, faculty, potential, potentiality *formal* ☒ **1** subjection **3** impotence, weakness **4** inability

powerful *adj* **1** *a powerful figure in the industry:* all-powerful, authoritative, commanding, compelling, convincing, dominant, effective, energetic, forceful, high-powered, impressive, influential, leading, overwhelming, persuasive, potent, prevailing, telling, winning **2** *a powerful physique:* brawny, burly, hardy, mighty, muscular, robust, strapping, strong, tough ☒ **1** impotent, ineffective, powerless **2** weak

powerfully *adv* cogently *formal*, convincingly, forcefully, forcibly, hard, impressively, mightily *formal*, persuasively, potently, strongly, tellingly, vigorously, with might and main *formal*

powerless *adj* defenceless, having no say, helpless, impotent, incapable, ineffectual *formal*, unable, unfit, vulnerable, weak ☒ able, influential, powerful

practicability *n* feasibility, handiness, operability, possibility, practicality, use, usefulness, utility, value, viability, workability, workableness ☒ impracticability

practicable *adj* achievable, attainable, doable, feasible, performable, possible, practical, realistic, viable, workable ☒ impracticable

---

practicable or *practical? Practicable* means 'able to be done, used, carried out, etc': *a practicable plan. Practical* when applied to things, suggestions, etc also means 'able to be done, used, or carried out' but has the further connotation of 'efficient, sensible, useful': *Both these suggested courses of action are practicable, but John's is certainly the more practical of the two; High heels aren't very practical for hill-walking.* Applied to people, *practical* means 'able to do, make, or deal with things well or efficiently': *He's not a very practical person: he has lots of ideas for redesigning the bathroom but he doesn't have a clue how to put up a shelf.*

---

practical *adj* **1** *put to practical use:* actual, applied, hands on, real **2** *let's be practical:* businesslike,

down-to-earth, hard-headed, hard-nosed *colloq*, having both feet on the ground *colloq*, matter-of-fact, pragmatic, realistic, sensible **3** *practical experience:* accomplished, efficient, experienced, proficient, qualified, skilled, trained **4** *practical ideas:* applied, commonsense, feasible, practicable, realistic, sensible, workable **5** *practical shoes:* everyday, functional, handy, ordinary, sensible, serviceable, strong, suitable, useful, utilitarian, workaday, working **6** *a practical walkover:* effective, essential, virtual ☒ **1** theoretical **2** impractical **3** impractical, unskilled **5** impractical

practicality *n* **1** *the practicality of the idea:* feasibility, practicability, practicalness, soundness, utility, workability **2** *she lacks practicality:* common sense, experience, practicalness, practice, pragmatism, realism, sense **3** *the practicality of this simple tool:* functionalism, functionality, practicalness, serviceability, usefulness, utility **4** *get down to practicalities:* basics, nitty-gritty *colloq*, nuts and bolts *colloq*

practically *adv* **1** *they're practically bankrupt:* all but, almost, essentially, fundamentally, in effect, in principle, just about, nearly, pretty much *colloq*, pretty well *colloq*, to all intents and purposes, virtually, well-nigh **2** *deal with a problem practically:* matter-of-factly, pragmatically, rationally, realistically, reasonably, sensibly

practice *n* **1** *it is the shop's practice to refuse credit:* convention, custom, habit, method, policy, procedure, routine, system, tradition, usage, way, wont *formal* **2** *football practice:* drill, dry run, dummy run, exercise, experience, preparation, rehearsal, run-through, study, training, try-out, warm-up, work-out **3** *in practice:* action, actuality, application, effect, exercise, operation, performance, reality, use **4** *the practice of medicine:* business, career, employment, following, job, occupation, profession, pursuit, work **5** *working in a legal practice:* business, company, firm, office ☒ **3** principle, theory

practise *v* **1** *practise what you preach:* apply, carry out, do, engage in, execute *formal*, follow, implement, observe, perform, pursue, put into practice, undertake **2** *practise a piece on the piano:* go over, go through, perfect, polish, prepare, refine, rehearse, repeat, run through, study, work at, work on **3** *practise for a concert:* drill, exercise, prepare, rehearse, study, train

practised *adj* able, accomplished, adept, consummate *formal*, experienced, expert, knowing, knowledgeable, masterly, proficient, qualified, seasoned, skilful, skilled, trained, versed, veteran ☒ inexperienced, inexpert, unpractised

pragmatic *adj* businesslike, efficient, hard-headed, hard-nosed *colloq*, matter-of-fact, practical, realistic, sensible, unsentimental, utilitarian ☒ idealistic, romantic, unrealistic

pragmatism *n* hard-headedness, humanism, opportunism, practicalism, practicality, realism, unidealism, utilitarianism ☒ idealism, romanticism

pragmatist *n* opportunist, practicalist, realist, utilitarian
 idealist, romantic

praise *v* **1** *praised him for his bravery:* acclaim, acknowledge, admire, applaud, cheer, commend, compliment, congratulate, eulogize *formal*, express approval of, extol, hail, honour, laud *formal*, pay tribute to, rave over *colloq*, recognize, sing the praises of, speak highly of, speak well of, wax lyrical **2** *praise God in prayer:* adore, bless, exalt, glorify, magnify, worship
 1 criticize, revile
♦ *n* **1** *be full of praise for someone:* acclaim, accolade, admiration, adulation, applause, approbation *formal*, approval, bouquets *colloq*, cheering, commendation, compliment, congratulation, encomium *formal*, eulogy *formal*, homage, honour, laudation *formal*, ovation, panegyric *formal*, plaudits, puff *colloq*, recognition, testimonial, tribute **2** *a hymn of praise:* adoration, glory, hallelujah, homage, thanks, thanksgiving, worship
 1 criticism, revilement

praiseworthy *adj* admirable, commendable, deserving, estimable, excellent, exemplary, fine, honourable, laudable *formal*, reputable, sterling, worthy
 blameworthy, dishonourable, ignoble

praising *adj* adulatory, approbatory *formal*, approving, commendatory, complimentary, congratulatory, encomiastic *formal*, eulogistic *formal*, favourable, laudative *formal*, laudatory *formal*, panegyric *formal*, plauditory *formal*, recommendatory
 condemnatory, critical

prance *v* **1** *the children pranced around the hall:* bound, caper, cavort, curvet, dance, frisk, frolic, gambol, jump, leap, romp, skip, spring **2** *prancing around in her designer clothes:* parade, show off, strut, swagger, swank *colloq*

prank *n* antic, caper, escapade, frolic, joke, lark, practical joke, stunt, trick

prattle *v* babble *colloq*, blather, blether, chat, chatter, drivel, gabble, gossip, jabber *colloq*, patter, rattle, twaddle, twattle, twitter, witter
♦ *n* babble, blather, blether, chat, chatter, drivel, foolishness, gab, gibberish, gossip, hot air *colloq*, jaw, nonsense, prating, talk, tattle

prattler *n* babbler *colloq*, blabbermouth *colloq*, bletherer, chatterbox *colloq*, chatterer, gabbler, gossip, magpie, talker, tatler, tattler, windbag *colloq*

pray *v* **1** *they pray and meditate all day:* be at prayer, say a prayer, say your prayers **2** *pray to God:* adore, call on, commune with, invoke, praise, say a prayer to, speak to, talk to, thank, worship **3** *he prayed for mercy:* ask, beg, beseech *formal*, crave, entreat, implore, petition, plead, request, solicit, supplicate *formal*

prayer *n* **1** *prayer to God:* devotion, intercession, invocation, mantra **2** *a prayer for justice:* appeal, entreaty, petition, plea, request, supplication *formal*

prayer-book *n* breviary, euchologion, euchology, formulary, mahzor, missal, ordinal, service-book, Triodion

preach *v* **1** *preaching to a congregation:* address, evangelize, exhort, give a sermon, sermonize,

spread the gospel **2** *preach the gospel:* proclaim, spread, teach **3** *preach tolerance:* advise, advocate, exhort, teach, urge **4** *please don't preach at me:* admonish, harangue, lecture, moralize, pontificate, sermonize

preacher *n* clergyman, evangelist, homilist, minister, missionary, moralizer, parson, pontificater, pulpite(e)r, ranter, revivalist, sermonizer, televangelist

preaching *n* **1** *the preaching of the gospel:* evangelism, exhortation *formal*, instruction, kerygma, pontificating, sermonizing, teaching **2** *his preachings are recorded in the scriptures:* doctrine, dogma, evangel *technical*, gospel, homiletics, homilies, kerygma, message, precepts, sermons, teaching

preachy *adj* didactic, dogmatic, edifying, exhortatory *formal*, holier-than-thou *colloq*, homiletic, hortatory *formal*, moralizing, pharisaic, pietistic, pontifical, pontificating, religiose, sanctimonious, self-righteous, sermonizing

preamble *n* exordium *formal*, foreword, introduction, lead-in, overture, preface, preliminaries, prelude, proem *formal*, prolegomenon *formal*, prologue
 epilogue, postscript

precarious *adj* **1** *a precarious ladder:* dangerous, insecure, shaky, unreliable, unsafe, unstable, unsteady, wobbly **2** *in a precarious position:* chancy *colloq*, dangerous, dicey *colloq*, dicky *colloq*, dodgy *colloq*, doubtful, dubious, hairy *colloq*, hazardous, iffy *colloq*, insecure, risky, uncertain, undependable, unpredictable, unsafe, unsettled, unstable, unsure, vulnerable
 1 safe, secure, stable **2** certain, safe, secure, stable

precaution *n* **1** *safety precautions:* insurance, preparation, preventive/preventative measure, protection, provision, safeguard, security measure **2** *use precaution when handling fireworks:* anticipation, attentiveness, care, caution, circumspection *formal*, farsightedness, foresight, forethought, providence, prudence *formal*

precautionary *adj* cautious, far-sighted, judicious *formal*, preliminary, preparatory, preventative, preventive, protective, provident, prudent *formal*, safety

precede *v* **1** *the event which preceded the ceremony:* antecede *formal*, antedate *formal*, come before, come first, herald, introduce, prevene *formal*, usher in **2** *she preceded him into the church:* go ahead of, go before, lead, take precedence **3** *the quote which precedes the main article:* come before, go before, head, introduce, preface
 1 follow, succeed **2** follow, succeed **3** follow, succeed

precedence *n* ascendancy *formal*, eminence, first place, lead, pre-eminence, preference, pride of place, priority, rank, seniority, superiority, supremacy

precedent *n* case, criterion, example, exemplar *formal*, instance, model, paradigm *formal*, parallel, pattern, standard, yardstick

preceding *adj* **1** *in the preceding paragraph:* above, aforementioned *formal*, aforesaid *formal*, earlier, foregoing, precedent, precursive *formal*,

previous, supra *formal* **2** *sales for the preceding month:* antecedent, earlier, foregoing, past, precedent, previous, prior
F **1** following, later **2** following, later

precept *n* **1** *the precepts of his religion:* canon, charge, command, commandment, convention, decree, dictum, direction, directive, guideline, injunction, institute, instruction, law, mandate, order, ordinance, principle, regulation, rubric, rule, statute **2** *the precept that an Englishman's home is his castle:* axiom, dictum, maxim, motto, principle, saying

precinct *n* **1** *a shopping precinct:* area, district, division, galleria, mall, quarter, section, sector, shopping centre, zone **2** *within the precincts of the university:* bound, boundary, close, confine, enclosure, environs, limit, locality, milieu, neighbourhood, purlieus, surrounds, vicinity

preciosity *n* affectation, artificiality, chichi, floweriness, over-refinement, pretentiousness, tweeness

precious *adj* **1** *his most precious memories:* adored, beloved, cherished, darling, dear, dearest, favourite, idolized, loved, prized, treasured, valued **2** *precious jewels:* choice, costly, dear, expensive, fine, high-priced, inestimable, priceless, rare, valuable **3** *method actors can be a very precious lot:* affected, artificial, chichi, contrived, flowery, mannered, overrefined, pretentious, twee

precipice *n* bluff, brink, cliff, cliff face, crag, drop, escarp, escarpment, height, krantz, scarp, steep

precipitate *v* **1** *the invasion which precipitated the war:* accelerate, advance, bring about, bring on, cause, expedite, further, hasten, hurry, induce, occasion, quicken, speed (up), trigger **2** *we were precipitated into the water:* fling, heave, hurl, throw
♦ *adj* **1** *his precipitate actions:* frantic, hasty, heedless, hot-headed, hurried, impatient, impetuous, impulsive, rash, reckless **2** *a precipitate increase in interest rates:* abrupt, breakneck, headlong, hurried, quick, rapid, speedy, sudden, swift, unexpected, violent
F **1** careful, cautious

---

precipitate or *precipitous*? *Precipitate* means 'hasty or too hasty': *a precipitate decision*. *Precipitous* means 'very steep, like a precipice': *The path through the mountains is narrow and precipitous*.

---

precipitation

Types of precipitation include:
dew, downpour, drizzle, fog, hail, mist, rain, rainfall, rainstorm, shower, sleet, snow, snowfall, snowflake

---

precipitous *adj* **1** *a precipitous rockface:* high, perpendicular, sheer, steep, vertical **2** *a precipitous departure:* abrupt, sharp, sudden
F **1** gradual **2** gradual

précis *n* abbreviation, abridgement, abstract, compendium, condensation, conspectus *formal*, contraction, digest, encapsulation *formal*, epitome, outline, résumé, run-down, sketch, summary, synopsis
♦ *v* abbreviate, abridge, abstract, compress,

condense, contract, digest, encapsulate, epitomize, outline, shorten, sum up, summarize, synopsize
F amplify, expand

precise *adj* **1** *give precise details:* accurate, actual, authentic, blow-by-blow, clear-cut, correct, definite, detailed, distinct, exact, explicit, express, factual, faithful, particular, specific, unambiguous, unequivocal, word-for-word **2** *his precise manners:* careful, conscientious, correct, exact, fastidious, fixed, literal, meticulous, minute, nice, particular, punctilious, right, rigid, rigorous, scrupulous, strict
F **1** ambiguous, imprecise, inexact **2** careless

precisely *adv* **1** *it's precisely noon:* accurately, bang on *colloq*, correctly, dead on *colloq*, exactly, on the dot, strictly **2** *landed precisely in the centre:* accurately, correctly, dead on *colloq*, exactly, plumb *colloq*, slap *colloq*, smack *colloq*, squarely **3** *repeat precisely what you heard:* exactly, literally, verbatim, word for word **4** *described him precisely:* absolutely, clearly, distinctly, exactly, minutely, to a T *colloq* **5** *'Am I right?' – 'Precisely':* absolutely, exactly, just so, on the button *US*, spot on *colloq*, to a T *colloq*

precision *n* **1** *the precision of the planning:* accuracy, care, conscientiousness, detail, distinctness, exactitude, exactness, explicitness, rigour **2** *the precision of his dress:* correctness, fastidiousness, meticulousness, neatness, particularity, punctiliousness, scrupulousness
F **1** imprecision, inaccuracy

preclude *v* **1** *her condition precludes air travel:* make impossible, obviate *formal*, prevent, rule out **2** *his prison record precludes him from finding a job:* check, debar, eliminate, exclude, forestall, hinder, inhibit, prevent, prohibit, stop
F **1** incur, involve

precocious *adj* advanced, bright, brilliant, clever, developed, early, fast, gifted, mature, quick, smart, talented
F backward, slow, stupid

preconceive *v* anticipate, assume, conceive, envisage, expect, imagine, picture, presume, presuppose, project, visualize

preconception *n* anticipation, assumption, bias, conjecture *formal*, expectation, notion, predisposition *formal*, prejudgement, prejudice, presumption, presupposition

precondition *n* condition, essential, must *colloq*, necessity, prerequisite, requirement, sine qua non *formal*, stipulation

precursor *n* **1** *our precursors were hunter-gatherers:* ancestor, forebear, progenitor *formal* **2** *the precursors of modern science:* antecedent, forerunner, pioneer, trail-blazer **3** *a precursor to a takeover:* curtain-raiser, forerunner, harbinger, herald, indication, prelude, sign
F **1** follower, successor **2** follower, successor

precursory *adj* antecedent, anterior, introductory, preambulatory *formal*, preceding, precursive *formal*, prefatory, preliminary, preludial *formal*, prelusive *formal*, preparatory, prevenient *formal*, previous, prior, prodromal *formal*
F following, resulting, subsequent

predatory *adj* **1** *predatory animals:* carnivorous, hunting, predacious *formal*, predative *formal*, preying, raptatorial *formal*, raptorial *formal* **2** *a target for predatory gangs*: despoiling, marauding, pillaging, plundering, preying, ravaging, thieving **3** *predatory businesses*: acquisitive, avaricious, covetous, greedy, lupine, rapacious *formal*, voracious, vulturine, vulturous, wolfish

predecessor *n* **1** *our predecessors lived in tribes*: ancestor, forebear, forefather, precursor, progenitor *formal* **2** *better at the job than his predecessor*: antecedent, forerunner, precursor
🖅 **1** descendant, successor **2** successor

predestination *n* destiny, doom, fate, foreordination, lot, predetermination *formal*

predestine *v* destine, doom, fate, foredoom, foreordain, intend, mean, predestinate *formal*, predetermine *formal*, pre-elect, preordain

predetermined *adj* **1** *his fate was predetermined*: destined, doomed, fated, foreordained, ordained, predestined **2** *meet at a predetermined time*: agreed, arranged, fixed, prearranged, set, settled

predicament *n* can of worms *colloq*, crisis, dilemma, emergency, fix, hiccup *colloq*, hole *colloq*, hot/deep water *colloq*, impasse, jam *colloq*, kettle of fish *colloq*, mess, pickle *colloq*, plight, quandary, scrape *colloq*, situation, spot *colloq*, stew *colloq*, tight spot *colloq*, trouble

predicate *v* **1** *predicate the existence of God*: affirm, assert, aver *formal*, avouch *formal*, avow *formal*, contend, declare, posit *formal*, postulate *formal*, premise *formal*, proclaim, state **2** *the theory is predicated on accurate information*: base, be dependent, build, establish, found, ground, maintain, rest

predict *v* augur *formal*, auspicate *formal*, divine *formal*, forecast, foresee, foretell, portend *formal*, presage *formal*, prognosticate *formal*, project, prophesy, second-guess *colloq*, vaticinate *formal*

predictable *adj* anticipated, certain, dependable, expected, foregone, foreseeable, foreseen, imaginable, likely, odds-on *colloq*, on the cards *colloq*, probable, reliable, sure
🖅 uncertain, unforeseeable, unpredictable

prediction *n* augury *formal*, auspication *formal*, divination *formal*, forecast, fortune-telling, prognosis, prognostication *formal*, prophecy, soothsaying

predictive *adj* augural *formal*, diagnostic, divinatory *formal*, foretelling, prognostic *formal*, prophetic

predilection *n* affection, affinity, bent, bias, enthusiasm, fancy, fondness, inclination, leaning, liking, love, partiality, penchant *formal*, predisposition *formal*, preference, proclivity *formal*, propensity *formal*, soft spot, taste, tendency, weakness
🖅 antipathy *formal*, disinclination, dislike

predispose *v* **1** *predispose someone to do something*: bias, dispose, incline, induce, influence, make, move, persuade, prejudice, prompt, sway **2** *predispose someone to a disease*: make liable

predisposed *adj* **1** *I felt predisposed to like him*: agreeable, amenable, biased, disposed, favourable, inclined, minded, not unwilling, prejudiced, prepared, ready, well-disposed,

willing **2** *people predisposed to the disease*: liable, prone, subject, susceptible
🖅 **1** loath, reluctant, unwilling

predisposition *n* **1** *a predisposition to think the best of people*: bent, bias, disposition, inclination, leaning, liability, likelihood, penchant *formal*, predilection *formal*, preference, prejudice, proclivity *formal*, propensity *formal*, tendency, willingness **2** *a predisposition to diabetes*: liability, proneness, propensity *formal*, susceptibility, tendency, vulnerability

predominance *n* **1** *the predominance of males in the profession*: numbers, preponderance *formal*, prevalence, weight **2** *achieve predominance in the industry*: ascendancy *formal*, control, dominance, dominion, edge *colloq*, hegemony *formal*, hold, influence, leadership, mastery, paramountcy *formal*, power, prepollence *formal*, prepollency *formal*, prepotence *formal*, prepotency *formal*, prevalence, supremacy, sway, upper hand *colloq*
🖅 **2** ineffectiveness, weakness

predominant *adj* **1** *my predominant feeling was relief*: chief, main, most noticeable, most obvious, preponderant *formal*, prevailing, primary, principal, strongest **2** *the company is predominant in the business world*: ascendant *formal*, capital, chief, controlling, dominant, forceful, important, in control, in the ascendancy *formal*, influential, leading, most important, paramount, potent, powerful, preponderant *formal*, prevailing, prime, principal, ruling, sovereign, supreme
🖅 **1** weak **2** lesser, minor

predominate *v* **1** *women predominate in the nursing profession*: be in the majority, obtain *formal*, outnumber, outweigh, preponderate *formal* **2** *one company predominates in the industry*: be dominant, dominate, preponderate *formal*, prevail, reign, rule

pre-eminence *n* distinction, excellence, fame, incomparability, matchlessness, paramountcy, peerlessness, predominance, prestige, prominence, renown, repute, superiority, supremacy, transcendence

pre-eminent *adj* chief, distinguished, eminent, excellent, exceptional, famous, first, foremost, incomparable, inimitable, leading, matchless, most important, outstanding, prominent, renowned, superior, superlative, supreme, transcendent, unequalled, unmatched, unrivalled, unsurpassed
🖅 inferior, unknown

pre-eminently *adv* conspicuously, eminently, emphatically, especially, exceptionally, exclusively, incomparably, inimitably, matchlessly, notably, par excellence, particularly, peerlessly, signally, singularly, strikingly, superlatively, supremely, surpassingly

pre-empt *v* **1** *pre-empt land*: acquire, appropriate *formal*, arrogate *formal*, assume, secure, seize, usurp **2** *pre-empt a move*: anticipate, forestall, prevent

preen *v* **1** *birds preening their feathers*: clean, groom, plume, slick, smooth, tidy, trim **2** *preening herself for her big night out*: adorn, array *formal*, beautify, deck, do up *colloq*, doll up, dress up, prettify, primp, prink, spruce up, tart up *colloq*, trick out **3** *preened himself on his intellect*:

bask, congratulate, exult, gloat, pat yourself on the back *colloq*, pique, plume, pride

preface *n* foreword, frontmatter, introduction, preamble, preliminaries, prelims *colloq*, prelude, proem *formal*, prolegomenon *formal*, prologue
F3 epilogue, postscript
♦ *v* begin, introduce, launch, lead up to, open, precede, prefix, start
F3 complete, end, finish

prefatory *adj* antecedent, exordial *formal*, explanatory, introductory, opening, preambulatory *formal*, precursory *formal*, prefatorial *formal*, preliminary, preludial *formal*, prelusive *formal*, prelusory *formal*, proemial *formal*, prolegomenal *formal*
F3 closing, final

prefect *n* administrator, monitor, praefect, praeposter, prepositor, supervisor

prefer *v* **1** *which candidate do you prefer?*: adopt, advocate, back, be partial to, choose, desire, elect, fancy *colloq*, favour, go for, like better, opt (for), pick (out), plump for *colloq*, recommend, select, single out, support, want, wish, would rather, would sooner **2** *prefer someone to a higher position*: advance, aggrandize *formal*, elevate, exalt, favour, honour, move up, promote, raise **3** *prefer charges*: bring, file, lodge, place, present, press
F3 **1** reject **2** demote

preferable *adj* advantageous, advisable, better, chosen, desirable, favoured, more desired, preferred, recommended, superior
F3 inferior, undesirable

preferably *adv* by/for preference, first, for choice, from choice, much rather, much sooner, rather, sooner

preference *n* **1** *which dish would be your preference?*: choice, cup of tea *colloq*, desire, favourite, first choice, option, pick, selection, wish **2** *we can accommodate your preferences*: bent, bias, fancy, inclination, leaning, liking, partiality, predilection **3** *give someone preference*: discrimination, favouritism, precedence, preferential treatment, priority

preferential *adj* advantageous, better, biased, favourable, favoured, partial, partisan, privileged, special, superior
F3 equal

preferment *n* advancement, aggrandizement *formal*, betterment, dignity, elevation, exaltation, furtherance, improvement, promotion, rise, step up, upgrading
F3 demotion

preferred *adj* approved, authorized, choice, chosen, desired, favoured, predilect *formal*, recommended, sanctioned, selected
F3 rejected, undesirable

pregnancy *n* child-bearing, conception, family way *colloq*, fertilization, gestation, gravidity *formal*, impregnation, parturition *technical*

pregnant *adj* **1** *a pregnant woman*: enceinte *formal*, expectant, expecting, in the club *colloq*, in the family way *colloq*, parturient *technical*, preggers *slang*, up the spout *slang*, with a bun in the oven *slang*, with child *formal* **2** *a pregnant pause*: charged, eloquent, expressive, loaded, meaningful, pointed, significant, suggestive, telling **3** *the air was pregnant with tension*:

charged, filled, fraught, full, heavy, loaded, replete *formal*, rich
F3 **2** jejune

prehistoric *adj* **1** *prehistoric times*: earliest, early, primeval, primitive, primordial **2** *my prehistoric old word processor*: ancient, antediluvian *colloq*, antiquated, archaic, before the flood *colloq*, obsolete, old, out of date, out of the ark *colloq*, outmoded
F3 **1** modern **2** modern

prejudge *v* anticipate, assume, forejudge, judge prematurely, predetermine *formal*, prejudicate *formal*, presume, presuppose

prejudice *n* **1** *a victim of prejudice*: ageism, anti-Semitism, bigotry, chauvinism, discrimination, injustice, intolerance, misanthropy, misogyny, narrow-mindedness, racism, sexism, unfairness, xenophobia **2** *his middle-class prejudices*: bias, narrow-mindedness, one-sidedness, partiality, partisanship, preference **3** *without prejudice to your rights*: damage, detriment, disadvantage, harm, hurt, impairment, injury, loss, ruin
F3 **1** fairness, tolerance **2** fairness **3** advantage, benefit
♦ *v* **1** *his experiences have prejudiced him*: bias, colour, condition, distort, incline, influence, jaundice, load, predispose *formal*, slant, sway, weight **2** *prejudice your chances*: be detrimental to, be disadvantageous to, damage, harm, hinder, hurt, impair, injure, mar, ruin, spoil, undermine, wreck
F3 **2** advance, benefit, help

prejudiced *adj* biased, bigoted, blinkered, chauvinist, chauvinistic, conditioned, discriminatory, distorted, influenced, insular, intolerant, jaundiced, narrow-minded, one-sided, parochial, partial, partisan, predisposed *formal*, subjective, unfair, unjust, warped
F3 fair, impartial, tolerant

prejudicial *adj* counter-productive, damaging, deleterious *formal*, detrimental, disadvantageous, harmful, hurtful, inimical, injurious, unfavourable
F3 advantageous, beneficial

preliminary *adj* **1** *preliminary meetings*: advance, beginning, earliest, early, exordial *formal*, experimental, exploratory, first, inaugural, initial, introductory, opening, pilot, precursory *formal*, prefatory, preparatory, primary, prior, test, trial **2** *the preliminary rounds*: eliminating, first, opening, qualifying
F3 **1** closing, final **2** closing, final
♦ *n* **1** *start with the preliminaries first*: basics, beginning, formalities, foundations, groundwork, introduction, opening, preparation, rudiments, start **2** *the preliminaries of the book*: exordium *formal*, foreword, introduction, opening, preamble, preface, prelude, prodrome *formal*, proem *formal*, prolegomenon *formal*

prelude *n* **1** *the prelude to the piece*: foreword, introduction, opening, overture, preamble, preface, preliminary, prodrome *formal*, proem *formal*, prolegomenon *formal*, prologue **2** *the prelude of the war*: beginning, commencement *formal*, curtain-raiser, forerunner, harbinger, herald, introduction, opener, opening, precursor, preliminary, preparation, start
F3 **1** epilogue, finale **2** finale

premature *adj* **1** *a premature birth:* abortive, immature, incomplete, too early, too soon, undeveloped, untimely **2** *premature baldness:* early, too early, too soon, untimely **3** *our celebrations were premature:* hasty, ill-considered, ill-timed, impetuous, impulsive, inopportune, jumping the gun *colloq*, precipitate, rash, soon, too early, too soon, untimely
🔁 **2** late, tardy *formal* **3** late, tardy *formal*

premeditated *adj* calculated, cold-blooded, conscious, considered, contrived, deliberate, intended, intentional, planned, prearranged, predetermined, preplanned, wilful
🔁 spontaneous, unpremeditated

premeditation *n* deliberateness, deliberation, design, determination, forethought, intention, malice aforethought *technical*, planning, plotting, prearrangement, predetermination *formal*, purpose, scheming
🔁 impulse, spontaneity

premier *n* chancellor, chief minister, first minister, head of government, prime minister, secretary of state
♦ *adj* cardinal, chief, first, foremost, head, highest, leading, main, paramount, pre-eminent, primary, prime, principal, supreme, top

première *n* début, first night, first performance, first showing, opening, opening night

premise *n* argument, assertion, assumption, basis, hypothesis, postulate *formal*, presupposition *formal*, proposition, statement, supposition, thesis
♦ *v* assert, assume, hypothesize *formal*, lay down, posit *formal*, postulate *formal*, predicate *formal*, presuppose, state, stipulate, take as true

premises *n* building, establishment, estate, grounds, office, place, property, site

premium *n* **1** *pay an insurance premium:* instalment, regular payment **2** *they charge a huge premium for emergency work:* an arm and a leg *colloq*, daylight robbery *colloq*, extra sum/charge, overcharging, surcharge

premonition *n* **1** *had a premonition something was wrong:* anxiety, apprehension, fear, feeling, feeling in your bones *colloq*, foreboding, funny feeling *colloq*, gut feeling *colloq*, hunch, idea, intuition, misgiving, presentiment *formal*, sixth sense, sneaking suspicion, suspicion, worry **2** *the raven was seen as a premonition of disaster:* omen, portent *formal*, presage *formal*, sign, warning

preoccupation *n* **1** *a preoccupation with steam engines:* bee in your bonnet *colloq*, enthusiasm, fixation, hang-up *colloq*, hobby-horse, interest, obsession, one-track mind *colloq*, thing *colloq* **2** *lost in preoccupation:* absent-mindedness, absorption, abstraction, daydreaming, distraction, engrossment, heedlessness, inattentiveness, oblivion, obliviousness, reverie

preoccupied *adj* **1** *preoccupied with her appearance:* absorbed, deep in thought, engaged, engrossed, immersed, intent, involved, obsessed, pensive, taken up, wrapped up **2** *too preoccupied to see what was happening:* absent-minded, absorbed, abstracted, daydreaming, distracted, distrait *formal*, faraway, heedless, oblivious

preoccupy *v* absorb, engage, involve, obsess, occupy, occupy the attention of, take up

preordain *v* destine, doom, fate, foreordain, prearrange, predestine *formal*, predetermine *formal*

preparation *n* **1** *preparations for the wedding:* arrangement, measure, plan, provision **2** *weeks of preparation:* assembly, composition, construction, development, equipping, foundation, groundwork, homework, organization, planning, preliminaries, production, spadework **3** *in preparation for the event:* provision, readiness **4** *preparation for an exam:* coaching, practice, revision, study, training **5** *a preparation for the skin:* application, composition, compound, concoction, cosmetic, lotion, medicine, mixture, potion

preparatory *adj* basic, elementary, fundamental, initial, introductory, opening, precursory *formal*, prefatory *formal*, preliminary, primary, rudimentary

prepare *v* **1** *prepare an action plan:* arrange, assemble, compose, concoct, construct, contrive, devise, draft, draw up, fashion, get ready, make ready, organize, plan, put together, set up **2** *prepare for an event:* adjust, do the spadework for, do your homework for, gear up *colloq*, get ready, lay the foundations for, lay the groundwork for, make preparations for, make ready, pave the way, plan, psych up *colloq*, set the scene for, take the necessary steps for, tee up *colloq* **3** *prepare a ship for a voyage:* equip, fit out, get ready, make ready, prime, provide, rig out, supply **4** *prepare for a match:* coach, exercise, get into shape, make ready, practise, prime, train, warm up **5** *prepare for an exam:* coach, make ready, prime, study **6** *prepare a meal:* concoct, fix *US*, get ready, make, produce, put together, throw together

prepared *adj* **1** *not prepared to wait:* disposed, inclined, predisposed *formal*, ready, willing **2** *everything is prepared for the journey:* arranged, fit, fixed, in order, organized, planned, ready, set, waiting
🔁 **2** unprepared, unready

preparedness *n* alertness, anticipation, expectancy, fitness, order, preparation, readiness
🔁 unreadiness

preponderance *n* **1** *the preponderance of men in this profession:* extensiveness, greater number, predominance, prevalence **2** *the preponderance of evidence supports his claim:* bulk, lion's share *colloq*, majority, mass, weight **3** *the country's preponderance over its neighbours:* ascendancy *formal*, dominance, domination, dominion, force, power, predominance, prevalence, superiority, supremacy, sway

preponderant *adj* **1** *industries where women are preponderant:* greater, larger, predominant, prevailing **2** *the government is preponderant over the opposition:* controlling, foremost, more important, overriding, overruling, predominant, prevailing, superior

preponderate *v* **1** *males preponderate in the bird population:* outnumber, predominate, prevail **2** *the evidence preponderates in her favour:* dominate, override, overrule, prevail, rule, tell, turn the balance, turn the scales, weigh

prepossessing *adj* alluring, appealing, attractive, beautiful, bewitching, captivating, charming, delightful, enchanting, engaging, fair, fascinating, fetching, good-looking, handsome, inviting, likeable, lovable, magnetic, pleasing, striking, taking, winning, winsome
🖭 unattractive, unprepossessing

preposterous *adj* absurd, asinine, crazy, farcical, foolish, impossible, incredible, intolerable, irrational, ludicrous, monstrous, nonsensical, outrageous, ridiculous, senseless, shocking, unbelievable, unreasonable, unthinkable
🖭 acceptable, reasonable, sensible

prerequisite *n* condition, essential, imperative, must *colloq*, necessity, precondition *formal*, proviso, qualification, requirement, requisite *formal*, sine qua non *formal*
🖭 extra
♦ *adj* basic, essential, fundamental, imperative, indispensable, mandatory *formal*, necessary, needed, needful, obligatory, required, requisite *formal*, vital
🖭 superfluous, unnecessary

prerogative *n* advantage, authority, birthright, carte blanche, choice, claim, droit *technical*, due, exemption, immunity, liberty, licence, privilege, right, sanction

presage *v* adumbrate *formal*, announce, augur *formal*, be a sign of, be an indication of, bespeak *formal*, betoken *formal*, bode *formal*, forebode *formal*, forecast, foreshadow *formal*, foretell, foretoken, forewarn *formal*, harbinger *formal*, herald, indicate, point to, portend *formal*, predict, prognosticate *formal*, promise, signify, threaten, warn of
♦ *n* augury *formal*, foreboding, forecast, forerunner, foreshadowing *formal*, forewarning *formal*, harbinger *formal*, indication, omen, portent *formal*, precursor, prefiguration, premonition, presentiment *formal*, prognostic *formal*, prognostication *formal*, sign, signification *formal*, threat, warning

prescience *n* clairvoyance, far-sightedness, foreknowledge, foresight, precognition *formal*, prevision *formal*, prophecy, propheticness, second sight

prescient *adj* clairvoyant, discerning, divinatory, divining, far-seeing, far-sighted, foreknowing, foresighted, perceptive, previsional *formal*, prophetic, psychic
🖭 imperceptive

prescribe *v* 1 *prescribe a medicine*: advise, specify, stipulate 2 *prescribe a duty*: appoint, command, decree, define, dictate, direct, fix, impose, lay down, limit, ordain, order, require, rule, set, specify, stipulate

prescribe or *proscribe*? To *prescribe* is to advise or order: *The doctor prescribed a course of antibiotics; The law prescribes severe penalties for such offences.* To *proscribe* is to ban, outlaw or forbid: *This book was formerly proscribed by the church; Such actions are proscribed by law.*

prescribed *adj* assigned, decreed, formulary *formal*, laid down, ordained, set, specified, stipulated

prescription *n* 1 *a new prescription for eczema*: drug, medicine, mixture, preparation, remedy, treatment 2 *a prescription for happiness*: advice, direction, formula, guideline(s), instruction, recipe, recommendation

prescriptive *adj* authoritarian, dictatorial, didactic, dogmatic, legislating, preceptive *formal*, prescribing, rigid

presence *n* 1 *your presence is required*: attendance, companionship, company, occupancy, residence 2 *the presence of bacteria in the water*: being, existence 3 *his considerable stage presence*: air, appeal, appearance, attraction, aura, bearing *formal*, carriage *formal*, charisma, demeanour *formal*, magnetism, personality, poise, self-assurance, self-confidence 4 *his presence made me nervous*: closeness, nearness, neighbourhood, propinquity *formal*, proximity, vicinity 5 *we sensed a ghostly presence*: apparition, ghost, phantom, shadow, spectre, spirit, visitant
🖭 1 absence 2 absence 4 distance, remoteness

present¹ *adj* 1 *no-one was present when it happened*: at hand, attending, available, close at hand, here, near, nearby, there, to hand 2 *oxygen is present in the atmosphere*: existent, existing, extant, in existence 3 *at the present time*: contemporary, current, existent, existing, immediate, instant, present-day
🖭 1 absent 2 absent 3 out of date, past

present² *v* 1 *present the OBE*: award, bestow *formal*, confer *formal*, donate, give, grant, hand over 2 *presented her hand*: extend, hold out 3 *presented a watch to her*: offer, proffer *formal*, submit, tender 4 *to present a play*: demonstrate, display, exhibit, host, mount, organize, perform, put on, put on display, show, stage 5 *presented to the queen*: introduce, make known 6 *she presents a television show*: announce, compère, host, introduce 7 *the story presents her sympathetically*: characterize, delineate *formal*, depict, describe, picture, portray, represent

present³ *n* benefaction *formal*, bounty, contribution, donation, endowment, freebie *colloq*, gift, grant, gratuity, handout, largesse, offering, perk *colloq*, prezzie *colloq*, sweetener *colloq*, tip

presentable *adj* 1 *try to look presentable*: clean, neat, smart, smartly dressed, spruce, tidy 2 *a presentable score*: acceptable, decent, proper, respectable, satisfactory, suitable, tolerable
🖭 1 shabby, unpresentable, untidy

presentation *n* 1 *the presentation of the document*: appearance, arrangement, form, format, layout, organization, structure, system 2 *the presentation of an award*: award, bestowal *formal*, conferral *formal*, donating, granting, investiture, presenting 3 *gave a presentation on his project*: address, disquisition *formal*, lecture, seminar, speech, talk 4 *a new presentation of the play*: demonstration, display, exhibition, mounting, performance, production, rendition, representation, show, showing, staging 5 *her presentation at the court*: introduction, launch, making known

present-day *adj* contemporary, current, existing, living, modern, present, up-to-date
🖭 future, past

presenter *n* anchorman, anchorwoman, announcer, compère, emcee *colloq*, frontman, host, master of ceremonies, MC

presentiment *n* anticipation, apprehension, bad vibes *colloq*, expectation, fear, feeling, forebodement *formal*, foreboding, forethought, hunch, intuition, misgiving, premonition, presage *formal*

presently *adv* **1** *she'll be along presently:* before long, by and by, in a minute, in a short time, in a short while, shortly, soon **2** *he's presently working in Beijing:* at present, at the moment, at the present time, at this moment in time, currently, now, these days

preservation *n* **1** *the preservation of the rainforests:* conservation, guarding, keeping, maintenance, protection, safeguarding, safekeeping, safety, upkeep **2** *the preservation of the status quo:* continuation, defence, guarding, keeping, maintenance, perpetuation, retention, security, support, upholding
🔁 **1** destruction, ruin **2** destruction, ruin

preserve *v* **1** *preserve endangered species:* care for, conserve, defend, guard, keep, look after, maintain, protect, safeguard, save, shelter, shield, take care of **2** *efforts to preserve order:* continue, keep, maintain, perpetuate, secure, sustain, uphold **3** *preserve food:* bottle, can, cure, dry, pickle, salt, smoke, store, tin
🔁 **1** destroy, ruin **2** destroy, ruin
♦ *n* **1** *home-made preserves:* conserve, jam, jelly, marmalade, pickle **2** *control of the budget is his preserve:* area, domain, field, realm, speciality, sphere **3** *a wildlife preserve:* game reserve, reservation, reserve, safari park, sanctuary

preside *v* **1** *preside at a meeting:* be in the chair, be the chairman/chairwoman/chairperson, call the shots *colloq*, chair, officiate **2** *preside over an inquiry:* administer, be in charge of, be responsible for, be the chairman/chairwoman/ chairperson of, chair, conduct, control, direct, govern, head, head up *colloq*, lead, manage, rule, run

president *n* **1** *the president of the United States:* chief of state, governor, head of state, ruler **2** *the company president:* boss *colloq*, chief, controller, director, head, leader, manager, principal

press *v* **1** *press grapes:* compress, crush, knead, mash, pinch, squash, squeeze, trample **2** *press a button:* depress, push (down) **3** *press the dough into the tin:* cram, jam, push (down), stuff **4** *the crowd pressed round him:* crowd, surge, swarm, throng **5** *press clothes:* flatten, iron, roll, smooth (out) **6** *pressed him to her bosom:* caress, clasp, crush, cuddle, embrace, enfold, grasp, hug, squeeze **7** *they are pressing me to resign:* besiege, coerce, compel, constrain, demand, exhort, force, harass, insist on, pressure, pressurize, put pressure on, trouble, vex, worry **8** *press for a change in the law:* call for, campaign, demand, entreat, implore, petition, plead, push for, push forward, supplicate *formal*, urge
♦ *n* **1** *the press of people:* crowd, crush, flock, horde, mob, multitude, pack, push, swarm, throng, troop **2** *talk to the press:* correspondents, Fleet Street, fourth estate, hacks *colloq*, journalists, news media, newspapermen, newspapers, newspaperwomen, paparazzi, papers, photographers, pressmen, presswomen,

reporters, the media **3** *shut down the presses:* printing press, printing-machine, rotary press **4** *get a good/bad press:* articles, coverage, criticism, praise, reviews, treatment
▶ **press on** carry on, continue, go ahead, go on, press ahead, proceed

pressed *adj* **1** *won't be pressed into a decision:* browbeaten, bullied, coerced, constrained, forced, harassed, hurried, pressured, pressurized, pushed, rushed **2** *be pressed for time:* deficient in, having little, lacking, not having enough, short of
🔁 **1** unhurried **2** well-off

pressing *adj* burning, critical, crucial, demanding, essential, exigent *formal*, high-priority, imperative, important, key, needing to be dealt with immediately, serious, urgent, vital
🔁 trivial, unimportant

pressure *n* **1** *burst under the pressure:* burden, compression, crushing, force, heaviness, load, power, squeezing, strain, stress, weight **2** *put pressure on someone:* bullying, coercion, compulsion, constraints, duress, force, harassment **3** *the pressures of the job:* adversity, aggro *colloq*, burden, constraint, demand, difficulty, hassle *colloq*, obligation, problem, stress, tension, trouble

pressurize *v* browbeat, bulldoze, bully, coerce, compel, constrain, dragoon, drive, force, lean on *colloq*, oblige, press, pressure, put pressure on, put the screws on *colloq*

prestige *n* authority, credit, distinction, eminence, esteem *formal*, fame, honour, importance, influence, kudos, regard, renown, reputation, standing, stature, status
🔁 humbleness, unimportance

prestigious *adj* blue-chip *colloq*, celebrated, distinguished, eminent, esteemed *formal*, exalted, famous, great, high-ranking, illustrious, important, imposing, impressive, influential, prominent, renowned, reputable, respected, up-market, well-known
🔁 humble, modest

presumably *adv* apparently, as like as not, doubtless, doubtlessly, in all likelihood, in all probability, most likely, no doubt, probably, seemingly, very likely

presume *v* **1** *I presume this is your first trip abroad:* assume, believe, deduce, hypothesize *formal*, imagine, infer, suppose, surmise, take it, think **2** *this theory presumes the existence of God:* assume, presuppose, take for granted **3** *presume to criticize:* dare, go so far, have the audacity, make so bold, take the liberty, undertake, venture
▶ **presume on** bank on, count on, depend on, exploit, rely on, take (unfair) advantage of, trust

presumption *n* **1** *your presumption that she is guilty:* assumption, belief, conjecture *formal*, deduction, guess, hypothesis *formal*, inference, opinion, presupposition *formal*, supposition *formal*, surmise **2** *a strong presumption that he is dead:* likelihood, probability **3** *had the presumption to argue with me:* arrogance, assurance, audacity, boldness, cheek *colloq*, effrontery, forwardness, impertinence, impudence, insolence, nerve *colloq*, presumptuousness, temerity
🔁 **3** humility

presumptive *adj* **1** *the heir presumptive to the throne:* assumed, believed, designate, expected, hypothetical *formal*, inferred, prospective, supposed, understood **2** *a presumptive reason for his absence:* believable, conceivable, credible, likely, plausible, possible, probable, reasonable
☒ **1** known **2** unlikely

presumptuous *adj* arrogant, audacious, big-headed *colloq*, bold, cheeky *colloq*, cocksure, cocky *colloq*, conceited, forward, impertinent, impudent, insolent, over-confident, over-familiar, pushy *colloq*, too big for your boots *colloq*
☒ humble, modest

presuppose *v* accept, assume, consider, imply, posit *formal*, postulate *formal*, premise *formal*, presume, suppose, take for granted

presupposition *n* assumption, belief, hypothesis *formal*, preconception, premise *formal*, premiss *formal*, presumption, supposition, theory

pretence *n* **1** *keep up a pretence of normality:* acting, appearance, charade, deceit, deception, display, fabrication, façade, faking, false show, falsehood, feigning, front, invention, lie, make-believe, masquerade, semblance, sham, show, simulation, veneer **2** *there is no pretence in him:* affectation *formal*, bluff, deceit, deception, display, dissembling *formal*, dissimulation *formal*, faking, false show, falsehood, hypocrisy, ostentation, play-acting, posing, posturing, pretentiousness, show, showiness, trickery, wile **3** *killed him under the pretence of self-defence:* cloak, cover, excuse, façade, guise, lie, mask, pretext, ruse, veil
☒ **1** honesty, openness **2** honesty, openness

pretend *v* **1** *pretend to be asleep:* act, affect *formal*, assume, bluff, counterfeit, dissemble *formal*, fabricate, fake, feign, go through the motions, impersonate, keep up appearances *colloq*, mime, pass yourself off, play-act, put on, put on an act, sham, simulate **2** *I can't pretend to follow your logic:* allege, claim, profess, purport *formal* **3** *let's pretend:* imagine, make believe, suppose

pretended *adj* affected *formal*, alleged, artificial, avowed *formal*, bogus, counterfeit, fake, false, feigned, fictitious, imaginary, ostensible, phoney *colloq*, pretend *colloq*, professed, pseudo *colloq*, purported *formal*, put-on, sham, so-called, specious, spurious, supposed, supposititious *formal*
☒ real

pretender *n* aspirant, candidate, claimant, claimer

pretension *n* **1** *I can't stand his pretension:* affectation *formal*, airs, conceit, hypocrisy, ostentation, pretence, pretentiousness, self-importance, show, showiness, snobbishness, vanity **2** *the pretension of his writing:* floweriness, magniloquence *formal*, pomposity, pretentiousness **3** *her pretensions to be an actress:* ambition, aspiration, claim, profession, purporting *formal*
☒ **1** humility, modesty **2** simplicity

pretentious *adj* **1** *his pretentious boasting:* conceited, exaggerated, extravagant, flamboyant, flaunting, immodest, ostentatious, self-important, showy, snobbish, vainglorious

formal **2** *a pretentious style of writing:* affected *formal*, artificial, bombastic, elaborate, extravagant, grandiose, high-sounding, inflated, magniloquent *formal*, mannered, pompous, twee
☒ **1** humble, modest **2** simple, straightforward

pretentiousness *n* **1** *the pretentiousness of her lifestyle:* attitudinizing, flamboyance, ostentation, posing, posturing *formal*, pretension, pseudery *colloq*, show, theatricality **2** *the pretentiousness of his speech:* floridness, floweriness, pretension, pseudery *colloq*
☒ **1** humbleness, modesty **2** simplicity, straightforwardness

preternatural *adj* abnormal, exceptional, extraordinary, unusual

pretext *n* alleged/ostensible reason, appearance, cloak, cover, excuse, guise, mask, ploy, pretence, red herring *colloq*, ruse, semblance, sham, show, veil

prettify *v* adorn, beautify, bedeck, deck, deck out, decorate, do up *colloq*, doll up *colloq*, embellish, garnish, gild, ornament, smarten up, tart up *colloq*, trick out, trim
☒ mar, uglify

pretty *adj* **1** *a pretty child:* appealing, attractive, beautiful, bonny *Scot*, cute, delightful, engaging, fair, good-looking, handsome, lovely, personable, prepossessing, winsome **2** *a pretty room:* dainty, delicate, delightful, elegant, fine, nice, pleasant, pleasing
☒ **1** plain, ugly, unattractive **2** plain, ugly, unattractive
♦ *adv* fairly, moderately, quite, rather, reasonably, somewhat, tolerably

prevail *v* **1** *his better nature prevailed:* be victorious, carry the day *colloq*, conquer, gain ascendancy *formal*, gain mastery, overcome, overrule, reign, rule, succeed, triumph, win **2** *the opinion which prevails in this country:* abound, be accepted, be common, be current, be customary, be normal, be present, hold sway, obtain *formal*, predominate, preponderate *formal*
☒ **1** lose
► **prevail upon** bring round, convince, incline, induce, influence, lean on *colloq*, persuade, pressure, pressurize, prompt, soft-soap *colloq*, sway, sweet-talk *colloq*, talk into, twist someone's arm *colloq*, urge, win over

prevailing *adj* **1** *the prevailing prejudice against travellers:* accepted, ascendant *formal*, common, current, customary, dominant, established, fashionable, general, in fashion, in style, in vogue, influential, mainstream, most common, most usual, popular, predominant, preponderant, prepotent *formal*, prevalent, reigning, supreme, usual, widespread **2** *the prevailing climate:* chief, main, predominant, preponderant, prepotent *formal*, prevalent, principal, ruling
☒ **1** minor, subordinate

prevalence *n* acceptance, ascendancy *formal*, commonness, currency, frequency, mastery, omnipresence *formal*, pervasiveness, popularity, predominance, preponderance *formal*, primacy *formal*, profusion, rule, sway, ubiquity *formal*, universality
☒ uncommonness

prevalent *adj* accepted, common, current, customary, dominant, established, everyday, extensive, frequent, general, pervasive, popular, prevailing, rampant, rife, ubiquitous, universal, usual, widespread
F₃ rare, uncommon

prevaricate *v* beat about the bush *colloq*, cavil *formal*, deceive, dodge *colloq*, equivocate, evade, hedge *colloq*, lie, pussy-foot *colloq*, quibble, shift, shilly-shally *colloq*, shuffle, sit on the fence *colloq*, tergiversate *formal*, waffle *colloq*

---

prevaricate or *procrastinate*? To *prevaricate* is 'to talk evasively in order to avoid telling the truth, coming to the point, or answering a question': *When faced with difficult questions, politicians usually prevaricate.* To *procrastinate* is 'to put off until later things that should be done immediately'.

---

prevarication *n* cavilling *formal*, deceit, deception, equivocation, evasion, falsehood, falsification, fib(s), fibbing, half-truth, lie, misrepresentation, pretence, quibbling, tergiversation *formal*, untruth

prevaricator *n* casuist *formal*, caviller *formal*, deceiver, dissembler *formal*, dodger *colloq*, equivocator, evader, fibber *colloq*, liar, quibbler, sophist *formal*

prevent *v* arrest, avert, avoid, balk, bar, block, check, deter, fend off, foil, forestall, frustrate, halt, hamper, head off, hinder, hold back, hold in check, impede, inhibit, intercept, keep from, obstruct, obviate *formal*, preclude *formal*, restrain, stave off, stop, thwart, ward off
F₃ allow, cause, encourage, foster, help

prevention *n* arresting, avoidance, balking, bar, check, deterrence, elimination, fending off, foiling, frustration, halting, hampering, heading off, hindrance, impediment, obstacle, obstruction, obviation *formal*, precaution, preclusion *formal*, prophylaxis *technical*, safeguard, staving off, warding off
F₃ cause, help

preventive *adj* counteractive, deterrent, inhibitory, obstructive, precautionary, pre-emptive, preventative, prophylactic *technical*, protective
F₃ causative, fostering
♦ *n* block, deterrent, hindrance, impediment, neutralizer, obstacle, obstruction, precautionary measure, prevention, prophylactic *technical*, protection, protective, remedy, safeguard, shield
F₃ cause, encouragement, incitement

previous *adj* **1** *his previous wife*: antecedent, earlier, erstwhile *formal*, ex-, former, one-time, past, preceding, quondam *formal*, sometime **2** *the previous week*: foregoing, past, preceding, prior
F₃ 1 following, later, subsequent **2** following, later, subsequent

previously *adv* at one time, before, beforehand, earlier, erst *formal*, erstwhile *formal*, formerly, heretofore *formal*, hitherto *formal*, in the past, once, until now
F₃ later

prey *n* **1** *the tiger's prey*: game, kill, quarry **2** *the con man's prey*: fall guy *colloq*, mug *colloq*, target, victim

▶ **prey on 1** *the owl preys on field mice*: catch, devour, eat, feed on, hunt, kill, live off **2** *prey on the elderly*: bleed *colloq*, con *colloq*, exploit, fleece *colloq*, take advantage of **3** *prey on one's mind*: burden, distress, hang over, haunt, oppress, plague, torment, trouble, weigh down, worry

price *n* **1** *the price of the repairs*: amount, assessment, bill, charge, cost, estimate, expenditure, expense(s), fee, figure, levy, outlay, payment, quotation, rate, sum, valuation, value, worth **2** *a price on his head*: bounty, reward **3** *pay the price*: consequences, forfeit, penalty, result, sacrifice
♦ *v* appraise *formal*, assess, cost, estimate, evaluate, rate, set/fix the price at, valorize *formal*, value

priceless *adj* **1** *a priceless antique*: cherished, costly, dear, expensive, inestimable, invaluable, irreplaceable, precious, prized, rare, treasured, valuable, worth its weight in gold *colloq* **2** *a priceless joke*: a scream *colloq*, amusing, comic, funny, hilarious, killing *colloq*, rich *colloq*, riotous, side-splitting
F₃ 1 cheap, run-of-the-mill

pricey *adj* costing an arm and a leg *colloq*, costly, dear, excessive, exorbitant, expensive, extortionate, high-priced, over the odds *colloq*, steep *colloq*
F₃ cheap

prick *v* **1** *the thorn pricked his finger*: jab, jag, nick, perforate, pierce, punch, puncture, spike, stab, sting, wound **2** *her eyes pricked with tears*: itch, prickle, smart, sting, tingle **3** *prick your conscience*: distress, gnaw at, harass, harry, plague, prey on, torment, trouble, worry
♦ *n* **1** *a slight prick of the needle*: jab, jag, nick, pain, pang, stab, sting, twinge **2** *a pin prick*: hole, perforation, pinhole, puncture, wound **3** *the prick of tears in his eyes*: smarting, stinging, sting, tingle

prickle *n* **1** *the stem is covered with prickles*: acantha *formal*, barb, needle, point, prong, spike, spine, spur, thorn, tine **2** *feel a prickle of fear*: formication *formal*, itching, pang, paraesthesia *technical*, pins and needles *colloq*, sensation, smarting, sting, stinging, tingle, twinge
♦ *v* itch, nip, prick, smart, sting, tingle

prickly *adj* **1** *prickly branches*: barbed, brambly, bristly, pronged, rough, scratchy, spiked, spiky, spiny, thorny **2** *a prickly old man*: bad-tempered, crabby *colloq*, crotchety *colloq*, edgy, grouchy *colloq*, grumpy, irritable, ratty *colloq*, short-tempered, stroppy *colloq*, touchy **3** *a prickly subject*: complicated, difficult, hard, problematical, thorny, tough, tricky, troublesome
F₃ 1 smooth **2** easy-going *colloq*, relaxed

pride *n* **1** *pride in your accomplishments*: delight, gratification, joy, pleasure, satisfaction, sense of achievement **2** *a blow to his pride*: dignity, ego, honour, self-esteem, self-image, self-respect, self-worth **3** *pride goes before a fall*: arrogance, big-headedness, boastfulness, conceit, egotism, haughtiness, presumption, pretentiousness, self-conceit, self-importance, smugness, snobbery, superciliousness, vanity
F₃ 1 shame **3** humility, modesty

priest *n* churchman, churchwoman, clergyman, clergywoman, deacon, deaconess, father, man/

woman of God, man/woman of the cloth, minister, padre, parson, pastor, vicar

priestess *n* abbess, beguine, canoness, clergywoman, deaconess, mambo, prioress, vestal

priestly *adj* Aaronic(al), canonical, clerical, ecclesiastical, hieratic *formal*, pastoral, priestlike, sacerdotal

prig *n* goody-goody *colloq*, holy Joe *colloq*, holy Willie *colloq*, killjoy, Mrs Grundy, old maid, precisian, prude, puritan

priggish *adj* goody-goody *colloq*, holier-than-thou *colloq*, narrow-minded, prim, prudish, puritanical, sanctimonious, self-righteous, starchy, strait-laced, stuffy
F3 broad-minded

prim *adj* demure, fastidious, formal, fussy, old-maidish, particular, precise, priggish, prissy, proper, prudish, puritanical, school-marmish, starchy, strait-laced, stuffy
F3 easy-going *colloq*, relaxed

primacy *n* ascendancy *formal*, command, dominance, dominion, leadership, paramountcy, pre-eminence, seniority, sovereignty, superiority, supremacy
F3 inferiority

primal *adj* 1 *a primal human urge*: basic, central, chief, fundamental, greatest, highest, main, major, paramount, primary, prime, principal 2 *primal societies*: earliest, first, initial, original, primary, prime, primeval *formal*, primitive, primordial *formal*
F3 1 minor 2 later

primarily *adv* 1 *this is primarily a software problem*: basically, chiefly, especially, essentially, fundamentally, in essence, in the main, mainly, mostly, particularly, predominantly, principally 2 *it was primarily designed as a toy*: at first, first, firstly, in the first place, initially, originally

primary *adj* 1 *our primary concern is the children's safety*: capital, cardinal, chief, dominant, foremost, greatest, highest, leading, main, paramount, predominant, prime, principal, supreme, ultimate 2 *the primary requirements for survival*: basic, elemental *formal*, elementary, essential, fundamental, radical 3 *a primary introduction to economics*: basic, beginning, elementary, first, initial, introductory, opening, rudimentary, simple
F3 1 minor, secondary, subsidiary

prime[1] *adj* 1 *a prime location for the office*: best, choice, excellent, first-class, first-rate, highest, pre-eminent, quality, select, supreme, top, top-grade 2 *our prime concern is safety*: chief, foremost, leading, main, predominant, principal, supreme 3 *a prime example*: characteristic, classic, paradigmatic *formal*, quintessential *formal*, standard, typical
F3 1 secondary, second-rate
♦ *n* acme *formal*, best part, bloom, blossom, culmination, flower, height, heyday, maturity, peak, perfection, pinnacle, zenith

prime[2] *v* 1 *prime a bomb*: equip, get ready, prepare 2 *primed him on what to say*: brief, clue up *colloq*, coach, fill, fill in, gen up *colloq*, inform, notify, train

primer *n* introduction, manual, prodrome *formal*, prodromus *formal*, textbook

primeval *adj* 1 *a primeval swamp*: ancient, earliest, early, first, old, original, prehistoric, primitive, primordial *formal* 2 *a primeval instinct*: basic, instinctive, primitive, primordial *formal*
F3 1 modern 2 modern

primitive *adj* 1 *primitive societies*: barbarian, savage, uncivilized, uncultured, undeveloped, unsophisticated 2 *primitive mammals*: ancient, earliest, early, elementary, first, original, primary, primeval *formal*, primordial *formal* 3 *primitive cave paintings*: crude, naïve, simple, undeveloped, unsophisticated 4 *a primitive cutting tool*: crude, rough, rudimentary, simple
F3 1 advanced, civilized, sophisticated 2 advanced 3 sophisticated

primordial *adj* 1 *primordial swamps*: ancient, earliest, early, first, old, prehistoric, primeval *formal*, primitive 2 *primordial urges*: basic, fundamental, instinctive, original, primeval *formal*
F3 1 modern

primp *v* beautify, doll up *colloq*, dress up, groom, preen, put on your best bib and tucker *colloq*, put on your glad rags *colloq*, smarten, spruce up, tart up *colloq*, tidy, titivate *colloq*

prince *n* lord, monarch, potentate, ruler, sovereign

princely *adj* 1 *a princely residence*: grand, imperial, imposing, magnificent, majestic, noble, regal, royal, sovereign, splendid, stately 2 *a princely sum*: bounteous *formal*, generous, handsome, lavish, liberal, magnanimous, magnificent, sumptuous

principal *adj* arch, cardinal, chief, controlling, dominant, essential, first, foremost, highest, in charge, key, leading, main, major, most important, paramount, pre-eminent, primary, prime, supreme
F3 least, lesser, minor, subsidiary
♦ *n* 1 *the principal of the college*: boss *colloq*, chief, controller, director, head, head teacher, headmaster, headmistress, leader, manager, rector, ruler, superintendent 2 *repay the principal on a debt*: assets, capital, capital funds, capital sum, money

> *principal* or *principle*? As an adjective, *principal* means 'most important': *Shipbuilding and coal-mining were two of Britain's principal industries*. As a noun, *principal* means 'the head of a school, college or university'. *Principle* can only be used as a noun. It means 'a general rule' or 'the theory underlying a method or way of working': *the principles of economic theory*.

principally *adv* above all, chiefly, especially, first and foremost, for the most part, in the main, mainly, mostly, particularly, predominantly, primarily

principle *n* 1 *the principles of Buddhism*: axiom, canon, code, creed, criterion, dictum, doctrine, dogma, idea, maxim, precept, rule, standard, tenet 2 *the principles of physics*: basis, essential, formula, fundamental, idea, law, postulate *formal*, precept, proposition, rule, theory, truth 3 *a man of principle*: conscience, decency, ethics, honour, integrity, morality, morals, rectitude *formal*, scruples, standards, uprightness, virtue

principled *adj* conscientious, decent, ethical, high-minded, honourable, just, moral, righteous, right-minded, scrupulous, upright, virtuous
🖪 unprincipled

print *v* 1 *print a document:* copy, put to bed *colloq*, reproduce, run off 2 *print a magazine:* issue, publish, release 3 *his name was printed on it:* engrave, etch, impress, imprint, mark, stamp
♦ *n* 1 *in bold print:* characters, fount, lettering, letters, type, typeface 2 *the print of a boot:* fingerprint, footprint, impression, mark 3 *Hogarth's prints:* design, engraving, etching, lithograph, picture 4 *a print of the painting:* copy, photo, picture, replica, reproduction 5 *a set of extra prints:* copy, photo, photograph, picture, snap *colloq*, snapshot

> **Printing methods include:**
> bubble-jet printing, collotype, colour-process printing, copper engraving, die-stamping, digital printing, duplicating, electrostatic printing, engraving, etching, flexography, gravure, ink-jet printing, intaglio, laser printing, letterpress, lino blocking, litho, lithography, offset lithography, offset printing, photoengraving, rotary press, screen printing, silk-screen printing, stencilling, thermography, twin-etching, xerography

prior *adj* earlier, foregoing, former, preceding, previous
🖪 later

priority *n* 1 *a top priority:* essential, first concern, main thing, matter of highest/greatest importance, most important thing, most urgent matter, pole position, primary issue, requirement, supreme matter, top of the tree *colloq* 2 *priority is given to the elderly:* first/highest place, precedence, preference 3 *health takes priority over education:* paramountcy, precedence, pre-eminence, rank, right of way, seniority, superiority, supremacy
🖪 2 inferiority 3 inferiority

priory *n* abbey, béguinage, cloister, convent, friary, monastery, nunnery, religious house

prise *v* dislodge, force, hoist, jemmy, lever, lift, move, pry, raise, shift, winkle

prison *n* cage, can *slang*, cell, choky *slang*, clink *slang*, confinement, cooler *slang*, custody, detention, dungeon, imprisonment, inside *colloq*, jail, jug *slang*, lock-up, nick *colloq*, penitentiary, quod *slang*, slammer *slang*

prisoner *n* captive, con *colloq*, convict, detainee, hostage, inmate, internee, jailbird *colloq*, lifer *colloq*, (old) lag *colloq*, POW, prisoner of war, recidivist, yardbird *colloq*

prissy *adj* demure, fastidious, finicky *colloq*, formal, fussy, old-maidish, particular, po-faced *colloq*, precise, priggish, prim, proper, prudish, puritanical, school-marmish, starchy, strait-laced, stuffy

pristine *adj* 1 *in pristine condition:* immaculate, uncorrupted, undefiled, unspoiled, unsullied, untouched, virgin 2 *the pristine swampland:* earliest, first, former, initial, original, primal,

primary, primeval *formal*, primigenial *formal*, primitive, primordial *formal*
🖪 1 spoiled 2 developed, later

privacy *n* 1 *a need for privacy:* isolation, privateness, quietness, retirement, retreat, seclusion, sequestration *formal*, solitude 2 *the privacy of the meeting:* concealment, confidentiality, privateness, secrecy
🖪 1 interference, interruption 2 publicness

private *adj* 1 *private discussions:* classified, confidential, hush-hush *colloq*, off the record, privileged, secret, unofficial 2 *your private life/feelings:* confidential, individual, innermost, intimate, personal, secret 3 *a private bathroom:* exclusive, individual, own, particular, personal, special 4 *a private person:* quiet, reserved, retiring, self-contained, separate, solitary, withdrawn 5 *a private place:* concealed, hidden, isolated, out-of-the-way, quiet, remote, secluded, secret, sequestered *formal*, undisturbed 6 *private industries:* commercial, denationalized, free-enterprise, independent, non-governmental, privatized, self-determining, self-governing
🖪 1 official, public 5 public 6 nationalized, public, state-controlled, state-run
♦ *n* enlisted man, private soldier, squaddy, swad, swaddy, Tommy, Tommy Atkins *colloq*

privateer *n* buccaneer, corsair, filibuster, freebooter, marque, pirate, sea robber, sea wolf

privation *n* austerity, deprivation, destitution, hardship, indigence *formal*, lack, loss, need, neediness, penury *formal*, poverty, want *formal*
🖪 affluence, wealth

privilege *n* 1 *citizens' privileges:* advantage, benefit, birthright, concession, due, entitlement, franchise, freedom, liberty, licence, prerogative, right, sanction 2 *diplomatic privileges:* authority, dispensation, exemption, immunity, liberty 3 *it's been a privilege to know you:* honour, pleasure
🖪 1 disadvantage 2 disadvantage

privileged *adj* 1 *a privileged few:* advantaged, elite, excepted, exempt, favoured, honoured, indulged, powerful, ruling, sanctioned, special 2 *privileged information:* classified, confidential, off the record, private, secret, unofficial
🖪 1 disadvantaged, under-privileged 2 public

privy *n* bog *colloq*, cloakroom, latrine, lavatory, loo *colloq*, public convenience, toilet, washroom, water closet, WC

prize *n* 1 *first prize:* accolade, award, honour, laurels, medal, reward, trophy 2 *a rollover prize of £1 million:* jackpot, premium, purse, stake(s), trophy, winnings 3 *a prize worth striving for:* aim, desire, gain, goal, honour, hope 4 *the pirates made off with their prize:* booty, capture, loot, pickings, pillage, plunder, spoils, trophy
♦ *adj* award-winning, best, champion, excellent, first-rate, out of this world *colloq*, outstanding, prize-winning, smashing *colloq*, terrific *colloq*, top, top-notch *colloq*, winning
🖪 second-rate
♦ *v* appreciate, cherish, esteem *formal*, hold dear, hold in high regard, love, revere, set great store by, think highly of, treasure, value
🖪 despise, undervalue

prize-winner *n* champ *colloq*, champion, cup-winner, dux, medallist, winner

probability *n* chance(s), expectation, likelihood, likeliness, odds, possibility, prospect
🔁 improbability

probable *adj* a fair bet *colloq*, anticipated, apparent, believable, credible, expected, feasible, foreseeable, likely, odds-on *colloq*, on the cards *colloq*, plausible, possible, predictable, seeming, to be expected
🔁 improbable, unlikely

probably *adv* a fair bet *colloq*, as likely as not, (as) like as not *colloq*, doubtless, in all likelihood, in all probability, it looks like, likely, maybe, most likely, perhaps, possibly, presumably, the chances are
🔁 improbably

probation *n* apprenticeship, experimental period, supervision, test, test period, trial, trial period

probe *v* 1 *probe into someone's background:* analyse, examine, go into, inquire, investigate, look into, research, scrutinize, search, sift, study, test 2 *probed her breasts for lumps:* check, examine, explore, poke, prod 3 *probed the soil for samples:* penetrate, pierce, plumb, sound
♦ *n* 1 *a probe into working conditions:* analysis, examination, exploration, inquest, inquiry, investigation, research, scrutinization, scrutiny, study, test 2 *sink a probe into the earth:* bore, drill

probity *n* goodness, honesty, honour, honourableness, integrity, justice, morality, rectitude *formal*, righteousness, trustworthiness, truthfulness, uprightness, virtue, worth
🔁 improbity *formal*

problem *n* 1 *an insurmountable problem:* catch-22 *colloq*, complication, difficulty, dilemma, dire straits *colloq*, fix *colloq*, hassle *colloq*, hole *colloq*, mess *colloq*, no-win situation *colloq*, pickle *colloq*, plight, predicament, quandary, snag, tight spot *colloq*, trouble, worry 2 *an intriguing logic problem:* brain-teaser, conundrum, enigma, poser, puzzle, question, riddle
♦ *adj* delinquent, difficult, disobedient, intransigent *formal*, recalcitrant *formal*, troublesome, uncontrollable, unmanageable, unruly
🔁 manageable, well-behaved

problematic *adj* 1 *the problematic question of abortion:* a can of worms *colloq*, a minefield *colloq*, awkward, difficult, enigmatic, fraught with difficulties, hard, intricate, involved, moot, perplexing, problematical, puzzling, thorny, tricky, troublesome 2 *the problematic future of the hospital:* debatable, doubtful, dubious, questionable, uncertain
🔁 1 easy, straightforward 2 certain

procedure *n* action, conduct, course, course of action, custom, formula, means, measure, method, methodology, modus operandi, move, operation, performance, plan of action, policy, practice, process, routine, scheme, step, strategy, system, technique, way

proceed *v* 1 *proceed to the next stage:* advance, carry on, continue, go ahead, go forward, go on, make your way, move on, press on, progress 2 *proceed with the tests:* begin, get under way, make a start, set in motion, start, take steps 3 *the health problems which proceed from smoking:* arise,

come, derive, emanate, ensue, flow, follow, issue, originate, result, spring, start, stem
🔁 1 retreat, stop

proceedings *n* 1 *publish the proceedings of the conference:* account, affairs, annals, archives, business, dealings, matters, minutes, records, report, transactions 2 *regarded the proceedings with disapproval:* action, activities, course of action, deeds, doings, events, happenings, manoeuvres, measures, moves, operations, procedures, steps 3 *legal proceedings:* action, case, lawsuit, litigation, process, trial

proceeds *n* earnings, gain, income, produce, profit(s), receipts, returns, revenue, takings, yield
🔁 expenditure, outlay

process *n* 1 *a process of trial and error:* action, manner, means, method, mode *formal*, operation, practice, procedure, system, way 2 *the manufacturing process:* method, procedure, system, technique 3 *the process of evolution:* action, advance, change(s), course, development, evolution, formation, growth, movement, proceeding, progress, progression
♦ *v* 1 *the factory where the coffee beans are processed:* alter, change, convert, prepare, refine, transform, treat 2 *process an application:* action, deal with, handle

procession *n* 1 *a procession through the streets:* cavalcade, column, cortège, file, march, motorcade, parade, train 2 *a procession of scandals:* course, run, sequence, series, stream, succession, train

proclaim *v* 1 *proclaimed his love for her:* advertise, affirm *formal*, announce, blazon, broadcast, circulate, declare, give out, indicate, make known, notify, profess, promulgate *formal*, publish, show, testify, trumpet 2 *proclaim a holiday:* announce, declare, pronounce

proclamation *n* 1 *a proclamation of emergency:* affirmation *formal*, announcement, command, declaration, decree, edict, manifesto, notice, order, pronouncement, rule 2 *the proclamation of the news:* advertisement, affirmation *formal*, announcement, broadcast, circulation, declaration, notification, promulgation *formal*, pronouncement, publication

proclivity *n* bent, bias, disposition, inclination, leaning, liability, liableness, penchant *formal*, predilection *formal*, predisposition *formal*, proneness, propensity *formal*, tendency, weakness
🔁 disinclination

procrastinate *v* dally, defer, delay, dilly-dally *colloq*, drag your feet, play for time, postpone, prolong, protract, put off, retard *formal*, stall, temporize *formal*
🔁 advance, proceed

---
procrastinate or *prevaricate*? See panel at **prevaricate**
---

procrastination *n* deferral, delaying, delaying tactics, dilly-dallying *colloq*, stalling, temporizing *formal*

procreate *v* beget *old use*, breed, conceive, engender, father, generate, mother, multiply, produce, propagate, reproduce, sire, spawn

procure v 1 *procure a passport:* acquire, appropriate *formal,* buy, come by, find, gain, get, get hold of, lay hands on, obtain, pick up, purchase, requisition *formal,* secure, win 2 *procure a prostitute:* hook *colloq,* hustle *colloq,* pander, pimp, solicit
▧ 1 lose

procurer n bawd, madam, pander, panderer, pimp, procuress, whoremonger

prod v 1 *prodded me in the ribs:* butt, dig, elbow, jab, nudge, poke, push, shove *colloq,* thrust 2 *prodded him into action:* egg on *colloq,* encourage, goad, incite, motivate, move, prompt, spur, stimulate, stir, urge
◆ n 1 *gave him a prod in the back:* dig, elbow, jab, nudge, poke, push, shove *colloq* 2 *he just needs a prod from you:* encouragement, goad, motivation, prompt, prompting, reminder, spur, stimulus

prodigal adj 1 *prodigal spending:* excessive, extravagant, immoderate, improvident, intemperate, lavish, profligate *formal,* spendthrift, squandering, unthrifty, wanton, wasteful 2 *prodigal with his time:* bounteous *formal,* bountiful *formal,* lavish, unsparing 3 *prodigal vegetation:* bounteous *formal,* bountiful *formal,* copious, exuberant, lavish, luxuriant *formal,* profuse
▧ 1 modest, parsimonious, thrifty 2 parsimonious, thrifty
◆ n big spender *colloq,* profligate *formal,* spendall, spendthrift, squanderer, waster, wastrel

prodigality n 1 *the prodigality of her lifestyle:* abandon, dissipation, excess, extravagance, immoderation, intemperance, lavishness, profligacy *formal,* squandering, sumptuousness, unthriftiness, wantonness, waste, wastefulness 2 *the prodigality of nature:* abundance, bounteousness *formal,* copiousness *formal,* exuberance, lavishness, luxuriance *formal,* plenteousness *formal,* plenty, profusion, richness
▧ 1 modesty, parsimony, thrift 2 parsimony, thrift

prodigious adj 1 *prodigious quantities:* colossal, enormous, giant, gigantic, huge, immeasurable, immense, mammoth, massive, vast 2 *prodigious talent:* abnormal, amazing, astounding, exceptional, extraordinary, fabulous, fantastic, flabbergasting, impressive, inordinate, marvellous, miraculous, monumental, phenomenal, remarkable, spectacular, staggering, startling, striking, stupendous, tremendous, unusual, wonderful
▧ 1 small 2 commonplace, unremarkable

prodigy n child genius, curiosity, freak, genius, gifted child, marvel, mastermind, miracle, phenomenon, rarity, sensation, virtuoso, whizz kid *colloq,* wonder, wonder child

produce v 1 *produce a result:* bring about, cause, create, effect *formal,* evoke, generate, give rise to, occasion, originate, provoke, result in 2 *the factory produces cars:* assemble, build, construct, create, fabricate, fashion, make, manufacture, put together 3 *produce a litter of puppies:* bear, beget, breed, bring forth, deliver, give birth to 4 *produce a piece of music:* compose, create, develop, invent, originate 5 *the tree produces fruit:* bear, give, grow, yield 6 *produce concrete evidence:* advance, bring forth, bring forward, bring out,

come up with, demonstrate, exhibit, furnish, give, offer, present, provide, put forward, supply 7 *produce your passport at customs:* display, exhibit, present, proffer *formal,* show 8 *produce a play:* arrange, direct, manage, mount, organize, perform, present, put on, stage
◆ n crop, dairy products, food, foodstuffs, fruit, harvest, output, product(s), vegetables, yield

producer n 1 *the play's producer:* director, impresario, manager, presenter, régisseur 2 *the world's largest car producer:* maker, manufacturer 3 *beef producers:* farmer, grower

product n 1 *electrical products:* artefact, article, commodity, creation, end-product, goods, invention, item, merchandise, wares 2 *farm products:* fruit, goods, produce, yield 3 *the product of hard work and perseverance:* by-product, consequence, effect, fruit, issue, legacy, offshoot, outcome, result, return, spin-off, upshot
▧ 3 cause

production n 1 *the production of the cars:* assembly, building, construction, creation, formation, making, manufacture, manufacturing, origination, producing 2 *the production of his paintings:* composition, creation, development, origination 3 *an increase in production:* achievement, fruit(s), harvest, manufacture, output, performance, productivity, return(s), yield 4 *the production of a play:* direction, management, mounting, organization, presentation, staging 5 *stars in a new production:* concert, drama, film, musical, opera, performance, play, presentation, revue, show
▧ 1 consumption

productive adj 1 *productive land:* fecund *formal,* fertile, fructiferous *formal,* fruitful, high-yielding, prolific, rich, teeming 2 *a productive meeting:* beneficial, constructive, effective, efficient, fruitful, gainful, profitable, rewarding, useful, valuable, worthwhile 3 *a productive artist:* busy, creative, energetic, inventive, prolific, vigorous
▧ 1 fruitless, unproductive, useless 2 fruitless, unproductive, useless 3 unproductive, useless

productivity n capacity, efficiency, output, production, productiveness, work rate, yield

profane adj 1 *profane language:* abusive, blasphemous, coarse, crude, disrespectful, filthy, foul, godless, idolatrous, impious, irreligious, irreverent, sacrilegious, unclean, ungodly, vulgar 2 *the dichotomy between the sacred and the profane worlds:* lay, secular, temporal, unconsecrated, unhallowed, unholy, unsanctified, worldly
▧ 1 sacred 2 religious, respectful
◆ v abuse, contaminate, debase, defile, desecrate, misemploy, misuse, pervert, pollute
▧ honour, revere

profanity n 1 *the profanity committed on the shrine:* abuse, blasphemy, impiety, irreverence, profaneness, sacrilege 2 *roaring profanities at passers-by:* abuse, blasphemy, curse, cursing, execration *formal,* expletive, four-letter word *colloq,* imprecation *formal,* malediction *formal,* obscenity, swearing, swear-word
▧ 1 politeness, reverence

profess v 1 *she professes to be psychic:* allege, claim, dissemble *formal,* lay claim to, maintain, make out, pretend 2 *professed his guilt:* acknowledge, admit, affirm, announce, assert, aver *formal*, avow *formal*, certify, confess, confirm, declare, own, proclaim, state

professed *adj* 1 *a professed feminist:* acknowledged, avowed *formal*, certified, confirmed, declared, proclaimed, self-acknowledged, self-confessed 2 *his professed love of animals:* alleged, ostensible, pretended, purported *formal*, self-styled, so-called, soi-disant, supposed, would-be

profession *n* 1 *the medical profession:* appointment, business, calling, career, craft, employment, job, line (of work), métier, occupation, trade, vocation, walk of life 2 *a profession of faith:* acknowledgement, admission, affirmation, announcement, assertion, averment *formal*, avowal *formal*, claim, confession, declaration, statement, testimony

professional *adj* 1 *make a professional job of something:* adept, businesslike, competent, efficient, experienced, expert, masterly, practised, proficient, skilful 2 *architects and other professional people:* educated, licensed, qualified, skilled, trained
🖹 1 amateur, unprofessional 2 amateur, unprofessional
♦ *n* ace *colloq*, authority, dab hand *colloq*, expert, master, past master, pro *colloq*, specialist, virtuoso, wizard *colloq*
🖹 amateur

proffer *v* 1 *proffered his hand:* extend, hand, hold out, offer, present 2 *proffer a suggestion:* advance, offer, propose, propound *formal*, submit, suggest, tender, volunteer

proficiency *n* ability, accomplishment, adeptness, aptitude, aptness, capability, competence, dexterity, experience, expertise, finesse, knack, mastery, skilfulness, skill, talent
🖹 incompetence

proficient *adj* able, accomplished, adept, apt, capable, clever, competent, effective, efficient, experienced, expert, gifted, masterly, qualified, skilful, skilled, talented, trained
🖹 incompetent, unskilled

profile *n* 1 *the profile of the building:* contour, figure, form, line(s), outline, shape, side view, silhouette 2 *a profile of the school's intake:* analysis, chart, diagram, examination, graph, review, study, survey 3 *a profile of each contestant:* biography, curriculum vitae, CV, portrait, sketch, thumbnail sketch, vignette

profit *n* 1 *the company's profits:* bonus, bottom line, dividend, earnings, excess, fast buck *colloq*, gain, gravy *colloq*, interest, killing *colloq*, proceeds, rake-off *colloq*, receipts, return, revenue, surplus, takings, winnings, yield 2 *there's no profit in arguing:* advantage, avail, benefit, gain, use, value, worth
🖹 1 loss 2 loss
♦ *v* 1 *profiting at the community's expense:* gain, line your pockets *colloq*, make money 2 *it won't profit us to complain:* avail, benefit, pay, serve
🖹 1 lose
▶ **profit by/from** capitalize on, cash in on *colloq*, exploit, gain a benefit from, gain an advantage from, milk *colloq*, put to good use, reap the benefit of, take advantage of, turn to advantage, use, utilize

profitable *adj* 1 *a profitable business:* commercial, cost-effective, economic, gainful *formal*, in the black *colloq*, lucrative, money-making, paying, remunerative, rewarding, successful 2 *a profitable discussion:* advantageous, beneficial, fruitful, productive, rewarding, successful, useful, valuable, worthwhile
🖹 1 loss-making, non-profit-making, unprofitable 2 unprofitable

profiteer *n* exploiter, extortioner, extortionist, racketeer
♦ *v* exploit, extort, fleece *colloq*, make a fast buck *colloq*, make a quick killing *colloq*, overcharge, racketeer

profiteering *n* exploitation, extortion, Rachmanism, racketeering

profitless *adj* 1 *a profitless business:* unproductive, unprofitable, unremunerative 2 *a profitless task:* fruitless, futile, gainless, idle, ineffective, ineffectual *formal*, pointless, thankless, unavailing, unproductive, unprofitable, useless, vain, worthless
🖹 1 profitable 2 profitable

profligacy *n* 1 *profligacy which led to bankruptcy:* excess, extravagance, improvidence, lavishness, prodigality, recklessness, squandering, unrestraint, unthriftiness, waste, wastefulness 2 *sexual profligacy:* corruption, debauchery, degeneracy, depravity, dissipation, dissoluteness, immorality, libertinism, licentiousness, promiscuity, wantonness
🖹 1 morality, parsimony, thrift, uprightness

profligate *adj* 1 *profligate spending:* excessive, extravagant, immoderate, improvident, prodigal, reckless, spendthrift, squandering, wasteful 2 *a man of profligate morals:* corrupt, debauched, degenerate, depraved, dissipated, dissolute, immoral, iniquitous, libertine, licentious, loose, promiscuous, unprincipled, wanton, wicked
🖹 1 parsimonious *formal*, thrifty 2 moral, upright
♦ *n* 1 *a profligate who squandered all he had:* prodigal, spendthrift, squanderer, waster, wastrel 2 *associating with whores and profligates:* debauchee, degenerate, libertine, rake, reprobate, roué

profound *adj* 1 *profound relief:* deep, extreme, great, heartfelt, intense, sincere 2 *a profound silence:* absolute, complete, deep, extreme, intense 3 *undergo a profound change:* exhaustive, extensive, far-reaching, marked, radical, thorough, thoroughgoing 4 *a profound remark:* abstruse *formal*, deep, discerning, erudite *formal*, esoteric *formal*, impenetrable, learned, penetrating, philosophical, sagacious *formal*, serious, thoughtful, weighty, wise
🖹 1 mild, shallow, slight 2 mild, slight 3 mild, slight 4 shallow

profoundly *adv* acutely, deeply, extremely, greatly, heartily, intensely, keenly, seriously, sincerely, thoroughly
🖹 slightly

profundity *n* 1 *the profundity of her writing:* abstruseness *formal*, acumen, depth, erudition *formal*, insight, intelligence, learning, penetration, perceptiveness, perspicacity *formal*, perspicuity

formal, profoundness, sagacity *formal*, seriousness, wisdom **2** *the profundity of her despair*: depth, extremity, intensity, profoundness, seriousness, severity, strength
▣ **1** shallowness **2** shallowness

profuse *adj* **1** *profuse thanks*: excessive, extravagant, fulsome, generous, immoderate, inordinate *formal*, lavish, liberal, over the top *colloq*, unstinting **2** *profuse vegetation*: abundant, ample, copious, luxuriant *formal*, overabundant, overflowing, plentiful, rich, superabundant
▣ **1** inadequate **2** sparse

profusion *n* abundance, copiousness, excess, extravagance, glut, heaps *colloq*, loads *colloq*, lots *colloq*, multitude, plenitude *formal*, plenty, plethora *formal*, riot, superabundance, superfluity, surplus, tons *colloq*, wealth
▣ inadequacy, scarcity

progenitor *n* *the living conditions of our progenitors*: ancestor, begetter *old use*, father, forebear, forefather, mother, parent, primogenitor *formal*, procreator *formal* **2** *the progenitors of modern art*: antecedent, forerunner, founder, instigator, originator, precursor, predecessor, source

progeny *n* **1** *provided for their progeny*: children, family, issue, offspring, quiverful, young **2** *the progeny of a noble race*: breed, descendants, lineage, posterity *formal*, race, scions *formal*, seed, stock

prognosis *n* assessment, diagnosis, evaluation, expectation, forecast, outlook, prediction, prognostication *formal*, projection, prospect, speculation, surmise

prognosticate *v* **1** *seers who prognosticated the future*: augur *formal*, divine, forecast, foretell, predict, presage *formal*, prophesy, soothsay **2** *the omens prognosticate disaster*: augur *formal*, betoken *formal*, foreshadow, harbinger *formal*, herald, indicate, portend *formal*, presage *formal*

prognostication *n* expectation, forecast, prediction, prognosis *formal*, projection, prophecy, speculation, surmise

programme *n* **1** *a programme of events*: agenda, calendar, line-up, list, listing, order of events, plan, schedule, timetable **2** *a programme for development*: plan, plan of action, project, scheme, strategy **3** *a study programme*: course, curriculum, plan, syllabus **4** *radio programme*: broadcast, episode, performance, presentation, production, show, simulcast, transmission
♦ *v* arrange, book, design, formulate, itemize, lay on, line up, list, map out, plan, prearrange, schedule, work out

progress *n* **1** *make slow progress*: advance, headway, journey, movement, passage, progression, way **2** *the progress of the project*: advancement *formal*, betterment, breakthrough, development, evolution, growth, headway, improvement, increase, movement, progression, step(s) forward **3** *his progress through the ranks*: advancement *formal*, betterment, progression, promotion, upgrading
▣ **2** decline, deterioration, recession
♦ *v* **1** *progress gradually*: advance, continue, go forward, go on, make headway, make progress, make your way, move forward, proceed **2** *our plans are progressing*: advance, be getting

there *colloq*, better, blossom, come on, develop, flourish, forge ahead, grow, improve, increase, make headway, make progress, make strides, mature, move forward, proceed, prosper, shape up *colloq*
▣ **2** decline, deteriorate

progression *n* **1** *the progression of the disease*: advance, advancement *formal*, development, forward movement, headway, passage, progress **2** *the natural progression of events*: chain, course, cycle, order, sequence, series, stream, string, succession, train

progressive *adj* **1** *a progressive company*: advanced, avant-garde, dynamic, enlightened, enterprising, forward-looking, forward-thinking, go-ahead, innovative, liberal, modern, radical, reformist, revolutionary, up-and-coming **2** *a progressive loss*: accelerating, advancing, continuing, developing, escalating, growing, increasing, intensifying
▣ **1** conservative **2** regressive

prohibit *v* **1** *trading is prohibited on a Sunday*: ban, bar, exclude, forbid, interdict *formal*, outlaw, proscribe *formal*, rule out, veto **2** *the lock prohibits movement of the door panel*: hamper, hinder, impede, obstruct, preclude *formal*, prevent, restrict, stop
▣ **1** allow, authorize, permit **2** allow, permit

prohibited *adj* banned, barred, disallowed *formal*, embargoed, forbidden, interdicted *formal*, proscribed *formal*, taboo, verboten, vetoed
▣ allowed, permitted

prohibition *n* ban, bar, constraint, disallowance *formal*, embargo, exclusion, forbiddal *formal*, forbiddance, forbidding, injunction, interdict *formal*, interdiction *formal*, negation, obstruction, prevention, proscription *formal*, restriction, veto
▣ permission

prohibitionist *n* abolitionist, dry, pussyfoot, teetotaller

prohibitive *adj* **1** *the cost would be prohibitive*: excessive, exorbitant, extortionate, impossible, preposterous, sky-high *colloq*, steep *colloq* **2** *prohibitive government policies*: forbidding, prohibiting, prohibitory, proscriptive *formal*, repressive, restraining, restrictive, suppressive
▣ **1** reasonable **2** encouraging, reasonable

project *n* **1** *a government-funded project*: activity, campaign, contract, enterprise, idea, job, occupation, plan, programme, proposal, scheme, undertaking, venture, work **2** *a history project*: assignment, homework, task
♦ *v* **1** *the building is projected to cost over £1million*: calculate, estimate, expect, extrapolate, forecast, gauge, predict, reckon **2** *her projected visit to America*: design, map out, plan, predetermine *formal*, propose **3** *weapons which project a missile*: cast, discharge, fling, hurl, launch, propel, throw **4** *cannons projected from the side of the ship*: bulge, extend, jut out, obtrude *formal*, overhang, protrude, stand out, stick out

projectile *n* ball, bullet, grenade, missile, mortar-bomb, rocket, shell, shot

projecting *adj* beetling, exsertile *formal*, extrusive *formal*, extrusory *formal*, overhanging, protrudent *formal*, protruding, protrusive

projection *n* **1** *sales projections for the next year*: calculation, computation, design, estimate, estimation, expectation, extrapolation, forecast, plan, prediction, reckoning **2** *a projection from the cliff face*: bulge, jutting, ledge, overhang, protuberance, ridge, shelf, sill

proletariat *n* canaille, common people, commonalty, commoners, great unwashed *colloq*, herd, hoi polloi, lower classes, masses, mob, plebs *colloq*, proles *colloq*, rabble, riff-raff *colloq*, working class

proliferate *v* breed, build up, burgeon *formal*, escalate, expand, extend, flourish, grow quickly, increase, intensify, multiply, mushroom, reproduce, rocket, snowball, spread, thrive
Fa dwindle

proliferation *n* build-up, concentration, escalation, expansion, extension, increase, intensification, multiplication, mushrooming, rocketing, snowballing, spread
Fa decrease

prolific *adj* **1** *a prolific artist*: creative, fertile, productive **2** *prolific crops*: abundant, copious, fecund *formal*, fertile, fruitful, luxuriant *formal*, productive, profuse, rank
Fa **1** unproductive **2** unproductive

prolix *adj* diffuse, digressive, discursive, lengthy, long, long-winded, pleonastic *technical*, prolonged, prosy, protracted *formal*, rambling, tedious, tiresome, verbose, wordy
Fa succinct

prolixity *n* boringness, diffuseness, discursiveness, long-windedness, pleonasm *technical*, prosiness, rambling, tediousness, verbiage, verboseness, verbosity, wandering, wordiness
Fa succinctness

prologue *n* exordium *formal*, foreword, introduction, preamble, preface, preliminary, prelude, proem *formal*, prolegomena *formal*, prooemion *formal*, prooemium *formal*

prolong *v* **1** *prolong the wait*: continue, delay, drag out, draw out, extend, lengthen, perpetuate, protract *formal*, spin out, stretch (out) **2** *prolong a line*: continue, elongate, extend, lengthen, protract *formal*
Fa **1** shorten **2** shorten

promenade *n* **1** *a walk along the promenade*: boulevard, esplanade, front, parade, prom, seafront, terrace, walkway **2** *when I take my morning promenade*: airing, breather, constitutional *formal*, saunter, stroll, turn, walk, walkabout
♦ *v* mosey *colloq*, parade, perambulate *formal*, sally forth, saunter, stroll, strut, swagger, walk

prominence *n* **1** *achieved prominence in a reality show*: celebrity, distinction, eminence, fame, greatness, illustriousness, importance, name, note, pre-eminence, prestige, rank, renown, reputation, standing, stature **2** *give a story prominence*: conspicuousness, pre-eminence, top billing, weight **3** *a painful prominence on the knee joint*: bulge, bump, hump, jutting, lump, mound, process, projection, protruding, protuberance, rise, swelling **4** *coastal prominences*: cliff, crag, crest, elevation, headland, height, pinnacle, promontory, rise
Fa **1** insignificance, unimportance **2** insignificance, unimportance

prominent *adj* **1** *a prominent feature*: conspicuous, eye-catching, noticeable, obtrusive, obvious, striking, unmistakable **2** *prominent eyes*: bulging, jutting (out), projecting, protruding, protrusive, protuberant, standing out, sticking out **3** *a prominent writer*: acclaimed, celebrated, chief, distinguished, eminent, famous, foremost, illustrious, important, leading, main, notable, noted, outstanding, popular, pre-eminent, renowned, respected, top, well-known
Fa **1** inconspicuous **3** insignificant, unimportant, unknown

promiscuity *n* debauchery, depravity, dissipation, dissoluteness, immorality, laxity, licentiousness, looseness, permissiveness, profligacy *formal*, protervity *formal*, wantonness
Fa chastity, morality

promiscuous *adj* **1** *a promiscuous lifestyle*: abandoned, debauched, dissipated, dissolute, fast, immoral, licentious, loose, of easy virtue, profligate *formal*, wanton **2** *a promiscuous jumble of items*: casual, haphazard, indiscriminate, random
Fa **1** chaste, moral

promise *v* **1** *I promise to pay you back*: assure, contract, give an assurance, give an undertaking, give your word, guarantee, pledge, swear, take an oath, undertake, vouch, vow, warrant **2** *clouds that promise rain*: augur *formal*, be a sign of, betoken *formal*, denote, hint at, indicate, presage *formal*, signify, suggest
♦ *n* **1** *a promise to marry*: assurance, bond, commitment, compact *formal*, contract, covenant *formal*, engagement, guarantee, oath, pledge, undertaking, vow, word, word of honour **2** *show great promise*: ability, aptitude, capability, flair, potential, talent **3** *a promise of autumn sunshine*: evidence, hint, indication, sign, suggestion

promising *adj* **1** *a promising student*: able, budding, gifted, talented, up-and-coming *colloq* **2** *a promising start*: auspicious *formal*, bright, encouraging, favourable, hopeful, optimistic, propitious *formal*, rosy
Fa **1** unpromising **2** discouraging, inauspicious, unpromising

promontory *n* bluff, cape, cliff, foreland, head, headland, naze, ness, peninsula, point, projection, prominence, ridge, spur

promote *v* **1** *promoted to colonel*: advance, aggrandize *formal*, elevate, exalt, honour, move up, prefer *formal*, raise, upgrade **2** *promote religious tolerance*: advance, advocate, aid, assist, back, boost, champion, contribute to, encourage, endorse, espouse *formal*, forward, foster, further, help, nurture, recommend, sponsor, stimulate, support, urge **3** *promote a new product*: advertise, hype *colloq*, market, plug *colloq*, popularize, publicize, puff up *colloq*, push, sell
Fa **1** demote, relegate **2** discourage, disparage *formal*, hinder

promotion *n* **1** *her promotion to manager*: advancement, aggrandizement *formal*, elevation, exaltation, move up, preferment *formal*, rise, upgrading **2** *the promotion of racial harmony*: advocacy, backing, boosting, contribution, development, encouragement, espousal *formal*, fostering, furtherance, recommendation, support, urging **3** *the promotion of a new line*: advertising, campaign, hype *colloq*, marketing,

plugging *colloq*, propaganda, publicity, pushing *colloq*
⊟ 1 demotion **2** discouragement, disparagement *formal*, obstruction

prompt *adj* **1** *requiring prompt attention:* direct, early, immediate, instant, instantaneous, on time, punctual, quick, rapid, speedy, swift, timely, unhesitating **2** *prompt and courteous service:* alert, eager, quick, ready, responsive, speedy, swift, unhesitating, willing
⊟ 1 hesitant, late, slow **2** hesitant, slow
♦ *adv* bang on *colloq*, dead on *colloq*, exactly, on the dot, on time, promptly, punctually, sharp, spot on *colloq*, to the minute
♦ *v* **1** *prompted an angry response:* call forth, cause, elicit, encourage, give rise to, impel, incite, induce, inspire, instigate, lead, make, motivate, move, occasion, produce, provoke, result in, spur, stimulate, urge **2** *prompted him:* cue, jog your memory, prod, remind
⊟ 1 deter, dissuade
♦ *n* **1** *took it as a prompt to keep going:* cue, encouragement, jolt, prod, spur, stimulus **2** *if I forget his name, give me a prompt:* cue, help, hint, prod, refresher, reminder

prompting *n* assistance, encouragement, hint, incitement, influence, jogging, persuasion, pressing, pressure, prodding, protreptic *formal*, pushing, suggestion, urging
⊟ dissuasion

promptly *adv* **1** *the ambulance arrived promptly:* as soon as possible, ASAP *colloq*, directly, forthwith *formal*, immediately, instantly, pdq *colloq*, posthaste, pretty damn quick *colloq*, pronto *colloq*, quickly, speedily, swiftly, unhesitatingly **2** *please be here promptly at eight:* bang on *colloq*, dead on *colloq*, exactly, on target, on the dot, on time, punctually, sharp, spot on *colloq*, to the minute

promptness *n* alacrity *formal*, briskness, dispatch, eagerness, expedition *formal*, haste, promptitude *formal*, punctuality, quickness, readiness, speed, swiftness, willingness
⊟ tardiness *formal*

promulgate *v* **1** *promulgate the message of universal peace:* advertise, announce, broadcast, circulate, communicate, disseminate *formal*, issue, notify, proclaim, promote, publicize, publish, spread **2** *promulgate a new law:* announce, declare, decree, proclaim

promulgation *n* **1** *the promulgation of this message:* announcement, communication, dissemination *formal*, issuance, proclamation, promulgating, publication, publicizing **2** *the promulgation of a statute:* announcement, declaration, decreeing, proclamation, promulgating

prone *adj* **1** *prone to migraines:* apt, bent, disposed, given, inclined, liable, likely, predisposed *formal*, subject, susceptible, vulnerable **2** *she lay prone:* face down, flat, full-length, horizontal, procumbent *formal*, prostrate, recumbent *formal*, stretched
⊟ 1 immune, unlikely **2** supine, upright

proneness *n* aptness, bent, bias, disposition, inclination, leaning, liability, penchant *formal*, proclivity *formal*, propensity *formal*, susceptibility, tendency, weakness
⊟ dislike

prong *n* fork, point, projection, spike, spur, tip

pronounce *v* **1** *pronounce your name:* articulate, enunciate, express, say, sound, speak, stress, utter, vocalize, voice **2** *pronounced dead:* affirm, announce, assert, declare, decree, judge, proclaim

pronounceable *adj* articulable, enunciable, expressible, sayable, speakable, utterable, vocable
⊟ unpronounceable

pronounced *adj* broad, clear, conspicuous, decided, definite, distinct, evident, marked, noticeable, obvious, positive, striking, strong, thick, unmistakable
⊟ faint, vague

pronouncement *n* announcement, assertion, declaration, decree, dictum, edict, ipse dixit *formal*, judgement, manifesto, notification, proclamation, promulgation *formal*, pronunciamento *formal*, statement

pronunciation *n* accent, articulation, delivery, diction, elocution, enunciation, inflection, intonation, modulation, saying, speech, stress, uttering, vocalization, voicing

proof *n* attestation *formal*, authentication, certification, confirmation, corroboration, demonstration, documentation, evidence, substantiation, validation, verification
♦ *adj* bombproof, bulletproof, childproof, fireproof, foolproof, impenetrable, impervious, leakproof, proofed, rainproof, repellent, resistant, soundproof, strong, tamperproof, tight, treated, waterproof, weatherproof, windproof
⊟ permeable, untreated

prop *v* **1** *propped up with scaffolding:* bolster (up), brace, buttress, hold up, maintain, set, shore (up), stay, support, sustain, underpin, uphold **2** *propped against the wall:* balance, lean, rest, stand, steady
♦ *n* **1** *held up with props:* bolster, brace, buttress, column, mainstay, post, shaft, stanchion, stay, stick, strut, support, truss, upright **2** *the central prop in his life:* anchor, column, mainstay, pillar, support, supporter

propaganda *n* advertising, brainwashing, disinformation, hype *colloq*, indoctrination, information, promotion, publicity

propagandist *n* advocate, canvasser, evangelist, indoctrinator, pamphleteer, plugger *colloq*, promoter, proponent *formal*, proselytizer, publicist

propagate *v* **1** *propagate a message:* broadcast, circulate, communicate, diffuse, disseminate *formal*, distribute, proclaim, promote, promulgate *formal*, publicize, publish, spread, transmit **2** *how plants propagate:* breed, generate, grow, increase, multiply, procreate *formal*, produce, proliferate, reproduce, spawn

propagation *n* **1** *the propagation of ideas:* circulation, communication, diffusion, dissemination *formal*, distribution, promotion, promulgation *formal*, spread, spreading, transmission **2** *the propagation of plants:* breeding, generation, increase, multiplication, procreation *old use*, proliferation, reproduction, spawning

propel *v* drive, force, impel, launch, move, push (forward), send, shoot, shove *colloq*, thrust
🔁 stop

propensity *n* aptness, bent, bias, disposition, foible, inclination, leaning, liability, penchant *formal*, predisposition *formal*, proclivity *formal*, proneness, readiness, susceptibility, tendency, weakness
🔁 disinclination

proper *adj* 1 *the proper answer:* accurate, actual, correct, exact, precise, right 2 *get a proper job:* actual, genuine, real, true 3 *not behaving in a proper manner:* acceptable, accepted, appropriate, conventional, correct, decent, established, fitting, genteel, gentlemanly, ladylike, orthodox, polite, refined, respectable, suitable 4 *very prim and proper:* formal, genteel, prim, prudish, strict
🔁 1 incorrect, wrong 3 improper, indecent 4 improper, indecent

property *n* 1 *lost all his property:* assets, belongings, capital, chattels, effects *formal*, gear *colloq*, goods, holding(s), means, paraphernalia, possessions, resources, riches, wealth 2 *buying up property:* acres, buildings, estate, holding(s), house(s), land, premises, real estate 3 *the chemical properties of mercury:* attribute, characteristic, feature, idiosyncrasy, mark, peculiarity, quality, quirk, trait

prophecy *n* 1 *the gift of prophecy:* augury *formal*, divination, fortune-telling, second sight, soothsaying 2 *his prophecies of disaster:* augury *formal*, forecast, prediction, prognosis, prognostication *formal*

prophesy *v* augur, forecast, foresee, foretell, forewarn, predict, prognosticate *formal*

prophet *n* clairvoyant, forecaster, foreteller, fortune-teller, oracle, prognosticator *formal*, seer, soothsayer

prophetic *adj* augural *formal*, divinatory *formal*, fatidical *formal*, fey, forecasting, foreshadowing, mantic *formal*, oracular, predictive, presaging *formal*, prescient *formal*, prognostic, sibylline *formal*, vatic *formal*, vaticidal *formal*
🔁 unprophetic

prophylactic *adj* anticipatory, counteractive, deterrent, inhibitory, obstructive, precautionary, pre-emptive, preventative, preventive, protective
🔁 causative, fostering

propinquity *n* 1 *the propinquity of the two countries:* adjacency, closeness, contiguity *formal*, nearness, neighbourhood, proximity, vicinity 2 *the propinquity of a blood relationship:* affiliation, affinity, blood, closeness, connection, consanguinity *formal*, kindredness *formal*, kindredship *formal*, kinship, nearness, relation, relationship, tie
🔁 1 remoteness 2 remoteness

propitiate *v* appease, conciliate, mollify, pacify, placate, reconcile, satisfy, soothe
🔁 anger, provoke

propitiation *n* appeasement, conciliation, mollification, pacification, pacifying, peacemaking, placation, reconciliation
🔁 angering, provocation

propitiatory *adj* appeasing, assuaging, conciliatory, mollifying, pacificatory, pacifying,
peacemaking, placative *formal*, placatory *formal*, propitiative *formal*, reconciliatory, soothing
🔁 provocative

propitious *adj* 1 *a propitious time to sell:* advantageous, auspicious *formal*, beneficial, bright, encouraging, favourable, fortunate, lucky, opportune, promising, prosperous, rosy, timely 2 *encouraged by his propitious attitude:* benevolent, benign, favourable, friendly, gracious, happy, kindly, reassuring, well-disposed
🔁 1 inauspicious 2 inauspicious

proponent *n* advocate, apologist, backer, champion, defender, enthusiast, exponent, friend, partisan, patron, proposer, propounder *formal*, subscriber, supporter, upholder, vindicator
🔁 enemy, opponent

proportion *n* 1 *a proportion of the tax goes on schools:* amount, cut *colloq*, division, fraction, measure, part, percentage, piece of the action *colloq*, portion, quota, segment, share, slice of the cake *colloq*, split *colloq*, whack *colloq* 2 *the proportion of men to women on the course:* balance, correspondence, distribution, quotient, ratio, relationship, symmetry 3 *a building of huge proportions:* breadth, bulk, capacity, depth, dimensions, extent, height, length, magnitude, mass, measurements, scale, size, volume, width
🔁 2 disproportion, imbalance

proportional *adj* analogous, commensurate, comparable, consistent, corresponding, equitable, equivalent, even, proportionate, relative
🔁 disproportionate

proportionally *adv* commensurately, comparably, correspondingly, evenly, pro rata, proportionately, relatively
🔁 disproportionately

proposal *n* bid, design, manifesto, motion, offer, plan, presentation, programme, project, proposition, recommendation, scheme, suggestion, tender, terms

propose *v* 1 *propose a suggestion:* advance, advocate, bring up, introduce, move, offer, present, proffer *formal*, propound *formal*, put forward, recommend, submit, suggest, table, tender 2 *what do you propose to do?:* aim, design, have in mind, intend, mean, plan, purpose 3 *proposed as chairman:* name, nominate, put up, recommend, suggest 4 *propose marriage:* ask for someone's hand in marriage, ask to marry, go down on bended knee *colloq*, pop the question *colloq*
🔁 1 withdraw

proposition *n* 1 *a business proposition:* manifesto, motion, plan, programme, project, proposal, recommendation, scheme, suggestion, tender 2 *a philosophical proposition:* theorem *formal*, theory 3 *doing it yourself is quite a different proposition:* activity, task, undertaking, venture 4 *a sexual proposition:* advance, approach, indecent proposal/suggestion, overture, pass
♦ *v* accost, make a pass at, make an indecent proposal to, make sexual advances/overtures to, solicit

propound *v* advance, advocate, contend, lay down, move *formal*, postulate *formal*, present, propose, put forward, set forth, submit, suggest
☒ oppose

proprietor, proprietress *n* deed holder, freeholder, landlady, landlord, landowner, leaseholder, owner, possessor, title-holder

propriety *n* 1 *lose all sense of propriety*: breeding, civility, courtesy, decency, decorum, delicacy, etiquette, gentlemanliness, good manners, ladylikeness, manners, modesty, politeness, protocol, punctilio *formal*, rectitude *formal*, refinement, respectability 2 *question the propriety of such behaviour*: appropriateness, aptness, becomingness, correctness, rightness, suitableness 3 *observe the proprieties*: civility, convention, decency, etiquette, nicety, p's and q's *colloq*, standard, the done thing *colloq*
☒ 2 impropriety

propulsion *n* drive, driving force, impetus, impulse, impulsion, momentum, motive force, power, pressure, push, thrust

prosaic *adj* banal, bland, boring, commonplace, dry, dull, everyday, flat, hackneyed, humdrum, matter-of-fact, monotonous, mundane, ordinary, pedestrian, routine, stale, tame, trite, unimaginative, uninspired, uninspiring, vacuous, vapid, workaday
☒ imaginative, interesting

proscribe *v* 1 *smoking is proscribed in pubs*: ban, bar, disallow *formal*, embargo, forbid, interdict *formal*, prohibit 2 *he was proscribed for alleged sedition*: banish, black, blackball, boycott, deport, exclude, excommunicate, exile, expatriate, expel, ostracize, outlaw, reject 3 *swearing was proscribed by my parents*: censure, condemn, damn, denounce, reject
☒ 1 allow, permit

---

proscribe or *prescribe*? See panel at **prescribe**

---

proscription *n* 1 *the proscription of alcohol at football matches*: ban, bar, barring, embargo, interdict *formal*, prohibition 2 *his proscription from politics*: banishment, boycott, deportation, ejection, eviction, exclusion, excommunication, exile, expatriation, expulsion, ostracism, outlawry, rejection 3 *the Church's proscription of contraception*: censure, condemnation, damning, denunciation, rejection
☒ 1 admission, allowing 2 admission

prosecute *v* accuse, arraign *formal*, bring an action against, bring charges, charge, indict *formal*, litigate, prefer charges, put on trial, sue, summon, take to court, try
☒ defend

proselytize *v* bring into the fold, bring to God, convert, evangelize, make converts, persuade, propagandize, spread the gospel, win over

prospect *n* 1 *the prospect of rain*: anticipation, chance(s), expectation, future, hope, likelihood, likeness, odds, outlook, possibility, probability, promise 2 *a prospect of the bay*: aspect, landscape, opening, outlook, panorama, perspective, scene, spectacle, view, vista
☒ 1 unlikelihood
♦ *v* examine, explore, fossick, inspect, look for, nose *colloq*, quest, search, seek, survey

prospective *adj* 1 *prospective buyers*: aspiring, possible, potential, probable, would-be 2 *the prospective agreement*: anticipated, approaching, awaited, coming, designate, destined, expected, forthcoming, future, hoped-for, imminent, intended, likely, -to-be

prospectus *n* brochure, catalogue, conspectus *formal*, leaflet, list, literature, manifesto, outline, pamphlet, plan, programme, scheme, syllabus, synopsis

prosper *v* advance, be successful, bloom, boom, burgeon *formal*, do well, flourish, flower, get ahead *colloq*, get on, get on in the world *colloq*, get on well, go up in the world *colloq*, grow rich, hit the big time *colloq*, hit the jackpot *colloq*, live on easy street *colloq*, make progress, make your pile *colloq*, progress, succeed, thrive, turn out well
☒ fail

prosperity *n* affluence, bed of roses *colloq*, boom, clover *colloq*, easy street *colloq*, fortune, good fortune, land of milk and honey *colloq*, lap of luxury *colloq*, luxury, plenty, riches, success, the good life *colloq*, the life of Riley *colloq*, wealth
☒ adversity, poverty

prosperous *adj* 1 *a prosperous businessman*: affluent, fortunate, lucky, opulent *formal*, rich, rolling in it *colloq*, wealthy, well-heeled *colloq*, well-off, well-to-do 2 *a prosperous business*: blooming, booming, burgeoning *formal*, flourishing, successful, thriving
☒ 1 poor, unfortunate

prostitute *n* bawd, brass, call-girl, cocotte, courtesan, drab, fallen woman, fille de joie, fille des rues, floosie, grande cocotte, harlot, hooker *colloq*, hustler *colloq*, loose woman, lorette, moll *colloq*, pro *colloq*, rent-boy, street-walker, strumpet, tart *colloq*, trollop, wench, whore, woman of ill repute, woman of the streets, woman of the town
♦ *v* cheapen, debase, degrade, demean, devalue, misapply, misuse, pervert, profane

prostitution *n* harlotry, meretriciousness, street-walking, the game *colloq*, the oldest profession *colloq*, vice, whoredom, whoring

prostrate *adj* 1 *be prostrate on the ground*: fallen, flat, horizontal, lying down, lying flat, prone 2 *be prostrate with grief*: crushed, devastated, overcome, overwhelmed 3 *be prostrate with illness*: brought to your knees, defenceless, helpless, laid low, overwhelmed, paralysed, powerless
☒ 1 erect 2 triumphant
♦ *v* 1 *be prostrated with exhaustion*: drain, exhaust, fatigue, sap, tire, wear out 2 *be prostrated by illness*: bring to your knees, lay low 3 *prostrated by civil war*: crush, flatten, knock down, level, overcome, overthrow, overwhelm, ruin
☒ 1 strengthen

prostration *n* 1 *his prostration after his wife's death*: dejection, depression, desolation, despair, despondency, grief, slough of despond *formal* 2 *prostration from the heat*: collapse, exhaustion, helplessness, paralysis, weakness, weariness 3 *his prostration before the emperor*: abasement, bow, genuflection *formal*, kneeling, kowtow, obeisance *formal*, submission
☒ 1 elation, exaltation, happiness, triumph

protagonist *n* **1** *a leading protagonist of the movement:* adherent, advocate, champion, exponent, leader, mainstay, moving spirit, prime mover, proponent *formal*, standard-bearer, supporter **2** *the protagonist of the film:* hero, heroine, lead, main/chief/leading character, principal, title role
🖪 **1** critic, opponent

protean *adj* amoebic, changeable, ever-changing, inconstant, many-sided, mercurial, multiform, mutable, polymorphic *technical*, polymorphous, variable, versatile, volatile
🖪 stable, unchanging

protect *v* care for, conserve, cover, defend, guard, harbour, keep, keep safe, look after, preserve, safeguard, save, screen, secure, shelter, shield, take care of, watch over
🖪 attack, neglect

protection *n* **1** *protection of the environment:* care, charge, conservation, custody, defence, guardianship, preservation, safeguard, safekeeping, safety, security **2** *protection from evil:* barrier, buffer, bulwark, cover, defence, guard, insurance, refuge, safeguard, screen, security, shelter, shield **3** *a flak vest as protection against bullets:* armour, barrier, cover, screen, shield
🖪 **1** attack, neglect

protective *adj* **1** *protective clothing:* covering, defensive, fireproof, insulating, shielding, waterproof **2** *very protective towards his daughters:* careful, defensive, fatherly, maternal, motherly, overprotective, paternal, possessive, vigilant, wary, watchful
🖪 **2** aggressive, threatening

protector *n* **1** *a protector of the weak:* advocate, benefactor, bodyguard, champion, defender, father-figure, guardian, minder, patron, protectress *formal*, protectrix *formal* **2** *wear eye protectors when playing squash:* bolster, buffer, cushion, guard, pad, safeguard, shield
🖪 **1** attacker, threat

protégé, protégée *n* blue-eyed boy *colloq*, charge, dependant, discovery, pupil, student, ward
🖪 guardian

protest *v* **1** *protest against a decision:* appeal, argue, complain, demonstrate, demur *formal*, disagree, disapprove, gripe *colloq*, kick up a fuss *colloq*, make/raise an objection to, object, oppose, reject, remonstrate *formal*, speak out, take exception, take issue, whinge *colloq* **2** *protest your innocence:* affirm *formal*, announce, assert, attest *formal*, avow *formal*, contend, declare, insist on, maintain, proclaim, profess
🖪 **1** accept
♦ *n* **1** *a protest against the ruling:* appeal, complaint, demurral *formal*, disagreement, disapproval, dissent, exception, fuss, objection, opposition, outcry, protestation, remonstration *formal* **2** *a protest in front of the town hall:* civil disobedience, demo *colloq*, demonstration, march, riot **3** *his protests that he was being persecuted:* affirmation *formal*, announcement, assertion, attestation *formal*, avowal *formal*, contention, declaration, proclamation
🖪 **1** acceptance

protestation *n* **1** *protestations against the arrests:* complaint, disagreement, dissent, expostulation *formal*, objection, outcry, protest, remonstrance

formal, remonstration *formal* **2** *protestations of loyalty:* affirmation *formal*, asseveration *formal*, assurance, avowal *formal*, declaration, oath, pledge, profession, statement, vow

protester *n* **1** *police clashed with protesters:* agitator, demonstrator, dissenter, dissident, rebel, striker **2** *protesters say the new law is unfair:* complainer, dissenter, objector, opponent, opposer

protocol *n* civilities, code of behaviour, convention, custom, decorum *formal*, etiquette, formalities, good form, manners, procedure, propriety *formal*, p's and q's *colloq*

prototype *n* archetype *formal*, example, exemplar *formal*, mock-up, model, original, paradigm *formal*, pattern, precedent, standard, type

protract *v* **1** *protract the war:* continue, drag out *colloq*, draw out, extend, keep going, lengthen, make longer, prolong, spin out, stretch out, sustain **2** *protract a line:* continue, extend, lengthen, make longer, prolong
🖪 **1** shorten **2** shorten

protracted *adj* drawn-out, endless, extended, interminable, lengthy, long, long-drawn-out, overlong, prolonged, spun out, stretched out
🖪 brief, shortened

protrude *v* beetle, bulge, come through, extend, jut out, obtrude *formal*, poke out, project, stand out, stick out

protruding *adj* exsertive *formal*, extrusive *formal*, extrusory *formal*, jutting, prominent, protrudent *formal*, protrusive *formal*, protuberant, proud
🖪 flat, flush

protrusion *n* bulge, bump, jut, knob, lump, obtrusion *formal*, outgrowth, process *formal*, projection, protuberance, swelling

protuberance *n* apophysis *technical*, bulb, bulge, bump, excrescence *formal*, knob, lump, outgrowth, process *formal*, projection, prominence, protrusion, swelling, tuber, tubercle, tumour, wart, welt

protuberant *adj* astrut *old use*, beetling, bulbous, bulging, exsertive *formal*, extrusive *formal*, extrusory *formal*, gibbous, jutting, popping, prominent, protrudent *formal*, protruding, protrusive *formal*, proud, swelling, swollen
🖪 flat

proud *adj* **1** *too proud to mix with ordinary people:* arrogant, big-headed, boastful, cocky, complacent, conceited, egotistical, full of yourself, haughty, high and mighty *colloq*, hubristic *formal*, jumped-up *colloq*, overbearing, overweening, pompous, presumptuous, puffed up, self-important, smug, snobbish, snooty *colloq*, stuck-up *colloq*, supercilious, toffee-nosed *colloq*, too big for your boots *colloq*, vain **2** *be proud of your achievements:* content, contented, delighted, glad, gratified, happy, honoured, pleased, satisfied, thrilled **3** *a proud and noble family:* dignified, honourable, noble, self-respecting, worthy **4** *a proud moment:* gratifying, marvellous, memorable, notable, pleasing, red-letter *colloq*, satisfying, splendid, wonderful **5** *a proud sight:* glorious, grand, imposing, magnificent, notable, outstanding, splendid, worthy

☰ 1 humble, modest, unassuming **2** ashamed **3** deferential, ignoble

provable *adj* attestable *formal*, confirmable, corroborable *formal*, demonstrable, establishable, evincible *formal*, testable, verifiable
☰ unprovable

prove *v* **1** *prove someone's innocence:* ascertain, attest *formal*, authenticate, bear out, bear witness to, certify, confirm, corroborate *formal*, demonstrate, determine, document, establish, justify, show, substantiate *formal*, validate, verify **2** *prove a new drug:* analyse, check, examine, test, try (out) **3** *it proved to be harder than I thought:* be the case, come about, eventuate *formal*, pan out *colloq*, transpire *formal*, turn out
☰ 1 discredit, disprove, falsify

proven *adj* accepted, attested *formal*, authentic, certified, checked, confirmed, corroborated *formal*, definite, dependable, established, proved, reliable, tested, tried, trustworthy, undoubted, valid, verified
☰ unproven

provenance *n* birthplace, derivation, origin, provenience *US*, source

provender *n* comestibles, eatables *colloq*, eats, edibles, fare, feed, fodder, food, foodstuffs, forage, groceries, grub *slang*, nosh *slang*, provisions, rations, supplies, sustenance, victuals *formal*

proverb *n* adage, aphorism, apophthegm *formal*, byword, dictum, gnome, maxim, paroemia *formal*, precept, saw, saying

proverbial *adj* accepted, acknowledged, archetypal, axiomatic, conventional, customary, famed, famous, infamous, legendary, notorious, renowned, time-honoured, traditional, typical, well-known

provide *v* **1** *provide you with what you need:* cater to, contribute, equip, furnish, give, kit out, offer, outfit, serve, stock, supply **2** *provide opportunity for growth:* add, afford *formal*, bring, give, impart *formal*, lend, offer, present, yield **3** *the contract provides that the landlord is responsible for repairs:* lay down, require, specify, state, stipulate
☰ 1 remove, take
▶ provide for 1 *provide for your family:* endow, fend for, keep, look after, maintain, support, sustain, take care of **2** *provide for every eventuality:* accommodate, allow for, anticipate, arrange for, make plans for, make provision for, plan for, prepare for, take measures/steps against, take precautions against

provided *conj* as/so long as, given, on condition, on the understanding, with the proviso

providence *n* **1** *it was only by providence that he survived:* destiny, divine intervention, fate, fortune, God's will, luck **2** *his providence in money matters:* care, caution, circumspection *formal*, economy, far-sightedness, foresight, forethought, judgement, judiciousness *formal*, prudence, sagacity *formal*, thrift, wisdom
☰ 2 improvidence

provident *adj* careful, cautious, circumspect *formal*, economical, far-sighted, frugal, judicious *formal*, prudent, sagacious *formal*, thrifty
☰ improvident

providential *adj* convenient, fortuitous, fortunate, happy, heaven-sent, lucky, opportune, timely, welcome
☰ untimely

provider *n* **1** *the main provider of aid to the country:* benefactor, donor, funder, giver, source, supplier **2** *a good provider for his family:* breadwinner, earner, mainstay, supporter, wage-earner

providing *conj* as long as, given, on condition that, on the understanding that, provided, with the proviso that

province *n* **1** *the country's eastern province:* area, colony, county, department, dependency, district, region, shire, state, territory, zone **2** *it is his province to deal with these matters:* area, business, charge, concern, department, domain, duty, field, function, line, office, pigeon *colloq*, responsibility, role, sphere

provincial *adj* **1** *a provincial theatre:* district, local, outlying, regional **2** *provincial attitudes:* hick *colloq*, home-grown, insular, intolerant, inward-looking, limited, narrow, narrow-minded, parish-pump, parochial, small-minded, small-town, unsophisticated
☰ 1 capital, cosmopolitan, metropolitan, national, urban **2** sophisticated
♦ *n* country bumpkin, hick *colloq*, hillbilly *colloq*, peasant, rustic, yokel

provincialism *n* insularity, localism, narrow-mindedness, parochialism, provinciality, regionalism, sectionalism
☰ sophistication

provision *n* **1** *the provision of supplies:* contribution, equipping, furnishing, giving, outfitting, service, supply **2** *no provision for wheelchair users:* amenities, facilities, resources, services **3** *make provisions for the future:* allowance, arrangement, concession, measure, plan, precaution, preparation, step **4** *a provision in the contract:* clause, condition, proviso, qualification, requirement, rider, specification, stipulation, term **5** *take provisions for the voyage:* eatables *colloq*, food, foodstuff, groceries, rations, stocks, stores, supplies, sustenance

provisional *adj* **1** *a provisional manager:* interim, makeshift, pro tem *colloq*, stopgap, temporary, transitional **2** *a provisional date:* conditional, provisory, tentative
☰ 1 permanent **2** definite, fixed

provisionally *adv* for the time being, interim, meanwhile, pro tem *colloq*

proviso *n* clause, condition, limitation, provision, qualification, requirement, reservation, restriction, rider, stipulation, strings *colloq*, term

provocation *n* **1** *kept her temper despite provocation:* affront, aggravation *colloq*, angering, annoyance, challenge, dare, enraging, exasperation, injury, insult, irritation, offence, taunt, vexation **2** *they attacked without provocation:* cause, grounds, incitement, inducement, instigation, justification, motivation, motive, reason, stimulus

provocative *adj* **1** *provocative behaviour:* abusive, aggravating *colloq*, annoying, exasperating, galling, infuriating, insulting, irritating, offensive, outrageous **2** *a provocative discussion:* challenging, exciting, stimulating **3** *a provocative*

outfit: alluring, arousing, erotic, inviting, seductive, sexually arousing, sexy, suggestive, tantalizing, teasing, tempting, titillating
🔁 **1** conciliatory

provoke *v* **1** *try not to provoke him:* aggravate *colloq*, anger, annoy, enrage, exasperate, get someone's back up *colloq*, harass, hassle *colloq*, incense, infuriate, irritate, madden, make someone's blood boil *colloq*, needle *colloq*, nettle, offend, rile, vex, wind up *colloq* **2** *they provoked him to fight:* egg on *colloq*, goad, incite, inflame, instigate, motivate, prod, prompt, rouse, spur, stimulate, stir **3** *provoke a reaction:* call forth, cause, elicit, engender, evoke, excite, generate, give rise to, induce, inspire, move, occasion, produce, promote
🔁 **1** pacify, please **3** result

provoking *adj* aggravating *colloq*, annoying, exasperating, galling, infuriating, irking, irksome, irritating, maddening, offensive, tiresome, vexatious, vexing
🔁 pleasing

prow *n* bow(s), cut-water, fore, forepart, front, head, nose, stem
🔁 stern

prowess *n* **1** *his prowess as a musician:* ability, accomplishment, adeptness, adroitness, aptitude, capability, command, dexterity, expertise, facility, genius, mastery, proficiency, skilfulness, skill, talent **2** *famed for their prowess in battle:* audacity, bottle *colloq*, courage, daring, dauntlessness, fearlessness, gallantry, grit *colloq*, guts *colloq*, heroism, intrepidity, nerve *colloq*, pluck, spunk *colloq*, valour

prowl *v* creep, cruise, hunt, lurk, move stealthily, nose, patrol, range, roam, rove, scavenge, search, skulk, slink, sneak, snoop, stalk, steal

proximity *n* adjacency, closeness, contiguity *formal*, juxtaposition, nearness, neighbourhood, propinquity *formal*, vicinity
🔁 remoteness

proxy *n* agent, delegate, deputy, factor, representative, stand-in, substitute, surrogate

prude *n* prig, puritan

prudence *n* **1** *I advise prudence:* canniness, care, caution, circumspection *formal*, discretion, heedfulness, precaution, preparedness, vigilance, wariness **2** *act with prudence:* common sense, far-sightedness, foresight, forethought, good sense, judgement, judiciousness *formal*, policy, sagacity *formal*, wisdom **3** *prudence in financial matters:* economy, frugality, husbandry, providence, saving, thrift
🔁 **1** imprudence, rashness **2** imprudence, rashness **3** imprudence

prudent *adj* **1** *a prudent approach:* careful, cautious, circumspect *formal*, discreet, vigilant, wary **2** *a prudent move:* discerning, far-sighted, judicious *formal*, politic, sagacious *formal*, sensible, shrewd, wise **3** *prudent to the point of meanness:* economical, frugal, provident, thrifty
🔁 **1** careless, imprudent, rash, unwise **2** careless, imprudent, rash, unwise **3** imprudent

prudery *n* Grundyism, old-maidisliuess, overmodesty, priggishness, primness, prissiness, puritanism, squeamishness, starchiness, strictness, stuffiness
🔁 laxness

prudish *adj* demure, narrow-minded, old-maidish, overmodest, overnice, po-faced *colloq*, priggish, prim, prissy, proper, puritanical, school-marmish, squeamish, starchy, strait-laced, stuffy, ultra-virtuous, Victorian
🔁 easy-going *colloq*, lax

prune *v* **1** *prune hedges:* clip, cut, dock, lop, pare, shape, shorten, snip, trim **2** *prune expenditure:* cut, cut back, reduce, trim

prurient *adj* **1** *prurient interest in her:* concupiscent *formal*, cupidinous *formal*, desirous, lascivious, lecherous, lewd, libidinous *formal*, lustful, salacious, voyeuristic **2** *prurient scenes:* blue *colloq*, dirty, erotic, indecent, lewd, obscene, pornographic, salacious, smutty *colloq*
🔁 **1** decent **2** decent

pry *v* delve, dig, ferret, interfere, intrude, meddle, nose, poke/stick your nose in *colloq*, put your oar in *colloq*, snoop *colloq*
🔁 mind your own business

prying *adj* curious, inquisitive, interfering, intrusive, meddlesome, meddling, nosy, snooping *colloq*, snoopy *colloq*, spying
🔁 uninquisitive

psalm *n* canticle, chant, hymn, paean, paraphrase, poem, prayer, song

pseud *n* fraud, humbug, phoney *colloq*, poser, poseur, trendy

pseudo *adj* artificial, bogus, counterfeit, ersatz, fake, false, imitation, mock, phoney *colloq*, pretended, pseud *colloq*, quasi-, sham, spurious, ungenuine
🔁 authentic, genuine, real

pseudonym *n* alias, allonym *formal*, assumed name, false name, incognito, nom-de-plume, pen-name, stage-name

psyche *n* anima *technical*, awareness, consciousness, deepest feelings, heart of hearts, individuality, intellect, intelligence, mind, personality, pneuma, self, soul, spirit, subconscious, understanding

psychiatrist *n* analyst, head doctor *colloq*, headshrinker *colloq*, person in a white coat *colloq*, psychoanalyser, psychoanalyst, psychologist, psychotherapist, shrink *colloq*, therapist, trick cyclist *colloq*

psychic *adj* **1** *psychic powers:* clairvoyant, extrasensory, mystic(al), occult, spiritual, supernatural, telekinetic, telepathic **2** *psychic energy:* cognitive, intellectual, mental, psychological, spiritual

psychological *adj* **1** *psychological wellbeing:* cerebral *formal*, cognitive, emotional, intellectual, mental, psychosomatic **2** *a psychological advantage:* emotional, imaginary, irrational, mental, subconscious, subjective, unconscious, unreal
🔁 **1** physical **2** real

psychology *n* **1** *to study psychology:* science of human/animal behaviour, science of the mind, study of mental processes, study of the mind **2** *the psychology of crowds:* attitudes, behavioural characteristics, habits, make-up, mental characteristics, mental chemistry, mind, mindset, motives, what makes someone tick *colloq*

psychopath *n* lunatic, mad person, maniac, psycho *colloq*, psychotic, sociopath

psychopathic *adj* demented, deranged, insane, lunatic, mad, maniacal, mentally disturbed, psychotic, unbalanced

pub *n* bar, boozer *slang*, brasserie, counter, grill, hostelry *colloq*, inn, local *colloq*, lounge, lounge bar, public house, saloon, table, taproom, tavern, watering-hole *colloq*

puberty *n* adolescence, growing up, maturity, pubescence, teenage years, teens, young adulthood, youth
🖪 childhood, immaturity, old age

public *adj* **1** *public buildings:* accessible, civic, civil, collective, common, communal, community, general, government, national, nationalized, official, open, popular, social, state, universal, unrestricted **2** *public knowledge:* acknowledged, celebrated, eminent, exposed, famous, illustrious, important, influential, known, obvious, open, overt, plain, popular, published, recognized, respected, well-known, widespread
🖪 **1** personal, private, privatized **2** exclusive, secret
♦ *n* audience, buyers, citizens, clientèle, community, consumers, country, customers, electorate, everyone, fans, followers, masses, multitude, nation, patrons, people, populace, population, society, spectators, supporters, voters

publican *n* barmaid, barman, hotelier, hotel-keeper, innkeeper, landlady, landlord, mine host, taverner

publication *n* **1** *the publication of a book:* circulation, distribution, issue, printing, production, publishing, release **2** *a glossy publication:* book, booklet, brochure, daily, handbill, journal, leaflet, magazine, monthly, newspaper, pamphlet, periodical, quarterly, weekly **3** *the publication of their engagement:* announcement, declaration, disclosure, notification, proclamation, reporting

publicity *n* advertising, attention, boost, build-up, hype *colloq*, limelight, marketing, plug *colloq*, promotion, propaganda, puff, splash

publicize *v* advertise, announce, blaze, bring to the public's attention, broadcast, disseminate *formal*, hype *colloq*, make known, make public, market, plug *colloq*, promote, promulgate *formal*, push *colloq*, spotlight

public-spirited *adj* altruistic, charitable, community-minded, conscientious, generous, humanitarian, philanthropic, unselfish
🖪 selfish

publish *v* **1** *publish a book:* bring out, circulate, diffuse, disseminate *formal*, distribute, issue, print, produce, promulgate *formal*, release, spread **2** *publish the news:* advertise, announce, communicate, declare, disclose, divulge, import, make known, make public, notify, proclaim, publicize, release, report, reveal

pucker *v* compress, contract, crease, crinkle, crumple, furrow, gather, pleat, purse, ruck, ruckle, ruffle, screw up, shrivel, wrinkle
♦ *n* crease, crinkle, crumple, fold, ruck, ruckle, shirr, wrinkle

puckered *adj* creased, gathered, pursy, rucked, ruckled, wrinkled
🖪 smooth

puckish *adj* frolicsome, impish, mischievous, naughty, playful, roguish, sly, sportive, teasing, waggish, whimsical
🖪 serious, solemn

pudding *n* afters *colloq*, dessert, pastry, pie, pud *colloq*, sweet, tart

puddle *n* plash, pool, slop, sop

puerile *adj* adolescent, babyish, childish, foolish, immature, inane, infantile, irresponsible, juvenile, silly, trivial
🖪 mature

puff *n* **1** *a puff of wind:* blast, breath, draught, flurry, gust, waft, whiff **2** *a puff on a cigarette:* drag, pull **3** *puff about that new movie:* advertisement, commendation, marketing, plug *colloq*, promotion, publicity, push
♦ *v* **1** *huffing and puffing:* blow, breathe, expand, gasp, gulp, inflate, pant, swell, waft, wheeze **2** *puff a cigarette:* drag, draw, pull, smoke, suck **3** *puffing up her new novel:* advertise, commend, market, plug *colloq*, praise, promote, publicize, push

puffed *adj* breathless, done in *colloq*, exhausted, gasping, out of breath, panting, winded

puffy *adj* bloated, dilated *formal*, distended *formal*, enlarged, inflated, oedematous *technical*, puffed up, swollen

pugilism *n* boxing, fighting, fistiana *colloq*, prize-fighting, the fancy *colloq*, the noble art, the noble science, the prize-ring, the ring

pugilist *n* boxer, bruiser *colloq*, fighter, prize-fighter

pugnacious *adj* aggressive, antagonistic, argumentative, bad-tempered, bellicose *formal*, belligerent, contentious, disputatious *formal*, hostile, hot-tempered, quarrelsome
🖪 peaceable

puke *v* disgorge, heave, regurgitate, retch, spew, throw up *colloq*, vomit

pull *v* **1** *pulling a tractor:* drag, draw, haul, heave, jerk, tow, trail, tug, yank *colloq* **2** *to pull a tooth:* draw out, extract, pluck, pull out, pull up, remove, rip, root out, take out, tear, uproot, wrench **3** *pulled in the crowds:* allure, attract, bring in, draw, entice, lure, magnetize, pull in, tempt **4** *pulled a muscle:* damage, dislocate, sprain, strain, tear, wrench
🖪 **1** press, push **3** deter, discourage, repel
♦ *n* **1** *a pull on the rope:* drag, jerk, tug, yank *colloq* **2** *his job gives him a lot of pull:* authority, clout *colloq*, forcefulness, influence, muscle *colloq*, power, weight **3** *the pull of the musicals:* allure, attraction, draw, drawing power, lure, magnetism
▶ **pull apart 1** *pull the old shed apart:* dismantle, dismember, part, separate, take to pieces, tear apart **2** *pulled apart her work:* attack, criticize, do a hatchet job on *colloq*, pick holes in *colloq*, pull to pieces *colloq*, run down *colloq*, slam *colloq*, slate *colloq*, take apart
▶ **pull back** back out, disengage, draw back, fall back, retire, retreat, withdraw
▶ **pull down** bulldoze, demolish, destroy, dismantle, knock down, raze to the ground
🖪 build, erect, put up
▶ **pull in 1** *pull in outside the bank:* arrive, draw in, park, pull up, stop **2** *pull in large audiences:* allure, attract, bring in, draw, entice, lure **3** *pulled in*

by the police: apprehend, arrest, book *colloq*, bust *colloq*, capture, collar *colloq*, detain, nab *colloq*, nick *colloq*, run in *colloq*, seize, take into custody **4** *she pulls in £50,000 a year:* be paid, clear, earn, make, rake in *colloq*, receive, take home
▶ **pull off 1** *how did you pull that off?:* accomplish, achieve, bring off, carry off, carry out, manage, succeed **2** *pull off the tab:* detach, remove, rip off, separate, take off, tear off
▶ **pull out** abandon, back out, depart, desert, evacuate, leave, move out, quit, retreat, withdraw
◪ arrive, join
▶ **pull through** come through, rally, recover, recuperate, survive, weather
▶ **pull together** collaborate, co-operate, team up, work together
◪ fight
▶ **pull up 1** *pull up at the lights:* brake, come to a halt, draw up, halt, park, pull in, pull over, stop **2** *pulled up for massaging the figures:* carpet *colloq*, criticize, rebuke, reprimand, scold, take to task, tell off *colloq*, tick off *colloq*

pulp *n* flesh, marrow, mash, mush, pap, paste, purée, triturate *formal*
♦ *v* crush, liquidize, mash, pulverize, purée, shred, squash

pulpit *n* dais, lectern, platform, rostrum, soapbox *colloq*

pulpy *adj* crushed, fleshy, mushy, pappy, sloppy, soft, squashy, succulent
◪ hard

pulsate *v* beat, drum, hammer, oscillate, pound, pulse, quiver, throb, thud, thump, vibrate

pulsating *adj* oscillating, palpitating, pulsatile *formal*, pulsative *formal*, pulsatory *formal*, pulsing, vibratile *formal*, vibrating, vibrative *formal*

pulsation *n* ictus *technical*, oscillation, palpitation, vibration, vibratiuncle

pulse *n* beat, beating, drumming, oscillation, pounding, pulsation, rhythm, stroke, throb, throbbing, thud, thudding, thump, thumping, vibration
♦ *v* beat, drum, pound, pulsate, throb, thud, tick, vibrate

pulverize *v* **1** *pulverize the substance into a fine powder:* crumble, crush, grind, mill, pound, powder, pulp, squash, triturate *formal* **2** *pulverize the opposing team:* annihilate, defeat, demolish, destroy, hammer *colloq*, smash, thrash *colloq*, vanquish *formal*, wipe the floor with *colloq*

pummel *v* bang, batter, beat, hammer, hit, knock, pound, punch, strike, thump

pump *v* **1** *pumped the water out:* drain, draw, drive, force, send, siphon **2** *pumped me for information:* cross-examine, cross-question, give someone the third degree *colloq*, grill *colloq*, interrogate, quiz
▶ **pump out** bail out, drain, draw off, empty, force out, siphon
▶ **pump up** blow up, fill, inflate, puff up

pun *n* double entendre, paronomasia *technical*, play on words, quip, witticism

punch¹ *v* **1** *punched him in the face:* bash, biff *colloq*, bop *colloq*, box, clout, cuff, hit, jab, knock, pummel, slug, sock *colloq*, strike, thump, thwack, wallop *colloq* **2** *punch a hole in the wall:* bore, cut,

drill, hole, make a hole in, perforate, pierce, prick, puncture, stamp
♦ *n* **1** *a punch in the face:* bash, biff *colloq*, blow, bop *colloq*, clout, hit, jab, knock, sock *colloq*, thump, thwack, wallop *colloq* **2** *he writes with real punch:* bite *colloq*, drive, effectiveness, force, forcefulness, impact, panache, pizzazz *colloq*, power, strength, verve, vigour

punch-drunk *adj* befuddled, confused, dazed, dizzy, groggy, reeling, staggering, stupefied, unsteady, woozy

punch-up *n* argument, brawl, ding-dong *colloq*, dust-up *colloq*, fight, free-for-all, row, ruckus, scrap *colloq*, set-to *colloq*, shindy *colloq*, stand-up fight

punchy *adj* aggressive, dynamic, effective, forceful, incisive, lively, powerful, spirited, vigorous, zappy *colloq*
◪ feeble, weak

punctilio *n* **1** *his insistence on military punctilio:* ceremony, convention, exactness, finickiness, formality, meticulousness, preciseness, precision, punctiliousness, refinement, scrupulousness, strictness **2** *a linguistic punctilio:* delicacy, detail, distinction, exactitude, fine point, nicety, particular, particularity
◪ **1** informality

punctilious *adj* careful, choosy *colloq*, conscientious, exact, finicky, formal, fussy, meticulous, nit-picking *colloq*, particular, pernickety *colloq*, picky *colloq*, precise, proper, scrupulous, strict
◪ informal, lax

punctual *adj* bang on time *colloq*, dead on time *colloq*, early, exact, in good time, on cue *colloq*, on the dot *colloq*, on time, precise, prompt, well-timed
◪ late, unpunctual

punctuality *n* promptitude, promptness, readiness, regularity, strictness
◪ unpunctuality

punctually *adv* bang on *colloq*, dead on *colloq*, exactly, on the dot, on time, precisely, prompt, promptly, sharp, spot on *colloq*, to the minute
◪ unpunctually

punctuate *v* accentuate, break, emphasize, interject *formal*, interrupt, intersperse, pepper, point, sprinkle

punctuation

Punctuation marks include:
apostrophe, asterisk, backslash, brackets, colon, comma, dash, exclamation mark, full stop, hyphen, inverted commas, oblique stroke, parentheses, period, question mark, quotation marks, quotes *colloq*, semicolon, solidus, speech marks, square brackets, star

---

puncture *n* **1** *got a puncture on the way home:* blow-out, flat *colloq*, flat tyre **2** *a puncture in the skin:* cut, hole, holing, leak, nick, perforation, piercing, prick, rupture, slit
♦ *v* **1** *punctured the skin:* bore, burst, cut, hole, nick, penetrate, perforate, pierce, prick, rupture, spike **2** *punctured my pride:* deflate, flatten, humiliate, let down, put down *colloq*

pundit *n* authority, buff *colloq*, expert, guru, maestro, master, sage, savant, teacher

pungent adj 1 *a pungent taste/smell:* acid, acrid, acute, aromatic, biting, bitter, burning, caustic, fiery, hot, keen, peppery, piquant, powerful, sharp, sour, spicy, stinging, strong, tangy, tart 2 *pungent comments:* biting, burning, caustic, cutting, incisive, penetrating, piercing, pointed, sarcastic, scathing, stinging
F3 1 bland, mild, tasteless 2 bland, mild

punish v 1 *punished them for their crimes:* beat, bring to book *colloq*, cane, castigate *formal*, chastise *formal*, correct, crucify, discipline, fine, flog, give someone hell *colloq*, hang, imprison, knee-cap, lash, make an example of *colloq*, make someone pay, penalize, scold, scourge, slap, smack, spank, teach someone a lesson *colloq*, throw the book at *colloq*, whip 2 *punished the other fighter:* batter, beat, defeat, hammer *colloq*, rough up *colloq*, thrash *colloq*, trounce 3 *his driving style really punishes the engine:* abuse, damage, harm, maltreat, misuse
F3 1 reward

punishable adj blameworthy, chargeable, convictable, criminal, culpable *formal*, indictable *formal*, unlawful

punishing adj arduous, backbreaking, burdensome, crippling, cruel, crushing, demanding, exhausting, fatiguing, grinding, gruelling, hard, harsh, severe, strenuous, taxing, tiring, wearying
F3 easy

punishment n chastisement, correction, deserts, discipline, penalty, retribution, revenge, sentence, short sharp shock *colloq*
F3 reward

Forms of punishment include:
banishment, beating, belting, the birch, borstal, the cane, capital punishment, cashiering, chain gang, confinement, confiscation, corporal punishment, defrocking, demotion, deportation, detention, dressing-down, excommunication, execution, exile, expulsion, fine, flaying, flogging, gaol, gating, grounding, hiding *colloq*, hitting, horsewhipping, house arrest, imprisonment, incarceration, internment, jail, jankers, keelhauling, larruping *colloq*, lashing, leathering, lines, penal colony, prison, probation, being put away *colloq*, the rack, rap across the knuckles, scourging, being sent down *colloq*, being sent to Coventry, sequestration, slapping, the slipper, smacking, spanking, the stocks, suspension, tanning someone's hide *colloq*, tarring and feathering, thrashing, torturing, transportation, unfrocking, walking the plank, walloping, whipping. See also **execution**

punitive adj 1 *take punitive action:* castigatory *formal*, chastising *formal*, disciplinary, penal, retaliatory, retributive, vindictive 2 *the heat was punitive:* burdensome, crippling, cruel, crushing, demanding, gruelling, hard, harsh, punishing, severe

punter n 1 *a regular punter:* backer, better, gambler, wagerer 2 *bring the punters in:* client, consumer, customer, individual, person

puny adj diminutive, feeble, frail, inconsequential, insignificant, little, measly *colloq*, minor, petty, piddling *colloq*, sickly, small, stunted, tiny, trifling, trivial, underdeveloped, undersized, undeveloped, weak
F3 important, large, strong, sturdy

pupil n apprentice, beginner, disciple, learner, novice, protégé(e), scholar, schoolboy, schoolgirl, student
F3 teacher

puppet n 1 *perform a show with puppets:* doll, finger puppet, glove puppet, marionette 2 *a mere puppet of a government:* cat's-paw, creature, dupe, figurehead, gull, instrument, mouthpiece, pawn, quisling, stooge, tool

purchase v acquire, buy, earn, gain, get, go shopping, invest in, obtain, pay for, pick up, procure *formal*, secure, shop for, snap up *colloq*, splash out on *colloq*, win
F3 sell
♦ n 1 *the purchase of the land:* acquisition, buying, emption *formal*, gain, possession 2 *pleased with my purchase:* bargain, buy, goods, investment, possessions, property 3 *unable to get any purchase on the stroke:* grasp, grip, hold, leverage
F3 1 sale

purchaser n buyer, client, consumer, customer, emptor *formal*, hirer, shopper, vendee *formal*
F3 seller, vendor

pure adj 1 *pure gold:* authentic, flawless, genuine, natural, neat, one hundred per cent, perfect, real, simple, solid, straight, true, unadulterated, unalloyed, undiluted, unmixed 2 *pure water:* antiseptic, aseptic, clean, clear, disinfected, fresh, germ-free, hygienic, immaculate, natural, sanitary, spotless, sterile, sterilized, uncontaminated, uninfected, unpolluted 3 *pure madness:* absolute, complete, downright, perfect, sheer, thorough, total, unmitigated, unqualified, utter 4 *a pure life:* chaste, decent, good, honest, honourable, innocent, moral, noble, righteous, unblemished, undefiled, unsullied, upright, virgin, virginal, virtuous, worthy 5 *pure mathematics:* abstract, academic, conjectural, speculative, theoretical
F3 1 adulterated, impure 2 contaminated, polluted 4 corrupt, defiled, immoral 5 applied

pure-bred adj blooded, full-blooded, pedigree, pedigreed, pure-blood, pure-blooded, thoroughbred
F3 cross-bred, hybrid, mixed, mongrel

purely adv 1 *focus purely on my work:* absolutely, completely, entirely, thoroughly, totally, utterly, wholly 2 *did it purely for fun:* exclusively, just, merely, only, simply, solely

purgative n aperient, cathartic, depurative *formal*, eccoprotic, emetic *technical*, enema, evacuant, laxative, purge
♦ adj abstersive *formal*, aperient *technical*, cathartic, cathartical, cleansing, depurative *formal*, eccoprotic, evacuant, laxative, purging

purge v 1 *purge the emotions:* absolve, clean out, cleanse, clear, purify, scour 2 *purged foreigners from the city:* clear (out), depose, dismiss, eject, eradicate, expel, get rid of, kill, oust, remove, rid, root out, wipe out
♦ n cleansing, disposal, ejection, eradication, expulsion, extermination, ousting, removal, rooting-out, witch hunt

purification n 1 *purification of water:* cleaning, cleansing, decontamination, deodorization, depuration *formal*, desalination, disinfection, epuration *formal*, filtration, fumigation, refinement, sanitization 2 *ritual purification:* absolution, cleansing, lustration *formal*, purgation *formal*, purge, redemption, sanctification

F3 1 contamination, defilement, pollution

purify v 1 *purify the water supply:* clarify, clean, cleanse, decontaminate, deodorize, depurate *formal*, disinfect, distil, filter, filtrate, freshen, fumigate, lustrate *formal*, refine, sanitize, sterilize 2 *purify their souls:* absolve, cleanse, lustrate *formal*, purge, redeem, sanctify, shrive

F3 1 contaminate, defile, pollute

purifying adj cathartic *technical*, cleansing, depurative *formal*, lustral *formal*, mundificative *formal*, purgative, purging, purificatory, refining

F3 contaminating, defiling, polluting

purism n Atticism, austerity, classicism, fastidiousness, formalism, fussiness, orthodoxy, over-precision, pedantry, restraint, strictness

F3 liberality, open-mindedness, tolerance

purist n dogmatist, formalist, literalist, nit-picker *colloq*, pedant, precisionist, quibbler, stickler

♦ adj captious, fastidious, finicky, fussy, hypercritical, nit-picking *colloq*, over-exact, over-fastidious, over-meticulous, over-particular, over-precise, pedantic, puristic, quibbling, strict, uncompromising

F3 liberal, open-minded, tolerant

puritan n disciplinarian, fanatic, killjoy, moralist, pietist, prude, rigorist, spoilsport, zealot

F3 hedonist, libertarian

puritanical adj abstemious, ascetic, austere, bigoted, disapproving, disciplinarian, fanatical, moralistic, narrow-minded, prim, proper, prudish, puritan, rigid, severe, stern, stiff, strait-laced, strict, stuffy, zealous

F3 broad-minded, hedonistic, indulgent, liberal

puritanism n abstemiousness, abstinence, asceticism, austerity, bigotry, fanaticism, narrow-mindedness, narrowness, priggishness, primness, propriety, prudishness, rigidity, rigorousness, self-denial, self-discipline, severity, sternness, stiffness, strictness, uncompromisingness, zealotry

F3 broad-mindedness, hedonism, indulgence, liberality

purity n 1 *the purity of the air:* clarity, cleanliness, cleanness, clearness, flawlessness, freshness, untaintedness, wholesomeness 2 *the purity of her accent:* authenticity, genuineness, perfection, simplicity, truth 3 *a life of great purity:* blamelessness, chastity, decency, goodness, honesty, honour, innocence, integrity, morality, nobility, rectitude, uprightness, virginity, virtue, virtuousness, worthiness

F3 1 contamination, impurity, pollution 3 immorality

purloin v appropriate *formal*, filch *colloq*, finger *colloq*, lift *colloq*, nick *colloq*, nobble *colloq*, pilfer, pinch *colloq*, pocket *colloq*, remove, rob, snaffle *colloq*, snatch *colloq*, steal, swipe *colloq*, take, thieve *colloq*

purport v allege, assert, betoken *formal*, claim, convey, declare, denote, express, imply, import *formal*, indicate, intend, maintain, mean, portend *formal*, pose as, pretend, proclaim, profess, seem, show, signify, suggest

♦ n bearing, direction, drift, gist, idea, implication, import *formal*, meaning, point, significance, spirit, substance, tendency, tenor, theme, thrust

purpose n 1 *the purpose of the exercise:* aim, ambition, aspiration, basis, design, desire, end, goal, hope, idea, intention, justification, motivation, motive, object, objective, outcome, plan, point, principle, rationale, reason, result, target, vision, wish 2 *strode forward with purpose:* constancy, dedication, determination, devotion, doggedness, drive, firmness, perseverance, persistence, resolution, resolve, single-mindedness, steadfastness, tenacity, zeal 3 *this tool has several purposes:* advantage, application, benefit, effect, function, gain, good, use, usefulness, value

♦ v aim, aspire, contemplate, decide, design, desire, determine, intend, mean, meditate, plan, propose, resolve, settle

purposeful adj constant, decided, deliberate, determined, dogged, firm, persevering, persistent, positive, resolute, resolved, single-minded, steadfast, strong-willed, tenacious, unfaltering, unwavering

F3 aimless, purposeless

purposefully adv perseveringly, persistently, resolutely, single-mindedly, steadfastly, tenaciously, unfalteringly, unwaveringly

> **purposefully** or **purposely**? *Purposefully* means 'obviously, or apparently, having some purpose': *She stole purposefully towards him, clearly intent on settling things once and for all. Purposely* means 'intentionally': *She didn't want to go to college so she purposely failed her exams.*

purposeless adj aimless, empty, goalless, gratuitous, motiveless, needless, nonsensical, objectless, pointless, senseless, thoughtless, unasked-for, uncalled-for, unnecessary, useless, vacuous, vain, wanton

F3 purposeful

purposely adv by design, calculatedly, consciously, deliberately, designedly, expressly, intentionally, knowingly, on purpose, premeditatedly, specifically, wilfully, with malice aforethought

F3 by accident, impulsively, spontaneously, unintentionally

purse n 1 *money in her purse:* money-bag, pouch, wallet 2 *a drain on the public purse:* coffers, exchequer, finances, funds, means, money, resources, treasury 3 *received a purse of a million dollars:* award, gift, present, prize, reward

♦ v close, compress, contract, draw together, pucker, tighten, wrinkle

pursuance n accomplishment, achievement, completion, discharge, effecting *formal*, effectuation *formal*, execution *formal*, following, fulfilment, performance, prosecution *formal*, pursuing, pursuit

pursue v 1 *pursue a fugitive:* chase, dog, follow, go after, harass, harry, hound, hunt, inquire into, investigate, run after, search for, seek, shadow, stalk, tail, track, trail **2** *pursue an activity:* apply yourself to, carry on, conduct, continue, engage in, follow, hold to, keep on, keep up, maintain, perform, persevere in, persist in, practise **3** *pursue happiness:* aim for, aspire to, have your goal, search for, seek, strive for, try for, work towards

pursuit *n* **1** *the pursuit of deer:* chase, hue and cry, hunt, pursuing, shadowing, stalking, tailing, tracking, trail **2** *the pursuit of liberty:* aim, aspiration, continuance, following, goal, investigation, perseverance, persistence, quest, search **3** *country pursuits:* activity, craft, hobby, interest, line, occupation, pastime, speciality, trade, vocation

purvey *v* **1** *to purvey fine cheeses:* cater, deal in, furnish, provide, provision *formal,* retail, sell, stock, supply, trade in, victual *formal* **2** *to purvey the news:* communicate, disseminate *formal,* pass on, propagate *formal,* publicize, publish, put about, spread, transmit

purveyor *n* **1** *a purveyor of meats:* dealer, provider, provisor, retailer, stockist, supplier, trader, victualler *formal* **2** *be the purveyor of good news:* communicator, disseminator *formal,* propagator *formal,* transmitter

push *v* **1** *push it into the crack:* cram, drive, force, plunge, press, propel, ram, shove, squeeze, thrust **2** *push someone in the back:* jolt, knock, nudge, poke, prod, shove **3** *push through the crowd:* butt, elbow, force, hustle, jostle, manhandle, shove, squeeze **4** *push someone into doing something:* bully, coerce, constrain, egg on *colloq,* encourage, force, goad, impel, incite, influence, persuade, press, press (for), pressurize, prod, put the screws on *colloq,* spur, twist someone's arm *colloq,* urge **5** *they are really pushing this new brand:* advertise, boost, hype *colloq,* market, plug *colloq,* promote, publicize

☒ **1** pull **4** discourage, dissuade
♦ *n* **1** *a push in the back:* butt, jolt, jostle, knock, nudge, poke, prod, ram, shove, thrust **2** *a push into enemy territory:* advance, assault, charge, foray, incursion, invasion, offensive, raid **3** *have a lot of push:* ambition, determination, drive, dynamism, effort, energy, enterprise, force, forcefulness, get-up-and-go *colloq,* go *colloq,* initiative, vigour, vitality
▶ **push around** bully, intimidate, pick on, terrorize, torment, victimize
▶ **push off** beat it *colloq,* buzz off *colloq,* clear off/out *colloq,* depart, go away, leave, make a move *colloq,* make tracks *colloq,* move, push along *colloq,* shove off *colloq*

pushed *adj* harassed, hard-pressed, hard-up, harried, hurried, in difficulties, pinched, pressed, rushed, short of, strapped, stretched, under pressure

pushover *n* **1** *he's a pushover:* dupe, fall guy *colloq,* gull, mug, sitting duck *colloq,* sitting target *colloq,* soft touch *colloq,* stooge, sucker **2** *the job's a pushover:* child's play *colloq,* cinch *colloq,* doddle *colloq,* picnic *colloq,* piece of cake *colloq,* walkover *colloq*
☒ **2** challenge, labour

pushy *adj* aggressive, ambitious, arrogant, assertive, assuming, bold, bossy *colloq,* brash,

forceful, forward, impertinent, over-confident, presumptuous, self-assertive
☒ unassertive, unassuming

pusillanimity *n* cowardliness, cravenness, faint-heartedness, fearfulness, feebleness, gutlessness *colloq,* poltroonery *formal,* spinelessness, timidity, timorousness, weakness

pusillanimous *adj* chicken *colloq,* chicken-hearted, cowardly, craven, faint-hearted, fearful, feeble, gutless *colloq,* lily-livered, scared, spineless, timid, timorous, weak, weak-kneed, wimpish *colloq,* yellow *colloq*
☒ brave, courageous, strong

pussyfoot *v* **1** *say what you mean and don't pussyfoot about:* beat about the bush *colloq,* equivocate, hedge, mess about *colloq,* prevaricate, tergiversate *formal* **2** *pussyfooting about in the dark:* creep, pad, prowl, slink, steal, tiptoe

pustule *n* abscess, blister, boil, carbuncle, eruption, fester, papule, pimple, pock, ulcer, whitlow

put *v* **1** *put it down over there:* deposit, dispose, dump *colloq,* establish, fix, lay (down), locate, place, plonk *colloq,* position, post, rest, set (down), settle, situate, stand, station **2** *put the children into groups:* arrange, categorize, class, classify, grade, group, place, rank, sort **3** *put a tax on bananas:* apply, assign, demand, exact, impose, inflict, levy, require, subject **4** *put the blame on someone:* ascribe, assign, attach, attribute, charge, fix, impute, lay, pin, place **5** *put your thoughts into words:* couch, express, formulate, frame, phrase, pronounce, say, speak, state, utter, voice, word **6** *put a suggestion:* bring forward, offer, present, proffer *formal,* propose, set forth, set/lay before, submit, suggest, tender **7** *put money/energy into a project:* contribute, dedicate, devote, give, invest, sink, spend **8** *put it in French:* convert, render, transcribe, translate, turn **9** *put money on a horse:* bet, chance, gamble, lay, place, risk
▶ **put about** announce, circulate, disseminate *formal,* make known, spread, tell
▶ **put across** bring home to, clarify, communicate, convey, explain, express, get across/over, get through to, make clear, make understood, put over, spell out
▶ **put aside** hoard, keep, keep in reserve, lay aside/by, put by, put to one side, reserve, retain, salt away, save, set aside, stash *colloq,* stockpile, store, stow
▶ **put away 1** *put away two hot dogs:* consume, devour, down, drink, eat (up), guzzle *colloq,* polish off *colloq,* scoff *colloq,* swallow, tuck in *colloq,* wolf *colloq* **2** *put away for five years:* bang up *colloq,* certify, commit, confine, imprison, jail, lock up, send down *colloq* **3** *put some away for emergencies:* keep, keep in reserve, lay aside/by, put aside/by, reserve, retain, save, set aside, stockpile, store, stow
▶ **put back 1** *put back the start time:* adjourn, defer, delay, freeze, postpone, procrastinate *formal,* put on ice *colloq,* reschedule, shelve, suspend **2** *put the jar back in the cupboard:* clear away/up, reinstate, replace, restore, return, return to its place, tidy away/up
▶ **put down 1** *put down your thoughts in a blog:* enter, jot down, list, log, note down, record, register, transcribe, write down **2** *put down the*

insurgency: crush, defeat, quash, quell, silence, stamp out, stop, suppress **3** *put down a sick dog*: destroy, kill, put out of its misery, put to sleep **4** *put his failure down to nerves*: ascribe, attach, attribute, blame, charge, fix, lay, set down **5** *always putting down his wife*: crush, deflate, deprecate *formal*, disparage *formal*, humble, humiliate, mortify, shame, slight, snub, squash, take down a peg *colloq*
▶ **put forward** advance, introduce, move, nominate, offer, present, proffer *formal*, propose, recommend, submit, suggest, table, tender
▶ **put in** enter, fit, input, insert, install, submit
▶ **put off 1** *put off our holidays*: adjourn, defer, delay, postpone, procrastinate *formal*, put on ice *colloq*, put on the back burner *colloq*, reschedule, shelve, suspend **2** *put off by a lot of figures*: confuse, daunt, demoralize, deter, disconcert, discourage, dishearten, dismay, dissuade, distract, intimidate, nauseate, sicken, talk out of **3** *try to put her off*: deflect, distract, divert, sidetrack, turn away/aside
▶ **put on 1** *put on new clothes*: change into, don, dress in, get dolled up in *colloq*, get dressed in, get into, slip into, throw on *colloq*, try on, wear **2** *put on a stamp*: add, affix, apply, attach, impose, place **3** *put on an accent*: affect, assume, fake, feign, pretend, sham, simulate **4** *put on a play*: do, mount, perform, present, produce, stage
▶ **put out 1** *put it out that they were going to leave*: announce, bring out, broadcast, circulate, disclose, issue, make known, publish **2** *put out a fire*: douse, extinguish, quench, smother, stamp out **3** *I don't want to put you out*: anger, annoy, bother, cause inconvenience to, discommode *formal*, disconcert, disturb, exasperate, faze *colloq*, hurt, impose on, inconvenience, infuriate, irk, irritate, offend, perturb *formal*, provoke, trouble, unsettle, upset
▶ **put through** accomplish, achieve, bring off, complete, conclude, execute, finalize, manage
▶ **put together** assemble, build, construct, fit/piece together, join
🔁 take apart
▶ **put up 1** *put up a tent*: assemble, build, construct, erect, raise **2** *put up guests*: accommodate, give a room to, house, lodge, provide with board and lodging, shelter **3** *put up prices*: bump up *colloq*, escalate, hike up *colloq*, increase, jack up *colloq*, raise **4** *put up the money for the venture*: advance, float, give, invest, offer, pay, pledge, provide, supply **5** *put up a candidate*: choose, nominate, propose, put forward, recommend, suggest
▶ **put upon** exploit, impose on, inconvenience, take advantage of, take for granted, take liberties
▶ **put up to** egg on *colloq*, encourage, goad, incite, persuade, prompt, urge
🔁 discourage, dissuade
▶ **put up with** abide, accept, allow, bear, brook, endure, stand, stand for, stomach, suffer, swallow *colloq*, take, take lying down *colloq*, tolerate
🔁 object to, reject

putative *adj* alleged, assumed, conjectural *formal*, hypothetical, presumed, reported, reputative, reputed, supposed, suppositional, suppositious *formal*, theoretical

put-down *n* affront, dig *colloq*, disparagement *formal*, gibe, humiliation, insult, rebuff, sarcasm, slap in the face *colloq*, slight, sneer, snub

put-off *n* constraint, curb, damper, deterrent, discouragement, disincentive, hindrance, obstacle, restraint
🔁 encouragement, incentive

putrefy *v* addle, corrupt, decay, decompose, deteriorate, fester, gangrene, go bad, mould, perish, rot, spoil, stink, taint

putrescent *adj* decaying, decomposing, festering, mephitic *formal*, perishing, putrefying, rotting, stinking

putrid *adj* addled, bad, contaminated, corrupt, decayed, decomposed, fetid, foul, mouldy, off, polluted, rancid, rank, rotten, stinking, tainted
🔁 fresh, wholesome

put-upon *adj* abused, exploited, imposed on, inconvenienced, maltreated, persecuted, taken advantage of, used

puzzle *v* **1** *I was completely puzzled*: baffle, beat *colloq*, bewilder, confound, confuse, floor *colloq*, flummox *colloq*, mystify, nonplus *colloq*, perplex, stagger, stump *colloq* **2** *puzzling over the latest developments*: brood, consider, deliberate, figure, meditate, mull over, muse over, ponder, rack your brains, think
♦ *n* brain-teaser, conundrum, dilemma, enigma, mind-bender, mystery, paradox, poser, question, riddle
▶ **puzzle out** clear up, crack *colloq*, decipher, decode, figure out, find the answer to, get *colloq*, piece together, resolve, solve, sort out, suss (out) *colloq*, think out, unravel, untangle, work out

puzzled *adj* at a loss, at sea *colloq*, baffled, beaten, bewildered, confounded, confused, floored *colloq*, flummoxed *colloq*, in a haze, lost, mystified, nonplussed *colloq*, perplexed, stumped *colloq*
🔁 clear

puzzlement *n* astonishment, bafflement, bamboozlement *colloq*, bewilderment, confusion, disorientation, doubt, doubtfulness, incertitude *formal*, mystification, perplexity, surprise, uncertainty, wonder
🔁 certainty, clarity, lucidity

puzzling *adj* abstruse *formal*, ambiguous, baffling, bewildering, bizarre, confusing, cryptic, curious, enigmatic, equivocal, impenetrable, inexplicable, intricate, involved, knotty, labyrinthine *formal*, mind-bending, mind-boggling, misleading, mysterious, mystical, mystifying, peculiar, perplexing, queer, Sphinx-like, strange, tortuous, unaccountable, unclear, unfathomable

pyromaniac *n* arsonist, firebug *colloq*, fire-raiser, incendiary

Q

quack n charlatan, cowboy, fake, fraud, humbug, impostor, masquerader, mountebank, phoney *colloq*, pretender, pseud *colloq*, quacksalver *old use*, sham, swindler, trickster
♦ *adj* bogus, counterfeit, fake, false, fraudulent, phoney *colloq*, pretended, sham, so-called, spurious, supposed, unqualified
☒ genuine, real

quackery n charlatanism, fraud, fraudulence, humbug *colloq*, imposture, mountebankery, phoniness *colloq*

quaff v down, drain, drink, gulp, guzzle *colloq*, imbibe *formal*, knock back, swallow, swig, swill, toss off

quagmire n 1 *rain turned the field into a quagmire:* bog, fen, marsh, mire, morass, quag, quicksand, slough, swamp 2 *a diplomatic quagmire:* deep water *colloq*, dilemma, fix *colloq*, hole *colloq*, hot water *colloq*, mess, perplexity, pickle *colloq*, problem, quandary, tight spot *colloq*

quail v back away, blench, cower, cringe, draw back, falter, flinch, pull back, quake, recoil, shake, shiver, shrink, shudder, shy away, tremble

quaint adj 1 *a quaint little cottage:* attractive, charming, olde-worlde *colloq*, old-fashioned, old-world, picturesque, sweet, twee *colloq* 2 *quaint notions of chivalry:* antiquated, bizarre, curious, droll, fanciful, odd, old-fashioned, strange, unusual, whimsical
☒ 2 modern

quake v convulse, heave, move, pulsate, quail, quiver, rock, shake, shiver, shudder, sway, throb, tremble, vibrate, wobble

qualification n 1 *excellent qualifications for the job:* ability, accomplishment, aptitude, capability, capacity, certificate, certification, competence, degree, diploma, eligibility, fitness, proficiency, skill, suitability, training 2 *added a qualification to her earlier statement:* adaptation, adjustment, allowance, caveat, condition, exception, exemption, limitation, modification, provision, proviso, reservation, restriction, rider, stipulation

qualified adj 1 *a fully qualified nurse:* able, accomplished, adept, capable, certified, chartered, competent, efficient, eligible, equipped, experienced, expert, fit, fitted, knowledgeable, licensed, practised, prepared, professional, proficient, skilful, skilled, talented, trained 2 *qualified praise:* bounded, cautious, circumscribed *formal*, conditional, contingent *formal*, equivocal, guarded, half-hearted, limited, modified, provisional, reserved, restricted
☒ 1 unqualified, unconditional, whole-hearted

qualify v 1 *qualify as a doctor:* graduate, pass 2 *having a degree qualifies her to teach:* allow, authorize, empower, entitle, equip, fit, license, make ready, permit, prepare, sanction 3 *qualify a statement:* adjust, alleviate *formal*, delimit, diminish, lessen, limit, make conditional, mitigate *formal*, moderate, modify, reduce, restrain, restrict, soften, temper, weaken
☒ 2 disqualify

quality n 1 *of poor quality:* calibre, class, condition, grade, kind, level, make, merit, rank, sort, standard, status, type, value, variety, worth 2 *a reputation for quality:* distinction, eminence, excellence, merit, pre-eminence, refinement, superiority, value, worth 3 *her voice has an unusual quality:* aspect, attribute, character, characteristic, feature, make-up, mark, nature, peculiarity, property, trait

qualm n anxiety, apprehension, compunction *formal*, concern, disinclination, disquiet, doubt, fear, hesitancy, hesitation, misgiving, reluctance, scruple, uncertainty, uneasiness, worry

quandary n bewilderment, confusion, difficulty, dilemma, fix *colloq*, hole *colloq*, impasse, jam *colloq*, mess, muddle, perplexity, pickle *colloq*, predicament, problem, tight spot *colloq*

quantity n 1 *a large quantity of sugar:* aggregate, allotment, amount, bulk, capacity, content, dose, expanse, extent, lot, magnitude, mass, measure, number, portion, proportion, quota, share, size, sum, total, volume 2 *quantities of food:* heaps *colloq*, loads *colloq*, lots, many, masses, much, stacks *colloq*

quarantine n detention, isolation, lazaret, lazaretto, segregation

quarrel n altercation *formal*, argument, clash, conflict, contention, controversy, difference, difference of opinion, disagreement, disputation *formal*, dispute, dissension, dust-up *colloq*, feud, fight, fracas, misunderstanding, row, schism, scrap *colloq*, set-to *colloq*, slanging match *colloq*, squabble, strife, tiff, vendetta, wrangle
☒ agreement, harmony
♦ *v* argue, be at loggerheads, be at odds, be at variance, bicker, clash, contend, differ, disagree, dispute, dissent, fall out, feud, fight, row, scrap, squabble, wrangle
☒ agree

quarrelling n altercations *formal*, arguments, argy-bargying *colloq*, bickering, contention, discord *formal*, disharmony, disputation *formal*, dissension, feuding, rowing, strife, vitilitigation *formal*, wrangling
☒ concord, harmony

quarrelsome adj argumentative, bellicose *formal*, belligerent, contentious, disputatious, hot-tempered, ill-tempered, irascible, irritable, pugnacious *formal*, ready for a fight
☒ peaceable, placid

quarry n game, goal, kill, object, prey, prize, target, victim

quarter n 1 *the city's French quarter:* area, district, division, locality, neighbourhood, part, province, region, section, sector, vicinity, zone 2 *no trouble from that quarter:* area, direction, place, point, side 3 *gave his enemies no quarter:* clemency, compassion, favour, forgiveness, grace, indulgence, leniency, mercy, pardon, pity 4 *living quarters:* accommodation, barracks, billet, digs *colloq*, domicile *formal*, dwelling

formal, habitation *formal*, lodgings, pad *colloq*, residence, rooms
♦ *v* accommodate, billet, board, house, lodge, post, put up, shelter, station

quash *v* **1** *his convictions were quashed on appeal:* abrogate *formal*, annul, cancel, countermand *formal*, invalidate, nullify *formal*, override, overrule, overturn, rescind, reverse, revoke, set aside, void **2** *quashed reports she is planning to quit:* dismiss, quell, refute, squash, subdue, suppress
 1 confirm, vindicate

quaver *v* flicker, flutter, oscillate, quake, quiver, shake, shudder, tremble, trill, vibrate, waver
♦ *n* break, quaveriness, quiver, shake, sob, throb, tremble, trembling, tremolo, tremor, trill, vibration, vibrato

quay *n* dock, harbour, jetty, pier, wharf

queasy *adj* bilious, dizzy, faint, giddy, green, groggy, ill, nauseated, out of sorts *colloq*, queer *colloq*, rough *colloq*, sick, sickened, squeamish, under the weather *colloq*, unwell

queen *n* **1** *kings and queens:* consort, empress, majesty, monarch, ruler, sovereign **2** *a fashion queen:* belle, idol, princess

queenly *adj* august *formal*, dignified, gracious, grand, imperial, imperious, majestic, monarchical *formal*, noble, regal, royal, sovereign, splendid, stately, sublime *formal*
 undignified

queer *adj* **1** *a queer thing happened:* abnormal, bizarre, curious, deviant, eccentric, extraordinary, funny, mysterious, odd, outlandish, peculiar, puzzling, remarkable, singular *formal*, strange, uncommon, unconventional, unnatural, unorthodox, unusual, weird **2** *I feel queer:* dizzy, faint, giddy, ill, light-headed, out of sorts *colloq*, queasy, rough *colloq*, sick, under the weather *colloq*, unwell **3** *something queer going on:* doubtful, dubious, fishy *colloq*, iffy *colloq*, irregular, peculiar, shady *colloq*, shifty, strange, suspect, suspicious **4** *transgender and queer culture:* bisexual, gay, homosexual, lesbian
 1 common, ordinary, usual **2** well **4** heterosexual, straight *colloq*
♦ *v* botch, endanger, foil, frustrate, harm, impair, jeopardize, mar, ruin, spoil, stymie, thwart, upset, wreck

queerness *n* abnormality, anomalousness, bizarreness, curiousness, eccentricity, irregularity, oddity, peculiarity, singularity *formal*, strangeness, uncommonness, unconventionality, unnaturalness, unorthodoxy, unusualness

quell *v* allay, alleviate *formal*, appease, calm, conquer, crush, defeat, extinguish, hush, mitigate *formal*, moderate, overcome, overpower, pacify, put down, quash, quiet, rout, silence, soothe, squash, stifle, subdue, suppress, vanquish *formal*

quench *v* **1** *quench one's thirst:* cool, sate, satiate *formal*, satisfy, slake **2** *quench the flames:* douse, extinguish, put out, smother, snuff out, stamp out, stifle

querulous *adj* cantankerous *formal*, captious, carping, complaining, critical, cross, discontented, dissatisfied, fault-finding, fractious, fretful, fussy, grouchy *colloq*,

grumbling, irascible, irritable, peevish, petulant *formal*, ratty *colloq*, shirty *colloq*, sour, testy
 contented, placid, uncomplaining

query *v* ask, be sceptical of, challenge, disbelieve, dispute, distrust, doubt, have suspicions about, inquire, mistrust, quarrel with, question, suspect, throw doubts on
 accept
♦ *n* doubt, hesitation, inquiry, problem, qualm, question, quibble, reservation, scepticism, suspicion, uncertainty, uneasiness

quest *n* **1** *a quest for buried treasure:* adventure, crusade, enterprise, expedition, exploration, hunt, inquiry, investigation, journey, mission, pilgrimage, search, seeking, undertaking, venture, voyage **2** *their ultimate quest is EU membership:* aim, goal, purpose, pursuit

question *v* **1** *questioned him about his involvement:* ask, catechize, cross-examine, cross-question, debrief, examine, give the third degree to *colloq*, grill, inquire of, interrogate, interview, investigate, probe, pump, quiz **2** *questioned the existence of God:* challenge, disbelieve, dispute, doubt, have doubts about, have qualms about, have reservations about, query
♦ *n* **1** *a tricky question:* difficulty, inquiry, poser, problem, query **2** *the burning questions of the day:* controversy, debate, dispute, issue, matter, motion, point, point at issue, problem, proposal, proposition, subject, theme, topic **3** *there is some question about his loyalty:* argument, controversy, debate, dispute, doubt, query, uncertainty

questionable *adj* arguable, controversial, debatable, disputable, doubtful, dubious, fishy *colloq*, iffy *colloq*, shady *colloq*, suspect, suspicious, uncertain, undetermined, unproven, unsettled, vexed
 certain, indisputable, unquestionable

questioner *n* catechist, examiner, inquisitor, interlocutor *formal*, interrogator, interviewer, investigator

questionnaire *n* form, opinion poll, quiz, survey, test

queue *n* chain, column, concatenation *formal*, crocodile, file, line, order, procession, row, sequence, series, string, succession, tailback, train
♦ *v* file, line up, tail back, wait

quibble *v* avoid the issue, carp, cavil, equivocate, nit-pick *colloq*, prevaricate, split hairs
♦ *n* cavil, complaint, criticism, equivocation, niggle, nit-picking *colloq*, objection, prevarication, protest, query

quick *adj* **1** *a quick runner:* brisk, express, fast, nippy, rapid, speedy, swift **2** *a quick response:* expeditious *formal*, express, immediate, instant, instantaneous, prompt, rapid, speedy, swift **3** *a quick glance:* brief, brisk, cursory, fleeting, hasty, hurried, perfunctory, sudden, swift **4** *a quick mind:* astute, clever, discerning, intelligent, keen, nimble, perceptive, quick-witted, receptive, responsive, sharp, sharp-witted, shrewd, smart
 1 slow **2** sluggish **3** leisurely **4** dull, unintelligent

quicken *v* **1** *the quickening pace of development:* accelerate, advance, hasten, hurry (up), speed (up) **2** *things that quicken her soul:* activate,

animate, arouse, energize, enliven, excite, galvanize, incite, inspire, instigate, invigorate, kindle, reactivate, refresh, reinvigorate, revitalize, revive, revivify *formal*, rouse, stimulate, stir (up), strengthen, whet
F₃ 1 retard, slow 2 dull

quickly *adv* 1 *ran quickly:* apace, at a rate of knots *colloq*, at the double *colloq*, briskly, fast, hell for leather *colloq*, like a bat out of hell *colloq*, like greased lightning *colloq*, like the clappers *colloq*, quick, rapidly, speedily, swiftly 2 *get the job finished quickly:* at the double *colloq*, before you can say Jack Robinson *colloq*, expeditiously *formal*, fast, immediately, instantaneously, instantly, lickety-split *colloq*, posthaste, prestissimo, presto *technical*, promptly, pronto *colloq*, quick, rapidly, soon, speedily, swiftly 3 *glanced quickly around the room:* abruptly, cursorily, hastily, hurriedly, perfunctorily *formal*
F₃ 1 slowly 2 slowly, tardily *formal*

quickness *n* 1 *moved with surprising quickness:* agility, briskness, expedition *formal*, hastiness, promptitude *formal*, promptness, rapidity, speed, speediness, swiftness 2 *quickness of understanding:* acuteness, alertness, astuteness, intelligence, keenness, penetration, quick-wittedness, sharpness, shrewdness
F₃ 1 slowness, tardiness *formal* 2 dullness

quick-tempered *adj* choleric, excitable, explosive, fiery, hot-tempered, impatient, impulsive, irascible, irritable, passionate, petulant *formal*, quarrelsome, shrewish, snappy, splenetic *formal*, temperamental, testy, touchy, volcanic, waspish
F₃ cool, dispassionate

quick-witted *adj* acute, alert, astute, bright, clever, crafty, ingenious, intelligent, keen, nimble-witted, penetrating, perceptive, ready-witted, resourceful, sharp, shrewd, smart, wide-awake, witty
F₃ dull, slow, stupid

quiescent *adj* 1 *lay quiescent on his back:* asleep, at rest, dormant, motionless, passive, reposeful *formal*, resting, silent, sleeping, still, undisturbed 2 *relatively quiescent in terms of hurricane activity:* calm, dormant, in abeyance *formal*, inactive, inert, peaceful, quiet, serene, tranquil, untroubled
F₃ 2 active

quiet *adj* 1 *a quiet buzzing noise:* faint, inaudible, indistinct, low, muffled, soft 2 *the room was quiet:* hushed, noiseless, silent, soundless 3 *a quiet night in:* calm, peaceful, placid, restrained, serene, still, tranquil, undisturbed, untroubled 4 *a quiet man:* discreet, gentle, imperturbable *formal*, introverted, meek, mild, phlegmatic, placid, reserved, reticent, retiring, shy, stoic, subdued, taciturn, thoughtful, uncommunicative, undemonstrative, unexcitable, unflappable *colloq*, unforthcoming, withdrawn 5 *a quiet spot:* isolated, lonely, off the beaten track *colloq*, peaceful, private, secluded, sequestered *formal*, sleepy, undisturbed, unfrequented 6 *quiet colours:* faint, low-key, muted, restrained, soft, subdued, subtle
F₃ 1 loud 2 noisy 4 excitable, extrovert 5 noisy 6 loud
♦ *n* calm, hush, lull, noiselessness, peace,

quietness, repose *formal*, rest, serenity, silence, soundlessness, stillness, tranquillity
F₃ bustle, disturbance, loudness, noise

quieten *v* 1 *quietened the child's screams:* deaden, diminish, dull, hush, lower, muffle, mute, reduce, shush, shut up *colloq*, silence, soften, stifle 2 *quietened the angry mob:* calm (down), compose, pacify, quell, quiet, smooth, sober, soothe, still, subdue, tranquillize
F₃ 2 agitate, disturb

quietly *adv* calmly, gently, inaudibly, meekly, mildly, modestly, mutely, noiselessly, peacefully, placidly, privately, secretly, silently, softly, soundlessly, surreptitiously, tranquilly, undemonstratively, unobtrusively, unostentatiously
F₃ noisily, obtrusively

quietness *n* calm, calmness, composure, dullness, hush, inactivity, inertia, lull, peace, placidity, quiescence *formal*, quiet, quietude *formal*, repose *formal*, serenity, silence, still, stillness, tranquillity, uneventfulness
F₃ activity, bustle, commotion, disturbance, noise

quilt *n* bedcover, bedspread, continental quilt, counterpane, coverlet, duvet, eiderdown

quintessence *n* core, distillation, embodiment, essence, exemplar *formal*, extract, gist, heart, kernel, marrow, pattern, pith, quiddity *formal*, soul, spirit, sum and substance

quintessential *adj* archetypal *formal*, complete, consummate *formal*, definitive, essential, ideal, perfect, prototypical *formal*, ultimate

quip *n* crack, epigram, gag *colloq*, gibe, jest, joke, one-liner *colloq*, pleasantry, retort, riposte, wisecrack, witticism
♦ *v* gag, gibe, jest, joke, retort, riposte, wisecrack

quirk *n* caprice, characteristic, curiosity, eccentricity, feature, foible, freak, habit, hang-up *colloq*, idiosyncrasy, kink, mannerism, obsession, oddity, peculiarity, thing *colloq*, trait, turn, twist, vagary, whim

quisling *n* betrayer, collaborator, fifth columnist, Judas, renegade, traitor, turncoat

quit *v* 1 *quit smoking:* abandon, abstain from *formal*, cease *formal*, desist *formal*, discontinue *formal*, drop, end, give up, leave off, pack in *colloq*, stop 2 *quit my job:* abandon, forsake *formal*, give up, leave, relinquish, renounce, resign, retire (from), surrender, withdraw (from) 3 *quit her native country:* decamp, depart, desert, exit, go (away) from, leave, withdraw (from)

quite *adv* 1 *quite fond of ballet:* comparatively, fairly, moderately, rather, reasonably, relatively, somewhat, to some extent/degree 2 *felt quite miserable:* absolutely, completely, entirely, exactly, fully, perfectly, precisely, totally, utterly, wholly

quits *adj* equal, even, level, square

quitter *n* apostate, defector, delinquent, deserter, rat *colloq*, recreant, renegade, shirker, skiver *colloq*

quiver *v* flutter, oscillate, palpitate, pulsate, quake, quaver, shake, shiver, shudder, tingle, tremble, vibrate, wobble

♦ *n* flutter, oscillation, palpitation, pulsation, quaver, shake, shiver, shudder, throb, tremble, tremor, vibration, wobble

quixotic *adj* **1** *quixotic ideas:* chivalrous, extravagant, fanciful, idealistic, impracticable, romantic, starry-eyed, unrealistic, unworldly, utopian, visionary **2** *a quixotic adventure:* fantastical, impetuous, impulsive, romantic ⊠ **1** hard-headed, practical, realistic

quiz *n* competition, cross-examination, cross-questioning, examination, questioning, questionnaire, test
♦ *v* cross-examine, cross-question, examine, give the third degree to *colloq*, grill *colloq*, interrogate, pump *colloq*, question

quizzical *adj* amused, baffled, curious, humorous, inquiring, mocking, mystified, perplexed, puzzled, questioning, sardonic, satirical, sceptical, teasing

quota *n* allocation, allowance, assignment, cut *colloq*, part, percentage, portion, proportion, ration, share, slice, slice of the cake *colloq*, whack *colloq*

quotation *n* **1** *a quotation from the Bible:* allusion, citation, cutting, excerpt, extract, line, passage, piece, quote *colloq*, reference, selection **2** *a quotation for building work:* charge, costing, estimate, figure, price, quote *colloq*, tender

quote *v* allude to, cite, echo, mention, name, recall, recite, recollect, refer to, repeat, reproduce

quotidian *adj* common, commonplace, customary, daily, day-to-day, diurnal *formal*, everyday, habitual, normal, ordinary, recurrent, regular, repeated, routine, workaday

R

rabbit *n* bunny, bunny rabbit, cony, cottontail
▶ **rabbit on** babble *colloq*, blather, blether, chatter, gab *colloq*, go on (and on), maunder (on), natter *colloq*, waffle *colloq*, witter (on) *colloq*

rabble *n* **1** *his rabble of fans:* crowd, herd, horde, mob, throng **2** *above the common rabble:* common people, crowd, herd, hoi polloi, masses, mob, plebs *colloq*, populace, proletariat, riff-raff *colloq*

rabble-rouser *n* agitator, demagogue, firebrand, incendiary, ringleader, troublemaker

rabid *adj* **1** *a rabid zealot:* ardent, bigoted, extreme, fanatical, fervent, intolerant, irrational, narrow-minded, obsessive, overzealous, unreasoning, zealous **2** *a rabid dog:* berserk, crazed, frenzied, hydrophobic, mad, violent, wild

race¹ *n* **1** *a horse race:* chase, competition, contest **2** *the race for the leadership:* competition, contention, contest, pursuit, quest, rivalry
♦ *v* bolt, career, dart, dash, fly, gallop, hasten, hurry, run, run like hell *colloq*, rush, speed, sprint, tear, zoom

---

Types of race and famous races include:
cycle race, cyclo-cross, road race, time trial, Tour de France; greyhound race, Greyhound Derby; horse race, Cheltenham Gold Cup, the Classics (Derby, Oaks, One Thousand Guineas, St Leger, Two Thousand Guineas), Grand National, Kentucky Derby, Melbourne Cup, Prix de l'Arc de Triomphe, steeplechase, trotting race, harness race *US*; motorcycle race, motocross, scramble, speedway, Isle of Man Tourist Trophy (TT); motor-race, Grand Prix, Indianapolis 500, Le Mans, Monte Carlo rally, RAC Rally, scramble, stock car race; rowing, regatta, Boat Race; running, cross-country, dash *US*, hurdles, marathon, London Marathon, relay, sprint, steeplechase, track event; ski race, downhill, slalom; swimming race; walking race, walkathon; yacht race, Admiral's Cup, America's Cup; egg-and-spoon race, pancake race, sack race, wheelbarrow race

---

race² *n* **1** *a race of people:* ancestry, blood, clan, dynasty, ethnic group, extraction, family, house, line, lineage, nation, parentage, people, racial group, stirps, stock, tribe **2** *a race of animals:* breed, family, genus, species, stirps, stock, strain

racecourse *n* circuit, course, racetrack, speedway, track, turf

racial *adj* ancestral, ethnic, ethnological, folk, genealogical, genetic, inherited, national, tribal

raciness *n* **1** *offended by the raciness of his humour:* bawdiness, coarseness, crudeness, indecency, indelicacy, lewdness, naughtiness, ribaldry, smuttiness, suggestiveness, vulgarity **2** *the vivid raciness of her writing:* animation, dynamism, ebullience *formal*, energy, freshness, liveliness, pep *colloq*, zest, zestfulness

racism *n* apartheid, bias, chauvinism, discrimination, jingoism, prejudice, racial discrimination, racial prejudice, racialism, xenophobia

racist *n* bigot, chauvinist, discriminator, racialist
♦ *adj* bigoted, discriminatory, intolerant, racialist

rack *n* **1** *a luggage rack:* frame, framework, holder, shelf, stand, structure, support, trestle **2** *rack and ruin:* affliction, agony, anguish, distress, misery, pain, pangs, suffering, torment, torture
♦ *v* afflict, agonize, convulse, crucify, distress, excruciate, harass, harrow, lacerate, oppress, pain, tear, torment, torture

racket *n* **1** *a dreadful racket:* clamour, commotion, din, disturbance, fuss, hubbub, hullabaloo, hurly-burly, noise, outcry, pandemonium, row, shouting, tumult, uproar, yelling **2** *a money-laundering racket:* con *colloq*, dodge, fiddle, fraud, game *colloq*, scheme, swindle

racy *adj* **1** *a racy novel:* bawdy, blue *colloq*, coarse, crude, dirty, indecent, indelicate, naughty, off-colour, ribald, risqué, rude, smutty, suggestive, vulgar **2** *written in a fast-moving, racy style:* animated, dynamic, ebullient *formal*, energetic, fast-moving, lively, peppy *colloq*, sparkling, spirited, vigorous, vivacious, zippy *colloq*

radiance *n* **1** *the radiance of the sun:* brightness, brilliance, effulgence *formal*, gleam, glitter, glow, incandescence *technical*, light, luminosity, lustre, refulgence *formal*, resplendence, shine **2** *the radiance of her expression:* bliss, delight, ecstasy, elation, happiness, joy, pleasure, rapture

radiant *adj* **1** *cast a radiant light:* beaming, bright, brilliant, effulgent *formal*, gleaming, glittering, glowing, illuminated, incandescent *technical*, luminous, refulgent *formal*, resplendent, shining, sparkling **2** *a radiant bride:* blissful, delighted, ecstatic, elated, happy, in raptures, in seventh heaven *colloq*, joyful, on top of the world *colloq*, over the moon *colloq*
🆉 **1** dull **2** miserable

radiate *v* **1** *radiate light:* diffuse, emit, give off, issue, pour, send out/forth, shed **2** *the light radiated through the fog:* beam, diffuse, emanate, gleam, glow, issue, pour, shine **3** *side streets radiating from the square:* branch, disperse, disseminate *formal*, divaricate *formal*, diverge, spread (out)

radiation *n* emanation, emission, insolation *technical*, rays, waves

radical *adj* **1** *radical differences:* basic, deep-seated, elemental, elementary, essential, fundamental, innate, intrinsic, native, natural, primary, profound, rudimentary **2** *radical changes:* absolute, complete, comprehensive, drastic, entire, exhaustive, far-reaching, profound, sweeping, thorough, thoroughgoing, total, utter **3** *a radical political outlook:* extreme, extremist, fanatical, militant, revolutionary
🆉 **1** superficial **3** moderate
♦ *n* extremist, fanatic, fundamentalist, militant, reformer, reformist, revolutionary

raffish *adj* bohemian, careless, casual, devil-may-care, disreputable, dissipated, dissolute,

flamboyant, flashy, jaunty, meretricious *formal*, rakish, showy, sporty
F3 decorous *formal*, proper, sedate, staid

raffle *n* draw, lottery, sweep, sweepstake, tombola

rag[1] *n* **1** *cleaned it with an old rag:* cloth, duster, flannel, floorcloth, towel **2** *dressed in rags:* clouts, duddery *colloq*, remnants, shreds, tats, tatters

rag[2] *v* bait, kid *colloq*, mock, rib *colloq*, ridicule, take the mickey out of *colloq*, taunt, tease, torment

ragamuffin *n* gamin, guttersnipe, urchin

ragbag *n* assemblage *formal*, assortment, confusion, hotchpotch, jumble, medley, miscellany, mix, mixture, omnium-gatherum *colloq*, pastiche, potpourri, salad

rage *n* **1** *filled with rage:* anger, fury, madness, wrath **2** *fly into a rage:* frenzy, fury, paroxysm, tantrum, temper
♦ *v* blow a fuse *colloq*, blow your cool *colloq*, blow your top *colloq*, boil over *colloq*, burst a blood vessel *colloq*, do your nut *colloq*, explode *colloq*, flip your lid *colloq*, fly off the handle *colloq*, foam at the mouth *colloq*, fume, go mad *colloq*, go off the deep end *colloq*, go up the wall *colloq*, hit the roof *colloq*, lose your cool *colloq*, lose your rag *colloq*, raise hell *colloq*, rampage, rant, rave, see red *colloq*, seethe, storm, thunder

ragged *adj* **1** *ragged clothes:* falling to pieces, frayed, holey, in holes, in tatters, rent *old use*, ripped, shabby, tattered, tatty, threadbare, torn, worn-out **2** *ragged children:* destitute, down and out, down-at-heel, indigent *formal*, poor, scruffy, unkempt, untidy **3** *a ragged edge:* irregular, jagged, notched, rough, rugged, serrated, uneven **4** *ragged cheers:* disorganized, erratic, fragmented **5** *a ragged queue:* disorganized, straggling

raging *adj* **1** *the raging sea:* stormy, tumultuous, turbulent, violent, wild **2** *raging at the delay:* angry, enraged, frenzied, fulminating *formal*, fuming, furibund *formal*, furious, incensed, infuriated, irate, ireful *formal*, mad, raving, seething, wrathful

raid *n* **1** *a raid on enemy territory:* assault, attack, blitz, charge, foray, incursion, inroad, invasion, onset, onslaught, sally, sortie, strike, swoop **2** *a bank raid:* break-in, hold-up, robbery, smash-and-grab raid **3** *a police raid:* bust *slang*, swoop
♦ *v* **1** *tribes who raided neighbouring villages:* assail, attack, descend on, invade, maraud, pillage, plunder, rush, sack, set upon, storm, swoop on **2** *the thieves who raided the gallery:* break into, loot, ransack, rifle **3** *police raided the house at dawn:* bust *slang*, descend on, swoop on

raider *n* **1** *raiders from the north:* attacker, brigand, invader, marauder, pillager, pirate, plunderer **2** *art raiders who stole a Van Gogh painting:* criminal, crook *colloq*, looter, ransacker, robber, shark *colloq*, thief

rail *v* abuse, arraign *formal*, attack, castigate *formal*, censure, criticize, decry, denounce *formal*, fulminate *formal*, inveigh *formal*, revile, upbraid, vituperate *formal*, vociferate

railing *n* balustrade, barrier, fence, fencing, paling, parapet, rail(s)

raillery *n* badinage, banter, chaff, chiacking *colloq*, dicacity *old use*, irony, jeering, jesting, joke, joking, kidding *colloq*, mockery, persiflage, pleasantry, ragging *colloq*, repartee, ribbing *colloq*, ridicule, satire, sport, teasing

rain *n* **1** *heavy rain:* cloudburst, deluge, downpour, drizzle, mizzle, precipitation, raindrops, rainfall, rainstorm, shower, squall, storm, thunderstorm, torrent **2** *a rain of stones:* deluge, shower, torrent, volley
♦ *v* bucket (down) *colloq*, come down in buckets/sheets/stair rods/torrents *colloq*, drizzle, mizzle, pelt, piss down *slang*, pour (down), rain cats and dogs *colloq*, shower, spit, teem, tipple down

rainbow *n* arc, arch, bow, iris
♦ *adj* iridescent *formal*, irisated *formal*, irised *formal*, kaleidoscopic, opalescent, prismatic, rainbow-like, spectral, variegated
F3 monochrome

The colours of the rainbow are:
red, orange, yellow, green, blue, indigo, violet
---

rainy *adj* damp, drizzly, showery, wet
F3 dry

raise *v* **1** *raise a building:* build, construct, erect, put up, set up **2** *raise something off the ground:* elevate, heave up, hoist, jack up, lift, lift up, uplift **3** *raise the volume:* amplify, augment *formal*, bump up *colloq*, escalate, increase, intensify, jack up *colloq*, magnify, put up, step up, strengthen **4** *raise standards:* boost, enhance, heighten, increase, strengthen, upgrade **5** *raise funds:* accumulate, amass, collect, gather, get, get together, obtain **6** *raise an army:* assemble, gather, get together, muster, rally, recruit **7** *raise children:* bring up, educate, nurture, rear **8** *raise livestock and crops:* breed, cultivate, develop, grow, nurture, produce, propagate, rear **9** *raise a subject:* bring up, broach, introduce, moot, present, put forward, suggest **10** *raise a smile:* activate, arouse, cause, create, evoke, excite, provoke, rouse, stir
F3 **2** lower **3** decrease, reduce **4** decrease, reduce **10** suppress

raised *adj* applied, appliqué, cameo, embossed, relief, relievo
F3 engraved, incised, intaglio

rake[1] *v* **1** *rake the soil:* comb, graze, hoe, level, scrape, scratch, smooth **2** *raking through her bag for the keys:* comb, hunt, ransack, rifle, rummage, scour, search **3** *rake the leaves together:* accumulate, amass, collect, gather

rake[2] *n* debauchee, degenerate, dissolute, hedonist, lecher, libertine, playboy, pleasure-seeker, profligate *formal*, roué, sensualist, swinger
F3 ascetic, puritan
▶ **rake in** bring in *colloq*, earn, get paid, make, pull in *colloq*, receive
▶ **rake up** bring up, drag up, introduce, mention, raise, revive

rake-off *n* cut, part, portion, share, slice

rakish *adj* **1** *a wild, rakish young man:* abandoned, debauched, degenerate, depraved, devil-may-care, dissipated, dissolute, immoral, lecherous, libertine, licentious, loose, prodigal *formal*, profligate *formal* **2** *wearing his hat at a rakish angle:*

rally *n* **1** *a political rally:* assemblage *formal*, assembly, conference, convention, convocation, demonstration, gathering, jamboree, march, mass meeting, meeting, reunion **2** *a sudden rally in the market:* comeback, improvement, recovery, recuperation, renewal, resurgence, revival
♦ *v* **1** *he rallied the troops:* assemble, bring together, collect, convene *formal*, gather, get together, marshal, mobilize, muster, organize, reassemble, reform, regroup, reorganize, round up, summon, unite **2** *his supporters rallied in the square:* assemble, band together, come together, congregate, convene *formal*, gather, get together, group, muster, reassemble, reform, regroup, unite **3** *she rallied after the operation:* be on the mend *colloq*, bounce back *colloq*, gain strength, get back on your feet *colloq*, get better, get well, improve, perk up *colloq*, pick up, pull through, recover, recuperate, revive

ram *v* **1** *a truck rammed the gates:* bump, butt, crash into, dash into, drive into, hit, slam into, smash, strike **2** *ramming the papers into her bag:* compress, cram, drive, force, jam, pack, squeeze, stuff, thrust, wedge

ramble *v* **1** *rambling across the moors:* amble, hike, jaunt, meander, range, roam, rove, saunter, stray, stroll, traipse, tramp, trek, walk, wander **2** *keeps rambling about her past:* babble, blather, blether, chatter, digress, expatiate *formal*, go off at a tangent *colloq*, rabbit (on) *colloq*, waffle *colloq*, witter (on) *colloq*
♦ *n* amble, excursion, hike, jaunt, roam, saunter, stroll, tour, tramp, trek, trip, walk, wander

rambler *n* drifter, hiker, roamer, rover, saunterer, stroller, traveller, walker, wanderer, wayfarer

rambling *adj* **1** *rambling ivy plants:* sprawling, spreading, straggling, trailing **2** *a rambling story:* circuitous *formal*, digressive, disconnected, disjointed, incoherent, long-drawn-out, long-winded, periphrastic *formal*, roundabout, verbose *formal*, wandering, wordy
◙ **2** direct

ramification *n* **1** *the ramifications of this decision:* complication, consequence, development, effect, implication, outcome, result, sequel, upshot **2** *small ramifications issuing from the stem:* branch, divarication *formal*, limb, offshoot, outgrowth

ramp *n* acclivity *formal*, grade, gradient, incline, rise, slope

rampage *v* charge, go berserk, rage, run amok, run riot, run wild, rush, rush violently/wildly, storm, tear
♦ *n* destruction, frenzy, furore, fury, mayhem, rage, storm, turmoil, uproar, violence

rampant *adj* **1** *rampant sexism in the military:* epidemic, prevalent, profuse, rank, rife, widespread **2** *rampant growth of weeds:* excessive, out of control, out of hand, pandemic, raging, riotous, spreading like wildfire *colloq*, unbridled, unchecked, uncontrolled, unrestrained, wanton, wild

rampart *n* bank, barricade, bastion, breastwork, bulwark, defence, earthwork, embankment, fence, fort, fortification, guard, parapet, security, stronghold, vallum, wall

ramshackle *adj* broken-down, crumbling, decrepit, derelict, dilapidated, flimsy, gone to rack and ruin, jerry-built, rickety, ruined, run-down, shaky, tottering, tumbledown, unsafe, unsteady
◙ solid, stable

ranch *n* estancia, estate, farm, hacienda, plantation, station

rancid *adj* bad, fetid, foul, high, malodorous *formal*, musty, noisome *formal*, noxious *formal*, off, overripe, putrid, rank, rotten, sour, stale, turned
◙ sweet

rancorous *adj* acerbic, acrimonious *formal*, bitter, hostile, malevolent *formal*, malignant, resentful, spiteful, splenetic *formal*, vengeful, venomous, vindictive, virulent

rancour *n* acrimony *formal*, animosity, animus *formal*, antipathy *formal*, bitterness, enmity, grudge, hate, hatred, hostility, ill-feeling, ill-will, malevolence *formal*, malice, malignity, resentfulness, resentment, spite, spleen, venom, vindictiveness

random *adj* **1** *random events:* accidental, arbitrary, casual, chance, fortuitous, incidental, serendipitous *formal*, stray, unarranged, unplanned **2** *random acts of violence:* aimless, arbitrary, casual, haphazard, hit-or-miss *colloq*, indiscriminate, irregular, purposeless, sporadic, unmethodical, unsystematic
◙ **1** deliberate **2** deliberate, systematic

randy *adj* amorous, aroused, concupiscent *formal*, goatish, horny, hot, lascivious, lecherous, lustful, raunchy, satyric, sexy, turned-on *colloq*

range *n* **1** *a range of products:* array, assortment, diversity, selection, series, variety **2** *a range of mountains:* chain, file, line, row, series, string **3** *the average age range:* confines, extent, gamut, limits, parameters, scale, span, spectrum, spread, sweep **4** *beyond our range of understanding:* area, bounds, compass, distance, domain, field, limits, orbit, province, radius, reach, scope, span, sphere **5** *a cooking range:* cooker, oven, stove
♦ *v* **1** *the anthology ranges across his entire career:* cover, extend, go, reach, run, spread, stretch **2** *temperatures range wildly:* fluctuate, vary **3** *range them according to size:* arrange, catalogue, categorize, class, classify, compartmentalize, grade, group, order, pigeonhole, rank **4** *armies ranged against each other:* align, arrange, dispose *formal*, draw up, line up, order, rank **5** *the hens range all over the farm:* amble, drift, ramble, roam, stray, stroll, wander

rangy *adj* gangling, lanky, leggy, long-legged
◙ compact, dumpy

rank[1] *n* **1** *social rank:* caste, class, classification, degree, division, echelon, estate, grade, group, level, mark, place in the pecking order *colloq*, position, sort, standing, station, status, stratum, tier, type **2** *ranks of soldiers:* column, file, formation, line, order, range, row, series, string
♦ *v* **1** *ranked according to size:* arrange, categorize, class, classify, grade, order, organize, place, position, range, rate, sort **2** *trees ranked along the riverbank:* align, arrange, dispose *formal*, draw up, line up, order

Ranks in the armed services include:
air force: aircraftsman, aircraftswoman, corporal, sergeant, warrant officer, pilot officer, flying officer, flight lieutenant, squadron-leader, wing commander, group-captain, air-commodore, air-vice-marshal, air-marshal, air-chief-marshal, marshal of the Royal Air Force; army: private, lance-corporal, corporal, sergeant, warrant officer, lieutenant, captain, major, lieutenant-colonel, colonel, brigadier, major general, lieutenant-general, general, field marshal; navy: able seaman, rating, petty officer, chief petty officer, sublieutenant, lieutenant, lieutenant-commander, commander, captain, commodore, rear admiral, vice-admiral, admiral, admiral of the fleet. See also **soldier**

rank² *adj* **1** *rank favouritism:* absolute, arrant, blatant, complete, downright, flagrant, glaring, gross, out-and-out, outrageous, sheer, thorough, total, unmitigated, unqualified, utter **2** *a rank smell:* acrid, disgusting, evil-smelling, fetid, foul, graveolent *formal*, malodorous *formal*, mephitic *formal*, offensive, pungent, putrid, rancid, repulsive, revolting, stale, stinking **3** *rank disobedience:* coarse, gross, outrageous, shocking, vile **4** *rank weeds:* abundant, dense, lush, luxuriant *formal*, overgrown, profuse, vigorous

rankle *v* anger, annoy, bug *colloq*, cause bitterness/resentment, embitter, gall, get your back up *colloq*, get your blood up *colloq*, irk, irritate, nettle, peeve *colloq*, rile, vex

ransack *v* **1** *the invaders ransacked the city:* depredate *formal*, despoil *formal*, devastate, loot, maraud, pillage, plunder, raid, ravage, sack, strip **2** *she ransacked her bag for the keys:* comb, go through, rifle, rummage through, scour, search, turn inside out, turn upside down

ransom *n* **1** *pay a ransom:* money, payment, pay-off, price **2** *the ransom of the hostages:* deliverance, freedom, liberation, redemption, release, rescue, restoration, setting free
♦ *v* buy/purchase the freedom of, deliver, free, liberate, redeem, release, rescue, set free

rant *v* bellow, bluster, declaim *formal*, harangue, rant and rave, rave, roar, shout, tub-thump *colloq*, vociferate *formal*, yell
♦ *n* bluster, bombast, declamation *formal*, diatribe *formal*, harangue, oration, philippic *formal*, roaring, shouting, storm, tirade, vociferation *formal*, yelling

rap *v* **1** *rapped on the head:* bang, batter, clip, clout, cuff, hammer, hit, knock, strike, tap, thump, whack **2** *rapped by his boss:* blame, castigate *formal*, censure, criticize, knock *colloq*, rail *colloq*, reprimand, reprove, scold, slam *colloq*, slate *colloq*
♦ *n* **1** *a rap on the knuckles:* bang, batter, blow, clip, clout, cuff, hammer, hit, knock, tap, thump, whack **2** *she took the rap for the mistake:* blame, castigation *formal*, censure, flak *colloq*, knocking *colloq*, rebuke, reprimand, slamming *colloq*, slating *colloq*, stick *colloq*

rapacious *adj* avaricious *formal*, esurient *formal*, grasping, greedy, insatiable, marauding, plundering, predatory, preying, ravening, ravenous, voracious, vulturish, vulturous, wolfish, wolvish

rapacity *n* avarice, avidity *formal*, esurience *formal*, esuriency *formal*, graspingness, greed, greediness, insatiableness, predatoriness, rapaciousness, ravenousness, shark's manners *colloq*, voraciousness, voracity, wolfishness

rape *v* **1** *rape a woman:* abuse, assault, assault sexually, defile, ravish, violate **2** *rape the land:* defile, depredate *formal*, despoil *formal*, devastate, loot, pillage, plunder, raid, ransack, ravage, rob, sack, spoliate *formal*, strip, violate
♦ *n* **1** *the rape of a young girl:* abuse, assault, ravishment, sexual assault, violation **2** *rape of the countryside:* defilement, depredation *formal*, despoliation *formal*, devastation, looting, plundering, raid, ransacking, rapine *formal*, ravaging, sacking, spoliation *formal*, stripping, violation

rapid *adj* brisk, expeditious *formal*, express, fast, hasty, headlong, hurried, like lightning *colloq*, lively, precipitate *formal*, prompt, quick, speedy, swift
▪ leisurely, slow, sluggish, tardy *formal*

rapidity *n* alacrity *formal*, briskness, celerity *formal*, dispatch, expedition *formal*, expeditiousness *formal*, fleetness, haste, hurry, precipitateness *formal*, promptitude *formal*, promptness, quickness, rush, speed, speediness, swiftness, velocity
▪ slowness

rapidly *adv* briskly, expeditiously *formal*, fast, hastily, hurriedly, lickety-split *colloq*, precipitately *formal*, promptly, quickly, speedily, swiftly
▪ slowly

rapine *n* defilement, depredation *formal*, despoliation *formal*, devastation, looting, plundering, raid, ransacking, ravaging, sacking, spoliation *formal*, stripping, violation

rapport *n* affinity, bond, empathy, good understanding, harmony, link, relationship, sympathy, understanding

rapprochement *n* agreement, détente, harmonization, increased friendliness, reconcilement, reconciliation, reunion

rapt *adj* **1** *rapt in contemplation:* absorbed, engrossed, fascinated, gripped, intent, preoccupied **2** *the audience was rapt:* bewitched, captivated, charmed, delighted, ecstatic, enchanted, enraptured, enthralled, entranced, ravished, spellbound, thrilled, transported

rapture *n* bliss, cloud nine *colloq*, delectation *formal*, delight, ecstasy, elation, enchantment, euphoria, exaltation, exhilaration, felicity *formal*, happiness, joy, seventh heaven *colloq*, top of the world *colloq*, transport

rapturous *adj* blissful, delighted, ecstatic, entranced, euphoric, exalted, happy, in seventh heaven *colloq*, joyful, joyous, on cloud nine *colloq*, on top of the world *colloq*, over the moon *colloq*, overjoyed, ravished, rhapsodic, transported

rare *adj* **1** *jobs like that are rare:* exceptional, few and far between *colloq*, infrequent, like gold dust *colloq*, scarce, sparse, sporadic, thin on the ground *colloq*, uncommon, unusual **2** *rare beauty:* choice, excellent, exceptional, exquisite, incomparable, matchless, outstanding,

remarkable, superb, superior, superlative, unparalleled
F₁ 1 abundant, common, frequent, ordinary, typical

rarefied *adj* esoteric, exclusive, private, refined, select, special, sublime

rarely *adv* hardly, hardly ever, infrequently, little, occasionally, once in a blue moon *colloq*, scarcely, scarcely ever, seldom
F₁ frequently, often

raring *adj* desperate, eager, enthusiastic, impatient, itching, keen, longing, ready, willing

rarity *n* **1** *a collection of rarities:* curio, curiosity, find, gem, marvel, pearl, treasure, wonder **2** *the rarity of these stamps:* infrequency, scarcity, shortage, sparseness, strangeness, uncommonness, unusualness
F₁ 2 frequency

rascal *n* devil, good-for-nothing, imp, mischief-maker, ne'er-do-well, rogue, scallywag, scamp, scoundrel, villain, wastrel

rascally *adj* bad, base, crooked, dishonest, disreputable, furciferous *colloq*, good-for-nothing, knavish, low, mean, reprobate, scoundrelly, unscrupulous, vicious, villainous, wicked

rash¹ *adj* careless, foolhardy, hare-brained, hasty, headlong, headstrong, heedless, hot-headed, ill-advised, ill-considered, impetuous, imprudent, impulsive, indiscreet, madcap, precipitate *formal*, premature, reckless, unguarded, unthinking, unwary
F₁ careful, cautious, wary

rash² *n* **1** *a rash on the skin:* eruption, hives, outbreak, pompholyx *technical*, urticaria **2** *a rash of burglaries:* deluge, epidemic, flood, outbreak, plague, run, rush, spate, torrent, wave

rashness *n* carelessness, foolhardiness, hastiness, heedlessness, impulsiveness, incaution, incautiousness, indiscretion, precipitance *formal*, precipitancy *formal*, precipitation *formal*, recklessness, thoughtlessness
F₁ carefulness, cautiousness, wariness

rasp *n* **1** *the rasp of fingernails on a blackboard:* grating, grinding, scrape, scratch **2** *the rasp of his voice:* croak, harshness, hoarseness
♦ *v* **1** *sandpaper rasping the wood:* abrade, excoriate *formal*, file, grate, grind, rub, sand, scour, scrape, scratch **2** *his voice rasped in her ear:* croak, screech, squawk

rasping *adj* creaking, croaking, croaky, grating, gravelly, gruff, harsh, hoarse, husky, jarring, raspy, rough, scratchy, stridulant *formal*

rate *n* **1** *the rate at which it travels:* speed, tempo, time, velocity **2** *the current rate of exchange:* degree, grade, measure, percentage, proportion, ratio, relation, scale, standard **3** *charged a fair rate for the work:* amount, charge, cost, fee, figure, pay, payment, price, value, worth
♦ *v* **1** *rate a performance as excellent:* adjudge *formal*, appraise *formal*, assess, categorize, class, classify, consider, count, deem, esteem *formal*, estimate, evaluate, grade, judge, measure, rank, reckon, regard, value, weigh (up) **2** *I don't rate him at all:* admire, esteem *formal*, have a high opinion of, prize, respect, value **3** *she rates a*

mention: be entitled to, be worthy of, deserve, have a right to, justify, merit, warrant

rather *adv* **1** *I'm rather tired:* a bit, a little, fairly, moderately, noticeably, pretty, quite, relatively, significantly, slightly, somewhat, to some degree/extent, very **2** *I'd rather stay here:* by/for preference, for/from choice, much rather, much sooner, preferably, sooner

ratify *v* affirm, agree to, approve, authenticate, authorize, certify, confirm, corroborate, countersign, endorse, establish, legalize, sanction, sign, uphold, validate, warrant
F₁ reject, repudiate

rating *n* adjudging *formal*, appraisal *formal*, assessment, category, class, classification, degree, evaluation, grade, grading, mark, order, placing, position, rank, score, standing, status

ratio *n* balance, correlation, correspondence, fraction, percentage, proportion, relation, relationship

ration *n* **1** *petrol rations:* allocation, allotment, allowance, amount, helping, lot, measure, part, portion, proportion, quota, share **2** *emergency rations:* food, foodstuffs, provisions, stores, supplies, viands *formal*, victuals *formal*
♦ *v* **1** *forced to ration food:* budget, conserve, control, limit, restrict, save **2** *I rationed out the water:* allocate, allot, apportion *formal*, deal out, dispense, distribute, divide out, dole out, hand out, issue, measure out, share out

rational *adj* **1** *a rational plan:* circumspect *formal*, judicious *formal*, logical, prudent *formal*, realistic, reasonable, sagacious *formal*, sensible, sound, well-founded, wise **2** *rational beings:* cerebral *formal*, cognitive *formal*, enlightened, intelligent, logical, ratiocinative *formal*, reasoning, sagacious *formal*, thinking **3** *she was barely rational:* balanced, clear-headed, lucid, normal, of sound mind, sane
F₁ 1 crazy, illogical, insane, irrational
2 irrational **3** crazy, insane, irrational

rationale *n* basis, explanation, grounds, hypothesis, logic, motivation, motive, philosophy, principle, purpose, raison d'être, reason(s), reasoning, theory, thesis

rationalize *v* **1** *trying to rationalize his actions:* account for, excuse, explain, explain away, justify, make allowances for, vindicate **2** *rationalize a business:* cut out waste in, make cutbacks in, make more efficient, modernize, reorganize, streamline, trim

rattle *v* **1** *rattled the cage:* bounce, bump, clank, clink, jangle, jingle, jolt, knock, shake, vibrate **2** *the bottles rattled:* bang, bounce, clang, clank, clatter, clink, jangle, jingle, shake, vibrate **3** *don't let him rattle you:* alarm, confuse, disconcert, disturb, faze *colloq*, put off/out, shake, throw off balance, unnerve, unsettle, upset
▶ **rattle off** list, list quickly, recite, reel off, repeat, run through
▶ **rattle on** blether, chatter, gab *colloq*, gabble, jabber, prate, prattle, rabbit on *colloq*, witter *colloq*, yack *colloq*

ratty *adj* angry, annoyed, crabbed, cross, impatient, irritable, peeved *colloq*, short, short-tempered, snappy, testy, touchy
F₁ calm, patient

raucous *adj* discordant, ear-piercing, grating, harsh, jarring, loud, noisy, piercing, rasping, rough, screeching, sharp, shrill, strident

ravage *v* damage, demolish, depredate, despoil *formal*, destroy, devastate, lay waste, leave in ruins, level, loot, maraud, pillage, plunder, raze, ruin, sack, spoil, wreck
♦ *n* damage, depredation *formal*, despoliation *formal*, destruction, devastation, havoc, looting, pillage, plunder, ransacking, ruin, ruination, spoliation *formal*, wreckage

ravaged *adj* battle-torn, destroyed, devastated, ransacked, shattered, spoilt, war-torn, war-wasted, war-worn, wrecked
🗷 unspoilt

rave *v* 1 *a madman raving in the streets*: babble, jabber, ramble, rant, roar, shout, talk wildly, yell 2 *raved at his staff*: boil over *colloq*, explode, flip your lid *colloq*, hit the roof *colloq*, lose your cool *colloq*, lose your temper, rage, rant, roar, storm, thunder 3 *raving about the film*: acclaim, be mad about *colloq*, enthuse, extol, hail, sing the praises of, wax lyrical
♦ *adj* ecstatic, enthusiastic, excellent, favourable, laudatory *formal*, praising, rapturous, wonderful
♦ *n* bash *colloq*, blow-out *colloq*, carousal, celebration, do *colloq*, knees-up *colloq*, party, rave-up *colloq*

ravenous *adj* 1 *I'm absolutely ravenous*: famished, hungry, starved, starving 2 *a ravenous appetite*: greedy, insatiable, voracious, wolfish

ravine *n* canyon, deep narrow valley, gap, gorge, gully, pass

raving *adj* barmy *colloq*, batty *colloq*, berserk, crazy *colloq*, delirious, demented, deranged, frenzied, hysterical, insane, irrational, loony *colloq*, loopy *colloq*, mad, out of your mind, round the bend/twist *colloq*, unbalanced, wild
🗷 balanced, rational, sane

ravish *v* 1 *ravished by the music*: bewitch, captivate, charm, delight, enchant, enrapture, enthral, entrance, fascinate, overjoy, spellbind 2 *ravish a woman*: abuse, assault, assault sexually, defile, rape, violate

ravishing *adj* alluring, beautiful, bewitching, charming, dazzling, delightful, enchanting, enthralling, gorgeous, lovely, radiant, seductive, stunning

raw *adj* 1 *raw vegetables*: fresh, uncooked 2 *raw materials*: crude, natural, rough, unfinished, unprepared, unprocessed, unrefined, untreated 3 *raw emotion*: bare, basic, blunt, brutal, candid, frank, harsh, naked, plain, realistic 4 *raw skin*: abraded, bloody, chafed, excoriated *formal*, exposed, grazed, open, scraped, scratched, sensitive, sore, tender 5 *a raw morning*: biting, bitter, bleak, chill, chilly, cold, damp, freezing, nippy, piercing, wet 6 *a raw recruit*: callow, green, ignorant, immature, inexperienced, naïve, new, unpractised, unskilled, untrained, untutored, wet behind the ears *colloq*
🗷 1 cooked, done 2 processed, refined, treated 5 warm 6 experienced, skilled

ray *n* 1 *a ray of light*: beam, flash, flicker, gleam, glimmer, glint, shaft, streak, stream, twinkle 2 *a ray of hope*: flicker, glimmer, glint, hint, indication, spark, suggestion, trace, twinkle

raze *v* bulldoze, demolish, destroy, fell, flatten, knock down, level, pull down, ruin, tear down

re *prep* about, concerning, on the subject of, regarding, with reference to, with regard to

reach *v* 1 *reached the end of the road*: arrive at, come to, get to, hit *colloq*, make, make it to 2 *the death toll could reach over 100*: amount to, come to, hit *colloq* 3 *reach a solution*: achieve, arrive at, attain, come to 4 *tried to reach his hand*: contact, extend to, grasp, hit, hold, strike, touch 5 *her hair reaches to her waist*: come down/up to, come to, continue, extend, go as far as, go down/up to, project, spread, stretch 6 *trying to reach you*: communicate with, contact, get hold of, get in touch with, get onto, get through to, speak to
♦ *n* 1 *just out of his reach*: distance, extension, extent, grasp, range, scope, span, spread, stretch 2 *beyond the reach of the police*: ambit, authority, command, compass, control, influence, jurisdiction, latitude, power

react *v* 1 *react to something*: acknowledge, act, answer, behave, reciprocate, reply, respond, retaliate 2 *react against something*: defy, dissent *formal*, oppose, rebel, resist, rise up against

reaction *n* 1 *his reaction to the news*: acknowledgement, answer, feedback *colloq*, reply, response 2 *a reaction against something*: backlash *colloq*, counteraction, counterbalance, kickback *colloq*, reciprocation, recoil, reflex, repercussion, retaliation, reversal, reversion

reactionary *adj* conservative, counter-revolutionary, diehard, rightist, right-wing, traditional, ultraconservative
🗷 progressive, revolutionary
♦ *n* conservative, counter-revolutionary, diehard, rightist, right-winger, traditionalist, ultraconservative
🗷 progressive, revolutionary

read *v* 1 *read a document*: browse through *colloq*, dip into *colloq*, examine, flick through *colloq*, leaf through *colloq*, look at, peruse *formal*, pore over, scan, scrutinize, skim, study, thumb through *colloq* 2 *his silence was read as defiance*: comprehend, construe *formal*, decipher, decode, interpret, understand 3 *reading a poem to the audience*: declaim, deliver, recite, speak, utter 4 *the gauge read zero*: display, indicate, measure, record, register, show
♦ *n* browsing, look, perusal, scan, scanning, scrutiny, skimming, study
▶ **read into** construe *formal*, deduce, infer, interpret, read between the lines *colloq*

readable *adj* 1 *readable handwriting*: clear, comprehensible, decipherable, easy to read, intelligible, legible, understandable 2 *a readable book*: captivating, enjoyable, entertaining, enthralling, gripping, interesting, stimulating, unputdownable *colloq*, worth reading
🗷 1 illegible 2 unreadable

readily *adv* 1 *he readily agreed*: eagerly, enthusiastically, freely, gladly, happily, unhesitatingly, willingly 2 *it can be readily done*: easily, effortlessly, promptly, quickly, rapidly, smoothly, speedily, swiftly, with ease
🗷 1 reluctantly, unwillingly 2 with difficulty

readiness *n* 1 *her readiness to help*: eagerness, gameness *colloq*, inclination, keenness, willingness 2 *in a state of readiness*: availability, fitness, handiness, preparation, preparedness **3** *readiness of wit:* aptitude, ease, facility, promptness, quickness, rapidity, skill

reading *n* **1** *a careful reading of the document:* browsing, examination, inspection, perusal, scan, scrutiny, study **2** *one reading of the situation:* deciphering, decoding, interpretation, understanding, version **3** *a poetry reading:* recital, rendering, rendition **4** *the reading on a meter:* display, figure, indication, measurement, record, register **5** *a reading from the Bible:* lesson, passage

ready *adj* **1** *ready to go:* all set, equipped, fit, fitted out, geared up *colloq,* prepared, rigged out, set, waiting **2** *everything's ready:* arranged, completed, finished, organized, prepared, set **3** *ready to help:* disposed, eager, enthusiastic, game *colloq,* happy, inclined, keen, predisposed *formal,* willing **4** *ready money:* accessible, at your fingertips *colloq,* available, convenient, handy, near, on hand, present, to hand, within reach **5** *looked ready to hit him:* about to, liable to, likely to, on the point of, on the verge of **6** *ready wit:* alert, astute, easy, immediate, perceptive, prompt, quick, rapid, resourceful, sharp, speedy, swift
🔁 **1** unprepared **3** disinclined, reluctant, unwilling **4** inaccessible, unavailable **6** slow
♦ *v* arrange, equip, order, organize, prepare, prime, set

real *adj* **1** *in the real world:* actual, concrete, existing, material, physical, substantial, tangible **2** *real leather:* authentic, bona fide, genuine **3** *the real facts:* certain, factual, genuine, positive, sure, true, veritable **4** *the real owner:* bona fide, genuine, legitimate, official, rightful, true, valid **5** *real repentance:* fervent, from the heart, genuine, heartfelt, honest, sincere, true, truthful, unaffected, unfeigned **6** *this is a real mess:* absolute, complete, right, thorough, utter
🔁 **1** imaginary, unreal **2** false, imitation **5** insincere

realism *n* **1** *his realism about the situation:* actuality, practicality, pragmatism, rationality, saneness, sanity, sensibleness **2** *the realism of the special effects:* authenticity, faithfulness, genuineness, lifelikeness, naturalness, truthfulness

realistic *adj* **1** *realistic about our goals:* businesslike, clear-sighted, commonsense, detached, down-to-earth, hard-boiled *colloq,* hard-headed, hard-nosed *colloq,* level-headed, logical, matter-of-fact, objective, practical, pragmatic, rational, sensible, unromantic, unsentimental **2** *a realistic image:* authentic, close, faithful, genuine, graphic, lifelike, natural, real, real-life, representational, true, true-to-life, truthful, vivid
🔁 **1** idealistic, impractical, irrational, unrealistic **2** fake, imitation, unrealistic

reality *n* **1** *lose touch with reality:* actuality, authenticity, certainty, corporeality *formal,* existence, fact, genuineness, materiality, real life, real world, realism, substantiality, tangibility, truth, validity **2** *the reality of the situation:* actuality, fact, truth
🔁 **1** fantasy, fiction

realization *n* **1** *gradual realization of the truth:* acceptance, appreciation, apprehension *formal,* awareness, cognizance *formal,* comprehension,

consciousness, discernment, grasp, perception, recognition, understanding **2** *the realization of her ambition:* accomplishment, achievement, completion, consummation *formal,* fulfilment, implementation **3** *the realization of over a million pounds:* clearing, earning, fetching, gain, making

realize *v* **1** *realize what is happening:* appreciate, apprehend *formal,* ascertain, become aware/conscious of, catch on, comprehend *formal,* cotton on *colloq,* discern, discover, glean, grasp, learn, perceive, recognize, take in, tumble to *colloq,* twig *colloq,* understand **2** *realize your goals:* accomplish, achieve, bring about, complete, consummate *formal,* effect *formal,* effectuate *formal,* fulfil, implement, perform **3** *the collection realized over £1000 at auction:* bring in, clear, earn, encash, fetch, gain, make, net, produce, sell for

really *adv* **1** *do you really believe him?:* absolutely, actually, categorically, certainly, genuinely, honestly, in fact, positively, sincerely, surely, truly, undoubtedly **2** *he's really angry:* exceptionally, extremely, highly, indeed, intensely, remarkably, very

realm *n* **1** *defence of the realm:* area, country, domain, empire, kingdom, land, monarchy, principality, province, region, state, territory **2** *the realm of politics:* area, department, domain, field, orbit, province, region, sphere, world

reap *v* **1** *reap a rich harvest:* garner *formal,* gather, harvest **2** *reap the rewards of hard work:* acquire, collect, derive, gain, get, obtain, realize, secure, win

rear *n* **1** *a woman with a huge rear:* backside *colloq,* behind, bottom, buttocks, posterior, rump, tail **2** *the rear of the queue:* back, end, stern, tail
🔁 **2** front
♦ *adj* back, hind, hindmost, rearmost, tail-end
🔁 front
♦ *v* **1** *rear a child:* bring up, care for, educate, foster, instruct, look after, nurse, nurture, parent, raise, train **2** *rear livestock:* breed, cultivate, grow, keep, raise **3** *the building reared above us:* loom, rise, rise up, soar, tower **4** *the horse reared its head:* elevate, hoist, lift (up), raise

rearrange *v* **1** *rearrange the ornaments:* adjust, reorder, reposition, shift **2** *rearrange plans:* adjust, alter, change, rejig, reorder, reschedule

reason *n* **1** *the reason for her behaviour:* aim, basis, cause, end, goal, ground(s), impetus, incentive, inducement, intention, motivation, motive, object, purpose, raison d'être *formal* **2** *what reason do you have for saying that?:* argument, basis, case, defence, excuse, explanation, ground(s), justification, rationale *formal,* warrant **3** *he's lost his reason:* brain, common sense, comprehension, gumption, intellect, intellectuality, intelligence, judgement, logic, mind, nous *colloq,* ratiocination *formal,* rationality, reasoning, sanity, sense, thought, understanding, wisdom, wit
♦ *v* cerebrate *formal,* cogitate *formal,* conclude, deduce, infer, ratiocinate *formal,* reckon, resolve, syllogize *formal,* think, use your brain, work out
▶ **reason with** argue with, coax, debate with, discuss with, move, persuade, plead with, remonstrate with *formal,* urge

reasonable *adj* **1** *a reasonable man:* fair, intelligent, judicious *formal,* practical, rational, sagacious *formal,* sane, sensible, sound, wise

2 *a reasonable conclusion*: credible, fair, logical, plausible, possible, rational, reasoned, sensible, sound, understandable, viable, well-advised, well-thought-out **3** *a reasonable price*: acceptable, average, fair, inexpensive, just, low, moderate, modest, satisfactory **4** *a reasonable standard of work*: acceptable, average, fair, moderate, no great shakes *colloq*, not a lot to write home about *colloq*, not to be sneezed at *colloq*, OK *colloq*, satisfactory, tolerable
🔁 **1** irrational, unreasonable **2** irrational, unreasonable **3** exorbitant, expensive **4** bad, poor

reasoned *adj* clear, judicious *formal*, logical, methodical, organized, rational, sensible, sound, systematic, well-thought-out
🔁 illogical, unsystematic

reasoning *n* **1** *powers of reasoning*: analysis, cerebration *formal*, deduction, logic, ratiocination *formal*, rationalization, supposition, thinking, thought **2** *I don't follow your reasoning*: argument, case, hypothesis, interpretation, logic, proof, rationale *formal*, supposition

reassure *v* bolster, brace, buoy up, cheer (up), comfort, encourage, hearten, inspirit *formal*, nerve, rally
🔁 alarm, unnerve

rebate *n* allowance, decrease, deduction, discount, reduction, refund, repayment

rebel *n* **1** *the rebels stormed the castle*: agitator, freedom fighter, guerrilla, insurgent, insurrectionary, mutineer, revolter, revolutionary **2** *the rebels in the party*: apostate, dissenter, heretic, nonconformist, recusant *old use*, schismatic
♦ *v* **1** *rebelling against the tyrant*: defy, disobey, dissent, mutiny, oppose, resist, revolt, riot, rise up, run riot **2** *rebel against your parents*: defy, disobey, dissent, resist **3** *rebelled at the thought of marriage*: flinch, pull back, recoil, shrink, shy away
🔁 **1** conform, obey **2** conform, obey
♦ *adj* defiant, disobedient, insubordinate *formal*, insurgent, insurrectionary, malcontent(ed), mutinous, rebellious, revolutionary

rebellion *n* **1** *the rebellion was put down by the soldiers*: civil disobedience, coup, coup d'état, insurgence, insurrection, military takeover, mutiny, resistance, revolt, revolution, riot, rising, uprising **2** *an act of rebellion*: defiance, disobedience, dissent, heresy, insubordination *formal*, opposition, resistance

rebellious *adj* **1** *the rebellious mob*: disorderly, insubordinate *formal*, insurgent, insurrectionary, mutinous, rebelling, revolutionary, rioting, seditious, ungovernable, unruly **2** *a rebellious teenager*: contumacious *formal*, defiant, disobedient, insubordinate *formal*, intractable *formal*, mutinous, obstinate, rebelling, recalcitrant *formal*, resistant, unmanageable
🔁 **1** obedient, submissive **2** obedient, submissive

rebirth *n* regeneration, reincarnation, rejuvenation, renaissance, renewal, restoration, resurrection, revitalization, revival

rebound *v* **1** *the ball rebounded*: bounce (back), recoil, return, ricochet, spring (back) **2** *his plan rebounded*: backfire, be self-defeating,

boomerang, come home to roost *colloq*, defeat itself, recoil, return, ricochet
♦ *n* backfiring, bounce, recoil, reflection, return, ricochet, spring

rebuff *v* cold-shoulder *colloq*, cut, decline, discourage, put down *colloq*, refuse, reject, repudiate, repulse, slight, snub, spurn, turn down
♦ *n* brush-off *colloq*, check, cold shoulder *colloq*, discouragement, kick in the teeth *colloq*, put-down *colloq*, refusal, rejection, repudiation, repulse, slap in the face *colloq*, slight, snub, spurning

rebuild *v* reassemble, reconstruct, refashion, remake, remodel, renovate, restore
🔁 demolish, destroy

rebuke *v* admonish *formal*, blame, castigate *formal*, censure, chide, come down on like a ton of bricks *colloq*, dress down *colloq*, give an earful *colloq*, rate, read the riot act to *colloq*, remonstrate with *formal*, reprimand, reproach, reprove, scold, tear off a strip *colloq*, tell off *colloq*, throw the book at *colloq*, tick off *colloq*, upbraid
🔁 compliment, praise
♦ *n* admonition *formal*, blame, carpeting *colloq*, castigation *formal*, censure, dressing-down *colloq*, lecture, remonstration *formal*, reprimand, reproach, reproof, scolding, telling-off *colloq*, ticking-off *colloq*
🔁 commendation, praise

rebut *v* confute *formal*, discredit, disprove, explode *colloq*, give the lie to, invalidate, negate, overturn, quash, refute

rebuttal *n* confutation *formal*, disproof, invalidation, negation, overthrow, refutation

recalcitrant *adj* contrary, contumacious *formal*, defiant, disobedient, insubordinate *formal*, intractable *formal*, obstinate, refractory *formal*, renitent *formal*, stubborn, uncontrollable, unco-operative, ungovernable, unmanageable, unruly, unsubmissive, unwilling, wayward, wilful
🔁 amenable, tractable

recall *v* **1** *recall the first time we met*: call to mind, call up, cast your mind back to, evoke, recollect, remember, reminisce about, summon up, think back to, think of **2** *recalled to hospital for tests*: call back, order back, order to return, summon (back) **3** *the order was recalled*: abrogate *formal*, annul, cancel, countermand *formal*, nullify *formal*, repeal, rescind *formal*, retract *formal*, revoke, withdraw
♦ *n* **1** *total recall*: memory, recollection, remembrance **2** *the recall of the order*: abrogation *formal*, annulment, cancellation, countermanding *formal*, nullification *formal*, recision *formal*, repeal, retraction *formal*, revocation *formal*, withdrawal

recant *v* abjure *formal*, abrogate *formal*, apostatize, deny, disavow *formal*, disclaim *formal*, disown, forswear *formal*, recall, renounce, repudiate, rescind, retract, revoke, unsay, withdraw

recantation *n* abjuration *formal*, apostasy, denial, disavowal *formal*, disclaimer *formal*, disownment, renunciation, repudiation, retractation *formal*, revocation, revoke, withdrawal

recapitulate *v* go over, recap, recount, reiterate, repeat, restate, review, run over, sum up, summarize

recede *v* **1** *recede into the distance:* go back, move away, retire, retreat, return, withdraw **2** *the storm receded:* abate *formal*, decline, decrease, diminish, drop, dwindle, ebb, fade, fall off, lessen, sink, slacken, subside, wane
🗷 **1** advance, approach **2** grow, increase

receipt *n* **1** *ask the salesman for a receipt:* acknowledgement, counterfoil, proof of purchase, slip, stub, voucher **2** *payment upon receipt of the goods:* acceptance, delivery, gaining, getting, obtaining, receiving, reception **3** *receipts are up this year:* earnings, gains, income, money received, proceeds, profits, return(s), takings, turnover

receive *v* **1** *receive a gift:* accept, acquire, collect, come by, gain, gather, get, obtain, pick up, take **2** *receive guests:* accommodate, admit, entertain, greet, let in, take in, welcome **3** *receive a nasty shock:* bear, encounter, experience, go through, meet with, suffer, sustain, undergo **4** *received the news well:* apprehend *formal*, be informed of, find out about, hear, learn about, react to, respond to
🗷 **1** donate, give

receiver *n* **1** *the receiver of the gift:* assignee, beneficiary, donee, grantee, legatee, recipient **2** *switch on the receiver:* handset, radio, tuner, wireless
🗷 **1** donor

recent *adj* contemporary, current, fresh, late, latest, modern, new, novel, present-day, up-to-date, up-to-the-minute, young
🗷 old, out of date

recently *adv* a little while back, a short time ago, freshly, in the last few days/weeks/months/years, lately, newly, not long ago, of late
🗷 long ago

receptacle *n* container, holder, repository *formal*, reservatory *formal*, vessel

reception *n* **1** *get a cool reception:* acknowledgement, greeting, reaction, recognition, response, treatment, welcome **2** *the reception of new ideas:* acceptance, admission, receipt, receiving **3** *a wedding reception:* at-home, bash *colloq*, beano *colloq*, do *colloq*, entertainment, function, gathering, get-together, party, rave-up *colloq*, shindig *colloq*, social

receptive *adj* **1** *receptive to new ideas:* accessible, accommodating, amenable, approachable, favourable, flexible, friendly, hospitable, interested, open, open to reason, open-minded, suggestible, susceptible, sympathetic, welcoming, willing **2** *receptive to treatment:* amenable, responsive, sensitive, susceptible
🗷 **1** narrow-minded, resistant **2** resistant, unresponsive

recess *n* **1** *the summer recess:* break, holiday, intermission, interval, respite, rest, time off, time out *colloq*, vacation **2** *a recess in the wall:* alcove, bay, cavity, corner, hollow, niche, nook, oriel **3** *the darkest recesses of the mind:* bowels, depths, heart, innards, interior, penetralia *formal*, reaches

recession *n* collapse, crash, decline, depression, downturn, failure, slide, slump, trough
🗷 boom, upturn

recherché *adj* **1** *recherché knowledge:* abstruse *formal*, arcane *formal*, esoteric *formal* **2** *recherché gifts:* choice, exotic, rare, refined, select
🗷 **1** commonplace **2** commonplace

recipe *n* **1** *a recipe for pumpkin soup:* directions, formula, guide, ingredients, instructions **2** *a recipe for success:* formula, means, method, prescription, procedure, process, system, technique, way

recipient *n* assignee, beneficiary, donee, grantee, legatee, receiver
🗷 donor, giver

reciprocal *adj* complementary, correlative *formal*, corresponding, equivalent, exchanged, give-and-take, interchangeable, interdependent, mutual, requited, returned

reciprocate *v* correspond, do the same *colloq*, equal, exchange, give as good as you get *colloq*, give in return, interchange, match, repay, reply, requite *formal*, respond, return, swap, trade

recital *n* **1** *a music recital:* concert, performance, show **2** *a recital of his grievances:* account, description, narration, report, telling **3** *the recital of a mantra:* declamation *formal*, reading, recitation, rendering, rendition, repetition

recitation *n* **1** *the recitation of a poem:* narration, reading, recital, rendering, telling **2** *perform a recitation:* monologue, party piece, piece, poem, story, tale, verse **3** *a recitation from the Bible:* passage, piece, reading, verse

recite *v* **1** *recite poetry:* articulate, declaim *formal*, deliver, perform, relate, repeat, say aloud, speak **2** *recite a list of names:* enumerate, itemize, rattle off, recount, reel off, repeat, tell

reckless *adj* careless, daredevil, devil-may-care, foolhardy, hasty, heedless, ill-advised, imprudent, incautious, indiscreet, irresponsible, madcap, mindless, negligent, precipitate *formal*, rash, tearaway, thoughtless, wild
🗷 careful, cautious, prudent, wary

recklessness *n* carelessness, foolhardiness, heedlessness, imprudence, incaution, irresponsibility, irresponsibleness, madness, mindlessness, negligence, rashness, thoughtlessness
🗷 carefulness, caution, prudence

reckon *v* **1** *I reckon he'll come:* assume, believe, conjecture *formal*, fancy, guess, imagine, suppose, surmise *formal*, think **2** *reckoned to be the best:* appraise *formal*, assess, consider, deem *formal*, esteem, estimate, evaluate, gauge, judge, look upon, rate, regard, think of, value **3** *reckon your total income:* add up, calculate, compute, count, enumerate, figure out, number, tally, total, work out
▶ **reckon on 1** *I didn't reckon on this:* anticipate, bargain for, expect, figure on, foresee, plan for, take into account **2** *reckoning on your help:* bank on, count on, depend on, hope for, rely on, take for granted, trust in
▶ **reckon with 1** *didn't reckon with his interference:* anticipate, bargain for, consider, expect, foresee, plan for, take into account **2** *a lot to reckon with:* consider, cope, deal, face, handle, treat

reckoning *n* **1** *by my reckoning:* addition, calculation, computation, enumeration, estimate, number, score, tally, total, working-out **2** *pay the* *reckoning*: account, bill, charge, due, paying, payment, score, settlement **3** *a reckoning of his work*: appraisal *formal*, assessment, estimation, evaluation, judgement, opinion **4** *the day of reckoning*: damnation, doom, judgement, punishment, retribution

reclaim *v* **1** *reclaim an inheritance*: claim back, get back, recover, regain, reinstate, retrieve, take back **2** *reclaim the wetlands*: recapture, recover, regain, regenerate, restore, retrieve, salvage, take back **3** *reclaim lost souls*: redeem, rescue

recline *v* lean back, lie (down), loll, lounge, repose *formal*, rest, sprawl, stretch out

recluse *n* anchoress, anchoret, anchorite, ascetic, eremite, hermit, loner, monk, solitaire, solitarian, solitary, stylite

reclusive *adj* anchoritic, ascetic, cloistered, eremitic, hermitical, isolated, monastic, recluse, retiring, secluded, sequestered *formal*, solitary, withdrawn

recognition *n* **1** *recognition of an old friend*: detection, discovery, identification, knowing, placing, recall, recollection, remembrance, spotting **2** *his recognition of the truth*: admission, awareness, cognizance *formal*, confession, consciousness, knowledge, perception, realization, understanding **3** *the recognition of the treaty*: acceptance, acknowledgement, admittance, allowing, approval, endorsement, granting, sanction, validation **4** *receive recognition for your work*: appreciation, gratitude, honour, respect, reward, salute, thankfulness

recognize *v* **1** *recognized him at once*: call to mind, identify, know, not miss, not mistake, notice, perceive, pick out, place, recall, recollect, remember, see, spot, tell **2** *recognize your faults*: accept, acknowledge, admit, allow, appreciate, apprehend *formal*, be aware of, be conscious of, concede, confess, discern, grant, own, perceive, realize, understand **3** *recognize a qualification*: accept, acknowledge, admit, allow, approve, endorse, grant, sanction, validate **4** *recognize someone's contribution*: appreciate, be thankful for, honour, respect, salute, show your gratitude/thankfulness

recoil *v* **1** *recoil in disgust*: falter, flinch, jump back, move back, quail, react, shrink, shy away, spring back **2** *the gun recoiled in his face*: backfire, kick, misfire, rebound, spring back ◆ *n* **1** *the powerful recoil of the rifle*: kick, rebound **2** *a recoil against an oppressive regime*: backlash, reaction, repercussion

recollect *v* call to mind, cast your mind back, recall, remember, reminisce

recollection *n* memory, (mental) impression, recall, remembrance, reminiscence

recommend *v* **1** *I recommend that you see a doctor*: advance, advise, counsel, exhort *formal*, propose, suggest, urge **2** *recommend a good plumber*: advocate, commend, endorse, plug *colloq*, propose, put in a good word for, suggest, vouch for **3** *recommended for promotion*: approve, commend, endorse, praise, propose, put forward ◼ **2** disapprove **3** disapprove

recommendation *n* **1** *the doctor's recommendation was rest*: advice, counsel, exhortations *formal*, guidance, proposal,

suggestion, tip, urging **2** *his personal recommendation*: advocacy, approval, blessing, commendation, endorsement, good word, plug *colloq*, praise, reference, sanction, special mention, testimonial ◼ **2** disapproval

recompense *n* amends, compensation, damages, guerdon *formal*, indemnification, pay, payment, remuneration, reparation, repayment, requital, restitution, satisfaction ◆ *v* compensate, guerdon *formal*, indemnify, pay, redress, reimburse, remunerate, repay, requite, satisfy

reconcile *v* **1** *be reconciled after an argument*: become friends again *colloq*, bury the hatchet *colloq*, forgive and forget *colloq*, make (your) peace, make up *colloq*, reunite, shake hands *colloq* **2** *reconcile a couple*: appease, bring together, conciliate, mollify, pacify, placate, propitiate *formal*, put on friendly terms, reunite **3** *reconcile different aims*: accord *formal*, harmonize, resolve, settle, square **4** *reconcile yourself to an unpleasant situation*: accept, come to accept, face up to, resign yourself to, submit to ◼ **2** alienate, estrange

reconciliation *n* **1** *a reconciliation between the couple*: accord *formal*, agreement, appeasement, conciliation, détente, mollification, pacification, peace, propitiation *formal*, rapprochement, reunion **2** *the reconciliation of two opposing aims*: accommodation, adjustment, compromise, harmonizing, harmony, resolution, settlement, squaring ◼ **1** estrangement, separation

recondite *adj* abstruse *formal*, arcane *formal*, concealed, dark, deep, esoteric *formal*, hidden, mysterious, mystical, obscure, profound, secret ◼ simple, straightforward

recondition *v* fix, overhaul, refurbish, remodel, renew, renovate, repair, restore, revamp

reconnaissance *n* examination, exploration, inspection, investigation, observation, patrol, probe, recce *colloq*, reconnoitring, scan, scouting, scrutiny, search, survey

reconnoitre *v* check out *colloq*, examine, explore, inspect, investigate, observe, patrol, recce *colloq*, scan, scrutinize, see how the land lies *colloq*, see the lie of the land *colloq*, spy out, survey

reconsider *v* have second thoughts, reassess, re-examine, rethink, review, revise, think better of, think over, think twice

reconstruct *v* reassemble, rebuild, recreate, redo, re-establish, refashion, reform, regenerate, remake, remodel, renovate, reorganize, restore, revamp

record *n* **1** *keep your records up-to-date*: account, annals, archives, chart, chronicle, data, diary, document(s), dossier, entry, file, history, journal, log, logbook, memoir, memorandum, memorial, minutes, notes, register, report **2** *there's no record of the transaction*: documentation, evidence, note, testimony, trace **3** *his Elvis records*: album, disc, LP, recording, release, single, vinyl *colloq* **4** *break the record*: best performance, fastest time, furthest distance, personal best, world record **5** *he has an unblemished record*: background, career, curriculum vitae, history, previous performance

♦ *v* **1** *record all the information:* catalogue, chart, chronicle, document, enter, inscribe, keep, list, log, minute, note, preserve, put down, put on record, register, report, take down, transcribe, write down **2** *record a concert:* cut, make a recording of, tape, tape-record, video, videotape **3** *the gauge records electrical activity:* display, indicate, read, register, show

recorder *n* annalist, archivist, chronicler, chronologer, clerk, diarist, historian, registrar, score-keeper, scorer, scribe, secretary, stenographer

recording

Types of recording include:
album, audiotape, cassette, CD, compact disc, digital recording, disc, DVD (digital versatile disc), EP (extended play), 45, gramophone record, long-playing record, LP, magnetic tape, mono recording, record, 78, single, stereo recording, tape, tape-recording, tele-recording, video, videocassette, video disc, videotape, vinyl *colloq*

recount *v* depict, describe, detail, impart, narrate, portray, recite, rehearse, relate, repeat, report, tell, unfold

recoup *v* get back, make good, recover, regain, repossess, retrieve, win back

recourse *n* alternative, choice, option, possibility, refuge, remedy, resort, way out

recover *v* **1** *recover from illness:* be on the mend *colloq*, bounce back *colloq*, come round, convalesce, feel better, feel yourself again, gain strength, get back on your feet *colloq*, get better, get over, get stronger, get well, heal, improve, mend, pick up, pull through *colloq*, rally, recuperate, respond to treatment, revive, turn the corner *colloq* **2** *recover lost property:* get back, recapture, reclaim, recoup, regain, repossess, restore, retake, retrieve, win back
Fa **1** worsen **2** forfeit, lose

recovery *n* **1** *make a complete recovery:* convalescence, healing, improvement, mending, rally, rallying, recuperation, rehabilitation, restoration, revival, upturn **2** *the recovery of the economy:* amelioration, improvement, rallying, restoration, revival **3** *the recovery of his fortune:* recapture, reclamation, recouping, regaining, repossession, retrieval, salvage
Fa **1** worsening **2** worsening **3** forfeit, loss

recreation *n* **1** *no time for recreation:* amusement, distraction, diversion, enjoyment, entertainment, fun, leisure, pastime, play, pleasure, relaxation, sport **2** *her favourite recreation is swimming:* diversion, entertainment, game, hobby, leisure activity, leisure pursuit, pastime, sport

recrimination *n* accusation, bickering, counter-attack, countercharge, quarrel, retort

recruit *v* **1** *recruit a team of helpers:* acquire, assemble, engage, enlist, gather, muster, obtain, procure *formal*, put together, raise, take on **2** *recruit soldiers:* conscript, draft, enlist, enrol, levy, mobilize, muster, sign up
♦ *n* **1** *the latest recruit:* apprentice, beginner, convert, greenhorn *colloq*, initiate, learner, new entrant, newcomer, novice, rookie *colloq*, tiro, trainee **2** *an army recruit:* conscript, draftee

rectify *v* adjust, ameliorate *formal*, amend, better, correct, cure, emend *formal*, fix, improve, make good, mend, put right, redress *formal*, reform, remedy, repair, right, set right

rectitude *n* **1** *a man of rectitude:* correctness, decency, goodness, honesty, honour, incorruptibility, integrity, irreproachability, justice, morality, probity *formal*, righteousness, scrupulousness, uprightness, virtue **2** *the rectitude of the statement:* accuracy, correctness, exactness, precision, soundness

recumbent *adj* horizontal, leaning, lounging, lying down, lying flat, prone, prostrate, reclining, resting, sprawling, supine *formal*
Fa erect, upright

recuperate *v* be on the mend *colloq*, bounce back *colloq*, convalesce, get back on your feet *colloq*, get better, get stronger, get well, improve, mend, pick up, pull through, rally, recover, regain your strength, revive, turn the corner *colloq*
Fa worsen

recur *v* happen again, persist, reappear, repeat itself, return

recurrent *adj* chronic, continual, cyclical, frequent, habitual, intermittent, periodic, persistent, recurring, regular, repeated, repetitive

recycle *v* reclaim, recover, reprocess, re-use, salvage, save

red *adj* **1** *red lipstick:* cherry, crimson, maroon, reddish, rose, ruby, russet, scarlet, vermilion **2** *red eyes:* bloodshot, inflamed **3** *a red face:* florid, flushed, glowing, rosy, rubicund *formal*, ruddy, rufescent *technical* **4** *red with humiliation:* blushing, embarrassed, flushed, shamefaced **5** *red hair:* auburn, carroty, chestnut, ginger, Titian **6** *accused of being Red:* Bolshevik, communist, leftist, revolutionary, socialist

red-blooded *adj* hearty, lusty, manly, robust, strong, vigorous, virile

redden *v* blush, colour, crimson, flush, go red

reddish *adj* **1** *a reddish complexion:* pink, red, rosy, rubicund *formal*, ruddy, rufescent *technical*, rufous *formal* **2** *reddish hair:* ginger, red, rufescent *technical*, rufous *formal*, russet, sandy

redeem *v* **1** *redeem a voucher:* cash (in), change, convert, exchange, give in exchange, trade, trade in **2** *redeem a pawned item:* buy back, get back, reclaim, recoup, recover, regain, repossess, repurchase, retrieve **3** *I redeemed my earlier mistake:* atone for, compensate for, make up for, offset, outweigh **4** *Christ redeems sinners:* absolve, acquit, deliver, discharge, emancipate, expiate *formal*, free, liberate, ransom, release, remove guilt from, rescue, save, set free

redemption *n* **1** *the redemption of a coupon:* exchange, trade-in **2** *the redemption of a pawned item:* reclamation, recovery, repossession, repurchase, retrieval **3** *make redemption for a sin:* amends, atonement, compensation, reparation **4** *Christ's redemption of sinners:* deliverance, emancipation, expiation, freedom, liberation, ransom, release, rescue, salvation

redolent *adj* **1** *redolent of that era:* evocative, remindful, reminiscent, suggestive **2** *the air was* *redolent with incense:* aromatic, fragrant, odorous *formal*, perfumed, scented, sweet-smelling

redoubtable *adj* fearsome, formidable, mighty, powerful, strong, terrible

redound *v* conduce *formal*, contribute, effect *formal*, ensue, reflect, result, tend

redress *v* 1 *redress a wrong:* avenge, make compensation for, put right, recompense, rectify, remedy, requite, right 2 *redress the balance:* adjust, amend, balance, correct, regulate
♦ *n* 1 *no redress for the harm they suffered:* aid, assistance, atonement, compensation, help, indemnification, justice, payment, recompense, relief, reparation, requital, restitution, satisfaction 2 *a redress of the balance of power:* adjustment, balance, correction, regulation

reduce *v* 1 *reduce the size/amount of something:* curtail, decrease, deplete, downsize, lessen, lower, make less, make smaller, minimize, moderate, shorten, shrink, trim 2 *reduce the effect of something:* curtail, decrease, dilute, diminish, impair, lessen, make less, minimize, mitigate *formal*, moderate, take the edge off, weaken 3 *people reduced to the status of animals:* bring down, degrade, demote, downgrade, humble, humiliate, lower 4 *reduced to begging for money:* drive, force 5 *reduce prices:* cut, decrease, discount, halve, knock down, lower, rebate, slash
🔁 1 boost, increase, raise 2 boost, increase, raise

reduction *n* 1 *a reduction in size:* abbreviation, compression, contraction, curtailment, cut, cutback, decline, decrease, deduction, devaluation, diminution *formal*, downsizing, drop, fall, lessening, limitation, loss, moderation, narrowing, restriction, shortening, shrinkage, weakening 2 *tax reductions:* allowance, concession, discount, discounting, rebate
🔁 1 enlargement, increase, rise 2 increase, rise

redundancy *n* 1 *employees facing redundancy:* boot *colloq*, discharge, dismissal, elbow *colloq*, expulsion, firing *colloq*, laying-off, marching-orders, notice, papers *colloq*, push *colloq*, removal, sack *colloq*, sacking *colloq* 2 *a redundancy of material:* excess, superfluity, surplus 3 *the redundancy of his language:* pleonasm *technical*, prolixity *formal*, repetition, tautology, verbosity *formal*, wordiness
🔁 1 appointment, hiring

redundant *adj* 1 *redundant workers:* dismissed, fired *colloq*, jobless, laid off, out of work, sacked *colloq*, unemployed 2 *redundant equipment:* excess, extra, inessential, superfluous, supernumerary *formal*, surplus, unnecessary, unneeded, unwanted 3 *redundant language:* padded, periphrastic *formal*, pleonastic *technical*, repetitious, tautological, verbose, wordy
🔁 2 essential, necessary, required 3 concise

reef *n* cay, key, ridge, sandbank, sandbar

reek *v* hum *colloq*, pong *colloq*, smell, stink
♦ *n* effluvium *formal*, fetor *formal*, fume(s), malodour *formal*, mephitis *formal*, odour, pong *colloq*, smell, stench, stink

reel *v* 1 *she reeled back:* falter, lurch, pitch, rock, totter, waver, wobble 2 *the room reeled about him:* revolve, roll, spin, swim, swirl, twirl, wheel, whirl

refer *v* 1 *refer to an earlier incident:* allude, bring up, cite, hint at, mention, speak of, touch on

2 *refer to a catalogue:* consult, look at, look up, resort to, turn to 3 *be referred to a specialist:* commit, deliver, hand on, pass on, remit *formal*, send, transfer 4 *refer someone to a textbook:* direct, guide, point 5 *the term refers to a computer process:* apply, be relevant, belong, concern, pertain *formal*, relate

referee *n* adjudicator, arbitrator, judge, mediator, ref *colloq*, umpire
♦ *v* adjudicate, arbitrate, judge, mediate, umpire

reference *n* 1 *make no reference to an incident:* allusion, hint, mention, remark 2 *references are listed at the foot of the page:* authority, citation, footnote, instance, note, quotation, source 3 *check someone's references:* character reference, credentials, endorsement, recommendation, testimonial 4 *what is your call in reference to?:* applicability, bearing, connection, pertinence *formal*, regard, relation, respect

referendum *n* plebiscite, poll, survey, vote

refine *v* 1 *refine a substance:* clarify, cleanse, clear, distil, filter, process, purify, sift, strain, treat 2 *refine a process:* elaborate, hone, improve, perfect, polish

refined *adj* 1 *refined manners:* civil, civilized, courtly, cultivated, cultured, elegant, genteel, gentlemanly, gracious, ladylike, polished, polite, urbane, well-bred, well-mannered 2 *refined tastes:* cultivated, cultured, delicate, discriminating, exact, fine, precise, sophisticated, stylish, subtle 3 *refined oil:* clear, distilled, filtered, processed, purified, treated
🔁 1 coarse, rude, vulgar 2 coarse, vulgar

refinement *n* 1 *refinements to the technique:* addition, alteration, amelioration *formal*, amendment, improvement, modification 2 *a man of refinement and taste:* breeding, civility, cultivation, culture, discrimination, finesse, gentility, good manners, grace, polish, sophistication, style, taste, urbanity
🔁 1 deterioration 2 coarseness, vulgarity

reflect *v* 1 *reflect an image:* echo, imitate, mirror, reproduce, send back, throw back 2 *her expression reflected her distaste:* bespeak *formal*, communicate, demonstrate, depict, display, exhibit, express, indicate, manifest *formal*, portray, reveal, show 3 *reflect on your future:* brood, cerebrate *formal*, cogitate *formal*, consider, contemplate, deliberate, dwell, meditate, mull (over), muse, ponder, ruminate *formal*, think 4 *it reflects on the school:* discredit, disgrace, give a bad name to, put in a bad light, tarnish

reflection *n* 1 *a reflection in a mirror:* echo, image, likeness, mirror image 2 *a reflection of his true feelings:* demonstration, display, expression, impression, indication, manifestation *formal*, portrayal, view 3 *time spent in reflection:* cerebration *formal*, cogitation *formal*, consideration, contemplation, deliberation, meditation, musing, rumination *formal*, study, thinking, thought 4 *reflections on life:* belief, feeling(s), idea, impression, meditation, musing, opinion, thinking, thought, view, viewpoint 5 *our policy is no reflection on her ability:* aspersion *formal*, blame, criticism, discredit, disgrace, disrepute, reproach, shame, slur

reflective *adj* absorbed, cogitating *formal*, contemplative, deliberative, dreamy,

meditative, pensive, pondering, reasoning, ruminative *formal*, thoughtful

reflex *adj* automatic, involuntary, knee-jerk *colloq*, natural, spontaneous, uncontrollable, unwilled, without thinking

reform *v* ameliorate *formal*, amend, better, change, correct, improve, mend, rebuild, reconstitute, reconstruct, rectify, refashion, regenerate, rehabilitate, remodel, renovate, reorganize, repair, restore, revamp, revise, revolutionize, shake up *colloq*
♦ *n* amendment, betterment, change, correction, improvement, rebuilding, reconstruction, rectification, rehabilitation, remodelling, renovation, reorganization, restoration, revision, shake-up *colloq*

reformer *n* agent of change, innovator, modernizer, new broom *colloq*, progressive, revolutionary

refractory *adj* contentious, contumacious *formal*, defiant, difficult, disobedient, disputatious *formal*, headstrong, intractable *formal*, mulish, obstinate, perverse, recalcitrant *formal*, resistant, restive *formal*, stubborn, uncontrollable, unco-operative, unmanageable, unruly, wilful
F3 co-operative, malleable, obedient

refrain[1] *v* abstain *formal*, avoid, cease *formal*, desist *formal*, do without, eschew *formal*, forbear *formal*, give up, leave off, quit *colloq*, renounce, stop

refrain[2] *n* burden, chorus, melody, response, song, strain, tune

refresh *v* 1 *a shower will refresh you*: brace, breathe new life into *colloq*, cool, energize, enliven, fortify *formal*, freshen, invigorate, reanimate, reinvigorate, rejuvenate, renew, restore, revitalize, revive, revivify *formal*, stimulate 2 *refresh your memory*: activate, jog, prod, prompt, remind, stimulate, stir
F3 1 exhaust, tire

refreshing *adj* 1 *a refreshing bath*: bracing, cool, energizing, invigorating, reviving, stimulating 2 *a refreshing change from routine*: different, fresh, new, novel, original

refreshment *n* invigoration, reanimation, reinvigoration, renewal, restoration, revitalization, revival, stimulation

refreshments *n* aliment, drinks, eats *colloq*, elevenses, food, grub *slang*, nosh *slang*, provisions, snacks, sustenance, titbits

refrigerate *v* chill, cool, freeze, keep cold
F3 heat, warm

refuge *n* 1 *find refuge*: asylum, protection, sanctuary, security, shelter 2 *get to a refuge*: bolthole, harbour, haven, hide-away, hideout, island, place of safety, resort, retreat, sanctuary, shelter

refugee *n* displaced person, émigré, escapee, exile, fugitive, runaway, stateless person

refulgent *adj* beaming, bright, brilliant, gleaming, glistening, glittering, irradiant *formal*, lambent *formal*, lustrous *formal*, radiant, resplendent *formal*, shining

refund *v* give back, pay back, rebate, reimburse, repay, restore, return
♦ *n* rebate, reimbursement, repayment, return

refurbish *v* do up *colloq*, mend, overhaul, recondition, redecorate, re-equip, refit, remodel, renovate, repair, restore, revamp

refusal *n* denial, negation, no, rebuff, rejection, repudiation, spurning, turning-down
F3 acceptance, agreement

refuse[1] *v* 1 *refuse to go*: decline *formal*, deny, dig your heels in *colloq*, draw the line at *colloq*, knock back *colloq*, pass up *colloq*, rebuff, reject, repel, repudiate, say no, shake your head *colloq*, spurn, turn down 2 *refuse permission*: decline *formal*, deny, say no, withhold
F3 1 accept, agree 2 allow, grant, permit

refuse[2] *n* debris, draff, dregs, dross, garbage, junk, litter, offscum, rubbish, scoria *technical*, scum, trash, waste

refutation *n* confutation *formal*, disproof, elenchus *technical*, negation, overthrow, rebuttal

refute *v* confute *formal*, counter, deny (strongly), discredit, disprove, give the lie to, negate, overthrow, rebut, silence

regain *v* 1 *regain lost property*: get back, recapture, reclaim, recoup, recover, repossess, retake, retrieve, take back, win back 2 *he regained his car and drove off*: get back to, return to

regal *adj* imperial, kingly, lordly, majestic, noble, princely, queenly, royal, sovereign, stately

regale *v* 1 *regaled us with stories*: amuse, captivate, delight, divert, entertain, fascinate 2 *regaled us with food and drink*: feast, ply, refresh, serve

regard *v* 1 *regarded as an expert*: appraise *formal*, believe, consider, deem *formal*, estimate, gauge, imagine, judge, rate, suppose, think, value 2 *regarded him closely*: behold *formal*, contemplate, eye, gaze at, give the once-over *colloq*, look at, look upon, observe, scrutinize, see, view, watch 3 *didn't regard his warning*: bear in mind, follow, heed, listen to, note, observe, pay attention to, take into account/consideration, take notice of
♦ *n* 1 *have the highest regard for her*: admiration, affection, approbation *formal*, approval, deference, esteem *formal*, honour, love, respect 2 *no regard for other people's feelings*: attention, care, concern, consideration, heed, notice, respect, sympathy 3 *in this regard*: aspect, detail, matter, particular, point, subject 4 *send her my regards*: best wishes, compliments, good wishes, greetings, respects, salutations
F3 1 contempt, disregard 2 contempt, disregard

regardful *adj* 1 *regardful of the consequences*: attentive, aware, careful, circumspect *formal*, considerate, heedful, mindful, thoughtful 2 *a regardful bow*: attentive, dutiful, respectful
F3 1 heedless, inattentive, regardless

regarding *prep* about, apropos, as regards, as to, concerning, in connection with, in regard to, in relation to, on the subject of, re, with reference to, with regard to, with respect to

regardless *adj* disregarding, heedless, inattentive, indifferent, neglectful, negligent, unconcerned, unmindful
F3 attentive, heedful, mindful
♦ *adv* anyhow, anyway, at any price/cost *colloq*,

come what may, despite everything, nevertheless, no matter what, nonetheless

regenerate *v* **1** *regenerate spiritually:* inspirit *formal*, invigorate, reawaken, refresh, reinvigorate, rejuvenate, rekindle, renew, restore, revive, revivify *formal*, uplift **2** *regenerate the city:* reconstitute, reconstruct, re-establish, renew, renovate, restore

regeneration *n* **1** *spiritual regeneration:* reinvigoration, rejuvenation, renewal **2** *regeneration of the area:* reconstitution, reconstruction, re-establishment, renewal, renovation, restoration **3** *regeneration of a limb:* homomorphosis *formal*, reproduction

regime *n* administration, command, control, direction, establishment, government, leadership, management, reign, rule, system

regiment *n* army, band, battery, body, brigade, cohort, company, crew, group, platoon, squadron

regimented *adj* controlled, disciplined, methodical, ordered, organized, regulated, standardized, strict, systematic, systematized ⊠ disorganized, free, lax

region *n* **1** *inhabitants of a region:* division, expanse, land, neighbourhood, part, place, section, sector, terrain **2** *beyond the region of our knowledge:* ambit, field, orbit, range, scope, sphere, world

regional *adj* district, local, localized, parochial, provincial, sectional, zonal ⊠ international, national, worldwide

register *n* almanac, annals, archives, catalogue, chronicle, diary, directory, file(s), index, journal, ledger, list, listing, log, record, roll, roster, schedule
♦ *v* **1** *register a birth:* catalogue, chronicle, enter, inscribe, list, log, mark, note, put down, put in writing, record, set down, take down **2** *register on a course:* check in, enlist, enrol, enter, sign on **3** *registered his disapproval:* betray, demonstrate, display, exhibit, express, indicate, manifest *formal*, reveal, show **4** *register a measurement:* display, indicate, read, record, show

registrar *n* administrator, annalist, archivist, cataloguer, chronicler, clerk, official, protocolist, recorder, secretary

regress *v* backslide, degenerate, deteriorate, ebb, lapse, recede, relapse, retreat, retrocede *formal*, retrogress *formal*, return, revert, wane ⊠ progress

regret *v* **1** *regret my hasty action:* be sorry about, deplore, feel sorry about, repent, rue, weep over, wish that you had not done **2** *regret lost opportunities:* be disappointed about, be distressed about, bemoan, grieve over, lament, mourn, weep over
♦ *n* **1** *regrets about leaving him:* bitterness, compunction *formal*, contrition, penitence, remorse, repentance, self-reproach, shame **2** *expressed her regret at his death:* disappointment, grief, sorrow

regretful *adj* **1** *regretful about what he did:* apologetic, ashamed, conscience-stricken, contrite, penitent, remorseful, repentant, rueful, sorry **2** *regretful about lost chances:* disappointed, sad, sorrowful

⊠ **1** impenitent, unashamed

---

regretful or *regrettable*? *Regretful* means 'full of regret'. *Regrettable* means 'causing regret': *It is regrettable that you have behaved so foolishly, and I feel regretful that I must now ask you to leave.*

---

regrettable *adj* deplorable, disappointing, disgraceful, distressing, ill-advised, lamentable, reprehensible *formal*, sad, shameful, sorry, unfortunate, unhappy, unlucky, upsetting, wrong ⊠ fortunate, happy

regular *adj* **1** *regular exercise:* daily, everyday, frequent, habitual **2** *our regular routine:* common, commonplace, customary, daily, established, everyday, habitual, normal, ordinary, routine, typical, usual **3** *looks just like a regular phone:* average, conventional, normal, ordinary, standard **4** *follow the regular method:* approved, classic, conventional, correct, established, official, orthodox, proper, standard, time-honoured **5** *regular appointments:* daily, fixed, frequent, hourly, monthly, periodic, recurring, regular as clockwork *colloq*, set, weekly, yearly **6** *set out in regular rows:* balanced, even, evenly spread, fixed, flat, level, orderly, set, symmetrical, uniform **7** *music with a regular beat:* consistent, constant, even, fixed, rhythmic, set, smooth, steady, unchanging, uniform, unvarying **8** *a very regular procedure:* consistent, fixed, methodical, orderly, set, steady, systematic, unchanging, uniform, unvarying, well-organized

⊠ **2** unconventional, unusual **3** unusual **4** unconventional, unusual **5** intermittent, irregular **6** irregular **7** intermittent, irregular **8** irregular

regulate *v* **1** *regulate the industry:* administer, arrange, conduct, control, direct, govern, guide, handle, manage, monitor, order, organize, oversee, rule, run, superintend, supervise **2** *regulate the controls:* adjust, balance, control, moderate, set, synchronize, tune

regulation *n* **1** *follow the regulations:* act, by-law, command, commandment, decree, dictate, dictum, directive, edict, law, order, ordinance, precept, procedure, pronouncement, requirement, rule, ruling, statute **2** *the regulation of the stock market:* administration, control, direction, guidance, management, rule, superintendence, supervision
♦ *adj* accepted, customary, fixed, mandatory *formal*, normal, obligatory, official, orthodox, prescribed *formal*, required, set, standard, statutory, usual

regurgitate *v* **1** *regurgitate food:* bring up, disgorge *formal*, puke *colloq*, spew, throw up *colloq*, vomit **2** *regurgitate facts:* recapitulate, reiterate *formal*, repeat, restate, say/tell again

rehabilitate *v* **1** *rehabilitated into the community:* normalize, re-establish, reinstate, reintegrate **2** *rehabilitate a criminal:* redeem, reform **3** *rehabilitate urban areas:* adjust, clear, convert, mend, rebuild, recondition, reconstitute, reconstruct, re-establish, reinstate, renew, renovate, restore, save

rehash *n* rearrangement, rejig, rejigging, reshuffle, restatement, reworking, rewrite
♦ *v* alter, change, rearrange, refashion, rejig, rejigger, reshuffle, restate, rework, rewrite

rehearsal *n* drill, dry run *colloq*, dummy run *colloq*, exercise, practice, preparation, reading, recital, run-through, trial run

rehearse *v* **1** *rehearse a new song:* go over, practise, prepare, run through, try out **2** *rehearsing the dancers:* drill, prepare, train **3** *rehearsed his reasons for leaving:* enumerate, go over, recite, recount, relate, repeat

reign *v* **1** *he reigned for forty years:* be in charge, be in command, be in control, be in government, be in power, be king/queen, command, govern, rule, sit on the throne **2** *silence reigns:* be present, exist, hold sway, obtain *formal*, occur, predominate, prevail
♦ *n* ascendancy *formal*, command, dominion, empire, government, monarchy, rule, sovereignty, supremacy, sway

reimburse *v* compensate, give back, indemnify, pay back, recompense, refund, remunerate, repay, restore, return

rein *n* **1** *a horse's reins:* brake, bridle, curb, harness, restraint **2** *a rein on spending:* brake, check, control, curb, restraint, restriction
♦ *v* **1** *rein a horse in:* bridle, check, halt, hold back, restrain, stop **2** *rein in expenditure:* arrest, check, control, curb, halt, limit, restrain, restrict, stop

reinforce *v* **1** *reinforce a roof:* brace, buttress, fortify *formal*, harden, prop, shore, stay, steel, stiffen, strengthen, support, toughen **2** *reinforce troops:* augment, strengthen, support **3** *reinforce a point:* consolidate, emphasize, stress, underline
🔁 **1** undermine, weaken

reinforcement *n* **1** *reinforcements on the doors:* brace, buttress, fortification *formal*, prop, shore, stay, support **2** *the reinforcement of the police:* addition, amplification, augmentation *formal*, enlargement, increase, strengthening, supplement **3** *the reinforcement of our goal:* emphasis, stress, underlining **4** *send reinforcements:* additional soldiers/police officers, auxiliaries, back-up, help, reserves, supplementaries, support

reinstate *v* bring back, reappoint, recall, re-establish, reinstall, replace, restore, return

reinstatement *n* bringing back, recall, re-establishment, replacement, restoration, return

reiterate *v* emphasize, iterate *formal*, recapitulate, repeat, resay, restate, retell, stress

reject *v* **1** *reject a proposal:* decline, deny, disallow, exclude, have nothing to do with *colloq*, not have anything to do with *colloq*, not touch with a barge pole *colloq*, refuse, repudiate, say no to, spurn, take a raincheck on *colloq*, turn down, turn your nose up at *colloq*, veto, wash your hands of *colloq* **2** *reject a person:* brush off *colloq*, despise, forsake *formal*, give the cold shoulder to *colloq*, have nothing to do with *colloq*, jilt, not have anything to do with *colloq*, rebuff, renounce *formal*, repel, say no to, spurn, turn down, turn your back on *colloq*, wash your hands of *colloq* **3** *faulty products are rejected by the inspectors:* cast off, discard, eliminate, jettison, scrap, set aside, throw away

🔁 **1** accept, agree to **2** accept **3** choose, select
♦ *n* **1** *factory rejects:* cast-off, discard, second **2** *a bunch of rejects and misfits:* failure, outcast

rejection *n* **1** *the rejection of the plan:* declining, denial, discarding, dismissal, elimination, exclusion, jettisoning, refusal, repudiation, turning-down, veto **2** *his humiliating rejection:* brush-off *colloq*, cold shoulder *colloq*, Dear John letter *colloq*, rebuff, refusal, renunciation *formal*, turning-down
🔁 **1** acceptance, choice, selection **2** acceptance, selection

rejoice *v* be delighted/pleased, be joyful/happy, celebrate, delight, exult, glory, jump for joy *colloq*, make merry *old use*, revel, take pleasure, triumph, whoop it up *colloq*

rejoicing *n* celebration, delight, elation, euphoria, exultation, festivity, gladness, happiness, joy, jubilation, merrymaking *old use*, revelry, triumph

rejoin *v* answer, quip, repartee, reply, respond, retort, riposte

rejoinder *n* answer, quip, repartee, reply, response, retort, riposte

rejuvenate *v* freshen up, reanimate, recharge, refresh, regenerate, reinvigorate, renew, restore, revitalize, revive, revivify *formal*

relapse *v* **1** *relapsed into his old habits:* backslide, degenerate, fall back, lapse, regress, retrogress *formal*, revert, sink **2** *patients often relapse:* deteriorate, fail, sink, weaken, worsen
♦ *n* **1** *a relapse into drug-taking:* backsliding, lapse, regression, retrogression *formal*, reversion **2** *the patient suffered a relapse:* deterioration, recurrence, setback, weakening, worsening

relate *v* **1** *relate one thing to another:* ally, associate, connect, correlate *formal*, couple, join, link **2** *this letter relates to your application:* appertain *formal*, apply, be relevant, concern, have a bearing on, pertain *formal*, refer **3** *relate an anecdote:* communicate, delineate *formal*, describe, detail, narrate, present, recite, recount, report, tell **4** *I can't relate to her at all:* be on the same wavelength *colloq*, empathize, feel for, get on (well) with, hit it off *colloq*, identify, speak the same language *colloq*, sympathize, understand

related *adj* **1** *related by marriage:* agnate *formal*, akin, connected, consanguineous *formal*, kindred **2** *related sciences:* accompanying, affiliated, agnate *formal*, allied, associated, cognate *formal*, concomitant *formal*, connected, correlated *formal*, interconnected, interrelated, linked, relevant
🔁 **1** unrelated **2** unconnected, unrelated

relation *n* **1** *price bears no relation to quality:* affiliation, alliance, bond, comparison, connection, correlation *formal*, interconnection, interdependence, interrelation, link, linking, relationship, similarity **2** *a question with relation to his health:* application, bearing, pertinence *formal*, reference, regard, relevance **3** *a relation by marriage:* family, kin, kindred, kinsfolk, kinsman, kinswoman, relative

relations *n* **1** *has no living relations:* family, folks *colloq*, kin, kindred, kinsfolk, kinsmen, kinswomen, relatives **2** *good relations with her colleagues:* affairs, associations, communications, connections, contact(s), dealings, interaction, intercourse *formal*, liaison, rapport, relationship, terms **3** *sexual relations:* carnal knowledge, coition *formal,* coitus *formal,* copulation, going to bed with someone *colloq,* intercourse, intimacy, intimate relations, love-making, sex, sleeping with someone *colloq*

relationship *n* **1** *no relationship between the two events:* association, connection, correlation *formal,* link, parallel, proportion, ratio, similarity, tie-up **2** *her relationship with her parents:* affinity, alliance, bond, chemistry *colloq,* closeness, connection, friendship, liaison, rapport, tie(s) **3** *an illicit relationship:* affair, fling *colloq,* intimacy, liaison, love affair, romance

relative *adj* **1** *live in relative poverty:* commensurate *formal,* comparable, comparative, correlative *formal,* corresponding, parallel, proportional, proportionate, reciprocal, respective **2** *the facts relative to his employment:* applicable, apposite *formal,* appropriate, connected, germane *formal,* interrelated, pertinent *formal,* related, relevant
♦ *n* family, kin, kindred, kinsfolk, kinsman, kinswoman, relation

relatively *adv* comparatively, fairly, in/by comparison, quite, rather, somewhat

relax *v* **1** *relax on holiday:* calm (down), chill out *colloq,* cool it *colloq,* hang loose *colloq,* let your hair down *colloq,* let yourself go *colloq,* loosen up, make yourself at home *colloq,* put your feet up *colloq,* rest, take it/things easy *colloq,* unwind, wind down **2** *meditation relaxes me:* calm (down), loosen up, sedate, tranquillize, unwind **3** *relax the rules:* abate *formal,* diminish, ease (off), lessen, loosen, lower, moderate, reduce, remit *formal,* slacken, soften, weaken
☒ **3** tighten

relaxation *n* **1** *time for relaxation:* amusement, enjoyment, entertainment, fun, leisure, loosening up, pleasure, recreation, refreshment, repose *formal,* rest, unwinding **2** *relaxation of the rules:* abatement *formal,* détente, easing, lessening, let-up *colloq,* loosening, moderation, reduction, slackening, softening, weakening
☒ **1** tension **2** intensification

relaxed *adj* **1** *feel relaxed:* at ease, calm, carefree, collected, comfortable, composed, cool, happy-go-lucky, leisurely, restful, unhurried, uninhibited **2** *a relaxed situation:* casual, easy-going, informal, laid-back *colloq,* restful
☒ **1** nervous, tense, worried **2** formal, tense

relay *n* **1** *a news relay:* broadcast, communication, dispatch, message, programme, transmission **2** *work in relays:* period, shift, spell, stint, time, turn
♦ *v* broadcast, carry, circulate, communicate, hand on, pass on, send, spread, transmit

release *v* **1** *release a prisoner:* deliver, emancipate, free, liberate, set free **2** *release someone from their bonds:* let go, loose, loosen, unbind, unchain, undo, unfasten, unleash, unlock, unloose, unshackle, untie **3** *release someone from a contract:* absolve, acquit, discharge, excuse, exempt, exonerate *formal,* let go, let off **4** *release the details:* announce, circulate, disclose, divulge, issue, make known, make public, present, publish, reveal **5** *release an album:* circulate, distribute, issue, launch, make available, present, publish, unveil

☒ **1** imprison **3** detain
♦ *n* *his release from captivity:* deliverance, emancipation, freedom, liberation, liberty, manumission *formal* **2** *a release from a promise:* absolution, acquittal, discharge, exemption, exoneration, let-off *colloq* **3** *a press release:* announcement, bulletin, declaration, disclosure, issue, proclamation, publication, publishing, revelation
☒ **1** detention, imprisonment

relegate *v* **1** *relegated to a minor division:* banish, consign, degrade, demote, deport, downgrade, eject, exile, expel, reduce, transfer **2** *relegate the question to a committee:* assign, consign, delegate, dispatch, entrust, refer, transfer
☒ **1** promote

relent *v* **1** *she relented and let him go:* capitulate, change your mind, come round, give in, give way, soften, weaken, yield **2** *the storm relented:* abate *formal,* die down, ease, let up, relax, slacken, weaken

relentless *adj* **1** *a relentless tyrant:* cold-hearted, cruel, fierce, grim, hard, hard-hearted, harsh, implacable, inexorable, inflexible, merciless, pitiless, remorseless, ruthless, uncompromising, unforgiving, unrelenting, unyielding **2** *relentless pressure:* incessant, inexorable, persistent, punishing, unceasing, unrelenting, unremitting
☒ **1** merciful, yielding

relevant *adj* admissible, applicable, apposite, appropriate, apropos *formal,* apt, congruous *formal,* fitting, germane *formal,* material, pertinent *formal,* proper, related, significant, suitable, to the point
☒ inapplicable, inappropriate, irrelevant, unsuitable

reliable *adj* **1** *a reliable worker:* conscientious, dependable, dutiful, honest, responsible, solid, sound, stable, trustworthy, unfailing **2** *a reliable friend:* constant, dependable, devoted, faithful, staunch, true, trusty, unfailing **3** *reliable equipment:* dependable, predictable, regular, safe, sound, tested, trustworthy **4** *reliable evidence:* certain, dependable, solid, sound, sure, true, trustworthy, well-founded, well-grounded
☒ **1** unreliable, untrustworthy **2** unreliable, untrustworthy **3** unreliable, untrustworthy **4** doubtful, unreliable, untrustworthy

reliance *n* **1** *her reliance on her husband for support:* dependence **2** *reliance in his abilities:* assurance, belief, confidence, conviction, credit, faith, trust

relic *n* antique, artefact, fragment, heirloom, keepsake, memento, remains, remembrance, reminder, remnant, scrap, souvenir, vestige

relief *n* **1** *the relief of pain:* abatement *formal,* allaying *formal,* alleviation, assuaging *formal,* cure, easing, lessening, mitigation *formal,* palliation *formal,* reduction, remedy, remission, soothing **2** *no relief from his agony:* deliverance, release, respite **3** *a sense of relief:* calmness, comfort, consolation, happiness, reassurance, relaxation **4** *some relief from work:* break, breather *colloq,* diversion, interruption, let-up *colloq,* refreshment, relaxation, repose *formal,* respite, rest **5** *famine relief:* aid, assistance, back-up, help, rescue, saving, succour *formal,* support, sustenance **6** *arrange relief for absent staff:* locum, proxy, replacement, reserve, stand-by, stand-in, substitute, supply, surrogate, understudy

relieve *v* **1** *relieve the pain:* abate *formal,* allay *formal,* alleviate, assuage *formal,* cure, heal, lessen, mitigate *formal,* palliate *formal,* reduce, slacken, soften, soothe **2** *relieved at the news:* comfort, console, reassure, soothe **3** *relieved of a burden:* deliver, discharge, liberate, release, set free, unburden **4** *the night porter relieves him at eight:* replace, stand in for, substitute, take over from, take the place of **5** *relieve poverty-stricken countries:* aid, assist, help, rescue, save, succour *formal,* support, sustain **6** *relieve someone of their duties:* discharge, dismiss, excuse, exempt, expel, free, release, remove **7** *relieve the tedium:* break (up), bring to an end, discontinue *formal,* interrupt, pause, punctuate, stop
1 aggravate, intensify **2** aggravate

religion

> *Religions include:*
> Christianity, Jehovah's Witnesses,
> Mormonism, Bahaism, Buddhism,
> Confucianism, Hinduism, Islam, Jainism,
> Judaism, Sikhism, Taoism, Shintoism,
> Zoroastrianism, voodoo, druidism. See also
> **scripture, worship**

religious *adj* **1** *religious writings:* devotional, divine, doctrinal, holy, sacred, scriptural, spiritual, theological **2** *a religious person:* believing, church-going, committed, devout, God-fearing, godly, having a living faith, pious, practising, reverent, righteous **3** *a religious attention to detail:* conscientious, meticulous, rigorous, scrupulous, strict
1 secular **2** irreligious, ungodly

relinquish *v* abandon, abdicate *formal,* abstain *formal,* cease *formal,* cede, desert, desist *formal,* discontinue *formal,* drop, forgo, forsake *formal,* give up, hand over, let go, quit *colloq,* release, renounce, repudiate, resign, surrender, waive, yield
keep, retain

relish *v* **1** *relish a meal:* enjoy, savour **2** *relish a challenge:* adore, appreciate, delight in, enjoy, like, love, revel in
♦ *n* **1** *served with a relish:* chutney, condiment, flavouring, garnish, pickle, sauce, seasoning **2** *the dish's delicate relish:* flavour, flavouring, piquancy, spice, tang **3** *he ate with relish:* appreciation, delight, enjoyment, gusto, liveliness, pleasure, satisfaction, vigour, zest

reluctance *n* aversion, backwardness, disinclination *formal,* dislike, distaste, hesitancy, hesitation, indisposition *formal,* loathing, recalcitrance *formal,* repugnance *formal,* unwillingness
eagerness, enthusiasm, willingness

reluctant *adj* averse, backward, disinclined *formal,* grudging, hesitant, indisposed, loath, slow, unenthusiastic, unwilling
eager, enthusiastic, ready, willing

rely *v* **1** *rely on your advice:* depend, lean **2** *can rely on him to help:* bank, be sure, count, depend, reckon, trust

remain *v* **1** *remain where you are:* bide *old use,* linger, rest, stand, stay, stay behind, tarry *formal,* wait **2** *remain silent:* bide *old use,* continue, stand,

stay **3** *nothing remains of the building:* abide *formal,* be left over, continue, endure, last, linger, persist, prevail, survive
1 depart, go, leave

remainder *n* balance, excess, leftovers, remains, remnant, residue, residuum *formal,* rest, superfluity *formal,* surplus, vestiges

remaining *adj* **1** *the remaining liquid:* left, left-over, outstanding, residual, spare, unfinished, unspent, unused **2** *the remaining traces:* abiding, last, lasting, left, lingering, persisting, surviving

remains *n* **1** *the remains of the meal:* crumbs, debris, detritus *formal,* dregs, fragments, leavings, leftovers, oddments, odds and ends *colloq,* remainder, remnants, residue, rest, scraps, traces, vestiges **2** *Egyptian remains found on the site:* relics, reliquiae *formal* **3** *human remains:* ashes, body, cadaver, carcase, corpse, dead body

remark *v* **1** *he remarked that he was leaving:* assert, comment, declare, mention, observe, pronounce, say, state **2** *did you remark how worried she looked?:* note, notice, observe
♦ *n* **1** *sarcastic remarks:* assertion, comment, declaration, observation, opinion, pronouncement, reflection, statement, utterance **2** *one incident is worthy of remark:* acknowledgement, comment, mention, notice, observation, reference

remarkable *adj* amazing, considerable, conspicuous, distinguished, exceptional, extraordinary, important, impressive, memorable, momentous, notable, noteworthy, odd, outstanding, phenomenal, pre-eminent, prominent, rare, signal, significant, singular *formal,* strange, striking, surpassing, surprising, uncommon, unusual
average, commonplace, ordinary, usual

remedy *n* **1** *a traditional remedy:* antidote, cure, medicament *formal,* medication, medicine, nostrum *formal,* panacea, physic *formal,* relief, restorative, therapy, treatment **2** *a remedy for the problem:* answer, antidote, corrective, countermeasure, cure, panacea, relief, solution
♦ *v* **1** *treatment to remedy the condition:* control, cure, ease, heal, help, mend, mitigate *formal,* relieve, soothe, treat **2** *remedy the situation:* correct, counteract, fix, help, mend, mitigate *formal,* put right, rectify *formal,* redress, relieve, repair, solve, sort (out)

remember *v* **1** *remember the old days:* call to mind, cast your mind back, hark back, look back, recall, recollect, reminisce, summon up, think back, think of **2** *remember someone's name:* call to mind, place, recall, recognize, recollect, think of **3** *remember your lines:* commit to memory, learn, learn by heart, make a mental note of, memorize, retain **4** *we remember him every year:* celebrate, commemorate, honour, mark, pay tribute to, recognize **5** *remember me to them:* send good/best wishes, send greetings, send regards/respects
1 forget **2** forget

remembrance *n* **1** *we do it in remembrance of his sacrifice:* commemoration, memorial, recognition, testimonial **2** *the remembrance of things past:* memory, nostalgia, recall, recollection, reminiscence, retrospect, thought **3** *kept it as a remembrance of her:* keepsake, memento, memorial, monument, relic, souvenir, token

remind v bring to mind, call to mind, call up, evoke, hint, jog your memory, make you think of, nudge, prompt, refresh your memory

reminder n 1 *a reminder to take his keys*: aide-mémoire, hint, memo *colloq*, memorandum, note, nudge, prompt, suggestion 2 *a reminder of our holiday*: memento, souvenir

reminisce v hark back, look back, recall, recollect, remember, review, think back

reminiscence n anecdote, memoir, memory, recall, recollection, reflection, remembrance, retrospection, review

reminiscent adj evocative, nostalgic, redolent *formal*, suggestive

remiss adj careless, casual, dilatory *formal*, forgetful, heedless, inattentive, indifferent, lackadaisical, lax, neglectful, negligent, slack, slipshod, sloppy, thoughtless, unmindful
Fa careful, scrupulous

remission n 1 *a remission of the cancer*: abatement *formal*, alleviation *formal*, ebb, lessening, moderation, respite 2 *snowed without remission*: abatement *formal*, decrease, diminution *formal*, ebb, lessening, let-up *colloq*, lull, reduction, relaxation, respite, slackening, weakening 3 *remission of a sentence*: abrogation *formal*, annulment, cancellation, repeal, reprieve, rescinding *formal*, revocation *formal*, suspension 4 *the remission of our sins*: absolution, acquittal, amnesty, discharge, excuse, exemption, exoneration *formal*, forgiveness, indulgence, pardon

---

remission or **remittance**? *Remission* means 'a lessening in force or effect', as in *Remissions in that form of cancer are not unknown*, 'the shortening of a prison sentence', 'the cancelling of a debt or punishment', and, in Christian theology, 'the forgiveness of sins'. *Remittance* is a formal word for the sending of money in payment for something, or for the money itself: *We are grateful for your remittance of the correct sum of money.*

---

remit v 1 *remit money to someone*: dispatch, forward, mail, pay, post, send, settle, transmit 2 *remit the matter to a tribunal*: direct, pass on, refer, transfer 3 *remit a sentence*: abrogate *formal*, cancel, hold over, repeal, rescind *formal*, revoke *formal*, set aside, suspend
♦ n authorization, brief, guidelines, instructions, orders, responsibility, scope, terms of reference

remittance n 1 *enclose a remittance for £10*: allowance, consideration, fee, payment 2 *the remittance of the fee*: dispatch, sending

remnant n balance, bit, end, fragment, leftover, oddment, offcut, piece, remainder, remains, residue, scrap, shred, trace, vestige

remonstrance n complaint, expostulation *formal*, grievance, objection, opposition, petition, protest, protestation, reprimand, reproof

remonstrate v argue, challenge, complain, dispute, dissent *formal*, expostulate *formal*, gripe *colloq*, object, oppose, protest, take exception to, take issue with

remorse n bad conscience, compunction *formal*, contrition, grief, guilt, penitence, regret, repentance, ruefulness, self-reproach, shame, sorrow

remorseful adj apologetic, ashamed, chastened *formal*, compunctious *formal*, conscience-stricken, contrite, guilt-ridden, guilty, penitent, regretful, repentant, rueful, sad, sorrowful, sorry
Fa impenitent, remorseless

remorseless adj 1 *a remorseless tyrant*: callous, cruel, hard, hard-hearted, harsh, implacable, inhumane, merciless, pitiless, relentless, ruthless, savage, stern, unforgiving, unmerciful, unrelenting 2 *the remorseless spread of the disease*: inexorable, relentless, undeviating, unrelenting, unremitting, unstoppable
Fa 1 remorseful, sorry

remote adj 1 *a remote location*: distant, far, faraway, far-off, God-forsaken, inaccessible, isolated, lonely, off the beaten track *colloq*, outlying, out-of-the-way, secluded 2 *she was chilly and remote*: aloof, detached, distant, reserved, standoffish, unapproachable, uncommunicative, unconcerned, uninvolved, withdrawn 3 *a remote possibility*: doubtful, dubious, faint, improbable, inconsiderable, insignificant, meagre, negligible, outside, poor, slender, slight, slim, small, unlikely
Fa 1 accessible, close, nearby 2 approachable, friendly 3 strong

removal n 1 *our removal to another location*: conveyance, departure, move, relocation, shift, shifting, transferral, transporting, uprooting 2 *the removal of a tooth*: detachment, extraction, taking away, withdrawal 3 *the removal of an error*: deletion, obliteration 4 *the removal of a ban*: abolition, taking away, withdrawal 5 *his withdrawal from office*: boot *colloq*, departure, discharge, dislodgement *formal*, dismissal, disposal, ejection, elbow *colloq*, eviction, expulsion, firing *colloq*, ousting, push *colloq*, relegation, sack *colloq*, sacking *colloq*

remove v 1 *removed the TV to another room*: carry, convey, move, relocate, shift, take away, transfer, transport, withdraw 2 *remove clothing*: doff, pull off, shed, strip, take off, tear off 3 *remove a tumour*: amputate, cut off, cut out, destroy, detach, excise, extract, get out, lop off, pull out, take away, take out 4 *remove a passage from a book*: abolish, blue-pencil, cross out, delete, eliminate, expurge *formal*, get rid of, strike out 5 *remove a mark*: efface *formal*, eliminate, erase, get rid of, obliterate, purge, rub out 6 *remove someone from office*: boot out *colloq*, cashier, cast out, depose, discharge, dislodge, dismiss, eject, evict, expel, fire *colloq*, get rid of, oust, relegate, sack *colloq*, throw out, unseat

remunerate v compensate, indemnify, pay, recompense, redress, reimburse, repay

remuneration n 1 *a remuneration for the inconvenience caused*: compensation, indemnity, payment, recompense, reimbursement, repayment 2 *remuneration for services*: earnings, emolument, fee, honorarium, income, pay, payment, profit, remittance, retainer, reward, salary, stipend, wages

remunerative adj (financially) worthwhile, fruitful, gainful, lucrative, moneymaking, paying, profitable, rewarding, rich

renaissance *n* awakening, new birth, new dawn, reappearance, reawakening, rebirth, recrudescence *formal*, re-emergence, regeneration, rejuvenation, renascence *formal*, renewal, restoration, resurgence, resurrection, revival

renascent *adj* born again *colloq*, reanimated, reawakened, reborn, re-emergent, renewed, resurgent, resurrected, revived

rend *v* break, burst, cleave *formal*, divide, fracture, lacerate, rip, rupture, separate, sever, shatter, smash, splinter, split, stab, tear

render *v* **1** *they rendered it harmless:* cause to be, leave, make, turn **2** *render payment:* contribute, deliver, furnish, give, hand over, present, proffer *formal*, provide, submit, supply, tender **3** *German lyrics rendered into English:* clarify, explain, interpret, represent, transcribe, translate **4** *render a song:* perform, play, sing **5** *the scenes are rendered beautifully:* depict, describe, display, exhibit, manifest *formal*, represent, show

rendezvous *n* **1** *a rendezvous with a friend:* appointment, assignation, date, engagement, meeting, tryst **2** *a favourite rendezvous for lovers:* haunt, meeting-place, resort, venue
♦ *v* assemble, collect, come together, convene *formal*, converge, gather, meet, muster, rally

rendition *n* **1** *a rendition of an old song:* arrangement, delivery, depiction, execution *formal*, interpretation, performance, portrayal, presentation, rendering, version **2** *a rendition of Ovid's poems:* explanation, interpretation, reading, transcription, translation, version

renegade *n* apostate, backslider, betrayer, defector, deserter, dissident, mutineer, outlaw, rebel, runaway, traitor, turncoat
🔁 adherent, disciple, follower
♦ *adj* apostate, backsliding, disloyal, dissident, mutinous, outlaw, perfidious *formal*, rebel, rebellious, recreant, runaway, traitorous, unfaithful
🔁 faithful, loyal

renege *v* apostatize, backslide, default, go back on your promise, repudiate, welsh

renew *v* **1** *renew a building:* mend, modernize, overhaul, recondition, reconstitute, re-create, refit, re-form, refurbish, remodel, renovate, repair, restore, transform **2** *renewed my faith:* regenerate, reinvigorate, rejuvenate, restore, resuscitate, revitalize, revive **3** *renew supplies:* refresh, replace, replenish, restock, restore **4** *renew hostilities:* continue, extend, prolong, reaffirm, recommence, re-establish, reiterate *formal*, repeat, restart, restate, resume

renewal *n* **1** *the renewal of slum housing:* reconditioning, reconstitution, reconstruction, re-creation, refurbishment, renovation, repair **2** *the renewal of life:* reinvigoration, rejuvenation, resurrection, resuscitation, revitalization, revivification *formal* **3** *the renewal of their marriage vows:* continuance, reaffirmation, recommencement, reiteration *formal*, repetition, restatement, resumption

renounce *v* **1** *renounce your faith:* abandon, abjure *formal*, abstain from *formal*, deny, desist *formal*, discard, disclaim *formal*, disown, eschew *formal*, forsake *formal*, give up, recant *formal*, reject, repudiate, shun, spurn, wash your hands

of *colloq* **2** *renounce a claim to the throne:* abandon, abdicate *formal*, abjure *formal*, abnegate *formal*, disclaim *formal*, forgo, forsake *formal*, give up, relinquish, resign, sign away, surrender, waive

renovate *v* do up *colloq*, give a facelift *colloq*, improve, modernize, overhaul, recondition, redecorate, refit, re-form, refurbish, rehabilitate, remodel, renew, repair, restore, revamp

renovation *n* facelift *colloq*, improvement, modernization, reconditioning, refit, refurbishment, renewal, repair, restoration

renown *n* acclaim, celebrity, distinction, eminence, esteem *formal*, fame, glory, honour, illustriousness, mark, note, pre-eminence, prestige, prominence, reputation, repute, stardom
🔁 anonymity, obscurity

renowned *adj* acclaimed, celebrated, distinguished, eminent, famed, famous, illustrious, notable, noted, of repute, pre-eminent, prestigious, prominent, well-known
🔁 obscure, unknown

rent¹ *n* fee, hire, lease, payment, rental
♦ *v* **1** *rent a flat from someone:* charter, hire, lease **2** *rent a flat to tenants:* hire out, lease, let (out), rent out, sublet

rent² *n* **1** *a rent in the cloth:* gash, hole, perforation, rip, slash, slit, split, tear **2** *a rent in the earth:* breach, break, chink, cleavage, crack, division, hole, opening, rift, rupture

renunciation *n* **1** *the renunciation of his faith:* abandonment, abnegation *formal*, abstinence *formal*, denial, desistance *formal*, discarding, disclaiming *formal*, disowning, forsaking *formal*, giving up, rejection, repudiation, shunning, spurning **2** *renunciation of his rights:* abandonment, abdication *formal*, disclaiming *formal*, forsaking *formal*, giving up, relinquishment, surrender, waiving

repair¹ *v* adjust, darn, fix, heal, maintain, make good, mend, overhaul, patch up, put right, rectify, redress, refit, renew, renovate, restore, service, sew
♦ *n* **1** *in need of repair:* improvement, maintenance, overhaul, refit, restoration, service **2** *there are no visible repairs:* darn, mend, patch **3** *in good/bad repair:* condition, fettle, form, kilter, nick *colloq*, shape, state, (working) order

repair² *v* go, move, remove, resort, retire, wend your way, withdraw

reparable *adj* corrigible, curable, recoverable, rectifiable, remediable, restorable, retrievable, salvageable, savable
🔁 irreparable

reparation *n* amends, atonement, compensation, damages, indemnity, propitiation *formal*, recompense, redress, requital, restitution, satisfaction, solatium *technical*

repartee *n* badinage, banter, jesting, retort, riposte, wit

repay *v* **1** *I'll repay you as soon as I can:* compensate, pay, pay back, recompense, refund, reimburse, remunerate, reward, settle, settle up with, square **2** *repay someone for an insult:* avenge, get back at, get even with, get your own back on *colloq*, give as good as you get *colloq*, not take it lying down *colloq*, reciprocate, retaliate, revenge, settle the score *colloq*

repayment *n* **1** *repayment of a loan*: payment, rebate, refund, reimbursement **2** *a repayment for the inconvenience caused*: amends, compensation, payment, recompense, redress, reparation, requital, restitution **3** *repayment for the wrong he had done me*: reciprocation, retaliation, retribution, revenge, tit for tat *colloq*, vengeance

repeal *v* abjure *formal*, abolish, abrogate *formal*, annul, cancel, countermand *formal*, invalidate, nullify *formal*, quash, recall, rescind *formal*, retract *formal*, reverse, revoke *formal*, set aside, void, withdraw
🔁 enact
♦ *n* abolition, abrogation *formal*, annulment, cancellation, invalidation, nullification *formal*, quashing, rescinding *formal*, rescindment *formal*, rescission *formal*, reversal, revocation *formal*, withdrawal
🔁 enactment, establishment

repeat *v* **1** *could you repeat that?*: iterate *formal*, recap *colloq*, recapitulate, reiterate *formal*, restate, say again **2** *repeat word for word*: duplicate, echo, parrot, quote, relate, retell **3** *repeat an old story*: quote, recite, rehearse *formal* **4** *the episode is repeated*: rebroadcast, replay, rerun, reshow **5** *repeat an action*: duplicate, redo, renew, reproduce
♦ *n* **1** *a repeat of my earlier comment*: recapitulation, repetition, restatement **2** *a repeat of last week's rioting*: duplicate, duplication, echo, repetition, reproduction **3** *the repeat is shown tomorrow*: rebroadcast, replay, rerun, reshowing

repeated *adj* constant, continual, frequent, periodic, persistent, recurrent, recurring, regular

repeatedly *adv* again and again, frequently, often, over and over, time after time, time and (time) again

repel *v* **1** *repel the attackers*: beat back, check, drive back, fight, force back, hold off, keep at bay, oppose, parry, push back, rebuff, reject, repulse, resist, spurn, ward off **2** *the smell repelled her*: be repugnant to *formal*, disgust, make you sick, nauseate, offend, revolt, sicken, turn off *colloq*, turn your stomach *colloq*
🔁 **1** attract **2** delight

repellent *adj* abhorrent, abominable, disagreeable, disgusting, distasteful, foul, hateful, horrid, loathsome, nasty, nauseating, objectionable, obnoxious, offensive, off-putting, repugnant *formal*, repulsive, revolting, shocking, sickening, unpleasant, vile
🔁 attractive, delightful, pleasant

repent *v* **1** *repent past misdeeds*: be ashamed of, be contrite about, be sorry for, beat your breast over *colloq*, deplore, feel remorse about, lament, regret, rue, sorrow over **2** *he repented and became a Christian*: be converted, do a U-turn *colloq*, recant *formal*, see the error of your ways *colloq*, see the light *colloq*, turn

repentance *n* **1** *repentance for their crimes*: compunction *formal*, contrition, grief, guilt, penitence, regret, remorse, shame, sorrow **2** *the belief that repentance guarantees salvation*: conversion, recantation *formal*, U-turn *colloq*

repentant *adj* apologetic, ashamed, chastened, conscience-stricken, contrite, guilty, penitent, regretful, remorseful, rueful, sorrowful, sorry
🔁 unrepentant

repercussion *n* backlash *colloq*, consequence, echo, effect, rebound, recoil, result, reverberation, ripple *colloq*, shock wave *colloq*

repertoire *n* collection, list, range, repertory, repository *formal*, reserve, reservoir, stock, store, supply

repetition *n* **1** *a repetition of the incident*: duplication, echo, reappearance, recurrence, reprise *formal*, return **2** *his repetition of her remarks*: copying, echo, echoing, quoting, restatement **3** *the report is full of repetition*: iterance *formal*, iteration *formal*, recapitulation, redundancy, reiteration *formal*, restatement, superfluity, tautology

repetitious *adj* long-winded, monotonous, pleonastic(al) *technical*, prolix *formal*, redundant, tautological, unchanging, unvaried, verbose, windy, wordy

repetitive *adj* automatic, mechanical, monotonous, recurrent, samey *colloq*, unchanging, unvaried

rephrase *v* ask/say differently, paraphrase, put in other/different words, recast, reword, rewrite

replace *v* **1** *replace the lid*: put back, re-establish, reinstate, restore, return **2** *she replaced him as manager*: act for, come after, deputize, fill in for, follow, oust, relieve, stand in for, substitute, succeed, supersede, supplant, take the place of

replacement *n* fill-in, proxy, reserve, stand-in, substitute, successor, surrogate, understudy

replenish *v* **1** *replenish supplies*: furnish, make up, provide, renew, replace, restore, supply **2** *replenish a glass*: fill, fill up, recharge, refill, reload, restock, stock, top up

replete *adj* abounding, brimful, brimming, charged, chock-a-block *colloq*, chock-full *colloq*, crammed, filled, full, full up, glutted, gorged, jammed, jam-packed *colloq*, sated, satiated *formal*, stuffed, teeming, well-provided, well-stocked

repletion *n* completeness, fullness, glut, overfullness, plethora *formal*, satiation *formal*, satiety *formal*, superabundance, superfluity

replica *n* clone, copy, duplicate, facsimile, imitation, model, reproduction

replicate *v* ape, clone, copy, duplicate, follow, mimic, recreate, reduplicate, repeat, reproduce

reply *v* acknowledge, answer, come back, counter, react, reciprocate, rejoin, respond, retaliate, retort, return, riposte, write back
♦ *n* acknowledgement, answer, comeback *colloq*, reaction, rejoinder, repartee, response, retaliation, retort, return, riposte

report *n* **1** *a vivid report*: account, communication, declaration, delineation *formal*, description, narrative, relation, statement, story, tale **2** *a news report*: article, bulletin, chronicle, communication, communiqué, item, piece, story, write-up **3** *no report on her progress*: announcement, communication, information, message, news, word **4** *submit a report*: brief,

dossier, file, minutes, note, record, register **5** *the report is that they have split up*: gossip, hearsay, rumour, talk **6** *a woman of good report*: character, credit, distinction, esteem *formal*, honour, name, renown, reputation, repute, standing, stature **7** *the report of a pistol*: bang, boom, crack, crash, explosion, noise, reverberation, shot
♦ *v* **1** *report a story*: air, announce, broadcast, chronicle, circulate, communicate, cover, delineate *formal*, describe, detail, disclose, divulge, document, narrate, pass on, proclaim, publish, record, recount, relate, relay, set forth, tell **2** *report the theft to the police*: communicate, declare, note, notify, tell **3** *reported him to his manager*: blow the whistle on *colloq*, complain about, grass on *slang*, inform on, rat on *colloq*, shop *colloq*, split on *colloq*, tell on *colloq*

reporter *n* announcer, columnist, commentator, correspondent, hack *colloq*, journalist, newscaster, newspaperman, newspaperwoman

repose *n* **1** *an atmosphere of repose*: calm, calmness, ease, peace, quiet, quietness, quietude *formal*, relaxation, respite, rest, restfulness, stillness, tranquillity **2** *his face looked younger in repose*: inactivity, relaxation, rest **3** *a noise disturbed his repose*: rest, sleep, slumber *formal*
⊟ 1 activity, strain, stress **2** activity
♦ *v* lay, laze *colloq*, lie, recline, relax, rest, sleep, slumber *formal*

repository *n* archive, bank, container, depository, depot, magazine, receptacle, safe, store, storehouse, treasury, vault, warehouse

reprehensible *adj* bad, blamable, blameworthy, censurable, condemnable, culpable *formal*, delinquent, discreditable, disgraceful, errant, erring, ignoble, objectionable, opprobrious *formal*, shameful, unworthy
⊟ creditable, good, praiseworthy

represent *v* **1** *this symbol represents danger*: amount to, be, be equivalent to, constitute, correspond to, denote, designate, mean, stand for, symbolize **2** *a lawyer representing a client*: act as representative of, act as spokesperson for, act for, act/speak in the name of, act/speak on behalf of, speak for, stand for **3** *he represents all that is noble*: embody, epitomize, exemplify, personify, show, stand for, typify **4** *represented as a villain in the story*: characterize, depict, describe, display, draw, evoke, exhibit, illustrate, picture, portray, sketch **5** *she represents Britannia in the film*: act as, appear as, enact, perform

representation *n* **1** *a lifelike representation in bronze*: bust, depiction, illustration, image, likeness, model, picture, portrait, sketch, statue **2** *a sympathetic representation of the Queen*: account, delineation *formal*, description, portrayal **3** *they have no representation in the House of Commons*: ambassador, councillor, delegate, delegation, deputation, deputy, envoy, member of parliament, mouthpiece, MP, proxy, representative, spokesman, spokesperson, spokeswoman, stand-in **4** *a spectacular representation*: performance, play, presentation, production, show, spectacle **5** *make representations to the council*: account, allegation, complaint, protest, report, request, statement

representative *n* **1** *our representative at the conference*: agent, ambassador, commissioner, councillor, delegate, delegation, deputation, deputy, envoy, mouthpiece, proxy, spokesman, spokesperson, spokeswoman, stand-in **2** *the representative for the constituency*: member of parliament, MP **3** *a sales representative*: agent, rep *colloq*, salesman, saleswoman, traveller
♦ *adj* **1** *a representative sample*: characteristic, exemplary, illustrative, indicative, normal, typical, usual **2** *an image representative of peace*: archetypal *formal*, emblematic, symbolic **3** *a representative parliament*: appointed, authorized, chosen, commissioned, delegated, elected, elective, nominated
⊟ 1 atypical, unrepresentative
2 unrepresentative

repress *v* **1** *repress a memory*: bottle up, check, control, curb, inhibit, restrain, suppress **2** *repress a giggle*: hold back, muffle, silence, smother, stifle, suppress **3** *repress a revolt*: crush, overcome, overpower, put down, quash, quell, subdue **4** *repress a people*: dominate, domineer, master, oppress, subjugate *formal*, vanquish *formal*

repressed *adj* frustrated, inhibited, introverted, self-restrained, uptight *colloq*, withdrawn
⊟ relaxed, uninhibited

repression *n* **1** *a reign of repression and terror*: authoritarianism, coercion, constraint, control, crushing, despotism, dictatorship, domination, oppression, quashing, quelling, subjugation *formal*, suppression, tyranny **2** *the government's repression of the press*: censorship, control, domination, gagging, suppression **3** *repression of your feelings*: control, inhibition, restraint, suppression **4** *repression of a laugh*: holding-back, muffling, smothering, stifling

repressive *adj* absolute, authoritarian, autocratic, coercive, cruel, despotic, dictatorial, dominating, harsh, oppressive, severe, strict, totalitarian, tough, tyrannical

reprieve *v* **1** *he has been reprieved*: acquit, give respite to, let off *colloq*, let off the hook *colloq*, pardon, show mercy/pity, spare **2** *jobs reprieved*: give respite to, redeem, relieve, rescue, save, spare
♦ *n* abatement *formal*, abeyance *formal*, amnesty, deferment, let-up *colloq*, pardon, postponement, relief, remission, respite, suspension

reprimand *v* admonish *formal*, berate *formal*, blame, castigate *formal*, censure, chide, criticize, give a dressing-down *colloq*, give a rap over the knuckles *colloq*, give a ticking-off *colloq*, haul over the coals *colloq*, lecture, rap over the knuckles *colloq*, read the riot act *colloq*, rebuke, reproach, reprove, scold, slate *colloq*, tell off *colloq*, tick off *colloq*
♦ *n* a flea in your ear *colloq*, admonition *formal*, blame, carpeting *colloq*, castigation *formal*, censure, dressing-down *colloq*, lecture, rebuke, reproach, reproof, rocket *colloq*, talking-to *colloq*, telling-off *colloq*, ticking-off *colloq*, upbraiding *formal*, wigging *colloq*

reprisal *n* a taste of your own medicine *colloq*, counter-attack, recrimination, redress, requital, retaliation, retribution, revenge, tit for tat *colloq*, vengeance

reproach *v* admonish *formal*, blame, censure, chide, condemn, criticize, defame, disparage *formal*, find fault with, give someone a dressing-down *colloq*, give someone a ticking-off *colloq*, haul over the coals *colloq*, rap over the knuckles *colloq*, rebuke, reprehend, reprimand, reprove, scold, upbraid

♦ *n* **1** *deserve a reproach*: admonition *formal*, blame, censure, condemnation, criticism, disapproval, rebuke, reprimand, reproof, scolding **2** *this tragedy is a reproach to our community*: blemish, blot, degradation, discredit, disgrace, dishonour, disrepute, ignominy *formal*, obloquy *formal*, opprobrium *formal*, shame, slur, smear, stain, stigma

reproachful *adj* castigating *formal*, censorious, critical, disapproving, fault-finding, opprobrious *formal*, reproving, scolding, upbraiding
🖾 complimentary

reprobate *adj* abandoned, bad, base, corrupt, degenerate, depraved, dissolute, hardened, immoral, profligate *formal*, reprobative *formal*, reprobatory *formal*, shameless, sinful, unprincipled, vile, wicked
🖾 upright, virtuous

♦ *n* criminal, dastard, degenerate, evildoer, knave, mischief-maker, miscreant, ne'er-do-well, profligate *formal*, rake, rascal, rogue, scallywag, scamp, scoundrel, sinner, troublemaker, villain, wretch, wrongdoer

reproduce *v* **1** *reproduce the original conditions*: ape, clone, copy, duplicate, echo, emulate, follow, imitate, match, mimic, mirror, reconstruct, recreate, redo, remake, repeat, replicate *formal*, simulate **2** *reproduce a document*: copy, duplicate, photocopy, Photostat®, print, replicate *formal*, transcribe, Xerox® **3** *unable to reproduce*: bear young, breed, generate, give birth, multiply, procreate *formal*, proliferate, propagate, spawn

reproduction *n* **1** *a reproduction of the scene*: clone, copy, duplicate, imitation, picture, replica **2** *a reproduction of the letter*: copy, duplicate, facsimile, photocopy, print, replica **3** *animals capable of reproduction*: breeding, generation, multiplication, procreation *formal*, propagation
🖾 **1** original **2** original

reproductive *adj* generative, genital, procreative *formal*, progenitive *formal*, propagative, sex, sexual

reproof *n* **1** *receive a reproof*: admonition *formal*, berating *formal*, carpeting *colloq*, castigation *formal*, censure, dressing-down *colloq*, rebuke, reprimand, reproach, rocket *colloq*, scolding, telling-off *colloq*, ticking-off *colloq*, upbraiding *formal*, wigging *colloq* **2** *gave me a look of reproof*: censure, condemnation, criticism, disapprobation *formal*, reproach
🖾 **1** praise **2** praise

reprove *v* admonish *formal*, berate *formal*, castigate *formal*, censure, chide, condemn, criticize, give someone a dressing-down *colloq*, give someone a ticking-off *colloq*, haul over the coals *colloq*, rap over the knuckles *colloq*, rebuke, reprehend, reprimand, reproach, scold, slate *colloq*, tell off *colloq*, tick off *colloq*, upbraid *formal*
🖾 praise

reptile

Reptiles include:
adder, puff adder, grass snake, tree snake, asp, viper, rattlesnake, sidewinder, anaconda, boa constrictor, cobra, king cobra, mamba, python; lizard, chameleon, gecko, iguana, skink, slow-worm; turtle, green turtle, hawksbill turtle, terrapin, tortoise, giant tortoise; alligator, crocodile. See also **dinosaurs**

repudiate *v* **1** *repudiate your religion*: abandon, abjure *formal*, cast off, desert, disavow *formal*, discard, disclaim *formal*, disown, disprofess *formal*, forsake *formal*, have nothing to do with *colloq*, not have anything to do with *colloq*, not touch with a barge pole *colloq*, reject, renounce, retract, turn your back on *colloq* **2** *repudiate an accusation*: deny, disaffirm *formal*, rebut, refute **3** *repudiate an agreement*: abandon, disaffirm *formal*, disclaim *formal*, reject, renounce, rescind *formal*, retract, reverse, revoke **4** *repudiate a spouse*: abandon, cast off, divorce, forsake *formal*
🖾 **1** admit, own **2** admit, own

repudiation *n* abjuration *formal*, denial, disaffirmance *formal*, disaffirmation *formal*, disavowal *formal*, disowning, recantation *formal*, rejection, renouncement, renunciation, retraction *formal*
🖾 acceptance

repugnance *n* abhorrence *formal*, antipathy *formal*, aversion, disgust, dislike, distaste, hatred, horror, loathing, nausea, odium *formal*, repulsion, revulsion
🖾 delight, liking, pleasure

repugnant *adj* **1** *a repugnant sight*: abhorrent *formal*, abominable, disgusting, distasteful, foul, hateful, horrid, loathsome, nauseating, objectionable, obnoxious, odious, offensive, repellent, revolting, sickening, vile **2** *repugnant to society*: adverse, antagonistic, antipathetic, averse, contradictory, hostile, incompatible, inconsistent, inimical *formal*, opposed, unacceptable
🖾 **1** pleasant **2** acceptable, consistent

repulse *v* **1** *the thought repulsed me*: disgust, nauseate, offend, repel, revolt, sicken **2** *repulse an attack*: beat off, check, defeat, drive back, rebuff, repel **3** *she repulsed his advances*: disdain, disregard, rebuff, refuse, reject, snub, spurn

♦ *n* **1** *the repulse of the Viking invaders*: check, defeat, rebuff **2** *her repulse of his proposal*: rebuff, refusal, rejection, repudiation, snub, spurning
🖾 acceptance

repulsion *n* abhorrence *formal*, aversion, detestation *formal*, disgust, disrelish *formal*, distaste, hatred, loathing, repellence *formal*, repellency *formal*, repugnance *formal*, revulsion
🖾 liking

repulsive *adj* abhorrent, abominable, disagreeable, disgusting, distasteful, foul, hateful, heinous *formal*, hideous, horrid, loathsome, nasty, nauseating, objectionable, obnoxious, offensive, off-putting, repellent, repugnant *formal*, revolting, sickening, ugly, unattractive, unpleasant, vile
🖾 attractive, delightful, pleasant

reputable *adj* admirable, creditable, dependable, esteemed *formal*, estimable *formal*, excellent, good, honest, honourable, irreproachable, of high/good repute, reliable, respectable, respected, trustworthy, upright, virtuous, well-thought-of, worthy
🖾 disreputable, infamous

reputation n 1 *a reputation for being hard to please:* celebrity, character, distinction, fame, infamy, name, notoriety, repute 2 *the scandal destroyed his reputation:* character, credit, esteem *formal,* estimation *formal,* good name, good standing, honour, image, position, prestige, renown, respect, respectability, standing, stature, status

repute n 1 *damaged his repute:* esteem *formal,* estimation *formal,* good name, name, renown, reputation, standing, stature 2 *ill repute:* celebrity, distinction, fame, name, reputation
🔁 1 infamy

reputed adj 1 *he is reputed to be living in Spain:* alleged, assumed, believed, considered, estimated, held, judged, presumed, reckoned, regarded, rumoured, said, supposed, thought 2 *sold the house for a reputed £1,000,000:* apparent, ostensible *formal,* putative, seeming, supposed
🔁 2 actual, true

reputedly adv allegedly, apparently, ostensibly *formal,* reputatively, seemingly, supposedly
🔁 actually

request v appeal, apply for, ask for, beg, beseech *formal,* call for, demand, desire, entreat *formal,* petition, put in for *colloq,* require, requisition *formal,* seek, solicit *formal,* supplicate *formal*
♦ n appeal, application, behest *formal,* call, demand, desire, entreaty *formal,* imploration *formal,* petition, petitioning, plea, pleading, prayer, requisition *formal,* solicitation *formal,* suit, supplication *formal*

require v 1 *let me know if you require anything:* be deficient in, be short of, crave, desire, lack, miss, need, want, wish 2 *you are required to attend:* ask, call on, command, compel, constrain *formal,* demand, direct, enjoin *formal,* force, insist on, instruct, make, oblige, order, request 3 *this requires careful thought:* demand, entail, involve, necessitate *formal,* take

required adj compulsory, demanded, essential, mandatory *formal,* necessary, needed, obligatory, prescribed *formal,* recommended, requisite *formal,* set, stipulated, unavoidable, vital
🔁 inessential, optional

requirement n 1 *meet all your requirements:* demand, essential, lack, must *colloq,* necessity, need, want 2 *a legal requirement:* condition, precondition *formal,* prerequisite *formal,* provision, proviso, qualification, requisite *formal,* sine qua non, specification, stipulation, term

requisite adj compulsory, essential, mandatory *formal,* necessary, needed, obligatory, prerequisite *formal,* prescribed *formal,* required, set, vital
♦ n 1 *legal requisites:* condition, precondition *formal,* prerequisite *formal,* qualification, requirement, specification, stipulation 2 *the basic requisites:* desiderative *formal,* desideratum *formal,* essential, must *colloq,* necessity, need, sine qua non
🔁 1 inessential 2 inessential

requisition v 1 *the soldiers requisitioned the lorry:* appropriate *formal,* commandeer, confiscate, occupy, seize, take, take over, take possession of, use 2 *requisition office equipment:* apply for, demand, order, put in for, request
♦ n 1 *the requisition of his vehicle:* appropriation

formal, commandeering, confiscation, occupation, seizure, takeover, use 2 *a requisition for a new PC:* application, call, demand, order, request

requital n amends, compensation, indemnification, indemnity, payment, pay-off, quittance *formal,* recompense, redress, reparation, repayment, restitution, satisfaction

requite v 1 *requited him for the inconvenience:* compensate, pay, recompense, redress, reimburse, remunerate, repay, satisfy 2 *requite an insult:* avenge, reciprocate, repay, respond to, retaliate, return

rescind v abrogate *formal,* annul, cancel, countermand *formal,* invalidate, negate, nullify *formal,* overturn, quash, recall, repeal, retract *formal,* reverse, revoke *formal,* set aside, void
🔁 enforce

rescue v 1 *rescue someone from danger:* deliver, emancipate, extricate, free, liberate, recover, release, save, set free 2 *rescued the fireplace from a skip:* recover, redeem, salvage, save
♦ n 1 *the rescue of the trapped miners:* deliverance, emancipation, freeing, liberation, recovery, release, salvation, saving 2 *the rescue of a historic building:* recovery, redemption, salvage, saving

research n analysis, assessment, examination, experiment, experimentation, exploration, fact-finding, groundwork, inquiry, inspection, investigation, probe, review, scrutiny, study, test(s), testing
♦ v analyse, assess, examine, experiment, explore, inspect, investigate, look into, probe, review, scrutinize, study, test

researcher n analyst, boffin, field worker, inquirer, inspector, investigator

resemblance n affinity, agreement, analogy, closeness, comparability, comparison, conformity, congruity *formal,* correspondence, likeness, nearness, parallel, parallelism, parity *formal,* sameness, similarity, similitude *formal,* uniformity
🔁 dissimilarity

resemble v approach, be like, be similar to, bear a resemblance to, duplicate, echo, favour, look like, mirror, parallel, take after
🔁 differ from

resent v be angry at, begrudge, dislike, feel aggrieved at, feel bitter about, grudge, grumble at, object to, take amiss, take exception to, take offence at, take umbrage at
🔁 accept, like

resentful adj aggrieved, angry, bitter, embittered, grudging, hurt, in high dudgeon, incensed, indignant, irked, irritated, miffed *colloq,* offended, peeved *colloq,* piqued, put out, wounded
🔁 contented, satisfied

resentment n anger, animosity, annoyance, bad feelings, bitterness, displeasure, grudge, hard feelings, (high) dudgeon, hostility, hurt, ill-feeling, ill-will, indignation, ire, irritation, offence, pique, umbrage, vexation
🔁 contentment, happiness

reservation n 1 *no reservations about employing him:* demur *formal,* doubt, hesitancy, hesitation, misgiving, qualm, scepticism, scruple, second thoughts 2 *a hotel reservation:* appointment, arrangement, booking, engagement, prearrangement **3** *a Native American reservation:* enclave, homeland, park, preserve, reserve, sanctuary, tract **4** *the reservation that you vacate the room by 10:* condition, limitation, proviso, qualification, stipulation

reserve *v* **1** *reserve a copy for me:* earmark, hold back, keep, keep back, lay aside, save, set apart, set aside **2** *reserve the liquid to make stock:* accumulate, hoard, keep, lay aside, retain, save, set aside, stockpile, store **3** *reserve a seat:* arrange for, book, engage, prearrange, secure **4** *reserve judgement:* adjourn, defer, delay, hold over, postpone, put off, shelve, suspend
🖬 **1** use up **2** use up
♦ *n* **1** *oil reserves:* accumulation, bank, cache, fund, hoard, pool, reservoir, savings, stock, stockpile, store, supply **2** *replaced him with one of the reserves:* fill-in, proxy, replacement, stand-in, substitute, supply, surrogate, understudy **3** *a nature reserve:* area, enclave, park, preserve, reservation, sanctuary, tract **4** *break through someone's reserve:* aloofness, coldness, coolness, detachment, remoteness, restraint, reticence, shyness, unapproachability, unresponsiveness
🖬 **4** approachability, friendliness, openness
♦ *adj* additional, alternative, auxiliary, extra, secondary, spare, substitute

reserved *adj* **1** *reserved seats:* arranged, booked, designated, destined, earmarked, engaged, held, intended, kept, meant, prearranged, retained, saved, set aside, spoken for, taken **2** *his reserved manner:* aloof, cold, cool, distant, remote, restrained, reticent, retiring, shy, silent, standoffish, taciturn, unapproachable, uncommunicative, unforthcoming, unresponsive, unsociable
🖬 **1** available, free, unreserved **2** friendly, open

reservoir *n* **1** *the reservoirs are drying up:* lake, loch *Scot*, pond, pool **2** *a reservoir for the fuel:* basin, cistern, container, holder, receptacle, repository *formal*, reservatory *formal*, tank, vat **3** *oil reservoirs:* accumulation, bank, fund, reserves, source, stock, stockpile, store, supply

reshuffle *n* change, interchange, realignment, rearrangement, redistribution, regrouping, reorganization, restructuring, revision, shake-up, upheaval
♦ *v* change, interchange, realign, rearrange, redistribute, regroup, reorganize, restructure, revise, shake up, shift, shuffle

reside *v* **1** *reside in the city:* board, dwell *formal*, inhabit, live, lodge, occupy, remain, settle, sojourn *formal*, stay **2** *the peace which resides in us all:* abide *formal*, be contained, be inherent, be present, dwell *formal*, exist, lie, rest

residence *n* **1** *a residence in the country:* abode *formal*, apartment, country house, country seat, digs *colloq*, domicile *formal*, dwelling *formal*, flat, habitation *formal*, hall, home, house, lodging, lodgings, manor, mansion, pad *colloq*, palace, place, quarters, seat, villa **2** *the duration of your residence:* sojourn *formal*, stay

resident *n* **1** *the city's residents:* citizen, dweller *formal*, householder, inhabitant, local, resider *formal* **2** *residents in the block:* dweller *formal*, lodger, occupant, occupier, resider *formal*, tenant

3 *parking is for hotel residents only:* client, guest, inmate, patient, resider *formal*, sojourner *formal*
🖬 **1** non-resident **2** non-resident **3** non-resident
♦ *adj* **1** *resident in the UK:* dwelling, gremial *old use*, inhabiting, settled **2** *the resident population:* local, neighbourhood **3** *the resident doctor:* en poste, live-in, living-in, permanent
🖬 **1** non-resident **2** non-resident **3** non-resident

residential *adj* commuter, dormitory, exurban *formal*, suburban

residual *adj* excess, left-over, net, remaining, surplus, unconsumed, unused

residue *n* balance, difference, dregs, excess, extra, lees, leftovers, overflow, remainder, remains, remnant, residuum *formal*, rest, surplus
🖬 core

resign *v* **1** *he resigned last week:* give in your notice, hand in your notice, leave, quit *colloq*, retire, stand down, step down **2** *resign a post:* abandon, abdicate, forgo, forsake *formal*, give up, leave, quit *colloq*, relinquish *formal*, renounce *formal*, surrender, vacate, yield

resignation *n* **1** *a letter of resignation:* abdication, departure, giving-up, notice, relinquishment *formal*, renunciation *formal*, retirement, standing-down, stepping-down, surrender **2** *accepted his fate with resignation:* acceptance, acquiescence *formal*, compliance *formal*, non-resistance, passivity, patience, reconciliation, stoicism, submission, yielding
🖬 **2** resistance

resigned *adj* acquiescent *formal*, long-suffering, passive, patient, philosophical, reconciled, stoical, submissive, unprotesting, unresisting, yielding
🖬 protesting, resistant

resilience *n* **1** *the resilience of the material:* bounce, elasticity, flexibility, give, plasticity, pliability, recoil, spring, springiness, suppleness **2** *she has shown great resilience:* adaptability, hardiness, strength, toughness
🖬 **1** inflexibility, rigidity

resilient *adj* **1** *resilient material:* bouncy, elastic, flexible, plastic, pliable, rubbery, springy, supple **2** *a resilient woman:* adaptable, hardy, strong, tough
🖬 **1** brittle, rigid **2** weak

resist *v* **1** *resist change:* battle, check, combat, confront, contend with, counter, counteract, curb, defy, fight, halt, hinder, hold out against, impede, obstruct, oppose, prevent, refuse, stem, stop, struggle against, thwart **2** *resist capture:* battle, combat, fight, hold out against, repel, stand up to, struggle against **3** *resist sweets:* abstain from, avoid, hold out against, refrain from, stop **4** *resist fire:* combat, counter, counteract, repel, stand up to, weather, withstand
🖬 **1** accept, submit to **2** submit to

resistance *n* **1** *a resistance to change:* avoidance, confrontation, contention, counteraction, hindrance, impedance, impediment, intransigence *formal*, obstruction, opposition, prevention, refusal, thwarting, withstanding **2** *surrendered without resistance:* battle, combat, confrontation, defiance, fight, fighting, obstruction, opposition, struggle
🖬 **1** acceptance, submission **2** submission

resistant *adj* **1** *resistant to new ideas:* antagonistic, defiant, intransigent *formal*, opposed, unwilling, unyielding **2** *resistant to high temperatures:* immune, impervious, invulnerable, proof, strong, tough, unaffected, unsusceptible   ⊠ **1** compliant, yielding

resolute *adj* adamant, bold, constant, decided, dedicated, determined, dogged, earnest, firm, fixed, inflexible, intent, obdurate *formal*, obstinate, persevering, relentless, resolved, serious, set, single-minded, stalwart, staunch, steadfast, strong-willed, stubborn, tenacious, undaunted, unflinching, unswerving, unwavering, unyielding   ⊠ half-hearted, irresolute, weak-willed

resolution *n* **1** *pass a resolution:* declaration, decree, finding, judgement, motion, proposition, verdict **2** *a New Year resolution:* decision, dedication **3** *his unshakeable resolution:* commitment, constancy, dedication, determination, devotion, doggedness, earnestness, firmness, inflexibility, intentness, perseverance, persistence, resolve, seriousness, steadfastness, tenacity, willpower, zeal **4** *the resolution of a puzzle:* answer, disentangling, solution, solving, sorting out, unravelling, working out   ⊠ **3** half-heartedness, indecision, uncertainty

resolve *v* **1** *resolve to do better:* conclude, decide, determine, fix, make up your mind, settle (on) **2** *resolve a problem:* answer, disentangle, solve, sort out, unravel, work out **3** *resolve something to its component parts:* analyse, anatomize, break down, break up, convert, detail, disintegrate, dissolve, divide, itemize, reduce, separate   ♦ *n* commitment, constancy, dedication, determination, devotion, doggedness, earnestness, firmness, inflexibility, intentness, perseverance, persistence, sense of purpose, seriousness, steadfastness, tenacity, willpower   ⊠ indecision

resonant *adj* booming, canorous *formal*, deep, echoing, full, plummy, resounding, reverberant, reverberating, rich, ringing, sonorous, strong, vibrant   ⊠ faint, weak

resort *n* **1** *a holiday resort:* centre, health resort, holiday centre, spa, spot **2** *our last resort:* alternative, chance, course (of action), expedient *formal*, measure, option, possibility, recourse, refuge, step   ▶ **resort to 1** *she resorted to tears:* avail yourself of, employ, exercise, fall back on, have recourse to, make use of, turn to, use, utilize **2** *we resort to the bar:* go to, patronize, repair to *formal*, visit

resound *v* boom, echo, re-echo, resonate, reverberate, ring, sound, thunder

resounding *adj* **1** *a resounding voice:* booming, echoing, loud, resonant, resonating, reverberating, ringing, sonorous, thunderous, vibrant **2** *a resounding victory:* conclusive, decisive, emphatic, great, impressive, notable, outstanding, remarkable, striking, thorough   ⊠ **1** faint

resource *n* **1** *a shortage of resources:* assets, capital, funds, holdings, materials, means, money, power, property, reserves, riches, supplies, wealth, wherewithal **2** *a resource of learning materials:* accumulation, fund, pool,

reserve, source, stockpile, store, supply **3** *our only resource is to call the police:* course, device, expedient *formal*, resort **4** *he showed great resource:* ability, capability, enterprise, imagination, ingenuity, initiative, inventiveness, resourcefulness

resourceful *adj* able, bright, capable, clever, creative, enterprising, imaginative, ingenious, innovative, inventive, original, quick-witted, sharp

resourceless *adj* feckless, feeble, helpless, hopeless, inadequate, shiftless, useless   ⊠ unimaginative

respect *v* **1** *respect your parents:* admire, appreciate, approve of, esteem *formal*, have a good opinion of, hold in high regard, honour, praise, regard, revere, set great store by, think highly of, value, venerate *formal* **2** *respect the rules:* adhere to, comply with *formal*, follow, fulfil, heed, honour, obey, observe **3** *respect other people's wishes:* consider, pay attention to, show consideration for, show regard for, take cognizance of *formal*, take into account   ⊠ **1** despise, scorn **2** disobey, ignore   ♦ *n* **1** *have great respect for her:* admiration, appreciation, approbation *formal*, esteem *formal*, high opinion, high regard, regard, reverence, veneration *formal* **2** *treat someone with respect:* attention, attentiveness, consideration, courtesy, notice, politeness, regard, thoughtfulness **3** *pay your respects:* best wishes, compliments, devoirs *formal*, good wishes, greetings, regards, salutations **4** *in every respect:* aspect, bearing, characteristic, connection, detail, facet, feature, matter, particular, point, reference, regard, relation, sense, way   ⊠ **1** disrespect

respectable *adj* **1** *a respectable woman:* above-board, clean-living, decent, decorous *formal*, dignified, good, honest, honourable, reputable, respected, upright, worthy **2** *wear something respectable:* clean, decent, neat, presentable, tidy **3** *a respectable amount:* acceptable, adequate, all right, appreciable, considerable, fair, not bad *colloq*, OK *colloq*, passable, reasonable, tolerable   ⊠ **1** dishonourable, disreputable **2** disreputable **3** inadequate, paltry

respected *adj* admired, esteemed *formal*, held in high regard, highly esteemed *formal*, highly regarded, highly valued, thought highly of, valued

respectful *adj* civil, courteous, courtly, deferential, humble, polite, reverent, reverential, subservient, well-mannered   ⊠ disrespectful

respective *adj* corresponding, individual, own, particular, personal, relevant, separate, several, special, specific, various

respite *n* **1** *work all day with no respite:* adjournment, break, breather *colloq*, cessation *formal*, gap, halt, hiatus *formal*, intermission, interruption, interval, let-up *colloq*, lull, pause, recess, relaxation, relief, rest **2** *these measures only provide a temporary respite:* abatement *formal*, deferment, delay, moratorium, postponement, remission, reprieve, stay, suspension

resplendent *adj* beaming, bright, brilliant, dazzling, effulgent *formal*, fulgent *formal*,

gleaming, glittering, irradiant, luminous, lustrous *formal*, radiant, refulgent *formal*, shining, splendid, splendiferous *colloq*
🖅 dull

respond *v* **1** *respond to a question:* answer, answer back, rejoin, reply, retort, return **2** *they have not responded to our offer:* acknowledge, answer, counter, reply **3** *respond to an attack:* counter, react, reciprocate, retaliate

response *n* **1** *response to a remark:* acknowledgement, answer, comeback *colloq*, feedback, rejoinder, reply, retort, return, riposte **2** *his response was to hit me:* reaction
🖅 **1** query

responsibility *n* **1** *it's your responsibility:* affair, baby *colloq*, burden, business, care, charge, concern, duty, obligation, onus, pidgin *colloq*, role, task **2** *a job with more responsibility:* authority, control, power **3** *admit responsibility:* accountability, answerability, blame, culpability *formal*, fault, guilt **4** *show responsibility:* conscientiousness, dependability, honesty, maturity, reliability, soundness, stability

responsible *adj* **1** *the person responsible for finance:* accountable, answerable, controlling, in charge of, in control of, leading, managing **2** *responsible for an accident:* accountable, answerable, at fault, blameworthy, culpable *formal*, guilty, liable, to blame **3** *a responsible citizen:* adult, conscientious, dependable, level-headed, mature, rational, reasonable, reliable, sane, sensible, sober, sound, stable, steady, trustworthy **4** *a responsible job:* authoritative, decision-making, executive, high-level *colloq*, important, powerful
🖅 **3** irresponsible, unreliable, untrustworthy

responsive *adj* alert, alive, amenable, awake, aware, forthcoming, on the ball *colloq*, open, perceptive, reactive, receptive, respondent, sensitive, sharp, with it *colloq*
🖅 unresponsive

rest[1] *n* **1** *a period of rest:* calm, ease, idleness, inactivity, leisure, motionlessness, quietude *formal*, relaxation, repose *formal*, stillness, tranquillity **2** *have a little rest:* lie-down, nap, siesta, sleep, slumber *formal*, snooze **3** *take a rest from working:* break, breather *colloq*, breathing-space, cessation *formal*, halt, holiday, interlude, intermission, interval, lull, pause, recess, respite, time off, vacation **4** *a pot rest:* base, holder, prop, stand, support
🖅 **1** action, activity **3** work
♦ *v* **1** *carry on without resting:* cease *formal*, halt, pause, stop **2** *you should rest for a while:* doze, laze, lie down, lounge, put your feet up *colloq*, recharge your batteries *colloq*, recline, relax, repose *formal*, sit (down), sleep, snooze, take it easy *colloq* **3** *what happens next rests on you:* be based, depend, hang, hinge, lie, rely **4** *rested her elbows on the desk:* lean, prop, stand, steady, support
🖅 **1** continue **2** work

rest[2] *n* balance, excess, leftovers, others, remainder, remains, remnant(s), residue, residuum *formal*, surplus
♦ *v* continue, endure, last, persist, remain, stay

restful *adj* calm, calming, comfortable, leisurely, peaceful, placid, quiet, relaxed, relaxing, serene, soothing, still, tranquil, undisturbed, unhurried

🖅 restless, tiring

restitution *n* amends, compensation, damages, indemnification, indemnity, recompense, redress, refund, reimbursement, remuneration, reparation, repayment, requital, restoration, restoring, return, satisfaction

restive *adj* **1** *a restive child:* recalcitrant *formal*, refractory *formal*, turbulent, uncontrollable, undisciplined, unmanageable, unruly, wayward, wilful **2** *the crowd grew restive:* agitated, anxious, edgy, fidgeting, fidgety, fretful, jumpy *colloq*, nervous, restless, tense, uneasy, unsettled, uptight *colloq*
🖅 **2** calm, relaxed

restless *adj* **1** *the crowd was getting restless:* impatient, restive *formal*, turbulent, unruly **2** *he seemed restless and uneasy:* agitated, anxious, edgy, fretful, jittery *colloq*, jumpy *colloq*, nervous, troubled, uneasy, unsettled, uptight *colloq*, worried **3** *the restless jiggling of his foot:* fidgeting, fidgety **4** *spent a restless night:* broken, disturbed, sleepless, tossing and turning, uncomfortable
🖅 **2** calm, relaxed **3** still **4** comfortable, restful

restlessness *n* **1** *the restlessness of the city:* activity, bustle, hurry, inconstancy, instability, movement, transience, turbulence, turmoil, unrest, unsettledness **2** *her increasing restlessness:* agitation, anxiety, disquiet, disturbance, edginess *colloq*, fitfulness, fretfulness, heebie-jeebies *colloq*, inquietude *formal*, jitters *colloq*, jumpiness *colloq*, nervousness, restiveness *formal*, uneasiness, unrest, unsettledness, worriedness
🖅 **1** calmness, relaxation **2** calmness, relaxation

restoration *n* **1** *the restoration of a building:* rebuilding, reconstruction, refurbishing, rehabilitation, renewal, renovation, repair **2** *restoration of strength after an illness:* recovery, refreshment, rejuvenation, revitalization, revival **3** *the restoration of the monarchy:* re-establishment, reinstallation, reinstatement, replacement, restitution, return
🖅 **1** damage **2** weakening **3** removal

restore *v* **1** *restore a building:* do up *colloq*, fix, mend, rebuild, recondition, reconstruct, redecorate, refurbish, rehabilitate, renew, renovate, repair, retouch, revamp **2** *restore your strength:* build up, recover, refresh, rejuvenate, revitalize, revive, revivify *formal*, strengthen **3** *restore lost property:* give back, hand back, replace, return **4** *restore order:* re-enforce, re-establish, re-impose, reinstate, reintroduce, return
🖅 **1** damage **2** weaken **3** remove

restrain *v* **1** *restrain someone from moving:* check, control, curb, detain, hinder, hold back, impede, obstruct, prevent, restrict, stop **2** *restrain a prisoner:* arrest, bind, chain, confine, detain, fetter, imprison, jail, manacle, tie **3** *restrain your feelings:* bottle up *colloq*, control, curb, govern, hold back, hold in check, inhibit, keep back, keep under control, regulate, repress, subdue, suppress
🖅 **2** liberate **3** encourage

restrained *adj* **1** *an unemotional and restrained person:* aloof, calm, cold, controlled, self-controlled, self-restrained, steady, unemotional **2** *restrained decorations:* discreet, low-key, mild, moderate, muted, quiet, soft, subdued, subtle, tasteful, temperate, unobtrusive
🖅 **1** demonstrative, emotional **2** loud *colloq*

restraint *n* **1** *restraints on spending:* barrier, block, bridle, check, constraint, control, curb, hindrance, inhibition, limit(s), limitation, prevention, rein, restriction(s), stint, suppression **2** *behave with restraint:* constraint, control, inhibition, judiciousness *formal*, moderation, prudence *formal*, self-control, self-discipline **3** *held under restraint:* bondage, captivity, confinement, constraint, duress, imprisonment **4** *kept in restraints:* bonds, chains, fetters, straitjacket, tie
ᴇ **1** liberty **3** liberty

restrict *v* **1** *restrict the number of entrants:* contain, control, curtail, demarcate, keep under control, keep within limits, limit, regulate **2** *restrict someone's movement:* bound, confine, constrain, cramp, curtail, hamper, handicap, hem in *colloq*, hinder, impede, restrain
ᴇ **1** broaden **2** free

restricted *adj* **1** *a restricted space:* confined, cramped, narrow, small, tight **2** *restricted information:* controlled, exclusive, limited, private, regulated, secret

restriction *n* **1** *restrictions on the use of the Internet:* bound, check, condition, constraint, control, curb, handicap, limit, limitation, proviso, qualification, regulation, restraint, rule, stipulation **2** *a total restriction on smoking:* ban, embargo
ᴇ **1** freedom **2** freedom

result *n* **1** *the result of overeating:* by-product, consequence, effect, end-product, fruit(s), issue, outcome, pay-off *colloq*, reaction, sequel, side effect, spin-off *colloq*, upshot **2** *the result of the tests:* answer, conclusion, decision, end, implication, judgement, verdict **3** *an exam result:* grade, mark, score
ᴇ **1** cause
♦ *v* **1** *result from alcohol abuse:* arise, come out of, derive, develop, emanate, emerge, ensue, eventuate *formal*, evolve, flow, follow, happen, issue, occur, proceed, spring, stem **2** *resulted in his paralysis:* culminate, end, finish, terminate
ᴇ **1** cause

resume *v* **1** *resume a search:* begin again, carry on, continue, go on with, proceed with, recommence, reopen, restart, start again, take up (again) **2** *classes resume soon:* begin again, carry on, continue, go on, proceed, recommence, reconvene, reopen, restart, start again
ᴇ **1** cease **2** cease

résumé *n* abstract, breakdown, digest, epitome, outline, overview, précis, recapitulation, review, run-down, sketch, summary, synopsis

resumption *n* continuation, proceeding, recommencement, re-establishment, renewal, reopening, restart, resurgence
ᴇ cessation

resurgence *n* reappearance, rebirth, recrudescence *formal*, re-emergence, renaissance, renascence *formal*, resumption, resurrection, return, revival, revivification *formal*, risorgimento *formal*
ᴇ decrease

resurrect *v* **1** *be resurrected from the dead:* bring back to life, raise from the dead, restore, restore to life, revive **2** *resurrect an old idea:* bring back,

reactivate, re-establish, re-install, reintroduce, renew, restore, resuscitate, revitalize, revive
ᴇ **1** bury, kill

resurrection *n* **1** *the resurrection of Jesus Christ:* bringing back to life, raising/rising from the dead, restoration to life, return from the dead **2** *resurrection of former procedures:* comeback, reappearance, rebirth, re-establishment, renaissance, renewal, restoration, resurgence, resuscitation, return, revitalization, revival

resuscitate *v* **1** *be resuscitated after an accident:* bring round, give the kiss of life to *colloq*, quicken, revive, revivify *formal*, save **2** *resuscitate a business:* breathe new life into, reanimate, reinvigorate, renew, rescue, restore, resurrect, revitalize, revive, revivify *formal*, save

resuscitated *adj* redintegrate(d) *formal*, redivivus *formal*, restored, resurrected, revived

retain *v* **1** *retain property:* grasp, grip, hang on to *colloq*, hold, hold back, hold fast to, keep, keep hold of, preserve, reserve, save **2** *retain feelings for:* continue to have, keep, maintain, preserve **3** *retain information:* bear in mind, call to mind, keep in mind, memorize, recall, recollect, remember **4** *retained as a consultant:* commission, employ, engage, hire, pay
ᴇ **1** release **3** forget **4** dismiss

retainer *n* **1** *be paid a retainer:* advance, deposit, fee, retaining fee **2** *his faithful retainer:* attendant, domestic, footman, lackey, menial, servant, valet, vassal

retaliate *v* avenge, counter-attack, fight back, get back at, get even with *colloq*, get your own back *colloq*, give as good as you get *colloq*, give someone a taste of their own medicine *colloq*, hit back, pay back, reciprocate, return like for like *colloq*, strike back, take revenge

retaliation *n* a taste of your own medicine *colloq*, an eye for an eye and a tooth for a tooth *colloq*, counter-attack, like for like *colloq*, reciprocation, reprisal, retribution, revenge, tit for tat *colloq*, ultion *formal*, vengeance

retard *v* brake, check, curb, decelerate, delay, handicap, hinder, hold up, impede, obstruct, put a/the brake on, restrict, slow down
ᴇ accelerate, speed up

retardation *n* **1** *the retardation of the process:* delay, hindering, hindrance, impeding, obstruction, retardment *formal*, slowing **2** *mental retardation:* deficiency, dullness, incapability, incapacity, mental handicap, retardment *formal*, slowness
ᴇ **1** advancement

retch *v* disgorge, gag, heave, puke *colloq*, reach, regurgitate, spew *colloq*, throw up *colloq*, vomit

reticence *n* muteness, quietness, reserve, restraint, secretiveness, silence, taciturnity, uncommunicativeness, unforthcomingness
ᴇ communicativeness, forwardness, frankness

reticent *adj* quiet, reserved, restrained, secretive, silent, taciturn, tight-lipped, uncommunicative, unforthcoming
ᴇ communicative, forward, frank

retinue *n* aides, attendants, cortège, entourage, escort, followers, following, personnel, servants, staff, suite, train

retire v **1** *retire at 65:* be put out to pasture *colloq*, give up work, leave work, stop work, stop working **2** *retired from the room:* depart, go, go away, leave, move, recede, withdraw **3** *retire from the battle:* decamp, retreat, withdraw
☒ **2** enter **3** advance, join

retired adj emeritus, ex-, former, past

retirement n **1** *retirement from the job:* departure, exit, giving up work, stopping work **2** *emerged from his retirement in the country:* loneliness, obscurity, privacy, retreat, seclusion, solitude, withdrawal

retiring adj bashful, coy, diffident, humble, modest, quiet, reserved, reticent, self-effacing, shrinking, shy, timid, unassertive, unassuming
☒ assertive, bold, forward

retort v answer, counter, rejoin, reply, respond, retaliate, return
♦ n answer, rejoinder, reply, response, riposte

retract v abjure *formal*, abrogate *formal*, cancel, deny, disavow *formal*, disclaim, disown, recant, renege, renounce, repeal, repudiate, rescind *formal*, reverse, revoke *formal*, take back, withdraw
☒ assert, maintain

retreat v decamp, depart, draw back, fall back, flee, give ground, give way, leave, pull back, quit *colloq*, recoil, retire, shrink, turn tail *colloq*, withdraw
☒ advance
♦ n **1** *the army's retreat from the city:* departure, drawing back, evacuation, falling back, flight, pulling back, withdrawal **2** *a remote mountain retreat:* asylum, den, harbour, haven, hide-away, hideout, refuge, sanctuary, shelter **3** *sought retreat from the world:* privacy, refuge, retirement, sanctuary, seclusion, shelter, solitude
☒ **1** advance, charge

retrench v **1** *need to retrench spending:* curtail, cut, cut back, decrease, diminish, lessen, limit, pare, prune, reduce, trim **2** *the crisis forced the company to retrench:* economize, husband, live more economically, save, slim down, tighten your belt *colloq*
☒ **1** increase

retrenchment n contraction, cost-cutting, curtailment, cut, cutback, cutting back, economy, pruning, reduction, run-down, shrinkage, tightening your belt *colloq*
☒ increase

retribution n compensation, just deserts *colloq*, justice, Nemesis, payment, punishment, reckoning, recompense, redress, repayment, reprisal, requital, retaliation, revenge, satisfaction, vengeance

retrieve v **1** *retrieved their ball from the garden:* bring back, fetch, get back, recapture, reclaim, recoup, recover, regain, repossess, rescue, restore **2** *somehow retrieved the situation:* make good, mend, put to rights, recoup, recover, redeem, remedy, repair, rescue, restore, salvage, save
☒ **1** lose

retrograde adj backward, declining, deteriorating, downward, negative, retrogressive, reverse, worsening
☒ progressive

retrogress v backslide, decline, degenerate, deteriorate, drop, ebb, fall, recede, regress, relapse, retreat, retrograde, return, revert, sink, wane, worsen
☒ advance, progress

retrogression n decline, deterioration, drop, ebb, fall, recidivism *formal*, regress, regression, relapse, retrogradation *formal*, return, worsening
☒ increase, progress

retrospect n afterthought, hindsight, recollection, re-examination, reflection, remembrance, review, survey, thinking back
☒ prospect

retrospective adj backward-looking, retro-active, retro-operative

return v **1** *return the way you came:* backtrack, come back, come home, get back, go back, revert **2** *see a doctor if the pains return:* come again, come back, reappear, recur **3** *return a library book:* deliver, give back, hand back, remit *formal*, send back, take back **4** *return the forests destroyed by development:* put back, reinstate, replace, restore **5** *return a favour:* do the same *colloq*, equal, exchange, match, reciprocate, repay, requite *formal* **6** *return a loan:* recompense, refund, reimburse, repay **7** *'and the same to you'*, *she returned:* answer, counter, rejoin, reply, respond, retort, riposte **8** *return a verdict:* announce, bring in, declare, deliver, pronounce
☒ **1** depart, leave **3** take
♦ n **1** *the return of the travellers:* comeback *colloq*, home-coming, reappearance **2** *the return of the symptoms:* reappearance, recurrence **3** *the return of a loan:* reciprocation, recompense, repayment **4** *the return of the wetlands:* reinstatement, replacement, restoration **5** *a good return on an investment:* advantage, benefit, gain, income, interest, proceeds, profit, revenue, reward, takings, yield **6** *the return of the books:* delivery, giving back, handing back, taking back
☒ **1** departure, disappearance **2** disappearance **4** removal **5** expense, loss, payment

re-use v reconstitute, recycle

revamp v do up *colloq*, overhaul, rebuild, recondition, reconstruct, refit, refurbish, rehabilitate, renovate, repair, restore

reveal v **1** *revealed her face:* display, exhibit, expose, expose to view, lay bare, manifest, show, uncover, unearth, unmask, unveil **2** *reveal a secret:* announce, betray, bring to light, broadcast, communicate, disclose, divulge, give away, impart, leak, let out, let slip, make known, make public, proclaim, publicize, publish, tell
☒ **1** conceal, hide, mask **2** conceal, hide

revealing adj **1** *a revealing remark:* give-away, indicative, revelatory, significant **2** *a revealing dress:* daring, diaphanous, low-cut, see-through, sheer

revel v **1** *revel in an experience:* bask, delight, enjoy, gloat, glory, indulge, joy, lap up, luxuriate, rejoice, relish, savour, take delight, take pleasure, thrive, wallow **2** *revelling through the night:* carouse, celebrate, have a party, live it up *colloq*, make merry, paint the town red *colloq*, push the boat out *colloq*, raise the roof *colloq*, roist, roister, whoop it up *colloq*
☒ **1** dislike
♦ n bacchanal, carousal, carouse, celebration, debauch, festivity, jollification, merrymaking,

party, rave *colloq*, rave-up *colloq*, saturnalia, spree

revelation *n* **1** *the revelation of his dark secret:* admission, betrayal, bringing to light, broadcasting, confession, disclosure, divulgence, exposure, leaking, uncovering, unearthing, unmasking, unveiling **2** *a shocking revelation:* announcement, communication, detail, fact, information, news, proclamation, publication, secreted/confidential information

reveller *n* bacchanal, carouser, celebrator, merrymaker, party-goer, pleasure-seeker, roisterer, wassailer

revelry *n* carousal, celebration, debauchery, festivity, fun, jollification, jollity, merrymaking, party
🖃 sobriety

revenge *n* eye for an eye and a tooth for a tooth *colloq*, redress, reprisal, requital, retaliation, retribution, satisfaction, tit for tat *colloq*, vendetta, vengeance
♦ *v* avenge, get back at someone for, get even with someone for *colloq*, get your own back for *colloq*, hit back at someone for, pay someone back for, repay, retaliate, settle a score/an old score

revengeful *adj* bitter, implacable, merciless, pitiless, resentful, spiteful, unforgiving, unmerciful, vengeful, vindictive
🖃 forgiving, merciful

revenue *n* gain, income, interest, proceeds, profit(s), receipts, return, rewards, takings, yield
🖃 expenditure

reverberate *v* boom, echo, re-echo, resonate, resound, ring, vibrate

reverberation *n* **1** *the reverberation of the sounds in the hall:* echo, rebound, recoil, re-echoing, reflection, resonance, resounding, ringing, vibration **2** *reverberations following the resignation:* consequence, effect, repercussion, result, ripple *colloq*, shock wave *colloq*

revere *v* admire, adore, esteem *formal*, exalt, honour, look up to, pay homage to, respect, reverence, think highly of, venerate *formal*, worship
🖃 despise, scorn

reverence *n* admiration, adoration, awe, deference, devotion, exaltation, (high) esteem *formal*, homage, honour, respect, veneration *formal*, worship
🖃 contempt, scorn
♦ *v* admire, adore, honour, respect, revere, venerate *formal*, worship
🖃 despise, scorn

reverent *adj* admiring, adoring, awed, deferential, devoted, devout, dutiful, humble, loving, respectful, reverential, solemn, worshipping
🖃 disrespectful, irreverent

reverie *n* absent-mindedness, abstraction, brown study, daydream, daydreaming, inattention, musing, preoccupation, trance, woolgathering

reversal *n* **1** *the reversal of the verdict:* annulment, cancellation, countermanding, negation, nullification, repeal, rescinding *formal*, reverse, revocation *formal*, turnabout, turnaround, upset,

U-turn *colloq*, volte-face **2** *suffer many reversals:* adversity, affliction, blow, check, defeat, difficulty, disappointment, failure, hardship, misadventure, misfortune, mishap, problem, setback, trial, upset
🖃 **1** advancement, progress

reverse *v* **1** *reversed away at high speed:* back, backtrack, drive backwards, move backwards, regress *formal*, retreat, withdraw **2** *reverse a decision:* annul, cancel, countermand *formal*, invalidate, negate, overrule, overthrow, quash, repeal, rescind *formal*, retract *formal*, revoke *formal*, set aside, undo **3** *reverse the position of the two ornaments:* alter, change, change round, swap, transpose **4** *reverse a glass:* invert, overturn, put back to front, turn round, turn upside-down, up-end, upset
🖃 **1** go forwards **2** advance, enforce
♦ *n* **1** *the reverse of a coin:* antithesis *formal*, back, contrary, converse, counter, inverse, opposite, other side, rear, underside **2** *suffer many reverses:* adversity, affliction, blow, check, defeat, difficulty, disappointment, failure, hardship, misadventure, misfortune, mishap, problem, reversal, setback, trial, upset, vicissitude *formal*
♦ *adj* back, backward, contrary, converse, inverse, inverted, opposite, rear, verso

revert *v* go back, lapse, regress, relapse, resume, return

review *n* **1** *a review of a film:* appraisal, assessment, commentary, criticism, critique, evaluation, judgement, notice, rating, report **2** *a review on climate change:* analysis, examination, report, scrutiny, study, survey **3** *a review of the process:* recapitulation, recension *formal*, re-evaluation, re-examination, rethink *colloq*, revision **4** *writes for the Literary Review:* journal, magazine, periodical
♦ *v* **1** *review a book:* appraise *formal*, assess, criticize, discuss, evaluate, judge, weigh (up) **2** *review soldiers on parade:* analyse, examine, inspect, scrutinize, study, survey, view **3** *review the situation:* reassess, recapitulate, reconsider, re-evaluate, re-examine, rethink, revise, size up *colloq*, take stock of, weigh (up)

reviewer *n* arbiter, commentator, connoisseur, critic, essayist, judge

revile *v* abuse, blackguard, calumniate *formal*, defame, denigrate *formal*, despise, hate, libel, malign, reproach, scorn, slander, smear, traduce *formal*, vilify *formal*, vituperate *formal*
🖃 praise

revise *v* **1** *revise your opinion:* alter, change, modify, reconsider, re-examine, review **2** *revise a text:* alter, amend, change, correct, edit, emend *formal*, recast, redraft, revamp, reword, rewrite, update **3** *revise a subject for an exam:* bone up on *colloq*, cram *colloq*, learn, memorize, mug up *colloq*, study, swot up *colloq*

revision *n* **1** *the revision of a policy:* alteration, amendment, change, modification, re-examination, review **2** *the revision of an article:* alteration, amendment, change, correction, editing, emendation *formal*, recast, recasting, reconstruction, rereading, rewriting **3** *doing revision for an exam:* homework, learning, memorizing, studying, swotting *colloq*, updating

revitalize *v* reactivate, reanimate, refresh, rejuvenate, renew, restore, resurrect, revive, revivify *formal*
⊟ dampen, suppress

revival *n* comeback *colloq*, reawakening, rebirth, re-establishment, reintroduction, renaissance, renewal, restoration, resurgence, resurrection, resuscitation, revitalization, the kiss of life *colloq*, upsurge, upturn

revive *v* 1 *the paramedics tried to revive him:* animate, awaken, bring round, give the kiss of life to *colloq*, quicken, reawaken, resuscitate, rouse 2 *she revived from her coma:* awaken, rally, reawaken, recover, rouse 3 *steps to revive the business:* animate, breathe new life into, invigorate, rally, reactivate, reanimate, re-establish, reintroduce, rekindle, renew, restore, revitalize 4 *revived by a hot meal:* breathe new life into, cheer up, comfort, invigorate, refresh, renew, restore, revitalize
⊟ 4 weary

revivify *v* inspirit *formal*, invigorate, reactivate, reanimate, refresh, renew, restore, resuscitate, revitalize, revive
⊟ dampen, depress

reviving *adj* bracing, enheartening, exhilarating, invigorating, reanimating, refreshening, regenerating, reinvigorating, revivescent *formal*, revivifying *formal*, reviviscent *formal*, stimulating, tonic
⊟ disheartening, exhausting

revocation *n* abolition, annulment, cancellation, countermanding *formal*, invalidation, negation, nullification, quashing, repeal, repealing, repudiation, rescinding *formal*, rescission *formal*, retractation *formal*, retraction *formal*, reversal, revoking, withdrawal
⊟ enforcement

revoke *v* abolish, abrogate *formal*, annul, cancel, countermand *formal*, invalidate, negate, nullify, quash, repeal, rescind *formal*, retract *formal*, reverse, withdraw
⊟ enforce

revolt *n* coup (d'état), defection, insurrection, mutiny, putsch, rebellion, revolution, rising, secession, uprising
♦ *v* 1 *the people revolted against their masters:* defect, dissent *formal*, mutiny, rebel, resist, riot, rise, rise up, take to the streets, take up arms 2 *the smell revolted me:* disgust, nauseate, offend, repel, sicken, turn your stomach
⊟ 1 submit 2 delight, please

revolting *adj* abhorrent, abominable, appalling, disgusting, distasteful, foul, hateful, horrible, loathsome, nasty, nauseating, obnoxious, offensive, off-putting, repellent, repugnant *formal*, repulsive, shocking, sickening, vile
⊟ attractive, delightful, palatable, pleasant

revolution *n* 1 *the French revolution:* coup (d'état), insurgence, insurrection, mutiny, putsch, rebellion, revolt, rising, uprising 2 *a revolution in communications:* cataclysm, change, innovation, metamorphosis *technical*, reformation, transformation, upheaval 3 *half a million revolutions per minute:* circle, circuit, cycle, gyration, orbit, rotation, round, spin, turn, wheel, whirl

revolutionary *n* anarchist, insurgent, insurrectionist, mutineer, rebel, revolutionist
♦ *adj* 1 *a revolutionary movement:* anarchistic, extremist, insurgent, insurrectionary, mutinous, rebel, rebellious, seditious, subversive 2 *revolutionary ideas:* avant-garde, different, drastic, experimental, innovative, new, progressive, radical
⊟ 1 conservative

revolutionize *v* cause radical changes in, reform, reorganize, restructure, transfigure, transform, turn upside-down

revolve *v* 1 *the planets revolve round the sun:* circle, go, gyrate, move, orbit, rotate 2 *the Earth revolves on its axis:* gyrate, pivot, rotate, spin, swivel, turn, wheel, whirl 3 *his life revolves around sport:* be preoccupied with, centre on, concentrate on, focus on, hang on, hinge on, turn on

revolver *n* firearm, gun, handgun, pistol, shooter *colloq*, six-shooter

revolving *adj* gyrating, gyratory, rotating, spinning, turning, whirling
⊟ stationary

revulsion *n* abhorrence, abomination, aversion, detestation *formal*, disgust, dislike, distaste, hate, hatred, loathing, nausea, repugnance *formal*, repulsion
⊟ approval, delight, pleasure

reward *n* 1 *a reward for long service:* decoration, desert, honour, medal, merit 2 *a reward for his capture:* benefit, bonus, bounty, compensation, gain, payment, pay-off, premium, present, prize, profit, recompense, remuneration, repayment, return 3 *a fitting reward for his crimes:* just deserts *colloq*, punishment, requital, retribution
♦ *v* 1 *rewarded for his valour:* decorate, honour 2 *you'll be rewarded for your help:* compensate, pay, recompense, remunerate, repay, requite
⊟ 1 punish

rewarding *adj* advantageous, beneficial, edifying, enriching, fruitful, fulfilling, gratifying, lucrative, pleasing, productive, profitable, remunerative, satisfying, valuable, worthwhile
⊟ unrewarding

rewording *n* metaphrase *technical*, metaphrasis, paraphrase, rephrasing, revision

rewrite *v* correct, edit, emend *formal*, recast, redraft, revise, reword, rework

rhetoric *n* 1 *the art of rhetoric:* eloquence, oratory 2 *a speech full of empty rhetoric:* bombast, fustian, grandiloquence *formal*, hyperbole, long-windedness, magniloquence *formal*, pomposity, prolixity *formal*, verbosity, wordiness

rhetorical *adj* 1 *a rhetorical device:* linguistic, oratorical, stylistic, verbal 2 *his pompous, rhetorical language:* artificial, bombastic, declamatory *formal*, flamboyant, florid, flowery, grand, grandiloquent *formal*, high-flown, high-sounding, long-winded, magniloquent *formal*, pompous, pretentious, prolix *formal*, showy, verbose, wordy
⊟ 2 simple

rhyme *n* ditty, jingle, limerick, ode, poem, poetry, song, verse

rhythm n **1** *the rhythm of the music:* beat, cadence, lilt, pulse, swing, tempo, throb, time **2** *the changing rhythms in the poem:* accent, cadence, measure, metre, tempo, time **3** *the rhythm of the seasons:* flow, movement, pattern

rhythmic adj flowing, lilting, metric, metrical, periodic, pulsating, regular, repeated, rhythmical, steady, throbbing

rib n **1** *a fractured rib:* bone, costa *formal* **2** *the structure is supported by metal ribs:* band, bar, moulding, ribbing, ridge, shaft, support, vein, wale, welt

ribald adj base, bawdy, blue *colloq,* coarse, earthy, filthy, foul-mouthed, gross, indecent, lewd, licentious, low, naughty *colloq,* obscene, off-colour, Rabelaisian, racy, risqué, rude, scurrilous, smutty, vulgar
🗷 polite

ribaldry n baseness, bawdiness, coarseness, earthiness, filth, grossness, indecency, licentiousness, lowness, naughtiness *colloq,* obscenity, raciness, rudeness, scurrility, smut, smuttiness, vulgarity

ribbon n **1** *ribbons in her hair:* band, braid, cord, fillet, hair-band, headband, sash, taenia **2** *cut to ribbons:* shred, strip, tatter

rich adj **1** *a rich man:* affluent, filthy rich *slang,* flush *colloq,* in the money *colloq,* loaded *slang,* made of money *colloq,* moneyed, prosperous, rolling in it *colloq,* stinking rich *slang,* wealthy, well-heeled *colloq,* well-off, well-to-do, with money to burn *colloq* **2** *rich costumes:* costly, elaborate, expensive, fine, gorgeous, grand, lavish, lush, luxurious, magnificent, opulent *formal,* ornate, precious, priceless, splendid, sumptuous, valuable **3** *rich in nutrients:* abounding, full, high, overflowing, packed, replete *formal,* steeped, well-provided, well-supplied **4** *a rich supply:* abundant, ample, copious, plenteous *formal,* plentiful, profuse **5** *rich soil:* fecund *formal,* fertile, fruitful, lush, productive **6** *rich food:* creamy, fatty, full-bodied, full-flavoured, heavy, savoury, spicy, strong **7** *rich colours:* bright, brilliant, deep, intense, strong, vibrant, vivid, warm **8** *that's rich!:* ironic, laughable, outrageous, preposterous, ridiculous **9** *a rich voice:* deep, full, mellifluous *formal,* mellow, resonant, sonorous
🗷 **1** impoverished, poor **2** plain **5** barren, infertile **6** bland, plain **7** dull, soft

riches n affluence, assets, (filthy) lucre *old use,* fortune, gold, means, money, opulence *formal,* property, prosperity, resources, substance, treasure, wealth
🗷 poverty

richly adv **1** *a richly furnished suite:* elaborately, elegantly, expensively, exquisitely, gorgeously, lavishly, luxuriously, opulently *formal,* palatially, splendidly, sumptuously **2** *she richly deserves her good fortune:* appropriately, completely, fully, properly, suitably, thoroughly, well
🗷 **1** poorly, scantily

rickety adj broken-down, decrepit, derelict, dilapidated, flimsy, insecure, jerry-built, ramshackle, shaky, unstable, unsteady, wobbly
🗷 stable, strong

rid v cleanse, clear, deliver, free, purge, purify, relieve, unburden

riddance n **1** *the riddance of household pests:* clearance, disposal, ejection, elimination, expulsion, extermination, purgation, removal **2** *riddance from ailments:* deliverance, freedom, release, relief
🗷 **2** burdening

riddle[1] n **1** *solve a riddle:* brainteaser, conundrum, koan *technical,* poser, problem, puzzle **2** *he's a riddle to me:* enigma, mystery, puzzle

riddle[2] v **1** *riddled with holes:* pepper, perforate, pierce, puncture **2** *riddled with cancer:* fill, infest, permeate, pervade **3** *riddle the soil and then rake it:* filter, sieve, sift, strain, winnow

ride v **1** *ride a horse:* control, gallop, handle, manage, sit, trot **2** *ride in a vehicle:* drive, go, journey, move, pedal, progress, sit, steer, travel
◆ n drive, jaunt, journey, lift, outing, spin, trip

ridge n **1** *clouds appeared over the ridge:* arête, drum, drumlin, escarpment, esker, hill, hog's back, hummock, reef, saddle, sastruga, yardang **2** *the surface is covered in small ridges:* band, costa *formal,* crinkle, knurl, lump, ripple, wale, welt

ridicule n badinage, banter, chaff, derision, irony, jeering, laughter, mockery, sarcasm, satire, scorn
🗷 praise
◆ v burlesque, caricature, deride, gibe, jeer, lampoon, laugh at, make fun of, mock, parody, pooh-pooh *colloq,* rag *colloq,* rib *colloq,* satirize, scoff, scorn, send up, sneer, take the mickey out of *colloq*
🗷 praise

ridiculous adj **1** *amused us with his ridiculous antics:* comical, droll, facetious, funny, hilarious, humorous, risible *formal* **2** *a ridiculous notion:* absurd, contemptible, derisory, farcical, foolish, incredible, laughable, ludicrous, nonsensical, outrageous, preposterous, risible *formal,* silly, stupid, unbelievable
🗷 **2** sensible

rife adj **1** *rife with cockroaches:* abounding, overflowing, swarming, teeming **2** *rumours are rife:* abundant, common, epidemic, extensive, frequent, general, predominant, prevalent, raging, rampant, ubiquitous, widespread
🗷 **2** scarce

riff-raff n canaille, dregs, hoi polloi, mob, rabble, rent-a-mob *colloq,* scum, undesirables

rifle[1] n airgun, bundook, carbine, firearm, firelock, flintlock, fusil, gun, musket, shotgun

rifle[2] v **1** *rifle through a desk:* rummage, search **2** *rifle a till:* burgle, loot, maraud, pillage, plunder, ransack, rob, sack, strip

rift n **1** *a rift in the rock:* breach, break, cavity, chink, cleft, crack, cranny, crevice, fault, fissure, fracture, gap, opening, slit, space, split **2** *the argument caused a rift between them:* alienation, breach, conflict, difference, disagreement, division, estrangement *formal,* schism, separation, split
🗷 **2** unity

rig n accoutrements *formal,* apparatus, equipment, fittings, fixtures, gear, kit, machinery, outfit, tackle
◆ v cook *colloq,* distort, doctor, fake, falsify, fiddle, forge, manipulate, massage, misrepresent, pervert, tamper with, twist

▶ **rig out 1** *rig a boat out:* equip, fit (out), furnish, kit out, make ready, outfit, provide, supply **2** *rigged out in designer clothes:* accoutre *formal,* array *formal,* attire *formal,* clothe, dress (up), garb, get up *colloq,* robe, turn out

▶ **rig up** arrange, assemble, build, cobble together *colloq,* construct, erect, fit up, fix up, improvise, knock up *colloq,* put together, throw together *colloq*

F3 dismantle

right *adj* **1** *the right answer:* accurate, actual, authentic, bang on *colloq,* correct, exact, factual, genuine, precise, real, spot on *colloq,* true, valid **2** *the right thing to do:* acceptable, accepted, admissible, appropriate, approved, becoming, correct, desirable, fit, fitting, proper, reasonable, satisfactory, suitable, the done thing *colloq* **3** *the right time to sell:* advantageous, appropriate, auspicious *formal,* convenient, favourable, opportune, preferable, propitious *formal* **4** *it's not right that he should have to pay:* equitable, ethical, fair, good, honest, honourable, just, lawful, legal, moral, principled, proper, righteous, upright, virtuous **5** *my right eye:* dextral *formal,* right-hand, starboard **6** *the right wing of the party:* conservative, reactionary **7** *he's a right fool:* absolute, complete, real, thorough, utter

F3 1 erroneous, incorrect, wrong **2** improper, unsuitable **3** unsuitable **4** unfair, wrong **5** left **6** left

♦ *adv* **1** *do everything right:* by the book *colloq,* correctly, precisely, properly, satisfactorily, well **2** *you've guessed right:* accurately, correctly, exactly, factually, precisely **3** *it's all turned out right for him:* favourably, satisfactorily, well **4** *didn't treat her right:* fairly, properly, well **5** *right to the bottom:* absolutely, all the way, as the crow flies, completely, directly, entirely, in a straight line, slap bang *colloq,* straight, totally, utterly, wholly **6** *I'll be right back:* immediately, straight, without delay

F3 1 incorrectly, wrongly **2** incorrectly, wrongly **3** wrongly **4** unfairly

♦ *n* **1** *know right from wrong:* ethics, fairness, good, goodness, honesty, honour, integrity, justice, lawfulness, legality, morality, propriety *formal,* rectitude *formal,* righteousness, truthfulness, uprightness, virtue **2** *know your rights:* authority, birthright, claim, droit *technical,* due, entitlement, freedom, licence, lien *formal,* permission, power, prerogative, privilege

F3 1 wrong

♦ *v* **1** *try to right a wrong:* avenge, correct, fix, put in order, put right, rectify, redress, repair, settle, straighten out, vindicate **2** *managed to right the canoe:* set upright, stand up, straighten up

righteous *adj* **1** *a righteous person/action:* blameless, equitable, ethical, fair, God-fearing, good, guiltless, honest, honourable, incorrupt, irreproachable, just, law-abiding, moral, pure, saintly, sinless, upright, virtuous, worthy **2** *righteous anger:* acceptable, defensible, excusable, explainable, justifiable, justified, legitimate, proper, reasonable, supportable, valid, warranted, well-founded

F3 1 unrighteous **2** unjustifiable

righteousness *n* blamelessness, dharma *technical,* equity, ethicalness, goodness, holiness, honesty, honour, integrity, justice, morality,

probity *formal,* purity, rectitude *formal,* sanctification, uprightness, virtue

F3 unrighteousness

rightful *adj* authorized, bona fide, correct, due, genuine, just, lawful, legal, legitimate, proper, real, suitable, true, valid

F3 unlawful, wrongful

rightfully *adv* by rights, correctly, de jure *technical,* justifiably, justly, lawfully, legally, legitimately, properly, rightly

F3 incorrectly, unjustifiably

rigid *adj* **1** *rigid plastic:* firm, hard, inelastic, inflexible, stiff, unbending, unyielding **2** *a rigid routine:* cast-iron, fixed, inflexible, invariable, set, unalterable, unbending, unyielding **3** *a rigid political system:* austere, harsh, inflexible, intransigent *formal,* rigorous, severe, Spartan, stern, strict, stringent, uncompromising, unrelenting, unyielding

F3 1 bending, elastic, flexible, malleable **2** flexible **3** variable, weak

rigmarole *n* **1** *go through the whole rigmarole again:* bother, carry-on *colloq,* fuss, hassle *colloq,* palaver, performance, process, red tape *colloq,* to-do *colloq* **2** *some rigmarole about her being psychic:* gibberish, jargon, nonsense, twaddle

rigorous *adj* **1** *rigorous checks:* accurate, conscientious, exact, laborious, meticulous, painstaking, precise, punctilious, scrupulous, thorough **2** *rigorous training:* austere, exacting, firm, hard, harsh, intransigent *formal,* rigid, severe, spartan, stern, strict, stringent, tough, uncompromising

F3 1 lax, superficial

rigour *n* **1** *the rigours of war:* hardship, ordeal, privation *formal,* suffering, trial **2** *the rigour of the tests:* accuracy, conscientiousness, exactness, meticulousness, preciseness, precision, punctiliousness, thoroughness **3** *a self-imposed rigour in budgetary matters:* austerity, firmness, hardness, harshness, inflexibility, intransigence *formal,* rigidity, severity, sternness, strictness, stringency, toughness

F3 3 leniency, mildness

rig-out *n* apparel *formal,* clobber *colloq,* clothes, clothing, costume, dress, garb *colloq,* garments, gear *colloq,* get-up *colloq,* habit, livery, outfit, raiment *formal,* togs *colloq,* uniform

rile *v* aggravate *colloq,* anger, annoy, bug *colloq,* exasperate, irk, irritate, nettle, peeve *colloq,* pique, put out, upset, vex

F3 calm, soothe

rim *n* border, brim, brink, circumference, edge, lip, margin, verge

F3 centre, middle

rind *n* crust, epicarp *formal,* husk, integument *formal,* peel, skin

ring¹ *n* **1** *a ring of islands:* atoll, band, belt, circle, circlet, circuit, girdle, halo, hoop, loop, round **2** *a boxing ring:* area, arena, circle, enclosure **3** *a ring of drug smugglers:* alliance, association, band, cartel, cell, circle, clique, club, combine, coterie, crew, fraternity, gang, gathering, group, league, mob, organization, society, sorority, syndicate

♦ *v* circumscribe *formal,* encircle, enclose, encompass, gird, hem in, loop, surround

ring² *v* **1** *a bell rang:* buzz, chime, clang, clink, ding, ding-dong, jingle, knell, peal, sound, tinkle,

toll **2** *his voice rang:* echo, resonate, resound, reverberate, sound **3** *I'll ring you later:* call, give a bell *colloq*, give a buzz *colloq*, give a tinkle *colloq*, phone, ring up, telephone
♦ *n* **1** *the ring of the bells:* chime, clang, clink, ding-dong, jingle, knell, peal, tinkle, toll **2** *give me a ring:* bell *colloq*, buzz *colloq*, call, phone call, tinkle *colloq*

ringleader *n* bell-wether, brains *colloq*, chief, fugleman, leader, mouthpiece, spokesman, spokesperson, spokeswoman

rinse *v* bathe, clean, cleanse, dip, swill, wash, wash clean, wet

riot *n* **1** *a riot in the streets:* affray, anarchy, brawl, commotion, confusion, disorder, disturbance, fight, fracas, fray, insurgence, insurrection, lawlessness, mêlée, quarrel, rebellion, revolt, rising, row, strife, tumult, turbulence, turmoil, uprising, uproar **2** *a drunken riot:* debauchery, feasting, indulgence, merrymaking *old use*, orgy, partying, rave *colloq*, rave-up *colloq*, revelry **3** *a riot of colour:* display, exhibition, extravaganza, flourish, show **4** *this show is a riot:* hoot *colloq*, laugh, scream *colloq*
🄴 **1** calm, order
♦ *v* go berserk, go on the rampage, mutiny, rampage, rebel, revolt, rise up, run amok, run riot, run wild, rush wildly, storm, tear

riotous *adj* **1** *a riotous mob:* disorderly, insubordinate, insurrectionary, lawless, mutinous, rebellious, uncontrollable, ungovernable, unruly, violent **2** *riotous living:* unrestrained, wanton, wild **3** *a riotous party:* boisterous, loud, noisy, rowdy, tumultuous, uproarious
🄴 **1** orderly **2** restrained

rip *v* **1** *rip the material:* burst, cut, gash, hack, lacerate, rend, rupture, shred, slash, slit, split, tear **2** *the paper ripped:* be torn, burst, rupture, separate, split, tear
♦ *n* cleavage, cut, gash, hole, rent, rupture, slash, slit, split, tear
▶ **rip off** cheat, con *colloq*, defraud, diddle, do *colloq*, dupe, exploit, fleece *colloq*, overcharge, sting *slang*, swindle, trick

ripe *adj* **1** *ripe fruit:* complete, developed, finished, fully-developed, fully-grown, grown, mature, mellow, perfect, ripened, seasoned **2** *the time is ripe for change:* advantageous, auspicious *formal*, favourable, fit, opportune, propitious *formal*, ready, right, suitable, timely
🄴 **2** inauspicious *formal*, inopportune, untimely

ripen *v* age, come to maturity, develop, mature, mellow, season

rip-off *n* cheat, con *colloq*, con trick *colloq*, daylight robbery *colloq*, diddle, exploitation, fraud, robbery, sting *slang*, swindle, theft

riposte *n* answer, comeback, quip, rejoinder, repartee, reply, response, retort, return, sally

ripple *n* **1** *ripples in the water:* disturbance, eddy, ripplet, undulation, wave **2** *the gentle ripple of the stream:* babble, burble, gurgle, lapping, purl **3** *the firm's collapse caused ripples in the City:* consequence, effect, repercussion, result, reverberation, shock wave *colloq*
♦ *v* **1** *the wind rippled the fabric:* crease, crumple, pucker, ruffle, wimple, wrinkle **2** *the flag rippled*

in the breeze: ruffle, undulate, wimple **3** *the brook rippled through the forest:* flow, purl

rise *v* **1** *the sun was rising:* ascend, get higher, go up, move upwards **2** *the land rose in front of us:* ascend, climb (up), get steeper, go uphill, mount, rocket **3** *the castle rose before them:* loom, soar, tower **4** *prices keep rising:* escalate, get higher, go up, grow, increase, intensify, mount, rocket, soar, swell **5** *he rises at 7:* arise, get out of bed, get up **6** *she rose when he entered:* arise, get to your feet, get up, jump up, leap up, spring up, stand up **7** *he is rising in the world:* advance, be promoted, improve, make progress, progress, prosper **8** *the problems which rise from poverty:* appear, begin, commence *formal*, emanate, emerge, flow, issue, originate, spring, start **9** *the people rose against this tyranny:* defect, dissent *formal*, mutiny, rebel, resist, revolt, riot, take to the streets, take up arms **10** *rise to the challenge:* attempt, do your best, exert yourself, react to, respond to, try
🄴 **1** descend, fall **2** descend, fall **4** fall **5** go to bed **6** sit down **7** decline
♦ *n* **1** *a steep rise:* acclivity *formal*, ascent, climb, elevation, hill, incline, slope **2** *the rise in crime:* escalation, growth, increase, increment, leap, upsurge, upturn **3** *his rise to power:* advance, advancement, aggrandizement *formal*, improvement, progress, promotion, raise *US*
🄴 **1** descent, valley **2** fall **3** fall

risible *adj* absurd, amusing, comic, comical, droll, farcical, funny, hilarious, humorous, laughable, ludicrous, rib-tickling *colloq*, ridiculous, side-splitting *colloq*
🄴 serious, unfunny

rising *n* insurrection, revolt, revolution, riot, uprising
♦ *adj* **1** *the rising of costs:* ascending, growing, increasing, intensifying, mounting, soaring, swelling **2** *the rising of fascism:* advancing, approaching, emerging
🄴 **1** decreasing

risk *n* **1** *there is some risk of side-effects:* chance, danger, hazard, possibility, threat, uncertainty **2** *lives are at risk:* danger, hazard, jeopardy, peril, threat **3** *take a risk:* adventure, chance, gamble, hazard, speculation, venture
🄴 **1** certainty **2** safety **3** certainty
♦ *v* **1** *risk your life:* endanger, gamble, hazard, imperil, jeopardize, put in jeopardy, put on the line *colloq*, take a chance on **2** *risk punishment:* chance, dare, take the risk of, venture

risky *adj* chancy, dangerous, dicey *colloq*, dodgy *colloq*, hazardous, high-risk, iffy *colloq*, perilous, precarious, touch-and-go, tricky, uncertain, unsafe
🄴 safe

risqué *adj* adult *colloq*, bawdy, blue *colloq*, coarse, crude, dirty, earthy, immodest, improper, indecent, indelicate, naughty, near the knuckle *colloq*, off-colour, racy, ribald, rude, smutty, suggestive
🄴 decent, proper

rite *n* act, ceremonial, ceremony, custom, form, formality, liturgy, observance, office, ordinance, practice, procedure, ritual, sacrament, service, usage

ritual *n* **1** *a religious ritual:* celebration, ceremonial, ceremony, liturgy, observance, ordinance, rite, sacrament, service, solemnity

2 *her bedtime ritual:* act, convention, custom, form, formality, habit, practice, procedure, routine, tradition, usage, wont
♦ *adj* ceremonial, conventional, customary, formal, habitual, prescribed, procedural, routine, set, traditional
 informal

rival *n* **1** *defeated his rivals:* adversary, antagonist, challenger, competitor, contender, contestant, opponent, opposition, vier **2** *a pianist without rival:* equal, fellow, match, peer
 1 associate, colleague
♦ *adj* competing, competitive, conflicting, in competition, in conflict, in opposition, opposed, opposing
 associate
♦ *v* compare with, compete with, contend with, emulate, equal, match, measure up to, oppose, parallel, vie with

rivalry *n* antagonism, competition, competitiveness, conflict, contention, contest, opposition, strife, struggle, vying
 co-operation

river *n* watercourse, waterway

Forms of river or watercourse include:
beck, billabong, bourn, broads, brook, burn, canal, channel, confluence, creek, cut, delta, estuary, firth, frith, inlet, mountain stream, mouth, rill, rillet, rivulet, runnel, source, stream, tributary, wadi, waterway

---

riveting *adj* absorbing, arresting, captivating, engrossing, enthralling, exciting, fascinating, gripping, hypnotic, interesting, magnetic, spellbinding
 boring

roam *v* amble, ambulate *formal*, drift, meander, perambulate *formal*, peregrinate *formal*, prowl, ramble, range, rove, stray, stroll, tramp, travel, traverse, trek, walk, wander
 stay

roar *v* **1** *he roared in fury:* bawl, bellow, cry, howl, scream, shout, shriek, thunder, yell **2** *the waterfall roared:* crash, rumble, thunder **3** *roar with laughter:* break up *colloq*, burst out laughing, crease up *colloq*, fall about *colloq*, guffaw, hoot, howl, laugh, laugh like a drain *colloq*, shriek with laughter, split your sides *colloq*
 1 whisper
♦ *n* **1** *a roar of pain:* bawl, bellow, cry, howl, scream, shout, shriek, yell **2** *the roar of the waters:* rumble, thunder **3** *a roar of laughter:* guffaw, hoot, howl, shriek

rob *v* **1** *rob a bank:* burgle, do *colloq*, heist *slang*, hold up, loot, pillage, plunder, raid, ransack, rifle, sack, steal from **2** *rob an old lady:* cheat, defraud, deprive, do *colloq*, hold up, mug *colloq*, rip off *colloq*, steal from, sting *slang*, swindle

robber *n* bandit, brigand, burglar, cheat, con man *colloq*, embezzler, highwayman, looter, mugger *colloq*, pirate, plunderer, raider, stealer, swindler, thief

robbery *n* **1** *a robbery at a factory:* break-in, burglary, heist *slang*, hold-up, raid, stick-up *slang*, theft **2** *charged with robbery:* burglary, embezzlement, fraud, housebreaking, larceny, mugging *colloq*, pilferage, pillage, plunder, rip-off *colloq*, stealing, swindle, theft

robe *n* **1** *wearing a loose robe:* bathrobe, dressing-gown, gown, habit, housecoat, peignoir, wrap, wrapper **2** *dressed in fine robes:* costume, vestment
♦ *v* apparel *formal*, attire *formal*, clothe, drape, dress, garb, vest

robot *n* android, automaton, machine

robust *adj* **1** *a robust constitution:* athletic, energetic, fit, hardy, healthy, muscular, powerful, stalwart, strapping, strong, sturdy, tough, vigorous, well-built **2** *robust opinions:* direct, forceful, no-nonsense *colloq*, straightforward, strong, vigorous **3** *robust talk:* coarse, crude, earthy, raw, ribald, risqué, rude
 1 feeble, unhealthy, weak

rock¹ *n* **1** *falling rocks:* boulder, pebble, stone **2** *a lighthouse on a rock:* crag, outcrop

---

Rocks include:
basalt, breccia, chalk, coal, conglomerate, flint, gabbro, gneiss, granite, lava, limestone, marble, marl, obsidian, ore, porphyry, pumice stone, sandstone, schist, serpentine, slate

---

rock² *v* **1** *rock backwards and forwards:* lurch, move to and fro, oscillate, pitch, reel, roll, stagger, sway, swing, tilt, tip, toss, totter, undulate, wobble **2** *news that rocked the nation:* astonish, astound, bewilder, daze, dumbfound, shake, shock, stagger, startle, stun, surprise, take aback

rocket *v* escalate, increase quickly/suddenly, shoot up, soar

rocky¹ *adj* craggy, flinty, pebbly, rough, rugged, stony
 smooth

rocky² *adj* shaky, tottering, uncertain, unreliable, unstable, unsteady, weak, wobbly
 dependable, stable, steady, strong

rod *n* bar, baton, cane, mace, pole, sceptre, shaft, staff, stick, strut, switch, wand

rodent *n*

Kinds of rodent include:
agouti, bandicoot, beaver, black rat, brown rat, cane rat, capybara, cavy, chinchilla, chipmunk, cony, coypu, dormouse, ferret, fieldmouse, gerbil, gopher, grey squirrel, groundhog, guinea pig, hamster, hare, harvest mouse, hedgehog, jerboa, kangaroo rat, lemming, marmot, meerkat, mouse, muskrat, musquash, pika, porcupine, prairie dog, rabbit, rat, red squirrel, sewer-rat, squirrel, vole, water rat, water vole, woodchuck

---

rogue *n* **1** *a despicable rogue:* cheat, con man *colloq*, crook *colloq*, deceiver, fraud, fraudster, good-for-nothing, miscreant, nasty piece of work *colloq*, ne'er-do-well, reprobate, scoundrel, swindler, villain **2** *a loveable rogue:* rascal, scamp

roguish *adj* **1** *a roguish smile:* cheeky, coquettish, frolicsome, impish, mischievous, playful, waggish **2** *a roguish con man:* criminal, crooked, deceitful, deceiving, dishonest, fraudulent, knavish, rascally, shady, swindling, unprincipled, unscrupulous, villainous
 1 serious **2** honest

roisterous *adj* boisterous, clamorous, disorderly, exuberant, loud, noisy, obstreperous, rowdy, uproarious, wild
 orderly, restrained

role *n* **1** *his role as manager:* capacity, duty, function, job, place, position, post, situation, task **2** *his role as Hamlet:* character, impersonation, part, portrayal, representation

roll *v* **1** *the wheels rolled:* go round, gyrate, revolve, rotate, spin, turn (round), twirl, wheel, whirl **2** *a car rolled past:* go, move, pass, run **3** *rolled the baby in a blanket:* bind, enfold, envelop, fold, wind, wrap **4** *rolled the paper into a ball:* coil, curl, fold, furl, twist, wind **5** *the ship rolled:* lurch, pitch, reel, rock, stagger, sway, swing, toss, tumble, wallow **6** *the waves rolled:* billow, toss, tumble, undulate **7** *roll the pastry flat:* crush, flatten, level, press, press down, smooth **8** *the thunder rolled:* boom, resound, reverberate, roar, rumble, thunder
♦ *n* **1** *the film is wound on a roll:* bobbin, cylinder, drum, reel, roller, scroll, spool **2** *the electoral roll:* annals, catalogue, census, chronicle, directory, file, index, inventory, list, record, register, roster, schedule **3** *the roll of the wheels:* cycle, gyration, revolution, rotation, spin, turn, twirl, wheel, whirl **4** *a roll of thunder:* boom, resonance, reverberation, roar, rumble, thunder **5** *the roll of the ship:* pitching, reeling, rocking, tossing **6** *the roll of the waves:* billowing, swell, tossing, undulation
▶ **roll up** arrive, assemble, congregate, convene, gather
F⊒ leave

rollicking *adj* boisterous, carefree, cavorting, devil-may-care, exuberant, frisky, frolicsome, hearty, jaunty, jovial, joyous, light-hearted, lively, merry, noisy, playful, rip-roaring, roisterous, roisting, romping, spirited, sportive, sprightly, swashbuckling
F⊒ restrained, serious

rolling *adj* heaving, rippling, surging, undulant, undulating, waving
F⊒ flat

roly-poly *adj* chubby, fat, overweight, plump, podgy, pudgy, rotund *formal*, rounded, tubby
F⊒ slim

romance *n* **1** *a secret romance:* affair, amour, attachment, intrigue, liaison, love affair, relationship **2** *a medieval romance:* fairytale, fantasy, fiction, idyll, legend, love story, novel, romantic fiction, story, tale **3** *the romance of foreign travel:* adventure, charm, excitement, fascination, glamour, melodrama, mystery
♦ *v* court, date *colloq*, go out with, go steady with *colloq*, see, woo

romantic *adj* **1** *a romantic legend:* extravagant, fairy-tale, fanciful, fantastic, fictitious, imaginary, improbable, legendary, unlikely, wild **2** *a romantic idea of life in the country:* dreamy, idealistic, idyllic, impractical, optimistic, quixotic, starry-eyed, unrealistic, utopian, visionary **3** *travelling to romantic locations:* exciting, fascinating, mysterious **4** *a romantic night in:* amorous, fond, lovey-dovey *colloq*, loving, mushy, passionate, sentimental, sloppy, soppy, tender
F⊒ **1** real **2** practical, realistic **4** unromantic, unsentimental
♦ *n* dreamer, idealist, sentimentalist, utopian, visionary
F⊒ realist

Romeo *n* Casanova, Don Juan, gigolo, ladies' man, lady-killer, lover

romp *v* caper, cavort, frisk, frolic, gambol, revel, roister, rollick, skip, sport
♦ *n* caper, frolic, lark, rig, spree

rook *v* bilk *colloq*, cheat, con *colloq*, defraud, diddle *colloq*, do *colloq*, fleece *colloq*, overcharge, rip off *colloq*, sting *colloq*, swindle

room *n* **1** *no room for a bookcase:* area, capacity, elbow-room, expanse, extent, headroom, legroom, space, volume **2** *a lot of room for improvement:* allowance, chance, latitude, leeway, margin, opportunity, range, scope

roomy *adj* ample, broad, capacious *formal*, commodious *formal*, extensive, generous, large, sizeable, spacious, voluminous *formal*, wide
F⊒ cramped, small, tiny

root¹ *n* **1** *the plant's roots:* radical, radicle, radix, rhizome, stem, tuber **2** *the root of the problem:* base, basis, bottom, cause, core, derivation, essence, foundation, fount, fountainhead, fundamental, germ, heart, kernel, nub, nucleus, origin, reason, seat, seed, source, starting point **3** *trace your roots:* background, beginning(s), family, heritage, origins
♦ *v* anchor, base, embed, entrench, establish, fasten, fix, ground, implant, moor, set, stick
▶ **root out 1** *root out the cause of the problem:* dig out, discover, uncover, unearth **2** *root out the troublemakers:* abolish, clear away, destroy, eliminate, eradicate, exterminate, extirpate *formal*, get rid of, put an end to, remove

root²
▶ **root around** burrow, delve, dig, ferret, forage, hunt, nose, poke, pry, rummage

root³ *v* applaud, cheer (on), encourage, pull *US*, shout, support

rooted *adj* **1** *a story rooted in reality:* established, fixed **2** *deeply rooted beliefs:* confirmed, deep, deeply felt, deep-seated, entrenched, felt, firm, fixed, ingrained, radical, rigid
F⊒ **2** superficial, temporary

rope *v* bind, fasten, hitch, lash, moor, tether, tie
▶ **rope in** engage, enlist, inveigle *formal*, involve, persuade, talk into

ropy *adj* **1** *his performance was ropy:* below par *colloq*, deficient, inadequate, inferior, poor, rough, substandard, unsatisfactory **2** *feeling a bit ropy:* below par *colloq*, off-colour, rough, unwell
F⊒ **1** good **2** well

roster *n* directory, index, list, listing, register, roll, rota, schedule

rostrum *n* dais, platform, podium, stage

rosy *adj* **1** *rosy skin:* bloodshot, blooming, blushing, florid, flushed, fresh, glowing, healthy-looking, inflamed, pink, red, reddish, rose, roseate, rose-coloured, rose-hued, roselike, rose-pink, rose-red, rubicund *formal*, ruddy **2** *a rosy future:* auspicious *formal*, bright, cheerful, encouraging, favourable, hopeful, optimistic, promising, reassuring, sunny
F⊒ **2** depressing, sad, unhappy

rot *v* **1** *the fruit has rotted:* decay, decompose, degenerate, fester, go bad, go off, go sour, perish, putrefy *formal*, spoil, taint **2** *the wood is rotting:* corrode, crumble, decay, decompose, degenerate, deteriorate, disintegrate, perish
♦ *n* **1** *rot has set in:* corrosion, decay,

decomposition, deterioration, disintegration, mould, putrefaction *formal*, rust **2** *he's talking rot*: baloney *colloq*, bosh *colloq*, bunk *colloq*, bunkum *colloq*, claptrap, codswallop *colloq*, drivel, humbug *colloq*, nonsense, piffle *colloq*, poppycock *colloq*, rubbish, tosh *colloq*

rotary *adj* gyrating, gyratory, revolving, rotating, spinning, turning, whirling
◼ fixed

rotate *v* **1** *the wheels rotate*: go round, gyrate, pivot, reel, revolve, roll, spin (round), swivel, turn (round), whirl **2** *the planets rotate around the sun*: go round, move round, orbit, revolve **3** *the committee members rotate*: alternate, interchange, reciprocate, take (it) in turns

rotation *n* **1** *the rotation of the wheel*: cycle, gyration, revolution, spin, spinning, swivel, swivelling, turn, turning, whirl **2** *the rotation of the planets round the sun*: orbit, revolution, turning **3** *the rotation of crops*: alternation, cycle, sequence, succession

rotten *adj* **1** *rotten meat*: addled, bad, decayed, decaying, decomposed, fetid, foul, mouldering, mouldy, off, putrescent *formal*, putrid, rank, rotting, sour, spoilt, stinking, tainted **2** *a rotten singer*: bad, crummy *colloq*, inadequate, inferior, lousy, low-grade, mean, poor, ropy *colloq* **3** *a rotten thing to do*: beastly, contemptible, corrupt, despicable, dirty, dishonest, dishonourable, evil, horrible, immoral, nasty, unprincipled, wicked **4** *feel rotten*: awful, grotty *colloq*, ill, off-colour, poorly, ropy *colloq*, rough *colloq*, sick, unwell
◼ **1** fresh **3** good **4** well

rotter *n* blackguard, blighter *colloq*, bounder *colloq*, cad, cur, dastard, fink *colloq*, louse *colloq*, rat *colloq*, scoundrel, stinker *colloq*, swine *colloq*

rotund *adj* **1** *a rotund little woman*: chubby, corpulent *formal*, fat, fleshy, heavy, obese, plump, podgy, portly, roly-poly, round, stout, tubby **2** *rotund shapes*: bulbous, globular, orbicular *formal*, rotundate *formal*, round, spheral, spheric, spherical, spherular **3** *rotund prose*: grandiloquent *formal*, magniloquent *formal*, orotund *formal* **4** *a rotund voice*: full, resonant, rich, rounded, sonorous
◼ **1** gaunt, slim **2** flat

rough *adj* **1** *rough terrain*: bumpy, craggy, gnarled, irregular, jagged, lumpy, rugged, stony, uneven **2** *his chin felt rough*: bristly, coarse, hairy, prickly, scaly, scratchy, shaggy **3** *a rough crowd*: boisterous, disorderly, energetic, forceful, lively, noisy, raucous, rowdy, violent, wild **4** *subjected to rough treatment*: brusque, brutal, brutish, coarse, cruel, curt, difficult, drastic, extreme, hard, harsh, impolite, insensitive, merciless, severe, sharp, stern, tough, unfeeling, vulgar **5** *in a rough voice*: croaking, discordant, gruff, guttural, harsh, hoarse, husky, rasping, raucous, strident, throaty **6** *a rough guess*: approximate, estimated, imprecise, inexact, vague **7** *a rough idea*: general, hazy, sketchy, vague **8** *a rough drawing*: basic, crude, cursory, hasty, incomplete, quick, rudimentary, sketchy, unfinished, unpolished, unrefined **9** *a rough sea*: agitated, choppy, stormy, tempestuous, turbulent, violent, wild **10** *feeling rough*: below par *colloq*, grotty *colloq*, ill, off-colour, poorly, rotten *colloq*, sick, unhealthy, unwell

◼ **1** smooth **2** smooth **3** gentle **4** mild **6** accurate, exact **7** accurate, exact **9** calm, smooth **10** well
◆ *n* **1** *the cover roughs*: draft, mock-up, model, outline, sketch **2** *a bunch of drunken roughs*: bruiser, bully, hooligan, roughneck, rowdy, ruffian, thug, tough, yob *slang*, yobbo *slang*
▸ **rough out** draft, draw in rough, give a summary of, mock up, outline, sketch
▸ **rough up** bash *colloq*, beat up, do in *colloq*, knock about *colloq*, maltreat, manhandle, mistreat, mug *colloq*

rough-and-ready *adj* approximate, crude, hurried, make-do, makeshift, provisional, simple, sketchy, stop-gap, unpolished, unrefined
◼ exact, refined

rough-and-tumble *n* affray, brawl, dust-up *colloq*, fight, fracas, mêlée, punch-up *colloq*, rumpus, scrap *colloq*, scuffle, struggle

roughen *v* abrade, asperate, chafe, chap, coarsen, graze, harshen, rasp, rough, scuff
◼ smooth

roughneck *n* bruiser, bully boy, hooligan, keelie, lout, rough, rowdy, ruffian, thug, tough

round *adj* **1** *a round object*: ball-shaped, circular, curved, cylindrical, dislike, discoid *formal*, discoidal *formal*, disc-shaped, globate *formal*, globelike, globular, hooplike, orbicular *formal*, ring-shaped, rounded, spherical, spheroid *formal* **2** *a round little woman*: ample, corpulent *formal*, plump, portly, rotund, stout **3** *that's just a round figure*: approximate, estimated, imprecise, rough
◆ *n* **1** *small rounds of dough*: ball, band, circle, circlet, cylinder, disc, globe, hoop, orb, ring, sphere **2** *the final round*: game, heat, level, period, session, stage **3** *a round of redundancies*: bout, cycle, sequence, series, succession **4** *on his round*: beat, circuit, course, lap, path, route, routine
◆ *v* bypass, circle, go round, move past, skirt, travel round
▸ **round off** cap, close, complete, conclude, crown, end, finish (off), top off
◼ begin
▸ **round on** abuse, attack, lay into, set upon, turn on
▸ **round up** assemble, bring together, collect, gather, group, herd, marshal, muster, rally
◼ disperse, scatter

roundabout *adj* **1** *a roundabout route*: circuitous, circumlocutory *formal*, devious, indirect, meandering, tortuous, twisting, winding **2** *told me in a roundabout way*: circuitous, circumlocutory *formal*, evasive, indirect, oblique, periphrastic *formal*
◼ **1** direct, straight **2** direct, straight

roundly *adv* bluntly, completely, fiercely, forcefully, frankly, intensely, openly, outspokenly, rigorously, severely, sharply, thoroughly, vehemently, violently
◼ mildly

round-up *n* **1** *a round-up of the local news*: collation, overview, précis, summary, survey **2** *a cattle round-up*: assembly, collection, gathering, herding, marshalling, muster, rally
◼ **2** dispersal

rouse *v* **1** *he's hard to rouse in the morning*: arouse, awaken, call, get up, wake (up) **2** *rouse a mob*: agitate, anger, disturb, excite, galvanize, impel,

incite, inflame, move, provoke, whip up **3** *roused feelings of anger in him:* call up, evoke, incite, induce, instigate, kindle, provoke, start, stimulate
🖃 **2** calm

rousing *adj* brisk, electrifying, exciting, exhilarating, inspiring, lively, moving, spirited, stimulating, stirring, vigorous
🖃 boring, calming, dull

rout *n* beating, conquest, defeat, drubbing, overthrow, retreat, subjugation *formal*, thrashing *colloq*, trouncing
🖃 win
♦ *v* beat, chase, conquer, crush, defeat, hammer *colloq*, lick *colloq*, overthrow, put to flight, scatter, slaughter *colloq*, subjugate *formal*, thrash *colloq*, trounce, vanquish *formal*, wipe the floor with *colloq*

route *n* **1** *go by a different route:* avenue, course, direction, flight path, itinerary, journey, passage, path, road, way **2** *the postman's route:* beat, circuit, itinerary, round, run
♦ *v* **1** *traffic being routed into a single lane:* direct, guide, steer **2** *mail is routed through a server:* convey, dispatch, forward, send

routine *n* **1** *followed his usual routine:* custom, formula, method, order, pattern, practice, procedure, programme, schedule, system, usage, way, wont **2** *stuck in a routine:* habit, rut **3** *a comedy routine:* act, lines, patter *colloq*, performance, piece, programme, spiel *colloq*, yak *colloq*
♦ *adj* **1** *a routine procedure:* common, conventional, customary, everyday, familiar, habitual, normal, ordinary, standard, typical, usual, wonted, workaday **2** *brightened a routine day:* banal, boring, dull, hackneyed, humdrum, monotonous, predictable, run-of-the-mill, tedious, tiresome, unoriginal
🖃 **1** different, unusual **2** different, exciting, inspiring, unusual

rove *v* cruise, drift, gallivant, meander, ramble, range, roam, stravaig *Scot*, stray, stroll, traipse, wander
🖃 stay

row¹ *n* bank, chain, column, file, line, queue, range, rank, sequence, series, string, tier

row² *n* **1** *a row about a parking space:* altercation *formal*, argument, brawl, conflict, controversy, disagreement, dispute, dust-up *colloq*, falling-out *colloq*, fight, fracas, quarrel, scrap *colloq*, set-to *colloq*, slanging match *colloq*, squabble, tiff **2** *heard a row out in the street:* clamour, commotion, din, disturbance, hubbub, noise, racket, rumpus, tumult, uproar
🖃 **2** calm
♦ *v* argue, bicker, fight, quarrel, scrap *colloq*, squabble, wrangle

rowdy *adj* boisterous, disorderly, loud, noisy, obstreperous, riotous, rough, unruly, wild
🖃 peaceful, quiet, restrained
♦ *n* brawler, hoodlum *colloq*, hooligan, keelie, lout, rough, ruffian, tearaway, tough, yahoo *slang*, yob *slang*, yobbo *slang*

royal *adj* **1** *the royal family:* imperial, kinglike, kingly, monarchical, princely, queenlike, queenly, regal, sovereign **2** *a royal welcome:*

august, grand, imposing, impressive, magnificent, majestic

rub *v* **1** *rubbed the cat's ears:* caress, fondle, knead, massage, pat, scratch, stroke **2** *rub the surface with a duster:* buff (up), burnish, clean, polish, shine, smooth, wipe **3** *rub the wood with sandpaper:* abrade, clean, scour, scrape, scratch, scrub **4** *rub lotion into the skin:* apply, embrocate *formal*, put on, smear, spread, work in **5** *my shoes are rubbing my heels:* chafe, grate, pinch, scrape
♦ *n* **1** *give my shoulders a rub:* caress, kneading, massage, stroke **2** *a quick rub with a cloth:* clean, polish, shine, wipe **3** *there's the rub:* catch, difficulty, drawback, hindrance, hitch, impediment, obstacle, problem, snag *colloq*, trouble
▶ **rub in** emphasize, harp on, highlight, insist on, make much of, stress, underline
▶ **rub off on** affect, alter, change, have an effect on, influence, transform
▶ **rub out 1** *rub out a mistake:* cancel, delete, efface *formal*, erase, obliterate **2** *hired a hit man to rub him out:* assassinate, bump off *colloq*, do away with, do in *colloq*, eliminate *colloq*, finish off, kill, liquidate *colloq*, murder, put to death

rubbish *n* **1** *streets littered with rubbish:* debris, detritus *formal*, dross, flotsam and jetsam, garbage *US*, junk, litter, refuse, rubble, scrap, trash, waste **2** *he's talking rubbish:* balderdash, bosh *colloq*, bull *slang*, bullshit *slang*, bunk *colloq*, bunkum *colloq*, claptrap *colloq*, cobblers *colloq*, crap *slang*, drivel, gibberish, gobbledegook, nonsense, piffle *colloq*, poppycock *colloq*, rot *colloq*, shit *slang*, stuff and nonsense *colloq*, tosh *colloq*, tripe *colloq*, twaddle
🖃 **2** sense

rubbishy *adj* cheap, gimcrack, grotty, shoddy, tatty, tawdry, third-rate, throw-away, trashy, twopenny-halfpenny, valueless, worthless
🖃 classy, high-quality

ruction *n* altercation *formal*, brawl, commotion, dispute, disturbance, fracas, fuss, protest, quarrel, racket, rookery *colloq*, rout, row, ruffle, rumpus, scrap *colloq*, storm, to-do *colloq*, trouble, uproar
🖃 calm

ruddy *adj* blooming, blushing, crimson, florid, flushed, fresh, glowing, healthy, red, reddish, rosy, rubicund *formal*, scarlet, sunburnt
🖃 pale, unhealthy

rude *adj* **1** *a rude reply:* abrupt, abusive, brusque, cheeky *colloq*, curt, discourteous, disrespectful, ill-bred, ill-mannered, impertinent, impolite, impudent, insolent, insulting, offensive, sharp, short, uncivil, unpleasant **2** *a rude joke:* bawdy, coarse, dirty, filthy, gross, improper, indecent, indelicate, lewd, naughty, near the bone *colloq*, obscene, ribald, risqué, vulgar **3** *get a rude shock:* disagreeable, harsh, nasty, sudden, unexpected, unpleasant **4** *a rude shelter:* crude, primitive, rough, rough-and-ready, rudimentary, simple **5** *regarded as rude barbarians:* ignorant, illiterate, rough, uncivilized, uncouth, uneducated, unpolished, unrefined, untutored
🖃 **1** civil, courteous, polite **2** clean, decent **3** pleasant **4** advanced, well-developed **5** educated

rudimentary *adj* **1** *rudimentary music theory:* basic, elementary, fundamental, initial,

introductory, primary **2** *a rudimentary shelter:* crude, primitive, rough, simple **3** *a creature with rudimentary wings:* embryonic, undeveloped

F3 1 advanced **3** developed

rudiments *n* ABC, basics, beginnings, elements, essentials, foundations, fundamentals, principles

rue *v* be regretful for, be sorry for, bemoan, bewail, deplore, feel remorse for, grieve, lament, mourn, regret, repent

F3 rejoice

rueful *adj* apologetic, conscience-stricken, contrite *formal*, dismal, doleful, lugubrious *formal*, melancholy, mournful, penitent, plaintive, regretful, remorseful, repentant, sad, self-reproachful, sorrowful, sorry, woebegone *formal*, woeful *formal*

F3 glad, joyful

ruffian *n* bruiser, brute, bully, cut-throat, hoodlum *colloq*, hooligan, lout, miscreant *formal*, rascal, rogue, roughneck, rowdy, scoundrel, thug, tough *colloq*, villain, yob *slang*

ruffle *v* **1** *ruffle the sheets:* crease, crumple, disarrange *formal*, dishevel, ripple, rumple, tangle, tousle, wrinkle **2** *don't let him ruffle you:* aggravate *colloq*, anger, annoy, bug *colloq*, discompose *formal*, exasperate, fluster, hassle *colloq*, irk, irritate, nettle, put out, rattle *colloq*, rile, trouble, upset, vex

F3 1 smooth **2** pacify

rugged *adj* **1** *rugged terrain:* bumpy, craggy, irregular, jagged, rocky, rough, stony, uneven **2** *a rugged lumberjack:* burly, hardy, muscular, robust, sinewy, stalwart, strong, sturdy, tough, vigorous, weather-beaten, well-built **3** *rugged determination:* determined, firm, resolute, strong, tenacious, tough, unflinching, unwavering

F3 1 smooth

ruin *n* **1** *the ruin of civilized society:* breakdown, collapse, defeat, destruction, devastation, disintegration, downfall, failure, fall, overthrow, undoing **2** *buildings falling into ruin:* decay, disintegration, disrepair, ruination, wreckage **3** *financial ruin:* bankruptcy, crash, disaster, failure, indigence *formal*, insolvency, loss, penury *formal* **4** *castle ruins:* debris, detritus *formal*, fragments, relics, remains, remnants, rubble

F3 1 development, reconstruction **2** development, reconstruction

♦ *v* **1** *the tornado which ruined the town:* cripple, crush, damage, demolish, destroy, devastate, lay waste, overthrow, overwhelm, raze, shatter, smash, wreak havoc on, wreck **2** *ruin someone's chances:* botch, damage, harm, injure, mar, mess up *colloq*, spoil, wreck **3** *ruined him financially:* bankrupt, cripple, impoverish, make bankrupt, make insolvent

F3 1 develop, restore

ruinous *adj* **1** *ruinous costs:* crippling, excessive, exorbitant, extortionate, immoderate, unreasonable **2** *the building was in a ruinous condition:* broken-down, damaged, decrepit, destroyed, devastated, dilapidated, in ruins, ramshackle, ruined, shattered, wrecked **3** *the ruinous effects of the storm:* calamitous, cataclysmic, catastrophic, devastating

F3 1 low

rule *n* **1** *follow the rules:* canon, command, commandment, corrective, decree, direction, guide, guideline, instruction, law, order, ordinance, regulation, restriction, ruling, statute **2** *the rules of physics:* formula, law, principle, standard, truth **3** *my golden rule:* axiom, canon, criterion, maxim, precept, principle, tenet, truism **4** *foreign rule:* administration, authority, command, control, direction, dominion, government, influence, jurisdiction, kingship, leadership, mastery, power, queenship, regime, reign, sovereignty, supremacy, sway **5** *it was his rule to walk five miles a day:* convention, custom, form, habit, practice, procedure, protocol, routine, standard, wont

♦ *v* **1** *rule a country:* administer, be in control of, command, control, direct, dominate, govern, guide, lead, manage, preside over, regulate **2** *she ruled for forty years:* be in control, call the shots *colloq*, officiate, prevail, reign, sit in the driving seat *colloq* **3** *the court ruled that he was guilty:* adjudicate, decide, decree, determine, direct, establish, find, judge, lay down, order, pronounce, resolve, settle

▶ **rule out 1** *rule out suicide:* dismiss, eliminate, exclude, preclude *formal*, reject **2** *ruled out of playing:* ban, disallow, exclude, forbid, preclude *formal*, prevent, prohibit

ruler

Titles of rulers include:

aga, begum, caesar, caliph, commander, consul, controller, duce, emir, emperor, empress, Führer, governor, governor-general, head, head of state, kaiser, khan, king, leader, lord, maharajah, maharani, mikado, monarch, nawab, nizam, overlord, pharaoh, potentate, president, prince, princess, queen, rajah, rani, regent, shah, sheikh, shogun, sovereign, sultan, sultana, suzerain, tsar, viceroy

---

ruling *n* adjudication, decision, decree, finding, judgement, pronouncement, resolution, verdict

♦ *adj* **1** *the ruling monarch:* commanding, controlling, governing, in charge, in control, leading, on the throne, reigning, sovereign, supreme **2** *money is the ruling factor in his life:* chief, dominant, leading, main, most influential, predominant, principal

rum *adj* abnormal, bizarre, curious, freakish, funny, funny-peculiar *colloq*, odd, peculiar, queer, singular *formal*, strange, suspect, suspicious, unusual, weird

rumbustious *adj* boisterous, clamorous, disorderly, exuberant, loud, noisy, obstreperous *formal*, roisterous, roisting, rough, rowdy, unmanageable, unruly, uproarious, wayward, wild, wilful

F3 quiet, restrained, sensible

ruminate *v* brood, chew over, cogitate *formal*, consider, contemplate, deliberate, meditate, mull over, muse, ponder, reflect, think

rummage *v* delve, examine, explore, forage, hunt, poke around, ransack, rifle, root (around), search, turn over

♦ *n* bric-à-brac, jumble, junk, odds and ends, tat

rumour *n* bush telegraph *colloq*, buzz *colloq*, gossip, grapevine *colloq*, hearsay, information, news, report, scandal, speculation, story, talk,

tidings *formal*, whisper, word
♦ *v* bruit, circulate, gossip, hint, noise abroad, publish, put about, report, say, tell, whisper

rump *n* **1** *slapped him on the rump*: backside, bottom, bum *colloq*, butt *US colloq*, buttocks, croup, dock, haunch, hindquarters, nache, posterior *colloq*, rear, seat **2** *the rump of a political party*: leftovers, remainder, remains, residue, trace, vestige

rumple *v* crease, crinkle, crumple, crush, derange, dishevel, disorder, ruffle, scrunch, tousle, wrinkle
🖪 smooth

rumpus *n* brawl, brouhaha, commotion, confusion, disruption, disturbance, fracas, furore, fuss, kerfuffle *colloq*, noise, rout, row, ruction, tumult, uproar
🖪 calm

run *v* **1** *she ran out*: bolt, career, charge, dart, dash, gallop, hurry, jog, race, rush, scamper, scoot, scurry, scuttle, speed, sprint, step on it *colloq*, tear, trot **2** *the river runs through the forest*: flow, go, issue, move, pass, proceed, travel **3** *the engine is running*: be in operation, function, go, operate, perform, progress, work **4** *run a company*: administer, be in charge of, be in control of, carry on, carry out, conduct, control, co-ordinate, direct, head, lead, manage, operate, organize, oversee, own, regulate, superintend, supervise **5** *run in an election*: challenge, compete, contend, enter, put yourself forward, stand, take part in **6** *the path runs to the stream*: continue, extend, go, go on, last, proceed, range, reach, spread, stretch **7** *water was running down the wall*: cascade, course, drip, flow, glide, gush, issue, jet, pour, roll, spurt, stream, trickle **8** *run your hand over*: move, pass, slide, spread **9** *run you to the station*: convey, drive, give a lift, take, transport **10** *run a car*: drive, have, keep, maintain, own, possess, use **11** *the play ran for years*: be mounted, be performed, be played, be presented, be produced, be staged, go on, last **12** *run a story*: broadcast, carry, communicate, feature, include, print, publish
♦ *n* **1** *break into a run*: dash, gallop, hurry, jog, race, rush, sprint, spurt **2** *go for a run in the car*: drive, excursion, jaunt, journey, outing, ride, spin *colloq*, trip **3** *a run of bad luck*: chain, course, cycle, period, round, sequence, series, spell, stretch, string, succession **4** *the ship's regular run*: course, flight path, line, road, route, track, way **5** *built a run for the dogs*: coop, enclosure, fold, paddock, pen, pound, sty, yard **6** *a run on a currency*: call, clamour, demand, need, rush **7** *fifteen runs*: goal, hit, mark, point, score **8** *the average run of things*: category, class, kind, set, sort, type, variety **9** *a run in a stocking*: cut, gash, hole, ladder, rip, slash, slit, snag, split, tear
▶ **run across** bump into *colloq*, chance upon *formal*, come across, encounter, meet, run into
▶ **run after** chase, follow, pursue, tail
🖪 flee
▶ **run away 1** *the thief ran away*: abscond, beat it *colloq*, bolt, clear off *colloq*, decamp, escape, flee, make a run for it *colloq*, make off, run off, scarper *colloq* **2** *run away from problems*: avoid, brush aside, disregard, evade, ignore, neglect, shut your eyes to *colloq*, take no notice of, turn your back on *colloq* **3** *run away with your neighbour's wife*: elope, leave, make off, run off **4** *run away*

with the money: appropriate *formal*, lift *colloq*, make off with, nick *colloq*, pinch *colloq*, pocket, purloin *formal*, steal, walk off with
▶ **run down 1** *she's always running him down in public*: attack, belittle, criticize, defame, denigrate *formal*, denounce, disparage, knock *colloq*, rubbish *colloq*, slag off *colloq*, slate *colloq* **2** *he ran down a child*: hit, knock down, knock over, knock to the ground, run over **3** *he's completely run down*: exhaust, tire, weaken, weary **4** *run down production*: curtail, cut, cut back on, decrease, drop, reduce, trim
▶ **run in** apprehend *formal*, arrest, bust *colloq*, collar *colloq*, jail, lift *colloq*, nab *colloq*, nick *colloq*, pick up *colloq*, pinch *colloq*
▶ **run into 1** *ran into an old friend in town*: bump into *colloq*, chance upon *formal*, encounter, meet, run across **2** *his car ran into a tree*: bump into, collide with, crash, hit, ram, strike
▶ **run off 1** *the mugger ran off*: abscond, bolt, decamp, escape, make off, run away, scarper *colloq*, skedaddle *colloq* **2** *run off a few copies*: duplicate, Photostat®, print, produce, Xerox®
▶ **run off with** elope with, make off with, run away with
▶ **run on** carry on, continue, extend, go on, last, reach
▶ **run out** be exhausted, be finished, cease *formal*, dry up, end, exhaust, expire, fail, finish, give out, terminate
▶ **run out on** abandon, chuck *colloq*, ditch *colloq*, dump *colloq*, forsake *formal*, jilt *colloq*, leave, leave in the lurch *colloq*, maroon, strand, walk out on *colloq*
▶ **run over 1** *the driver ran over a child*: hit, knock down, run down **2** *run over your lines*: go over, practise, rehearse, reiterate *formal*, repeat, review, run through, survey
▶ **run through 1** *run through the instructions again*: examine, go through, practise, read, rehearse, review, run over, survey **2** *ran through his entire fortune*: dissipate *formal*, exhaust, fritter away, spend, squander, waste
▶ **run to 1** *the cost will run to over a million pounds*: add up to, amount to, come to, equal, total **2** *we can't run to another car*: afford, have enough for
▶ **run together** amalgamate, blend, coalesce, combine, commingle *formal*, fuse, join, merge, mingle, mix, unite
🖪 separate

runaway *n* absconder, deserter, escapee, escaper, fugitive, refugee, truant
♦ *adj* **1** *a runaway horse*: escaped, fugitive, loose, out of control, uncontrolled, wild **2** *a runaway car*: out of control, uncontrolled

run-down *n* **1** *a run-down in the number of troops*: curtailment, cut, cutback, decline, decrease, drop, reduction **2** *a run-down of the proposal*: analysis, briefing, outline, recap, résumé, review, run-through, sketch, summary, synopsis
♦ *adj* **1** *she's feeling run-down and needs a holiday*: debilitated *formal*, drained, enervated *formal*, exhausted, fatigued, tired, unhealthy, weak, weary, worn-out *colloq* **2** *run-down buildings*: broken-down, decrepit, dilapidated, neglected, ramshackle, shabby, tumbledown, uncared-for
🖪 **1** healthy **2** well-kept

run-in *n* altercation *formal*, argument, brush, confrontation, contretemps, difference of opinion, dispute, dust-up *colloq*, fight, quarrel, set-to, skirmish, tussle, wrangle

runner *n* **1** *runners in the race*: athlete, competitor, jogger, participant, racer, sprinter **2** *a runner brought the news*: bearer, courier, dispatch rider, messenger **3** *the plant's runners*: flagellum *technical*, offshoot, sarmentum *technical*, shoot, sprig, sprout, stem, stolon *technical*, tendril

running *n* **1** *long-distance running*: jogging, racing, sprinting **2** *the running of the company*: administration, charge, conduct, control, controlling, co-ordination, direction, leadership, management, organization, regulation, superintendency, supervision **3** *the smooth running of the engines*: functioning, operation, performance, working **4** *out of the running*: competition, contention, contest
♦ *adj* **1** *a running argument with my neighbours*: ceaseless, constant, continuous, incessant, perpetual, unbroken, unceasing *formal*, uninterrupted **2** *running water*: flowing, moving **3** *he was late three days running*: consecutive, in a row, in succession, on the trot *colloq*, successive
🅴 **1** broken, occasional

runny *adj* diluted, flowing, fluid, liquefied, liquid, melted, molten, watery
🅴 solid

run-of-the-mill *adj* average, common, everyday, fair, mediocre, middling, no great shakes *colloq*, normal, not up to much *colloq*, ordinary, so-so *colloq*, tolerable, undistinguished, unexceptional, unimpressive, unremarkable
🅴 exceptional, remarkable

rupture *n* **1** *a rupture in the pipe*: breach, break, breaking, burst, crack, fracture, puncture, split, tear **2** *a rupture between the two parties*: bust-up *colloq*, disagreement, division, estrangement *formal*, falling-out, quarrel, rift, schism, separation, split
♦ *v* **1** *the impact ruptured the fuel tank*: break, burst, crack, fracture, puncture, split, tear **2** *the pipeline had ruptured*: break, burst, crack, divide, fracture, separate, split, tear

rural *adj* agrarian, agricultural, bucolic, country, pastoral, rustic, sylvan
🅴 urban

ruse *n* artifice, blind, deception, device, dodge *colloq*, hoax, imposture, manoeuvre, plan, plot, ploy, scheme, sham, stratagem, subterfuge, tactic, trick, wile

rush *v* **1** *she rushed out*: bolt, career, charge, dart, dash, fly, gallop, get a move on *colloq*, hasten, hurry, race, run, scramble, shoot, speed (up), sprint, stampede, tear **2** *I'll have to rush you*: accelerate, dispatch, hurry, hustle, press, push, quicken, speed (up) **3** *they rushed the gates*: assault, attack, charge, raid, storm, strike
♦ *n* **1** *a mad rush*: charge, dash, race, scramble, stampede, surge **2** *why all the rush?*: haste, hurry, rapidity, speed, swiftness, urgency **3** *a rush of*

water: flood, flow, gush, stream, surge **4** *the Christmas rush*: activity, bustle, comings and goings *colloq*, commotion, excitement, flurry, hive of activity *colloq*, hurly-burly, hurry, hustle and bustle, stir **5** *a rush on the enemy*: assault, attack, charge, onslaught, raid, storm, strike **6** *a rush for tickets*: call, clamour, demand, need, run

rushed *adj* brisk, busy, careless, cursory, emergency, expeditious *formal*, fast, hasty, hurried, prompt, quick, rapid, superficial, swift, urgent

rust *n* corrosion, decay, oxidation, stain, verdigris
♦ *v* corrode, decay, oxidize, rot, tarnish

rustic *adj* **1** *a rustic scene*: bucolic, countrified, country, countryside, pastoral, rural, sylvan **2** *rustic handicrafts*: artless, homespun, plain, simple, unsophisticated **3** *dismissed him as a rustic boor*: awkward, boorish, clodhopping, clumsy, coarse, crude, graceless, indelicate, maladroit *formal*, oafish, provincial, rough, rude, uncouth, uncultured, unrefined, unsophisticated
🅴 **1** urban **2** sophisticated **3** cultivated, polished, sophisticated, urbane
♦ *n* boor, bumpkin, churl, clod, clodhopper, country cousin, countryman, countrywoman, hayseed *colloq*, hick *colloq*, hillbilly *colloq*, oaf, peasant, provincial, yokel
🅴 dandy, sophisticate

rustle *v* crackle, sigh, susurrate *formal*, swish, whisper, whoosh
♦ *n* crackle, crepitation *formal*, crepitus *formal*, crinkling, rustling, susurration *formal*, susurrus *formal*, swish, whisper, whispering, whoosh

rusty *adj* **1** *rusty iron*: corroded, discoloured, dull, oxidized, rust-covered, rusted, tarnished **2** *rusty hair*: auburn, brown, chestnut, copper, coppery, ginger, gingery, red, reddish, reddish-brown, russet, rust-coloured, sandy, tawny, Titian **3** *my Spanish is rusty*: deficient, impaired, out of practice, poor, unpractised, weak **4** *rusty ideas about teaching*: antiquated, creaking, dated, old-fashioned, outmoded, stale

rut *n* **1** *the wheel got stuck in a rut*: channel, ditch, furrow, gouge, groove, gutter, indentation, pothole, track, trough, wheelmark **2** *feel as if I'm stuck in a rut*: daily grind, grind, habit, humdrum, no change of scenery, pattern, routine, same old round/place, system, treadmill

ruthless *adj* **1** *a ruthless tyrant*: barbarous, brutal, callous, cruel, draconian, ferocious, fierce, hard, hard-hearted, harsh, heartless, implacable, inexorable, inhuman, merciless, pitiless, relentless, remorseless, savage, severe, stern, unfeeling, unforgiving, unmerciful, unrelenting, unsparing, vicious **2** *a ruthless business*: cut-throat *colloq*, dog-eat-dog *colloq*, grim, hard
🅴 **1** compassionate, merciful

S

sable *adj* black, coal-black, dark, dusky, ebony, inky, jet, midnight, pitch-black, pitch-dark, pitchy

sabotage *v* **1** *the parachute had been sabotaged:* damage, destroy, disable, impair, incapacitate, mar, ruin, spoil, undermine, vandalize, weaken, wreck **2** *bad weather sabotaged their plans:* disrupt, impair, mar, scupper, spoil, thwart, undermine ♦ *n* damage, destruction, disruption, impairment, ruin, spoiling, vandalism, weakening, wrecking

sac *n* bag, bladder, bursa *technical*, capsule, cyst, follicle, pocket, pod, pouch, saccule, theca *technical*, vesica *technical*, vesicle *technical*, vesicula *technical*

saccharine *adj* cloying, gushy *colloq*, honeyed, maudlin, mawkish, mushy *colloq*, nauseating, oversweet, schmaltzy *colloq*, sentimental, sickly, sickly-sweet, sloppy *colloq*, soppy *colloq*, sugary, sweet, syrupy
🗉 bitter, tart

sack¹ *v* axe *colloq*, boot out *colloq*, discharge, dismiss, fire, give someone the sack/push/ boot/elbow *colloq*, give someone their cards *colloq*, lay off, make redundant, send packing *colloq*, show someone the door *colloq* ♦ *n* discharge, dismissal, firing *colloq*, marching orders, notice, sacking, the axe *colloq*, the boot *colloq*, the chop *colloq*, the elbow *colloq*, the push *colloq*

sack² *v* demolish, depredate *formal*, desecrate, despoil *formal*, destroy, devastate, lay waste, level, loot, maraud, pillage, plunder, raid, rape, ravage, raze, rifle, rob, ruin, spoil, strip, waste ♦ *n* depredation *formal*, desecration, despoliation *formal*, destruction, devastation, levelling, looting, marauding, pillage, plunder, plundering, rape, rapine *formal*, ravage, razing, ruin, waste

sacred *adj* **1** *a sacred temple:* blessed, consecrated, dedicated, divine, hallowed, heavenly, holy, sanctified **2** *sacred music:* devotional, ecclesiastical, religious, spiritual **3** *sacred institution of marriage:* defended, hallowed, impregnable, inviolable, protected, respected, revered, sacrosanct, secure, untouchable, venerable
🗉 **1** profane, secular **2** temporal

sacredness *n* divinity, godliness, holiness, saintliness, sanctity
🗉 profaneness, worldliness

sacrifice *v* **1** *sacrificed an animal in a religious ceremony:* immolate, offer, offer up, slaughter **2** *she sacrificed a normal childhood to find fame:* abandon, forgo, forfeit, give up, let go, relinquish ♦ *n* **1** *a sacrifice to the gods:* immolation, oblation *formal*, offering **2** *sacrifice of personal liberties:* abandonment, giving-up, loss, renunciation, surrender

sacrificial *adj* atoning, expiatory *formal*, oblatory *formal*, piacular *formal*, propitiatory *formal*, reparative *formal*, votive

sacrilege *n* blasphemy, desecration, disrespect, heresy, impiety, irreligion, irreverence, mockery, outrage, profanation, profanity, violation
🗉 piety, respect, reverence

sacrilegious *adj* blasphemous, desecrating, disrespectful, godless, heretical, impious, irreligious, irreverent, profanatory *formal*, profane, ungodly, unholy
🗉 pious, respectful, reverent

sacrosanct *adj* hallowed, impregnable, inviolable, protected, sacred, secure, untouchable

sad *adj* **1** *felt sad after saying goodbye:* (at) rock bottom *colloq*, blue *colloq*, crestfallen, dejected, depressed, despondent, disconsolate *formal*, dismal, distressed, doleful, down *colloq*, down in the dumps *colloq*, downcast, down-hearted, fed up *colloq*, gloomy, glum, grief-stricken, heavy-hearted, in low spirits, joyless, long-faced, low *colloq*, low-spirited, melancholy, miserable, mournful, sorrowful, tearful, unhappy, upset, wistful, woebegone *formal*, wretched **2** *sad news:* calamitous, depressing, disastrous, distressing, grave, grievous, heart-breaking, heart-rending, lamentable, miserable, painful, poignant, regrettable, serious, sorrowful, sorry, touching, tragic, unfortunate, unhappy, upsetting **3** *in a sad state:* deplorable, disgraceful, grievous, lamentable, pathetic *colloq*, pitiable, pitiful, regrettable, shameful, sorry, unfortunate, wretched
🗉 **1** cheerful, happy **2** fortunate, lucky **3** good

sadden *v* break your heart, cast down, deject, depress, discourage, dishearten, dismay, dispirit, distress, drive to despair, get someone down *colloq*, grieve, upset
🗉 cheer, delight, gratify, please

saddle *v* burden, charge, encumber, impose, land, load, lumber, tax

sadism *n* barbarity, bestiality, brutality, callousness, cruelty, heartlessness, inhumanity, malevolence *formal*, ruthlessness, savagery, spite, viciousness

sadistic *adj* barbarous, bestial, brutal, cruel, inhuman, merciless, perverted, pitiless, savage, vicious

sadness *n* bleakness, cheerlessness, dejection, depression, desolation, despondency, disconsolateness *formal*, dismalness, distress, dolefulness, gloominess, glumness, grief, heartache *colloq*, joylessness, low spirits, lugubriousness *formal*, melancholy *formal*, misery, misfortune, mournfulness, pain, regret, sombreness, sorrow, sorrowfulness, tearfulness, unhappiness, woe *formal*, wretchedness
🗉 cheerfulness, delight, happiness

safe *adj* **1** *safe to drink:* harmless, innocuous, non-poisonous, non-toxic, uncontaminated **2** *kept her belongings safe:* defended, guarded, immune, impregnable, in good hands *colloq*, intact, invulnerable, out of danger, out of harm's way *colloq*, protected, safe and sound *colloq*, safe as

houses *colloq*, secure, sheltered, sound, unassailable, undamaged, unharmed, unhurt, uninjured, unscathed **3** *a safe choice for the post*: dependable, honest, honourable, proven, reliable, responsible, sound, sure, tested, tried, trustworthy, upright **4** *opted for the safe route*: cautious, circumspect *formal*, conservative, prudent *formal*, unadventurous, unenterprising
F3 1 dangerous, harmful **2** at risk, exposed, vulnerable **3** risky **4** adventurous
♦ *n* cash box, chest, coffer, deposit box, depository, repository, safety-deposit box, strongbox, vault

safe-conduct *n* authorization, laissez-passer, licence, pass, passport, permit, safeguard, warrant

safeguard *v* defend, guard, look after, preserve, protect, screen, secure, shelter, shield, take care of
F3 endanger, jeopardize
♦ *n* assurance, cover, defence, guarantee, insurance, precaution, preventative, preventive, protection, security, shield, surety

safekeeping *n* care, charge, custody, guardianship, protection, supervision, surveillance, trust, ward, wardship

safety *n* **1** *demanded greater public safety*: immunity, protection, safeness, security, soundness, welfare **2** *led his family to safety*: cover, refuge, sanctuary, shelter
F3 1 danger, jeopardy, risk
♦ *adj* precautionary, preventative, preventive, protective

sag *v* **1** *sagged under the weight of the snow*: bag, bend, droop, give, hang, hang loosely **2** *her spirits started to sag*: dip, drop, fail, fall, falter, flag, flop, sink, slump, subside, weaken, wilt
F3 1 bulge **2** rise
♦ *n* decline, depression, dip, downturn, drop, dwindling, fall, low, reduction, slide, slip, slump
F3 peak, rise

saga *n* adventure, chronicle, epic, epopee *formal*, epopeia *formal*, epos *formal*, history, narrative, roman fleuve, romance, soap opera, story, tale, yarn

sagacious *adj* able, acute, astute, canny, discerning, far-sighted, insightful, intelligent, judicious *formal*, knowing, penetrating, perceptive, percipient *formal*, perspicacious *formal*, prudent *formal*, quick, sage *formal*, sapient *formal*, sharp, shrewd, smart, wide-awake, wise
F3 foolish, obtuse

sagacity *n* acumen, acuteness, astuteness, canniness, discernment, foresight, insight, judgement, judiciousness *formal*, knowingness, percipience *formal*, perspicacity *formal*, prudence *formal*, sapience *formal*, sense, sharpness, shrewdness, understanding, wariness, wiliness, wisdom
F3 foolishness, obtuseness

sage *n* authority, elder, expert, guru, hakam, maharishi, mahatma, master, oracle, philosopher, pundit, savant, Solomon, teacher, wise man, wise person, wise woman
F3 ignoramus
♦ *adj* astute, canny, discerning, intelligent,

judicious *formal*, knowing, knowledgeable, learned, perspicacious *formal*, prudent *formal*, sagacious *formal*, sapient *formal*, wise
F3 foolish

sail *v* **1** *the boat sailed at 8.00pm*: embark, leave port, put off, put to sea, set out, set sail, weigh anchor **2** *her husband sailed their catamaran to Australia*: captain, navigate, pilot, skipper, steer **3** *they sailed around the island*: coast, drift, float, glide, scud, skim, soar, sweep **4** *she sailed into the room*: drift, float, fly, glide, scud, skim, soar, sweep **5** *clouds sailed through the sky*: drift, float, fly, glide, scud, skim, soar, sweep
▶ **sail through** deal with successfully, pass easily, romp through, succeed in
F3 scrape through

Types of sail include:
canvas, course, foreroyal, foresail, forestaysail, foretop, fore-topgallant, fore-topsail, gaff sail, gaff-topsail, gennaker, genoa, headsail, jib, jigger, kite, lateen sail, lugsail, main course, mainsail, maintopsail, mizzen, moonraker, royal, skysail, spanker, spinnaker, spritsail, square sail, staysail, studdingsail, topgallant, topsail, trysail

sailing

Terms used in sailing include:
abaft, across the wind, alongside, astern, backing, bearing, beat, beating, bending on (a sail), blanketing effect, breaking out (the anchor), casting off/letting go, close-hauled, coming about, downwind, fetch, fitting out, fixing a position, going about, gybe, handing (a sail), hard on the wind, heeling (to the wind), in irons/in stays, knockdown (by the wind), laying off (a course), lay up, lee helm, lee-oh!, leeway, lift, points of sailing, port, reaching, beam reach, broad reach, close reach, ready about!, running, running goose-winged, sailing by the lee, sail trimming, sheeting in a sail, spilling wind, standing on, starboard, stepping/unstepping (the mast), tacking, port tack, starboard tack, steerage way, taking soundings, unbending (a sail), under way, upwind, veer (the anchor cable), weather helm, weathering, windward, yawing. See also **knot**

Types and classes of modern sailing boat include:
sloop, cutter, yawl, ketch, schooner; formula class, one-design class, restricted class; 420, 470, 49er, 5-0-5, Cadet, Conway One, Dragon, Enterprise, Finn, Fireball, Firefly, Fisher, Flying Dutchman, Flying Fifteen, Fourteen, Laser, Maxi, Minisail, Mirror, Moody, Moth, Optimist, Rival, Solo, Star, Topper, Tornado, Trapper, Twelve, Wayfarer, Westerley, Yngling

sailor *n* mariner, seafarer, seaman

Types of sailor include:
AB, able seaman, bargee, bluejacket, boatman, boatswain, bosun, buccaneer, cabin boy, captain, cox, coxswain, crewman, deck hand, fisherman, galiongee, gob *US slang*, hearty, helmsman, Jack tar, lascar, leatherneck, limey *US colloq*, marine, master, mate, matelot *slang*,

navigator, oarsman, pilot, pirate, purser, rating, rower, salt, sculler, sea dog, skipper, tar *colloq*, tarry-breeks *Scot*, water rat, Wren, yachtsman, yachtswoman

saintliness *n* asceticism, blamelessness, blessedness, chastity, devoutness, godliness, goodness, holiness, innocence, morality, piety, purity, righteousness, sanctity, self-denial, selflessness, self-sacrifice, sinlessness, spirituality, spotlessness, unselfishness, uprightness
⊟ godlessness, unholiness, wickedness

saintly *adj* angelic, blameless, blessed, devout, ethical, God-fearing, godly, good, holy, innocent, moral, pious, pure, religious, righteous, saintlike, sinless, spiritual, spotless, upright, virtuous, worthy
⊟ godless, unholy, wicked

sake *n* **1** *decided to give up smoking for the sake of his health*: advantage, behalf, benefit, good, interest, profit, regard, respect, welfare, wellbeing **2** *he's only complaining for the sake of it*: account, cause, goal, object, objective, purpose, reason

salacious *adj* bawdy, blue *colloq*, carnal, coarse, concupiscent *formal*, erotic, horny, improper, indecent, lascivious *formal*, lecherous, lewd, libidinous *formal*, lubricious *formal*, lustful, obscene, pornographic, prurient, randy, raunchy, ribald, scurrilous, smutty *colloq*, steamy *colloq*, wanton
⊟ clean, decent, proper

salaried *adj* emolumental *formal*, emolumentary *formal*, paid, remunerated, stipendiary, waged
⊟ honorary, unpaid, voluntary

salary *n* earnings, emolument, fee, honorarium, income, pay, remuneration, stipend, wages

sale *n* bargaining, deal, disposal, market, marketing, selling, trade, traffic, transaction, vending

Types of sale include:
auction, autumn sale, bargain offer, bazaar, bazumble, boot-sale, bring-and-buy, car-boot sale, charity sale, church bazaar, clearance sale, closing-down sale, cold-call, end-of-line sale, end-of-season sale, exhibition, exposition, fair, fleamarket, forced sale, garage sale, grand opening sale, introductory offer, January sale, jumble sale, mail order, market, mid-season sale, on-promotion, open market, pre-season sale, private sale, public sale, pyramid selling, remainder sale, rummage sale, sale of bankrupt stock, sale of the century, sale of work, second-hand sale, special offer, spring sale, stocktaking sale, summer sale, tabletop sale, telesales, trade show, trash and treasure sale, winter sale

saleable *adj* desirable, marketable, merchantable, sought-after, vendible *formal*
⊟ unmarketable, unsaleable

salesperson *n* clerk *US*, rep *colloq*, representative, sales assistant, salesclerk *US*, salesman, saleswoman, shop assistant, shopkeeper

salient *adj* arresting, chief, conspicuous, important, main, noticeable, obvious,

outstanding, principal, prominent, pronounced, remarkable, signal, significant, striking

sallow *adj* anaemic, colourless, jaundiced, pale, pallid, pasty, sickly, unhealthy, wan, waxen, yellowish
⊟ healthy, rosy

sally[1] *v* **1** *troops sally forth towards the enemy*: attack, charge, erupt, foray, issue, rush, sortie, surge, venture **2** *sallied into town*: mosey *colloq*, promenade, saunter, stroll, wander
⊟ **1** retreat
♦ *n* **1** *the army's sudden sally gained them ground*: assault, attack, dash, foray, incursion, offensive, raid, rush, sortie, surge, thrust, venture **2** *fond memories of sallies to the country*: drive, escapade, excursion, frolic, jaunt, trip, wander
⊟ **1** retire, retreat

sally[2] *n* bon mot, crack, jest, jeu d'esprit, joke, quip, retort, riposte, wisecrack, witticism

salt *n* **1** *a pinch of salt*: flavour, relish, rock-salt, savour, sea-salt, seasoning, taste **2** *add a bit of salt to the conversation*: liveliness, piquancy, punch, pungency, trenchancy *formal*, vigour, wit, zest, zip **3** *an old salt*: marine, mariner, rating, sailor, seafarer, seaman
♦ *adj* salty, brackish, briny, saline, salted, saltish
⊟ fresh
▶ **salt away** accumulate, amass, bank, cache, collect, hide, hoard, save, stash, stockpile, store up
⊟ spend, squander

salty *adj* **1** *salty water*: brackish, briny, saline, salt **2** *salty snacks*: piquant, salted, savoury, tangy **3** *salty comments*: animated, exciting, lively, piquant, racy, stimulating, trenchant *formal*, vigorous, witty
⊟ **1** fresh **2** sweet

salubrious *adj* beneficial, healthful, health-giving, healthy, invigorating, pleasant, refreshing, salutary, sanitary, wholesome

salutary *adj* **1** *a salutary reminder*: advantageous, beneficial, good, helpful, practical, profitable, timely, useful, valuable **2** *a salutary walk*: health-giving, healthy, hygienic, invigorating, refreshing, sanitary

salutation *n* address, greeting, respects, salute, welcome

salute *v* **1** *the children saluted him warmly*: acknowledge, address, greet, recognize, wave **2** *the captain saluted and marched away*: acknowledge, bow, hail, honour, present arms **3** *he saluted his son's achievements*: acknowledge, celebrate, honour, mark, pay tribute to, recognize
♦ *n* **1** *greeted the woman with a courteous salute*: acknowledgement, address, bow, gesture, greeting, handshake, nod, reverence, wave, welcome **2** *the concert was held as a salute to the musician*: acknowledgement, celebration, homage, honour, recognition, tribute

salvage *v* conserve, get back, preserve, reclaim, recover, recuperate, redeem, repair, rescue, restore, retain, retrieve, save
⊟ abandon, waste

salvation *n* deliverance, liberation, preservation, reclamation, redemption, rescue
⊟ damnation, loss

salve *n* application, balm, cream, embrocation *formal*, liniment, lotion, medication, ointment,

preparation
♦ *v* calm, comfort, ease, lighten, relieve, soothe

same *adj* *we have the same name:* alike, carbon copy, comparable, corresponding, duplicate, equal, equivalent, identical, indistinguishable, interchangeable, like, matching, mutual, one and the same, selfsame, similar, substitutable, synonymous, the very same, twin, very **2** *the situation remains the same:* changeless, consistent, unchanged, unchanging, uniform, unvariable, unvarying
Ⅎ **1** different **2** changeable, inconsistent, variable

sameness *n* changelessness, consistency, duplication, identicalness, indistinguishability, invariability, likeness, monotony, oneness, predictability, repetition, resemblance, similarity, standardization, uniformity
Ⅎ difference, variety

sample *n* cross-section, demonstration, example, foretaste, illustration, indication, instance, model, pattern, piece, representative, sampling, specimen, swatch, test
♦ *v* examine, experience, inspect, sip, taste, test, try
♦ *adj* demonstrative, dummy, illustrative, pilot, representative, specimen, test, trial, typical

sanctify *v* anoint, bless, canonize, cleanse, consecrate, dedicate, exalt, hallow, make holy, make sacred, purify, set apart, wash
Ⅎ defile, desecrate

sanctimonious *adj* goody-goody *colloq*, holier-than-thou, hypocritical, moralizing, pharisaical, pietistic, pious, priggish, self-righteous, smug, superior
Ⅎ humble

sanctimoniousness *n* cant, complacency, humbug, hypocrisy, moralizing, pharisaism, pietism, preachiness, priggishness, righteousness, self-righteousness, self-satisfaction, smugness
Ⅎ humility

sanction *n* **1** *received their official sanction:* accreditation *formal*, agreement, approbation *formal*, approval, authority, authorization, backing, confirmation, endorsement, go-ahead *colloq*, green light *colloq*, licence, OK *colloq*, permission, ratification, support, thumbs-up *colloq* **2** *impose sanctions on a country:* ban, boycott, embargo, penalty, punishment, restriction
♦ *v* accredit *formal*, allow, approve, authorize, back, confirm, endorse, give the go-ahead to *colloq*, give the green light to *colloq*, give the thumbs-up to *colloq*, legitimize, license, OK *colloq*, permit, ratify, support, underwrite, warrant
Ⅎ disapprove, forbid, veto

sanctity *n* blessedness, godliness, goodness, holiness, inviolability, purity, righteousness, sacredness, saintliness, spirituality, virtue
Ⅎ godlessness, impurity, secularity, unholiness, worldliness

sanctuary *n* **1** *a holy sanctuary:* altar, church, holy of holies, holy place, place of worship, sanctum *formal*, sanctum sanctorum *formal*, shrine, tabernacle, temple **2** *the flat became a sanctuary for his followers:* asylum, haven, hideaway, hideout, refuge, retreat, shelter **3** *the system provides sanctuary to those who need it:* asylum, immunity, protection, safeguard, safety, security **4** *a wildlife sanctuary:* enclave, park, reservation, reserve

sanctum *n* **1** *the temple's inner sanctum:* holy of holies, holy place, sanctuary, sanctum sanctorum *formal*, shrine **2** *escaped to his sanctum:* cubbyhole, den, hideaway, hideout, refuge, retreat, study

sand *n* beach, desert, sands, seashore, shore, strand

sandbank *n* bar, hurst, reef, sand bar, yardang

sandy *adj* **1** *sandy hair and blue eyes:* auburn, coppery, ginger, gingery, red, reddish, reddish-yellow, rusty, tawny, Titian, yellow, yellowish, yellowy **2** *sandy terrain:* arenaceous *technical*, gritty, psammitic *technical*

sane *adj* all there *colloq*, balanced, in your right mind, judicious *formal*, level-headed, lucid, moderate, normal, of sound mind, rational, reasonable, responsible, right-minded, sensible, sober, sound, stable, wise
Ⅎ crazy, foolish, insane, mad

sangfroid *n* aplomb *formal*, assurance, calmness, composure, cool *colloq*, cool-headedness, coolness, dispassion, equanimity, imperturbability, nerve *colloq*, nonchalance, phlegm *formal*, poise, self-control, self-possession, unflappability *colloq*
Ⅎ discomposure, excitability, hysteria, panic

sanguinary *adj* bloodied, bloodthirsty, bloody, brutal, cruel, gory, grim, merciless, murderous, pitiless, ruthless, savage

sanguine *adj* **1** *he is sanguine about his chances:* ardent, assured, buoyant, cheerful, confident, expectant, hopeful, optimistic, over-confident, over-optimistic, unabashed, unbowed **2** *a sanguine complexion:* florid, flushed, fresh, fresh-complexioned, pink, red, rosy, rubicund *formal*, ruddy
Ⅎ **1** cynical, depressive, gloomy, melancholy, pessimistic **2** pale, sallow

sanitary *adj* antiseptic, aseptic, clean, disinfected, germ-free, healthy, hygienic, pure, salubrious *formal*, sterile, uncontaminated, unpolluted, wholesome
Ⅎ insanitary, unwholesome

sanity *n* balance of mind, common sense, good sense, judiciousness *formal*, level-headedness, lucidity, normality, prudence *formal*, rationality, reason, responsibility, right-mindedness, sense, soundness, soundness of mind, stability, wisdom
Ⅎ insanity, madness

sap *v* debilitate *formal*, deplete, diminish, drain, enervate *formal*, enfeeble, erode, exhaust, impair, reduce, undermine, weaken, wear down/away
Ⅎ build up, increase, strengthen
♦ *n* **1** *sap in a plant:* energy, essence, juice, lifeblood, vital fluid **2** *he's such a sap:* clot *colloq*, fink *slang*, fool, git *slang*, idiot, imbecile, jerk *slang*, moron, nit *colloq*, nitwit *colloq*, prat *slang*, twit *colloq*

sarcasm *n* acidity, acrimony *formal*, bitterness, contempt, cynicism, derision, gibing, irony, mockery, resentment, ridicule, satire, scoffing, scorn, sneering, spitefulness, trenchancy *formal*

sarcastic *adj* acerbic *formal*, acrimonious *formal*, biting, caustic, cutting, cynical, derisive, derisory, disparaging *formal*, incisive, ironical, jeering, mocking, mordant *formal*, sardonic, sarky *colloq*, satirical, scathing, scoffing, scornful, sneering, snide, taunting

sardonic *adj* acerbic *formal*, acrimonious *formal*, biting, bitter, contemptuous, cruel, cynical, derisive, dry, heartless, jeering, malicious, mocking, mordant *formal*, sarcastic, scornful, sneering

Satan *n* Abaddon, Apollyon, Beelzebub, Belial, Lucifer, Mephistopheles, Old Nick, Prince of Darkness, the Adversary, the Devil, the Enemy, the Evil One, the Tempter

satanic *adj* abominable, accursed, black, damned, dark, demonic, devilish, diabolical, evil, fiendish, hellish, infernal, inhuman, malevolent *formal*, satanical, sinful, wicked
🔁 benevolent, divine, godly, holy, saintly

sate *v* cloy, fill, glut, gorge, gratify, overfill, satiate *formal*, satisfy, saturate, slake, surfeit
🔁 deprive, dissatisfy, starve

satellite *n* 1 *send a satellite into orbit*: artificial satellite, orbiting body, spacecraft, spaceship 2 *a satellite of Mars*: moon, natural satellite, orbiting body, planet 3 *a satellite of the Soviet Union*: adherent, aide, attendant, dependant, disciple, follower, hanger-on, lackey, minion, parasite, puppet *colloq*, retainer, sidekick, subordinate, sycophant, vassal

satiate *v* cloy, engorge, glut, gorge, nauseate, overfeed, overfill, sate, satisfy, slake, stuff, surfeit
🔁 deprive, dissatisfy, underfeed

satiety *n* fullness, gratification, over-fullness, overindulgence, repleteness *formal*, repletion *formal*, satiation, satisfaction, saturation, surfeit

satire *n* burlesque, caricature, irony, lampoon, mickey-taking *colloq*, parody, piss-taking *slang*, ridicule, sarcasm, send-up *colloq*, skit, spoof *colloq*, take-off *colloq*, travesty, wit

satirical *adj* acerbic *formal*, acrimonious *formal*, biting, bitter, caustic, cutting, cynical, derisive, incisive, ironical, irreverent, mocking, mordant *formal*, ridiculing, sarcastic, sardonic, taunting, trenchant *formal*

satirist *n* caricaturist, cartoonist, lampooner, lampoonist, mocker, parodist, pasquilant *formal*, pasquiler *formal*, pasquinader *formal*, ridiculer

satirize *v* burlesque, caricature, criticize, deride *formal*, lampoon, make fun of, mock, parody, poke fun at, ridicule, send up *colloq*, take off *colloq*, take the mickey out of *colloq*, take the piss out of *slang*
🔁 acclaim, honour

satisfaction *n* 1 *great satisfaction from her work*: comfort, contentment, delight, enjoyment, fulfilment, gratification, happiness, pleasure, pride, self-satisfaction, sense of achievement, well-being 2 *demand due satisfaction*: amends, compensation, damages, indemnification, indemnity, recompense, redress, reimbursement, reparation, requital, restitution, settlement, vindication
🔁 1 displeasure, dissatisfaction

satisfactory *adj* acceptable, adequate, all right, average, competent, fair, fine, OK *colloq*, passable, sufficient, up to scratch *colloq*, up to the mark
🔁 inadequate, unacceptable, unsatisfactory

satisfied *adj* 1 *she is completely satisfied with her life*: content, contented, happy, pleased 2 *I was satisfied that he had done a good job*: certain, convinced, persuaded, positive, reassured, sure 3 *left the dinner table feeling satisfied*: full, replete *formal*, sated, satiated
🔁 1 disgruntled *colloq*, dissatisfied 2 unconvinced 3 hungry

satisfy *v* 1 *the breakfast was enough to satisfy his appetite*: appease, assuage *formal*, content, delight, gratify, indulge, please, quench, sate, satiate, slake, surfeit 2 *satisfies the requirements of the government agenda*: answer, be adequate for, be sufficient for, comply with *formal*, discharge, fill, fulfil, meet, qualify, serve, settle, suffice *formal* 3 *we were satisfied that the proper arrangements were in place*: assure, convince, persuade, reassure
🔁 1 dissatisfy 2 fail

satisfying *adj* 1 *a satisfying meal*: cheering, filling, fulfilling, gratifying, pleasing, pleasurable, refreshing, satisfactory 2 *a satisfying argument*: convincing, cool, persuasive, satisfactory
🔁 1 unsatisfactory 2 dissatisfying, frustrating, unsatisfactory

saturate *v* drench, fill, flood, glut, imbue, impregnate, make wet through, overfill, permeate, pervade, soak, souse, steep, suffuse, waterlog, wet

saturated *adj* 1 *absolutely saturated with water*: drenched, dripping, flooded, soaked, soaking, sodden, sopping, soused, steeped, waterlogged, wringing 2 *saturated in a golden light*: imbued, permeated, suffused

saturnine *adj* austere, dismal, dour, dull, gloomy, glum, grave, heavy, melancholy, moody, morose, phlegmatic, severe, sombre, stern, sullen, taciturn, uncommunicative, unfriendly, withdrawn
🔁 cheerful, jovial

sauce *n* 1 *served with a creamy sauce*: condiment, dip, dressing, flavouring, mayonnaise, relish 2 *was shocked at his sauce*: audacity, backchat, brass *colloq*, brazenness, cheek, cheekiness, disrespect, disrespectfulness, flippancy, freshness, impertinence, impudence, insolence, irreverence, lip *colloq*, mouth *colloq*, nerve *colloq*, pertness, presumption, presumptuousness, rudeness, sass
🔁 2 politeness, respectfulness

saucy *adj* brazen, cheeky *colloq*, disrespectful, flippant, forward, fresh *colloq*, impertinent, impudent, insolent, irreverent, lippy *colloq*, pert, presumptuous, rude, sassy *US colloq*
🔁 polite, respectful

saunter *v* amble, meander, mooch *colloq*, mosey *colloq*, ramble, stroll, wander
♦ *n* amble, constitutional, mooch *colloq*, mosey *colloq*, ramble, stroll, walk

savage *adj* 1 *a depiction of savage violence*: barbaric, barbarous, beastly, bloodthirsty, bloody, brutal, cruel, cut-throat *colloq*, dog-eat-dog *colloq*, ferocious, fierce, grim, harsh, inhuman, merciless, murderous, pitiless, ruthless, sadistic, terrible, vicious, wild **2** *fought through savage jungle terrain:* feral *formal*, primitive, uncivilized, undomesticated, untamed, wild

⧉ 1 humane, mild **2** civilized, tame

♦ *n* barbarian, beast, boor, brute, churl, monster, wild man, wild person, wild woman

♦ *v* **1** *savaged by a dog:* attack, bite, claw, lacerate, mangle, maul, tear, tear to pieces **2** *savaged by the critics:* attack, denounce, run down *colloq*, slam *colloq*, slate *colloq*, tear to pieces *colloq*, tear to shreds *colloq*

savagery *n* barbarity, bestiality, bloodthirstiness, brutality, brutishness, cruelty, ferity *formal*, ferocity, fierceness, inhumanity, mercilessness, murderousness, pitilessness, primitiveness, roughness, ruthlessness, sadism, viciousness, wildness

⧉ civility, civilization, humanity

savant *n* authority, guru, intellectual, man/woman of letters, master, mastermind, philosopher, pundit, sage *formal*, scholar

⧉ amateur, ignoramus

save *v* **1** *saved by a firefighter:* bail out *colloq*, deliver, free, get someone out of, liberate, recover, redeem, release, rescue, salvage, set free **2** *save food:* collect, conserve, gather, hoard, hold, keep, lay up, preserve, put aside, put by, reserve, retain, set aside, stash *colloq*, stockpile, store **3** *has been saving for years:* be thrifty, budget, buy cheaply, cut back, cut costs, cut your coat according to your cloth *colloq*, economize, live on the cheap, scrimp and save, tighten your belt *colloq*, use less **4** *save the whale:* guard, keep, keep safe, preserve, protect, safeguard, screen, shield, spare

⧉ 2 discard, waste **3** spend, squander

saving *adj* compensatory, extenuating, mitigating, qualifying, redeeming

♦ *n* **1** *resulted in a saving of around £10:* cut, discount, economy, reduction **2** *put your savings in the bank:* capital, fund, investments, nest egg, reserves, resources

⧉ 1 expense, loss, waste **2** expenditure

saviour *n* **1** *is considered the company's saviour:* champion, defender, deliverer, emancipator, guardian, liberator, protector, redeemer, rescuer **2** *accept Jesus Christ as my Saviour:* Deliverer, Emmanuel, Lamb of God, Mediator, Redeemer

⧉ 1 destroyer

savoir-faire *n* ability, accomplishment, assurance, capability, confidence, diplomacy, discretion, expertise, finesse, know-how *colloq*, poise, tact, urbanity

⧉ awkwardness, clumsiness, incompetence, inexperience

savour *n* **1** *lost its savour:* flavour, piquancy, relish, salt, smack, spice, tang, taste, zest **2** *the savour of cooking hung thick in the air:* aroma, bouquet, fragrance, perfume, scent, smell **3** *just a savour of garlic:* hint, smattering, suggestion, touch, trace

♦ *v* **1** *she savoured every moment:* appreciate, delight in, enjoy, enjoy to the full, like, relish, revel in, take pleasure in, taste to the full **2** *his tone savoured of familiarity:* have all the signs of, have the hallmarks of, seem like, smack, speak, spell, suggest

⧉ 1 shrink from

savoury *adj* **1** *prepared some savoury treats:* appetizing, delicious, flavoursome, luscious, mouthwatering, palatable, scrumptious *colloq*, tasty, yummy *colloq* **2** *prefers savoury foods:* aromatic, piquant, salty, spicy, tangy

⧉ 1 insipid, tasteless, unappetizing **2** sweet

♦ *n* appetizer, bonne-bouche, canapé, hors d'oeuvre, snack

say *v* **1** *I can't say how proud I am:* articulate, deliver, enunciate, express, orate *formal*, perform, phrase, pronounce, put, put into words, read, recite, render, repeat, speak, utter, voice **2** *'OK', he said:* add, answer, comment, drawl, ejaculate *formal*, exclaim, grunt, mention, mutter, observe, rejoin, remark, reply, respond, retort **3** *a report says that universities must collaborate more:* affirm, allege, announce, assert, claim, communicate, convey, declare, disclose, divulge, imply, intimate, maintain, report, reveal, rumour, state, suggest **4** *I would say she's likely to win the race:* assume, estimate, guess, imagine, judge, presume, reckon, suppose, surmise

♦ *n* **1** *determined to have his say at the meeting:* opinion, right to express yourself, turn/chance to speak, voice **2** *have no say in the matter:* authority, clout *colloq*, influence, power, sway, weight

---

Other words for say include:

accuse, acknowledge, add, admit, admonish, advise, affirm, agree, allege, announce, answer, argue, ask, assert, assume, aver *formal*, avow *formal*, babble, banter, bark, bawl, beg, begin, bellow, blare, blaspheme, blurt, boast, brag, call, chant, chatter, claim, coax, come out with *colloq*, command, comment, communicate, complain, conclude, contradict, convey, conjecture, continue, correct, counter, croak, cry, curse, declare, demand, deny, describe, detail, disclose, dispute, divulge, echo, elaborate, elucidate, emphasize, enjoin, estimate, exclaim, expostulate, express, falter, finish, flounder, gasp, greet, groan, growl, grumble, grunt, guess, hint, howl, imagine, implore, imply, indicate, infer, inform, inquire, insinuate, insist, instruct, interrogate, interrupt, intervene, intimate, jeer, jest, joke, laugh, lecture, lie, maintain, make known, make public, mention, mimic, moan, mock, mouth, mumble, murmur, mutter, nag, observe, offer, orate, order, persist, persuade, phrase, pipe, plead, point out, predict, press, presume, proclaim, profess, proffer, prompt, pronounce, propose, protest, put about *colloq*, query, question, quote, rage, rail, rant, read, reassure, rebuke, recite, reckon, recommend, rehearse, reiterate, rejoice, relate, remark, remonstrate, renounce, repeat, reply, report, request, resolve, respond, retaliate, retort, retract, reveal, roar, rumour, scoff, scold, scream, screech, shout, shriek, snap, snarl, speak, specify, speculate, squeak, stammer, state, storm, stutter, submit, suggest, suppose, surmise, swear, sympathize, taunt, tease, tell, testify, thunder, urge, utter, venture, voice, volunteer, vow, whine, whisper, wonder, yell

---

saying *n* adage, aphorism, apophthegm *formal*, axiom, catch phrase, cliché, dictum, epigram, expression, maxim, motto, phrase, platitude, precept, proverb, quotation, remark, slogan, statement, word/pearl of wisdom

say-so *n* affirmation, agreement, approval, assertion, asseveration *formal*, assurance, authority, authorization, backing, consent *formal*, dictum *formal*, guarantee, OK *colloq*, permission, ratification, sanction, word

scaffold *n* **1** *the building was covered by a scaffold:* framework, platform, scaffolding **2** *he was taken to the scaffold for execution:* gallows, gibbet

scald *v* blister, brand, burn, cauterize *formal*, scorch, sear

scale¹ *n* **1** *the Richter scale:* calibration, graduation, measuring system, register, system of measurement **2** *the scale of the damage:* degree, extent, level, measure, range, reach, scope, spread **3** *the scale of the map:* proportion, ratio, relative size **4** *lower down the social scale:* hierarchy, ladder, order, pecking order *colloq*, progression, ranking, sequence, series
♦ *v* ascend, climb, conquer, go up, mount
► **scale down** contract, cut back/down, decrease, drop, lessen, make less, reduce, shrink

scale² *n* coat, coating, crust, deposit, encrustation, film, lamina, layer, limescale, plaque, plate, tartar

scaly *adj* desquamative *formal*, desquamatory *formal*, flaky, furfuraceous *formal*, furfurous *formal*, lepidote *formal*, rough, scabby, scabrous, scurfy, squamose *formal*, squamous *formal*, squamulose *formal*

scamp *n* devil, imp, mischief-maker, monkey, rascal, rogue, scallywag, troublemaker, whippersnapper *colloq*, wretch

scamper *v* dart, dash, fly, frolic, gambol, hasten *formal*, hurry, race, romp, run, rush, scoot, scramble, scurry, scuttle, sprint

scan *v* **1** *scan the horizon:* check, examine, inspect, investigate, scrutinize, search, study, survey **2** *scan the text:* browse through, flick through, flip through, glance at, go over, have a quick look at, leaf through, run over, run through, run your eye over, skim, thumb through
♦ *n* check, examination, inspection, investigation, probe, review, screening, scrutiny, search, study, survey, test

scandal *n* **1** *the politician's behaviour caused a scandal:* discredit, disgrace, dishonour, embarrassment, furore, ignominy, obloquy *formal*, offence, opprobrium *formal*, outcry, outrage, shame, uproar **2** *newspapers full of celebrity scandal:* calumny *formal*, defamation *formal*, dirt, dirty linen/washing/laundry *colloq*, gossip, rumours, skeleton in the cupboard *colloq*, smear **3** *his actions brought scandal on the family:* black mark, blot, crying shame *colloq*, disgrace, pity, reproach, shame, slur, smear, stain

scandalize *v* affront, appal, disgust, dismay, horrify, insult, offend, outrage, repel, revolt, shock

scandalmonger *n* busybody, calumniator *formal*, defamer *formal*, gossip, gossip-monger, muck-raker *colloq*, nosy parker *colloq*, quidnunc, talebearer, tattler, traducer *formal*

scandalous *adj* abominable, appalling, atrocious, disgraceful, dishonourable, disreputable, flagrant, improper, infamous,

juicy *colloq*, libellous, malicious, monstrous, opprobrious *formal*, outrageous, scurrilous, shameful, shocking, unseemly *formal*, unspeakable

scant *adj* bare, deficient, exiguous *formal*, hardly any, inadequate, insufficient, limited, little, little or no, measly *colloq*, minimal, sparse
☒ adequate, ample, sufficient

scanty *adj* bare, deficient, inadequate, insubstantial, insufficient, limited, little, meagre, narrow, poor, restricted, scant, short, skimpy, sparse, thin
☒ adequate, ample, plentiful, substantial, sufficient

scapegoat *n* fall guy *colloq*, patsy *US slang*, victim, whipping-boy

scar *n* blemish, blotch, defacement, discolouration, disfigurement, injury, lesion, mark, shock, stigma, trauma, wound
♦ *v* brand, damage, deface, disfigure, injure, mark, shock, spoil, stigmatize, traumatize

scarce *adj* deficient, few, few and far between *colloq*, in short supply, inadequate, infrequent, insufficient, lacking, like gold dust *colloq*, meagre, not enough, rare, scant, scanty, sparse, too little, uncommon, unusual
☒ common, plentiful

scarcely *adv* **1** *I can scarcely hear you:* barely, hardly, only just **2** *that is scarcely a reason to hit him:* certainly not, definitely not, hardly, not

scarcity *n* dearth, deficiency, exiguity *formal*, infrequency, insufficiency, lack, paucity *formal*, rareness, rarity, scantiness, scantness, shortage, sparseness, uncommonness, want *formal*
☒ abundance, enough, glut, plenty, sufficiency

scare *v* alarm, appal, daunt, dismay, frighten, intimidate, make afraid, make frightened, make someone jump out of their skin *colloq*, make your blood run cold *colloq*, make your flesh creep *colloq*, make your hair stand on end *colloq*, menace, panic, perturb *formal*, petrify, put the frighteners on *colloq*, put the wind up *colloq*, rattle *colloq*, scare out of your wits *colloq*, scare the living daylights out of *colloq*, scare the shit out of *slang*, shock, startle, terrify, terrorize, threaten, unnerve
☒ calm, reassure
♦ *n* alarm, fearfulness, fright, horror, hysteria, panic, shock, start, terror
☒ comfort, reassurance

scared *adj* afraid, alarmed, anxious, cowed, fearful, frightened, having kittens *colloq*, in a blue funk *colloq*, jittery, nervous, panicky, panic-stricken, petrified, quivery, scared out of your wits *colloq*, scared to death *colloq*, shaken, shaking like a leaf *colloq*, startled, terrified, terrorized, terror-stricken, unnerved, with your heart in your mouth *colloq*, worried
☒ confident, reassured

scaremonger *n* alarmist, Cassandra, doom and gloom merchant, doomwatcher, jitterbug, pessimist, prophet of doom

scarf *n* babushka, headscarf, headsquare, kerchief, muffler, neckerchief, shawl, stole

scarper *v* abscond, beat it *colloq*, bolt, bunk off *colloq*, clear off *colloq*, decamp, depart, disappear, do a bunk *colloq*, escape, flee, flit, go, hightail it *colloq*, leave, run away, run for it *colloq*, scram *colloq*, skedaddle *colloq*, vamoose *colloq*, vanish

scary *adj* alarming, bloodcurdling, chilling, creepy, daunting, disturbing, eerie, fearsome, forbidding, formidable, frightening, hair-raising, hairy *colloq*, horrifying, intimidating, petrifying, shocking, spine-chilling, spooky *colloq*, terrifying

scathing *adj* acid, biting, bitter, brutal, caustic, critical, cutting, ferocious, fierce, harsh, mordant *formal*, sarcastic, savage, scornful, severe, stinging, trenchant *formal*, unsparing, vitriolic
F3 complimentary

scatter *v* diffuse, disband, dispel, disperse, disseminate *formal*, dissipate, disunite, fling, shower, sow, spread, sprinkle, strew
F3 collect, gather

scatterbrained *adj* absent-minded, carefree, careless, empty-headed, feather-brained, forgetful, frivolous, hare-brained, having your head in the clouds *colloq*, impulsive, inattentive, irresponsible, scatty *colloq*, slap-happy, thoughtless, unreliable, wool-gathering
F3 careful, efficient, sensible, sober

scattering *n* few, handful, smattering, sprinkling
F3 abundance, mass

scavenge *v* forage, hunt, look for, rake, rummage, scrounge, search

scavenger *n* forager, raker, rummager, scavager, scrounger

scenario *n* **1** *the worst-case scenario:* circumstances, scene, sequence of events, situation, state, state of affairs **2** *the government devised a detailed scenario:* plan, plot, programme, projection, scheme **3** *showed the actor a scenario of the film:* outline, plan, plot, résumé, screenplay, script, sequence, storyline, summary, synopsis

scene *n* **1** *scene of the action:* area, arena, backdrop, background, context, environment, locale, locality, location, milieu, place, position, set, setting, site, situation, spot, stage, whereabouts **2** *admired the beautiful scene:* landscape, outlook, pageant, panorama, picture, prospect, scenery, sight, spectacle, tableau, view, vista **3** *filmed the scene several times:* act, clip, episode, incident, part **4** *don't make a scene:* commotion, display, drama, exhibition, furore, fuss, kerfuffle *colloq*, outburst, performance, show, to-do *colloq* **5** *not my scene:* area, area of activity, area of interest, field, speciality

scenery *n* **1** *beautiful mountainous scenery:* landscape, outlook, panorama, prospect, setting, surroundings, terrain, view, vista **2** *scenery in a theatre:* backdrop, background, mise-en-scène, scene, set

scenic *adj* attractive, awe-inspiring, beautiful, breathtaking, grand, impressive, panoramic, picturesque, pretty, spectacular, striking
F3 dreary, dull

scent *n* **1** *the delicious scent of flowers:* aroma, bouquet, fragrance, odour, perfume, redolence *formal*, smell **2** *bought some scent in the duty-free shop:* cologne, eau-de-cologne, eau-de-toilette, perfume, toilet water **3** *follow the scent:* smell, spoor, trace, track, trail

F3 1 stink
♦ *v* **1** *a tiger scenting its prey:* nose (out), smell, sniff (out), trace, track **2** *scenting victory:* become aware of, become conscious of, detect, discern, perceive, recognize, sense

scented *adj* aromatic, fragrant, perfumed, sweet-smelling
F3 malodorous, stinking

sceptic *n* agnostic, atheist, cynic, disbeliever, doubter, doubting Thomas, questioner, rationalist, scoffer, unbeliever
F3 believer

sceptical *adj* cynical, disbelieving, distrustful, doubtful, doubting, dubious, hesitant, hesitating, incredulous, mistrustful, pessimistic, questioning, scoffing, suspicious, unbelieving, unconvinced
F3 confident, convinced, trusting

scepticism *n* agnosticism, atheism, cynicism, disbelief, distrust, doubt, doubtfulness, dubiety, hesitancy, incredulity, pessimism, rationalism, suspicion, unbelief
F3 belief, faith

schedule *n* agenda, calendar, catalogue, diary, form, inventory, itinerary, list, plan, programme, scheme, syllabus, table, timetable
♦ *v* appoint, arrange, assign, book, list, organize, plan, programme, table, time, timetable

schematic *adj* diagrammatic, graphic, illustrative, representational, symbolic

scheme *n* **1** *an innovative recycling scheme:* arrangement, configuration *formal*, course of action, device, disposition *formal*, method, plan, procedure, programme, project, schedule, strategy, system **2** *showed them the early schemes:* blueprint, chart, delineation *formal*, design, diagram, draft, idea, layout, map, outline, pattern, plan, project, proposal, proposition, schedule, schema, sketch **3** *took part in the evil scheme:* conspiracy, intrigue, machinations *formal*, manoeuvre, plot, ploy, ruse, stratagem, strategy, tactic(s)
♦ *v* collude, connive, conspire, contrive, devise, frame, intrigue, machinate *formal*, manipulate, manoeuvre, mastermind, plan, plot, project

schemer *n* conniver, deceiver, fox, intrig(u)ant(e), intriguer, Machiavellian, machinator *formal*, mastermind, plotter, wangler *colloq*, wheeler-dealer *colloq*, wire-puller *colloq*

scheming *adj* artful, calculating, conniving, crafty, cunning, deceitful, designing, devious, duplicitous *formal*, insidious, Machiavellian, slippery, sly, tricky, underhand, unscrupulous, wily
F3 artless, honest, open, transparent

schism *n* **1** *a widening schism between the two factions:* breach, break, discord, disunion, division, estrangement *formal*, rift, rupture, separation, severance, split **2** *left the church and joined the schism:* detachment, faction, group, sect

scholar *n* **1** *several scholars failed the exam:* learner, pupil, schoolboy, schoolchild, schoolgirl, student **2** *a leading scholar and university professor:* academic, authority, egghead *colloq*, expert, intellectual, mastermind, philosopher, pundit

scholarly *adj* academic, analytical, bookish, conscientious, erudite, highbrow, intellectual,

knowledgeable, learned, lettered, scholastic, studious, well-read
🔁 illiterate, uneducated

scholarship *n* **1** *the book is a fine example of modern scholarship:* academic achievements/attainments, education, erudition *formal,* knowledge, learnedness, learning, wisdom **2** *a scholarship to a public school:* award, bursary, endowment, exhibition, fellowship, foundation, grant

scholastic *adj* **1** *scholastic institutions:* academic, educational, learned, lettered, literary, pedagogic, scholarly **2** *scholastic disputes:* analytical, pedantic, precise

school *n* **1** *go to school:* academy, college, institute, institution, madrasa, seminary, university, yeshiva(h) **2** *school of medicine:* department, division, faculty, institute **3** *a school of artists:* association, circle, clique, club, company, coterie, faction, group, guild, league, set, society
♦ *v* coach, educate, instruct, prepare, prime, teach, train, tutor, verse

schooling *n* book-learning, coaching, drill, education, grounding, guidance, indoctrination, instruction, learning, preparation, teaching, training, tuition

schoolteacher *n* educator, instructor, master, mistress, pedagogue, schoolmarm, schoolmaster, schoolmistress, teacher

science *n* dexterity, discipline, expertise, knowledge, proficiency, skill, specialization, technique, technology

Sciences include:
acoustics, aerodynamics, aeronautics, agricultural science, anatomy, anthropology, archaeology, astronomy, astrophysics, behavioural science, biochemistry, biology, biophysics, botany, chemistry, chemurgy, climatology, computer science, cybernetics, diagnostics, dietetics, domestic science, dynamics, earth science, ecology, economics, electrodynamics, electronics, engineering, entomology, environmental science, food science, genetics, geochemistry, geographical science, geology, geophysics, graphology, hydraulics, information technology, inorganic chemistry, life science, linguistics, macrobiotics, materials science, mathematics, mechanical engineering, mechanics, medical science, metallurgy, meteorology, microbiology, mineralogy, morphology, natural science, nuclear physics, organic chemistry, ornithology, pathology, pharmacology, physics, physiology, political science, psychology, radiochemistry, robotics, sociology, space technology, telecommunications, thermodynamics, toxicology, ultrasonics, veterinary science, zoology

scientific *adj* accurate, analytical, controlled, exact, mathematical, methodical, orderly, precise, regulated, scholarly, systematic, thorough

scintillate *v* blaze, coruscate *formal,* flash, gleam, glint, glisten, glitter, shine, spark, sparkle, twinkle, wink

scintillating *adj* **1** *a scintillating star:* bright, brilliant, dazzling, flashing, glittering, shining, sparkling **2** *scintillating conversation:* animated, bright, brilliant, dazzling, ebullient *formal,* exciting, exhilarating, glittering, invigorating, lively, shining, sparkling, stimulating, vivacious, witty
🔁 **1** dull **2** dull

scion *n* child, descendant, heir, offspring, successor

scoff [1] *v* belittle, deride *formal,* despise, disparage *formal,* gibe, jeer, knock *colloq,* laugh at, mock, poke fun, pooh-pooh *colloq,* revile, rib *colloq,* ridicule, scorn, sneer, taunt, tease
🔁 compliment, flatter, praise

scoff [2] *v* bolt, consume, devour, eat, finish off, gobble, gulp, guzzle, put away *colloq,* wolf *colloq*
♦ *n* chow *US slang,* comestibles, eatables *colloq,* eats *colloq,* food, foodstuffs, grub *slang,* meal, nosh *slang,* nosh-up *slang,* nourishment, nutriment, nutrition, provisions, refreshments, subsistence, sustenance, tuck *colloq*

scoffing *adj* cynical, derisive, disparaging *formal,* Mephistophelian, mocking, sarcastic, scathing, sneering, taunting

scold *v* admonish *formal,* berate *formal,* castigate *formal,* censure, chide, give a dressing-down *colloq,* give someone a piece of your mind *colloq,* haul over the coals *colloq,* lambaste *formal,* lecture, nag, rap over the knuckles *colloq,* read the riot act to *colloq,* rebuke, reprimand, reproach, reprove, take to task, tell off *colloq,* tick off *colloq,* upbraid *formal*
🔁 commend, praise

scolding *n* a piece of your mind *colloq,* carpeting *colloq,* castigation *formal,* dressing-down *colloq,* earful *colloq,* lecture, rebuke, reprimand, reproof, talking-to, telling-off, ticking-off *colloq,* upbraiding *formal,* wigging *colloq*
🔁 commendation, praise

scoop *n* **1** *used a metal scoop:* bailer, bucket, dipper, ladle, shovel, spoon **2** *journalists hunting for a scoop:* coup, exclusive, exposé, inside story, latest *colloq,* revelation, sensation
♦ *v* bail, dig, empty, excavate, gouge, hollow, ladle, remove, scrape, shovel, spoon

scoot *v* beat it *colloq,* bolt, career, dart, dash, hurry, run, rush, scarper *colloq,* scud, scurry, scuttle, shoot, skedaddle *colloq,* sprint, tootle, vamoose *colloq,* zip

scope *n* **1** *the scope of his knowledge:* ambit, area, breadth, compass, confines, coverage, extent, field, limits, range, reach, realm, span, sphere **2** *scope for improvement:* capacity, elbow-room, freedom, latitude, leeway, opportunity, room, space

scorch *v* **1** *wildfires scorched hundreds of acres of grassland:* blacken, burn, char, roast, scald, sear, singe **2** *the grass was scorched after a long, dry summer:* discolour, dry up, parch, wither

scorching *adj* baking *colloq,* blistering, boiling *colloq,* burning, red-hot, roasting, searing, sizzling, sweltering, torrid, tropical

score *n* **1** *the score was even at half-time:* goals, hits, marks, outcome, points, record, result, runs, sum, tally, total **2** *made a score on the surface:* cut, gash, gouge, groove, incision, line, mark, nick,

notch, scrape, scratch, slit **3** *scores of people:* crowds, droves, hosts, hundreds, legions, lots, masses, millions, multitudes, myriads, shoals, swarms, thousands **4** *don't worry on that score:* account, argument, basis, case, explanation, grounds, motives, reason **5** *he knew the score:* facts, issue, matter, question, situation, subject **6** *settle old scores:* argument, bone of contention, complaint, dispute, grievance, grudge, quarrel
♦ *v* **1** *score a goal:* achieve, attain, chalk up *colloq*, earn, gain, get, make, notch up *colloq*, register **2** *this car scores well on reliability:* be one up, have the advantage, have the edge, hit the jackpot *colloq*, win **3** *to score a piece of card:* cut, engrave, gash, gouge, graze, groove, incise, indent, mark, nick, notch, scrape, scratch, slash, slit **4** *to score a piece of music:* adapt, arrange, instrument, orchestrate, set, write
► **score off** gain an advantage over, get one over on *colloq*, get the better of, have the edge, humiliate, make a clever reply to
► **score out** cancel, cross out, delete, efface *formal*, erase, expunge *formal*, obliterate *formal*, remove, strike out
🔁 reinstate, restore

scorn *n* contempt, contumely *formal*, derision, disdain, disgust, disparagement *formal*, haughtiness, mockery, ridicule, sarcasm, scornfulness, sneering
🔁 admiration, respect
♦ *v* deride *formal*, despise, disdain, dismiss, disparage *formal*, laugh at, look down on, mock, rebuff, refuse, reject, scoff at, shun, slight, sneer at, sniff at, spurn
🔁 admire, respect

scornful *adj* contemptuous, derisive, disdainful, dismissive, disparaging *formal*, insulting, jeering, mocking, sarcastic, scathing, scoffing, slighting, sneering
🔁 admiring, respectful

scornfully *adv* arrogantly, contemptuously, derisively, disdainfully, dismissively, disparagingly *formal*, haughtily, scathingly, slightingly, sneeringly, superciliously, witheringly
🔁 admiringly, respectfully

scot-free *adj* clear, safe, undamaged, unharmed, unhurt, uninjured, unpunished, unrebuked, unreprimanded, unreproached, unscathed, without a scratch

scoundrel *n* cheat, good-for-nothing, louse *slang*, miscreant, ne'er-do-well, rascal, rat *colloq*, reprobate, rogue, rotter, ruffian, scab *slang*, scallywag, scamp, swine *colloq*, vagabond, villain

scour¹ *v* abrade *formal*, burnish, clean, cleanse, flush, polish, purge, rub, scrape, scrub, wash, wipe

scour² *v* comb, drag, forage, hunt, rake, ransack, rummage, search, turn upside-down

scourge *n* **1** *a terrible scourge on the community:* affliction, bane, curse, evil, menace, nuisance, plague, thorn in your side, torment **2** *he was beaten with a scourge:* birch, cat-o'-nine-tails, flagellum, flail, lash, strap, switch, whip
🔁 **1** blessing, boon, godsend
♦ *v* **1** *scourging society:* afflict, burden, curse, devastate, plague **2** *criminals were cruelly*

scourged: beat, birch, cane, flail, flog, lash, punish, strap, thrash, torment, torture, whip

scout *v* case *slang*, check out, explore, hunt, inspect, investigate, look (for), observe, probe, recce *colloq*, reconnoitre, search, seek, snoop, spy, spy out, survey, watch
♦ *n* advance guard, escort, lookout, outrider, reconnoitre, recruiter, spotter, spy, talent spotter, vanguard

scowl *v* frown, glare, glower, grimace, look daggers at, lour, pout
🔁 beam, grin, smile
♦ *n* dirty/black look *colloq*, frown, glare, glower, grimace, pout
🔁 beam, grin, smile

scrabble *v* clamber, claw, dig, grope, grub, paw, root, scramble, scrape, scratch

scraggy *adj* angular, bony, emaciated, gaunt, lanky, lean, raw-boned, scrawny, skinny, thin, undernourished, wasted
🔁 plump, sleek

scram *v* beat it *colloq*, bolt *colloq*, clear off *colloq*, clear out *colloq*, depart, disappear, do a bunk *colloq*, flee, go away, leave, quit *colloq*, scarper *colloq*, scoot *colloq*, shove off *colloq*, skedaddle *colloq*, take to your heels *colloq*, vamoose *colloq*

scramble *v* **1** *they scrambled up the hillside:* clamber, climb, crawl, grope, scale, scrabble **2** *photographers scrambled for a better view:* battle, compete, contend, jockey, jostle, push, strive, struggle, tussle, vie **3** *scrambled the data:* disorganize, disturb, jumble, mix, mix up
♦ *n* **1** *the scramble up the rocks took her breath away:* clamber, climb, scaling, scrabble **2** *a mad scramble for bargains:* bustle, commotion, competition, dash, free-for-all, hurry, hustle, mêlée, race, rush, scurry, stampede, struggle, tussle, vying

scrap¹ *n* **1** *a scrap of material:* bit, fragment, particle, piece, remnant, shred, sliver, snippet, tatter, trace **2** *a scrap of truth:* bit, fraction, grain, iota, mite, particle, piece, shred, trace, vestige **3** *scraps of food:* bits, bits and pieces *colloq*, crumbs, leavings, leftovers, odds and ends *colloq*, odds and sods *slang*, remains, residue, scrapings, waste
♦ *v* **1** *the authorities have scrapped their plans:* abandon, axe, cancel, discard, ditch *colloq*, drop, write off **2** *the owner decided to scrap the car:* break up, chuck out *colloq*, demolish, discard, ditch *colloq*, dump, get rid of, junk *colloq*, throw away, write off
🔁 **2** recover, restore

scrap² *n* argument, brawl, disagreement, dispute, dust-up *colloq*, fight, fracas, punch-up *colloq*, quarrel, row, scuffle, set-to *colloq*, squabble, tiff, wrangle
🔁 agreement, peace
♦ *v* argue, bicker, brawl, disagree, fall out, fight, quarrel, row, squabble, wrangle
🔁 agree

scrape *v* **1** *scraped the old paint off the walls:* abrade *formal*, clean, erase, file, grate, rasp, remove, rub, scour **2** *he fell and scraped his knees:* bark, cut, graze, scratch, scuff, skin
♦ *n* **1** *escaped with only scrapes and bruises:* abrasion, graze, scratch, scuff **2** *got himself into a scrape:* difficulty, dilemma, distress, fix *colloq*,

mess *colloq*, pickle *colloq*, predicament, tight spot *colloq*, trouble
▶ **scrape by** get by, just manage to live, scarcely have enough to live on
▶ **scrape through** get through by a whisker *colloq*, just pass, just succeed in, only just/barely win
▶ **scrape together** collect with difficulty, get together, get with difficulty, just manage to get, obtain with difficulty, pool together

scrappy *adj* bitty, disjointed, disorganized, fragmentary, incomplete, piecemeal, sketchy, slapdash, slipshod, superficial, untidy
🎱 complete, finished

scratch *v* abrade *formal*, claw, cut, engrave, etch, gash, gouge, graze, incise, lacerate, mark, nick, rub, score, scrape, scuff, skin
♦ *n* abrasion, gash, graze, laceration, line, mark, scrape, scuff, wound
♦ *adj* haphazard, impromptu, improvised, rough, rough-and-ready, unrehearsed
🎱 polished

scrawl *v* dash off, doodle, jot (down), scribble, write quickly
♦ *n* bad/illegible handwriting, cacography *formal*, scrabble, scribble, squiggle

scrawny *adj* angular, bony, emaciated, lanky, lean, raw-boned, scraggy, skinny, thin, underfed, undernourished
🎱 fat, plump

scream *v* bawl, cry, holler *colloq*, howl, roar, screech, shout, shriek, squawk, squeal, wail, yawp *US colloq*, yell, yelp
🎱 whisper
♦ *n* 1 *let out a piercing scream:* bawl, cry, holler *colloq*, howl, roar, screech, shout, shriek, squawk, squeal, wail, yawp *US colloq*, yell, yelp 2 *he's a scream:* character *colloq*, comedian, comic, hoot *colloq*, joker, laugh *colloq*, riot *colloq*, wit
🎱 1 whisper 2 bore

screech *v* cry, howl, shriek, squawk, squeal
♦ *n* cry, howl, scream, shriek, squawk, squeal, yell, yelp
🎱 whisper

screen *n* 1 *a screen in the middle of the room:* divider, partition 2 *they observed from behind a screen:* blind, cover, curtain, façade, front, guard, mesh, net, netting, protection, shade, shelter, shield
♦ *v* 1 *screen a film:* broadcast, present, show 2 *house is screened from the street by hedges:* camouflage, conceal, cover, hide, mask, protect, shade, shelter, shield 3 *the containers were screened by customs officials:* check, evaluate, examine, filter, gauge, grade, investigate, process, scan, sift, sort, test, vet
🎱 2 expose, uncover
▶ **screen off** conceal, divide (off), fence off, hide, partition (off), separate (off)

screw *n* bolt, brad, fastener, nail, pin, rivet, tack
♦ *v* 1 *screw the lid on:* clamp, fasten, fix, tighten, turn, twist 2 *screw the cloth into a ball:* compress, distort, squeeze, turn, twist, wind, wring, wrinkle 3 *screw money out of him:* bleed *colloq*, extort, extract, force, pressurize
🎱 1 unscrew 2 unscrew
▶ **screw up 1** *screwed up his face:* contort, contract, crumple, distort, knot, pucker, tighten, wrinkle 2 *screwed up his chances:* botch, bungle,

cock up *slang*, louse up *slang*, make a hash of *colloq*, mess up, mishandle, mismanage, spoil

screwy *adj* batty *colloq*, crackers *colloq*, crazy, daft *colloq*, dotty *colloq*, eccentric, mad, nutty *colloq*, odd, queer, round the bend *colloq*, round the twist *colloq*, weird
🎱 sane

scribble *v* dash off, doodle, jot (down), pen, scrawl, write
♦ *n* bad/illegible handwriting, cacography *formal*, handwriting, scrabble, scratch, squiggle, writing

scrimmage *n* affray, bovver *colloq*, brawl, disturbance, dust-up *colloq*, fight, fray, free-for-all, mêlée, riot, row, scrap *colloq*, scuffle, set-to *colloq*, shindy, skirmish, squabble, struggle

scrimp *v* curtail, cut back on, cut your coat according to your cloth *colloq*, economize, limit, pinch, reduce, restrict, save, scrape, shorten, skimp, stint, tighten your belt *colloq*
🎱 spend

script *n* 1 *a film script:* book, libretto, lines, manuscript, screenplay, text, words 2 *her beautiful italic script:* calligraphy, copy, hand, handwriting, longhand, manuscript, writing

scripture

The sacred writings of religions include: the word of God, the word, Holy Bible, the Gospel, Old Testament, New Testament, Epistle, Torah, Pentateuch, Talmud, Koran, Bhagavad-Gita, Veda, Granth, Zend-Avesta

Scrooge *n* cheapskate *colloq*, meanie *colloq*, miser, money-grubber *colloq*, niggard, penny-pincher *colloq*, skinflint, tightwad *colloq*
🎱 spendthrift

scrounge *v* beg, bludge *colloq*, borrow, bum *colloq*, cadge, sponge *colloq*

scrounger *n* beggar, bludger *colloq*, borrower, bum *colloq*, cadger, freeloader *colloq*, moocher *colloq*, parasite, sponger *colloq*

scrub¹ *v* 1 *scrub the floor:* brush, clean, cleanse, rub, scour, wash, wipe 2 *they scrubbed their plans at the last minute:* abandon, axe *colloq*, cancel, discontinue *formal*, drop, forget, give up

scrub² *n* backwoods, brush, bush, scrubland

scruffy *adj* bedraggled, dishevelled, disreputable, down-at-heel, messy, ragged, run-down, seedy, shabby, slatternly, sloppy *colloq*, slovenly, sluttish *slang*, squalid, tattered, ungroomed, unkempt, untidy, worn-out
🎱 tidy, well-dressed

scrumptious *adj* appetising, delectable *formal*, delicious, delightful, exquisite, luscious, magnificent, morish *colloq*, mouth-watering, scrummy *colloq*, succulent, tasty, yummy *colloq*
🎱 unappetizing, yucky *colloq*

scrunch *v* champ, chew, crumple, crunch, crush, grate, grind, mash, screw (up), squash, twist

scruple *n* 1 *I have some artistic scruples about the piece:* difficulty, doubt, hesitation, misgiving, perplexity, qualm, reservation, second thoughts, uneasiness, vacillation *formal* 2 *she has no scruples:* ethics, morals, principles, standards

♦ *v* balk, be reluctant, hesitate, hold back, shrink, think twice, vacillate *formal*

scrupulous *adj* 1 *worked with scrupulous attention to detail:* careful, conscientious, exact, fastidious, meticulous, minute, nice, painstaking, precise, punctilious *formal*, rigorous, strict, thorough 2 *a scrupulous lawyer:* ethical, high-principled, honest, honourable, moral, principled, upright
🇫 1 careless, reckless, superficial 2 unprincipled, unscrupulous

scrutinize *v* analyse, examine, explore, go over, go through, inspect, investigate, look over, look through, peruse *formal*, probe, run over, run through, scan, search, sift, study

scrutiny *n* analysis, examination, exploration, inquiry, inspection, investigation, perusal *formal*, probe, search, study

scuff *v* abrade *formal*, brush, drag, graze, rub, scrape, scratch

scuffle *v* brawl, clash, come to blows, contend, fight, grapple, quarrel, scrap *colloq*, struggle, tussle
♦ *n* affray, brawl, commotion, disturbance, dust-up *colloq*, fight, fray, quarrel, row, rumpus, scrap *colloq*, set-to *colloq*, tussle

sculpt *v* carve, cast, chisel, cut, fashion, form, hew, model, mould, represent, sculpture, shape

sculpture

Types of sculpture include:
bas-relief, bronze, bust, carving, cast, effigy, figure, figurine, group, head, high-relief, maquette, marble, moulding, plaster cast, relief, statue, statuette, telamon, waxwork

---

scum *n* 1 *the scum floated to the surface:* dross, film, foam, froth, impurities 2 *the scum of the earth:* dregs of society, lowest of the low, plebs *colloq*, rabble, riff-raff *colloq*, rubbish, the great unwashed *colloq*, trash, undesirables

scupper *v* 1 *scuppered our plans:* destroy, foil, overthrow, put a spanner in the works *colloq*, ruin, scuttle, wreck 2 *scupper a ship:* destroy, sink, submerge
🇫 1 advance, promote

scurrility *n* abuse, abusiveness, coarseness, foulness, grossness, indecency, invective *formal*, nastiness, obloquy *formal*, obscenity, offensiveness, rudeness, scurrilousness, vituperation *formal*, vulgarity
🇫 politeness

scurrilous *adj* abusive, coarse, defamatory *formal*, disparaging *formal*, foul, indecent, insulting, libellous, obscene, offensive, rude, salacious, scandalous, slanderous, vituperative *formal*, vulgar
🇫 complimentary, courteous, polite

scurry *v* bustle, dart, dash, fly, hasten *formal*, hurry, race, run, rush, scamper, scoot, scramble, scud, scuttle, skim, sprint, trot
♦ *n* bustling, flurry, hurry, hustle and bustle *colloq*, rush, scampering, whirl
🇫 calm

scurvy *adj* abject *formal*, bad, base, contemptible, despicable, dirty, dishonourable, ignoble, low, low-down *colloq*, mean, pitiful, rotten, shabby, sorry, vile, worthless
🇫 good, honourable

scuttle *v* bustle, hasten *formal*, hurry, run, rush, scamper, scramble, scud, scurry, scutter

sea *n* 1 *the deep blue sea:* briny *colloq*, deep, main, ocean 2 *a sea of faces:* abundance, expanse, host, large number, mass, multitude, profusion
♦ *adj* aquatic, marine, ocean, oceanic, saltwater, seafaring
🇫 air, land

seafaring *adj* marine, maritime, nautical, naval, ocean-going, oceanic, sailing, sea-going

seal *v* 1 *seal a jar:* close (up), cork, fasten, make airtight/watertight, plug, secure, shut, stop (up), stopper, tighten, waterproof 2 *they shook hands to seal the bargain:* clinch *colloq*, conclude, confirm, finalize, ratify, settle
🇫 1 unseal
♦ *n* insignia, signet, stamp
► **seal off** block up, close off, cordon off, cut off, fence off, isolate, quarantine, segregate, shut off
🇫 open up

sealed *adj* closed, corked, hermetic, plugged, shut
🇫 unsealed

seam *n* 1 *breaking apart at the seams:* closure, join, joint, junction, line, weld 2 *coal seam:* layer, lode, stratum, vein

seaman *n* AB, deck hand, Jack tar, matelot *slang*, rating, sailor, sea dog, seafarer, steersman, tar

seamy *adj* dark, disreputable, low, nasty, rough, sleazy *colloq*, sordid, squalid, unpleasant, unsavoury
🇫 pleasant, respectable, wholesome

sear *v* brand, brown, burn, cauterize *formal*, char, dry-up, fry, parch, scorch, seal, shrivel, singe, sizzle, wilt, wither

search *v* 1 *search for their passports:* comb, forage, go through, go through with a fine-tooth comb *colloq*, hunt, look, look through, ransack, rifle, rummage, scour, seek, sift, turn upside-down/inside-out *colloq* 2 *search the evidence for clues:* check, examine, explore, inquire, inspect, investigate, probe, pry, scrutinize
♦ *n* 1 *an ongoing search for the missing dog:* forage, hunt, pursuit, quest 2 *a thorough search of the data:* examination, exploration, inquiry, inspection, investigation, probe, research, scrutiny, survey

searching *adj* alert, close, discerning, intent, keen, minute, observant, penetrating, piercing, probing, sharp, thorough
🇫 superficial, vague

seaside *n* beach, coast, sands, seashore, shore

season *n* interval, period, phase, span, spell, term, time
♦ *v* 1 *season food:* add flavouring, add herbs to, add pepper to, add relish/sauce to, flavour, pep up *colloq*, salt, spice 2 *season wood:* age, condition, harden, mature, mellow, prepare, prime, ripen, toughen, train, treat 3 *season your behaviour:* moderate, temper, tone down

seasonable *adj* appropriate, convenient, fitting, opportune, providential, suitable, timely, welcome, well-timed
🇫 inopportune, unseasonable

seasoned *adj* acclimatized, battle-scarred, conditioned, established, experienced, habituated *formal*, hardened, long-serving, mature, old, practised, toughened, veteran, weathered, well-versed ⊞ inexperienced, novice

seasoning *n* condiment, dressing, flavouring, herbs, pepper, relish, salt, sauce, spice

seat *n* **1** *we were shown to our seats*: bench, chair, pew, settle, stall, stool, throne **2** *country seat*: abode *formal*, house, mansion, residence, stately home **3** *the nation's seat of power*: axis, base, centre, foundation, headquarters, heart, hub, location, place, site, situation, source ♦ *v* **1** *were seated at the back*: deposit, install, locate, place, position, put, set, settle, sit **2** *the theatre seats 1000*: accommodate, contain, have room for, hold, take

seating *n* accommodation, chairs, places, room, seats

secede *v* apostatize *formal*, break, break away, disaffiliate, leave, quit *colloq*, resign, retire, separate, split off, turn your back on, withdraw ⊞ join, unite with

secession *n* apostasy *formal*, break, breakaway, defection, disaffiliation, schism, seceding, split, withdrawal ⊞ amalgamation, unification

secluded *adj* cloistered, concealed, cut off, hidden, isolated, lonely, out-of-the-way, private, remote, sequestered *formal*, sheltered, shut away, solitary, unfrequented ⊞ accessible, public

seclusion *n* concealment, hiding, isolation, privacy, remoteness, retirement, retreat, secrecy, sequestration *formal*, shelter, solitude, withdrawal

second¹ *adj* **1** *second course*: following, next, subsequent, succeeding **2** *a second car*: additional, alternate, alternative, back-up, extra, further, other, supplementary **3** *second class*: inferior, lesser, lower, secondary, subordinate, supporting ♦ *n* assistant, attendant, backer, helper, right-hand man/woman, second-in-command, supporter ♦ *v* advance, agree with, aid, approve, assist, back, back up, encourage, endorse, forward, further, help, promote, support

second² *n* flash, instant, jiffy *colloq*, minute, moment, split second, tick *colloq*, trice, twinkling, twinkling of an eye, two shakes of a lamb's tail *colloq*

second³ *v* assign, change, move, relocate, send, shift, transfer

secondary *adj* alternative, ancillary, auxiliary, back-up, derivative, derived, extra, indirect, inferior, lesser, lower, minor, non-essential, relief, reserve, resulting, second, spare, subordinate, subsidiary, supporting, unimportant ⊞ essential, main, major, primary

second-class *adj* indifferent, inferior, mediocre, second-best, second-rate, undistinguished, unimportant, uninspired, uninspiring ⊞ valuable

second-hand *adj* borrowed, derivative, hand-me-down, indirect, nearly-new, old, secondary, used, vicarious, worn ⊞ brand-new

second-in-command *n* assistant, attendant, backer, helper, right-hand man/woman, supporter

second-rate *adj* cheap, inferior, lesser, lousy *colloq*, low-grade, mediocre, poor, ropy *colloq*, second-best, second-class, shoddy, substandard, tacky *colloq*, tawdry, tinpot *colloq*, undistinguished, unimportant, uninspired, uninspiring ⊞ first-rate

secrecy *n* camouflage, concealment, confidence, confidentiality, covertness, disguise, furtiveness, mystery, privacy, seclusion, stealth, stealthiness, surreptitiousness ⊞ openness

secret *adj* **1** *a secret operation*: back-door, backstairs, camouflaged, clandestine *formal*, cloak-and-dagger *colloq*, closet *colloq*, concealed, covered, covert, discreet, disguised, furtive, hidden, hole-and-corner *colloq*, private, shrouded, sly, stealthy, surreptitious, undercover, underground, underhand, under-the-counter, unseen **2** *secret information*: between you and me *colloq*, classified, confidential, hush-hush *colloq*, restricted, sensitive, top secret *colloq*, undisclosed, unknown, unpublished, unrevealed **3** *secret rites*: abstruse *formal*, arcane *formal*, cryptic, deep, mysterious, occult, recondite *formal* **4** *a secret garden*: cloistered, concealed, cut off, hidden, isolated, lonely, out-of-the-way, private, remote, secluded, sequestered *formal*, sheltered, shut away, solitary, unfrequented ⊞ **1** open, public **2** well-known **4** accessible, public ♦ *n* **1** *it's a secret*: confidence, confidential matter, enigma, inside story *colloq*, mystery, private matter **2** *the secret of eternal youth*: answer, code, formula, key, recipe, solution

secretary *n* amanuensis, clerk, executive assistant, office administrator, PA, person Friday, personal assistant, stenographer, typist

secrete¹ *v* appropriate, bury, cache, conceal, cover, cover up, disguise, hide, screen, sequester *formal*, shroud, stash away *colloq*, take, veil ⊞ disclose, reveal, uncover

secrete² *v* discharge, emanate, emit, excrete, exude, give off, leach, leak, ooze, produce, release, send out

secretion *n* discharge, emanation, emission, exudation, leakage, oozing, osmosis *technical*, release

secretive *adj* cagey *colloq*, close, cryptic, deep, enigmatic, intent, playing your cards close to your chest *colloq*, quiet, reserved, reticent, taciturn, tight-lipped, uncommunicative, unforthcoming, withdrawn ⊞ communicative, forthcoming, open

secretly *adv* behind closed doors *colloq*, clandestinely *formal*, confidentially, covertly, furtively, in camera *formal*, in confidence, in private, in secret, on the q.t. *colloq*, on the quiet, on the sly *colloq*, privately, privily *formal*, quietly, stealthily, surreptitiously, under cover, unobserved ⊞ openly

sect *n* camp, cult, denomination, division, faction, group, order, party, school, splinter group, subdivision, wing

sectarian *adj* bigoted, cliquish, doctrinaire, dogmatic, exclusive, extreme, factional, fanatical, hidebound, insular, limited, narrow, narrow-minded, parochial, partisan, prejudiced, rigid
🔁 broad-minded, non-sectarian
♦ *n* bigot, dogmatist, extremist, fanatic, fractionalist, partisan, zealot

section *n* area, bit, branch, chapter, component, department, district, division, fraction, fragment, instalment, paragraph, part, passage, piece, portion, region, sector, segment, slice, subdivision, wing, zone
🔁 whole

sectional *adj* class, divided, exclusive, factional, local, localized, partial, racial, regional, sectarian, separate, separatist
🔁 general, universal

sector *n* area, branch, category, district, division, field, part, quarter, region, section, subdivision, zone
🔁 whole

secular *adj* civil, earthly, lay, non-religious, non-spiritual, profane, state, temporal, worldly
🔁 religious, spiritual

secure *adj* 1 *kept their valuables secure in a strongbox:* closed, fast, fastened, fortified *formal*, immune, impregnable, locked, out of harm's way *colloq*, protected, safe, sealed, sheltered, shielded, tight, undamaged, unharmed 2 *a secure personality:* assured, comfortable, confident, contented, happy, reassured, relaxed, safe 3 *the bookshelves are absolutely secure:* firm, fixed, immovable, solid, stable, steady, sturdy 4 *secure evidence:* certain, conclusive, definite, dependable, established, reliable, settled, steadfast, sure, well-founded
🔁 1 insecure, vulnerable 2 embarrassed, ill at ease, uncomfortable, uneasy
♦ *v* 1 *secured the best tickets for the show:* acquire, come by *colloq*, gain, get, get hold of, land *colloq*, obtain, procure *formal* 2 *secured the doors and windows:* attach, batten down, bolt, chain, close, fasten, fix, lash, lock (up), make fast, moor, nail, padlock, rivet, shut, tie (up) 3 *secured the property against intruders:* cover, defend, guard, make safe, protect, safeguard, screen, shield, strengthen 4 *secure a loan:* assure, confirm, endorse, ensure, establish, guarantee, sponsor, underwrite
🔁 1 lose 2 unfasten

security *n* 1 *police could not provide adequate security:* asylum, care, cover, custody, defence, immunity, invulnerability, preservation, protection, refuge, safe-keeping, safety, sanctuary, surveillance 2 *security for a loan:* assurance, collateral, guarantee, insurance, pledge, precaution(s), protection, safeguard(s), surety, warranty 3 *security in his own abilities:* assurance, certainty, confidence, conviction, ease, peace of mind, positiveness
🔁 1 danger, insecurity 3 anxiety, embarrassment, worry

sedate *adj* calm, collected, composed, cool, decorous *formal*, deliberate, demure, dignified, dull, earnest, grave, imperturbable *formal*, proper, quiet, serene, serious, slow-moving, sober, solemn, staid, stiff, tranquil, unexciting, unflappable *colloq*, unruffled

🔁 agitated, lively, undignified
♦ *v* calm, calm down, pacify, quieten down, relax, soothe, tranquillize

sedative *adj* anodyne, calming, depressant, lenitive, relaxing, soothing, soporific, tranquillizing
🔁 rousing
♦ *n* barbiturate, calmative, depressant, downer *colloq*, narcotic, opiate, sleeping-pill, tranquillizer

sedentary *adj* desk-bound, immobile, inactive, seated, sitting, stationary, still, unmoving
🔁 active

sediment *n* deposit, dregs, grounds, lees, precipitate *formal*, residue, residuum *formal*, silt

sedition *n* agitation, disloyalty, fomentation *formal*, incitement to riot *formal*, insubordination *formal*, mutiny, rabble-rousing, rebellion, revolt, subversion, treachery, treason
🔁 calm, loyalty

seditious *adj* agitating, disloyal, dissident *formal*, fomenting *formal*, inciting, insubordinate *formal*, insurrectionist *formal*, mutinous, rabble-rousing, rebellious, refractory *formal*, revolutionary, subversive, traitorous
🔁 calm, loyal

seduce *v* allure, attract, beguile, charm, corrupt, deceive, deprave, dishonour, ensnare, entice, get into bed *colloq*, inveigle *formal*, lead astray, lure, mislead, ruin, tempt
🔁 repel

seducer *n* Casanova, charmer, deceiver, Don Juan, flirt, goat *colloq*, libertine, Lothario, philanderer, wolf *colloq*, womanizer

seduction *n* allure, allurement, appeal, attraction, beguilement, charm, come-on *colloq*, corruption, deception, enticement, lure, misleading, ruin, temptation

seductive *adj* alluring, appealing, attractive, beguiling, bewitching, captivating, charming, come-hither *colloq*, deceiving, enticing, flirtatious, inviting, irresistible, luring, misleading, provocative, sexy, sultry, tantalizing, tempting
🔁 repulsive, unattractive

seductress *n* Circe, femme fatale, Lorelei, siren, temptress, vamp *colloq*

sedulous *adj* assiduous, busy, conscientious, constant, determined, diligent, industrious, laborious, painstaking, persevering, persistent, resolved, tireless, unflagging, unremitting, untiring
🔁 half-hearted

see *v* 1 *I can see the mountains from my window:* catch sight of, discern, distinguish, get a look at, glimpse, identify, look at, make out, mark, note, notice, observe, perceive, regard, set eyes on, sight, spot, view, watch, witness 2 *I see what you mean:* appreciate, comprehend, cotton onto *colloq*, follow, get *colloq*, grasp, know, latch onto *colloq*, make out, realize, recognize, understand 3 *economists see better times ahead:* anticipate, envisage, forecast, foresee, imagine, picture, predict, visualize 4 *need to see whether it works:* ascertain, decide, determine, discover, find out, inquire, investigate, learn 5 *I'll see you to your car:* accompany, escort, lead, show, take, usher 6 *I saw Bill the other day:* bump into *colloq*, chance

upon *formal*, come across *colloq*, encounter, meet, run into *colloq* **7** *she's seeing John now*: court, date, go out with, keep company with, take out
▶ **see about** arrange, attend to, be responsible for, deal with, do, fix, look after, manage, organize, sort out, take care of
▶ **see through 1** *see through a trick*: fathom, get wise to *colloq*, not be deceived by, not be taken in by **2** *see a task through*: continue, hang in *colloq*, not give up, persevere, persist, stick out
▶ **see to** arrange, attend to, be responsible for, deal with, do, fix, look after, manage, mind, organize, sort out, take care of

seed *n* **1** *the seeds of a plant*: germ, grain, kernel, nucleus, pip, stone **2** *the seeds of rebellion*: beginning, cause, origin, reason(s), root, source, start **3** *seed of Abraham*: child, children, descendants, family, heirs, offspring, successors, young, young one(s)

seedy *adj* **1** *a seedy establishment*: crummy *colloq*, decaying, dilapidated, dirty, grotty *colloq*, mangy, run-down, scruffy, shabby, sleazy *colloq*, squalid, tatty, untidy **2** *felt seedy the next morning*: groggy *colloq*, ill, off-colour, out of sorts *colloq*, poorly, rough *colloq*, sick, under the weather *colloq*, unwell
🔁 **2** well

seek *v* aim, ask, aspire *formal*, attempt, beg, desire, endeavour, entreat *formal*, follow, hunt for, inquire, invite, look for, petition, pursue, request, search for, solicit *formal*, strive, try, try to find, want

seem *v* appear, come across as, feel, give the impression of being, have the look of, give the appearance of being, look, look like, pretend to be, show signs of, sound, strike you as

seeming *adj* apparent, assumed *formal*, external, ostensible *formal*, outward, pretended, pseudo, quasi-, specious, superficial, supposed, surface
🔁 real

seemingly *adv* allegedly, apparently, as far as you can see, on the face of it, on the surface, ostensibly *formal*, outwardly, superficially
🔁 really

seemly *adj* appropriate, attractive, becoming, befitting, comme il faut, decent, decorous *formal*, fit, fitting, handsome, maidenly, nice, proper, suitable, suited
🔁 unseemly

seep *v* drain, dribble, drip, exude, leak, ooze, percolate, permeate, soak, trickle, well

seepage *n* dripping, exudation, leak, leakage, oozing, osmosis *technical*, percolation

seer *n* augur, prophet, sibyl, soothsayer, spaeman, spaewife

seesaw *v* alternate, fluctuate, go from one extreme to the other, oscillate, pitch, swing, teeter, yo-yo *colloq*

seethe *v* **1** *full of seething liquid*: boil, bubble, effervesce, ferment, fizz, foam, froth, simmer, surge, swell **2** *mother was seething*: be furious, be incensed, be livid, be outraged, boil over *colloq*, explode *colloq*, foam at the mouth *colloq*, fume, rage, see red *colloq*

see-through *adj* filmy, flimsy, gauzy, gossamer(y), sheer, translucent, transparent
🔁 opaque

segment *n* bit, compartment, division, part, piece, portion, section, slice, wedge
🔁 whole
◆ *v* anatomize, cut up, divide, halve, separate, slice, split

segregate *v* cut off, dissociate, exclude, isolate, keep apart, ostracize, quarantine, separate, sequester *formal*, set apart
🔁 join, unite

segregation *n* apartheid, discrimination, dissociation, isolation, quarantine, separation, sequestration *formal*, setting apart
🔁 unification

seize *v* **1** *the boy seized the toy*: clutch, get/take hold of, grab, grab hold of, grasp, grip, hold, snatch **2** *the authorities seized the property*: annex, commandeer, confiscate, impound, sequestrate *formal*, take **3** *the criminals seized the plane*: abduct, appropriate, commandeer, hijack, kidnap, take, usurp **4** *the police seized the criminal*: apprehend, arrest, capture, catch, collar *colloq*, nab *colloq*, nail *colloq*, nobble *colloq*
🔁 **2** hand back, release **3** hand back, let go, release

seizure *n* **1** *suffered a seizure and was transferred to hospital*: attack, convulsion, fit, paroxysm, spasm **2** *a tip-off led to the seizure of illegal weapons*: annexation, apprehension, capture, commandeering, confiscation, sequestration *formal* **3** *condemned the seizure of military personnel*: abduction, capture, hijack, snatching, taking
🔁 **3** liberation, release

seldom *adv* hardly ever, infrequently, occasionally, once in a blue moon *colloq*, rarely, scarcely ever
🔁 often, usually

select *v* appoint, choose, decide on, elect, favour, invite, opt for, pick, prefer, settle on, single out
◆ *adj* best, choice, élite, excellent, exclusive, finest, first-class, first-rate, hand-picked, high-quality, limited, posh *colloq*, prime, privileged, selected, special, superior, supreme, top
🔁 general, ordinary, second-rate

selection *n* **1** *selection of a new candidate*: choice, preference **2** *a fantastic selection of pastries*: assortment, choice, collection, line-up, medley, miscellany, range, variety

selective *adj* careful, choosy *colloq*, discerning, discriminating, fastidious, finicky, fussy, particular, pernickety *colloq*, picky *colloq*
🔁 indiscriminate

self *n* ego, heart of hearts *colloq*, I, identity, inner being, person, personality, soul, the real me *colloq*

self-assertive *adj* aggressive, authoritarian, bossy *colloq*, commanding, dictatorial, domineering, forceful, heavy-handed, high-handed, not backward in coming forward *colloq*, overbearing, overweening, peremptory *formal*, pushing, pushy *colloq*
🔁 compliant

self-assurance *n* aplomb, assurance, belief in yourself, cockiness *colloq*, cocksureness, confidence, overconfidence, positiveness, self-confidence, self-possession
🔁 humility, unsureness

self-assured *adj* assured, cocksure, cocky *colloq*, confident, overconfident, self-collected, self-confident, self-possessed, sure of oneself
Ⓕ humble, unsure

self-centred *adj* egocentric, egotistic(al), narcissistic, self-absorbed, self-interested, selfish, self-seeking, self-serving, thinking only of yourself, wrapped up in yourself
Ⓕ altruistic

self-confident *adj* assured, bold, composed, confident, cool, fearless, positive, self-assured, self-possessed, self-reliant, unabashed
Ⓕ self-conscious, unsure

self-conscious *adj* awkward, bashful, blushing, coy, diffident, embarrassed, ill at ease, insecure, nervous, retiring, self-effacing, shamefaced, sheepish, shrinking, shy, timid, timorous *formal*, uncomfortable
Ⓕ confident, natural, unaffected

self-control *n* calmness, composure, cool *colloq*, patience, restraint, self-denial, self-discipline, self-mastery, self-restraint, temperance, willpower

self-denial *n* abstemiousness, asceticism, moderation, self-abnegation *formal*, selflessness, self-renunciation *formal*, self-sacrifice, temperance, unselfishness
Ⓕ self-indulgence

self-esteem *n* amour-propre, dignity, ego, pride, self-assurance, self-confidence, self-pride, self-regard, self-respect
Ⓕ inferiority complex

self-evident *adj* axiomatic, clear, incontrovertible, inescapable, manifest *formal*, obvious, undeniable, unquestionable

self-glorification *n* egotheism, egotism, self-admiration, self-advertisement, self-aggrandizement, self-exaltation
Ⓕ humility

self-government *n* autarchy *formal*, autonomy, democracy, home rule, independence, self-sovereignty
Ⓕ subjection

self-importance *n* arrogance, big-headedness, bumptiousness *colloq*, cockiness *colloq*, conceit, conceitedness, donnism, pomposity, pompousness, pushiness *colloq*, self-consequence, self-opinion, vanity
Ⓕ humility

self-important *adj* arrogant, big-headed, bumptious *colloq*, cocky *colloq*, conceited, egoistic, overbearing, pompous, proud, pushy *colloq*, self-consequent, strutting, swaggering, swollen-headed, vain
Ⓕ humble

self-indulgence *n* dissipation *formal*, dissoluteness, excess, extravagance, hedonism, high living, intemperance, profligacy *formal*, self-gratification, sensualism
Ⓕ self-denial

self-indulgent *adj* dissipated *formal*, dissolute, extravagant, hedonistic, immoderate, intemperate, profligate *formal*
Ⓕ abstemious

self-interest *n* self, selfishness, self-love, self-regard, self-serving
Ⓕ selflessness

selfish *adj* covetous, egocentric, egotistic(al), greedy, inconsiderate, mean, mercenary, miserly, self-centred, self-interested, self-seeking, self-serving, thinking of nobody except yourself *colloq*
Ⓕ considerate, generous, selfless, unselfish

selfishness *n* egotism, greed, meanness, self-centredness, self-interest, self-love, self-regard, self-seeking, self-serving
Ⓕ selflessness

selfless *adj* altruistic, generous, magnanimous *formal*, philanthropic, self-denying, self-sacrificing, unselfish
Ⓕ self-centred, selfish

self-possessed *adj* calm, collected, composed, confident, cool *colloq*, poised, self-assured, self-collected, together *colloq*, unflappable *colloq*, unruffled
Ⓕ worried

self-possession *n* aplomb *formal*, calmness, composure, confidence, cool *colloq*, coolness, poise, sangfroid *formal*, self-command, self-confidence, unflappability *colloq*

self-reliance *n* autarky *technical*, independence, self-sufficiency, self-support, self-sustainment, self-sustenance, self-sustentation *formal*
Ⓕ dependence

self-reliant *adj* autarkic(al) *technical*, independent, self-sufficient, self-supporting, self-sustaining
Ⓕ dependent

self-respect *n* amour-propre, dignity, pride, self-assurance, self-confidence, self-esteem, self-regard
Ⓕ inferiority complex

self-restraint *n* abstemiousness, encraty *formal*, forbearance, moderation, patience, self-command, self-control, self-denial, self-discipline, self-government, temperance, willpower
Ⓕ licence

self-righteous *adj* complacent, goody-goody *colloq*, holier-than-thou, hypocritical, pharisaical, pi *colloq*, pietistic, pious, priggish, sanctimonious, smug, superior
Ⓕ humble

self-righteousness *n* goodiness, goody-goodiness *colloq*, pharisaicalness, pharisaism, piousness, priggishness, sanctimoniousness
Ⓕ humility

self-sacrifice *n* altruism, generosity, self-abnegation *formal*, self-denial, selflessness, self-renunciation *formal*, unselfishness
Ⓕ selfishness

self-satisfaction *n* complacency, contentment, pride, self-appreciation, self-approbation *formal*, self-approval, smugness
Ⓕ humility

self-satisfied *adj* complacent, proud, puffed up *colloq*, self-congratulatory, self-righteous, smug
Ⓕ humble

self-seeking *adj* acquisitive, calculating, careerist, fortune-hunting, gold-digging, mercenary, on the make *colloq*, opportunistic, self-endeared, self-interested, selfish, self-loving, self-serving
Ⓕ altruistic

self-styled *adj* pretended, professed, self-appointed, self-titled, so-called, soi-disant, would-be

self-supporting *adj* independent, self-financing, self-reliant, self-sufficient, self-sustaining
F∃ dependent

self-willed *adj* bloody-minded, cussed *colloq*, headstrong, intractable *formal*, obstinate, opinionated, pig-headed, refractory *formal*, self-opinionated, self-opinionative, stiff-necked, stubborn, ungovernable, wilful
F∃ complaisant

sell *v* **1** *I want to sell my car:* auction, barter, dispose of, exchange, flog *colloq*, hawk, peddle, retail, tout, trade, vend **2** *the shop sells a fine selection of teas:* carry, deal in, export, handle, import, market, merchandise, stock, trade in **3** *on tour to sell his new film:* advertise, get support/approval for, hype *colloq*, market, promote, push *colloq*
F∃ **1** buy
▶ **sell out** be out of stock, have none left, run out of

seller *n* merchant, stockist, supplier, trader, vendor
F∃ buyer, purchaser

selling *n* dealing, marketing, merchandising, promotion, salesmanship, trading, traffic, trafficking, transactions, vendition *formal*
F∃ buying

semblance *n* air, apparition *formal*, appearance, aspect, façade, front, guise, image, likeness, look, mask, pretence, resemblance, show, similarity, veneer

seminal *adj* creative, formative, imaginative, important, influential, innovative, major, original, productive, seminary
F∃ derivative

seminary *n* academy, college, institute, institution, school, training-college

send *v* **1** *sent a letter:* address, consign, convey, deliver, dispatch, forward, mail, post, put in the post/mail, redirect **2** *sent a message:* beam, broadcast, communicate, convey, radio, relay, televise, transmit **3** *a new satellite sent into space:* cast, direct, discharge, drive, fire, fling, hurl, launch, move, project, propel, shoot, throw
▶ **send for** call for, summon
▶ **send up** make fun of, mimic, mock, parody, ridicule, satirize, take off *colloq*, take the mickey out of *colloq*, take the piss out of *slang*

send-off *n* departure, farewell, goodbye, leave-taking, start
F∃ arrival

send-up *n* imitation, mickey-take *colloq*, mockery, parody, satire, skit, spoof *colloq*, take-off *colloq*

senile *adj* aged, confused, decrepit, doddering, failing, gaga *colloq*, old, senescent *formal*

senility *n* anility, caducity *formal*, decrepitude, dotage, infirmity, old age, paracme *formal*, second childhood, senescence *formal*, senile dementia

senior *adj* aîné(e) *formal*, chief, doyen(ne) *formal*, elder, first, higher, high-ranking, major, older, superior
F∃ junior

seniority *n* age, importance, precedence, priority, rank, standing, status, superiority

sensation *n* **1** *a sensation of of cold:* awareness, consciousness, feeling, impression, perception, sense **2** *the report caused a sensation:* agitation, commotion, excitement, furore, outrage, scandal, stir, thrill **3** *the new pop sensation:* hit, success, triumph

sensational *adj* **1** *a sensational meal:* amazing, astounding, breathtaking, dramatic, electrifying, excellent, exceptional, exciting, fabulous *colloq*, fantastic *colloq*, impressive, marvellous, smashing *colloq*, spectacular, staggering, startling, stirring, superb, terrific *colloq*, thrilling, wonderful **2** *sensational headlines:* lurid, melodramatic, scandalous
F∃ **1** ordinary, run-of-the-mill

sense *n* **1** *sense of touch:* appreciation, awareness, consciousness, faculty, feeling, impression, perception, sensation, sensibility *formal* **2** *a mature woman with a great deal of sense:* appreciation, apprehension, brain(s), cleverness, common sense, comprehension, discernment, gumption *colloq*, intelligence, intuition, judgement, judiciousness *formal*, logic, mind, nous *colloq*, prudence *formal*, reason, savvy *colloq*, understanding, wisdom, wit(s) **3** *the sense of what he was saying:* definition, denotation *formal*, drift, implication, import *formal*, interpretation, meaning, nuance, point, purport *formal*, purpose, significance, substance, tenor
F∃ **2** foolishness **3** nonsense
♦ *v* appreciate, be aware of, be conscious of, comprehend, detect, discern, divine *formal*, experience, feel, grasp, intuit *formal*, notice, observe, perceive, pick up *colloq*, realize, recognize, suspect, understand

senseless *adj* **1** *senseless act of vandalism:* absurd, crazy, daft *colloq*, fatuous, foolish, futile, idiotic, illogical, irrational, ludicrous, mad, meaningless, mindless, moronic, nonsensical, pointless, purposeless, ridiculous, silly, stupid, unreasonable **2** *was knocked senseless:* deadened, insensate *formal*, insensible *formal*, out *colloq*, out cold *colloq*, stunned, unconscious
F∃ **1** intelligent, meaningful, sensible
2 conscious

sensibility *n* **1** *show sensibility:* awareness, delicacy, discernment, insight, intuition, perceptiveness, responsiveness, sensitiveness, sensitivity, taste **2** *offend someone's sensibilities:* emotions, feelings, sensitivities, sentiments, susceptibilities
F∃ **1** insensibility

sensible *adj* **1** *a level-headed, sensible girl:* clever, commonsense, commonsensical, down-to-earth, far-sighted, functional, intelligent, judicious *formal*, level-headed, logical, mature, practical, prudent *formal*, rational, realistic, reasonable, sagacious *formal*, sane, sharp, shrewd, sober, sound, well-advised, wise, with both feet on the ground *colloq*, with your head screwed on (the right way) *colloq* **2** *he was sensible of his mother's situation:* aware, perceptive, responsive, sensitive **3** *wearing sensible shoes:* everyday, hard-wearing, ordinary, practical, serviceable, strong, tough, working

F 1 foolish, senseless, unwise 2 insensitive 3 decorative, fashionable, impractical

sensitive *adj* 1 *a sensitive child:* appreciative, aware, discerning, emotional, impressionable, irritable, perceptive, reactive, responsive, sensitized, susceptible, temperamental, tender, thin-skinned, touchy, vulnerable 2 *carried sensitive instruments on board:* delicate, exact, precise 3 *a sensitive issue:* awkward, controversial, delicate, difficult, problematic, touchy, tricky 4 *needs sensitive handling:* careful, considerate, delicate, diplomatic, discerning, discreet, sympathetic, tactful, well-thought-out

F 1 insensitive, thick-skinned 2 approximate, imprecise

sensitivity *n* 1 *sensitivity to the problems of others:* appreciation, awareness, perceptiveness, reactiveness, receptiveness, responsiveness, sympathy 2 *sensitivity to the arts:* appreciation, discernment, receptiveness, responsiveness 3 *sensitivity of character:* delicacy, fragility, susceptibility, vulnerability

F 1 insensitivity

sensual *adj* animal, bodily, carnal, erotic, fleshly, lecherous, lewd, licentious, lustful, physical, randy *colloq*, self-indulgent, sexual, sexy, sultry, voluptuous, worldly

F ascetic

---

sensual or **sensuous**? *Sensual* means 'of or concerning the physical senses and the body rather than the mind', and is used especially with a connotation of sexuality or sexual arousal: *a full, sensual mouth; a strong desire for sensual pleasure. Sensuous* means 'perceived by or affecting the senses, especially in a pleasant way', as in I *find his music very sensuous; Her sculptures have a certain sensuous quality to them*.

---

sensuality *n* animalism, carnality, debauchery, eroticism, gourmandize, lasciviousness, lecherousness, lewdness, libertinism, licentiousness, lustfulness, profligacy *formal*, prurience *formal*, salaciousness, sexiness, voluptuousness

F asceticism, Puritanism

sensuous *adj* aesthetic, gratifying, lush, luxurious, pleasant, pleasing, pleasurable, rich, sumptuous, voluptuous

F ascetic, plain, simple

sentence *n* condemnation, decision, decree, judgement, order, pronouncement, punishment, ruling, verdict

♦ *v* condemn, doom, impose a sentence on, judge, pass judgement on, penalize, punish

sententious *adj* 1 *a sententious, interfering old woman:* canting, judgemental, moralistic, moralizing, pompous, preachy *colloq*, sanctimonious 2 *a sententious statement:* aphoristic, brief, compact, concise, epigrammatic, gnomic, laconic, pithy, pointed, short, succinct, terse

F 1 humble 2 verbose

sentient *adj* aware, conscious, live, living, reactive, responsive, sensitive

F insentient *formal*

sentiment *n* 1 *the report is an indicator of consumer sentiment:* attitude, belief, feeling, idea, judgement, opinion, persuasion, point of view, thought, view 2 *he kept the animal out of sentiment:* emotion, romanticism, sensibility, sentimentality, soft-heartedness, softness, tenderness

sentimental *adj* affectionate, corny *colloq*, emotional, gushing, gushy *colloq*, lovey-dovey *colloq*, loving, maudlin, mawkish, mushy *colloq*, nostalgic, pathetic, romantic, schmaltzy *colloq*, sickly *colloq*, sloppy, slushy *colloq*, soft-hearted, soppy, sugary, tear-jerking, tender, touching, weepy *colloq*

F cynical, realistic, unsentimental

sentimentality *n* bathos *formal*, corniness *colloq*, emotionalism, gush *colloq*, mawkishness, mush *colloq*, nostalgia, pulp *colloq*, romanticism, schmaltz *colloq*, sentimentalism, sloppiness *colloq*, slush *colloq*, tenderness

sentry *n* guard, lookout, picket, sentinel, watch, watchman

separable *adj* detachable, different, distinct, distinguishable, divisible, independent, particular, removable

F inseparable

separate *v* abstract, become estranged *formal*, break off, break up, cut off, detach, disaffiliate, disconnect, disentangle, disjoin *formal*, dismantle, disunite, diverge, divide, divorce, isolate, keep apart, part, part company, partition, remove, secede, segregate, sever, single out, split (up), sunder *old use*, take/come apart, uncouple, withdraw

F combine, join, unite

♦ *adj* alone, apart, autonomous *formal*, detached, different, disconnected, discrete *formal*, disjointed, disparate *formal*, distinct, disunited, divided, divorced, independent, individual, isolated, particular, segregated, several *formal*, single, solitary, sundry, unattached, unconnected, unrelated

F attached, together

separated *adj* apart, disassociated, disconnected, disunited, divided, isolated, parted, segregated, separate, split up

F attached, together

separately *adv* alone, apart, discretely, discriminately, independently, individually, personally, severally *formal*, singly

F together

separating *adj* dividing, divisive, intervening, isolating, partitioning, segregating

F unifying

separation *n* apartheid, break-up, detachment, disconnection, disengagement, disseverment *formal*, dissociation, divergence, division, divorce, estrangement *formal*, farewell, gap, isolation, leave-taking, parting, parting of the ways, rift, schism, segregation, severance *formal*, split, split-up, uncoupling

F unification

septic *adj* festering, infected, poisoned, putrefactive *formal*, putrefying, putrid, suppurating *formal*

sepulchral *adj* cheerless, deep, dismal, funereal, gloomy, grave, hollow, lugubrious *formal*, melancholy, morbid, mournful, sad,

sepulchrous *formal*, solemn, sombre, woeful *formal*
☒ cheerful, happy

sepulchre *n* burial place, grave, mausoleum, tomb, vault

sequel *n* conclusion, consequence, continuation, development, end, follow-up, issue, outcome, pay-off, result, upshot

sequence *n* arrangement, chain, consequence, course, cycle, line, order, procession, progression, run, series, set, string, succession, track, train

sequester *v* **1** *sequestered the children from public view*: detach, insulate, isolate, remove, seclude, set apart, shut away, shut off **2** *the authorities sequestered the aircraft*: appropriate *formal*, commandeer, confiscate, impound, seize, sequestrate, take

sequestered *adj* cloistered, isolated, lonely, outback, out-of-the-way, private, quiet, remote, retired, secluded, unfrequented
☒ busy, frequented, public

sequestrate *v* appropriate *formal*, commandeer, confiscate, impound, seize, sequester, take

seraphic *adj* angelic, beatific *formal*, blissful, celestial, divine, heavenly, holy, innocent, pure, saintly, seraphical, sublime *formal*
☒ demonic

serendipity *n* accident, chance, coincidence, fortuity *formal*, fortune, good fortune, happy coincidence, luck

serene *adj* calm, composed, cool, halcyon *formal*, imperturbable *formal*, peaceful, placid, quiet, still, tranquil, unclouded, undisturbed, unflappable *colloq*, unruffled, untroubled
☒ disturbed, troubled

serenity *n* calm, calmness, composure, cool, peace, peacefulness, placidity, quietness, quietude *formal*, stillness, tranquillity, unflappability *colloq*
☒ anxiety, disruption

series *n* arrangement, chain, concatenation *formal*, course, cycle, line, order, progression, row, run, sequence, set, stream, string, succession, train

serious *adj* **1** *corruption is a serious problem*: acute, critical, crucial, deep, difficult, far-reaching, grave, grim, important, life-and-death, momentous, no joke *colloq*, no laughing matter *colloq*, of consequence *formal*, pressing, severe, significant, urgent, weighty, worrying **2** *watched with a serious expression*: dour, grave, grim, heavy *colloq*, humourless, long-faced, preoccupied, sober, solemn, sombre, stern, unlaughing, unsmiling **3** *the job requires a serious individual*: earnest, genuine, honest, pensive, quiet, sincere, thoughtful **4** *serious injuries*: acute, bad, critical, dangerous, grave, grievous, life-and-death, severe
☒ **1** trivial **2** facetious, joking, laughing, light-hearted, smiling **3** frivolous **4** slight, trivial

seriously *adv* **1** *he was seriously considering retirement*: earnestly, sincerely, solemnly, thoughtfully **2** *several passengers were seriously injured*: acutely, badly, critically, dangerously, gravely, grievously, severely
☒ **1** casually **2** slightly

seriousness *n* **1** *must not underestimate the seriousness of the problem*: gravity, importance, moment *formal*, significance, urgency, weight **2** *managers were impressed by his seriousness and commitment*: earnestness, gravitas *formal*, humourlessness, sedateness, sobriety *formal*, solemnity, staidness, sternness
☒ **1** slightness, triviality **2** casualness

sermon *n* address, declamation *formal*, discourse, exhortation *formal*, harangue, homily, lecture, message, oration *formal*, talk, talking-to *colloq*

serpentine *adj* coiling, crooked, meandering, serpentiform *formal*, sinuous, snakelike, snaking, snaky, tortuous, twisting, winding
☒ straight

serrated *adj* indented, jagged, notched, saw-edged, sawlike, saw-toothed, serratulate *formal*, serrulated *formal*, toothed
☒ smooth

serried *adj* close, close-set, compact, crowded, dense, massed
☒ scattered

servant *n* ancillary, assistant, attendant, help, helper, hireling, retainer
☒ master, mistress

serve *v* **1** *serving the community*: aid, assist, attend, be employed by, be of assistance to, be of benefit to, be of use to, benefit, do a good turn to *colloq*, further, help, minister to, succour *formal*, support, work for **2** *serve an important function*: answer, carry out, complete, fulfil, go through, perform, satisfy, suffice *formal* **3** *served the evening meal*: deliver, dish up, distribute, dole out, give out, present, supply, take care of

service *n* **1** *retired after thirty years of service*: activity, assistance, business, duties, duty, employment, labour, performance, work **2** *can I be of service?*: assistance, benefit, help, use, usefulness, utility **3** *dropped the car for a service*: check, maintenance, overhaul, repair(s), servicing **4** *attended the church service*: ceremony, observance, ordinance, rite, ritual, sacrament, worship **5** *a member of the armed services*: air force, army, forces, navy **6** *efficient postal services*: amenities, facilities, resources, utilities
♦ *v* check, go over, maintain, overhaul, recondition, repair, tune

serviceable *adj* advantageous, beneficial, convenient, dependable, durable, efficient, functional, hard-wearing, helpful, plain, practical, profitable, sensible, simple, strong, tough, unadorned, usable, useful, utilitarian
☒ unserviceable, unusable

servile *adj* abject, base, bootlicking, cringing, fawning, grovelling, humble, low, lowly, mean, menial, obsequious, slavish, subject, submissive, subservient, sycophantic *formal*, toadying
☒ aggressive, assertive

servility *n* abjection, abjectness, baseness, bootlicking, fawning, grovelling, meanness, obsequiousness, self-abasement, slavishness, submissiveness, subservience, sycophancy *formal*, toadyism, unctuousness
☒ aggressiveness, boldness

serving *n* amount, bowlful, helping, plateful, portion, ration, share, spoonful

servitude *n* bondage, bonds, chains, enslavement, obedience, serfdom, slavery, subjugation *formal*, thraldom, thrall, vassalage, villeinage

🔀 freedom, liberty

session *n* **1** *the judge resumed the session:* assembly, conference, discussion, hearing, meeting, sitting **2** *a new school session:* period, semester, term, year

set *v* **1** *set his luggage on the floor:* arrange, deposit, dump *colloq*, lay (down), locate, lodge, park, place, plonk *colloq*, position, put **2** *set a time for the meeting:* agree on, allocate, appoint, arrange, assign, confirm, decide, designate, determine, establish, fix, impose, name, ordain, organize, prescribe, schedule, settle, specify, stipulate **3** *set your watches:* adjust, co-ordinate, harmonize, put right, regulate, synchronize **4** *set the table:* arrange, get ready, lay, prepare, set out **5** *set something in motion:* begin, bring about, cause, give rise to, lead to, occasion, produce, prompt, result in, set off, start, trigger (off) **6** *set someone a task:* allocate, assign, choose, delegate, give **7** *set a precedent:* begin, bring into being, create, establish, inaugurate, provide, start **8** *set a trap:* arrange, devise, lay, organize, plan, prepare, set up **9** *set words to music:* adapt, arrange, harmonize, orchestrate, score, write **10** *the sun sets:* decline, dip, disappear, go below the horizon, go down, sink, subside, vanish **11** *allow the mixture to set:* become firm/hard, coagulate, congeal, crystallize, gel, harden, solidify, stiffen, thicken **12** *set the alarm:* activate, initiate, prompt, set in motion

🔀 **10** rise

♦ *n* **1** *had acquired the complete set:* array *formal*, assemblage *formal*, assortment, batch, collection, kit, outfit, sequence, series **2** *a set of people:* band, circle, clique, crowd, faction, gang, group **3** *the set of a film:* backdrop, background, mise-en-scène, scene, scenery, setting **4** *the set of someone's face/body:* bearing *formal*, expression, form, look, position, posture, turn

♦ *adj* **1** *following a set procedure:* agreed, appointed, arranged, decided, entrenched, established, firm, fixed, inflexible, ingrained, ordained *formal*, prearranged, predetermined *formal*, prescribed *formal*, rigid, scheduled, settled, specified, strict **2** *has very set ideas:* conventional, customary, everyday, habitual, regular, routine, standard, stereotyped, stock, traditional, usual **3** *everything was set for the wedding:* all set, arranged, completed, equipped, finished, organized, prepared, ready

🔀 **1** movable, undecided **2** spontaneous **3** unprepared

▶ **set about** begin, commence *formal*, embark on, get down to, set the ball rolling *colloq*, start, tackle, undertake

▶ **set against 1** *the outcome of the war will be set against its human cost:* balance, compare, contrast, juxtapose *formal*, weigh **2** *the two sides of the family have been set against each other:* alienate, disunite, divide, estrange *formal*, oppose

▶ **set apart** differentiate, distinguish, make different, mark off

▶ **set aside 1** *money will be set aside for an emergency fund:* earmark, keep (back), keep in reserve, lay aside, lay by, mothball, put aside, put away, reserve, save, select, separate, set apart, stash away *colloq* **2** *the initial contract was finally set aside:* abrogate *formal*, annul, cancel,

discard, discount, ignore, overrule, overturn, reject, reverse, revoke *formal*

▶ **set back** check, delay, hinder, hold up, impede, retard *formal*, slow, thwart

▶ **set down 1** *the government has set down precise rules:* affirm, assert, establish, formulate, lay down, prescribe, stipulate **2** *they set down the information in notebooks:* note (down), put in writing, record, write down

▶ **set forth 1** *the report set forth in detail the company's plans:* clarify, delineate *formal*, describe, elucidate *formal*, explain, explicate *formal*, expound, present, set out **2** *set forth on a journey:* depart, leave, set off, set out, start out

▶ **set in** arrive, begin, come, commence *formal*, start

▶ **set off 1** *set off for France:* depart, leave, set forth, set out, start (out) **2** *the movement set off the bomb:* detonate, ignite, light, touch off, trigger off **3** *the grey dress sets off the blue of her eyes:* enhance, heighten, intensify, show off, throw into relief

▶ **set on** assault, attack, beat up *colloq*, fall upon, go for, lay into, mug, set upon, turn on

▶ **set out 1** *set out on her journey:* begin, depart, leave, set off, start (out) **2** *plans were clearly set out:* arrange, describe, display, exhibit, explain, lay out, present

▶ **set up 1** *set up a new factory on the site:* assemble, build, construct, elevate, erect, raise **2** *set up new businesses:* arrange, begin, bring into being, create, establish, form, found, inaugurate, initiate, institute, introduce, organize, prepare, start **3** *the criminal claimed he had been set up:* fit up *colloq*, frame, incriminate, trap

setback *n* blow *colloq*, defeat, delay, disappointment, hiccup, hindrance, hitch, hold-up *colloq*, impediment, misfortune, obstruction, problem, reversal, reverse, snag *colloq*, stumbling-block, upset

🔀 advance, advantage, boost, help

setting *n* background, context, environment, frame, locale, location, milieu, mise-en-scène, mounting, period, perspective, position, scene, scenery, site, surroundings

setting-up *n* creation, establishment, foundation, founding, inauguration, inception *formal*, initiation, institution, introduction, start

🔀 abolition, termination

settle *v* **1** *we settled on a time to meet:* agree (on), appoint, arrange, choose, confirm, decide, decide (on), determine, establish, fix **2** *I'd like to settle arrangements:* arrange, complete, conclude, order, organize, put in order **3** *leaves settled all around:* alight, come down, descend, drop, fall, land, light upon, sink **4** *early migrants settled in Scotland:* colonize, make your home, occupy, people, populate, put down roots **5** *settle a bill:* clear, cough up *colloq*, foot *colloq*, fork out *colloq*, pay, settle up, square (up)

▶ **settle down** calm down, compose, quieten, still

settlement *n* **1** *negotiated a peaceful settlement:* agreement, conclusion, patching up *colloq*, reconciliation, resolution, termination *formal* **2** *was offered a settlement of £20,000:* defrayal *formal*, liquidation, payment **3** *early settlements grew up inland:* camp, colony, community, encampment, establishment, hamlet, kibbutz, outpost, plantation, village

settler *n* colonist, colonizer, frontiersman, frontierswoman, immigrant, incomer, newcomer, pioneer, planter, squatter
☒ native

set-to *n* altercation *formal*, argument, argy-bargy *colloq*, barney *colloq*, brush, conflict, contest, disagreement, dust-up *colloq*, exchange, fight, fracas, quarrel, row, scrap *colloq*, slanging-match, spat *colloq*, squabble, wrangle

set-up *n* arrangement, business, circumstances, composition, conditions, disposition *formal*, format, framework, organization, structure, system

sever *v* 1 *her ring finger was severed*: amputate, break off, chop (off), cleave *formal*, cut off, detach, disconnect, disjoin, disunite, divide, lop off, rend *old use*, split, tear off 2 *severed their relationship*: break off, cease *formal*, dissolve, end, estrange *formal*, terminate *formal*
☒ 1 attach, join, unite

several *adj* a number of, assorted, different, disparate *formal*, distinct, diverse, individual, many, particular, (quite) a few, separate, some, sundry, various

severally *adv* apiece, discretely, individually, particularly, respectively, separately, seriatim, singly, specifically
☒ simultaneously, together

severe *adj* 1 *were forced to take severe measures*: acute, difficult, drastic, extreme, fierce, forceful, hard, harsh, merciless, pitiless, powerful, relentless, stringent, strong, tough 2 *an unpopular and severe teacher*: cold, cruel, disapproving, dour, draconian, rigid, serious, sober, stern, strait-laced, strict, tyrannical, unbending, unsmiling, unsympathetic 3 *a simple and rather severe dress*: ascetic, austere, functional, modest, plain, simple, Spartan, unadorned, undecorated, unembellished 4 *a severe illness*: acute, critical, dangerous, grave, perilous, serious 5 *endured a severe training regime*: hard, arduous, burdensome, demanding, difficult, exacting, punishing, rigorous, taxing
☒ 1 compassionate, kind, mild, sympathetic 2 lenient 3 decorated, ornate 4 minor 5 easy, simple

severely *adv* 1 *the child is severely ill*: acutely, badly, critically, dangerously, extremely, gravely, intensely 2 *as a boy he was treated severely*: coldly, disapprovingly, harshly, sternly, strictly, unsympathetically

severity *n* 1 *doctors were surprised at the severity of his symptoms*: acuteness, extremity, fierceness, forcefulness, intensity, severeness, strength 2 *exhibited a severity of character*: coldness, gravity, grimness, hardness, harshness, mercilessness, pitilessness, ruthlessness, seriousness, sharpness, sternness, strictness, stringency, toughness, ungentleness 3 *was known for the severity of her dress*: asceticism, austerity, bareness, plainness, rigour, simplicity, Spartanism
☒ 1 mildness 2 compassion, kindness, leniency

sew *v* baste, darn, embroider, hem, mend, seam, stitch, tack

sex *n* 1 *we welcome applicants of either sex*: gender 2 *obsessed with sex*: coition *formal*, coitus *formal*, consummation *formal*, copulation, fornication, fucking *taboo slang*, going to bed with someone

colloq, intercourse, intimacy, intimate relations, lovemaking, reproduction, screwing *taboo slang*, sexual intercourse, sexual relations, shagging *taboo slang*, sleeping with someone *colloq*, union

sexless *adj* asexual, neuter, parthenogenetic *technical*, undersexed, unfeminine, unmasculine, unsexed, unsexual

sexton *n* caretaker, fossor, grave-digger, grave-maker, sacristan, verger

sexual *adj* carnal, coital, erotic, genital, procreative, reproductive, sensual, sex, venereal

sexuality *n* carnality, desire, eroticism, lust, sensuality, sexiness, sexual desire, sexual instincts, sexual orientation, sexual urge, virility, voluptuousness

sexy *adj* alluring, arousing, attractive, beddable *colloq*, desirable, erotic, flirtatious, inviting, nubile, pornographic, provocative, provoking, raunchy *colloq*, salacious, seductive, sensual, slinky, stimulating, suggestive, titillating, voluptuous
☒ sexless

shabby *adj* 1 *wearing shabby clothes*: faded, frayed, mangy, moth-eaten, ragged, scruffy, tattered, tatty, threadbare, worn, worn-out 2 *a shabby apartment block*: broken-down, dilapidated, dingy, dirty, in disrepair, ramshackle, run-down, seedy, squalid, tacky *colloq*, tumbledown 3 *a shabby trick*: cheap, contemptible, despicable, dishonourable, low, mean, rotten, shameful, shoddy, unfair, unworthy
☒ 1 smart 2 smart 3 fair, honourable

shack *n* cabin, dump *colloq*, hole *colloq*, hovel, hut, hutch, lean-to, shanty, shed

shackle *v* 1 *the policies could shackle economic growth*: constrain, encumber, hamper, handicap, impede, inhibit, limit, obstruct, restrain, restrict, thwart 2 *shackled the prisoners*: bind, chain, fetter, handcuff, manacle, restrain, tether, tie, trammel
♦ *n* bond, chain, fetter, handcuff, iron, manacle, rope, tether, trammel

shade *n* 1 *she was practically invisible in the shade*: darkness, dimness, dusk, gloaming, gloom, gloominess, murkiness, obscurity, semi-darkness, shadiness, shadow(s), twilight 2 *draw the shades to keep out the sun*: awning, blind, canopy, cover, covering, curtain, protection, screen, shield 3 *a deep shade of green*: colour, hue, tinge, tint, tone 4 *there was a shade of relief in his voice*: amount, dash, degree, gradation, hint, memory, nuance, reminder, suggestion, suspicion, tad *colloq*, touch, trace 5 *the area is haunted by the shade of a young serving girl*: apparition, ghost, phantom, semblance, spectre, spirit
♦ *v* block light from, cover, darken, overshadow, protect, screen, shadow, shield

shadow *n* 1 *concealed in shadow*: darkness, dimness, dusk, gloaming, gloom, semi-darkness, shade, tenebrosity *formal*, twilight 2 *the pine trees cast long shadows on the grass*: image, outline, shape, silhouette 3 *cast a shadow over the proceedings*: cloud, foreboding, gloom, sadness 4 *was my constant shadow for twelve years*: companion, constant companion, pal, sidekick *colloq* 5 *hired a shadow to follow her*: detective, follower, sleuth 6 *without a shadow of a doubt*:

hint, remnant, suggestion, suspicion, trace, vestige
♦ *v* **1** *wearing a hat that shadowed his face:* darken, obscure, overhang, overshadow, screen, shade, shield **2** *he shadowed her every move:* follow, tail, trail, watch

shadowy *adj* **1** *hidden in the shadowy forest:* crepuscular *formal*, dark, dim, gloomy, murky, obscure, tenebrious *formal*, tenebrose *formal*, tenebrous *formal* **2** *glimpsed a shadowy figure:* dreamlike, ethereal, faint, ghostly, hazy, ill-defined, illusory, imaginary, indeterminate, indistinct, indistinguishable, intangible, mysterious, nebulous, phantom, spectral, unclear, unreal, unsubstantial, vague

shady *adj* **1** *keep the plant in a shady spot:* bowery, cool, covered, dark, dim, leafy, obscure, protected, screened, shaded, shadowy, shielded, tenebrious *formal*, tenebrose *formal*, tenebrous *formal*, umbrageous *formal*, umbratile *formal*, umbratilous *formal*, umbriferous *formal*, umbrose *formal*, umbrous *formal* **2** *frequented by an assortment of shady characters:* crooked, dishonest, disreputable, dubious, fishy *colloq*, iffy *colloq*, questionable, slippery *colloq*, suspect, suspicious, unethical, unreliable, unscrupulous, untrustworthy
🔁 **1** bright, sunlit, sunny **2** honest, honourable, trustworthy

shaft *n* **1** *trapped in a mine shaft:* duct, flue, passage, tunnel **2** *the shaft of the wheel:* arrow, bar, handle, pillar, pole, rod, shank, stem, stick, upright **3** *a shaft of light:* beam, dart, ray

shaggy *adj* bushy, crinose *formal*, dishevelled, hairy, hirsute, long-haired, unkempt, unshorn, woolly
🔁 bald, close-cropped, shorn

shake *v* **1** *the plane shook in the turbulence:* bounce, bump, convulse, heave, jerk, jolt, judder, oscillate, rattle, roll, throb, vibrate **2** *he was shaking with nerves:* convulse, judder, quake, quiver, rock, shiver, shudder, sway, tremble, twitch, wobble **3** *he emerged, shaking a stick:* brandish, flourish, swing, wave, wield **4** *the news shook her:* agitate, alarm, discompose *formal*, distress, disturb, faze *colloq*, frighten, perturb *formal*, rattle *colloq*, shake up, shock, stir, unnerve, unsettle, upset **5** *shake someone's confidence:* diminish, lessen, lower, reduce, undermine, weaken
♦ *n* **1** *the train gave a shake:* bounce, jerk, jolt, judder, rattle, rocking, roll, throbbing, twitch, vibration **2** *she awoke with a shake:* convulsion, quake, quaking, quiver, shiver, shivering, shudder, shuddering, trembling **3** *the noise gave him a shake:* alarm, jolt, shock, upset
▶ **shake off** elude, escape, get rid of, give the slip, leave behind, lose, outdistance, outstrip
▶ **shake up 1** *the accident shook me up:* alarm, distress, rattle *colloq*, shock, unnerve, unsettle, upset **2** *shake up an organization:* rearrange, reorganize, reshuffle *colloq*

shake-up *n* disturbance, rearrangement, reorganization, reshuffle *colloq*, upheaval

shaky *adj* **1** *edged forward with shaky steps:* doddering, faltering, quavery, quivering, staggering, tottering, tottery, trembling, tremulous *formal*, unsteady, wobbly **2** *a shaky restaurant table:* insecure, precarious, rickety,

rocky, tottery, unstable, unsteady, weak, wobbly **3** *the trial centred on shaky evidence:* dubious, flimsy, questionable, suspect, unfounded, ungrounded, unreliable, unsound, unsupported, untrustworthy, weak
🔁 **2** firm, strong

shallow *adj* **1** *a shallow argument:* skin-deep, superficial, surface **2** *a shallow person:* empty, flimsy, foolish, frivolous, idle, ignorant, insincere, meaningless, petty, simple, slight, superficial, trifling, trivial, unscholarly
🔁 **1** deep, profound **2** careful, deep, profound, serious

sham *n* **1** *the elections proved later to be a sham:* fake, feigning, fraud, imitation, imposture, pretence **2** *the 'vet' was exposed as a sham:* charlatan, cheat, con man *colloq*, deceiver, fake, fraud, impersonator, impostor, phoney *colloq*, pretender, swindler
♦ *adj* artificial, bogus, counterfeit, fake, false, feigned, imitation, make-believe, mock, phoney *colloq*, pretended, put-on, simulated, spurious, synthetic
🔁 authentic, genuine, real
♦ *v* affect *formal*, counterfeit, dissemble *formal*, fake, feign, imitate, pretend, put on, simulate

shaman *n* angekok, magician, medicine man, medicine woman, pawaw, powwow, sorcerer, witch doctor

shamble *v* doddle, drag, falter, hobble, limp, scrape, shuffle, toddle

shambles *n* anarchy, bedlam, chaos, confusion, disarray *formal*, disorder, disorganization, havoc, madhouse *colloq*, mess, muddle, pigsty *colloq*, wreck

shambling *adj* awkward, clumsy, disjointed, loose, lumbering, lurching, shuffling, unco-ordinated, ungainly, unsteady
🔁 agile, neat, nimble, spry

shame *n* **1** *felt deep shame at what she'd done:* degradation, embarrassment, guilt, humiliation, mortification, remorse, shamefacedness **2** *his actions brought shame on his profession:* discredit, disgrace, dishonour, disrepute, ignominy *formal*, infamy, opprobrium *formal*, scandal, stain **3** *what a shame:* bad luck, disappointment, misfortune, pity, unfortunate thing
🔁 **1** pride **2** credit, distinction, honour
♦ *v* abash, confound, debase, degrade, discredit, disgrace, dishonour, embarrass, humiliate, put to shame, show up, stain, sully, taint

shamefaced *adj* abashed, apologetic, ashamed, blushing, conscience-stricken, contrite, embarrassed, guilty, humiliated, mortified, penitent, red-faced, regretful, remorseful, sheepish *colloq*, sorry, uncomfortable
🔁 proud, unashamed

shameful *adj* **1** *a shameful waste of money:* abominable, atrocious, base, contemptible, discreditable, disgraceful, dishonourable, heinous *formal*, ignoble, indecent, inglorious, low, mean, outrageous, reprehensible, scandalous, shocking, unworthy, vile, wicked **2** *found his financial situation shameful:* embarrassing, humiliating, ignominious *formal*, mortifying, shaming
🔁 **1** creditable, honourable, worthy

shameless *adj* **1** *a shameless self-promoter:* audacious, barefaced, blatant, brash, brazen, defiant, flagrant, hardened, impenitent, imprudent, incorrigible, unabashed, unashamed, unregretful, unrepentant **2** *shameless conduct:* corrupt, depraved, dissolute, immodest, improper, indecent, indecorous *formal*, unbecoming *formal*, unprincipled, unseemly *formal*, wanton
➋ **1** ashamed, contrite, shamefaced **2** modest

shanty *n* bothy, cabin, hovel, hut, hutch, lean-to, shack, shed

shape *n* **1** *a square shape:* build, configuration *formal*, contours, cut, design, figure, form, format, frame, lines, model, mould, outline, outward appearance, pattern, physique, profile, silhouette, structure **2** *took on the shape of:* air, appearance, aspect, form, guise, image, likeness, look, semblance **3** *in good shape:* condition, fettle, form, health, kilter, state, trim **4** *changed the shape of the nation:* character, configuration *formal*, format, model, mould, pattern, structure
♦ *v* **1** *shaped the clay into a bowl:* carve, cast, fashion, forge, form, make, model, mould, remodel, sculpt, sculpture, whittle **2** *the media shapes public opinion:* adjust, alter, determine, form, guide, influence, modify, mould, regulate **3** *they shaped their defence meticulously:* adapt, construct, create, define, design, develop, devise, organize, plan, prepare, produce
▶ **shape up** come on, develop, flourish, make headway, make progress, move forward, progress, prove, take shape

Geometrical shapes include:
circle, semicircle, quadrant, oval, ellipse, crescent, triangle, equilateral triangle, isosceles triangle, scalene triangle, quadrilateral, square, rectangle, oblong, rhombus, diamond, kite, trapezium, parallelogram, polygon, pentagon, hexagon, heptagon, octagon, nonagon, decagon, polyhedron, cube, cuboid, prism, pyramid, tetrahedron, pentahedron, octahedron, cylinder, cone, sphere, hemisphere

shapeless *adj* amorphous, badly proportioned, deformed, dumpy, formless, ill-proportioned, irregular, misshapen, nebulous, undeveloped, unfashioned, unformed, unframed, unstructured

shapely *adj* attractive, curvaceous, elegant, gainly, graceful, neat, pretty, trim, voluptuous, well-formed, well-proportioned, well-turned

shard *n* bit, chip, fragment, part, particle, piece, shiver, splinter

share *v* allocate, allot, apportion *formal*, assign, carve up *colloq*, deal out, distribute, divide, dole out, give out, go Dutch *colloq*, go fifty-fifty *colloq*, go halves, hand out, have a share in, partake, participate, share out, split
♦ *n* allocation, allotment, allowance, contribution, cut *colloq*, dividend, division, due, lot, part, percentage, piece/slice of the action *colloq*, portion, proportion, quota, rake-off *colloq*, ration, slice of the cake *colloq*, whack *colloq*
▶ **share out** allot, apportion, assign, distribute, divide up, give out, hand out, mete out, parcel out
➋ monopolize

shark *n* crook, extortioner, fleecer *colloq*, parasite, slicker, sponger *colloq*, swindler, wheeler-dealer *colloq*

Types of shark include:
basking, blue, dogfish, fox, ghost, goblin, great white, Greenland, grey reef, hammerhead, leopard, mackerel, mako, nurse, porbeagle, requiem, saw, thresher, tiger, whale

sharp *adj* **1** *a sharp blade:* barbed, cutting, jagged, keen, knife-edged, needle-like, pointed, razor-edged, razor-sharp, serrated **2** *exercises keep them mentally sharp:* alert, astute, bright, clever, intelligent, observant, penetrating, perceptive, quick, quick-witted, shrewd **3** *the minister is famous for his sharp tongue:* acrimonious *formal*, biting, brusque, caustic, cruel, cutting, harsh, hurtful, incisive, malicious, sarcastic, sardonic, scathing, trenchant *formal*, venomous, vitriolic **4** *the camera takes sharp, bright pictures:* clear, clear-cut, crisp, distinct, well-defined **5** *he felt a sharp pain:* abrupt, acute, extreme, fierce, intense, keen, piercing, severe, shooting, stabbing, stinging, sudden, tight, unexpected, violent **6** *a sharp smell of smoke filled the air:* acerbic, acid, acidic, acrid, biting, bitter, burning, piquant, pungent, sour, strong **7** *a sharp businessman:* artful, clever, crafty, cunning, deceptive, dishonest, sly, wily **8** *she has always been a sharp dresser:* elegant, fashionable, natty *colloq*, neat, smart, snappy *colloq*, stylish, tidy
➋ **1** blunt **2** slow, stupid **3** mild **4** blurred **5** gentle **6** bland **8** shabby
♦ *adv* **1** *meet at eight o'clock sharp:* exactly, on the dot, precisely, promptly, punctually **2** *the car pulled up sharp:* abruptly, suddenly, unexpectedly
➋ **1** approximately, roughly **2** approximately, roughly

sharpen *v* acuminate *formal*, edge, file, grind, hone, keen, strop, whet
➋ blunt, blur

sharp-eyed *adj* eagle-eyed, hawk-eyed, keen-sighted, noticing, observant, perceptive
➋ short-sighted, unobservant

sharpness *n* **1** *displayed a sharpness in his business dealings:* acuteness, astuteness, discernment, incisiveness, keenness, observation, penetration, shrewdness **2** *a lack of sharpness on the pitch:* eagerness, fierceness, intensity, perceptiveness, quick-wittedness **3** *the defensive sharpness in his tone:* brusqueness, cruelty, harshness, incisiveness, sarcasm, venom **4** *the photographer was pleased with the sharpness of the images:* clarity, crispness, definition, precision

shatter *v* **1** *the blast shattered the windows:* break, crack, crush, demolish, shiver, smash, smash/blow to smithereens, splinter **2** *shatter your hopes:* crush, dash, destroy, devastate, disappoint, overturn, ruin, wreck **3** *shattered by her death:* break your heart, crush, devastate, overwhelm, upset

shattered *adj* **1** *he was shattered by what he had heard:* broken, crushed, devastated, overwhelmed **2** *felt shattered after the race:* all in *colloq*, dead beat *colloq*, dog-tired *colloq*, done in *colloq*, exhausted, knackered *colloq*, tired out, weary, worn out, zonked *colloq*

shattering *adj* crushing, damaging, devastating, overwhelming, paralysing, severe

shave *v* barber, brush, crop, cut, graze, pare, plane, scrape, shear, touch, trim

sheaf *n* armful, bunch, bundle, truss

sheath *n* **1** *pulled a knife from a sheath on his belt:* case, casing, covering, envelope, scabbard, shell, sleeve, wrapping **2** *bought a packet of sheaths:* condom, French letter *slang*, johnnie *slang*, prophylactic *US*, protective contraceptive, rubber *slang*

shed[1] *v* **1** *the snake shed its skin:* cast (off), discard, drop, get rid of, moult, slough **2** *shed a golden glow over the fields:* cast, diffuse, emit, give out, pour, radiate, scatter, send out, shine, shower, spill, throw

shed[2] *n* building, hut, lean-to, outhouse, shack

sheen *n* brightness, brilliance, burnish, gleam, gloss, lustre, patina *formal*, polish, shimmer, shine, shininess, sparkle
F3 dullness, tarnish

sheep *n* bell-wether, ewe, jumbuck *Austral colloq*, lamb, ram, tup, wether

sheepish *adj* abashed, ashamed, chastened, embarrassed, foolish, mortified, self-conscious, shamefaced, silly, uncomfortable
F3 bold, brazen, unabashed

sheer[1] *adj* **1** *she laughed for sheer joy:* absolute, complete, downright, out-and-out, pure, total, unadulterated, unconditional, unmitigated *formal*, unqualified, utter, veritable **2** *on the edge of a sheer drop:* abrupt, perpendicular, precipitous, sharp, steep, vertical **3** *a sheer silk scarf:* delicate, diaphanous *formal*, fine, flimsy, gauzy, gossamer, light, see-through, thin, translucent, transparent
F3 **2** gentle, gradual **3** heavy, thick

sheer[2] *v* bend, deflect, deviate, diverge, drift, shift, swerve, swing, turn, veer

sheet *n* **1** *thick cotton sheets:* bed-linen, cover **2** *topped with a sheet of plastic:* coating, covering, film, lamina *formal*, layer, membrane, overlay, piece, plate, veneer **3** *a sheet of paper:* folio, leaf, page **4** *a sheet of ice:* expanse, reach, stretch, sweep

shelf *n* **1** *put books on the shelf:* bench, bracket, counter, ledge, mantelpiece, mantelshelf, sill **2** *a shelf on the seabed:* bank, bar, continental shelf, ledge, reef, sand bar, sandbank, shoal, step, terrace

shell *n* **1** *protected by a thick external shell:* carapace, case, casing, covering, hull, husk, integument *technical*, pod, rind, shuck *US* **2** *the racing car's lightweight shell:* body, chassis, frame, framework, skeleton, structure **3** *the army launched artillery shells:* explosive, grenade, missile
◆ *v* **1** *spent hours shelling the nuts:* hull, husk, peel, pod, shuck *US* **2** *the enemy were shelling the area:* attack, blitz, bomb, bombard, fire on
▶ **shell out** cough up *colloq*, fork out *colloq*, lay out, pay out, spend

shelter *n* accommodation, asylum, cover, defence, guard, harbour, haven, lodging, protection, refuge, retreat, roof, safety, sanctuary, screen, security, shade, shadow, shield
F3 exposure
◆ *v* accommodate, conceal, cover, defend, guard, harbour, hide, protect, put up, safeguard, screen, shade, shadow, shield, shroud
F3 expose

sheltered *adj* cloistered, cosy, covered, isolated, protected, quiet, reclusive, retired, screened, secluded, shaded, shady, shielded, snug, unworldly, warm, withdrawn
F3 exposed

shelve *v* defer, halt, lay aside, mothball, pigeonhole, postpone, put aside, put off, put on ice *colloq*, put on the back burner *colloq*, suspend
F3 expedite, implement

shepherd *n* guardian, herdboy, herdess, herdsman, protector, shepherd boy, shepherdess, shepherdling
◆ *v* conduct, convoy, escort, guide, herd, lead, marshal, steer, usher

shield *n* buckler, bulwark, cover, defence, escutcheon *technical*, guard, protection, protector, rampart, safeguard, screen, shelter, support, targe
◆ *v* cover, defend, guard, protect, safeguard, screen, shade, shadow, shelter
F3 expose

shift *v* **1** *they shifted the furniture together:* budge, carry, move, rearrange, relocate, reposition **2** *the mood shifted from upbeat to pessimistic:* adjust, alter, change, fluctuate, modify, swerve, switch, transfer, vary, veer
◆ *n* **1** *a major shift in public opinion:* alteration, change, displacement, fluctuation, modification, switch, transfer, transposition *formal*, U-turn *colloq*, variation **2** *tired after a twelve-hour shift:* period, span, spell, stint, stretch, time

shiftless *adj* aimless, directionless, feckless, goalless, good-for-nothing *colloq*, idle, incompetent, indolent *formal*, ineffectual *formal*, inefficient, inept, irresponsible, lackadaisical *colloq*, lazy, resourceless, slothful *formal*, unambitious, unenterprising
F3 ambitious, aspiring, eager, enterprising

shifty *adj* contriving, crafty, cunning, deceitful, devious, dishonest, dubious, duplicitous *formal*, evasive, furtive, iffy *colloq*, scheming, shady *colloq*, slippery *colloq*, tricky, underhand, untrustworthy, wily
F3 dependable, honest, open

shilly-shally *v* dilly-dally *colloq*, dither, falter, fluctuate, hem and haw *colloq*, hesitate, mess about *colloq*, prevaricate *formal*, seesaw, teeter, vacillate, waver

shimmer *v* flicker, gleam, glimmer, glint, glisten, glitter, glow, scintillate, sparkle, twinkle
◆ *n* flicker, gleam, glimmer, glint, glistening, glitter, glow, iridescence *formal*, lustre, sparkle, twinkle

shimmering *adj* aventurine *technical*, gleaming, glistening, glittering, glowing, incandescent *formal*, iridescent *formal*, luminous, lustrous, shining, shiny
F3 dull, matt

shin *v* ascend, clamber, climb, mount, scale, scramble, shoot, soar, swarm

shine *v* **1** *a delicate chandelier shone brightly:* beam, dazzle, glare, gleam, glimmer, glint, glisten,

glitter, glow, incandesce *formal*, radiate, shimmer, sparkle, twinkle **2** *he shines his shoes every Sunday*: brush, buff, burnish, gloss, polish, rub (up), wax **3** *she really shines at tennis*: be brilliant, be excellent, be outstanding, be pre-eminent, excel, stand out
♦ *n* **1** *the sun's shine*: brightness, dazzle, effulgence *formal*, flash, flicker, glare, gleam, glint, glitter, glow, incandescence *formal*, lambency *formal*, light, luminescence *formal*, radiance, shimmer, sparkle, twinkle **2** *the wax gave the wood a wonderful shine*: burnish, glaze, gleam, gloss, lustre, patina *formal*, polish, sheen

shiniess *n* brightness, burnish, effulgence *formal*, gleam, glitter, glossiness, lustre, polish, sheen, shine
🔁 dullness

shining *adj* **1** *a shining diamond tiara*: beaming, bright, brilliant, effulgent *formal*, flashing, flickering, gleaming, glinting, glistening, glittering, glorious, glowing, incandescent *formal*, luminous, phosphorescent *formal*, radiant, resplendent *formal*, shimmering, sparkling, splendid, twinkling **2** *a shining example of the writer's art*: brilliant, celebrated, conspicuous, distinguished, eminent, excellent, glorious, illustrious, leading, magnificent, outstanding, pre-eminent, splendid
🔁 **1** dark

shiny *adj* bright, burnished, gleaming, glistening, glossy, lustrous, polished, sheeny, shimmering, shining, silky, sleek
🔁 dull, matt

ship *n* boat, craft, ferry, liner, steamer, tanker, trawler, vessel, yacht

Parts of a ship include:
anchor, berth, bilge, boiler room, bollard, bridge, brig, bulkhead, bulwarks, bunk, cabin, capstan, chain locker, chart room, cleat, companion ladder, companion way, crow's nest, davit; deck, after deck, boat deck, flight deck, gun deck, lower deck, main deck, poop deck, promenade deck, quarter deck, top deck; engine room, figurehead, forecastle (fo'c'sle), funnel, galley, gangplank, gangway, gunwale (gunnel), hammock, hatch, hatchway, hawser, head, hold, keel, landing, mast, oar, paddle wheel, pilot house, Plimsoll line, port, porthole, prow, quarter, radio room, rigger, rowlock, rudder, sail, stabilizer, stanchion, starboard, stateroom, stern, superstructure, tiller, transom, wardroom, waterline, wheel, winch. See also **boat, sail**

shipshape *adj* businesslike, neat, orderly, spick and span, spruce, tidy, trig, trim, well-organized, well-planned, well-regulated
🔁 disorderly, untidy

shirk *v* avoid, dodge, duck *colloq*, evade, get out of, play truant, shrink from, shun, skive *colloq*, slack

shirker *n* absentee, dodger, idler, layabout, loafer, malingerer, quitter *colloq*, shirk, skiver *colloq*, slacker, truant

shiver¹ *v* flutter, palpitate, quake, quiver, shake, shudder, tremble, vibrate
♦ *n* flutter, quiver, shake, shudder, start, tremor, twitch, vibration

shiver² *n* bit, chip, fragment, piece, shard, shaving, shred, sliver, smithereen(s) *colloq*, splinter
♦ *v* break, crack, shatter, smash, splinter, split

shivery *adj* chilled, chilly, cold, fluttery, nervous, quaking, quivery, shaking, shuddery, trembly

shoal *n* assemblage *formal*, flock, group, horde, mass, mob, multitude, swarm, throng

shock *v* agitate, amaze, appal, astound, bewilder, bowl over *colloq*, confound, daze, disgust, dismay, disquiet, distress, dumbfound, horrify, nauseate, numb, offend, outrage, paralyse, perturb *formal*, repel, revolt, scandalize, shake, sicken, stagger, startle, stun, stupefy, surprise, take aback, traumatize, unnerve, unsettle, upset
🔁 delight, gratify, please, reassure
♦ *n* **1** *was a terrible shock for the boy*: blow, bolt from the blue *colloq*, bombshell *colloq*, fright, jolt, perturbation *formal*, rude awakening *colloq*, start, surprise, thunderbolt *colloq*, trauma, upset **2** *designed with cushioning to absorb shock*: blow, collision, crash, impact, jarring, jerk, jolt, shake
🔁 **1** delight, pleasure, reassurance

shocking *adj* abhorrent, abominable, appalling, atrocious, awful, deplorable, detestable, disgraceful, disgusting, disquieting, distressing, dreadful, foul, frightful, ghastly, hideous, horrible, horrific, horrifying, intolerable, loathsome, monstrous, nauseating, offensive, outrageous, perturbing *formal*, repugnant *formal*, repulsive, revolting, scandalous, sickening, terrible, unbearable, unsettling, unspeakable, vile
🔁 acceptable, delightful, pleasant, satisfactory

shoddy *adj* careless, cheap, cheapjack, inferior, poor, poor-quality, ropy *colloq*, rubbish *colloq*, rubbishy, second-rate, slapdash, slipshod, tacky *colloq*, tatty, tawdry, trashy
🔁 superior, well-made

shoe see **footwear**

shoot *v* **1** *shoot a missile*: aim, direct, discharge, fire, fling, hit, hurl, launch, let off, lob, propel, throw **2** *shoot the enemy fighters*: blast, bombard, gun down, hit, injure, kill, open fire, pick off, shell, snipe at, wound, zap *colloq* **3** *he shot off down the road*: bolt, charge, dart, dash, fly, hurry, hurtle, race, rush, speed, sprint, streak, tear, whisk, whiz **4** *shoot a scene*: film, photograph, snap *colloq*, take photographs of, video **5** *the new plants are shooting through the earth*: bolt, bud, burgeon, germinate, grow, shoot up, sprout
♦ *n* branch, bud, offshoot, scion, sprig, sprout, tendron

shop *n* emporium *formal*, retail outlet, store
♦ *v* **1** *shopping for food*: buy, do the shopping, get, go shopping, purchase, stock up on **2** *shopped his accomplice*: betray, blow the whistle on *colloq*, grass up *slang*, inform on, rat on *colloq*, split on *colloq*, squeal *colloq*, tell on *colloq*

Types of shop include:
bazaar, market, indoor market, stall, mini-market, general store, corner shop, shopping precinct, shopping mall, arcade, complex, mall, plaza, galleria, chain store, department store, supermarket, superstore, hypermarket, cash-and-carry; butcher, baker, grocer, greengrocer, fishmonger, dairy, delicatessen,

health-food shop, farm shop, fish and chip shop, take-away, off-licence, tobacconist, sweet shop, confectioner, tuck shop; bookshop, newsagent, stationer, chemist, pharmacy, tailor, outfitter, dress shop, boutique, milliner, shoe shop, haberdasher, draper, florist, jeweller, toy shop, hardware shop, ironmonger, saddler, radio and TV shop, video shop; launderette, hairdresser, barber, betting shop, bookmaker, bookie *colloq*, pawnbroker, post office

shore[1] *n* bank, beach, coast, foreshore, front, lakeside, promenade, sand(s), seaboard, seashore, seaside, shingle, strand, waterfront

shore[2] *v* brace, buttress, hold (up), prop (up), reinforce, stay, strengthen, support, underpin

shorn *adj* bald, beardless, crew-cut, cropped, cut, deprived, shaved, shaven, stripped

short *adj* 1 *a short interview:* abbreviated, abridged, brief, compact, compressed, concise, condensed, crisp, cursory, curtailed, ephemeral *formal*, evanescent *formal*, fleeting, momentary, pithy, shortened, short-lived, succinct, summarized, summary, temporary, terse, to the point, transitory, truncated 2 *she had always been very short:* diminutive, dumpy, little, low, minuscule, petite, pint-size(d) *colloq*, slight, small, squat, stubby, teeny *colloq*, wee *Scot* 3 *qualified tradesmen are in short supply:* deficient, inadequate, insufficient, lacking, low, meagre, poor, scant, scanty, scarce, sparse, tight *colloq*, wanting 4 *his manner was extremely short:* abrupt, blunt, brusque, curt, direct, discourteous, gruff, impolite, rude, sharp, snappy, terse, uncivil
⊟ 1 lasting, long 2 tall 3 adequate, ample 4 polite
♦ *adv* abruptly, suddenly, unexpectedly

shortage *n* absence, dearth, deficiency, deficit, inadequacy, insufficiency, lack, need, paucity *formal*, poverty, scarcity, shortfall, want
⊟ abundance, sufficiency, surplus

shortcoming *n* defect, drawback, failing, fault, flaw, foible, frailty, imperfection, weak point, weakness

shorten *v* abbreviate, abridge, compress, condense, contract, crop, curtail, cut (down), decrease, diminish, dock, lessen, pare (down), prune, reduce, sum up, take up, trim, truncate
⊟ amplify, enlarge, lengthen

shortened *adj* abbreviated, abbreviatory *formal*, abridged, abstracted, condensed, summarized
⊟ amplified

short-lived *adj* brief, caducous *technical*, ephemeral *formal*, evanescent *formal*, fleeting, fugacious *formal*, impermanent, momentary, passing, short, temporary, transient, transitory
⊟ abiding, enduring, lasting, long-lived

shortly *adv* 1 *I'll be there shortly:* before long, by and by, in a little while, in a while, presently, soon 2 *he responded rather shortly:* abruptly, bluntly, brusquely, curtly, directly, discourteously, gruffly, impolitely, rudely, sharply, tersely, uncivilly

short-sighted *adj* 1 *I wear glasses because I'm short-sighted:* myopic, near-sighted 2 *a short-sighted policy decision:* careless, hasty, heedless, ill-advised, ill-considered, impolitic, improvident,

imprudent *formal*, injudicious *formal*, rash, thoughtless, uncircumspect *formal*, unthinking, unwise
⊟ 1 far-sighted, long-sighted

short-staffed *adj* below strength, shorthanded, understaffed, with insufficient staff

short-tempered *adj* bad-tempered, choleric, crusty, fiery, hot-tempered, impatient, irascible, irritable, quick-tempered, ratty *colloq*, testy *colloq*, touchy *colloq*
⊟ calm, patient, placid

short-winded *adj* breathless, gasping, panting, puffing

shot[1] *n* 1 *after he left the restaurant a shot was heard:* bang, blast, crack, discharge, explosion, gunfire 2 *filled with lead shot:* ammunition, ball, bullet, missile, pellet, projectile, slug *colloq* 3 *the shot went wide of the goal:* fling, hit, kick, lob, throw 4 *my holiday shots:* image, photo, photograph, picture, print, snap, snapshot 5 *have a shot at this puzzle:* attempt, bash *colloq*, crack *colloq*, go *colloq*, guess, stab *colloq*, try, turn, whack *colloq* 6 *was given a tetanus shot:* dose, fix *slang*, immunization, injection, inoculation, jab *colloq*, vaccination

shot[2] *adj* iridescent, moiré, mottled, variegated, watered

shoulder *v* 1 *they shouldered the responsibility:* accept, assume, bear, carry, support, sustain, take on, take upon yourself 2 *he shouldered his way through the crowd:* elbow, force, jostle, press, push, shove, thrust

shout *v* bawl, bay, bellow, call (out), cheer, cry (out), holler *colloq*, howl, raise your voice, rant and rave, roar, scream, shriek, squawk, yawp *US colloq*, yell
♦ *n* bawl, bay, bellow, call, cheer, cry, holler *colloq*, howl, roar, scream, shriek, squawk, yawp *US colloq*, yell

shove *v* barge, crowd, drive, elbow, force, jolt, jostle, press, propel, push, shoulder, thrust
♦ *n* elbow, jolt, jostle, push, shoulder, thrust
▶ **shove off** beat it *colloq*, clear off *colloq*, clear out *colloq*, depart, do a bunk *colloq*, get lost *colloq*, leave, push off *colloq*, scarper *colloq*, scram *colloq*, skedaddle *colloq*, vamoose *colloq*

shovel *n* bucket, scoop, spade
♦ *v* clear, dig, dredge, excavate, heap, move, scoop, shift, spade

show *v* 1 *showed her true feelings:* disclose, divulge, expose, make clear, make known, make plain, make visible, manifest *formal*, reveal, uncover 2 *statistics show a sharp rise in claims:* be evidence, bear witness to, depict, express, indicate, make it clear, portray, record, register, signify, suggest 3 *the teacher showed us the technique:* demonstrate, elucidate, explain, expound *formal*, illustrate, instruct, teach 4 *showed his work in a local gallery:* demonstrate, display, exhibit, offer, present, produce, set out 5 *show him around:* accompany, attend, conduct, direct, escort, guide, lead, steer, take, usher 6 *for some reason he didn't show:* appear, arrive, come, materialize *colloq*, turn up
⊟ 1 cover (up), hide
♦ *n* 1 *a long-running Broadway show:* entertainment, extravaganza, performance, production, programme, showing, spectacle, staging 2 *a horticultural trade show:*

demonstration, display, exhibition, expo *colloq*, exposition *formal*, fair, presentation **3** *the flowers give a wonderful show of colour:* demonstration, display, indication, manifestation *formal*, presentation, representation, sign **4** *his displays of affection are just show:* affectation *formal*, exhibitionism, façade, flamboyance, front, illusion, ostentation, panache, parade, pizzazz *colloq*, play-acting *colloq*, pose, pretence, semblance, showiness, window dressing *colloq* **5** *gave a false show of wealth:* air, appearance, display, guise, impression **6** *who's running the show?:* affair, operation, organization, proceedings, undertaking

▶ **show off** advertise, boast, demonstrate, display, exhibit, flaunt, parade, show to advantage

▶ **show up 1** *a scan will show up the infected tissue:* expose, highlight, lay bare, make visible, pinpoint, reveal, show, unmask **2** *afraid he would show himself up:* disgrace, embarrass, humiliate, let down, put to shame, shame

showdown *n* clash, climax, confrontation, crisis, culmination, dénouement, face-off, moment of truth

shower *n* barrage, deluge, drizzling, hail, rain, sprinkling, stream, torrent, volley
♦ *v* deluge, fall, heap, inundate, lavish, load, overwhelm, pour, rain, spray, sprinkle

showiness *n* flamboyance, flashiness *colloq*, glitter, glitz, ostentation, pizzazz *colloq*, pretentiousness, razzle-dazzle, razzmatazz *colloq*, swank *colloq*
⊟ restraint

showing *n* account, appearance, display, evidence, exhibition, impression, past performance, performance, presentation, record, representation, show, staging, statement, track record *colloq*
♦ *adj* demonstrative, descriptive, elucidative *formal*, explanatory, explicatory *formal*, illustrative, indicative, representative, revelatory *formal*, significant, symbolic

showing-off *n* boasting, braggadocio, bragging, egotism, exhibitionism, peacockery, self-advertisement, swagger, swank *colloq*, vainglory *formal*
⊟ modesty

showman *n* entertainer, impresario, performer, publicist, ring-master

show-off *n* boaster, braggart, egotist, exhibitionist, know-all *colloq*, peacock, poser, poseur, swaggerer, swanker *colloq*

showy *adj* fancy, flamboyant, flash *colloq*, flashy, garish, gaudy, glittering, loud, ornate, ostentatious, pompous, pretentious, swanky *colloq*, tawdry
⊟ quiet, restrained

shred *n* **1** *a shred of material:* bit, fragment, particle, piece, rag, remnant, ribbon, scrap, sliver, snippet, speck, tatter **2** *there is not a shred of evidence:* atom, grain, iota, jot, mite, trace, whisp, whit

shred *v* chop, cut (up), rip (up), slice, tear (up)

shrew *n* bitch *slang*, dragon, Fury, harridan, henpecker, nag, scold, spitfire, termagant, virago, vixen, Xanthippe

shrewd *adj* acute, alert, artful, astute, calculated, calculating, callid *formal*, canny, clever, crafty, cunning, discerning, discriminating, far-sighted, intelligent, judicious *formal*, keen, knowing, observant, perceptive, perspicacious *formal*, sagacious *formal*, sharp, sly, smart, well-advised, wily
⊟ naïve, obtuse, unsophisticated, unwise

shrewdly *adv* artfully, astutely, cannily, cleverly, craftily, far-sightedly, judiciously *formal*, knowingly, perceptively, perspicaciously *formal*, sagaciously *formal*, slyly, wisely

shrewdness *n* acumen, acuteness, astucity *formal*, astuteness, callidity *formal*, canniness, discernment, grasp, intelligence, judgement, penetration, perceptiveness, perspicacity *formal*, sagacity *formal*, sharpness, smartness *colloq*, wisdom
⊟ foolishness, naïvety, obtuseness

shrewish *adj* bad-tempered, captious, complaining, discontented, fault-finding, henpecking, ill-humoured, ill-natured, ill-tempered, nagging, peevish, petulant, quarrelsome, querulous *formal*, scolding, sharp-tongued, vixenish
⊟ affectionate, peaceable, placid, supportive

shriek *v* cry (out), howl, scream, screech, shout, squawk, squeal, wail, yell
♦ *n* cry, howl, scream, screech, shout, squawk, squeal, wail, yell

shrill *adj* acute, ear-splitting, high, high-pitched, penetrating, piercing, screaming, screeching, sharp, strident, treble
⊟ deep, gentle, low, soft

shrine *n* chapel, church, dagoba, darga, delubrum, dome, fane, holy place, martyry, sacred place, sanctuary, stupa, tabernacle, temple, tope, vimana

shrink *v* **1** *the clothes had shrunk in the wash:* contract, decrease, diminish, dwindle, grow/become smaller, lessen, narrow, reduce, shorten, shrivel, wither, wrinkle **2** *they shrank back in fear:* back away, balk, cower, cringe, draw back, flinch, quail, recoil, shy away, start back, wince, withdraw
⊟ **1** expand, stretch **2** accept, embrace

shrivel *v* burn, dehydrate, desiccate, dry (up), dwindle, frizzle, gizzen *Scot*, parch, pucker (up), scorch, sear, shrink, wilt, wither, wrinkle

shrivelled *adj* desiccated, dried up, dry, emaciated, gizzen *Scot*, puckered, sere *formal*, shrunken, withered, wizened, wrinkled

shroud *v* blanket, cloak, cloud, conceal, cover, enshroud, envelop, hide, screen, swathe, veil, wrap
⊟ expose, uncover
♦ *n* blanket, cerecloth, cerement, cloak, cloth, cloud, covering, graveclothes, mantle, pall, screen, veil, winding-sheet

shrouded *adj* blanketed, cloaked, clouded, concealed, covered, enshrouded, enveloped, hidden, swathed, veiled, wrapped
⊟ exposed, uncovered

shrub

Shrubs include:
azalea, berberis, broom, buddleia, camellia, clematis, cotoneaster, daphne, dogwood,

euonymus, firethorn, flowering currant, forsythia, fuchsia, heather, hebe, holly, honeysuckle, hydrangea, ivy, japonica, jasmine, laburnum, laurel, lavender, lilac, magnolia, mallow, mimosa, mock orange, peony, privet, musk rose, rhododendron, rose, spiraea, viburnum, weigela, wistaria, witch hazel. See also **flower, plant**

shrug
▶ **shrug off** brush off, dismiss, disregard, ignore, neglect, take no notice of

shrunken *adj* cadaverous *formal*, contracted, emaciated, gaunt, reduced, shrivelled, shrunk
Ⓕ full, generous, rounded, sleek

shudder *v* convulse, heave, quake, quiver, shake, shiver, tremble
♦ *n* convulsion, heave, quake, quiver, shiver, spasm, tremble, tremor

shuffle *v* 1 *he shuffled the cards:* confuse, disorder, intermix, jumble (up), mix (up), move around, rearrange, reorganize, shift around 2 *she shuffled across the room:* doddle, drag, falter, hobble, limp, scuffle, shamble, toddle

shun *v* avoid, cold-shoulder *colloq*, elude, eschew *formal*, evade, give a wide berth to *colloq*, ignore, keep away from, ostracize, shy away from, spurn, steer clear of
Ⓕ accept, embrace

shut *v* bar, bolt, close, fasten, latch, lock, seal, secure, slam
Ⓕ open
▶ **shut down** cease *formal*, close (down), discontinue *formal*, halt, inactivate, stop, suspend, switch off, terminate *formal*
▶ **shut in** box in, cage (in), confine, enclose, fence in, hem in, immure *formal*, imprison, keep in
▶ **shut off** cut off, isolate, seclude, separate
▶ **shut out 1** *she felt shut out from society:* banish, bar, debar, exclude, exile, lock out, ostracize, outlaw 2 *ferns shut out the daylight:* block out, cover (up), hide, mask, screen, veil
▶ **shut up 1** *told the boys to shut up and listen:* be quiet, hold your tongue, hush, keep mum *colloq*, keep silence, pipe down *colloq*, quieten 2 *was shut up in a dark room:* cage in, confine, coop up, immure *formal*, imprison, incarcerate *formal*, intern, jail, lock up

shuttle *v* alternate, commute, go to and fro, ply, seesaw, shunt, shuttlecock, travel

shy *adj* backward in coming forward *colloq*, bashful, cautious, chary, coy, demure, diffident, embarrassed, hesitant, inhibited, introverted, modest, mousy *colloq*, nervous, reserved, reticent, retiring, self-conscious, self-effacing, shrinking, suspicious, timid, timorous *formal*, withdrawn
Ⓕ assertive, bold, confident
▶ **shy away** avoid, back away, balk, buck, flinch, quail, rear, recoil, shrink, start, swerve, wince

shyness *n* bashfulness, constraint, coyness, diffidence, embarrassment, hesitancy, inhibition, modesty, mousiness *colloq*, nervousness, reticence, self-consciousness, timidity, timidness, timorousness *formal*
Ⓕ assertiveness, boldness, confidence

sibling *n* brother, german, sister, twin

sick *adj* **1** *a sick patient:* ailing, feeble, groggy *colloq*, ill, laid up, off colour *colloq*, out of sorts *colloq*, poorly, rough *colloq*, sickly, under the weather *colloq*, unwell, weak **2** *spent the journey feeling sick:* airsick, bilious, carsick, nauseous, queasy, seasick, travel-sick **3** *sick of waiting:* bored, fed up *colloq*, tired, weary **4** *his actions make me sick:* angry, annoyed, browned off *colloq*, cheesed off *colloq*, disgruntled, disgusted, enraged, fed up *colloq*, hacked off *colloq*, pissed off *slang*, sick and tired *colloq* **5** *a sick joke:* black, cruel, gross, in bad taste, tasteless, vulgar
Ⓕ **1** healthy, well

sicken *v* **1** *her behaviour sickens me:* appal, disgust, nauseate, put off, repel, revolt, turn off *colloq* **2** *cattle and sheep sickened and died:* become ill, become ill with, become infected with, catch, come down with, contract *formal*, develop, get, go down with, pick up, succumb to *formal*
Ⓕ **1** attract, delight

sickening *adj* appalling, disgusting, distasteful, foul, loathsome, nauseating, nauseous, offensive, off-putting, repellent, repulsive, revolting, shocking, stomach-turning, vile
Ⓕ attractive, delightful, pleasing

sickly *adj* **1** *a sickly child:* ailing, bilious, delicate, faint, feeble, frail, indisposed, infirm, pale, pallid, sick, unhealthy, wan, washed out *colloq*, weak **2** *a sickly love song:* cloying, gushy *colloq*, mawkish, mushy *colloq*, nauseating, schmaltzy *colloq*, slushy *colloq*, soppy *colloq*, sweet, syrupy
Ⓕ **1** healthy, robust, strong, sturdy

sickness *n* **1** *the footballer is fighting off sickness:* affliction *formal*, ailment, bug *colloq*, complaint, disease, disorder, ill-health, illness, infirmity, malady *formal*, virus *colloq* **2** *symptoms include sickness and diarrhoea:* airsickness, biliousness, carsickness, morning sickness, motion sickness, nausea, puking *colloq*, queasiness, retching, seasickness, spewing up *colloq*, throwing up *colloq*, travel sickness, vomiting
Ⓕ **1** health

side *n* **1** *the side of an object:* end, face, facet, profile, surface **2** *the side of the road:* bank, border, boundary, edge, fringe, limit, margin, periphery, verge **3** *the other side of the city:* area, district, neighbourhood, quarter, region, section, sector, zone **4** *try to see it from my side:* angle, aspect, facet, point of view, profile, slant, standpoint, view, viewpoint **5** *the opposing side:* camp, cause, faction, interest, party, sect, splinter group, team, wing
♦ *adj* **1** *used the side entrance:* flanking, lateral, wing **2** *explore the side streets:* incidental, lesser, marginal, minor, secondary, subordinate, subsidiary
▶ **side with** agree with, back, be on the side of, favour, give your backing, give your support, join with, prefer, support, take someone's side, team up with, vote for

sidelong *adj* covert, indirect, oblique, sideward, sideways
Ⓕ direct, overt

sidestep *v* avoid, bypass, circumvent *formal*, dodge, duck *colloq*, elude, evade, find a way around, give a miss *colloq*, shirk *colloq*, skirt
Ⓕ deal with, tackle

sidetrack *v* deflect, distract, divert, head off, lead away from

sideways *adv* askance, athwart, crabwise, edgeways, edgewise, from side to side, laterally, obliquely, sidewards
♦ *adj* indirect, lateral, oblique, side, sidelong, sideward, slanted

sidle *v* creep, edge, inch, slink, sneak

siege *n* beleaguerment, besiegement, blockade, encirclement

siesta *n* catnap *colloq*, doze, forty winks *colloq*, nap, relaxation, repose *formal*, rest, sleep, snooze *colloq*

sieve *v* filter, remove, riddle, screen, separate, sift, sort, strain, winnow
♦ *n* colander, filter, riddle, screen, sifter, strainer

sift *v* 1 *sifted the ingredients:* filter, riddle, screen, separate, sieve, sort, strain, winnow 2 *sifted through the results:* analyse, examine, investigate, pore over, probe, review, scrutinize, study

sigh *v* 1 *she sighed happily:* breathe, exhale *formal*, moan 2 *the wind sighing through the valley:* rustle, susurrate *formal*, swish, whisper
▶ **sigh for** languish over, long for, pine for, weep for, yearn for

sight *n* 1 *his sight slowly deteriorated:* ability to see, eyesight, faculty/sense of sight, vision 2 *caught a sight of the bear:* glance, glimpse, look, view 3 *the twin waterfalls are a spectacular sight:* display, exhibition, scene, show, spectacle 4 *the new building is a sight:* eyesore *colloq*, fright *colloq*, monstrosity, spectacle 5 *see the sights of London:* beauties, curiosities, features, marvels, places of interest, splendours, wonders
♦ *v* discern, distinguish, glimpse, make out, observe, perceive, see, spot

sightseer *n* excursionist, holidaymaker, rubberneck *US*, tourist, tripper, visitor

sign *n* 1 *this sign means 'stop':* character, cipher, code, emblem, figure, insignia, logo, representation, symbol 2 *they held the meeting as a sign of their unity:* clue, evidence, indication, manifestation *formal*, mark, pointer, proof, signal, suggestion, token 3 *made a sign behind her back:* act, action, gesticulation, gesture, indication, motion, movement, signal 4 *placed a sign outside the shop:* board, indicator, marker, notice, placard, poster 5 *a sign from the gods:* augury *formal*, foreboding, forewarning, harbinger *formal*, omen, portent, presage *formal*, prognostication *formal*
♦ *v* 1 *sign your name in the book:* autograph, countersign, endorse, initial, inscribe *formal*, write 2 *he signed to the waiter to bring the bill:* beckon, communicate, express, gesticulate, gesture, indicate, motion, nod, signal, wave, wink
▶ **sign over** consign, convey, deliver, entrust, make over, surrender, transfer, turn over
▶ **sign up** employ, engage, enlist, enrol, join (up), join the services, put your name down for, register, sign on, take on, volunteer

signal *n* alert, clue, evidence, gesture, hint, indication, light, mark, message, pointer, shot across the bows *colloq*, sign, symptom, tip-off, token, warning
♦ *v* beckon, communicate, express, gesticulate, gesture, indicate, mark, motion, nod, show, sign, signify *formal*, wave, wink
♦ *adj* conspicuous, distinguished, eminent,

exceptional, extraordinary, famous, glorious, important, impressive, memorable, momentous, notable, noteworthy, outstanding, remarkable, significant, striking

signature *n* autograph, endorsement, initials, inscription, John Hancock *US colloq*, mark, name

significance *n* consequence, consideration, essence, force, gist, implication(s), import *formal*, importance, interest, magnitude, matter, meaning, message, point, purport *formal*, relevance, sense, seriousness, solemnity, weight
🔁 insignificance, pettiness, unimportance

significant *adj* 1 *the bank reported significant losses:* appreciable, consequential, considerable, critical, crucial, fateful, important, key, marked, material, memorable, momentous, noteworthy, relevant, serious, vital, weighty 2 *gave me a significant look:* eloquent, expressive, indicative, meaningful, ominous, pregnant, suggestive, symbolic, symptomatic
🔁 1 insignificant, trivial, unimportant 2 meaningless

significantly *adj* 1 *temperatures have dropped significantly:* appreciably, considerably, critically, crucially, materially, noticeably, perceptibly 2 *significantly, all their talk was of weddings:* eloquently, knowingly, meaningfully, suggestively

signify *v* 1 *buoys signified the presence of rocks below the water:* be a sign of, betoken *formal*, communicate, convey, denote *formal*, exhibit, express, imply, indicate, intimate, mean, proclaim, represent, show, signal, stand for, suggest, symbolize 2 *it doesn't signify:* be important, be of importance, be relevant, carry weight, count, have influence, make waves *colloq*, matter

signpost *n* clue, finger-post, guidepost, handpost, indicator, marker, placard, pointer, sign, waypost

silence *n* calm, calmness, dumbness, hush, lull, muteness, noiselessness, peace, peacefulness, quiet, quietness, reserve, reticence, secretiveness, soundlessness, speechlessness, still, stillness, taciturnity, tranquillity, uncommunicativeness, voicelessness, wordlessness
🔁 din, noise, sound, uproar
♦ *v* abate *formal*, be able to hear a pin drop *colloq*, deaden, dumbfound, gag, hush, muffle, mute, muzzle, quell, quiet, quieten, stifle, still, strike dumb, subdue, suppress

silent *adj* calm, dumb, hushed, implicit, implied, inaudible, mum *colloq*, mute, muted, noiseless, peaceful, quiet, reserved, reticent, secretive, soundless, speechless, still, tacit, taciturn, tight-lipped, tongue-tied, understood, unexpressed, unspoken, unvoiced, voiceless, wordless
🔁 loud, noisy, talkative

silently *adv* calmly, dumbly, inaudibly, mutely, noiselessly, quietly, soundlessly, speechlessly, tacitly, unheard, wordlessly

silhouette *n* configuration *formal*, contour, delineation *formal*, form, outline, profile, shadow, shape
♦ *v* configurate *formal*, configure *formal*, delineate *formal*, outline, profile, shadow, shape, stand out

silky *adj* diaphanous *formal*, fine, glossy, lustrous, satiny, silken, sleek, smooth, soft, velvety

silly *adj* absurd, barmy *colloq*, childish, daft *colloq*, dotty *colloq*, fatuous, foolhardy, foolish, frivolous, idiotic, illogical, immature, imprudent *formal*, inane, injudicious *formal*, irrational, irresponsible, loony *colloq*, loopy *colloq*, ludicrous, meaningless, nutty *colloq*, pointless, potty *colloq*, preposterous, puerile, rash, reckless, ridiculous, scatterbrained, senseless, soft *colloq*, stupid, thoughtless, unintelligent, unreasonable, unwise
☒ clever, intelligent, mature, sane, sensible, wise
♦ *n* clot *colloq*, dope *colloq*, duffer *colloq*, dumbo *colloq*, fool, goose *colloq*, half-wit, idiot, ignoramus, ninny, silly-billy *colloq*, simpleton, twit *colloq*, wally *colloq*

silt *n* alluvium *formal*, deposit, mud, ooze, residue, sediment, sludge
▶ **silt up** block, choke, clog, congest, dam

silvan *adj* arboreous *formal*, forestal *formal*, forested *formal*, forestine *formal*, leafy, tree-covered, wooded, woodland
☒ treeless

similar *adj* akin, alike, analogous *formal*, close, comparable, corresponding, equivalent, homogeneous *formal*, homologous *technical*, like, much the same, related, uniform
☒ different, dissimilar

similarity *n* affinity, agreement, analogy *formal*, closeness, comparability, compatibility, concordance *formal*, congruence *formal*, correspondence, equivalence, homogeneity *formal*, kinship, likeness, parallelism, relation, resemblance, sameness, similitude *formal*, uniformity
☒ clash, difference, dissimilarity

similarly *adv* by analogy, by the same token, correspondingly, in the same way, likewise, uniformly
☒ differently

similitude *n* affinity, agreement, analogy *formal*, closeness, comparability, compatibility, congruence *formal*, correspondence, equivalence, likeness, parallelism, relation, resemblance, sameness, similarity, uniformity

simmer *v* 1 *the soup simmered in the saucepan:* boil gently, bubble, cook gently 2 *she was simmering with anger:* burn, fume, rage, seethe, smoulder
▶ **simmer down** calm down, collect yourself, control yourself, cool down, lessen, subside

simpering *adj* affected *formal*, coy, giggling, missish, schoolgirlish, silly

simple *adj* 1 *the test was very simple:* a cinch *colloq*, a doddle *colloq*, a piece of cake *colloq*, a pushover *colloq*, as easy as falling off a log *colloq*, clear, comprehensible, easy, easy-peasy *colloq*, effortless, elementary, straightforward, uncomplicated, understandable, uninvolved 2 *the architecture had a simple, elegant style:* austere, basic, classic, low-tech *colloq*, natural, no-frills *colloq*, ordinary, plain, primitive, rudimentary, Spartan, stark, unadorned, undecorated, unembellished, unfussy, unpretentious, unsophisticated 3 *the simple fact is...:* bald, basic, blunt, candid, direct, honest,

open, plain, sincere, stark, straightforward, unambiguous 4 *a down-to-earth, simple character:* artless, green, guileless, ingenuous, innocent, naïve, natural, unsophisticated 5 *the teacher regarded him as simple:* backward, feeble-minded, foolish, half-witted, idiotic, retarded, silly, simple-minded, slow, stupid
☒ 1 complicated, difficult, hard, intricate 2 elaborate, fancy, luxurious 4 artful, sophisticated, worldly 5 clever

simple-minded *adj* addle-brained, artless, backward, brainless, cretinous, dim-witted, dopey *colloq*, feeble-minded, foolish, goofy *colloq*, idiot, idiotic, imbecile, moronic, natural, retarded, simple, stupid, unsophisticated
☒ bright, clever

simpleton *n* blockhead *colloq*, booby *colloq*, clot *colloq*, dolt, dope *colloq*, dullard, dunce, dupe, flathead, fool, goose *colloq*, greenhorn *colloq*, idiot, imbecile, jackass, moron, nincompoop *colloq*, ninny, nitwit *colloq*, numskull *colloq*, softhead *colloq*, stupid *colloq*, twerp *colloq*, twit *colloq*
☒ brain

simplicity *n* 1 *the simplicity of the exercise:* clarity, ease, easiness, elementariness, facility, intelligibility, lucidity, simpleness, straightforwardness, uncomplicatedness 2 *the elegant simplicity of the design:* clean lines, plainness, purity, restraint, starkness 3 *the simplicity of a young child:* artlessness, candour, directness, frankness, guilelessness, honesty, innocence, naïvety, naturalness, openness, purity, simpleness, sincerity
☒ 1 complexity, difficulty 2 elaborateness, intricacy 3 sophistication

simplify *v* abridge, clarify, decipher, disentangle, explain, make (more) comprehensible, make easier to understand, make easy/easier, paraphrase, reduce, remove complexities in, sort out, streamline, unravel, untangle
☒ complicate, elaborate

simplistic *adj* facile, naïve, oversimplified, pat, shallow, simple, superficial, sweeping
☒ analytical, detailed

simply *adv* 1 *that meal was simply delicious:* absolutely, altogether, clearly, completely, obviously, plainly, positively, purely, quite, really, totally, unconditionally, undeniably, unquestionably, unreservedly, utterly, wholly 2 *the hoax was simply a bit of fun:* just, merely, only, solely 3 *the problem can be solved quite simply:* easily, naturally, plainly, straightforwardly

simulate *v* act, affect *formal*, assume, copy, counterfeit, duplicate, echo, fake, feign, imitate, make believe *colloq*, mimic, parallel, parrot, pretend, put on, reflect, reproduce, sham

simulated *adj* artificial, assumed, bogus, fake, feigned, imitation, inauthentic, insincere, make-believe, man-made, mock, phoney *colloq*, pretended, pseudo *colloq*, put-on, sham, spurious, substitute, synthetic
☒ genuine, real

simultaneous *adj* coexistent, coinciding, concomitant *formal*, concurrent *formal*, contemporaneous *formal*, done at the same time,

sin *n* badness, crime, error, evil, fault, guilt, immorality, impiety, iniquity *formal*, irreligiousness, lapse, misdeed, misdemeanour *formal*, offence, sinfulness, transgression *formal*, trespass *formal*, ungodliness, unrighteousness, wickedness, wrong, wrongdoing
♦ *v* commit a sin, do wrong, err, fall, fall from grace, go astray, go wrong, lapse, misbehave, offend, stray, transgress *formal*, trespass *formal*

sincere *adj* above board *colloq*, artless, bona fide, candid, direct, earnest, fervent, frank, genuine, guileless, heartfelt, honest, ingenuous, natural, no-nonsense *colloq*, open, plain-spoken, pure, real, serious, simple, straightforward, true, trustworthy, truthful, unadulterated, unaffected *formal*, unfeigned, unmixed, up front *colloq*, wholehearted
▄ affected, hypocritical, insincere

sincerely *adv* earnestly, genuinely, honestly, in earnest, really, seriously, simply, truly, truthfully, unaffectedly *formal*, unfeignedly, wholeheartedly

sincerity *n* artlessness, candour, directness, earnestness, frankness, genuineness, guilelessness, honesty, honour, ingenuousness, integrity, openness, probity, seriousness, straightforwardness, trustworthiness, truth, truthfulness, uprightness, wholeheartedness
▄ insincerity

sinecure *n* cinch *colloq*, cushy job *colloq*, doddle *colloq*, gravy train *colloq*, money for jam *colloq*, money for old rope *colloq*, picnic *colloq*, plum job *colloq*, soft option

sinewy *adj* athletic, brawny, burly, muscular, robust, stalwart, strapping, stringy, strong, sturdy, vigorous, wiry

sinful *adj* bad, corrupt, criminal, depraved, erring, evil, fallen, guilty, immoral, impious, iniquitous *formal*, irreligious, ungodly, unholy, unrighteous, wicked, wrong, wrongful
▄ godly, righteous, sinless

sinfulness *n* corruption, depravity *formal*, guilt, immorality, impiety, iniquity *formal*, peccability *formal*, peccancy *formal*, sin, transgression *formal*, ungodliness, unrighteousness, wickedness
▄ righteousness

sing *v* burst into song, chant, chirp, croon, hum, intone, pipe, quaver, serenade, trill, vocalize, warble, whistle, yodel
▶ **sing out** bawl, bellow, call, cooee, cry (out), holler *colloq*, shout, yell

singe *v* blacken, burn, char, scorch, sear

singer

Singers include:
chanteuse, songster, songstress, vocalist, warbler, balladeer, minstrel, troubadour, opera singer, diva, prima donna, soloist, precentor, choirboy, choirgirl, chorister, chorus, folk-singer, pop star, pop singer, rapper, crooner, carol-singer; soprano, coloratura soprano, castrato, tenor, treble, contralto, alto, baritone, bass

existing at the same time, happening at the same time, parallel, synchronic, synchronous
▄ asynchronous

single *adj* **1** *found a single earring on the floor:* by itself, distinct, individual, isolated, lone, one, one and only, particular, separate, sole, solitary, unique **2** *he has been single since his partner left:* available, by yourself, celibate, free, on your own, unattached, unmarried, unwed
▄ **1** multiple **2** married
▶ **single out** choose, decide on, hand-pick, identify, isolate, pick, pinpoint, select, separate (out), set apart

single-handed *adj* independent, lone, solo, unaccompanied, unaided, unassisted
♦ *adv* alone, by yourself, independently, on your own, solo, unaccompanied, unaided, unassisted, without help

single-minded *adj* committed, dedicated, determined, devoted, dogged, fixed, monomaniacal, obsessive, persevering, resolute, set, steadfast, tireless, undeviating, unswerving, unwavering

singly *adv* distinctly, independently, individually, on their own, one at a time, one by one, separately, solely

singular *adj* **1** *a singular achievement in the field of science:* conspicuous, eminent, exceptional, extraordinary, noteworthy, outstanding, pre-eminent, remarkable, unique, unparalleled, unusual **2** *he is a singular character:* atypical, curious, eccentric, odd, peculiar, queer, strange, uncommon, unusual
▄ **1** usual **2** normal

singularity *n* abnormality, curiousness, eccentricity, extraordinariness, idiosyncrasy, irregularity, oddity, oddness, oneness, particularity, peculiarity, queerness, quirk, strangeness, twist, uniqueness
▄ normality

singularly *adv* bizarrely, conspicuously, especially, exceptionally, extraordinarily, notably, outstandingly, particularly, prodigiously, remarkably, signally, surprisingly, uncommonly, unusually

sinister *adj* cruel, disquieting, disturbing, evil, frightening, harmful, inauspicious *formal*, malevolent *formal*, menacing, ominous, portentous *formal*, terrifying, threatening, unlucky, vicious, wicked
▄ auspicious *formal*, harmless, innocent

sink *v* **1** *water levels sank:* descend, dip, disappear, droop, drop, fall, go down, go lower, lower, plummet, plunge, slip, slump, vanish **2** *my hopes sank:* abate *formal*, collapse, decay, decline, decrease, diminish, dwindle, ebb, fade, fail, fall (in), flag, go downhill *colloq*, go to pot *colloq*, lessen, subside, weaken **3** *the boat began to sink into the sea:* dive, drown, founder, immerse, plummet, plunge, submerge **4** *sink a well:* bore, dig, drill, drive, excavate, penetrate, put down **5** *sink money into a project:* invest, lay out, plough, put in, risk **6** *sunk any chance of a deal:* demolish, destroy, devastate, foil, put a spanner in the works *colloq*, ruin, scupper, scuttle, wreck
▄ **1** rise **2** improve, increase **3** float

sinless *adj* faultless, guiltless, immaculate, impeccable, innocent, pure, unblemished, uncorrupted, undefiled, unspotted, unsullied, virtuous
▄ sinful

sinner *n* backslider, criminal, evil-doer, malefactor *formal*, miscreant *formal*, offender, reprobate, transgressor *formal*, trespasser *formal*, wrongdoer

sinuous *adj* bending, coiling, curling, curved, curving, lithe, meandering, ogee, serpentine, slinky, tortuous, turning, twisting, undulating, wavy, winding
Ⓕ straight

sip *v* drink, drink slowly, sample, sup, taste
◆ *n* drink, drop, mouthful, spoonful, taste

siren *n* **1** *could hear a distant siren*: alarm, burglar alarm, car alarm, fire alarm, personal alarm, security alarm, tocsin **2** *1960s screen siren*: charmer, femme fatale, seductress, temptress, vamp

sissy *n* baby, coward, milksop, mummy's boy, namby-pamby *colloq*, pansy, softy, weakling, wet *colloq*, wimp *colloq*
◆ *adj* cowardly, effeminate, feeble, namby-pamby *colloq*, pansy, soft, unmanly, weak, wet *colloq*, wimpish *colloq*

sister *n* **1** *brothers and sisters*: blood-sister, relation, relative, sibling **2** *sisters in the struggle against injustice*: associate, colleague, companion, comrade, fellow, friend, partner **3** *sisters in a convent*: abbess, nun, prioress, vowess

sit *v* **1** *she sat at her desk*: be seated, perch, rest, settle, sit down, squat (down), take your seat **2** *the table sits twelve people*: accommodate, have room/space for, seat **3** *the group sits every Wednesday*: assemble, be in session, consult, convene, deliberate, gather, meet

site *n* **1** *a popular site for birdwatchers*: locality, location, place, position, scene, setting, situation, spot, station **2** *the site was earmarked for development*: area, ground, lot, plot
◆ *v* locate, place, position, put, set, situate

sitting *n* assembly, consultation, hearing, meeting, period, session, spell

situate *v* install, locate, place, position, put, set, station

situation *n* **1** *the house has a beautiful situation*: environment, locale, locality, location, milieu, place, position, seat, setting **2** *taking steps to improve the situation*: affairs, case, circumstances, climate, condition(s), environment, lie of the land *colloq*, picture *colloq*, predicament, scenario *colloq*, score *colloq*, set-up, state, state of affairs, state of play, what's going on *colloq* **3** *looking for a new situation*: employment, job, place, position, post

size *n* amount, area, bigness, bulk, dimensions, expanse, extent, greatness, height, immensity, largeness, length, magnitude, mass, measurement(s), proportions, range, scale, vastness, volume
▶ **size up** appraise *formal*, assess, estimate, evaluate, gauge, judge, measure, rate, suss out *colloq*, weigh up

sizeable *adj* biggish, considerable, decent, fairly large, generous, goodly, largish, respectable, substantial
Ⓕ small, tiny

sizzle *v* crackle, frizzle, fry, hiss, spit, sputter

skeletal *adj* cadaverous *formal*, drawn, emaciated, fleshless, gaunt, haggard, hollow-cheeked, shrunken, skin-and-bone, wasted

skeleton *n* bare bones, blueprint, bones, draft, frame, framework, outline, plan, sketch, structure, support
◆ *adj* basic, lowest, minimum, reduced, smallest

sketch *v* block out, delineate, depict, draft, draw, outline, paint, pencil, portray, represent, rough out
◆ *n* abstract, croquis *formal*, delineation *formal*, description, design, diagram, draft, drawing, ébauche *formal*, esquisse *formal*, outline, plan, representation, skeleton, vignette

sketchily *adv* cursorily, hastily, imperfectly, inadequately, incompletely, patchily, perfunctorily, roughly, vaguely
Ⓕ fully

sketchy *adj* bitty, crude, cursory, defective, deficient, hasty, imperfect, inadequate, incomplete, insufficient, meagre, patchy, perfunctory, provisional, rough, scrappy, slight, superficial, unfinished, unpolished, vague
Ⓕ complete, full

skilful *adj* able, accomplished, adept, adroit, capable, clever, competent, cunning, deft, dexterous, efficient, experienced, expert, gifted, good, handy, masterly, practised, professional, proficient, skilled, smart, tactical, talented, trained, (well-)versed
Ⓕ awkward, clumsy, inept

skill *n* ability, accomplishment, adeptness, adroitness, aptitude, art, cleverness, competence, deftness, efficiency, experience, expertise, expertness, facility, finesse, handiness, intelligence, knack, mastery, professionalism, proficiency, skilfulness, smartness, talent, technique, training

skilled *adj* able, accomplished, adept, capable, competent, efficient, experienced, expert, gifted, good, masterly, practised, professional, proficient, qualified, schooled, skilful, talented, trained
Ⓕ inexperienced, unskilled

skim *v* **1** *skim over the water*: bounce, brush, fly, glide, graze, plane, sail, skate, skip **2** *skim a text*: browse through, flick through, flip through, glance at, have a quick look at, leaf through, look through, read (through) quickly, run through/over, scan, thumb through **3** *skim milk*: cream, despumate *formal*, separate

skimp *v* be economical, cut back on, cut corners *colloq*, cut your coat according to your cloth *colloq*, economize, pinch, scrimp, stint, tighten your belt *colloq*, withhold
Ⓕ squander, waste

skimpy *adj* beggarly, exiguous *formal*, inadequate, insubstantial, insufficient, meagre, measly *colloq*, miserly, niggardly, scanty, short, sketchy, small, sparse, thin, tight
Ⓕ generous

skin *n* casing, coating, corium *technical*, cover, covering, crust, cuticle *formal*, cutis, derma, dermis, epidermis, fell, film, fleece, hide, hull, husk, integument, layer, membrane, outside, peel, pelt, pod, rind, surface, tegument
◆ *v* flay, fleece, graze, peel, scrape, strip

skin-deep *adj* artificial, empty, external, meaningless, outward, shallow, superficial, surface

skinflint *n* cheeseparer, meanie *colloq*, miser, niggard, penny-pincher *colloq*, Scrooge
🗲 spendthrift

skinny *adj* (all) skin-and-bone *colloq*, emaciated, lean, scraggy, scrawny, skeletal, thin, underfed, undernourished
🗲 fat, plump

skip *v* 1 *skip down the street:* bob, bounce, bound, caper, cavort, dance, frisk, gambol, hop, jump, leap, prance, spring 2 *skip a page:* cut *colloq*, leave out, miss (out), omit 3 *skip from one thing to another:* dart, jump, move quickly, pass, race, rush, tear

skirmish *n* affray, altercation *formal*, argument, battle, brush, clash, combat, conflict, confrontation, difference of opinion, dispute, dust-up *colloq*, encounter, engagement, fight, fracas, mêlée, punch-up *colloq*, scrap *colloq*, set-to *colloq*, tussle
♦ *v* argue, battle, be at each other's throats *colloq*, brawl, clash, combat, contend, fall out *colloq*, fight, quarrel, scrap *colloq*, scuffle, tussle, wrangle

skirt *v* 1 *a small stream skirts his field:* border, circle, circumnavigate *formal*, circumvent *formal*, edge, flank, go round 2 *skirt a subject:* avoid, bypass, circumvent *formal*, evade, find a way round

skit *n* burlesque, caricature, mickey-taking *colloq*, parody, piss-taking *slang*, satire, send-up *colloq*, sketch, spoof *colloq*, take-off *colloq*

skittish *adj* excitable, fidgety, frivolous, highly-strung, jumpy, lively, nervous, playful, restive *formal*

skive *v* dodge, idle, laze, malinger, shirk, skulk, slack, swing the lead *colloq*

skiver *n* dodger, do-nothing, idler, loafer, malingerer, shirker, slacker

skulduggery *n* chicanery, double-dealing, duplicity *formal*, fraudulence, hanky-panky *colloq*, jiggery-pokery *colloq*, machinations *formal*, shenanigans *colloq*, swindling, trickery, underhandedness, unscrupulousness

skulk *v* creep, hide, lie in wait, loiter, lurk, pad, prowl, pussyfoot, slide, slink, sneak, steal

sky *n* air, atmosphere, empyrean *formal*, firmament, heavens, space, the blue, vault of heaven *formal*, welkin *formal*

slab *n* block, brick, briquette, chunk, hunk, lump, piece, portion, slice, wedge, wodge *colloq*

slack *adj* 1 *wearing a slack cotton dress:* baggy, flapping, hanging, limp, loose, sagging 2 *slack muscles:* flabby, flaccid *formal*, flexible, hanging, limp, loose, sagging 3 *a slack period:* idle, inactive, lazy, quiet, slow, sluggish 4 *Freya's slack attitude to motherhood:* careless, easy-going *colloq*, inattentive, lax, neglectful, negligent, permissive, relaxed, remiss *formal*, sloppy *colloq*, tardy *formal*
🗲 1 rigid, stiff, tight 2 taut, tight 3 busy 4 diligent
♦ *n* excess, give, leeway, looseness, play, room, spare capacity
♦ *v* idle, malinger, shirk, skive *colloq*

slacken *v*
▶ **slacken off** abate *formal*, become less intense/active, become slower, decrease, diminish, ease, get less, lessen, loosen, moderate, reduce, relax, release, slow (down), take it easy *colloq*
🗲 increase, intensify, quicken, tighten

slacker *n* clock-watcher, dawdler, good-for-nothing, idler, layabout, loafer, malingerer, shirker, skiver *colloq*

slag
▶ **slag off** abuse, berate *formal*, criticize, deride *formal*, insult, lambaste *formal*, malign, mock, slam *colloq*, slate *colloq*

slake *v* abate *formal*, allay, assuage *formal*, extinguish, gratify, mitigate *formal*, moderate, moisten, quench, reduce, sate, satiate, satisfy

slam *v* 1 *slammed the door behind him:* bang, crash, dash, smash, thump 2 *critics slammed the show:* attack, criticize, denounce, do a hatchet job on *colloq*, find fault with, pan *colloq*, pull/tear to pieces *colloq*, rubbish *colloq*, run down *colloq*, slate *colloq*, tear to shreds *colloq*

slander *n* aspersion *formal*, backbiting, calumny *formal*, defamation, denigration, disparagement *formal*, libel, misrepresentation, muck-raking *colloq*, mudslinging *colloq*, obloquy *formal*, scandal, slur, smear, smear campaign, traducement *formal*, vilification *formal*
♦ *v* backbite, badmouth *US colloq*, blacken the name of, calumniate *formal*, cast aspersions on *formal*, defame, denigrate *formal*, disparage, drag someone's name through the mud *colloq*, libel, malign, sling/throw mud at *colloq*, slur, smear, traduce *formal*, vilify *formal*, vilipend *formal*
🗲 compliment, praise

slander or *libel*? See panel at **libel**

slanderous *adj* abusive, aspersive *formal*, aspersory *formal*, backbiting, calumniatory *formal*, calumnious *formal*, damaging, defamatory, false, insulting, libellous, malicious, untrue

slang *n* argot, cant, colloquialism, doublespeak, informal expressions, jargon, lingo *colloq*, patois, patter, vulgarism

slanging match *n* altercation *formal*, argument, argy-bargy *colloq*, barney *colloq*, dispute, quarrel, row, set-to *colloq*, shouting match, spat *colloq*

slant *v* 1 *the cabin walls slanted at an angle:* angle, be askew, dip, incline, lean, list, shelve, skew, slope, tilt 2 *slanted the story in favour of the government:* bend, bias, colour, distort, skew, twist, warp, weight
♦ *n* 1 *the slant of the roof:* angle, camber, diagonal, dip, gradient, inclination, incline, leaning, pitch, slope, tilt 2 *putting a positive slant on the situation:* angle, attitude, bias, distortion, emphasis, one-sidedness, opinion, point of view, prejudice, twist, view, viewpoint

slanting *adj* askew, at a slant, diagonal, dipping, inclining, leaning, listing, oblique, on an incline, sloping, tilted, tilting

slap *n* bang, biff *colloq*, blow, clap, clobber *colloq*, clout *colloq*, cuff, hit, smack, sock *colloq*, spank, thump, wallop *colloq*, whack
♦ *v* 1 *slapped his colleague on the back:* bang, biff *colloq*, clap, clobber *colloq*, clout *colloq*, cuff, hit, smack, sock *colloq*, spank, strike, thump, wallop

colloq, whack **2** *slapped the cards on the table:* plonk, plump, put down, set (down), slam, stick **3** *slapped the plaster on the walls:* apply, daub, spread
♦ *adv* bang *colloq*, dead, directly, exactly, plumb, precisely, right, slap-bang *colloq*, smack *colloq*, straight

slapdash *adj* careless, clumsy, disorderly, haphazard, hasty, hurried, last-minute, messy, negligent, offhand, perfunctory, rash, slipshod, sloppy *formal*, slovenly, thoughtless, throwntogether, untidy
🔁 careful, orderly

slap-happy *adj* boisterous, casual, dazed, giddy, haphazard, happy-go-lucky, hit-or-miss, irresponsible, nonchalant, punch-drunk, reckless, reeling, slapdash, woozy

slapstick *n* buffoonery, comedy, farce, horseplay, knockabout, tomfoolery

slap-up *adj* elaborate, excellent, first-class, firstrate, lavish, luxurious, magnificent, princely, splendid, sumptuous, superb, superlative

slash *v* **1** *slash your wrists:* cut, gash, hack, knife, lacerate, rip, score, slit, tear **2** *slash costs:* curb, curtail, cut, decrease, prune, reduce
♦ *n* cut, gash, incision, laceration, rent, rip, score, slit, tear

slate *v* berate, blame, censure, criticize, do a hatchet job on *colloq*, pan *colloq*, pull/tear to pieces *colloq*, rebuke, reprimand, rubbish *colloq*, run down *colloq*, scold, slam *colloq*, tear to shreds *colloq*
🔁 praise

slatternly *adj* bedraggled, dirty, dowdy, frowzy, frumpish, frumpy, slipshod, sloppy, slovenly, sluttish, unclean, unkempt, untidy

slaughter *v* annihilate, butcher, exterminate, kill, liquidate, massacre, murder, put to death, slay
♦ *n* annihilation, blood-bath, bloodshed, butchery, carnage, extermination, killing, liquidation, massacre, murder, putting to death

slave *n* bond(s)man, bond(s)woman, captive, drudge, lackey, menial, serf, servant, skivvy *colloq*, thrall, vassal, villein
♦ *v* drudge, grind, labour, slog, sweat, toil, work your fingers to the bone, work your guts out

slavery *n* bondage, captivity, enslavement, serfdom, servitude, subjugation *formal*, thraldom, thrall, vassalage, yoke
🔁 freedom, liberty

slavish *adj* **1** *a slavish imitation:* imitative, literal, strict, unimaginative, uninspired, unoriginal **2** *a slavish relationship:* abject, cringing, deferential, fawning, grovelling, low, mean, menial, obsequious, servile, submissive, sycophantic
🔁 **1** imaginative, original **2** assertive, independent

slay *v* annihilate, assassinate, butcher, destroy, dispatch, eliminate, execute, exterminate, kill, massacre, murder, rub out *colloq*, slaughter

slaying *n* annihilation, assassination, butchery, destruction, dispatch, elimination, extermination, killing, mactation *formal*, massacre, murder, slaughter

sleazy *adj* crummy, disreputable, low, rundown, seedy, sordid, squalid, tacky *colloq*

sleek *adj* glossy, lustrous, prosperous, shiny, silken, silky, smooth, soft, stylish, thriving, wellgroomed
🔁 rough, unkempt

sleep *v* be asleep, be in the land of Nod *colloq*, crash out *colloq*, doss (down) *slang*, doze, drift off, drop off, fall asleep, flake out *colloq*, get some sleep, go off, go out like a light *colloq*, have a snooze *colloq*, have forty winks *colloq*, hibernate, kip *slang*, nap, nod off, repose *formal*, rest, sleep like a log *colloq*, slumber *formal*, snooze *colloq*
♦ *n* catnap, doze, forty winks *colloq*, hibernation, kip *slang*, nap, repose *formal*, rest, shut-eye *colloq*, siesta, slumber *formal*, snooze *colloq*

sleepiness *n* doziness, drowsiness, heaviness, languor *formal*, lethargy, oscitancy *formal*, oscitation *formal*, somnolence *formal*, torpor
🔁 alertness, wakefulness

sleeping *adj* asleep, becalmed, daydreaming, dormant, hibernating, idle, inactive, inattentive, off guard, passive, slumbering *formal*, unaware
🔁 alert, awake

sleepless *adj* alert, awake, disturbed, insomniac, restless, unsleeping, vigilant, wakeful, watchful, wide-awake

sleeplessness *n* insomnia, insomnolence *formal*, wakefulness

sleepwalker *n* noctambulist, somnambulist

sleepwalking *n* noctambulation, noctambulism, somnambulation, somnambulism

sleepy *adj* **1** *felt sleepy in the afternoons:* comatose *technical*, drowsy, dull, heavy, hypnotic, inactive, languid *formal*, languorous *formal*, lethargic, quiet, slow, sluggish, somnolent *formal*, soporific, tired, torpid, weary **2** *a sleepy little village:* dull, isolated, lonely, off the beaten track *colloq*, peaceful, quiet, sequestered *formal*, still, undisturbed, unfrequented
🔁 **1** alert, awake, restless, wakeful

sleight of hand *n* adroitness, artifice, deception, dexterity, legerdemain, magic, manipulation, prestidigitation *formal*, skill, trickery

slender *adj* **1** *a slender figure:* graceful, lean, slight, slim, svelte, sylphlike, thin, trim, willowish, willowy **2** *a slender chance:* faint, feeble, flimsy, inadequate, inconsiderable, insufficient, little, meagre, remote, scant, scanty, slight, slim, small, tenuous
🔁 **1** fat **2** ample, appreciable, considerable

sleuth *n* bloodhound *colloq*, detective, dick *colloq*, gumshoe *colloq*, private eye *colloq*, private investigator, shadow, tail, tracker

slice *n* allocation, allotment, chunk, cut *colloq*, helping, hunk, part, piece, portion, rasher, section, segment, share, slab, slice of the cake *colloq*, sliver, tranche, wafer, wedge, whack *colloq*
♦ *v* carve, chop, cut (up), divide, segment, separate, sever

slick *adj* **1** *a slick marketing campaign:* adroit, deft, dexterous, easy, efficient, glib, masterly, plausible, polished, professional, sharp, simplistic, skilful, smooth, sophisticated, well-organized **2** *a slick surface:* glossy, polished, shiny, sleek, smooth, streamlined, well-oiled **3** *a slick salesman:* glib, insincere, persuasive, smarmy, smooth-speaking, smooth-talking, suave, unctuous

slide *v* **1** *they slid down the hill:* coast, glide, go smoothly, move smoothly, plane, skate, ski, skid, skim, slip, slither, toboggan **2** *house prices sliding and interest rates rising:* decline, decrease, depreciate, deteriorate, drop, fall, get worse, lapse, lessen, plummet, plunge, worsen

slight *adj* **1** *a slight problem:* imperceptible, inappreciable, inconsequential, inconsiderable, insignificant, insubstantial, little, minor, minute, modest, negligible, paltry, petty, scant, small, subtle, trivial, unimportant **2** *of slight build:* dainty, delicate, diminutive, elfin, fragile, frail, petite, slender, slim, small
F₃ 1 considerable, major, noticeable, significant **2** large, muscular
◆ *v* **1** *slighted by her former colleagues:* cold-shoulder *colloq,* disregard, giving the cold shoulder to *colloq,* ignore, neglect, snub, spurn **2** *the article slighted friend and foe alike:* affront, disparage *formal,* insult, offend, scorn, slur
F₃ 2 compliment, flatter, praise, respect
◆ *n* affront, cold shoulder *colloq,* contempt, discourtesy, disdain, disregard, disrespect, indifference, insult, kick in the teeth *colloq,* neglect, rebuff, rudeness, scorn, slap in the face *colloq,* slur, snub

slighting *adj* abusive, belittling, defamatory, derogatory, disdainful, disparaging *formal,* disrespectful, insulting, offensive, scornful, slanderous, supercilious, uncomplimentary
F₃ complimentary

slightly *adv* a bit, a little, quite, rather, to some degree, to some extent

slim *adj* **1** *a slim woman:* graceful, lean, slender, slight, svelte, sylphlike, thin, trim, willowish, willowy **2** *a slim chance of success:* faint, flimsy, inadequate, inconsiderable, insufficient, little, meagre, poor, remote, scant, scanty, slight, small, tenuous
F₃ 1 chubby, fat **2** considerable, strong
◆ *v* diet, go on a diet, lose weight

slime *n* goo *colloq,* gunk *colloq,* mess, muck, mud, ooze, yuck *colloq*

slimy *adj* **1** *stepped in some slimy mud:* greasy, miry, mucous, muddy, oily, oozy, slippery, sludgy, sticky, viscous **2** *the slimy shop assistant:* creeping, grovelling, ingratiating, obsequious, oily, servile, smarmy *colloq,* sycophantic, toadying, unctuous

sling *v* **1** *slung the ball into the crowd:* catapult, chuck *colloq,* fling, heave, hurl, lob, pitch, shy, throw, toss **2** *slung the hammock from the tree:* dangle, hang, suspend, swing
◆ *n* band, bandage, catapult, loop, strap, support

slink *v* creep, lurk, prowl, sidle, skulk, slip, sneak, steal

slinky *adj* clinging, close-fitting, figure-hugging, sinuous, skin-tight, sleek

slip¹ *v* **1** *slipped on the ice:* fall, lose your balance, lose your footing, skid, slide, stumble, trip **2** *slipped into the side entrance:* creep, glide, slink, slither, sneak, steal **3** *slip into/out of clothes:*

change into, change out of, don, get dressed in, get into, pull on, put on, take off, wear **4** *standards are slipping:* decline, decrease, deteriorate, drop, fall, get worse, go down the tube *colloq,* go to pot *colloq,* go to the dogs *colloq,* lapse, plummet, plunge, sink, slump, worsen
◆ *n* bloomer *colloq,* blunder, boob *colloq,* booboo *colloq,* clanger *colloq,* cock-up *slang,* error, failure, howler *colloq,* indiscretion, mistake, omission, oversight, slip-up *colloq*
▶ **slip up** blunder, boob *colloq,* botch *colloq,* bungle, cock up *slang,* fluff *colloq,* get wrong, go wrong, goof *colloq,* make a mistake, miscalculate, screw up *slang,* stumble

slip² *n* certificate, chit, coupon, note, paper, piece, strip, voucher

slippery *adj* **1** *be careful on the slippery pavements:* dangerous, glassy, greasy, icy, oily, perilous, skiddy *colloq,* slimy, slippy, smooth, treacherous, wet **2** *a slippery character:* crafty, cunning, deceitful, devious, dishonest, duplicitous *formal,* evasive, false, foxy, perfidious *formal,* shifty, smarmy, smooth, two-faced, unreliable, untrustworthy
F₃ 1 rough **2** reliable, trustworthy

slipshod *adj* careless, casual, disorganized, lax, negligent, slapdash, sloppy, slovenly, untidy
F₃ careful, fastidious, methodical, neat, organized, tidy

slip-up *n* bloomer *colloq,* blunder, boob *colloq,* booboo *colloq,* clanger *colloq,* cock-up *slang,* error, failure, fault, howler *colloq,* indiscretion, mistake, omission, oversight, slip

slit *v* cut, gash, knife, lance, pierce, rend *formal,* rip, slash, slice, split, tear
◆ *n* aperture, cut, fissure, gash, incision, opening, rent *formal,* rip, slash, split, tear, vent

slither *v* creep, glide, skid, slide, slink, slip, snake, undulate, worm

sliver *n* bit, chip, flake, fragment, paring, piece, scrap, shard, shaving, shiver, shred, slice, splinter, wafer

slob *n* boor, churl, lout, oaf, philistine, sloven, yob *colloq*

slobber *v* dribble, drivel, drool, foam at the mouth, salivate *formal,* slaver

slog *v* **1** *slogged the ball:* bash *colloq,* belt, hit, slosh *colloq,* slug *colloq,* smite *formal,* sock *colloq,* strike, thump, wallop *colloq* **2** *slogged through the forest:* labour, persevere, plod, plough through, slave, toil, tramp, trek, trudge
◆ *n* effort, exertion, grind, hike, labour, struggle, tramp, trek, trudge

slogan *n* battle-cry, catch phrase, catchword, jingle, logo, motto, rallying cry, war cry, watchword

slop *v* overflow, slosh, spatter, spill, splash, splatter

slope *v* dip, drop, fall (away), incline, lean, pitch, rise, slant, tilt, tip
▶ **slope off** leave quietly, slip away, sneak off, steal away

sloping *adj* acclivitous *formal,* acclivous *formal,* angled, askew, bevelled, canting, declivitous *formal,* declivous *formal,* inclined, inclining, leaning, oblique, slanting, tilting
F₃ level

sloppy *adj* **1** *sloppy porridge:* liquid, mushy, runny, slushy, soggy, splashy, watery, wet **2** *sloppy work:* amateurish, careless, clumsy, disorganized, hasty, hit-or-miss, hurried, messy, slapdash, slipshod, slovenly, untidy **3** *a sloppy film:* corny *colloq*, gushing, gushy, maudlin, mawkish, mushy *colloq*, schmaltzy *colloq*, sentimental, sickly *colloq*, slushy *colloq*, soppy *colloq*
🔁 **1** solid **2** careful, exact, methodical, organized, precise

slosh *v* **1** *I sloshed the water around:* flounder, pour, slop, splash, spray, swash, wade **2** *sloshed him in the face:* bash *colloq*, biff *colloq*, hit, punch, slap, slug *colloq*, sock *colloq*, strike, swipe, thump, thwack, wallop *colloq*

slot *n* **1** *pushed money into the slot:* aperture, groove, hole, opening, slit **2** *a slot in your schedule:* gap, niche, opening, place, position, space, spot, time, window *colloq*
♦ *v* assign, fit, insert, install, pigeonhole, place, position, put

sloth *n* accidie *formal*, acedia *formal*, fainéance *formal*, idleness, inactivity, indolence *formal*, inertia, laziness, listlessness, slackness, slothfulness, sluggishness, torpor
🔁 diligence, industriousness, sedulity *formal*

slothful *adj* do-nothing, fainéant *formal*, idle, inactive, indolent *formal*, inert, lazy, listless, skiving *colloq*, slack, sluggish, torpid, workshy
🔁 diligent, industrious, sedulous *formal*

slouch *v* bend, droop, hunch, loll, lounge, shamble, shuffle, slump, stoop

slovenly *adj* careless, dirty, disorganized, messy, scruffy, slatternly, slipshod, sloppy, sluttish, unclean, unkempt, untidy
🔁 careful, neat, smart, tidy

slow *adj* **1** *a slow drive in the country:* at a snail's pace, creeping, dawdling, dilatory *formal*, lagging, lazy, leisurely, lingering, measured, plodding, ponderous, slow-motion, slow-moving, sluggish, tardy *formal*, unhurried **2** *the child was rather slow:* daft, dense, dim, dopey *colloq*, dull, dull-witted, dumb *colloq*, retarded, slow-witted, stupid, thick *colloq*, unintelligent **3** *the plot of this book is very slow:* boring, dull, long-drawn-out, prolonged, protracted, tedious, time-consuming, tiresome, uneventful, uninteresting, wearisome **4** *business is very slow:* dead, dull, quiet, slack, sluggish, stagnant **5** *slow to anger:* averse, disinclined, hesitant, indisposed, loath, reluctant, unwilling
🔁 **1** fast, quick, rapid, speedy, swift **2** bright, clever, intelligent **3** exciting **4** brisk, lively
♦ *v* brake, check, decelerate, ease up, keep/hold back, put the brakes on, reduce speed
🔁 accelerate, speed

slowly *adv* adagio, at a leisurely pace, at a snail's pace, by degrees, gradually, larghetto, largo, lazily, leisurely, lento *technical*, little by little, ploddingly, ponderously, slowly but surely, sluggishly, steadily, unhurriedly
🔁 fast, quickly

sludge *n* dregs, gunge *colloq*, gunk *colloq*, mire, muck, mud, ooze, residue, sediment, silt, slag, slime, slop, slush, swill

sluggish *adj* apathetic, dull, heavy, idle, inactive, indolent *formal*, languid, languorous,

formal, lazy, lethargic, lifeless, listless, phlegmatic, slothful, slow, slow-moving, somnolent *formal*, torpid, unresponsive
🔁 brisk, dynamic, lively, vigorous

sluggishness *n* apathy, drowsiness, dullness, fainéance *formal*, heaviness, indolence *formal*, inertia, languor *formal*, lassitude, lethargy, listlessness, phlegm, slothfulness, slowness, somnolence *formal*, stagnation, torpor
🔁 dynamism, eagerness, quickness

sluice *v* cleanse, drain, drench, flush, irrigate, slosh, swill, wash

slumber *n* doze, forty winks *colloq*, kip *slang*, nap, repose *formal*, rest, shut-eye *colloq*, sleep, snooze *colloq*
♦ *v* doze, drowse, nap, repose *formal*, rest, sleep, snooze *colloq*

slummy *adj* decayed, dirty, overcrowded, ramshackle, run-down, seedy, sleazy, sordid, squalid, wretched

slump *v* **1** *cigarette sales have slumped:* collapse, crash, decline, decrease, deteriorate, drop, fail, fall, go down, nosedive, plummet, plunge, sink, subside, worsen **2** *he slumped on the sofa:* droop, flop, loll, lounge, sag, slouch
♦ *n* collapse, crash, decline, decrease, depression, deterioration, devaluation, downswing, downturn, fall, low, lowering, plunge, recession, slide, stagnation, trough, worsening
🔁 boom, upturn

slur *n* affront, aspersion *formal*, blot, calumny *formal*, discredit, disgrace, innuendo, insinuation, insult, libel, reproach, slander, slight, smear, stain, stigma
♦ *v* mumble, speak unclearly, splutter, stumble

slush *n* **1** *the snow soon turned to slush:* melting snow, wet snow **2** *the love song was pure slush:* emotionalism, gush *colloq*, mawkishness, mush *colloq*, pulp *colloq*, romanticism, schmaltz *colloq*, sentimentality, sloppiness *colloq*, soppiness *colloq*

slut *n* drab, floosie *colloq*, hooker *colloq*, hussy, loose woman, prostitute, scrubber *slang*, slag *slang*, slattern, sloven, tart *slang*, trollop

sly *adj* artful, astute, canny, clandestine *formal*, clever, conniving, covert, crafty, cunning, devious, foxy, furtive, guileful, impish, insidious, knowing, mischievous, roguish, scheming, secret, secretive, shifty, shrewd, smart, sneaky *colloq*, stealthy, subtle, surreptitious, tricky, underhand, wily
🔁 candid, frank, honest, open

smack¹ *v* belt *colloq*, biff *colloq*, box, clobber *colloq*, clout *colloq*, cuff, give a hiding to *colloq*, hit, punch, slap, sock *colloq*, spank, strike, thump, thwack *colloq*, wallop *colloq*, whack *colloq*
♦ *n* belt *colloq*, biff *colloq*, blow, box, clobber *colloq*, clout *colloq*, cuff, punch, slap, sock *colloq*, spank, thud, thump, thwack *colloq*, wallop *colloq*, whack *colloq*
♦ *adv* bang, directly, exactly, plumb, precisely, right, slap-bang, straight

smack² *v* bring to mind, evoke, give the impression of, hint at, intimate, remind you of, suggest
♦ *n* **1** *a smack of lemon:* flavour, piquancy, relish, savour, tang, taste, zest **2** *she spoke with a smack of sarcasm:* dash, hint, impression, intimation,

nuance, speck, suggestion, tinge, touch, trace, whiff

small *adj* **1** *a small room/person*: compact, cramped, diminutive, infinitesimal, knee-high to a grasshopper *colloq*, little, microscopic, mini, miniature, minuscule, minute, petite, pint-size(d) *colloq*, pocket, pocket-sized, poky, puny, short, slight, teeny, tiny, wee *Scot* **2** *a small matter*: inappreciable, inconsiderable, insignificant, minor, negligible, petty, trifling, trivial, unimportant **3** *a small amount*: inadequate, insufficient, limited, meagre, mean, paltry, scanty **4** *make you feel small*: ashamed, broken, crushed, deflated, degraded, disgraced, embarrassed, humiliated, insignificant, stupid, unimportant
F3 **1** big, huge, large, tall **2** considerable, great, major **3** ample

small-minded *adj* biased, bigoted, hidebound, illiberal, insular, intolerant, mean, narrow-minded, parochial, petty, prejudiced, rigid, ungenerous
F3 broad-minded, generous, liberal, open-minded, tolerant

small-time *adj* inconsequential, insignificant, minor, no-account, petty, piddling, unimportant
F3 big-time, important, major

smarminess *n* obsequiousness, oiliness, servility, suavity, sycophancy, toadying, unctuosity *formal*, unctuousness

smarmy *adj* bootlicking, crawling, fawning, ingratiating, obsequious, oily, servile, smooth, suave, sycophantic, toadying, unctuous

smart *adj* **1** *he always looks smart*: chic, cool *colloq*, dapper, elegant, fashionable, modish, natty *colloq*, neat, presentable, snazzy *colloq*, spruce, stylish, tidy, trim, well-dressed, well-groomed, well-turned-out **2** *Alex is a smart businesswoman*: acute, astute, bright, clever, intelligent, sharp, shrewd **3** *they booked a smart hotel*: chic, elegant, expensive, fashionable, glitzy *colloq*, modish, posh *colloq*, ritzy *colloq*, stylish
F3 **1** dowdy, scruffy, unfashionable, untidy **2** slow, stupid **3** cheap
♦ *v* ache, burn, hurt, nip, prick, sting, throb, tingle, twinge

smarten *v* beautify, clean, groom, make neat, make tidy, neaten, polish, spruce up, tidy (up)

smash *v* **1** *smash a vase*: break, crack, crush, dash, demolish, destroy, ruin, shatter, splinter, wreck **2** *smash into a wall*: bang, bash, bump, collide, crash, drive, go, hit, knock, plough, run, strike, thump, wreck
♦ *n* accident, bump, collision, crash, pile-up, prang *colloq*, smash-up *colloq*

smashing *adj* excellent, exhilarating, fabulous, fantastic, first-class, first-rate, great, magnificent, marvellous, sensational, stupendous, super, superb, superlative, terrific, tremendous, wonderful

smattering *n* basics, bit, dash, elements, modicum, rudiments, sprinkling

smear *v* **1** *smear ointment on the wound*: coat, cover, daub, plaster, rub, slap, spread **2** *trying to smear his reputation*: badmouth *US colloq*, blacken, calumniate *formal*, defame *formal*, drag someone's name through the mud *colloq*, malign *formal*, slur, stain, sully, taint, tarnish, vilify *formal*

♦ *n* **1** *a smear of paint*: blot, blotch, daub, patch, smudge, splodge, splotch, spot, streak **2** *a true story or a political smear?*: aspersion *formal*, defamation *formal*, libel, muck-raking *colloq*, mudslinging *colloq*, obloquy *formal*, slander, slur, stain, taint, vilification *formal*

smell *n* aroma, fragrance, odour, stench, stink

Words used for types of smell include:
pleasant: aroma, bouquet, fragrance, incense, nose, potpourri, perfume, redolence, scent; *unpleasant*: b.o. (body odour), fetor, funk *US*, hum, malodour, mephitis, miasma *slang*, niff *colloq*, pong, pungency, reek, sniff, stench, stink, whiff

---

smelly *adj* bad, fetid *formal*, foul, high, humming *colloq*, malodorous *formal*, mephitic *formal*, noisome *formal*, off, pongy *colloq*, putrid, reeking, stinking, strong-smelling

smile *n* be all smiles *colloq*, beam, chuckle, giggle, grin, laugh, leer, simper, smirk, sneer, snigger, someone's face lights up *colloq*, titter

smirk *n* grin, leer, simper, sneer, snigger

smitten *adj* afflicted, attracted, beguiled, beset, bewitched, bowled over *colloq*, burdened, captivated, charmed, enamoured, enthusiastic, infatuated, obsessed, plagued, struck, troubled

smog *n* fog, fumes, haze, mist, pea-souper, pollution, smoke, vapour

smoke *n* exhaust, fog, fumes, gas, mist, smog, vapour
♦ *v* **1** *smoke a pipe*: draw on, light up, puff **2** *smoke salmon*: cure, dry, preserve

smoky *adj* black, cloudy, dark, foggy, grey, grimy, hazy, murky, smoggy, sooty

smooth *adj* **1** *a smooth surface*: even, flat, horizontal, level, plane **2** *a smooth journey*: continuous, easy, effortless, even, flowing, plain sailing *colloq*, problem-free, regular, rhythmic, simple, steady, trouble-free, unbroken, uniform, uninterrupted **3** *smooth hair*: burnished, glassy, glossy, like a mirror, polished, shiny, silken, silky, sleek, velvety **4** *smooth waters*: calm, peaceful, serene, still, tranquil, undisturbed **5** *a smooth salesperson*: crawling, fawning, glib, ingratiating, over-confident, persuasive, plausible, slick, smarmy *colloq*, smooth-talking, sophisticated, suave, unctuous, urbane
F3 **1** coarse, lumpy, rough **2** erratic, irregular, troublesome, unsteady **4** bumpy, choppy, rough
♦ *v* **1** *smooth the surface*: flatten, even (out), file, grind, iron, level, plane, plaster (down), polish, press (down), rub down, sand, slick **2** *smooth political tensions*: allay, alleviate, appease *formal*, assuage *formal*, calm (down), ease, mitigate *formal*, mollify, pacify, palliate, soothe **3** *smooth the path to an agreement*: aid, assist, clear the way for, ease, encourage, facilitate, help, make easier
F3 **1** crease, roughen, wrinkle

smoothly *adv* calmly, easily, effortlessly, equably, evenly, fluently, mildly, peacefully, pleasantly, serenely, soothingly, steadily, tranquilly

smoothness *n* **1** *the smoothness of the stones*: evenness, flatness, levelness **2** *the smoothness of the ride*: calmness, ease, efficiency, effortlessness,

evenness, facility, flow, fluency, regularity, rhythm, serenity, steadiness, stillness, unbrokenness **3** *the smoothness of the silk:* glassiness, polish, shine, silkiness, sleekness, softness, velvetiness
F3 1 coarseness, roughness

smooth-talking *adj* bland, facile, glib, persuasive, plausible, silver-tongued, slick, smooth *colloq*, suave

smother *v* asphyxiate, choke, cocoon, conceal, cover, damp (down), dampen, envelop, extinguish, hide, inundate, keep back, muffle, overwhelm, put out, repress, shroud, snuff, stifle, strangle, suffocate, suppress, surround, throttle, wrap

smoulder *v* **1** *the fire smouldered:* burn, fume, smoke **2** *she smouldered with rage:* boil, fester, foam, fume, rage, seethe, simmer

smudge *n* blemish, blot, blotch, blur, (dirty) mark, smear, smutch, spot, stain, streak
♦ *v* besmirch, blacken, blur, daub, dirty, make dirty, mark, smear, soil, spot, stain, streak

smug *adj* complacent, conceited, holier-than-thou, pleased with yourself, priggish, self-righteous, self-satisfied, superior
F3 humble, modest

smuggler *n* bootlegger *colloq*, contrabandist, courier, moonshiner, mule *colloq*, runner

smutty *adj* bawdy, blue *colloq*, coarse, crude, dirty, filthy, gross, improper, indecent, indelicate, lewd, obscene, off colour *colloq*, pornographic, prurient *formal*, racy, raunchy *colloq*, ribald, risqué, salacious, sleazy *colloq*, suggestive, vulgar
F3 clean, decent

snack *n* bite, bite to eat *colloq*, buffet, elevenses *colloq*, light meal, nibble(s), pick-me-up *colloq*, refreshment(s), sandwich, titbit

snag *n* catch, complication, difficulty, disadvantage, drawback, hitch, inconvenience, obstacle, problem, setback, stumbling-block
♦ *v* catch, hole, ladder, rip, tear

snap *v* **1** *the twig snapped:* break, crack, fracture, separate, splinter, split **2** *the dog snapped:* bark, bite, growl, nip, snarl **3** *I was so angry I snapped at my friend:* bark at, growl at, lash out at, snarl at, speak angrily to, speak sharply/brusquely to **4** *a photographer came up and snapped our picture:* film, photograph, record, shoot, take
♦ *n* **1** *I heard the branch snap:* break, crack, crackle **2** *a snap of the fingers:* crack, fillip, flick **3** *a cold snap:* period, span, spell, stint, stretch, time **4** *looking at an old holiday snap:* photo, photograph, picture, print, shot, snapshot, still
♦ *adj* abrupt, immediate, instant, on-the-spot, sudden
► **snap up** grab, grasp, nab *colloq*, pick up, pluck, pounce on, seize, snatch

snappy *adj* **1** *a snappy dresser:* chic, elegant, fashionable, modish, natty *colloq*, smart, snazzy *colloq*, stylish, trendy *colloq*, up-to-date, up-to-the-minute **2** *come on, make it snappy!:* brisk, energetic, hasty, lively, quick **3** *she was tired, and started to become snappy:* bad-tempered, brusque, crabbed, cross, crotchety, edgy, ill-natured, ill-tempered, irascible, irritable, quick-tempered, testy, touchy
F3 1 dowdy **2** slow

snare *v* capture, catch, ensnare, entrap, net, seize, trap
♦ *n* catch, gin, net, noose, pitfall, springe, trap, wire

snarl¹ *v* bark, complain, growl, grumble, howl, lash out at, show your teeth, snap, yelp

snarl² *v* complicate, confuse, embroil, enmesh, entangle, entwine, jumble, knot, muddle, ravel, tangle, twist

snarl-up *n* confusion, entanglement, gridlock, jumble, mess, mix-up, muddle, tangle, traffic jam

snatch *v* abduct, bag *colloq*, clutch, collar *colloq*, gain, grab, grasp, grip, kidnap, make off with, nab *colloq*, nail *colloq*, pluck, pounce on, pull, secure, seize, steal, swipe *colloq*, take, take as hostage, take/get hold of, win, wrench, wrest
♦ *n* bit, fraction, fragment, part, piece, section, segment, smattering, snippet, spell

snazzy *adj* attractive, dashing, fashionable, flamboyant, flashy *colloq*, jazzy *colloq*, raffish, ritzy *colloq*, showy, smart, snappy *colloq*, sophisticated, sporty, stylish, swinging *colloq*, with it *colloq*
F3 drab, unfashionable

sneak *v* **1** *sneak around the house:* creep, lurk, pad, prowl, sidle, skulk, slink, steal **2** *go sneaking to the boss:* blow the whistle on *colloq*, grass on *slang*, inform on, rat *colloq*, shop *colloq*, snitch *colloq*, split *colloq*, squeal *colloq*, tell tales
♦ *n* grass *slang*, informer, mole *colloq*, rat *colloq*, squealer *colloq*, tell-tale, whistle-blower *colloq*
♦ *adj* clandestine *formal*, covert, furtive, quick, secret, stealthy, surprise, surreptitious

sneaking *adj* furtive, grudging, hidden, intuitive, lurking, nagging, niggling, persistent, private, secret, suppressed, surreptitious, uncomfortable, unexpressed, unvoiced, worrying

sneaky *adj* base, contemptible, cowardly, deceitful, devious, dishonest, disingenuous *formal*, double-dealing, furtive, guileful, low, low-down, malicious, mean, nasty, shady, shifty, slippery *colloq*, sly, snide, unethical, unreliable, unscrupulous, untrustworthy
F3 honest, open, up front *colloq*

sneer *v* deride *formal*, disdain, gibe, insult, jeer, laugh, look down on, mock, ridicule, scoff, scorn, slight, smirk, snicker, snigger, taunt
♦ *n* derision, disdain, gibe, insult, jeer, mockery, ridicule, scorn, slight, smirk, snicker, snigger, taunt

snide *adj* biting, caustic, cynical, derisive, derogatory, disparaging *formal*, hurtful, ill-natured, jeering, malicious, mean, mocking, nasty, sarcastic, scathing, scoffing, scornful, sneering, spiteful, taunting, unkind
F3 complimentary

sniff *v* **1** *sniffed deeply:* breathe, inhale, snuff, snuffle **2** *sniffed the perfume:* get a whiff of, nose, scent, smell, whiff
♦ *n* **1** *caught a sniff of chocolate:* aroma, scent, smell, whiff **2** *the barest sniff of a chance:* hint, impression, intimation, suggestion, trace, whiff
► **sniff at** deride *formal*, disdain, dismiss, disparage *formal*, disregard, laugh at, look down on, mock, overlook, reject, scoff at, shun, slight, sneer at, spurn
F3 admire, respect

sniffy *adj* condescending, contemptuous, disdainful, haughty, scoffing, scornful, sneering, snobbish, snobby, supercilious, superior

snigger *v* chortle, chuckle, giggle, laugh, smirk, sneer, snicker, titter

snip *v* clip, crop, cut, dock, incise, nick, notch, prune, slit, snick, trim
 ♦ *n* **1** *a snip here, a cut there:* clip, crop, cut, prune, slit, trim **2** *a snip of paper:* bit, fragment, piece, scrap, shred, snippet **3** *it's a snip at £3.99:* bargain, giveaway, good buy, special offer, steal *colloq*, value for money

snippet *n* bit, clipping, cutting, fragment, part, particle, piece, portion, scrap, section, segment, shred, snatch

snivel *v* bawl, blub, blubber, cry, grizzle, moan, sniff, sniffle, snuffle, sob, weep, whimper, whine, whinge

snivelling *adj* blubbering, crying, grizzling, moaning, sniffling, snuffling, weeping, whimpering, whingeing, whining

snobbery *n* airs, airs and graces, arrogance, condescension, disdain, haughtiness, loftiness, pretension, pride, side *colloq*, snobbishness, snootiness *colloq*, superciliousness, superiority, uppishness *colloq*

snobbish *adj* affected, arrogant, condescending, disdainful, haughty, high and mighty, hoity-toity *colloq*, jumped-up *colloq*, lofty, patronizing, pretentious, proud, snobby, snooty *colloq*, stuck-up *colloq*, supercilious, superior, toffee-nosed *colloq*, too big for your boots *colloq*, uppity *colloq*

snoop *v* interfere, meddle, nose, poke/stick your nose in *colloq*, pry, sneak, spy, stick/put your oar in *colloq*
 ♦ *n* **1** *have a snoop around:* nose, pry, sneak **2** *he is a vicious-tongued snoop:* busybody, meddler, nosy parker *colloq*, Paul Pry *colloq*, pry, snooper, spy

snooze *v* catnap, doze, drop off, have forty winks *colloq*, kip *slang*, nap, nod off, sleep, slumber *formal*
 ♦ *n* catnap, doze, forty winks *colloq*, kip *slang*, nap, repose *formal*, shut-eye *colloq*, siesta, sleep, slumber *formal*

snout *n* muzzle, neb, nose, proboscis *formal*, schnozzle *colloq*, snitch *colloq*, trunk

snow *n* blizzard, ice, sleet, slush, snow flurries, snowdrift, snowfall, snowflakes, snowstorm

snub *v* affront *formal*, brush off, cold-shoulder *colloq*, cut, disregard, give the cold-shoulder to *colloq*, humble, humiliate, ignore, insult, kick in the teeth *colloq*, mortify, put down, rebuff, rebuke, shame, shun, slap in the face *colloq*, slight, spurn, squash
 ♦ *n* affront, brush-off, humiliation, insult, kick in the teeth *colloq*, put-down, rebuff, rebuke, slap in the face *colloq*, slight

snug *adj* close-fitting, comfortable, comfy *colloq*, cosy, figure-hugging, friendly, homely, intimate, secure, sheltered, skintight, snug as a bug in a rug *colloq*, tight, warm

snuggle *v* cuddle, curl up, embrace, hug, nestle, nuzzle

soak *v* bathe, drench, imbue, immerse, infuse, marinate, penetrate, permeate, ret, saturate, souse, steep, submerge, wet

soaking *adj* drenched, dripping, saturated, soaked, soaked to the skin, sodden, sopping, sopping wet, streaming, waterlogged, wet through, wringing
 ⊟ dry

soar *v* ascend, climb, escalate, fly, glide, mount, plane, rise, rocket, skyrocket, spiral, take off, tower, wing
 ⊟ fall, plummet

sob *v* bawl, blubber, boohoo *colloq*, cry, howl, shed tears, snivel, weep

sober *adj* **1** *she was the only sober person at the party:* abstemious, abstinent, clear-headed, dry *colloq*, having signed the pledge *colloq*, moderate, off the bottle *colloq*, on the wagon *colloq*, sober as a judge *colloq*, stone-cold sober *colloq*, teetotal, temperate **2** *was more sober, serious and conscientious than his father:* calm, clear-headed, composed, cool, dignified, dispassionate, earnest, grave, level-headed, practical, quiet, rational, realistic, reasonable, sedate, self-controlled, serene, serious, solemn, staid, steady, thoughtful, unexcited, unruffled **3** *sober dress:* austere, dark, drab, dull, plain, restrained, severe, sombre, staid, subdued
 ⊟ **1** drunk, intemperate **2** excited, frivolous, irrational, unrealistic **3** flashy, garish

sobriety *n* **1** *resigning herself to an evening of sobriety:* abstemiousness, abstinence, moderation, soberness, teetotalism, temperance **2** *issues were handled with stark sobriety:* calmness, composure, coolness, gravity, level-headedness, restraint, sedateness, self-restraint, seriousness, solemnity, staidness, steadiness
 ⊟ **1** drunkenness **2** excitement, frivolity

so-called *adj* alleged, nominal, ostensible, pretended, professed, purported *formal*, self-styled, soi-disant, supposed, would-be

sociability *n* affability, chumminess *colloq*, companionability, congeniality, conviviality, cordiality, friendliness, gregariousness, neighbourliness

sociable *adj* accessible, affable, approachable, chummy *colloq*, companionable, convivial, cordial, familiar, friendly, genial, gregarious, hospitable, neighbourly, outgoing, warm
 ⊟ hostile, unfriendly, unsociable, withdrawn

sociable or *social*? *Sociable* is usually applied to people and means 'friendly, fond of the company of others': *Our new neighbours aren't very sociable; He's a cheerful, sociable sort of bloke. Social* means 'of or concerning society': *Problems such as this are social rather than medical in origin; social class. Social* also means 'concerning the gathering together or meeting of people for recreation and amusement': *a social club; His reasons for calling round were purely social.*

social *adj* **1** *social policies:* civic, collective, common, communal, community, general, group, organized, public **2** *social activities:* amusement, entertainment, leisure
 ♦ *n* dance, do *colloq*, event, gathering, get-together, party

socialism *n* communism, leftism, Leninism, Marxism, Stalinism, Trotskyism, welfarism

socialist *adj* commie *colloq*, communist, leftie *colloq*, leftist, left-wing, red *colloq*, Trot *colloq*, Trotskyist, Trotskyite
♦ *n* commie *colloq*, communist, leftie *colloq*, leftist, left-winger, red *colloq*, Trot *colloq*, Trotskyist, Trotskyite, welfarist

socialize *v* be sociable, entertain, fraternize, get together, go out, hobnob *colloq*, meet people, meet socially, mingle, mix

society *n* **1** *projects which benefit society:* civilization, community, culture, human race, humanity, humankind, mankind, nation, people, population, public **2** *joined the local music society:* alliance, association, band, body, brotherhood, circle, club, company, federation, fellowship, fraternity, group, guild, league, organization, sisterhood, sorority, union **3** *enjoyed their society:* camaraderie, companionship, company, fellowship, friendship **4** *a stunning entrance into London society:* aristocracy, elite, gentry, nobility, nobs *colloq*, Sloane Rangers *colloq*, swells *colloq*, the smart set *colloq*, the upper crust *colloq*, toffs *colloq*, top drawer *colloq*, upper classes

sodden *adj* boggy, drenched, drookit *Scot*, marshy, miry, saturated, soaked, soaking, soggy, sopping, waterlogged, wet
🔁 dry

soft *adj* **1** *soft ground:* ductile *formal*, elastic, flexible, malleable, mushy, plastic, pliable, pliant, pulpy, spongy, springy, squashy, squelchy, squishy *colloq*, supple, tender, yielding **2** *a soft voice:* delicate, dulcet, faint, gentle, hushed, low, mellifluous *formal*, mellow, melodious, mild, muted, quiet, restrained, soothing, subdued, sweet, whispered **3** *soft colours:* bland, delicate, diffuse, dim, gentle, light, low-key, mellow, muted, pale, pastel, quiet, restrained, shaded, soothing, subdued **4** *soft skin:* downy, fleecy, furry, silken, silky, smooth, velvety **5** *a soft teacher:* easy-going *colloq*, forbearing, forgiving, indulgent, lax, lenient, liberal, permissive, spineless *colloq*, tolerant, weak **6** *soft words:* affectionate, generous, gentle, kind, sensitive, sympathetic, tender **7** *a soft life:* a bed of roses *colloq*, comfortable, cushy *colloq*, easy, luxurious, prosperous, successful
🔁 **1** firm, hard **2** hard, harsh, loud, sharp **3** bright, harsh **4** rough **5** hard, severe, strict **6** cruel, unsympathetic **7** hard

soften *v* **1** *soften their opposition to the measures:* abate *formal*, alleviate, appease, assuage *formal*, calm (down), diminish, ease, lessen, lighten, lower, mitigate *formal*, moderate, mollify, palliate, quell, relax, soothe, still, subdue, temper **2** *soften the butter over a low heat:* dissolve, liquefy, melt, reduce
▶ **soften up** butter up *colloq*, conciliate, disarm, melt, persuade, soft-soap *colloq*, weaken, win over

soft-hearted *adj* affectionate, benevolent, charitable, compassionate, generous, gentle, kind, sentimental, sympathetic, tender, warm-hearted
🔁 callous, hard-hearted

soft-pedal *v* go easy, moderate, play down, subdue, tone down
🔁 emphasize, highlight

soggy *adj* boggy, damp, drenched, dripping, heavy, moist, pulpy, saturated, soaked, soaking, sodden, sopping, sopping wet, spongy, waterlogged, wet

soil[1] *n* **1** *rich, chalky soil:* clay, dirt, dust, earth, ground, humus, loam **2** *companies operating on UK soil:* country, land, region, territory

soil[2] *v* **1** *soiled her hands:* begrime, dirty, muddy, smear, smudge, spot, stain **2** *soil your reputation:* besmirch, defile, smear, stain, sully, tarnish

soiled *adj* dirty, grimy, maculate *formal*, manky *colloq*, polluted, spotted, stained, sullied, tarnished
🔁 clean, immaculate

sojourn *n* peregrination *formal*, rest, stay, stop, stopover, visit
♦ *v* abide *formal*, dwell *formal*, lodge, reside *formal*, rest, stay, stop, tabernacle *formal*, tarry *formal*

solace *n* alleviation, cheer, comfort, condolence, consolation, relief, succour *formal*, support
♦ *v* allay, alleviate, comfort, console, mitigate *formal*, soften, soothe, succour *formal*, support

soldier
▶ **soldier on** continue, hang on, hold on, keep at it *colloq*, keep going, keep on, persevere, plug away *colloq*, remain, stick at it *colloq*

Types of soldier include:
cadet, private, sapper, NCO, orderly, officer, gunner, infantryman, trooper, fusilier, rifleman, paratrooper, sentry, guardsman, marine, commando, tommy, dragoon, cavalryman, lancer, hussar, conscript, recruit, regular, private, Territorial, GI *US*, warrior, mercenary, legionnaire, guerrilla, partisan, centurion; fighter, serviceman, troops. See also **rank**[1]

---

sole *adj* alone, exclusive, individual, lone, one, only, single, singular, solitary, unique
🔁 multiple, shared

solecism *n* absurdity, anacoluthon *technical*, blunder, boob *colloq*, booboo *colloq*, cacology, error, faux pas, gaffe *colloq*, gaucherie, howler *colloq*, impropriety, incongruity *formal*, indecorum *formal*, lapse, mistake

solely *adv* alone, completely, entirely, exclusively, merely, only, single-handedly, singly, uniquely

solemn *adj* **1** *wore a solemn expression:* earnest, formal, glum, grave, reverential, serious, sober, sombre, thoughtful **2** *a solemn ceremony:* august, awe-inspiring, ceremonial, ceremonious, dignified, formal, grand, imposing, impressive, majestic, momentous, pompous, ritual, stately, venerable **3** *a solemn promise:* committed, earnest, formal, genuine, grave, sincere, wholehearted
🔁 **1** light-hearted **2** frivolous

solemnity *n* dignity, grandeur, gravity, impressiveness, momentousness, portentousness *formal*, seriousness, stateliness
🔁 frivolity

solemnize *v* celebrate, commemorate, dignify, honour, keep, observe

solicit *v* apply (for), ask (for), beg, beseech *formal*, canvass, crave, entreat *formal*, hustle *colloq*, implore, importune *formal*, petition, plead, pray, request, seek *formal*, sue *formal*, supplicate *formal*, tout *colloq*

solicitor *n* advocate, attorney, barrister, lawyer, QC

solicitous *adj* anxious, apprehensive, attentive, caring, concerned, considerate, eager, earnest, troubled, uneasy, worried, zealous

solicitude *n* anxiety, attentiveness, care, concern, considerateness, consideration, disquiet, regard, trouble, uneasiness, worry

solid *adj* **1** *built on solid foundations:* compact, compressed, concrete, dense, durable, firm, hard, long-lasting, sound, stable, strong, sturdy, substantial, thick, unshakable, well-built **2** *a solid, respectable citizen:* decent, dependable, level-headed, reliable, respectable, sensible, serious, sober, stable, steadfast, trustworthy, trusty, upright, upstanding, worthy **3** *solid evidence:* authoritative, cogent *formal*, firm, reliable, sound, strong, valid, weighty, well-founded, well-grounded **4** *a solid object:* concrete, genuine, pure, real, tangible **5** *a solid white line:* continuous, unbroken, undivided, uninterrupted
🔁 **1** gaseous, hollow, liquid **2** unreliable, unstable **3** unreliable, unsound **4** unreal **5** broken, dotted

solidarity *n* accord, agreement, camaraderie, cohesion, concord, consensus, esprit de corps, harmony, like-mindedness, single-mindedness, soundness, stability, team spirit, unanimity, unity
🔁 discord, division, schism

solidify *v* cake, clot, coagulate, congeal, crystallize, gel, go/become hard, harden, jell, set
🔁 dissolve, liquefy, soften

solitary *adj* **1** *he's always been a solitary person:* alone, by yourself, companionless, friendless, hermitical, introverted, lone, lonely, lonesome, reclusive, retired, retiring, unsociable, withdrawn **2** *walked to a solitary cove:* cloistered, desolate, inaccessible, isolated, lonely, out-of-the-way, remote, secluded, separate, sequestered *formal*, unfrequented, untrodden, unvisited
🔁 **1** accompanied, busy, gregarious **2** accessible
♦ *n* anchoress, anchorite, ancress, ascetic, eremite, hermit, individualist, lone wolf *colloq*, loner, monk, recluse, stylite

solitude *n* aloneness, desolation, friendlessness, introversion, isolation, loneliness, lonesomeness, privacy, reclusiveness, remoteness, retirement, seclusion, singleness, unsociability
🔁 companionship

solution *n* **1** *need to find the solution:* answer, clarification, decipherment, elucidation *formal*, explanation, key, remedy, resolution, result, way out **2** *dilute the solution:* blend, compound, emulsion, liquid, mix, mixture, solvent, suspension

solve *v* answer, clarify, clear up, crack *colloq*, decipher, disentangle, explain, expound *formal*, fathom *colloq*, figure out, get to the bottom of, interpret, put right, puzzle out, rectify *formal*, remedy, resolve, settle, unfold, unravel, work out

solvent *adj* able to pay, creditworthy, financially sound, in the black *colloq*, out of debt, sound, unindebted
🔁 insolvent

sombre *adj* dark, depressed, dim, dingy, dismal, doleful, drab, dull, funereal, gloomy, grave, joyless, lugubrious *formal*, melancholy, morose, mournful, obscure, sad, serious, shadowy, shady, sober, solemn
🔁 bright, cheerful, happy

somebody *n* big noise *colloq*, big shot *colloq*, big wheel *colloq*, bigwig *colloq*, celebrity, dignitary, heavyweight, household name *colloq*, luminary, magnate, mogul, nabob, name, notable, panjandrum, personage, someone, star, superstar, VIP
🔁 nobody

someday *adv* at some time in the future, by and by, eventually, in due course, later, later on, one day, one of these (fine) days, sometime, sooner or later, ultimately
🔁 never

somehow *adv* by fair means or foul *colloq*, by hook or by crook *colloq*, by some means, come hell or high water *colloq*, come what may, one way or another

sometime *adv* another time, at some time in the future, at some time in the past, earlier, in the past, one day, previously, someday, then
♦ *adj* emeritus, erstwhile *formal*, ex *colloq*, former, late, one-time, previous, quondam *formal*, retired

sometimes *adv* at times, every so often, from time to time, now and again, now and then, occasionally, off and on, on and off, on occasion(s), once in a while
🔁 always, never

somnolent *adj* comatose *technical*, dozy, drowsy, half-awake, heavy-eyed, oscitant *formal*, sleepy, soporific, torpid

son *n* boy, child, descendant, disciple, inhabitant, lad(die), native, offspring

song

Types of song include:
air, anthem, aria, ballad, barcarole, blues, calypso, cantata, canticle, cantilena, canzone, canzonet, carol, chanson, chansonette, chant, chorus, descant, dirge, dithyramb, ditty, elegy, epinikion, epithalamium, folk-song, gospel song, hymn, jingle, lay, love-song, lied, lullaby, madrigal, nursery rhyme, ode, plainchant, plainsong, pop song, psalm, recitative, refrain, requiem, roundelay, serenade, shanty, spiritual, Negro spiritual, threnody, war song, wassail, yodel. See also **poem**

songster *n* balladeer, chanteuse, chorister, crooner, minstrel, singer, troubadour, vocalist, warbler

sonorous *adj* full, full-mouthed, full-throated, full-voiced, grandiloquent *formal*, high-flown, high-sounding, loud, ororotund, orotund, plangent *formal*, resonant, resounding, rich, ringing, rounded, sounding

soon *adv* any minute (now), before long, before you can say Jack Robinson *colloq*, in a jiffy *colloq*, in a little while, in a minute, in a moment (or two), in a short time, in a tick *colloq*, in no time (at all), in the near future, in two shakes of a lamb's tail *colloq*, presently, pronto *colloq*, shortly

soothe *v* allay, alleviate, appease *formal*, assuage *formal*, calm (down), comfort, compose, ease, hush, lull, mitigate *formal*, mollify, pacify, palliate, quiet, quieten (down), relieve, salve, settle (down), soften, still, temper, tranquillize
🖅 aggravate, annoy, irritate, vex

soothing *adj* anetic *technical*, assuasive *formal*, balmy, balsamic, calming, demulcent *formal*, easeful, emollient, lenitive, palliative, relaxing, restful
🖅 annoying, irritating, vexing

soothsayer *n* augur, Chaldee, diviner, foreteller, haruspex *formal*, prophet, seer, sibyl

sophisticated *adj* **1** *took me to meet her sophisticated friends:* cosmopolitan, cultivated, cultured, elegant, experienced, polished, refined, seasoned, stylish, suave, urbane, worldly, worldly-wise **2** *sophisticated technology:* advanced, complex, complicated, elaborate, highly-developed, intricate, subtle
🖅 **1** naïve, unsophisticated **2** primitive, simple

sophistication *n* culture, elegance, experience, finesse, poise, savoir-faire, savoir-vivre, urbanity, worldliness
🖅 naïvety, simplicity

sophistry *n* casuistry, elenchus, fallacy, paralogism *technical*, quibble, sophism

soporific *adj* hypnotic, narcotic, opiate, sedative, sleep-inducing, sleepy, somnolent *formal*, tranquillizing
🖅 invigorating, stimulating
♦ *n* anaesthetic, hypnic, hypnotic, narcotic, opiate, sedative, sleeping pill, sleeping tablet, tranquillizer
🖅 stimulant

soppy *adj* cloying, corny *colloq*, crazy, daft *colloq*, lovey-dovey *colloq*, maudlin, mawkish, mushy *colloq*, overemotional, schmaltzy *colloq*, sentimental, silly, sloppy *colloq*, slushy *colloq*, soft, weepy *colloq*, wet *colloq*, wild, wimpish *colloq*

sorcerer *n* angek(k)ok, enchanter, mage, magian, magician, magus, necromancer, reim-kennar, sorceress, thaumaturgist *formal*, voodoo, warlock, witch, wizard

sorcery *n* black magic, charm, enchantment, incantation, magic, necromancy, pishogue, spell, thaumaturgy *formal*, voodoo, witchcraft, wizardry

sordid *adj* **1** *lived in a sordid basement flat:* dirty, filthy, foul, grimy, mucky, seamy, seedy, shabby, sleazy, soiled, squalid, stained, tawdry, unclean, vile **2** *the more that emerges, the more sordid the affair appears:* abhorrent *formal*, base, corrupt, debased, debauched, degenerate, degraded, despicable, dishonest, dishonourable, disreputable, foul, ignominious *formal*, immoral, low, mean, mercenary, shameful, vile, wretched
🖅 **1** clean, pure **2** honourable, upright

sore *adj* **1** *suffering from a sore neck:* aching, bruised, burning, chafed, hurting, inflamed, injured, painful, raw, red, reddened, sensitive, smarting, stinging, tender, wounded **2** *I was still very sore about the experience:* aggrieved, angry,

annoyed, bitter, distressed, hurt, irritated, offended, resentful, upset, vexed, wounded
🖅 **2** happy, pleased
♦ *n* abrasion, abscess, boil, inflammation, laceration, lesion, swelling, ulcer, wound

sorrow *n* **1** *her sorrow did not last long:* anguish, dejection, disconsolateness *formal*, distress, dolour *formal*, grief, heartache, heartbreak, misery, misfortune, mourning, pain, regret, remorse, sadness, suffering, unhappiness, woe, wretchedness **2** *a hard life full of sorrows:* affliction *formal*, hardship, misfortune, trial, tribulation *formal*, trouble, worry
🖅 **1** happiness, joy **2** joy
♦ *v* agonize, be/feel miserable, be/feel sad, bemoan, grieve, lament, moan, mourn, pine, weep
🖅 rejoice

sorrowful *adj* afflicted *formal*, dejected, depressed, disconsolate *formal*, distressing, doleful, grievous, heartbroken, heart-rending, heavy-hearted, lamentable, lugubrious *formal*, melancholy, miserable, mournful, painful, piteous, rueful, sad, sorry, tearful, unhappy, wae *Scot*, woebegone *formal*, woeful, wretched
🖅 happy, joyful

sorry *adj* **1** *was sorry for his actions:* apologetic, ashamed, conscience-stricken, contrite, guilt-ridden, penitent, regretful, remorseful, repentant, shamefaced **2** *sorry to hear the news:* distressed, down *colloq*, sad, unhappy, upset **3** *felt sorry for the child:* compassionate, concerned, moved, pitying, sympathetic, understanding **4** *in a sorry state:* dismal, grievous, heart-rending, miserable, pathetic, pitiful, poor, sad, shameful, unhappy, wretched
🖅 **1** impenitent, unashamed **2** happy, pleased **3** uncaring **4** cheerful, happy

sort *n* brand, breed, category, character, class, denomination, description, family, genre *formal*, genus *technical*, group, ilk, kind, make, nature, order, quality, race, species, style, type, variety
♦ *v* arrange, catalogue, categorize, class, classify, distribute, divide, grade, group, order, organize, put in order, rank, screen, segregate, separate, sift, systematize
▶ **sort out 1** *sort out their finances:* arrange, order, organize, put in order, work out **2** *sort them out by colour:* categorize, class, classify, divide, grade, group, order, rank, segregate, select, separate **3** *sort out your problems:* clear up, put right, resolve, solve, work out

sortie *n* assault, attack, charge, foray, invasion, offensive, raid, rush, sally, swoop

so-so *adj* adequate, average, fair, fair to middling *colloq*, indifferent, middling, moderate, neutral, not bad *colloq*, OK *colloq*, ordinary, passable, respectable, run-of-the-mill *colloq*, tolerable, undistinguished, unexceptional

soul *n* **1** *perform rituals believed to purify their souls:* character, essence, heart of hearts *colloq*, inner being, inner self, intellect, life-giving principle, mind, psyche, reason, spirit, vital force **2** *not a soul for miles around:* creature, human being, individual, man, person, woman **3** *a singer with no soul:* compassion, feeling, humanity, inspiration, sensitivity, tenderness **4** *he's the soul of discretion:* embodiment, epitome, essence, example, model, personification
🖅 **1** body

soulful *adj* eloquent, emotional, expressive, heartfelt, meaningful, mournful, moving, profound, sensitive
✗ soulless

soulless *adj* callous, cold, cruel, dead, ignoble, inhuman, lifeless, mean, mean-spirited, mechanical, soul-destroying, spiritless, unfeeling, uninteresting, unkind, unsympathetic
✗ soulful

sound¹ *n* din, noise, resonance, reverberation, tenor, timbre, tone
♦ *v* **1** *she was still asleep when the bells sounded:* chime, echo, go off, peal, resonate, resound, reverberate, ring, toll **2** *sounded his opinions:* announce, articulate, declare, enunciate, express, pronounce, say, utter, voice

---

Sounds include:
bang, beep, blare, blast, bleep, boom, buzz, chime, chink, chug, clack, clang, clank, clap, clash, clatter, click, clink, crack, crackle, crash, creak, crunch, cry, drone, echo, fizz, groan, gurgle, hiccup, hiss, honk, hoot, hum, jangle, jingle, knock, moan, murmur, patter, peal, ping, pip, plop, pop, rattle, report, ring, roar, rumble, rustle, scrape, scream, screech, sigh, sizzle, skirl, slam, slurp, smack, snap, snore, snort, sob, splash, splutter, squeak, squeal, squelch, swish, tap, thud, thump, thunder, tick, ting, tinkle, toot, twang, wail, whimper, whine, whirr, whistle, whoop, yell

---

Animal sounds include:
bark, bay, bellow, bleat, bray, cackle, caw, chirp, chirrup, cluck, coo, croak, crow, gobble, growl, grunt, hiss, hoot, howl, low, mew, miaow, moo, neigh, purr, quack, roar, screech, snarl, squawk, squeak, tweet, twitter, warble, whinny, woof, yap, yelp, yowl

---

sound² *adj* **1** *the doctor confirmed his patient was sound:* disease-free, fit, healthy, in fine fettle *colloq*, in good condition/shape, in good health, perfect, robust, sane, sound as a bell *colloq*, undamaged, unhurt, unimpaired, uninjured, vigorous, well **2** *built on sound foundations:* firm, intact, robust, solid, sturdy, substantial **3** *a sound argument:* authoritative, cogent *formal*, complete, dependable, good, judicious *formal*, logical, orthodox, proven, rational, reasonable, reliable, right, secure, solid, thorough, trustworthy, valid, weighty, well-founded, well-grounded
✗ **1** ill, shaky, unfit **2** shaky **3** poor, unreliable, unsound

sound³ *v* examine, fathom, inspect, investigate, measure, plumb, probe, test
▶ **sound out** ask, canvass, examine, investigate, probe, pump, question, research, survey, suss out *colloq*

sound⁴ *n* channel, estuary, firth, fjord, inlet, passage, strait, voe

soup *n* broth, chowder, consommé, julienne, potage, stock

sour *adj* **1** *a sour fruit:* acetic, acid, aciduous, acidy, bitter, pungent, sharp, tangy, tart, vinegary **2** *sour milk:* curdled, off *colloq*, rancid, turned **3** *the boss was in a sour mood:* acrimonious *formal*, bad-tempered, churlish, crabbed *colloq*, crusty, disagreeable, embittered, grouchy *colloq*, ill-tempered, nasty, peevish, ratty *colloq*, resentful, shirty *colloq*, surly, unpleasant
✗ **1** sugary, sweet **2** fresh **3** generous, good-natured
♦ *v* embitter, envenom, exasperate, make bitter, spoil

source *n* author, authority, beginning, cause, commencement *formal*, derivation, fons et origo *formal*, fountainhead, informant, mine, origin, originator, primordium *formal*, provenance *formal*, rise, root, spring, start, supply, wellhead, wellspring, ylem *technical*

sourpuss *n* crosspatch *colloq*, grouse *colloq*, grumbler, grump *colloq*, killjoy, kvetch, misery, shrew, whiner, whinger *colloq*

souse *v* dip, douse, drench, dunk, immerse, marinade, marinate, pickle, plunge, saturate, sink, soak, steep, submerge

souvenir *n* keepsake, memento, relic, remembrance, reminder, token, trophy

sovereign *n* chief, emperor, empress, king, monarch, potentate *formal*, queen, ruler, tsar
♦ *adj* **1** *a sovereign monarch:* absolute, chief, dominant, imperial, kingly, majestic, paramount, predominant, princely, principal, queenly, royal, ruling, supreme, unlimited **2** *a sovereign nation:* autonomous, independent, self-governing, self-ruling **3** *a sovereign method:* extreme, outstanding, unequalled, unrivalled, utmost

sovereignty *n* ascendancy *formal*, autonomy, domination, dominion, imperium *formal*, independence, kingship, primacy, queenship, raj, regality, supremacy, suzerainty *formal*, sway

sow *v* bestrew, broadcast, disperse, disseminate *formal*, distribute, implant, lodge, plant, scatter, seed, spread, strew

space *n* **1** *there's plenty of space:* accommodation, amplitude *formal*, area, capacity, clearance, elbow-room, expanse, expansion, extent, latitude, leeway, margin, place, play, range, room, scope, seat, stretch, sweep, volume **2** *space between two objects:* blank, break, chasm, empty space, gap, intermission, interstice *formal*, interval, lacuna *formal*, omission, opening **3** *in a short space of time:* period, shift, span, spell, stint, stretch, time **4** *launched the rocket into space:* cosmos, deep space, galaxy, outer space, solar system, the Milky Way, universe
♦ *v* arrange, array *formal*, order, place at intervals, put in order, range, set apart, space out, stretch out, string out

spacious *adj* ample, big, broad, capacious *formal*, commodious *formal*, expansive, extensive, huge, immense, large, open, roomy, sizeable, uncrowded, vast, wide
✗ confined, cramped, narrow, poky *colloq*, small

spadework *n* donkey-work *colloq*, drudgery, foundation, groundwork, homework, labour, preparation

span *n* compass, distance, duration, extent, interval, length, period, range, reach, scope, spell, spread, stretch, term, time
♦ *v* arch, bestride *formal*, bridge, cover, cross, extend, include, last, link, range, stretch, traverse, vault

spank v cane, put over your knee *colloq*, slap, slipper, smack, tan *colloq*, thrash, thwack *colloq*, wallop *colloq*, whack *colloq*

spanking adj brisk, energetic, fast, fine, gleaming, invigorating, lively, quick, smart, snappy, speedy, swift, vigorous
☒ slow
♦ adv absolutely, brand, completely, exactly, positively, strikingly, totally, utterly

spar v argue, bicker, box, contend, contest, dispute, fall out, scrap *colloq*, skirmish, spat *colloq*, squabble, tiff *colloq*, wrangle, wrestle

spare adj **1** *used the spare batteries:* additional, auxiliary, emergency, extra, leftover, over, remaining, reserve, superfluous, supernumerary, supplementary, surplus, surplus to requirements, unused, unwanted **2** *spare time:* free, leisure, unoccupied **3** *a small, spare figure in a dark coat:* all skin and bones *colloq*, bony, gaunt, lank, lean, scraggy, scrawny, skinny, slender, slim, thin **4** *provided only spare information:* frugal, meagre, modest, scant, scanty, sparing
☒ **1** necessary, used, vital **3** fat
♦ v **1** *the judge spared the accused:* forgive, free, let off, pardon, release, reprieve, show mercy to **2** *could you spare some money?:* afford, allow, dispense with *formal*, do without, give, grant, manage without, part with, provide **3** *he spared your life:* defend, guard, not harm, protect, safeguard, save, secure, take care of

sparing adj careful, close-fisted, economical, frugal, meagre, mingy *colloq*, miserly, penurious *formal*, prudent *formal*, stingy *colloq*, thrifty, tight-fisted
☒ lavish, liberal, unsparing

spark n **1** *a spark of light:* flare, flash, flicker, gleam, glimmer, glint **2** *not a spark of intelligence:* atom, bit, flicker, hint, iota, jot, scrap, suggestion, touch, trace, vestige
▶ **spark off** cause, excite, incite, inspire, kindle, occasion, precipitate *formal*, prompt, provoke, set off, start (off), stimulate, stir, touch off, trigger (off)

sparkle v **1** *stars sparkled in the sky:* beam, coruscate *formal*, flash, flicker, gleam, glimmer, glint, glisten, glitter, glow, scintillate, shimmer, shine, twinkle **2** *champagne sparkled in the glass:* bubble, effervesce, fizz **3** *she sparkled at the party:* be animated, be bubbly *colloq*, be ebullient *formal*, be effervescent, be enthusiastic, be lively, be spirited, be vivacious, be witty
♦ n **1** *the sparkle of gold:* brilliance, coruscation *formal*, dazzle, flash, flicker, gleam, glint, glitter, glow, radiance, shimmer, shine, spark, twinkle **2** *a lovely woman who brought a sparkle to the office:* animation, dash, ebullience *formal*, energy, enthusiasm, get-up-and-go *colloq*, life, liveliness, pizzazz *colloq*, spirit, vim *colloq*, vitality, vivacity

sparkling adj **1** *a glass of sparkling water:* bubbly, carbonated, effervescent, fizzy **2** *a sparkling diamond ring:* coruscating *formal*, gleaming, glistening, glittering, twinkling **3** *sparkling conversation:* animated, lively, scintillating, witty
☒ **1** flat **3** dull

sparse adj infrequent, meagre, scanty, scarce, scattered, slight, sporadic
☒ dense, plentiful, thick

spartan adj abstemious, ascetic, austere, bleak, disciplined, frugal, harsh, joyless, plain, rigorous, self-denying, severe, simple, strict, stringent, temperate
☒ luxurious, self-indulgent

spasm n access *formal*, attack, bout, burst, contraction, convulsion, cramp, eruption, fit, frenzy, jerk, outburst, paroxysm, seizure, tic, twitch

spasmodic adj erratic, fitful, intermittent, irregular, jerky, occasional, periodic, sporadic
☒ continuous, uninterrupted

spate n deluge, flood, flow, outpouring, rush, torrent

spatter v bedaub, bespatter, besprinkle, bestrew, daub, dirty, scatter, shower, soil, speckle, splash, splatter, splodge, spray, sprinkle

spay n castrate, doctor, emasculate, geld, neuter, sterilize

speak v address, argue, articulate, chat, chatter *colloq*, communicate, converse *formal*, declaim *formal*, declare, discuss, enunciate, express, gab *colloq*, harangue, have a word with *colloq*, hold forth, lecture, pronounce, say, state, talk, tell, utter, voice, witter *colloq*, yak *colloq*
▶ **speak for** act as spokesperson for, act for, represent, speak on behalf of, stand for
▶ **speak of** discuss, make mention of, make reference to, mention, refer to
▶ **speak out/up** defend, protest, say publicly, speak openly, stand up and be counted *colloq*, support
▶ **speak to** accost, address, admonish *formal*, bring to book *colloq*, dress down *colloq*, lecture, rebuke, reprimand, scold, tell off *colloq*, tick off *colloq*, upbraid *formal*, warn
▶ **speak up** make yourself heard, raise your voice, talk (more) loudly

speaker n lecturer, mouthpiece, orator, prolocutor *formal*, spokesman, spokesperson, spokeswoman, talker

spearhead v front, head, initiate, launch, lead, pioneer
♦ n cutting edge *colloq*, front line, guide, leader, leading position, overseer, pioneer, trailblazer, van *colloq*, vanguard

special adj **1** *a special occasion:* distinctive, distinguished, exceptional, extraordinary, important, major, memorable, momentous, notable, noteworthy, out of the ordinary *colloq*, outstanding, red-letter *colloq*, remarkable, significant, unusual **2** *his special interest is the environment:* characteristic, choice, detailed, distinctive, exclusive, individual, particular, peculiar, precise, select, singular *formal*, specific, unique
☒ **1** normal, ordinary, run of the mill *colloq*, usual **2** common, general

specialist n authority, brains *colloq*, connoisseur, consultant, expert, master, professional

speciality n feature, field, field/area of study, forte, gift, pièce de résistance, specialty *US*, strength, talent

specially adv distinctly, exclusively, explicitly, expressly, for a particular purpose, for a special purpose, in particular, particularly, specifically, uniquely

species *n* breed, category, class, collection, description, genus, group, kind, sort, type, variety

specific *adj* clear-cut, definite, detailed, determined, exact, explicit, express, fixed, limited, particular, precise, set, special, unambiguous, unequivocal, well-defined
≠ approximate, unspecific, vague

specification *n* condition, delineation *formal*, description, designation, detail, instruction, item, listing, naming, particular, qualification, requirement, statement, stipulation

specify *v* cite, define, delineate *formal*, describe, designate, detail, enumerate, indicate, itemize, list, mention, name, particularize, set out, spell out, state, stipulate

specimen *n* copy, example, exemplar *formal*, exhibit, illustration, instance, model, paradigm *formal*, pattern, representative, sample, type

specious *adj* casuistic *formal*, deceptive, fallacious *formal*, false, misleading, plausible, sophistic *formal*, sophistical *formal*, unsound, untrue
≠ true, valid

speck *n* atom, bit, blemish, blot, defect, dot, fault, flaw, fleck, grain, iota, jot, mark, mite, particle, shred, speckle, spot, stain, tittle, trace, whit

speckled *adj* brinded, brindle(d), dappled, dotted, flecked, fleckered, freckled, lentiginous *technical*, mottled, spotted, spotty, sprinkled, stippled

spectacle *n* curiosity, display, exhibition, extravaganza, marvel, pageant, parade, performance, phenomenon, picture, scene, show, sight, wonder

spectacles

Types of spectacles include:
bifocals, diving mask, eyeglass, goggles, half-glasses, lorgnette, monocle, pince-nez, Polaroid® glasses, quizzing glass, reading glasses, safety glasses, shooting glasses, sports spex, sunglasses, trifocals, varifocals

spectacular *adj* amazing, astonishing, breathtaking, colourful, daring, dazzling, dramatic, extraordinary, eye-catching, flamboyant, glorious, grand, impressive, magnificent, opulent *formal*, ostentatious, outstanding, remarkable, resplendent *formal*, sensational, splendid, staggering, striking, stunning
≠ ordinary, unimpressive
♦ *n* display, exhibition, extravaganza, pageant, show, spectacle

spectator *n* beholder *formal*, bystander, eye-witness, looker-on, observer, onlooker, passer-by, rubberneck *US slang*, viewer, watcher, witness
≠ participant, player

spectral *adj* disembodied, eerie, ghostly, incorporeal, insubstantial, phantom, shadowy, spooky *colloq*, supernatural, uncanny, unearthly, weird

spectre *n* **1** *a spectre appeared over his bed:* apparition, ghost, phantom, presence, revenant, shade, shadow, spirit, spook *colloq*, vision, visitant, wraith **2** *raised the spectre of a renewed conflict:* dread, fear, menace, threat

spectrum see **rainbow**

speculate *v* **1** *it's too early to speculate about the cause:* cogitate *formal*, conjecture *formal*, consider, contemplate, deliberate, guess, hypothesize *formal*, meditate, muse, reflect, suppose, surmise *formal*, theorize, wonder **2** *speculated in the land market:* gamble, hazard, risk, venture

speculation *n* **1** *it's pure speculation at this point:* conjecture *formal*, contemplation, flight of fancy, guess, guesswork, hypothesis, supposition, surmise *formal*, theory **2** *financial speculation:* gamble, gambling, hazard, risk

speculative *adj* abstract, academic, chancy *colloq*, conjectural, dicey *colloq*, hazardous, hypothetical, iffy *colloq*, indefinite, notional, risky, suppositional *formal*, tentative, theoretical, uncertain, unpredictable, unproven, vague

speech *n* **1** *a relaxed style of speech:* accent, articulation, communication, conversation, delivery, dialect, dialogue, diction, elocution, enunciation, language, parlance, pronunciation, spoken communication, talk, tongue, utterance, voice **2** *gave a lengthy speech at the meeting:* address, conversation, dialogue, diatribe *formal*, discourse, harangue, lecture, monologue, oration, patter, philippic *formal*, soliloquy, spiel *colloq*, talk, tirade

speechless *adj* aghast, amazed, astounded, dumb, dumbfounded, dumbstruck, inarticulate, mum, mute, obmutescent *formal*, shocked, silent, thunderstruck, tongue-tied
≠ talkative

speed *n* acceleration, alacrity, celerity *formal*, dispatch, expeditiousness *formal*, haste, hurry, momentum, pace, promptness, quickness, rapidity, rate, rush, swiftness, tempo, velocity
≠ delay, slowness
♦ *v* accelerate, belt *colloq*, bowl along, career, dash, gallop, hasten *formal*, hurry, hurtle *colloq*, pelt *colloq*, put your foot down *colloq*, quicken, race, rush, sprint, step on it/the gas/the juice *colloq*, tear, zoom
≠ delay, slow
▶ **speed up 1** *speeding up as he got onto the motorway:* accelerate, drive faster, gain momentum, go faster, open up *colloq*, pick up/gather speed, put on a spurt *colloq*, put your foot down *colloq*, quicken, step on it/the gas/the juice *colloq* **2** *to speed up a process:* advance, expedite *formal*, facilitate, forward, further, hasten *formal*, hurry, precipitate *formal*, promote, quicken, spur on, step up, stimulate

speedily *adv* fast, hastily, hurriedly, posthaste, promptly, quickly, rapidly, swiftly
≠ slowly

speedy *adj* cursory, expeditious *formal*, express, fast, hasty, hurried, immediate, nimble, nippy *colloq*, precipitate *formal*, prompt, quick, rapid, summary, swift, zippy *colloq*
≠ leisurely, slow

spell[1] *v* augur *formal*, herald, imply, indicate, mean, portend *formal*, presage *formal*, promise, signal, signify, suggest

▶ **spell out** clarify, detail, elucidate, emphasize, explain, make clear, specify, stipulate

spell² *n* bout, course, extent, interval, patch, period, season, session, shift, span, stint, stretch, term, time, turn

spell³ *n* 1 *a magician's spell:* abracadabra, bewitchment, charm, enchantment, incantation, magic, sorcery, trance, witchery 2 *the character cast his spell over the audience:* allure, attraction, charm, drawing power, fascination, glamour, magnetism, pull

spellbinding *adj* bewitching, captivating, enchanting, enthralling, entrancing, fascinating, gripping, mesmerizing, riveting

spellbound *adj* bewitched, captivated, charmed, enchanted, enraptured, enthralled, entranced, fascinated, gripped, hypnotized, mesmerized, rapt, riveted, transfixed, transported

spend *v* 1 *spend money:* blow *colloq,* consume, dip/dig into your pocket *colloq,* disburse *formal,* exhaust, expend, finish, fork out *colloq,* fritter, invest, lay out, pay out, shell out *colloq,* spend like water *colloq,* splash out *colloq,* squander, use up, waste 2 *spend time:* apply, devote, employ, fill, kill *colloq,* occupy, pass, put in, take up, use (up), while away
◼ 1 hoard, save

spendthrift *n* prodigal, profligate *formal,* squanderer, wastrel
◼ hoarder, miser, saver
◆ *adj* extravagant, improvident, prodigal, profligate *formal,* squandering, wasteful

spent *adj* 1 *spent matches:* consumed, exhausted, expended, finished, gone, used (up) 2 *was left feeling spent and lethargic:* all in *colloq,* burnt out *colloq,* bushed *colloq,* dead beat *colloq,* debilitated *formal,* dog-tired *colloq,* done in *colloq,* drained, effete *formal,* exhausted, fagged (out) *colloq,* jiggered *colloq,* knackered *colloq,* shattered *colloq,* tired out, weakened, wearied, weary, whacked *colloq,* worn out *colloq,* zonked *colloq*

spew *v* belch, disgorge, gush, issue, puke *colloq,* regurgitate, retch, spit out, spurt, throw up *colloq,* vomit

sphere *n* 1 *the pearl was a perfect sphere:* ball, globe, globule, orb, round 2 *her sphere of influence:* area, compass, domain, extent, field, province, range, realm, scope 3 *his sphere of friends:* band, circle, class, clique, crowd, group, set

spherical *adj* ball-shaped, globate *formal,* globe-shaped, globoid *formal,* globose *formal,* globular, orbicular *formal,* rotund *formal,* round

spice *n* 1 *added spice to the dish:* flavouring, piquancy, relish, savour, seasoning, tang 2 *inject a little spice into your life:* colour, excitement, gusto, kick *colloq,* life, pep *colloq,* zap *colloq,* zest, zip *colloq*
◆ *v* animate, brighten, buck up *colloq,* energize, enliven, hot up *colloq,* invigorate, liven (up), pep up *colloq,* perk up *colloq,* put life into, rouse, stir (up), vitalize

spicy *adj* 1 *enjoys spicy food:* aromatic, flavoured, flavoursome, fragrant, hot, peppery, piquant, pungent, seasoned, sharp, strongly flavoured, tangy, tart, well-seasoned 2 *he told me every spicy*

detail: adult *colloq,* blue *colloq,* improper, indecent, indecorous *formal,* indelicate, juicy *colloq,* near the bone/knuckle *colloq,* racy, raunchy *colloq,* ribald, risqué, scandalous, sensational, suggestive, unseemly *formal*
◼ 1 bland, insipid 2 decent

spiel *n* oration *formal,* patter, pitch, recital, sales patter, speech

spike *n* barb, nail, point, projection, prong, rowel, spine, stake, tine
◆ *v* 1 *spike the meat onto the skewer:* impale, prick, skewer, spear, stick 2 *spike a drink:* add to, contaminate, drug, lace, mix in

spill *v* discharge, disgorge, flow, overflow, overturn, pour, run (out/over), scatter, shed, slop, tip, upset, well
◆ *n* accident, cropper *colloq,* fall, overturn, tumble, upset

spin *v* 1 *spin around:* circle, go round, gyrate, pirouette, reel, revolve, rotate, swirl, swivel, turn (round), twirl, twist, wheel, whirl, whirr 2 *spin a yarn:* dream up, fabricate, invent, make up, narrate, relate, tell
◆ *n* 1 *a spin of the wheel:* circle, gyration, pirouette, reel, revolution, rotation, swirl, swivel, turn, twirl, twist, wheel, whirl 2 *threw the academics into a spin:* agitation, commotion, dither *colloq,* flap *colloq,* fluster *colloq,* panic, state *colloq,* tizz *colloq,* tizzy *colloq* 3 *go for a spin in the car:* drive, jaunt, journey, outing, ride, run, trip
▶ **spin out** amplify, extend, lengthen, pad out, prolong, protract *formal*

spindle *n* arbor *technical,* axis, axle, fusee, pin, pivot, rod

spindly *adj* attenuate(d) *formal,* gangling, gangly, lanky, long, skeletal, skinny, spidery, spindle-shanked, thin, weedy *colloq*
◼ stocky, thickset

spine *n* 1 *she straightened her spine:* backbone, dorsum, rachis, spinal column, vertebrae, vertebral column 2 *scratched by a cactus spine:* barb, bristle, needle, prickle, quill, rachis, spike, thorn 3 *he has the spine to face his critics:* bottle *colloq,* bravery, courage, determination, fortitude *formal,* grit *colloq,* guts *colloq,* mettle, pluck, resolution, spirit, spunk *colloq,* strength of character

spine-chilling *adj* bloodcurdling, eerie, frightening, hair-raising, horrifying, scary, spooky *colloq,* terrifying

spineless *adj* chicken *colloq,* cowardly, faint-hearted, feeble, indecisive, ineffective, irresolute, lily-livered, soft, spiritless, submissive, timid, timorous *formal,* weak, weak-kneed, wet *colloq,* wimpish *colloq,* yellow *colloq*
◼ brave, courageous, strong

spiny *adj* acanthaceous *formal,* acanthous *formal,* briery, prickly, spicular *formal,* spiculate *formal,* spiniferous *formal,* spinigerous *formal,* spinose *formal,* spinous *formal,* thistly, thorny

spiral *adj* circular, cochleate(d) *formal,* coiled, corkscrew, helical, scrolled, twisting, whorled, winding
◆ *n* cochlea *technical,* coil, convolution, corkscrew, curlicue, gyre *formal,* helix, screw, twist, volute *formal,* volution *formal,* whorl
◆ *v* 1 *the spiralling stairwell:* circle, coil, gyrate, gyre, screw, twist, whorl, wind, wreathe 2 costs

were spiralling: climb, escalate, go up, increase, rise, rocket, skyrocket, soar

spire *n* belfry, crest, peak, pinnacle, point, spike, steeple, summit, tip, top, tower, turret

spirit *n* **1** *she believes in the immortality of the spirit:* breath, élan vital, inner being, inner self, life-giving principle, mind, psyche, soul, vital force **2** *the house is haunted by spirits:* angel, apparition, demon, devil, fairy, fiend, ghost, phantom, presence, renevant, shade, shadow, spectre, spook *colloq,* sprite, supernatural being, visitant, wraith **3** *showed great spirit through the whole battle:* backbone, bottle *colloq,* bravery, courage, dauntlessness, determination, grit *colloq,* guts *colloq,* mettle, pluck, resolution, spunk *colloq,* stoutheartedness, strength of character, willpower **4** *the band played the music with tremendous spirit:* animation, ardour, energy, enterprise, enthusiasm, fire, kick *colloq,* liveliness, motivation, pizzazz *colloq,* sparkle, vigour, vivacity, zeal, zest, zip *colloq* **5** *the photo captures the spirit of the times:* air, atmosphere, character, essence, essential quality, mood, quality **6** *she has an independent spirit:* attitude, character, disposition, humour, make-up, outlook, temperament **7** *the crowd are in good spirits:* frame of mind, humour, mood, morale, temper **8** *the spirit of the law:* character, drift, essence, gist, substance, tenor

▶ **spirit away** abduct *colloq,* capture, carry, convey, kidnap, purloin *formal,* remove, seize, snaffle *colloq,* steal, take, whisk

spirited *adj* active, animated, ardent, bold, confident, courageous, determined, energetic, feisty *colloq,* fiery, high-spirited, lively, mettlesome, passionate, plucky, resolute, sparkling, valiant, valorous *formal,* vigorous, vivacious, zealous

🔁 cowardly, lethargic, spiritless

spiritless *adj* anaemic, apathetic, dejected, depressed, despondent, dispirited, droopy, dull, lacklustre, languid *formal,* lifeless, listless, low, melancholy, torpid, unenthusiastic, unmoved, weak, wishy-washy *colloq*

🔁 spirited

spirits *n* **1** *liked drinking spirits:* alcohol, fire-water *colloq,* hooch *colloq,* liquor, moonshine, strong drink, strong liquor, the hard stuff *colloq* **2** *everyone was in good spirits:* attitude, emotions, feelings, humour, mood, temper, temperament

spiritual *adj* **1** *sensed a spiritual presence:* ethereal, immaterial, incorporeal, intangible, otherworldly, unworldly **2** *a spiritual leader:* devotional, divine, ecclesiastical, heavenly, holy, religious, sacred

🔁 **1** material, physical, temporal **2** secular

spit *v* discharge, eject, expectorate *formal,* hawk, hiss, issue, rasp, splutter
♦ *n* dribble, drool, expectoration *formal,* phlegm, saliva, slaver, spittle, sputum

spite *n* animosity, bitterness, evil, gall, grudge, hard feelings *colloq,* hate, hatred, hostility, ill nature, ill-feeling, ill-will, malevolence *formal,* malice, maliciousness, malignity *formal,* rancour, resentment, spitefulness, vengeance, venom, vindictiveness

🔁 affection, compassion, goodwill
♦ *v* annoy, gall, hurt, injure, irk, irritate, offend, provoke, put out, upset, vex, wound

spiteful *adj* barbed, bitchy *colloq,* bitter, catty *colloq,* cruel, hostile, ill-disposed, ill-natured, malevolent *formal,* malicious, malignant *formal,* nasty, rancorous, resentful, snide, vengeful, venomous, vindictive

🔁 affectionate, charitable

splash *v* **1** *water splashed over the boat:* batter, beat, break, buffet, dabble, dash, daub, shower, slop, slosh, smack, spatter, splatter, splodge, splotch, spray, sprinkle, squirt, strike, surge, wash, wet **2** *splashed around in the water:* bathe, dabble, paddle, plunge, slosh, wade, wallow **3** *scandal was splashed across the front of every newspaper:* blazon, display, exhibit, flaunt, plaster, publicize, show, trumpet
♦ *n* **1** *a splash of paint:* burst, dash, patch, splatter, splodge, splotch, splurge, spot, stain, streak, touch **2** *the film created a splash on its release:* effect, excitement, impact, impression, publicity, sensation, stir
▶ **splash out** be extravagant, invest in, push the boat out *colloq,* spend, splurge

spleen *n* acrimony *formal,* anger, animosity, animus *formal,* bad temper, bile, biliousness, bitterness, gall, hatred, hostility, ill-humour, ill-will, malevolence *formal,* malice *formal,* malignity, peevishness, petulance *formal,* pique, rancour, resentment, spite, spitefulness, venom, vindictiveness, wrath

splendid *adj* admirable, bright, brilliant, celebrated, dazzling, distinguished, excellent, exceptional, fabulous *colloq,* fine, first-class, glittering, glorious, glowing, gorgeous, grand, great, illustrious, imposing, impressive, lavish, lustrous, luxurious, magnificent, marvellous, opulent *formal,* outstanding, radiant, refulgent *formal,* remarkable, renowned, resplendent *formal,* rich, stately, sublime, sumptuous, super *colloq,* superb, supreme, terrific *colloq,* wonderful

🔁 drab, ordinary, run-of-the-mill

splendour *n* brightness, brilliance, ceremony, dazzle, display, gleam, glory, glow, grandeur, illustriousness, lustre, luxury, magnificence, majesty, opulence *formal,* pomp, radiance, resplendence *formal,* richness, show, solemnity, spectacle, sumptuousness

🔁 drabness, squalor

splenetic *adj* acid, angry, bad-tempered, bilious, bitchy *colloq,* choleric, churlish, crabbed *colloq,* crabby, cross, envenomed, fretful, irascible, irritable, morose, peevish, petulant *formal,* rancorous *formal,* ratty *colloq,* sour, spiteful, sullen, testy, touchy

splice *v* bind, braid, connect, entwine, fasten, graft, interlace, intertwine, interweave, join, knit, marry, mesh, plait, tie

splinter *n* bit, chip, flake, fragment, paring, piece, shard, shaving, shiver, shred, sliver, smithereens *colloq*
♦ *v* break, break into pieces, cleave *formal,* crumble, disintegrate, fracture, fragment, shatter, shiver, smash, split

split *v* **1** *split the logs:* break, chop, cleave *formal,* crack, cut, open, rend *old use,* rip, rupture, shiver, slash, slit, splinter, tear **2** *split in two:* bisect,

divide, halve, partition, separate **3** *split the profits*: allocate, allot, apportion, carve up *colloq*, distribute, divide, dole out, halve, hand out, parcel out, separate, share **4** *split from her partner*: become alienated, become estranged, break up, disband, dissociate from, disunite, divide, divorce, part, part company, separate, set apart **5** *split on his colleagues*: betray, blow the whistle on *colloq*, grass *slang*, incriminate, inform on, rat *colloq*, shop *colloq*, squeal *colloq*, tell on *colloq*
♦ *n* **1** *a split in the wooden beam*: breach, break, cleft, crack, crevice, cut, division, fissure, gap, partition, rift, rip, rupture, separation, slash, slit, tear **2** *a split within the political party*: alienation, break-up, difference, discord, dissension, disunion, divergence, division, estrangement, rupture, schism, separation
♦ *adj* bisected, broken, cleft, cloven *formal*, cracked, divided, fractured, ruptured
▶ **split up** break up, disband, divorce, get divorced, part, part company, separate

split-up *n* alienation, break-up, divorce, estrangement, parting, parting of the ways, separation

spoil *v* **1** *his behaviour spoiled the evening*: cast a shadow over *colloq*, louse up *slang*, mar, mess up *colloq*, pour cold water on *colloq*, put a damper on *colloq*, ruin, screw up *slang*, taint, throw a spanner in the works *colloq*, upset, wreck **2** *the new tower block spoils the view*: blemish, contaminate, damage, deface, deform, destroy, disfigure, foul, harm, impair, obliterate, ruin, taint, tarnish **3** *spoil a child*: baby, coddle, cosset, indulge, mollycoddle, overindulge, pamper, spoon-feed, wait on hand and foot *colloq* **4** *the milk will spoil if you don't put it in the fridge*: curdle, deteriorate, go bad, go off, go sour, go/become rotten, rot, sour, turn
▶ **spoil for** be eager for, be intent on, be keen on, long for, yearn for

spoils *n* acquisitions, benefit, booty, gain, haul, loot, pickings *colloq*, plunder, prizes, profit, spoliation *formal*, swag *slang*, winnings

spoilsport *n* damper, dog in the manger *colloq*, killjoy, meddler, misery, party-pooper, wet blanket *colloq*, wowser *colloq*

spoken *adj* declared, expressed, oral, phonetic, said, stated, told, unwritten, uttered, verbal, viva voce, voiced
⊟ unexpressed, unspoken, written

spokesman, spokeswoman *n* agent, arbitrator, broker, delegate, go-between, intermediary, mediator, mouthpiece, negotiator, propagandist, representative, spokesperson, voice

sponge *v* **1** *sponged the floor*: clean, mop, swab, wash, wipe **2** *sponge off other people*: beg, bludge *colloq*, borrow, bum *colloq*, cadge, freeload *colloq*, scrounge

sponger *n* beggar, bludger *colloq*, borrower, bum *colloq*, cadger, freeloader *colloq*, hanger-on, moocher *colloq*, parasite, scrounger

spongy *adj* absorbent, cushioned, cushiony, elastic, light, porous, resilient, soft, springy, squashy, yielding

sponsor *n* angel *colloq*, backer, friend, guarantor, patron, promoter, subsidizer, supporter, surety, underwriter
♦ *v* back, bankroll, be a patron of, finance, fund, guarantee, patronize, promote, put up the money for, subsidize, support, underwrite

spontaneous *adj* **1** *a spontaneous performance*: extempore, free, impromptu, spur of the moment *colloq*, uncompelled, unplanned, unpremeditated, unprompted, unrehearsed **2** *a spontaneous wit*: impulsive, instinctive, natural, unforced, untaught
⊟ **1** deliberate, planned **2** forced, studied

spontaneously *adv* extempore, freely, impromptu, impulsively, instinctively, of your own accord, off the cuff *colloq*, off the top of your head *colloq*, on impulse, on the spur of the moment, unplanned, unprompted, voluntarily, willingly

spoof *n* bluff, burlesque, caricature, con *colloq*, deception, fake, game, hoax, joke, lampoon, leg-pull *colloq*, mockery, parody, prank, satire, send-up *colloq*, take-off *colloq*, travesty, trick

spooky *adj* chilling, creepy, eerie, frightening, ghostly, hair-raising, mysterious, scary, spine-chilling, supernatural, uncanny, unearthly, weird

spoon-feed *v* baby, cosset, featherbed, indulge, mollycoddle, overindulge, pamper, spoil, wait on hand and foot *colloq*

sporadic *adj* erratic, infrequent, intermittent, irregular, isolated, occasional, random, scattered, spasmodic, uneven
⊟ frequent, regular

sport *n* **1** *encouraging children to take up a sport*: activity, amusement, diversion, entertainment, exercise, game, pastime, physical activity, play, pleasure, recreation **2** *made the comments in sport*: banter, fun, humour, jesting, joking, kidding *colloq*, mirth, mockery, ridicule, sneering, teasing
♦ *v* display, exhibit, show off, wear

Sports include:
badminton, fives, lacrosse, squash, table-tennis, ping-pong *colloq*, tennis; American football, baseball, basketball, billiards, boules, bowls, cricket, croquet, football, golf, handball, hockey, netball, pétanque, pitch and putt, polo, pool, putting, rounders, Rugby, snooker, soccer, tenpin bowling, volleyball; athletics, cross-country, decathlon, discus, high-jump, hurdling, javelin, long-jump, marathon, pentathlon, pole vault, running, shot put, triple-jump; angling, canoeing, diving, fishing, rowing, sailing, skin-diving, surfing, swimming, synchronized swimming, water polo, water-skiing, windsurfing, yachting; bobsleigh, curling, ice-hockey, ice-skating, skiing, speed skating, tobogganing (luging); aerobics, fencing, gymnastics, jogging, keep-fit, roller-skating, trampolining; archery, darts, quoits; boxing, judo, jujitsu, karate, kung fu, tae kwon do, weightlifting, wrestling; climbing, mountaineering, rock-climbing, walking, orienteering, pot-holing; cycle racing, drag-racing, go-karting, motor racing, speedway racing, stock-car racing, greyhound-racing, horse-racing, show-jumping, trotting, hunting, shooting, clay-pigeon shooting; gliding, sky-diving

sporting *adj* considerate, decent, fair, honourable, just, modest, reasonable, respectable, sportsmanlike
 ✗ unfair, ungentlemanly, unsporting

sportive *adj* coltish, frisky, frolicsome, gamesome, gay, jaunty, kittenish, lively, merry, playful, prankish, rollicking, skittish, sprightly

sporty *adj* **1** *a sporty child*: athletic, energetic, fit, outdoor **2** *a sporty jacket*: casual, flashy, informal, jaunty, loud, natty *colloq*, showy, snazzy *colloq*, stylish, trendy *colloq*

spot *n* **1** *a spot on the page*: blemish, blot, blotch, daub, discoloration, dot, flaw, fleck, mark, smudge, speck, speckle, splash, splodge, splotch, stain **2** *a spot on your face*: blackhead, blemish, boil, papula, papule, pimple, pock, pustule **3** *a pleasant spot*: area, locality, location, place, point, position, scene, setting, site, situation **4** *have a spot of lunch*: bit, bite, little, morsel, small amount, some **5** *have a spot on television*: airtime, niche, opening, place, position, programme, show, slot, time **6** *in a tight spot*: difficulty, fix *colloq*, hole *colloq*, jam *colloq*, mess, pickle *colloq*, plight, predicament, quandary, scrape *colloq*, trouble
 ♦ *v* **1** *spotted her friends in the crowd*: catch sight of, descry *formal*, detect, discern, espy *formal*, identify, make out, notice, observe, recognize, see **2** *spotted the paper with ink*: blemish, dot, fleck, mark, soil, speckle, stain, taint

spotless *adj* blameless, chaste, clean, faultless, gleaming, immaculate, innocent, irreproachable, pure, shining, spick and span, unblemished, unmarked, unstained, unsullied, untainted, untouched, virgin, virginal, white
 ✗ dirty, impure

spotlight *v* accentuate, draw attention to, emphasize, feature, focus on, give prominence to, highlight, illuminate, point up, stress, throw into relief, underline
 ✗ play down, tone down
 ♦ *n* attention, emphasis, fame, interest, limelight *colloq*, notoriety, public attention, public eye

spotted *adj* brindled, dappled, dotted, flecked, guttate(d) *formal*, macular *formal*, mottled, piebald, pied, polka-dot, speckled, spotty

spotty *adj* **1** *teenager with spotty skin*: blotchy, pimpled, pimply, spotted **2** *a horse with a spotty coat*: dappled, dotted, flecked, mottled, piebald, pied, speckled, spotted **3** *planes with spotty safety records*: bitty, erratic, inconsistent, patchy, uneven, varying

spouse *n* better half *colloq*, companion, consort, hubby *colloq*, husband, mate, missus *colloq*, other half *colloq*, partner, wife

spout *v* **1** *water spouts ten metres in the air*: discharge, disgorge, emit, erupt, flow, gush, jet, pour, shoot, spew, spray, spurt, squirt, stream, surge **2** *spouting poetry*: expatiate *formal*, go on, hold forth, orate *formal*, pontificate, rabbit on *colloq*, rant, recite, sermonize *formal*, spiel *colloq*, spout off/forth, waffle *colloq*, witter (on) *colloq*
 ♦ *n* **1** *a spout of water streamed out*: fountain, geyser, jet, spray, stream **2** *water poured from the spout*: gargoyle, nozzle, outlet, rose

sprawl *v* **1** *sprawl on the couch*: flop, loll *colloq*, lounge *colloq*, recline, repose *formal*, slouch, slump, stretch **2** *a sprawl of new public buildings*: spread, straggle, stretch, trail

spray[1] *n* **1** *covered with a fine spray*: drizzle, foam, froth, jet, mist, moisture, shower, spindrift, spume **2** *a pine-scented bathroom spray*: aerosol, atomizer, sprinkler, vaporizer
 ♦ *v* diffuse, disperse, disseminate *formal*, drench, gush, shower, spatter, spout, sprinkle

spray[2] *n* bouquet, branch, corsage, garland, nosegay, posy, sprig, wreath

spread *v* **1** *fires spread over a wide area*: advance, broaden, cover, develop, escalate, expand, extend, fan out, grow, grow/become bigger, increase, mushroom, open (out), proliferate, spill over, sprawl, stretch, swell, unfold, unfurl, unroll, widen **2** *spread the news*: advertise, broadcast, circulate, communicate, diffuse, disseminate *formal*, distribute, get round, make known, make public, promulgate *formal*, propagate, publicize, publish, radiate, scatter, strew, transmit **3** *spread the bread with butter*: apply, coat, cover, layer, put on, smear
 ✗ **1** close, fold **2** suppress
 ♦ *n* **1** *a large spread of land*: compass, expanse, extent, reach, span, stretch, sweep **2** *the spread of knowledge*: advance, broadcasting, communication, development, diffusion, dispersion, dissemination *formal*, distribution, escalation, expansion, increase, mushrooming, proliferation, propagation, transmission **3** *put on a wonderful spread*: banquet, blow-out *colloq*, dinner, dinner party, feast, large meal, party, repast *formal*, treat

spree *n* bender *colloq*, binge *colloq*, bout, carouse, debauch, fling, orgy, razzle *colloq*, razzle-dazzle *colloq*, revel, splurge *colloq*

sprig *n* bough, branch, shoot, spray, stem, twig

sprightly *adj* active, agile, airy, animated, blithe, brisk, cheerful, energetic, frolicsome, hearty, jaunty, light-hearted, lively, nimble, perky *colloq*, playful, spirited, spry, vivacious
 ✗ doddering, inactive, lifeless

spring *v* **1** *lambs springing around the field*: bounce, bound, hop, jump, leap, vault **2** *his inspiration springs from traditional music*: appear, arise, come, derive, descend, develop, emanate, emerge, grow, issue, originate, proceed, sprout, start, stem **3** *spring the news on someone*: present without warning, reveal suddenly, tell unexpectedly
 ♦ *n* **1** *she gives a spring and runs towards him*: bounce, bound, hop, jump, leap **2** *the old sofa has lost its spring*: bounciness, buoyancy, elasticity, flexibility, give, resilience, springiness **3** *he walked away with a spring in his step*: animation, briskness, cheerfulness, energy, light-heartedness, liveliness, spirit **4** *the new school was a spring of hope for the community*: basis, beginning, cause, fountainhead, origin, root, source, wellhead, wellspring **5** *took water from a spring*: geyser, source, spa, well, wellhead, wellspring
 ▶ **spring up** appear suddenly, come into being, come into existence, develop, grow, mushroom, proliferate, shoot up, sprout up

springy *adj* bouncy, buoyant, elastic, flexible, resilient, rubbery, spongy, stretchy, tensible, tensile
 ✗ hard, rigid, stiff

sprinkle *v* dot, dust, pepper, powder, scatter, shower, spatter, splash, spray, strew, trickle

sprinkling *n* admixture *formal*, dash, dusting, few, handful, scatter, scattering, smattering, sprinkle, touch, trace, trickle

sprint *v* belt *colloq*, career, dart, dash, fly, race, run, scoot *colloq*, shoot, tear, zip *colloq*

sprite *n* apparition, brownie, dryad, elf, fairy, goblin, imp, kelpie, leprechaun, naiad, nymph, pixie, pouke, puck, spirit, sylph

sprout *v* bud, come up, develop, germinate, grow, put forth, shoot, spring up

spruce *adj* chic, cool *colloq*, dapper, elegant, natty *colloq*, neat, sleek, smart, snazzy *colloq*, trim, well-dressed, well-groomed, well-turned-out
🖅 scruffy, untidy
▶ **spruce up** groom, neaten, preen, primp, smarten up, tidy (up), titivate

spry *adj* active, agile, alert, brisk, energetic, nimble, nippy *colloq*, peppy *colloq*, quick, ready, sprightly, supple
🖅 doddering, inactive, lethargic

spume *n* bubbles, effervescence, fizz, foam, froth, head, lather, suds

spunk *n* backbone *colloq*, bottle *colloq*, chutzpah, courage, gameness, grit *colloq*, guts *colloq*, heart, mettle, nerve, pluck, resolution, spirit, toughness
🖅 funk *colloq*

spur *v* drive, encourage, goad, impel, incite, induce, motivate, poke, prick, prod, prompt, propel, stimulate, urge
🖅 curb, discourage
♦ *n* encouragement, fillip, impetus, incentive, incitement, inducement, motivation, motive, prompt, stimulant, stimulus, urge
🖅 curb, discouragement, disincentive

spurious *adj* artificial, bogus, contrived, counterfeit, deceitful, fake, false, feigned, forged, fraudulent, imitation, make-believe *colloq*, mock, phoney *colloq*, pretended, pseudo *colloq*, sham, simulated, trumped-up *colloq*
🖅 authentic, genuine, real

spurn *v* cold-shoulder *colloq*, condemn, despise, disdain, disregard, ignore, look down on *colloq*, rebuff, reject, repudiate, repulse, say no to, scorn, slight, snub, turn away, turn down
🖅 accept, embrace

spurt *v* burst, erupt, gush, issue, jet, pour, shoot, spout, spray, squirt, stream, surge, well
♦ *n* 1 *a spurt of water*: eruption, gush, jet, outpouring, spray, squirt, stream, welling 2 *a spurt of activity*: burst, fit, increase, rush, spate, surge

spy *n* double agent, enemy agent, fifth columnist, foreign agent, mole *colloq*, scout, secret agent, snooper, undercover agent
♦ *v* catch sight of, descry *formal*, discern, discover, espy *formal*, glimpse, make out, notice, observe, see, spot
▶ **spy on** keep an eye on, keep tabs on, keep under surveillance, observe (closely), watch

squabble *v* argue, bicker, brawl, clash, dispute, fight, have words, quarrel, row, scrap *colloq*, set to *colloq*, wrangle
♦ *n* argument, barney *colloq*, clash,

disagreement, dispute, fight, row, scrap *colloq*, set-to *colloq*, spat, tiff *colloq*

squad *n* band, brigade, company, crew, force, gang, group, outfit, platoon, team, troop, unit

squalid *adj* 1 *living in squalid conditions*: broken-down, dilapidated, dingy, dirty, disgusting, filthy, foul, grimy, grotty *colloq*, grubby, mucky, neglected, ramshackle, repulsive, run-down, seedy, sleazy *colloq*, slovenly, sordid, uncared-for, unclean, unkempt, untidy 2 *a squalid atmosphere*: disgraceful, low, mean, nasty, obscene, offensive, repulsive, shameful, sordid, unpleasant, vile, wretched
🖅 1 attractive, clean 2 pleasant

squall *n* blow, gale, gust, hurricane, storm, tempest, wind, windstorm
♦ *v* cry, groan, howl, moan, wail, yell, yowl

squally *adj* blowy, blustery, gusty, rough, stormy, tempestuous, turbulent, wild, windy

squalor *n* decay, dinginess, dirt, dirtiness, filth, filthiness, foulness, grime, griminess, grubbiness, meanness, muckiness, neglect, sleaziness *colloq*, squalidness, uncleanness, wretchedness

squander *v* blow *slang*, consume, dissipate, expend, fritter away, lavish, misspend, misuse, scatter, spend, spend money as if it grows on trees *colloq*, spend money as if it's going out of style/fashion *colloq*, spend money like there's no tomorrow *colloq*, spend money like water *colloq*, splash out on *colloq*, splurge *colloq*, throw away, throw/pour down the drain *colloq*, waste

square *n* 1 *meet me in the square*: market square, plaza, quad *colloq*, quadrangle, town square 2 *he's a bit of a square*: conformer, conformist, conservative, conventionalist, diehard, fuddy-duddy *colloq*, (old) fogey *colloq*, stick-in-the-mud *colloq*, traditionalist
♦ *v* 1 *their evidence does not square with the facts*: agree, be compatible with, be congruous with *formal*, conform, correspond, fit, harmonize, match, reconcile, tally 2 *square the bill*: pay (up), set/put right, settle (up) 3 *your figures square with mine*: accord *formal*, balance, be compatible, be congruous *formal*, conform, correspond, even, fit, harmonize, level, make equal, match, reconcile, regulate, tally
♦ *adj* 1 *a square box*: quadrilateral, rectangular 2 *a square deal*: above-board, equitable, ethical, fair, genuine, honest, honourable, just, on the level *colloq*, straight, upright 3 *thought he was a real square*: conformist, conservative, conventionalist, diehard, fuddy-duddy *colloq*, old-fashioned, strait-laced, traditionalist

squash *v* 1 *squashed the fruit*: compress, crush, flatten, grind, jam, macerate *formal*, mash, pound, press, pulp, pulverize *formal*, smash, squeeze, squelch, stamp, trample 2 *attempts to squash the insurrection*: annihilate, crush, humiliate, put down, quash, quell, silence, suppress
🖅 1 expand, stretch

squashy *adj* mushy, pappy, pulpy, soft, spongy, squelchy, squishy, yielding
🖅 firm

squat *v* bend, crouch, hunch, kneel, sit, sit on your haunches, stoop

♦ *adj* chunky, dumpy, short, stocky, stubby, thickset

☒ lanky, slender, slim

squawk *v* cackle, croak, crow, cry, hoot, scream, screech, shriek, yelp

squeak *v* cheep, creak, peep, pipe, squeal, whine

squeal *v* **1** *teenagers squealed on showground rides:* cry, howl, scream, screech, shout, shriek, squawk, wail, yell, yelp **2** *do you know who squealed on him?:* betray, grass *slang*, inform, rat *colloq*, shop *colloq*, sneak, snitch *colloq*, split *colloq*, tell *colloq*, tell tales
♦ *n* cry, howl, scream, screech, shout, shriek, squawk, wail, yell, yelp

squeamish *adj* delicate, fastidious, finicky, nauseated, nauseous, particular, prudish, punctilious, queasy, scrupulous, sick, strait-laced

squeeze *v* **1** *squeeze his hands:* clasp, clutch, compress, crush, cuddle, embrace, enfold, grip, hold tight, hug, nip, pinch, press, pulp, squash, tighten, twist, wring **2** *squeeze into a corner:* cram, crowd, crush, force, jam, jostle, pack, push, ram, shove, squash, stuff, thrust, wedge **3** *squeeze him for money:* bleed *colloq*, extort, force, lean on *colloq*, milk, pressure, pressurize, put the screws on *colloq*, wrest, wring
♦ *n* **1** *a tight squeeze:* congestion, crowd, crush, jam, press, squash **2** *her father gave her an affectionate squeeze:* cuddle, embrace, hug

squint *adj* askew, aslant, awry, cock-eyed, crooked, indirect, oblique, off-centre, skew-whiff *colloq*

☒ straight

squirm *v* fidget, flounder, move, shift, twist, wiggle, wriggle, writhe

squirt *v* discharge, ejaculate, eject, emit, expel, gush, issue, jet, pour, shoot, spew (out), spout, spray, spurt, stream, surge, well
♦ *n* gush, jet, spray, spurt, stream, surge

stab *v* bayonet, cut, gore, injure, jab, knife, pierce, puncture, skewer, slash, spear, stick, wound
♦ *n* **1** *felt a stab in her side:* ache, pain, pang, prick, spasm, throb, twinge **2** *received a stab from a knife:* cut, gash, incision, injury, jab, puncture, slash, wound **3** *have a stab at playing the violin:* attempt, bash *colloq*, crack *colloq*, endeavour, essay *formal*, go, shot *colloq*, try, venture, whirl *colloq*

stabbing *adj* acute, painful, piercing, shooting, stinging, throbbing

stability *n* constancy, durability, firmness, regularity, reliability, secureness, solidity, soundness, steadiness, sturdiness, unchangeability, uniformity

☒ insecurity, instability, unsteadiness, weakness

stable *adj* **1** *a stable structure:* balanced, fast, firm, fixed, reliable, secure, solid, sound, static, steady, strong, sturdy, sure **2** *a stable government/ relationship:* abiding, deep-rooted, dependable, durable, enduring, established, invariable, lasting, long-lasting, permanent, reliable, unchangeable, unswerving, unwavering, well-founded **3** *the patient's condition is stable:* constant, regular, steady, unchanging, uniform

☒ **1** shaky, unstable, weak, wobbly **2** unstable **3** erratic, irregular, unstable

stack *n* **1** *stacks of dirty plates littered the floor:* accumulation, heap, hoard, load, mass, mound, pile **2** *stacks of money:* a good/great deal, a large amount, great numbers, heaps *colloq*, loads *colloq*, lot, many, masses *colloq*, oodles *colloq*, piles *colloq*, tons *colloq*
♦ *v* accumulate, amass, assemble, gather, heap, pile

stadium *n* arena, bowl, field, pitch, ring, sports field, sports ground, track

staff *n* **1** *ask one of the staff for assistance:* crew, employees, officers, personnel, team, workers, workforce **2** *carrying a wooden staff:* baton, cane, crook, crosier, crutch, pole, prop, rod, stick, truncheon, wand
♦ *v* equip, man, operate

stage *n* **1** *talks are at an early stage:* juncture, leg, level, period, phase, point, step, time **2** *performing on the stage:* apron, dais, platform, podium, rostrum, soapbox *colloq*, stand **3** *the course will provide the stage for this year's golf tournament:* arena, backdrop, background, field, realm, scene, setting, sphere
♦ *v* arrange, direct, do, engineer, give, lay on, mount, orchestrate, organize, perform, present, produce, put on, put together, stage-manage

stagger *v* **1** *staggered out of the building:* falter, hesitate, lurch, pitch, reel, rock, roll, sway, teeter, totter, waver, wobble **2** *the news staggered her:* amaze, astonish, astound, bowl over *colloq*, confound, dumbfound, flabbergast *colloq*, overwhelm, shake, shock, stun, stupefy, surprise

staggering *adj* amazing, astonishing, astounding, dramatic, mind-boggling *colloq*, shocking, stunning, stupefying, surprising, unexpected, unforeseen

stagnant *adj* **1** *stagnant water:* dirty, filthy, foul, motionless, smelly, stale, standing, still, unflowing, unhealthy **2** *a stagnant economy:* dull, inactive, lethargic, quiet, slow, sluggish, torpid

☒ **1** fresh, moving **2** busy

stagnate *v* become stagnant, decay, decline, degenerate, deteriorate, do nothing, fester, idle, languish, putrefy, rot, rust, vegetate

staid *adj* calm, composed, decorous *formal*, demure, formal, grave, prim, proper, quiet, sedate, serious, serious-minded, sober, solemn, sombre, starchy, steady, stiff

☒ adventurous, debonair, frivolous, jaunty

stain *v* **1** *she had stained the carpet with red wine:* blemish, blot, blotch, dirty, discolour, mark, soil, spot **2** *these incidents stain the reputation of our military:* besmirch *formal*, blacken, blemish, contaminate, corrupt, damage, disgrace, injure, sully, taint, tarnish **3** *the wooden floors were stained and polished:* colour, dye, paint, tinge, tint, varnish
♦ *n* **1** *covered with stains:* blemish, blot, blotch, discoloration, mark, smear, smudge, splodge, spot **2** *decent woman with no stain on her character:* blemish, disgrace, dishonour, mark, shame, slur, taint

stake[1] *n* pale, paling, picket, pole, post, rod, spike, standard, stick
♦ *v* **1** *staked the tomato plants:* brace, fasten, hold (up), prop (up), secure, support, tether, tie, tie up

2 *stake a claim:* declare, demand, establish, lay claim to, put in, requisition *formal*, state
▶ **stake out 1** *staked out their plot:* define, delimit, demarcate, mark out, outline, reserve, stake off **2** *photographers who stake out her London home:* keep an eye on, survey, watch

stake² *n* **1** *the consortium retained a stake in the company:* claim, concern, (financial) interest, investment, involvement, share **2** *a £20 stake:* ante *colloq*, bet, pledge, wager **3** *the leadership stakes:* competition, contest, prize, race
♦ *v* ante *colloq*, bet, chance, hazard, pledge, risk, venture, wager

stale *adj* **1** *stale bread:* dry, fusty, (gone) off *colloq*, hard, hardened, mouldy, musty, old, sour **2** *it has become a stale joke:* banal, clichéed, cliché-ridden, commonplace, corny, flat, hackneyed, insipid, jaded, over-familiar, overused, platitudinous *formal*, run of the mill *colloq*, stereotyped, stock, tired, trite, uninspired, unoriginal, worn-out
☒ **1** crisp, fresh **2** imaginative, new, original

stalemate *n* blockade, deadlock, draw, halt, impasse, stand-off, standstill, tie, zugzwang
☒ progress

stalk¹ *n* branch, peduncle *technical*, petiole, shoot, stem, trunk, twig

stalk² *v* **1** *stalk a person/an animal:* chase, follow, give chase, haunt, hunt, pursue, shadow, tail, track, track down, trail **2** *pushes past me and stalks off down the street:* march, pace, step, stride, walk

stall¹ *v* beat about the bush *colloq*, defer, delay, drag your feet *colloq*, equivocate, hedge, hold up, obstruct, play for time, postpone, put off, put on ice *colloq*, put on the back burner *colloq*, stonewall, temporize

stall² *n* **1** *a stall selling cakes:* booth, counter, kiosk, stand, table **2** *a cattle stall:* compartment, coop, cubicle, enclosure, pen

stalwart *adj* **1** *a stalwart supporter of the team:* committed, dependable, determined, devoted, faithful, indomitable, intrepid, loyal, reliable, resolute, staunch, steadfast, steady, supportive, trusty, valiant, vigorous **2** *a stalwart sportsperson:* athletic, brawny, burly, hardy, muscular, robust, rugged, stout, strapping, strong, sturdy, vigorous
☒ **1** disloyal, unfaithful **2** feeble, timid, weak

stamina *n* endurance, energy, force, fortitude *formal*, grit *colloq*, indefatigability, power, resilience, resistance, staying power, strength, vigour
☒ weakness

stammer *v* babble, falter, gibber, hesitate, lisp, mumble, splutter, stumble, stutter
♦ *n* speech defect, speech impediment, stutter

stamp *v* **1** *stamped on the insects:* crush, mash, pound, pulp, squash, trample, tread **2** *stamped their logo on the documents:* brand, emboss, engrave, fix, impress, imprint, inscribe, label, mark, print
♦ *n* **1** *marked with a stamp to show its origin:* attestation *formal*, authorization, character, hallmark, impression, imprint, label, mark, print, seal, signature, tag **2** *others of her stamp:* brand, breed, cast, character, cut, description, fashion, form, kind, mould, quality, sort, type, variety

▶ **stamp out** crush, destroy, eliminate, end, eradicate, extinguish, extirpate *formal*, quash, quell, scotch, suppress

stampede *n* charge, dash, flight, onrush, rout, rush, scattering, sprint
♦ *v* charge, dash, flee, fly, gallop, race, run, rush, scatter, shoot, sprint, tear

stance *n* angle, attitude, bearing, carriage, deportment, line, opinion, point of view, policy, position, posture, slant, stand, standpoint, viewpoint

stanch *v* arrest, block, check, dam, halt, plug, stay, stem, stop
☒ increase, promote

---

stanch or *staunch*? In the sense of 'to stop the flow of', either form is correct, but *staunch* is the commoner: *staunched the flow of blood from the wound; staunch the decline of royal authority; This helped to staunch the Danish invasion.* As an adjective, the form to use is *staunch*, meaning 'loyal, trusty, steadfast': *a staunch ally.*

---

stand *v* **1** *please stand:* be erect, be on your feet, be upright, get on/to your feet, get up, rise, rise to your feet, stand up, straighten up **2** *stand the wardrobe over here:* erect, locate, place, position, put, set, station, up-end **3** *I can't stand it:* abide *formal*, bear, brook, cope with, endure, live with, put up with, stomach *colloq*, suffer, tolerate, weather, withstand **4** *the offer still stands:* be in effect, be in force, be valid, exist, hold, obtain *formal*, prevail *formal*, remain
♦ *n* **1** *placed the pot on a stand:* base, frame, pedestal, rack, shelf, support **2** *set up a stand at the exhibition:* booth, counter, stall, table **3** *take a tough stand:* angle, attitude, line, opinion, point of view, policy, position, slant, stance, standpoint, viewpoint
▶ **stand by** adhere to, back, champion, defend, hold to, stand up for, stick by, stick up for, uphold
☒ let down
▶ **stand down** abdicate, give up, quit, resign, retire, step down, withdraw
☒ join
▶ **stand for 1** *what does that symbol stand for?:* betoken *formal*, denote, indicate, mean, represent, signify, symbolize **2** *will not stand for such nonsense:* allow, bear, brook, endure, put up with, stomach *colloq*, tolerate
▶ **stand in for** cover for, deputize for, hold the fort for *colloq*, replace, substitute for, take the place of, understudy
▶ **stand out** be conspicuous, be noticeable, be obvious, catch the eye *colloq*, show, stick out, stick out a mile *colloq*
▶ **stand up 1** *the students stood up when the tutor came into the room:* get to your feet, get up, rise, rise to your feet, stand **2** *that argument simply doesn't stand up:* cohere, hold up, hold water, stand, wash *colloq*
▶ **stand up for** champion, defend, fight for, protect, side with, stand by, stick up for, support, uphold
☒ attack
▶ **stand up to** brave, challenge, confront, defy, endure, face, face up to, oppose, resist, withstand
☒ give in to

standard *n* **1** *the industry standard:* archetype *formal*, average, benchmark, example, exemplar *formal*, gauge, grade, guide, guideline, level, measure, model, norm, paradigm *formal*, pattern, principle, quality, requirement, rule, sample, specification, touchstone, type, yardstick **2** *will not compromise my standards:* code, ethic, ideal, moral, principle, scruple **3** *the regimental standard flew overhead:* banner, colours, ensign, flag, gonfalon, pennant, pennon, streamer, vexillum *technical*
♦ *adj* accepted, approved, basic, conventional, customary, definitive, established, fixed, habitual, normal, official, ordinary, orthodox, popular, prevailing, recognized, regular, set, staple, stock, typical, usual
🗲 abnormal, irregular, unusual

standardize *v* equalize, homogenize, mass-produce, normalize, regiment, regularize, stereotype, systematize
🗲 differentiate

stand-in *n* delegate, deputy, locum, proxy, representative, second, second-in-command, substitute, surrogate, understudy

standing *n* **1** *enhanced his standing as a manager:* eminence, position, rank, reputation, repute, seniority, station, status **2** *friend of over thirty years' standing:* continuance, duration, existence
♦ *adj* **1** *in a standing position:* erect, on your feet, perpendicular, up-ended, upright, vertical **2** *a standing joke in our household:* fixed, lasting, permanent, perpetual, regular, repeated
🗲 **1** horizontal, lying **2** temporary

stand-off *n* blockade, deadlock, halt, impasse, standstill

standoffish *adj* aloof, cold, cool, detached, distant, remote, reserved, unapproachable, uncommunicative, unfriendly, unsociable, withdrawn
🗲 approachable, friendly

standpoint *n* angle, perspective, point of view, position, slant, stance, station, vantage point, viewpoint

standstill *n* cessation *formal*, dead stop, deadlock, halt, hold-up, impasse, jam, log-jam, lull, pause, rest, stalemate, stop, stoppage
🗲 advance, progress

staple *adj* basic, chief, essential, foremost, fundamental, important, indispensable, key, main, major, necessary, primary, principal, standard, vital
🗲 dispensable, minor

star *n* **1** *the stars in the sky:* asteroid, heavenly/celestial body, moon, orb, planet, satellite, sphere, sun **2** *one of Hollywood's biggest stars:* big name *colloq*, big shot *colloq*, bigwig *colloq*, celebrity, household name *colloq*, idol, lead, leading lady, leading light *colloq*, leading man, luminary, personage, principal, superstar
♦ *adj* brilliant, celebrated, famous, illustrious, leading, major, paramount, pre-eminent, principal, prominent, talented, well-known
🗲 minor

Types of star include:
nova, supernova, pulsar, quasar, falling-star, shooting-star, meteor, comet, Halley's comet, red giant, supergiant, white dwarf, red dwarf, brown dwarf, neutron star, Pole Star, Polaris, North Star. See also **constellation**

starchy *adj* ceremonious, conventional, formal, prim, punctilious, stiff, strait-laced, stuffy
🗲 informal

stare *v* gape, gawk, gawp, gaze, glare, goggle, look, watch
♦ *n* gawp, gaze, glare, look

stark *adj* **1** *faced with the stark reality:* bald, bare, blunt, grim, harsh, plain, severe, simple, unadorned, undecorated, unembellished **2** *a stark landscape:* austere, bare, barren, bleak, depressing, desolate, dreary, empty, forsaken, gloomy, grim, harsh, severe **3** *stark inequality:* absolute, arrant, complete, consummate *formal*, downright, flagrant, out-and-out, pure, sheer, thorough, total, unmitigated, unqualified, utter
♦ *adv* absolutely, altogether, clean, completely, entirely, quite, totally, utterly, wholly
🗲 mildly, slightly

stark-naked *adj* in the altogether *colloq*, in the buff *colloq*, in the nude, in the raw *colloq*, in your birthday suit *colloq*, naked, nude, starkers *colloq*, stripped, unclad *formal*, undressed
🗲 clothed, dressed

start *v* **1** *it started early:* activate, appear, arise, begin, bring/come into being, bring/come into existence, commence *formal*, create, depart, embark on/upon, establish, fire away *colloq*, get cracking *colloq*, get going, get things moving *colloq*, get under way, inaugurate, initiate, instigate, institute, kick off *colloq*, launch, leave, open, set off, set out, set the ball rolling *colloq*, set up, trigger (off), turn on **2** *started at the loud noise:* flinch, jerk, jump, leap, recoil, shrink, twitch, wince
🗲 **1** end, finish, stop
♦ *n* **1** *waited patiently for the start:* beginning, commencement *formal*, dawn, emergence, foundation, inauguration, inception *formal*, initiation, kick-off *colloq*, launch, onset, opening, origin, origination, outset **2** *woke up with a start:* convulsion, fit, flinch, jerk, jump, leap, spasm, twitch, wince
🗲 **1** end, finish, stop

startle *v* agitate, alarm, amaze, astonish, astound, disturb, frighten, make you jump, perturb *formal*, scare, shock, surprise, unsettle, upset
🗲 calm

startling *adj* alarming, astonishing, astounding, dramatic, electrifying, extraordinary, shocking, staggering, sudden, surprising, unexpected, unforeseen
🗲 boring, calming, ordinary

starvation *n* death, extreme hunger, famine, fasting, hunger, malnutrition, undernourishment
🗲 excess, plenty

starve *v* deny, deprive, die, diet, faint, fast, hunger, perish
🗲 feed, gorge

starving *adj* dying, faint, famished, ravenous, underfed, undernourished, (very) hungry

stash *v* cache, closet, conceal, hide, hoard, lay up, salt away *colloq*, save up, secrete *formal*, stockpile, store, stow

⊟ bring out, uncover
♦ *n* accumulation, cache, collection, fund, heap, hoard, mass, pile, reserve, reservoir, stockpile, store

state *n* 1 *in a terrible state:* circumstances, condition, position, predicament, shape, situation 2 *agreement between neighbouring states:* country, federation, government, kingdom, land, nation, realm, republic, territory 3 *got into a state about her results:* bother, flap *colloq*, fluster *colloq*, panic, plight, predicament, tizzy *colloq* 4 *relied on help from the state:* administration, authorities, council, Establishment, government, parliament 5 *the monarch travelled in state:* ceremony, dignity, glory, grandeur, majesty, pomp, splendour
♦ *v* affirm, announce, articulate, assert, aver *formal*, communicate, declare, disclose, divulge, express, formulate, make known, present, proclaim, promulgate *formal*, put, report, reveal, say, set out, specify, tell, utter, voice
♦ *adj* 1 *a state banquet:* ceremonial, formal, official, pompous, stately 2 *state funding:* governmental, national, parliamentary, public
⊟ 2 commercial, private

stately *adj* august *formal*, ceremonial, ceremonious, deliberate, dignified, elegant, glorious, graceful, grand, imperial, imposing, impressive, lofty, magnificent, majestic, measured, noble, pompous, regal, royal, solemn, splendid
⊟ informal, unimpressive

statement *n* account, affirmation *formal*, announcement, assertion, averment *formal*, bulletin, communication, communiqué, declaration, disclosure, divulgence, presentation, proclamation, promulgation *formal*, report, revelation, testimony, utterance

statesman, stateswoman *n* diplomat, elder statesman, GOM, grand old man *colloq*, leader, politician

static *adj* at a standstill, changeless, constant, fixed, immobile, inert, motionless, resting, stable, stationary, steady, still, unchanging, undeviating, unmoving, unvarying
⊟ dynamic, mobile, varying

station *n* 1 *a bus/railway station:* exchange, fare-stage, halt, park-and-ride, stop, stopping-place, terminus 2 *went to the local police station:* base, depot, headquarters, office 3 *your station in life:* class, grade, level, position, rank, standing, status 4 *took up stations along the road:* place, place of duty, position, post
♦ *v* establish, garrison, install, locate, post, send, set

stationary *adj* at a standstill, constant, fixed, immobile, inert, moored, motionless, parked, resting, standing, static, still, unmoving
⊟ active, mobile, moving

stationery

Items of stationery include:
account book, address book, adhesive tape, blotter, bulldog clip, calendar, carbon paper, card index, cartridge ribbon, cash book, clipboard, computer disk, copying paper, correcting paper, correction fluid, correction ribbon, desk-diary, diary, divider, document folder, document wallet, drawing pin, dry-transfer lettering, elastic band, envelope, brown manila envelope, reply-paid envelope,

self-seal envelope, window envelope, eraser, expanding file, file, file tab, filing tray, Filofax®, flip chart, floppy disk, folder, graph paper, headed notepaper, index card, ink, Jiffy bag®, label, lever arch file, marker, memo pad, notepaper, paper clip, paper fastener, paper knife, pen, pencil, pencil-sharpener, personal organizer, pin, pocket calculator, pocket folder, Post-it note®, printer label, printer paper, printer ribbon, reinforcement ring, ring binder, rubber, rubber band, rubber stamp, ruler, scissors, Sellotape®, shorthand notebook, spiral notebook, stamp pad, staple, suspension file, tape dispenser, Tipp-Ex®, toner, treasury tag, typewriter ribbon, wall chart, writing paper. See also **paper**

statue *n* bronze, bust, carving, effigy, figure, figurine, head, idol, image, representation, sculpture, statuette

statuesque *adj* dignified, handsome, imposing, impressive, majestic, regal, stately
⊟ small

stature *n* 1 *of small stature:* height, size, tallness 2 *China's growing stature as an economic and military power:* consequence, eminence, fame, importance, prestige, prominence, rank, renown, reputation, standing, weight
⊟ 2 unimportance

status *n* 1 *raised to the status of director:* class, condition, degree, grade, level, position, rank, standing, state, station 2 *has a high status within the group:* consequence, distinction, eminence, importance, prestige, reputation, weight
⊟ 2 insignificance, unimportance

statute *n* act, decree, edict, enactment, interlocution *formal*, law, ordinance, regulation, rule, ukase

staunch[1] *adj* committed, constant, dependable, devoted, faithful, firm, hearty, loyal, reliable, resolute, sound, steadfast, stout, strong, sure, true, trustworthy, trusty
⊟ unfaithful, unreliable, weak

staunch[2] *v* arrest, block, check, halt, plug, stay, stem, stop
⊟ increase, promote

staunch or *stanch*? See panel at **stanch**

stave
▶ **stave off** avert, avoid, deflect, fend off, foil, keep at bay, keep back, parry, repel, repulse, turn aside, ward off
⊟ cause, encourage

stay[1] *v* 1 *she stayed there a while:* abide *formal*, keep, linger, remain, stay put, tarry *formal* 2 *stay in a hotel:* be accommodated at, board, dwell *formal*, halt, live, lodge, pause, put up, reside *formal*, rest, settle, sojourn *formal*, stop, take a room at, visit 3 *stay judgement:* adjourn, defer, delay, halt, postpone, prorogue *formal*, put off, reprieve, suspend 4 *stay your anger:* arrest, block, check, control, curb, halt, hinder, obstruct, prevent, restrain, stop, suppress
♦ *n* 1 *enjoy your stay!:* holiday, sojourn *formal*, stopover, vacation, visit 2 *a stay of execution:* deferment, delay, postponement, remission *formal*, reprieve, suspension

stay² *n* brace, buttress, prop, reinforcement, shoring, stanchion, support

steadfast *adj* constant, dedicated, dependable, established, faithful, firm, fixed, implacable, intent, loyal, persevering, reliable, resolute, single-minded, stable, staunch, steady, stout-hearted, sturdy, unfaltering, unflinching, unswerving, unwavering
☒ unreliable, wavering, weak

steady *adj* **1** *hold the camera steady:* balanced, firm, fixed, immovable, motionless, poised, secure, stable, unmoving, well-balanced **2** *make steady progress:* ceaseless, consistent, constant, even, gradual, incessant *formal,* perpetual, persistent, regular, unbroken, unchanging, unfaltering, uniform, uninterrupted, unremitting *formal,* unvariable, unvarying, unwavering **3** *steady nerves:* calm, controlled, imperturbable, self-controlled, settled, stable, still, unexcitable, unexcited, unflappable *colloq,* well-balanced **4** *a steady friend:* balanced, dependable, reliable, sensible, serious, sober, steadfast, trustworthy **5** *a steady boyfriend:* constant, customary, established, habitual, regular, usual
☒ 1 shaky, unsteady, wobbly **2** irregular, uneven, variable, wavering **3** excitable, worried **4** unreliable
♦ *v* **1** *he steadied the ladder:* balance, brace, fix, secure, stabilize, support **2** *he steadied his nerves:* check, compose, control, relax, restrain, soothe, still, subdue, tranquillize

steal *v* **1** *steal the goods:* appropriate *formal,* embezzle, filch, go/walk off with *colloq,* have your fingers in the till *colloq,* heist *slang,* help yourself to *colloq,* knock off *colloq,* knock up *colloq,* lift *colloq,* make off/away with *colloq,* misappropriate, nick *colloq,* nobble *colloq,* peculate *formal,* pilfer, pinch *colloq,* poach, pocket, purloin *formal,* rip off *colloq,* run off with *colloq,* shoplift, snaffle *colloq,* snatch, swipe, take, thieve **2** *steal into the room:* creep, slide, slink, slip, slither, sneak, tiptoe
☒ 1 give back, return
♦ *n* bargain, discount, giveaway, good buy, reduction, snip *colloq,* special offer, value for money

stealing *n* appropriation *formal,* break-in, burglary, embezzlement, filching *colloq,* larceny, misappropriation, nicking *colloq,* peculation *formal,* pilferage, pilfering, pinching *colloq,* piracy, plagiarism, poaching, purloining *formal,* rip-off *colloq,* robbery, shoplifting, stick-up job *colloq,* theft, thievery, thieving

stealth *n* covertness, furtiveness, secrecy, slyness, sneakiness, stealthiness, surreptitiousness, unobtrusiveness

stealthy *adj* clandestine *formal,* covert, cunning, furtive, quiet, secret, secretive, sly, sneaky, surreptitious, underhand, unobtrusive

steam *n* **1** *the room was filled with steam:* condensation, dampness, mist, moisture, vapour **2** *run out of steam:* eagerness, energy, enthusiasm, liveliness, stamina, vigour
▶ **steam up** become covered with mist, become covered with steam, fog up, mist up

steamy *adj* **1** *a steamy jungle:* close, damp, hazy, hot, humid, misty, muggy, steaming, stewy, sticky, sultry, sweaty, sweltering, vaporous,

vapourish, vapoury **2** *a steamy romance:* amorous, blue *colloq,* erotic, lustful, passionate, raunchy *colloq,* seductive, sensual, sexy *colloq*

steel *v* brace, fortify *formal,* harden, nerve, prepare, toughen
☒ weaken

steely *adj* **1** *steely eyes:* blue-grey, grey, steel-blue, steel-coloured **2** *a steely resolve to succeed:* determined, firm, hard, harsh, inflexible, merciless, pitiless, resolute, strong, unyielding

steep¹ *adj* **1** *a steep slope:* abrupt, acclivitous *formal,* declivitous *formal,* perpendicular, precipitous, sharp, sheer, sudden, vertical **2** *their fees are too steep:* costly, dear, excessive, exorbitant, expensive, extortionate, extreme, high, over the top *colloq,* overpriced, stiff, unreasonable
☒ 1 gentle, gradual **2** low, moderate

steep² *v* drench, imbrue, imbue, immerse, infuse, macerate, marinate, moisten, pickle, saturate, seethe, soak, souse, submerge, suffuse

steeple *n* belfry, spire, tower, turret

steer *v* conduct, control, cox, direct, drive, govern, guide, lead, navigate, pilot, usher

stem¹ *n* branch, peduncle *technical,* shoot, stalk, stock, trunk
♦ *v* arise, come, derive, develop, emanate, flow, issue, originate, spring
☒ cause, give rise to

stem² *v* arrest, block, check, contain, curb, dam, halt, oppose, resist, restrain, stanch, staunch, stop
☒ encourage

stench *n* mephitis *formal,* miasma *formal,* niff *slang,* odour, pong *colloq,* reek, smell, stink, whiff

step *n* **1** *take three steps forward:* footstep, pace, stride **2** *saw her steps in the snow:* footprint, impression, print, trace, track **3** *taking steps to calm the situation:* act, action, course of action, deed, effort, manoeuvre, measure, move **4** *a further step towards finding a solution:* advance, development, grade, level, phase, procedure, proceeding, process, progression, stage **5** *climb up the steps:* rung, stair
♦ *v* advance, move, pace, progress, stamp, stride, tread, walk
▶ **step down** abdicate, give up your post, leave, quit, resign, retire, stand down, withdraw
▶ **step in** arbitrate, intercede, interfere, interrupt, intervene, involve yourself in, mediate
▶ **step up** accelerate, augment *formal,* boost, build up, escalate, increase, intensify, speed up
☒ decrease

stereotype *n* cliché, convention, conventional/standardized image, fixed set of ideas, formula, hackneyed expression, model, mould, pattern
♦ *v* categorize, conventionalize, formalize, label, mass-produce, pigeonhole, standardize, tag, typecast
☒ differentiate

stereotyped *adj* banal, clichéed, cliché-ridden, conventional, corny, hackneyed, mass-produced, overused, platitudinous *formal,* stale, standard, standardized, stereotypical, stock, threadbare, tired, trite, unoriginal
☒ different, unconventional

sterile adj **1** *using sterile instruments:* aseptic, clean, disinfected, germ-free, germless, sterilized, uncontaminated, uninfected **2** *the farmland has become sterile:* arid, bare, barren, fruitless, ineffectual *formal,* infecund *formal,* infertile, unfruitful, unproductive, unprofitable, unyielding, useless
🗷 **1** septic **2** fertile, fruitful

sterility n **1** *sterility of the needles:* asepsis *technical,* cleanness, purity **2** *the illness can cause sterility:* atocia *technical,* barrenness, impotence, infertility, unfecundity *formal,* unfruitfulness, unproductiveness
🗷 **1** contamination, infection **2** fertility, fruitfulness

sterilize v **1** *sterilized the area thoroughly:* clean, cleanse, disinfect, fumigate, purify **2** *a vet sterilized the animal:* castrate, doctor, geld, make infertile, neuter, spay
🗷 **1** contaminate, infect

sterling adj authentic, excellent, first-class, genuine, great, pure, real, sound, standard, superlative, true, worthy
🗷 false, poor

stern¹ adj austere, authoritarian, cruel, demanding, draconian, exacting, forbidding, grim, hard, harsh, inflexible, relentless, rigid, rigorous, severe, sombre, stark, strict, stringent, tough, tyrannical, unrelenting, unsparing, unyielding
🗷 gentle, kind, lenient, mild

stern² n back, poop, rear, tail, tail end
🗷 bow

stew v **1** *stew the meat:* boil, braise, casserole, cook, simmer **2** *let him stew about it for a while:* agonize, fret, fuss, sweat, worry
♦ n **1** *prepared a stew for dinner:* casserole, chowder, daube, goulash, hash, lobscouse, pot-au-feu, ragout **2** *he was in a stew:* bother, fluster, tizzy *colloq*

steward n air hostess, attendant, butler, caretaker, chamberlain, custodian, factor, flight attendant, homme d'affaires, maître d'hôtel, major-domo, manciple, marshal, official, overseer, supervisor, waiter, waitress

stick¹ v **1** *stuck a needle into her arm:* insert, jab, penetrate, pierce, poke, prick, puncture, push, spear, stab, thrust **2** *stick the pieces together:* adhere, affix, attach, bind, bond, cement, fasten, fix, fuse, glue, gum, hold, join, paste, pin, secure, solder, tack, tape, weld **3** *stick your things on the table for now:* deposit, drop, lay, locate, place, position, put, set (down), site **4** *the car's stuck in the mud:* come to a halt, come to a standstill, fix, get bogged down, jam, stop, trap **5** *stick with us:* abide *formal,* carry on, continue, dwell *formal,* endure, last, linger, persist, remain, rest, stay **6** *I can't stick that sort of music:* abide *formal,* bear, endure, put up with, stand, stomach *colloq,* tolerate
▶ **stick at 1** *decided to stick at the job for a while:* continue, keep at, persevere, persist, plug away *colloq* **2** *he would stick at nothing to achieve his ambitions:* balk, demur *formal,* doubt, draw the line at *colloq,* hesitate, pause, recoil, scruple, shrink from, stop at
▶ **stick by** back, champion, defend, side with, stand by, stand up for, stick up for, support
🗷 let down

▶ **stick out 1** *he really sticks out in those clothes:* be conspicuous, be noticeable, be obvious **2** *a nail was sticking out of the wall:* bulge, extend, jut out, poke out, project, protrude
▶ **stick up for** champion, defend, fight for, protect, speak up for, stand by, stand up for, support, take the side/part of
🗷 attack

stick² n **1** *gather dry sticks:* branch, switch, twig **2** *give a person stick:* abuse, blame, criticism, flak *colloq,* hostility, punishment, reproof
🗷 **2** praise

stickiness n adhesiveness, glueyness, glutinousness *formal,* goo *colloq,* gooeyness *colloq,* gumminess, syrupiness, tackiness, viscidity *formal*

stick-in-the-mud adj antediluvian, antiquated, conservative, fogeyish, fossilized, fuddy-duddy, outmoded, square *colloq,* unadventurous, Victorian
🗷 adventurous, modern
♦ n back number *colloq,* conservative, fossil *colloq,* fuddy-duddy, (old) fogey *colloq*

stickler n fanatic, fusspot, maniac, nut *colloq,* pedant, perfectionist, precisionist, purist

sticky adj **1** *a sticky mess on the kitchen floor:* adhesive, gluey, glutinous *formal,* gooey *colloq,* gummed, gummy, tacky, viscoid *formal,* viscous **2** *a sticky situation:* awkward, delicate, difficult, embarrassing, sensitive, thorny, tricky, unpleasant **3** *hot, sticky weather:* clammy, close, humid, muggy, oppressive, sultry, sweltering
🗷 **1** dry **2** easy **3** cool, fresh

stiff adj **1** *a piece of stiff cardboard:* firm, hard, hardened, inelastic, inflexible, rigid, solid, solidified, unbending, unyielding **2** *my muscles were stiff:* aching, arthritic, rheumatic, rheumaticky, tense, tight **3** *a stiff challenge:* arduous, awkward, challenging, demanding, difficult, exacting, hard, harsh, laborious, rigorous, tiring, tough **4** *a stiff, unsmiling character:* awkward, ceremonial, ceremonious, chilly, cold, decorous *formal,* formal, pompous, priggish, prim, reserved, stand-offish **5** *stiff penalties for carrying knives:* austere, demanding, draconian, drastic, extreme, hard, harsh, rigorous, severe, strict, stringent, tough **6** *a stiff breeze:* brisk, forceful, fresh, strong, vigorous **7** *a stiff drink:* alcoholic, intoxicating, strong
🗷 **1** flexible, supple **3** easy **4** friendly, informal, relaxed **6** light

stiffen v **1** *beat the mixture until it stiffens:* coagulate, congeal, harden, jell, set, solidify, thicken **2** *stiffened the resin sculptures with fibreglass:* brace, fortify *formal,* harden, reinforce, steel, strengthen

stiff-necked adj arrogant, contumacious *formal,* haughty, obstinate, opinionated, proud, stubborn, uncompromising
🗷 flexible, humble

stifle v **1** *stifle opposition:* check, crush, curb, dampen, deaden, extinguish, hold back, hush, keep in, muffle, quash, quell, repress, restrain, silence, smother, subdue, suppress **2** *he stifled his victim with a pillow:* asphyxiate, smother, suffocate
🗷 **1** encourage

stigma *n* blemish, blot, brand, disgrace, dishonour, mark, shame, slur, spot, stain, taint
🔁 credit, honour

stigmatize *v* blemish, brand, condemn, denounce, discredit, disgrace, label, mark, shame, stain, vilify *formal*, vilipend *formal*
🔁 praise

still *adj* 1 *they kept perfectly still for the photograph*: immobile, inactive, inert, lifeless, motionless, sedentary, stagnant, static, stationary, stock-still, unmoving, unstirring 2 *a still afternoon*: calm, hushed, mild, noiseless, peaceful, quiet, restful, serene, silent, smooth, tranquil, undisturbed, unruffled
🔁 1 active, moving 2 agitated, disturbed, noisy
♦ *v* abate *formal*, allay, appease *formal*, assuage *formal*, calm, hush, moderate, pacify, quiet, quieten, restrain, settle, silence, smooth, soothe, subdue, tranquillize
🔁 agitate, stir up
♦ *adv* 1 *they are still married*: until now, up to the present time, up to this time 2 *Jack still managed to win*: even so, for all that, however, in spite of this/that, nevertheless, nonetheless
♦ *n* calm, hush, noiselessness, peace, peacefulness, quiet, quietness, serenity, silence, stillness, tranquillity
🔁 agitation, disturbance, noise

stilted *adj* artificial, constrained, forced, laboured, stiff, unnatural, wooden
🔁 flowing, fluent, natural, relaxed

stimulant *n* analeptic *technical*, pep pill *colloq*, pick-me-up *colloq*, restorative, reviver, tonic

stimulate *v* animate, arouse, encourage, excite, fan, fillip, fire, goad, impel, incite, induce, inflame, inspire, instigate, kindle, motivate, prompt, provoke, quicken, rouse, spur, trigger (off), urge, whip up *colloq*
🔁 discourage, hinder, prevent

stimulating *adj* exciting, exhilarating, galvanic, inspiring, interesting, intriguing, provocative, provoking, rousing, stirring, thought-provoking
🔁 boring, depressing, uninspiring

stimulus *n* drive, encouragement, fillip, goad, impetus, incentive, incitement, inducement, jog, jolt, prod, provocation, push, shot in the arm *colloq*, spur
🔁 discouragement

sting *v* 1 *stung by a scorpion*: bite, hurt, injure, prick, wound 2 *her eyes stung as she chopped the onions*: burn, irritate, smart, tingle 3 *the players were stung by the criticism*: annoy, distress, exasperate, grieve, hurt, incense, needle, nettle, offend, pain, provoke, torment, upset, wound 4 *stung them for their life savings*: cheat, con *colloq*, deceive, defraud, do *colloq*, fiddle, fleece *colloq*, rip off *colloq*, swindle, take for a ride *colloq*, take to the cleaners *colloq*, trick
♦ *n* 1 *an agonizing sting on the arm*: bite, nip, pain, prick, smart, tingle, wound 2 *in time the memory lost its sting*: bite, causticity, causticness, edge, incisiveness, malice, pungency, sarcasm, sharpness, spite, viciousness

stinging *adj* aculeate(d) *formal*, burning, distressing, hurtful, injurious, irritating, offensive, smarting, tingling, urent *formal*, urticant *formal*, wounding
🔁 comforting, mild, soothing

stingy *adj* mean, mingy *colloq*, miserly, niggardly, parsimonious *formal*, penny-pinching *colloq*, penurious *formal*, tight-fisted *colloq*
🔁 generous, liberal

stink *v* 1 *that place really stinks*: hum *colloq*, pong *colloq*, reek, smell 2 *the whole set-up stinks*: be awful, be bad, be despicable, be nasty, be unpleasant
♦ *n* 1 *what a stink!*: bad/foul smell, malodour *formal*, niff *slang*, odour, pong *colloq*, smell, stench 2 *the controversial exhibition caused a stink*: bother, commotion, flap *colloq*, fluster, furore, fuss, hassle *colloq*, hoo-ha *colloq*, row, song and dance *colloq*, stir, trouble

stinker *n* 1 *that exam was a real stinker*: horror, problem, shocker 2 *described her ex as a stinker*: creep, cur, rat *slang*, rotter, scoundrel, swine *slang*

stinking *adj* awful, bad, contemptible, disgusting, foul, nasty, rotten, unpleasant, vile
🔁 good, pleasant

stint *n* bit, period, quota, share, shift, spell, stretch, time, turn
♦ *v* begrudge, economize, pinch, save, scrimp, skimp on *colloq*, withhold

stipulate *v* demand, insist on, lay down, require, set down, specify

stipulation *n* condition, demand, point, precondition *formal*, prerequisite *formal*, proviso, requirement, specification

stir *v* 1 *the leaves stirred in the breeze*: agitate, flutter, move, quiver, rouse, rustle, shake, shift, tremble, twitch 2 *stir the ingredients until combined*: beat, blend, mix, whip 3 *the audience were stirred by his performance*: affect, excite, inspire, thrill, touch
♦ *n* activity, ado, agitation, bustle, commotion, disorder, disturbance, excitement, ferment, flap *colloq*, flurry, fuss, hoo-ha *colloq*, kerfuffle *colloq*, song and dance *colloq*, tizzy *colloq*, to-do *colloq*, tumult, uproar
🔁 calm
▶ **stir up** arouse, awaken, encourage, excite, fire, galvanize, incite, inflame, inspire, instigate, kindle, prompt, provoke, rouse, spur, stimulate, waken
🔁 calm, discourage

stirring *adj* animating, dramatic, emotive, exciting, exhilarating, heady, impassioned, inspiring, intoxicating, lively, moving, rousing, spirited, stimulating, thrilling
🔁 calming, uninspiring

stitch *v* darn, embroider, hem, mend, repair, seam, sew, tack

stock *n* 1 *a wide range of stock*: commodities, goods, merchandise, wares 2 *a stock of fruits and vegetables*: accumulation, amassment, assortment, cache, collection, fund, heap, hoard, pile, quantity, range, repertoire, reserve, reservoir, selection, source, stockpile, store, supply, variety 3 *stocks and shares*: assets, bonds, capital, equities, funds, holding, investment, money, portfolio, securities, shares 4 *of aristocratic stock*: ancestry, background, blood, descent, extraction, family, genealogy, line, lineage, parentage, pedigree, relatives 5 *vaccinated all their stock*: animals, cattle, cows, farm animals, flocks, herds, horses, livestock, pigs, sheep

♦ *adj* average, banal, basic, clichéd, common, conventional, customary, essential, hackneyed, ordinary, overused, regular, routine, run-of-the-mill, set, standard, stereotyped, tired, traditional, trite, usual, worn-out
🗷 original, unusual
♦ *v* carry, deal in, handle, keep, market, merchandise, provide, sell, supply, trade in, traffic in
▶ **stock up** accumulate, amass, buy (up), fill (up), heap (up), hoard, lay in, provision *formal*, put aside, put away, replenish *formal*, salt away *colloq*, stack up, stash away *colloq*, stockpile, store (up)

stockpile *v* accumulate, amass, gather, heap (up), hoard, keep, pile up, put aside, put away, save, store (up)
♦ *n* accumulation, amassment, cache, fund, heap, hoard, pile, reserve, reservoir, store

stock-still *adj* immobile, inactive, inert, motionless, static, stationary, still, unmoving, unstirring

stocky *adj* broad, chunky, dumpy, mesomorphic *formal*, short, solid, squat, stubby, stumpy, sturdy, thickset
🗷 skinny, tall

stodgy *adj* 1 *stodgy food*: filling, heavy, indigestible, solid, starchy, substantial 2 *a stodgy though respected journal*: boring, dull, formal, fuddy-duddy *colloq*, heavy, laboured, leaden, solemn, spiritless, staid, stuffy, tedious, turgid, unenterprising, unexciting, unimaginative, uninspired
🗷 1 light 2 exciting, informal

stoical *adj* accepting, calm, cool, dispassionate, forbearing, impassive, imperturbable, indifferent, long-suffering, patient, philosophical, phlegmatic *formal*, resigned, self-controlled, self-disciplined, uncomplaining, unemotional, unexcitable
🗷 anxious, excitable

stoicism *n* acceptance, ataraxia *formal*, ataraxy *formal*, calmness, dispassion, fatalism, forbearance, fortitude *formal*, impassivity, imperturbability, indifference, long-suffering, patience, resignation, stolidity, unexcitability
🗷 anxiety, depression, fury

stolid *adj* apathetic, blockish, bovine, dull, heavy, impassive, indifferent, lumpish, phlegmatic *formal*, slow, solemn, unemotional, unimaginative, uninspiring, wooden
🗷 interested, lively

stomach *n* 1 *a pain in the stomach*: abdomen, belly, bread basket *slang*, gut, inside(s), tummy *colloq* 2 *he didn't have the stomach for a fight*: appetite, courage, desire, determination, guts *colloq*, inclination, liking, passion
♦ *v* abide *formal*, bear, brook, endure, put up with, stand, submit to, take, tolerate

stone *n* 1 *the beach was covered with stones*: boulder, cobble, concretion *formal*, pebble, rock 2 *precious stones*: gem, gemstone, jewel 3 *carved an inscription on the stone*: gravestone, headstone, tombstone 4 *removed the stones from the plums before making the jam*: endocarp *technical*, kernel, pip, pit, seed

stony *adj* 1 *a stony beach*: gravelly, gritty, pebbly, rocky, shingly 2 *a stony stare*: adamant, blank,

callous, chilly, cold, deadpan, expressionless, frigid, frosty, hard, heartless, hostile, icy, indifferent, inexorable, merciless, pitiless, poker-faced, severe, steely, stern, unfeeling, unforgiving, unresponsive
🗷 2 friendly, soft-hearted, warm

stooge *n* butt, cat's paw *colloq*, dupe, fall guy *colloq*, foil, henchman, lackey, pawn, puppet

stoop *v* 1 *she stooped and picked up the dog*: bend, bow, crouch, duck, hunch, incline, kneel, lean, lower, squat 2 *I can't believe he could stoop to blackmail*: descend, go so far as, go so low as, lower yourself, resort, sink
♦ *n* droop, hunching, inclination, round-shoulderedness, sag, slouch, slump

stop *v* 1 *they stopped play due to bad weather*: abandon, arrest *formal*, bring/come to an end, cease *formal*, conclude, desist *formal*, discontinue, end, finish, halt, interrupt, knock off *colloq*, leave off *colloq*, pause, quit, refrain *formal*, suspend, terminate *formal*, wind up *colloq* 2 *he managed to stop smoking after twenty years*: kick *colloq*, pack in *colloq*, quit 3 *they stopped the group from marching further*: bar, block, check, frustrate, hinder, impede, intercept, obstruct, prevent, restrain, stall, thwart 4 *they stopped the leak with old rags until the plumber arrived*: arrest, block, bung, close, cover, obstruct, plug, seal, stanch, staunch, stem, stop up 5 *they stopped at the hotel for two nights*: board, break your journey, lodge, pause, put up, rest, sojourn *formal*, stay, visit
🗷 1 begin, continue, start 2 start
♦ *n* 1 *the proceedings finally came to a stop*: cessation *formal*, close, conclusion, discontinuance *formal*, discontinuation *formal*, end, finish, halt, standstill, stoppage, termination *formal* 2 *I'm getting off at the next stop*: bus stop, fare stage, halt, station, stopping-place, terminus 3 *an unscheduled overnight stop*: break, pause, rest, sojourn *formal*, stage, stay, stopover, visit
🗷 1 beginning, continuation, start

stopgap *n* expedient, improvisation, makeshift, resort, shift, substitute, temporary substitute
♦ *adj* emergency, expediential *formal*, impromptu, improvised, makeshift, provisional, rough-and-ready *colloq*, temporary
🗷 finished, permanent

stopover *n* break, overnight stay, rest, sojourn *formal*, stop, stop-off, visit

stoppage *n* 1 *contamination lead to the stoppage of water supplies*: arrest, cessation *formal*, check, discontinuance *formal*, discontinuation *formal*, halt, interruption, standstill, stop, termination *formal* 2 *called in a plumber to investigate the stoppage in a pipe*: blockage, obstacle, obstruction, occlusion *formal* 3 *the union staged a 24-hour stoppage over a wage dispute*: closure, industrial action, shutdown, sit-in, strike, walk-out 4 *the payslip detailed stoppages from his salary*: allowance, deduction, subtraction, taking away/off
🗷 1 continuation, start

store *v* accumulate, bank, collect, deposit, gather, hoard, keep, lay by, lay down, lay in, lay up, put aside, put down, reserve, salt away *colloq*, save, save for a rainy day *colloq*, stash *colloq*, stock, stock up with, stockpile
🗷 use
♦ *n* 1 *keeps a store of wine in his cellar*: abundance, accumulation, amassment, cache, heap, hoard,

load, lot, mine, plenty, provision, quantity, reserve, stock, stockpile, supply **2** *went to the store to buy supplies:* chain store, corner shop, department store, hypermarket, retail outlet, shop, supermarket **3** *kept any excess goods in the store:* buttery, depository, larder, repository, storehouse, storeroom, warehouse

ஒ 1 scarcity

storehouse *n* armoury, arsenal, barn, buttery, cellar, depository, depot, entrepot, fund, garner, granary, hold, larder, pantry, repertory, repository, silo, treasury, vault, warehouse, wealth

storey *n* deck, flight, floor, level, stage, tier

storm *n* agitation, brouhaha, clamour, commotion, disturbance, furore, kerfuffle *colloq*, offensive, onslaught, outbreak, outburst, outcry, rage, row, rumpus, stir, to-do *colloq*, tumult, turmoil, uproar

ஒ calm

♦ *v* **1** *storm a citadel:* assail, assault, attack, charge, rush **2** *he stormed at his students:* explode, foam at the mouth *colloq*, fume, hit the roof *colloq*, lose your cool *colloq*, rage, rant, rave, roar, seethe, shout, thunder **3** *storm out of the room:* charge, flounce, rush, stamp, tear

---

Kinds of storm include:
blizzard, buran, cloudburst, cyclone, downpour, dust-devil, dust-storm, electrical storm, gale, haboob, hailstorm, hurricane, monsoon, rainstorm, sand storm, snow storm, squall, tempest, thunderstorm, tornado, typhoon, whirlwind. See also **wind**

---

stormy *adj* blustery, choppy, foul, gusty, raging, rainy, rough, squally, tempestuous, turbulent, wild, windy

ஒ calm, peaceful

story *n* **1** *a bedtime story:* account, anecdote, chronicle, fiction, history, narrative, plot, recital, tale **2** *a news story:* account, article, feature, item, report **3** *he's telling stories again:* falsehood, lie, rib *colloq*, untruth

---

Types of story include:
adventure story, anecdote, bedtime story, blockbuster *colloq*, children's story, comedy, black comedy, crime story, detective story, fable, fairy story, fairy tale, fantasy, folk tale, ghost story, historical novel, horror story, legend, love story, mystery, myth, novel, novella, parable, romance, saga, science fiction, sci-fi *colloq*, short story, spiel, spine-chiller, spy story, supernatural tale, tall story, thriller, western, whodunit *colloq*, yarn *colloq*

---

storyteller *n* anecdotist, author, bard, chronicler, narrator, novelist, raconteur, raconteuse, romancer, tell-tale, writer

stout *adj* **1** *a stout man with grey hair:* athletic, beefy, big, brawny, bulky, burly, corpulent *formal*, fat, fleshy, heavy, hulking, muscular, obese, overweight, plump, portly, stocky, thickset, tubby **2** *stout shoes:* durable, hardy, heavy, robust, solid, strong, sturdy, substantial, thick, tough **3** *a stout ally of the state:* bold, brave, courageous, dauntless, determined, fearless, fierce, forceful, gallant, gritty *colloq*, gutsy *colloq*,

---

heroic, intrepid, plucky, resolute, spunky *colloq*, stalwart, strong, tough, valiant, valorous *formal*

ஒ 1 lean, slim, thin **2** weak **3** afraid, cowardly, timid

stow *v* bundle, cram, deposit, load, pack, place, put away, stash *colloq*, store, stuff

ஒ unload

straggle *v* amble, dilly-dally *colloq*, drift, lag, loiter, ramble, range, roam, rove, scatter, spread, stray, string out, trail, wander

straggly *adj* aimless, disorganized, drifting, irregular, loose, rambling, random, spreading, straggling, straying, strung out, untidy

ஒ grouped, organized, tidy

straight *adj* **1** *a straight line:* direct, unbending, unbent, uncurving, undeviating, unswerving **2** *that picture isn't quite straight:* aligned, horizontal, level, right, true, upright, vertical **3** *just be straight with me:* blunt, candid, direct, forthright, frank, honest, outspoken, straightforward **4** *their fifth straight win:* consecutive, one after the other, successive, unbroken, uninterrupted **5** *make sure the house is straight:* in order, neat, orderly, organized, shipshape, tidy **6** *a straight and honest way of life:* conventional, decent, fair, faithful, honest, honourable, just, law-abiding, reliable, respectable, sincere, straightforward, trustworthy, upright, upstanding **7** *gay and straight men:* heterosexual **8** *straight whisky:* neat, pure, unadulterated, undiluted, unmixed

ஒ 1 bent, crooked, curly, curved, wavy **2** sloping **3** evasive **5** untidy **6** dishonest **7** gay, homosexual **8** diluted

♦ *adv* **1** *walk straight down the road:* as the crow flies, directly, with no changes of direction, without deviating **2** *go straight to the headmaster's office:* as soon as possible, at once, directly, immediately, instantly, promptly, pronto *colloq*, right away, without delay **3** *tell someone straight:* bluntly, candidly, clearly, directly, forthrightly, frankly, honestly, not pulling any punches *colloq*, plainly, point-blank, straight from the shoulder *colloq*, straightforwardly **4** *he worked for 20 hours straight:* consecutively, continuously, on the trot *colloq*, one after the other, successively, uninterruptedly

straighten *v* adjust, align, arrange, neaten, order, put in order, put right, tidy (up), unbend

ஒ bend, twist

▶ **straighten out** clear up, correct, disentangle, put in order, put right, realign, rectify *formal*, regularize, resolve, settle, sort out, tidy up

ஒ confuse, muddle

▶ **straighten up** stand, stand erect, stand up, stand upright, straighten your back/body

straightforward *adj* **1** *this cake recipe is very straightforward:* a piece of cake *colloq*, child's play *colloq*, clear, easy, elementary, like falling off a log *colloq*, simple, uncomplicated, undemanding, unexacting **2** *he gave a straightforward answer to my question:* candid, direct, forthright, frank, genuine, honest, open, plain-speaking, sincere, truthful

ஒ 1 complicated, difficult, tricky **2** devious, evasive

strain¹ *v* **1** *I've strained a muscle in my leg:* distend *formal*, hurt, injure, pull, sprain, stretch, tauten, tear, tighten, tug, twist, wrench, wrick **2** *strain*

the mixture: drain, express, filter, percolate, purify, riddle, screen, separate, sieve, sift **3** *I strained to finish on time:* do your utmost, drive, endeavour, exert, fatigue, force, go all out *colloq*, labour, make every effort, overtax, overwork, pressure, pull out all the stops *colloq*, push to/beyond the limit, put your heart and soul into *colloq*, strive, struggle, tax, try ♦ *n* **1** *suffered a strain in his wrist:* injury, pull, sprain, twist, wrench, wrick **2** *she has a massage when the strain of work gets too much:* anxiety, burden, demand, duress, effort, exertion, exhaustion, fatigue, force, overwork, pressure, stress, struggle, tension, tiredness, weariness, worry
🔁 **2** relaxation

strain² *n* **1** *from a noble strain:* ancestry, blood, breed, descent, extraction, family, kind, lineage, pedigree, sort, stock, type, variety **2** *a stoic strain in the national character:* characteristic, disposition *formal*, element, proclivity *formal*, quality, streak, tendency, trace, trait, vein **3** *the strain of the pipes:* air, melody, song, theme, tune

strained *adj* artificial, awkward, constrained, embarrassed, false, forced, laboured, self-conscious, stiff, tense, uncomfortable, uneasy, unnatural, unrelaxed, wooden
🔁 natural, relaxed

strainer *n* colander, filter, riddle, sieve, sifter

strait *n* **1** *the Straits of Gibraltar:* channel, inlet, kyle, narrows, sound **2** *in desperate straits:* crisis, difficulty, dilemma, distress, fix *colloq*, hardship, hole *colloq*, mess *colloq*, pickle *colloq*, plight, predicament

straitened *adj* difficult, distressed, embarrassed, impoverished, limited, poor, reduced, restricted
🔁 easy, well-off

strait-laced *adj* moralistic, narrow, narrow-minded, priggish, prim, proper, prudish, puritanical, starchy, strict, stuffy
🔁 broad-minded

strand¹ *n* **1** *strands of material:* fibre, filament, piece, string, thread, wire **2** *the strands of a narrative:* component, element, feature, ingredient

strand² *n* beach, foreshore, front, sand(s), seashore, shore, waterfront

stranded *adj* abandoned, aground, beached, forsaken *formal*, grounded, helpless, high and dry, (left) in the lurch *colloq*, marooned, penniless, shipwrecked, wrecked

strange *adj* **1** *her behaviour was very strange:* abnormal, bizarre, curious, eccentric, exceptional, extraordinary, fantastic, freaky *colloq*, funny *colloq*, inexplicable, irregular, kinky *colloq*, mystifying, odd, oddball *colloq*, offbeat *colloq*, peculiar, perplexing, queer, remarkable, singular *formal*, surreal, uncanny, uncommon, unexpected, unexplained, unreal, unusual, wacky *colloq*, weird **2** *alone in a strange land:* alien, exotic, foreign, new, novel, unaccustomed, unacquainted, unfamiliar, unheard-of, unknown, untried
🔁 **1** common, ordinary **2** familiar, well-known

strangeness *n* abnormality, bizarreness, eccentricity, eeriness, exoticness, extraordinariness, irregularity, oddity, oddness,

peculiarity, queerness, singularity *formal*, uncanniness
🔁 ordinariness

stranger *n* alien, foreigner, guest, incomer, new arrival, newcomer, non-member, outsider, visitor
🔁 local, native

strangle *v* **1** *tried to strangle her:* asphyxiate, choke, smother, stifle, suffocate, throttle **2** *the leader is strangling democracy:* check, gag, hold back, inhibit, keep in, repress, restrain, stifle, suppress

strap *n* band, belt, cord, tie ♦ *v* **1** *was strapped for his misdemeanours:* beat, belt, flog, lash, scourge, whip **2** *securely strapped into position:* bandage, bind, fasten, lash, secure, tie

strapping *adj* beefy, big, brawny, burly, hefty, hulking, hunky *colloq*, husky, robust, strong, sturdy, well-built
🔁 puny

stratagem *n* artifice, deception, device, dodge, intrigue, machination *formal*, manoeuvre, plan, plot, ploy, ruse, scheme, subterfuge, tactic, trick, wile

---

stratagem or *strategy*? A *stratagem* is a plan or trick, intended to deceive someone or gain an advantage over them: *He was a master of the cunning stratagem and the bare-faced lie. Strategy* is used to describe tactics, especially in a long-term plan of campaign: *adopt a strategy of civil disobedience; guerrilla tactics were replaced by a strategy of conventional warfare.*

---

strategic *adj* calculated, critical, crucial, decisive, deliberate, diplomatic, essential, important, key, planned, politic, tactical, vital
🔁 unimportant

strategy *n* approach, blueprint *colloq*, design, game plan *colloq*, plan, plan of action, planning, policy, procedure, programme, schedule, scheme, tactics

stratum *n* **1** *a stratum of society:* bracket, caste, category, class, grade, group, level, rank, station, tier **2** *geological stratum:* bed, layer, lode, seam, stratification, vein

stray *v* amble, deviate, diverge, drift, err, get lost, go astray, go off at a tangent *colloq*, meander, ramble, range, roam, rove, saunter, straggle, wander (off) ♦ *adj* **1** *a stray dog:* abandoned, homeless, lost, roaming, wandering **2** *it was only one stray incident:* accidental, chance, erratic, freak, isolated, odd, random

streak *n* **1** *streaks on the window:* band, layer, line, smear, stripe **2** *a streak of cruelty in his character:* dash, element, strain, touch, trace **3** *on a lucky streak:* period, spell, stint, stretch, time ♦ *v* **1** *his face streaked with dirt:* band, daub, fleck, mark, smear, smudge, striate *formal*, stripe **2** *he streaked across the playing field:* dart, dash, flash, fly, gallop, hurtle, race, rush, scurry, speed, sprint, sweep, tear, whistle, whizz, zoom

streaked *adj* banded, barred, brinded, brindle(d), flecked, fleckered, lined, streaky, striate *formal*

stream *n* **1** *a mountain stream:* beck, brook, burn, creek, rill, rillet, river, rivulet, tributary **2** *a stream of traffic:* burst, cascade, course, current, deluge, drift, efflux *formal*, flood, flow, gush, jet, outpouring, run, rush, surge, tide, torrent, volley
♦ *v* **1** *water streamed from the opening:* cascade, course, flood, flow, gush, issue, pour, run, spill, spout, surge, well **2** *streaming in the wind:* flap, float, flutter, fly, trail, wave

streamlined *adj* **1** *a streamlined car:* aerodynamic, graceful, sleek, smooth **2** *a streamlined organization:* efficient, modernized, organized, rationalized, slick, smooth-running, up-to-the-minute *colloq*, well-run
🗷 **2** clumsy, inefficient

street *n* avenue, boulevard, lane, road, thoroughfare

strength *n* **1** *he had the strength to carry the wardrobe upstairs:* brawn, clout *colloq*, energy, fitness, force, health, muscle, power, sinew, stamina, stoutness, toughness, vigour **2** *X-rays can be used to measure bone strength:* durability, firmness, hardiness, impregnability, resilience, resistance, robustness, solidity, solidness, soundness, sturdiness, toughness **3** *summoned the strength to make a decision:* assertiveness, bravery, courage, determination, firmness, forcefulness, fortitude *formal*, guts *colloq*, persistence, resolution, spirit **4** *the strength of popular feeling was plain to see:* ardour, depth, fervency, graphicness, intensity, keenness, passion, sharpness, vehemence, vividness **5** *the prime minister's growing strength:* cogency *formal*, effectiveness, force, forcefulness, persuasiveness, potency, power, soundness, validity, weight **6** *compassion is one of his strengths:* advantage, aptitude, asset, bent, forte, gift, métier, speciality, specialty, strong point, talent
🗷 **1** frailty, weakness **2** weakness **3** feebleness, weakness **4** faintness, mildness **5** ineffectiveness, weakness **6** weakness

strengthen *v* back up, beef up *colloq*, bolster, brace, build up, buttress, confirm, consolidate, corroborate, encourage, fortify *formal*, harden, hearten, heighten, increase, intensify, invigorate, nourish, prop up, rally, refresh, reinforce, restore, shore up, steel, stiffen, substantiate, support, toughen
🗷 undermine, weaken

strenuous *adj* **1** *strenuous work:* arduous, demanding, difficult, exhausting, gruelling, hard, heavy, laborious, taxing, tiring, tough, uphill, weighty **2** *despite strenuous opposition:* active, bold, determined, eager, earnest, energetic, forceful, indefatigable, keen, resolute, spirited, tenacious, tireless, vigorous
🗷 **1** easy, effortless

stress *n* **1** *caused high levels of stress:* anxiety, apprehension, difficulty, distress, hassle *colloq*, pressure, strain, tension, trauma, trouble, uneasiness, worry **2** *he puts the stress on the last word in a sentence:* accent, accentuation, beat, emphasis, force, ictus *technical*, weight
🗷 relaxation
♦ *v* accentuate, emphasize, highlight, point up, repeat, spotlight, underline, underscore
🗷 downplay, moderate, play down, tone down, understate

stretch *v* **1** *stretching the balloon's thin rubber:* broaden, draw out, elongate, expand, extend, lengthen, make/become longer, make/become wider, spread, widen **2** *stretch from one point to another:* continue, extend, go as far as, go/come down/up to, last, project, range, reach, spread, unfold, unroll **3** *stretched a muscle:* pull, strain, tauten, tighten **4** *she stretched out her arms towards him:* extend, hold out, offer, present, proffer *formal*, reach out, straighten **5** *the job will stretch you:* challenge, push, tax, test, try
🗷 **1** compress, condense, shorten
♦ *n* **1** *a wide open stretch of scrubland:* area, expanse, space, spread, sweep, tract **2** *a stretch in prison:* period, run, spell, stint, term, time
▶ **stretch out** extend, lie down, recline *formal*, relax, sprawl

strew *v* bestrew, disperse, litter, scatter, spread, sprinkle, toss
🗷 gather

stricken *adj* affected, afflicted, hit, injured, smitten, struck, wounded
🗷 unaffected

strict *adj* **1** *a strict teacher:* austere, authoritarian, disciplinarian, firm, hard, harsh, inflexible, no-nonsense, rigid, rigorous, severe, stern, stringent, tough, uncompromising **2** *impose strict conditions:* absolute, accurate, clear, clear-cut, close, complete, exact, meticulous, particular, precise, scrupulous **3** *a strict vegetarian:* complete, conscientious, faithful, orthodox, scrupulous
🗷 **1** easy-going *colloq*, flexible, liberal, soft **2** loose

strictness *n* **1** *parents were surprised at the strictness of the teacher's regime:* austerity, authoritarianism, firmness, harshness, rigidity, rigidness, severity, sternness, stringency, stringentness **2** *the strictness of their selection criteria:* accuracy, exactness, meticulousness, precision, rigorousness, rigour, scrupulousness
🗷 **1** flexibility, mildness

stricture *n* **1** *they decided to continue despite the government's strictures:* animadversion *formal*, censure, criticism, flak *colloq*, rebuke, reproof **2** *was dictated by the strictures of prison life:* bound, confine, constraint, control, limit, restraint, restriction
🗷 **1** praise

stride *v* advance, pace, progress, step, tread, walk
♦ *n* advance, movement, pace, progression, step, tread, walk

strident *adj* booming, clamorous, clashing, discordant, grating, harsh, jangling, jarring, loud, rasping, raucous, roaring, rough, screeching, shrill, stentorian *formal*, stridulant *formal*, stridulous *formal*, thundering, unmusical, vociferous
🗷 quiet, soft

strife *n* animosity, argument, battle, bickering, combat, conflict, contention, controversy, disagreement, discord, dispute, dissension, fighting, friction, hostility, ill-feeling, ill-will, quarrel, quarrelling, rivalry, row, struggle, warfare, wrangling
🗷 peace

strike *n* **1** *a three-day strike:* go-slow, industrial action, mutiny, revolt, sit-in, stoppage, walk-out, work-to-rule **2** *a magnificent strike of the ball:* belt *colloq*, biff *colloq*, blow, clobber *colloq*, hit, slap, smack, thump, thwack, wallop *colloq*, whack *colloq* **3** *the possibility of military strikes:* ambush, assault, attack, charge, storming
♦ *v* **1** *employees voted to strike:* down tools, mutiny, protest, revolt, stop work, take industrial action, walk out, work to rule **2** *struck him about the head:* bang, batter, beat, belt *colloq*, biff *colloq*, box, buffet, clobber *colloq*, clout *colloq*, cuff, hammer, hit, knock, pound, punch, rap, slap, smack, sock *colloq*, swipe *colloq*, thrash, thump, thwack, wallop *colloq*, whack *colloq* **3** *the enemy struck during the night:* ambush, assail, assault, attack, charge, pounce on, raid, set about, storm, trap **4** *strike gold:* chance upon *formal*, come upon, discover, find, happen upon *formal*, reach, uncover, unearth **5** *the idea suddenly struck me:* come to, come to mind, dawn on, hit, occur to, register **6** *it strikes me as odd:* appear, feel, give the impression, have the look of, look, look like, seem **7** *strike a pose:* adopt, affect, assume, take on **8** *strike an agreement:* achieve, agree on, arrive at, clinch *colloq*, come to, come to an agreement on, make, reach, settle on
▶ **strike back** fight back, get back at, get even with *colloq*, get your own back *colloq*, hit back, pay someone back, reciprocate, retaliate
▶ **strike down** afflict, assassinate, destroy, fell, kill, murder, ruin, slay *formal*, smite *formal*
▶ **strike out** cancel, cross out, delete, erase, obliterate, remove, rub out, strike off, strike through
ⓔ add
▶ **strike up** begin, commence *formal*, establish, initiate, instigate, introduce, kick off *colloq*, start

striking *adj* **1** *a striking example of Gothic architecture:* arresting, astonishing, conspicuous, dazzling, distinct, evident, extraordinary, impressive, memorable, noticeable, obvious, outstanding, remarkable, salient, stunning, visible **2** *a striking young woman:* attractive, beautiful, glamorous, good-looking, gorgeous, pretty, stunning
ⓔ **1** unimpressive **2** ugly

string *n* **1** *a piece of string:* cable, cord, fibre, line, rope, twine, yarn **2** *a string of events:* chain, procession, sequence, series, stream, succession, train **3** *a string of characters:* column, file, line, row, sequence **4** *with no strings attached:* catches, conditions, limitations, obligations, prerequisites *formal*, provisos, qualifications, requirements, restrictions, stipulations
♦ *v* festoon, hang, link, loop, sling, suspend, thread, tie up
▶ **string along** bluff, deceive, dupe, fool, hoax, play (someone) false, play fast and loose with *colloq*, put one over on *colloq*, take for a ride *colloq*
▶ **string out** extend, lengthen, protract *formal*, stretch out
ⓔ shorten
▶ **string up** hang, kill, lynch, send to the gallows/scaffold/gibbet, top *colloq*

stringent *adj* binding, demanding, exacting, firm, hard, harsh, inflexible, rigid, rigorous, severe, strict, tight, tough, uncompromising
ⓔ flexible, lax

stringy *adj* chewy, fibrous, gristly, leathery, ropy, sinewy, tough, wiry
ⓔ tender

strip *v* **1** *he stripped before getting into bed:* denude *formal*, disrobe *formal*, lay bare, remove your clothes, take your clothes off, unclothe, uncover, undress **2** *looters stripped a government warehouse:* clean out, clear, divest, empty, gut, loot, pillage, plunder, ransack **3** *goats had stripped the branches:* peel, skin **4** *stripped the car to its constituent pieces:* disassemble, dismantle, pull apart, separate, take apart, take to pieces
ⓔ **1** clothe, dress, get dressed **2** fill **4** assemble, put together
♦ *n* band, bar, belt, bit, lath, piece, ribbon, sash, shred, slat, slip, strap, stripe, swathe, thong

stripe *n* band, bar, belt, chevron, flash, fleck, line, streak, strip

striped *adj* banded, barred, streaky, striated, stripy, variegated, vittate

stripling *n* adolescent, boy, fledgling, lad, teenager, youngster, young'un *colloq*, youth

strive *v* **1** *staff work together as a team and strive for excellence:* attempt, do your best, do your utmost, endeavour, exert yourself, give your all, labour, strain, struggle, toil, try, try hard, work **2** *heroic ballads about men striving against insuperable odds:* battle, combat, compete, contend, contest, do battle, engage, fight, vie

stroke *n* **1** *the soft stroke of her hand:* caress, pat, rub **2** *a well-aimed stroke to the boundary:* belt *colloq*, biff *colloq*, blow, clobber *colloq*, hit, knock, smack, swipe, thump, thwack, wallop *colloq*, whack *colloq* **3** *with a single stroke of his sword:* action, flourish, line, motion, move, movement, sweep **4** *a stroke of political genius:* accomplishment, achievement, coup **5** *suffered a series of strokes in her seventies:* attack, cerebral haemorrhage, collapse, seizure, spasm, thrombosis
♦ *v* caress, fondle, massage, pat, pet, rub, touch

stroll *v* amble, dawdle, go for a walk, meander, ramble, saunter, stretch your legs *colloq*, wander
♦ *n* amble, constitutional, ramble, saunter, turn, walk

stroller *n* dawdler, rambler, saunterer, walker, wanderer

strong *adj* **1** *a strong man:* athletic, beefy, brawny, burly, fit, healthy, lusty, mighty, muscular, powerful, sinewy, stout, strapping, sturdy, well-built **2** *strong boots:* durable, hard-wearing, hardy, heavy-duty, long-lasting, reinforced, resilient, robust, rugged, solid, stalwart, sturdy, tough, vigorous, well-built, well-protected **3** *a strong personality:* aggressive, assertive, brave, confident, courageous, determined, firm, forceful, formidable, gutsy *colloq*, persistent, resolute, single-minded, strong-minded, strong-willed **4** *a strong colour:* bright, deep, fierce, graphic, heady, intense, powerful, violent, vivid **5** *a strong taste:* highly-flavoured, highly-seasoned, hot, intense, keen, piquant, powerful, pungent, sharp, spicy **6** *make a strong impression:* clear, clear-cut, evident, marked, obvious, pronounced, remarkable **7** *take strong action:* active, decisive, firm, forceful, positive, resolute, severe **8** *a strong interest in railways:* committed, devoted, eager, enthusiastic, keen, passionate

9 *a strong case/argument:* compelling, convincing, effective, efficacious *formal*, forceful, persuasive, plausible, potent, powerful, sound, telling, valid, weighty **10** *strong feelings:* ardent, deep, fervent, great, intense, passionate, powerful, profound, vehement **11** *strong liquor:* concentrated, potent, undiluted

F3 **1** frail, sickly, unhealthy, weak **2** insubstantial, weak **3** feeble, weak **4** faint, weak **5** bland, faint, mild, weak **7** indecisive, weak **9** unconvincing, weak **10** feeble, weak **11** diluted

strongarm *adj* aggressive, bullying, coercive, forceful, intimidatory, oppressive, physical, terror, threatening, thuggish, violent
F3 gentle

stronghold *n* bastion, castle, citadel, fort, fortress, keep, refuge, tower

strong-minded *adj* determined, firm, independent, iron-willed, resolute, steadfast, strong-willed, tenacious, unbending, uncompromising, unwavering
F3 weak-willed

strong-willed *adj* inflexible, intractable, intransigent *formal*, obdurate *formal*, obstinate, recalcitrant *formal*, refractory *formal*, self-willed, stubborn, wayward, wilful

stroppy *adj* awkward, bad-tempered, bloody-minded, cantankerous, difficult, obstreperous, perverse, quarrelsome, refractory *formal*, rowdy, unco-operative, unhelpful
F3 co-operative, sweet-tempered

structural *adj* configurational *formal*, constructional, design, formational *formal*, organizational, tectonic *technical*

structure *n* **1** *the structure of society:* arrangement, composition, configuration *formal*, conformation *formal*, constitution, construction, design, fabric, form, formation, frame, framework, make-up, organization, set-up, shape, system **2** *a traditional wooden structure:* building, construction, edifice, erection
♦ *v* arrange, assemble, build, construct, design, form, organize, shape

struggle *v* **1** *struggled for recognition:* agonize, do your best, do your utmost, exert yourself, give your all, labour, strain, strive, toil, try hard, work **2** *struggled with his attacker:* battle, combat, compete, contend, contest, engage, fight, grapple, vie, wrestle
F3 **2** give in, yield
♦ *n* **1** *the struggle for survival:* battle, competition, conflict, contest, effort, exertion, strife, toil, work **2** *a struggle between police and protesters:* battle, brawl, clash, combat, conflict, encounter, exertion, fight, scuffle, skirmish
F3 **1** co-operation, ease **2** submission

strut *v* parade, peacock, prance, stalk, swagger, swank *colloq*

stub *n* butt, counterfoil, dog-end *colloq*, end, fag end *colloq*, remnant, stump

stubborn *adj* adamant, difficult, dogged, headstrong, hidebound, inflexible, intractable *formal*, intransigent *formal*, mulish, not listening/open to reason, obdurate *formal*, obstinate, persistent, pig-headed, recalcitrant *formal*, refractory *formal*, rigid, self-willed, stiff-necked, strong-willed, stubborn as a mule,

tenacious, unbending, uncompromising, unmanageable, unyielding, wilful
F3 compliant, flexible, yielding

stubby *adj* chunky, dumpy, short, squat, stumpy, thickset
F3 long, tall, thin

stuck *adj* **1** *the car is stuck in the mud:* bogged down *colloq*, cemented, embedded, fast, fastened, firm, fixed, glued, immobile, jammed, joined, rooted, unmovable **2** *I can't finish this crossword – I'm completely stuck:* at a loss *colloq*, at your wits' end *colloq*, baffled, beaten, perplexed *colloq*, stumped *colloq*
F3 **1** loose

stuck-up *adj* arrogant, bigheaded *colloq*, conceited, condescending, haughty, high and mighty *colloq*, hoity-toity *colloq*, patronizing, proud, snobbish, snooty *colloq*, supercilious, toffee-nosed *colloq*, uppish *colloq*
F3 humble, modest

studded *adj* dotted, flecked, ornamented, scattered, set, spangled, speckled, spotted, sprinkled

student *n* apprentice, disciple, learner, postgraduate, probationer, pupil, scholar, schoolboy, schoolgirl, trainee, undergraduate

studied *adj* affected, artificial, calculated, conscious, contrived, deliberate, forced, intentional, over-elaborate, planned, premeditated, purposeful, unnatural, wilful
F3 impulsive, natural, unplanned

studio *n* atelier, school, workroom, workshop

studious *adj* academic, assiduous, attentive, bookish, careful, diligent, eager, earnest, hard-working, industrious, intellectual, meticulous, reflective, scholarly, sedulous *formal*, serious, thorough, thoughtful
F3 idle, lazy, negligent

study *v* **1** *she's studying French literature:* analyse, contemplate, examine, investigate, learn, major in, meditate, peruse, ponder, pore over, read, read up, research, scan, scrutinize, survey, train **2** *she's studying hard for her exams:* bone up, cram, mug up *colloq*, read up, research, revise, swot *colloq*
♦ *n* **1** *his study of religion and psychology:* analysis, consideration, contemplation, examination, inquiry, inspection, investigation, learning, preparation, reading, research, revision, scholarship, scrutiny **2** *the study revealed some astonishing findings:* critique, essay, monograph, paper, report, review, survey, thesis, work **3** *your mother's in the study:* den *colloq*, library, office, studio, workroom

---

Subjects of study include:
accountancy, agriculture, anatomy, anthropology, archaeology, architecture, art, astrology, astronomy, biology, botany, building studies, business studies, calligraphy, chemistry, CDT (craft, design and technology), civil engineering, the Classics, commerce, computer studies, cosmology, craft, dance, design, domestic science, drama, dressmaking, driving, ecology, economics, education, electronics, engineering, environmental studies, ethnology, eugenics, fashion, fitness, food technology, forensics, genetics,

geography, geology, heraldry, history, home economics, horticulture, information technology (IT), journalism, languages, law, leisure studies, lexicography, linguistics, literature, logistics, management studies, marketing, mathematics, mechanics, media studies, medicine, metallurgy, metaphysics, meteorology, music, mythology, natural history, oceanography, ornithology, pathology, penology, personal and social education (PSE), personal, social and health education (PSHE), pharmacology, philosophy, photography, physics, physiology, politics, pottery, psychology, religious studies, science, shorthand, social sciences, sociology, sport, statistics, surveying, technology, theology, typewriting, visual arts, word processing, writing, zoology

stuff *v* **1** *stuffed our clothes into the suitcase*: compress, cram, crowd, force, jam, pack, pad, press, push, ram, shove *colloq*, squeeze, stow, thrust, wedge **2** *I stuffed myself with as much food as I could*: gobble, gorge, gormandize, gross out *colloq*, guzzle, make a pig of yourself *colloq*, overindulge, pig out *colloq*, sate, satiate
F3 1 empty, unload **2** nibble
♦ *n* **1** *what is this stuff?*: essence, fabric, material, matter, substance **2** *I felt at home once I'd unpacked my stuff*: articles, belongings, clobber *colloq*, equipment, gear *colloq*, goods, items, kit, luggage, materials, objects, paraphernalia, possessions, tackle, things

stuffing *n* farce, filling, forcemeat, kapok, packing, padding, quilting, wadding

stuffy *adj* **1** *a stuffy room*: airless, close, fuggy, heavy, muggy, musty, oppressive, stale, stifling, suffocating, sultry, unventilated **2** *trying to get rid of his stuffy image*: conventional, dreary, dull, fuddy-duddy *colloq*, old-fashioned, pompous, prim, staid, starchy, stiff, stodgy, strait-laced, uninteresting
F3 1 airy, well-ventilated **2** informal, lively, modern

stultify *v* blunt, dull, hebetate *formal*, invalidate, negate, nullify, numb, smother, stifle, stupefy, suppress, thwart
F3 electrify, prove, sharpen

stumble *v* **1** *he stumbled on the uneven path*: blunder, fall, flounder, lose your balance, lurch, reel, slip, stagger, trip **2** *stumbled over the words*: falter, hesitate, stammer, stutter
▶ **stumble on** chance upon *formal*, come across, discover, encounter, find, happen upon *formal*

stumbling-block *n* bar, barrier, difficulty, hindrance, hurdle, impediment, obstacle, obstruction, snag

stump *n* butt, dog-end *colloq*, end, fag end *colloq*, remains, remnant, stub, trunk
♦ *v* baffle, bamboozle *colloq*, bewilder, confound, confuse, defeat, dumbfound, flummox *colloq*, foil, mystify, nonplus *colloq*, outwit, perplex, puzzle
F3 assist
▶ **stump up** chip in *colloq*, contribute, cough up *colloq*, donate, fork out *colloq*, hand over, pay, pay out/up, shell out *colloq*
F3 receive

stumped *adj* baffled, bamboozled *colloq*, floored *colloq*, flummoxed *colloq*, nonplussed *colloq*, perplexed, stuck, stymied *colloq*

stumpy *adj* chunky, dumpy, heavy, short, squat, stocky, stubby, thick, thickset
F3 long, tall, thin

stun *v* amaze, astonish, astound, bewilder, bowl over *colloq*, confound, confuse, daze, dumbfound, flabbergast *colloq*, knock for six *colloq*, knock out *colloq*, overcome, overpower, shock, stagger, stupefy, take your breath away *colloq*

stunned *adj* amazed, astounded, dazed, devastated, dumbfounded, flabbergasted *colloq*, floored *colloq*, gobsmacked *colloq*, numb, shocked, staggered, stupefied
F3 indifferent

stunner *n* beauty, charmer, dazzler, eye-catcher *colloq*, femme fatale, good-looker, heart-throb, knock-out *colloq*, looker, lovely, peach *colloq*, sensation, siren, smasher *colloq*, wow *colloq*

stunning *adj* amazing, beautiful, brilliant, dazzling, extraordinary, fabulous *colloq*, gorgeous, great, impressive, incredible, lovely, marvellous, ravishing, remarkable, sensational, smashing *colloq*, spectacular, staggering, striking, wonderful
F3 awful, ugly

stunt[1] *n* act, action, deed, enterprise, exploit, feat, performance, trick, turn, wheeze *colloq*

stunt[2] *v* arrest, check, curb, dwarf, hamper, hinder, impede, restrict, retard *formal*, slow, stop
F3 encourage, promote

stunted *adj* diminutive, dwarfed, dwarfish, little, small, tiny, undersized
F3 large, sturdy

stupefaction *n* amazement, astonishment, bafflement, bewilderment, blackout, daze, numbness, senselessness, state of shock, wonder

stupefy *v* amaze, astound, bowl over *colloq*, daze, devastate, dull, dumbfound, knock for six *colloq*, knock out *colloq*, numb, shock, stagger, stun

stupendous *adj* amazing, astounding, breathtaking, colossal, enormous, extraordinary, fabulous, fantastic *colloq*, gigantic, huge, immense, marvellous, overwhelming, phenomenal, prodigious *formal*, staggering, stunning, superb, tremendous, vast, wonderful
F3 ordinary, unimpressive

stupid *adj* **1** *how could you be so stupid?*: absurd, brainless, crass, dense, dim, dopey *colloq*, dull, dull-witted, dumb *colloq*, fatuous, feeble-minded, foolhardy, foolish, gormless *colloq*, half-witted, idiotic, ill-advised, imbecilic, inane, indiscreet, injudicious *formal*, irresponsible, laughable, ludicrous, lunatic, mad, meaningless, mindless, moronic, nonsensical, pointless, puerile, rash, senseless, silly, simple-minded, slow, slow on the uptake *colloq*, thick *colloq*, thick as a plank/two short planks *colloq* **2** *the illness left him feeling stupid*: dazed, groggy, semiconscious, sluggish, stunned, stupefied, unconscious
F3 1 clever, intelligent, sensible, wise **2** alert

stupidity *n* absurdity, asininity, brainlessness, crassness, denseness, dimness, dopiness *colloq*,

doziness *colloq*, dullness, dumbness *colloq*, fatuity, fatuousness, feeble-mindedness, folly, foolhardiness, foolishness, futility, idiocy, imbecility, impracticality, inanity, indiscretion, ineptitude, irresponsibility, ludicrousness, lunacy, madness, naïvety, obtuseness, pointlessness, puerility, rashness, senselessness, silliness, slowness, thickness *colloq*
🔄 alertness, cleverness, intelligence

stupor *n* blackout, coma, daze, inertia, insensibility, lethargy, numbness, oblivion, state of shock, stupefaction, torpor *formal*, trance, unconsciousness
🔄 alertness, consciousness

sturdy *adj* athletic, determined, durable, firm, flourishing, hardy, hearty, mighty *formal*, muscular, powerful, resolute, robust, solid, stalwart, staunch, steadfast, stout, strong, substantial, tenacious, vigorous, well-built, well-made
🔄 flimsy, puny, weak

stutter *v* falter, hesitate, mumble, splutter, stammer, stumble

style *n* **1** *a style of shoe:* appearance, category, cut, design, form, genre *formal*, kind, pattern, shape, sort, type, variety **2** *she has always dressed with impeccable style:* chic, dash, dressiness, elegance, fashion, flair, flamboyance, grandeur, luxury, panache, polish, refinement, smartness, sophistication, stylishness, suaveness, taste, urbanity **3** *he has a relaxed style of management:* approach, custom, fashion, manner, method, methodology, mode *formal*, technique, way **4** *the distinctive style of each written piece:* expression, language, phrasing, tenor, tone, wording
🔄 **2** inelegance, tastelessness
♦ *v* **1** *styled a beautiful dress for her:* adapt, design, fashion, make, produce, shape, tailor **2** *a gifted conman, he styled himself 'Count':* address, call, denominate *formal*, designate, dub, label, name, tag, term, title

stylish *adj* à la mode, chic, classy *colloq*, dressy, elegant, fashionable, in vogue, modish, natty *colloq*, polished, refined, ritzy *colloq*, smart, snappy, snazzy *colloq*, sophisticated, trendy *colloq*, urbane, voguish
🔄 old-fashioned, shabby

stylus *n* graphium *formal*, hand, index, needle, pen, pointer, probe, style

stymie *v* baffle, balk, bamboozle *colloq*, confound, defeat, flummox *colloq*, foil, frustrate, hinder, mystify, nonplus *colloq*, puzzle, snooker *colloq*, stump, thwart
🔄 assist, help

suave *adj* affable, agreeable, bland, charming, civil, civilized, courteous, debonair, glib, polished, polite, refined, smooth, soft-spoken, sophisticated, unctuous, urbane, worldly
🔄 rude, unsophisticated

suavity *n* agreeability, blandness, charm, civility, courtesy, politeness, refinement, smoothness, sophistication, unctuousness, urbanity, worldliness
🔄 coarseness

subaquatic *adj* demersal *formal*, subaqua *formal*, subaqueous *formal*, submarine, submersed, undersea, underwater

subconscious *adj* deep, hidden, inner, innermost, instinctive, intuitive, latent, repressed, subliminal, suppressed, unconscious, underlying
🔄 conscious
♦ *n* ego, id, psyche, super-ego, unconscious, unconscious self

subdue *v* break, check, conquer, control, crush, damp, defeat, discipline, gain mastery over, get the better of, humble, master, mellow, moderate, overcome, overpower, overrun, quash, quell, quieten, reduce, repress, restrain, soften, stifle, subject, subjugate *formal*, suppress, tame, vanquish *formal*
🔄 arouse, awaken

subdued *adj* **1** *the news left her feeling subdued:* crestfallen, dejected, depressed, down in the dumps *colloq*, downcast, grave, quiet, sad, serious, solemn, unexcited **2** *a subdued atmosphere after the match:* dim, hushed, low-key, muted, noiseless, quiet, restrained, silent, sober, sombre, toned down **3** *painted in subdued tones:* delicate, muted, pastel, soft, sombre, subtle
🔄 **1** cheerful, excited, lively **2** loud, obtrusive **3** bright, loud, striking

subject *n* **1** *a sensitive subject:* affair, issue, matter, point, question, theme, topic **2** *my favourite subject at school:* area of study, discipline, field, field of study, topic **3** *a British subject:* citizen, inhabitant, national, native, resident **4** *the subject of the experiment:* participant, patient, victim **5** *a subject of the king:* dependant, inferior, liegeman, subordinate, underling *colloq*, vassal
🔄 **5** master, monarch, ruler
♦ *adj* **1** *subject to mood swings:* apt, disposed, exposed, liable, likely, open, prone, susceptible, vulnerable **2** *subject states:* accountable, answerable, bound, constrained, inferior, obedient, subjugated *formal*, submissive, subordinate, subservient **3** *she has been offered a place, subject to her exam results:* conditional, contingent *formal*, dependent
🔄 **1** invulnerable **2** free, superior **3** unconditional
♦ *v* **1** *invaders subjected the local population:* subdue, subjugate *formal*, subordinate **2** *subjected them to vicious attacks:* expose, lay open, submit

subjection *n* bondage, captivity, chains, defeat, domination, enslavement, mastery, oppression, shackles, slavery, subjugation *formal*

subjective *adj* biased, bigoted, emotional, idiosyncratic, individual, instinctive, intuitive, personal, prejudiced
🔄 impartial, objective, unbiased

subjugate *v* conquer, crush, defeat, enslave, gain mastery over, get the better of, master, oppress, overcome, overpower, overthrow, quell, reduce, subdue, suppress, tame, thrall, vanquish *formal*
🔄 free, liberate

sublimate *v* channel, divert, elevate, exalt, heighten, purify, redirect, refine, transfer, transmute *formal*, turn
🔄 let out

sublime *adj* **1** *the sublime architecture of Venice:* beautiful, elevated, exalted, glorious, grand, great, high, imposing, lofty, magnificent, majestic, noble, spiritual, transcendent **2** *a writer*

of sublime talent: complete, extreme, great, intense, supreme, utter
🖪 1 base, lowly

submerge *v* bury, deluge, dip, drown, duck, dunk, engulf, flood, go down, go/put under water, immerse, inundate, overflow, overwhelm, plummet, plunge, sink, submerse, swamp
🖪 surface

submerged *adj* cloaked, concealed, drowned, hidden, immersed, inundated, submersed, sunk, sunken, swamped, underwater, unseen, veiled

submission *n* **1** *forced into submission:* acquiescence, agreement, assent *formal*, capitulation, compliance, deference, giving in, meekness, obedience, passivity, resignation, submissiveness, surrender **2** *a written submission:* assertion, averment *formal*, contribution, entry, introduction, offering, presentation, proposal, statement, suggestion, tabling, tender, tendering
🖪 **1** intractability, intransigence, opposition, resistance

submissive *adj* accommodating, acquiescent, biddable, compliant, deferential, docile, downtrodden, humble, ingratiating, malleable, meek, obedient, passive, patient, resigned, resisting, self-effacing, servile, subdued, subservient, supine *formal*, uncomplaining, unresisting, weak, weak-willed, yielding
🖪 assertive, intractable, intransigent *formal*

submit *v* **1** *submit to demands:* accede *formal*, acquiesce, agree, bend, bow, capitulate, comply, defer, give in, give way, knuckle under, succumb, surrender, yield **2** *submit a proposal:* argue, assert, aver *formal*, claim, introduce, move, offer, present, proffer *formal*, propose, propound *formal*, put forward, state, suggest, table, tender
🖪 **1** oppose, resist **2** withdraw

subnormal *adj* backward, below average, below normal, feeble-minded, inferior, low, retarded, slow
🖪 gifted

subordinate *adj* ancillary, auxiliary, dependent, inferior, junior, lesser, lower, lower in rank, lower-ranking, lowly, minor, secondary, subservient, subsidiary
🖪 senior, superior
♦ *n* aide, assistant, attendant, dependant, deputy, dogsbody *colloq*, inferior, junior, menial, second, second fiddle *colloq*, sidekick *colloq*, skivvy *colloq*, underling *colloq*, vassal
🖪 boss, superior

subordination *n* dependence, inferiority, servitude, subjection, submission, subservience
🖪 superiority

subscribe *v* **1** *subscribe to a magazine:* buy regularly, pay for regularly, receive/take regularly **2** *subscribe to a charity:* contribute, donate, fork out *colloq*, give, pledge, shell out *colloq* **3** *subscribe to a theory:* advocate *formal*, agree, approve, back, consent *formal*, endorse, support, underwrite

subscription *n* contribution, donation, dues, gift, membership fee, offering, payment

subsequent *adj* consequent, ensuing, following, future, later, next, resulting, succeeding
🖪 earlier, previous, prior

subsequently *adv* after, afterwards, consequently, later
🖪 previously

subservient *adj* ancillary, auxiliary, dependent, inferior, junior, less important, lesser, lower, minor, secondary, subordinate, subsidiary
🖪 more important, senior, superior

subside *v* **1** *interest in the case has subsided:* abate *formal*, decline, decrease, die down, diminish, dwindle, ease, ebb, fall, get lower, lessen, let up, lower, moderate, peter out *colloq*, quieten, recede, slacken, wane **2** *the survey revealed that the house was subsiding:* cave in, collapse, descend, drop, fall, lower, settle, sink
🖪 **1** increase, rise

subsidence *n* abatement *formal*, decline, decrease, de-escalation, descent, detumescence *formal*, diminution *formal*, ebb, lessening, settlement, settling, sinking, slackening
🖪 increase

subsidiary *adj* additional, ancillary, assistant, auxiliary, lesser, minor, secondary, subordinate, subservient, supplementary, supporting
🖪 chief, major, primary
♦ *n* branch, division, offshoot, part, section, wing

subsidize *v* aid, back, contribute to, endorse, finance, fund, give a subsidy to, invest in, pay part of the cost of, promote, sponsor, support, underwrite

subsidy *n* aid, allowance, assistance, backing, contribution, endorsement, finance, funding, grant, help, investment, sponsorship, subvention *formal*, support, underwriting

subsist *v* continue, eke out an existence, endure, exist, hold out, last, live, remain, survive

subsistence *n* aliment, continuance, existence, food, keep, livelihood, living, maintenance, nourishment, provisions, rations, support, survival, sustenance

substance *n* **1** *a harmless substance:* fabric, material, matter, medium, stuff **2** *has no material substance:* actuality, concreteness, corporeality *formal*, essence, mass, materiality, reality, solidity, tangibility **3** *the substance of the complaint:* basis, burden, force, foundation, gist, ground, import *formal*, importance, matter, meaning, meaningfulness, pith, power, significance, subject, subject matter, text, theme, topic, truth, validity, weight **4** *a person of substance:* affluence, assets, influence, means, money, power, prosperity, resources, riches, wealth

substandard *adj* below par *colloq*, damaged, imperfect, inadequate, inferior, not up to scratch *colloq*, poor, second-rate, shoddy, unacceptable
🖪 first-rate, perfect, superior

substantial *adj* **1** *a substantial donation:* ample, big, considerable, generous, great, important, large, meaningful, notable, remarkable, significant, sizeable, tidy *colloq*, valuable, weighty, worthwhile **2** *a substantial structure:* durable, solid, sound, stout, strong, sturdy, tough, well-built **3** *substantial matter:* actual, concrete, corporeal *formal*, existing, material, real, tangible **4** *the substantial facts of the situation:* basic, central, essential, fundamental, inherent, intrinsic, main, primary, principal **5** *a substantial*

businesswoman: affluent, influential, powerful, prosperous, rich, successful, wealthy
🔁 1 insignificant, small 2 flimsy 3 imaginary, insubstantial 5 poor

substantially *adv* 1 *the new version is substantially smaller than its predecessor:* considerably, largely, significantly, to a great extent 2 *the allegations are substantially true:* essentially, fundamentally, in the main, mainly, materially, to all intents and purposes
🔁 1 slightly

substantiate *v* authenticate, back up, bear out, confirm, corroborate *formal*, prove, support, uphold, validate, verify
🔁 disprove, refute

substitute *v* 1 *he substituted lime for lemon in the recipe:* change, exchange, interchange, replace, swap, switch, use instead 2 *Hodgson substituted for Wilson:* act instead of, cover, deputize, double, fill in *colloq*, relieve, stand in, sub *colloq*, take over, take the place of, understudy
♦ *n* agent, deputy, locum, locum tenens *formal*, proxy, relief, replacement, reserve, stand-by, stand-in, stopgap, supply, surrogate, temp *colloq*, understudy
♦ *adj* acting, alternative, deputy, proxy, relief, replacement, reserve, stand-by, stand-in, surrogate, temporary

substitution *n* change, exchange, interchange, replacement, swap, swapping, switch, switching

subterfuge *n* artifice, deception, deviousness, dodge *colloq*, duplicity *formal*, evasion, excuse, expedient, intrigue, machination *formal*, manoeuvre, ploy, pretence, pretext, ruse, scheme, stratagem, trick, wile
🔁 honesty, openness

subtle *adj* 1 *a subtle change of tone:* deep, delicate, elusive, faint, fine, implied, indefinite, indirect, indistinct, low-key, mild, minute, refined, slight, tenuous, toned down, understated 2 *a subtle plan:* artful, astute, clever, complex, crafty, cunning, devious, discreet, indirect, intricate, shrewd, sly, strategic, tactful, wily
🔁 1 blatant, obvious 2 artless, indiscreet, open, tactless

subtlety *n* 1 *writes with subtlety and grace:* delicacy, finesse, nicety, nuance, refinement, sophistication 2 *the subtlety of his plot:* acuteness, artfulness, astuteness, cleverness, craftiness, cunning, deviousness, guile, intricacy, sagacity *formal*, skill, slyness, wiliness

subtract *v* debit, deduct, detract, diminish, dock, remove, take away, withdraw
🔁 add

suburb *n* commuter belt, dormitory town, outskirts, purlieus *formal*, residential area, suburbia
🔁 centre, heart

suburban *adj* 1 *a suburban railway:* commuter, residential 2 *suburban attitudes:* bourgeois, conventional, dull, insular, middle-class, narrow, narrow-minded, parochial, provincial, unimaginative

subversive *adj* destructive, discrediting, disruptive, incendiary, inflammatory, revolutionary, riotous, seditious, traitorous,

treacherous, treasonous, troublemaking, undermining, weakening
🔁 loyal
♦ *n* dissident, fifth columnist *colloq*, freedom fighter *colloq*, quisling, seditionist, terrorist, traitor

subvert *v* confound, contaminate, corrupt, debase, demolish, demoralize, deprave, destroy, disrupt, invalidate, overturn, pervert, poison, raze, ruin, sabotage, undermine, upset, vitiate *formal*, wreck
🔁 boost, uphold

subway *n* 1 *the subway train service was disrupted:* metro, tube *colloq*, underground, underground railway 2 *used the subway to pass under the busy road:* pedestrian tunnel, tunnel, underground passage, underpass

succeed *v* 1 *after several attempts she has finally succeeded:* accomplish, achieve, attain, be successful, bring home the bacon *colloq*, bring off *colloq*, carry out, complete, do well, flourish, fulfil, get on *colloq*, get results, go places *colloq*, hit the jackpot *colloq*, land/fall on your feet *colloq*, make good, make it *colloq*, manage, prevail, prosper, pull off *colloq*, reach, realize, strike gold *colloq*, thrive, triumph, turn up trumps *colloq*, win the day *colloq*, work, work out 2 *winter succeeds autumn:* come after, ensue, follow, replace, take the place of
🔁 1 fail, flop *colloq* 2 precede
▶ **succeed to** accede *formal*, assume *formal*, come into, enter upon, inherit, replace, supersede, take over
🔁 abdicate, precede

succeeding *adj* coming, ensuing, following, later, next, subsequent, successive, to come
🔁 earlier, previous, prior

success *n* 1 *they owe their success to hard work and enthusiasm:* accomplishment, achievement, attainment, eminence, fame, fortune, fulfilment, happiness, luck, positive result, prosperity, triumph, victory 2 *became an overnight success:* bestseller, big name *colloq*, big shot *colloq*, bigwig *colloq*, box-office hit *colloq*, celebrity, hit, sell-out *colloq*, sensation, somebody *colloq*, star, VIP *colloq*, winner, wow *colloq*
🔁 1 disaster, failure 2 dead loss *colloq*, failure, flop *colloq*, loser, write-off *colloq*

successful *adj* 1 *a successful business:* affluent, booming, flourishing, fruitful, lucrative, moneymaking, productive, profitable, prosperous, rewarding, satisfying, thriving, triumphant, victorious, wealthy, winning 2 *a successful writer:* bestselling, famous, leading, popular, top, unbeaten, well-known
🔁 1 fruitless, unprofitable, unsuccessful 2 unknown

successfully *adv* beautifully, famously, fine, great, swimmingly *colloq*, victoriously, well
🔁 unsuccessfully

succession *n* 1 *a succession of unfortunate incidents:* chain, continuation, course, cycle, line, procession, progression, run, sequence, series, string, train 2 *the succession to the throne:* accession, assumption *formal*, attaining, elevation, inheritance

successive *adj* consecutive, following, running, sequential, serial, succeeding

successively *adv* consecutively, in succession, on the trot *colloq*, one after the other, running, sequentially, uninterruptedly

successor *n* beneficiary, co-heir, descendant, heir, inheritor, next in line, relief, replacement, substitute

succinct *adj* brief, compact, concise, condensed, crisp, in a word, pithy, short, summary, terse, to the point
◨ lengthy, long, verbose, wordy

succour *n* aid, assistance, comfort, help, helping hand *colloq*, ministrations *formal*, relief, support
♦ *v* aid, assist, befriend, comfort, encourage, foster, help, help out, minister to, nurse, relieve, support
◨ undermine

succulent *adj* fleshy, juicy, luscious, lush, mellow, moist, mouthwatering, rich
◨ dry

succumb *v* 1 *succumb to peer pressure*: capitulate, collapse, fall, give in, give way, submit, surrender, yield 2 *succumb to an illness*: catch, contract *formal*, die of, go down with, pick up
◨ 1 master, overcome, overwhelm

suck *v* absorb, blot up, drain, draw (in), extract, imbibe, soak up
▶ **suck up to** curry favour, fawn, flatter, ingratiate, lick someone's boots *colloq*, toady, truckle

sucker *n* butt *colloq*, cat's-paw *colloq*, dupe, fool, leech, mug *colloq*, pushover *colloq*, sap, stooge, victim

suckle *v* breastfeed, feed, nurse

sudden *adj* abrupt, dramatic, fast, hasty, hurried, immediate, impetuous, impulsive, instantaneous, meteoric, prompt, quick, rapid, rash, sharp, snap *colloq*, speedy, spur-of-the-moment *colloq*, startling, surprising, swift, unanticipated, unexpected, unforeseen
◨ expected, gradual, predictable, slow

suddenly *adv* abruptly, all of a sudden, from out of nowhere *colloq*, immediately, instantaneously, out of the blue *colloq*, quickly, sharply, unexpectedly, without warning

suddenness *n* abruptness, haste, hastiness, hurriedness, impulsiveness, unexpectedness
◨ slowness

sue *v* 1 *sued a former employer for wrongful dismissal*: bring charges against, bring to trial, charge, indict, prosecute, take (legal) action against, take to court 2 *they sued for peace*: appeal, beg, beseech *formal*, petition, plead, solicit

suffer *v* 1 *suffering from serious injuries*: ache, agonize, be afflicted, be in pain, go through the mill *colloq*, hurt 2 *suffered great hardship*: endure, experience, feel, go through, meet with, sustain, undergo 3 *does not suffer fools gladly*: abide *formal*, bear, endure, put up with, stand, support, tolerate

suffering *n* adversity, affliction, agony, anguish, discomfort, distress, hardship, hurt, hurting, misery, ordeal, pain, plight, torment, torture, wretchedness
◨ comfort, ease

suffice *v* answer, be adequate, be sufficient, content, do, fit/fill the bill *colloq*, measure up, satisfy, serve

sufficiency *n* adequacy, adequateness, competence, enough, plenty, satiety
◨ inadequacy, insufficiency

sufficient *adj* adequate, ample, decent *colloq*, effective, enough, plenty, satisfactory
◨ inadequate, insufficient

suffocate *v* asphyxiate, be/make breathless, choke, smother, stifle, strangle, throttle

suffrage *n* enfranchisement *formal*, franchise, right of representation, right to vote

suffuse *v* bathe, colour, cover, flood, imbue, infuse, mantle, permeate, pervade, redden, spread, steep, transfuse

sugar

> *Kinds of sugar include:*
> beet sugar, brown sugar, cane sugar, caster sugar, crystallized sugar, demerara, dextrose, fructose, glucose, golden syrup, granulated sugar, icing sugar, invert sugar, jaggery, lactose, maltose, maple syrup, molasses, powdered sugar, refined sugar, sucrose, sugar loaf, sugar lump, sweets, candy *US*, sugar candy *US*, syrup, treacle, unrefined sugar

sugary *adj* corny *colloq*, emotional, gushing, gushy *colloq*, lovey-dovey *colloq*, maudlin, mawkish, mushy *colloq*, schmaltzy *colloq*, sentimental, sickly *colloq*, sloppy, slushy *colloq*, soppy, touching

suggest *v* 1 *I suggested that we should redefine our goals*: advise, advocate, counsel, propose, put forward, recommend, submit 2 *evidence suggests mobile phones are safe to use*: give the impression, hint, imply, indicate, insinuate, intimate

suggestion *n* 1 *made a sensible suggestion to the group*: idea, motion, piece of advice, plan, pointer, proposal, proposition, recommendation, submission 2 *the suggestion is that we are not able to decide matters for ourselves*: implication, innuendo, insinuation, intimation 3 *a suggestion of make-up on her face*: hint, suspicion, touch, trace

suggestive *adj* 1 *thick vegetation, suggestive of a forest or a jungle*: evocative, indicative, meaning, redolent *formal*, reminiscent 2 *a suggestive remark*: bawdy, blue *colloq*, dirty, immodest, improper, indecent, indelicate, lewd, off-colour, provocative, ribald, risqué, sexual, smutty, titillating
◨ 1 inexpressive 2 clean, decent

suicide *n* ending it all *colloq*, felo de se *formal*, hara-kiri, killing yourself, self-destruction, self-immolation *formal*, self-murder, self-slaughter, suttee, taking of your (own) life, topping yourself *colloq*

suit *n* 1 *wear a suit*: clothing, costume, dress, ensemble, outfit, set of clothes 2 *a paternity suit*: action, argument, case, cause, contest, dispute, lawsuit, litigation, proceedings, process, prosecution, trial
♦ *v* 1 *that dress suits you perfectly*: become, befit, complement, fit, flatter, go well with, harmonize with, look good/attractive on, match 2 *a holiday by the sea would suit all of us*: gratify, please, satisfy 3 *an early appointment would suit me*: be

acceptable, be applicable, be appropriate, be convenient for, be satisfactory, be suitable for, fit/fill the bill *colloq*
☒ 1 clash 2 displease 3 be inconvenient for, be unsuitable for

suitability *n* appositeness *formal*, appropriateness, aptness, convenience, fitness, fittingness, opportuneness, rightness, timeliness
☒ inappropriateness, unsuitability

suitable *adj* acceptable, adequate, applicable, apposite *formal*, appropriate, apt, becoming, befitting, compatible, fit, fitting, in keeping, opportune, pertinent *formal*, proper, relevant, right, (right/just) up someone's street *colloq*, satisfactory, suited, well-matched, well-suited
☒ inappropriate, unsuitable

suitably *adv* acceptably, accordingly, appropriately, fitly, fittingly, properly, quite
☒ unsuitably

suitcase *n* attaché case, bag, case, flight bag, hand-luggage, holdall, overnight-bag, portfolio, portmanteau, travel bag, trunk, valise

suite *n* 1 *a palatial penthouse suite:* apartment, household, rooms, set of rooms 2 *a new bathroom suite:* collection, furniture, set 3 *the king and his suite:* attendants, entourage, escort, followers, retainers, retinue, servants

suitor *n* admirer, beau, boyfriend, follower, lover, pretendant, wooer, young man

sulk *v* be in a huff *colloq*, be miffed *colloq*, brood, grouse, grump, mope, pout
♦ *n* bad mood, bad temper, huff *colloq*, miff *colloq*, mood, pique, temper

sulky *adj* aloof, bad-tempered, brooding, cross, disgruntled, grudging, grumpy, huffy *colloq*, miffed *colloq*, moody, moping, morose, out of sorts, put out, ratty *colloq*, resentful, sullen, unsociable
☒ cheerful, good-tempered, sociable

sullen *adj* 1 *a sullen teenager:* churlish, cross, gloomy, glum, moody, morose, obstinate, perverse, resentful, silent, sour, stubborn, sulky, surly, uncommunicative 2 *a sullen sky:* cheerless, dark, dismal, dull, gloomy, heavy, leaden, sombre
☒ 1 cheerful, happy 2 clear, fine

sullenness *n* brooding, glowering, glumness, heaviness, moodiness, moroseness, sourness, sulkiness, surliness
☒ cheerfulness

sully *v* besmirch, blemish, contaminate, damage, defile, dirty, disgrace, dishonour, mar, pollute, soil, spoil, spot, stain, taint, tarnish
☒ cleanse, honour

sultry *adj* 1 *sultry weather:* airless, close, hot, humid, muggy, oppressive, sticky, stifling, stuffy, suffocating, sweltering 2 *a sultry beauty:* alluring, attractive, passionate, provocative, seductive, sensual, sexy, tempting, voluptuous
☒ 1 cold, cool

sum *n* aggregate, amount, answer, culmination, entirety, number, quantity, reckoning, result, score, sum total, summary, tally, total, whole
▶ **sum up** 1 *summed up the meeting in a few words:* close, conclude, put in a nutshell *colloq*, recapitulate, review, summarize 2 *the picture*

sums up the whole day: embody, encapsulate, epitomize, exemplify

summarily *adv* abruptly, arbitrarily, expeditiously *formal*, forthwith *formal*, hastily, immediately, peremptorily *formal*, promptly, speedily, swiftly, without delay

summarize *v* abbreviate, abridge, condense, encapsulate, epitomize, outline, précis, recap *colloq*, review, shorten, sketch, sum up
☒ expand (on)

summary *n* abridgement, abstract, compendium, condensation, digest, main points, outline, overview, plan, précis, recapitulation, résumé, review, rundown *colloq*, summing-up, synopsis
♦ *adj* arbitrary, brief, cursory, direct, hasty, immediate, instant, instantaneous, peremptory *formal*, prompt, short, speedy, succinct, swift, unceremonious, without delay, without formality
☒ careful, lengthy

summerhouse *n* belvedere, gazebo, pavilion

summit *n* acme, apex *formal*, apogee *formal*, climax, crest, crown, culmination, head, height, peak, pinnacle, point, top, vertex, zenith *formal*
☒ bottom, foot, nadir

summon *v* arouse, assemble, beckon, bid, call, convene, convoke *formal*, demand, gather, invite, mobilize, muster, order, rally, rouse, send for
☒ dismiss
▶ **summon up** arouse, assemble, call to mind, convene, evoke, gather, mobilize, muster, rally, revive, rouse

summons *n* call, citation, injunction, order, subpoena, writ

sumptuous *adj* costly, de luxe, dear, expensive, extravagant, gorgeous, grand, lavish, luxurious, magnificent, opulent *formal*, plush, rich, splendid, superb
☒ plain, poor

sun *n* daylight, daystar, light, star, sunlight, sunshine
♦ *v* bake, bask, brown, insolate *formal*, sunbathe, tan

sunbathe *v* bake, bask, brown, insolate *formal*, sun, tan

sunburnt *adj* blistered, blistering, bronzed, brown, burnt, inflamed, peeling, red, sun-tanned, tanned, weather-beaten
☒ pale

sunder *v* chop, cleave *formal*, cut, dissever *formal*, dissunder *formal*, divide, part, separate, sever, split
☒ join

sundry *adj* a few, assorted, different, diverse, miscellaneous, several, some, varied, various

sunk *adj* done for *colloq*, doomed, failed, finished, in a fix/jam *colloq*, lost, ruined, up the creek *colloq*, up the spout *colloq*

sunken *adj* 1 *sunken treasure:* below ground level, buried, submerged 2 *sunken eyes:* concave, depressed, drawn, haggard, hollow

sunless *adj* bleak, cheerless, cloudy, dark, depressing, dismal, dreary, gloomy, grey, hazy, overcast, sombre
☒ bright, sunny

sunny *adj* **1** *a beautiful sunny day:* bright, brilliant, clear, cloudless, fine, summery, sunlit, sunshiny, unclouded **2** *a sunny disposition:* beaming, blithe *formal*, bouncy, bright, bubbly, buoyant, cheerful, cheery, glad, happy, hopeful, joyful, light-hearted, merry, optimistic, pleasant, radiant, smiling
🗲 **1** cloudy, dull, sunless **2** gloomy

sunrise *n* aurora, break of day, cock-crow, crack of dawn, dawn, daybreak, daylight, first light, sun-up

sunset *n* close of day, dusk, evening, gloaming, nightfall, sundown, twilight

super *adj* ace *colloq*, brill *colloq*, cool *slang*, excellent, glorious, great, incomparable, magnificent, marvellous, matchless, mega *slang*, neat *colloq*, outstanding, peerless, sensational, smashing *colloq*, superb, terrific *colloq*, top-notch *colloq*, wicked *slang*, wonderful
🗲 lousy *colloq*, poor

superannuated *adj* aged, antiquated, decrepit, elderly, moribund *formal*, obsolete, old, past it *colloq*, pensioned off, put out to grass *colloq*, retired, senile
🗲 young

superb *adj* ace *colloq*, admirable, breathtaking, brill *colloq*, brilliant, choice, dazzling, excellent, exquisite, fabulous *colloq*, fine, first-class, first-rate, gorgeous, grand, great, impressive, lavish, magnificent, marvellous, neat *colloq*, outstanding, remarkable, smashing *colloq*, splendid, superior, superlative, terrific *colloq*, unrivalled, unsurpassed, wonderful
🗲 bad, inferior, poor

supercilious *adj* arrogant, condescending, contemptuous, disdainful, haughty, hoity-toity *colloq*, imperious, insolent, jumped up *colloq*, lofty, lordly, overbearing, patronizing, proud, scornful, snooty *colloq*, snotty *colloq*, stuck-up *colloq*, toffee-nosed *colloq*, too big for your boots *colloq*, uppish *colloq*, uppity *colloq*, vainglorious *formal*
🗲 humble, self-effacing

superficial *adj* alleged, apparent, careless, casual, cosmetic, cursory, exterior, external, facile, frivolous, hasty, hurried, insignificant, lightweight, ostensible *formal*, outer, outward, passing, perfunctory, peripheral, seeming, shallow, sketchy, skin-deep, slapdash, slight, surface, trivial
🗲 deep, internal, thorough

superficially *adv* apparently, carelessly, casually, externally, hurriedly, on the surface, ostensibly *formal*, seemingly
🗲 in depth

superfluity *n* excess, excessiveness, extra, exuberance, glut, pleonasm *technical*, plethora *formal*, redundancy, superabundance, surfeit, surplus
🗲 lack

superfluous *adj* excess, excessive, extra, gratuitous, needless, redundant, remaining, spare, supernumerary *formal*, surplus, to spare, uncalled-for, unnecessary, unneeded, unwanted, unwarranted
🗲 essential, necessary, needed, required, wanted

superhuman *adj* divine, great, herculean, heroic, immense, paranormal, phenomenal, preternatural *formal*, prodigious *formal*, stupendous, supernatural
🗲 average, ordinary

superintend *v* administer, be in charge of, be in control of, be responsible for, control, direct, handle, inspect, manage, overlook, oversee, run, steer, supervise

superintendence *n* administration, care, charge, control, direction, government, guidance, inspection, management, oversight, running, supervision, surveillance

superintendent *n* administrator, boss *colloq*, chief, conductor, controller, curator, director, gaffer *colloq*, governor, inspector, manager, overseer, supervisor

superior *adj* **1** *superior goods:* admirable, choice, de luxe, distinguished, excellent, exceptional, exclusive, fine, first-class, first-rate, high-class, high-quality, par excellence, prime, prize, quality, select, top-flight *colloq*, top-notch *colloq*, unrivalled **2** *complained to his superior officer:* higher, higher in rank, senior **3** *I can't stand my colleague, she's so superior:* condescending, disdainful, haughty, jumped up *colloq*, lofty, lordly, patronizing, pretentious, snobbish, snooty *colloq*, stuck-up *colloq*, supercilious, toffee-nosed *colloq*, too big for your boots *colloq*, uppish *colloq*, uppity *colloq*
🗲 **1** average, inferior **2** inferior, lower, worse **3** humble, self-effacing
♦ *n* better, boss, chief, director, elder, foreman, manager, principal, senior, supervisor
🗲 assistant, inferior, junior, subordinate

superiority *n* advantage, ascendancy *formal*, dominance, edge, eminence, lead, predominance, pre-eminence, supremacy
🗲 inferiority

superlative *adj* ace *colloq*, best, brill *colloq*, brilliant, consummate *formal*, excellent, first-class, first-rate, greatest, highest, magnificent, matchless, outstanding, peerless, supreme, transcendent *formal*, unbeatable, unbeaten, unparalleled, unrivalled, unsurpassed
🗲 average, mediocre, poor

supernatural *adj* abnormal, eerie, ghostly, hidden, magic, magical, metaphysical, miraculous, mysterious, mystic, mystical, occult, otherworldly, paranormal, phantom, preternatural *formal*, psychic, spiritual, unnatural, weird
🗲 natural, normal

supernumerary *adj* excess, excessive, extra, extraordinary, redundant, spare, superfluous, surplus
🗲 necessary

supersede *v* displace, oust, remove, replace, succeed, supplant, take over from, take the place of, usurp

superstition *n* delusion, fallacy, illusion, magic, myth, old wives' tale

superstitious *adj* delusive, fallacious, false, groundless, illusory, irrational, mythical
🗲 factual, logical, rational

supervise *v* administer, be in charge of, be in control of, be responsible for, conduct, control, direct, guide, handle, inspect, keep an eye on, look after, manage, oversee, preside over, run, superintend, watch (over)

supervision *n* administration, care, charge, control, direction, guidance, inspection, instruction, management, oversight, running, superintendence, surveillance

supervisor *n* administrator, boss, chief, director, foreman, forewoman, inspector, manager, overseer, steward, superintendent

supervisory *adj* administrative, directorial *formal*, executive, managerial, overseeing, superintendent

supine *adj* **1** *lying in a supine position:* flat, horizontal, prostrate, recumbent *formal* **2** *a supine approach to pay negotiations:* apathetic, bored, careless, heedless, idle, inactive, indifferent, indolent *formal*, inert, languid, lazy, lethargic, listless, negligent, passive, resigned, slothful, sluggish, spineless *colloq*, spiritless, torpid *formal*, uninterested, unresisting
⟐ 1 upright **2** alert

supper *n* dinner, evening meal, snack, tea

supplant *v* displace, oust, overthrow, remove, replace, supersede, take over from, take the place of, topple, unseat, usurp

supple *adj* bending, double-jointed, elastic, flexible, graceful, limber, lithe, loose-limbed, plastic, pliable, pliant, stretching
⟐ inflexible, rigid, stiff

supplement *n* addendum, addition, additive, add-on, appendix, codicil *technical*, extra, insert, postscript, pull-out, rider, sequel
◆ *v* add to, augment *formal*, boost, complement, eke out, extend, fill up, increase, reinforce, top up
⟐ deplete, use up

> *supplement*, *complement* or *compliment*? See panel at **complement**

supplementary *adj* accompanying, added, additional, attached, auxiliary, complementary, extra, secondary

> *supplementary*, *complementary* or *complimentary*? See panel at **complementary**

suppliant *adj* begging, beseeching *formal*, craving, entreating, imploring, importunate *formal*, supplicating

supplicant *n* applicant, petitioner, pleader, postulant *formal*, suitor, suppliant

supplicate *v* appeal, beseech *formal*, entreat, invoke *formal*, petition, plead, pray, request, solicit

supplication *n* appeal, entreaty, imploration *formal*, invocation *formal*, orison, petition, plea, pleading, prayer, request, rogation *formal*, solicitation *formal*, suit

supplicatory *adj* begging, beseeching *formal*, imploring, imprecatory *formal*, petitioning, precative *formal*, precatory *formal*, supplicating

supplier *n* contributor, dealer, donor, outfitter, provider, retailer, seller, vendor, wholesaler

supply *v* contribute, donate, endow, endue *formal*, equip, fit out, furnish, give, grant, proffer *formal*, provide, replenish, sell, yield
⟐ receive, take
◆ *n* **1** *a plentiful supply of flour:* amount, cache,

fund, heap, hoard, mass, pile, quantity, reserve, reservoir, source, stock, stockpile, store **2** *put away enough supplies for the winter:* equipment, food, materials, necessities, provisions, rations, stores

support *v* **1** *supported the protest:* advocate, aid, assist, back, be behind/with, be in favour of, be in sympathy with, champion, defend, espouse *formal*, foster, further, help, promote, rally round, run with *colloq*, second, throw your weight behind *colloq* **2** *supported her through a difficult period:* be kind to, be supportive to, befriend, care for, comfort, encourage, give moral support to, give strength to, help, motivate, sympathize with **3** *supporting the fabric of the building:* bear, bolster (up), brace, buttress, carry, hold up, prop (up), reinforce, shore up, strengthen, sustain, take the weight of, underpin **4** *supports a wife and three young children:* feed, keep, look after, maintain, nourish, provide for, sustain, take care of **5** *support a statement:* authenticate, back up, bear out, confirm, corroborate *formal*, document, endorse, ratify, substantiate, validate, verify **6** *supporting a good cause:* back, contribute to, finance, fund, give a donation to, sponsor, subsidize, underwrite
⟐ 1 oppose **4** live off **5** contradict
◆ *n* **1** *the campaign has attracted a lot of support in the local community:* aid, allegiance, approval, assistance, backing, defence, encouragement, espousal *formal*, help, loyalty, patronage, protection **2** *the supports gave way:* base, bolster, brace, buttress, crutch, foundation(s), pillar, post, prop, skeleton, stay, substructure, trestle, underpinning **3** *your support helped me through a crisis:* care, comfort, encouragement, friendship, help, moral support, motivation, strength, sympathy **4** *they depend on the state for support:* food, keep, maintenance, provision, subsistence, sustenance **5** *the benefactor's continued support enables to charity to carry out its work:* contribution, donation, finance, funding, grant, patronage, sponsorship, subsidy **6** *the latest findings give support to my case:* authentication, backing, confirmation, evidence, ratification, substantiation, validation, verification
⟐ 1 hostility, opposition

supporter *n* adherent, advocate, ally, apologist, champion, contributor, co-worker, defender, donor, fan, follower, friend, helper, partner, patron, promoter, seconder, sponsor, sympathizer, voter, well-wisher
⟐ opponent

supportive *adj* attentive, caring, comforting, encouraging, helpful, reassuring, sympathetic, understanding
⟐ discouraging

suppose *v* **1** *I suppose they'll get married eventually:* believe, conclude, conjecture *formal*, consider, expect, fancy, guess, imagine, infer, judge, reckon, surmise *formal*, take for granted, think **2** *their theory supposes an increased demand for organic produce:* assume, hypothesize *formal*, imply, posit *formal*, postulate *formal*, presume, presuppose *formal*, require

supposed *adj* alleged, assumed, believed, hypothetical, imagined, presumed, putative *formal*, reported, reputed, rumoured, so-called

supposition *n* assumption, conjecture *formal*, guess, hypothesis *formal*, idea, notion, postulation *formal*, presumption, presupposition *formal*, speculation, surmise *formal*, theory
🔹 knowledge

suppress *v* censor, check, conceal, contain, control, crack/clamp down on *colloq*, crush, hold back, inhibit, keep in check, keep under control, put an end to, quash, quell, repress, restrain, silence, smother, squash, stamp out, stifle, stop, strangle, subdue, vanquish *formal*, withhold
🔹 encourage, incite

suppression *n* censorship, check, clampdown *colloq*, cover-up, crackdown *colloq*, crushing, dissolution, elimination, extinction, inhibition, prohibition, quashing, quelling, smothering, termination
🔹 encouragement, incitement

suppurate *v* discharge, fester, gather, maturate *technical*, ooze, weep

suppuration *n* diapyesis *technical*, festering, mattering, pus

supremacy *n* ascendancy *formal*, control, dominance, domination, dominion, hegemony *formal*, lordship, mastery, paramountcy *formal*, power, predominance, pre-eminence, primacy, rule, sovereignty, sway

supreme *adj* **1** *the supreme actress of her generation:* best, chief, consummate, crowning, excellent, first, first-class, first-rate, foremost, greatest, head, highest, incomparable, leading, matchless, peerless, predominant, pre-eminent, prevailing, prime, principal, second-to-none, sovereign, superlative, top, transcendent, unsurpassed, world-beating **2** *the supreme sacrifice:* extreme, final, greatest, highest, last, ultimate, utmost
🔹 **1** lowly, poor

sure *adj* **1** *my team is sure to win:* assured, bound, certain, clear, guaranteed, inevitable **2** *I'm sure you'll manage:* assured, confident, convinced, positive **3** *the only sure way of preventing an outbreak:* effective, efficacious *formal*, foolproof, guaranteed, proven, sure-fire *colloq*, tested **4** *a sure footing:* dependable, fast, firm, infallible, reliable, safe, safe as houses *colloq*, secure, solid, stable, steadfast, steady, unerring, unfailing, unfaltering, unwavering **5** *a sure sign of success:* accurate, clear, decided, definite, indisputable, irrevocable, undeniable, undoubted, unmistakable, unquestionable **6** *a sure friend:* dependable, faithful, firm, infallible, loyal, never-failing, reliable, solid, stable, steadfast, steady, trustworthy, unfaltering, unquestionable
🔹 **1** doubtful, uncertain **2** doubtful, uncertain, unsure **4** insecure, unsafe **5** uncertain, unsure

surely *adv* assuredly, certainly, confidently, definitely, doubtlessly, firmly, indubitably, inevitably, inexorably, undoubtedly, unquestionably, without doubt

surety *n* bail, bond, bondsman, certainty, deposit, guarantee, guarantor, hostage, indemnity, insurance, mortgagor, pledge, safety, security, sponsor, warrant, warranty

surface *n* covering, exterior, façade, face, outside, outward appearance, plane, side, skin, top, veneer
🔹 inside, interior
🔹 *v* appear, arise, come to light, come to the surface, come up, emerge, materialize, reappear, rise
🔹 disappear, sink, vanish
🔹 *adj* apparent, exterior, external, outer, outside, outward, superficial
🔹 interior

surfeit *n* bellyful *colloq*, excess, glut, overindulgence, plethora *formal*, satiety, superabundance, superfluity, surplus
🔹 lack
🔹 *v* cram, fill, glut, gorge, overfeed, overfill, satiate, stuff

surge *n* **1** *a sudden surge hit the sea defences:* billow, breaker, eddy, efflux *formal*, flow, gush, pouring, roller, rush, stream, sweep, swell, wave(s) **2** *a surge of support for the MP:* escalation, increase, intensification, rise, upsurge, upswing
🔹 *v* **1** *water surged over the barriers:* break, eddy, flow, gush, heave, pour, roll, rush, seethe, stream, sweep, swell, swirl **2** *share prices surging ahead:* escalate, increase, rise

surly *adj* bad-tempered, brusque, cantankerous, churlish, crabbed *colloq*, cross, crotchety *colloq*, crusty, grouchy, gruff, grumpy, ill-natured, irascible, morose, sulky, sullen, testy, uncivil, ungracious
🔹 friendly, polite

surmise *v* assume, conclude, conjecture *formal*, consider, deduce, fancy, guess, imagine, infer, opine *formal*, presume, speculate, suppose, suspect
🔹 know
🔹 *n* assumption, conclusion, conjecture *formal*, deduction, guess, hypothesis *formal*, idea, inference, notion, opinion, possibility, presumption, speculation, supposition *formal*, suspicion, thought
🔹 certainty

surmount *v* conquer, exceed, get over, master, overcome, prevail over, surpass, triumph over, vanquish *formal*

surpass *v* beat, better, eclipse, exceed, excel, outclass, outdo, outshine, outstrip, overshadow, tower above, transcend

surpassing *adj* exceptional, extraordinary, incomparable, inimitable, matchless, outstanding, phenomenal, rare, supreme, transcendent, unrivalled, unsurpassed
🔹 poor

surplus *n* balance, excess, glut, leftovers, remainder, residue, superfluity, surfeit
🔹 lack, shortage
🔹 *adj* excess, extra, left over, redundant, remaining, spare, superfluous, unused

surprise *v* **1** *she was surprised by the warm welcome she received:* amaze, astonish, astound, bewilder, bowl over *colloq*, confuse, disconcert, flabbergast *colloq*, knock for six *colloq*, knock someone down with a feather *colloq*, stagger, startle, stun, take aback, take someone's breath away *colloq*, wow *colloq* **2** *came home early and surprised the burglar:* burst in on, catch in the act, catch red-handed, catch someone with their pants/trousers down *colloq*, catch unawares, expose, find (out), startle, unmask
🔹 *n* **1** *looked at him in complete surprise:* amazement, astonishment, bewilderment, bolt

from the blue *colloq*, bombshell *colloq*, dismay, incredulity, revelation, shock, start, thunderbolt *colloq*, wonder **2** *the news came as a surprise:* bolt from the blue *colloq*, bombshell *colloq*, revelation, shock, thunderbolt *colloq*
F **1** composure

surprised *adj* amazed, astonished, astounded, dumbfounded, flabbergasted *colloq*, gobsmacked *colloq*, lost for words, nonplussed *colloq*, open-mouthed, shocked, speechless, staggered, startled, stunned, thunderstruck
F composed, unsurprised

surprising *adj* amazing, astonishing, astounding, extraordinary, incredible, remarkable, staggering, startling, stunning, unexpected, unforeseen, unlooked-for, wonderful
F expected, unsurprising

surrender *v* abandon, abdicate, capitulate, cede, concede, forgo, give in, give up, leave behind, let go of, quit *colloq*, relinquish, renounce, resign, submit, succumb *formal*, throw in the towel/sponge *colloq*, waive, yield
♦ *n* abandonment, abdication, capitulation, cession *formal*, relinquishment, renunciation, resignation, submission, waiving, yielding

surreptitious *adj* clandestine *formal*, covert, furtive, hidden, secret, sly, sneaky *colloq*, stealthy, unauthorized, underhand, veiled
F obvious, open

surrogate *n* deputy, proxy, replacement, representative, stand-in, substitute

surround *v* beset, besiege, confine, encase, encircle, enclose, encompass, envelop, environ *formal*, fence in, gird, girdle, go round, hem in, ring

surrounding *adj* adjacent, adjoining, bordering, encircling, nearby, neighbouring

surroundings *n* ambience, background, element, environment, environs, habitat, locality, milieu, neighbourhood, scene, setting, vicinity

surveillance *n* care, charge, check, control, direction, guardianship, inspection, monitoring, observation, regulation, scrutiny, stewardship, superintendence, supervision, vigilance, watch

survey *v* **1** *survey the panorama:* consider, contemplate, examine, inspect, look at, look over, observe, poll, research, review, scan, scrutinize, study, view **2** *survey the opinions of female voters:* canvass, poll, research, review, study **3** *survey the results:* appraise *formal*, assess, chart, evaluate, map, measure, size up *colloq*
♦ *n* **1** *a survey of the company's finances:* appraisal, assessment, consideration, examination, inspection, measurement, overview, poll, review, scrutiny, study, valuation **2** *a survey of public opinion:* form, market research, opinion poll, probe, questionnaire, quiz, study, test

surveyor *n* assessor, examiner, geodesist *technical*, inspector

survive *v* be extant *formal*, continue, cope, endure, exist, hold out, keep your head above water *colloq*, last, live (on), make it *colloq*, manage, outlast, outlive, persist, pull through *colloq*, rally, recover, remain, stay, weather, withstand
F die, succumb

susceptibility *n* defencelessness, gullibility, liability, openness, predisposition *formal*, proclivity *formal*, proneness, propensity *formal*, responsiveness, sensitivity, suggestibility, tendency, vulnerability, weakness
F impregnability, resistance

susceptible *adj* credulous, defenceless, disposed, easily led, given, gullible, impressionable, inclined, liable, open, prone, receptive, responsive, sensitive, subject, suggestible, tender, vulnerable, weak
F immune, resistant

suspect *v* **1** *I suspect his motives:* be uneasy about, be wary of, call into question, distrust, doubt, have doubts about, have misgivings/qualms about, mistrust **2** *I suspect you're right:* believe, conclude, conjecture *formal*, consider, fancy, feel, get it into your head *colloq*, guess, have a hunch *colloq*, infer, speculate, suppose, surmise *formal*
♦ *adj* debatable, dodgy *colloq*, doubtful, dubious, fishy *colloq*, iffy *colloq*, questionable, suspicious, unreliable
F acceptable, reliable

suspend *v* **1** *lights suspended from a tree:* dangle, hang, swing **2** *the judge suspended the case:* adjourn, arrest, cease *formal*, defer, delay, discontinue *formal*, interrupt, postpone, prorogue *formal*, put in abeyance *formal*, put off, put on ice *colloq*, put on the back burner *colloq*, shelve, take a raincheck on *colloq* **3** *suspended from his position for bad behaviour:* debar, dismiss, exclude, expel, keep out, remove, shut out, unfrock
F **2** carry on, continue **3** reinstate, restore

suspended *adj* **1** *suspended from the ceiling:* dangling, hanging, pendent *formal*, pensile *formal* **2** *plans were suspended while an investigation was carried out:* deferred, delayed, pending, postponed, put off, put on ice *colloq*, shelved

suspense *n* anticipation, anxiety, apprehension, doubt, excitement, expectancy, expectation, insecurity, nervousness, tension, uncertainty
F certainty, knowledge

suspension *n* **1** *the suspension of the meeting:* abeyance *formal*, adjournment, break, cessation *formal*, deferment, deferral, delay, intermission, interruption, moratorium, postponement, remission, respite, stay **2** *suspension from school:* debarment, dismissal, exclusion, expulsion, removal
F **1** continuation

suspicion *n* **1** *made her suspicions about him clear:* apprehension, caution, chariness, distrust, doubt, misgiving(s), mistrust, qualm(s), scepticism, wariness **2** *a suspicion of anger in his voice:* glimmer, hint, scintilla, shade, shadow, soupçon, suggestion, tinge, touch, trace **3** *I had a suspicion you'd be here:* belief, feeling, funny feeling *colloq*, hunch *colloq*, idea, notion, opinion, sixth sense *colloq*
F **1** trust

suspicious *adj* **1** *she has a naturally suspicious character:* apprehensive, chary, disbelieving, distrustful, doubtful, mistrustful, sceptical, suspecting, unbelieving, uneasy, unsure, wary **2** *suspicious behaviour:* dishonest, dodgy *colloq*, dubious, fishy *colloq*, funny, guilty, iffy *colloq*, irregular, odd, peculiar, questionable, shady *colloq*, shifty, strange, suspect
F **1** confident, trustful **2** innocent, trustworthy

sustain *v* **1** *sustains a large population:* bear, carry, feed, foster, give strength to, help, nourish, nurture, provide for, relieve, support **2** *managed to sustain a steady pace throughout the race:* carry on, continue, hold, keep going, keep up, maintain, uphold **3** *sustained extensive injuries:* endure, experience, go through, receive, suffer, undergo

sustained *adj* constant, continuing, continuous, long-drawn-out, ongoing, perpetual, prolonged, protracted *formal*, steady, unremitting *formal*
◨ broken, intermittent, interrupted, spasmodic

sustenance *n* aliment *formal*, comestibles *formal*, fare, food, grub *colloq*, livelihood, maintenance, nosh *colloq*, nourishment, provender *formal*, provisions, refection *formal*, scoff *colloq*, subsistence, support, viands *formal*, victuals *formal*

svelte *adj* elegant, graceful, lissom, lithe, polished, shapely, slender, slim, sophisticated, sylphlike, urbane, willowy
◨ bulky, ungainly

swagger *v* bluster, boast, brag, crow, go over the top *colloq*, make an exhibition of yourself *colloq*, parade, play to the gallery *colloq*, prance, show off *colloq*, strut, swank *colloq*
♦ *n* arrogance, bluster, ostentation, parading, prancing, show

swallow *v* **1** *swallow food and drink:* consume, devour, down *colloq*, drink, eat, gobble up, gulp, guzzle *colloq*, ingest *formal*, knock back *colloq*, polish off *colloq*, quaff, scoff *colloq*, swig *colloq* **2** *swallow a story:* accept, be certain of, believe, buy *colloq*, fall for *colloq*, swallow hook line and sinker *colloq*, trust **3** *swallow his laughter:* contain, hold back, repress, smother, stifle, suppress **4** *he swallowed their insults:* abide, accept, bear, endure, put up with, stand, stomach *colloq*, take, tolerate
▶ **swallow up** assimilate, enfold, engulf, envelop, overrun, overwhelm

swamp *n* bog, fen, marsh, mire, morass, mud, quag, quagmire, quicksand, slough
♦ *v* beset, besiege, deluge, drench, engulf, flood, inundate, overload, overwhelm, saturate, sink, submerge, wash out, waterlog, weigh down

swampy *adj* boggy, fenny, marshy, miry, paludal *formal*, quaggy, soggy, squelchy, uliginous *formal*, waterlogged, wet
◨ arid, dehydrated, dry

swank *v* attitudinize, boast, brag, parade, posture, preen yourself, show off, strut, swagger
♦ *n* boastfulness, bragging, conceit, conceitedness, display, ostentation, pretentiousness, self-advertisement, show, showing-off, swagger, vainglory *formal*
◨ modesty, restraint

swanky *adj* de luxe, exclusive, expensive, fancy, fashionable, flash *colloq*, flashy *colloq*, glamorous, grand, lavish, luxurious, ostentatious, plush *colloq*, plushy *colloq*, posh *colloq*, pretentious, rich, ritzy *colloq*, showy, smart, stylish, sumptuous, swish *colloq*
◨ discreet, unobtrusive

swap, swop *v* bandy, barter, exchange, interchange, substitute, switch, trade, traffic, transpose

swarm *n* army, body, crowd, drove, flock, herd, horde, host, mass, mob, multitude, myriad, pack, shoal, stream, throng
♦ *v* congregate, crowd, flock, flood, mass, stream, surge, throng

swarthy *adj* black, brown, dark, dark-complexioned, dark-skinned, dusky, tanned
◨ fair, pale

swashbuckling *adj* adventurous, bold, courageous, dare-devil, daring, dashing, exciting, flamboyant, gallant, robust, spirited, swaggering
◨ tame, unadventurous, unexciting

swathe *v* bandage, bind, cloak, drape, enshroud, envelop, enwrap, fold, furl, lap, sheathe, shroud, swaddle, wind, wrap
◨ unwind, unwrap

sway *v* **1** *sway from side to side:* bend, lean, lurch, oscillate, reel, rock, roll, shake, stagger, swerve, swing, veer, wave, wobble **2** *sway opinion:* affect, bring round, convert, convince, direct, dominate, govern, induce, influence, overrule, persuade, prevail upon *formal*, rule, win over
♦ *n* ascendancy *formal*, authority, clout *colloq*, command, control, dominion, government, hegemony *technical*, influence, jurisdiction, leadership, power, predominance, preponderance *formal*, rule, sovereignty

swear *v* **1** *I swear it's the truth:* abjure *formal*, affirm, assert, asseverate *formal*, attest *formal*, aver *formal*, avow *formal*, be on/under oath, declare, insist, pledge, pledge yourself, promise, promise solemnly, take an oath, testify, vow **2** *he swore loudly:* blaspheme, blind, curse, cuss *colloq*, eff *colloq*, eff and blind *colloq*, imprecate *formal*, maledict *formal*, take the Lord's name in vain, turn the air blue, use bad language, utter profanities
▶ **swear by** believe in, depend on, have confidence in, have faith in, rely on, trust in

swearing *n* bad language, blasphemy, coprolalia *technical*, cursing, cussing *colloq*, effing and blinding *colloq*, expletives, foul language, imprecations *formal*, maledictions *formal*, profanity

swear-word *n* bad language, blasphemy, curse, expletive, foul language, four-letter word, imprecation *formal*, oath, obscenity, profanity, swearing

sweat *n* **1** *covered in sweat after the match:* diaphoresis, hidrosis, moisture, perspiration, stickiness, sudor *technical* **2** *he's in a sweat about his exam results:* agitation, anxiety, dither, flap *colloq*, fluster *colloq*, fuss, panic, tizzy *colloq*, worry **3** *this work is such a sweat:* chore, drudgery, effort, labour, toil
♦ *v* break out in a sweat, drip, exude *formal*, perspire, secrete, sudate *technical*, sweat buckets *colloq*, sweat like a pig *colloq*

sweaty *adj* clammy, damp, moist, perspiring, sticky, sweating
◨ cool, dry

sweep *v* **1** *sweep the floor:* brush, clean (up), clear (up), dust, vacuum **2** *swept the children into the car:* drag, drive, elbow, force, jostle, move quickly, poke, push, shove, spread quickly, thrust **3** *she swept past them out of the room:* fly, glance, glide, hurtle, pass, race, sail, scud, skim, tear, whip, whisk

♦ *n* **1** *a sweep of the arm:* action, arc, bend, curvature *formal,* curve, gesture, move, movement, stroke, swing **2** *the vast sweep of her ambition:* compass, expanse, extent, immensity, range, scope, span, stretch, vastness, vista

sweeping *adj* across-the-board *colloq,* all-embracing, all-inclusive, blanket *colloq,* broad, comprehensive, extensive, far-reaching, general, global, indiscriminate, oversimplified, radical, simplistic, thorough, thoroughgoing, wholesale, wide, wide-ranging

🔄 narrow, specific

sweepstake *n* draw, gambling, lottery, sweep, sweepstakes

sweet *adj* **1** *my son prefers sweet things to savoury:* candied, delicious, glacé, honeyed, luscious, ripe, saccharine, sickly, sickly sweet, sugary, sweetened, syrupy **2** *the sweet perfume of sandalwood:* ambrosial *formal,* aromatic, balmy, fragrant, odoriferous *formal,* odorous *formal,* perfumed, redolent *formal,* sweet-scented **3** *sweet music:* dulcet, euphonious, harmonious, mellifluous *formal,* mellow, melodious, musical, soft, sweet-sounding, tuneful **4** *a sweet child:* adorable, affectionate, agreeable, amiable, appealing, attractive, beautiful, charming, cherished, cute, darling, dear, delightful, engaging, kind, kindly, likeable, lovable, lovely, pleasant, pleasing, precious, pretty, tender, treasured, winning, winsome **5** *sweet air:* clean, clear, fresh, pure, wholesome

🔄 **1** bitter, salty, savoury, sour **2** foul **3** discordant **4** nasty, ugly, unpleasant **5** foul

♦ *n* **1** *they served a sweet after the main course:* afters *colloq,* dessert, pudding **2** *she passed around the sweets:* bonbon, candy, confection *formal,* confectionery, sweetie *colloq,* sweetmeat

Sweets include:
barley sugar, bull's eye, butterscotch, caramel, chewing-gum, chocolate, fondant, fruit pastille, fudge, gobstopper, gumdrop, humbug, jelly, jelly bean, liquorice, liquorice allsort, lollipop, marshmallow, marzipan, nougat, peppermint, praline, rock, toffee, toffee apple, truffle, Turkish delight

sweeten *v* **1** *sweeten a cup of tea:* add sugar to, honey, sugar **2** *sweeten a bad mood:* appease, mellow, mollify, soften, soothe **3** *sweeten a blow:* alleviate, cushion, ease, mitigate *formal,* relieve, temper

🔄 **2** embitter, sour

sweetheart *n* admirer, beloved, betrothed, boyfriend, darling, dear, flame *colloq,* follower, girlfriend, inamorata, inamorato, love, lover, Romeo, steady *colloq,* suitor, sweetie *colloq,* truelove, valentine

sweetness *n* **1** *the cloying sweetness of the pastries:* lusciousness, succulence, sugariness, syrup **2** *the sweetness of summer meadows:* aroma, balminess, fragrance **3** *the sweetness of her personality:* amiability, charm, kindness, loveliness, sweet temper, tenderness,

winsomeness **4** *the sweetness of the piece of music:* dulcitude *formal,* euphony, harmony

🔄 **1** acidity, bitterness, saltness, sourness **2** foulness **3** nastiness **4** cacophony

sweet-smelling *adj* ambrosial *formal,* aromatic, balmy, fragrant, odoriferous *formal,* odorous *formal,* perfumed, redolent *formal,* sweet-scented

🔄 fetid, malodorous

swell *v* **1** *her stomach began to swell:* balloon, billow, bloat, blow up, bulge, dilate *formal,* distend *formal,* enlarge, expand, extend, fatten, grow larger, inflate, puff up **2** *the tension swelled:* accelerate, augment *formal,* escalate, grow, heighten, increase, intensify, mount, mushroom, proliferate, rise, skyrocket, snowball, step up, surge

🔄 **1** contract, shrink **2** decrease, dwindle

♦ *n* **1** *rocked by the swell of the ocean:* billow, rise, surge, undulation, wave **2** *he considers himself a swell:* beau, bigwig *colloq,* cockscomb, dandy, dude, fop

🔄 **2** down-and-out, scarecrow, tramp

♦ *adj* de luxe, excellent, exclusive, fashionable, flashy *colloq,* grand, great, posh *colloq,* ritzy *colloq,* smart, stylish, swanky *colloq,* wonderful

🔄 seedy, shabby

swelling *n* blister, boil, bruise, bulge, bump, distension *formal,* enlargement, inflammation, lump, protuberance, puffiness, tumescence *formal,* tumour

sweltering *adj* airless, baking *colloq,* boiling, clammy, hot, humid, muggy, oppressive, roasting *colloq,* scorching, sizzling *colloq,* steamy, sticky, stifling, suffocating, sultry, torrid, tropical

🔄 airy, breezy, cold, cool, fresh

swerve *v* bend, change direction suddenly, deflect, deviate, diverge, incline, sheer, shift, skew, stray, swing, turn, twist, veer, wander

swift *adj* abrupt, agile, brief, brisk, expeditious *formal,* express, fast, flying, hasty, hurried, immediate, lively, nimble, nippy *colloq,* prompt, quick, rapid, ready, short, speedy, sudden

🔄 slow, sluggish, unhurried

swiftly *adj* at full tilt, double-quick *colloq,* expeditiously *formal,* express, fast, hotfoot *colloq,* hurriedly, instantly, posthaste, promptly, quickly, rapidly, speedily

🔄 slowly, tardily *formal*

swiftness *n* alacrity *formal,* celerity *formal,* dispatch, expedition *formal,* immediacy, immediateness, instantaneity, promptness, quickness, rapidity, readiness, speed, speediness, suddenness, velocity

🔄 delay, slowness, tardiness *formal*

swill *v* consume, drain, drink, gulp, guzzle, imbibe *formal,* knock back *colloq,* quaff, swallow, swig

♦ *n* **1** *consumed the contents of the cup in one swill:* drink, gulp, swallow, swig **2** *fed the swill to the pigs:* hogwash, pigswill, refuse, scourings, slops, waste

▶ **swill out** clean, cleanse, drench, flush, rinse, sluice, wash down, wash out

swim *v* bathe, bob, float, snorkel, take a dip, tread water

The main swimming strokes include:
backstroke, breaststroke, butterfly, crawl,
doggy-paddle, sidestroke

swimming-pool *n* leisure pool, lido,
swimming-bath, swimming-pond
swimsuit *n* bathing costume, bathing suit,
bikini, swimming costume, trunks
swindle *v* bamboozle *colloq*, cheat, con *colloq*,
deceive, defraud, diddle, do *colloq*, dupe,
exploit, fleece, overcharge, pull the wool over
someone's eyes *colloq*, put one over on *colloq*, rip
off *colloq*, rook *colloq*, sting *colloq*, take for a ride
colloq, take to the cleaners *colloq*, trick
♦ *n* con *colloq*, deception, diddle, double-
dealing, fiddle, fraud, racket, rip-off *colloq*, scam
colloq, sharp practice, trickery
swindler *n* charlatan, cheat, con man *colloq*,
fiddler, fraud, hood *colloq*, hoodlum *colloq*,
hustler *colloq*, impostor, mountebank, rascal,
rogue, rook *colloq*, shark *colloq*, trickster
swine *n* **1** *feed the swine:* beast, boar, hog, pig
2 *her husband behaves like an absolute swine:* boor,
brute, good-for-nothing, rascal, rogue, scoundrel
swing *v* **1** *lights swinging from the trees:* dangle,
hang, pendulate *formal*, pivot, rock, rotate, spin,
sway, wave **2** *the road swung to the left:* bend,
curve, incline, lean, swerve, turn, twist, vary,
veer, wind **3** *it will be difficult but I think we can
swing it:* achieve, arrange, fix (up) *colloq*, get,
make, organize, set up
♦ *n* **1** *a swing of the bat:* motion, move, movement,
oscillation, rock, stroke, sway, waving **2** *a swing
in voting patterns:* change, fluctuation, move,
shift, sway, variation
swingeing *adj* devastating, draconian, drastic,
excessive, exorbitant, extortionate, harsh, heavy,
oppressive, punishing, serious, severe,
stringent, thumping *colloq*
🔁 mild
swinging *adj* contemporary, dynamic, exciting,
fashionable, hip *slang*, jet-setting *colloq*, lively,
modern, stylish, trendy *colloq*, up-to-date, up-to-
the-minute, with it *colloq*
🔁 fuddy-duddy, old-fashioned
swipe *v* **1** *swiped his brother in the mouth:* biff
colloq, clout *colloq*, hit, lash out, lunge, slap, sock
colloq, strike, wallop *colloq*, whack *colloq* **2** *swiped
the takings from the till:* filch *colloq*, lift, nick *colloq*,
pilfer, pinch *colloq*, steal, whip *colloq*
♦ *n* biff *colloq*, blow, clout *colloq*, slap, smack,
strike, stroke, wallop *colloq*, whack *colloq*
swirl *v* agitate, churn, circulate, curl, eddy,
revolve, spin, twirl, twist, wheel, whirl
swish[1] *v* birch, brandish, flog, flourish, lash,
rustle, swing, swirl, swoosh, thrash, twirl, wave,
whip, whirl, whisk, whistle, whizz, whoosh
swish[2] *adj* de luxe, elegant, exclusive,
fashionable, flash *colloq*, grand, plush, posh
colloq, ritzy *colloq*, smart, stylish, sumptuous,
swanky *colloq*, swell *colloq*
🔁 seedy, shabby
switch *v* change, chop and change *colloq*,
exchange, interchange, rearrange, replace, shift,
substitute, swap, trade, transpose *formal*, turn
♦ *n* **1** *a sudden switch:* about-turn, alteration,
change, exchange, interchange, replacement,

reversal, shift, substitution, swap **2** *hit with a
switch:* birch, branch, cane, lash, rod, thong, twig,
whip, whisk
swivel *v* gyrate, pirouette, pivot, revolve, rotate,
spin, turn, twirl, wheel
swollen *adj* bloated, bulbous, bulging, dilated
formal, distended *formal*, enlarged, expanded,
inflamed, inflated, puffed up, puffy, tumescent
formal, tumid
🔁 shrivelled, shrunken
swoop *v* descend, dive, drop, fall, lunge,
plunge, pounce, rush, stoop
♦ *n* attack, descent, dive, drop, lunge,
onslaught, plunge, pounce, rush
swop see **swap**
sword *n* blade, épée, foil, katana, rapier, sabre,
scimitar, steel
sworn *adj* attested *formal*, confirmed, devoted,
eternal, implacable, inveterate, relentless
swot *v* bone up *colloq*, burn the midnight oil
colloq, cram, learn, memorize, mug up *colloq*,
revise, study, work
sybarite *n* bon vivant, epicure, epicurean,
hedonist, one of the idle rich, parasite, playboy,
pleasurer, pleasure-seeker, sensualist,
voluptuary
🔁 ascetic, toiler
sybaritic *adj* easy, epicurean, hedonistic,
luxurious, parasitic, pleasure-loving, pleasure-
seeking, self-indulgent, sensual, voluptuous
🔁 ascetic
sycophancy *n* adulation, arse-licking *slang*,
backscratching, bootlicking *colloq*, cringing,
fawning, flattery, grovelling, kowtowing,
obsequiousness *formal*, servility, slavishness,
toadyism, truckling
sycophant *n* arse-licker *slang*, backscratcher,
bootlicker *colloq*, cringer, fawner, flatterer,
groveller, hanger-on, parasite, slave, sponger
colloq, toad-eater, toady, truckler, yes-man *colloq*
sycophantic *adj* arse-licking *slang*,
backscratching, bootlicking *colloq*, cringing,
fawning, flattering, grovelling, ingratiating,
obsequious *formal*, parasitical, servile, slavish,
slimy, smarmy *colloq*, time-serving, toad-eating,
toadying, truckling, unctuous
syllabus *n* course, curriculum, outline, plan,
programme, schedule
sylphlike *adj* elegant, graceful, lithe, slender,
slight, slim, streamlined, svelte, willowy
🔁 bulky, plump
symbiotic *adj* commensal *formal*, co-operative,
endophytic *technical*, epizoan, epizoic, epizootic,
interactive, interdependent, synergetic *formal*
symbol *n* badge, character, emblem, figure,
ideograph, image, logo, mark, representation,
sign, token, type *formal*
symbolic *adj* allegorical, emblematic, figurative,
illustrative, meaningful, metaphorical,
representative, significant, symbolical, token,
typical
symbolize *v* betoken *formal*, denote, epitomize,
exemplify, mean, personify, represent, signify,
stand for, typify
symmetrical *adj* balanced, consistent,
corresponding, even, harmonious, parallel,

proportional, regular, uniform, well-proportioned

☒ asymmetrical, irregular

symmetry *n* agreement, balance, congruity *formal*, consistency, correspondence, evenness, harmony, parallelism, proportion(s), regularity, uniformity

☒ asymmetry, irregularity

sympathetic *adj* affectionate, agreeable, appreciative, caring, comforting, commiserating, companionable, compassionate, compatible, concerned, congenial, considerate, consoling, encouraging, favourable, friendly, interested, kind, kind-hearted, kindly, likeable, like-minded, neighbourly, pitying, pleasant, sociable, solicitous *formal*, supportive, tender, tolerant, understanding, warm, warm-hearted, well-disposed

☒ antipathetic, callous, indifferent, unsympathetic

sympathetically *adv* appreciatively, comfortingly, compassionately, consolingly, feelingly, kindly, pityingly, responsively, sensitively, supportively, understandingly, warm-heartedly, warmly

sympathize *v* appreciate, be supportive, care for, comfort, commiserate, console, empathize, encourage, feel for, feel sorry for, identify with, offer condolences, pity, respond to, show concern/interest, understand, your heart goes out

☒ disregard, ignore

sympathizer *n* adherent, admirer, backer, condoler, fan, fellow-traveller, friend in need, partisan, supporter, well-wisher

☒ adversary, enemy, opponent

sympathy *n* 1 *show sympathy for a friend:* affinity, appreciation, closeness, comfort, commiseration, compassion, condolences, consideration, consolation, empathy, encouragement, fellow-feeling, kindness, pity, solace *formal*, support, tenderness, thoughtfulness, understanding, warm-heartedness, warmth 2 *sympathy for a cause:* accord *formal*, agreement, approbation *formal*, approval, correspondence, harmony, support

☒ 1 callousness, indifference, insensitivity 2 disagreement

symptom *n* characteristic, demonstration, display, evidence, expression, feature, indication, manifestation *formal*, mark, note, prodrome *technical*, prodromus, sign, signal, token, warning

symptomatic *adj* associated, characteristic, indicative, suggesting, suggestive, typical

syndicate *n* alliance, association, bloc, cartel, combination, combine, group, ring

synonymous *adj* comparable, corresponding, equivalent, identical, interchangeable, similar, substitutable, tantamount, the same

☒ antonymous, opposite

synopsis *n* abridgement, abstract, compendium, condensation, conspectus *formal*, digest, outline, précis, recapitulation, résumé, review, run-down *colloq*, sketch, summary, summation *formal*

synthesis *n* alloy, amalgam, amalgamation, blend, coalescence, combination, composite, compound, fusion, integration, pastiche, unification *formal*, union, welding

synthesize *v* alloy, amalgamate, blend, coalesce, combine, compound, fuse, integrate, merge, unify, unite, weld

☒ analyse, resolve, separate

synthetic *adj* artificial, bogus, ersatz, fake, imitation, man-made, manufactured, mock, pseudo, sham, simulated

☒ genuine, natural, real

syrupy *adj* 1 *a syrupy dessert wine:* honeyed, saccharine, sickly sweet, sugary, sweet, sweetened 2 *a syrupy love song:* affectionate, corny *colloq*, emotional, gushing, gushy *colloq*, lovey-dovey *colloq*, loving, maudlin, mawkish, mushy *colloq*, pathetic, romantic, schmaltzy *colloq*, sentimental, sickly *colloq*, sloppy, slushy *colloq*, soppy, sugary, tear-jerking, weepy *colloq*

system *n* 1 *the capitalist system:* approach, means, method, mode *formal*, modus operandi, practice, procedure, process, routine, rule, technique, usage, way 2 *a computer system:* apparatus, arrangement, classification, co-ordination, framework, logic, mechanism, methodology, network, order, orderliness, organization, plan, scheme, set-up, structure, systematization

systematic *adj* businesslike, efficient, logical, methodical, ordered, orderly, organized, planned, scientific, standardized, structured, systematized, well-ordered, well-organized, well-planned

☒ arbitrary, disorderly, inefficient, unsystematic

systematize *v* arrange, classify, dispose *formal*, make uniform, methodize, order, organize, plan, rationalize, regiment, regulate, schematize, standardize, structure, tabulate

T

tab *n* flap, label, marker, sticker, tag, ticket

tabby *adj* banded, brindled, mottled, streaked, striped, stripy, variegated

table *n* **1** *put the tray on a table:* bar, bench, board, counter, desk, slab, stand, worktop **2** *a table of results:* catalogue, chart, diagram, figure, graph, index, inventory, list, plan, programme, record, register, schedule, tabulation, timetable **3** *keeps a good table:* board, chow *US slang*, diet, dish, fare, food, grub *slang*, menu, nosh *slang*
♦ *v* move, propose, put forward, submit, suggest

tableau *n* diorama, picture, portrayal, representation, scene, spectacle, tableau vivant, vignette

tablet *n* ball, bolus, capsule, lozenge, pellet, pill

taboo *adj* banned, forbidden, prohibited, proscribed *formal*, ruled out, unacceptable, unmentionable, unthinkable, vetoed
🔁 acceptable, permitted
♦ *n* anathema, ban, curse, interdiction *formal*, prohibition, proscription *formal*, restriction, veto
🔁 acceptance, permission

tabulate *v* arrange, arrange in columns, catalogue, categorize, chart, classify, codify, index, list, order, range, sort, systematize, table, tabularize

tacit *adj* implicit, implied, inferred, silent, understood, unexpressed, unspoken, unstated, unvoiced, wordless
🔁 explicit, express

taciturn *adj* close-mouthed, dumb, mute, quiet, reserved, reticent, silent, tight-lipped, uncommunicative, unforthcoming, withdrawn
🔁 communicative, forthcoming, talkative

tack *n* **1** *fixed to the board with a tack:* drawing-pin, nail, pin, staple, thumbtack *US* **2** *try a different tack:* approach, attack, course, course of action, direction, line of action, method, plan, policy, procedure, process, strategy, tactic, technique, way **3** *the boat changed tack:* bearing, course, direction, heading, line, path, track
♦ *v* **1** *tacked the notice to the board:* add, affix, append, attach, fasten, fix, nail, pin, staple **2** *tack the lace round the hem:* baste, sew, stitch

tackle *n* **1** *a rugby tackle:* attack, block, challenge, interception, intervention **2** *fishing tackle:* accoutrements *formal*, apparatus, equipment, gear, harness, implements, outfit, paraphernalia, rig, stuff *colloq*, things, tools, trappings
♦ *v* **1** *tackle a problem:* address, attend to, deal with, face up to, get to grips with, grapple with, handle, take on **2** *tackle a job:* apply yourself to, attempt, attend to, begin, deal with, embark on, go about, set about, take on, try, undertake **3** *tackled him about his drinking:* challenge, confront, encounter, face up to **4** *tackled by another player:* block, challenge, deflect, halt, intercept, obstruct, stop **5** *tackled the mugger:* catch, grab, grapple with, grasp, seize, take, take hold of
🔁 **1** avoid, sidestep **2** avoid, sidestep

tacky[1] *adj* adhesive, gluey, gooey *colloq*, gummy, sticky

tacky[2] *adj* **1** *a tacky old sofa:* dingy, grotty *colloq*, messy, ragged, scruffy, shabby, shoddy, tattered, tatty, threadbare **2** *tacky souvenirs:* flashy, gaudy, kitschy, naff *colloq*, tasteless, tawdry, vulgar

tact *n* adroitness, consideration, delicacy, diplomacy, discretion, finesse, judgement, judiciousness *formal*, perception, savoir-faire, sensitivity, skill, subtlety, tactfulness, thoughtfulness, understanding
🔁 indiscretion, tactlessness

tactful *adj* adroit, careful, considerate, delicate, diplomatic, discreet, judicious *formal*, perceptive, polite, politic, sensitive, skilful, subtle, thoughtful, understanding
🔁 indiscreet, rude, tactless, thoughtless

tactic *n* **1** *his tactic was to deny everything:* approach, course, course of action, device, expedient, manoeuvre, means, method, move, plan, ploy, procedure, ruse, scheme, shift, stratagem, subterfuge, trick, way **2** *military tactics:* approach, campaign, line of attack, manoeuvres, moves, plan, policy, strategy

tactical *adj* adroit, artful, calculated, clever, cunning, judicious *formal*, politic, prudent, shrewd, skilful, smart, strategic

tactician *n* brain *colloq*, campaigner, co-ordinator, director, mastermind, orchestrator, planner, strategist

tactless *adj* blundering, careless, clumsy, discourteous, gauche, impolite, impolitic, imprudent, inappropriate, inconsiderate, indelicate, indiscreet, injudicious *formal*, insensitive, maladroit *formal*, rude, thoughtless, undiplomatic, unfeeling, unkind, unsubtle
🔁 diplomatic, discreet, tactful

tactlessness *n* bad timing, boorishness, clumsiness, discourtesy, gaucherie, impoliteness, indelicacy, indiscretion, ineptitude, insensitivity, maladroitness *formal*, rudeness, thoughtlessness
🔁 diplomacy, tact, tactfulness

tag *n* **1** *a luggage tag:* docket, identification, label, marker, note, slip, sticker, tab, ticket **2** *earned him the tag 'Mr Nice Guy':* badge, description, epithet, identification, label, name, nickname, title **3** *the old tag 'where there's life, there's hope':* allusion, dictum, epithet, expression, maxim, moral, motto, phrase, proverb, quotation, quote *colloq*, saying, stock phrase
♦ *v* **1** *she was tagged 'the Brazilian Bombshell':* call, christen, designate, dub, entitle, label, name, nickname, style, term, title **2** *tagged an extra paragraph on to the letter:* add, adjoin, affix, annex, append, attach, fasten, tack
▶ **tag along** accompany, follow, shadow, tail, trail

tail *n* **1** *the horse's tail:* appendage, backside *colloq*, behind *colloq*, bottom, extremity, posterior *colloq*, rear, rear end, rump **2** *the tail of the comet:* back, end, extremity, rear, termination *formal* **3** *she put a tail on her husband:* detective, gumshoe *colloq*, private eye *colloq*, (private) investigator, shamus *colloq*, sleuth *colloq*

♦ *v* dog, follow, pursue, shadow, stalk, track, trail

▶ **tail off** decline, decrease, die (out), drop (off), dwindle, fade, fall away, peter out, taper off, wane

🔁 grow, increase

tailor *n* clothier, costumer, costumier, couturier, dressmaker, modiste, outfitter, seamster, seamstress

♦ *v* accommodate, adapt, adjust, alter, convert, cut, fashion, fit, modify, mould, shape, style, suit, trim

tailor-made *adj* **1** *wears only tailor-made suits:* bespoke, custom-made, fitted, made-to-measure **2** *this job is tailor-made for you:* fitted, ideal, perfect, right, suited

🔁 **1** off the peg, ready-made

taint *v* **1** *food tainted by bacteria:* adulterate, befoul *formal*, blight, contaminate, corrupt, defile, dirty, infect, pollute, ruin, soil, spoil **2** *the scandal has tainted his name:* befoul *formal*, blacken, blemish, blot, damage, defile, deprave, disgrace, dishonour, harm, injure, muddy, ruin, shame, smear, stain, sully, tarnish

♦ *n* **1** *a taint in the water supply:* adulteration, contagion, contamination, corruption, infection, pollution **2** *a taint on his reputation:* blemish, blot, defect, disgrace, dishonour, fault, flaw, shame, smear, spot, stain, stigma

take *v* **1** *take first prize:* get, obtain, receive, secure, win **2** *takes its name from its inventor:* acquire, derive, get, obtain, receive **3** *he took the job:* accept, adopt, assume, take on **4** *I'll take this one:* choose, decide on, have, pick, select, settle on **5** *he took her hand:* catch, clutch, grab, grasp, grip, hold, seize, snatch, take hold of **6** *caught taking money from the till:* appropriate *formal*, carry off, filch *colloq*, lift *colloq*, nick *colloq*, pinch *colloq*, purloin *formal*, remove, seize, steal, take away **7** *someone took the child from his pram:* abduct, carry off, kidnap, lift *colloq*, remove, seize, steal **8** *take me home:* accompany, bear *formal*, bring, carry, conduct, convey, deliver, drive, escort, ferry, fetch, guide, lead, shepherd, show, transport, usher, whisk *colloq* **9** *she can't take criticism:* abide, bear, endure, experience, put up with, stand, stomach, suffer, tolerate, undergo, withstand **10** *the journey takes 6 hours:* continue for, go on for, last **11** *it will take all my spare time:* call for, demand, necessitate, need, require, use (up) **12** *the invaders took the city:* capture, conquer, occupy, seize, vanquish *formal*, win **13** *take pleasure in something:* achieve, attain, be given, come by, derive, draw, gain, get, obtain, procure *formal*, receive **14** *take the blame/responsibility:* accept, acknowledge, admit, be responsible for, bear, undertake **15** *let's take each point in turn:* consider, examine, note **16** *I take it you agree?:* assume, believe, presume, suppose **17** *do you take my meaning?:* apprehend, comprehend, cotton on *colloq*, fathom (out), follow, gather, grasp, twig *colloq*, understand **18** *take the news badly:* accept, cope with, deal with, handle, react to, respond to **19** *take him for a fool:* believe, consider, deem *formal*, hold, look upon, reckon, regard, suppose, think, view **20** *the hall takes 400 people:* accommodate, contain, have a capacity of, have room for, have space for, hold, seat **21** *take a measurement:* ascertain, determine, discover,

establish, find out, measure **22** *took the cottage for the summer:* book, hire, lease, pay for, rent **23** *I take this paper every day:* buy, purchase, receive **24** *take a subject at university:* be taught, learn, major in, pursue, read, research, study **25** *take the new road:* drive along, follow, go along, travel along, use **26** *take food/drink:* consume, devour, drink, eat, guzzle *colloq*, imbibe *formal*, scoff *colloq*, swallow, tuck in *colloq* **27** *will the drug take?:* be effective, be efficacious *formal*, produce results, succeed, work **28** *take six from ten:* deduct, discount, remove, subtract, take away

🔁 **3** refuse **4** leave, refuse **6** put back, replace **7** put back, replace **12** lose **22** sell **23** sell **27** fail

♦ *n* **1** *the day's take of grouse:* bag, catch, haul, yield **2** *the total take for the week:* gate, gate-money, income, proceeds, profit(s), receipts, return(s), revenue, takings, yield

▶ **take aback** astonish, astound, bewilder, disconcert, dismay, shock, stagger, startle, stun, surprise, upset

▶ **take after** be like, be similar to, echo, favour, look like, mirror, resemble

▶ **take against** despise, disapprove of, dislike, object to, regard with distaste

🔁 take to

▶ **take apart** disassemble *formal*, dismantle, separate, take to pieces

▶ **take back 1** *take back what you said:* deny, disclaim, eat one's words *colloq*, recant, renounce, repudiate, retract, withdraw **2** *take it back and ask for a refund:* give back, hand back, replace, restore, return, send back **3** *he took back his CDs when we split up:* get back, reclaim, regain, repossess

▶ **take down 1** *took down the scaffolding:* demolish, disassemble, dismantle, level, lower, raze **2** *take down everything he says:* get down, make a note of, note, put down, put on paper, record, set down, transcribe, write down

▶ **take in 1** *couldn't take in what he said:* absorb, appreciate, assimilate, comprehend, digest, grasp, realize, understand **2** *they took us in for the night:* accommodate, admit, receive, shelter, welcome **3** *the course takes in three main topics:* comprise, contain, cover, embrace, encompass, include, incorporate **4** *taken in by con men:* bamboozle *colloq*, cheat, con *colloq*, deceive, dupe, fool, hoodwink, lead up the garden path *colloq*, mislead, swindle, trick

▶ **take off 1** *watch the plane take off:* ascend, become airborne, climb, depart, fly, lift off, mount, rise, soar **2** *take off your clothes:* detach, discard, divest, doff, drop, pull off, remove, shed, strip, tear off, throw off **3** *they took off in the middle of the night:* abscond, bunk off *colloq*, decamp, depart, disappear, do a runner *colloq*, flee, go, leave, run away, scarper *colloq*, skedaddle *colloq* **4** *he took off the prime minister:* caricature, imitate, mimic, mock, parody, satirize, send up *colloq* **5** *the project has really taken off:* become all the rage *colloq*, become fashionable, become popular, catch on, do well, flourish, go places *colloq*, hit the jackpot *colloq*, make it *colloq*, prosper, strike gold *colloq*, succeed, work

▶ **take on 1** *take on a challenge:* accept, assume, face, tackle, undertake **2** *take someone on in a fight:* compete with, contend with, fight, oppose, tackle, vie with **3** *take on staff:* employ, engage, enlist, enrol, hire, recruit, retain

▸ **take out 1** *take out a tumour:* cut out, detach, excise, extract, get out, pull out, remove **2** *he's been taking her out for a while now:* go out with, go with, see **3** *take someone out to a restaurant:* accompany, escort **4** *take out a loan:* arrange, fix *colloq,* organize, set up **5** *take out a book from the library:* be lent, borrow, have on loan, use temporarily

▸ **take over** assume responsibility for, become responsible for, buy out, gain control of, take charge of

▸ **take to 1** *I took to him right away:* become friendly with, become keen on, find attractive, find pleasant, like **2** *he's taken to staying up late:* begin, start

▸ **take up 1** *the job takes up all my time:* absorb, consume, engage, engross, fill, monopolize, occupy, use (up) **2** *took the child up in her arms:* lift, pick up, raise **3** *take up a hobby:* begin, commence *formal,* embark on, pursue, start **4** *take up where you left off:* carry on, continue, pick up, pick up the threads *colloq,* resume **5** *take up an offer:* accept, adopt, agree to

take-off *n* **1** *the plane's takeoff:* ascent, climbing, departure, flight, flying, lift-off **2** *a take-off of the president:* caricature, imitation, impersonation, mimicry, parody, send-up *colloq,* spoof *colloq,* travesty

takeover *n* amalgamation, buyout, coalition, combination, coup, gaining of control, incorporation, merger

taking *adj* alluring, appealing, attractive, beguiling, captivating, charming, delightful, enchanting, engaging, fascinating, fetching, pleasing, prepossessing, winning, winsome ☒ repellent, repulsive, unattractive
♦ *n* earnings, gain, gate, gate money, income, pickings, proceeds, profits, receipts, returns, revenue, winnings, yield

tale *n* **1** *a fairy tale:* account, allegory, anecdote, epic, fable, legend, myth, narrative, old wives' tale, parable, rumour, saga, spiel *colloq,* story, superstition, yarn **2** *surely you didn't fall for a tale like that?:* cock-and-bull story *colloq,* fabrication, falsehood, fib *colloq,* lie, porky *colloq,* tall story *colloq,* untruth, whopper *colloq*

talent *n* ability, aptitude, aptness, bent, capacity, endowment, facility, faculty, feel, flair, forte, genius, gift, knack, power, skill, strength, strong point ☒ inability, weakness

talented *adj* able, accomplished, adept, adroit, brilliant, capable, clever, deft, gifted, proficient, skilful ☒ inept

talisman *n* abraxas, amulet, charm, fetish, idol, ju-ju, mascot, periapt, phylactery, totem

talk *v* **1** *she never stops talking:* articulate, babble *colloq,* chatter, communicate, express yourself, jabber *colloq,* jaw *colloq,* natter *colloq,* prattle *colloq,* say, speak, utter, voice **2** *we were talking only yesterday:* chat, chinwag *colloq,* communicate, confer *formal,* converse *formal,* have a conversation/discussion, natter *colloq,* speak **3** *the two sides have agreed to talk:* bargain, discuss, negotiate, work out an agreement **4** *people will talk:* gossip, spread rumours **5** *it didn't take long to make him talk:* blab *colloq,* confess, give (secret)

information, give the game away *colloq,* grass *slang,* let the cat out of the bag *colloq,* spill the beans *colloq,* squeal *colloq,* tell, tell tales *colloq*
♦ *n* **1** *we need to have a talk:* chat, chatter, chinwag *colloq,* confab *colloq,* conversation, dialogue, discussion, jaw *colloq,* natter *colloq,* tête-à-tête **2** *give a talk:* address, discourse, disquisition *formal,* lecture, oration *formal,* seminar, sermon, speech, spiel *colloq,* symposium **3** *ignore all the talk about him:* gossip, hearsay, rumour, tittle-tattle **4** *the two sides are holding talks:* bargaining, conclave *formal,* conference, consultation, debate, dialogue, discussion, meeting, negotiation, seminar, summit conference, symposium **5** *indulge in baby talk:* cant, dialect, idiolect technical, jargon, language, lingo *colloq,* slang, speech, utterance, words

▸ **talk back** answer back, answer rudely, be cheeky to, retaliate, retort, riposte

▸ **talk down to** look down on, patronize, speak condescendingly towards

▸ **talk into** bring round, coax, convince, encourage, persuade, sway, win over ☒ dissuade, talk out of

▸ **talk out of** deter, discourage, dissuade, prevent, put off, stop ☒ convince, persuade, talk into

talkative *adj* can talk the hind legs of a donkey *colloq,* chatty, communicative, expansive, forthcoming, gabby *colloq,* garrulous, gassy *colloq,* gossipy, longwinded, loquacious *formal,* mouthy *colloq,* unreserved, verbose, vocal, voluble *formal,* wordy ☒ quiet, reserved, taciturn

talker *n* **1** *a fluent talker:* chatterbox *colloq,* communicator, conversationalist, speaker **2** *a professional talker:* lecturer, orator *formal,* speaker, speech-maker

talking-to *n* carpeting *colloq,* criticism, dressing-down *colloq,* lecture, rebuke, reprimand, reproach, reproof, scolding, telling-off *colloq,* ticking-off *colloq* ☒ commendation, praise

tall *adj* **1** *a tall building:* big, elevated, giant, gigantic, great, high, lofty, sky-high, soaring, towering **2** *a tall man:* big, giant, gigantic, lanky, lofty **3** *a tall story:* absurd, dubious, exaggerated, far-fetched, implausible, improbable, incredible, overblown, preposterous, remarkable, unbelievable, unlikely **4** *a tall order:* challenging, demanding, difficult, exacting, hard, taxing, trying ☒ **1** low, small **2** short, small **3** reasonable **4** easy

tallness *n* altitude, height, loftiness, stature

tally *n* **1** *a tally of how much you spend:* account, count, enumeration, list, reckoning, record, register, roll, score, sum, total **2** *kept the tallies in a box:* counterfoil, counterpart, duplicate, stub, tab, tag, ticket
♦ *v* **1** *the two stories don't tally:* accord, agree, coincide, concur *formal,* conform, correspond, fit, harmonize, match, square, suit, tie in **2** *tally the month's sales:* add (up), count, figure, reckon, total ☒ **1** differ, disagree

tame *adj* **1** *a tame rabbit:* broken in, disciplined, docile, domesticated, gentle, tractable, trained **2** *a tame and submissive wife:* amenable, biddable, docile, manageable, meek, obedient, subdued, submissive, unresisting **3** *my life is tame compared to yours:* bland, boring, dull, feeble, flat, humdrum, insipid, lifeless, spiritless, tedious, unadventurous, unenterprising, unexciting, uninspired, uninteresting, vapid, wearisome

1 wild **2** rebellious, unmanageable **3** adventurous, exciting

♦ *v* **1** *tame a horse:* break in, bridle, bring to heel, discipline, domesticate, house-train, train **2** *tame a crowd:* calm, curb, master, overcome, pacify, quell, repress, subdue, subjugate *formal*, suppress

tamper *v* **1** *tamper with a machine:* fiddle, interfere, meddle, mess about *colloq*, monkey *colloq*, muck about *colloq*, tinker **2** *tamper with the evidence:* alter, fix *colloq*, manipulate, rig *colloq*

tan *adj* brown, light brown, yellowish brown
♦ *v* **1** *she tans easily:* bronze, brown, go/turn brown, make/become darker, sunburn **2** *tan someone's backside:* beat, belt *colloq*, birch, cane, clout *colloq*, flay, flog, lash, spank, strap, thrash, wallop *colloq*, whack *colloq*, whip

tang *n* **1** *the tang of citrus:* bite *colloq*, edge *colloq*, flavour, kick *colloq*, pep *colloq*, piquancy, punch *colloq*, pungency, savour, sharpness, spice, taste **2** *smell the tang of the sea:* aroma, scent, smack, smell, whiff **3** *a tang of irritation in his voice:* hint, overtone, suggestion, tinge, touch, trace, whiff

tangible *adj* actual, concrete, definite, discernible, evident, hard, manifest *formal*, material, palpable, perceptible, physical, positive, real, solid, substantial, tactile *formal*, touchable, unmistakable, visible, well-defined

abstract, intangible, unreal

tangle *n* **1** *a tangle of cables:* coil, convolution *formal*, knot, mat, mesh, snarl-up, twist, web **2** *got myself into a real tangle:* complication, confusion, embroilment, entanglement, imbroglio, jumble, labyrinth, maze, mess, mix-up, muddle
♦ *v* **1** *tangle the wires up:* coil, convolve *formal*, entangle, interlace, intertwine, intertwist, interweave, knot, ravel, snarl, twist **2** *an animal tangled in a net:* catch, enmesh, ensnare, entangle, entrap **3** *getting his facts tangled:* confuse, muddle **4** *get tangled in a bad situation:* embroil, enmesh, ensnare, entrap, implicate, involve

3 disentangle **4** disentangle

tangled *adj* **1** *tangled hair:* dishevelled, entangled, knotted, knotty, matted, messy, snarled, tousled, twisted **2** *a tangled story:* complex, complicated, confused, convoluted *formal*, intricate, involved, jumbled, mixed up, muddled, tortuous, twisted

tangy *adj* acid, biting, piquant, pungent, sharp, spicy, strong, tart

insipid, tasteless

tank *n* **1** *a hot-water tank:* basin, cistern, container, receptacle, reservoir, vat **2** *tanks rolled into the town:* armoured car, armoured vehicle, panzer

tantalize *v* entice, frustrate, lead on, provoke, taunt, tease, titillate, torment, torture

fulfil, gratify, satisfy

tantamount *adj* as good as, commensurate with *formal*, equal to, equivalent to, synonymous with, the same as

tantrum *n* fit, fit of temper, flare-up, fury, outburst, paddy *colloq*, paroxysm, pet, rage, storm, temper

tap¹ *v* beat, drum, hit, knock, pat, rap, strike, touch
♦ *n* beat, knock, light blow, pat, rap, touch

tap² *n* **1** *turn on the tap:* faucet, spigot, spout, stopcock, valve **2** *put the tap in the barrel:* bung, plug, stopper **3** *a tap on someone's phone:* bug, hidden microphone, listening device, receiver
♦ *v* bleed, drain, exploit, milk, mine, quarry, siphon, use, utilize

tape *n* **1** *a parcel tied with tape:* band, binding, ribbon, string, strip **2** *have a tape of a concert:* audiotape, cassette, magnetic tape, recording, tape-recording, video, video recording, videocassette, videotape **3** *with tape over their mouths:* adhesive tape, masking tape, Sellotape®, sticky tape
♦ *v* **1** *tape the ends down:* bind, fasten, seal, secure, stick, tie **2** *tape a programme:* record, tape-record, video, video-record

taper *v* attenuate *formal*, become narrow, become thin, narrow, slim, thin

flare, swell, widen
♦ *n* candle, spill, wick
► **taper off** decrease, die away/off, diminish, dwindle, fade, lessen, peter out, reduce, tail off, thin out, wane

increase

tardily *adv* **1** *help arrived tardily:* at the eleventh hour *colloq*, at the last minute, belatedly *formal*, late, late in the day, unpunctually **2** *walked tardily to school:* slowly

1 promptly, punctually

tardiness *n* **1** *reprimanded for habitual tardiness:* belatedness *formal*, lateness, unpunctuality **2** *her tardiness in fulfilling her duties:* dawdling, delay, dilatoriness *formal*, procrastination *formal*, slowness, sluggishness

1 punctuality **2** promptness

tardy *adj* **1** *always tardy for meetings:* belated *formal*, late, overdue, unpunctual **2** *tardy in settling bills:* backward, behindhand, dawdling, delayed, dilatory *formal*, eleventh-hour, last-minute, loitering, procrastinating *formal*, slack, slow, sluggish

1 prompt, punctual **2** prompt

target *n* **1** *hit a target:* aim, bull's eye, goal, mark **2** *the target of a racist attack:* butt, prey, quarry, victim **3** *meet sales targets:* aim, ambition, end, goal, intention, object, objective, purpose

tariff *n* **1** *impose tariffs on imported goods:* customs, duty, excise, levy, tax, toll **2** *energy tariffs:* (list of) charges, price list, schedule **3** *the café's tariff:* bill of fare, menu

tarnish *v* **1** *the silver is tarnished:* blemish, blot, corrode, darken, dim, discolour, dull, mar, rust, spoil, spot, stain, taint **2** *tarnished his reputation:* befoul *formal*, besmirch *formal*, blacken, mar, stain, sully, taint

1 brighten, polish
♦ *n* blackening, blemish, blot, discoloration, film, patina, rust, spot, stain, taint

brightness, polish

tarry *v* abide *formal*, bide *formal*, dally, dawdle, delay, lag, linger, loiter, pause, remain, rest, stay, stop, wait

tart[1] *n* **1** *cherry tart:* flan, pastry, patty, pie, quiche, strudel, tartlet **2** *she's just a cheap tart:* broad, call girl, drab, fallen woman, fille de joie, floosie *colloq*, harlot, hooker *colloq*, loose woman, prostitute, scarlet woman, scrubber *slang*, slut, street-walker, strumpet, tramp *slang*, trollop, whore
▶ **tart up** decorate, do up *colloq*, embellish, redecorate, renovate, smarten (up)

tart[2] *adj* **1** *the food tastes tart:* acid, acidulous *formal*, bitter, piquant, pungent, sharp, sour, tangy, vinegary **2** *tart remarks:* acerbic, acid, astringent *formal*, biting, caustic, cutting, incisive, sarcastic, sardonic, scathing, sharp, trenchant *formal*
🆎 **1** bland, sweet **2** kind

task *n* activity, assignment, burden, business, charge, chore, commission, duty, employment, engagement, enterprise, errand, exercise, job, labour, mission, occupation, piece of work, toil, undertaking, work

taste *n* **1** *the taste of lemon:* flavour, relish, savour, smack, tang **2** *have a taste of this dessert:* bit, bite, dash, drop, morsel, mouthful, nibble, piece, sample, sip, soupçon, titbit **3** *a taste for adventure:* appetite, bent, desire, fondness, hankering, hunger, inclination, leaning, liking, partiality, penchant *formal*, predilection *formal*, preference, thirst **4** *good taste in music:* appreciation, cultivation, culture, discernment, discrimination, elegance, grace, judgement, perception, polish, refinement, style, stylishness, tastefulness **5** *your remarks were not in good taste:* decorum, etiquette, finesse, judgement, propriety, sensitivity, tastefulness
🆎 **1** blandness
♦ *v* **1** *taste the wine:* nibble, sample, sip, test, try **2** *it tastes of mint:* relish, savour, smack **3** *he had tasted freedom:* encounter, experience, feel, know, meet, undergo **4** *taste the garlic in this:* differentiate, discern, distinguish, make out, perceive

---

Ways of describing taste include:
acid, acrid, appetizing, bitter, bittersweet, citrus, creamy, delicious, flavoursome, fruity, hot, meaty, moreish, mouth-watering *colloq*, peppery, piquant, pungent, salty, sapid, savoury, scrumptious *colloq*, sharp, sour, spicy, sugary, sweet, tangy, tart, tasty, vinegary, yummy *colloq*

---

tasteful *adj* aesthetic, artistic, beautiful, charming, cultivated, cultured, delicate, discriminating, elegant, exquisite, graceful, harmonious, pleasing, polished, pretty, refined, restrained, smart, stylish, well-judged
🆎 garish, tasteless, tawdry

tasteless *adj* **1** *tasteless soup:* bland, boring, dull, flat, flavourless, insipid, mild, plain, thin, uninteresting, vapid, watered-down, watery, weak **2** *tasteless ornaments:* cheap, flashy, garish, gaudy, inelegant, kitsch, loud, naff *slang*, showy, tacky *colloq*, tawdry, vulgar **3** *a tasteless comment:* crass, crude, graceless, improper, indiscreet, rude, tactless, uncouth, unfitting, unseemly, vulgar
🆎 **1** tasty **2** elegant, tasteful **3** tasteful

tasting *n* assay, assessment, gustation *formal*, sampling, testing, trial

tasty *adj* appetizing, delectable, delicious, flavorous *formal*, flavoursome, luscious, mouth-watering, palatable, piquant, savoury, scrumptious *colloq*, spicy, succulent, sweet, tangy, yummy *slang*
🆎 insipid, tasteless

tattered *adj* frayed, ragged, ripped, scruffy, shabby, tatty, threadbare, torn
🆎 neat, smart

tattler *n* busybody, gossip, newsmonger, rumour-monger, scandalmonger, talebearer, tale-teller, tell-tale

taunt *v* bait, deride, gibe, goad, insult, jeer, make fun of, mock, poke fun at, provoke, revile, rib *colloq*, ridicule, sneer, tease, torment
♦ *n* barb, brickbat *colloq*, catcall, derision, dig, gibe, insult, jeer, mockery, provocation, ridicule, sarcasm, sneer, taunting, teasing

taut *adj* contracted, rigid, stiff, strained, stretched, tense, tensed, tight, tightened, unrelaxed
🆎 loose, relaxed, slack

tautological *adj* pleonastic *technical*, redundant, repetitive, superfluous, verbose *formal*, wordy
🆎 economical, succinct

tautology *n* duplication, iteration *formal*, perissology, pleonasm *technical*, redundancy, repetition, repetitiveness, superfluity, verbosity *formal*

tavern *n* alehouse, bar, boozer *slang*, hostelry *colloq*, inn, joint *colloq*, local, pub *colloq*, public house, roadhouse, tap-house

tawdry *adj* cheap, fancy, flashy, garish, gaudy, glittering, showy, tacky *colloq*, tasteless, tinselly, vulgar
🆎 fine, tasteful

tawny *adj* fawn, fulvid *formal*, fulvous *formal*, golden, golden brown, khaki, sandy, tan, xanthous *formal*, yellow

tax *n* **1** *a tax on imported goods:* charge, contribution, customs, duty, imposte *formal*, levy, rate, tariff **2** *a tax on his patience:* burden, imposition, load, pressure, strain, stress, weight
♦ *v* **1** *to tax imported oil:* charge a tax on, exact a tax on, impose a tax on, levy a tax on **2** *taxing her strength:* burden, drain, encumber, enervate *formal*, exhaust, impose on, load, make demands on, overload, sap, strain, stretch, test, tire, try, weaken, wear out, weary, weigh (down)

Taxes include:
airport tax, capital gains tax, capital transfer tax, capitation, community charge, corporation tax, council tax, customs, death duty, estate duty, excise, income tax, inheritance tax, insurance tax, PAYE, poll tax, property tax, rates, surtax, tithe, toll, value added tax (VAT)

---

taxi *n* cab, hackney cab, hansom-cab, minicab, taxicab

taxing *adj* burdensome, demanding, draining, enervating *formal*, exacting, exhausting, hard, heavy, onerous, punishing, stressful, tiring, tough, trying, wearing, wearisome, wearying
🆎 easy, gentle, mild

teach *v* **1** *teach at a primary school:* coach, direct, drill, edify, educate, enlighten, give lessons,

ground, guide, inform, instruct, lecture, school, train, tutor, verse **2** *teach music:* give instruction in, give lessons in, instruct in, lecture in, tutor **3** *teach me how to swim:* demonstrate, show, train **4** *taught to fear him:* brainwash, condition, inculcate *formal*, indoctrinate, train
F3 **1** learn **2** learn **3** learn **4** learn

teacher *n* educator, guide, schoolteacher
F3 pupil

> **Kinds of teacher include:**
> adviser, coach, college lecturer, counsellor, crammer, dean, demonstrator, deputy head, doctor, don, duenna, fellow, form teacher, governess, guru, head of department, head of year, headmaster, headmistress, headteacher, housemaster, housemistress, instructor, lecturer, maharishi, master, mentor, middle school teacher, mistress, nursery school teacher, pastoral head, pedagogue, pedant, preceptor, preceptress, primary school teacher, principal, private tutor, professor, pundit, reception teacher, school-ma'am, schoolmaster, schoolmistress, schoolteacher, secondary school teacher, senior lecturer, student teacher, subject co-ordinator, supply teacher, trainer, tutor, university lecturer, upper school teacher

teaching *n* **1** *teaching in schools:* education, instruction, pedagogy, tuition **2** *the teachings of the church:* doctrine, dogma, precept, principle, tenet

> **Methods of teaching include:**
> apprenticeship, briefing, coaching, computer-aided learning, correspondence course, counselling, demonstration, distance learning, drilling, familiarization, grounding, guidance, hands-on training, home-learning, indoctrination, induction training, in-service training, instruction, job training, lecturing, lesson, master-class, on-the-job training, practical, preaching, private tuition, role play, rote learning, schooling, seminar, shadowing, special tuition, theory, training, tuition, tutelage, tutorial, vocational training, work experience

team *n* **1** *a football team:* line-up, side, squad **2** *a team of workers:* band, bunch, company, crew, gang, group, set, shift, squad, stable, troupe
▶ **team up** band together, collaborate, combine, co-operate, couple, join, unite, work together

teamwork *n* collaboration, co-operation, co-ordination, esprit de corps, fellowship, joint effort, team spirit
F3 disharmony, disunity

tear[1] *v* **1** *tore the fabric:* ladder, rend, rip, shred, slash, split **2** *its claws tore his flesh:* claw, gash, injure, lacerate, mangle, mutilate, pull apart, rend, rip, rupture, scratch, slash, wound **3** *civil war tore the country:* break apart, divide, rupture, split **4** *tore the book out of my hands:* grab, pluck, pull, seize, snatch, wrest, yank *colloq* **5** *tear down the street:* belt *colloq*, bolt, career, charge, dart, dash, fly, gallop, hurry, nip *colloq*, race, rip *colloq*, run, rush, shoot, speed, sprint, step on it *colloq*, vroom *colloq*, whizz *colloq*, zap *colloq*, zing *colloq*, zip *colloq*, zoom *colloq*

♦ *n* **1** *a tear in the skin:* gash, injury, laceration, mutilation, rupture, scratch, slash, wound **2** *a tear in the material:* gash, hole, rent, rip, run, slash, slit, split

tearaway *n* delinquent, good-for-nothing *colloq*, hoodlum, hooligan, hothead, madcap, rascal, rough, roughneck, rowdy, ruffian, tough

tearful *adj* **1** *parted from his tearful wife:* blubbering, crying, distressed, lachrymose *formal*, sobbing, sorrowful, upset, weeping, weepy *colloq*, whimpering **2** *a tearful scene:* distressing, doleful, emotional, mournful, sad, sorrowful, upsetting
F3 **1** happy, laughing, smiling **2** happy

tears *n* blubbering, crying, sobbing, weeping

tease *v* **1** *teased him about his height:* banter, gibe, kid *colloq*, mock, needle *colloq*, rag *colloq*, rib *colloq*, ridicule, taunt, vex **2** *if you tease the dog it will bite you:* aggravate *colloq*, annoy, badger, bait, goad, irritate, pester, plague, provoke, torment, worry **3** *teased him with promises:* lead on, tantalize, torment

technical *adj* **1** *a job which needs technical knowledge:* applied, expert, practical, professional, scientific, specialist, specialized, technological **2** *a technical fault:* computer, electronic, mechanical, technological

technique *n* **1** *the latest techniques:* approach, course, fashion, manner, means, method, mode *formal*, modus operandi, procedure, style, system, way **2** *improve his piano technique:* ability, art, artistry, capability, craft, craftsmanship, delivery, dexterity, execution, expertise, facility, knack, know-how *colloq*, mastery, performance, proficiency, skilfulness, skill, touch

tedious *adj* banal, boring, drab, dreary, dull, flat, humdrum, laborious, lifeless, long-drawn-out, long-winded, monotonous, prosaic *formal*, routine, run-of-the-mill *colloq*, samey *colloq*, tiresome, tiring, unexciting, uninspired, uninteresting, unvaried, wearisome, wearying
F3 exciting, interesting, lively

tedium *n* banality, boredom, drabness, dreariness, dullness, ennui, lifelessness, monotony, prosiness, routine, sameness, tediousness, vapidity
F3 excitement, interest

teem *v* **1** *a flat teeming with vermin:* abound, brim, bristle, burst, crawl, overflow, pullulate *formal*, swarm **2** *wildlife teemed on the plains:* bear, increase, multiply, produce, proliferate, pullulate *formal*
F3 **1** lack, want

teeming *adj* **1** *teeming with tourists:* alive, brimming, bristling, bursting, chock-a-block *colloq*, chock-full *colloq*, crawling, full, overflowing, packed, pullulating *formal*, replete *formal*, seething, swarming, thick **2** *teeming wildlife:* abundant, fruitful, full, numerous, pullulating *formal*
F3 **1** lacking **2** rare, sparse

teenage *adj* adolescent, immature, juvenile, teenaged, young, youthful

teenager *n* adolescent, boy, girl, juvenile, minor, young adult, young person, youth

teeny *adj* diminutive, microscopic, miniature, minuscule, minute, teensy-weensy *colloq*, teeny-weeny *colloq*, tiny, titchy *colloq*, wee *Scot*

teeter *v* **1** *teeter on the edge of a cliff:* balance, pivot, rock, seesaw, shake, sway, totter, tremble, waver, wobble **2** *teeter along on high heels:* lurch, pitch, reel, stagger, totter

teetotal *adj* abstemious, abstinent, on the wagon *colloq*, sober, temperate

teetotaller *n* abstainer, nephalist, non-drinker, Rechabite, water-drinker

telegram *n* cable, fax, telegraph, Telemessage®, telex, wire *colloq*

telegraph *n* cable, radiotelegraph, telegram, telex, wire *colloq*
♦ *v* cable, send, signal, telex, transmit, wire *colloq*

telepathy *n* clairvoyance, ESP, extrasensory perception, mind-reading, sixth sense, thought transference

telephone *n* blower *colloq*, handset, hot line *colloq*, phone, receiver
♦ *v* buzz *colloq*, call (up), contact, dial, get in touch with, give a bell *colloq*, give a buzz *colloq*, give a tinkle *colloq*, phone, ring (up)

Types of telephone include:
Ansaphone®, answering machine, caller display phone, camera phone, carphone, cashphone, cellphone, cellular phone, clamshell phone, cordless phone, fax, fax-phone, flip phone, hazardous area phone, Minicom®, mobile phone, pager, payphone, push-button telephone, system phone, textphone, tone-dialling phone, Touchtone®, Uniphone®, videophone

telescope *v* abbreviate, abridge, compact, compress, concertina, condense, contract, curtail, cut, reduce, shorten, shrink, squash, squeeze, trim, truncate

televise *v* air, beam, broadcast, put on, relay, screen, show, transmit

television *n* boob tube *US colloq*, goggle-box *colloq*, idiot box *colloq*, receiver, set, small screen, telly *colloq*, the box *colloq*, the tube *colloq*, TV

Parts of a television set include:
aerial, aerial socket, amplifier, cathode-ray tube, chrominance signal extractor, colour decoder module, deflector coil, electron gun, horizontal synchronizing module, intermediate frequency amplifier module, loudspeaker, luminance signal amplifier, phosphor dots, picture tube, remote control, scanning current generator, screen, set-top-box, shadow mask, sound demodulator, stand-by switch, synchronizing pulse separator, tuner

tell *v* **1** *tell me what's going on:* acquaint with, apprise of *formal*, brief, give the low-down *colloq*, inform, let know, notify **2** *tell a secret:* announce, broadcast, communicate, confess, declare, disclose, divulge, impart, make known, mention, proclaim, report, reveal, say, speak, state, utter **3** *tell a story:* delineate *formal*, describe, narrate, portray, recite, recount, relate, report, sketch **4** *tell someone to leave:* advise, bid, charge,

command, direct, instruct, order, require **5** *I can't tell what's happened:* comprehend, discern, discover, make out, perceive, see, understand **6** *can't tell him from his brother:* differentiate, discern, discriminate, distinguish, identify, recognize, tell apart **7** *the strain is telling on her:* affect, have an effect on, take its toll of **8** *you promised not to tell:* blab *colloq*, give the game away *colloq*, grass *slang*, let the cat out of the bag *colloq*, spill the beans *colloq*, squeal *colloq*, talk, tell tales *colloq*
▶ **tell off** berate *formal*, censure, chide, dress down *colloq*, give a talking-to *colloq*, lecture, rebuke, reprimand, reproach, reprove, scold, tick off *colloq*, upbraid *formal*
▶ **tell on** betray, blow the whistle on *colloq*, denounce, grass on *slang*, inform on *formal*, rat on *colloq*, shop *slang*

telling *adj* **1** *a telling argument:* cogent *formal*, convincing, effective, impressive, persuasive, powerful **2** *a telling remark:* revealing, significant

telling-off *n* bawling-out *colloq*, castigation *formal*, chiding, dressing-down *colloq*, lecture, rebuke, reprimand, reproach, reproof, row, scolding, ticking-off *colloq*, upbraiding *formal*

tell-tale *adj* give-away *colloq*, meaningful, noticeable, perceptible, revealing, revelatory, unmistakable
♦ *n* clype *Scot*, grass *slang*, informer, snake in the grass *colloq*, sneak, snitch *colloq*, snitcher *colloq*, squealer *colloq*

temerity *n* audacity, boldness, cheek *colloq*, daring, effrontery, gall, impertinence, impudence, nerve *colloq*, presumption, rashness, recklessness
🗲 caution, prudence

temper *n* **1** *his usual good temper:* attitude, character, constitution, disposition, frame/state of mind, humour, mood, nature, temperament **2** *control your temper:* anger, annoyance, fury, ill-humour, irritability, petulance, rage **3** *in a temper:* bad mood, fit of temper, flare-up *colloq*, fury, paddy *colloq*, passion, rage, storm, tantrum, wax *colloq* **4** *lose your temper:* calm, calmness, composure, cool *slang*, self-control, tranquillity
🗲 **2** calmness, self-control **3** calmness, self-control **4** anger, rage
♦ *v* **1** *temper your language:* lessen, moderate, modify, reduce, soften, tone down *colloq*, weaken **2** *nothing would temper his anger:* allay, alleviate, assuage *formal*, calm, lessen, mitigate *formal*, palliate, reduce, soften, soothe **3** *the steel is tempered in the forge:* anneal *technical*, fortify *formal*, harden, strengthen, toughen

temperament *n* **1** *a sunny temperament:* attitude, bent, character, complexion, constitution, disposition, frame/state of mind, humour, make-up, mood, nature, outlook, personality, soul, spirit, temper, tendency **2** *a fit of temperament:* excitability, explosiveness, fieriness, hot-headedness, impatience, irritability, moodiness, touchiness, volatility

temperamental *adj* **1** *I can't bear temperamental people:* capricious, emotional, excitable, explosive, fiery, highly-strung, hot-blooded, hot-headed, hypersensitive, impatient, irritable, mercurial, moody, neurotic, over-emotional, passionate, sensitive, touchy, volatile **2** *this printer's a bit temperamental:* erratic,

undependable, unpredictable, unreliable
3 *temperamental characteristics:* congenital,
constitutional, inborn, ingrained, inherent,
innate, natural
🔁 **1** calm, level-headed, steady

temperance *n* **1** *a society which promotes
temperance:* abstemiousness, abstinence,
prohibition, sobriety, teetotalism **2** *practice
temperance in all things:* abstemiousness,
continence, moderation, restraint, self-control,
self-denial, self-discipline, self-restraint
🔁 **1** intemperance **2** excess, intemperance

temperate *adj* **1** *a temperate climate:* agreeable,
balmy, clement, fair, gentle, mild, moderate,
pleasant **2** *temperate remarks:* balanced, calm,
composed, controlled, equable, even-tempered,
moderate, reasonable, restrained, sensible, stable
3 *temperate habits:* abstemious, continent,
restrained, self-controlled, self-denying, self-
restrained, sensible, sober, stable
🔁 **2** excessive, extreme, intemperate
3 excessive, extreme, intemperate

tempest *n* **1** *the tempest raged outside:* cyclone,
gale, hurricane, squall, storm, tornado, typhoon
2 *a financial tempest was brewing:* commotion,
disturbance, ferment, furore, tumult, upheaval,
uproar

tempestuous *adj* **1** *tempestuous weather:*
blustery, boisterous, gusty, raging, rough,
squally, stormy, tumultuous, turbulent, wild,
windy **2** *a tempestuous relationship:* feverish,
fierce, furious, heated, impassioned, intense,
passionate, stormy, tumultuous, turbulent,
uncontrolled, violent, wild
🔁 **1** calm, peaceful, quiet **2** calm, peaceful, quiet

temple *n* church, mosque, pagoda, place of
worship, sanctuary, shrine, tabernacle

tempo *n* **1** *the tempo of the music:* beat, cadence,
measure, metre, pace, rate, rhythm, speed, time
2 *they upped the tempo of the match:* pace, speed,
velocity

temporal *adj* carnal, earthly, fleshly, material,
mortal, profane, secular, terrestrial, worldly
🔁 spiritual

temporarily *adv* briefly, fleetingly, for the time
being, in the interim, momentarily, pro tem,
transiently, transitorily
🔁 permanently

temporary *adj* **1** *a temporary problem:* brief,
ephemeral *formal,* evanescent *formal,* fleeting,
fugacious *formal,* impermanent, momentary,
passing, short-lived, temporal, transient,
transitory **2** *a temporary secretary:* fill-in, interim,
makeshift, pro tem, provisional, short-term,
stopgap
🔁 **1** everlasting, permanent **2** permanent

temporize *v* delay, equivocate, hang back, hum
and haw *colloq,* pause, play for time,
procrastinate *formal,* stall, tergiversate *formal*

tempt *v* **1** *the ads tempt customers to buy:* bait,
cajole, coax, egg on, entice, incite, inveigle *formal,*
lure, persuade, seduce, woo **2** *tempted by the
cakes:* allure, attract, draw, invite, make
someone's mouth water *colloq,* tantalize **3** *tempt
fate by bragging about your luck:* provoke, test, try
🔁 **1** discourage, dissuade **2** repel

temptation *n* **1** *open to many temptations:*
allurement, bait, cajolery, coaxing, enticement,

incitement, inducement, influence, invitation,
lure, persuasion, seduction, urging **2** *the
temptation of gambling:* allure, appeal, attraction,
pull, seduction

tempting *adj* alluring, appetizing, attractive,
enticing, inviting, mouthwatering, seductive,
tantalizing
🔁 unattractive, uninviting

temptress *n* coquette, Delilah, enchantress,
femme fatale, flirt, seductress, siren, sorceress,
vamp

tenable *adj* arguable, believable, credible,
defendable, defensible, feasible, justifiable,
maintainable, plausible, rational, reasonable,
sound, supportable, viable
🔁 indefensible, unjustifiable, untenable

tenacious *adj* **1** *a tenacious player:* adamant,
determined, dogged, intransigent *formal,*
obdurate *formal,* obstinate, persistent,
purposeful, relentless, resolute, single-minded,
steadfast, stubborn, unswerving, unyielding
2 *his tenacious belief in an afterlife:* dogged, firm,
unshakeable, unswerving, unyielding **3** *a
tenacious grip:* clinging, fast, firm, secure, tight
🔁 **1** weak **2** weak **3** loose, slack, weak

tenacity *n* **1** *succeeded thanks to his tenacity:*
application, determination, diligence,
doggedness, indomitability, inflexibility,
intransigence *formal,* obduracy *formal,* obstinacy,
perseverance, persistence, pertinacity *formal,*
resoluteness, resolution, resolve, single-
mindedness, staunchness, steadfastness,
stubbornness, toughness **2** *the tenacity of his grip:*
fastness, firmness, force, forcefulness, power,
strength
🔁 **1** weakness **2** looseness, slackness, weakness

tenancy *n* **1** *tenancy of a building:* holding, lease,
leasehold, occupancy, occupation, possession,
renting, residence **2** *the president's tenancy:*
incumbency, period of office, tenure, time in
office

tenant *n* inhabitant, landholder, leaseholder,
lessee, occupant, occupier, renter, resident

tend[1] *v* **1** *tends to arrive late:* be apt, be inclined,
be liable, be likely, be prone, have a habit, have a
tendency, show a tendency **2** *tend toward liberal
views:* gravitate, incline, lean, show a tendency
3 *the path tends to the left:* aim, bear, bend, go,
head, lead, move, point

tend[2] *v* **1** *tend someone who is ill:* attend (to), care
for, guard, handle, keep, keep an eye on, look
after, mind, minister to, nurse, protect, see to,
serve, take care of, wait on, watch (over) **2** *tend a
garden:* cultivate, maintain, manage, nurture
🔁 **1** ignore, neglect **2** ignore, neglect

tendency *n* **1** *the government's tendency toward
nannyism:* bearing, bias, course, direction, drift,
heading, movement, trend **2** *his tendency to blame
others:* aptness, bent, conatus *formal,* disposition,
inclination, leaning, liability, partiality,
predisposition *formal,* proclivity *formal,*
proneness, propensity *formal,* readiness,
susceptibility

tender[1] *adj* **1** *tender loving care:* affectionate,
benevolent, caring, compassionate, considerate,
fond, generous, gentle, humane, kind, kindly,
loving, sensitive, soft-hearted, sympathetic,
tender-hearted, warm **2** *a tender love story:*

emotional, evocative, moving, romantic, sentimental, touching **3** *at the tender age of nine:* callow, early, green, immature, impressionable, inexperienced, new, raw, vulnerable, young, youthful **4** *tender skin:* dainty, delicate, fragile, frail, sensitive, soft, vulnerable, weak **5** *a tender steak:* juicy, soft, succulent **6** *a tender spot:* aching, bruised, inflamed, painful, raw, red, sensitive, smarting, sore, throbbing
F3 1 callous, hard-hearted **3** mature **4** hard, tough **5** hard, tough

tender² *v* advance, bid, extend, give, offer, present, proffer, propose, submit, suggest, volunteer
♦ *n* **1** *legal tender:* currency, money **2** *submit a tender for the work:* bid, estimate, offer, price, proposal, proposition, quotation, submission, suggestion

tender-hearted *adj* affectionate, benevolent, benign, caring, compassionate, considerate, feeling, fond, gentle, humane, kind, kind-hearted, kindly, loving, merciful, mild, pitying, responsive, sensitive, sentimental, soft-hearted, sympathetic, warm, warm-hearted
F3 callous, cruel, hard-hearted, unfeeling

tenderness *n* **1** *the tenderness of his feelings for her:* affection, attachment, benevolence, care, compassion, consideration, devotion, fondness, gentleness, humaneness, humanity, kindness, liking, love, loving-kindness, mercy, pity, sensitivity, sentimentality, soft-heartedness, sweetness, sympathy, tender-heartedness, warm-heartedness, warmth **2** *wise beyond the tenderness of his years:* callowness, greenness, immaturity, inexperience, youth, youthfulness **3** *the tenderness of a baby's skin:* delicateness, fragility, frailness, softness, vulnerability, weakness **4** *a tenderness in the gums:* ache, aching, bruising, inflammation, irritation, pain, painfulness, rawness, sensitiveness, soreness
F3 1 cruelty, hardness, harshness **2** maturity **3** hardness, toughness

tenet *n* article of faith, belief, canon, conviction, credo, creed, doctrine, dogma, maxim, opinion, precept, presumption, principle, rule, teaching, thesis, view

tenor *n* aim, burden, course, direction, drift, essence, gist, intent, meaning, path, point, purport *formal*, purpose, sense, spirit, substance, tendency, theme, trend, way

tense *adj* **1** *tense muscles:* rigid, stiff, strained, stretched, taut, tight **2** *she was feeling tense:* anxious, apprehensive, distraught, edgy *colloq*, fidgety, jittery, jumpy, keyed up, nervous, overwrought, restless, screwed up *slang*, strained, stressed out *colloq*, under pressure, uneasy, uptight *colloq*, worried **3** *this is a tense time:* charged, exciting, fraught, nail-biting, nerve-racking, strained, stressful, uneasy, worrying
F3 1 loose, slack **2** calm, relaxed
♦ *v* brace, contract, stiffen, strain, stretch, tighten
F3 loosen, relax

tension *n* **1** *tension in the muscles:* pressure, rigidity, stiffness, strain, straining, stress, stretching, tautness, tightness **2** *the tension was getting to me:* agitation, anxiety, apprehension, disquiet, distress, edginess, nerves *colloq*,

nervousness, pressure, restlessness, strain, stress, suspense, uneasiness, worry **3** *the tension between the neighbouring states:* antagonism, antipathy *formal*, clash, conflict, confrontation, contention, difference of opinion, disagreement, discord, dispute, dissension, feud, friction, hostility, ill-will, opposition, quarrel, strife, unrest, variance
F3 1 looseness **2** calm(ness), relaxation **3** harmony

tentative *adj* **1** *a tentative plan:* conjectural *formal*, experimental, exploratory, indefinite, pilot, provisional, speculative, test, trial, unconfirmed, unproven **2** *a tentative smile:* cautious, doubtful, faltering, hesitant, timid, uncertain, undecided, unsure, wavering
F3 1 conclusive, definite, final, firm **2** confident, decisive

tenuous *adj* **1** *a tenuous connection:* doubtful, dubious, hazy, indefinite, insubstantial, questionable, shaky, slight, vague, weak **2** *a tenuous thread:* delicate, fine, flimsy, fragile, slender, slim, thin, weak
F3 1 strong, substantial **2** strong

tenure *n* **1** *our tenure of the site:* habitation *formal*, holding, occupancy, occupation, possession, proprietorship, residence, tenancy **2** *his tenure as manager:* incumbency, tenancy, term, time

tepid *adj* **1** *tepid water:* cool, lukewarm, warmish **2** *a tepid reception:* apathetic, cool, half-hearted, indifferent, lukewarm, unenthusiastic
F3 1 cold, hot **2** passionate

term *n* **1** *a technical term:* appellation *formal*, denomination *formal*, designation *formal*, epithet, expression, locution *formal*, name, phrase, title, word **2** *the school term:* semester, session **3** *a term of office:* course, duration, interval, period, season, space, span, spell, stretch, time **4** *on good terms:* footing, position, relations, relationship, standing **5** *the terms of the contract:* clauses, conditions, details, particulars, points, provisions, provisos, qualifications, specifications, stipulations **6** *buy something on easy terms:* charges, costs, fees, prices, rates, tariff **7** *carry a baby to term:* close, conclusion, culmination, end, finish, fruition
♦ *v* call, denominate *formal*, designate, dub, entitle, label, name, style, tag, title

terminal *adj* **1** *the terminal moments of the match:* concluding, ending, final, ultimate **2** *the terminal part of the route:* end, extreme, last, utmost **3** *terminal illness:* deadly, dying, fatal, incurable, killing, lethal, mortal
F3 1 first, initial **2** first, initial
♦ *n* **1** *a bus terminal:* depot, terminus **2** *the terminal of the route:* boundary, end, extremity, limit, termination **3** *a computer terminal:* computer workstation, console, input-output device, keyboard, monitor, VDU

terminate *v* **1** *terminate a discussion:* bring to an end, close, complete, conclude, cut off, discontinue *formal*, end, finish, put an end to, stop, wind up *colloq* **2** *my contract terminates next month:* cease *formal*, come to an end, conclude, end, expire, finish, lapse, run out, stop **3** *the train terminates here:* end its journey, finish, stop **4** *terminate a pregnancy:* abort, end
F3 1 begin, initiate, start **2** begin, start **3** start

termination *n* 1 *the termination of a contract:* cessation *formal*, close, completion, conclusion, demise *formal*, discontinuation *formal*, end, ending, expiry, finis, finish 2 *the successful termination of their efforts:* conclusion, consequence, dénouement, effect, end, finale, issue, result 3 *the termination of a pregnancy:* abortion, ending
⊠ 1 beginning, initiation, start

terminology *n* expressions, jargon, language, nomenclature, phraseology, terms, vocabulary, words

terminus *n* 1 *a bus terminus:* depot, garage, station, terminal 2 *the terminus of the journey:* close, destination, end, goal, target, termination 3 *the western terminus of the island:* boundary, end, extremity, limit, termination

terrain *n* country, countryside, ground, land, landscape, territory, topography

terrestrial *adj* earthly, global, mundane, worldly
⊠ cosmic, heavenly

terrible *adj* 1 *terrible injuries:* appalling, awful, distressing, dreadful, grave, gruesome, harrowing, horrible, horrific, shocking, unspeakable 2 *a terrible smell:* abhorrent, awful, bad, disgusting, dreadful, foul, frightful, hateful, hideous, horrible, horrid, nasty, obnoxious, offensive, repulsive, revolting, shocking, unpleasant, unspeakable, vile 3 *his playing is terrible:* appalling, awful, bad, dreadful, frightful, incompetent, poor, shocking 4 *a terrible situation:* awful, bad, desperate, dreadful, extreme, frightful, grave, grim, serious
⊠ 2 wonderful 3 excellent, superb, wonderful

terribly *adv* awfully *colloq*, decidedly, desperately, exceedingly, extremely, frightfully *colloq*, greatly, much, seriously, thoroughly, very

terrific *adj* 1 *a terrific guitarist:* ace *colloq*, amazing, awesome *slang*, breathtaking, brill *colloq*, brilliant, cool *slang*, crack *colloq*, crucial *slang*, excellent, fabulous *colloq*, fantastic *colloq*, great, magnificent, marvellous, mega *slang*, neat *colloq*, out of this world *colloq*, outstanding, remarkable, sensational, smashing *colloq*, stupendous, super, superb, wicked *slang*, wonderful 2 *a terrific sum of money:* enormous, gigantic, great, huge, tremendous 3 *a terrific explosion:* enormous, excessive, extraordinary, extreme, gigantic, great, huge, intense, tremendous
⊠ 1 appalling, awful, terrible

terrified *adj* alarmed, appalled, frightened, having kittens *colloq*, horrified, horror-struck, in a blue funk *colloq*, intimidated, panic-stricken, petrified, scared, scared out of your wits *colloq*, scared stiff, scared to death *colloq*

terrify *v* alarm, appal, frighten, intimidate, make you jump out of your skin *colloq*, make your blood run cold *colloq*, make your hair stand on end *colloq*, numb, panic, paralyse, petrify, put the frighteners on *colloq*, put the wind up *colloq*, rattle *colloq*, scare, scare out of your wits *colloq*, scare stiff, scare the living daylights out of *colloq*, scare the shit out of *slang*, terrorize

territorial *adj* area, district, domainal *formal*, geographical, localized, regional, sectional, topographic, zonal

territory *n* area, country, county, dependency, district, domain, jurisdiction, land, preserve, province, region, sector, state, terrain, tract, zone

terror *n* 1 *fill someone with terror:* alarm, blue funk *colloq*, dread, fear, fright, horror, intimidation, panic, trepidation 2 *that child's a terror:* horror, rascal, rogue, tearaway 3 *the terrors of his imagination:* demon, devil, fiend, monster

terrorize *v* 1 *thugs terrorizing the locals:* alarm, frighten, intimidate, menace, oppress, petrify, put the frighteners on *colloq*, put the wind up *colloq*, scare, shock, terrify 2 *terrorized us into agreeing:* browbeat, bully, coerce, intimidate, strongarm *colloq*, threaten

terse *adj* 1 *a terse tone of voice:* abrupt, blunt, brusque, curt, short, snappy 2 *a terse statement to the press:* brief, compact, concise, condensed, crisp, elliptical *formal*, epigrammatic *formal*, gnomic *formal*, incisive, laconic, pithy, short, succinct, to the point
⊠ 2 long-winded, verbose

test *v* 1 *test a new drug:* analyse, assay *formal*, assess, check, evaluate, experiment with, inspect, investigate, probe *colloq*, prove, sample, screen, scrutinize, study, try (out), verify 2 *test someone on spelling:* appraise *formal*, assess, check, examine, try (out) 3 *test someone's patience:* burden, drain, encumber, exact, exhaust, impose on, make demands on, overload, sap, strain, stretch, tire, try, weaken, wear out, weary
♦ *n* 1 *tests of the product:* analysis, assessment, check, check-up, evaluation, experiment, exploration, inspection, investigation, pilot study, proof, scrutinization, trial, try-out 2 *a French test:* assessment, audition, examination, questionnaire, questions, quiz, try-out

testament *n* 1 *a testament to her loyalty:* attestation *formal*, demonstration, earnest, evidence, exemplification, proof, testimony, tribute, witness 2 *his last will and testament:* will

testicles *n* balls *taboo slang*, bollocks *taboo slang*, goolies *taboo slang*, nuts *taboo slang*, rocks *taboo slang*

testify *v* 1 *they testified that he had started the fight:* affirm *formal*, assert, attest *formal*, avow *formal*, bear witness, certify, declare, state, swear, vouch 2 *willing to testify in court:* attest *formal*, bear witness, depose *formal*, give evidence, give testimony 3 *all the evidence testifies to this point:* attest to *formal*, back up, bear witness to, confirm, corroborate *formal*, demonstrate, endorse, establish, show, substantiate, support, verify

testimonial *n* certificate, character, commendation, credential, endorsement, (letter of) recommendation, reference, tribute

---

testimonial or *testimony?* A *testimonial* is a letter describing a person's character and abilities. A *testimony* is a statement of evidence, for example that of a witness at a trial: *He was convicted mainly by the testimony of his former partner; Her book is a remarkable testimony to her vision for the future of her country.*

testimony *n* **1** *his sworn testimony:* affidavit *technical*, affirmation *formal*, assertion, attestation *formal*, confirmation, declaration, deposition, evidence, profession, statement, submission **2** *testimony to her loyalty:* corroboration *formal*, demonstration, evidence, indication, manifestation *formal*, proof, support, verification

testy *adj* bad-tempered, cantankerous *formal*, captious, crabbed *colloq*, cross, crotchety *colloq*, crusty, fretful, grumpy, impatient, irascible, irritable, peevish, petulant, quick-tempered, ratty *colloq*, shirty *colloq*, short-tempered, snappish, snappy, splenetic, stroppy *colloq*, tetchy *colloq*, touchy *colloq*, waspish
🔁 even-tempered, good-humoured

tetchy *adj* bad-tempered, crotchety *colloq*, crusty, grumpy, irascible, irritable, peevish, ratty *colloq*, shirty *colloq*, short-tempered, snappish, touchy *colloq*

tête-à-tête *n* chat, confab *colloq*, conversation, dialogue, heart-to-heart, natter *colloq*, talk

tether *n* bond, chain, cord, fastening, fetter, lead, leash, line, restraint, rope, shackle
♦ *v* bind, chain, fasten, fetter, lash, leash, manacle, restrain, rope, secure, shackle, tie

text *n* **1** *the text of the manual:* body, content, main matter, matter, wording, words **2** *the text for his sermon:* issue, point, subject, subject matter, theme, topic **3** *read out a text from the Bible:* chapter, paragraph, passage, reading, sentence, verse **4** *set texts for the course:* book, set book, source, textbook

texture *n* character, composition, consistency, constitution, fabric, feel, finish, grain, quality, structure, surface, tissue, touch, weave

thank *v* acknowledge, appreciate, be grateful, credit, express your thanks, recognize, say thank you, show your appreciation, show / express your gratitude

thankful *adj* **1** *thankful to you for your help:* appreciative, beholden *formal*, grateful, indebted, obliged **2** *be thankful it was no worse:* appreciative, contented, grateful, pleased, relieved
🔁 **1** unappreciative, ungrateful **2** unappreciative, ungrateful

thankless *adj* fruitless, unacknowledged, unappreciated, unprofitable, unrecognized, unrequited, unrewarded, unrewarding, useless
🔁 rewarding, worthwhile

thanks *n* acknowledgement, appreciation, credit, gratefulness, gratitude, recognition, thanksgiving

thaw *v* **1** *the snow has thawed:* defreeze, defrost, de-ice, dissolve, heat up, liquefy, melt, soften, warm **2** *relations thawed somewhat:* become friendlier, become more relaxed, loosen up, relax
🔁 **1** freeze

theatre *n* **1** *go to the theatre:* amphitheatre, auditorium, hall, lyceum, odeon, opera house, playhouse **2** *a career in the theatre:* drama, dramatics, rep *colloq*, show business, the boards *colloq*, the footlights *colloq*, the stage, theatrics, Thespian art *formal*

Parts of a theatre include:
apron, auditorium, backstage, balcony, border, box, bridge, catwalk, circle, coulisse, cut drop, cyclorama, decor, downstage, flat, flies, forestage, fourth wall, gallery, the gods *colloq*, green room, grid, leg drop, lights, floats, floods, footlights, spots, loge, loggia, logum, mezzanine, open stage, opposite prompt, orchestra pit, picture-frame stage, pit, prompt side, proscenium, proscenium arch, revolving stage, rostrum, safety curtain, scruto, set, stage, stalls, tormentor, trapdoor, upper circle, upstage, wings

theatrical *adj* **1** *the theatrical arts:* dramatic, thespian **2** *a theatrical gesture:* affected, artificial, dramatic, exaggerated, extravagant, forced, histrionic, mannered, melodramatic, ostentatious, overdone, pompous, showy, unreal

Theatrical forms include:
ballet, burlesque, cabaret, circus, comedy, black comedy, comedy of humours, comedy of manners, comedy of menace, commedia dell'arte, duologue, farce, fringe theatre, Grand Guignol, kabuki, Kitchen-Sink, legitimate drama, masque, melodrama, mime, miracle play, monologue, morality play, mummery, music hall, musical, musical comedy, mystery play, Noh, opera, operetta, pageant, pantomime, play, Punch and Judy, puppet theatre, revue, street theatre, tableau, theatre-in-the-round, Theatre of the Absurd, Theatre of Cruelty, tragedy

theft *n* burglary, embezzlement, fraud, kleptomania, larceny, lifting *colloq*, nicking *colloq*, nobbling *colloq*, pilfering, pinching *colloq*, purloining *formal*, robbery, shoplifting, stealing, swindling, swiping *colloq*, thieving

thematic *adj* classificatory, conceptual, notional, taxonomic *formal*

theme *n* **1** *the theme of the novel:* argument, burden, essence, gist, idea, keynote, leitmotif *formal*, motif, subject, subject matter, thread, topic **2** *write a theme on a topic:* composition, dissertation, essay, matter, paper, text, thesis **3** *the main theme of the concerto:* melody, motif, tune

then *adv* **1** *we were happier then:* at that moment, at that point, at that time, in those days **2** *do the house up and then sell it:* after, afterwards, at a later date, next, soon, subsequently **3** *he works all day and then studies all evening:* additionally, also, as well, besides, further, furthermore, in addition, moreover, too **4** *then you leave me no choice:* accordingly, as a result, consequently, therefore, thus *formal*

theological *adj* divine, doctrinal, ecclesiastical, hierological *technical*, religious, scriptural

theorem *n* deduction, dictum *formal*, formula, hypothesis, postulate *formal*, principle, proposition, rule, statement

theoretical *adj* **1** *theoretical mathematics:* abstract, conceptual, doctrinaire, ideal, on paper *colloq*, pure, speculative **2** *a theoretical case:* academic, conjectural *formal*, hypothetical, notional, suppositional *formal*
🔁 **1** applied, practical **2** concrete

theorize *v* conjecture *formal*, formulate, guess, hypothesize *formal*, postulate *formal*, propound *formal*, speculate, suppose

theory *n* **1** *the theory of evolution*: hypothesis, philosophy, plan, proposal, scheme, system, thesis **2** *a theory that he was guilty*: abstraction, assumption, conjecture *formal*, guess, idea, notion, opinion, postulation *formal*, presumption, speculation, supposition, surmise, view
🖃 **1** practice **2** certainty

therapeutic *adj* advantageous, ameliorative *formal*, beneficial, corrective, curative, curing, good, healing, health-giving, medicinal, remedial, restorative, salutary, sanative *formal*, tonic
🖃 detrimental, harmful

therapy *n* cure, healing, remedy, tonic, treatment

Types of therapy include:
acupressure, acupuncture, Alexander technique, aromatherapy, art therapy, aversion therapy, beauty therapy, behaviour therapy, biofeedback, chemotherapy, chiropractic, cognitive therapy, confrontation therapy, crystal healing, drama therapy, electro-convulsive therapy, electrotherapy, faith healing, family therapy, Gestalt therapy, group therapy, heat treatment, herbalism, homeopathy, hormone-replacement therapy, horticulture therapy, hydrotherapy, hypnotherapy, irradiation, moxibustion, music therapy, naturopathy, occupational therapy, osteopathy, phototherapy, physiotherapy, play therapy, primal therapy, psychotherapy, radiotherapy, reflexology, regression therapy, reminiscence therapy, reiki, Rolfing, sex therapy, shiatsu, speech therapy, thalassotherapy, ultrasound, zone therapy

thereabouts *adv* about, approximately, near that date, near that number, roughly

thereafter *adv* after that, after that time, afterwards, next, subsequently

therefore *adv* accordingly, and so, as a result, consequently, ergo *formal*, so, then, thus *formal*

thesaurus *n* dictionary, encyclopedia, lexicon, synonymy, treasury, vocabulary, wordbook

thesis *n* **1** *doctoral thesis*: composition, disquisition *formal*, dissertation, essay, monograph, paper, treatise **2** *the main thesis of the novel*: argument, contention, hypothesis, idea, opinion, premise, proposal, proposition, statement, subject, theme, theory, topic, view

thick *adj* **1** *a thick body*: big, broad, bulky, chunky, fat, heavy, solid, stout, substantial, wide **2** *thick forest*: close, compact, deep, dense, impenetrable **3** *a thick sauce*: clotted, coagulated, concentrated, condensed, creamy, heavy, lumpy, stiff, substantial, viscous **4** *thick hair*: abundant, dense, heavy, lush, luxuriant **5** *the place is thick with tourists*: abounding, brimming, bristling, bursting, chock-a-block *colloq*, crawling, crowded, filled, full, overflowing, packed, swarming, teeming **6** *thick crowds of people*: abundant, numerous **7** *thick fog*: concentrated, dense, heavy, impenetrable, murky, opaque, smoggy, soupy **8** *a thick voice*: croaking, croaky, gravelly, gruff, guttural, husky, indistinct, rasping, rough, throaty, unclear **9** *a thick accent*: broad, definite, marked, noticeable, obvious,

pronounced, striking, strong **10** *he's really thick*: brainless, dense, dim-witted, dopey *colloq*, dull, dumb *colloq*, foolish, gormless *colloq*, simple, slow, stupid, thick as a plank/two short planks *colloq*
🖃 **1** slender, slight, slim, thin **2** thin **3** thin **4** thin **6** sparse **8** clear **9** faint, vague **10** brainy *colloq*, clever, intelligent
♦ *n* centre, focus, heart, hub, middle, midst

thicken *v* **1** *stir till the sauce thickens*: become more solid, cake, clot, coagulate, condense, congeal, gel, jell, set, solidify, stiffen **2** *the plot thickens*: become more complicated, become more intricate, become more involved, become more mysterious
🖃 **1** thin

thickhead *n* blockhead *colloq*, chump *colloq*, clot *colloq*, dimwit *colloq*, dope *colloq*, dummy *colloq*, dunce, fathead *colloq*, fool, idiot, imbecile *colloq*, moron *colloq*, nitwit *colloq*, numskull *colloq*, pinhead *colloq*, twit *colloq*

thick-headed *adj* asinine, blockheaded *colloq*, brainless, dense, dim-witted, doltish, dopey *colloq*, dull-witted, foolish, gormless *colloq*, idiotic, imbecilic, moronic, obtuse, slow, slow-witted, stupid, thick *colloq*
🖃 brainy *colloq*, clever, intelligent, sharp

thickness *n* **1** *the thickness of the glass*: breadth, density, diameter, extent, width **2** *the thickness of the undergrowth*: closeness, density **3** *the thickness of his body*: body, breadth, bulk, bulkiness, solidness, width **4** *the thickness of the sauce*: consistency, density, viscosity **5** *several thicknesses of wool*: band, bed, coat, deposit, film, lamina, layer, ply, seam, sheet, stratum, vein
🖃 **1** thinness **2** thinness **3** thinness **4** thinness

thickset *adj* beefy *colloq*, brawny *colloq*, bulky, burly, dense, heavily built, heavy, muscular, powerful, solid, squabby, squat, stocky, strong, sturdy, well-built
🖃 lanky

thick-skinned *adj* callous, case-hardened, hard-boiled *colloq*, hardened, hard-nosed *colloq*, insensitive, inured, invulnerable, tough, tough as old boots *colloq*, unfeeling
🖃 sensitive, thin-skinned, vulnerable

thief *n* bandit, brigand, burglar, embezzler, filcher *colloq*, house-breaker, kleptomaniac, mugger *colloq*, nicker *colloq*, pickpocket, pilferer, plunderer, poacher, robber, shoplifter, stealer, swindler

thieve *v* abstract, embezzle, filch *colloq*, heist *slang*, knock off *colloq*, lift *colloq*, make/run off with *colloq*, misappropriate, nick *colloq*, peculate *formal*, pilfer, pinch, plunder, poach, purloin *formal*, rip off *colloq*, rob, snaffle *colloq*, steal, swindle, swipe *colloq*

thieving *n* banditry, burglary, embezzlement, filching *colloq*, knocking off *colloq*, larceny, lifting *colloq*, mugging *colloq*, nicking *colloq*, peculation *formal*, pilferage, pilfering, piracy, plundering, ripping off *colloq*, robbery, shoplifting, stealing, theft, thievery

thin *adj* **1** *she's too thin*: anorexic, bony, emaciated, gaunt, lanky, lean, light, scraggy, scrawny, shrunken, skeletal, skinny, slender, slight, slim, spare, spindly, svelte, thin as a rake *colloq*, undernourished, underweight, wasted

2 *a thin layer:* attenuated, fine, narrow, paper-thin, wafer-thin **3** *thin fabric:* delicate, diaphanous *formal*, filmy, fine, flimsy, gauzy, gossamer, light, see-through, sheer, translucent, transparent **4** *his hair's getting thin:* deficient, inadequate, meagre, paltry, poor, scant, scanty, scarce, scattered, skimpy, sparse, straggly, wispy **5** *a thin liquid:* dilute, diluted, runny, watery, weak, wishy-washy *colloq* **6** *the evidence is thin:* defective, deficient, feeble, flimsy, implausible, inadequate, inconclusive, lame, unconvincing, untenable, weak **7** *a thin voice:* faint, quiet, soft, weak

F **1** broad, fat **2** broad **3** dense, solid, substantial, thick **4** abundant, plentiful, thick **5** strong, thick **6** strong, substantial

♦ *v* **1** *thin the plants in summer:* attenuate *formal*, decrease, lessen, make less in number, reduce, trim, weed out **2** *the crowds thinned:* become less in number, decrease, diminish, dwindle, lessen, reduce **3** *thin the soup with water:* dilute, make more watery, rarefy, refine, water down, weaken

thing *n* **1** *what's that thing in the bath?:* article, body, creature, entity, item, object **2** *the thing you change channels with:* apparatus, contrivance, device, doodah *colloq*, gadget, gismo *colloq*, implement, instrument, machine, mechanism, thingamy *colloq*, thingummy *colloq*, thingummybob *colloq*, thingummyjig *colloq*, thingy *colloq*, tool, what-d'you-call-it *colloq*, whatsit *colloq*, what's-its-name *colloq* **3** *camping things:* apparatus, apparel *formal*, baggage, belongings, bits and bobs *colloq*, bits and pieces, clobber *colloq*, effects *formal*, equipment, gear *colloq*, goods, luggage, oddments, odds and ends, paraphernalia, possessions, stuff *colloq*, tackle, tools **4** *take those wet things off:* apparel *formal*, attire *formal*, clobber *colloq*, clothes, clothing, garments, gear *colloq*, togs *colloq* **5** *the best thing about him:* aspect, attribute, characteristic, element, feature, property, quality, trait **6** *I just want to know one thing:* detail, fact, factor, particular, point **7** *don't talk about such depressing things:* concept, idea, notion, thought **8** *loads of things to do:* act, action, chore, deed, exploit, feat, job, problem, responsibility, task, undertaking **9** *the worst thing that can happen:* episode, event, eventuality, happening, incident, occurrence, phenomenon **10** *the whole thing is getting to me:* affair, circumstance, condition, matter, proceeding, situation **11** *a thing about flying:* aversion, dislike, fear, hang-up *colloq*, horror, phobia **12** *she has a thing about tall men:* affection, affinity, appreciation, attraction, bent, bias, desire, fancy, fetish, fixation, fondness, idée fixe, inclination, leaning, liking, love, obsession, one-track mind *colloq*, partiality, penchant *formal*, predilection *formal*, preference, preoccupation, proclivity *formal*, proneness, propensity *formal*, soft spot *colloq*, taste, tendency, weakness

think *v* **1** *I think you're right:* believe, conclude, consider, esteem *formal*, hold that, judge, opine *formal*, reckon, regard **2** *let's think what to do:* conclude, consider, determine, judge, reason **3** *I think he's lost:* calculate, consider, deem *formal*, estimate, figure *colloq*, judge, reckon **4** *I thought this would happen:* anticipate, conceive, conjecture *formal*, envisage, expect, foresee, guess, imagine, presume, suppose, surmise *formal*, visualize **5** *think before you act:* brood, cerebrate *formal*,

cogitate *formal*, concentrate, deliberate, meditate, muse, ponder, reflect, review, ruminate, sleep on it *colloq*, take stock **6** *thinking of moving house:* chew over, consider, contemplate, deliberate about, weigh up **7** *can't think what his name is:* recall, recollect, remember

♦ *n* assessment, cogitation *formal*, consideration, contemplation, deliberation, evaluation, meditation, reflection

▶ **think over** chew over, consider, contemplate, meditate, mull over, ponder, reflect upon, ruminate, weigh up

▶ **think up** conceive, concoct, contrive, create, design, devise, dream up, imagine, invent, visualize

thinkable *adj* cogitable *formal*, conceivable, feasible, imaginable, likely, possible, reasonable, supposable

F unthinkable

thinker *n* brain *colloq*, ideologist, intellect, mastermind, philosopher, sage, scholar, theorist

thinking *n* appraisal, assessment, conclusion(s), evaluation, idea, judgement, opinion, outlook, philosophy, position, reasoning, theory, thought(s), view

♦ *adj* analytical, contemplative, cultured, intellectual, intelligent, logical, meditative, philosophical, rational, reasoning, reflective, sensible, sophisticated, thoughtful

thin-skinned *adj* easily upset, hypersensitive, sensitive, soft, susceptible, tender, touchy *colloq*, vulnerable

F callous, thick-skinned, unfeeling

third-rate *adj* awful, bad, cheap and nasty, indifferent, inferior, low-grade, low-quality, mediocre, naff *slang*, poor, ropy *colloq*, shoddy, slipshod, unsatisfactory

F first-rate

thirst *n* **1** *a raging thirst:* drought, drouth, drouthiness, dryness, parchedness, thirstiness **2** *a thirst for adventure:* appetite, craving, desire, eagerness, hankering, hunger, keenness, longing, lust, passion, yearning, yen *colloq*

♦ *v* crave, desire, hanker, hunger, long, lust, yearn

thirsty *adj* **1** *I'm really thirsty:* dehydrated, dry, gasping *colloq*, parched *colloq* **2** *thirsty for knowledge:* avid, burning, craving, desirous, dying, eager, greedy, hankering, hungry, itching, keen, longing, thirsting, yearning

thorn *n* barb, bristle, needle, point, prickle, spike, spine

thorny *adj* **1** *thorny plants:* acanthous *formal*, barbed, bristly, pointed, prickly, sharp, spiky, spinose *formal*, spinous *formal*, spiny **2** *a thorny problem:* awkward, complex, convoluted *formal*, delicate, difficult, intricate, irksome, knotty, problematic, ticklish, tough, tricky, troublesome, trying, vexed, worrying

thorough *adj* **1** *a thorough worker:* careful, conscientious, efficient, methodical, meticulous, painstaking, scrupulous **2** *thorough research:* all-embracing, all-inclusive, comprehensive, deep, exhaustive, extensive, in-depth, intensive, meticulous, scrupulous, sweeping, thoroughgoing, widespread **3** *a thorough waste of time:* absolute, complete, downright, entire, full,

out-and-out, perfect, pure, sheer, total, unmitigated, unqualified, utter
Ⅎ 2 careless, partial, superficial

thoroughbred *adj* blooded, full-blooded, pedigree, pedigreed, pure-blood, pure-blooded
Ⅎ cross-bred, hybrid, mixed, mongrel

thoroughfare *n* access, avenue, boulevard, concourse, highway, motorway, passage, passageway, road, roadway, street, turnpike, way

thoroughly *adv* **1** *searched thoroughly:* assiduously, carefully, comprehensively, conscientiously, efficiently, exhaustively, inside out, intensively, meticulously, painstakingly, root and branch, scrupulously, sweepingly, with a fine-tooth comb *colloq* **2** *thoroughly exhausted:* absolutely, completely, downright, entirely, every inch *colloq*, fully, perfectly, quite, totally, utterly
Ⅎ 1 carelessly, haphazardly **2** partially

though *conj* allowing for the fact that, although, but, even if, granted, notwithstanding *formal*, while, yet
♦ *adv* all the same *colloq*, even so, for all that, however, nevertheless, nonetheless, still, yet

thought *n* **1** *lost in thought:* cerebration *formal*, cogitation *formal*, contemplation, introspection, meditation, musing, pondering, reflection, thinking **2** *give it some thought:* attention, care, consideration, deliberation, heed, pondering, reasoning, regard, rumination, scrutiny, study, thinking **3** *what are your thoughts about this?:* appraisal, assessment, belief, concept, conception, conclusion, conviction, estimation, feeling, idea, judgement, notion, opinion, point of view, reasoning, theory, view **4** *I had no thought of leaving:* aim, design, idea, intention, notion, plan, purpose **5** *give up all thoughts of winning:* anticipation, aspiration, dream, expectation, hope, idea, prospect **6** *no thought for other people:* care, compassion, concern, consideration, kindness, regard, solicitude *formal*, sympathy, tenderness, thoughtfulness

thoughtful *adj* **1** *you're looking thoughtful:* absorbed, abstracted, cogitative *formal*, contemplative, dreamy, in a brown study *colloq*, introspective, lost in thought, pensive, quiet, reflective, serious, solemn, thinking, wistful **2** *a thoughtful novel:* deep, profound, serious, studious **3** *so kind and thoughtful:* attentive, caring, compassionate, considerate, helpful, kind, solicitous *formal*, sympathetic, tender, unselfish **4** *thoughtful of how she appears to others:* careful, cautious, heedful *formal*, mindful, prudent, wary
Ⅎ 3 insensitive, selfish, thoughtless
4 thoughtless

thoughtless *adj* **1** *a thoughtless remark:* impolite, inconsiderate, indiscreet, insensitive, rude, selfish, tactless, uncaring, undiplomatic, unfeeling, unkind, unthinking **2** *her actions were thoughtless rather than wicked:* absent-minded, careless, foolish, hasty, heedless, ill-advised, ill-considered, imprudent, mindless, negligent, precipitate *formal*, rash, reckless, remiss, silly, stupid, unwise
Ⅎ 1 considerate, thoughtful **2** careful

thrall *n* bondage, enslavement, serfdom, servitude, slavery, subjection, subjugation *formal*, thraldom, vassalage
Ⅎ freedom

thrash *v* **1** *thrashed him with a slipper:* beat, belt *colloq*, cane, clobber, flog, lash, lay into, punish, scourge, spank, tan *colloq*, wallop *colloq*, whack *colloq*, whip **2** *they thrashed the opposition:* be more than a match for, beat, clobber *colloq*, crush, defeat, drub, hammer *colloq*, have the edge on, lick *colloq*, overwhelm, rout, slaughter *colloq*, trounce, vanquish *formal*, wipe the floor with *colloq* **3** *thrashing about on the floor:* flail, jerk, swish, thresh, toss, writhe
▶ **thrash out** debate, discuss, hammer out, negotiate, resolve, settle

thrashing *n* **1** *he deserves a thrashing:* beating, belting *colloq*, caning, chastisement *formal*, flogging, hiding, lashing, leathering, pasting, punishment, tanning, whipping **2** *we got a thrashing in the finals:* beating, clobbering *colloq*, crushing, defeat, drubbing, hammering *colloq*, lamming, licking *colloq*, rout, trouncing

thread *n* **1** *fine cotton thread:* fibre, filament, line, strand, string, strip, yarn **2** *follow the thread of the discussion:* course, direction, drift, motif, plot, storyline, subject, tenor, theme, train of thought
♦ *v* **1** *thread the beads on to the wire:* move, pass, push, string, weave **2** *thread your way through the crowd:* ease, inch, meander, move, pass, push, wind

threadbare *adj* **1** *threadbare clothes:* frayed, moth-eaten, ragged, scruffy, shabby, tattered, tatty, worn **2** *threadbare platitudes:* commonplace, corny *colloq*, hackneyed, overused, stereotyped, stock
Ⅎ 1 new **2** fresh

threat *n* **1** *the threat of a nuclear attack:* danger, hazard, menace, peril, risk **2** *felt a sense of threat:* foreboding, menace, omen, portent *formal*, presage *formal*, warning **3** *carry out a threat:* commination *formal*, menace, ultimatum

threaten *v* **1** *he threatened us into agreeing:* blackmail, browbeat, bully, comminate *formal*, cow, intimidate, lean on *colloq*, menace, pressurize, push around *colloq*, put the frighteners on *colloq*, put the screws on *colloq*, terrorize **2** *threaten the health of children:* endanger, imperil, jeopardize, menace, put at risk **3** *a storm is threatening:* approach, be imminent, be in the offing, loom (up) **4** *omens threatening disaster:* augur *formal*, forebode, foreshadow, portend *formal*, presage *formal*, warn of

threatening *adj* **1** *threatening letters:* bullying, intimidatory, menacing, minacious *formal*, minatory *formal* **2** *threatening signs:* cautionary, foreboding, grim, inauspicious *formal*, ominous, sinister, warning **3** *the threatening storm:* impending *formal*, looming

threesome *n* triad, trilogy, trinity, trio, triple, triplet, triptych, triumvirate, triune, troika

threshold *n* **1** *stood at the threshold:* door, doorstep, doorway, entrance, entry, opening, sill **2** *the threshold of a new age:* beginning, brink, commencement, dawn, opening, outset, start, starting-point, verge

thrift n carefulness, conservation, economy, frugality, husbandry, parsimony *formal,* prudence *formal,* saving, scrimping and saving *colloq*
⊟ extravagance, waste

thriftless adj dissipative *formal,* extravagant, improvident *formal,* imprudent *formal,* lavish, prodigal, profligate *formal,* spendthrift, unthrifty, wasteful
⊟ thrifty

thrifty adj careful, conserving, economical, frugal, parsimonious *formal,* prudent *formal,* saving, sparing
⊟ extravagant, prodigal, profligate, wasteful

thrill n 1 *the thrill of a rollercoaster ride:* adventure, buzz *colloq,* charge, delight, excitement, frisson, glow, joy, kick *colloq,* pleasure, stimulation 2 *a thrill of horror:* feeling, flutter, frisson, quiver, sensation, shudder, throb, tingle, tremor, vibration
♦ v arouse, electrify, excite, exhilarate, flush, galvanize, give a buzz/kick to *colloq,* move, rouse, stimulate, stir
⊟ bore

thrilling adj electrifying, exciting, exhilarating, gripping, hair-raising *colloq,* heart-stirring, rip-roaring, riveting, rousing, sensational, soul-stirring, stimulating, stirring

thrive v advance, bloom, blossom, boom, burgeon *formal,* develop, do well, flourish, gain, grow, increase, make headway, make progress, profit, prosper, succeed
⊟ die, fail, languish, stagnate

thriving adj affluent, blooming, blossoming, booming, burgeoning *formal,* comfortable, developing, flourishing, growing, healthy, prosperous, successful, wealthy, well
⊟ ailing, dying, failing, languishing, stagnating

throat n craw, fauces, gorge, gullet, halse, oesophagus, the Red Lane *colloq,* thrapple *Scot,* thropple, throttle, windpipe

throaty adj deep, gruff, guttural, hoarse, husky, low, rasping, thick

throb v 1 *my head's throbbing:* beat, palpitate, pound, pulsate, thump 2 *the engine throbbed:* beat, pulsate, pulse, thump, vibrate
♦ n 1 *the dull throb in his head:* beat, palpitation, pounding, pulsation, pulse, thumping 2 *the steady throb of the motor:* beat, pulsation, pulse, thumping, vibration

throe n agony, anguish, convulsion, distress, fit, pain, pang, paroxysm, seizure, spasm, stab, suffering, torture, travail *formal*

throng n assemblage *formal,* bevy, congregation, crowd, crush, flock, herd, horde, host, jam, mass, mob, multitude, pack, press, swarm
♦ v 1 *the fans thronged round him:* bunch, congregate, converge, crowd, flock, herd, mill around *colloq,* press, swarm 2 *the tourists who thronged the square:* crowd, fill, jam, pack

throttle v 1 *he had been throttled with his tie:* choke, strangle, strangulate 2 *the government throttled the press:* check, gag, hold back, inhibit, restrain, silence, smother, stifle, strangle, suppress

through prep 1 *through the tunnel:* across, all the way across, from one end of to the other, from

one side of to the other 2 *complained through his MP:* by, by means of, by virtue of *formal,* by way of, through the agency of, through the good offices of *formal,* using, via, with the help of 3 *all through the night:* during, from the beginning to the end of, in, throughout, to/until the end of, without a break/interruption in 4 *injured through my neglect:* as a result of, because of, by virtue of, due to, on account of, owing to, thanks to
♦ adj 1 *his training is through now:* completed, done, ended, finished, terminated *formal* 2 *I'm through with him:* done, finished, no longer having anything to do with, no longer involved with 3 *the through train:* direct, express, non-stop

throughout adv 1 *the house is painted in green throughout:* completely, everywhere, extensively, in every part, ubiquitously *formal,* widely 2 *she complained throughout:* from beginning to end, from start to finish, right through, the whole time
♦ prep 1 *he talked throughout the film:* all through, during, during/in the whole of, for the duration of, in the course of 2 *branches throughout the country:* all over, all round, everywhere, in all parts of, in every part of

throw v 1 *threw stones at him:* cast, catapult, chuck *colloq,* fling, heave, hurl, launch, lob, pitch, project, propel, send, shy, sling, toss 2 *throw light:* cast, cause to fall, direct, emit, give off, project, radiate, send, shed 3 *he threw me to the ground:* bring down, fell, floor, prostrate 4 *the horse threw its rider:* dislodge, overturn, unhorse, unsaddle, unseat, upset 5 *throw a switch:* operate, put on, switch on, work 6 *his question threw me:* astonish, baffle, confound, confuse, discomfit *formal,* disconcert, disturb, dumbfound, floor *colloq,* perplex, put out, surprise 7 *throw a party:* arrange, give, lay on, organize, put on
♦ n cast, chuck *colloq,* fling, heave, lob, pitch, sling, toss

▶ **throw away** 1 *he never throws anything away:* chuck away/out *colloq,* discard, dispense with *formal,* dispose of, ditch *colloq,* dump *colloq,* get rid of, jettison, reject, scrap, throw out 2 *throw away a chance:* blow *slang,* fritter away, lose, squander, waste

▶ **throw off** 1 *threw off his pursuers:* elude, escape from, get rid of, shake off 2 *throw off your inhibitions:* abandon, cast off, discard, drop, free yourself from, get rid of, jettison, shed

▶ **throw out** 1 *threw him out of the building:* eject, evict, expel, turf out *colloq,* turn out 2 *throw out rubbish:* discard, ditch, dump *colloq,* jettison, scrap, throw away 3 *they threw out our first idea:* dismiss, dispense with *formal,* reject, turn down 4 *can I just throw out a suggestion?:* bring up, introduce, mention, point out, refer to, speak about 5 *throw out light:* diffuse, emanate, emit, exude, give off, produce, radiate, send out

▶ **throw over** abandon, chuck *colloq,* desert, discard, drop, finish with, forsake *formal,* jilt, leave, quit *colloq,* reject

▶ **throw up** 1 *I think I'm going to throw up:* disgorge, gag, heave, puke *colloq,* regurgitate, retch, spew, vomit 2 *threw up his job at the bank:* abandon, chuck in *colloq,* jack in *colloq,* leave, pack in *colloq,* quit, relinquish *formal,* renounce, resign

throwaway adj 1 *throwaway comments:* careless, casual, offhand, passing, undramatic, unemphatic 2 *a throwaway product:*

biodegradable, cheap, disposable, expendable, non-returnable

thrust *v* **1** *he thrust me out of the way:* butt, drive, force, impel, press, prod, propel, push, shove **2** *thrust the paper through the letterbox:* jam, press, push, ram, shove, stick, wedge **3** *thrust a knife into his back:* drive, jab, lunge, pierce, plunge, poke, push, shove, stab, stick **4** *the job was thrust on him:* burden, encumber, foist, force, impose, inflict, press
♦ *n* **1** *the fatal thrust:* jab, lunge, poke, prod, stab **2** *gave the door a sharp thrust:* push, shove **3** *the engine's thrust:* drive, force, impetus, momentum, power, pressure **4** *the thrust of an argument:* drift, essence, gist, message, point, substance, tenor, theme

thud *n* bang, bash, clonk, clump, clunk, crash, knock, smack, thump, wallop *colloq,* wham *colloq*

thug *n* assassin, bandit, cut-throat, gangster, hoodlum, hooligan, killer, mugger *colloq,* murderer, robber, rough, roughneck, ruffian, tough, villain

thumb
▶ **thumb through** browse through, flick through, flip through, glance at, leaf through, peruse, scan, skim

thumbnail *adj* brief, compact, concise, miniature, pithy, quick, short, small, succinct

thumbs-down *n* disapproval, negation, no, rebuff, refusal, rejection, turn-down
⊟ thumbs-up

thumbs-up *v* acceptance, affirmation *formal,* approval, encouragement, go-ahead *colloq,* green light *colloq,* OK *colloq,* sanction, yes
⊟ thumbs-down

thump *v* **1** *I'll thump you if you keep doing that:* batter, box, clout *colloq,* cuff, hit, punch, slap, smack, strike, thrash, thwack, wallop *colloq,* whack *colloq* **2** *he thumped the door:* bang, crash, knock, rap, thud **3** *her heart thumped wildly:* beat, hammer, palpitate, pound, pulsate, throb
♦ *n* **1** *a thump in the face:* blow, box, clout *colloq,* cuff, knock, punch, rap, smack, thwack, wallop *colloq,* whack *colloq* **2** *heard a loud thump:* bang, beat, crash, knock, rap, smack, throb, thud

thumping *adj* **1** *a thumping price:* big, colossal, enormous, excessive, exorbitant, gargantuan, gigantic, great, huge, immense, impressive, mammoth, massive, monumental, terrific, titanic, tremendous, whopping *colloq* **2** *a thumping headache:* extreme, intense, severe, thundering
⊟ **1** insignificant, petty, piddling *colloq,* trivial
♦ *adv* extremely, greatly, intensely, really, severely, unusually, very

thunder *n* **1** *the thunder of the cannons:* blast, boom, clap, crack, explosion, outburst, peal **2** *the thunder of the ocean:* boom, crash, crashing, reverberation, roar, rumble
♦ *v* **1** *the big guns thundered:* bang, blast, boom, clap, crack, peal, resound **2** *the sea thundered in the distance:* boom, crash, reverberate, roll, rumble **3** *he thundered at us to stand still:* bellow, boom, roar

thundering *adj* enormous, excessive, great, monumental, remarkable, tremendous, unmitigated

♦ *adv* extremely, greatly, intensely, really, severely, unusually, very

thunderous *adj* booming, deafening, ear-splitting, loud, noisy, resounding, reverberating, roaring, rumbling, tumultuous

thunderstruck *adj* agape, aghast, amazed, astonished, astounded, bowled over *colloq,* dazed, dumbfounded, flabbergasted *colloq,* floored *colloq,* flummoxed *colloq,* knocked for six *colloq,* nonplussed *colloq,* open-mouthed, paralysed, petrified, shocked, staggered, stunned

thus *adv* **1** *she ruled the king and thus the country:* accordingly, consequently, ergo *formal,* hence *formal,* so, then, therefore **2** *hold it thus:* as follows, in this way, like this, so

thwack *v* bash, beat, buffet, clout *colloq,* cuff, flog, hit, slap, smack, thump, wallop *colloq,* whack *colloq*
♦ *n* bash, blow, buffet, cuff, slap, smack, thump, wallop *colloq,* whack *colloq*

thwart *v* baffle, balk, block, check, cross, defeat, foil, frustrate, hamper, hinder, impede, nobble, obstruct, oppose, prevent, stop, stymie *colloq*
⊟ aid, assist, help

tic *n* jerk, spasm, tic douloureux, twitch

tick *n* **1** *the tick of his watch:* beat, click, stroke, tap, tick-tock **2** *wait a tick:* flash, instant, jiffy *colloq,* minute, moment, sec *colloq,* second, trice *colloq,* twinkling **3** *put a tick against her name:* check *US,* line, mark, stroke
♦ *v* **1** *tick the correct box:* check *US,* choose, indicate, mark, select **2** *the clock ticked:* beat, click, tap
▶ **tick off 1** *tick off items on a list:* check (off) *US,* indicate, mark, put a tick against **2** *ticked us off for slacking:* chide, give someone a dressing-down *colloq,* haul over the coals *colloq,* rebuke, reprimand, reproach, reprove, scold, tear off a strip *colloq,* tell off *colloq,* upbraid *formal*

ticket *n* **1** *tickets for the concert:* card, certificate, counterfoil, coupon, pass, slip, stub, token, voucher **2** *a price ticket:* docket, label, slip, sticker, tag

tickle *v* **1** *tickling the baby's feet:* stroke, touch **2** *the idea tickled me:* amuse, delight, divert, entertain, gratify, please, thrill **3** *tickle your imagination:* excite, interest, stimulate

ticklish *adj* awkward, critical, delicate, difficult, dodgy *colloq,* hazardous, knotty, precarious, problematic, risky, sensitive, thorny, touchy, tricky
⊟ easy, simple, straightforward

tide *n* **1** *swim against the tide:* current, ebb, flow, flux, movement, stream **2** *the tide of events:* course, direction, drift, movement, run, tendency, tenor, trend
▶ **tide over** aid, assist, help, help out, keep going, see through

tidings *n* bulletin, communication, dope *colloq,* gen *colloq,* information, intelligence, message, news, report, word

tidy *adj* **1** *a tidy house:* businesslike, clean, immaculate, in order, neat, ordered, orderly, shipshape, spick-and-span, spruce, trim, uncluttered, well-kept, well-ordered **2** *a tidy person:* businesslike, clean, efficient, methodical, neat, organized, smart, spruce, systematic, trim, well-groomed **3** *a tidy sum:* ample, considerable, fair, generous, good, large, respectable, sizeable, substantial

▨ **1** disorganized, messy, untidy **2** disorganized, messy, untidy **3** insignificant, small

♦ *v* arrange, clean (up), clear up, neaten, order, smarten, spruce up, straighten (out), straighten up

tie *v* **1** *tie the boat to the jetty:* attach, bind, chain, connect, couple, fasten, fix, join, knot, lash, link, moor, rope, secure, strap, tether, unite **2** *don't want to be tied to a schedule:* confine, constrain, cramp, curb, hamper, hinder, impede, limit, restrain, restrict, shackle **3** *the two teams tied:* be all square *colloq,* be equal, be even, draw
♦ *n* **1** *fastened with a tie:* band, bond, clip, fastening, knot, link, ribbon, tape **2** *I have no ties with him:* affiliation, allegiance, bond, connection, friendship, kinship, liaison, link, relationship **3** *the ties of duty:* commitment, constraint, duty, hindrance, limit, limitation, obligation, restraint, restriction **4** *the match ended in a tie:* dead heat, deadlock, draw, stalemate
▶ **tie down** confine, constrain, hamper, hinder, limit, restrain, restrict
▶ **tie up 1** *tied up to a post:* attach, connect, fasten, lash, moor, rope, secure, tether **2** *he had to be tied up:* bind, restrain, truss **3** *tie up a parcel:* do up, wrap up **4** *tie up a deal:* conclude, finalize, settle, terminate *formal,* wind up *colloq,* wrap up *colloq* **5** *tied up with work:* engage, engross, keep busy, occupy

tie-in *n* affiliation, association, connection, co-ordination, hook-up *colloq,* liaison, link, relation, relationship, tie-up

tier *n* band, bank, belt, echelon, floor, layer, level, line, rank, row, stage, storey, stratum, zone

tiff *n* **1** *a lovers' tiff:* barney *colloq,* difference, difference of opinion, disagreement, dispute, falling-out *colloq,* quarrel, row, scrap *colloq,* set-to *colloq,* spat *colloq,* squabble, words **2** *went off in a tiff:* huff *colloq,* ill-humour, pet *colloq,* sulk, tantrum, temper

tight *adj* **1** *a tight skirt:* close-fitting, figure-hugging, skin-tight, snug **2** *a tight hold:* clenched, fast, firm, fixed, secure **3** *the rope is pulled tight:* rigid, stiff, strained, stretched, taut, tense **4** *a tight space:* close, compact, compressed, constricted, cramped, limited, restricted **5** *all the seals are tight:* airtight, hermetic, impenetrable, impervious, proof, sound, watertight **6** *tight security:* firm, hard, harsh, inflexible, rigid, rigorous, severe, strict, stringent, tough **7** *money is tight:* in short supply, inadequate, insufficient, limited, not enough, scarce, too little **8** *a tight contest:* close, evenly matched, hard-fought, neck and neck *colloq,* well-matched **9** *in a tight corner/ spot:* awkward, delicate, difficult, dodgy *colloq,* problematic, tricky **10** *too tight to buy a drink:* mean, miserly, niggardly, parsimonious *formal,* penny-pinching, stingy, tight-fisted *colloq* **11** *too tight to drive:* drunk, intoxicated, legless *colloq,* merry *colloq,* pissed *slang,* plastered *colloq,* sloshed *colloq,* smashed *slang,* sozzled *colloq,* stoned *slang,* tanked up *slang,* tiddly *colloq,* tipsy, under the influence *colloq,* well-oiled *colloq*

▨ **1** loose, slack **2** loose, slack **3** loose, slack **5** open **6** lax **7** plentiful **9** easy **10** generous **11** sober

tighten *v* **1** *tighten your grip:* close, constrict, squeeze **2** *tighten a rope:* pull tight, rigidify *formal,* stiffen, stretch, tauten, tense **3** *tighten a bolt:* fasten, fix, make fast, secure **4** *tighten the space between them:* close, constrict, constringe *formal,* cramp, narrow

▨ **1** loosen, relax **2** loosen, relax **3** loosen

tight-fisted *adj* grasping, mean, mingy *colloq,* miserly, niggardly, parsimonious *formal,* penny-pinching, sparing, stingy, tight *colloq*

▨ charitable, generous

tight-lipped *adj* close-lipped, close-mouthed, mum, mute, quiet, reserved, reticent, secretive, silent, taciturn, uncommunicative, unforthcoming

▨ forthcoming, garrulous, talkative

till[1] *prep* all through, through *US,* to, until, up to, up to the time of

till[2] *v* cultivate, dig, farm, plough, work

tilt *v* cant, incline, lean, list, pitch, slant, slope, tip
♦ *n* angle, inclination, incline, list, pitch, slant, slope

timber *n* **1** *an area farmed for timber:* lumber *US,* trees, wood **2** *the timbers of the ship:* beam, board, lath, log, plank, pole, spar

timbre *n* colour, klang *technical,* quality, resonance, ring, tonality, tone, voice quality

time *n* **1** *worked there for a time:* duration, interval, period, season, session, space, span, spell, stretch, term, while **2** *a song in waltz time:* beat, measure, metre, rhythm, tempo **3** *is this a good time to talk?:* instance, instant, juncture, moment, occasion, point, stage **4** *the time of the ancient Romans:* age, epoch, era **5** *the greatest composer of his time:* generation, lifetime **6** *I wish I had my time over again:* life, lifespan, lifetime **7** *in her time, she was a great beauty:* heyday, peak
♦ *v* **1** *timed our holiday to miss the crowds:* arrange, fix, programme, schedule, set, timetable **2** *timed each lap:* clock, count, measure, meter **3** *the alarm's timed to go off at seven:* adjust, control, regulate

---

Periods of time include:
eternity, eon, era, age, generation, period, epoch, millennium, chiliad, century, lifetime, decade, decennium, quinquennium, year, light-year, yesteryear, quarter, month, fortnight, week, midweek, weekend, long weekend, day, today, tonight, yesterday, tomorrow, morrow, weekday, hour, minute, second, moment, instant, millisecond, microsecond, nanosecond; dawn, sunrise, sun-up, the early hours, wee small hours *colloq,* morning, morn, am, daytime, midday, noon, high noon, pm, afternoon, tea-time, evening, twilight, dusk, sunset, nightfall, bedtime, night, night-time; season, spring, summer, midsummer, autumn, fall *US,* winter

---

time-honoured *adj* accustomed, age-old, ancient, conventional, customary, established, fixed, historic, long-established, old, traditional, usual, venerable

timeless *adj* abiding *formal*, ageless, changeless, deathless, endless, enduring, eternal, everlasting, immortal, immutable *formal*, imperishable, indestructible, lasting, permanent, unchanging, unending

timely *adj* appropriate, at the right time, convenient, felicitous *formal*, opportune, propitious *formal*, seasonable, suitable, well-timed
☒ ill-timed, inappropriate, unsuitable

timetable *n* **1** *our timetable for the week:* agenda, calendar, diary, list, listing, programme, roster, rota, schedule **2** *subjects on the timetable:* course, curriculum, programme, syllabus
♦ *v* arrange, diarize, fix, list, programme, schedule, set

time-worn *adj* **1** *time-worn toys:* aged, ancient, broken-down, dated, decrepit, dog-eared, old, out of date, outworn, ragged, ruined, run-down, shabby, threadbare, weathered, well-worn, worn **2** *time-worn clichés:* bromidic, clichéd, hackneyed, hoary, passé, stale, stock, threadbare, tired, trite, well-worn
☒ **1** fresh, new **2** fresh, new

timid *adj* **1** *a timid child:* apprehensive, bashful, retiring, shrinking, shy **2** *too timid to stand up for himself:* afraid, chicken *colloq*, cowardly, faint-hearted, fearful, frightened, gutless *colloq*, lily-livered *colloq*, nervous, pusillanimous *formal*, scared, spineless, timorous *formal*, wimpish *colloq*, yellow *colloq*
☒ **1** bold, confident **2** bold, brave

timorous *adj* **1** *a timorous little woman:* apprehensive, bashful, diffident, mousy *colloq*, retiring, shrinking, shy, tentative, timid, unadventurous **2** *too timorous to fight:* afraid, cowardly, faint-hearted, fearful, frightened, nervous, pusillanimous *formal*, scared, timid, unadventurous
☒ **1** assertive, assured, bold **2** bold

tincture *n* **1** *a tincture of cloves:* aroma, dash, flavour, seasoning **2** *a tincture of blue:* colour, dash, hint, hue, shade, stain, tinge, tint **3** *a tincture of mockery in his voice:* dash, hint, shade, smack, suggestion, tinge, touch, trace
♦ *v* **1** *tinctured with garlic:* flavour, imbue, infuse, permeate, scent, season **2** *tinctured with green:* colour, dye, suffuse, tinge, tint

tinge *n* **1** *a tinge of ginger:* dash, drop, flavour, hint, pinch, smattering, sprinkling **2** *a tinge of mockery in her voice:* bit, hint, smack, suggestion, touch, trace **3** *a blue tinge:* colour, dye, shade, tincture, tint, wash
♦ *v* **1** *oil tinged with basil:* flavour, imbue, shade, suffuse **2** *pride tinged with sadness:* imbue, suffuse, touch **3** *tinged with green:* colour, dye, shade, stain, tint

tingle *v* **1** *his skin tingled:* itch, prick, prickle, sting, tickle **2** *her body tingled with excitement:* quiver, thrill, tremble, vibrate
♦ *n* **1** *felt a tingle on my scalp:* gooseflesh, goose-pimples, itch, itching, pins and needles *colloq*, prickling, stinging, tickle, tickling **2** *a tingle of excitement:* quiver, shiver, thrill, throb, tremor

tinker *v* dabble, fiddle, fool about/around, meddle, mess about/around *colloq*, play, potter, tamper, toy, trifle
♦ *n* Gypsy, itinerant, traveller

tinkle *v* chime, chink, clink, ding, jangle, jingle, peal, ring
♦ *n* **1** *the tinkle of the bell:* chime, chink, clink, ding, jangle, jingle, peal, ring **2** *give you a tinkle:* bell *colloq*, buzz *colloq*, call, phone call, ring

tinsel *n* artificiality, display, flamboyance, frippery, garishness, gaudiness, glitter, insignificance, meaninglessness, ostentation, pretension, sham, show, spangle, triviality, worthlessness

tint *n* **1** *a slight tint of blue:* cast, colour, hue, shade, tincture, tinge, tone, touch, trace **2** *had a tint put in her hair:* colour, dye, rinse, stain, streak, tincture, wash
♦ *v* **1** *tinted her hair:* colour, dye, stain, streak, tinge **2** *the experience tinted his view of the world:* affect, colour, taint, tinge

tiny *adj* diminutive, dwarfish, infinitesimal, insignificant, itsy-bitsy *colloq*, Lilliputian, little, microscopic, midget, mini *colloq*, miniature, minuscule, minute, negligible, petite, pint-sized *colloq*, pocket, slight, small, teeny *colloq*, teeny-weeny *colloq*, trifling, wee *Scot*
☒ enormous, huge, immense

tip¹ *n* **1** *the tip of a finger:* end, extremity, head, nib, point **2** *the tip of Everest:* acme, apex, cap, crown, peak, pinnacle, point, summit, top
♦ *v* cap, crown, surmount, top

tip² *v* **1** *tip your head:* cant, incline, lean, list, slant, tilt **2** *the boat tipped over:* capsize, overturn, topple (over), upset **3** *tip the water down the sink:* dump, empty, pour (out), spill, unload
♦ *n* dump, midden, refuse-heap, rubbish-heap, slag heap

tip³ *n* **1** *a useful tip:* advice, clue, forecast, hint, information, inside information, pointer, recommendation, suggestion, tip-off, warning **2** *gave the waiter a tip:* baksheesh, bonus, gift, gratuity, perk *colloq*, perquisite *formal*, pourboire, present, reward
♦ *v* **1** *he tipped me about the speed cameras:* advise, caution, forewarn, inform, tell, tip off, warn **2** *tip the driver:* remunerate, reward

tip-off *n* clue, hint, information, inside information, pointer, suggestion, warning

tipple *v* bib, booze *colloq*, drink, imbibe, quaff, swig *colloq*
♦ *n* alcohol, booze *colloq*, drink, favourite drink, liquor, poison *colloq*, regular drink, usual *colloq*

tippler *n* bibber, boozer *colloq*, dipso(maniac), drinker, drunk, drunkard, hard drinker, inebriate, lush *slang*, soak *slang*, sot *slang*, sponge *colloq*, toper *slang*, wine-bag, wino *slang*

tipsy *adj* drunk, happy *colloq*, mellow *colloq*, merry *colloq*, squiff(y) *colloq*, tiddly *colloq*, tight *colloq*, under the influence
☒ sober

tirade *n* abuse, denunciation, diatribe, fulmination *formal*, harangue, invective *formal*, outburst, philippic *formal*, rant

tire *v* **1** *the walk tired me:* drain, enervate *formal*, exhaust, fatigue, strain, tax, tire out, wear out, weary **2** *she tires easily:* become tired, drop, fatigue, flag, tire out, weary **3** *his endless bragging tires me:* bore, tax, tire out, weary
☒ **1** enliven, invigorate, refresh

tired *adj* **1** *too tired to go out*: all in *colloq*, beat *colloq*, bushed *colloq*, dead-beat *colloq*, dog-tired, drained, drowsy, enervated *formal*, exhausted, fagged out *colloq*, fatigued, flagging, hardly able to keep your eyes open *colloq*, knackered *colloq*, ready to drop *colloq*, shattered *colloq*, sleepy, washed-out *colloq*, wearied, weary, whacked *colloq*, worn out **2** *tired of waiting*: bored, fed up *colloq*, jaded, sick, sick and tired *colloq* **3** *the same tired reasons*: clichéd, corny *colloq*, hackneyed, old, past its sell-by date *colloq*, stale, trite, worn-out
➤ **1** energetic, lively, refreshed, rested **3** new

tireless *adj* determined, diligent, energetic, indefatigable, industrious, resolute, unflagging, untiring, unwearied, vigorous
➤ lazy, tired, unenthusiastic

tiresome *adj* annoying, boring, dull, exasperating, fatiguing, humdrum, irksome, irritating, laborious, monotonous, routine, tedious, tiring, troublesome, trying, unexciting, uninteresting, vexatious, wearisome
➤ easy, interesting, stimulating

tiring *adj* arduous, demanding, difficult, draining, enervating *formal*, exacting, exhausting, fatiguing, hard, laborious, strenuous, taxing, tough, wearisome, wearying

tiro, tyro *n* apprentice, beginner, catechumen, freshman, greenhorn, initiate, learner, neophyte, novice, novitiate, pupil, starter, student, tenderfoot, trainee
➤ old hand *colloq*, veteran

tissue *n* **1** *skin tissue*: material, matter, substance **2** *a box of tissues*: disposable handkerchief, facial tissue, Kleenex®, paper handkerchief, toilet paper, toilet tissue **3** *covered in gold tissue*: fabric, gauze, gossamer, stuff **4** *a tissue of lies*: mesh, network, structure, web

titanic *adj* colossal, cyclopean, enormous, giant, gigantic, herculean, huge, immense, jumbo, mammoth, massive, mighty *formal*, monstrous, monumental, mountainous, prodigious, stupendous, towering, vast
➤ insignificant, small

titbit *n* appetizer, bonne-bouche, dainty, delicacy, morsel, snack, treat

tithe *n* duty, impost, levy, tariff, tax, tenth, toll, tribute
♦ *v* **1** *ten per cent of the donations are tithed*: charge, levy, take in, tax **2** *members tithe a proportion of their earnings*: give, hand over, pay

titillate *v* arouse, excite, interest, intrigue, provoke, stimulate, tantalize, tease, thrill, tickle, turn on *colloq*

titillating *adj* arousing, captivating, erotic, exciting, lewd, lurid, provocative, seductive, sensational, sexy, stimulating, suggestive, teasing, thrilling

titivate *v* doll up *colloq*, make up, preen, primp, prink, smarten up, tart up *colloq*, touch up

title *n* **1** *the title 'Grand Master'*: appellation *formal*, denomination *formal*, designation, epithet, form of address, handle *colloq*, label, moniker *colloq*, name, nickname, nom-de-plume, office, position, pseudonym, rank, sobriquet, status, term **2** *the title of the painting*: caption, credit(s), heading, headline, inscription, legend **3** *legal title to the property*: claim, deeds, entitlement, ownership, prerogative, privilege, proprietorship, right **4** *the heavyweight title*: championship, competition, crown, game, laurels, match, prize, stakes, trophy
♦ *v* call, designate, dub, entitle, label, name, style, tag, term

titter *v* chortle, chuckle, giggle, laugh, snicker, snigger
♦ *n* chortle, chuckle, giggle, laugh, snicker, snigger

tittle-tattle *n* babble *colloq*, blather *colloq*, blether *colloq*, cackle, chatter, chitchat *colloq*, gossip, hearsay, jaw *colloq*, natter *colloq*, prattle, rumour, twaddle *colloq*, ya(c)k *colloq*, yackety-yak *colloq*
♦ *v* babble *colloq*, blather *colloq*, blether *colloq*, chat, chatter, chitchat *colloq*, gossip, jaw *colloq*, natter *colloq*, prattle, witter *colloq*, ya(c)k *colloq*, yackety-yak *colloq*

titular *adj* formal, honorary, nominal, official, puppet *colloq*, putative *formal*, self-styled, so-called, token

toady *n* arse-licker *slang*, bootlicker *colloq*, crawler *colloq*, creep *colloq*, fawner, flatterer, flunkey, groveller, hanger-on *colloq*, jackal, lackey, minion, parasite, sucker *colloq*, sycophant, truckler *colloq*, yes-man *colloq*
♦ *v* bootlick *colloq*, bow and scrape *colloq*, butter up *colloq*, crawl, creep, curry favour, fawn, flatter, grovel, kiss the feet *colloq*, kowtow, suck up *colloq*, truckle *colloq*

toast *v* **1** *toast the nuts for five minutes*: bake, barbecue, brown, crisp, grill, heat (up), roast, warm (up) **2** *toast the bride and groom*: drink the health of, drink to, honour, pledge, salute
♦ *n* best wishes, compliment(s), drink, health, pledge, salutation, salute, tribute

Toasts include:
all the best!, *auf Ihre Gesundheit, à votre santé,* bottoms up!, cheers!, down the hatch!, good health!, good luck!, happy landings!, here's how!, here's looking at you!, here's mud in your eye!, here's to...!, here's to you!, *prosit!,* *skoal!, slàinte!,* to absent friends!, your health!

tobacco

Forms of tobacco include:
baccy *colloq*, cheroot, chewing tobacco; cigar, Havana cigar, cigarette, cork-tipped cigarette, filter-tip cigarette, king-size cigarette, menthol cigarette, Russian cigarette; ciggie *colloq*, coffin nail *slang*, fag *colloq*; cigarette end, cigarette butt, dog-end *slang*, fag end *slang*; cigarillo, corona, high-tar, low-tar, panatella, plug, snuff, flake tobacco, pipe tobacco, shag tobacco, Turkish tobacco, Virginia tobacco, the weed *colloq*

Tobacco accessories include:
ashtray, cigar box, cigar case, cigar cutter, cigar-holder, cigarette box, cigarette case, cigarette-holder, cigarette lighter, gas lighter, petrol lighter, cigarette machine, cigarette paper, cigarette roller, humidor, match, matchbook, box of matches, match striker, pipe, chibouk, church-warden, clay pipe,

hookah, meerschaum, narghile, peace pipe (pipe of peace), tobacco pipe, pipe-cleaner, pipe-rack, pipe-rest, smoker's companion, snuffbox, tobacco-pouch, vesta

today *n* the present day, the present time, this afternoon, this day, this evening, this morning
♦ *adv* at the present time, at this moment, at this moment in time, just now, now, nowadays, right now, these days, this very day

toddle *v* falter, lurch, reel, stagger, stumble, sway, teeter, totter, waddle, walk/move unsteadily, waver, wobble

to-do *n* agitation, bother, brouhaha *colloq*, bustle, commotion, disturbance, excitement, flap *colloq*, flurry, furore, fuss, hoo-ha *colloq*, performance *colloq*, quarrel, ruction, rumpus, stew *colloq*, stir, tumult, turmoil, unrest, uproar

together *adv* 1 *working together:* as a partnership, as a team, as one, collectively, in collaboration, in concert, in conjunction, in unison, jointly, mutually, united, working together 2 *marching together:* hand in hand, in a row, shoulder to shoulder, side by side 3 *all spoke together:* all at once, at one time, at the same time, concurrently *formal*, simultaneously 4 *for three days together:* back to back *colloq*, consecutively, continuously, in succession, on end, on the trot *colloq*, successively, without a break, without interruption
Fa 1 individually, separately 2 alone
♦ *adj* calm, commonsensical, composed, cool *colloq*, down-to-earth, level-headed, organized, sensible, stable, well-adjusted, well-balanced, well-organized

toil *n* application, donkey-work *colloq*, drudgery, effort, elbow grease *colloq*, exertion, graft *colloq*, hard work, industry, labour, slaving, slog, sweat
♦ *v* drudge, graft *colloq*, grind, labour, plug away *colloq*, push yourself, slave, slog, strive, struggle, sweat, work, work like a Trojan *colloq*, work your fingers to the bone *colloq*

toiler *n* drudge, grafter, labourer, menial, navvy, slave, slogger, struggler, workaholic, worker, workhorse
Fa idler, loafer, shirker

toilet *n* bathroom, bog *colloq*, cloakroom, convenience, john *US slang*, kazi *slang*, latrine, lavatory, loo *colloq*, powder room, public convenience, rest room *US*, the gents *colloq*, the ladies *colloq*, urinal, washroom, WC

toilsome *adj* arduous, backbreaking, burdensome, difficult, fatiguing, hard, herculean, laborious, painful, severe, strenuous, taxing, tedious, tiresome, tough, uphill, wearisome

token *n* 1 *a token of my gratitude:* clue, demonstration, emblem, evidence, expression, index, indication, keepsake, manifestation *formal*, mark, memento, memorial, proof, recognition, remembrance, reminder, representation, sign, signal, souvenir, symbol 2 *gift token:* counter, coupon, disc, voucher
♦ *adj* cosmetic, emblematic, hollow, insincere, minimal, nominal, perfunctory, slight, superficial, symbolic

tolerable *adj* 1 *the pain was barely tolerable:* bearable, endurable, sufferable 2 *the meal was tolerable:* acceptable, adequate, all right, average, fair, fairly good, indifferent, mediocre, middling, no great shakes *colloq*, not bad *colloq*, not much cop *colloq*, nothing (much) to write home about *colloq*, OK *colloq*, ordinary, passable, reasonable, run-of-the-mill *colloq*, satisfactory, so-so *colloq*, unexceptional
Fa 1 insufferable, intolerable, unbearable

tolerance *n* 1 *known for his tolerance:* broad-mindedness, forbearance, indulgence, leniency, lenity, liberalism, magnanimity *formal*, open-mindedness, patience, permissiveness, sympathy, toleration, understanding 2 *a tolerance of plus or minus 5%:* allowance, clearance, fluctuation, give *colloq*, play *colloq*, swing *colloq*, variation 3 *tolerance to pain:* endurance, fortitude *formal*, resilience, resistance, stamina, toughness
Fa 1 bias, bigotry, intolerance, narrow-mindedness, prejudice

tolerant *adj* broad-minded, catholic, charitable, compliant, easy-going *colloq*, fair, forbearing, forgiving, indulgent, kind-hearted, lenient, liberal, long-suffering, magnanimous *formal*, open-minded, patient, permissive, sympathetic, understanding, unprejudiced
Fa biased, bigoted, intolerant, prejudiced, unsympathetic

tolerate *v* 1 *can't tolerate the pain:* abide *formal*, bear, endure, put up with, stand, stomach *colloq*, suffer, swallow, take 2 *won't tolerate this behaviour:* accept, admit, allow, condone, countenance *formal*, indulge, permit, put up with, receive, sanction, stand for, swallow, take, warrant

toleration *n* 1 *exercise toleration:* broad-mindedness, forbearance, indulgence, leniency, lenity, liberalism, magnanimity *formal*, open-mindedness, patience, permissiveness, sympathy, understanding 2 *toleration to heat:* endurance, fortitude *formal*, resilience, resistance, stamina, toughness 3 *his toleration of her spending:* acceptance, allowance, endurance, indulgence, sanction, sufferance

toll[1] *v* 1 *the bell tolls:* chime, clang, knell, peal, ring, sound, strike 2 *the clock tolled midnight:* announce, call, herald, sound, warn

toll[2] *n* 1 *motorway tolls:* charge, cost, demand, duty, fee, levy, payment, penalty, rate, tariff, tax 2 *the casualty toll:* cost, damage, death, injury, loss

tomb *n* burial-place, catacomb, cenotaph, crypt, grave, mausoleum, sepulchre, vault

tombstone *n* gravestone, headstone, memorial, monument, stone

tome *n* book, opus, volume, work

tomfoolery *n* buffoonery, childishness, clowning, foolishness, hooey *colloq*, horseplay, idiocy, inanity, larking about *colloq*, larks *colloq*, messing about, messing on, mischief, shenanigans *colloq*, silliness, skylarking, stupidity

tone *n* 1 *tone of voice:* accent, accentuation, emphasis, expression, force, inflection, intonation, modulation, note, pitch, quality,

sound, strength, stress, timbre, volume **2** *delicate tones of peach:* cast, colour, hue, shade, tincture, tinge, tint, tonality **3** *the tone of the letter was formal:* air, attitude, character, drift, effect, feel, humour, manner, mood, quality, spirit, style, temper, tenor, vein
♦ *v* blend, co-ordinate, go (well) with, harmonize, match, suit
▶ **tone down** alleviate, dampen, dim, lighten, mitigate *formal*, moderate, play down, reduce, restrain, soften, soft-pedal *colloq*, subdue, temper
▶ **tone up** invigorate, limber up, shape up, sharpen up, trim, tune up

tongue *n* **1** *learn a foreign tongue:* argot, cant, dialect, idiom, jargon, language, lingo *colloq*, parlance *formal*, patois, slang, talk, vernacular **2** *her ready tongue:* articulation, discourse, speech, talk, utterance

tongue-tied *adj* dumb, dumbstruck, inarticulate, lost for words, mute, silent, speechless, voiceless, wordless
🔁 garrulous, talkative, voluble

tonic *n* analeptic, boost, bracer, cordial, fillip, pick-me-up, refresher, restorative, shot in the arm *colloq*, stimulant

too *adv* **1** *he acts, and he writes too:* also, as well, besides, furthermore, in addition, likewise, moreover **2** *it's too expensive:* excessively, extremely, inordinately, over, overly, ridiculously, unduly, unreasonably, very

tool *n* **1** *a useful little tool:* apparatus, appliance, artefact, contraption, contrivance, device, gadget, gismo *colloq*, implement, instrument, machine, utensil **2** *a training tool:* agency, agent, intermediary, means, medium, vehicle **3** *a tool of the government:* cat's paw, dupe, flunkey, hireling, minion, pawn, puppet, stooge
♦ *v* chase, cut, decorate, fashion, machine, ornament, shape, work

---

Types of tool include:
axe, bolster, caulking-iron, crowbar, hod, jackhammer, jointer, mattock, pick, pick-axe, plumb-line, sledgehammer; chaser, clamp, dividers, dolly, drill, hacksaw, jack, pincers, pliers, protractor, punch, rule, sander, scriber, snips, socket-wrench, soldering-iron, spraygun, tommy bar, vice, wrench; auger, awl, bevel, brace and bit, bradawl, chisel, file, fretsaw, hammer, handsaw, jack-plane, jigsaw, level, mallet, plane, rasp, saw, screwdriver, set-square, spirit level, tenon-saw, T-square; billhook, chainsaw, chopper, dibber, fork, grass-rake, hay fork, hoe, pitchfork, plough, pruning-knife, pruning-shears, rake, scythe, secateurs, shears, shovel, sickle, spade, thresher, trowel; needle, scissors, pinking-shears, bodkin, crochet hook, forceps, scalpel, tweezers, tongs, cleaver, steel, gimlet, mace, mortar, pestle, paper-cutter, paper-knife, stapler, pocket-knife, penknife

---

tooth *n* denticle, denticulation, dentil, fang, incisor, masticator, molar, tush, tusk

---

Types of tooth include:
baby tooth, back tooth, bicuspid, bucktooth, canine, carnassial, dog-tooth, eye tooth, fang, first tooth, gold tooth, grinder, incisor, central incisor, lateral incisor, milk tooth, molar, first molar, second molar, third molar, premolar, first premolar, second premolar, snaggletooth, tush, tusk, wisdom tooth; false tooth, false teeth, bridge, cap, crown, denture, dentures, plate

---

toothsome *adj* agreeable, appetizing, dainty, delectable, delicious, flavoursome, luscious, mouth-watering, nice, palatable, savoury, scrumptious *colloq*, sweet, tasty, tempting, yummy *colloq*
🔁 disagreeable, unpleasant

top *n* **1** *the top of the hill:* acme, apex, apogee, crest, crown, culmination, head, height, highest point, peak, pinnacle, summit, tip, vertex *technical*, zenith **2** *at the top of his career:* acme, apex, apogee, climax, crest, culmination, height, highest point, peak, pinnacle, summit, zenith **3** *bottle tops:* cap, cork, cover, lid, stopper **4** *a sleeveless top:* blouse, jersey, jumper, pullover, shirt, smock, sweater, sweatshirt, tank top, tee shirt, T-shirt
🔁 **1** base, bottom, nadir **2** base, bottom, nadir **4** bottoms
♦ *adj* **1** *the top man in the business:* best, chief, dominant, finest, first, foremost, greatest, head, highest, leading, main, paramount, pre-eminent, prime, principal, ruling, sovereign, superior, supreme **2** *the top moment in the game:* best, crowning, culminating, finest, greatest, paramount, supreme **3** *the top layer:* highest, topmost, upmost, upper, uppermost **4** *the car's top speed:* greatest, highest, maximum, topmost, utmost
🔁 **1** bottom, inferior, lowest **2** lowest **3** bottom, lowest **4** lowest
♦ *v* **1** *topped with fresh cream:* cap, cover, crown, decorate, finish (off), garnish, top **2** *top their score:* beat, best, better, eclipse, exceed, excel, outdo, outshine, outstrip, surmount, surpass, transcend **3** *topped a poll:* be first in, head, lead
▶ **top up** add to, augment *formal*, boost, increase, recharge, refill, reload, replenish *formal*, supplement

topic *n* argument, issue, matter, point, question, subject, subject matter, talking point, text, theme, thesis

topical *adj* contemporary, current, familiar, newsworthy, popular, recent, relevant, up-to-date, up-to-the-minute

topmost *adj* **1** *the topmost floor of the building:* apical *technical*, highest, loftiest, top, upper, uppermost **2** *the topmost players:* dominant, first, foremost, leading, paramount, principal, supreme, top **3** *its topmost speed:* highest, maximum, top, uppermost
🔁 **1** bottom, bottommost, lowest **2** bottom, lowest **3** bottommost, lowest

top-notch *adj* A1 *colloq*, ace *colloq*, admirable, crack *colloq*, excellent, exceptional, fine, first rate, first-class, leading, matchless, out of this world *colloq*, outstanding, peerless, premier, prime, second-to-none, splendid, super *colloq*, superb, superior, superlative, supreme, top, top-flight

topple *v* **1** *the wind toppled our fence:* knock over/down, overturn, tip over, upset **2** *toppled off the ladder:* capsize, collapse, fall (over), keel over, overbalance, totter, tumble **3** *topple a dictator:* bring down, dethrone, displace, oust, overthrow, unseat

topsy-turvy *adj* chaotic, confused, disarranged, disorderly, disorganized, in confusion, in disorder, inside out, jumbled, messy, mixed-up, untidy, upside down
🔲 ordered, tidy

torch *n* brand, firebrand, flambeau, flashlight *US*, light

torment *n* **1** *suffered terrible torment:* affliction, agony, anguish, distress, misery, ordeal, pain, suffering, torture, worry **2** *our son is a torment to us:* annoyance, bane, bother, curse, harassment, irritation, nuisance, pain in the neck *colloq*, pest, provocation, scourge, thorn in the flesh *colloq*, trouble, vexation, worry
♦ *v* **1** *the memory tormented her:* afflict, distress, harrow, pain, plague, torture, trouble **2** *stop tormenting your sister:* annoy, badger, bedevil, bother, harass, hound, irritate, pester, plague, provoke, tease, trouble, vex, worry

torn *adj* **1** *torn material:* cut, lacerated, ragged, rent, ripped, slit, split **2** *torn between two options:* dithering, divided, irresolute, uncertain, undecided, unsure, vacillating, wavering

tornado *n* cyclone, gale, hurricane, monsoon, squall, storm, tempest, twister *colloq*, typhoon, whirlwind

torpid *adj* apathetic, dead, deadened, drowsy, dull, inactive, indolent *formal*, inert, insensible, languorous *formal*, lazy, lethargic, lifeless, listless, numb, passive, sleepy, slow, sluggish, somnolent *formal*, supine *formal*
🔲 active, lively, vigorous

torpor *n* apathy, drowsiness, dullness, hebetude *formal*, inactivity, indolence *formal*, inertia, inertness, languor *formal*, laziness, lethargy, lifelessness, listlessness, numbness, passivity, sleepiness, sloth, slowness, sluggishness, somnolence *formal*, torpidity
🔲 activity, enthusiasm, vigour

torrent *n* **1** *a torrent of water:* barrage, cascade, deluge, downpour, flood, gush, inundation, outburst, rush, spate, storm, stream, volley **2** *a torrent of abuse:* barrage, flood, outburst, rush, spate, storm, stream, volley
🔲 **1** trickle

torrid *adj* **1** *torrid regions:* arid, desert, hot, parched, scorched, tropical, waterless **2** *torrid heat:* arid, blazing, blistering, boiling, hot, scorching, sizzling, stifling, sweltering, tropical **3** *a torrid love scene:* amorous, erotic, passionate, red-hot, sexy, steamy *colloq*

tortuous *adj* **1** *a tortuous road:* circuitous, curving, indirect, meandering, roundabout, serpentine, sinuous *formal*, twisting, winding, zigzag **2** *a slow and tortuous method:* circuitous, complicated, convoluted *formal*, indirect, involved, roundabout
🔲 **1** straight **2** straightforward

torture *v* **1** *tortured them to extract a confession:* abuse, afflict, agonize, crucify, excruciate, ill-treat, mistreat, pain, persecute, rack, torment **2** *tortured herself with guilt:* distress, harrow, pain, plague, rack, torment, trouble, worry
♦ *n* **1** *the torture of prisoners:* abuse, ill-treatment, mistreatment, persecution, torment **2** *the torture*

of not knowing: agony, anguish, distress, misery, pain, suffering, torment

toss *v* **1** *tossed it into the bin:* cast, chuck *colloq*, fling, flip, heave, hurl, lob, pitch, shy, sling, throw **2** *a boat tossing on the sea:* heave, lurch, pitch, rock, roll, sway **3** *toss the pieces in olive oil:* agitate, roll, shake, stir **4** *the horse tossed its head back:* jerk, jolt **5** *he tossed and turned in his sleep:* squirm, thrash, wriggle, writhe
♦ *n* cast, chuck *colloq*, fling, flip, pitch, throw

tot[1] *n* **1** *when he was just a tot:* baby, bairn *Scot*, child, infant, mite, toddler **2** *a tot of whisky:* dram, finger, measure, nip, shot, slug

tot[2]
▶ **tot up** add (up), calculate, compute, count (up), reckon, sum, tally, total

total *n* aggregate *formal*, amount, entirety, grand total, lot, mass, sum, totality, whole
♦ *adj* **1** *the total amount:* complete, comprehensive, entire, full, whole **2** *a total disaster:* absolute, all-out, complete, consummate *formal*, downright, outright, perfect, rank, sheer, thorough, thoroughgoing, unconditional, undisputed, unmitigated *formal*, unqualified, utter
🔲 **1** partial **2** limited, partial, restricted
♦ *v* **1** *totalled over a million dollars:* add up to, amount to, come to, make, reach **2** *total the scores:* add (up), count (up), reckon, sum (up), tot (up)

totalitarian *adj* authoritarian, despotic, dictatorial, monocratic *formal*, monolithic, omnipotent *formal*, one-party, oppressive, tyrannous, undemocratic
🔲 democratic

totality *n* **1** *revise the scheme in its totality:* entirety, fullness, pleroma *formal*, wholeness **2** *the totality of human experience:* aggregate *formal*, all, entirety, everything, sum, total, whole **3** *the totality of the destruction:* completeness, entireness

totally *adv* absolutely, completely, comprehensively, consummately *formal*, entirely, fully, perfectly, quite, thoroughly, unconditionally, undisputedly, undividedly, unmitigatedly *formal*, utterly, wholeheartedly, wholly
🔲 partially

totter *v* **1** *he tottered across the road:* falter, lurch, move unsteadily, reel, stagger, stumble, sway, waddle, wobble **2** *the ladder began to totter:* lurch, quiver, rock, shake, sway, teeter, tremble, waver, wobble **3** *the economy is tottering:* be about to collapse, be insecure, be precarious, be shaky, be unstable, be unsteady, wobble *colloq*

touch *v* **1** *he touched her face gently:* brush, caress, feel, finger, fondle, handle, pat, pet, run your finger over, skim, stroke, tickle **2** *the car touched him as it passed:* brush, contact, graze, hit, strike, tap **3** *where their land touches ours:* abut, adjoin, be contiguous *formal*, border, come into contact, impinge, meet **4** *her story touched me:* affect, disturb, have an effect on, have an influence/ impact on, impress, inspire, move, sadden, stir, upset **5** *a matter which touches us all:* affect, concern, have an effect on, have an influence/ impact on, influence, involve, regard **6** *nobody can touch him as a chef:* approach, better, come near, equal, hold a candle to *colloq*, match, rival **7** *gales touching 100 mph:* attain, come to, hit

colloq, make, reach **8** *not touch alcohol:* consume, devour, drink, eat, take, use
♦ *n* **1** *the slightest touch:* brush, caress, contact, feel, pat, stroke, tap **2** *the sense of touch:* feel, feeling, tactility **3** *material with a silky touch:* feel, finish, grain, surface, texture, weave **4** *a masterly touch:* approach, art, craftsmanship, dexterity, flair, knack, manner, method, skill, style, technique **5** *finishing touches:* addition, aspect, detail, feature, minutiae, nicety, point **6** *keep/lose touch:* association, communication, connection, contact, correspondence **7** *a touch of garlic:* bit, dash, hint, jot, pinch, smack, soupçon, speck, spot, suggestion, suspicion, taste, tinge, trace, whiff *colloq*
▶ **touch off 1** *the attack which touched off the riot:* actuate *formal*, arouse, begin, cause, foment, ignite, inflame, initiate, provoke, set off, spark off, trigger (off) **2** *the spark that touched off the explosion:* fire, ignite, light, set off, spark off, trigger (off)
▶ **touch on** allude to, broach, cover, deal with, mention *formal*, refer to, remark on, speak of
▶ **touch up** brush up, enhance, finish off, improve, patch up, perfect, polish up, renovate, retouch, revamp

touch-and-go *adj* close, critical, dangerous, dire, dodgy *colloq*, hairy *colloq*, hazardous, near, nerve-racking, parlous *formal*, perilous, precarious, risky, sticky, tricky, uncertain

touched *adj* **1** *I was touched by her story:* affected, disturbed, impressed, influenced, inspired, moved, stirred, upset **2** *he's a bit touched:* barmy *colloq*, batty *colloq*, bonkers *colloq*, crazy, daft *colloq*, deranged, disturbed, dotty *colloq*, eccentric, insane, loopy *colloq*, mad, nutty *colloq*, unbalanced

touchiness *n* bad temper, captiousness, crabbedness, grouchiness, grumpiness, irascibility, irritability, peevishness, pettishness, petulance, surliness, testiness, tetchiness

touching *adj* affecting, disturbing, emotional, heart-breaking, heart-rending, moving, pathetic, piteous *formal*, pitiable, pitiful, poignant, sad, stirring, tender, upsetting

touchstone *n* benchmark, criterion, gauge, guide, measure, model, norm, pattern, proof, standard, template, test, yardstick

touchy *adj* bad-tempered, captious, crabbed, cross, grouchy, grumpy, irascible, irritable, over-sensitive, peevish, prickly *colloq*, quick-tempered, thin-skinned
F≡ calm, imperturbable

tough *adj* **1** *made of tough material:* durable, firm, hard, hardy, inflexible, leathery, resilient, resistant, rigid, solid, stiff, strong, sturdy **2** *a tough criminal:* callous, disorderly, hardened, rough, rowdy, vicious, violent **3** *a tough line on crime:* adamant, determined, firm, harsh, resolute, severe, stern, strict, tenacious, uncompromising, unyielding **4** *a tough job:* arduous, difficult, exacting, grim, hard, laborious, strenuous, taxing, uphill *colloq* **5** *a tough problem:* baffling, difficult, hard, knotty, perplexing, puzzling, thorny, troublesome **6** *tough rugby players:* burly, fit, hardy, muscular, robust, rugged, stalwart, sturdy, vigorous, well-built **7** *the meat is tough:* chewy, fibrous, gristly, rubbery, tough as leather *colloq* **8** *a tough time:*

distressing, hard, uncomfortable, unfortunate, unlucky, unpleasant
F≡ **1** delicate, fragile, tender, weak **2** gentle, soft **3** gentle **4** easy, simple **5** easy, simple **6** weak **7** tender **8** good
♦ *n* brute, bully, hooligan, lout, roughneck, rowdy, ruffian, thug, yob *slang*

toughen *v* **1** *the steel is toughened with boron:* brace, fortify *formal*, harden, reinforce, stiffen, strengthen **2** *toughen his stance:* consolidate, harden, make stricter, reinforce, strengthen, substantiate

toughness *n* **1** *the toughness of the material:* inflexibility, resilience, resistance, ruggedness, strength, sturdiness **2** *his toughness in dealing with terrorists:* determination, firmness, grit *colloq*, hardiness, inflexibility, obduracy, strength, tenacity
F≡ **1** softness, weakness **2** liberality, softness, vulnerability, weakness

tour *n* **1** *a tour round the island:* drive, excursion, expedition, jaunt, journey, outing, peregrination *formal*, ride, trip **2** *a guided tour of the museum:* inspection, peregrination *formal*, visit, walkabout *colloq* **3** *a cricket tour of South Africa:* circuit, course, round
♦ *v* **1** *toured the countryside:* drive through, go round, journey through, ride round, travel round **2** *toured the castle:* explore, go round, sightsee, visit

tourist *n* day-tripper, excursionist, globetrotter, holidaymaker, rubberneck *US slang*, sightseer, traveller, tripper, visitor, voyager

tournament *n* championship, competition, contest, event, match, meet, meeting, series

tousled *adj* disarranged, dishevelled, disordered, messed up, ruffled, rumpled, tangled, tumbled

tout *v* **1** *touting tickets:* hawk, peddle, sell, trade **2** *being touted as the new Sinatra:* advertise, hype *colloq*, market, plug *colloq*, promote, push *colloq* **3** *touting for donations:* appeal, ask, petition, seek, solicit

tow *v* drag, draw, haul, lug, pull, trail, transport, tug
♦ *n* haul, lug, pull, tug

towards *prep* **1** *move towards the front:* approaching, in the direction of, on the way to, to, -wards **2** *towards the end of the year:* almost, approaching, close to, nearing, nearly **3** *his feelings towards her:* about, concerning, for, regarding, with regard to, with respect to

tower *v* **1** *the cliffs towered over us:* ascend, loom, mount, overlook, overshadow, rear, rise, soar **2** *towered over his contemporaries:* dominate, eclipse, exceed, excel, overshadow, surpass, top, transcend

towering *adj* **1** *towering skyscrapers:* colossal, elevated, gigantic, great, high, lofty, monumental, soaring, tall **2** *a towering genius:* extraordinary, imposing, impressive, incomparable, magnificent, outstanding, sublime, supreme, surpassing, unrivalled **3** *in a towering rage:* extreme, inordinate, overpowering
F≡ **1** low, small, tiny **2** minor, trivial **3** minor, trivial

town n borough, burgh, city, conurbation, county town, market town, metropolis, municipality, new town, pueblo, settlement, suburbs, township, urban district
F₃ country

town-dweller n burgher, citizen, oppidan formal, townsman, townswoman, towny colloq, urbanite
F₃ country-dweller, rustic

toxic adj baneful, dangerous, deadly, harmful, lethal, noxious, poisonous, unhealthy
F₃ harmless, safe

toy n 1 children's toys: plaything 2 a toy for the rich: bauble, knick-knack, trifle, trinket
♦ v 1 toyed with his affections: dally, flirt, mess about/around colloq, play, sport, trifle 2 toyed with her necklace as she spoke: fiddle, play, tinker

Kinds of toy include:
Action Man®, activity centre, aeroplane, baby-bouncer, baby-walker, ball, balloon; bicycle, bike colloq, mountain bike; blackboard and easel, boxing-gloves, building-block, building-brick, catapult, climbing-frame, computer game, crayon; doll, Barbie doll®, kewpie doll, rag-doll, doll's buggy, doll's cot, doll's house, doll's pram; drum set, electronic game, executive toy, farm, fivestones, football, fort, Frisbee®, game, garage, glove puppet, go-kart, golliwog, guitar, gun, cap-gun, pop-gun, gyroscope, hobby-horse, hula-hoop, jack-in-the-box, jigsaw puzzle, kaleidoscope, kite, box-kite, Lego®, marble, Meccano®, model car, model kit, model railway, modelling clay, musical box, ocarina, paddling-pool, paints, pantograph, pedal-car, peashooter, Plasticene®, Play-Doh®, playhouse, pogo stick, puzzle, rattle, rocker, rocking-horse, Rubik's Cube®, sandpit, scooter, seesaw, sewing machine, skateboard, skipping-rope, slide, soft-toy, spacehopper, spinning top, swing, swingball, teaset, teddy-bear, toy soldier, train set, trampoline, tricycle, trike colloq, typewriter; video game; walkie-talkie, water pistol, Wendy house, yo-yo. See also **game**

trace n 1 I detected a trace of orange: bit, dash, drop, hint, jot, pinch, shadow, smack, soupçon, spot, suggestion, suspicion, tinge, touch 2 the intruder left no traces: footmark, footprint, mark, scent, spoor, track, trail 3 traces of an ancient civilization: evidence, indication, record, relic, remains, remnant, sign, token, vestige
♦ v 1 trace your family tree: dig up, discover, find, seek, uncover, unearth 2 the police traced him to an apartment: detect, dog, follow, hunt, pursue, run down colloq, shadow, stalk, track (down), trail 3 tracing pictures from a book: copy, draft, draw, map, outline, sketch 4 traced the course of the ship: chart, delineate formal, depict, draw, map, mark (out), outline, record, show

track n 1 a track through the woods: path, route, trail, way 2 the track of the satellite: course, drift, line, orbit, path, route, trajectory 3 railways tracks: groove, line, rail, slot 4 animal tracks in the snow: footmark, footprint, footstep, mark, scent, spoor, trace, trail, wake
♦ v chase, dog, follow, hunt, pursue, shadow, stalk, tail, trace, trail

▶ **track down 1** track down the killers: capture, catch, find, hunt down, run down colloq, run to earth 2 track down the cause of the problem: dig up, discover, expose, ferret out, find, nose out, sniff out, trace, turn up, uncover, unearth

tract n 1 a tract of land: area, district, expanse, extent, lot, plot, quarter, region, stretch, territory, zone 2 a religious tract: booklet, brochure, discourse, disquisition formal, dissertation, essay, homily, leaflet, monograph, pamphlet, sermon, treatise

tractable adj amenable, biddable, complaisant formal, compliant, controllable, docile, governable, malleable, manageable, obedient, persuadable, pliable, pliant, submissive, tame, tractile, willing, yielding
F₃ headstrong, intractable, obstinate, refractory, stubborn, unruly, wilful

traction n 1 tyres with good traction in the snow: adhesion, drag, friction, grip, purchase 2 the traction of railway carriages: draught, drawing, haulage, propulsion, pull, pulling

trade n 1 foreign trade: business, buying, commerce, dealing, marketing, selling, shopkeeping, traffic, trafficking, transactions 2 losing trade because of the strike: business, custom 3 a fair trade: barter, exchange, swap, switch 4 in the building trade: business, calling, career, craft, employment, job, line (of work), métier, occupation, profession, skill, vocation, work
♦ v 1 they trade with other countries: bargain, barter, buy, deal, do business, sell, transact 2 trade arms: peddle, run, sell, traffic 3 I'll trade mine for yours: barter, exchange, swap, switch

trademark n 1 a registered trademark: badge, brand, brand name, crest, emblem, insignia, label, logo, name, proprietary brand, proprietary name, sign, symbol, tradename 2 a trademark of his films: attribute, characteristic, (distinctive) feature, hallmark, idiosyncrasy, mark, peculiarity, quirk, speciality, stamp, typical quality

trader n broker, buyer, dealer, marketeer, marketer, merchant, peddler, retailer, seller, shopkeeper, supplier, tradesman, tradeswoman, trafficker, vendor, wholesaler

tradesman, tradeswoman n 1 tradesmen selling their wares: buyer, dealer, merchant, retailer, seller, shopkeeper, vendor 2 a time-served tradesman: artisan, craftsman, craftswoman, journeyman, mechanic, worker

tradition n 1 a revival of the ancient traditions: belief, ceremony, custom, folklore, institution, observance, practice, praxis formal, rite, ritual, usage, way 2 a family tradition: convention, custom, habit, practice, routine

traditional adj 1 using traditional methods: accustomed, age-old, conventional, customary, established, fixed, habitual, historic, long-established, old, routine, set, time-honoured, usual 2 traditional stories: folk, old, oral, unwritten
F₃ 1 contemporary, innovative, modern, new, unconventional

traduce v abuse, asperse formal, blacken, calumniate formal, decry, defame, denigrate formal, deprecate formal, depreciate formal, detract *formal*, disparage *formal*, insult, knock *colloq*, malign, misrepresent, revile, run down *colloq*, slag *colloq*, slander, smear, vilify *formal*

traffic *n* **1** *heavy traffic:* cars, freight, passengers, transport, vehicles **2** *the traffic of goods:* freight, shipping, transport, transportation **3** *the traffic in drugs:* barter, business, buying and selling, commerce, dealing, exchange, peddling, trade, trading, trafficking **4** *have no traffic with him:* communication, contact, dealings, intercourse *formal*, relations
♦ *v* bargain, barter, buy, deal, do business, exchange, peddle, sell, trade

trafficker *n* broker, dealer, merchant, monger, peddler, trader

tragedy *n* adversity, affliction, blow, calamity, catastrophe, disaster, misfortune, unhappiness
🖅 success, triumph

tragic *adj* **1** *a tragic accident:* appalling, awful, calamitous, catastrophic, dire, disastrous, dreadful, fatal, ill-fated, shocking, terrible, unfortunate, unlucky **2** *a tragic waste:* appalling, awful, deplorable, dreadful, shocking, terrible **3** *a tragic figure:* heartbreaking, miserable, pathetic, pitiable, sad, sorrowful, unhappy, wretched
🖅 **1** happy **3** comic, happy, successful

trail *n* **1** *a trail through the woods:* path, road, route, track, way **2** *followed the animal's trail:* footmarks, footpath, footprints, scent, sign, spoor, trace, tracks, wake **3** *the ship's trail:* wake
♦ *v* **1** *she trailed her shawl behind her:* dangle, drag, draw, haul, pull, sweep, tow **2** *his scarf trailing on the ground:* dangle, drag, droop, hang, reach, stream, sweep **3** *he trailed along behind us:* dawdle, lag, linger, loiter, straggle, tow **4** *police trailed him to an apartment:* chase, dog, follow, hunt, pursue, shadow, stalk, tail, track
▶ **trail away** decrease, die away, diminish, disappear, dwindle, fade (away), fall away, lessen, melt away, peter out, sink, subside, tail off, taper off, trail off, weaken

train *n* **1** *a train of events:* chain, concatenation *formal*, order, progression, sequence, series, set, string, succession **2** *a train of vehicles:* caravan, column, convoy, cortège, file, line, procession, stream, string, succession **3** *we followed in his train:* path, trail **4** *his train of attendants:* attendants, cortège, court, entourage, followers, following, household, retinue, staff, suite
♦ *v* **1** *training them in various skills:* coach, discipline, drill, educate, groom, ground, improve, instruct, prepare, rehearse, school, teach, tutor **2** *he trains at a gym:* exercise, practise, work out **3** *training to be a doctor:* be prepared, be taught, be trained, learn, study **4** *trained the gun on him:* aim, direct, focus, level, point

trainer *n* coach, educator, handler, instructor, teacher, tutor

training *n* **1** *his training as an electrician:* apprenticeship, coaching, discipline, drill, education, grounding, instruction, learning, lessons, preparation, schooling, teaching, tuition, tutoring **2** *martial arts training:* exercise, practice, working-out, workout

traipse *v* plod, slouch, trail, tramp, trudge
♦ *n* plod, slog, tramp, trek, trudge

trait *n* attribute, characteristic, feature, idiosyncrasy, peculiarity, property, quality, quirk

traitor *n* back-stabber *colloq*, betrayer, deceiver, defector, deserter, double-crosser, double-dealer, fifth columnist, informer, Judas, quisling, renegade, turncoat, two-timer *colloq*
🖅 defender, loyalist, supporter

traitorous *adj* apostate, disloyal, double-crossing, double-dealing, faithless, false, perfidious *formal*, renegade, treacherous, treasonable, unfaithful, untrue
🖅 faithful, loyal, patriotic

trajectory *n* course, flight, flight path, line, orbit, path, route, track, trail

tramp *n* **1** *living like a tramp:* bum *slang*, derelict, dosser *slang*, down-and-out, hobo, vagabond, vagrant **2** *a tramp through the woods:* hike, march, ramble, tread, trek, trudge, walk **3** *she's a cheap tramp:* loose woman, prostitute, scrubber *slang*, slut *slang*, tart *slang*, trollop, wench, whore
♦ *v* **1** *tramping for miles:* hike, march, plod, ramble, roam, rove, stump, trail, traipse, trek, trudge, walk **2** *don't tramp on the flowers:* stamp, stomp, tread, walk

trample *v* crush, flatten, squash, stamp, tread

trance *n* catalepsy, daze, dream, ecstasy, rapture, reverie, spell, stupor, unconsciousness

tranquil *adj* **1** *a tranquil scene:* calm, hushed, peaceful, quiet, reposeful *formal*, restful, sedate, serene, silent, still, undisturbed **2** *he remained tranquil in adversity:* calm, composed, cool, even-tempered, imperturbable, laid-back *colloq*, placid, relaxed, sedate, serene, undisturbed, unexcited, unflappable *colloq*, untroubled
🖅 **1** disturbed, noisy **2** agitated, disturbed, troubled

tranquillity *n* **1** *the tranquillity of the lake:* calm, calmness, hush, peace, peacefulness, placidity, quiet, quietness, quietude *formal*, repose *formal*, rest, restfulness, sedateness, serenity, silence, stillness **2** *nothing disturbed her tranquillity:* ataraxia *technical*, ataraxy *technical*, calm, calmness, composure, coolness, equanimity, imperturbability, peace, peacefulness, placidity, quietude *formal*, sedateness, serenity
🖅 **1** agitation, disturbance, noise **2** agitation, disturbance

tranquillize *v* calm, compose, lull, narcotize *technical*, opiate, pacify, quell, quiet, relax, sedate, soothe
🖅 agitate, disturb, upset

tranquillizer *n* barbiturate, calmative, downer *colloq*, narcotic, opiate, sedative, sleeping pill

transact *v* accomplish, carry on, carry out, conclude, conduct, discharge, dispatch, do, enact, execute, handle, manage, negotiate, perform, prosecute *formal*, settle

transaction *n* **1** *bank transactions:* action, affair, agreement, arrangement, bargain, business, deal, deed, enactment, enterprise, matter, negotiation, proceeding, settlement, undertaking **2** *the transaction of business:* discharge, enactment, execution, handling, negotiation **3** *the transactions of the Philosophical Society:* affairs, annals, concerns, doings, goings-on *colloq*, minutes, proceedings, record, reports

transcend *v* beat, eclipse, exceed, excel, go beyond, leave behind, outdo, outshine, outstrip, overstep, rise above, surmount, surpass

transcendence *n* ascendancy *formal*, excellence, greatness, incomparability, matchlessness, paramoun(t)cy, predominance, pre-eminence, sublimity *formal*, superiority, supremacy, transcendency

transcendent *adj* **1** *transcendent beauty:* excellent, excelling, incomparable, magnificent, matchless, peerless, sublime, superlative, supreme, surpassing, unparalleled, unsurpassable **2** *a transcendent being:* ineffable *formal*, numinous *formal*, spiritual, superhuman, supernatural

transcendental *adj* metaphysical, mysterious, mystical, otherworldly, preternatural *formal*, spiritual, supernatural

transcribe *v* **1** *transcribed the interview:* copy out, copy up, note, record, reproduce, take down, write out, write up **2** *Hebrew transcribed into Latin letters:* render, rewrite, translate, transliterate

transcript *n* copy, duplicate, manuscript, note, record, reproduction, transcription, translation, transliteration, version

transfer *v* **1** *transferred us from the bus to the train:* carry, change, convey, move, relocate, remove, shift, take, transplant, transport, transpose **2** *transfer land:* assign, consign, convey, grant, hand over, transmit
♦ *n* **1** *the transfer of the money:* change, changeover, conveyance *technical*, displacement, handover, move, relocation, removal, shift, transference, transmission, transposition **2** *a transfer to another department:* assignment, move, relocation

transfigure *v* alter, change, convert, metamorphose *formal*, transform, translate *formal*, transmute *formal*

transfix *v* **1** *transfixed by the sight:* engross, fascinate, hold, hypnotize, mesmerize, paralyse, petrify, rivet, spellbind, stun **2** *a butterfly transfixed with a pin:* impale, pierce, run through, skewer, spear, spike, stick

transform *v* **1** *the caterpillar transformed into a butterfly:* adapt, alter, change, convert, metamorphose *formal*, transfigure, transmogrify *colloq*, transmute *formal* **2** *transformed the room:* convert, rebuild, reconstruct, remodel, renew, revolutionize, transfigure
Ⓕ **2** maintain, preserve

transformation *n* alteration, change, conversion, metamorphosis *formal*, metastasis *technical*, mutation *formal*, sea change *colloq*, transfiguration, transmogrification *colloq*, transmutation *formal*

transfuse *v* imbue, instil, permeate, pervade, suffuse, transfer

transgress *v* **1** *transgress a law:* breach, break, contravene, defy, disobey, violate **2** *those who transgress will be punished:* err, lapse, misbehave, offend, sin, trespass *formal* **3** *transgress the bounds of acceptable behaviour:* encroach, exceed, infringe, overstep
Ⓕ **1** keep, obey **3** keep, obey

transgression *n* **1** *forgive his transgressions:* breach, contravention, crime, error, fault, infraction *formal*, iniquity, lapse, misbehaviour, misdeed, misdemeanour, offence, peccadillo, sin, trespass *formal*, violation, wrong, wrongdoing **2** *the transgression of boundaries:* encroachment, infringement

transgressor *n* criminal, culprit, debtor, delinquent, evil-doer, felon, lawbreaker, malefactor *formal*, miscreant, offender, sinner, trespasser *formal*, villain, wrongdoer

transience *n* brevity, briefness, caducity *technical*, deciduousness, ephemerality *formal*, evanescence *formal*, fleetingness *colloq*, fugacity *formal*, fugitiveness *formal*, impermanence, shortness, transitoriness
Ⓕ permanence

transient *adj* brief, ephemeral *formal*, evanescent *formal*, fleeting, flying, fugacious *formal*, impermanent, momentary, passing, short, short-lived, short-term, temporary, transitory
Ⓕ lasting, permanent

transit *n* carriage, conveyance, crossing, haulage, journey, journeying, movement, passage, shipment, transfer, transportation, travel

transition *n* alteration, change, change-over, conversion, development, evolution, flux, metamorphosis *formal*, move, movement, passage, passing, progress, progression, shift, switch, transformation, transmutation *formal*

transitional *adj* **1** *a transitional phase:* changing, developmental, evolutionary, fluid, intermediate, passing, unsettled **2** *the transitional manager of the project:* interim, provisional, temporary
Ⓕ **1** final, initial

transitory *adj* brief, ephemeral *formal*, evanescent *formal*, fleeting, flying, fugacious *formal*, impermanent, momentary, passing, short, short-lived, short-term, temporary, transient
Ⓕ lasting, permanent

translate *v* **1** *translate into German:* construe *formal*, decipher, decode, interpret, put, render, transcribe, transliterate **2** *translated into layman's language:* decipher, decode, explain, interpret, paraphrase, put, reword, simplify **3** *translated his words into actions:* alter, change, convert, transform, transmogrify *colloq*, transmute *formal* **4** *translated to another branch:* move, relocate, shift, transfer

translation *n* **1** *a translation from Spanish:* crib, gloss, interpretation, rendering, rendition, transcription, transliteration, version **2** *a translation into simple language:* explanation, metaphrasis *formal*, paraphrase, rephrasing, rewording, simplification **3** *his translation into a star:* alteration, change, conversion, metamorphosis *formal*, transformation, transmogrification *colloq*, transmutation *formal* **4** *her translation to another department:* move, shift, transfer

translator *n* dragoman, exegete *formal*, exegetist *formal*, glossarist *formal*, glossator *formal*, glosser, interpreter, linguist, metaphrast *formal*, paraphraser, paraphrast *formal*

translucent *adj* clear, diaphanous *formal*, limpid, pellucid, see-through, translucid, transparent

ᴲ opaque

transmission *n* **1** *the transmission of goods*: carriage, conveyance, dispatch, sending, shipment, transfer, transference, transport **2** *the transmission of information*: communication, conveyance, diffusion, dispatch, dissemination *formal*, imparting, sending, spread, transfer, transference **3** *the transmission of the programme*: airing, broadcasting, relaying, sending, showing **4** *a live transmission*: broadcast, episode, performance, presentation, production, programme, show, simulcast

ᴲ **1** reception **3** reception

transmit *v* **1** *goods transmitted by air*: bear, carry, convey, dispatch, forward, remit *formal*, send, transfer, transport **2** *transmit a disease*: communicate, convey, diffuse, disseminate *formal*, impart, pass on, relay, spread, transfer **3** *transmit a programme*: air, broadcast, network, radio, relay

ᴲ **1** receive **2** receive **3** receive

transmute *v* alter, change, convert, metamorphose *formal*, remake, transfigure, transform, translate *formal*, transmogrify *colloq*, transverse

ᴲ retain

transparency *n* **1** *the transparency of the material*: clarity, clearness, diaphanousness *formal*, filminess, gauziness, limpidity, limpidness, pellucidity, pellucidness, perspicuousness, sheerness, translucence, translucency, translucidity **2** *the transparency of the system*: candidness, clarity, clearness, directness, forthrightness, frankness, openness, straightforwardness **3** *the transparency of his language*: apparentness, clarity, clearness, distinctness, explicitness, obviousness, patentness, plainness, straightforwardness, unambiguousness **4** *holiday transparencies*: photo, photograph, picture, slide

ᴲ **1** opacity **2** unclearness **3** ambiguity, unclearness

transparent *adj* **1** *transparent plastic*: clear, diaphanous, filmy, gauzy, pellucid, see-through, sheer, translucent **2** *a transparent electoral process*: candid, clear, direct, forthright, lucid, open, straightforward, unambiguous, unequivocal **3** *his motives are transparent*: apparent, candid, clear, discernible, distinct, evident, explicit, manifest *formal*, noticeable, obvious, patent, perceptible, plain, unambiguous, undisguised, unequivocal, unmistakable, visible

ᴲ **1** opaque **2** ambiguous, unclear **3** ambiguous, unclear

transpire *v* **1** *it transpired that he was guilty*: appear, be disclosed, become apparent, become known, come out, come to light, prove, turn out **2** *let's see what transpires*: arise, befall *formal*, come about, come to pass, ensue, happen, occur, take place

transplant *v* displace, graft, move, relocate, remove, replant, repot, resettle, shift, transfer, uproot

ᴲ leave

transport *v* **1** *transport goods*: bear, bring, carry, convey, fetch, haul, move, remove, run, shift, ship, take, transfer **2** *he was transported to Australia*: deport, exile **3** *transported by the sight*: captivate, carry away *colloq*, delight, electrify, enrapture, entrance, spellbind

♦ *n* **1** *public transport*: conveyance, transportation, vehicle **2** *the transport of goods*: carriage, conveyance, freight, haulage, removal, shipment, shipping, transfer, transit, transportation **3** *transports of delight*: bliss, ecstasy, elation, euphoria, exhilaration, fit, frenzy, rapture, seventh heaven *colloq*

transportation *n* carriage, conveyance, freight, haulage, shipment, shipping, transfer, transit

transpose *v* alter, change, convert, exchange, interchange, move, rearrange, reorder, shift, substitute, swap, switch, transfer

transverse *adj* cross, crossways, crosswise, diagonal, oblique, transversal

trap *n* **1** *catching animals in a trap*: booby-trap, gin, mesh, net, noose, pitfall, snare, springe **2** *the police had set up a trap*: ambush **3** *her question was a trap*: artifice, deception, device, ploy, ruse, stratagem, subterfuge, trick, trickery, wile

♦ *v* **1** *trapping birds in a net*: catch, confine, enmesh, ensnare, entrap, net, snare, take **2** *he was trapped in an alley*: ambush, catch, corner, entrap **3** *trapped him into telling the truth*: beguile, deceive, dupe, entrap, inveigle *formal*, lure, trick **4** *her legs were trapped under the car*: catch, confine

trappings *n* accompaniments, accoutrements *formal*, adornments, clothes, decorations, dress, equipment, finery, fittings, fixtures, fripperies, furnishings, gear, housings, livery, ornaments, panoply *formal*, paraphernalia, raiment *formal*, things *colloq*, trimmings

trash *n* **1** *throw out the trash*: dregs, garbage, junk, litter, offscourings, refuse, rubbish, scum, sweepings, waste **2** *he's talking trash*: balderdash, bull *colloq*, bunk *colloq*, drivel, garbage, gibberish, gobbledygook, junk, nonsense, rot *colloq*, rubbish, tripe *colloq* **3** *poor white trash*: canaille, dregs, rabble, riff-raff, scum, undesirables

trashy *adj* cheap, cheap-jack, inferior, kitschy, meretricious *formal*, naff *colloq*, rubbishy, tawdry, third-rate, tinsel, worthless

ᴲ first-rate

trauma *n* **1** *the trauma of losing a parent*: agony, anguish, distress, disturbance, jolt, ordeal, pain, shock, strain, stress, suffering, torture, upheaval, upset **2** *severe trauma to the spine*: damage, hurt, injury, lesion, wound

ᴲ **2** healing

traumatic *adj* **1** *a traumatic experience*: agonizing, distressing, disturbing, frightening, harmful, painful, shocking, stressful, unpleasant, upsetting **2** *a traumatic injury*: harmful, hurtful, injurious, wounding

ᴲ **1** relaxing **2** healing

travail *n* **1** *a life of travail*: distress, drudgery, effort, exertion, grind, hardship, slog, strain, stress, suffering, sweat, tears, toil, tribulation *formal* **2** *women in travail*: birth pangs, childbirth, labour, labour pains, throes

ᴲ **1** rest

travel *v* **1** *travel to London*: go, journey, make a trip, make your way, proceed, progress, ramble,

roam, rove, voyage, wander **2** *travel vast distances:* advance, cover, cross, move, proceed, traverse **3** *I've always wanted to travel:* explore, go abroad/overseas, journey, make a trip, roam, rove, see the world *colloq*, tour
🔁 **1** remain, stay **3** remain, stay
♦ *n* **1** *travel broadens the mind:* globetrotting *colloq*, journeying, touring, tourism, travelling **2** *an account of his travels around Spain:* excursion, expedition, globetrotting *colloq*, journey, passage, sightseeing, tour, trip, voyage, wanderings

> **Forms of travel include:**
> flight, cruise, sail, voyage, ride, drive, march, walk, hike, ramble, excursion, holiday, jaunt, outing, tour, trip, visit, expedition, safari, trek, circumnavigation, exploration, journey, migration, mission, pilgrimage

traveller *n* **1** *travellers on the Underground:* commuter, passenger **2** *a traveller to foreign parts:* excursionist, explorer, globetrotter, hiker, holidaymaker, rambler, sightseer, tourer, tourist, tripper *colloq*, voyager, wanderer **3** *travellers are banned from the pub:* drifter, Gypsy, itinerant, migrant, nomad, tinker, tramp, vagrant, wanderer, wayfarer **4** *a traveller for the company:* agent, commercial traveller, rep *colloq*, representative, sales representative, salesman, saleswoman

travelling *adj* itinerant, migrant, migrating, migratory, mobile, moving, nomadic, peripatetic *formal*, roaming, roving, touring, unsettled, vagrant, wandering, wayfaring
🔁 fixed, settled

traverse *v* **1** *we traversed a stream:* cross, ford, go across/through, negotiate, pass over/through, travel across/through **2** *the bridge which traverses the river:* bridge, cross, go across, pass over, span **3** *he traversed the country:* cross, go across/through, pass over/through, peregrinate *formal*, ply, range, roam, travel across/through, wander

travesty *n* apology, burlesque, caricature, corruption, distortion, farce, misrepresentation, mockery, parody, perversion, send-up *colloq*, sham, spoof *colloq*, take-off *colloq*, wind-up *colloq*

treacherous *adj* **1** *betrayed by his treacherous friend:* back-stabbing *colloq*, deceitful, disloyal, double-crossing *colloq*, duplicitous *formal*, faithless, false, perfidious *formal*, traitorous, two-timing *colloq*, unfaithful, unreliable, untrue, untrustworthy **2** *treacherous roads:* dangerous, hazardous, icy, perilous, precarious, risky, slippery, unsafe
🔁 **1** dependable, faithful, loyal **2** safe, stable

treacherously *adv* deceitfully, disloyally, faithlessly, falsely, perfidiously *formal*
🔁 loyally

treachery *n* back-stabbing *colloq*, betrayal, deceitfulness, disloyalty, double-crossing *colloq*, double-dealing *colloq*, duplicity *formal*, faithlessness, falseness, infidelity, perfidity *formal*, treason, two-timing *colloq*, unfaithfulness
🔁 dependability, loyalty

tread *v* **1** *tread carefully:* go, hike, march, pace, plod, step, stride, tramp, trek, trudge, walk **2** *don't tread on the flowers:* crush, flatten, press (down), squash, stamp, step, trample, walk on

♦ *n* footfall, footstep, gait, pace, step, stride, tramp, walk

treason *n* disaffection, disloyalty, duplicity *formal*, lese-majesty, mutiny, perfidy *formal*, rebellion, sedition *formal*, subversion, treachery
🔁 loyalty

treasonable *adj* disloyal, faithless, false, mutinous, perfidious *formal*, rebellious, seditious, subversive, traitorous, unfaithful
🔁 loyal

treasure *n* **1** *hidden treasure:* cache, cash, fortune, gems, gold, hoard, jewels, money, riches, valuables, wealth **2** *the treasure of the collection:* crème de la crème, gem, masterpiece, pièce de résistance, pride and joy, prize
♦ *v* adore, cherish, dote on, esteem *formal*, guard, hold dear, idolize, love, preserve, prize, revere, think highly of, value, worship
🔁 belittle, disparage

treasurer *n* bursar, cashier, purser

treasury *n* **1** *his personal treasury:* assets, cache, capital, coffers, finances, funds, hoard, money, resources, revenues **2** *money in the treasury:* bank, coffers, exchequer, repository, store, storehouse, vault **3** *a treasury of folk songs:* corpus, fund, hoard, repository, resource, storehouse, thesaurus

treat *n* **1** *a Sunday school treat:* amusement, banquet, celebration, entertainment, excursion, feast, outing, party, surprise **2** *brought the children a treat:* gift, indulgence, present, surprise **3** *it's always a treat to see you:* delight, enjoyment, fun, gratification, pleasure, thrill
♦ *v* **1** *treat women as second-class citizens:* behave towards, consider, deal with, handle, manage, regard, use, view **2** *he treats the subject with sensitivity:* consider, cover, deal with, discuss, handle, manage, review, study, view **3** *treat a patient:* attend to, care for, cure, heal, look after, medicate, minister to, nurse, tend **4** *treated us to a meal:* buy, entertain, feast, give, pay for, pay/foot the bill, provide, regale, stand, take out **5** *wood treated with creosote:* apply, cover with, lay on, paint, put on, rub, smear, spread on

treatise *n* discourse, disquisition *formal*, dissertation, essay, exposition *formal*, monograph, pamphlet, paper, prodrome *formal*, study, thesis, tract

treatment *n* **1** *a condition which requires treatment:* care, healing, nursing, surgery, therapeutics, therapy **2** *a new treatment for diabetes:* cure, medicament, medication, remedy **3** *his treatment of his wife:* action, behaviour, conduct, dealing(s), handling, usage, use **4** *the paper's treatment of the story:* coverage, dealing(s), discussion, handling, management

treaty *n* agreement, alliance, bargain, bond, compact, concordat *formal*, contract, convention, covenant, deal, negotiation, pact, pledge

treble *adj* **1** *a treble voice:* high, high-pitched, piping, sharp, shrill **2** *a treble crochet stitch:* threefold, triple
🔁 **1** deep

tree *n* bush, conifer, evergreen, shrub

> **Trees include:**
> acacia, acer, alder, almond, apple, ash, aspen,

balsa, bay, beech, birch, blackthorn, blue gum, box, cedar, cherry, chestnut, coconut palm, cottonwood, cypress, date palm, dogwood, Dutch elm, ebony, elder, elm, eucalyptus, fig, fir, gum, hawthorn, hazel, hickory, hornbeam, horse chestnut, jacaranda, Japanese maple, larch, laurel, lime, linden, mahogany, maple, monkey puzzle, mountain ash, oak, palm, pear, pine, plane, plum, poplar, prunus, pussy willow, redwood, rowan, rubber tree, sandalwood, sapele, sequoia, silver birch, silver maple, spruce, sycamore, tamarisk, teak, walnut, weeping willow, whitebeam, willow, witch hazel, yew, yucca; bonsai, conifer, deciduous, evergreen, fruit, hardwood, ornamental, palm, softwood

trek *v* **1** *trekked across the Himalayas:* hike, journey, march, ramble, roam, rove **2** *we trekked all round the shops:* plod, slog, traipse, tramp, trudge ♦ *n* **1** *a trek through the jungle:* expedition, hike, journey, march, odyssey, ramble, safari **2** *it's a long trek to the station:* slog, tramp, walk

trellis *n* framework, grate, grating, grid, grille, lattice, mesh, net, network, reticulation *formal*

tremble *v* **1** *tremble in fear:* quake, shake, shiver, shudder **2** *the earth trembled:* judder, quake, rock, shake, vibrate, wobble ♦ *n* judder, quake, quiver, shake, shiver, shudder, tremor, vibration, wobble 🖪 steadiness

trembling *n* **1** *the trembling of his hands:* oscillation, quavering, quivering, shakes *colloq*, shaking, shivering, shuddering **2** *the trembling of the earth:* juddering, quaking, rocking, vibration 🖪 **1** steadiness **2** steadiness

tremendous *adj* **1** *a tremendous player:* amazing, exceptional, extraordinary, great, impressive, incredible, marvellous, out of this world *colloq*, remarkable, sensational, smashing *colloq*, spectacular, stupendous, terrific *colloq*, wicked *slang*, wonderful **2** *a tremendous building:* colossal, enormous, formidable, gigantic, great, huge, immense, massive, towering, vast 🖪 **1** ordinary, unimpressive

tremor *n* **1** *the tremor in his voice:* agitation, quake, quaver, quiver, shake, shiver, thrill, tremble, trembling, wobble **2** *an earth tremor:* earthquake, quake, shock, vibration 🖪 **1** steadiness **2** steadiness

tremulous *adj* **1** *a tremulous voice:* quavering, quivering, quivery, shaking, shivering, trembling, trembly, unsteady, vibrating, wavering **2** *a tremulous smile:* afraid, agitated, anxious, fearful, frightened, jittery, jumpy, nervous, scared, timid 🖪 **1** firm, steady **2** calm

trench *n* channel, cut, ditch, drain, earthwork, entrenchment, excavation, fosse, furrow, gutter, pit, rill, sap, trough, waterway

trenchant *adj* **1** *a trenchant observation:* acerbic, acute, astute, biting, caustic, incisive, mordant *formal*, penetrating, perceptive, perspicacious *formal*, pungent, scathing, sharp **2** *a trenchant argument:* blunt, clear, clear-cut, effective, emphatic, forceful, forthright, no-nonsense *colloq*, terse, unequivocal, vigorous 🖪 **1** woolly

trend *n* **1** *the trend towards socialism:* bearing, course, current, direction, drift, flow, inclination, leaning, tendency **2** *the latest trends:* craze, fad *colloq*, fashion, latest *colloq*, look, mode, rage *colloq*, style, vogue

trendy *adj* all the rage *colloq*, cool *colloq*, fashionable, funky *colloq*, groovy *colloq*, hip *colloq*, in *colloq*, latest, modish, natty *colloq*, stylish, up to the minute, voguish, with it *colloq* 🖪 unfashionable

trepidation *n* agitation, alarm, anxiety, apprehension, butterflies *colloq*, cold sweat *colloq*, consternation *formal*, dismay, disquiet, dread, fear, fright, jitters *colloq*, misgivings, nerves *colloq*, nervousness, palpitation, perturbation *formal*, qualms, quivering, shaking, trembling, tremor, unease, uneasiness, worry 🖪 calm

trespass *v* **1** *trespass on someone's property:* encroach, impinge, infringe, intrude, invade, obtrude *formal*, poach, violate **2** *trespass against others:* do wrong, offend, sin, transgress *formal* ♦ *n* **1** *charged with trespass:* encroachment, infringement, intrusion, invasion, poaching, violation **2** *forgiven his trespasses:* contravention, misdemeanour, offence, sin, transgression *formal*, wrongdoing

trespasser *n* **1** *trespassers will be shot:* encroacher, intruder, poacher **2** *trespassers against others:* criminal, delinquent, evil-doer, offender, sinner, transgressor *formal*

tress *n* braid, bunch, curl, hair, lock, pigtail, plait, ringlet, tail

trial *n* **1** *gave evidence at the trial:* appeal, case, examination, hearing, inquiry, lawsuit, litigation, retrial, tribunal **2** *a trial of the new drug:* assay *formal*, check, dry run *colloq*, dummy run, examination, experiment, test, try-out **3** *his trial for the team:* audition, practice, probation, rehearsal, selection, test, try-out **4** *suffered many trials:* adversity, affliction *formal*, burden, cross, cross to bear, distress, grief, hardship, misery, ordeal, suffering, tribulation *formal*, trouble, vexation **5** *it's been a trial dealing with him:* annoyance, bane, bother, hassle *colloq*, nuisance, pain in the neck *colloq*, pest *colloq*, thorn in the flesh *colloq* 🖪 **4** happiness, relief **5** happiness, relief ♦ *adj* dry *colloq*, dummy, experimental, exploratory, pilot, probationary, provisional, test, testing

triangle

Types of triangle include:
acute-angled, congruent, equilateral, isosceles, obtuse-angled, right-angled, scalene, similar

triangular *adj* three-cornered, three-sided, triangle-shaped, trigonal *formal*, trigonic *formal*, trigonous *technical*, trilateral

tribal *adj* class, ethnic, family, group, indigenous, native

tribe *n* blood, branch, caste, clan, class, division, dynasty, ethnic group, family, group, house, nation, people, race, sept, stock

tribulation *n* adversity, affliction *formal*, blow, burden, care, curse, distress, grief, hardship, heartache, misery, misfortune, ordeal, pain, reverse, sorrow, suffering, travail *formal*, trial, trouble, unhappiness, vexation, woe, worry

F3 happiness

tribunal *n* bar, bench, committee, court, examination, hearing, inquisition, trial

tribute *n* **1** *tributes from his colleagues*: accolade, acknowledgement, applause, commendation, compliment, credit, enconium *formal*, eulogy *formal*, good word, high/good opinion, homage, honour, paean *formal*, panegyric *formal*, praise, recognition, respect, testimonial **2** *her success is a tribute to her dedication*: evidence, proof, testimony **3** *the flowers were a tribute from an admirer*: gift, present **4** *tribute imposed on conquered nations*: charge, contribution, duty, levy, payment, tariff, tax

trice *n* flash, instant, jiffy *colloq*, minute, moment, sec *colloq*, second, shake *colloq*, tick *colloq*, twinkling

trick *n* **1** *a trick to con tourists*: artifice, con *colloq*, deceit, deception, device, diddle *colloq*, dodge, fast one *colloq*, fraud, manoeuvre, ploy, rip-off *colloq*, ruse, scam *colloq*, subterfuge, swindle, trap **2** *let's play a trick on him*: caper, frame-up *colloq*, gag, hoax, jape, joke, leg-pull *colloq*, practical joke, prank, stunt **3** *a conjuring trick*: feat, illusion, legerdemain, sleight of hand **4** *a trick of the light*: apparition, illusion, mirage **5** *has the trick of writing for both children and adults*: ability, art, capability, capacity, facility, faculty, flair, gift, hang *colloq*, knack, know-how *colloq*, secret, skill, talent, technique

♦ *adj* artificial, bogus, counterfeit, ersatz, fake, false, forged, imitation, mock, sham

F3 genuine, real

♦ *v* **1** *tricked her into giving him money*: beguile, bluff, cheat, con *colloq*, deceive, defraud, delude, diddle, do *colloq*, dupe, fool, hoodwink, lead up the garden path *colloq*, mislead, outwit, pull a fast one on *colloq*, pull one over *colloq*, pull the wool over someone's eyes *colloq*, swindle, take for a ride *colloq*, take in, trap **2** *a show in which members of the public are tricked*: fool, have on *colloq*, hoax, kid *colloq*, pull someone's leg *colloq*, take in

trickery *n* **1** *the trickery used by scam artists*: artifice, cheating, chicanery, cunning, deceit, deception, dishonesty, double-dealing, duplicity *formal*, fraud, funny business *colloq*, guile, hanky-panky *colloq*, imposture, jiggery-pokery *colloq*, monkey business, pretence, shenanigans *colloq*, skulduggery, subterfuge, swindling, wiliness **2** *entertained us with trickery*: hocus-pocus *colloq*, illusion, sleight of hand

F3 1 honesty, straightforwardness

trickle *v* dribble, drip, drop, exude, filter, flow slowly, leak, ooze, percolate, run, seep

F3 gush, stream

♦ *n* dribble, drip, drop, leak, seepage

F3 gush, stream

trickster *n* cheat, con man *colloq*, cozener, deceiver, diddler *colloq*, dissembler *formal*, fraud, hoaxer, impostor, pretender, swindler, tricker

tricky *adj* **1** *a tricky problem*: awkward, complicated, delicate, difficult, dodgy *colloq*, knotty, problematic, sensitive, thorny, ticklish **2** *he's a tricky old devil*: artful, crafty, cunning, deceitful, devious, dodgy *colloq*, foxy, scheming, slippery, sly, subtle, wily

F3 1 easy, simple **2** honest

tried *adj* dependable, established, proved, reliable, tested, trusted, trustworthy

trifle *n* **1** *have a trifle more*: bit, dash, drop, little, small amount, spot, touch, trace **2** *insignificant trifles*: bauble, inessential, knick-knack, minor consideration, nothing, plaything, toy, trinket, trivia, triviality

♦ *v* dabble, dally, fiddle, flirt, meddle, mess about/around *colloq*, play, sport, toy, treat frivolously

trifling *adj* foolish, inconsequential *formal*, inconsiderable, insignificant, minor, negligible, paltry, petty, slight, small, trivial, unimportant, worthless

F3 important, serious, significant

trigger *v* **1** *trigger a reaction*: bring about, cause, elicit, generate, initiate, produce, prompt, provoke, set in motion, set off, spark off, start **2** *trigger a car alarm*: activate, set going, set off, start off

♦ *n* **1** *pulled the trigger*: catch, lever, switch **2** *the trigger for the fight*: spur, stimulus

trim *adj* **1** *trim gardens*: in good order, neat, orderly, presentable, shipshape, smart, spick-and-span, spruce, tidy **2** *looking trim in a new suit*: dapper, natty *colloq*, neat, presentable, smart, snazzy *colloq*, spick-and-span, spruce, tidy, well-dressed, well-groomed, well-turned-out **3** *a trim figure*: fit, slender, slim, svelte **4** *a trim handset*: compact, slim, streamlined

F3 1 scruffy, untidy **2** scruffy, untidy

♦ *v* **1** *trim the hedges*: chop, clip, crop, cut, dock, neaten, pare, prune, shave, shear, snip, tidy (up) **2** *try to trim costs*: contract, curtail, cut (down), cut back on, decrease, diminish, reduce, scale down **3** *a satin dress trimmed with lace*: adorn, array *formal*, decorate, dress, edge, embellish, festoon, fringe, garnish, ornament

♦ *n* **1** *in good trim for her age*: condition, fettle, fitness, form, health, order, shape, state **2** *a lace trim*: border, braid, edging, frill, fringe, trimming

trimming *n* **1** *a blouse with lace trimming*: adornment, border, braid, decoration, edging, embellishment, falbala, fimbriation *technical*, frill, fringe, frou-frou, garnish, ornamentation, passement, passementerie, piping, trim **2** *turkey with all the trimmings*: accessory, accompaniment, extra, garnish **3** *fingernail trimmings*: clipping, cutting, end, paring

trinket *n* bagatelle, bauble, gewgaw, gimcrack, jewel, knick-knack, ornament, trifle, whim-wham

trio *n* threesome, triad, trilogy, trinity, triplet, triplicity, triumvirate *formal*, triune, triunity, troika *formal*

trip *n* **1** *a trip to London*: drive, excursion, expedition, foray, jaunt, journey, outing, ride, run, spin, tour, voyage **2** *a trip which sprained her ankle*: fall, false step, slip, stumble, tumble **3** *a magic mushroom trip*: apparition, buzz *slang*, dream, fantasy, freak-out *slang*, hallucination, illusion, vision

♦ *v* **1** *tripped on the stairs*: fall, lose your footing, slide, slip, stagger, stumble, totter, tumble **2** *tripped lightly across the room*: caper, dance, gambol, hop, skip, spring, tiptoe

▶ **trip up** catch (out), ensnare, outsmart, outwit, snare, trap, trick

tripe *n* balderdash *colloq*, balls *slang*, blah *colloq*, bosh *colloq*, bullshit *slang*, bunkum, claptrap, drivel, garbage, guff, hogwash *colloq*, inanity, nonsense, poppycock *colloq*, rot *colloq*, rubbish, tosh *colloq*, trash, twaddle *colloq*
☒ sense

triple *adj* **1** *a triple sized bottle:* three times, threefold, treble, triplicate **2** *a triple layer cake:* three-ply, three-way, tripartite
♦ *v* treble, triplicate

tripper *n* excursionist, grockle *colloq*, holidaymaker, sightseer, tourist, traveller, voyager

trite *adj* banal, clichéd, common, commonplace, corny *colloq*, dull, hackneyed, ordinary, overdone, overused, platitudinous *formal*, routine, run-of-the-mill, stale, stereotyped, stock, threadbare, tired, uninspired, unoriginal, worn, worn-out
☒ fresh, imaginative, inspired, new, original

triumph *n* **1** *a triumph over his rivals:* accomplishment, achievement, attainment, conquest, coup, feat, hit, masterstroke, mastery, sensation, success, victory, walkover *colloq*, win **2** *they yelled in triumph:* celebration, elation, exultation, happiness, joy, jubilation, rejoicing
☒ **1** failure
♦ *v* **1** *good triumphed over evil:* beat, conquer, defeat, dominate, gain mastery, overcome, overwhelm, prevail *formal*, prosper, succeed, vanquish *formal*, win, win the day *colloq* **2** *we triumphed in the streets:* celebrate, crow, exult, gloat, glory, jubilate *formal*, rejoice, revel
☒ **1** fail, lose

triumphant *adj* **1** *the triumphant side:* conquering, prize-winning, successful, victorious, winning **2** *the triumphant fans:* boastful, celebratory, cock-a-hoop *colloq*, elated, exultant, gloating, joyful, jubilant, proud, rejoicing
☒ **1** defeated **2** humble

trivia *n* details, irrelevancies, minutiae, pap *colloq*, trifles, trivialities
☒ essentials

trivial *adj* banal, commonplace, cutting no ice *colloq*, everyday, flimsy, frivolous, incidental, inconsequential *formal*, inconsiderable, insignificant, little, meaningless, measly *colloq*, minor, negligible, no great shakes *colloq*, paltry, petty, piddling *colloq*, small, trifling, trite, unimportant, worthless
☒ important, profound, significant, substantial

triviality *n* **1** *the triviality of the problem:* foolishness, frivolity, insignificance, meaninglessness, pettiness, smallness, unimportance, worthlessness **2** *wasting time on trivialities:* detail, frivolity, technicality, trifle
☒ **1** importance **2** essential

trivialize *v* belittle, depreciate, devalue, minimize, play down, scoff at, underestimate, underplay, undervalue
☒ exalt

troop *n* **1** *send in troops:* armed forces, army, military, servicemen, servicewomen, soldiers **2** *a troop of soldiers:* band, company, contingent, division, squad, squadron, team, unit **3** *a troop of children:* assemblage *formal*, band, body, bunch, company, crew, crowd, flock, gang, gathering, group, herd, horde, mob, multitude, pack, throng
♦ *v* flock, go, march, parade, stream, swarm, throng, traipse, trudge

trophy *n* **1** *won the swimming trophy:* award, cup, laurels, prize **2** *kept the head as a trophy:* memento, souvenir, spoils

tropical *adj* boiling, hot, humid, steamy, stifling, sultry, sweltering, torrid
☒ arctic, cold, cool, temperate

trot *v* bustle, canter, jog, pace, run, scamper, scurry, scuttle
♦ *n* canter, jog, run
▶ **trot out** adduce *formal*, bring forward, bring out, bring up, drag up, exhibit, recite *formal*, rehearse *formal*, reiterate, relate, repeat

trouble *n* **1** *cause a lot of trouble:* agitation, annoyance, anxiety, bother, difficulty, disquiet *formal*, distress, hassle *colloq*, inconvenience, irritation, nuisance, pain, problem, vexation **2** *talk about your troubles:* adversity, affliction *formal*, anxiety, burden, concern, difficulty, disquiet *formal*, distress, grief, hardship, hassle *colloq*, headache *colloq*, heartache, misfortune, pain, problem, struggle, suffering, torment, trial, tribulation *formal*, unease, uneasiness, vexation, woe, worry **3** *we're in trouble now:* adversity, corner *colloq*, difficulty, fix *colloq*, hot water *colloq*, jam *colloq*, mess *colloq*, pickle *colloq*, scrape *colloq*, tight spot *colloq* **4** *trouble in the streets:* commotion, disorder, disturbance, fighting, strife, tumult, unrest, upheaval **5** *suffer from back trouble:* affliction *formal*, ailment, complaint, defect, disability, disease, disorder, illness **6** *engine trouble:* breakdown, conking-out *slang*, cutting-out, failure, malfunction *formal*, packing-up *colloq*, problem(s), shutdown, stalling, stopping **7** *take trouble over something:* attention, bother, care, effort, exertion, pains, thought, thoughtfulness **8** *it's no trouble:* ado, bother, fuss, hassle *colloq*, inconvenience
☒ **1** calm, relief **2** calm, relief **4** order **5** health
♦ *v* **1** *is something troubling you?:* agitate, annoy, bother, disconcert, distress, disturb, harass, hassle *colloq*, irritate, pain, perturb *formal*, sadden, torment, upset, vex, weigh (down), worry **2** *I'm sorry to trouble you:* bother, burden, discommode *formal*, hassle *colloq*, inconvenience, put out **3** *don't trouble to get up:* bother, make the effort **4** *troubled by back pain:* afflict, bother, pain, torment
☒ **1** help, reassure **2** help

troublemaker *n* agent provocateur, agitator, incendiary, inciter, instigator, mischief-maker, rabble-rouser, ringleader, stirrer
☒ peacemaker

troublesome *adj* **1** *a troublesome problem:* annoying, awkward, bothersome, demanding, difficult, disturbing, exacting, hard, inconvenient, irksome, irritating, laborious, perturbing *formal*, taxing, thorny, tiresome, tricky, vexatious, wearisome, worrisome **2** *troublesome children:* insubordinate, mischievous, rebellious, rowdy, trying, turbulent, unco-operative, unruly
☒ **1** easy, simple

trough *n* **1** *pigs feeding from a trough:* crib, feeder, feeding trough, manger **2** *the water flows through a trough:* channel, conduit, depression, ditch, drain, duct, flame, furrow, groove, gully, gutter, hollow, trench

trounce *v* beat, best, clobber *colloq*, crush, defeat, drub *colloq*, hammer *colloq*, lick *colloq*, overwhelm, paste, punish, rout, slaughter *colloq*, thrash, wallop *colloq*, wipe the floor with *colloq*

troupe *n* band, cast, company, group, set, troop

trouper *n* **1** *the troupers who toured in the company*: actor, artiste, entertainer, performer, player, theatrical, thespian *formal* **2** *he handled the problem like a trouper*: old hand *colloq*, veteran

trousers *n* breeches, denims, dungarees, flannels, jeans, Levis®, pants *US*, shorts, slacks

truancy *n* absence, absenteeism, French leave, shirking, skiving *colloq*
🔁 attendance

truant *n* absentee, deserter, dodger, runaway, shirker, skiver *colloq*
♦ *adj* absent, missing, runaway
♦ *v* desert, dodge, play hooky *colloq*, play truant, shirk, skive *colloq*, skive off *colloq*

truce *n* armistice, break, cease-fire, cessation, intermission, interval, let-up *colloq*, lull, moratorium, peace, respite, rest, stay, suspension
🔁 hostilities, war

truck[1] *n* float, heavy goods vehicle (HGV), lorry, van, wagon

truck[2] *n* business, commerce, communication, connection, contact, dealings, exchange, intercourse *formal*, relations, trade, traffic

truculent *adj* aggressive, antagonistic, argumentative, bad-tempered, bellicose *formal*, belligerent, combative, contentious, cross, defiant, fierce, hostile, ill-tempered, obstreperous, pugnacious *formal*, quarrelsome, sullen, violent
🔁 co-operative, good-natured

trudge *v* clump, hike, labour, lumber, march, plod, shuffle, slog, stump, toil, traipse, tramp, trek, walk
♦ *n* haul, hike, march, slog, traipse, tramp, trek, walk

true *adj* **1** *what he says is true*: accurate, correct, exact, factual, right, truthful, valid, veracious *formal*, veritable **2** *a true reading*: accurate, close, correct, exact, faithful, precise, unerring, valid **3** *the true reason for his resignation*: actual, authentic, genuine, proper, real **4** *the true owner*: actual, genuine, legitimate, real, rightful, valid **5** *showed true remorse*: genuine, honest, real, sincere **6** *a true friend*: constant, dedicated, dependable, devoted, faithful, fast, firm, honourable, loyal, reliable, sincere, staunch, steadfast, trustworthy, trusty
🔁 **1** false, inaccurate, incorrect, untrue, wrong **2** false, inaccurate, incorrect **3** false, untrue **4** false **5** false **6** faithless, unfaithful
♦ *adv* **1** *he speaks true*: correctly, honestly, rightly, truly, truthfully, veraciously *formal*, veritably **2** *the arrow flew true*: accurately, correctly, exactly, perfectly, precisely, properly, rightly, unerringly
🔁 **1** falsely, inaccurately **2** inaccurately

true-blue *adj* card-carrying, committed, confirmed, constant, dedicated, devoted,

dyed-in-the-wool, faithful, loyal, staunch, true, trusty, uncompromising, unwavering
🔁 superficial, wavering

truism *n* axiom, bromide, cliché, commonplace, platitude, self-evident truth, truth

truly *adv* **1** *the system is truly fair*: exactly, genuinely, in fact, in reality, indubitably *formal*, precisely, properly, really, rightly, truthfully, undeniably, undoubtedly **2** *he truly cares for her*: constantly, genuinely, honestly, sincerely, steadfastly **3** *I truly believe him*: actually, certainly, definitely, genuinely, honestly, indeed, really, sincerely, surely **4** *a truly awful film*: exceptionally, extremely, greatly, indeed, really, very
🔁 **1** falsely, incorrectly, slightly **2** falsely, slightly **3** slightly **4** slightly

trumped-up *adj* concocted, contrived, cooked-up, fabricated, fake, faked, false, falsified, invented, made-up, phoney *colloq*, spurious, untrue
🔁 actual, authentic, bona fide, genuine, real, sound, true, veritable

trumpet *n* **1** *play the trumpet*: bugle, clarion, horn **2** *heard the trumpet of elephants*: bellow, blare, blast, call, cry, roar
♦ *v* **1** *being trumpeted as the next big thing*: advertise, announce, broadcast, herald, proclaim **2** *elephants trumpeted loudly*: bay, bellow, blare, blast, roar, shout

truncate *v* abbreviate, clip, crop, curtail, cut, diminish, dock, lop, pare, prune, reduce, shorten, trim
🔁 extend, lengthen

truncheon *n* baton, club, cosh, cudgel, knobkerrie, shillelagh, staff, stick

trunk *n* **1** *a tree trunk*: shaft, stalk, stem, stock **2** *pack your trunks*: box, case, chest, coffer, crate, portmanteau, suitcase **3** *an elephant's trunk*: nose, proboscis *technical*, snout **4** *exercises to strengthen the trunk*: body, frame, torso

truss *v* bind, fasten, pinion, secure, strap, tie, wrap
🔁 loosen, untie
♦ *n* **1** *had to wear a truss*: bandage, binding, brace, pad, stay, support **2** *a bridge supported by trusses*: brace, buttress, joist, prop, shore, stay, strut, support

trust *n* **1** *I have every trust in him*: assurance, belief, certainty, confidence, conviction, credence, credit, expectation, faith, hope, reliance **2** *left him in your trust*: care, charge, custody, guardianship, protection, safekeeping, trusteeship **3** *in a position of trust*: commitment, duty, obligation, responsibility, trusteeship
🔁 **1** distrust, doubt, mistrust, scepticism
♦ *v* **1** *I trust her completely*: bank on, be sure of, count on, depend on, have confidence in, put your confidence in, rely on, swear by **2** *I trust you're going to pay for the damage*: assume, believe, expect, hope, imagine, presume, suppose, surmise *formal* **3** *trusted my secrets to her*: confide, entrust **4** *trusted my money to him*: assign, commit, consign, delegate, entrust, give, turn over
🔁 **2** disbelieve, distrust, doubt, mistrust

trustee *n* administrator, agent, custodian, depositary, executor, executrix, fiduciary, guardian, keeper

trusting *adj* credulous, gullible, ingenuous, innocent, naïve, trustful, unguarded, unquestioning, unsuspecting, unwary
🔁 cautious, distrustful, suspicious

trustworthy *adj* 1 *a trustworthy friend:* (as) good as your word *colloq*, committed, dependable, devoted, faithful, honest, honourable, loyal, principled, reliable, staunch, steadfast, true, upright 2 *a trustworthy adult:* dependable, level headed, reliable, responsible, sensible, stable
🔁 1 dishonest, unreliable, untrustworthy 2 irresponsible, unreliable, untrustworthy

trusty *adj* 1 *a trusty friend:* dependable, faithful, firm, loyal, staunch, strong, supportive, true, trustworthy 2 *a trusy employee:* dependable, honest, reliable, responsible, solid, steady, trustworthy, upright
🔁 1 unreliable 2 unreliable

truth *n* 1 *there's some truth in what you say:* accuracy, authenticity, correctness, exactness, genuineness, honesty, legitimacy, precision, realism, rightness, sincerity, truthfulness, validity, veracity *formal* 2 *his devotion to truth:* candour, frankness, genuineness, honesty, honour, honourableness, integrity, truthfulness, uprightness 3 *the truth of her love for him:* constancy, fidelity *formal*, loyalty 4 *tell the truth:* actuality, fact, facts, home truth *colloq*, reality, the gospel truth 5 *a universal truth:* axiom, fact, maxim, principle, reality, truism
🔁 1 deceit, dishonesty, falseness 2 deceit, dishonesty, falseness 3 falseness 4 falsehood, lie

truthful *adj* 1 *a truthful child:* candid, forthright, frank, honest, open, sincere, straight, trustworthy, veracious *formal* 2 *a truthful account:* accurate, correct, exact, factual, faithful, honest, precise, realistic, reliable, right, true, valid, veracious *formal*, veritable
🔁 1 deceitful, untruthful 2 false, untrue, untruthful

truthfulness *n* candour, frankness, honesty, openness, righteousness, sincerity, straightness, uprightness, veracity *formal*
🔁 untruthfulness

try *v* 1 *try to learn the piano:* aim, assay *formal*, attempt, endeavour, give something a whirl *colloq*, give something your best shot *colloq*, have a bash/crack/shot/stab *colloq*, have a go *colloq*, seek, strive, undertake, venture 2 *try a case in court:* examine, hear, investigate, judge 3 *try this recipe:* experiment with, sample, taste, test, try out 4 *try someone's patience:* drain, exhaust, make demands on, sap, strain, stress, stretch, tax, tire, weaken, wear out, weary
♦ *n* 1 *give windsurfing a try:* attempt, bash *colloq*, crack *colloq*, effort, endeavour, go *colloq*, shot *colloq*, stab *colloq*, whirl *colloq* 2 *a try with the new camera:* appraisal *formal*, evaluation, experiment, sample, taste, test, trial
▶ **try out** appraise *formal*, check out, evaluate, inspect, sample, taste, test, try on

trying *adj* aggravating *colloq*, annoying, arduous, bothersome, demanding, difficult, exasperating, hard, irritating, taxing, testing, tiresome, tough, troublesome, vexatious, wearisome
🔁 easy

tub *n* 1 *a tub of water:* barrel, butt, cask, keg, tun, vat 2 *a long soak in the tub:* basin, bath, bathtub

tubby *adj* buxom, chubby, corpulent *formal*, fat, obese, overweight, paunchy, plump, podgy, portly, pudgy, roly-poly, rotund *formal*, stout, well-upholstered
🔁 slim

tube *n* 1 *water flows along the tube:* channel, conduit, duct, hose, inlet, outlet, pipe, shaft, spout 2 *a tube of toothpaste:* cylinder

tubular *adj* pipelike, pipy, tubate *formal*, tubelike, tubiform *formal*, tubulate *formal*, tubulous *formal*, vasiform *formal*

tuck *v* 1 *tuck your shirt inside your waistband:* cram, ease, insert, push, stuff, thrust 2 *tuck the material into a seam:* crease, fold, gather, pleat, ruffle
♦ *n* 1 *a blouse with tucks in front:* crease, fold, gather, pleat, pucker 2 *bring some tuck to school:* comestibles, eats *colloq*, food, grub *slang*, meals, nosh *slang*, scoff *slang*, snack(s)
▶ **tuck away** conceal, hide, hoard, save (up), stash away, store
▶ **tuck in** *I tucked the children in:* cover up, make comfortable, make snug, put to bed, tuck up, wrap up 2 *don't wait for me – just tuck in!:* eat, eat up, get stuck in *colloq*, wire in *colloq*
▶ **tuck into** devour, dine on, eat, eat up, feast on, gobble *colloq*, gorge on, scoff *colloq*, wolf down *colloq*

tuft *n* bunch, clump, cluster, crest, flocculus *formal*, knot, tassel, truss, wisp

tug *v* drag, draw, haul, heave, jerk, lug, pull, tow, wrench, yank *colloq*
♦ *n* haul, heave, jerk, pluck, pull, wrench, yank *colloq*

tuition *n* coaching, education, guidance, instruction, lessons, schooling, teaching, training

tumble *v* 1 *he tumbled off the ladder:* drop, fall, flop, stumble, topple 2 *they tumbled him off his bicycle:* knock down, overthrow, topple, trip (up), unseat 3 *the ship tumbled about on the waves:* heave, lurch, pitch, reel, roll, sway, toss 4 *prices are tumbling:* collapse, decline, decrease, dive, fall, fall headlong, nosedive, plummet, plunge, slide
♦ *n* 1 *a tumble down the stairs:* drop, fall, roll, stumble, toss, trip 2 *a tumble in share prices:* collapse, decline, decrease, dive, fall, nosedive, slide
▶ **tumble to** become aware of, cotton on to *colloq*, grasp, perceive, realize, twig *colloq*, understand

tumbledown *adj* broken-down, crumbling, crumbly, decrepit, dilapidated, disintegrating, ramshackle, rickety, ruined, ruinous, shaky, tottering, unsafe, unstable, unsteady
🔁 well-kept

tumbler *n* 1 *the tumblers in the circus:* acrobat, contortionist, gymnast 2 *drink from a tumbler:* beaker, cup, drinking-glass, glass, goblet, mug

tumid *adj* bloated, bulbous, bulging, distended *formal*, enlarged, protuberant, puffed up, swollen, tumescent *formal*

tumour *n* cancer, carcinoma *technical*, growth, lump, lymphoma, melanoma, myeloma, neoplasm, sarcoma, swelling

tumult *n* **1** *heard a tumult outside:* affray, babel, brawl, clamour, commotion, din, disorder, disturbance, fracas, hubbub, hullabaloo, noise, pandemonium, racket, row, rumpus, shouting, uproar **2** *caused a tumult in the scientific community:* agitation, bedlam, chaos, commotion, confusion, disarray *formal*, disorder, disturbance, pandemonium, riot, row, stir, strife, turmoil, unrest, upheaval
🔁 **1** calm, peace **2** calm, composure

tumultuous *adj* **1** *tumultuous applause:* boisterous, clamorous, deafening, disorderly, excited, fervent, fierce, frenzied, loud, noisy, raging, riotous, rowdy, uncontrolled, unruly, vehement, wild **2** *these are tumultuous times:* agitated, disturbed, exciting, hectic, stormy, troubled, turbulent, violent, wild
🔁 **1** calm, peaceful, quiet **2** calm, peaceful, quiet

tune *n* air, melody, motif, song, strain, theme
♦ *v* **1** *tune an instrument:* adjust, attune *formal*, harmonize, pitch, temper **2** *tune a radio:* adapt, adjust, attune *formal*, regulate, set, synchronize

tuneful *adj* agreeable, catchy, euphonious, harmonious, mellifluous *formal*, mellow, melodic, melodious, musical, pleasant, sonorous
🔁 discordant, tuneless

tuneless *adj* atonal *formal*, cacophonous, clashing, disagreeable, discordant, dissonant, harsh, horrisonant *formal*, unmelodic, unmelodious, unmusical, unpleasant
🔁 tuneful

tunnel *n* burrow, hole, mine, passage, passageway, shaft, subway, underground passage, underpass
♦ *v* bore, burrow, dig, excavate, mine, penetrate, sap, undermine

turbid *adj* **1** *turbid waters:* clouded, cloudy, dense, dim, feculent *formal*, foggy, foul, fuzzy, hazy, impure, muddy, murky, opaque, thick, turbulent, unclear, unsettled **2** *a turbid description:* confused, disordered, incoherent, muddled
🔁 **1** clear **2** clear

turbulence *n* **1** *the plane hit some turbulence:* agitation, roughness, storm **2** *turbulence in the cities:* agitation, chaos, commotion, confusion, disorder, disruption, instability, pandemonium, tumult, turmoil, unrest, upheaval
🔁 **1** calm **2** calm

turbulent *adj* **1** *turbulent seas:* agitated, blustery, boisterous, choppy, foaming, furious, raging, rough, stormy, tempestuous, tumultuous, unsettled, unstable, violent, wild **2** *a turbulent mob:* agitated, boisterous, confused, disordered, disorderly, furious, in turmoil, mutinous, obstreperous, raging, rebellious, riotous, rowdy, tumultuous, unbridled, undisciplined, unruly, unsettled, violent, wild
🔁 **1** calm **2** calm, composed

turf *n* **1** *a lawn of green turf:* grass, green, lawn, sward **2** *dig up turfs:* clod, divot, glebe, sod
▶ **turf out 1** *turfed out of the house:* banish, chuck out *colloq*, dispossess *formal*, eject, evict, expel, fling out, kick out *colloq*, throw out, turn out **2** *turfed out of his job:* discharge, dismiss, elbow *colloq*, expel, fire *colloq*, give the elbow to *colloq*, kick out *colloq*, oust, sack *colloq*, throw out

turgid *adj* affected, bombastic, extravagant, flowery, fulsome, grandiloquent *formal*, grandiose, high-flown, inflated, magniloquent *formal*, ostentatious, overblown, pompous, pretentious, stilted
🔁 simple

turmoil *n* **1** *heard a turmoil from next door:* agitation, bedlam, bustle, commotion, din, disturbance, hubbub, noise, pandemonium, row, tumult, uproar **2** *political turmoil:* agitation, bedlam, chaos, confusion, disarray *formal*, disorder, disquiet, ferment, flurry, pandemonium, row, stir, trouble, tumult, turbulence, upheaval, uproar
🔁 **1** calm, peace, quiet **2** calm, peace

turn *v* **1** *the wheels turned:* circle, go round, go round and round, go round in circles, gyrate, move, pivot, reel, revolve, roll, rotate, spin, spiral, swivel, twirl, twist, whirl **2** *we'll have to turn and go back:* change course, divert, reverse, shift, swerve, swing round, veer **3** *the car turned the corner:* come round, go round, pass, round **4** *the road turns to the right:* bend, curve, swing, twist, veer, wind **5** *turned the gun on me:* aim, direct, point, swing **6** *turn the attic into a bedroom:* adapt, alter, change, convert, fashion, fit up, form, make, metamorphose *formal*, modify, mould, remodel, shape, transform, transmute *formal* **7** *the caterpillar turned into a butterfly:* change, metamorphose *formal*, mutate *formal*, transform **8** *ornaments made by turning wood:* cast, fashion, form, model, mould, shape **9** *turn cold:* become, come to be, go, grow **10** *no-one else to turn to:* appeal, apply, have recourse, resort **11** *the milk has turned:* become rancid, curdle, go bad, go off, sour, spoil **12** *the heat has turned the milk:* curdle, make rancid, sour, spoil
♦ *n* **1** *several turns of the wheel:* circle, cycle, gyration, revolution, rotation, round, spin, swivel, twirl, twist, whirl **2** *make a left turn:* bend, curve, reversal **3** *a sharp turn in the road:* bend, corner, curve, loop, twist **4** *a sudden turn in the weather:* alteration, change, deviation, difference, divergence, shift, variation **5** *it's your turn:* bash *colloq*, chance, crack *colloq*, go, occasion, opportunity, period, spell, stab *colloq*, stint, time **6** *a comedy turn:* act, performer **7** *did a turn on the stage:* act, appearance, performance, routine **8** *take a sinister turn:* bias, direction, drift, tendency, trend **9** *his mind has an artistic turn:* inclination, leaning, propensity *formal* **10** *you gave me a turn:* fright, scare, shock, start **11** *she's had a turn:* dizzy spell, faintness, illness
▶ **turn against** become hostile to, disapprove of, dislike
🔁 like, support
▶ **turn aside 1** *tried to turn the blow aside:* avert, deflect, fend off, parry, ward off **2** *turn aside from his course:* deflect, depart, deviate, diverge
▶ **turn away 1** *he was turned away by his father:* cold shoulder *colloq*, reject **2** *turned away the attack:* avert, repulse **3** *turn away from the original course:* deflect, depart, deviate, move away
▶ **turn down 1** *turn down an offer:* decline, rebuff, refuse, reject, repudiate, spurn, veto **2** *turn down*

the volume: decrease, lessen, lower, make quieter, muffle, mute, quieten, reduce, soften

▶ **turn in 1** *turn in for the night:* go to bed, hit the hay *colloq,* hit the sack *colloq,* retire **2** *turn in an essay:* deliver, give in, hand in, hand over, submit **3** *turn in a library book:* give back, give in, hand in, return **4** *turned himself in to the police:* deliver, give up, hand in, hand over, surrender

▶ **turn off 1** *turn off the motorway:* depart from, leave, quit *colloq* **2** *turned off along a side road:* branch off, deviate, divert, go along a different road **3** *turn off the TV:* disconnect, pull off, shut down, stop, switch off, turn out, unplug **4** *violence turns me off:* alienate, discourage, disenchant, disgust, displease, nauseate, offend, put off, repel, sicken

▶ **turn on 1** *turn on the computer:* activate, connect, plug (in), start (up), switch on **2** *leather turns me on:* arouse, attract, excite, please, stimulate, thrill **3** *the whole plan turns on you:* be contingent on *formal,* depend on, hang on, hinge on, rest on **4** *the gang turned on him:* attack, fall on, lay into, round on, set upon

▶ **turn out 1** *it turns out you were right:* become, come about, develop, emerge, end up, ensue, happen, pan out *colloq,* result, transpire *formal* **2** *turn out the lights:* disconnect, switch off, turn off, unplug **3** *she turns her children out beautifully:* clothe, dress, present **4** *they all turned out for the premiere:* appear, arrive, attend, be present, come, go, show up *colloq,* turn up **5** *the factory turns out DVD players:* assemble, churn out *colloq,* fabricate, make, manufacture, produce **6** *turned out of his job for stealing:* banish, chuck out *colloq,* deport, discharge, dismiss, drum out, evict, expel, fire *colloq,* kick out *colloq,* sack *colloq,* throw out, turf out *colloq* **7** *turn out the attic:* clean out, clear (out), empty

▶ **turn over 1** *turning things over in my mind:* consider, contemplate, deliberate, examine, mull over, ponder, reflect on, ruminate *formal,* think about, think over **2** *turned over to the authorities:* assign, consign, deliver, hand over, surrender, transfer **3** *the boat turned over:* be upset, capsize, invert, keel over, overturn, reverse, turn turtle, upend

▶ **turn up 1** *hardly anyone turned up:* appear, arrive, attend, be present, come, show up *colloq,* turn out **2** *turn up the volume:* amplify, increase, intensify, make louder, raise **3** *turn up new evidence:* bring to light, dig up, disclose, discover, expose, find, reveal, show, uncover, unearth

turning *n* bend, crossroads, curve, fork, junction, turn, turn-off

turning-point *n* crisis, critical/decisive moment, crossroads, crux, moment of truth, watershed

turnout *n* **1** *a huge turnout for the premiere:* assemblage *formal,* assembly, attendance, audience, congregation, crowd, gate, gathering, number **2** *a stylish turnout:* appearance, array *formal,* attire, clobber *colloq,* clothes, dress, gear *colloq,* get-up *colloq,* outfit, togs *colloq*

turnover *n* **1** *a turnover of £3 million a year:* business, flow, income, output, outturn, production, productivity, profits, volume, yield **2** *an increase in staff turnover:* change, movement, replacement

turpitude *n* badness, baseness, corruption, corruptness, criminality, degeneracy, depravity, evil, flagitiousness *formal,* foulness, immorality, iniquity *formal,* nefariousness *formal,* sinfulness, viciousness, vileness, villainy, wickedness
▣ honour

tussle *v* battle, brawl, contend, fight, grapple, scramble, scrap, scuffle, struggle, wrestle
♦ *n* battle, bout, brawl, conflict, contention, dust-up *colloq,* fight, fracas, fray, mêlée, punch-up, scramble, scrap, scrimmage, scrum, scuffle, set-to, struggle

tutelage *n* **1** *left under his grandparents' tutelage:* aegis *formal,* care, charge, custody, eye, guardianship, protection, vigilance, wardship **2** *his tutelage under a great master:* education, guidance, instruction, patronage, preparation, schooling, teaching, tuition

tutor *n* coach, educator, guide, guru, instructor, lecturer, mentor, supervisor, teacher
♦ *v* coach, direct, drill, educate, guide, instruct, lecture, school, teach, train

tutorial *n* class, lesson, seminar, teach-in
♦ *adj* coaching, didactic, educative, educatory, guiding, instructional, teaching

TV *n* boob tube *US colloq,* goggle-box *colloq,* idiot box *colloq,* receiver, set, small screen, television, telly *colloq,* the box *colloq,* the tube *colloq*

twaddle *n* balderdash, balls *colloq,* blather, blether, bunk, bunkum, claptrap, drivel, gabble, garbage, gobbledygook, gossip, guff, hogwash *colloq,* hot air *colloq,* inanity, nonsense, piffle *colloq,* poppycock, rot *colloq,* rubbish, stuff, tattle, tosh *colloq,* trash, waffle
▣ sense

tweak *v* jerk, nip, pinch, pull, squeeze, tug, twist, twitch

twee *adj* affected, cute, dainty, precious, pretty, quaint, sentimental, sweet

twiddle *v* adjust, fiddle, finger, play with, swivel, turn, twirl, twist, wiggle

twig[1] *n* branch, offshoot, ramulus *formal,* shoot, spray, sprig, stick, wattle, whip, withe, withy

twig[2] *v* catch on *colloq,* comprehend, cotton on *colloq,* fathom, get, grasp, rumble, see, tumble to *colloq,* understand

twilight *n* **1** *the bats come out at twilight:* crepuscule *formal,* dimness, dusk, evening, gloaming, gloom, half-light, sunset **2** *the twilight of her life:* decline, ebb, evening
♦ *adj* **1** *stars in a twilight sky:* crepuscular *formal,* darkening, dim, evening, shadowy **2** *his twilight years:* declining, dying, ebbing, final, last

twin *n* clone, complement, counterpart, (dead) ringer *colloq,* double, duplicate, equivalent, fellow, likeness, look-alike, match, mate
♦ *adj* corresponding, double, dual, duplicate, identical, matched, matching, paired, parallel, symmetrical, twofold
♦ *v* couple, join, link, match, pair, yoke

twine *n* cord, string, thread, yarn
♦ *v* **1** *her fingers were twined in his:* braid, entwine, knit, plait, tangle, twist, weave **2** *the python twined round its prey:* bend, coil, curl, encircle, loop, spiral, surround, twist, wind, wrap, wreathe

twinge n 1 *a twinge of pain:* ache, cramp, pain, pang, prick, spasm, stab, stitch, throb, throe 2 *a twinge of remorse:* pang, prick, spasm, stab

twinkle v coruscate *formal*, flash, flicker, gleam, glimmer, glint, glisten, glitter, scintillate, shimmer, shine, sparkle, wink
♦ n coruscation *formal*, flash, flicker, gleam, glimmer, glint, glisten, glitter, light, scintillation, shimmer, shining, sparkle, wink

twinkling adj blinking, bright, coruscating *formal*, flashing, flickering, gleaming, glimmering, glistening, glittering, nitid *formal*, scintillating, shimmering, shining, sparkling, winking
♦ n flash, instant, jiff *colloq*, jiffy *colloq*, mo *colloq*, moment, no time *colloq*, sec *colloq*, second, shake *colloq*, tick *colloq*, trice *colloq*, two shakes of a lamb's tail *colloq*

twirl v 1 *twirling round on the spot:* gyrate, pirouette, pivot, revolve, rotate, spin, swivel, turn, twist, wheel, whirl 2 *twirled the key around her finger:* revolve, rotate, spin, turn, whirl, wind
♦ n 1 *a twirl of the baton:* gyration, pirouette, revolution, rotation, spin, turn, twist, whirl 2 *patterned in twirls of red and yellow:* coil, convolution, curl, spiral, whirl

twist v 1 *twisted her hair on top of her head:* coil, curl, screw, twirl, wind 2 *the wires were twisted together:* braid, entangle, entwine, intertwine, plait, twine, weave, wind, wreathe 3 *twisted round to look at her:* pivot, revolve, rotate, skew, spin, swivel, turn 4 *the road twists through the hills:* bend, curve, turn, weave, wind, zigzag 5 *twisted in her grasp:* squirm, wriggle, writhe 6 *twist your ankle:* rick, sprain, strain, wrench 7 *twisting my words:* alter, change, distort, falsify, garble, misquote, misreport, misrepresent, pervert 8 *twist something out of shape:* bend, contort, deform, distort, misshape, warp
♦ n 1 *give the knob a twist:* screw, spin, turn, twirl 2 *a road full of twists and turns:* arc, bend, convolution, curve, kink, loop, squiggle, turn, zigzag 3 *a twist of rope:* coil, curl, curve, loop, roll, tangle 4 *gave his ankle a nasty twist:* rick, sprain, strain, wrench 5 *the story ends with a twist:* change, development, surprise, turnabout 6 *a twist on an old idea:* break, change, turn, variation 7 *a dark twist in his psyche:* aberration *formal*, defect, flaw, imperfection, perversion 8 *a twist in her personality:* foible, freak, idiosyncrasy, oddity, peculiarity, quirk

twisted adj 1 *a twisted line:* sinuous *formal*, squiggly, wavy, winding 2 *a twisted sense of humour:* deviant, odd, peculiar, perverted, strange, unnatural, warped
🔁 1 straight

twister n blackguard, cheat, con man *colloq*, crook, deceiver, fraud, phoney *colloq*, rogue, scoundrel, swindler, trickster

twit n ass *colloq*, blockhead, chump *colloq*, clot *colloq*, clown, dope *colloq*, fool, halfwit *colloq*, idiot, nincompoop *colloq*, ninny *colloq*, nitwit *colloq*, simpleton, twerp *colloq*

twitch v blink, flutter, jerk, jump, quiver, shake, tremble
♦ n convulsion, flutter, jerk, jump, quiver, shiver, spasm, tic, tremor

twitter v 1 *sparrows twittering:* chatter, cheep, chirp, chirrup, sing, tweet, warble, whistle 2 *she twittered on about her boyfriend:* blather, blether, gabble, gossip, prattle, twaddle, witter
♦ n chatter, chirping, chirruping, cry, song, tweeting, warble

two-faced adj deceitful, devious, dissembling *formal*, double-dealing, duplicitous *formal*, false, hypocritical, insincere, Janus-faced, lying, perfidious *formal*, treacherous, untrustworthy
🔁 candid, frank, honest

tycoon n baron, big cheese *colloq*, big noise *colloq*, capitalist, captain of industry, entrepreneur, fat cat *colloq*, financier, industrialist, magnate, mogul, moneybags *colloq*, moneyspinner *colloq*, supremo

type n 1 *there are many types to choose from:* brand, breed, category, class, classification, description, designation, form, genre *formal*, genus *technical*, group, kind, make, mark, model, order, set, sort, species, stamp, strain, style, subdivision, variety 2 *the very type of a country squire:* archetype *formal*, embodiment, example, exemplar *formal*, model, original, pattern, prototype, quintessence *formal*, specimen 3 *printed in bold type:* character(s), face, font, fount, letter(s), lettering, number(s), print, printing, symbol(s)

typhoon n cyclone, hurricane, squall, storm, tempest, tornado, twister *colloq*, whirlwind

typical adj 1 *typical teenage hobbies:* archetypal *formal*, characteristic, classic, conventional, illustrative, indicative, model, normal, ordinary, orthodox, quintessential *formal*, representative, standard, stereotypical, stock, usual 2 *just a typical day at work:* average, normal, ordinary, run-of-the-mill *colloq*, standard, usual 3 *it's typical of her to be so lazy:* characteristic, in character, in keeping, true to type, usual
🔁 1 atypical, unusual 2 atypical, unusual 3 atypical, unusual

typically adv as a rule, characteristically, customarily, habitually, normally, ordinarily, quintessentially *formal*, routinely, usually

typify v characterize, embody, encapsulate, epitomize, exemplify, illustrate, personify, represent, symbolize

tyrannical adj absolute, arbitrary, authoritarian, autocratic, cruel, despotic, dictatorial, domineering, harsh, high-handed, imperious, oppressive, overbearing, overpowering, peremptory *formal*, repressive, ruthless, severe, strict, totalitarian, unjust, unreasonable
🔁 liberal, tolerant

tyrannize v browbeat, bully, coerce, crush, dictate, domineer, enslave, intimidate, lord it over, oppress, repress, subjugate *formal*, suppress, terrorize

tyranny n absolutism, authoritarianism, autocracy, cruelty, despotism, dictatorship, harshness, high-handedness, imperiousness, injustice, oppression, ruthlessness, severity, strictness
🔁 democracy, freedom

tyrant n absolutist, authoritarian, autocrat, bully, despot, dictator, martinet, oppressor, slave-driver, taskmaster

tyro see **tiro**

U

ubiquitous *adj* common, ever-present, everywhere, frequent, global, omnipresent *formal*, pervasive, universal
🖪 rare, scarce

ugly *adj* **1** *an ugly person*: deformed, grotesque, hideous, homely *US*, ill-favoured, misshapen, monstrous, plain, repulsive, revolting, ugly as sin *colloq*, unattractive, unlovely, unprepossessing, unsightly **2** *ugly behaviour*: disagreeable, disgusting, foul, frightful, hideous, horrid, loathsome, nasty, objectionable, obnoxious, offensive, repulsive, revolting, shocking, terrible, unpleasant, vile **3** *the situation could turn ugly*: alarming, dangerous, evil, grave, hostile, nasty, sinister, threatening
🖪 **1** attractive, beautiful, good-looking, handsome, pretty **2** pleasant

ulcer *n* abscess, boil, canker, fester, noma, open sore, sore, ulceration

ulterior *adj* concealed, covert, hidden, personal, private, secondary, secret, selfish, undisclosed, unexpressed, unrevealed
🖪 declared, overt

ultimate *adj* **1** *my ultimate goal*: closing, concluding, end, eventual, extreme, final, furthest, last, remotest, terminal **2** *the ultimate truth*: basic, elemental *formal*, fundamental, primary, radical **3** *the ultimate sports car*: best, greatest, highest, maximum, perfect, superlative, supreme, topmost, utmost
♦ *n* best, chef d'oeuvre, consummation *formal*, culmination, daddy of them all *colloq*, epitome *formal*, extreme, greatest, greatest achievement, height, last word *colloq*, masterpiece, peak, perfection, summit

ultimately *adv* **1** *ultimately ended in triumph*: after all, at last, eventually, finally, in the end, sooner or later **2** *ultimately responsible*: basically, fundamentally, primarily

ultra- *prefix* especially, exceptionally, excessively, extra, extraordinarily, extremely, remarkably, unusually

ululate *v* cry, holler, hoot, howl, keen, lament, moan, mourn, scream, screech, sob, wail, weep

umbrella *n* **1** *put up your umbrella*: brolly *colloq*, gamp *colloq*, parasol, sunshade **2** *came under the umbrella of the Scottish Executive*: aegis *formal*, agency, cover, patronage, protection

umpire *n* adjudicator, arbiter, arbitrator, judge, linesman, mediator, moderator, ref *colloq*, referee
♦ *v* adjudicate, arbitrate, control, judge, mediate, moderate, referee

umpteen *adj* a good many *colloq*, countless, innumerable, numerous, plenty, very many
🖪 few

unabashed *adj* blatant, bold, brazen, confident, unashamed, unconcerned, undaunted, undismayed, unembarrassed
🖪 abashed, sheepish

unable *adj* impotent, inadequate, incapable, incompetent, ineffectual *formal*, powerless, unequipped, unfit, unqualified
🖪 able, capable, up to *colloq*

unabridged *adj* complete, entire, full, full-length, uncondensed, uncut, unexpurgated, unshortened, whole
🖪 abridged, shortened

unacceptable *adj* disagreeable, disappointing, inadmissible, intolerable, objectionable, obnoxious, offensive, undesirable, unpleasant, unsatisfactory, unsuitable, unwelcome
🖪 acceptable, satisfactory

unaccommodating *adj* disobliging, inflexible, intransigent *formal*, obstinate, perverse, rigid, stubborn, unbending, uncomplaisant *formal*, uncompromising, unco-operative, unyielding
🖪 flexible, obliging

unaccompanied *adj* alone, by yourself, lone, on your own, single, single-handed, solo, unattended, unescorted
🖪 accompanied

unaccountable *adj* **1** *for some unaccountable reason*: astonishing, baffling, bizarre, curious, extraordinary, impenetrable, incomprehensible, inexplicable, insoluble, mysterious, odd, peculiar, puzzling, queer, singular, strange, uncommon, unexplainable, unfathomable, unheard-of, unusual **2** *unaccountable to the public*: free, immune, not answerable, not responsible
🖪 **1** explainable, explicable **2** accountable, bound

unaccustomed *adj* **1** *unaccustomed to such luxury*: inexperienced, unacquainted, unfamiliar, unpractised, unused, unwonted *formal* **2** *found myself in an unaccustomed environment*: different, extraordinary, new, remarkable, strange, surprising, uncharacteristic, uncommon, unexpected, unfamiliar, unprecedented, unusual
🖪 **1** accustomed, familiar **2** customary

unacquainted *adj* ignorant, inexperienced, strange, unaccustomed, unfamiliar, unused

unadorned *adj* plain, restrained, severe, simple, stark, straightforward, undecorated, unembellished, unornamented, unvarnished
🖪 decorated, embellished, ornate

unaffected *adj* **1** *unaffected by criticism*: impervious, indifferent, unaltered, unchanged, unconcerned, unmoved, untouched **2** *an unaffected personality*: artless, candid, genuine, guileless, honest, ingenuous, naïve, natural, plain, simple, sincere, straightforward, true, unassuming, unpretentious, unsophisticated, unspoilt
🖪 **1** impressed, influenced, moved **2** affected, insincere, pretentious

unafraid *adj* brave, confident, courageous, daring, dauntless, fearless, imperturbable, intrepid, unshakable
🖪 afraid, fearful, nervous

unalterable *adj* final, fixed, immutable, inflexible, invariable, permanent, rigid, unchangeable, unchanging, unyielding

◳ alterable, flexible

unanimity *n* accord *formal*, agreement, concert, concord *formal*, concurrence, congruence *formal*, consensus, consistency, harmony, like-mindedness, unison, unity
◳ disagreement, disunity

unanimous *adj* 1 *we were unanimous in our support:* as one, concerted, concordant *formal*, harmonious, in accord *formal*, in agreement, like-minded, united 2 *our unanimous opinion:* common, consistent, joint
◳ 1 disunited, divided 2 divided

unanimously *adv* as one, by common consent, conjointly *formal*, in concert, nem con, of one mind, unopposed, with one voice, without exception, without opposition

unanswerable *adj* absolute, conclusive, final, incontestable, incontrovertible, indisputable, irrefragable *formal*, irrefutable *formal*, unarguable, undeniable
◳ answerable, refutable

unappetizing *adj* disagreeable, distasteful, insipid, off-putting, tasteless, unappealing, unattractive, unexciting, uninteresting, uninviting, unpalatable, unpleasant, unsavoury
◳ appetising

unapproachable *adj* aloof, cold, cool, distant, forbidding, inaccessible, remote, reserved, standoffish, uncommunicative, unfriendly, unresponsive, unsociable, withdrawn
◳ approachable, friendly

unapt *adj* inapplicable, inapposite *formal*, inappropriate, inapt, malapropos *formal*, unfit, unfitted, unseasonable, unsuitable, unsuited, untimely
◳ apt

unarmed *adj* defenceless, exposed, helpless, open, unprotected, vulnerable, weak
◳ armed, protected

unashamed *adj* blatant, honest, impenitent, open, shameless, unabashed, unconcealed, undisguised, unrepentant
◳ abashed, ashamed

unasked *adj* spontaneous, unannounced, unbidden, uninvited, unrequested, unsolicited, unsought, unwanted, voluntary
◳ invited, wanted

unassailable *adj* absolute, conclusive, impregnable, incontestable, incontrovertible, indisputable, invincible, inviolable, invulnerable, irrefutable *formal*, secure, sound, undeniable
◳ assailable

unassertive *adj* backward, bashful, diffident, meek, mousy, quiet, reticent, retiring, self-effacing, shy, timid, timorous, unassuming
◳ assertive

unassuming *adj* demure, humble, meek, modest, natural, quiet, restrained, reticent, retiring, self-effacing, shy, simple, unassertive, unobtrusive, unpretentious
◳ assertive, presumptuous, pretentious

unattached *adj* available, by yourself, fancy-free, footloose, free, independent, on your own, single, unaffiliated, uncommitted, unengaged, unmarried
◳ committed, engaged

unattended *adj* abandoned, alone, disregarded, forgotten, forsaken *formal*, ignored, neglected, unaccompanied, unescorted, unguarded, unsupervised, unwatched
◳ attended, escorted, looked after

unauthorized *adj* forbidden, illegal, illegitimate, illicit, irregular, prohibited, unapproved, unlawful, unlicensed, unofficial, unsanctioned, unwarranted
◳ accredited *formal*, authorized, legal

unavailing *adj* abortive, beaten, defeated, failed, fruitless, frustrated, futile, ineffective, losing, luckless, sterile, thwarted, unfortunate, unlucky, unproductive, unprofitable, unsuccessful, useless, vain
◳ effective, successful

unavoidable *adj* certain, compulsory, destined, fated, ineluctable *formal*, inescapable, inevitable, inexorable, mandatory *formal*, necessary, obligatory, predestined, required, sure
◳ avoidable

unaware *adj* blind, deaf, heedless, ignorant, in the dark, insentient *formal*, oblivious, unconscious, unenlightened, uninformed, unknowing, unmindful, unsuspecting
◳ aware, conscious

unawares *adv* aback, abruptly, accidentally, by surprise, inadvertently, insidiously, mistakenly, off guard, on the hop *colloq*, suddenly, unconsciously, unexpectedly, unintentionally, unknowingly, unprepared, unthinkingly, unwittingly

unbalanced *adj* 1 *he seems a little unbalanced:* barmy *colloq*, crackers *colloq*, crazy *colloq*, demented, deranged, disturbed, insane, irrational, lunatic, mad, mentally ill, needing your head examining *colloq*, round the bend *colloq*, round the twist *colloq*, unsound, unstable 2 *an unbalanced report:* asymmetrical, biased, inequitable *formal*, lopsided, one-sided, partisan, prejudiced, unequal, uneven, unfair, unjust, unstable, unsteady
◳ 1 sane, sound 2 unbiased

unbearable *adj* excruciating, insufferable, insupportable, intolerable, unacceptable, unendurable
◳ acceptable, bearable

unbeatable *adj* best, excellent, indomitable *formal*, invincible, matchless, supreme, unconquerable, unstoppable, unsurpassable

unbeaten *adj* supreme, triumphant, unbowed, unconquered, undefeated, unsubdued, unsurpassed, unvanquished *formal*, victorious, winning
◳ defeated, vanquished *formal*

unbecoming *adj* improper, inappropriate, indecorous *formal*, indelicate, unattractive, unbefitting, ungentlemanly, unladylike, unseemly, unsightly, unsuitable
◳ attractive, suitable

unbelief *n* agnosticism, atheism, disbelief, doubt, incredulity, scepticism
◳ belief, faith

unbelievable *adj* 1 *I found the plot unbelievable:* far-fetched, implausible, improbable, incredible, outlandish, preposterous, unconvincing, unlikely 2 *an unbelievable success:* amazing,

astonishing, extraordinary, incredible, staggering, unimaginable, unthinkable
F∃ 1 believable, credible

unbeliever *n* agnostic, atheist, disbeliever, doubter, doubting Thomas, infidel, nullifidian *formal*, sceptic
F∃ believer, supporter

unbelieving *adj* disbelieving, distrustful, doubtful, doubting, dubious, incredulous, nullifidian *formal*, sceptical, suspicious, unconvinced, unpersuaded
F∃ credulous, trustful

unbend *v* become less formal/strict, loosen up, relax, straighten, thaw, unbutton, uncoil, uncurl, unfreeze
F∃ stiffen, withdraw

unbending *adj* aloof, distant, firm, forbidding, formal, formidable, hard-line, inflexible, intransigent *formal*, reserved, resolute, rigid, severe, stern, stiff, strict, stubborn, tough, uncompromising, unyielding
F∃ approachable, friendly, relaxed

unbiased *adj* disinterested, dispassionate, equitable, even-handed, fair, fair-minded, impartial, independent, just, neutral, objective, open-minded, uncoloured, uninfluenced, unprejudiced
F∃ biased

unbidden *adj* free, spontaneous, unasked, unforced, uninvited, unprompted, unsolicited, unwanted, unwelcome, voluntary, willing
F∃ invited, solicited

unbind *v* free, liberate, loose, loosen, release, unchain, undo, unfasten, unfetter, unloose, unloosen, unshackle, untie, unyoke
F∃ bind, restrain

unblemished *adj* clear, flawless, immaculate, irreproachable, perfect, pure, spotless, unflawed, unimpeachable, unspotted, unstained, unsullied, untarnished
F∃ blemished, flawed, imperfect

unblinking *adj* assured, calm, composed, cool, emotionless, fearless, impassive, imperturbable, steady, unafraid, unemotional, unfaltering, unflinching, unshrinking, unwavering
F∃ cowed, fearful

unblushing *adj* amoral, blatant, bold, brazen, conscience-proof, immodest, shameless, unabashed, unashamed, unembarrassed
F∃ abashed, ashamed

unborn *adj* awaited, coming, embryonic, expected, future, in utero, subsequent, succeeding, to-come

unbosom *v* bare, confide, disclose, divulge, lay bare, unburden, uncover

unbounded *adj* boundless, endless, immeasurable, infinite, limitless, unbridled, unchecked, uncontrolled, unlimited, unrestrained, unrestricted, vast
F∃ limited, restrained

unbreakable *adj* durable, indestructible, infrangible *formal*, resistant, rugged, shatterproof, solid, strong, tough, toughened
F∃ breakable, fragile

unbridled *adj* excessive, immoderate, intemperate, licentious, profligate, rampant, riotous, unchecked, unconstrained,

uncontrolled, uncurbed, ungoverned, unrestrained, wild

unbroken *adj* **1** *the surface remained unbroken:* complete, entire, intact, solid, undivided, whole **2** *a week of unbroken sunshine:* ceaseless, constant, continuous, endless, incessant, non-stop, perpetual, successive, unceasing, uninterrupted, unremitting *formal* **3** *unbroken record:* unbeaten, unequalled, unmatched, unrivalled, unsurpassed
F∃ 1 broken, damaged **2** fitful, intermittent

unburden *v* bare, lay bare, offload, pour out, reveal, uncover

uncalled-for *adj* gratuitous, needless, unasked-for, undeserved, unjustified, unnecessary, unprompted, unprovoked, unsolicited, unsought, unwarranted, unwelcome
F∃ timely

uncanny *adj* bizarre, creepy, eerie, eldritch *Scot*, exceptional, extraordinary, fantastic, incredible, mysterious, odd, preternatural *formal*, queer, remarkable, spooky *colloq*, strange, supernatural, unaccountable, unearthly, unnatural, weird

uncaring *adj* callous, cold, inconsiderate, indifferent, unconcerned, unfeeling, uninterested, unmoved, unsympathetic
F∃ caring, concerned

unceasing *adj* ceaseless, constant, continual, continuous, endless, incessant, never-ending, non-stop, perpetual, persistent, relentless, unbroken, unending, unrelenting, unremitting
F∃ intermittent, spasmodic

uncertain *adj* **1** *uncertain what to do:* ambivalent, doubtful, dubious, equivocating, hesitant, in two minds *colloq*, open, unconvinced, undecided, unresolved, unsure, vacillating, wavering **2** *an uncertain grip on reality:* changeable, erratic, fitful, inconstant, irregular, shaky, unreliable, unsteady, variable **3** *an uncertain fate:* hanging in the balance *colloq*, iffy *colloq*, in the lap of the gods *colloq*, indefinite, insecure, risky, speculative, touch and go *colloq*, unclear, unconfirmed, undetermined, unforeseeable, unknown, unpredictable, unresolved, unsettled, up in the air *colloq*, vague
F∃ 1 certain, sure **2** steady **3** predictable

uncertainty *n* **1** *uncertainty about what to do:* ambiguity, ambivalence, bewilderment, confusion, dilemma, doubt, hesitation, irresolution, misgiving, perplexity, puzzlement, qualm(s), scepticism, uneasiness, vagueness **2** *greater uncertainty in the stock market:* insecurity, riskiness, unpredictability, unreliability
F∃ 1 certainty

unchangeable *adj* changeless, eternal, final, immutable *formal*, intransmutable *formal*, invariable, irreversible, permanent, unchanging
F∃ changeable

unchanging *adj* abiding, constant, enduring, eternal, invariable, lasting, permanent, perpetual, same, steadfast, steady, unvarying
F∃ changeable, changing

uncharitable *adj* callous, cruel, hard, hard-hearted, harsh, insensitive, mean, severe, stern, uncompassionate, unfeeling, unforgiving, unfriendly, ungenerous, unkind, unsympathetic
F∃ charitable, generous, kind, sensitive

uncharted *adj* alien, foreign, new, strange, undiscovered, unexplored, unfamiliar, unknown, unplumbed, unsurveyed, virgin
F3 familiar

unchaste *adj* defiled, depraved, dishonest, dissolute, fallen, immodest, immoral, impure, lewd, licentious, loose, promiscuous, wanton
F3 chaste

uncivil *adj* abrupt, bad-mannered, bearish, boorish, brusque, churlish, curt, discourteous, disrespectful, gruff, ill-bred, ill-mannered, impolite, rude, surly, uncouth, ungracious, unmannerly
F3 civil, polite

uncivilized *adj* antisocial, barbarian, barbaric, benighted, boorish, brutish, illiterate, primitive, rough, savage, uncouth, uncultured, uneducated, unenlightened, unrefined, unsophisticated, untamed, wild
F3 civilized, cultured

unclassifiable *adj* indefinable, indefinite, indescribable, indeterminate, indistinct, uncertain, undefinable, unidentifiable, vague
F3 definable, identifiable

unclean *adj* adulterated, bad, contaminated, defiled, dirty, filthy, foul, grimy, grubby, impure, polluted, soiled, sullied, tainted, unhygienic, unwholesome
F3 clean, hygienic

unclear *adj* **1** *the situation is unclear:* ambiguous, doubtful, dubious, equivocal, hazy, iffy *colloq*, indefinite, indistinct, uncertain, undetermined, unsettled, unsure, vague **2** *unclear skies:* dim, foggy, hazy, obscure
F3 **1** clear, evident **2** clear

unclothed *adj* bare, disrobed *formal*, in the altogether *colloq*, in the buff *colloq*, in your birthday suit *colloq*, naked, nude, stark naked *colloq*, starkers *colloq*, stripped, unclad *formal*, undressed
F3 clothed, dressed

uncomfortable *adj* **1** *uncomfortable conditions:* cold, cramped, disagreeable, hard, tough **2** *uncomfortable shoes:* ill-fitting, irritating, painful, tight **3** *felt uncomfortable in crowds:* anxious, awkward, conscience-stricken, discomfited *formal*, disquieted, distressed, disturbed, embarrassed, nervous, on edge *colloq*, self-conscious, tense, troubled, uneasy, worried
F3 **1** comfortable **2** comfortable **3** relaxed

uncommitted *adj* available, fancy-free, floating, free, neutral, non-aligned, non-partisan, unattached, undecided, uninvolved
F3 committed

uncommon *adj* abnormal, atypical, bizarre, curious, distinctive, exceptional, extraordinary, few and far between *colloq*, infrequent, like gold dust *colloq*, notable, odd, outstanding, peculiar, queer, rare, remarkable, scarce, singular, special, strange, striking, thin on the ground *colloq*, unfamiliar, unusual
F3 common, normal, usual

uncommonly *adv* **1** *uncommonly fond of cheese:* abnormally, exceptionally, extremely, occasionally, outstandingly, particularly, peculiarly, remarkably, singularly, strangely,

unusually, very **2** *they occur uncommonly:* infrequently, occasionally, rarely, seldom
F3 **2** commonly, frequently

uncommunicative *adj* aloof, brief, close, curt, diffident, quiet, reserved, reticent, retiring, secretive, shy, silent, taciturn, tight-lipped, unforthcoming, unresponsive, unsociable, withdrawn
F3 communicative, forthcoming, talkative

uncomplicated *adj* clear, direct, easy, simple, straightforward, undemanding, uninvolved
F3 complex, complicated, involved

uncompromising *adj* die-hard, firm, hard-line, immovable, inexorable, inflexible, intransigent *formal*, obdurate *formal*, obstinate, rigid, stiff, strict, stubborn, tough, unaccommodating, unbending, unyielding
F3 flexible, yielding

unconcealed *adj* admitted, apparent, blatant, conspicuous, evident, ill-concealed, manifest *formal*, noticeable, obvious, open, overt, patent, self-confessed, unashamed, undisguised, visible
F3 hidden, secret

unconcern *n* aloofness, apathy, callousness, detachment, indifference, insouciance *formal*, negligence, nonchalance, pococurantism *formal*, remoteness, uninterestedness
F3 concern

unconcerned *adj* aloof, apathetic, callous, carefree, casual, complacent, composed, cool, detached, dispassionate, distant, indifferent, insouciant *formal*, nonchalant, oblivious, pococurante *formal*, relaxed, remote, uncaring, uninterested, uninvolved, unmoved, unperturbed *formal*, unruffled, unsympathetic, untroubled, unworried
F3 concerned, interested, worried

unconditional *adj* absolute, categorical, complete, conclusive, definite, downright, entire, full, out-and-out, outright, thoroughgoing, total, unequivocal, unlimited, unqualified, unreserved, unrestricted, utter, whole-hearted
F3 conditional, limited, qualified

unconfirmed *adj* unauthenticated, uncorroborated *formal*, unproved, unproven, unsubstantiated, unverified
F3 confirmed

uncongenial *adj* antagonistic, antipathetic *formal*, disagreeable, discordant, displeasing, distasteful, incompatible, unappealing, unattractive, unfriendly, uninviting, unpleasant, unsavoury, unsuited, unsympathetic
F3 congenial

unconnected *adj* **1** *unconnected to the earlier events:* beside/off the point, independent, irrelevant, neither here nor there *colloq*, separate, unrelated **2** *unconnected to the wall:* detached, separate, unattached **3** *unconnected thoughts:* confused, disconnected, disjointed, illogical, incoherent, irrational, unco-ordinated
F3 **1** connected, relevant **2** connected, integral

unconquerable *adj* enduring, indomitable *formal*, ingrained, insuperable, insurmountable, inveterate, invincible, irrepressible, irresistible, overpowering, unbeatable, undefeatable, unyielding
F3 weak, yielding

unconscionable *adj* amoral, criminal, excessive, exorbitant, extravagant, extreme, immoderate, inordinate, outrageous, preposterous, unethical, unjustifiable, unpardonable, unprincipled, unreasonable, unscrupulous, unwarrantable

unconscious *adj* **1** *in an unconscious state:* asleep, blacked out, collapsed, comatose *technical*, concussed, dazed, dead to the world *colloq*, drugged, fainted, in a coma, insensible *formal*, knocked out, out, out cold *colloq*, out for the count *colloq*, senseless, stunned, zonked *colloq* **2** *unconscious of the warning:* blind, deaf, heedless, ignorant, incognizant *formal*, insensible *formal*, oblivious, unaware, unmindful **3** *an unconscious reaction:* accidental, automatic, impulsive, inadvertent, innate, instinctive, involuntary, latent, reflex, repressed, subconscious, subliminal, suppressed, unintentional, unthinking, unwitting
⊠ **1** conscious **2** aware **3** intentional

unconstraint *n* abandon, freedom, laissez-faire, liberality, openness, relaxation, unreserve, unrestraint

uncontrollable *adj* disorderly, furious, intractable *formal*, irrepressible, mad, out of control, strong, ungovernable, unmanageable, unruly, violent, wild
⊠ controllable, manageable

uncontrolled *adj* boisterous, rampant, riotous, unbridled, unchecked, uncurbed, undisciplined, unhindered, unrestrained, unruly, violent, wild
⊠ controlled, restrained

unconventional *adj* abnormal, alternative, bizarre, bohemian, different, eccentric, far-out *slang*, freaky *colloq*, fringe *colloq*, idiosyncratic, irregular, odd, offbeat, original, out of the ordinary *colloq*, rare, uncommon, unorthodox, unusual, wacky *colloq*, way-out *slang*
⊠ conventional, orthodox

unconvincing *adj* doubtful, dubious, feeble, fishy *colloq*, flimsy, implausible, improbable, lame, questionable, suspect, unlikely, weak
⊠ convincing, plausible

unco-ordinated *adj* awkward, bumbling, bungling, clodhopping, clumsy, disjointed, inept, maladroit *formal*, ungainly, ungraceful
⊠ graceful

uncouth *adj* awkward, bad-mannered, boorish, clumsy, coarse, crude, gauche, graceless, ill-mannered, impolite, improper, loutish, rough, rude, uncivilized, uncultivated, uncultured, unrefined, unseemly *formal*, unsophisticated, vulgar
⊠ polite, refined, urbane

uncover *v* **1** *to uncover a plot:* bring to light, detect, dig up, disclose, discover, divulge, expose, lay bare, leak, make known, reveal, show, unearth, unmask, unveil **2** *left the food uncovered:* bare, expose, open, peel, unwrap **3** *to uncover human remains:* dig up, exhume, unearth
⊠ **1** conceal, suppress **2** cover

uncritical *adj* accepting, credulous, gullible, naïve, non-judgemental, trusting, undiscerning, undiscriminating, unfussy, unquestioning, unselective
⊠ discerning, discriminating, sceptical

unctuous *adj* **1** *an unctuous smile:* fawning, glib, gushing, ingratiating, insincere, obsequious, pietistic, plausible, sanctimonious, servile, slick, smarmy *colloq*, smooth, suave, sycophantic **2** *something unctuous and gooey:* creamy, greasy, oily

uncultivated *adj* fallow, natural, rough, wild
⊠ cultivated

uncultured *adj* boorish, coarse, crude, hick, ill-bred, rough, rustic, uncivilized, uncouth, uncultivated, unintellectual, unrefined, unsophisticated
⊠ cultured, sophisticated

undaunted *adj* bold, brave, courageous, dauntless, fearless, indomitable, intrepid, resolute, steadfast, unalarmed, unbowed, undeterred, undiscouraged, undismayed, unflagging
⊠ discouraged, timorous

undecided *adj* ambivalent, debatable, dithering, doubtful, dubious, equivocating, hesitant, in two minds *colloq*, indefinite, irresolute, moot, open, uncertain, uncommitted, unestablished, unknown, unresolved, unsettled, unsure, up in the air *colloq*, vague, wavering
⊠ certain, decided, definite

undefeated *adj* supreme, triumphant, unbeaten, unbowed, unconquered, unsubdued, unsurpassed, unvanquished *formal*, victorious, winning
⊠ defeated, vanquished *formal*

undefended *adj* defenceless, exposed, naked, open, pregnable, unarmed, unfortified *formal*, unguarded, unprotected, vulnerable
⊠ armed, defended, fortified *formal*

undefiled *adj* chaste, clean, clear, flawless, immaculate, intact, inviolate *formal*, pure, sinless, spotless, unblemished, unsoiled, unspotted, unstained, unsullied, virginal

undefined *adj* formless, hazy, ill-defined, imprecise, indefinite, indeterminate *formal*, indistinct, inexact, nebulous, shadowy, tenuous, unclear, unexplained, unspecified, vague, woolly
⊠ definite, precise

undemonstrative *adj* aloof, cold, cool, distant, formal, impassive, phlegmatic, remote, reserved, restrained, reticent, stiff, uncommunicative, unemotional, unresponsive, withdrawn
⊠ communicative, demonstrative

undeniable *adj* beyond doubt, beyond question, certain, clear, definite, evident, incontrovertible, indisputable, indubitable, irrefutable *formal*, manifest *formal*, obvious, patent, positive, proven, sure, undoubted, unmistakable, unquestionable
⊠ questionable

undependable *adj* capricious, changeable, erratic, fair-weather, fickle, inconsistent, inconstant, irresponsible, mercurial, treacherous, uncertain, unpredictable, unreliable, unstable, untrustworthy, variable
⊠ dependable, reliable

under *prep* **1** *under the chair:* below, beneath, underneath **2** *under thirty:* below, less than, lower than **3** *served under two prime ministers:*

inferior to, junior to, secondary to, subordinate to, subservient to
🔁 **1** above, on top of **2** above, more than, over
♦ *adv* below, beneath, down, downward, less, lower, underneath

underclothes *n* frillies, lingerie, smalls *colloq*, underclothing, undergarments, underlinen, underwear, undies *colloq*, unmentionables *colloq*

undercover *adj* clandestine *formal*, concealed, confidential, covert, furtive, hidden, hush-hush *colloq*, intelligence, private, secret, sly, stealthy, surreptitious, underground
🔁 open, unconcealed

undercurrent *n* **1** *an undercurrent in the sea:* riptide, underflow, undertow **2** *an undercurrent of criticism:* atmosphere, aura, drift, feeling, flavour, hint, movement, overtone, sense, suggestion, tendency, tinge, trend, undertone, undertow

undercut *v* underbid, undercharge, undermine, underprice, undersell

underestimate *v* belittle, dismiss, disparage *formal*, fail to appreciate, look down on, minimize, miscalculate, misjudge, play down *colloq*, sell short, trivialize, underrate, undervalue
🔁 exaggerate, overestimate

undergo *v* bear, endure, experience, go through, put up with, stand, submit to, suffer, sustain, tolerate, weather, withstand

underground *adj* **1** *an underground passage:* buried, concealed, covered, hidden, subterranean, sunken **2** *an underground protest movement:* alternative, avant-garde, clandestine *formal*, covert, experimental, furtive, illegal, secret, subversive, surreptitious, undercover, unofficial, unorthodox
♦ *n* metro, subway, tube *colloq*
♦ *adv* below ground, below ground level, below the surface

undergrowth *n* bracken, brambles, briars, brush, brushwood, bushes, ground cover, scrub, thicket, vegetation

underhand *adj* clandestine *formal*, crafty, crooked *colloq*, deceitful, deceptive, devious, dishonest, fraudulent, furtive, immoral, improper, scheming, secret, shady *colloq*, sly, sneaky, stealthy, surreptitious, unethical, unscrupulous
🔁 above board *colloq*, honest, open

underline *v* accentuate, draw attention to, emphasize, highlight, italicize, mark, point up, stress, underscore
🔁 play down, soft-pedal

underling *n* flunkey, hireling, inferior, lackey, menial, minion, nobody, nonentity, servant, slave, subordinate
🔁 boss, leader, master

underlying *adj* basal *formal*, basic, concealed, elementary, essential, fundamental, hidden, intrinsic, latent, lurking, primary, root, veiled

undermine *v* **1** *undermine someone's position:* damage, destroy, erode, impair, injure, make less secure, mar, sabotage, sap, subvert, vitiate *formal*, weaken, wear away **2** *undermine the enemy defences:* dig, excavate, mine, tunnel
🔁 **1** fortify, strengthen

underprivileged *adj* deprived, destitute, disadvantaged, impecunious *formal*, impoverished, in distress, in need, in want, needy, oppressed, poor
🔁 affluent, fortunate, privileged

underrate *v* belittle, depreciate, dismiss, disparage *formal*, fail to appreciate, look down on, sell short, underestimate, undervalue
🔁 exaggerate, overrate

undersell *v* cut, depreciate, disparage *formal*, mark down, play down, reduce, sell short, undercut, understate

undersized *adj* achondroplastic *technical*, atrophied, dwarf, little, miniature, minute, pint-(sized) *colloq*, puny, pygmy, runtish, small, stunted, tiny, underdeveloped, underweight
🔁 big, oversized, overweight

understand *v* **1** *I don't understand it:* accept, appreciate, apprehend *formal*, click *colloq*, comprehend, cotton on *colloq*, discern, fathom, figure out, follow, get *colloq*, get the hang of *colloq*, get the message *colloq*, get the picture *colloq*, get wise *colloq*, get your head/mind round *colloq*, grasp, latch onto *colloq*, make out, penetrate, perceive, realize, recognize, rumble *colloq*, savvy *slang*, see, suss out *colloq*, take in, tumble to *colloq*, twig *colloq* **2** *no one understands me:* comfort, commiserate with, empathize with, feel for, feel sorry for, identify with, support, sympathize with **3** *I understand you are leaving:* assume, believe, conclude, gather, hear, know, learn, presume, suppose, think
🔁 **1** misunderstand

understanding *n* **1** *a good understanding of maths:* appreciation, apprehension *formal*, awareness, belief, comprehension *formal*, discernment, feeling, grasp, idea, impression, insight, intelligence, interpretation, judgement, knowledge, notion, opinion, perception, sense, view, wisdom **2** *come to an understanding:* accord *formal*, agreement, arrangement, bargain, compact *formal*, entente *formal*, harmony, pact **3** *treated me with understanding:* comfort, commiseration, compassion, consolation, empathy, support, sympathy, trust
♦ *adj* compassionate, considerate, forbearing, forgiving, kind, lenient, loving, patient, sensitive, supportive, sympathetic, tender, thoughtful, tolerant
🔁 impatient, insensitive, intolerant, unsympathetic

understate *v* belittle, dismiss, make light of, minimize, play down, soft-pedal *colloq*, underplay
🔁 emphasize, exaggerate

understood *adj* accepted, assumed, implicit, implied, inferred, presumed, tacit, unspoken, unstated, unwritten

understudy *n* deputy, double, fill-in *colloq*, locum, relief, replacement, reserve, stand-in, substitute

undertake *v* **1** *undertake to finish the job:* agree, contract, covenant, guarantee, pledge, promise **2** *undertake a huge project:* accept, assume, attempt, begin, commence *formal*, embark on, set about, tackle, take on, try

undertaker *n* funeral director, funeral furnisher, mortician *US*

undertaking *n* **1** *a momentous undertaking:* affair, attempt, business, campaign, effort, endeavour, enterprise, job, operation, plan, project, scheme, task, venture **2** *give a solemn undertaking:* assurance, commitment, guarantee, pledge, promise, vow, warrant, word

undertone *n* atmosphere, aura, feeling, flavour, hint, intimation, murmur, suggestion, tinge, touch, trace, undercurrent, whisper

undervalue *v* depreciate, dismiss, disparage *formal*, look down on, minimize, misjudge, sell short, underestimate, underrate
🖅 exaggerate, overrate

underwater *adj* immersed, subaquatic, subaqueous *formal*, submarine, submerged, sunken, undersea

underwear *n* frillies, lingerie, smalls *colloq*, underclothes, undergarments, undies *colloq*

underweight *adj* half-starved, thin, underfed, undernourished, undersized
🖅 overweight

underworld *n* **1** *a police campaign against the underworld:* criminal world, gangland, organized crime, the mob *slang* **2** *the Greek god of the underworld:* Hades, hell, infernal regions, nether world, the Inferno

underwrite *v* **1** *underwrite a deal:* approve, authorize, back, confirm, endorse, finance, fund, guarantee, insure, sanction, sponsor, subscribe, subsidize, support **2** *underwrite a cheque:* countersign, endorse, initial, sign

undesirable *adj* disagreeable, disliked, distasteful, foul, nasty, objectionable, obnoxious, offensive, repugnant *formal*, unacceptable, unpleasant, unsuitable, unwanted, unwelcome, unwished-for
🖅 desirable, pleasant

undeveloped *adj* **1** *undeveloped nations:* developing, less advanced, Third World, underdeveloped **2** *an undeveloped fetus:* embryonic, immature, inchoate *formal*, latent, potential, primordial *formal*, stunted, unformed
🖅 **1** advanced, industrialized **2** developed, mature

undignified *adj* clumsy, foolish, improper, inappropriate, indecorous *formal*, inelegant, unbecoming, ungainly, unseemly *formal*, unsuitable
🖅 dignified, elegant

undisciplined *adj* disobedient, disorganized, obstreperous, uncontrolled, unpredictable, unreliable, unrestrained, unruly, unschooled, unsteady, unsystematic, untrained, wayward, wild, wilful
🖅 disciplined, self-controlled

undisguised *adj* apparent, blatant, evident, explicit, frank, genuine, manifest *formal*, naked, obvious, open, outright, overt, patent, stark, thoroughgoing, transparent, unadorned, unconcealed, utter
🖅 concealed, hidden, secret

undisputed *adj* accepted, acknowledged, certain, conclusive, incontrovertible, indisputable, irrefutable *formal*, recognized, sure, unchallenged, uncontested, undeniable, undoubted, unquestioned
🖅 debatable, uncertain

undistinguished *adj* banal, common, everyday, indifferent, inferior, mediocre, no great shakes *colloq*, not all that it is cracked up to be *colloq*, not much cop *colloq*, not up to much *colloq*, nothing much to write about *colloq*, ordinary, pedestrian, run-of-the-mill *colloq*, so-so *colloq*, unexceptional, unimpressive, unremarkable
🖅 distinguished, exceptional, remarkable

undisturbed *adj* calm, collected, composed, equable, even, motionless, placid, quiet, serene, tranquil, unaffected, unconcerned, uninterrupted, unperturbed *formal*, unruffled, untouched, untroubled
🖅 disturbed, interrupted

undivided *adj* combined, complete, concentrated, dedicated, entire, exclusive, full, intact, serious, sincere, solid, total, unanimous, unbroken, united, unqualified, unreserved, whole, wholehearted

undo *v* **1** *undo a fastening:* disentangle, free, loose, loosen, open, release, separate, unbuckle, unbutton, unfasten, unhook, unlock, untie, unwind, unwrap, unzip **2** *undo all my good work:* defeat, destroy, mar, obliterate, ruin, spoil, subvert, undermine, upset, wreck **3** *undo the court's judgement:* annul, cancel, invalidate, nullify *formal*, overturn, quash, repeal, reverse, revoke, set aside
🖅 **1** do up, fasten

undoing *n* collapse, defeat, destruction, disgrace, downfall, overthrow, reversal, ruin, ruination, shame, weakness

undone *adj* **1** *things left undone:* forgotten, ignored, incomplete, left, neglected, omitted, outstanding, passed over, uncompleted, unfinished, unfulfilled **2** *his trousers were undone:* loose, open, unbuttoned, unfastened, unlaced, unlocked, untied **3** *we are utterly undone!:* betrayed, destroyed, lost, ruined
🖅 **1** accomplished, complete, done **2** fastened

undoubted *adj* acknowledged, certain, definite, incontrovertible, indisputable, indubitable *formal*, irrefutable *formal*, obvious, patent, sure, unchallenged, uncontested, undeniable, undisputed, unquestionable

undoubtedly *adv* assuredly, beyond doubt, certainly, definitely, doubtless, indubitably *formal*, no doubt, of course, surely, undeniably, unmistakably, unquestionably, without doubt

undreamed-of *adj* amazing, astonishing, inconceivable, incredible, miraculous, undreamt, unexpected, unforeseen, unheard-of, unhoped-for, unimagined, unsuspected, unthought-of

undress *v* disrobe, divest *formal*, peel off *colloq*, remove, shed, strip, take off, unclothe
♦ *n* déshabillé, disarray *formal*, dishabille, nakedness, nudity

undressed *adj* disrobed, naked, nude, stark naked, stripped, unclothed
🖅 clothed

undue *adj* disproportionate, excessive, extravagant, extreme, immoderate, improper, inappropriate, inordinate, needless, superfluous, uncalled-for, undeserved,

unjustified, unnecessary, unreasonable, unwarranted
F3 moderate, proper, reasonable

undulate *v* billow, heave, ripple, rise and fall, roll, surge, swell, wave

undulating *adj* billowing, flexuose *formal*, flexuous *formal*, rippling, rolling, sinuous, undate *formal*, undulant *formal*, wavy
F3 flat

unduly *adv* disproportionately, excessively, immoderately, inordinately, out of all proportion, over, too, unjustifiably, unnecessarily, unreasonably
F3 moderately, reasonably

undying *adj* abiding *formal*, constant, continuing, deathless, eternal, everlasting, immortal, imperishable, indestructible, inextinguishable, infinite, lasting, perennial, permanent, perpetual, sempiternal *formal*, undiminished, unending, unfading
F3 impermanent, inconstant

unearth *v* bring to light, detect, dig up, discover, disinter, excavate, exhume, expose, find, reveal, uncover
F3 bury

unearthly *adj* 1 *unearthly sounds:* creepy *colloq*, eerie, eldritch *Scot*, ghostly, other-worldly, phantom, preternatural *formal*, spine-chilling, strange, supernatural, uncanny, weird 2 *at this unearthly hour:* appalling, horrendous *colloq*, outrageous, preposterous, ungodly, unreasonable
F3 2 reasonable

uneasiness *n* agitation, alarm, anxiety, apprehension, apprehensiveness, dis-ease, disquiet, doubt, inquietude *formal*, misgiving, nervousness, perturbation *formal*, qualms, suspicion, unease, worry
F3 calm, composure

uneasy *adj* 1 *uneasy at the prospect of change:* agitated, alarmed, anxious, apprehensive, disturbed, edgy, impatient, insecure, jittery *colloq*, keyed up *colloq*, nervous, nervy *colloq*, on edge *colloq*, perturbed *formal*, restless, shaky, strained, tense, troubled, twitchy *colloq*, uncomfortable, unsettled, unsure, upset, worried, wound up *colloq* 2 *an uneasy silence:* disconcerting, disturbing, perturbing *formal*, troubling, unnerving, unsettling, worrying
F3 1 calm, composed

uneconomic *adj* loss-making, non-profit-making, uncommercial, unprofitable
F3 economic, profitable, profit-making, remunerative

uneducated *adj* benighted, ignorant, illiterate, philistine, uncultivated, uncultured, unread, unschooled, untaught
F3 educated

unemotional *adj* apathetic, cold, cool, detached, dispassionate, impassive, indifferent, objective, passionless, phlegmatic, reserved, undemonstrative, unexcitable, unfeeling, unresponsive
F3 emotional, excitable

unemphatic *adj* down-beat *colloq*, played-down, underplayed, understated, unobtrusive, unostentatious

unemployed *adj* idle, jobless, laid off, on the dole *colloq*, out of work, redundant, unoccupied, unwaged
F3 employed, occupied

unending *adj* ceaseless, constant, continual, continuous, endless, eternal, everlasting, incessant, interminable, never-ending, perpetual, unceasing, undying, uninterrupted, unremitting *formal*
F3 intermittent, transient

unendurable *adj* insufferable, insupportable, intolerable, overwhelming, shattering, unbearable
F3 bearable, endurable

unenthusiastic *adj* apathetic, blasé, bored, cool, half-hearted, indifferent, Laodicean, lukewarm, neutral, nonchalant, unimpressed, uninterested, unmoved, unresponsive
F3 enthusiastic

unenviable *adj* difficult, disagreeable, thankless, uncomfortable, uncongenial, undesirable, unpleasant
F3 desirable, enviable

unequal *adj* 1 *unequal treatment:* biased, different, discriminatory, dissimilar, inequitable, unfair, unjust, unlike, varying 2 *an unequal contest:* lopsided, unbalanced, uneven, unfair 3 *unequal to a task:* inadequate, incapable, incompetent, not cut out for *colloq*, not up to *colloq*, unfitted, unqualified, unsuited
F3 2 even, fair 3 equal

unequalled *adj* incomparable, inimitable, matchless, nonpareil *formal*, paramount, peerless, pre-eminent, supreme, surpassing, transcendent, unique, unmatched, unparalleled, unrivalled, unsurpassed

unequivocal *adj* absolute, categorical, clear, definite, direct, distinct, evident, explicit, express, incontrovertible, outright, plain, positive, straight, straightforward, unambiguous, unmistakable, unqualified, unreserved
F3 ambiguous, qualified, vague

unerring *adj* accurate, certain, dead *colloq*, exact, faultless, impeccable, infallible, perfect, sure, uncanny, unfailing
F3 fallible

unethical *adj* dishonest, dishonourable, disreputable, evil, illegal, illicit, immoral, improper, shady *colloq*, underhand, unprincipled, unprofessional, unscrupulous, wicked, wrong
F3 ethical

uneven *adj* 1 *uneven ground:* bumpy, coarse, craggy, irregular, jagged, lumpy, rough, rugged, stony 2 *uneven shapes:* asymmetrical, crooked, lopsided, odd 3 *an uneven contest:* ill-matched, inequitable, lopsided, one-sided, unbalanced, unequal, unfair 4 *uneven progress:* changeable, erratic, fitful, fluctuating, inconsistent, intermittent, irregular, jerky, patchy, spasmodic, unsteady, variable
F3 1 even, flat, level 2 even 3 equal, even 4 consistent, regular

uneventful *adj* boring, commonplace, dull, everyday, humdrum, monotonous, ordinary, quiet, routine, run-of-the-mill *colloq*, tedious,

unexceptional, unexciting, uninteresting, unmemorable, unremarkable, unvaried
☒ eventful, memorable, remarkable

unexampled *adj* incomparable, never before seen, novel, unequalled, unheard-of, unique, unmatched, unparalleled, unprecedented

unexceptional *adj* average, common, everyday, indifferent, mediocre, no great shakes *colloq*, normal, not all that it is cracked up to be *colloq*, not much cop *colloq*, not up to much *colloq*, nothing much to write about *colloq*, ordinary, run-of-the-mill *colloq*, so-so *colloq*, typical, undistinguished, unimpressive, unmemorable, unremarkable, usual
☒ exceptional, impressive

unexpected *adj* abrupt, accidental, amazing, astonishing, chance, fortuitous, startling, sudden, surprising, unanticipated, unforeseen, unlooked-for, unpredictable, unusual
☒ expected, predictable

unexpectedly *adv* abruptly, by chance, fortuitously, out of the blue *colloq*, suddenly, surprisingly, unpredictably, without warning

unexpressive *adj* blank, dead-pan, emotionless, expressionless, immobile, impassive, inexpressive, inscrutable, vacant
☒ expressive, mobile

unfading *adj* abiding *formal*, durable, enduring, evergreen, fadeless, fast, imperishable, lasting, undying, unfailing
☒ changeable, transient

unfailing *adj* certain, constant, dependable, faithful, inexhaustible, infallible, loyal, reliable, staunch, steadfast, steady, sure, true, undying, unfading
☒ fickle, impermanent, transient

unfair *adj* **1** *an unfair decision*: arbitrary, biased, bigoted, discriminatory, inequitable *formal*, one-sided, partial, partisan, prejudiced, slanted, unbalanced, uncalled-for, undeserved, unjust, unmerited, unreasonable, unwarranted, weighted **2** *unfair treatment*: below the belt *colloq*, bent *colloq*, crooked *colloq*, deceitful, dishonest, shady *colloq*, unethical, unprincipled, unscrupulous, wrongful
☒ **1** deserved, fair, just, unbiased **2** ethical, honest

unfairness *n* bias, bigotry, discrimination, inequity, injustice, one-sidedness, partiality, partisanship, prejudice
☒ equity, fairness

unfaithful *adj* **1** *a friend who proved unfaithful*: deceitful, dishonest, disloyal, double-dealing, duplicitous *formal*, faithless, false, inconstant, insincere, perfidious *formal*, treacherous, unbelieving, unreliable, untrue, untrustworthy **2** *an unfaithful lover*: adulterous, cheating, deceitful, faithless, false, fickle, inconstant, two-timing *colloq*
☒ **1** faithful, loyal, reliable **2** faithful

unfaltering *adj* constant, firm, fixed, indefatigable, pertinacious *formal*, resolute, steadfast, steady, tireless, unfailing, unflagging, unflinching, unswerving, untiring, unwavering, unyielding
☒ faltering, uncertain, wavering

unfamiliar *adj* **1** *unfamiliar territory*: alien, curious, different, foreign, new, novel, strange,

uncharted, uncommon, unexplored, unknown, unusual **2** *unfamiliar with this software*: inexperienced, unaccustomed, unacquainted, unconversant, uninformed, unpractised, unskilled, unversed
☒ **1** familiar **2** conversant

unfashionable *adj* antiquated, dated, démodé, obsolete, old hat *colloq*, old-fashioned, out, out of date, outmoded, passé, square *colloq*, unpopular
☒ fashionable

unfasten *v* detach, disconnect, loosen, open, separate, unclasp, uncouple, undo, unlock, untie, unwrap
☒ bolt, do up, fasten, lock

unfathomable *adj* **1** *for some unfathomable reason*: abstruse *formal*, baffling, esoteric *formal*, hidden, impenetrable, incomprehensible, indecipherable, inexplicable, inscrutable, mysterious, unknowable **2** *the unfathomable ocean*: bottomless, deep, fathomless, immeasurable, impenetrable, profound, unplumbed, unsounded
☒ **1** comprehensible, explicable **2** penetrable

unfavourable *adj* **1** *an unfavourable sign*: adverse, bad, contrary, disadvantageous, discouraging, inauspicious *formal*, inopportune, negative, ominous, poor, threatening, unfortunate, unlucky, unpromising, unseasonable, untimely **2** *unfavourable reviews of her work*: adverse, bad, critical, hostile, inimical *formal*, negative, poor, uncomplimentary
☒ **1** auspicious *formal*, favourable, promising **2** complimentary, friendly, good

unfeeling *adj* apathetic, callous, cold, cruel, hard, hard-hearted, harsh, heartless, inhuman, insensitive, pitiless, stony, uncaring, unsympathetic
☒ sensitive, sympathetic

unfeigned *adj* frank, genuine, heartfelt, natural, pure, real, sincere, spontaneous, unaffected, unforced, wholehearted
☒ feigned, insincere, pretended

unfettered *adj* free, unbridled, unchecked, unconfined, unconstrained, unhampered, unhindered, uninhibited, unrestrained, unshackled, untrammelled
☒ constrained, fettered

unfinished *adj* **1** *the job remained unfinished*: deficient, half-done, imperfect, incomplete, lacking, unaccomplished, uncompleted, undone, unfulfilled, wanting **2** *an unfinished draft*: crude, imperfect, incomplete, rough, sketchy
☒ **1** finished **2** finished, perfect

unfit *adj* **1** *unfit for the task*: ill-equipped, inadequate, inappropriate, inapt, incapable, incompetent, ineffective, ineligible, unable, unequal, unprepared, unqualified, unsuitable, unsuited, untrained, useless **2** *I'm so unfit these days!*: debilitated *formal*, decrepit, feeble, flabby, out of condition, unhealthy, weak
☒ **1** competent, fit, suitable **2** fit, healthy

unflagging *adj* constant, fixed, indefatigable, never-failing, persevering, persistent, single-minded, staunch, steady, tireless, unceasing, undeviating, unfailing, unfaltering, unremitting *formal*, unswerving, untiring
☒ faltering, inconstant

unflappable *adj* calm, collected, composed, cool, equable, impassive, imperturbable *formal*, level-headed, phlegmatic, self-possessed, unexcitable, unruffled, unworried
🔁 excitable, nervous, panicky *colloq*, temperamental

unflattering *adj* blunt, candid, critical, honest, outspoken, unbecoming, uncomplimentary, unfavourable, unprepossessing
🔁 complimentary, flattering

unflinching *adj* bold, constant, determined, firm, fixed, resolute, stalwart, staunch, steadfast, steady, sure, unblinking, unfaltering, unshaken, unshrinking, unswerving, unwavering
🔁 scared, unsteady

unfold *v* 1 *watch events unfold:* come about, develop, emerge, evolve, grow, result, work out 2 *unfolded her plans:* clarify, describe, disclose, elaborate, explain, make known, narrate, present, relate, reveal, show, tell 3 *unfold a map:* flatten, open (out), spread out, straighten (out), stretch out, uncoil, uncover, undo, unfurl, unravel, unroll, unwrap
🔁 2 suppress, withhold 3 fold, wrap

unforeseen *adj* startling, sudden, surprising, unanticipated, unexpected, unlooked-for, unpredictable, unpredicted, unusual
🔁 expected, predictable

unforgettable *adj* distinctive, exceptional, extraordinary, historic, important, impressive, indelible, memorable, momentous, notable, noteworthy, remarkable, significant, special, striking
🔁 unexceptional, unmemorable

unforgivable *adj* contemptible, deplorable, disgraceful, indefensible, inexcusable, intolerable, outrageous, reprehensible *formal*, shameful, unjustifiable, unpardonable
🔁 forgivable, venial

unforgiven *adj* unabsolved, unredeemed, unregenerate
🔁 absolved, forgiven

unfortunate *adj* 1 *an unfortunate accident:* adverse, calamitous, disadvantageous, disastrous, doomed, hapless *formal*, hopeless, ill-fated, luckless, poor, ruinous, unhappy, unlucky, unpleasant, unsuccessful, untoward, wretched 2 *an unfortunate decision:* adverse, deplorable, ill-advised, ill-timed, inappropriate, injudicious *formal*, inopportune, lamentable, regrettable, unfavourable, unsuitable, untimely
🔁 1 fortunate, happy 2 appropriate, favourable

unfortunately *adv* alas, regrettably, sad to relate, sad to say, sadly, unhappily, unluckily, worse luck *colloq*
🔁 fortunately

unfounded *adj* baseless, conjectural *formal*, fabricated, false, groundless, idle, spurious, trumped-up, uncorroborated *formal*, unjustified, unproven, unsubstantiated, unsupported, without foundation
🔁 justified, substantiated

unfrequented *adj* deserted, desolate, God-forsaken, isolated, lone, lonely, remote, secluded, sequestered *formal*, solitary, uninhabited, unvisited
🔁 busy, crowded, populous

unfriendly *adj* aggressive, aloof, antagonistic, chilly, cold, cool, disagreeable, distant, frosty, hostile, ill-disposed, inhospitable, inimical *formal*, quarrelsome, sour, standoffish, strained, surly, unapproachable, uncongenial, unkind, unneighbourly, unpleasant, unsociable, unwelcoming
🔁 agreeable, amiable, friendly

unfruitful *adj* arid, barren, fruitless, impoverished, infecund *formal*, infertile, infructuous *formal*, sterile, unproductive, unprofitable, unprolific, unrewarding
🔁 fruitful, productive

ungainly *adj* awkward, clumsy, gangling, gauche, gawky, inelegant, loutish, lumbering, maladroit *formal*, unco-ordinated, uncouth, ungraceful, unwieldy
🔁 elegant, graceful

ungodly *adj* 1 *an ungodly hour:* horrendous *colloq*, intolerable, outrageous, preposterous, unearthly, unreasonable, unsocial 2 *ungodly men:* blasphemous, corrupt, depraved, godless, immoral, impious, iniquitous *formal*, irreligious, profane, sinful, wicked

ungovernable *adj* disorderly, masterless, rebellious, refractory *formal*, uncontrollable, ungoverned, unmanageable, unrestrainable, unruly, wild

ungracious *adj* bad-mannered, boorish, churlish, discourteous, disrespectful, graceless, ill-bred, impolite, offhand, rude, uncivil, unmannerly
🔁 gracious, polite

ungrateful *adj* ill-mannered, impolite, rude, selfish, unappreciative, uncivil, ungracious, unthankful
🔁 grateful, thankful

unguarded *adj* 1 *in an unguarded moment:* careless, foolhardy, foolish, heedless, ill-considered, impolitic *formal*, imprudent *formal*, inattentive, incautious, indiscreet, off guard, rash, thoughtless, uncircumspect *formal*, undiplomatic, unthinking, unwary 2 *an unguarded fort:* defenceless, exposed, undefended, unpatrolled, unprotected, vulnerable
🔁 1 cautious, guarded 2 defended, protected

unhappily *adv* alas, regrettably, sad to relate, sad to say, sadly, unfortunately, unluckily, worse luck *colloq*
🔁 fortunately

unhappy *adj* 1 *an unhappy person:* blue *colloq*, crestfallen, dejected, depressed, despondent, disconsolate *formal*, dispirited, down *colloq*, down in the dumps *colloq*, downcast, fed up *colloq*, gloomy, glum, long-faced, low *colloq*, melancholy, miserable, mournful, sad, sorrowful, woebegone *formal* 2 *an unhappy knack of getting lost:* awkward, clumsy, hapless *formal*, ill-advised, ill-chosen, ill-fated, ill-starred, inappropriate, inapt, injudicious *formal*, tactless, unfortunate, unlucky, unsuitable
🔁 1 happy 2 fortunate, suitable.

unharmed *adj* intact, safe, sound, undamaged, unhurt, uninjured, unscathed, untouched, whole
🔁 harmed, hurt, injured

unhealthy *adj* **1** *an unhealthy child:* ailing, debilitated *formal*, feeble, frail, ill, indisposed *formal*, infirm, invalid, poorly, sick, sickly, unsound, unwell, weak **2** *unhealthy living conditions:* insalubrious *formal*, insanitary, noxious, unhygienic **3** *an unhealthy interest in guns:* detrimental, harmful, injurious, insalutary, morbid, unnatural, unwholesome
☞ **1** fit, healthy **2** hygienic **3** natural, wholesome

unheard-of *adj* **1** *unheard-of behaviour:* exceptional, extraordinary, inconceivable, offensive, outrageous, preposterous, shocking, unacceptable, unbelievable, undreamed-of, unimaginable, unprecedented, unthinkable **2** *an unheard-of composer:* new, obscure, undiscovered, unfamiliar, unheralded, unknown, unsung
☞ **1** acceptable, normal **2** famous

unheeded *adj* disobeyed, disregarded, forgotten, ignored, neglected, overlooked, unnoted, unnoticed, unobserved, unremarked
☞ noted, observed

unheralded *adj* surprise, unadvertised, unannounced, unexpected, unforeseen, unnoticed, unproclaimed, unpublicized, unrecognized, unsung
☞ acclaimed, advertised, publicized, trumpeted

unhesitating *adj* automatic, confident, immediate, implicit, instant, instantaneous, prompt, ready, spontaneous, unfaltering, unquestioning, unwavering, wholehearted
☞ hesitant, tentative

unhinge *v* confuse, craze, derange, disorder, distract, drive mad, madden, unbalance, unnerve, unsettle, upset

unholy *adj* **1** *unholy thoughts:* blasphemous, corrupt, depraved, evil, godless, immoral, impious, iniquitous *formal*, irreligious, sinful, ungodly, wicked **2** *an unholy mess:* horrendous *colloq*, outrageous, shocking, unearthly, ungodly, unreasonable
☞ **1** godly, holy, pious **2** reasonable

unhoped-for *adj* surprising, unanticipated, unbelievable, undreamed-of, unexpected, unforeseen, unimagined, unlooked-for

unhurried *adj* calm, deliberate, easy, easy-going *colloq*, laid-back *colloq*, leisurely, relaxed, sedate, slow
☞ hasty, hurried, rushed

unhurt *adj* intact, safe, sound, unharmed, uninjured, unscathed, untouched, whole
☞ hurt, injured

unidentified *adj* anonymous, incognito, mysterious, nameless, obscure, strange, unclassified, unfamiliar, unknown, unmarked, unnamed, unrecognized
☞ identified, known, named

unification *n* alliance, amalgamation, coalescence, coalition, combination, confederation, enosis *formal*, federation, fusion, incorporation, merger, union, uniting
☞ division, separation, split

uniform *n* costume, dress, garb *colloq*, livery, outfit, regalia, regimentals, rig *colloq*, robes, suit
♦ *adj* **1** *uniform patterns:* alike, consistent, equal, homogeneous, identical, invariable, like, monotonous, similar, the same, unchanging, unvarying **2** *uniform progress:* consistent,

constant, even, flat, regular, smooth, stable, unbroken, undeviating
☞ **1** changing, different, variable **2** irregular

uniformity *n* constancy, evenness, flatness, homogeneity *formal*, homomorphism *formal*, invariability, monotony, regularity, sameness, similarity, similitude *formal*
☞ difference, dissimilarity, variation

unify *v* amalgamate, bind, blend, bring/come together, coalesce, combine, consolidate, fuse, integrate, join, merge, mix, unite, weld
☞ divide, separate, split

unimaginable *adj* amazing, astonishing, extraordinary, fantastic, far-fetched, inconceivable, incredible, mind-boggling *colloq*, outlandish, preposterous, staggering, unbelievable, unconvincing, undreamed-of, unheard-of, unlikely, unthinkable

unimaginative *adj* banal, barren, boring, dry, dull, hackneyed, lifeless, matter-of-fact *colloq*, mundane, ordinary, pedestrian, predictable, routine, samey *colloq*, stale, tame, unexciting, uninspired, unoriginal, usual
☞ creative, imaginative, original

unimpeachable *adj* blameless, dependable, faultless, immaculate, impeccable, irreproachable, perfect, reliable, spotless, unassailable, unblemished, unchallengeable, unquestionable
☞ blameworthy, faulty

unimpeded *adj* clear, free, open, unblocked, unchecked, unconstrained, unhampered, unhindered, uninhibited, unrestrained, untrammelled
☞ hampered, impeded

unimportant *adj* immaterial, incidental, inconsequential, insignificant, insubstantial, irrelevant, marginal, minor, negligible, no big deal *colloq*, no great shakes *colloq*, not worth mentioning *colloq*, nugatory *formal*, peripheral, petty, secondary, slight, trifling, trivial, worthless
☞ important, relevant, significant, vital

uninhabited *adj* abandoned, deserted, desolate, empty, unoccupied, unpeopled, unpopulated, unsettled, vacant

uninhibited *adj* abandoned, candid, frank, free, informal, liberated, natural, open, outspoken, relaxed, spontaneous, unconstrained, uncontrolled, unreserved, unrestrained, unrestricted, unselfconscious
☞ constrained, inhibited, repressed, restrained

uninspired *adj* boring, commonplace, dull, humdrum, indifferent, ordinary, pedestrian, prosaic, stale, stock, trite, undistinguished, unexciting, unimaginative, uninspiring, uninteresting, unoriginal
☞ exciting, inspired, original

unintelligent *adj* brainless, dense, dull, dumb *colloq*, empty-headed, fatuous, foolish, gormless *colloq*, half-witted, obtuse, silly, slow, stupid, thick *colloq*, unreasoning, unthinking
☞ intelligent

unintelligible *adj* complex, complicated, double Dutch *colloq*, garbled, illegible, impenetrable, inarticulate, incoherent, incomprehensible, indecipherable, involved,

jumbled, muddled, mysterious, obscure, puzzling, scrambled, unfathomable, unreadable
Ⓔ clear, comprehensible, intelligible

unintentional *adj* accidental, careless, fortuitous *formal*, inadvertent, involuntary, uncalculated, unconscious, unintended, unplanned, unpremeditated, unwitting
Ⓔ deliberate, intentional

uninterested *adj* apathetic, blasé, bored, distant, impassive, indifferent, listless, unconcerned, unenthusiastic, uninvolved, unresponsive
Ⓔ concerned, curious, enthusiastic, interested, responsive

---

uninterested or *disinterested*? See panel at **disinterested**

---

uninteresting *adj* boring, drab, dreary, dry, dull, flat, humdrum, monotonous, pedestrian, prosaic, stale, tame, tedious, tiresome, uneventful, unexciting, unimpressive, uninspiring, wearisome
Ⓔ entertaining, exciting, interesting

uninterrupted *adj* ceaseless, constant, continual, continuous, endless, non-stop, peaceful, steady, sustained, unbroken, unceasing, undisturbed, unending, unremitting *formal*
Ⓔ broken, intermittent

uninvited *adj* unasked, unsolicited, unsought, unwanted, unwelcome
Ⓔ invited

uninviting *adj* disagreeable, distasteful, offensive, off-putting, repellent, repulsive, unappealing, unappetizing, unattractive, undesirable, unpleasant, unsavoury, unwelcoming
Ⓔ inviting, welcome

union *n* **1** *a union of two parts:* alliance, amalgamation, association, blend, coalition, combination, confederation, consolidation, fusion, joining, junction, league, merger, mixture, synthesis, unification, unity **2** *the steelworkers' union:* alliance, association, club, coalition, confederacy, consortium, federation, league, trade union **3** *we are all in union:* accord *formal*, agreement, concurrence *formal*, harmony, unanimity, unity **4** *the union of Andrew and Claire:* marriage, matrimony *formal*, nuptials *formal*, wedding
Ⓔ **1** separation **4** divorce

unique *adj* incomparable, inimitable, matchless, nonpareil *formal*, one and only, one of a kind, one-off, only, peerless, single, sole, solitary, sui generis *formal*, unequalled, unmatched, unparalleled, unprecedented, unrivalled
Ⓔ common

unison *n* accord *formal*, concert, concord *formal*, unanimity, unity

unit *n* assembly, component, constituent, element, entity, item, module, one, part, piece, portion, section, segment, system, whole

unite *v* **1** *unite the warring factions:* amalgamate, blend, combine, connect, consolidate, couple, fuse, join, link together, marry, pull together *colloq*, unify, weld together **2** *the clubs agreed to unite:* ally together, band together, coalesce, confederate, co-operate, federate, form an

alliance, join forces, link up, merge, pull together *colloq*
Ⓔ **1** separate, sever **2** separate, split up

united *adj* affiliated, agreed, allied, amalgamated, collective, combined, concerted, co-operative, corporate, in accord *formal*, in agreement, like-minded, one, pooled, unanimous, unified
Ⓔ disunited

unity *n* **1** *unity among the workforce:* accord *formal*, agreement, concert *formal*, concord *formal*, consensus, harmony, peace, solidarity, togetherness *colloq*, unanimity **2** *act with unity of purpose:* integrity, oneness, unification, wholeness
Ⓔ **1** disagreement, discord, disunity, strife

universal *adj* across-the-board, all-embracing, all-inclusive, all-round, common, comprehensive, cosmic, entire, general, global, omnipresent *formal*, total, ubiquitous *formal*, unlimited, whole, worldwide

universality *n* all-inclusiveness, commonness, completeness, comprehensiveness, entirety, generality, prevalence, totality, ubiquity *formal*

universally *adv* always, everywhere, invariably, ubiquitously *formal*, uniformly

universe *n* cosmos, creation, firmament, heavens, macrocosm *formal*, nature, world

university *n* academia *formal*, academy, college, institute, varsity *colloq*

unjust *adj* biased, inequitable *formal*, one-sided, partial, partisan, prejudiced, undeserved, unfair, unjustified, unreasonable, wrong
Ⓔ fair, just, reasonable

unjustifiable *adj* excessive, immoderate, indefensible, inexcusable, outrageous, unacceptable, uncalled-for, unforgivable, unpardonable, unreasonable, unwarranted
Ⓔ acceptable, justifiable

unkempt *adj* dishevelled, disordered, messy, rumpled, scruffy, shabby, shambolic *colloq*, slobbish *colloq*, sloppy *colloq*, slovenly, tousled, uncombed, ungroomed, untidy
Ⓔ tidy, well-groomed

unkind *adj* bitchy *colloq*, callous, cold-hearted, cruel, hard-hearted, harsh, heartless, inconsiderate, inhuman, inhumane, insensitive, malevolent *formal*, malicious, mean, nasty, pitiless, ruthless, shabby *colloq*, snide, spiteful, thoughtless, uncaring, uncharitable, unfeeling, unfriendly, unsympathetic, vicious
Ⓔ considerate, generous, kind, kindly, sympathetic

unkindness *n* callousness, cruelty, hard-heartedness, harshness, inhumanity, insensitivity, maliciousness, meanness, spite, uncharitableness, unfriendliness
Ⓔ friendship, kindness

unknown *adj* alien, anonymous, concealed, dark, foreign, hidden, incognito, mysterious, nameless, new, obscure, secret, strange, uncharted, undisclosed, undiscovered, undivulged, unexplored, unfamiliar, unheard-of, unidentified, unnamed, unrevealed, untold
Ⓔ familiar, known

unlawful *adj* against the law, banned, criminal, forbidden, illegal, illegitimate, illicit, outlawed,

prohibited, unauthorized, unconstitutional, unlicensed, unsanctioned
▣ allowed, lawful, legal, permitted

unleash *v* free, let loose, loose, release, unloose, untether, untie
▣ restrain

unlettered *adj* ignorant, illiterate, uneducated, unlearned, unlessoned, unschooled, untaught, untutored
▣ educated

unlike *adj* contrasted, different, disparate *formal*, dissimilar, distinct, divergent, diverse, ill-matched, incompatible, opposed, opposite, unequal, unrelated
▣ related, similar
◆ *prep* as against, as opposed to, different from, dissimilar to, in contrast to
▣ like

unlikely *adj* 1 *an unlikely outcome*: doubtful, dubious, far-fetched, implausible, improbable, inconceivable, incredible, questionable, suspect, suspicious, unbelievable, unexpected, unimaginable 2 *an unlikely chance of success*: distant, faint, inconsiderable, remote, slight, slim, small
▣ 1 likely, plausible

unlimited *adj* absolute, all-encompassing, boundless, complete, countless, endless, extensive, full, great, illimitable, immeasurable, immense, incalculable, indefinite, infinite, limitless, total, unbounded, unchecked, unconditional, unconstrained, uncontrolled, unhampered, unimpeded, unqualified, unrestricted, untold, vast
▣ limited

unload *v* discharge, dump, empty, offload, relieve, unburden, unpack
▣ load

unlock *v* free, open, release, unbar, unbolt, undo, unfasten, unlatch
▣ fasten, lock

unlooked-for *adj* chance, fortuitous *formal*, fortunate, lucky, surprise, surprising, unanticipated, undreamed-of, unexpected, unforeseen, unhoped-for, unpredicted, unthought-of
▣ expected, predictable

unloved *adj* detested, disliked, hated, loveless, neglected, rejected, spurned, uncared-for, unpopular, unwanted
▣ loved

unlucky *adj* 1 *an unlucky person*: cursed, doomed, down on your luck *colloq*, hapless *formal*, ill-fated, ill-starred, jinxed, luckless, miserable, poor, star-crossed, unfortunate, unhappy, unsuccessful, wretched 2 *an unlucky omen*: adverse, calamitous, catastrophic, disadvantageous, disastrous, doomed, ill-fated, inauspicious *formal*, ominous, unfavourable, unfortunate, unpleasant, unpromising, unpropitious *formal*, untoward
▣ 1 fortunate, lucky 2 favourable, lucky

unmanageable *adj* 1 *unmanageable suitcases*: awkward, bulky, cumbersome, incommodious *formal*, inconvenient, unhandy, unwieldy 2 *unmanageable children*: difficult, disorderly, obstreperous, recalcitrant *formal*, refractory

formal, uncontrollable, ungovernable, unruly, wild
▣ 1 manageable 2 controllable

unmanly *adj* chicken-hearted, cowardly, craven, dishonourable, effeminate, namby-pamby, soft, weak, weak-kneed, wet *colloq*, wimpish *colloq*, yellow *colloq*
▣ manly

unmannerly *adj* badly-behaved, bad-mannered, boorish, discourteous, disrespectful, graceless, ill-bred, ill-mannered, impolite, low-bred, rude, uncivil, uncouth, ungracious
▣ polite

unmarried *adj* available, celibate, divorced, lone, on your own, single, unattached, unwed
▣ married

unmask *v* bare, detect, disclose, discover, expose, reveal, show, uncloak, uncover, unveil
▣ conceal, mask

unmatched *adj* beyond compare, consummate *formal*, incomparable, matchless, nonpareil *formal*, paramount, peerless, supreme, unequalled, unexampled, unique, unparalleled, unrivalled, unsurpassed

unmentionable *adj* abominable, disgraceful, embarrassing, immodest, indecent, scandalous, shameful, shocking, taboo, unpleasant, unspeakable, unutterable

unmerciful *adj* brutal, callous, cruel, hard, heartless, implacable, merciless, pitiless, relentless, remorseless, ruthless, sadistic, uncaring, unfeeling, unrelenting, unsparing
▣ merciful

unmethodical *adj* confused, desultory *formal*, disorderly, haphazard, illogical, irregular, muddled, random, unco-ordinated, unorganized, unsystematic
▣ methodical

unmindful *adj* blind, careless, deaf, forgetful, heedless, inattentive, indifferent, lax, neglectful, negligent, oblivious, regardless, remiss, slack, unaware, unconscious, unheeding
▣ aware, heedful, mindful

unmistakable *adj* beyond question, blatant, certain, clear, clear-cut, conspicuous, definite, distinct, evident, explicit, glaring, indisputable, indubitable *formal*, manifest *formal*, obvious, patent, plain, positive, pronounced, striking, sure, unambiguous, undeniable, unequivocal, unquestionable, well-defined
▣ ambiguous, unclear

unmitigated *adj* absolute, arrant *formal*, complete, consummate *formal*, downright, out-and-out, outright, perfect, pure, rank, relentless, sheer, thorough, thoroughgoing, unabated *formal*, unalleviated, unbroken, undiminished, unmodified, unqualified, unredeemed, unrelenting, unrelieved, unremitting *formal*, utter

unmoved *adj* adamant, cold, determined, dispassionate, dry-eyed, firm, impassive, indifferent, inflexible, resolute, resolved, steady, unaffected, unbending, unchanged, unconcerned, undeviating, unfeeling, unimpressed, unresponsive, unshaken, unstirred, untouched, unwavering
▣ affected, moved, shaken

unnatural adj 1 unnatural sounds: abnormal, anomalous, bizarre, extraordinary, freakish, inhuman, irregular, odd, peculiar, perverted, queer, strange, supernatural, uncanny, uncommon, unusual 2 an unnatural manner: affected, artificial, contrived, false, feigned, forced, insincere, laboured, self-conscious, staged, stiff, stilted, strained, unspontaneous **F3** 1 natural, normal 2 natural, spontaneous

unnecessary adj dispensable, expendable, gratuitous, inessential, needless, non-essential, redundant, superfluous, uncalled-for, unneeded, unrequired, unwanted, wasted **F3** essential, indispensable, necessary

unnerve v alarm, confound, daunt, deject, demoralize, disconcert, discourage, dishearten, dismay, disquiet, fluster, frighten, intimidate, perturb formal, put out, rattle colloq, scare, shake, unman, unsettle, upset, worry **F3** brace, nerve, steel

unnoticed adj disregarded, ignored, neglected, overlooked, undiscovered, unheeded, unobserved, unrecognized, unremarked, unseen **F3** noted, noticed

unobtrusive adj humble, inconspicuous, low-key, modest, quiet, restrained, retiring, self-effacing, subdued, unaggressive, unassertive, unassuming, unnoticeable, unostentatious, unpretentious **F3** obtrusive, ostentatious, prominent

unobtrusively adv humbly, inconspicuously, modestly, on the quiet, quietly, surreptitiously, unostentatiously, unpretentiously **F3** aggressively, obtrusively, ostentatiously, showily

unoccupied adj 1 unoccupied houses: deserted, empty, forsaken formal, uninhabited, vacant 2 I was unoccupied for the summer: free, idle, inactive, jobless, unemployed, workless **F3** 1 occupied 2 busy

unofficial adj confidential, illegal, informal, off-the-record, personal, private, unauthorized, unconfirmed, undeclared, unratified **F3** accredited formal, corroborated formal, official, ratified, substantiated formal

unoriginal adj cliché-ridden, copied, cribbed, derivative, derived, hackneyed, second-hand, stale, trite, unimaginative, uninspired **F3** creative, fresh, imaginative, innovative, original

unorthodox adj abnormal, alternative, creative, eccentric, fresh, fringe, heterodox, innovative, irregular, new, nonconformist, novel, unconventional, unusual **F3** conventional, orthodox

unpaid adj 1 unpaid bills: due, outstanding, overdue, owing, payable, pending, remaining, uncollected, unsettled 2 unpaid work: free, honorary, unremunerative, unsalaried, unwaged, voluntary **F3** 1 paid 2 paid

unpalatable adj 1 an unpalatable combination of ingredients: bitter, disgusting, distasteful, inedible, insipid, unappetizing, uneatable, unsavoury 2 her views were unpalatable to the party leadership: disagreeable, distasteful, nasty, offensive, repellent, repugnant formal, unattractive, unpleasant, unsavoury **F3** 1 palatable 2 pleasant

unparalleled adj beyond compare, exceptional, incomparable, matchless, peerless, superlative, supreme, unequalled, unique, unmatched, unprecedented, unrivalled, unsurpassed, without equal

unpardonable adj deplorable, disgraceful, indefensible, inexcusable, irremissible formal, outrageous, reprehensible formal, scandalous, shameful, shocking, unconscionable formal, unforgivable, unjustifiable **F3** forgivable, understandable

unperturbed adj calm, collected, composed, cool, impassive, placid, poised, self-possessed, serene, tranquil, undisturbed, unexcited, unflinching, unflustered, unruffled, untroubled, unworried **F3** anxious, perturbed

unpleasant adj 1 an unpleasant smell: bad, disagreeable, disgusting, distasteful, foul, nasty, noisome formal, objectionable, offensive, repugnant formal, repulsive, unappetizing, unattractive, undesirable, unpalatable 2 an unpleasant person: aggressive, bad-tempered, disagreeable, discourteous, hostile, ill-natured, impolite, mean, nasty, objectionable, quarrelsome, rude, sour, surly, unfriendly, unkind **F3** 2 agreeable, nice, pleasant

unpleasantness n annoyance, bother, embarrassment, furore, fuss, ill-feeling, nastiness, scandal, trouble, upset

unpolished adj 1 unpolished work: rough, sketchy, unfashioned, unfinished, unrefined, unsophisticated, unworked 2 unpolished manners: coarse, crude, home-bred, rough, rough and ready, rude, uncivilized, uncouth, uncultivated, uncultured, unrefined, unsophisticated, vulgar **F3** 1 finished, polished 2 polished, refined

unpopular adj avoided, detested, disliked, friendless, hated, shunned, unattractive, undesirable, unfashionable, unloved, unsought-after, unwanted, unwelcome **F3** fashionable, popular

unprecedented adj abnormal, exceptional, extraordinary, freakish, remarkable, revolutionary, unequalled, unheard-of, unknown, unparalleled, unrivalled, unusual, without parallel

unpredictable adj capricious formal, chance, changeable, erratic, fickle, inconstant, mercurial formal, random, unexpected, unforeseeable, unreliable, unstable, variable, volatile **F3** constant, foreseeable, predictable, reliable

unprejudiced adj balanced, detached, dispassionate, enlightened, even-handed, fair, fair-minded, impartial, just, non-partisan, objective, open-minded, unbiased, uncoloured **F3** narrow-minded, prejudiced

unpremeditated adj extempore, fortuitous formal, impromptu, impulsive, offhand, off-the-cuff colloq, spontaneous, spur-of-the-moment colloq, unintentional, unplanned, unprepared, unrehearsed **F3** premeditated

unprepared *adj* **1** *an unprepared speech:* ad-lib, half-baked, improvised, off-the-cuff *colloq,* spontaneous, unplanned, unrehearsed **2** *totally unprepared for what happened:* ill-equipped, surprised, unready, unsuspecting
F3 1 prepared **2** prepared, ready

unpretentious *adj* honest, humble, modest, natural, ordinary, plain, simple, straightforward, unaffected, unassuming, unobtrusive, unostentatious
F3 ostentatious, pretentious, show

unprincipled *adj* corrupt, crooked *colloq,* deceitful, devious, discreditable, dishonest, dishonourable, immoral, underhand, unethical, unprofessional, unscrupulous
F3 ethical, principled

unproductive *adj* **1** *unproductive work:* fruitless, futile, idle, ineffective, inefficacious *formal,* otiose *formal,* unfruitful, unprofitable, unremunerative, unrewarding, useless, vain, worthless **2** *unproductive land:* arid, barren, dry, infertile, sterile, unfruitful, unprofitable
F3 1 productive **2** fertile, productive

unprofessional *adj* **1** *did an unprofessional job:* amateurish, casual, incompetent, inefficient, inexperienced, inexpert, lax, negligent, sloppy *colloq,* unskilled, untrained **2** *unprofessional behaviour:* improper, inadmissible, indecorous *formal,* unacceptable, unethical, unprincipled, unscrupulous, unseemly *formal*
F3 1 professional, skilful **2** professional

unpromising *adj* adverse, depressing, discouraging, dispiriting, doubtful, gloomy, inauspicious, ominous, unfavourable, unpropitious *formal*
F3 auspicious, favourable, promising

unprotected *adj* defenceless, exposed, helpless, liable, naked, open, unarmed, unattended, uncovered, undefended, unfortified, unguarded, unsheltered, unshielded, vulnerable
F3 immune, protected, safe

unqualified *adj* **1** *unqualified to do the work:* amateur, ill-equipped, incapable, incompetent, ineligible, inexperienced, unfit, unlicensed, unprepared, untrained **2** *an unqualified success:* absolute, categorical, complete, consummate *formal,* downright, out and out, outright, perfect, positive, thorough, total, unconditional, unequivocal, unmitigated, unreserved, unrestricted, utter, wholehearted
F3 1 professional, qualified **2** conditional, tentative

unquestionable *adj* absolute, beyond question, certain, clear, conclusive, definite, faultless, flawless, incontestable, incontrovertible *formal,* indisputable, indubitable *formal,* irrefutable *formal,* manifest *formal,* obvious, patent, self-evident, sure, unchallenged, undeniable, unequivocal, unmistakable
F3 dubious, questionable

unquestioning *adj* implicit, questionless, unconditional, unhesitating, unqualified, wholehearted
F3 doubtful

unravel *v* **1** *unravel a mystery:* clear up, explain, figure out, interpret, penetrate, puzzle out, resolve, solve, sort out, straighten out, work out

2 *unravel a thread:* disentangle, extricate, free, sort out, undo, unknot, untangle, unwind
F3 1 complicate **2** tangle

unreadable *adj* complex, complicated, double Dutch *colloq,* garbled, illegible, impenetrable, inarticulate, incoherent, incomprehensible, indecipherable, involved, jumbled, muddled, mysterious, obscure, puzzling, scrambled, too difficult to read, unfathomable, unintelligible
F3 clear, comprehensible, intelligible

unreal *adj* artificial, bizarre, chimerical *formal,* fairy-tale, fake, false, fanciful, fantastic, fictitious, hypothetical, illusory, imaginary, immaterial, insubstantial, legendary, made-up, make-believe, mock, mythical, nebulous, non-existent, phantasmagorical *formal,* pretend *colloq,* sham, synthetic, visionary
F3 authentic, genuine, real

unrealistic *adj* idealistic, impossible, impracticable, impractical, over-optimistic, quixotic, romantic, theoretical, unreasonable, unworkable
F3 pragmatic, realistic

unreasonable *adj* **1** *an unreasonable decision:* biased, unacceptable, uncalled-for, undue, unfair, unjust, unjustifiable, unjustified, unwarranted **2** *unreasonable behaviour:* absurd, arbitrary, far-fetched, foolish, headstrong, illogical, inconsistent, irrational, ludicrous, mad, nonsensical, opinionated, outrageous, perverse, preposterous, senseless, silly, stupid **3** *unreasonable prices:* excessive, exorbitant, expensive, extortionate, extravagant, immoderate, outrageous, steep *colloq,* undue
F3 1 fair, reasonable **2** rational, sensible **3** moderate

unrecognizable *adj* altered, changed, disguised, incognito, incognizable *formal,* unidentifiable, unknowable

unrecognized *adj* disregarded, ignored, neglected, overlooked, undiscovered, unheeded, unnoticed, unobserved, unremarked, unseen
F3 noted, noticed, recognized

unrefined *adj* **1** *an unrefined person:* coarse, crude, uncultivated, uncultured, unpolished, unsophisticated, vulgar **2** *unrefined sugar:* crude, raw, unprocessed, unpurified, untreated
F3 1 refined **2** processed, refined

unregenerate *adj* abandoned, hardened, impenitent, incorrigible *formal,* intractable *formal,* obdurate *formal,* obstinate, persistent, recalcitrant *formal,* refractory *formal,* shameless, stubborn, unconverted, unreformed, unrepentant
F3 reformed, repentant

unrelated *adj* beside/off the point, different, disparate *formal,* dissimilar, distinct, extraneous, foreign, independent, irrelevant, neither here nor there *colloq,* separate, unassociated, unconnected, unlike
F3 related, similar

unrelenting *adj* ceaseless, constant, continual, continuous, endless, incessant *formal,* inexorable, perpetual, relentless, remorseless, ruthless, steady, unabated *formal,* unbroken, unceasing, uncompromising, unforgiving, unremitting *formal,* unsparing
F3 intermittent, spasmodic

unreliable *adj* deceptive, doubtful, fallible, fickle, iffy *colloq*, inaccurate, irresponsible, slippery *colloq*, uncertain, unconvincing, undependable, unsound, unstable, untrustworthy
🔁 dependable, reliable, sound, trustworthy

unremitting *adj* ceaseless, constant, continual, continuous, incessant *formal*, perpetual, relentless, remorseless, tireless, unabated *formal*, unbroken, unceasing, unrelenting
🔁 intermittent, spasmodic

unrepentant *adj* callous, confirmed, hardened, impenitent, incorrigible *formal*, obdurate *formal*, shameless, unabashed, unapologetic, unashamed
🔁 ashamed, penitent, repentant

unreserved *adj* **1** *my unreserved approval*: absolute, complete, entire, full, total, unconditional, unhesitating, unlimited, unqualified, unrestrained, wholehearted **2** *an unreserved personality*: candid, demonstrative, extrovert, forthright, frank, open, outgoing, outspoken, uninhibited
🔁 **1** hesitant, tentative **2** inhibited

unreservedly *adv* completely, entirely, outright, unhesitatingly, utterly, wholeheartedly

unresolved *adj* doubtful, indefinite, moot, pending, problematical, unanswered, undecided, undetermined, unsettled, unsolved, up in the air *colloq*, vague, vexed
🔁 definite, determined

unresponsive *adj* aloof, apathetic, cool, indifferent, unaffected, uninterested, unmoved, unsympathetic
🔁 responsive

unrest *n* agitation, disaffection *formal*, discontent, discord *formal*, disorder, disquiet, dissatisfaction, dissension, perturbation *formal*, protest, rebellion, restlessness, turmoil, unease, uneasiness, worry
🔁 calm, peace

unrestrained *adj* abandoned, boisterous, free, immoderate, inordinate, intemperate, irrepressible, natural, rampant, unbounded, unbridled, unchecked, unconstrained, uncontrolled, unhindered, uninhibited, unrepressed, unreserved
🔁 inhibited, restrained

unrestricted *adj* absolute, clear, free, free-for-all *colloq*, open, public, unbounded, unconditional, unhindered, unimpeded, unlimited, unobstructed, unopposed
🔁 limited, restricted

unrivalled *adj* beyond compare, incomparable, inimitable *formal*, matchless, nonpareil *formal*, peerless, superlative, supreme, unequalled, unmatched, unparalleled, unsurpassed, without equal

unruffled *adj* calm, collected, composed, cool, even, imperturbable, level, peaceful, serene, smooth, tranquil, undisturbed, unperturbed *formal*, untroubled
🔁 anxious, troubled

unruly *adj* disobedient, disorderly, headstrong, insubordinate, intractable *formal*, lawless, mutinous, obstreperous, rebellious, recalcitrant *formal*, refractory *formal*, riotous, rowdy,

uncontrollable, ungovernable, unmanageable, wayward, wild, wilful
🔁 manageable, orderly

unsafe *adj* **1** *an unsafe course of action*: chancy, dangerous, dicey *colloq*, hairy *colloq*, hazardous, high-risk, perilous, precarious, risky, treacherous, uncertain, unreliable **2** *the building is unsafe*: dangerous, exposed, insecure, unsound, unstable
🔁 **1** safe **2** safe, secure

unsaid *adj* undeclared, unexpressed, unmentioned, unpronounced, unspoken, unstated, unuttered, unvoiced
🔁 spoken

unsatisfactory *adj* defective, deficient, disappointing, displeasing, dissatisfying, faulty, frustrating, imperfect, inadequate, inferior, insufficient, leaving a lot to be desired *colloq*, mediocre, poor, unacceptable, unsatisfying, unsuitable, weak
🔁 adequate, pleasing, satisfactory

unsavoury *adj* disagreeable, disgusting, distasteful, nasty, nauseating, objectionable, obnoxious, offensive, repellent, repugnant *formal*, repulsive, revolting, sickening, sordid, squalid, unappetizing, unattractive, undesirable, unpalatable, unpleasant
🔁 palatable, pleasant

unscathed *adj* intact, safe, sound, undamaged, unharmed, unhurt, uninjured, untouched, whole
🔁 harmed, hurt, injured

unscrupulous *adj* corrupt, crooked *colloq*, dishonest, dishonourable, immoral, improper, ruthless, shameless, unethical, unprincipled
🔁 ethical, proper, scrupulous

unseasonable *adj* ill-timed, inappropriate, inopportune *formal*, intempestive *formal*, malapropos *formal*, mistimed, unsuitable, untimely
🔁 seasonable, timely

unseat *v* **1** *unseat the incumbent president*: depose, dethrone, discharge, dismiss, displace, oust, overthrow, remove, topple **2** *the horse unseated its rider*: dishorse, dismount, throw, unhorse, unsaddle

unseemly *adj* discreditable, disreputable, improper, in poor taste, inappropriate, indecorous *formal*, indelicate, unbecoming, unbefitting, undignified, undue, unrefined, unsuitable
🔁 decorous, seemly

unseen *adj* concealed, hidden, invisible, lurking, obscure, undetected, unnoticed, unobserved, unobtrusive, veiled
🔁 visible

unselfish *adj* altruistic, charitable, disinterested, generous, humanitarian, kind, liberal, magnanimous *formal*, noble, open-handed, philanthropic, public-spirited, self-denying, self-forgetting, selfless, self-sacrificing
🔁 selfish

unsettle *v* agitate, bother, confuse, destabilize, discomfit *formal*, discompose, disconcert, disturb, fluster, perturb *formal*, rattle *colloq*, ruffle, shake, throw *colloq*, trouble, unbalance, upset

unsettled *adj* **1** *unsettled by the turn of events:* agitated, anxious, confused, disoriented, disturbed, edgy, fidgety, flustered, on edge *colloq*, shaken, tense, troubled, uneasy, unnerved, upset **2** *the point was still unsettled:* doubtful, in the balance *colloq*, open, to be decided, uncertain, undecided, undetermined, unresolved, up in the air *colloq* **3** *unsettled weather:* changeable, inconstant, insecure, shaky, uncertain, unpredictable, unstable, unsteady, variable **4** *unsettled bills:* in arrears, outstanding, overdue, owing, payable, unpaid **5** *an unsettled region:* abandoned, deserted, desolate, uninhabited, unoccupied, unpeopled, unpopulated
🔁 **1** composed **2** certain, decided **3** settled **4** paid **5** peopled, settled

unshakable *adj* constant, determined, firm, fixed, immovable, resolute, stable, staunch, steadfast, sure, unassailable, unswerving, unwavering, well-founded
🔁 insecure

unsightly *adj* disagreeable, hideous, off-putting, repugnant, repulsive, revolting, ugly, unattractive, unpleasant, unprepossessing
🔁 attractive

unskilful *adj* amateurish, awkward, bungling, clumsy, fumbling, gauche, incompetent, inept, inexperienced, inexpert, maladroit *formal*, uneducated, unpractised, unprofessional, unqualified, unskilled, untalented, untaught, untrained
🔁 skilful, skilled

unskilled *adj* amateurish, incompetent, inexperienced, inexpert, unpractised, unprofessional, unqualified, untrained
🔁 professional, skilled

unsociable *adj* aloof, chilly, cold, cool, distant, hostile, inhospitable, introverted, reclusive, reserved, retiring, solitary, standoffish, taciturn, uncommunicative, uncongenial, unforthcoming, unfriendly, unneighbourly, withdrawn
🔁 congenial, friendly, sociable

unsolicited *adj* gratuitous, spontaneous, unasked, unasked-for, uncalled-for, uninvited, unrequested, unsought, unwanted, unwelcome, voluntary
🔁 invited, requested

unsophisticated *adj* **1** *an unsophisticated person:* artless, childlike, guileless, inexperienced, ingenuous, innocent, naïve, natural, simple, unaffected, unpretentious, unworldly **2** *an unsophisticated approach to the problem:* basic, crude, plain, rudimentary, simple, straightforward, uncomplicated, undeveloped, uninvolved, unrefined
🔁 **1** sophisticated, worldly **2** complex

unsound *adj* **1** *unsound reasoning:* defective, erroneous, fallacious *formal*, false, faulty, flawed, ill-founded, illogical, invalid, shaky, unfounded, weak **2** *of unsound mind:* ailing, delicate, deranged, diseased, frail, ill, unbalanced, unhealthy, unhinged, unwell, weak **3** *that chair looks unsound:* broken, dangerous, insecure, rickety, shaky, unreliable, unsafe, unstable, unsteady, wobbly
🔁 **1** sound **2** well **3** stable

unsparing *adj* **1** *unsparing in their hospitality:* abundant, bountiful, generous, lavish, liberal, munificent *formal*, open-handed, plenteous, profuse, ungrudging, unstinting **2** *unsparing criticism:* hard, harsh, implacable, merciless, relentless, ruthless, severe, stern, uncompromising, unforgiving, unmerciful
🔁 **1** mean, sparing **2** forgiving

unspeakable *adj* appalling, awful, dreadful, execrable *formal*, frightful, horrible, inconceivable, indescribable, inexpressible, monstrous, shocking, terrible, unbelievable, unimaginable, unthinkable, unutterable

unspoilt *adj* **1** *unspoilt countryside:* natural, preserved, unchanged, untouched **2** *an unspoilt record:* perfect, unblemished, unimpaired **3** *she has an unspoilt nature:* natural, unaffected, unsophisticated
🔁 **3** affected, spoilt

unspoken *adj* assumed, implicit, implied, inferred, silent, tacit, undeclared, understood, unexpressed, unsaid, unstated, unuttered, voiceless, wordless
🔁 explicit, stated

unstable *adj* **1** *unstable prices:* changeable, erratic, fluctuating, inconsistent, inconstant, unpredictable, variable, volatile, wavering **2** *unstable rock formations:* insecure, precarious, rickety, shaky, tottering, unbalanced, unsafe, unsteady, wobbly **3** *an unstable personality:* capricious *formal*, erratic, mercurial *formal*, moody, unpredictable, unreliable, untrustworthy, vacillating, volatile **4** *became unstable after his wife died:* barmy *colloq*, crackers *colloq*, crazy *colloq*, deranged, disturbed, insane, mad, unhinged, unsound
🔁 **1** stable **2** steady **3** stable **4** sane, stable

unsteady *adj* **1** *unsteady on his feet:* doddery, rickety, shaky, tottering, unstable **2** *an unsteady flame:* flickering, inconstant, irregular **3** *an unsteady foothold:* insecure, precarious, shaky, treacherous, unreliable, unsafe, unstable, wobbly
🔁 **1** stable, steady **3** stable, steady

unstinting *adj* abounding, abundant, ample, bountiful, full, generous, large, lavish, liberal, munificent *formal*, plentiful, prodigal *formal*, profuse, ungrudging, unsparing
🔁 grudging, mean

unsubstantiated *adj* debatable, disputable, dubious, questionable, unattested *formal*, unconfirmed, uncorroborated *formal*, unestablished, unproved, unproven, unsupported, unverified
🔁 proved, proven

unsuccessful *adj* abortive, beaten, defeated, failed, fruitless, frustrated, futile, ineffective, ineffectual *formal*, losing, luckless, thwarted, unavailing, unfortunate, unlucky, unproductive, unprofitable, useless, vain
🔁 effective, fortunate, successful, winning

unsuitable *adj* improper, inapposite *formal*, inappropriate, inapt, incompatible, incongruous, formal, infelicitous *formal*, malapropos *formal*, out of place, unacceptable, unbecoming *formal*, unfit, unseemly *formal*, unsuited
🔁 appropriate, suitable

unsullied *adj* clean, immaculate, intact, perfect, pristine *formal*, pure, spotless, stainless,

unblackened, unblemished, uncorrupted, undefiled, unsoiled, unspoiled, unspotted, unstained, untainted, untarnished, untouched
✳ dirty, stained

unsung *adj* anonymous, disregarded, forgotten, neglected, obscure, overlooked, unacclaimed, unacknowledged, uncelebrated, unhailed, unhonoured, unknown, unpraised, unrecognized
✳ famous, honoured, renowned

unsure *adj* 1 *unsure of yourself:* doubtful, dubious, hesitant, insecure, lacking self-confidence, sceptical, suspicious, tentative, uncertain, unconvinced, undecided, unpersuaded 2 *unsure about what to do:* ambivalent, dithering, doubtful, equivocating, hesitant, in two minds *colloq*, indefinite, irresolute, uncertain, uncommitted, undecided, vague, wavering
✳ 1 certain, confident, sure 2 certain, decided, sure

unsurpassed *adj* exceptional, incomparable, matchless, superlative, supreme, surpassing, transcendent, unbeaten, unequalled, unexcelled, unparalleled, unrivalled
✳ surpassed

unsuspecting *adj* credulous, gullible, ingenuous, innocent, naïve, off guard, trustful, trusting, unaware, unconscious, unsuspicious, unwary
✳ knowing, suspicious

unswerving *adj* constant, dedicated, devoted, direct, firm, fixed, immovable, resolute, single-minded, staunch, steadfast, steady, sure, true, undeviating, unfaltering, unflagging, untiring, unwavering
✳ irresolute, tentative

unsympathetic *adj* antagonistic, callous, cold, cruel, hard, hard-hearted, harsh, heartless, hostile, indifferent, inhuman, insensitive, pitiless, soulless, stony, uncaring, unconcerned, unfeeling, unkind, unmoved, unpitying, unresponsive
✳ compassionate, sympathetic

unsystematic *adj* chaotic, confused, disorderly, disorganized, haphazard, illogical, indiscriminate, irregular, jumbled, muddled, random, shambolic, slapdash, sloppy *colloq*, unco-ordinated, unmethodical, unorganized, unplanned, untidy
✳ logical, systematic

untamed *adj* barbarous, feral *formal*, fierce, savage, undomesticated, unmellowed, untameable, wild
✳ domesticated, tame

untangle *v* disentangle, extricate, resolve, solve, straighten out, undo, unravel, work out
✳ complicate, tangle

untarnished *adj* 1 *untarnished silver:* bright, burnished, clean, glowing, immaculate, polished, pristine *formal*, pure, shining, spotless, stainless, unsoiled, unspotted, unstained 2 *an untarnished record:* immaculate, impeccable, intact, spotless, unblemished, unimpeachable, unspoilt, unsullied
✳ 1 tarnished 2 blemished, tarnished

untenable *adj* fallacious, flawed, illogical, indefensible, inexcusable, insupportable, rocky,

shaky, unjustifiable, unmaintainable, unreasonable, unsound, unsustainable
✳ sound, tenable

unthinkable *adj* absurd, illogical, implausible, impossible, improbable, inconceivable, incredible, outrageous, preposterous, shocking, staggering, unbelievable, unheard-of, unimaginable, unlikely, unreasonable

unthinking *adj* 1 *an unthinking reaction:* automatic, impulsive, instinctive, involuntary, mechanical, unconscious 2 *how could she be so unthinking?:* impolite, inconsiderate, indiscreet, insensitive, rude, tactless, thoughtless, undiplomatic, unkind
✳ 1 conscious 2 considerate

untidy *adj* 1 *an untidy office:* chaotic, cluttered, disorderly, disorganized, haywire, higgledy-piggledy *colloq*, jumbled, messy, muddled, shambolic, slipshod, sloppy *colloq*, topsy-turvy, unsystematic 2 *untidy hair:* bedraggled, dishevelled, messy, rumpled, scruffy, slovenly, unkempt
✳ 1 neat, tidy 2 neat, tidy

untie *v* free, loose, loosen, release, unbind, undo, unfasten, unhitch, unknot, unwrap
✳ fasten, tie

untimely *adj* 1 *an untimely action:* awkward, ill-timed, inappropriate, inauspicious *formal*, inconvenient, infelicitous *formal*, inopportune, malapropos *formal*, unfortunate, unseasonable, unsuitable 2 *her untimely death:* early, premature
✳ 1 opportune, timely

untiring *adj* constant, dedicated, determined, devoted, dogged, incessant, indefatigable, persevering, persistent, resolute, staunch, steady, tenacious, tireless, unceasing, unfailing, unfaltering, unflagging, unremitting *formal*
✳ inconstant, wavering

untold *adj* 1 *cause untold damage:* inconceivable, indescribable, inexpressible, unimaginable, unutterable 2 *untold numbers of innocent people:* boundless, countless, immeasurable, incalculable, inexhaustible, infinite, innumerable, measureless, uncountable, uncounted, undreamed-of, unimaginable, unnumbered, unreckoned

untouched *adj* intact, safe, unaffected, unaltered, unchanged, undamaged, unharmed, unhurt, unimpaired, unimpressed, uninjured, unscathed, unstirred
✳ affected, damaged

untoward *adj* adverse, annoying, awkward, contrary, disastrous, ill-timed, improper, inappropriate, inauspicious, inconvenient, indecorous *formal*, inopportune *formal*, irritating, ominous, troublesome, unbecoming *formal*, unexpected, unfavourable, unfitting, unfortunate, unlucky, unpropitious *formal*, unseemly *formal*, unsuitable, untimely, vexatious, worrying
✳ auspicious, suitable

untrained *adj* amateur, incompetent, inexperienced, inexpert, uneducated, unpractised, unprofessional, unqualified, unschooled, unskilled, untaught
✳ expert, trained

untried *adj* experimental, exploratory, innovative, innovatory, new, novel, unestablished, unproved, untested
🔃 proven, tested, tried

untroubled *adj* calm, composed, cool, impassive, peaceful, placid, serene, steady, tranquil, unconcerned, undisturbed, unexcited, unflappable *colloq*, unflustered, unperturbed *formal*, unruffled, unstirred, unworried
🔃 anxious, troubled

untrue *adj* 1 *an untrue statement:* deceptive, erroneous, fabricated, fallacious, false, inaccurate, incorrect, inexact, made-up *colloq*, misleading, mistaken, trumped-up *colloq*, wrong 2 *untrue to his wife:* deceitful, dishonest, disloyal, fraudulent, perfidious *formal*, two-faced *colloq*, unfaithful, untrustworthy, untruthful
🔃 1 correct, true 2 faithful, honest

untrustworthy *adj* capricious, deceitful, dishonest, dishonourable, disloyal, duplicitous *formal*, faithless, false, fickle, fly-by-night, treacherous, two-faced *colloq*, unfaithful, unreliable, untrue, untrusty, untruthful
🔃 reliable, trustworthy

untruth *n* cock-and-bull story *colloq*, deceit, fabrication, falsehood, fib *colloq*, fiction, invention, lie, lying, made-up story *colloq*, perjury, porky *colloq*, story, tale, tall story *colloq*, untruthfulness, whopper *colloq*
🔃 truth

untruthful *adj* crooked *colloq*, deceitful, dishonest, erroneous, fabricated, fallacious, false, fictional, hypocritical, insincere, invented, lying, mendacious *formal*, two-faced *colloq*, untrue, unveracious *formal*
🔃 honest, truthful

untutored *adj* artless, ignorant, illiterate, inexperienced, inexpert, simple, uneducated, unlearned, unlessoned, unpractised, unrefined, unschooled, unsophisticated, untrained, unversed
🔃 educated, trained

unused *adj* 1 *unused resources:* available, extra, idle, leftover, remaining, spare, surplus, unemployed, unexploited, untapped, untouched 2 *an unused envelope:* blank, clean, fresh, new 3 *unused to the sun:* inexperienced, unaccustomed, unacquainted, unfamiliar, unpractised
🔃 2 used 3 used

unusual *adj* abnormal, anomalous, atypical, bizarre, curious, different, exceptional, extraordinary, irregular, odd, offbeat *colloq*, out of the ordinary, phenomenal, queer, rare, remarkable, singular *formal*, special, strange, surprising, uncommon, unconventional, unexpected, unfamiliar, unorthodox, unprecedented, weird
🔃 normal, ordinary, usual

unutterable *adj* egregious *formal*, extreme, indescribable, ineffable, nefandous *formal*, overwhelming, unimaginable, unspeakable

unvarnished *adj* bare, candid, frank, honest, naked, plain, pure, sheer, simple, sincere, stark, straightforward, unadorned, undisguised, unembellished
🔃 disguised, embellished, exaggerated

unveil *v* bare, betray, bring out into the open, bring to light, disclose, discover, divulge, expose, lay bare, lay open, make known, reveal, take the lid off *colloq*, uncover, unmask
🔃 cover, hide

unwanted *adj* 1 *unwanted food:* extra, otiose *technical*, outcast, redundant, rejected, superfluous, surplus, unnecessary, unneeded, unrequired, useless 2 *an unwanted guest:* undesired, uninvited, unsolicited *formal*, unwelcome
🔃 1 necessary, needed, wanted

unwarranted *adj* gratuitous, groundless, indefensible, inexcusable, uncalled-for, undeserved, unjust, unjustifiable, unjustified, unnecessary, unprovoked, unreasonable, wrong
🔃 deserved, justifiable, warranted

unwary *adj* careless, hasty, heedless, imprudent *formal*, incautious, indiscreet, off guard, rash, reckless, thoughtless, unguarded, unthinking
🔃 cautious, wary

unwavering *adj* consistent, dedicated, determined, resolute, single-minded, staunch, steadfast, steady, tenacious, undeviating, unfaltering, unflagging, unquestioning, unshakable, unshaken, unswerving, untiring
🔃 fickle, wavering

unwelcome *adj* 1 *unwelcome in our house:* excluded, rejected, undesirable, uninvited, unpopular, unwanted 2 *unwelcome news:* disagreeable, distasteful, unacceptable, unpalatable, unpleasant, upsetting, worrying
🔃 1 desirable, welcome 2 pleasant

unwell *adj* ailing, debilitated *formal*, dicky *colloq*, groggy *colloq*, ill, in a bad way *colloq*, indisposed *formal*, like death warmed up *colloq*, off-colour, out of sorts *colloq*, poorly, rough *colloq*, run down *colloq*, sick, sickly, under the weather *colloq*, unfit, unhealthy
🔃 healthy, well

unwholesome *adj* anaemic, bad, corrupting, degrading, demoralizing, depraving, evil, harmful, immoral, innutritious, insalubrious *formal*, insalutary *formal*, insanitary, junk *colloq*, noxious, pale, pallid, pasty, perverting, poisonous, sickly, tainted, unhealthy, unhygienic, wan, wicked
🔃 salubrious, wholesome

unwieldy *adj* awkward, bulky, clumsy, cumbersome, hefty, hulking, incommodious *formal*, inconvenient, massive, ponderous, ungainly, unmanageable, weighty
🔃 dainty, handy

unwilling *adj* averse, disinclined, grudging, hesitant, indisposed *formal*, loath, loathful *formal*, opposed, reluctant, resistant, slow, unenthusiastic
🔃 enthusiastic, willing

unwind *v* 1 *he unwound his scarf:* disentangle, uncoil, undo, unravel, unreel, unroll, untwist, unwrap 2 *unwind after a day's work:* calm down, chill out *colloq*, cool it *colloq*, hang loose *colloq*, kick back *colloq*, let your hair down *colloq*, let yourself go *colloq*, make yourself at home *colloq*, put your feet up *colloq*, relax, take it/things easy *colloq*, wind down
🔃 1 roll, wind

unwise *adj* foolhardy, foolish, ill-advised, ill-considered, ill-judged, impolitic *formal*, improvident, imprudent *formal*, inadvisable, indiscreet, inexpedient, injudicious *formal*, irresponsible, rash, reckless, senseless, short-sighted, silly, stupid, thoughtless
🖪 prudent *formal*, sensible, wise

unwitting *adj* 1 *an unwitting victim*: involuntary, unaware, unconscious, unknowing, unsuspecting, unthinking 2 *an unwitting reference to Hitchcock*: accidental, chance, inadvertent, unintended, unintentional, unplanned
🖪 1 knowing 2 conscious, deliberate

unwonted *adj* atypical, exceptional, extraordinary, infrequent, peculiar, rare, singular *formal*, strange, unaccustomed, uncommon, uncustomary, unexpected, unfamiliar, unheard-of, unusual
🖪 usual, wonted

unworldly *adj* 1 *an unworldly child*: green *colloq*, gullible, idealistic, impractical, inexperienced, ingenuous, innocent, naïve, unsophisticated, visionary 2 *had an unworldly air about her*: extra-terrestrial, metaphysical, otherworldly, spiritual, transcendental
🖪 1 sophisticated, worldly 2 materialistic, worldly

unworthy *adj* base, contemptible, despicable, discreditable, disgraceful, dishonourable, disreputable, ignoble, improper, inappropriate, incongruous *formal*, inferior, shameful, unbecoming *formal*, unbefitting *formal*, undeserving, unfitting, unseemly *formal*, unsuitable
🖪 commendable, worthy

unwritten *adj* accepted, conventional, customary, implicit, oral, recognized, tacit, traditional, understood, unrecorded, verbal, word-of-mouth
🖪 recorded, written

unyielding *adj* adamant, determined, firm, hard-line, immovable, implacable *formal*, inexorable *formal*, inflexible, intractable *formal*, intransigent *formal*, obdurate *formal*, obstinate, relentless, resolute, rigid, solid, staunch, steadfast, stubborn, tough, unbending, uncompromising, unrelenting, unwavering
🖪 flexible, yielding

up-and-coming *adj* ambitious, eager, enterprising, go-getting *colloq*, promising, pushing *colloq*

upbeat *adj* bright, bullish *colloq*, buoyant, cheerful, cheery, encouraging, favourable, forward-looking, heartening, hopeful, optimistic, positive, promising, rosy
🖪 downbeat, gloomy

upbraid *v* admonish, berate *formal*, castigate *formal*, censure, chide, criticize, rebuke, reprimand, reproach, reprove, scold
🖪 commend, praise

upbringing *n* breeding, bringing-up, care, cultivation, education, instruction, nurture, parenting, raising, rearing, teaching, tending, training

update *v* amend, correct, modernize, renew, renovate, revamp, revise, upgrade

upgrade *v* advance, ameliorate *formal*, better, elevate, enhance, improve, make better, modernize, promote, raise
🖪 demote, downgrade

upheaval *n* chaos, confusion, disorder, disruption, disturbance, overthrow, revolution, shake-up *colloq*, turmoil, upset

uphill *adj* arduous, burdensome, difficult, exhausting, gruelling, hard, laborious, onerous, punishing, strenuous, taxing, tiring, tough, wearisome
🖪 downhill, easy

uphold *v* advocate, back, champion, confirm, defend, endorse, fortify *formal*, hold to, justify, keep, maintain, promote, stand by, strengthen, support, sustain, vindicate
🖪 abandon, reject

upkeep *n* 1 *the upkeep of public buildings*: care, conservation, keep, maintenance, preservation, repair, running, subsistence, support, sustenance 2 *a cheque for my general upkeep*: expenditure, expenses, oncosts, operating costs, outlay, overheads, running costs
🖪 1 neglect

uplift *v* advance, ameliorate *formal*, better, boost, elate, elevate, enlighten, exalt, improve, inspire, lift, raise
♦ *n* advancement, boost, enhancement, improvement, lift

upper *adj* elevated, eminent, exalted, greater, high, higher, important, loftier, senior, superior, top, topmost, uppermost
🖪 inferior, junior, lower

upper-class *adj* 1 *an upper-class person*: aristocratic, blue-blooded, high-born, high-class, noble, patrician, well-born, well-bred 2 *an upper-class restaurant*: elite, exclusive, high-class, swanky *colloq*, top-drawer *colloq*
🖪 1 working-class 2 humble

uppermost *adj* chief, dominant, first, foremost, greatest, highest, leading, loftiest, main, major, paramount, predominant, pre-eminent, primary, principal, supreme, top, topmost
🖪 lowest

uppity *adj* affected, arrogant, assuming, big-headed, bumptious, cocky, conceited, hoity-toity *colloq*, impertinent, overweening, presumptuous, self-important, snobbish, stuck-up *colloq*, supercilious, swanky *colloq*, toffee-nosed *colloq*
🖪 diffident, unassertive

upright *adj* 1 *stood in an upright position*: at right angles, erect, perpendicular, sheer, steep, straight, vertical 2 *an upright man*: decent, ethical, good, high-minded, honest, honourable, incorruptible, moral, noble, principled, reputable, respectable, righteous, trustworthy, upstanding, virtuous, worthy
🖪 1 flat, horizontal 2 dishonest

uprising *n* coup d'état, insurgence, insurrection, mutiny, overthrow, putsch, rebellion, revolt, revolution, rising

uproar *n* bedlam, brouhaha, clamour, commotion, confusion, din, disorder, fracas, furore, hubbub, hullabaloo, mayhem, noise, outcry, pandemonium, racket, riot, ruction, rumpus, tumult, turbulence, turmoil

uproarious *adj* boisterous, clamorous, confused, deafening, hilarious, hysterical, killing *colloq*, loud, noisy, rib-tickling *colloq*, riotous, rip-roaring, rollicking, rowdy, side-splitting, unrestrained, wild
🗷 quiet

uproot *v* destroy, displace, eradicate, pull up, remove, rip up, root out, weed out, wipe out

upset *v* 1 *I don't want to upset you:* agitate, bother, confuse, discompose *formal*, disconcert, dismay, distress, disturb, fluster, grieve, hurt, perturb *formal*, put out, ruffle, sadden, shake (up), trouble, unnerve, worry 2 *they upset the boat:* capsize, destabilize, knock over, overthrow, overturn, tip over, topple
♦ *n* 1 *recovering from the upset:* agitation, bother, disruption, distress, disturbance, perturbation *formal*, reverse, shake-up *colloq*, shock, surprise, trouble, upheaval, worry 2 *a stomach upset:* ailment, bug *colloq*, complaint, disorder, illness, malady *formal*, sickness
♦ *adj* agitated, annoyed, bothered, confused, discomposed *formal*, disconcerted, dismayed, distressed, disturbed, flustered, grieved, het up *colloq*, hurt, in a state *colloq*, perturbed *formal*, put out, shaken, troubled, unsettled, uptight *colloq*, worked up *colloq*, worried

upshot *n* conclusion, consequence, culmination, dénouement, end, finish, issue, outcome, pay-off *colloq*, result

upside-down *adj* 1 *the room was left upside-down:* chaotic, confused, disordered, jumbled, messed up *colloq*, muddled, topsy-turvy, up-ended 2 *an upside-down glass:* inverted, overturned, up-ended, upset, upturned, wrong side up, wrong way up

upstanding *adj* ethical, firm, good, honest, honourable, incorruptible, moral, principled, strong, true, trustworthy, upright, virtuous
🗷 untrustworthy

upstart *n* arriviste, nobody, nouveau riche, parvenu, parvenue, social climber

uptight *adj* anxious, edgy, hung-up, irritated, nervy, on edge *colloq*, prickly *colloq*, tense, uneasy
🗷 calm, cool, relaxed

up-to-date *adj* all the rage *colloq*, contemporary, cool *colloq*, current, fashionable, hip *colloq*, in *colloq*, in fashion, latest, modern, new, present-day, prevalent, recent, state-of-the-art *colloq*, trendy *colloq*
🗷 old-fashioned, out of date

upturn *n* amelioration *formal*, betterment, boost, improvement, increase, recovery, revival, rise, upsurge, upswing
🗷 downturn, drop

urban *adj* built-up, city, civic, inner-city, metropolitan, municipal, oppidan *formal*, town
🗷 country, rural

> **urban** or **urbane**? *Urban* means 'of a town': *urban development; urban life; urban violence.* *Urbane* means 'cultured, elegant, refined': *urbane wit.*

urbane *adj* civil, civilized, courteous, cultivated, cultured, debonair, elegant, mannerly, polished, refined, smooth, sophisticated, suave, well-bred, well-mannered
🗷 gauche, uncouth

urbanity *n* charm, civility, courtesy, cultivation, culture, ease, elegance, grace, mannerliness, polish, refinement, smoothness, sophistication, suavity, worldliness
🗷 awkwardness, gaucheness

urchin *n* brat, gamin, guttersnipe, kid, ragamuffin, street Arab, waif

urge *v* 1 *urged on by his mates:* compel, drive, egg on *colloq*, encourage, force, goad, hasten, impel, incite, induce, instigate, persuade, press, prod, push, spur, stimulate 2 *I urged them to stop:* appeal, beg, beseech *formal*, entreat, implore, plead with 3 *she urged caution:* advise, advocate, counsel, encourage, exhort *formal*, recommend
🗷 1 deter, discourage, dissuade, hinder
♦ *n* compulsion, desire, drive, eagerness, fancy, impetus, impulse, inclination, itch *colloq*, longing, need, wish, yearning, yen *colloq*
🗷 disinclination

urgency *n* exigency *formal*, extremity, gravity, haste, hurry, imperativeness, importance, importunity *formal*, necessity, need, pressure, priority, seriousness, stress

urgent *adj* 1 *in urgent need of help:* critical, crucial, essential, exigent *formal*, immediate, imperative, important, instant, necessary, pressing, top-priority, vital 2 *spoke in an urgent whisper:* compelling, eager, earnest, grave, insistent, persistent, persuasive, serious
🗷 1 unimportant

urinate *v* leak *colloq*, micturate *formal*, pass water, pee *colloq*, piddle *colloq*, piss *slang*, relieve yourself, spend a penny *colloq*, tinkle *colloq*, wee *colloq*

usable *adj* available, current, exploitable, fit to use, functional, operational, practical, serviceable, valid, working
🗷 unusable, useless

usage *n* 1 *usage of steroids:* application, employment, handling, management, operation, treatment, use 2 *according to local usage:* convention, custom, etiquette, form, habit, method, mode *formal*, practice, procedure, regulation, routine, rule, tradition

use *v* 1 *use the latest techniques:* apply, bring into play, deal with, draw on, employ, enjoy, exercise, handle, make use of, manoeuvre, operate, ply, practise, put to use, resort to, service, take advantage of, treat, utilize, wield, work 2 *they are just using her to make money:* abuse, bleed *colloq*, cash in on *colloq*, exploit, impose on, manipulate, milk *colloq*, misuse, take advantage of, take liberties with 3 *used my last five dollars:* expend, go through, spend, squander
♦ *n* 1 *the use of medicines:* application, employment, exercise, exploitation, manipulation, operation, usage, utilization 2 *of no practical use:* advantage, avail, benefit, end, good, help, object, point, profit, purpose, service, usefulness, value, worth
▶ **use up** absorb, consume, deplete, devour, drain, exhaust, finish, get through, sap, waste

used *adj* cast-off, dog-eared, hand-me-down, nearly new, second-hand, soiled, worn
🗷 fresh, new, unused

useful *adj* **1** *a useful gadget:* advantageous, all-purpose, beneficial, convenient, effective, fruitful, functional, general-purpose, handy, helpful, nifty *colloq*, practical, productive, profitable, rewarding, valuable, worthwhile **2** *quite a useful tennis player:* able, experienced, expert, handy, practised, proficient, skilful, skilled
▣ **1** ineffective, useless, worthless

useless *adj* **1** *useless advice:* broken-down, clapped-out *colloq*, fruitless, futile, hopeless, idle, impractical, ineffectual *formal*, inefficacious *formal*, pointless, to no avail, unavailing, unhelpful, unproductive, unprofitable, unusable, unworkable, vain, worthless **2** *useless at football:* bad, hopeless *colloq*, incapable, incompetent, ineffective, inefficient, weak
▣ **1** effective, helpful, useful **2** good

usher *n* attendant, doorkeeper, escort, guide, usherette
♦ *v* accompany, conduct, direct, escort, guide, lead, pilot, show, steer
▶ **usher in** announce, herald, inaugurate, initiate, introduce, launch, pave the way for, precede, ring in

usual *adj* accepted, accustomed, average, common, conventional, customary, established, everyday, expected, familiar, general, habitual, normal, ordinary, orthodox, predictable, recognized, regular, routine, standard, stock, traditional, typical, unexceptional, wonted *formal*
▣ rare, strange, unusual

usually *adv* as a rule, by and large, chiefly, commonly, for the most part, generally, in the main, mainly, mostly, nine times out of ten *colloq*, normally, on average, on the whole, ordinarily, regularly, routinely, traditionally, typically
▣ exceptionally

usurer *n* extortionist, loan-shark *colloq*, money-lender, Shylock

usurp *v* annex, appropriate, arrogate, assume, commandeer, seize, steal, take, take over, take possession of

usury *n* extortion, interest, money-lending

utensil *n* apparatus, appliance, contrivance, device, gadget, implement, instrument, tool

utilitarian *adj* convenient, effective, efficient, functional, practical, pragmatic, sensible, serviceable, unpretentious, useful
▣ decorative, impractical

utility *n* advantage, avail, benefit, convenience, efficacy *formal*, efficiency, fitness, good, help, practicality, profit, service, serviceableness, use, usefulness, value, worth

utilize *v* adapt, employ, exploit, make use of, put to use, resort to, take advantage of, turn to account, use

utmost *adj* **1** *with the utmost care:* extreme, greatest, highest, maximum, most, paramount, supreme **2** *the utmost ends of the earth:* farthest, final, furthermost, furthest, last, outermost, remotest, ultimate
♦ *n* best, hardest, maximum, most, peak, top

utopia *n* bliss, Eden, Elysium, Garden of Eden, heaven, heaven on earth, paradise, seventh heaven *colloq*, Shangri-la

utopian *adj* airy, chimerical *formal*, Elysian, fanciful, fantastic, ideal, idealistic, illusory, imaginary, impractical, perfect, romantic, unrealistic, unworkable, visionary, wishful

utter[1] *v* announce, articulate, declare, deliver, divulge, enunciate, express, proclaim, pronounce, put into words, reveal, say, sound, speak, state, tell, verbalize, vocalize, voice

utter[2] *adj* absolute, arrant, categorical, complete, consummate, downright, entire, out-and-out, perfect, positive, sheer, stark, thorough, thoroughgoing, total, unmitigated, unqualified

utterance *n* announcement, articulation, comment, declaration, delivery, enunciation, expression, opinion, proclamation, pronouncement, remark, speech, statement, word

utterly *adv* absolutely, categorically, completely, downright, entirely, fully, perfectly, thoroughly, totally, wholly

U-turn *n* about-turn, backtrack, reversal, volte-face

V

vacancy *n* job, opening, opportunity, place, position, post, room, situation

vacant *adj* **1** *a vacant property:* abandoned, available, deserted, empty, free, not in use, unfilled, uninhabited, unoccupied, unused, void **2** *a vacant expression:* absent, absent-minded, blank, deadpan, dreaming, dreamy, expressionless, impassive, inane, inattentive, poker-faced, straight-faced, unthinking, vacuous 🗷 **1** busy, engaged, in use, occupied

vacate *v* abandon, depart, evacuate, leave, quit *colloq,* withdraw

vacation *n* break, furlough, holiday, leave, leave of absence, recess, rest, time off, trip

vacillate *v* dither, fluctuate, haver, hesitate, keep changing your mind, oscillate, shilly-shally, sway, temporize, tergiversate *formal,* waver

vacillating *adj* dithering, hesitant, irresolute, oscillating, shilly-shallying, shuffling, uncertain, unresolved, wavering 🗷 resolute, unhesitating

vacillation *n* fluctuation, hesitancy, hesitation, inconstancy, indecision, indecisiveness, irresolution, shilly-shallying, temporization, tergiversation *formal,* unsteadiness, wavering

vacuity *n* apathy, blankness, emptiness, inanity, incognizance *formal,* incomprehension, incuriosity, nothingness, space, vacuousness, vacuum, void

vacuous *adj* apathetic, blank, empty, idle, inane, incurious, stupid, uncomprehending, unfilled, unintelligent, vacant, void

vacuum *n* chasm, emptiness, gap, hollowness, lacuna *formal,* nothingness, space, vacuity, void

vagabond *n* beggar, bum *slang,* down-and-out, hobo, itinerant, migrant, nomad, outcast, rover, runabout, tramp, vagrant, wanderer, wayfarer

vagary *n* caprice *formal,* crotchet, fancy, humour, megrim *Scot,* notion, prank, quirk, whim, whimsy

vagrant *n* beggar, bum *slang,* drifter, gangrel *Scot,* hobo, itinerant, rolling stone *colloq,* stroller, tramp, wanderer
♦ *adj* homeless, itinerant, nomadic, roaming, rootless, roving, shiftless, travelling, unsettled, vagabond, wandering

vague *adj* **1** *a vague shape:* amorphous *formal,* blurred, dim, faint, foggy, fuzzy, hazy, ill-defined, indistinct, misty, nebulous, obscure, out of focus, shadowy, unfocused **2** *a vague recollection:* ambiguous, approximate, evasive, generalized, imprecise, indefinite, indeterminate *formal,* inexact, lax, loose, rough, uncertain, unclear, undefined, undetermined, unspecific, unspecified, unsure, woolly 🗷 **1** clear **2** definite, precise, specific

vaguely *adv* absent-mindedly, dimly, faintly, imprecisely, inexactly, obscurely, slightly

vagueness *n* ambiguity, amorphousness *formal,* dimness, faintness, fuzziness, haziness, imprecision, inexactitude, looseness, obscurity, uncertainty, unclearness, woolliness 🗷 clarity, precision

vain *adj* **1** *a vain attempt:* abortive *formal,* empty, fruitless, futile, groundless, hollow, idle, insignificant, insubstantial, nugatory *formal,* pointless, trivial, unavailing, unimportant, unproductive, unprofitable, useless, worthless **2** *a vain prima donna:* affected, arrogant, big-headed *colloq,* conceited, egotistical, haughty, high and mighty *colloq,* narcissistic, ostentatious, peacockish, pretentious, proud, self-conceited, self-glorious, self-important, self-satisfied, swaggering, swollen-headed *colloq* 🗷 **1** fruitful, successful **2** modest, self-effacing

valediction *n* adieu, farewell, goodbye, leave-taking, send-off *colloq* 🗷 greeting, welcome

valedictory *adj* departing, farewell, final, last, parting

valetudinarian *adj* delicate, feeble, frail, hypochondriac, infirm, invalid, neurotic, sickly, weakly

valiant *adj* audacious, bold, brave, courageous, dauntless, fearless, gallant, heroic, indomitable *formal,* intrepid, lion-hearted, plucky, staunch, stout-hearted, valorous *formal* 🗷 cowardly, fearful

valid *adj* **1** *valid criticism:* cogent *formal,* conclusive, convincing, credible, forceful, good, just, justifiable, logical, powerful, reasonable, reliable, sound, substantial, telling, weighty, well-founded, well-grounded **2** *a valid passport:* authentic, binding, bona fide, contractual, effective, genuine, lawful, legal, legitimate, official, proper 🗷 **1** false, weak **2** invalid, unofficial

validate *v* **1** *validates our decision:* attest *formal,* authenticate, confirm, corroborate *formal,* endorse, substantiate, underwrite **2** *validate pilot licences:* authenticate, authorize, certify, legalize, ratify

validity *n* **1** *the validity of her claims:* authority, cogency *formal,* force, foundation, grounds, justifiability, legitimacy, logic, point, power, soundness, strength, substance, weight **2** *the validity of their documents:* authority, lawfulness, legality, legitimacy, soundness 🗷 **1** invalidity **2** invalidity

valley *n* cwm, dale, dell, depression, glen, gulch, hollow, slade, strath *Scot,* vale

valorous *adj* bold, brave, courageous, dauntless, doughty, fearless, gallant, hardy, heroic, intrepid, lion-hearted, mettlesome, plucky, stalwart, stout-hearted, valiant 🗷 cowardly, weak

valour *n* boldness, bravery, courage, doughtiness, fearlessness, fortitude *formal,* gallantry, hardiness, heroism, intrepidity, lion-heartedness, mettle, spirit 🗷 cowardice, weakness

valuable *adj* **1** *a valuable necklace:* cherished, costly, dear, estimable, expensive, high-priced, precious, priceless, prized, treasured, valued, worth a pretty penny *colloq*, worth its weight in gold *colloq* **2** *valuable suggestions:* advantageous, beneficial, constructive, fruitful, handy, helpful, important, invaluable, profitable, serviceable, useful, worthwhile, worthy
Fa 1 worthless **2** useless

valuation *n* appraisement *formal*, assessment, computation, estimate, evaluation, survey

value *n* **1** *property values:* cost, price, rate, worth **2** *the value of his experience:* advantage, avail, benefit, desirability, gain, good, importance, merit, profit, significance, use, usefulness, utility, worth **3** *moral values:* ethics, morals, principles, standards
♦ *v* **1** *value your opinion:* admire, appreciate, cherish, esteem *formal*, hold dear, prize, respect, set great store by, treasure **2** *value the company at several million:* appraise *formal*, assess, estimate, evaluate, price, put a price on, rate, survey
Fa 1 disregard, neglect **2** undervalue

valued *adj* beloved, cherished, dear, esteemed *formal*, highly regarded, loved, prized, respected, treasured

vanguard *n* firing line, fore, forefront, front, front line, lead, leading/foremost position, most advanced part, spearhead

vanish *v* **1** *they vanished from view:* depart, disappear, dissolve, evanesce *formal*, exit, fade, fade away/out, leave **2** *her patience rapidly vanished:* die out, dissolve, dwindle, evanesce *formal*, evaporate, fade, fade away/out, fizzle out, melt (away), peter out
Fa 1 appear, materialize **2** increase, materialize

vanity *n* **1** *her one flaw was a certain vanity:* affectation, airs, arrogance, big-headedness *colloq*, conceit, conceitedness, egotism, haughtiness, narcissism, ostentation, pretension, pride, self-conceit, self-glorification, self-love, self-satisfaction, swollen-headedness *colloq* **2** *the vanity of her hopes:* emptiness, fruitlessness, futility, hollowness, idleness, insignificance, pointlessness, triviality, unimportance, unproductiveness, unprofitableness, unreality, uselessness, worthlessness
Fa 1 modesty, worth

vanquish *v* beat, clobber *colloq*, confound, conquer, crush, defeat, hammer *colloq*, humble, master, overcome, overpower, overwhelm, quell, repress, rout, slaughter *colloq*, subdue, subjugate *formal*, triumph over, wipe the floor with *colloq*

vapid *adj* banal, bland, boring, colourless, dead, dull, flat, flavourless, insipid, lifeless, limp, stale, tame, tasteless, tedious, tiresome, trite, uninspiring, uninteresting, vacuous, watery, weak, wishy-washy
Fa interesting, vigorous

vapour *n* breath, damp, dampness, exhalation, fog, fumes, haze, mist, smoke, steam

variable *adj* chameleonic *formal*, changeable, fickle, fitful, flexible, fluctuating, inconstant, mutable, protean *formal*, shifting, temperamental, uneven, unpredictable, unstable, unsteady, vacillating, varying, wavering
Fa fixed, invariable, stable
♦ *n* factor, parameter

variance *n* **1** *variance in delivery times:* difference, discrepancy, divergence, inconsistency, variation **2** *at variance with popular opinion:* conflict, disagreement, discord, disharmony, dissension, dissent, division, odds, opposition, quarrelling, strife
Fa 1 agreement **2** agreement, harmony

variant *n* alternative, development, deviant, modification, rogue, variation
♦ *adj* alternative, derived, deviant, different, divergent, modified
Fa normal, standard, usual

variation *n* alteration, change, departure, deviation, difference, discrepancy, diversification, diversity, fluctuation, inflection, innovation, modification, modulation, novelty, vacillation, variety
Fa monotony, uniformity

varied *adj* assorted, different, diverse, heterogeneous *formal*, miscellaneous, mixed, motley, multifarious *formal*, sundry, various, wide-ranging
Fa standardized, uniform

variegated *adj* dappled, jaspe, many-coloured, marbled, motley, mottled, multicoloured, particoloured, pied, poikilitic *technical*, speckled, streaked, varicoloured
Fa monochrome, plain

variety *n* **1** *a variety of foods:* assortment, collection, medley, miscellany, mixture, potpourri, range **2** *a variety of opinions:* difference, discrepancy, dissimilarity, diversity, multifariousness *formal*, multiplicity *formal*, variation **3** *different varieties of fish:* brand, breed, category, class, classification, kind, make, sort, species, strain, type
Fa 2 similitude *formal*, uniformity

various *adj* assorted, different, differing, disparate *formal*, dissimilar, distinct, diverse, diversified, heterogeneous *formal*, many, miscellaneous, mixed, motley, several, unlike, varied, variegated *formal*, varying

varnish *n* coating, enamel, glaze, gloss, japan, lac, lacquer, polish, resin, shellac, veneer
♦ *v* coat, enamel, glaze, gloss, japan, lacquer, polish, shellac, veneer

vary *v* **1** *vary the menu:* alter, alternate, change, diversify, inflect, metamorphose *formal*, modify, modulate, permutate, reorder, transform **2** *varies from town to town:* be at odds, be dissimilar, be in conflict, depart, differ, diverge, fluctuate

vase *n* amphora, container, ewer, hydria, jar, jug, pitcher, urn, vessel

vassal *n* bondman, bondservant, bondsman, liege, liegeman, retainer, serf, slave, subject, thrall, villein

vast *adj* boundless, colossal, enormous, extensive, far-flung, fathomless, gigantic, great, huge, immeasurable, immense, limitless, massive, monstrous, monumental, never-ending, prodigious *formal*, sweeping, tremendous, unlimited

vault[1] v bound, clear, hurdle, jump, leap, leap-frog, spring

vault[2] n 1 *the bank vaults:* basement, cavern, cellar, crypt, depository, mausoleum, repository, strongroom, tomb, underground chamber, wine-cellar 2 *the vaults of the frescoed celing:* arch, concave, roof, span

vaunt v blow your own horn *US colloq,* blow your own trumpet *colloq,* boast, brag, crow, exult in, flaunt, parade, show off *colloq,* swank *colloq,* trumpet
◳ belittle, minimize

veer v change, deviate, diverge, sheer, shift, swerve, swing, tack, turn, wheel

vegetable

Vegetables include:
artichoke, asparagus, aubergine, bean, beetroot, broad bean, broccoli, Brussels sprout, butter bean, cabbage, calabrese, capsicum, carrot, cauliflower, celeriac, celery, chicory, courgette, cress, cucumber, eggplant *US,* endive, fennel, French bean, garlic, kale, leek, lentil, lettuce, mange tout, marrow, mushroom, okra, onion, parsnip, pea, pepper, petit pois, potato, spud *colloq,* pumpkin, radish, runner bean, shallot, soya bean, spinach, spring onion, swede, sweetcorn, sweet-potato, turnip, watercress, yam, zucchini *US*

vegetate v degenerate, deteriorate, do nothing, go to seed, idle, languish, moulder, rust, rusticate, stagnate

vegetation n flora, flowers, green plants, greenery, herbage *formal,* plants, trees, verdure *formal*

vehemence n animation, ardour, eagerness, earnestness, emphasis, energy, enthusiasm, fervency, fervour, fire, force, forcefulness, heat, intensity, keenness, passion, power, strength, urgency, verve, vigour, violence, warmth, zeal
◳ indifference

vehement adj animated, ardent, eager, earnest, emphatic, enthusiastic, fervent, fervid *formal,* fierce, forceful, forcible, heated, impassioned, intense, keen, passionate, powerful, spirited, strong, urgent, vigorous, violent, zealous
◳ apathetic, indifferent

vehicle n 1 *fuel-efficient vehicles:* conveyance, transport 2 *a vehicle for her talents:* agency, channel, instrument, means, mechanism, medium, organ

Vehicles include:
plane, boat, ship, car, taxi, hackney-carriage; bicycle, bike *colloq,* cycle, tandem, tricycle, boneshaker *colloq,* penny-farthing, motor-cycle, motor-bike, scooter; bus, omnibus, minibus, double-decker *colloq,* coach, charabanc, caravan, caravanette, camper; train, Pullman, sleeper, wagon-lit, tube, tram, monorail, maglev, trolleybus; van, Transit®, lorry, truck, juggernaut, pantechnicon, trailer, tractor, fork-lift truck, steam-roller, tank, wagon; bobsleigh, sled, sledge, sleigh, toboggan, troika; barouche, brougham, dog-cart, dray, four-in-hand, gig, hansom, landau, phaeton, post-chaise, stagecoach, sulky,

surrey, trap; rickshaw, sedan-chair, litter. See also **aircraft, boat, car**

veil v blanket, camouflage, cloak, conceal, cover (up), disguise, hide, mantle, mask, obscure, screen, shade, shadow, shield, shroud
◳ expose, uncover
◆ n blanket, blind, canopy, cloak, cover, covering, curtain, disguise, film, mantle, mask, purdah, screen, shade, shroud

vein n 1 *varicose vein:* blood vessel 2 *cheese with blue veins:* lode, seam, stratum, streak, stripe 3 *in a similar vein:* attitude, bent, disposition, frame of mind, humour, inclination, mode, mood, strain, style, temper, temperament, tendency, tenor, tone

velocity n celerity *formal,* impetus, pace, quickness, rapidity, rate, speed, swiftness

venal adj bent *colloq,* bribable, buyable *colloq,* corrupt, corruptible, grafting, mercenary, simoniacal
◳ incorruptible

vendetta n bad blood, bitterness, blood-feud, enmity, feud, quarrel, rivalry

vendor n merchant, salesperson, seller, stockist, supplier, trader

veneer n 1 *a veneer of respectability:* appearance, camouflage, display, façade, front, gloss, guise, mask, pretence, show 2 *an oak veneer:* coating, covering, finish, gloss, layer, surface

venerable adj aged, august, dignified, esteemed *formal,* grave, hallowed *formal,* honoured, respected, revered, venerated, wise, worshipped

venerate v adore, esteem *formal,* hallow *formal,* honour, respect, revere, worship
◳ anathematize, despise

veneration n adoration, awe, deference, devotion, esteem *formal,* respect, reverence, worship

vengeance n an eye for an eye and a tooth for a tooth *colloq,* reprisal, requital, retaliation, retribution, revenge, tit for tat *colloq*
◳ absolution, forgiveness, mercy, pardon

vengeful adj avenging, implacable, punitive, rancorous *formal,* relentless, retaliatory, retributive, revengeful, spiteful, unforgiving, vindictive
◳ forgiving

venial adj excusable, forgivable, insignificant, minor, negligible, pardonable, slight, trifling, trivial
◳ mortal, unforgivable, unpardonable

venom n 1 *snake venom:* poison, toxin 2 *he spoke with venom:* acrimony *formal,* animosity, bitterness, enmity, hate, hostility, ill-will, malevolence *formal,* malice, rancour, resentment, spite, vindictiveness, virulence

venomous adj 1 *a venomous sting:* deadly, fatal, harmful, lethal, noxious *formal,* poisonous, toxic, virulent 2 *a venomous look:* baleful, baneful, bitter, hostile, malevolent *formal,* malicious, malignant, rancorous *formal,* resentful, spiteful, vicious, vindictive
◳ 1 harmless

vent n aperture, duct, gap, hole, opening, orifice, outlet, passage

♦ *v* air, discharge, emit, express, let out, pour out, release, utter, voice

ventilate *v* **1** *ventilate a room:* aerate, air, cool, freshen **2** *ventilate your feelings:* air, bring out into the open, broadcast, debate, discuss, express

venture *v* **1** *venture to make a suggestion:* advance, dare, go, make bold, presume, put forward, suggest, volunteer **2** *venture a fortune on the outcome:* chance, endanger, gamble, hazard, imperil, jeopardize, put in jeopardy, risk, speculate, stake, wager
♦ *n* adventure, chance, endeavour, enterprise, exploit, fling, gamble, hazard, operation, project, risk, speculation, undertaking

venturesome *adj* adventurous, audacious, bold, brave, courageous, daredevil *colloq*, daring, dauntless, doughty, enterprising, fearless, intrepid, plucky, spirited
▣ cowardly, unenterprising

veracious *adj* accurate, credible, dependable, exact, factual, faithful, frank, genuine, honest, reliable, straightforward, true, trustworthy, truthful
▣ untruthful

veracity *n* accuracy, candour, credibility, exactitude, frankness, honesty, integrity, precision, probity *formal*, rectitude *formal*, trustworthiness, truth, truthfulness
▣ untruthfulness

verbal *adj* linguistic, oral, said, spoken, unwritten, uttered, verbatim, vocal, word-of-mouth
▣ written

verbatim *adv* closely, exactly, literally, precisely, to the letter, word for word

verbiage *n* circumlocution *formal*, periphrasis *formal*, pleonasm *formal*, prolixity *formal*, repetition, verbosity, waffle
▣ briefness, succinctness

verbose *adj* circumlocutory *formal*, diffuse, garrulous, long-winded, loquacious *formal*, periphrastic *formal*, pleonastic *formal*, prolix *formal*, windy, wordy
▣ brief, succinct

verbosity *n* garrulity, logorrhoea, long-windedness, loquaciousness *formal*, loquacity *formal*, multiloquy *formal*, prolixity *formal*, verbiage, verboseness, windiness, wordiness
▣ economy, succinctness

verdant *adj* fresh, graminaceous *formal*, gramineous *formal*, grassy, green, leafy, lush, virid *formal*, viridescent *formal*

verdict *n* adjudication, assessment, conclusion, decision, finding, judgement, opinion, ruling, sentence

verge *n* **1** *the grass verge:* border, boundary, edge, edging, extremity, limit, margin, rim **2** *on the verge of civil war:* brim, brink, edge, rim, threshold
▶ **verge on** approach, border on, come close to, near, tend towards

verification *n* attestation *formal*, authentication, checking, confirmation, corroboration *formal*, proof, substantiation, validation

verify *v* accredit *formal*, attest *formal*, authenticate, bear out, confirm, corroborate

formal, endorse, prove, substantiate, support, testify, validate
▣ discredit, invalidate

verisimilitude *n* authenticity, colour, credibility, likeliness, plausibility, realism, resemblance, ring of truth *colloq*, semblance
▣ implausibility

verity *n* actuality, authenticity, factuality, soundness, truth, truthfulness, validity, veracity *formal*
▣ untruth

vernacular *adj* colloquial, common, indigenous, informal, local, native, popular, vulgar
♦ *n* cant, dialect, idiom, jargon, language, lingo *colloq*, parlance, speech, tongue

versatile *adj* adaptable, adjustable, all-purpose, all-round, flexible, functional, general-purpose, handy, many-sided, multifaceted, multipurpose, resourceful, variable
▣ inflexible

versed *adj* accomplished, acquainted, competent, conversant, experienced, familiar, knowledgeable, learned, practised, proficient, qualified, read, seasoned, skilled

version *n* **1** *his version of events:* account, adaptation, interpretation, paraphrase, portrayal, reading, rendering, report, translation, understanding **2** *the film version:* design, form, kind, model, reproduction, style, type, variant

vertex *n* acme *technical*, apex, apogee, crown, culmination, extremity, height, highest point, peak, pinnacle, summit, top, zenith
▣ nadir

vertical *adj* erect, on end, perpendicular, sheer, straight up, upright, upstanding
▣ horizontal

vertigo *n* dizziness, giddiness, light-headedness, sickness

verve *n* animation, brio, dash, élan, energy, enthusiasm, fervour, force, gusto, life, liveliness, passion, pizzazz *colloq*, relish, sparkle, spirit, vigour, vitality, vivacity, zip *colloq*
▣ apathy, lethargy

very *adv* absolutely, acutely, awfully *colloq*, deeply, dreadfully *colloq*, exceeding(ly), exceptionally, excessively, extremely, greatly, highly, incredibly, noticeably, particularly, really, remarkably, terribly *colloq*, truly, unbelievably, uncommonly, unusually
▣ scarcely, slightly
♦ *adj* **1** *the very essence of rural life:* actual, exact, genuine, perfect, pure, real, sheer, true, utter **2** *the very one I was looking for:* actual, exact, same, selfsame

vessel *n* **1** *a naval vessel:* barque, boat, craft, ship **2** *empty vessels:* bowl, container, holder, jar, jug, pitcher, pot, receptacle

vest *v* authorize, bestow, confer *formal*, empower, endow, give, grant, sanction, supply

vestibule *n* anteroom, entrance, entrance hall, entranceway, foyer, hall, lobby, porch, portico

vestige *n* evidence, glimmer, hint, impression, indication, inkling, mark, print, relics, remainder, remains, remnant, residue, scrap, sign, suspicion, token, touch, trace, track, whiff *colloq*

vestigial *adj* 1 *vestigial danger:* reduced, remaining, surviving 2 *vestigial wings:* functionless, imperfect, incomplete, rudimentary, undeveloped

vet *v* appraise *formal*, audit, check (out), examine, inspect, investigate, review, scan, scrutinize, survey

veteran *n* master, old hand, old stager, old-timer, pastmaster, pro *colloq*, warhorse
☒ novice, recruit
♦ *adj* adept, battle-scarred, experienced, expert, long-serving, old, practised, proficient, seasoned
☒ inexperienced

veto *v* ban, block, disallow *formal*, forbid, give the thumbs-down to *colloq*, interdict *formal*, prohibit, proscribe *formal*, reject, rule out, turn down
☒ approve, sanction
♦ *n* ban, embargo, prohibition, proscription *formal*, rejection, thumbs-down *colloq*
☒ approval, assent

vex *v* aggravate *colloq*, agitate, annoy, bother, bug *colloq*, distress, disturb, enrage, exasperate, fret, get someone's back up *colloq*, get someone's blood up *colloq*, harass, hassle *colloq*, irritate, needle *colloq*, perturb *formal*, pester, provoke, put out *colloq*, torment, trouble, upset, worry
☒ calm, soothe

vexation *n* aggravation *colloq*, anger, annoyance, bore, bother, chagrin, difficulty, displeasure, dissatisfaction, exasperation, frustration, fury, headache *colloq*, irritant, nuisance, pain *colloq*, pain in the ass/butt *US slang*, pain in the backside/arse *slang*, pique, problem, thorn in the flesh *colloq*, trouble, upset, worry

vexatious *adj* afflicting, aggravating *colloq*, annoying, bothersome, burdensome, disagreeable, disappointing, distressing, exasperating, infuriating, irksome, irritating, nagging, pesky *colloq*, pestiferous *formal*, provoking, teasing, tormenting, troublesome, trying, unpleasant, upsetting, worrisome, worrying
☒ pleasant, soothing

vexed *adj* 1 *feeling vexed:* aggravated *colloq*, agitated, annoyed, bothered, confused, displeased, distressed, disturbed, exasperated, flustered, harassed, hassled *colloq*, incensed, infuriated, irate, irritated, miffed *colloq*, narked *colloq*, nettled *colloq*, peeved *colloq*, perplexed, provoked, put out, riled, ruffled, troubled, upset, worried 2 *a vexed question:* contested, controversial, debated, difficult, disputed, in dispute, moot *formal*

viable *adj* achievable, feasible, operable, possible, practicable, sound, sustainable, usable, workable
☒ impossible, unworkable

vibes *n* ambience, atmosphere, aura, emanation, emotions, feel, feelings, reaction, response, vibrations

vibrant *adj* 1 *a vibrant community:* animated, dynamic, electric, electrifying, energetic, lively, responsive, sensitive, sparkling, spirited, thrilling, vigorous, vivacious 2 *vibrant colours:* bright, brilliant, colourful, striking, vivid

vibrate *v* oscillate, pulsate, quiver, resonate, resound, reverberate, shake, shiver, shudder, sway, swing, throb, tremble, undulate

vibration *n* frisson, judder, juddering, oscillation, pulsation, pulse, quiver, resonance, resounding, reverberation, shaking, shudder, throb, throbbing, trembling, tremor

vicarious *adj* acting, commissioned, delegated, deputed, empathetic *formal*, indirect, second-hand, substituted, surrogate

vice *n* 1 *the vice of drug-trafficking:* corruption, degeneracy, depravity, evil, evil-doing, immorality, iniquity *formal*, profligacy *formal*, sin, transgression *formal*, wickedness, wrongdoing 2 *chocolate is her secret vice:* bad habit, besetting sin, blemish, defect, failing, fault, flaw, foible, imperfection, shortcoming, weakness
☒ 1 morality, virtue

vice versa *adj* contrariwise, conversely, inversely, oppositely, reciprocally, the other way round

vicinity *n* area, district, environs, locality, neighbourhood, precincts, propinquity *formal*, proximity, surroundings

vicious *adj* 1 *a vicious dog:* barbarous, brutal, cruel, dangerous, ferocious, fierce, savage, violent, wild 2 *a vicious smear campaign:* bitchy *colloq*, catty *colloq*, caustic, cruel, defamatory, malevolent *formal*, malicious, mean, nasty, slanderous, spiteful, venomous, vindictive, virulent 3 *a vicious cycle of sectarian violence:* bad, corrupt, debased, degenerate, depraved, diabolical, heinous, immoral, perverted, profligate *formal*, unprincipled, vile, wicked, wrong
☒ 1 gentle 2 kind 3 virtuous

viciousness *n* badness, bitchiness *colloq*, brutality, corruption, cruelty, depravity, ferocity, immorality, malice, profligacy *formal*, rancour *formal*, savagery, sinfulness, spite, spitefulness, venom, virulence, wickedness
☒ gentleness, goodness, virtue

vicissitude *n* alteration, alternation, change, deviation, divergence, fluctuation, mutation *formal*, revolution, shift, turn, twist, variation

victim *n* 1 *a victim of the attack:* casualty, fatality, martyr, sacrifice, sufferer 2 *victims of the fraud:* dupe *colloq*, fall guy *colloq*, prey, quarry, scapegoat, sitting target *colloq*, sucker *colloq*
☒ 1 attacker, offender

victimize *v* 1 *victimized by violence:* bully, discriminate against, exploit, oppress, persecute, pick on, prey on, take (unfair) advantage of 2 *victimized by identity theft:* cheat, deceive, defraud, dupe, fool, hoodwink, swindle *colloq*, trick

victor *n* champ *colloq*, champion, conqueror, first, prize-winner, subjugator *formal*, top dog *colloq*, vanquisher *formal*, victor ludorum *formal*, winner
☒ loser, vanquished *formal*

victorious *adj* champion, conquering, first, prize-winning, successful, top, triumphant, unbeaten, vanquishing *formal*, winning
☒ defeated, unsuccessful

victory n conquest, mastery, overcoming, subjugation, success, superiority, triumph, vanquishment, win
🖅 defeat, failure, loss

victuals n aliment *formal*, bread, comestibles, eatables *colloq*, eats *colloq*, edibles, food, grub *slang*, nosh *slang*, provisions, rations, stores, supplies, sustenance, tuck *colloq*, viands *formal*

vie v compete, contend, contest, fight, rival, strive, struggle

view n 1 *in my view:* angle, attitude, belief, conviction, estimation, feeling, idea, impression, judgement, notion, opinion, point of view, sentiment, thought, viewpoint 2 *a view of the sea:* composition, landscape, outlook, panorama, perspective, prospect, range of vision, scene, sight, spectacle, vision, vista 3 *open to public view:* assessment, contemplation, examination, inspection, observation, review, scan, scrutiny, study, survey
♦ v 1 *view the scene:* examine, gaze at, inspect, look at, observe, perceive, scan, scrutinize, see, survey, watch, witness 2 *view the consequences:* consider, contemplate, judge, reflect on, regard, speculate, think about

viewer n observer, onlooker, spectator, watcher

viewpoint n angle, attitude, feeling, opinion, perspective, position, slant, stance, standpoint

vigil n lookout, pernoctation *formal*, stake-out, wake, wakefulness, watch

vigilance n alertness, attentiveness, carefulness, caution, circumspection *formal*, guardedness, observation, wakefulness, watchfulness

vigilant adj alert, attentive, aware, careful, cautious, circumspect *formal*, observant, on the lookout, on your guard, watchful, wide-awake
🖅 careless

vigorous adj 1 *a vigorous wholesome life:* active, athletic, energetic, healthy, lively, lusty, robust, sound, strenuous, strong, tough, vital 2 *a vigorous defence of his legacy:* animated, brisk, dynamic, effective, efficient, enterprising, flourishing, forceful, forcible, full-blooded, intense, lively, powerful, sparkling, spirited, stout
🖅 2 feeble, weak

vigorously adv briskly, eagerly, energetically, forcefully, hard, heartily, lustily, powerfully, strenuously, strongly
🖅 feebly, weakly

vigour n activity, animation, brio *colloq*, dash, dynamism, energy, force, forcefulness, gusto, health, liveliness, might, oomph *colloq*, pep *colloq*, potency, power, resilience, robustness, soundness, spirit, stamina, strength, sturdiness, toughness, verve, vitality, vivacity *formal*, zip *colloq*
🖅 weakness

vile adj 1 *a vile meal:* disagreeable, disgusting, distasteful, foul, horrible, horrid, loathsome, nasty, nauseating, noxious *formal*, obnoxious, offensive, repugnant, repulsive, revolting, sickening, unpleasant 2 *vile depravity:* appalling, bad, base, contemptible, corrupt, debased, degenerate, degrading, depraved, despicable, disgraceful, evil, impure, iniquitous *formal*, low,

mean, miserable, sinful, vicious, wicked, worthless, wretched
🖅 1 lovely, pleasant 2 pure, worthy

vilification n abuse, aspersion *formal*, calumniation *formal*, calumny *formal*, contumely *formal*, criticism, defamation, denigration, disparagement *formal*, invective *formal*, mud-slinging *colloq*, revilement *formal*, scurrility, vituperation *formal*

vilify v abuse, asperse *formal*, badmouth *colloq*, berate *formal*, calumniate *formal*, criticize, debase, decry *formal*, defame, denigrate, denounce, disparage *formal*, malign *formal*, revile, slam *colloq*, slander, slate *colloq*, smear, stigmatize, traduce *formal*, vilipend *formal*, vituperate *formal*
🖅 adore, compliment, eulogize, glorify, praise

village n community, hamlet, one-horse town *colloq*, settlement, town

villain n baddy *colloq*, criminal, devil, evildoer, knave, malefactor *formal*, miscreant *formal*, rascal, reprobate, rogue, scoundrel, wretch, wrongdoer
🖅 goody *colloq*, hero, heroine

villainous adj bad, criminal, cruel, debased, degenerate, depraved, disgraceful, evil, fiendish, heinous *formal*, inhuman, iniquitous *formal*, nefarious *formal*, notorious, opprobrious *formal*, sinful, terrible, vicious, vile, wicked
🖅 good

villainy n atrocity, badness, baseness, crime, criminality, delinquency, depravity, iniquity *formal*, knavery, rascality, roguery, sin, turpitude *formal*, vice, viciousness, wickedness

vindicate v 1 *posthumously vindicated:* absolve, acquit, clear, exculpate *formal*, excuse, exonerate *formal*, rehabilitate 2 *the report vindicated his actions:* advocate, assert, back, champion, confirm, corroborate *formal*, defend, establish, justify, maintain, support, sustain, uphold, verify, warrant

vindication n 1 *a vindication of their position:* assertion, defence, extenuation, justification, maintenance, rehabilitation, substantiation, support, verification 2 *this pardon is a measure of vindication:* apology, exculpation *formal*, excuse, exoneration *formal*, extenuation, plea
🖅 2 accusation, conviction

vindictive adj implacable, malevolent *formal*, malicious, punitive, rancorous *formal*, resentful, revengeful, spiteful, unforgiving, vengeful, venomous
🖅 forgiving

vintage n 1 *of the same vintage:* epoch, era, generation, origin, period, time, year 2 *this year's record vintage:* crop, gathering, generation, harvest
♦ adj 1 *vintage Sinatra:* best, choice, classic, enduring, fine, high-quality, prime, quality, ripe, select, superior, supreme 2 *a vintage gown:* classic, mature, old, venerable, veteran

violate v 1 *violate civil liberties:* breach, break, contravene, disobey, disregard, flout, infract *formal*, infringe, transgress *formal* 2 *violate the sacred sites:* defile, desecrate, dishonour, disrupt, disturb, invade, profane 3 *she was cruelly violated:* debauch, defile, interfere with, molest, rape, ravish
🖅 1 observe

violation *n* abuse, breach, contravention, defilement, desecration, disruption, encroachment, infraction *formal*, infringement, offence, outrage, profanation, sacrilege, spoliation *formal*, transgression *formal*, trespass
🔁 obedience, observance

violence *n* **1** *the violence of his performance:* ferocity, fierceness, force, forcefulness, intensity, might *formal*, passion, power, severity, strength, tumult, turbulence, vehemence, wildness **2** *domestic violence:* aggression, bloodshed, brutality, cruelty, destructiveness, fighting, frenzy, fury, hostilities, murderousness, passion, roughness, savagery, wildness

violent *adj* **1** *a violent reaction to the drug:* acute, agonizing, destructive, devastating, dramatic, excruciating, extreme, forceful, forcible, great, harmful, harsh, injurious, intense, painful, passionate, powerful, rough, ruinous, severe, sharp, strong, tumultuous, turbulent, vehement **2** *violent criminals:* aggressive, bloodthirsty, brutal, cruel, destructive, ferocious, fierce, fiery, furious, headstrong, hot-headed, impetuous, intemperate, maddened, murderous, outrageous, passionate, riotous, savage, uncontrollable, ungovernable, unrestrained, vicious, wild
🔁 **1** calm, moderate **2** gentle, peaceful

VIP *n* big cheese *colloq*, big name *colloq*, big noise *colloq*, big shot *colloq*, bigwig *colloq*, celebrity, dignitary, headliner, heavyweight *colloq*, lion, luminary, magnate, notable, personage, somebody, star
🔁 nobody, nonentity

virago *n* battle-axe *colloq*, dragon, fury, gorgon, harridan, scold, shrew, tartar, termagant, vixen, Xanthippe

virgin *n* celibate, girl, maiden, vestal
♦ *adj* chaste, fresh, immaculate, intact, new, pure, spotless, stainless, unblemished, undefiled, unspoilt, unsullied, untainted, untouched, virginal

virginal *adj* celibate, chaste, fresh, immaculate, maidenly, pristine *formal*, pure, snowy, spotless, stainless, uncorrupted, undefiled, undisturbed, untouched, vestal, virgin, white

virginity *n* chasteness, chastity, maidenhood, purity, virtue

virile *adj* forceful, lusty, macho *colloq*, male, man-like, manly, masculine, muscular, potent, red-blooded, robust, rugged, strapping, strong, vigorous
🔁 effeminate, impotent

virility *n* machismo, manhood, manliness, masculinity, potency, ruggedness, vigour
🔁 effeminacy, impotence, weakness

virtual *adj* effective, essential, for all practical purposes, implicit, implied, in all but name, in effect, potential, practical, prospective

virtually *adv* almost, as good as, conceivably, effectively, for all practical purposes, in all but name, in effect, in essence, more or less, nearly, practically

virtue *n* **1** *patience is a virtue:* excellence, goodness, high-mindedness, honesty, honour, incorruptibility, integrity, justice, morality, probity *formal*, rectitude *formal*, righteousness,

uprightness, worthiness **2** *the virtues of education:* advantage, asset, benefit, credit, merit, plus *colloq*, quality, strength, worth
🔁 **1** vice

virtuosity *n* artistry, bravura, brilliance, éclat, expertise, finesse, finish, flair, mastery, panache, polish, skill, wizardry

virtuoso *n* expert, genius, maestro, master, prodigy
♦ *adj* brilliant, dazzling, excellent, expert, masterly, skilful

virtuous *adj* angelic, blameless, clean-living, decent, ethical, excellent, exemplary, good, high-principled, honest, honourable, incorruptible, innocent, irreproachable, moral, respectable, righteous, unimpeachable, upright, upstanding, worthy
🔁 immoral, vicious

virulence *n* **1** *the virulence of racism:* deadliness, poison, toxicity, venom **2** *the virulence of the campaign:* acrimony, antagonism, bitterness, harmfulness, hatred, hostility, hurtfulness, malevolence, malice, malignancy, rancour *formal*, resentment, spite, spleen, viciousness, vindictiveness, vitriol

virulent *adj* **1** *virulent influenza viruses:* communicable, contagious, epidemic, infectious, spreading, transmittable **2** *a virulent boil:* deadly, extreme, fatal, injurious, intense, lethal, malignant, pernicious, poisonous, severe, toxic, venomous **3** *virulent detractors:* acrimonious, bitter, hostile, malevolent *formal*, malicious, rancorous *formal*, resentful, spiteful, vicious, vindictive, vitriolic
🔁 **2** harmless

viscous *adj* adhesive, gelatinous *formal*, gluey, glutinous *formal*, gooey *colloq*, gummy, mucilaginous *formal*, mucous, sticky, syrupy, tacky, tenacious, thick, treacly, viscid
🔁 runny, thin, watery

visible *adj* apparent, clear, conspicuous, detectable, discernible, discoverable, distinguishable, evident, exposed, manifest *formal*, noticeable, observable, obvious, open, overt, palpable, patent, perceivable, perceptible, plain, recognizable, showing, unconcealed, undisguised, unmistakable
🔁 hidden, indiscernible, invisible

vision *n* **1** *perfect vision:* discernment, eyesight, far-sightedness, foresight, penetration, perception, seeing, sight **2** *her vision for the future:* conception, daydream, dream, fantasy, idea, ideal, image, imagination, insight, intuition, mental image, mental picture, perception, picture, view **3** *a sudden vision appeared:* apparition, chimera, delusion, dream, ghost, hallucination, illusion, mirage, optical illusion, phantom, spectre, wraith

visionary *adj* discerning, dreamy, fanciful, far-sighted, idealistic, imaginative, impractical, perceptive, prophetic, quixotic, romantic, speculative, unreal, unrealistic, unworkable, utopian
♦ *n* daydreamer, Don Quixote, dreamer, fantasist, idealist, mystic, prophet, rainbow-chaser, romantic, seer, theorist, utopian
🔁 pragmatist

visit *v* **1** *visit her brother:* call in, call on, drop by *colloq,* drop in on *colloq,* go and see, go round/ over to, look in, look up, pop in *colloq,* see, spend time with, stay at, stay with, stop by *colloq* **2** *visited by tragedy:* afflict, curse, inflict, plague, punish, trouble
♦ *n* call, excursion, sojourn *formal,* stay, stop

visitation *n* **1** *a visitation by inspectors:* examination, inspection, visit **2** *a visitation of bad luck:* bane, blight, calamity, cataclysm, catastrophe, disaster, infliction, ordeal, punishment, retribution, scourge, trial **3** *ghostly visitations:* appearance, manifestation

visitor *n* **1** *a regular visitor:* caller, company, guest **2** *foreign visitors:* holidaymaker, tourist, traveller

vista *n* outlook, panorama, perspective, prospect, scene, view, vision

visual *adj* **1** *a visual image:* discernible, observable, perceptible, specular *formal,* visible **2** *visual impairment:* ocular *formal,* optic *formal,* optical

visualize *v* conceive, conceive of, contemplate, envisage, imagine, picture, see

vital *adj* **1** *vital repairs:* basic, critical, crucial, decisive, essential, forceful, fundamental, imperative, important, indispensable, key, life-and-death, necessary, requisite *formal,* significant, urgent **2** *a vital and fun performance:* alive, animated, dynamic, energetic, forceful, invigorating, life-giving, lively, living, quickening *formal,* spirited, vibrant, vigorous, vivacious
ⅷ **1** inessential, peripheral **2** dead

vitality *n* animation, energy, exuberance, get-up-and-go *colloq,* go *colloq,* life, liveliness, oomph *colloq,* pizzazz *colloq,* sparkle, spirit, stamina, strength, vigour, vivacity, zest

vitiate *v* blemish, blight, contaminate, corrupt, debase, defile, deprave, deteriorate, devalue, harm, impair, injure, invalidate, mar, nullify, pervert, pollute, ruin, spoil, sully, taint, undermine, weaken

vitriolic *adj* abusive, acerbic *formal,* acrimonious *formal,* biting, bitter, caustic, destructive, malicious, mordant *formal,* sardonic, scathing, trenchant *formal,* venomous, vicious, virulent, vituperative *formal*

vituperate *v* abuse, berate *formal,* blame, castigate *formal,* censure, denounce, reproach, revile, slag off *colloq,* slam *colloq,* slate *colloq,* upbraid *formal,* vilify *formal*
ⅷ applaud, extol, praise

vituperation *n* abuse, blame, castigation *formal,* censure, contumely *formal,* diatribe *formal,* fault-finding, flak *colloq,* invective *formal,* objurgation *formal,* obloquy *formal,* philippic *formal,* rebuke, reprimand, reproach, revilement *formal,* scurrility, stick *colloq,* vilification *formal*
ⅷ acclaim, praise

vituperative *adj* abusive, belittling, calumniatory *formal,* censorious, defamatory, denunciatory *formal,* derogatory, fulminatory *formal,* harsh, insulting, opprobrious *formal,* scornful, withering
ⅷ laudatory

vivacious *adj* animated, bubbly *colloq,* cheerful, ebullient *formal,* effervescent, high-spirited,

jolly, light-hearted, lively, merry, sparkling, spirited

vivacity *n* activity, animation, brio *colloq,* dynamism, ebullience *formal,* effervescence, élan, energy, light-heartedness, liveliness, merriness, quickness, spirit, vitality

vivid *adj* **1** *vivid colours:* animated, bright, brilliant, colourful, dazzling, dramatic, dynamic, expressive, flamboyant, glaring, glowing, intense, lifelike, lively, lurid, rich, spirited, strong, vibrant, vigorous **2** *vivid memories:* clear, distinct, dramatic, graphic, lively, memorable, powerful, realistic, sharp, striking
ⅷ **1** colourless, dull **2** vague

vividness *n* **1** *the vividness of her green eyes:* brightness, brilliancy, glow, intensity, life, liveliness, radiance, refulgence *formal,* resplendence *formal* **2** *the vividness of her feelings:* clarity, distinctness, immediacy, intensity, lucidity, realism, sharpness, strength
ⅷ **1** dullness, lifelessness

vocabulary *n* language, lexicon, lexis *technical,* words

vocal *adj* **1** *vocal exercises:* expressed, oral, said, spoken, uttered, voiced **2** *a vocal opponent:* articulate, blunt, clamorous, eloquent, expressive, forthright, frank, noisy, outspoken, plain-spoken, shrill, strident, vociferous
ⅷ **1** unspoken **2** inarticulate

vocation *n* business, calling, career, craft, employment, job, line, métier, mission, occupation, office, post, profession, pursuit, role, trade, work

vociferous *adj* blunt, clamorous, forthright, frank, loud, noisy, obstreperous, outspoken, shouting, strident, thundering, vehement, vocal
ⅷ quiet

vogue *n* acceptance, craze, custom, fad *colloq,* fashion, mode *formal,* popularity, prevalence, style, taste, the latest *colloq,* the rage *colloq,* the thing *colloq,* trend

voice *n* **1** *a shrill voice:* agency, articulation, expression, inflection, instrument, intonation, medium, mouthpiece, organ, sound, speech, tone, utterance, words **2** *have a voice in the matter:* airing, decision, desire, opinion, option, say, view, vote, will, wish
♦ *v* air, articulate, assert, convey, declare, disclose, divulge, enunciate, express, mention, say, speak of, talk of, utter, verbalize

void *adj* **1** *void of emotion:* bare, blank, clear, devoid, drained, emptied, empty, free, lacking, unfilled, unoccupied, vacant **2** *the election was declared null and void:* annulled, cancelled, futile, ineffective, inoperative, invalid, nugatory, nullified, useless, vain, worthless
ⅷ **1** full **2** binding, valid
♦ *n* abyss, blank, blankness, cavity, chasm, emptiness, gap, hollow, lack, lacuna *formal,* opening, space, vacuity, vacuum, want
♦ *v* **1** *the votes were voided:* abnegate *formal,* annul, cancel, invalidate, nullify, rescind **2** *they voided their bowels:* defecate, discharge, eject, emit, empty, evacuate
ⅷ **1** validate **2** fill

volatile *adj* **1** *volatile energy prices:* capricious *formal,* changeable, erratic, fickle, fitful, flighty, giddy, inconstant, irregular, restless,

unpredictable, unsettled, unstable, unsteady, up and down *colloq*, variable **2** *a volatile marriage:* charged, explosive, lively, mercurial *formal*, temperamental, unpredictable, unsettled, unstable, unsteady, up and down *colloq*, volcanic
Ⓕ 1 constant, steady **2** calm, steady

volcano

The world's active volcanoes include:
Mayon, Hudson, Kilauea, Mount Pinatubo, Vulcano, Mount St Helens, Etna, Ruapehu, Stromboli, Klyuchevskoy, Mauna Loa, Nyamuragira, Hekla, Krakatoa, Taal, Vesuvius

---

volition *n* choice, choosing, determination, discretion, election, free will, option, preference, purpose, resolution, will

volley *n* barrage, blast, bombardment, burst, cannonade, discharge, explosion, fusillade, hail, salvo, shower

voluble *adj* articulate, chatty *colloq*, fluent, forthcoming, garrulous, glib, loquacious *formal*, talkative

volume *n* **1** *the volume of imports:* aggregate, amount, amplitude, body, bulk, capacity, dimensions, loudness, mass, quantity, size, sound, space **2** *turn the volume up:* loudness, sound **3** *a slim volume:* book, omnibus *formal*, publication, tome

voluminous *adj* ample, big, billowing, bulky, capacious *formal*, full, huge, large, roomy, spacious, vast

voluntarily *adv* by choice, consciously, deliberately, freely, intentionally, of your own accord, of your own free will, on your own initiative, purposely, spontaneously, willingly
Ⓕ involuntarily, unwillingly

voluntary *adj* **1** *voluntary work:* free, gratuitous, honorary, spontaneous, unforced, unpaid, volunteer, willing **2** *voluntary redundancy:* conscious, deliberate, intended, intentional, of your own free will, of your own volition *formal*, purposeful, wilful
Ⓕ 1 compulsory, obligatory **2** involuntary

volunteer *v* advance, offer, present, proffer *formal*, propose, put forward, step forward, suggest, tender

voluptuary *n* bon vivant, debauchee, epicurean, hedonist, libertine, playboy *colloq*, pleasure-seeker, profligate *formal*, sensualist, sybarite
Ⓕ ascetic

voluptuous *adj* **1** *voluptuous sensations:* hedonistic, licentious, luxurious, opulent, self-indulgent, sensual, sensuous **2** *a voluptuous screen goddess:* buxom, enticing, erotic, full-figured, provocative, seductive, sexy *colloq*, shapely

vomit *v* barf *US slang*, be sick, bring up, fetch up *colloq*, heave, puke *colloq*, regurgitate, retch, spew *colloq*, throw up *colloq*

voracious *adj* avid, devouring, edacious *formal*, gluttonous, greedy, hungry, insatiable,

omnivorous *formal*, prodigious *formal*, rapacious *formal*, ravening, ravenous, uncontrolled, unquenchable

voracity *n* acquisitiveness, avidity, eagerness, edacity *formal*, greed, hunger, rapacity *formal*, ravenousness

vortex *n* eddy, maelstrom, whirl, whirlpool, whirlwind

votary *n* addict, adherent, believer, devotee, disciple, follower

vote *n* **1** *to cast your vote:* ballot, election, franchise, plebiscite, poll, referendum **2** *give everyone the vote:* enfranchisement, franchise, suffrage
Ⓕ 2 disenfranchisement
♦ *v* **1** *only seventy per cent voted:* cast your vote, go to the polls **2** *voted to go on strike:* ballot, choose, declare, elect, opt, plump

vouch
▶ **vouch for** affirm, answer for, assert, asseverate *formal*, assure, attest to *formal*, back, certify, confirm, endorse, guarantee, speak for, support, swear to, uphold, verify, warrant

voucher *n* coupon, document, paper, ticket, token

vouchsafe *v* accord *formal*, bestow *formal*, cede, confer *formal*, deign, give, grant, impart, yield

vow *v* affirm, dedicate, devote, give your word, pledge, profess, promise, swear, undertake
♦ *n* oath, pledge, promise

voyage *n* crossing, cruise, expedition, journey, odyssey *formal*, passage, safari, sail, tour, travel(s), trip
♦ *v* cruise, go, journey, sail, tour, travel

vulgar *adj* **1** *vulgar language:* bawdy, coarse, crude, dirty, distasteful, filthy, impolite, improper, indecent, indelicate, lewd, near the bone *colloq*, obscene, off-colour, offensive, ribald, risqué, rude, suggestive **2** *vulgar breeding:* boorish, coarse, common, crude, ill-bred, impolite, indecorous *formal*, rough, rude, uncouth, unrefined **3** *a vulgar gift:* cheap and nasty *colloq*, flashy, garish, gaudy, glitzy *colloq*, kitsch, loud, ostentatious, showy, tacky *colloq*, tasteless, tawdry **4** *the vulgar hordes:* common, general, low, ordinary, popular, uncultured, unsophisticated, vernacular
Ⓕ 1 decent, polite **2** refined **3** tasteful
4 sophisticated

vulgarity *n* **1** *the vulgarity of his words:* coarseness, crudeness, crudity, dirtiness, indecency, ribaldry, rudeness, suggestiveness **2** *their brash vulgarity:* garishness, gaudiness, ostentation, showiness, tastelessness, tawdriness
Ⓕ 1 decency, politeness **2** tastefulness

vulnerable *adj* defenceless, exposed, helpless, insecure, open, open to attack, powerless, sensitive, susceptible, unguarded, unprotected, weak, wide open
Ⓕ protected, safe, strong

W

wacky *adj* crazy, daft, eccentric, erratic, goofy *colloq*, irrational, loony *colloq*, loopy *colloq*, nutty *colloq*, odd, off beat *colloq*, screwy *colloq*, silly, unpredictable, wild, zany
☲ sensible

wad *n* ball, block, bundle, chunk, hunk, lump, mass, plug, roll, wodge *colloq*

wadding *n* cottonwool, filler, filling, lining, packing, padding, stuffing

waddle *v* rock, shuffle, sway, toddle, totter, wobble

wade *v* cross, ford, lurch, plough, splash, traverse *formal*
▶ **wade in** get stuck in, launch in, pitch in, set to, tear in

waffle *v* babble, blather, jabber, prattle, rabbit on *colloq*, witter on *colloq*
♦ *n* blather, gobbledygook *colloq*, guff *colloq*, hot air *colloq*, nonsense, padding, prattle, verbosity *formal*, wordiness

waft *v* blow, carry, drift, float, glide, transmit, transport
♦ *n* breath, breeze, current, draught, puff, scent, whiff

wag *v* bob, flutter, nod, oscillate, quiver, rock, shake, sway, swing, vibrate, waggle, wave, wiggle, wobble
♦ *n* banterer, clown, comedian, comic, droll, fool, humorist, jester, joker, wit

wage *n* allowance, compensation, earnings, emolument *formal*, fee, hire, pay, payment, recompense, remuneration, returns, reward, salary, stipend, wage-packet
♦ *v* carry on, conduct, engage in, execute, practise, pursue, undertake

wager *v* bet, chance, gamble, hazard, lay odds, pledge, punt, risk, speculate, stake, venture
♦ *n* bet, flutter, gamble, hazard, pledge, punt, speculation, stake, venture

waggish *adj* amusing, bantering, comical, droll, facetious, frolicsome, funny, humorous, impish, jesting, jocose, jocular, merry, mischievous, playful, puckish, risible *formal*, roguish, sportive, witty
☲ grave, serious, staid

waggle *v* bobble, flutter, jiggle, oscillate, shake, wag, wave, wiggle, wobble

waif *n* foundling, orphan, stray

wail *v* complain, cry, groan, howl, keen, lament, moan, sob, ululate *formal*, weep, yowl *colloq*
♦ *n* complaint, cry, groan, howl, lament, moan, sob, ululation *formal*, weeping

wait *v* abide *formal*, await, bide your time *formal*, delay, hang around *colloq*, hang fire *colloq*, hang on *colloq*, hesitate, hold back, linger, pause, remain, rest, sit out, stand by, stay, tarry *formal*
☲ go ahead, proceed
♦ *n* delay, halt, hesitation, hold-up, interval, pause
▶ **wait on** attend to, look after, minister to, serve, take care of, tend, work for

---

Colloquial ways of telling someone to wait include:
all in good time, bear with me, half a mo, half a moment, half a tick, hang on, hold on, hold your horses, I'll be right with you, just a jiffy, just a minute, just a moment, just a second, just a tick, wait a minute, wait a moment

---

waiter, waitress *n* attendant, butler, host, hostess, server, steward, stewardess

waive *v* abandon, cede, defer, do without, forgo *formal*, give up, postpone, relinquish *formal*, renounce *formal*, resign, set aside, surrender, yield
☲ claim, enforce, maintain

waiver *n* abandonment, abdication *formal*, deferral *formal*, disclaimer, postponement, relinquishment *formal*, remission *formal*, renunciation *formal*, resignation, surrender

wake¹ *v* **1** *woken by a strange noise:* arise, awake, awaken, bring round, come to, get up, rise, rouse, stir, waken **2** *her comments woke the diva in me:* activate, animate, arouse, egg on *colloq*, excite, fire, galvanize, goad, prod, stimulate, stir, whet **3** *woke me to his lies:* alert, make/become aware of, make/become conscious of, notify, signal, warn
☲ **1** sleep
♦ *n* death-watch, funeral, vigil, watch

wake² *n* aftermath, backwash, path, rear, track, trail, train, wash, waves

wakeful *adj* alert, attentive, heedful, insomniac, observant, restless, sleepless, unsleeping, vigilant, wary, watchful
☲ inattentive, sleepy, unwary

waken *v* activate, animate, arouse, awake, awaken, enliven, fire, galvanize, ignite, kindle, quicken, rise, rouse, stimulate, stir, wake

walk *v* **1** *walk along the street:* amble, go, march, roam, stride, stroll **2** *walk me to my car:* accompany, conduct, escort, guide, lead, shepherd, usher
♦ *n* **1** *he has an odd walk:* carriage, gait, pace, step, stride **2** *go for a walk:* amble, hike, march, promenade, ramble, saunter, stroll, trail, traipse, tramp, trek, trudge **3** *a tree-lined walk:* alley, avenue, drive, esplanade, footpath, lane, path, pathway, pavement, promenade, sidewalk, track, walkway **4** *signposted forest walks:* beat, circuit, path, round, rounds, route, trail, way
▶ **walk off/away with** go off with, lift *colloq*, make off with, nick *colloq*, pinch *colloq*, pocket, run off with, steal
▶ **walk out** down tools, go on strike, mutiny, protest, revolt, stop work, strike, take industrial action
▶ **walk out on** abandon, desert, dump *colloq*, forsake *formal*, jilt *colloq*, leave high and dry *colloq*, leave in the lurch *colloq*, run out on *colloq*

Ways of walking include:
amble, clump, crawl, creep, dodder, go by

shanks's pony *colloq*, hike, hobble, hoof it *colloq*, limp, lope, lurch, march, mince, mooch *colloq*, pace, pad, paddle, parade, patter, perambulate *formal*, plod, potter, promenade, prowl, ramble, roam, saunter, scuttle, shamble, shuffle, slink, sneak, stagger, stalk, steal, step, stomp, stretch your legs *colloq*, stride, stroll, strut, stumble, swagger, tiptoe, toddle *colloq*, totter, traipse, tramp, trample, tread, trek, trip, troop, trot, trudge, trundle, waddle, wade, wander, yomp *colloq*

walker *n* hiker, pedestrian, rambler

walk-out *n* industrial action, protest, rebellion, revolt, stoppage, strike

walk-over *n* child's play *colloq*, cinch *colloq*, doddle *colloq*, piece of cake *colloq*, pushover *colloq*

wall

Types of wall and famous walls include:
abutment, bailey, barricade, barrier, block, breeze-block wall, brick wall, bulkhead, bulwark, buttress, cavity wall, curtain wall, dam, dike, divider, embankment, enclosure wall, fence, flying buttress, fortification, garden wall, Great Wall of China, Hadrian's Wall, hedge, inner wall, load-bearing wall, mural, obstacle, outer bailey, paling, palisade, parapet, partition, party wall, rampart, retaining wall, screen, sea-wall, shield wall, stockade, stud partition, wall of death

wallet *n* bill-fold *US*, case, folder, holder, notecase, pochette, pouch, purse

wallop *v* bash, batter, beat, belt *colloq*, buffet, clobber, clout *colloq*, crush, defeat, drub, hammer, hit, lick *colloq*, paste *colloq*, pound, pummel, punch, rout, smack, strike, swat, swipe, thrash, thump, thwack, trounce, vanquish *formal*, whack *colloq*
♦ *n* bash, blow, hit, kick, punch, smack, swat, swipe, thump, thwack, whack

wallow *v* 1 *wallow in mud*: flounder, lie, loll, lurch, roll, splash, wade, welter 2 *wallow in nostalgia*: bask, delight, enjoy, glory, indulge, luxuriate *formal*, relish, revel

wan *adj* anaemic, ashen, bleak, colourless, discoloured, faint, feeble, ghastly, mournful, pale, pallid, pasty, sickly, washed out, waxen, weak, weary, whey-faced, white

wand *n* baton, mace, rod, sceptre, sprig, staff, stick, twig

wander *v* 1 *he wandered round the town*: drift, meander, peregrinate *formal*, prowl, ramble, range, roam, rove, saunter, straggle, stray, stroll, traipse 2 *your mind is wandering*: depart, deviate, digress, diverge, err, go astray, lose your way, stray, swerve, veer 3 *they thought she was wandering and went away*: babble, gibber, ramble, rave, talk nonsense
♦ *n* amble, cruise, excursion, meander, prowl, ramble, saunter, stroll

wanderer *n* drifter, Gypsy, itinerant, nomad, rambler, ranger, rolling stone *colloq*, rover, straggler, stray, stroller, traveller, vagabond, vagrant, voyager, wayfarer

wandering *adj* drifting, homeless, itinerant, migratory, nomadic, peripatetic *formal*, rambling, rootless, roving, strolling, travelling, unsettled, vagabond, vagrant, voyaging, wayfaring
♦ *n* drift(ing), journey(ing), meander(ing), odyssey *formal*, peregrination *formal*, travels, walkabout

wane *v* abate, contract, decline, decrease, dim, diminish, droop, drop, dwindle, ebb, fade (away), fail, lessen, peter out, shrink, sink, subside, taper off, vanish, weaken, wither
■ increase, wax
♦ *n* abatement *formal*, atrophy, contraction, decay, decline, decrease, degeneration, diminution *formal*, drop, dwindling, ebb, fading, failure, fall, lessening, sinking, subsidence, tapering off, weakening
■ increase

wangle *v* arrange, contrive, engineer, fiddle *colloq*, fix, manage, manipulate, manoeuvre, pull off, scheme, wheel and deal *colloq*, work

want *v* 1 *I want a new dress for the party*: covet, crave, desire, fancy, feel like, hope for, hunger for, like, long for, pine for, thirst for, wish, yearn for 2 *he wants for nothing*: be deficient in, be without, call for, demand, lack, miss, need, require
♦ *n* 1 *ruled by his wants and emotions*: appetite, coveting, craving, demand, desire, hunger, longing, lust, need, pining, requirement, thirst, wish, yearning 2 *suffered for want of funding*: absence, dearth, deficiency, inadequacy, insufficiency, lack, paucity *formal*, scantiness, scarcity, shortage 3 *whether living in plenty or in want*: destitution, indigence *formal*, penury *formal*, poverty, privation *formal*

wanting *adj* defective, deficient, disappointing, faulty, imperfect, inadequate, not up to scratch *colloq*, poor, substandard, unacceptable, unsatisfactory
■ adequate

wanton *adj* 1 *wanton brutality*: arbitrary, extravagant, gratuitous, groundless, malevolent *formal*, malicious, pointless, rash, reckless, unjustifiable, unprovoked, unrestrained, wild, wilful 2 *a wanton woman*: abandoned, dissipated, dissolute, immodest, immoral, impure, lecherous, lewd, promiscuous, shameless
♦ *n* Casanova, debauchee, Don Juan, harlot, lecher, libertine, prostitute, rake, roué, slut, strumpet, tart *slang*, trollop, voluptuary, whore

war *n* antagonism, battle, bloodshed, campaign, clash, combat, conflict, confrontation, contention, contest, enmity, fight, fighting, hostilities, ill-will, skirmish, strife, struggle, warfare
■ cease-fire, peace
♦ *v* battle, clash, combat, contend, contest, cross swords, fight, make war, skirmish, strive, struggle, take up arms, wage war

Types of war include:
ambush, armed conflict, assault, attack, battle, biological warfare, blitz, blitzkrieg, bombardment, chemical warfare, civil war, cold war, counter-attack, engagement, germ warfare, guerrilla warfare, holy war, hot war, invasion, jihad, jungle warfare, limited war,

manoeuvres, nuclear war, private war, resistance, skirmish, state of siege, struggle, total war, trade war, war of attrition, war of nerves, world war

Famous wars include:
American Civil War (Second American Revolution), American Revolution (War of Independence), Boer War, Cod Wars, Crimean War, Crusades, English Civil War, Falklands War, Franco-Prussian War, Gulf War, Hundred Years War, Indian Wars, Iran-Iraq War, Korean War, Mexican War, Napoleonic War, Opium Wars, Peasants' War, Russo-Finnish War (Winter War), Russo-Japanese War, Russo-Turkish Wars, Seven Years War, Six-Day War, Spanish-American War, Spanish-American Wars of Independence, Spanish Civil War, Suez Crisis, Thirty Years War, Vietnam War, War of 1812, War of the Pacific, Wars of the Roses, World War I (the Great War), World War II

warble *v* chirp, chirrup, quaver, sing, trill, twitter, yodel
♦ *n* call, chirp, chirrup, cry, quaver, song, trill, twitter

ward *n* **1** *work on a medical ward:* apartment, compartment, cubicle, room, unit **2** *contact your ward councillor:* area, district, division, precinct, quarter, zone **3** *a guardian and his former ward:* charge, dependant, minor, protégé(e), pupil
► **ward off** avert, avoid, beat off, block, deflect, dodge *colloq,* drive back, evade, fend off, forestall, parry, repel, stave off, thwart, turn aside, turn away

warden *n* administrator, caretaker, curator, custodian, guardian, janitor, keeper, overseer, protector, ranger, steward, superintendent, supervisor, warder, watchman

warder *n* custodian, guard, jailer, keeper, prison officer, screw *slang,* warden, wardress

wardrobe *n* **1** *her dress hung from the wardrobe door:* closet, cupboard **2** *she bought a whole new wardrobe when she lost weight:* apparel *formal,* attire *formal,* clothes, outfit

warehouse *n* depository, depot, entrepot, repository, stockroom, store, storehouse

wares *n* commodities, goods, merchandise, produce, products, stock, stuff

warfare *n* arms, battle, blows, campaign, combat, conflict, confrontation, contention, contest, discord, fighting, hostilities, passage of arms, strife, struggle, war
🔁 peace

warily *adv* apprehensively, cagily, carefully, cautiously, charily, circumspectly *formal,* distrustfully, gingerly, guardedly, hesitantly, suspiciously, uneasily, vigilantly, watchfully
🔁 heedlessly, recklessly, thoughtlessly, unwarily

wariness *n* alertness, apprehension, attention, caginess, care, carefulness, caution, circumspection *formal,* discretion, distrust, foresight, heedfulness, hesitancy, mindfulness, prudence *formal,* suspicion, unease, vigilance, watchfulness
🔁 heedlessness, recklessness, thoughtlessness

warlike *adj* aggressive, antagonistic, bellicose *formal,* belligerent, bloodthirsty, combative, hawkish, hostile, martial, militant, militaristic, pugnacious *formal,* unfriendly, war-mongering
🔁 friendly, peaceable

warlock *n* conjurer, demon, enchanter, magician, necromancer *formal,* sorcerer, witch, wizard

warm *adj* **1** *warm milk helps you sleep:* heated, lukewarm, tepid **2** *give her my warmest wishes:* ardent, eager, earnest, enthusiastic, fervent, heart-felt, intense, passionate, sincere, vehement, zealous **3** *warm colours:* cheerful, intense, mellow, relaxing, rich **4** *a warm welcome:* affable, affectionate, amiable, caring, cordial, friendly, genial, hearty, hospitable, kind, kindly, loving, sympathetic, tender **5** *in warm weather:* balmy, close, fine, sunny, temperate
🔁 **1** cool **2** indifferent **3** cold, cool **4** unfriendly **5** cool
♦ *v* **1** *warm the baby's bottle:* heat (up), make warm, melt, reheat, thaw **2** *warms the hearts of men:* animate, cheer up, delight, enliven, excite, interest, liven up, please, put some life into, rouse, stimulate, stir
🔁 **1** cool

warm-blooded *adj* ardent, earnest, emotional, enthusiastic, excitable, fervent, hot-blooded, impetuous, lively, passionate, rash, spirited, vivacious

warm-hearted *adj* affectionate, ardent, compassionate, cordial, generous, genial, kind, kind-hearted, kindly, loving, sympathetic, tender, tender-hearted
🔁 cold, unsympathetic

warmth *n* **1** *the warmth of the fireside:* fire, heat, hotness, warmness **2** *he has such warmth, such charisma:* affection, care, compassion, cordiality, friendliness, hospitality, kindliness, kindness, love, sympathy, tenderness **3** *the warmth of your praise:* ardour, eagerness, enthusiasm, fervour, intensity, passion, sincerity, vehemence, zeal
🔁 **1** coldness **2** unfriendliness **3** indifference

warn *v* **1** *warned about the health risks of smoking:* advise, alert, forewarn *formal,* give (advance) notice, inform, let know, notify, put on your guard, sound the alarm, tell, tip off *colloq* **2** *he warned us not to jump on the sofa:* advise, caution, counsel, exhort, urge **3** *he was warned for throwing his racket:* admonish *formal,* caution, rebuke, reprimand, reprove

warning *n* **1** *provide ample warning:* admonition *formal,* advance notice, advice, alarm, alert, counsel, hint, information, lesson, notice, notification, shot across the bows *colloq,* tip-off *colloq* **2** *a warning of a serious illness:* augury *formal,* omen, portent *formal,* premonition *formal,* presage *formal,* sign, signal, threat
♦ *adj* admonitory *formal,* cautionary, monitory *formal,* ominous, premonitory *formal,* threatening

warp *v* bend, contort, corrupt, deform, deviate, distort, kink, misshape, pervert, twist
🔁 straighten
♦ *n* bend, bent, bias, contortion, defect, deformation, deviation, distortion, irregularity, kink, perversion, quirk, turn, twist

warrant *n* authority, authorization, commission, consent *formal,* guarantee, licence,

permission, permit, pledge, sanction, security, validation, voucher, warranty
♦ *v* **1** *to warrant that the report is accurate:* affirm, answer for, assure, avouch *formal*, back, certify, declare, endorse, guarantee, pledge, support, swear, underwrite, uphold, vouch for **2** *new data that warrants investigation:* allow, approve, authorize, call for, commission, consent to *formal*, empower, entitle, excuse, justify, license, necessitate *formal*, permit, require, sanction, support

warrantable *adj* accountable, allowable, defensible, excusable, justifiable, lawful, legal, necessary, permissible, proper, reasonable, right
🔄 indefensible, unjustifiable, unwarrantable

warranty *n* assurance, authorization, bond, certificate, contract, covenant *formal*, guarantee, justification, pledge

warring *adj* at daggers drawn, at war, belligerent, combatant, conflicting, contending, embattled, fighting, hostile, opposed, opposing

warrior *n* champion, combatant, fighter, fighting man, soldier, wardog, warhorse

wary *adj* alert, attentive, cagey, careful, cautious, chary, circumspect *formal*, distrustful, guarded, heedful, on the alert, on the lookout, on your guard, prudent *formal*, suspicious, vigilant, watchful, wide-awake
🔄 careless, heedless, unwary

wash *v* **1** *wash your hair:* clean, cleanse, launder, mop, rinse, scrub, shampoo, soak, sponge, swab down, swill, wipe **2** *I need to wash and change:* bath, bathe, douche, freshen up, get cleaned up, have a bath, have a shower, have a wash, shampoo, shower **3** *the wash of high tide:* beat, dash, flow, splash, stream, sweep, swell, wave **4** *that excuse won't wash:* be accepted, be believable, be plausible, bear examination, bear scrutiny, carry weight, hold, pass muster, stand up, stick *colloq*
♦ *n* **1** *did you have a wash?:* bath, bathe, cleansing, shampoo, shower, washing **2** *give my jeans a quick wash:* cleaning, laundering, laundry, rinse, washing **3** *the wash caused by the speedboat:* flow, roll, surge, sweep, swell, wave **4** *a wash of blue glaze:* coat, coating, layer, rinse, stain

washed-out *adj* all in *colloq*, blanched, bleached, colourless, dead on your feet *colloq*, dog-tired *colloq*, drained, drawn, exhausted, faded, fatigued, flat, haggard, knackered *colloq*, lacklustre, pale, pallid, spent, tired-out, wan, weary, worn-out

washout *n* debacle, disappointment, disaster, failure, fiasco, flop *colloq*, lead balloon *colloq*, messy
🔄 success, triumph

waspish *adj* bad-tempered, bitchy *colloq*, cantankerous *formal*, captious, crabbed *colloq*, crabby *colloq*, critical, cross, crotchety *colloq*, grouchy *colloq*, grumpy, ill-tempered, irascible, irritable, peevish, petulant *formal*, prickly *colloq*, snappish, testy, touchy *colloq*

waste *v* **1** *don't waste your money on sweets:* blow *colloq*, dissipate *formal*, fritter away, get through, go through, lavish, misspend, misuse, spend, splurge *colloq*, squander, throw away **2** *wasting our natural resources:* consume, destroy, devastate, drain, erode, exhaust, spoil **3** *his*

muscles just wasted after the accident: atrophy *formal*, become emaciated, debilitate *formal*, shrink, shrivel, wither **4** *seizing and wasting church property:* depredate *formal*, desolate, despoil *formal*, destroy, devastate, lay waste, pillage, rape, ravage, raze, ruin, sack, spoil
🔄 **1** economize **2** preserve
♦ *n* **1** *the report condemned government waste:* dissipation *formal*, extravagance, loss, prodigality *formal*, squandering, wastefulness **2** *a waste of funds:* abuse, misapplication, misuse, neglect **3** *kitchen waste:* debris, dregs, dross, effluent, garbage, leftovers, litter, offscouring(s), refuse, rubbish, scrap, slops, trash *US*
🔄 **1** thriftiness
♦ *adj* **1** *pile the waste branches into heaps for burning:* extra, left-over, superfluous, supernumerary *formal*, unused, unwanted, useless, worthless **2** *rubbish dumps on waste land nearby:* bare, barren, bleak, desolate, devastated, dismal, dreary, empty, uncultivated, uninhabited, unproductive, unprofitable, wild

wasteful *adj* extravagant, improvident, lavish, prodigal, profligate *formal*, ruinous, spendthrift, thriftless, uneconomical, unthrifty
🔄 economical, thrifty

wasteland *n* barrenness, desert, emptiness, void, waste, wild(s), wilderness

wastrel *n* good-for-nothing, idler, layabout, loafer, lounger *colloq*, malingerer, ne'er-do-well, profligate *formal*, shirker *colloq*, skiver *colloq*, spendthrift

watch *v* **1** *we don't watch television:* contemplate, gape at, gaze at, look at, look on, mark, note, notice, observe, peer at, regard, scan, see, stare at, survey, view **2** *watch my bag for me:* guard, inspect, keep, keep an eye on, keep tabs on *colloq*, look after, mind, not take your eyes off *colloq*, protect, superintend, take care of **3** *I'm watching what I eat:* be careful about, look out for, pay attention to, take care about, take heed of
♦ *n* **1** *glanced to check his watch:* chronometer *formal*, clock, timepiece, wristwatch **2** *someone should be on watch:* alertness, attention, guard, heed, inspection, lookout, notice, observation, supervision, surveillance, vigil, vigilance, watchfulness
► **watch out** be vigilant, keep a lookout, keep your eyes open, keep your eyes peeled *colloq*, keep your eyes skinned *colloq*, look out, notice
► **watch over** defend, guard, keep an eye on, look after, mind, preserve, protect, shelter, shield, stand guard over, take care of

watchdog *n* **1** *German Shepherds are good watchdogs:* guard dog, house-dog **2** *investment watchdog:* custodian, guardian, inspector, monitor, ombudsman, protector, scrutineer, vigilante

watcher *n* looker-on, lookout, (member of the) audience, observer, onlooker, spectator, spy, viewer, witness

watchful *adj* alert, attentive, cautious, chary, circumspect *formal*, guarded, heedful, keep your eyes open/peeled/skinned, observant, on the lookout, on the qui vive *formal*, on your guard, suspicious, vigilant, wary, wide awake
🔄 inattentive, unobservant

watchfulness *n* alertness, attention, attentiveness, caution, cautiousness,

circumspection, heedfulness, suspicion, suspiciousness, vigilance, wariness
🖪 inattention

watchman *n* caretaker, custodian, guard, security guard

watchword *n* battle-cry, buzz word, byword, catch phrase, catchword, magic word, maxim, motto, password, rallying-cry, shibboleth, signal, slogan

water *n* current, flooding, lake, moisture, ocean, rain, river, sea, stream, torrent
♦ *v* dampen, douse, drench, flood, hose, irrigate, moisten, saturate, soak, spray, sprinkle, wet
🖪 dry out, parch
▶ **water down** adulterate, dilute, mitigate *formal*, mix, play down, qualify, soften, soft-pedal *colloq*, thin, tone down, weaken

waterfall *n* cascade, cataract, chute, fall, falls, torrent

waterproof *adj* coated, damp-proof, impermeable, impervious, proofed, rubberized, water-repellent, water-resistant
🖪 leaky

watertight *adj* 1 *make sure the seal is watertight:* hermetic, sound, waterproof 2 *that argument is not watertight:* airtight, firm, flawless, foolproof, impregnable, incontrovertible, indisputable, sound, unassailable
🖪 1 leaky

watery *adj* 1 *red, watery eyes:* aqueous *formal*, damp, fluid, hydrous *technical*, liquid, moist, wet 2 *she makes tasteless watery tea:* adulterated, diluted, flavourless, insipid, runny, tasteless, thin, watered-down, weak, wishy-washy *colloq* 3 *amongst catkins and watery ditches:* soggy, squelchy, washy, wet
🖪 1 dry

wave *v* 1 *he waved to us from the car:* beckon, direct, gesticulate, gesture, indicate, sign, signal 2 *waving a large brown envelope at me:* brandish, flap, flourish, move from side to side, shake, swing 3 *Icelandic flags wave in the breeze:* flap, flutter, move from side to side, quiver, ripple, stir, surge, sway, undulate *formal*, waft
♦ *n* 1 *white-fringed Atlantic waves:* billow, breaker, comber, foam, froth, ripple, roller, surf, swell, tidal wave, undulation, wavelet, white horse *colloq* 2 *waves of immigrants:* current, drift, flood, flow, ground swell, rash, rush, stream, surge, sweep, swell, upsurge 3 *wave of popular patriotism:* movement, outbreak, rash, rush, stream, tendency, trend, upsurge
▶ **wave aside** brush aside, dismiss, disregard, pour cold water on *colloq*, reject, set aside, shelve, spurn

waver *v* 1 *one ambition from which I never wavered:* dither, equivocate, falter, fluctuate, hesitate, hum and haw *colloq*, seesaw, shilly-shally *colloq*, vacillate, vary 2 *his voice wavered:* oscillate, rock, shake, stagger, sway, teeter, totter, tremble, wobble
🖪 1 decide

wavy *adj* curling, curly, curving, curvy, ridged, rippled, sinuous, undulating, winding, zigzag

wax *v* become, broaden, develop, enlarge, expand, extend, fill out, get bigger, grow, increase, magnify, mount, rise, spread, swell, widen
🖪 decrease, wane

waxen *adj* anaemic, ashen, bloodless, colourless, ghastly, livid, pale, pallid, wan, white, whitish
🖪 ruddy

waxy *adj* ceraceous *formal*, cereous *formal*, impressible, impressionable, pallid, pasty, soft, waxen

way *n* 1 *one way of doing it:* approach, course of action, fashion, instrument, instrumentality *formal*, lines, manner, means, method, mode *formal*, plan, procedure, process, strategy, style, system, technique, tool 2 *her funny ways:* behaviour, characteristic, conduct, custom, disposition, habit, idiosyncrasy, manner, mannerism, nature, peculiarity, personality, practice, style, temper, temperament, trait, usage, wont *formal* 3 *heading that way:* course, direction, path, route 4 *there were trees all along the way:* avenue, channel, highway, lane, passage, path, pathway, road, roadway, route, street, thoroughfare, track

wayfarer *n* globetrotter, Gypsy, itinerant, journeyer, nomad, rover, traveller, trekker, voyager, walker, wanderer
🖪 resident, stay-at-home

wayfaring *adj* drifting, itinerant, journeying, nomadic, peripatetic *formal*, rambling, roving, travelling, voyaging, walking, wandering
🖪 resident, stay-at-home

waylay *v* accost, ambush, attack, buttonhole, catch, hold up, intercept, lie in wait for, seize, set upon, surprise

way-out *adj* avant-garde, bizarre, crazy, eccentric, experimental, fantastic, far-out *colloq*, freaky *colloq*, off-beat *colloq*, outlandish, progressive, unconventional, unorthodox, unusual, weird, wild
🖪 ordinary

wayward *adj* capricious *formal*, changeable, contrary, contumacious *formal*, disobedient, fickle, headstrong, incorrigible, insubordinate, intractable *formal*, obdurate *formal*, obstinate, perverse, rebellious, refractory *formal*, self-willed, stubborn, ungovernable, unmanageable, unpredictable, unruly, wilful
🖪 good-natured, tractable

weak *adj* 1 *weak from hunger:* debilitated *formal*, delicate, enervated *formal*, exhausted, fatigued, feeble, flimsy, fragile, frail, indisposed *formal*, infirm, puny, shaky, sickly, unhealthy, weedy *colloq*, worn out 2 *a weak pound:* defenceless, exposed, unguarded, unprotected, vulnerable 3 *a weak, second-rate man:* feeble, impotent, inadequate, indecisive, ineffectual *formal*, irresolute, lacking, poor, powerless, spineless, useless 4 *a weak heart:* defective, deficient, feeble, impotent, inadequate, lacking, poor 5 *a weak argument:* deficient, feeble, flimsy, imperfect, inconclusive, lacking, lame, poor, unconvincing, unsound, untenable 6 *a weak voice:* dim, dull, faint, imperceptible, low, muffled, slight, soft, stifled 7 *this coffee is too weak:* adulterated, diluted, insipid, runny, tasteless, thin, watery
🖪 1 strong 2 secure 3 determined, powerful 4 powerful 6 strong 7 strong

weaken *v* **1** *weakens the government:* diminish, lessen, lower, mitigate, moderate, reduce, soften (up), temper, undermine **2** *weakened with age:* cripple, debilitate *formal*, disable, enervate *formal*, enfeeble, exhaust, incapacitate, paralyse, sap, soften (up), temper, tire **3** *just a touch of tonic in my gin, don't weaken it:* dilute, thin, water down **4** *weakening in her resolve:* abate *formal*, droop, dwindle, ease up, fade, fail, flag, give way, tire
🖃 **1** strengthen **2** strengthen **3** strengthen

weakling *n* coward, doormat *colloq*, drip *colloq*, mouse, sissy *colloq*, underdog, underling, wally *colloq*, weed *colloq*, wet *colloq*, wimp *colloq*
🖃 hero, stalwart

weak-minded *adj* complaisant *formal*, compliant, faint-hearted, irresolute, persuadable, persuasible, pliable, pusillanimous *formal*, spineless *colloq*, submissive, weak-kneed
🖃 strong-willed

weakness *n* **1** *muscle weakness:* debility *formal*, delicateness, enervation *formal*, feebleness, frailty, impotence, incapacity, infirmity, powerlessness, vulnerability **2** *showing emotion isn't a weakness:* Achilles' heel, blemish, defect, deficiency, failing, fault, flaw, foible, imperfection, shortcoming, weak point **3** *I have a bit of a weakness for red wine:* fondness, inclination, liking, passion, penchant *formal*, predilection *formal*, predisposition *formal*, proclivity *formal*, soft spot *colloq*
🖃 **1** strength **2** strength **3** dislike

weal *n* cicatrice, cicatrix, contusion, mark, ridge, scar, streak, stripe, welt, wound

wealth *n* **1** *she dreams of great wealth:* affluence, assets, capital, cash, estate, finance, fortune, funds, goods, mammon, means, money, opulence *formal*, possessions, property, prosperity, resources, riches, substance, treasure **2** *a wealth of research:* abundance, bounty, copiousness, cornucopia *formal*, fullness, mass, plenitude *formal*, plenty, profusion *formal*, store
🖃 **1** poverty

wealthy *adj* affluent, comfortable, filthy rich *slang*, flush *colloq*, loaded *slang*, made of money *colloq*, moneyed, opulent *formal*, prosperous, rich, rolling in it *colloq*, stinking rich *slang*, well-heeled, well-off, well-to-do
🖃 impoverished, poor

weapon

Weapons include:
gun, airgun, pistol, revolver, automatic, Colt®, Luger®, magnum, Mauser, six-gun, six-shooter, rifle, air rifle, Winchester® rifle, carbine, shotgun, blunderbuss, musket, elephant gun, machine-gun, kalashnikov, submachine-gun, tommy-gun, sten gun, Bren gun, cannon, field gun, gatling-gun, howitzer, mortar, turret-gun; knife, bowie knife, flick-knife, stiletto, dagger, dirk, poniard, sword, épée, foil, rapier, sabre, scimitar, bayonet, broadsword, claymore, lance, spear, pike, machete; bomb, atom bomb, H-bomb, cluster-bomb, depth-charge, incendiary bomb, Mills bomb, mine, land-mine, napalm bomb, time-bomb; bow and arrow, longbow, crossbow, blowpipe, catapult, boomerang, sling, harpoon, bolas, rocket, bazooka, ballistic missile, Cruise missile, Exocet®, Scud *colloq*, torpedo, hand grenade, flame-thrower; battleaxe, pole-axe, halberd, tomahawk, cosh, cudgel, knuckleduster, shillelagh, truncheon; gas, Agent Orange, CS gas, Mace® *US*, mustard gas, tear-gas

wear *v* **1** *wear your blue tie:* assume, be clothed in, be dressed in, bear, carry, display, don, dress in, exhibit, have, have on, put on, show, sport **2** *the brakes have worn:* abrade, become thinner, become threadbare, become weaker, consume, corrode, deteriorate, erode, fray, grind, rub, waste
◆ *n* **1** *glamorous evening wear:* attire *formal*, clothes, clothing, costume, dress, garments, outfit **2** *distinct signs of wear:* abrasion, corrosion, damage, deterioration, erosion, friction, wear and tear **3** *you get no wear out of kids' shoes:* durability, employment, service, use, usefulness, utility
▶ **wear down** chip away at, consume, corrode, diminish, erode, grind down, lessen, macerate *formal*, overcome, reduce, rub away
▶ **wear down** chip away at, grind down, overcome, reduce, undermine
▶ **wear off** abate *formal*, decrease, diminish, disappear, dwindle, ebb, fade, lessen, peter out, subside, wane, weaken
🖃 increase
▶ **wear on** elapse, go by, go on, pass
▶ **wear out 1** *pain makes you feel depressed and worn out:* drain, enervate *formal*, exhaust, fatigue, sap, strain, stress, tire (out) **2** *with the front tyres worn out:* consume, deteriorate, erode, fray, impair, wear through

weariness *n* drowsiness, enervation *formal*, ennui, exhaustion, fatigue, languor *formal*, lassitude, lethargy, listlessness, prostration, sleepiness, tiredness
🖃 freshness

wearing *adj* erosive, exasperating, exhausting, fatiguing, irksome, oppressive, taxing, tiresome, tiring, trying, wearisome
🖃 refreshing

wearisome *adj* annoying, boring, bothersome, burdensome, dreary, dull, exasperating, exhausting, fatiguing, humdrum, irksome, monotonous, tedious, tiresome, troublesome, trying, vexatious, wearing
🖃 refreshing

weary *adj* **1** *weary from the labour:* all in *colloq*, bushed *colloq*, dead beat *colloq*, dog-tired *colloq*, done in *colloq*, drained, drowsy, exhausted, fagged out *colloq*, fatigued, jaded, knackered *colloq*, pooped *colloq*, sleepy, tired, whacked *colloq*, worn out **2** *weary of trying to please him:* bored, bored to tears *colloq*, brassed off *colloq*, browned off *colloq*, cheesed off *colloq*, fed up *colloq*, sick and tired *colloq*, tired, unenthusiastic, unexcited, uninterested
🖃 **1** refreshed **2** excited, interested
◆ *v* **1** *she was wearied by a persistent cough:* burden, debilitate *formal*, drain, enervate *formal*, fade, fag *colloq*, fail, fatigue, jade, sap, sicken, tax, tire, tire out, wear out **2** *wearying me with your complaints:* annoy, bore, bug *colloq*, drain, exasperate, irk, irritate, sicken, tax, tire

weather *n* atmospheric conditions, climate, cloudiness, conditions, dryness, forecast, humidity, meteorological reports, outlook, sunniness, temperature, windiness

♦ *v* 1 *we'll have to weather the financial problems:* brave, come through, endure, get through, live through, overcome, pull through, resist, ride out, rise above, stand, stick out, suffer, surmount, survive, withstand 2 *weathered wood is beautiful:* dry, expose, harden, season, toughen
🖅 1 succumb

weave *v* 1 *new methods of weaving textiles:* braid, entwine, fuse, intercross, interlace, intertwine, interwork, knit, lace, merge, plait, spin, unite 2 *weaving stories for his grandson:* compose, construct, contrive, create, fabricate, make up, put together 3 *weaving in and out of traffic:* criss-cross, twist, wind, zigzag

web *n* complex, interlacing, knot, lacework, lattice, mesh, net, netting, network, snare, tangle, trap, webbing, weft

wed *v* 1 *he wants to wed:* espouse *formal*, get hitched *colloq*, get married, marry, splice *colloq*, tie the knot *colloq*, yoke 2 *a traditional text wedded to a well-loved tune:* ally, blend, coalesce, combine, commingle *formal*, fuse, interweave, join, link, merge, unify, unite
🖅 1 divorce

wedded *adj* conjugal *formal*, connubial *formal*, husbandly, joined, marital, married, matrimonial *formal*, nuptial *formal*, spousal *formal*, wifely

wedding *n* celebration of marriage, marriage, marriage ceremony, marriage service, matrimony *formal*, nuptials *formal*, union
🖅 divorce
♦ *adj* bridal *formal*, epithalamic *formal*, hymeneal *formal*, hymenean *formal*, marriage, matrimonial *formal*, nuptial *formal*

wedge *n* block, chock, chunk, lump, piece, triangle, wodge
♦ *v* block, cram, crowd, fit, force, jam, lodge, pack, push, ram, squeeze, stuff, thrust

wedlock *n* holy matrimony *formal*, marriage, matrimony *formal*, union

wee *adj* diminutive, insignificant, itsy-bitsy *colloq*, Lilliputian, little, microscopic, midget, miniature, minuscule, minute, negligible, small, teeny *colloq*, teeny-weeny *colloq*, tiny, weeny *colloq*
🖅 big, large

weed *v*
▶ **weed out** eliminate, eradicate, extirpate *formal*, get rid of, purge, remove, root out
🖅 add, fix, infiltrate

weedy *adj* feeble, frail, gangling, insipid, puny, scrawny, skinny, thin, undersized, weak, weak-kneed, wet *colloq*, wimpish *colloq*
🖅 strong

weekly *adv* by the week, every week, hebdomadally *formal*, once a week
♦ *adj* hebdomadal *formal*, hebdomadary *formal*

weep *v* bawl, be in tears, blub *colloq*, blubber, cry, grieve, lament, moan, mourn, shed tears, snivel, sob, wail, whimper, whine
🖅 rejoice
♦ *n* blub, cry, lament, moan, snivel, sob

weepy *adj* blubbering, crying, labile *formal*, lachrymose *formal*, sobbing, tearful, teary, weeping
♦ *n* melodrama, sob-stuff, tear-jerker

weigh *v* 1 *weigh the apples:* measure the weight of, see/measure how heavy something is 2 *his illness weighed on her:* afflict, bear down, burden, depress, get down *colloq*, oppress, trouble, worry 3 *he was right to weigh the evidence:* consider, contemplate, deliberate, evaluate, examine, meditate on, mull over, ponder, reflect on, think over
▶ **weigh down** 1 *weighed down by pressure of debts:* afflict, bear down, depress, get down *colloq*, oppress, press down, trouble, weigh upon, worry 2 *weighed down by shopping bags:* burden, load, overload
▶ **weigh up** assess, balance, chew over *colloq*, compare, consider, contemplate, deliberate, discuss, evaluate, examine, mull over, ponder, size up, think over

weight *n* 1 *put on several pounds in weight:* avoirdupois *formal*, ballast, burden, force, gravity, heaviness, load, mass, poundage, pressure, quantity, tonnage 2 *lends weight to their allegations:* authority, clout *colloq*, consequence, consideration, force, impact, importance, influence, moment, power, preponderance *formal*, significance, substance, value 3 *the weight of the world on your shoulders:* burden, duty, encumbrance, load, onus, responsibility, strain, trouble, worry
🖅 1 lightness
♦ *v* 1 *her illness has weighted him down for months:* burden, handicap, load, oppress, weigh down 2 *tended to weight the case in their favour:* angle, bias, load, prejudice, slant, sway, twist, unbalance

weightless *adj* airy, imponderous *formal*, insubstantial, light
🖅 heavy

weighty *adj* 1 *a weighty volume:* bulky, heavy, hefty, massive, substantial 2 *weighty problems we can't understand:* authoritative, consequential, critical, crucial, grave, important, influential, momentous, serious, significant, solemn, vital 3 *a rather weighty responsibility:* burdensome, demanding, difficult, exacting, onerous, taxing
🖅 1 light 2 insignificant, unimportant

weird *adj* bizarre, creepy, eerie, far-out *colloq*, freakish, ghostly, grotesque, mysterious, preternatural *formal*, queer, spooky *colloq*, strange, supernatural, uncanny, unnatural, way-out *colloq*
🖅 normal, usual

weirdo *n* crackpot *colloq*, crank, cure, eccentric, freak, fruitcake *colloq*, loony *colloq*, nut *colloq*, nutcase *colloq*, nutter *colloq*, oddball *colloq*, queer fish *colloq*

welcome *adj* acceptable, agreeable, appreciated, delightful, desirable, gratifying, pleasant, pleasing, popular, refreshing
🖅 unwelcome
♦ *n* acceptance, greeting, hospitality, reception, red carpet *colloq*, salutation *colloq*
♦ *v* accept, approve of, be pleased with, be satisfied with, embrace, greet, hail, meet, receive, roll out the red carpet for *colloq*, salute
🖅 reject, snub

weld *v* bind, bond, cement, connect, fuse, join, link, seal, solder, unite
🖅 separate
♦ *n* bond, joint, seal, seam

welfare *n* **1** *your welfare is most important:* advantage, benefit, comfort, fortune, good, happiness, health, interest, profit, prosperity, security, soundness, success, well-being **2** *live off welfare:* allowance, benefit, income, payment, pension, sick pay

well¹ *adv* **1** *speak Czech well:* ably, adeptly, competently, correctly, effectively, excellently, expertly, proficiently, properly, rightly, skilfully, successfully **2** *everything turned out well:* adequately, fittingly, satisfactorily, sufficiently, suitably **3** *treat someone well:* agreeably, generously, genially, happily, hospitably, kindly, pleasantly **4** *did you know her well?:* carefully, closely, completely, considerably, deeply, fully, greatly, industriously, profoundly, properly, thoroughly **5** *live well:* comfortably, fortunately, luckily, prosperously, splendidly, successfully **6** *think/speak well of someone:* approvingly, favourably, glowingly, highly, warmly **7** *well over a thousand people:* considerably, far, substantially, to a great extent, very much **8** *you may well be right:* certainly, conceivably, probably, quite possibly, very likely

⊠ **1** badly, inadequately, incompetently, wrongly **3** badly **5** poorly **6** unfavourably ♦ *adj* **1** *not a well man:* able-bodied, fit, flourishing, hale and hearty, healthy, in good health, robust, sound, strong, thriving **2** *all was well:* agreeable, all right, fine, fortunate, good, lucky, OK *colloq*, pleasing, proper, right, satisfactory

⊠ **1** ill **2** bad

well² *n* fount, fountain, pool, reservoir, source, spring, well-head, well-spring ♦ *v* brim over, flood, flow, gush, issue, jet, ooze, pour, rise, run, rush, seep, spout, spring, spurt, stream, surge, swell, trickle

---

Types of well include: artesian well, borehole, draw-well, gas well, geyser, gusher, hot spring, inkwell, lift-shaft, mineral spring, oil-well, pump-well, stairwell, thermal spring, waterhole, wishing-well

---

well-balanced *adj* **1** *she is a well-balanced young woman:* level-headed, rational, reasonable, sane, sensible, sober, sound, stable, together *colloq*, well-adjusted **2** *a well-balanced diet:* balanced, healthy, regulated, well-proportioned **3** *a well-balanced programme of growth:* balanced, even, harmonious, symmetrical, well-ordered, well-proportioned

⊠ **1** maladjusted, unbalanced **3** asymmetrical, disordered

well-behaved *adj* compliant *formal*, considerate, co-operative, good, good as gold *colloq*, obedient, polite, respectful, under control, well-mannered

⊠ disobedient, naughty

well-being *n* comfort, good, good health, happiness, health, welfare

well-bred *adj* aristocratic, blue-blooded, civil, courteous, cultivated, cultured, gallant, genteel, gentlemanly, ladylike, mannerly, polite, refined, upper-crust, urbane, well-brought-up, well-mannered

⊠ ill-bred

well-built *adj* beefy, brawny, burly, muscular, stout, strapping, strong

well-disposed *adj* agreeable, amicable, favourable, friendly, sympathetic, well-aimed, well-arranged, well-minded, well-placed

⊠ ill-disposed

well-dressed *adj* chic, dapper, elegant, fashionable, natty *colloq*, neat, smart, spruce, stylish, tidy, trim, well-groomed

⊠ badly dressed, scruffy

well-founded *adj* acceptance, fit, justifiable, plausible, proper, reasonable, right, sensible, sound, sustainable, valid, warranted

well-groomed *adj* dapper, neat, smart, spruce, tidy, trim, well-dressed, well-turned-out

well-known *adj* celebrated, eminent, famed, familiar, famous, illustrious, notable, noted, renowned, widely-known

⊠ unknown

well-nigh *adv* all but, almost, just about, nearly, practically, to all intents and purposes, virtually

well-off *adj* **1** *well-off families:* affluent, comfortable, filthy rich *slang*, flush *colloq*, loaded *slang*, moneyed, prosperous, rich, rolling in it *colloq*, stinking rich *slang*, successful, thriving, wealthy, well-heeled *colloq*, well-to-do **2** *made me realize how well-off I am:* comfortable, fortunate, lucky

⊠ **1** badly-off, poor **2** unfortunate, unlucky

well-spoken *adj* articulate, clear, coherent, eloquent, fluent, well-expressed

well-thought-of *adj* admired, esteemed *formal*, highly regarded, honoured, looked up to, respected, revered, venerated *formal*

⊠ despised, looked down on

well-to-do *adj* affluent, comfortable, flush *colloq*, loaded *slang*, moneyed, prosperous, rich, rolling in it *colloq*, wealthy, well-heeled *colloq*, well-off

⊠ poor

well-worn *adj* **1** *a well-worn phrase:* commonplace, corny *colloq*, hackneyed, overused, stale, stereotyped, threadbare, timeworn, tired, trite, unoriginal **2** *well-worn clothing:* frayed, ragged, scruffy, shabby, threadbare, worn, worn out

⊠ **1** original **2** new

welsh *v* cheat, defraud, diddle *colloq*, do *colloq*, swindle

welter *v* flounder, heave, lurch, pitch, roll, splash, toss, wade, wallow ♦ *n* confusion, hotchpotch, jumble, mess, mishmash *colloq*, muddle, tangle, web

wet *adj* **1** *my socks are wet:* clammy, damp, dank, drenched, dripping, moist, saturated, soaked, soaking, sodden, soggy, sopping, sopping wet, spongy, waterlogged, watery **2** *I'm tired of this wet weather:* damp, dank, drizzling, humid, pouring, raining, rainy, showery, teeming **3** *don't be so wet, it's only a spider:* effete *formal*, feeble, ineffectual *formal*, irresolute, namby-pamby, pathetic *colloq*, soft, spineless, timorous *formal*, weak, weedy, wimpish *colloq*

⊠ **1** dry **2** dry **3** strong ♦ *n* **1** *the car isn't good in the wet:* clamminess, condensation, damp, dampness, drizzle, humidity, liquid, moistness, moisture, rain,

water, wetness **2** *you're such a wet*: drip *colloq*, fool, idiot, jerk *slang*, milksop, nerd *slang*, softy, wally *colloq*, weakling, wimp *colloq*
🔁 **1** dryness
♦ *v* damp, dampen, dip, douse, drench, flood, imbue, irrigate, moisten, saturate, soak, splash, spray, sprinkle, steep, swamp, water
🔁 dry

wetness *n* clamminess, condensation, damp, dampness, dankness, humidity, liquid, moisture, soddenness, sogginess, water, wet
🔁 dryness

whack *v* bang, bash *colloq*, beat, belt *colloq*, box, buffet, clobber *colloq*, clout *colloq*, cuff, hit, rap, slap, smack, sock *colloq*, strike, thrash, thump, wallop *colloq*
♦ *n* **1** *he gave me a whack*: bang, bash *colloq*, blow, box, clout *colloq*, cuff, hit, rap, slap, smack, stroke, thump, wallop *colloq* **2** *a fair whack of acting ability*: allocation, allowance, cut *colloq*, division, lot, part, percentage, portion, proportion, quota, rake-off *colloq*, share, slice of the cake *colloq*, stint

wharf *n* dock, dockyard, jetty, landing-stage, marina, pier, quay, quayside

what's-its-name *n* doodah *colloq*, thingummy, thingummybob, thingummyjig, what-d'you-call-it, whatnot *colloq*, whatsit *colloq*

wheedle *v* beguile, cajole, charm, coax, court, draw, entice, flatter, induce, inveigle *formal*, persuade, talk into, win over
🔁 force

wheel *n* circle, gyration, pivot, revolution, roll, rotation, spin, turn, twirl, whirl
♦ *v* circle, go round, gyrate, orbit, pivot, revolve, roll, rotate, spin, swing, swivel, turn, twirl, whirl

wheeze *v* cough, gasp, hiss, pant, rasp, whistle
♦ *n* **1** *his bronchial wheeze*: cough, gasp, hiss, rasp, whistle **2** *a brilliant wheeze he dreamt up*: anecdote, catch phrase, chestnut *colloq*, crack, gag, idea, joke, one-liner *colloq*, plan, ploy, practical joke, prank, ruse, scheme, story, stunt, trick, wrinkle *colloq*

whereabouts *n* location, place, position, site, situation, vicinity

wherewithal *n* capital, cash, funds, means, money, necessary, readies *colloq*, resources, supplies

whet *v* **1** *whet the blade on the stone*: edge, file, grind, hone, sharpen **2** *her curiosity had been whetted*: arouse, awaken, excite, incite, increase, kindle, provoke, quicken, rouse, stimulate, stir, titillate
🔁 **1** blunt **2** dampen

whiff *n* **1** *a whiff of fresh air*: blast, breath, draught, gust, puff, trace **2** *a faint whiff of lemon*: aroma, hint, odour, reek, scent, smell, sniff, stench, stink **3** *a whiff of scandal/danger*: hint, suggestion, suspicion, touch, trace

while *n* interval, period, season, span, spell, stretch, time
▶ **while away** devote, occupy, pass, spend

whim *n* caprice, conceit, craze, fad, fancy, freak, humour, idea, impulse, notion, passion, quirk, urge, vagary

whimper *v* cry, grizzle, groan, mewl, moan, sniffle, snivel, sob, weep, whine, whinge *colloq*
♦ *n* cry, groan, moan, snivel, sob, whine

whimsical *adj* capricious *formal*, curious, dotty *colloq*, droll, eccentric, fanciful, funny, impulsive, mischievous, odd, peculiar, playful, quaint, queer, quirky, unpredictable, unusual, weird

whine *v* **1** *the pup was whining*: cry, grizzle, moan, sob, wail, whimper **2** *a spoiled young woman who was always whining*: beef *colloq*, belly-ache *colloq*, carp, complain, gripe *colloq*, groan, grouch *colloq*, grouse, grumble, moan, whinge *colloq*
♦ *n* **1** *a high-pitched whine*: cry, moan, sob, wail, whimper **2** *had a whine about the referee*: beef *colloq*, belly-ache *colloq*, complaint, gripe *colloq*, groan, grouch *colloq*, grouse, grumble, moan

whinge *v* beef *colloq*, belly-ache *colloq*, carp, complain, gripe *colloq*, grouse *colloq*, grumble, moan
♦ *n* beef *colloq*, belly-ache *colloq*, complaint, gripe *colloq*, groan, grouse, grumble, moan

whip *v* **1** *cab driver whipping a lazy horse*: beat, belt *colloq*, birch, cane, castigate *formal*, chastise *formal*, clout *colloq*, discipline, flagellate *formal*, flog, give someone a good hiding *colloq*, lash, punish, scourge, strap, tan *colloq*, thrash, wallop *colloq*, whack *colloq* **2** *whipped the rug from under her feet*: flash, jerk, pull, snatch, whisk, yank *colloq* **3** *my mind whipped back to the crash*: dart, dash, flit, fly, rush, tear **4** *whip the cream*: beat, mix, stir, whisk **5** *he could whip them into a frenzy*: agitate, drive, goad, incite, instigate, prod, prompt, provoke, push, rouse, spur, stir, urge
♦ *n* birch, cane, cat-o'-nine-tails, crop, horsewhip, lash, riding-crop, scourge, switch
▶ **whip up** agitate, arouse, excite, foment, incite, inflame, instigate, kindle, provoke, psych up *colloq*, stir up, work up
🔁 dampen, deter

whipping *n* beating, belting *colloq*, birching, caning, castigation *formal*, flagellation *formal*, flogging, hiding *colloq*, lashing, punishment, spanking, tanning *colloq*, thrashing, walloping *colloq*

whirl *v* circle, gyrate, pirouette, pivot, reel, revolve, roll, rotate, spin, swirl, swivel, turn, turn round, twirl, twist, wheel
♦ *n* **1** *a whirl around the track*: circle, gyration, pirouette, pivot, reel, revolution, roll, rotation, spin, swirl, turn, twirl, twist, wheel **2** *the social whirl of Mayfair*: agitation, bustle, commotion, flurry, hubbub, hurly-burly, jumble, merry-go-round, round, series, succession, tumult, uproar **3** *his mind was in a whirl*: agitation, confusion, daze, giddiness, muddle

whirlpool *n* eddy, maelstrom, vortex, weel *Scot*

whirlwind *n* cyclone, tornado, vortex
♦ *adj* hasty, headlong, impetuous, impulsive, lightning, quick, rapid, rash, speedy, swift
🔁 deliberate, slow

whisk *v* **1** *whisk the eggwhites to soft peaks*: beat, mix, stir, whip **2** *he whisked backwards out of sight*: bolt, dart, dash, dive, fly, hasten, hurry, race, rush, shoot, speed, tear, whip **3** *she whisked a blanket off the bed*: tear, whip **4** *whisking their tails*

in excitement: brush, flick, sweep, twitch, wipe
♦ *n* beater, brush, swizzle-stick

whisky *n* bourbon, malt, moonshine, rye, Scotch, usquebaugh, whiskey

whisper *v* 1 *it's rude to whisper:* breathe, mumble, murmur, mutter, say/speak quietly 2 *the wind whispering in the trees:* hiss, mumble, murmur, rustle, sigh, sough, susurrate *formal* 3 *my enemies were whispering that I had gambling debts:* divulge, gossip, hint, insinuate, intimate
Fǝ 1 shout
♦ *n* 1 *her voice dropped to a weary whisper:* hiss, murmur, rustle, sigh, soft/quiet/low voice, sough, undertone 2 *a whisper of lilac:* hint, soupçon, suggestion, tinge, trace, whiff 3 *a whisper of an early election:* breath, buzz, innuendo, insinuation, report, rumour, suspicion

whistle *v* call, cheep, chirp, pipe, sing, warble
♦ *n* call, cheep, chirp, hooter, siren, song, warble

whit *n* atom, bit, crumb, dash, drop, fragment, grain, hoot, iota, jot, little, mite, modicum, particle, piece, pinch, scrap, shred, speck, trace
Fǝ lot

white *adj* 1 *her face was as white as a sheet:* anaemic, ashen, colourless, creamy, light-skinned, milky, pale, pallid, pasty, wan, waxen 2 *a man with a thick white beard:* grey, hoary, ivory, light, silver, snowy 3 *white as the driven snow:* immaculate, pure, spotless, stainless, undefiled
Fǝ 1 black, dark, ruddy 2 dark 3 defiled

white-collar *adj* clerical, executive, non-manual, office, professional, salaried
Fǝ blue-collar, manual

whiten *v* blanch, bleach, etiolate *formal*, fade, pale, whitewash
Fǝ blacken, darken

whitewash *n* camouflage, concealment, cover-up, deception
Fǝ exposure
♦ *v* 1 *wanted to whitewash his reputation:* camouflage, conceal, cover up, gloss over, hide, make light of, suppress 2 *whitewashed 5-0 in the test series:* beat, best, clobber *colloq*, crush, drub, hammer *colloq*, lick *colloq*, paste *colloq*, thrash, trounce *colloq*
Fǝ 1 expose

whittle *v* 1 *whitish sticks which he has whittled:* carve, cut, hew, pare, scrape, shape, shave, trim 2 *whittled the lead down to just one point:* consume, diminish, eat away, erode, reduce, undermine, use (up), wear away

whole *adj* 1 *the whole world:* complete, entire, full, integral, total, unabridged, uncut, undivided, unedited 2 *you have to swallow it whole:* in one piece, intact, inviolate *formal*, mint, perfect, sound, unbroken, undamaged, unharmed, unhurt, uninjured 3 *to heal her wounds and make her whole:* fit, healthy, sound, strong, well
Fǝ 1 partial 2 damaged 3 ill
♦ *n* aggregate, all, ensemble, entirety, entity, everything, fullness, lot, piece, sum total, total, totality, unit
Fǝ part

wholehearted *adj* committed, complete, dedicated, devoted, earnest, emphatic, enthusiastic, genuine, heartfelt, hearty, passionate, real, sincere, true, unfeigned,

unqualified, unreserved, unstinting, warm, zealous
Fǝ half-hearted

wholesale *adj* all-inclusive, broad, comprehensive, extensive, far-reaching, indiscriminate, mass, massive, outright, sweeping, total, wide-ranging
Fǝ partial
♦ *adv* comprehensively, en bloc, extensively, indiscriminately, massively, totally
Fǝ partially

wholesome *adj* 1 *wholesome food:* beneficial, bracing, good, healthful, healthy, hygienic, invigorating, nourishing, nutritious, refreshing, salubrious *formal*, salutary, sanitary 2 *wholesome entertainment:* beneficial, clean, decent, edifying, ethical, helpful, honourable, improving, moral, proper, pure, respectable, righteous, uplifting, virtuous
Fǝ 1 unhealthy 2 immoral, unwholesome

wholly *adv* absolutely, all, altogether, completely, comprehensively, entirely, exclusively, fully, in every respect, one hundred per cent *colloq*, only, perfectly, purely, thoroughly, totally, utterly
Fǝ partly

whoop *v* cheer, cry, holler *colloq*, hoop, hoot, hurrah, roar, scream, shout, shriek, yell

whopper *n* 1 *the fish was a whopper:* behemoth, giant, monster, prodigy 2 *told a whopper:* fable, fabrication, fairy story *colloq*, falsehood, lie, tall story *colloq*, untruth

whopping *adj* big, enormous, extraordinary, giant, gigantic, great, huge, immense, large, mammoth, massive, monumental, prodigious *formal*, staggering, tremendous, vast, whacking
Fǝ tiny

whore *n* call girl, courtesan, fallen woman, fille de joie, harlot, hooker *colloq*, hustler *colloq*, prostitute, scarlet woman, street-walker, strumpet, tart *slang*, trollop, wench, woman of the town

whorehouse *n* bagnio, bawdy-house, bordello, brothel, cat-house *US slang*, house of ill repute, knocking-shop *slang*

whorl *n* coil, convolution *formal*, corkscrew, helix, spiral, turn, twist, vortex

wicked *adj* 1 *a cold, wicked woman:* abominable, bad, black-hearted, corrupt, debased, depraved, devilish, dissolute *formal*, egregious *formal*, evil, heinous *formal*, immoral, iniquitous *formal*, nasty, nefarious *formal*, offensive, scandalous, shameful, sinful, ungodly, unprincipled, unrighteous, vicious, villainous 2 *a wicked lie:* atrocious, awful, bad, difficult, distressing, dreadful, foul, harmful, injurious, nasty, severe, terrible, troublesome, unpleasant, vile, worthless 3 *a wicked headache:* awful, dreadful, fierce, intense, severe, terrible 4 *a wicked grin:* impish, mischievous, naughty, rascally, roguish 5 *this new game is wicked!:* admirable, cool *colloq*, excellent
Fǝ 1 good, upright 2 harmless 3 mild

wickedness *n* abomination, amorality, atrocity, corruption, corruptness, depravity, devilishness, dissoluteness *formal*, enormity, evil, fiendishness, foulness, heinousness *formal*, immorality, impiety, iniquity *formal*, reprobacy

formal, shamefulness, sin, sinfulness,
unrighteousness, vileness
☒ uprightness

wide *adj* **1** *wide expanses of heathland:* ample,
broad, extensive, immense, roomy, spacious,
vast **2** *her wide eyes stared:* dilated, expanded, full
3 *a wide range of references:* broad,
comprehensive, extensive, far-reaching, general,
great, immense, vast, wide-ranging **4** *men in
vests and wide trousers:* baggy, capacious *formal*,
full, loose, roomy **5** *his shot was only inches wide:*
distant, off the mark, off-course, off-target,
remote
☒ **1** narrow **3** restricted **5** near
♦ *adv* **1** *he sliced his shot wide and hit a bunker:*
astray, off course, off target, off the mark **2** *she
opened her arms as wide as she could:* all the way,
completely, fully, to the full extent
☒ **1** on target

wide or *broad*? See panel at **broad**

wide-awake *adj* alert, astute, aware, conscious,
fully awake, heedful, keen, observant, on the
alert, on the ball *colloq*, on the qui vive, on your
toes, quick-witted, roused, sharp, vigilant,
wakened, wary, watchful
☒ asleep

widely *adv* broadly, comprehensively,
extensively, generally

widen *v* broaden, dilate *formal*, distend *formal*,
enlarge, expand, extend, increase, spread,
stretch
☒ narrow

wide-open *adj* defenceless, exposed, gaping,
open, outspread, outstretched, spread,
susceptible, unfortified *formal*, unprotected,
vulnerable, wide
☒ closed, narrow

wide-ranging *adj* broad, comprehensive,
extensive, far-reaching, important, momentous,
significant, sweeping, thorough, widespread

widespread *adj* broad, common, extensive,
far-flung, far-reaching, general, pervasive,
prevalent, rife, sweeping, universal, unlimited,
wholesale
☒ limited

width *n* amplitude, beam, breadth, broadness,
compass, diameter, extensiveness, extent, girth,
largeness, measure, range, reach, scope, span,
thickness, wideness

wield *v* **1** *wield a weapon:* brandish, flourish,
handle, manage, manipulate, ply, shake, swing,
wave **2** *wield power:* command, control, employ,
exercise, exert, have, hold, maintain, possess,
use, utilize

wife *n* better half *colloq*, bride, companion, mate,
missus *colloq*, other half *colloq*, partner, spouse

wiggle *v* jerk, jiggle, shake, twist, twitch, wag,
waggle, wriggle
♦ *n* jerk, jiggle, shake, twist, wag, waggle

wild *adj* **1** *overrun with wild cats:* barbarous,
brutish, feral *formal*, ferocious, fierce, natural,
primitive, savage, unbroken, uncivilized,
undomesticated, untamed **2** *wild tribes from the
north:* barbarous, brutish, natural, primitive,
savage, uncivilized **3** *wild mountainous regions
of the Pashtuns:* barren, desolate, forsaken,

inhospitable, natural, rugged, uncultivated,
uninhabited, unpopulated, unsettled, waste
4 *teenagers running wild through the streets:*
boisterous, disorderly, lawless, out of control,
rampant, riotous, rowdy, turbulent,
uncontrollable, undisciplined, ungovernable,
unmanageable, unrestrained, unruly, violent **5** *a
wild wintry night:* blustery, choppy, furious,
raging, rough, stormy, tempestuous, turbulent,
violent **6** *wild hair and wilder emotions:*
dishevelled, messy, tousled, uncombed,
unkempt, untidy **7** *he made all sorts of wild plans:*
extravagant, fantastic, foolhardy, foolish,
impracticable, imprudent *formal*, impulsive,
irrational, outrageous, preposterous, rash,
reckless, unwise, wayward **8** *the crowd went wild
when the final whistle blew:* bananas *colloq*, berserk,
beside yourself, bonkers *colloq*, crazy *colloq*,
demented, distraught, frantic, frenzied, mad,
nuts *colloq*, nutty *colloq* **9** *she'll be wild with rage if
she sees you:* angry, blazing, crazy *colloq*, enraged,
foaming at the mouth *colloq*, fuming, furious,
hopping mad *colloq*, incensed, infuriated, mad
colloq, raging **10** *he's wild about racing cars:* crazy
colloq, daft *colloq*, enthusiastic, excited, fanatical,
fervent, keen, mad *colloq*, nuts *colloq*, passionate,
potty *colloq*, vehement
☒ **1** civilized, tame **2** civilized **3** cultivated
4 restrained **5** calm **6** tidy **7** sensible **8** sane

wilderness *n* desert, jungle, waste, wasteland,
wilds

wild flower

Wild flowers include:
Aaron's rod, ale hoof, bird's foot trefoil,
birthwort, bistort, black-eyed susan, bladder
campion, bluebell, broomrape, butter-and-
eggs, buttercup, campion, celandine, clary,
clustered bellflower, clover, columbine,
comfrey, common evening-primrose, common
mallow, common toadflax, cowslip, crane's
bill, crowfoot, cuckoo flower, daisy, edelweiss,
field cow-wheat, foxglove, goatsbeard,
goldcup, goldenrod, great mullein, harebell,
heartsease, heather, horsetail, lady's slipper,
lady's smock, lungwort, marguerite,
masterwort, moneywort, multiflora rose, New
England aster, oxeye daisy, oxslip,
pennyroyal, poppy, primrose, ragged robin,
rock rose, rough-fruited cinquefoil, self-heal,
shepherd's club, solomon's seal, stiff-haired
sunflower, stonecrop, teasel, toadflax, violet,
water lily, white campion, wild chicory, wild
endive, wild gladiolus, wild iris, wild orchid,
wild pansy, wood anemone, yarrow, yellow
rocket

wildlife *n* animals, fauna

wilds *n* desert, outback, remote areas, the back
of beyond *colloq*, the boondocks *colloq*, the
middle of nowhere *colloq*, the sticks *colloq*,
wasteland, wilderness

wiles *n* artfulness, cheating, chicanery,
contrivance, craftiness, cunning, deceit,
deception, device, dodge *colloq*, fraud, guile,
manoeuvre, ploy, ruse, stratagem, subterfuge,
trick, trickery
☒ guilelessness

wilful *adj* **1** *wilful destructiveness:* calculated, conscious, deliberate, intentional, planned, premeditated, voluntary **2** *petulant and wilful child:* contrary, determined, dogged, headstrong, inflexible, intractable *formal*, intransigent *formal*, mulish, obdurate *formal*, obstinate, perverse, pig-headed, refractory *formal*, self-willed, stubborn, uncompromising, unyielding, wayward
F3 1 spontaneous, unintentional **2** good-natured

will *n* **1** *exercise free will:* choice, decision, discretion, option, preference, volition **2** *imposed his will on everyone:* desire, disposition, fancy, feeling, inclination, mind, wish **3** *sheer endurance and the will to survive:* aim, command, determination, intention, purpose, purposefulness, resolution, resolve, single-mindedness, willpower
♦ *v* **1** *she willed her husband to live:* command, compel, decree, direct, intend, ordain, order, want **2** *you must do as you will:* choose, desire, want, wish **3** *my gran willed her ring to me:* bequeath, confer *formal*, dispose of, hand down, leave, pass down, pass on, transfer *formal*

willing *adj* **1** *willing to go along with them:* agreeable, amenable, consenting, content, disposed, eager, enthusiastic, favourable, game *colloq*, glad, happy, inclined, keen, pleased, prepared, ready, so-minded, well-disposed **2** *a very willing worker:* biddable, compliant *formal*, co-operative, eager, enthusiastic, game *colloq*, keen
F3 1 disinclined, reluctant, unwilling **2** reluctant

willingly *adv* by choice, cheerfully, eagerly, freely, gladly, happily, nothing loth, readily, unhesitatingly, voluntarily
F3 unwillingly

willingness *n* agreeableness, agreement, complaisance *formal*, compliance *formal*, consent, desire, disposition, enthusiasm, favour, inclination, readiness, volition, will, wish
F3 unwillingness

willowy *adj* graceful, limber, lissom, lithe, lithesome, slender, slim, supple, svelte, sylphlike
F3 buxom

willpower *n* commitment, determination, doggedness, drive, grit *colloq*, persistence, resolution, resolve, self-command, self-control, self-discipline, self-mastery, single-mindedness, will

willy-nilly *adv* compulsorily, necessarily, of necessity, perforce *formal*

wilt *v* diminish, droop, dwindle, ebb, fade, fail, faint, flag, flop, grow less, languish, lessen, sag, shrivel, sink, wane, weaken, wither
F3 perk up

wily *adj* artful, astute, cheating, crafty, crooked, cunning, deceitful, deceptive, designing, fly *colloq*, foxy, guileful, intriguing, scheming, sharp, shifty, shrewd, sly, tricky, underhand
F3 guileless

wimp *n* clot *colloq*, clown, drip *colloq*, fool, jerk *slang*, milksop, nerd *slang*, softy, wally *colloq*, wet *colloq*

win *v* **1** *I never tire of winning:* achieve, be victorious, carry off, come (in) first, come out on top *colloq*, conquer, finish first, hit the jackpot *colloq*, overcome, prevail, strike gold *colloq*, succeed, triumph, turn up trumps *colloq*, win hands down *colloq*, win the day *colloq* **2** *win a promotion:* accomplish, achieve, acquire, attain, catch, collect, earn, gain, get, net, obtain, procure *formal*, receive, secure
F3 1 fail, lose
♦ *n* conquest, mastery, success, triumph, victory
F3 defeat
► **win over** allure, attract, bring round, charm, convert, convince, influence, persuade, prevail upon *formal*, sway, talk round

wince *v* blench, cower, cringe, draw back, flinch, jerk, jump, quail, recoil, shrink, start
♦ *n* cringe, flinch, jerk, start

wind¹ *n* air, air-current, blast, bluster, breath, breeze, current, draught, gale, gust, hurricane, puff, tornado

---

Types of wind include:
anticyclone, austral wind, berg wind, bise, bora, Cape doctor, chinook, cyclone, doctor, east wind, El Niño, etesian, Favonian wind, föhn, gregale, harmattan, helm wind, khamsin, levant, libeccio, meltemi, mistral, monsoon, north wind, nor'wester, pampero, prevailing wind, samiel, simoom, sirocco, snow eater, southerly, southerly buster, trade wind, tramontana, westerly, wet chinook, williwaw, willy-willy, zephyr, zonda

---

wind² *v* **1** *the river winds lazily for miles:* bend, curve, deviate, loop, meander, ramble, snake, spiral, twine, zigzag **2** *wind the spun yarn on the bobbin:* coil, curl, encircle, furl, reel, roll, turn, twine, twist, wrap, wreathe
♦ *n* bend, curve, meander, turn, twist, zigzag
► **wind down 1** *he gradually wound down his involvement in sport:* bring/come to an end, decline, diminish, dwindle, lessen, reduce, slacken off, slow (down), stop, subside **2** *she had a bath to help her wind down:* calm down, ease up, quieten down, relax, unwind
► **wind up 1** *we will have to wind up the business:* bring to a close, bring to an end, close (down), conclude *formal*, end, finalize, finish, liquidate, stop, terminate *formal* **2** *he wound up in Devon:* end up, find yourself, finish up, settle **3** *you get wound up too easily:* annoy, disconcert, irritate, rub someone up the wrong way *colloq* **4** *they were always winding each other up:* fool, kid *colloq*, make fun of, pull someone's leg *colloq*, trick

windbag *n* big-mouth *colloq*, blether, boaster, bore, braggart, gasbag *colloq*, gossip

winded *adj* breathless, out of breath, out of puff, panting, puffed, puffed out
F3 fresh

windfall *n* bonanza, find, godsend, jackpot, manna, pennies from heaven, stroke of luck, treasure-trove

winding *adj* anfractuous *formal*, bending, circuitous, convoluted *formal*, crooked, curving, flexuose *formal*, flexuous *formal*, indirect, meandering, roundabout, serpentine, sinuate(d) *formal*, sinuous *formal*, spiral, tortuous, turning, twisting
F3 straight

windy *adj* **1** *windy weather:* blowy, blustery, breezy, gusty, squally, stormy, tempestuous, wild, windswept **2** *windy speech:* bombastic,

garrulous, long-winded, pompous, prolix *formal*, rambling, turgid, verbose, wordy **3** *even grown men can get a bit windy about him:* afraid, chicken *colloq*, frightened, nervous, nervy *colloq*, on edge *colloq*, scared, timid, uneasy
Fa 1 calm, windless **3** fearless

wine

Types of wine include:
alcohol-free, dry, brut, sec, demi-sec, sweet, sparkling, table wine, house wine, red wine, house red *colloq*, white wine, house white *colloq*, rosé, blush wine, fortified wine, mulled wine, tonic wine, vintage wine, plonk *colloq*; sherry, dry sherry, fino, medium sherry, amontillado, sweet sherry, oloroso; port, ruby, tawny, white port, vintage port

---

Varieties of wine include:
Alsace, Asti, Auslese, Barolo, Beaujolais, Beaujolais Nouveau, Beaune, Bordeaux, Burgundy, cabernet sauvignon, Cava, Chablis, Chambertin, champagne, Chardonnay, Chianti, claret, Côtes du Rhône, Dao, Douro, Frascati, Graves, Grenache, hock, Lambrusco, Liebfraumilch, Mâcon, Madeira, Malaga, Marsala, Mateus Rosé, Médoc, Merlot, moselle, Muscadet, muscatel, Niersteiner, Piesporter, Pinot grigio, Pinot noir, retsina, Riesling, Rioja, Sancerre, Sauterne, Sauvignon, Sekt, Shiraz, Soave, Spätlese, Tarragona, Valpolicella, vinho verde, Zinfandel

---

Sizes of wine-bottles include:
magnum, flagon, jeroboam, methuselah, rehoboam, salmanazar, balthazar, nebuchadnezzar

---

wing *n* **1** *the organization's military wing:* arm, branch, circle, coterie, faction, flank, group, grouping, section, segment, set, side **2** *in the 16th century, an east wing was added:* adjunct, annexe, attachment, extension, side
♦ *v* **1** *winging its way across the Atlantic:* hasten *formal*, hurry, move, pass, race, soar, speed, travel, zoom **2** *birds winging their way across the sky:* flit, fly, glide, soar

wink *v* **1** *laughing and winking at me:* blink, flutter, nictate *formal*, nictitate *formal* **2** *the brilliant winking lights of the cafés:* flash, flicker, gleam, glimmer, glint, glitter, sparkle, twinkle
♦ *n* **1** *he gave me a teasing wink:* blink, flutter, nictation *formal*, nictitation *formal* **2** *the answering machine winked cheerfully:* flash, gleam, glimmer, glint, glitter, sparkle, twinkle **3** *the food disappeared in a wink:* flash, instant, moment, second, split second
► **wink at** condone, disregard, ignore, neglect, overlook, pass over, take no notice of, turn a blind eye to *colloq*

winkle *v* draw out, extract, extricate, flush, force, prise, worm

winner *n* champ *colloq*, champion, conqueror, medallist, prizewinner, title-holder, vanquisher *formal*, victor, world-beater
Fa loser

winning *adj* **1** *the winning team:* conquering, successful, triumphant, unbeaten, undefeated, vanquishing *formal*, victorious **2** *he has such a*

winning smile: alluring, amiable, attractive, beguiling, bewitching, captivating, charming, delightful, enchanting, endearing, engaging, fetching, lovely, pleasing, sweet, winsome
Fa 1 losing **2** unappealing

winnings *n* booty, gains, jackpot, prize(s), proceeds, profits, spoils, takings
Fa losses

winnow *v* comb, cull, divide, fan, part, screen, select, separate, sift, sort

winsome *adj* alluring, amiable, attractive, beguiling, bewitching, captivating, charming, delectable *formal*, delightful, enchanting, endearing, engaging, fetching, lovely, pleasing, prepossessing, pretty, sweet
Fa unattractive

wintry *adj* **1** *wintry weather:* arctic, biting, bleak, cheerless, chilly, cold, desolate, dismal, freezing, frosty, frozen, glacial, harsh, hibernal *formal*, hiemal *formal*, icy, piercing, raw, snowy **2** *she gave a wintry smile:* bleak, cheerless, cold, cool, desolate, dismal, frosty, harsh, hostile, icy, unfriendly

wipe *v* **1** *wipe the table top:* brush, clean, clear, dry, dust, mop, rub, sponge, swab **2** *wipe the file from the computer:* erase, get rid of, remove, take away, take off
♦ *n* brush, clean, dry, dust, mop, rub, sponge, swab
► **wipe out** abolish, annihilate, blot out, demolish, destroy, efface *formal*, eradicate, erase, expunge, exterminate, extirpate *formal*, massacre, obliterate, raze

wiry *adj* **1** *a wiry physique:* lean, muscular, sinewy, strong, tough **2** *wiry hair:* coarse, rough
Fa 1 flabby, puny **2** soft

wisdom *n* astuteness, circumspection *formal*, common sense, comprehension, discernment, enlightenment, erudition *formal*, foresight, insight, intelligence, judgement, judiciousness *formal*, knowledge, learning, penetration, prudence *formal*, reason, sagacity *formal*, sapience *formal*, sense, understanding
Fa folly, stupidity

wise *adj* **1** *the wise men from Harvard fly in:* aware, clever, discerning, educated, enlightened, erudite *formal*, experienced, informed, intelligent, knowing, knowledgeable, perceptive, rational, sagacious *formal*, sapient *formal*, understanding, well-informed **2** *a wise decision:* circumspect *formal*, far-sighted, judicious *formal*, long-sighted, politic, prudent *formal*, reasonable, sagacious *formal*, sensible, shrewd, sound, well-advised
Fa 1 foolish, stupid **2** ill-advised

wisecrack *n* barb, funny, gag, gibe, in-joke, jest, joke, one-liner *colloq*, pun, quip, witticism

wish *v* **1** *nobody wishes to be exploited:* aspire, covet, crave, desire, fancy, hanker, hope, hunger, long, lust, need, pine, prefer, thirst, want, yearn, yen *colloq* **2** *he will do as you wish:* ask, bid, command, direct, instruct, order, require
♦ *n* **1** *it was not my wish to be here:* aspiration, craving, desire, fancy, fondness, hankering, hope, hunger, inclination, liking, longing, preference, thirst, urge, want, whim, yearning, yen *colloq* **2** *against my express wish:* bidding, command, desire, instruction, order, request, will

wishy-washy *adj* bland, feeble, flat, ineffective, ineffectual *formal*, insipid, namby-pamby *colloq*, tasteless, thin, vapid, watered-down, watery, weak
F3 firm, strong

wisp *n* lock, piece, shred, strand, thread, twist

wispy *adj* attenuated *formal*, delicate, ethereal, faint, fine, flimsy, fragile, frail, gossamer, insubstantial, light, straggly, thin
F3 substantial

wistful *adj* 1 *a wistful smile on her face:* contemplative, dreaming, dreamy, meditative, musing, pensive, reflective, thoughtful, wishful 2 *with delicate wistful flute playing:* disconsolate *formal*, forlorn, longing, melancholy, mournful, sad, yearning

wit *n* 1 *full of tongue-in-cheek wit:* badinage, banter, drollery, facetiousness, funniness, humour, jocularity, levity, repartee, waggishness 2 *battle of wits:* astuteness, brains *colloq*, cleverness, common sense, faculties, gumption *colloq*, insight, intellect, intelligence, judgement, marbles *colloq*, nous *colloq*, reason, sagacity *formal*, sense, shrewdness, understanding, wisdom 3 *he is a dandy, a wit and a connoisseur:* comedian, comic, humorist, joker, satirist, wag
F3 1 seriousness 2 stupidity

witch *n* enchantress, hag, hex, magician, necromancer *formal*, occultist, sorceress

witchcraft *n* black magic, conjuration *formal*, divination, enchantment, incantation, magic, necromancy *formal*, occultism, sorcery, spell, the black art, the occult, voodoo, wizardry

withdraw *v* 1 *he withdrew a few coins from his pocket:* draw back, draw out, extract, pull back, pull out, remove, take away 2 *French troops had to be withdrawn from Brittany:* back out, draw back, drop out, fall back, recede, remove, retreat, scratch, secede 3 *he then withdrew from the meeting:* absent yourself, depart, go (away), leave, retire 4 *he withdrew claims for defamation of character:* abjure *formal*, annul *formal*, cancel, disclaim, nullify *formal*, recall, recant, rescind *formal*, retract, revoke, take away, take back 5 *he withdrew his hand sharply:* draw back, pull back, recoil, shrink back

withdrawal *n* 1 *withdrawal of Intercity services:* drawing back/out, extraction, pulling back, removal, taking away 2 *withdrawal of enemy forces:* departure, disengagement, evacuation, exit, exodus, falling back, retirement, retreat 3 *insisted on the immediate withdrawal of his statement:* abjuration *formal*, disavowal *formal*, disclaimer, recall, recantation, repudiation, revocation, secession

withdrawn *adj* 1 *her withdrawn, uncommunicative state:* aloof, detached, introvert, introverted, private, quiet, reserved, retiring, shrinking, shy, silent, taciturn, uncommunicative, unforthcoming, unsociable 2 *a withdrawn area:* distant, hidden, isolated, out-of-the-way, private, remote, secluded, solitary
F3 1 extrovert, forthcoming, outgoing

wither *v* decay, decline, die (off), disappear, disintegrate, droop, dry (up), dwindle, fade (away), languish, perish, shrink, shrivel, wane, waste, weaken, wilt
F3 flourish, thrive

withering *adj* contemptuous, deadly, death-dealing, destructive, devastating, humiliating, mortifying, scathing, scornful, snubbing, wounding
F3 encouraging, supportive

withhold *v* check, conceal, control, curb, decline *formal*, deduct, hide, hold back, keep back, keep in check, refuse, repress, reserve, restrain, retain, suppress
F3 accord, give

withstand *v* bear, brave, confront, cope with, defy, endure, face, fight, hold off, hold out, hold your ground, last out, oppose, put up with, resist, stand, stand fast, stand firm, stand up to, stand your ground, survive, take on, thwart, tolerate, weather
F3 give in, yield

witless *adj* crazy, cretinous, daft, dull, empty-headed, foolish, gormless, half-witted, idiotic, imbecilic, inane, mindless, moronic, senseless, silly, stupid
F3 intelligent

witness *n* 1 *witness in a court:* attestant *formal*, deponent *formal*, testifier 2 *witnesses to the accident:* bystander, eye-witness, looker-on, observer, onlooker, spectator, viewer, watcher ♦ *v* 1 *I have never witnessed anything so awful:* look on, mark, note, notice, observe, perceive, see, view, watch 2 *witnessed that he saw the crime:* affirm *formal*, attest *formal*, be evidence of, bear out, bear witness, confirm, corroborate *formal*, depose *formal*, endorse, give evidence, prove, support, testify, verify 3 *to witness a will:* countersign, endorse, sign

witticism *n* bon mot, epigram, one-liner *colloq*, pleasantry, pun, quip, repartee, riposte, wisecrack

witty *adj* amusing, brilliant, clever, comic, droll, facetious, fanciful, funny, humorous, ingenious, jocular, lively, original, sharp-witted, sparkling, waggish, whimsical
F3 dull, unamusing

wizard *n* 1 *Islay also had its wizards and witches:* conjurer, enchanter, magician, necromancer *formal*, occultist, sorcerer, thaumaturge *formal*, warlock, witch 2 *a technical wizard:* ace, adept, expert, genius, hotshot *colloq*, maestro, master, prodigy, star *colloq*, virtuoso, whiz *colloq* ♦ *adj* brilliant, enjoyable, fab *colloq*, fantastic, good, great, marvellous, sensational, smashing *colloq*, super, superb, terrific *colloq*, tremendous, wonderful

wizened *adj* dried up, gnarled, lined, shrivelled, shrunken, thin, withered, worn, wrinkled

wobble *v* 1 *his legs began to wobble:* dodder, fluctuate, oscillate, quake, quiver, rock, seesaw, shake, stagger, sway, teeter, totter, tremble, vibrate 2 *wobbled a bit before completing the victory:* dither, hesitate, shilly-shally *colloq*, vacillate, waver ♦ *n* oscillation, quaking, rock, shake, tremble, tremor, unsteadiness, vibration

wobbly *adj* doddering, doddery, quavering, rickety, shaky, teetering, tottering, trembling, unbalanced, uneven, unsafe, unstable, unsteady, wonky *colloq*
F3 stable, steady

woe *n* adversity, affliction *formal*, agony, anguish, burden, calamity, curse, dejection, depression, disaster, distress, gloom, grief, hardship, heartache, heartbreak, melancholy, misery, misfortune, pain, sadness, sorrow, suffering, tears, trial, tribulation *formal*, trouble, unhappiness, wretchedness
🖪 joy

woebegone *adj* blue *colloq*, crestfallen, dejected, disconsolate *formal*, dispirited, doleful, down in the mouth *colloq*, downcast, downhearted, forlorn, gloomy, grief-stricken, long-faced, lugubrious *formal*, miserable, mournful, sad, sorrowful, tearful, tear-stained, troubled, wretched
🖪 joyful

woeful *adj* 1 *woeful tales of broken romances:* disconsolate *formal*, doleful *formal*, gloomy, grieving, grievous, heartbreaking, heart-rending, miserable, mournful, sad, unhappy, wretched 2 *woeful mothers with their young babes:* catastrophic, cruel, deplorable, distressing, dreadful, hopeless, lamentable, shocking, sorrowful, terrible, tragic 3 *a woeful backpass:* appalling, awful, bad, calamitous, deplorable, disappointing, disastrous, disgraceful, dreadful, feeble, hopeless, inadequate, lamentable, lousy *colloq*, mean, paltry, pathetic *colloq*, pitiable, poor, rotten, shocking
🖪 1 joyful

wolf *n* Casanova, Don Juan, ladies' man, lady-killer, lecher, philanderer, Romeo, seducer, womanizer
▶ **wolf down** bolt, cram, devour, gobble, gorge, gulp, pack away, put away, scoff, stuff
🖪 nibble

woman *n* female, girl, lady, maid, maiden

womanhood *n* 1 *they blossom into womanhood:* adulthood, maturity, muliebrity *formal* 2 *respect for womanhood:* woman, womankind, womenfolk(s), womenkind

womanizer *n* Casanova, Don Juan, ladies' man, lady-killer, lecher, philanderer, Romeo, seducer, wolf

womanly *adj* effeminate, female, feminine, kind, ladylike, motherly, tender, warm, womanish

wonder *n* 1 *sense of wonder and awe:* admiration, amazement, astonishment, awe, bewilderment, fascination, pleasure, surprise, wonderment 2 *the botanical gardens of Egypt were a wonder to behold:* curiosity, marvel, miracle, nonpareil *formal*, phenomenon, prodigy, rarity, sight, spectacle
♦ *v* 1 *she laughed and wondered what to say:* ask yourself, conjecture *formal*, doubt, meditate, ponder, puzzle, query, question, reflect, speculate, think 2 *wondered at the prescience of his words:* be amazed, be astonished, be astounded, be dumbfounded, be lost for words, be surprised, gape, marvel, stand in awe

The seven wonders of the world are:
Pyramids of Egypt, Hanging Gardens of Babylon, Statue of Zeus at Olympia, Temple of Artemis at Ephesus, Mausoleum of Halicarnassus, Colossus of Rhodes, Pharos of Alexandria

wonderful *adj* 1 *wonderful weather:* ace *colloq*, admirable, brilliant *colloq*, cool *slang*, delightful, excellent, fabulous *colloq*, fantastic *colloq*, great *colloq*, magnificent, marvellous, out of this world *colloq*, outstanding, phenomenal, sensational, smashing *colloq*, stupendous, super *colloq*, superb, terrific *colloq*, tremendous, wicked *slang* 2 *this wonderful young singer from Dresden:* amazing, astonishing, astounding, awesome, extraordinary, incredible, remarkable, staggering, startling, strange, surprising
🖪 1 appalling, awful, dreadful 2 ordinary

wonky *adj* amiss, askew, shaky, skew-whiff, unsound, unsteady, weak, wobbly, wrong
🖪 balanced, stable, straight

wont *adj* accustomed, given, habituated *formal*, inclined, used
♦ *n* custom, habit, practice, routine, rule, use, way

wonted *adj* accustomed, common, conventional, customary, daily, familiar, frequent, habitual *formal*, normal, regular, routine, usual
🖪 unwonted

woo *v* 1 *woo a lover:* chase, court, pay court to, pursue, seek the hand of 2 *woo custom:* attract, cultivate, encourage, look for, pursue, seek

wood *n* 1 *carving a figure from wood:* lumber, planks, timber 2 *he wanders through the wood:* coppice, copse, forest, grove, plantation, spinney, thicket, trees, woodland, woods

Types of wood include:
timber, lumber *US*, hardwood, softwood, heartwood, sapwood, seasoned wood, green wood, bitterwood, brushwood, cordwood, firewood, kindling, matchwood, plywood, pulpwood, whitewood, chipboard, hardboard, wood veneer; afrormosia, ash, balsa, beech, cedar, cherry, chestnut, cottonwood, deal, ebony, elm, mahogany, African mahogany, maple, oak, pine, redwood, rosewood, sandalwood, sapele, satinwood, teak, walnut, willow. See also **tree**

wooded *adj* forested, sylvan *formal*, timbered, tree-covered, woody
🖪 open

wooden *adj* 1 *a small wooden peg:* timber, woody 2 *her expression wooden and unyielding:* blank, deadpan, emotionless, expressionless, unemotional, unresponsive, vacant, vacuous 3 *try and cover the terrible, wooden silence:* awkward, clumsy, graceless, impassive, leaden, lifeless, rigid, slow, spiritless, stiff, stilted, stodgy
🖪 2 lively

wool *n* down, fleece, floccus, hair, yarn

wool-gathering *n* absent-mindedness, day-dreaming, distraction, forgetfulness, inattention, preoccupation

woolly *adj* 1 *I wish I had my woolly hat on:* fleecy, made of wool, woollen 2 *woolly caterpillars:* downy, flocculent *formal*, fluffy, frizzy, fuzzy, hairy, shaggy, woolly-haired 3 *the woolly nature of these claims:* blurred, cloudy, confused, foggy, fuzzy, hazy, ill-defined, indefinite, indistinct, muddled, nebulous, unclear, vague
🖪 3 clear, distinct
♦ *n* cardigan, jersey, jumper, pullover, sweater

woozy *adj* befuddled, bemused, blurred, confused, dazed, dizzy, fuddled, nauseated, rocky, tipsy, unsteady, wobbly
F3 alert

word *n* **1** *the word 'forte' on a label is an indication of strength:* designation, expression, name, term, utterance, vocable *formal* **2** *I want a word with your father:* chat, consultation, conversation, discussion, talk, tête-à-tête **3** *but there's still no word from the doctor:* account, advice, assertion, bulletin, comment, communication, communiqué, declaration, dispatch, dope *colloq*, gen *colloq*, info *colloq*, information, intelligence, low-down *colloq*, message, news, notice, remark, report, statement, tidings *formal*, utterance, warning **4** *I'm not going back on my word:* assurance, guarantee, honour, oath, pledge, promise, undertaking, vow **5** *just say the word and we'll leave:* command, commandment, decree, go-ahead *colloq*, green light *colloq*, mandate, order, signal, thumbs-up *colloq*, will **6** *the word is that she's been sacked:* gossip, hearsay, rumour, scandal, speculation, talk, whisper **7** *the words of a song:* book, libretto, lyrics, script, text
♦ *v* couch, explain, express, phrase, put, say, state, write

wording *n* choice of words, diction, expression, language, phraseology, phrasing, style, terminology, verbiage, wordage, words

word-perfect *adj* accurate, exact, faithful, letter-perfect, spot-on
F3 inaccurate

wordplay *n* paronomasia *technical*, punning, puns, repartee, wit, witticisms

wordy *adj* diffuse, discursive, garrulous, long-winded, loquacious *formal*, prolix *formal*, rambling, verbose
F3 concise

work *n* **1** *the study helped him in his work as a teacher:* art, business, calling, career, craft, employment, field, job, line, line of business, livelihood, métier, occupation, profession, pursuit, skill, trade, vocation, workmanship **2** *I've got a lot of work to get through before my holiday:* assignment, charge, chore, commission, duty, job, mission, responsibility, task, undertaking **3** *farming is really hard work:* drudgery, effort, elbow grease *colloq*, exertion, graft *colloq*, industry, labour, slog *colloq*, toil, travail *formal*, trouble **4** *I'm not familiar with his work:* accomplishment, achievement, book, composition, creation, œuvre, opus, painting, piece, play, poem, production, writing **5** *steel works:* factory, foundry, mill, plant, shop, workshop **6** *good works:* actions, acts, deeds, doings **7** *the works of a clock:* action, guts *colloq*, innards *colloq*, installations, machinery, mechanism, movement, parts, working parts, workings
F3 **1** hobby, play, rest
♦ *v* **1** *he works as a cook:* be employed, earn a living, have a job **2** *she works much too hard:* drudge, exert yourself, labour, peg away *colloq*, plug away *colloq*, slave, slog *colloq*, slog your guts out *colloq*, toil, work your fingers to the bone *colloq* **3** *I can't get the DVD player to work:* function, go, handle, operate, perform, run **4** *sails rotate to work the grinding stones:* control, drive, handle, manage, operate, run, use **5** *the*

green staff worked miracles to get the course ready: accomplish, achieve, bring about, cause, create, do, effect *formal*, execute, perform, pull off *colloq* **6** *a complete ban will not work:* be effective, be satisfactory, be successful, go well, have the desired effect, prosper, succeed **7** *he'd have to somehow work it so he stayed behind:* arrange, contrive, engineer, fiddle *colloq*, fix *colloq*, manipulate, manoeuvre, wangle *colloq* **8** *work your way to the front:* edge, guide, make, manoeuvre, move, penetrate, shift **9** *nobody wants to work the land:* cultivate, dig, farm, till **10** *work the dough as little as possible:* fashion, form, knead, make, manipulate, model, mould, process, shape
F3 **1** be unemployed **2** play, rest **3** fail

▶ **work out 1** *we can't work out how they could have hidden the child for so long:* calculate, clear up, figure out, puzzle out, resolve, solve, sort out, understand **2** *things didn't seem to work out somehow:* be effective, develop, evolve, go well, pan out *colloq*, prosper, succeed, turn out **3** *work out a sound crop rotation:* arrange, construct, contrive, develop, devise, formulate, invent, organize, plan, put together **4** *that works out at about £16 an hour:* add up to, amount to, come out, come to, total **5** *she works out five times a week:* drill, exercise, keep fit, practise, train, warm up

▶ **work up 1** *work up a crowd:* agitate, arouse, excite, incite, move, stir up **2** *work up an appetite:* agitate, animate, arouse, build up, generate, incite, inflame, instigate, kindle, move, rouse, spur, stimulate, stir up, whet

workable *adj* doable, feasible, possible, practicable, practical, realistic, viable
F3 unworkable

workaday *adj* common, commonplace, dull, everyday, familiar, humdrum, labouring, mundane, ordinary, practical, routine, run-of-the-mill *colloq*, toiling, work-day, working
F3 exciting

worker *n* artisan, breadwinner, craftsman, craftswoman, employee, hand, labourer, member of staff, operative, proletarian, tradesman, wage-earner, workaholic *colloq*, workhorse *colloq*, working man, working woman, workman, workwoman

workforce *n* employees, labour, labour force, manpower, personnel, shop floor, staff, workers, work-people

working *n* **1** *the normal working of the kidney:* action, functioning, manner, method, operation, process, routine, running, system **2** *mine workings:* diggings, excavations, mine, pit, quarry, shaft **3** *the workings of a clock:* action, guts *colloq*, innards *colloq*, installations, machinery, mechanism, movement, parts, working parts, works
♦ *adj* **1** *a working mill:* functioning, going, in working order, operating, operational, operative, running, up and running *colloq* **2** *the aims of the working class:* active, employed
F3 **1** inoperative **2** idle

workman, workwoman *n* artificer, artisan, craftsman, craftswoman, employee, hand, journeyman, labourer, mechanic, navvy, operative, tradesperson, worker

workmanlike adj adept, careful, efficient, expert, masterly, painstaking, professional, proficient, satisfactory, skilful, skilled, thorough
☒ amateurish

workmanship n art, artistry, craft, craftsmanship, execution, expertise, finish, handicraft, handiwork, manufacture, skill, technique, work

workmate n associate, colleague, co-worker, fellow-worker, work-fellow, yoke-fellow

workout n aerobic, callisthenics, drill, eurhythmics, exercise, gymnastics, isometrics, practice, training, warm-up

workshop n 1 *he's busy in his workshop*: atelier, factory, garage, mill, plant, shop, studio, workroom, works 2 *a theatre workshop*: class, discussion group, seminar, study group, symposium

world n 1 *anywhere in the world*: cosmos, creation, earth, globe, heavenly body, nature, planet, sphere, star, universe 2 *the whole world is interested*: everybody, everyone, human race, humanity, humankind, man, mankind, people 3 *the world of rock music*: area, department, division, domain, field, group, kingdom, province, realm, section, society, sphere, system 4 *the Victorian world*: age, days, epoch, era, life, period, times 5 *her world is completely different from mine*: existence, experience, life, reality, situation, way of life

worldly adj 1 *concerned with the wordly dimensions*: carnal, corporeal *formal*, earthly, material, mundane, physical, profane, secular, temporal, terrestrial, unspiritual 2 *she has a wordly, knowing air*: cosmopolitan, experienced, knowing, sophisticated, streetwise *colloq*, urbane, worldly-wise 3 *worldly ambition*: ambitious, avaricious, covetous, grasping, greedy, materialistic, selfish
☒ 1 eternal, spiritual 2 unsophisticated

worldwide adj catholic, general, global, international, mondial *formal*, ubiquitous *formal*, universal
☒ local

worn adj frayed, in tatters, ragged, shabby, tattered, tatty, threadbare, worn-out
☒ new, unused

worried adj afraid, agonized, (all) hot and bothered *colloq*, anxious, apprehensive, bothered, concerned, dismayed, disquieted, distracted, distraught, distressed, disturbed, fearful, fretful, frightened, ill at ease, nervous, on edge *colloq*, overwrought, perturbed *formal*, strained, tense, troubled, uneasy, upset, uptight *colloq*, wired *slang*
☒ calm, unconcerned, unworried

worrisome adj agonizing, anxious, apprehensive, bothersome, disquieting, distressing, disturbing, fretful, frightening, insecure, irksome, jittery, nail-biting *colloq*, perturbing *formal*, troublesome, uneasy, upsetting, vexing, worrying
☒ calm, reassuring

worry v 1 *try not to worry*: agonize, be anxious, be distressed, be troubled, fret 2 *his carelessness has always worried me*: aggravate *colloq*, agitate, annoy, bother, bug *colloq*, concern, disturb, harass, harry, hassle *colloq*, irritate, nag, perturb

formal, pester, plague, tease, torment, trouble, unsettle, upset, vex 3 *dogs can chase and worry sheep*: attack, bite, go for, savage, tear at
☒ 1 be unconcerned 2 comfort
♦ n 1 *he's always had money worries*: annoyance, burden, care, concern, irritation, nuisance, pest, plague, problem, responsibility, trial, trouble, vexation 2 *body image is a worry – even if you're five*: agitation, anguish, anxiety, apprehension, concern, disquiet, distress, disturbance, fear, fearfulness, hang-up *colloq*, misery, misgiving, perplexity, perturbation *formal*, stew *colloq*, strain, stress, tension, tiz *colloq*, tizzy *colloq*, torment, trouble, unease
☒ 2 comfort, reassurance

worrying adj anxious, disquieting, distressing, disturbing, harassing, nail-biting *colloq*, niggling, perturbing *formal*, troublesome, trying, uneasy, unsettling, upsetting, worrisome
☒ calm, reassuring

worsen v 1 *worsen the outlook for employment*: aggravate, exacerbate, heighten, increase, intensify 2 *causes the condition to worsen*: decline, degenerate, deteriorate, get worse, go down the tube(s) *colloq*, go downhill *colloq*, go from bad to worse *colloq*, go to pot *colloq*, sink, slip, weaken
☒ 1 improve

worship v admire, adore, adulate, deify, exalt, extol, glorify, honour, idolize, laud *formal*, love, praise, pray to, respect, revere, reverence, venerate *formal*
☒ despise, hate
♦ n adoration, adulation, deification, devotion(s), exaltation, glorification, glory, homage, honour, idolatry, laudation *formal*, love, praise, prayer(s), regard, respect, reverence, veneration *formal*

> **Places of worship include:**
> abbey, bethel, cathedral, chantry, church, fane, kirk, masjid, meeting-house, minster, mosque, pagoda, shrine, shul, synagogue, tabernacle, temple, wat

worst v beat, best, conquer, crush, defeat, drub, get the better of, master, overcome, overpower, overthrow, subdue, subjugate *formal*, vanquish *formal*, whitewash

worth n advantage, assistance, avail, benefit, cost, credit, desert(s), eminence, excellence, gain, good, help, importance, merit, price, profit, quality, rate, service, significance, use, usefulness, utility, value, virtue, worthiness
☒ worthlessness

worthless adj 1 *worthless railway shares*: cheap, paltry, poor, trashy, trifling, trivial, unusable, useless, valueless 2 *the effort involved was worthless*: futile, ineffectual *formal*, insignificant, meaningless, naff *slang*, nugatory *formal*, pointless, rubbishy, unavailing, unimportant, useless 3 *a worthless human being*: contemptible, corrupt, despicable, good-for-nothing, low, useless, vile
☒ 1 valuable 2 significant 3 worthy

worthwhile adj advantageous, beneficial, constructive, gainful, good, helpful, justifiable, productive, profitable, useful, valuable, worthy
☒ worthless

worthy *adj* admirable, appropriate, commendable, creditable, decent, deserving, excellent, fit, good, honest, honourable, laudable *formal*, meritorious *formal*, moral, praiseworthy, reliable, reputable, respectable, righteous, trustworthy, upright, valuable, virtuous, worthwhile
◼ disreputable, unworthy
♦ *n* big cheese *colloq*, big noise *colloq*, big shot *colloq*, bigwig *colloq*, dignitary, luminary, name, notable, personage

would-be *adj* ambitious, aspiring, budding, eager, endeavouring, enterprising, hopeful, keen, longing, optimistic, striving, wishful

wound *n* **1** *a superficial wound:* cut, gash, graze, hurt, injury, laceration, lesion, scar, scratch, trauma **2** *seeing him again reopened old wounds:* ache, anguish, blow, damage, distress, grief, harm, heartbreak, hurt, pain, shock, torment, trauma
♦ *v* **1** *wounded in clashes with police:* cut, damage, gash, graze, harm, hit, hurt, injure, lacerate, pierce, puncture, scratch, slash, stab, tear **2** *what wounded her was her husband's indifference:* distress, grieve, hurt, insult, mortify, offend, pain, shock, slight, traumatize, upset

wraith *n* apparition, ghost, phantom, revenant, shade, spectre, spirit, spook *colloq*

wrangle *n* altercation *formal*, argument, argy-bargy *colloq*, barney *colloq*, bickering, clash, contest, controversy, disagreement, dispute, quarrel, row *colloq*, set-to *colloq*, slanging match *colloq*, squabble, tiff, tussle
◼ agreement
♦ *v* altercate *formal*, argue, bicker, clash, contend, disagree, dispute, fall out *colloq*, fight, have words, quarrel, row, scrap, spar, squabble
◼ agree

wrap *v* **1** *she wrapped the parcels carefully:* pack, package, parcel (up) **2** *umbilical cord was wrapped round the windpipe:* bind, fold, swathe, wind **3** *they spotted the baby wrapped in a towel:* bundle up, cloak, cocoon, cover, encase, enclose, enfold, envelop, fold, muffle, roll up, shroud, surround, swathe **4** *wrap it or you'll be sorry!:* belt up *colloq*, dry up *colloq*, give it a rest *colloq*, hold your tongue *colloq*, pipe down *colloq*, put a sock in it *colloq*, shut up, shut your mouth *colloq*
◼ **3** unwrap
♦ *n* cape, cloak, mantle, robe, shawl, stole
▶ **wrap up 1** *wrapping up presents:* pack up, package, parcel (up) **2** *the home side had wrapped up the game early:* bring to a close, complete, conclude, end, finish off, round off, terminate, wind up

wrapper *n* case, casing, cover, covering, dust jacket, envelope, jacket, Jiffy bag®, packaging, paper, sheath, sleeve, wrapping

wrath *n* anger, annoyance, bitterness, choler, displeasure, exasperation, fury, indignation, ire *formal*, irritation, passion, rage, resentment, spleen, temper
◼ calm, pleasure

wrathful *adj* angry, bitter, displeased, enraged, furibund *formal*, furious, in a paddy *colloq*, incensed, indignant, infuriated, irate, ireful, on the warpath *colloq*, raging
◼ calm, pleased

wreak *v* bestow *formal*, bring about, carry out, cause, create, execute, exercise, express, inflict, perpetrate, unleash, vent

wreath *n* band, chaplet, circle, circlet, coronet, crown, festoon, garland, loop, ring

wreathe *v* adorn, coil, crown, encircle, enfold, entwine, envelop, enwrap, festoon, intertwine, interweave, shroud, surround, twine, twist, wind, wrap

wreck *v* break, demolish, destroy, devastate, mar, play havoc with, ravage, ruin, shatter, sink, smash, spoil, torpedo, write off
◼ conserve, repair
♦ *n* breaking, debris, demolition, derelict, destruction, devastation, disaster, disruption, flotsam, fragments, loss, mess, pieces, remains, rubble, ruin, ruination, shattering, shipwreck, smashing, undoing, write-off

wreckage *n* debris, detritus *formal*, flotsam, fragments, pieces, remains, rubble, ruin

wrench *v* **1** *wrenched back the door:* force, jerk, pull, rip, tear, tug, twist, wrest, wring, yank **2** *he wrenched his back:* distort, rick, sprain, strain
♦ *n* **1** *they X-rayed his ankle but it was just a wrench:* ache, jerk, pain, pang, pull, sprain, tear, tug, twist **2** *leaving home was a real wrench for her:* blow, sadness, shock, sorrow, upheaval, uprooting

wrest *v* extract, force, pull, seize, strain, take, twist, win, wrench, wring

wrestle *v* battle, combat, contend, contest, fight, grapple, scuffle, strive, struggle, tussle, vie

wretch *n* devil, good-for-nothing, miscreant, outcast, rascal, rat *colloq*, rogue, ruffian, scoundrel, swine *colloq*, vagabond, villain, worm *colloq*

wretched *adj* **1** *his mother felt wretched about the matter:* broken-hearted, crestfallen, dejected, depressed, disconsolate, distressed, doleful, downcast, forlorn, gloomy, melancholy, miserable, sad, sorry, unhappy **2** *their wretched pups caged in hellholes:* hapless *formal*, hopeless, miserable, pathetic, piteous, pitiable, pitiful, poor, sad, sorry, unfortunate, unhappy, unlucky **3** *wretched coward that he was:* bad, base, contemptible, despicable, inferior, low, mean, paltry, shameful, vile, worthless **4** *until this wretched tax is repealed:* appalling, atrocious, awful, deplorable, dreadful, horrible, outrageous, shocking, terrible
◼ **1** happy **2** enviable **3** worthy **4** excellent

wriggle *v* crawl, dodge, edge, extricate, manoeuvre, sidle, slink, snake, squiggle, squirm, turn, twist, waggle, wiggle, worm, writhe, zigzag
♦ *n* jerk, jiggle, squirm, turn, twist, twitch, wiggle, writhe

wring *v* **1** *wring out the mop:* extract, mangle, screw, squeeze, twist, wrench, wrest **2** *a successful way to wring money out of people:* coerce, exact, extort, force **3** *Ruth felt wrung with fear:* distress, hurt, lacerate, pain, pierce, rack, rend, stab, tear, torture, wound

wrinkle *n* corrugation, crease, crumple, fold, frounce, furrow, gather, line, pucker, ridge, rumple, wimple
♦ *v* corrugate, crease, crinkle, crumple, fold, furrow, gather, line, pucker, rumple, shrivel

wrinkled *adj* creased, crinkled, crinkly, crumpled, furrowed, puckered, ridged, rivelled, rugate *formal*, rugose *formal*, rugous *formal*, rumpled, wrinkly
🖹 smooth

writ *n* court order, decree, subpoena, summons

write *v* **1** *she writes poems and short stories:* compose, create, dash off *colloq*, draft, draw up, pen **2** *write your questions down before you go:* copy, inscribe, jot down, make a note of, note (down), print, put down, put down in black and white *colloq*, record, register, scrawl, scribble, set down, take down, transcribe **3** *she wrote to invite me to her party:* communicate, correspond
▶ **write off 1** *write off the value of the shares against capital:* annul *formal*, cancel, cross out, delete, disregard, nullify *formal*, wipe out **2** *the second car he's written off:* crash, demolish, destroy, smash (up), wreck

writer

Writers include:
annalist, author, autobiographer, bard, biographer, calligraphist, chronicler, clerk, columnist, composer, contributor, copyist, copywriter, correspondent, court reporter, diarist, dramatist, editor, essayist, fabler, fiction writer, ghost writer, hack, historian, journalist, leader-writer, lexicographer, librettist, lyricist, novelist, pen-friend, penman, pen-pal, penpusher *colloq*, penwoman, playwright, poet, poet laureate, reporter, rhymer, satirist, scribbler, scribe, scriptwriter, short-story writer, sonneteer, stenographer, storyteller *colloq*

---

writhe *v* coil, contort, jerk, squirm, struggle, thrash, thresh, toss, twist, twist and turn *colloq*, wiggle, wriggle

writing *n* **1** *I can't read his writing:* calligraphy, hand, handwriting, penmanship, print, scrawl, scribble, script, text, words **2** *teaching and writing of Raymond Williams:* composition, document, opus, publication, volume, work

---

Types of writing instruments include:
pen, ballpoint, Biro®, calligraphy pen, cartridge pen, dip pen, eraser pen, felt-tip pen, fountain pen; marker pen, rollerball pen; writing brush, pencil, chinagraph pencil, coloured pencil, crayon, ink pencil, lead pencil, propelling pencil, board marker, laundry marker, permanent marker, highlighter; cane pen, quill, reed, Roman metal pen, steel pen, stylus; brailler, typewriter, word-processor

---

written *adj* documental *formal*, documentary, documented, drawn up, recorded, set down, transcribed
🖹 unwritten, verbal

wrong *adj* **1** *a wrong answer:* erroneous, fallacious *formal*, false, imprecise, in error, inaccurate,
incorrect, mistaken, off beam *colloq*, off target *colloq*, wide of the mark *colloq* **2** *take the wrong approach:* improper, inapposite *formal*, inappropriate, inapt, incongruous *formal*, indecorous *formal*, infelicitous *formal*, malapropos *formal*, unconventional, unfitting, unseemly *formal*, unsuitable **3** *their actions were unquestionably wrong:* bad, blameworthy, criminal, crooked *colloq*, dishonest, dishonourable, evil, felonious *formal*, illegal, illicit, immoral, iniquitous *formal*, reprehensible *formal*, sinful, to blame, unethical, unfair, unjust, unjustified, unlawful, wicked **4** *a wrong judgement:* amiss, awry, defective, faulty, out of order, up the spout *colloq* **5** *the wrong end of the telescope:* back, contrary, inside, inverse, inverted, opposite, reverse
🖹 **1** correct, right **2** right, suitable **3** good, moral **4** in order **5** front, right
♦ *adv* amiss, astray, awry, badly, erroneously, faultily, imprecisely, improperly, inaccurately, incorrectly, inexactly, mistakenly, wrongly
🖹 right
♦ *n* abuse, crime, error, grievance, infringement, injury *formal*, injustice, misdeed, offence, sin, transgression *formal*, trespass *formal*, wrongdoing
🖹 right
♦ *n* immorality, inequity, iniquity, injustice, sinfulness, unfairness, unlawfulness, wickedness
🖹 right
♦ *v* abuse, cheat, discredit, dishonour, harm, hurt, ill-treat, ill-use, injure, malign, maltreat, misrepresent, mistreat, oppress

wrongdoer *n* criminal, culprit, delinquent, evil-doer, felon, law-breaker, malefactor *formal*, miscreant, offender, sinner, transgressor *formal*, trespasser

wrongdoing *n* crime, delinquency, error, evil, fault, felony, immorality, iniquity *formal*, maleficence *formal*, mischief, misdeed, offence, sin, sinfulness, transgression *formal*, wickedness

wrongful *adj* blameworthy, criminal, dishonest, dishonourable, evil, illegal, illegitimate, illicit, immoral, improper, reprehensible, unethical, unfair, unjust, unjustified, unlawful, unwarranted, wicked, wrong
🖹 rightful

wrongly *adv* badly, by mistake, erroneously, in error, inaccurately, incorrectly, mistakenly
🖹 rightly

wrought *adj* beaten, decorative, fashioned, hammered, made, manufactured, ornamental, ornamented, ornate, shaped

wry *adj* **1** *wry humour:* droll, dry, ironic, mocking, sarcastic, sardonic, witty **2** *he pulled a wry face:* askew, contorted, crooked, deformed, distorted, twisted, uneven, warped
🖹 **2** straight

X,Y,Z

xenophobia *n* ethnocentrism, racialism, racism
☐ xenomania

xenophobic *adj* ethnocentrist, parochial, racialist, racist

xerox *v* copy, duplicate, photocopy, Photostat®, print, reproduce, run off

Xerox® *n* duplicate, facsimile, photocopy, Photostat®

yack *v* blather, chatter, gab *colloq*, gossip, harp on, jabber, jaw *colloq*, prattle, tattle, witter on, yap *colloq*
♦ *n* **1** *a good yack with my mates*: blather, chat, chinwag *colloq*, confab *colloq*, gossip, jaw, prattle, rant, yackety-yack *colloq* **2** *just a load of yack*: blah *colloq*, hot air

yank *v* haul, heave, jerk, pull, snatch, tug, wrench
♦ *n* haul, heave, jerk, pull, snatch, tug, wrench

yap *v* **1** *yapping poodles*: bark, yelp **2** *stop yapping and get a move on*: babble, chatter, gab *colloq*, jabber, jaw *colloq*, prattle, yatter

yard *n* court, courtyard, garden, quad *colloq*, quadrangle

yardstick *n* benchmark, criterion, gauge, guideline, measure, standard, touchstone

yarn *n* **1** *nylon yarn*: fibre, strand, thread **2** *an adventure yarn*: anecdote, cock-and-bull story *colloq*, fable, fabrication, story, tale, tall story *colloq*

yawning *adj* cavernous, gaping, huge, vast, wide, wide-open

yearly *adj* annual, per annum, per year, perennial
♦ *adv* annually, every year, once a year, perennially

yearn *v* ache, covet, crave, desire, fancy, hanker, hunger, itch, languish, long, pine, thirst, want, wish, yen *colloq*

yearning *n* craving, desire, fancy, hankering, hunger, longing, pining, thirst, wish, yen *colloq*

yell *v* bawl, bellow, cry (out), holler *colloq*, howl, roar, scream, screech, shout, shriek, squall, squeal, whoop, yelp, yowl
☐ whisper
♦ *n* bellow, cry, holler *colloq*, howl, roar, scream, screech, shout, shriek, squeal, whoop
☐ whisper

yellow *adj* buff, canary, flavescent *formal*, flaxen, fulvid *formal*, fulvous *formal*, gold, golden, lemon, primrose, saffron, tawny, vitellary, vitelline, xanthic, xanthous *technical*

yelp *v* bark, bay, cry, squeal, yap, yell, yowl
♦ *n* bark, cry, squeal, yap, yell, yip, yowl

yen *n* craving, desire, hankering, hunger, itch, longing, lust, passion, thing *colloq*, yearning
☐ dislike

yes *adv* absolutely, affirmative, agreed, certainly, of course, quite, right, yeah *colloq*, yep *colloq*
☐ no

yes-man *n* arse-licker *slang*, bootlicker, crawler, lackey, minion, sycophant, toady

yet *adv* **1** *not over yet*: already, as yet, by now, by then, heretofore *formal*, hitherto *formal*, now, thus far *formal*, until now, up till now, up till then, up to this time **2** *yet more rain*: also, besides, even, furthermore, in addition, into the bargain *colloq*, moreover, still, too
♦ *conj* all the same, but, even so, for all that, however, just the same, nevertheless, nonetheless, notwithstanding *formal*

yield *v* **1** *yielded good profits*: bear, bring forth, bring in, earn, fetch, fructify *formal*, fructuate *formal*, furnish, generate, give, gross, net, pay, produce, provide, return, supply **2** *yielded to pressure*: accede, acquiesce *formal*, admit defeat, agree, allow, bow, capitulate, cave in, comply, concede, consent, give in, give way, go along with, knuckle under, permit, resign yourself, submit, succumb, surrender, throw in the towel/sponge *colloq* **3** *yielded his title*: abandon, abdicate, cede, give up, part with, relinquish *formal*, renounce *formal*, surrender
☐ **2** resist, withstand **3** hold on to, retain
♦ *n* **1** *yield on investments*: earnings, income, proceeds, profit, return, revenue, takings **2** *a fine yield of corn*: crop, harvest, haul, output, produce, product

yielding *adj* **1** *a soft, yielding surface*: elastic, flexible, pliable, pliant, quaggy, resilient, soft, spongy, springy, supple **2** *a more yielding character*: accommodating, acquiescent *formal*, amenable, biddable, complaisant *formal*, compliant *formal*, easy, obedient, obliging, submissive, tractable *formal*, unresisting
☐ **1** solid **2** obstinate

yoke *n* **1** *trudged along with yokes on their shoulders*: bond, coupling, harness, link, tie **2** *the yoke of dictatorship*: bondage, burden, enslavement, oppression, servility, servitude *formal*, slavery, subjugation *formal*, tyranny
♦ *v* bond, bracket, connect, couple, harness, hitch, join, link, tie, unite

yokel *n* boor, bucolic, clodhopper, country bumpkin, country cousin, hick, hillbilly *colloq*, peasant, rustic
☐ sophisticate, towny

young *adj* **1** *two young girls*: adolescent, baby, childlike, infant, junior, juvenile, kid *colloq*, little, small, teenage, youthful **2** *young for his age*: childish, fledgling, green, growing, immature, inexperienced, undeveloped, unfledged **3** *the night is young*: early, new, recent
☐ **1** adult, old **2** mature, old
♦ *n* babies, brood, children, family, issue, litter, little ones, offspring, progeny *formal*

youngster *n* adolescent, boy, child, girl, kid *colloq*, lad, lass, shaver *colloq*, teenager, toddler, young adult, young man, young person, young woman, youth

youth *n* **1** *an aggressive youth:* adolescent, boy, juvenile, kid *colloq*, lad, teenager, young man, youngster **2** *the youth of today:* the young, young people, younger generation **3** *my misspent youth:* adolescence, boyhood, childhood, girlhood, immaturity, inexperience, teenage years, teens
F3 adulthood, maturity

youthful *adj* **1** *a youthful complexion:* boyish, childish, fresh, girlish, well-preserved, young **2** *youthful exuberance:* boyish, childish, girlish, immature, inexperienced, juvenile

youthfulness *n* boyishness, childishness, girlishness, immaturity, inexperience, juvenility

yowl *v* bay, caterwaul, cry, howl, screech, squall, ululate *formal*, wail, yell, yelp
♦ *n* cry, howl, screech, wail, yell, yelp

yucky *adj* **1** *a yucky mess:* dirty, disgusting, filthy, foul, grotty *colloq*, horrible, messy, mucky, revolting, unpleasant **2** *a yucky romantic comedy:* saccharine, sentimental, sickly
F3 1 pleasant

zany *adj* absurd, amusing, clownish, comical, crazy *colloq*, daft *colloq*, droll, eccentric, funny, kooky *US colloq*, loony *colloq*, odd, ridiculous, wacky *colloq*
F3 serious

zap *v* hit, kill, shoot

zeal *n* ardour, commitment, dedication, devotion, eagerness, earnestness, energy, enthusiasm, fanaticism, fervour, fire, gusto, intensity, keenness, passion, spirit, vehemence, verve, vigour, warmth, zest
F3 apathy, indifference

zealot *n* bigot, extremist, fanatic, militant, partisan, radical

zealous *adj* ardent, burning, committed, dedicated, devoted, eager, earnest, enthusiastic, fanatical, fervent, fervid *formal*, fiery, impassioned, intense, keen, militant, passionate, spirited, warm
F3 apathetic, indifferent

zenith *n* acme *technical*, apex, apogee, climax, culmination, height, high point, highest point, meridian, optimum, peak, pinnacle, summit, top, vertex

F3 nadir

zero *n* cipher, duck, love, naught, nil, nothing, nought, zilch *colloq*
► **zero in on** aim for, concentrate on, converge on, direct at, fix on, focus on, head for, home in on, level at, pinpoint, train on, zoom in on

zest *n* appetite, eagerness, enjoyment, enthusiasm, exuberance, gusto, interest, joie de vivre, keenness, liveliness, relish, vigour, zeal, zing *colloq*
F3 apathy

zigzag *v* curve, meander, snake, twist, wind
♦ *adj* crooked, meandering, serpentine, sinuous, twisting, winding
F3 straight

zing *n* animation, brio *colloq*, dash *colloq*, élan, energy, go *colloq*, joie de vivre, life, liveliness, oomph *colloq*, pizzazz *colloq*, sparkle, spirit, vigour, vitality, zest, zip *colloq*
F3 listlessness

zip *n* drive, élan, energy, enthusiasm, get-up-and-go *colloq*, go *colloq*, gusto, life, liveliness, oomph *colloq*, pep *colloq*, pizzazz *colloq*, punch *colloq*, sparkle, spirit, verve, vigour, vitality, zest, zing *colloq*
F3 listlessness
♦ *v* dash, flash, fly, hurry, race, rush, scoot, shoot, speed, tear, whiz *colloq*, whoosh *colloq*, zoom

zodiac

The signs of the zodiac (with their symbols) are:
Aries (Ram), Taurus (Bull), Gemini (Twins), Cancer (Crab), Leo (Lion), Virgo (Virgin), Libra (Balance), Scorpio (Scorpion), Sagittarius (Archer), Capricorn (Goat), Aquarius (Water-bearer), Pisces (Fishes)

zone *n* area, belt, district, province, region, section, sector, sphere, stratum, territory, tract

zoo *n* animal park, menagerie, safari park, zoological gardens

zoom *v* dash, dive, flash, fly, go all out *colloq*, hurtle, race, rush, shoot, speed, streak, tear, vroom *colloq*, whirl, whiz *colloq*, zip

Words grouped by ending

This supplementary feature collects together words which share the same ending. Endings which are found in a large number of words are listed, starting with *-cide* and ending with *-urgy*, together with a brief account of their meaning and origin. Then an alphabetical list of words that use the ending is given, each one having a definition or explanation in brackets. Some of the word endings (*-graphy*, for example) have a number of senses, so their lists have been further divided by meaning to make it easier to find related words.

-cide

A combining form meaning killer or (the act of) killing. Many of the words listed can have either meaning (eg homicide, fratricide), whereas others (eg pesticide) demonstrate only the meaning of killer. Borrowed into Middle English via French, from Latin *-cida* meaning 'agent' and *-cidium* meaning 'act of killing'. Words in brackets refer to the thing killed.

acaricide (mites)
algicide (algae)
aphicide (aphids)
aphidicide (aphids)
bacillicide (bacilli)
bactericide (bacteria)
biocide (living material)
deicide (a god)
ecocide (an environment)
feticide (a fetus)
filicide (one's own child)
fratricide (a brother)
fungicide (fungi)
genocide (racial, national, ethnic or
   religious group)
germicide (germs)
herbicide (weeds)
homicide (a person)
infanticide (a child)
insecticide (insects)
larvicide (larvae)
matricide (one's mother)
miticide (mites)
ovicide (sheep)
parasiticide (parasites)
parricide (parent or near relative)
patricide (one's father)
pesticide (pests)
prolicide (offspring or the human race)
pulicide (fleas)
regicide (a king)
rodenticide (rodents)
sororicide (a sister)
speciocide (a species)
spermicide (sperm)

suicide (oneself)
tyrannicide (a tyrant)
uxoricide (one's wife)
vaticide (a prophet)
vermicide (worms)
viricide (virus)
viticide (vines)
vulpicide (a fox)

-cracy

A combining form denoting rule, government or domination by a particular group, from Greek *kratos* meaning 'power', 'rule' or 'strength'. Words in brackets refer to the ruling group.

aristocracy (aristocrats)
autocracy (one person)
bureaucracy (bureaucrats)
chrysocracy (the wealthy)
democracy (the whole population)
doulocracy (slaves)
ergatocracy (workers)
gerontocracy (old people)
gynaecocracy (women)
hagiocracy (holy men)
hierocracy (priests or ministers)
isocracy (equals)
kakistocracy (the worst)
kleptocracy (thieves)
meritocracy (the meritorious)
mobocracy (the mob)
monocracy (one individual)
nomocracy (rule of law)
ochlocracy (mobs)
pantisocracy (all equally)
pedantocracy (pedants)
physiocracy (natural laws)
plantocracy (plantation owners)
plutocracy (the wealthy)
pornocracy (prostitutes)
ptochocracy (beggars)
slavocracy (slave owners)
stratocracy (the military)
technocracy (technical experts)

theocracy (priests or religious law)
timocracy (property owners)

-culture

An ending that forms words relating to the cultivation of living things for commercial purposes, from Latin *cultura*, from *colere* 'to cherish or practise'. Words in brackets refer to the thing cultivated.

agriculture (crops and livestock)
apiculture (honey bees)
aquaculture (seafood and sea plants)
arboriculture (trees and shrubs)
aviculture (birds)
citriculture (citrus fruit)
floriculture (flowers)
horticulture (fruit, vegetables, flowers)
mariculture (aquatic flora and fauna)
monoculture (one crop)
permaculture (sustainable ecosystems)
pisciculture (fish in artificial conditions)
polyculture (more than one crop or kind of animal)
pomiculture (fruit)
sericulture (silkworms)
silviculture (trees)
stirpiculture (special stocks or strains)
vermiculture (earthworms)
viniculture (grapevines for winemaking)
viticulture (grapevines)
zooculture (animals)

-graphy

A combining form signifying the process of recording or representing something in graphic form or a descriptive science or art, from Greek *graphein* meaning 'to draw' or 'to write'.

Words in brackets refer to the type of writing, reproduction, or representation:

autobiography (people's lives as recorded by themselves)
autography (one's own handwriting)
biography (people's lives as recorded by others)
cacography (bad handwriting or spelling)
calligraphy (decorative handwriting)
cerography (engraving on wax)
chalcography (engraving on copper or brass)
chirography (handwriting)
chromotypography (printing in colours from wooden blocks)
dactyliography (engraving on gems)

ectypography (etching in relief)
epigraphy (ancient inscriptions)
epistolography (letter-writing)
ideography (ideograms in writing)
lithography (printing using metal or stone plates treated with ink)
nomography (graphic representation of numerical relationships)
petrography (writing on stone)
phonography (representation of spoken sounds by written characters)
photography (recording of images using light-sensitive film)
pornography (sexually arousing images)
psalligraphy (paper-cutting to make pictures)
serigraphy (silk-screening)
steganography (writing in cipher)
stenography (writing in shorthand)
stylography (mode of writing with a pen)
tachygraphy (shorthand)
typography (setting of texts for printing)
xerography (photocopying)
xylography (engraving on wood)

Words in brackets refer to the subject studied or described:

aerography (air or the atmosphere)
ampelography (vines)
anemography (wind)
angiography (blood vessels by X-ray)
anthropogeography (geographical distribution of humans)
arteriography (arteries)
bibliography (books)
biogeography (distribution of living things)
cardiography (movements of the heart)
cartography (maps)
choreography (representation of dancing)
chorography (mapping of a region)
chronography (history)
cinematography (motion pictures)
climatography (climate)
cometography (comets)
cosmography (the universe)
cryptography (codes)
dactylography (fingerprints)
demography (population statistics)
discography (musical recordings)
ethnography (culture of a society)
fractography (fractures in metal surfaces)
geography (the earth's surface)
glossography (glossaries)
glyptography (gem-carving)
hagiography (lives of saints)
heliography (the sun)
historiography (writing history)

holography (holograms)
horography (clocks)
hydrography (charting seas, lakes, etc)
hymnography (writing hymns)
hypsography (measuring heights)
iconography (images and symbols in visual
   arts)
lexicography (dictionaries)
lexigraphy (representation of words by
   signs)
metallography (metals)
myography (muscles)
mythography (myths)
nosography (diseases)
oceanography (the oceans)
odontography (teeth)
orography (mountains)
orthography (spelling)
osteography (bones)
palaeogeography (geography of ancient
   epochs)
palaeography (ancient writing systems)
physiography (physical geography)
phytogeography (geographical distribution
   of plants)
phytography (description of plants)
radiography (the body's interior by X-ray)
radiotelegraphy (telegraphy by radio
   transmission)
seismography (earthquakes)
selenography (the moon's surface)
stratigraphy (geological strata)
telegraphy (sending of messages by
   telegraph)
thalassography (marine organisms)
topography (features on land surface)
uranography (mapping of the heavens)
venography (veins by X-ray)
zoogeography (distribution of animals)

-latry

A combining form denoting worship of a
specified person or thing, from Greek *-latria*
meaning 'worship'. Words in brackets refer
to the person or thing worshipped.

angelolatry (angels)
anthropolatry (human beings)
astrolatry (planets and stars)
autolatry (oneself)
bardolatry (William Shakespeare)
bibliolatry (the Bible)
Christolatry (Jesus Christ)
cosmolatry (the cosmos)
demonolatry (devils)
dendrolatry (trees)
ecclesiolatry (church tradition)
epeolatry (words)

geolatry (the earth)
gyniolatry (women)
hagiolatry (saints)
heliolatry (the sun)
hierolatry (saints)
ichthyolatry (fish)
iconolatry (sacred images)
idolatry (images that are not God)
litholatry (a stone or stones)
lordolatry (nobility)
Maryolatry (the Virgin Mary)
monolatry (one god)
necrolatry (the dead)
ophiolatry (snakes)
physiolatry (nature)
plutolatry (wealth)
pyrolatry (fire)
symbololatry (symbols)
thaumatolatry (miracles)
theriolatry (animals)
zoolatry (animals or pets)

-lysis

A combining form denoting disintegration
or breaking down, from Greek *lysis*
meaning 'dissolution'. Words in brackets
refer to the nature of the disintegration.

analysis (examination of the structure or
   elements of something)
atmolysis (separation of gases of different
   densities)
autolysis (destruction of tissues or cells by
   their own enzymes)
bacteriolysis (rupturing of bacterial cells)
biolysis (disintegration of organic matter)
catalysis (speeding up of a chemical
   reaction by a catalyst)
cryptanalysis (deciphering of a coded
   message without the key)
cyclodialysis (detachment of the ciliary
   body from the sclera in the eye)
cytolysis (dissolution of cells)
dialysis (separation of particles in a liquid)
electroanalysis (chemical analysis by
   electrochemical methods)
electrolysis (decomposition of a chemical
   solution by electric current)
frontolysis (disruption of a weather front)
glycolysis (breakdown of glucose by
   enzymes)
haemodialysis (kidney dialysis)
haemolysis (destruction of red blood cells)
histolysis (breaking down of tissues)
homolysis (decomposition of a compound
   into two uncharged atoms)
hydrolysis (breakdown of a compound by
   reaction with water)

karyolysis (dissolution of a cell nucleus)
lipolysis (breakdown of fats by hydrolysis)
microanalysis (analysis of very small samples of substances)
narcoanalysis (use of truth drugs)
neurolysis (disintegration of nerve tissue)
oncolysis (destruction of a tumour)
paralysis (loss of ability to move following injury)
photocatalysis (acceleration of a chemical reaction by light)
photolysis (separation of molecules by action of light)
plasmolysis (contraction of plant cell protoplast as a result of water loss)
pneumatolysis (chemical alteration of rocks by action of hot magmatic gases)
proteolysis (breakdown of proteins into amino acids by action of enzymes)
psychoanalysis (examination of conscious and unconscious elements of the mind)
pyrolysis (decomposition brought about by high temperatures)
radiolysis (molecular disintegration resulting from radiation)
thermolysis (breakdown of molecules by action of heat)
uranalysis (analysis of urine)

-mancy

A combining form denoting divination by a specified method, from Greek *manteia* meaning 'divination'. Words in brackets refer to the means of divination.

aeromancy (weather)
axinomancy (an axe)
belomancy (arrows)
bibliomancy (opening a book at random)
botanomancy (burning branches or plants)
capnomancy (smoke)
cartomancy (playing cards)
ceromancy (wax drippings)
chiromancy (lines on the palm of the hand)
cleromancy (dice)
coscinomancy (sieve and a pair of shears)
crithomancy (strewing meal over sacrifices)
crystallomancy (crystal globe)
dactyliomancy (a finger)
gastromancy (sounds from the stomach)
geomancy (casting earth onto a surface)
gyromancy (falling from dizziness)
hieromancy (objects offered in a sacrifice)
hydromancy (water)
lampadomancy (flame)
lithomancy (stones or meteorites)
myomancy (movements of mice)

necromancy (communication with the dead)
oenomancy (appearance of wine)
omphalomancy (knots in the umbilical cord)
oneiromancy (dreams)
onychomancy (fingernails)
ornithomancy (flight of birds)
pyromancy (fire)
rhabdomancy (stick or rod)
scapulimancy (burnt shoulder blade)
tephromancy (ashes)
theomancy (oracles)
zoomancy (observing animals)

-mania

A combining form denoting an exaggerated desire or extreme enthusiasm for a specified thing, from Greek mania meaning 'madness', related to *mainesthai* 'to rage'. Words in brackets refer to the things desired or enthused over.

ablutomania (washing)
ailuromania (cats)
anglomania (England)
anthomania (flowers)
arithmomania (counting)
balletomania (ballet)
bibliomania (books)
cynomania (dogs)
dipsomania (alcohol)
dromomania (travelling)
egomania (oneself)
eleutheromania (freedom)
ergomania (work)
erotomania (sex)
flagellomania (flogging)
francomania (France)
gallomania (France or the French)
graphomania (writing)
hedonomania (pleasure)
hippomania (horses)
hydromania (water)
kleptomania (stealing)
logomania (talking)
megalomania (one's own importance)
melomania (music)
methomania (alcohol)
metromania (writing verse)
monomania (one thing)
morphinomania (morphine)
mythomania (lies)
narcomania (drugs)
necromania (death)
nostomania (returning to familiar places)
nymphomania (sex)
oenomania (wine)

opsomania (food of one kind)
orchidomania (testicles)
phagomania (eating)
pteridomania (ferns)
pyromania (fire)
technomania (technology)
thanatomania (death)
theatromania (technology)
theomania (God)
timbromania (stamps)
tomomania (performing surgery)
toxicomania (poison)
trichotillomania (pulling out one's hair)
tulipomania (tulips)
verbomania (words)
xenomania (foreigners)

-metry

A combining form creating nouns denoting
the science or process of measurement,
from Greek
-metria, from *metron* meaning 'a measure'.
Words in brackets refer to the thing
measured.

acidimetry (strength of an acid)
aerometry (air)
alcoholometry (concentration of alcohol)
alkalimetry (strength of an alkali)
allometry (growth of body parts)
altimetry (altitude)
anthropometry (human body)
archaeometry (dating of archaeological
    remains)
astrometry (motions and magnitudes of the
    stars)
barometry (atmospheric pressure)
bathymetry (depth of water)
biometry (biological data)
bolometry (radiant energy)
calorimetry (heat involved in a reaction)
campimetry (eye's field of vision)
cephalometry (proportions of head and
    face)
chronometry (time)
clinometry (elevation of a slope)
colorimetry (intensity of colour)
craniometry (skull dimensions)
cytometry (number of cells)
cytophotometry (light let through by a cell
    after staining)
densimetry (density, esp. of liquids)
densitometry (photographic density)
dosimetry (ionizing radiation)
dynamometry (engine's power output)
electrometry (electrical potential)
galvanometry (small electric currents)
gasometry (quantity of gas)

geometry (lines, angles, and shapes)
goniometry (angles)
gravimetry (variations in gravity)
hodometry (distance of a sea voyage)
horometry (time)
hydrometry (density of liquids)
hygrometry (humidity of air or a gas)
hypsometry (calibration of thermometers)
iconometry (size of an object)
interferometry (length of displacement in
    terms of wavelength)
isoperimetry (figures having equal
    boundaries or perimeters)
magnetometry (magnetic forces)
micrometry (small distances)
microseismometry (small earthquakes)
nanometry (distances in the nanometre
    range)
nephelometry (particles suspended in
    liquid or gas)
noometry (the mind)
odometry (distance travelled by a wheeled
    vehicle)
odorimetry (strength of odours)
olfactometry (intensity of an odour)
ophthalmometry (corneal curvatures of the
    eye)
optometry (eyesight)
pelvimetry (pelvis)
perimetry (person's field of vision)
photogrammetry (distances between
    objects, by means of photography)
photometry (intensity of light)
planimetry (area of a plane figure)
polarimetry (rotation of the plane of
    polarization of polarized light)
psychrometry (atmospheric humidity)
pyrometry (high temperatures, esp in
    furnaces)
seismometry (earthquakes)
sociometry (relationships within a group of
    people)
spectrometry (spectra)
spectrophotometry (intensity of light in a
    part of the spectrum)
spirometry (air capacity of the lungs)
stalagmometry (surface tension)
stereometry (solid bodies)
stichometry (lines in documents)
stoichiometry (relative quantities of
    substances involved in a reaction)
stylometry (variations in literary style)
symmetry (similarity between parts or
    halves)
tachometry (working speed of an engine)
tachymetry (distances)
telemetry (readings of an instrument)
tensiometry (surface tension)

thermometry (temperature)
tonometry (musical pitch)
trigonometry (sides and angles of triangles)
udometry (quantity of precipitation)
uranometry (distances between heavenly
   bodies)
velocimetry (velocity of fluids)
viscometry (viscosity of liquids)
zoometry (comparative measurement of
   animal parts)

-pathy

A combining form creating words denoting
feeling, suffering or emotion; often, in words
of a more modern origin it denotes a disease
or disorder, and thus methods of treating
disease. It comes from the Greek pathos
meaning 'suffering' or 'feeling'.

Words in brackets denote a feeling:

anthropopathy (ascription of human
   feelings to inanimate objects)
antipathy (feeling of strong dislike)
apathy (lack of interest or enthusiasm)
dyspathy (feeling of strong dislike)
empathy (ability to understand another
   person's feelings)
enantiopathy (feeling of strong dislike)
nostopathy (fear of returning to familiar
   places)
protopathy (first or direct experience)
sympathy (understanding of the suffering
   of others)
telepathy (apparent communication
   between minds)
theopathy (emotions brought on by religious
   belief)

*Words in brackets denote a disease or disorder
or a method of treatment:*

allopathy (treatment of disease by
   conventional means)
arthropathy (disease of the joints)
cardiomyopathy (disorder of the heart
   muscle)
encephalopathy (disorder of the brain)
enteropathy (disease of the intestinal tract)
haemoglobinopathy (type of blood disease)
homeopathy (treatment by small doses of
   drugs producing symptoms similar to the
   disease itself)
hydropathy (use of water in treatment of
   disease)
idiopathy (disease of unknown cause)
kinesipathy (treatment of illness with
   exercise)

lymphadenopathy (abnormal enlargement
   of the lymph nodes)
myocardiopathy (disorder of the heart
   muscle)
myopathy (abnormality of muscle tissue)
naturopathy (treatment of disease by diet,
   massage, and exercise)
nephropathy (disease affecting the kidneys)
neuropathy (disorder of the nervous
   system)
osteopathy (therapy involving
   manipulation of the skeleton)
psychopathy (mental disorder or illness)
sociopathy (condition characterised by
   extreme antisocial behaviour)

-phagy

A combining form forming words denoting
the eating of a specified substance,
especially as a practice or habit, from Greek
phagein meaning 'to eat'. Words in brackets
refer to the thing eaten.

anthropophagy (human flesh)
autocoprophagy (one's own excrement)
autophagy (body's own tissues)
coprophagy (excrement)
endophagy (the flesh of those within one's
   tribe)
entomophagy (insects)
exophagy (the flesh of those outside one's
   tribe)
geophagy (earth or clay)
hippophagy (horseflesh)
ichthyophagy (fish)
monophagy (one kind of food)
mycophagy (fungi)
omophagy (raw flesh)
onychophagy (fingernails)
pantophagy (all kinds of food)
polyphagy (many kinds of food)
scatophagy (excrement)
theophagy (a god, as part of a religious
   sacrament)
xerophagy (dry food, esp. during Lent)
zoophagy (animals)

-philia

A combining form denoting an admiration,
fondness or affinity for, and sometimes an
abnormal and usually sexual liking or love
of a specified thing. It derives from Greek
philia meaning 'affection', from *philos*
meaning 'loving'. Words in brackets refer
to the thing loved.

acrophilia (heights)
ailurophilia (cats)

arctophilia ((teddy) bears)
biophilia (living things)
coprophilia (excrement)
cynophilia (dogs)
entomophilia (insects)
ephebophilia (pubescent adolescents)
gerontophilia (the elderly)
necrophilia (dead bodies)
neophilia (newness)
paedophilia (children)
paraphilia (sexual deviancy)
retrophilia (the past)
stigmatophilia (tattooing or branding)
technophilia (technology)
topophilia (a particular place)
zoophilia (animals)

-phily

A combining form creating words that
denote a love of something, from Greek
philos 'loving'. Words in brackets refer to
the thing loved.

Anglophily (England)
arctophily (collecting teddy bears)
bibliophily (books)
cartophily (collecting cigarette cards)
Francophily (France)
Germanophily (Germany)
notaphily (collecting banknotes and
   cheques)
oenophily (wine)
scripophily (collecting share certificates)
Sinophily (China)
timbrophily (collecting stamps)
toxophily (archery)

-phobia

A combining form denoting obsessive and
persistent fear of something, from Greek
phobos meaning 'fear'. Words in brackets
are the things feared.

acrophobia (heights)
aerophobia (air)
agoraphobia (open spaces)
aichmophobia (points)
ailurophobia (cats)
algophobia (pain)
anemophobia (wind)
anglophobia (England)
anthropophobia (man)
apiphobia (bees)
aquaphobia (water)
arachnophobia (spiders)
arithmophobia (numbers)
astraphobia (lightning)

autophobia (solitude)
bathophobia (depths)
batrachophobia (reptiles)
bibliophobia (books)
brontophobia (thunder)
cancerophobia (cancer)
claustrophobia (closed spaces)
clinophobia (going to bed)
cynophobia (dogs)
dromophobia (crossing streets)
dysmorphophobia (physical deformities)
ecophobia (home)
eleutherophobia (freedom)
emetophobia (vomiting)
entomophobia (insects)
ergophobia (work)
erotophobia (sex)
erythrophobia (red lights or blushing)
euphobia (good news)
Francophobia (France)
gallophobia (France or the French)
genophobia (sex)
gerontophobia (the elderly)
graphophobia (writing)
gynophobia (women)
herpetophobia (snakes)
hierophobia (sacred things)
hippophobia (horses)
homophobia (homosexuals)
hydrophobia (water)
hypsophobia (high places)
kenophobia (void)
misophobia (contamination)
monophobia (one thing)
necrophobia (corpses)
negrophobia (blacks)
neophobia (newness)
nosophobia (disease)
nyctophobia (night)
ochlophobia (crowds)
odontophobia (teeth)
ophthalmophobia (being stared at)
ornithophobia (birds)
panphobia (everything)
pantophobia (everything)
pathophobia (disease)
phagophobia (eating)
phasmophobia (ghosts)
phengophobia (daylight)
phonophobia (noise or speaking aloud)
photophobia (light)
pyrophobia (fire)
Russophobia (Russia)
satanophobia (Satan)
scopophobia (being looked at)
Scotophobia (Scotland)
sitophobia (food)
symmetrophobia (symmetry)

syphilophobia (syphilis)
tachophobia (speed)
taphephobia (being buried alive)
technophobia (technology)
thanatophobia (death)
theophobia (God)
toxicophobia (poison)
toxiphobia (poison)
triskaidecaphobia (thirteen)
xenophopbia (foreigners)
zelophobia (jealousy)
zoophobia (animals)

-phony

A combining form denoting sound, from
Greek *phone* meaning 'sound' or 'voice'.
Words in brackets refer to the sound
produced.

antiphony (alternative singing by choir
  divided in two)
cacophony (disagreeable combination of
  loud noises)
dodecaphony (twelve-tone music)
euphony (harmonious sounds)
homophony (music with one dominant
  voice)

polyphony (music with two or more
  independent parts)
quadraphony (sound through four
  channels)
radiotelephony (telephony using radio
  transmission)
stereophony (sound through two channels)
symphony (unison of simultaneous
  sounds)
tautophony (repetition of the same sound)
telephony (use of telephones to transmit
  speech)

-urgy

A combining form used to refer to a
technology, a process or technique, from
Greek *-ourgia* meaning 'working'. Words in
brackets indicate the thing being worked or
the process involved.

chemurgy (organic raw materials)
metallurgy (metals)
micrurgy (minute tools in a magnified
  field)
zymurgy (fermentation)